Teacher's Edition

Needham, Massachusetts
Upper Saddle River, New Jersey
Glenview, Illinois

ISBN 0-13-115419-2
1 2 3 4 5 6 7 8 9 10 08 07 06 05 04

ADVENTURES

Table of Contents

Nature of Science: Reducing Hurricane Damage

What Is Science?

A NEW three-book series!

A balance of Life, Earth, and Physical Science in each book.

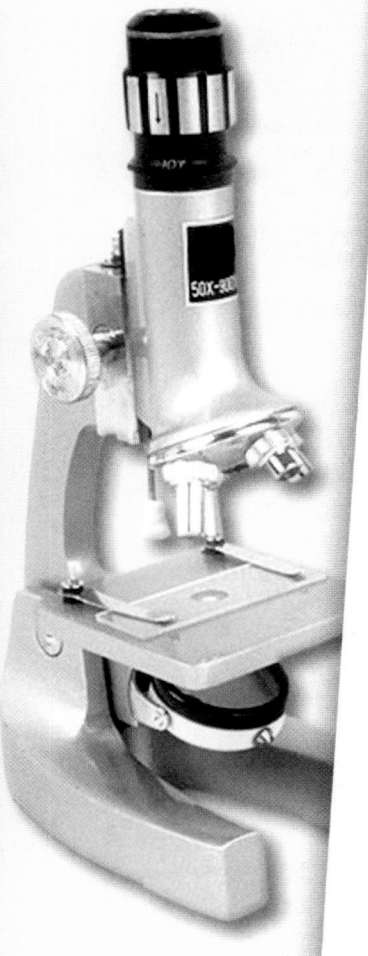

Dear Science Educator:

Welcome to the world of *Science Explorer*!

Prentice Hall is offering students and teachers the best in educational textbooks and software. Continuing our commitment to publishing materials that align with the National Science Education Standards, we are proud to introduce *Science Explorer: Discoveries, Investigations, and Adventures in Life, Earth, and Physical Science*.

Each text was developed exclusively to include a balance of Life, Earth, and Physical Sciences, with accessible content and a rich assortment of hands-on activities—providing numerous opportunities for investigations, inquiry, and experimentation.

In addition to rich content and hands-on activities, the texts contain a variety of ways to attract and maintain your students' attention. A student-friendly writing style, integrated reading strategies, ongoing assessment, and an unsurpassed art program make the texts accessible to all students.

I am very excited about our new middle grades science program, and I think you and your students will be too!

Sincerely,

Michael J. Padilla

Michael Padilla
Lead Author of *Science Explorer*

Student Edition and Teacher's Edition

Each text provides a complete balance of Life, Earth, and Physical Science for grades 6–8. The three-step lesson plan—Engage/Explore, Facilitate, and Assess—is ideal for reaching all students.

Teaching Support

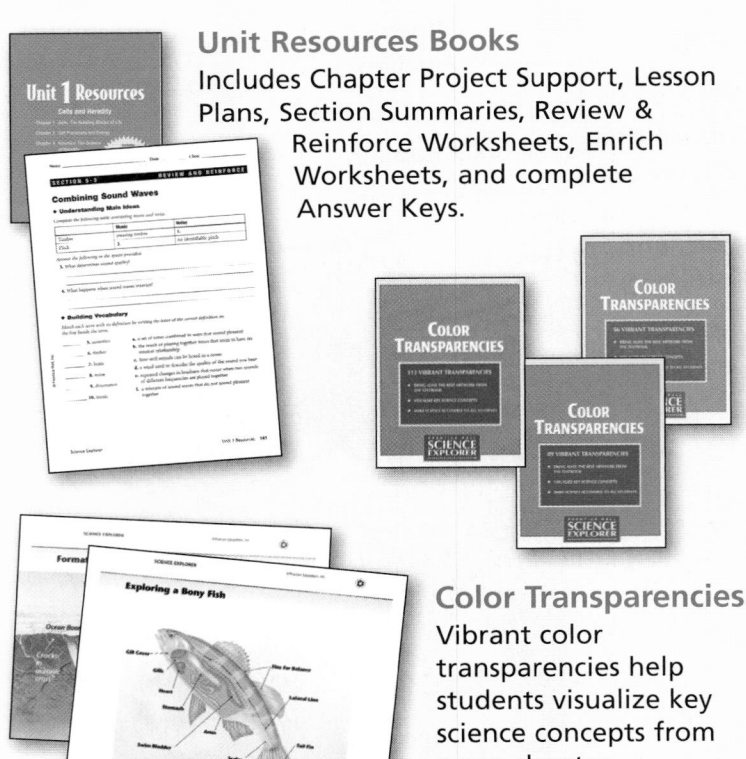

Unit Resources Books

Includes Chapter Project Support, Lesson Plans, Section Summaries, Review & Reinforce Worksheets, Enrich Worksheets, and complete Answer Keys.

Color Transparencies

Vibrant color transparencies help students visualize key science concepts from every chapter.

Resource Pro® CD-ROM

All of the teaching resources are available electronically including unit resources, project support, color transparencies and Computer Test Bank, all organized by chapter to save you time.

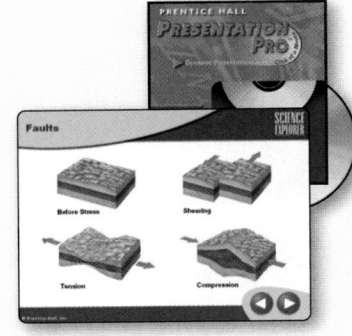

Presentation Pro CD-ROM

Easy-to-use instructional tool assists in delivering visually exciting content. Slide-show presentations include engaging questions, colorful art, and graphic organizers.

Teacher's ELL Handbook

Provides multiple strategies for reaching students who lack fluency in English.

Reading Support

Guided Reading and Study Workbook

Section-by-section questions encourage active reading and help build study skills.

Reading in the Content Area with Literature Connections

Provides strategies for improving comprehension and can be applied to any textbook section.

Section Summaries on Audio CD

Section summaries of every chapter provide additional reading support for students.

Lab Activity Video Libraries

Every full-period lab from the text is performed step-by-step providing support for students who have trouble reading lab instructions or are absent on lab day.

Concept Video Libraries

Short documentaries contain animations and footage of scientific events connected to the content of each chapter in the student text.

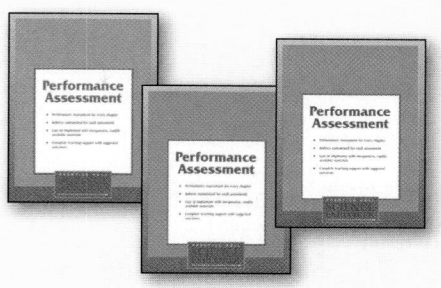

Performance Assessment

Assessment for every chapter along with teacher notes, scoring rubrics, and worksheets.

ExamView® Computer Test Bank Books with CD-ROM

Provides thousands of test questions with options to create new questions or edit existing ones with an easy-to-use word processor.

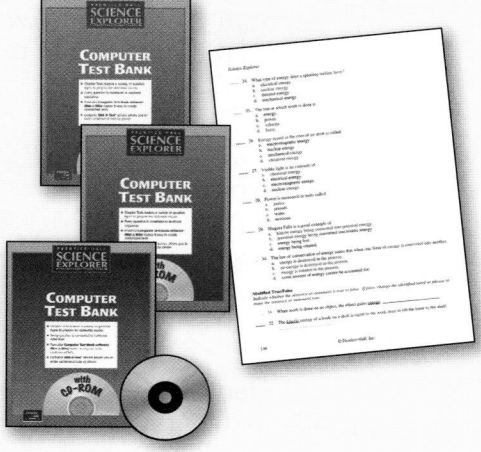

Test Preparation Workbook

Includes tests based on the National Science Education Standards and on SAT9, ITBS, and Terra Nova test objectives. The Teacher's Guide provides answers to all practice tests.

Assessment

Chapter Tests

Contains test strategies, abundant sample problems, and blackline master practice worksheets and tests.

Test-Taking Tips with Transparencies

Provides practice exercises to reinforce the test-taking tips and helps middle grades students overcome test-taking anxiety.

Labs and Activities

Laboratory Manual

Contains in-depth labs, covering the entire curriculum, with complete teaching support.

Probeware Lab Manual with CD-ROM

Incorporates labs from the program to help students explore with sensors and software from three major manufacturers.

Computer Microscope and Lab Manual

Labs and activities from the student text work directly with the Intel® QX3™ computer microscope. Students can capture, manipulate, and export microscopic images for use in reports and presentations.

Inquiry Skills Activity Book

Contains minds-on activities that can be used at any time of the year, providing additional flexibility in assessing science skills.

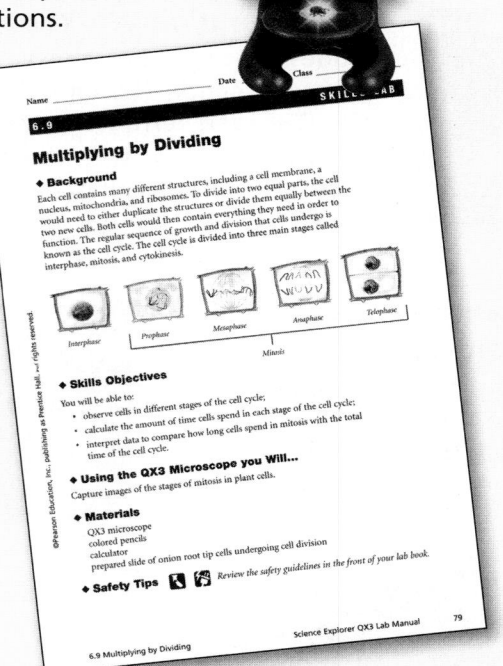

Exclusively from Prentice Hall...

Exclusive catalog for teachers adopting Prentice Hall Science Programs

Discovery Channel

An exclusive partnership provides the opportunity to receive 2 free videotapes and/or CD-ROMs upon adoption of the program.

PHSchool.com

Companion Web site

Provides teaching ideas, activities, and self-tests for every chapter. Stay current in the world of science through recently published articles from *Science News*® linked by topic.

Options for Pacing *Adventures*

The Pacing Chart below suggests one way to schedule your instructional time. The ***Science Explorer*** program offers many other aids to help you plan your instructional time, whether regular class periods or **block scheduling.** Refer to the Chapter Planning Guide before each chapter to view all program resources with suggested times for Student Edition activities.

Pacing Chart

	Periods	Blocks		Periods	Blocks
Introduction to Science	2	1	**Chapter 4 Motion**		
Chapter 1 Genetics: The Science of Heredity			Chapter 4 Project	Ongoing	Ongoing
Chapter 1 Project	Ongoing	Ongoing	**1** Describing and Measuring Motion	2	1
1 Mendel's Work	2	1	**2** Integrating Earth Science: Slow Motion on Planet Earth	1	$\frac{1}{2}$
2 Integrating Mathematics: Probability and Genetics	2	1	**3** Acceleration	1	$\frac{1}{2}$
3 The Cell and Inheritance	1	$\frac{1}{2}$	Chapter 4 Review and Assessment	1	$\frac{1}{2}$
4 The DNA Connection	1	$\frac{1}{2}$	**Chapter 5 Forces**		
Chapter 1 Review and Assessment	1	$\frac{1}{2}$	Chapter 5 Project	Ongoing	Ongoing
Chapter 2 Modern Genetics			**1** The Nature of Force	2	1
Chapter 2 Project	Ongoing	Ongoing	**2** Force, Mass, and Acceleration	1	$\frac{1}{2}$
1 Human Inheritance	1	$\frac{1}{2}$	**3** Friction and Gravity	2	1
2 Human Genetic Disorders	2	1	**4** Action and Reaction	1	$\frac{1}{2}$
3 Integrating Technology: Advances in Genetics	2	1	**5** Integrating Space Science: Orbiting Satellites	1	$\frac{1}{2}$
Chapter 2 Review and Assessment	1	$\frac{1}{2}$	Chapter 5 Review and Assessment	1	$\frac{1}{2}$
Chapter 3 Changes Over Time			**Chapter 6 Forces in Fluids**		
Chapter 3 Project	Ongoing	Ongoing	Chapter 6 Project	Ongoing	Ongoing
1 Darwin's Voyage	2	1	**1** Pressure	2	1
2 Integrating Earth Science: The Fossil Record	1	$\frac{1}{2}$	**2** Transmitting Pressure in a Fluid	1	$\frac{1}{2}$
3 Other Evidence for Evolution	2	1	**3** Floating and Sinking	1	$\frac{1}{2}$
Chapter 3 Review and Assessment	1	$\frac{1}{2}$	**4** Integrating Technology: Applying Bernoulli's Principle	1	$\frac{1}{2}$
Integrated Exploration: Dogs, Loyal Companions	1	$\frac{1}{2}$	Chapter 6 Review and Assessment	1	$\frac{1}{2}$

Pacing Chart

	Periods	Blocks		Periods	Blocks
Chapter 7 Work and Machines			**Chapter 10 Electric Current and Magnetic Fields**		
Chapter 7 Project	Ongoing	Ongoing	Chapter 10 Project	Ongoing	Ongoing
1 What is Work?	1	$\frac{1}{2}$	**1** Electricity, Magnetism, and Motion	2	1
2 Mechanical Advantage and Efficiency	2	1	**2** Generating Electric Current	1	$\frac{1}{2}$
3 Simple Machines	2	1	**3** Using Electric Power	1	$\frac{1}{2}$
4 Integrating Life Science: Machines in the Human Body	1	$\frac{1}{2}$	**4** Integrating Chemistry: Batteries	1	$\frac{1}{2}$
Chapter 7 Review and Assessment	1	$\frac{1}{2}$	Chapter 10 Review and Assessment	1	$\frac{1}{2}$
Chapter 8 Magnetism and Electromagnetism			Nature of Science: Electrical Engineer in Outer Space	1	$\frac{1}{2}$
Chapter 8 Project	Ongoing	Ongoing	**Chapter 11 Plate Tectonics**		
1 The Nature of Magnetism	1	$\frac{1}{2}$	Chapter 11 Project	Ongoing	Ongoing
2 Integrating Earth Science: Magnetic Earth	1	$\frac{1}{2}$	**1** Earth's Interior	1	$\frac{1}{2}$
3 Electric Current and Magnetic Fields	2	1	**2** Integrating Physics: Convection Currents and the Mantle	1	$\frac{1}{2}$
4 Electromagnets	1	$\frac{1}{2}$	**3** Drifting Continents	1	$\frac{1}{2}$
Chapter 8 Review and Assessment	1	$\frac{1}{2}$	**4** Sea-Floor Spreading	2	1
Chapter 9 Electric Charges and Current			**5** The Theory of Plate Tectonics	2	1
Chapter 9 Project	Ongoing	Ongoing	Chapter 11 Review and Assessment	1	$\frac{1}{2}$
1 Electric Charge and Static Electricity	1	$\frac{1}{2}$	**Chapter 12 Earthquakes**		
2 Circuit Measurements	2	1	Chapter 12 Project	Ongoing	Ongoing
3 Series and Parallel Circuits	1	$\frac{1}{2}$	**1** Earth's Crust in Motion	2	1
4 Integrating Health: Electrical Safety	1	$\frac{1}{2}$	**2** Measuring Earthquakes	2	1
Chapter 9 Review and Assessment	1	$\frac{1}{2}$	**3** Earthquake Hazards and Safety	1	$\frac{1}{2}$
			4 Integrating Technology: Monitoring Faults	1	$\frac{1}{2}$
			Chapter 12 Review and Assessment	1	$\frac{1}{2}$

Options for Pacing *Adventures*

Pacing Chart

Chapter 13 Volcanoes	Periods	Blocks	Chapter 16 The Atmosphere	Periods	Blocks
Chapter 13 Project	Ongoing	Ongoing	Chapter 16 Project	Ongoing	Ongoing
1 Volcanoes and Plate Tectonics	2	1	1 The Air Around You	2	1
2 Volcanic Activity	1	$\frac{1}{2}$	2 Integrating Environmental Science: Air Quality	1	$\frac{1}{2}$
3 Volcanic Landforms	2	1	3 Air Pressure	2	1
4 Integrating Space Science: Volcanoes in the Solar System	1	$\frac{1}{2}$	4 Layers of the Atmosphere	1	$\frac{1}{2}$
Chapter 13 Review and Assessment	1	$\frac{1}{2}$	Chapter 16 Review and Assessment	1	$\frac{1}{2}$
Chapter 14 Minerals			**Chapter 17 Weather Factors**		
Chapter 14 Project	Ongoing	Ongoing	Chapter 17 Project	Ongoing	Ongoing
1 Properties of Minerals	2	1	1 Energy in the Atmosphere	2	1
2 How Minerals Form	1	$\frac{1}{2}$	2 Integrating Physics: Heat Transfer	1	$\frac{1}{2}$
3 Integrating Technology: Mineral Resources	2	1	3 Winds	2	1
Chapter 14 Review and Assessment	1	$\frac{1}{2}$	4 Water in the Atmosphere	1	$\frac{1}{2}$
Chapter 15 Rocks			5 Precipitation	1	$\frac{1}{2}$
Chapter 15 Project	Ongoing	Ongoing	Chapter 17 Review and Assessment	1	$\frac{1}{2}$
1 Classifying Rocks	1	$\frac{1}{2}$	**Chapter 18 Weather Patterns**		
2 Igneous Rocks	1	$\frac{1}{2}$	Chapter 18 Project	Ongoing	Ongoing
3 Sedimentary Rocks	1	$\frac{1}{2}$	1 Air Masses and Fronts	1	$\frac{1}{2}$
4 Integrating Life Science: Rocks From Reefs	1	$\frac{1}{2}$	2 Storms	2	1
5 Metamorphic Rocks	2	1	3 Integrating Health: Floods	1	$\frac{1}{2}$
6 The Rock Cycle	2	1	4 Predicting the Weather	1	$\frac{1}{2}$
Chapter 15 Review and Assessment	1	$\frac{1}{2}$	Chapter 18 Review and Assessment	1	$\frac{1}{2}$
Nature of Science: Focus on Faults	1	$\frac{1}{2}$			

Pacing Chart

	Periods	Blocks		Periods	Blocks
Chapter 19 Climate and Climate Change			**Chapter 23 Energy Resources**		
Chapter 19 Project	Ongoing	Ongoing	Chapter 23 Project	Ongoing	Ongoing
1 What Causes Climate?	2	1	**1** Fossil Fuels	1	$\frac{1}{2}$
2 Climate Regions	1	$\frac{1}{2}$	**2** Renewable Sources of Energy	2	1
3 Long-Term Changes in Climate	1	$\frac{1}{2}$	**3** Integrating Chemistry: Nuclear Energy	1	$\frac{1}{2}$
4 Integrating Environmental Science: Global Changes in the Atmosphere	1	$\frac{1}{2}$	**4** Energy Conservation	2	1
Chapter 19 Review and Assessment	1	$\frac{1}{2}$	Chapter 23 Review and Assessment	1	$\frac{1}{2}$
Nature of Science: Eyes on Earth	1	$\frac{1}{2}$	Integrated Exploration: Antarctica	1	$\frac{1}{2}$
Chapter 20 Living Resources					
Chapter 20 Project	Ongoing	Ongoing			
1 Environmental Issues	2	1			
2 Forests and Fisheries	2	1			
3 Biodiversity	1	$\frac{1}{2}$			
4 Integrating Health: The Search for New Medicines	1	$\frac{1}{2}$			
Chapter 20 Review and Assessment	1	$\frac{1}{2}$			
Chapter 21 Land and Soil Resources					
Chapter 21 Project	Ongoing	Ongoing			
1 Conserving Land and Soil	2	1			
2 Solid Waste	2	1			
3 Integrating Chemistry: Hazardous Wastes	1	$\frac{1}{2}$			
Chapter 21 Review and Assessment	1	$\frac{1}{2}$			
Chapter 22 Air and Water Resources					
Chapter 22 Project	Ongoing	Ongoing			
1 Air Pollution	2	1			
2 The Water Supply	2	1			
3 Integrating Technology: Finding Pollution Solutions	1	$\frac{1}{2}$			
Chapter 22 Review and Assessment	1	$\frac{1}{2}$			

RESOURCE◉PRO®

The Resource Pro® CD-ROM is the ultimate scheduling and lesson planning tool. Resource Pro® allows you to preview all the resources in the *Science Explorer* program, organize your chosen materials, and print out any teaching resource. You can follow the suggested lessons or create your own, using resources from anywhere in the program.

Project 2061 was established by the American Association for the Advancement of Science (AAAS) as a long-term project to improve science education nationwide. A primary goal of Project 2061 is to define a "common core of learning"—the knowledge and skills we want all students to achieve. Project 2061 published *Science for All Americans* in 1989 and followed this with *Benchmarks for Science Literacy* in 1993. *Benchmarks* recommends what students should know and be able to do by the end of grades 2, 5, 8, and 12. Project 2061 clearly states that *Benchmarks* is not a curriculum, but a tool for designing successful curricula.

The National Research Council (NRC) utilized *Science for All Americans* and *Benchmarks* to develop the National Science Education Standards (NSES), which were published in 1996. The NSES are organized into six categories (Content, Teaching, Assessment, Professional Development, Program, and System) to help schools establish the conditions necessary to achieve scientific literacy for all students.

Michael Padilla, the lead author of *Science Explorer*, guided one of six teams of teachers whose work led to the publication of *Benchmarks*. He also was a contributing writer of the National Science Education Standards. Under his guidance, *Science Explorer* has implemented these standards through its inquiry approach, a focus on student learning of important concepts and skills, and teacher support aligned with the NSES teaching standards.

Neither *Benchmarks* nor the NSES requires a single, uniform national curriculum, and in fact there is a great diversity nationwide in science curricula. The correlations that follow are designed to help you utilize the *Science Explorer* program to meet your particular curriculum needs.

National Science Education Standards Correlation

National Science Education Standards	*Discoveries* Sections	*Investigations* Sections	*Adventures* Sections
CONTENT STANDARD A: SCIENCE AS INQUIRY			
A-1 Identify Questions that Can Be Answered Through Scientific Investigations.	5.2, 5.3, 8.2, 8.4, 9.1; Chapter Projects: 1, 9, 12, 15	3.3, 3.4, 4.1, 4.3, 5.2, 5.3, 6.1; Chapter Project: 20	8.1
A-2 Design and Conduct a Scientific Investigation.	Introduction, 3.2, 6.1, 8.4, 10.2, 11.3, 17.4, 21.3; Chapter Projects: 1, 3, 5, 9, 15	Introduction, 8.1, 12.1, 13.2, 13.3, 14.1, 14.3, 16.2, 18.1; Chapter Projects: 1, 2, 8, 15, 18	Introduction, 4.2, 15.6, 16.1, 19.1, 21.1, 22.1, 23.2, 23.4; Chapter Project: 20
A-3 Use Appropriate Tools and Techniques to Gather, Analyze, and Interpret Data.	Introduction, 2.2, 2.3, 3.3, 4.2, 18.1, 18.2, 20.1	Introduction, 1.1, 2.4, 2.5; Chapter Projects: 13, 17	Introduction, 1.1, 4.1, 12.2, 14.1, 14.3, 15.5, 16.3, 17.3, 18.4, 19.2, 22.2; Chapter Projects: 4, 14, 15, 17, 18, 19, 23
A-4 Develop Descriptions, Explanations, Predictions, and Models Using Evidence.	13.2, 21.4, 22.4; Chapter Projects: 14, 22	7.2, 11.1–11.5, 17.2, 17.4, 18.2, 19.1, 19.2, 21.4; Chapter Projects: 5, 11, 19, 21	1.2, 2.2, 2.3, 3.1, 3.3, 11.4, 11.5, 13.1, 13.3, 20.1, 20.2, 21.2; Chapter Projects: 1, 2, 3, 11, 16
A-5 Think Critically and Logically to Make the Relationships between Evidence and Explanations.	Introduction, 7.4, 12.2, 13.2, 19.1, 19.3, 20.2; Chapter Project: 2	Introduction, 8.4	Introduction, 17.1; Chapter Project: 10
A-6 Recognize and Analyze Alternative Explanations and Predictions.	Chapter Projects: 11		10.3
A-7 Communicate Scientific Procedures and Explanations.	Introduction, 10.2; Chapter Projects: 1, 6	Introduction, 10.1; Chapter Projects: 1, 20	Introduction, 6.3, 8.3; Chapter Projects: 8, 13, 22
A-8 Use Mathematics in All Aspects of Scientific Inquiry.	4.1, 5.2, 5.3, 14.2, 14.3, 17.1, 17.4	7.4, 9.4, 22.2	1.2, 4.1, 4.2, 6.3; Chapter Projects: 1, 4

National Science Education Standards Correlation

National Science Education Standards	*Discoveries* Sections	*Investigations* Sections	*Adventures* Sections
CONTENT STANDARD B: PHYSICAL SCIENCE			
B-1 Properties and Changes of Properties in Matter	13.1, 13.2, 14.1, 14.4, 15.1, 15.2, 16.1, 16.2, 18.1, 18.3, 21.3	6.1, 10.1, 10.2, 11.3, 11.4, 12.1–12.3, 22.1	6.3, 10.4, 14.1, 14.2, 16.1–16.3
B-2 Motions and Forces	9.4, 11.2	11.3, 13.2, 13.3	4.1, 4.3, 5.1–5.4
B-3 Transfer of Energy	6.1, 6.2, 14.4, 17.1–17.3, 18.1–18.4, 19.1, 19.2, 21.1, 21.2, 21.4; Chapter Projects: 17, 18	10.1, 10.3, 13.1, 15.2, 16.1, 16.3, 16.4, 19.3, 19.5, 21.2; Chapter Project: 16	6.1–6.3, 8.3, 8.4, 9.1–9.3, 10.1–10.4, 11.2, 11.5, 12.1, 12.2, 17.1, 17.2, 23.1, 23.3; Chapter Projects: 6, 9
CONTENT STANDARD C: LIFE SCIENCE			
C-1 Structure and Function in Living Systems	2.1–2.3, 3.1–3.4, 4.2, 4.3, 5.1, 5.3, 6.1–6.4, 7.1–7.4, 8.2, 10.1–10.4, 11.1–11.4, 16.3; Chapter Projects: 3, 5, 6	3.1–3.4, 4.3, 4.4, 5.1, 5.2, 6.1, 6.3, 7.2, 8.1, 12.4, 14.4, 16.4	1.3, 1.4, 6.4
C-2 Reproduction and Heredity	1.1, 6.3, 6.4, 7.1–7.3; Chapter Project: 7	9.2	1.1, 1.3, 1.4, 2.1–2.3; Chapter Projects: 1, 2
C-3 Regulation and Behavior	2.4, 12.1–12.4	8.2, 8.3, 9.1, 9.2, 14.5; Chapter Project: 8	
C-4 Populations and Ecosystems	3.1, 3.2, 4.2, 5.2, 8.3, 9.3, 12.1–12.3, 19.2, 19.4, 22.2, 22.3, 22	2.1–2.5, 18.2; Chapter Project: 2	15.4, 19.2
C-5 Diversity and Adaptations of Organisms	4.1, 4.2, 5.1, 5.2, 6.1, 6.3, 6.4, 8.1, 8.3, 8.4, 9.1–9.5, 10.1–10.4, 11.1–11.4, 12.2, 12.3; Chapter Projects: 1, 8		3.1–3.3, 20.3, 20.4; Chapter Project: 20
CONTENT STANDARD D: EARTH AND SPACE SCIENCE			
D-1 Structure of the Earth System	19.1–19.4, 22.1	2.2, 2.5, 11.5, 13.4, 18.1–18.3, 19.1, 19.2, 21.3; Chapter Projects: 18, 19	4.2, 8.2, 11.1, 11.4, 11.5, 12.1, 12.2, 13.1–13.3, 14.2, 15.1–15.6, 16.4, 17.3–17.5, 18.1–18.3, 19.1, 19.2, 21.1, 22.1, 22.2
D-2 Earth's History	10.5	20.4	3.2, 11.3, 11.5, 19.3; Chapter Project: 3
D-3 Earth in the Solar System	21.2	20.1, 20.2, 20.4, 21.1, 22.5	5.3, 5.5, 13.4, 17.1, 17.3, 17.4, 19.1

National Science Education Standards Correlation

National Science Education Standards	*Discoveries* Sections	*Investigations* Sections	*Adventures* Sections
CONTENT STANDARD E: SCIENCE AND TECHNOLOGY			
E-1 Abilities of Technological Design	13.4, 16.3; Chapter Projects: 16, 18, 20, 21	10.4, 15.4, 20.3, 22.1; Chapter Projects: 12, 14, 16	5.3, 7.2, 7.3, 9.2, 10.1, 10.4, 16.2; Chapter Projects: 6, 7, 9, 12, 21
E-2 Understandings about Science and Technology	2.1, 17.4, 20.1, 20.4, 22.1, 22.4	15.3, 15.4, 17.2–17.4; Chapter Project: 15	2.2, 2.3, 14.3, 15.2, 15.3, 15.5, 15.6, 23.1–23.3
CONTENT STANDARD F: SCIENCE IN PERSONAL AND SOCIAL PERSPECTIVES			
F-1 Personal Health	16.3, 18.2, 20.1, 20.3; Chapter Project: 16	4.1, 5.4, 6.2, 7.5, 8.4, 14.4	18.2, 18.3, 21.3, 22.1, 22.2
F-2 Populations, Resources, and Environments	7.5, 20.1, 22.4		10.2, 20.3
F-3 Natural Hazards			12.3, 13.2. 9.1, 9.4, 18.3, 21.1
F-4 Risks and Benefits		8.2, 19.2, 14.4, 15.2	18.3, 22.3; Chapter Projects: 13, 22
F-5 Science and Technology in Society	3.4, 19.1, 20.2, 20.3; Chapter Project: 19	1.2, 10.4, 14.5, 16.518.1	2.3, 7.3, 7.412.3, 12.4, 18.4, 19.4, 20.1, 21.2; Chapter Projects: 12, 21
CONTENT STANDARD G: HISTORY AND NATURE OF SCIENCE			
G-1 Science as a Human Endeavor	Introduction, 15.1	Introduction	Introduction
G-2 Nature of Science	Introduction	Introduction, 11.2	Introduction
G-3 History of Science	1.1–1.3, 15.1	5.4, 17.2, 21.1, 22.1	1.1, 1.2, 3.1, 9.4, 20.1

Benchmarks Correlation

Benchmarks for Science Literacy	*Discoveries* Chapters	*Investigations* Chapters	*Adventures* Chapters
1 THE NATURE OF SCIENCE			
1A The Scientific World View		Introduction, 4, 7, 10, 15, 16, 21	10, 11
1B Scientific Inquiry	Introduction, 1–6, 8, 9, 12–17, 19–22	Introduction, 1, 2, 5, 8, 12, 13, 17–19	Introduction, 1–3, 11, 13, 15–23
1C The Scientific Enterprise	Introduction, 2	7, 17, 22	Introduction, 1, 3, 6, 8, 9, 11, 20
2 THE NATURE OF MATHEMATICS			
2A Patterns and Relationships		11, 13	
2B Mathematics, Science, and Technology		1	7
2C Mathematical Inquiry		14, 21, 22	9, 10
3 THE NATURE OF TECHNOLOGY			
3A Technology and Science	2, 12, 20, 22	10, 16, 17, 20, 22	2, 4, 11, 12, 14–18, 20–23
3B Design and Systems	17, 18	20	5, 6, 9, 10, 12, 22, 23
3C Issues in Technology	3, 4, 7, 13, 18, 19, 20, 22	5, 14, 15, 18	2, 16, 19–23
4 THE PHYSICAL SETTING			
4A The Universe		13, 21, 22	13
4B The Earth	17, 19–21	2, 17–21	16–22
4C Processes that Shape the Earth	21, 22	2, 18–20	3, 11–15, 19
4D Structure of Matter	13–16, 18, 21	6, 10–12	6, 10, 14, 16
4E Energy Transformations	14, 15, 18, 21	10, 11, 15, 19, 21, 22	7, 9–11, 16, 17
4F Motion	9	13, 14, 16, 20	4, 5, 12, 17
4G Forces of Nature	15	21	8
5 THE LIVING ENVIRONMENT			
5A Diversity of Life	1, 4–11, 22		3, 15, 20
5B Heredity			1, 2
5C Cells	11	3, 8, 16	1
5D Interdependence of Life	8–10, 19, 22	1, 2, 18	19
5E Flow of Matter and Energy	16, 17	2, 4, 6, 12	
5F Evolution of Life	10, 11		3
6 THE HUMAN ORGANISM			
6A Human Identity			
6B Human Development		3, 9	
6C Basic Functions	16	3–6, 8, 12, 14	
6D Learning		8	
6E Physical Health	3, 16	4–8	18, 22
6F Mental Health			
7 HUMAN SOCIETY			
7A Cultural Effects on Behavior		6	
7B Group Behavior			
7C Social Change		1	18
7D Social Trade-Offs	20	19	12, 13, 18, 22

Benchmarks Correlation			
Benchmarks for Science Literacy	*Discoveries* **Chapters**	*Investigations* **Chapters**	*Adventures* **Chapters**
7 HUMAN SOCIETY *(continued)*			
7E Political and Economic Systems			
7F Social Conflict			
7G Global Interdependence			
8 THE DESIGNED WORLD			
8A Agriculture	7		
8B Materials and Manufacturing			
8C Energy Sources and Use	17, 18, 20, 21		7–10, 16, 23
8D Communication		15, 16, 20	
8E Information Processing		17	
8F Health Technology			
9 THE MATHEMATICAL WORLD			
9A Numbers			
9B Symbolic Relationships	14, 17, 22	13	4, 7, 19
9C Shapes			
9D Uncertainty			1
9E Reasoning			
10 HISTORICAL PERSPECTIVES			
10A Displacing the Earth from the Center of the Universe			4
10B Uniting the Heavens and Earth			
10C Relating Matter & Energy and Time & Space			
10D Extending Time			
10E Moving the Continents			
10F Understanding Fire			
10G Splitting the Atom			
10H Explaining the Diversity of Life			
10I Discovering Germs		7	
10J Harnessing Power	17, 18		
11 COMMON THEMES			
11A Systems		5, 14, 22	7, 9
11B Models	10, 13, 19, 21, 22	11, 21	6, 12, 13
11C Constancy and Change	7, 8	3, 6, 10, 12, 13, 20	12
11D Scale			
12 HABITS OF MIND			
12A Values and Attitudes		12	10
12B Computation and Estimation	14	17	4, 12
12C Manipulation and Observation			5, 17
12D Communication Skills	Introduction, 1, 4, 5, 9–11, 13, 19	Introduction, 4, 7	Introduction, 2, 5, 13, 16, 19, 22
12E Critical-Response Skills			5

Inquiry Skills Chart

The Prentice Hall *Science Explorer* program provides comprehensive teaching, practice, and assessment of science skills, with an emphasis on the process skills necessary for inquiry. The chart lists the skills covered in the program and cites the page numbers where each skill is covered.

Basic Process SKILLS

	Student Text: Projects and Labs	Student Text: Activities	Student Text: Caption and Review Questions
Observing	72, 84–85, 148–149, 268–269, 294–295, 309, 372–373, 380, 424, 440–441, 449, 472, 511, 526–527, 639, 656, 662, 686, 720, 789	64, 70, 116, 142, 150, 189, 230, 246, 248, 256, 296, 327, 331, 361, 365, 396, 398, 450, 457, 518, 551, 581, 597, 610, 672, 715, 730	98, 263, 349, 421, 453, 475, 567, 587, 599, 628, 709, 719
Inferring	17, 130–131, 148–149, 254–255, 268–269, 314–315, 372–373, 380, 394–395, 424, 472, 526–527, 618–619, 649, 678	18, 34, 50, 57, 81, 83, 89, 91, 114, 132, 146, 195, 206, 262, 278, 282, 288, 310, 348, 357, 512, 525, 546, 565, 593, 613, 615, 632, 637, 657, 663, 706, 738, 749, 753	22, 74, 105, 155, 157, 173, 178, 180, 185, 207, 232, 234, 274, 341, 362, 364, 383, 389, 408, 423, 429, 447, 461, 475, 519, 521, 667, 674, 699
Predicting	17, 32–33, 49, 84–85, 141, 214–215, 254–255, 286–287, 314–315, 385, 472, 539, 573, 590–591, 745	26, 31, 41, 127, 153, 166, 216, 298, 375, 386, 404, 520, 529, 679	46, 56, 75, 104, 136, 154, 156, 169, 188, 201, 235, 272, 275, 307, 333, 341, 359, 371, 379, 383, 393, 416, 417, 423, 447, 474, 514, 524, 528, 536, 558, 562, 564, 596, 603, 636, 640, 676, 690, 713, 726, 744, 756, 758
Classifying	394–395, 419, 694–695	78, 97, 225, 266, 319, 387, 453, 579, 627, 691	15, 31, 38, 133, 187, 234, 247, 306, 307, 341, 382, 416, 447, 458, 474, 536, 564, 570, 571, 580, 606, 629, 679, 703, 751, 758, 759
Making Models	17, 32–33, 49, 72, 77, 84–85, 141, 175, 182–183, 203, 228–229, 245, 268–269, 314–315, 347, 373–373, 380, 385, 394–395, 440–441, 539, 694–695	54, 96, 252, 291, 363, 369, 423, 426, 435, 550, 716	219, 290, 307, 607
Communicating	17, 49, 77, 113, 141, 175, 203, 277, 309, 347, 385, 419, 449, 539, 609, 649, 678, 705, 729	69, 594, 654, 655, 710	138, 172, 200, 234, 382, 416, 446, 474, 536, 570, 606, 642, 676, 702, 726, 758
Measuring	113, 124–125, 130–131, 160–161, 228–229, 309, 449, 459, 472, 516–517, 526–527, 539, 544–545, 547, 552–553, 618–619, 714, 720, 752	189, 257, 391, 540, 709	117, 139, 401, 643
Calculating	77, 130–131, 203, 228–229, 537, 720	92, 158, 292, 406, 567, 582, 660, 749	27, 29, 74, 105, 139, 173, 201, 235, 293, 571, 651, 727, 759
Creating Data Tables	449, 511, 539, 544–545, 609, 649, 729	353	
Graphing	148–149, 539, 609, 618–619, 630–631	651, 689, 722, 732	235, 537, 571, 677, 703

Inquiry Skills Chart

Advanced Process SKILLS

	Student Text: Projects and Labs	Student Text: Activities	Student Text: Caption and Review Questions
Posing Questions		324, 360, 442, 466	4, 378, 405, 444, 607
Developing Hypotheses	24–25, 190–191, 286–287, 440–441, 544–559, 609, 686	162, 176, 178, 204, 211, 300, 316, 420, 425, 514, 574, 721, 737	6, 200, 261, 436, 447, 617, 677, 703, 727
Designing Experiments	11, 182–183, 277, 294–295, 656, 735, 752	52	173, 200, 275
Controlling Variables	11, 141, 160–161, 182–183, 214–215, 245, 618–619, 686, 714		275, 307
Forming Operational Definitions	160–161, 745	39, 126, 168, 208, 270, 620, 650, 696	554
Interpreting Data	24–25, 32–33, 62–63, 347, 402–403, 424, 516–517, 552–553, 590–591, 604, 609, 630–631, 714, 729	29, 98, 318, 548, 561, 600, 687	75, 105, 139, 193, 235, 456, 513, 607, 643, 677, 692, 727, 759
Drawing Conclusions	11, 24–25, 62–63, 72, 102, 214–215, 336–337, 402–403, 419, 459, 472, 544–545, 552–553, 604, 630–631, 662, 678, 694–695, 729	98, 155, 192, 259, 280, 374, 410, 417, 639	75, 105, 201, 274, 370, 434, 454, 475, 523, 534, 571

Critical Thinking SKILLS

	Student Text: Projects and Labs	Student Text: Activities	Student Text: Caption and Review Questions
Comparing and Contrasting	32–33, 449, 539, 573, 649	98	74, 80, 96, 104, 115, 119, 159, 167, 172, 181, 187, 192, 213, 251, 271, 274, 285, 299, 323, 327, 340, 351, 356, 382, 411, 416, 438, 444, 446, 451, 474, 570, 606, 624, 626, 642, 655, 661, 693, 726, 742, 758
Applying Concepts	49, 254–255, 268–269, 277, 294–295, 314–315, 342, 385, 402–403, 440–441, 472, 516–517, 552–553, 590–591, 630–631	70	10, 19, 23, 35, 46, 55, 66, 74, 88, 104, 138, 144, 147, 163, 170, 172, 181, 187, 189, 194, 198, 200, 201, 207, 210, 234, 250, 252, 253, 274, 292, 303, 304, 306, 318, 325, 335, 340, 359, 367, 399, 416, 446, 457, 474, 515, 530, 536, 543, 549, 556, 558, 568, 575, 582, 589, 595, 606, 612, 629, 638, 654, 664, 679, 693, 702, 712, 723, 726, 736, 756
Interpreting Diagrams, Graphs, Photographs, and Maps	573, 590–591		7, 8, 21, 28, 36, 40, 51, 53, 75, 87, 90, 92, 105, 127, 128, 166, 170, 181, 204, 209, 224, 248, 267, 274, 285, 293, 301, 313, 317, 368, 383, 397, 413, 417, 462, 464, 518, 537, 541, 555, 578, 580, 586, 589, 602, 607, 611, 636, 643, 658, 663, 667, 707, 711, 733, 734, 749, 750
Relating Cause and Effect	385, 705	460	15, 44, 58, 104, 132, 146, 198, 200, 217, 218, 234, 356, 371, 382, 387, 401, 416, 439, 446, 464, 470, 474, 536, 570, 606, 621, 642, 676, 685, 717, 719, 736
Making Generalizations			65, 82, 134, 138, 143, 196, 226, 382, 413, 416, 446, 458, 671, 676, 724, 726, 740
Making Judgments	590–591, 705		15, 68, 70, 101, 606, 642, 676, 700, 702, 758
Problem Solving	326–327		15, 46, 61, 74, 123, 129, 136, 138, 152, 159, 172, 177, 274, 306, 330, 340, 409, 570, 702, 726, 758

Inquiry Skills Chart

	Student Text: Projects and Labs	Student Text: Activities	Student Text: Caption and Review Questions
Information Organizing SKILLS			
Concept Maps			73, 137, 273, 339, 415, 445, 535, 569, 641, 675, 725
Compare/ Contrast Tables			45, 171, 233, 605, 701, 757
Venn Diagrams			305, 473
Flowcharts			103, 199
Cycle Diagrams			381

Master Materials List

To make ordering supplies easier, the Master Materials List cross-references by chapter and section, the materials needed for activities. You can use the Materials List CD-ROM, which Science Kit and Boreal Laboratories developed to create an electronic list of the materials. Science Kit produces both Consumable Kits and Nonconsumable Kits for *Science Explorer* activities. For more information call 1-800-848-9500.

Consumable Materials

*	Description	Qty per class	Textbook Section(s)	*	Description	Qty per class	Textbook Section(s)
C	Aluminum Foil, Roll, 12" × 25'	2	8-3 (SYS), 8-3 (Lab), 9-1 (Lab), 10-4 (DIS), 23-2 (Lab)	C	Candle, Warming	5	14-2 (DIS), 16-1 (DIS), 16-2 (DIS), 17-2 (DIS)
SS	Apples	10	10-4 (Lab)	C	Candle, White, 10 cm × 1.75 cm	10	11-5 (Lab)
C	Bag, Paper, 10 cm × 20 cm × 7.5 cm	20	1-2 (Lab), 2-1 (TT)	SS	Cardboard	1	4-1 (Lab)
C	Bag, Plastic Zip Lip, 6" × 8"	50	16-4 (DIS), 17-1 (DIS), 21-2 (Lab), 23-2 (DIS)	C	Cardboard, Corrugated, 10 cm × 20 cm	10	17-3 (Lab), 18-1 (DIS)
C	Bags, Plastic (Sandwich), Pkg/80	1	19-4 (TT)	C	Cards, Index, Blank, 3" × 5", Pkg/100	1	(INT), 2-2 (Lab), 15-6 (DIS)
C	Baking Soda, 454 g	1	13-2 (TT)	C	Charcoal Pieces, 16 oz	1	22-3 (DIS)
C	Balloon, Round, 9", Pkg/35	1	6-1 (DIS), 9-1 (DIS), 13-3 (DIS)	C	Cheesecloth, 2 M Piece	1	21-2 (Lab)
C	Balloons, Round, 15", Pkg/8	2	16-3 (DIS), 16-3 (Lab)	C	Clay, Modeling (Cream) lb (water-resistant)	4	6-3 (DIS), 9-2 (DIS), 10-1 (Lab), 10-2 (DIS), 10-4 (Lab), 11-5 (Lab), 15-5 (TT), 16-1 (DIS). 16-2 (DIS), 16-3 (TT), 16-3 (Lab)
C	Battery, Alkaline, Size D	10	8-3 (DIS), 8-3 (SYS), 8-3 (Lab), 8-4 (DIS), 9-2 (DIS), 9-2 (Lab), 9-3 (DIS), 9-3 (SYS), 9-4 (DIS), 10-1 (DIS), 10-1 (Lab), 19-1 (DIS), 22-2 (DIS)	C	Clay, Modeling (four colors) lb (Red, Blue, Green, Yellow)	2	12-1 (Lab)
				SS	Cracker	5	7-4 (DIS)
SS	Bird Seed, 1 lb	1	3-1 (TT)	SS	Crayons	5	15-6 (Lab)
SS	Bread, Slice	10	15-3 (DIS)	C	Cup, Paper, 200 mL, Pkg/25	1	8-3 (Lab), 21-1 (Lab), 23-3 (Lab)
SS	Bulb, Fluorescent, 15 Watt, Pkg	5	23-4 (DIS)				
C	Bulb, Incandescent, 100 Watt	5	(INT), 17-1 (Lab), 19-1 (Lab)	C	Cup, Styrofoam, 6 oz., Pkg/25	1	8-1 (SYS), 9-1 (Lab), 23-3 (Lab)
SS	Bulb, Incandescent, 60 Watt, Pkg	5	23-4 (DIS)	C	Cupric Sulfate, 100 g	1	14-3 (Lab)
SS	Butter	1	15-6 (Lab)	C	Cups, Plastic, Clear, 300 mL, Pkg/50	1	6-3 (DIS), 18-3 (DIS), 22-3 (DIS), 23-3 (Lab)

KEY: **DIS**: Discover; **SYS**: Sharpen Your Skills; **TT**: Try This; **Lab**: Lab

Quantities based on 5 lab groups per class

* Items designated **C** are in the Consumable Kit, **N** are in the Nonconsumable Kit, and **SS** are School Supplied.

Master Materials List

Consumable Materials (continued)

*	Description	Qty per class	Textbook Section(s)	*	Description	Qty per class	Textbook Section(s)
C	Cups, Plastic, Clear, 9 oz, Pkg/50	1	3-1 (TT), 3-2 (TT), 10-4 (DIS), 11-2 (DIS), 13-3 (Lab), 16-1 (TT), 20-3 (DIS), 20-4 (DIS), 22-1 (TT), 22-2 (DIS), 22-2 (TT), 22-3 (DIS)	C	Lamp, Miniature, #14 (2.47 V), Pkg/12	2	8-3 (DIS), 8-3 (SYS), 8-3 (Lab), 9-2 (DIS), 9-2 (Lab), 9-3 (DIS), 9-3 (SYS), 9-4 (DIS), 10-3 (DIS)
				C	Lead (Graphite Rod) 4", Pkg/6	2	8-3 (SYS), 9-2 (Lab)
C	Detergent, Household, 14.7 oz (dish detergent)	1	8-2 (DIS), 18-2 (DIS), 22-1 (Lab)	C	Lid for 200 mL Paper Cup	25	23-3 (Lab)
C	Epsom Salt, 500 g	1	14-1 (TT)	C	Lid for Styrofoam Cup, 6 oz	25	23-3 (Lab)
C	Filter Paper, 15 cm Diam, Pkg/100	1	20-4 (DIS), 22-3 (DIS)	C	Lid, Clear, for 300 mL Cup	50	23-3 (Lab)
C	Filters, Coffee, Box/100	1	16-1 (Lab)	C	Limewater Solution Mix, 5 g, Calcium Hydroxide, To Prepare 1 Gallon	1	16-1 (TT)
C	Food Coloring, Blue 30 mL In Dropper Bottle	1	18-1 (DIS)	SS	Map, World Outline Showing Longitude and Latitude	5	13-1 (Lab)
C	Food Coloring, Dark Red, 30 mL In Dropper Bottle	2	11-2 (DIS), 13-1 (TT), 13-3 (Lab), 18-1 (DIS), 21-2 (Lab), 22-2 (TT), 22-2 (Lab)	C	Marker, Black, Permanent	5	1-2 (Lab), 6-1 (Lab), 6-3 (DIS), 7-3 (Lab), 12-1 (Lab)
C	Forks, Plastic, Pkg/24	1	6-4 (DIS)	SS	Marker, Black, Soluble	5	17-3 (DIS), 20-4 (DIS)
SS	Fresh Fruit, Assortment	5	3-2 (TT)	SS	Markers	10	2-2 (Lab), 3-1 (Lab), 11-4 (Lab)
C	Gelatin, Box of 4 Packets	2	13-3 (Lab)	C	Marking Pencil, Black Wax	5	1-2 (Lab), 22-1 (Lab)
SS	Glue	5	16-3 (Lab), 23-2 (Lab)	SS	Marshmallows, Bag	1	23-2 (Lab)
SS	Graph Paper, Metric Coordinates, pk/100, 1 cm grid	1	2-1 (DIS), 17-1 (Lab), 17-2 (TT), 19-1 (Lab), 19-2 (Lab), 20-2 (DIS), 21-2 (DIS), 22-3 (SYS)	C	Matches, Wood Safety, Box/30	5	14-2 (DIS), 16-1 (DIS), 16-2 (DIS), 17-2 (DIS)
				SS	Milk	1	22-2 (DIS)
SS	Honey	1	4-2 (DIS)	SS	Newspaper	6	11-3 (TT), 20-1 (Lab), 21-1 (Lab), 21-2 (Lab)
C	Hydrochloric Acid, 1 M, 500 mL	1	15-4 (DIS)	C	Oil, Vegetable, 16 oz	1	22-1 (Lab)
SS	Ice Cubes, Bucket	3	14-2 (DIS), 17-4 (DIS), 17-5 (DIS)	C	Paint, Tempera Red, 8 oz	1	15-6 (Lab)
SS	Ink	5	15-6 (Lab)	SS	Paper Towel Roll	1	(INT), 6-3 (Lab), 10-4 (DIS)
C	Ink Pad, Washable (Black)	5	2-3 (DIS)	SS	Paper, Construction, Asst, Pkg/50	1	3-1 (Lab)
C	Juice, Lemon, 15 oz	1	22-1 (TT)				
C	Knives, Plastic, Pkg/24	1	12-1 (Lab), 13-3 (Lab)	SS	Paper, Construction, Black, Pkg/50	1	14-1 (TT), 17-3 (TT), 19-1 (Lab), 19-4 (DIS)

KEY: **DIS**: Discover; **SYS**: Sharpen Your Skills; **TT**: Try This; **Lab**: Lab
* Items designated **C** are in the Consumable Kit, **N** are in the Nonconsumable Kit, and **SS** are School Supplied.

Consumable Materials (continued)

*	Description	Qty per class	Textbook Section(s)	*	Description	Qty per class	Textbook Section(s)
SS	Paper, Oaktag, Sheet	15	23-2 (Lab)	C	Salt, Non-Iodized, 737 g	2	6-3 (Lab), 10-4 (DIS), 14-1 (TT), 17-5 (DIS), 18-1 (DIS), 22-1 (Lab)
SS	Paper, Sheet	70	1-3 (DIS), 2-3 (DIS), 3-1 (SYS), 7-3 (TT), 8-2 (TT), 9-1 (Lab), 11-4 (Lab), 11-5 (DIS), 13-3 (Lab), 15-3 (DIS), 17-1 (DIS), 20-1 (DIS)	C	Sand, Fine, 2.5 kg	2	13-3 (DIS), 17-1 (Lab), 21-1 (DIS)
				C	Seeds, Radish, 15 g	1	22-1 (Lab)
				C	Seeds, Sunflower, 30 g	1	3-1 (DIS), 21-1 DIS)
C	Paper, Tissue, Assorted Colors/20, 20" × 30"	1	9-1 (SYS)	SS	Sequins, Pkg	1	15-5 (TT)
SS	Paper, Tracing, 9" × 12", Pad/50	1	18-2 (Lab)	SS	Sod, Small Square	5	21-1 (Lab)
C	Pebbles/Gravel, 1 kg	3	21-2 (Lab)	SS	Soda Cans, Empty, with Tabs Attached	30	6-1 (Lab)
SS	Pen	5	12-2 (TT), 17-3 (Lab)	C	Soil, Potting, 4 lb	1	22-1 (Lab)
SS	Pencil	5	7-2 (TT), 7-3 (TT), 8-1 (SYS), 8-1 (Lab), 9-1 (Lab), 12-2 (TT), 14-3 (DIS), 16-3 (Lab), 17-3 (DIS), 17-3 (TT), 19-1 (Lab), 20-4 (DIS), 21-1 (DIS)	C	Soil, Sandy, 2.5 kg	2	21-1 (DIS), 21-1 (Lab), 21-2 (Lab)
				C	Splints, Wooden, 15 cm, Pkg/25	1	17-3 (Lab)
				C	Spoons, Plastic, Pkg/24	1	4-2 (DIS), 6-3 (DIS), 6-4 (DIS), 14-2 (DIS), 21-1 (DIS), 22-2 (TT)
SS	Pencils, Colored, Pkg/12	5	13-1 (Lab), 13-3 (Lab), 18-2 (Lab), 19-2 (Lab), 20-2 (Lab)	C	Sticks, Craft, Pkg/50	1	1-3 (DIS), 8-1 (Lab), 12-1 (DIS)
SS	Pens, Variety	40	3-3 (DIS)	C	Straws, Plastic, Flexible, Pkg/50	1	6-3 (TT)
SS	Perfume, Bottle	1	22-1 (DIS)	C	Straws, Plastic, Pkg/250	1	5-4 (DIS), 6-1 (DIS), 12-3 (DIS), 13-3 (DIS), 16-1 (TT), 16-3 (TT), 16-3 (Lab), 17-3 (TT)
C	pH Test Paper-Wide Range, 100/Vial	5	22-1 (TT)				
C	Phenyl Salicylate (Salol) 100g	1	14-2 (DIS)	C	String, Cotton, 200 ft	1	5-1 (Lab), 5-5 (DIS), 7-2 (TT), 15-5 (TT), 17-1 (Lab)
C	Plastic Wrap Roll, 50 sq ft	1	19-2 (TT), 19-4 (DIS), 20-1 (Lab), 21-2 (Lab)				
C	Plates, Paper, 9", Pkg/50	1	3-1 (TT), 4-2 (DIS), 20-3 (DIS)	C	Sugar, Granulated, 454 g	1	6-3 (DIS), 22-2 (TT)
				SS	Suncsreen, 2 Different SPFs	2	19-4 (TT)
C	Plates, Styrofoam, 9", Pkg/35	1	9-1 (TT), 9-1 (Lab)	C	Sunprint Paper, 12 Sheets	2	19-4 (TT)
SS	Raisins, Box	2	3-1 (TT), 13-2 (TT)	C	Tagboard, 9" × 12", Pkg/25	1	8-1 (Lab), 16-3 (Lab)
C	Rubber Band, Asst. Colors & Sizes, 1-1/2 oz Pkg	1	5-4 (DIS), 7-1 (DIS), 16-1 (Lab), 16-3 (Lab), 16-4 (DIS), 19-2 (TT), 21-2 (Lab)	C	Tape, Adding Machine Roll, 2-1/4" Width (100 ft length)	1	12-2 (TT), 19-1 (DIS)
				C	Tape, Cassette, Blank	1	11-4 (TT)
				C	Tape, Duct, 10 yds	1	8-3 (Lab)

KEY: **DIS**: Discover; **SYS**: Sharpen Your Skills; **TT**: Try This; **Lab**: Lab
* Items designated **C** are in the Consumable Kit, **N** are in the Nonconsumable Kit, and **SS** are School Supplied.

Master Materials List

Consumable Materials (continued)

*	Description	Qty per class	Textbook Section(s)
SS	Tape, Masking 3/4" × 60 yd	5	1-2 (TT), 4-1 (Lab), 4-2 (DIS), 4-3 (DIS), 5-1 (TT), 5-1 (Lab), 5-3 (Lab), 5-4 (TT), 7-2 (Lab), 7-3 (TT), 8-1 (Lab), 8-2 (SYS), 9-1 (TT), 9-2 (DIS), 11-1 (DIS), 11-5 (DIS), 12-1 (SYS), 12-3 (DIS), 13-3 (DIS), 16-3 (Lab), 17-2 (DIS), 17-3 (DIS), 17-3 (TT), 17-3 (Lab), 19-1 (DIS), 19-1 (Lab), 20-4 (DIS), 22-1 (Lab), 23-2 (Lab)
SS	Tape, Transparent Dispenser Roll	1	11-4 (TT)
SS	Tea, Herbal, Cup	5	22-3 (DIS)
C	Thread, White, 200 yd Spool	1	5-1 (TT), 17-2 (DIS)
SS	Tissues, Facial	5	12-4 (DIS)
C	Toothpicks, Round, Pkg/250	1	17-3 (Lab)
SS	Trash Bag, Filled	5	21-2 (DIS)
C	Tray, Styrofoam, 8" × 10"	2	13-1 (TT)
C	Vinegar, 500 mL	1	10-4 (DIS), 13-2 (TT), 22-1 (Lab)
C	Wax Paper, Roll, 75 sq ft	1	8-3 (SYS)

Nonconsumable Materials

*	Description	Qty per class	Textbook Section(s)
N	Alligator Clip with 3/8" Jaw	10	8-3 (SYS), 9-2 (Lab), 9-4 (DIS)
SS	Aluminum Can, Empty	5	9-1 (DIS)
SS	Appliances, Electrical	5	10-3 (SYS)
SS	Atlas	5	11-5 (DIS)
N	Ball, Inflatable (Beach Ball)	5	17-3 (DIS)
N	Ball, Styrofoam, 1"	5	8-2 (DIS)
N	Balls, Table Tennis, Pkg/6	1	5-1 (TT)
SS	Bar Codes, Set	5	2-3 (Lab)
SS	Basin, Large	5	6-1 (Lab)
N	Battery Holder w/Fahnestock Clips, D-Cell	10	8-3 (DIS), 8-3 (SYS), 8-4 (DIS), 9-2 (DIS), 9-2 (Lab), 9-3 (DIS), 9-3 (SYS), 9-4 (DIS), 10-1 (DIS)
N	Beads, Plastic, 3/8", Pkg/144 (Assorted Colors)	1	1-2 (Lab), 2-1 (TT)
N	Beaker, 250 mL	5	6-3 (Lab)
N	Beaker, 400 mL	10	14-3 (Lab), 17-1 (Lab), 17-5 (DIS)
N	Beaker, 600 mL	5	6-1 (Lab), 6-3 (Lab), 9-2 (TT), 23-3 (Lab)
N	Bin, C-Thru, 13" × 7-1/4" × 4-1/2" w/Lid	5	18-1 (DIS), 18-3 (DIS)
SS	Board, Flat, about 1.5 m Long	5	4-1 (Lab)
SS	Board, Wood	5	7-3 (Lab)

KEY: **DIS**: Discover; **SYS**: Sharpen Your Skills; **TT**: Try This; **Lab**: Lab
* Items designated **C** are in the Consumable Kit, **N** are in the Nonconsumable Kit, and **SS** are School Supplied.

Nonconsumable Materials (continued)

*	Description	Qty per class	Textbook Section(s)	*	Description	Qty per class	Textbook Section(s)
N	Bolt, Long, Round Head, 10-32, 4"	10	8-4 (DIS), 10-1 (DIS), 10-4 (Lab)	SS	Compass with Pencil	5	12-2 (Lab), 21-2 (SYS)
SS	Book	40	4-1 (Lab), 5-4 (DIS), 7-3 (Lab), 10-1 (DIS), 12-2 (TT), 13-3 (Lab), 15-3 (DIS), 19-1 (Lab), 20-1 (Lab)	N	Compass, Pocket, 40 mm	15	8-2 (SYS), 8-2 (TT), 8-3 (DIS), 9-2 (DIS)
				SS	Container and Lid, Glass	5	23-3 (Lab)
				SS	Container and Lid, Metal	5	23-3 (Lab)
SS	Bottle, 2 L Plastic with Cap	5	6-1 (DIS), 6-2 (DIS), 6-3 (TT), 13-2 (TT), 16-3 (TT), 17-4 (DIS)	N	Cup, Measuring, Polypropylene, 8 oz	5	21-2 (Lab)
N	Bottle, Flint Glass, Narrow Mouth w/Screw Cap, 2 oz	5	13-1 (TT)	N	Cylinder, Graduated, Plastic, 10 mL	5	22-2 (Lab)
N	Bowl, Opaque, 2 L	5	13-3 (Lab), 20-1 (Lab)	N	Cylinder, Graduated, Plastic, 100 mL	5	13-2 (TT), 14-1 (Lab), 14-3 (Lab), 22-1 (Lab), 22-2 (TT), 23-2 (DIS)
N	Bowl, Plastic, Translucent, 16 oz	10	19-2 (TT)				
SS	Box, Plastic	5	13-1 (TT)	SS	Dime	5	5-3 (DIS)
SS	Brick	30	5-1 (Lab), 11-5 (Lab), 21-1 (Lab)	SS	Dish	5	8-2 (DIS)
				N	Dominoes, Box of 28	3	23-3 (DIS)
N	Brick Veneer, 1/4" Thick (used as "mystery rock")	1	15-5 (Lab)	N	Dowel, Wood, 12" × 1/4"	15	23-2 (Lab)
SS	Broomsticks	10	7-3 (DIS)	N	Dowel, Wood, 8" × 1"	5	7-2 (Lab)
SS	Brush, Wire	5	15-6 (Lab)	N	Droppers, Plastic, Pkg/6	1	(INT), 11-2 (DIS), 15-4 (DIS), 15-6 (Lab), 22-2 (DIS)
SS	Calculator, Light-Powered	5	19-2 (Lab), 20-2 (Lab)				
SS	Can, Aluminum	5	14-3 (DIS)	SS	Egg Beater	5	20-1 (Lab)
N	Canister, Film Type w/Snap Cap	15	10-1 (Lab), 11-1 (DIS)	N	Fishing Line, 8 lb Test 100 yd	1	6-1 (Lab)
N	Car, Toy	10	5-1 (DIS), 5-4 (TT)	N	Flashlight, Plastic (Size D)	5	19-1 (DIS), 22-2 (DIS)
N	Chips, Black Opaque, Pkg/100	2	3-1 (SYS)	SS	Foam	5	8-3 (SYS)
N	Chips, White, Pkg/400	1	3-1 (SYS)	N	Forceps, Fine Tip, 115 mm	5	3-1 (TT), 21-1 (DIS), 21-2 (Lab)
N	Cloth, Wool, 12" × 24"	1	9-1 (Lab)				
N	Clothespins, Spring Type, Pkg/18	2	3-1 (TT), 10-4 (Lab)	N	Friction Block 7.5 × 16 × 2 cm	5	7-3 (Lab)
				N	Funnel, Plastic, 3.25"	5	9-2 (TT), 17-5 (SYS), 18-3 (DIS), 22-3 (DIS)
SS	Coins, Various	30	1-2 (DIS), 1-2 (TT), 8-1 (Lab)	SS	Hair Clips	5	3-1 (TT)
				N	Iron Filings (Shaker Top) 8 oz	2	8-1 (TT)
N	Comb, Plastic, 15 cm	5	9-1 (SYS)	N	Jar, Clear, Styrene, 850 mL	15	21-2 (Lab)

KEY: **DIS**: Discover; **SYS**: Sharpen Your Skills; **TT**: Try This; **Lab**: Lab
* Items designated **C** are in the Consumable Kit, **N** are in the Nonconsumable Kit, and **SS** are School Supplied.

Master Materials List

Nonconsumable Materials (continued)

*	Description	Qty per class	Textbook Section(s)	*	Description	Qty per class	Textbook Section(s)
N	Jar, Plastic (Tall) 12 oz	5	17-5 (SYS), 18-2 (DIS)	N	Marbles, 5/8", Pkg/20	5	5-3 (TT), 5-4 (DIS), 18-2 (DIS), 23-3 (TT)
N	Jar, Plastic, 60 mL	5	6-3 (Lab)	SS	Meter Stick, Wood, Plain Ends	5	2-1 (DIS), 4-1 (DIS), 4-1 (Lab), 4-2 (Lab), 4-3 (DIS), 5-1 (Lab), 7-2 (Lab), 17-2 (TT), 17-3 (Lab)
N	Jar, Wide Mouth, 16 oz, Flint Glass	5	16-1 (DIS), 16-3 (Lab), 16-4 (DIS)				
N	Jar, Wide Mouth, 4 oz, Flint Glass	5	16-1 (DIS), 16-2 (DIS)	N	Mineral Kit #1 (11 specimens/ 6 each) (Includes calcite, feldspar, talc, gypsum, pyrite, quartz, fluorite, apatite, microcline, magnetite, graphite)	1	14-1 (DIS), 14-1 (SYS), 14-1 (Lab), 14-3 (DIS)
SS	Key	5	8-3 (SYS)				
SS	Labels from Hazardous Household Products, Assortment	5	21-3 (DIS)				
N	Lid for 12 oz Jar	5	18-2 (DIS)	N	Mineral, Bauxite, Tenpack	1	14-3 (DIS)
N	Lid, Metal 53 mm (60 mL Jar)	5	6-3 (Lab)	N	Mineral, Galena Specimen Pak (6 pieces)	1	14-1 (Lab)
N	Light Socket, Clamp On w/Shade	5	(INT), 17-1 (Lab), 19-1 (Lab)	N	Mineral, Hematite Specimen Pak (6 pieces)	1	14-1 (DIS)
N	Light Socket, Mini w/Fahnstock Clips	20	8-3 (DIS), 8-3 (SYS), 9-2 (DIS), 9-2 (Lab), 9-3 (DIS), 9-3 (SYS), 9-4 (DIS), 10-3 (DIS)	N	Mirrors, Plastic, 7.5 cm × 12.5 cm, Pkg/6	1	1-1 (Lab)
				SS	Mug	5	7-1 (DIS)
N	Magnet, Bar, Alnico w/Marked Poles, 3"	6	8-1 (DIS), 8-1 (TT), 8-1 (Lab), 8-2 (DIS), 8-2 (TT), 10-2 (TT), 11-4 (TT)	N	Nails, 20D, Pkg/15	1	6-1 (Lab)
				N	Nails, 3.75 cm, 4D, 500 g	1	6-1 (Lab)
N	Magnet, Donut, 3 cm OD, 1 cm ID	10	8-1 (SYS), 10-1 (Lab)	N	Nails, 7.5 cm, 10D, 500 g	1	6-1 (Lab), 14-3 (Lab), 15-6 (Lab)
N	Magnet, Horseshoe, 7.5 cm, Pkg/6	1	8-1 (DIS), 10-1 (DIS), 10-2 (DIS)	N	Needles, Metal, Blunt, Pkg/7	1	8-2 (DIS)
				SS	Nickel	5	5-3 (DIS)
N	Magnet, Steel Bar (pair in box) 150 mm × 19 mm × 7 mm	1	10-2 (TT)	SS	Object, Small, Mass about 50 g	5	7-2 (Lab)
				SS	Objects, Assortment	5	7-2 (DIS)
N	Magnifying Glasses, Pkg/6	1	2-3 (Lab), 3-1 (DIS), 13-2 (DIS), 14-1 (TT), 14-2 (DIS), 15-1 (DIS), 15-2 (DIS), 15-3 (TT), 15-4 (DIS), 15-5 (DIS), 15-5 (Lab), 15-6 (Lab), 20-2 (Lab), 23-1 (DIS)	N	Pan, Aluminum Foil, 13" × 9" × 2"	10	11-5 (Lab), 21-1 (DIS), 21-1 (Lab)
				N	Pan, Aluminum Foil, 22.5 cm Diam	10	5-3 (TT), 6-3 (Lab), 9-1 (TT), 11-2 (DIS), 13-3 (DIS), 13-3 (Lab), 14-1 (TT), 15-3 (TT), 16-1 (DIS), 16-2 (DIS), 17-2 (DIS)
SS	Map, Local	5	8-2 (DIS), 8-2 (SYS)				
SS	Map, U. S. with City Names and Latitude Lines	5	19-2 (Lab)	N	Pan, Aluminum Foil, 8" × 8" × 1-1/4"	5	20-1 (Lab)

KEY: **DIS**: Discover; **SYS**: Sharpen Your Skills; **TT**: Try This; **Lab**: Lab
* Items designated **C** are in the Consumable Kit, **N** are in the Nonconsumable Kit, and **SS** are School Supplied.

Nonconsumable Materials (continued)

*	Description	Qty per class	Textbook Section(s)	*	Description	Qty per class	Textbook Section(s)
N	Paper Clips, Box/100	2	6-3 (TT), 8-1 (DIS), 8-3 (SYS), 8-4 (DIS)	SS	Rocks	30	5-2 (DIS)
N	Paper Clips, Jumbo, Box/100	1	5-3 (Lab), 10-1 (Lab)	N	Rope, Clothesline, 7/32" × 50'	1	7-3 (DIS)
SS	Pegboard	5	13-3 (Lab)	SS	Ruler, Plastic, 12"/30 cm	5	3-1 (DIS), 4-2 (DIS), 5-3 (DIS), 6-3 (DIS), 7-2 (TT), 7-3 (Lab), 8-1 (Lab), 10-1 (DIS), 11-4 (Lab), 12-4 (DIS), 16-3 (Lab), 17-1 (Lab), 18-2 (Lab), 19-1 (Lab), 19-2 (Lab), 20-2 (Lab), 21-2 (Lab), 22-1 (Lab)
SS	Pennies, Post-1982	140	7-2 (Lab)				
SS	Penny	5	10-4 (DIS), 14-1 (SYS), 15-1 (DIS)				
N	Petri Dishes, 100 mm, Pkg/6	2	(INT), 22-1 (Lab)				
N	Pins, Hair Pkg/100, 1-3/4"	1	3-1 (TT)				
N	Pins, Map, Assorted Colors Pkg/100	1	11-5 (Lab)	N	Sandpaper, Medium, 9" × 11"	7	10-1 (Lab), 12-1 (SYS)
N	Pins, Straight, Steel, Pkg/150	1	17-3 (TT)	SS	Scissors	5	2-2 (Lab), 3-1 (Lab), 7-3 (TT), 8-3 (Lab), 9-1 (Lab), 10-4 (DIS), 11-4 (TT), 11-4 (Lab), 11-5 (DIS), 16-3 (Lab), 17-3 (TT), 19-1 (Lab), 19-4 (DIS), 21-2 (Lab), 23-2 (Lab)
SS	Plastic Products, Assortment	5	21-2 (TT)				
SS	Pliers	5	10-1 (Lab)				
SS	Pot, Cooking	5	7-2 (TT)				
SS	Protractor, 6", Plastic	5	4-1 (Lab), 8-1 (Lab), 8-2 (SYS), 19-1 (Lab), 21-2 (SYS)				
N	Putty, Plastic	5	12-1 (TT)	N	Screen, Window, 12" × 24"	2	20-1 (Lab)
SS	Quarter	5	5-3 (DIS)	N	Seeds, Bean (White) 4 oz	1	20-3 (DIS)
N	Rack, Test Tube Support, Double Row, Wood	5	22-2 (Lab)	N	Seeds, Bean, Kidney, lb	1	20-3 (DIS)
				N	Seeds, Black Bean, lb	1	20-3 (DIS)
N	Rock Specimen Kit/72 (12 types/6 ea) (Includes quartzite, pumice, slate, sandstone, granite, limestone, marble, basalt, shale, obsidian, rhyolite, gneiss)	1	13-2 (DIS), 15-1 (DIS), 15-2 (DIS), 15-3 (TT), 15-4 (DIS), 15-5 (DIS), 15-5 (Lab), 15-6 (Lab)	SS	Shoebox	10	19-4 (DIS)
				N	Sinker, Lead Fishing, 4 oz	5	12-1 (SYS)
				SS	Skateboard	5	4-1 (Lab), 5-1 (Lab)
				N	Slides, Microscope, Box/72	1	14-2 (DIS), 20-1 (Lab)
				N	Slinky, Plastic	5	12-2 (DIS)
N	Rock, Coal (Bituminous) (6 pieces)	1	23-1 (DIS)	SS	Sneakers, Different Types	15	5-3 (Lab)
				N	Soup Mix, 15 Bean, 20 oz Pkg	1	20-3 (DIS)
N	Rock, Conglomerate Specimen Pak (6 pieces)	1	15-1 (DIS)	N	Sponge, 15 cm × 7.5 cm × 1.8 cm	15	11-5 (Lab), 21-2 (Lab)
N	Rock, Limestone (Coquina) Pak (6 pieces)	1	15-4 (DIS)	N	Spool, Plastic	5	5-5 (DIS)
				N	Spring Scale 2 kg/20 N	5	5-2 (DIS), 5-3 (Lab)

KEY: **DIS**: Discover; **SYS**: Sharpen Your Skills; **TT**: Try This; **Lab**: Lab
* Items designated **C** are in the Consumable Kit, **N** are in the Nonconsumable Kit, and **SS** are School Supplied.

Master Materials List

Nonconsumable Materials (continued)

*	Description	Qty per class	Textbook Section(s)	*	Description	Qty per class	Textbook Section(s)
N	Spring Scale 500 g/5 N	5	5-1 (Lab), 5-3 (Lab), 7-2 (TT), 7-3 (Lab), 12-1 (SYS)	N	Tree Cross-Sections, Approx 4" Diam	5	20-2 (Lab)
N	Steel Wool Pads, Pkg/6	1	9-4 (DIS)	SS	Truck, Toy Dump	5	5-2 (DIS)
N	Stopwatch, Electronic LED	10	(INT), 3-1 (TT), 3-1 (SYS), 4-1 (DIS), 4-1 (Lab), 4-2 (DIS), 4-2 (Lab), 4-3 (DIS), 5-1 (Lab), 6-1 (Lab), 9-2 (TT), 16-1 (DIS), 17-1 (Lab), 19-1 (Lab), 23-2 (Lab), 23-3 (Lab)	N	Tube, Cardboard, 7.5 cm × 4 cm OD	5	19-1 (DIS)
				N	Tube, Cardboard, 13 cm × 5.5 cm OD	5	8-3 (Lab)
				N	Tubing, Rubber, Black, 1/8" × 1/16", Foot	2	9-2 (Lab)
				N	Tubing, Vinyl Plastic, 3/8" × 1/16", Foot	5	9-2 (TT)
N	Streak Plates, Pkg/8	1	14-1 (DIS)	SS	Vacuum Cleaner with Intake Hose	1	16-1 (Lab)
N	Switch, Single Pole, Single Throw, Plastic	10	9-2 (DIS), 9-3 (DIS), 9-3 (SYS), 10-1 (DIS)	SS	Washcloth	5	11-4 (DIS)
N	Syringe, Disposable, 10 cc	5	13-3 (Lab)	N	Washer, Metal, 3/4" OD × 5/16" ID	20	5-1 (DIS), 8-1 (Lab)
N	Tape Measures, 1.5 m, Dual Scale, Pkg/6	1	4-2 (Lab)	SS	Wind Vane	5	17-3 (Lab)
N	Test Tube, 16 mm × 150 mm, 20 mL	45	17-5 (DIS), 22-2 (Lab)	N	Wire, Copper, Bare, 16 Gauge, 4 oz	1	9-2 (Lab), 10-4 (Lab)
N	Test Tube, Plastic w/Cap, 16 mm × 150 mm	5	8-1 (TT)	N	Wire, Enameled Copper, 24 Gauge, 4 oz (Approx 200 ft)	1	10-1 (Lab)
N	Thermometer, −20 to 110°C, 30 cm	5	23-2 (DIS), 23-3 (Lab), 23-4 (DIS)	N	Wire, Insulated Copper, 22 Gauge, 25 m	2	8-3 (DIS), 8-3 (SYS), 8-3 (Lab), 8-4 (DIS), 9-2 (DIS), 9-2 (Lab), 9-3 (DIS), 9-3 (SYS), 9-4 (DIS), 10-1 (DIS), 10-1 (Lab), 10-2 (DIS), 10-2 (TT), 10-4 (Lab)
N	Thermometer, −40C - 50°C/ −40F - 120°F, Pkg/6	3	16-1 (Lab), 17-1 (DIS), 17-1 (Lab), 17-2 (TT), 19-1 (Lab), 19-4 (DIS), 23-2 (Lab)				
N	Tongs, Flask and Test Tube	5	14-2 (DIS)	N	Wood, Block, 3" × 4" × 3/4"	10	15-5 (TT)

KEY: **DIS**: Discover; **SYS**: Sharpen Your Skills; **TT**: Try This; **Lab**: Lab
* Items designated **C** are in the Consumable Kit, **N** are in the Nonconsumable Kit, and **SS** are School Supplied.

Equipment

*	Description	Qty per class	Textbook Section(s)	*	Description	Qty per class	Textbook Section(s)
E	Apron, Vinyl	30	several activities	E	Goggles, Chemical Splash-Class Set	1	several activities
E	Balance, Triple Beam, Single Pan	5	5-3 (SYS), 5-3 (Lab), 6-3 (Lab), 11-1 (DIS), 13-2 (TT), 14-1 (Lab), 14-3 (Lab), 15-3 (TT), 16-3 (DIS)	E	Hand Generator, Genecon	10	10-2 (SYS), 10-3 (DIS)
				E	Mass Set, Gram, Brass 12-Piece	5	5-3 (Lab)
				E	Microscope, Inclined with Sub-Stage Illuminator	5	16-1 (Lab), 20-1 (Lab)
E	Galvanometer, −35 mV to +35 mV DC	5	10-2 (DIS), 10-2 (TT)	E	Mitten, Oven, Adult Size	5	16-1 (DIS), 16-2 (DIS)
E	Globe, Raised Relief, Political, 12" w/Semi-Meridian	5	11-3 (DIS), 19-1 (DIS)	E	Support Base with Rod	5	9-2 (TT), 17-1 (Lab)
				E	Support Ring with Clamp	5	9-2 (TT), 17-1 (Lab)
E	Gloves, Medium Latex Laboratory, Box/100	1	13-3 (Lab), 21-2 (DIS)	E	Voltmeter, Single Range, DC, 0 to 1 V	5	10-4 (DIS)

KEY: **DIS**: Discover; **SYS**: Sharpen Your Skills; **TT**: Try This; **Lab**: Lab
* Items designated **C** are in the Consumable Kit, **N** are in the Nonconsumable Kit, and **SS** are School Supplied.

Adventures in Life, Earth, and Physical Science

Print Resources
Student Edition
Annotated Teacher's Edition
Unit Resource Books, including:
- Chapter Project Support
- Lesson Plans
- Section Summaries
- Review and Reinforce Worksheets
- Enrich Workshops
- Student Edition Lab Worksheets
- Answer Keys

Color Transparencies
Chapter Tests
Performance Assessments
Standardized Test Preparation Workbook
Test-Taking Tips With Transparencies
Laboratory Manual, Student Edition
Laboratory Manual, Teacher's Edition
Guided Reading and Study Workbook
Guided Reading and Study Workbook, Teacher's Edition
Inquiry Skills Activity Book
Student-Centered Science Activity Books

Reading in the Content Area With
Literature Connections
How to Assess Student Work
How to Manage Instruction in the Block
Teacher's ELL Handbook

Media/Technology
Resource Pro® CD-ROM
Exam View®Computer Test Bank Book
  with CD-ROM
Probeware Laboratory Manual with
  CD-ROM
Section Summaries on Audio CD
Presentation Pro CD-ROM
Order Assistant Plus CD-ROM
Computer Microscope and Lab Manual
Lab Activity Video Library
Concept Video Library
Companion Web site at PHSchool.com

Materials Kits
Consumable Materials Kit
Nonconsumable Materials Kit

Acknowledgments

Excerpt on page 110 from *James Herriot's Dog Stories* by James Herriot. Copyright © 1986 by James Herriot. Published by St. Martin's Press.

Activity on pages 440–441 is from *Exploring Planets in the Classroom*. Copyright by Hawaii Space Grant Consortium, based on experiments done by R. Fisk and D. Jackson, U.S. Geological Survey.

Excerpt on pages 764–765 from *Alone* by Richard E. Byrd. Copyright © 1938 by Richard E. Byrd.

Note: Every effort has been made to locate the copyright owner of material used in this textbook. Omission brought to our attention will be corrected in subsequent editions.

ISBN 0-13-115416-8   1 2 3 4 5 6 7 8 9 10 08 07 06 05 04

Teacher's Edition ISBN 0-13-115419-2

Program Authors

Michael J. Padilla, Ph.D.
Professor
Department of Science Education
University of Georgia
Athens, Georgia

Michael Padilla is a leader in middle school science education. He has served as an editor and elected officer for the National Science Teachers Association. He has been principal investigator of several National Science Foundation and Eisenhower grants and served as a writer of the National Science Education Standards.

As lead author of *Science Explorer,* Mike has inspired the team in developing a program that meets the needs of middle grades students, promotes science inquiry, and is aligned with the National Science Education Standards.

Ioannis Miaoulis, Ph.D.
Dean of Engineering
College of Engineering
Tufts University
Medford, Massachusetts

Martha Cyr, Ph.D.
Director, Engineering
    Educational Outreach
College of Engineering
Tufts University
Medford, Massachusetts

Science Explorer was created in collaboration with the College of Engineering at Tufts University. Tufts has an extensive engineering outreach program that uses engineering design and construction to excite and motivate students and teachers in science and technology education.

Faculty from Tufts University participated in the development of *Science Explorer* chapter projects, reviewed the student books for content accuracy, and helped coordinate field testing.

CHAPTER PROJECT

Series Authors

Elizabeth Coolidge-Stolz, M.D.
Medical Writer
North Reading, Massachusetts

Linda Cronin-Jones, Ph.D.
Professor, College of Education
University of Florida
Gainesville, Florida

Donald Cronkite, Ph.D.
Professor of Biology
Hope College
Holland, Michigan

Joseph D. Exline, M.A., Ed.D.
President
Exline Consulting Services, Inc.
Beaverdam, Virginia

David V, Frank, Ph.D.
Head, Department of Physical Sciences
Ferris State University
Big Rapids, Michigan

Dawn Graff-Haight, Ph.D., CHES
Associate Professor, Health Education
Linfield College
McMinnville, Oregon

Fred Holtzclaw
Science Instructor
Oak Ridge High School
Oak Ridge, Tennessee

Jan Jenner, Ph.D.
Science Writer
Talladega, Alabama

John G. Little
Science Teacher
St. Mary's High School
Stockton, California

Steve Miller
Science Writer
State College, Pennsylvania

Jay M. Pasachoff, Ph.D.
Professor of Astronomy
Williams College
Williamstown, Massachusetts

Barbara Brooks Simons
Science Writer
Boston, Massachusetts

Carole Garbuny Vogel, M.A.T.
Science Writer
Lexington, Massachusetts

Camille L. Wainwright, Ph.D.
Professor of Science Education
Pacific University
Forest Grove, Oregon

Thomas R. Wellnitz
Science Teacher
The Paideia School
Atlanta, Georgia

Contributing Writers

W. Russell Blake, Ph.D.
Planetarium Director
Plymouth Community Intermediate
    School
Plymouth, Massachusetts

Alfred B. Bortz, Ph.D.
School of Education
Duquesne University
Pittsburgh, Pennsylvania

Rose-Marie Botting
Science Teacher
Broward County School District
Fort Lauderdale, Florida

Doug E. Bowman
Health/Physical Education Teacher
Welches Middle School
Welches, Oregon

Mary Sue Burns
Science Teacher
Pocahontas County High School
Dunmore, West Virginia

Jeffrey C. Callister
Science Instructor
Newburgh Free Academy
Newburgh, New York

Colleen Campos
Science Teacher
Laredo Middle School
Aurora, Colorado

John Coffey
Science/Mathmatics Teacher
Venice Area Middle School
Venice, Florida

Patricia M. Doran
Science Teacher
Rondout Valley Junior High School
Stone Ridge, New York

Holly Estes
Science Instructor
Hale Middle School
Stow, Massachusetts

Edward Evans
Former Science Teacher
Hilton Central School
Hilton, New York

Theresa K. Holtzclaw
Former Science Instructor
Clinton, Tennesse

Jorie Hunken
Science Consultant
Woodstock, Connecticut

Greg Hutton
Science and Health Curriculum
    Coordinator
School Board of Sarasota County
Sarasota, Florida

Mark Illingworth
Teacher
Hollis Public Schools
Hollis, New Hampshire

James Robert Kaczynski, Jr.
Science Teacher
Barrington Middle School
Barrington, Rhode Island

Lauren Magruder
Science Instructor
St. Michael's Country Day School
Newport, Rhode Island

Thomas L. Messer
Science Teacher
Cape Cod Academy
Osterville, Massachusetts

Susan Offner
Biology Teacher
Milton High School
Milton, Massachusetts

Warren Phillips
Science Teacher
Plymouth Community Intermediate
    School
Plymouth, Massachusetts

Emery Pineo
Science Teacher
Barrington Middle School
Barrington Rhode Island

Linda Shoulberg
Science Teacher
Millbrook High School
Raleigh, North Carolina

Karen Riley Sievers
Science Teacher
Callanan Middle School
Des Moines, Iowa

Evan P. Silberstein
Science Teacher
Spring Valley High School
Spring Valley, New York

Sharon M. Stroud
Science Teacher
Widefield High School
Colorado Springs, Colorado

Joseph Stukey, Ph.D.
Department of Biology
Hope College
Holland, Michigan

Reading Consultant

Bonnie B. Armbruster, Ph.D.
Department of Curriculum
    and Instruction
University of Illinois
Champaign, Illinois

Interdisciplinary Consultant

Heidi Hayes Jacobs, Ed.D.
Teachers College
Columbia University
New York, New York

Safety Consultants

W. H. Breazeale, Ph.D.
Department of Chemistry
College of Charleston
Charleston, South Carolina

Ruth Hathaway, Ph.D.
Hathaway Consulting
Cape Girardeau, Missouri

Content Reviewers

Activity Field Testers

Nicki Bibbo
Russell Street School
Littleton, Massachusetts

Connie Boone
Fletcher Middle School
Jacksonville Beach, Florida

Rose-Marie Botting
Broward County
    School District
Fort Lauderdale, Florida

Colleen Campos
Laredo Middle School
Aurora, Colorado

Elizabeth Chait
W. L. Chenery Middle
    School
Belmont, Massachusetts

Holly Estes
Hale Middle School
Stow, Massachusetts

Laura Hapgood
Plymouth Community
    Intermediate School
Plymouth, Massachusetts

Sandra M. Harris
Winman Junior High
    School
Warwick, Rhode Island

Jason Ho
Walter Reed Middle School
Los Angeles, California

Joanne Jackson
Winman Junior High
    School
Warwick, Rhode Island

Mary F. Lavin
Plymouth Community
    Intermediate School
Plymouth, Massachusetts

James MacNeil, Ph.D.
Concord Public Schools
Concord, Massachusetts

Lauren Magruder
St. Michael's Country
    Day School
Newport, Rhode Island

Jeanne Maurand
Glen Urquhart School
Beverly Farms, Massachusetts

Warren Phillips
Plymouth Community
    Intermediate School
Plymouth, Massachusetts

Carol Pirtle
Hale Middle School
Stow, Massachusetts

Kathleen M. Poe
Kirby-Smith Middle
    School
Jacksonville, Florida

Cynthia B. Pope
Ruffner Middle School
Norfolk, Virginia

Anne Scammell
Geneva Middle School
Geneva, New York

Karen Riley Sievers
Callanan Middle School
Des Moines, Iowa

David M. Smith
Howard A. Eyer Middle
    School
Macungie, Pennsylvania

Derek Strohschneider
Plymouth Community
    Intermediate School
Plymouth, Massachusetts

Sallie Teames
Rosemont Middle School
Fort Worth, Texas

Gene Vitale
Parkland Middle School
McHenry, Illinois

Zenovia Young
Meyer Levin Junior
    High School (IS 285)
Brooklyn, New York

Contents

Adventures in Life, Earth, and Physical Science

Unit 2 Motion, Forces, and Energy

ix

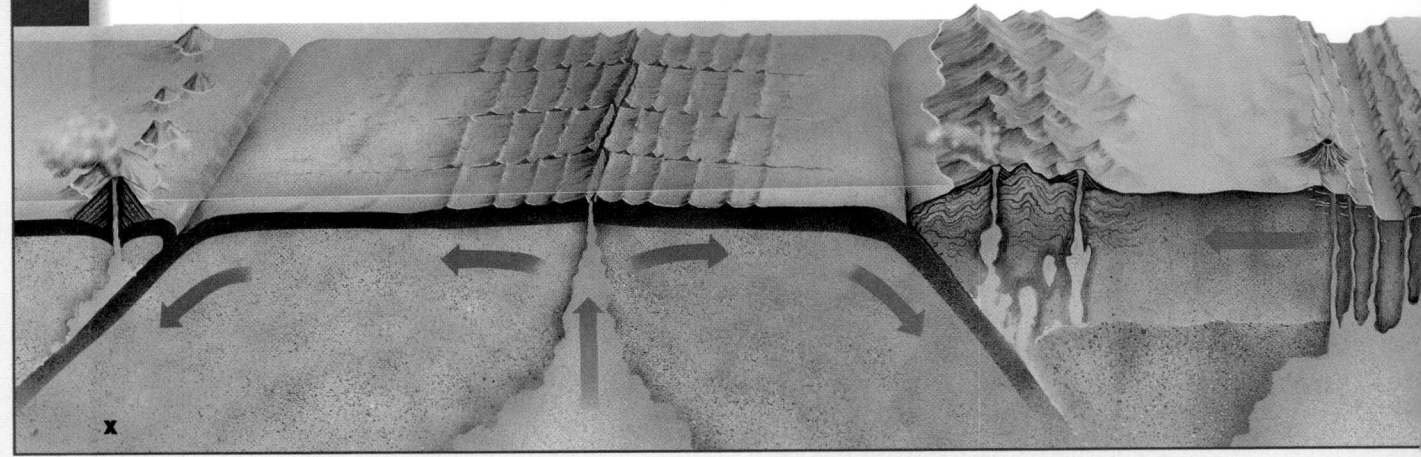

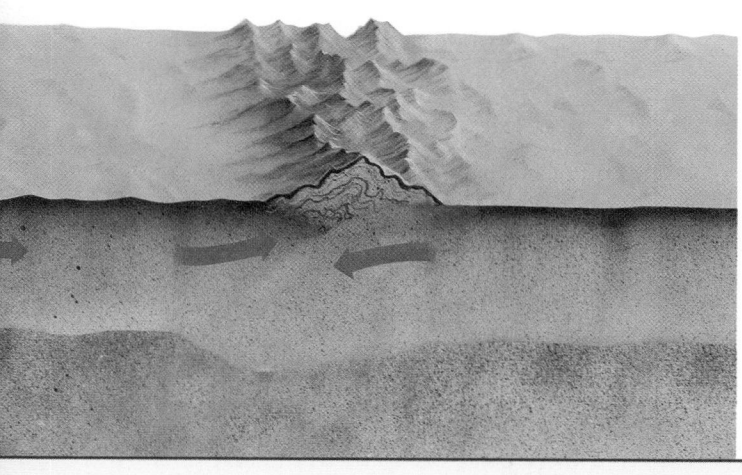

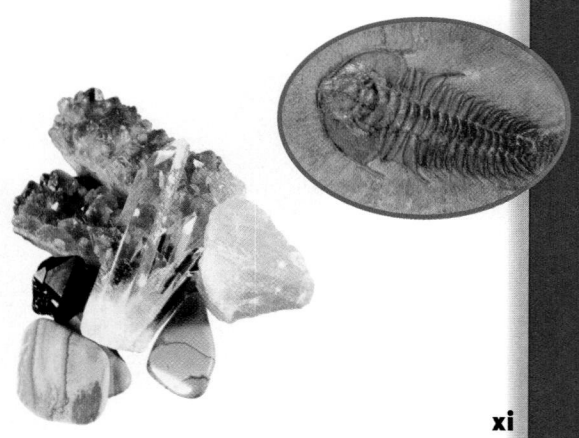

Unit 6 Environmental Science

PRENTICE HALL
SCIENCE EXPLORER
ADVENTURES
in Life, Earth, and
Physical Science

Activities

Inquiry Activities

CHAPTER PROJECT
Opportunities for long-term inquiry

DISCOVER
Exploration and inquiry before reading

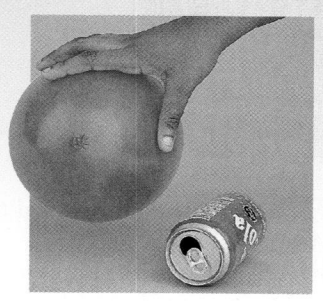

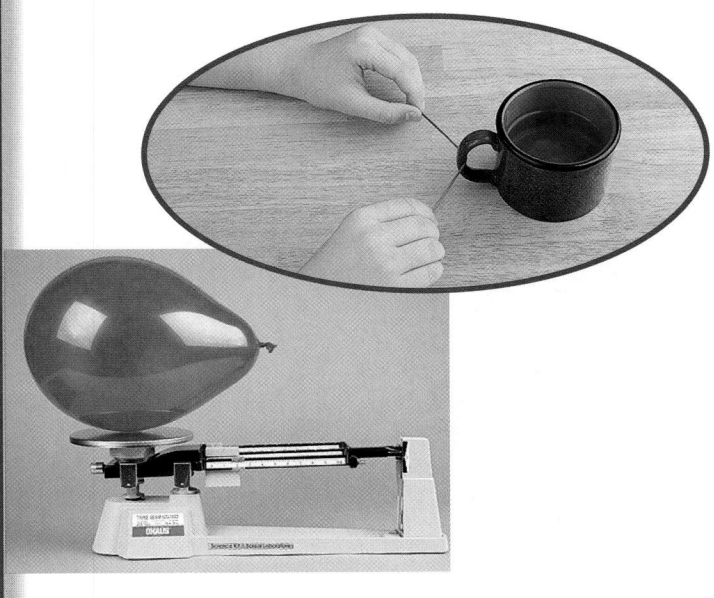

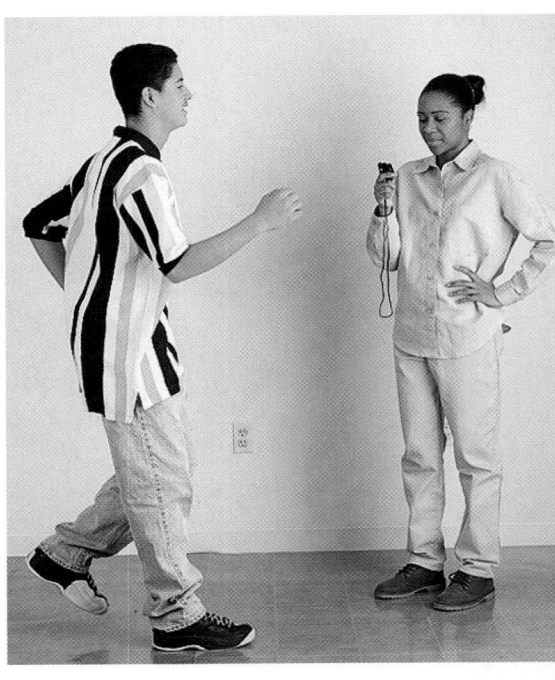

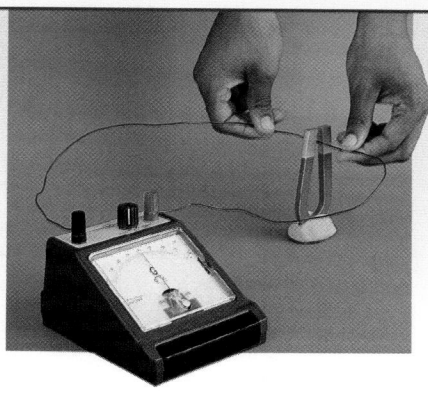

Sharpen your *Skills*

Practice of specific science inquiry skills

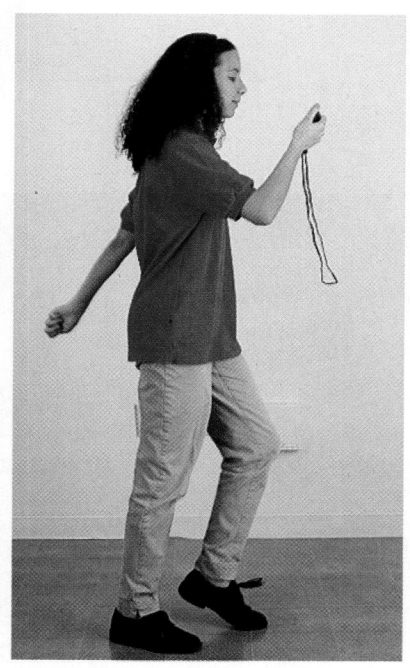

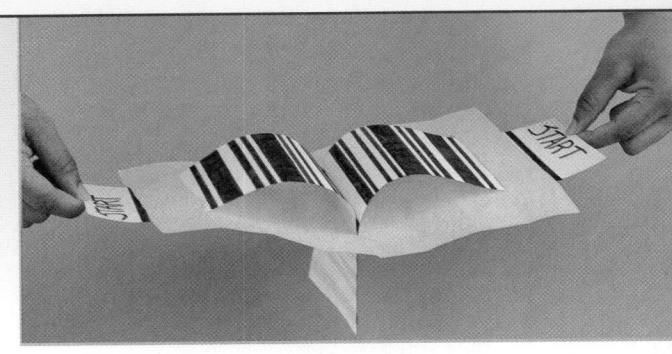

TRY THIS

Reinforcement of key concepts

Interdisciplinary Activities

xx

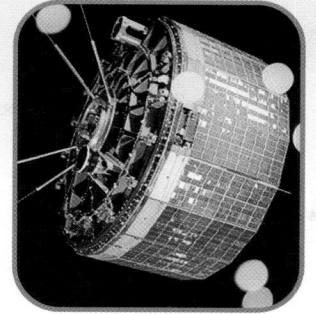

EXPLORING

Visual exploration of concepts

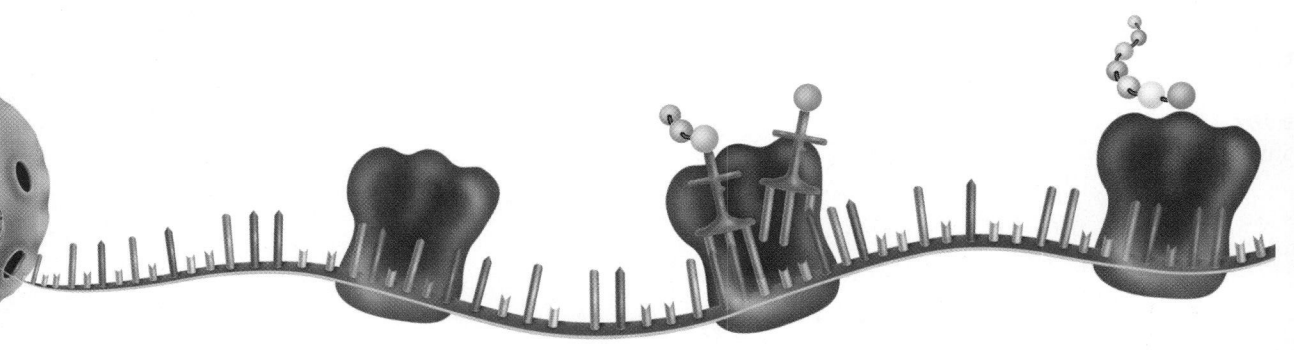

Introduction to Science

Objectives	Time	Student Edition Activities	Other Activities	
0.0.1 Explain the nature of scientific inquiry. 0.0.2 Identify and describe the skills used by scientists in their work. 0.0.3 Explain how scientific hypotheses can be tested through controlled experiments. 0.0.4 Distinguish among a scientific hypothesis, theory, and law. 0.0.5 Explain the importance of laboratory safety.	2 periods/ 1 block	**Skills Lab: Designing Experiments** Speeding Up Evaporation, p. 11	TE TE TE TE	Addressing Naive Conceptions, p. 5 Building Inquiry Skills; Developing Hypotheses, p. 6 Demonstration, p. 12 Including All Students, p. 13

 For Standard or Block Schedule The Resource Pro® CD-ROM gives you maximum flexibility for planning your instruction for any type of schedule. Resource Pro® contains Planning Express®, an advanced scheduling program, as well as the entire contents of the Teaching Resources and the Computer Test Bank.

Key: **CTB** Computer Test Bank
CT Chapter Tests
ELL Teacher's ELL Handbook

Meeting the National Science Education Standards and AAAS Benchmarks

National Science Education Standards	Benchmarks for Science Literacy	Unifying Themes
Science as Inquiry (Content Standard A) ◆ **Design and conduct a scientific investigation** Students design an experiment about the rate of evaporation of water. *(Skills Lab)* ◆ **Use appropriate tools and techniques to gather, analyze, and interpret data** Students collect and analyze data about evaporation. *(Skills Lab)* ◆ **Think critically and logically to make the relationships between evidence and explanation** Students use their data to draw a conclusion about the relationship between environmental conditions and the rate of evaporation of water. *(Skills Lab)* ◆ **Communicate scientific procedures and explanations** Students describe their experimental designs. *(Skills Lab)* **History and Nature of Science** (Content Standard G) ◆ **Science as a human endeavor** Many different types of people are involved in science and its related fields. ◆ **Nature of science** Scientists use observation and experimentation to explain the living world around them.	**1B Scientific Inquiry** Students investigate the scientific process. **1C The Scientific Enterprise** Scientists work in many different places throughout the world. **12D Communication Skills** Students record data and identify the relationships they indicate. *(Skills Lab)*	◆ **Systems and Interactions** Environmental factors such as heat and air movement affect the rate at which water evaporates.

CHAPTER PLANNING GUIDE

 The Resource Pro® CD-ROM provides flexibility for planning the instruction for any type of schedule.

Program Resources	Assessment Strategies	Media and Technology
UR Introduction Lesson Plan, p. 2 UR Introduction Section Summary, p. 3 UR Introduction Review and Reinforce, p. 4 UR Introduction Enrich, p. 5 UR Introduction Skills Lab, pp. 6–7	TE Ongoing Assessment, pp. 5, 7, 9 TE Performance Assessment, p. 13 SE Study Guide/Assessment, pp. 14–15 PA Performance Assessment, pp. 2–4 CT Introduction Test, pp. 2–3 CTB Introduction Test PHAS Provides standardized test preparation	🌐 Science Explorer Internet Site 🎧 Audio CDs, Section Summaries 📼 Lab Activity Videotape, *Tape 1* 💽 Computer Test Bank, Introduction Test

GRSW Guided Reading and Study Workbook
ISAB Inquiry Skills Activity Book
LM Laboratory Manual

PA Performance Assessment
PHAS Prentice Hall Assessment System
PLM Probeware Lab Manual

RCA Reading in the Content Area
SE Student Edition

TE Teacher's Edition
UR Unit Resources

Student Edition Activities Planner

ACTIVITY	Time (minutes)	Materials *Quantities for one work group*	Skills
Skills Lab, p. 11	40 min Day 1, 5–10 min Days 2–5	**Consumable** water, 3 index cards, paper towels **Nonconsumable** 2 plastic petri dishes, plastic dropper, 1 petri dish cover, stopwatch, lamp	Designing Experiments, Controlling Variables, Drawing Conclusions

A list of all materials required for the Student Edition activities can be found starting on page T23. You can obtain information about ordering materials by calling 1-800-848-9500 or by accessing the Science Explorer Internet site at **www.phschool.com**.

Take It to the Net

The **www.phschool.com** Web site provides you with multiple opportunities to incorporate the internet into your instruction. Go to **www.phschool.com** and click on the Science icon. Then select Science Explorer Integrated.

Internet Activities provide opportunities for students to review, extend, or assess a concept from the chapter.

■ Have students use the chapter Self-Test to get instant feedback.

■ Hot Links and Reference Links provide opportunities for online research.

STAY CURRENT with **SCIENCE NEWS**®

Find out the latest research and information about the nature of science at: **www.phschool.com**

Reducing Hurricane Damage

Focus on Weather

This four-page article features Kishor Mehta, a civil engineer working and teaching at the University of Texas in Austin. Dr. Mehta works primarily on wind research, and the article describes some of the projects he and his team have tackled. Using Dr. Mehta's research, the article focuses on experimentation as a scientific tool.

Students will learn more about weather factors in Chapter 17, and weather patterns in Chapter 18. They do not need that knowledge to understand and appreciate the information in this article.

Scientific Inquiry

◆ Ask students to think of ways that the wind is helpful, and ways that it can be destructive. *(Responses might include: (helpful) powers windmills, useful for sailboats, flying kites, helps disperse seeds of plants; (destructive) breaks limbs off trees, damages structures, blows topsoil away.)* Keep a list on the board as students make suggestions, dividing the list into appropriate categories.

◆ Ask students why a structural engineer would need to understand the effects of wind on buildings and other structures. *(They need to know how strong a building must be to withstand winds.)*

REDUCING HURRICANE DAMAGE

▲ Kishor Mehta grew up in India, and moved to the United States to go to college. He remembers that his greatest challenge in learning English was learning how to think in a new language. After college, he received his Ph.D. in civil engineering from the University of Texas in Austin.

Hurricane winds roar through a coastal city, tearing off roof tiles and metal sidings from houses. An entire roof rips into the air. Flying tree limbs, street signs, and debris from broken houses crash into the windows and doors of other buildings, opening them to even more damage by wind and water. What can be done to change the fate of buildings in the path of heavy winds? At the Wind Engineering Research Center at Texas Tech University in Lubbock, people are trying to answer this question.

Kishor Mehta (KEE-shour MEH-tah) is the center's director and an expert on the effects of hurricane winds. "Hurricanes cause damage. We can't stop them, but we can learn to live with them. We can prevent them from disrupting the life of the community. That's our goal."

Studying the Wind

Kishor started his studies in the field of civil engineering—which focuses on the design and construction of public buildings, bridges, and other structures. He later became more interested in structural engineering—the branch of civil engineering that concentrates on design. A few years after arriving at Texas Tech, Kishor started to think about doing wind research. He thought that he and his colleagues might investigate wind power, but a tornado gave them an even better idea.

Background

Facts and Figures The Swiss scientist Daniel Bernoulli (1700–1782) studied the flow of fluids, both liquids and gases. He formulated the theory that the pressure exerted by a fluid is inversely proportional to its rate of flow. This is the basis of the Bernoulli effect, or Bernoulli's Principle. According to Bernoulli's Principle, a fast-moving fluid causes an area of low pressure. For example, gusts of wind moving past a building can decrease the air pressure outside the building, which can cause the glass panes to pop out of large windows. When this happens, the relatively higher air pressure inside the building presses outward on walls and windows. If the Bernoulli effect created by the wind outside is strong enough, the air pressure inside the building can push the glass out of the windows.

◄ High winds can rip apart buildings, leaving them battered or destroyed. The instrumented movable test building (shown below) at the Texas Tech Field Laboratory helps researchers study the effects of high winds on buildings.

Starting an Investigation

A devastating tornado had just torn through downtown Lubbock. "We began to study how structures perform under high wind conditions," explains Kishor. "At the time, very little research had been done in this area." Kishor and his team analyzed how the tornado had affected local buildings. Then they traveled to other towns and cities that had been struck by tornadoes or hurricanes to study damage that had happened in those places.

Their early data showed that the winds from tornadoes and hurricanes affect buildings in very similar ways. Once the engineers understood how and why damage was occurring, they began to think about ways to design buildings that could withstand high winds.

Broadening the Research

Lubbock is in a very windy part of Texas, so it is a good place to study how wind affects the structure of a building. Currently, under Kishor's leadership, students and teachers at the university's Wind Engineering Research Field Laboratory carry out a wide variety of wind experiments. In addition to a movable tower that measures wind speed, the center has an instrumented tower that is used to measure other weather conditions. Nearby, there is even a movable building! Depending on wind direction, researchers can turn the building to orient the instruments in the direction of the wind and see how the roof and walls are affected.

◆ Have students look at the photograph at the top of page 1. Ask students to describe the damage that is shown. Then invite students to suggest changes in construction that might have reduced the damage.

◆ The shape of a building can affect the flow of air around it. To demonstrate how air flows over smooth contours, place a lighted candle on the desk. **CAUTION:** *Tie back loose hair and clothing, wear safety goggles, and exercise care in lighting and extinguishing the candle.* Hold a small paper, such as a note card, in front of the candle and blow from a distance of about 8 to 10 inches. Students should see that the candle flame bends towards the back of the note card. As you blow on the card, air flows towards the card, but has to shift direction and go around the card. Since the air pressure of the moving air is less than the pressure of the still air, the moving air flows backward to balance the pressure. Now bend the note card into a teardrop shape, and use tape to hold the ends together. Hold the card in front of the candle, with the closed end facing the candle. Again, blow toward the card. Students should see that the flame bends away from the card. Air flow is much smoother, and the pressure is generally balanced without major points of backdraft.

1

Background

Facts and Figures The instrumented tower at Wind Engineering Research Field Laboratory is about 50 m tall. The tower has groups of instruments at intervals from near the ground to its top. These instruments measure and record the wind profile, wind turbulence level, density of the air, ground roughness, and the stability of the atmosphere.

The field laboratory's test building is mounted on a circular track. The building can be rotated to face the wind at a desired angle. The surface of the building has taps that record pressures using differential pressure transducers.

Scientists at the laboratory study the effects of wind pressures on buildings and roofing, and wind flow around buildings. They also use the site to gain field data during high winds and thunderstorms.

◆ Have students reread the last paragraph under "Working in Teams." Discuss with students the concept of cost-benefit analysis. Ask students what sort of information the team might need before they can recommend specific building standards. *(They would need to know what typical "normal" winds are like in the area, and they would need wind data for severe storms that have occurred in that area. This information would help the team understand the forces that would affect a building in the area.)*

◆ In the Northern hemisphere, wind generally blows from west to east. Differences in air pressure and temperatures, as well as surrounding terrain, may change this direction slightly. Winds are named for the direction from which the wind is blowing. Have students keep a record of the wind direction around the school for two weeks. Using a compass, select a place that is as open as possible, and chalk the positions of the compass on the ground. Always take the wind direction in this same place, and as close as possible to the same time every day. Ask: **How can you determine the direction of the wind?** *(Responses may include suggestions such as wetting a finger and holding it in the air, tossing light objects to see which way they blow, or holding a handkerchief by one end to see which way it blows.)* **How can you compare the speed of the wind from one day to another?** *(Students might suggest measuring the distance a tossed object is carried, how close to horizontal a handkerchief or ribbon becomes when held in the wind.)* Allow small groups of students to decide how they will determine the direction and speed of the wind. Groups can compare their records at the end of two weeks.

Working in Teams

Kishor sometimes works with researchers from other fields. For example, he and a professor from Texas Tech's economics department conducted a study of property damage from hurricanes in Galveston. "I like working in teams," Kishor explains. "Each person brings a different set of skills, a different point of view. Keeping costs in mind, we can work together to decide where to put the most effort into design."

Designing buildings that resist severe weather is not a problem. Engineers know how, and they do just that for nuclear power plants. "But when it comes to building houses, the costs are too high" says Kishor "So what we do is sit down with a group of people—economists, architects, city planners—and decide how we can do the most good with the resources available."

Solving a Problem

While the Texas Tech researchers spend quite a bit of time in the field, they also use equipment and devices at the school's Wind Engineering Research Field Laboratory to solve specific problems.

A few years ago, the Texas Department of Transportation noticed something troubling about certain traffic lights. Some of the lights that were attached to horizontal poles hanging over the street would vibrate. State officials were concerned about the danger to cars passing under the lights. "They wanted to know what kind of wind was causing the problem and why it affected some poles but not others," says Kishor. Was there any way to reinforce the poles or the lights?

The school's field laboratory was set up to test how wind affects traffic light poles. Kishor and his colleagues discovered that serious

Kishor and another researcher watch as wind data from the instrumented tower and test building are recorded by computer. ▶

2

Background

Facts and Figures Steady winds can cause problems, if engineers do not consider the effects of wind on a structure. The classic example of such a problem was the Tacoma Narrows Bridge near Seattle, Washington. While the bridge was still under construction, people noticed that it swayed in the wind. Engineers were called in to study the problem. Months before the bridge's completion in 1940, winds of 64 kph caused the bridge to undulate and twist violently.

The bridge was literally torn apart by its own movements. Fortunately, the bridge had been closed to traffic before it collapsed.

The designers of the bridge had not considered the possibility of wind damage, and they had not done any wind-tunnel tests on the design. Engineers designed the second Tacoma Narrows Bridge to resist swaying. The bridge's structure was strengthened and a grating in the bridge's deck allowed wind to pass through.

(A) A traffic light was erected at the field laboratory to test vibration of the pole in natural wind. (B) The solution to the problem was a metal plate above the traffic lights to prevent dangerous vibrations of the pole.

◆ Have students look at the photographs on page 3. Ask volunteers to describe the shape, size, and position of the metal plate on top of the horizontal pole. Encourage students to suggest other shapes, sizes, or positions that might have been tested. Point out that scientists do not necessarily find the best design on the first test. Help students understand that testing a design that does not have the desired effect is still a valuable learning experience.

In Your Journal Encourage students to think of a time when the change in plans was dramatic, or at least serious. You may want to discuss what kinds of changes are appropriate for this journal entry before allowing students to proceed with their assignment.

vibrations occur when the backs of the lights face into steady winds blowing from about 15 to 50 kilometers per hour. The team looked for a way to reduce the vibrations. They found that attaching a horizontal metal plate to the pole on top of the light eased the problem. Grateful for the suggestion, the state added the plates to the traffic lights. They also passed the study results on to other parts of the United States where high winds pose risks.

Reaching His Goals

Early in his career, Kishor realized that he enjoyed teaching. The opportunity to teach and do research led him to Texas Tech. In recent years, Kishor has spent more than half his time teaching.

He also continues to direct the overall research and management of the center, work with colleagues, and speak publicly about how wind affects buildings and other structures. As a result of the efforts of Kishor and his colleagues, the Texas Tech Wind Engineering Research Field Laboratory has become recognized as a place where people can find out how to live more safely.

In Your Journal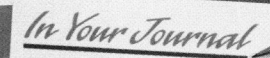

Kishor Mehta changed his plan for studying the wind when a tornado gave him another idea. Think about an example in your life when you switched to another plan for a project, trip, social event, or other activity. How did you feel about giving up your idea for a new one? What factors convinced you to change?

3

READING STRATEGIES

Further Reading

◆ *Do Tornadoes Really Twist?: Questions and Answers About Tornadoes and Hurricanes* Melvin Berger, et al. (Scholastic, 2000)
◆ *Eye of the Storm: Inside the World's Deadliest Hurricanes, Tornadoes, and Blizzards* Jeffery P. Rosenfield (Plenum Press, 1999)
◆ *Galveston and the 1900 Storm* Patricia Bellis Bixel Elizabeth Hayes Turner (University of Texas Press, 2000)
◆ *Hurricanes and Tornadoes (Natural Disasters)* Neil Morris (Barron's, 1999)
◆ *Hurricanes (Disasters in Nature)* Catherine Chambers (Heineman Library)
◆ *Isaac's Storm: A Man, a Time, and the Deadliest Hurricane in History* Erik Larson, (G. K. Hall & Co., 2000)

What is Science?

Objectives

After completing this introduction, students will be able to
- explain the nature of scientific inquiry;
- identify and describe the skills used by scientists in their work;
- explain how scientific hypotheses can be tested through controlled experiments;
- distinguish among a scientific hypothesis, theory, and law;
- explain the importance of laboratory safety.

Key Terms science, scientific inquiry, observation, inference, hypothesis, variable, manipulated variable, responding variable, controlled experiment, data, scientific law, scientific theory

1 Engage/Explore

Activating Prior Knowledge

Ask students what they think scientists do. Students will likely say that scientists work in a laboratory and carry out experiments. Have students preview pages 12–13. Then discuss that scientists work in many kinds of places.

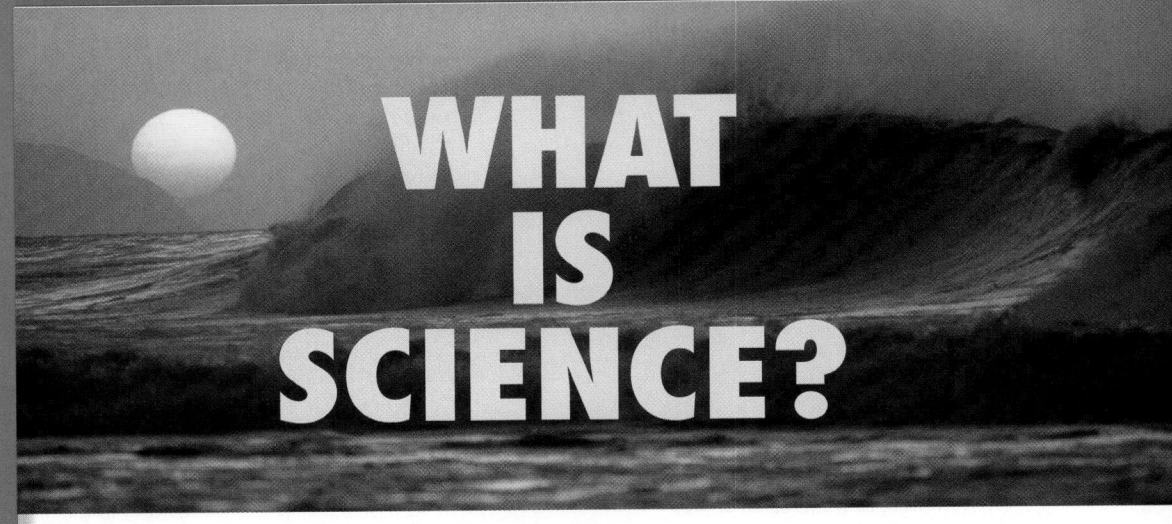

WHAT IS SCIENCE?

GUIDE FOR READING

- **What skills do scientists use?**
- **How can you work safely in the laboratory?**

Reading Tip Before you begin reading, make a list of the boldfaced terms. As you read, write the definition for each term.

As a structural engineer, Kishor Mehta asks a lot of questions. Is the pole that holds up a traffic signal sturdy enough to stand up to strong winds? How can we design buildings so that they can withstand tornadoes and hurricanes? Asking questions is an important part of science.

Science is a way of learning about the natural world. Science also includes all the knowledge gained through the process of exploring the natural world. This body of knowledge is always growing and changing as scientists ask new questions and explore new ideas.

Another term for the many ways in which scientists study the world around them is **scientific inquiry.** Scientific inquiry is used every day by the engineers at the Wind Engineering Research Center at Texas Tech University.

You do not have to be a scientist to use scientific inquiry. In fact, you may not realize that you probably have used the process of scientific inquiry. If you have tried to find the best conditions for fish in a fish tank or the correct way to throw a curve ball, you have used scientific inquiry.

Figure 1 This student is using the skills of scientific inquiry as she monitors conditions in this fish tank. *Posing Questions What questions would you have about the conditions needed to keep fish alive and healthy in a fish tank?*

4

READING STRATEGIES

Reading Tip Have students write a question for each of the terms they list. They may combine terms in a compare-and-contrast statement. Sample answer: How does a manipulated variable differ from a responding variable?

Program Resources

- **Unit 1 Resources** Introduction Lesson Plan, p. 2; Introduction Section Summary, p. 3
- **Guided Reading and Study Workbook** Introduction

Thinking Like a Scientist

Kishor Mehta uses many skills as he investigates the effects of strong winds on buildings. You may have used some of these skills, while others will be new to you.

Some of the skills that scientists use are posing questions, making observations and inferences, developing hypotheses, designing experiments, collecting data and making measurements, interpreting data, and drawing conclusions. Sometimes scientists make models to help them understand the problem they are trying to solve. Scientists also must use the skill of communication in their work.

Posing Questions In the 1800s, scientists used scientific inquiry to study glaciers. Glaciers are huge masses of ice. They are usually found on and around high mountains, such as the Alps in Switzerland.

Two hundred years ago, scientists knew very little about glaciers. Some scientists thought that glaciers could move. Others doubted that these huge masses of ice could move at all. So some scientists in Switzerland decided to investigate.

Scientists usually begin an investigation with a question about something that is unexplained. The Swiss scientists studying glaciers asked, "Do glaciers move?"

Making Observations and Inferences Look at the glacier in Figure 2. What color is it? What does its surface look like? As you answer these questions, you are using a science skill. You are making observations. The skill of **observation** involves using one or more of your senses—sight, hearing, smell, and sometimes taste—to gather information. In this case, you used your sense of sight to gather information about glaciers.

You may have observed a dark band in the glacier. If you could travel to this glacier and make more-detailed observations, you would find that this dark band is due to rocks in the ice. Where did the rocks come from? You might think that they came from nearby mountains. This statement is an **inference,** an interpretation based on observations and prior knowledge.

☑ *Checkpoint* What is the difference between an observation and an inference?

Figure 2 The Gorner glacier winds down from high peaks in the Swiss Alps. The dark bands in the glacier are pieces of rock broken off and picked up by the moving ice.

---

2 Facilitate

Thinking Like a Scientist

Addressing Naive Conceptions

Materials *beaker, water, hot plate*

Help students distinguish between making observations and inferences. Heat a beaker of water on a hot plate until the water boils. When the water has reached the boiling point, ask students to describe what they see. Students will likely say that the water is boiling. Ask them to describe what they see without using the word *boiling*. Students should describe observing bubbles forming inside the water, rising, and breaking at the surface. Students may also be able to observe a fog-like layer above the surface of the water. Point out that these are observations, and the statement that the water is boiling is an inference based on observing the hot, bubbling water and using what they know about boiling. **learning modality: visual**

Using the Visuals: Figure 2

Have students identify the glacier and the dark bands in the photograph. Ask how the glacier differs from the mountains around it. **learning modality: visual**

Background

For students, the most important task is learning to distinguish *observations* (evidence gathered through the senses) from *inferences* (logical thinking about those observations). Students often mistake one for the other. By making the distinction, they take a major step in modeling the way scientists think. Use the Addressing Naive Conceptions activity on this page to help students practice making the distinction.

Answers to Self-Assessment

Caption Question

Figure 1 Questions may include, "What do fish need to eat?", "Is the temperature of the water important?", and similar questions.

☑ *Checkpoint*

An observation is information that is gathered by the senses. An inference is an interpretation of an observation and involves a person's prior knowledge.

Ongoing Assessment

Skills Check Place a glass of ice water on a table at the front of the class. Have students write 3 observations and 3 inferences about it.

Thinking Like a Scientist, continued

Building Inquiry Skills: Developing Hypotheses

Materials *beaker, water, hot plate, ice cube, tongs*

Heat water in a beaker on a hot plate. When the water is boiling, ask students: **What does boiling water feel like?** (*Very hot*) Show students an ice cube. Ask: **What does an ice cube feel like?** (*Very cold*) On the board write, "When an ice cube is placed into boiling water…" and invite students to suggest endings for the sentence. List the endings on the board. Tell students that these statements are hypotheses. Discuss how the hypotheses can be tested. Then use the tongs to place the ice cube into the boiling water so that students can see if their hypotheses are supported. **learning modality: visual**

Including All Students

At the time that the first humans landed on the moon, several areas of the United States had heavy rains. Some people said that the rain was caused by the moon landing. Ask students if this is a valid hypothesis. (*No, because it is based on a coincidence, and even if the observation was repeated, this would not support the hypothesis. Also, this is not a testable hypothesis because all the relevant variables could never be controlled in a way that would establish a causal relationship between moon landings and rain.*) **learning modality: logical/ mathematical**

Building Inquiry Skills: Communicating

Divide students into two groups. Have one group take the part of the Swiss scientists who believed that glaciers did not move. Have the other group take the part of the Swiss scientists who believed that glaciers did move. Have each group list observations that led to its point of view. **learning modality: verbal**

Developing Hypotheses After posing a question, scientists often gather information or make observations. They then use this information to form a hypothesis. A **hypothesis** is a possible explanation for a set of observations or answer to a scientific question. In science, a hypothesis must be something that can be tested. A hypothesis can be tested by observation or experimentation. Scientists do not accept a hypothesis after just one test. Repeated tests must provide evidence that supports the hypothesis.

People in the Alps had long observed boulders in the valleys below glaciers. Did that mean that moving ice had carried the boulders? Such observations led scientists to propose the following hypothesis: *Glaciers move slowly over the land.*

Designing Controlled Experiments How do scientists test a hypothesis? In many cases, they carry out experiments. In setting up an experiment, scientists think about all the factors that could affect the outcome of the experiment. These factors are called **variables.** The scientists change one variable, called the **manipulated variable,** or independent variable. They then observe how this change affects another variable. The variable that changes as a result is called the **responding variable,** or dependent variable.

There can be many variables in an experiment. To be sure that changes in the manipulated variable alone are responsible for any changes in the responding variable, scientists must test only one variable at a time. They control all of the other variables so that they do not change. An experiment in which there is only one manipulated variable and all other variables are kept constant is called a **controlled experiment.**

Figure 3 shows an example of a controlled experiment. The student is investigating whether the shape of an ice block affects how quickly it melts. The manipulated variable in the experiment is the shape of the ice. The responding variable is the time it takes for the ice to melt. Notice that all other variables are kept constant. The two blocks of ice are exposed to identical sources of heat, contain the same volume of water, and are on identical surfaces. Because all other variables have been controlled, any difference in melting times must be due to the difference in shape.

Figure 3 In this controlled experiment, the shape of the ice block is the manipulated variable. The time it takes for melting to occur is the responding variable. *Developing Hypotheses What hypothesis is being investigated?*

6

Background

The term *hypothesis* refers to a proposed explanation that can be tested. In science, many hypotheses are developed as inferences, that is, through logical thinking. But some hypotheses have resulted from imagination, creative leaps, chance events, and even dreams. The key characteristic of a hypothesis is that it is testable. Use the Building Inquiry Skills and the Including All Students activities on this page to help students practice identifying a valid hypothesis.

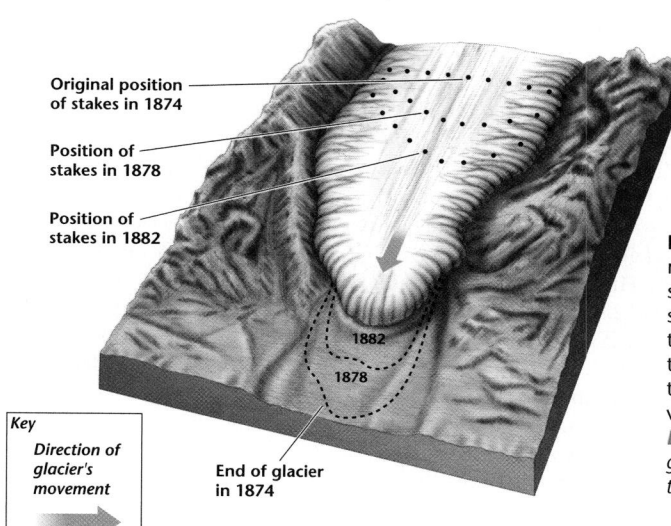

Original position of stakes in 1874

Position of stakes in 1878

Position of stakes in 1882

Key
Direction of glacier's movement

1882

1878

End of glacier in 1874

Figure 4 To measure the movement of a glacier, scientists drove a row of stakes into the glacier. They then measured how much the stakes moved in relation to the rocky sides of the valley. *Interpreting Diagrams Which part of the glacier appears to be moving the fastest? How can you tell?*

In the real world, conducting a controlled experiment can be difficult or impossible. The objects studied by some scientists can be very large. And some processes that scientists study can take millions of years. In cases like these, scientists test hypotheses through observation and measurement, as did the scientists who studied glaciers.

Figure 4 shows how the Swiss scientists investigated the movement of a glacier. They placed a row of stakes across the glacier, and went back over time to see if the stakes moved.

✓ *Checkpoint* **What is a variable?**

Collecting Data and Making Measurements The facts, figures, and other evidence collected in an experiment are called **data.** Scientists know that it is important to record all data carefully. That way they have a permanent account of what happened in an experiment.

Some data can be in the form of descriptions. For example, the scientists studying glaciers may have examined rocks and compared them with rocks from nearby mountains.

Much of the data collected in experiments is in the form of measurements. The scientists studying the glacier noted the original positions of the stakes in the glacier and then measured how far the stakes moved from these positions.

Scientists around the world all use the same system of measurement. This system is called the International System of Units. The name is abbreviated as SI, which comes from the French name for the system (*Système International d'Unités*).

SI is based on the metric system of measurements. If you have ever measured length in meters, you have used SI units. To learn about making measurements in science, see pages 768–769 in the Skills Handbook.

Ask students: **How did the edge of the glacier change from 1874 to 1882?** *(The glacier's edge appeared to move back.)* **Suggest hypotheses that could explain this observation.** *(Possible hypotheses: the glacier is moving backward; the glacier is melting at its edge.)* Then direct students to look at the stakes in the glacier. Ask: **How have the positions of the stakes in the glacier changed?** *(They moved downhill.)* **How does this observation affect hypotheses about the change at the edge of the glacier?** *(If the stakes moved downhill, the hypothesis that the glacier moved uphill is unlikely.)* **learning modality: visual**

Answers to Self-Assessment

Caption Questions

Figure 3 Thin ice melts faster than thick ice.

Figure 4 The area just to the right of center appears to be moving fastest because the stakes moved farther in that location.

✓ *Checkpoint*

A variable is one of the factors in an experiment that can change.

Ongoing Assessment

Writing Have students write definitions in their own words for the terms *manipulated variable* and *responding variable*.

7

Thinking Like a Scientist, continued

Using the Visuals: Figure 5

Have students look at the data table and line graph. Ask: **What kind of information is shown?** *(How the size of the glacier changed.)* **How is the size of the glacier recorded?** *(Its area is recorded in hectares.)* **How did the area change?** *(It decreased.)* **Was the rate of change always the same?** *(No)* **How can you tell?** *(The line on the graph falls more steeply between 1900 and 1945 than it does in any other time span.)* **learning modality: logical/mathematical**

Addressing Naive Conceptions

Ask students: **Do you think every experiment allows the scientist to draw a conclusion?** *(Responses may vary, but most students may believe this is true.)* Help students understand that not all experiments or data collections will lead to a firm conclusion. Some can be labeled as "inconclusive." This, as well as negative support of a hypothesis, can be a good result. Scientists must then look for other factors and other ways to test their hypotheses. Sometimes a different approach can lead to a new discovery. **learning modality: verbal**

Interpreting Data After scientists collect their data, they then need to interpret, or find the meaning of, these data. Finding a way to display the data is part of interpreting it. One way to display data is in the form of a diagram, such as the one in Figure 4. Another way to display data is in data tables and graphs, as in Figure 5.

Interpreting data involves looking for patterns, or trends. The study of the Swiss glacier produced two sets of data. The positions of the stakes at three different times make up one set of data. Look back at Figure 4. What pattern do you see in these positions?

The other set of data is the three positions of the lower end of the glacier. There's a pattern here, too. How did the end of the glacier change over the years of the study?

Drawing Conclusions Once scientists have reviewed their data, they are ready to draw a conclusion. The data may support the hypothesis.

Or the data may show that the hypothesis was incorrect. Sometimes, no conclusion can be reached, and more data must be collected.

The Swiss scientists studying glaciers concluded that their data supported their hypothesis. But the data also revealed a surprise. As the glacier was moving downhill, it was also getting shorter at its lower end. A surprising find like this one can lead scientists to form new hypotheses and try new experiments. What hypothesis could you propose to explain the change at the lower end of the glacier?

In the example of the glacier, the evidence collected by the scientists supported their hypothesis. But what if it hadn't supported the hypothesis? Would that mean the experiment was a failure? Definitely not! Eliminating a false hypothesis is as important as supporting another hypothesis. And what may seem like a failure often turns out to be the first step on the path to a new discovery.

Change in Size of a Glacier Over Time	
Year	Area of Glacier (hectares*)
1850	380
1900	370
1927	240
1945	160
1993	135

*1 hectare = 10,000 square meters

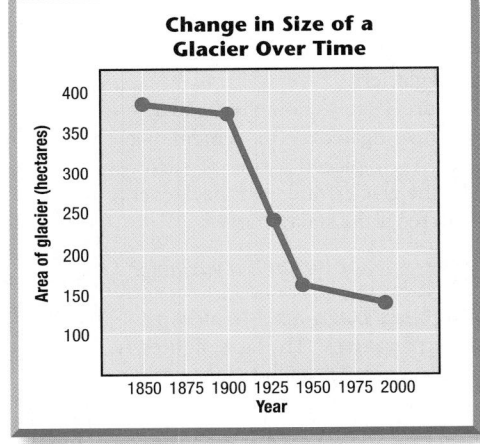

Figure 5 The data in this data table were collected by scientists studying a glacier in Glacier National Park in Montana. When the data are graphed, the graph reveals a pattern or trend. *Interpreting Graphs* What pattern do you see in the graph?

8

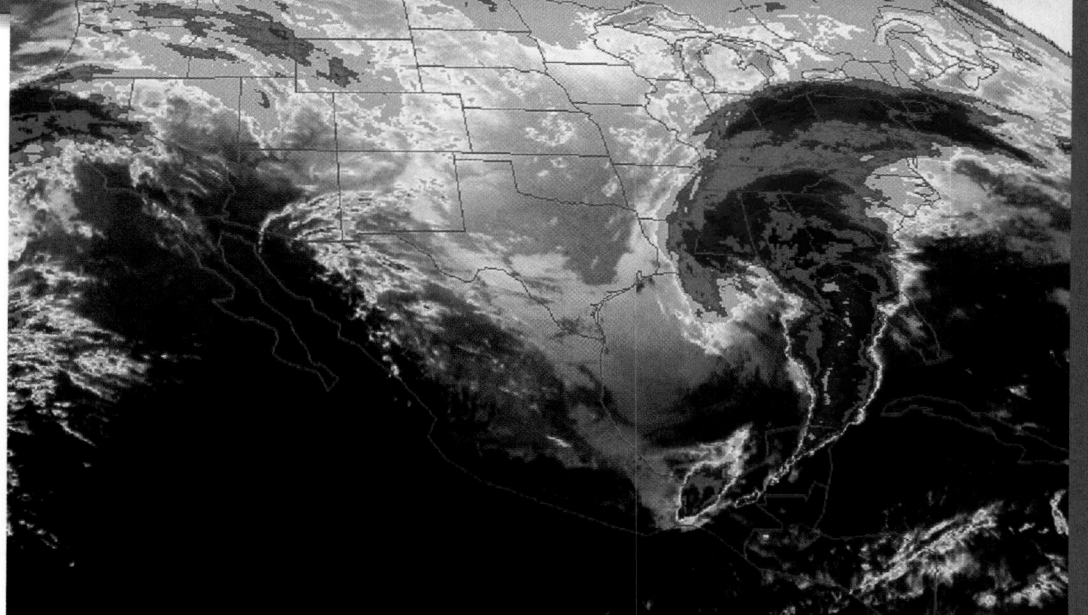

Including all Students
Ask students to list objects that are too large to study in the classroom. (*Answers will vary, but may include skyscrapers, airplanes, ships, the moon, or planets.*) Than ask what kinds of models might help students to study these objects? (*Three-dimensional models, drawings, maps, blueprints of buildings, ships, or planes.*) **learning modality: verbal**

Cultural Diversity
Ask students why studying one or more languages other than English might be useful to scientists. (*Possible answers: To communicate with scientists from other places in the world, to study work done by scientists in other languages, to facilitate field work or research in another country.*) **learning modality: verbal**

Making Models and Simulations What would you do if you wanted to show your classmates what a glacier looks like? You can't take a glacier into your classroom, but you can use a model to show what the glacier looks like. The model could be a three-dimensional scale model. It could also be a diagram or a map. Many scientists today use computers to make models of complex objects or events.

Sometimes scientists use simulations to test a hypothesis. A simulation is a model that imitates a real-world situation.

Scientists working in modern laboratories have used simulations to study how glaciers move. The scientists studied samples of hot metal to see how the metal changes shape when under great pressure. The changes in the metal simulate the movement of the slowly flowing ice in a glacier. Using such simulations helps scientists develop new hypotheses and new ways of testing them.

Communicating Information
For scientists, communicating information is an important part of scientific inquiry. By sharing ideas and experimental findings, scientists learn from each other.

Scientists communicate with each other by writing articles for scientific journals. Scientists also go to scientific meetings. There they talk about their own research and listen to talks about the research of other scientists. Scientists also use the Internet to communicate with one another.

Scientific discoveries also are shared with the general public—people who are not scientists. In these communications, scientists must use simpler terms that can be easily understood by everyone. Communicating with nonscientists is especially important in areas that affect people's health and safety.

☑ *Checkpoint* **What are some ways in which scientists communicate information?**

Figure 6 A weather map is a model of changing conditions in Earth's atmosphere. This map, based on satellite data, shows a storm over the eastern United States.

Answers to Self-Assessment
Caption Question
Figure 5 The size of the glacier decreased over time.

☑ *Checkpoint*
Scientists communicate by writing articles, attending scientific meetings, and by using the Internet.

Ongoing Assessment

Skills Check Have students draw flowcharts that show how scientists test a hypothesis. (*Sample flowchart: design a controlled experiment → collect data → interpret data → draw conclusions*)

Scientific Laws and Theories

Addressing Naive Conceptions

Some students may think that a theory that has been tested and supported is now a law. Point out that a theory is an explanation, and is always subject to change. A law describes a pattern that occurs in nature. **learning modality: logical/mathematical**

Laboratory Safety

Including all Students

Remind students that electrical devices should not be used near water unless they are specifically designed for such purposes. When using both electricity and water as in the Skills Lab on page 11, be sure to keep the two far apart. Also, be sure that all electrical equipment has GFI switches. **learning modality: verbal**

Scientific Laws and Theories

Scientific inquiry often begins with observations. Scientists have noticed that some events in nature always happen the same way. What happens if you hold a ball in your hand and let go of it? Has this happened every time you've tried it? You have made the same observation over and over again—the ball falls to the ground.

When scientists have observed an event so often that they are sure it will always happen, they call the observation a scientific law. A **scientific law** is a statement that describes what scientists expect to happen every time under a particular set of conditions. In the case of the falling ball, the scientific law has to do with gravity.

Sometimes a large body of related information can be explained by a single major idea. If that idea is supported by many tests, it may develop into a scientific theory. A **scientific theory** is a well-tested scientific concept that explains a wide range of observations. An accepted

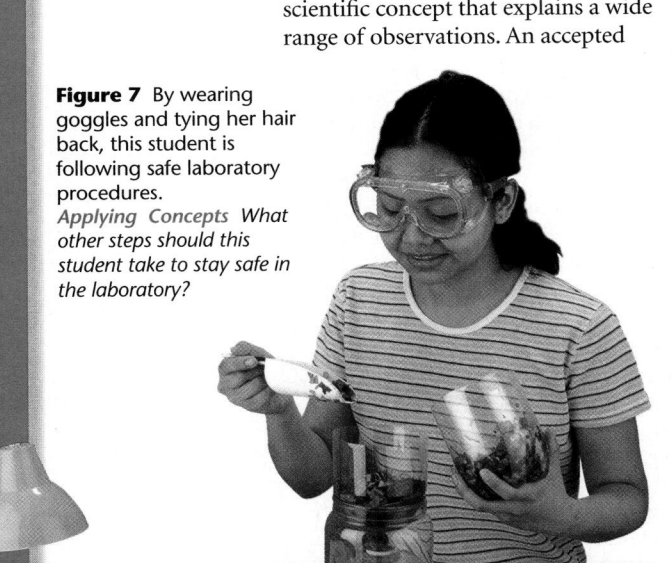

Figure 7 By wearing goggles and tying her hair back, this student is following safe laboratory procedures. *Applying Concepts What other steps should this student take to stay safe in the laboratory?*

scientific theory has withstood repeated tests. However, it is possible that additional tests could contradict the theory. If that happens, scientists will change the theory or abandon it.

Have you ever heard someone say, "Well, my theory is . . ."? In everyday language, people often use the word *theory* to refer to any explanation or personal opinion. Remember that, in science, a theory is an explanation that has been thoroughly tested. It is not merely a guess.

☑ *Checkpoint What is a scientific theory?*

Laboratory Safety

An important part of scientific inquiry is carrying out experiments. Scientists don't just go into a laboratory and start experimenting. They plan their steps carefully and make sure their procedures are safe.

As you use this textbook, you will conduct many experiments. As you do this, it is very important to think about safety. Always follow your teacher's instructions. Follow the steps you are given and use only the materials your teacher tells you to use. **Safe laboratory practices protect both you and your classmates from injury. In addition, your lab investigations will be more successful if you follow safety guidelines.**

Before conducting any experiments, review Appendix A on pages 779–781. Be sure that you understand the safety symbols and rules.

10

Program Resources

◆ **Unit 1 Resources** Introduction Skills Lab blackline masters, pp. 6–7
◆ **Inquiry Skills Activity Book** provides teaching and practice of all inquiry skills

Media and Technology

 Lab Activity Videotapes
Tape 1

Speeding Up Evaporation

Evaporation is the process by which water vapor enters Earth's atmosphere from the ocean and other surface waters. Rates of evaporation determine the amount of moisture in the atmosphere. Atmospheric moisture in turn affects the formation of clouds and helps to determine whether it will rain.

Problem

What factors increase the rate at which water evaporates?

Materials

water	plastic dropper
2 plastic petri dishes	1 petri dish cover
3 index cards	paper towels
stopwatch	lamp

Procedure

Part 1 Effect of Heat

1. How do you think heating a water sample will affect how fast it evaporates? Record your hypothesis.
2. Place each petri dish on an index card.
3. Add a single drop of water to each of the petri dishes. Try to make the two drops the same size.
4. Position the lamp over one of the dishes as a heat source. Turn on the light. Make sure the light does not shine on the other dish. **CAUTION:** *The light bulb will become very hot. Avoid touching the bulb or getting water on it.*
5. Observe the dishes every 3 minutes to see which sample evaporates faster. Record your result.

Part 2 Effect of Wind

6. How do you think fanning the water will affect how fast it evaporates? Record your hypothesis.
7. Dry both petri dishes and place them over the index cards. Add a drop of water to each dish as you did in Step 3.
8. Use an index card to fan one of the dishes for 5 minutes. Be careful not to fan the other dish.
9. Observe the dishes to see which sample evaporates faster. Record your result.

Analyze and Conclude

1. Did the evidence support both hypotheses? If not, which hypothesis was not supported?
2. Make a general statement about factors that increase the rate at which water evaporates.
3. **Think About It** What everyday experiences helped you make your hypotheses at the beginning of each experiment? Explain how hypotheses differ from guesses.

Design an Experiment

How do you think increasing the surface area of a water sample will affect how fast it evaporates? Write your hypothesis and then design an experiment to test it. Check your plan with your teacher before you begin.

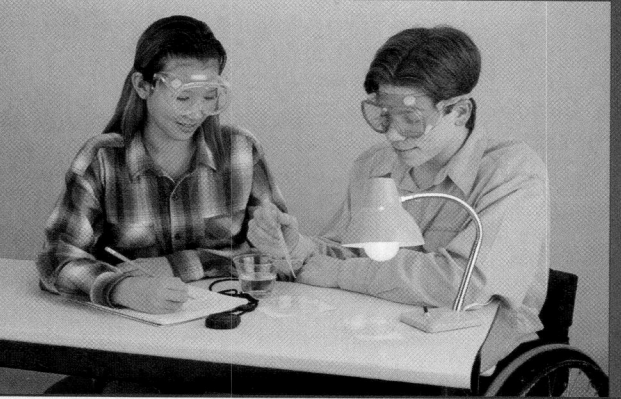

11

---

3. Think About It Sample response: how quickly a puddle dries in the sun or wind. Hypotheses are based on information gathered through study or experience, whereas guesses are based only on feelings.

Safety

Caution students to be careful when handling a lamp, because the bulb gets hot and can explode if splashed with water. Review the safety guidelines in Appendix A.

Design an Experiment

A typical hypothesis might suggest that increasing the surface area of a water sample increases the rate of evaporation. A typical design might suggest pouring equal amounts of water into a deep bowl and a shallow pan and then exposing both to the same amount of heat or wind.

Speeding Up Evaporation

Preparing for Inquiry

Key Concept Various factors influence the rate at which water evaporates, including exposure to a heat source and the presence of wind.

Skills Objectives Students will be able to:
◆ develop hypotheses about factors affecting the evaporation of water;
◆ control variables to determine the effect of different factors;
◆ draw conclusions about how various factors affect evaporation.

Time 40 minutes

Advance Planning Choose locations for each group's dishes for each part.

Guiding Inquiry

Invitation Ask: **Do you think evaporation occurs faster in a desert or a forest?** (*In a desert*) **Does it occur faster on a windy day or a calm day?** (*On a windy day*)

Introducing the Procedure
Have students read through the complete procedure. Then ask: **What variable is being tested in each part?** (*In Part 1, exposure to a heat source; in Part 2, the presence of wind*)

Troubleshooting the Experiment
Emphasize that in each part, both dishes should contain drops of water that are the same size.

Expected Outcome
In Part 1, water under a lamp evaporates faster. In Part 2 water fanned by the index card evaporates faster.

Analyze and Conclude
1. Answers will vary. Some students may have foreseen the results correctly in each case and confirmed their hypothesis through the experiment.
2. Factors that increase the rate of evaporation of water include exposure to a heat source and exposure to wind.

Branches of Science

Building Inquiry Skills: Inferring

Have students look at the photographs of the scientists on pages 12 and 13, and ask them to identify the branch of science for each career. Ask volunteers to describe the activites shown and infer the purpose of each activity. **learning modality: visual**

Addressing Naive Conceptions

The names of various careers may be misleading to some students. Point out that a meteorologist, for example, does not study meteors, but weather and weather patterns. An oceanographer may not study the ocean at all, but rather fresh water and climate. Ask students to name some careers and what scientists in that field study. Be sure to correct any misconceptions. **learning modality: auditory/verbal**

Technology and the Internet

Demonstration

ACTIVITY

Demonstrate, or have a computer teacher or math teacher demonstrate, how a computer can be used to plot the points of a scatter plot graph and draw the line of best fit. Before the actual demonstration, give students the coordinates of the points and have them make their own scatter plots on graph paper. Then ask them to draw the line of best fit themselves. Later they can compare their graphs to the graph drawn by the computer. Discuss also the relative ease of obtaining the results by hand and through the computer. Which was faster? Which was more reliable? **learning modality: logical/mathematical**

Branches of Science

There are four main branches of science—physical science, Earth science, life science, and environmental science. Physical science includes the study of motion, energy, sound, light, electricity, magnetism, and the matter that makes up everything around you.

Earth science is the study of Earth and its place in the universe. This includes studying landforms, oceans, rocks and minerals, weather, and the planets that make up the solar system.

Life science is the study of living things, including plants, animals, and microscopic life forms. Life scientists also study how living things interact with each other and with their surroundings.

Environmental science is the study of how human activities affect Earth's land, air, water, and living things. Environmental scientists try to find solutions for problems that result from the use of Earth's natural resources. Some problems that environmental scientists study are pollution and global warming.

The branches of science are not separate from one another. For example, Kishor Mehta and the other engineers he works with are mainly physical scientists. They study the effects of the force of wind on various objects. But to understand wind, they have to study weather, which is part of Earth science.

In Figure 8, you can see some of the work that scientists do. You may think of scientists as people who work in laboratories. But as you can see, scientists work in all kinds of places—from the bottom of the ocean to outer space. Scientists test water supplies to make sure the water is clean enough to drink. They design safer cars and buildings. They search the rain forests to find new plants and animals. Wherever people are asking questions and searching for answers, they are using the skills of scientific inquiry.

☑ *Checkpoint* **Which branch of science would be involved in studying volcanoes and earthquakes?**

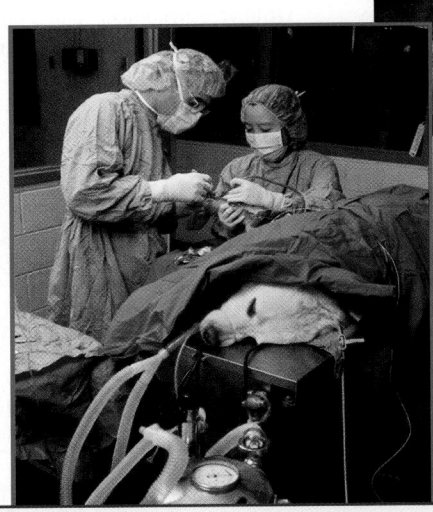

Figure 8 Scientists seek answers to questions in a wide variety of places using diverse skills and tools.

Veterinarians ▶
Veterinarians are doctors that treat animals. They care for animals ranging from house pets to farm and zoo animals.

Astronomers ▲
Astronomers study the universe. These astronomers are using a radio telescope to detect radio signals from distant stars and galaxies.

12

Background

Facts and Figures Most careers in science require at least a college degree, and many require a Master's, a Doctorate, or further training for a specified number of years.

Veterinarians, for example, attend a specialized veterinary school for four years after they have earned their degree. They must complete the course and pass a state licensing exam before they can practice.

Many companies will hire people who have completed college only, but require that they continue their education as they work.

There are also many assistant positions in all scientific fields that do not require a college degree. Some do require certification from a technical school, which can usually be accomplished in less than two years.

Technology and the Internet

Today, many scientists use the latest technology in their research. From high-powered microscopes that can look at tiny viruses to huge telescopes that search the sky for faraway stars, scientists have many tools that they can use.

Most modern scientific instruments are connected to computers, which allow scientists to quickly record, store, and analyze the data they collect. You have already read how important computers are for creating models and simulations of scientific events.

Computers also help scientists communicate information to each other and to the public. You can find large amounts of information about current research and discoveries in science on the Internet. Many government agencies maintain Web sites that are excellent sources of scientific information. Hospitals and universities that have research centers often have Web sites, too. The publisher of this textbook maintains a Web site, **www.phschool.com**. This site includes links to other Web sites that may help you as you study science.

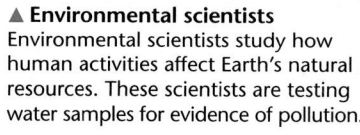

▲ Environmental scientists
Environmental scientists study how human activities affect Earth's natural resources. These scientists are testing water samples for evidence of pollution.

▼ Research chemists
Research chemists study the compositon and structure of matter as well as matter's physical and chemical properties. Their applied research is often aimed at developing new materials for a wide range of uses.

Answers to Self-Assessment

☑ *Checkpoint*
The study of volcanoes and earthquakes is included in Earth science.

---

3 Assess

Including All Students

Have students form four groups and assign each group one of the careers highlighted on the pages. Encourage each group to list what they know about the work "their" scientist does and what they would like to learn about the career. Have groups share their knowledge and questions with the whole class. Some questions might be: What kind of education is needed by each scientist? Where might each scientist work? What is the pay scale for jobs in this type of science? Have each group prepare a notebook with information about their scientist's career. **cooperative learning**

Performance Assessment

Writing Have students select a scientific career, name the branch of science, and list the scientific skills needed for that career. Be sure students give examples for each skill, such as: observing—the chemist would observe the reaction of the chemicals to the tested substance.

Reviewing Content

Multiple Choice

1. b 2. d 3. a 4. d 5. b

True or False

6. inference 7. true 8. true
9. simulation 10. true

Checking Concepts

11. Students should describe science as a way of knowing about the natural world based on observations and logical reasoning.

12. Scientists cannot always use controlled experiments because some of the things that they study are very large, or are located in space, or may involve processes that take a very long time or happened millions of years ago.

13. A hypothesis is a possible explanation for an observation or an answer to a scientific question. A hypothesis can be tested by observation or experiment. A scientific theory is a concept that explains a wide range of observations. If scientists test a hypothesis repeatedly and find that the evidence supports the hypothesis, that hypothesis may be accepted as a scientific theory.

14. Scientists interpret the data collected during an experiment to determine whether the data support their hypothesis. Scientists can then draw a conclusion about the hypothesis.

15. Following safety rules ensures that nobody involved in the experiment will be injured. It also protects equipment from damage.

16. The four main branches of science are Earth science, life science, physical science, and environmental science. Earth scientists study Earth and its place in the universe. Life scientists study all living things. Physical scientists study motion, energy, sound, light, and particles. Environmental scientists study how human activity affects the Earth.

17. Answers may vary. An example might be: I saw baby geese flapping their wings before they could fly. I think they do this to build up strength in their flying muscles, so when they can start to fly they will be able to.

Study Guide

Key Ideas

◆ Science is both a way of learning about the natural world and the knowledge gained from that process.

◆ Scientific methods generally include posing questions, making observations and inferences, developing hypotheses, designing experiments, collecting data and making measurements, interpreting data, and drawing conclusions. Scientists also may make models and use the skill of communication in their work.

◆ The System of International Units (SI) is the standard system of measurement in science.

◆ A scientific law describes what scientists expect to happen every time under a particular set of conditions. A scientific theory is a well-tested scientific concept that explains a wide range of observations.

◆ In experiments and activities, it is very important to think about safety. Always follow your teacher's instructions on safety in the laboratory.

Key Terms

science	manipulated variable
scientific inquiry	responding variable
observation	controlled experiment
inference	scientific law
hypothesis	scientific theory
variable	

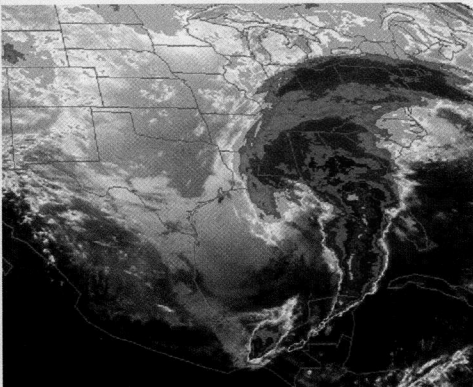

Reviewing Content

Multiple Choice

Choose the letter of the best answer.

1. Scientists seek to answer questions about the natural world in a process of
   a. modeling.   b. scientific inquiry.
   c. predicting.   d. developing hypotheses.

2. An explanation that can be tested by observation or experimentation is a(n)
   a. experiment.   b. scientific theory.
   c. scientific fact. d. hypothesis.

3. One of the factors that can change in an experiment is called a(n)
   a. variable.   b. theory.
   c. hypothesis.   d. observation.

4. One way in which scientists test a hypothesis is by
   a. asking questions.
   b. drawing conclusions.
   c. interpreting data.
   d. conducting a controlled experiment.

5. A scientist who studies weather and climate is a(n)
   a. life scientist.
   b. Earth scientist.
   c. physical scientist.
   d. environmental scientist.

True or False

If the statement is true, write true. If it is false, change the underlined word or words to make the statement true.

6. A <u>variable</u> is an interpretation of an observation.

7. The facts and figures that a scientist collects in an experiment are called <u>data</u>.

8. If an experiment fails to support a <u>scientific theory</u>, scientists will change the theory or abandon it.

9. A <u>hypothesis</u> is a model that imitates a real-world situation.

10. <u>Environmental scientists</u> study the effects of human activities on Earth's land, air, water, and living things.

Program Resources

◆ **Unit 1 Resources** Introduction Review and Reinforce, p. 4; Introduction Enrich, p. 5

◆ **Performance Assessment** Introduction, pp. 2–4

◆ **Chapter Tests** Introduction Test, pp. 2–3

Media and Technology

 Computer Test Bank
Introduction Test

Checking Concepts

11. In your own words, explain briefly what science is.
12. Why is it sometimes difficult to use controlled experiments to test hypotheses?
13. What is the difference between a hypothesis and a scientific theory?
14. Explain how a scientist would use the data gathered through a controlled experiment.
15. Explain the importance of following safety rules in laboratory experiments.
16. What are the four main branches of science? Briefly describe what each type of scientist studies.
17. **Writing to Learn** Give an example of an observation of the natural world that you have made. Then give an example of an inference that you made based on that observation. Explain.

Thinking Critically

18. **Problem Solving** You may have heard the saying, "Red sky at night/Sailor's delight." This expression is a hypothesis: A colorful red sunset means there will be fair weather the next day. Describe a scientific method of testing this hypothesis.
19. **Relating Cause and Effect** In a controlled experiment, why do scientists try to control all of the variables except one?
20. **Making Judgments** As a result of just one experiment, a scientist finds evidence that supports a hypothesis. Should other scientists around the world accept this hypothesis? Explain your answer.
21. **Classifying** Which branch of science would investigate the surface temperature of a star? Which branch would investigate the chemical makeup of a food?

Test Preparation
Use these questions to prepare for standardized tests.

Read the passage. Then answer Questions 22–25.

It may surprise you to learn that the climate in a large city can be different from the climate just outside the city. Climate is the average, year-to-year weather conditions in a region. Meteorologists have collected data on these climate differences. The data show that the climate in a city is often warmer and wetter than the climate in the nearby countryside. Cities are also less sunny and less windy than the country around them.

Why are cities warmer? One reason is that buildings and paved surfaces absorb and store more of the sun's energy than do grass, crops, and trees. Another reason is that cars, factories, heating, and air conditioning in cities all give off heat.

Scientists think several factors cause increased rainfall in cities. One hypothesis is that the built-up areas of a city form an obstacle to passing storms. As a result, the storms take longer to move over the city, allowing more rain to fall.

22. The best title for this reading selection is
   a. Sunny Weather Ahead
   b. Meteorologists at Work
   c. City Climates
   d. What Causes Storms?
23. Meteorologists found that the climate in a city differs from the climate in the country by
   a. asking city residents.
   b. collecting data.
   c. observing clouds.
   d. performing controlled experiments.
24. How would you predict a city could lower its outdoor temperature in the summer?
   a. by building more factories
   b. by having more parks with grass and trees
   c. by putting more cars on the road
   d. by adding more air conditioners
25. The idea that a city's buildings can increase rainfall by slowing down a passing storm is an example of a
   a. variable.   b. scientific theory.
   c. determining factor. d. hypothesis.

Thinking Critically

18. Answers may vary. Students may say that you would need to observe the color of sunsets over time and then record what kinds of weather occurred on each following day. If fair weather consistently followed a colorful sunset, then you could conclude that the evidence supported the hypothesis.
19. By controlling all variables but one, scientists can draw a valid conclusion. If more than one variable is changing, scientists cannot tell which variable is the cause of the results that are observed.
20. Other scientists should not accept the hypothesis. For a hypothesis to be accepted, other scientists must be able to repeat the experiment many times and obtain the same results.
21. Investigating the temperature of a star involves Earth science; the chemical make up of a food is a subject for life science.

Test Preparation

22. c **23.** b **24.** b **25.** d

Program Resources

◆ **Inquiry Skills Activity Book** Provides teaching and review of all inquiry skills
◆ **Prentice Hall Assessment System** Provides standardized test practice
◆ **Reading in the Content Area** Provides strategies to improve science reading skills
◆ **Teacher's ELL Handbook** Provides multiple strategies for English language learners

Genetics: The Science of Heredity

Sections	Time	Student Edition Activities	Other Activities	
CHAPTER PROJECT 1 **All in The Family** p. 17	Ongoing (2–3 weeks)	Check Your Progress, pp. 23, 38, 44 Project Wrap Up, p. 47	TE	Chapter 1 Project Notes, pp. 16–17
1 Mendel's Work pp. 18–25 ◆ 1.1.1 Describe Mendel's genetics experiments. ◆ 1.1.2 Identify the factors that control the inheritance of traits in organisms. ◆ 1.1.3 Explain how geneticists use symbols to represent alleles.	2 periods/ 1 block	**Discover** What Does the Father Look Like?, p. 18 **Skills Lab: Developing Hypotheses** Take a Class Survey, pp. 24–25	TE TE TE TE	Building Inquiry Skills: Observing, p. 19 Inquiry Challenge, p. 19 Demonstration, p. 21 Inquiry Challenge, p. 22
2 ⬤ **INTEGRATING MATHEMATICS** **Probability and Genetics** pp. 26–33 ◆ 1.2.1 Describe the principles of probability and how Mendel applied them to inheritance. ◆ 1.2.2 State how geneticists use Punnett squares. ◆ 1.2.3 Explain the meanings of the terms *phenotype, genotype, homozygous, heterozygous,* and *codominance.*	2 periods/ 1 block	**Discover** What's the Chance?, p. 26 **Try This** Coin Crosses, p. 29 **Science at Home,** p. 31 **Skills Lab: Making Models** Make the Right Call!, pp. 32–33	TE TE TE TE	Including All Students, p. 27 Inquiry Challenge, p. 27 Inquiry Challenge, p. 28 Demonstration, p. 29
3 The Cell and Inheritance pp. 34–38 ◆ 1.3.1 Describe the role of chromosomes in inheritance. ◆ 1.3.2 Identify and describe the events that occur during meiosis.	1 period/ ½ block	**Discover** Which Chromosome Is Which?, p. 34	TE TE TE LM	Inquiry Challenge, p. 35 Building Inquiry Skills: Making Models, p. 36 Observing, p. 37 Including All Students, p. 38 1, "Chromosomes and Inheritance"
4 The DNA Connection pp. 39–44 ◆ 1.4.1 Explain the term "genetic code." ◆ 1.4.2 Describe the process by which a cell produces proteins. ◆ 1.4.3 Describe the different types of mutations.	1 period/ ½ block	**Discover** Can You Crack the Code?, p. 39 **Sharpen Your Skills** Predicting, p. 41	TE TE	Inquiry Challenge, p. 41 Building Inquiry Skills: Making Models, p. 43
Study Guide/Assessment pp. 45–47	1 period/ ½ block		ISAB	Provides teaching and review of all inquiry skills

For Standard or Block Schedule The Resource Pro® CD-ROM gives you maximum flexibility for planning your instruction for any type of schedule. Resource Pro® contains Planning Express®, an advanced scheduling program, as well as the entire contents of the Teaching Resources and the Computer Test Bank.

Key: **CTB** Computer Test Bank
CT Chapter Tests
ELL Teacher's ELL Handbook

CHAPTER PLANNING GUIDE

Program Resources	Assessment Strategies	Media and Technology
UR Chapter 1 Project Teacher Notes, pp. 8–9 **UR** Chapter 1 Project Overview and Worksheets, Materials, pp. 10–13	**TE** Check Your Progress, pp. 23, 38, 44 **TE** Performance Assessment: Chapter 1 Project Wrap Up, p. 47 **UR** Chapter 1 Project Scoring Rubric, p. 14	Science Explorer Internet Site Audio CDs, Section Summaries
UR 1-1 Lesson Plan, p. 15 **UR** 1-1 Section Summary, p. 16 **UR** 1-1 Review and Reinforce, p. 17 **UR** 1-1 Enrich, p. 18 **UR** Skills Lab blackline masters, pp. 31–32	**SE** Section 1 Review, p. 29 **SE** Analyze and Conclude, p. 31 **TE** Ongoing Assessment, pp. 25, 27 **TE** Performance Assessment, p. 29	Concept Videotape Library, *Adventures, Tape 1,* "We Are All Heirs" Presentation Pro, "Mendel and Genetics" Transparency 1, "Genetics of Pea Plants" Lab Activity Videotape, *Tape 1*
UR 1-2 Lesson Plan, p. 19 **UR** 1-2 Section Summary, p. 20 **UR** 1-2 Review and Reinforce, p. 21 **UR** 1-2 Enrich, p. 22 **UR** Skills Lab blackline masters, pp. 33–35	**SE** Section 2 Review, p. 31 **SE** Analyze and Conclude, p. 33 **TE** Ongoing Assessment, pp. 27, 29 **TE** Performance Assessment, p. 31	Transparency 2, "Punnett Square—Pea Plants" Lab Activity Videotape, *Tape 1*
UR 1-3 Lesson Plan, p. 23 **UR** 1-3 Section Summary, p. 24 **UR** 1-3 Review and Reinforce, p. 25 **UR** 1-3 Enrich, p. 26	**SE** Section 3 Review, p. 38 **TE** Ongoing Assessment, pp. 35, 37 **TE** Performance Assessment, p. 38	Concept Videotape Library, *Adventures, Tape 1,* "The Chromosome Theory" Presentation Pro, "Meiosis" Transparency 3, "Exploring Meiosis"
UR 1-4 Lesson Plan, p. 27 **UR** 1-4 Section Summary, p. 28 **UR** 1-4 Review and Reinforce, p. 29 **UR** 1-4 Enrich, p. 30	**SE** Section 4 Review, p. 44 **TE** Ongoing Assessment, pp. 41, 43 **TE** Performance Assessment, p. 45	Concept Videotape Library, *Adventures, Tape 1,* "Protein Synthesis" Presentation Pro, "DNA"; "Protein Synthesis" Transparency 4, "Exploring Protein Synthesis"
GRSW Provides worksheets to promote student comprehension of content **RCA** Provides strategies to improve science reading skills **ELL** Provides multiple strategies for English language learners	**SE** Study Guide/Assessment, pp. 45–47 **PA** Performance Assessment, pp. 4–6 **CT** Chapter 1 Test, pp. 3–6 **CTB** Chapter 1 Test **PHAS** Provides standardized test preparation	Computer Test Bank, Chapter 1 Test

GRSW Guided Reading and Study Workbook
ISAB Inquiry Skills Activity Book
LM Laboratory Manual

PA Performance Assessment
PHAS Prentice Hall Assessment System
PLM Probeware Lab Manual

RCA Reading in the Content Area
SE Student Edition

TE Teacher's Edition
UR Unit Resources

Meeting the National Science Education Standards and AAAS Benchmarks

National Science Education Standards	Benchmarks for Science Literacy	Unifying Themes
Science As Inquiry (Content Standard A) ◆ **Use appropriate tools and technology to gather, analyze, and interpret data** Students investigate genetic traits among classmates. *(Skills Lab)* ◆ **Develop descriptions, explanations, predictions, and models using evidence** Students model genetic crosses. Students predict the possible results of genetic crosses. *(Chapter Project; Skills Lab)* ◆ **Use mathematics in all aspects of scientific inquiry** Geneticists use Punnett squares to determine the probability of a particular outcome. *(Chapter Project; Section 2; Skills Lab)* **Life Science** (Content Standard C) ◆ **Structure and function in living systems** Meiosis is the process by which the number of chromosomes is reduced by half to form sex cells. During protein synthesis, the cell uses information from genes to produce proteins. *(Sections 3, 4)* ◆ **Reproduction and heredity** The passing of traits from parents to offspring is called heredity. Genes are carried from parents to offspring on chromosomes. Mutations can be a source of genetic variety. *(Chapter Project; Sections 1, 3, 4; Skills Lab)* **History and Nature of Science** (Content Standard G) ◆ **History of science** Many of the genetic principles that Mendel discovered still stand to this day. *(Sections 1, 2)*	**1B Scientific Inquiry** Students model genetic crosses, investigate genetic traits among classmates, and predict the possible results of genetic crosses. *(Chapter Project; Skills Lab)* **1C The Scientific Enterprise** Many of the genetic principles that Gregor Mendel discovered still stand to this day. Mendel was the first scientist to recognize that the principles of probability can be used to predict the results of genetic crosses. Walter Sutton concluded that chromosomes carry genes from one generation to the next. *(Sections 1, 2, 3)* **5B Heredity** The passing of traits from parents to offspring is called heredity. Genes are carried from parents to offspring on chromosomes. Mutations can be a source of genetic variety. *(Chapter Project; Sections 1, 3, 4; Skills Lab)* **5C Cells** Meiosis is the process by which the number of chromosomes is reduced by half to form sex cells. During protein synthesis, the cell uses information from a gene to produce a specific protein. *(Sections 3, 4)* **9D Uncertainty** Geneticists use Punnett squares to show all the possible outcomes of a genetic cross and to determine the probability of a particular outcome. *(Chapter Project; Section 2; Skills Lab)*	◆ **Evolution** Genes are the basic units of heredity. Genes are carried from parents to offspring on chromosomes. Mutations can be a source of genetic variety. *(Sections 1, 3, 4)* ◆ **Modeling** Students model genetic crosses. *(Chapter Project; Skills Lab)* ◆ **Patterns of Change** Individual alleles control the inheritance of traits. During meiosis, a cell undergoes two divisions to produce sex cells with half the number of chromosomes. Mutations can cause a cell to produce an incorrect protein. *(Sections 1, 3, 4)* ◆ **Scale and Structure** Genes are located on chromosomes. Sex cells have half the normal number of chromosomes. DNA and RNA are made up of nitrogen bases. *(Sections 3, 4)* ◆ **Stability** Heredity is the passing of traits from parents to offspring. A dominant allele is one whose trait always shows up in the organism when the allele is present. Before meiosis begins, every chromosome in the cell is copied. In the genetic code, a group of three bases codes for the attachment of a specific amino acid. *(Sections 1, 3, 4)* ◆ **Systems and Interactions** During meiosis, chromosome pairs separate and are distributed to two different cells. During protein synthesis, the cells use information from a gene to produce specific proteins. *(Sections 2, 3, 4)* ◆ **Unity and Diversity** The different forms of a gene are called alleles. *(Section 1)*

Take It to the Net

The **www.phschool.com** Web site provides you with multiple opportunities to incorporate the internet into your instruction. Go to **www.phschool.com** and click on the Science icon. Then select Science Explorer Integrated.

- Have students use the chapter Self-Test to get instant feedback.
- Hot Links and Reference Links provide opportunities for online research.

WEB ACTIVITY www.phschool.com

Internet Activities provide opportunities for students to review, extend, or assess a concept from the chapter.

STAY CURRENT with **SCIENCE NEWS** ®

Find out the latest research and information about genetics at: **www.phschool.com**

ACTIVITY	Time (minutes)	Materials Quantities for one work group	Skills
Section 1			
Discover, p. 18	10	No special materials are required.	Inferring
Skills Lab, pp. 24–25	40	**Nonconsumable** mirror (optional)	Developing Hypotheses, Interpreting Data, Drawing Conclusions
Section 2			
Discover, p. 26	15	**Nonconsumable** coin	Predicting
Try This, p. 29	15	**Consumable** masking tape **Nonconsumable** 2 coins, scissors	Interpreting Data
Science at Home, p. 31	home	No special materials are required.	Predicting
Skills Lab, pp. 32–33	40	**Consumable** 2 small paper bags **Nonconsumable** marking pen, 3 blue marbles, 3 white marbles	Making Models, Predicting, Interpreting Data, Comparing and Contrasting
Section 3			
Discover, p. 34	10	**Consumable** 4 craft sticks **Nonconsumable** 3 pieces of paper, marking pen	Inferring
Section 4			
Discover, p. 39	15	No special materials are required.	Forming Operational Definitions
Sharpen Your Skills, p. 41	10	No special materials are required.	Predicting

A list of all materials required for the Student Edition activities can be found beginning on page T23. You can obtain information about ordering materials by calling 1-800-848-9500 or by accessing the Science Explorer Internet site at **www.phschool.com.**

All In The Family

Most students are curious about why family members share some physical similarities. Some might even have their own ideas about how physical traits run in families.

Purpose In the Chapter 1 Project, students will create a family of "paper pets" based on phenotypes they have selected. In doing so, students will learn about phenotypes, genotypes, traits, and alleles. They will also learn how traits are passed from parent to offspring and how it is possible to predict the outcomes of genetic crosses.

Skills Focus After completing the Chapter 1 Project, students will be able to
◆ model the inheritance of traits using a paper pet;
◆ infer their pets' genotypes;
◆ predict the genotypes and phenotypes of their pets' offspring;
◆ communicate the results of genetic crosses in a class presentation.

Project Time Line The entire project will require about two or three weeks. See Chapter 1 Project Teacher Notes on pages 8–9 in Unit 1 Resources for more detailed instructions. Begin the project by distributing Chapter 1 Project Overview, pages 10–11 in Unit 1 Resources. Discuss the project with students and begin talking about the materials they will need to decorate their pets. Students will use Chapter 1 Project Worksheet 1, page 12 in Unit 1 Resources, to help them create their pets.

Once they have created their pets, allow class time for students to set up crosses with another pet. After students have found partners, distribute Chapter 1 Project Worksheet 2, page 13 in Unit 1 Resources, to help students determine the results of the crosses between their pets and create the offspring. Student pairs might need class time to prepare displays of their pet families.

Suggested Shortcuts You can simplify this project by having students record the phenotype and genotype of their pets on paper. Student pairs can set up Punnett squares for the crosses without making paper models of the pet parents and

Genetics: The Science of Heredity

WEB ACTIVITY www.phschool.com

Integrating Mathematics

SECTION 1	Mendel's Work	SECTION 2	Probability and Genetics	SECTION 3	The Cell and Inheritance
Discover	What Does the Father Look Like?	**Discover**	What's the Chance?	**Discover**	Which Chromosome Is Which?
Skills Lab	Take a Class Survey	**Try This**	Coin Crosses		
		Skills Lab	Make the Right Call!		

16

offspring. Each pair can simply assume that one of their pets is female and the other is male.

Possible Materials Students need blue or yellow construction paper for the pet's body. They will also need scissors, colored pencils, glue, and markers to create their pets. Encourage students to decorate their pets with additional materials. You can provide these materials or have students use materials from home. Materials students might use include

glitter, beads, feathers, sequins, yarn, and buttons. Students will need a coin to toss to determine the offspring's genotypes and poster board or other large paper to display their pet families.

Launching the Project To introduce the Chapter 1 Project, invite students to look at the photo of the boxer puppies on these pages. Ask: **How are these puppies similar to each other and to their mother? How are they different?** *(Accept all answers. Most students will describe*

PROJECT 1

All In The Family

Did you ever wonder why some offspring resemble their parents while others do not? In this chapter, you'll learn how offspring come to have traits similar to those of their parents. In this project, you'll create a family of "paper pets" to explore how traits pass from parents to offspring.

Your Goal To create a "paper pet" that will be crossed with a pet belonging to a classmate, and to determine what traits the offspring will have.

To complete this project successfully, you must
◆ create your own unique paper pet with five different traits
◆ cross your pet with another pet to produce six offspring
◆ determine what traits the offspring will have, and explain how they came to have those traits

Get Started Cut out your pet from either blue or yellow construction paper. Choose other traits for your pet from this list: female or male; square eyes or round eyes; oval nose or triangular nose; pointed teeth or square teeth. Then create your pet using materials of your choice.

Check Your Progress You'll be working on this project as you study this chapter. To keep your project on track, look for Check Your Progress boxes at the following points.
Section 1 Review, page 23: Identify your pet's genotype.
Section 3 Review, page 38: Determine what traits your pet's offspring have.
Section 4 Review, page 44: Make a display of your pet's family.

Wrap Up At the end of the chapter (page 47), you and your partner will display your pet's family and analyze the inheritance patterns.

These boxer puppies and their mother resemble each other in many ways. However, there are also noticeable differences between one dog and the next.

SECTION 4 The DNA Connection
Discover Can You Crack the Code?
Sharpen Your Skills Predicting

17

Program Resources

◆ **Unit 1 Resources** Chapter 1 Project Teacher Notes, pp. 8–9; Project Overview and Worksheets, pp. 10–13; Project Scoring Rubric, p. 14

Media and Technology

 Audio CDs Section Summaries

WEB ACTIVITY www.phschool.com

You will find an Internet activity, chapter self-tests for students, and links to other chapter topics at this site.

---

similarities in the shape of the nose and ears and differences in color.) Encourage students to offer explanations for these similarities and differences.

Finally, have students read the description of the project in their text and in the Chapter 1 Project Overview. Encourage students to begin thinking about what traits their pets will have without considering which alleles are dominant or recessive.

Performance Assessment

The Chapter 1 Project Scoring Rubric on page 14 of Unit 1 Resources will help you evaluate how well students complete the Chapter 1 Project. Students will be assessed on
◆ how neatly and creatively they design their paper pets and how correctly they identify the phenotypes and genotypes;
◆ how accurately they identify the genotypes and phenotypes of their pets' offspring;
◆ how accurately and completely they design a display of their pets' families.

By sharing the Chapter 1 Project Scoring Rubric with students at the beginning of the project, you will make it clear to them what they are expected to do.

17

Objectives

After completing the lesson, students will be able to

◆ describe Mendel's genetics experiments;

◆ identify the factors that control the inheritance of traits in organisms;

◆ explain how geneticists use symbols to represent alleles.

Key Terms trait, heredity, genetics, purebred, gene, allele, dominant allele, recessive allele, hybrid

1 Engage/Explore

Activating Prior Knowledge

Invite students to share observations they have made about the physical similarities and differences among family members. Ask: **Have you ever wondered why some family members look very similar while others look very different?** *(Many students will have considered this in one way or another.)* Encourage students to share their ideas about the inheritance of traits in families. Be alert for misconceptions students might have, and address these throughout the section.

•••••••• **DISCOVER** •••••••

Skills Focus inferring
Time 10 minutes
Expected Outcome Two kittens are mostly white with some black. The third kitten is dark grey with some white. The mother is black with some white.
Think It Over Students will probably infer that the father may be mostly white. They may infer that the white kittens may have inherited their color pattern from the father. They may also infer that the grey kitten is a mixture of the mostly white father and mostly black mother.

SECTION 1 Mendel's Work

DISCOVER •• **ACTIVITY**

What Does the Father Look Like?

1. Observe the colors of each kitten in the photo. Record each kitten's coat colors and patterns. Include as many details as you can.

2. Observe the mother cat in the photo. Record her coat color and pattern.

Think It Over
Inferring Based on your observations, describe what you think the kittens' father might look like. Identify the evidence on which you based your inference.

GUIDE FOR READING

◆ What factors control the inheritance of traits in organisms?

Reading Tip Before you read, preview the section and make a list of the boldfaced terms. As you read, write a definition for each term in your own words.

Gregor Mendel in the monastery garden ▼

The year was 1851. Gregor Mendel, a young priest from a monastery in Central Europe, entered the University of Vienna to study mathematics and science. Two years later, Mendel returned to the monastery and began teaching at a nearby high school.

Mendel also cared for the monastery's garden, where he grew hundreds of pea plants. He became curious about why some of the plants had different physical characteristics, or **traits.** Some pea plants grew tall while others were short. Some plants produced green seeds, while others had yellow seeds.

Mendel observed that the pea plants' traits were often similar to those of their parents. Sometimes, however, the pea plants had different traits than their parents. The passing of traits from parents to offspring is called **heredity.** For more than ten years, Mendel experimented with thousands of pea plants to understand the process of heredity. Mendel's work formed the foundation of **genetics,** the scientific study of heredity.

Mendel's Peas

Mendel made a wise decision when he chose to study peas rather than other plants in the monastery garden. Pea plants are easy to study because they have many traits that exist in only two forms. For example, pea plant stems are either tall or short, but not medium height. Also, garden peas produce a large number of offspring in one generation. Thus, it is easy to collect large amounts of data to analyze.

READING STRATEGIES

Reading Tip Make sure students use their own words to define each boldfaced term. After students have previewed the section, pronounce each boldfaced term for the class to make sure that students are pronouncing them correctly. Students could write each term on one side of an index card and the definition on the other side. They can then use these cards as study aids.

Concept Mapping Have students make a concept map in which they show the relationships among the terms in the section. Students may include their definitions on the concept maps, if they wish.

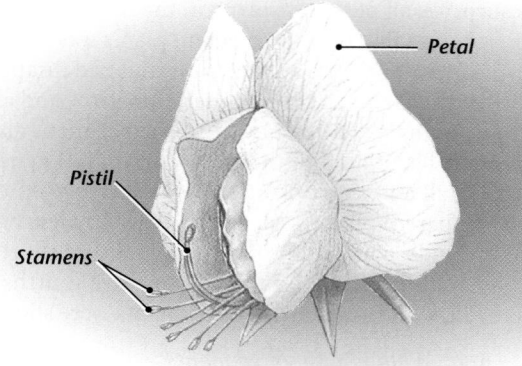

Petal

Pistil

Stamens

Figure 1 Garden peas usually reproduce by self-pollination. Pollen from a flower's stamens lands on the pistil of the same flower. Plants that result from self-pollination inherit all of their characteristics from the single parent plant. *Applying Concepts How did Mendel prevent his pea plants from self-pollinating?*

Figure 1 shows a flowering pea plant. Notice that the flower's petals surround the pistil and the stamens. The pistil produces female sex cells, or eggs, while the stamens produce pollen, which contains the male sex cells.

In nature, pea plants are usually self-pollinating. This means that pollen from one flower lands on the pistil of the same flower. Mendel developed a method by which he could cross-pollinate, or "cross," pea plants. To cross two plants, he removed pollen from a flower on one plant and brushed it onto a flower on a second plant. To prevent the pea plants from self-pollinating, he carefully removed the stamens from the flowers on the second plant.

Mendel's Experiments

Suppose you had a garden full of pea plants, and you wanted to study the inheritance of traits. What would you do? Mendel decided to cross plants with opposite forms of a trait, for example, tall plants and short plants. He started his experiments with purebred plants. A **purebred** plant is one that always produces offspring with the same form of a trait as the parent. For example, purebred short pea plants always produce short offspring. Purebred tall pea plants always produce tall offspring. To produce purebred plants, Mendel allowed peas with one particular trait to self-pollinate for many generations. By using purebred plants, Mendel knew that the offspring's trait would always be identical to that of the parents.

In his first experiment, Mendel crossed purebred tall plants with purebred short plants. He called these parent plants the parental generation, or P generation. He called the offspring from this cross the first filial (FIL ee ul) generation, or the F_1 generation. The word *filial* means "son" in Latin.

Answers to Self-Assessment

Caption Question

Figure 1 Mendel removed the stamens from the flowers that he cross-pollinated.

2 Facilitate

Mendel's Peas

Building Inquiry Skills: Observing

Materials *tulip or lily flower, hand lens, small blunt-tipped scissors*
Time 15 minutes

ACTIVITY

Encourage students to closely observe the intact flower with a hand lens. Then instruct students to snip apart the pistil and stamens with scissors and examine these parts individually. Have students draw a labeled diagram of the flower and its parts. Then have them compare their diagrams with the pea flower in Figure 1. Ask: **What makes the pea flower well suited for self-pollination?** *(The petals almost completely enclose the pistil and stamen.)* Tell students that self-pollinating plants are a better choice for studying inheritance because it is easier to obtain purebreeding plants.
learning modality: kinesthetic

Mendel's Experiments

Inquiry Challenge

Materials *posterboard*
Time 20 minutes

ACTIVITY

Challenge small groups to evaluate Mendel's experimental procedure. Groups should create a poster on which they identify Mendel's question and hypothesis and outline his experimental design. Groups should also include a summary of their opinions about Mendel's procedures. Have them consider why Mendel allowed the F_1 plants to self-pollinate. *(To see if they were purebred)* Groups can present their posters to the class. **cooperative learning**

Ongoing Assessment

Writing Have students identify three characteristics of pea plants that make them useful for studying inheritance. *(Only two forms of many traits, large number of offspring, self-pollinating)*

Language Arts
CONNECTION

Have students compare Mendel's description with the round and wrinkled peas in Figure 3. Invite them to suggest changes to Mendel's description. Then ask: **Why do you think detailed descriptions are important in scientific papers?** *(So readers will clearly understand the author's ideas)*

In Your Journal Before students list the features of their objects, discuss adjectives and adverbs, the kinds of words used to describe objects. Tell students not to use the name of their objects in their paragraphs. Then have students trade paragraphs and guess their partners' objects. **learning modality: verbal**

Dominant and Recessive Alleles

Using the Visuals: Figure 3
Review with students the forms of each trait in the peas that Mendel studied. Ask: **Why are these traits well suited for studying inheritance?** *(The traits are easy to observe and have two distinct forms.)* Then have students solve simple genetic crosses between peas that differ in one trait. For example: **What color seeds will the offspring have when a purebred pea plant with yellow seeds is crossed with a purebred plant with green seeds?** *(yellow seeds)* **learning modality: visual**

Including All Students
Students can add the following terms to their lists of boldfaced terms from the Reading Tip activity to create their own genetics dictionary: *factor, characteristic, self-pollination, cross-pollination, cross, filial, F₁ generation, P generation, inheritance,* and *purebred.* Students should write their own definitions of these words and include drawings if needed. Allow students whose native language is not English to write definitions in their own language. **limited English proficiency**

Language Arts
CONNECTION

Gregor Mendel presented a detailed description of his observations in a scientific paper in 1866. In the excerpt that follows, notice how clearly he describes his observations of the two different seed shapes in peas.

"These are either round or roundish, the depressions, if any, occur on the surface, being always only shallow; or they are irregularly angular and deeply wrinkled."

In Your Journal

Choose an everyday object, such as a piece of fruit or a pen. Make a list of the object's features. Then write a short paragraph describing the object. Use clear, precise language in your description.

You can see the results of Mendel's first cross in Figure 2. To Mendel's surprise, all of the offspring in the F_1 generation were tall. Despite the fact that one of the parent plants was short, none of the offspring were short. The shortness trait had disappeared!

Mendel let the plants in the F_1 generation grow and allowed them to self-pollinate. The results of this experiment also surprised Mendel. The plants in the F_2 (second filial) generation were a mix of tall and short plants. This occurred even though none of the F_1 parent plants were short. The shortness trait had reappeared. Mendel counted the number of tall and short plants in the F_2 generation. He found that about three fourths of the plants were tall, while one fourth of the plants were short.

☑ *Checkpoint* **What is a purebred plant?**

Other Traits

In addition to stem height, Mendel studied six other traits in garden peas: seed shape, seed color, seed coat color, pod shape, pod color, and flower position. Compare the two forms of each trait in Figure 3. Mendel crossed plants with these traits in the same manner as he did for stem height. The results in each experiment were similar to those that he observed with stem height. Only one form of the trait appeared in the F_1 generation. However, in the F_2 generation the "lost" form of the trait always reappeared in about one fourth of the plants.

Figure 2 When Mendel crossed purebred tall and short pea plants, all the offspring in the F_1 generation were tall. In the F_2 generation, three fourths of the plants were tall, while one fourth were short.

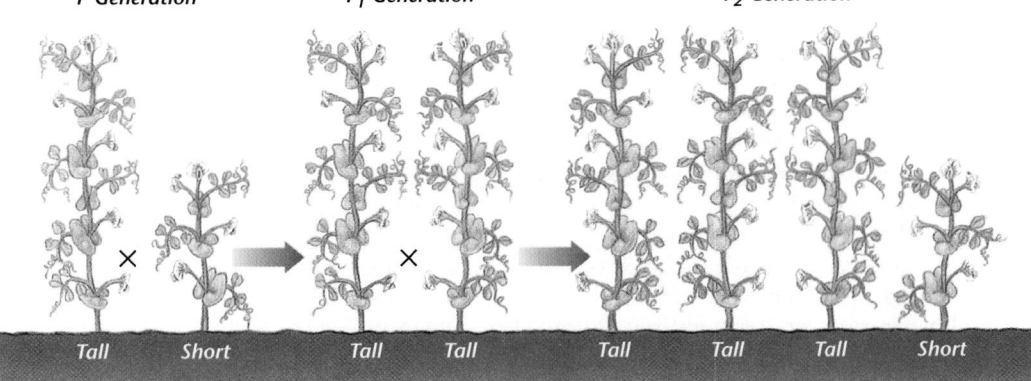

P Generation   **F_1 Generation**   **F_2 Generation**

Tall   Short   Tall   Tall   Tall   Tall   Tall   Short

Background

History of Science Mendel's work is relevant today because of his careful experimental design. Unlike other scientists and plant and animal breeders of his time, Mendel carefully chose to study distinct traits. He allowed plants to self-pollinate until he was certain that the plants he used were purebreeding. Most importantly, he applied the principles of statistics when setting up his crosses and interpreting his results. This prevented him from interpreting his results using his personal opinions and beliefs. Other scientists and breeders at that time set up their crosses randomly with parents of unknown breeding and often tried to follow more than one trait at a time. They also thought that inheritance was much too complicated to analyze using the principles of statistics.

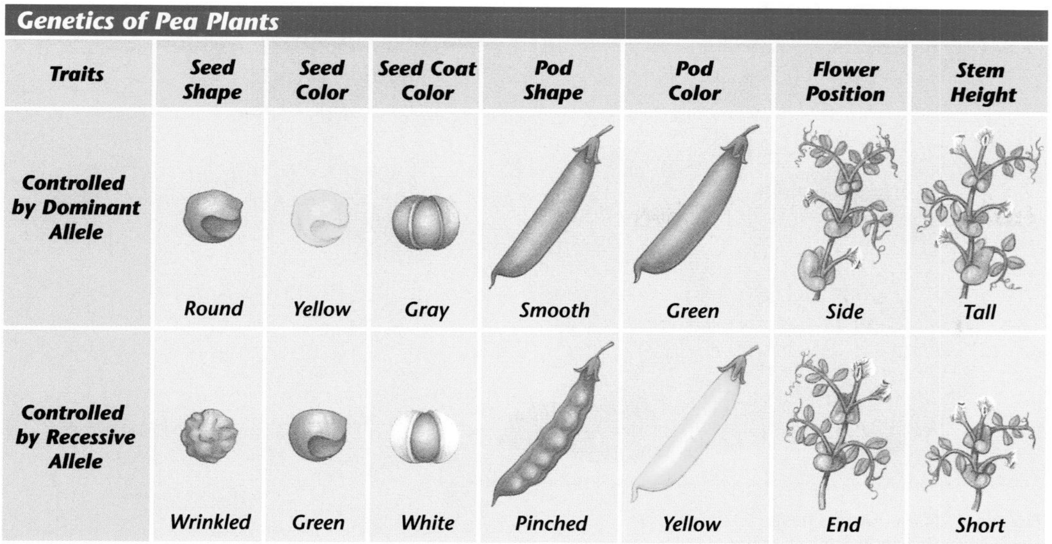

Genetics of Pea Plants

Traits	Seed Shape	Seed Color	Seed Coat Color	Pod Shape	Pod Color	Flower Position	Stem Height
Controlled by Dominant Allele	Round	Yellow	Gray	Smooth	Green	Side	Tall
Controlled by Recessive Allele	Wrinkled	Green	White	Pinched	Yellow	End	Short

Figure 3 Mendel studied seven different traits in pea plants. Each trait has two different forms. *Interpreting Diagrams Is yellow seed color controlled by a dominant allele or a recessive allele? What type of allele controls pinched pod shape?*

Dominant and Recessive Alleles

From his results, Mendel reasoned that individual factors must control the inheritance of traits in peas. The factors that control each trait exist in pairs. The female parent contributes one factor, while the male parent contributes the other factor.

Mendel went on to reason that one factor in a pair can mask, or hide, the other factor. The tallness factor, for example, masked the shortness factor in the F_1 generation.

Today, scientists call the factors that control traits **genes.** They call the different forms of a gene **alleles** (uh LEELZ). The gene that controls stem height in peas, for example, has one allele for tall stems and one allele for short stems. Each pea plant inherits a combination of two alleles from its parents—either two alleles for tall stems, two alleles for short stems, or one of each.

Individual alleles control the inheritance of traits. Some alleles are dominant, while other alleles are recessive. A **dominant allele** is one whose trait always shows up in the organism when the allele is present. A **recessive allele,** on the other hand, is masked, or covered up, whenever the dominant allele is present. A trait controlled by a recessive allele will only show up if the organism does not have the dominant allele.

In pea plants, the allele for tall stems is dominant over the allele for short stems. Pea plants with one allele for tall stems and one allele for short stems will be tall. The allele for tall stems masks the allele for short stems. Only pea plants that inherit two recessive alleles for short stems will be short.

Media and Technology

Transparencies "Genetics of Pea Plants," Transparency 1

Concept Videotape Library *Adventures, Tape 1,* "We Are All Heirs"

Answers to Self-Assessment

Checkpoint

A plant that always produces offspring with the same form of a trait as the parent

Caption Question

Figure 3 a dominant allele; recessive

Demonstration

ACTIVITY

Materials *2* Drosophila melanogaster *cultures—wild-type and ebony, culture vials and plugs,* Drosophila *media, nonether anesthesia kit, hand lens, paint brush, white index card, marking pen* (NOTE: Drosophila *cultures are available from science supply companies.)*

Time 20 minutes

Advance Preparation Set up the parental cross about two weeks in advance by placing 2 to 3 ebony males with 2 to 3 wild-type virgin females in each of three vials. To collect virgin females, remove all adult flies from the culture vial. Then, within 4 to 6 hours, collect the newly emerged females. Females have pointed abdomens with stripes almost to the end. Males have rounded abdomens that are black at the end. Anesthetize flies to sort them and to set up the crosses. Place vials on their sides until the flies wake up. Remove parent flies from the vials when pupae begin to develop. When F_1 adults begin to emerge, remove the flies daily to prevent F_2 offspring from mixing with F_1 offspring. Dispose of flies in a jar of mineral oil. Empty this "morgue" into a garbage disposal.

Tips Anesthetize the parent flies and place them on index cards for students to examine. Ask: **How do these flies differ?** *(Ebony flies have darker bodies than wild-type flies.)* Challenge students to predict which trait is controlled by a dominant allele and which is controlled by a recessive allele. Then anesthetize the F_1 flies and place them on index cards for students to count. Ask: **Which trait is controlled by a dominant allele?** *(lighter body color)* **How do you know?** *(None of the F_1 flies have ebony bodies.)* **What body color will F_2 flies have?** *(Some will have ebony bodies, but most will have lighter bodies.)* **learning modality: logical/mathematical**

Ongoing Assessment

Drawing Have students diagram Mendel's crosses between tall and short pea plants. Tell them to label the traits controlled by dominant and recessive alleles.

Portfolio Students can save their drawings in their portfolios.

Understanding Mendel's Crosses

Building Inquiry Skills: Applying Concepts

Have students choose a pea trait from Figure 3, and challenge them to diagram the crosses that Mendel made. In their diagrams, students should show how dominant and recessive alleles are inherited from the P generation through the F_1 generation to the F_2 generation. Encourage students to share their diagrams with the class. **learning modality: logical/mathematical**

Using Symbols in Genetics

Including All Students

Students who need more help can practice using genetic symbols by assigning letters to the dominant and recessive alleles for each trait that Mendel studied. Students can use any letter to represent each trait, although the convention is to use the letter that begins the word of the dominant allele. For example, *R* stands for round seeds and *r* stands for wrinkled. Dominant alleles must have a capital letter; recessive alleles, lower-case. **learning modality: verbal**

Inquiry Challenge

Materials F_2 *ear of corn with purple and yellow kernels (available from science supply companies)*

Time 15 minutes

Give each small group an ear of corn. Explain that the ears were produced by F_2 generation plants and that kernel color is controlled by dominant and recessive alleles—purple is controlled by the dominant allele, and yellow is controlled by the recessive allele. Then challenge students to trace the inheritance of the dominant and recessive alleles for kernel color by working backward from the F_2 ear to the F_1 cross and finally to the parental cross. Students should use symbols to represent the alleles for kernel color. (*F_1 parents: both purple (Pp); P parents: one purple (PP), one yellow (pp)*) **learning modality: logical/mathematical**

Figure 4 These rabbits have some traits controlled by dominant alleles and other traits controlled by recessive alleles. For example, the allele for black fur is dominant over the allele for white fur. *Inferring What combination of alleles must the white rabbit have?*

Understanding Mendel's Crosses

You can understand Mendel's results by tracing the inheritance of alleles in his experiments. The purebred plants in the P generation had two identical alleles for stem height. The purebred tall plants had two alleles for tall stems. The purebred short plants had two alleles for short stems. In the F_1 generation, all of the plants received one allele for tall stems from the tall parent. They received one allele for short stems from the short parent. The F_1 plants are called **hybrids** (HY bridz) because they have two different alleles for the trait. All the F_1 plants are tall because the dominant allele for tall stems masks the recessive allele for short stems.

When Mendel crossed the hybrid plants in the F_1 generation, some of the plants inherited two dominant alleles for tall stems. These plants were tall. Other plants inherited one dominant allele for tall stems and one recessive allele for short stems. These plants were also tall. Other plants inherited two recessive alleles for short stems. These plants were short.

☑ *Checkpoint* *If a pea plant has a tall stem, what possible combinations of alleles could it have?*

Using Symbols in Genetics

Geneticists today use a standard shorthand method to write about alleles in genetic crosses. Instead of using words such as "tall stems" to represent alleles, they simply use letters. A

Background

History of Science At the time of Mendel's studies of inheritance, most of the scientific community believed in the blending theory of inheritance. This theory assumed that both parents contributed equally to the characteristics of the offspring. According to the theory, parents of contrasting appearance always produced offspring with an intermediate appearance. When parental traits reappeared in the offspring, it was thought to be due to some genetic disturbance. Mendel also subscribed to the blending theory. When he started working on his experiments with peas, he was not trying to discover the laws of inheritance. Rather, he was trying to find a hybrid that would breed true. This is one reason why his results went unnoticed for some time. The scientific community could not interpret them for what they really showed.

dominant allele is represented by a capital letter. For example, the allele for tall stems is represented by *T*. A recessive allele is represented by the lowercase version of the letter. So, the allele for short stems would be represented by *t*. When a plant inherits two dominant alleles for tall stems, its alleles are written as *TT*. When a plant inherits two recessive alleles for short stems, its alleles are written as *tt*. When a plant inherits one allele for tall stems and one allele for short stems, its alleles are written as *Tt*.

Mendel's Contribution

In 1866, Mendel presented his results to a scientific society that met regularly near the monastery. In his paper, Mendel described the principles of heredity he had discovered. Unfortunately, other scientists did not understand the importance of Mendel's work. Some scientists thought that Mendel had oversimplified the process of inheritance. Others never read his paper, or even heard about his work. At that time, scientists in different parts of the world were isolated from each other. Mendel was especially isolated because he wasn't at a university. Remember, there were no telephones, and no computers to send electronic mail.

Mendel's work was forgotten for 34 years. In 1900, three different scientists rediscovered Mendel's work. They had made many of the same observations as Mendel had. The scientists quickly recognized the importance of Mendel's work. Many of the genetic principles that Mendel discovered still stand to this day. Because of his work, Mendel is often called the Father of Genetics.

Figure 5 The dominant allele for yellow skin color in summer squash is represented by the letter *Y*. The recessive allele for green skin color is represented by the letter *y*.

Section 1 Review

1. Explain how the inheritance of traits is controlled in organisms. Use the terms *genes* and *alleles* in your explanation.
2. What is a dominant allele? What is a recessive allele? Give an example of each.
3. The allele for round seeds is represented by *R*. Suppose that a pea plant inherited two recessive alleles for wrinkled seeds. How would you write the symbols for its alleles?
4. **Thinking Critically** **Applying Concepts** Can a short pea plant ever be a hybrid? Why or why not?

Check Your Progress

CHAPTER PROJECT 1

By now you should have constructed your paper pet. On the back, write what alleles your pet has for each trait. Use XX for a female, and XY for a male. The dominant alleles for the other four traits are: *B* (blue skin), *R* (round eyes), *T* (triangular nose), and *P* (pointed teeth). (*Hint:* If your pet has a trait controlled by a dominant allele, you can choose which of the possible combinations of alleles your pet has.)

Program Resources

◆ **Unit 1 Resources** 1-1 Review and Reinforce, p. 17; 1-1 Enrich, p. 18

Answers to Self-Assessment

Caption Question

Figure 4 two alleles for white fur

☑ *Checkpoint*

Two alleles for tall stems or one allele for tall stems and one allele for short stems

---

Mendel's Contribution

Real-Life Learning

Explain to students that it is not unusual for scientists who have discovered new ideas to be misunderstood or even ridiculed. It is very difficult to change popular opinion. Some ideas that were once controversial include that Earth orbits the sun and that Earth is round. Challenge student groups to work together to write a broadcast news story about a scientific idea that is controversial. Students might choose Mendel's results or another idea, either current or historical. You might wish to videotape the groups' broadcasts in a pretend news show. **cooperative learning**

3 Assess

Section 1 Review Answers

1. Each allele of a gene controls the inheritance of a specific trait.
2. *Dominant:* trait always shows up when the allele is present; tall stems in peas. *Recessive:* trait is covered up whenever dominant allele is present; short pea stems.
3. The symbols would be *rr*.
4. No, it has two recessive alleles *(tt)*; hybrids have two different alleles for a trait.

Check Your Progress

CHAPTER PROJECT 1

Check each paper pet to make sure students have correctly assigned pairs of alleles based on the traits they chose. Monitor the number of male and female pets so that there is an equal number of each. If the class has an odd number of students, create an extra pet. Encourage students to be creative when they decorate their pets.

Performance Assessment

Writing Have students summarize Mendel's experiments and his conclusions about the inheritance of traits.

 Students can save their summaries in their portfolios.

Take a Class Survey

Preparing for Inquiry

Key Concept Human traits are controlled by dominant and recessive alleles, causing many different combinations of traits among a group of people.

Skills Objectives Students will be able to
- develop hypotheses about whether traits controlled by dominant alleles are more common than traits controlled by recessive alleles;
- interpret data about certain traits controlled by dominant and recessive alleles in humans;
- draw conclusions about the frequency and the variation of certain traits in the class.

Time 40 minutes

Advance Planning Gather mirrors, or invite students to bring some from home. You might wish to make photocopies of the circle chart and the data table.

Alternative Materials If you do not have mirrors, students can observe each other.

Guided Inquiry

Invitation Help students relate Mendel's conclusions to their own physical characteristics. Ask: **Why do you think people often look very similar to other family members, but also different?** *(Some students might realize that children inherit both dominant and recessive alleles from each parent. The combination of these alleles determines the child's physical appearance.)*

Introducing the Procedure
- Have students read through the entire procedure. Then review with them what each trait looks like. Refer students to the illustrations in the text, or find examples of each trait among the class. Tell students that curly hair includes wavy hair or any hair that is not straight.

Skills Lab

Developing Hypotheses

Take a Class Survey

In this lab, you'll explore how greatly traits can vary in a group of people—your classmates.

Problem

Are traits controlled by dominant alleles more common than traits controlled by recessive alleles?

Materials

mirror (optional)

Procedure

Part 1 Dominant and Recessive Alleles

1. Write a hypothesis reflecting your ideas about the problem question. Then copy the data table.
2. For each of the traits listed in the data table, work with a partner to determine which trait you have. Circle that trait in your data table.
3. Count the number of students who have each trait. Record that number in your data table. Also record the total number of students.

DATA TABLE
Total Number _____

	Trait 1	Number	Trait 2	Number
A	Free ear lobes		Attached ear lobes	
B	Hair on fingers		No hair on fingers	
C	Widow's peak		No widow's peak	
D	Curly hair		Straight hair	
E	Cleft chin		Smooth chin	
F	Smile dimples		No smile dimples	

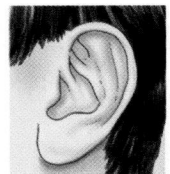 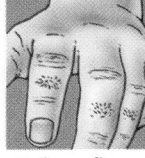 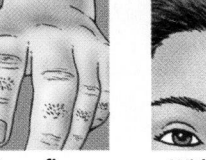 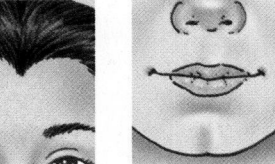 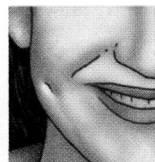

Free ear lobe *Hair on fingers* *Widow's peak* *Cleft chin* *Smile dimples*

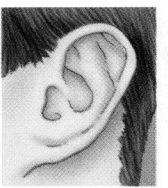 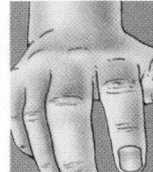 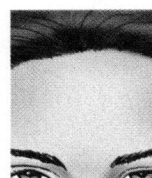 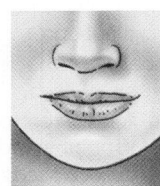 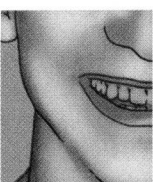

Attached ear lobe *No hair on fingers* *No widow's peak* *No cleft chin* *No smile dimples*

- Make sure students know how to use the circle of traits in Part 2. Point out how to use the color-coding, starting at the center of the circle.

Troubleshooting the Experiment
- Monitor students as they work to make sure they correctly identify each trait.
- The class can record their results on a large data table on the chalkboard by writing their initials in the appropriate columns.

Expected Outcome
Students will show a great variation in traits. Few, if any, will have the same number on the circle of traits.

Analyze and Conclude
1. One trait controlled by a dominant allele that is usually more common is free earlobes. Some traits controlled by recessive alleles that are usually more common include smooth chin, straight hair, no widow's peak, and no mid-finger hair. However, any class's results

Part 2 Are Your Traits Unique?

4. Look at the circle of traits below. All the traits in your data table appear in the circle. Place the eraser end of your pencil on the trait in the small central circle that applies to you—either free ear lobes or attached ear lobes.

5. Look at the two traits touching the space your eraser is on. Move your eraser onto the next description that applies to you. Continue using your eraser to trace your traits until you reach a number on the outside rim of the circle. Share that number with your classmates.

Analyze and Conclude

1. The traits listed under Trait 1 in the data table are controlled by dominant alleles. The traits listed under Trait 2 are controlled by recessive alleles. Which traits controlled by dominant alleles were shown by a majority of students? Which traits controlled by recessive alleles were shown by a majority of students?

2. How many students ended up on the same number on the circle of traits? How many students were the only ones to have their number? What do the results suggest about each person's combination of traits?

3. Think About It Do your data support the hypothesis you proposed in Step 1? Explain your answer with examples.

Design an Experiment

Do people who are related to each other show more genetic similarity than unrelated people? Write a hypothesis. Then design an experiment to test your hypothesis.

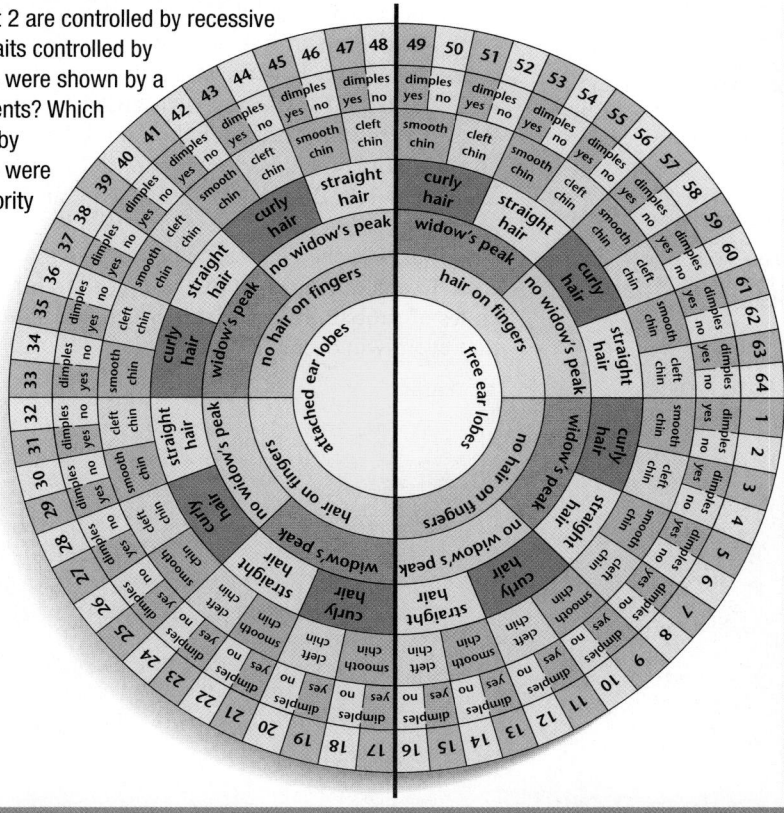

may vary from the overall population patterns because of the small sample size.

2. Answers will vary, but usually few or no students have the same number when six traits are studied. As more traits are considered, the smaller the chance that any two people in a class will have the same number. Even siblings, except for identical twins, have different combinations of traits.

3. Answers will vary, but students should describe, using examples from the lab, that neither traits controlled by dominant alleles nor traits controlled by recessive alleles are automatically more common in a population.

Extending the Inquiry

Design an Experiment Students' hypotheses will vary. *Sample hypothesis:* A group of related people will share more numbers on the circle of traits than a group of unrelated people. Student experiments can follow the same procedure as this lab, except students should observe the traits in people from a single family.

Program Resources

◆ **Unit 1 Resources** Skills Lab blackline masters, pp. 31–32

Media and Technology

 Lab Activity Videotape
Tape 1

Safety

Review the safety guidelines in Appendix A.

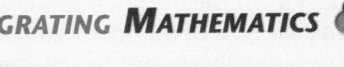

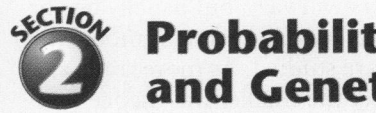

SECTION 2 Probability and Genetics

Objectives

After completing the lesson, students will be able to

◆ describe the principles of probability and how Mendel applied them to inheritance;

◆ state how geneticists use Punnett squares;

◆ explain the meanings of the terms *phenotype, genotype, homozygous, heterozygous,* and *codominance.*

Key Terms probability, Punnett square, phenotype, genotype, homozygous, heterozygous, codominance

1 Engage/Explore

Activating Prior Knowledge

Invite students to describe situations in which they have used a coin toss to decide an issue. Ask: **Why did you toss a coin in these situations?** *(Students might mention that it was the fairest way to make a decision.)* **Why is a coin toss fair?** *(Each person has a 50–50 chance of winning.)*

Skills Focus predicting
Materials *coin*
Time 15 minutes
Expected Outcome The actual outcome of the coin tosses will vary. The more data, the closer the outcome will be to the expected ratio of 1 head: 1 tail.
Think It Over For most students, their results were slightly different from their predictions. The combined class data should be closer to the expected ratio of 1 head to 1 tail. Students might infer that the difference is due to chance or that the more coin tosses they make, the closer they will come to the predicted outcome.

SECTION 2 Probability and Genetics

DISCOVER ·························ACTIVITY

What's the Chance?

1. Suppose you were to toss a coin 20 times. Predict how many times the coin would land "heads up" and how many times it would land "tails up."

2. Now test your prediction by tossing a coin 20 times. Record the number of times the coin lands heads up and the number of times it lands tails up.

3. Combine the data from the entire class. Record the total number of tosses, the number of heads, and the number of tails.

Think It Over
Predicting How did your results in Step 2 compare to your prediction? How can you account for any differences between your results and the class results?

GUIDE FOR READING

◆ How do the principles of probability help explain Mendel's results?

◆ How do geneticists use Punnett squares?

Reading Tip Before you read, rewrite the headings in the section as questions that begin with *how, what,* or *why.* As you read, look for answers to these questions.

The city of Portland, Oregon, was founded in the mid-1800s. Two men, Asa L. Lovejoy and Francis W. Pettygrove, owned the land on which the new city was built. Lovejoy, who was from Massachusetts, wanted to name the new town Boston. Pettygrove, however, thought the town should be named after his hometown, Portland, Maine. To settle the dispute, they decided to toss a coin. Pettygrove won, and the new town was named Portland.

What was the chance that Pettygrove would win the coin toss? To answer this question, you need to understand the principles of probability. **Probability** is the likelihood that a particular event will occur.

26

READING STRATEGIES

Reading Tip Students can write questions for both the major headings and the subheads in the section. Questions may included, "What are the principles of heredity?" Remind students to leave space after each question to allow room for their answers. Encourage students to keep their questions nearby so they can write the answers as they read.

Vocabulary Show students that the term *homozygous* is made up of the Greek words *homos,* meaning "same," and *zygos,* meaning "yoked or paired." Taken together, these words describe a cell formed from two gametes that have the same genetic makeup. In *heterozygous, heteros* is the Greek word meaning "other or different." This word describes a cell formed from two gametes that have a different genetic makeup.

Principles of Probability

If you did the Discover activity, you used the principles of probability to predict the results of a particular event. Each time you toss a coin, there are two possible ways that the coin can land—heads up or tails up. Each of these two events is equally likely to occur. In mathematical terms, you can say that the probability that a tossed coin will land heads up is 1 in 2. There is also a 1 in 2 probability that the coin will land tails up. A 1 in 2 probability can also be expressed as the fraction $\frac{1}{2}$ or as a percent—50 percent.

If you tossed a coin 20 times, you might expect it to land heads up 10 times and tails up 10 times. However, you might not actually get these results. You might get 11 heads and 9 tails, or 8 heads and 12 tails. Remember that the laws of probability predict what is likely to occur, not necessarily what will occur. However, the more tosses you make, the closer your actual results will be to the results predicted by probability.

When you toss a coin more than once, the results of one toss do not affect the results of the next toss. Each event occurs independently. For example, suppose you toss a coin five times and it lands heads up each time. What is the probability that it will land heads up on the next toss? Because the coin landed heads up on the previous five tosses, you might think that it would be likely to land heads up on the next toss. However, this is not the case. The probability of the coin landing heads up on the next toss is still 1 in 2, or 50 percent. The results of the first five tosses do not affect the results of the sixth toss.

☑ *Checkpoint* *Why is there a 1 in 2 probability that a tossed coin will land heads up?*

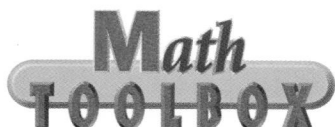

Math TOOLBOX

Calculating Percent

One way you can express a probability is as a percent. A percent (%) is a number compared to 100. For example, 50% means 50 out of 100.

Suppose that 3 out of 5 tossed coins landed heads up. Here's how you can calculate what percent of the coins landed heads up.

1. Write the comparison as a fraction.

$$3 \text{ out of } 5 = \frac{3}{5}$$

2. Multiply the fraction by 100% to express it as a percent.

$$\frac{3}{5} \times \frac{100\%}{1} = 60\%$$

60% of the coins landed heads up.

Now, suppose 3 out of 12 coins landed tails up. How can you express this as a percent?

Figure 6 According to the laws of probability, there is a 50 percent probability that the coin will land heads up. *Calculating* *What is the probability that the coin will land tails up?*

Answers to Self-Assessment

☑ *Checkpoint*

There are two possible ways that the coin can land, and each one has an equal chance of occurring.

Caption Question

Figure 6 50%

2 Facilitate

Principles of Probability

Including All Students

Materials *4 pipe cleaners of different lengths, but all the same color*

To help reinforce the concept of probability, challenge student pairs to use the pipe cleaners to illustrate the two principles of probability: each event has equal chance of occurring and each event occurs independently. Then ask: **What is the chance that the longest pipe cleaner will be chosen?** *(1 out of 4 or 25%)* **If the longest pipe cleaner is chosen the first time and is replaced, what is the chance that it will be chosen again?** *(Also 25%; each event occurs independently of the results of other events.)* **learning modality: kinesthetic**

Inquiry Challenge

Challenge small groups of students to create a game that uses the principles of probability. Students may use coin tosses in the game, use a spinner, or anything else that gives players an equal chance at winning the game. Each group should write rules for its game and teach another group how to play the game. **cooperative learning**

Math TOOLBOX

Time 10 minutes
Tips Remind students that in fractions, the line separating the numbers stands for "divided by." For the problem, students should set up the fraction $\frac{3}{12}$, or calculate 3 "divided by" 12 to get 0.25. To calculate the percent, students should then multiply 0.25 by 100% to get 25%. **learning modality: logical/ mathematical**

Ongoing Assessment

Oral Presentation Call on students at random to describe the two principles of probability using a coin toss as an example.

Make the Right Call!

Preparing for Inquiry

Key Concepts Punnett squares can predict the results of a genetic cross when the genotypes of both parents are known.

Skills Objectives Students will be able to

◆ model the combination of alleles in a genetic cross;

◆ predict the offspring of a genetic cross;

◆ analyze data from models of genetic crosses;

◆ compare actual data with predicted outcomes.

Time 40 minutes

Alternative Materials Marbles of other colors may be substituted, but use two easily distinguished colors. (Some students may be colorblind.) Other small colored objects that have the same shape and texture, such as buttons, can also be used.

Guiding Inquiry

Invitation Discuss circumstances in which students make predictions in their lives. Talk about the different evidence and ideas that lead to various predictions. Then ask: **Why is it helpful to scientists to make accurate predictions in their experiments?** *(Accurate predictions make scientists more confident that they are asking the right questions and correctly understanding the phenomena that they are studying; they also help scientists to better plan their experiments.)*

Introducing the Procedure

◆ Have students read the entire procedure. Then ask: **What do the marbles represent?** *(The alleles from each parent)* **Why should you not look inside the bag when you remove the marbles?** *(To make sure the allele combinations occur randomly)*

◆ Make sure students know the meanings of *homozygous* and *heterozygous.*

MAKE THE RIGHT CALL!

You know that making predictions is an important part of science. An accurate prediction can be a sign that you understand the event you are studying. In this lab, you will make predictions as you model the events involved in genetic crosses.

Problem

How can you predict the possible results of genetic crosses?

Materials

2 small paper bags
marking pen
3 blue marbles
3 white marbles

Procedure

1. Label one bag "Bag 1, Female Parent." Label the other bag "Bag 2, Male Parent." Then read over Part 1, Part 2, and Part 3 of this lab. Write a prediction about the kinds of offspring you expect from each cross.

Part 1 Crossing Two Homozygous Parents

2. Copy the data table and label it *Data Table Number 1.* Then place two blue marbles in Bag 1. This pair of marbles represents the female parent's alleles. Use the letter *B* to represent the dominant allele for blue color.

3. Place two white marbles in Bag 2. Use the letter *b* to represent the recessive allele for white color.

4. For Trial 1, remove one marble from Bag 1 without looking in the bag. Record the result in your data table. Return the marble to the bag. Again, without looking in the bag, remove one marble from Bag 2. Record the result in your data table. Return the marble to the bag.

5. In the column labeled *Offspring's Alleles,* write *BB* if you removed two blue marbles, *bb* if you removed two white marbles, or *Bb* if you removed one blue marble and one white marble.

6. Repeat Steps 4 and 5 nine more times.

DATA TABLE

Number _____

Trial	Allele From Bag 1 (Female Parent)	Allele From Bag 2 (Male Parent)	Offspring's Alleles
1			
2			
3			
4			
5			
6			

Troubleshooting the Experiment

◆ As students perform the different crosses, encourage them to discuss whether only one type of allele can be passed on by a parent or whether either of two alleles can be passed on.

◆ Monitor students to make sure they correctly identify the dominant and recessive alleles.

Expected Outcome

In the first cross (*BB* × *bb*), students should observe that all offspring are *Bb*. In the second cross (*BB* × *Bb*), all offspring are blue, but some are homozygous (*BB*) and some are heterozygous (*Bb*). In the third cross (*Bb* × *Bb*), some offspring are blue and some are white. All white offspring are homozygous (*bb*). Blue offspring are either homozygous (*BB*) or heterozygous (*Bb*).

BAG 1
Female
Parent

BAG 2
Male
Parent

Part 2 Crossing a Homozygous Parent With a Heterozygous Parent

7. Place two blue marbles in Bag 1. Place one white marble and one blue marble in Bag 2. Copy the data table again, and label it *Data Table Number 2.*

8. Repeat Steps 4 and 5 ten times.

Part 3 Crossing Two Heterozygous Parents

9. Place one blue marble and one white marble in Bag 1. Place one blue marble and one white marble in Bag 2. Copy the data table again and label it *Data Table Number 3.*

10. Repeat Steps 4 and 5 ten times.

Analyze and Conclude

1. Make a Punnett square for each of the crosses you modeled in Part 1, Part 2, and Part 3.

2. According to your results in Part 1, how many different kinds of offspring are possible when the homozygous parents (*BB* and *bb*) are crossed? Do the results you obtained using the marble model agree with the results shown by a Punnett square?

3. According to your results in Part 2, what percent of offspring are likely to be homozygous when a homozygous parent (*BB*) and a heterozygous parent (*Bb*) are crossed? What percent of offspring are likely to be heterozygous? Does the model agree with the results shown by a Punnett square?

4. According to your results in Part 3, what different kinds of offspring are possible when two heterozygous parents (*Bb* × *Bb*) are crossed? What percent of each type of offspring are likely to be produced? Does the model agree with the results of a Punnett square?

5. For Part 3, if you did 100 trials instead of 10 trials, would your results be closer to the results shown in a Punnett square? Explain.

6. **Think About It** How does the marble model compare with a Punnett square? How are the two methods alike? How are they different?

More to Explore

In peas, the allele for yellow seeds (*Y*) is dominant over the allele for green seeds (*y*). What possible crosses do you think could produce a heterozygous plant with yellow seeds (*Yy*)? Use the marble model and Punnett squares to test your predictions.

Punnett square for Part 3:

	B	b
B	BB	Bb
b	Bb	bb

2. Only heterozygous blue offspring (*Bb*) are possible. The Punnett square shows the same results.

3. Student results may produce slightly different answers. As the number of trials increases, the more closely it will show that 50 percent of the offspring are likely to be homozygous (*BB*), while 50 percent are likely to be heterozygous (*Bb*). The Punnett square shows that 50 percent will be homozygous and 50 percent will be heterozygous.

4. Student results may vary due to chance, but all should observe that three different kinds of offspring are possible: *BB*, *Bb*, and *bb*. From the Punnett square, students can predict that 25 percent are likely to be *BB*, 50 percent are likely to be *Bb*, and 25 percent are likely to be *bb*. The marble model will probably not totally agree with the Punnett square due to chance.

5. Probably, as the number of trials is increased, the results are more likely to match those predicted in a Punnett square because of chance.

6. The marble model and the Punnett square both show the genotypes of the parents and offspring and demonstrate how the parent can donate one of two possible alleles to the offspring. The Punnett square gives all the possible genotypes of the offspring and their probabilities of occurring. The model gives the genotypes of the offspring based on chance, much like the actual combining of alleles in a real genetic cross.

Extending the Inquiry

More to Explore Crosses that will produce a heterozygous plant (*Yy*) include *YY* × *yy*, *YY* × *Yy*, *Yy* × *Yy*, and *Yy* × *yy*.

Analyze and Conclude

1. Punnett square for Part 1:

	b	b
B	Bb	Bb
B	Bb	Bb

Punnett square for Part 2:

	B	b
B	BB	Bb
B	BB	Bb

Program Resources

◆ **Unit 1 Resources** Skills Lab blackline masters, pp. 33–35

Media and Technology

 Lab Activity Videotape
Tape 1

Objectives

After completing the lesson, students will be able to

◆ describe the role of chromosomes in inheritance;

◆ identify and describe the events that occur during meiosis.

Key Term meiosis

1 Engage/Explore

Activating Prior Knowledge

Have students recall what they know about cells and cell structure. Based on their knowledge of cell structure, challenge them to predict the location of Mendel's hereditary factors, or genes, within the cell. You might wish to record students' predictions on the board and have the class evaluate them as you study the section.

DISCOVER

Skills Focus inferring
Materials *4 craft sticks, 3 pieces of paper, marking pen*
Time 10 minutes
Expected Outcome Students should realize that parents contribute only one of their two chromosomes to the offspring. The idea is to get students thinking about genes being carried on chromosomes and the cell has some kind of process to make sure only one allele of a gene is contributed to offspring.
Think It Over Students might infer that genes are located on chromosomes and chromosomes must divide and separate in a certain way so that the offspring get only one chromosome, or one allele, from each parent.

SECTION 3 — The Cell and Inheritance

DISCOVER ··············· ACTIVITY

Which Chromosome Is Which?

Mendel did not know that chromosomes play a role in genetics. Today we know that genes are located on chromosomes.

1. Label two craft sticks with the letter *A*. The craft sticks represent a pair of chromosomes in the female parent. Turn the sticks face down on a piece of paper.

2. Label two more craft sticks with the letter *a*. These represent a pair of chromosomes in the male parent. Turn the sticks face down on another piece of paper.

3. Turn over one craft stick "chromosome" from each piece of paper. Move both sticks to a third piece of paper. These represent a pair of chromosomes in the offspring. Note the allele combination that the offspring received.

Think It Over
Inferring Use this model to explain how chromosomes are involved in the inheritance of alleles.

GUIDE FOR READING

◆ What role do chromosomes play in inheritance?

◆ What events occur during meiosis?

Reading Tip Before you read, preview *Exploring Meiosis* on page 37. Predict what role chromosomes play in the inheritance of traits.

Sperm cells ▼

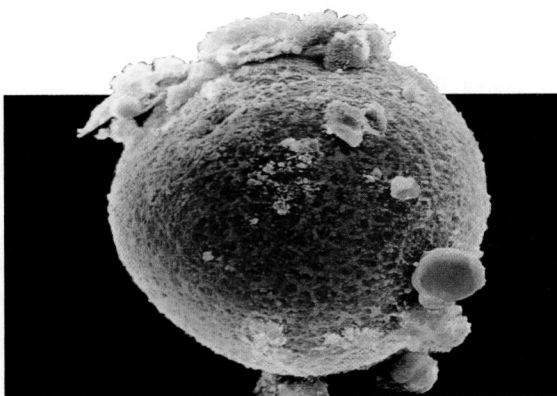

◀ Egg cell

When Mendel's results were rediscovered in 1900, scientists around the world became excited about Mendel's principles of inheritance. They were eager to identify the structures inside of cells that carried Mendel's hereditary factors, or genes.

In 1903, Walter Sutton, an American geneticist, added an important piece of information to scientists' understanding of genetics. Sutton was studying the cells of grasshoppers. He was trying to understand how sex cells—sperm and egg—form. During his studies, Sutton examined sex cells in many different stages of formation. He became particularly interested in the movement of chromosomes during the formation of sex cells. Sutton hypothesized that chromosomes were the key to understanding how offspring come to have traits similar to those of their parents.

READING STRATEGIES

Reading Tip Instruct students to record their predictions on a piece of paper and place that piece of paper in their books at the end of this section. When students have finished reading the section, have them review their predictions and revise them, if necessary. Explain that scientists make many predictions while setting up experiments and often revise them after completing the experiments.

Vocabulary While studying the process of meiosis, explain to students that the term *meiosis* is a Greek word that means "to diminish or make less." Discuss with students what objects are diminishing during the process of meiosis. *(the number of chromosomes)*

Figure 12 Grasshoppers have 24 chromosomes in each of their body cells. *Applying Concepts How many chromosomes did Sutton observe in the sperm cells and egg cells of grasshoppers?*

Chromosomes and Inheritance

Sutton knew that structures inside cells must be responsible for the inheritance of genes. He needed evidence to support his hypothesis that chromosomes were those structures. Sutton compared the number of chromosomes in a grasshopper's sex cells with the number of chromosomes in the other cells in the grasshopper's body. As you can see in Figure 12, the body cells of grasshoppers have 24 chromosomes. To his surprise, Sutton found that the grasshopper's sex cells have only 12 chromosomes. In other words, a grasshopper's sex cells have exactly half the number of chromosomes found in its body cells.

Sutton knew that he had discovered something important. He observed what happened when a sperm cell (with 12 chromosomes) and an egg cell (with 12 chromosomes) joined. The fertilized egg that formed had 24 chromosomes—the original number. As a result, the grasshopper offspring had exactly the same number of chromosomes in its cells as did each of its parents. The 24 chromosomes existed in 12 pairs. One chromosome in each pair came from the male parent, while the other chromosome came from the female parent.

Sutton concluded that the chromosomes carried Mendel's hereditary factors, or genes, from one generation to the next. In other words, genes are located on chromosomes. Sutton's idea came to be known as the chromosome theory of inheritance. **According to the chromosome theory of inheritance, genes are carried from parents to their offspring on chromosomes.**

Checkpoint How does the number of chromosomes in a grasshopper's sex cells compare to the number in its body cells?

2 Facilitate

Chromosomes and Inheritance

Addressing Naive Conceptions

Students might have difficulty visualizing exactly where genes are located on chromosomes and how chromosomes fit inside cells. Review cell structure and encourage students to draw diagrams of the cell in which they show the chromosomes inside the cell nucleus. Until students learn the composition of chromosomes (in Section 4), it will be difficult for them to visualize what kind of structure a gene actually has. Explain that chromosomes are made up of many, many genes lined up one after the other. Genes are not separate structures "stuck to" chromosomes; rather, chromosomes are long chains of genes. **learning modality: visual**

Inquiry Challenge

Challenge small groups of students to conclude what might happen if sex cells did not have half the number of chromosomes as body cells. Groups should develop a model that illustrates their conclusions. Provide various art materials for students to use, or encourage them to bring materials from home. Have groups present their models to the class and explain why sex cells must have half the chromosomes as body cells. **learning modality: logical/mathematical**

ACTIVITY

Program Resources

◆ **Unit 1 Resources** 1-3 Lesson Plan, p. 23; 1-3 Section Summary, p. 24
◆ **Guided Reading and Study Workbook** Section 1-3

Answers to Self-Assessment

Caption Question

Figure 12 12 chromosomes in each

Checkpoint

The sex cells have exactly half the number of chromosomes as the body cells.

Ongoing Assessment

Drawing Have students draw a diagram of a grasshopper body cell and sex cell and show the number of chromosomes in each of these cells.

EXPLORING
Meiosis

Walk students through each stage in meiosis. Point out that before meiosis occurs, every chromosome is copied, so the cell actually has four copies of each chromosome. Emphasize that during Meiosis I, the chromosome pairs separate. The centromeres are still holding together the chromosome copies. When discussing Meiosis II, point out that this division is similar to the division that occurs during mitosis—the centromeres split and the chromosome copies separate. Ask: **How many sex cells are produced at the end of the meiosis?** *(four)* **How do the sex cells differ from the parent cell?** *(The sex cells have half the number of chromosomes of the parent cell.)* **learning modality: visual**

Building Inquiry Skills: Making Models

Materials *8 pipe cleaners—4 of one color and 4 of another, 4 beads*
Time 15 minutes

Challenge students to model the steps in meiosis using the pipe cleaners to represent two chromosomes in a cell. Students should use pipe cleaners of the same color to represent chromosome pairs, with different chromosome pairs having different colors. Monitor students to make sure they double each chromosome before meiosis begins. (They should add another pipe cleaner of the same color to each pipe cleaner chromosome.) Students can use beads to hold the chromosome copies together, or they can simply twist the pipe cleaners together at one point. Make sure students separate the chromosome pairs during Meiosis I and the chromosome copies during Meiosis II. **learning modality: kinesthetic**

Meiosis

How do sex cells end up with half the number of chromosomes as body cells? To answer this question, you need to understand the events that occur during meiosis. **Meiosis** (my OH sis) is the process by which the number of chromosomes is reduced by half to form sex cells—sperm and eggs.

You can trace the events of meiosis in *Exploring Meiosis*. In this example, each parent cell has four chromosomes arranged in two pairs. **During meiosis, the chromosome pairs separate and are distributed to two different cells. The resulting sex cells have only half as many chromosomes as the other cells in the organism.** In *Exploring Meiosis,* notice that the sex cells end up with only two chromosomes each—half the number found in the parent cell. Only one chromosome from each chromosome pair ends up in each sex cell.

When sex cells combine to produce offspring, each sex cell will contribute half the normal number of chromosomes. Thus, the offspring gets the normal number of chromosomes—half from each parent.

✓ *Checkpoint* *What types of cells form by meiosis?*

Meiosis and Punnett Squares

The Punnett squares that you learned about earlier in this chapter are actually a shorthand way to show the events that occur at meiosis. When the chromosome pairs separate into two different sex cells, so do the alleles carried on each chromosome. One allele from each pair goes to each sex cell. In Figure 13, you can see how the Punnett square accounts for the separation of alleles during meiosis.

As shown across the top of the Punnett square, half of the sperm cells from the male parent will receive the chromosome with the *T* allele. The other half of the sperm cells will receive the chromosome with the *t* allele. In this example, the same is true for the egg cells from the female parent, as shown down the left side of the Punnett square. Depending on which sperm cell combines with which egg cell, one of the allele combinations shown in the boxes will result.

Figure 13 This Punnett square shows how alleles separate when sex cells form during meiosis. It also shows the possible allele combinations that can result after fertilization occurs. *Interpreting Charts* *What is the probability that a sperm cell will contain a T allele?*

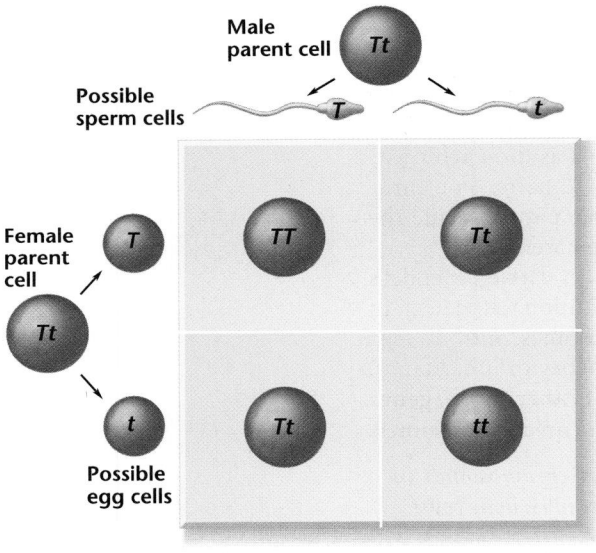

Male parent cell — Tt
Possible sperm cells — T, t
Female parent cell — Tt
Possible egg cells — T, t
TT, Tt, Tt, tt

EXPLORING Meiosis

During meiosis, a cell undergoes two divisions to produce sex cells that have half the number of chromosomes.

① Beginning of Meiosis
Before meiosis begins, every chromosome in the cell is copied. As in mitosis, centromeres hold the double-stranded chromosomes together.

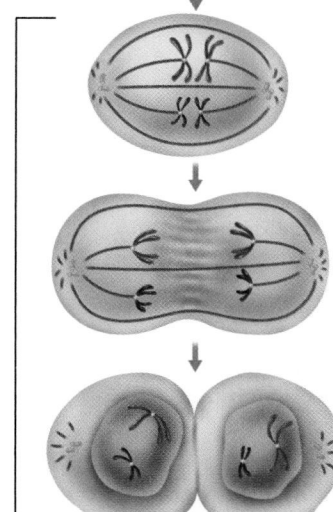

② Meiosis I
The chromosome pairs line up next to each other in the center of the cell. The pairs then separate from each other and move to opposite ends of the cell. Two cells form, each with half the number of chromosomes. Each chromosome is still double-stranded.

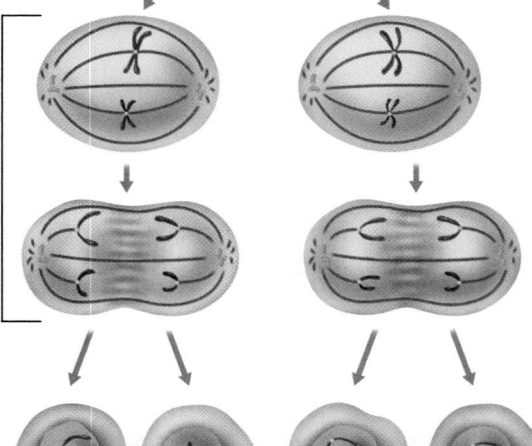

③ Meiosis II
The double-stranded chromosomes move to the center of the cell. The centromeres split and the two strands of each chromosome separate. The two strands move to opposite ends of the cell.

④ End of Meiosis
Four sex cells have been produced. Each cell has only half the number of chromosomes that the parent cell had at the beginning of meiosis. Each cell has only one chromosome from each original pair.

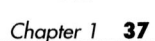

Chapter 1 **37**

Media and Technology

 Transparency "Exploring Meiosis," Transparency 3

 Concept Videotape Library *Adventures, Tape 1,* "The Chromosome Theory"

Answers to Self-Assessment

☑ *Checkpoint*
Sex cells form by meiosis.

Caption Question
Figure 13 $\frac{1}{2} \times 100\% = 50\%$

Building Inquiry Skills: Observing

Materials *a set of prepared slides showing the stages of meiosis, microscopes*

ACTIVITY

Set up microscope stations at which you place the prepared slides. Depending on the number of microscopes you have and the ability of your students to use microscopes, you could place a whole set of slides at each microscope and allow students to change the slides themselves, or you could place the microscopes in a row with individual slides from a set positioned and focused for students to simply look at. As students examine the slides, encourage them to compare the *Exploring Meiosis* diagram to what they see. Have students draw their observations, labeling the chromosomes. Emphasize that meiosis is a dynamic process. Each slide represents a snapshot in a continuous event, much like a photograph captures an instant of time in a parade or a soccer game.
learning modality: visual

Meiosis and Punnett Squares

Using the Visuals: Figure 13

Point out that like other Punnett squares they have studied, the one in Figure 13 also shows all possible allele combinations for the offspring. Make it clear that the cells inside the boxes of the Punnett square represent the body cells of the offspring. This Punnett square goes one step further in showing the genotypes of the parents' body cells. Ask: **What are the possible sex cells produced by each offspring?** (TT *would only produce sex cells with* T; Tt *would produce both* T *and* t *sex cells; and* tt *would produce only sex cells with* t.) **learning modality: visual**

Ongoing Assessment

Writing Have students write an outline of meiosis in which each major step is a main heading in the outline.
 Students can save their outlines in their portfolios.

Chromosomes

Including All Students

Give students who need more help craft sticks to make a model of a chromosome pair based on the diagram in Figure 14. Each chromosome model should have at least six different genes, either homozygous or heterozygous. **learning modality: kinesthetic**

ACTIVITY

3 Assess

Section 3 Review Answers

1. Chromosomes carry the information for the inheritance of traits.
2. Chromosome pairs separate to form sex cells with half the number of chromosomes in each.
3. Genes are located on chromosomes.
4. It shows how the alleles separate when sex cells form during meiosis.
5. 22 chromosomes

CHAPTER PROJECT 1

Check Your Progress

Students can choose mates for their pets based on phenotypes or by you randomly choosing names out of a hat for males and one for females. Suggest that students first toss the coin to determine the color of each offspring and cut out each offspring from paper of the appropriate color. Then students can determine the genotypes of the other traits and write the genotypes directly on the backs of each offspring.

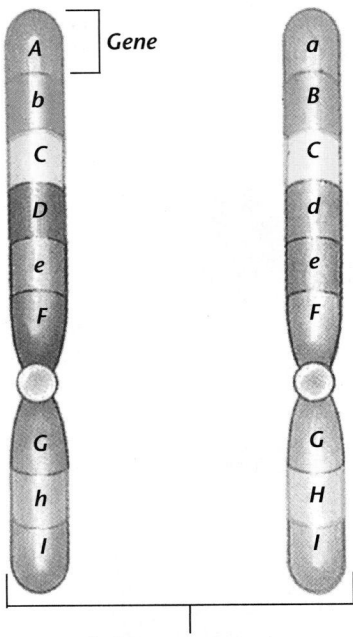

Figure 14 Genes are located on chromosomes. The chromosomes in a pair may have different alleles for some genes and the same alleles for others. *Classifying For which genes is this organism homozygous? For which genes is it heterozygous?*

A chromosome pair

Chromosomes

Since Sutton's time, scientists have studied the chromosomes of many different organisms. The body cells of humans, for example, contain 23 pairs, or 46 chromosomes. The body cells of dogs have 78 chromosomes, while the body cells of silkworms have 56 chromosomes. As you can see, larger organisms don't always have more chromosomes.

Chromosomes are made up of many genes joined together like beads on a string. Sutton reasoned that chromosomes must contain a large number of genes because organisms have so many traits. Although you have only 23 pairs of chromosomes, your body cells contain more than 60,000 genes. Each of the genes controls a particular trait.

Look at the pair of chromosomes in Figure 14. One chromosome in the pair came from the female parent. The other chromosome came from the male parent. Notice that each chromosome in the pair has the same genes. The genes are lined up in the same order from one end of the chromosome to the other. However, the alleles for some of the genes might be different. For example, the organism has the *A* allele on one chromosome and the *a* allele on the other. As you can see, this organism is heterozygous for some traits and homozygous for others.

Section 3 Review

1. Explain the role that chromosomes play in inheritance.
2. Briefly describe what happens to chromosomes during meiosis.
3. On what structures in a cell are genes located?
4. How is a Punnett square a model for what happens during meiosis?
5. **Thinking Critically Inferring** The body cells of hamsters have 44 chromosomes. How many chromosomes would the sex cells of a hamster have?

CHAPTER PROJECT 1

Check Your Progress

At this point, you should find a classmate with a paper pet of the opposite sex. Suppose the two pets were crossed and produced six offspring. For each trait, use coin tosses to determine which allele the offspring will inherit from each parent. Construct a paper pet for each offspring, showing the traits that each one has inherited. Write the genotype for each trait on their backs.

Performance Assessment

Drawing Have students make a Punnett square for a cross between two heterozygous black guinea pigs, *Bb × Bb*. Before they make the Punnett square, students should make a diagram similar to Figure 13, showing how the four sex cells formed for each parent.

Answers to Self-Assessment

Caption Question

Figure 14 The organism is homozygous for genes C, E, F, G, and I. The organism is heterozygous for genes A, B, D, and H.

Program Resources

◆ **Laboratory Manual** 1, "Chromosomes and Inheritance"
◆ **Unit 1 Resources** 1-3 Review and Reinforce, p. 25; 1-3 Enrich, p. 26

DISCOVER ••

A •–	N –•
B –•••	O –––
C –•–•	P •––•
D –••	Q ––•–
E •	R •–•
F ••–•	S •••
G ––•	T –
H ••••	U ••–
I ••	V •••–
J •–––	W •––
K –•–	X –••–
L •–••	Y –•––
M ––	Z ––••

Can You Crack the Code?

1. Use the Morse code in the chart to decode the question in the message below. The letters are separated by slash marks.

•––/••••/•/•–•/•/••–/•–•/•/––•/•/–•/
•/•••/•–••/––•/–•–•/•–/–/•/–••/

2. Write your answer to the question in Morse code.

3. Exchange your coded answer with a partner. Then decode your partner's answer.

Think It Over

Forming Operational Definitions Based on your results from this activity, write a definition of the word *code*. Then compare your definition to one in a dictionary.

A white buffalo calf was born on Childs Place Farm near Hanover, Michigan, in 1998. White buffaloes are extremely rare, occurring only once in every 10 million births. Why was this calf born with such an uncommon phenotype? To answer this question, you need to know how the genes on a chromosome control an organism's traits.

The Genetic Code

Today scientists know that the main function of genes is to control the production of proteins in the organism's cells. Proteins help to determine the size, shape, and many other traits of an organism.

Figure 15 The white color of this buffalo calf is very unusual. Both of the calf's parents had brown coats.

GUIDE FOR READING

♦ **What is meant by the term "genetic code"?**

♦ **How does a cell produce proteins?**

♦ **How do mutations affect an organism?**

Reading Tip As you read, create a flowchart that shows how a cell produces proteins.

Objectives

After completing the lesson, students will be able to

♦ explain the term "genetic code";

♦ describe the process by which a cell produces proteins;

♦ describe different types of mutations and how they affect an organism.

Key Terms messenger RNA, transfer RNA

1 Engage/Explore

Activating Prior Knowledge

Invite students to recall what they have learned about inheritance, DNA, and cell division up to this point. Then ask: **How do genes determine the traits of an organism?** (*Accept all answers without comment.*) Explain that students will learn more about this process in the section.

••••••• DISCOVER •••••••

Skills Focus forming operational definitions
Time 15 minutes
Expected Outcome The coded question is "Where are genes located?" The answer, "on chromosomes," is encoded below.

–––/–•/–•••/••••/•••/–––/––/
–––/•••/–––/––/•/•••/

Think It Over Students might define *code* as set of symbols with specific meanings used to send messages. Some dictionaries define *code* as a system of symbols, letters, or words given arbitrary meanings, used for transmitting messages requiring secrecy or brevity.

Program Resources

♦ **Unit 1 Resources** 1-4 Lesson Plan, p. 27; 1-4 Section Summary, p. 28
♦ **Guided Reading and Study Workbook** Section 1-4

READING STRATEGIES

Reading Tip Student flowcharts should begin with genes on a chromosome in the nucleus of a cell. Next they should include the production of messenger RNA and its entrance into the cytoplasm to attach to a ribosome. Then transfer RNA brings the amino acid to the growing protein chain. Encourage students to illustrate their flowcharts, define terms, and explain processes that are new to them.

2 Facilitate

The Genetic Code

Using the Visuals: Figure 16

Have students trace the relationship between DNA and chromosomes in Figure 16. Explain that a gene is a segment of DNA with a specific sequence of nitrogen bases that codes for a certain protein. Start students thinking about protein synthesis by pointing out that although DNA is located in the cell nucleus, proteins are made in the cytoplasm. **learning modality: visual**

Including All Students

To help students bring together everything they have studied so far, explain that the traits Mendel observed, such as tall plants and short plants, are the results of the action of proteins in an organism. Challenge students to draw a diagram or a concept map that shows the relationships among DNA, genes, proteins, genotypes, and phenotypes. **learning modality: visual**

How Cells Make Proteins

Building Inquiry Skills: Inferring

Discuss the role of messenger RNA. Then ask: **Why do you think the cell sends a coded message for a gene into the cytoplasm instead of sending the gene itself?** *(Some students might infer that by using a coded message for a gene, the cell protects its DNA from possible damage, ensuring that it will always produce the proper proteins throughout its life.)* **learning modality: logical/mathematical**

A cell's chromosomes are composed mostly of the genetic material DNA. In Figure 16, you can see the relationship between chromosomes and DNA. Notice that a DNA molecule is made up of four different nitrogen bases—adenine (A), thymine (T), guanine (G), and cytosine (C). These bases form the rungs of the DNA "ladder." A single gene on a chromosome may contain anywhere from several hundred to a million or more of these bases. The bases are arranged in a specific order—for example, ATGACGTAC.

The order of the nitrogen bases along a gene forms a genetic code that specifies what type of protein will be produced. In the genetic code, a group of three bases codes for the attachment of a specific amino acid. Amino acids are the building blocks of proteins. The order of the bases determines the order in which amino acids are put together to form a protein. You can think of the bases as three-letter code words. The code words tell the cell which amino acid to add to the growing protein chain.

☑ *Checkpoint* *What is the main function of genes?*

How Cells Make Proteins

The production of proteins is called protein synthesis. **During protein synthesis, the cell uses information from a gene on a chromosome to produce a specific protein.** Protein synthesis takes place on the ribosomes in the cytoplasm of the cell. As you know, the cytoplasm is outside the nucleus. The chromosomes, however, are found inside the nucleus. How, then, does the information needed to produce proteins get out of the nucleus and into the cytoplasm?

Figure 16 A chromosome contains thousands of genes along its length. The sequence of bases along a gene forms a code that tells the cell what protein to produce. *Interpreting Diagrams Where in the cell are the chromosomes located?*

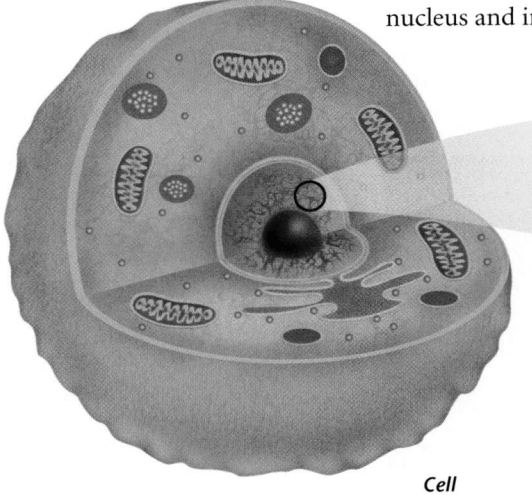

Cell

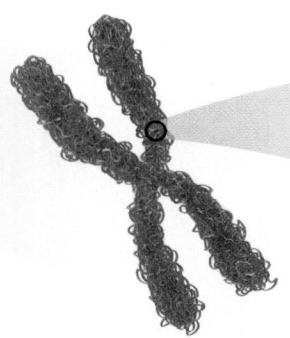

Chromosome

40

Background

Facts and Figures *Transcription* is the process by which RNA is produced using a single-stranded DNA template. Messenger RNA, transfer RNA, and ribosomal RNA are all transcribed in the nuclei of eukaryotic cells and then pass into the cytoplasms. Ribosomal RNA and proteins make up the structures of ribosomes, the organelles where proteins are made.

Translation is the production of protein in the ribosomes. Often, several ribosomes are attached to the same messenger RNA molecule. The ribosome holds both the messenger RNA with its genetic information and the transfer RNAs with their attached amino acids in position to allow a specific protein chain to form.

The Role of RNA Before protein synthesis can take place, a "messenger" must first carry the genetic code from the DNA inside the nucleus into the cytoplasm. This genetic messenger is called ribonucleic acid, or RNA.

Although RNA is similar to DNA, the two molecules differ in some important ways. Unlike DNA, which looks like a twisted ladder, an RNA molecule almost always looks like only one side, or strand, of the ladder. RNA also contains a different sugar molecule from the sugar found in DNA. Another difference between DNA and RNA is in their nitrogen bases. Like DNA, RNA contains adenine, guanine, and cytosine. However, instead of thymine, RNA contains uracil (YOOR uh sil).

There are several types of RNA involved in protein synthesis. **Messenger RNA** copies the coded message from the DNA in the nucleus, and carries the message into the cytoplasm. Another type of RNA, called **transfer RNA,** carries amino acids and adds them to the growing protein.

Translating the Code The process of protein synthesis is shown in *Exploring Protein Synthesis* on the next page. The first step is for a DNA molecule to "unzip" between its base pairs. Then one of the strands of DNA directs the production of a strand of messenger RNA. To form the RNA strand, RNA bases pair up with the DNA bases. Instead of thymine, however, uracil pairs with adenine. The messenger RNA then leaves the nucleus and attaches to a ribosome in the cytoplasm. There, molecules of transfer RNA pick up the amino acids specified by each three-letter code word. Each transfer RNA molecule puts the amino acid it is carrying in the correct order along the growing protein chain.

☑ *Checkpoint* **What is the function of transfer RNA?**

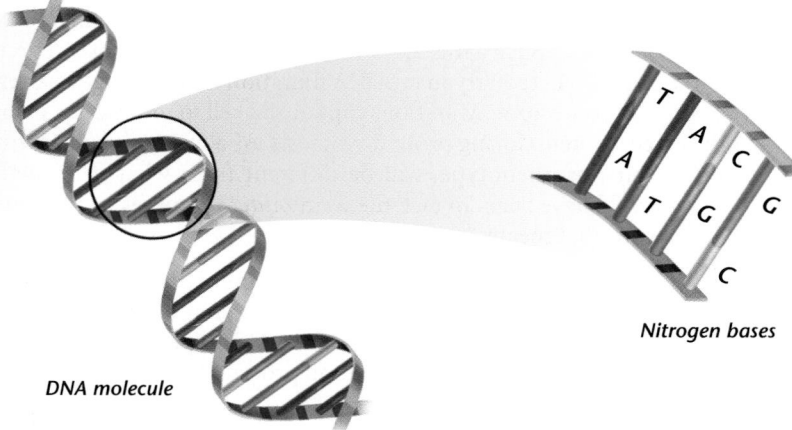

DNA molecule

Nitrogen bases

Sharpen your Skills

Predicting

The following is a sequence of nitrogen bases on a DNA molecule.

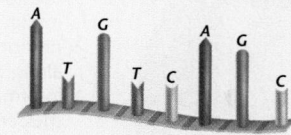

Write out the sequence of RNA bases that would pair up with the DNA bases.

Answers to Self-Assessment

Caption Question

Figure 16 in the nucleus

☑ *Checkpoint*

(p. 40) To control the production of proteins

(p. 41) To carry amino acids and add them to the growing protein chain

---

Sharpen your Skills

Predicting

Time 10 minutes

Expected Outcome The sequence of RNA bases is U A C A G U C G.

Extend Ask students: **What is the DNA sequence that pairs to this DNA sequence?** (*T A C A G T C G. Uracil is present in RNA in place of thymine.*)

What RNA bases would pair up with the strand of DNA you just identified? (*A U G U C A G C*) Point out that this is different from the RNA sequence they first identified. Explain that these two RNA sequences would code for different proteins. The cell uses only one of the two DNA strands to make a protein.

learning modality: logical/ mathematical

Inquiry Challenge

Materials *building blocks*
Time 20 minutes

Construct a structure from building blocks in a place where students cannot see it. Then challenge student groups to build the same structure as yours with these stipulations: Only two people from each group may look at the structure, and they may look at it only once; no verbal communication is allowed between the group members who observe the structure and the rest of the group; only group members who did not see the structure may build it; all building blocks must be gathered from a central point. Suggest to students that they may use a code to communicate instructions on how to build the structure. When each group has completed its structure, bring your structure into view and allow students to make comparisons. Discuss the characteristics of a good "code" and what groups might have done to improve theirs. Then relate the activity to protein synthesis. Talk about the importance of the cell building perfect proteins.
cooperative learning

Ongoing Assessment

Writing Have students describe the role of RNA in making proteins.

EXPLORING
Protein Synthesis

Review each step in the process of protein synthesis using the Exploring. Emphasize in Step 1 that DNA always stays inside the cell nucleus. In Step 2, explain that the ribosome has special sites that hold messenger RNA as the ribosome moves along it. The ribosome also has special sites that hold transfer RNA so its amino acid can easily join the growing protein chain. In Step 3, explain that transfer RNA is made in the same way as messenger RNA, but has a region to which amino acids bond. In Step 4, explain that more than one ribosome can attach to a single messenger RNA at one time. **learning modality: visual**

Including All Students

Some students may have difficulty with the terms related to protein synthesis. Help students identify these words and have them add the words to the glossary of genetics terms that they began in Section 1. **learning modality: verbal**

EXPLORING *Protein Synthesis*

To make proteins, messenger RNA copies information from DNA in the nucleus. Transfer RNA then uses this information to produce proteins in the ribosomes.

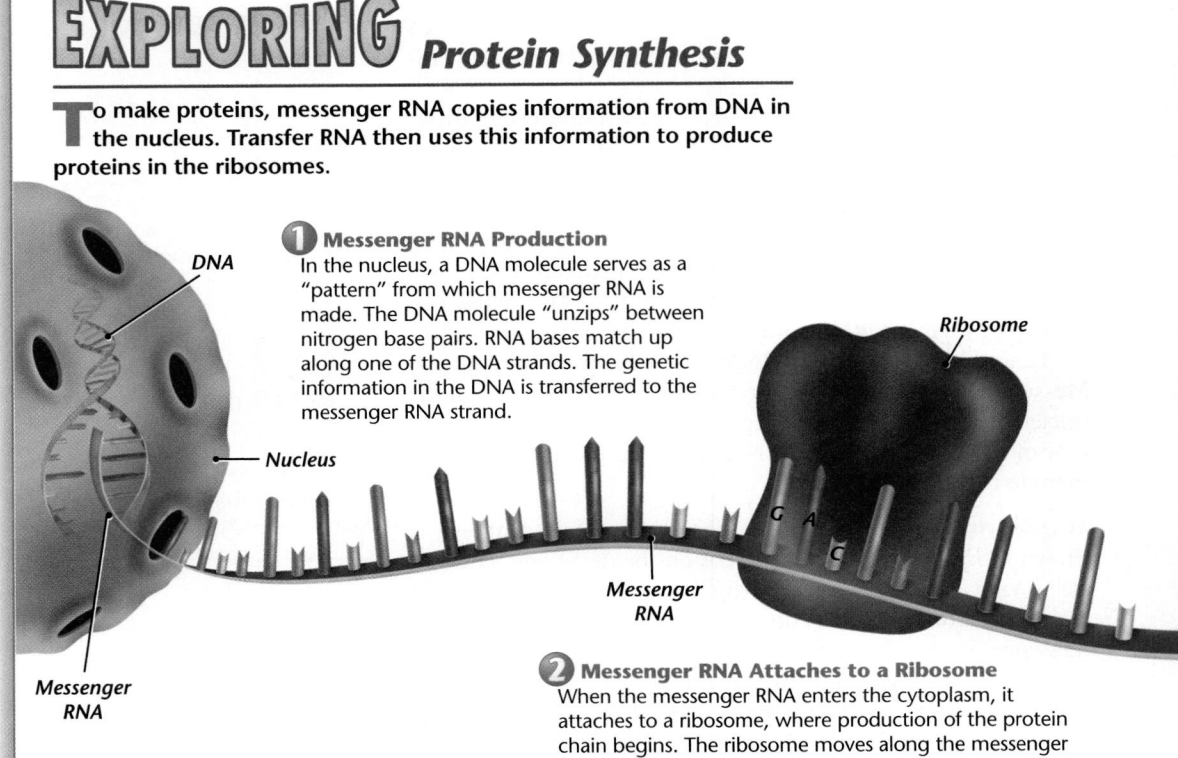

1 Messenger RNA Production
In the nucleus, a DNA molecule serves as a "pattern" from which messenger RNA is made. The DNA molecule "unzips" between nitrogen base pairs. RNA bases match up along one of the DNA strands. The genetic information in the DNA is transferred to the messenger RNA strand.

DNA

Nucleus

Ribosome

Messenger RNA

Messenger RNA

2 Messenger RNA Attaches to a Ribosome
When the messenger RNA enters the cytoplasm, it attaches to a ribosome, where production of the protein chain begins. The ribosome moves along the messenger RNA strand and "reads" each three-letter code of bases.

Mutations

Suppose that a mistake occurred in one gene of a chromosome. Instead of the base A, for example, the DNA molecule might have the base G. Such a mistake is one type of mutation that can occur in a cell's hereditary material. A mutation is any change in a gene or chromosome. Mutations can cause a cell to produce an incorrect protein during protein synthesis. As a result, the organism's traits, or phenotype, will be different from what it normally would have been. In fact, the term *mutation* comes from a Latin word that means "change."

Types of Mutations Some mutations are the result of small changes in an organism's hereditary material, such as the substitution of a single base for another. This type of mutation can occur during the DNA replication process. The white coat on the

Background

Facts and Figures Different types of changes in the base sequence of DNA affect the organism in different ways. If a base is inserted or deleted from a gene, the reading frame for three-letter base code, or codon, is shifted. The result of a frame-shift mutation is a nonfunctional protein.

A point mutation occurs when one base is substituted for another. This kind of mutation affects only one codon, which has variable affects on the protein product. Sometimes it has no effect because most amino acids are encoded by more than one codon. Sometimes the protein will have a reduced function because one amino acid is substituted for the correct one. Other times, the protein will not work at all, either because the codon has been changed to a stop codon or the amino acid that is substituted completely changes the nature of the protein.

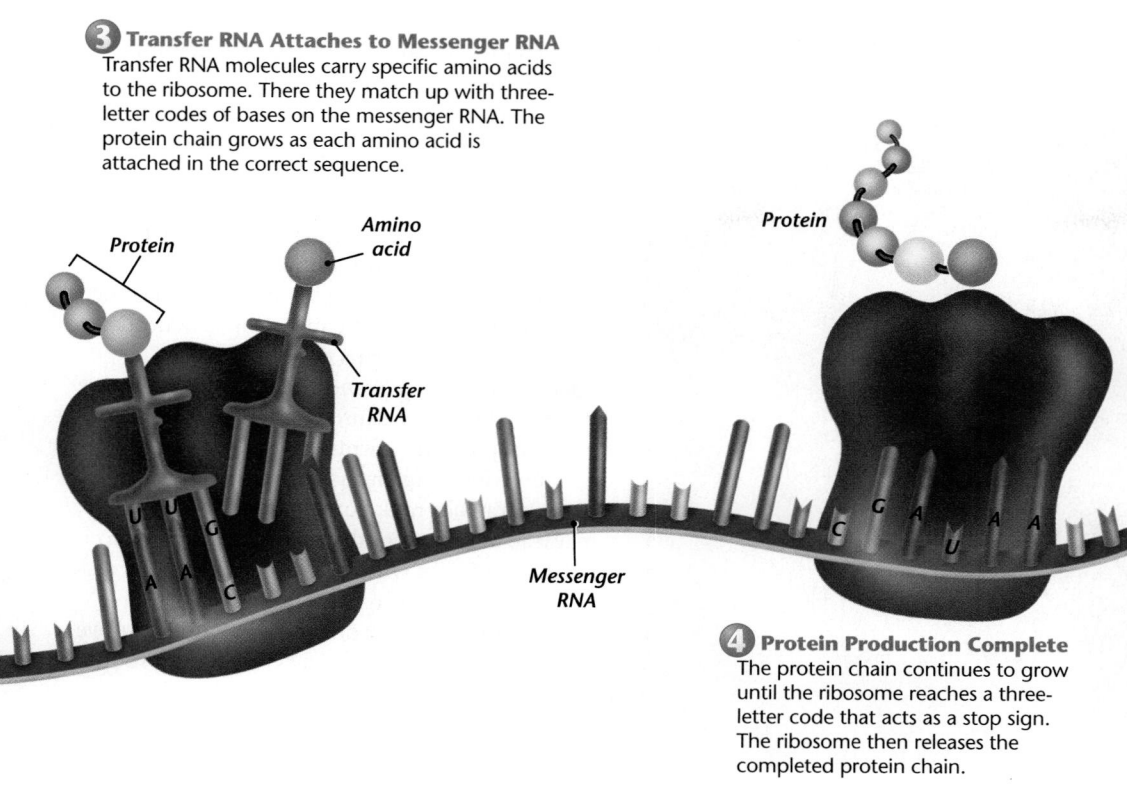

3 **Transfer RNA Attaches to Messenger RNA**
Transfer RNA molecules carry specific amino acids to the ribosome. There they match up with three-letter codes of bases on the messenger RNA. The protein chain grows as each amino acid is attached in the correct sequence.

Protein

Amino acid

Protein

Transfer RNA

Messenger RNA

4 **Protein Production Complete**
The protein chain continues to grow until the ribosome reaches a three-letter code that acts as a stop sign. The ribosome then releases the completed protein chain.

buffalo calf you read about at the start of this section might have resulted from this type of mutation. Other mutations may occur when chromosomes don't separate correctly during meiosis. When this type of mutation occurs, a cell can end up with too many or too few chromosomes. The cell could also end up with extra segments of chromosomes.

If a mutation occurs in a body cell, such as a skin cell, the mutation will affect only the cell that carries it. If, however, a mutation occurs in a sex cell, the mutation can be passed on to an offspring and affect the offspring's phenotype.

The Effects of Mutations Because mutations can introduce changes in an organism, they can be a source of genetic variety. **Some of the changes brought about by mutations are harmful to an organism. Other mutations, however, are helpful, and still others are neither harmful nor helpful.** A mutation is

Mutations

Building Inquiry Skills: Making Models

Materials *beads of different colors, pipe cleaners*
Time 15 minutes

Challenge students to use the materials to model the two types of mutations described in the text: a point mutation, in which a single base is substituted for another, and a chromosomal mutation, in which chromosomes do not separate correctly during meiosis. The beads should represent nitrogen bases, and the pipe cleaners should be the chromosomes. Check students' models to make sure they are accurate. Remind students that organisms have two copies of each chromosome. You might also challenge students to model why mutations in body cells do not affect offspring. **learning modality: kinesthetic**

Addressing Naive Conceptions

Some students might think that mutations can only harm an organism. To help dispel this misconception, explain that mutations can also provide organisms a means to better adapt to their environment. Then display pictures of a monarch and a viceroy butterfly. Tell students that birds learn to avoid monarchs because of their bitter taste. Birds like the taste of viceroy butterflies, and many years ago, viceroys looked different from monarchs. However over time, various mutations in the appearance of viceroy butterflies have made them look similar to monarchs. Ask: **How have these mutations helped viceroys?** *(Birds also avoid viceroys because they associate their appearance with a bitter taste.)* **learning modality: visual**

Ongoing Assessment

Oral Presentation Call on students at random to explain what a mutation is and how mutations affect organisms.

Mutations, continued

Integrating Health

Ask students: **What is cancer?** *(A disease in which mutated body cells grow out of control)* Explain that the mutation that causes a particular cancer may occur either in a gene that causes cancer cells to grow or in a gene that prevents cancer cells from growing. Emphasize that one of the best ways to stop cancer is by prevention. Eating a healthful diet that is low in fat, high in fiber, and includes plenty of fruits and vegetables is one way to reduce the risk of cancer. Other ways include regular physical exams and cancer screenings and avoiding smoking, sunbathing, and alcohol. **learning modality: verbal**

3 Assess

Section 4 Answers

1. The order of the nitrogen bases forms a genetic code that specifies what type of protein will be produced. Groups of three bases code for specific amino acids, the building blocks of proteins.

2. First, messenger RNA is produced using a strand of DNA as a pattern. Messenger RNA moves into the cytoplasm where it attaches to a ribosome. The ribosome helps match the three-letter code of bases in the messenger RNA to the transfer RNA that carries the specified amino acid. The protein chain continues to grow until the ribosome comes to a stop signal, and then the completed protein chain is released.

3. Some mutations can be helpful to the organism, some are harmful, and others are neither helpful nor harmful.

4. in the cytoplasm

5. Only sex cells can pass on their chromosomes to the offspring. Body cells are not passed to offspring, they remain a part of the parent.

Figure 17 Mutations can affect an organism's traits, or phenotype. The unusually large strawberries on the left are the result of a mutation. The cells of these strawberries have extra sets of chromosomes.

harmful to an organism if it reduces the organism's chance for survival and reproduction.

Whether a mutation is harmful or not depends partly on the organism's environment. The mutation that led to the production of a white buffalo calf would probably be harmful to an organism in the wild. Its white color would make it more visible, and thus easier for predators to find. However, a white buffalo calf raised on a farm has the same chance for survival as a brown buffalo. On the farm, the mutation is neutral—it neither helps nor harms the buffalo.

INTEGRATING HEALTH Some diseases in humans are caused by harmful mutations. For example, some forms of cancer are caused by mutations in an organism's body cells. Overexposure to the ultraviolet radiation in sunlight, for example, may lead to mutations that could cause skin cancer. In Chapter 2, you will learn more about other diseases that result from harmful mutations.

Helpful mutations, on the other hand, improve an organism's chances for survival and reproduction. Antibiotic resistance in bacteria is an example. Antibiotics are chemicals that kill bacteria. Gene mutations have enabled some kinds of bacteria to become resistant to certain antibiotics— that is, the antibiotics do not kill the bacteria that have the mutations. Since the antibiotic-resistant bacteria are not killed by the antibiotics, the mutations have improved the bacteria's ability to survive and reproduce.

Section 4 Review

1. How do the nitrogen bases along a gene serve as a genetic code?
2. Briefly describe the process by which a cell produces proteins.
3. What possible effects can a mutation have on an organism?
4. Where in a cell does protein synthesis take place?
5. **Thinking Critically** Relating Cause and Effect Why are mutations that occur in an organism's body cells not passed on to its offspring?

44

Check Your Progress

CHAPTER PROJECT 1

With your partner, plan a display of your pet's family. Label the parents the P generation. Label the offspring the F₁ generation. Construct a Punnett square for each trait to help explain the inheritance pattern in your pet's family. *(Hint: Attach your pets to the display in a way that lets viewers turn the pets over to read their genotypes.)*

Program Resources

♦ **Unit 1 Resources** 1-4 Review and Reinforce, p. 29; 1-4 Enrich, p. 30

SECTION 1 — Mendel's Work

Key Ideas
◆ Gregor Mendel's work was the foundation for understanding why offspring have traits similar to those of their parents.
◆ Traits are controlled by alleles of genes. Organisms inherit one allele from each parent.
◆ Some alleles are dominant and some alleles are recessive.

Key Terms
trait   purebred   dominant allele
heredity   gene   recessive allele
genetics   allele   hybrid

SECTION 2 — Probability and Genetics
INTEGRATING MATHEMATICS

Key Ideas
◆ Probability is the likelihood that a particular event will happen.
◆ Mendel was the first scientist to interpret his data using the principles of probability.
◆ Geneticists use Punnett squares to show all the possible outcomes of a genetic cross.

Key Terms
probability   homozygous
Punnett square   heterozygous
phenotype   codominance
genotype

SECTION 3 — The Cell and Inheritance

Key Ideas
◆ According to the chromosome theory of inheritance, genes are carried from parents to their offspring on chromosomes.
◆ During meiosis, chromosome pairs separate to form sex cells. Only one chromosome from each pair ends up in each sex cell. The sex cells have half the number of chromosomes as the body cells.

Key Term
meiosis

SECTION 4 — The DNA Connection

Key Ideas
◆ The nitrogen bases along a gene form a code that specifies the order in which amino acids will be put together to produce a protein.
◆ During protein synthesis, messenger RNA copies the coded message from the DNA in the nucleus and carries the message into the cytoplasm. Transfer RNA adds amino acids to the growing protein.
◆ A mutation is a change in a gene or chromosome. Some mutations are harmful, some are helpful, and some are neutral.

Key Terms
messenger RNA
transfer RNA

Organizing Information

Compare/Contrast Table Copy the table comparing DNA and messenger RNA onto a separate sheet of paper. Then complete the table. (For more about compare/contrast tables, see the Skills Handbook.)

Characteristic	DNA	Messenger RNA
Nitrogen bases	a. _?_ , b. _?_ , c. _?_ , d. _?_	Adenine, uracil, guanine, cytosine
Structure	Twisted ladder	e. _?_
Function	Forms a genetic code that specifies what type of protein will be produced	f. _?_

CHAPTER PROJECT 1

Check Your Progress
Give each pair of students a poster board on which they can display their pet family. If students don't understand the hint, show them how to attach the pets to the poster board by taping down the left side of the pet so people can easily turn over the pet to read their genotypes, much like turning a page in a book. Check Punnett squares to make sure students have correctly shown all the possible genotypes and phenotypes of the F_1 pets, based on the genotypes of the two parents. Each student pair should construct five Punnett squares, one for each trait—sex, body color, eye shape, nose shape, and teeth shape.

Organizing Information

Compare/Contrast Table
a.–d. adenine, thymine, guanine, cytosine **e.** one strand of the ladder **f.** carries the genetic code from the DNA inside the nucleus into the cytoplasm

Program Resources

◆ **Unit 1 Resources** Chapter 1 Project Scoring Rubric, p. 14
◆ **Performance Assessment** Chapter 1, pp. 4–6
◆ **Chapter Tests** Chapter 1 Test, pp. 3–6

Media and Technology

Computer Test Bank
Chapter 1 Test

Performance Assessment

Drawing Have students draw a diagram that shows the process by which a cell produces proteins. In their diagrams, have students indicate where mistakes could occur, leading to mutations.

 Students can save their diagrams in their portfolios.

Reviewing Content
Multiple Choice
1. a 2. c 3. b 4. a 5. c

True or False
6. true 7. phenotype 8. true
9. meiosis 10. cytoplasm

Checking Concepts
11. All the first generation offspring were tall.
12. There is a 1 in 2, or 50 percent chance, that the coin will land heads up on the sixth toss because each coin toss is an independent event—the result of one toss does not affect the following coin tosses.
13. Punnett squares should look like the following:

	B	b
b	Bb	bb
b	Bb	bb

There is a 50 percent (2 in 4) chance that an offspring will have a white coat (bb).
14. Before meiosis begins, the chromosomes make copies of themselves. During Meiosis I, chromosome pairs separate from each other. In Meiosis II, the chromosome copies separate from each other to form four sex cells, each with half the number of chromosomes as the parent cell.
15. Transfer RNA carries the amino acid that corresponds to the code in the messenger RNA and adds it to the growing protein chain.
16. Student letters should describe Mendel's experiments as outlined in Section 1.

Thinking Critically
17. The solid-colored parent must be homozygous for the recessive allele (ss), and the spotted parent must be homozygous for the dominant allele (SS). If the spotted parent were heterozygous (Ss), then 50 percent of the offspring would have been solid-colored.
18. The allele for the striped trait is dominant. If it were recessive, all of the offspring would have been solid green.
19. A thicker coat is a helpful mutation in a very cold environment, because it provides extra insulation to keep the mouse warm. It would be harmful in a

---

Reviewing Content
Multiple Choice
Choose the letter of the best answer.

1. The different forms of a gene are called
   a. alleles.   b. chromosomes.
   c. phenotypes.   d. genotypes.
2. In a coin toss, the probability of the coin landing heads up is
   a. 100 percent.   b. 75 percent.
   c. 50 percent.   d. 25 percent.
3. An organism with two identical alleles for a trait is
   a. heterozygous.
   b. homozygous.
   c. recessive.
   d. dominant.
4. If the body cells of an organism have 10 chromosomes, then its sex cells would have
   a. 5 chromosomes.
   b. 10 chromosomes.
   c. 15 chromosomes.
   d. 20 chromosomes.
5. During protein synthesis, messenger RNA
   a. "reads" each three-letter code of bases.
   b. releases the completed protein chain.
   c. copies information from DNA in the nucleus.
   d. carries amino acids to the ribosome.

True or False
If the statement is true, write true. If it is false, change the underlined word or words to make the statement true.

6. The scientific study of heredity is called <u>genetics</u>.
7. An organism's physical appearance is its <u>genotype</u>.
8. In <u>codominance</u>, neither of the alleles is dominant or recessive.
9. <u>Heredity</u> is the process by which sex cells form.
10. Proteins are made in the <u>nucleus</u> of the cell.

Checking Concepts
11. Describe what happened when Mendel crossed purebred tall pea plants with purebred short pea plants.
12. You toss a coin five times and it lands heads up each time. What is the probability that it will land heads up on the sixth toss? Explain your answer.
13. In guinea pigs, the allele for black fur (B) is dominant over the allele for white fur (b). In a cross between a heterozygous black guinea pig (Bb) and a homozygous white guinea pig (bb), what is the probability that an offspring will have white fur? Use a Punnett square to answer the question.
14. In your own words, describe the sequence of steps in the process of meiosis.
15. Describe the role of transfer RNA in protein synthesis.
16. **Writing to Learn** Imagine that you are a student in the 1860s visiting Gregor Mendel in his garden. Write a letter to a friend describing Mendel's experiments.

Thinking Critically
17. **Applying Concepts** In rabbits, the allele for a spotted coat is dominant over the allele for a solid-colored coat. A spotted rabbit was crossed with a solid-colored rabbit. The offspring all had spotted coats. What were the genotypes of the parents? Explain.
18. **Problem Solving** Suppose you are growing purebred green-skinned watermelons. One day you find a mutant striped watermelon. You cross the striped watermelon with a purebred green watermelon. Fifty percent of the offspring are striped, while fifty percent are green. Is the allele for the striped trait dominant or recessive? Explain.
19. **Predicting** A new mutation in mice causes the coat to be twice as thick as normal. In what environments would this mutation be helpful?

---

very warm environment, because the mouse would not be able to easily lose heat.

Applying Skills
20. $\frac{9}{12} \times 100\% = 75\%$ green pods;
$\frac{3}{12} \times 100\% = 25\%$ yellow pods
21. Yellow pods: gg; green pods: GG or Gg

22. Both parents are Gg. If both parents were GG, then none of the offspring would have yellow pods. If one parent were GG and the other were Gg, then, again, none of the offspring would have yellow pods. Neither parent could be gg, because both parents have green pods, and g is a recessive allele for yellow pods.

Applying Skills

In peas, the allele for green pods (G) is dominant over the allele for yellow pods (g). The table shows the phenotypes of the offspring produced from a cross of two plants with green pods. Use the data to answer Questions 20–22.

Phenotype	Number of Offspring
Green pods	9
Yellow pods	3

20. **Calculating** Calculate what percent of the offspring have green pods. Calculate what percent have yellow pods.
21. **Inferring** What is the genotype of the offspring with yellow pods? What are the possible genotypes of the offspring with green pods?

22. **Drawing Conclusions** What are the genotypes of the parents? How do you know?

Performance CHAPTER PROJECT 1 Assessment

Project Wrap Up Finalize your display of your pet's family. Be prepared to discuss the inheritance patterns in your pet's family. Examine your classmates' exhibits, and see which offspring look most like, and least like, their parents. Can you find any offspring that "break the laws" of inheritance?

Reflect and Record How did your paper pets help you learn about genetics? How do the inheritance patterns in your pet's family resemble real-life patterns? How could you use paper pets to help you understand other topics in genetics?

Test Preparation
Use these questions to prepare for standardized tests.

Use the information to answer Questions 23–26.
A pet store's customers prefer pet mice with black fur over mice with white fur. With this in mind, the owner crossed a female with black fur and a male with black fur. When the mice were born, she was surprised that three of the ten offspring had white fur. She did not know that the parents were heterozygous for fur color.

23. Which letters represent the genotype of the female parent?
  a. BB
  b. Bb
  c. B
  d. bb
24. Which letters represent the genotype of the male parent?
  a. BB
  b. Bb
  c. B
  d. bb

25. How could the pet store owner breed a litter of only white mice?
  a. by making sure that either the mother or the father has white fur
  b. by making sure that both the mother and the father have white fur
  c. by making sure that at least one of the grandparents has white fur
  d. She could not breed a litter of only white mice.
26. If the pet store owner were to cross one homozygous black mouse with a heterozygous black mouse, what percentage of the mice would you expect to have white fur?
  a. 0%
  b. 25%
  c. 50%
  d. 75%

Performance CHAPTER PROJECT 1 Assessment

Project Wrap Up Make sure students understand that "breaking the laws" of inheritance refers to proposed inheritance patterns that violate the principles of heredity. This could happen, for example, when students propose that two homozygous recessive parents produce offspring with one or two dominant alleles. Students should review each other's Punnett squares to make sure that no offspring "break the inheritance laws."
Reflect and Record Students should record in their journals how their paper pets helped them understand specific concepts and principles of genetics. For example, students should describe how the inheritance patterns of their paper pets demonstrated the inheritance of dominant and recessive alleles, or showed the relationship between genotype and phenotype. They should also explain how paper pets could be used as models to study other topics in genetics.

Test Preparation
23. b **24.** b **25.** b **26.** a

Program Resources

- ◆ **Inquiry Skills Activity Book** Provides teaching and review of all inquiry skills
- ◆ **Prentice Hall Assessment System** Provides standardized test practice
- ◆ **Reading in the Content Area** Provides strategies to improve science reading skills
- ◆ **Teachers ELL Handbook** Provides multiple strategies for English language learners

47

Modern Genetics

Sections	Time	Student Edition Activities	Other Activities	
CHAPTER PROJECT 2 **A Family Portrait** p. 49	Ongoing (2 weeks)	Check Your Progress, pp. 56, 61 Project Wrap Up, p. 75	**TE**	Chapter 2 Project Notes, pp. 48–49
1 Human Inheritance pp. 50–56 ◆ 2.1.1 Explain what multiple alleles are. ◆ 2.1.2 Explain why some human traits show a large variety of phenotypes. ◆ 2.1.3 Explain how environmental factors can alter the effects of a gene. ◆ 2.1.4 Explain what determines sex and why some sex-linked traits are more common in males than in females. ◆ 2.1.5 Describe how geneticists use pedigrees.	1 period/ ½ block	**Discover** How Tall Is Tall?, p. 50 **Try This** The Eyes Have It, p. 52 **Try This** Girl or Boy?, p. 54	**TE** **LM**	Including All Students, p 55 2, "How Are Genes on Sex Chromosomes Inherited?"
2 Human Genetic Disorders pp. 57–63 ◆ 2.2.1 Describe the causes and symptoms of four human genetic disorders. ◆ 2.2.2 Explain how genetic disorders are diagnosed.	2 periods/ 1 block	**Discover** How Many Chromosomes?, p. 57 **Real-World Lab: Careers in Science** Family Puzzles, pp. 62–63	**TE** **TE**	Including All Students, p. 58 Demonstration, p. 60
3 INTEGRATING TECHNOLOGY **Advances in Genetics** pp. 64–72 ◆ 2.3.1 Describe three ways in which people have developed organisms with desired traits. ◆ 2.3.2 Explain how DNA fingerprinting is used. ◆ 2.3.3 State the goal of the Human Genome Project.	2 periods/ 1 block	**Discover** What Do Fingerprints Reveal?, p. 64 **Sharpen Your Skills** Communicating, p. 69 **Science at Home,** p. 70 **Real-World Lab: You Solve the Mystery** Guilty or Innocent?, p. 72	**TE** **TE** **TE**	Real-Life Learning, p. 65 Demonstration, p. 66 Inquiry Challenge, p. 67
Study Guide/Assessment pp. 73–75	1 period/ ½ block		**ISAB**	Provides teaching and review of all inquiry skills

 For Standard or Block Schedule The Resource Pro® CD-ROM gives you maximum flexibility for planning your instruction for any type of schedule. Resource Pro® contains Planning Express®, an advanced scheduling program, as well as the entire contents of the Teaching Resources and the Computer Test Bank.

Key: **CTB** Computer Test Bank
CT Chapter Tests
ELL Teacher's ELL Handbook

CHAPTER PLANNING GUIDE

Program Resources	Assessment Strategies	Media and Technology
UR Chapter 2 Project Teacher Notes, pp. 36–37 **UR** Chapter 2 Project Overview and Worksheets, pp. 38–41	**TE** Check Your Progress, pp. 56, 61 **TE** Performance Assessment: Chapter 2 Project Wrap Up, p. 75 **UR** Chapter 2 Project Scoring Rubric, p. 42	Science Explorer Internet Site Audio CDs, Section Summaries
UR 2-1 Lesson Plan, p. 43 **UR** 2-1 Section Summary, p. 44 **UR** 2-1 Review and Reinforce, p. 45 **UR** 2-1 Enrich, p. 46	**SE** Section 1 Review, p. 56 **TE** Ongoing Assessment, pp. 51, 53, 55 **TE** Performance Assessment, p. 52	Presentation Pro, "Human Inheritance" Transparency 5, "Punnett Square—Male or Female?"; Transparency 6, "Exploring a Pedigree"
UR 2-2 Lesson Plan, p. 47 **UR** 2-2 Section Summary, p. 48 **UR** 2-2 Review and Reinforce, p. 49 **UR** 2-2 Enrich, p. 50 **UR** Real-World Lab blackline masters, pp. 55–57	**SE** Section 2 Review, p. 61 **SE** Analyze and Conclude, p. 63 **TE** Ongoing Assessment, p. 59 **TE** Performance Assessment, p. 61	Concept Videotape Library, *Adventures, Tape 1,* "An Unusual Mutation" Lab Activity Videotape, *Tape 1*
UR 2-3 Lesson Plan, p. 51 **UR** 2-3 Section Summary, p. 52 **UR** 2-3 Review and Reinforce, p. 53 **UR** 2-3 Enrich, p. 54 **UR** Real-World Lab blackline masters, pp. 58–59	**SE** Section 3 Review, p. 70 **SE** Analyze and Conclude, p. 72 **TE** Ongoing Assessment, pp. 65, 67, 69 **TE** Performance Assessment, p. 70	Concept Videotape Library, *Adventures, Tape 1,* "Breeding for Dollars" Presentation Pro, "Advances in Genetics" Transparency 7, "Exploring Genetic Engineering" Lab Activity Videotape, *Tape 1*
GRSW Provides worksheets to promote student comprehension of content **RCA** Provides strategies to improve science reading skills **ELL** Provides multiple strategies for English language learners	**SE** Study Guide/Assessment, pp. 73–75 **PA** Performance Assessment, pp. 7–9 **CT** Chapter 2 Test, pp. 7–10 **CTB** Chapter 2 Test **PHAS** Provides standardized test preparation	Computer Test Bank, Chapter 2 Test

GRSW Guided Reading and Study Workbook
ISAB Inquiry Skills Activity Book
LM Laboratory Manual

PA Performance Assessment
PHAS Prentice Hall Assessment System
PLM Probeware Lab Manual

RCA Reading in the Content Area
SE Student Edition

TE Teacher's Edition
UR Unit Resources

Meeting the National Science Education Standards and AAAS Benchmarks

National Science Education Standards	Benchmarks for Science Literacy	Unifying Themes

National Science Education Standards

Science As Inquiry (Content Standard A)

◆ **Develop descriptions, explanations, predictions, and models using evidence** Students create a pedigree for an imaginary family, investigate inheritance patterns in families and model DNA finger-printing. (*Chapter Project; Real-World Lab*)

Life Science (Content Standard C)

◆ **Reproduction and heredity** Human traits can be controlled by single genes, multiple alleles, or many genes. A pedi-gree is used to trace the inheritance of traits. Genetic disorders are caused by mutations. People have used selective breeding, cloning, and genetic engineering to develop organisms with desirable traits. (*Chapter Project; Sections 1, 2, 3; Real-World Lab*)

Science and Technology (Content Standard E)

◆ **Understandings about science and technology** Doctors use such tools as amniocentesis and karyotypes to help detect genetic disorders. In genetic engineering, genes from one organism are transferred into the DNA of another organism. DNA can be used to identify individuals. (*Sections 2, 3; Real-World Lab*)

Science in Personal and Social Perspectives (Content Standard F)

◆ **Science and technology in society** Students examine the issue of who should have access to genetic test results. (*Science and Society*)

Benchmarks for Science Literacy

1B Scientific Inquiry Students create a pedigree for an imaginary family. Students investigate inheritance patterns in families. Students model DNA fingerprinting. (*Chapter Project; Real-World Lab*)

3A Technology and Science Doctors use such tools as amniocentesis and karyotypes to help detect genetic disorders. In genetic engineering, genes from one organism are transferred into the DNA of another organism. DNA can be used to identify individuals. (*Sections 2, 3; Real-World Lab*)

3C Issues in Technology Students examine the issue of who should have access to genetic test results. (*Science and Society*)

5B Heredity Human traits can be controlled by single genes, multiple alleles, or many genes. A pedigree is used to trace the inheritance of traits. Genetic disorders are caused by mutations. People have used selective breeding, cloning, and genetic engineering to develop organisms with desirable traits. (*Chapter Project; Sections 1, 2, 3; Real-World Lab*)

12D Communication Skills Students present their pedigrees and "photo" albums to the class. (*Chapter Project*)

Unifying Themes

◆ **Evolution** Geneticists use a pedigree to trace the inheritance of traits in humans. People have used selective breeding, cloning, and genetic engineering to develop organisms with desirable traits. (*Chapter Project; Sections 1, 3; Real-World Lab*)

◆ **Patterns of Change** The effects of genes are often altered by the environment. Genetic disorders are caused by mutations. Selective-breeding methods can be used to produce desired characteristics in plants and animals. (*Sections 1, 2, 3*)

◆ **Scale and Structure** The Y chromosome is much smaller than the X chromosome. The 23 pairs of human chromosomes that make up the human genome contain about 60,000 to 80,000 genes. (*Sections 1, 3*)

◆ **Stability** A clone is an organism that is genetically identical to the organism from which it was produced. (*Section 3*)

◆ **Systems and Interactions** Because males have only one X chromosome, males are more likely than females to inherit sex-linked traits controlled by recessive alleles. Doctors use tools such as amniocentesis and karyotypes to help detect genetic disorders. In genetic engineering, genes from one organism are transferred into the DNA of another organism. (*Sections 1, 2, 3*)

◆ **Unity and Diversity** Human traits can be controlled by single genes, multiple alleles, or many genes. A genetic disorder is an abnormal condition that a person inherits through genes or chromosomes. (*Sections 1, 2, 3; Real-World Lab*)

Take It to the Net

The **www.phschool.com** Web site provides you with multiple opportunities to incorporate the internet into your instruction. Go to **www.phschool.com** and click on the Science icon. Then select Science Explorer Integrated.

www.phschool.com

Internet Activities provide opportunities for students to review, extend, or assess a concept from the chapter.

■ Have students use the chapter Self-Test to get instant feedback.

■ Hot Links and Reference Links provide opportunities for online research.

STAY CURRENT with **SCIENCE NEWS** ®

Find out the latest research and information about genetics at: **www.phschool.com**

Student Edition Activities Planner

ACTIVITY	Time (minutes)	Materials Quantities for one work group	Skills
Section 1			
Discover, p. 50	15	**Consumable** graph paper **Nonconsumable** tape measure	Inferring
Try This, p. 52	10	No special materials are required.	Designing Experiments
Try This, p. 54	10	**Nonconsumable** 2 paper bags, 3 red marbles, 1 white marble	Making Models
Section 2			
Discover, p. 57	10	No special materials are required.	Inferring
Real-World Lab, pp. 62–63	40	**Consumable** 12 index cards **Nonconsumable** scissors, marker	Interpreting Data, Drawing Conclusions
Section 3			
Discover, p. 64	15	**Consumable** plain white paper **Nonconsumable** ink pad, hand lens	Observing
Sharpen Your Skills, p. 69	15	No special materials are required.	Communicating
Science at Home, p. 70	home	No special materials are required.	Observing, Applying Concepts
Real-World Lab, p. 72	20	**Consumable** 4–6 bar codes **Nonconsumable** hand lens	Observing, Making Models, Drawing Conclusions

A list of all materials required for the Student Edition activities can be found beginning on page T23. You can obtain information about ordering materials by calling 1-800-848-9500 or by accessing the Science Explorer Internet site at **www.phschool.com.**

A Family Portrait

In Chapter 2, students will learn more about human traits and how they are inherited. They also will learn how pedigrees can be used to trace the inheritance of traits in families. The Chapter 2 Project will give students an opportunity to use pedigrees to demonstrate different types of inheritance.

Purpose In the Chapter 2 Project, students will create a pedigree for an imaginary family and use it to show how two different traits have been passed from generation to generation within the family. Students also will create a family album showing how the traits appear in individual family members. Successfully completing the Chapter 2 Project will require students to understand different patterns of inheritance and the concepts of genotype and phenotype.

Skills Focus After completing the Chapter 2 Project, students will be able to
◆ create a model pedigree for an imaginary family;
◆ apply genetic concepts to show the inheritance of two different traits in the family's pedigree;
◆ predict phenotypes of individuals with different genotypes to create a family album;
◆ communicate their work in a class presentation.

Project Time Line The Chapter 2 Project will take about two weeks to complete. On the first day, have students read about the project on page 49 in the text. Review the traits controlled by a single gene that are described in Chapters 1 and 2. Tell students to select two of the traits for the project. Distribute the Chapter 2 Project Overview, pages 38–39 in Unit 1 Resources, and give students a chance to read through it and ask questions. Hand out the Chapter 2 Project Scoring Rubric, page 42 in Unit 1 Resources, so students will know how their work will be evaluated.

If you want students to work in groups, assign them to groups at this time as well, and give groups a chance to meet and plan the project. Distribute Chapter 2 Project Worksheet 1, page 40 in Unit 1 Resources, and instruct

CHAPTER 2 Modern Genetics

www.phschool.com

SECTION 1 Human Inheritance
Discover How Tall Is Tall?
Try This The Eyes Have It
Try This Girl or Boy?

SECTION 2 Human Genetic Disorders
Discover How Many Chromosomes?
Real-World Lab Family Puzzles

SECTION 3 *Integrating Technology* Advances in Genetics
Discover What Do Fingerprints Reveal?
Sharpen Your Skills Communicating
Real-World Lab Guilty or Innocent?

48

students to complete it before they begin their pedigrees.

Give students two or three days to create a pedigree for their imaginary families, following the specifications in Exploring a Pedigree on page 56 in their text. After students have completed their pedigrees, check them for errors. Then hand out Chapter 2 Project Worksheet 2, page 41 in Unit 1 Resources, and instruct students to complete the worksheet before they create their pedigrees for the two traits. When students have finished their

pedigrees, check their work before they begin their family albums.

Students may need several days to create their family albums, depending on how they choose to represent their selected traits. Finally, set aside at least one class period at the end of the project for students to present their work to the rest of the class. Consider having students present their work in a poster-session format, where half the class at a time is available to discuss results and answer questions with the other half of the class.

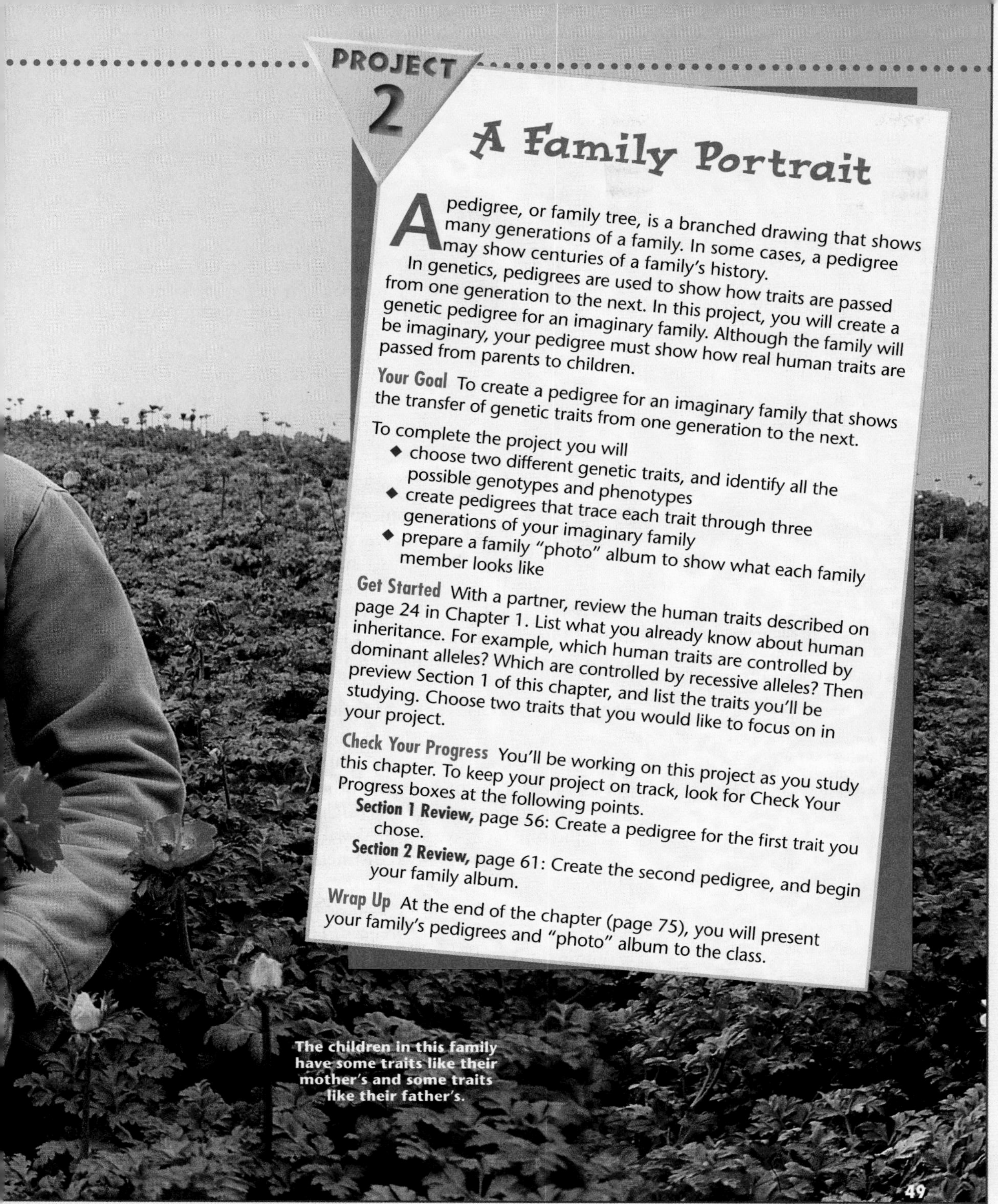

PROJECT 2

A Family Portrait

A pedigree, or family tree, is a branched drawing that shows many generations of a family. In some cases, a pedigree may show centuries of a family's history.

In genetics, pedigrees are used to show how traits are passed from one generation to the next. In this project, you will create a genetic pedigree for an imaginary family. Although the family will be imaginary, your pedigree must show how real human traits are passed from parents to children.

Your Goal To create a pedigree for an imaginary family that shows the transfer of genetic traits from one generation to the next.

To complete the project you will

- choose two different genetic traits, and identify all the possible genotypes and phenotypes
- create pedigrees that trace each trait through three generations of your imaginary family
- prepare a family "photo" album to show what each family member looks like

Get Started With a partner, review the human traits described on page 24 in Chapter 1. List what you already know about human inheritance. For example, which human traits are controlled by dominant alleles? Which are controlled by recessive alleles? Then preview Section 1 of this chapter, and list the traits you'll be studying. Choose two traits that you would like to focus on in your project.

Check Your Progress You'll be working on this project as you study this chapter. To keep your project on track, look for Check Your Progress boxes at the following points.

Section 1 Review, page 56: Create a pedigree for the first trait you chose.

Section 2 Review, page 61: Create the second pedigree, and begin your family album.

Wrap Up At the end of the chapter (page 75), you will present your family's pedigrees and "photo" album to the class.

The children in this family have some traits like their mother's and some traits like their father's.

49

For more detailed information on the chapter project, see Chapter 2 Project Teacher Notes, pages 36–37 in Unit 1 Resources.

Suggested Shortcuts Before students fill in the basic pedigree for specific traits, make sure it is accurate. Then have students make a photocopy of their pedigree. This will save them the time and effort of copying it over for the second trait.

Possible Materials For their pedigrees, students can use large sheets of white paper or poster board. For their family albums, students can use a variety of different materials. The album itself may be a real photo album or scrapbook or a sheet of poster board. For pictures, students can use drawings or photographs from magazines or newspapers or sketches of their own. To show traits that are not visible, such as colorblindness or hemophilia, urge students to think of creative ways of depicting individuals with different phenotypes, such as fictitious newspaper articles or letters.

Launching the Project Introduce the project by calling students' attention to the family photograph on these pages and asking: **What are some traits that the children in this family appear to share with their parents?** *(Students are likely to name obvious physical traits such as hair color or nose shape.)* Point out that, in addition to traits such as these, children inherit thousands of other traits from their parents, including many traits that are not so apparent. Tell students that, in the Chapter 2 Project, they will create a family tree for an imaginary family and show how genetic traits pass from one generation to the next.

Program Resources

- **Unit 1 Resources** Chapter 2 Project Teacher Notes, pp. 36–37; Project Overview and Worksheets, pp. 38–41; Project Scoring Rubric, p. 42

Media and Technology

Audio CDs Section Summaries

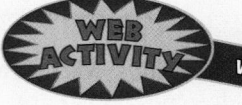

WEB ACTIVITY www.phschool.com

You will find an Internet activity, chapter self-tests for students, and links to other chapter topics at this site.

Performance Assessment

To assess students' performance in this project, use the Chapter 2 Project Scoring Rubric on page 42 of Unit 1 Resources. Students will be assessed on

- the accuracy of their pedigrees;
- how accurately and creatively they depict the phenotypes of the individuals in their family albums;
- how complete and prepared their class presentation is;
- their group participation, if they worked in groups.

Objectives

After completing the lesson, students will be able to

◆ explain what multiple alleles are;
◆ explain why some human traits show a large variety of phenotypes;
◆ explain how environmental factors can alter the effects of a gene;
◆ explain what determines sex and why some sex-linked traits are more common in males than in females;
◆ describe how geneticists use pedigrees.

Key Terms multiple alleles, sex-linked gene, carrier, pedigree

1 Engage/Explore

Activating Prior Knowledge

Help students think of examples of inherited traits by asking: **What are some traits that children may share with one or both of their parents?** (*Students are likely to identify traits such as hair color, nose shape, or eye color.*)

········ **DISCOVER** ·········

Skills Focus inferring
Materials *metric ruler, graph paper*
Time 15 minutes
Tips If any students are in wheelchairs, you might want to have the class measure sitting height, which is the height from the base of the spine to the top of the head.
Expected Outcome The graph of students' heights is likely to include several bars, but not as many as there are students in the class.
Think It Over Students may infer that height in humans is controlled by more than one gene because the graph of students' heights has more bars than the two-bar graph Mendel would have drawn.

DISCOVER ·············· **ACTIVITY**

How Tall Is Tall?

1. Choose a partner. Measure each other's height to the nearest 5 centimeters. Record your measurements on the chalkboard.

2. Create a bar graph showing the number of students at each height. Plot the heights on the horizontal axis and the number of students on the vertical axis.

Think It Over
Inferring If Gregor Mendel had graphed the heights of his pea plants, the graph would have had two bars—one for tall stems and one for short stems. Do you think height in humans is controlled by a single gene, as it is in peas? Explain your answer.

GUIDE FOR READING

◆ Why do some human traits show a large variety of phenotypes?

◆ Why are some sex-linked traits more common in males than in females?

◆ How do geneticists use pedigrees?

Reading Tip Before you read, rewrite the headings in this section as *how, why,* or *what* questions. As you read, write answers to the questions.

Have you ever heard someone say "He's the spitting image of his dad" or "She has her mother's eyes"? Children often resemble their parents. The reason for this is that alleles for eye color, hair color, and thousands of other traits are passed from parents to their children. People inherit some alleles from their mother and some from their father. This is why most people look a little like their mother and a little like their father.

Traits Controlled by Single Genes

In Chapter 1, you learned that many traits in peas and other organisms are controlled by a single gene with two alleles. Often one allele is dominant, while the other is recessive. Many human traits are also controlled by a single gene with one dominant allele and one recessive allele. As with tall and short pea plants, these human traits have two distinctly different phenotypes, or physical appearances.

For example, a widow's peak is a hairline that comes to a point in the middle of the forehead. The allele for a widow's peak is dominant over the allele for a straight hairline. The Punnett square in Figure 1 illustrates a cross between two parents who are heterozygous for a widow's peak. Trace the possible combinations of alleles that a child may inherit. Notice that each child has a 3 in 4, or 75 percent, probability of having a widow's peak. There is only a 1 in 4, or 25 percent, probability that a child will have a straight hairline. Recall from Chapter 3 that when Mendel crossed peas that were heterozygous for a trait, he obtained similar percentages in the offspring.

READING STRATEGIES

Reading Tip *Sample questions:* What traits are controlled by single genes? What are multiple alleles? Which traits are controlled by many genes? How does the environment affect phenotypes? What determines whether you are male or female? How are sex-linked genes different from other genes? What is a pedigree? Advise students to save their questions and answers and use them to quiz themselves on the material when they prepare for assessments.

Study and Comprehension Before students begin the section, you may want to have them review several of the key terms from Chapter 1 that are important for understanding the concepts in this section. Have them find and read the definition of each of the following: *allele, dominant allele, recessive allele, phenotype, genotype,* and *codominance.*

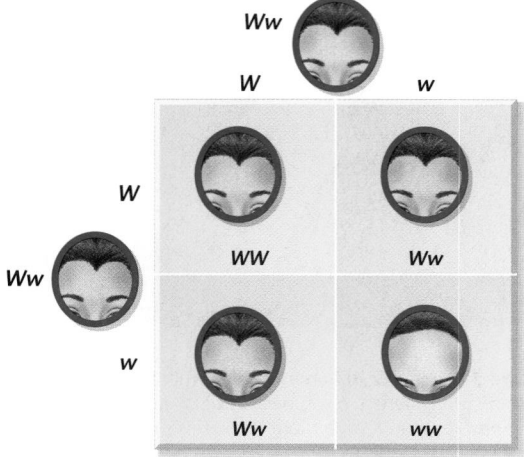

Figure 1 This Punnett square shows a cross between two parents with widow's peaks. *Interpreting Diagrams What are the possible genotypes of the offspring? What percent of the offspring will have each genotype?*

Do you have dimples when you smile? If so, then you have the dominant allele for this trait. Like having a widow's peak, having smile dimples is controlled by a single gene. People who have two recessive alleles do not have smile dimples.

Multiple Alleles

Some human traits are controlled by a single gene that has more than two alleles. Such a gene is said to have **multiple alleles**—three or more forms of a gene that code for a single trait. You can think of multiple alleles as being like flavors of pudding. Pudding usually comes in more flavors than just chocolate and vanilla!

Even though a gene may have multiple alleles, a person can carry only two of those alleles. This is because chromosomes exist in pairs. Each chromosome in a pair carries only one allele for each gene.

One human trait that is controlled by a gene with multiple alleles is blood type. There are four main blood types—A, B, AB, and O. Three alleles control the inheritance of blood types. The allele for blood type A and the allele for blood type B are codominant. The codominant alleles are written as capital letters with superscripts—I^A for blood type A and I^B for blood type B. The allele for blood type O—written i—is recessive. Recall that when two codominant alleles are inherited, neither allele is masked. A person who inherits an I^A allele from one parent and an I^B allele from the other parent will have type AB blood. Figure 2 shows the allele combinations that result in each blood type. Notice that only people who inherit two i alleles have type O blood.

☑ *Checkpoint* *If a gene has multiple alleles, why can a person only have two of the alleles for the gene?*

Blood Types	
Blood Type	**Combination of Alleles**
A	$I^A I^A$ or $I^A i$
B	$I^B I^B$ or $I^B i$
AB	$I^A I^B$
O	ii

Figure 2 Blood type is determined by a single gene with three alleles. This chart shows which combinations of alleles result in each blood type.

2 Facilitate

Traits Controlled by Single Genes

Addressing Naive Conceptions

Help students avoid the naive conception that the children in families always have genotypes that are in the ratios predicted by Punnett squares. Ask: **Could two parents with a widow's peak have three children without widow's peaks, and only one child with a widow's peak?** *(Students may say that three of the four children should have a widow's peak because the allele for the trait is dominant.)* Explain that three out of four children with a widow's peak is the most likely outcome for this mating. However, due to chance and the small number of offspring, any given family can deviate significantly from ratio determined by a Punnett square, as in the example given here. **learning modality: verbal**

Multiple Alleles

Using the Visuals: Figure 2

Make sure that students understand that the superscripts are not exponents but just labels used to distinguish the two codominant alleles, I^A and I^B. Then check that students understand the relationship between genotype and phenotype for traits controlled by multiple alleles, such as blood type, by asking: **Which column in the table lists the genotypes? Which lists the phenotypes?** *(The right column lists the genotypes; the left column the phenotypes.)* **Why are there more genotypes than phenotypes?** *(Because two different genotypes—I^{A}I^A and I^{A}i—result in the A phenotype and two other genotypes—I^{B}I^B and I^{B}i—result in the B phenotype.)* **learning modality: visual**

Ongoing Assessment

Drawing Have students draw a Punnett square that shows a cross between two heterozygotes for smile dimples (a trait controlled by a dominant allele).

Program Resources

◆ **Unit 1 Resources** 2-1 Lesson Plan, p. 43; 2-1 Section Summary, p. 44
◆ **Guided Reading and Study Workbook** Section 2-1

Answers to Self-Assessment

Caption Question

Figure 1 The possible genotypes of the offspring are *WW, Ww,* and *ww;* 25% should have the *WW* genotype, 50% the *Ww* genotype, and 25% the *ww* genotype.

☑ *Checkpoint*

Chromosomes exist in pairs, and each chromosome in a pair carries only one allele for each gene.

Traits Controlled by Many Genes

Building Inquiry Skills: Calculating

Challenge students to identify all the possible genotypes for a hypothetical trait controlled by two genes, each having two alleles, with *A* and *a* representing the two alleles for one gene and *B* and *b* representing the two alleles for the other gene. Ask a volunteer to record students' responses on the chalkboard as they identify all the possible genotypes. (*The possible genotypes are AABB, AABb, AAbb, AaBB, AaBb, Aabb, aaBB, aaBb, and aabb.*) After the list is complete, ask: **How many more genotypes are there for a trait controlled by two genes than for a trait controlled by one gene, if each gene has two alleles?** (*Three times as many*) **learning modality: logical/ mathematical**

The Effect of Environment

Skills Focus designing experiments
Time 10 minutes
Tips Make sure students focus on an object that is at least a few meters away from them.
Expected Outcome Students should find that when they close one eye their finger appears to be stationary, but when they close the other eye their finger appears to move. For some students the finger will appear stationary when they look at it with their right eye, meaning their right eye is dominant. For other students the finger will appear stationary when they look at it with their left eye, meaning their left eye is dominant. To test the relationship between eye and hand dominance, students might determine eye and hand dominance for a large sample of people, and then inspect the data to see if a pattern emerges.
Extend Ask: **How is a dominant eye different than a dominant allele?** (*A dominant eye is a trait, whereas a dominant allele controls the inheritance of a trait.*) **learning modality: kinesthetic**

Figure 3 Skin color in humans is determined by three or more genes. Different combinations of alleles at each of the genes result in a wide range of possible skin colors.

The Eyes Have It

One inherited trait is eye dominance—the tendency to use one eye more than the other. Here's how you can test yourself for this trait.

1. Hold your hand out in front of you at arm's length. Point your finger at an object across the room.
2. Close your right eye. With only your left eye open, observe how far your finger appears to move.
3. Repeat Step 2 with the right eye open. With which eye did your finger seem to remain closer to the object? That eye is dominant.

Designing Experiments Is eye dominance related to hand dominance—whether a person is right-handed or left-handed? Design an experiment to find out. Obtain your teacher's permission before carrying out your experiment.

Traits Controlled by Many Genes

If you did the Discover activity, you observed that height in humans has more than two distinct phenotypes. In fact, there is an enormous variety of phenotypes for height. What causes this wide range of phenotypes? **Some human traits show a large number of phenotypes because the traits are controlled by many genes. The genes act together as a group to produce a single trait.** At least four genes control height in humans, so there are many possible combinations of genes and alleles.

Like height, skin color is determined by many genes. Human skin color ranges from almost white to nearly black, with many shades in between. Skin color is controlled by at least three genes. Each gene, in turn, has at least two possible alleles. Various combinations of alleles at each of the genes determine the amount of pigment that a person's skin cells produce. Thus, a wide variety of skin colors is possible.

The Effect of Environment

The effects of genes are often altered by the environment—the organism's surroundings. For example, people's diets can affect their height. A diet lacking in protein, minerals, and vitamins can prevent a person from growing to his or her potential maximum height. Since the late 1800s, the average height of adults in the United States has increased by almost 10 centimeters. During that time, American diets have become more healthful. Other environmental factors, such as medical care and living conditions, have also improved since the late 1800s.

✓ *Checkpoint* *How can environmental factors affect a person's height?*

Background

History of Science The existence of sex chromosomes was discovered in the late 1800s by Hermann Henking. While studying wasp cells, Henking observed an "accessory chromosome" in each dividing cell that did not have a matching chromosome at prophase. He also noted that male wasps had an uneven number of chromosomes, but females had an even number.

In the early 1900s, the American zoologist Clarence McClung observed "accessory chromosomes" in cells of grasshoppers. McClung's work revealed the significance of the "accessory chromosome," the X chromosome, as a mechanism for the determination of an organism's sex.

Male or Female?

"Congratulations, Mr. and Mrs. Gonzales. It's a baby girl!" What factors determine whether a baby is a boy or a girl? As with other traits, the sex of a baby is determined by genes on chromosomes. Among the 23 pairs of chromosomes in each body cell is a single pair of chromosomes called the sex chromosomes. The sex chromosomes determine whether a person is male or female.

The sex chromosomes are the only pair of chromosomes that do not always match. If you are female, your two sex chromosomes match. The two chromosomes are called X chromosomes. If you are male, your sex chromosomes do not match. One of your sex chromosomes is an X chromosome. The other chromosome is a Y chromosome. The Y chromosome is much smaller than the X chromosome.

What happens to the sex chromosomes when egg and sperm cells form? As you know, each egg and sperm cell has only one chromosome from each pair. Since both of a female's sex chromosomes are X chromosomes, all eggs carry one X chromosome. Males, however, have two different sex chromosomes. This means that half of a male's sperm cells carry an X chromosome, while half carry a Y chromosome.

When a sperm cell with an X chromosome fertilizes an egg, the egg has two X chromosomes. The fertilized egg will develop into a girl. When a sperm with a Y chromosome fertilizes an egg, the egg has one X chromosome and one Y chromosome. The fertilized egg will develop into a boy. Thus it is the sperm that determines the sex of the child, as you can see in Figure 4.

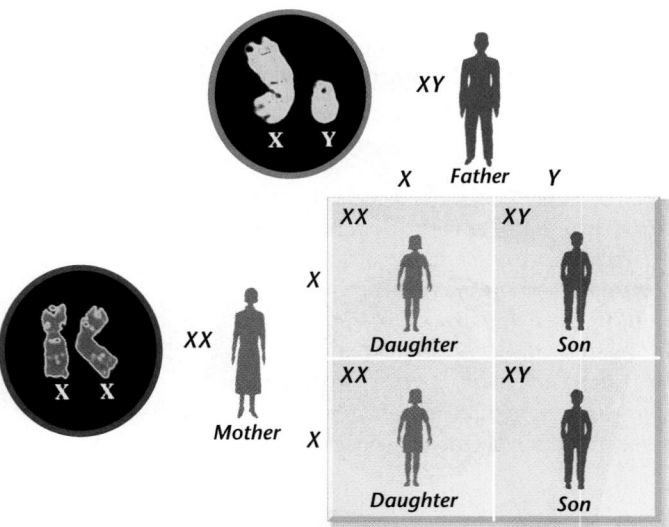

Figure 4 As this Punnett square shows, there is a 50 percent probability that a child will be a girl and a 50 percent probability that a child will be a boy. *Interpreting Diagrams What sex will the child be if a sperm with a Y chromosome fertilizes an egg?*

Building Inquiry Skills: Drawing Diagrams

Challenge students to draw two simple diagrams of meiosis, contrasting the formation of sex cells in males and females. Their drawings should show clearly which type of sex chromosome each of the sex cells contains. If students do not remember the details of meiosis, suggest that they refer to *Exploring Meiosis* on page 37, Chapter 1. Explain that the X and Y chromosomes pair up during meiosis. After students have finished their drawings, ask: **How do your drawings demonstrate that it is the father's sperm that determines the sex of a child?** (*The drawings should show that the sex cells produced by a male may contain either an X or a Y chromosome, whereas the sex cells produced by a female may contain only an X chromosome. Thus, the sex of a child is determined by whether an egg is fertilized by an X-bearing or a Y-bearing sperm produced by the father.*)
learning modality: kinesthetic

Using the Visuals: Figure 4

Use the visual to help students understand why an allele on a man's X chromosome cannot be inherited by his sons. Ask: **If the man in the figure had an allele *A* on his X chromosome, which of his offspring—his sons or his daughters—would inherit the allele?** (*The man's daughters*) **Why wouldn't his sons inherit the allele?** (*Because the man's sons inherit only the Y chromosome from their father.*)
learning modality: visual

Ongoing Assessment

Writing Have students explain, in their own words, why about half of all babies are boys and about half are girls. (*Sample answer: A baby's sex depends on whether it receives an X or a Y chromosome from the father. Half the sperm produced by males contain an X chromosome, and the other half contain a Y chromosome. Therefore, about half the time eggs are fertilized by Y-bearing sperm and about half the time they are fertilized by X-bearing sperm. This results in about half the babies being boys and about half being girls.*)

 Transparencies "Punnett Square–Male or Female?," Transparency 5

Answers to Self-Assessment

✓ *Checkpoint*
Environmental factors such as a poor diet can affect a person's height by preventing the person from reaching his or her potential maximum height.

Caption Question
Figure 4 The child will be male.

Male or Female?, continued

Skills Focus making models

Materials *two paper bags, three red marbles, one white marble*

Time 10 minutes

Tips Remind students to replace the two marbles in the correct bags each time before they make their next draw.

Expected Outcome About half the time students will draw two red marbles, representing a female, and about half the time they will draw one red and one white marble, representing a male. If you add up the numbers of females and males produced by the whole class, the totals are likely to be even closer to half female and half male.

Extend Ask: **How could you use the same setup to model the inheritance of a trait controlled by a single gene, such as widow's peak?** (*The most likely way is to assume that one color marble represents the dominant allele and the other color represents the recessive allele for the same gene. Students would draw one marble from each bag, as in the original activity.*)

learning modality: kinesthetic

Sex-Linked Genes

Building Inquiry Skills: Inferring

Challenge students to infer how the inheritance of a sex-linked trait controlled by a dominant allele would differ from the inheritance of a sex-linked trait controlled by a recessive allele. First, remind students that a sex-linked trait controlled by a recessive allele is more common in males because males need to inherit just one recessive allele to have the trait. Then ask: **If a sex-linked trait is controlled by a dominant allele, would the trait be more common in males than in females? Why or why not?** (*A trait controlled by a dominant allele would not be more common in males because females, like males, would need to inherit just one dominant allele to have the trait.*) **learning modality: logical/mathematical**

Girl or Boy?

You can model how the sex of an offspring is determined.

1. Label one paper bag "female." Label another paper bag "male."

2. Place two red marbles in the bag labeled "female." The red marbles represent X chromosomes.

3. Place one red marble and one white marble in the bag labeled "male." The white marble represents a Y chromosome.

4. Without looking, pick one marble from each bag. Two red marbles represent a female offspring. One red marble and one white marble represent a male offspring. Record the sex of the "offspring."

5. Put the marbles back in the correct bags. Repeat Step 4 nine more times.

Making Models How many males were produced? How many females? How close were your results to the expected probabilities for male and female offspring?

Sex-Linked Genes

Some human traits occur more often in one sex than the other. The genes for these traits are often carried on the sex chromosomes. Genes on the X and Y chromosomes are often called **sex-linked genes** because their alleles are passed from parent to child on a sex chromosome. Traits controlled by sex-linked genes are called sex-linked traits.

Like other genes, sex-linked genes can have dominant and recessive alleles. Recall that females have two X chromosomes, whereas males have one X chromosome and one Y chromosome. In females, a dominant allele on one X chromosome will mask a recessive allele on the other X chromosome. The situation is not the same in males, however. In males, there is no matching allele on the Y chromosome to mask, or hide, the allele on the X chromosome. As a result, any allele on the X chromosome—even a recessive allele—will produce the trait in a male who inherits it. **Because males have only one X chromosome, males are more likely than females to have a sex-linked trait that is controlled by a recessive allele.**

One example of a sex-linked trait that is controlled by a recessive allele is red-green colorblindness. A person with red-green colorblindness cannot distinguish between red and green. A common test for red-green colorblindness is shown in Figure 5.

Many more males than females have red-green colorblindness. You can understand why this is the case by examining the Punnett square in Figure 6. Both parents in this example have normal color vision. Notice, however, that the mother is a carrier of colorblindness. A **carrier** is a person who has one recessive allele for a trait and one dominant allele. Although a carrier does not have the trait, the carrier can pass the recessive allele on to his or her offspring. In the case of sex-linked traits, only females can be carriers.

Figure 5 A person with red-green colorblindness cannot see the loop of red and pink dots in this test chart.

Program Resources

◆ **Laboratory Manual** 2, "How Are Genes on Sex Chromosomes Inherited?"

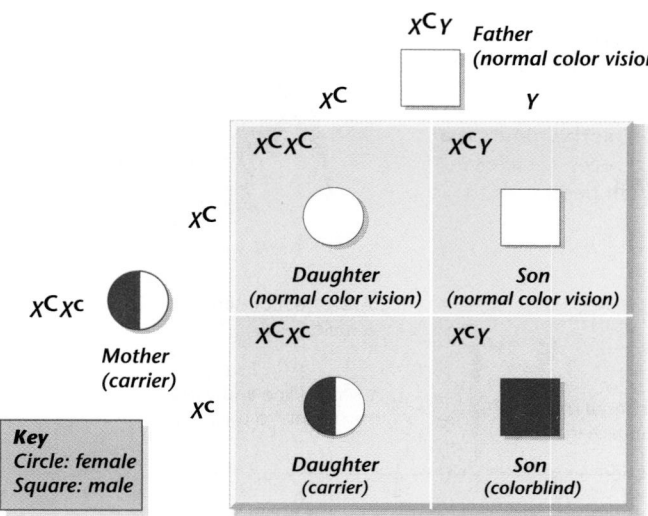

Key
Circle: female
Square: male

Father
(normal color vision)

Daughter
(normal color vision)

Son
(normal color vision)

Mother
(carrier)

Daughter
(carrier)

Son
(colorblind)

Figure 6 Red-green colorblindness is a sex-linked trait. A girl who receives only one recessive allele (written X^c) for red-green colorblindness will not have the trait. However, a boy who receives one recessive allele will be colorblind. *Applying Concepts What allele combination would a daughter need to inherit to be colorblind?*

As you can see in Figure 6, there is a 25 percent probability that this couple will have a colorblind child. Notice that none of the couple's daughters will be colorblind. On the other hand, the sons have a 50 percent probability of being colorblind. For a female to be colorblind, she must inherit two recessive alleles for colorblindness, one from each parent. A male needs to inherit only one recessive allele. This is because there is no gene for color vision on the Y chromosome. Thus, there is no allele that could mask the recessive allele on the X chromosome.

Pedigrees

Imagine that you are a geneticist interested in studying inheritance patterns in humans. What would you do? You can't set up crosses with people as Mendel did with peas. Instead, you would need to trace the inheritance of traits through many generations in a number of families.

One important tool that geneticists use to trace the inheritance of traits in humans is a pedigree. A **pedigree** is a chart or "family tree" that tracks which members of a family have a particular trait. The trait recorded in a pedigree can be an ordinary trait such as widow's peak, or it could be a sex-linked trait such as colorblindness. In *Exploring a Pedigree* on page 56, you can trace the inheritance of colorblindness through three generations of a family.

✓ *Checkpoint* How is a pedigree like a "family tree"?

Answers to Self-Assessment

Caption Question

Figure 6 A daughter would need to inherit two X^c alleles.

✓ *Checkpoint*

A pedigree is like a "family tree" in that it traces the inheritance of a trait through the generations of a family.

Including All Students

Materials *white, red, and green pipe cleaners*
Time 15 minutes

Provide hands-on learners with an opportunity to make a three-dimensional model to help them understand sex-linked inheritance. Have students twist together two white pipe cleaners to represent a normal X chromosome, a red pipe cleaner and a green pipe cleaner to represent an X chromosome with the allele for red-green colorblindness, and a single white pipe cleaner to represent a Y chromosome. Encourage students to use their models to represent several different matings and their expected outcomes. Then ask: **What is the phenotype of each individual represented in your model?** *(Students' answers should show that they understand that males are colorblind when they inherit just one allele for colorblindness.)* **learning modality: kinesthetic**

Pedigrees

EXPLORING
a Pedigree

Check that students understand the symbols in the pedigree by asking: **How many married couples are there in the second generation?** *(three)* **In all three generations, how many males are colorblind?** *(two)* **How many females are carriers?** *(four)* Then check that students understand sex-linked recessive inheritance by asking: **Which third-generation individuals could have colorblind daughters?** *(The two carrier females and the colorblind male, if he marries a colorblind female.)* **learning modality: visual**

Ongoing Assessment

Skills Check Have students solve the following problem: Mary and her mother are both colorblind. Is Mary's father colorblind, too? How do you know? *(Because Mary is colorblind, she must have inherited an X^c allele from each parent. Therefore, Mary's father's genotype must be X^cY, so he is colorblind, too.)*

3 Assess

Section 1 Review Answers

1. Such traits are controlled by many genes and influenced by environment.

2. It is controlled by a recessive allele on the X chromosome, and males need to inherit only one recessive allele to have the trait.

3. It is a chart that tracks which members of a family have a particular trait. They are used by geneticists as tools for tracing inheritance.

4. Yes, if both parents are heterozygous for widow's peak and the child inherits a recessive allele for straight hairline from each parent. No, because the parents each have two recessive alleles for straight hairline, so the child will inherit two recessive alleles.

Check Your Progress

CHAPTER PROJECT 2

Check that students' pedigrees cover at least three generations and that the second generation consists of five children. Make sure the pedigrees do not contain any errors before students start using them to show inheritance patterns. Also check that students have chosen traits controlled by single genes to represent in their pedigrees.

Performance Assessment

Drawing Have students draw a pedigree showing the inheritance of a single recessive allele, starting with first generation genotypes of $Aa \times Aa$ and continuing for three generations.

EXPLORING *a Pedigree*

This pedigree traces the occurrence of colorblindness in three generations of a family. Colorblindness is a sex-linked trait that is controlled by a recessive allele. Notice that specific symbols are used in pedigrees to communicate genetic information.

A circle represents a female.

A square represents a male.

A horizontal line connecting a male and female represents a marriage.

A vertical line and a bracket connect the parents to their children.

A half-shaded circle or square indicates that a person is a carrier of the trait.

A completely shaded circle or square indicates that a person has the trait.

A circle or square that is not shaded indicates that a person neither has the trait nor is a carrier of the trait.

Section 1 Review

1. Why do human traits such as height and skin color have many different phenotypes?

2. Explain why red-green colorblindness is more common in males than in females.

3. What is a pedigree? How are pedigrees used?

4. Thinking Critically **Predicting** Could two people with widow's peaks have a child with a straight hairline? Could two people with straight hairlines have a child with a widow's peak? Explain.

56

Check Your Progress

CHAPTER PROJECT 2

By now, you should be creating your pedigree for the first trait you chose. Start with one couple, and show two generations of offspring. The couple should have five children. It is up to you to decide how many children each of those children has. Use Punnett squares to make sure that your imaginary family's inheritance pattern follows the laws of genetics.

Background

Facts and Figures Traits controlled by sex-linked recessive alleles are unique in appearing to skip generations in a pedigree. Such traits do not pass from a man to his sons. Instead they pass from a man through his daughters, who do not have the trait but are carriers, to his grandsons. When a trait shows this inheritance pattern, it is likely to be controlled by a sex-linked recessive allele.

Program Resources

◆ **Unit 1 Resources** 2-1 Review and Reinforce, p. 45; 2-1 Enrich, p. 46

2 Human Genetic Disorders

DISCOVER •• ACTIVITY

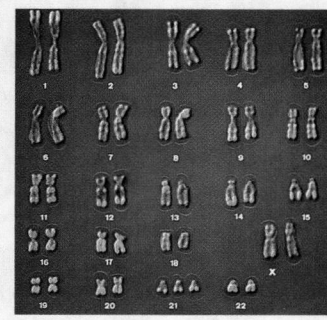

How Many Chromosomes?

The photo at the left shows the chromosomes from a cell of a person with Down syndrome, a genetic disorder. The chromosomes have been sorted into pairs.

1. Count the number of chromosomes in the photo.

2. How does the number of chromosomes compare to the usual number of chromosomes in human cells?

Think It Over

Inferring How do you think a cell could have ended up with this number of chromosomes? (*Hint:* Think about the events that occur during meiosis.)

The air inside the stadium was hot and still. The crowd cheered loudly as eight runners approached the starting blocks. The runners shook out their arms and legs to loosen up their muscles and calm their jitters. When the starter raised the gun, all eyes focused on the runners. At the crack of the starter's gun, the runners leaped into motion and sprinted down the track.

Seconds later, the race was over. The runners, bursting with pride, hugged each other and their coaches. It didn't matter where each of the runners placed. All that mattered was that they had finished the race and done their best. These athletes were running in the Special Olympics, a competition for people with disabilities.

Many of the athletes who compete in the Special Olympics have disabilities that result from genetic disorders. A **genetic disorder** is an abnormal condition that a person inherits through genes or chromosomes. **Genetic disorders are caused by mutations, or changes in a person's DNA.** In some cases, a mutation occurs when sex cells form during meiosis. In other cases, a mutation that is already present in a parent's cells is passed on to the offspring. In this section, you will learn about some common genetic disorders.

GUIDE FOR READING

◆ What causes genetic disorders?

◆ How are genetic disorders diagnosed?

Reading Tip As you read, make a list of different types of genetic disorders. Write a sentence about each disorder.

A runner at the Special Olympics ▶

Chapter 2 **57**

Program Resources

◆ **Unit 1 Resources** 2-2 Lesson Plan, p. 47; 2-2 Section Summary, p. 48
◆ **Guided Reading and Study Workbook** Section 2-2

READING STRATEGIES

Vocabulary Students may find several terms in this section difficult to spell and pronounce. Before students read the section, write the following terms on the board: *cystic fibrosis, sickle-cell, hemophilia, amniocentesis,* and *karyotype.* Pronounce each term clearly, and have students repeat it after you. Also have students write and rewrite each term until they can spell it correctly.

Human Genetic Disorders

Objectives

After completing the lesson, students will be able to
◆ describe the causes and symptoms of four human genetic disorders;
◆ explain how genetic disorders are diagnosed.

Key Terms genetic disorder, amniocentesis, karyotype

1 Engage/Explore

Activating Prior Knowledge

Introduce human genetic disorders by asking: **What do you think is a genetic disorder?** (*An abnormal condition that is inherited*) **What are some genetic disorders you have heard about?** (*Accept all student responses without comment at this time.*) Write students' suggestions of genetic disorders on the board, so students can reevaluate the list at the end of the section.

•••••••• DISCOVER ••••••••

Skills Focus inferring
Time 10 minutes
Tips Provide any students who have vision problems with a hand lens for examining the photo.
Expected Outcome Students should count 47 chromosomes in the photo, or one more than the 46 chromosomes normally found in human cells, because there is an extra copy of chromosome 21.
Think It Over Students may correctly say that the extra chromosome is due to failure of the chromosomes to separate during meiosis.

Cystic Fibrosis

Building Inquiry Skills: Relating Cause and Effect

Point out that cystic fibrosis, like most genetic disorders, can be treated but not cured. Then ask: **What is the difference between a treatment and a cure for a disease like cystic fibrosis?** *(A cure eliminates the disease, and therefore the symptoms, whereas a treatment controls the symptoms without eliminating the disease.)* **What are some ways that cystic fibrosis can be treated?** *(Possible ways include drugs to prevent infections and physical therapy to break up mucus in the lungs.)* **How could a genetic disorder like cystic fibrosis be cured?** *(By changing or replacing the gene that causes the symptoms)* **learning modality: verbal**

Sickle-Cell Disease

Including All Students

Materials *poster board, marker*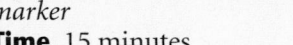

Time 15 minutes

Reinforce the concept of codominance for hands-on learners by having them draw a two-generation pedigree for sickle-cell disease, starting with the genotypes of *Ss* × *Ss*. Remind students to include a key indicating which individuals in the pedigree have normal hemoglobin, one sickle-cell allele, and sickle-cell disease. Invite students to share their pedigrees with the rest of the class. Follow up by asking: **In terms of the genetics, why is having one sickle-cell allele different from being a carrier of cystic fibrosis?** *(People with one sickle-cell allele have both normal hemoglobin and sickle-cell hemoglobin because the allele for abnormal hemoglobin is codominant with the allele for normal hemoglobin. In contrast, people who are carriers of cystic fibrosis have no signs or symptoms of cystic fibrosis because the allele for cystic fibrosis is recessive to the normal allele.)* **learning modality: logical/mathematical**

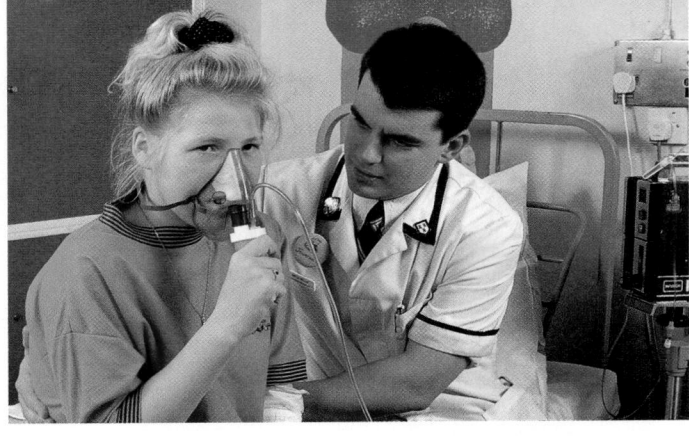

Figure 7 Cystic fibrosis is a genetic disorder that causes thick mucus to build up in a person's lungs and intestines. This patient is inhaling a fine mist that will help loosen the mucus in her lungs.

Figure 8 Normally, red blood cells are shaped like round disks (top). In a person with sickle-cell disease, red blood cells can become sickle-shaped (bottom). *Relating Cause and Effect What combination of alleles leads to sickle-cell disease?*

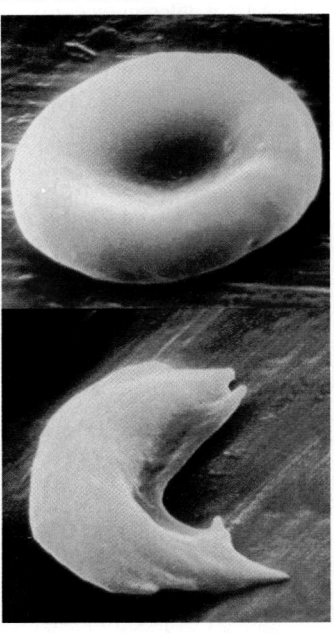

Cystic Fibrosis

Cystic fibrosis is a genetic disorder in which the body produces abnormally thick mucus in the lungs and intestines. The thick mucus fills the lungs, making it hard for the affected person to breathe. Bacteria that grow in the mucus can cause infections and, eventually, lung damage. In the intestines, the mucus makes it difficult for digestion to occur.

The mutation that leads to cystic fibrosis is carried on a recessive allele. The cystic fibrosis allele is most common among people whose ancestors are from Northern Europe. Every day in this country, four babies are born with cystic fibrosis.

Currently there is no cure for cystic fibrosis. Medical treatments include drugs to prevent infections and physical therapy to break up mucus in the lungs. Recent advances in scientists' understanding of the disease may lead to better treatments and longer lifespans for people with cystic fibrosis.

☑ *Checkpoint* What are some symptoms of cystic fibrosis?

Sickle-Cell Disease

Sickle-cell disease is a genetic disorder that affects the blood. The mutation that causes the disorder affects the production of an important protein called hemoglobin. Hemoglobin is the protein in red blood cells that carries oxygen. People with sickle-cell disease produce an abnormal form of hemoglobin. When oxygen concentrations are low, their red blood cells have an unusual sickle shape, as you can see in Figure 8.

Sickle-shaped red blood cells cannot carry as much oxygen as normal-shaped cells. Because of their shape, the cells become stuck in narrow blood vessels, blocking them. People with sickle-cell disease suffer from lack of oxygen in the blood and experience pain and weakness.

58

Background

Integrating Science Another example of a genetic disorder controlled by a recessive allele is Tay-Sachs disease, found primarily in Jews from central or eastern Europe. People with Tay-Sachs disease are missing an enzyme needed to break down fats in the brain. As a result, fatty substances accumulate in the brain, leading to blindness, deafness, and paralysis. Death usually occurs by age four or five.

The allele for the sickle-cell trait is most common in people of African ancestry. About 9 percent of African Americans carry the sickle-cell allele. The allele for the sickle-cell trait is codominant with the normal allele. A person with two sickle-cell alleles will have the disease. A person with one sickle-cell allele will produce both normal hemoglobin and abnormal hemoglobin. This person usually will not have symptoms of the disease.

Currently, there is no cure for sickle-cell disease. People with sickle-cell disease are given drugs to relieve their painful symptoms and to prevent blockages in blood vessels. As with cystic fibrosis, scientists are hopeful that new, successful treatments will soon be found.

Hemophilia

Hemophilia is a genetic disorder in which a person's blood clots very slowly or not at all. People with the disorder do not produce one of the proteins needed for normal blood clotting. A person with hemophilia can bleed to death from a minor cut or scrape. The danger of internal bleeding from small bumps and bruises is also very high.

Hemophilia is an example of a disorder that is caused by a recessive allele on the X chromosome. Because hemophilia is a sex-linked disorder, it occurs more frequently in males than in females. **INTEGRATING HEALTH** People with hemophilia must get regular doses of the missing clotting protein. In general, people with hemophilia can lead normal lives. However, they are advised to avoid contact sports and other activities that could cause internal injuries.

Figure 9 Empress Alexandra of Russia (center row, left) passed the allele for hemophilia to her son Alexis (front).

Social Studies CONNECTION

Hemophilia has affected European history. Queen Victoria of England had a son and three grandsons with hemophilia. Victoria, at least two of her daughters, and four of her granddaughters were carriers of the disease.

As Victoria's descendants passed the hemophilia allele to their offspring, hemophilia spread through the royal families of Europe. For example, Empress Alexandra, Queen Victoria's grand-daughter, married the Russian Czar Nicholas II in 1894. Alexandra, a carrier of hemophilia, passed the disease to her son Alexis, who was heir to the throne.

A monk named Rasputin convinced Alexandra that he could cure Alexis. As a result of his control over Alexandra, Rasputin was able to control the Czar as well. The people's anger at Rasputin's influence may have played a part in the Russian Revolution of 1917, in which the Czar was overthrown.

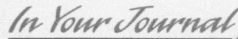

In Your Journal

Imagine that you are Empress Alexandra. Write a diary entry expressing your feelings and unanswered questions about Alexis's condition.

Media and Technology

Concept Videotape Library
Adventures, Tape 1, "An Unusual Mutation"

Answers to Self-Assessment

Caption Question

Figure 8 The combination of two recessive alleles leads to sickle-cell disease.

 Checkpoint

Some symptoms of cystic fibrosis are difficulty breathing, frequent infections, and difficulty digesting food.

Hemophilia

 Integrating Health

Give a group of students who need extra challenges a chance to research and create a flowchart showing how blood clots form. Each group member should research at least one source. Group members should then compile their information and collaborate on creating the flowchart. Have one or more group members explain the flowchart to the rest of the class. Then ask: **How does the hemophilia allele interfere with blood clotting?** (*By leading to the lack of a protein, which is essential for blood to clot*) Challenge group members to point out this step in the flowchart. **cooperative learning**

Social Studies CONNECTION

Provide background for the feature by informing students that the presence of the hemophilia allele in Queen Victoria is believed to have been created by a new mutation. This is based on the fact that neither Victoria's husband nor any of her male relatives in earlier generations had the disorder.

In Your Journal Help students put themselves in Alexandra's place by urging them to imagine what it was like for a child to live with hemophilia, especially in the late 1800s before the development of blood transfusions and blood-clotting proteins. Every cut or nosebleed could cause a life-threatening loss of blood. Ask: **How do you think her son's hemophilia might have affected Alexandra's relationship with him?** (*Alexandra might have been overly protective of her son and very focused on caring for his health and safety.*) Point out that this could have made Alexandra fall more easily under the influence of Rasputin. **learning modality: verbal**

Ongoing Assessment

Skills Check Have students create a table comparing and contrasting cystic fibrosis, sickle-cell disease, and hemophilia.

Down Syndrome

Demonstration

Materials *colored chalk*
Time 10 minutes

Demonstrate with a simple drawing how the production of sex cells with an abnormal number of chromosomes can lead to genetic disorders like Down syndrome. Use circles to represent cells and short lines to represent chromosomes. Start with one parent cell containing two colored X's to represent a pair of chromosomes that has replicated. Illustrate these chromosomes as the cell goes through Meiosis I and Meiosis II, as shown in *Exploring Meiosis* on page 37. Point out that the chromosome pairs can fail to separate correctly in either stage. Then draw four smaller circles to represent four sex cells. Distribute the colored chromosomes among the sex cells unequally, so that one of the sex cells contains two chromosomes and one contains none. Beside each sex cell, draw another small circle containing one white line, to represent a normal sex cell with one chromosome from the other parent. Finally, draw four circles to represent the possible individuals formed when sex cells unite. Two individuals should be normal, one should contain only one white chromosome, and one should contain one white and two colored chromosomes. Ask: **Which individual will have Down syndrome?** *(The one with three chromosomes)* **learning modality: visual**

Diagnosing Genetic Disorders

 Integrating Technology

Tell students that amniocentesis is not performed routinely in every pregnancy because there are risks involved. Amniocentesis often is recommended for older mothers because they have a substantially greater risk of having babies with Down syndrome. Ask: **For what other women do you think amniocentesis is recommended?** *(Women who have, or whose husbands have, a family history of genetic disorders.)* **learning modality: logical/mathematical**

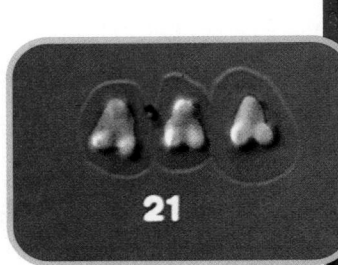

Figure 10 Down syndrome is a genetic disorder in which a person's cells have an extra copy of chromosome 21. Although people with Down syndrome have some mental and physical limitations, they can lead active, productive lives.

Down Syndrome

Some genetic disorders are the result of too many or too few chromosomes. In one such disorder, called Down syndrome, a person's cells have an extra copy of chromosome 21. The extra chromosome is the result of an error during meiosis. Recall that in meiosis, cells divide and chromosomes separate to produce sex cells with half the normal chromosome number. Down syndrome most often occurs when chromosomes fail to separate properly during meiosis.

People with Down syndrome have a distinctive physical appearance, and have some degree of mental retardation. Heart defects are also common, but can be treated. Despite their limitations, many people with Down syndrome lead full, active lives.

Diagnosing Genetic Disorders

INTEGRATING TECHNOLOGY   Years ago, doctors had only Punnett squares and pedigrees to help them predict whether a child might have a genetic disorder. **Today doctors use tools such as amniocentesis and karyotypes to help detect genetic disorders.**

Before a baby is born, doctors can use a procedure called **amniocentesis** (am nee oh sen TEE sis) to determine whether the baby will have some genetic disorders. During amniocentesis, a doctor uses a very long needle to remove a small amount of the fluid that surrounds the developing baby. The fluid contains cells from the baby.

Background

Facts and Figures In addition to Down syndrome, there are a number of other syndromes caused by too many chromosomes. Edwards syndrome is caused by an extra copy of chromosome 18. It occurs about once in every 8,000 live births. Symptoms include mental retardation and malformations of the head, heart, and kidneys. Death usually occurs in the first year. Patau syndrome is caused by an extra copy of chromosome 13. It occurs about once in every 20,000 live births. Symptoms include mental retardation and defects of the hands, heart, and genitals. Death typically occurs by age one. Klinefelter's syndrome is caused by an extra X chromosome in males. It occurs about once in every 500 male live births. Symptoms may include feminine features, sterility, and behavioral problems.

The doctor then examines the chromosomes from the cells. To do this, the doctor creates a karyotype. A **karyotype** (KA ree uh typ) is a picture of all the chromosomes in a cell. The chromosomes in a karyotype are arranged in pairs. A karyotype can reveal whether a developing baby has the correct number of chromosomes in its cells and whether it is a boy or a girl. If you did the Discover activity, you saw a karyotype from a girl with Down syndrome.

Genetic Counseling

A couple that has a family history or concern about a genetic disorder may turn to a genetic counselor for advice. Genetic counselors help couples understand their chances of having a child with a particular genetic disorder. Genetic counselors use tools such as karyotypes, pedigree charts, and Punnett squares to help them in their work.

Suppose, for example, that a husband and wife both have a history of cystic fibrosis in their families. If they are considering having children, they might seek the advice of a genetic counselor. The genetic counselor might order a test to determine whether they are carriers of the allele for cystic fibrosis. The genetic counselor would then apply the same principles of probability that you learned about in Chapter 1 to calculate the couple's chances of having a child with cystic fibrosis.

Figure 11 Couples may meet with a genetic counselor and their doctor in order to understand their chances of having a child with a genetic disorder.

 Section 2 Review

1. Explain how genetic disorders occur in humans. Give two examples of genetic disorders.
2. Describe two tools that doctors use to detect genetic disorders.
3. How do the cells of people with Down syndrome differ from those of others? How might this difference arise?
4. **Thinking Critically** **Problem Solving**
   A couple with a family history of hemophilia is about to have a baby girl. What information about the parents would you want to know? How would this information help you determine whether the baby will have hemophilia?

Check Your Progress CHAPTER PROJECT 2

At this point, you should begin to trace the inheritance of another trait through the same family members that are in your first pedigree. Also, start making your family "photo" album. Will you use drawings or some other method to show what the family members look like? (*Hint:* Photo albums show phenotypes. Remember that more than one genotype can have the same phenotype.)

Program Resources

◆ **Unit 1 Resources** 2-2 Review and Reinforce, p. 49; 2-2 Enrich, p. 50

Genetic Counseling

Inquiry Challenge

Challenge students to assume they are genetic counselors who must determine the chance of a couple having a child with cystic fibrosis, when both husband and wife are carriers. (*Students should draw a Punnett square for two heterozygotes. The Punnett square should show that 25% of the couple's children would be likely to inherit two recessive alleles.*) Ask: **If the couple already has three normal children, what is the chance that their fourth child will have cystic fibrosis?** (*25%; each child has a 25% chance of having cystic fibrosis.*) **learning modality: logical/mathematical**

3 Assess

Section 2 Review Answers

1. Genetic disorders occur when mutations cause changes in DNA. Cystic fibrosis, sickle-cell disease, hemophilia
2. In amniocentesis, cells are removed from the fluid surrounding the baby; in karyotypes, a picture of the chromosomes is analyzed for abnormal chromosomes.
3. They have an extra copy of chromosome 21, which might arise if the chromosomes fail to separate properly during meiosis.
4. You would want to know if the parents have hemophilia or are carriers. This would help you predict the chances of their baby girl having hemophilia.

Check Your Progress CHAPTER PROJECT 2

By now students should be working on their pedigrees for the second trait. Remind them to use the same basic pedigree as they did for the first trait. Ask students how they plan to show individuals in the family album.

Performance Assessment

Skills Check Have students explain how amniocentesis and a karyotype can be used to determine whether a developing baby will have Down syndrome.

Family Puzzles

Preparing for Inquiry

Key Concept By analyzing pedigrees, you can determine the pattern of inheritance of a trait and the chance of any given individual inheriting specific alleles.

Skills Objectives Students will be able to
◆ interpret data on phenotypes to construct family pedigrees;
◆ draw conclusions from the pedigrees about the type of alleles controlling the traits and the chances of given individuals inheriting specific alleles for the traits.

Time 40 minutes

Advance Planning To save time, you can cut and label the index cards for students before class begins.

Alternative Materials Instead of index cards to represent alleles, students can use marbles, game chips, beads, or other similar objects, with different colors representing the two different alleles in each case study.

Guiding Inquiry

Invitation Before students begin, draw a simple pedigree on the chalkboard showing a wife with a genetic disorder and a healthy husband who have an affected daughter and a healthy son. Ask: **Can you tell if the trait shown in this pedigree is controlled by a dominant or recessive allele?** *(No, there isn't enough information.)* Extend the pedigree back one generation by adding two healthy parents for the wife. Then ask: **Now can you tell if the trait is controlled by a dominant or recessive allele?** *(The trait must be controlled by a recessive allele; otherwise, at least one of the wife's parents would also have the trait.)* Point out to students that the more generations there are in a pedigree, the more obvious the pattern of inheritance becomes, as they will see when the do this lab.

Introducing the Procedure

◆ Check that students remember how to draw pedigrees. For example, ask: **How do you show in a pedigree that**

Family Puzzles

Imagine that you are a genetic counselor. Two couples come to you for advice. Their family histories are summarized in the boxes labeled *Case Study 1* and *Case Study 2*. They want to understand the probability that their children might inherit certain genetic disorders. In this lab, you will find answers to their questions.

Problem

How can you investigate inheritance patterns in families?

Materials

12 index cards
scissors
marker

Procedure ✂

Part 1 Investigating Case Study 1

1. Read over Case Study 1. In your notebook, draw a pedigree that shows all the family members. Use circles to represent the females, and squares to represent the males. Shade in the circles or squares representing the individuals who have cystic fibrosis.

> **Case Study 1: Joshua and Bella**
> ◆ Joshua and Bella have a son named Ian. Ian has been diagnosed with cystic fibrosis.
> ◆ Joshua and Bella are both healthy.
> ◆ Bella's parents are both healthy.
> ◆ Joshua's parents are both healthy.
> ◆ Joshua's sister, Sara, has cystic fibrosis.

2. You know that cystic fibrosis is controlled by a recessive allele. To help you figure out Joshua and Bella's family pattern, create a set of cards to represent the alleles. Cut each of six index cards into four smaller cards. On 12 of the small cards, write *N* to represent the dominant normal allele. On the other 12 small cards, write *n* for the recessive allele.

3. Begin by using the cards to represent Ian's alleles. Since he has cystic fibrosis, what alleles must he have? Write in this genotype next to the pedigree symbol for Ian.

4. Joshua's sister, Sara, also has cystic fibrosis. What alleles does she have? Write in this genotype next to the pedigree symbol that represents Sara.

---

a man and woman are married? *(By linking their symbols with a horizontal line)* If necessary, suggest students review *Exploring a Pedigree* on page 56.

Troubleshooting the Experiment

◆ Before students answer the questions, check that they have drawn their pedigrees correctly and labeled each individual with the appropriate genotype(s). You may want to have pairs of students compare pedigrees to detect any errors.

◆ Tell students they will need to draw Punnett squares to find the answers to Questions 2 and 4.

Expected Outcome

Students should be able to use the data provided to construct a pedigree for each family. From the pedigrees, students should be able to determine the type of allele controlling the skin condition and the probability of particular individuals inheriting each condition.

Case Study 2: Li and Mai

- ◆ The father, Li, has a skin condition. The mother, Mai, has normal skin.
- ◆ Li and Mai's first child, a girl named Gemma, has the same skin condition as Li.
- ◆ Mai's sister has a similar skin condition, but Mai's parents do not.

- ◆ Li has one brother whose skin is normal, and one sister who has the skin condition.
- ◆ Li's mother has the skin condition. His father does not.
- ◆ Li's family lives in a heavily wooded area. His family has always thought the skin condition was a type of allergy.

5. Now use the cards to figure out what genotypes Joshua and Bella must have. Write their genotypes next to their symbols in the pedigree.

6. Work with the cards to figure out the genotypes of all other family members. Fill in each person's genotype next to his or her symbol in the pedigree. If more than one genotype is possible, write in both genotypes.

Part 2 Investigating Case Study 2

7. Read over Case Study 2.

8. You suspect that Gemma and Li's skin condition is caused by an inherited recessive allele. Begin to investigate this possibility by drawing a family pedigree in your notebook. Use shading to indicate which individuals have the skin condition.

9. Fill in the genotype ss beside each individual who has the skin condition. Then use cards as you did in Case Study 1 to figure out each family member's genotype. If more than one genotype is possible, fill in both genotypes.

Analyze and Conclude

1. In Case Study 1, what were the genotypes of Joshua's parents? What were the genotypes of Bella's parents?

2. In Case Study 1, Joshua also has a brother. What is the probability that he has cystic fibrosis? Explain.

3. Can you conclude that the skin condition in Case Study 2 is most likely an inherited trait controlled by a recessive allele? Explain.

4. What is the probability that Mai and Li's next child will have the skin condition? Explain.

5. **Apply** Why do genetic counselors need information about many generations of a family in order to draw conclusions about a hereditary condition?

More to Explore

Review the two pedigrees that you just studied. What data suggests that the traits are not sex-linked? Explain.

Analyze and Conclude

1. Joshua's parents are both heterozygous (Nn). The genotypes of Bella's parents cannot be determined for certain, but at least one must be heterozygous; the other could be either heterozygous or homozygous (NN).

2. Because both parents are heterozygous (Nn), there is a 25 percent chance of each child inheriting two n alleles and having cystic fibrosis.

3. All the evidence in the family's pedigree supports the conclusion that the skin

Program Resources

◆ **Unit 1 Resources** Real-World Lab blackline masters, pp. 55–57

Media and Technology

 Lab Activity Videotape *Tape 1*

---

condition is controlled by a recessive allele. At least one of Mai's parents would have the skin condition if the allele were dominant, but both of the parents have normal skin.

4. Because one of the parents is heterozygous *(Ss)* and one is homozygous *(ss)* for the skin condition, there is a 50 percent chance of each child inheriting two *s* alleles and having the skin condition.

5. Genetic counselors cannot usually draw firm conclusions about a hereditary condition with information about just one or two generations, because more than one inheritance pattern may explain the facts when the information is so limited. For example, if the only information in Case Study 2 were the phenotypes of Li, Mai, and Gemma, sex-linked inheritance could not be ruled out.

Extending the Inquiry

More to Explore Data showing that the traits are not sex-linked include the observation that the traits affect males and females about equally. If the skin condition in Case Study 2 were sex-linked, Li's brother also would have inherited the condition from their mother, but he did not. If cystic fibrosis in Case Study 1 were sex-linked, Ian would have inherited the disorder from his mother's side of the family, not his father's side of the family, as appears to have been the case.

Case Study 1: Joshua and Bella

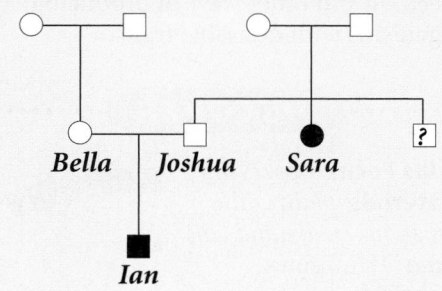

Case Study 2: Li and Mai

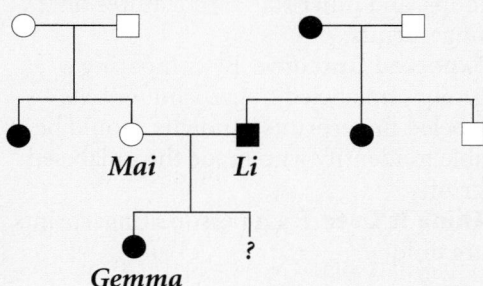

SECTION 3 Advances in Genetics

Objectives

After completing the lesson, students will be able to
◆ describe three ways in which people have developed organisms with desired traits;
◆ explain how DNA fingerprinting is used;
◆ state the goal of the Human Genome Project.

Key Terms selective breeding, inbreeding, hybridization, clone, genetic engineering, gene therapy, genome

1 Engage/Explore

Activating Prior Knowledge

Introduce the section by helping students appreciate the variation that has been selectively bred into dogs. Ask: **What are some breeds of dogs that have very different characteristics?** *(Possible answers might include dachshund, Chihuahua, and Great Dane.)* Explain that the different breeds were produced by mating animals that have certain desirable traits. In this section, students will learn about selective breeding and other ways of producing organisms with desirable traits.

DISCOVER

Skills Focus observing
Materials *plain white paper, ink pad, hand lens*
Time 15 minutes
Tips Help students recognize similarities and differences among the fingerprints by pointing out examples of whirls, loops, and other standard features of fingerprints.
Expected Outcome By comparing a group's unlabeled fingerprint with its labeled fingerprints, students should be able to identify who made the unlabeled print.
Think It Over Each person's fingerprints are unique.

SECTION 3 Advances in Genetics

DISCOVER .... ACTIVITY

What Do Fingerprints Reveal?

1. Label a sheet of paper with your name. Then roll one of your fingers from side to side on an ink pad. Make a fingerprint by carefully rolling your inked finger from side to side on the paper.

2. Divide into groups. Each group should choose one member to use the same finger to make a second fingerprint on a sheet of paper. Leave the paper unlabeled.

3. Exchange your group's fingerprints with those from another group. Compare each labeled fingerprint with the fingerprint on the unlabeled paper. Decide whose fingerprint it is.

4. Wash your hands after completing this activity.

Think It Over
Observing Why are fingerprints a useful tool for identifying people?

GUIDE FOR READING

◆ What are three ways in which an organism's traits can be altered?

◆ What is the goal of the Human Genome Project?

Reading Tip As you read, make a concept map of the methods used to produce organisms with desirable traits. Include at least one example of each technique.

Dolly ▼

In the summer of 1996, a lamb named Dolly was born in Scotland. Dolly was an ordinary lamb in every way except one. The fertilized cell that developed into Dolly was produced in a laboratory by geneticists using experimental techniques. You will learn more about the techniques used by the geneticists later in the section.

Although the techniques used to create Dolly are new, the idea of producing organisms with specific traits is not. For thousands of years, people have tried to produce plants and animals with desirable traits. **Three methods that people have used to develop organisms with desirable traits are selective breeding, cloning, and genetic engineering.**

Selective Breeding

More than 5,000 years ago, people living in what is now central Mexico discovered that a type of wild grass could be used as food. They saved the seeds from those plants that produced the best food, and planted them to grow new plants. By repeating this process over many generations of plants, they developed an early variety of the food crop we now call corn. The process of selecting a few organisms with desired traits to serve as parents of the next generation is called **selective breeding.**

People have used selective breeding with many different plants and animals. Breeding programs usually focus on increasing the value of the plant or animal to people. For

---

READING STRATEGIES

Reading Tip Students' concept maps should show that inbreeding and hybridization are two types of selective breeding and that cloning and genetic engineering are additional methods used to produce organisms with desirable traits.

Study and Comprehension Before students read the section, suggest that they make an outline using the boldfaced headings and subheadings. Then, as students read the section, urge them to add a sentence or two under each heading to summarize the main points. Encourage visual learners to preview the section by looking at the figures and reading the captions.

Vocabulary Help students understand the technical material presented in the section by having them write definitions of the bold-faced terms as they read.

example, dairy cows are bred to produce larger quantities of milk. Many varieties of fruits and vegetables are bred to resist diseases and insect pests.

Inbreeding One useful selective breeding technique is called inbreeding. **Inbreeding** involves crossing two individuals that have identical or similar sets of alleles. The organisms that result from inbreeding have alleles that are very similar to those of their parents. Mendel used inbreeding to produce purebred pea plants to use in his experiments.

One goal of inbreeding is to produce breeds of animals with specific traits. For example, by only crossing horses with exceptional speed, breeders can produce purebred horses that can run very fast. Purebred dogs, such as Labrador retrievers and German shepherds, were produced by inbreeding.

Unfortunately, because inbred organisms are genetically very similar, inbreeding reduces an offspring's chances of inheriting new allele combinations. Inbreeding also increases the probability that organisms may inherit alleles that lead to genetic disorders. For example, inherited hip problems are common in many breeds of dogs.

Hybridization Another selective breeding technique is called hybridization. In **hybridization** (hy brid ih ZAY shun), breeders cross two genetically different individuals. The hybrid organism that results is bred to have the best traits from both parents. For example, a farmer might cross corn that produces many kernels with corn that is resistant to disease. The result might be a hybrid corn plant with both of the desired traits. Today, most crops grown on farms and in gardens were produced by hybridization.

Figure 12 For thousands of years, people have used selective breeding to produce plants and animals with desirable traits. *Making Generalizations What are some traits for which corn may be bred?*

Program Resources

◆ **Unit 1 Resources** 2-3 Lesson Plan, p. 51; 2-3 Section Summary, p. 52
◆ **Guided Reading and Study Workbook** Section 2-3

Media and Technology

 Concept Videotape Library *Adventures, Tape 1, "Breeding for Dollars"*

Answers to Self-Assessment

Caption Question

Figure 12 Some traits include resistance to disease and the production of ears with many kernels.

---

2 Facilitate

Selective Breeding

Cultural Diversity

Provide students with additional information about selective breeding to help them appreciate its significance throughout human history. For example, thousands of years ago, some Native Americans began domesticating plant species. They genetically changed plant species by cross-pollinating plants with desired traits. Eventually, more than 100 different species of plants were domesticated, of which maize, or corn, is probably the most important. Maize was selectively bred by Native Americans to have larger, more numerous kernels. Conclude by asking: **How do you think the selective breeding of plants such as maize would have affected the people who depended on the plants for food?** *(It would have increased the amount of food available, so people could have been better fed or more people could have been fed.)* **learning modality: verbal**

Real-Life Learning

Materials *seed catalogs*
Time 10 minutes

Help students appreciate the importance of hybridization in real life by giving them an opportunity to examine seed catalogs and read about hybrid varieties of flowers, vegetables, and fruits that have been developed by plant breeders. Ask: **What are some traits for which hybrids have been bred?** *(Students might name rapid growth or improved flavor, among many other possible traits.)* **learning modality: verbal**

Ongoing Assessment

Drawing Have students draw two Punnett squares, one to represent inbreeding and one to represent hybridization. *(To represent inbreeding, students should show a cross between individuals with the same genotype, such as AA × AA. To represent hybridization, students should show a cross between individuals with different genotypes, such as AA × aa.)*

65

Cloning

Figure 13 Plants can be easily cloned by making a cutting. Once the cutting has grown roots, it can be planted and will grow into a new plant. *Applying Concepts Why is the new plant considered to be a clone of the original plant?*

Cloning

One problem with selective breeding is that the breeder cannot control whether the desired allele will be passed from the parent to its offspring. This is because the transmission of alleles is determined by probability, as you learned in Chapter 1. For some organisms, another technique, called cloning, can be used to produce offspring with desired traits. A **clone** is an organism that is genetically identical to the organism from which it was produced. This means that a clone has exactly the same genes as the organism from which it was produced. Cloning can be done in plants and animals, as well as other organisms.

Cloning Plants One way to produce a clone of a plant is through a cutting. A cutting is a small part of a plant, such as a leaf or a stem, that is cut from the plant. The cutting can grow into an entire new plant. The new plant is genetically identical to the plant from which the cutting was taken.

Cloning Animals Remember Dolly, the lamb described at the beginning of this section? Dolly was the first clone of an adult mammal ever produced. To create Dolly, researchers removed an egg cell from one sheep. The cell's nucleus was replaced with the nucleus from a cell of a six-year-old sheep. The egg was then implanted into the uterus of a third sheep. Five months later, Dolly was born. Dolly is genetically identical to the six-year-old sheep that supplied the nucleus. Dolly is a clone of that sheep.

Since scientists first cloned Dolly, pigs and calves have also been cloned. Scientists hope that cloning animals will allow humans to live healthier lives. For example, pigs that are being cloned have genes that will make their organs suitable for organ transplant into humans.

Checkpoint How can a clone of a plant be produced?

Genetic Engineering

In the past few decades, geneticists have developed another powerful technique for producing organisms with desired traits. In this process, called **genetic engineering,** genes from one organism are transferred into the DNA of another organism. Genetic engineering is sometimes called "gene splicing" because a DNA molecule is cut open and a gene from another organism is spliced into it. Genetic engineering can produce medicines and improve food crops, and may cure human genetic disorders.

EXPLORING Genetic Engineering

Scientists use genetic engineering to create bacterial cells that produce important human proteins, such as insulin.

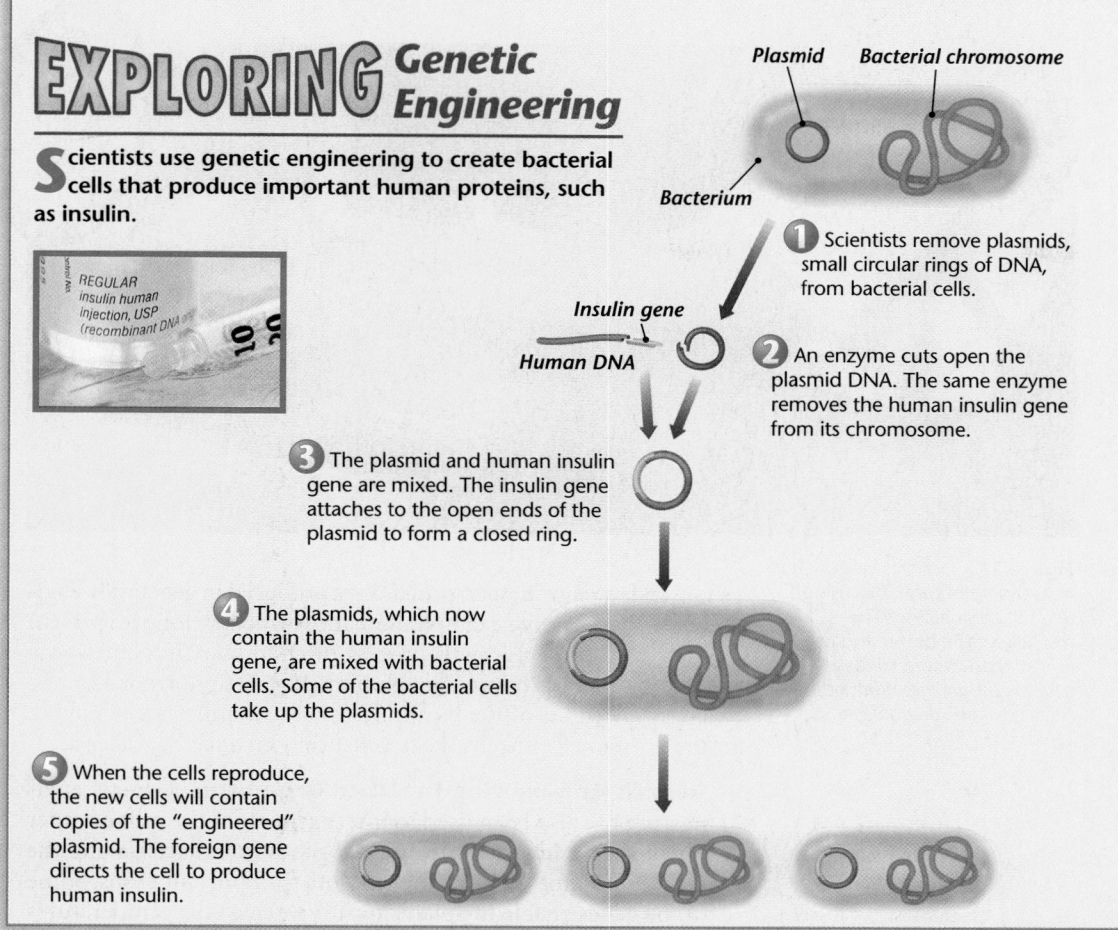

Plasmid   **Bacterial chromosome**

Bacterium

1 Scientists remove plasmids, small circular rings of DNA, from bacterial cells.

Insulin gene

Human DNA

2 An enzyme cuts open the plasmid DNA. The same enzyme removes the human insulin gene from its chromosome.

REGULAR
insulin human
injection, USP
(recombinant DNA)

3 The plasmid and human insulin gene are mixed. The insulin gene attaches to the open ends of the plasmid to form a closed ring.

4 The plasmids, which now contain the human insulin gene, are mixed with bacterial cells. Some of the bacterial cells take up the plasmids.

5 When the cells reproduce, the new cells will contain copies of the "engineered" plasmid. The foreign gene directs the cell to produce human insulin.

Genetic Engineering in Bacteria Researchers had their first successes with genetic engineering when they inserted DNA from other organisms into bacteria. Recall that the single DNA molecule of bacterial cells is found in the cytoplasm. Some bacterial cells also contain small circular pieces of DNA called plasmids.

In *Exploring Genetic Engineering,* you can see how scientists insert a human gene into the plasmid of a bacterium. Once the DNA is spliced into the plasmid, the bacterial cell and all its offspring will contain this human gene. As a result, the bacteria produce the protein that the human gene codes for, in this case insulin. Because bacteria reproduce quickly, large amounts of insulin can be produced in a short time. The insulin can be collected and used to treat people with diabetes, a disorder in which the body does not produce enough of this protein.

Answers to Self-Assessment
Caption Question
Figure 13 The new plant is genetically identical to the original plant.

☑ *Checkpoint*
By growing a cutting of the original plant

EXPLORING
Genetic Engineering

Provide students with background information about diabetes so they can appreciate the importance of genetically engineering bacteria to produce human insulin. Insulin is a hormone that cells need to absorb sugar from the blood for energy. People with Type I, or juvenile onset diabetes cannot produce insulin. As a result, their cells are unable to absorb sugar from the blood, and the sugar level in their blood can become dangerously high. Taking insulin helps control the level of sugar in the blood, which helps prevent life-threatening complications of the disease.

Guide students who need more help by asking questions that will require them to read the captions carefully. For example, ask: **What is a plasmid, and where is it found?** (*A small circular ring of DNA in a bacterial cell*) **Why are the bacteria in Step 5 able to produce human insulin?** (*Because they contain copies of the human insulin gene.*)
limited English proficiency

Inquiry Challenge
Materials *two pieces of yarn of different colors, blunt scissors, tape*
Time 10 minutes

Challenge students to create a simple model of DNA with yarn and then to use the model to simulate gene splicing, as illustrated in *Exploring Genetic Engineering.* (*The most likely way is to arrange a piece of yarn of one color in a circle to represent a bacterial plasmid and to use the piece of yarn of the other color to represent a small section of human DNA. Gene splicing can be simulated by cutting both pieces of yarn, taping a piece of the "DNA" yarn to the piece of "plasmid" yarn, and reforming the circle.*) Ask: **What do the scissors represent in your model?** (*The enzyme that cuts the DNA*)
learning modality: kinesthetic

Ongoing Assessment

Skills Check Have students compare and contrast cloning and genetic engineering.

Genetic Engineering, continued

Inquiry Challenge

Challenge students to think of ways that plants could be genetically engineered to increase the production of food. Ask: **How could you genetically engineer a fruit, vegetable, or other food plant so that it would be more likely to survive and thrive?** *(Ways that food plants actually have been genetically engineered include making plants that are able to tolerate poor soil or resist disease.)* **learning modality: logical/mathematical**

Real-Life Learning

Point out that genetic engineering, particularly of food plants, has led to public concern about the potential consequences to consumers and the environment. Urge students who need extra challenges to learn more about the issues and form their own opinions. Then call on these students to debate the issues, with students on one side arguing that the genetic engineering of food plants should be unregulated and students on the other side arguing that the genetic engineering of food plants should be closely regulated or even outlawed. The debate should address such questions as: **What are the potential dangers of genetically engineered foods?** *(Potential dangers include the short and long term human health risks and the ecological impact that genetically engineered foods might have.)* **What are the potential benefits?** *(Foods might be more nutritious, keep longer, or be easier to transport. Also plants and animals can be genetically engineered to be raised under a wider range of conditions.)* After the debate, encourage the rest of the class to comment on which side was more convincing and why. **cooperative learning**

Figure 14 Scientists created this new variety of tomatoes using genetic engineering. The tomatoes taste better and keep longer than other varieties. *Making Judgments What other traits would be desirable in tomatoes?*

Today, many human proteins are produced in genetically engineered bacteria. For example, human growth hormone is a protein that controls the growth process in children. Children whose bodies do not produce enough human growth hormone can be given injections of the hormone. Today, an unlimited supply of the hormone exists, thanks to genetically engineered bacteria.

Genetic Engineering in Other Organisms Genetic engineering has also been used to insert genes into the cells of other organisms. Scientists have inserted genes from bacteria into the cells of tomatoes, wheat, rice, and other important crops. Some of the genes enable the plants to survive in colder temperatures or in poor soil conditions, and to resist insect pests.

Genetic engineering techniques can also be used to insert genes into animals, which then produce important medicines for humans. For example, scientists can insert human genes into the cells of cows. The cows then produce the human protein for which the gene codes. Scientists have used this technique to produce the blood clotting protein needed by people with hemophilia. The protein is produced in the cows' milk, and can easily be extracted and used to treat people with the disorder.

Gene Therapy Researchers are also using genetic engineering to try to correct some genetic disorders. This process, called **gene therapy,** involves inserting working copies of a gene directly into the cells of a person with a genetic disorder. For example, people with cystic fibrosis do not produce a protein that is needed for proper lung function. Both copies of the gene that codes for the protein are defective in these people.

Background

Facts and Figures Two major problems must be solved in developing gene therapy for a particular genetic disorder. The first problem is finding the best way to correct the genetic defect that is causing the disorder. Options may include correcting or increasing the defective cell product, making diseased cells weaker or more vulnerable, or blocking the operation of diseased cells. The other problem that must be solved is finding a way to carry the genetically engineered DNA to target cells. Because of their ability to infect living cells, viruses make excellent candidates for this role. However, before a virus can be used safely, the viral DNA must be genetically engineered to make the virus harmless to the human patient.

Scientists can insert working copies of the gene into harmless viruses. The "engineered" viruses can then be sprayed into the lungs of patients with cystic fibrosis. Researchers hope that the working copies of the gene in the viruses will function in the patient to produce the protein. Gene therapy is still an experimental method for treating genetic disorders. Researchers are working hard to improve this promising technique.

DNA Fingerprinting

In courtrooms across the country, a genetic technique called DNA fingerprinting is being used to help solve crimes. If you did the Discover activity, you know that fingerprints can help to identify people. No two people have the same fingerprints. Detectives routinely use fingerprints found at a crime scene to help identify the person who committed the crime. In a similar way, DNA from samples of hair, skin, and blood can also be used to identify a person. No two people, except for identical twins, have the same DNA.

In DNA fingerprinting, enzymes are used to cut the DNA in the sample found at a crime scene into fragments. An electrical current then separates the fragments by size to form a pattern of bands, like the ones you see in Figure 15. Each person's pattern of DNA bands is unique. The DNA pattern can then be compared to the pattern produced by DNA taken from people suspected of committing the crime.

☑ *Checkpoint* *In what way is DNA like fingerprints?*

Figure 15 This scientist is explaining how DNA fingerprinting can be used to help solve crimes. DNA from blood or other substances collected at a crime scene can be compared to DNA from a suspect's blood.

Addressing Naive Conceptions

Students may develop the naive conception that all genetic disorders will soon be cured with gene therapy. Point out that gene therapy is unlikely to be developed, at least not any time soon, for diabetes, heart disease, or most types of cancer, because these diseases are also influenced by the environment. Conclude by asking: **Besides cystic fibrosis, which genetic disorders are good candidates for gene therapy?** (*Students' responses should reflect their understanding that gene therapy is most likely to lead to cures for genetic disorders caused by single genes, such as hemophilia or sickle-cell disease.*) **learning modality: logical/ mathematical**

DNA Fingerprinting

Sharpen your Skills

Communicating

Time 15 minutes
Tips Advise students to pretend they are explaining DNA fingerprinting to a friend who has no knowledge of genetics.
Expected Outcome Students should write a paragraph explaining the process of DNA fingerprinting in simple terms. Their paragraph should make it clear that each cell contains a complete set of a person's DNA and that each person, with the exception of identical twins, has DNA that is unique.
Extend Tell students that before DNA fingerprinting was developed, blood typing often was used for identification purposes. Ask: **Why is blood typing a less accurate way of identifying an individual?** (*Because many people have the same blood type*) **learning modality: verbal**

Answers to Self-Assessment

Caption Question

Figure 14 Other traits might include deep red color, large size, and firmness.

☑ *Checkpoint*

DNA, like fingerprints, is unique to each person, except for identical twins.

Ongoing Assessment

Oral Presentation Call on students at random to describe ways that genetic engineering has been used to treat human disorders.

The Human Genome Project

3 Assess

Section 3 Review Answers

1. Inbreeding, hybridization, and cloning
2. To learn what makes the body work and what causes things to go wrong
3. The process of transferring genes from one organism into the DNA of another organism; produce medicines, improve food crops, treat human genetic disorders
4. It is produced by cutting the DNA from a sample of hair, skin, or blood into fragments and separating the fragments by size to form a pattern of bands. It can reveal who committed a crime by identifying the person who left the sample at the crime scene.
5. Answers may vary. Make sure students give logical, well-founded reasons to support their position.

Science at Home

Other vegetables and fruits that students might focus on because of their variety are squash and pears. Suggest that students ask the store's produce manager what traits each variety is known for.

Figure 16 The goal of the Human Genome Project is to identify the sequence of every DNA base pair in the human genome.

The Human Genome Project

Imagine trying to crack a code that is 3 billion characters long. Then imagine working with people all over the world to accomplish this task. That's exactly what scientists working on the Human Genome Project are doing. A **genome** is all the DNA in one cell of an organism. Researchers estimate that the 23 pairs of chromosomes that make up the human genome contain about 3 billion DNA base pairs—or about 30,000 to 35,000 genes.

The main goal of the Human Genome Project is to identify the DNA sequence of every gene in the human genome. The Human Genome Project will provide scientists with an encyclopedia of genetic information about humans. Scientists will know the DNA sequence of every human gene, and thus the amino acid sequence of every protein.

With the information from the Human Genome Project, researchers may gain a better understanding of how humans develop from a fertilized egg to an adult. They may also learn more about what makes the body work, and what causes things to go wrong. New understandings may lead to new treatments and prevention strategies for many genetic disorders and for diseases such as cancer.

Section 3 Review

1. Name three techniques that people have used to produce organisms with desired traits.
2. Why do scientists want to identify the DNA sequence of every human gene?
3. What is genetic engineering? Describe three possible benefits of this technique.
4. Explain how a DNA fingerprint is produced. What information can a DNA fingerprint reveal?
5. **Thinking Critically Making Judgments** Do you think there should be any limitations on genetic engineering? Give reasons to support your position.

70

Science at Home

With a parent or other adult family member, go to a grocery store. Look at the different varieties of potatoes, apples, and other fruits and vegetables. Discuss how these varieties were created by selective breeding. Then chose one type of fruit or vegetable and make a list of different varieties. If possible, find out what traits each variety was bred for.

Who Should Have Access to Genetic Test Results?

Scientists working on the Human Genome Project have identified many alleles that put people at risk for certain diseases, such as breast cancer and Alzheimer's disease. Through techniques known as genetic testing, people can have their DNA analyzed to find out whether they have any of these alleles. If they do, they may be able to take steps to prevent the illness or to seek early treatment.

Some health insurance companies and employers want access to this type of genetic information. However, many people believe that genetic testing results should be kept private.

The Issues

Why Do Insurance Companies Want Genetic Information? Health insurance companies set their rates based on a person's risk of health problems. To determine a person's insurance rate, insurance companies often require that a person have a physical examination. If the examination reveals a condition such as high blood pressure, the company may charge that person more for an insurance policy. This is because he or she would be more likely to need expensive medical care.

Insurance companies view genetic testing as an additional way to gather information about a person's health status. Insurers argue that if they were unable to gather this information, they would need to raise rates for everyone. This would be unfair to people who are in good health.

Why Do Employers Want Genetic Information? Federal laws forbid employers with 15 or more workers from choosing job applicants based on their health status. These laws

do not apply to smaller companies, however. Employers may not want to hire employees with health problems because they often miss more work time than other employees. In addition, employers who hire people with health problems may be charged higher health insurance rates. Many small companies cannot afford to pay these higher rates.

Should Genetic Information Be Kept Private? Some people think that the government should prohibit all access to genetic information. Today, some people fear that they will be discriminated against as a result of genetic test results. Because of this fear, some people avoid genetic testing—even though testing might allow them to seek early treatment for a disorder. These people want tighter control of genetic information. They want to be sure that insurers and employers will not have access to genetic test results.

You Decide

1. Identify the Problem
In your own words, explain the problem of deciding who should have access to genetic test results.

2. Analyze the Options
Examine the pros and cons of keeping genetic test results private. List reasons to maintain privacy. List reasons why test results should be shared.

3. Find a Solution
Create a list of rules to control access to genetic information. Who should have access, and under what circumstances? Explain your reasoning.

Who Should Have Access to Genetic Test Results?

Purpose To provide students with an introduction to the ethical problems raised by genetic testing.

Panel Discussion

Time a day to prepare; 30 minutes for panel discussion

Choose students to play the following roles in a panel discussion: the CEO of a health insurance company, the president of an association of small business owners, the doctor who presides over the American Medical Association, the spokesperson for a patients' rights group, the director of a diabetes foundation, and the president of a worker's union. Urge each panel member to take the point of view they believe the person they represent would actually take on issues relating to genetic testing. Other students should take notes during the discussion and ask questions afterward. The panel discussion should begin with each panel member briefly stating his or her position regarding who should have access to genetic test results. Then panel members should take turns presenting arguments in support of their statements.

Extend Challenge students to find out more about genetic testing by interviewing a lab technician, nurse, or doctor. Suggest that they ask such questions as: **What genetic tests are commonly performed today? What are some reasons genetic testing is done?**

You Decide

Help students keep to the point by challenging them to explain the problem in a single sentence. Reasons for sharing genetic test results can be found in the first two paragraphs. Reasons for keeping genetic test results private can be found in the last paragraph. In addition, encourage students to think of reasons of their own. If students are having difficulty creating a list of rules, suggest that they first decide what they believe are acceptable uses for genetic information. This will help them decide who should control it and under what circumstances.

Guilty or Innocent?

Preparing for Inquiry

Key Concept A person's DNA forms a unique pattern of bands that can be used to identify the person.

Skills Objectives Students will be able to
◆ use bar codes as models of DNA fingerprints;
◆ observe similarities and differences in the patterns of bands on the bar codes;
◆ draw conclusions about which suspect was present at the crime scene based on the comparisons.

Time 20 minutes

Advance Planning Remove bar codes from commercial products and cut the numbers from them. Each students' set of bar codes should contain one that is identical to the bar code from the crime scene. You could mount the bar codes on heavy paper so they can be reused.

Alternative Materials If you can obtain actual DNA fingerprints, the lab will be more realistic. Provide a hand lens for any student who has vision problems.

Guiding Inquiry

Troubleshooting the Experiment
◆ Advise students to examine the patterns of bands very carefully, because the differences may be minor and easily overlooked.

Expected Outcome
Students should find that one of the suspect DNA samples is identical to the DNA sample from the crime scene.

Analyze and Conclude
1. The suspect whose DNA sample matches the DNA sample from the crime scene must have been present at the crime scene.
2. DNA patterns differ so greatly because no two people, except for identical twins, have the same sequence of bases in their DNA.
3. The twin's DNA pattern would be identical to the suspect's, making it impossible to conclude which individual

---

Guilty or Innocent?

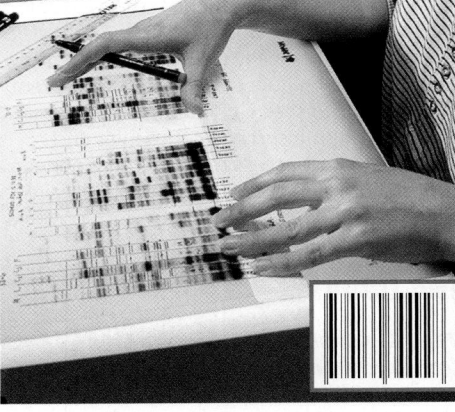

In this lab, you will investigate how DNA fingerprinting can be used to provide evidence related to a crime.

Problem
How can DNA be used to identify individuals?

Skills Focus
observing, making models, drawing conclusions

Materials
4–6 bar codes   hand lens

Procedure
1. Look at the photograph of DNA band patterns shown at right. Each person's DNA produces a unique pattern of these bands.
2. Now look at the Universal Product Code, also called a bar code, shown below the DNA bands. A bar code can be used as a model of a DNA band pattern. Compare the bar code with the DNA bands to see what they have in common. Record your observations.
3. Suppose that a burglary has taken place, and you're the detective leading the investigation. Your teacher will give you a bar code that represents DNA from blood found at the crime scene. You arrange to have DNA samples taken from several suspects. Write a sentence describing what you will look for as you try to match each suspect's DNA to the DNA sample from the crime scene.
4. You will now be given bar codes representing DNA samples taken from the suspects. Compare those bar codes with the bar code that represents DNA from the crime scene.

5. Use your comparisons to determine whether any of the suspects was present at the crime scene.

Analyze and Conclude
1. Based on your findings, were any of the suspects present at the crime scene? Support your conclusion with specific evidence.
2. Why do people's DNA patterns differ so greatly?
3. How would your conclusions be affected if you learned that the suspect whose DNA matched the evidence had an identical twin?
4. **Apply** In everyday life, do you think that DNA evidence is enough to determine that a suspect committed the crime? Explain.

More to Explore
Do you think the DNA fingerprints of a parent and a child would show any similarities? Draw what you think they would look like. Then explain your thinking.

---

had been at the crime scene.
4. Students may say that DNA evidence alone is not enough, because it only identifies who was at the crime scene and not who actually committed the crime. Students also may say that errors can be made in analyzing the DNA evidence.

Extending the Inquiry

More to Explore The DNA fingerprints of a parent and a child should look more similar than the DNA fingerprints of unrelated people,

because parents and children share many of the same genes.

Program Resources
◆ **Unit 1 Resources** Real-World Lab blackline masters, pp. 58–59

Media and Technology
 Lab Activity Videotape
Tape 1

SECTION 1 Human Inheritance

Key Ideas

◆ Some human traits are controlled by a single gene that has multiple alleles—three or more forms.

◆ Some human traits show a wide range of phenotypes because these traits are controlled by many genes. The genes act together as a group to produce a single trait.

◆ Traits are often influenced by the organism's environment.

◆ Males have one X chromosome and one Y chromosome. Females have two X chromosomes. Males are more likely than females to have a sex-linked trait controlled by a recessive allele.

◆ Geneticists use pedigrees to trace the inheritance pattern of a particular trait through a number of generations of a family.

Key Terms

multiple alleles   carrier
sex-linked gene   pedigree

SECTION 2 Human Genetic Disorders

Key Ideas

◆ Genetic disorders are abnormal conditions that are caused by mutations, or DNA changes, in genes or chromosomes.

◆ Common genetic disorders include cystic fibrosis, sickle-cell disease, hemophilia, and Down syndrome.

◆ Amniocentesis and karyotypes are tools used to diagnose genetic disorders.

◆ Genetic counselors help couples understand their chances of having a child with a genetic disorder.

Key Terms

genetic disorder   karyotype
amniocentesis

SECTION 3 Advances in Genetics

INTEGRATING TECHNOLOGY

Key Ideas

◆ Selective breeding is the process of selecting a few organisms with desired traits to serve as parents of the next generation.

◆ Cloning is a technique used to produce genetically identical organisms.

◆ Genetic engineering can be used to produce medicines and to improve food crops. Researchers are also using genetic engineering to try to cure human genetic disorders.

◆ DNA fingerprinting can be used to help determine whether material found at a crime scene came from a particular suspect.

◆ The goal of the Human Genome Project is to identify the DNA sequence of every gene in the human genome.

Key Terms

selective breeding   genetic engineering
inbreeding   gene therapy
hybridization   genome
clone

Organizing Information

Concept Map Copy the concept map about human traits onto a separate sheet of paper. Then complete it and add a title. (For more on concept maps, see the Skills Handbook.)

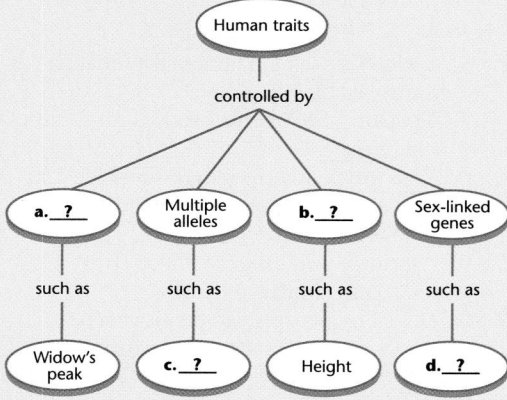

Organizing Information

Concept Map **a.** Single genes **b.** Many genes **c.** Blood type **d.** Colorblindness (or Hemophilia) *Sample title:* The Inheritance of Human Traits

Program Resources

◆ **Unit 1 Resources** Chapter 2 Project Scoring Rubric, p. 42

◆ **Performance Assessment** Chapter 2, pp. 7–9

◆ **Chapter Tests** Chapter 2 Test, pp. 7–10

Media and Technology

Computer Test Bank Chapter 2 Test

Reviewing Content
Multiple Choice
1. b 2. c 3. a 4. d 5. c

True or False
6. true 7. female 8. pedigree
9. Inbreeding 10. true

Checking Concepts
11. The four or more genes that control height determine the maximum height that a person can attain. The environment, particularly diet, medical care, and living conditions, determines whether or not the person reaches the potential maximum height.
12. Traits controlled by recessive alleles on the X chromosome are more common in males than in females because males need to inherit just one allele to have the trait, whereas females need to inherit two alleles.
13. Sickle-cell disease is a genetic disorder in which red blood cells contain an abnormal form of hemoglobin. People who have the disease inherit a copy of the affected allele from each parent.
14. In amniocentesis, a doctor removes fluid surrounding a growing baby so that the baby's chromosomes can be analyzed. Down syndrome is present if there is an extra copy of chromosome 21.
15. The horse breeder would mate only horses that have golden coats.
16. To treat hemophilia with gene therapy, doctors would give the person with hemophilia a virus containing the normal gene for the missing blood-clotting protein. The viral DNA would infect the person's cells and lead to the production of the missing protein.
17. Students should identify the genetic disorder they chose and then describe its symptoms, how it is inherited, and how it is treated. Check that students' answers accurately reflect the information provided in the text.

Thinking Critically
18. Two alleles are needed for the trait to be expressed. If the person has only one recessive allele for the trait, he or she will not have the trait, but will be a carrier. However, a person cannot be a carrier of a trait caused by a dominant allele

Reviewing Content
Multiple Choice
Choose the letter of the best answer.

1. A human trait that is controlled by multiple alleles is
   a. dimples.   b. blood type.
   c. height.   d. skin color.
2. A genetic disorder caused by a sex-linked gene is
   a. cystic fibrosis.
   b. sickle-cell disease.
   c. hemophilia.
   d. Down syndrome.
3. Sickle-cell disease is characterized by
   a. abnormally shaped red blood cells.
   b. abnormally thick body fluids.
   c. abnormal blood clotting.
   d. an extra copy of chromosome 21.
4. Inserting a human gene into a bacterial plasmid is an example of
   a. inbreeding.
   b. selective breeding.
   c. DNA fingerprinting.
   d. genetic engineering.
5. DNA fingerprinting is a way to
   a. clone organisms.
   b. breed organisms with desirable traits.
   c. identify people.
   d. map and sequence human genes.

True or False
If the statement is true, write true. If it is false, change the underlined word or words to make the statement true.

6. A widow's peak is a human trait that is controlled by a single gene.
7. A person who inherits two X chromosomes will be male.
8. A karyotype is a chart that shows the relationships between the generations of a family.
9. Hybridization is the crossing of two genetically similar organisms.
10. A clone is an organism that is genetically identical to another organism.

Checking Concepts
11. Explain how both genes and the environment determine how tall a person will be.
12. Explain why traits controlled by recessive alleles on the X chromosome are more common in males than in females.
13. What is sickle-cell disease? How is this disorder inherited?
14. How can amniocentesis be used to detect a disorder such as Down syndrome?
15. Explain how a horse breeder might use selective breeding to produce horses that have golden coats.
16. Describe how gene therapy might be used in the future to treat a person with hemophilia.
17. **Writing to Learn** As the webmaster for a national genetics foundation, you must create a Web site to inform the public about genetic disorders. Choose one human genetic disorder discussed in this chapter. Write a description of the disorder that you will use for the Web site.

Thinking Critically
18. **Applying Concepts** Why can a person be a carrier of a trait caused by a recessive allele but not of a trait caused by a dominant allele?
19. **Problem Solving** A woman with normal color vision has a colorblind daughter. What are the genotypes and phenotypes of both parents?
20. **Calculating** If a mother is a carrier of hemophilia, what is the probability that her son will have the trait? Explain your answer.
21. **Inferring** How could ancient people selectively breed corn if they didn't know about genes and inheritance?
22. **Comparing and Contrasting** How are selective breeding and genetic engineering different? How are they similar?

because if the person has only one dominant allele, he or she will have the trait.
19. The mother has normal color vision but is a carrier of the colorblindness allele. Her genotype is $X^C X^c$. The father is colorblind. His genotype is $X^c Y$.
20. If the mother is a carrier of hemophilia, one of her X chromosomes has the allele for normal clotting and the other X chromosome has the allele for hemophilia. The son has a 50

percent chance of inheriting an X chromosome that carries the allele for hemophilia, and therefore of having hemophilia.
21. Selective breeding is based on phenotypes. Therefore, ancient people could selectively breed corn without knowing about genes and inheritance by using seeds only from the plants that had the traits they desired.

Applying Skills

Use the information below to answer Questions 23–25.

- Bob and Helen have three children.
- Bob and Helen have one son who has albinism, an inherited condition in which the skin does not have brown pigments.
- Bob and Helen have two daughters who do not have albinism.
- Neither Bob nor Helen has albinism.
- Albinism is neither sex-linked nor codominant.

23. Interpreting Data Use the information to construct a pedigree. If you don't know whether someone is a carrier, leave their symbol empty. If you decide later that a person is a carrier, change your pedigree.

24. Drawing Conclusions Is albinism controlled by a dominant allele or by a recessive allele? Explain your answer.

25. Predicting Suppose Bob and Helen were to have another child. What is the probability that the child will have albinism? Explain.

Performance **CHAPTER PROJECT 2** **Assessment**

Project Wrap Up Before displaying your project, exchange it with another group to check each other's work. Make any necessary corrections, and then display your materials to the class. Be ready to explain the inheritance patterns shown in your pedigrees.

Reflect and Record In your journal, describe what you learned by creating the pedigrees. What questions do you have as a result of the project?

Test Preparation

Use these questions to prepare for standardized tests.

Use the information to answer Questions 26–29. The Punnett square below shows how muscular dystrophy, a sex-linked recessive disorder, is inherited.

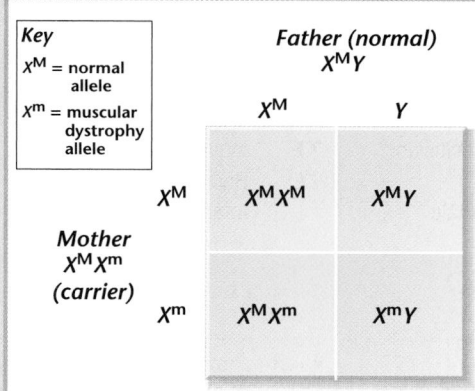

26. What is the probability that a daughter of these parents will have muscular dystrophy?
- **a.** 0%   **b.** 25%
- **c.** 50%   **d.** 100%

27. What is the probability that a son of these parents will have muscular dystrophy?
- **a.** 0%   **b.** 25%
- **c.** 50%   **d.** 100%

28. What is the probability that a daughter of these parents will be a carrier of the disease?
- **a.** 0%   **b.** 25%
- **c.** 50%   **d.** 100%

29. Which of the following statements is true of muscular dystrophy?
- **a.** More men than women have muscular dystrophy.
- **b.** More women than men have muscular dystrophy.
- **c.** More men than women are carriers of muscular dystrophy.
- **d.** No women can have muscular dystrophy.

---

22. Both selective breeding and genetic engineering are ways of producing organisms with desirable traits. Selective breeding involves restricting matings to those individuals who have the desirable traits. Genetic engineering involves inserting genes for the desirable traits into an individual's genome.

Program Resources

- **Inquiry Skills Activity Book** Provides teaching and review of all inquiry skills
- **Prentice Hall Assessment System** Provides standardized test practice
- **Reading in the Content Area** Provides strategies to improve science reading skills
- **Teacher's ELL Handbook** Provides multiple strategies for English language learners

---

Applying Skills

23. The top row of the pedigree should show a half-shaded circle (Helen) connected with a half-shaded square (Bob), indicating that both parents are carriers for albinism. The second row should show two unshaded circles (the two daughters) and a shaded square (the affected son).

24. Albinism must be controlled by a recessive allele, because otherwise either Bob or Helen also would have the condition.

25. Both Bob and Helen must be carriers of the albinism allele in order to have an affected child, so there is a 25 percent chance that any child born to them would have albinism.

Performance **CHAPTER PROJECT 2** **Assessment**

Project Wrap Up Before students make their presentations, give them a chance to exchange their pedigrees and family albums with other students for feedback and to make any corrections or other changes. Have each student trace each of their family's traits through the pedigree from generation to generation and point out individuals in the family album with each possible phenotype for the two traits. Make sure that the family album is consistent with the information in the pedigrees.

Reflect and Record After all the students have presented their projects, encourage students to compare the different patterns of inheritance shown in the pedigrees. Challenge them to identify ways that the patterns differ. Conclude by saying that detecting such patterns in pedigrees is how geneticists have determined which type of gene controls different traits.

Test Preparation

26. a **27.** c **28.** c **29.** a

CHAPTER 3 Changes Over Time

Sections	Time	Student Edition Activities	Other Activities	
CHAPTER PROJECT 3 **Life's Long Calendar** p. 77	Ongoing (2 weeks)	Check Your Progress, pp. 88, 101 Project Wrap Up, p. 105	**TE**	Chapter 3 Project Notes, pp. 76–77
1 Darwin's Voyage pp. 78–88 ◆ 3.1.1 State how Darwin explained variations among similar species. ◆ 3.1.2 Explain how natural selection leads to evolution and the role of genes in evolution. ◆ 3.1.3 Describe how new species form.	2 periods/ 1 block	**Discover** How Do Living Things Vary?, p. 78 **Try This** Bird Beak Adaptations, p. 81 **Sharpen Your Skills** Inferring, p. 83 **Skills Lab: Making Models** Nature at Work, pp. 84–85	**TE** **TE** **TE** **LM**	Demonstration, p. 79 Building Inquiry Skills: Observing, p. 80 Inquiry Challenge, p. 86 3, "Variation in a Population"
2 *INTEGRATING EARTH SCIENCE* **The Fossil Record** pp. 89–96 ◆ 3.2.1 Describe how most fossils form. ◆ 3.2.2 Explain how a scientist determines a fossil's age. ◆ 3.2.3 Describe the main events of the Geologic Time Scale. ◆ 3.2.4 Describe two theories of how fast evolution occurs.	1 period/ $\frac{1}{2}$ block	**Discover** What Can You Learn From Fossils?, p. 89 **Try This** Preservation in Ice, p. 91 **Sharpen Your Skills** Calculating, p. 92 **Science at Home,** p. 96	**TE** **TE** **TE** **TE**	Demonstration, p. 90 Including All Students, p. 90 Inquiry Challenge, p. 95 Including All Students, p. 95
3 Other Evidence for Evolution pp. 97–102 ◆ 3.3.1 State evidence from modern-day organisms that scientists use to determine evolutionary relationships among groups. ◆ 3.3.2 Describe how scientists classify organisms and place them on branching trees.	2 periods/ 1 block	**Discover** How Can You Classify Species?, p. 97 **Sharpen Your Skills** Drawing Conclusions, p. 98 **Skills Lab: Interpreting Data** Telltale Molecules, p. 102	**TE** **TE** **TE**	Building Inquiry Skills: Observing, p. 98 Inquiry Challenge, p. 99 Building Inquiry Skills: Interpreting Data, p. 100
Study Guide/Assessment pp. 103–105	1 period/ $\frac{1}{2}$ block		**ISAB**	Provides teaching and review of all inquiry skills

For Standard or Block Schedule The Resource Pro® CD-ROM gives you maximum flexibility for planning your instruction for any type of schedule. Resource Pro® contains Planning Express®, an advanced scheduling program, as well as the entire contents of the Teaching Resources and the Computer Test Bank.

Key: **CTB** Computer Test Bank
CT Chapter Tests
ELL Teacher's ELL Handbook

CHAPTER PLANNING GUIDE

Program Resources	Assessment Strategies	Media and Technology
UR Chapter 3 Project Teacher Notes, pp. 60–61 **UR** Chapter 3 Project Overview and Worksheets, pp. 62–65	**TE** Check Your Progress, pp. 88, 101 **TE** Performance Assessment: Chapter 3 Project Wrap Up, p. 105 **UR** Chapter 3 Project Scoring Rubric, p. 66	Science Explorer Internet Site Audio CDs, Section Summaries
UR 3-1 Lesson Plan, p. 67 **UR** 3-1 Section Summary, p. 68 **UR** 3-1 Review and Reinforce, p. 69 **UR** 3-1 Enrich, p. 70 **UR** Skills Lab blackline masters, pp. 79–81	**SE** Analyze and Conclude, p. 85 **SE** Section 1 Review, p. 88 **TE** Ongoing Assessment, pp. 79, 81, 83, 87 **TE** Performance Assessment, p. 88	Presentation Pro, "Evolution" Lab Activity Videotape, *Tape 1*
UR 3-2 Lesson Plan, p. 71 **UR** 3-2 Section Summary, p. 72 **UR** 3-2 Review and Reinforce, p. 73 **UR** 3-2 Enrich, p. 74	**SE** Section 2 Review, p. 96 **TE** Ongoing Assessment, pp. 91, 93, 95 **TE** Performance Assessment, p. 96	Concept Videotape Library, *Adventures, Tape 1,* "Fossils"; "Extinction"; "Mummification"; "Geologic Time" Presentation Pro, "The History of Life"; "Fossils and Other Evidence for Evolution" Transparencies 8, "How Fossils Form"; 9, "Exploring Life's History (1)"; 10, "Exploring Life's History (2)"
UR 3-3 Lesson Plan, p. 75 **UR** 3-3 Section Summary, p. 76 **UR** 3-3 Review and Reinforce, p. 77 **UR** 3-3 Enrich, p. 78 **UR** Skills Lab blackline masters, pp. 82–83	**SE** Section 3 Review, p. 101 **SE** Analyze and Conclude, p. 102 **TE** Ongoing Assessment, p. 99 **TE** Performance Assessment, p. 101	Concept Videotape Library, *Adventures, Tape 1,* "Primate Evolution" Presentation Pro, "Fossils and Other Evidence for Evolution" Transparency 11, "Homologous Structures" Lab Activity Videotape, *Tape 1*
GRSW Provides worksheets to promote student comprehension of content **RCA** Provides strategies to improve science reading skills **ELL** Provides multiple strategies for English language learners	**SE** Study Guide/Assessment, pp. 103–105 **PA** Performance Assessment, pp. 10–12 **CT** Chapter 3 Test, pp. 11–14 **CTB** Chapter 3 Test **PHAS** Provides standardized test preparation	Computer Test Bank, Chapter 3 Test

GRSW Guided Reading and Study Workbook
ISAB Inquiry Skills Activity Book
LM Laboratory Manual

PA Performance Assessment
PHAS Prentice Hall Assessment System
PLM Probeware Lab Manual

RCA Reading in the Content Area
SE Student Edition

TE Teacher's Edition
UR Unit Resources

Meeting the National Science Education Standards and AAAS Benchmarks

National Science Education Standards	Benchmarks for Science Literacy	Unifying Themes

Science As Inquiry (Content Standard A)

◆ **Develop descriptions, explanations, predictions, and models using evidence** Students create time lines of Earth's history. Students model how natural selection leads to changes in a species over time. Students compare the structure of a protein in several animals to determine their evolutionary relationships. *(Chapter Project; Skills Lab)*

Life Science (Content Standard C)

◆ **Diversity and adaptations of organisms** Over a long period of time, natural selection can lead to evolution. A species is extinct if no members of that species are still alive. Scientists compare body structures, early development, and DNA sequences to determine evolutionary relationships. *(Sections 1, 2, 3; Skills Lab)*

Earth and Space Science (Content Standard D)

◆ **Earth's history** The fossil record provides clues about how and when new groups of organisms evolved. *(Chapter Project; Section 2)*

History and Nature of Science (Content Standard G)

◆ **History of science** Charles Darwin explained that evolution occurs by means of natural selection. *(Section 1)*

1B Scientific Inquiry Students create time lines of Earth's history. Students model how natural selection leads to changes in a species over time. Students compare the structure of a protein in several animals to determine their evolutionary relationships. *(Chapter Project; Skills Lab)*

1C The Scientific Enterprise Charles Darwin explained that evolution occurs by means of natural selection. *(Section 1)*

4C Processes that Shape the Earth Most fossils form when organisms that die become buried in sediments. *(Section 2)*

5A Diversity of Life Any difference between individuals of the same species is called a variation. *(Section 1)*

5F Evolution of Life Over a long period of time, natural selection can lead to evolution. The fossil record provides clues about how and when new groups of organisms evolved. Scientists compare body structures, early development, and DNA sequences to determine the evolutionary relationships among organisms. *(Chapter Project, Sections 1, 2, 3; Skills Lab)*

◆ **Evolution** Over a long period of time, natural selection can lead to evolution. The fossil record provides clues about how and when new groups of organisms evolved. Scientists compare body structures, early development, and DNA sequences to determine evolutionary relationships. *(Chapter Project, Sections 1, 2, 3; Skills Lab)*

◆ **Patterns of Change** A new species can form when a group of individuals is isolated from the rest of the species. Most fossils form when organisms that die become buried in sediments. *(Sections 1, 2)*

◆ **Scale and Structure** Scientists can determine a fossil's age through relative dating and absolute dating. Similar structures that related species have inherited from a common ancestor are called homologous structures. Protein structures can reveal evolutionary relationships among organisms. *(Sections 2, 3; Skills Lab)*

◆ **Stability** Natural selection is the survival and reproduction of those organisms best adapted to their environment. The half-life of a radioactive element is the time it takes for half of the atoms in a sample to decay. *(Sections 1, 2)*

◆ **Unity and Diversity** A species is a group of similar organisms that can mate and produce fertile offspring. Two theories of how quickly evolution occurs are gradualism and punctuated equilibria. *(Sections 1, 2)*

Take It to the Net

The **www.phschool.com** Web site provides you with multiple opportunities to incorporate the internet into your instruction. Go to **www.phschool.com** and click on the Science icon. Then select Science Explorer Integrated.

■ Have students use the chapter Self-Test to get instant feedback.

■ Hot Links and Reference Links provide opportunities for online research.

Internet Activities provide opportunities for students to review, extend, or assess a concept from the chapter.

STAY CURRENT with **SCIENCE NEWS** ®

Find out the latest research and information about evolution at: **www.phschool.com**

ACTIVITY	Time (minutes)	Materials Quantities for one work group	Skills
Section 1			
Discover, p. 78	15	**Consumable** 10 sunflower seeds **Nonconsumable** metric ruler, hand lens	Classifying
Try This, p. 81	10	**Consumable** bird seed, paper plate, 20 raisins, paper cup **Nonconsumable** tweezers, hair clips, hairpins, clothespins, stopwatch	Inferring
Sharpen Your Skills, p. 83	10	**Consumable** large sheet of plain white paper **Nonconsumable** 15 black buttons, 15 white buttons, stopwatch	Inferring
Skills Lab, pp. 84–85	40	**Consumable** 2 colors of construction paper **Nonconsumable** scissors, marking pen	Making Models, Observing, Predicting
Section 2			
Discover, p. 89	5	No special materials are required.	Inferring
Try This, p. 91	10	**Consumable** fresh fruit, water **Nonconsumable** 2 plastic containers	Inferring
Sharpen Your Skills, p. 92	10	**Nonconsumable** calculator	Calculating
Science at Home, p. 96	home	**Consumable** mud **Nonconsumable** shallow, flat-bottomed pan	Making Models
Section 3			
Discover, p. 97	10	**Nonconsumable** 6-8 pens	Classifying
Sharpen Your Skills, p. 98	5	No special materials are required.	Drawing Conclusions
Skills Lab, p. 102	30	No special materials are required.	Interpreting Data, Comparing and Contrasting, Drawing Conclusions

A list of all materials required for the Student Edition activities can be found beginning on page T23. You can obtain information about ordering materials by calling 1-800-848-9500 or by accessing the Science Explorer Internet site at **www.phschool.com**.

Life's Long Calendar

Understanding evolution through natural selection requires an appreciation for the vast spans of time involved in the development of Earth's diverse species. The Chapter 3 Project is designed to help students understand the large numbers involved in geologic time, and place significant evolutionary events within an accurate model of Earth's history: a time line drawn to scale. The project works best as a small-group activity.

Sometimes illustrations of the history of life on Earth, including the main section on pages 94–95 of this book, are not drawn to scale. (The time line that runs across the top of the spread *is* drawn to scale.) Illustrations that are not drawn to scale do not give an accurate image of the relative amounts of time occupied by different eras and periods in geologic history. However, a single time line to scale would devote most of the line to the Precambrian and squeeze the evolution of all plants and animals into a very small portion. To avoid this problem, students will make two time lines in this project: one showing Earth's history from 5 billion years ago to the present, and the other from 600 million years ago to the present. Students will then be able to see the relative sizes of time spans and the comparative placement of events in Earth's evolutionary history.

Purpose Students will construct scale models of Earth's history by converting geological units of millions of years to more familiar and manageable units of either length or time. Students will mark both lines to show important events in Earth's history.

Skills Focus After completing the Chapter 3 Project, students will be able to make scale models representing the history of life on Earth, with major evolutionary events included.

Project Time Line If students label only the major evolutionary events shown on the textbook's time line, less than two weeks' time should be sufficient. If you want students to add other important events, allow additional time to complete the project.

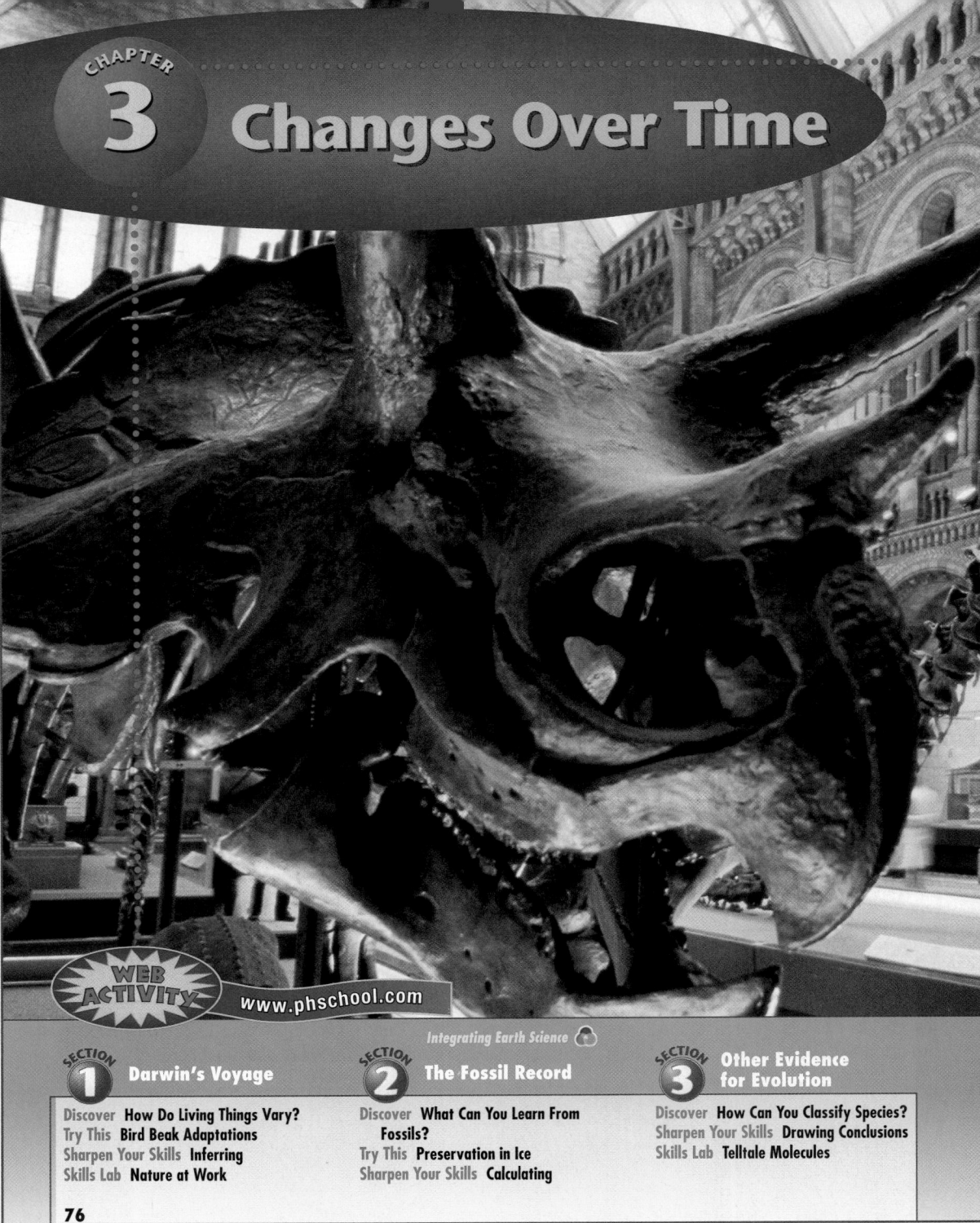

3 Changes Over Time

WEB ACTIVITY www.phschool.com

Integrating Earth Science

SECTION
1 Darwin's Voyage

Discover **How Do Living Things Vary?**
Try This **Bird Beak Adaptations**
Sharpen Your Skills **Inferring**
Skills Lab **Nature at Work**

SECTION
2 The Fossil Record

Discover **What Can You Learn From Fossils?**
Try This **Preservation in Ice**
Sharpen Your Skills **Calculating**

SECTION
3 Other Evidence for Evolution

Discover **How Can You Classify Species?**
Sharpen Your Skills **Drawing Conclusions**
Skills Lab **Telltale Molecules**

76

Possible Materials
◆ Students could use calculators to determine the scale of each model and the placement of each evolutionary event.
◆ Meter sticks and metric tape measures will be needed to construct all models that use units of length to represent millions of years.
◆ Other materials will vary depending on the formats that students choose.
◆ If you want students to research additional evolutionary events to include in their time lines, provide a variety of source materials.

Launching the Project Invite students to read the project description on page 77 and examine the time line on pages 94–95. Then draw a long line across the board, and label the left end *Beginning of Earth* and the right end *Present*. Ask: **How long ago did Earth begin?** (*4.6 billion years ago*) Write *4,600,000,000* on the board. **When did the first animals appear on Earth?** (*600 million years ago*) Write *600,000,000* below the first number with the place values aligned. Ask: **Where should the line be marked to show when the first animals**

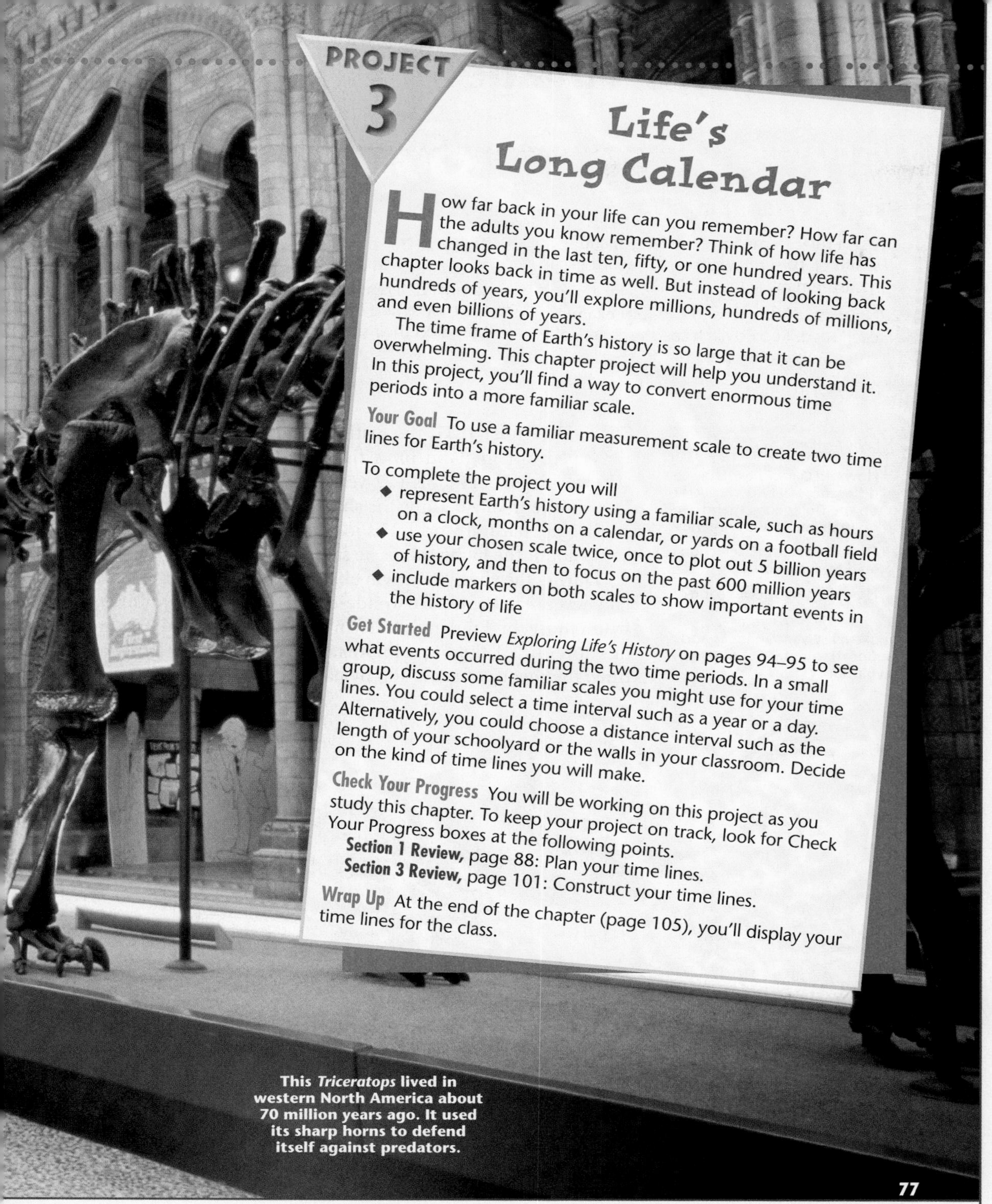

PROJECT 3

Life's Long Calendar

How far back in your life can you remember? How far can the adults you know remember? Think of how life has changed in the last ten, fifty, or one hundred years. This chapter looks back in time as well. But instead of looking back hundreds of years, you'll explore millions, hundreds of millions, and even billions of years.

The time frame of Earth's history is so large that it can be overwhelming. This chapter project will help you understand it. In this project, you'll find a way to convert enormous time periods into a more familiar scale.

Your Goal To use a familiar measurement scale to create two time lines for Earth's history.

To complete the project you will
- ◆ represent Earth's history using a familiar scale, such as hours on a clock, months on a calendar, or yards on a football field
- ◆ use your chosen scale twice, once to plot out 5 billion years of history, and then to focus on the past 600 million years
- ◆ include markers on both scales to show important events in the history of life

Get Started Preview *Exploring Life's History* on pages 94–95 to see what events occurred during the two time periods. In a small group, discuss some familiar scales you might use for your time lines. You could select a time interval such as a year or a day. Alternatively, you could choose a distance interval such as the length of your schoolyard or the walls in your classroom. Decide on the kind of time lines you will make.

Check Your Progress You will be working on this project as you study this chapter. To keep your project on track, look for Check Your Progress boxes at the following points.
Section 1 Review, page 88: Plan your time lines.
Section 3 Review, page 101: Construct your time lines.

Wrap Up At the end of the chapter (page 105), you'll display your time lines for the class.

This *Triceratops* lived in western North America about 70 million years ago. It used its sharp horns to defend itself against predators.

77

appeared on Earth? Have a volunteer mark the line. *(The mark should be close to the "Present" end of the line. If it is not, ask the rest of the class to comment on the mark's placement.)* Point out that if students made only one time line to scale, all the events that happened from the beginning of the Paleozoic Era to the present would have to be crowded into a very small section of the line. Explain that this is the reason they will make two time lines in this project.

Distribute the Chapter 3 Project Overview on pages 62–63 of Unit 1 Resources, and have students review the project rules and procedures. Invite questions and comments. Then divide the class into groups of three or four students each, and let the groups meet to discuss the types of time lines they could make.

When students are ready to make the first time line at the end of Section 1, distribute Worksheet 1 on page 64 of Unit 1 Resources. This worksheet will provide practice in making a time line to scale. At the end of Section 3, distribute Worksheet 2, on page 65 in Unit 1 Resources. This worksheet lists other evolutionary events that could be included in the time lines.

Additional information on guiding the project is provided in Chapter 3 Project Teacher Notes on pages 60–61 of Unit 1 Resources.

Program Resources

◆ **Unit 1 Resources** Chapter 3 Project Teacher Notes, pp. 60–61; Project Overview and Worksheets, pp. 62–65; Project Scoring Rubric, p. 66

Media and Technology

 Audio CDs Section Summaries

 **WEB ACTIVITY** www.phschool.com

You will find an Internet activity, chapter self-tests for students, and links to other chapter topics at this site.

Performance Assessment

The Chapter 3 Project Scoring Rubric on page 66 in Unit 1 Resources will help you evaluate how well students complete the Chapter 3 Project. You may want to share the scoring rubric with students so they are clear about what will be expected of them. Students will be assessed on
- ◆ their accuracy in calculating the scales for the two models;
- ◆ their ability to construct two scale models of Earth's history with important evolutionary events accurately marked;
- ◆ their effectiveness in communicating the model-making process and results to others;
- ◆ their participation in their groups.

Objectives

After completing the lesson, students will be able to

◆ state how Darwin explained variations among similar species;

◆ explain how natural selection leads to evolution, and explain the role of genes in evolution;

◆ describe how new species form.

Key Terms species, adaptation, evolution, scientific theory, natural selection, variation

1 Engage/Explore

Activating Prior Knowledge

Most students will have read articles or seen television specials about Darwin or the Galapagos Islands. Help them recall what they know by asking: **Who was Charles Darwin?** *(A scientist who came up with the idea of evolution by natural selection)* **What is special about the Galapagos Islands?** *(They have a lot of unusual organisms, such as giant lizards and tortoises.)*

DISCOVER

Skills Focus classifying
Materials *metric ruler, 10 sunflower seeds, hand lens*
Time 15 minutes
Tips Tell students that differences among seeds in their sample may be slight and hard to detect, so they should examine the seeds very carefully.
Expected Outcome Students should observe that the seeds in their sample differ in such traits as size, shape, color, or number of stripes.
Think It Over The seeds in each sample may differ in some traits and be similar in others. Depending on the makeup of their sample, students may group together seeds that are similar in size, shape, color, number of stripes, or other traits.

SECTION 1 Darwin's Voyage

DISCOVER ⋯⋯⋯⋯⋯⋯⋯⋯⋯⋯⋯⋯⋯ ACTIVITY

How Do Living Things Vary?

1. Use a ruler to measure the length and width of 10 sunflower seeds. Record each measurement.

2. Now use a hand lens to carefully examine each seed. Record each seed's shape, color, and number of stripes.

Think It Over
Classifying In what ways are the seeds in your sample different from one another? In what ways are they similar? How could you group the seeds based on their similarities and differences?

GUIDE FOR READING

◆ How did Darwin explain the differences between species on the Galapagos Islands and on mainland South America?

◆ How does natural selection lead to evolution?

◆ How do new species form?

Reading Tip As you read, make a list of main ideas and supporting details about evolution.

In December 1831, the British naval ship HMS *Beagle* set sail from England on a five-year-long trip around the world. On board was a 22-year-old named Charles Darwin. Darwin eventually became the ship's naturalist—a person who studies the natural world. His job was to learn as much as he could about the living things he saw on the voyage.

During the voyage, Darwin observed plants and animals he had never seen before. He wondered why they were so different from those in England. Darwin's observations led him to develop one of the most important scientific theories of all time: the theory of evolution by natural selection.

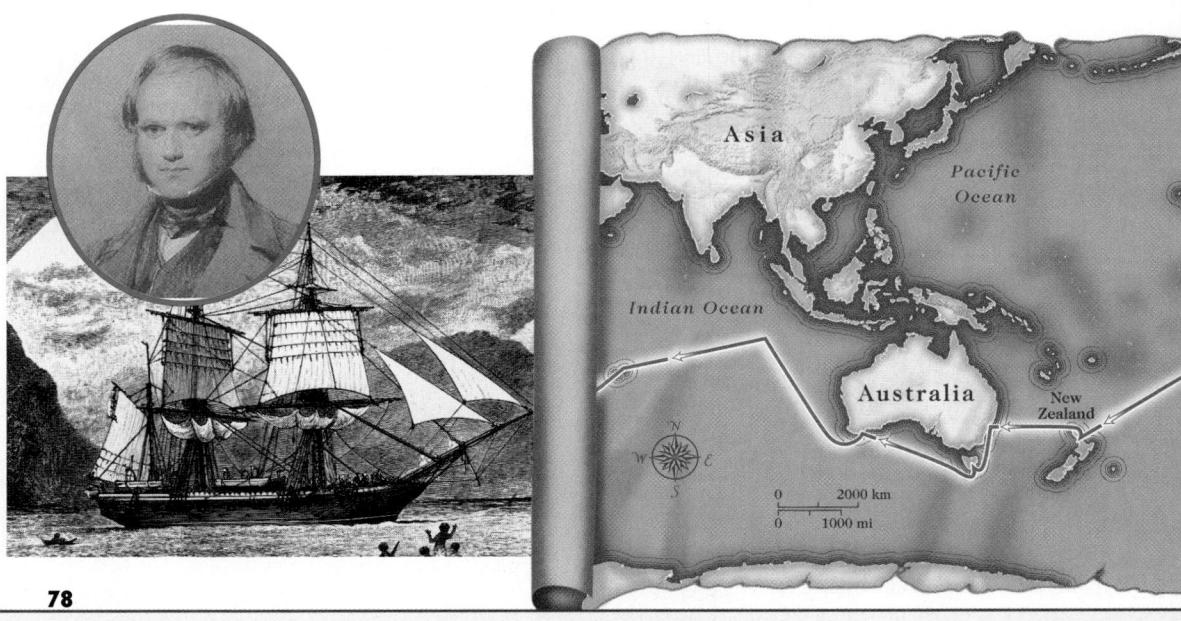

READING STRATEGIES

Reading Tip Help students find the main ideas by advising them to try to answer the Guide for Reading questions as they read the section.

Vocabulary Students may think that the term *species* is plural and that the singular form is *specie.* Explain that the term *species* is both singular and plural. Then use the word in a sentence to illustrate. For example, say: "All humans belong to one species, but humans and chimpanzees belong to two different species."

Study and Comprehension As students read the section, have them rewrite as a question each of the boldfaced statements and the statements defining key terms. After students have finished reading the section, have pairs of students exchange and answer each other's questions.

Darwin's Observations

One of the *Beagle's* first stops was the coast of South America. In Brazil, Darwin saw insects that looked like flowers, and ants that marched across the forest floor like huge armies. In Argentina, he saw armadillos—burrowing animals covered with small, bony plates. He also saw sloths, animals that moved very slowly and spent much of their time hanging upside down in trees.

Darwin was amazed by the tremendous diversity, or variety, of living things he saw. Today scientists know that living things are even more diverse than Darwin could ever have imagined. Scientists have identified more than 1.7 million species of organisms on Earth. A **species** is a group of similar organisms that can mate with each other and produce fertile offspring.

Darwin saw something else in Argentina that puzzled him: the bones of animals that had died long ago. From the bones, Darwin inferred that the animals had looked like the sloths he had seen. However, the bones were much larger than those of the living sloths. He wondered why only smaller sloths were alive today. What had happened to the giant creatures from the past?

In 1835, the *Beagle* reached the Galapagos Islands, a group of small islands in the Pacific Ocean off the west coast of South America. It was on the Galapagos Islands that Darwin observed some of the greatest diversity of life forms. He saw large numbers of giant tortoises, or land turtles, which he described as immense in size. There were also seals covered with fur, and lizards that ate cactus for food and water.

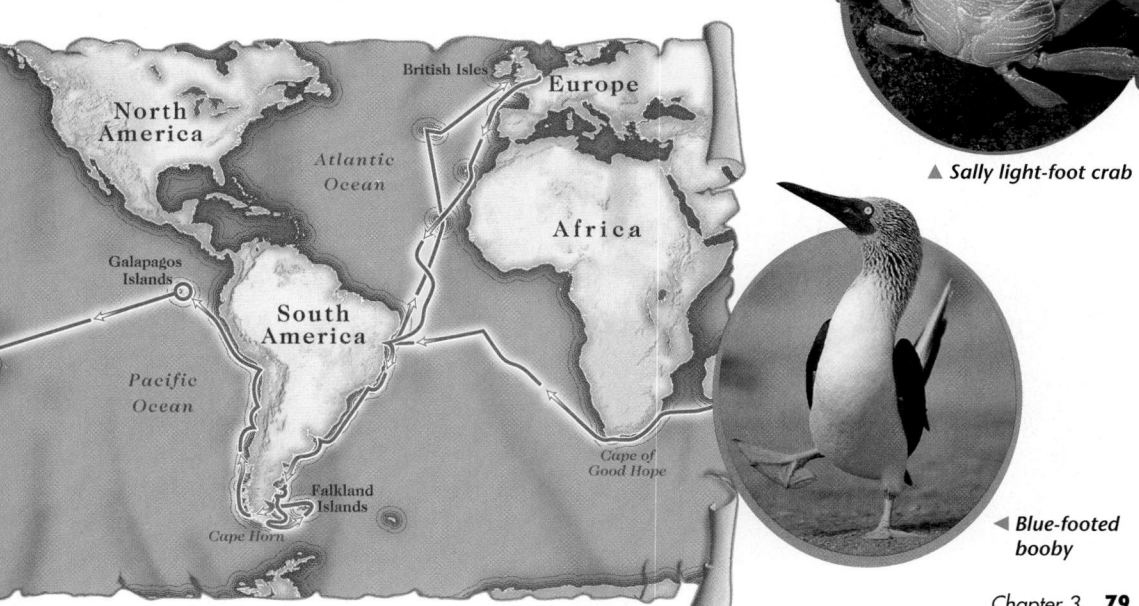

Figure 1 Charles Darwin sailed on HMS *Beagle* from England to South America and then to the Galapagos Islands. He saw many unusual organisms on the Galapagos Islands.

Galapagos hawk ▼

▲ *Giant tortoise*

▲ *Sally light-foot crab*

◄ *Blue-footed booby*

Chapter 3 **79**

Program Resources

◆ **Unit 1 Resources** 3-1 Lesson Plan, p. 67; 3-1 Section Summary, p. 68
◆ **Guided Reading and Study Workbook** Section 3-1

2 Facilitate

Darwin's Observations

Using the Visuals: Figure 1

Have students trace on the map with their finger the route that Darwin took on his voyage. When they have traced Darwin's route as far as the Galapagos Islands, ask: **About how far are the Galapagos Islands from mainland South America?** *(About 1,000 km)* Help students appreciate how far away from the mainland that is, and therefore how isolated the islands are, by equating the distance to a distance with which they are more familiar, such as from Seattle to Sacramento, Detroit to Boston, or Indianapolis to Washington, D.C. **learning modality: kinesthetic**

Demonstration

Materials *taxonomic chart*
Time 10 minutes

Show students a taxonomic chart, either a chart from a biology book or encyclopedia or a simple chart that you have drawn on the chalkboard. Point out that the taxonomic categories group together organisms based on the degree to which they are similar, with the largest, most inclusive category being the kingdom. Explain that humans belong to the animal kingdom, because, like other animals, humans are multicellular and do not make their own food. Ask: **What other organisms are in the animal kingdom?** *(Accept any type of animal in response, and use students' responses to illustrate how diverse the animal kingdom is.)* Then point out that at the other end of the taxonomy is the species, the smallest, most exclusive category, containing only those organisms that can reproduce together. **learning modality: visual**

Ongoing Assessment

Writing Have students describe in their own words the insights that Darwin gained from his voyage.

Similarities and Differences

Building Inquiry Skills: Observing

Materials *drawings of related bird species from a field identification guide*

Time 10 minutes

Point out to students that much of Darwin's time during the voyage of the *Beagle* was spent observing and comparing different organisms. Add that Darwin was a keen observer, and he noticed many details that other people might overlook. Give students a chance to see how difficult Darwin's job was, as well as to improve their own observation skills. Provide students with drawings from a field guide that show several related species of birds, such as several species of ducks, warblers, herons, or woodpeckers. Have students examine the drawings carefully and make lists of all the similarities and differences they observe among the species pictured. Then, have pairs of students compare lists. Emphasize that being a good observer requires care and skill. Be sensitive to visually-challenged students by asking: **What are some other ways these birds might be similar or different that you cannot observe visually?** *(Possible ways include their songs and the texture of their feathers.)* **learning modality: visual**

Using the Visuals: Figure 2

Call students' attention to the figure and have them answer the caption question. Most students will respond that one way the two species differ is in color. Point out that variations in a trait such as this may make organisms better suited for their environment. Ask: **What difference in the environment do you think might explain the difference in color between the two species of iguanas?** *(Students may say the colors in the environment: the green iguana's color helps it blend in with its leafy environment, and the marine iguana's color helps it blend in with its rocky environment.)* **learning modality: logical/mathematical**

Similarities and Differences

Darwin was surprised that many of the plants and animals on the Galapagos Islands were similar to organisms on mainland South America. For example, many of the birds on the islands, including hawks, mockingbirds, and finches, resembled those on the mainland. Many of the plants were also similar to plants Darwin had collected on the mainland.

However, there were also important differences between the organisms on the islands and those on the mainland. Large sea birds called cormorants, for example, lived in both places. The cormorants on the mainland were able to fly, while those on the Galapagos Islands were unable to fly. The iguanas on the Galapagos Islands had large claws that allowed them to keep their grip on slippery rocks, where they fed on seaweed. The iguanas on the mainland had smaller claws. Smaller claws allowed the mainland iguanas to climb trees, where they ate leaves.

From his observations, Darwin inferred that a small number of different plant and animal species had come to the Galapagos Islands from the mainland. They might have been blown out to sea during a storm or set adrift on a fallen log. Once the plants and animals reached the islands, they reproduced. Eventually, their offspring became different from their mainland relatives.

Darwin also noticed many differences among similar organisms as he traveled from one Galapagos island to the next. For example, the tortoises on one island had dome-shaped shells. Those on another island had saddle-shaped shells. The governor of one of the islands told Darwin that he could tell which island a tortoise came from just by looking at its shell.

☑ *Checkpoint* How did Darwin think plants and animals had originally come to the Galapagos Islands?

Figure 2 Darwin observed many differences between organisms in South America and similar organisms on the Galapagos Islands. For example, green iguanas (left) live in South America. Marine iguanas (right) live on the Galapagos Islands. *Comparing and Contrasting How are the two species similar? How are they different?*

Facts and Figures Ever since Darwin's time, scientists have suggested that one way species can become dispersed around the world is on natural rafts of fallen trees blown out to sea during storms. However, until recently there was virtually no direct evidence to support this idea. Then, in 1995, two powerful hurricanes passed through the Caribbean Sea, and a large clump of trees was blown into the sea from the island of Guadeloupe. Storm winds blew the natural raft across more than 300 km of sea, and it eventually washed ashore on the island of Anguilla. On the raft were 15 green iguanas, native to Guadeloupe but, until that time, not found on Anguilla. Most of the iguanas survived the journey and within a few months started reproducing. Scientists speculate that green iguanas eventually will become established on Anguilla.

Figure 3 Darwin made these drawings of four species of Galapagos finches. The beak of each finch is adapted to the type of food it eats.

Adaptations

Like the tortoises, the finches on the Galapagos Islands were noticeably different from one island to another. The most obvious differences were the varied sizes and shapes of the birds' beaks. As Darwin studied the different finches, he noticed that each species was well suited to the life it led. Finches that ate insects had sharp, needlelike beaks. Finches that ate seeds had strong, wide beaks. Beak shape is an example of an **adaptation,** a trait that helps an organism survive and reproduce.

Evolution

After he returned home to England, Darwin continued to think about what he had seen during his voyage on the *Beagle.* Darwin spent the next 20 years consulting with many other scientists, gathering more information, and thinking through his ideas. He especially wanted to understand how the variety of organisms with different adaptations arose on the Galapagos Islands.

Darwin reasoned that plants or animals that arrived on one of the Galapagos Islands faced conditions that were different from those on the mainland. **Perhaps, Darwin thought, the species gradually changed over many generations and became better adapted to the new conditions.** The gradual change in a species over time is called **evolution.**

Darwin's ideas are often referred to as the theory of evolution. A **scientific theory** is a well-tested concept that explains a wide range of observations.

It was clear to Darwin that evolution had occurred on the Galapagos Islands. He did not know, however, how this process had occurred. Darwin had to draw on other examples of changes in living things to help him understand how evolution occurs.

Bird Beak Adaptations

Use this activity to explore adaptations in birds.

1. Scatter a small amount of bird seed on a paper plate. Scatter 20 raisins on the plate to represent insects.
2. Obtain a variety of objects such as tweezers, hair clips, clothes pins, and hairpins. Pick one object to use as a "beak."
3. See how many seeds you can pick up and drop into a cup in 10 seconds.
4. Now see how many "insects" you can pick up and drop into a cup in 10 seconds.
5. Use a different "beak" and repeat Steps 3 and 4.

Inferring What type of beak worked well for seeds? For insects? How are different-shaped beaks useful for eating different foods?

Adaptations

Skills Focus inferring
Materials *bird seed, paper plate, 20 raisins, tweezers, hair clips, hairpins, clothes pins, stopwatch, paper cup*
Time 10 minutes
Tips Have students work with partners so one student can pick up the seeds or raisins while the partner watches the clock.
Expected Outcome Students will find that some objects are better for picking up seeds and others for picking up raisins. Students should infer that some bird beaks are better for picking up seeds and others for picking up insects.
Extend Ask: **Which species in Figure 3 appear to be adapted to a diet of seeds, and which to a diet of insects?** *(Species 1, 2, and possibly 3 appear to be adapted to a diet of seeds, and species 4 to a diet of insects.)* **learning modality: kinesthetic**

Evolution

Addressing Naive Conceptions

People often say, "It's only a theory," and this may lead students to believe that a theory is just any idea. Address this naive conception by asking: **What makes an idea a theory?** *(It is well-tested and explains many observations.)* **How is a theory different from a fact?** *(A fact is a specific observation, known to be true; a theory is a broad concept, thought to be true because it explains many facts.)* **Upon which facts did Darwin base his theory of evolution?** *(The similarities and differences he observed among living things)* **learning modality: verbal**

Answers to Self-Assessment

Caption Question

Figure 2 Both species have spines, claws, and scaly skin. Green iguanas are green, have smaller claws, and live in trees. Marine iguanas are gray, have larger claws, and live on rocks near the ocean.

☑ *Checkpoint*

Perhaps by being blown out to sea during a storm or set adrift on a fallen log

Ongoing Assessment

Oral Presentation Call on students at random to define each term in their own words: *species, adaptation, evolution,* and *scientific theory.*

Evolution, continued

Including All Students

Support students who need more help in understanding natural selection by relating it to selective breeding, which they learned about in Chapter 2. Create a simple compare/contrast table on the chalkboard and call on students to help you complete it. The table should have two rows, one for selective breeding and one for natural selection. It also should have columns such as: **Type of Traits Selected** (*Selective breeding: traits that benefit humans; natural selection: traits that benefit the organism*); **Examples of Traits Selected** (*Selective breeding: fine wool in sheep or many kernels in corn; natural selection: ability to escape predators or resist drought*); **How Traits Are Selected** (*Selective breeding: by humans, who allow only organisms with the traits to reproduce; natural selection: by natural events, which allow organisms with the traits to produce more offspring*) After the table is completed, ask: **Why would *artificial* selection be a good term for selective breeding?** (*Because, like natural selection, selective breeding leads to changes in a species' traits, but artificial human choices, not natural events, control the process*) **learning modality: logical/mathematical**

Natural Selection

Building Inquiry Skills: Communicating

Encourage students who need extra challenges to learn about and then communicate to the rest of the class how natural selection has resulted in the viceroy butterfly bearing a close but superficial resemblance to the monarch butterfly. Urge students to use diagrams and illustrations to communicate what they learn. After students have communicated their findings, ask: **Why is this type of natural selection called mimicry?** (*Because natural selection results in one species looking like, or mimicking, another species*) **learning modality: verbal**

Darwin knew that people used selective breeding to produce organisms with desired traits. For example, English farmers used selective breeding to produce sheep with fine wool. Darwin himself had bred pigeons with large, fan-shaped tails. By repeatedly allowing only those pigeons with many tail feathers to mate, Darwin produced pigeons with two or three times the usual number of tail feathers. Darwin thought that a process similar to selective breeding must happen in nature. But he wondered why certain traits were selected for, and how.

✓ *Checkpoint* **What observations led Darwin to propose his theory of evolution?**

Natural Selection

In 1858, Darwin and another British biologist, Alfred Russel Wallace, proposed an explanation for how evolution occurs. The next year, Darwin described this mechanism in a book entitled *The Origin of Species*. In his book, Darwin explained that evolution occurs by means of natural selection. **Natural selection** is the process by which individuals that are better adapted to their environment are more likely to survive and reproduce than other members of the same species. Darwin identified a number of factors that affect the process of natural selection: overproduction, competition, and variations.

Overproduction Most species produce far more offspring than can possibly survive. In many species, so many offspring are produced that there are not enough resources—food, water, and living space—for all of them. For example, each year a female sea turtle may lay more than 100 eggs. If all the young turtles survived, the sea would soon be full of turtles. Darwin knew that this doesn't happen. Why not?

Figure 4 Most newborn loggerhead sea turtles will not survive to adulthood. *Making Generalizations What factors limit the number of young that survive?*

Figure 5 The walruses lying on this rocky beach in Alaska must compete for resources. All organisms compete for limited resources such as food.

Competition Since food and other resources are limited, the offspring must compete with each other to survive. Competition does not usually involve direct physical fights between members of a species. Instead, competition is usually indirect. For example, some turtles may fail to find enough to eat. Others may not be able to escape from predators. Only a few turtles will survive long enough to reproduce.

Variations As you learned in your study of genetics, members of a species differ from one another in many of their traits. Any difference between individuals of the same species is called a **variation.** For example, some newly hatched turtles are able to swim faster than other turtles.

Selection Some variations make certain individuals better adapted to their environment. Those individuals are more likely to survive and reproduce. When those individuals reproduce, their offspring may inherit the allele for the helpful trait. The offspring, in turn, will be more likely to survive and reproduce, and thus pass on the allele to their offspring. After many generations, more members of the species will have the helpful trait. In effect, the environment has "selected" organisms with helpful traits to be the parents of the next generation—hence the term "natural selection." **Over a long period of time, natural selection can lead to evolution. Helpful variations gradually accumulate in a species, while unfavorable ones disappear.**

For example, suppose a new fast-swimming predator moves into the turtles' habitat. Turtles that are able to swim faster would be more likely to escape from the new predator. The faster turtles would thus be more likely to survive and reproduce. Over time, more and more turtles in the species would have the "fast-swimmer" trait.

Sharpen your Skills

Inferring

Scatter 15 black buttons and 15 white buttons on a sheet of white paper. Have a partner time you to see how many buttons you can pick up in 10 seconds. Pick up the buttons one at a time.

Did you collect more buttons of one color than the other? Why? How can a variation such as color affect the process of natural selection?

Program Resources

◆ **Laboratory Manual** 3, "Variation in a Population"

Answers to Self-Assessment

☑ Checkpoint

Darwin proposed his theory of evolution based on observations of similarities and differences among species in nature and observations of domestic animals selectively bred to have desired traits.

Caption Question

Figure 4 Factors include predators and limited resources.

Cultural Diversity

Point out to students that human beings are unusual among living things in the variation of their behavior. Explain that the ability of humans to adapt their behavior has allowed them to move into a wide range of environments without evolving specific physical adaptations. In very cold climates, for example, animals such as polar bears have evolved thick fur to stay warm. Humans, on the other hand, have been able to use behavioral means, such as making and wearing clothing, to stay warm. As a result, humans do not have any special physical adaptations to extreme cold. Ask: **What are some behavioral means that humans use to protect themselves from predators?** *(Possible ways might include making and using weapons and living in groups.)* **learning modality: verbal**

Sharpen your Skills

Inferring

Materials *15 black buttons, 15 white buttons, large sheet of plain white paper, stopwatch*
Time 10 minutes
Tips Have students work in pairs so one student can focus on picking up buttons while the other keeps track of the time. All the buttons should be identical except for color.
Expected Outcome Students are likely to pick up more black buttons than white buttons. They should infer that a variation such as color can affect natural selection by making an organism more or less likely to be seen and captured by a predator.
Extend Ask: **Besides color, what are some other variations that might affect whether or not an organism is seen and captured by a predator?** *(Accept any reasonable responses, such as other physical traits, intelligence, and acuteness of senses.)* **learning modality: kinesthetic**

Ongoing Assessment

Writing Have students explain how overproduction, competition, and variations lead to natural selection.

Nature at Work

Preparing for Inquiry

Key Concept Natural selection can lead to changes in a species' traits over time.
Skills Objectives Students will be able to
- make a dynamic model of natural selection in mice;
- observe how selection changes a species;
- predict how changing environmental conditions will affect natural selection in the model.

Time 40 minutes
Advance Planning To save time, before class begins you can prepare enough mouse and event cards so there is a complete set of cards for each group of students.

Guiding Inquiry

Invitation Tell students that in this lab they will simulate natural selection in mice of two different colors. Ask: **How do you think variation of color in a species might affect natural selection?** *(Some colors might make individuals better able to hide from predators, making them more likely to survive and reproduce. Other colors might make it more difficult for individuals to hide from predators, making them less likely to survive and reproduce.)*

Introducing the Procedure

Make sure students understand the rationale behind each step of the procedure. It may not be obvious to them, for example, why they cannot simply use cards representing mice of each color, rather than cards representing alleles. Ask: **Why do the mouse cards represent alleles rather than phenotypes?** *(Because alleles are passed on to the next generation, not phenotypes)* Point out that choosing alleles to make up the next generation is a realistic way to model reproduction and the inheritance of traits while choosing phenotypes is not.

Nature at Work

I n this lab, you will investigate how natural selection can lead to changes in a species over time. You'll explore how both genetic and environmental factors play a part in natural selection.

Problem

How do species change over time?

Materials

scissors
marking pen
construction paper, 2 colors

Procedure

1. Work on this lab with two other students. One student should choose construction paper of one color and make the team's 50 "mouse" cards, as described in Table 1. The second student should choose a different color construction paper and make the team's 25 "event" cards, as described in Table 2. The third student should copy the data table and record all the data.

Part 1 A White Sand Environment

2. Mix up the mouse cards.
3. Begin by using the cards to model what might happen to a group of mice in an environment of white sand dunes. Choose two mouse cards. Allele pairs *WW* and *Ww* produce a white mouse. Allele pair *ww* produces a brown mouse. Record the color of the mouse with a tally mark in the data table.

4. Choose an event card. An "S" card means the mouse survives. A "D" or a "P" card means the mouse dies. A "C" card means the mouse dies if its color contrasts with the white sand dunes. (Only brown mice will die when a "C" card is drawn.) Record each death with a tally mark in the data table.
5. If the mouse lives, put the two mouse cards in a "live mice" pile. If the mouse dies, put the cards in a "dead mice" pile. Put the event card at the bottom of its pack.
6. Repeat Steps 3 through 5 with the remaining mouse cards to study the first generation of mice. Record your results.
7. Leave the dead mice cards untouched. Mix up the cards from the live mice pile. Mix up the events cards.
8. Repeat Steps 3 through 7 for the second generation. Then repeat Steps 3 through 6 for the third generation.

Table 1: "Mouse" Cards

Number	Label	Meaning
25	W	Dominant allele for white fur
25	w	Recessive allele for brown fur

Table 2: "Event" Cards

Number	Label	Meaning
5	S	Mouse survives.
1	D	Disease kills mouse.
1	P	Predator kills mice of all colors.
18	C	Predator kills mice that contrast with the environment.

84

Troubleshooting the Experiment

- Divide students into groups of three before they start the lab, and make sure group members divide the tasks as specified in the text.
- Check that students are assigning the right phenotype to each genotype. Remind them that the *W* allele for white fur is dominant to the *w* allele for brown fur.

Expected Outcome

Groups should find that the number of mice declines each generation, with the number of brown mice declining faster than the number of white mice in Part 1, and the number of white mice declining faster than the number of brown mice in Part 2.

DATA TABLE				
Type of Environment:				
Generation	White Mice	Brown Mice	Deaths	
			White Mice	Brown Mice
1				
2				
3				

Part 2 A Forest Floor Environment

9. How would the data differ if the mice in this model lived on a dark brown forest floor? Record your prediction in your notebook.

10. Make a new copy of the data table. Then use the cards to test your prediction. Remember that a "C" card now means that any mouse with white fur will die.

Analyze and Conclude

1. In Part 1, how many white mice were there in each generation? How many brown mice? In each generation, which color mouse had the higher death rate? (*Hint:* To calculate the death rate for white mice, divide the number of white mice that died by the total number of white mice, then multiply by 100%.)

2. If the events in Part 1 occurred in nature, how would the group of mice change over time?

3. How did the results in Part 2 differ from those in Part 1?

4. What are some ways in which this investigation models natural selection? What are some ways in which natural selection differs from this model?

5. **Think About It** How would it affect your model if you increased the number of "C" cards? If you decreased the number?

Design an Experiment

Choose a different species with a trait that interests you. Make a set of cards similar to these cards to investigate how natural selection might bring about the evolution of that species.

Sample Data Table				
Type of Environment: White Sand				
Generation	White Mice	Brown Mice	Deaths of White Mice	Deaths of Brown Mice
1	18	7	2	5
2	16	2	2	1
3	14	1	1	1

Program Resources

◆ **Unit 1 Resources** Skills Lab blackline masters, pp. 79–81

Media and Technology

 Lab Activity Videotape
Tape 1

Analyze and Conclude

1. Answers will depend on the genotypes of the mice in each generation and the order in which the mouse and event cards are drawn. For the sample data, there were 18 white mice in the first generation, of which 2 died, yielding a death rate of 11% for the white mice. There were also 7 brown mice in the first generation, of which 5 died, yielding a death rate of 71% for the brown mice.

2. The population of mice would contain more and more mice with white fur.

3. In Part 2, the population contains more brown mice each generation because white mice are selected against, whereas in Part 1, the population contains more white mice each generation because the brown mice are selected against.

4. This investigation models natural selection in that an organism's chances of surviving and reproducing depend both on the organism's inherited traits and on the environment in which the organism lives. Natural selection differs from the model in that other environmental factors besides predators and disease, and other traits besides fur color, are likely to influence an organism's chances of surviving and reproducing.

5. If you increased the number of "C" cards, natural selection against mice that contrast with the environment would be stronger and contrasting-color mice would decrease in number more quickly. If you decreased the number of "C" cards, natural selection against mice that contrast with the environment would be weaker and contrasting-color mice would decrease in number more slowly.

Extending the Inquiry

Design an Experiment Urge students to select a trait that is controlled by a recessive allele so they can see how dominance affects the rate at which natural selection changes the genetic makeup of the population. The trait they choose to model may be real or hypothetical.

Safety
Review the safety guidelines in Appendix A.

The Role of Genes in Evolution

Inquiry Challenge

Time 10 minutes

Divide the class into groups, and challenge students in each group to brainstorm an experiment to demonstrate that only inherited traits are affected by natural selection. You may wish to share the information on Lamarck in the Background below to stimulate students' thinking. (*One way is to change experimental organisms in some way, for example, by dyeing the hair of lab rats, and then observing whether the changed trait appears in their offspring.*) Have each group elect a spokesperson to describe its plan to the rest of the class, and urge the class to give the group feedback on its ideas. Then ask: **Why are only inherited traits affected by natural selection?** (*Because only genes are passed from parents to their offspring*)
cooperative learning

Evolution in Action

Social Studies
CONNECTION

Give students a context for the feature by explaining that the type of natural selection it describes is called *industrial melanism.* Explain that melanism refers to the pigment melanin, which gives many organisms—from peppered moths to humans—their color. The change in color of moths was documented in several unrelated species and in several different places, all of which were heavily industrialized. Point out that industrial melanism is one of the best analyzed examples of natural selection in action in the real world.

In Your Journal Students should (correctly) predict that strict pollution laws since the 1950s would lead to trees returning to their light gray color and natural selection favoring light-colored moths. This, in turn, would result in peppered moth populations becoming mostly light-colored again. **learning modality: logical/mathematical**

Social Studies
CONNECTION

The case of the English peppered moth is an example of how human actions can affect natural selection. In the late 1700s, most English peppered moths were light gray in color. The light-colored moths had an advantage over black peppered moths because birds could not see them against the light-gray trees. Natural selection favored the light-colored moths over the black moths.

The Industrial Revolution began in England in the late 1700s. People built factories to make cloth and other goods. Over time, smoke from the factories blackened the trunks of the trees. Now the light-colored moths were easier to see than the black ones. As a result, birds caught more light-colored moths. Natural selection favored the black moths. By about 1850, almost all the peppered moths were black.

In Your Journal

Since the 1950s, strict pollution laws have reduced the amount of smoke released into the air in England. Predict how this has affected the trees and the moths.

Figure 6 The Industrial Revolution affected natural selection in peppered moths in England. As pollution blackened the tree trunks, black moths became more likely to survive and reproduce.

The Role of Genes in Evolution

Without variations, all the members of a species would have the same traits. Evolution by natural selection would not occur because all individuals would have an equal chance of surviving and reproducing. But where do variations come from? How are they passed on from parents to offspring? Darwin could not answer these questions.

Darwin did not know anything about genes or mutations. It is not surprising that he could not explain what caused variations or how they were passed on. As scientists later learned, variations can result from mutations in genes or from the shuffling of alleles during meiosis. Only genes are passed from parents to their offspring. Because of this, only traits that are inherited, or controlled by genes, can be acted upon by natural selection.

Evolution in Action

Since Darwin published his book, scientists have observed many examples of evolution in action. In a 1977 study of the finches on Daphne Major, one of the Galapagos Islands, scientists observed that beak size could change very quickly by natural selection. That year, little rain fell on the island—only 25 millimeters instead of the usual 130 millimeters or so. Because of the lack of rain, many plants died. Fewer of the seeds that the finches usually ate were available. Instead, the birds had to eat large seeds that were enclosed in tough, thorny seed pods.

Finches with larger and stronger beaks were better able to open the tough pods than were finches with smaller, weaker beaks. Many of the finches with smaller beaks did not survive the drought. The next year, more finches on the island had larger and stronger beaks. Evolution by natural selection had occurred in just one year.

How Do New Species Form?

Darwin's theory of evolution by natural selection explains how variations can lead to changes in a species. But how does an entirely new species evolve? Since Darwin's time, scientists have come to understand that geographic isolation is one of the main ways that new species form. Isolation, or complete separation, occurs when some members of a species become cut off from the rest of the species.

Sometimes a group is separated from the rest of its species by a river, volcano, or mountain range. Even an ocean wave can separate a few individuals from the rest of their species by sweeping them out to sea and later washing them ashore on an island. This may have happened on the Galapagos Islands. Once a group becomes isolated, members of the isolated group can no longer mate with members of the rest of the species.

A new species can form when a group of individuals remains separated from the rest of its species long enough to evolve different traits. The longer the group remains isolated from the rest of the species, the more likely it is to evolve into a new species. For example, the Abert's squirrel and the Kaibab squirrel live in forests in the Southwest. About 10,000 years ago both types of squirrels were members of the same species. About that time, however, a small group of squirrels became isolated in a forest on the north side of the Grand Canyon in Arizona. Over time, this group evolved into the Kaibab squirrel, which has a distinctive black belly. Scientists are not sure whether the Kaibab squirrel has become different enough from the Abert's squirrel to be considered a separate species.

☑ *Checkpoint* How did geographic isolation affect the Kaibab squirrel?

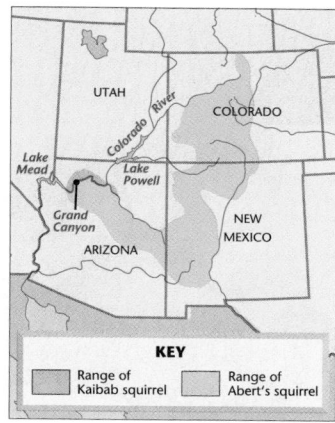

Figure 7 About 10,000 years ago, a group of squirrels became isolated from the rest of the species. As a result, the Kaibab squirrel (left) has evolved to become different from the Abert's squirrel (right). *Interpreting Maps What geographic feature separates the range of the Kaibab squirrel from that of the Abert's squirrel?*

KEY
Range of Kaibab squirrel
Range of Abert's squirrel

How Do New Species Form?

Inquiry Challenge

Divide the class into groups, and challenge each group to brainstorm a way that geographic isolation could arise and lead to the formation of a new species. *(A natural event such as an earthquake or a human activity such as the construction of a road could isolate some members of a species and keep them isolated long enough to evolve new traits.)* After groups have shared their ideas, ask: **Why must a group become isolated to develop into a new species?** *(Without isolation, matings could occur between the group and the rest of the species. As a result, any new traits would evolve not just in the group but throughout the entire species.)* **cooperative learning**

Using the Visuals: Figure 7

Use the figure to reinforce the information in the text for students who are still mastering English. First have students find the words *Arizona* and *Grand Canyon* on the map. Point out that the Grand Canyon is almost 30 km wide and 2 km deep. Stress how effectively a canyon of that size would isolate animals living on either side. Next have students carefully read the map key and the figure caption to locate the range of each type of squirrel on the map and identify which of the squirrels pictured above the map lives in each range. Finally, have students find the line in the text that answers the question: **What trait has evolved in the Kaibab squirrel that makes it different from the Abert's squirrel?** *(A black belly)* **limited English proficiency**

Answers to Self-Assessment

Caption Question

Figure 7 The Grand Canyon

☑ *Checkpoint*

Geographic isolation led to the Kaibab squirrel developing some traits that are different from the traits of the Abert squirrel, including a black belly.

Ongoing Assessment

Writing Have students explain how species can change, using the finches on Daphne Major as an example. *(Students should explain how evolution by natural selection changed an isolated group of finches.)*

Continental Drift

Demonstration

Display a map of Pangaea. Point out that Australia broke away from Pangaea 250 million years ago, while other continents were still joined as recently as 50 million years ago. This isolated marsupials in Australia from competition with other mammals. Ask: **What are some other Australian marsupials?** *(kangaroo, koala, wombat)* **learning modality: visual**

3 Assess

Section 1 Review Answers

1. Evolution is the gradual change in a species over time. Darwin observed different adaptations among organisms.
2. Otherwise all individuals would be equally adapted to their environment and equally likely to survive and reproduce.
3. A new species can form when a group of individuals becomes isolated from the rest of its species and remains separated long enough to evolve different traits.
4. Insects that look like sticks are camouflaged among twigs and may be overlooked by predators. If the trait increases the insect's chances of surviving and reproducing, then insects with the trait would become more common than insects without it.

Check Your Progress
CHAPTER PROJECT 3

Review students' plans to make sure they have chosen workable models. Distribute Worksheet 1, and guide students through the procedure of making a scale model of their own life history to date. When students are comfortable with the process, let each group start its first time line.

Performance Assessment

Skills Check Have students explain how continental drift led to the evolution of many different marsupials in Australia.

Continental Drift

Geographic isolation has also occurred on a worldwide scale. For example, hundreds of millions of years ago all of Earth's landmasses were connected as one landmass. It formed a supercontinent called Pangaea. Organisms could migrate from one part of the supercontinent to another. Over millions of years, Pangaea gradually split apart in a process called continental drift. As the continents separated, species became isolated from one another and began to evolve independently.

Perhaps the most striking example of how continental drift affected the evolution of species is on the continent of Australia. The organisms living in Australia have been isolated from all other organisms on Earth for millions of years. Because of this, unique organisms have evolved in Australia. For example, most mammals in Australia belong to the group known as marsupials. Unlike other mammals, a marsupial gives birth to very small young that continue to develop in a pouch on the mother's body. Figure 8 shows two of the many marsupial species that exist in Australia. In contrast, few species of marsupials exist on other continents.

Figure 8 As a result of continental drift, many species of marsupials evolved in Australia. Australian marsupials include the numbat (top) and the spotted cuscus (bottom).

Section 1 Review

1. What is evolution? What did Darwin observe on the Galapagos Islands that he thought was the result of evolution?
2. Explain why variations are needed for natural selection to occur.
3. Describe how geographic isolation can result in the formation of a new species.
4. Thinking Critically Applying Concepts Some insects look just like sticks. How could this be an advantage to the insects? How could this trait have evolved through natural selection?

88

Check Your Progress
CHAPTER PROJECT 3

You should now be ready to submit your plans for your time lines to your teacher. Include a list of the major events you will include on your time lines. Remember, you want to emphasize the life forms that were present at each period. When your plans are approved, begin to construct your time lines. (*Hint:* You will need to divide your time lines into equal-sized intervals. For example, if you use a 12-month calendar to represent 5 billion years, calculate how many months will represent 1 billion years.)

Program Resources

◆ **Unit 1 Resources** 3-1 Review and Reinforce, p. 69; 3-1 Enrich, p. 70

SECTION 2 The Fossil Record

DISCOVER

What Can You Learn From Fossils?

1. Look at the fossil in the photograph. Describe the fossil's characteristics in as much detail as you can.

2. From your description in Step 1, try to figure out how the organism lived. How did it move? Where did it live?

Think It Over

Inferring What type of present-day organism do you think is related to the fossil? Why?

A crime has been committed. You and another detective arrive at the crime scene after the burglar has fled. To piece together what happened, you begin searching for clues. First you notice a broken first-floor window. Leading up to the window are footprints in the mud. From the prints, you can infer the size and type of shoes the burglar wore. As you gather these and other clues, you slowly piece together a picture of what happened and who the burglar might be.

To understand events that occurred long ago, scientists act like detectives. Some of the most important clues to Earth's past are fossils. A **fossil** is the preserved remains or traces of an organism that lived in the past. A fossil can be formed from a bone, tooth, shell, or other part of an organism. Other fossils can be traces of the organism, such as footprints or worm burrows left in mud that later turned to stone.

How Do Fossils Form?

Very few fossils are of complete organisms. Often when an animal dies, the soft parts of its body either decay or are eaten before a fossil can form. Usually only the hard parts of the animal, such as the bones or shells, remain. Plants also form fossils. The parts of plants that are most often preserved as fossils include leaves, stems, roots, and seeds.

The formation of any fossil is a rare event. The conditions must be just right for a fossil to form. **Most fossils form when organisms that die become buried in sediments.** Sediments are

GUIDE FOR READING

◆ How do most fossils form?

◆ How can scientists determine a fossil's age?

Reading Tip Before you read, preview *Exploring Life's History* on pages 94–95. Make a list of questions you have about geologic time and the evolution of life.

A fossilized shark tooth ▼

Chapter 3 **89**

SECTION 2 The Fossil Record

Objectives

After completing the lesson, students will be able to

◆ describe how most fossils form;

◆ explain how a scientist determines a fossil's age;

◆ describe the main events of the Geologic Time Scale;

◆ describe two theories of how fast evolution occurs.

Key Terms fossil, sedimentary rock, petrified fossil, mold, cast, relative dating, absolute dating, radioactive element, half-life, fossil record, extinct, gradualism, punctuated equilibria

1 Engage/Explore

Activating Prior Knowledge

Most students are likely to know a lot about dinosaurs. Ask: **How do we know so much about dinosaurs if there are no longer any of them left alive?** *(From their remains, which have been preserved as fossils)* Tell students they will learn in this section how fossils are formed and how they are used by scientists to understand extinct organisms and their evolution.

DISCOVER

Skills Focus inferring
Time 5 minutes
Tips It may be helpful to provide a hand lens for any students with vision problems. After the activity, inform students that the fossil pictured is a trilobite, an ocean-bottom-dwelling animal that existed about 540 to 250 million years ago.
Expected Outcome Students are likely to describe the overall shape and obvious physical features of the fossil, including what appear to be a shell and numerous legs.
Think It Over Students may say the fossil is related to present-day insects or crabs, because it resembles them in its physical features.

Program Resources

◆ **Unit 1 Resources** 3-2 Lesson Plan, p. 71; 3-2 Section Summary, p. 72
◆ **Guided Reading and Study Workbook** Section 3-2

Media and Technology

 Transparencies "How Fossils Form," Transparency 8

READING STRATEGIES

Reading Tip Questions may include, "Why aren't periods all the same length?" If students write questions that are not answered in the text, challenge them to use encyclopedias or other sources to find the answers and to share them with the class.

2 Facilitate

How Do Fossils Form?

Demonstration

Materials *clear plastic container, sand, soil, shells, other small objects*

Time 10 minutes

Demonstrate how most fossils form by gradually layering sand and soil in a clear container and scattering small shells or other objects throughout the layers to represent organic remains. As you add the layers of sediment, point out to students how the gradual accumulation of sediment buries and helps preserve the remains of organisms. Relate the demonstration to the actual formation of fossils by asking: **How would real animal remains become buried in this way?** *(By wind or water dropping sand and soil on them)* **How might the fossils become uncovered again?** *(Answers may vary. Usually erosion wears away layers of rock.)* **learning modality: visual**

Including All Students

Materials *baking sheet, modeling clay, prepared gelatin, shell or other small object*

Time 5 minutes one day; 5 minutes the next day

Give hands-on learners an opportunity to experience how molds and casts are formed. Instruct students to lay a flat piece of clay on a baking sheet and make an impression in the clay with a small object such as a shell. Then have students pour a small amount of prepared gelatin into the depression and put the baking sheet in a refrigerator overnight. The next day, advise students to gently dislodge the hardened gelatin from the clay. The gelatin should have the same shape as the object that made the depression in the clay. Ask: **Which part of your model represents a mold? Which part represents a cast?** *(The depression in the clay represents a mold; the gelatin shape represents a cast.)* **learning modality: kinesthetic**

1. Two dinosaurs are buried by ash from an erupting volcano.

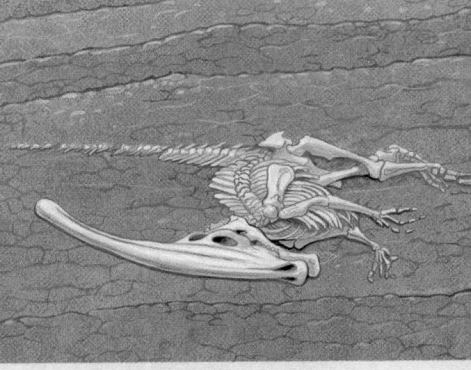

2. Minerals gradually replace the remains. Over millions of years, the fossils become buried by sediments.

Figure 9 Fossils are the preserved remains or traces of organisms that lived in the past. Fossils can form when organisms that die become buried in sediments. *Interpreting Diagrams What is one way in which a buried fossil can become uncovered?*

particles of soil and rock. When a river flows into a lake or ocean, the sediments carried by the river settle to the bottom. Layers of sediments build up and cover the dead organisms. Over millions of years, the layers harden to become **sedimentary rock.**

Petrified Fossils Some remains that become buried in sediments are actually changed to rock. Minerals dissolved in the water soak into the buried remains. Gradually, the minerals replace the remains, changing them into rock. Fossils that form in this way are called **petrified fossils.**

Molds and Casts Sometimes shells or other hard parts buried by sediments are gradually dissolved. An empty space remains in the place the part once occupied. A hollow space in sediment in the shape of an organism or part of an organism is called a **mold.**

Sometimes a mold becomes filled in with hardened minerals, forming a **cast.** A cast is a copy of the shape of the organism that made the mold. If you have ever made a gelatin dessert in a plastic mold, then you can understand how a cast forms.

Preserved Remains Organisms can also be preserved in substances other than sediments. Entire organisms, such as the huge elephant-like mammoths that lived thousands of years ago, have been preserved in ice. The low temperatures preserved the mammoths' soft parts.

The bones and teeth of other ancient animals have been preserved in tar pits. Tar is a dark, sticky form of oil. Tar pits formed when tar seeped up from under the ground to the surface. The tar pits were often covered with water. Animals that came to drink the water became stuck in the tar.

Background

Facts and Figures Some of the most useful fossils for reconstructing the behavior of extinct animals are fossilized footprints. Fossilized footprints are relatively common because a single organism can leave a great many footprints and also because footprints tend to fossilize well if they are made in sand or mud. Fossilized footprints of dinosaurs, for example, have been found at more than 1,000 sites. Fossilized footprints can reveal a great deal about the animal that left them. For example, they provide evidence of the speed and length of the animal's stride, whether the animal walked on two or four legs, the bone structure of the animal's feet, and whether the animal traveled in a herd.

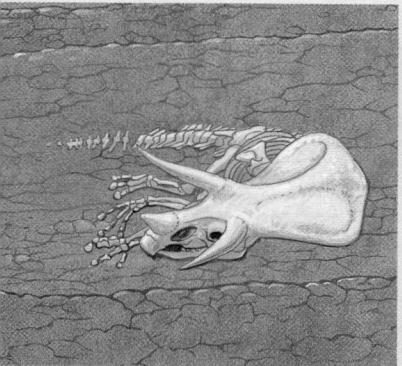

3. Running water cuts through the sedimentary rock layers, exposing the fossils.

Insects and some other organisms can become stuck in the sticky sap that some evergreen trees produce. The sap then hardens, forming amber. The amber protects the organism's body from decay.

Determining a Fossil's Age

To understand how living things have changed through time, scientists need to be able to determine the ages of fossils. They can then determine the sequence in which past events occurred. This information can be used to reconstruct the history of life on Earth. **Scientists can determine a fossil's age in two ways: relative dating and absolute dating.**

Relative Dating Scientists use **relative dating** to determine which of two fossils is older. To understand how relative dating works, imagine that a river has cut down through layers of sedimentary rock to form a canyon. If you look at the canyon walls, you can see the layers of sedimentary rock piled up one on top of another. The layers near the top of the canyon were formed most recently. These layers are the youngest rock layers. The lower down the canyon wall you go, the older the layers are. Therefore, fossils found in layers near the top of the canyon are younger than fossils found near the bottom of the canyon.

Relative dating can only be used when the rock layers have been preserved in their original sequence. Relative dating can help scientists determine whether one fossil is older than another. However, relative dating does not tell scientists the fossil's actual age.

Checkpoint *Which rock layers contain younger fossils?*

TRY THIS

Preservation in Ice

1. Place fresh fruit, such as apple slices, strawberries, and blueberries, in an open plastic container.

2. Completely cover the fruit with water. Put the container in a freezer.

3. Place the same type and amount of fresh fruit in another open container. Leave it somewhere where no one will disturb it.

4. After three days, observe the fruit in both containers.

Inferring Use your observations to explain why fossils preserved in ice are more likely to include soft, fleshy body parts.

Skills Focus inferring
Materials *fresh fruit, two plastic containers, water*
Time 10 minutes
Tips Make sure students find a place to put the container of fruit that is left out so it will not be disturbed. Warn students not to eat the fruit that has been left out.
Expected Outcome The frozen fruit is well preserved, whereas the fruit that was left out is starting to spoil. Students should infer that freezing prevents the soft parts from drying out and/or rotting.
Extend Ask: **How do you think a mammoth or other animal might get preserved in this way?** *(Accept any reasonable response, such as an avalanche burying the animal or the animal falling into a crevasse in a glacier.)* **learning modality: kinesthetic**

Determining a Fossil's Age

Building Inquiry Skills: Problem Solving

Have students assume they are scientists who have excavated two fossil reptile skulls. Tell them that one skull was found 20 m below the surface and the other was found 30 m below the surface. Then ask: **Based on this information alone, what can you infer about the age of the two skulls?** *(The skull found nearer the surface is most likely younger than the skull found farther down in the ground.)* Urge students to draw a diagram to illustrate the problem and its solution. **learning modality: logical/mathematical**

Media and Technology

Concept Videotape Library
 Adventures, Tape 1, "Fossils"; "Mummification"

Answers to Self-Assessment

Caption Question

Figure 9 A buried fossil can become uncovered when running water cuts through sedimentary rock layers.

Checkpoint

The rock layers nearer the surface contain younger fossils.

Ongoing Assessment

Oral Presentation Call on students at random to describe how petrified fossils, molds, and casts form.

Integrating Chemistry

Reinforce students' understanding of absolute dating by calling their attention to Figure 10 and asking: **If the sample contains one eighth of the original amount of potassium-40, how old is it?** *(Three half-lives, or 3.9 billion years, old)* **What proportion of the same sample would be argon-40?** *(seven eighths)* **learning modality: logical/mathematical**

Sharpen your Skills

Calculating

Materials *calculator*
Time 10 minutes
Tips Remind students that for each half-life that passes, half of the sample will break down.
Expected Outcome Three half-lives will have gone by after 2,139 million years (2,139 ÷ 713 = 3). One-eighth ($\frac{1}{2} \times \frac{1}{2} \times \frac{1}{2}$) of the original 16-gram sample, or 2 grams, will remain after 2,139 million years.
Extend Explain that other radioactive elements have longer or shorter half-lives than potassium-40. Ask: **How does the length of an element's half-life relate to its usefulness for dating purposes?** *(Very old rocks can be dated using an element with a long half-life.)* **learning modality: logical/mathematical**

What Do Fossils Reveal?

Addressing Naive Conceptions

Explain that of the millions of extinct species, only a fraction of one percent are likely to have been preserved as fossils. Ask: **Which organisms are most likely to be found as fossils: those that lived when much of Earth was covered by shallow seas or those that lived when Earth's mountain ranges were being formed?** *(Those that lived when much of Earth was covered by shallow seas)* **learning modality: verbal**

Figure 10 The half-life of potassium-40, a radioactive element, is 1.3 billion years. This means that half of the potassium-40 in a sample will break down into argon-40 every 1.3 billion years. *Interpreting Charts If a sample contains one fourth of the original amount of potassium-40, how old is the sample?*

Decay of Potassium-40 (Half-life = 1.3 billion years)		
Time	**Amount of Potassium-40**	**Amount of Argon-40**
2.6 billion years ago	4 g	0 g
1.3 billion years ago	2 g	2 g
Present	1 g	3 g

Absolute Dating Another technique, called **absolute dating,** allows scientists to determine the actual age of fossils. The rocks that fossils are found near contain **radioactive elements,** unstable elements that decay, or break down, into different elements. The **half-life** of a radioactive element is the time it takes for half of the atoms in a sample to decay. Figure 10 shows how a sample of potassium-40, a radioactive element, breaks down into argon-40 over time.

Scientists can compare the amount of a radioactive element in a sample to the amount of the element into which it breaks down. As you can see in Figure 10, this information can be used to calculate the age of the rock, and thus the age of the fossil.

☑ *Checkpoint* What is a half-life?

What Do Fossils Reveal?

Like pieces in a jigsaw puzzle, fossils help scientists piece together information about Earth's past. The millions of fossils that scientists have collected are called the **fossil record.** The fossil record, however, is incomplete. Many organisms die without leaving fossils behind. Despite gaps in the fossil record, it has given scientists a lot of important information about past life on Earth.

Almost all of the species preserved as fossils are now extinct. A species is **extinct** if no members of that species are still alive. Most of what scientists know about extinct species is based on the fossil record. Scientists use fossils of bones and teeth to build models of extinct animals. Fossil footprints provide clues about how fast an animal could move and how tall it was.

Sharpen your Skills

Calculating

A radioactive element has a half-life of 713 million years. After 2,139 million years, how many half-lives will have gone by?

Calculate how much of a 16-gram sample of the element will remain after 2,139 million years.

Background

Facts and Figures Another element used in absolute dating is carbon-14. All plants and animals contain some radioactive carbon-14. As plants and animals grow, carbon atoms are added to their tissues. After the organism dies, no more carbon-14 is added and the carbon-14 in the organism's body decays. To determine the absolute age of a sample, scientists measure the amount of carbon-14 that is left in the organism's remains.

Carbon-14 has been used to date frozen mammoths and the skeletons of prehistoric humans, as well as pieces of wood and bone.

Carbon-14 is very useful in dating materials from plants and animals that lived up to about 50,000 years ago. Since carbon-14 has a half-life of only 5,730 years, it can't be used to date really ancient fossils or rocks. The amount of carbon-14 left would be too small to measure accurately.

The fossil record also provides clues about how and when new groups of organisms evolved. The first animals appeared in the seas about 540 million years ago. These animals included worms, sponges, and other invertebrates—animals without backbones. About 500 million years ago, fishes evolved. These early fishes were the first vertebrates—animals with backbones.

The first land plants, which were similar to mosses, evolved around 410 million years ago. Land plants gradually evolved strong stems that held them upright. These plants were similar to modern ferns and cone-bearing trees. Look at *Exploring Life's History* on pages 94 and 95 to see when other groups of organisms evolved.

The Geologic Time Scale

Using absolute dating, scientists have calculated the ages of many different fossils and rocks. From this information, scientists have created a "calendar" of Earth's history that spans more than 4.6 billion years. Scientists have divided this large time period into smaller units called eras and periods. This calendar of Earth's history is sometimes called the Geologic Time Scale.

The largest span of time in the Geologic Time Scale is Precambrian Time, also called the Precambrian (pree KAM bree un). It covers the first 4 billion years of Earth's history. Scientists know very little about the Precambrian because there are few fossils from these ancient times. After the Precambrian, the Geologic Time Scale is divided into three major blocks of time, or eras. Each era is further divided into shorter periods. In *Exploring Life's History,* you can see the events that occurred during each time period.

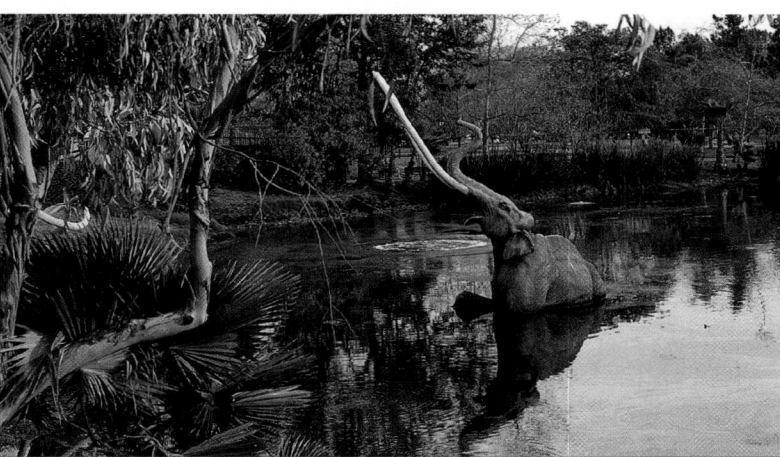

Figure 11 Complete skeletons of animals that lived thousands of years ago have been found in the Rancho La Brea tar pits in Los Angeles, California. The photo shows a model of an elephant-like animal. Scientists created the model based on information learned from the fossils.

Building Inquiry Skills: Interpreting Diagrams

Students are referred in the text to the *Exploring Life's History* on pages 94 and 95. Check that they are interpreting the diagram correctly and extracting the most important information from the feature by asking them the following series of questions: **When did the first amphibians evolve?** *(During the Devonian Period, about 380 million years ago)* **When did the earliest reptiles appear on Earth?** *(During the Carboniferous Period, about 320 million years ago)* **When did the first dinosaurs and mammals evolve?** *(In the Triassic Period, about 220 million years ago)* **When did the first birds appear?** *(During the Jurassic Period, about 150 million years ago)* **When did the first primates appear?** *(During the Tertiary Period, about 66 million years ago)* **When did humans evolve?** *(During the Quaternary Period, about 1.5 million years ago)* **learning modality: verbal**

The Geologic Time Scale

Including All Students

Support students who need more help in learning the names of the eras in the Geologic Time Scale by explaining the words' roots. The combining form *-zoic* comes from the Greek word for "life," *paleo-* from the Greek word for "ancient," *meso-* from the Greek word for "middle," and *ceno-* from the Greek word for "recent." After students have learned the meanings of the combining forms, check their understanding by asking: **What do the terms *Paleozoic, Mesozoic,* and *Cenozoic* mean?** *(Ancient life, middle life, and recent life, respectively)* **learning modality: verbal**

Media and Technology

Concept Videotape Library
Adventures, Tape 1, "Extinction"; "Geologic Time"

Answers to Self-Assessment

Caption Question

Figure 10 The sample is two half-lives, or 2.6 billion years, old.

Checkpoint

A half-life is the time it takes for half the atoms in a sample of a radioactive element to break down, or decay.

Ongoing Assessment

Skills Check Have students create a table that compares and contrasts relative and absolute dating.

Portfolio Students can save their tables in their portfolios.

The Geologic Time Scale, continued

EXPLORING
Life's History

Call students' attention to the feature and stress that the captions at the bottom summarize the important evolutionary events in each time period. Make sure that students understand the time line that runs across the top of the feature. Explain that the Precambrian actually covers most of Earth's *total* history, but because there were few living things during the Precambrian, it makes up very little of Earth's *life* history. Add that almost one-quarter of Earth's history passed before the first life forms appeared around 3.5 billion years ago. Inform students that the earliest life forms on Earth were confined to the water. Then ask: **When did the first land plants and animals appear on Earth?** *(During the Silurian Period, about 430 million years ago)* The amount of detail in the feature may overwhelm some students, so make sure you are clear about how much detail you expect them to learn. **learning modality: visual**

Building Inquiry Skills: Communicating

Challenge students to imagine that they are in a machine traveling back in time from the present to another period in Earth's history. Then have them write an eyewitness report, modeled on a television or newspaper story, relaying what they might observe in their time travels. In their report, they should address such questions as: **What would it be like to live during another time period? What type of organisms would you see? What familiar species of today would you not see?** Encourage students who need extra challenges to use outside sources in addition to *Exploring Life's History* for more information, such as descriptions of climate or land forms. Ask volunteers to share their reports with the rest of the class, and challenge other students to identify each time period as it is described in the reports. **learning modality: verbal**

EXPLORING Life's History

Take a trip through time to see how life on Earth has changed.

PRECAMBRIAN TIME The Precambrian covers about 87 percent of Earth's history.

4.6 billion years ago

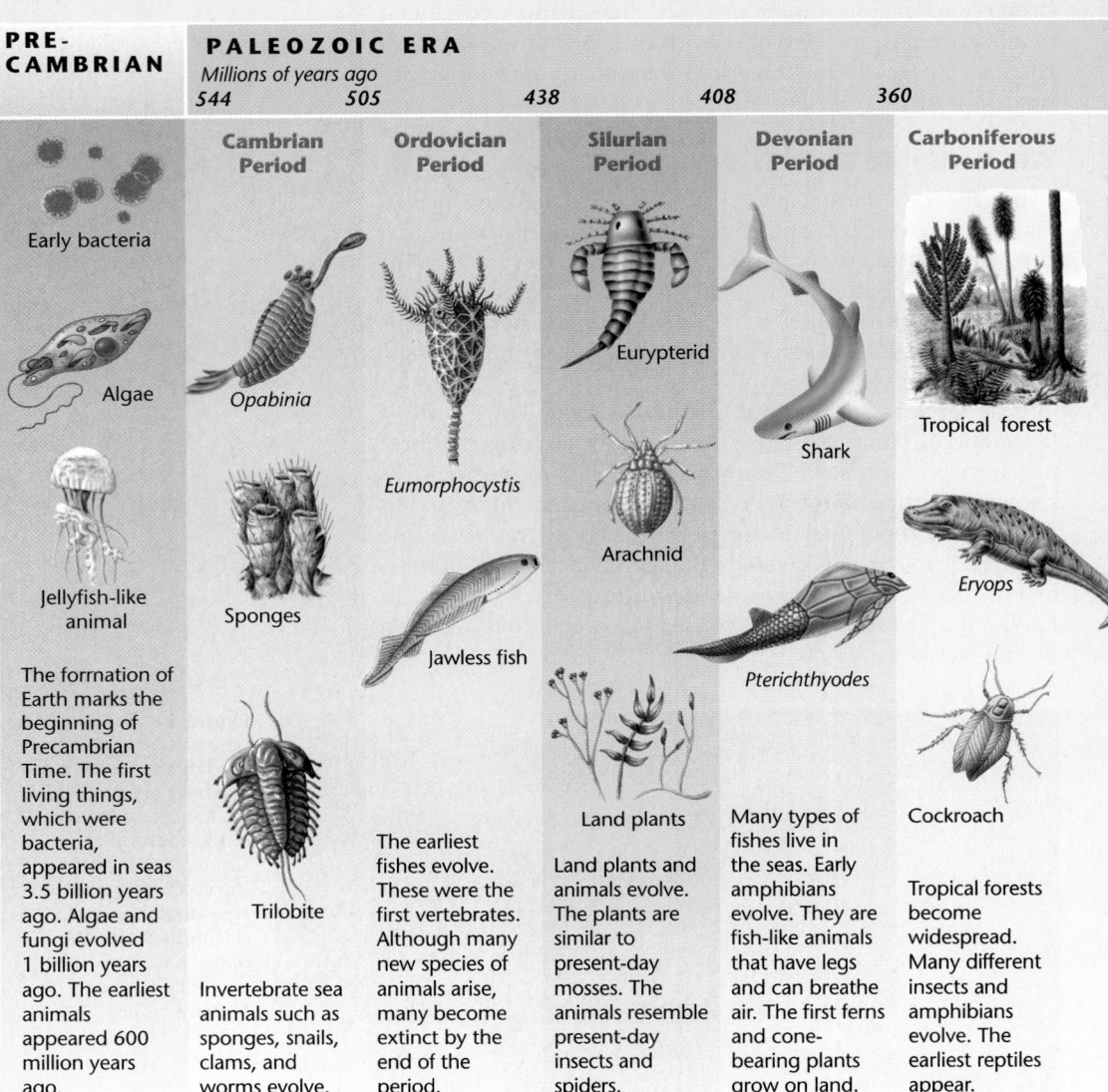

PRE-CAMBRIAN	PALEOZOIC ERA

Millions of years ago
544   505   438   408   360

Early bacteria

Algae

Jellyfish-like animal

The formation of Earth marks the beginning of Precambrian Time. The first living things, which were bacteria, appeared in seas 3.5 billion years ago. Algae and fungi evolved 1 billion years ago. The earliest animals appeared 600 million years ago.

Cambrian Period

Opabinia

Sponges

Trilobite

Invertebrate sea animals such as sponges, snails, clams, and worms evolve.

Ordovician Period

Eumorphocystis

Jawless fish

The earliest fishes evolve. These were the first vertebrates. Although many new species of animals arise, many become extinct by the end of the period.

Silurian Period

Eurypterid

Arachnid

Land plants

Land plants and animals evolve. The plants are similar to present-day mosses. The animals resemble present-day insects and spiders.

Devonian Period

Shark

Pterichthyodes

Many types of fishes live in the seas. Early amphibians evolve. They are fish-like animals that have legs and can breathe air. The first ferns and cone-bearing plants grow on land.

Carboniferous Period

Tropical forest

Eryops

Cockroach

Tropical forests become widespread. Many different insects and amphibians evolve. The earliest reptiles appear.

94

Background

Facts and Figures Scientists have concluded that there were mass extinctions at the end of the Cretaceous Period, including the extinction of the dinosaurs, but there is still debate about the cause. Many theories have been proposed, ranging from climatic changes to predators. In the early 1980s, scientists at the University of California proposed another theory—that a giant asteroid or comet struck Earth and sent so much dust into the atmosphere that it blocked sunlight for more than two years. This event would have greatly reduced photosynthesis and led to the collapse of food chains and to mass extinctions. This theory is based on direct evidence of a collision crater in the Yucatan and the presence at Cretaceous sites of the element iridium, rare on Earth but plentiful in asteroids.

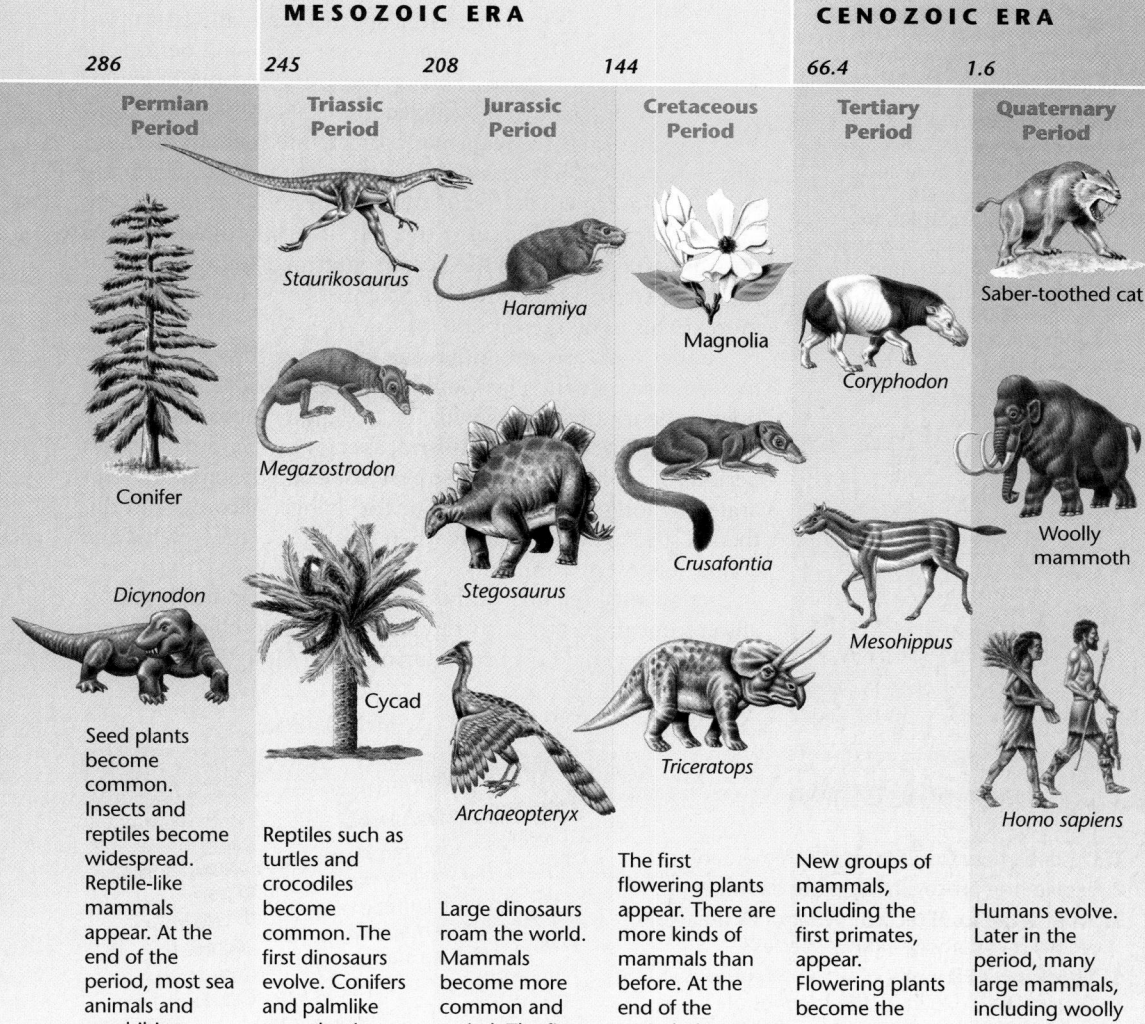

PALEOZOIC · MESOZOIC · CENOZOIC

544 million years ago   245 million years ago   66.4 million years ago

MESOZOIC ERA

286   245   208   144

CENOZOIC ERA

66.4   1.6

Permian Period

Conifer

Dicynodon

Seed plants become common. Insects and reptiles become widespread. Reptile-like mammals appear. At the end of the period, most sea animals and amphibians become extinct.

Triassic Period

Staurikosaurus

Megazostrodon

Cycad

Reptiles such as turtles and crocodiles become common. The first dinosaurs evolve. Conifers and palmlike trees dominate forests.

Jurassic Period

Haramiya

Stegosaurus

Archaeopteryx

Large dinosaurs roam the world. Mammals become more common and varied. The first birds appear.

Cretaceous Period

Magnolia

Crusafontia

Triceratops

The first flowering plants appear. There are more kinds of mammals than before. At the end of the period, dinosaurs become extinct.

Tertiary Period

Coryphodon

Mesohippus

New groups of mammals, including the first primates, appear. Flowering plants become the most common kind of plant.

Quaternary Period

Saber-toothed cat

Woolly mammoth

Homo sapiens

Humans evolve. Later in the period, many large mammals, including woolly mammoths, become extinct.

Chapter 3 **95**

Inquiry Challenge

Materials *poster board, dice, index cards, markers, small toys or other items for game tokens*
Time 30 minutes

 ACTIVITY

Divide the class into groups, and challenge each group to create a board game, called *A Trip Through Geologic Time,* to reinforce their knowledge of Earth's life history. The game board should start in the Precambrian and continue on to the present. To advance around the game board (and through time), players should be required to answer questions, perhaps written on chance cards, about each period. Escaping from carnivorous dinosaurs, skirting around treacherous tar pits, or avoiding similar relevant obstacles in particular time periods might be included on the game board to add excitement to the game and require students to apply more of the information from *Exploring Life's History.* After students have created their games, urge groups to exchange and play each other's games. **cooperative learning**

Including All Students

Materials *index cards*
Time 30 minutes

ACTIVITY

Pair students who are having difficulty or who are still mastering English with other students who have strong verbal skills. Then have the members of each pair work together to make flash cards for the periods of the Geologic Time Scale. On each card, they should include the dates for the period and the most important life history events. Challenge pairs to exchange flash cards and use them to quiz each other on the material. **limited English proficiency**

Ongoing Assessment

Oral Presentation Call on students at random to each describe an event in the evolution of plants or animals, based on the information in *Exploring Life's History.*

How Fast Does Evolution Occur?

Building Inquiry Skills: Inferring

Ask students: **Why are fossils of intermediate life forms likely to be rare if the theory of punctuated equilibria explains how evolution occurs?** *(The theory proposes that new species evolve rapidly over a short period of time, so the chances of fossils of intermediate species forming are greatly reduced.)* **learning modality: logical/mathematical**

3 Assess

Section 2 Review Answers

1. Most fossils form when organisms that die become buried in layers of sediment and the layers harden to become sedimentary rock.

2. Scientists compare the amount of a radioactive element in a sample to the amount of the element into which it breaks down and then calculate the age of the fossil based on the element's constant rate of decay.

3. The fossil record refers to the millions of fossils scientists have collected. It reveals how extinct species looked, behaved, and evolved.

4. Both theories attempt to explain the fossil record. Gradualism proposes that evolution occurs slowly and steadily. Punctuated equilibria proposes that evolution occurs during short periods of rapid change separated by long periods of little or no change.

Science at Home

Advise students to use mud that contains a lot of clay and enough water to make it the consistency of yogurt or pudding.

Performance Assessment

Skills Check Have students make a table to compare and contrast the theories of gradualism and punctuated equilibria.

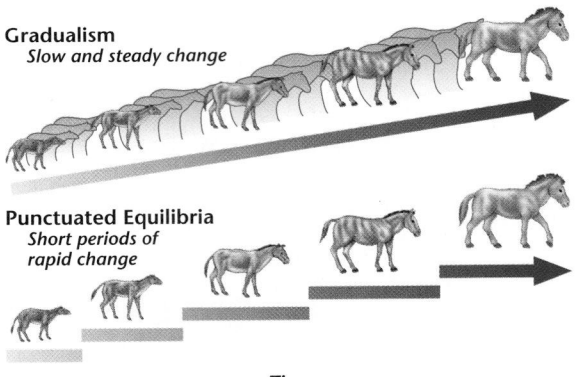

Gradualism
Slow and steady change

Punctuated Equilibria
Short periods of rapid change

Time

Figure 12 According to the theory of gradualism, new species of horses evolved slowly and continuously. Intermediate forms were common. According to punctuated equilibria, new species evolved rapidly during short periods of time. Intermediate forms were rare.

How Fast Does Evolution Occur?

Because the fossil record is incomplete, many questions about evolution remain unanswered. For example, scientists cannot always tell from the fossil record how quickly a particular species evolved.

One theory, called **gradualism,** proposes that evolution occurs slowly but steadily. According to this theory, tiny changes in a species gradually add up to major changes over very long periods of time. This is how Darwin thought evolution occurred.

If the theory of gradualism is correct, intermediate forms of all species should have existed. However, the fossil record often shows no intermediate forms for long periods of time. Then, quite suddenly, fossils appear that are distinctly different. One possible explanation for the lack of intermediate forms is that the fossil record is incomplete. Scientists may eventually find more fossils to fill the gaps.

Rather than assuming that the fossil record is incomplete, two scientists, Stephen Jay Gould and Niles Eldridge, have developed a theory that agrees with the fossil data. According to the theory of **punctuated equilibria,** species evolve during short periods of rapid change. These periods of rapid change are separated by long periods of little or no change. According to this theory, species evolve quickly when groups become isolated and adapt to new environments.

Today most scientists think that evolution can occur gradually at some times and fairly rapidly at others. Both forms of evolution seem to have occurred during Earth's long history.

Section 2 Review

1. Describe how fossils form in sedimentary rock.
2. Explain the process of absolute dating.
3. What is the fossil record? What does the fossil record reveal about extinct species?
4. **Thinking Critically** *Comparing and Contrasting* How are the theories of gradualism and punctuated equilibria similar? How are they different?

Science at Home

With an adult family member, spread some mud in a shallow flat-bottomed pan. Smooth the surface of the mud. Use your fingertips to make "footprints" across the mud. Let the mud dry and harden, so that the footprints become permanent. Explain to your family how this is similar to the way some fossils form.

Background

Facts and Figures Just how short are the periods of rapid change proposed by supporters of the punctuated equilibria theory? Generally, they are on the order of 50,000 to 100,000 years, which is very short indeed compared with the billions of years of the Geologic Time Scale. The best data in support of the theory come from the fossilized remains of invertebrates, or animals without backbones, such as snails.

Program Resources

◆ **Unit 1 Resources** 3-2 Review and Reinforce, p. 73; 3-2 Enrich, p. 74

SECTION 3 Other Evidence for Evolution

DISCOVER ··· ACTIVITY

How Can You Classify Species?

1. Collect six to eight different pens. Each pen will represent a different species of similar organisms.

2. Choose a trait that varies among your pen species, such as size or ink color. Using this trait, try to divide the pen species into two groups.

3. Now choose another trait. Divide each group into two smaller groups.

Think It Over
Classifying Which of the pen species share the most characteristics? What might the similarities suggest about how the pen species evolved?

Do you know anyone who has had their appendix out? The appendix is a tiny organ attached to the large intestine. You might think that having a part of the body removed might cause a problem. After all, you need your heart, lungs, stomach and other body parts to live. However, this is not the case with the appendix. In humans, the appendix does not seem to have much function. In some other species of mammals, though, the appendix is much larger and plays an important role in digestion. To scientists, this information about modern-day organisms provides clues about their ancestors and their relationships.

The appendix is just one example of how modern-day organisms can provide clues about evolution. By comparing organisms, scientists can infer how closely related the organisms are in an evolutionary sense. **Scientists compare body structures, development before birth, and DNA sequences to determine the evolutionary relationships among organisms.**

Similarities in Body Structure

Scientists long ago began to compare the body structures of living species to look for clues about evolution. In fact, this is how Darwin came to understand that evolution had occurred on the Galapagos Islands. An organism's body structure is its basic body plan, such as how its bones are arranged. Fishes, amphibians, reptiles, birds, and mammals, for example, all have a similar body

> ### GUIDE FOR READING
>
> ◆ What evidence from modern-day organisms can help scientists determine evolutionary relationships among groups?
>
> *Reading Tip* As you read, use the headings to make an outline about the different types of evidence for evolution.

Chapter 3 **97**

Program Resources

◆ **Unit 1 Resources** 3-3 Lesson Plan, p. 75; 3-3 Section Summary, p. 76
◆ **Guided Reading and Study Workbook** Section 3-3

Media and Technology

 Transparencies "Homologous Structures," Transparency 11

READING STRATEGIES

Reading Tip Suggest that students fill in their outline with details as they read the section. Sample outline (partial):
I   Other Evidence for Evolution
   A. Similarities in Body Structure
   B. Similarities in Early Development

SECTION 3 Other Evidence for Evolution

Objectives

After completing the lesson, students will be able to
◆ state evidence from modern-day organisms that scientists use to show evolutionary relationships among groups;
◆ describe how scientists classify organisms and place them on branching trees.

Key Terms homologous structure, branching tree

1 Engage/Explore

Activating Prior Knowledge

On the chalkboard write the following list: *horse, rabbit, zebra, squirrel, donkey, deer, chipmunk,* and *mouse.* Then ask: **Which animals would you group together based on their similarities?** (*Students are likely to place the horse, zebra, donkey, and deer in one group and the rabbit, squirrel, chipmunk, and mouse in another.*) Tell students that, in this section, they will see how scientists use similarities among living species to infer how the species evolved.

·········· DISCOVER ··········

Skills Focus classifying
Materials *6 to 8 pens*
Time 10 minutes
Tips Have extra pens to guarantee that each student has enough. Include pens that are somewhat different from each other.

Expected Outcome How students classify their pens will depend on their particular sample of pens and the traits they choose for classification.

Think It Over Students may say that the pen species that are most similar evolved from a common ancestor.

97

Similarities in Body Structure

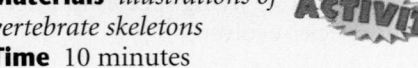
Sharpen your Skills

Drawing Conclusions

Time 5 minutes
Tips If students have difficulty identifying similarities between the crocodile's leg and the legs of the animals shown in Figure 13, advise them to focus on the number and arrangement of bones.

Expected Outcome Students are likely to say that crocodiles share a common ancestor with birds, dolphins, and dogs because of the similar structure of the bones in their legs.

Extend Ask: **What other animals do you think would have forelimbs similar in structure to those of crocodiles, birds, dolphins, and dogs?** (*Possible answers include any reptile, bird, or mammal.*) **learning modality: logical/mathematical**

Building Inquiry Skills: Observing

Materials *illustrations of vertebrate skeletons*
Time 10 minutes

Show students illustrations of skeletons from a variety of vertebrates, such as fish, reptiles, birds, and mammals. (Illustrations can be found in zoology and anatomy textbooks, as well as in general reference books such as encyclopedias.) Challenge students to compare the skeletal structures, then ask: **What evidence suggests that all of these animals share a common ancestor?** (*Students should point out ways that the skeletal structures are similar in the number and arrangement of bones. They should also explain how such similarities are used to infer evolutionary relationships.*) **learning modality: visual**

Sharpen your Skills

Drawing Conclusions

Look at the drawing below of the bones in a crocodile's leg. Compare this drawing to Figure 13. Do you think that crocodiles share a common ancestor with birds, dolphins, and dogs? Support your answer with evidence.

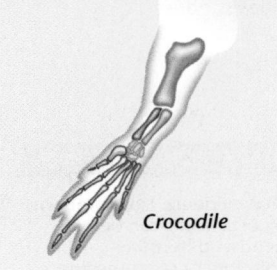
Crocodile

Figure 13 A bird's wing, dolphin's flipper, and dog's leg are all adapted to performing different tasks. However, the structure of the bones in each forelimb is very similar. These homologous structures provide evidence that these animals evolved from a common ancestor. *Observing What similarities in structure do the three forelimbs share?*

structure—an internal skeleton with a backbone. This is why scientists classify all five groups of animals together as vertebrates. Presumably, these groups all inherited these similarities in structure from an early vertebrate ancestor that they shared.

Look closely at the structure of the bones in the bird's wing, dolphin's flipper, and dog's leg shown in Figure 13. Notice that the bones in the forelimbs of these three animals are arranged in a similar way. These similarities provide evidence that these three organisms all evolved from a common ancestor. Similar structures that related species have inherited from a common ancestor are called **homologous structures** (hoh MAHL uh gus).

Sometimes scientists find fossil evidence that supports the evidence provided by homologous structures. For example, scientists have recently found fossils of ancient whale-like creatures. The fossils show that the ancestors of today's whales had legs and walked on land. This evidence supports other evidence that whales and humans share a common ancestor.

☑ *Checkpoint* *What information do homologous structures reveal?*

Similarities in Early Development

Scientists can also make inferences about evolutionary relationships by comparing the early development of different organisms. Suppose you were asked to compare an adult turtle, a chicken, and a rat. You would probably say they look quite different from each other. However, during early development, these three organisms go through similar stages, as you can see

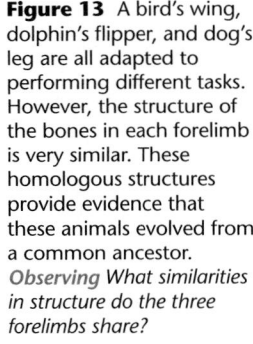
Bird

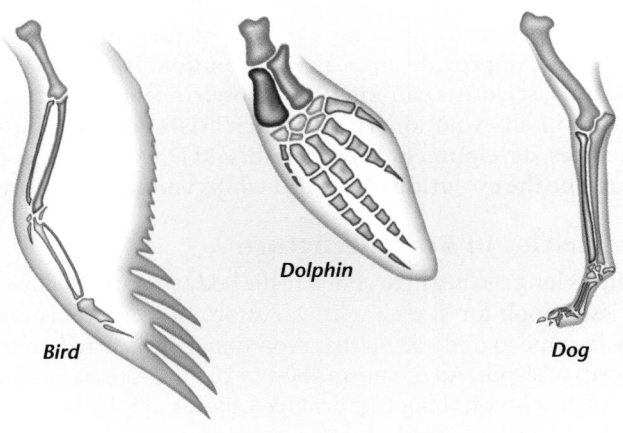
Dolphin

Dog

Background

Facts and Figures The system of classification based on homologous structures is believed to have been developed by Carolus Linnaeus, the eighteenth century Swedish botanist who developed the taxonomic system for classifying living things that is still in use today. Based on homologous structures, humans are classified as primates along with monkeys and apes, and lions are classified as cats

along with tigers and leopards.

Sometimes species have similar structures that reflect parallel adaptations but not a common ancestor. Such structures are called analogous structures. A good example is the wing of a bird and the wing of a butterfly. The wings of both animals perform the same function, but their internal structures are quite different because the animals evolved from different ancestors.

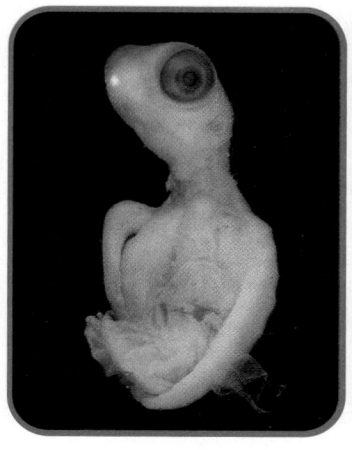 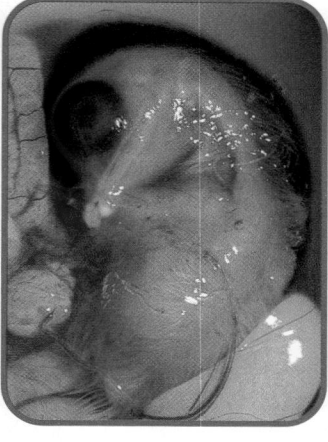 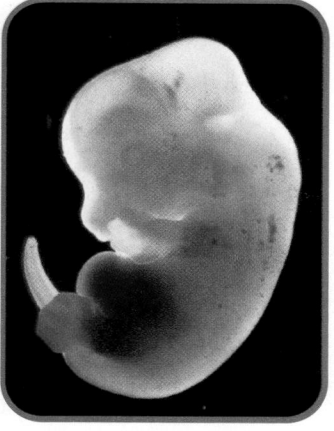

in Figure 14. For example, during the early stages of development all three organisms have a tail and tiny gill slits in their throats. These similarities suggest that these three vertebrate species are related and share a common ancestor.

When scientists study early development more closely, they notice that the turtle appears more similar to the chicken than it does to the rat. This evidence supports the conclusion that turtles are more closely related to chickens than they are to rats.

Figure 14 Turtles (left), chickens (center), and rats (right) look similar during the earliest stages of development. These similarities provide evidence that these three animals evolved from a common ancestor.

Similarities in DNA

Why do related species have similar body structures and development patterns? Scientists infer that the species inherited many of the same genes from a common ancestor. Recently, scientists have begun to compare the genes of different species to determine how closely related the species are.

Recall that genes are made of DNA. By comparing the sequence of nitrogen bases in the DNA of different species, scientists can infer how closely related the species are. The more similar the sequences, the more closely related the species are.

Recall also that the DNA bases along a gene specify what type of protein will be produced. Thus, scientists can also compare the order of amino acids in a protein to see how closely related two species are.

Sometimes DNA evidence does not confirm earlier conclusions about relationships between species. For example, aside from its long nose, the tiny elephant shrew looks very similar to rodents such as mice. Because of this, biologists used to think that the elephant shrew was closely related to rodents. But when scientists compared DNA from elephant shrews to that of both

Chapter 3 **99**

Media and Technology

 Concept Videotape Library
Adventures, Tape 1, "Primate Evolution"

Answers to Self-Assessment

☑ *Checkpoint*
Homologous structures reveal that organisms share a common ancestor.

Caption Question
Figure 13 The three forelimbs share a similar number and arrangement of bones.

Similarities in Early Development

Using the Visuals: Figure 14
Challenge students to detect ways that the three embryos are similar and different. *(Similarities might include tails and a curved shape; differences might include shape of head and body.)* Point out that scientists have concluded, on the basis of such similarities and differences, that turtles are more closely related to chickens than to rats. Then ask: **In what ways do the turtle and chicken appear to be more similar than the turtle and rat?** *(Students may say that the turtle and chicken both have large eyes and a pointed mouth.)* **learning modality: visual**

Similarities in DNA

Inquiry Challenge
Challenge pairs of students to draw short sections of DNA base sequences for three hypothetical related species to illustrate how DNA similarities can be used to infer evolutionary relationships. Remind students that there are four bases in DNA: adenine, thymine, guanine, and cytosine, which they can abbreviate as A, T, G, and C, respectively. After students have finished their drawings, urge volunteers to share their work with the class. Have other students try to infer from the DNA base sequences how the three species are related. *(They should infer that the more similar the DNA base sequences, the more closely related the species.)* Conclude by asking: **How do you think the amino acid sequences in the proteins of the three species would compare? Why?** *(Students should say that the amino acid sequences in the proteins would reflect the same evolutionary relationships as the DNA base sequences. This is because the amino acid sequences are encoded in the DNA.)* **learning modality: logical/mathematical**

Ongoing Assessment

Oral Presentation Call on students at random to describe the three kinds of similarities in living species that scientists use to reconstruct evolutionary relationships.

99

Similarities in DNA, continued

Integrating Technology

Encourage students to think about how recent advances in DNA technology may affect the way scientists study evolutionary relationships. Ask: **What can scientists learn from fossil DNA that they could not learn by studying the physical structure of the fossils?** *(DNA provides more direct evidence of genetic relationships.)* **Will the ability to extract DNA from fossils mean that scientists will no longer have to compare living species in order to reconstruct evolutionary relationships?** *(The fossil record is incomplete, so being able to extract DNA from fossils will not add any new information about many extinct species. Therefore, scientists will still have to compare living species to reconstruct evolutionary relationships.)* **learning modality: logical/mathematical**

Combining the Evidence

Building Inquiry Skills: Interpreting Data

Time 10 minutes

ACTIVITY

Have students interpret data to infer how three hypothetical species—A, B, and C—are related. First tell students that A and C appear to be more similar in body structure than A and B or B and C. Then tell students that A and B appear to be more similar in their early development than A and C or B and C. Finally, tell students that the DNA base sequences of A and B are more similar than the DNA base sequences of A and C or B and C. After providing students with this information, challenge them to combine and weigh the evidence. Then ask: **What are the evolutionary relationships among the three species?** *(Species A and B are more closely related to each other than either species is related to species C because of the similarities in their early development and DNA.)* Challenge students to draw a branching tree to illustrate the evolutionary relationships among the three species. **learning modality: logical/mathematical**

Figure 15 Because of its appearance, the tiny elephant shrew was thought to be closely related to mice and other rodents. Surprisingly, DNA comparisons showed that the elephant shrew is actually more closely related to elephants.

rodents and elephants, they got a surprise. The elephant shrew's DNA was more similar to the elephant's DNA than it was to the rodent's DNA. Scientists now think that elephant shrews are more closely related to elephants than to rodents.

INTEGRATING TECHNOLOGY Recently, scientists have developed techniques that allow them to extract, or remove, DNA from fossils. Using these techniques, scientists have now extracted DNA from fossils of bones, teeth, and plants, and from insects trapped in amber. The DNA from fossils has provided scientists with new evidence about evolution.

Combining the Evidence

Scientists have combined evidence from fossils, body structures, early development, and DNA and protein sequences to determine the evolutionary relationships among species. In most cases, DNA and protein sequences have confirmed conclusions based on earlier evidence. For example, recent DNA comparisons show that dogs are more similar to wolves than they are to coyotes. Scientists had already reached this conclusion based on similarities in the structure and development of these three species.

Another example of how scientists combined evidence from different sources is shown in the branching tree in Figure 16. A **branching tree** is a diagram that shows how scientists think different groups of organisms are related. Based on similar body structures, lesser pandas were thought to be closely related to giant pandas. The two panda species also resemble both bears and raccoons. Until recently, scientists were not sure how these four groups were related. DNA analysis and other methods have shown that giant pandas and lesser pandas are not closely related. Instead, giant pandas are more closely related to bears, while lesser pandas are more closely related to raccoons.

Background

Integrating Science Similarities and differences in DNA base sequences are assessed using a technique called DNA hybridization. In this technique, double strands of DNA from two different species are separated and then recombined into a new molecule called hybrid DNA. The

genetic similarity of the two species is then measured by calculating the number of base pairs that do not match along the hybrid sequence, that is, pairs in which adenine is not matched with thymine or cytosine is not matched with guanine.

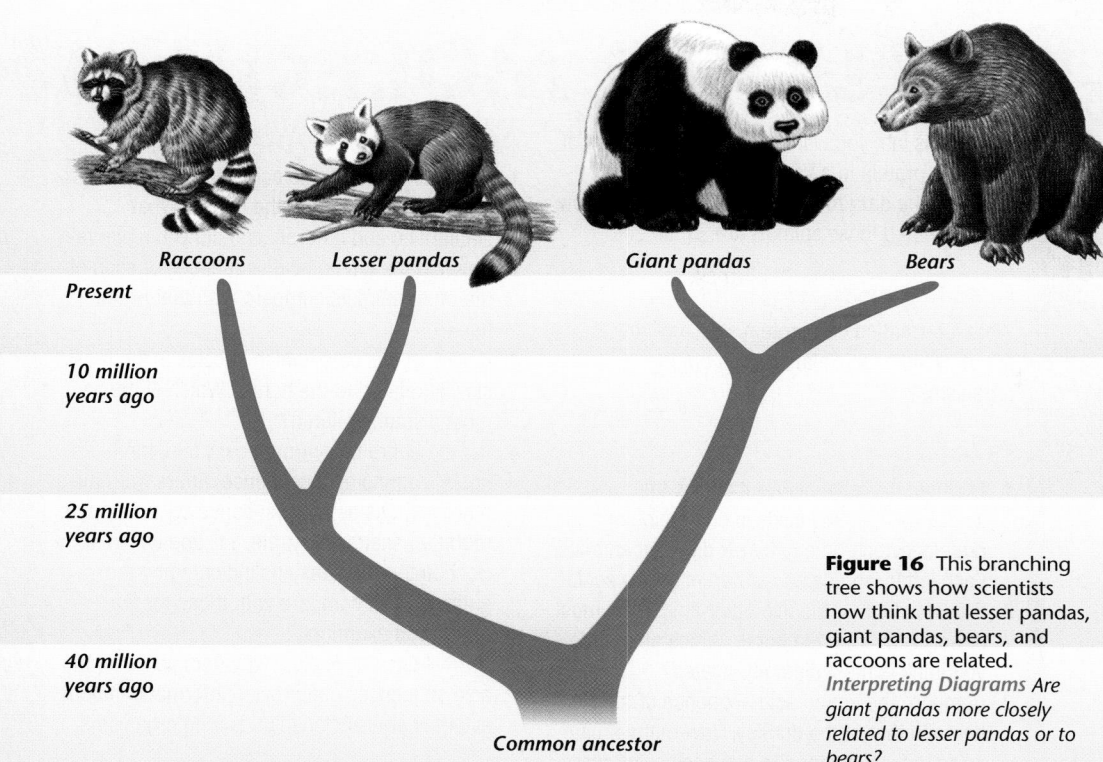

Raccoons   Lesser pandas   Giant pandas   Bears

Present

10 million years ago

25 million years ago

40 million years ago

Common ancestor

Figure 16 This branching tree shows how scientists now think that lesser pandas, giant pandas, bears, and raccoons are related. *Interpreting Diagrams Are giant pandas more closely related to lesser pandas or to bears?*

Using the Visuals: Figure 16

Reinforce students' understanding of branching trees and evolutionary relationships. Ask: **When did giant pandas and bears evolve from their common ancestor?** *(About 10 million years ago)* **When did raccoons and lesser pandas evolve from their common ancestor?** *(About 25 million years ago)* **Which are more closely related, raccoons and lesser pandas, or giant pandas and bears?** *(Giant pandas and bears)* **learning modality: visual**

3 Assess

Section 3 Review Answers

1. Similarities in body structure, similarities in early development, and similarities in DNA base sequences
2. Similar structures that related species have inherited from a common ancestor
3. Scientists learned that these animals evolved from a common ancestor.
4. You would expect the base sequences to be very similar.
5. DNA similarities are the most direct indicator that species inherited their genes from a common ancestor.

Check Your Progress

CHAPTER PROJECT 3

Review each group's first time line, and offer comments before the group starts its second time line. Make sure students understand that because the second time line is an enlargement of one section of the first time line, its scale will be different. Distribute Worksheet 2, which lists additional evolutionary events not in the text. Provide source materials for students to use.

Section 3 Review

1. Name three types of evidence from modern-day organisms that scientists use to determine evolutionary relationships.
2. What are homologous structures?
3. What information did scientists learn by comparing the early developmental stages of turtles, chickens, and rats?
4. If two species are closely related, what would you expect a comparison of their DNA base sequences to reveal?
5. **Thinking Critically Making Judgments** Most scientists today consider similarities in DNA to be the best indicator of how closely two species are related. Why do you think this is the case?

Check Your Progress

CHAPTER PROJECT 3

You should be completing construction of the time line that covers 5 billion years. Now begin work on the time line showing 600 million years. This version is a magnified view of one part of the first time line. It will give you additional space to show what happened in the more recent years of Earth's history. (*Hint:* Prepare drawings to show how life forms on Earth were changing. Also, try to include three or more events not mentioned in the text.)

Program Resources

◆ **Unit 1 Resources** 3-3 Review and Reinforce, p. 77; 3-3 Enrich, p. 78

Answers to Self-Assessment

Caption Question

Figure 16 Giant pandas are more closely related to bears than to lesser pandas.

Performance Assessment

Drawing Have students draw a branching tree that shows how dogs, wolves, and coyotes are related. *(Students' drawings should show that dogs and wolves shared a common ancestor more recently than either species did with coyotes.)*

Telltale Molecules

Preparing for Inquiry

Key Concept The more similar the amino acid sequence in proteins of different species, the more closely the species are related.

Skills Objectives Students will be able to
- interpret data on amino acid sequences in proteins;
- compare and contrast amino acid sequences in the same protein for different species;
- draw conclusions about how the species are related based on the amino acid comparisons.

Time 30 minutes

Advance Planning You may need to review with students what they learned about protein synthesis in Chapter 1.

Alternative Materials You may want to provide students with copies of tables comparing actual amino acid sequences from a genetics textbook to show how similar the data in the lab are to data scientists actually use to reconstruct evolutionary relationships.

Guiding Inquiry

Invitation Ask students: **What is a genetic code?** *(It is the order of the nitrogen bases along a gene.)* **How do cells use a genetic code to make proteins?** *(The nitrogen bases code for the production of specific amino acids, which are the building blocks of proteins.)* **What are genes made of?** *(DNA)*

Introducing the Procedure

- Have students read the entire lab, then ask: **What is the objective of this lab activity?** *(To use the amino acid sequence of a protein to determine the evolutionary relationship among several animals)* **What do the letters in the table represent?** *(Each letter represents a different amino acid.)*
- Suggest that students create a table to record the number of differences between the horse and each of the other animals.

TELLTALE MOLECULES

In this lab, you will compare the structure of one protein in a variety of animals. You'll use the data to draw conclusions about how closely related those animals are.

Problem

What information can protein structure reveal about evolutionary relationships among organisms?

Procedure

1. Examine the table below. It shows the sequence of amino acids in one region of a protein, cytochrome c, for six different animals. Each letter represents a different amino acid.
2. Predict which of the five other animals is most closely related to the horse. Which animal do you think is most distantly related?
3. Compare the amino acid sequence of the horse to that of the donkey. How many amino acids differ between the two species? Record that number in your notebook.
4. Compare the amino acid sequences of each of the other animals to that of the horse. Record the number of differences in your notebook.

Analyze and Conclude

1. Which animal's amino acid sequence was most similar to that of the horse? What similarities and difference(s) did you observe?
2. How did the amino acid sequences of each of the other animals compare with that of the horse?
3. Based on this data, which species is the most closely related to the horse? Which is the most distantly related?
4. For the entire cytochrome c protein, the horse's amino acid sequence differs from the other animals as follows: donkey, 1 difference; rabbit, 6; snake, 22; turtle, 11; and whale, 5. How do the relationships indicated by the entire protein compare with those for the region you examined?
5. **Think About It** Explain why data about amino acid sequences can provide information about evolutionary relationships among organisms.

More to Explore

Use the amino acid data to construct a branching tree that includes horses, donkeys, and snakes. The tree should show one way that the three species could have evolved from a common ancestor.

Section of Cytochrome c Protein in Animals															
Animal	Amino Acid Position														
	39	40	41	42	43	44	45	46	47	48	49	50	51	52	53
Horse	A	B	C	D	E	F	G	H	I	J	K	L	M	N	O
Donkey	A	B	C	D	E	F	G	H	Z	J	K	L	M	N	O
Rabbit	A	B	C	D	E	Y	G	H	Z	J	K	L	M	N	O
Snake	A	B	C	D	E	Y	G	H	Z	J	K	W	M	N	O
Turtle	A	B	C	D	E	V	G	H	Z	J	K	U	M	N	O
Whale	A	B	C	D	E	Y	G	H	Z	J	K	L	M	N	O

Troubleshooting the Experiment

- Make sure students understand how to read the table correctly before they compare the different species.

Expected Outcome

Students should infer from the amino acid comparisons which species are most closely related and which are least closely related to the horse.

Program Resources

- **Unit 1 Resources** Skills Lab blackline masters, pp. 82–83

Media and Technology

 Lab Activity Videotape
Tape 1

Darwin's Voyage

Key Ideas

◆ Darwin thought that species gradually changed over many generations as they became better adapted to new conditions. This process is called evolution.

◆ Darwin's observations led him to propose that evolution occurs through natural selection. Natural selection occurs due to overproduction, competition, and variations.

◆ Only traits controlled by genes can change over time as a result of natural selection.

◆ If a group of individuals remains separated from the rest of its species long enough to evolve different traits, a new species can form.

Key Terms

species	evolution	natural selection
adaptation	scientific theory	variation

 The Fossil Record

INTEGRATING EARTH SCIENCE

Key Ideas

◆ Most fossils form when organisms die and sediments bury them. The sediments harden, preserving parts of the organisms.

◆ Relative dating determines which of two fossils is older and which is younger. Absolute dating determines the actual age of a fossil.

◆ Fossils help scientists understand how extinct organisms looked and evolved.

◆ The Geologic Time Scale shows when during Earth's 4.6-billion-year history major groups of organisms evolved.

◆ Evolution has occurred gradually at some times and fairly rapidly at other times.

Key Terms

fossil	radioactive element
sedimentary rock	half-life
petrified fossil	fossil record
mold	extinct
cast	gradualism
relative dating	punctuated equilibria
absolute dating	

Other Evidence for Evolution

Key Ideas

◆ By comparing modern-day organisms, scientists can infer how closely related they are in an evolutionary sense.

◆ Homologous structures can provide evidence of how species are related and of how they evolved from a common ancestor.

◆ Similarities in early developmental stages are evidence that species are related and shared a common ancestor.

◆ Scientists can compare DNA and protein sequences to determine more precisely how species are related.

◆ A branching tree is a diagram that shows how scientists think different groups of organisms are related.

Key Terms
homologous structure
branching tree

Organizing Information

Flowchart Copy the flowchart about natural selection onto a separate sheet of paper. Complete the flowchart by writing a sentence describing each factor that leads to natural selection. Then add a title. (For more on flowcharts, see the Skills Handbook.)

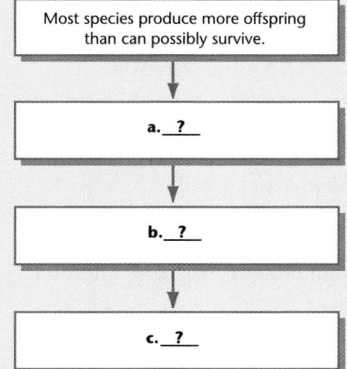

Analyze and Conclude

1. The donkey's amino acid sequence was most similar to that of the horse, differing only in the amino acid in position 47.

2. The rabbit and whale differed from the horse in two amino acids. The snake and turtle differed from the horse in three amino acids.

3. Based on this data, the donkey is most closely related to the horse and the turtle and snake are least closely related to the horse.

4. The relationships indicated by the entire protein are similar to the relationships indicated by the region of the protein examined in the lab.

5. As two or more species evolve from a common ancestor, their DNA may undergo different mutations, causing changes in the amino acids making up common proteins. The fewer differences in the amino acids, the more closely the given species are related.

Extending the Inquiry

More to Explore Students' branching trees should show that the horse and donkey have the most recent common ancestor and that the horse and snake have the most distant common ancestor.

Organizing Information

Flowchart *Sample title:* How Natural Selection Works

a. Since food and other resources are limited, the offspring must compete with each other to survive.

b. The offspring will have variations that make some of them better adapted to their environment.

c. Better adapted offspring are more likely to survive and reproduce, and after many generations more members of the species will have the adaptive variations.

Program Resources

◆ **Unit 1 Resources** Chapter 3 Project Scoring Rubric, p. 66

◆ **Performance Assessment** Chapter 3, pp. 10–12

◆ **Chapter Tests** Chapter 3 Test, pp. 11–14

Media and Technology

 Computer Test Bank
Chapter 3 Test

Reviewing Content

Multiple Choice

1. b 2. b 3. b 4. c 5. c

True or False

6. true 7. true 8. true
9. absolute dating 10. true

Checking Concepts

11. The overproduction of offspring leads to competition in which only the better adapted organisms survive and reproduce.

12. Examples will vary. *Sample answer:* A large number of turtles are born every year but only a few will be able to swim fast enough to escape predators. Because being able to swim faster makes the turtles more likely to survive and reproduce, natural selection leads to an increase through time in the fast-swimming trait.

13. Fossils found in layers of rock nearer the surface are younger than fossils found in deeper layers.

14. According to the theory of punctuated equilibria, the fossil record includes very few intermediate forms because new species evolve so rapidly that there is very little chance that such intermediate forms will be preserved as fossils.

15. Related species inherit the same basic developmental plan from their common ancestor.

16. Students' questions and answers will vary, but they should demonstrate clearly that students understand Darwin's theory of evolution by natural selection.

Thinking Critically

17. The islands were characterized by a great diversity of species that had developed different adaptations.

18. Natural selection would favor members of the species that were better adapted to the new climate. For example, in a species of mammal, a colder climate might lead to natural selection for animals with thicker fur.

19. Geographic isolation prevents mating between members of the isolated population and the rest of the species. This, in turn, allows natural selection to lead to the evolution of different traits in the isolated population.

Reviewing Content

Multiple Choice

Choose the letter of the best answer.

1. Changes in a species over long periods of time are called
   a. relative dating.
   b. evolution.
   c. homologous structures.
   d. developmental stages.

2. A trait that helps an organism survive and reproduce is called a(n)
   a. variation.   b. adaptation.
   c. species.   d. selection.

3. The type of fossil formed when an organism dissolves and leaves an empty space in a rock is called a
   a. cast.   b. mold.
   c. trace.   d. petrified fossil.

4. The rate of decay of a radioactive element is measured by its
   a. year.   b. era.
   c. half-life.   d. period.

5. Which of these is *not* used as evidence for evolution?
   a. DNA sequences
   b. stages of development
   c. body size
   d. body structures

True or False

If the statement is true, write true. If it is false, change the underlined word or words to make the statement true.

6. Darwin's idea about how evolution occurs is called <u>natural selection</u>.

7. Most members of a species show differences, or <u>variations</u>.

8. A footprint of an extinct dinosaur is an example of a <u>fossil</u>.

9. The technique of <u>relative dating</u> can be used to determine the actual age of a fossil.

10. <u>Homologous structures</u> are similar structures in related organisms.

Checking Concepts

11. What role does the overproduction of offspring play in the process of natural selection?

12. Use an example to explain how natural selection can lead to evolution.

13. How are rock layers used to determine the relative ages of fossils?

14. According to the theory of punctuated equilibria, why does the fossil record include very few intermediate forms?

15. Explain why similarities in the early development of different species suggest that the species are related.

16. **Writing to Learn** You are a young reporter for a local newspaper near the home of Charles Darwin. You have been asked to interview Darwin about his theory of evolution. Write three questions that you would ask Darwin. Then choose one question and answer it as Darwin would have.

Thinking Critically

17. **Applying Concepts** Why did Darwin's visit to the Galapagos Islands have such an important influence on his development of the theory of evolution by natural selection?

18. **Predicting** Predict how an extreme change in climate might affect natural selection in a species.

19. **Relating Cause and Effect** What is the role of geographic isolation in the formation of new species?

20. **Comparing and Contrasting** How does relative dating differ from absolute dating?

21. **Applying Concepts** A seal's flipper and a human arm have very different functions. What evidence might scientists look for to determine whether both structures evolved from the forelimb of a common ancestor?

20. Relative dating determines which of two fossils is older and which is younger based on their relative positions in layers of sedimentary rock. Absolute dating determines the actual age of fossils in years based on the amount of decay of radioactive elements in the fossils.

21. Scientists might look for evidence that the structures are homologous, for example, whether they have the same number and arrangement of bones.

Applying Skills

22. Based on the positions of the fossils in the rock layers, B is the youngest, C is intermediate in age, and A is the oldest.

23. Based on the carbon-14 and nitrogen data, A is 17,190 years old, B is 5,730 years old, and C is 11,460 years old.

24. Students should say that the answers based on the two methods of dating are in agreement.

Applying Skills

Radioactive carbon-14 decays to nitrogen with a half-life of 5,730 years. Use this information and the table below to answer Questions 22–24.

Fossil	Amount of Carbon-14 in Fossil	Amount of Nitrogen in Fossil	Position of Fossil in Rock Layers
A	1 gram	7 grams	bottom layer
B	4 grams	4 grams	top layer
C	2 grams	6 grams	middle layer

22. Inferring Use the positions of the fossils in the rock layers to put the fossils in order from youngest to oldest.

23. Calculating Calculate the age of each fossil using the data about carbon-14 and nitrogen.

24. Drawing Conclusions Do your answers to Questions 22 and 23 agree or disagree with each other? Explain.

Performance CHAPTER PROJECT 3 Assessment

Project Wrap Up Display your completed time lines for the class. Be prepared to explain why you chose the scale that you did. Also, describe how your time lines are related to each other.

Reflect and Record In your notebook, describe how the time lines helped you understand the long periods involved in the evolution of life. Were you surprised to see how far apart some of the events were? What surprised you the most? What did making two time lines enable you to see that you might have missed with only one?

Test Preparation

Use these questions to prepare for standardized tests.

Use the illustration to answer Questions 25–28.

25. What is the best title for this illustration?
  a. Plant Growth Over Time
  b. Branching Tree of Plant Evolution
  c. Mosses and Ferns, the Oldest Plants
  d. Flowering Plants, the Youngest Plants

26. About how long ago did mosses evolve?
  a. 100 million years ago
  b. 150 million years ago
  c. 350 million years ago
  d. 450 million years ago

27. Which group of plants would have DNA that is most similar to the DNA of flowering plants?
  a. mosses
  b. ferns
  c. conifers
  d. They would all be equally alike.

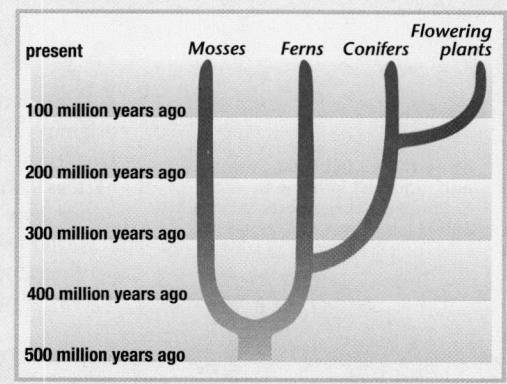

28. Which group of plants would have DNA that is least similar to the DNA of flowering plants?
  a. mosses
  b. ferns
  c. conifers
  d. They would all be equally alike.

Performance CHAPTER PROJECT 3 Assessment

Project Wrap Up Give each group an opportunity to show its two time lines to the rest of the class, describe how the models were made, and explain how the second time line relates to the first time line. Ask each group to point out any evolutionary events that were not included in the textbook's time line. Encourage the rest of the class to ask questions.

Reflect and Record Students' responses to these questions will vary, but students should realize that making a second time line for the past 600 millions years allowed them to see the time spans and placements of evolutionary events much more clearly. Let students share their ideas in a class discussion.

Test Preparation

25. b **26.** d **27.** c **28.** a

Program Resources

◆ **Inquiry Skills Activity Book** Provides teaching and review of all inquiry skills
◆ **Prentice Hall Assessment System** Provides standardized test practice
◆ **Reading in the Content Area** Provides strategies to improve science reading skills
◆ **Teacher's ELL Handbook** Provides multiple strategies for English language learners

Dogs—Loyal Companions

This interdisciplinary feature presents the central theme of dogs and the traits of various breeds that make them similar and different by connecting four different disciplines: science, social studies, language arts, and mathematics. The four explorations are designed to capture students' interest and help them see how the content they are studying in science relates to other school subjects and to real-world events. The unit is particularly suitable for team teaching.

1 Engage/Explore

Activating Prior Knowledge

Help students recall what they learned in Chapter 1, Genetics: The Science of Heredity, by asking questions such as: **How are traits inherited from parent to offspring?** *(The alleles of genes are carried from parents to their offspring on chromosomes.)* **Why do offspring sometimes look different from parents?** *(Offspring inherit different combinations of alleles from parents so they might express a trait controlled by a recessive allele that is masked in the parents or inherit a trait controlled by a dominant allele that is expressed in one parent, but not the other.)*

Introducing the Unit

Invite students who own dogs to share the characteristics of their dogs with the class. Separately list on the board each dog's characteristics, and have students compare the characteristics of each dog. Ask: **How are these dogs different?** *(Differences might include size, temperament, length and color of fur, type of ears, and length of tail.)* **What causes these differences?** *(The combination of alleles that each dog inherited from its parents)*

DOGS
LOYAL COMPANIONS

WHAT'S YOUR IMAGE OF A DOG?

- ✦ A small, floppy-eared spaniel?
- ✦ A large, powerful Great Dane?
- ✦ A protective German shepherd guide dog?
- ✦ A shaggy sheepdog?
- ✦ A tiny, lively Chihuahua?
- ✦ A friendly, lovable mutt?

The gray wolf is the ancestor of most modern breeds of dogs.

More than 3,000 years ago, an artist in ancient Egypt drew three dogs chasing a hyena. ▼

Most dogs are descendants of the gray wolf, which was originally found throughout Europe, Asia, and North America. Dogs were the first animals to be domesticated, or tamed. As far back as 9,000 years ago, farmers who raised sheep, cattle, and goats tamed dogs to herd and guard the livestock.

After taming dogs, people began to breed them for traits that people valued. Early herding dogs helped shepherds. Speedy hunting dogs learned to chase deer and other game. Strong, sturdy working dogs pulled sleds and even rescued people. Small, quick terriers hunted animals, such as rats. "Toy" dogs were companions to people of wealth and leisure. More recently, sporting dogs were trained to flush out and retrieve birds. Still others were bred to be guard dogs. But perhaps the real reason people bred dogs was for their loyalty and companionship.

106

Program Resources

◆ **Unit 1 Resources** Interdisciplinary Exploration, Science, pp. 84–86; Social Studies, pp. 87–89; Language Arts, pp. 90–92; Mathematics, pp. 93–95

From Wolf to Purebred

About ten thousand years ago, some wolves may have been attracted to human settlements. They may have found it easier to feed on food scraps than to hunt for themselves. Gradually the wolves came to depend on people for food. The wolves, in turn, kept the campsites clean and safe. They ate the garbage and barked to warn of approaching strangers. These wolves were the ancestors of the dogs you know today.

Over time dogs became more and more a part of human society. People began to breed dogs for the traits needed for tasks such as herding sheep and hunting. Large, aggressive dogs, for example, were bred to be herding dogs, while fast dogs with a keen sense of smell were bred to be hunting dogs. Today there are hundreds of breeds. They range from the tiny Chihuahua to the massive Saint Bernard, one of which can weigh as much as fifty Chihuahuas.

Today, people breed dogs mostly for their appearance and personality. Physical features such as long ears or a narrow snout are valued in particular breeds of dogs. To create "pure" breeds of dogs, breeders use a method known as inbreeding. Inbreeding involves mating dogs that are genetically very similar. Inbreeding is the surest way to produce dogs with a uniform physical appearance.

One undesirable result of inbreeding is an increase in genetic disorders. Experts estimate that 25 percent of all purebred dogs have a genetic disorder. Dalmatians, for example, often inherit deafness. German shepherds may develop severe hip problems. Mixed-breed dogs, in contrast, are less likely to inherit genetic disorders.

In Labrador retrievers, the allele for dark-colored fur is dominant over the allele for yellow fur.

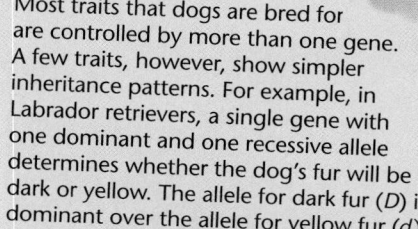

Science Activity

Most traits that dogs are bred for are controlled by more than one gene. A few traits, however, show simpler inheritance patterns. For example, in Labrador retrievers, a single gene with one dominant and one recessive allele determines whether the dog's fur will be dark or yellow. The allele for dark fur (*D*) is dominant over the allele for yellow fur (*d*).

- Construct a Punnett square for a cross between 2 Labrador retrievers that are both heterozygous for dark fur (*Dd*).

- Suppose there were 8 puppies in the litter. Predict how many would have dark fur and how many would have yellow fur.

- Construct a second Punnett square for a cross between a Labrador retriever with yellow fur (*dd*) and one with dark fur (*Dd*). In a litter with 6 puppies, predict how many would have dark fur and how many would have yellow fur.

107

2 Facilitate

- Point out the role of genetics in the development of dog breeds. Ask: **What are some traits that people choose when breeding dogs?** (*Size, sense of smell, aggressiveness, personality, speed, appearance*) Remind students that genes control these traits.

- Ask students: **Why does inbreeding cause an increase in genetic disorders?** (*Since inbred dogs are genetically similar, there is a greater chance that breeders will unknowingly cross two carriers to produce offspring with the disorder.*) **Why are mixed-breed dogs less likely to have genetic disorders?** (*Mixed breeds are hybrids. They usually have two different alleles for most traits, so an allele for a genetic disorder would probably be masked by the normal allele.*)

- **Unit 1 Resources** The following worksheets correlate with page 107: Developing a Classification System, page 84; Breeding Spinoni, page 85; Identifying Dog Adaptations, page 86

Science Activity

Have students complete the activity on their own. Suggest that students calculate the probability for each color of offspring before they calculate the number of puppies with a certain color.

3 Assess

Activity Assessment

Punnett square for *Dd* × *Dd* has offspring *DD*, *Dd*, *Dd*, *dd*. Out of 8 puppies, the ratio is 6 with dark fur (8 × 0.75) and 2 with yellow fur (8 × 0.25). Punnett square for *dd* × *Dd* has offspring *Dd*, *dd*, *Dd*, *dd*. Out of 6 puppies, the ratio is 3 with dark fur (6 × 0.5) and 3 with yellow fur (6 × 0.5).

Background

Facts and Figures Some people still hand raise wild wolf puppies to keep in captivity. For example, Aleuts in Alaska and northern Canada often breed wolves with their own dogs to improve their stamina. They also use tamed wolves, as well as wolf-dog mixes, for their dog sled teams. A tamed wolf, however, can be very dangerous. Because they are still instinctively wild animals, they tend to react defensively in unfamiliar situations—being around new people or in a new place. When a wolf reacts defensively, it usually attacks whatever or whomever it feels is threatening it. It takes several generations of selective breeding for gentleness among wolves in captivity to remove this defensive instinct.

2 Facilitate

◆ After students have read about each dog breed, discuss how people have developed each breed to fit a particular role. Ask: **Which breeds are hunters?** *(Golden retriever, chow chow, Akita, basset hound, dachshund, greyhound)* **Which were bred for herding?** *(Border collie, chow chow)* **Which were bred for guarding?** *(Chow chow, Akita, Lhaso apso)* **Which were bred for pulling sleds?** *(Siberian husky)* **Which were bred for companionship?** *(Pekingese)* Point out that each breed has certain traits that make it well suited for its role in people's lives. Some dogs are still used as working dogs, but most dogs now are simply companions.

◆ Invite students to locate on the map the places of origin for each breed shown. Explain that breeds have also originated in the United States, such as the Alaskan malamute and the bluetick coonhound, and in Australia, such as the silky terrier and the Australian kelpie. Point out that the origins of the older breeds coincide with the locations of ancient civilizations. **Which breed is the oldest?** *(greyhound)* **In which ancient civilization did it originate?** *(ancient Egypt)*

◆ Encourage students to identify working roles that dogs play in the lives of people today. *(Modern roles played by dogs include search and rescue; finding drugs, explosives, or weapons; assisting people with disabilities; tracking criminals; hunting game; herding livestock; and guarding property or people.)* As students identify roles, challenge them to identify traits that make the dogs well suited for their roles.

Golden Retriever
Great Britain, A.D. 1870s
Lord Tweedsmouth developed this breed to help hunters retrieve waterfowl and other small animals.

Border Collie
Great Britain, after A.D. 1100
This breed was developed in the counties near the border of England and Scotland for herding sheep. The Border collie's ancestors were cross-breeds of local sheepdogs and dogs brought to Scotland by the Vikings.

Dachshund
Germany, A.D. 1700s
These dogs were bred to catch badgers or rats. Their short legs and long body can fit into a badger's burrow. In fact, in German the word *Dachshund* means "badger dog."

Basset Hound
France, A.D. 1600s
Second only to the bloodhound at following a scent, the basset hound has short legs and a compact body that help it run through underbrush.

Greyhound
Egypt, 3500 B.C.
These speedy, slender hounds were bred for chasing prey. Today, greyhounds are famous as racers.

108

Background

Facts and Figures The American Kennel Club divides dog breeds into seven groups. These groups are sporting dogs, hounds, working dogs, terriers, toy dogs, nonsporting dogs, and herding dogs. Sporting dogs were bred to assist hunters who use guns. Hounds were bred to hunt for prey by catching it themselves or by cornering it until the hunter arrives. Working dogs were bred for specific jobs, such as guarding, hauling, pulling sleds, or rescuing people and other animals. Terriers were bred to dig into the ground in pursuit of prey, mostly rodents. Toy dogs are small dogs that are companions. Nonsporting dogs are large companion dogs. Herding dogs were bred to protect and herd livestock, such as sheep.

Dogs and People

Over thousands of years, people have developed many different breeds of dogs. Each of the dogs shown on the map was bred for a purpose—hunting, herding, guarding, pulling sleds—as well as companionship. Every breed has its own story.

Siberian Husky
Siberia, 1000 B.C.
The Chukchi people of northeastern Siberia used these strong working dogs to pull sleds long distances across the snow.

Pekingese
China, A.D. 700s
These lapdogs were bred as pets in ancient China. One Chinese name for a Pekingese means "lion dog," which refers to the dog's long, golden mane.

Chow Chow
China, 150 B.C.
Chow chows, the working dogs of ancient China, worked as hunters, herders, and guard dogs.

Akita
Japan, A.D. 1600s
This breed was developed in the cold mountains of northern Japan as a guard dog and hunting dog. The Akita is able to hunt in deep snow and is also a powerful swimmer.

Lhasa Apso
Tibet, A.D. 1100
This breed has a long, thick coat to protect it from the cold air of the high Tibetan plateau. In spite of its small size, the Lhasa apso guarded homes and temples.

Social Studies Activity

Draw a time line that shows the approximate date of origin of different breeds of domestic dogs from 7000 B.C. to the present. Use the information on the map to fill out your time line. Include information about where each breed was developed.

109

◆ Extend this exploration by encouraging interested students to find the place and time of origin for their favorite breed of dog. Students can find this kind of information in encyclopedias of dog breeds.

◆ **Unit 1 Resources** The following worksheets correlate with pages 108–109: Reading a Data Table, page 87; Finding Your Way Around a Sheepdog Trial, page 88; The Responsibilities of Owning a Dog, page 89.

Social Studies Activity

Students can work individually or in small groups. Provide students with shelf paper or butcher's paper so that they have adequate space to draw and label the time lines. Encourage students to add drawings or pictures of the different dog breeds. Remind students to make the divisions in time equal in length on the time line. They can do this by first calculating the total number of years in the time line.

3 Assess

Activity Assessment

Display the time lines in the classroom and in the hallway. You might consider allowing class time for students to present their time lines. Each time line should be divided into equal increments with the origins of all dog breeds clearly and accurately labeled. Students should also include information about each dog breed as presented in the text, especially where each breed was developed. Excellent time lines will also be illustrated with the dog breeds.

2 Facilitate

- Before students read this section, ask if they are familiar with James Herriot and have read any of his books or watched the television series based on his books. If so, let these students describe what the books are about.
- After students have read the excerpt, ask: **How does Herriot feel about getting a Border terrier?** (*He was happy, excited, and content.*) **What do you think Herriot meant when he wrote, "The wheel had indeed turned?"** (*He finally felt complete because he finally found the dog that he had wanted for so long.*)
- **Unit 1 Resources** The following worksheets correlate with page 110: Developing Dialog, page 90; Practicing Point of View, page 91; Researching for the Right Dog, page 92.

Language Arts Activity

Before students begin writing their narratives, encourage them to think about their lives and choose one event that is particularly memorable to them. Instruct students to write down why this particular event was so memorable to them. Did they overcome a problem, for example, or were they recognized for their special efforts? Then encourage students to list the emotions they felt during this event and record why they felt those emotions.

3 Assess

Activity Assessment

Invite students to read their narratives aloud to the rest of the class. Evaluate students' narratives based on their use of first-person point of view, the use of dialog, and the clarity with which they expressed their emotions.

Picking a Puppy

People look for different traits in the dogs they choose. Here is how one expert selected his dog based on good breeding and personality.

James Herriot, a veterinarian in England, had owned several dogs during his lifetime. But he had always wanted a Border terrier. These small, sturdy dogs are descendants of working terrier breeds that lived on the border of England and Scotland. For centuries they were used to hunt foxes, rats, and other small animals. In this story, Herriot and his wife Helen follow up on an advertisement for Border terrier puppies.

Language Arts Activity

James Herriot describes this scene using dialog and first-person narrative. The narrative describes Herriot's feelings about a memorable event—finally finding the dog he had wanted for so long. Write a first-person narrative describing a memorable event in your life. You might choose a childhood memory or a personal achievement at school. What emotions did you feel? How did you make your decision? If possible, use dialog in your writing.

Border terrier ▶

S he [Helen, his wife] turned to me and spoke agitatedly, "I've got Mrs. Mason on the line now. There's only one pup left out of the litter and there are people coming from as far as eighty miles away to see it. We'll have to hurry. What a long time you've been out there!"

We bolted our lunch and Helen, Rosie, granddaughter Emma and I drove out to Bedale. Mrs. Mason led us into the kitchen and pointed to a tiny brindle creature twisting and writhing under the table.

"That's him," she said.

I reached down and lifted the puppy as he curled his little body round, apparently trying to touch his tail with his nose. But that tail wagged furiously and the pink tongue was busy at my hand. I knew he was ours before my quick examination for hernia and overshot jaw.

The deal was quickly struck and we went outside to inspect the puppy's relations. His mother and grandmother were out there. They lived in little barrels which served as kennels and both of them darted out and stood up at our legs, tails lashing, mouths panting in delight. I felt vastly reassured. With happy, healthy ancestors like those I knew we had every chance of a first rate dog.

As we drove home with the puppy in Emma's arms, the warm thought came to me. The wheel had indeed turned. After nearly fifty years I had my Border terrier.

James Herriot was a country veterinarian in Yorkshire, England. In several popular books published in the 1970s and 1980s, he wrote warm, humorous stories about the animals he cared for. His book *All Creatures Great and Small* was the basis for a television series.

110

Background

Facts and Figures James Herriot was the pen name of James Alfred Wight, a British veterinarian and writer. Herriot began practicing veterinary medicine in North Yorkshire, England, after he graduated from veterinary school in 1937. In his practice, he cared for cows, horses, and sheep, as well as dogs and cats. He began writing about his experiences with people and animals in his practice when he was 50 years old. His first book, *All Creatures Great and Small,* was published in 1972. He published three other books *All Things Bright and Beautiful, All Things Wise and Wonderful,* and *The Lord God Made Them All,* as well as children's stories and a book of photographs describing the Yorkshire countryside. James Herriot died in 1995 at the age of 78.

Breed	1970	1980	1990	1997
Poodle	265,879	92,250	71,757	54,773
Labrador Retriever	25,667	52,398	99,776	158,366
Cocker Spaniel	21,811	76,113	105,642	41,439

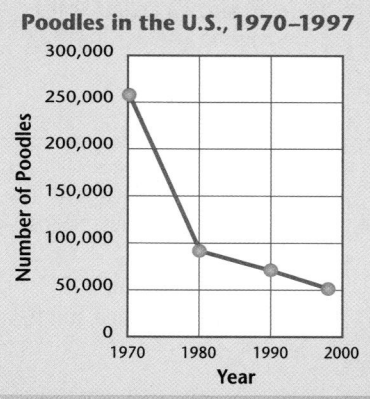

Poodles in the U.S., 1970–1997

Math Activity

The popularity of different breeds of dogs changes over time. For example, the line graph shows how the number of poodles registered with the American Kennel Club changed between 1970 and 1997. Use the table to create your own line graph for Labrador retrievers and cocker spaniels.

Which breed was more popular in 1980, Labrador retrievers or cocker spaniels? How has the number of Labrador retrievers changed from 1970 to 1997? How has the number of cocker spaniels changed over the same time?

Tie It Together

Best of Breed Show

In many places proud dog owners of all ages bring their animals to compete in dog shows. Organize your own dog show. With a partner, choose one specific breed of dog. Pick a breed shown on the map on pages 108–109, or use library resources to research another breed.

◆ Find out what the breed looks like, the time and place where it originated, and what traits it was first bred for.

◆ List your breed's characteristics, height, weight, and coloring.

◆ Research the breed's personality and behavior.

◆ Find out your breed's strengths. Learn what weakness may develop as a result of inbreeding.

◆ Make a poster for your breed. Include a drawing or photo and the information that you researched.

◆ With your class, organize the dog displays into categories of breeds, such as hunting dogs, herding dogs, and toy dogs.

111

2 Facilitate

◆ To assess students' understanding of the data, ask questions such as: **What breed was most popular in 1980?** *(poodle)* **Which breed is most popular now?** *(Labrador retriever)*

◆ Ask students questions about the graph, such as: **How has the number of poodles changed from 1970 to 1997?** *(There has been a sharp decrease.)*

◆ **Unit 1 Resources** The following Worksheets correlate with page 111: Making a Bar Graph, page 93; The Cost of Owning a Dog, page 94; Calculating Points in an Obedience Trial, page 95.

Mathematics Activity

Have students complete the activity on their own. Provide them with graph paper. Students may draw separate graphs for each breed or combine the breeds on one graph. Encourage students to use the graph on this page as a guide for their own graphs.

3 Assess

Activity Assessment

Students' graphs should look similar to the graph for poodles on this page. In 1980, cocker spaniels were more popular. Labrador retrievers have increased steadily in popularity from 1970 to 1997. Cocker spaniel popularity increased steadily until 1990, when it began to decrease sharply.

Tie It Together

Time 1 week (2 days for research, 2 days for the poster, 1 day for the show)

Tips Students can learn about specific dog breeds on the Internet. They can use the breed name as the search word. Have the class vote for their favorite breed to determine "Best of Show."

Motion

Sections	Time	Student Edition Activities	Other Activities	
CHAPTER PROJECT 4 **Speeds à la Carte** p. 113	Ongoing (2 weeks)	Check Your Progress, pp. 127, 136 Project Wrap Up, p. 139	TE	Chapter 4 Project Notes, pp. 112–113
1 Describing and Measuring Motion pp. 114–125 ◆ 4.1.1 Explain when an object is in motion and how motion is relative to a reference point. ◆ 4.1.2 Calculate an object's speed and velocity using SI units of distance. ◆ 4.1.3 Graph motion showing changes in distance as a function of time.	2 periods/ 1 block	**Discover** How Fast and How Far?, p. 114 **Try This** Sunrise, Sunset, p. 116 **Skills Lab: Measuring** Inclined to Roll, pp. 124–125	TE TE TE TE	Building Inquiry Skills: Applying Concepts, p. 115 Integrating Mathematics, p. 117 Math Toolbox, p. 117 Inquiry Challenge, p. 119
2 INTEGRATING EARTH SCIENCE **Slow Motion on Planet Earth** pp. 126–131 ◆ 4.2.1 Explain the slow movement of Earth's plates and calculate their speed.	1 period/ $\frac{1}{2}$ block	**Discover** How Slow Can It Flow?, p. 126 **Sharpen Your Skills** Predicting, p. 127 **Science at Home** p. 129 **Real-World Lab: You and Your Community** Stopping on a Dime, pp. 130–131	TE	Building Inquiry Skills: Problem Solving, p. 128
3 Acceleration pp. 132–136 ◆ 4.3.1 Describe what happens to the motion of an object as it accelerates. ◆ 4.3.2 Calculate the acceleration of an object and graph changing speed and distance of an accelerating object.	1 period/ $\frac{1}{2}$ block	**Discover** Will You Hurry Up?, p. 132	TE TE LM	Inquiry Challenge, p. 133 Integrating Space Science, p. 134 4 Speed"
Study Guide/Assessment pp. 137–139	1 period/ $\frac{1}{2}$ block		ISAB	Provides teaching and review of all inquiry skills

For Standard or Block Schedule The Resource Pro® CD-ROM gives you maximum flexibility for planning your instruction for any type of schedule. Resource Pro® contains Planning Express®, an advanced scheduling program, as well as the entire contents of the Teaching Resources and the Computer Test Bank.

Key: **CTB** Computer Test Bank
 CT Chapter Tests
 ELL Teacher's ELL Handbook

CHAPTER PLANNING GUIDE

Program Resources	Assessment Strategies	Media and Technology
UR Chapter 4 Project Teacher Notes, pp. 2–3 **UR** Chapter 4 Project Overview and Worksheets, pp. 4–7	**TE** Check Your Progress, pp. 127, 136 **TE** Performance Assessment: Chapter 4 Project Wrap Up, p. 139 **UR** Chapter 4 Project Scoring Rubric, p. 8	Science Explorer Internet Site Audio CDs, Section Summaries
UR 4-1 Lesson Plan, p. 9 **UR** 4-1 Section Summary, p. 10 **UR** 4-1 Review and Reinforce, p. 11 **UR** 4-1 Enrich, p. 12 **UR** Skills Lab blackline masters, pp. 21–22	**SE** Section 1 Review, p. 123 **SE** Analyze and Conclude, p. 125 **TE** Ongoing Assessment, pp. 117, 119, 121 **TE** Performance Assessment, p. 123	Concept Videotape Library, *Adventures, Tape 1,* "Travel"; "The Age of Invention" Presentation Pro, "Motion" Transparency 12, "Exploring Motion Graphs" Lab Activity Videotape, *Tape 1*
UR 4-2 Lesson Plan, p. 13 **UR** 4-2 Section Summary, p. 14 **UR** 4-2 Review and Reinforce, p. 15 **UR** 4-2 Enrich, p. 16 **UR** Real-World Lab blackline masters, pp. 23–25	**SE** Section 2 Review, p. 129 **SE** Analyze and Conclude, p. 131 **TE** Ongoing Assessment, p. 127 **TE** Performance Assessment, p. 129	Lab Activity Videotape, *Tape 1*
UR 4-3 Lesson Plan, p. 17 **UR** 4-3 Section Summary, p. 18 **UR** 4-3 Review and Reinforce, p. 19 **UR** 4-3 Enrich, p. 20	**SE** Section 3 Review, p. 136 **TE** Ongoing Assessment, pp. 133, 135 **TE** Performance Assessment, p. 136	
GRSW Provides worksheets to promote student comprehension of content **RCA** Provides strategies to improve science reading skills **ELL** Provides multiple strategies for English language learners	**SE** Study Guide/Assessment, pp. 137–139 **PA** Performance Assessment, pp. 13–15 **CT** Chapter 4 Test, pp. 15–18 **CTB** Chapter 4 Test **PHAS** Provides standardized test preparation	Computer Test Bank, Chapter 4 Test

GRSW Guided Reading and Study Workbook
ISAB Inquiry Skills Activity Book
LM Laboratory Manual

PA Performance Assessment
PHAS Prentice Hall Assessment System
PLM Probeware Lab Manual

RCA Reading in the Content Area
SE Student Edition

TE Teacher's Edition
UR Unit Resources

Meeting the National Science Education Standards and AAAS Benchmarks

National Science Education Standards	Benchmarks for Science Literacy	Unifying Themes

Science as Inquiry (Content Standard A)

◆ **Use appropriate tools and techniques to gather, analyze, and interpret data** Students make distance and time measurements, then analyze and interpret their data. *(Chapter Project; Skills Lab)*

◆ **Design and conduct an experiment** An experiment is designed and conducted to determine what distance is necessary beyond the out-of-bounds line on a basketball court. *(Real-World Lab)*

◆ **Use mathematics in all aspects of scientific inquiry** Students measure time and distance and calculate speed. *(Chapter Project; Section 1, 2; Skills Lab; Real-World Lab)* Students calculate acceleration. *(Section 3)*

Physical Science (Content Standard B)

◆ **Motions and forces** Students learn how to describe the motion of an object. They also learn to represent motion on a graph. *(Section 1)* Students learn how to calculate acceleration. *(Section 3)*

Earth and Space Science (Content Standard C)

◆ **Structure of the earth system** Students apply knowledge about the Earth's moving plates and calculate the speed and distance of their motion. *(Section 2)*

3A Technology and Science The history of speed and transportation is discussed with emphasis on the progress of technology. *(Section 1)*

4F Motion Objects in motion have a direction and speed that can be changed. *(Sections 1, 3)*

9B Symbolic Relationships Students quantify speed and acceleration using equations and graph the motion of various objects. *(Sections 1, 2; 3; Skills Lab)*

10A Displacing the Earth from the Center of the Universe Students learn that motion is relative to a given reference point. *(Section 1)*

12B Computation and Estimation Students determine units of measurement, estimate distances, and compare numbers in measurements of speed and acceleration. *(Sections 2, 3; Chapter Project, Real-World Lab)*

◆ **Evolution** The Earth's plates move at a measurable velocity so scientists can predict how they will change over time. *(Section 2)*

◆ **Patterns of Change** As an object accelerates, its motion changes as it slows down, speeds up, or changes direction. *(Sections 1, 2, 3; Real-World Lab)*

◆ **Scale and Structure** The idea of scale is emphasized with SI units and unit conversions. SI units can be used for very large and very small speeds. *(Sections 1 and 2)*

◆ **Systems and interactions** Earth's tectonic plates comprise a complex system with many different types of interactions as plates collide, pull apart, or slide past each other. *(Sections 1 and 2)*

◆ **Modeling** Students conduct an activity to measure speed. An experiment is designed and conducted to determine what distance is necessary between the out-of-bounds line and a wall so that a basketball player can stop before hitting the wall. *(Skills Lab, Real-World Lab)*

Take It to the Net

The www.phschool.com Web site provides you with multiple opportunities to incorporate the internet into your instruction. Go to www.phschool.com and click on the Science icon. Then select Science Explorer Integrated.

Internet Activities provide opportunities for students to review, extend, or assess a concept from the chapter.

■ Have students use the chapter Self-Test to get instant feedback.

■ Hot Links and Reference Links provide opportunities for online research.

STAY CURRENT with **SCIENCE NEWS** ®

Find out the latest research and information about mechanics at: **www.phschool.com**

ACTIVITY	Time (minutes)	Materials Quantities for one work group	Skills
Section 1			
Discover, p. 114	15	**Consumable** masking tape **Nonconsumable** meter stick, stopwatch	Inferring
Try This, p. 116	5 min, 6–8 times during 1 day	No special materials are required.	Observing, Interpreting Data, Drawing Conclusions
Skills Lab, pp. 124–125	40	**Consumable** masking tape **Nonconsumable** skateboard, meter stick, protractor, flat board about 1.5 m long, small piece of sturdy cardboard, supports to prop up the board (books, boxes), 2 stopwatches or wristwatches with a stopwatch function	Measuring
Section 2			
Discover, p. 126	20	**Consumable** honey, masking tape, damp cloths or paper towels **Nonconsumable** spoon, plate, books or blocks, metric ruler, stopwatch or clock	Observing, Inferring, Forming Operational Definitions
Sharpen Your Skills, p. 127	15	No special materials are required.	Predicting
Science at Home, p. 129	home	**Nonconsumable** metric ruler	Measuring
Real-World Lab, pp. 130–131	50	**Nonconsumable** wooden meter stick, tape measure, 2 stopwatches or watches with second hands	Measuring, Calculating, Inferring
Section 3			
Discover, p. 132	15	**Consumable** masking tape **Nonconsumable** meter stick, stopwatch	Inferring

A list of all materials required for the Student Edition activities can be found beginning on page T23. You can obtain information about ordering materials by calling 1-800-848-9500 or by accessing the *Science Explorer* Internet site at: **www.phschool.com**

CHAPTER
4 Motion

CHAPTER PROJECT 4

Speeds à la Carte

While moving objects are very common in our daily lives, measuring the motion of an object is a very sophisticated notion. In this chapter, students will be introduced to three of the useful ways of measuring and describing motion: speed, velocity, and acceleration. The Chapter Project allows students to develop and practice techniques used to measure motion.

Purpose In this project, students will identify and measure the motion of several different objects.

Skills Focus Students will be able to
- measure distance and time accurately;
- record data in lists or tables;
- apply concepts learned in class to calculate speed;
- communicate their work on display cards.

Project Time Line Students can begin measuring speeds the first week. Some measurements can be completed in a very short period of time, although others, such as the rate at which grass grows, may take longer. Most students should be able to complete all of their measurements within one week. Allow another week for students to prepare display cards for presenting the speeds that they measured. Before beginning the project, see Chapter 4 Project Teacher Notes on pages 2–3 in Unit 2 Resources for more details on carrying out the project. Also, distribute the students' Chapter 4 Project Student Overview and Worksheets and Scoring Rubric on pages 4–8 in Unit 2 Resources.

Suggested Shortcuts Although the project is written to be completed by students individually at home, they could complete parts of the project in groups in the classroom. You may wish to adjust the requirements of each level of success to better match the cooperative capabilities of small groups of students. To ensure that all students have ample opportunities to measure speed, have each student measure at least one speed at home and in class.

WEB ACTIVITY www.phschool.com

SECTION 1 Describing and Measuring Motion	*Integrating Earth Science* SECTION 2 Slow Motion on Planet Earth	SECTION 3 Acceleration
Discover **How Fast and How Far?** Try This **Sunrise, Sunset** Skills Lab **Inclined to Roll**	Discover **How Slow Can It Flow?** Sharpen Your Skills **Predicting** Real-World Lab **Stopping on a Dime**	Discover **Will You Hurry Up?**

Possible Materials
- metric ruler to measure centimeters and millimeters
- device to measure meters such as meter sticks, tape measures, or strings marked in meters
- timing device such as a stop watch or clock

Launching the Project To introduce the project and to stimulate student interest, show students several toys that move in various ways, such as wind up cars or other toys. Some of these should move in straight lines with

112

Speeds à la Carte

Imagine that you have traveled thousands of miles to visit the tropics of South America. Suddenly, vivid reds and blues brighten the green of the rain forest as a group of macaws swoop down and perch above you in a nut tree. They squawk at each other as they crack nuts with their powerful jaws and eat the meat. In a few minutes they spread their wings to take off, and vanish from sight. The macaws cracking nuts, flapping their wings, and flying through the forest are all examples of motion. Your plane flight to South America is another.

In this chapter, you will learn how to describe and measure motion. You will find examples of motion and describe how fast different objects move. You will measure the speeds of various common moving things.

Your Goal To identify several examples of motion and measure how fast each one moves. You will arrange your results from slowest to fastest.

Your project must
- ◆ include careful distance and time measurements
- ◆ use your data to calculate the speed of each example
- ◆ provide display cards that show data, diagrams, and calculations
- ◆ follow the safety guidelines in Appendix A

Get Started Brainstorm with a group of your classmates several examples of motion. For example, you might consider a feather falling, your friend riding a bicycle, or the minute hand moving on a clock. Which examples will be easy to measure? Which will be more challenging?

Check Your Progress You'll be working on this project as you study this chapter. To keep your project on track, look for Check Your Progress boxes at the following points.
Section 1 Review, page 123: Create a data table.
Section 3 Review, page 136: Repeat measurements and make calculations.

Wrap Up At the end of the chapter (page 139), you will compare the speeds recorded by the class.

113

These red-and-green macaws live in the Amazon River basin in Peru.

Program Resources

- ◆ **Unit 2 Resources** Chapter 4 Project Teacher's Notes, pp. 2–3; Project Overview and Worksheets, pp. 4–7; Project Scoring Rubric, p. 8

Media and Technology

 Audio CDs Section Summaries

WEB ACTIVITY www.phschool.com

You will find an Internet activity, chapter self-tests for students, and links to other chapter topics at this site.

constant speed, some can move in other ways. Or have one volunteer walk in a straight line, another walk in a circle, while a third walks randomly. Ask: **What are some other examples of motion?** *(Sample: a cloud moving in the sky, an acorn falling from an oak tree, a sprinter running down a track)* **How can we describe different types of motion?** *(Measure distance and time, create a map showing the various positions)*

Allow time for students to read the Chapter Project Overview on pages 4–5 in Unit 2 Resources. Then encourage discussions on measuring speed and answer any initial questions students may have. Pass out copies of the Chapter 4 Project Worksheets on pages 6–7 in Unit 2 Resources for students to review. Make sure students understand the the requirements. Have students review the rubric and set goals for their work.

Performance Assessment

The Chapter 4 Project Scoring Rubric on page 8 of Unit 2 Resources will help you evaluate how well students complete the Chapter 4 Project. You may wish to share the scoring rubric with your students so they are clear about what will be expected of them. Students will be assessed on
- ◆ how carefully they measured and how thoroughly they recorded data;
- ◆ their explanations of how they calculated the speeds;
- ◆ the clarity of their data and the associated units of measurement in each step of their written displays;
- ◆ the thoroughness and organization of their display cards.

SECTION 1 Describing and Measuring Motion

Objectives

After completing the lesson, students will be able to

◆ explain when an object is in motion and how motion is relative to a reference point;

◆ calculate an object's speed and velocity using SI units of distance;

◆ graph motion showing changes in distance as a function of time.

Key Terms motion, reference point, International System of Units (SI), meter, speed, velocity

1 Engage/Explore

Activating Prior Knowledge

Invite students to list various kinds of movement. Ask: **How did you know the object moved?** (*Sample: Because I saw it change position.*) Then ask: **Did the object appear to move slowly or quickly? How could you tell?** (*Sample: It appeared to move slowly because it moved a short distance in a fairly long time.*)

······· DISCOVER ·········

Skills Focus inferring
Materials *meter stick, stopwatch, masking tape*
Time 15 minutes
Tips Tape a long piece of masking tape to the ground as a starting line. Place another piece of tape 5 m from the first piece for Step 1. Tell students to use a third piece of tape to mark their location after 5 seconds for Step 2. Remind students to walk at a normal pace for the first two measurements. Ask: **How can you change the distance that you travel in 5 seconds?** (*Walk or run faster or slower, take larger or smaller steps.*)
Think It Over The faster you walk, the less time it takes to walk a certain distance. The faster you walk, the farther you will travel in a given time. If you walk a longer distance in a given amount of time, you are walking faster.

SECTION 1 Describing and Measuring Motion

DISCOVER ·· ACTIVITY

How Fast and How Far?

1. Find out how long it takes you to walk 5 meters at a normal pace. Record your time.

2. Now find out how far you can walk in 5 seconds if you walk at a normal pace. Record your distance.

3. Repeat Steps 1 and 2, walking slower than your normal pace. Then repeat Steps 1 and 2, walking faster than your normal pace.

Think It Over
Inferring What is the relationship between the distance you walk, the time it takes you to walk, and your walking speed?

GUIDE FOR READING

◆ When is an object in motion?

◆ How can you find the speed and velocity of an object?

Reading Tip Before you read, rewrite the headings in the section as questions. As you read, look for answers.

▼ Gray squirrels

It's three o'clock and school is over! You hurry out of class to enjoy the bright afternoon. A light breeze is blowing. A few clouds are lazily drifting across the sky, and colorful leaves float down from the trees. Two birds fly playfully over your head. A bunch of frisky squirrels chase one another up a tree. You spend a few minutes with some friends who are kicking a ball around. Then you head home.

Does anything strike you about this afternoon scene? It is filled with all kinds of motion: blowing, drifting, fluttering, flying, and chasing. There are simple motions and complicated motions, motions

READING STRATEGIES

Reading Tip Discuss with students how they might rewrite each heading as a question. For example, they could write "How do I know when something is in motion?" for *Recognizing Motion*. Have students write down their questions and leave space by each question to add answers as they read.

Study and Comprehension Suggest students write new definitions and formulas on note cards while they are working on the section. Make sure they include the formulas for calculating constant speed and average speed as well as the definition of velocity.

Figure 1 Whether or not an object is in motion depends on the reference point you choose. *Comparing and Contrasting* Which people are moving if you compare them to the escalator? Which people are moving if you compare them to Earth?

that are over in a moment, and motions that continue all afternoon. How else can you describe all of these examples of motion? There is actually a great deal to understand about how and why all these things move as they do. In this section, you will learn how scientists describe and measure motion.

Recognizing Motion

Deciding if an object is in motion isn't as easy as it sounds. For example, you are probably sitting as you read this paragraph. Are you moving? Other than your eyes blinking and your chest moving up and down, you would probably say that you (and this book) are not moving. An object is in **motion** when its distance from another object is changing. Since the distance between you and this book is not changing, you conclude that neither you nor the book is moving.

At the same time that you think you are sitting still, you are actually moving about 30 kilometers every second. At that speed, you could travel from New York City to Los Angeles in about 2 minutes! You are moving because you are on planet Earth, which is orbiting the sun. Earth moves about 30 kilometers every second, so you and everything else on Earth are moving at that speed as well.

Whether an object is moving or not depends on your point of view. If you compare the books on a desk to the floor beneath them, they are not moving.

Program Resources

◆ **Unit 2 Resources** 4-1 Lesson Plan, p. 9; 4-1 Section Summary, p. 10
◆ **Guided Reading and Study Workbook** Section 4-1

Answers to Self-Assessment

Caption Question

Figure 1 The people walking on the escalator are moving with respect to the escalator. All the people are moving with respect to Earth.

2 Facilitate

Recognizing Motion

Language Arts Connection

Read aloud an action-filled poem such as "Paul Revere's Ride" by Longfellow. Ask: **What words and phrases does the poet use to describe motion?** *(Sample: raced, crept)* Explain that poets use descriptive language to help readers and listeners understand the poem. **learning modality: verbal**

Building Inquiry Skills: Applying Concepts

Materials *globes, measuring tape*
Time 15 minutes

Have students work in small groups. Ask them to locate their home state on the globe. Then ask them to locate Tokyo, Japan. Have them use the measuring tape to find the distance on the globe between their state and Tokyo. Have a volunteer rotate the globe one-half turn starting from the home state. **Why doesn't our state get closer to or farther away from Japan when the globe turns?** *(Japan is moving at the same rate as everything else on the globe.)* **cooperative learning**

Using the Visuals: Figure 1

Draw students' attention to the person at the top of the "up" escalator. Ask: **Which people are moving relative to this person?** *(The people on the "down" escalator)* Then ask: **Why isn't this person at the top moving from the point of view of the person a few steps behind him?** *(The distance between them stays the same.)* **learning modality: visual**

Ongoing Assessment

Writing Have students write a paragraph about their trip to school in the morning describing everything they saw that was moving.

Recognizing Motion, continued

TRY THIS

Skills Focus observing
Time 5 minutes, 6 to 8 times during 1 day
Tips Students should pick a place for their observations that they can visit throughout the day, and mark the spot. Have students draw a sketch of their observation area from their reference point, complete with buildings and trees. Direct students to record the position of the sun on their sketches. Remind them to include the time of observation. Ask: **How did the position of the sun at lunch time compare with the position of the sun in the morning and late afternoon?** (*The sun appeared higher in the sky at lunch time than it appeared at other times.*)

Expected Outcome Students should observe that the sun moves across the sky throughout the day. However, they should conclude that they see the sun as moving because they use the things around them as reference points. If they view the same information, but use the sun as a reference point, they can show that Earth is moving.

Extend Using a flashlight and a globe or large ball, have students model the motion of Earth and the sun. By marking a spot on the ball, students can demonstrate how the sun appears to move from the perspective of someone on Earth. **learning modality: visual**

Including all Students

Students who are still mastering English may have increased difficulty understanding the words in this section that indicate motion. Pair them with native English speakers and have partners find such words, list them, then form sentences using the words.
limited English proficiency

Figure 2 Both the Hubble Space Telescope and the astronaut are actually moving rapidly through space. But compared to the Hubble Space Telescope, the astronaut is not moving and can therefore complete necessary repairs.

Sunrise, Sunset

Earth rotates as it moves around the sun. But to you, the sun appears to move.

1. Choose a spot from which you can observe the sky throughout one day.

2. From the same spot, observe the sun at 6 to 8 different times during the day. **CAUTION:** *Be careful not to look directly at the sun.* Describe its position by comparing it with things around you, such as trees and buildings.

3. Draw a diagram showing the sun's positions throughout the day.

Observing What reference point(s) did you use? Did the sun appear to move when compared with those reference points? Did it really move?

But if you compare them to the sun, the books are moving quite rapidly. Earth and the sun are different reference points. A **reference point** is a place or object used for comparison to determine if something is in motion. **An object is in motion if it changes position relative to a reference point.** You assume that the reference point is stationary, or not moving.

If you have ever been on a slow-moving train, you know that you may not be able to tell the train is moving unless you look out the window. A nearby building is a good reference point, and a glance at it will tell you if you and the train are moving. But it is important to choose your reference point carefully. Have you ever been in a school bus stopped right next to another school bus? Suddenly, you think your bus is moving backward. When you look out the window on the other side, you find that your bus isn't moving at all. Actually, the other bus is moving forward! Your bus seemed to be moving backward because you used the other bus as a reference point. You assumed your reference point was stationary. But in fact, your reference point—the other bus—was really moving.

Describing Distance

INTEGRATING MATHEMATICS To describe motion further, you need to use units of measurement. Whether you realize it or not, you use units, or standard quantities, all the time. You might, for example, measure 2 cups of milk for a recipe, swim 100 yards after school, or buy 3 pounds of fruit at the store. Cups, yards, and pounds are all units.

Scientists all over the world use the same system of units so that they can communicate information clearly. This system of

---

Background

Integrating Science Throughout recorded time, civilizations have devised methods of measurement. Units of measurement are often based on parts of the human body. For example, the Egyptians called the distance from the fingertips to the elbow a *cubit*. Even our own U.S. system has some units based on body parts. One example is the *foot*. The standard system of units we use today is a relatively modern innovation. At one time, practically every nation on Earth used a different system of units. This made commerce and trade between nations very difficult. Today, even when different units of measurement are used (such as feet or gallons) they are defined in terms of the standard system of units.

measurement is called the **International System of Units,** or in French, Système International (SI). SI is a system based on the number ten. This makes calculations with the system relatively easy.

The basic SI unit of length is the **meter** (m). A meter is a little longer than a yard. The Eiffel Tower in Figure 3 is measured in meters. To measure the length of an object smaller than a meter, scientists use the metric unit called the centimeter (cm). The prefix *centi-* means "one hundredth." A centimeter is one hundredth of a meter, so there are 100 centimeters in a meter. The beautiful butterfly in Figure 3 is measured in centimeters. For even smaller lengths, the millimeter (mm) is used. The prefix *milli-* means "one thousandth," so there are 1,000 millimeters in a meter. In the International System, long distances are measured in kilometers (km). The prefix *kilo-* means "one thousand." There are 1,000 meters in a kilometer.

SI units are also used to describe quantities other than length. You can find more information about SI units in the Skills Handbook on pages 768–769 of this textbook.

☑ *Checkpoint* *What unit would you use to describe the width of your thumb?*

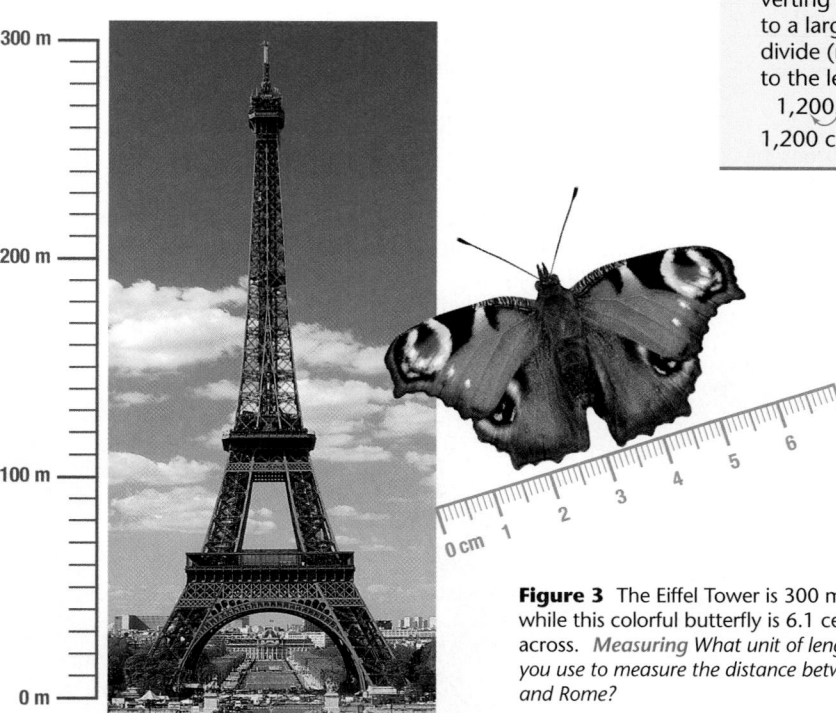

300 m
200 m
100 m
0 m

Figure 3 The Eiffel Tower is 300 meters tall, while this colorful butterfly is 6.1 centimeters across. *Measuring What unit of length would you use to measure the distance between Paris and Rome?*

Math TOOLBOX

Converting Units

When you convert one metric unit to another, you must move the decimal point.

1. How many millimeters are in 14.5 meters? You are converting from a larger unit to a smaller one, so you multiply. There are 1,000 millimeters in a meter. To multiply by 1,000, move the decimal to the right three places.

   14.500 m = 14,500. mm

   There are 14,500 mm in 14.5 m.

2. Convert 1,200 centimeters to meters. You are converting from a smaller unit to a larger one, so you divide (move the decimal to the left).

   1,200. cm = 12.00 m

   1,200 cm equals 12 m.

Describing Distance

Integrating Mathematics

Materials *meter sticks, classroom items such as a chalkboard, desk, chair, eraser, stapler, sheet of paper*
Time 20 minutes

ACTIVITY

Challenge students to create a metric measurement inventory of the classroom. Students can measure a variety of 10 or more objects. Have them determine the appropriate unit of measurement for each object and record their findings. Ask: **What was the smallest object you measured? What unit did you use?** *(Sample: paper clip, staple, push pin; millimeter)* **Then ask: What was the largest object you measured? What unit did you use?** *(Sample: chalkboard, bookshelf; meter)* **learning modality: logical/mathematical**

Math TOOLBOX

Time 15 minutes
Tips For Problem 1, show students a meter stick that is divided into millimeters. Ask: **If there are 1,000 mm on 1 meter stick, then how many mm are on 2 meter sticks?** *(2,000)* **On 7.5 meter sticks?** *(7,500)* Then write out the problem 14.5 m × 1,000 mm/m = 14,500 mm. Ask: **Where is the decimal point in the number 14,500? How many places did it move?** *(To the right of the last zero; 3 places to the right)* For Problem 2, ask: **How many centimeters are in 1 meter?** *(100)* Then write out the problem 1,200 cm ÷ 100 cm/m = 12 m. Ask: **If the decimal point for 1,200 centimeters is to the right of the zero, which direction did it move when you converted from centimeters to meters?** *(To the left)* **learning modality: logical/mathematical**

ACTIVITY

Ongoing Assessment

Skills Check Have students measure the width and length of their index finger in millimeters and convert the answer to centimeters.

Answers to Self-Assessment

Caption Question

Figure 3 The distance between Paris and Rome would be measured in kilometers.

☑ *Checkpoint*

You would measure the width of your thumb in millimeters or centimeters

Calculating Speed

Social Studies
CONNECTION

After students have read the feature, point out that cities are not symmetrical and the "spokes" may be several different widths. City growth is also limited by geographic constraints and legal requirements as well as transportation needs.

In Your Journal Ask students how many kilometers a person could go in one hour along each of the routes. That distance represents the greatest distance people are willing to drive. Students should realize that they would expect to find homes built farther from the center of the city on Highway 1 and Red Rail. Each transportation route should extend away from the city center in a different direction. Have students choose a scale (for example, 1 mm = 1 km) and measure the distance in mm along the transportation route equal to the number of kilometers a person could travel in one hour. Since these distances represent the maximum distance a person is willing to travel, they mark the city boundaries. **learning modality: logical/mathematical**

Students can save their maps in their portfolios.

Addressing Naive Conceptions

Some students may think objects that have "speed" must move fast. Direct their attention to a clock. Explain that even though the tip of the hour hand on the clock may move very slowly, it still travels at a measurable speed. Have students measure the circumference of a clock by wrapping a piece of string around the clock and measuring the string with a ruler. Ask: **How long does it take the tip of the hour hand to travel around the clock's face one time?** *(12 hours)* **What is its speed?** *(Answers should be the length of the circumference divided by 12 hours.)* Students can also calculate the speed of the minute and second hands. **learning modality: visual**

Social Studies
CONNECTION

Does speed affect the shape of cities? Because people want to travel quickly, they live close to major transportation routes—highways and railroads. Thus a city often looks like a hub with spokes coming out of it along the transportation routes.

In Your Journal

People prefer not to travel more than one hour from home to work. The table shows a city's travel routes.

Route	Average Speed
Highway 1	75 km/h
Highway 2	55 km/h
Blue Rail	60 km/h
Red Rail	75 km/h
Main Street	35 km/h

Along which two routes would you expect to find people living farther from the center of the city? Explain why. Draw a map of what you think this city might look like.

Calculating Speed

Scientists use SI units to describe the distance an object travels. A car, for example, might travel 90 kilometers. An ant might travel 2 centimeters. If you know the distance an object travels in a certain amount of time, you know the speed of the object. To be more exact, the **speed** of an object is the distance the object travels per unit of time. Speed is a type of rate. A rate tells you the amount of something that occurs or changes in one unit of time.

To calculate the speed of an object, divide the distance the object travels by the amount of time it takes to travel that distance. This relationship can be written as follows.

$$Speed = \frac{Distance}{Time}$$

Speed measurements consist of a unit of distance divided by a unit of time. If you measure distance in meters and time in seconds, you express speed in meters per second (m/s). (The slash is read as "per.") If you measure distance in kilometers and time in hours, you express speed in kilometers per hour (km/h).

If a car travels 90 kilometers in one hour, the car is traveling at a speed of 90 km/h. An ant that moves 2 centimeters in one second is moving at a speed of 2 centimeters per second, or 2 cm/s. The ant is much slower than the car.

Constant Speed A ship traveling across the ocean may move at the same speed for several hours. Or a horse cantering across a field may keep a steady pace for several minutes. If so, the ship and the horse travel at constant speeds. If the speed of an object does not change, the object is traveling at a constant speed. When an object travels at a constant speed, you know that its speed is the same at all times during its motion.

Figure 4 This horse is cantering at a constant speed. *Problem Solving* What information do you need to calculate the horse's speed?

118

Background

History of Science Sundials, invented about 3,500 years ago, measure time by the shadow cast by the sun as it crosses the sky. Water clocks, which measure time by the movement of dripping water, came into use about 3,500 years ago. By the early eighteenth century, mechanical clocks with cogs and wheels gained or lost only about a second per day. Today, most clocks and watches are powered by a vibrating quartz crystal and are extremely accurate.

Figure 5 The cyclists do not travel at a constant speed throughout this cross-country race. *Comparing and Contrasting How does average speed differ from constant speed?*

If you know the distance an object travels in a given amount of time, you can use the formula for speed to calculate the object's constant speed. Suppose, for example, that the horse in Figure 4 is moving at a constant speed. Find the horse's speed if it canters 21 meters in 3 seconds. Divide the distance traveled, 21 meters, by the time, 3 seconds, to find the horse's speed.

$$Speed = \frac{21 \text{ m}}{3 \text{ s}} = 7 \text{ m/s}$$

The horse's speed is 7 meters per second, or 7 m/s.

Average Speed Most objects do not move at constant speeds for very long. The cyclists in Figure 5, for example, change their speeds many times during the race. They might glide along on level ground, move more slowly as they climb steep inclines, and dash down hills. Occasionally, they stop to fix a tire.

Unlike the horse described earlier, you cannot use any one speed to describe the motion of the cyclists at every point during the race. You can, however, find the average speed of a cyclist throughout the entire race. To find the average speed, divide the total distance traveled by the total time.

Suppose a cyclist travels 32 kilometers during the first two hours of riding, and 13 kilometers during the next hour. The average speed of the cyclist during the trip is the total distance divided by the total time.

$$Total\ distance = 32 \text{ km} + 13 \text{ km} = 45 \text{ km}$$

$$Total\ time = \quad 2 \text{ h} + 1 \text{ h} \quad = 3 \text{ h}$$

$$Average\ speed = \quad \frac{45 \text{ km}}{3 \text{ h}} \quad = 15 \text{ km/h}$$

The average speed of the cyclist is 15 kilometers per hour.

☑ *Checkpoint* How do you calculate average speed?

Building Inquiry Skills: Calculating

Ask students what information they need to know to determine the speed of an object. (*The distance it moved and the amount of time it took to move that distance*) Then have them calculate the speed of the following objects:
◆ a baseball that moves 11 m in 1 s (*11 m ÷ 1 sec = 11 m/s*)
◆ a car that travels 70 km in 1.75 h (*70 km ÷ 1.75 hr = 40 km/hr*)
learning modality: logical/ mathematical

Inquiry Challenge

Materials *two or three wind-up toys per group, stopwatches, metric rulers, masking tape*
Time 40 minutes
Tips Have students bring toys from home. Challenge students to discover which wind-up toy reaches the highest speed. Students can work in small groups. Have students mark off a "test track" on the floor with masking tape, then measure how long it takes for each toy to travel the length of the track. Suggest students perform at least three trials for each toy and calculate an average speed from the results. To determine if the toy is changing speed during the run, students can compare the average speed of a certain toy measured over two or three different distances. Ask students to describe any changes in each toy's speed during each trial. (*The toys may slow down as they move down the track.*) Ask: **For each trial, are you measuring constant speed or average speed?** (*average speed*) After students complete their trials, have a final race with each group choosing one toy that they think will go fastest over a distance chosen by you. **cooperative learning**

Answers to Self-Assessment

Caption Questions
Figure 4 The distance the horse traveled and the time it took to travel that distance
Figure 5 Average speed is the total distance traveled divided by the total time. During a trip, the speed can change many times. Constant speed means that the speed never changes.

☑ *Checkpoint*
Divide the total distance traveled by the total time.

Ongoing Assessment

Skills Check Have students find the speed of an asteroid that travels 4,500 km in 60 s. (*4,500 km ÷ 60 s = 75 km/s*)

Describing Velocity

Real-Life Learning

Obtain a set of hurricane-tracking charts from your local weather service. Have students follow weather reports to track the daily progress of any hurricanes. Have students calculate the average speed of a hurricane based on the data they gather. If hurricane charts are unavailable, charts showing the movement of high- or low-pressure systems can be substituted. Ask: **How is this type of information useful to weather forecasters?** *(It helps them predict how long it will take for a hurricane to reach a region so they can warn people who live there.)* **learning modality: visual**

Describing Velocity

Knowing the speed at which something travels does not tell you everything about its motion. For example, if a weather forecaster announces that a severe storm is traveling at 25 km/h, would you prepare for the storm? Storms usually travel from west to east. If you live to the west of the storm and the storm is traveling to the east, you need not worry. But if you live to the east of the storm, take cover.

It is important to know not only the speed of the storm, but also its direction. **When you know both the speed and direction of an object's motion, you know the velocity of the object.**

SCIENCE & History

The Speed of Transportation

The speed with which people can travel from one place to another has increased over the years.

1885
Benz Tricycle Car Introduced

This odd-looking vehicle was the first internal combustion (gasoline-powered) automobile sold to the public. Although it is an ancestor of the modern automobile, its top speed was only about 15 km/h— not much faster than a horse-drawn carriage.

1800　　　　　　　　　**1850**

1818
National Road Constructed

The speed of transportation has been limited largely by the quality of roadways. The U.S. government paid for the construction of a highway named the Cumberland Road. It ran from Cumberland, Maryland, to Wheeling, in present-day West Virginia. Travel by horse and carriage on the roadway was at a speed of about 11 km/h.

1869
Transcontinental Railroad

After more than six and a half years of work, railroad tracks from each side of the country met in Utah, just north of Great Salt Lake. Passengers could now travel across the United States by steam-powered trains. A cross-country trip took about a week at an average speed of 30 km/h.

Speed in a given direction is called **velocity**. If you know the velocity at which an object is moving, you know two different things about the object's motion—its speed and its direction. A weather forecaster may give the speed of the storm as 25 km/h, but you don't know its velocity unless you know that the storm is moving 25 km/h eastward.

Air traffic controllers must keep very close track of the velocities of all of the aircraft under their control. These velocities change more often than the velocities of storm systems. An error in determining a velocity, either in speed or in direction, could lead to a collision.

In Your Journal

The distance between Wheeling, West Virginia, and Cumberland, Maryland, is 258 kilometers. How many hours would it take to travel this distance for each of the vehicles in the time line if they each traveled at the speed shown? Record your results on a bar graph.

1908
Ford Model T Mass-Produced

Between 1908 and 1927, over 15 million of these automobiles were sold. The Model T had a top speed of 65 km/h.

1956
Inauguration of the Interstate Highway System

The passage of the Federal Aid Highway Act established the Highway Trust Fund. This act allowed the construction of the Interstate and Defense Highways. Nonstop transcontinental auto travel became possible. Speed limits in many parts of the system were more than 100 km/h.

1900   **1950**   **2000**

1936
***Pioneer Zephyr* Introduced**

The first diesel passenger train in the United States was the *Pioneer Zephyr*. The *Zephyr* set a long-distance record, traveling from Chicago to Denver at an average speed of 125 km/h for more than 1,633 km.

1983
TGV in Motion

First introduced in 1983, this French high-speed train now has a top speed of 300 km/h. On its route from Paris to Lyon, it averages 152.6 km/h.

Chapter 4   **121**

SCIENCE & History

Review each item along the timeline with students. Ask: **How do you think improvements in transportation affected the lives of people living at that time?** *(Sample: They could go farther to find a job, get supplies, or visit relatives.)* Then ask: **What do you think are some negative effects of widespread rapid transportation?** *(Sample: increased pollution, damage to the environment, accidents at high speeds may be deadlier)*

In Your Journal Allow students to use calculators to calculate how long the journeys would take. *(Horse and Carriage on Cumberland Road—23.5 hours; Transcontinental Railroad—8.6 hours; Benz tricycle car—17.2 hours; Ford Model T —4.0 hours; Pioneer Zephyr— 2.0 hours; Interstate Highway—2.6 hours; TGV—0.86 hours (51.6 mins) at 300 km/h or 1.7 hours at 152.6 km/h)* **learning modality: logical/ mathematical**

Cultural Diversity

The United States has built an elaborate system of highways for public and freight transportation, while the rail system is primarily used for transportation of heavy freight. Other countries, such as France and Japan, have constructed sophisticated high speed rail systems for public transportation. In small groups, allow students to discuss the relative advantages and disadvantages of primarily using automobiles for public transportation (as opposed to high-speed rail). Have students relate the contrasting systems of public transportation to the availability of natural resources, such as petroleum. Students may also relate preferences for different modes of public transportation to cultural differences. **cooperative learning**

EXPLORING
Motion Graphs

Draw students' attention to the first graph. They should recognize that the jogger travels 170 m each minute. To show that speed is constant, show that the average speed between any two points is 170 m/min. Have students copy the graph and extend the line to predict how long she would have to jog to travel 2,550 m. *(15 min)* As students examine the second graph, ask: **What happened during the sixth through eighth minutes?** *(The jogger stopped.)* Then ask students: **What effect did the stop have on the jogger's average speed?** *(Average speed was lowered: 1,190 m ÷ 10 min = 119 m/min.)* Ask: **What was the difference in the jogger's average speed between the first and second day?** *(51 m/min)* Compare the slope of the first and third graphs. *(The slope of the first graph is greater.)* Ask: **How fast would the jogger be traveling if the graph were flat?** *(0 m/min)*

Extend Take students to a running track. Pair students. Ask each pair to create motion graphs based on their own actual motion. For example, one student jogs, then walks, and rests (1 min for each). The partner records what the other student is doing and the distance he or she travels. Then partners reverse roles. They then work together to graph their data. Pairs share their graphs with the class and ask the class to describe the student's motion. **learning modality: logical/mathematical**

EXPLORING *Motion Graphs*

Motion graphs provide an opportunity to analyze changes in distance and time.

FIRST DAY
Start with Enthusiasm.
The jogger travels at a constant speed of 170 m/min. The graph of constant speed is a slanted straight line. Notice that the speed is the same at every point on the graph. You can use the graph to analyze the jogger's motion. How far does the jogger run in 10 minutes? (1,700 m) How long does she run to travel 680 meters? (4 min)

SECOND DAY
Take a Break.
The jogger again runs at a constant speed of 170 m/min, but she takes a break after running 850 m. The horizontal line shows that distance did not change during the break—thus there is no motion. What is the jogger's average speed if she ran a total distance of 1190 m? (119 m/min)

THIRD DAY
Slow Down.
As on the first day, the jogger runs at a constant speed, but this time she runs at a slower speed— 100 m/min. Notice that the slant, or slope, of the graph is not as steep as it was on the first day. The steepness of the slope is related to the speed. The faster the speed, the steeper the slope. How far does the jogger run in 10 minutes on this day? (1,000 m)

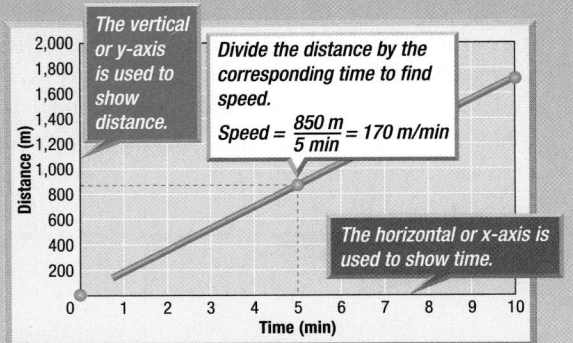

The vertical or y-axis is used to show distance.

Divide the distance by the corresponding time to find speed.

$$Speed = \frac{850 \text{ m}}{5 \text{ min}} = 170 \text{ m/min}$$

The horizontal or x-axis is used to show time.

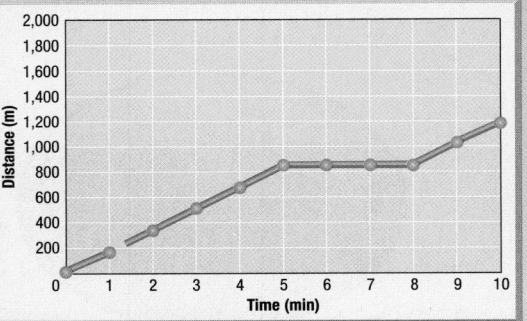

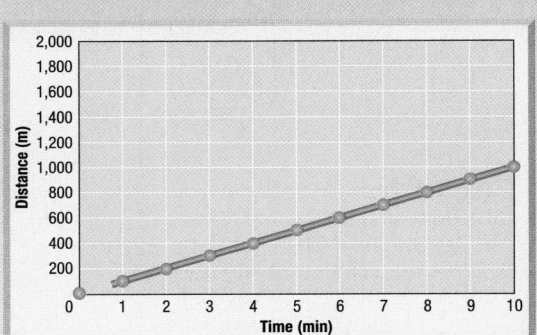

122

Stunt pilots make spectacular use of their control over the velocity of their aircraft. To avoid colliding with other aircraft, these skilled pilots must have precise control of both speed and direction. Stunt pilots use this control to stay in close formation while flying graceful maneuvers.

Graphing Motion

You can show the motion of an object on a line graph in which you plot distance against time. A point on the graph represents the location of an object at a particular time. By tradition, time is shown on the *x*-axis and distance on the *y*-axis. A straight line (a line with a constant slant, or slope) represents motion at a constant speed. The steepness of the slope depends on how quickly or slowly the object is moving. The faster the motion, the steeper the slope, because the object moves a greater distance in a given amount of time. A horizontal line represents an object that is not moving at all. To see examples of how graphs represent motion, read about the jogger in *Exploring Motion Graphs* on page 122.

Figure 6 During a complicated maneuver an airplane's direction changes continuously, along with its speed.

Section 1 Review

1. Why do you need a reference point to know if an object is moving?
2. What is the difference between an object's speed and an object's velocity?
3. A bamboo plant grows 15 centimeters in 4 hours. At what average speed does the plant grow?
4. **Thinking Critically Problem Solving** The distance traveled by two crawling babies is shown in the table. Graph the information and determine which baby moves at constant speed throughout the entire trip. What is that baby's speed? Describe the speed of the other baby.

Time (s)	Baby Scott Distance (m)	Baby Sarah Distance (m)
1	0.5	1
2	1	2
3	1.5	2.5
4	2	2.5
5	2.5	3.5

Check Your Progress

CHAPTER PROJECT 4

To measure each object's speed, you will need to know how far it moves in a certain amount of time. Create a data table to record your measurements and to show the speeds you calculate. Be sure to choose the best units for each speed measurement. To measure fast speeds, you may choose to measure distance in meters and time in seconds. For slower speeds you may choose to measure distance in centimeters or millimeters, and time in minutes or hours.

Inclined to Roll

Preparing for Inquiry

Key Concept After an object rolls down a ramp, it will be going faster if the incline is steeper.

Skills Objectives Students will be able to

◆ measure speed using time taken to travel a certain distance;

◆ measure the effect of the incline of the ramp on the speed an object attains at the end of the incline;

◆ begin to think about acceleration.

Time 40 minutes

Advance Planning If you have not yet taught the skill of measuring, see pages 188–189 of the Skills Handbook. Buy 4 ft × 8 ft sheets of 1/2-in. plywood or pegboard and have them cut crosswise into six ramps 16 in. wide. Many hardware stores will cut the sheets for you. Since these ramps would be 4 feet long, the starting line on the ramp would be at 1 m. This lab requires plenty of space and may need to be done in a gym or outdoors.

Alternative Materials If no student in a group has a skateboard, ask other students to bring extras. Students can also use four-wheeled toys. If protractors are unavailable, have students measure the height of the ramp at the starting line. This height can be used instead of angle to measure ramp incline.

Guiding Inquiry

Invitation Have students predict what they think they will find. Ask: **Have you ever ridden a roller coaster or bicycled down a hill? How did the incline of the hill affect your average speed?** (Faster on a steeper hill) **How did you judge how fast you were traveling?** (Samples: Trees appeared to go by faster; air rushed by faster) Emphasize that speed is measured relative to an object.

Introducing the Procedure

◆ Refer students to the photo illustrating the experimental setup.

◆ Show students how to use the stopwatches. Have students roll the

Inclined to Roll

In this lab, you will practice the skills of measuring time and distance to find the speed of a moving object.

Problem

How does the steepness of a ramp affect how fast an object moves across the floor?

Materials

skateboard
protractor
flat board, about 1.5 m long
small piece of sturdy cardboard
supports to prop up the board (books, boxes)
two stopwatches
meter stick
masking tape

Procedure

1. In your notebook, make a data table like the sample. Include space for five angles.

2. Lay the board flat on the floor. Using masking tape, mark a starting line in the middle of the board. Mark a finish line on the floor 1.5 m beyond one end of the board. Place a barrier after the finish line.

3. Prop up the other end of the board to make a slight incline. Use a protractor to measure the angle that the board makes with the ground. Record the angle in your data table.

4. Working in groups of three, have one person hold the skateboard so that its front wheels are even with the starting line. As the holder releases the skateboard, the other two students should start their stopwatches.

5. One timer should stop his or her stopwatch when the front wheels of the skateboard reach the end of the incline.

6. The second timer should stop his or her stopwatch when the front wheels reach the finish line. Record the times to the bottom of the ramp and to the finish line in the columns labeled Time 1 and Time 2.

DATA TABLE							
Angle (degrees)	Trial Number	Time 1 (to bottom) (s)	Time 2 (to finish) (s)	Avg Time 1 (s)	Avg Time 2 (s)	Avg Time 2 – Avg Time 1 (s)	Avg Speed (m/s)
	1						
	2						
	3						
	1						
	2						
	3						
	1						
	2						

skateboard down the ramp a few times to practice using the stopwatches before they collect data.

Troubleshooting the Experiment

◆ Make sure students begin with a very small incline.

◆ Make sure the skateboard rolls smoothly at the transition from the ramp to the ground.

Sample Data Table				
Angle (degrees)	Time 1 (to bottom) (s)	Time 2 (to finish) (s)	Avg Time 2 – Avg Time 1 (s)	Avg Speed (m/s)
6	1.47	2.75	1.28	1.17
9	1.31	2.40	1.09	1.38
12	1.06	1.88	0.82	1.83
18	0.87	1.58	0.71	2.11
27	0.71	1.28	0.57	2.63

7. Repeat Steps 4–6 two more times. If your results for the three times aren't within 0.2 seconds of one another, carry out more trials.
8. Repeat Steps 3–7 four more times, making the ramp gradually steeper each time.
9. For each angle of the incline, complete the following calculations and record them in your data table.
   a. Find the average time the skateboard takes to get to the bottom of the ramp (Time 1).
   b. Find the average time the skateboard takes to get to the finish line (Time 2).
   c. Subtract the average Time 1 from the average Time 2.

Analyze and Conclude

1. How can you find the average speed of the skateboard across the floor for each angle of incline? Determine the average speed for each angle and record it in your data table.
2. Which is your manipulated variable and which is your responding variable in this experiment? Explain why. (For a discussion of manipulated and responding variables, see the Skills Handbook.)
3. On a graph, plot the speed of the skateboard (on the *y*-axis) against the angle of the ramp (on the *x*-axis). Connect the points on your graph.
4. What does the shape of your graph show about the relationship between the speed and the angle of the ramp?
5. **Think About It** Do you think your method of timing was accurate? Did the timers start and stop their stopwatches exactly at the appropriate points? How could the accuracy of the timing be improved?

Design an Experiment

A truck driver transporting new cars needs to roll the cars off the truck. You offer to design a ramp to help with the task. What measurements might you make that would be useful? Design an experiment to test your ideas.

Program Resources

◆ **Unit 2 Resources** Skills Lab blackline masters, pp. 21–22

Media and Technology

Lab Activity Videotape
Tape 1

Expected Outcome

◆ As the ramp incline increases, the time taken to travel from starting line to bottom of ramp (Average Time 1) will decrease.
◆ As the ramp incline increases, the time taken to travel from bottom of ramp to finish line (Average Time 2 – Average Time 1) will decrease. Thus, average speed will increase as ramp incline increases.

Analyze and Conclude

1. Average speed is distance traveled on floor (distance from bottom of ramp to finish line or 1.5 m) divided by time on floor (Average Time 2 – Average Time 1).
2. The manipulated variable is ramp incline and the responding variable is average speed.
3.

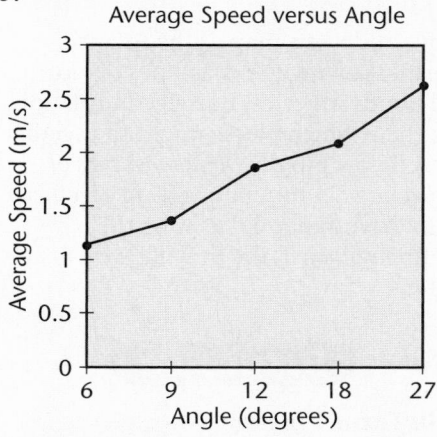

4. Speed will increase as the incline goes from small (0 degrees) to large (45 or more degrees).
5. Many students could time a particular run. The average of all students could then be used. Alternatively, an electric timing device as used during athletic events such as downhill skiing could be utilized.

Extending the Inquiry

Design An Experiment Students need to know the weight of the cars and the distance between the left and right wheels so that the ramp could be wide enough and strong enough.

SECTION 2 Slow Motion on Planet Earth

Objective
After completing the lesson, students will be able to
◆ explain the slow movement of Earth's plates and calculate their speed.

Key Term plates

1 Engage/Explore

Activating Prior Knowledge
Show students a map of the Atlantic Ocean, showing the coastlines of North and South America, Europe, and Africa. Ask them which pieces might fit together like a jigsaw puzzle. (*The coastlines of Africa and South America do fit together.*) If you have a map that shows the continental shelf, the fit will be even better.

 **DISCOVER**

Skills Focus observing, inferring

Materials *spoon, plate, honey, books or blocks, masking tape, metric ruler, stopwatch or clock, damp cloths or paper towels*

Time 20 minutes

Tips Refrigerate the honey if possible. Students should prop up the plates using books or blocks. Provide damp cloths or paper towels to clean up any spilled honey. Write the equation for calculating speed on the board: Speed = Distance ÷ Time. Ask: **What distance will you use to complete the calculation?** (*4 cm*) Divide the class into groups of two or three. Allow students to complete their calculations and compare results.

Think It Over You can tell an object is moving if it changes position over a period of time. If the object moves too slowly, you need to observe it over longer periods of time. The growth of hair and the movement of the hour hand on a clock are too slow to see.

SECTION 2 Slow Motion on Planet Earth

DISCOVER •••••••••••••••••••• **ACTIVITY**

How Slow Can It Flow?

1. Put a spoonful of honey on a plate.
2. Lift one side of the plate just high enough that the honey is visibly flowing.
3. Reduce the angle of the plate a small amount so that the honey appears to be barely moving. Prop up the plate at this angle.
4. Using a ruler, place a piece of tape 4 cm from the bottom edge of the honey.
5. Time how long it takes the honey to flow to the tape. Use this information to calculate the speed of the honey.

Think It Over
Forming Operational Definitions
How can you tell that an object is moving if it doesn't appear to be moving at first glance? Can you think of some other examples of motion that are too slow to see?

 **GUIDE FOR READING**

◆ How does the theory of plate tectonics describe the movement of Earth's continents?

Reading Tip Before you read, preview Figure 8, and describe what you think is happening.

Satellite photo of Africa and the Arabian Peninsula ▼

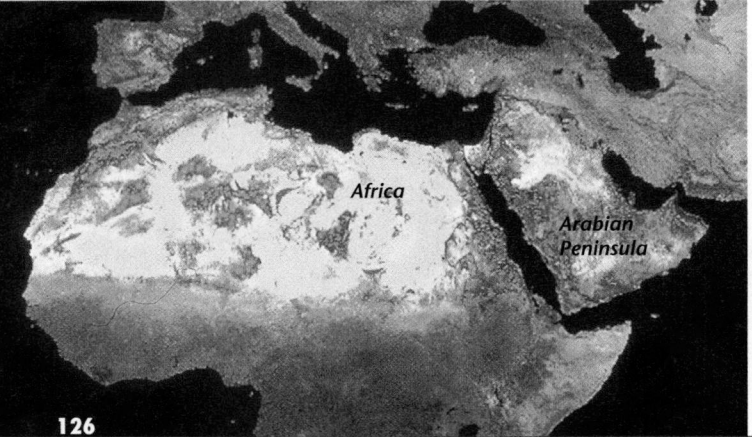

Africa

Arabian Peninsula

126

Have you ever noticed that Earth's landmasses resemble pieces of a giant jigsaw puzzle? It's true—take a look at a map of the world. The east coast of South America, for example, would fit nicely with the west coast of Africa. The Arabian Peninsula, as shown in the satellite photo below, would fit fairly well with the northeastern coast of Africa. Since the 1600s, people have wondered why Earth's landmasses look as if they would fit together. After all, land can't move—or can it?

What Are Earth's Plates?
Earth's rocky outer shell consists of broken pieces that fit together like a jigsaw puzzle. The upper layer of Earth consists of more than a dozen major pieces called **plates.** The boundaries between the plates are cracks in Earth's crust. The various plates are shown in Figure 7.

Scientists use this concept of plates to explain how landmasses have changed over time. **According to their explanation, known as the theory of plate tectonics, Earth's plates move ever so slowly in various directions.**

READING STRATEGIES

Reading Tip As students preview Figure 8, elicit their predictions about the speed of the continents. Point out that there is an enormous amount of time between the pictures. Ask students to think of other objects that might move as slowly.

Study and Comprehension Tell students there are three important things for them to learn from this section. Have them glance over the text and identify what they are. Guide them to see that they should learn
◆ what the theory of plate tectonics is;
◆ how to calculate distance from speed and time; and
◆ how to convert units using a conversion factor.

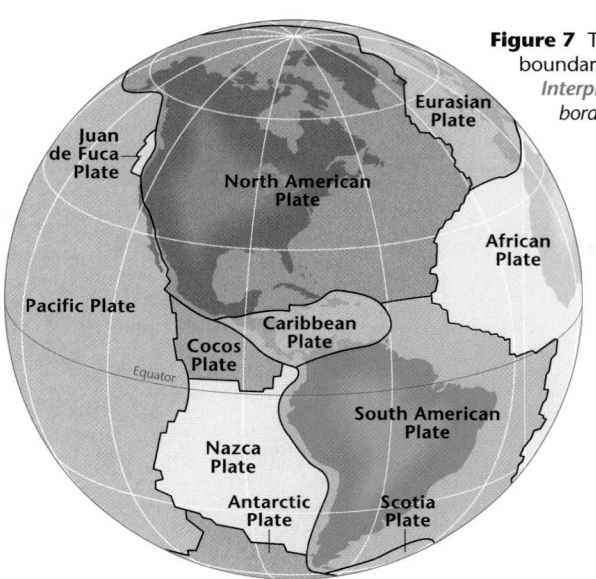

Figure 7 The black outlines show the boundaries of some of Earth's plates. *Interpreting Maps* Which plates border the Nazca plate?

Some plates pull away from each other, some plates push toward each other, and some plates slide past each other.

☑ *Checkpoint* *What is the name scientists use for pieces of Earth's upper layer?*

How Fast Do Plates Move?

The speed with which Earth's plates move is very slow indeed. Some small plates can move as much as several centimeters per year, whereas others move only a few millimeters per year.

Knowing how far a plate moves in a certain amount of time enables scientists to calculate the average speed of the plate. This, in turn, enables scientists to explain how Earth's surface has changed over time. And it helps them to predict how it will change in the future. Figure 8 on pages 128–129 shows an estimate of how the continents have moved in the past and how they may move in the future.

Calculating Distance Suppose scientists study a particular plate over the course of a year. They find that the plate moves a distance of 5 centimeters. Thus the speed at which the plate moves is 5 centimeters divided by one year, or 5 cm/yr.

How can you use the speed of a plate to predict how far the plate will move in 1,000 years? To find distance, rearrange the speed formula to look like this: Distance = Speed × Time.

Sharpen your Skills

Predicting

Los Angeles, on the Pacific Plate, is slowly moving northwest. San Francisco, on the North American plate, is slowly moving southeast. These two cities are moving toward each other at a rate of about 5 cm/yr. If the two cities are now 554,000 m apart, how long will it take for the two cities to meet each other?

Answers to Self-Assessment

Caption Question

Figure 7 Antarctic, South American, Cocos, Caribbean, Pacific

☑ *Checkpoint*

Pieces of Earth's crust are called plates.

---

2 Facilitate

What Are Earth's Plates?

Using the Visuals: Figure 7

Have students examine the map. Find a plate boundary. Ask: **What would happen at a boundary where plates are pushing together?** (*Answers may vary. Sample: Mountains may form.*) **learning modality: visual**

How Fast Do Plates Move?

Sharpen your Skills

Predicting

Time 15 minutes
Tips Write the formula for speed on the board: Speed = Distance ÷ Time. Ask: **How does distance depend on time?** (*A greater distance takes a greater time.*) **How does time depend on speed?** (*A greater speed means less time for a certain distance.*) Write the formula for time on the board (Time = Distance ÷ Speed). Remind students that all distances in the equation must first be changed to the same unit. Guide students' calculations using these steps:

554,000 m × 100 cm/m = 55,400,000 cm
Time = 55,400,000 cm ÷ 5 cm/yr
Time = 11,080,000 yr

Extend Give students a map of California and ask them to find San Francisco and Los Angeles. Have them try to figure out where the fault runs based on the information in the text. **learning modality: logical/ mathematical**

Ongoing Assessment

Writing Calculate the distance that a plate will move if it moves at a speed of 4 cm/yr for 8,000,000 years (*32,000,000 cm*)

How Fast Do Plates Move?, continued

Using the Visuals: Figure 8

Help students identify the portions of the southern land mass that became South America, Africa, and India. Have students trace the movement of these land masses between 135 million years ago to 100 million years ago. Ask: **How did the movements of the plates affect South America, Africa and India between 100 million years ago and now?** *(All three moved north. India collided with Eurasia.)* **If South America, Africa and India continue moving in the same direction, predict what will happen?** *(South America will move north, the Mediterranean will disappear as Africa crashes into Europe, and the Himalayas will continue to pile up.)* **learning modality: visual**

Building Inquiry Skills: Problem Solving

Materials *number cubes, index cards, poster board, markers, tokens to use as game pieces*

ACTIVITY

Time 1 class period

Before class, prepare sufficient game cards so that each group will have at least 10 cards. Create conversion problems using units of time, distance, and speed and create other problems solving for speed, reading graphs, and so on. Print each problem on one side of an index card and write the answer on the other side. You may wish to have some of your more capable students help you create cards. Allow students to work in groups to design the game board. Some students in each group can create the board, including spaces such as "Lose a Turn," "Roll Again," and "Go Back 2 Spaces." The remaining students can write down the game rules. The basic rule should be that players must correctly answer a conversion problem before rolling the number cubes and advancing across the board. **learning modality: logical/mathematical**

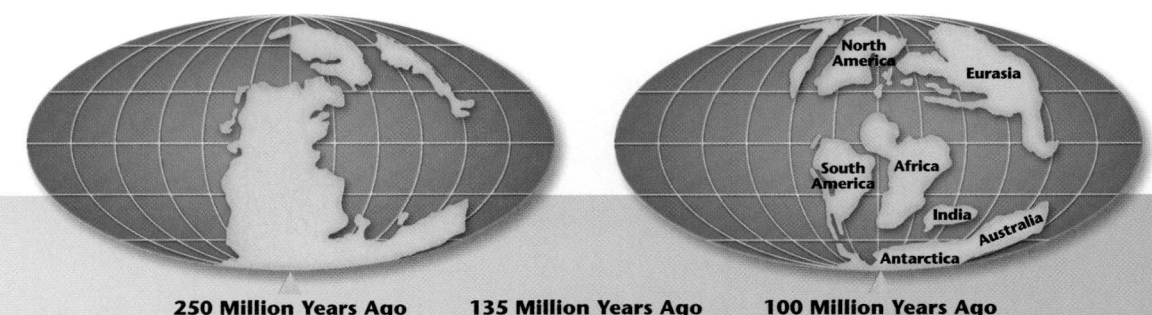

250 Million Years Ago   **135 Million Years Ago**   **100 Million Years Ago**

Figure 8 The shapes and positions of Earth's continents have changed greatly over time and will continue to change in the future. *Interpreting Maps Locate Australia on the map. How does its position change over time?*

This formula tells you to multiply the speed of the plate by the time during which the plate travels at that speed.

$$Distance = \frac{5\ cm}{1\ yr} \times 1,000\ yr = 5,000\ cm$$

The plate moves 5,000 centimeters in 1,000 years. Since 5,000 is a large number, try expressing this distance in meters. Recall that there are 100 centimeters in 1 meter, so you can divide by 100 by moving the decimal to the left two places.

$$5,000.\ cm = 50.00\ m$$

So in 1,000 years, which is well over ten average lifetimes, this plate moves only 50 meters. Walking at a brisk pace, you can probably travel the same distance in about 30 seconds!

Converting Units Suppose you want to know the speed of the plate in centimeters per day rather than centimeters per year. You can convert from one unit of measurement to another by using a conversion factor, a fraction in which the numerator and denominator are equal. In this example, 1 year is equal to 365 days. So you choose a conversion factor from these two possibilities.

$$\frac{1\ yr}{365\ d} = 1 \quad or \quad \frac{365\ d}{1\ yr} = 1$$

Background

History of Science In the 1960s, Harry Hess proposed the hypothesis of sea-floor spreading. His hypothesis stated that rising volcanic material along a mid-ocean ridge pushed the older hardened rock away from the ridge in two directions. This movement, in turn, acted like a conveyor belt for the floating continents. Hess's discovery led to an understanding of how the continents moved.

Earth's continents and other landmasses also move as the plates that carry them move toward or away from each other. When plates collide or split apart, new land features, such as mountains, form.

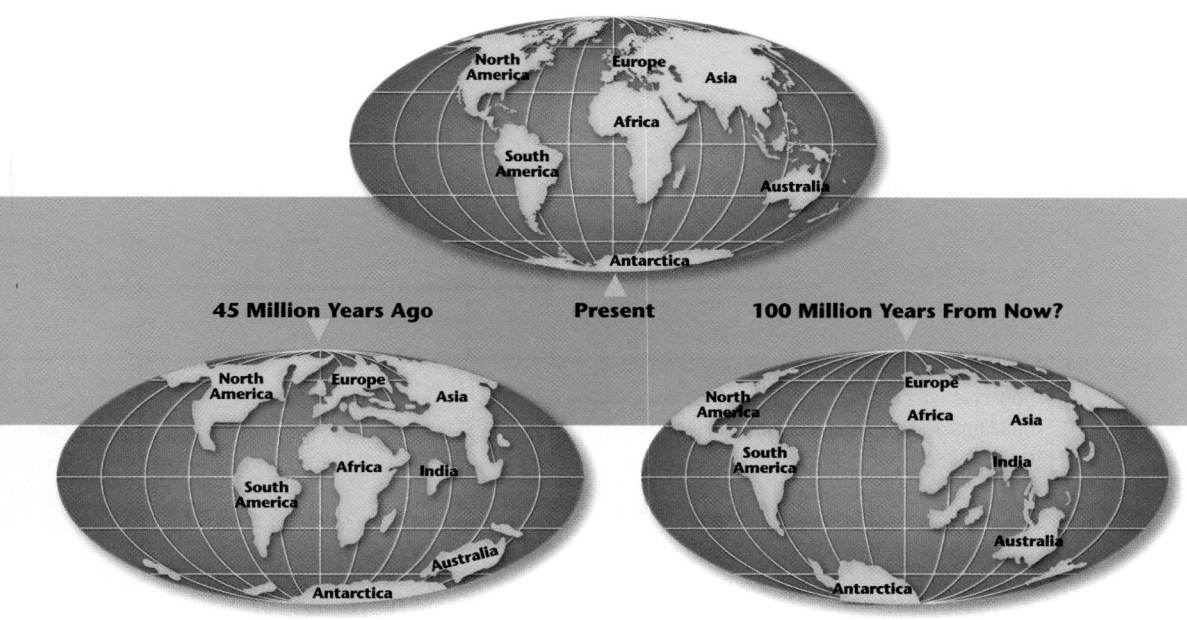

45 Million Years Ago   **Present**   **100 Million Years From Now?**

The conversion factor you need is the one that will allow you to cancel the years units. This factor is the one that has years in the numerator.

$$\frac{5\ cm}{1\ yr} \times \frac{1\ yr}{365\ d} = 0.0137\ cm/d$$

So you can describe the speed of this plate as 5 centimeters per year or as 0.0137 centimeters per day.

Section 2 Review

1. What is the theory that explains the slow movement of continents on Earth's surface?
2. Give two reasons why you don't notice the land moving beneath you. (*Hint*: Remember reference points.)
3. Suppose you are studying the motion of one of Earth's plates. What units would you probably use to describe its speed? Explain why.
4. **Thinking Critically Problem Solving** A certain plate moves 5 mm in 100 days. What is its speed in mm/d? What is its speed in mm/yr?

Science at Home

Have each member of your family measure the length of the white part at the end of one fingernail. Write down the results (and which finger you used) and mark your calendar for a date in exactly three weeks. On that day, measure the new length of the white part of the same fingernail. Then calculate the speed, in millimeters per day, at which your fingernail grew. Discuss with your family how your results compare with the typical speed with which continents move.

Program Resources

◆ **Unit 2 Resources** 4-2 Review and Reinforce, p. 15; 4-2 Enrich, p. 16

Answers to Self-Assessment

Caption Question

Figure 8 Over time, Australia moved north.

Section 2 Review Answers

1. The theory of plate tectonics
2. Because the movement is slow and because you do not change position relative to the reference point, the plate
3. Use cm/yr or mm/yr because plates travel very slowly.
4. 0.05 mm/d; 18.25 mm/yr

Science at Home

Materials *metric ruler*
Encourage students to involve at least one or two family members of different ages. Students should record the measurements in millimeters. Suggest that students and family members take measurements of more than one finger in case a particular fingernail breaks during the three-week period. Students should find that fingernail growth rate is similar to the movement of Earth's plates.

Performance Assessment

Skills Check Calculate the distance in meters that a continental plate will travel if it moves at a speed of 2 cm/yr for 5 million years. *(100,000 m)*

Stopping on a Dime

Preparing for Inquiry

Key Concept Students will use measurements of reaction times, running speeds, and stopping distances to help them decide where a basketball court should be located.

Skills Objectives Students will be able to
◆ measure reaction time, maximum speed, and stopping distance;
◆ use reaction time, maximum speed, and stopping distance to calculate the total distance a student could travel after crossing an out-of-bounds line;
◆ infer how reaction time, speed, and stopping distance influence total distance.

Time 50 minutes

Advance Planning Reserve time and space on the school field or in the gymnasium for Part II of the lab.

Guiding Inquiry

Invitation Have students think about the importance of using measurements and calculations to infer a suitable location of a basketball court. Ask: **When you run out of bounds on a basketball court, what determines how long it takes you to stop?** (*Sample: running speed*)

Introducing the Procedure

◆ Tell students that the distance a basketball player will run past an out-of-bounds line depends on three things. First, on how fast the player is running when he or she goes out of bounds (maximum running speed). Second, on how long it takes the player to realize that he or she is out of bounds (reaction time). Third, on how far a player travels after realizing that he or she needs to stop (stopping distance).

◆ Give students specific instructions concerning where running speed and stopping distance will be measured. Show them where the timer should stand, where the runner will begin, and in which direction the runner should run. If possible, go through a sample calculation on the board.

Stopping on a Dime

The school has decided to put in a new basketball court in a small area between two buildings. Safety is an important consideration in the design of the court. You and your friends volunteer to find out experimentally how close the out-of-bounds lines can be to the buildings and still allow players to stop without running into a wall.

Problem

What is the distance needed between an out-of-bounds line and a wall so that a player can stop before hitting the wall?

Skills Focus

measuring, calculating, inferring

Materials

wooden meter stick · · · · tape measure
2 stopwatches or watches with second hands

Procedure

Part I Reaction Time

1. Have your partner suspend a wooden meter stick, zero end down, between your thumb and index finger, as shown. Your thumb and index finger should be about 3 cm apart.
2. Your partner will drop the meter stick without giving you any warning. You will try to grab it with your thumb and index finger.
3. Note the level at which you grabbed the meter stick and use the chart shown to determine your reaction time. Record the time in the class data table.
4. Reverse roles with your partner and repeat Steps 1 through 3.

Reaction Time

Distance (cm)	Time (s)	Distance (cm)	Time (s)
15	0.175	25	0.226
16	0.181	26	0.230
17	0.186	27	0.235
18	0.192	28	0.239
19	0.197	29	0.243
20	0.202	30	0.247
21	0.207	31	0.252
22	0.212	32	0.256
23	0.217	33	0.260
24	0.221	34	0.263

Expected Outcome

A typical reaction time is about 0.2 seconds. A typical running speed is about 5 m/s, which produces a stopping distance of about 3 m. Reaction time plus stopping distance means that there should be a safety margin of around 4 m.

Troubleshooting the Experiment

Make sure students do not slow down before reaching the 25-meter mark. Be sure that the person dropping the meter stick does not inadvertently signal the person catching.

Analyze and Conclude

1. Find the student with the lowest time for running the course. Divide the distance (25 m) by this time to get the maximum running speed in meters per second.

2. The maximum running speed multiplied by the slowest reaction time tells how far the

CLASS DATA TABLE

Student Name	Reaction Time (s)	Running Time (s)	Stopping Distance (m)

Part II Stopping Distance

5. On the school field or in the gymnasium, mark off a distance of 25 m. **CAUTION:** *Be sure to remove any obstacles from the course.*

6. Have your partner time how long it takes you to run the course at full speed. After you pass the 25-m mark, come to a stop as quickly as possible and remain standing. You must not slow down before the mark.

7. Have your partner measure the distance from the 25-m mark to your final position. This is the distance you need to come to a complete stop. Enter your time and distance into the class data table.

8. Reverse roles with your partner. Enter your partner's time and distance into the class data table.

Analyze and Conclude

1. How can you calculate the average speed of the student who ran the 25-m course the fastest? Find this speed.

2. Multiply the speed of the fastest student (calculated in Question 1) by the slowest reaction time listed in the class data table. Why would you be interested in this product?

3. Add the distance calculated in Question 2 to the longest stopping distance in the class data table. What does this total distance represent?

4. Explain why it is important to use the fastest speed, the slowest reaction time, and the longest stopping distance in your calculations.

5. What other factors should you take into account to get results that apply to a real basketball court?

6. **Apply** Suppose the distance between the out-of-bounds line and the wall in a playground or gymnasium is, according to your calculations, too short for safety. Suggest some strategies that could be used (other than moving the wall) for making that playground safer.

Getting Involved

Visit a local playground and examine it from the viewpoint of safety. Use what you learned about stopping distance as one of your guidelines, but also try to identify other potentially unsafe conditions. Write a letter to the department of parks or to the officials of your town informing them of your findings.

---

3. Adding the longest stopping distance tells how much farther the student in Question 2 will travel before coming to a complete stop if that student also had the longest measured stopping distance.

4. It's the "worst case scenario." You are calculating the maximum distance it could take a student to stop. In reality, students will either be slower runners or will react faster or will have a shorter stopping distance. Thus all students should be able to stop in a distance that is shorter than you have calculated. To show that this is true, students can calculate how far they would travel given their own measured maximum speed, reaction time, and stopping distance.

5. A player may go out of bounds running sideways, jumping, or stumbling. A player might not immediately realize that he or she is out of bounds. These factors might increase the distance the player traveled.

6. You could add a wide yellow line to let players know when they are approaching the out of bounds. This would alert them to react sooner. You could also place cushions on the wall to reduce the risk of injury in a collision.

Extending the Inquiry

Getting Involved Students should check to make sure that there is enough distance between the out-of-bounds line and any obstructions (trees, walls, parking areas, roads). Students should realize that lines indicating where spectators should sit or stand would prevent a possible collision with a player. Students should note that basketball posts are very close to the court and perhaps should be wrapped in foam. Students should look for cracks in the playing surface.

Safety

All students should run in the same direction. Students should not be allowed to walk across the area where running speeds are being measured. Review the safety guidelines in Appendix A.

Program Resources

◆ **Unit 2 Resources** Real-World Lab blackline masters, pp. 23–25

Media and Technology

 Lab Activity Videotape
Tape 1

Objectives

After completing the lesson, students will be able to
- describe what happens to the motion of an object as it accelerates;
- calculate the acceleration of an object and graph changing speed and distance of an accelerating object.

Key Term acceleration

1 Engage/Explore

Activating Prior Knowledge

Ask a volunteer to blow up a balloon and hold the opening firmly shut. Say: **Describe the motion of the balloon right now.** *(The balloon is not moving.)* Then ask: **What could you do to make the balloon move?** *(Release it.)* Now have the volunteer release the balloon. Make sure it is released toward a wall, well away from other students. Ask students to describe when the balloon changed speed or direction as it flew. *(More or less continuously, from the moment of release until it landed)* Tell students in this section they investigate changing speed and direction.

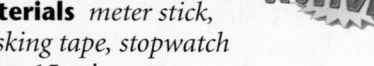

Skills Focus inferring
Materials *meter stick, masking tape, stopwatch*
Time 15 minutes
Tips Take students to a large open area or a long hallway where they will not disturb others. When students begin walking, suggest they walk very slowly, and gradually increase their speed until they are moving as fast as they can without running. Caution them not to run.
Think It Over The faster you speed up, the less time it takes to walk the course.

132

DISCOVER ······························ACTIVITY

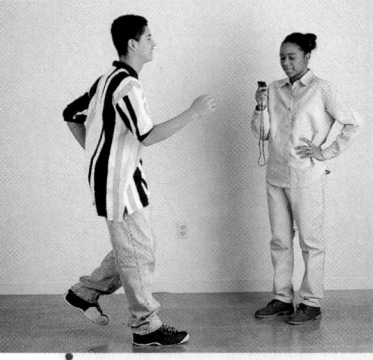

Will You Hurry Up?

1. Measure 10 meters in an area in which you can walk freely. Mark the distance with a piece of masking tape.

2. Walk the 10 meters in such way that you keep moving faster throughout the entire distance. Have a partner time you.

3. Repeat Step 2, but try to walk the 10 meters in less time than you did before. Try it again, but this time walk it in twice the amount of time as the first. Remember that you must keep speeding up throughout the entire 10 meters.

Think It Over
Inferring How is the change in your speed related to the time in which you walk the 10-meter course?

GUIDE FOR READING

- What happens to the motion of an object as it accelerates?
- How is acceleration calculated?

Reading Tip As you read, list the three different types of acceleration. Then give several examples of each.

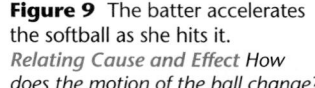

Figure 9 The batter accelerates the softball as she hits it.
Relating Cause and Effect How does the motion of the ball change?

The pitcher winds up. She throws. The ball speeds to the batter and, *crack*—off the bat it goes. It's going, it's going, it's gone—a home run!

Before landing, the ball went through several changes in motion. It started moving when it left the pitcher's hand, sped up, stopped when it hit the bat, changed direction, sped up again, and eventually slowed down. Most examples of motion involve similar changes. In fact, it is rare for any motion to stay the same for very long. You can describe changes in motion in much the same way as you did when you learned how to describe motion in terms of speed and velocity.

Acceleration in Science

Consider a car stopped at a red light. When the light changes to green, the driver of the car gently steps on the accelerator. As a result, the car speeds up, or accelerates. In everyday language, *acceleration* means "the process of speeding up."

Acceleration has a more precise definition in science. **Acceleration** is the rate at which velocity changes. Recall that velocity has two components (speed and direction). Acceleration involves a change in either of these components. **In science, acceleration refers to increasing speed, decreasing speed, or changing direction.**

READING STRATEGIES

Reading Tip For each kind of acceleration, challenge students to identify at least three examples of objects in motion not in the text. *(Sample: Increasing speed—car starting from stopped position; decreasing speed—jet landing on a runway; changing direction—moon orbiting Earth)* Once students' lists are complete, invite them to share ideas with each other.

Concept Mapping As they complete the section, students can form a concept map using the following terms: *acceleration, time, speed, direction, distance.*

Increasing Speed Any time the speed of an object increases, the object experiences acceleration. Can you think of examples of acceleration? A softball accelerates when the pitcher throws it, and again when a bat hits it. A car that begins to move from a stopped position or speeds up to pass another car is accelerating.

People can experience acceleration as well. The runners in Figure 10 increase their speed to sprint down the track. A figure skater will accelerate as he speeds up before jumping into the air. Similarly, a gymnast might accelerate as she runs into a tumbling routine. You accelerate as you speed up to catch the bus for school.

Decreasing Speed Just as objects can speed up, they can also slow down. Motion in which speed decreases is also considered acceleration in science. This change in speed is sometimes called deceleration, or negative acceleration.

Can you think of examples of deceleration? A softball decelerates as it rolls to a stop. A car decelerates when it comes to a stop at a red light. A jet decelerates as it lands on an aircraft carrier. The diver in Figure 10 decelerates when traveling through the water.

Changing Direction A car on a highway may be traveling at constant speed. Thus you may be tempted to conclude that it is not accelerating. Recall, however, that velocity involves *both* speed and direction. Therefore, an object can be accelerating even if its speed is constant. The car, for example, will be accelerating if it follows a gentle curve in the road or changes lanes. The skaters in Figure 10 accelerate as they round the turns on the track.

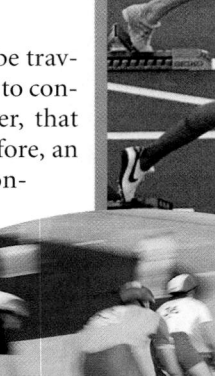

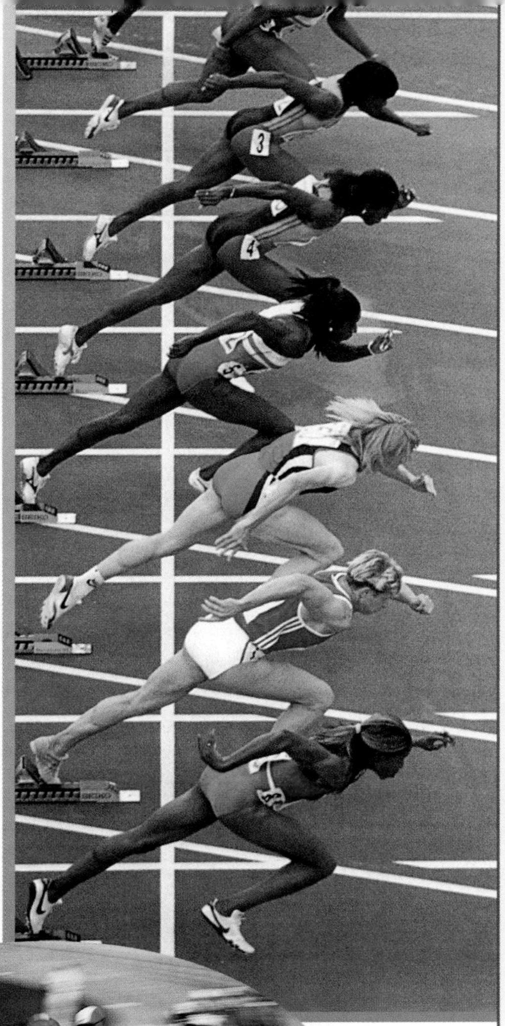

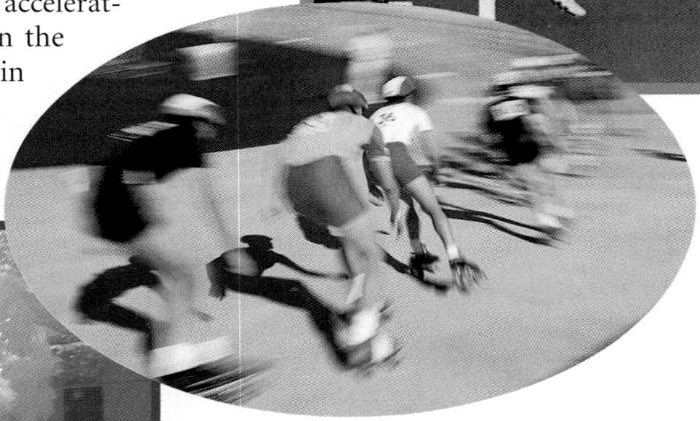

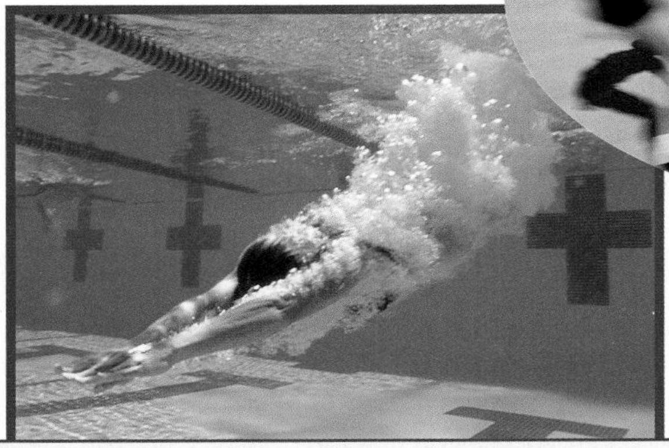

Figure 10 The diver, the skaters, and the runners are all accelerating. *Classifying Can you identify the change in motion in each example?*

2 Facilitate

Acceleration in Science

Addressing Naive Conceptions

Students may not realize that acceleration can involve speeding up or slowing down. Ask students which of these statements could be true:

- When you step on the gas, the car accelerates.
- When you step on the brake, the car accelerates.

Explain that both statements are correct, because acceleration is defined as any change in velocity. Slowing down, or deceleration, is negative acceleration. **learning modality: verbal**

Inquiry Challenge

ACTIVITY

Materials *marble, cardboard tubes, scissors, masking tape, books or blocks*
Time 40 minutes
Tips To demonstrate the ways an object can accelerate, invite students to construct tracks for marbles. Organize students in small groups. They can cut the cardboard tubes in half lengthwise and join the sections with masking tape. Tracks must be long enough for the marble to show all forms of acceleration. Tell students the tracks must make the marble speed up, slow down, and change direction. Ask: **How can you arrange the track so that the marble speeds up?** *(Make it so that the marble rolls downward.)* **Slows down?** *(Make it so that it has an upward-sloping section.)* **Changes direction?** *(Make it have a curve.)* **learning modality: kinesthetic**

Program Resources

- **Unit 2 Resources** 4-3 Lesson Plan, p. 17; 4-3 Section Summary, p. 18
- **Guided Reading and Study Workbook** Section 4-3
- **Laboratory Manual** 4, "Measuring Speed"

Answers to Self-Assessment

Caption Questions

Figure 9 The ball approaches the bat at almost constant speed, stops momentarily while in contact with the bat, then accelerates in the opposite direction just as the bat pushes it forward.
Figure 10 The runners are speeding up, the diver is changing direction and slowing down, and the skaters are changing direction.

Ongoing Assessment

Drawing Have students make sketches that show three ways an object can accelerate. *(Sketches should show acceleration by speeding up, slowing down, and changing direction.)*

Acceleration in Science, continued

Integrating Space Science

Materials *bicycle, tape, construction paper, scissors*
Time 5 minutes

Make a construction-paper arrow. Tape it to the bicycle wheel so that it points in the direction the wheel will move when spinning. Slowly spin the wheel. Ask: **In what direction is the arrow pointing?** (*In different directions*) Ask: **Does the arrow have acceleration? Explain.** (*Yes, because it changes direction.*) Point out that just like the arrow, the moon, Earth, and satellites accelerate because they constantly change direction. **learning modality: visual**

Calculating Acceleration

Using the Visuals: Figure 12

Have students draw a line graph plotting the data for the airplane. Ask students to describe the graph. (*The graph is a straight line sloping up to the right.*) Ask students what this tells them about constant acceleration. (*The speed changes by the same amount each second.*)
learning modality: logical/ mathematical

Building Inquiry Skills: Calculating

Students may have difficulty understanding units of acceleration. Ask them to imagine that they are riding in a car traveling at 30 km/h. Exactly 1 minute later, the speedometer reads 50 km/h. Ask: **What was the change in speed?** (*20 km/h*) Then ask: **What was the change in time?** (*1 min*) Finally, ask: **If you watched the speedometer during that minute, what would you expect to see?** (*The needle moving slowly from 30 km/h to 50 km/h*) Since acceleration is the change in speed over a period of time, the acceleration is written as 20 km/h per min, or 20 km/h/min.
learning modality: logical/ mathematical

Figure 11 The Ferris wheel is accelerating because it is changing direction. *Making Generalizations* What path does the Ferris wheel follow?

Many objects continuously change direction without changing speed. The simplest example of this type of motion is circular motion, or motion along a circular path. The seats on the Ferris wheel accelerate because they move in a circle.

 INTEGRATING SPACE SCIENCE In a similar way, the moon accelerates because it is continuously changing direction. Just as Earth revolves around the sun, the moon revolves around Earth. Another object that continuously accelerates is an artificial satellite orbiting Earth.

☑ *Checkpoint* How is it possible for a car to be accelerating if its speed is a steady 65 km/h?

Calculating Acceleration

Acceleration describes the rate at which velocity changes. **To determine the acceleration of an object, you must calculate the change in velocity during each unit of time.** This is summarized by the following formula.

$$\text{Acceleration} = \frac{\text{Final velocity} - \text{Initial velocity}}{\text{Time}}$$

If velocity is measured in meters/second and time is measured in seconds, the unit of acceleration is meters per second per second. This unit is written as m/s^2. This unit may sound peculiar at first. But acceleration is the change in velocity per unit of time and velocity is the change in distance per unit of time. Therefore, acceleration has two units of time. Suppose velocity is measured in kilometers/hour and time is measured in hours. Then the unit of acceleration becomes kilometers per hour per hour, or km/h^2.

Background

Facts and Figures All objects in the solar system are accelerating in some way or another.

Comets travel in elliptical orbits. As they approach the sun, comets accelerate because their speed increases and their direction of motion changes. After a comet has moved past the sun and is headed back toward deep space, it is still accelerating because it is slowing down and changing direction.

Geostationary satellites appear to remain suspended above a spot on Earth's equator. However, they are not really stationary because, to stay over the same spot on the equator, they must move with constant speed completely around Earth once in 24 hours. Geostationary satellites are still accelerating because their direction of motion is constantly changing.

If the object's speed changes by the same amount during each unit of time, the acceleration at any time during its motion is the same. If, however, the acceleration varies, you can describe only the average acceleration.

For an object moving without changing direction, the acceleration of the object is the change in its speed during one unit of time. Consider, for example, a small airplane moving on a runway. The speed of the airplane at the end of each of the first 5 seconds of its motion is shown in Figure 12.

To calculate the acceleration of the airplane, you must first subtract the initial speed (0 m/s) from the final speed (40 m/s). This gives the change in speed, 40 m/s. Then divide the change in speed by the time, 5 seconds. The acceleration is 40 m/s divided by 5 seconds, which is 8 m/s^2.

The acceleration tells you how the speed of the airplane in Figure 12 changes during each second. Notice that after each interval of one second, the speed of the airplane is 8 m/s greater

Change in Speed Over Time

Time (s)	Speed (m/s)
0	0
1	8
2	16
3	24
4	32
5	40

Figure 12 The speed of the airplane increases by the same amount each second.

Sample Problem

A roller coaster car rapidly picks up speed as it rolls down a slope. As it starts down the slope, its speed is 4 m/s. But 3 seconds later, at the bottom of the slope, its speed is 22 m/s. What is its average acceleration?

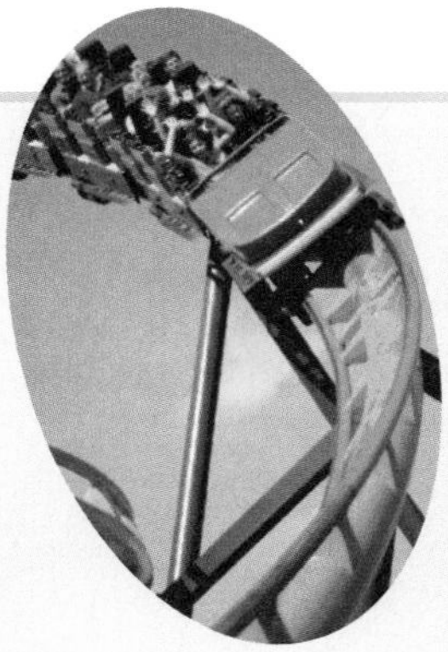

Analyze. You know the initial velocity and final velocity of the car, and the length of time during which its velocity changed. You are looking for its acceleration.

Write the formula.
$$\text{Acceleration} = \frac{\text{Final velocity} - \text{Initial velocity}}{\text{Time}}$$

Substitute and solve.
$$\text{Acceleration} = \frac{22 \text{ m/s} - 4 \text{ m/s}}{3 \text{ s}}$$
$$\text{Acceleration} = \frac{18 \text{ m/s}}{3 \text{ s}}$$
$$\text{Acceleration} = 6 \text{ m/s}^2$$

Think about it. The answer is reasonable. If the car's velocity increases by 6 m/s each second, its velocity will be 10 m/s after one second, 16 m/s after two seconds, and 22 m/s after three seconds.

Practice Problems

1. A car advertisement states that a certain car can accelerate from rest to 90 km/h in 9 seconds. Find the car's average acceleration.
2. An eagle accelerates from 15 m/s to 22 m/s in 4 seconds. What is the eagle's average acceleration?

Answers to Self-Assessment

Caption Question

Figure 11 The Ferris wheel follows a circular path.

✓ Checkpoint

If the car is turning, it would be changing direction and therefore accelerating.

Including All Students

Students who are still mastering English may not understand the difference between speed and acceleration. When students say a car is "fast," they usually mean the car accelerates rapidly. Have students use speed and acceleration words in sentences such as: *The runner ____ quickly at the start, but could not keep up her ____ to the finish line.* **limited English proficiency**

Sample Problem

Identify the main parts of the problem for students. Ask: **What is the initial velocity?** *(4 m/s)* **What is the final velocity?** *(22 m/s)* **How long did it take for the roller coaster to get from the top to the bottom of the slope?** *(3 s)* Ask students to complete the calculation. Follow up by asking: **What happens to the velocity each second?** *(It increases by 6 m/s.)* **learning modality: logical/mathematical**

Practice Problems

1. 10 km/hr/s
2. 1.75 m/s^2

Real-Life Learning

Ask students to describe what happens when they ride a bike down a steep hill. *(You move faster and faster.)* Then ask: **Suppose you reach the bottom of a hill traveling 20 km/hr. What additional information do you need to find your acceleration rate?** *(Speed at the top of the hill; time it took to go from the top to the bottom of the hill)* **learning modality: logical/mathematical**

Ongoing Assessment

Skills Check A badminton shuttlecock leaves the racquet traveling 30 m/s. It goes over the net 0.5 seconds later with a speed of 10 m/s. Calculate the average acceleration.

Graphing Acceleration

Using the Visuals: Figure 13

Draw student's attention to the line graphs in the figure. Ask: **How is the graph of change in distance over time different from the graph of change in speed over time?** *(The distance-time graph curves upward instead of being a straight line.)* Then ask: **What would happen to the curved graph if the acceleration were less?** *(The graph would curve upward less.)* **learning modality: logical/mathematical**

3 Assess

Section 3 Review Answers

1. Increasing speed—a plane taking off; decreasing speed—a car braking; changing direction—a bicycle turning
2. Acceleration = (Final velocity − Initial velocity) ÷ Time
3. The horse is accelerating because it is continually changing direction.
4. The car could have accelerated at 2 m/s^2 for 12 s, 4 m/s^2 for 6 s, or 6 m/s^2 for 4 s. There are an infinite number of ways for the speed increase to have happened.

Check Your Progress
CHAPTER PROJECT 4

Talk with the whole class about ways to make measurements more accurately. Explain to students why taking several measurements and then calculating the average improves accuracy. Show students ways to organize their calculations to model good problem-solving techniques.

Changes in Speed and Distance Over Time

Time (s)	Speed (m/s)	Distance (m)
0	0	0
1	10	5
2	20	20
3	30	45
4	40	80
5	50	125

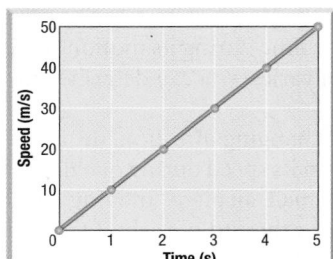 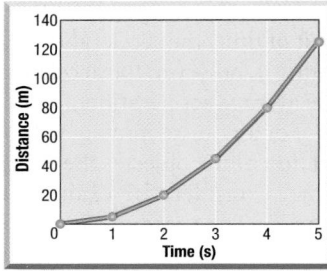

Figure 13 These graphs plot the motion of an accelerating object. *Predicting How would the slope of the speed and time graph change if the object were accelerating more rapidly? More slowly? What do you think the graph of a decelerating object would look like?*

than during the previous interval. So after one second, its speed is 8 m/s. After two seconds, its speed is 8 m/s + 8 m/s, or 16 m/s, and so on. Since the acceleration of the airplane does not change during the 5 seconds, you can use this formula for any time interval during the five seconds. Try it.

Graphing Acceleration

You can use a graph to analyze the motion of an object that is accelerating. Figure 13 shows the data for an object that is accelerating at 10 m/s^2. The graph showing speed versus time is a slanted straight line. The straight line shows that acceleration is constant. For every increase of one second, the speed increases by 10 m/s. Thus the graphed line rises the same amount each second. If the object accelerated by a different amount each second, the graph would not be a straight line.

The graph of distance versus time is a curved line. This tells you that the distance traveled by the accelerating object varies each second. As the speed increases, the graph curves upward.

Section 3 Review

1. What three kinds of change in motion are called acceleration? Give an example of each.
2. What formula is used to calculate acceleration?
3. A horse trots around a large circular track, maintaining a constant speed of 5 m/s. Is the horse accelerating? Explain.
4. **Thinking Critically Problem Solving** A car is creeping down a deserted highway at 1 m/s. Sometime later, its speed is 25 m/s. This could have happened if the car accelerated at 3 m/s^2 for 8 seconds. Is this the only way the increase in speed could have happened? Explain.

Check Your Progress
CHAPTER PROJECT 4

You can improve the accuracy of your speed estimations by repeating measurements and by using averaged data. Make all your calculations in an organized, step-by-step manner. Prepare display cards that show how you calculated each speed.

Performance Assessment

Oral Presentation Divide the class into small groups. Have each group write a short scenario involving an object being accelerated, then exchange scenarios with another group and sketch a graph of speed versus time for the scenario. Finally, have each group present its findings to the class.

Program Resources

◆ **Unit 2 Resources** 4-3 Review and Reinforce, p. 19; 4-3 Enrich, p. 20

Answers to Self-Assessment

Caption Question

Figure 13 If the object were accelerating more rapidly, then the slope of the speed and time line would be steeper. If it were accelerating more slowly, then the slope of the line would less steep. A decelerating object would produce a speed and time graph with a line that falls instead of rises.

Describing and Measuring Motion

Key Ideas

◆ The motion of an object is determined by its change of position relative to a reference point.

◆ Speed is the distance an object travels in one unit of time. If an object moves at constant speed, its speed can be determined by dividing the distance it travels by the time taken. If an object's speed varies, then dividing distance by time gives you the object's average speed.

◆ When you state both the speed of an object and the direction in which it is moving, you are describing the object's velocity.

◆ The slope of a distance-time graph represents speed. The steeper the slope, the faster the speed.

Key Terms

motion	meter
reference point	speed
International System of Units (SI)	velocity

 Slow Motion on Planet Earth

INTEGRATING EARTH SCIENCE

Key Idea

◆ The plates that make up Earth's outer layer move very slowly, only centimeters per year, in various directions.

Key Term

plate

Acceleration

Key Ideas

◆ Acceleration is the rate at which velocity changes. It involves increasing speed, decreasing speed, or changing direction.

◆ Acceleration can be calculated by dividing the change in velocity by the amount of time it took that change to occur.

Key Term

acceleration

Organizing Information

Concept Map Copy the concept map about motion onto a separate sheet of paper. Then complete it and add a title. (For more on concept maps, see the Skills Handbook.)

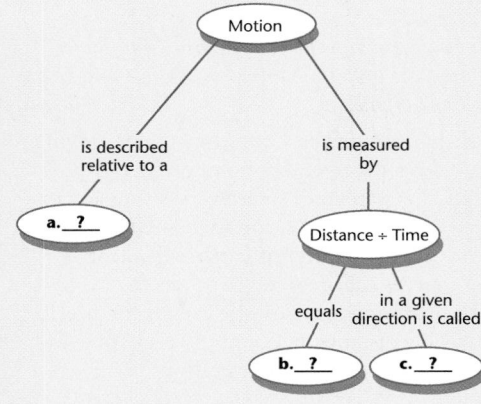

Chapter 4 **137**

Organizing Information

Concept Map Sample title: Describing and Measuring Motion
a. reference point **b.** speed **c.** velocity

Reviewing Content
Multiple Choice
1. d **2.** b **3.** b **4.** d **5.** a

True or False
6. true **7.** straight line **8.** plates **9.** true
10. speed

Checking Concepts
11. From the reference point of the train, you are moving toward the rear of the train at walking speed. From the reference point of the ground, you are moving in the same direction as the train at a speed slightly less than the speed of the train.
12. The warbler has a greater speed, 12 m/s, compared to the hawk's 10 m/s.
13. The greater the slope, the greater the speed.
14. You could make a mark where it is today (a reference point), then come back after a certain period of time and make a mark to show where it is now. If it is still at the same reference point, it is not moving.
15. The insect is accelerating because the direction of its motion is always changing.
16. This assignment should generate interesting and useful responses. Check that the actual speeds students use are reasonable values for what they are describing.

Thinking Critically
17. Compare the times it takes to travel each block. If they are the same, the car probably stayed at a constant speed. If they are different, then the car accelerated.
18. Since they left at the same time, the first driver had the greater average speed since that driver drove the same distance in less time.
19. The family traveled a total distance of 160 km (80 km/hr × 1 hr + 40 km/hr × 2 hr) in 3 hours. So their average speed is 53.3 km/hr (160 km ÷ 3 hr = 53.3 km/hr). Simply adding the two speeds and dividing by 2 gives an incorrect answer because the family spent more time driving at the slower speed.

Reviewing Content
Multiple Choice
Choose the letter of the best answer.

1. A change in position with respect to a reference point is
  a. acceleration.   **b.** velocity.
  c. direction.   **d.** motion.

2. To find the average speed of an object,
  a. add together its different speeds and divide by the number of speeds.
  b. divide the distance it travels by the time taken to travel that distance.
  c. divide the time it takes to travel a distance by the distance traveled.
  d. multiply the acceleration by the time.

3. If you know a car travels 30 km in 20 minutes, you can find its
  a. acceleration.   **b.** average speed.
  c. direction.   **d.** graph.

4. A child on a merry-go-round is accelerating because the child
  a. is moving relative to the ground.
  b. does not change speed.
  c. is moving relative to the sun.
  d. is always changing direction.

5. If you divide the increase in an object's speed by the time taken for that increase, you are determining the object's
  a. acceleration.   **b.** constant speed.
  c. average speed.   **d.** velocity.

True or False
If the statement is true, write true. If it is false, change the underlined word or words to make the statement true.

6. In a moving elevator, you are not moving from the reference point of the <u>elevator</u>.
7. The graph of distance versus time for an object moving at constant speed is a <u>curve</u>.
8. The upper layer of Earth is made of pieces called <u>reference points</u>.
9. Acceleration is a change in speed or <u>direction</u>.
10. The distance an object travels in one unit of time is called <u>acceleration</u>.

Applying Skills
20. Starting line to line B = 2.0 cm; line B to finish line = 5.0 cm
21. 2 cm/s
22. 1.0 cm/s^2

Checking Concepts
11. Suppose you walk toward the rear of a moving train. Describe your motion as seen from a reference point on the train. Then describe it from a reference point on the ground.
12. Which has a greater speed, a hawk that travels 600 meters in 60 seconds or a tiny warbler that travels 60 meters in 5 seconds? Explain.
13. You have a motion graph for an object that shows distance and time. How does the slope of the graph relate to the object's speed?
14. How can you tell if an object is moving if its motion is too slow to see?
15. An insect is on a compact disc that is put into a compact disc player. The disc spins around and the insect hangs on for dear life. Is the insect accelerating? Explain why or why not.
16. **Writing to Learn** Suppose that one day some of the things that usually move very slowly start to go faster, while some things that usually move quickly slow to a snail's pace. Write a description of some of the strange events that might occur during this weird day. Include a few actual speeds as part of your description.

Thinking Critically
17. **Making Generalizations** Suppose you make two measurements. One is the time that a car takes to travel a city block. The other is the time the car takes to travel the next city block. From these measurements, explain how you decide if the car is moving at a steady speed or if it is accelerating.
18. **Problem Solving** Two drivers start at the same time to make a 100-km trip. Driver 1 takes 2 hours to complete the trip. Driver 2 takes 3 hours, but stops for an hour at the halfway point. Which driver had a greater average speed for the whole trip? Explain.
19. **Applying Concepts** A family takes a car trip. They travel for an hour at 80 km/h and then for 2 hours at 40 km/h. Find the average speed. (*Hint:* Remember to consider the total distance and the total amount of time.)

Applying Skills

Use the illustration of the motion of a ladybug to answer Questions 20–22.

A — Start   B   C — Finish

20. **Measuring** Measure the distance from the starting line to line B, and from line B to the finish line. Measure to the nearest tenth of a centimeter.

21. **Calculating** Starting at rest, the ladybug accelerated to line B and then moved at constant speed until she reached the finish line. If she took 2.5 seconds to move from line B to the finish line, calculate her constant speed during that time.

22. **Interpreting Data** The speed you calculated in Question 21 is also the speed the ladybug had at line B (at the end of her acceleration). If she took 2 seconds to accelerate from the start line to line B, what is her acceleration during that time?

Performance CHAPTER PROJECT 4 Assessment

Project Wrap Up Organize your display cards so that they are easy to follow. Remember to put a title on each card stating the speed that was being measured. Place them in order from the slowest speed to the fastest. Then display your cards to your class. Compare your results with those of other students.

Reflect and Record When you measured the same speed more than once, were the data always the same? Explain. What factors make measuring a speed difficult?

Test Preparation

Use these questions to prepare for standardized tests.

Study the graph. Then answer Questions 23–27.

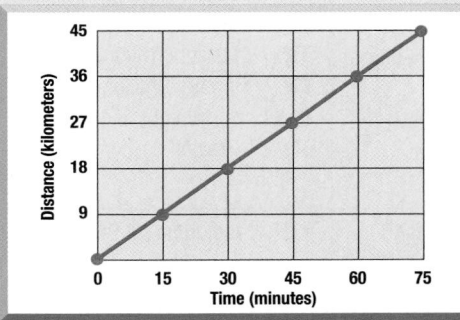

23. What would be the best title for this graph?
    a. Train at Rest
    b. Train Moving at Constant Acceleration
    c. Train Moving at Constant Speed
    d. Train Slowing to a Stop

24. During each 15-minute interval, the train travels a distance of
    a. 9 kilometers.   b. 18 kilometers.
    c. 36 kilometers.   d. 45 kilometers.

25. According to the graph, how long does it take for the train to travel 27 kilometers?
    a. 15 minutes   b. 30 minutes
    c. 45 minutes   d. 1 hour

26. What is the train's speed?
    a. 9 km/h   b. 18 km/h
    c. 36 km/h   d. 72 km/h

27. After 75 minutes, the train stops for 5 minutes to pick up passengers. How would the graph look during this period?
    a. The line would slant downward.
    b. The line would be horizontal.
    c. The line would be broken.
    d. The line would stop at a point and continue from the same point once the train begins to move again.

Performance CHAPTER PROJECT 4 Assessment

Project Wrap Up
- Have students review each other's display cards in small groups for the easy and medium categories. Prepare a table on which students can record and compare their different values.
- Have individual students present their methods on the board for calculating the speeds from the difficult category. Share alternate methods for each measurement, and discuss discrepancies in students' answers.
- Have students convert all the speed measurements to m/s. The class can then put all the display cards in order from slowest to fastest, and the display can be put on the wall or made into a booklet showing a spectrum of speeds.

Reflect and Record The students probably got slightly different answers when they measured the same speed more than once. Multiple measurements improve accuracy. Measuring speed is difficult because it involves measuring two different things, distance and time, accurately.

Test Preparation

23. c 24. a 25. c 26. c 27. b

Program Resources

- **Inquiry Skills Activity Book** Provides teaching and review of all inquiry skills
- **Prentice Hall Assessment System** Provides standardized test practice
- **Reading in the Content Area** Provides strategies to improve science reading skills
- **Teacher's ELL Handbook** Provides multiple strategies for English language learners

Forces

Sections	Time	Student Edition Activities	Other Activities	
CHAPTER PROJECT 5 **Newton Scooters** p. 141	Ongoing (3 weeks)	Check Your Progress, pp. 152, 159, 167 Project Wrap Up, p. 173	TE	Chapter 5 Project Notes, pp. 140–141
1 The Nature of Force pp. 142–149 ◆ 5.1.1 Explain how balanced and unbalanced forces are related to motion. ◆ 5.1.2 State Newton's first law of motion and define inertia.	2 periods/ 1 block	**Discover** What Changes Motion?, p. 142 **Try This** Around and Around, p. 146 **Science at Home** p. 147 **Skills Lab: Interpreting Data** Forced to Accelerate, pp. 148–149	TE TE	Including All Students, p. 143 Demonstration, p. 146
2 Force, Mass, and Acceleration pp. 150–152 ◆ 5.2.1 State Newton's second law of motion and explain how force and mass are related to acceleration.	1 period/ $\frac{1}{2}$ block	**Discover** How do the Rocks Roll?, p. 150	TE	Demonstration, p. 151
3 Friction and Gravity pp. 153–161 ◆ 5.3.1 Describe friction and identify the factors that determine the friction force between two surfaces. ◆ 5.3.2 Explain how mass differs from weight. ◆ 5.3.3 State the law of universal gravitation. ◆ 5.3.4 Describe the effects of gravity and air resistance on an object in free fall.	2 periods/ 1 block	**Discover** Which Lands First?, p. 153 **Try This** Spinning Plates, p. 155 **Sharpen Your Skills** Calculating, p. 158 **Real-World Lab: You, the Consumer** Sticky Sneakers, pp. 160–161 **PLM** Provides instructions for the probeware version of the lab	TE TE TE LM	Building Inquiry Skills: Designing Experiments, p. 154 Demonstration, p. 156 Inquiry Challenge, p. 157 5, "Weight and the Force of Gravity"
4 Action and Reaction pp. 162–167 ◆ 5.4.1 State Newton's third law of motion. ◆ 5.4.2 Define and calculate momentum and state the law of conservation of momentum.	1 period/ $\frac{1}{2}$ block	**Discover** How Pushy Is a Straw?, p. 162 **Try This** Colliding Cars, p. 166	TE	Including All Students, p. 163
5 *INTEGRATING SPACE SCIENCE* **Orbiting Satellites** pp. 168–170 ◆ 5.5.1 Explain how a rocket lifts off the ground. ◆ 5.5.2 Describe the forces that keep a satellite in orbit.	1 period/ $\frac{1}{2}$ block	**Discover** What Makes an Object Move in a Circle?, p. 168 **Science at Home** p. 170	TE	Demonstration, p. 169
Study Guide/Assessment pp. 171–173	1 period/ $\frac{1}{2}$ block		ISAB	Provides teaching and review of all inquiry skills

 For Standard or Block Schedule The Resource Pro® CD-ROM gives you maximum flexibility for planning your instruction for any type of schedule. Resource Pro® contains Planning Express®, an advanced scheduling program, as well as the entire contents of the Teaching Resources and the Computer Test Bank.

Key: **CTB** Computer Test Bank
CT Chapter Tests
ELL Teacher's ELL Handbook

CHAPTER PLANNING GUIDE

Program Resources	Assessment Strategies	Media and Technology
UR Chapter 5 Project Teacher Notes, pp. 26–27 **UR** Chapter 5 Project Overview and Worksheets, pp. 28–31	**TE** Check Your Progress, pp. 152, 159, 167 **TE** Performance Assessment: Chapter 5 Project Wrap Up, p. 173 **UR** Chapter 5 Project Scoring Rubric, p. 32	Science Explorer Internet Site Audio CDs, Section Summaries
UR 5-1 Lesson Plan, p. 33 **UR** 5-1 Section Summary, p. 34 **UR** 5-1 Review and Reinforce, p. 35 **UR** 5-1 Enrich, p. 36 **UR** Skills Lab blackline masters, pp. 53–54	**SE** Section 1 Review, p. 147 **SE** Analyze and Conclude, p. 149 **TE** Ongoing Assessment, pp. 143, 145 **TE** Performance Assessment, p. 147	Concept Videotape Library, *Adventures, Tape 1,* "Sir Isaac Newton" Transparency 13, "Exploring Combined Forces" Lab Activity Videotape, *Tape 1*
UR 5-2 Lesson Plan, p. 37 **UR** 5-2 Section Summary, p. 38 **UR** 5-2 Review and Reinforce, p. 39 **UR** 5-2 Enrich, p. 40	**SE** Section 2 Review, p. 152 **TE** Ongoing Assessment, p. 151 **TE** Performance Assessment, p. 152	Concept Videotape Library, *Adventures, Tape 1,* "Amusement Parks"
UR 5-3 Lesson Plan, p. 41 **UR** 5-3 Section Summary, p. 42 **UR** 5-3 Review and Reinforce, p. 43 **UR** 5-3 Enrich, p. 44 **UR** Real-World Lab blackline masters, pp. 55–57	**SE** Section 3 Review, p. 159 **SE** Analyze and Conclude, p. 161 **TE** Ongoing Assessment, pp. 155, 157 **TE** Performance Assessment, p. 159	Concept Videotape Library, *Adventures, Tape 1,* "Light as a Feather" Presentation Pro, "Friction and Gravity" Transparencies 14, "Air Resistance"; 15, "Law of Universal Gravitation" Lab Activity Videotape, *Tape 1*
UR 5-4 Lesson Plan, p. 45 **UR** 5-4 Section Summary, p. 46 **UR** 5-4 Review and Reinforce, p. 47 **UR** 5-4 Enrich, p. 48	**SE** Section 4 Review, p. 167 **TE** Ongoing Assessment, p. 165 **TE** Performance Assessment, p. 167	Presentation Pro, "Momentum" Transparency 16, "Conservation of Momentum"
UR 5-5 Lesson Plan, p. 49 **UR** 5-5 Section Summary, p. 50 **UR** 5-5 Review and Reinforce, p. 51 **UR** 5-5 Enrich, p. 52	**SE** Section 5 Review, p. 170 **TE** Ongoing Assessment, p. 169 **TE** Performance Assessment, p. 170	Concept Videotape Library, *Adventures, Tape 1,* "We Have Lift Off"
GRSW Provides worksheets to promote student comprehension of content **RCA** Provides strategies to improve science reading skills **ELL** Provides multiple strategies for English language learners	**SE** Study Guide/Assessment, pp. 171–173 **PA** Performance Assessment, pp. 16–18 **CT** Chapter 5 Test, pp. 19–22 **CTB** Chapter 5 Test **PHAS** Provides standardized test preparation	Computer Test Bank, Chapter 5 Test

GRSW Guided Reading and Study Workbook
ISAB Inquiry Skills Activity Book
LM Laboratory Manual

PA Performance Assessment
PHAS Prentice Hall Assessment System
PLM Probeware Lab Manual

RCA Reading in the Content Area
SE Student Edition

TE Teacher's Edition
UR Unit Resources

Meeting the National Science Education Standards and AAAS Benchmarks

National Science Education Standards	Benchmarks for Science Literacy	Unifying Themes
Physical Science (Content Standard B) ◆ **Motions and forces** Balanced forces, unbalanced forces, inertia, and Newton's first law of motion are presented for student analysis. *(Section 1)* Students learn how Newton's second law of motion explains the relationship between force, mass, and acceleration. *(Section 2)* Students examine the effect of friction and gravity on motion. *(Section 3)* Students learn Newton's third law of motion and the law of conservation of momentum. *(Section 4)* **Earth and Space Science** (Content Standard D) ◆ **Earth in the solar system** The idea that gravity attracts all objects in the universe is discussed. *(Section 3)* Students examine the forces affecting orbiting satellites. *(Section 5)* **Science and Technology** (Content Standard E) ◆ **Design a solution or a product** Students are challenged to design and build a vehicle powered only through Newton's third law of motion. *(Chapter Project)* ◆ **Evaluate completed technological designs or products** The amount of friction generated by different types of sneakers is measured. *(Real-World Lab)*	**3B Design and Systems** Students design a scooter based on Newton's principles of motion. *(Chapter Project)* **4F Motion** Balanced and unbalanced forces, inertia, friction, and momentum are discussed as students apply Newton's three laws of motion. *(Sections 1, 2, 3, 4)* **12C Manipulation and Observation** Students use force meters to calculate acceleration and weight. They assemble a scooter of their own design. *(Chapter Project, Skills Lab, Real-World Lab)* **12D Communication Skills** Students organize data in tables and graphs. *(Skills Lab, Real-World Lab)* **12E Critical-Response Skills** Students compare different types of sneakers and evaluate their usefulness for different activities. *(Real-World Lab)*	◆ **Systems and Interactions** Interactions between systems of objects are summarized in Newton's three laws of motion and the law of gravity. This includes interactions within the system of objects known as the Solar System. *(Chapter Project, Sections 1, 2, 3, 4, 5, Skills Lab)* ◆ **Stability** A system is stable and will remain stable as long as there are no unbalanced forces acting on it. *(Section 1)* ◆ **Patterns of Change** When change in a system occurs, the nature and magnitude of the change is determined by Newton's laws, especially Newton's second law relating force, mass, and acceleration. *(Sections 1, 2, 3, 4, Chapter Project, Skills Lab, Real-World Lab)* ◆ **Modeling** Students create models of vehicles. *(Chapter Project)*

Take It to the Net

The **www.phschool.com** Web site provides you with multiple opportunities to incorporate the internet into your instruction. Go to **www.phschool.com** and click on the Science icon. Then select Science Explorer Integrated.

www.phschool.com

Internet Activities provide opportunities for students to review, extend, or assess a concept from the chapter.

■ Have students use the chapter Self-Test to get instant feedback.

■ Hot Links and Reference Links provide opportunities for online research.

STAY CURRENT with **SCIENCE NEWS** ®

Find out the latest research and information about mechanics at: **www.phschool.com**

ACTIVITY	Time (minutes)	Materials Quantities for one work group	Skills
Section 1			
Discover, p. 142	10	**Nonconsumable** toy car, metal washers, heavy book	Observing
Try This, p. 146	15	**Consumable** thread, masking or cellophane tape **Nonconsumable** table tennis ball	Inferring
Science at Home, p. 147	home	**Consumable** paper cup, water, index card **Nonconsumable** coin or large paper clip	Communicating
Skills Lab, p. 148–149	45	**Consumable** string, masking tape **Nonconsumable** skateboard; meter stick; spring scale, 5 N; stopwatch; several bricks or other large mass(es)	Interpreting Data
Section 2			
Discover, p. 150	10	**Nonconsumable** toy dump truck, several small rocks, spring scale	Observing
Section 3			
Discover, p. 153	15	**Nonconsumable** dime, nickel, quarter, ruler	Predicting
Try This, p. 155		**Nonconsumable** two identical pie plates, marbles	Drawing Conclusions
Sharpen Your Skills, p. 158	20	**Nonconsumable** four objects, such as a shoe, a book, a spiral notebook, a pair of scissors; scale balance	Calculating
Real-World Lab, p. 160–161	45	**Consumable** tape **Nonconsumable** three or more different types of sneakers; 2 spring scales, 5 N and 20 N (or force sensors); mass set(s); 3 large paper clips; balance	Forming Operational Definitions, Measuring, Controlling Variables
Section 4			
Discover, p. 162	15	**Consumable** plastic straw **Nonconsumable** rubber band, hard cover book, 4 marbles	Developing Hypotheses
Try This, p. 166	10	**Consumable** masking tape **Nonconsumable** two toy cars that are about the same mass and roll with relatively little friction	Predicting
Section 5			
Discover, p. 168	10	**Consumable** length of string no more than 1 m long **Nonconsumable** small object such as an empty thread spool, safety goggles	Forming Operational Definitions
Science at Home, p. 170	home	**Consumable** water **Nonconsumable** child's plastic bucket	Communicating

A list of all materials required for the Student Edition activities can be found beginning on page T23. You can obtain information about ordering materials by calling 1-800-848-9500 or by accessing the *Science Explorer* Internet site at: **www.phschool.com**

Newton Scooters

In this chapter, students will be introduced to Newton's three laws of motion and learn how forces change all kinds of motion. The project has students design a vehicle that is propelled by an application of Newton's laws.

Purpose In this project, students will apply Newton's third law of motion by building a vehicle that moves forward by pushing back on something else.

Skills Focus Students will be able to
◆ identify and manipulate variables that affect the performance of the scooter;
◆ make a model of the scooter by drawing a diagram of the design;
◆ predict how the scooter will work based on the model;
◆ communicate the results of the activity to classmates through a demonstration.

Project Time Line Allow at least one week for students to brainstorm possible ideas for a vehicle. Drawing all the forces acting on the vehicle requires that they have read most of the chapter. Once given permission to begin building their vehicle, allow two or three weeks for students to build their vehicle and then troubleshoot problems that they encounter. Before beginning the project, see Chapter 5 Project Teacher Notes on pages 26–27 in Unit 2 Resources for more details on carrying out the project. Also distribute the Chapter 5 Project Overview and Worksheets and Scoring Rubric on pages 28–32 in Unit 2 Resources.

Possible Materials Provide a wide variety of materials from which students can choose. Some possibilities are listed below. Encourage students to suggest and use other materials as well. For example, an effective vehicle can be made from a milk carton with a balloon inside, floating in a basin of water.
◆ recycled materials from home
◆ toys or building block sets
◆ balloons
◆ straws
◆ fishing lines
◆ paper towel rolls
◆ a basin of water

CHAPTER 5 Forces

WEB ACTIVITY www.phschool.com

SECTION 1 The Nature of Force
Discover **What Changes Motion?**
Try This **Around and Around**
Skills Lab **Forced to Accelerate**

SECTION 2 Force, Mass, and Acceleration
Discover **How Do the Rocks Roll?**

SECTION 3 Friction and Gravity
Discover **Which Lands First?**
Try This **Spinning Plates**
Sharpen Your Skills **Calculating**
Real-World Lab **Sticky Sneakers**

140

Launching the Project

Demonstrate the concept of Newton's third law of motion by releasing an inflated balloon into the air. Have the class discuss what makes the balloon move. Also discuss how a car moves forward when the wheels of the car push backward on the road. Allow time for students to read the description of the project in their text and the Chapter Project Overview on pages 28–29 in Unit 2 Resources. Pass out copies of the Chapter 5 Project Worksheets on pages 30–31 in Unit 2 Resources for students.

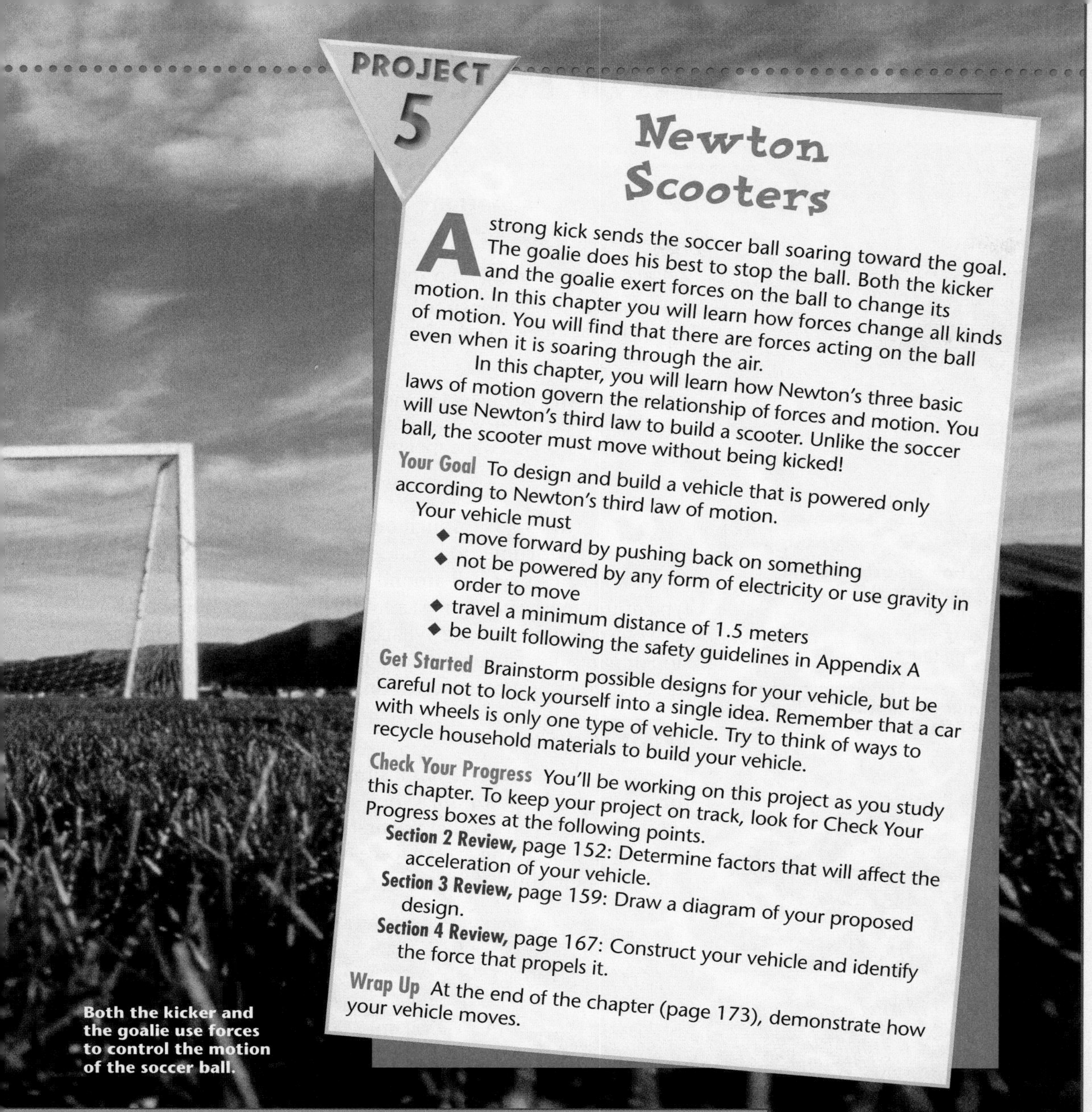

Newton Scooters

A strong kick sends the soccer ball soaring toward the goal. The goalie does his best to stop the ball. Both the kicker and the goalie exert forces on the ball to change its motion. In this chapter you will learn how forces change all kinds of motion. You will find that there are forces acting on the ball even when it is soaring through the air.

In this chapter, you will learn how Newton's three basic laws of motion govern the relationship of forces and motion. You will use Newton's third law to build a scooter. Unlike the soccer ball, the scooter must move without being kicked!

Your Goal To design and build a vehicle that is powered only according to Newton's third law of motion.

Your vehicle must
- move forward by pushing back on something
- not be powered by any form of electricity or use gravity in order to move
- travel a minimum distance of 1.5 meters
- be built following the safety guidelines in Appendix A

Get Started Brainstorm possible designs for your vehicle, but be careful not to lock yourself into a single idea. Remember that a car with wheels is only one type of vehicle. Try to think of ways to recycle household materials to build your vehicle.

Check Your Progress You'll be working on this project as you study this chapter. To keep your project on track, look for Check Your Progress boxes at the following points.

Section 2 Review, page 152: Determine factors that will affect the acceleration of your vehicle.

Section 3 Review, page 159: Draw a diagram of your proposed design.

Section 4 Review, page 167: Construct your vehicle and identify the force that propels it.

Wrap Up At the end of the chapter (page 173), demonstrate how your vehicle moves.

Both the kicker and the goalie use forces to control the motion of the soccer ball.

SECTION **4** **Action and Reaction**

Discover **How Pushy Is a Straw?**
Try This **Colliding Cars**

SECTION **5** *Integrating Space Science* **Orbiting Satellites**

Discover **What Makes an Object Move in a Circle?**

141

Program Resources

- **Unit 2 Resources** Chapter 5 Project Teacher's Notes, pp. 26–27; Project Overview and Worksheets, pp. 28–31; Project Scoring Rubric, p. 32

Media and Technology

 Audio CDs Section Summaries

 WEB ACTIVITY www.phschool.com

You will find an Internet activity, chapter self-tests for students, and links to other chapter topics at this site.

Allow the students to form groups. Have each group brainstorm vehicles other than four-wheeled cars and how they might power such vehicles without using any form of electricity or the force of gravity. Also have the students think about ways that they can keep vehicles going in a straight line. Tell students to apply what they learn about the forces in the chapter to their designs. Once they have acceptable designs, they may begin to build and test their vehicles.

To conclude this project, students will present their vehicles to the class. They will demonstrate how their vehicles move and indicate all the forces that act on them.

Performance Assessment

The Chapter 5 Project Scoring Rubric on page 32 of Unit 2 Resources will help you evaluate how well students complete the Chapter 5 Project. You may wish to share the scoring rubric with your students so they are clear about what will be expected of them. Students will be assessed on
- how well they planned their vehicle before building it, including consideration of all of the forces acting on it;
- the care with which the vehicle was built and the ability to modify the design after testing;
- the thoroughness and organization of their presentation, including explanations for all of the features of the vehicle.

Objectives

After completing the lesson, students will be able to
- explain how balanced and unbalanced forces are related to motion;
- state Newton's first law of motion and define inertia.

Key Terms force, net force, unbalanced force, balanced force, inertia, mass

1 Engage/Explore

Activating Prior Knowledge

Place a book in the middle of a table. Have students take turns moving the book, each using a different method. As obvious methods are used up, students will need to get more creative. They may use rubber bands, magnets, and springs. Ask the rest of the students to classify each method as a push or a pull. Ask: **What was required to make the book move?** *(A push or a pull)* **Did the book move when there was no push or pull?** *(no)*

DISCOVER

Skills Focus observing
Materials *toy car, metal washers, heavy book*

Time 10 minutes
Tips Make sure students understand they should not fasten the washers to the top of the car. Have students record their predictions before they roll the car. Advise them not to push the car too hard or the washers will fall off the back.
Expected Outcome The car stops or bounces backward when it hits while the washers continue to move forward. The activity demonstrates inertia.
Think It Over The car stopped or bounced back while the washers kept moving forward. The force of the book stopped the forward motion of the car, but nothing stopped the forward motion of the washers.

SECTION 1 The Nature of Force

DISCOVER • ACTIVITY

What Changes Motion?

1. Stack several metal washers on top of a toy car.
2. Place a heavy book on the floor near the car.
3. Predict what will happen to both the car and the washers if you roll the car into the book. Test your prediction.

Think It Over
Observing What happened to the car when it hit the book? What happened to the washers? What might be the reason for any difference between the motions of the car and the washers?

GUIDE FOR READING

- How are balanced and unbalanced forces related to motion?
- What is Newton's first law of motion?

Reading Tip As you read, use your own words to define each boldfaced word.

An arrow soars through the air to its distant target. A long jumper comes to a sudden stop in a cloud of sand. You kick a soccer ball around your opponent. There is some type of motion involved in each of these activities. But why does each object move as it does? What causes an object to start moving, stop moving, or change direction? The answer is a force. In each of these activities, a force is exerted on, or applied to, an object.

What Is a Force?

In science the word *force* has a simple and specific meaning. A **force** is a push or a pull. When one object pushes or pulls another object, you say that the first object is exerting a force on the second object. You exert a force on a pen when you write, on a book when you lift it, and on a zipper when you pull it.

142

READING STRATEGIES

Reading Tip Have partners work together to define this section's boldfaced words. Partners can take turns defining the terms in his or her own words. Give students index cards so that they can write a term on one side and its definition on the other. Then partners can quiz each other on the term he or she did *not* define.

Study and Comprehension Reinforce concepts presented in this section by having students write descriptive captions for photographs shown. Instruct students to choose three photographs. Then direct them to write a new caption for each photograph. Suggest that students use up to three sentences for each caption. Invite volunteers to read aloud their completed captions while classmates study the photographs.

You exert a force on a pebble when you skim it across a pond, on a wagon when you pull it, and on a nail when you hammer it into a piece of wood.

Like velocity and acceleration, forces are described not only by how strong they are, but also by the *direction* in which they act. If you push on a door, you exert a force in a different direction than if you pull on the door.

Unbalanced Forces

Suppose you need to push a heavy box across a floor. When you push on the box, you exert a force on it. If a friend helps you, the total force exerted on the box is the sum of your force plus your friend's force. When two forces act in the same direction, they add together.

Figure 1 uses arrows to show the addition of forces. The head of each arrow points in the direction of a force. The width of each arrow tells you the strength of a force. A wider arrow shows a greater force. (When forces are shown in this book, the strength of a force will usually be shown by the width of an arrow.)

When forces act in opposite directions, they also add together. However, you must pay attention to the direction of each force. Adding a force acting in one direction to a force acting in the opposite direction is the same as adding a positive number and a negative number. So when two forces act in opposite directions, they combine by subtraction. If one force is greater than the other force, the overall force is in the direction of the greater force.

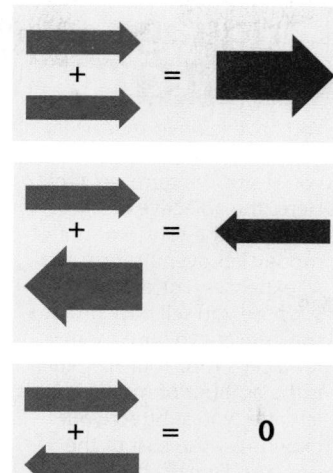

Figure 1 Two forces can combine so that they add together (top), or subtract from each other (center). They may also cancel each other (bottom).

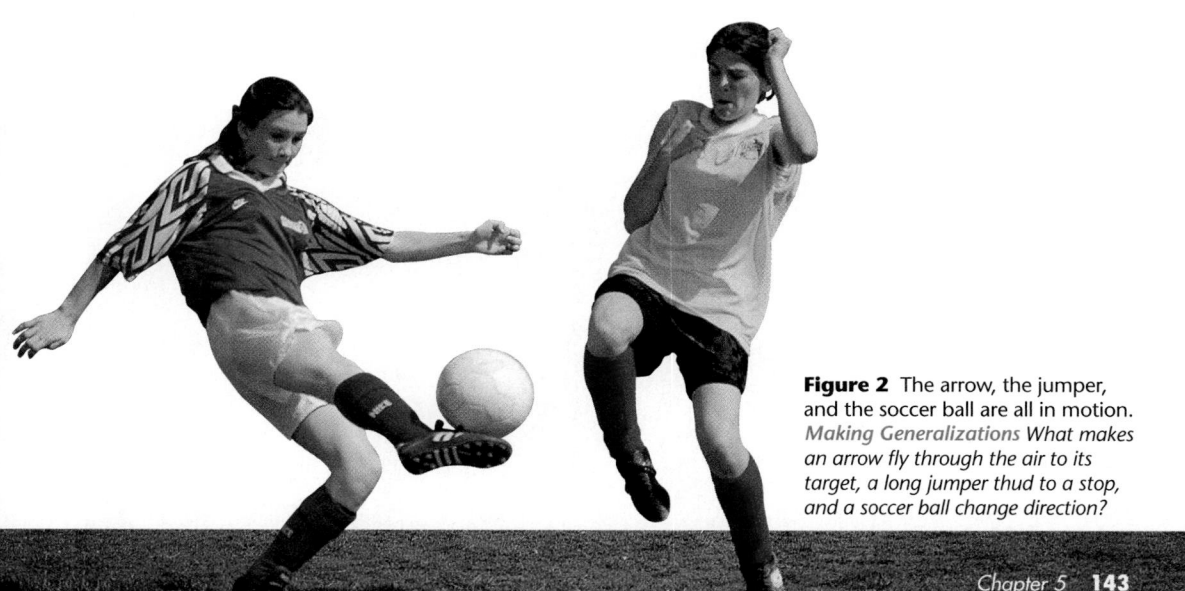

Figure 2 The arrow, the jumper, and the soccer ball are all in motion. *Making Generalizations What makes an arrow fly through the air to its target, a long jumper thud to a stop, and a soccer ball change direction?*

Program Resources

◆ **Unit 2 Resources** 5-1 Lesson Plan, p. 33; 5-1 Section Summary, p. 34
◆ **Guided Reading and Study Workbook** Section 5-1

Answers to Self-Assessment

Caption Question

Figure 2 The force of the bow string on the arrow makes the arrow fly, the force of the ground on the jumper makes the long jumper stop, and the force of a toe on the ball makes the soccer ball change direction.

2 Facilitate

What Is a Force?

Building Inquiry Skills: Applying Concepts

Have each student select a classroom object (such as a stapler, 3-hole punch, scissors, or desk drawer). Ask students to demonstrate how force is typically applied to each object and explain what happens when the force is applied. Help students recognize that all objects require a push or pull to put them into motion or to stop or change their motion. **learning modality: kinesthetic**

Unbalanced Forces

Including All Students

Assign students to two groups. Then have each group divide into two teams. Make sure teams consist of students that are matched in strength and height but unequal in number. For example, one team could have six students, the other four. The two teams will pull on opposite ends of a rope until one team moves forward and the other backward. Inform students that, unlike many tug of wars they may have seen, this is not a competition, but a scientific experiment. Caution the team with more students not to pull so hard that the other team falls over. They should continue to pull only until one team moves forward. Ask: **Were both teams exerting forces?** (*Yes.*) **Which team exerted more force?** (*The larger team*) Since the forces are unbalanced, the net force moves both the rope and the teams. **cooperative learning**

Ongoing Assessment

Writing Have students give two examples of force they have seen today. (*Answers will vary. Sample: I saw my dog push his food bowl and the teacher pick up a book.*)

Unbalanced Forces, continued

Language Arts
CONNECTION

The word *net* has several meanings. Some of the meanings are similar to net force (net profit, net effect) and some are different (fishing net). Pair native English speakers with students of limited English proficiency. Have partners take turns constructing sentences using the word *net* and giving the definition of the word as used in the sentence. To help students get started, write sample sentences on the board.

In Your Journal Encourage students to include other words that have multiple meanings as well as the terms in the book. Be sure students include the parts of speech. Students can use dictionaries as references. Sample: spring—a season (noun), a coil (noun); pound—a measurement of weight (noun), to smash something (verb); bat—a flying mammal (noun), to brush away (verb); bowl—a concave vessel for holding liquids (noun), to take part in the game of bowling (verb); row—a horizontal line (noun), to push oars through water and move a boat (verb) **limited English proficiency**

Balanced Forces

Using the Visuals: Figure 3

Direct students' attention to the stocking the dogs are pulling. Ask: **In what direction are forces being applied?** (*Toward each dog*) **If neither the dogs nor the stocking is moving, what can you infer about the amount of force each dog is placing on the stocking?** (*The force exerted by the dog on the left is balanced by the force exerted by the three dogs on the right.*) **What would happen to the stocking if the dog on the left suddenly let go? Why?** (*The stocking would move to the right because the forces would be unbalanced.*) **learning modality: visual**

Language Arts
CONNECTION

You have learned that *net force* means "overall force." Have you heard the term *net profit?* Here, the adjective *net* describes the total amount of money left over after paying all expenses. For example, suppose you sell popcorn at a sports event to raise money for a class trip. Your *net profit* is the amount of money that is left after you subtract your expenses—the cost of the popcorn kernels, butter, salt, bags, and posters.

In Your Journal

Can you think of another meaning for the word *net?* Many words have more than one meaning. Here are just a few: *spring, pound, bat, bowl,* and *row.* Think of two meanings for each word. Use at least two of these words in sentences that show their different meanings. Add more words to the list.

You can see what happens when the students in the center of the next page exert unequal forces in opposite directions.

In any situation, the overall force on an object after all the forces are added together is called the **net force.** When there is a net force acting on an object, the forces are said to be unbalanced. **Unbalanced forces** can cause an object to start moving, stop moving, or change direction. **Unbalanced forces acting on an object will change the object's motion.** In other words, an unbalanced force will cause an object to accelerate. For example, if two unequal forces acting in opposite directions are applied to a box, the box will accelerate in the direction of the greater force.

Balanced Forces

Forces exerted on an object do not always change the object's motion. Consider the forces involved when the dogs in Figure 3 pull on a stocking in opposite directions. Even though there are forces acting on it, the motion of the stocking does not change. While one dog exerts a force on the stocking in one direction, the other dogs exert an equal force on the stocking in the opposite direction.

Equal forces acting on one object in opposite directions are called **balanced forces.** One force is exactly balanced by the other force. **Balanced forces acting on an object will not change the object's motion.** When you add equal forces exerted in opposite directions, the net force is zero. You can also see how balanced forces cancel in the example at the bottom of the next page. The box does not move at all.

☑ *Checkpoint* **Which cause change in motion—balanced forces or unbalanced forces?**

Figure 3 These dogs are exerting a great deal of force, but they aren't moving. *Applying Concepts What would happen if one of the dogs pulled harder? Explain why.*

144

Background

Integrating Science In the *Science Explorer* series, forces are represented by arrows whose width is proportional to the size of the force. Students who go on to take physics in high school will encounter forces represented by arrows whose length is proportional to the size of the force. There are advantages to both methods. For middle school students, width seems more intuitive as a means of representing sizes of forces. However, with geometric (graphical or trigonometric) methods of addition and subtraction of force vectors that are not in line, arrows with proportional length must be used to preserve the size and direction of resultant forces.

EXPLORING Combined Forces

What happens when two friends push on the same object? The forces they exert combine in different ways, depending on the directions in which they push.

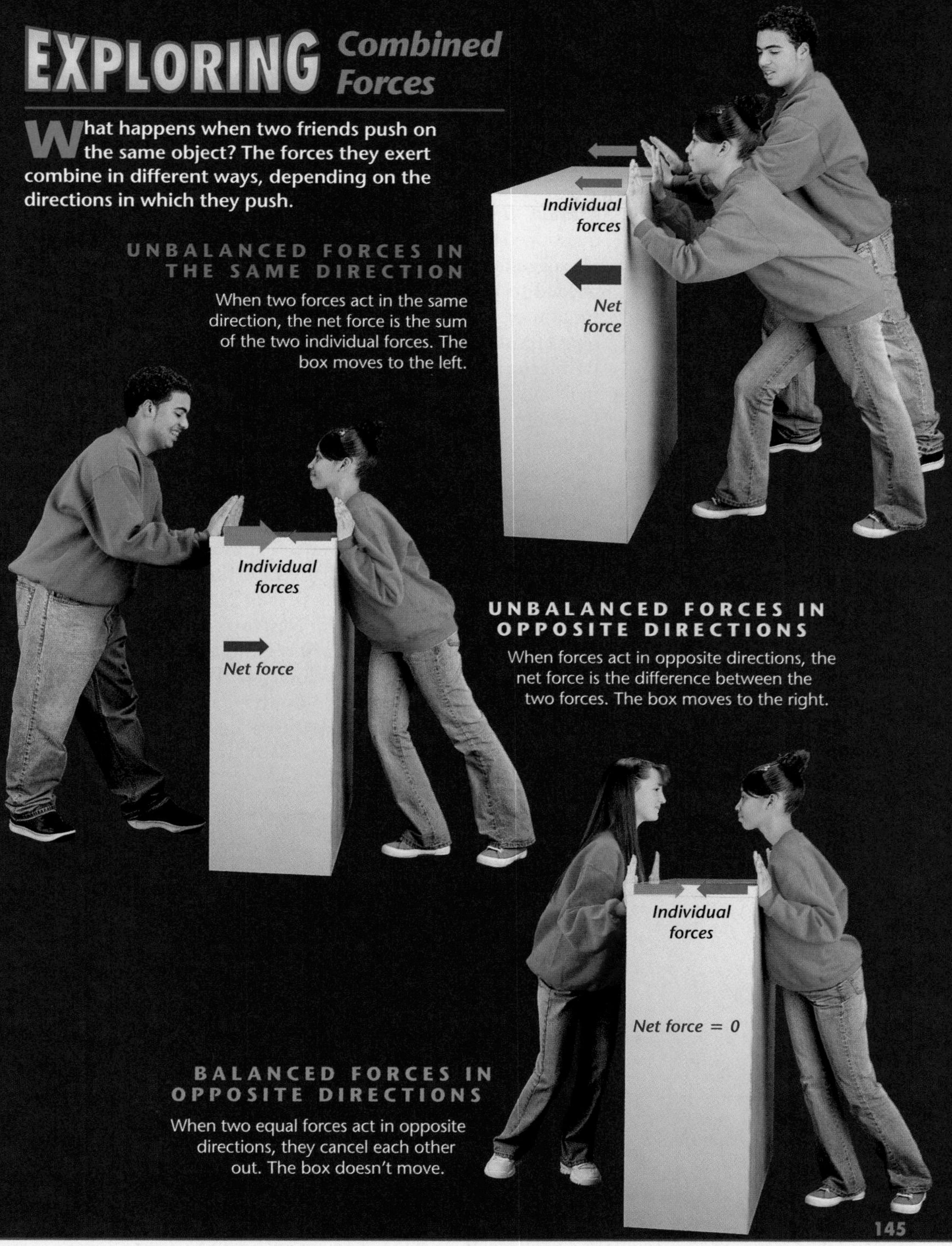

UNBALANCED FORCES IN THE SAME DIRECTION

When two forces act in the same direction, the net force is the sum of the two individual forces. The box moves to the left.

Individual forces

Net force

UNBALANCED FORCES IN OPPOSITE DIRECTIONS

When forces act in opposite directions, the net force is the difference between the two forces. The box moves to the right.

Individual forces

Net force

BALANCED FORCES IN OPPOSITE DIRECTIONS

When two equal forces act in opposite directions, they cancel each other out. The box doesn't move.

Individual forces

Net force = 0

145

EXPLORING
Combined Forces

Guide students through the explanations in the visual by calling on volunteers to demonstrate the concepts. A student desk can be substituted for the heavy box shown. Some students may identify friction as a force acting on the box or desk. Tell them that in this activity, frictional force is ignored. To represent two forces in the same direction, have two students push the desk at the same time and in the same direction. Ask: **What is the net force acting on the desk?** (*The force of the first student's push added to the force of the second student's push*) Then have two other volunteers demonstrate two unequal forces in opposite directions. Suggest that one student push with one hand while the other pushes with two hands. Ask: **How would you calculate the net force?** (*Find the difference between the force of the first student's push and the force of the second student's push*) Then ask: **What happens to the desk when the forces acting on it are unequal?** (*The desk moves in the direction of the greater force.*) Finally, have two new volunteers demonstrate two equal forces acting in opposite directions. Ask: **What is the net force acting on the desk?** (*zero*) Then ask: **What happened to the desk when two equal forces push it from opposite directions?** (*The desk did not move.*)

Extend Have students identify other objects acted upon by equal and unequal forces and sketch the objects with arrows that represent the direction and strength of forces.

Portfolio Students can save their sketches in their portfolios.

learning modality: visual

Media and Technology

 Transparencies "Exploring Combined Forces," Transparency 13

 Concept Videotape Library *Adventures, Tape 1,* "Sir Isaac Newton"

Answers to Self-Assessment

Caption Question

Figure 3 The forces will become unbalanced and the stocking, and perhaps one or two of the dogs, will move toward the dog that pulls harder. An object that is not moving will move when acted upon by an unbalanced force.

☑ *Checkpoint*
unbalanced forces

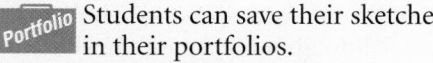

Ongoing Assessment

Drawing Have student sketch arm-wrestling matches in which balanced and unbalanced forces are demonstrated.

145

Newton's First Law of Motion

TRY THIS

Skills Focus inferring

Materials *thread, masking or cellophane tape, table tennis ball*

Time 15 minutes

Tips Caution students to avoid releasing the table tennis ball so that it hits another person. Consider taking students outdoors or to an open area to reduce the chance that someone will get hit by a ball.

Inferring The ball will roll away if you let go of the thread when the ball is moving away from you. The ball will roll toward you if you let go of the thread when the ball is moving toward you. The inertia of the ball causes it to continue moving in the same direction that it was moving when it was released.

Extend Involve students in a game of tetherball and have them point out the effects of inertia on the movement of the ball. **learning modality: kinesthetic**

Demonstration

Materials *large, smooth cloth with no edge seam; several large, chrome-plated sockets from a wrench set (19–23 mm sizes work well)*

Time 10 minutes

Practice this demonstration before performing it in front of the class. Explain that this trick is not magic, just science. Place the cloth on a smooth table and arrange the sockets so that they are about 10 cm from the front edge of the cloth. The sockets should be placed so that the end with the square hole is down. Allow about 20 cm of the cloth to hang over the back edge of the table. Firmly grasp the edge of the cloth, lift your hands slightly, then snap the cloth straight down. Do not pull the cloth toward you, because you may lift it and you cannot pull it fast enough. The sockets should stay in place with little noticeable movement. Ask: **What kept the sockets in place?** *(inertia)* **learning modality: visual**

TRY THIS

Around and Around

An object moving in a circle has inertia.

1. Tape one end of a length of thread (about 1 m) to a table tennis ball.
2. Suspend the ball in front of you and swing it in a horizontal circle. Keep the ball about 2 or 3 cm above the floor.
3. Let go of the thread and observe the direction in which the ball rolls.
4. Repeat this several times, letting go of the thread at different points.

Inferring At what point do you need to let go of the thread if you want the ball to roll directly away from you? Toward you? Draw a diagram as part of your answer.

Figure 4 These crash-test dummies weren't wearing safety belts. *Relating Cause and Effect What caused them to move forward even after the car stopped?*

Newton's First Law of Motion

The ancient Greeks observed that objects have natural resting places. Objects move toward those places. A rock falls to the ground. A ball rolls to the bottom of a hill. Once an object is in its natural resting place, it cannot move by itself. For an object to start moving, a force has to act on it.

Inertia In the early 1600s, the Italian astronomer Galileo Galilei questioned the idea that a force is needed to keep an object moving. He suggested that once an object is in motion, no push or pull is needed to keep it moving. Force is needed only to change the motion of an object. But whether it is moving or at rest, every object resists any change to its motion. This resistance is called inertia. **Inertia** (in UR shuh) is the tendency of an object to resist change in its motion.

You may have observed this yourself. A puck that rides on a cushion of air in an "air-hockey" game glides along quite freely once you push it. Similarly, a tennis ball flies through the air once you hit it with a racket. In both cases, the object continues to move even after you remove the force.

Galileo's ideas paved the way for the English mathematican Sir Isaac Newton. Newton discovered the three basic laws of motion in the late 1600s. The first of Newton's three laws of motion restates Galileo's idea. **Newton's first law of motion states that an object at rest will remain at rest, and an object that is moving at constant velocity will continue moving at constant velocity unless acted upon by an unbalanced force.** Newton's first law of motion is also called the law of inertia.

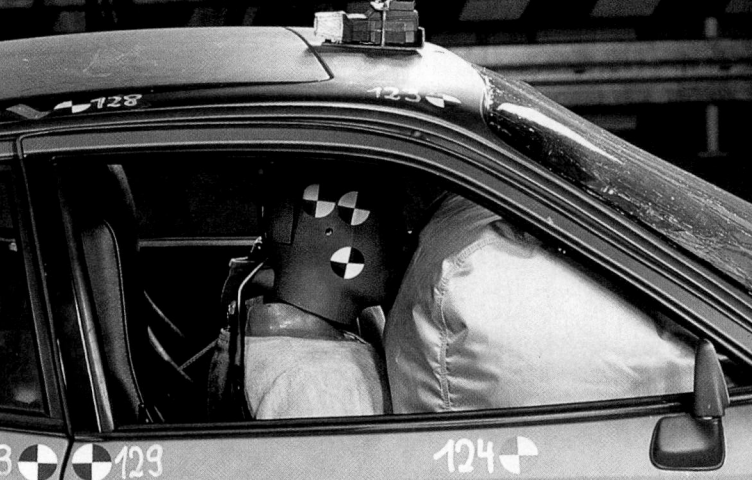

Background

History of Science Aristotle, Eratosthenes, Democritus, Thales, and many other ancient Greeks made important discoveries about science and nature. Beginning in the 1500s and through the late 1700s, philosophers and scientists reexamined their perceptions of the world around them and began to use the scientific method—experimentation and careful observation. It was during this time that Kepler and Galileo started to think and write about how things move. Kepler correctly described the motions of the planets, and Galileo first stated the most useful descriptions of what causes objects to accelerate. Sir Isaac Newton (1642–1727) restated and formalized these ideas about motion in his three laws of motion and the law of universal gravitation.

Inertia explains many common events. For example, if you are in a car that stops suddenly, inertia causes you to continue moving forward. The crash test dummies in Figure 4 don't stop when the car does. Passengers in a moving car have inertia. Therefore a force is required to change their motion. That force is exerted by the safety belt. If the safety belt is not worn, that force may be exerted by the windshield instead!

Mass Which is more difficult to move, a jar of pennies or a jar of plastic foam "peanuts"? Obviously, the jar of pennies is harder to move. What is the difference between the jar of pennies and the jar of plastic peanuts? After all, you can see in Figure 5 that both jars occupy the same amount of space, and so have the same volume. The difference is the amount of mass each one has. **Mass** is the amount of matter in an object. The jar of pennies has more mass than the jar of plastic peanuts.

The SI unit of mass is the kilogram (kg). A small car might have a mass of 1,000 kilograms. A bicycle without a rider might have a mass of about 10 kilograms, and a student might have a mass of 45 kilograms. You describe the mass of smaller objects in terms of grams (1 kilogram = 1,000 grams). The mass of a nickel is about 5 grams.

The amount of inertia an object has depends on its mass. The greater the mass of an object, the greater its inertia. Mass, then, can also be defined as a measure of the inertia of an object.

Figure 5 The two jars have the same volume, but very different masses.

Section 1 Review

1. What are the differences in how balanced and unbalanced forces affect motion?
2. What is inertia? How is it involved in Newton's first law of motion?
3. Two children who are fighting over a toy pull on it from opposite sides. The result is a stand-off. Explain this in terms of the net force.
4. **Thinking Critically** **Applying Concepts** Draw a diagram in which two forces acting on an object are unbalanced and a diagram in which two balanced forces act on an object. Use arrows to show the forces.

Science at Home

Fill a paper cup with water. Cover the cup with an index card and place a coin or paper clip in the center of the index card. Challenge your family members to move the coin from the card to the cup without touching the coin or holding on to the card. If they cannot think how to do it, show them how. Hold the cup and use your finger to flick the card with a sharp sideways force. The force doesn't have to be very strong, but it must be sharp. Explain what happens to the coin in terms of inertia.

Program Resources

◆ **Unit 2 Resources** 5-1 Review and Reinforce, p. 35; 5-1 Enrich, p. 36

Answers to Self-Assessment

Caption Question

Figure 4 The inertia of the dummies caused them to continue moving forward after the car stopped. The dummies stop only after a force from the airbag changes their motion.

3 Assess

Section 1 Review Answers

1. Balanced forces cancel out and do not change the motion of the object. Unbalanced forces cause an object to start moving, stop moving, or change speed or direction.
2. Inertia is the tendency of an object to resist any change in its motion. Newton's first law is called the law of inertia. The law states that an object at rest will remain at rest, and an object moving at constant speed will continue at a constant speed unless an unbalanced force acts on the object.
3. Because the toy does not move, each child must be pulling with the same amount of force. Because the forces are balanced, the net force equals zero.
4. Students' diagrams should resemble the force diagrams in *Exploring Combined Forces.*

Science at Home

Materials *paper cup, water, index card, coin or large paper clip*
ACTIVITY
Suggest students practice the activity once or twice before challenging family members. Make sure students understand that the force applied to the card by flicking the edge of the card is not significantly transferred to the coin or paper clip. When the card is no longer there to counteract the force of gravity, no force holds up the object and it falls into the water.

Performance Assessment

Drawing Have students draw cartoon strips or diagrams of ball games that illustrate Newton's first law of motion. Students can save their cartoons in their portfolios.

Forced to Accelerate

Preparing for Inquiry

Key Concept An unbalanced force causes an object to accelerate.

Skills Objectives Students will be able to
- make observations of time and distance and calculate velocity and acceleration;
- graph data of acceleration vs. force;
- infer the relationship between force and acceleration for constant mass.

Time 45 minutes

Advance Planning Ask volunteers to bring skateboards from home. Check calibration of the spring scales. Practice the experiment.

Alternative Materials You may be able to borrow carts or use old-fashioned roller skates in place of skateboards.

Guiding Inquiry

Invitation Put a skateboard on the floor and put a brick on it. Have a student accelerate it for about 1 meter using a spring scale. Ask students why the skateboard accelerated. Ask the students how they could investigate how acceleration depends on force.

Introducing the Procedure
- If needed, demonstrate how to zero and use a spring scale.
- Review the concepts of average speed and acceleration.
- Ask the students: **What are the manipulated and responding variables in this experiment?** *(Manipulated variable: force with which they pull the skateboard; responding variable: acceleration of the skateboard)*

Troubleshooting the Experiment
- If more mass is needed to keep the final velocity low, add bricks. Keep mass constant during the experiment.
- Be sure students zero the spring scale each time they use it. Point out that the scale must be held horizontal and pulled straight.

Forced to Accelerate

In this lab, you will practice the skill of interpreting data as you explore the relationship between force and acceleration.

Problem

How is the acceleration of a skateboard related to the force that is pulling it?

Materials

skateboard	meter stick
string	stopwatch
masking tape	spring scale, 5 N
several bricks or other large mass(es)	

Procedure

1. Attach a loop of string to a skateboard. Place the bricks on the skateboard.
2. Using masking tape, mark off a one-meter distance on a level floor. Label one end "Start" and the other "Finish."
3. Attach a spring scale to the loop of string. Pull it so that you maintain a force of 2.0 N. Be sure to pull with the scale straight out in front. Practice applying a steady force to the skateboard as it moves.
4. Copy the data table into your notebook.
5. Find the smallest force needed to pull the skateboard at a slow, constant speed. Do not accelerate the skateboard. Record this force on the first line of the table.
6. Add 0.5 N to the force in Step 5. This will be enough to accelerate the skateboard. Record this force on the second line of the table.
7. Have one of your partners hold the front edge of the skateboard at the starting line. Then pull on the spring scale with the force you found in Step 6.
8. When your partner says "Go" and releases the skateboard, maintain a constant force until the skateboard reaches the finish line. A third partner should time how long it takes the skateboard to go from start to finish. Record the time in the column labeled Trial 1.
9. Repeat Steps 7 and 8 twice more. Record your results in the columns labeled Trial 2 and Trial 3.
10. Repeat Steps 7, 8, and 9 using a force 1.0 N greater than the force you found in Step 5.
11. Repeat Steps 7, 8, and 9 twice more. Use forces that are 1.5 N and 2.0 N greater than the force you found in Step 5.

DATA TABLE							
Force (N)	Trial 1 Time (s)	Trial 2 Time (s)	Trial 3 Time (s)	Avg Time (s)	Avg Speed (m/s)	Final Speed (m/s)	Acceleration (m/s²)

- If the spring scale is calibrated in grams, multiply by 0.01 to obtain newtons.
- Remind students that, for Steps 6–11, they should try to pull with constant force, not at a constant speed. Students should practice this before starting to record data.
- Be sure students round off their results to an appropriate number of digits.
- Remind students to measure force when the skateboard is moving, not the initial force to get it started moving (which will be higher).

- Students may want to pull using forces of 0.5 N, 1.0 N, and so on. Be sure to add the force reading from Step 5. For example, if it takes 0.2 N to keep the skateboard moving at constant speed, then the students should pull with 0.7 N, 1.2 N, and so on.
- In Question 3, students calculate the final speed from the average speed. They can do this because the acceleration is constant. Average speed = (Final speed − initial speed)/2. Since the initial speed is zero, Final speed = Average speed × 2.

Analyze and Conclude

1. For each force you used, find the average of the three times that you measured. Record the average in your data table.

2. Find the average speed of the skateboard for each force. Use this formula:

   Average speed = 1 m ÷ Average time

   Record this value for each force.

3. To obtain the final speed of the skateboard, multiply each average speed by 2. Record the result in your data table.

4. To obtain the acceleration, divide each final speed you found by the average time. Record the acceleration in your data table.

5. Make a line graph. Show the acceleration on the *y*-axis and the force on the *x*-axis. The *y*-axis scale should go from zero to about 1 m/s^2. The *x*-axis should go from zero to 3.0 newtons.

6. If your data points seem to form a straight line, draw a line through them.

7. Your first data point is the force required for an acceleration of zero. How do you know the force for an acceleration of zero?

8. According to your graph, how is the acceleration of the skateboard related to the pulling force?

9. **Think About It** Which variable is the manipulated variable? Which is the responding variable?

Design an Experiment

Design an experiment to test how the acceleration of the loaded skateboard depends on its mass. Think about how you would vary the mass of the skateboard. What quantity would you need to measure that you did not measure in this experiment? Do you have the equipment to make that measurement? If not, what other equipment would you need?

Sample Data Table

Force for zero acceleration: _0.2_ N

Force (N)	0.7	1.2	1.7	2.2
Trial 1 Time (s)				
Trial 2 Time (s)				
Trial 3 Time (s)				
Avg. Time (s)	4.4	3.2	2.5	2.0
Avg. Speed (m/s)	0.23	0.31	0.40	0.50
Final Speed (m/s)	0.46	0.62	0.80	1.00
Acceleration (m/s^2)	0.11	0.19	0.32	0.50

Program Resources

◆ **Unit 2 Resources** Skills Lab blackline masters, pp. 53–54

Media and Technology

Lab Activity Videotape
Tape 1

Expected Outcome

◆ The students should complete a data table similar to the sample provided.

◆ After calculating acceleration, the students should produce a graph showing that acceleration is proportional to force.

◆ Possible sources of error include improper use of the spring scale, calculating errors, and failing to pull with a constant force.

Analyze and Conclude

1. Answers may vary. If the mass is about 4 kg, and the force is 2.2 N, the time to accelerate for 1.0 m will be approximately 2 s.

2. Answers may vary. For the same combination, the average speed will be around 0.5 m/s.

3. Answers may vary. For the same combination, the final speed will be around 1 m/s.

4. Answers may vary. For the same combination, the acceleration will be around 0.5 m/s^2.

5. Answers may vary. Be sure to check for accuracy of graphing and comprehension of what the graph results mean.

6. Show students how to draw a "best-fit" line. Do not allow them to "connect the dots."

7. The force for an acceleration of zero was measured in Step 5 (at constant speed).

8. Acceleration is proportional to accelerating force.

9. The manipulated variable is the force; the responding variable is the acceleration.

Extending the Inquiry

Design an Experiment The new experiment should be essentially the same except that students should vary the mass (change the number of bricks) and keep the force constant.

Safety

The skateboard can achieve a significant speed. It is safest to perform the experiment on the floor rather than on tables. Review the safety guidelines in Appendix A.

SECTION 2 Force, Mass, and Acceleration

Objective

After completing the lesson, students will be able to
◆ state Newton's second law of motion and explain how force and mass are related to acceleration.

Key Term newton

1 Engage/Explore

Activating Prior Knowledge

Give pairs of students a flexible ruler and a small ball such as a golf ball. Have one student place one end of the ruler next to the ball. Ask the student to bend the ruler back, then release it to exert a small force against the ball on the floor. Once the ruler is released, have the pairs observe the motion of the ball. Students can repeat the activity, bending the ruler more and exerting a greater force against the ball. Have students compare the two forces and the motion of the ball. Ask: **How does changing the force of the ruler against the ball affect the motion of the ball?** *(The larger force causes more acceleration.)*

.... DISCOVER ....

Skills Focus observing
Materials *toy dump truck, several small rocks, spring scale*
Time 10 minutes
Tips Encourage students to pull the truck with a steady force to get a reading on the spring scale that stays constant. Remind students to record the reading on the spring scale each time they remove the rocks. Students should record their measurements in a data table.
Expected Outcome The students will probably notice that the same force causes the truck to accelerate more as rocks are removed. (They may say it goes faster.)
Think It Over Students should observe that as mass decreases, acceleration increases.

150

DISCOVER ....ACTIVITY

How Do the Rocks Roll?

1. Place several small rocks in a toy dump truck. Hook a spring scale to the bumper of the truck.

2. Practice pulling the truck with the spring scale so that the reading on the scale stays constant.

3. Pull the truck with a constant force and observe its motion. Then remove a few rocks from the truck and pull it again with the same force.

4. Remove a few more rocks and pull the truck again. Finally, empty the truck and observe how it moves with the same constant force.

Think It Over
Observing How did changing the mass of the loaded truck affect its motion?

GUIDE FOR READING

◆ How are force and mass related to acceleration?

Reading Tip As you read, use your own words to describe the relationship among force, mass, and acceleration.

On a sunny afternoon you are baby-sitting for two boys who love wagon rides. You soon find that they enjoy the ride most if you accelerate quickly. They shout "Faster, faster!" and after a few minutes you sit down in the wagon to catch your breath. The smaller boy takes a turn pulling, but finds that he can't make the wagon accelerate nearly as fast as you can. How is the acceleration of the wagon related to the force pulling it? How is the acceleration related to the mass of the wagon?

Newton's Second Law of Motion

Newton's second law of motion explains how force, mass, and acceleration are related. **The net force on an object is equal to the product of its acceleration and its mass.** The relationship

150

READING STRATEGIES

Reading Tip Suggest students review the meanings of the terms *force, mass,* and *acceleration* before they begin to read. Sample description: A force acting on a mass causes the mass to accelerate.

Vocabulary Explain to students that the word *mass* has several meanings other than its scientific meaning. Organize students in small groups. Provide each group with a dictionary and direct group members to read the various meanings of *mass*. Then challenge students in each group to write an original sentence for each of the different meanings.

among the quantities force, mass, and acceleration can be written in one equation.

$$Force = Mass \times Acceleration$$

People often refer to this equation itself as Newton's second law of motion.

As with any equation, you must pay attention to the units of measurement. When acceleration is measured in meters per second per second (m/s^2) and mass is measured in kilograms, force is measured in kilograms × meters per second per second ($kg \cdot m/s^2$). This long unit is called the newton (N), in honor of Isaac Newton. One **newton** equals the force required to accelerate one kilogram of mass at 1 meter per second per second.

$$1\ N = 1\ kg \times 1\ m/s^2$$

A student might have a mass of 40 kilograms. Suppose she is walking, and accelerates at $1\ m/s^2$. You can easily find the force exerted on her by substituting mass and acceleration into the equation. You find that 40 kilograms × $1\ m/s^2$ is 40 newtons.

Sometimes you may want to write the relationship among acceleration, force, and mass in a different form.

$$Acceleration = \frac{Force}{Mass}$$

This form is found by rearranging the equation for Newton's second law.

Sample Problem

A 52-kg water-skier is being pulled by a speedboat. The force causes her to accelerate at $2\ m/s^2$. Calculate the net force that causes this acceleration.

Analyze.	You know the acceleration and the mass. You want to find the force.
Write the equation.	$Force = Mass \times Acceleration$
Substitute and solve.	$Force = 52\ kg \times 2\ m/s^2$
	$Force = 104\ kg \times m/s^2 = 104\ kg \cdot m/s^2$
	$Force = 104\ N$
Think about it.	The answer tells you that a force of 104 N is required to accelerate the water-skier. This is not a large force, but it does not include the force that overcomes friction.
Practice Problems	**1.** What is the net force on a 1,000-kg elevator accelerating at $2\ m/s^2$? **2.** What net force is needed to accelerate a 55-kg cart at $15\ m/s^2$?

Program Resources

◆ **Unit 2 Resources** 5-2 Lesson Plan, p. 37; 5-2 Section Summary, p. 38
◆ **Guided Reading and Study Workbook** Section 5-2

Media and Technology

Concept Videotape Library
Adventures, Tape 1, "Amusement Parks"

---

2 Facilitate

Newton's Second Law of Motion

Demonstration

Materials *spring scale, 1-kg mass*

Time 15 minutes
Tips Remind students that a newton is a unit of force, and that 1 N equals the force needed to accelerate a 1-kg mass at a rate of $1\ m/s^2$. Demonstrate 1 N of force by attaching the spring scale to the 1-kg mass and dragging the mass along a table. You can minimize friction by pulling the mass over oil or beads. Ask: **How can you tell the amount of force it took to pull the mass?** *(Look at the measurement on the spring scale)* Have volunteers demonstrate forces less than and greater than 1 N. Ask: **What happens to the acceleration when the force on the mass increases?** *(It increases.)* Then write the equation Acceleration = Force/Mass on the board. Ask: **How does Newton's equation represent what you observed?** *(In the equation, as the value of the force gets larger, the value for acceleration also gets larger.)* **learning modality: visual**

Sample Problem

Make sure that students practice good problem-solving skills. Have them write out the formula, substitute the known quantities, cancel the units and do the multiplication. Remind students that whatever mathematical operations are performed on the values are also performed on the units. Remind them that the $kg \cdot m/s^2$ has a special name, the newton (N).

Practice Problems
1. $1{,}000\ kg \times 2\ m/s^2 = 2{,}000\ N$
2. $55\ kg \times 15\ m/s^2 = 825\ N$

Ongoing Assessment

Skills Check Have students calculate the force needed to accelerate a 25-kg crate of bananas at a rate of $1.5\ m/s^2$. *(Force = $25\ kg \times 1.5\ m/s^2 = 37.5\ N$)*

Changes in Force and Mass

Using the Visuals: Figure 6

Draw attention to this photograph to help students visualize how mass and acceleration are related. Ask:

◆ **How could you decrease the mass so that acceleration could increase?** *(Ask a child to step out of the wagon.)*
◆ **How could you increase acceleration without changing mass?** *(Increase force by pulling harder.)*
◆ **How could you apply what you learned about mass, force, and acceleration to make the wagon accelerate as much as possible?** *(Increase force and decrease mass at the same time.)*

learning modality: visual

3 Assess

Section 2 Review Answers

1. Force, mass, and acceleration; Force = Mass × Acceleration.
2. The acceleration increases.
3. You need to know the mass of the shopping cart.
4. If you double the force acting on an object, you have to double the mass of the object to keep the acceleration unchanged.

Check Your Progress
CHAPTER PROJECT 5

At this point, students should begin to sketch possible vehicle designs. Allow them to discuss their designs in small groups so that they can improve their vehicles. Have them brainstorm ways of increasing force or decreasing mass. For example: three wheels have less mass than four.

Performance Assessment

Oral Presentation Have students explain why the same force accelerates an empty wagon more than a wagon full of bricks. *(According to Newton's second law, if the mass is smaller, acceleration is larger for the same force.)*

Figure 6 The acceleration of an object depends on the force acting on it and the object's mass.

Changes in Force and Mass

How can you increase the acceleration of the wagon? Look again at the equation for acceleration: Acceleration = Force ÷ Mass. One way to increase acceleration is by changing the force. According to the equation, acceleration and force change in the same way. An increase in force causes an increase in acceleration. So to increase the acceleration of the wagon, you can increase the force you use to pull it. You can pull harder.

Another way to increase acceleration is to change the mass. According to the equation, acceleration and mass change in opposite ways. This means that an increase in mass causes a decrease in acceleration. It also means that a decrease in mass causes an increase in acceleration. So to increase the acceleration of the wagon, you can decrease its mass. Instead of you, the boys should ride in the wagon.

Section 2 Review

1. What three quantities are related in Newton's second law of motion? What is the relationship among them?
2. When the net force on an object increases, how does the object's acceleration change?
3. Suppose you know the acceleration of a shopping cart as it rolls down a supermarket aisle. You want to find the net force with which it was pushed. What other information do you need in order to find the force?
4. **Thinking Critically** **Problem Solving** Suppose you doubled the force acting on an object. In what way could you change its mass to keep its acceleration unchanged?

Check Your Progress
CHAPTER PROJECT 5

The vehicle for your project will need to accelerate from a resting position. From Newton's second law of motion, you know that Acceleration = Force ÷ Mass. This means you have two ways of increasing acceleration: increasing force or decreasing mass. How can you either increase the force acting on your vehicle or decrease its mass?

Background

Facts and Figures In the U.S. Customary system of measurement, the pound is a unit of force, not mass. In this system, the unit for mass is the *slug*. The weight of an object that has a mass of 1 slug is 32.17 pounds. This unit of mass measurement is used widely by engineers but is rarely used by anybody else. When people say they want to take off a few "pounds," they probably mean they want to lose mass.

Program Resources

◆ **Unit 2 Resources** 5-2 Review and Reinforce, p. 39; 5-2 Enrich, p. 40

SECTION 3 Friction and Gravity

DISCOVER

Which Lands First?

Do you think a quarter will fall more quickly than a dime? More quickly than a nickel? Record your predictions and find out!

1. Place a dime, a nickel, and a quarter along the edge of a desk.

2. Put a ruler behind the coins. Line it up with the edge of the desk.

3. Keeping the ruler parallel to the edge of the desk, push all three coins over the edge at the same time. Observe any time difference when the coins land.

Think It Over

Predicting Did you see a pattern in the time the coins took to fall? Use your observations about the coins to predict whether a soccer ball will fall more quickly than a marble. Will a pencil fall more quickly than a book? How can you test your predictions?

What happens if you push a book slowly across your desk and then stop pushing? Will it keep moving? Without actually pushing a book, you can predict that it will come to a stop. Now think about lifting a book above your desk and letting it go. Again, without actually dropping the book, you can predict that it will fall. In both of these situations, you first exert a force to change the motion of a book, and then you remove the force.

According to Newton's first law of motion, the book's motion changes only if unbalanced forces act on it. A force should not be necessary to keep the book moving at a constant speed. So why does the book stop sliding after you push it? And why does the book fall back to the ground once you stop exerting a force to hold it up?

From Newton's first law of motion, we know that in each case other forces must be acting on the book. Two other forces do indeed act on the book. When the book slides, the force of friction causes it to slow to a stop. When the book falls, the force of the gravity causes it to accelerate downward. In this section you will learn that these two forces affect nearly all motion.

GUIDE FOR READING

◆ What factors determine the friction force between two surfaces?

◆ How does mass differ from weight?

◆ What is the law of universal gravitation?

Reading Tip As you read, compare and contrast friction and gravity.

Chapter 5 **153**

READING STRATEGIES

Reading Tip Remind students that comparing is finding similarities and contrasting is finding differences. Suggest that students write *Friction* and *Gravity* as column headings on a sheet of paper. They can list information about each force as they read the section. You may wish to have students use a Venn diagram to show the similarities and differences.

Program Resources

◆ **Unit 2 Resources** 5-3 Lesson Plan, p. 41; 5-3 Section Summary, p. 42
◆ **Guided Reading and Study Workbook** Section 5-3
◆ **Laboratory Manual** 5, "Weight and the Force of Gravity"

SECTION 3 Friction and Gravity

Objectives

After completing the lesson, students will be able to

◆ describe friction and identify the factors that determine the friction force between two surfaces;

◆ explain how mass differs from weight;

◆ state the law of universal gravitation;

◆ describe the effects of gravity and air resistance on an object in free fall.

Key Terms friction, sliding friction, rolling friction, fluid friction, gravity, free fall, projectile, air resistance, terminal velocity, weight

1 Engage/Explore

Activating Prior Knowledge

Stack two books on a table and tie a string around the bottom book. Attach a long elastic band to the string. Move the stack of books a short distance by pulling the elastic band. Have students observe how much the elastic band stretches. Now place several round pencils under the books. Move the books with the elastic band. Have students observe how much the elastic band stretches. Encourage the students to discuss what is happening in both cases.

DISCOVER

Skills Focus predicting
Materials *dime, nickel, quarter, ruler*
Time 15 minutes
Tips Caution students to keep rulers parallel to the edge rather than lining up edge of coin with edge of desk.
Think It Over Students should observe that all the coins took the same time to fall. They should predict that the soccer ball and the marble, and the pencil and the book will all take the same time to fall. They can test their predictions by holding two of the objects at the same height, releasing them at the same time, and observing whether they land at the same time.

153

2 Facilitate

Friction

Using the Visuals: Figure 8

Have students measure the widths of the two friction arrows and the force exerted on the skiers and decide if the forces are balanced. (Have them refer to Figure 1 for a refresher on balanced and unbalanced forces.) If the forces are balanced, what is happening to the skiers? *(They have constant speed)* If the forces are not balanced, what is happening to the skiers? *(They are accelerating)* **learning modality: logical/mathematical**

Building Inquiry Skills: Designing Experiments

Materials *spring scale, wooden block, wooden board, various materials such as sandpaper, carpeting, and aluminum foil.*
Time 20 minutes

Allow students to compare the friction generated by a rough and smooth surface. Have them run their fingers over the sandpaper or carpet and compare with the table top. Ask: **How would you describe the texture of a surface that produces a lot of friction?** *(Rough or gritty)* Suggest students design an experiment to investigate the friction created by different surfaces. If the small wooden blocks don't have hooks, wrap rubber bands around the blocks and attach paper clips to the rubber bands to serve as connectors. The students will attach the spring scale to the block and drag it across a smooth surface and then across a rough surface. If students drag the block at a constant speed, then the forces are balanced and the spring scale reading is equal to the friction force. Encourage students to collect various materials to test different surfaces. Students should conclude that the rougher the surfaces of the two objects, the greater the friction between them.
learning modality: kinesthetic

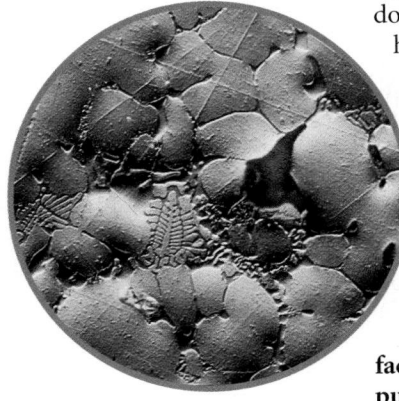

Figure 7 If you look at a polished metal surface under a special microscope, you'll find that it is actually quite rough. *Predicting What would a rough surface look like?*

Friction

When you push a book across a table, the surface of the book rubs against the surface of the table. In the same way, the skin of a firefighter's hands rubs against the polished metal pole as she slides down. Although surfaces may seem quite smooth, they actually have many irregularities. When two surfaces rub, the irregularities of one surface get caught on those of the other surface. The force that one surface exerts on another when the two rub against each other is called **friction.**

The Nature of Friction Friction acts in a direction opposite to the object's direction of motion. Without friction, the object would continue to move at constant speed forever. Friction, however, opposes motion. Eventually friction will cause an object to come to a stop.

The strength of the force of friction depends on two factors: the types of surfaces involved and how hard the surfaces push together. Rough surfaces produce greater friction than smooth surfaces. The skiers in Figure 8 get a fast ride because there is very little friction between their skis and the snow. The reindeer would not be able to pull them easily over a rough surface such as sand. The force of friction also increases if the surfaces push harder against each other. If you rub your hands together forcefully, there is more friction than if you rub your hands together lightly.

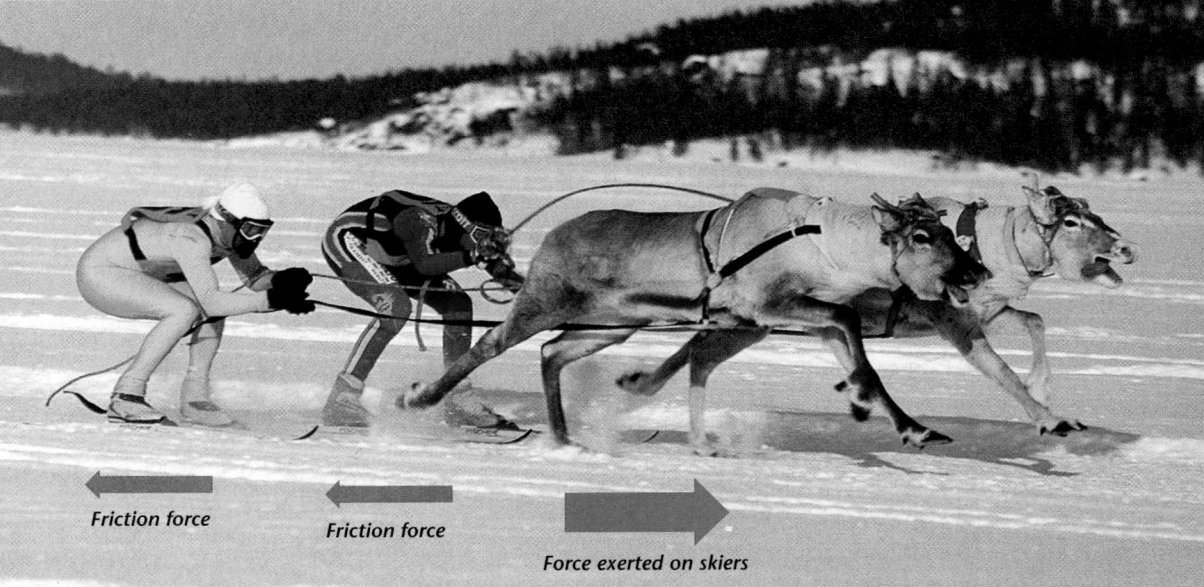

Figure 8 These reindeer can't fly. But they can give an exciting ride to the two Finlanders on skis.

Friction force

Friction force

Force exerted on skiers

154

Background

Integrating Science Earth's surface is made up of separate plates that move relative to one another. At some boundaries, the plates are slowly sliding past each other at the rate of 10 centimeters or so a year. However, friction sometimes temporarily prevents the plate boundaries from sliding. Thus stress can build up over a long time until the force gets large enough to overcome the friction. When the plates finally do slip, the shaking of Earth's crust can cause earthquake waves that spread over a large area. Some scientists have suggested drilling wells and pumping water into the plate boundaries. This would lubricate the boundaries and reduce friction, thus allowing the plates to slide past each other more easily.

Figure 9 Friction enables these students to draw on the pavement. Friction also enables the metalworker to smooth a metal surface. *Inferring How can you tell that the grinder is producing heat?*

Is Friction Useful or Not? Is friction necessarily a bad thing? No—whether or not friction is useful depends on the situation. You are able to walk, for example, because friction acts between the soles of your shoes and the floor. Without friction your shoes would only slide across the floor, and you would never move forward. An automobile moves because of friction between its tires and the road. Thanks to friction you can light a match and you can walk on a sidewalk.

Friction is so useful that at times people want to increase it. If you are walking down a snow-covered hill, you might wear rubber boots or spread sand to increase the friction and slow you down. Ballet dancers spread a sticky powder on the soles of their shoes so that they do not slip on the dance floor.

Controlling Friction There are different kinds of friction. When solid surfaces slide over each other, the kind of friction that occurs is called **sliding friction.** When an object rolls over a surface, the kind of friction that occurs is **rolling friction.** The force needed to overcome rolling friction is much less than the force needed to overcome sliding friction.

Ball bearings are one way of reducing friction between two surfaces. Ball bearings are small, smooth steel balls. The balls roll between rotating metal parts. The wheels of in-line skates, skateboards, and bicycles all have ball bearings. Many automobile parts have ball bearings as well.

The friction that occurs when an object moves through a liquid or a gas is called **fluid friction.** The force needed to overcome fluid friction is usually less than that needed to overcome sliding friction. The fluid keeps surfaces from making direct contact and thus reduces friction. The moving parts of machines are bathed in oil so that they can slide past each other with less friction.

☑ *Checkpoint* *What are two ways to reduce friction?*

Spinning Plates

Find out if the force of rolling friction is really less than the force of sliding friction.

1. Stack two identical pie plates together. Try to spin the top plate.
2. Now separate the plates and fill the bottom of one pie plate loosely with marbles.
3. Place the second plate in the plate with marbles.
4. Try to spin the top plate again. Observe the results.

Drawing Conclusions What applications are there for the rolling friction modeled in this activity?

Skills Focus drawing conclusions
ACTIVITY
Materials *two identical pie plates, marbles*
Time 10 minutes
Tips Shallow bowls may be substituted for the pie plates. Allow students to work in groups to complete the activity. After students complete Step 1, ask: **What kind of friction occurred?** *(Sliding friction)* In Step 2, 10 to 20 marbles are sufficient. Students should not fill the pie plate. After Step 4, ask: **What kind of friction occurred?** *(Rolling friction)*
Drawing Conclusions Applications include wheels with ball bearings and some types of Lazy Susans.
Extend Students can put enough water in the bottom pie plate to make the top plate float, then repeat the experiment. The result of this activity will be similar to that of the activity with marbles, because the water acts as a lubricant to reduce friction. **learning modality: visual**

Real-Life Learning

Ask students to name several lubricants that they have encountered. *(Sample: motor oil in a car, grease for a bicycle chain)* Ask: **Why do lubricants reduce friction?** *(Lubricants replace sliding friction with fluid friction.)* **limited English proficiency**

Media and Technology

📼 **Concept Videotape Library**
Adventures, Tape 1, "Light as a Feather"

Answers to Self-Assessment

Caption Questions

Figure 7 A rough surface would look even rougher under a microscope, with more hills and valleys than a smooth surface.

Figure 9 The metal surface is glowing and sparks are flying.

☑ *Checkpoint*

Ball bearings and oil or other lubricants

Ongoing Assessment

Writing Have students write a sentence or two describing a situation where friction is both a help and a hindrance. *(Sample: Friction slows a car and increases gasoline use but also allows the wheels to push the car forward and helps to keep the car on the road.)*

 Portfolio Students can save their sentences in their portfolios.

155

Gravity

Gravity, continued

Sharpen your Skills

Calculating

Materials *four distinct objects, such as a shoe, a book, a spiral notebook, a pair of scissors; scale balance*
Time 20 minutes
Tips This activity can help reinforce the difference between weight and mass. Have students create a data table for their estimates, measurements, and calculations. You may wish to provide a sample calculation for converting mass to weight.
Extend Suggest students use a newton spring scale to determine the weight of an object in newtons, then divide by 9.8 m/s² to calculate the object's mass in kilograms. They can then check the mass on the scale balance. **learning modality: logical/mathematical**

Universal Gravitation

Using the Visuals: Figure 13

Ask students: **Why do the arrows in the figure point toward each other?** (*The force attracts the objects toward each other, so each force arrow points to the other object.*) Point out to students the parts of the diagram with the thickest arrows. Ask: **How could you increase the gravitational force between the objects?** (*Add mass to the objects or decrease the distance between the objects.*) Have students draw their own diagrams to indicate what decreasing the mass of the objects might look like. **learning modality: logical/mathematical**

 Integrating Space Science

Discuss the problems created by humans living for an extended period in a low or zero gravity environment during space flight. **learning modality: verbal**

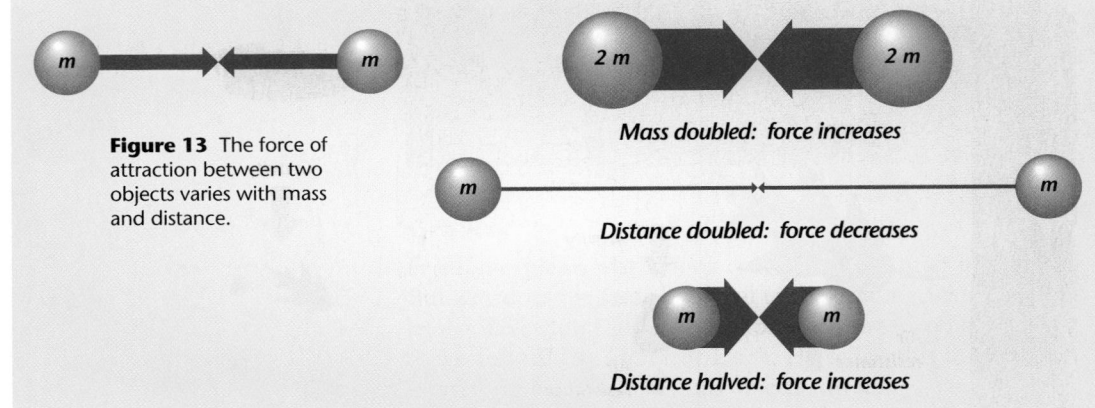

Figure 13 The force of attraction between two objects varies with mass and distance.

Mass doubled: force increases

Distance doubled: force decreases

Distance halved: force increases

Since weight is a force, you can rewrite Newton's second law of motion, Force = Mass × Acceleration, to find weight.

Weight = Mass × Acceleration due to gravity

Weight is usually measured in newtons, mass in kilograms, and acceleration due to gravity in m/s². So a 50-kilogram person weighs 50 kg × 9.8 m/s² = 490 newtons on Earth's surface.

Universal Gravitation

Newton realized that Earth is not the only object that exerts a gravitational force. Instead, gravity acts everywhere in the universe. Gravity is the force that makes an apple fall to the ground. It is the force that keeps the moon orbiting around Earth. It is also the force that keeps all the planets orbiting around the sun.

What Newton discovered is now called the law of universal gravitation. **The law of universal gravitation states that the force of gravity acts between all objects in the universe.** Any two objects in the universe, without exception, attract each other. This means that you are not only attracted to Earth, but you are also attracted to all the other objects around you! Earth and the objects around you are attracted to you as well.

Why don't you notice that the objects around you are pulling on you? After all, this book exerts a gravitational force on you. The reason is that the strength of the force depends on the masses of the objects involved. The force of gravity is much greater between you and Earth than between you and your book. **INTEGRATING SPACE SCIENCE** Although your mass would remain the same on another planet or moon, your weight would be different. For example, the force of gravity on Earth's moon is about one sixth that on Earth. Your weight on

Sharpen your Skills

Calculating ACTIVITY

You can determine the weight of an object if you measure its mass.

1. Estimate the weight of four objects. (*Hint:* An apple weighs about 1 N.)
2. Find the mass of each object. If the measurements are not in kilograms, convert them to kilograms.
3. Multiply each mass by 9.8 m/s² to find the weight in newtons.

How close to actual values were your estimates?

Background

Facts and Figures Gravity is much weaker than electrical, magnetic, or any other forces in nature. Magnetic and electric forces can both attract and repel, but as far as we know, gravity only attracts. Gravity is not blocked by anything. Even though gravity is the weakest of the forces, it is the force that holds the universe together.

Program Resources

◆ **Unit 2 Resources** 5-3 Review and Reinforce, p. 43; 5-3 Enrich, p. 44

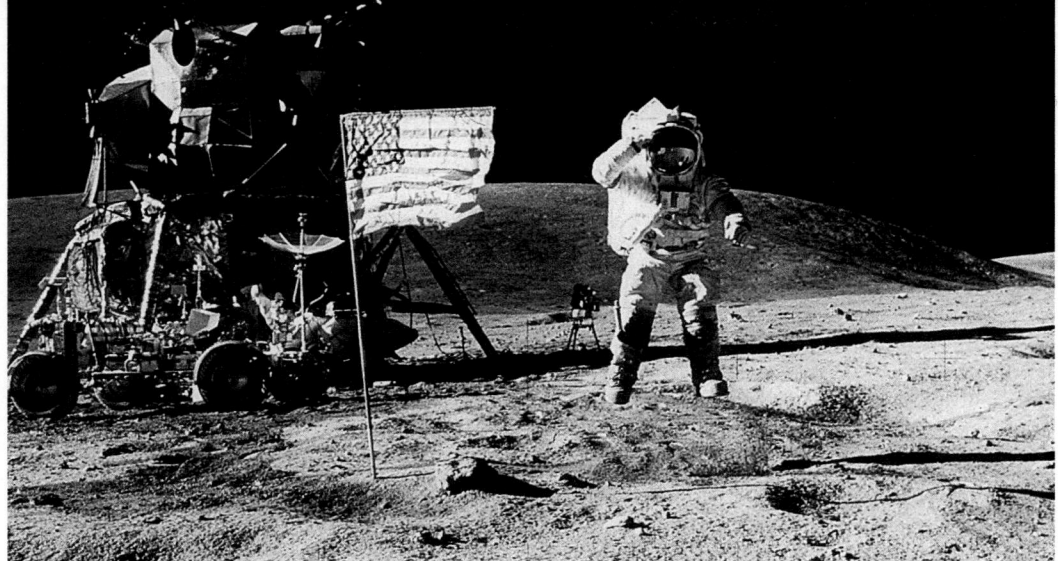

Figure 14 This astronaut jumps easily on the moon. *Comparing and Contrasting How do his mass and weight on the moon compare to his mass and weight on Earth?*

the moon, then, would be about a sixth of what it is on Earth. That is why the astronaut in Figure 14 can leap so easily.

If the gravitational force depends on mass, you might then expect to notice a force of attraction from a massive object, such as the moon or the sun. But you do not. The reason is that the gravitational force also depends on the distance between the objects. The farther apart the objects are, the weaker the force.

Astronauts travel great distances from Earth. As they travel from Earth toward the moon, Earth's gravitational pull becomes weaker. At the same time, the moon's gravitational pull becomes stronger. At the surface of the moon an astronaut feels the pull of the moon's gravity, but no longer notices the pull of Earth's gravity.

 Section 3 Review

1. What factors determine the strength of the friction force when two surfaces slide against each other?
2. What is the difference between weight and mass?
3. State the law of universal gravitation in your own words.
4. **Thinking Critically Problem Solving** A squirrel drops a nut over a cliff. What is the velocity of the nut after 3 seconds? After 5 seconds? After 10 seconds? (Ignore air resistance. Remember that the acceleration due to gravity is 9.8 m/s².)

CHAPTER PROJECT 5

Check Your Progress
Draw a diagram of your vehicle. Use labeled arrows to show each place that a force is acting on it. Be sure to include friction forces in your diagram. Brainstorm ways to reduce forces that slow down your vehicle.

Media and Technology

📺 **Transparencies** "Law of Universal Gravitation," Transparency 15

Answers to Self-Assessment

Caption Question

Figure 14 Although his mass is the same, his weight is lower on the moon.

3 Assess

Section 3 Review Answers

1. The types of surfaces, and how hard the surfaces push together.
2. Weight is a measure of the force of gravity acting on an object. Mass is a measure of the amount of matter in that object.
3. Every object exerts a force of gravity on every other object in the universe. This force is proportional to both objects' mass, and inversely proportional to the square of the distance between them. This means that the force decreases significantly as the distance between the objects increases and vice versa.
4. After 3 seconds: 29.4 m/s; after 5 seconds: 49 m/s; after 10 seconds: 98 m/s

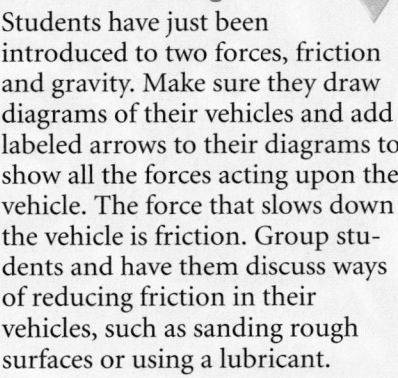 **CHAPTER PROJECT 5**

Check Your Progress
Students have just been introduced to two forces, friction and gravity. Make sure they draw diagrams of their vehicles and add labeled arrows to their diagrams to show all the forces acting upon the vehicle. The force that slows down the vehicle is friction. Group students and have them discuss ways of reducing friction in their vehicles, such as sanding rough surfaces or using a lubricant.

Performance Assessment

Writing Ask students to imagine they are playing basketball on a planet with either less friction or lower gravity than on Earth. Have students write paragraphs that describe how the motion of the players and the ball would be different from a game on Earth.

 Portfolio Students can save their paragraphs in their portfolios.

159

You, the Consumer

Sticky Sneakers

Preparing for Inquiry

Key Concept Sneaker soles illustrate three kinds of friction.

Skills Objectives Students will be able to
◆ form operational definitions of starting friction, forward-stopping friction, and sideways-stopping friction;
◆ measure the force required to overcome friction;
◆ control variables such as total mass.

Time 45 minutes

Advance Planning Assemble the spring scales, paper clips, tape, balance and mass sets. Bring in an assortment of sneakers or ask students to volunteer their sneakers.

 If using probeware, refer to the *Probeware Lab Manual*.

Guiding Inquiry

Invitation Have a student in sneakers demonstrate three types of friction forces: stopping, starting, and sideways. Ask:
What does friction depend on? *(The kinds of surfaces involved and how hard the surfaces push together)* Ask students to discuss how different kinds of sneakers might have different kinds of friction.

Introducing the Procedure
◆ If necessary, demonstrate how to zero and use a spring scale.
◆ Show students how to measure the force of sliding friction with a spring scale by pulling an object with a slow, constant speed.
◆ Ask students which way they should pull a sneaker to measure stopping friction. *(Forward, so that the friction force on the shoe is toward the back of the shoe)* Ask similar questions about starting friction and sideways-stopping friction.

Troubleshooting the Experiment
◆ Be sure students check the zero of the spring scale each time they use it. If the spring scale is calibrated in grams, students can multiply by 0.01 to obtain a reading in newtons.

Sticky Sneakers

The appropriate sneaker for an activity should have a specific type of tread to grip the floor or the ground. In this lab you will test different sneakers by measuring the amount of friction between the sneakers and a table.

Problem

How does the amount of friction between a sneaker and a surface compare for different types of sneakers?

Skills Focus

forming operational definitions, measuring, controlling variables

Materials

three or more different types of sneakers
2 spring scales, 5 N and 20 N, or force sensors
mass set(s)   tape
3 large paper clips   balance

Procedure

1. Sneakers are designed to deal with various friction forces, including these:
   ◆ starting friction, which is involved when you start from a stopped position
   ◆ forward-stopping friction, which is involved when you come to a forward stop
   ◆ sideways-stopping friction, which is involved when you come to a sideways stop

2. Prepare a data table in which you can record each type of friction for each sneaker.
3. Place each sneaker on a balance. Then put masses in each sneaker so that the total mass of the sneaker plus the masses is 1,000 g. Spread the masses out evenly inside the sneaker.
4. You will need to tape a paper clip to each sneaker and then attach a spring scale to the paper clip. (If you are using force sensors, see your teacher for instructions.) To measure
   ◆ starting friction, attach the paper clip to the back of the sneaker.
   ◆ forward-stopping friction, attach the paper clip to the front of the sneaker.
   ◆ sideways-stopping friction, attach the paper clip to the side of the sneaker.

DATA TABLE

Sneaker	Starting friction (N)	Sideways-stopping friction (N)	Forward-stopping friction (N)
A			
B			

◆ Point out that the scale must not be angled to the side or up or down while it is used, as this changes the reading.

Expected Outcome

Students should have a table with a column for each kind of friction, showing the force of friction for each kind of sneaker.

Analyze and Conclude

1. Manipulated variable: the sneaker sole. Responding variable: the amount of friction.

2. For stopping friction: the sneaker is moving at a constant speed, therefore, the friction force and the pulling force must be balanced (equal). The pulling force is indicated by the spring scale. For starting friction, the pulling force must overcome the friction force in order to make the sneaker move. At the point where the sneaker starts to move, the two forces are almost equal.

3. It is a fair test of the friction as long as the amount of friction in each sneaker depends on mass in the same way.

5. To measure starting friction, pull the sneaker backward until it starts to move. Use the 20-N spring scale first. If the reading is less than 5 N, use a 5-N scale. The force necessary to make the sneaker start moving is equal to the friction force. Record the starting friction force in your data table.

6. To measure either type of stopping friction, use the spring scale to pull each sneaker at a slow, constant speed. Record the stopping friction force in your data table.

7. Repeat Steps 4–6 for the remaining sneakers.

Analyze and Conclude

1. What are the manipulated and responding variables in this experiment? Explain. (See the Skills Handbook for a discussion of experimental variables.)

2. Why is the reading on the spring scale equal to the friction force in each case?

3. Do you think that using a sneaker with a small amount of mass in it is a fair test of the friction of the sneakers? (Consider the fact that sneakers are used with people's feet inside them.) Explain your answer.

4. Draw a diagram that shows the forces acting on the sneaker for each type of motion.

5. Why did you pull the sneaker at a slow speed to test for stopping friction? For starting friction, why did you pull a sneaker that wasn't moving?

6. Which sneaker had the most starting friction? Which had the most forward stopping friction? Which had the most sideways stopping friction?

7. Can you identify a relationship between the type of sneaker and the type of friction you observed? What do you observe about the sneakers that would cause one to have better traction than another?

8. **Apply** Wear a pair of your own sneakers. Start running and notice how you press against the floor with your sneaker. How do you think this affects the friction between the sneaker and the floor? How can you test for this variable?

Getting Involved

Go to a store that sells sneakers. If possible take a spring scale and, with the clerk's permission, do a quick friction test on sneakers designed for different activities. Also, note the materials they are made of, the support they provide for your feet, and other features. Then decide whether it is necessary to buy specific sneakers for different activities.

Sample Data Table

Sneaker	Starting friction (N)	Sideways-stopping friction (N)	Forward-stopping friction (N)
A	6.3	4.5	4.8
B	4.6	3.7	3.6
C	4.4	3.3	3.4

Program Resources

◆ **Unit 2 Resources** Real-World Lab blackline masters, pp. 55–57
◆ **Probeware Lab Manual** Blackline masters

Media and Technology

 Lab Activity Videotape
Tape 1

4. See students' diagrams. Diagrams should be clearly labeled with force arrows reflecting the size of the force and the direction.

5. You pull the sneaker at a slow speed to test stopping friction because when you stop, the sneaker is sliding slowly along the ground. You pull a sneaker that is not moving for starting friction because when you start running the sneaker is not moving yet.

6. Answers will vary. Running sneakers tend to exhibit more starting friction. Basketball sneakers tend to exert more stopping friction. Tennis shoes tend to exert more sideways-stopping friction.

7. One type of sneaker may provide better traction than another because the soles are made of a different material, they have different treads, or have worn treads or rubber soles hardened with age.

8. When you press against the floor when starting to run, you increase the force with which the sneaker and floor press against each other, increasing the friction force. To test for this variable, students could repeat the lab after adding weights to each sneaker. A suitable weight could be made by filling several resealable plastic bags with sand. These could be stuffed into the sneaker before measuring each type of friction.

Extending the Inquiry

Getting Involved Remind students they must go to the store with an adult supervisor and ask permission from the store clerk before carrying out the friction test. Remind students to compare sneakers of about the same mass. Students will probably find there are not big differences in friction between different types of sneakers. The same type of sneakers should exhibit about the same amount of each type of friction.

Objectives

After completing the lesson, students will be able to
◆ state Newton's third law of motion;
◆ define and calculate momentum and state the law of conservation of momentum.

Key Terms momentum, law of conservation of momentum

1 Engage/Explore

Activating Prior Knowledge

Invite a volunteer to sit facing forward on a wide skateboard with his or her feet up. Once the student is steady on the board, give him or her a basketball to toss to you. Ask students: **What happened to the student on the skateboard when he or she tossed the ball?** *(The student moved backward as he or she tossed the ball.)* Ask: **What made the ball move?** *(a force)* **Where did the force come from?** *(The person on the skateboard)* **What made the person on the skateboard move?** *(a force)* **Where did this force come from?** *(It must have come from the ball.)*

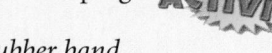
DISCOVER

Skills Focus developing hypotheses
Materials *rubber band, hard cover book, marbles, plastic straw*
Time 15 minutes
Tips Have students work in pairs. Make sure that they do not produce a twisting motion and that they release the straw and the book at the same time. Allow several attempts to master the technique.
Think It Over Students should observe that the book and straw moved in opposite directions, and the straw moved faster than the book. One hypothesis might be that the straw exerted a force on the book and the book exerted a force on the straw.

162

DISCOVER ·· **ACTIVITY**

How Pushy Is a Straw?

1. Stretch a rubber band around the middle of the front cover of a small or medium-size hardcover book.

2. Place four marbles in a small square on a table. Carefully place the book on the marbles so that the cover with the rubber band is on top.

3. Hold the book steady by placing one index finger on the center of the binding. Then, as shown in the illustration, push a straw against the rubber band with your other index finger.

4. Push the straw so that the rubber band stretches about ten centimeters. Then let go of both the book and the straw at the same time.

Think It Over
Developing Hypotheses What did you observe about the motion of the book and the straw? Write a hypothesis to explain what happened in terms of the forces on the book and the straw.

GUIDE FOR READING

◆ What is Newton's third law of motion?

◆ What is the law of conservation of momentum?

Reading Tip Before you read, preview the illustrations and predict what *action* and *reaction* mean.

Imagine that you are an astronaut making a space walk outside your space station. In your excitement about your walk, you lose track of time and use up all the fuel in your jet pack. How do you get back to the station? Your jet pack is empty, but it can still get you back to the station if you throw it away. To understand how, you need to know Newton's third law of motion.

Newton's Third Law of Motion

Newton realized that forces are not "one-sided." Whenever one object exerts a force on a second object, the second object exerts a force back on the first object. The force exerted by the second object is equal in strength and opposite in direction to the first force. The first force is called the "action" and the other force the "reaction." **Newton's third law of motion states that if one object exerts a force on another object, then the second object exerts a force of equal strength in the opposite direction on the first object.**

Figure 15 A hammer exerts a force on a nail, pushing it into a piece of wood. At the same time, the nail exerts a force back on the hammer, causing its motion to come to a sudden stop.

162

READING STRATEGIES

Reading Tip Indicate to students that illustrations and their captions can give them an idea of the content. Encourage students to preview the illustrations in this section and then predict what this section covers. Have students record any questions that come to mind as they view the illustrations.

Study and Comprehension Write the four major headings in the section on separate note cards. Place the cards face down and invite volunteers to choose a card and summarize the information presented under that heading.

Vocabulary Emphasize to students that *conservation* has a special meaning in physical science. Have partners take turns explaining the terms *conservation of momentum* and *conservation of natural resources* and give examples of each.

Equal but Opposite You may already be familiar with examples of Newton's third law of motion. Perhaps you have watched figure skaters and have seen one skater push on the other. As a result, both skaters move—not only the skater who was pushed. The skater who pushed is pushed back with an equal force, but in the opposite direction.

The speeds with which the two skaters move depend on their masses. If they have the same mass, they will move at the same speed. But if one skater has a greater mass than the other, she will move backward more slowly. Although the action and reaction forces will be equal and opposite, the same force acting on a greater mass results in a smaller acceleration. Recall that this is Newton's second law of motion.

Now can you figure out how to return from your space walk? In order to get a push back to the space station, you need to push on some object. You can remove your empty jet pack and push it away from you. In return, the jet pack will exert an equal force on you, sending you back to the safety of the space station.

Action-Reaction in Action Newton's third law is in action all around you. When you walk, you push the ground with your feet. The ground pushes back on your feet with an equal and opposite force. You go forward when you walk because the ground is pushing you! A bird flies forward by exerting a force on the air with its wings. The air pushes back on those wings with an equal force that propels the bird forward.

 INTEGRATING LIFE SCIENCE A squid applies Newton's third law of motion to move itself through the water. The squid exerts a force on the water that it expels from its body cavity. At the same time, the water exerts an equal and opposite force on the squid, causing it to move.

Figure 16 One skater pushes gently on the other. The result is that the other skater pushes back with an equal force—even if she isn't trying. *Applying Concepts Which of Newton's laws describes this phenomenon?*

Figure 17 When a squid pushes water out, the expelled water pushes back and forces the squid to move ahead (to the right). The force the squid exerts on the water is the action force.

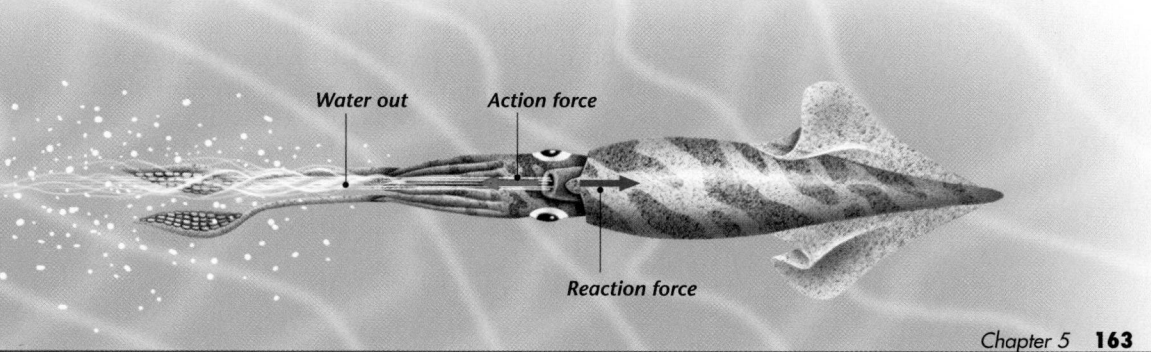

Water out   Action force

Reaction force

Program Resources

◆ **Unit 2 Resources** 5-4 Lesson Plan, p. 45; 5-4 Section Summary, p. 46
◆ **Guided Reading and Study Workbook** Section 5-4

Answers to Self-Assessment
Caption Question
Figure 16 Newton's third law of motion

---

2 Facilitate

Newton's Third Law of Motion

Building Inquiry Skills: Interpreting Illustrations

Have students collect examples of action and reaction forces from daily life. They can draw a picture of the example or use photographs from magazines. Have students use a marker to draw arrows on pictures to indicate the direction of action and reaction forces. Ask: **What two characteristics describe action and reaction forces?** (*They are equal and opposite.*) **learning modality: logical/mathematical**

Integrating Life Science

Inform students that several sea animals other than squid employ action and reaction forces as they move. These animals use a similar form of jet propulsion to move around. Scallops escape danger by snapping their shells together and forcing out water. This action pushes the scallops backward in a burst of speed. **learning modality: verbal**

Including All Students

Some students may wonder how we can show that the action-reaction forces are equal. Obtain a plastic ruler with a groove down the middle. Have students work in pairs to experiment with two marbles by rolling them along this groove. When a rolling marble collides with a stationary marble, the rolling marble stops and the stationary marble starts rolling. Students should recognize that the force required to stop the rolling marble is the same size as the force required to start the stationary marble. **learning modality: kinesthetic**

ACTIVITY

Ongoing Assessment

Skills Check Have students apply Newton's third law of motion to a pogo stick. Ask: **What are the action and reaction forces in a pogo stick jump?**

163

Newton's Third Law of Motion, continued

Using the Visuals: Figure 18B

Have students indicate the direction in which each player in Figure 18B applies a force. Then have them indicate the direction of the reaction force. *(There are two pairs of action and reaction forces.)* Challenge students to describe the size of all four forces illustrated. What happens to all the forces if the player on the left exerts a larger force on the ball than the player on the right. *(The action reaction pairs are still equal, but the forces exerted by the hands on the ball would be unbalanced. The ball would move to the right.)* **learning modality: visual**

Addressing Naive Conceptions

Some students may confuse balanced forces with action and reaction forces. Place a book on the table. Ask students to list all of the forces acting on the book. Ask: **Why doesn't the book move?** *(The forces are balanced.)* **What is pulling down on the book?** *(gravity).* **What is pushing up on the book?** *(the table)* **If the table is pushing up on the book, what is the book doing to the table?** *(pushing down)* The force of gravity on the book and the force of the table on the book are balanced forces. They both act on the book. The force of the book on the table and the force of the table on the book are an action-reaction pair. One acts on the book, the other acts on the table. **learning modality: visual**

Including All Students

Students whose first language is not English may not recognize the difference between the words *action* and *reaction* or *balanced* and *unbalanced*. Ask all students to supply other instances of words using the prefixes *un-* and *re-* with which they are familiar. *(Sample: tie— untie, do—redo, play—replay)* **limited English proficiency**

Figure 18 In these photographs, red arrows show action forces and blue arrows show reaction forces. **A.** The player's wrists exert the action force. **B.** As two players jump for the ball, the ball exerts reaction forces on both of them.

Do Action-Reaction Forces Cancel? In Section 1 you learned that balanced forces, which are equal and opposite, add up to zero. In other words, balanced forces cancel out. They produce no change in motion. Why then don't the action and reaction forces in Newton's third law of motion cancel out as well? After all, they are equal and opposite.

To answer this question, you have to consider the object on which the forces are acting. Look, for example, at the two volleyball players in Figure 18B. When they hit the ball from opposite directions, each of their hands exerts a force on the ball. If the forces are equal in strength, but opposite in direction, the forces cancel out. The ball does not move either to the left or to the right.

Newton's third law, however, refers to forces on two different objects. If only one player hits the ball, as shown in Figure 18A, the player exerts an upward action force on the ball. In return, the ball exerts an equal but opposite downward reaction force back on her wrists. One force is on the ball, and the other is on the player. The action and reaction forces cannot be added together because they are acting on different objects. Forces can be added together only if they are acting on the same object.

☑ *Checkpoint* *Why don't action and reaction forces cancel each other?*

Background

Integrating Science Personal watercraft (jet skis) are also propelled with action-and-reaction force pairs. The watercraft pushes a strong jet of water backward, and this jet of water pushes the watercraft forward. An exposed propeller would be dangerous in the event of an accident, so the propeller is concealed in a pump for safety reasons. Water is drawn in through an intake and expelled at the back. Jet airplanes use a similar principle by drawing air in through the engine intake, mixing the air with hot combustion gases, and expelling the mixture through the rear of the engine. In both cases, the craft is propelled forward by a reaction to the force required to expel a fluid backwards.

Momentum

When Newton presented his three laws of motion, he used two different words to describe moving objects. He used the word velocity, but he also wrote about something that he called the "quantity of motion." What is this quantity of motion? Today we call it momentum. The **momentum** (moh MEN tum) of an object is the product of its mass and its velocity.

Momentum = Mass × Velocity

What is the unit of measurement for momentum? Since mass is measured in kilograms and velocity is measured in meters per second, the unit for momentum is kilogram-meters per second (kg·m/s). Like velocity and acceleration, momentum is described by its direction as well as its quantity. The momentum of an object is in the same direction as its velocity.

The more momentum an object has, the harder it is to stop. You can catch a baseball moving at 20 m/s, for example, but you cannot stop a car moving at the same speed. Why does the car have more momentum than the ball? The car has more momentum because it has a greater mass.

A high velocity also can produce a large momentum, even when mass is small. A bullet shot from a rifle, for example, has a large momentum. Even though it has a small mass, it travels at a high speed.

Sample Problem

Which has more momentum: a 3-kg sledgehammer swung at 1.5 m/s or an 4-kg sledgehammer swung at 0.9 m/s?

Analyze.   You know the mass and velocity of two different objects. You need to determine the momentum of each.

Write the formula.   *Momentum = Mass × Velocity*

Substitute and solve.   *(a) 3 kg × 1.5 m/s = 4.5 kg·m/s*

      (b) 4 kg × 0.9 m/s = 3.6 kg·m/s

Think about it.   The lighter hammer has more momentum than the heavier one, because it is swung at a greater velocity—almost twice as fast.

Practice Problems   1. A golf ball travels at 16 m/s, while a baseball moves at 7 m/s. The mass of the golf ball is 0.045 kg and the mass of the baseball is 0.14 kg. Which has greater momentum?
      2. What is the momentum of a bird with a mass of 0.018 kg flying at 15 m/s?

Answers to Self-Assessment

☑ Checkpoint

The forces are acting on different objects.

Momentum

Building Inquiry Skills: Inferring

To help students understand that momentum depends upon the mass and velocity of a moving object, ask: **If a fire engine and a tricycle are rolling at a speed of 5 km/h, which would be easier to stop? Why?** *(The tricycle; it has less mass and less momentum.)* **Can a bullet and an automobile have the same momentum? Explain.** *(Yes, a bullet with a small mass that is moving very fast can have the same momentum as a car with a greater mass that is moving very slowly.)* **When a truck driver begins to brake, what happens to the momentum of the truck? Explain.** *(The truck's momentum decreases because its velocity decreases.)* **learning modality: logical/ mathematical**

Sample Problem

When working through mathematical problems, always model good techniques. Write the formula, substitute known quantities, then perform the mathematical operations. Remind students to manipulate the units as well. There is no special name for the unit of momentum, it is always written as kg·m/s.

Practice Problems
1. 0.045 kg × 16 m/s = 0.72 kg·m/s
    0.14 kg × 7 m/s = 0.98 kg·m/s
The baseball has greater momentum.
2. 0.018 kg × 15 m/s = 0.27 kg·m/s

Ongoing Assessment

Drawing Direct students to draw a diagram showing the direction and relative size of the action and reaction forces exerted when a person jumps. Students' diagrams should include force arrows showing a downward force from the person to the ground and an upward force from the ground to the person.

Conservation of Momentum

Figure 19 In the absence of friction, momentum is conserved when two train cars collide. This is true regardless of whether the train cars bounce off each other or couple together during the collision.
Interpreting Diagrams In which diagram is all of the momentum transferred from car X to car Y?

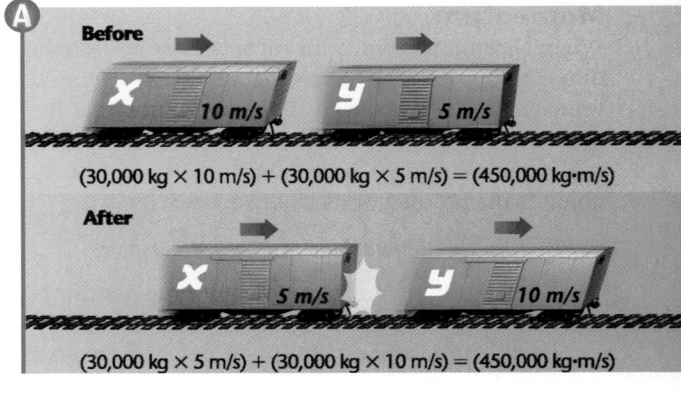

$(30{,}000 \text{ kg} \times 10 \text{ m/s}) + (30{,}000 \text{ kg} \times 5 \text{ m/s}) = (450{,}000 \text{ kg·m/s})$

$(30{,}000 \text{ kg} \times 5 \text{ m/s}) + (30{,}000 \text{ kg} \times 10 \text{ m/s}) = (450{,}000 \text{ kg·m/s})$

Conservation of Momentum

You know that if someone bumps into you from behind, you gain momentum in the forward direction. Momentum is useful for understanding what happens when an object collides with another object. When two objects collide in the absence of friction, momentum is not lost. This fact is called the law of conservation of momentum. The **law of conservation of momentum** states that the total momentum of the objects that interact does not change. The quantity of momentum is the same before and after they interact. **The total momentum of any group of objects remains the same unless outside forces act on the objects.** Friction is an example of an outside force.

Before you hear the details of this law, you should know that the word *conservation* means something different in physical science than in everyday usage. In everyday usage, conservation means saving resources. You might conserve water or fossil fuels, for example. In physical science, the word conservation refers to conditions before and after some event. A quantity that is conserved is the same after an event as it was before the event.

Two Moving Objects Look at the two train cars traveling in the same direction on a track shown in Figure 19A. Car X is traveling at 10 m/s and car Y is traveling at 5 m/s. Eventually, car X will catch up with car Y and bump into it. During this collision, the speed of each car changes. Car X slows down to 5 m/s, and car Y speeds up to 10 m/s. Momentum is conserved—the momentum of one train car decreases while the momentum of the other increases.

One Moving Object Suppose that car X moves down the track at 10 m/s and hits car Y, which is not moving. Figure 19B shows that after the collision, car X is no longer moving, but car Y is moving.

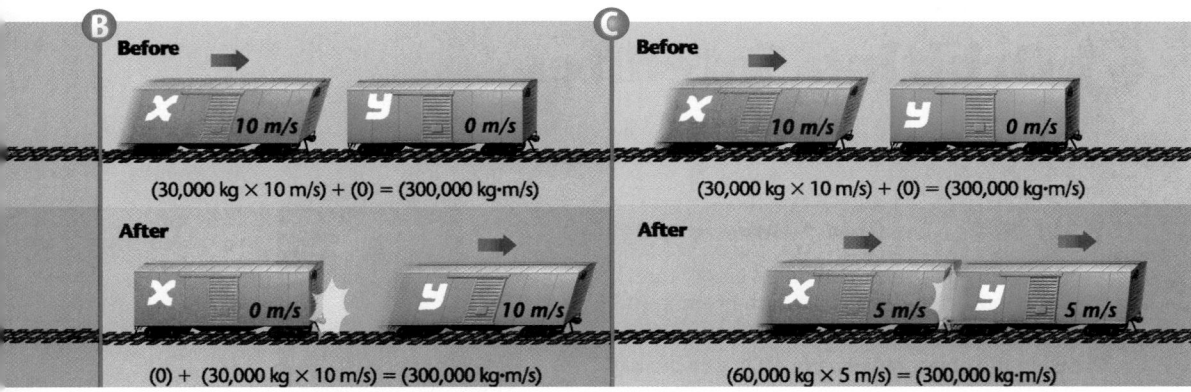

B Before
X 10 m/s   Y 0 m/s

(30,000 kg × 10 m/s) + (0) = (300,000 kg·m/s)

After
X 0 m/s   Y 10 m/s

(0) + (30,000 kg × 10 m/s) = (300,000 kg·m/s)

C Before
X 10 m/s   Y 0 m/s

(30,000 kg × 10 m/s) + (0) = (300,000 kg·m/s)

After
X 5 m/s   Y 5 m/s

(60,000 kg × 5 m/s) = (300,000 kg·m/s)

Even though the situation has changed, momentum is still conserved. The total momentum is the same before and after the collision. This time, all of the momentum has been transferred from car X to car Y.

Two Connected Objects Now suppose that, instead of bouncing off each other, the two train cars couple together when they hit. Is momentum still conserved? The answer is yes. You can see in Figure 19C that the total momentum before the collision is again 300,000 kg·m/s. But after the collision, the coupled train cars make one object with a total mass of 60,000 kilograms (30,000 kilograms + 30,000 kilograms). The velocity of the coupled trains is 5 m/s—half the velocity of car X before the collision. Since the mass is doubled, the velocity must be divided in half in order for momentum to be conserved.

 **Section 4 Review**

1. According to Newton's third law of motion, how are action and reaction forces related?
2. What is meant by "conservation of momentum"?
3. Suppose you and a friend, who has exactly twice your mass, are on skates. You push away from your friend. How does the force with which you push your friend compare to the force with which your friend pushes you? How do your accelerations compare?
4. **Thinking Critically** **Comparing and Contrasting** Which has more momentum, a 250-kg dolphin swimming at 6 m/s, or a 450-kg manatee swimming at 2 m/s?

Check Your Progress CHAPTER PROJECT 5

Construct your vehicle. Is your vehicle powered according to Newton's third law of motion? Add to your diagram so that it shows the force exerted by your vehicle and the force exerted on your vehicle to make it move. What exerts the force that moves your vehicle? Be ready to explain the diagram to other students.

Chapter 5 **167**

Answers to Self-Assessment

Caption Question
Figure 19 Diagram B

Section 4 Review Answers

1. Action and reaction forces are equal but act in opposite directions.
2. The total momentum is exactly the same before and after a collision.
3. The force with which you push your friend is equal and opposite to the force with which your friend pushes you (even if your friend is not deliberately "pushing"). You accelerate faster than your friend and roll back further because your mass is less.
4. The dolphin has a greater momentum (1,500 kg·m/s) than the manatee (900 kg·m/s).

Check Your Progress CHAPTER PROJECT 5

Allow students to work in pairs as they add force arrows to their diagrams and verify that they are using Newton's third law. They should be able to explain to their partner how each force acts and how this is in accord with the third law. Working in pairs and explaining to their partner gives students practice for the class presentation.

Performance Assessment

Skills Check Have students write and solve a problem in which they must calculate the momentum of two objects before and after a collision. Have students compare their problems and solutions in small groups.

 Students can save their problems and solutions in their portfolios.

SECTION 5 Orbiting Satellites

Objectives

After completing the lesson, students will be able to

◆ explain how a rocket lifts off the ground;

◆ describe the forces that keep a satellite in orbit.

Key Terms satellite, centripetal force

1 Engage/Explore

Activating Prior Knowledge

Ask students if they have seen a launching of the space shuttle on television. Encourage a volunteer to describe the launch. Invite students who enjoy model rocketry to tell about their hobby to the class. Compare the launching of a rocket to the way a squid propels itself. Call students' attention to the photograph of a shuttle launch and have them describe the action-reaction force pair that produces lift.

••••••• **DISCOVER** •••••••

Skills Focus forming operational definitions

Materials *small object such as an empty thread spool, length of string no more than 1 m long, safety goggles*

Time 10 minutes

Tips Caution students not to swing the object near another person. Have them wear safety goggles during the activity. In Step 3, students may predict that the spool will move more slowly or that it won't make it over the top. In Step 4, several variables are related to the length of the string. Students may find that the object moves faster (for the same force) when the length of the string is increased.

Think It Over The object is moving in a circle and is constantly accelerating. The force that keeps the object accelerating in a circle is the pulling force, or tension, of the string.

SECTION 5 Orbiting Satellites

DISCOVER •••••••••••••••••••••••••••••• ACTIVITY

What Makes an Object Move in a Circle?

1. Tie a small mass, such as an empty thread spool, to the end of a length of string (no more than one meter long).

2. Swing the object rapidly around in a circle that is perpendicular to the floor. Make sure no one is near the swinging object, and don't let it go!

3. Predict what will happen if you decrease the speed of the object. Test your prediction.

4. Predict how the length of the string affects the motion of the object. Test your prediction.

Think It Over

Forming Operational Definitions Describe the motion of the object. How do you know that the string exerts a force?

GUIDE FOR READING

◆ How does a rocket lift off the ground?

◆ What keeps a satellite in orbit?

Reading Tip As you read, make a list of main ideas and supporting details about rockets and satellites.

What would it be like to be at Cape Canaveral in Florida for a space shuttle launch? The countdown is broadcast over a loudspeaker—ten—nine—eight—seven—six—five—four. White steam comes out of the base of the rocket—three—two—one. The rocket rises into space and begins to turn slightly and roll. The noise hits you, and the ground shakes. With an astonishingly loud rumble, the rocket rises in the distance. Everyone cheers. You watch the rocket until it is too far away to see.

How Do Rockets Lift Off?

The awesome achievement of lifting a rocket into space against the force of gravity can be explained using Newton's third law of motion. As a rocket burns fuel, it expels exhaust gases. When the gases are forced out of the rocket, they exert an equal and opposite force back on

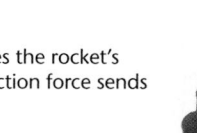

Figure 20 The action force pushes the rocket's exhaust gases downward. The reaction force sends the rocket into space.

168

READING STRATEGIES

Reading Tip Remind students that a main idea is an important point an author makes about a topic. Supporting details are the facts that support a main idea. Suggest that students use this format to list main ideas and supporting details.

Main idea 1: _____

  Supporting detail: _____

  Supporting detail: _____

Sample answer:

Main idea 1: *The motion of a rocket can be explained by Newton's third law.*

Supporting detail: *Exhaust gases are pushed out of the rocket.*

Supporting detail: *The exhaust gases exert a force on the rocket.*

the rocket. **A rocket can rise into the air because the gases it expels with a downward force exert an equal but opposite force on the rocket.** As long as this upward pushing force, called thrust, is greater than the downward pull of gravity, there is a net force in the upward direction. As a result, the rocket accelerates upward.

☑ Checkpoint *When a rocket is launched, what is the direction of the reaction force?*

What Is a Satellite?

Rockets are often used to carry satellites into space. A **satellite** is any object that travels around another object in space. An artificial satellite is a device that is launched into orbit around Earth. Artificial satellites are designed for many purposes. They are used in space research, communications, military intelligence, weather analysis, and geographical surveys.

Circular Motion Artificial satellites travel around Earth in an almost circular path. Recall that an object traveling in a circle is accelerating because it is constantly changing direction. If an object is accelerating, there must be a force acting on it to change its motion. Any force that causes an object to move in a circle is called a **centripetal force** (sen TRIP ih tul). The word *centripetal* means "center-seeking." For a satellite, the centripetal force is the gravitational force that pulls the satellite toward the center of Earth.

Satellite Motion If gravity pulls satellites toward Earth, why doesn't a satellite fall, as a ball thrown into the air would? The answer is that satellites do not travel straight up into the air. Instead, they move around Earth. If you throw a ball horizontally, for example, it will move out in front of you at the same time that it is pulled to the ground. If you throw the ball faster, it will land even farther in front of you. The faster you throw a projectile, the farther it travels before it lands.

Figure 21 As this rocket moves higher, its path tilts more and more. Eventually its path is parallel to Earth's surface. *Predicting How will the direction of the accelerating force change?*

Figure 22 The faster a projectile like this ball is thrown, the farther it travels before it hits the ground.

Answers to Self-Assessment

Caption Question

Figure 21 The direction of the force gradually changes from vertical to horizontal.

☑ Checkpoint

The direction of a rocket's reaction force is upward.

2 *Facilitate*

How Do Rockets Lift Off?

Demonstration

Materials *plastic water rocket, hand air pump, safety goggles*
Time 15 minutes plus time for rocket assembly

This demonstration uses a plastic water rocket and must be done outdoors. Water rockets can be purchased from science supply companies. The rocket uses compressed air to expel a mixture of water and air from the rocket nozzle. CAUTION: *These water rockets are safe, but the manufacturer's recommendations must be followed exactly. Students should wear goggles and observe from a safe distance.* After the launch, challenge students to identify the action and reaction forces that acted as the rocket lifted off the ground. (*The compressed air exerted a downward force on the water, expelling it from the rocket. The water exerted an upward force on the rocket.*) Then ask students which unbalanced forces are responsible for the rocket's upward movement. (*The upward force of the water on the rocket is greater than the downward pull of gravity.*) **learning modality: visual**

What Is a Satellite?

Building Inquiry Skills: Inferring

Ensure that students grasp how forces act on a satellite by asking: **Earth travels around the sun, so there must be a force acting on it to change the direction of its motion. What is that force?** (*The sun's gravity*) **learning modality: logical/mathematical**

Ongoing Assessment

Drawing Have students draw a diagram of the Earth-moon system and draw and label the centripetal force acting on the moon.

3 Assess

Section 5 Review Answers

1. According to Newton's third law, since the rocket exerts a force when it pushes the gas out backward, the gas exerts an equal and opposite force on the rocket, pushing it upward.

2. As the satellite falls, the surface of Earth curves away.

3. No. For satellites in low orbit, the force of gravity is almost as large as it would be on the surface. Satellites stay in orbit because they fall and move along the orbit at the same time.

4. All three factors increase acceleration. The decrease in air resistance allows the rocket to accelerate faster because there is less air resistance pushing the rocket in the opposite direction. The decrease in gravity allows the rocket to accelerate faster because there is less gravity pulling the rocket back toward Earth. The decrease in the rocket's mass increases acceleration because the same force acting on a smaller mass causes a greater acceleration.

Science at Home

Materials *child's plastic bucket, water*

If students have difficulty spinning the bucket, suggest they tie a rope to the handle. Warn students that if they spin the bucket too slowly, the water will spill out when the bucket gets to the top of the circle. If they spin the bucket fast enough, the bucket will "catch" the water before the water spills out due to gravity.

Performance Assessment

Writing Tell students they have received a letter from a person wondering about what will happen when the geostationary communications satellites orbiting Earth run out of fuel. Have students write paragraphs explaining why the communications satellites are not really stationary and why they don't need fuel to stay in orbit.

Portfolio Students can save their paragraphs in their portfolios.

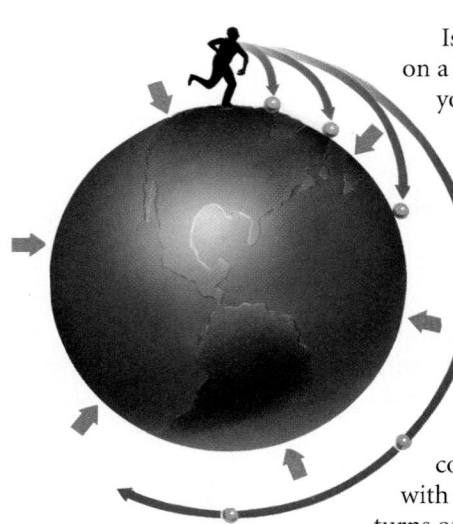

Figure 23 A projectile with enough velocity will move in a circular orbit around Earth. *Interpreting Diagrams The force of gravity is always toward the center of Earth. How does the direction of gravity compare to the direction of the projectile's motion at any point?*

Isaac Newton wondered what would happen if you were on a high mountain and were able to throw a stone as fast as you wanted. The faster you threw it, the farther away it would land. At a certain speed, the path of the object would match the curve of Earth. Although the stone would keep falling due to gravity, Earth's surface would curve away from the stone at the same rate. Thus the object would circle Earth, as in Figure 23. **Satellites in orbit around Earth continually fall toward Earth, but because Earth is curved they travel around it.** In other words, a satellite is a projectile that falls around Earth rather than into it. A satellite does not need fuel because it continues to move ahead due to its inertia. At the same time, gravity continuously changes the satellite's direction. The speed with which an object must be thrown in order to orbit Earth turns out to be about 7,900 m/s! This speed is almost 200 times as fast as a pitcher can throw a baseball.

Satellite Location Some satellites, such as the space shuttle, are put into low orbits. The time to complete a trip around Earth in a low orbit is about 90 minutes. Other satellites are sent into higher orbits. At these distances, the satellite travels more slowly and takes longer to circle Earth. For example, communications satellites travel about 36,000 kilometers above the surface. At this height they circle Earth once every 24 hours. Since Earth rotates once every 24 hours, a satellite above the equator always stays above the same point on Earth as it orbits.

Section 5 Review

1. Use action-reaction forces to explain why a rocket can lift off the ground.
2. Why doesn't an orbiting satellite fall back to Earth?
3. Is it correct to say that satellites stay in orbit rather than falling to Earth because they are beyond the pull of Earth's gravity? Explain.
4. **Thinking Critically** **Applying Concepts** When a rocket travels higher, air resistance decreases as the air becomes less dense. The force of gravity also decreases because the rocket is farther from Earth, and the rocket's mass decreases as its fuel is used up. Explain how acceleration is affected.

Science at Home

Fill a small plastic bucket halfway with water and take it outdoors. Challenge a family member to swing the bucket in a vertical circle. Explain that the water won't fall out at the top if the bucket is moving fast enough. Tell your family member that if the bucket falls as fast as the water, the water will stay in the bucket. Relate this activity to a satellite that also falls due to gravity, yet remains in orbit.

Program Resources

◆ **Unit 2 Resources** 5-5 Review and Reinforce, p. 51; 5-5 Enrich, p. 52

Media and Technology

Concept Videotape Library
Adventures, Tape 1, "We Have Lift Off"

Answers to Self-Assessment

Caption Question

Figure 23 For a projectile in orbit, the direction of the force of gravity is perpendicular to the projectile's motion.

CHAPTER 5 STUDY GUIDE

SECTION 1 The Nature of Force

Key Ideas
- The sum of all the forces acting on an object is the net force.
- Unbalanced forces change the motion of an object, whereas balanced forces do not.
- According to Newton's first law of motion, an object at rest will remain at rest and an object in motion will continue in motion at constant speed unless the object is acted upon by an unbalanced force.

Key Terms

force	balanced forces
net force	inertia
unbalanced forces	mass

SECTION 2 Force, Mass, and Acceleration

Key Idea
- Newton's second law of motion states that the net force on an object is the product of its acceleration and its mass.

Key Term
newton

SECTION 3 Friction and Gravity

Key Ideas
- Friction is a force that one surface exerts on another when they rub against each other.
- Weight is a measure of the force of gravity on an object, and mass is a measure of the amount of matter that an object contains.
- The force of gravity acts between all objects in the universe.

Key Terms

friction	free fall
sliding friction	projectile
rolling friction	air resistance
fluid friction	terminal velocity
gravity	weight

SECTION 4 Action and Reaction

Key Ideas
- Newton's third law of motion states that every time there is an action force on an object, the object will exert an equal and opposite reaction force.
- The momentum of an object is the product of its mass and its velocity.
- The law of conservation of momentum states that the total momentum is the same before and after an event, as long as there are no outside forces.

Key Terms
momentum
law of conservation of momentum

SECTION 5 Orbiting Satellites
INTEGRATING SPACE SCIENCE

Key Ideas
- A rocket burns fuel and produces gases. The rocket pushes these gases downward. At the same time, the gases apply an equal force to the rocket, pushing it upward.
- Even though a satellite is pulled downward by gravity, it stays in orbit because it is moving so quickly. Earth's surface curves away from the satellite as the satellite falls.

Key Terms
satellite   centripetal force

Organizing Information

Compare/Contrast Table Copy the compare/contrast table below on a separate sheet of paper. Complete the table to compare and contrast friction and gravity. (For more information on compare/contrast tables see the Skills Handbook.)

Force	Direction of Force	Force Depends Upon
Friction	a. ?	b. ?
Gravity	c. ?	d. ?

Chapter 5 **171**

Organizing Information

Compare/Contrast Table
a. opposite to the direction of the motion b. types of surfaces involved and how hard the surfaces push together c. between any two objects d. masses and distance

Program Resources
- **Unit 2 Resources** Chapter 5 Project Scoring Rubric, p. 32
- **Performance Assessment** Chapter 5, pp. 16–18
- **Chapter Tests** Chapter 5 Test, pp. 19–22

Media and Technology
Computer Test Bank
Chapter 5 Test

Reviewing Content
Multiple Choice
1. a **2.** b **3.** a **4.** d **5.** c

True or False
6. equal and opposite to **7.** matter or inertia **8.** true **9.** true **10.** true

Checking Concepts
11. The net force on an object equals mass times acceleration.

12. The fluids keep surfaces from making direct contact and thus reduce friction.

13. Both erasers hit the ground at the same time. While one is thrown horizontally, they both accelerate downward at the same rate.

14. Air resistance on the flat sheet is greater than the air resistance on the crumpled paper.

15. The cleats dig into the ground and prevent sliding.

16. Your mass would stay the same, but your weight on the asteroid would be less because the asteroid pulls you less strongly than the Earth.

17. Yes. The pavement exerts a force on the ball.

18. Answers will vary. Drawing should resemble the art on Figure 23. The satellite is accelerating since it is changing direction.

19. Students write original material. The answer should include a description of each kind of force involved in the event, how those forces changed the motion of objects involved in the event, and how the objects interacted.

Thinking Critically
20. When walking on land, you push the ground and the ground pushes back with an equal force on you. On the boat, you push the boat and the boat pushes back with an equal force on you. You move forward but the boat is also free to move backward.

21. 30 N

22. The skateboard stops, but you will keep moving forward because of inertia.

Reviewing Content
Multiple Choice
Choose the letter of the best answer.

1. When an unbalanced force acts on an object, the force
  a. changes the motion of the object.
  b. is canceled by another force.
  c. does not change the motion of the object.
  d. is equal to the weight of the object.

2. When two equal forces act in opposite directions on an object, they are called
  a. friction forces.   **b.** balanced forces.
  c. centripetal forces.   **d.** gravitational forces.

3. The resistance of an object to any change in its motion is called
  a. inertia.   **b.** friction.
  c. gravity.   **d.** weight.

4. According to Newton's second law of motion, force is equal to mass times
  a. inertia.   **b.** weight.
  c. direction.   **d.** acceleration.

5. The product of an object's mass and its velocity is called the object's
  a. net force.   **b.** weight.
  c. momentum.   **d.** gravitation.

True or False
If the statement is true, write true. If it is false, change the underlined word or words to make the statement true.

6. According to Newton's third law of motion, whenever you exert a force on an object, the object exerts a force back on you that is <u>greater than</u> your force.

7. Mass is a measure of the amount of <u>force</u> that an object has.

8. <u>Weight</u> is the measure of the force of gravity exerted on an object.

9. <u>Conservation</u> in science refers to the amount of some quantity staying the same before and after an event.

10. The force that causes a satellite to orbit Earth is <u>gravity</u>.

Checking Concepts
11. Explain how force, mass, and acceleration are related.

12. Why do slippery fluids such as oil reduce sliding friction?

13. One student tosses a chalkboard eraser horizontally so that the eraser hits the ground 5 meters away. At exactly the same time, another student drops an eraser. Which eraser hits the ground first? Explain.

14. Explain why a flat sheet of paper dropped from a height of 2 meters will not accelerate at the same rate as a sheet of paper crumpled into a ball.

15. Why do athletes' shoes often have cleats?

16. Compare your mass and weight on Earth with your mass and weight on an asteroid, which is much smaller than Earth.

17. When you drop a golf ball to the pavement, it bounces up. Is a force needed to make it bounce up? If so, what exerts the force?

18. Draw a diagram showing the motion of a satellite around Earth. Is the satellite accelerating?

19. **Writing to Learn** You are a reporter for a local television station, and you like to give your stories a physical-science twist. Write a story for the evening news in which you describe an event in terms of the forces involved. Use a catchy title.

Thinking Critically
20. **Comparing and Contrasting** If you stand up in a rowboat and take a step toward the dock, you may fall in the water. Explain what happens in this situation. How is it similar to what happens when you take a step on land? How is it different?

21. **Problem Solving** If a toy train has a mass of 1.5 kg and accelerates at a rate of 20 m/s^2, calculate the force acting on it.

22. **Applying Concepts** You are riding fast on a skateboard when your wheel suddenly gets stuck in a crack on the sidewalk. Using the term *inertia,* explain what happens.

Applying Skills
23. Left ball before: 0.4 kg $\times$ 2 m/s = 0.8 kg·m/s; right ball before: 0.4 kg $\times$ 0 m/s = 0 kg·m/s; left ball after: 0.4 kg $\times$ 0.5 m/s = 0.2 kg·m/s; right ball after: 0.4 kg $\times$ 1.5 m/s = 0.6 kg·m/s

24. Total momentum before: 0.8 kg·m/s + 0 kg·m/s = 0.8 kg·m/s; total momentum after: 0.2 kg·m/s + 0.6 kg·m/s = 0.8 kg·m/s; yes, the law of conservation is satisfied. Total momentum before the collision is equal to total momentum after the collision.

25. Students' designs will vary, but should include a high-friction surface to demonstrate how friction will decrease the momentum.

Applying Skills

Use the illustration showing a collision between two balls to answer Questions 23–25.

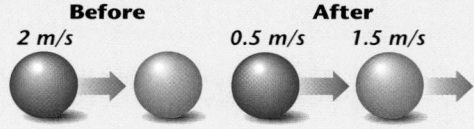

Before 2 m/s **After** 0.5 m/s 1.5 m/s

23. **Calculating** Use the formula for momentum to find the momentum of each ball before and after the collision. Assume the mass of each ball is 0.4 kg.
24. **Inferring** Find the total momentum before and after collision. Is the law of conservation of momentum satisfied in this collision? Explain.
25. **Designing Experiments** Design an experiment in which you could show that momentum is not conserved between the balls when friction is strong.

Project Wrap Up Test your vehicle to make sure it will work on the type of floor in your classroom. Will the vehicle stay within the bounds set by your teacher? Identify all the forces acting on the vehicle. List at least three features you included in the design of the vehicle that led to an improvement in its performance. For example, did you give it a smooth shape for low air resistance?

Reflect and Record What was the most significant source of friction for your vehicle? What was the most successful way to overcome the friction? In your journal, describe the features of your vehicle that led to its success or that kept it from succeeding.

Test Preparation

Use these questions to prepare for standardized tests.

Read the information. Then answer Questions 26–30.

Two students are pulling the volleyball equipment with the forces indicated. The friction force between the bag and the floor is 15 N.

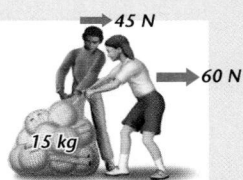

45 N
60 N
15 kg

26. What law can you use to calculate the acceleration of the bag?
    a. Newton's first law of motion
    b. Newton's second law of motion
    c. Newton's third law of motion
    d. the law of universal gravitation

27. What is the net force on the bag?
    a. 90 N   b. 105 N
    c. 120 N   d. 15 N
28. What is the acceleration of the bag?
    a. 6.0 m/s   b. 6.0 m/s^2
    c. 6.5 m/s^2 d. 7.0 m/s
29. How could they make the bag accelerate more?
    a. They could move it a shorter distance.
    b. They could add mass to it.
    c. They could exert a smaller force.
    d. They could exert a greater force.
30. What would happen to the motion if a third student pulled the bag in the opposite direction with a force of 40 N?
    a. The bag will move in the opposite direction.
    b. The bag will stop moving.
    c. The bag will continue to move in the same direction, but it will accelerate more slowly.
    d. The bag will continue to move in the same direction, but it will accelerate more quickly.

Chapter 5   **173**

Project Wrap Up Allow time for students to test their vehicles. Remind students to include a diagram identifying the forces. Encourage students to incorporate Newton's first two laws of motion when they explain the features of their design that improved performance.

Reflect and Record After all presentations have been completed, have students discuss the sources of friction for the different vehicles. Encourage them to compare design features with their classmates as they evaluate their own vehicles.

Test Preparation

26. b 27. a 28. b 29. d 30. c

Program Resources

◆ **Inquiry Skills Activity Book** Provides teaching and review of all inquiry skills
◆ **Prentice Hall Assessment System** Provides standardized test practice
◆ **Reading in the Content Area** Provides strategies to improve science reading skills
◆ **Teacher's ELL Handbook** Provides multiple strategies for English language learners

CHAPTER 6 Forces in Fluids

Sections	Time	Student Edition Activities	Other Activities
CHAPTER PROJECT 6 **Staying Afloat** p. 175	Ongoing (2 weeks)	Check Your Progress, pp. 187, 194 Project Wrap Up, p. 201	**TE** Chapter 6 Project Notes, pp. 174–175
1 Pressure pp. 176–183 ◆ 6.1.1 Define and calculate pressure. ◆ 6.1.2 State how pressure changes with altitude and depth. ◆ 6.1.3 Identify and explain examples of balanced pressures.	2 periods/ 1 block	**Discover** Can You Blow Up a Balloon in a Bottle?, p. 176 **Sharpen Your Skills** Developing Hypotheses, p. 178 **Science at Home** p. 181 **Real-World Lab: How It Works** Spinning Sprinklers, pp. 182–183	**TE** Building Inquiry Skills: Controlling Variables, p. 177 **TE** Math Toolbox, p. 177 **TE** Addressing Naive Conceptions, p. 178 **TE** Demonstration, p. 179 **TE** Real-Life Learning, p. 180 **TE** Using the Visuals, p. 180
2 Transmitting Pressure in a Fluid pp. 184–187 ◆ 6.2.1 State Pascal's principle and recognize applications of the principle. ◆ 6.2.2 Explain how a hydraulic device can multiply force.	1 period/ $\frac{1}{2}$ block	**Discover** How Does Pressure Change?, p. 184	**TE** Building Inquiry Skills: Making Models, p. 186 **TE** Integrating Life Science, p. 186
3 Floating and Sinking pp. 188–194 ◆ 6.3.1 Define the buoyant force and its effect. ◆ 6.3.2 State Archimedes' principle. ◆ 6.3.3 Explain how the density of an object determines whether it floats or sinks.	1 period/ $\frac{1}{2}$ block	**Discover** What Can You Measure With a Straw?, p. 188 **Sharpen Your Skills** Measuring, p. 189 **Skills Lab: Drawing Conclusions** Sink and Spill, pp. 190–191 **Try This** Dive!, p. 192	**TE** Inquiry Challenge, p. 189 **TE** Demonstration, p. 192 **TE** Demonstration, p. 193 **LM** 6 "Raising a Sunken Ship"
4 *INTEGRATING TECHNOLOGY* **Applying Bernoulli's Principle** pp. 195–198 ◆ 6.4.1 State Bernoulli's principle. ◆ 6.4.2 Explain the application of Bernoulli's principle to flight.	1 period/ $\frac{1}{2}$ block	**Discover** Does Water Push or Pull?, p. 195 **Science at Home** p. 198	**TE** Demonstration, p. 196 **TE** Inquiry Challenge, p. 196
Study Guide/Assessment pp. 199–201	1 period/ $\frac{1}{2}$ block		**ISAB** Provides teaching and review of all inquiry skills

 For Standard or Block Schedule The Resource Pro® CD-ROM gives you maximum flexibility for planning your instruction for any type of schedule. Resource Pro® contains Planning Express®, an advanced scheduling program, as well as the entire contents of the Teaching Resources and the Computer Test Bank.

Key: **CTB** Computer Test Bank
CT Chapter Tests
ELL Teacher's ELL Handbook

CHAPTER PLANNING GUIDE

Program Resources	Assessment Strategies	Media and Technology
UR Chapter 6 Project Teacher Notes, pp. 58–59 **UR** Chapter 6 Project Overview and Worksheets, pp. 60–63	**TE** Check Your Progress, pp. 187, 194 **TE** Performance Assessment: Chapter 6 Project Wrap Up, p. 201 **UR** Chapter 6 Project Scoring Rubric, p. 64	🌐 Science Explorer Internet Site 🎧 Audio CDs, Section Summaries
UR 6-1 Lesson Plan, p. 65 **UR** 6-1 Section Summary, p. 66 **UR** 6-1 Review and Reinforce, p. 67 **UR** 6-1 Enrich, p. 68 **UR** Real-World Lab blackline masters, pp. 81–83	**SE** Section 1 Review, p. 181 **SE** Analyze and Conclude, p. 183 **TE** Ongoing Assessment, pp. 177, 179 **TE** Performance Assessment, p. 181	📼 Lab Activity Videotape, *Tape 2*
UR 6-2 Lesson Plan, p. 69 **UR** 6-2 Section Summary, p. 70 **UR** 6-2 Review and Reinforce, p. 71 **UR** 6-2 Enrich, p. 72	**SE** Section 2 Review, p. 187 **TE** Ongoing Assessment, pp. 185 **TE** Performance Assessment, p. 187	💿 Presentation Pro, "Forces in Fluids"
UR 6-3 Lesson Plan, p. 73 **UR** 6-3 Section Summary, p. 74 **UR** 6-3 Review and Reinforce, p. 75 **UR** 6-3 Enrich, p. 76 **UR** Skills Lab blackline masters, pp. 84–85	**SE** Section 3 Review, p. 194 **SE** Analyze and Conclude, p. 191 **TE** Ongoing Assessment, pp. 189, 193 **TE** Performance Assessment, p. 194	📼 Concept Videotape Library, *Adventures, Tape 2,* "Isto What?"; "Density" 💿 Presentation Pro, "Density" 📽 Transparencies 17, "Floating and Sinking"; 18, "Density" 📼 Lab Activity Videotape, *Tape 2*
UR 6-4 Lesson Plan, p. 77 **UR** 6-4 Section Summary, p. 78 **UR** 6-4 Review and Reinforce, p. 79 **UR** 6-4 Enrich, p. 80	**SE** Section 4 Review, p. 198 **TE** Ongoing Assessment, p. 197 **TE** Performance Assessment, p. 198	📼 Concept Videotape Library, *Adventures, Tape 2,* "How an Airplane Flies" 📽 Transparency 19, "Exploring Wings"
GRSW Provides worksheets to promote student comprehension of content **RCA** Provides strategies to improve science reading skills **ELL** Provides multiple strategies for English language learners	**SE** Study Guide/Assessment, pp. 199–201 **PA** Performance Assessment, pp. 19–21 **CT** Chapter 6 Test, pp. 23–26 **CTB** Chapter 6 Test **PHAS** Provides standardized test preparation	💿 Computer Test Bank, Chapter 6 Test

GRSW Guided Reading and Study Workbook
ISAB Inquiry Skills Activity Book
LM Laboratory Manual

PA Performance Assessment
PHAS Prentice Hall Assessment System
PLM Probeware Lab Manual

RCA Reading in the Content Area
SE Student Edition

TE Teacher's Edition
UR Unit Resources

Meeting the National Science Education Standards and AAAS Benchmarks

National Science Education Standards	Benchmarks for Science Literacy	Unifying Themes
Science as Inquiry (Content Standard A) ◆ **Develop descriptions, explanations, predictions, and models using evidence** Students model a rotating lawn sprinkler to determine the factors that affect the speed of its rotation. *(Real-World Lab)* ◆ **Communicate scientific procedures and explanations** Students follow a scientific procedure and communicate their findings as they examine the relationship between the buoyant force on an object and the weight of the water the object displaces. *(Skills Lab)* ◆ **Using mathematics in all aspects of scientific inquiry** Students calculate pressure. *(Section 1)* Measurements of force and volume are taken and buoyant force is calculated. *(Skills Lab)* **Physical Science** (Content Standard B) ◆ **Properties and changes of properties in matter** Students explore the densities of specific objects and determine why objects float or sink. *(Section 3)* **Science and Technology** (Content Standard E) ◆ **Implement a proposed design** Students construct a small-scale boat that can carry cargo and float. *(Chapter Project)*	**1C The Scientific Enterprise** Students learn how the contributions of scientists Blaise Pascal and Daniel Bernoulli improved our understanding of fluid pressure and the motion of fluids. *(Sections 2, 4)* **3B Design and Systems** As students design small-scale boats they take constraints into account and propose solutions to improve their designs. *(Chapter Project)* **4D The Structure of Matter** Matter is composed of moving particles. A liquid or fluid is a form of matter with distinct properties. Different forms of matter have different physical properties, such as pressure and density. *(Sections 1, 2, 3, 4; Skills Lab)* **11B Models** Modeling the rotation of a lawn sprinkler allows students to think about the application of pressure and force to making sprinklers spin. *(Real-World Lab)*	◆ **Systems and Interactions** The movement of a fluid affects its pressure on an object. When the forces of fluid pressure are confined they are equally transmitted to objects. *(Sections 1, 2, 4)* ◆ **Scale and Structure** Different forms of matter have different densities. The buoyant force on an object is equal to the weight of the fluid displaced by the object. *(Section 3; Chapter Project; Skills Lab)* ◆ **Modeling** Students model the effects of pressure on the motion of fluids. *(Section 4; Real-World Lab)*

Take It to the Net

The **www.phschool.com** Web site provides you with multiple opportunities to incorporate the internet into your instruction. Go to **www.phschool.com** and click on the Science icon. Then select Science Explorer Integrated.

Internet Activities provide opportunities for students to review, extend, or assess a concept from the chapter.

■ Have students use the chapter Self-Test to get instant feedback.

■ Hot Links and Reference Links provide opportunities for online research.

STAY CURRENT with **SCIENCE NEWS** ®

Find out the latest research and information about mechanics at: **www.phschool.com**

ACTIVITY	Time (minutes)	Materials Quantities for one work group	Skills
Section 1			
Discover, p. 176	10	**Consumable** small balloon **Nonconsumable** 2-L plastic bottle, straw	Developing Hypotheses
Sharpen Your Skills, p. 178	10	No special materials are required.	Developing Hypotheses
Science at Home, p. 181	home	**Consumable** water, index card **Nonconsumable** small plastic container	Communicating
Real-World Lab, pp. 182–183	45	**Consumable** fishing line, 30 cm **Nonconsumable** 6 empty soda cans with tabs, waterproof marker, beaker or wide-mouth jar, stopwatch or clock with second hand, 4d common nail, 10d common nail, 20d common nail, large basin to catch water	Making Models, Designing Experiments, Controlling Variables
Section 2			
Discover, p. 184	10	**Consumable** water **Nonconsumable** 2-L plastic bottle with cap	Observing
Section 3			
Discover, p. 188	20	**Consumable** plastic straw, water, sugar **Nonconsumable** metric ruler, scissors, waterproof clay, waterproof marker, glass, spoon	Predicting
Sharpen your Skills, p. 189	5	**Nonconsumable** wooden block, metric ruler	Measuring
Skills Lab, pp. 190–191	45	**Consumable** table salt, paper towels, water **Nonconsumable** beaker, 600-mL; pie pan; triple-beam balance; jar with watertight lid, about 30 mL	Drawing Conclusions
Try This, p. 192	20	**Consumable** plastic straw **Nonconsumable** scissors, paper clips, jar, 2-L plastic bottle	Drawing Conclusions
Section 4			
Discover, p. 195	10	**Nonconsumable** plastic spoon, plastic fork, faucet	Inferring
Science at Home, p. 198	home	**Consumable** plastic straw, water **Nonconsumable** scissors, drinking glass or jar	Making Models

A list of all materials required for the Student Edition activities can be found beginning on page T23. You can obtain information about ordering materials by calling 1-800-848-9500 or by accessing the *Science Explorer* Internet site at: **www.phschool.com**

Staying Afloat

In this chapter, students will be introduced to the principles of buoyancy that allow some objects to float while others sink. They will apply these principles to design a boat that will float even though it is made of metal and loaded with heavy cargo.

Purpose Students will have the opportunity to design, build, test, and modify a boat. Then students will test their boats' ability to carry cargo without capsizing.

Skills Focus After completing the Chapter 6 Project, students will be able to
◆ build a boat out of metal;
◆ design and test the boat so that it can hold 50 pennies for 10 seconds;
◆ describe the scientific reasoning behind design modifications to the rest of the class.

Project Time Line The entire project will require at least two weeks. Set aside one or two class periods at the end of the project for students to present their boats in class.

For more detailed information on planning and supervising the chapter project, see Chapter 6 Project Teacher Notes, pages 58–59 in Unit 1 Resources.

Possible Materials cans, metal plates or bowls, aluminum foil, sheet metal, wire, tin snips, pennies, dishpan or bath tub, meter stick, string

Suggested Shortcuts You may wish to divide the class into small groups to carry out the project. You can make this project less involved by specifying the materials that should be used by all students. For example, limit the choices of materials to aluminum foil and metal plates or bowls.

WEB ACTIVITY www.phschool.com

SECTION 1 Pressure	SECTION 2 Transmitting Pressure in a Fluid	SECTION 3 Floating and Sinking
Discover Can You Blow Up a Balloon in a Bottle? Sharpen Your Skills Developing Hypotheses Real-World Lab Spinning Sprinklers	Discover How Does Pressure Change?	Discover What Can You Measure With a Straw? Sharpen Your Skills Measuring Skills Lab Sink and Spill Try This Dive!

174

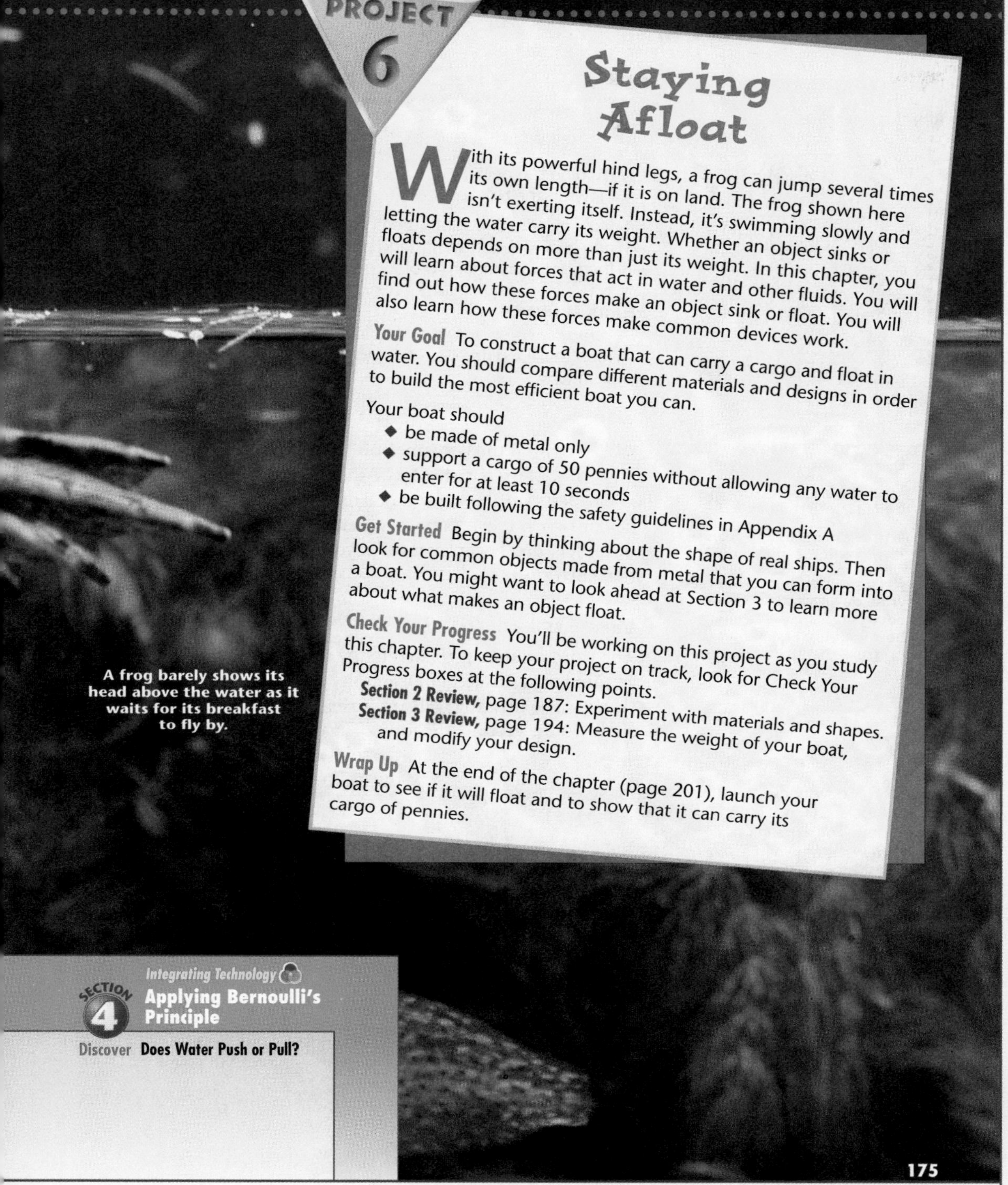

Staying Afloat

With its powerful hind legs, a frog can jump several times its own length—if it is on land. The frog shown here isn't exerting itself. Instead, it's swimming slowly and letting the water carry its weight. Whether an object sinks or floats depends on more than just its weight. In this chapter, you will learn about forces that act in water and other fluids. You will find out how these forces make an object sink or float. You will also learn how these forces make common devices work.

Your Goal To construct a boat that can carry a cargo and float in water. You should compare different materials and designs in order to build the most efficient boat you can.

Your boat should
- ◆ be made of metal only
- ◆ support a cargo of 50 pennies without allowing any water to enter for at least 10 seconds
- ◆ be built following the safety guidelines in Appendix A

Get Started Begin by thinking about the shape of real ships. Then look for common objects made from metal that you can form into a boat. You might want to look ahead at Section 3 to learn more about what makes an object float.

Check Your Progress You'll be working on this project as you study this chapter. To keep your project on track, look for Check Your Progress boxes at the following points.
Section 2 Review, page 187: Experiment with materials and shapes.
Section 3 Review, page 194: Measure the weight of your boat, and modify your design.

Wrap Up At the end of the chapter (page 201), launch your boat to see if it will float and to show that it can carry its cargo of pennies.

A frog barely shows its head above the water as it waits for its breakfast to fly by.

SECTION **4**
Integrating Technology
Applying Bernoulli's Principle

Discover **Does Water Push or Pull?**

175

Program Resources

- ◆ **Unit 2 Resources** Chapter 6 Project Teacher Notes, pp. 58–59; Project Overview and Worksheets, pp. 60–63; Project Scoring Rubric, p. 64

Media and Technology

 Audio CDs Section Summaries

 www.phschool.com

You will find an Internet activity, chapter self-tests for students, and links to other chapter topics at this site.

Launching the Project Fill a 500-mL beaker halfway with water. Place the beaker where all students can see it. Choose a laboratory cork and a small stone that have the same mass. Ask: **What will happen when these are dropped in the water?** *(Many students will predict that the stone will sink and the cork will float.)* Demonstrate by placing the cork and the stone in the water. Ask students to explain why the stone sank. *(At the beginning of this chapter, most students will say that the stone is heavier rather than denser.)* Place the stone and the cork on a balance to demonstrate that they are the same weight. Explain to students that very heavy things can still float if they are shaped to hold a lot of air. Explain to students that in the Chapter 6 Project, they will design and test boats made out of metal that can carry a cargo of 50 pennies without sinking. To help students get started, hand out Chapter 6 Project Overview and Worksheets, pages 60–63 in Unit 2 Resources. You may also wish to pass out the Chapter 6 Project Scoring Rubric, page 64, at this time.

Performance Assessment

Use the Chapter 6 Project Scoring Rubric to assess students' work. Students will be assessed on
- ◆ how well the boat meets the size and material specifications;
- ◆ how well they document the testing procedure and observations;
- ◆ how well they revise the design of the boat based on the results of testing;
- ◆ how well the boat performs;
- ◆ the clarity and organization of the presentation to the class.

Objectives

After completing the lesson, students will be able to

◆ define and calculate pressure;
◆ state how pressure changes with altitude and depth;
◆ identify and explain examples of balanced pressures.

Key Terms pressure, pascal, fluid

1 Engage/Explore

Activating Prior Knowledge

Have students take turns placing one hand inside a plastic bag and plunging the covered hand into clean water at room temperature. The water should be in a container deep enough for students to submerge their arms up to the elbow and the plastic bag should be long enough to cover the student's arm to above the elbow. A new garbage can and a tall kitchen bag would work well. Ask: **What did it feel like?** (*Most students will say that the water exerted pressure on their arms.*) **How did the plastic bag affect what you felt?** (*The bag allowed students to feel pressure without feeling the water on their skin.*)

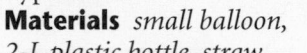 **DISCOVER**

Skills Focus developing hypotheses
Materials *small balloon, 2-L plastic bottle, straw*
Time 10 minutes
Tips Make sure the mouth of the balloon is outside the bottle. Caution students not to hold the straw near their eyes in Step 2.
Expected Outcome In Step 1 the balloon will inflate until it seals the neck of the bottle. With the straw, the balloon will continue to inflate easily.
Think It Over Blowing up the balloon compressed the air trapped inside the bottle, which made it difficult to blow up the balloon any farther. Inserting the straw allowed air inside the bottle to escape.

DISCOVER • **ACTIVITY**

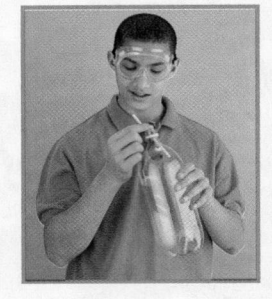

Can You Blow Up a Balloon in a Bottle?

1. Holding the neck, insert a balloon into an empty bottle. Try to blow up the balloon.

2. Now insert a straw into the bottle, next to the balloon. Keep one end of the straw sticking out of the container as shown in the photo. Try again to blow up the balloon.

Think It Over
Developing Hypotheses Did holding the straw next to the balloon make a difference? If it did, develop a hypothesis to explain why.

GUIDE FOR READING

◆ **What causes pressure in fluids?**

◆ **How does pressure change with altitude and depth?**

Reading Tip Before you read, write down what you know about pressure. Then check how your understanding of pressure changes as you read.

Think of the last time you heard a friend say "I'm under a lot of pressure!" Maybe she was talking about having two tests on the same day. That sort of pressure is over in a day or two. But everyone is under another kind of pressure that never lets up. This pressure, as you will learn, is due to the air that surrounds you!

What Is Pressure?

The word *pressure* is related to the word *press*. It refers to a force pushing on a surface. For example, when you lean against a wall, you push against the wall and so exert pressure on it. When you stand on the ground, the force of gravity pulls you downward. So the soles of your shoes push down on the ground and exert pressure on it.

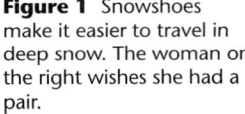
Figure 1 Snowshoes make it easier to travel in deep snow. The woman on the right wishes she had a pair.

READING STRATEGIES

Reading Tip Before students read the section, have them create charts with three columns, with the headings *What I Know, What I Want to Know,* and *What I Learned.* Have students fill in the first two columns with information and questions about pressure. As students read the section, have them fill in the third column. Invite volunteers to share the information on their charts.

Study and Comprehension Pair students. Give one student in each pair a notecard that says, *Describe what causes pressure in fluids.* Give the other student a card that says, *Tell how pressure changes with altitude and depth.* Have students review the section. Encourage them to make notes on information that relates to the instructions on their notecards. Then direct partners to take turns giving oral summaries of the information called for on their notecards.

Force and Pressure Suppose you try to walk on top of deep snow. Most likely you will sink into the snow, much as the woman on the right in Figure 1. But if you walk with snowshoes, you will be able to walk without sinking. The downward force you exert on the snow—your weight—doesn't change. Your weight is the same whether you wear boots or snowshoes. So what's the difference?

The difference is the size of the area over which your weight is distributed. When your weight is distributed over the smaller area of the soles of your boots, you sink. When your weight is distributed over the much larger area of the snowshoes, you don't sink. The larger area results in less downward pressure on the snow under the snowshoes. So force and pressure are closely related, but they are not the same thing.

Calculating Pressure The relationship of force, area, and pressure is summarized by this formula.

$$\text{Pressure} = \frac{\text{Force}}{\text{Area}}$$

Pressure is equal to the force exerted on a surface divided by the total area over which the force is exerted. Force is measured in newtons (N). When area is measured in square meters (m²), the SI unit of pressure is the newton per square meter (N/m²). This unit of pressure is also called the **pascal** (Pa): 1 N/m² = 1 Pa.

A smaller unit of measure for area is often more practical to use, such as a square centimeter instead of a square meter. When square centimeters are used, the unit of pressure is N/cm².

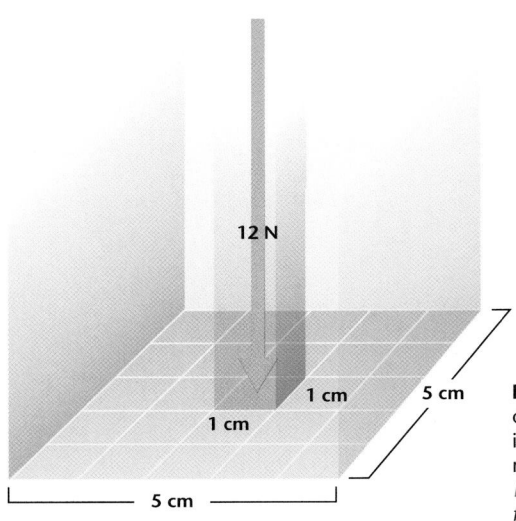

Figure 2 The force a fluid exerts on each square centimeter in the illustration is 12 N. So the resulting pressure is 12 N/cm². *Problem Solving What is the total force on the entire bottom surface?*

Math TOOLBOX

Area

Area is a measure of a surface. The area of a rectangle is found by multiplying the length by the width. The area of the rectangle below is 2 cm × 3 cm, or 6 cm².

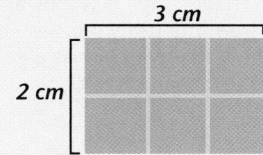

Notice that area is written as cm². This is read as "square centimeter."

Answers to Self-Assessment

Caption Question

Figure 2 300 N (12 N/cm² × 5 cm × 5 cm) = 12 N/cm² × 25 cm² = 300 N

---

2 Facilitate

What Is Pressure?

Building Inquiry Skills: Controlling Variables

Materials *modeling clay; assortment of rigid container lids; waxed paper; 100-g and 500-g masses or other small, heavy objects*
Time 15 minutes

Organize students into small groups and have them spread a 1.0 cm layer of modeling clay onto sheets of waxed paper. Show students lids from bottled drinks, baby food jars, or similar containers, and ask them to predict which lids will leave deeper dents. Students should place a lid on the clay, set the 100-g mass on top, and observe how the clay looks after 5 seconds. Ask: **Did smaller lids exert more or less pressure?** *(Smaller lids left a deeper mark; they exerted more pressure under the same force.)* Repeat the activity with a heavier mass and compare the results. **learning modality: kinesthetic**

Math TOOLBOX

Time 15 minutes
Tips Draw a 2 cm × 3 cm rectangle on an overhead projector and divide it into 1-cm squares. Have students count the squares to verify that the rectangle is 6 cm². Then have students find the areas of several rectangular objects.

Ongoing Assessment

Skills Check Have students perform the following calculations:
◆ A solid block of wood has a square base 1 m × 1 m and weighs 5,000 N. How much pressure does it exert on the floor underneath. *(Pressure = 5,000 N/1 m² = 5,000 Pa)*
◆ A baseball strikes a catcher's mitt with a force of 200 N. If the area the ball strikes is 0.003 m², what is the pressure exerted on the mitt? *(Pressure = 200 N/0.003 m² = 66,667 Pa)*

Fluid Pressure

Addressing Naive Conceptions

Some students may think that only liquids are fluids. Have students partially blow up one balloon and fill a second balloon partway with water. Both balloons should be tied. Have students squeeze the balloons and observe what happens. Ask: **What happens to the fluid inside the air-filled balloon when it is squeezed?** *(The air moves or flows from one side to the other.)* **What happens to the fluid inside the water-filled balloon?** *(The water moves or flows from one side to the other.)* Guide students to infer that both the gas and the liquid are fluids because they flow. **learning modality: kinesthetic**

Building Inquiry Skills: Relating Cause and Effect

Ask students: **If you decreased the number of molecules in a gas and kept the gas in the same container, what would happen to the pressure?** *(It would decrease. The force of fewer molecules would be added to make up the pressure exerted by the gas.)* **learning modality: logical/mathematical**

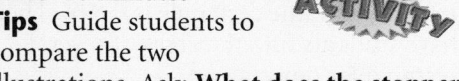

Developing Hypotheses

Time 10 minutes

Tips Guide students to compare the two illustrations. Ask: **What does the stopper on the right do?** *(Keeps air from entering the bottle)*

Expected Outcome A typical hypothesis states that when air cannot get in the bottle, as fluid starts to rise up the straw, the volume of air in the bottle increases, thus decreasing the pressure. When the pressure of air in the lungs is equal to the pressure of air in the bottle, the fluid will no longer rise in the straw.

Extend Challenge students to explain why it is necessary to pierce the lid of a large juice can in two places to make the juice pour out easily. **learning modality: visual**

Developing Hypotheses

If you took a sip from the straw on the left, you would be able to drink the lemonade. But if you took a sip from the straw on the right, you would not be able to quench your thirst.

What is the difference between the two illustrations? What can you conclude about how you drink through a straw? Write a hypothesis that explains why you can drink through one straw and not the other.

You can produce a lower pressure by increasing the area a force acts on. Or you can work the other way around. You can produce a much higher pressure by decreasing the area a force acts on. For instance, the blades of ice skates have a very small surface area. They exert a much higher pressure on the ice than ordinary shoes would.

Fluid Pressure

In this chapter, you will learn about the pressure exerted by fluids. A **fluid** is a substance that can easily flow. As a result, a fluid is able to change shape. Both liquids and gases have this property. Air, helium, water, and oil are all fluids.

Fluids exert pressure against the surfaces they touch. To understand how fluids exert forces on surfaces, you must think about the particles that make up the fluid. Fluids, like all matter, are made up of molecules. These molecules are tiny particles that are much too small to be seen using your eyes or even a good microscope. One liter of water contains about 33 trillion trillion molecules (that's 33 followed by 24 zeros)!

In fluids, molecules are constantly moving in all directions. In air, for example, molecules are moving around at high speeds. They are constantly colliding with each other and with any surface that they meet.

As each molecule collides with a surface, it exerts a force on the surface. **All of the forces exerted by the individual molecules in a fluid add together to make up the pressure exerted by the fluid.** The number of particles is so large that you can consider the fluid as if it were not made up of individual particles. Thus fluid pressure is the total force exerted by the fluid divided by the area over which the force is exerted.

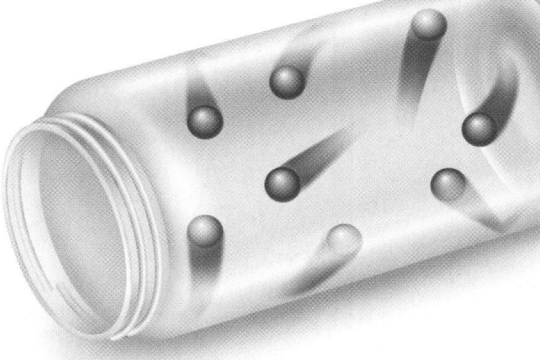

Figure 3 In a gas, molecules move at different speeds in all directions. As they hit surfaces, the molecules exert forces on those surfaces. The total force divided by the area of the surface gives the pressure of the gas. *Inferring Do you think that the pressure inside the jar is the same as the pressure outside the jar? How can you tell?*

Background

Facts and Figures The fluids in the human body exert pressure that balances the pressure of Earth's atmosphere. To travel beyond Earth, astronauts wear pressurized suits to balance the pressure of their bodies. Without these suits, their body fluids would boil and evaporate. In orbit, the pressure in the space shuttle can be kept constant, so astronauts do not have to wear the suits. But during launch and	re-entry, cabin pressure may drop, so astronauts wear partially pressurized suits. These suits contain air bladders that automatically fill with air to maintain pressure on the astronauts' bodies. On a spacewalk, astronauts are not protected by the controlled pressure of the shuttle. Spacewalking astronauts must wear suits that maintain a pressure high enough to balance the pressure of their bodies.

Fluid Pressure All Around

Hold your hand out in front of you, palm up. You are holding up a weight equivalent to that of a washing machine. How can this be? You are surrounded by a fluid that presses down on you all the time. This fluid is the mixture of gases that makes up Earth's atmosphere. The pressure exerted by the air is usually referred to as air pressure, or atmospheric pressure.

Air exerts pressure because it has mass. You may forget that air has mass, but each cubic meter of air around you has a mass of about 1 kilogram. The force of gravity on this mass produces air pressure. The pressure from the weight of air in the atmosphere is great because the atmosphere is over 100 kilometers high.

Average air pressure at sea level is 10.13 N/cm². Think about a square measuring one centimeter by one centimeter on the palm of your hand. Air is pushing against that small square with a force of 10.13 newtons. The total surface area of your hand is probably about 100 square centimeters. So the total force due to the air pressure on your hand is about 1,000 newtons.

☑ *Checkpoint* **Why does the atmosphere exert pressure on you?**

Balanced Pressures

How could your hand possibly support the weight of the atmosphere when you don't feel a thing? In a fluid that is not moving, pressure at a given point is exerted equally in all directions. Air is pushing down on the palm of your hand with 10.13 N/cm² of pressure. It is also pushing up on the back of your hand with the same 10.13 N/cm² of pressure. These two pressures balance each other exactly.

 INTEGRATING LIFE SCIENCE So why aren't you crushed even though the air pressure outside your body is so great? The reason again has to do with a balance of pressures. Pressure inside your body balances the air pressure outside your body. But where does the pressure inside your body come from? It comes from fluids within your body. Some parts of your body, such as your lungs, sinus cavities, and your inner ear, contain air. Other parts of your body, such as your cells and your blood vessels, contain liquids.

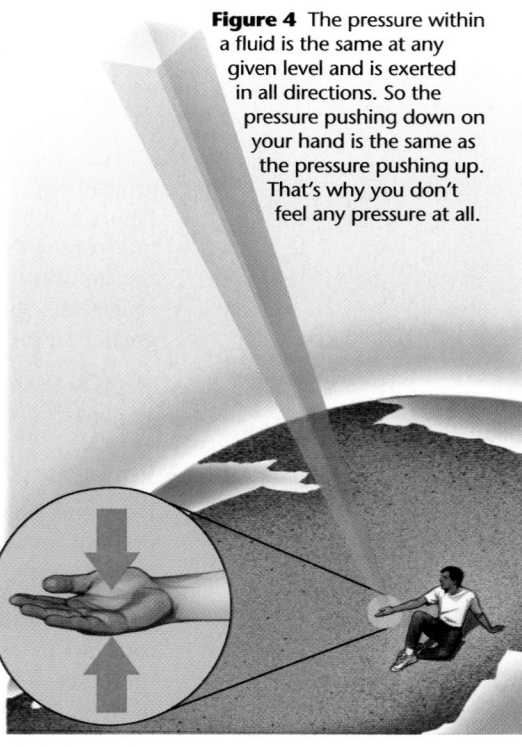

Figure 4 The pressure within a fluid is the same at any given level and is exerted in all directions. So the pressure pushing down on your hand is the same as the pressure pushing up. That's why you don't feel any pressure at all.

Demonstration

Materials *unopened jar with cap that says "Safety button will pop up if seal is broken."* **ACTIVITY**
Time 10 minutes

Explain that the pressure inside the jar is less than the pressure outside. Before the seal is broken, the greater pressure outside the jar pushes the cap down. Have students press the button on the jar, noting that it does not move. Direct them to listen closely as you open the jar. Ask them to infer what happens when the seal is broken. (*The inside pressure becomes the same as the outside pressure.*) Ask: **How could you tell the seal was broken?** (*The button moved; you could hear air rush into the jar.*) **learning modality: visual**

Balanced Pressures

Integrating Life Science

Point out that astronauts and deep-sea divers explore areas where the pressure is much greater or smaller than normal atmospheric pressure. Encourage interested students to contact a local diving shop or certified diving instructor to find out how the special equipment worn by deep-sea divers controls the pressure. **learning modality: verbal**

Answers to Self-Assessment

Caption Question

Figure 3 Yes. The jar is open so that the molecules are free to move in and out of the jar, making the pressure equal.

☑ *Checkpoint*

The atmosphere is a large mass of air, and the force of gravity on the air above an object produces air pressure on the object.

Ongoing Assessment

Drawing Have students draw diagrams showing beakers of water and label the fluid pressures acting on the beakers. (*Student diagrams should include the fluid pressure of water on the bottom and sides of the beaker, and air pressure on the surface of the water and on the outside of the beaker.*)

Balanced Pressures,
continued

Real-Life Learning

Materials *daily newspapers from the previous week or so*
Time 10 minutes

Have students save weather maps from a local newspaper for one week. Point out the high- and low-pressure areas marked on the maps. Explain that the air pressure is measured in inches of mercury, which refers to how high the air can push a column of mercury. Have students analyze their maps and compare the pressure readings to the weather conditions. Have pairs of students prepare a weather forecast and present it to the class. Encourage interested students to participate in weather school programs offered by local weather service offices or television stations.
learning modality: logical/ mathematical

Variations in Fluid Pressure

Using the Visuals: Figure 6

Materials $\frac{1}{2}$ *gallon plastic milk jug or similar container*
Time 20 minutes

Have students examine the water streams in the photograph. Ask: **How can you tell which stream has more pressure?** *(The one with more pressure will have more force. It will be able to move farther.)* Make a vertical line of equally spaced holes in the side of a plastic milk jug. The easiest way to make the holes is to use tongs to hold a nail in a bunsen burner flame for a few moments, then poke the heated nail through the side of the plastic jug. Use caution when heating the nail. Fill the jug with water (while holding it over the sink) and have students draw the escaping streams of water and label them from least to greatest pressure. *(Students' drawings should show the greatest pressure at the bottom.)*
learning modality: visual

Figure 5 A vacuum pump removes the air from a metal can. The pump produces dramatic results in a few moments. *Inferring Can you think of a way to crush the can without pumping out the air inside it? Explain why your idea works.*

Are you still having trouble believing that the air pressure around you is so high? Take a look at the metal container in Figure 5. When the can is filled with air, the air pressure pushing out from within the can balances the air pressure pushing in on the can. But when the air is removed from the can, there is no longer the same pressure pushing from within the can. The greater air pressure outside the can crushes it.

☑ *Checkpoint* **What is the effect of balanced pressures acting on an object?**

Variations in Fluid Pressure

Does the pressure of a fluid ever change? What happens to pressure as you move up to a higher elevation or down to a deeper depth within a fluid?

Pressure and Elevation Have your ears ever "popped" as you rode up in an elevator? **Air pressure decreases as elevation increases.** Remember that air pressure at a given point results from the weight of air above that point. At higher elevations, there is less air above and therefore less weight of air to support.

Background

Integrating Science Scuba divers have to be careful not to rise to the surface too quickly. When atmospheric pressure decreases rapidly, humans can experience decompression sickness, a dangerous condition also known as *the bends*. This occurs when gases in their tissues come out of solution. Although oxygen is absorbed quickly, nitrogen bubbles form in the blood and cause severe muscle pain.

A different condition, known as *altitude sickness*, can occur when a person travels to high altitudes. This reaction can be severe and, unless the person returns to low altitude, possibly fatal. A person with altitude sickness may experience breathlessness, racing heartbeat, giddiness, headache, swelling of the legs and feet, gastrointestinal upsets, and weakness.

The fact that air pressure decreases as you move up in elevation explains why your ears pop. When the air pressure outside your body changes, the air pressure inside will adjust too, but more slowly. For a moment, the air pressure behind your eardrums is greater than it is outside. Your body releases this pressure with a "pop" so that the pressures are once again balanced.

Pressure and Depth Fluid pressure depends on depth. The pressure at one meter below the surface of a swimming pool is the same as the pressure one meter below the surface of a lake. But if you dive deeper into the water in either case, pressure becomes greater as you descend. The deeper you swim, the greater the pressure you feel. **Water pressure increases as depth increases.**

As with air, you can think of water pressure as being due to the weight of the water above a particular point. At greater depths, there is more water above that point and therefore more weight to support. In addition, air in the atmosphere pushes down on the water. Therefore, the total pressure at a given point beneath the water results from the weight of the water plus the weight of the air above it. In the deepest parts of the ocean, the pressure is more than 1,000 times the air pressure you experience every day.

Figure 6 The strength of the stream of water coming out of the holes in the jug depends on the water pressure at each level. *Interpreting Photos At which hole is the pressure greatest?*

Section 1 Review

1. Explain how fluids exert pressure.
2. How does air pressure change as you move farther away from the surface of Earth? Explain why it changes.
3. Why aren't deep-sea fish crushed by the tremendous pressure of the water above them?
4. **Thinking Critically Applying Concepts** Why do you think an astronaut must wear a pressurized suit in space?
5. **Thinking Critically Comparing and Contrasting** Suppose two women each have a mass of 50 kg. If one woman is wearing shoes with spiked heels and the other is wearing work boots, which one exerts more pressure on the floor with each step? Explain.

Science at Home

Fill a small plastic container—a bottle or a cup—to the brim with water. Place an index card over the entire opening of the container. Ask your family to predict what would happen if the container were turned upside down. Test the predictions by slowly turning the container upside down while holding the card in place. Let go of the card and see what happens. Without touching the card, turn the container on its side. Use air pressure to explain why the card stays in place and why the water stays in the container.

Program Resources

◆ **Unit 2 Resources** 6-1 Review and Reinforce, p. 67; 6-1 Enrich, p. 68

Answers to Self-Assessment

Caption Questions

Figure 5 The can will be crushed if enough additional pressure is applied from the outside, for example by putting it deep underwater.

Figure 6 The bottom hole has the greatest pressure.

✓ *Checkpoint*

Balanced pressures cancel each other out.

3 Assess

Section 1 Review Answers

1. The molecules of a fluid exert force when they collide with surfaces. The fluid pressure is the total force exerted divided by the area.
2. It decreases. As you move farther away from the Earth, there is less fluid above you. Less fluid has less weight, so pressure decreases.
3. Deep-sea fish are not crushed because their internal fluids and organs are at a pressure similar to those of their surroundings.
4. Space contains no air, so it exerts no air pressure on the astronaut's body. Astronauts wear pressurized suits to balance the pressure inside their bodies.
5. The woman wearing spike-heeled shoes exerts force over a smaller area than the woman wearing work boots. Because pressure depends on area, the woman in spike-heeled shoes, which cover less area of the floor than the work boots, exerts more pressure on the floor.

Science at Home

Materials *small plastic container, water, index card*

Suggest that students first practice this activity outdoors or over a sink. Make sure there are no air bubbles in the cup with the index card and that the student presses the card down so it touches the entire rim. Encourage interested students to present this activity to their families as an illusion. The index card will remain on the cup and the water will remain inside. Students should explain that the air pushing up on the index card exerts pressure equal to that of the water pushing down.

Performance Assessment

Writing Have students write and illustrate a story describing the changes in fluid pressure experienced by a diver as he or she rises from the ocean floor to the surface. *(Students' stories should describe a decrease in water pressure as the diver rises.)*

Spinning Sprinklers

Preparing for Inquiry

Key Concept The operation of a rotating lawn sprinkler can be explained by examining the factors that affect the pressure of water escaping from a can.

Skills Objectives Students will be able to

◆ make a model of a sprinkler;

◆ design an experiment to test factors affecting water pressure;

◆ control variables such as the size and number of the holes in the can.

Time 45 minutes

Advance Planning Obtain fishing line and nails. Rinse the soda cans to remove any residue that will attract insects. Obtain a sample sprinkler, or make a diagram of one.

Alternative Materials The lab can be done using clean one-quart or half-gallon milk containers. Follow the same procedure as with the cans, but have students count the number of spins in 30 seconds because the larger containers will not spin as fast as the cans.

Guiding Inquiry

Invitation Bring in a lawn sprinkler that operates by forcing water in one direction while spinning in the opposite direction. Ask: **What factors will affect how fast the sprinkler spins?** *(Pressure of escaping water, size and number of holes)* If a sprinkler of this type is not available, draw a diagram of one on the board and have the same discussion.

Introducing the Procedure Ask students to predict what factors will affect the can's rate of spinning based on the discussion about the sprinkler. *(Amount of water in the can, size and number of nail holes)*

Spinning Sprinklers

T here's nothing like running through a lawn sprinkler on a hot summer day. One type of sprinkler uses the pressure of the escaping water to cause it to spin. Its operation is similar to an ancient device known as Hero's engine. Hero's engine used the pressure of escaping steam to cause a sphere to spin.

Problem

What factors affect the speed of rotation of a lawn sprinkler?

Skills Focus

making models, designing experiments, controlling variables

Materials

3 empty soda cans with tabs attached
fishing line, 30 cm
waterproof marker
wide-mouth jar or beaker
stopwatch or clock with second hand
small nail
medium nail
large nail
large basin to catch water

Procedure

1. Fill the jar with enough water to completely cover a can. Place it in the basin.

2. Bend up the tab of a can and tie the end of a length of fishing line to it. **CAUTION:** *Be careful not to cut yourself on the edge of the can opening.*

3. Place a mark on the can to help you keep track of how many times the can spins. Copy the data table into your notebook.

4. Using the small nail, make a hole in the side of the can about 1 cm up from the bottom. Poke the nail straight in. Then twist the nail until it makes a right angle with the radius of the can. See the diagram below. **CAUTION:** *Nails are sharp and should be used only to puncture the cans.*

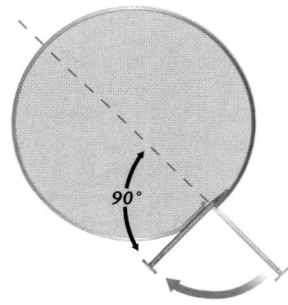

90°

Sample Data Table

Nail Size	# of Holes	# of spins in 15 seconds
small	1	3
small	2	13
medium	1	18
medium	2	21
large	1	16 in 10 sec
large	2	11 in 6 sec

Nail Size	# of Holes	# of spins in 15 seconds
small	1	
small	2	
medium	1	
medium	2	
large	1	
large	2	

DATA TABLE

5. Submerge the can in the jar and fill the can to the top with water.

6. Quickly lift the can with the fishing line so that it is 1–2 cm above the water level in the jar. Count how many spins the can completes in 15 seconds. Record the result.

7. Design a way to investigate how the size of the hole affects the number of spins made by the can. Propose a hypothesis and then test the relationship. Record your results.

8. Design a way to investigate how the number of holes affects the number of spins made by the can. Propose a hypothesis and then test the relationship. Record your results.

Analyze and Conclude

1. How does the size of the hole affect the rate of spin of the can?
2. How does the number of holes affect the rate of spin of the can?
3. Explain the motion of the can in terms of water pressure.
4. Explain the motion of the can in terms of Newton's third law of motion (Chapter 5).
5. How could you make the can spin in the opposite direction?
6. What will cause the can to stop spinning?
7. You made a hole in the can at about 1 cm above the bottom of the can. Predict what would happen if you made the hole at a higher point on the can. How could you test your prediction?
8. **Apply** Use your observations to explain why a spinning lawn sprinkler spins.

Getting Involved

Many sprinkler systems use water pressure to spin the sprinklers. Examine one of these sprinklers to see the size, direction, and number of holes. What would happen if you put a second sprinkler in line with the first? If possible, try it.

Program Resources

◆ **Unit 2 Resources** Real-World Lab blackline masters, pp. 81–83

Media and Technology

 Lab Activity Videotape
Tape 2

Troubleshooting the Experiment

◆ Students must be sure to hold the cans over the large basin as the water escapes.
◆ The angle of the holes must be the same for all trials, as shown in the diagram.
◆ If the can drains in less than 15 seconds for any trial, students can use a proportion to find out how many spins there would have been if it had gone for 15 seconds. For example, if a can spins 16 times in 10 seconds, use the proportion $\frac{16}{10} = \frac{x}{15}$ to find $x = 24$.
◆ Be sure to use new cans when investigating what might happen if the hole angles are reversed.

Expected Outcome

Results should illustrate that the more holes there are in the can, and the larger the holes are, the faster the can spins.

Analyze and Conclude

1. The larger the hole, the faster the spin.
2. The greater the number of holes, the faster the rate of spin.
3. The water exerts a pressure due to its weight. The force of the water escaping from the hole in the can causes the can to spin in the opposite direction.
4. A force equal and opposite to the force of the water is exerted on the can, so the can spins in the direction opposite to the direction of the water.
5. Bending the hole in the opposite direction will cause the can to spin in the opposite direction.
6. The can will stop spinning when the water level falls below the holes.
7. Holes made at a higher point on the can will reduce the water pressure, thus reducing the speed of spinning.
8. Students should use Newton's third law of motion to explain why a spinning lawn sprinkler spins. They should explain that the water pressure and the size and number of holes will affect the speed of rotation.

Extending the Inquiry

Getting Involved A second sprinkler on the same line will reduce the pressure in each. The water from the second sprinkler may interfere with the water from the first, so some factors that need to be considered include the distance between sprinklers and the directions of their rotations.

SECTION 2 Transmitting Pressure in a Fluid

Objectives

After completing the lesson, students will be able to

◆ state Pascal's principle and recognize applications of the principle;
◆ explain how a hydraulic device can multiply force.

Key Terms Pascal's principle, hydraulic system

1 Engage/Explore

Activating Prior Knowledge

Show students a sealed bag of water. Ask: **What will happen if you squeeze one side of the bag?** (*The water will move to the other side of the bag.*) Encourage students to describe what happens to the fluid in the bag when you push on one part of it. (*It all moves.*)

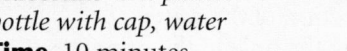 **DISCOVER**

Skills Focus observing
Materials *2-L plastic bottle with cap, water*
Time 10 minutes
Tips Remove the label from the plastic bottle. Remind students to maintain a constant, firm pressure with their left thumbs. Encourage students to push in several different places on the bottle.
Think It Over The water pressure increases when you push in the bottle with your right thumb. You can tell because you can feel the pressure being exerted on your left thumb.

DISCOVER ⋯⋯⋯⋯⋯⋯⋯⋯⋯⋯⋯ **ACTIVITY**

How Does Pressure Change?

1. Fill an empty two-liter plastic bottle to the top with water. Then screw on the cap tightly. There should be no bubbles in the bottle (or only very small bubbles).

2. Lay the bottle on its side. Pick a spot on the bottle, and push in with your left thumb.

3. With your right thumb, push in fairly hard on a spot at the other end of the bottle, as shown in the diagram. What does your left thumb feel?

4. Pick another spot on the bottle for your left thumb and repeat Step 3.

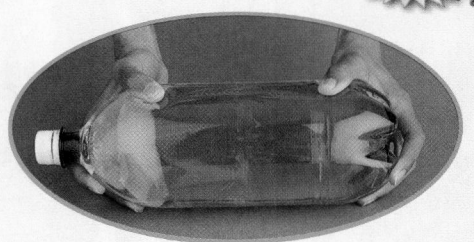

Think It Over
Observing When you push in with your right thumb, does the water pressure in the bottle increase, decrease, or remain the same? How do you know?

GUIDE FOR READING

◆ What does Pascal's principle say about an increase in fluid pressure?

◆ How does a hydraulic device work?

Reading Tip As you read, make a list of devices that apply Pascal's principle. Write one sentence describing each device.

Piercing sirens shatter the morning quiet. Dark smoke rolls into the air. Bright flames shoot from a burning building. Firefighters arrive on the scene. Quickly, with the push of a button, a huge ladder is raised to the top floor. The firefighters climb up the ladder and soon have the blaze under control.

Thanks to equipment on the firetruck, this story has a happy ending. You might be surprised to discover that the truck is capable of using fluids to lift the ladder and its equipment to great heights. As you read on, you'll find out how.

Figure 7 A fire truck uses fluids under high pressure both to lift its ladder and to put out a fire.

184

READING STRATEGIES

Reading Tip Students should list force pumps, hydraulic lifts, and hydraulic brake systems. Sample description: In a hydraulic lift a force on a small piston produces a larger force on a larger piston.

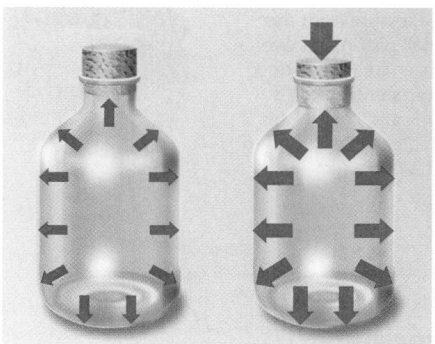

Figure 8 A liquid completely filling a bottle exerts pressure in all directions. When the stopper is pushed farther into the bottle, the pressure increases. *Predicting Suppose you poked a hole in the side of the bottle. What would happen when you pushed down on the stopper? Explain why.*

Pascal's Principle

As you learned in the last section, a fluid exerts pressure on any surface in contact with it. For example, the water in each bottle in Figure 8 exerts pressure on the entire inside surface of the bottle—up, down, and sideways.

What happens if you push the stopper down even farther? The water has nowhere to go, so it presses harder on the inside surface of the bottle. The pressure in the water increases everywhere in the bottle. This is shown by the increased width of the arrows on the right in Figure 8.

Pressure increases by the same amount throughout an enclosed, or confined, fluid. This fact was discovered in the 1600s by a French mathematician named Blaise Pascal. (Pascal's name is used for the unit of pressure.) **When force is applied to a confined fluid, an increase in pressure is transmitted equally to all parts of the fluid.** This relationship is known as **Pascal's principle.**

Force Pumps

What would happen if you increased the pressure at one end of a fluid in a container with a hole at the other end? If you have ever used a squeeze bottle or a medicine dropper, you already know what happens. Because it is not confined by the container, the fluid is pushed out of the opening. This simple example shows you how a force pump works. A force pump causes a fluid to move from one place to another by increasing the pressure in the fluid.

Your heart consists of two force pumps. One of them pumps blood to the lungs, where it can pick up oxygen from the air you breathe. This blood, now carrying oxygen, returns to your heart. It is then pumped to the rest of the body by the second pump.

✓ *Checkpoint* What is the effect on fluid pressure if you press down on the stopper of a bottle full of water?

Social Studies CONNECTION

The French mathematician and philosopher Blaise Pascal lived from 1623 until 1662. He first became famous for a mechanical calculator he designed before he was 21. He later explored the behavior of fluids, and was a pioneer in the mathematics of probability. Near the end of his life, he wrote about philosophical and religious subjects.

In Your Journal

Create a time line showing when the following people lived and worked: Galileo, Archimedes, Newton, Pascal, and Bernoulli. On your time line, write a brief description of each one's work.

Pascal's Principle

Using the Visuals: Figure 8

After students examine the diagram, ask: **As force is applied to the stopper, what happens?** *(Pressure increases inside the bottle and stays the same outside the bottle.)* **What will happen if the force on the stopper continues to increase?** *(The pressure inside will increase and the bottle could break.)* **learning modality: logical/mathematical**

Force Pumps

Real-Life Learning

Invite a nurse or certified CPR instructor to demonstrate the Heimlich maneuver. Explain that the diaphragm is a muscle under the lungs. Exerting force on the diaphragm increases lung pressure. Ask: **How does the Heimlich maneuver help a choking person?** *(It increases the lung pressure and forces the object out of the person's windpipe.)* **learning modality: visual**

Social Studies CONNECTION

Pascal began to write philosophical treatments of religious faith in 1655 and eventually joined a religious group at the monastery of Port Royal. While he continued to write scientific and religious works, they were published in the name of the monastery.

In Your Journal Encourage students to include interesting anecdotes on their time lines. Possible resources include biographies, the Internet, and encyclopedias. **learning modality: verbal**

Ongoing Assessment

Oral Presentation Ask students to identify two force pumps they have used. *(Sample answers include toothpaste tubes or ketchup squeeze bottles.)*

Program Resources

◆ **Unit 2 Resources** 6-2 Lesson Plan, p. 69; 6-2 Section Summary, p. 70
◆ **Guided Reading and Study Workbook** Section 6-2

Answers to Self-Assessment

Caption Question

Figure 8 When you push on the stopper, the water will spurt out of the hole with more force because there is more pressure acting on the water in the bottle.

✓ *Checkpoint*

The pressure increases throughout the water in the bottle.

Using Pascal's Principle

Including All Students

Have students brainstorm a list of English words that use the root *hydr-* (or *hydro*) which means "water." *(Sample: hydrant, hydroelectric, dehydrate, hydrothermal)* Write the words students suggest on the board. Then have volunteers give the dictionary definitions of the words. **limited English proficiency**

Building Inquiry Skills: Making Models

Materials *two different sizes of plastic "air pistons" or similar devices, short piece of clear plastic tubing*

Time 20 minutes

Turkey basters or other similar devices could also be used in place of the air pistons. Fill the smaller air piston with water. Fill the larger air piston about half way. Attach the plastic tubing to the end of the larger air piston. Squeeze a small amount of water into the tubing. Attach the other end of the plastic tubing to the smaller air piston. The combination is now a working hydraulic system. Either piston can be depressed, forcing water through the tube into the other cylinder. If the larger piston is depressed, the displacement of the smaller piston will be larger. If the smaller piston is depressed, the larger piston will move a smaller distance but be capable of exerting a larger force. **learning modality: kinesthetic**

Integrating Life Science

You can demonstrate the suction of the tube foot with a small plastic dropper. Fill the dropper with water, squeeze out most of the water, and let the last drop fall on your skin. Still squeezing the bulb, hold the dropper tip against your wet skin and release it. Air pressure will hold the dropper in place. If you gently pull on the dropper, it will pull up the skin under the tip. **learning modality: visual**

Figure 9 A. In a hydraulic device, a force applied to one piston increases the pressure in the fluid.

Force

A

B. Pressure from the small piston acts over a larger area to produce a greater force. In a hydraulic car lift, this greater force is used to lift a car.

B

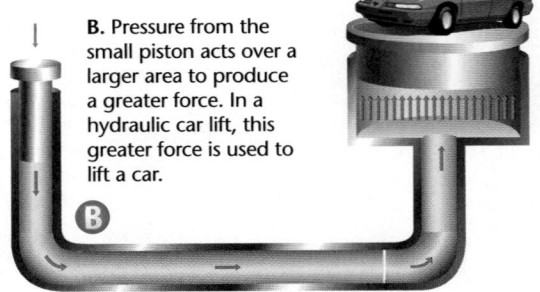

Using Pascal's Principle

Suppose you fill the small U-shaped tube shown in Figure 9A with water and push down on the piston on the left side. (A piston is similar to a stopper that can slide up and down inside the tube.) The increase in pressure will be transmitted to the piston on the right.

What can you determine about the force exerted on the right piston? According to Pascal's principle, both pistons will experience the same fluid pressure. If both pistons have the same area, then they will also experience the same force.

Now suppose that the right piston has a greater area than the left piston. For example, the small piston in the U-shaped tube in Figure 9B has an area of 1 square meter. The large piston has an area of 20 square meters. If you push down on the left piston with a force of 500 newtons, the increase in pressure on the fluid is 500 N/m². A pressure increase of 500 N/m² means that the force on every square meter of the piston's surface increases by 500 newtons. Since the surface area of the right piston is 20 square meters, the total increase in force on the right piston is 10,000 newtons. The push exerted on the left piston is multiplied twenty times on the right piston! By changing the size of the pistons, you can multiply force by almost any amount you wish.

Hydraulic Systems **Hydraulic systems** are designed to take advantage of Pascal's principle. **A hydraulic system multiplies a force by applying the force to a small surface area. The increase in pressure is then transmitted to another part of a confined fluid, which pushes on a larger surface area.** In this way, the force is multiplied. A common hydraulic system is used to lift the heavy ladder on a fire truck.

You also rely on Pascal's principle every time you ride in a car. The brake system of a car is a hydraulic system. A brake system with disc brakes is shown in simplified form in Figure 10. When a driver pushes down on

Figure 10 The hydraulic brake system of a car multiplies the force exerted on the brake pedal.

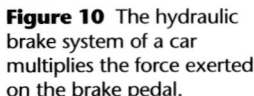
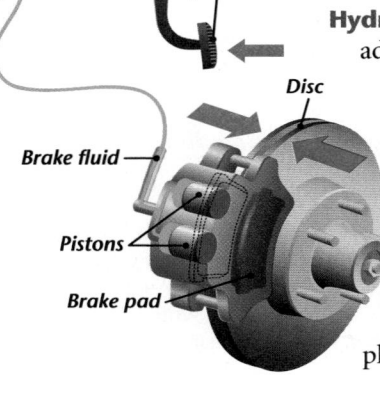

Pistons

Brake lines

Brake pedal

Disc

Brake fluid

Pistons

Brake pad

Background

Facts and Figures None of the hydraulic devices in modern aircraft and automobiles would have been possible without the work of Pascal. In fact, in the late 1800s engineers began to develop many applications based on Pascal's work with fluids.

One of the first hydraulic systems was built in 1882 in London, England. This system delivered pressurized water throughout the city in a system of pipes

and provided the power to run factory machinery. In 1906, sailors on the *Virginia* used an oil hydraulic system to raise and lower the guns. The biggest advance came in the 1920s, when individual hydraulic units were developed. These units had a pump, controls, and a motor. They allowed people to develop hydraulic systems for transportation, farm machinery, and spacecraft.

the brake pedal, he or she pushes a piston. The piston exerts pressure on the brake fluid. The increased pressure is transmitted through the brake lines to pistons within the wheels of the car. Each of these pistons pushes on a brake pad. The brake pad then rubs against the brake disc, and the wheel's motion is slowed down by the force of friction. Because the brake system multiplies force, a person can stop a very large car with only a light push on the brake pedal.

Pascal's Principle in Nature The sea stars shown in Figure 11

INTEGRATING LIFE SCIENCE use a natural hydraulic system called the water vascular system in order to move. Sea stars have rows of small suckers at the ends of their hollow tube feet. Each tube foot is filled with fluid. A valve is located at each foot. When the valve closes, the foot becomes a hydraulic container. As the sea star contracts different muscles, it changes the pressure in the fluid. The change in pressure causes the tube foot to either push down or pull up on the sucker. By the coordinated action of all of its tube feet, a sea star is able to move—even to climb straight up rock surfaces!

Fluid

Tube foot

Figure 11 A sea star exerts pressure on fluids in its cavities in order to move around. *Classifying Why are the tube feet considered part of a hydraulic device?*

Section 2 Review

1. Explain Pascal's principle in your own words.
2. How does a hydraulic device multiply force?
3. What fluid is pumped by your heart?
4. **Thinking Critically Applying Concepts** How can you increase the force a hydraulic device produces without increasing the size of the force you apply to the small piston?
5. **Thinking Critically Comparing and Contrasting** How is the braking system of a car similar to the water vascular system of a sea star?

Check Your Progress **CHAPTER PROJECT 6**

Experiment with various metal items in your home to see how they work as boats. Keep in mind that your designs don't have to look like real boats. Experiment with various shapes. Determine how the material and the shape relate to whether or not the boat floats or sinks. What works better: a wide but shallow boat or a narrow but deep boat? Keep a log that describes the material, the shape, and your results.

Program Resources

◆ **Unit 2 Resources** 6-2 Review and Reinforce, p. 71; 6-2 Enrich, p. 72

Answers to Self-Assessment

Caption Question

Figure 11 When the tube feet are closed, they enclose a fluid. The sea star moves by exerting pressure on this fluid so that the tube feet act like hydraulic devices.

3 Assess

Section 2 Review Answers

1. If a force is exerted on a confined fluid, the pressure is transferred equally to all parts of the fluid.
2. The pressure on the smaller piston is transferred to the larger one. Because the pressure is the same and the area is larger, the force on the large piston is greater.
3. blood
4. Either decrease the size of the smaller piston, or increase the size of the larger piston.
5. In the brake system, pressure on a small area is transferred to pistons in the car's wheels. The sea star uses muscles to change the pressure in its tube feet so that they can push down on its suckers.

Check Your Progress **CHAPTER PROJECT 6**

Encourage students to record sketches of their designs and observations from their tests in their design log. Discuss how to experiment scientifically by altering and testing the effects of one variable at a time. For instance, students making aluminum foil boats might build and test three boats that are different heights but that are identical in every other way. Look for evidence of scientific experimentation in students' design logs.

Performance Assessment

Drawing Challenge students to invent a new hydraulic device. Instruct students to draw their new device on a sheet of notebook paper. Have them use labels and arrows to indicate a force applied to one area of the device and the effect of the force. (*Sample: A device to raise an elevator*)

 Students can save their designs in their portfolios.

SECTION 3 Floating and Sinking

Objectives

After completing the lesson, students will be able to
- define the buoyant force and its effect;
- state Archimedes' principle;
- explain how the density of an object determines whether it floats or sinks.

Key Terms buoyant force, Archimedes' principle, density

1 Engage/Explore

Activating Prior Knowledge

Fill a large basin with water and show students a variety of common objects, such as soap, blocks of wood, rubber duckies or other toys, cans of diet and regular soda (diet soda will float, regular soda will sink). Ask students to predict whether each object will float or sink. Record their predictions, then have volunteers test their predictions by putting each object into the water. Tell students that in this section, they learn why objects sink and float.

········ **DISCOVER** ········

Skills Focus predicting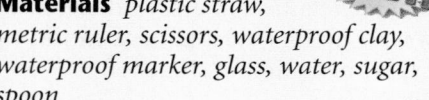
Materials *plastic straw, metric ruler, scissors, waterproof clay, waterproof marker, glass, water, sugar, spoon*
Time 20 minutes
Tips Make sure students place the straw firmly in the clay so that water cannot leak into the straw. Help students realize they should count the marks above the water to take measurements.
Expected Outcome In plain water, the hydrometer will float lower in the water. In sugar water, the hydrometer will float higher out of the water.
Think It Over Students should predict that the hydrometer will float higher out of the water when more sugar is added to the water.

SECTION 3 Floating and Sinking

DISCOVER ··· ACTIVITY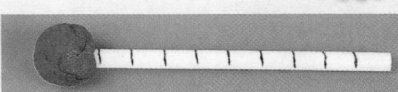

What Can You Measure With a Straw?

1. Cut a plastic straw to a 10-centimeter length.
2. Use a waterproof marker to make marks on the straw that are 1 centimeter apart.
3. Roll a ball of modeling clay about 1.5 centimeters in diameter. Stick one end of the straw in the clay. You have constructed a hydrometer.
4. Place the hydrometer in a glass of water. About half of the straw should remain above water. If it sinks, remove some clay. Make sure no water gets into the straw.
5. Dissolve 10 spoonfuls of sugar in a glass of water. Try out your hydrometer in this liquid.

Think It Over
Predicting Compare your observations in Steps 4 and 5. Then predict what will happen if you use 20 spoonfuls of sugar in a glass of water. Test your prediction.

GUIDE FOR READING

- What is the efffect of the buoyant force?
- What is Archimedes' principle?
- How does the density of an object determine whether it floats or sinks?

Reading Tip As you read, write a paragraph explaining how buoyancy and Archimedes' principle are related.

In April of 1912, the *Titanic* departed from England on its first and only voyage. It was as long as three football fields and as tall as a twelve-story building. It was the largest ship that had been built as of that time, and its furnishings were the finest and most luxurious. The *Titanic* was also the most technologically advanced ship afloat. Its hull was divided into compartments, and it was considered to be unsinkable.

Yet a few days into the voyage, the *Titanic* struck an iceberg. Two hours and forty minutes later, the bow of the great ship slipped underwater. As the stern rose high into the air, the ship broke in two. Both pieces sank to the bottom of the Atlantic Ocean. More than a thousand people died.

Figure 12 This painting shows the bow section of the *Titanic* resting on the sea floor.

188

READING STRATEGIES

Reading Tip Suggest students make notes or draw diagrams before they write paragraphs on the relationship between buoyancy and Archimedes' principle. Remind students that a paragraph is a group of related sentences that develop one main idea. A paragraph should have a topic sentence that states the main idea, supporting sentences, and a concluding sentence.

Program Resources

- **Unit 2 Resources** 6-3 Lesson Plan, p. 73; 6-3 Section Summary, p. 74
- **Guided Reading and Study Workbook** Section 6-3
- **Laboratory Manual** 6, "Raising a Sunken Ship"

How is it possible that a huge ship can float easily in water under certain conditions, and then in a few hours become a sunken wreck? And why does most of an iceberg lie hidden beneath the surface of the water? To answer these questions, you need to find out what makes an object float and what makes an object sink.

Buoyancy

If you have ever picked up an object under water, you know that it seems lighter in water than in air. Water exerts a force called the **buoyant force** that acts on a submerged object. **The buoyant force acts in the upward direction, against the force of gravity, so it makes an object feel lighter.**

As you can see in Figure 13, a fluid exerts pressure on all surfaces of a submerged object. Since the pressure in a fluid increases with depth, the upward pressure on the bottom of the object is greater than the downward pressure on the top. The result is a net force acting upward on the submerged object. This is the buoyant force.

A submerged object displaces, or takes the place of, a volume of fluid equal to its own volume. You can see this by looking at Figure 14. An object that floats on the surface of a fluid, however, displaces a smaller volume. It displaces a volume of fluid equal to the portion of the object that is submerged.

Archimedes' principle relates the amount of fluid a submerged object displaces to the buoyant force on the object. This relationship is named for its discoverer, the ancient Greek mathematician Archimedes. **Archimedes' principle states that the buoyant force on an object is equal to the weight of the fluid displaced by the object.**

☑ *Checkpoint* Compare the direction of the buoyant force to the direction of the force of gravity.

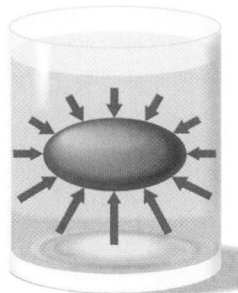

Figure 13 The pressure at the bottom of a submerged object is greater than the pressure at the top. The result is a net force in the upward direction. *Applying Concepts What is this upward force called?*

Figure 14 The volume of water displaced by an object is equal to the volume of the object. If the object floats, the volume of displaced water is equal to the volume of the portion of the object that is under water.

Measuring

How can you measure an object's volume? Measure in centimeters (cm) the length, width, and height of a wooden block. Then multiply length times width times height. The product is the volume. Volume has units of cubic centimeters (cm^3).

Answers to Self-Assessment

Caption Question

Figure 13 The upward force is called buoyant force.

☑ *Checkpoint*

The buoyant force acts upward, and the force of gravity acts downward.

---

2 *Facilitate*

Buoyancy

Including All Students

Students who are still mastering English may need extra help to understand the term *buoyancy*. Ask students to describe a buoy. *(Sample: a buoy is a large floating object used to mark channels or water hazards.)* Have students draw pictures of buoys that include arrows showing the buoyant force. **limited English proficiency**

Sharpen your Skills

Measuring

Materials *wooden block, metric ruler*
Time 5 minutes
Tips Suggest students create a data table to record their measurements and volumes.
Expected Outcome Students should find the volume of the block in cm^3.
Extend Challenge students to calculate the volume of the room using a meter stick. **learning modality: logical/mathematical**

Inquiry Challenge

Materials *assorted small classroom objects, graduated cylinder or beaker, water, metric ruler*
Time 15 minutes
Tips Challenge groups of students to find the volumes of regularly shaped objects by measuring them with a ruler and comparing the resultant calculation of volume with the measured volume of water they displace.
Extend Challenge students to find the volume of irregularly shaped objects. **learning modality: kinesthetic**

Ongoing Assessment

Skills Check Ask students to describe the relationship between the weight of the water an object displaces and the buoyant force.

Sink and Spill

Preparing for Inquiry

Key Concept The buoyant force on an object is equal to the weight of the fluid displaced by the object (Archimedes' principle).

Skills Objectives Students will be able to:
- perform calculations;
- interpret data;
- draw conclusions on how the buoyant force on a floating object is related to the weight of the displaced water.

Time 45 minutes

Advance Planning Assemble the beakers, balance, salt, paper towels, and small jars with lids. Baby food jars may serve as small watertight jars. Prepare any solutions you will need if you plan to use a liquid other than water.

Alternative Materials Instead of water, part of the class can use sugar water, salt water, or vegetable oil. A denser material than salt, such as iron filings, could be used to fill the jar.

Guiding Inquiry

Invitation You may want to perform this lab before you cover Archimedes' principle in class. Tell students that in this lab they will compare the buoyant force of the water to the weight of the water displaced, a comparison first made by Archimedes.

Introducing the Procedure

Discuss ways students might determine the weight of water displaced when an object sinks or floats. Explain the method used in this lab—subtracting the weight of the dry paper towel and 250-mL beaker from their weight *after* the spill.

Sink and Spill

In this lab, you will use data on floating objects to practice the skill of drawing conclusions.

Problem

How is the buoyant force on a floating object related to the weight of the water it displaces?

Materials

paper towels   water
pie pan
triple-beam balance
beaker, 600 mL
table salt
jar with watertight lid, about 30 mL

Procedure

1. Preview the procedure and copy the data table into your notebook.
2. Find the mass, in grams, of a dry paper towel and the pie pan together. Multiply the mass by 0.01. This gives you the weight in newtons. Record it in your data table.
3. Place the 600-mL beaker, with the dry paper towel under it, in the middle of the pie pan. Fill the beaker to the very top with water.
4. Fill the jar about halfway with salt. (The jar and salt must be able to float in water.) Then find the mass of the dry jar (with its cover on) in grams. Multiply the mass by 0.01. Record this weight in your data table.
5. Gently lower the jar into the 600-mL beaker. (If the jar sinks, take it out and remove some salt. Repeat Steps 2, 3, and 4.) Estimate the fraction of the jar that is underwater, and record it.
6. Once all of the displaced water has been spilled, find the total mass of the paper towel and pie pan containing the water. Multiply the mass by 0.01 and record the result in your data table.
7. Empty the pie pan. Dry off the pan and the jar.
8. Repeat Steps 2 through 7 several more times. Each time fill the jar with a different amount of salt, but make sure the jar still floats.

	DATA TABLE					
Jar	Weight of Empty Pie Pan and Dry Paper Towel (N)	Weight of Jar, Salt, and Cover (N)	Weight of Pie Pan with Displaced Water and Paper Towel (N)	Fraction of Jar Submerged in Water	Buoyant Force (N)	Weight of Displaced Water (N)
1						
2						
3						

Safety

Caution students not to spill liquid on the floor, as it could become slippery. Caution students to use care handling glass objects. Review the safety guidelines in Appendix A.

Program Resources

- **Unit 2 Resources** Skills Lab blackline masters, pp. 84–85

Media and Technology

 Lab Activity Videotape
Tape 2

9. Calculate the buoyant force for each trial and record it in your data table. (*Hint:* When an object floats, the buoyant force is equal to the weight of the object.)
10. Calculate the weight of the displaced water in each case. Record it in your data table.

Analyze and Conclude

1. In each trial, the jar had a different weight. How did this affect the way that the jar floated?
2. The jar had the same volume in every trial. Why did the volume of displaced water vary?
3. What can you conclude about the relationship between the buoyant force and the weight of the displaced water?
4. Can you suggest places where errors may have been introduced?

5. **Think About It** If you put too much salt in the jar, it will sink. What can you conclude about the buoyant force in this case? How can you determine the buoyant force for an object that sinks?

Design an Experiment

How do you think your results would change if you used a different liquid that is more dense or less dense than water? Design an experiment to test your hypothesis. What liquid or liquids will you use? Will you need equipment other than what you have used for this experiment? If so, what will you need? If you carry out your new experiment, be sure to have your teacher check your design before you begin.

Sample Data Table

Jar	Weight of Empty Pie Pan and Dry Paper Towel (N)	Weight of Jar, Salt, and Cover (N)	Weight of Pie Pan with Displaced Water and Paper Towel (N)	Fraction of Jar Submerged in Water	Buoyant Force (N)	Weight of Displaced Water (N)
1	1.08	0.26	1.33	1/4	0.26	0.25
2						
3						

Troubleshooting the Experiment
◆ Make sure students perform the lab on a level surface.
◆ Remind students to multiply their mass readings by 0.01 (actually 0.0098, rounded for simplicity) to convert them to newtons. They can round the forces to the nearest hundredth of a newton.
◆ Make sure students capture all the displaced water. If they do not, errors will be introduced.
◆ Tell students that the same paper towel can be used to wipe any water that clings to the 600-mL beaker so it can be included in the mass.

Expected Outcome
The weight of the displaced water will be equal to the buoyant force, which in turn is equal to the weight of the jar, salt, and cover.

Analyze and Conclude
1. Because the volume remains constant, the lighter the jar, the higher it floated.
2. The amount of displaced water depends only on the volume of jar that is submerged. Since this varied each time, so did the amount of displaced water.
3. The buoyant force is the same as (or close to) the weight of the displaced water.
4. Errors may be introduced in capturing all of the spilled water. If any of the water is lost, the measured weight of the displaced water will be less than the actual amount.
5. If a jar sinks, the buoyant force is less than the weight of the jar. However, the buoyant force will still be equal to the weight of the displaced water, which can be found using the method from this lab.

Extending the Inquiry
Design an Experiment A typical hypothesis states that if a liquid that is denser than water is used, then the same jar would float higher and a smaller volume of liquid would be displaced. Students should plan to repeat this lab using a liquid denser than water, such as corn syrup or glycerin, to test this hypothesis.

Floating and Sinking

Using the Visuals: Figure 15

Draw students' attention to the relative sizes of the force arrows in the images. Ask: **What information do the arrows give you about the forces involved?** (*In the diagrams on the left and right, the weight of the displaced water is equal to the object's weight. In the middle, the object's weight is greater.*) **learning modality: visual**

Density

Demonstration

Materials *modeling clay, clear plastic container, water, paper towels*
Time 15 minutes

Have students who have difficulty understanding the text examine Figure 17 on page 96. Then fill a clear plastic container three-quarters full of water. Make a small clay ball. Have students predict whether the ball will float, then drop it into the water. Remove the ball, dry it, and shape it into a small boat. Have students predict whether the boat will float, then try it. Elicit the fact that the ball sinks because it is more dense than water. The boat floats because its overall density is less than water. Since it displaces more water, it floats.
limited English proficiency

TRY THIS

Skills Focus drawing conclusions

Materials *plastic straw, scissors, paper clips, jar, 1–2 L plastic bottle*
Time 20 minutes
Tips Have students test the diver in the jar. If the diver is less than 0.5 cm above the water, it may sink in the bottle.
Expected Outcome When the bottle is squeezed, the pressure on the water increases, causing it to enter the straw. Students may conclude that the diver sinks because it has greater density.
Extend Challenge students to find a way to remove the diver from the bottle without emptying the bottle. (*Fill the bottle to the top and the diver will rise to the surface.*) **learning modality: kinesthetic**

192

Figure 15 The illustration shows the forces on three different cubes. All three cubes have the same volume. *Comparing and Contrasting Why don't all three cubes float?*

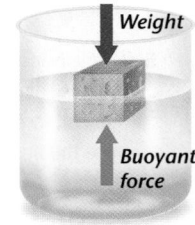
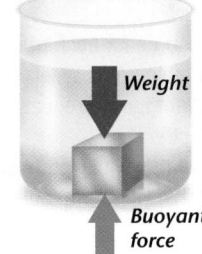
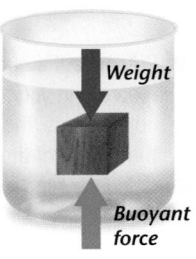

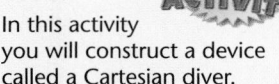

Dive!

In this activity you will construct a device called a Cartesian diver.

1. Bend a plastic straw into a U shape and cut the ends so that each side is about 4 cm long. Attach the ends with a paper clip.
2. Attach additional paper clips to the first paper clip. The straw should float with its top about half a centimeter above the surface. This is the diver.
3. Fill a plastic jar or bottle almost completely with water. Drop the diver in, paper clips first. Then put the lid on the jar.
4. Slowly squeeze and release the jar several times.

Drawing Conclusions Explain the behavior of the diver.

192

Floating and Sinking

Remember that there is always a downward force on a submerged object. That force is the weight of the object. If the weight of the object is greater than the buoyant force, the net force on a submerged object will be downward. The object will sink. If the weight of the object is less than the buoyant force, the object will begin to sink. It will only sink deep enough to displace a volume of fluid with a weight equal to its own. At that level, it will stop sinking deeper, and will float. If the weight of the object is exactly equal to the buoyant force, the two forces are balanced.

Density

Exactly why do some objects float and others sink? By comparing the density of an object to the density of a fluid, you can decide if it will float. But what is density?

The **density** of a substance is its mass per unit volume.

$$Density = \frac{Mass}{Volume}$$

For example, one cubic centimeter (cm^3) of lead has a mass of 11.3 grams, so its density is 11.3 g/cm^3.

$$Density\ of\ lead = \frac{11.3\ g}{1\ cm^3} = 11.3\ g/cm^3$$

In contrast, one cubic centimeter of cork has a mass of only about 0.25 gram. So its density is about 0.25 g/cm^3. You would say that lead is more dense than cork. The density of water is 1.0 g/cm^3, so it is less dense than lead but more dense than cork.

By comparing densities, you can explain the behavior of the objects shown in Figure 15. **An object that is more dense than the fluid in which it is immersed sinks. An object that is less dense than the fluid in which it is immersed floats to the surface.** And if the density of an object is equal to the density of the

---

fluid in which it is immersed, the object neither rises nor sinks in the fluid. Instead it floats at a constant level.

Now you know why lead sinks: It is several times denser than water. Cork, which is less dense than water, floats. An ice cube floats in water because the density of ice is less than the density of water. But it's just a little less! So most of a floating ice cube is below the surface. Since an iceberg is really a very large ice cube, the part that you see above water is only a small fraction of the entire iceberg. This is one reason why icebergs are so dangerous to ships.

 Checkpoint *To calculate the density of a substance, what two properties of the substance do you need to know?*

Densities of Substances Figure 16 shows several substances and their densities. Notice that liquids can float on top of other liquids. (You may have seen that salad oil floats on top of vinegar.) Notice also that the substances with the greatest densities are near the bottom of the cylinder.

Don't forget that air is also a fluid. Objects float in air if their densities are less than the density of air. A helium balloon rises because helium is less dense than air. An ordinary balloon filled with air, however, is more dense than the surrounding air because it is under pressure. So the balloon falls to the ground once you let go of it.

Changing the density of an object can make it float or sink in a given fluid. The density of a submarine, for example, is decreased when water is pumped out of its flotation tanks. The overall mass of the submarine decreases. Since its volume remains the same, its density decreases when its mass decreases. So the submarine will float to the surface. To dive, the submarine takes in water. In this way, it increases its mass (and thus its density), and sinks.

Figure 16 You can use density to predict whether an object will sink or float when placed in a liquid. *Interpreting Data Will a rubber washer sink or float in corn oil?*

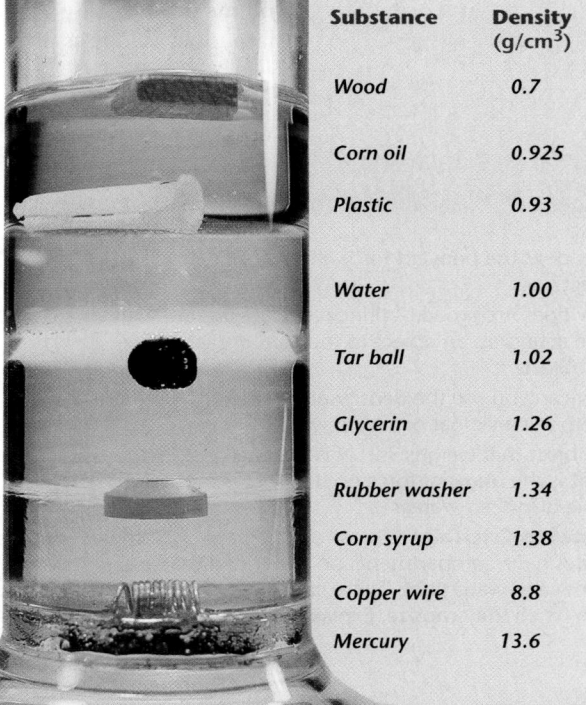

Substance	Density (g/cm^3)
Wood	0.7
Corn oil	0.925
Plastic	0.93
Water	1.00
Tar ball	1.02
Glycerin	1.26
Rubber washer	1.34
Corn syrup	1.38
Copper wire	8.8
Mercury	13.6

193

Media and Technology

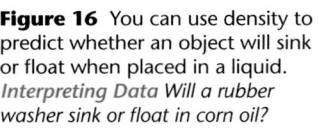 **Transparencies** "Floating and Sinking," Transparency 17

Concept Videotape Library *Adventures, Tape 2, "Density Column"*

Answers to Self-Assessment

Caption Questions

Figure 15 For a cube to float, the buoyant force must be greater than the weight of the cube.

Figure 16 A rubber washer will sink in corn oil.

 Checkpoint

To calculate density, you must know the mass and the volume.

Demonstration

Materials *tall, clear container; water; food coloring; rubbing alcohol; vegetable oil; corn syrup; glycerin*

Demonstration

Materials *tall, clear container; water; food coloring; rubbing alcohol; vegetable oil; corn syrup; glycerin*
Time 15 minutes
Tips As a class, explore the densities of different solutions by floating liquids in a container similar to the one in Figure 16. Pour a layer of corn syrup, then pour in the glycerin. When the glycerin has settled, add liquids in this order—colored water, vegetable oil, and colored rubbing alcohol. Pour gently to avoid mixing. Ask: **How do the different liquids float on each other ?** (*The lightest or less dense liquids float on top of the heaviest or more dense liquids.*) **Which liquids have a density greater than water?** (*Corn syrup and glycerin*) **learning modality: visual**

Addressing Naive Conceptions

Many students may believe that whether an object sinks or floats depends on its weight, not its density. Ask students to look at Figure 16. Ask: **Why are the liquids in layers rather than mixed?** (*They have different densities.*) **What would happen if a tar ball twice as large as the one in the illustration were placed in the liquids?** (*It would rest in the same position.*) Ask students to explain how they can determine whether an object will sink or float. (*If the object is less dense than the fluid, it will float. If it is more dense, it will sink.*) **learning modality: visual**

Ongoing Assessment

Skills Check Have students design an experiment that uses water to tell whether a substance is corn oil or corn syrup. (*Pour the unknown substance into a glass of water. If it floats on the water, it is corn oil, it if sinks, it is corn syrup.*)

Section 3 Review Answers

1. The buoyant force acts upward on a submerged object. This makes the object seem lighter.
2. The buoyant force on an object equals the weight of the fluid displaced by the object.
3. If the density of the object is greater than that of water, the object will sink; if the object's density is less than the density of water, it will float.
4. The buoyant force equals the weight of the object, so the buoyant force is 340 N. The weight of the displaced water is equal to the weight of the object, so it is also 340 N.
5. The air pockets increase the volume of the canoe, but not its mass. This makes the canoe less dense than water even if the material the canoe is made of is more dense than water.

Check Your Progress CHAPTER PROJECT 6

Make balances available for students to check the weights of their different designs. Students should add weight data to their design logs. Encourage students to brainstorm ideas for improving their designs. Help them to determine whether a boat sank because it was too dense, or if it capsized because it was unstable. Encourage students to find creative ways to solve the problems. Remind them to record everything they try in their design logs.

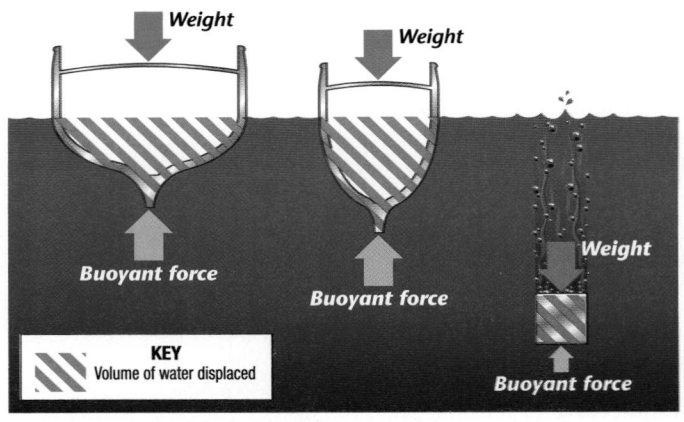

Figure 17 A solid cube of steel sinks when placed in water. A steel ship with the same weight floats.

KEY
Volume of water displaced

Buoyancy and Density Another way of changing density is to change volume. In Figure 17, the amount of steel present in the three objects is the same. Yet two of the figures float, and one sinks. Solid steel sinks rapidly in water, and so will the hull of a ship that is full of water. Usually, however, the hull of a ship contains a large volume of air. This air reduces the ship's overall density, and so allows it to float.

You can explain why a ship floats not just in terms of density, but also by means of the force of buoyancy. Since the buoyant force is equal to the weight of the displaced fluid, the buoyant force will increase if more fluid is displaced. The amount of fluid displaced depends on the volume of a submerged object. A large object displaces more fluid than a small object. Therefore, the object with greater volume has a greater buoyant force acting on it—even if the objects have the same weight.

The shape of a ship causes it to displace a greater volume of water than a solid piece of steel of the same mass. The greater the volume of water displaced, the greater the buoyant force. A ship stays afloat as long as the buoyant force is greater than its weight.

Section 3 Review

1. How does the buoyant force affect a submerged object?
2. How does Archimedes' principle relate the buoyant force acting on an object to the fluid displaced by the object?
3. How can you use the density of an object to predict whether it will float or sink in water?
4. An object that weighs 340 N is floating on a lake. What is the buoyant force on it? What is the weight of the displaced water?
5. **Thinking Critically** **Applying Concepts** Some canoes have compartments on either end that are hollow and watertight. These canoes won't sink, even when they capsize. Explain why.

Check Your Progress CHAPTER PROJECT 6

Don't be content with the first design that floats. Try several more, considering the characteristics that make your boat useful. How much space does your boat have for cargo? How does the weight of your boat affect the amount of cargo it can carry? (*Hint:* To measure the weight of each boat, see how many pennies will balance it on a double-pan balance.) Select your best boat and determine the number of pennies it can carry as it floats.

Performance Assessment

Writing Ask students to imagine that they are newspaper reporters the day after the *Titanic* sank. Have them write a column explaining why the unsinkable ship sank after striking an iceberg. (*Students' columns should describe how the water entering the ship increased the ship's density and caused it to sink.*)

Media and Technology

 Transparencies "Density," Transparency 18

Program Resources

◆ **Unit 2 Resources** 6-3 Review and Reinforce, p. 75; 6-3 Enrich, p. 76

SECTION 4 Applying Bernoulli's Principle

DISCOVER

ACTIVITY

Does Water Push or Pull?

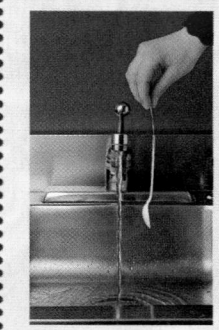

1. Hold a plastic spoon loosely by the edges of its handle so it is swinging freely between your fingers.

2. Turn on a faucet to produce a steady stream of water. Predict what will happen if you bring the curved back of the spoon into contact with the stream of water.

3. Test your prediction. Repeat the test several times.

4. Predict how your observations might change if you were to use a plastic fork instead of a spoon.

5. Test your prediction.

Think It Over

Inferring On what side of the spoon is the pressure lower? How do you know? Does the fork behave any differently from the spoon? If so, develop a hypothesis to explain why.

I n December of 1903, Wilbur and Orville Wright brought an odd-looking vehicle to a deserted beach in Kitty Hawk, North Carolina. People had flown in balloons for more than a hundred years, but the Wright brothers' goal was something no one had ever done before. They flew a plane that was heavier (denser) than air! They had spent years experimenting with different wing shapes and surfaces, and they had carefully studied the flight of birds. Their first flight at Kitty Hawk lasted just 12 seconds. The plane flew 36 meters and made history.

What did the Wright brothers know about flying that allowed them to construct the first airplane? And how can the principles they used explain how a jumbo jet can fly across the country? The answer has to do with fluid pressure and what happens when a fluid moves.

Bernoulli's Principle

So far in this chapter you have learned about fluids that are not moving. But what happens when a fluid, such as air or water, moves? Consider what happens if you hold a plastic spoon in a stream of running water. You might predict that the spoon would be pushed away by the water. But it is not. Surprisingly, the spoon is pushed toward the stream of water.

GUIDE FOR READING

◆ How is fluid pressure related to the motion of a fluid?

Reading Tip Before you read, preview *Exploring Wings* and predict how you can explain flight in terms of fluid pressure.

Figure 18 On December 17, 1903, Wilbur Wright watched his brother Orville take off in *Flyer I*, the first successful airplane.

READING STRATEGIES

Reading Tip Guide students in previewing *Exploring Wings*. Have students read the sentence under the main heading. Then ask what the paragraph headings and the pictures suggest. Students may predict that the shape of a wing causes unbalanced fluid pressure.

Program Resources

◆ **Unit 2 Resources** 6-4 Lesson Plan, p. 77; 6-4 Section Summary, p. 78
◆ **Guided Reading and Study Workbook** Section 6-4

SECTION 4 Applying Bernoulli's Principle

Objectives

After completing the lesson, students will be able to
◆ state Bernoulli's principle;
◆ explain the application of Bernoulli's principle to flight.

Key Term Bernoulli's principle

1 Engage/Explore

Activating Prior Knowledge

Have students tear a strip of newspaper about 30 cm long and 3 cm wide, then hold one end of the strip near their bottom lip so that the strip hangs loosely down. Then blow gently across the top of the strip. Ask students to describe what happens. *(The strip rises)* **What force is pushing on the strip to make it rise?** *(The force must be from air pressure since nothing else is touching the strip.)* Explain to students that in this lesson, they will learn about the principles relating fluid motion to pressure.

DISCOVER

Skills Focus inferring
Materials *plastic spoon, plastic fork, faucet*
Time 10 minutes
Tips Elicit students' predictions before the activity. Remind students to hold the back of the spoon facing the stream of water. After Step 3, ask: **What happened to the spoon?** *(It moved toward the water.)* Then ask about the fork. *(It did not move.)*
Expected Outcome The spoon will move toward the stream of water. The fork will not.
Think It Over Students may conclude that the pressure is lower on the back of the spoon, but the fork does not move toward the water as much because the tines of the fork allow the air pressure to equalize.

2 Facilitate

Bernoulli's Principle

Demonstration

Inflate two small balloons and knot each  one. Hang the balloons on strings so they hang with about 1 or 2 centimeters space between them. Have a volunteer gently blow air between the balloons. Ask students to observe what happens. (*The balloons move closer together.*) Ask: **Where do you think the pressure is the greatest?** (*On the outside, because the moving air between the balloons reduces the pressure.*) **learning modality: visual**

Objects in Flight

Inquiry Challenge

Materials *craft sticks, thin dowels, tissue paper, string, masking tape*
Time 40 minutes to design and build
Tips Have small groups design airplanes or gliders. Assign each student a task such as designer, assembler, and flight analyst. Allow students to test their designs outdoors. Challenge students to explain how the design of the plane or glider causes air to move more quickly over the top. **cooperative learning**

The behavior of the spoon demonstrates **Bernoulli's principle.** The Swiss scientist Daniel Bernoulli (bur NOO lee) found that the faster a fluid moves, the less pressure the fluid exerts. **Bernoulli's principle states that the pressure exerted by a moving stream of fluid is less than the pressure of the surrounding fluid.** The water running along the spoon is moving but the air on the other side of the spoon is not. The moving water exerts less pressure than the still air. The result is that the greater pressure of the still air on one side of the spoon pushes the spoon into the stream of water.

Similarly, if you blow above a sheet of tissue paper, the paper will rise. Moving air blown over the tissue paper exerts less pressure than the still air below the paper. The greater pressure below the paper pushes it upward.

☑ *Checkpoint* How is the pressure exerted by a fluid related to how fast the fluid moves?

Objects in Flight

Bernoulli's principle is one factor that can help explain flight—from a small bird to a huge airplane. Objects can be designed so that their shapes cause air to move at different speeds above and below them. If the air moves faster above the object, pressure pushes the object upward. But if the air moves faster below the object, pressure pushes it downward. The shape of the sail of a ship is somewhat like an airplane wing. The difference in the pressure on the two sides of the sail moves the ship forward. Look through *Exploring Wings* to see how Bernoulli's principle can be applied to airplanes, birds, and race cars.

Bernoulli's Principle at Home

Bernoulli's principle can help you understand many common occurrences. For example, you can sit next to a fireplace enjoying a cozy fire thanks in part to Bernoulli's principle. Smoke rises up the chimney partly because hot air rises, and partly because it is pushed. Wind blowing across the top of a chimney lowers the air pressure there. The higher pressure at the bottom then pushes air and smoke up the chimney.

Figure 19 Thanks to Bernoulli's principle, you can enjoy an evening by a warm fireplace without having the room fill up with smoke. *Making Generalizations Why does the smoke rise up the chimney?*

Background

History of Science Daniel Bernoulli (1700–1782) came from a family of esteemed scientists and mathematicians in Switzerland. His father, Johann Bernoulli, made many important contributions to mathematics, especially to the development of calculus. Johann and his brother Jakob were very competitive, and a new field of mathematical study called the calculus of variations developed from their arguments.

At the age of 25, Daniel Bernoulli and his brother Nicolaus joined the prestigious faculty of the St. Petersburg Academy of Sciences to teach mathematics. Later in life Daniel was elected to the Royal Society of London. Although most famous for his work on fluids, during his lifetime Daniel held academic posts in botany, anatomy, physiology, and physics. His work included studies in medicine, mechanics, mathematics, and oceanography.

EXPLORING Wings

Bernoulli's principle helps explain how air moving around a wing produces a force.

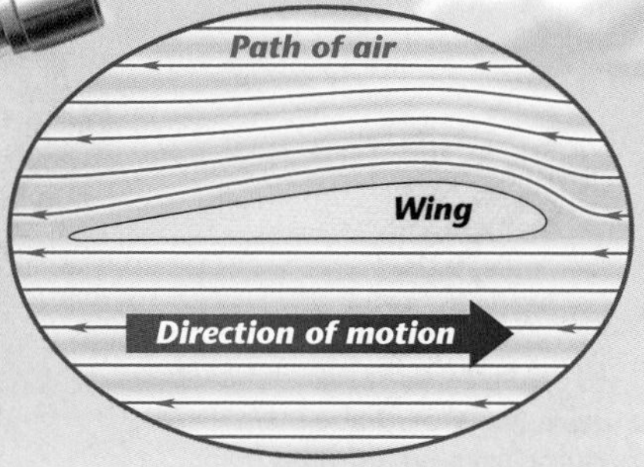

Airplane Wings

The top of this airplane wing is curved. Air that moves over the top of the wing must travel farther than air that moves along the bottom of the wing. Also, the air moving over the top moves faster and exerts less pressure than the air on the bottom. This difference in pressure creates an upward force on the wing, called lift.

Path of air

Wing

Direction of motion

Bird Wings

Like the airplane wing above, a bird's wing is curved on the top. A bird's wing is flexible, allowing it to propel the bird as well as producing lift.

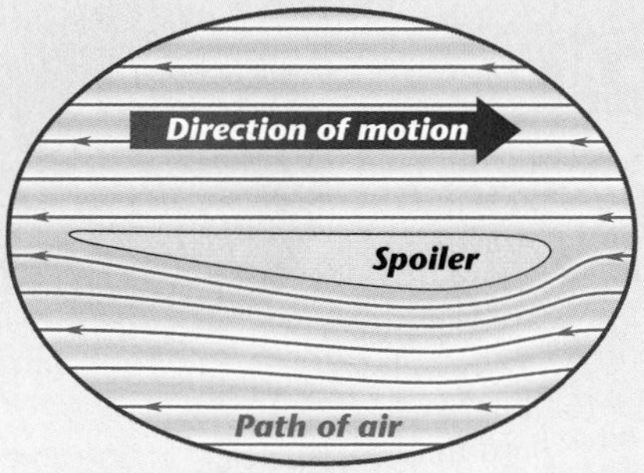

Direction of motion

Spoiler

Path of air

Spoilers

The spoiler on the back of a racing car is curved on the lower side, so a spoiler is an upside-down version of the airplane wing above. The greater pressure pushing downward on a spoiler gives the car better traction from its rear wheels.

EXPLORING
Wings

After students have had time to examine the visual, ask: **What fluid is moving?** *(air)* Ask: **How does the force exerted by the air on the top of the wing compare with the force exerted by the air on the bottom of the wing when the airplane takes off?** *(It is less.)* Ask: **How is this related to Bernoulli's principle?** *(The faster-moving air exerts less pressure.)* Have students explain why a spoiler on the back of a race car acts like an "upside down" wing. Direct students' attention to the cross section of the wing and ask them how a bird's wing is like an airplane wing and how it is different.

Extend Ask: **What would happen if an airplane flew into turbulent air?** *(Since the air would not flow smoothly above and below the wing, the wing might lose lift.)*
learning modality: visual

Bernoulli's Principle at Home

Real-Life Learning

Use Figure 19 and the description of fireplaces in the text to start a discussion of fire. Invite a member of the fire department to talk to the class about applications of Bernoulli's principle in fire fighting, such as backdrafts, updrafts, and fire safety. Encourage students to develop a list of questions before the talk. Prompt students to think about issues such as chimney flues, sparks and burning paper rising from a fire, and blowing on a fire to help it burn. Have students ask the speaker to explain how air pressure differences affect fire.
learning modality: verbal

Media and Technology

 Transparencies "Exploring Wings," Transparency 19

 Concept Videotape Library *Adventures, Tape 2,* "How an Airplane Flies"

Answers to Self-Assessment

Caption Question

Figure 19 Hot air rises on its own. In addition, the wind across the top of the chimney lowers air pressure at the top of the chimney. This allows air to be pushed up from the bottom of the chimney.

☑ *Checkpoint*

The faster a fluid moves, the less pressure it exerts.

Ongoing Assessment

Writing Have students give three examples of Bernoulli's principle.

3 Assess

Section 4 Review Answers

1. The pressure exerted by a moving fluid is lower than the pressure of the same fluid when it is not moving.

2. The air traveling above the wing is moving faster than the air traveling below the wing. The result is that air pressure above the wing is lower than air pressure below the wing. This causes an upward force, or lift, that allows the plane to fly.

3. Wind blowing over the roof exerts less pressure than the still air inside the house. The greater pressure inside the house pushes the roof upward.

4. The truck pulls air along with it. Because the air is moving at a greater speed than the air on the other side of your car, the greater pressure on the side of your car pushes your car toward the truck.

Science at Home

Materials *plastic straw, scissors, drinking glass or jar, water*

Caution students to follow the directions carefully. Student must blow forcefully to make the atomizer work. Students should explain that the device works because the air blown over the straw lowers the pressure at the top of the straw. The greater pressure outside the straw pushes the water up the straw.

Performance Assessment

Writing Native Americans of many different tribes have built temporary and permanent dwellings that use a simple hole in the roof to allow smoke from a fire to escape. Have students write a paragraph using Bernoulli's principle to explain how this works. They should include a prediction of whether the smoke outlet works better with no wind or with wind.

 Students can save their paragraphs in their portfolios.

Figure 20 The spray of perfume from an atomizer is an application of Bernoulli's principle. *Applying Concepts Why is the perfume pushed up and out of the flask?*

Bernoulli's principle can help you understand the operation of other familiar devices. In the atomizer shown in Figure 20, you squeeze a rubber bulb. Squeezing the bulb causes air to move quickly past the top of the tube. The bottom of the tube is in the liquid in the flask. The moving air lowers the pressure at the top of the tube. The greater pressure in the flask pushes the liquid up into the tube. When the liquid reaches the air stream, the action of the air stream breaks it into small drops. The liquid comes out as a fine mist.

Section 4 Review

1. What does Bernoulli's principle say about the pressure exerted by a moving fluid?
2. Why does the air pressure above an airplane wing differ from the pressure below it? How is this pressure difference involved in flight?
3. **Thinking Critically** **Relating Cause and Effect** A roof is lifted off a building during a severe windstorm. Explain this in terms of Bernoulli's principle.
4. **Thinking Critically** **Applying Concepts** You are riding in a car on a highway when a large truck speeds by you. Explain why your car is forced toward the truck.

Science at Home

You can make your own atomizer using a straw. Cut a plastic straw partway through. Hold one end of the straw in a glass of water and bend the other half of the straw at a right angle at the cut, as shown. Blow hard through the straw, making sure that no one is in the way! Show your device to your family. See if they know what it is and why it works. Explain the device to them in terms of Bernoulli's principle.

Program Resources

◆ **Unit 2 Resources** 6-4 Review and Reinforce, p. 79; 6-4 Enrich, p. 80

Answers to Self-Assessment

Caption Question

Figure 20 Air moves over the top of the tube when the bulb is squeezed. This lowers the pressure at the top of the tube. The higher pressure at the bottom of the tube pushes the perfume up the tube.

SECTION 1 Pressure

Key Ideas

◆ Pressure is the force per unit area on a surface.

◆ Fluid pressure results from the motion of the atoms or molecules that make up the fluid.

◆ Pressure at a given level in a fluid is the same in all directions. Pressure decreases with altitude and increases with depth.

Key Terms

pressure
pascal
fluid

 SECTION 2 Transmitting Pressure in a Fluid

Key Ideas

◆ According to Pascal's principle, an increase in pressure on a confined fluid is transmitted equally to all parts of the fluid.

◆ A hydraulic device works by transmitting an increase in pressure from one part of a confined fluid to the other. A small force exerted over a small area at one place results in a large force exerted by a larger area at another place.

Key Terms

Pascal's principle   hydraulic system

 SECTION 3 Floating and Sinking

Key Ideas

◆ The upward force on an object submerged in a fluid is called the buoyant force.

◆ The buoyant force on an object is equal to the weight of the fluid displaced by the object. This is Archimedes' principle.

◆ An object will sink, rise to the surface, or stay where it is in a fluid depending on whether its density is less than, greater than, or equal to the density of the fluid.

Key Terms

buoyant force   density
Archimedes' principle

 SECTION 4 Applying Bernoulli's Principle

INTEGRATING TECHNOLOGY

Key Idea

◆ The pressure in a fluid decreases as the speed of the fluid increases. This is Bernoulli's principle.

Key Term

Bernoulli's principle

Organizing Information

Flowchart Create a flowchart that shows how a hydraulic device multiplies force. (For more on flowcharts, see the Skills Handbook.)

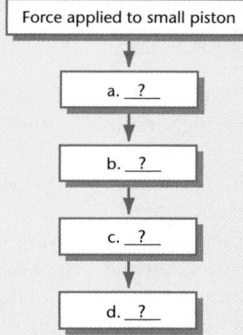

```
┌────────────────────────────┐
│ Force applied to small piston │
└────────────────────────────┘
              ↓
        ┌──────────┐
        │  a.  ?   │
        └──────────┘
              ↓
        ┌──────────┐
        │  b.  ?   │
        └──────────┘
              ↓
        ┌──────────┐
        │  c.  ?   │
        └──────────┘
              ↓
        ┌──────────┐
        │  d.  ?   │
        └──────────┘
```

Chapter 6   **199**

Organizing Information

Flowchart **a.** pressure on fluid increases; **b.** pressure is transmitted throughout fluid; **c.** pressure pushes on larger piston; **d.** same pressure over greater area results in greater force ($P = F/A$)

Program Resources

◆ **Unit 2 Resources** Chapter 6 Project Scoring Rubric, p. 64
◆ **Performance Assessment** Chapter 6, pp. 19–21
◆ **Chapter Tests** Chapter 6 Test, pp. 23–26

Media and Technology

Computer Test Bank
Chapter 6 Test

Reviewing Content

Multiple Choice

1. b 2. a 3. c 4. d 5. b

True or False

6. area 7. decreases 8. true 9. displaced fluid 10. true

Checking Concepts

11. You exert less pressure lying down. When you lie down, you spread the force of your weight out over a larger area, thus exerting less pressure.
12. Pressure = Force/Area = 14 N/7 cm² = 2 N/cm²
13. The braking system of a car and the hydraulic lift in an auto shop are examples of hydraulic systems.
14. In water, a greater upward force (the buoyant force) acts in the opposite direction of your weight. The net downward force, then, is less than in air.
15. Air moves faster above a bird's curved wings, so the greater pressure below the wings pushes the bird upward.
16. Students should explain that pressure increases with depth.

Thinking Critically

17. The sphere must be hollow.
18. This method will increase the volume of displaced water, increasing the buoyant force. It will also decrease the ship's overall density.
19. Take an object that floats in either of the liquids. If it sinks in the other liquid, the one it floats in is the denser liquid. If it floats in both, the one it floats higher in is the denser liquid.
20. The pressure above the kite is less than the pressure below it.

Applying Skills

21. The object weighs less in water because the buoyant force on it in water is opposite to the force of gravity.
22. The buoyant force is 2.0 N (9.8 N − 7.8 N).
23. The volume of water is equal to the volume of the object. The weight of the volume of water is equal to the buoyant force on the object, 2.0 N.
24. The object will sink because the buoyant force is less than its weight.

Reviewing Content

Multiple Choice

Choose the letter of the answer that best completes each statement.

1. Pressure can be measured in units of
   a. N.
   b. N/cm².
   c. N/cm.
   d. N/cm³.
2. The operation of a hydraulic device can be explained in terms of
   a. Pascal's principle.
   b. Bernoulli's principle.
   c. Archimedes' principle.
   d. Newton's third law.
3. If the buoyant force on an object in water is greater than the object's weight, the object will
   a. sink.
   b. hover beneath the surface of the water.
   c. rise to the surface and float.
   d. be crushed by the water pressure.
4. A stone will sink in water because
   a. it is very heavy.
   b. its density is less than that of water.
   c. it has a small buoyant force on it.
   d. its density is greater than that of water.
5. Much of the lift that enables an airplane to fly can be explained using
   a. Pascal's principle.
   b. Bernoulli's principle.
   c. Archimedes' principle.
   d. Newton's first law.

True or False

If the statement is true, write true. If it is false, change the underlined word or words to make the statement true.

6. Pressure is force per unit of <u>mass</u>.
7. As you rise higher into the atmosphere, the air pressure <u>increases</u>.
8. The braking system of a car is an example of a <u>hydraulic device</u>.
9. You can determine the buoyant force on an object if you know the weight of the <u>object</u>.
10. The pressure exerted by a moving stream of fluid is <u>less than</u> the pressure exerted by the same fluid when it is not moving.

Checking Concepts

11. How does the amount of pressure you exert on the floor when you are lying down compare with the amount of pressure you exert when you are standing up?
12. You have a closed bottle of soda. The force on the bottle cap due to the carbonation of the soda is 14 N. If the area of the bottle cap is 7 cm², what is the pressure on the cap?
13. Name two hydraulic devices that an auto mechanic is familiar with.
14. Why do you seem to weigh more in air than you do in water?
15. Explain how Bernoulli's principle can keep a bird in the air.
16. **Writing to Learn** You have a job greeting vacationers who are learning to scuba dive. Prepare a brochure or handout explaining the pressure changes they should expect to experience as they dive. Be sure to describe the reasons for the changes.

Thinking Critically

17. **Developing Hypotheses** A sphere made of steel is put in water and, surprisingly, it floats. Develop a hypothesis to explain this observation.
18. **Applying Concepts** One method of raising a sunken ship to the surface is to inflate large bags or balloons inside its hull. Explain why this procedure could work.
19. **Designing Experiments** You have two fluids of unknown density. Suggest an experiment to determine which is denser without mixing the two fluids.
20. **Relating Cause and Effect** Your kite rises into the air as you run quickly on a windy day. Is the air pressure greater above the kite or below it? Explain your answer.

Applying Skills

Use the illustration to answer Questions 21–24. It shows an object being supported by a spring scale in and out of water.

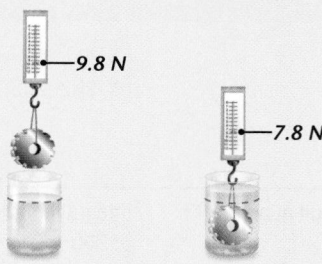

9.8 N

7.8 N

21. **Applying Concepts** Why is there a difference between the weight of the object in air and its weight in water?
22. **Calculating** What is the buoyant force on the object?
23. **Drawing Conclusions** What can you conclude about the water above the dotted line in the right half of the illustration?

24. **Predicting** If the spring scale were removed, would the object float or sink? How do you know?

Performance CHAPTER PROJECT 6 Assessment

Project Wrap Up Test your boat to make sure it does not leak. Then display it for the class and demonstrate how it floats. Be sure to include the diagrams you drew of the different designs you tried. Display the observations and data you recorded for each design. Point out to your classmates the features you incorporated into your final design.

Reflect and Record Suppose you had no limitations on what materials you could use for your boat. Also suppose you could form your material into any shape you choose. In your journal, sketch and describe the boat you would design.

Performance CHAPTER PROJECT 6 Assessment

Project Wrap Up Encourage students to describe the design features of their boats and explain why they were included.

Prepare a basin of water in which students can test their boats. Use a basin large enough to test two boats at one time. To test the boats, have students float them and add pennies gently so that the momentum of the falling pennies doesn't push the lip of the boat underwater. The number of pennies supported by the boat is one less than the number required to sink it. After testing the boats, collect the students' design logs.

Reflect and Record Ask students to sketch and describe in their journal the boat they would design if material limitations were removed.

Test Preparation

25. b 26. a 27. c 28. b

Test Preparation

Use these questions to prepare for standardized tests.

Read the passage. Then answer Questions 25–28.
Luis has a small stone. He fills a large beaker to the top with water and places a small beaker below the spout of the large beaker. Luis drops the stone into the large beaker and it sinks to the bottom. He then notes the volume of water that spills into the small beaker.

25. What does Luis learn about the stone?
    a. its mass   b. its volume
    c. its density   d. its composition
26. Luis can find the buoyant force on the stone by finding the
    a. weight of the displaced water.
    b. weight of the small beaker and the displaced water.
    c. weight of the large beaker with the water and stone in it.
    d. increase in the weight of the large beaker after the stone is dropped into it.

27. What conclusion can Luis draw about the density of the stone?
    a. It is less than the density of the water.
    b. It is equal to the density of the water.
    c. It is greater than the density of the water.
    d. It depends on the initial volume of water in the large beaker.
28. Luis chips a piece off the stone and repeats his experiment. What does he notice?
    a. The density of the stone decreases.
    b. The volume of displaced water decreases.
    c. The density of the stone increases.
    d. The volume of displaced water increases.

Chapter 6 **201**

Program Resources

- ◆ **Inquiry Skills Activity Book** Provides teaching and review of all inquiry skills
- ◆ **Prentice Hall Assessment System** Provides standardized test practice
- ◆ **Reading in the Content Area** Provides strategies to improve science reading skills
- ◆ **Teacher's ELL Handbook** Provides multiple strategies for English language learners

CHAPTER 7

Work and Machines

Sections	Time	Student Edition Activities	Other Activities	
CHAPTER PROJECT 7 **The Nifty Lifting Machine** p. 203	Ongoing (2 weeks)	Check Your Progress, pp. 207, 226 Project Wrap Up, p. 235	**TE**	Chapter 7 Project Notes, pp. 202–203
1 **What Is Work?** pp. 204–207 ◆ 7.1.1 Identify when work is done on an object. ◆ 7.1.2 Calculate the work done on an object.	1 period/ ½ block	**Discover** What Happens When You Pull at an Angle?, p. 204 **Sharpen Your Skills** Inferring, p. 206	**TE**	Integrating Mathematics, p. 206
2 **Mechanical Advantage and Efficiency** pp. 208–215 ◆ 7.2.1 Explain what machines do and how they make work easier. ◆ 7.2.2 Identify the difference between actual and ideal mechanical advantage. ◆ 7.2.3 Calculate the efficiency of a machine.	2 periods/ 1 block	**Discover** Is It a Machine?, p. 208 **Try This** Going Up, p. 211 **Science at Home** p. 213 **Skills Lab: Controlling Variables** Seesaw Science, pp. 214–215	**TE** **TE**	Including All Students, p. 210 Inquiry Challenge, p. 210
3 **Simple Machines** pp. 216–229 ◆ 7.3.1 Describe the six types of simple machines. ◆ 7.3.2 Calculate the ideal mechanical advantage of four types of simple machines. ◆ 7.3.3 Define compound machines.	2 periods/ 1 block	**Discover** How Can You Increase Your Force?, p. 216 **Try This** Modeling a Screw, p. 219 **Sharpen Your Skills** Classifying, p. 225 **Real-World Lab: You and Your Community** Angling for Access, pp. 228–229 **PLM** Provides instructions for the probeware version of the lab	**TE** **TE** **TE** **TE** **TE** **TE** **TE** **LM**	Real-Life Learning, p. 217 Demonstration, p. 218 Building Inquiry Skills: Predicting, p. 218; Measuring, p. 222; Interpreting Diagrams, p. 224 Visual Arts Connection, p. 220 Cultural Diversity, p. 220 Exploring the Three Classes of Levers, p. 221 Inquiry Challenge, p. 225 7, "Pulleys as Simple Machines"
4 **INTEGRATING LIFE SCIENCE** **Machines in the Human Body** pp. 230–232 ◆ 7.4.1 Explain how the body uses levers and wedges.	1 period/ ½ block	**Discover** Are You an Eating Machine?, p. 230 **Science at Home** p. 232	**TE**	Building Inquiry Skills: Observing, p. 231
Study Guide/Assessment pp. 233–235	1 period/ ½ block		**ISAB**	Provides teaching and review of all inquiry skills

For Standard or Block Schedule The Resource Pro® CD-ROM gives you maximum flexibility for planning your instruction for any type of schedule. Resource Pro® contains Planning Express®, an advanced scheduling program, as well as the entire contents of the Teaching Resources and the Computer Test Bank.

Key: **CTB** Computer Test Bank
CT Chapter Tests
ELL Teacher's ELL Handbook

CHAPTER PLANNING GUIDE

Program Resources	Assessment Strategies	Media and Technology
UR Chapter 7 Project Teacher Notes, pp. 86–87 **UR** Chapter 7 Project Overview and Worksheets, pp. 88–91	**TE** Check Your Progress, pp. 207, 226 **TE** Performance Assessment: Chapter 7 Project Wrap Up, p. 235 **UR** Chapter 7 Project Scoring Rubric, p. 92	Science Explorer Internet Site Audio CDs, Section Summaries
UR 7-1 Lesson Plan, p. 93 **UR** 7-1 Section Summary, p. 94 **UR** 7-1 Review and Reinforce, p. 95 **UR** 7-1 Enrich, p. 96	**SE** Section 1 Review, p. 207 **TE** Ongoing Assessment, p. 205 **TE** Performance Assessment, p. 207	Presentation Pro, "Work" Transparency 20, "Work and Force"
UR 7-2 Lesson Plan, p. 97 **UR** 7-2 Section Summary, p. 98 **UR** 7-2 Review and Reinforce, p. 99 **UR** 7-2 Enrich, p. 100 **UR** Skills Lab blackline masters, pp. 109–111	**SE** Section 2 Review, p. 213 **SE** Analyze and Conclude, p. 215 **TE** Ongoing Assessment, pp. 209, 211 **TE** Performance Assessment, p. 213	Concept Videotape Library, *Adventures, Tape 2*, "Work, Work, Work" Transparency 21, "Machines" Lab Activity Videotape, *Tape 2*
UR 7-3 Lesson Plan, p. 101 **UR** 7-3 Section Summary, p. 102 **UR** 7-3 Review and Reinforce, p. 103 **UR** 7-3 Enrich, p. 104 **UR** Real-World Lab blackline masters, pp. 112–113	**SE** Section 3 Review, p. 226 **SE** Analyze and Conclude, p. 229 **TE** Ongoing Assessment, pp. 217, 219, 221, 223, 225 **TE** Performance Assessment, p. 226	Concept Videotape Library, *Adventures, Tape 2,* "Simple Machines" Presentation Pro, "Simple Machines" Transparency 22, "Exploring the Three Classes of Levers" Transparency 23, "Pulleys" Lab Activity Videotape, *Tape 2*
UR 7-4 Lesson Plan, p. 105 **UR** 7-4 Section Summary, p. 106 **UR** 7-4 Review and Reinforce, p. 107 **UR** 7-4 Enrich, p. 108	**SE** Section 4 Review, p. 232 **TE** Ongoing Assessment, pp. 231 **TE** Performance Assessment, p. 232	Concept Videotape Library, *Adventures, Tape 2*, "Muscles and Bones" Transparency 24, "Exploring Levers in the Body"
GRSW Provides worksheets to promote student comprehension of content **RCA** Provides strategies to improve science reading skills **ELL** Provides multiple strategies for English language learners	**SE** Study Guide/Assessment, pp. 233–235 **PA** Performance Assessment, pp. 22–24 **CT** Chapter 7 Test, pp. 27–30 **CTB** Chapter 7 Test **PHAS** Provides standardized test preparation	Computer Test Bank, Chapter 7 Test

GRSW Guided Reading and Study Workbook
ISAB Inquiry Skills Activity Book
LM Laboratory Manual

PA Performance Assessment
PHAS Prentice Hall Assessment System
PLM Probeware Lab Manual

RCA Reading in the Content Area
SE Student Edition

TE Teacher's Edition
UR Unit Resources

Meeting the National Science Education Standards and AAAS Benchmarks

National Science Education Standards	Benchmarks for Science Literacy	Unifying Themes

National Science Education Standards

Physical Science (Content Standard B)

◆ **Transfer of energy** Energy is transferred by the work of simple machines. (*Sections 1, 2, 3; Skills Lab; Chapter Project*)

Life Science (Content Standard C)

◆ **Structure and function in living systems** Simple machines in the human body are a part of the muscular system, jaws, and teeth. (*Section 4*)

Science and Technology (Content Standard E)

◆ **Design a solution or a product** Students use a combination of simple machines to build a machine that can lift a soup can. (*Chapter Project*) Students evaluate how the angle of a wheelchair access ramp affects its usefulness. (*Real-World Lab*)

◆ **Evaluate completed technological designs or products** Students calculate the mechanical advantage and efficiency of different machines. (*Sections 2, 3*)

Science in Personal and Social Perspectives (Content Standard F)

◆ **Science and technology in society** Students learn about ancient engineering marvels and how they were built using simple machines. (*Section 3*) Some of the ethical problems posed by automation in the work place are discussed. (*Science and Society*) Students design a ramp system that will provide wheelchair access to a public library. (*Real-World Lab*)

Benchmarks for Science Literacy

2B Mathematics, Science, and Technology The use of mathematics to analyze work and machines has led to more-efficient machines and improved mechanical technology. (*Sections 1, 2, 3; Real-World Lab*)

3C Issues in Technology Students study how simple machines were used to make some of the most beautiful and useful structures in the world as well as how technology can improve life. The benefits and drawbacks of automation are discussed. (*Section 3; Real-World Lab; Science and Society*)

4E Energy Transformations How simple machines transfer input force into output force is described. Students examine the relationship between force, distance, and direction in simple machines. (*Sections 1, 2, 3; Skills Lab*)

8C Energy Sources and Use Students examine how some energy is lost in all simple machines. (*Sections 2, 3*)

9B Symbolic Relationships Students use equations to calculate work, mechanical advantage, and efficiency and determine how a change in one quantity affects other quantities in these equations. (*Sections 1, 2, 3; Skills Lab; Real-World Lab*)

11A Systems Students examine the interconnectedness of simple machines in compound machines and systems such as the human body. (*Chapter Project; Sections 3, 4*)

Unifying Themes

◆ **Energy** Simple machines convert input force or energy to output force or energy. Simple machines may increase force, increase distance, or change direction. (*Sections 1, 2, 3, 4; Skills Lab; Real-World Lab*)

◆ **Scale and Structure** Simple machines can be found in the human body. Compound machines are made up of more than one simple machine. (*Sections 3, 4; Chapter Project*)

◆ **Unity and Diversity** Although simple machines differ in appearance or use, they all make work easier. (*Sections 1, 3, 4*)

◆ **Systems and Interactions** Compound machines are systems of simple machines that interact to increase mechanical advantage. (*Chapter Project*)

◆ **Modeling** Students model a compound machine by constructing a "lifting machine" consisting of two simple machines that work together. (*Chapter Project*)

Take It to the Net

The **www.phschool.com** Web site provides you with multiple opportunities to incorporate the internet into your instruction. Go to **www.phschool.com** and click on the Science icon. Then select Science Explorer Integrated.

www.phschool.com

Internet Activities provide opportunities for students to review, extend, or assess a concept from the chapter.

■ Have students use the chapter Self-Test to get instant feedback.

■ Hot Links and Reference Links provide opportunities for online research.

STAY CURRENT with **SCIENCE NEWS** ®

Find out the latest research and information about mechanics at: **www.phschool.com**

ACTIVITY	Time (minutes)	Materials Quantities for one work group	Skills
Section 1			
Discover, p. 204	10	**Consumable** thin rubber band **Nonconsumable** mug	Developing Hypotheses
Sharpen Your Skills, p. 206	10	No special materials are required.	Inferring
Section 2			
Discover, p. 208	20	**Nonconsumable** objects that are machines, such as pliers, corkscrew, blunt knife, can opener, screwdriver, hammer, jar lid, scissors, pencil sharpener, broom, hole punch, staple remover; objects that are not machines, such as eraser, pencil, chalk, paper, ruler, ball, book, dishcloth, coin, straw, salt shaker	Forming Operational Definitions
Try This, p. 211	15	**Consumable** 50-cm string or twine **Nonconsumable** small cooking pot, 20-N spring scale, pencil	Developing Hypotheses
Science at Home, p. 213	home	**Nonconsumable** hand tools or utensil	Observing
Skills Lab, pp. 214–215	30	**Consumable** masking tape **Nonconsumable** meter stick; 28 pennies, post-1982; small object, mass about 50 g; dowel or other cylindrical object for pivot point, about 10 cm long and 3 cm in diameter	Controlling Variables
Section 3			
Discover, p. 216	15	**Nonconsumable** 2 broomsticks or dowels, long rope	Predicting
Try This, p. 219	10	**Consumable** sheet of paper, tape, string **Nonconsumable** long pencils, scissors, markers, ruler	Making Models
Sharpen Your Skills, p. 225	10	**Nonconsumable** first-class lever, single fixed pulley	Classifying
Real-World Lab, p. 228–229	55	**Nonconsumable** board, at least 10 cm wide and 50 cm long; wooden block with eye-hook; spring scale, 0–10 N (or force sensor); metric ruler; 4 books, about 2 cm thick; marker	Making Models, Measuring, Calculating
Section 4			
Discover, p. 230	10	**Consumable** crackers	Observing
Science at Home, p. 232	home	**Consumable** wooden toothpicks	Communicating

A list of all materials required for the Student Edition activities can be found beginning on page T23. You can obtain information about ordering materials by calling 1-800-848-9500 or by accessing the *Science Explorer* Internet site at: **www.phschool.com**

The Nifty Lifting Machine

Modern society depends on complex machines, but even the most complex of machines can be thought of as a series of interconnected simple machines.

Purpose Students will demonstrate their understanding of simple machines by designing and building a device to reduce the input force required to lift a 600-g soup can 5 centimeters.

Skills Focus Students will be able to
◆ design a device that is a compound machine able to lift a 600-g load using less than a 600-g mass as an input force;
◆ build the device that they designed;
◆ calculate actual and ideal mechanical advantage
◆ explain to others how their device incorporates simple machines in its construction.

Project Time Line The project requires about four weeks. Before beginning the project, see Chapter 7 Project Teacher Notes on pages 86–87 in Unit 2 Resources for more details on carrying out the project. During week one, students should design their devices. In weeks two and three, students build and modify their prototypes. In week four, students should write short descriptions of their devices and demonstrate them to the class. Also distribute the Chapter 7 Project Student Overview and Worksheets and Scoring Rubric on pages 88–92 in Unit 2 Resources.

Suggested Shortcuts Have students work in small groups as a cooperative learning task. To ensure that every student will have ample opportunity to participate in the design of a compound machine, have them work alone during the first phase of the project. Students can then get together as a group to build one or more of the devices that group members have designed. Each group should consist of no more than four students.

Possible Materials Provide a wide variety of materials students can use to build their devices. Suitable materials include: wood scraps of all sizes, cardboard and plastic tubes, nails and screws, coat hangers, straws, spools, cups, cans, wire, toy wheels, toy cars, string, paper clips, and cardboard. Encourage students to suggest and use other materials as well. Have sanding paper and a light lubricating oil available for students to use when they build their devices. Sand will be needed to fill soup cans to 600 g for the load and to fill soup cans for input force.

CHAPTER 7
Work and Machines

WEB ACTIVITY   www.phschool.com

202

PROJECT 7

The Nifty Lifting Machine

For thousands of years, machines have helped people do work. Whether a person is using a diesel-powered crane to unload a lumber truck, or a shovel to dig in the garden, any task is made easier by using machines. Even complex machines such as automobiles accomplish a given task by combining the action of many simple machines.

In this chapter, you will learn about the different types of machines and how you use them in your daily life. As you work through this chapter, you will build your own lifting machine and demonstrate it at work.

Your Goal To use a combination of at least two simple machines to build a machine that can lift a 600-gram soup can 5 centimeters.

Your machine must
- consist of at least two simple machines working in combination
- use another soup can gradually filled with sand as the input force
- be built following the safety guidelines in Appendix A

Get Started Brainstorm with your classmates ideas for different designs of machines. Discuss possible materials that might be useful for constructing each machine.

Check Your Progress You'll be working on the project as you study this chapter. To keep your project on track, look for Check Your Progress boxes at the following points.
- **Section 1 Review,** page 207: Determine the amount of work your machine must do.
- **Section 3 Review,** page 226: Analyze factors affecting efficiency and mechanical advantage, and construct your machine.

Wrap Up At the end of the chapter (page 235), demonstrate your machine.

Horses or oxen would once have done the work of this machine.

SECTION 4
Integrating Life Science
Machines in the Human Body

Discover **Are You an Eating Machine?**

203

Program Resources

- **Unit 2 Resource**s Chapter 7 Project Teacher Notes, pp. 86–87; Project Overview and Worksheets, pp. 88–91; Project Scoring Rubric, p. 92

Media and Technology

 Audio CDs Section Summaries

 www.phschool.com

You will find an Internet activity, chapter self-tests for students, and links to other chapter topics at this site.

Launching the Project To introduce the project and stimulate student interest, load an empty soup can with sand until its mass is 600 g. Show students how the input force to lift this load can be reduced using a meter stick as a lever and a chalkboard eraser as a fulcrum. Invite students to lift the can with and without the lever. You may also wish to use an incline plane and/or a set of pulleys to lift the load.

Allow students to read the description of the project in their text and the Chapter Project Overview on pages 88–89 in Unit 2 Resources. Then encourage discussions on simple machines, how one might build a machine, how one could combine two machines into one, materials that could be used, and any initial questions students may have. Pass out copies of the Chapter 7 Project Worksheets on pages 90–91 in Unit 2 Resources for students to review.

Performance Assessment

The Chapter 7 Project Scoring Rubric on page 92 in Unit 2 Resources will help you evaluate how well students complete the Chapter 7 Project. Students will be assessed on
- the clarity, simplicity, and completeness of their designs;
- the progress they make when constructing their devices;
- how well their written explanations of how their devices work exhibit an understanding of the machines involved;
- How well their devices perform during the demonstration.

By sharing the Chapter 7 Project Scoring Rubric with students at the beginning of the project, you will make it clear to them what they are expected to do.

Objectives

After completing the lesson, students will be able to
◆ identify when work is done on an object;
◆ calculate the work done on an object.

Key Terms work, joule

1 Engage/Explore

Activating Prior Knowledge

Ask a volunteer to hold a book in his or her hand while standing perfectly still. Ask another volunteer to lift a book from the floor and place it on a table. Ask: **Which volunteer is exerting force?** *(both)* Ask: **But which student is doing work?** *(the lifter, not the stander)*

DISCOVER

Skills Focus developing hypotheses

Materials *mug, thin rubber band*

Time 10 minutes

Tips Students should fill the mug halfway with water so that it will not turn over when it is pulled. Provide paper towels to clean up any spills. Students can use sand instead of water or place a book on top of the mug if they want to use more weight.

Think It Over The pull in which the halves of elastic were held parallel was more effective. Students may say it was more effective because the force was in the same direction as the motion of the mug. Students may also say that if they increased the angle, they would have to pull harder to get the mug to move, because much of the pull does not help move the mug.

DISCOVER ·· ACTIVITY

What Happens When You Pull at an Angle?

1. Fill a mug half full with water.
2. Cut a rubber band so that you have a medium-weight piece of elastic. Loop the elastic through the handle of the mug. You can pull on the elastic to move the mug at constant speed across a table.
3. You can hold the two halves of elastic parallel to each other or at an angle to each other as shown. Predict which way will be more effective in moving the mug.
4. Pull on the elastic both ways. Observe any differences.

Think It Over
Developing Hypotheses Which of the two pulls was more effective in moving the mug? Can you explain why? What do you think would happen if you increased the angle?

GUIDE FOR READING

◆ When is work done on an object?
◆ How do you calculate the work done on an object?

Reading Tip Before you read, preview the headings and turn them into questions. As you read, write brief answers to the questions.

After a heavy snowstorm, a neighbor's car gets stuck in a snowdrift. You shovel some snow away from the car, and then try to push it backward. The spinning tires whine as the driver attempts to move. Although you try as hard as you can, the car just won't budge. After 10 minutes of strenuous pushing, you are nearly exhausted. Unfortunately, the car is still lodged in the snow. That was sure hard work, wasn't it? You exerted a lot of force. You did some work shoveling the snow. But you might be surprised to discover that in scientific terms you didn't do any work at all on the car!

The Meaning of Work

In science you do **work** on an object when you exert a force on the object that causes the object to move some distance. If you push a child on a swing, for example, you are doing work on the child. If you pull your books out of your

Force Motion

Force Motion

Figure 1 Lifting a bin full of newspapers is work, but carrying the bin is not.
Interpreting Photos Why does the girl do no work when she carries the bin?

204

READING STRATEGIES

Reading Tip Remind students to begin their questions with words such as *What, How,* and *Why.* Sample question: What is the meaning of work? After students read the section, have them meet with a study partner to compare questions and discuss their answers.

Study and Comprehension Before students read the section, remind them of

these strategies for breaking down information to make it easier to understand:
◆ Read the title, headings, subheadings, and captions to get an overview.
◆ Read one section of text at a time, line by line. Reread parts you did not understand.
◆ Jot down unfamiliar words. Try to figure out their meanings or look the words up in a dictionary.

book bag, you do work on the books. If you lift a bag of groceries out of a shopping cart, you do work on the bag of groceries.

No Work Without Motion So why didn't you do work when trying to push the car out of the snow? The car didn't move. **In order for you to do work on an object, the object must move some distance as a result of your force.** If the object does not move, no work is done no matter how much force is exerted.

There are many situations in which you exert a force but don't do any work. Suppose, for example, you are asked to hold a piece of wood while you are helping on a construction project. You definitely exert a force to hold the wood in place, so it might seem as if you do work. But because the force you exert does not make the wood move, you are not doing any work on it.

Only Force in the Same Direction How much work do you do when you carry your heavy books to school? You may think you do a lot of work, but actually you don't. **In order to do work on an object, the force you exert must be in the same direction as the object's motion.** When you carry an object at constant velocity, you exert an upward force to hold the object so that it doesn't fall to the ground. The motion of the object, however, is in the horizontal direction. Since the force is vertical and the motion is horizontal, you don't do any work on the object as you carry it.

How much work do you do when you pull a sled? When you pull a sled, you pull on the rope at an angle to the ground. Therefore your force has both a horizontal part (to the right in Figure 3) and a vertical part (upward). When you pull this way, only part of your force does work—the part in the same direction as the motion of the sled. The rest of your force does not help pull the sled forward.

Figure 2 You may be making a great effort, but if the car doesn't move, you do no work.

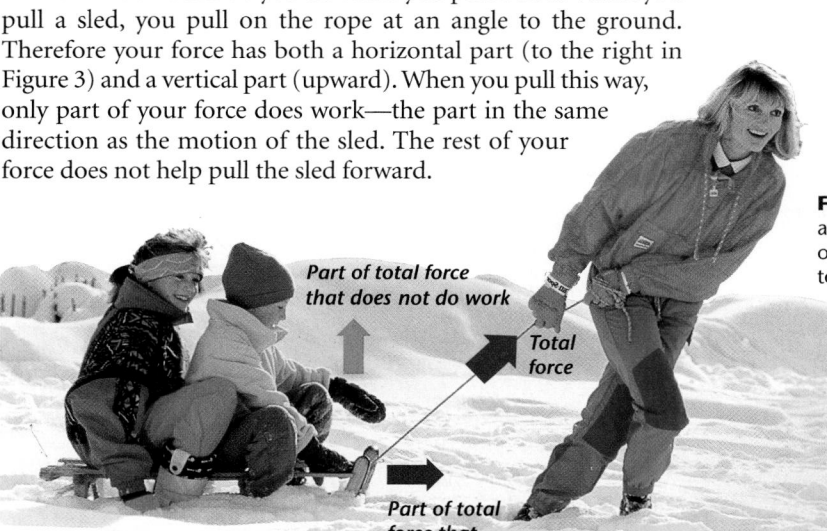

Part of total force that does not do work

Total force

Part of total force that pulls sled

Figure 3 When you pull a sled with a rope, not all of your force does work to move the sled.

The Meaning of Work

Including All Students

To assist students who are still mastering English, have all students assemble several pictures that illustrate the various meanings of the word *work*. For example, in Figure 1, one picture shows the girl exerting a force to do work, and the other picture shows the girl exerting a force but doing no work. Ask students to indicate which pictures reflect the scientific definition of work. (*Students should indicate pictures in which an object is moved by a force acting in the direction of the motion.*) **limited English proficiency**

Using the Visuals: Figure 3

As students examine the photograph, have them point to the forces that are exerted on the sled. (*Some force pulls the sled upward and some force pulls the sled forward.*) Have students consider how much work it takes to move the sled. Explain that whatever direction the woman pulls, only the portion of the force in the direction of motion does work. Ask: **What could the woman do to increase the part of the force that does work on the sled?** (*She could pull the rope horizontally.*) **learning modality: visual**

Program Resources

◆ **Unit 2 Resources** 7-1 Lesson Plan, p. 93; 7-1 Section Summary, p. 94
◆ **Guided Reading and Study Workbook** Section 7-1

Answers to Self-Assessment

Caption Question

Figure 1 When she carries the bin, the girl exerts a force on the bin. However, because none of the force is in the same direction as the bin is moving, no work is done.

Ongoing Assessment

Drawing Have students draw two diagrams that show a person exerting force on a ball. In one diagram, the person should do work on the ball; in the other the person should *not* do work on the ball.

 Students can save their diagrams in their portfolios.

The Meaning of Work, continued

Inferring

Time 10 minutes

Tips No work is done by Earth on the satellite because the force is always at right angles to the motion. Diagrams should indicate the satellite's motion (tangential to Earth) and the force of gravity (down toward the center of Earth).

Extend Ask students: **When an object speeds up or slows down, is work being done? Why?** *(Yes, because force is in the same direction as motion.)* **learning modality: logical/mathematical**

Calculating Work

Integrating Mathematics

Materials *spring scale; meter stick; three objects of different weights*

Time 15 minutes

Tips Pair students and have them find the force necessary to lift several objects a distance of 1 meter. Students should then calculate the amount of work done when each object is lifted and record the answer in joules. Ask: **What happens to the amount of work done when the force needed to lift up an object increases?** *(The amount of work increases.)* **learning modality: logical/mathematical**

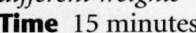

Sample Problem

Encourage good problem-solving techniques by making sure students always write the formula first, substitute known values, then solve.

Practice Problems
1. 12,000 N × 2 m = 24,000 J
2. 0.2 N × 1.5 m = 0.3 J

Inferring ACTIVITY

You do work when you drag your family's trash cans out to the curb. You exert a force and the trash cans move. Does this mean that work is always done on an object if the object is moving? Recall how a satellite orbits Earth. Is work done on the satellite as it orbits? Draw a diagram to support your answer.

If you did the Discover activity, you know that your effort will be more effective when you reduce the angle at which you push or pull an object. That is, exert as much of your force as possible in the direction of the object's motion. Keep this in mind the next time you rake a pile of leaves or vacuum a floor.

☑ *Checkpoint* How can you determine if work is done on an object?

Calculating Work

Which do you think involves more work: exerting a force of 100 N to lift a potted tree a meter off the ground or exerting a force of 200 N to lift a heavier tree to the same height? Is it more work to lift a tree from the ground to a wheelbarrow or from the ground to the top story of a building? Your common sense may suggest that lifting a heavier object, which demands a greater force, requires more work than lifting a lighter object. Also, moving an object a greater distance requires more work than moving the object a shorter distance. Both of these are true.

The amount of work you do depends on both the amount of force you exert and the distance the object moves:

$$\text{Work} = \text{Force} \times \text{Distance}$$

The amount of work done on an object can be determined by multiplying force times distance.

Sample Problem

To help rearrange the furniture in your classroom, you exert a force of 20 N to push a desk 10 m. How much work do you do?

Analyze. You know the force exerted on the desk and the distance the desk moved. You want to find the amount of work done. Draw a diagram similar to the one shown to help you.

Write the formula. Work = Force × Distance

Substitute and solve. Work = 20 N × 10 m

Work = 200 N·m, which is 200 J

Force = 20 N

Think about it. The answer tells you that the work you do on the desk is 200 J.

Distance = 10 m

Practice Problems

1. A hydraulic lift exerts a force of 12,000 N to lift a car 2 m. How much work is done on the car?
2. You exert a force of 0.2 N to lift a pencil off the floor. How much work do you do if you lift it 1.5 m?

Background

History of Science The metric unit *joule* is named after James Prescott Joule (1818–1889). Joule was born in Salford, England. After training as a scientist Joule built a laboratory in his father's house and used it to conduct experiments and try out new inventions. Among other important discoveries, he calculated the amount of work needed to produce a unit of heat. By performing increasingly precise experiments with many different materials, he was able to show that the same amount of mechanical work always produced the same amount of heat. This is usually called the "mechanical equivalent of heat."

INTEGRATING MATHEMATICS When force is measured in newtons and distance is measured in meters, the SI unit of work is the newton × meter (N·m). This unit is also called a joule (JOOL) in honor of James Prescott Joule, a physicist who studied work in the middle 1800s. One **joule** (J) is the amount of work you do when you exert a force of 1 newton to move an object a distance of 1 meter.

With the work formula, you can compare the amount of work you do to lift the trees. When you lift an object at constant speed, the upward force you exert must be equal to the object's weight. To lift the first tree, you would have to exert a force of 100 newtons. If you were to raise it 1 meter, you would do 100 newtons × 1 meter, or 100 joules of work. To lift the heavier tree, you would have to exert a force of 200 newtons. So the amount of work you do would be 200 newtons × 1 meter, or 200 joules. Thus you do more work to move the heavier object.

Now think about lifting the tree higher. You did 100 joules of work lifting it 1 meter. Suppose an elevator lifted the same tree to the top floor of a building 40 meters tall. The elevator would exert the same force on the tree for a greater distance. The work done would be 100 newtons × 40 meters, or 4,000 joules. The elevator would do 40 times as much work as you did.

Figure 4 These students are doing work as they transplant a tree. *Inferring How much work would they do if the tree weighed twice as much? If they had to lift it four times as far?*

Section 1 Review

1. If you exert a force, do you always do work? Explain your answer.
2. What is the formula for calculating work?
3. Compare the amount of work done when a force of 2 N moves an object 3 meters with the work done when a force of 3 N moves an object 2 meters.
4. **Thinking Critically** **Applying Concepts** You need to move five large cans of paint from the basement to the second floor of a house. Will you do more work on the cans of paint if you take them up all at once (if possible) or if you take them up individually? Explain.

CHAPTER PROJECT 7

Check Your Progress
Determine the amount of work that your machine must do to lift a 600-g soup can 5 cm. Draw a diagram showing the forces involved and the direction of those forces. Jot down some suggestions for accomplishing this work. Brainstorm with classmates about what materials you could use to build your machine.

Chapter 7 **207**

Program Resources

◆ **Unit 2 Resources** 7-1 Review and Reinforce, p. 95; 7-1 Enrich, p. 96

Media and Technology

 Transparencies "Work and Force," Transparency 20

Answers to Self-Assessment

Caption Question

Figure 4 If the tree weighed twice as much, they would do twice as much work. If they lifted it four times as far, they would do four times as much work.

☑ *Checkpoint*

The object moves some distance in the direction of the force that you exerted on it.

---

3 Assess

Section 1 Review Answers

1. No. Force must cause motion that is in the same direction as the force.
2. Work = Force × Distance
3. The same amount of work is done because work is the product of force and distance. Both equal 6 J of work.
4. You will do the same amount of work whether you take the cans up all at once or individually. The total force and the total distance are the same.

CHAPTER PROJECT 7

Check Your Progress
In order to determine the amount of work their machine must do, students will need to convert 600 g to newtons, and 5 cm to m *(5.88 N, 0.05 m)*. Remind students of the difference between weight and mass (Chapter 2), and show them how to do the conversion.

600 g / 1,000 g/kg = 0.6 kg
0.6 kg × 9.8 m/s^2 = 5.88 N
5.88 N × 0.05 m = 0.29 J

To draw diagrams with force arrows, students will need to consider the direction of the force and whether force is applied to their machine from the top, side, or bottom. Once they have decided what simple machine to use to lift the soup can, they can choose another simple machine to apply force to the first.

Performance Assessment

Oral Presentation Have students work in groups of three. One student performs an activity, such as holding a book, walking around while holding a book, moving a book across a table, or lifting a book from the floor. The second student states whether work is being done. The third students either agrees or disagrees, and explains why.

207

Objectives

After completing the lesson, students will be able to
◆ explain what machines do and how they make work easier;
◆ identify the difference between actual and ideal mechanical advantage;
◆ calculate the efficiency of a machine.

Key Terms machine, input force, output force, mechanical advantage, efficiency, actual mechanical advantage, ideal mechanical advantage

1 Engage/Explore

Activating Prior Knowledge

Show the class a kitchen spoon, a whisk, and an egg beater. Ask: **Which tool do you think is the best one to use to mix cake batter? Why?** *(Most students will infer that all the tools can be used, but that the egg beater makes the work easier, particularly if the batter is heavy.)*

•••••••• **DISCOVER** ••••••••

Skills Focus forming **ACTIVITY**
operational definitions
Materials *objects that are machines—pliers, corkscrew, blunt knife, can opener, screwdriver, broom; objects that are not machines—eraser, pencil, chalk, paper, ruler, ball, book*
Time 20 minutes
Tips Assign students to small groups and give them a few objects to examine. Once a group has classified an object, they should pass it along to another group. Make sure students list the criteria they used to classify the objects. Allow students to classify machines based on their own criteria.
Think It Over Students may say that objects that were machines could do work or make work easier. Or they may say a machine helps you to exert force.

DISCOVER •••••••••••••••••••••••••••••••••••• **ACTIVITY••••**

Is It a Machine?

1. Your teacher will give you an assortment of objects. Examine each object closely.

2. Sort the objects into those that you think are machines and those you think are not machines.

3. Determine how each object that you have identified as a machine functions. Explain each object to another student.

Think It Over
Forming Operational Definitions Why did you decide certain objects were machines while other objects were not?

GUIDE FOR READING

◆ **How do machines make work easier?**

◆ **What is the difference between actual and ideal mechanical advantage?**

◆ **How can you calculate the efficiency of a machine?**

Reading Tip As you read, use the headings to make an outline showing what machines do.

A truckload of mulch for your new garden has just arrived. The only problem is that the pile of mulch has been dumped 10 meters from where it belongs. What can you do? You could move the mulch by handfuls, but that would take a very long time. You could use a shovel and a wheelbarrow, which would make the job much easier. Or you could have a bulldozer move it. That would make the job easier still.

What Is a Machine?

Shovels and bulldozers are examples of machines. A **machine** is a device with which you can do work in a way that is easier or more effective. You may be used to thinking of machines as complex gadgets that run on electricity, but a machine can be as simple as a shovel or even a ramp.

Perhaps you think that a machine decreases the amount of work that is done. But it doesn't. Moving the pile of mulch, for example, will involve the same amount of work no matter how you do it. Similarly, you have to do the same amount of work to lift a piano whether you lift it by hand or push it up a ramp.

208

READING STRATEGIES

Reading Tip Write the following outline guide on the board. Review each item with students before they create outlines that show what machines do.
I. First Main Idea
   A. First supporting idea or fact.
      1. detail or example
      2. detail or example
   B. Second supporting idea or fact.
II. Second Main Idea (outline will continue)

Vocabulary Lead a discussion of the terms *input force* and *output force*. Then have students name other uses of *input* and *output* with which they are familiar.

Study and Comprehension Assign each of three students in a group one of the Guide for Reading questions. Allow time for students to reread the section to make notes on the answer to their question. Then have students present their answers to the group.

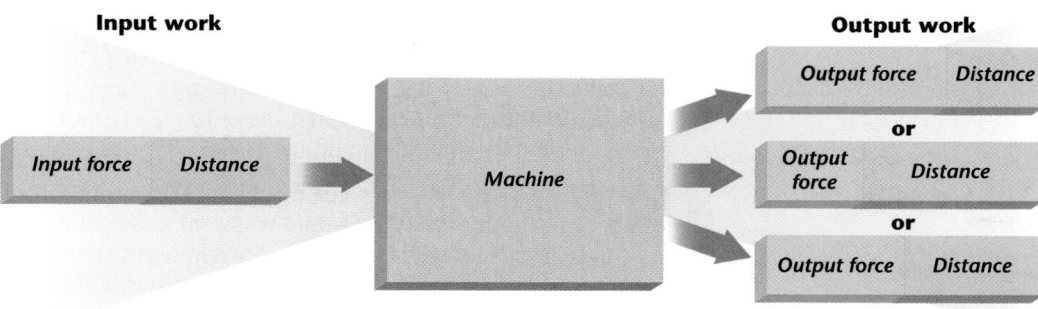

Input work

Input force | Distance

Output work

Output force | Distance

or

Output force | Distance

or

Output force | Distance

Machine

Figure 5 A machine can make a task easier in one of three ways. *Interpreting Diagrams How does the output force compare to the input force in each type of machine?*

What the shovel and the ramp do is to change the way in which you do the work. **A machine makes work easier by changing the amount of force you exert, the distance over which you exert your force, or the direction in which you exert your force.** You might say that a machine makes work easier by multiplying either force or distance, or by changing direction.

When you do work with a machine, you exert a force over some distance. For example, you exert a force on the handle when you use a shovel to lift mulch. The force you exert on the machine is called the **input force,** or sometimes the effort force. The machine then does work, by exerting a force over some distance. The shovel, in this case, exerts a force to lift the mulch. The force exerted by the machine is called the **output force.** Sometimes the term resistance force is used instead, because the machine must overcome some resistance.

Multiplying Force In some machines, the output force is greater than the input force. How can you exert a smaller force than is necessary for a job if the amount of work is the same? Remember the formula for work: Work = Force × Distance. If the amount of work stays the same, a decrease in force must mean an increase in distance. So if a machine allows you to use less force to do some amount of work, you must apply the input force over a greater distance. In the end, you do as much work with the machine as you would without the machine, but the work is easier to do.

What kind of device might allow you to exert a smaller force over a longer distance? Think about a ramp. Suppose you have to lift a piano onto the stage in your school auditorium. You could try to lift it vertically, or you could push it up a ramp.

Input force

Output force

Figure 6 The input force exerted on the shovel is greater than the output force exerted by the shovel.

Program Resources

◆ **Unit 2 Resources** 7-2 Lesson Plan, p. 97; 7-2 Section Summary, p. 98
◆ **Guided Reading and Study Workbook** Section 7-2

Answers to Self-Assessment

Caption Question

Figure 5 In the top machine, output force is greater than input force. In the middle machine, output force is less than input force. In the bottom machine, output force is equal to input force.

2 Facilitate

What Is a Machine?

Using the Visuals: Figure 5

Have students compare the total amount of input work with the total amount of output work. Ask students: **How does the total input work compare to the total output work in each type of machine?** (*The same*) **How do the distances compare?** (*different for the top two machines, the same for the bottom machine, where only the direction of the force changes*) Ask: **If you wanted to exert more force, which machine should you use?** (*The machine with the smaller distance*) Reinforce that a machine does not change the amount of work required—only force, distance, or direction. **learning modality: visual**

Building Inquiry Skills: Interpreting Illustrations

To help students understand the difference between input and output force, give them five pictures of machines taken from magazines or newspapers. Pair students and have them label the pictures with a marker, identifying the machine, the input force, and the output force. To further challenge students, ask them to infer whether the machine multiplies the input force, multiplies the distance over which the input force is exerted, or changes the direction of the input force. **learning modality: logical/mathematical**

Ongoing Assessment

Oral Presentation Ask students to explain how a snow shovel makes clearing a sidewalk easier. Students' explanations should use the terms input force and output force. (*The snow shovel takes the input force exerted on the handle and multiplies it to lift and move the snow.*)

209

What is a Machine?, continued

Including All Students

Some students may need extra help with understanding what happens when a machine multiplies force. Allow students to work in pairs to build a ramp with a board and a wooden block. Have students measure the length of their ramps and the height of their blocks. Ask: **Which measurement is greater?** *(The length of the ramp)* Fasten a string around a book and give students a spring scale to weigh the book. Then ask students to predict whether they would use more force lifting the book or pulling it up a ramp. *(Lifting it)* Allow students to test their predictions. Guide them to conclude that a ramp allows them to use less input force to do the work; thus, it multiplies the input force. **learning modality: kinesthetic**

Inquiry Challenge

Materials *meter stick, ruler, 2-cm stack of newspapers, desk or table*
Time 15 minutes
Tips In this activity, students compare the mechanical advantage of two machines by making observations about the force needed to operate each. Organize students in small groups. To carry out the activity, have students place a 2-cm stack of newspapers on the edge of a desk or table. Students should slip a ruler under the stack so that 15 cm of the ruler is resting on the table. Then they can lift the stack of newspapers by pressing down on the end of the ruler with one finger. Next have students repeat the procedure with the meter stick. Ask: **Which lifter has the greater mechanical advantage?** *(The meter stick.)*
Extend Challenge students to design a method to calculate the output force, input force, and mechanical advantage for the ruler and meter stick.
cooperative learning

If you use the ramp, the distance over which you must exert your force is greater than if you lift the piano directly. This is because the length of the ramp is greater than the height of the stage. The advantage of the ramp, then, is that it allows you to exert a smaller force to push the piano than to lift it.

Multiplying Distance In some machines, the output force is less than the input force. Why would you want to use a machine like this? The advantage of this kind of machine is that it allows you to exert your input force over a shorter distance than you would without the machine. For you to apply a force over a shorter distance, you need to apply a greater force.

When do you use this kind of machine? Think about taking a shot with a hockey stick. You move your hands a short distance, but the other end of the stick moves a greater distance to hit the puck. The hockey puck moves much faster than your hands. What happens when you fold up a sheet of paper and wave it back and forth to fan yourself? You move your hand a short distance, but the other end of the paper moves a longer distance to cool you off on a warm day. And when you ride a bicycle in high gear, you apply a large force to the pedals over a short distance. The bicycle, meanwhile, moves a much longer distance.

Changing Direction Some machines don't multiply either force or distance. What could be the advantage of these machines? Well, think about raising the sail in Figure 7. You could raise the sail by climbing the mast of the boat and pulling up on the sail with a rope. But it is much easier to stand on the deck and pull down than to lift up. By running a rope through the top of the mast as shown, you can raise the sail by pulling down on the rope. This rope system is a machine that makes your job easier by changing the direction in which you exert your force.

☑ *Checkpoint* **What are three ways in which a machine can make work easier?**

Figure 7 One, two, three, pull! Up goes the sail. This sailor pulls down on the rope in order to hoist the sail into position. *Applying Concepts Why is the rope system considered a machine?*

210

Background

Facts and Figures Many machines make work easier because of automation—they are automatically controlled by mechanical or electronic devices.

Unlike machines such as shovels, axes, or even hockey sticks, automated machines usually don't require human effort, other than the initial effort required to turn them on. Today, machines such as dishwashers, washing machines, bread machines, video recorders, and CD players are controlled by tiny computers called microprocessors. All the operator has to do is to program the controller to carry out the function of the machine.

However automated they are, machines are still machines. They do not change the amount of work to be done, they just make the work easier.

Figure 8 Chop, chop, chop. A knife is a machine that makes your work easier when you prepare a tasty meal.

Mechanical Advantage

If you compare the input force to the output force, you can determine the advantage of using a machine. **A machine's mechanical advantage is the number of times a force exerted on a machine is multiplied by the machine.** Finding the ratio of output force to input force gives you the **mechanical advantage** of a machine.

$$\text{Mechanical advantage} = \frac{\text{Output force}}{\text{Input force}}$$

Mechanical Advantage of Multiplying Force For a machine that multiplies force, the mechanical advantage is greater than 1. That is because the output force is greater than the input force. For example, consider a manual can opener. If you exert a force of 20 newtons on the opener, and the opener exerts a force of 60 newtons on a can, the mechanical advantage of the can opener is 60 newtons ÷ 20 newtons, or 3. The can opener tripled your force! Or suppose you would have to exert 3,200 newtons to lift a piano. If you use a ramp, you might need to exert only 1,600 newtons. The mechanical advantage of this ramp is 3,200 newtons ÷ 1,600 newtons, or 2. The ramp doubles the force that you exert.

Mechanical Advantage of Multiplying Distance For a machine that multiplies distance, the output force is less than the input force. So in this case, the mechanical advantage is less than 1. If, for example, you exert an input force of 20 newtons and the machine produces an output force of 10 newtons, the mechanical advantage is 10 newtons ÷ 20 newtons, or 0.5. The output force of the machine is half your input force, but the machine exerts that force over a longer distance.

Mechanical Advantage of Changing Direction What can you predict about the mechanical advantage of a machine that changes the direction of the force? If only the direction changes, the input force will be the same as the output force. The mechanical advantage will be 1.

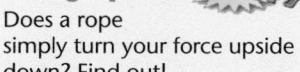

Going Up **ACTIVITY**

Does a rope simply turn your force upside down? Find out!

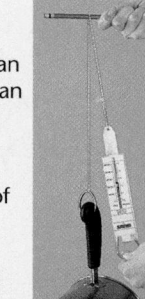

1. Tie a piece of string about 50 cm long to an object, such as an empty cooking pot. Make a small loop on the other end of the string.
2. Using a spring scale, slowly lift the pot 20 cm. Note the reading on the scale.
3. Now loop the string over a pencil and pull down on the spring scale to lift the pot 20 cm. Predict the reading on the scale. Were you correct?

Developing Hypotheses How did the readings on the spring scale compare? If the readings were different, suggest a reason why. What might be an advantage to using this system?

Chapter 7 **211**

Media and Technology

 Transparencies "Machines," Transparency 21

 Concept Videotape Library *Adventures, Tape 2,* "Work, Work, Work"

Answers to Self-Assessment

Caption Question

Figure 7 The rope system is considered a machine because it changes the direction of force to make work easier.

☑ *Checkpoint*

Machines can make work easier by multiplying input force, by increasing the output distance, or by changing the direction of the input force.

Mechanical Advantage

Addressing Naïve Conceptions

Some students may incorrectly assume that a machine with a mechanical advantage less than 1 is not a useful machine. Ask students to name a machine that makes work easier by multiplying the distance over which the input force acts. *(Sample: baseball bat, wooden spoon, bicycle)* Then ask them to describe the mechanical advantage of a machine that increases distance. *(Less than 1)* Help students conclude that a machine with an mechanical advantage of less than 1 may still be a useful machine. **learning modality: logical/mathematical**

TRY THIS

Skills Focus developing hypotheses
Materials *small cooking pot, 50-cm string or twine, 20-N spring scale, pencil*
Time 15 minutes
Tips Pair students. Before the activity, invite students to infer what they think will happen with the rope system. Students should find that it takes about 3 N to lift the pot directly with the spring scale, and about 6 N to lift the pot by looping the string over the pencil. Help students analyze their results by asking them to compare the amount of friction on the string in Steps 2 and 3.
Developing Hypotheses The reading on the spring scale was higher when the pot was lifted by a string looped over a pencil. Students may say that the readings were different because additional force was needed to overcome the friction between the pencil and the string in order to lift the pot in Step 3. The advantage to using the pencil is that it is easier to pull down than to pull up.
Extend Have students find the force needed to raise another pot when a pulley is used, then compare their results with the first activity. **learning modality: visual**

Ongoing Assessment

Skills Check Have students find the mechanical advantage of a lever if they exert 10 N to push it down and it exerts a force of 30 N to raise a box. *(3)*

Efficiency of Machines

Including All Students

Students whose native language is not English may have difficulty pronouncing the term *efficiency*. Provide all students with a phonetic spelling, such as *e FI shuhn see*. **limited English proficiency**

 Integrating Mathematics

Guide students in interpreting the equation for efficiency. Ask: **Will the fraction output work/input work ever equal a value higher than 1? Why or why not?** (*No, output work is always less than input work because some work is always used to overcome friction.*) Then ask students to analyze the following machine: When the machine is properly maintained, it has an output work of 12 J for every 24 J of input work. When the machine is not properly maintained (needs to sharpened, lubricated, cleaned, etc.), the machine has an output work of 8 J. Ask: **How efficient is the machine when it is properly maintained? When it is not properly maintained?** (*properly maintained = (12/24) × 100% = 50%; not properly maintained: = (8/24) × 100% = 33%*) **learning modality: logical/mathematical**

Sample Problem

Be sure students are careful to divide the output work by the input work, otherwise they will calculate efficiencies over 100%. Reemphasize writing the formula first before substituting values. Some students may need a brief refresher in the meaning of percent and why the fraction is multiplied by 100.

Practice Problems

1. Efficiency = (825/1,500) × 100% = 55%
2. 40%

Efficiency of Machines

So far you have learned that the work you put into a machine (input work) is exactly equal to the work done by the machine (output work). In an ideal situation, this is true. In real situations, however, the output work is always less than the input work. If you have ever tried to cut something with scissors that barely open and close, you know that a large part of your work is wasted overcoming the tightness, or friction, between the parts of the scissors.

In any machine, some work is wasted overcoming friction. The less friction there is, the closer the output work is to the input work. The **efficiency** of a machine compares the output work to the input work. Efficiency is expressed as a percent. The higher the percent, the more efficient the machine is.

If the tight scissors described above have an efficiency of 60%, a little more than half of the work you do goes into cutting the paper. The rest is wasted overcoming the friction in the scissors. A machine that has an efficiency of 95% loses very little work. An ideal machine would have an efficiency of 100%.

You cut the lawn with a hand lawn mower. You do 250,000 J of work to move the mower. If the work done by the mower in cutting the lawn is 200,000 J, what is the efficiency of the lawn mower?

Analyze. You are given the input work and the output work. You are asked to find the efficiency.

Write the formula.
$$\text{Efficiency} = \frac{\text{Output work}}{\text{Input work}} \times 100\%$$

Substitute and solve.
$$\text{Efficiency} = \frac{200,000}{250,000} \times 100\%$$

$$\text{Efficiency} = 0.8 \times 100\% = 80\%$$

Think about it. An efficiency of 80% means that 80 out of every 100 joules of work went into cutting the lawn. This answer makes sense, because most of the input work is converted to output work.

Practice Problems

1. You do 1,500 J of work in using a hammer. The hammer does 825 J of work on a nail. What is the efficiency of the hammer?
2. Suppose you left your lawn mower outdoors all winter. It's now rusty. Of your 250,000 joules of work, only 100,000 go to cutting the lawn. What is the efficiency of the lawn mower now?

Background

History of Science For many years, inventors and scientists were fascinated with the idea of a perpetual motion machine, which is a machine that runs continually with no input work. In 1150, a Hindu mathematician described a wheel that spun continually as weights swung outward on one side and inward on the other. Although many tried to build such a machine, it always failed. A perpetual motion machine of this kind will not work because all machines have efficiencies of less than 100%. Some work is always wasted in overcoming friction.

In the 18th century, James Cox designed a self-winding clock that used a barometer to drive the clockworks. It appeared to be a perpetual motion machine, but it actually received additional power from changes in the atmosphere.

Calculating Efficiency If you know the input work and output work for a machine, you can calculate a machine's efficiency. **To calculate the efficiency of a machine, divide the output work by the input work and multiply the result by 100 percent.** This is summarized by the following formula.

$$\text{Efficiency} = \frac{\text{Output work}}{\text{Input work}} \times 100\%$$

Actual and Ideal Mechanical Advantage The mechanical advantage that a machine provides in a real situation is called the **actual mechanical advantage.** You can only determine the actual mechanical advantage by measuring the true input and output forces. It cannot be determined in advance because the actual values depend on the efficiency of the machine.

You cannot predict the actual mechanical advantage of a machine. But you can predict a quantity related to the actual mechanical advantage if you ignore losses due to friction. In other words, you can consider the machine under ideal conditions. **The mechanical advantage of a machine without friction is called the ideal mechanical advantage of the machine.** The more efficient a machine is, the closer the actual mechanical advantage is to the **ideal mechanical advantage.** By keeping a machine clean and well lubricated, you can make its operation closer to the ideal. In this way you can increase the machine's efficiency and make your own work easier.

Math TOOLBOX

Percents

When you compare a number to 100, you are finding a percent. For example, 25 out of 100 can be written as 25 ÷ 100 or 25%.

Any ratio can be written as a percent by multiplying the fraction by 100 ÷ 1 and expressing the answer with a percent symbol. For example,

$$\frac{11}{20} \times \frac{100}{1} = 55\%$$

$$\frac{3}{4} \times \frac{100}{1} = 75\%$$

The efficiency of a machine is compared to an ideal machine, which would be 100% efficient.

Section 2 Review

1. Explain how machines make work easier if they do not decrease the amount of work you need to do.
2. Why is the actual mechanical advantage of a machine different from a machine's ideal mechanical advantage?
3. What do you need to know to calculate the efficiency of a machine?
4. Can a machine increase both force and distance? Explain why or why not.
5. **Thinking Critically** Comparing and Contrasting Make a comparison table for two machines: one that increases force and one that increases distance. For each machine, compare input and output force, input and output distance, and input and output work.

Science at Home

Have a family member examine a hand-powered device around your home. You might pick a hand tool such as a shovel, hammer, or screwdriver, or a kitchen utensil such as a knife or egg beater. Explain the idea of input and output forces. Then have him or her identify the input and output forces for the device you picked.

Program Resources

◆ **Unit 2 Resources** 7-2 Review and Reinforce, p. 99; 7-2 Enrich, p. 100

Math TOOLBOX

Explain to students that *percent* comes from the Latin words meaning "by the hundreds." Point out that students can find the percent of a number written as a decimal by moving the decimal two places to the right. **learning modality: logical/mathematical**

3 Assess

Section 2 Review Answers

1. Machines change the amount of an input force required, the input distance required, and/or the direction of a force.
2. Some work is used to overcome friction.
3. Output work and input work
4. No, if one is increased the other is decreased.
5.

Sample Answer Table			
For a machine that	Force	Distance	Work
increases force	input less than output	input greater than output	input greater than output
increases distance	input greater than output	input less than output	input greater than output

Science at Home

Sample answers: You exert input force on a hammer when you swing it; the hammer exerts output force when it hits a nail.

Performance Assessment

Writing Have students imagine that they are engineering consultants for a lawn-mower manufacturer. They must explain why the actual mechanical advantage of their latest lawn mower is only 80% of its ideal mechanical advantage.

Seesaw Science

Preparing for Inquiry

Key Concept Distance from the pivot point and the amount of input force play equal roles in determining the effect of the force on each side of a seesaw ($w_1d_1 = w_2d_2$).

Skills Objectives Students will be able to
- control variables to determine the effect of a particular variable;
- make predictions about where to place a load to balance a seesaw;
- draw conclusions about how various factors affect a seesaw.

Time 30 minutes

Advance Planning Gather meter sticks, masking tape, pennies (or washers, hex nuts, or other standard sized objects), 50-g masses, and dowels or other cylindrical objects for pivot point.

Guiding Inquiry

Invitation Ask students: **What happens when an adult gets on one end of a seesaw and a child on the other?** Model this for students using a meter stick. Place the dowel at 50 cm for the pivot point. Put ten pennies on one end of the meter stick and five pennies on the other. Then ask students: **What can we do to make the meter stick balance?** Students may suggest that you could move the ten pennies closer to the dowel. Do this, then ask students if there is another way to balance the meter stick. They may suggest moving the pivot point closer to the ten pennies.

Introducing the Procedure

Have the students read the procedure. Then ask them what variables are being changed and what variables are being held constant. (*Changed: number of pennies; held constant: pivot point, position of eight pennies*)

Troubleshooting the Experiment

- Students should position the meter stick so that the pivot point is on the center of the dowel. The meter stick will tend to move as it is used, and should be readjusted before each trial.

214

Seesaw Science

In this lab, you will use the skill of controlling variables as you investigate the properties of seesaws.

Problem

What is the relationship between distance and weight for a balanced seesaw?

Materials

meter stick
masking tape
28 pennies, post-1982
small object, mass about 50 g
dowel or other cylindrical object for pivot point, about 10 cm long and 3 cm in diameter

Procedure

1. Begin by using the dowel and meter stick to build a seesaw. Tape the dowel firmly to the table so that it does not roll.

2. Choose the meter stick mark that will rest on the dowel from the following: 55 cm or 65 cm. Record your choice. Position your meter stick so that it is on your chosen pivot point with the 100-cm mark on your right.

3. Slide the 50-g mass along the shorter end of the meter stick until the meter stick is balanced, with both sides in the air. (This is called "zeroing" your meter stick.)

4. Copy the data table into your notebook.

5. Place a stack of 8 pennies exactly over the 80-cm mark. Determine the distance, in centimeters, from the pivot point to the pennies. Record this distance in the "Distance to Pivot" column for the right side of the seesaw.

6. Predict where you must place a stack of 5 pennies in order to balance the meter stick. Test your prediction and record the actual position in the "Position of Pennies" column for the left side of the seesaw.

DATA TABLE

Your group's pivot point position: _____ cm

Trial #	Side of Seesaw	# of Pennies or Weight of Pennies (pw)	Position of Pennies (cm)	Distance to Pivot (cm)	Weight of Pennies × Distance
1	right				
	left				
2	right				
	left				
3	right				

214

Sample Data Table

Your group's pivot point position: 55 cm

Trial #	Side of Seesaw	# of Pennies	Position of Pennies (cm mark)	Distance to Pivot (cm)	Weight of Pennies x Distance
1	right	8	80	25	200
	left	5	15	40	200
2	right	8	80	25	200
	left	7	26.4	28.6	200.2
3	right	8	80	25	200
	left	12	38.3	16.7	200.4
4	right	8	80	25	200
	left	16	42.5	12.5	200
5	right	8	80	25	200
	left	20	45	10.0	200

7. Determine the distance, in centimeters, from the pivot point to the left stack of pennies. Record this distance in the "Distance to Pivot" column for the left side of the seesaw.

8. If you use an imaginary unit of weight, the pennyweight (pw), then one penny weighs 1 pw. Multiply the weight of each stack of pennies by the distance to the pivot point. Record the result in the last column of the data table.

9. Predict how the position of the pennies in Step 6 would change if you used 7, 12, 16, and 20 pennies instead of 5 pennies. Test your predictions.

Analyze and Conclude

1. In this experiment, what is the manipulated variable? The responding variable? How do you know which is which?

2. As you increase the number of pennies on the right, what happens to the distance at which you must place the stack in order to balance the meter stick?

3. What conclusion can you draw about the relationship between distances and weights needed to balance a seesaw?

4. Why was it important to zero the meter stick with the 50-g mass?

5. Compare your results with the other groups. How do different positions of the pivot point affect the results?

6. **Think About It** Name two other variables that could be manipulated in this experiment.

Design an Experiment

Suppose you have a seesaw with a movable pivot. You want to use it with a friend who weighs half what you weigh. You and your friend want to sit on the two ends of the seesaw. Make a hypothesis about where you should position the pivot point. Explain how you could modify the pennies experiment to see if you are right.

◆ Students should measure the position of the center of the stack of pennies to the nearest tenth of a centimeter.

Expected Outcome
Students' data should illustrate that a large weight close to the pivot point can be compensated by a small weight far from the pivot point (and vice versa).

Analyze and Conclude
1. Manipulated variable: the weight on the left side of the pivot point, because it is the variable that is being changed in each trial; responding variable: distance of that weight from the pivot point needed to achieve balance, because it changes as a result of the change in weight

2. As the number of pennies on the left increases, the distance must be decreased to balance the seesaw.

3. For a balanced seesaw, the product of weight and distance from the pivot point on the left is equal to the product of weight and distance from the pivot point on the right ($w_1d_1 = w_2d_2$). Weight and distance have equal importance in balancing the seesaw.

4. To ensure that the meter stick is balanced before you begin

5. For all groups, ($w_1d_1 = w_2d_2$). Different positions of the pivot point do not affect the result.

6. Accept any two: the distance of the weight on the left, the pivot point, the weight on the right, the distance on the left.

Design an Experiment
Students should hypothesize that the distance of the smaller student from the pivot point should be twice the distance of the larger student from the pivot point. For example, for a seesaw 3 m long, the distance of the smaller student from the pivot point should be 2 m, and the distance of the larger student from the pivot point should be 1 m. To test the ideal value (neglecting the weight of the seesaw), students could first zero the balance. One way a student could modify the experiment to test his or her hypothesis is to place five weights at 95 cm, ten weights at 5 cm, and the pivot point at 35 cm.

Objectives

After completing the lesson, students will be able to

◆ describe the six types of simple machines;

◆ calculate the ideal mechanical advantage of four types of simple machines;

◆ define compound machines.

Key Terms inclined plane, wedge, screw, lever, fulcrum, wheel and axle, pulley, compound machine, gears

1 Engage/Explore

Activating Prior Knowledge

From a selection of ordinary household objects, such as chopsticks, table knives, screwdrivers, and so on, show students examples of each kind of simple machine. Have students describe how each machine works and how it differs from the others.

DISCOVER

Skills Focus predicting
Materials *2 broomsticks or dowels, long rope*
Time 15 minutes
Tips After students have pulled the broomsticks together using the rope, ask: **What did the rope do to the force?** *(It multiplied the force exerted on the rope.)* Encourage students to test the predictions they make in Think It Over.
Expected Outcome Students should find it extremely difficult, if not impossible, to bring the students together by pulling on the broomsticks. They will be able to bring the brooms together by pulling on the rope.
Think It Over Wrapping the rope several more times will increase the force exerted on the broomsticks. However, at some point the friction will become too great. Lubricating the sticks with vegetable oil or using a nylon rope will reduce friction.

216

DISCOVER ·· ACTIVITY

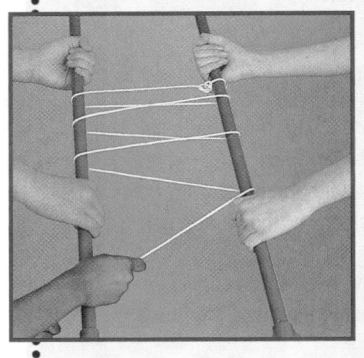

How Can You Increase Your Force?

1. Working with two partners, wrap a rope around two broomsticks as shown.

2. Your two partners should try to hold the brooms apart with the same amount of force throughout the activity. For safety, they should hold firmly, but not with all their strength.

3. Try to pull the two students together by pulling on the broomsticks. Can you do it?

4. Can you pull them together by pulling on the rope?

Think It Over

Predicting What do you think will be the effect of wrapping the rope around the broomstick several more times?

GUIDE FOR READING

◆ What are the six kinds of simple machines?

◆ How can you calculate the mechanical advantage of simple machines?

Reading Tip As you read, make a list of the six kinds of simple machines. Describe each one in your own words.

Look at the objects shown on these pages. Which of them would you call machines? Would it surprise you to find out that each is an example of a simple machine? As you learned in the last section, a machine helps you do work by changing the amount or direction of the force you need to apply.

There are six basic kinds of simple machines: the inclined plane, the wedge, the screw, the lever, the wheel and axle, and the pulley. In this section you will learn how the different types of simple machines help you.

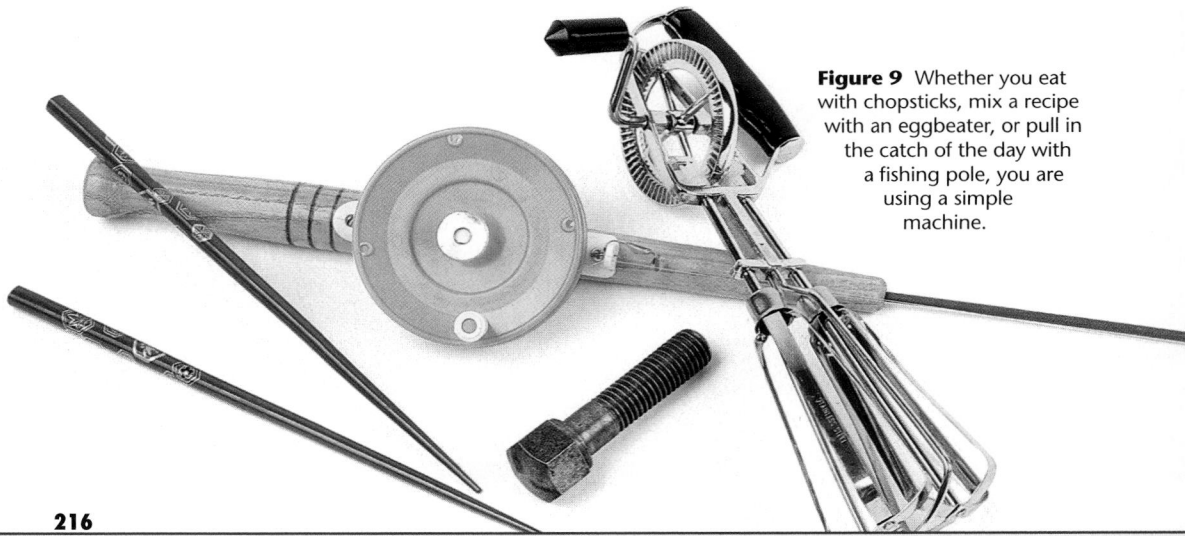

Figure 9 Whether you eat with chopsticks, mix a recipe with an eggbeater, or pull in the catch of the day with a fishing pole, you are using a simple machine.

216

READING STRATEGIES

Reading Tip Give each student six notecards. After students read the second paragraph, have them write the name of one type of simple machine on each notecard. As students read the section, instruct them to use their own words to write a description of each type of machine on the back of the card and at least one example of the machine. Pair students and have partners use the cards to quiz each other.

Study and Comprehension Before students read the section, have them preview each figure and caption. Suggest they answer these questions for each figure:

◆ What is being shown in this picture?

◆ What is the main idea of the picture?

◆ How does the information in the caption relate to what I already know?

◆ What new information did I learn from the caption?

Inclined Plane

Have you ever faced the task of lifting something from a lower level to a higher level? You probably know that the job is much easier if you have a ramp. For example, a ramp makes it much easier to push a grocery cart over a curb or a cart into a truck. A ramp is an example of a simple machine called an inclined plane. An **inclined plane** is a flat, slanted surface.

An inclined plane allows you to exert your input force over a longer distance. The input force necessary will then be less than the output force. The input force that you use on an inclined plane is the force with which you push or pull an object. The output force is the force that you would need to lift the object without the inclined plane. This force is equal to the weight of the object.

Advantage of an Inclined Plane You can determine the ideal mechanical advantage of an inclined plane by dividing the length of the incline by its height.

$$\text{Ideal mechanical advantage} = \frac{\text{Length of incline}}{\text{Height of incline}}$$

Suppose you are loading a truck that is 1 meter high and you set up a ramp 3.0 meters long, as shown in Figure 11. The ideal mechanical advantage of this inclined plane is 3.0 meters ÷ 1 meter, or 3.0. This inclined plane multiplies your input force three times.

What can you conclude about how the length of the inclined plane affects the ideal mechanical advantage? If the height of the incline does not change, increasing the length of the incline causes the ideal mechanical advantage to increase. So the longer the incline (the less steep the incline), the less input force you need to push or pull an object.

Efficiency of an Inclined Plane Even though an inclined plane has no moving parts, work is lost due to friction just as it is in any machine. The friction in this case is between the object and the inclined plane. For example, if you pull a crate up an

Figure 10 Although the amount of work is the same whether you lift the loaded cart or push it up the ramp to the truck, you need less force when you use an inclined plane.
Relating Cause and Effect What happens to the distance over which you exert your force?

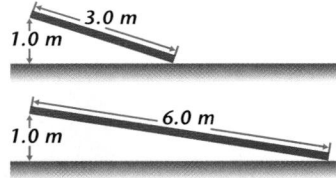

3.0 m
1.0 m

6.0 m
1.0 m

Figure 11 If you double the length of a ramp and leave its height unchanged, you double the mechanical advantage.

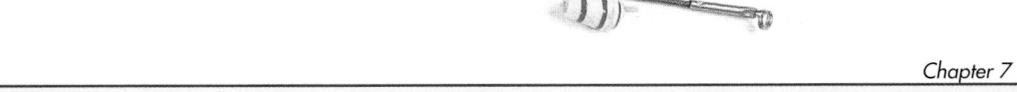

Answers to Self-Assessment

Caption Question
Figure 10 The distance increases.

2 Facilitate

Inclined Plane

Real-Life Learning

Time 20 minutes

ACTIVITY

Inform students that professional furniture movers often use ramps when they move heavy objects onto a truck or up steps into a house. Group students and challenge them to design on paper a model ramp that could be used to move a piano from a driveway into a house. Make sure the design includes control of variables. Have students calculate the ideal mechanical advantage of their ramps and prepare drawings that show where the ramp would be installed as well as its dimensions. Then have them summarize and report on their design. As a follow-up to the activity, ask: **How does increasing the length of the ramp make it easier to move the piano into the house?** *(The longer the ramp, the less effort it takes to move an object, such as a piano, up the ramp.)* **learning modality: logical/mathematical**

Portfolio Students can save their drawings in their portfolios.

Building Inquiry Skills: Problem Solving

Have students identify ways to increase the efficiency of an inclined plane. *(Sample: Put the object on wheels, put a lubricant between the plane and the object, build the inclined plane out of a smooth material)* Then ask: **Does reducing friction on an inclined plane always make it more useful?** *(Sample: No, if there is too little friction on a ramp, a person walking on the ramp may slip and fall. Also, friction can help keep an object under control if the ramp is being used to move something down.)* **learning modality: verbal**

Ongoing Assessment

Drawing Tell students to draw several different inclined planes and calculate the mechanical advantage for each plane. Drawings should include the length and height of the incline.

Wedge

Demonstration

Help students understand how a wedge can make work easier by demonstrating that a can opener is an effective machine. Begin by showing students a large, unopened juice can. Then show students the following tools: a hammer, butter knife, nail, and a hand-held can opener. Ask: **Which of these tools are wedges?** *(Nail, can opener, butter knife, claw part of hammer)* If students do not recognize the can opener as a wedge, show them the sharp-edged wheel and explain why it is a wedge. Ask: **Which tool should we use to open the can?** Ask students to describe how the wedge on the can opener uses your input force to open the can. *(The input force exerted on the handle of the can opener is multiplied by the wedge. The larger output force from the thin edge punctured the can.)* **learning modality: visual**

Building Inquiry Skills: Predicting

Materials *3 chisels of different sizes, metric ruler*
Time 10 minutes
Tips Challenge students to predict which chisel requires the least input force to achieve a desired result. After they observe the length and width of each chisel head, ask them to predict which chisel uses input force most efficiently and explain their reasoning. *(The chisel head that is the longest in length and the thinnest in width; accuracy of predictions may vary.)* **learning modality: logical/mathematical**

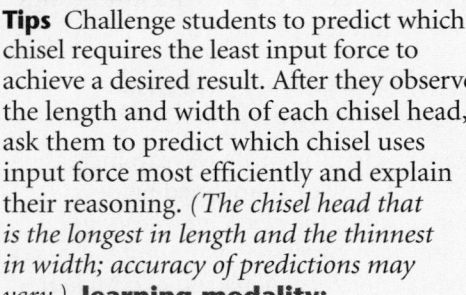

Figure 12 A large force is required to split a log in two. But with the use of a wedge, a small force is multiplied to do the job.

incline, friction acts between the bottom of the crate and the surface of the incline. You can increase the efficiency of an inclined plane by decreasing this friction. There would be less friction, for example, if you put the crate on a dolly with wheels and rolled it up the inclined plane instead of sliding it.

Wedge

If you've ever sliced an apple with a knife or seen someone chop wood with an ax, you are familiar with another simple machine known as a wedge. A **wedge** is a device that is thick at one end and tapers to a thin edge at the other end. It might be helpful to think of a wedge as an inclined plane (or two inclined planes back to back) that can move. As in the case of the inclined plane, the longer and thinner a wedge is, the less input force is required to do the same work.

In a wedge, instead of an object moving along the inclined plane, the inclined plane itself moves. For example, when someone uses an ax to split wood, the person applies an input force to the ax handle. The ax handle exerts a force on the thicker end of the wedge. That force pushes the wedge down into the wood. The wedge in turn exerts an output force that pushes through the wood, splitting it in two.

A zipper is another device that depends on the wedge. Have you ever tried to interlock the two sides of a zipper with your hands? It is almost impossible to create enough force with your fingers to join the two rows of teeth. But when you close a zipper, the part that you pull contains small wedges that multiply your input force. The result is a strong output force that either closes or separates the two sides of the zipper.

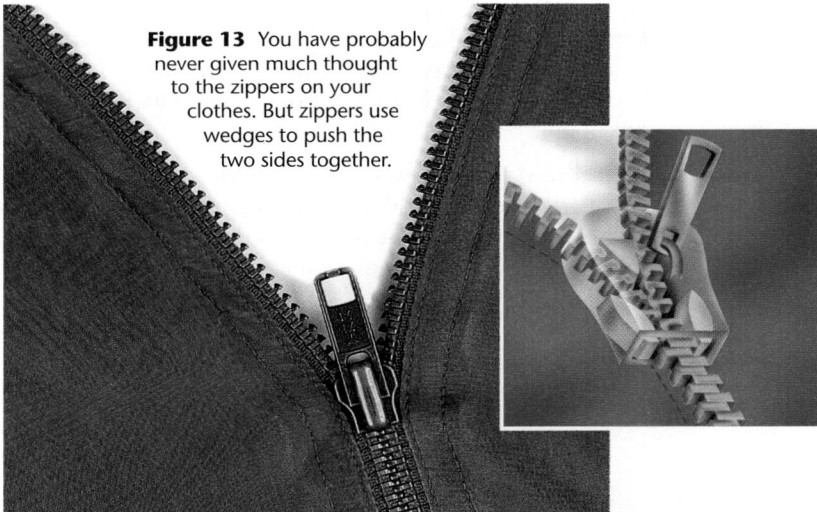

Figure 13 You have probably never given much thought to the zippers on your clothes. But zippers use wedges to push the two sides together.

Background

Facts and Figures The first tool thought to be made and used by human beings was a wedge. This tool, called a pebble tool, or chopper, dates back to the beginning of the Paleolithic Era, over 2.5 million years ago. The chopper was used for almost 2 million years, until the development of the hand axe.

When Neanderthals evolved about 110,000 years ago, they used many different hand axes, as well as the first knives and spears. About 40,000 years ago, the first modern humans invented another wedged tool called a burin, or graver. The graver could make narrow cuts into bone, and the Cro-Magnons used it to manufacture needles, hooks, and darts for spears and arrows.

Ground tools, including axe heads and chisels, appeared during the Neolithic Period, which began about 7000 B.C.

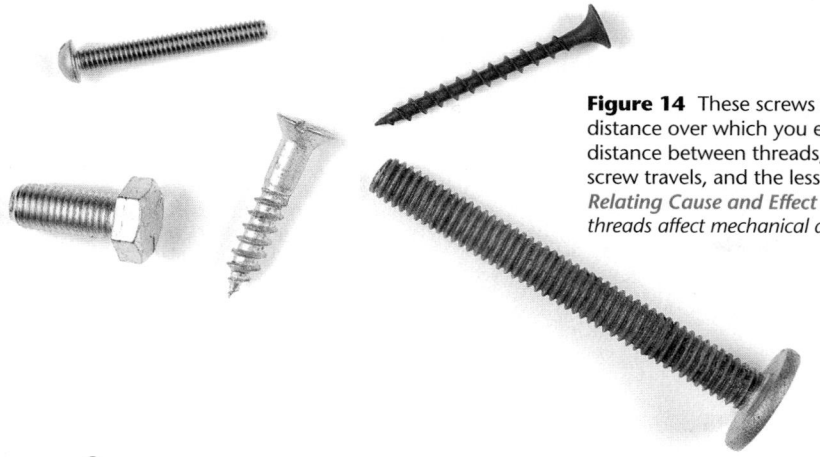

Figure 14 These screws multiply force by increasing the distance over which you exert your force. The smaller the distance between threads, the greater the distance the screw travels, and the less force you have to exert. *Relating Cause and Effect* How does the distance between threads affect mechanical advantage?

Screws

Like a wedge, a screw is a simple machine that is related to the inclined plane. A **screw** can be thought of as an inclined plane wrapped around a cylinder. This spiral inclined plane forms the threads of the screw.

When you use a screwdriver to twist a screw into a piece of wood, you exert an input force on the screw. As the threads of the screw turn, they exert an output force on the wood. If the threads of a screw are close together, you need to turn the screw many times in order to screw it into something. In other words, you apply your input force over a long distance. As with all machines, this increased distance results in an increased output force. The closer together the threads are, the greater is the mechanical advantage.

There are many other devices besides ordinary screws that take advantage of this principle. Examples include bolts, faucets, and jar lids. Think about a jar lid for a moment. You exert a relatively small input force when you turn the lid, but this force is greatly increased because of the screw threads on the lid (which fit into matching threads on the jar). The result is that the lid is pulled against the top of the jar with a strong enough output force to make a tight seal.

☑ *Checkpoint* How are wedges and screws related?

Levers

Have you ever ridden on a seesaw or pried open a paint can with an opener? If so, then you are already familiar with another simple machine called a lever. A **lever** is a rigid bar that is free to pivot, or rotate, about a fixed point. The fixed point that a lever pivots around is called the **fulcrum.**

TRY THIS

Modeling a Screw

Here's how to make a paper model of a screw.

ACTIVITY

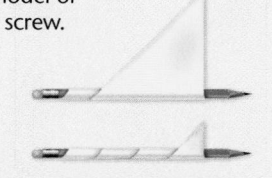

1. Cut out a triangle from a piece of paper.
2. Tape the wide end of the triangle to a pencil. Then wind the paper around the pencil.

Making Models How does this model represent a real screw? Can you think of a way to calculate the ideal mechanical advantage of your model screw?

Program Resources

◆ **Laboratory Manual** 7 "Pulleys as Simple Machines"

Answers to Self-Assessment

Caption Question

Figure 14 The smaller the distance between the threads, the greater the mechanical advantage.

☑ *Checkpoint*

Both wedges and screws are related to inclined planes. A wedge is an inclined plane that moves. A screw is an inclined plane wrapped around a central cylinder.

Screws

Using the Visuals: Figure 14

Guide students in analyzing which characteristics allow input force to be used most efficiently. Ask: **Which screw appears to have the largest diameter (requires the largest hole)? The smallest diameter (requires the smallest hole)?** *(Large screw on the lower right; screw on the top left)* Then ask: **Which screw appears to have the largest distance between threads? The smallest distance?** *(Screw at the top right; screw at the top left)* Tell students that the input force is used most efficiently when the diameter of the screw is large and the distance between the threads is small. **learning modality: visual**

TRY THIS

Skills Focus making models  **ACTIVITY**

Materials *sheet of paper, long pencils, scissors, markers, ruler, tape, string*

Time 10 minutes

Tips Be sure students use right triangles. Keep the short sides of the triangles the same length. The short sides should be about the same length as the pencil. Have students mark the diagonal edge of the triangle with a marker. This will make the edge easier to see. As students examine paper triangles of different shapes, they should draw the conclusion that triangles with small angles and longer edges form model screws with tighter threads.

Making Models The paper edge forms a spiral around the pencil, just like a real screw. To calculate ideal mechanical advantage, divide length of long side of paper triangle by length of side of paper parallel to pencil. **learning modality: kinesthetic**

Ongoing Assessment

Oral Presentation Ask students to explain why a lid that requires eight twists to seal a jar requires less input force than a similar lid that requires four twists. *(The first jar lid exerts the output force over a longer distance, so it requires a lower input force.)*

Levers

Calder trained as a mechanical engineer before beginning a career in art. Thus, he understood how simple machines work. As students examine the picture of Calder's mobile, ask them to point out one fulcrum and one lever. Ask: **What would happen if you pressed down on one end of the lever?** *(The other end of the lever will rise and exert a force on a connected lever; the whole mobile will begin to move.)* **learning modality: visual**

Visual Arts
CONNECTION

Materials *construction paper, string, wire hanger*
Time 20 minutes

Students may need assistance constructing their mobile. Students will have more success working from the bottom up. It may be helpful to have students first sketch the mobile. Stress creativity and imagination in design.

In Your Journal Make sure students include a description of how the mobile was constructed and balanced. **Portfolio** Students can save their sketches or mobiles in their portfolios.

Cultural Diversity

Materials *chopsticks, dried beans*
Time 10 minutes

Identify the chopsticks in Figure 9. Discuss how these are used. *(One chopstick is held still while the other is moved back and forth.)* Ask: **What simple machine is used here?** *(lever)* Encourage students with experience using chopsticks to demonstrate how they are used by picking up the beans. Challenge students to identify the fulcrum, the source of the input force, and direction of the output force. *(fulcrum: finger on which moving chopstick rests; input force: pointer finger; output force: the tip of the moving chopstick closing down on the bean)* Ask: **What kind of lever is this? How do you know?** *(third-class lever; both forces are on one side of the fulcrum, with the input force between the output force and the fulcrum)* **learning modality: kinesthetic**

220

Visual Arts
CONNECTION

Imagine creating a new form of art. Alexander Calder (1898–1976) did just that! Calder developed the art of mobiles. "A mobile is a piece of poetry that dances with the joy of life," he once said.

Calder combined his artistic flair with his knowledge of levers to express beauty through mobiles. You can, too.

In Your Journal

Make a mobile using construction paper, string, and a wire hanger. Write a description of your mobile and explain how you balanced it. Point out any adjustments you made to your design to balance the mobile.

Figure 16 The mechanical advantage of this lever is greater than 1.

Output distance   *Input distance*

220

Figure 15 This Calder mobile, entitled "Lobster Trap and Fish Tail," is in the Museum of Modern Art in New York City.

To understand how levers work, think about using a paint can opener. The opener acts as a lever. The opener rests against the edge of the can, which acts as the fulcrum. The tip of the opener is under the lid of the can. When you push down, you exert an input force on the handle and the opener pivots about the fulcrum. As a result, the tip of the opener pushes up, thereby exerting an output force on the lid.

The lever helps you in two ways. First, it increases the effect of your input force. Second, the lever changes the direction of your input force. You push down and the lid is pried up.

Different Types of Levers When a paint can opener is used as a lever, the fulcrum is located between the input and output forces. But this is not always the case. There are three different types of levers, classified according to the location of the fulcrum relative to the input and output forces. Examples are described in *Exploring the Three Classes of Levers*.

Advantage of a Lever When you used the paint can opener, you had to push the handle for a long distance in order to move the lid a short distance. However, you were able to apply a smaller force than you would have without the opener.

You can calculate the ideal mechanical advantage of a lever using the distances between the forces and the fulcrum.

$$\text{Ideal mechanical advantage} = \frac{\text{Distance from fulcrum to input force}}{\text{Distance from fulcrum to output force}}$$

Remember the case of the paint can opener. The distance from the fulcrum to the input force was greater than the distance from the fulcrum to the output force. This means that the ideal mechanical advantage was greater than 1. A typical ideal mechanical advantage for a paint can opener is 16 centimeters ÷ 0.8 centimeter = 20. That's a big advantage!

✓ *Checkpoint* *What point on a lever does not move?*

Background

Facts and Figures Archimedes, a scientist and philosopher who lived in ancient Greece, is believed to have said this about the lever, a simple machine, "Give me a place to stand and I will move the Earth." Whether or not he actually said this, Archimedes clearly understood that a lever could be used to multiply force.

It is hard to think of a machine of any kind that does not involve levers. Some automobiles engines use levers to activate the valves. Some automobile clutches work with levers. The arms of construction cranes are levers, and lift immense loads. Pianos have levers for keys and pedals. The jaws of some vises open and close with levers. Some organs use levers to control the flow of air to the pipes.

EXPLORING the Three Classes of Levers

The three classes of levers differ in the positions of the fulcrum, input force, and output force. Note the locations of the labels in each example.

FIRST-CLASS LEVERS

If the distance from the fulcrum to the input force is greater than the distance from the fulcrum to the output force, these levers multiply force. Otherwise, they multiply distance. Note that this kind of lever also changes the direction of the input force. Other examples include scissors, pliers, and seesaws.

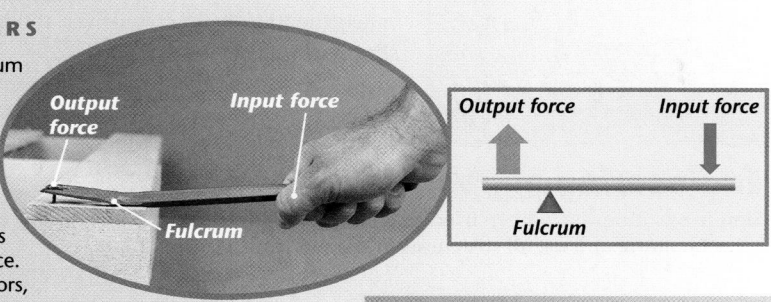

Output force   Input force   Fulcrum

Output force   Input force   Fulcrum

SECOND-CLASS LEVERS

Output force   Input force   Fulcrum

Output force   Input force   Fulcrum

These levers always multiply force. They do not, however, change the direction of the input force. Other examples include doors, nutcrackers, and bottle openers.

THIRD-CLASS LEVERS

Input force   Output force   Fulcrum

Fulcrum   Input force   Output force

These levers multiply distance, but do not change the direction of the input force. Other examples include fishing poles, shovels, and baseball bats.

Materials *plastic spoons, raisins*   **ACTIVITY**

Time 10 minutes

To compare the three classes of levers, students can model each one using plastic spoons and raisins. Organize students in pairs. Have one student place an index finger flat down on a table and balance the spoon on the finger. Another student can place a raisin in the bowl of the spoon and demonstrate how pressing on the spoon handle allows them to lift the raisin. Ask each group to identify the location of the input force, output force, and fulcrum. (*Input force—spoon handle, output force—bowl of spoon, fulcrum—finger*) Ask: **Did this first-class lever multiply force or distance?** (*Force—the students probably had to place their finger closer to the bowl than to the handle.*) Next, have one group member place the bowl of the spoon on the table and balance a raisin on the middle of spoon's handle. Another can carefully lift the edge of the handle. Ask: **How is this a second-class lever?** (*The fulcrum is at one end, the output force is in the middle, and the input force is at the other end of the lever.*) Finally, challenge groups to create a model of a third-class lever. Ask: **Where is the input force, output force, and fulcrum located in this lever?** (*Input force—in the center of the spoon handle, output force—at the bowl of the spoon, fulcrum—at the top of the spoon's handle.*) **Extend** Challenge students to design and construct other models to demonstrate the 3 kinds of levers. **cooperative learning**

Answers to Self-Assessment

☑ *Checkpoint*

The point touching the fulcrum

Ongoing Assessment

Skills Check Have students prepare compare/contrast tables that analyze the three classes of levers.

Wheel and Axle

Building Inquiry Skills: Measuring

Materials *plastic lid from coffee can, piece of cardboard or poster board, long pencil, scissors, measuring tape, marker, white paper*

Time 15 minutes

Tips In this activity, students explore the relationship between a wheel and axle by designing cardboard wheels. Have students trace the coffee-can lid onto the cardboard and cut out the circle. Then have them make a hole in the center of the circle with scissors, and insert the pencil through the hole. Have students measure the circumference of the cardboard circle (wheel) and the pencil (axle) with the measuring tape. This equals the distance that the wheel and axle travel during one rotation. Ask: **How does the distance traveled by the wheel compare to that traveled by the axle?** *(It is greater.)* Then ask: **Based on your measurements, what will happen to an input force exerted on the wheel? On the axle?** *(An input force exerted on the wheel will cause the output force to be greater. An input force exerted on the axle will cause the distance that the force travels to be multiplied.)* **learning modality: kinesthetic**

Could you insert a screw into a piece of wood using nothing more than your fingers? You would find it almost impossible. But with a screwdriver, you can turn the screw with ease.

A screwdriver makes use of a simple machine known as the wheel and axle. A **wheel and axle** is a simple machine made of two circular or cylindrical objects that are fastened together and that rotate about a common axis. The object with the larger diameter is called the wheel and the object with the smaller diameter is called the axle. In a screwdriver, the handle is the wheel and the shaft is the axle.

SCIENCE & History

Engineering Marvels

Simple machines have been used to create some of the most beautiful and useful structures in the world.

2550 B.C. Great Pyramid, Giza, Egypt
Workers used wooden wedges to cut 2.3 million blocks of stone to build the pyramid. At the quarry, the wedges were driven into cracks in the rock. The rock split into pieces. Workers hauled the massive blocks up inclined planes to the tops of pyramid walls.

| 2000 B.C. | 1000 B.C. | A.D. 1 |

500 B.C.
Theater at Epidaurus, Greece
Instead of ramps, the Greeks relied on a crane powered by pulleys to lift the stone blocks to build this theater. The crane was also used to lower actors to the stage during performances.

222

Background

Facts and Figures
◆ The wheel was most likely invented in Mesopotamia during the Bronze Age, around 3500 B.C.
◆ The spinning wheel was probably invented in India, but reached Europe in the Middle Ages.
◆ The first practical four-wheeled roller skates were designed in 1863 by James Plimpton, who lived in Massachusetts.

◆ The kinetoscope, the predecessor to the motion-picture projector, was invented in 1891 by Thomas Edison and William Dickson. The viewer looked through peephole in front of a spinning wheel with a narrow slit that acted as a shutter.
◆ The world's first true automobile, a steam-powered tricycle, was invented in France in 1869 by Nicolas-Joseph Cugnot.

Every time you turn a doorknob, you are using a wheel and axle. The knob is the wheel and the shaft is the axle. The water wheel of a mill, the steering wheel of a car, and the handle of an eggbeater are also examples of a wheel and axle.

Advantage of a Wheel and Axle How does a wheel and axle make work easier? You apply an input force to turn the wheel, which is larger than the axle. As a result, the axle rotates and exerts an output force to turn something such as a screw. The wheel and axle multiplies your force, but you must exert your force over a longer distance—in this case a circular distance.

In Your Journal

Imagine that you are the person who first thought of using a simple machine at one of the construction sites in the time line. Write out your proposal. You'll need to research the time and place. Explain to the people in charge why the simple machine you suggest will give workers a mechanical advantage.

A.D. 1056
Yingxian Pagoda, China

Slanted wooden beams called *ang* act as first-class levers to hold up the roof of this pagoda. The weight of the center of the roof presses down on one end of the beam. The other end of the beam swings up to support the outer edge of the roof.

A.D. 1000

A.D. 2000

A.D. 1000
Brihadeshrava Temple, India

The temple's tower at Thanjavur rises to a height of more than 60 meters. Workers dragged the dome-shaped capstone, a mass of over 70,000 kilograms, to the top of the structure along an inclined plane several kilometers long.

A.D. 1994
The Chunnel, United Kingdom to France

Special drilling equipment was built to tunnel under the English Channel. Opened in May of 1994, the tunnel is 50 kilometers long. It carries only railway traffic.

223

List some simple machines on the board. Then ask student volunteers to read the description of each engineering marvel shown in the time line. After each paragraph, ask a volunteer to name the simple machines used in the construction of the structure. Write the name of the structure beneath the name of that machine on the board. Then ask students to speculate on the tools that might be used to build similar structures today. (*Samples: jackhammers instead of a wooden wedges, motor-driven cranes in place of a hand-powered pulley or a ramp*)

In Your Journal Encourage students to prepare their journal entries as formal letters to the architects and construction leaders of particular projects. When they explain why the simple machine gives workers a mechanical advantage, students should mention how the machine makes work easier by multiplying input force, multiplying the distance the force is exerted, or changing the direction of the force.

Portfolio Students can save their letters in their portfolios. **learning modality: verbal**

Extend Ask students to list common hand tools that they have used. (*hammers, pliers, screwdrivers, crow bars, etc.*) Discuss how these tools are used. (Remind them that a hammer can be used to pull out nails as well as hammer them in.) Ask the students to identify the simple machines these tools represent.

Ongoing Assessment

Writing Have students prepare magazine advertisements for a museum exhibit called *Ancient Engineering*. Students should describe at least three simple machines in their advertisements.

Wheel and Axle, continued

Addressing Naïve Conceptions

Some students may confuse the radius of a circle with its diameter or circumference. While any of these three may be used to calculate mechanical advantage of a wheel and axle, using the radius assures consistency. Draw a large circle on the board. Invite volunteers to draw in the radius, circumference, and diameter. Ask: **What is the relationship between the radius and diameter?** (*The radius is one half the diameter.*) Draw a large diagram of a wheel and axle on the board. Have students measure the radii and calculate the ideal mechanical advantage. **learning modality: visual**

Pulley

Building Inquiry Skills: Interpreting Diagrams

Materials *2 pulleys, rope, 1-kg mass, spring scale*
Time 30 minutes
Tips Allow pairs of students to assemble the pulleys shown in Figure 18. You may wish to provide a clothesline, wire, or wooden dowel between two chairs for students to hang their pulleys. For each set-up, students should raise the mass using a spring scale, record the force needed to lift it, and record the ideal mechanical advantage. Ask:
- **In which set-ups did you change the direction of force?** (*A and C*)
- **In which set-up did you have to exert the least input force to raise the pulley?** (*D*)

Encourage students to form hypotheses about the number of sections of rope supporting the mass and the ideal mechanical advantage of a pulley system. Allow them to test their hypotheses. (*Sample hypothesis: If the number of sections supporting the mass increases, the mechanical advantage will increase.*)
learning modality: kinesthetic

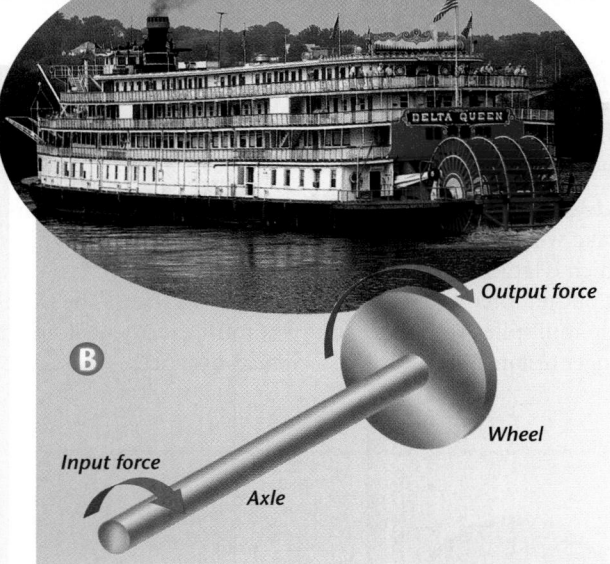

Figure 17 **A.** In some devices, such as a screwdriver, the wheel turns an axle. **B.** In the case of the riverboat paddle wheel, the axle turns the wheel. *Interpreting Photos How is work made easier by the wheel and axle on the riverboat?*

You can calculate the ideal mechanical advantage of a wheel and axle using the radius of the wheel and the radius of the axle. (Each radius is the distance from the outside to the common center of the wheel and axle.)

$$\text{Ideal mechanical advantage} = \frac{\text{Radius of wheel}}{\text{Radius of axle}}$$

For a screwdriver, a typical ideal mechanical advantage would be 1.5 centimeters ÷ 0.3 centimeter, or 5.

A Variation on the Wheel and Axle What would happen if the input force were applied to the axle rather than the wheel? For the riverboat in Figure 17, the force of the engine is applied to the axle of the large paddle wheel. The large paddle wheel in turn pushes against the water. In this case, the input force is exerted over a short distance while the output force is exerted over a long distance. So when the input force is applied to the axle, a wheel and axle multiplies distance. This means that the ideal mechanical advantage of the paddle wheel is less than 1.

☑ *Checkpoint* How does a doorknob work?

Pulley

When you raise or lower a flag on a flagpole or open and close window blinds, you are using a simple machine known as a pulley. A **pulley** is a grooved wheel with a rope (or a chain, or even a steel cable) wrapped around it. You use a pulley by pulling on the rope. As a result, you can change the amount and direction of your input force.

Background

Facts and Figures Many kinds of cranes use pulley systems to lift heavy objects and shift them horizontally.

Derricks are one class of crane. Derrick cranes consist of a boom called a jib, along which runs a pulley system. The cables or chains of the pulley system are wound and unwound around a drum at the base of the jib. The drum is turned by a motor. One type of derrick crane, a floating crane, is built onto a barge and used for constructing bridges or salvaging sunken objects. The *Musachi*, a floating crane built in Japan in 1974, can lift 3,000 tons.

Derrick is actually the name for the combination of a flexible rope or cable and pulleys used in cranes. The derrick was named after a famous seventeenth-century hangman in Tyburn, England.

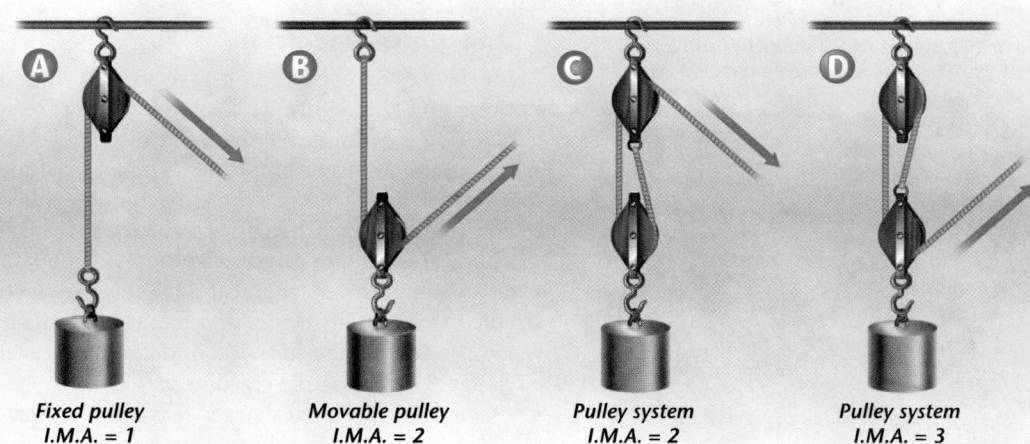

A Fixed pulley
I.M.A. = 1

B Movable pulley
I.M.A. = 2

C Pulley system
I.M.A. = 2

D Pulley system
I.M.A. = 3

Figure 18 **A.** A fixed pulley changes the direction of your force. **B.** A movable pulley multiplies your force. **C, D.** You can combine fixed and movable pulleys to increase the mechanical advantage.

Fixed Pulleys A pulley that you attach to a structure is called a fixed pulley. A single fixed pulley, as shown in Figure 18A, does not change the amount of force you apply. Instead it changes the direction of the input force. The ideal mechanical advantage of a single fixed pulley is 1. A single fixed pulley can be used to raise a sail, as you read in the previous section.

Movable Pulleys If you attach a pulley to the object you wish to move, then you are using a movable pulley. As you see in Figure 18B, the object is then supported by each side of the rope that is looped around the pulley. As a result, the ideal mechanical advantage of a movable pulley is 2. The output force on the object is twice the input force that you exert on the rope. You can also see that you must exert your force over a greater distance. For every meter you lift the object with a movable pulley, you need to pull the rope two meters.

Notice that with the movable pulley, your input force is in the same direction as the output force. A movable pulley is especially useful when you are lifting an object from above. Large construction cranes often work with a movable pulley. A hook fastened to the pulley carries the building materials.

Pulley Systems If you combine fixed and movable pulleys, you can make a pulley system. Such a pulley system is also called a "block and tackle." The pulley system pictured in Figure 18C has an ideal mechanical advantage of 2. The pulley system in Figure 18D has an ideal mechanical advantage of 3. **The ideal mechanical advantage of a pulley system is equal to the number of sections of the rope that support the object.** (Don't include the rope on which you pull downward, because it does not support the object.)

Classifying
Even though levers and pulleys may seem very different, pulleys can be classified as levers.

When you pull down on a fixed pulley, the object rises. In other words, the pulley changes the direction of your input force. This is what happens with a first-class lever. Instead of a bar, you apply your force to a rope. The center of the pulley acts like the fulcrum of the lever.

Draw a diagram showing how a single fixed pulley is like a first-class lever. Why is the mechanical advantage 1?

Classifying

Materials *first-class lever, single fixed pulley*
Time 10 minutes
Tips Provide students with a first-class lever and a single fixed pulley to observe. Have them diagram both the pulley and the lever and label the diagrams to indicate the location and direction of input and output forces.
Expected Outcome Students should conclude that a single fixed pulley changes only the direction of the force, so the input and output forces are the same and the ideal mechanical advantage equals 1.
Extend Have students suggest why single fixed pulleys have an actual mechanical advantage less than 1. (*Some effort is used to overcome friction.*)
learning modality: logical/ mathematical

Portfolio Students can save their diagrams in their portfolios.

Compound Machines

Inquiry Challenge

Materials *2 or 3 bicycles*
Time 15 minutes

Students can investigate how a compound machine works by observing simple machines in a multi-speed bicycle. Group students and have the groups identify and report on the number of simple machines they find in each bicycle. Encourage students to label drawings showing the different simple machines and how the machines are connected to the bicycle. **cooperative learning**

Answers to Self-Assessment

Caption Question

Figure 17 The input force is exerted over a short distance and the output force is exerted over a long distance, so turning the paddle is easier.

✓ *Checkpoint*

You apply an input force to the knob, or wheel, which causes the shaft, or axle, to rotate.

Ongoing Assessment

Oral Presentation Have students compare and contrast a single fixed pulley with a single moveable pulley.

3 Assess

Section 3 Review Answers

1. Sample answer: Inclined plane—ramp; wedge—knife; screw—jar lid; lever—see-saw; wheel and axle—doorknob; pulley—clothesline
2. inclined plane: length of incline/height of incline; lever: distance from fulcrum to input force/distance from fulcrum to output force; wheel and axle: radius of wheel/radius of axle; pulley: number of sections of rope that support the object
3. A flip-top opener is a first-class lever. You lift up on the metal tab (input force), the flip-top rotates around the point where it is connected to the can (fulcrum) and pushes in on the part of the top of the can where it is partially pre-cut (output force).
4. A machine with a mechanical advantage less than 1 allows you to increase the distance over which the input force acts. This is useful for a paddle wheel on a steamboat.

> ### Check Your Progress ▷ CHAPTER PROJECT 7
> Measurements to make for calculating actual mechanical advantage are the weight of the load can (5.88 N) and the amount of input force needed to lift the load. Discuss how lengthening a lever, adding a pulley, or changing the angle of an inclined plane increases ideal mechanical advantage. Note that the ideal mechanical advantage of a compound machine is the product of the ideal mechanical advantages of its components.

Performance Assessment

Drawing Have students draw blueprints for a design of a compound machine that allows them to open their bedroom door while still lying in bed.

226

Figure 19 Both a pencil sharpener and a clock are examples of compound machines that use gears. *Applying Concepts What is a compound machine?*

Compound Machines

Many devices that you can observe around you do not resemble the six simple machines you just read about. That is because more complex machines consist of combinations of simple machines. A machine that utilizes two or more simple machines is called a **compound machine.** To calculate the ideal mechanical advantage of a compound machine, you need to know the mechanical advantage of each simple machine. The overall mechanical advantage is the product of the individual ideal mechanical advantages of the simple machines.

A mechanical pencil sharpener is a good example of a compound machine. When you turn the handle, you are using a wheel and axle to turn the mechanism inside the sharpener. The two cutting wheels inside are screws that whittle away at the end of the pencil until it is sharp.

Inside the pencil sharpener in Figure 19 is an axle that turns **gears.** The gears then turn the cutting wheels. A system of gears is a device with toothed wheels that fit into one another. Turning one wheel causes another to turn. Gears form a compound machine with one wheel and axle linked to another wheel and axle. Sometimes this link is direct, as in the gears shown in Figure 19. In other devices, such as a bicycle, this link is through a chain.

Section 3 Review

1. List and give an example of each of the six kinds of simple machines.
2. Explain how to find the ideal mechanical advantage of four types of simple machines.
3. What kind of lever is the flip-top opener on a soda can? Explain your answer with the help of a diagram.
4. **Thinking Critically Making Generalizations** Some machines give a mechanical advantage less than 1. Explain why you might want to use such a machine.

> ### Check Your Progress ▷ CHAPTER PROJECT 7
> Think about whether force or distance is multiplied by each simple machine in your design. Consider how making levers longer, adding pulleys, or changing the angle of your inclined planes will affect the mechanical advantage. What measurements will you need to know to calculate the ideal mechanical advantage of your lifting machine? Finalize your design, and build your machine. As you build, consider how you can use lubrication or polishing to improve its efficiency.

Background

Facts and Figures Micromachines range in size from half a micron to 500 microns. Usually made from silicon, these machines are often simple gears and levers built at a tiny scale. Scientists envision one micromachine that could attack viruses in blood cells; such a machine might have gears the size of a protein molecule. Equipped with tiny sensors, micromachines may improve the manufacturing of all kinds of products.

Answers to Self-Assessment

Caption Question

Figure 19 A compound machine is a machine that uses two or more simple machines to do work.

SCIENCE AND SOCIETY

Automation in the Workplace— Lost Jobs or New Jobs?

Workers 150 years ago spent long days stitching clothes by hand. In a modern American factory, a worker makes a shirt with a sewing machine and much less effort. Since ancient times, people have invented machines to help with work. Today, factories can use automated machines to perform jobs that are difficult, dangerous, or even just boring. Like science-fiction robots, these machines can do a whole series of different tasks.

But if a machine does work instead of a person, then someone loses a job. How can society use machines to make work easier and more productive without having some people lose their chance to work?

The Issues

What Are the Effects of Automation?
New machines replace some jobs, but they also can create jobs. Suppose an automobile factory starts using machines instead of people to paint cars. At first, some workers may lose their jobs. But the factory may be able to produce more cars. Then it may need to hire more workers—to handle old tasks as well as some new ones. New jobs are created for people who are educated and skilled in operating and taking care of the new machines.

Still, some workers whose skills are no longer needed lose their jobs. Some are forced to work in different jobs for less money. Others may be unable to find new jobs. The challenge to society is to provide workers who have lost jobs with the skills needed for good new jobs.

What Can People Do? Education programs can train young people for new jobs and give older

workers new skills. Those who learn how to use computers and other new machines can take on new jobs. Learning how to sell or design a product can also prepare workers for new jobs. Workers who have lost jobs can train for very different types of work—work that cannot be done by machines. A machine, for example, cannot replace human skill in day care or medical care.

Who Should Pay? Teaching young people how to work in new kinds of jobs costs money. So do training programs for adult workers who have lost jobs. What is the fairest way to pay these costs? Businesses might share some of the costs. Some businesses give workers full pay until they are retrained or find new work. The government might provide unemployment pay or training for the unemployed. Then all taxpayers would share the costs.

You Decide

1. Identify the Problem
Describe in your own words the benefits and drawbacks of workplace automation.

2. Analyze the Options
List ways society could deal with the effects of automation. For each plan, give the benefits and drawbacks and tell how it would be paid for.

3. Find a Solution
The owner of the pizza shop in your neighborhood has bought an automated pizza-making system. Make a plan for the shop to use the system without having to fire workers.

You Decide

◆ Students' responses to Identify the Problem and Analyze the Options should be based on the concepts and issues presented in the text and in the class presentation. In response to Find a Solution, students may discuss issues raised in the debates.

◆ Make sure students understand that there are no "correct" opinions or solutions. As with many complex issues in our society, there are no easy answers.

Extend Have students contact and interview representatives from local industries about how much automation has affected their business. Students can ask if workers were displaced, and if so, whether the industries retrained displaced workers.

SCIENCE AND SOCIETY

Automation in the Workplace—Lost Jobs or New Jobs?

Purpose

To provide students with an understanding of the problems created by worker dislocations as a result of increased automation in industry.

Debate

Time one class period for research and preparation, 30 minutes to conduct the debate

◆ Begin a discussion by asking students if they know anyone who has had to change jobs as a result of automation in the workplace. (Use caution. This may be a sensitive subject!) Work through an example of automation-induced changes with students. For example, in the automobile industry, robots now do most of the body welding formerly done by individual workers.

◆ Explain to students that they will be debating the proposition that "It is the responsibility of the local, state, or federal government to fund retraining for workers displaced by automation." Inform them that a debate is not an argument. In a debate, two groups discuss a proposition by presenting reasons that support their position.

◆ Separate the class into two groups: one to support the proposition, the other to oppose it. Have groups review and investigate the issue from their respective points of view.

◆ Both groups should critically and constructively support their viewpoints. Encourage students in the group supporting government-funded training to explore ideas such as who else could ultimately pay for worker retraining. Encourage students in the other group to consider the consequences if workers are not retrained, as well as alternatives to government training.

Real-World Lab

You and Your Community

Angling for Access

Preparing for Inquiry

Key Concept The actual and ideal mechanical advantages of an inclined plane, such as a wheelchair-access ramp, vary with steepness.

Skills Objectives Students will be able to
◆ model a wheelchair ramp and relate it to a real ramp;
◆ measure distances and forces;
◆ calculate ideal and actual mechanical advantages.

Time 55 minutes

Advance Planning Gather boards for inclined planes, wooden blocks with eye hooks, spring scales, metric rulers, and markers. Any board about half a meter in length will do for an inclined plane. Make sure enough books are available.

Alternative Materials A ballistic cart, which you may be able to borrow from the physics department, can be substituted for the wooden block. The forces needed to pull the cart and block are comparable because the cart has less friction, but generally is much heavier. You can use a 20-N spring scale to weigh the cart, or find its mass in grams with a balance scale and multiply by 0.01.

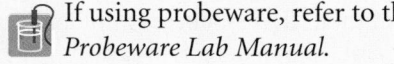 If using probeware, refer to the *Probeware Lab Manual.*

Guiding Inquiry

Invitation Have the boards, spring scales, and blocks or carts in the room. Ask students if they have seen or used a wheelchair ramp. Then ask how they might make a model to investigate these ramps using materials in the room. Let students brainstorm things they might investigate using the model. Ask: **What variables can you manipulate?** *(Weight of the block or cart, steepness of the ramp, type of material the ramp is made of, height of the ramp, length of the ramp)* Then ask: **What are some responding variables?** *(Force needed to pull the block or cart up the ramp, amount of friction)* In this experiment, the manipulated variable will be the steepness of the ramp and the responding variable will be the

---

ANGLING FOR ACCESS

You and your friends have volunteered to help build a wheelchair-access ramp for the local public library. The design of the ramp has not been decided upon yet, so you need to build a model inclined plane. The model will help you determine what the steepness of the ramp should be.

Problem

How does the steepness of a wheelchair-access ramp affect its usefulness?

Skills Focus

making models, measuring, calculating

Materials

4 books, about 2 cm thick   metric ruler
wooden block with eye-hook   marker
board, at least 10 cm wide and 50 cm long
spring scale, 0–10 N, or force sensor

Procedure

1. Preview the following steps that describe how you can construct and use a ramp. Then copy the data table into your notebook.

2. The output force with an inclined plane is equal to the weight of the object. Lift the block with the spring scale to measure its weight. Record this value in the data table. If you are using a force sensor, see your teacher for instructions.

3. Make a mark on the side of the board about 3 cm from one end. Measure the length from the other end of the board to the mark and record it in the data table.

4. Place one end of the board on top of a book. The mark you made on the board should be even with the edge of the book.

DATA TABLE

Number of Books	Output Force (N)	Length of Incline (cm)	Height of Incline (cm)	Input Force (N)	Ideal Mechanical Advantage	Actual Mechanical Advantage
1						
2						
3						
4						

---

force needed to pull the block or cart up the ramp at constant speed.

Introducing the Procedure
◆ Show students how to use and zero a spring scale. Stress the importance of pulling the spring scale parallel to the inclined plane to prevent inaccurate readings.
◆ Be sure the students are clear about what distances to measure. They are measuring from the table to the bottom of the ramp instead of the top to compensate for the fact

that the top of the ramp doesn't go all the way to the table.

Troubleshooting the Experiment
◆ If the spring scale is calibrated in grams, the students can multiply by 0.01 to obtain a reading in newtons.
◆ Be sure students pull the block or cart at a slow, constant speed to measure the pulling force. The force needed to get the block or cart started will be more than this and should not be used.

5. Measure the vertical distance in centimeters from the top of the table to where the underside of the incline touches the book. Record this value in the data table as "Height of Incline."

6. Lay the block on its largest side and use the spring scale to pull the block straight up the incline at a slow, steady speed. Be sure to hold the spring scale parallel to the incline, as shown in the photograph. Measure the force needed and record it in the data table.

7. Predict how your results will change if you repeat the investigation using two, three, and four books. Test your predictions.

8. For each trial, calculate the ideal mechanical advantage and the actual mechanical advantage. Record the calculations in your data table.

Analyze and Conclude

1. How did the ideal mechanical advantage and the actual mechanical advantage compare each time you repeated the experiment? Explain your answer.

2. Why do you write ideal and actual mechanical advantage without units?

3. What happens to the mechanical advantage as the inclined plane gets steeper? On the basis of this fact alone, which of the four inclined planes models the best steepness for a wheelchair-access ramp?

4. What other factors, besides mechanical advantage, should you consider when deciding on the steepness of the ramp?

5. **Apply** Suppose the door of the local public library is 2 m above the ground and the distance from the door to the parking lot is 15 m. How would these conditions affect your decision about how steep to make the ramp?

Getting Involved

Find actual ramps that provide access for people with disabilities. Measure the heights and lengths of these ramps and calculate their ideal mechanical advantages. Find out what the requirements are for access ramps in your area. Should your ramp be made of a particular material? Should it level off before it reaches the door? How wide should it be? How does it provide water drainage?

Sample Data Table

Number of Books	Output Force (N)	Length of Incline (cm)	Height of Incline (cm)	Input Force (N)	Ideal Mech. Adv.	Actual Mech. Adv.
1	3.0	47	3.5	1.6	13.4	1.9
2	3.0	47	6.4	1.9	7.3	1.6
3	3.0	47	9.6	2.1	4.9	1.4
4	3.0	47	13.0	2.4	3.6	1.3

Program Resources

◆ **Unit 2 Resources** Real-World Lab blackline masters, pp. 112–113
◆ **Probeware Lab Manual** Blackline masters

Media and Technology

 Lab Activity Videotape
Tape 2

Expected Outcome

◆ The actual mechanical advantage will always be less than the ideal mechanical advantage. The actual advantage decreases with increased height.

◆ If both carts and blocks are used, the actual mechanical advantages for the cart will be much higher than for the block.

Analyze and Conclude

1. The ideal mechanical advantage is always more than the actual mechanical advantage because of the friction between the block or cart and the incline.

2. Ideal mechanical advantage is obtained by dividing the length of incline by the height of incline. The units of distance (cm) cancel out. Actual mechanical advantage is obtained by dividing the output force by the input force. The units of force (newtons) cancel out.

3. The mechanical advantage decreases as the ramp gets steeper. On this basis alone, one would choose the least steep ramp.

4. Answers may vary. Sample: If the ramp is too gradual it may be too long to be feasible. If the ramp is too steep, it will be dangerous.

5. Unless the ramp doubled back on itself, the shallowness of the ramp would be limited by those conditions. The best possible ideal mechanical advantage would be 15/2 = 7.5.

Extending the Inquiry

Getting Involved Students may have difficulty measuring the length and height of their ramps. Explain that only the ratio of length to height determines the ideal mechanical advantage, and that this ratio is the same for all or part of the ramp. Students can work with only part of the ramp if that is more feasible. When interviewing people who use access ramps, students should prepare a series of questions in advance. Students should explain what they are doing and why, so that people will be more inclined to respond to their requests for an interview.

SECTION 4 Machines in the Human Body

Objective

After completing the lesson, students will be able to
◆ explain how the body uses levers and wedges.

Key Term tendons

1 Engage/Explore

Activating Prior Knowledge

Have two student volunteers kick a soccer ball back and forth. Ask: **Is work being done? How can you tell?** (*Yes; the ball is moving and changing direction.*) Then ask: **What is doing the work on the ball?** (*The student's feet and legs*) Challenge students to infer how legs are related to simple machines. Explain that legs can be considered to be levers.

DISCOVER

Skills Focus observing
Materials *crackers*
Time 10 minutes
Tips Tell students to take a bite of the cracker using their front teeth, rather than placing the entire cracker into their mouths at one time. Allow students to repeat the exercise until they are sure they can determine how their jaws move. If your school has one, a model of the jaw would be helpful.
Expected Outcome Students should not have difficulty recognizing that their front teeth are wedges. The recognition that their jaws are levers may be more difficult. But by opening their mouths wide so that the front of the jaw moves down, students should be able to feel the back of the jaw move up.
Think It Over The jaw is a lever; the teeth are wedges.

SECTION 4 Machines in the Human Body

DISCOVER ⋯⋯⋯⋯⋯⋯⋯⋯⋯⋯⋯⋯⋯⋯ ACTIVITY

Are You an Eating Machine?

1. Using your front teeth, bite off a piece of a cracker. As you bite, observe how your teeth are breaking the cracker. Also think about the shape of your front teeth.

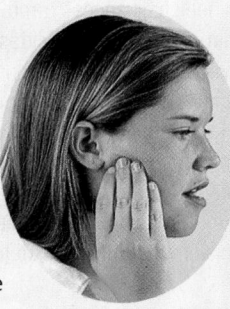

2. Now chew the cracker. Pay attention to how your lower jaw moves. Touch your jaw below your ear, as shown in the photo. As you chew, push in slightly there so that you can feel how your jaw moves. If the structure is still not clear, try opening your mouth wide while you feel the back of the jaw.

Think It Over
Observing When you bite and chew, your teeth and jaws serve as two kinds of machines. What are they?

GUIDE FOR READING

◆ How does the body use levers and wedges?

Reading Tip Before you read, preview the illustrations and predict how simple machines are related to the human body.

It's Saturday night, and you and your friends are taking a well-deserved break from your school work. You're watching a great movie, happily eating popcorn from a big bowl. Are you doing any work? Surprisingly, you are!

Every time you reach for the popcorn, your muscles exert a force that causes your arm to move. And when you chew on the popcorn, breaking it into bits that you can easily swallow, you are again doing work.

How are you able to do all this work without even noticing? The answer is machines! You probably don't think of the human body as being made of machines. But believe it or not, machines are involved in much of the work that your body does.

Living Levers

Most of the machines in your body are levers that consist of bones and muscles. Every time you move, you use a muscle. Your muscles are attached to your bones by tough connective tissue called **tendons.** Tendons and muscles pull on bones, making them work as levers. The joint, near where the tendon is attached to the bone, acts as the fulcrum of the lever. The muscles produce the input force. The output force is used for everything from lifting your hand to swinging a hammer.

230

READING STRATEGIES

Reading Tip Have partners work together to preview the illustrations and predict ways that simple machines are related to the human body. Suggest that they return to Section 3 for a quick review of simple machines. Encourage students to imitate the actions being shown in the illustrations as they make their predictions.

Compare/Contrast Tables Have students make compare/contrast tables that indicate the characteristics of levers and wedges and give examples of human-made machines and of machines in the body.

Compare/Contrast

	Levers	Wedges
Characteristics	bar that pivots about a fulcrum	tapered edge
Examples	scissors, pliers, neck, arm, foot	axe, zipper, teeth

A muscle by itself cannot push; it can only pull. When a muscle contracts, or becomes shorter, it pulls the bone to which it is attached. So how can you bend your arm as shown in *Exploring Levers in the Body?* The answer is that most muscles work in pairs. For example, when your biceps muscle (on the front of the upper arm) contracts, it exerts a force on the bone in your forearm. The result is that your arm bends at the elbow joint, which in this case is the fulcrum of the lever. When the triceps muscle (on the back of the upper arm) contracts, it opens the elbow joint.

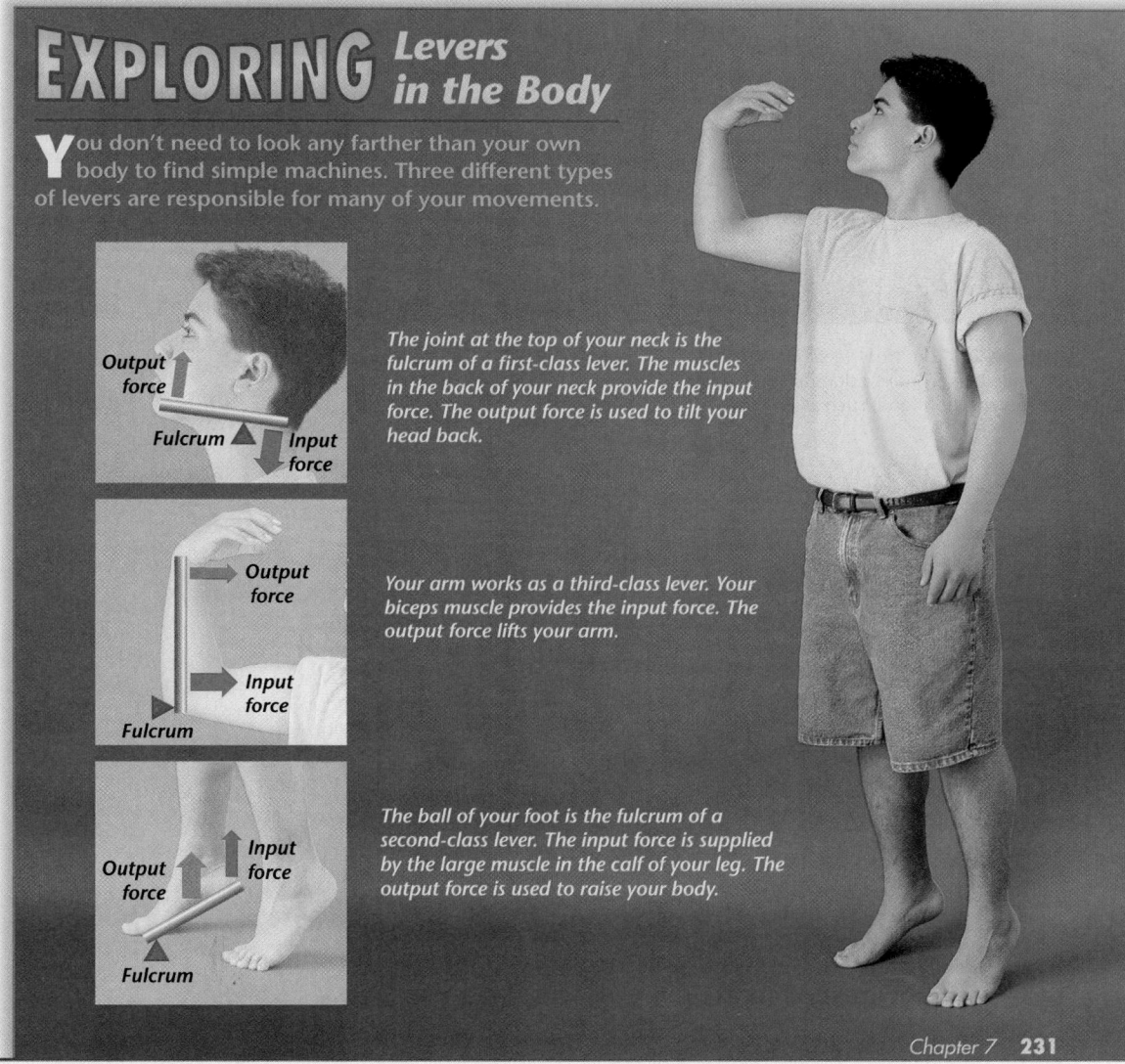

EXPLORING *Levers in the Body*

You don't need to look any farther than your own body to find simple machines. Three different types of levers are responsible for many of your movements.

The joint at the top of your neck is the fulcrum of a first-class lever. The muscles in the back of your neck provide the input force. The output force is used to tilt your head back.

Output force · Fulcrum · Input force

Your arm works as a third-class lever. Your biceps muscle provides the input force. The output force lifts your arm.

Output force · Input force · Fulcrum

The ball of your foot is the fulcrum of a second-class lever. The input force is supplied by the large muscle in the calf of your leg. The output force is used to raise your body.

Input force · Output force · Fulcrum

Chapter 7 **231**

Program Resources

◆ **Unit 2 Resources** 7-4 Lesson Plan, p. 105; 7-4 Section Summary, p. 160
◆ **Guided Reading and Study Workbook** Section 7-4

Media and Technology

Concept Videotape Library
Adventures, Tape 2, "Muscles and Bones"

Living Levers

Building Inquiry Skills: Observing

Materials *skinned chicken wings, antibacterial wipes*
Time 20 minutes
CAUTION: Make sure students use antibacterial wipes or wash their hands with antibacterial soap after handling the chicken wings. Have students diagram the wings, label the muscles, tendons, and bones, and label the input force, output force, and fulcrum of one lever in the wing. After the activity, have students properly dispose of the wings. **learning modality: kinesthetic**

EXPLORING

Levers in the Body

Have students copy motions shown in the photos. Pair students and allow each to feel their partner's muscles contract as force is applied. As they look at the first photo, one student can place a hand on the back of his or her partner's neck. Ask: **What do you feel as your partner lowers and raises his or her head?** *(The muscles tighten and contract)* As students examine the photo of the arm and move their arms as shown, ask: **What other joints work as third-class levers?** *(knuckles, knees)*
Extend Challenge students to draw a diagram or construct a model that shows how the motion of the arm would be affected if a tendon was injured.
learning modality: visual

Ongoing Assessment

Oral Presentation Have students describe how their arms function as simple machines when they raise light dumbbells. *(The arm is a lever. The biceps provide the input force, the elbow is the fulcrum, and the lower hand and arm provide the output force to move the barbell.)*

Working Wedges

Including All Students

Suggest that all students use their tongue to feel the shape of their teeth. Then provide students with a model of a human jaw and teeth. Allow them to feel the difference between the wedge-shaped incisors and the broad back teeth. Ask: **How would you find the mechanical advantage of the incisors?** (*Divide the length of the tooth by the width of the tooth at the point where it is attached to the jaw.*) **learning modality: kinesthetic**

3 Assess

Section 4 Review Answers

1. The bones are levers. The muscles exert the input force.
2. Some teeth are wedges. They are used to bite into foods.
3. The fulcrum is at the base of the index finger, where the finger meets the hand. The input force is the contraction of a muscle attached partway up the finger. The finger is a third-class lever.
4. You use the triceps muscle to straighten your arm. It is a third-class lever.

Science at Home

Materials *wooden toothpicks*

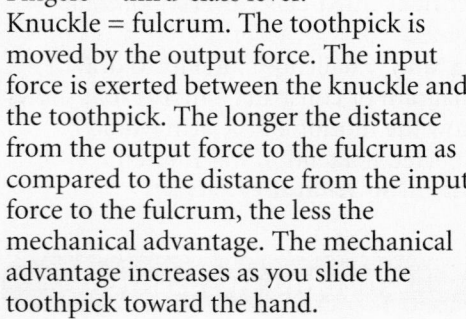

Fingers = third-class lever. Knuckle = fulcrum. The toothpick is moved by the output force. The input force is exerted between the knuckle and the toothpick. The longer the distance from the output force to the fulcrum as compared to the distance from the input force to the fulcrum, the less the mechanical advantage. The mechanical advantage increases as you slide the toothpick toward the hand.

Performance Assessment

Drawing Have students trace their hands onto a piece of paper. They should identify all the levers in the hand, then label the fulcrums, output forces, and input forces.

Figure 20 Your front teeth are shaped like wedges. These wedges allow you to cut through food, such as an apple.

Look again at the different levers in *Exploring Levers in the Body*. You will see that you can find a lever in your neck and another lever in your leg and foot. Just as you found with shovels, wheelbarrows, and fishing poles, the type of lever you find in the human body depends on the locations of the fulcrum, input force, and output force.

Working Wedges

Have you ever paid attention to the shape of your teeth? Some of your teeth are wedge-shaped, others are pointed, and still others are relatively flat. This is because they have different uses.

When you bite into an apple, you use your sharp front teeth, called incisors. These teeth are shaped to enable you to bite off pieces of food. What simple machine do these teeth resemble? **Your incisors are shaped like wedges.** When you bite down on something, the wedge shape of your front teeth produces enough force to break it in half, just as an ax is used to split a log. Your rear teeth, or molars, are more flat. These teeth are used to grind your food into pieces that are small enough to be swallowed and digested.

There's a lot more to chewing than you may have realized. The next time you take a bite of a crunchy apple, think about the machines in your mouth!

 **Section 4 Review**

1. In what way do your bones and muscles operate as levers?
2. Where in your body can you identify wedges? What role do they play in your daily life?
3. Point your left index finger (your pointing finger) in front of you. Then move it to the right. Where is the fulcrum? Where is the input force? What kind of lever is your finger?
4. **Thinking Critically** **Inferring** Make a motion as if you were going to throw a ball. What muscle do you think you use to straighten out your arm when you throw? What kind of lever are you using?

232

Science at Home

Have a family member place a wooden toothpick between the ends of his or her fingers as shown in the upper photograph. Ask that person to try to break the toothpick by pressing down with the first and third fingers. Now repeat the procedure, but this time have the person hold the toothpick as shown in the lower photograph. Explain to your family why the toothpick was easier to break on the second try. How were the positions of the forces and fulcrum different in each case?

Background

Integrating Science Many animals have adaptations that are wedges. A woodpecker's bill functions as a wedge when it drills into the bark of trees. Carnivores such as lions have sharply pointed teeth that help them pierce the flesh of prey. Similarly, the pointed talons of eagles and other birds of prey also function as wedges when they sink into the bodies of prey.

Program Resources

◆ **Unit 2 Resources** 7-4 Review and Reinforce, p. 107; 7-4 Enrich, p. 108

Media and Technology

Transparencies "Exploring Levers in the Body," Transparency 24

232

SECTION 1

What Is Work?

Key Ideas
◆ Work is done on an object when a force causes that object to move some distance.
◆ The amount of work done on an object is equal to the force on the object in the direction of its motion multiplied by the distance the object moves.

$$Work = Force \times Distance$$

Key Terms
work   joule

 SECTION 2

Mechanical Advantage and Efficiency

Key Ideas
◆ A machine makes work easier by changing the direction or amount of force needed to accomplish a task.
◆ The efficiency of a machine is the percentage of the input work that is changed to output work.

$$Efficiency = \frac{Output\ work}{Input\ work} \times 100\%$$

◆ The mechanical advantage of a machine is obtained by dividing the output force by the input force.

$$Mechanical\ advantage = \frac{Output\ force}{Input\ force}$$

◆ The ideal mechanical advantage of a machine is the mechanical advantage that it would have if there were no friction.

Key Terms
machine
input force
output force
mechanical advantage
efficiency
actual mechanical advantage
ideal mechanical advantage

 SECTION 3

Simple Machines

Key Ideas
◆ There are six basic kinds of simple machines: the inclined plane, the wedge, the screw, the lever, the wheel and axle, and the pulley.
◆ A compound machine is a machine that is made from two or more simple machines.

Key Terms
inclined plane   wheel and axle
wedge   pulley
screw   compound machine
lever   gears
fulcrum

 SECTION 4

Machines in the Human Body

INTEGRATING LIFE SCIENCE

Key Ideas
◆ Most of the machines in your body are levers that consist of bones with muscles attached to them.
◆ When you bite into something, your front teeth use the principle of the wedge.

Key Term
tendon

Organizing Information

Compare/Contrast Table Complete a compare/contrast table similar to the one shown below. For each of three other basic types of simple machines, you should show how to calculate the ideal mechanical advantage and give an example. (For more on compare/contrast tables, see the Skills Handbook.)

Simple Machine	Mechanical Advantage	Example
Inclined Plane	Length of incline ÷ Height of incline	Ramp

Organizing Information

Compare/Contrast Table

Simple Machine	Mechanical Advantage	Example
Inclined Plane	Length of incline ÷ height of incline	Ramp
Lever	Distance from fulcrum to input force ÷ distance from fulcrum to output force	Seesaw, crowbar, fishing pole, wheelbarrow
Wheel and Axle	Distance from center of wheel to outside of wheel ÷ distance from center of axle to outside of axle	Hand-mixer, screwdriver, doorknob, steering wheel
Pulley	Number of sections of rope supporting the load	Block and tackle, flag-pole lifting

Program Resources

◆ **Unit 2 Resources** Chapter 7 Project Scoring Rubric, p. 92
◆ **Performance Assessment** Chapter 7, pp. 22–24
◆ **Chapter Tests** Chapter 7 Test, pp. 27–30

Media and Technology

Computer Test Bank
Chapter 7 Test

Reviewing Content
Multiple Choice
1. b 2. b 3. a 4. d 5. c

True or False
6. true 7. true 8. efficiency
9. screw 10. wedge

Checking Concepts
11. No, because he does not move the Earth, he only holds it. There is no work without motion.
12. 50%
13. 15 N (input force × actual mechanical advantage.)
14. The longer ramp has a greater ideal mechanical advantage (6 as opposed to 3) because ideal mechanical advantage = length of incline ÷ height.
15. A wheel and axle
16. Answers may vary. Students might suggest the lower leg is a lever, with the knee as the fulcrum and the thigh muscle supplying the input force.
17. Students' responses should be creative and should incorporate what they learn in this chapter .

Thinking Critically
18. A door is a lever. The hinge is a fulcrum. The distance between the fulcrum and the output force remains the same. So if you decrease the distance between the effort force and the fulcrum (by pushing in the center of the door rather than the edge), you decrease the mechanical advantage.
19. A pulley or a wheel and axle
20. As friction increases, efficiency decreases.
21. Sharpening a knife makes the mechanical advantage greater by making the narrow edge of the wedge thinner.

Reviewing Content
Multiple Choice
Choose the letter of the answer that best completes each statement.

1. The amount of work done on an object is obtained by multiplying
   a. input force and output force.
   b. force and distance.
   c. time and force.
   d. efficiency and work.
2. One way a machine can make work easier for you is by
   a. decreasing the amount of work you do.
   b. changing the direction of your force.
   c. increasing the amount of work required for a task.
   d. decreasing the friction you encounter.
3. The output force is greater than the input force for a
   a. nutcracker.
   b. fishing pole.
   c. single fixed pulley.
   d. rake.
4. An example of a second-class lever is a
   a. seesaw.   b. shovel.
   c. paddle.   d. wheelbarrow.
5. An example of a compound machine is a
   a. screwdriver.   b. crowbar.
   c. bicycle.   d. ramp.

True or False
If the statement is true, write true. If it is false, change the underlined word or words to make the statement true.

6. If none of the force on an object is in the direction of the object's <u>motion</u>, no work is done.
7. <u>Friction</u> reduces the efficiency of a machine.
8. The comparison between output work and input work is <u>ideal mechanical advantage</u>.
9. A <u>pulley</u> can be thought of as an inclined plane wrapped around a central cylinder.
10. Your front teeth act as a <u>fulcrum</u> when you bite into something.

Checking Concepts
11. The mythical god Atlas was supposed to hold the stationary Earth on his shoulders. Was Atlas performing any work? Explain your answer.
12. Suppose that you do 1,000 joules of work when you operate an old can opener. However, the can opener does only 500 joules of work in opening the can. What is the efficiency of the can opener?
13. The actual mechanical advantage of a machine is 3. If you exert an input force of 5 N, what output force is exerted by the machine?
14. Which has a greater ideal mechanical advantage, a ramp that is 12 m long and 2 m high or a ramp that is 6 m long and 2 m high? Explain your answer.
15. When you let water into a bathtub, what kind of machine helps you open the tap?
16. Describe a lever in your body. Locate the input force, output force and fulcrum.
17. **Writing to Learn** You are a brilliant inventor. Recently you completed your most outstanding project—an odd-looking, but very important machine. Write an explanation describing your machine, how you built it, what it is made of, and what it does. You may wish to illustrate your explanation.

Thinking Critically
18. **Applying Concepts** To open a door, you push on the part farthest from the hinges. Why would it be harder to open the door if you pushed on the center?
19. **Classifying** What type of simple machine would be used to lower an empty bucket into a well and then lift the bucket full of water?
20. **Relating Cause and Effect** Describe the relationship between friction and the efficiency of a machine.
21. **Inferring** Why would sharpening a knife or ax blade improve its mechanical advantage?

Applying Skills
22. Ideal mechanical advantage = distance from fulcrum to input force ÷ distance from fulcrum to output force = 60 cm ÷ 20 cm = 3
23. 1; 2; 4
24. The graph describes the line $y = (1/20)x$.
25. The ideal mechanical advantage increases as the distance between the fulcrum and input force increases. They are directly proportional.

Applying Skills

Use the illustration to answer Questions 22–25.

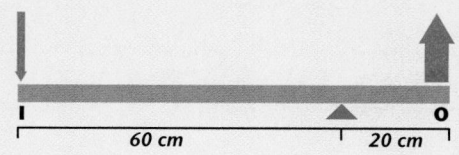

60 cm   20 cm

22. Calculating The figure shows the distance from the fulcrum to the input force (point I) and from the fulcrum to the output force (point O). Use the distance to calculate the ideal mechanical advantage of the lever.

23. Predicting What would the ideal mechanical advantage be if the distance from the fulcrum to the input force were 20 cm, 40 cm, or 80 cm?

24. Graphing Use your answers to Questions 22 and 23 to graph the distance from the fulcrum to the input force on the *x*-axis and the ideal mechanical advantage of the lever on the *y*-axis.

25. Interpreting Data What does your graph show you about the relationship between the ideal mechanical advantage of a first-class lever and the distance between the fulcrum and the input force.

Performance · CHAPTER PROJECT 7 · Assessment

Project Wrap Up Ask a classmate to review your project with you. Does your machine lift the loaded can 5 cm? Is it made up of two or more simple machines? Check all measurements and calculations. When you demonstrate your nifty lifting machine to the class, explain why you built it as you did. Describe any other designs that you considered along the way.

Reflect and Record If you were just beginning this project, you could use the knowledge you've gained to build an even better machine. Draw diagrams and write a short paragraph in your journal to explain how you would improve the machine you built.

Test Preparation

Use these questions to prepare for standardized tests.

Use the diagram to answer Questions 26–28.

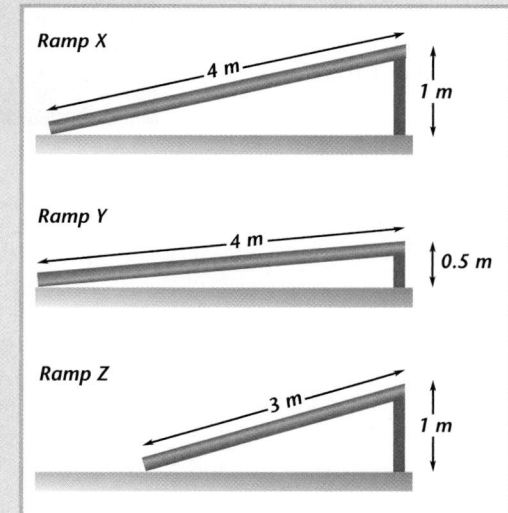

Ramp X — 4 m — 1 m

Ramp Y — 4 m — 0.5 m

Ramp Z — 3 m — 1 m

26. Which ramp has the greatest ideal mechanical advantage?
  a. X
  b. Y
  c. Z
  d. X and Y are the same.

27. To increase the ideal mechanical advantage of a ramp, you can
  a. increase the length and the height by the same amount.
  b. increase the length or decrease the height.
  c. decrease the length or increase the height.
  d. decrease the length and the height by the same amount.

28. What would the ideal mechanical advantage of Ramp Z become if the height were changed to 0.5 m and the length remained the same?
  a. 1.5   **b.** 3.5
  c. 6   **d.** 15

Project Wrap Up Review the rules with students the day before presentations to prevent students from missing their goals because they overlooked a restriction of the project. For instance, students may not remember that their machines must lift the load at least 5 cm because they were so focused on the mechanical advantage of their devices.

Any student who reached any level of success is indeed successful. A cooperative climate makes this project a positive experience for more students than does a competitive climate. You can set the example by stressing each student's success rather than comparing students' results.

Reflect and Record This step, sometimes called feedback, is an essential part of any design process. Encourage students to use their knowledge to improve their designs, not to just design another machine.

Test Preparation

26. b **27.** b **28.** c

Program Resources

◆ **Inquiry Skills Activity Book** Provides teaching and review of all inquiry skills
◆ **Prentice Hall Assessment System** Provides standardized test practice
◆ **Reading in the Content Area** Provides strategies to improve science reading skills
◆ **Teacher's ELL Handbook** Provides multiple strategies for English language learners

Bridges from Vines to Steel

This interdisciplinary feature presents the central theme of bridges by connecting four different disciplines: science, social studies, mathematics, and language arts. The four explorations are designed to capture students' interest and help them see how the content they are studying in science relates to other school subjects and to real-world events. The unit is particularly suitable for team teaching.

1 Engage/Explore

Activating Prior Knowledge

Help students recall what they learned in Chapter 5, Section 1, Balanced and Unbalanced Forces and Section 4, Action and Reaction, by asking questions such as: **What does Newton's third law say about action and reaction forces?** *(For every action force, there is an equal and opposite reaction force.)* and **If the weight of a truck pushes down on a bridge, what is the reaction force?** *(The bridge pushes up on the truck.)* Invite students to sketch on the board outlines of bridges they have seen.

Introducing the Unit

A bridge can save you from having to make a very long journey around an obstacle or from having to take a boat. Ask students the basic purposes of a bridge. Point out that bridges must be strong enough to support the weight of vehicles. Many bridges cross rivers used by water craft, so the design of the bridge must allow the craft to pass under the bridge. Refer students to the picture of the arch bridge. Ask: **What is holding this bridge up in the center of the arches?** *(Accept all reasonable responses.)*

Ask: **How do bridges encourage trade?** *(Write all reasonable responses on the board. Sample: The bridge makes it easier to transport goods.)*

B·R·I·D·G·E·S
FROM VINES TO STEEL

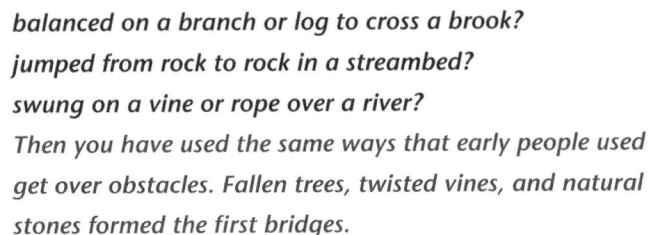

HAVE YOU EVER . . .

balanced on a branch or log to cross a brook?

jumped from rock to rock in a streambed?

swung on a vine or rope over a river?

Then you have used the same ways that early people used to get over obstacles. Fallen trees, twisted vines, and natural stones formed the first bridges.

Bridges provide easy ways of getting over difficult obstacles. For thousands of years, bridges have also served as forts for defense, scenes of great battles, and homes for shops and churches. They have also been sites of mystery, love, and intrigue. They span history—linking cities, nations, and empires and encouraging trade and travel.

But bridges have not always been as elaborate as they are today. The earliest ones were made of materials that were free and plentiful. In deep forests, people used beams made from small trees. In tropical regions where vegetation was thick, people wove together vines and grasses, then hung them to make walkways over rivers and gorges.

No matter what the structures or materials, bridges reflect the people who built them. Each of the ancient civilizations of China, Egypt, Greece, and Rome designed strong, graceful bridges to connect and control its empire.

**The Roman arch bridge
Ponte Sant'Angelo in Rome**

236

Program Resources

◆ **Unit 2 Resources** Interdisciplinary Explorations, Science, pp. 114–116; Social Studies, pp. 117–119; Language Arts, pp. 120–122; Mathematics, pp. 123–125

The Balance of Forces

What keeps a bridge from falling down? How does it support its own weight and the weight of people and traffic on it? Builders found the answers by considering the various forces that act on a bridge.

The weight of the bridge and the traffic on it are called the *load*. When a heavy truck crosses a beam bridge, the weight of the load forces the beam to curve downward. This creates a tension force that stretches the bottom of the beam. At the same time, the load also creates a compression force at the top of the beam.

Since the bridge doesn't collapse under the load, there must be upward forces to balance the downward forces. In simple beam bridges, builders attached the beam to the ground or to end supports called abutments. To cross longer spans or distances, they construct piers under the middle span. Piers and abutments are structures that act as upward forces—reaction forces.

Another type of bridge, the arch bridge, supports its load by compression. A heavy load on a stone arch bridge squeezes or pushes the stones together, creating compression throughout the structure. Weight on the arch bridge pushes down to the ends of the arch. The side walls and abutments act as reaction forces.

Early engineers discovered that arch bridges made of stone could span wider distances than simple beam bridges. Arch bridges were also stronger and more durable. Although the Romans were not the first to build arch bridges, they perfected the form in their massive, elegant structures. Early Roman arch bridges were built without mortar, or "glue." The arch held together because the stones were skillfully shaped to work in compression. After nearly 2,000 years, some of these Roman arch bridges are still standing.

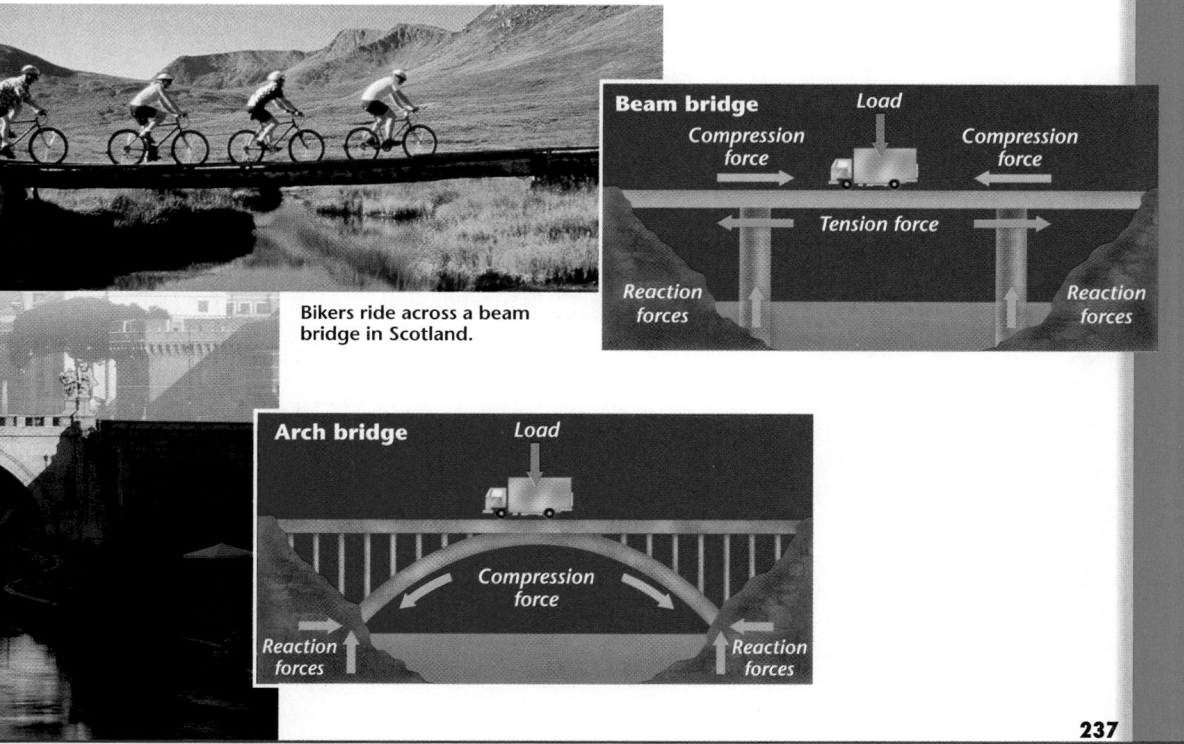

Bikers ride across a beam bridge in Scotland.

Beam bridge — Load — Compression force — Compression force — Tension force — Reaction forces — Reaction forces

Arch bridge — Load — Compression force — Reaction forces — Reaction forces

237

Background

Facts and Figures The oldest bridge still in use whose construction date can be accurately determined is in Turkey. This stone arch bridge over the River Meles in Izmir dates from about 850 B.C.

The longest stone arch bridge in the world is the Rockville Bridge in Pennsylvania. The bridge has 48 spans and is 1,161 meters long. This type of bridge is no longer built in the United States because of the expense.

Early bridge builders worked with stone, which is very strong in compression but very weak when bent. So early bridges were designed so that the forces of the load could be transferred to compression forces in the stone. Bridges, buildings, and aqueducts were all built by the Romans using arches, because arches take advantage of the high compression strength of stone.

2 Facilitate

- Have volunteers each read one paragraph aloud. As they are reading, direct students' attention to the diagrams.
- Point out that traffic does not necessarily refer to vehicles. Traffic can also mean people and animals.
- Challenge interested students to make a list of the different types of bridges. Then have students illustrate them with pictures or sketches and make a bulletin board display for the class.
- Invite a volunteer to find a diagram of the parts of a bridge in an encyclopedia or visual dictionary. In particular, have the student find illustrations of abutments to share with the class.
- Point out that bridges are too expensive and it would be too dangerous for builders to find out by trial and error how many supports a bridge needs. Ask students: **How do builders know how many supports a bridge needs?** (Answers will vary. Samples: they calculate the forces mathematically; they build scale models and test them; they use computer simulations)
- Model a beam bridge by laying a meter stick between two desks. Show how the meter stick bends as you add weight to the center of the stick.
- If there is a bridge in or near your town, encourage students to find out more about the bridge. Ask students to research when the bridge was built, why it was needed, how much it cost, why the design was chosen, and how people got around or across the obstacle before the bridge was built.
- Point out that this page is titled "The Balance of Forces." Ask: **What does this mean?** (The force of the load on the bridge is balanced by upward forces.) Ask: **What might happen if the forces were not balanced?** (The bridge could move or collapse.)

2 Facilitate

- Ask: **Why do trains need flat bridges?** *(Trains are very heavy. A train needs a huge amount of power to go uphill so railroads are built as flat as possible.)*
- Ask: **Why would builders prefer working with steel than iron?** *(Answers may vary. Sample: A bridge of a given strength can be built with lighter materials.)*
- As the class reads the text, direct students' attention to the bridge diagrams.
- Challenge an interested student to find a drawing or photograph of a tropical woven bridge. Have students compare the designs of the bridges. Ask: **Woven bridges sway in the wind. What does that tell you about suspension bridges?** *(They probably sway in the wind also.)* Point out that suspension bridges are designed to allow for some movement in high winds. The shape of some valleys cause them to be windy so bridge designers have to include wind factors in their design.
- Clarify that the road hangs from the wires. The towers do not support the road. The towers support the giant cables from which the road hangs.
- Ask: **What does the phrase "golden age" mean?** *(a very fortunate period)* **Why were the 1800s a golden age for bridges?** *(Many bridges were built because they were needed for railroads.)*
- On the photograph of the Brooklyn Bridge, point out the span while you explain that a span is one section of a bridge. A bridge may have several spans.

The Golden Age of Bridges

In the 1800s in the United States, the invention of the steam locomotive and the expansion of railroads increased the demand for bridges. Trains pulling heavy freight needed strong, flat bridges. Builders began to use cast iron instead of stone and wood. By the late 1800s, they were using steel, which was strong and relatively lightweight.

The use of new building materials was not the only change. Engineers began designing different types of bridges as well. They found that they could build longer, larger bridges by using a suspension structure.

Suspension bridges are modern versions of long, narrow, woven bridges found in tropical regions. These simple, woven suspension bridges can span long distances. Crossing one of these natural structures is like walking a tightrope. The weight of people and animals traveling over the bridge pushes down on the ropes, stretching them and creating tension forces.

Modern suspension bridges follow the same principles of tension as do woven bridges. A suspension bridge is strong in tension. In suspension bridges, parallel cables are stretched the entire length of the bridge—over giant towers. The cables are anchored at each end of the bridge. The roadway hangs from the cables, attached by wire suspenders. The weight of the bridge and the load on it act to pull apart or stretch the cables. This pulling apart creates tension force.

The towers act as supports for the bridge cables. The abutments that anchor the cables exert reaction forces as well. So forces in balance keep a suspension bridge from collapsing.

Brooklyn Bridge today

Suspension bridge — Tension force — Load — Reaction forces — Reaction forces

238

Background

Facts and Figures Iron, steel, and other metals are more flexible than stone but they are also very strong in tension. So it is possible to design a bridge that takes advantage of the strength of wire in tension to build higher and longer bridges than would be practical with stone (or the modern equivalent of stone, concrete).

Suspension bridges can span greater distances than beam or arch bridges because the strong steel cables transfer force to the tall towers. The towers can be built high enough to allow huge ocean liners to sail underneath. The tallest masted ships could still sail beneath the Brooklyn Bridge.

Each of the smaller cables that hang from the four main cables of the Brooklyn Bridge is made up of seven bundles of seven steel wires.

A Great Engineering Feat

When it opened in 1883, the Brooklyn Bridge was the longest suspension bridge in the world—one half span longer than any other. It connected Brooklyn and Manhattan. Yet when the idea was first proposed, people said it couldn't be done.

In the mid-1800s, many people from Brooklyn had jobs across the East River in Manhattan. But the only way to get there was by ferry. Fierce ocean tides, stormy weather, and ice chunks in winter could make the journey risky. In 1868 John Augustus Roebling, a German immigrant engineer, was hired to build a bridge.

An engineering genius, Roebling designed a suspension bridge using four cables stretched over two giant granite towers. Roebling was the first engineer to design bridge cables of strong, flexible steel instead of cast iron.

Each cable, about 16 inches in diameter, would contain nearly 5,300 wires. After the cables were in place, 1,500 smaller suspension cables would be attached to the main cables to support the roadway. It's not surprising that people didn't believe that it could be done.

It was impossible to lift heavy cables over the towers. So builders had to reel wire back and forth across the East River to create the cables. There are 3,515 miles of wire for each cable! To "spin the cables" John Roebling invented a traveling wheel that could carry the wire in a continuous loop, from one side of the river over the towers to the other side and back. It's an invention that is still used today.

Science Activity

Work in groups to make a suspension bridge, using 2 chairs, a wooden plank, rope, and some books.

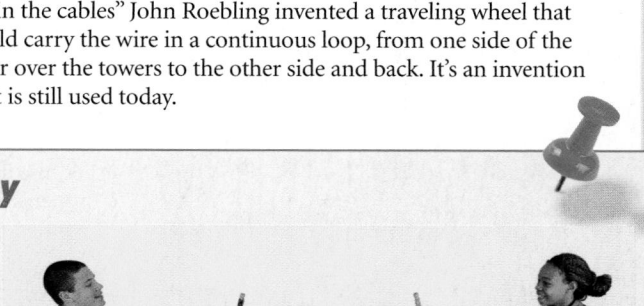

- Place 2 chairs back to back and stretch 2 ropes over the backs of the chairs. Hold the ropes at both ends.

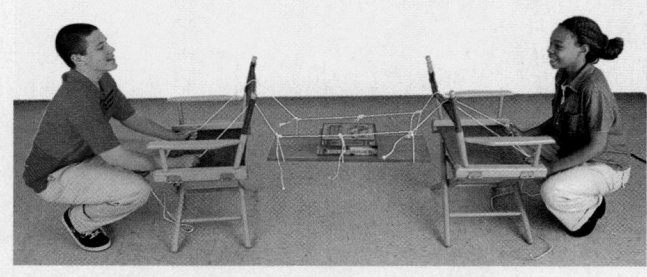

- Tie 3 pieces of rope to the longer ropes. Place the plank through the loops.
- With a partner, hold the ropes tightly at each end. Load books on top of the plank to see how much it will hold.

Why is it important to anchor the ropes tightly at each end?

239

Background

History John Roebling never lived to see his bridge reach completion. On June 28, 1869, he was inspecting the site of a bridge tower while standing on a ferry slip. Pilings on the slip shifted, and Roebling's foot was crushed between two pilings. Tetanus developed and Roebling was dead within a month. Washington Roebling, his son, took over the construction.

Some years later, Washington Roebling became disabled by caisson disease ("the bends"). In those days, the cause of the disease was not understood. Partly paralyzed, Washington supervised construction by telescope from his bedroom window in Brooklyn Heights.

- Ask: **In the 1990s, the record for the world's longest suspension bridge span has been exceeded several times. Do you think the record will continue to be broken?** *(Answers may vary. Sample: No; there must be some limit to how much weight a single span can support.)* If possible, find a civil engineer to discuss bridge design with the class.
- Point out that the Brooklyn Bridge was successfully built even though many people believed it was impossible. Ask students to suggest inventions or achievements that some people today feel are impossible but that are likely to be achieved in the future.
- Point out that the cranes you see on construction sites today did not exist when the Brooklyn Bridge was being built.
- **Unit 2 Resources** The following worksheets correlate with this page: Build an Arch Bridge, page 114; Move That Bridge!, page 115; and How Rainbow Bridge was Formed, page 116.

Science Activity

Materials *2 chairs, thin rope, wooden plank about 50 cm × 20 cm × 1 cm, several books for load*

Time 20 minutes

Have two students in each group hold the ends of the ropes while the other group members attach the vertical ropes and place the plank. Since the load is transferred to tension in the ropes, they must be anchored or held securely.

To extend this activity, invite students to experiment with changing the distance between the chairs or changing where students attach the vertical ropes.

Have students demonstrate for themselves that their suspension bridge can sway slightly in wind without damage.

3 Assess

Activity Assessment

Ask students what to describe the function of each part of their "chair bridge" and what structure in the Brooklyn Bridge performs the same

2 Facilitate

◆ Ask students: **How might bridge workers die on the job?** (*Answers may vary. Sample: falling from the bridge*) Explain that several bridge workers suffered from caisson disease ("the bends"), which is usually associated with scuba divers. The caissons had to be pressurized to prevent water from flowing in. When workers ascended to the surface too quickly, bubbles of nitrogen gas sometimes formed in the blood stream, causing excruciating pain or permanent paralysis.

◆ Ask students: **Why did Roebling have workers twist the wires together?** (*Twisting the strands of wire together gave them the strength of a single thick wire while still remaining flexible.*)

◆ **Unit 2 Resources** The following worksheets correlate with this page: Pros and Cons, page 117; Comparing Bridges, page 118; and Find the Bridges, page 119.

Social Studies Activity

Assign each group a different kind of famous bridge to research (for example, suspension, arch, beam). Tell students to begin by planning what questions each student will be responsible for researching. Suggest that students locate information about the bridge they are researching by reading about the city in which it is located.

Events connected to the bridge may be famous accidents, annual celebrations, or significant historical dates. Schedule time for students to make their presentations to the class.

3 Assess

Activity Assessment

Evaluate students' research procedures, particularly note-taking. Make sure students' presentations include the points on the student page.

Against All Odds

When John Roebling was hired in 1868 to build the Brooklyn Bridge, he was already an experienced suspension bridge engineer. He had plans for the bridge that he'd been working on since 1855.

But before bridge construction even began in 1869, John Roebling died in a bridge-related accident. Fortunately, he had worked out his bridge design to the last detail. His son, Colonel Washington Roebling, who was also a skilled engineer, dedicated himself to carrying out his father's plans.

The construction dragged on for 14 years and cost nearly 30 lives. Colonel Roebling himself became so disabled that he was forced to direct construction from his home. Using a telescope, Colonel Roebling followed every detail. His remarkable, energetic wife, Emily Warren Roebling, learned enough engineering principles to deliver and explain his orders to the workers.

The dedication of the Roebling family—John (left), Washington (center), and Emily (right)—ensured the success of the Brooklyn Bridge.

As soon as the giant towers were up, workers unrolled the steel wire back and forth across the towers to weave the cables. The next step was to twist the wires together. But the workmen were terrified of hanging so high on the bridge and refused to work. Finally, Frank Farrington, the chief mechanic, crossed the river on a small chair dangling from a wheel that ran across an overhead line. Farrington completed his journey to the roar of the crowd. This feat was billed as the greatest trapeze act of all time. Somewhat reassured, the builders returned to work. But it took two more years to string the cables. The bridge was one of the greatest engineering achievements of its time.

In the end, the Brooklyn Bridge project succeeded only because of the determination and sacrifices of the Roebling family. It became the model for hundreds of other suspension bridges.

Workers building the Brooklyn Bridge

Social Studies Activity

How do you think the Brooklyn Bridge changed the lives of New Yorkers? In groups, research the history of another famous bridge. Present your findings to your class along with drawings and photos. Find out

◆ when and why the bridge was built
◆ the type of bridge
◆ how peoples' lives changed after it was built—include effects on trade, travel, and population
◆ how landforms affected the bridge building
◆ about events connected to the bridge

Background

Integrating Science and Technology

Roebling designed his bridge using steel wire instead of the iron wire that had traditionally been used. Steel wire was a relatively new material then and had not yet proven itself. The wire for the Brooklyn Bridge was supplied by a contractor. After the workers had begun reeling the wire to make cables, they discovered that the wire did not match the bid specifications. The contractor had committed fraud by substituting cheaper and weaker wire. Fortunately, Roebling initially designed the bridge using steel wire that would be six times stronger than necessary. The cheaper wire that had been substituted was still five times stronger than necessary so the weaker wire remained in the bridge.

The New York Times   *May 25, 1883*

Two Great Cities United

The Brooklyn bridge was successfully opened yesterday. The pleasant weather brought visitors by the thousands from all around. Spectators were packed in masses through which it was almost impossible to pass, and those who had tickets to attend the ceremonies had hard work to reach the bridge. Every available house-top and window was filled, and an adventurous party occupied a tall telegraph pole. It required the utmost efforts of the police to keep clear the necessary space.

After the exercises at the bridge were completed the Brooklyn procession was immediately re-formed and the march was taken up to Col. Roebling's residence. From the back study on the second floor of his house Col. Roebling had watched through his telescope the procession as it proceeded along from the New York side until the Brooklyn tower was reached. Mrs. Roebling received at her husband's side and accepted her share of the honors of the bridge.

For blocks and blocks on either side of the bridge there was scarcely a foot of room to spare. Many persons crossed and re-crossed the river on the ferry boats, and in that way watched the display. Almost every ship along the river front was converted into a grand stand.

The final ceremonies of the opening of the great bridge began at eight o'clock, when the first rocket was sent from the center of the great structure, and ended at 9 o'clock, when a flight of 500 rockets illuminated the sky. The river-front was one blaze of light, and on the yachts and smaller vessels blue fires were burning and illuminating dark waters around them.

Story adapted from *The New York Times*, May 25, 1883.

THE GRAND DISPLAY OF FIREWORKS AND ILLUMINATIONS

This historic painting shows fireworks at the opening of the Brooklyn Bridge in 1883.

Language Arts Activity

A reporter's goal is to inform and entertain the reader. Using a catchy opening line draws interest. Then the reader wants to know the facts—what, who, where, when, why, and how (5 Ws and H).

You are a school reporter. Write about the opening of a bridge in your area. It could be a highway overpass or a bridge over water, a valley, or railroad tracks.

◆ Include some of the 5 Ws and H.
◆ Add interesting details and descriptions.

241

Background

Integrating Science and Technology In the summer of 1940, a new bridge was built over the narrows of Puget Sound, uniting two other cities, Tacoma and Seattle. Four months later, on November 7, 1940, the bridge collapsed. The aerodynamic forces of wind on bridges was not well understood in 1940. The bridge was simply too flexible. It was also built with plate girders, which provided a flat, eight foot high wall of steel on which the wind could blow. The combination proved disastrous when a 42-mile-an-hour wind set up torsional vibrations of the bridge that eventually tore the suspenders, causing the bridge to collapse.

When the bridge was rebuilt, open trusses were used instead of plate girders. The trusses are stiffer than girders and the wind can blow through the trusses, thus reducing the force exerted by the wind on the bridge.

2 Facilitate

◆ Ask: **Why was every house-top and window filled?** *(People wanted to see the procession and the fireworks.)* **Why was the bridge opening such a huge event?** *(Answers may vary. Samples: the bridge had taken years to build; many people believed it could never be built)*

◆ Clarify that the word "party" in the first paragraph can mean one person. Students may imagine that a whole group of people climbed to the top of a telegraph pole.

◆ To extend this exploration, have students think about where in or near your town they think a bridge would be useful. Have students consider what type of bridge would be most suitable for the location.

◆ **Unit 2 Resources** The following worksheets correlate with this page: Letter to the Editor, page 120; Many Kinds of Bridges, page 121; and A Poem Written on a Bridge, page 122.

Language Arts Activity

Students were probably not present when a bridge was opened, so have them think of a bridge in or near your town. Then have them imagine how the town was different before the bridge was built. Students could talk to long-term residents to find out what public opinion was during the construction and how town life changed as a result. Or you may wish to have students write about another civic event. Have pairs of students check each other's work to ensure that the main facts are included in the article.

3 Assess

Activity Assessment

Make sure students' writing is in the form of a newspaper article. Check that the major facts (5 Ws and H) are included. Students' stories should be informative but also interesting.

2 Facilitate

- ◆ To extend this exploration, cut four 10-cm × 1-cm strips of heavy cardboard. Punch a hole 0.5-cm from the end of each strip. Attach the strips end-to-end with brads to form a closed figure. Show the students how the shape of the figure can be altered. Now remove one of the strips so that a triangle is formed. Show the students how the triangle has a fixed shape. Ask students which shape would be better to use in bridge supports. (*The triangle, because of its fixed shape*)

- ◆ **Unit 2 Resources** The following worksheets correlate with this page: Graphing Bridge Data, page 123; and Konigsberg Bridge Problem, pages 124–125.

Math Activity

Urge students to record their answers slowly and carefully. They can easily write down the wrong letters if they work too hastily.

3 Assess

Activity Assessment

1. AE and IF are parallel. AI, BH, CG, and DF are parallel to each other. BG and CF are parallel. CH, DG, and EF are parallel.

2. All pairs of lines that are not parallel intersect.

3. rectangle

4. triangle

5. obtuse

6. acute

7. right triangle; It has a 90° angle.

8. A square does not have a rigid shape.

Bridge Geometry

As railroad traffic increased in the late 1800s, truss bridges became popular. Designed with thin vertical and diagonal supports to add strength, truss bridges were really reinforced beam bridge structures. Many of the early wood truss bridges couldn't support the trains that rumbled over them. Cast iron and steel trusses soon replaced wood trusses.

Using basic triangular structures, engineers went to work on more scientific truss bridge designs. The accuracy of the design is crucial to handling the stress from heavy train loads and constant vibrations. As in all bridge structures, each steel piece has to be measured and fitted accurately—including widths, lengths, angles, and points of intersection and attachment.

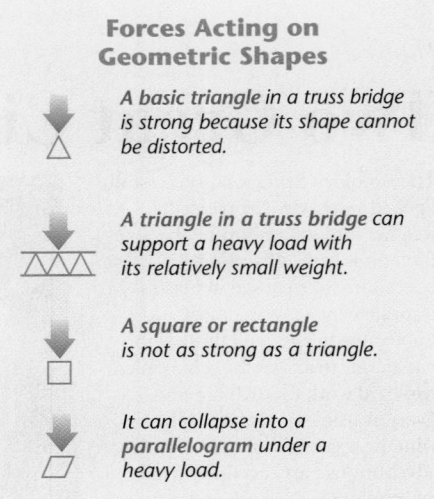

Forces Acting on Geometric Shapes

A basic triangle in a truss bridge is strong because its shape cannot be distorted.

A triangle in a truss bridge can support a heavy load with its relatively small weight.

A square or rectangle is not as strong as a triangle.

It can collapse into a parallelogram under a heavy load.

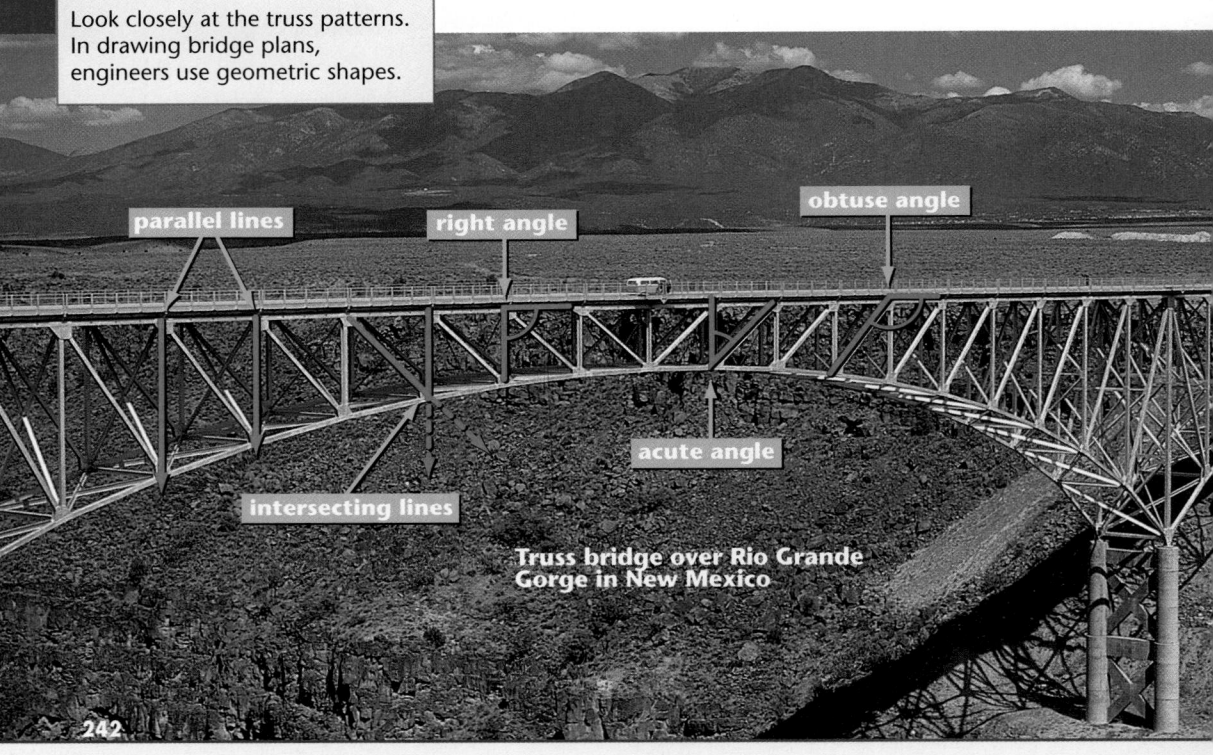

Look closely at the truss patterns. In drawing bridge plans, engineers use geometric shapes.

parallel lines

right angle

obtuse angle

intersecting lines

acute angle

Truss bridge over Rio Grande Gorge in New Mexico

242

Background

Integrating Science and Technology

When engineers have distances to measure that cannot be measured directly, they use trigonometry. Trigonometry is a branch of mathematics that deals with relationships between the sides and angles of triangles. A distance can be measured by representing it with one side of a triangle, measuring other sides or angles in the triangle, and then using trigonometric formulas to calculate the length of the side to be measured. Trigonometry has many applications in engineering, for example, studying vibrations in a building or a bridge.

Math Activity

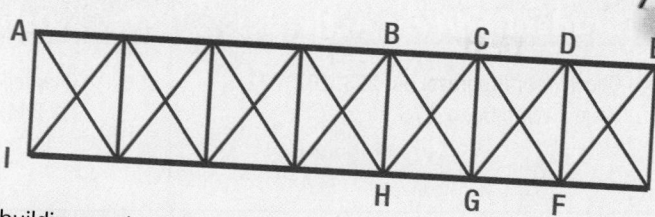

The chief building engineer has asked you to draw up exact plans for a new truss bridge. How well will you do as an assistant? You will soon find out by answering these questions:

1. Which lines are parallel?
2. Which lines intersect?
3. What kind of figure is formed by ABHI?
4. What kind of figure is formed by HCF?
5. What kind of angle is BGF—obtuse or right?
6. What kind of angle is CHG?
7. What kind of triangle is BHG? What makes it this kind of triangle?
8. Why is a triangle stronger than a square?

Tie It Together

Bridge the Gap

Work in small groups to build a model of a bridge out of a box of spaghetti and a roll of masking tape. Meet as a group to choose the type of bridge you will build. Each bridge should be strong enough to hold a brick. You can build—

◆ a beam bridge
◆ a truss bridge
◆ an arch bridge
◆ a suspension bridge (This one is challenging.)

After drawing a sketch of the bridge design, assign jobs for each team member. Then

◆ decide how long the bridge span will be
◆ measure and cut the materials
◆ build the roadway first for beam, truss, and suspension bridges
◆ build the arch first in an arch bridge

When your bridge is complete, display it in the classroom. Test the strength of each bridge by placing a brick on the roadway. Discuss the difference in bridge structures. Determine which bridge design is the strongest.

243

READING STRATEGIES

Further Reading Oxlade, Chris, *Bridges,* Raintree/Steck Vaughn, 1997.
Mann, Elizabeth B. and Alan Witschonke, *The Brooklyn Bridge: A Wonders of the World Book,* Mikaya Press, 1996.

Tie It Together

Time 2 class periods (1 period for planning and building; 1 period for finishing building, testing the design, examining other groups' work, and cleaning up) You may want to add an extra day so students can test whether their bridges could stay standing overnight.

Tips Divide the class into four groups. Assign each group a type of bridge.

◆ Make sure students understand that because their bridges are different designs, some groups will take longer than others. Students should not try to race.

◆ Have students spend 15 minutes planning their designs before you hand out the building materials. Urge students to plan first, not begin building by trial and error.

◆ You may wish to line each work area with newspaper to make cleanup easier.

◆ If the bridges will be sitting overnight, have students work in parts of the room where their constructions may be left.

◆ To discourage groups from using excessive amounts of masking tape to reinforce the spaghetti, you may wish to give each group a limited amount of tape rather than an entire roll.

◆ Groups making suspension bridges may need the most help. Suggest that they make the towers from spaghetti and the cables from rolled lengths of tape.

Extend As an alternative to building four different types of bridges, have all groups build the same type of bridge. To encourage them to use their materials as efficiently as possible, assign costs to all materials (such as $1 million for each length of spaghetti and $5 million for each meter of masking tape). Assign a volunteer to "sell" materials and keep track of how much money each group spends on materials.

CHAPTER 8 Magnetism and Electromagnetism

Sections	Time	Student Edition Activities	Other Activities
CHAPTER PROJECT 8 **Electromagnetic Fishing Derby** p. 244	Ongoing (3 weeks)	Check Your Progress, pp. 253, 267, 272 Project Wrap Up, p. 275	**TE** Chapter 8 Project Notes, pp. 244–245
1 **The Nature of Magnetism** pp. 246–255 ◆ 8.1.1 Define magnetic poles and describe the interaction between like and unlike magnetic poles. ◆ 8.1.2 Define magnetic fields and describe magnetic field lines. ◆ 8.1.3 Define magnetic domain and state how magnetic domains are lined up in magnetized material.	1 period/ ½ block	**Discover** What Do All Magnets Have in Common?, p. 246 **Sharpen Your Skills** Observing, p. 248 **Try This** How Attractive!, p. 252 **Real-World Lab: You Solve the Mystery** Detecting Fake Coins, pp. 254–255	**TE** Building Inquiry Skills: Predicting, p. 247 **TE** Building Inquiry Skills: Observing, p. 248 **TE** Including All Students, p. 251
2 **INTEGRATING EARTH SCIENCE** **Magnetic Earth** pp. 256–261 ◆ 8.2.1 Identify the magnetic properties of Earth and compare the magnetic and geographic poles. ◆ 8.2.2 Describe some of the effects of Earth's magnetic fields.	1 period/ ½ block	**Discover** Can You Use a Needle to Make a Compass?, p. 256 **Sharpen Your Skills** Measuring, p. 257 **Try This** Spinning in Circles, p. 259 **Science at Home** p. 261	**TE** Including All Students, p. 258 **TE** Demonstration, p. 260
3 **Electric Current and Magnetic Fields** pp. 262-269 ◆ 8.3.1 Describe the relationship between electric current and a magnetic field. ◆ 8.3.2 Define and give examples of conductors and insulators. ◆ 8.3.3 Identify the characteristics of an electric circuit.	2 periods/ 1 block	**Discover** Are Magnetic Fields Limited to Magnets?, p. 262 **Sharpen Your Skills** Classifying, p. 266 **Real-World Lab: How It Works** Build a Flashlight, pp. 268–269	**TE** Demonstration, p. 264 **TE** Integrating Technology, p. 266
4 **Electromagnets** pp. 270–272 ◆ 8.4.1 Identify characteristics and cite uses of an electromagnet.	1 period/ ½ block	**Discover** How Do You Turn a Magnet On and Off?, p. 270	**TE** Building Inquiry Skills: Making Models, p. 271 **TE** Inquiry Challenge, p. 271 **TE** Integrating Technology, p. 272 **LM** 8, "Electromagnetism"
Study Guide/Assessment pp. 273–275	1 period/ ½ block		**ISAB** Provides teaching and review of all inquiry skills

For Standard or Block Schedule The Resource Pro® CD-ROM gives you maximum flexibility for planning your instruction for any type of schedule. Resource Pro® contains Planning Express®, an advanced scheduling program, as well as the entire contents of the Teaching Resources and the Computer Test Bank.

Key: **CTB** Computer Test Bank
CT Chapter Tests
ELL Teacher's ELL Handbook

CHAPTER PLANNING GUIDE

Program Resources	Assessment Strategies	Media and Technology
UR Chapter 8 Project Teacher Notes, pp. 2–3 **UR** Chapter 8 Project Overview and Worksheets, pp. 4–7	**TE** Check Your Progress, pp. 253, 267, 272 **TE** Performance Assessment: Chapter 8 Project Wrap Up, p. 275 **UR** Chapter 8 Project Scoring Rubric, p. 8	Science Explorer Internet Site Audio CDs, Section Summaries
UR 8-1 Lesson Plan, p. 9 **UR** 8-1 Section Summary, p. 10 **UR** 8-1 Review and Reinforce, p. 11 **UR** 8-1 Enrich, p. 12 **UR** Real-World Lab blackline masters, pp. 25–27	**SE** Section 1 Review, p. 253 **SE** Analyze and Conclude, p. 255 **TE** Ongoing Assessment, pp. 247, 249, 251 **TE** Performance Assessment, p. 253	Presentation Pro, "Magnetism" Transparency 25, "Magnetic Fields" Transparency 26, "Dividing Magnets" Lab Activity Videotape, *Tape 2*
UR 8-2 Lesson Plan, p. 13 **UR** 8-2 Section Summary, p. 14 **UR** 8-2 Review and Reinforce, p. 15 **UR** 8-2 Enrich, p. 16	**SE** Section 2 Review, p. 261 **TE** Ongoing Assessment, pp. 257, 259 **TE** Performance Assessment, p. 261	Concept Videotape Library, *Adventures, Tape 2,* "The Northern Lights" Transparency 27, "The Magnetosphere"
UR 8-3 Lesson Plan, p. 17 **UR** 8-3 Section Summary, p. 18 **UR** 8-3 Review and Reinforce, p. 19 **UR** 8-3 Enrich, p. 20 **UR** Real-World Lab blackline masters, pp. 28–29	**SE** Section 3 Review, p. 267 **SE** Analyze and Conclude, p. 269 **TE** Ongoing Assessment, pp. 263, 265 **TE** Performance Assessment, p. 267	Concept Videotape Library, *Adventures, Tape 2,* "What Is Electricity?" Transparency 28, "Exploring Electric Circuits" Lab Activity Videotape, *Tape 2*
UR 8-4 Lesson Plan, p. 21 **UR** 8-4 Section Summary, p. 22 **UR** 8-4 Review and Reinforce, p. 23 **UR** 8-4 Enrich, p. 24	**SE** Section 4 Review, p. 272 **TE** Ongoing Assessment, p. 271 **TE** Performance Assessment, p. 272	Transparency 29, "Electromagnetism" Transparency 30, "Doorbell"
GRSW Provides worksheets to promote student comprehension of content **RCA** Provides strategies to improve science reading skills **ELL** Provides multiple strategies for English language learners	**SE** Study Guide/Assessment, pp. 273–275 **PA** Performance Assessment, pp. 25–27 **CT** Chapter 8 Test, pp. 31–34 **CTB** Chapter 8 Test **PHAS** Provides standardized test preparation	Computer Test Bank, Chapter 8 Test

GRSW Guided Reading and Study Workbook
ISAB Inquiry Skills Activity Book
LM Laboratory Manual

PA Performance Assessment
PHAS Prentice Hall Assessment System
PLM Probeware Lab Manual

RCA Reading in the Content Area
SE Student Edition

TE Teacher's Edition
UR Unit Resources

Meeting the National Science Education Standards and AAAS Benchmarks

National Science Education Standards	Benchmarks for Science Literacy	Unifying Themes
Science as Inquiry (Content Standard A) ◆ **Ask questions that can be answered by scientific investigations** How can you use a magnet to tell the difference between real and fake coins? *(Real-World Lab)* ◆ **Communicate scientific procedures and explanations** Students build a flashlight that works. Students build an electromagnet. *(Real-World Lab; Chapter Project)* **Physical Science** (Content Standard B) ◆ **Transfer of energy** An electric current is the flow of charge through a material. *(Section 3)* An electromagnet is a magnet that can be turned on and off. *(Section 4)* **Earth Science** (Content Standard D) ◆ **Structure of the earth system** Earth is surrounded by an immense magnetic field that is similar to the magnetic field around a bar magnet. *(Section 2)*	**1C The Scientific Enterprise** Students learn about the development of the electric light bulb and the different materials that Edison used in its development. *(Section 3)* **4G Forces of Nature** Magnetism is the attraction of a magnet for iron. A magnet has two ends called magnetic poles where the magnetic effect is the strongest. The magnetic force around a magnet is known as its magnetic field. Earth's magnetic poles differ from Earth's geographic north and south. *(Sections 1, 2)* **8C Energy Sources and Use** Electric currents flow though metal wires. The charges of electric currents move freely through materials called *conductors*. Charges are not able to move freely through materials called *insulators*. *(Section 2)*	◆ **Stability** Conductors are materials through which electric charges flow; electric charges do not flow through insulators. A magnetic field will always exist around a magnet and a current. *(Sections 1, 3)* ◆ **Scale and Structure** Every magnet regardless of size or shape has two poles where the magnetic effects are usually the strongest. *(Sections 2, 3, 4)* ◆ **Systems and Interactions** Properties of the atoms in a substance determine whether it will conduct electricity or not. The opposition to the movement of charges flowing through a material is called resistance. A magnetic field will exert a force on a wire that is carrying current. *(Sections 1, 2, 3)*

Take It to the Net

The www.phschool.com Web site provides you with multiple opportunities to incorporate the internet into your instruction. Go to www.phschool.com and click on the Science icon. Then select Science Explorer Integrated.

Internet Activities provide opportunities for students to review, extend, or assess a concept from the chapter.

■ Have students use the chapter Self-Test to get instant feedback.

■ Hot Links and Reference Links provide opportunities for online research.

STAY CURRENT with **SCIENCE NEWS** ®

Find out the latest research and information about magnetism at: **www.phschool.com**

ACTIVITY	Time (minutes)	Materials Quantities for one work group	Skills
Section 1			
Discover, p. 246	15	**Nonconsumable** bar magnet, horseshoe magnet, paper clips	Observing
Sharpen Your Skills, p. 248	10	**Nonconsumable** pencil, foam cup, 2 circular magnets	Observing
Try This, p. 252	20	**Nonconsumable** clear plastic tube, iron filings, strong bar magnet	Making Models
Real-World Lab, pp. 254–255	45	**Consumable** craft stick; tape; thin, stiff cardboard, about 25 cm × 30 cm **Nonconsumable** various coins; metric ruler; pencil; protractor; coin-sized steel washers; small bar magnet, about 2 cm wide	Predicting, Inferring
Section 2			
Discover, p. 256	20	**Consumable** water, dishwashing soap **Nonconsumable** large needle, strong bar magnet, dish, cork or foam ball, pliers	Observing
Sharpen Your Skills, p. 257	15	**Nonconsumable** local map, compass, protractor	Measuring
Try This, p. 259	20	**Consumable** sheet of paper **Nonconsumable** bar magnet, compass, centimeter ruler	Drawing Conclusions
Science at Home, p. 261	home	**Nonconsumable** compass	Classifying, Drawing Conclusions
Section 3			
Discover, p. 262	25	**Nonconsumable** 2 wires (20 cm long with insulation stripped from ends), light bulb, bulb holder, 3 compasses, D cell (1.5 volt)	Inferring
Sharpen Your Skills, p. 266	20	**Nonconsumable** 3 10-cm wires with insulation stripped from ends; 2 alligator clips; light bulb; D cell; conductors and insulators to test such as keys, foam, erasers, pencil lead, foil, wax paper, and paper clips	Classifying
Real-World Lab, pp. 268–269	40	**Consumable** cardboard tube, aluminum foil, paper cup, duct tape **Nonconsumable** D cell; flashlight bulb; scissors; 2 lengths of wire about 10 cm, with the insulation stripped off about 2 cm at each end; length of wire, 15–20 cm, with the insulation stripped off each end	Making Models, Observing, Inferring
Section 4			
Discover, p. 270	20	**Nonconsumable** 1 m bell wire or magnet wire, iron nail, D cell, paper clips	Forming Operational Definitions

A list of all materials required for the Student Edition activities can be found beginning on page T23. You can obtain information about ordering materials by calling 1-800-848-9500 or by accessing the Science Explorer Internet site at: **www.phschool.com**

Electro-magnetic Fishing Derby

Electromagnets can be turned on and off using the switch of an electric circuit. This allows electromagnets to perform complicated tasks such as lifting and releasing objects.

Purpose In this project, students will apply concepts about magnetism and electricity from the chapter to design a circuit and build electromagnetic fishing rods. They will use their fishing rods to lift paper clips and move them from one container to another.

Skills Focus After completing the Chapter 8 Project, students will be able to

- make model fishing rods using permanent magnets;
- design a switch for an electric circuit;
- identify and experiment with variables that affect the strength of an electromagnet.

Project Time Line This project will take about three weeks. Spend the first day discussing magnetism and electro-magnetic devices. Students should spend the next two or three days designing their model fishing rods using permanent magnets. Allow three or four days for students to experiment with electric circuits and develop a working switch. By the end of the second week, students should begin testing their electromagnets and incorporating them into their devices. At the end of the project, allow one class period for students to practice and fine-tune their fishing techniques. On the final day, allow students to present their fishing rods and "fish" for one minute. Before beginning the project, see Chapter 8 Project Teacher Notes on pages 2–3 in Unit 3 Resources for more details on carrying out the project. Also distribute to students the Chapter 8 Project Overview, Worksheets, and Scoring Rubric on pages 4–8 in Unit 3 Resources.

Possible Shortcuts This project can be completed in class by groups of four students rather than by individuals. Give each group a dowel, 12 m of wire, paper clips, a large nail, and tape. Two group

members can make the electromagnet while the other two devise a switch mechanism to be mounted on the fishing rod's handle. Students in a group can fish in relay style—they take turns lifting a batch of "fish" out of the pond and then pass the rod to the next person.

Possible Materials

- Each student will need 12–15 m of thin insulated wire and one fresh 1.5-volt D cell.
- Students can use meter sticks, dowels, broom handles, or plain sticks for the 1-m fishing rods.
- Students will use string for suspending the electromagnets and masking or electrical tape for connecting wires or attaching parts to the rod.
- Provide one large plastic container to serve as a fishing "pond." Provide an additional container for each group (Note: up to three groups at a time) to serve as "catch" basins. The pond should contain 50 paper clips for each group.

Magnetism and Electromagnetism

WEB ACTIVITY www.phschool.com

Integrating Earth Science

SECTION 1 **The Nature of Magnetism**	SECTION 2 **Magnetic Earth**	SECTION 3 **Electric Current and Magnetic Fields**
Discover What Do All Magnets Have in Common?	Discover Can You Use a Needle to Make a Compass?	Discover Are Magnetic Fields Limited to Magnets?
Sharpen Your Skills Observing	Sharpen Your Skills Measuring	Sharpen Your Skills Classifying
Try This How Attractive!	Try This Spinning in Circles	Real-World Lab Build a Flashlight
Real-World Lab Detecting Fake Coins		

244

Electromagnetic Fishing Derby

If you went fishing for cars, what kind of hook would you use—a ship's anchor? Though they resemble giant fishing rods, the cranes used in junkyards to move scrap cars don't use hooks—they use electromagnets.

In this chapter, you will learn what magnets are and how they are used. You will learn about electric current. And you will find out how electric current can be used to produce strong magnets, called electromagnets, that can be turned on and off. As you read the chapter, you will use what you learn to construct an electromagnetic fishing rod. Now go fish!

Your Goal To build an electromagnetic fishing rod that can lift paper clips from one container and drop them into another.

To complete your project you must

◆ make a model of a fishing rod that has a magnet as its hook
◆ design an on-off switch for an electromagnet suspended by string from the end of the rod and powered by a single D cell
◆ modify variables so you can move as many paper clips as possible from one container to another in one minute
◆ follow the safety guidelines in Appendix A

Get Started Think about fishing rods. Discuss some of their features. Then think about how you could catch and let go of a paper clip with a similar fishing device. Brainstorm ideas for using a magnet as a "hook."

Check Your Progress You'll be working on this project as you study this chapter. To keep your project on track, look for Check Your Progress boxes at the following points.

Section 1 Review, page 253: Make an initial model with a permanent magnet.
Section 3 Review, page 267: Design a switch.
Section 4 Review, page 272: Construct and improve your electromagnet by experimenting with variables.

Wrap Up At the end of the chapter (page 275), you will use your rod to fish alongside classmates in an electromagnetic fishing derby.

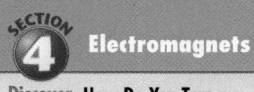
A crane uses an electromagnet to move iron and steel in a junkyard.

SECTION 4 Electromagnets

Discover **How Do You Turn a Magnet On and Off?**

Program Resources

◆ **Unit 3 Resources** Chapter 8 Project Teacher Notes, pp. 2–3; Project Overview and Worksheets, pp. 4–7; Project Scoring Rubric, p. 8

Media and Technology

 Audio CDs Section Summaries

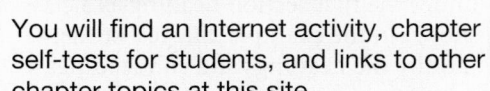 www.phschool.com

You will find an Internet activity, chapter self-tests for students, and links to other chapter topics at this site.

Launching the Project

Electromagnetism is discussed in Section 1-4, but you should give students a preview of this topic before introducing the Chapter Project. Build and demonstrate a basic electromagnet: Wrap about 100 turns of insulated wire around a large nail, and tape one bare end of the wire to one end of a 1.5-volt battery. Demonstrate how touching the other end of the wire to the other end of the battery produces an electromagnet that can be used to pick up small pieces of metal such as staples or paper clips.

Pass out copies of the Chapter 8 Project Overview and Worksheets on pages 4–7 in Unit 3 Resources for students to review. Allow time for students to read the description of the project in their text and in the Chapter Project Overview. Then encourage discussions on electric circuits and electromagnetism, materials that could be used, and any initial questions students may have.

Performance Assessment

The Chapter 8 Project Scoring Rubric on page 8 of Unit 3 Resources will help you evaluate how well students complete the Chapter 8 Project. Students will be assessed on

◆ how well they apply chapter concepts to their design of a fishing rod, electric circuit, and switch;
◆ how well they identify and experiment with variables and how well they apply the results of their tests to improve the strength of their electromagnets;
◆ how well their electromagnetic fishing rod works in an electromagnetic fishing derby;
◆ the thoroughness and organization of their presentation.

By sharing the Chapter 8 Scoring Rubric with students at the beginning of the project, you will make it clear to them what they are expected to do.

SECTION 1 The Nature of Magnetism

Objectives

After completing the lesson, students will be able to
- define magnetic poles and describe the interaction between like and unlike magnetic poles;
- define magnetic fields and describe magnetic field lines;
- define magnetic domain and state how magnetic domains are lined up in magnetized material.

Key Terms magnetism, magnetic pole, magnetic field, magnetic field line, atom, element, nucleus, proton, electron, magnetic domain, ferromagnetic material, permanent magnet

1 Engage/Explore

Activating Prior Knowledge

Challenge students to think how magnets are used in the kitchen. Ask: **What keeps cabinet, refrigerator, and freezer doors tightly closed? What holds the top of a can to an electric can opener after it has been cut off the can?** (*Students should infer magnets do these functions.*)

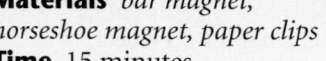
······· DISCOVER ·········

Skills Focus observing
Materials *bar magnet, horseshoe magnet, paper clips*
Time 15 minutes
Tips Tell students they will observe how two different types of magnets attract materials.
Expected Outcome Most paper clips will be attracted to the magnets' poles. Few or none will be attracted to the middle of the bar magnet, or to the curved part of the horseshoe magnet.
Think It Over Students should note that most of the magnetic pull comes from the poles, or ends, of each magnet.

SECTION 1 The Nature of Magnetism

DISCOVER ·· **ACTIVITY**

What Do All Magnets Have in Common?

1. Obtain a bar magnet and a horseshoe magnet.
2. See how many paper clips you can make stick to different parts of each magnet.
3. Draw a diagram showing the number and location of paper clips on each magnet.

Think It Over

Observing Where does each magnet hold the greatest number of paper clips? What similarities do you observe between the two magnets?

GUIDE FOR READING

- How do magnetic poles interact?
- What is the shape of magnetic field lines?
- How are the domains of a magnet arranged?

Reading Tip As you read, use the headings to make an outline of the main ideas and supporting details about magnetism and electricity.

Figure 1 This Japanese high-speed train is moved by strong magnets instead of wheels. It is called a magnetically levitating train, or maglev train.

Imagine zooming along in a train that glides without even touching the ground. You feel no vibration and hear no noise from solid steel tracks. You can just sit back and relax as you speed toward your destination at nearly 400 kilometers per hour.

Are you dreaming? No, you are not. Although you have probably not ridden on such a train, trains capable of floating a few centimeters in air do exist. What makes them float? Believe it or not, magnets make them float.

HSST

246

READING STRATEGIES

Reading Tip Outline the information under the first section heading as a class, as shown in the example. Suggest students modify the headings and subheadings as necessary to create phrases or sentences.
I. Magnets
  A. Magnetic rocks found in Magnesia 2,000 years ago
  B. Magnetic rocks contain magnetite
  C. Magnetic rocks known as lodestones

Study and Comprehension Before students begin reading, have them preview the section by reading the headings, subheadings, and captions and by looking at the pictures and diagrams. Invite students to ask questions they may have about the nature of magnets, magnetic poles, and magnetic fields. Write the questions on the board. After students read the section, have them work as a class to answer the questions on the board.

Magnets

When you think of magnets, you might think about the magnets that hold notes on your refrigerator. But magnets can also be found in many familiar devices, such as doorbells, televisions, and computers.

Magnets have many modern uses, but they are not new. More than 2000 years ago, people living in a region known as Magnesia discovered an unusual rock. (Magnesia is in Greece.) The rock attracted materials that contained iron. It contained a mineral that we call magnetite. Both the word *magnetite* and the word *magnet* come from the name "Magnesia." **Magnetism** is the attraction of a magnet for another object.

About a thousand years ago, people in other parts of the world discovered another interesting property of magnets. If they allowed the magnetic rock to swing freely from a string, one part of the rock would always point in the same direction. That direction was toward a certain northern star, called the leading star, or lodestar. For this reason, magnetic rocks also became known as lodestones.

Figure 2 Magnetic rocks contain the mineral magnetite.

Magnetic Poles

The magnets with which you are familiar are not found in nature, but they are made to have the same properties as lodestone. Any magnet, no matter what its shape, has two ends, each one called a **magnetic pole.** A pole is the area of a magnet where the magnetic effect is strongest. Just as one end of a piece of magnetite always points toward the north star, one pole of a magnet will also point north and is labeled the north pole. The other pole is labeled the south pole. Two north poles or two south poles are a pair of like poles. A north pole and a south pole are a pair of unlike, or opposite poles.

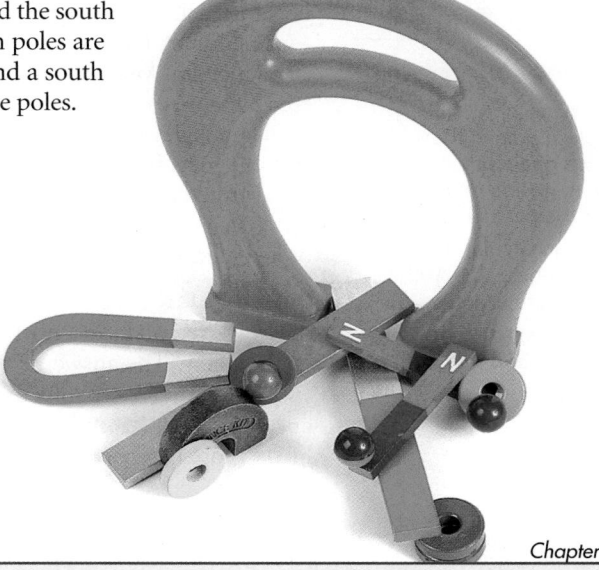

Figure 3 Modern magnets come in a variety of shapes and sizes. *Classifying How many different shapes of magnets can you identify in the photograph?*

Answers to Self-Assessment

Caption Question

Figure 3 Students should be able to see horseshoe, bar, spherical, semicircular, and circular magnets.

---

2 Facilitate

Magnets

Building Inquiry Skills: Predicting

Materials *bar magnets, items for testing (assorted materials including nails, screws, coins, paper, plastic, plastic foam packing, cans)*
Time 20 minutes

ACTIVITY

Have students predict which materials will be attracted to the magnets. Then have students test their predictions. Objects that contain the element iron will be attracted. Students might be surprised to find that most coins are not magnetic. Note that a "tin" can is attracted to a magnet because it is made of steel, not tin. Any nails attracted to a magnet have iron in them. Some nails are made of brass or aluminum and are not attracted to magnets. **learning modality: kinesthetic**

Magnetic Poles

Using the Visuals: Figure 3

Have students identify the poles of each magnet shown in the figure. Ask: **Where are the poles on the circular magnets? How can you tell?** (*The flat sides, or the top and bottom, of the circular magnets are the poles. These sides are where the magnets are attracted to the other magnets in the photo.*) **learning modality: visual**

Ongoing Assessment

Writing Have students define magnetism in their own words.

Magnetic Poles, continued

Building Inquiry Skills: Observing

Materials *2 bar magnets*
Time 5 minutes

Have students place the magnets on their desks. Then have them slide the poles of the magnets together until they can first feel the attraction between the magnets and then the repulsion. Encourage students to find out how close they can put the magnets before they are "pulled" together and how close before they are "pushed" apart. **limited English proficiency**

Sharpen your *Skills*

Observing

Materials *pencil, foam cup, 2 circular magnets*
Time 10 minutes
Tips Have students predict what will happen when they place the two magnets together on the pencil.
Expected Outcome In the first case, the top magnet will levitate. The levitation is caused by the repulsion between like poles. In the second case, the top magnet will be pulled down. This is caused by the attraction of unlike poles.
Extend Have students use more magnets to increase the height of the levitating magnet. Ask: **What happens when more magnets are used?** *(Adding more magnets increases the strength of the field.)*
learning modality: visual

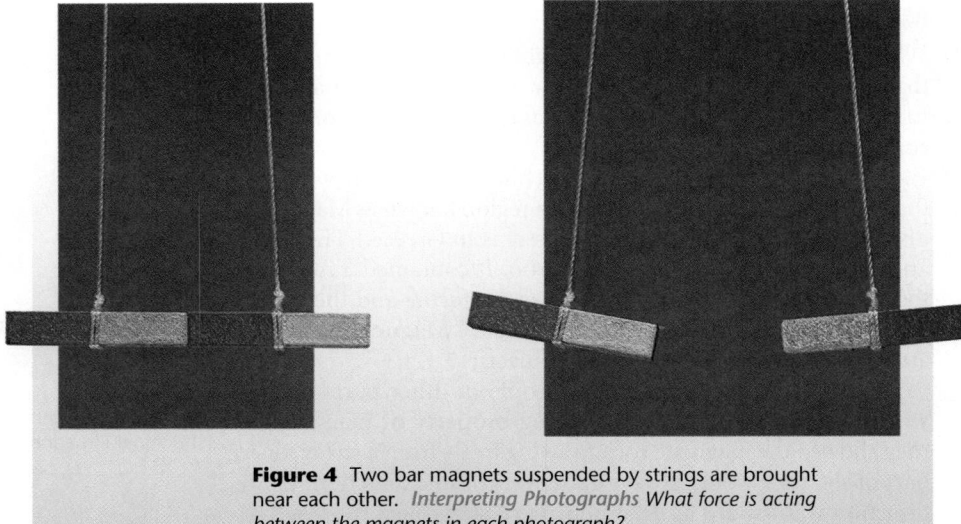

Figure 4 Two bar magnets suspended by strings are brought near each other. *Interpreting Photographs What force is acting between the magnets in each photograph?*

Sharpen your Skills

Observing

1. Use a pencil to poke a hole in the bottom of a foam cup. Turn the cup upside-down and stand the pencil in the hole.
2. Place two circular magnets on the pencil, so that their like sides are together.
3. Remove the top magnet. Flip it over and replace it on the pencil.

What happens to the magnets in each case? Explain your observations.

Interactions Between Magnetic Poles What happens if you bring two magnets together? The answer depends on how you hold the poles of the magnets. If you bring two north poles together, the magnets push away from each other. The same is true if two south poles are brought together. However, if you bring the north pole of one magnet near the south pole of another, the two magnets attract one another. **Magnetic poles that are alike repel each other and magnetic poles that are unlike attract each other.** Figure 4 shows how two bar magnets interact.

The force of attraction or repulsion between magnetic poles is magnetism. Any material that exerts magnetic forces is considered a magnet.

The maglev train you read about earlier depends on magnetism. Magnets in the bottom of the train and in the guideway on the ground have like poles. Since like poles repel, the two magnets push each other away. The result is that the train car is lifted up, or levitated. Other magnets push and pull the train forward.

Paired Poles What do you think happens if you break a magnet in two? Will you have a north pole in one hand and a south pole in the other? The answer is no. Rather than two separate poles, you will have two separate magnets. Each smaller magnet will be complete with its own north pole and south pole. And if you break those two halves again, you will then have four magnets.

☑ *Checkpoint* *What is a magnetic pole?*

248

| Background |

Facts and Figures Both Germany and Japan have worked on maglev prototypes since the early 1970s.

The first successful test of levitation and propulsion was made on a 200-meter track in 1975. By the mid 1980s, maglev trains were making demonstration runs and carrying passengers. In March 1989, the HSST-05, a two-car, 158-passenger maglev train operated at the Yokohama Expo in Japan. Currently, projects for developing intra-urban and inter-city trains are underway. Using maglev technology, these trains could reach speeds of up to 200 to 300 kilometers per hour.

Magnetic Fields

The magnetic force is strongest at the poles of a magnet, but it is not limited to the poles. Magnetic forces are exerted all around a magnet. The region of magnetic force around a magnet is known as its **magnetic field.** Magnetic fields allow magnets to interact without touching.

Figure 5A shows the magnetic field of a bar magnet. The lines, called **magnetic field lines,** map out the magnetic field around a magnet. **Magnetic field lines spread out from one pole, curve around a magnet, and return to the other pole.** The lines form complete loops from pole to pole and never cross.

Although you can't actually see a magnetic field, you can see its effects, as shown in Figure 5B. This photograph shows iron filings sprinkled on a sheet of plastic over a magnet. The magnetic forces act on the iron filings so that they point toward the poles of the magnet. The result is that the iron filings form a pattern similar to the magnetic field lines in Figure 5A.

The iron filings and the diagram are both on flat surfaces. But a magnetic field exists in three dimensions. You can see in Figure 5C that the magnetic field completely surrounds the magnet.

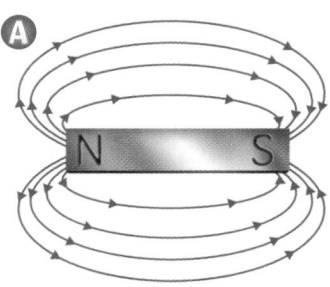

Figure 5 A magnetic field surrounds a magnet. **A.** In this diagram, magnetic field lines are shown in red. **B.** You can see the same magnetic field mapped out by iron filings. **C.** Iron filings also show that a magnetic field has three dimensions.

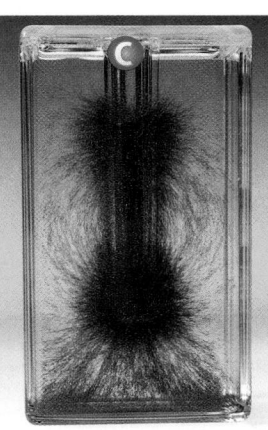

Chapter 8 **249**

Building Inquiry Skills: Inferring

Ask students to observe the magnetic field lines in the photos in Figure 5. Have students describe where the field seems to be the strongest. *(Around the poles)* Ask them to explain the evidence for this. *(The lines of iron filings are densest near the poles.)* Have students use their fingers to trace the field lines in the photo. Challenge students to explain why the lines curve between the two poles. Prompt them by asking: **Find an iron filing that is on the curve about halfway between the two poles. Describe the forces acting at that point.** *(At that point, the filing is equally attracted to both poles.)* **learning modality: logical/ mathematical**

Addressing Naive Conceptions

Students may be confused by the concept of a magnetic field. Explain that scientists recognize two kinds of forces, contact forces and field forces. Contact forces act when two objects are in physical contact, but field forces can act without physically touching. Ask: **If the filings were not present around the magnet in Figure 5B, would the field forces still be present around the poles of the magnet?** *(Yes, the field forces are always present. The iron filings are used to make the effects of the field visible.)* **learning modality: verbal**

Answers to Self-Assessment

Caption Question

Figure 4 In the first photo, the unlike poles attract each other. In the second photo, the like poles repel each other.

☑ *Checkpoint*

A magnetic pole is one of the two ends of the magnet where the magnetic effect is the strongest.

Ongoing Assessment

Drawing Challenge students to draw the pattern iron filings would make around the poles of a bar magnet and a horseshoe magnet. *(Note: The lines of force in their drawings of the horseshoe magnet should be closer together than those lines around the poles of a bar magnet because the poles of the horseshoe magnet are closer together.)*

Magnetic Fields,
continued

Using the Visuals: Figure 6

Have students compare the magnetic fields created by placing bar magnets near each other. Ask: **When like poles are placed near each other, where is the field weakest? Explain.** *(At the point exactly between the two magnets; there are no field lines there.)* **When unlike poles are placed near each other, where is the field strongest?** *(At the center point between the poles)* Discuss the field lines and have students determine where a compass needle would point at different places in the magnetic field. **learning modality: logical/mathematical**

Inside a Magnet

Building Inquiry Skills: Making Models

Encourage students to read the description of atomic structure in the text and use the description to diagram an atom. Clarify to students how tiny atoms really are. You may wish to refer students to a model of the atom that includes protons and electrons. Have students label the parts of the atom and indicate positive and negative charges. Ask: **How can an atom become a tiny magnet?** *(Because the motion of the electrons produces a magnetic field.)* **learning modality: visual**

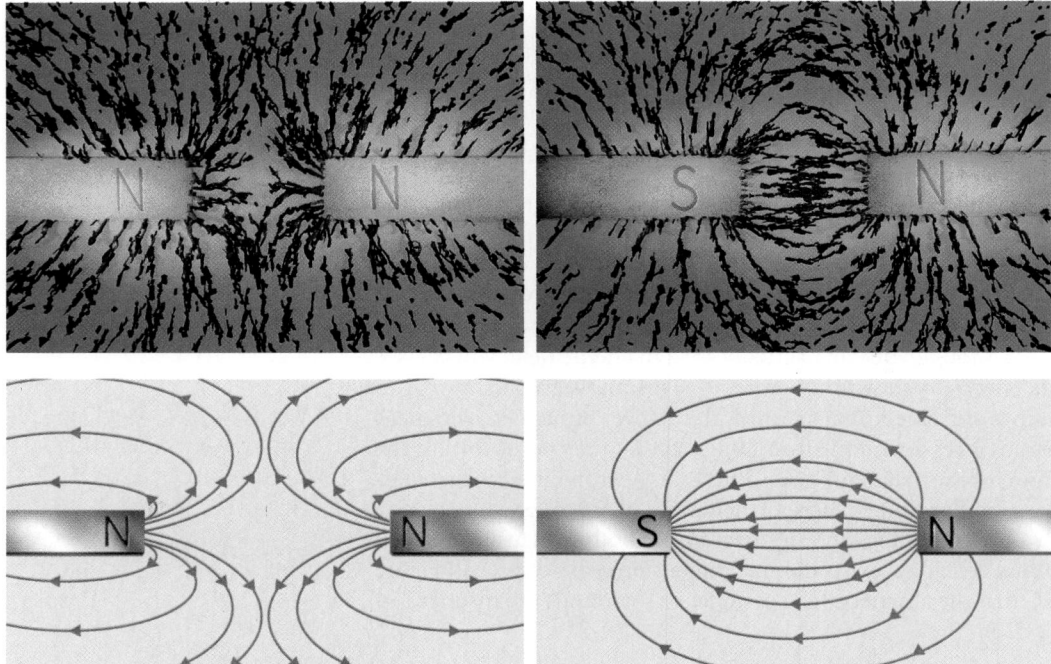

Figure 6 The magnetic field of each bar magnet is altered when two bar magnets are brought together.
Applying Concepts What do these photos and diagrams show about the interaction between magnetic poles?

When the magnetic fields of two or more magnets overlap, the result is a combined field. Figure 6 shows the magnetic fields produced when the poles of two bar magnets are brought near each other.

Inside a Magnet

What happens if you bring a piece of wood, glass, or plastic near a pile of paper clips? Nothing happens. These materials have no effect on the paper clips. But if you bring a bar magnet near the same pile, the paper clips will cling to the magnet. Why do some materials have strong magnetic fields while others do not?

Electron Spin The magnetic properties of a material depend on the structure of its atoms. All matter is made up of atoms. An **atom** is the smallest particle of an element that has the properties of that element. An **element** is one of about 100 basic materials that make up all matter.

The center of every atom is called a **nucleus.** The nucleus contains particles within it. **Protons** are nuclear particles that carry a positive charge. Orbiting the nucleus are other tiny particles called **electrons,** which carry a negative charge. Each of the

Background

History of Science When scientists first discovered the relationship between the electric charge on electrons and magnetic fields, they began searching for a single particle with a magnetic charge. These particles, called monopoles because they would have only one magnetic pole, have never been found. Physicists continue to look for monopoles. When a new source of matter is discovered, as in 1969 when astronauts brought back moon rocks, physicists examine it to look for monopoles.

Magnetic monopoles are consistent with certain theories. In 1931, P.A.M. Dirac, an English physicist, stated that if there were only one monopole in the universe, it would explain why electric charge only occurs in multiples of the charge on an electron. Theories to explain the origin of the universe also involve monopoles.

electrons in an atom acts as if it is spinning as it orbits the nucleus. A moving electron produces a magnetic field. The spinning and orbiting motion of the electrons make each atom a tiny magnet.

Magnetic Domains In most materials the magnetic fields of the atoms point in random directions. The result is that the magnetic fields cancel one another almost entirely. The magnetism of most materials is so weak that you cannot usually detect it.

In certain materials, the magnetic fields of the spinning electrons of many atoms are aligned with one another. A cluster of billions of atoms that all have magnetic fields that are lined up in the same way is known as a **magnetic domain.** The entire domain acts like a bar magnet with a north pole and a south pole.

In a material that is not magnetized, the domains point in random directions as shown in Figure 7. The magnetic fields exerted by some of the domains cancel the magnetic fields exerted by other domains. The result is that the material is not a magnet. **In a magnetized material all or most of the domains are arranged in the same direction.** In other words, the domains are aligned.

Magnetic Materials A material can be a strong magnet if it forms magnetic domains. A material that shows strong magnetic effects is said to be a **ferromagnetic material.** The word *ferromagnetic* comes from the Latin *ferrum*, which means "iron." Iron, nickel, and cobalt are the common ferromagnetic materials. Others include the rare elements samarium and neodymium, which can be made into magnets that are extremely powerful. Some very strong magnets are also made from mixtures, or alloys, of several metals.

☑ *Checkpoint* How is magnetism related to domains?

Figure 7 The arrows represent the domains of a material. The arrows point toward the north pole of each domain. *Comparing and Contrasting How does the arrangement of domains differ between magnetized iron and unmagnetized iron?*

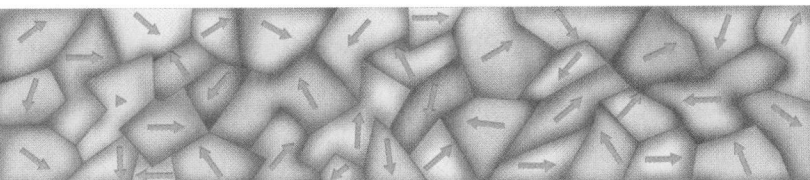

Unmagnetized Iron

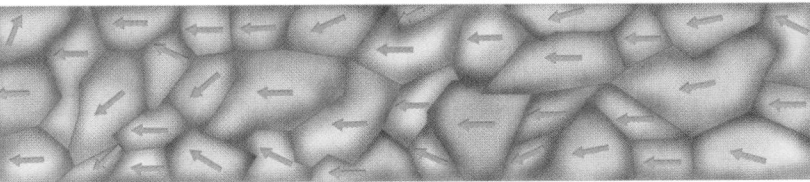

Magnetized Iron

Chapter 8   **251**

Including All Students

Materials *10 cm by 4 cm strips of construction paper, enough for each student to have at least 12 strips*

Time 15 minutes

This activity will assist students who need additional help to understand the concept of magnetic domains. Prepare the paper strips. (One sheet of construction paper should yield about 14 strips.) Give each student at least 12 strips, and tell them to label the ends of each strip N and S to represent the magnetic poles of the individual domains. First have students arrange the strips to show an unmagnetized substance. Then have them arrange the strips to show a magnetized substance. Ask: **How are the domains of the magnetic material aligned?** *(The north poles all point in the same direction.)*
learning modality: kinesthetic

Ongoing Assessment

Writing Have students explain what causes a material to have magnetic properties. Then have them name one ferromagnetic material.

Making Magnets

Destroying Magnets

Building Inquiry Skills: Applying Concepts

Tell students that the temperature above which a magnetic material loses its ferromagnetic properties is called the Curie temperature. This temperature is named for Pierre Curie, a French physicist who discovered the relationship between magnetic properties and changes in temperature. Each magnetic material loses its ferromagnetism at a different Curie temperature. Ask students: **What happens to a ferromagnetic material above its Curie temperature?** *(The domains lose their alignment and the material loses its magnetic properties.)* Ask students to infer what happens when the material cools to below its Curie temperature. *(The domains realign, and the material becomes magnetic again.)* **learning modality: verbal**

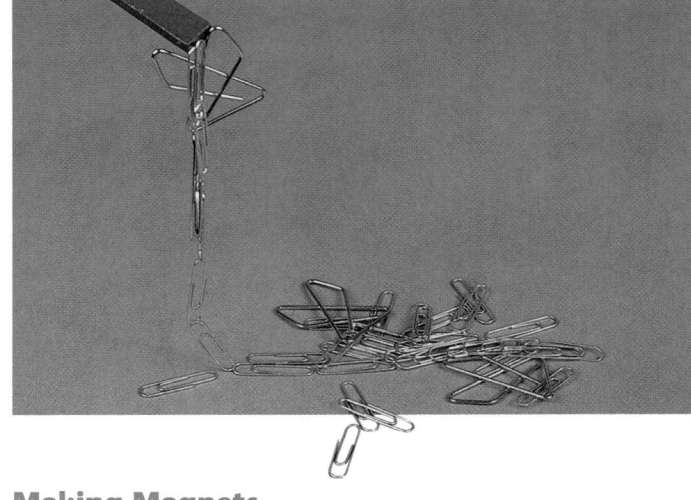

Figure 8 The magnet attracts the metal paper clips. *Applying Concepts How can a paper clip be attracted to a magnet?*

How Attractive!

You can use iron filings to find out how materials become magnetic.

1. Fill a clear plastic tube about two-thirds full with iron filings. Seal the tube.
2. Observe the arrangement of the filings.
3. Rub the tube lengthwise about 30 times in the same direction with one end of a strong magnet.
4. Again observe the arrangement of the filings.

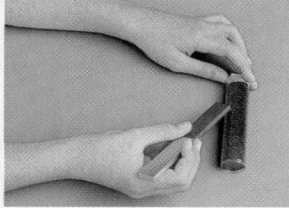

Making Models How do the iron filings in the tube model magnetic domains?

Making Magnets

You know that magnetite exists in nature. The magnets you use everyday, however, are made by people. A magnet can be made from a ferromagnetic material. This is done by placing the unmagnetized material in a strong magnetic field or by rubbing it with one pole of a strong magnet.

If the magnetic field is strong enough, two processes take place. First, the domains that point in the direction of the magnetic field become larger by lining up the fields of neighboring domains. Second, domains that are not pointing in the same direction as the magnetic field rotate toward the magnetic field. The result is that the majority of domains line up in the same direction. With its domains aligned, the material is a magnet.

The ability to make a magnet explains why an unmagnetized object, such as a paper clip, can be attracted to a magnet. Paper clips are made of steel, which is mostly iron. The magnet's field causes domains in the paper clip to line up slightly so that the clip becomes a magnet. Its north pole faces the south pole of the magnet. The paper clip can attract other paper clips for the same reason. After the magnet is removed, however, the domains of the paper clips return to their random arrangements. Thus the paper clips are no longer magnetic.

Some metals, such as the ordinary steel that paper clips are made of, are easy to magnetize but lose their magnetism quickly. Magnets made from these materials are called temporary magnets. Harder metals, such as other types of steel, are more difficult to magnetize but tend to stay magnetized. A magnet made of a material that keeps its magnetism is called a **permanent magnet.**

Checkpoint *How does a magnet attract another object?*

Destroying Magnets

Just as paper clips lose their magnetism when their domains become randomly arranged, a permanent magnet can also become unmagnetized. One way is to drop it or strike it hard. If a magnet is hit hard, its domains can be knocked out of alignment. Heating a magnet will also destroy its magnetism. When an object is heated, its particles vibrate faster and more randomly. This makes it more difficult for all the domains to stay lined up. In fact, above a certain temperature a material loses the property of ferromagnetism. The temperature depends on the material.

Breaking Magnets

Now that you know about domains, you can understand why breaking a magnet in half does not result in two pieces that are individual poles. Within the original bar magnet shown in Figure 9, there are many north and south poles facing each other. These poles balance each other.

At the ends of the magnet, there are many poles that are not facing an opposite pole. This produces strong magnetic effects at the north and south poles. If the magnet is cut in half, the domains will still be lined up in the same way. So the shorter pieces will still have strong ends made up of many north or south poles. Figure 9 shows the results of dividing a magnet into four pieces.

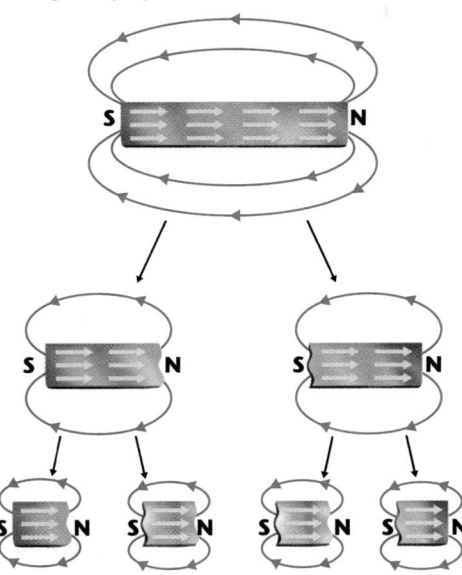

Figure 9 No matter how many times a magnet is cut in half, each piece retains its magnetic properties.

Section 1 Review

1. What happens if you bring together two like poles? Two unlike poles?
2. How are magnetic domains arranged in a magnet? How are they arranged in an unmagnetized object?
3. What parts of an atom produce magnetism?
4. How is a magnet made?
5. **Thinking Critically** Applying Concepts Iron filings align with the magnetic field of a bar magnet. What must be happening to the domains in the iron filings in the magnetic field?

Check Your Progress
CHAPTER PROJECT 8

Gather materials for the different parts of your fishing rod. Consider such items as a broom handle, dowel, or meter stick for the rod. You'll also need a string. Draw a basic design for your fishing rod. Make a model of the rod with a permanent magnet. Test how easily you can maneuver your model.

Chapter 8 **253**

Program Resources

◆ **Unit 3 Resources** 8-1 Review and Reinforce, p. 11; 8-1 Enrich, p. 12

Answers to Self-Assessment

Caption Question

Figure 8 A paper clip has its magnetic domains arranged in the same direction by the magnetic field so that the clip too becomes a magnet that is attracted to the larger magnet.

☑ *Checkpoint*

The magnet's field causes the object to become a magnet.

Breaking Magnets

Using the Visuals: Figure 9

Point out that each new magnet has a north and a south pole. Explain that this process can continue until the magnets are extremely small. Ask students to infer what is the smallest thing that has the properties of the larger magnet. (*A domain or an atom*) **learning modality: visual**

3 Assess

Section 1 Review Answers

1. Two like poles repel each other. Two unlike poles attract each other.
2. Most of the domains in a magnet are aligned. In an unmagnetized material, they are not aligned.
3. The spinning motions of electrons produce magnetism.
4. A magnet is made when an unmagnetized ferromagnetic material is placed in a strong magnetic field or rubbed in one direction with one pole of a magnet.
5. Most of the domains in the filings are moving into alignment.

Check Your Progress
CHAPTER PROJECT 8

Provide small permanent magnets so students can test the designs of their rods to make sure they will work when the electromagnet is attached. If possible, set up a sample showing the containers of paper clips that will be used to test the rods at the end of the project.

Performance Assessment

Drawing Have students draw a bar magnet and label its poles. Then have students sketch the magnetic fields around the poles and indicate the alignment of the domains in the magnet.

Detecting Fake Coins

Preparing for Inquiry

Key Concept In the United States, coins are made of nonmagnetic metals. They can be separated from magnetic metal slugs using a magnet.

Skills Objectives Students will be able to

◆ predict how different metals will react to the presence of a magnetic field;

◆ make inferences about the content of metallic objects based on their reaction to a magnetic field.

Time 45 minutes

Advance Planning You will need the type of cardboard used to make file folders, as well as craft sticks, washers of various sizes, and small bar magnets. Make sure the washers are attracted to the magnet. Supply coins or have students bring in their own.

Alternative Materials The magnet can be replaced with an electromagnet made by wrapping 50 loops of insulated wire around a nail and connecting the ends of the wire to a battery. If students use electromagnets, do not allow them to close the circuit for more than a few seconds, in order to avoid overheating.

Guiding Inquiry

Invitation Ask students if they have ever wondered how a vending machine can tell the difference between a real coin and a fake coin, or slug. Discuss different ways that a machine might be able to distinguish between one coin and another. *(Students may list properties of metals or of coins, such as size and shape, mass or density, magnetic properties.)*

Introducing the Procedure

Place a pile of coins and washers mixed together on a desk. Move a magnet around the top of the pile and pick up the magnet. The washers will stick to the magnet and the coins will be left behind.

Troubleshooting the Experiment

The effectiveness of students' devices can

Detecting Fake Coins

Suppose there has been a rash of fake steel coins used in vending machines. The machines may be removed by the owners unless someone can prevent the fake coins from being used. What can you do?

Problem

How can you use a magnet to tell the difference between real and fake coins?

Skills Focus

predicting, inferring

Materials

various coins   craft stick   tape
metric ruler   pencil   protractor
coin-size steel washers
small bar magnet, about 2 cm wide
thin, stiff cardboard, about 25 cm × 30 cm

Procedure

1. Mark a piece of cardboard to show its front, back, top, and bottom.
2. Draw a line lengthwise down the middle of both sides of the cardboard.
3. On the back of the cardboard, draw a line parallel to the first and about 2 cm to the right.
4. Place a magnet vertically about a third of the way down the line you drew in Step 3. Tape the magnet in place.
5. Place a craft stick on the front of the cardboard. The stick's upper end should be about 1 cm to the left of the center line and about 8 cm from the bottom of the cardboard.
6. Tape the stick at an angle, as shown in the photograph.
7. Prop the cardboard against something that will hold it at an angle of about 45°. Predict what will happen when you slide a coin down the front of the cardboard.
8. Place a coin on the center line and slide the coin down the front of the cardboard. (*Hint:* If the coin gets stuck, slowly increase the angle.)
9. Predict what will happen when you slide a steel washer.
10. Test your prediction by sliding a washer down the cardboard. Again, if the washer gets stuck, slowly increase the angle and try again.
11. Once you have reached an angle at which the objects slide easily, send down a randomly mixed group of coins and washers.

be affected by several factors. Probably the easiest for students to control is the angle of the inclined cardboard. When the angle of the incline is increased, the coins and washers will move down more quickly, decreasing a washer's chance of becoming stuck at the magnet. The other factor is the strength of the magnet. If a strong magnet is used, a steeper angle of incline or placing the magnet farther from the center line will allow coins and washers to slide down.

Expected Outcome

Coins should slide straight down the center line on the cardboard and be deposited in a pile. Washers should be pulled to the side by the magnet, then slide down along the craft stick and be deposited in a separate pile.

Analyze and Conclude

1. What was your prediction from Step 7? Explain your reasoning.
2. What was your prediction from Step 9? Explain your reasoning.
3. Describe how observations made during the lab either supported or did not support your predictions.
4. What is the role of the magnet in this lab?
5. What is the role of the craft stick?
6. Why did you have to use thin cardboard?
7. What can you conclude about the metals from which the coins are made? About the metals in the washers?
8. Why does the steepness of the cardboard affect how the coin separating device works?

9. **Apply** Some Canadian coins contain metals that are attracted to magnets. Would this device be useful in Canada to detect fake coins? Explain your answer.

Getting Involved

Go to a store that has vending machines. Find out who owns the vending machines. Ask the owners if they have a problem with counterfeit coins (sometimes called "slugs"). Ask how they or the makers of the vending machines solve the problem. How is their solution related to the device you built in this lab?

Analyze and Conclude

1. Students' predictions will vary. Sample: The coins will slide straight down.
2. Sample: The washers will be deflected and will slide along the stick.
3. Answers will depend on students' predictions. When the coins and washers slid down the incline, the coins slid straight down and the washers were deflected.
4. The magnet attracts any iron and other magnetic materials in the objects as they slide down the incline.
5. The craft stick serves to separate the two groups into piles at the bottom of the incline.
6. Other materials, such as thick cardboard or wood, increase the distance from the magnet so that the objects would be in a weaker part of the magnetic field.
7. The coins do not contain detectable amounts of magnetic metal. The washers contain a significant amount of magnetic metal.
8. The angle of the incline affects the speed of the objects sliding down the incline. When they are moving slowly, washers may stick to the magnet.
9. The device would not be useful in Canada because some Canadian coins are magnetic and would be deflected from the straight path.

Extending the Inquiry

Getting Involved This device is similar to the device that was used in many vending machines long ago. Today, magnetic fields are set up using electromagnets and the size and mass of the coins are analyzed very closely to differentiate real coins from fake coins.

Program Resources

◆ **Unit 3 Resources** Real-World Lab blackline masters, pp. 25–27

Media and Technology

 Lab Activity Videotape *Tape 2*

SECTION 2 Magnetic Earth

Objectives

After completing the lesson, students will be able to
◆ identify the magnetic properties of Earth and compare the magnetic and geographic poles;
◆ describe some of the effects of Earth's magnetic fields.

Key Terms compass, magnetic declination, Van Allen belts, solar wind, magnetosphere, aurora

1 Engage/Explore

Activating Prior Knowledge

Ask students which way is north. Some students may be able to point in the correct direction. Encourage students to discuss different ways to determine direction. Students may mention using the location and motion of the sun or using a compass. Challenge students to explain how to use a compass.

DISCOVER

Skills Focus observing
Materials *large needle, strong bar magnet, dish, water, dishwashing soap, cork or foam ball, pliers*
Time 20 minutes
Tips CAUTION: *Warn students to handle the needle carefully.* Students should rub the needle in only one direction. Have students use pliers to hold the needles when pushing them through the foam. Objects in the room may be magnetized and may attract the needle. Use a compass to find areas in the classroom where the compass needle will point north.
Expected Outcome The needle will point north.
Think It Over The needle will always point north, because Earth has a magnetic field.

SECTION 2 Magnetic Earth

DISCOVER · ACTIVITY

Can You Use a Needle to Make a Compass?

1. Magnetize a large needle by rubbing it several times in the same direction with one end of a strong bar magnet. Push the needle through a ball of foam or tape it to a small piece of cork.
2. Place a drop of dishwashing soap in a dish of water. Then float the foam or cork in the water. Adjust the needle until it floats horizontally.
3. Allow the needle to stop moving. Which way does it point?
4. Use a local map to determine the direction in which it points.

Think It Over

Observing In what direction did the needle point? Will it always point in the same direction? What does this tell you about Earth?

GUIDE FOR READING

◆ What are the magnetic properties of Earth?
◆ What are the effects of Earth's magnetic field?

Reading Tip As you read, make a table that compares the magnetic fields of Earth and a bar magnet.

W hen Christopher Columbus sighted land in 1492, he didn't really know what he had found. He was trying to find a shortcut from Europe to India. Where he landed, however, was on an island in the Caribbean Sea just south of the present-day United States. He had no idea that such an island even existed.

In spite of his error, Columbus had successfully followed a course west to the Americas without the help of an accurate map. Instead, Columbus used a compass for navigation. A **compass** is a device that has a magnetized needle that can spin freely. The compass needle usually points north, and as you read you'll find out why.

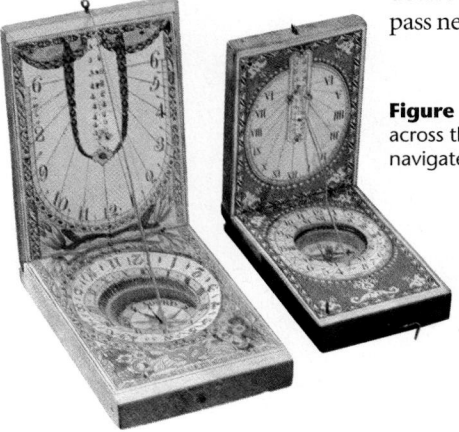

Figure 10 In 1492, Columbus set sail across the Atlantic Ocean. He and his crews navigated using compasses like these.

READING STRATEGIES

Reading Tip Tables should include information on poles and magnetic fields. After students prepare their tables comparing Earth to a bar magnet, invite volunteers to write the tables on the board and explain the information in them. Students should ask questions and have discussions to clarify any differences between their tables.

Vocabulary As students read, have them write boldfaced terms on note cards, one term per card. Instruct them to write definitions on the other side of the cards. After students have finished reading, have partners quiz each other, using the note cards as flashcards.

Figure 11 William Gilbert demonstrates his research to Queen Elizabeth I.

Earth as a Magnet

In the late 1500s, the English physician Sir William Gilbert became interested in compasses. He spoke with several navigators and experimented with his own compass. Gilbert confirmed that a compass always points in the same direction, no matter where you are. But no one knew why.

Gilbert suggested that a compass behaves as it does because Earth acts as a giant magnet. Although many educated people of his time laughed at this idea, Gilbert turned out to be correct. **Earth has an immense magnetic field surrounding it, just as there is a magnetic field around a bar magnet.**

Gilbert believed that the center of Earth contains magnetic rock. Scientists now believe that this is not the case, since Earth's core is too hot for the rock to be solid. Earth's magnetism is still not completely understood. Scientists do know that it is due to the circulation of molten metal (iron and nickel) within Earth's core.

The fact that Earth has a magnetic field explains why a compass works as it does. The poles of the magnetized needle on the compass align themselves with Earth's magnetic field.

✓ *Checkpoint* *What was Gilbert's new idea about Earth?*

Magnetic Declination

Earth's magnetic poles are not the same as the geographic poles. For example, the magnetic north pole (in northern Canada) is about 1,250 kilometers from the geographic north pole. The geographic north pole is sometimes called true north. The magnetic south pole is located near the coast of Antarctica.

Sharpen your Skills

Measuring ACTIVITY

1. Use a local map to locate geographic north relative to your school. Mark the direction on the floor with tape or chalk.
2. Use a compass to find magnetic north. Again mark the direction.
3. Use a protractor to measure the number of degrees between the two marks.

Compare the directions of magnetic and geographic north. Is magnetic north to the east or west of geographic north?

Program Resources

◆ **Unit 3 Resources** 8-2 Lesson Plan, p. 13; 8-2 Section Summary, p. 14
◆ **Guided Reading and Study Workbook** Section 8-2

Answers to Self-Assessment

✓ *Checkpoint*

Gilbert suggested that Earth acted as a giant magnet.

2 Facilitate

Earth as a Magnet

Cultural Diversity

Note for students that compasses were used by Chinese navigators as early as A.D. 1100. By the 1300s, they were used by western European, Arabic, and Scandinavian sailors as well. Early compasses were magnetized needles floating with a piece of wood or reed on water. Ask students: **Why can people all over the world use compasses of the same design?** *(Because Earth's magnetic field surrounds Earth.)* Encourage some students to prepare a class report on how various cultures built and used compasses. **cooperative learning**

Magnetic Declination

Sharpen your Skills

Measuring

Materials *local map, compass, protractor* ACTIVITY
Time 15 minutes
Tips If possible, do this activity outdoors, away from power lines or other magnetic materials.
Expected Outcome Students should find that the compass needle points at an angle to true north.
Extend Have students identify the direction the compass points on a local map and compare it to true north. Encourage students to identify landmarks in each direction. **learning modality: logical/mathematical**

Ongoing Assessment

Writing Have students explain why the needle of a compass always points in the same direction.

Magnetic Declination, continued

Including All Students

Materials *world map, compass*

Time 15 minutes

To reinforce the concept of magnetic declination, give students flat maps of the world. Have students find and mark true north on the maps. If the map has a compass "rose," suggest they use this to find true north. Then have students place the marked end of their maps toward true north for your location. Have each student place a compass on the map and mark the position of the needle. Students should be able to see the difference between true north and the position of the needle on the compass. **limited English proficiency**

Building Inquiry Skills: Interpreting Diagrams

Have students examine the map in Figure 13. Ask: **Does the compass needle always point to the same place? Where?** *(Yes, to the magnetic north pole.)* Then ask: **Does the compass needle always point in the same direction? Explain.** *(No, it depends where you are in relation to the pole. If you were standing at the geographic north pole, it would point south.)* **learning modality: logical/mathematical**

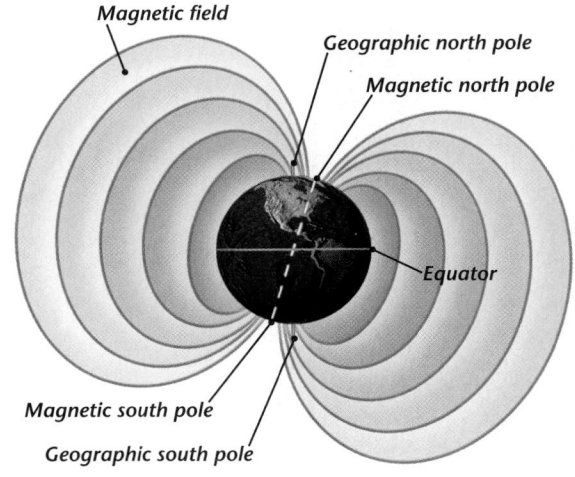

Figure 12 The magnetic poles are not located exactly at the geographic poles.

You can see the difference between the magnetic and geographic poles more clearly by imagining lines that connect each set of poles together. Figure 12 shows that the line connecting Earth's magnetic poles is tipped slightly from Earth's axis—the imaginary line around which Earth rotates.

If you use a compass you have to account for the fact that the geographic and magnetic poles are different. Suppose you could draw a line between you and the geographic north pole. The direction of this line is geographic north. Then imagine a second line between you and the magnetic pole. The angle between these two lines is the angle between geographic north and the north to which a compass needle points. This angle is known as **magnetic declination.**

Magnetic declination differs depending on where you are. Figure 13 shows magnetic declination in various locations in the United States. In North Carolina, for example, a hiker must head about 8 degrees east of the compass reading to get to a place that

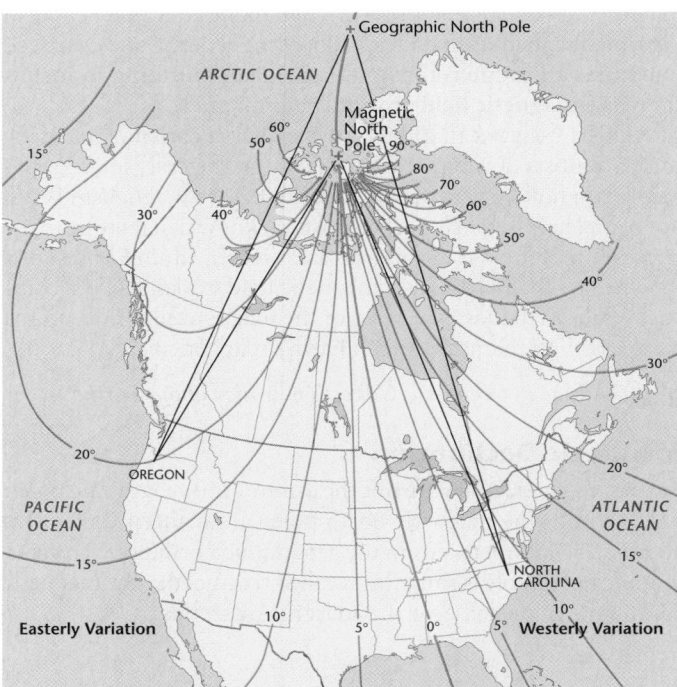

Figure 13 Magnetic declination varies with location.
Interpreting Maps What is the magnetic declination where you live?

Background

Facts and Figures Because Earth's magnetic field is generally detected with a horizontally mounted compass, it would seem that Earth's magnetic field lies only along the surface. The magnetic field is actually three-dimensional and extends throughout Earth and into space around Earth. A vertically mounted compass shows the angle Earth's magnetic field makes with the surface, called magnetic "dip." The instrument used to measure magnetic dip is called a "dipping needle." If a dipping needle were used directly over Earth's magnetic pole, the needle would point straight down. Locating the precise position of the north magnetic pole using this technique is complicated because the pole is located far below Earth's surface. The dipping needle would point straight down over an area in northeastern Canada.

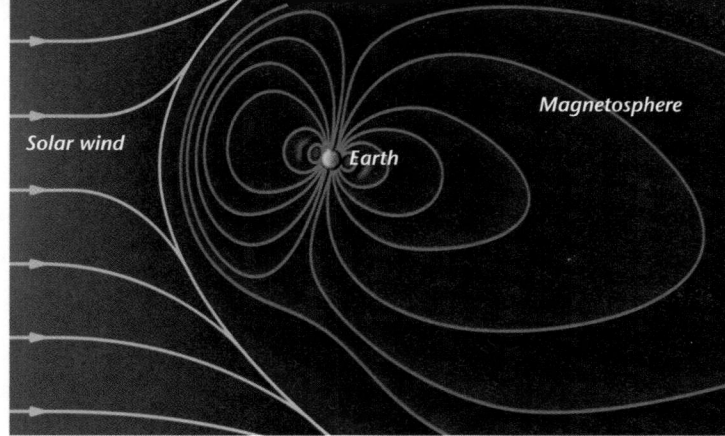

Figure 14 Earth's magnetic field differs from that of a bar magnet due to the solar wind. The solar wind causes the magnetic field to stretch out on the side of Earth experiencing night.

is directly north on a map. A hiker in Oregon would have to head about 20 degrees west of the compass reading.

Magnetic declination changes over time because the magnetic poles move slowly. Between 1580 and 1820, for example, the direction of magnetic north in London changed by 35 degrees.

☑ *Checkpoint* *What is magnetic declination?*

The Magnetosphere

Earth's magnetic field extends into space, which contains electrically charged particles. **Earth's magnetic field affects the movements of electrically charged particles in space. Charged particles also affect Earth's magnetic field.**

Between 1,000 and 25,000 kilometers above Earth's surface are two doughnut-shaped regions called the **Van Allen belts.** They are named after their discoverer, J. A. Van Allen. These regions contain electrons and protons traveling at very high speeds. At one time it was feared the particles would be dangerous for spacecraft passing through them, but this has not been the case.

Other electrically charged particles in space come from the sun. Earth and the other planets experience a solar wind. The **solar wind** is a stream of electrically charged particles flowing at high speeds from the sun. The solar wind pushes against Earth's magnetic field, and surrounds the field, as shown in Figure 14. The region of Earth's magnetic field shaped by the solar wind is called the **magnetosphere.** The solar wind constantly reshapes the magnetosphere as Earth rotates on its axis.

Although most particles in the solar wind cannot penetrate Earth's magnetic field, some particles do. They follow the lines of Earth's magnetic field to the magnetic poles. At the poles the magnetic field lines dip down to Earth's surface.

Spinning in Circles

Which way will a compass point?

1. Place a bar magnet in the center of a sheet of paper.
2. Place a compass about 2 cm beyond the north pole of the magnet. Draw a small arrow showing the direction of the compass needle.
3. Repeat Step 2 at 20 to 30 different positions around the magnet.
4. Remove the magnet and observe the pattern of arrows you drew.

Drawing Conclusions What does your pattern of arrows represent? Do compasses respond only to Earth's magnetic field?

The Magnetosphere

Using the Visuals: Figure 14

Have students compare the magnetosphere shown in Figure 14 to the magnetic field of a bar magnet. (*The bar magnet's field has a regular symmetrical shape, but the magnetosphere is compressed on one side and spread out on the other.*) Make sure students understand that the shape of the magnetosphere depends on the solar wind. **learning modality: visual**

Building Inquiry Skills: Inferring

Ask students: **Where do the auroral lights occur?** (*Almost exclusively at latitudes near the magnetic poles of Earth*) Ask students to infer why there would be more activity at these places than at others. (*Because the magnetic force is stronger at the poles, the charged particles cluster near the poles.*) **learning modality: verbal**

TRY THIS

Skills Focus drawing conclusions
Materials *bar magnet, sheet of paper, compass, centimeter ruler*
Time 20 minutes
Tips Use a bar magnet that is much larger than the compass to give the most accurate results.
Drawing Conclusions The pattern of arrows represents the magnetic field. Compasses also respond to magnetic material near them.
Extend Students can repeat the activity using a horseshoe magnet. Before they begin, ask students to predict how the arrows will appear around the horseshoe magnet based on their results with the bar magnet. **learning modality: kinesthetic**

Media and Technology

 Transparencies "The Magnetosphere," Transparency 27

Answers to Self-Assessment

Caption Question

Figure 13 Students should use the map to find the magnetic declination at their location.

☑ *Checkpoint*

Magnetic declination is the angle between a line pointing at the magnetic north pole and a line pointing at the geographic north pole.

Ongoing Assessment

Drawing Have students make captioned sketches to explain why a compass does not point to true north. Students can save their sketches in their portfolios.

Language Arts
CONNECTION

If possible, show students images or read a description of the auroral lights. Ask volunteers who have seen the lights to describe them. Encourage students to imagine living with the people described in the feature and hearing stories about the aurora.

In Your Journal Students' stories should be creative and descriptive. Encourage students to speculate on what could be the result of whistling at the aurora. **learning modality: verbal**

Effects of Earth's Magnetic Field

Demonstration

Materials *metal filing cabinet or other large metal object that has been in one place for a long time, such as a locker; compass*

ACTIVITY

Time 5 minutes

Hold the compass parallel to the ground and move it slowly from the top of the filing cabinet down to the bottom. If the needle turns and points in a different direction, the filing cabinet is magnetized. Allow students to move the compass around the cabinet and watch for the deflection of the needle. Ask: **How did this filing cabinet become magnetized?** *(Earth's magnetic field caused the domains to line up in the same direction.)* **learning modality: kinesthetic**

Figure 15 A band of colors called an aurora appears in the sky near the magnetic poles. *Relating Cause and Effect What causes an aurora?*

Language Arts
CONNECTION

From ancient times, people have sought to explain what they observe in nature. Imagine trying to explain the auroras without knowing that Earth is magnetic.

The Fox people in Wisconsin feared that the aurora was made up of the ghosts of their dead enemies.

A common belief among Eskimos in the Hudson Bay area of North America is that the aurora can be attracted by whistling to it. A hand clap will cause it to move away.

In Your Journal

Imagine that the aurora could really be attracted by whistling to it. Write a story about what might happen. Before you write the story, plan who the characters will be and what events will happen.

When charged particles get close to Earth's surface, they interact with atoms in the atmosphere. This causes the atoms to give off light. The result is one of Earth's most spectacular displays—a curtain of shimmering bright light in the atmosphere. A glowing region caused by charged particles from the sun is called an **aurora.** In the northern hemisphere, an aurora is called the Northern Lights, or aurora borealis. In the southern hemisphere, it is called the Southern Lights, or aurora australis.

Effects of Earth's Magnetic Field

You learned that a material such as iron can be made into a magnet by a strong magnetic field. **Since Earth produces a strong magnetic field, Earth itself can make magnets.**

Earth as a Magnet Maker Suppose you leave an iron bar lying in a north-south direction for many years. Earth's magnetic field can attract the domains strongly enough to cause them to line up in the same direction. (Recall that a strong magnetic field can cause the magnetic domains of a ferromagnetic material to increase in size or to line up in the same direction.) To speed the process, you could gently tap on the bar with a hammer. This vibrates the domains and they can then be aligned by the magnetic field.

What objects might be lying in Earth's magnetic field for many years? Consider metal objects or appliances that are left in the same position for many years, such as filing cabinets in your school. Even though no one has tried to make them into magnets, Earth might have done so anyway.

Background

Integrating Science Where magnetic lines of force break through the sun's surface, the temperature of the surface gases is lowered somewhat. These cooler areas appear as dark areas known as sunspots. Whenever sunspots appear in pairs, each sunspot in the pair represents a pole of the magnetic field. The annual number of sunspots increases and decreases in an 11-year cycle.

Program Resources

◆ **Unit 3 Resources** 8-2 Review and Reinforcement, p. 15; 8-2 Enrich, p. 16

Earth Leaves a Record Earth's magnetic field also acts on rocks that contain magnetic material, such as rock on the ocean floor. The ocean floor is produced from molten material that seeps up through a long crack in the ocean floor, known as the mid-ocean ridge. When the rock is molten, the iron it contains lines up in the direction of Earth's magnetic field. As the rock cools and hardens, the iron is locked in place. This creates a permanent record of the magnetic field.

As scientists studied such rock, they discovered that the direction and strength of Earth's magnetic field has changed over time. Earth's magnetic poles periodically reverse themselves. This last happened about 780,000 years ago.

The yellow arrows in Figure 16 indicate the direction of Earth's magnetic field. Notice that the patterns of bands on either side of the ridge are mirror images. This is because the sea floor spreads apart from the mid-ocean ridge. So rocks farther from the ridge are older than rocks near the ridge. The magnetic record in the rock depends on when the rock was formed.

You might be wondering why Earth's magnetic field changes direction. If so, you're not alone. Scientists have asked the same question. Earth's magnetic field arises from the motion of molten metal in Earth's core. Changes in the flow of that metal result in changes in Earth's magnetic field. But the details of this theory have not been worked out, and so scientists cannot explain why the flow changes. Maybe someday you will be able to shed light on this area.

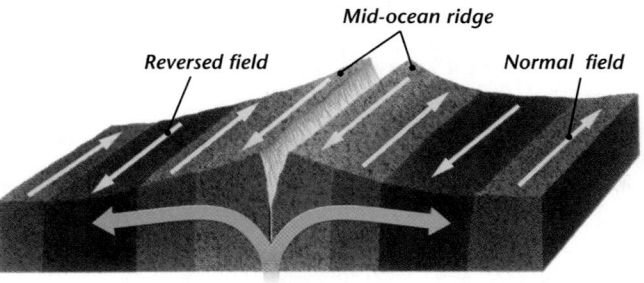

Mid-ocean ridge

Reversed field　　　*Normal field*

Figure 16 When volcanic lava on the ocean floor hardens into rock, the direction of Earth's magnetic field at that time is permanently recorded.

 Section 2 Review

1. How is Earth like a magnet?
2. Compare Earth's geographic poles with its magnetic poles.
3. How does a compass work?
4. What evidence of changes in Earth's magnetic field is found in rocks?
5. **Thinking Critically** Developing Hypotheses Some insects and birds have tiny particles of iron in parts of their body that are connected by nerves to their brain. What could be the function of the iron particles?

Science at Home

Explore your home with a compass. Use the compass to discover objects that are magnetized. For example, test the top and bottom of the stove, refrigerator, or a metal filing cabinet. Try metal objects that have been in the same position over a long period of time. Explain why these objects attract or repel a compass needle.

Chapter 8 **261**

Answers to Self-Assessment

Caption Question

Figure 15 An aurora is caused by charged particles from the sun entering Earth's magnetic field and interacting with atoms in the atmosphere.

---

3 Assess

Section 2 Review Answers

1. Earth has a magnetic field and has a north magnetic pole and a south magnetic pole.
2. Earth's geographic poles mark the ends of Earth's axis and are fixed in place. The magnetic poles attract the needle of a compass and move with time.
3. A compass has a magnetic needle that can spin freely. The north pole of the compass always points toward Earth's north magnetic pole.
4. When rocks are in a molten state, the magnetic material is free to move. Because it is attracted to Earth's magnetic field, the domains align with Earth's magnetic field. When the rocks cool and harden, the magnetic material is locked in place. By examining the pattern of magnetic material, scientists can study the magnetic history of Earth.
5. The iron particles in their bodies might be used for navigation, like a compass.

Science at Home

Materials *compass*
Prior to the activity, have students look at Figure 13 and imagine a refrigerator sitting on the surface of North America. Ask students to predict which side of the refrigerator will be the north-seeking side. *(The side facing north)* Some students may find that the top and bottom of the refrigerator are opposite poles. This is due to magnetic lines that are not parallel to Earth's surface but are at an angle to Earth's surface (magnetic "dip").

Performance Assessment

Oral Presentation Have students create presentations on an aspect of Earth's magnetic properties. Encourage students to create visual aids such as diagrams and charts to accompany their presentations.

261

SECTION 3 — Electric Current and Magnetic Fields

Objectives

After completing the lesson, students will be able to
- describe the relationship between electric current and a magnetic field;
- define and give examples of conductors and insulators;
- identify the characteristics of an electric circuit.

Key Terms electric charge, electric current, electric circuit, conductor, insulator, resistor, resistance, superconductor

1 Engage/Explore

Activating Prior Knowledge

Ask a volunteer to describe what he or she does when they want to use an electrical appliance such as a hairdryer. (*Plug it in, then switch it on.*) Tell students that when they do this, they are creating and closing an electrical circuit.

DISCOVER

Skills Focus inferring
Materials *2 wires (20 cm long with insulation stripped from ends), light bulb, bulb holder; 3 compasses, D cell (1.5 volt)*
Time 25 minutes
Tips Tell students that they are going to construct an electric circuit and that electricity will flow through the circuit when it is closed.
Expected Outcome The light bulb lights and some of the compass needles move when students touch the free end of the wire to the battery, thus closing the circuit.
Think It Over Students should infer that electricity in the wire creates a magnetic field.

SECTION 3 — Electric Current and Magnetic Fields

DISCOVER — ACTIVITY

Are Magnetic Fields Limited to Magnets?

1. Obtain two wires with the insulation removed from both ends. Each wire should be 20 to 30 cm long.
2. Connect one end of each wire to a socket containing a small light bulb.
3. Connect the other end of one of those wires to a D cell.
4. Place 3 compasses near the wire at any 3 positions. Note the direction in which the compasses are pointing.
5. Center the wire over the compasses. Make sure the compass needles are free to turn.
6. Touch the free end of the remaining wire to the battery. Observe the compasses as current flows through the wire. Move the wire away from the battery, and then touch it to the battery again. Watch the compasses.

Think It Over
Inferring What happened to the compasses? What can you infer about electricity and magnetism?

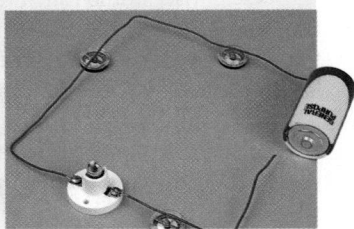

GUIDE FOR READING

- How is an electric current related to a magnetic field?
- How are conductors different from insulators?
- What are the characteristics of an electric circuit?

Reading Tip As you read, use the headings to make an outline.

262

In 1820, the Danish scientist Hans Christian Oersted (UR sted) was teaching a class at the University of Copenhagen. During his lecture, he allowed electricity to flow through a wire, just as electricity flows through wires to your electrical appliances. When electricity flowed, he noticed that the needle of a compass near the wire changed direction.

Oersted's observations surprised him. He could have assumed that something was wrong with his equipment. Instead, he investigated further. He set up several compasses around a wire. Oersted discovered that whenever he turned on the electricity, the compass needles lined up in a circle around the wire.

Oersted's discovery showed that magnetism and electricity are related. But just how are they related? To find out, you must learn about electric current.

Electric Current

You learned in Section 1 that all matter contains particles called electrons and protons. Electrons and protons have a property called **electric charge.** Electrons are negatively charged, and protons are positively charged.

◄ Oersted's demonstration

READING STRATEGIES

Reading Tip You may want to have students work with partners to outline the section as they read. Suggest students preview the section and write the headings in outline form, as shown here. Students should leave extra space to add information as they read.

I. Electric Current and Magnetic Fields
   A. Electric Current
   B. Moving Charge and Magnetism
   C. Electric Circuits
   D. Conductors and Insulators
   E. Electrical Resistance

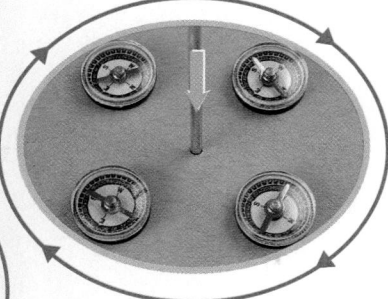

B. Compass needles align themselves with the magnetic field of a current moving upward (blue arrow).

Figure 17 Current in a wire affects a compass needle. **A.** With no current flowing, the compass needles all point to magnetic north.

C. Compass needles reverse their directions to align with the magnetic field of a current moving downward.

When electric charges flow through a wire or similar material, they create an electric current. **Electric current** is the flow of charge through a material. The amount of charge that passes through the wire in a unit of time is the rate at which electric current flows. The unit of current is the ampere (amp or A), named for André-Marie Ampère. You will often see the name of the unit shortened to "amp." The number of amps tells the amount of charge flowing past a given point each second.

What does all of this have to do with magnetism? **An electric current produces a magnetic field.** The lines of the magnetic field produced by a current in a straight wire are in the shape of circles with the wire at their center. You can see in Figure 17 that compasses placed around a wire line up with the magnetic field. The iron filings in Figure 18 map out the same field. The direction of the current determines the direction of the magnetic field. If the current is reversed, the magnetic field reverses as well. You can see this from the compasses in Figure 17C.

Moving Charge and Magnetism

Ampère carried out many experiments with electricity and magnetism. He hypothesized that all magnetism is a result of circulating charges. Atoms, for example, can become magnets because of the motion of the electrons. Based on modern knowledge of magnetism, Ampère's hypothesis is correct. All magnetism is caused by the movement of charges.

☑ *Checkpoint* What particles have electric charge?

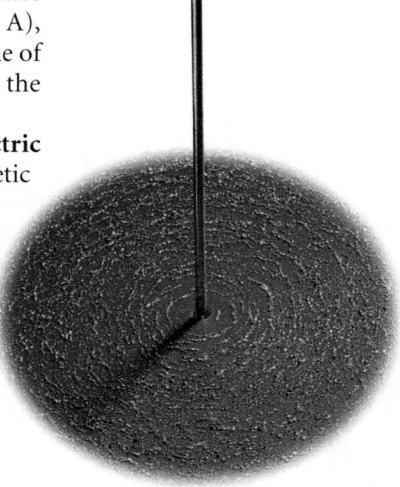

Figure 18 Iron filings show the field lines around a wire that carries a current.
Observing What is the shape of the field lines?

Program Resources

◆ **Unit 3 Resources** 8-3 Lesson Plan, p. 17; 8-3 Section Summary, p. 18
◆ **Guided Reading and Study Workbook** Section 8-3

Answers to Self-Assessment

Caption Question

Figure 18 The field lines are in the shape of circles.

☑ *Checkpoint*
Electrons and protons

---

2 Facilitate

Electric Current

Using the Visuals: Figure 17

Ask students to note the directions in which the compass needles are pointing in each photo in Figure 17. Point out that in the first photo, there is no current in the wire. Direct attention to the photo in the center. Ask: **How can you tell there is current in the wire?** (*The compass needles react to the magnetic field of the wire.*) Point out that the third photo shows what happens when the direction of the current is reversed and ask students to explain how they can tell. (*The compass needles are reversed.*) **learning modality: visual**

Moving Charge and Magnetism

Addressing Naive Conceptions

Students may be confused by the idea that magnetism is caused by moving charges because permanent magnets such as bar magnets do not seem to have moving parts. Ask: **Why can't you see moving particles in a magnet?** (*Moving particles are too tiny to see. In a solid, vibrating particles stay in the same relative positions.*) **learning modality: verbal**

Ongoing Assessment

Oral Presentation Call on students at random to state in their own words how magnetism and electricity are related according to Oersted's observations. Remind them to refer to compasses and electrical wire in their explanations.

Electric Circuits

Electric Circuits

An electric current will not flow automatically through every wire. Current flows only through electric circuits. An **electric circuit** is a complete path through which electric charges can flow. All electrical devices, from toasters to radios to electric guitars and televisions, contain electric circuits.

All circuits have the same basic features. **First, a circuit has a source of electrical energy.** Energy is the ability to do work. **Second, circuits have devices that are run by electrical energy.** A radio, a computer, a light bulb, and a refrigerator are all devices that convert electrical energy into another form of energy. A light bulb, for example, converts electrical energy to electromagnetic energy (it gives off light) and thermal energy (it gives off heat).

Third, electric circuits are connected by conducting wires and a switch. In order to describe a circuit, you can draw a circuit diagram. *Exploring Electric Circuits* on the next page shows a circuit diagram along with the symbols that represent the parts of the circuit. As you read, identify the parts of a circuit and their symbols.

Conductors and Insulators

Electric current flows through metal wires. Will it also flow through plastic or paper? The answer is no. Electric current does not flow through every material.

Electric currents move freely through materials called **conductors.** Metals, such as copper, silver, iron, and aluminum, are good conductors. **In a conductor, some of the electrons are only loosely bound to their atoms.** These electrons, called conduction electrons, are able to move throughout the conductor. As these electrons flow through a conductor, they form an electric current.

Did you ever wonder why a light goes on the instant you flip the switch? How do the electrons get to your lamp from the electric company so fast? The answer is that electrons are not created and sent to you when you flip a switch. They are present all along in the conductors that make up the circuit. When you flip the switch, conduction electrons at one end of the wire are pulled while those at the other end are pushed. The result is a continuous flow of electrons as soon as the circuit is completed.

Insulators are a different kind of material in which charges are not able to move freely. **The electrons in an insulator are bound tightly to their atoms and do not flow easily.** Examples of insulators are rubber, glass, sand, plastic, and wood.

✓ *Checkpoint* *What moves freely in a conductor?*

Figure 19 Charges behave like the chairs on a ski lift. Charges in all parts of a conducting wire begin to flow at the same time.

EXPLORING Electric Circuits

Electric circuits are all around you. They are so common that you probably don't think about them. An electric circuit has several basic features.

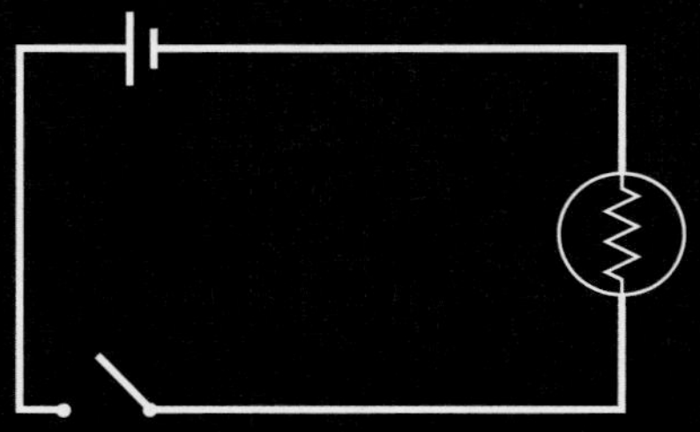

This circuit diagram represents the circuit shown in the photograph. Special symbols are used for the parts of the circuit.

Circuit Symbols

—∕ — Switch

—|⊢— Energy source

⊛ Resistor

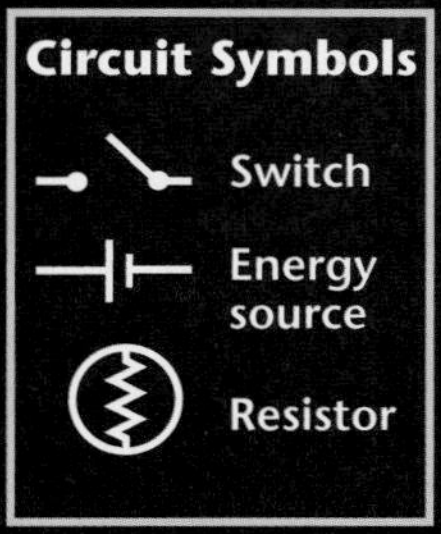

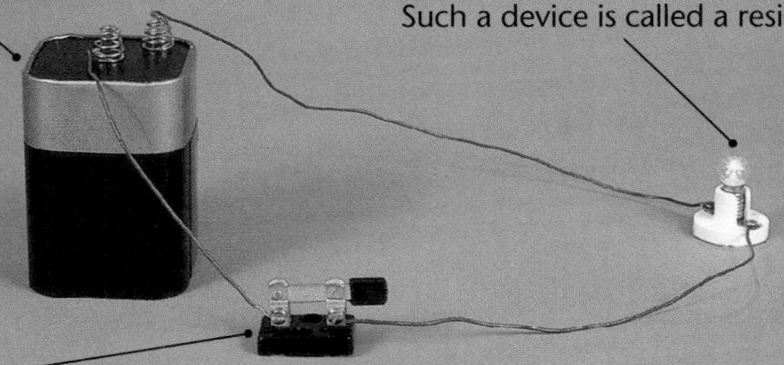

Battery
A source of electrical energy makes charges move around a circuit.

Resistor
A device such as a light bulb, appliance, or computer converts electrical energy to another form. Such a device is called a resistor.

Switch
A switch is used to open and close the circuit. When the switch is closed, the electric circuit is complete. When the switch is open, the circuit is broken. Charges cannot flow through a broken path.

Ask students to describe how the symbols used in circuit diagrams are useful for engineers. *(Sample: Using symbols allows engineers to describe only the parts of the circuit that are important. For example, light bulbs, toasters, and computers have resistors, so they are represented by the same symbol.)*

Extend Have students bring in circuit diagrams of small appliances to review the symbols. **learning modality: visual**

Media and Technology

Transparencies "Exploring Electric Circuits," Transparency 28

Concept Videotape Library *Adventures,* Tape 2, "What Is Electricity?"

Answers to Self-Assessment

☑ *Checkpoint*
In a conductor, electrons (or charges) move freely.

Ongoing Assessment

Oral Presentation Have students give one example of a conductor and one of an insulator and describe the difference between them.

265

Conductors and Insulators, continued

Classifying

Materials *3 10-cm wires*  *with insulation stripped from ends; 2 alligator clips; light bulb; D cell; conductors and insulators to test such as keys, foam, erasers, pencil lead, foil, wax paper, and paper clips*

Time 20 minutes

Tips Remove the insulation from the wires. You may want to construct circuits yourself before the activity. Students can then work in groups to test the materials. Students should open the circuits when they are not testing materials to conserve batteries.

Expected Outcome Conductors—metal objects, graphite in pencil lead; insulators—paper, foam, wooden objects. Students will know which materials are conductors because the bulb will light as the circuit is completed. The bulb will not light when insulators are tested.

Extend Ask students to explain why it is important not to use an appliance that has a cord with broken or cracked insulation. *(The rubber around a cord acts as an insulator. If there is no insulation, students may receive electric shocks.)*

learning modality: kinesthetic

Electrical Resistance

 Integrating Technology

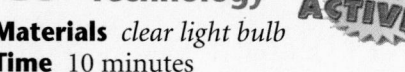

Materials *clear light bulb*

Time 10 minutes

Have students look closely at a light bulb and compare it to the one in Figure 20. Use a magnifying lens to observe the two ends of the filament. Note that one end is attached at the tip at the bottom of the bulb, and the other is soldered to the side of the threaded section. Therefore, for a bulb to light, the tip and the threaded section must be part of the complete circuit so current flows through the filament. **learning modality: visual**

266

Figure 20 Electric current passes through the tungsten filament of a light bulb. As it resists the flow of charge, the filament heats up until it glows.

Sharpen your Skills

Classifying

Gather several objects such as keys, foam, pencil lead, aluminum foil, wax paper, and paper clips. Predict which items will be conductors.

1. Obtain three 10-cm wires with the insulation removed from both ends.

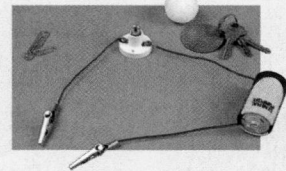

2. Construct a circuit like the one shown. Use the wires, a light bulb, a D cell, and two alligator clips.

3. Insert a test object between the two clips. Observe the light bulb. Repeat the test with each of the other objects.

Which objects are conductors? Which are insulators? How do you know?

266

Electrical Resistance

As charges flow through a circuit, they pass through resistors. A **resistor** uses electrical energy as it interferes with, or resists, the flow of charge. The opposition to the movement of charges flowing through a material is called **resistance.**

The resistance of a material depends on its atomic structure. Think about walking through a room with people in it. If the people are spread out, you can easily walk through the room without bumping into anyone. But if the people are crowded together, you will bump into people as you move through the room. In a similar way, an electron collides with particles in a material. During each collision, some of the electron's energy is converted to thermal energy (felt as heat) or electromagnetic energy (seen as light). The more collisions, the more electrical energy is converted.

The Light Bulb Thomas Edison used resistance when he was **INTEGRATING TECHNOLOGY** developing his electric light bulb. Edison experimented with many materials. He needed one that would conduct electric current, but would offer enough resistance to make the material heat up and glow. Edison tried copper wires, silk fibers, shredded corn husks, and even human hair. He had some success with cotton threads, then later he settled on charcoal made from bamboo slivers. Eventually, bamboo was replaced with wire made from tungsten. Tungsten is a metal that can get hot enough to glow without melting.

Figure 21 The magnetic field of the superconductor repels the magnetic cube. Thus the cube floats above the superconductor, much like the maglev train in Section 1.

Superconductors Scientists have discovered that some materials become superconductors at very low temperatures. A **superconductor** is a material that has no electrical resistance. A superconductor is very different from an ordinary conductor. Without resistance, a current flows through a superconductor with no loss of energy. Using superconducting wires would reduce wasted electrical energy and make electrical devices more efficient. Superconductors strongly repel magnets, as you can see in Figure 21. But their use as magnets is limited. A strong magnetic field destroys the superconductivity of a substance, turning it back into an ordinary conductor!

The greatest problem with superconductors is that very low temperatures are required. However, new materials have been found that become superconducting at higher temperatures. At the present time, researchers are working to make superconductors practical.

Section 3 Review

1. Are electricity and magnetism related? Explain.
2. What is the difference between a conductor and an insulator? Give an example of each.
3. What is an electric circuit?
4. **Thinking Critically Relating Cause and Effect** Why does a compass needle move when placed near a wire carrying an electric current? What do you think happens to the compass needle when the circuit is shut off?

Check Your Progress

CHAPTER
PROJECT
8

Construct an electric circuit for your fishing rod with a D cell and a piece of insulated wire about 12 meters long. Your fishing rod will need a switch. Making a switch is a matter of closing a circuit. One way to do this is to tape one end of your wire to one end of the battery and then to touch the other end of the wire to the other end of the battery. Think of a less awkward way of controlling the fishing rod.

3 Assess

Section 3 Review Answers

1. Yes; an electric current in a wire creates a magnetic field.
2. A conductor allows charge to flow through it. Examples are copper and other metals. An insulator does not allow charge to pass through it easily. Examples are paper, wood, and plastic.
3. An electric circuit is a complete path through which electric charges can flow.
4. The electric current sets up a magnetic field that is much stronger than Earth's magnetic field. When the circuit is shut off, the compass will point toward Earth's magnetic north pole.

Check Your Progress

CHAPTER
PROJECT
8

Provide materials so that students can experiment with different designs for switches. Encourage students to keep design logs with sketches of each switch they try and detailed notes of how well it works. Students should plan how their circuits will be attached to their fishing rods.

How It Works

Build a Flashlight

Preparing for Inquiry

Key Concept In order for bulbs to light, they must be part of a complete current. The bulb must be connected so that the current travels through the filament.

Skills Objectives Students will be able to
- make model flashlights that include a complete electric circuit;
- predict the arrangement of circuit components that will function as the best flashlight circuit;
- design a better switch.

Time 40 minutes

Advance Planning Have students collect and bring in cardboard tubes from paper towels and/or bathroom tissue. Have several different types of commercial flashlights available for students to examine.

Alternative Materials Provide aluminum foil baking cups instead of having students make their own reflectors.

Guiding Inquiry

Invitation Ask students if they have ever had an experience when the flashlight they were using failed. Have volunteers describe what they did to make the flashlight work again. *(Samples: Unscrewed the cap and put it back on, took out the batteries and put them back in, removed the cap and cleaned the connections, replaced the bulb or batteries.)* Have a class discussion about how these repairs relate to the structure of an electric circuit.

Introducing the Procedure

Have students examine the photo of the students working on the flashlight. Make sure students can identify all the components needed to construct a complete circuit.

Troubleshooting the Experiment

- If the bulb does not light, check to see that connections are making firm contact. Test the bulb to be certain it is not burned out. Test the battery to make sure it can light the bulb.

BUILD A FLASHLIGHT

I magine that you are camping in a forest. You hear noises outside your tent; something is rustling and bumping around nearby. At this moment, there is one device you might *really* appreciate having—a flashlight. Have you ever examined one to determine how it works?

Problem

How can you build a working flashlight?

Skills Focus

making models, observing, inferring

Materials

one cardboard tube	one D cell
flashlight bulb	aluminum foil
paper cup	duct tape
scissors	

2 lengths of wire, about 10 cm, with the insulation stripped off about 2 cm at each end
1 length of wire, 15–20 cm, with the insulation stripped off each end

Procedure

1. Check that the D cell fits inside the cardboard tube. Make two holes in the side of the tube about 2–3 cm apart. The holes should be near the middle of the tube.
2. Use duct tape to connect a 10-cm wire to each terminal of the battery. Touch the other ends of the wires to a flashlight bulb in order to find where to connect them. (*Hint:* Most bulbs have a bottom contact and a side contact. If there is no obvious side contact, try touching the metal on the side of the base.)

3. Line a paper cup with aluminum foil. Use a pencil to poke a hole in the bottom of the paper cup. The hole should be slightly smaller than the bulb, but large enough to allow the base of the bulb through.
4. Insert the base of the light bulb through the hole. Be sure the bulb fits securely.
5. Pass the long wire through one of the holes in the tube. Tape it to the inside of the tube, leaving about 2 cm outside the tube. The other end should reach the end of the tube.
6. Place the battery in the tube. Pass the wire attached to the bottom of the battery through the other hole in the tube. (Make sure the two wires outside the tube can touch.)
7. Make a sling from duct tape to hold the battery inside the tube.

- Students may find it easier to construct the flashlight if they cut the tube open lengthwise on the side opposite the two wire holes. This will help them see the relative positioning of the various components. This may also help in fitting the battery in the tube.

Analyze and Conclude

1. The aluminum foil is the reflector for this flashlight. It reflects some of the light forward for better illumination.

2. No. The orientation of the battery affects only the direction of the current. The bulb will light if current is flowing in either direction.
3. The circuit must include the bulb filament, so the bulb must be connected at both contact points.
4. To make a brighter bulb, add more batteries or use a different type of bulb. To make the flashlight stronger, use a plastic or metal case, or wrap something around the cardboard for more strength.

8. Attach the wires from the end of the tube to the contact points on the bulb.
9. Tape the cup on top of the tube, keeping all connections tight.
10. Touch the two free ends of the wires together to see if the bulb lights. If it doesn't, check to be sure all connections are taped together securely.

Analyze and Conclude

1. What is the purpose of lining the cup with aluminum foil?
2. Does it matter which way the battery is placed in the tube? Explain.
3. Why does the bulb have to be connected at two points in order for it to light?
4. How could you make your flashlight brighter? How could you make it more rugged?

5. Compare your flashlight to a manufactured one. Explain the differences.
6. **Apply** Design a more convenient switch for your flashlight. You may want to use materials such as paper clips, brass fasteners, or aluminum foil. Have your teacher approve your switch design and then build and test the switch.

Getting Involved

People use different types of flashlights for different purposes. Some are narrow and flexible while others are wide and sturdy. Compare several different flashlights. Describe the flashlights. Note the type and number of batteries required, the type of switch used, and any other features that you observe. Suggest useful applications for each flashlight. Then design a new flashlight based on a need that you observe.

5. In the commercial flashlight, there is a permanent switch that is easy to operate; the case is plastic or metal; the bulb can be easily removed and replaced. Commercial flashlights must be durable and reliable, and operate in a variety of situations.
6. Students' designs should have a convenient way to make contact between the two free ends of the wires coming out of the tube. Make sure they do not close the circuit for more than a few seconds, to avoid overheating.

Extending the Inquiry

Getting Involved Ask students to describe situations in which people rely on flashlights. *(Sample: Camping trips, power outages, emergencies)* Show them a variety of flashlights (disposable, common hand-held, camping lantern). Ask students to compare and contrast the flashlights by observing them closely and carefully. Encourage students to determine which flashlights would be best for each situation. Students should use what they learn in this discussion to design a flashlight for a specific purpose.

Safety

Remind students to be careful when using scissors. Make sure they wear safety goggles throughout the lab. Caution students to handle the glass light bulbs gently, as broken bulbs can produce serious cuts. Review the safety guidelines in Appendix A.

Program Resources

◆ **Unit 3 Resources** Real-World Lab blackline masters, pp. 28–29

Media and Technology

 Lab Activity Videotape
Tape 2

269

Objective

After completing the lesson, students will be able to

◆ identify characteristics and cite uses of an electromagnet.

Key Terms solenoid, electromagnet

1 Engage/Explore

Activating Prior Knowledge

Remind students that magnetic fields occur around moving charges, such as those in a current-carrying wire. Ask students to brainstorm a list of machines or appliances that generate magnetic fields. (*Samples: junkyard cranes, televisions*) Challenge students to think of some ways that the relationship between electricity and magnetism could be useful.

·········· DISCOVER ·········

Skills Focus forming operational definitions
Materials *1 m bell wire or magnet wire, iron nail, D cell, paper clips*
Time 20 minutes
Tips Use wire with very thin enamel insulation so that a large number of turns fit easily in a compact space around the nail. Caution students not to close the circuit for too long. If the current flows for too long, the nail may become magnetized and attract paper clips when the current is turned off. If this happens, reverse the wire connections to the battery. This will reverse the magnetic effect.
Expected Outcome The device will attract paper clips when the circuit is complete, but not when the circuit is open.
Think It Over Like a bar magnet—attracts paper clips; unlike a bar magnet—magnetism can be "switched off." Definition of electromagnet—magnet that can be turned on and off because an electric current is used to create the magnetic field.

SECTION
4 Electromagnets

DISCOVER ·· ACTIVITY

How Do You Turn a Magnet On and Off?

1. Wind one meter of wire tightly around an iron nail so that you have at least 25 turns. Leave about 15 centimeters of wire on each end.
2. Attach one end of the wire to one terminal of a D cell.
3. Briefly touch the other end of the wire to the other terminal of the D cell. **CAUTION:** *Do not leave the switch closed for more than two or three seconds at a time. The wire will heat up.*
4. With the circuit complete, bring a paper clip near the nail.
5. Add paper clips one at a time and repeat Steps 3 and 4.

Think It Over

Forming Operational Definitions The device you constructed is called an electromagnet. How does it compare with a bar magnet? Based on your observations, define "electromagnet."

GUIDE FOR READING

◆ What are the characteristics of an electromagnet?

Reading Tip Before you read, preview the illustrations. Write down any questions you have about the illustrations. Answer them as you read the section.

You learned in Section 3 that a current in a wire creates a magnetic field around the wire. By turning the current on and off, you can turn the magnetic field on and off. So by using an electric current to create a magnet, you produce a magnetic field that you can control.

Solenoids

The magnetic field around a current-carrying wire forms a cylinder around the wire. If the wire is twisted into a loop, the magnetic field lines become bunched up inside the loop. You can see this by looking at the iron filings in Figure 22. The strength of the

Figure 22 The magnetic field around a loop of wire bunches up in the center.

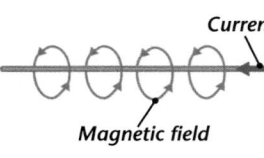

Current

Magnetic field

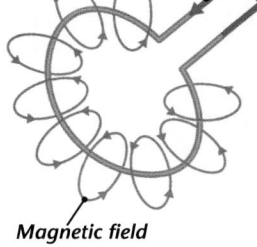

Current

Magnetic field

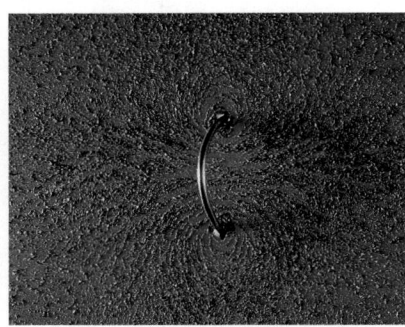

270

READING STRATEGIES

Reading Tip Questions may include, "What is a solenoid?" and "How does a solenoid make a bell ring?" After students have read the section, invite volunteers to read their questions and then answer them, based on information in the section.

Program Resources

◆ **Unit 3 Resources** 8-4 Lesson Plan, p. 21; 8-4 Section Summary, p. 22
◆ **Guided Reading and Study Workbook** Section 8-4

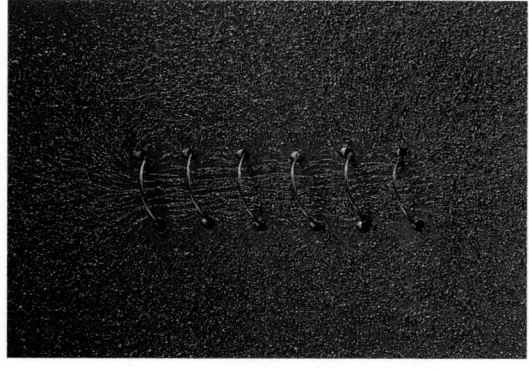

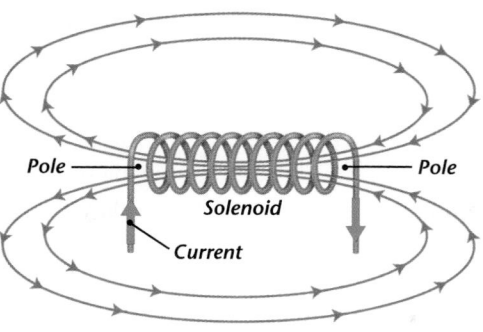

Figure 23 The magnetic field around a solenoid resembles that of a bar magnet. *Comparing and Contrasting How is a solenoid different from a bar magnet?*

magnetic field increases as the number of loops is increased. If the wire is bent into a second loop, the concentration of magnetic field lines within the loop is twice as great.

By winding a current-carrying wire into a coil you have strengthened the magnetic field in the center of the coil. The two ends of the coil act like poles. The iron filings around the loops of wire in Figure 23 line up much as they would around a bar magnet. A current-carrying coil of wire with many loops is called a **solenoid.** A solenoid creates a magnetic field that can be turned on and off by switching the current on and off. The north and south poles change with the direction of the current.

Multiplying Magnetism

If a ferromagnetic material such as iron is placed inside a solenoid, the magnetic field is increased. Recall how a ferromagnetic material acts. When iron is placed within the solenoid's magnetic field, it becomes a magnet as well. A solenoid with a ferromagnetic core is called an **electromagnet.** The temporary magnetic field of an electromagnet is produced by the current in the wire and the magnetized core. The overall magnetic field can be hundreds or thousands of times stronger than the magnetic field produced by the current alone. **An electromagnet is a strong magnet that can be turned on and off.**

An electromagnet is ideal for lifting heavy pieces of scrap metal. Have you ever seen stacks of junked cars? The flattened auto bodies are shredded into small metal fragments. The iron and steel fragments are picked up by a huge electromagnet on a crane. When the switch is turned on, current flows and the electromagnet lifts the metallic scrap and the crane moves it. When the switch is turned off, the pieces of scrap fall from the magnet.

☑ *Checkpoint* What is a solenoid?

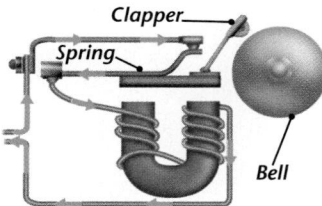

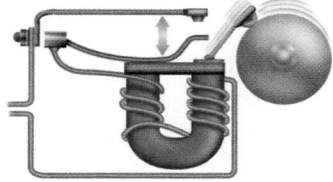

Figure 24 A solenoid is used to ring an alarm bell. When current flows through the circuit, the coil acts as a magnet. The strip of iron on the spring is attracted to the electromagnet and the clapper strikes the bell. At the same time, the spring opens the circuit and stops the current. The spring returns the clapper to its resting position.

Chapter 8 **271**

Answers to Self-Assessment

Caption Question

Figure 23 The magnetic field of a solenoid can be turned on and off.

☑ *Checkpoint*

A solenoid is a current-carrying coil of wire with many loops, which can be part of an electromagnet.

---

2 Facilitate

Solenoids

Building Inquiry Skills: Making Models

Materials *coiled spring toy, long thin rope*
Time 10 minutes

Have students place the rope inside the spring toy so the spring makes a cylinder around the cord, then tie the ends of the rope to the outermost links of the spring toy. Students can bend the cord into a loop and observe what happens to the spring toy. Ask: **How does this model the magnetic field around a current-carrying wire in an electromagnet?** (*The field lines in the electromagnet—coils in the spring toy—bunch up inside a loop in the wire—the current-carrying wire.*) **limited English proficiency**

Multiplying Magnetism

Inquiry Challenge

Materials *wooden dowel, insulated connecting wire, several identical iron nails, 1.5-V battery, iron objects*
Time 20 minutes

Have groups of students construct electromagnets and develop hypotheses on how the addition of iron nails might affect their strength. **cooperative learning**

Increasing the Strength of an Electromagnet

Building Inquiry Skills: Relating Cause and Effect

Ask: **What would happen if you increased the number of coils in a solenoid?** (*The magnetic field of the solenoid would be strengthened.*)
learning modality: logical/mathematical

Ongoing Assessment

Drawing Have each student draw a diagram of an electromagnet and explain how it works.

Recording Information

Integrating Technology

Challenge students to work in small groups and make a flowchart showing how the sound of their voice is recorded on audiotape and played back. Once the flowchart is complete, groups can evaluate one another's work.
cooperative learning

3 Assess

Section 4 Review Answers

1. Sample: An electromagnet is a coil of current-carrying wire that acts as a magnet when the current is turned on.
2. An electromagnet can be turned on and off; its strength can be increased by adding loops of coil, using more current, or using a different core.
3. Electromagnets are used in doorbells, video and audio recording equipment, and scrap metal separators.
4. Yes. A strong magnet will alter the magnetic pattern on the computer disk or in the metal powder on the tape.

CHAPTER PROJECT 8

Check Your Progress
Make sure students know how to connect the electromagnets to the circuits. To make testing easier, encourage students to create two or three different solenoid coils of 100, 175, and 250 turns, and test them all. Remind students to keep the switch open unless they are making direct observations. Students should make several trials with each electromagnet.

Increasing the Strength of an Electromagnet

There are a number of ways you can increase the strength of an electromagnet's field. You can increase the current in the solenoid. You can add more loops of wire to the solenoid. You can wind the coils of the solenoid closer together. Also, you can increase the strength of an electromagnet by using a stronger ferromagnetic material for the core.

Recording Information

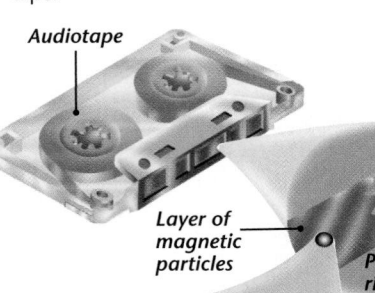

Figure 25 A magnified photograph shows a pattern of magnetic domains on a cassette tape.

Audiotape

Layer of magnetic particles

Plastic ribbon

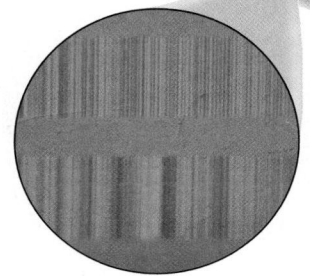

Magnified photograph of tape

INTEGRATING TECHNOLOGY When you record information on audiotapes, videotapes, computer disks, or credit cards, you are using electromagnets. Think about recording your voice with a tape recorder. When you talk into a microphone, the vibrations of your voice are changed into an electric current that varies with your voice. That current is used in an electromagnet in the recording head of the tape recorder to produce a magnetic field. Since the current changes, the magnetic field of the electromagnet changes as well.

A recording tape consists of a plastic ribbon coated with a thin layer of metal powder. The metal particles of the powder are magnetized by the magnetic field of the electromagnet in the recording head. As the tape moves past the electromagnet, the metal particles are magnetized more or less by the electromagnet. The strength of magnetization of the particles changes with the changing strength of the magnetic field. The magnetic pattern in the tape becomes a code for your voice. When you play the tape back, the code is converted back into sound. In a similar way, electromagnets are used to record images and sounds on videotape and all sorts of information on computer disks.

Section 4 Review

1. Describe an electromagnet in your own words.
2. How is an electromagnet different from a permanent magnet?
3. What are some uses for electromagnets?
4. **Thinking Critically** **Predicting** Will bringing a strong magnet near a computer disk or videotape cause damage to the recorded information? Explain.

272

Check Your Progress **CHAPTER PROJECT 8**
Construct an electromagnet by wrapping a length of insulated wire around one or more iron nails. Attach the ends of the wire to the circuit containing your switch. Test your electromagnet by dipping it into a pile of paper clips to see how many it can pick up at one time. Experiment with the strength of your electromagnet by changing one variable at a time.

Performance Assessment

Writing Ask students to design an electromagnet for a specific purpose. Students should describe how the electromagnet works and name one way it can be strengthened.

 Students can save their designs in their portfolios.

Background

Integrating Science Magnetic Resonance Imaging (MRI) uses powerful electromagnets. The magnetic fields needed for this procedure are so strong that people in the room cannot wear magnetic materials such as jewelry, pens, and watches. These materials would be attracted to the huge electromagnet and fly across the room at dangerous velocities.

Program Resources

- **Unit 3 Resources** 8-4 Review and Reinforce, p. 23; 8-4 Enrich, p. 24
- **Laboratory Manual** 8, "Electromagnetism"

SECTION 1 The Nature of Magnetism

Key Ideas

◆ Unlike magnetic poles attract; like magnetic poles repel.
◆ A magnetic field is a region around a magnet in which magnetic attraction acts.
◆ Magnetic domains are regions in which the magnetic fields of atoms are aligned.
◆ In a magnetized material, most of the domains are lined up in the same direction.

Key Terms

magnetism	nucleus
magnetic pole	proton
magnetic field	electron
magnetic field lines	magnetic domain
atom	ferromagnetic material
element	permanent magnet

SECTION 2 Magnetic Earth

INTEGRATING EARTH SCIENCE

Key Ideas

◆ Earth has a north magnetic pole and a south magnetic pole.
◆ A compass can be used to find directions because its needle lines up with Earth's magnetic poles.
◆ Earth's magnetic poles are not at exactly the same locations as the geographic poles.
◆ The magnetosphere is the magnetic field of Earth as shaped by the solar wind.

Key Terms

compass	solar wind
magnetic declination	magnetosphere
Van Allen belts	aurora

SECTION 3 Electric Current and Magnetic Fields

Key Ideas

◆ Electric current is electric charge in motion.
◆ An electric current produces a magnetic field.
◆ Electric charges flow freely through materials called conductors but not through insulators.
◆ Resistance is the opposition to the movement of charges flowing through a material.

Key Terms

electric charge	insulator
electric current	resistor
electric circuit	resistance
conductor	superconductor

SECTION 4 Electromagnets

Key Ideas

◆ A solenoid creates a magnetic field by means of a current flowing through a coil of wire.
◆ The strength of an electromagnet depends on the amount of current, the number of turns of wire in the coil, how close together the turns of wire are, and the type of magnetic core.

Key Terms

solenoid	electromagnet

Organizing Information

Concept Map Copy the concept map about magnetism onto a separate sheet of paper. Then complete it and add a title. (For more on concept maps, see the Skills Handbook.)

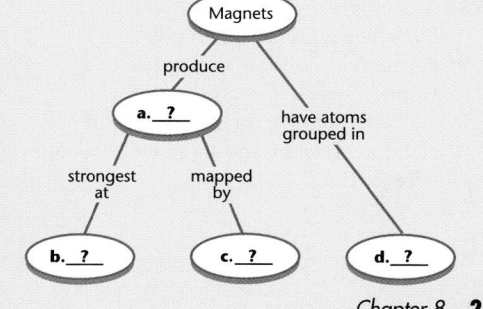

Magnets
produce
a. ?
strongest at
mapped by
have atoms grouped in
b. ? c. ? d. ?

Organizing Information

Concept Map **a.** Magnetic fields **b.** The poles **c.** Magnetic field lines **d.** Domains
Sample title: Magnetism

Program Resources

◆ **Unit 3 Resources** Chapter 8 Project Scoring Rubric, p. 8
◆ **Performance Assessment** Chapter 8, pp. 25–27
◆ **Chapter Tests** Chapter 8 Test, pp. 31–34

Media and Technology

Computer Test Bank
Chapter 8 Test

Review Content

Multiple Choice

1. c **2.** d **3.** c **4.** d **5.** b

True or False

6. true **7.** magnetite, or lodestone
8. magnetic **9.** electric charge, electricity, or current **10.** true

Checking Concepts

11. In a magnetic material, the domains (which act as tiny magnets) are aligned. In the middle of the magnet, north and south poles balance each other, but the ends of a magnet are unpaired poles. Diagrams should show that a magnet broken in half will have a north and south pole.

12. A material becomes a magnet when the domains of the material are turned to point in the same direction.

13. Earth acts like a magnet because it produces a magnetic field and has magnetic poles.

14. An aurora is a region of bright colored light produced by the interaction of particles from the solar wind and particles in Earth's atmosphere. Most of the solar wind is deflected by Earth's magnetic field, but some particles penetrate the field and enter Earth's atmosphere near the poles, where the magnetic forces are strongest.

15. Charges, or current, flowing through a wire set up a magnetic field that is stronger than Earth's magnetic field.

16. Students' drawings should show an electric circuit with a source of electrical energy and a device that is run by electrical energy, connected by connecting wires and a switch.

17. Electric charges move easily through conductors. Insulators do not allow electric charges to pass through them easily. Graphite and most metals are good conductors. Wood, plastic, and rubber are good insulators.

18. Sample: Magnets in your clothes could be attracted to electromagnets in your laundry hamper, so your clothes would pick themselves up. Students should mention whether their device depends on like poles repelling or unlike poles attracting one another. When they use an electromagnet, they should describe the source of electric current.

Reviewing Content

Multiple Choice

Choose the letter of the answer that best completes each statement.

1. The region in which magnetic forces act is called a
  a. line of force.   **b.** pole.
  c. magnetic field.   **d.** field of attraction.

2. An example of a ferromagnetic material is
  a. plastic.   **b.** wood.
  c. copper.   **d.** iron.

3. The person who first suggested that Earth behaves as a magnet was
  a. Ampère.
  b. Oersted.
  c. Gilbert.
  d. Columbus.

4. The region in which Earth's magnetic field is found is called the
  a. atmosphere.
  b. stratosphere.
  c. aurora.
  d. magnetosphere.

5. A coil of current-carrying wire with an iron core is called a(an)
  a. ferromagnet.
  b. electromagnet.
  c. compass.
  d. maglev.

True or False

If the statement is true, write true. If it is false, change the underlined word or words to make the statement true.

6. Like poles of magnets <u>repel</u> each other.

7. The type of magnetic mineral found in nature is called <u>platinum</u>.

8. A compass needle points in the direction of Earth's <u>geographic</u> north pole.

9. An electric circuit is a complete path through which <u>domains</u> can flow.

10. You can <u>increase</u> the strength of an electromagnet by adding more turns of a wire to it.

Checking Concepts

11. Explain why you are not left with one north pole and one south pole if you break a magnet in half. Draw a diagram to support your answer.

12. How does a material become a magnet?

13. How does Earth act like a magnet?

14. What is an aurora? How is it produced?

15. Why does a compass needle change direction when it is placed near a current-carrying wire?

16. Draw a simple electric circuit. Label and define the basic parts.

17. How is a conductor different from an insulator? Give two examples of each.

18. Writing to Learn Did you ever think of a chore that would be much easier if you only had some futuristic device? Here's your chance. Describe a task that you would like to make easier. Then think about how you could use an electromagnet to carry out the task. Be creative in describing your design.

Thinking Critically

19. Problem Solving Cassia borrowed her brother's magnet. When she returned it, it was barely magnetic. What might Cassia have done to the magnet?

20. Comparing and Contrasting What is the difference between a magnetized iron bar and an unmagnetized one?

21. Drawing Conclusions Why might an inexperienced explorer get lost using a compass?

22. Inferring A compass points north until a bar magnet is brought next to it. The compass needle is then attracted or repelled by the magnet. What inference can you make about the strengths of the magnetic fields of Earth and the bar magnet?

23. Relating Cause and Effect Why does opening a switch in an electric circuit stop the flow of current?

24. Applying Concepts How are the uses of an electromagnet different from those of a permanent bar magnet?

Although it is important that the idea utilize the properties of magnets, devices do not have to be realistic.

Thinking Critically

19. Cassia could have dropped the magnet or exposed it to heat. Either action can jostle the domains out of alignment.

20. The domains in a magnetized iron bar are all arranged in the same direction. The domains in the unmagnetized iron bar are not aligned.

21. The explorer might not know about magnetic declination. If the explorer follows the compass direction exactly, he or she will wind up off course. The amount of declination depends on the geographic location.

22. Although Earth's magnetic field covers a larger area, its local effect is less than that of the bar magnet and the effects of the bar magnet on the compass are more detectable. So the bar magnet has a stronger field.

23. Only with a closed switch will a circuit have a complete path for current to flow.

Applying Skills

Use the illustration of four electromagnets to answer Questions 25–27.

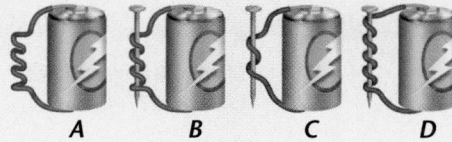

A   B   C   D

25. **Predicting** Will device A or B produce a stronger magnetic field? Will device B or C produce a stronger magnetic field? Explain your choices.
26. **Controlling Variables** Can you tell which electromagnet is the strongest of the four? Explain why or why not.
27. **Designing Experiments** Without changing the number of turns of wire, how could you change the strength of each electromagnet?

Performance CHAPTER PROJECT 8 **Assessment**

Project Wrap Up Test your final electromagnet. Cut the tops off two empty plastic milk containers. Practice moving paper clips from one container to the other until you are ready for a "fishing" competition. After your teacher gives you a one-minute opportunity to fish, compare the most successful designs in the class.

Reflect and Record In your journal, describe the features of other students' designs that worked well. Which switch designs were easiest to operate? What contributed to making the strongest magnets?

Test Preparation

Use these questions to prepare for standardized tests.

Read the passage. Then answer Questions 28–30.
Substances can be classified according to their ability to conduct electric charges. Those that conduct charges well are conductors, and those that do not are insulators.

Whether a substance is classified as a conductor or an insulator depends on how tightly the electrons are bound to the atoms of the substance. Outer electrons of the atoms in a metal, for example, are not tightly bound to the nuclei of particular atoms. Instead, they are free to roam in the material. This makes metals good conductors. The electrons in other materials, such as rubber, plastic, and glass, are tightly bound and remain with particular atoms. These materials are insulators.

28. What is this passage mostly about?
    a. how electric current flows through materials
    b. the characteristics of conductors and insulators
    c. the difference between atoms and electrons
    d. how atoms move in different materials
29. Conductors are different from insulators in that they
    a. have electrons that are free to move within the material.
    b. contain more electrons.
    c. contain more atoms.
    d. are missing some electrons.
30. Based on the passage, which substance do you think might be used to cover electrical wires in a building?
    a. steel   b. copper
    c. plastic   d. aluminum

---

24. Electromagnets can be turned on and off and can be very strong, so they are used for applications that require making patterns, such as data storage, or that require lifting and releasing.

Applying Skills

25. B produces a stronger magnetic field than A because it has a core. B produces a stronger magnetic field than C because there are more turns of wire.
26. D is the strongest due to the number of turns and the core.
27. Experiments could involve changing the size of the core or adding a stronger battery.

Performance CHAPTER PROJECT 8 **Assessment**

Project Wrap Up Organize the class into groups and allow them to practice using their devices and work cooperatively to improve their designs before the final presentation. Set up plastic containers and allow each student or team to "fish"—lift paper clips out of one container and drop them into another—for one minute. If you wish, add iron nails to the first container. Before students fish, have them describe their designs to the class. Determine whether the success of the design will be measured by how many paper clips the electromagnet can pick up each time, or by how many paper clips are transferred over the entire minute.

Reflect and Record Students should compare their designs with those of other students and determine what combination of features would make the best design.

Test Preparation

28. b **29.** a **30.** c

Program Resources

- **Inquiry Skills Activity Book** Provides teaching and review of all inquiry skills
- **Prentice Hall Assessment System** Provides standardized test practice
- **Reading in the Content Area** Provides strategies to improve science reading skills
- **Teacher's ELL Handbook** Provides multiple strategies for English language learners

Electric Charges and Current

Sections	Time	Student Edition Activities		Other Activities
CHAPTER PROJECT 9 **Cause for Alarm** p. 277	Ongoing (2–3 weeks)	Check Your Progress, pp. 293, 299 Project Wrap Up, p. 307	**TE**	Chapter 9 Project Notes, pp. 276–277
1 **Electric Charge and Static Electricity** pp. 278–287 ◆ 9.1.1 Describe the interaction of like and unlike electric charges. ◆ 9.1.2 Define and describe static electricity and state how it differs from electric current. ◆ 9.1.3 Describe lightning and other forms of static discharge.	1 period/ ½ block	**Discover** Can You Move a Can Without Touching It?, p. 278 **Sharpen Your Skills** Drawing Conclusions, p. 280 **Try This** Sparks Are Flying, p. 282 **Science at Home** p. 285 **Skills Lab: Predicting** The Versorium, pp. 286–287	**TE** **TE** **TE** **TE**	Demonstration, p. 279 Including All Students, p. 281 Real-Life Learning, p. 282 Building Inquiry Skills: Drawing Conclusions, p. 284
2 **Circuit Measurements** pp. 288–295 ◆ 9.2.1 Explain what causes flow of electric current in terms of electrical potential, potential difference, and voltage. ◆ 9.2.2 Describe the relationship between voltage and the flow of electric current. ◆ 9.2.3 Define resistance and state how it affects the flow of current. ◆ 9.2.4 Calculate resistance using Ohm's law.	2 periods/ 1 block	**Discover** How Can Current Be Measured?, p. 288 **Try This** Down the Tubes, p. 291 **Sharpen Your Skills** Calculating, p. 292 **Real-World Lab: How It Works** Constructing a Dimmer Switch, pp. 294–295	**TE** **TE** **TE** **LM**	Building Inquiry Skills: Making Models, p. 289 Inquiry Challenge, p. 290 Demonstration, p. 291 9, "Building Electric Circuits"
3 **Series and Parallel Circuits** pp. 296–299 ◆ 9.3.1 Describe and construct a series circuit. ◆ 9.3.2 Describe and construct a parallel circuit.	1 period/ ½ block	**Discover** Do the Lights Keep Shining?, p. 296 **Sharpen Your Skills** Predicting, p. 298	**TE** **TE**	Inquiry Challenge, p. 297 Building Inquiry Skills: Inferring, p. 298
4 *INTEGRATING HEALTH* **Electrical Safety** pp. 300–304 ◆ 9.4.1 Identify the safety devices used to protect people from common electrical hazards. ◆ 9.4.2 Describe how a lightning rod protects a building. ◆ 9.4.3 Explain how the severity of an electric shock is related to current, voltage, and resistance.	1 period/ ½ block	**Discover** How Can You Blow a Fuse?, p. 300 **Science at Home** p. 304	**TE** **TE** **TE** **TE**	Real-Life Learning, p. 301 Including All Students, p. 301 Demonstration, p. 302 Building Inquiry Skills: Comparing and Contrasting, p. 303
Study Guide/Assessment pp. 305–307	1 period/ ½ block		**ISAB**	Provides teaching and review of all inquiry skills

 For Standard or Block Schedule The Resource Pro® CD-ROM gives you maximum flexibility for planning your instruction for any type of schedule. Resource Pro® contains Planning Express®, an advanced scheduling program, as well as the entire contents of the Teaching Resources and the Computer Test Bank.

Key: **CTB** Computer Test Bank
CT Chapter Tests
ELL Teacher's ELL Handbook

CHAPTER PLANNING GUIDE

Program Resources	Assessment Strategies	Media and Technology
UR Chapter 8 Project Teacher Notes, pp. 30–31 UR Chapter 8 Project Overview and Worksheets, pp. 32–35	TE Check Your Progress, pp. 293, 299 TE Performance Assessment: Chapter 9 Project Wrap Up, p. 307 UR Chapter 9 Project Scoring Rubric, p. 36	Science Explorer Internet Site Audio CDs, Section Summaries
UR 8-1 Lesson Plan, p. 37 UR 8-1 Section Summary, p. 38 UR 8-1 Review and Reinforce, p. 39 UR 8-1 Enrich, p. 40 UR Skills Lab blackline masters, pp. 53–55	SE Section 1 Review, p. 285 SE Analyze and Conclude, p. 287 TE Ongoing Assessment, pp. 279, 281, 283 TE Performance Assessment, p. 285	Transparency 31, "Electric Fields" Transparency 32, "Exploring Static Electricity" Transparency 33, "Electroscope" Lab Activity Videotape, *Tape 2*
UR 8-2 Lesson Plan, p. 41 UR 8-2 Section Summary, p. 42 UR 8-2 Review and Reinforce, p. 43 UR 8-2 Enrich, p. 44 UR Real-World Lab blackline masters, pp. 56–57	SE Section 2 Review, p. 293 SE Analyze and Conclude, p. 295 TE Ongoing Assessment, pp. 289, 291 TE Performance Assessment, p. 293	Concept Videotape Library, *Adventures, Tape 2,* "What Is Electricity?" Lab Activity Videotape, *Tape 2*
UR 8-3 Lesson Plan, p. 45 UR 8-3 Section Summary, p. 46 UR 8-3 Review and Reinforce, p. 47 UR 8-3 Enrich, p. 48	SE Section 3 Review, p. 299 TE Ongoing Assessment, p. 297 TE Performance Assessment, p. 299	Presentation Pro, "Electric Currents"; "Series and Parallel Circuits" Transparency 34, "Series and Parallel Circuits" Transparency 35, "Household Circuits"
UR 8-4 Lesson Plan, p. 49 UR 8-4 Section Summary, p. 50 UR 8-4 Review and Reinforce, p. 51 UR 8-4 Enrich, p. 52	SE Section 4 Review, p. 304 TE Ongoing Assessment, pp. 301, 303 TE Performance Assessment, p. 304	Concept Videotape Library, *Adventures, Tape 2,* "Electric Bodies" Concept Videotape Library, *Adventures, Tape 2,* "Lightning Strikes"
GRSW Provides worksheets to promote student comprehension of content RCA Provides strategies to improve science reading skills ELL Provides multiple strategies for English language learners	SE Study Guide/Assessment, pp. 305–307 PA Performance Assessment, pp. 28–30 CT Chapter 9 Test, pp. 35–38 CTB Chapter 9 Test PHAS Provides standardized test preparation	Computer Test Bank, Chapter 9 Test

GRSW Guided Reading and Study Workbook
ISAB Inquiry Skills Activity Book
LM Laboratory Manual

PA Performance Assessment
PHAS Prentice Hall Assessment System
PLM Probeware Lab Manual

RCA Reading in the Content Area
SE Student Edition

TE Teacher's Edition
UR Unit Resources

Meeting the National Science Education Standards and AAAS Benchmarks

National Science Education Standards	Benchmarks for Science Literacy	Unifying Themes
Physical Science (Content Standard B) ◆ **Transfer of energy** Static electricity can be transferred through friction, conduction, and induction. *(Section 1)* Electrical circuits conduct electric current when a potential difference allows current to flow. *(Sections 2, 3; Chapter Project; Real-World Lab)* **Life Science** (Content Standard C) ◆ **Structure and function in living systems** Various structures, such as the heart and nervous system, rely on electrical charges to function; electric shock can damage these systems. *(Section 4)* **Science and Technology** (Content Standard E) ◆ **Design a solution or a product** Students design an alarm circuit and a dimmer switch. *(Chapter Project; Real-World Lab)* **Science in Personal and Social Perspectives** (Content Standard F) ◆ **Natural hazards** Lightning strikes are caused by a massive discharge of static electricity. To reduce the risk of being struck by lightning, avoid water and lie low if outside during a storm. *(Sections 1, 4)* **History and Nature of Science** (Content Standard G) ◆ **History of Science** Benjamin Franklin contributed to our understanding of electricity in addition to his many other endeavors. *(Section 4)*	**1B Scientific Inquiry** Students control variables as they construct a versorium and design a dimmer switch. *(Skills Lab; Real-World Lab)* **2C Mathematical Inquiry** Students use Ohm's law to determine the relationship among resistance, current, and voltage. *(Section 2)* **3B Design and Systems** Students use their understanding of currents and electricity to create an alarm circuit and a dimmer switch. *(Chapter Project; Real-World Lab)* **4E Energy Transformation** Electrical charges cannot be created or destroyed, but only transferred from one object to another. *(Section 1)* Electrical energy is the attraction of opposite charges and the repulsion of like charges. Electrons flow according to the potential difference between parts of a circuit. In a circuit, electrons flow from a voltage source through wire and resistors. *(Sections 1, 2, 3; Chapter Project; Skills Lab)* **8C Energy Sources and Use** Electrical energy flows from a voltage source. *(Section 2)* Circuit breakers and fuses are used to protect circuits in which current becomes too high. *(Section 4)* **11A Systems** Current increases when resistors are added to a parallel circuit and decreases when resistors are added to a series circuit. *(Section 3)*	◆ **Energy** Electricity is a form of energy caused by the flow of electrons. Interactions between electric fields can cause electrons to flow. Voltage, resistance, and current are measurements of electrical energy. In the human body, energy from a high current can disrupt normal electrical activity. *(Sections 1, 2, 4; Chapter Project; Skills Lab; Real-World Lab)* ◆ **Systems and Interactions** Electrons flow from an area of high potential energy to an area of lower potential energy. Electrons in a series circuit stop flowing when any part of the circuit is broken; electrons in a parallel circuit continue flowing through remaining paths when a single path is broken. *(Sections 1, 3; Chapter Project; Skills Lab; Real-World Lab)*

Take It to the Net

The **www.phschool.com** Web site provides you with multiple opportunities to incorporate the internet into your instruction. Go to **www.phschool.com** and click on the Science icon. Then select Science Explorer Integrated.

■ Have students use the chapter Self-Test to get instant feedback.

■ Hot Links and Reference Links provide opportunities for online research.

Internet Activities provide opportunities for students to review, extend, or assess a concept from the chapter.

STAY CURRENT with **SCIENCE NEWS** ®

Find out the latest research and information about electricity at: **www.phschool.com**

ACTIVity	Time (minutes)	Materials Quantities for one work group	Skills
Section 1			
Discover, p. 278	10	**Consumable** balloon **Nonconsumable** empty aluminum can	Inferring
Sharpen Your Skills, p. 280	10	**Consumable** tissue paper **Nonconsumable** hole punch, plastic comb	Drawing Conclusions
Try This, p. 282	10	**Consumable** 2 foam plates, tape **Nonconsumable** scissors, aluminum pie plate	Inferring
Science at Home, p. 285	home	**Consumable** balloon **Nonconsumable** television set	Observing, Applying Concepts
Skills Lab, pp. 286–287	30	**Consumable** foam cup, aluminum foil, paper **Nonconsumable** plastic foam plate, pencil, wool fabric, scissors	Predicting, Developing Hypotheses
Section 2			
Discover, p. 288	25	**Consumable** electrical tape **Nonconsumable** 1 meter bell wire, wire cutters and strippers, metric ruler, magnetic compass, two 1.5-volt bulbs and sockets, D cell and holder, modeling clay	Inferring
Try This, p. 291	15	**Consumable** water **Nonconsumable** two 200-mL beakers, funnel, ring stand, clear tubing of various lengths and widths, stopwatch	Making Models
Sharpen Your Skills, p. 292	15	No special materials are required.	Calculating
Real-World Lab, pp. 294–295	30	**Consumable** thick lead from mechanical pencil, masking tape **Nonconsumable** flashlight bulb in socket; D cell; uninsulated copper wire, the same length as the pencil lead; rubber tubing, the same length as the pencil lead; 1 wire 10–15 cm long; 2 wires 20–30 cm long; 2 alligator clips	Observing, Predicting, Designing Experiments
Section 3			
Discover, p. 296	15	**Nonconsumable** 4 light bulbs with sockets, 2 dry cells with holders, several lengths of insulated wire	Observing
Sharpen Your Skills, p. 298	20	**Nonconsumable** dry cell, 3 light bulbs, insulated wire, switch	Predicting
Section 4			
Discover, p. 300	15	**Nonconsumable** dry cell, light bulb, 2 alligator clips, very fine steel wool (00 or 000 grade)	Developing Hypotheses
Science at Home, p. 304	home	**Nonconsumable** fuse box or circuit breaker	Observing, Applying Concepts

A list of all materials required for the Student Edition activities can be found beginning on page T23. You can obtain information about ordering materials by calling 1-800-848-9500 or by accessing the Science Explorer Internet site at: **www.phschool.com**

CHAPTER PROJECT 9

Cause for Alarm

For students who have difficulty learning technical concepts, the chance to build an alarm will provide a fun and firsthand look at electric charges and parallel and series circuits.

Purpose In this project, students will have the opportunity to design and construct an alarm circuit that will be triggered by an outside event.

Skills Focus After completing the Chapter 9 Project, students will be able to
- apply concepts related to electric current;
- relate cause and effect to solve problems related to basic circuit design;
- design experiments in which they test their circuits;
- communicate their findings about circuitry to their classmates.

Project Time Line This project will take approximately two weeks to complete. Students will begin by brainstorming possible events to which their detector switches will respond. Then they will plan their detector switches and draw diagrams of their designs. Once you have approved their plans, they may construct their alarms. The students will then conduct several tests of their circuits, modifying them if necessary. At the conclusion of this project, students will demonstrate their alarms to the class, describing how their circuits work. Before beginning the project, see Chapter 9 Project Teacher Notes on pages 30–31 in Unit 3 Resources for more details on carrying out the project. Also distribute to students the Chapter 9 Project Overview, Worksheets, and Scoring Rubric on pages 32–36 in Unit 3 Resources.

Suggested Shortcuts Limit the number of choices students have for events to detect. Students could work in groups to reduce the amount of time required for presentations. Alternatively, you could use a few generic setups consisting of a light bulb or buzzer, one or two dry cells, and about 3 meters of wire. Have individual students connect their detector switches to the wire during the presentation part of the project.

CHAPTER 9

Electric Charges and Current

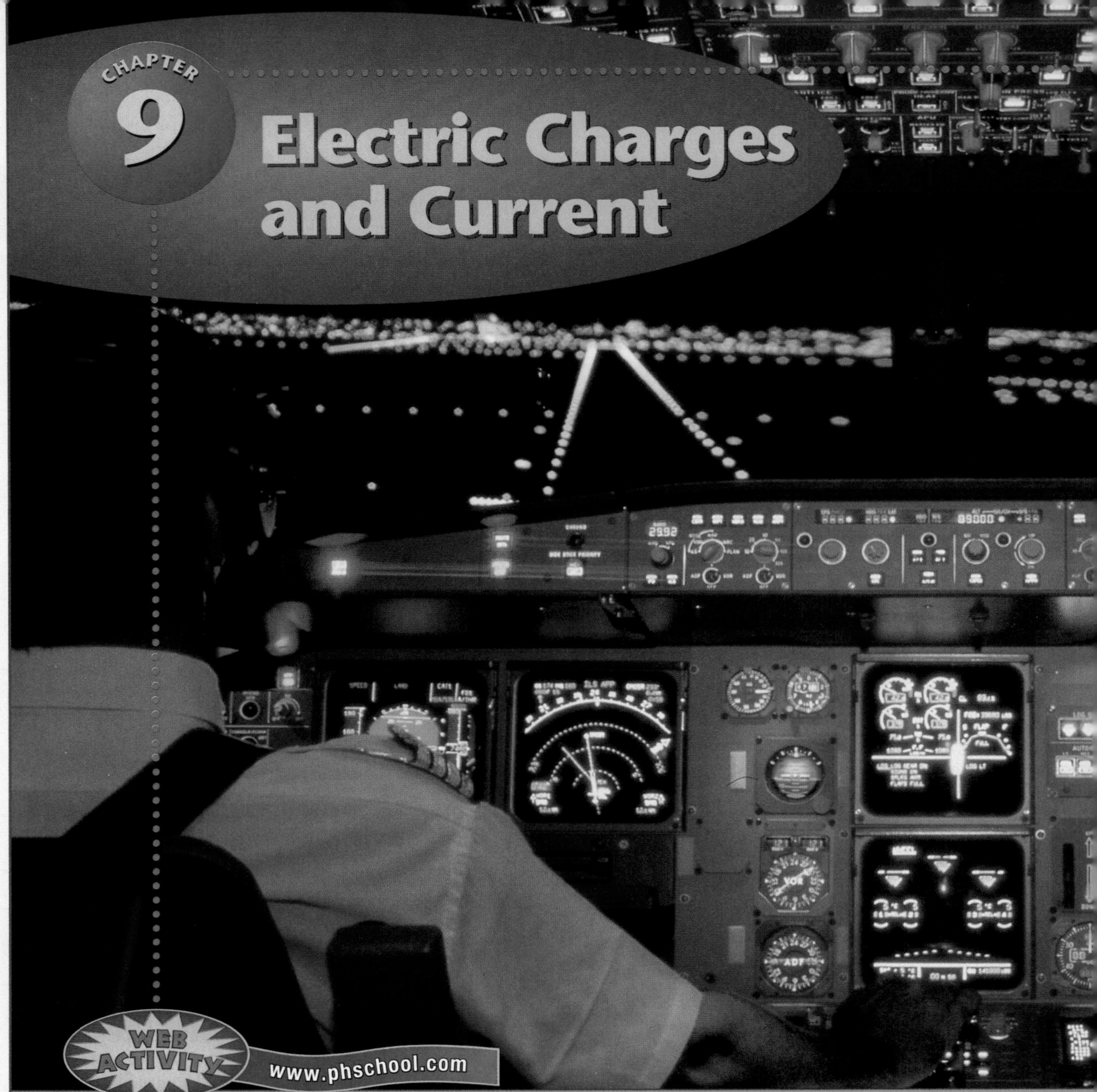

WEB ACTIVITY www.phschool.com

SECTION 1 **Electric Charge and Static Electricity**

Discover **Can You Make a Can Move Without Touching It?**
Sharpen Your Skills **Drawing Conclusions**
Try This **Sparks Are Flying**
Skills Lab **The Versorium**

SECTION 2 **Circuit Measurements**

Discover **How Can Current Be Measured?**
Try This **Down the Tubes**
Sharpen Your Skills **Calculating**
Real-World Lab **Constructing a Dimmer Switch**

SECTION 3 **Series and Parallel Circuits**

Discover **Do the Lights Keep Shining?**
Sharpen Your Skills **Predicting**

276

Possible Materials Provide a wide variety of materials from which students can choose, and encourage students to suggest and use other materials as well. Each student will need one or two 1.5-volt dry cells, about 3 meters of insulated wire, and a light bulb. Make sure to select bulbs that require only 1.5 volts for a single battery, or 3 volts for two batteries connected in series. Additionally, students may need aluminum foil, paper clips, screws, washers, nails, metal cans, electrical tape, basins or bowls, water, or salt.

Launching the Project Tape an uninsulated end of a piece of wire to a penny. Connect the other end of the wire to a light bulb. Use another piece of wire to connect the light bulb to a dry cell. Tape the other pole of the dry cell to an empty metal can. Ask the students what will happen if you drop the penny into the can. *(The light will go on.)* Tell them that this device is a Penny Detector; it shows one way that contact can be made between the ends of two wires.

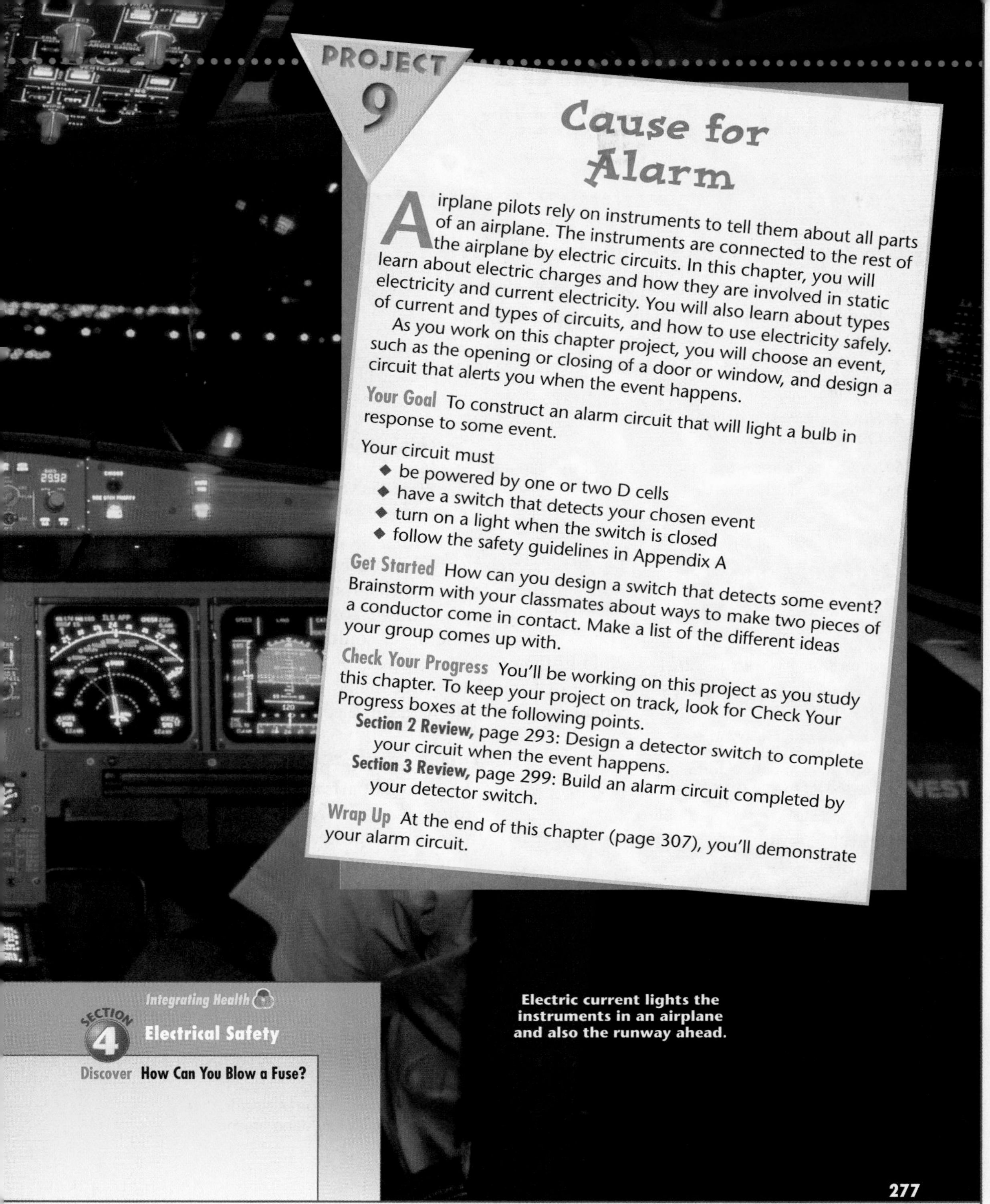

PROJECT 9

Cause for Alarm

Airplane pilots rely on instruments to tell them about all parts of an airplane. The instruments are connected to the rest of the airplane by electric circuits. In this chapter, you will learn about electric charges and how they are involved in static electricity and current electricity. You will also learn about types of current and types of circuits, and how to use electricity safely.

As you work on this chapter project, you will choose an event, such as the opening or closing of a door or window, and design a circuit that alerts you when the event happens.

Your Goal To construct an alarm circuit that will light a bulb in response to some event.

Your circuit must
- be powered by one or two D cells
- have a switch that detects your chosen event
- turn on a light when the switch is closed
- follow the safety guidelines in Appendix A

Get Started How can you design a switch that detects some event? Brainstorm with your classmates about ways to make two pieces of a conductor come in contact. Make a list of the different ideas your group comes up with.

Check Your Progress You'll be working on this project as you study this chapter. To keep your project on track, look for Check Your Progress boxes at the following points.
> **Section 2 Review, page 293:** Design a detector switch to complete your circuit when the event happens.
> **Section 3 Review, page 299:** Build an alarm circuit completed by your detector switch.

Wrap Up At the end of this chapter (page 307), you'll demonstrate your alarm circuit.

Electric current lights the instruments in an airplane and also the runway ahead.

SECTION
4 **Integrating Health** 🌐
Electrical Safety

Discover **How Can You Blow a Fuse?**

277

Program Resources

- **Unit 3 Resources** Chapter 9 Project Teacher Notes, pp. 30–31; Project Overview and Worksheets, pp. 32–35; Project Scoring Rubric, p. 36

Media and Technology

 Audio CDs Section Summaries

 **WEB ACTIVITY** www.phschool.com

You will find an Internet activity, chapter self-tests for students, and links to other chapter topics at this site.

Performance Assessment

The Chapter 9 Project Scoring Rubric on page 36 of Unit 3 Resources will help you evaluate how well students complete the Chapter 9 Project. Students will be assessed on
- how well they apply concepts related to electric currents and circuits;
- the clarity of the circuit diagram they draw of their device;;
- how well they conduct experiments to test and revise their circuits;
- the thoroughness and organization of their presentation.

By sharing the Chapter 9 Scoring Rubric with students at the beginning of the project, you will make it clear to them what they are expected to do.

SECTION 1 Electric Charge and Static Electricity

Objectives

After completing the lesson, students will be able to

◆ describe the interaction of like and unlike electric charges;

◆ define and describe static electricity and state how it differs from electric current;

◆ describe lightning and other forms of static discharge.

Key Terms electric field, static electricity, friction, conduction, induction, conservation of charge, static discharge, electroscope

1 Engage/Explore

Activating Prior Knowledge

Before class, rub together a piece of polyester fabric and nylon sock so that they stick together. Show students the fabric and sock clinging to each other. Ask: **Would you expect to find glue or some other form of matter between these two fabrics?** *(no)* Then ask: **What holds the fabrics together?** *(Sample: Electricity; static cling)* Explain that students will learn more about the forces that hold two fabrics together as they explore electric charges.

• • • • • • • DISCOVER • • • • • • •

Skills Focus inferring
Materials *empty aluminum can, balloon*
Time 10 minutes
Tips Make sure students rub the balloon vigorously. Avoid doing this activity on a damp or rainy day.
Expected Outcome The can follows the balloon in either direction.
Think It Over Students may suggest that an invisible force is attracting the can. If the balloon is charged, then opposite charges in the can are attracted to it.

SECTION 1 Electric Charge and Static Electricity

DISCOVER • ACTIVITY

Can You Move a Can Without Touching It?

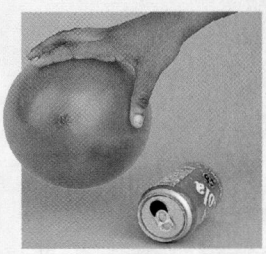

1. Place an empty aluminum can on its side on the floor.

2. Blow up a balloon. Then rub the balloon back and forth on your hair several times.

3. Hold the balloon about 3 to 4 centimeters away from the can.

4. Slowly move the balloon farther away from the can. Observe what happens.

5. Move the balloon to the other side of the can and observe what happens.

Think It Over
Inferring What happens to the can? What can you infer from your observation?

GUIDE FOR READING

◆ How do electric charges interact?

◆ How does static electricity differ from electric current?

◆ How are electrons transferred in static discharge?

Reading Tip Before you read, preview the headings and record them in outline form. Fill in details as you read.

You're in a hurry to get dressed for school, but you can't find one of your socks. You quickly head for the pile of clean laundry. You've gone through everything, but where's the sock? The dryer couldn't have really destroyed it, could it? Oh no, there it is. Your sister has found the sock stuck to one of her shirts. What makes clothes stick together? The explanation has to do with tiny electric charges.

Types of Electric Charge

The charged parts of atoms are electrons and protons. As you have learned, protons and electrons are charged particles. When two protons come close, they push one another apart. In other words, they repel each other. But if a proton and an electron come close, they attract one another.

Why do protons repel protons but attract electrons? The reason is that they have different types of charge. Protons and electrons have opposite charges. The charge on the proton is

Figure 1 The interaction of electric charges is making this girl's hair stand on end.

READING STRATEGIES

Reading Tip Before students write the section headings in outline form, ask them how many major headings they will have in the outline. *(six)* Explain that subheadings such as *Electric Fields Around Single Charges* will appear as subheads of the outline, preceded by capital letters. Have students leave room for additional information under each heading. As students read, they can fill in the supporting information.

Study and Comprehension After students read the section, have them review their outlines. Then instruct them to use the outlines to write questions based on the information about electric charge and static electricity. Have students form pairs and take turns asking and answering each other's questions.

No charge *Like charges repel* *Like charges repel* *Unlike charges attract*

called positive (+), and the charge on the electron is called negative (−). The names positive and negative were given to charges by Benjamin Franklin in the 1700s. They have been used by scientists ever since.

Interactions Between Charges

The two types of charges interact in specific ways. **Charges that are the same repel each other. Charges that are different attract each other.**

Does this sound familiar to you? This rule is the same as the rule for interactions between magnetic poles. Recall that magnetic poles that are alike repel each other and magnetic poles that are different attract each other.

There is one important thing about electric charges that is different from magnetic poles. Recall that magnetic poles do not exist alone. Whenever there is a south pole, there is always a north pole. Electric charges can exist alone. In other words, a negative charge can exist without a positive charge.

☑ *Checkpoint* How are the interactions between electric charges similar to the interactions between magnetic poles?

Electric Fields

Just as magnetic poles exert their forces over a distance, so do electric charges. An electric charge exerts a force through the **electric field** that surrounds the charge. An electric field extends outward from every charged particle.

When a charged particle is placed in the electric field of another charged particle, it is either pushed or pulled. It is pushed away if the two charges are the same. It is pulled toward the other charge if the two charges are different.

Figure 2 Charged objects exert forces on each other. They can either attract or repel.
Interpreting Diagrams What is the rule for the interaction of electric charges?

Chapter 9 **279**

Answers to Self-Assessment

Caption Question
Figure 2 Charges that are the same repel; charges that are different attract each other.

☑ *Checkpoint*
Like magnetic poles, electric charges that are alike repel each other, and electric charges that are unlike attract each other.

2 Facilitate

Types of Electric Charge

Addressing Naive Conceptions

Some students may think that neutral objects cannot interact with charged objects because they do not have an overall net charge. Explain that neutral objects contain equal numbers of positive and negative charges and can be attracted to both negatively and positively charged objects. **learning modality: verbal**

Interactions Between Charges

Using the Visuals: Figure 2

As students examine the visual, have them point their index fingers downward to represent the suspended objects in the diagram. Ask them to show two neutrally charged objects, two objects with the same charge, and two objects with opposite charges. *(Students should hold their fingers still; move their fingers apart; move their fingers together.)* **learning modality: kinesthetic**

Electric Fields

Demonstration

Materials *inflated balloon, wool cloth, faucet*
Time 15 minutes

Allow students to observe how a charge exerts a force through an electric field. Vigorously rub the balloon with the wool cloth, then turn on the faucet so that water flows in a steady stream. Have students observe what happens as you bring the charged balloon near the stream of water. *(The neutral water will bend toward the balloon.)* **learning modality: visual**

Ongoing Assessment

Writing Have students describe the types of electric charges and the kinds of interactions between them.

Electric Fields, continued

Using the Visuals: Figure 3

Direct students to place a finger on the negatively charged particle. Ask: **Why are the arrows facing toward your finger?** (*The arrows show the direction that a positive charge would move—toward a negative charge.*) Then have students place a finger on the center of the positively charged particle. Encourage them to trace a circle around the area of the strongest electric field. (*Students should trace the area nearest the particle.*) Finally, have students describe how the electric fields are altered in 3B. Ask: **How does the field between + and − differ from the field between + and +?** (*Attraction instead of repulsion*)
learning modality: visual

Sharpen your Skills

Drawing Conclusions

Materials *tissue paper, hole punch, plastic comb*

Time 10 minutes
Tips Avoid performing this activity on a damp or rainy day. The tissue paper should be attracted to the comb. Students should conclude that the comb and tissue paper are unlike—the tissue paper is neutral (it has no charge).
Extend Have students find out what happens if they run a comb through their hair several times and then hold it a short distance from their hair. The comb and hair become oppositely charged.
learning modality: visual

Static Charge

Language Arts Connection

Help students understand static electricity by explaining that the term *static* comes from the Greek word *statikos,* which means "standing still." Ask: **How does static electricity differ from electric currents?** (*Static electricity does not flow continuously. It can stay in one place, or stand still.*) **learning modality: verbal**

Drawing Conclusions

1. Tear tissue paper into small pieces, or cut circles out of it with a hole punch.
2. Run a plastic comb through your hair several times.
3. Place the comb close to, but not touching, the tissue paper pieces. What do you observe?

What can you conclude about the electric charges on the comb and the tissue paper?

Figure 3 Electric charges can attract or repel one another.
A. The arrows show that a positive charge repels another positive charge. A negative charge attracts a positive charge. **B.** When two charged particles come near each other, the electric fields of both particles are altered.

Electric Fields Around Single Charges You will recall using magnetic field lines to picture a magnetic field in an earlier chapter. In a similar way, you can use electric field lines to visualize the electric field. Electric field lines are drawn with arrows to show the direction of the force on a positive charge.

The electric fields in Figure 3A are strongest where the lines are closest together. You can see that the strength of the electric field is greatest near the charged particle. The field decreases as you move away from the charge.

Electric Fields Around Multiple Charges When there are two or more charges, the resulting electric field is altered. The electric fields due to the individual charges combine. Figure 3B shows the electric fields from two sets of charges.

☑ *Checkpoint* *Where is an electric field strongest?*

Static Charge

If matter consists of charged particles that produce electric fields, why aren't you attracted to or repelled by every object around you—your book, your desk, or your pen? The reason is that each atom has an equal number of protons and electrons. And the size, or magnitude, of the charge on an electron is the same as the size of the charge on a proton. So each positive charge is balanced by a negative charge. The charges cancel out and the object as a whole is neutral. As a result there is no overall electrical force.

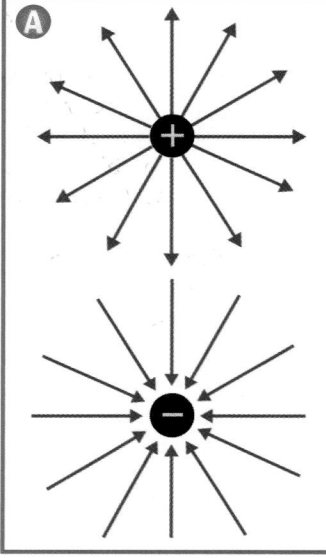
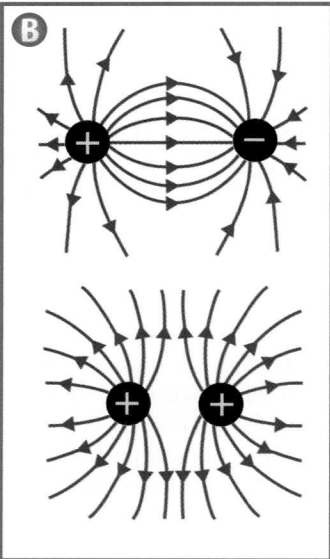

Background

History of Science The early study of electricity was hindered because generating and storing electricity was difficult. In 1745 and 1746, a German scientist, Ewald von Kleist, and a Dutch scientist, Pieter van Musschenbroek, developed the *Leyden jar.* The jar was named in honor of van Musschenbroek, who lived in the city of Leiden. The first Leyden jars consisted of a glass vial or jar that was partially filled with water. On the outside, the jar had a layer or band of metal. The jar was sealed with a cork, and the cork was pierced with a thick conducting wire or nail so that one end of the wire or nail was in the water. The jar was charged by bringing the end of the wire or nail into contact with a device that generated static electricity. Scientists could then use the stored static electricity at a later time in their experiments.

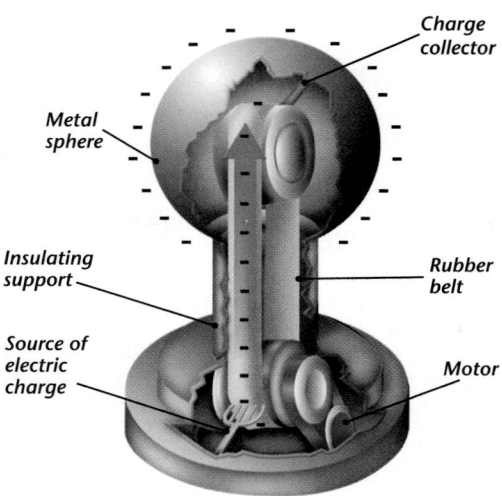

Figure 4 A Van de Graaff generator produces static electricity. Electrons are carried up a rubber belt and are transferred to the metal sphere. The charge built up on the sphere is enough to send a spark several meters through the air.

Charged Objects Protons are bound tightly in the center of an atom, but electrons can sometimes leave their atoms. Whether or not an electron will move depends on the material. Atoms in insulators, such as wood, rubber, plastic, and glass, hold their electrons tightly. Atoms in conductors, such as gold, silver, copper, and aluminum, hold some of their electrons loosely. These electrons move freely from atom to atom within the material.

A neutral object can become charged by gaining or losing electrons. If an object loses electrons, it is left with more protons (positive charge) than electrons (negative charge). Thus the object is positively charged overall. If, instead, an object gains electrons, it has more electrons than protons. Thus it has an overall negative charge.

The buildup of charges on an object is called **static electricity.** Static electricity behaves quite differently from electric currents. In an electric current, charges move continuously. **In static electricity, charges build up, but they do not flow.**

Transferring Charge Exactly how do charges build up? Charges must be transferred from one object to another. There are three methods by which charges are transferred: friction, conduction, and induction. **Friction** is the transfer of electrons from one object to another by rubbing. **Conduction** is the transfer of electrons from a charged object to another object by direct contact.

Media and Technology

 Transparencies "Electric Fields," Transparency 31

Answers to Self-Assessment

☑ *Checkpoint*
An electric field is strongest where the lines are closest together.

Addressing Naive Conceptions

Some students may assume that a negatively charged object has fewer charges than its positively charged counterpart. Explain that neutral atoms lose electrons to become positive and gain electrons to become negative. The gain or loss of electrons is very temporary and affects only a tiny percentage of the total number of atoms.
learning modality: verbal

Including All Students

Materials *plastic jar, 6 red marbles, 3 blue marbles*
Time 10 minutes
Tips The following activity will help students who are having difficulty understanding how objects become charged. Explain that red marbles represent electrons and blue marbles represent protons. Place the three blue marbles in the jar. Then ask: **If this jar is an atom, how many electrons, or red marbles, must you add to give the atom a neutral charge?** *(three)* Once students have added the marbles, have them demonstrate how to make the atom positively charged and negatively charged. *(Take electrons out of the jar; add electrons to the jar.)* **limited English proficiency**

Building Inquiry Skills: Classifying

Challenge students to identify the method of transferring charge in each of the following examples: rubbing a glass rod with a wool cloth *(friction)*; touching the glass rod to a metal door knob *(conduction)*; holding a charged rod near a metal rod *(induction)*. **learning modality: logical/mathematical**

Ongoing Assessment

Writing Have students describe the buildup of static electricity.

Static Charge, continued

Real-Life Learning

Materials *fabric softener sheets*
Time 30 minutes

Have students investigate how well the fabric softener sheets reduce static cling. Ask them to predict what will happen if they use one sheet, half of a sheet, or no sheet in the dryer. Encourage students to check their predictions by helping with the family laundry. Then have them briefly describe their conclusions.
learning modality: kinesthetic

Static Discharge

TRY THIS

Skills Focus inferring
Materials *2 foam plates, scissors, tape, aluminum pie plate*
Time 10 minutes

Tips You may want to prepare the plates in advance. Perform this activity on a dry day, and, if possible, in the dark. Students should observe that each time they touch the pie plate, they see a spark. (The spark is a transfer of a tiny amount of charge and is very safe.) They should explain their observations by saying that when they put the pie plate on the foam, the electrons in the foam repel the electrons in the metal. When they touch the pie plate, the electrons leap to their hand, making a spark. After the electrons jump to their hand, the pie plate is short of electrons and it attracts electrons when they touch it again. This causes another spark. When they put the pie plate back on the foam, the process starts all over again.
Extend Have students experiment to see how changing the length of time they rub the foam plate on their hair affects the outcome of this activity. **learning modality: visual**

TRY THIS

Sparks Are Flying

You can make your own lightning.

1. Cut a strip 3 cm wide from the middle of a foam plate. Fold the strip to form a T. Tape it to the center of an aluminum pie plate as a handle.

2. Rub a second foam plate on your hair. Put it upside down on a table.
3. Use the handle to pick up the pie plate. Hold the pie plate about 30 cm over the foam plate and drop it.
4. Now, very slowly, touch the tip of your finger to the pie plate. Be careful not to touch the foam plate. Then take your finger away.
5. Use the handle to pick up the pie plate again. Slowly touch the pie plate again.

Inferring What did you observe each time you touched the pie plate? How can you explain your observations?

Induction is the movement of electrons to one part of an object caused by the electric field of another object. The three methods of transferring charge are illustrated in *Exploring Static Electricity*.

Keep in mind that charges are not created or destroyed. If an object gives up electrons, another object gains those electrons. Electrons are only transferred from one location to another. This is known as the law of **conservation of charge.**

Static Cling Static electricity explains why clothes stick together in the clothes dryer. In a dryer, different fabrics rub together. Electrons from one fabric rub off onto another. In this way, the clothes become charged. A positively charged sock might then be attracted to a negatively charged shirt—the clothes stick together.

Your clothes are less likely to stick together if you use a fabric softener sheet. These sheets add a thin coating to your clothes as they bounce around in the dryer. The coating prevents electrons from rubbing off the clothing, so the clothes don't become charged.

Can you think of situations in which you might want to increase static electricity? Think about wrapping leftover food in plastic wrap. Plastic wrap picks up a charge when you unroll it. Since plastic is an insulator, the charge cannot easily move off it. So the wrap keeps its charge. When you place the plastic wrap on a container, it charges the edges of the container by induction. The force between the opposite charges on the wrap and the container causes the wrap to cling.

Static electricity allows you to make copies quickly. In a photocopier, a drum is given a negative static charge that is the image of the page to be copied. This charged image picks up positively charged particles of a very fine black powder. The drum then rolls against a negatively charged piece of paper, and the powder is transferred to the paper. Finally, the paper is heated to melt the powder, and the powder sticks to the paper.

✓ *Checkpoint* What is the law of conservation of charge?

Static Discharge

An object that gains a static charge doesn't hold the charge forever. Electrons tend to move, returning the object to its neutral condition. **When a negatively charged object and a positively charged object are brought together, electrons move until both objects have the same charge.** The loss of static electricity as electric charges move off an object is called **static discharge.**

Humidity If you rub a balloon on your clothing and then hold it next to a wall, it should stick. But the balloon may not always stick. Why is that? The answer could have to do with the weather.

Background

Facts and Figures When the textile industry began to produce synthetic materials such as nylon, polyester, and acrylic, consumers began to demand products to reduce static cling. Anti-static agents can be applied to textiles as they are being produced. Additionally, people can add liquid fabric softeners to their wash or put fabric softening sheets in their dryers.

The molecules of the active ingredient in both liquid and sheet fabric softeners are charged at one end and uncharged at the other. The charged end is attracted to the fabric surface. In this way, the softeners coat the surface of the clothing and reduce the electrical charge transferred due to the friction between clothes in the dryer.

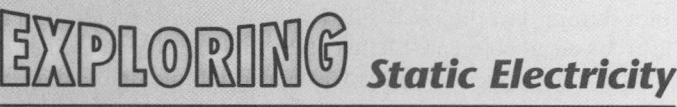

EXPLORING *Static Electricity*

Static electricity involves the transfer of electrons from one object to another. Electrons are transferred by friction, conduction, or induction.

CHARGING BY FRICTION

When you rub two objects together, electrons move from one object to the other. This is known as charging by friction.

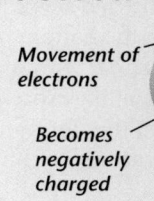

CHARGING BY CONDUCTION

When the charged rod or cloth touches the sphere, electrons are transferred by direct contact. This is known as conduction.

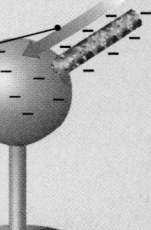

Movement of electrons

Becomes negatively charged

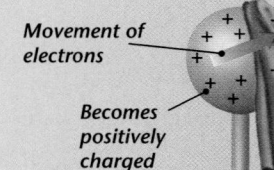

Movement of electrons

Becomes positively charged

CHARGING BY INDUCTION

During induction, charges within the spheres are rearranged without direct contact with the charged rod.

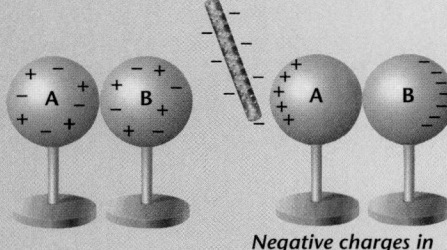

Neutral charge

Negative charges in the rod repel negative charges in the spheres.

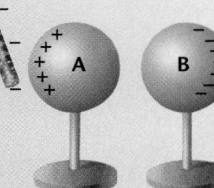

When the spheres are separated, each one is charged.

Removing the charged rod leaves two charged spheres.

As students examine each method of electron transfer, have them trace the flow of electrons away from or toward the objects involved. For Charging by Friction, ask: **Which object gains electrons?** *(The rod)* **Which object loses electrons?** *(The cloth)* For Charging by Conduction, ask: **Which object gains electrons?** *(Left: the sphere; right: the cloth)* **Which object loses electrons?** *(Left: the rod; right: the sphere)* Then ask: **Which example shows movement of electrons without direct contact?** *(Charging by Induction)* **How do spheres A and B become charged without direct contact with the rod?** *(The rod repels negative charges on sphere A. Since the spheres are touching, electrons travel to sphere B. When the spheres are separated, there is a positive charge (deficit of electrons) on sphere A and a negative charge (surplus of electrons) on sphere B.)*

Extend Have students demonstrate charge by friction by transferring charge to a thin strip of plastic wrap. If small pieces of tissue paper stick to the plastic wrap, then the transfer was successful.

learning modality: visual

Media and Technology

Transparencies "Exploring Static Electricity," Transparency 32

Answers to Self-Assessment

✓ *Checkpoint*

The law of conservation of charge states that electrons are only transferred from one location to another; they are never destroyed.

Ongoing Assessment

Skills Check Have students use a wool cloth and plastic comb to demonstrate how to place static charge on an object and how to cause static discharge.

Static Discharge, continued

Cultural Diversity

Many ancient cultures had myths about lightning. Some students will be familiar with the Greek god, Zeus, who hurled lightning bolts from the sky when he was angry. Norse mythology refers to the god Thor, who threw lightning bolts as weapons against demons. The Hindu religion has a god of lightning and thunder—Indra. The Bantu of Africa have a lightning-bird god called Umpundulo that threatens during storms. The Navajo people believed that lightning bolts held tremendous spiritual and healing powers. Ask students: **Why do you think so many ancient cultures explain lightning as a weapon of powerful gods?** *(Samples: It looks sharp; it can start fires; it comes with a loud noise.)* **learning modality: verbal**

Detecting Charge

Building Inquiry Skills: Drawing Conclusions

Materials *newspaper*
Time 15 minutes

Guide students in detecting charge. Have them tear two long strips from a sheet of newspaper. Tell students to hold the strips together at one end with one hand. Ask: **Do the strips contain an electric charge? How can you tell?** *(The strips do not appear to have a charge because they do not attract or repel each other.)* Using the thumb and forefinger of the other hand, students should lightly stroke downward on the strips for 1 minute. Ask: **What do you observe when you stop stroking the strips?** *(They repel each other.)* Finally, ask: **How are the strips similar to an electroscope?** *(They both indicate the presence of a charge.)*
learning modality: kinesthetic

On a humid day, the air is filled with water molecules. Extra electrons on an object are carried off by molecules of water in the air. Thus the charges do not have a chance to build up on objects such as the balloon.

Sparks and Lightning Have you ever felt a shock from touching a doorknob after walking across a carpet? That shock is the result of static discharge. For example, as you walk across the carpet, electrons may rub off the soles of your shoes. This gives you a slight positive charge. When you touch the doorknob, electrons jump from the doorknob to your finger, making you neutral again.

Lightning is a dramatic example of static discharge. Lightning is basically a huge spark. During thunderstorms, air swirls violently. Water droplets within the clouds become electrically charged. Notice in Figure 5 that electrons collect in the lower parts of the cloud. To restore a neutral condition, electrons move from areas of negative charge to areas of positive charge. As electrons jump, they produce an intense spark. You see that spark as lightning.

Much of the lightning in a storm occurs between different regions of a cloud or between different clouds. But some lightning reaches Earth. This is because the cloud causes the surface of Earth to become charged by induction, as shown in Figure 5. Negative charges on the bottom of a cloud repel electrons, leaving the surface of Earth with a positive charge. If the charge buildup is sufficient, a huge spark of lightning is produced. The spark jumps between the cloud and Earth's surface or tall objects on the surface, such as trees or buildings.

Figure 5 Lightning is a spectacular discharge of static electricity. Lightning can occur within a cloud, between two clouds, or between a cloud and Earth.

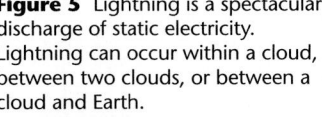

☑ *Checkpoint* *How can you get a shock from a doorknob?*

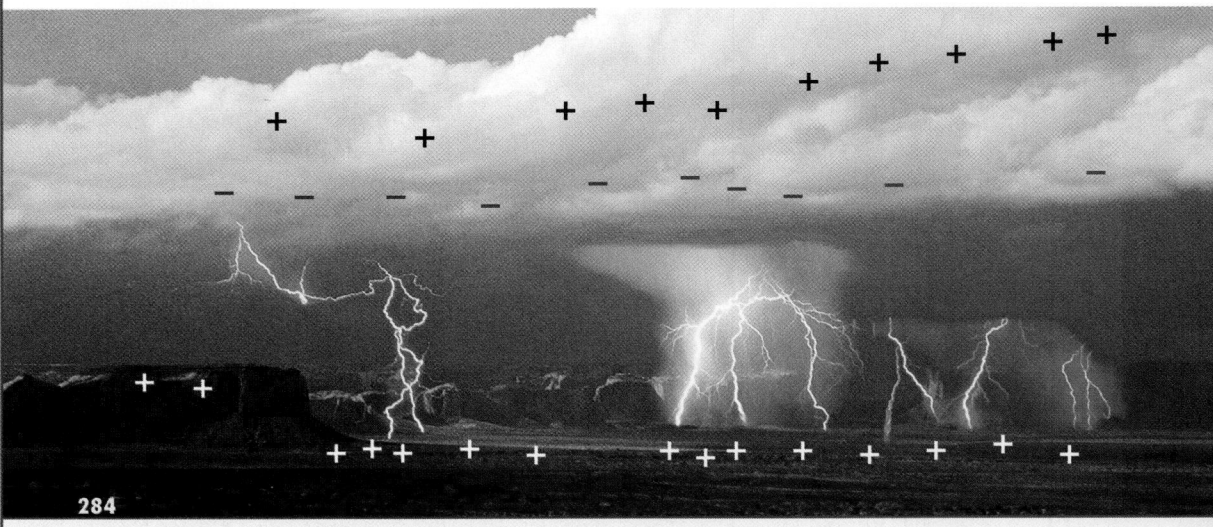

284

Background

Facts and Figures While scientists have a clear understanding of cloud-to-ground lightning strikes, they are still learning more about an unusual electrical phenomenon called ball lightning. Ball lightning appears as a colored, moving sphere of electricity several inches in diameter. Most frequent sightings have occurred near the ground and during thunderstorms that typically produce atmospheric lightning. The ball can look red, orange, or yellow. Sometimes a viewer hears a hissing sound when near the ball, and the ball can produce a distinct smell. The ball lightning only lasts a short time. Sometimes it explodes, other times it fizzles out quickly. Ball lightning can cause damage by burning or melting. Scientists do not know if, or how, ball lightning is related to normal lightning.

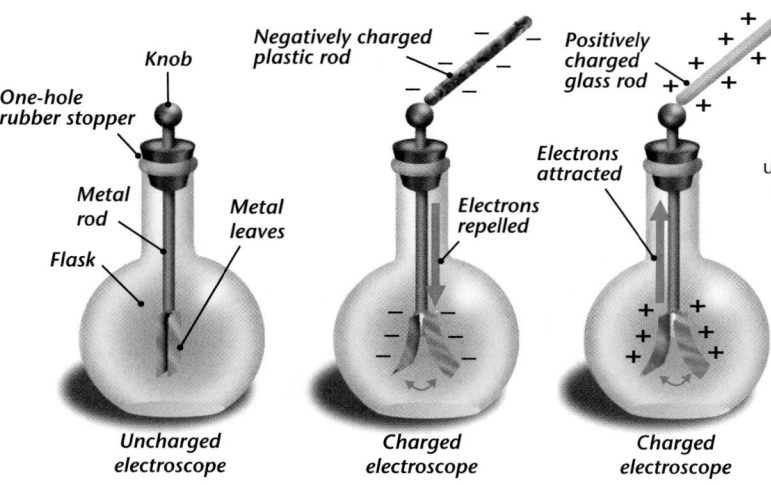

Knob

One-hole rubber stopper

Metal rod

Flask

Metal leaves

Negatively charged plastic rod

Electrons repelled

Positively charged glass rod

Electrons attracted

Uncharged electroscope

Charged electroscope

Charged electroscope

Figure 6 An electroscope is used to detect electric charges. *Relating Cause and Effect Why do the leaves in an electroscope move apart when either a positively charged object or a negatively charged object touches the knob?*

Detecting Charge

Electric charge is invisible, but it can be detected by a special instrument called an **electroscope**. A typical electroscope consists of a metal rod with a knob at the top. At the bottom of the rod are two sheets, or leaves, of very thin metal (aluminum, silver, or gold). When the electroscope is uncharged, the leaves hang straight down.

When a charged object touches the metal knob, electric charge travels along the rod and into or out of the leaves. The leaves then have a net charge. Since the charge on both leaves is the same, the leaves repel each other and spread apart.

The leaves of an electroscope move apart in response to either negative charge or positive charge, so you cannot use an electroscope to determine the type of charge. You can use an electroscope only to detect the presence of charge.

 Section 1 Review

Science at Home

1. How do particles with the same charge interact? How do particles with opposite charges interact?
2. What is static electricity?
3. What are the three ways by which static charge is produced?
4. How is static electricity discharged?
5. How does an electroscope detect charge?
6. **Thinking Critically Comparing and Contrasting** How are electric charges similar to magnetic poles? How are they different?

Science at Home

Rub a balloon against your hair and bring the balloon near one of your arms. Then bring your other arm near the front of a television screen that is turned on. Ask a family member to explain why the hairs on your arms are attracted to the balloon and to the screen. Explain that this is evidence that there is a static charge on both the balloon and the screen.

Program Resources

♦ **Unit 3 Resources** 9-1 Review and Reinforce, p. 39; 9-1 Enrich, p. 40

Media and Technology

 Transparencies "Electroscope," Transparency 33

Answers to Self-Assessment

Caption Question

Figure 6 Because both leaves contain the same charge, they repel each other.

✓ *Checkpoint*

A shock from a doorknob results from static charge. When you walk across carpet, electrons rub onto your shoes and give you a positive charge. When you touch the doorknob, electrons jump from the knob to your finger.

3 Assess

Section 1 Review Answers

1. Particles with the same charge repel each other. Particles with opposite charges attract each other.

2. Static electricity is the buildup of charge.

3. Static charge can build up by friction, conduction, or induction.

4. During electric discharge, charges escape the charged object by jumping from one object to another or by attaching to water or dust particles.

5. When a charged object touches the knob of an electroscope, electrons travel from an area of high electron density to an area of low electron density—through the electroscope to the leaves. The leaves of the electroscope acquire the same charge and repel each other.

6. Electric charges and magnetic poles both act over a distance, are surrounded by a field, and exert attractive and repulsive forces. Electric charges exist separately, while magnetic poles cannot be isolated.

Science at Home

Materials *balloon, television set*

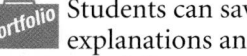

Students should avoid doing this activity on humid days. Students should readily feel the hairs of their arm attracted to the screen or observe that their hair is attracted. They may even feel very tiny sparks jump from the screen.

Performance Assessment

Writing Have students explain how an electroscope works. Students may include an illustration if they wish.

Portfolio Students can save their explanations and illustrations in their portfolios.

285

The Versorium

Preparing for Inquiry

Key Concept A neutral object (the versorium) is attracted to a charged object.

Skills Objectives Students will be able to
◆ develop hypotheses to explain observed behavior of the foil versorium;
◆ predict the behavior of the paper versorium and design an experiment to test it.

Time 30 minutes

Advance Planning
◆ On the day of the lab, test the plastic foam plates and wool to be sure they develop adequate static charge. To save time, cut the 3-cm by 10-cm strips of aluminum foil and paper in advance. Buy wool fabric at fabric or craft stores.
◆ To prepare the meter stick and balloon for the Invitation, push a thumbtack into the center of the narrow edge of a meter stick at the 50-cm mark. Test it to see if it balances. If not, add bits of clay to make it balance.

Alternative Materials Any set of materials that develops a static charge will work. Examples: wool fabric and balloon, plastic bag and plastic foam plate, acetate transparency and plastic foam plate, fur and balloon.

Guiding Inquiry

Invitation Place the balanced meter stick on the thumbtack on a table in front of the class and rub a plastic balloon on a student's hair. Ask the students what the charge on the meter stick is. *(neutral)* Bring the balloon close to the meter stick. It will be attracted to the balloon. Ask students to explain what is happening. *(Most students probably will not know. The electric charge on the balloon is attracting the oppositely charged particles in the meter stick.)*

Introducing the Procedure

◆ Show students how to construct the versorium. Tell them to make sure the tent is balanced loosely on the top of the pencil so that the tent can turn freely.

THE VERSORIUM

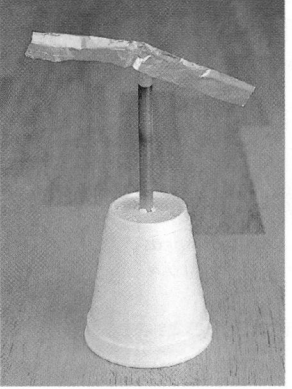

You are going to build a device that was first described in 1600 by Sir William Gilbert. He called this device a *versorium,* which is a Latin word meaning "turnabout." As you construct a versorium, you will use the skill of predicting.

Problem

Why does a versorium turn?

Materials

foam cup	plastic foam plate	pencil
aluminum foil	wool fabric	paper
scissors		

Procedure ✂

1. Cut a piece of aluminum foil approximately 3 cm by 10 cm.
2. Make a tent out of the foil strip by gently folding it in half in both directions.
3. Push a pencil up through the bottom of an inverted cup. **CAUTION:** *Avoid pushing the sharpened pencil against your skin.* Balance the center point of the foil tent on the point of the pencil as shown.
4. Make a copy of the data table.
5. Predict what will happen if you bring a foam plate near the foil tent. Record your prediction in the data table.
6. Predict what will happen if you rub the foam plate with a piece of wool fabric and then bring it near the foil tent. Record your prediction.
7. Predict what will happen if you bring the rubbed wool near the foil tent. Again record your prediction.
8. Test each of your three predictions and record your observations in the data table.

DATA TABLE

	Unrubbed Foam Plate	Rubbed Foam Plate	Rubbed Wool Fabric
Aluminum tent: Prediction			
Aluminum tent: Observation			
Paper tent: Prediction			
Paper tent: Observation			

◆ Remind students to slowly bring the plastic foam plate or the wool fabric near—but not touching—the top of the versorium tent.

Troubleshooting the Experiment
◆ Make sure the objects you choose develop sufficient static charge to attract the tent.
◆ Humidity may affect the static charge.
◆ The tent must be approached from the side.

Expected Outcome
Both the foil versorium and the paper versorium should be attracted to the rubbed foam plate and rubbed wool fabric. The foam plate that was not rubbed with wool fabric should cause no change.

Analyze and Conclude
1. Neutral. In its original state, the foil has not gained or lost any electrons.
2. The foam plate and the wool fabric acquired a static electric charge because electrons were transferred between them by rubbing.
3. The foil is attracted to the foam plate and

9. What do you think would happen if you used a paper tent versorium instead of the aluminum foil? Record your prediction.
10. Test your prediction and record your observation.

Analyze and Conclude

1. At the beginning of the lab, is the foil negatively charged, positively charged, or neutral? Explain your answer.
2. What was the effect of rubbing the foam plate with the wool fabric?
3. Explain the behavior of the aluminum foil as the foam plate is brought near it. Explain the behavior as the wool fabric is brought near it.
4. After you bring the materials near it, is the foil negatively charged, positively charged, or neutral? Explain your answer.
5. Now think about the paper tent. How is it charged before and after you bring the objects near it? How do you know?
6. Explain the behavior of the paper versorium as the foam plate is brought near it, and as the wool fabric is brought near it.

7. Can you use a versorium to determine whether an object is positively or negatively charged? Explain.
8. Why should you avoid touching the foam plate or the wool fabric to your clothing or any other object while you are using it to test a versorium?
9. **Think About It** Did the aluminum foil and paper tent versoriums behave the way you predicted? What did you learn that could help you improve your predictions?

Design an Experiment

What other materials besides foam or wool might have an effect on the versorium? Think of other materials you could use to make the versorium tent. Make predictions, and test the materials to see if they respond in a fashion similar to the aluminum foil and paper tents.

4. The tent remains neutral because the foil does not touch the plate or wool and no charges are transferred. Students may say that the foil is oppositely charged compared to the plate or wool. Tell them the electrons in the foil are repelled by the presence of a negatively charged object (plate), leaving the positive end of the foil near the plate. The positive end of the foil is attracted to the negatively charged plate. When the positively charged wool is brought near the foil, it attracts electrons, creating a negative end on the versorium that is attracted to the wool.
5. The paper tent remains neutral. This is evident because the versorium is attracted by both positively and negatively charged objects.
6. The paper versorium is attracted to the foam plate and the wool fabric. Electrons are not free to move in the paper, but the paper is attracted to a positively charged object (fabric) because the electrons cluster on one side of the molecules. A negatively charged object (plate) attracts the positively charged side of the molecules.
7. No. The versorium cannot detect the sign of the charge on an object since the tent is equally attracted to any charged object.
8. Touching the foam plate or wool fabric to clothing will redistribute the charges, allowing all or most of the charge to leak off. The plate would become neutral and lose its effect.
9. Students who hypothesized that the paper tent would not be affected by the plate or fabric could not have predicted the results. Students who hypothesized correctly probably predicted the results.

Extending the Inquiry

Design an Experiment Students may want to try materials such as inflated balloons, plastic rulers that have been rubbed with plastic sandwich bags, or objects charged with a Van de Graff generator, if available. Other materials for the versorium tent might be plastic, cardboard, wood, or other metal foils.

Sample Data Table

	Unrubbed foam plate	Rubbed foam plate	Rubbed wool fabric
Aluminum tent: prediction	No effect	Attracted	Attracted
Aluminum tent: observation	No effect	Attracted	Attracted
Paper tent: prediction	No effect	Attracted	Attracted
Paper tent: observation	No effect	Attracted	Attracted

Objectives

After completing the lesson, students will be able to

◆ explain what causes the flow of electric current in terms of electrical potential, potential difference, and voltage;
◆ describe the relationship between voltage and the flow of electric current;
◆ define resistance and state how it affects the flow of current;
◆ calculate resistance using Ohm's law.

Key Terms electrical potential, potential difference, voltage, voltage source, voltmeter, ammeter, Ohm's law

1 Engage/Explore

Activating Prior Knowledge

Hold up a drinking straw and a straw-type coffee stirrer. Ask: **Is it easier to drink a milkshake through a narrow straw or a wide straw?** *(Wide straw)* Explain that the narrow straw is more resistant to the flow of milkshake; therefore, you have to suck harder to get the milkshake to flow through the straw. Tell students they will learn about analogous concepts of resistance, voltage, and electric current in this chapter.

• • • • • • • • DISCOVER • • • • • • • •

Skills Focus inferring  **ACTIVITY**
Materials *1 m bell wire, wire cutters and strippers, metric ruler, magnetic compass, electrical tape, 2 1.5-volt bulbs and sockets, D cell and holder, modeling clay*
Time 25 minutes
✂ ♻ 🔧 **Tips** Remove the insulation from the ends of the wire. Demonstrate how to connect the batteries and then how to rewire the circuit in Step 6 each time a bulb and socket are removed.
Expected Outcome The compass deflects more as bulbs and sockets are removed from the circuit.
Think It Over The most current flowed when no bulbs were in the circuit. Students may explain that removing bulbs increases current.

288

DISCOVER • ACTIVITY

How Can Current Be Measured?

1. Obtain four pieces of wire with the insulation removed from both ends. Each piece should be about 25 cm long.
2. Wrap one of the wires four times around the compass as shown. You may use tape to keep the wire in place.
3. Build a circuit using the remaining wire, wrapped compass, two bulbs, and a D cell as shown. Adjust the compass so that the wire is directly over the compass needle.
4. Make sure the compass is level. If it is not, place it on a lump of modeling clay, so that the needle swings freely.
5. Observe the compass needle as you complete the circuit. Record the number of degrees the needle turns.
6. Repeat the activity using only one bulb, and again with no bulb. Record the number of degrees the needle turns.

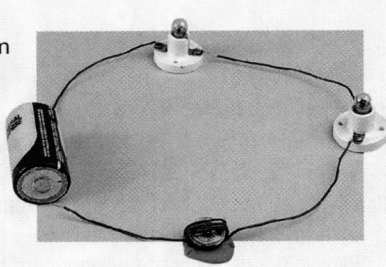

Think It Over
Inferring Based on your observations of the compass, when did the most current flow in your circuit? How can you explain your observations?

GUIDE FOR READING

◆ What causes electric current to flow?
◆ How does increasing voltage affect current?
◆ How does increasing resistance affect current?

Reading Tip Before you read, preview the boldfaced vocabulary terms. Write them down, leaving spaces between them for notes.

288

You're on a visit to a botanical garden. After a walk through the plush greenery, you rest by an artificial waterfall constructed in the middle of the garden. The continuous flow of water over the falls is soothing. You might be wondering what a waterfall could possibly have to do with electricity. Although there is an electric pump that keeps the water flowing, it is not the kind of pump that matters. The falling water itself, or any flowing liquid, is similar in some ways to the current in an electric circuit.

Electrical Potential

When water gets to the top of a waterfall it starts to fall down. When you lift something, you give it energy by doing work against the force of gravity. The type of energy that depends on position is called potential energy.

An object will move from a place of high potential energy to a place of low potential energy. The potential energy of the water is greater at the top of the waterfall than at the bottom. So water flows from the top to the bottom.

In a similar way, electrons in a circuit have potential energy. This potential energy, however, is related not to height but rather to the force exerted by electric fields. The potential energy per unit of electric charge is called **electrical potential.**

READING STRATEGIES

Reading Tip After students write down the boldfaced terms, discuss what they already know about each term's meaning. Have students speculate about the meanings of unfamiliar words or terms, based on word roots or affixes. With a term such as *potential difference,* have students speculate about its meaning based on definitions of each word in the term. Then have students read the section, making notes for each term.

Study and Comprehension Divide the class into five groups. Assign each group one of the five major headings. Suggest students summarize the information in the heading. Encourage students to prepare drawings or diagrams to accompany their summaries. Have each group rehearse, then give, its presentation. Have a question-and-answer session after each presentation, in which "audience" members ask questions based on the summaries.

Voltage

Just as water flows downhill, electrons flow from places of higher potential to places of lower potential. The difference in electrical potential between two places is called the **potential difference.** It provides the force that pushes charge through a circuit. The unit of measure of potential difference is the volt (V). For this reason, potential difference is also called **voltage.** Electrons will flow as long as there is a potential difference, or voltage between two parts of a circuit.

Recall that the flow of electrons through a material is called electric current. Now you know what causes current to flow. **Voltage causes current to flow through an electric circuit.**

Figure 7 The diagram shows how a hidden pump feeds the waterfall in the photo. The movement of the water is similar to the current in an electric circuit.

Program Resources

- ◆ **Unit 3 Resources** 9-2 Lesson Plan, p. 41; 9-2 Section Summary, p. 42
- ◆ **Laboratory Manual,** 9, "Building Electric Circuits"
- ◆ **Guided Reading and Study Workbook** Section 9-2

2 Facilitate

Electrical Potential

Including All Students

Students may have difficulty visualizing electrical potential. Refer students to Figure 7. Point out that the pump in the photo raises the water from the bottom of the waterfall to the top of the waterfall. Ask: **What happens when the water reaches the top of the waterfall?** *(It flows to the bottom.)* **Why?** *(Because potential energy at the top of the waterfall is higher than at the bottom, and objects move from a place of high potential energy to a place of low potential energy.)* Explain that electrons also flow from a place of high potential energy to low. Electrical potential, however, is related to force rather than height.* **learning modality: verbal**

Voltage

Building Inquiry Skills: Making Models

Materials *2 plastic cups, water, cotton string, stack of books*
Time 15 minutes

Have students set up a simple wick device to model voltage and current. They should fill a cup with water, stick one end of the string into the cup, and place the cup on the stack of books. Then, they should put the free end of the string into an empty cup that is positioned below the first cup. Have students observe the wick device after 15 minutes. Water should be visible in the second cup. Ask: **What part of the model is similar to voltage?** *(The difference in height between the two cups)* Then ask: **What represents current?** *(Water flowing from the first cup to the second)* **learning modality: kinesthetic**

Ongoing Assessment

Writing Have students write two or three sentences explaining why voltage is needed for current to flow.

Figure 8 As the difference in height between the two ends of the pipe increases, the flow of water increases. *Making Models How is the water pipe a model for voltage and current?*

Voltage Sources

Using the Visuals: Figure 8
Direct students to examine the potential difference in each image. Using a ruler, have students compare the difference in height of the ends of each pipe. Ask: **Which image represents the voltage source with the lowest potential difference?** *(The first image)* **learning modality: visual**

Inquiry Challenge
Materials *plastic bottle with small hole in bottom and cap removed, water, flexible plastic tubing, modeling clay*

Time 20 minutes

Ask groups to design a model that represents what happens as voltage, or potential difference, increases. Assign students specific tasks, such as manipulating potential difference, evaluating the force of the flowing water, and comparing the water model with electric current. Check student plans and then allow them to test their models. *(Sample model: Students could insert tubing through the hole in the bottom of the bottle, seal around the tubing with modeling clay if necessary, and fill the bottle with water. When the end of the plastic tube is at the same height as the top of the water bottle, no water flows—equal voltage. As the bottle is raised (or the end of the tubing lowered), the water flows faster and faster—higher and higher voltage difference.)* **cooperative learning**

Students can save their design plans in their portfolios.

Resistance

Language Arts Connection
The term *resistance* has several meanings. Challenge students to find the meaning of resistance in the phrases: "Resistance is futile," and "He belonged to the French Resistance." They may research the phrases in an encyclopedia or dictionary. Ask: **How is the scientific meaning of *resistance* similar to its meaning in these other phrases?** *(In all cases it means "to work against or to act in opposition.")* **learning modality: verbal**

Voltage Sources

What happens to the water when it gets to the bottom of the waterfall in the botanical garden? If nothing brings the water back to the top, the water flow will quickly stop. But this waterfall has a pump that pushes the water back up to the top. Once the water returns to the top, it can flow back down again. Another way to describe this process is to say that the pump maintains the potential difference between the top and bottom of the falls. As long as this difference exists, the water can continue to flow.

An electric circuit also requires a device to maintain a potential difference, or voltage. A **voltage source** creates a potential difference in an electric circuit. Batteries and generators are examples of voltage sources.

You will learn more about voltage sources in the next chapter. For now, all you need to know is that a voltage source has two terminals. The potential difference, or voltage, between the terminals causes charges to move around the circuit.

Some voltage sources are stronger than others. You can compare voltage to the downward slant of the pipe near the top of the waterfall. If a pipe is nearly level, the water just trickles out as shown in Figure 8. But if one end is much higher than the other, the rate of water flow is greater. The greater the difference in height, the greater the flow of water. **Just as an increase in the difference in height causes a greater flow of water, an increase in voltage causes a greater flow of electric current.**

Resistance

The amount of water that flows through a pipe in the waterfall depends on more than just the angle of the pipe. It also depends on the pipe through which the water travels. A long pipe will resist

Background

History of Science From the mid-eighteenth through the early nineteenth century, scientists believed that electricity was a fluid, just like water. In 1733, a French chemist named Charles DuFay proposed that electricity was made up of two fluids—vitreous electricity and resinous electricity. DuFay presumed that matter typically had a balanced amount of each type of electricity. When DuFay electrified a glass rod, it attracted pieces of cork. If he let the rod touch the cork pieces, the pieces were repelled from the rod and by each other. DuFay believed that when there was an excess of vitreous electricity, objects attracted each other. An excess of resinous electricity caused objects to repel each other. We now know that there are two types of charge, positive and negative, and that the negative charges move.

Figure 9 Water flows more easily through a short, wide pipe than through a long, narrow pipe. Similarly, electrons flow more easily through wires that are short and thick.

the flow of water more than a short pipe. And a thin pipe will resist the flow of water more than a wide pipe. In addition, a clogged pipe will offer more resistance than a clean pipe.

Current Depends on Resistance In a similar way, the amount of current that flows in a circuit depends on more than just the voltage. Current also depends on the resistance offered by the material through which it travels. Recall that electrical resistance is the opposition to the flow of charge. **The greater the resistance, the less current there is for a given voltage.**

The resistance of a wire depends on the thickness and length of the wire. Long wires have more resistance than short wires. Thin wires have more resistance than thick wires. Resistance also depends on how well the material conducts current. Electrons are slowed down by interactions with atoms of the wire. Electrons flow freely through conductors, but not through insulators.

One more factor, temperature, affects electrical resistance. In Chapter 8 you learned that electrical resistance can decrease as temperature decreases. You can also say that as the temperature of most conductors increases, resistance increases as well.

Path of Least Resistance Perhaps you have heard it said that someone is taking the "path of least resistance." This means that the person is doing something the easiest way. In a similar way, if an electric current can travel through either of two paths, more of the current will travel through the path with lower resistance.

Have you ever seen a flock of birds perched comfortably on high-voltage power lines? The reason the birds don't get hurt is that current flows through the path of least resistance. Since a bird's body offers more resistance than the wire, current continues to flow directly through the wire without harming the bird.

✓ *Checkpoint* *What two factors affect the flow of a current?*

Down the Tubes

Use water to make a model of an electric current.

1. Set up a funnel, tubing, beaker, and ring stand as shown.
2. Have a partner start a stopwatch as you pour 200 mL of water into the funnel. Be careful not to let it overflow.
3. Stop the stopwatch when all of the water has flowed into the beaker.

Making Models How did your model represent electric current, voltage, and resistance?

Skills Focus making models

Materials *water, two 200-mL beakers, funnel, ring stand, clear tubing of various lengths and widths, stopwatch*

Time 15 minutes

Tips Have students work in pairs. Keep paper towels handy to clean up any spills.

Making Models The water represents current. The length and width of the tubing determine the resistance. The height of the tube represents voltage or potential difference.

Extend Challenge students to find out what happens when they increase or decrease resistance by using tubing of different lengths and widths. **learning modality: kinesthetic**

Demonstration

Materials *latex glove, water, push pin, scissors, sink or basin*

Time 10 minutes

 To demonstrate for students the path of least resistance, fill the glove until the water is about 4–6 cm from the top of the wrist. Then tie the wrist. Hold the glove over the sink or basin with the fingers pointed upward, and put a single pinhole in one finger of the glove. Then snip the tip off a different finger. Ask students to predict what will happen if you turn the glove back over. Allow students to observe the water flowing out of the fingers of the glove. Ask: **Which path offered the least resistance? Why?** *(The path through the finger with the larger hole, because the water flowed out of it more quickly.)* **learning modality: visual**

Media and Technology

📼 **Concept Videotape Library**
Adventures, Tape 2, "What is Electricity?"

Answers to Self-Assessment

Caption Question

Figure 8 An increase in the difference in height between the ends of the water pipe causes a greater flow of water, just as an increase in voltage causes a greater flow of electric current.

✓ *Checkpoint*
Voltage and resistance

Ongoing Assessment

Drawing Have students sketch two wires and explain why one creates more resistance in a circuit than the other.

 Students can save their sketches in their portfolios.

Ohm's Law

Addressing Naive Conceptions

If an ammeter indicates a greater flow rate, some students may incorrectly infer that the electrons are traveling through the circuit at greater speeds. Explain that the ammeter shows an increase in flow rate if more electrons are flowing past a point even if their speed does not change. Therefore, a change in current should never be described as faster or slower; rather, students should describe a change in current as "more" or "less." **learning modality: verbal**

Including All Students

If students have difficulty applying Ohm's law, provide them with a memory device. Draw a circle on the board. Draw a horizontal line to divide the circle in half. In the top half, write the letter V. Divide the bottom half of the diagram with a vertical line. In the left side write the letter I and in the right, the letter R. Tell students to copy the diagram and to include the words *voltage, current,* and *resistance.* Tell students that to find any quantity if you know the other two, cover the unknown quantity with your finger. When the symbols are side by side, you multiply, and when they appear one over the other, you divide. Ask: **If you know voltage and resistance, how do you find current?** *(Cover the letter I (current). You get V over R; therefore, you divide voltage by resistance.)* **learning modality: visual**

Sharpen your Skills

Calculating

Time 15 minutes
The missing values are:
5 ohms; 1.5 volts; 0.1 amps; 30 ohms; 20 ohms; 6 volts. As voltage increases and resistance stays the same, current increases.
Extend Have students measure the voltage and current of a battery-powered clock or radio, using either a multimeter or voltmeter and ammeter, and calculate the resistance in the circuit.

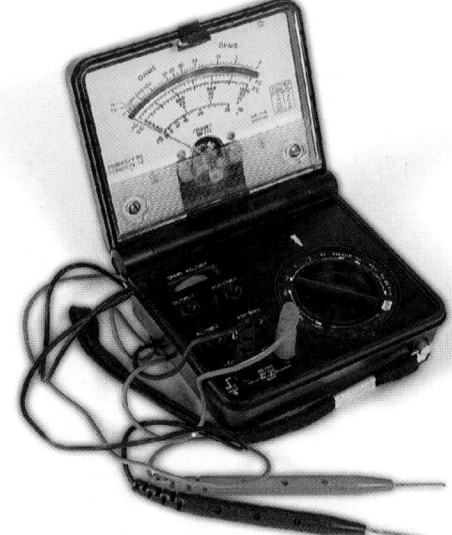

Figure 10 This multimeter can measure resistance, voltage, and small currents.

Sharpen your Skills

Calculating

Find the missing value in each row.

Voltage (V)	Current (A)	Resistance (Ω)
1.5	0.30	?
?	0.05	30
1.5	?	15
3.0	0.10	?
3.0	0.15	?
?	0.2	30

How are voltage, current, and resistance related?

Ohm's Law

In the 1820s, the German physicist Georg Ohm experimented with many substances to study electrical resistance. He analyzed various types of wire in order to determine the characteristics that affect a wire's resistance. As a result of Ohm's valuable experiments, the unit of resistance is named the ohm (Ω).

How can you measure the resistance of a wire? In order to measure resistance, Ohm set up a voltage between two points on a conductor. He then measured the current produced. Potential difference, or voltage, is measured with a device called a **voltmeter.** Current, which has units of amps, is measured with a device called an **ammeter.** Voltmeters and ammeters are often combined into a single device like the one in Figure 10.

Ohm found that the resistance for most conductors does not depend on the voltage across them. A conductor or any other device that has a constant resistance regardless of the voltage is said to obey **Ohm's law.** Most of the conductors that you will learn about do obey Ohm's law.

Ohm's law states that the resistance is equal to the voltage divided by the current.

$$\text{Resistance} = \frac{\text{Voltage}}{\text{Current}} \quad \text{or} \quad \text{Ohms} = \frac{\text{Volts}}{\text{Amps}}$$

The letter R can be used to represent resistance, I to represent current, and V to represent voltage. This formula is shorter.

$$R = \frac{V}{I}$$

You can rearrange the resistance formula as follows.

$$I = \frac{V}{R} \quad \text{or} \quad V = IR$$

If any two of the values in these formulas are known, you can solve for the third value.

You can use the formulas to see how changes in resistance, voltage, and current are related. For example, what happens to current if voltage is doubled without changing the resistance? For a constant resistance, if voltage is doubled, current is doubled as well. Thus the greater the voltage, the greater the current.

What happens if, instead, you double the resistance without changing the voltage? If resistance is doubled, the current will be cut in half. So for a greater resistance, the current is less.

It is sometimes important to increase the resistance in a circuit in order to prevent too much current from flowing. Specially constructed resistors, some no larger than a grain of rice, are

Background

Facts and Figures The symbol for the unit ohm is the capital Greek letter *omega* (Ω). Many Greek letters are used in math and science. The ancient Greeks had highly developed mathematics skills, particularly in geometry. Their early contributions led to a universal acceptance of the Greek alphabet to represent abstract ideas in math and science. The Greek letter *delta* (Δ) signifies the difference between two mathematical values.

Alpha (α), *beta* (β), and *gamma* (γ) are the first three letters of the Greek alphabet; they are used to represent radioactive emissions. The letter *sigma* (Σ) is used in mathematics to describe the sum of quantities in complicated equations. Perhaps the best known Greek letter is the letter *pi* (π), which stands for the ratio of the circumference of a circle to its diameter.

Sample Problem

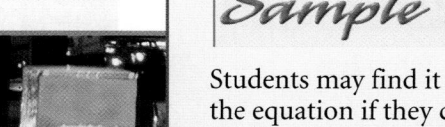

An automobile headlight is connected to a 12-volt battery. If the resulting current is 0.40 amps, what is the resistance of the headlight?

Analyze. You know the voltage and the current. You are looking for the resistance.

Write the formula.
$$R = \frac{V}{I}$$

Substitute and solve.
$$R = \frac{12\ V}{0.40\ A} = 30\ \Omega$$

Think about it. The answer makes sense because you are dividing the voltage by a decimal number. The answer should be greater than either number in the fraction, which it is.

Practice Problems

1. In a circuit, 0.5 A is flowing through the bulb. The voltage across the bulb is 4.0 V. What is the bulb's resistance?
2. In order for a waffle iron to operate efficiently, a current of 12 A must flow through its coils. If the resistance is 10 Ω, what must the voltage be?

added to circuits. Televisions, radios, and other similar devices contain dozens of such resistors.

Some resistors do not obey Ohm's law. For instance, the resistance of a light bulb increases when the bulb is turned on and the filament heats up. A filament has the lowest resistance before it heats up, and so a cold filament conducts the most current. That is one reason a bulb might burn out the instant you switch it on.

Section 2 Review

1. What is voltage?
2. How is voltage related to electric current?
3. How is resistance related to electric current?
4. **Thinking Critically Calculating** You light a light bulb with a 1.5-volt battery. If the bulb has a resistance of 10 ohms, how much current is flowing?
5. **Thinking Critically Relating Cause and Effect** In order to increase the amount of current flowing in a circuit, should you increase the voltage or the resistance? Explain.

Check Your Progress CHAPTER PROJECT 9

Pick the event that will close your switch, for example, the closing of a door. To make your switch, you might tape one of the free wires to a door and the other wire to the frame of the door. The wires will touch when the door closes. Here are some other ideas to explore: an object falling, a slight vibration or breeze, or a container filling with salt water. Draw a circuit diagram that includes a battery, a switch, and a light bulb.

Chapter 9 **293**

Program Resources

◆ **Unit 3 Resources** 9-2 Review and Reinforce, p. 43; 9-2 Enrich, p. 44

Sample Problem

Students may find it easier to interpret the equation if they can visualize the problem. Suggest they draw a battery, connecting wires, and a headlight. Have them label the battery "12 V" and the wire "0.4 A," then work through the steps of the problem. **learning modality: logical/mathematical**

Answers to Practice Problems
1. $R = \frac{4.0\ V}{0.5\ A} = 8\ \Omega$
2. $V = 10\ \Omega \times 12\ A = 120\ V$

3 Assess

Section 2 Review Answers

1. Voltage is the potential difference between two places in a circuit.
2. Voltage causes electrons to flow; in other words, voltage causes current. The greater the voltage for a given resistance, the greater the current.
3. The greater the resistance for a given voltage, the lower the current.
4. Current (I) = Volts (V)/Resistance (R): $I = \frac{1.5\ V}{10\ \Omega} = 0.15\ A$
5. To increase the amount of current, increase voltage or decrease resistance. Because $I = V \div R$, an increase in V or a decrease in R will cause an increase in I.

Check Your Progress CHAPTER PROJECT 9

Help students understand that a switch is simply a device that allows electricity to flow where it couldn't before. Be sure they realize that their choice will have a large influence on how their detector switch is designed.

Performance Assessment

Organizing Information Have students create concept maps using the terms *electrical potential, voltage, resistance, current, ohms, amperes,* and *volts.*

 Students can save their concept maps in their portfolios.

293

Constructing a Dimmer Switch

Preparing for Inquiry

Key Concept The brightness of a bulb is controlled by the amount of current flowing in the circuit, which in turn depends on the voltage and the resistance in the circuit.

Skills Objectives Students will be able to
◆ observe that the bulb gets dimmer as the amount of resistance in the circuit increases;
◆ predict what will happen if they increase or decrease the resistance in the circuit;
◆ adapt procedures to test their predictions.

Time 30 minutes

Advance Planning Cut the copper wire and rubber tubing to the same length as the pencil lead.

Alternative Materials Any non-conductor, such as wood or plastic, can be substituted for the rubber tubing.

Guiding Inquiry

Invitation Ask students to think about sitting in a movie theater just as the show is about to begin. Ask: **When people are arriving, are the lights on or off?** *(on)* **During the show are the lights on or off?** *(off)* **Do the lights all go off suddenly?** *(No. They gradually get dimmer.)*

Introducing the Procedure

◆ Explain that pencil lead is not made of lead at all, but graphite, a form of the element carbon. Inform students that the drawing part of a pencil is called lead because people used to draw on paper with the metal lead before pencils were invented.
◆ Refer students to the circuit in the photo.
◆ For a quantitative comparison, ask students to use small pieces of paper through which they view the bulb. They can compare the brightness by how many pieces of paper they can see the bulb through. This procedure will work best in a slightly darkened room.

Constructing a Dimmer Switch

Most light switches turn a light bulb on and off. There doesn't seem to be any setting in between. Suppose you wanted to find a way to dim lights slowly. Think about how you would design a switch that controls the brightness of a bulb.

▲ Engineer at a sound mixing board

Skills Focus

observing, predicting, designing experiments

Problem

What materials can be used to make a dimmer switch?

Materials

D cell   masking tape
flashlight bulb in a socket
thick lead from mechanical pencil
uninsulated copper wire, the same length as the pencil lead
rubber tubing, the same length as the pencil lead
1 wire 10–15 cm long
2 wires 20–30 cm long
2 alligator clips

Procedure

1. Construct the circuit shown in the photo. To begin, attach wires to the ends of the D cell.
2. Connect the other end of one of the wires to the bulb in a socket. Attach a wire with an alligator clip to the other side of the socket.
3. Attach an alligator clip to the other wire.
4. The pencil lead will serve as a resistor that can be varied—a variable resistor. Attach one alligator clip firmly to the tip of the pencil lead. Be sure the clip makes good contact with the lead. (*Note:* Pencil "lead" is actually graphite, a form of the element carbon.)
5. Predict how the brightness of the bulb will change as you slide the other alligator clip back and forth along the lead. Test your prediction.
6. What will happen to the brightness of the bulb if you replace the lead with a piece of uninsulated copper wire? Adapt your pencil-lead investigation to test the copper wire.

Troubleshooting the Experiment

◆ Poor contact between the alligator clips and the pencil lead can be improved by buffing the lead with sandpaper.

Expected Outcome

◆ As students include more pencil lead in the circuit, the total resistance increases and current decreases, so the bulb becomes dimmer. When they move the clips close together so the circuit contains less graphite, the total resistance decreases and the bulb becomes brighter.

◆ Students' results should show that the copper wire conducts well no matter its length. The rubber tubing doesn't conduct at all.

Analyze and Conclude

1. Resistance. The amount of resistance increased as the length of pencil lead in the circuit increased.
2. The bulb got dimmer as the length of lead in the circuit increased.

7. Predict what will happen to the brightness of the bulb if you replace the pencil lead with a piece of rubber tubing. Adapt your pencil-lead investigation to test the rubber tubing.

Analyze and Conclude

1. What variable did you manipulate by sliding the alligator clip along the pencil lead in Step 5?

2. What happened to the brightness of the bulb when you slid the alligator clip along the pencil lead?

3. Explain your reasoning in making predictions about the brightness of the bulb in Steps 6 and 7. Were your predictions supported by your observations?

4. Do you think that pencil lead has more or less resistance than copper? Do you think it has more or less resistance than rubber? Use your observations to explain your answers.

5. Which material tested in this lab would make the best dimmer switch? Explain your answer.

6. **Apply** If you wanted to sell your dimmer switch to the owner of a movie theater, how would you describe your device and explain how it works?

More to Explore

The volume controls on some car radios and television sets also contain variable resistors, called rheostats. The sliding volume controls on a sound mixing board are rheostats, as well. Homes and theaters may use rheostats to adjust lighting. Where else in your house would variable resistors be useful? (*Hint:* Look for applications where the output is graduated rather than all or nothing.)

3. Copper wire is an excellent conductor and rubber is an excellent insulator. The predictions should have been supported by the students' observations.

4. The tests show that pencil lead is a better resistor than copper wire; rubber tubing is a better resistor than pencil lead.

5. Pencil lead. Copper wire would have to be very long to offer enough resistance, and rubber does not conduct electricity at all.

6. Students should explain that the device is a switch that uses variable resistance to allow for full light for patrons to find their seats and safely exit the theater, and dim light for viewing the movie.

Extending the Inquiry

More to Explore Samples: electric heater controls, electric dryer, ceiling fan, exercise treadmill, variable-speed tools

---

Safety

Caution students to be careful not to break the flashlight bulb. Review the safety guidelines in Appendix A.

Program Resources

◆ **Unit 3 Resources** Real-World Lab blackline masters, pp. 56–57

Media and Technology

 Lab Activity Videotape
Tape 2

SECTION 3 Series and Parallel Circuits

Objectives

After completing the lesson, students will be able to
◆ describe and construct a series circuit;
◆ describe and construct a parallel circuit.

Key Terms series circuit, parallel circuit

1 Engage/Explore

Activating Prior Knowledge

Ask students what happens to the flow of electricity in a lamp when they turn the lamp switch on. *(Electricity flows from the socket, through the wire, and to the light bulb.)* Then ask: **If the wire between the switch and the light bulb is cut, what happens when you flick on the switch? Why?** *(Nothing happens because the electricity cannot flow to the bulb.)*

DISCOVER

Skills Focus observing
Materials *4 light bulbs with sockets, 2 dry cells with holders, several lengths of insulated wire*
Time 15 minutes
Tips Remove insulation from ends of wire. Students may need help reading the circuit diagrams. Point out the symbols for bulb, wire, and battery. You may want to have students include a switch in their circuits.
Think It Over The remaining bulb in the series circuit goes out; the remaining bulb in the parallel circuit does not. Students might recognize that the parallel circuit has two paths, so the current continues to flow through the remaining path. The series circuit has only one path.

DISCOVER ••••••••••••••••••••••••••••••• ACTIVITY

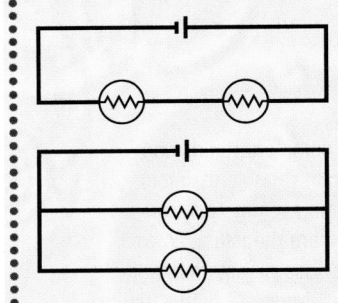

Do the Lights Keep Shining?

1. Construct both of the circuits shown using a battery, several insulated wires, and two light bulbs for each circuit.
2. Connect all wires and observe the light bulbs.
3. Now unscrew one bulb in each circuit. Observe the remaining bulbs.

Think It Over
Observing What happened to the remaining light bulbs when you unscrewed the first bulb? How can you account for your observations?

GUIDE FOR READING

◆ How many paths can current take in a series circuit?
◆ How does a parallel circuit differ from a series circuit?

Reading Tip As you read, create a table comparing series and parallel circuits.

It's a cool, clear night as you stroll by the harbor with your family. The night is dark, but the waterfront is bright thanks to the thousands of twinkling white lights that outline the tall ships. They make a striking view.

As you walk, you notice that a few of the lights are burned out. The rest of the lights, however, burn brightly. If one bulb is burned out, how can the rest of the lights continue to shine? The answer depends on how the electric circuit is designed. The parts of a circuit can be arranged in series or in parallel.

Figure 11 The lights that line the rigging of this ship are parts of a parallel circuit. If one goes out, the rest keep shining.

296

READING STRATEGIES

Reading Tip Help students create tables by writing a table such as the one shown on the board. Encourage students to copy the table and fill in the information as they read.

	Series Circuit	Parallel Circuit
Definition		
Paths		
Resistance		
Examples		

Study and Comprehension Have students preview the section by reading the headings and subheadings, and by looking at the photographs. Encourage students to suggest questions they have about series circuits, parallel circuits, and household circuits. Write the questions on the board. After students read the section, have them work as a class to answer the questions on the board. Encourage them to research answers not found in the section.

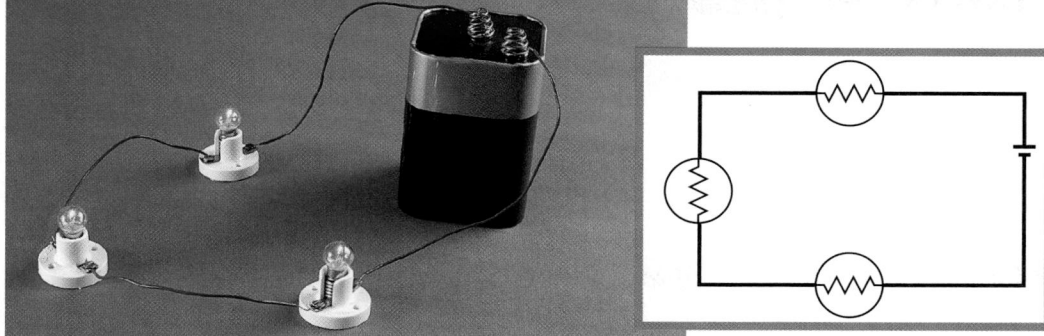

Figure 12 A series circuit provides only one path for the flow of electrons. *Applying Concepts What will happen to the other bulbs if one bulb burns out?*

Series Circuits

If all the parts of an electric circuit are connected one after another, the circuit is a **series circuit.** Figure 12 illustrates a series circuit. **In a series circuit, there is only one path for the current to take.** For example, a switch and the device it controls are connected in series with each other.

One Path A series circuit is very simple to design and build, but it has some disadvantages. What happens if a bulb in a series circuit burns out? A burned-out bulb is a break in the circuit, and there is no other path for the current to take. So if one light goes out, all the lights go out.

Added Resistors Another disadvantage of a series circuit is that the light bulbs in the circuit become dimmer as more bulbs are added. Why does that happen? Think about what happens to the overall resistance of a series circuit as you add more bulbs. The resistance increases. Remember that if resistance increases, current decreases. So as light bulbs are added to a series circuit, the current decreases. The result is that the bulbs burn less brightly.

Ammeters Different meters are wired into circuits in different ways. Recall from the previous section that an ammeter is used to measure current. If you want to measure the current through some device in a circuit, the ammeter should be connected in series with the device.

☑ *Checkpoint* How does resistance change as you add bulbs to a series circuit?

Parallel Circuits

Could the lights on the ships have been connected in series? No—if the lights were part of a series circuit, all of the lights would have gone off when one burned out. What you saw, however, was that a few lights were burned out and the rest were brightly lit.

Program Resources

◆ **Unit 3 Resources** 9-3 Lesson Plan, p. 45; 9-3 Section Summary, p. 46
◆ **Guided Reading and Study Workbook** Section 9-3

Media and Technology

 Transparencies "Series and Parallel Circuits," Transparency 34

Answers to Self-Assessment

Caption Question

Figure 12 If one bulb burns out, the other two bulbs will not light.

☑ *Checkpoint*

The more bulbs you add to a series circuit, the greater the resistance.

---

2 Facilitate

Series Circuits

Using the Visuals: Figure 12

Direct students to use their index fingers to trace the path of electricity through the circuit. Ask: **What happens to the electrons when they reach the bulbs?** *(They move through the filaments and cause the bulbs to glow.)* Have students infer what would happen to the electrons if a wire was cut. *(The electrons would stop flowing and the bulbs would not light.)* **learning modality: visual**

Inquiry Challenge

Materials *several insulated wires, light bulbs, dry cell*
Time 25 minutes

🔋 🔗 Challenge student groups to design experiments that show how adding resistors (light bulbs) to a series circuit decreases the brightness of the bulbs. Assign students specific tasks such as assembling materials, designing the circuit, building the circuit, and evaluating the brightness of the bulbs. Have students compile a list of materials and prepare a circuit design for your approval. Ask: **What will you use as a control for your experiment?** *(Sample: A series circuit with one light bulb)* Encourage students to formulate a general statement about the effect of resistors on current in a series circuit. *(Sample: Adding resistors reduces the current in a series circuit.)* **cooperative learning**

Ongoing Assessment

Oral Presentation Have students name one advantage and one disadvantage of series circuits.

Parallel Circuits

Including All Students

Encourage students who have difficulty distinguishing between parallel and series circuits to draw circuit diagrams of each. Students can add captions that explain the effect on current and resistance when bulbs (resistors) are added to the circuit.
learning modality: visual

 Students can save their diagrams in their portfolios.

Building Inquiry Skills: Inferring

Materials *strings of holiday lights*

Time 10 minutes

Challenge students to infer if a particular string of holiday lights is arranged in a series or a parallel circuit. Caution students to use care when plugging the lights into the wall. Ask: **How can you tell if the lights are arranged in a parallel circuit?** *(If you remove one light bulb and the rest of the string stays lit, then the bulbs are in a parallel circuit.)* To extend the activity, challenge students to create a circuit diagram for their string of lights.
learning modality: logical/ mathematical

Sharpen your Skills

Predicting

Materials *dry cell, 3 light bulbs, insulated wire, switch*

Time 20 minutes

Tips Help students recognize that this circuit contains one bulb in series and two bulbs in parallel. Students should observe that the series bulb is brighter than the bulbs in parallel, and that the bulbs in parallel are of the same brightness. The series bulb is brighter than the two parallel bulbs because it receives the same amount of current that the two bulbs in parallel share.

Extend Have students predict what would happen if another bulb (resistor) were added to the parallel circuit. *(The total current in the circuit increases; the bulb in series becomes brighter, the bulbs in parallel become dimmer.)* **learning modality: visual**

298

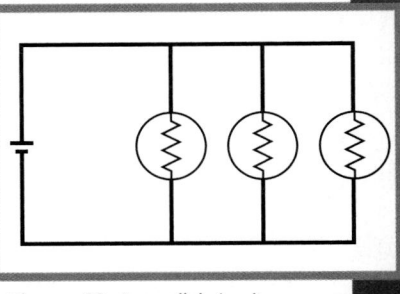
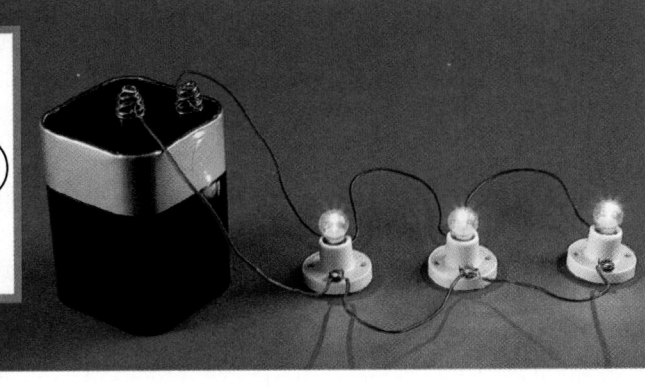

Figure 13 A parallel circuit provides several paths for the flow of electrons. More current flows, and the bulbs are brighter than in the series circuit.

Sharpen your Skills

Predicting

1. Look at the circuit diagram below. Predict whether all three light bulbs will shine with the same brightness.

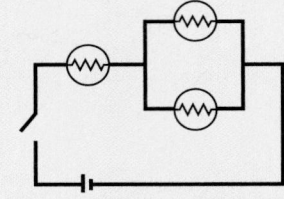

2. Construct the circuit using a dry cell and three identical light bulbs. Observe the brightness of the bulbs.

Does this circuit behave like either a parallel circuit or a series circuit? Explain.

298

The ships' lights were connected in parallel circuits. In a **parallel circuit,** the different parts of the circuit are on separate branches. Figure 13 shows a parallel circuit. **In a parallel circuit, there are several paths for current to take.** Notice that each bulb has its own path from one terminal of the battery to the other.

Several Paths What happens if a light burns out in a parallel circuit? If there is a break in one branch, current can still move through the other branches. So if one bulb goes out, the others remain lit. Switches can be placed along each branch so that individual bulbs can be turned on and off without affecting the others.

Added Branches What happens to the resistance of a parallel circuit when you add a branch? Although you might think that the overall resistance increases, it actually decreases. To understand this, consider the flow of water once again. Suppose water is being released from a reservoir held by a dam. If the water is allowed to flow through one pipe, a certain amount of water comes out. But if two pipes are used instead of one, twice as much water flows. The water will flow more easily because it has two paths to take. The same is true for a parallel circuit. As new paths, or branches, are added, the electric current has more paths to follow, and so total resistance decreases.

What does this tell you about current? If resistance decreases, the current must increase. The increased current travels along the new branch without affecting the original branches. So as you add branches to a parallel circuit, the brightness of the light bulbs does not change.

Voltmeters Recall from Section 2 that a voltmeter is used to measure voltage. When you measure the voltage across some device, the voltmeter and the device should be wired as parallel circuits.

Background

History of Science The first practical light bulb, or incandescent lamp, was developed in 1878 by the British chemist Sir Joseph Swan and in 1879 by the American inventor Thomas Edison. These bulbs had carbon filaments placed inside a glass that had been emptied using a vacuum. Edison went on to develop lighting systems using power lines to connect incandescent lamps. People did not immediately welcome electric lights. Before electricity, gas lighting was popular. As Edison and others developed electric appliances such as the light bulb, electric lamps began to replace gas lighting.

Figure 14 Parallel circuits are used in your home.
Interpreting Diagrams How many circuits does this house have?

Household Circuits

Would you want the circuits in your home to be series circuits? Of course you would not. With a series circuit, all the electrical devices in your home would go off every time a light bulb burned out or a switch was turned off. Instead, the circuits in your home are parallel circuits.

Electricity is fed into a home by heavy wires called lines. These lines have very low resistance. You can see in Figure 14 that parallel branches extend out from the lines to wall sockets, appliances, and lights in each room. The voltage in these household circuits is 120 volts. Switches are located in places where they can be used to control one branch of the circuit at a time.

 **Section 3 Review**

1. What are the two types of electric circuits? You can draw a diagram of each to explain your answer.
2. What happens to the bulbs in a series circuit if one of the bulbs burns out? Explain.
3. What happens to the bulbs in a parallel circuit if one of the bulbs burns out? Explain.
4. **Thinking Critically Comparing and Contrasting** You are building a string of lights using several bulbs. How is the brightness of the lights related to whether you connect the bulbs in series or in parallel?

Check Your Progress

CHAPTER PROJECT 9

Construct a circuit, either series or parallel, that lights a bulb when the switch is closed. Use the detector switch you designed earlier to close the circuit. Test the circuit to make sure that the switch closes when the event you are detecting occurs. Then make sure that the bulb lights when the switch is closed.

Program Resources

◆ **Unit 3 Resources** 9-3 Review and Reinforce, p. 47; 9-3 Enrich, p. 48

Media and Technology

 Transparencies "Household Circuits," Transparency 35

Answers to Self-Assessment

Caption Question
Figure 14 This house has four circuits.

Household Circuits

Real-Life Learning

Challenge students to design an electrical wiring plan for a room. They should include outlets and light fixtures in their drawings. Make sure the drawings show parallel circuits. **learning modality: visual**

3 Assess

Section 3 Review Answers

1. Series and parallel circuits. Diagrams should be labeled correctly.
2. The circuit is broken and all of the bulbs go out.
3. The bulbs in the other branches remain lit because the electricity can follow more than one complete path.
4. If the bulbs are connected in a series circuit, the bulbs will be dimmer than if each were used alone. If they are connected in a parallel circuit, adding bulbs will not change the brightness of the others.

Check Your Progress

CHAPTER PROJECT 9

If students are having a hard time getting their switches to work properly, help them along by providing hints on how to get the two ends of the wires to make electrical contact. Most of the completed circuits will be in the form of parts and wires that are held together in primitive ways and that just lie loosely on a tabletop. Encourage students to improve the durability and appearance of their designs.

Performance Assessment

Drawing Have students draw two circuit diagrams—one that shows three bulbs in a series circuit and one that shows three bulbs in a parallel circuit.

 Students can save their circuit diagrams in their portfolios.

SECTION 4 Electrical Safety

Objectives

After completing the lesson, students will be able to
◆ identify the safety devices used to protect people from common electrical hazards;
◆ describe how a lightning rod protects a building;
◆ explain how the severity of an electric shock is related to current, voltage, and resistance.

Key Terms short circuit, third prong, grounded, lightning rod, fuse, circuit breaker

1 Engage/Explore

Activating Prior Knowledge

Show students the symbol for electrical hazard. Ask: **What does this symbol indicate?** *(There is a danger of shock.)* Ask students to name one or two ways that they can avoid electrical shock dangers. *(Sample: Keep electrical appliances away from water; do not overload outlets; do not touch or cut electrical wires.)*

········ **DISCOVER** ········

Skills Focus developing hypotheses
Materials *dry cell, light bulb, 2 alligator clips, very fine steel wool (00 or 000 grade)*
Time 15 minutes
Tips Use unrusted, unsoaped steel wool. If students cannot make a good contact between the steel wool fiber and the alligator clips, suggest they wrap a small piece of aluminum foil around the end of the fiber, crimp it, then clamp the alligator jaws on it.
Expected Outcome The steel wire will flash and burn; the bulb will go out.
Think It Over If the steel wool becomes so hot it melts or burns, then the circuit will be broken.

SECTION 4 Electrical Safety

 **DISCOVER** ·············· **ACTIVITY**

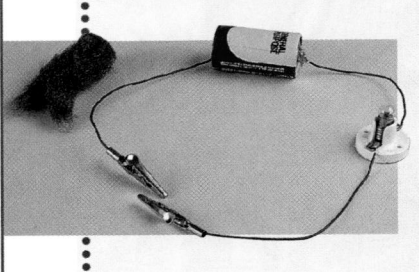

How Can You Blow a Fuse?

1. Begin by constructing the circuit shown using a D cell, a light bulb, and two alligator clips.
2. Pull a steel fiber out of a piece of steel wool. Wrap the ends of the steel fiber around the alligator clips.
3. Complete the circuit and observe the steel fiber and the bulb.

Think It Over
Developing Hypotheses Write a hypothesis to explain your observations.

GUIDE FOR READING

◆ How does a lightning rod protect a building?
◆ What safety devices are used in electric circuits?
◆ How is injury from an electric shock on the human body related to current?

Reading Tip As you read, make a list of ways that you can protect yourself from an electric shock.

The ice storm has ended, but it has left a great deal of destruction in its wake. Trees have been stripped of their branches, and a thick coating of ice covers the countryside. Perhaps the greatest danger is from the downed high-voltage lines left sparking in the streets. Residents are being warned to stay far away from them. What makes these power lines so dangerous?

Becoming Part of a Circuit

The sparks from those power lines should give you a clue as to what the danger is. One of the two parts of an electric company's circuit is a "live" wire carrying energy from the generating plant. The other part is a return or "ground" from the customer back to the generating plant. If a power line is damaged, the ground connection may be made through Earth itself. A person who touches a downed power line could create a short circuit to Earth through his or her body. A **short circuit** is a connection that allows current to take an unintended path. Rather than flowing through the return, or ground wire, the current would flow through the person.

The unintended path in a short circuit may offer less resistance than the intended path. So the current through a short circuit can be high. The result is a potentially fatal electric shock.

Exposed Wires Fallen high-voltage power lines are not the only potential source of electric shocks. Many people are hurt or killed by shocks from common household circuits. If you touch your hand to a 120-volt circuit, a potential difference, or voltage, is created between your hand and Earth. Since current flows when there is voltage, current will flow through your body.

READING STRATEGIES

Reading Tip Lists will include avoiding downed power lines, making sure home appliances don't have damaged wires, and not handling electrical appliances when you are wet. Summarize students' lists in a class chart with the headings *Way to Prevent Shock* and *Why This Prevents Shock.*

Study and Comprehension After students read the section, have them work with partners to list main ideas and supporting details for the information under each heading of the section. Provide students with examples of graphic organizers that students can use to record the main ideas and details.

Figure 15 Power must be shut off while work crews repair damaged lines.

The wires to the electrical devices in your home are protected by insulation. Sometimes that insulation wears off, leaving the wire exposed. If you touch such a wire, you become part of the circuit. You will get a painful, possibly harmful shock.

In some cases, the exposed wire is inside an electrical device such as a toaster. If the wire comes in contact with the outside metal case of the toaster, the entire toaster will conduct electricity. Then you could receive a shock from simply touching the toaster.

Resisting Current Is there any way to protect yourself if you become part of a circuit? The soles of your shoes will normally provide a large resistance between your feet and the surface of Earth. As a result, the current would not be enough to cause serious injury. But what happens if you're barefoot, or are standing in the bathtub when you touch the circuit? In either case, your resistance will be smaller. Ordinary tap water is not a very good conductor of electricity, but it does decrease your resistance. This means that the voltage can still produce enough current to seriously injure you.

Grounding

Additional grounding wires protect people from shocks. If a short circuit occurs in a device, current will go directly into Earth through a low-resistance grounding wire. In this way a person who touches the device will be protected.

Third Prong Have you ever noticed that some plugs have a third prong on them, as shown in Figure 16? The two flat prongs connect the appliance to the household circuit. This **third prong,** which is round, connects the metal shell of an appliance to the ground wire of a building.

In order to protect people from shocks, electrical systems are grounded. A circuit is electrically **grounded** when charges are able to flow directly from the circuit into the ground connection in the event of a short circuit.

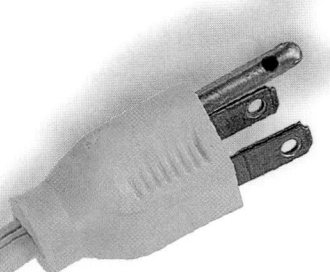

Figure 16 The rounded prong on this plug is a safety device.
Relating Cause and Effect How does the third prong protect you if the appliance is faulty?

Chapter 9 **301**

Answers to Self-Assessment
Caption Question
Figure 16 The third prong sends current directly into the ground if a short circuit occurs.

Becoming Part of a Circuit

Building Inquiry Skills: Applying Concepts

Have students draw a circuit diagram that a shows a circuit with an exposed wire. Ask: **Why does touching the exposed wire create a short circuit?** (*By touching the wire, the person creates a new path with less resistance for the current to follow.*) **learning modality: visual**

Real-Life Learning

Materials *appliances commonly used in the bathroom, such as hair dryers, curling irons, and electric shavers*
Time 15 minutes

ACTIVITY

Direct students to examine the labels on the appliances. Ask: **Why do the labels caution users against operating the appliances near water?** (*Tap water can decrease resistance to current. If you become part of the circuit while in contact with water, you can be seriously injured.*) **learning modality: verbal**

Grounding

Including All Students

Materials *two- and three-prong plugs, electrical outlet hardware (not wired to wall)*
Time 10 minutes

ACTIVITY

Allow students who are visually impaired to feel the difference between the plugs. Have students locate the grounding prong. Allow them to examine the electrical outlet to find out how the wires in the plugs fit into the circuit.
learning modality: kinesthetic

Ongoing Assessment

Writing Have students write a definition of a short circuit and describe examples of three short circuits.

Grounding, continued

Building Inquiry Skills: Inferring

Ask students to infer why people playing golf during a thunderstorm are in danger. *(The golf club could act as a lightning rod. The golf club attracts the electrons in a lightning bolt just as lightning rods do.)* Ask: **What is the safest thing to do if you are caught in a storm while golfing?** *(Go indoors as quickly as possible or lie flat on the ground away from tall objects.)* **learning modality: logical/mathematical**

Social Studies CONNECTION

Have reference materials available for students to research Benjamin Franklin's life story. Encourage them to share one interesting fact or anecdote with the class.

In Your Journal Encourage students to create a headline and an illustration to accompany their articles. Compile students' articles in a Ben Franklin Portfolio to display in the classroom or school library. **learning modality: verbal**

Fuses and Circuit Breakers

Demonstration

Materials *dry cell, 4 light bulbs, insulating wire, ammeter, switch*
Time 15 minutes

Demonstrate how adding resistors increases current. Build a parallel circuit using two light bulbs; place an ammeter between the last light bulb and the dry cell. Have students check the ammeter reading. Ask them to predict what will happen if you add resistors (light bulbs). *(The current will increase.)* Then add two more branches to the parallel circuit by attaching two more light bulbs. Allow students to compare a second ammeter reading with the first to check their predictions. **learning modality: visual**

Figure 17 A lightning rod attracts charges from a lightning bolt and carries them to Earth.

Social Studies CONNECTION

Benjamin Franklin was not only a talented experimenter, but also an inventor, statesman, philosopher, printer, musician, and economist.

In Your Journal

Read about the life and work of Benjamin Franklin. Choose one event or aspect of his life and write a newspaper article describing his work to your readers. For example, you might write about how Franklin founded the first lending library so that people who couldn't afford to buy books could read them.

Lightning Rods With the idea of grounding, Benjamin Franklin was able to invent the lightning rod. A **lightning rod** is a metal rod mounted on the roof of a building in order to protect a building. Recall from Section 1 that charge is induced on Earth's surface during a thunderstorm. Lightning results from the transfer of charge from a charged cloud to an oppositely charged object on Earth. Franklin realized that charges are more crowded on pointed objects than on flat ones. So electrons in a lightning bolt are attracted to a pointed object such as a lightning rod.

A lightning rod is connected to a grounding wire. When lightning strikes the rod, charges flow through the rod, into the wire, and then into Earth. This protects the building.

If you think about how a lightning rod works, you will understand how to stay safe during a thunderstorm. It is not safe to stand under a tall conductor, such as a tall, wet tree. Even worse would be to hold a pointed metal object, such as an umbrella. If you are outside during a storm, the best way to protect yourself from lightning is to stay low and dry.

Checkpoint *Why does lightning strike a lightning rod?*

Fuses and Circuit Breakers

A wire that carries more current than it is designed to carry will become hot. If it becomes too hot, it can melt the insulation on the wire. The hot wire can then come in contact with flammable materials in the walls of a building, causing a fire.

Electric current can become too high if a circuit is overloaded. Recall that as you add branches to a parallel circuit, the total resistance decreases and the current increases. If you use too many appliances at once, the current can become dangerously high. Overloading a circuit might result in a fire. **In order to prevent circuits from overheating, devices called fuses and circuit breakers are added to circuits.**

A **fuse** is a device that contains a thin strip of metal that will melt if too much current flows through it. When the strip of metal melts, or "blows," it breaks the circuit and stops the flow of current. If you have ever plugged in too many appliances at once, the electricity might have gone out because a fuse was blown. Once the overload is corrected, the fuse can be replaced and the electricity restored.

Background

Integrating Science Doctors often treat electric shock with a *defibrillator*. *Fibrillation* is the irregular and uncontrolled contraction of the heart muscle fibers. *De*fibrillators use two "paddles" to send an electric current across the muscles of the victim's ventricles. This "jump starts" the natural electrical impulses and restarts the heartbeat. Treatment with a defibrillator within 4 minutes can prevent permanent brain damage or death.

In 1996, a U.S. company won FDA approval for a portable defibrillator that uses paddles to analyze a patient's heart rhythm, then calculates the correct current and voltage. The device delivers spoken instructions, and can be used in public places, like airplanes. In November 1998, Michael Tighe became the first passenger on a domestic airplane flight to have his life saved by a portable defibrillator.

When a fuse burns out, it cannot be used again. To avoid the problem of having to replace fuses, circuits in new buildings are protected by devices called circuit breakers. A **circuit breaker** is a safety device that uses an electromagnet to shut off the circuit when the current gets too high. It's easy to reset the circuit breaker. All you have to do is pull back a switch—but only after turning off some of the appliances that are causing the high current in the circuit.

Electric Shocks

Why is it so important to protect the human body from electric shocks? The human body depends on electrical signals. Tiny electrical pulses, for example, control the beating of your heart. Similarly, electrical signals control your breathing and the movement of your muscles. If your body receives an electric current from a source outside it, the current will interfere with the normal processes within your body.

Current in the Body The shock you feel from static discharge after walking across a carpet on a dry day is not the same as the shock from touching a fallen power line. **The severity of an electric shock depends on the current.**

A current of less than 0.01 amp is almost unnoticeable. Between 0.1 amp and 0.2 amp, however, a current can be dangerous. Such a current might cause an irregular heartbeat and disrupt the flow of blood to your body. A current entering your hand can travel through your arm and across your heart. Currents greater than 0.2 amp cause burns and can stop your heart.

Resistance in the Body The current of an electric shock is related to voltage and resistance. The voltage is determined by the source of the shock. You can safely handle the 1.5-volt batteries for a radio, but you could be killed by touching power lines that carry thousands of volts.

The current that results from that voltage depends on the resistance of the human body. Resistance in the human body is affected by several factors. One factor is the conducting ability of body tissue. Living cells have a low resistance to electric current.

Figure 18 Both fuses and circuit breakers open a circuit when current gets too high.
Applying Concepts What is the maximum current that the yellow fuse can carry?

Chapter 9 **303**

Media and Technology

Concept Videotape Library
Adventures, Tape 2, "Electric Bodies"

 Answers to Self-Assessment

Caption Question

Figure 18 The yellow fuse can carry a maximum current of 20 amps.

☑ *Checkpoint*

The charges on the pointed lightning rod are crowded, so electricity in a lightning bolt is extremely attracted to the lightning rod.

303

Reviewing Content
Multiple Choice
1. d **2.** b **3.** a **4.** b **5.** c

True or False
6. true **7.** gains **8.** Induction **9.** true
10. fuse

Checking Concepts
11. The electric field enables a charge to exert an electric force at a distance. The field surrounding a positive charge exerts a repulsive force on other positive charges and an attractive force on negative charges.

12. Static electricity is a buildup of charges.

13. An object is charged if it has more or less than its normal number of electrons. An object can become charged by friction, conduction, or induction. Friction: Electrons are rubbed off one object onto another object. Conduction: One charged object touches another and transfers charges. Induction: A charged object is near a neutral object, causing a rearrangement of charges in the neutral object.

14. Once static electricity builds up, objects can return to their neutral state by releasing electrons. Lightning is the sudden discharge of electrons.

15. Ohm's Law states that resistance equals the voltage divided by current. Ohm's Law relates current, resistance, and voltage.

16. Volts, amperes (amps), and ohms

17. An ammeter measures current. A voltmeter measures voltage. Ammeters are wired in series. Voltmeters are wired in parallel.

18. Samples: Never handle electric appliances while in water, since some water contains ions which conduct electricity; never handle frayed wires; never overload a circuit; never touch power lines.

19. Both fuses and circuit breakers open a circuit when the current is too great. A fuse does so by melting, thereby breaking the path of electrons. A circuit breaker does so by opening a switch.

20. Students' letters should describe the features of both types of circuits. They should point out that a parallel circuit will enable them to switch off certain

---

Reviewing Content

Multiple Choice
Choose the letter of the answer that best completes each statement.

1. A particle that carries a negative electric charge is called a(n)
  a. neutron. **b.** atom.
  c. proton. **d.** electron.

2. When you charge an electroscope by touching it with a charged balloon, the process is called
  a. friction. **b.** conduction.
  c. induction. **d.** grounding.

3. The potential difference that causes charges to move in a circuit is
  a. voltage.
  b. resistance.
  c. current.
  d. electric discharge.

4. An example of a voltage source is a
  a. voltmeter. **b.** battery.
  c. resistance. **d.** switch.

5. A circuit that is connected to Earth is said to be
  a. series. **b.** parallel.
  c. grounded. **d.** discharged.

True or False
If the statement is true, write true. If it is false, change the underlined word or words to make the statement true.

6. Your hair might be attracted to your comb as your hair and the comb become <u>oppositely</u> charged.

7. A neutral object becomes negatively charged when it <u>loses</u> electrons.

8. <u>Conduction</u> is the process of charging an object without touching it.

9. Electrical resistance is low in a good <u>conductor</u>.

10. A <u>circuit breaker</u> contains a thin strip of metal that melts if too much current passes through it.

Checking Concepts
11. Describe the electric field surrounding a charge.

12. What is static electricity?

13. What does it mean to say that an object is charged? Describe the three ways in which an object can become charged.

14. How is lightning related to static electricity?

15. State and describe Ohm's Law.

16. What units are used to measure voltage, current, and resistance?

17. What type of meter is used to measure current? To measure voltage? How should each meter be connected in a circuit?

18. Discuss three safety rules to follow while using electricity.

19. How do fuses and circuit breakers act as safety devices in a circuit?

20. **Writing to Learn** You are an electrician about to design the electrical wiring system for a new house. Your plans call for parallel circuits, but the owners insist that a series circuit will be simpler and cheaper. Write a letter, with diagrams, to the owners explaining why you need to use parallel circuits.

Thinking Critically

21. **Problem Solving** A toaster is plugged into a 120-volt socket. If it has a resistance of 20 ohms, how much current will flow through the toaster coils? Show your work.

22. **Classifying** Identify each of the following statements as characteristic of series circuits, parallel circuits, or both:
  a. $I = V \div R$
  b. Total resistance increases as more light bulbs are added.
  c. Total resistance decreases as more branches are added.
  d. Current in each part of the circuit is the same.
  e. A break in any part of the circuit will cause current to stop.

23. **Applying Concepts** Explain why the third prong of a grounded plug should not be removed.

---

devices without shutting off all the others. Students should illustrate a parallel circuit as it might be designed for a home.

Thinking Critically
21. $\frac{120 \text{ volts}}{20 \text{ ohms}} = 6$ amperes

22. a. both **b.** series **c.** parallel **d.** series
e. series

23. The third prong is designed to send any stray current into the ground. A faulty device might have a casing at a high voltage. A person touching the device would then receive a shock.

Applying Skills
24. Both. Bulbs 2 and 3 are parallel to each other, and in series with Bulb 1.

25. If Bulb 1 were removed, the others would go out because the circuit would be broken. If Bulb 2 were removed, the others would remain lit because the current has another route to follow.

26. None of the bulbs would be lit if the switch were open because the switch breaks the flow of current back to the battery.

27. Students' drawings should show the switch either before or after Bulb 3.

Applying Skills

Use the illustration of an electric circuit to answer Questions 24–27.

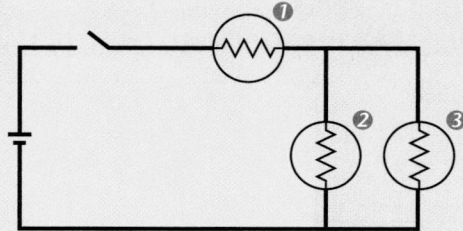

24. Classifying Is the circuit in the illustration series or parallel? Explain.

25. Controlling Variables Would the other bulbs continue to shine if you removed Bulb 1? Would they shine if you removed Bulb 2 instead? Explain your reasoning.

26. Predicting Will any of the bulbs be lit if you open the switch? Explain.

27. Making Models Redraw the circuit diagram to include a switch that controls only Bulb 3.

Performance CHAPTER PROJECT 9 Assessment

Project Wrap Up Prepare a description and circuit diagram for your display. If any parts of your alarm circuit are not visible, you should draw a second diagram showing how all the parts are assembled. Then present your alarm to your class and explain how it could be used.

Reflect and Record Describe the reliability of your switch. Does it work most of the time? All of the time? If your alarm circuit were to be used for a full year, would it still work? Draw sketches in your journal of parts of your alarm that would need to be redesigned so that it would last longer.

Test Preparation
Use these questions to prepare for standardized tests.

Use the diagram to answer Questions 28–30.

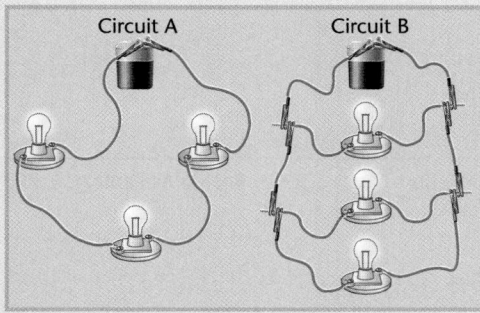

28. What will happen to the remaining bulbs in Circuit A if one of the bulbs burns out?
  a. They will continue to light, but they will be brighter.
  b. They will continue to light, but they will be dimmer.
  c. They will all go out.
  d. They will stay on until the current in the wire is used up and then go out.

29. Which of the following will happen if you add a fourth light to Circuit A?
  a. All of the lights will become brighter.
  b. The brightness of the lights will not change.
  c. The brightness of the lights located after the new light will become dimmer.
  d. All of the lights will become dimmer.

30. What will happen to the remaining bulbs in Circuit B if one of the bulbs burns out?
  a. They will remain lit with the same brightness.
  b. They will go out as well.
  c. They will continue to light, but they will be brighter.
  d. They will continue to light, but they will be dimmer.

Project Wrap Up Many students will need to make final connections and adjustments when they set up their projects. Have four students at a time set up their projects at separate stations. Then the class can move from station to station to see a demonstration of each project. If one student requires more time to set up than others, encourage students to visit the other three stations first. The presenter should ask other students if they can explain how the device works. Then the presenter can fill in the missing pieces of the explanation with remarks and diagrams. Following the demonstration, presenters should turn in one-page descriptions.

Reflect and Record The reliability of an alarm circuit will be affected by the performance of the switch and the effectiveness of the wiring. The batteries and light bulb may not last a year. This could be remedied by using a buzzer rather than a light bulb and using power from an electrical outlet rather than from batteries.

Test Preparation

28. c **29.** d **30.** a

Program Resources

- ◆ **Inquiry Skills Activity Book** Provides teaching and review of all inquiry skills
- ◆ **Prentice Hall Assessment System** Provides standardized test practice
- ◆ **Reading in the Content Area** Provides strategies to improve science reading skills
- ◆ **Teacher's ELL Handbook** Provides multiple strategies for English language learners

CHAPTER 10 Electric Current and Magnetic Fields

Sections	Time	Student Edition Activities	Other Activities
CHAPTER PROJECT 10 **Electrical Energy Audit** p. 309	Ongoing (2–3 weeks)	Check Your Progress, pp. 313, 323, 330 Project Wrap Up, p. 341	**TE** Chapter 10 Project Notes, pp. 308–309
1 Electricity, Magnetism, and Motion pp. 310–315 ◆ 10.1.1 Describe how electrical energy can be converted into mechanical energy. ◆ 10.1.2 Explain how a galvanometer measures current and how an electric motor converts electrical energy to mechanical energy.	2 periods/ 1 block	**Discover** How Does a Magnet Move a Wire?, p. 310 **Real-World Lab: How It Works** Building an Electric Motor, pp. 314–315	**TE** Demonstration, p. 311 **LM** 10, "Electricity From a Lemon"
2 Generating Electric Current pp. 316–323 ◆ 10.2.1 Describe how an electric current can be induced. ◆ 10.2.2 Explain how a generator induces electric current and compare it to a motor. ◆ 10.2.3 Identify the main sources of energy for generating electricity.	1 period/ ½ block	**Discover** Can You Produce Electric Current Without a Battery?, p. 316 **Try This** Keeping Current, p. 318 **Sharpen Your Skills** Classifying, p. 319	**TE** Inquiry Challenge, p. 317 **TE** Demonstration, p. 318 **TE** Including All Students, p. 319
3 Using Electric Power pp. 324–330 ◆ 10.3.1 Define and calculate electric power and usage of electrical energy. ◆ 10.3.2 Describe how transformers increase and decrease the voltage of electric current. ◆ 10.3.3 Describe the transmission of electric current from power station to users.	1 period/ ½ block	**Discover** How Can You Make a Bulb Burn More Brightly?, p. 324 **Sharpen Your Skills** Observing, p. 327	**TE** Real-Life Learning, p. 325
4 *INTEGRATING CHEMISTRY* **Batteries** pp. 331–338 ◆ 10.4.1 Describe how chemical reactions in electrochemical cells produce electric current. ◆ 10.4.2 Explain how electrochemical cells can be combined to make a battery.	1 period/ ½ block	**Discover** Can You Make Electricity With Spare Change?, p. 331 **Science at Home** p. 335 **Skills Lab: Drawing Conclusions** Electricity Grows on Trees, pp. 336–337	**TE** Inquiry Challenge, p. 333 **TE** Demonstration, p. 334 **TE** Real-Life Learning, p. 334
Study Guide/Assessment pp. 339–341	1 period/ ½ block		**ISAB** Provides teaching and review of all inquiry skills

For Standard or Block Schedule The Resource Pro® CD-ROM gives you maximum flexibility for planning your instruction for any type of schedule. Resource Pro® contains Planning Express®, an advanced scheduling program, as well as the entire contents of the Teaching Resources and the Computer Test Bank.

Key: **CTB** Computer Test Bank
      CT Chapter Tests
      ELL Teacher's ELL Handbook

CHAPTER PLANNING GUIDE

Program Resources	Assessment Strategies	Media and Technology
UR Chapter 10 Project Teacher Notes, pp. 58–59 **UR** Chapter 10 Project Overview and Worksheets, pp. 60–63	**TE** Check Your Progress, pp. 313, 323, 330 **TE** Performance Assessment: Chapter 10 Project Wrap Up, p. 341 **UR** Chapter 10 Project Scoring Rubric, p. 64	Science Explorer Internet Site Audio CDs, Section Summaries
UR 10-1 Lesson Plan, p. 65 **UR** 10-1 Section Summary, p. 66 **UR** 10-1 Review and Reinforce, p. 67 **UR** 10-1 Enrich, p. 68 **UR** Real-World Lab blackline masters, pp. 81–83	**SE** Section 1 Review, p. 313 **SE** Analyze and Conclude, p. 315 **TE** Ongoing Assessment, p. 311 **TE** Performance Assessment, p. 313	Presentation Pro, "Electric Charge"; "Electric Motors" Transparency 36, "Electric Motor" Lab Activity Videotape, *Tape 2*
UR 10-2 Lesson Plan, p. 69 **UR** 10-2 Section Summary, p. 70 **UR** 10-2 Review and Reinforce, p. 71 **UR** 10-2 Enrich, p. 72	**SE** Section 2 Review, p. 323 **TE** Ongoing Assessment, pp. 317, 319, 321 **TE** Performance Assessment, p. 323	Concept Videotape Library, *Adventures, Tape 2,* "Generating Electricity"; "Wired to the Sun" Presentation Pro, "Electricity, Transmission and Storage"; "Electromagnets"; "Electricity Generation" Transparency 37, "Induction of Electric Current"; "AC Generator"
UR 10-3 Lesson Plan, p. 73 **UR** 10-3 Section Summary, p. 74 **UR** 10-3 Review and Reinforce, p. 75 **UR** 10-3 Enrich, p. 76	**SE** Section 3 Review, p. 330 **TE** Ongoing Assessment, pp. 325, 327, 329 **TE** Performance Assessment, p. 330	Transparency 39, "Transmission of Electric Power"
UR 10-4 Lesson Plan, p. 77 **UR** 10-4 Section Summary, p. 78 **UR** 10-4 Review and Reinforce, p. 79 **UR** 10-4 Enrich, p. 80 **UR** Skills Lab blackline masters, pp. 84–85	**SE** Section 4 Review, p. 335 **SE** Analyze and Conclude, p. 337 **TE** Ongoing Assessment, p. 333 **TE** Performance Assessment, p. 335	Concept Videotape Library, *Adventures, Tape 2,* "Batteries" Transparency 40, "Dry Cell and Car Battery" Lab Activity Videotape, *Tape 2*
GRSW Provides worksheets to promote student comprehension of content **RCA** Provides strategies to improve science reading skills **ELL** Provides multiple strategies for English language learners	**SE** Study Guide/Assessment, pp. 339–341 **PA** Performance Assessment, pp. 31–33 **CT** Chapter 10 Test, pp. 39–42 **CTB** Chapter 10 Test **PHAS** Provides standardized test preparation	Computer Test Bank, Chapter 10 Test

GRSW Guided Reading and Study Workbook
ISAB Inquiry Skills Activity Book
LM Laboratory Manual

PA Performance Assessment
PHAS Prentice Hall Assessment System
PLM Probeware Lab Manual

RCA Reading in the Content Area
SE Student Edition

TE Teacher's Edition
UR Unit Resources

Meeting the National Science Education Standards and AAAS Benchmarks

National Science Education Standards	Benchmarks for Science Literacy	Unifying Themes
Science as Inquiry (Content Standard A) ◆ **Think critically and logically to make the relationships between evidence and explanations** Students carry out a home electrical energy audit to determine electrical energy use. (*Chapter Project*) Students evaluate the safety of disposing of dead batteries. (*Science and Society*) ◆ **Recognize and analyze alternative explanations and predictions** The dispute between Edison and Tesla involved using AC or DC current. (*Section 3*) **Physical Science** (Content Standard B) ◆ **Properties and changes of properties in matter** In an electrochemical cell, one electrode loses electrons while the other gains electrons. (*Section 4; Skills Lab*) ◆ **Transfer of energy** Motors and generators convert between electrical and mechanical energy. (*Sections 1–3; Real-World Lab*) In a wet or dry cell, chemical energy is converted into electrical energy. (*Section 4; Skills Lab*) **Science and Technology** (Content Standard E) ◆ **Implement a proposed design** Students build a motor and a cell. (*Real-World Lab; Skills Lab*) **Science in Personal and Social Perspectives** (Content Standard F) ◆ **Populations, resources, and environments** Some electrical energy resources are renewable while others are nonrenewable. (*Section 2*)	**1A The Scientific World View** Edison believed the high voltages of AC current would harm people, while Tesla believed the efficiency of AC current outweighed its risks. Tesla's system prevailed. (*Section 3*) **2B Mathematical Inquiry** Students calculate power and the cost of electrical energy using equations. (*Section 2; Chapter Project*) **3B Design and Systems** Students learn how an electric motor works and build an electrochemical cell. (*Real-World Lab; Skills Lab*) **3C Issues in Technology** The inexpensive production of batteries has led to a disposal problem. (*Science and Society*) **4D The Structure of Matter** In electrochemical cells, current is generated as reactants are converted into products. In a rechargeable battery, this current reverses the reaction. (*Section 4; Skills Lab*) **4E Energy Transformation** Electrical energy can be induced by passing a conductor through a magnetic field. (*Section 1*) Electrical energy can be converted into mechanical energy. Mechanical energy can be converted into electrical energy. A galvanometer measures the amount of electrical energy flowing through a circuit. (*Sections 1, 2; Real-World Lab*) Transformers alter the voltage of electrical energy in an alternating current. (*Section 3*) **8C Energy Sources and Use** Electrical energy can be generated from a variety of resources. (*Section 2*) **12A Values and Attitudes** Students examine the controversy between Tesla and Edison. (*Section 3*)	◆ **Energy** Electricity can be converted into many forms of energy, including mechanical and thermal. Energy from a magnetic field can induce electric current. Electrical energy can be generated from many sources, including solar energy, falling water, geothermal energy, and nuclear energy. Transformers can increase or decrease the voltage of electrical energy. Electrochemical cells store energy chemically and convert it into electricity. (*Sections 1, 2, 3, 4; Skills Lab; Real-World Lab; Chapter Project*) ◆ **Unity and Diversity** Electric motors and electric generators both use electromagnets to convert one form of energy into another form. Electric motors convert electric energy into mechanical energy; electric generators convert mechanical energy into electric energy. (*Sections 1, 2; Real-World Lab*) ◆ **Systems and Interactions** When a loop of wire spins inside a magnetic field, current is generated. Electric current can be alternating or direct, depending on the type of generator that produces the current. Wet and dry cells pass electrons from a positive to a negative terminal; a cell is made up of two electrodes submerged in an electrolyte. (*Sections 1, 2, 3, 4; Skills Lab; Real-World Lab*) ◆ **Stability** A magnetic field always exists around a current-carrying wire. (*Section 1*)

Take It to the Net

The **www.phschool.com** Web site provides you with multiple opportunities to incorporate the internet into your instruction.
Go to **www.phschool.com** and click on the Science icon.
Then select Science Explorer Integrated.

Internet Activities provide opportunities for students to review, extend, or assess a concept from the chapter.

■ Have students use the chapter Self-Test to get instant feedback.

■ Hot Links and Reference Links provide opportunities for online research.

STAY CURRENT with **SCIENCE NEWS**®

Find out the latest research and information about electricity at:
www.phschool.com

ACTIVITY	Time (minutes)	Materials Quantities for one work group	Skills
Section 1			
Discover, p. 310	20	**Nonconsumable** books, ruler, insulated or enameled copper wire, steel nail, horseshoe magnet, circuit wire, switch, battery	Inferring
Real-World Lab, pp. 314–315	45	**Consumable** 2 large paper clips, empty film canister, sandpaper **Nonconsumable** D cell; permanent disk magnet; 3 balls of clay; pliers; 2 insulated wires, approximately 15 cm each; enamel-coated wire, 22–24 gauge, approximately 1 meter	Making Models, Inferring
Section 2			
Discover, p. 316	10	**Nonconsumable** 1-m wire, galvanometer or multimeter, horseshoe magnet	Developing Hypotheses
Try This, p. 318	20	**Nonconsumable** 1-m wire, galvanometer or multimeter, bar magnet	Interpreting Data
Sharpen Your Skills, p. 319	10	**Nonconsumable** 2 identical hand generators	Classifying
Section 3			
Discover, p. 324	15	**Nonconsumable** light bulb in socket, hand generator, 1-m insulated copper wire	Posing Questions
Sharpen Your Skills, p. 327	10	**Nonconsumable** household appliances such as toasters, microwaves, mixers, and blenders	Observing
Section 4			
Discover, p. 331	15	**Consumable** paper towels, salt, water **Nonconsumable** penny, dime, metal polish, scissors, stirring rod, mixing cup, voltmeter	Observing
Science at Home, p. 335	home	**Nonconsumable** 2 old D cells, flashlight	Observing, Communicating, Drawing Conclusions
Skills Lab, pp. 336–337	30	**Consumable** 2 apples **Nonconsumable** 2 galvanized (zinc coated) nails about 10-cm long, 2 pieces of copper about the same size as the nails, 4 30-cm pieces of insulated wire with about 2 cm of insulation removed from each end, 2 marble-sized lumps of clay, 4 clothes pins (the "pinch" type with springs), calculator powered by one 1.5-volt dry cell	Drawing Conclusions, Problem Solving

A list of all materials required for the Student Edition activities can be found beginning on page T23. You can obtain information about ordering materials by calling 1-800-848-9500 or by accessing the Science Explorer Internet site at: **www.phschool.com**

Electrical Energy Audit

Students rely on electrical energy every day but often regard it as an invisible, inexhaustible quantity. This project gives them an opportunity to calculate the amount of energy that is used in their homes.

Purpose In this project, students have the opportunity to apply chapter concepts to their daily lives by analyzing energy use in their homes. By the end of the project, they should understand which appliances are heavy electrical energy users and cost the most to operate.

Skills Focus After completing the Chapter 10 Project, students will be able to
◆ observe and measure electrical energy use;
◆ analyze data to determine how much energy is used in an average week;
◆ communicate their findings about the consumption and cost of electricity to their classmates.

Project Time Line This project will take approximately two weeks to complete. Students begin by brainstorming a list of appliances in their homes and making data tables in which they can monitor the use of these items. After recording the amount of time each appliance was used during a one-week period, students calculate energy in kilowatt-hours for all items monitored. Students should then interpret their data, display their observations in a visual format such as a graph, and present their findings to the class. Before beginning the project, see Chapter 10 Project Teacher Notes on pages 58–59 in Unit 3 Resources for more details on carrying out the project. Also distribute to students the Chapter 10 Project Overview, Worksheets, and Scoring Rubric on pages 60–64 in Unit 3 Resources.

Possible Materials Students will need paper for their data tables, writing tools, and calculators. Students may want to use poster board, colored markers, or other materials to prepare their presentations.

Launching the Project Lead a class discussion in which students consider

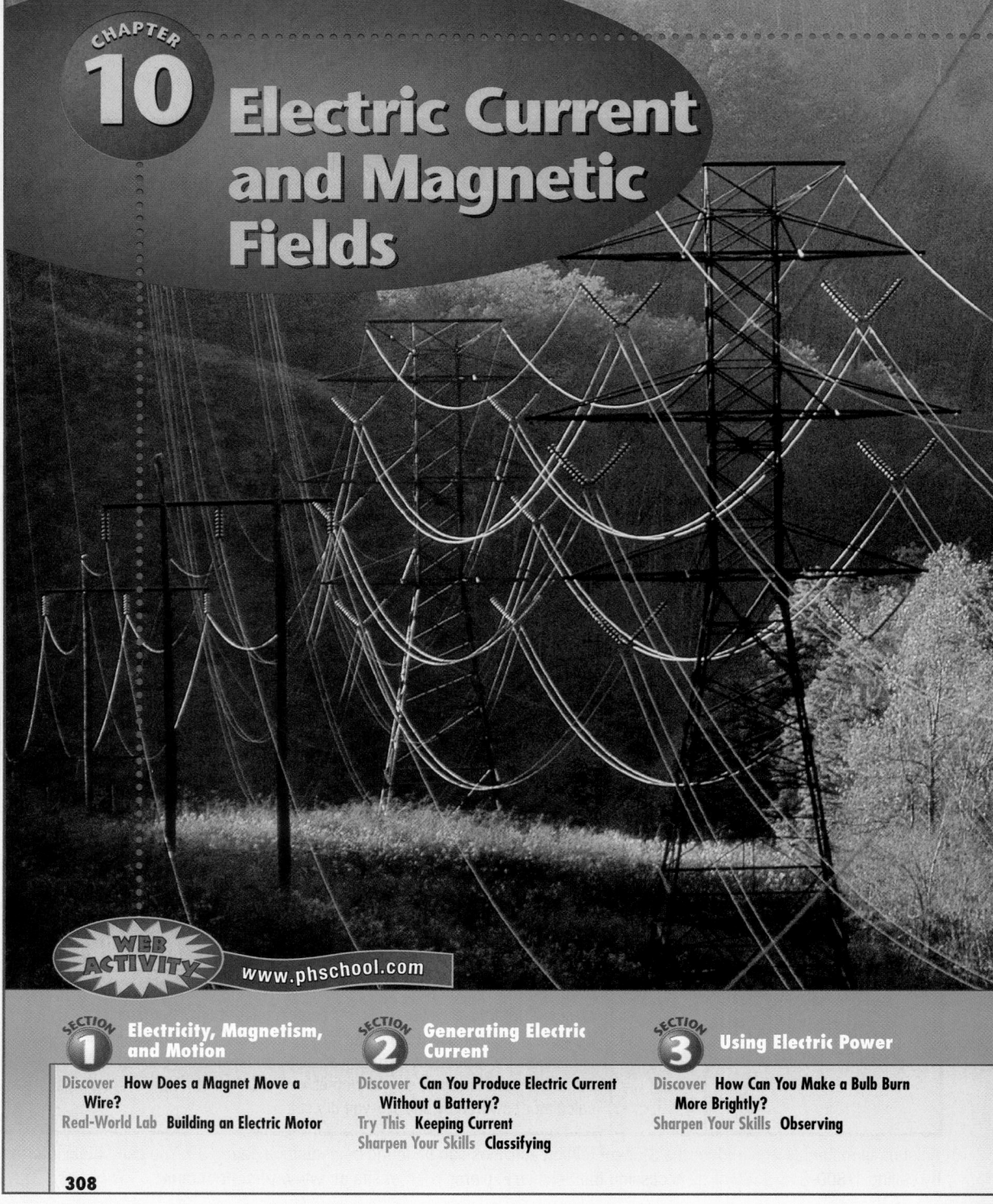

CHAPTER
10 Electric Current and Magnetic Fields

WEB ACTIVITY www.phschool.com

308

which appliances in their homes require the most power to operate and which appliances use the most energy every week.

Allow time for students to read the description of the project in their text and the Chapter Project Overview on pages 60–61 in Unit 3 Resources. Then encourage discussions on the appliances students will monitor. Answer any initial questions students may have and allow time for students to review the Chapter 10 Project Worksheets on pages 62–63 in Unit 3 Resources.

Electrical Energy Audit

Have you ever heard someone complain about high electric bills? Electricity can be expensive, but there are good reasons why. Generating electricity and delivering it to customers is a complicated business.

In this chapter, you will discover how electricity is generated and used. As you work through the chapter, you will study electrical energy consumption in your home.

Your Goal To analyze the ways you use electricity at home and to determine how much electricity you and your family use.

To complete the project you will
◆ prepare a list of appliances in your home, including lights, that use electricity
◆ record the length of time each appliance is used during an average week
◆ calculate how much electrical energy is used to operate each appliance
◆ follow the safety guidelines in Appendix A

Get Started Begin by preparing a data table you can use to keep track of your observations. You should include columns for the name of the appliance, whether it is plugged in or battery operated, the primary use of the appliance, and the number of hours it is used each day.

Check Your Progress You'll be working on this project as you study this chapter. To keep your project on track, look for Check Your Progress boxes at the following points.

Section 1 Review, page 313: List all of the electric appliances in your home.
Section 2 Review, page 323: Calculate the amount of time each appliance is used during a week.
Section 3 Review, page 330: Calculate the amount of energy consumed by each appliance.

Wrap Up At the end of the chapter (page 341), you will calculate the total amount of electrical energy consumed and determine which appliance in your home uses the most electrical energy.

High-voltage transmission lines glisten in the sunlight.

SECTION
4
Integrating Chemistry
Batteries

Discover **Can You Make Electricity With Spare Change?**
Skills Lab **Electricity Grows on Trees**

309

Program Resources

◆ **Unit 3 Resources** Chapter 10 Project Teacher Notes, pp. 58–59; Project Overview and Worksheets, pp. 60–63; Project Scoring Rubric, p. 64

Media and Technology

 Audio CDs Section Summaries

 **WEB ACTIVITY** www.phschool.com

You will find an Internet activity, chapter self-tests for students, and links to other chapter topics at this site.

Performance Assessment

The Chapter 10 Project Scoring Rubric on page 64 of Unit 3 Resources will help you evaluate how well students complete the Chapter 10 Project. Students will be assessed on
◆ the completeness of their data table entries, including the total amount of time each appliance was used during the week and the number of kilowatt-hours each used;
◆ the graphical presentation of their data including style, neatness, labeling, and accuracy;
◆ the thoroughness and organization of their presentations and how well they demonstrate their understanding of the main ideas behind their data.

By sharing the Chapter 10 Scoring Rubric with students at the beginning of the project, you will make it clear to them what they are expected to do.

309

Objectives

After completing the lesson, students will be able to
◆ describe how electrical energy can be converted into mechanical energy;
◆ explain how a galvanometer measures current and how an electric motor converts electrical energy to mechanical energy.

Key Terms energy, electrical energy, mechanical energy, galvanometer, electric motor, commutator, brushes, armature

1 Engage/Explore

Activating Prior Knowledge

Ask students to list devices that use electricity. Then ask: **Which of these devices produce sound? Light? Movement?** (*Student answers will vary depending on the items.*) **What is the energy source?** (*electricity*)

·········· DISCOVER ··········

Skills Focus inferring
Materials *books, ruler, insulated or enameled copper wire, steel nail, horseshoe magnet, circuit wire, switch, battery*
Time 20 minutes
Tips The nail should be parallel to the horseshoe magnet. Test the device in advance to be sure the magnet is strong enough to attract the electromagnet.
Think It Over The electromagnet swings when the switch is closed. It swings in the opposite direction when the battery connections are reversed. Electricity in a wire creates a magnetic field that interacts with the magnet. The force between them causes the wire to move.

SECTION 1 Electricity, Magnetism, and Motion

DISCOVER ···················· ACTIVITY

How Does a Magnet Move a Wire?

1. Make an electromagnet by winding insulated copper wire around a steel nail.

2. Make a pile of books, and place a ruler between the top two books.

3. Hang the electromagnet over the ruler so that it hangs free.

4. Complete the circuit by connecting the electromagnet to a switch and a battery.

5. Set a horseshoe magnet near the electromagnet. Then close the switch briefly and observe what happens to the electromagnet.

6. Reverse the wires connected to the battery and repeat Step 5.

Think It Over
Inferring What happened to the electromagnet when you closed the switch? Was anything different when you reversed the wires? How can you use electricity to produce motion?

GUIDE FOR READING

◆ How can electrical energy be converted into mechanical energy?

◆ What do galvanometers and electric motors do?

Reading Tip Preview the figures and captions. Then read to find out how magnetic forces and electric current are related to motion.

What comes to mind when you think about electricity? You may think of the bright lights of a big city, or the music from the radio in your bedroom. If you are familiar with electric motors like the one in a movie projector, then you already know about a very important application of electricity. Electricity can produce motion.

Electrical and Mechanical Energy

As you have learned, magnets can produce motion. They can move together or move apart, depending on how their poles are arranged. You have also learned that an electric current in a wire produces a magnetic field similar to that of a magnet. So you can understand that a magnet can move a wire, as it would move another magnet.

The wire at the top of Figure 1 is placed in a magnetic field. When current flows through the wire, the magnetic force pushes the wire down. If the current is reversed, the magnetic force pulls the wire up. The direction in which the wire moves depends on the direction of the current.

READING STRATEGIES

Reading Tip Have students preview the figures and captions with partners. Ask them to list unfamiliar terms, leaving space to define the terms as they read the section. Then have them do the same with questions they have about the relationship between magnetic forces and electric current. After students finish reading, have them read their questions aloud and challenge classmates to answer them.

Study and Comprehension After students read the section, have them imagine they are newspaper or television reporters. Ask them to write news stories on one of these topics: Galvanometers, How an Electric Motor Works, the Parts of a Motor. Encourage students to answer the questions What? Why? and How? in their stories. Suggest students use information from the Reading Tip activity in their stories. Invite volunteers to read their stories aloud.

The interaction between electricity and magnetism can cause something to move—in this case, a wire. The ability to move an object some distance is called **energy.** The energy associated with electric currents is called **electrical energy.** And the energy an object has due to its movement or position is called **mechanical energy.**

Energy can be changed from one form into another. **When a current-carrying wire is placed in a magnetic field, electrical energy is converted into mechanical energy.** This happens because the magnetic field of the current makes the wire move.

☑ *Checkpoint* What is energy?

Galvanometers

The upper part of the wire in Figure 1 moves up or down in the magnetic field. What will happen if you place a loop in a magnetic field? Look at the rectangular loop of wire in Figure 2. The current in the wire travels up one side of the loop and down the other. In other words, current travels in opposite directions on the two sides of the loop.

Since the direction the wire moves depends on the direction of the current, the two sides move in opposite directions. Once each side has moved as far up or down as it can go, it will stop moving. The result is that the loop rotates half a turn.

The rotation of a loop of wire in a magnetic field is the basis of a device called a **galvanometer,** which is used to measure small currents. In a galvanometer several loops of wire are suspended between the poles of a magnet. The loops of wire are also attached to a pointer and to a spring, as in Figure 2. When current flows through the wire, the current produces a magnetic field. This field interacts with the field of the magnet, causing the loops of wire and the pointer to rotate. **Electric current is used to turn the pointer of a galvanometer.** The force of the

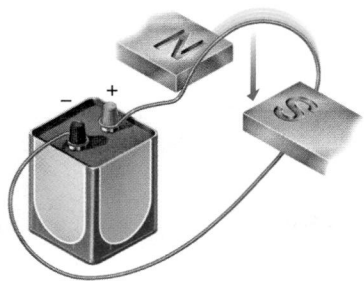

Force is down

Force is up

Figure 1 The magnetic field of the permanent magnet interacts with the magnetic field produced by the current in the wire. *Interpreting Diagrams How does the direction of the current affect the force on the wire?*

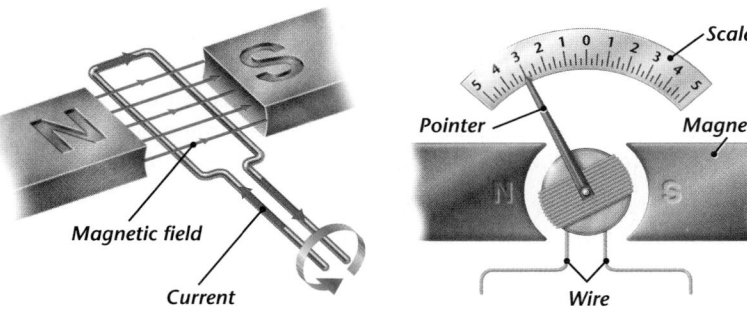

Magnetic field

Current

Scale

Pointer

Magnet

Wire

Figure 2 Since current travels in a different direction in each half of the wire loop (left), one side is pushed down while the other is pulled up. A galvanometer (right) uses loops of wire to move a pointer.

Program Resources

◆ **Unit 3 Resources** 10-1 Lesson Plan, p. 65; 10-1 Section Summary, p. 66
◆ **Laboratory Manual,** 10, "Electricity from a Lemon"
◆ **Guided Reading and Study Workbook** Section 10-1

Answers to Self-Assessment

Caption Question

Figure 1 When the direction of the current changes, the direction of the force changes.

☑ *Checkpoint*

Energy is the ability to move an object some distance.

---

2 *Facilitate*

Electrical and Mechanical Energy

Using the Visuals: Figure 1

Ask: **What is different in the two diagrams?** *(The direction of the current)* Have students describe what is happening in each diagram. *(First: There is a downward force on the wire. Second: There is an upward force on the wire.)* **learning modality: visual**

Galvanometers

Building Inquiry Skills: Interpreting Diagrams

As students examine Figure 2, have them hold one hand flat to represent the loop of wire, then trace the path of current around their hand. Have students move their hands to show what happens when the loop of wire is placed in a magnetic field like the one in the diagram. *(Students should turn their hands sideways.)* **limited English proficiency**

Demonstration

Materials *compass, electrical tape, insulated wire (1.2 m), board (10 × 15 cm), 12-V battery, wire strippers*
Time 20 minutes

ACTIVITY

To build a galvanometer, affix the underside of the compass to the wooden board with a loop of tape, then wrap the wire around the board and the compass, with stripped ends of the wire protruding from opposite sides of the board. Attach the wires to the battery. Ask: **How can you tell when current is flowing through the wire?** *(The compass needle is deflected.)* **learning modality: visual**

Ongoing Assessment

Writing Have students describe how electrical energy can be converted into mechanical energy.

Social Studies CONNECTION

Remind students that until about 100 years ago, electrical appliances did not exist. Encourage students to imagine how they would perform everyday tasks, such as vacuuming, washing clothes, and ironing, without electricity. Invite volunteers who have visited museums dedicated to reproducing early American life to describe some of the tools or methods used by people before electricity.

In Your Journal Students' posters should describe the advantages of using the new electrical appliance. You may want to provide examples of advertisements for students to refer to. Students may be interested in comparing modern newspaper ads to ads from the turn of the century. **learning modality: visual**

Using the Visuals: Figure 3

Have students examine the figure. Ask: **How does the motor convert electrical energy into mechanical energy?** (*The wire loop rotates in continuous half-turns, flipping over every time the current changes direction.*) **learning modality: visual**

Including All Students

Some students may have difficulty remembering the meanings of the terms *commutator* and *armature*. Have students look up the origins of the words. (Commutate—*Latin for "commute or exchange;"* armature—*Latin for "to arm"*) Challenge students to develop memory devices to help them recall the terms. (*Samples: Commute-mutator: the current commutes through the wire; the commutator mutates its direction of travel. An armature with many loops is heavily armed.*) **learning modality: verbal**

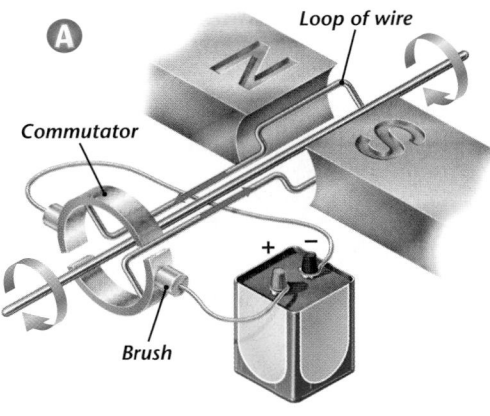

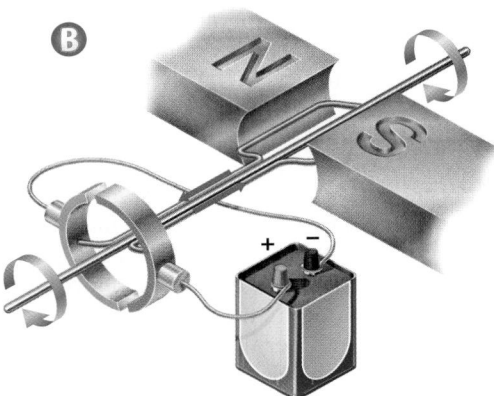

Figure 3 A loop of wire in a motor spins continuously. **A.** The magnetic field of the loop makes it rotate to a vertical position. **B.** As the loop of wire passes the vertical position, each half of the commutator makes contact with the opposite brush. The direction of current flow changes, and so does the direction of the magnetic force on the loop. The loop continues to spin in the same direction.

Loop of wire

Commutator

Brush

Social Studies CONNECTION

The sewing machine was invented before electricity came into general use. Find out about the sewing machine, the refrigerator, or some other household device that was originally operated without an electric motor.

In Your Journal

Sketch an advertising poster that could have been used to introduce the new, electrically operated version of the device. Be sure to show how electricity has improved the machine and the lives of its users.

interaction of the fields acts against the spring. So the amount of rotation of the loops of wire and the pointer depends on the amount of current in the wire. A galvanometer has a scale that is marked to show how much the pointer turns for a known current. An unknown current can then be measured with a galvanometer.

☑ *Checkpoint* How does a galvanometer work?

Electric Motors

The wire in the magnetic field of a galvanometer cannot rotate more than half a turn. Suppose you could make a loop of wire rotate continuously. Instead of moving a pointer, the wire could turn a rod, or axle. The axle could then turn something else, such as the blades of a fan or blender. Such a device would be an electric motor. An **electric motor** is a device that uses an electric current to turn an axle.

An electric motor converts electrical energy into mechanical energy. An electric motor is different from a galvanometer because in a motor, a loop of current-carrying wire spins continuously.

How a Motor Works How can you make a loop of wire continue to spin? The direction of the force on the wire depends on the current and the magnetic field surrounding the coil. In a motor, current is reversed just as the loop gets to the vertical position.

This reverses the force on each side of the loop. The side of the loop that was pushed up on the left is now pushed down on the right. The side of the loop that was pushed down on the right is now pushed up on the left. The current reverses after each half turn so that the loop spins continuously in the same direction.

Parts of a Motor A **commutator** is a device that reverses the flow of current through an electric motor. You can see in Figure 3 that a commutator consists of two parts of a ring. Each half of the commutator is attached to one end of the loop of wire. When the loop of wire rotates, the commutator rotates as well. As it moves, the commutator slides past two contact points called **brushes**. Each half of the commutator is connected to the current source by one of the brushes.

As the loop of wire gets to the vertical position, each half of the commutator makes contact with the other brush. Since the current runs through the brushes, changing brushes reverses the direction of the current in the loop. Changing the direction of the current causes the loop of wire to spin continuously.

Instead of a single loop of wire, practical electric motors have dozens or hundreds of loops of wire wrapped around an iron core. This arrangement of wires and iron core is called an **armature**. Using many loops increases the strength of the motor and allows it to rotate more smoothly. Large electric motors also use electromagnets in place of permanent magnets.

Figure 4 This armature contains hundreds of coils of wire. *Interpreting Photos Where is the axle of the motor?*

 Section 1 Review

1. How can electricity be used to produce motion?
2. What energy conversion takes place in an electric motor and a galvanometer?
3. What measurement can be made with a galvanometer?
4. Describe how the commutator and brushes of an electric motor operate.
5. **Thinking Critically** Relating Cause and Effect Why is it important to change the direction of the current in a motor?

Check Your Progress

CHAPTER PROJECT 10

List the appliances in your home that use electricity. Check your home room by room. Throughout the course of one week, keep a record of the amount of time each appliance is used. Make a row in your data table for each appliance. Each row in the table will contain a space for the amount of time the appliance is used each day. You may want to leave a small note pad and pencil next to appliances used by others.

Chapter 10 **313**

Program Resources

◆ **Unit 3 Resources** 10-1 Review and Reinforce, p. 67; 10-1 Enrich, p. 68

Media and Technology

Transparencies "Electric Motor," Transparency 36

Answers to Self-Assessment

Caption Question

Figure 4 It runs through the center of the armature.

✓ *Checkpoint*

Current passes through loops of wire in a magnetic field. The magnetic field from the wire interacts with the magnet's field, causing the loops of wire and a pointer attached to the loops to rotate.

Building Inquiry Skills: Inferring

Ask students to infer what would happen to a running motor if there were a gap between the brush and the commutator. (*The flow of electricity would be interrupted and the motor would stop turning.*) **learning modality: verbal**

3 Assess

Section 1 Review Answers

1. As current flows through an electromagnet in a magnetic field, a magnetic force will act on the electromagnet and cause it to move.
2. Electrical energy into mechanical energy
3. A galvanometer can measure small currents.
4. As the loop of wire rotates, the commutator rotates against the brushes, which are connected to the battery. The connection allows current to flow in the wire. When the wire reaches its vertical position, each side of the commutator contacts the opposite brush, causing the direction of the current to change.
5. When the wire in a motor turns halfway, it will stop moving. Since the direction of the magnetic field depends on the direction of current, reversing the current allows the loop to rotate a full circle.

Check Your Progress

CHAPTER PROJECT 10

Mention to students appliances they may not have thought about, such as an electric water heater or a furnace fan. Help students approximate electricity use for appliances that run discontinuously throughout the day. For example, a refrigerator uses about 2 kWh/day.

Performance Assessment

Drawing Have students draw a diagram of an electric motor and write captions to describe the relationship of the parts.

313

Building an Electric Motor

Preparing for Inquiry

Key Concept A motor is a device that converts electrical energy into mechanical energy.

Skills Objectives Students will be able to
- make a model of an electric motor;
- infer how the motor can be used to do useful work.

Time 45 minutes

Advance Planning Construct a motor yourself to make sure the materials you have available are appropriate and functional. Test the batteries to be certain they are strong enough to operate the motor.

Alternative Materials If film canisters are not available, use test tubes, glue sticks, thick markers, or any cylinder that is 1.5–3 cm in diameter as a guide for wrapping the coil.

Guiding Inquiry

Invitation Ask students to give examples of electric motors. *(Samples: Remote-control model cars, motors in electric appliances such as refrigerators or vacuum cleaners, electric clocks)* Point out that most electric motors are very similar, even though they may perform very different functions.

Introducing the Procedure
- Show students how to wrap the wire around the film canister.
- Demonstrate sanding the ends of the wire. For best results, hold the coil edgewise while sanding off the lower half of the insulation from one end of the wire.
- The ends of the coil wire are sharp; students must be careful not to poke themselves. If the coil is left on the paper clip supports for more than about 10 seconds, it may become very hot.

Troubleshooting the Experiment

If students have difficulty getting their motor to operate, try the following:
- Check both ends of the wire to see that

one end has all the insulation sanded off and the other has half the insulation sanded off.
- Check the balance of the coil. If it has more weight on one side, it will not spin freely.
- Make sure the paper clips make firm contact with the D cell.
- Try the coil on another group's apparatus.
- Move the paper clips downward so the coil is closer to the permanent magnet.
- Lift the coil, reverse its connections, then set it back on the supports.
- Substitute a stronger permanent magnet.

Building an Electric Motor

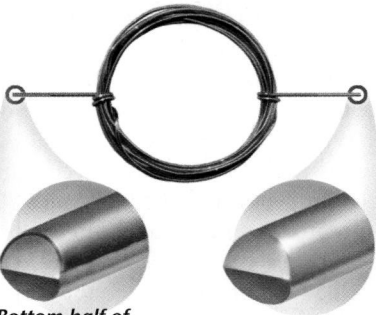

Bottom half of coating removed   *All coating removed*

What does an electric trolley car have in common with a food blender, a computer disk drive, and a garage door opener? At first glance, these things may appear to be unrelated, but each one contains an electric motor. Electric motors are devices that convert electrical energy into motion. In this lab, you will build an operating electric motor.

Problem

How does an electric motor operate?

Skills Focus

making models, inferring

Materials

D cell
2 large paper clips
permanent disk magnet
3 balls of clay
empty film canister
pliers
sandpaper
2 insulated wires, approximately 15 cm each
enamel-coated wire, 22–24 gauge,
    approximately 1 meter

Procedure ✂

1. Wrap about 1 meter of enamel-coated wire around a film canister. Leave approximately 5 cm free at each end.
2. Remove the film canister and wrap the two free ends three or four times around the wire coil to keep it from unwinding.
3. Use sandpaper to scrape off all the enamel from about 2 or 3 centimeters of one end of the coil of wire.

4. Scrape off *half* of the enamel from about 2 or 3 centimeters of the other end of the wire. To do so, hold the coil edgewise and sand off the bottom half. See the illustration above.
5. Bend two paper clips as shown in the photo at the right. Hold them down with clay.
6. Place the free ends of the wire on the paper clips. Make sure the coil of wire is perfectly balanced. Adjust the paper clips and wire so that the coil can rotate freely.
7. Use clay to hold a permanent magnet in place directly below the coil of wire. The coil needs to be able to rotate without hitting the magnet.
8. Remove the insulation from the ends of two insulated wires. Use these wires to attach the paper clips to a D cell.
9. Give the coil a gentle push to start it turning. If it does not spin or stops spinning after a few seconds, check the following:
   - Are the paper clips in good contact with the D cell?
   - Will the coil spin in the opposite direction?
   - Will the coil work on someone else's apparatus?

Analyze and Conclude

1. Current flows when both uninsulated ends of the wire are in contact with the paper clips. Current does not flow when the unsanded half of the wire is in contact with the paper clip.
2. A complete circuit allows current to flow through the motor. A flowing current produces a magnetic field.
3. When the coil becomes magnetic, it is either pulled or pushed by the force of the permanent magnet.

Analyze and Conclude

1. How is the flow of current through the coil related to how you sanded the ends of the enamel-coated wire in Steps 3 and 4?
2. A magnetic field is produced when the motor is connected to the D cell. Explain why.
3. Why does the coil of wire rotate?
4. What was the purpose of removing all the insulation from one end of the wire but only half from the other end?
5. Why did the coil have to be balanced in Step 6?
6. What factors did you find that affected the motion of the coil?
7. **Apply** Your motor is capable of producing motion, but it is not capable of doing much useful work. What are some ways you could modify your motor to make it capable of doing useful work?

Design an Experiment

You have demonstrated the principles of a simple electric motor. List three factors that may affect the motion of the coil. Design experiments to test these factors. What will happen to the motor if the connections to the voltage source are reversed? Try it and find out.

4. When both uninsulated ends are in contact with the supports, the current flows and the coil rotates. If the current did not change, the coil would be able to turn only half way. The insulated part of the wire turns the current off, so the coil is allowed to continue turning. As it turns, the uninsulated parts again complete the circuit. This allows current to flow and the coil turns completely around.

5. If the wires are not balanced, the coil will move unsteadily. This causes one or both wires to lose their connection in the circuit.

6. The direction of the current determined which way the coil moved.

7. Students might suggest adding a foam or cork cylinder at the end of the coil wire and attaching a string so that as the motor turns, it lifts a paper clip or other light object. Other attachments would allow the machine to perform other tasks. Students might suggest that the amount of work the motor performs can be increased by making it more rugged, or larger. Other improvements might include using more cells.

Extending the Inquiry

Design an Experiment Students' plans should identify factors that may affect the rotation of the coil, such as the voltage, whether the coil is balanced, and whether the ends of the wire are insulated. Students should describe experiments to test these variables. Before students perform any work in the lab, check their plans for safety.

Safety

Caution students not to poke themselves with the sharp ends of the coil wire. If coil is left on the paper clip supports for more than about 10 seconds, it may become very hot. Review the safety guidelines in Appendix A.

Program Resources

◆ **Unit 3 Resources** Real-World Lab blackline masters, pp. 81–83

Media and Technology

 Lab Activity Videotape
Tape 2

SECTION
2 Generating Electric Current

Objectives

After completing the lesson, students will be able to

◆ describe how an electric current can be induced;

◆ explain how a generator induces electric current and compare it to a motor;

◆ identify the main sources of energy for generating electricity.

Key Terms electromagnetic induction, alternating current, direct current, electric generator, slip rings, turbine, renewable resource, nonrenewable resource

1 Engage/Explore

Activating Prior Knowledge

Show students a hand-held calculator. Ask: **Where does this calculator get its energy?** *(Samples: A battery, the sun)* In this section, students learn more about ways to generate current in devices such as calculators.

DISCOVER

Skills Focus developing hypotheses
Materials *1-m wire, galvanometer or multimeter, horseshoe magnet*
Time 10 minutes
Tips To save time, set up the wires and galvanometer before the activity. Wear goggles and use wire strippers to remove the insulation from the ends of the wires.
Expected Outcome A current is produced when the wire moves. The faster the wire moves, the greater the current.
Think It Over Steps 4 and 5; if a wire is moved between the poles of a magnet, then electric current can be generated.

DISCOVER · ACTIVITY

Can You Produce Electric Current Without a Battery?

1. Obtain one meter of wire with the insulation removed from both ends.

2. Connect the wire to the terminals of a galvanometer or a sensitive multimeter.

3. Hold the wire between the poles of a strong horseshoe magnet. Observe the meter.

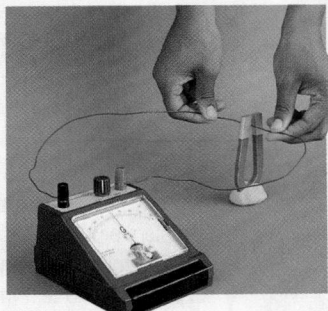

4. Move the wire up and down between the poles. Observe the meter.

5. Move the wire faster, and again observe the meter.

Think It Over
Developing Hypotheses In which steps does the meter indicate a current? Propose a hypothesis to explain how a current can exist without a battery. Be sure to use an "If . . . then . . ." statement.

GUIDE FOR READING

◆ What causes an electric current to be induced?

◆ How is a generator different from a motor?

◆ What are the main sources of energy for generating electricity?

Reading Tip Before you read, preview *Exploring Energy Resources* on pages 320 and 321. Write a list of any questions you have about generating electricity.

A n electric motor operates because electricity produces motion. Is the reverse true—can motion produce electricity? In 1831, scientists found out that motion of a wire in a magnetic field can cause an electric current to flow. That discovery has allowed electricity to be supplied to homes, schools, and businesses all over the world.

Induction of Electric Current

Before you can understand how electricity is supplied by your electric company, you need to know how electricity is produced. Figure 5 shows part of a wire coil placed in a magnetic field. The coil of wire is connected to a galvanometer.

Figure 5 When a coil of wire is moved up or down in a magnetic field, a current is induced in the wire.

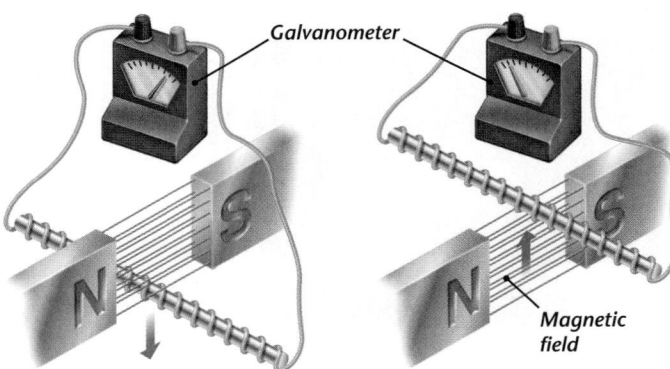

Galvanometer

Magnetic field

316

READING STRATEGIES

Reading Tip Questions may include, "Where is solar energy used?" and "Which energy resource is used the most?" After students read the section and answer their questions about generating energy, have them research one energy resource. Suggest they write facts about the power resource on note cards. Invite volunteers to give brief presentations on their findings.

Study and Comprehension Have students use Venn diagrams to compare and contrast alternating and direct currents. Write the main headings from the section on note cards, one heading per card. Place the cards in a container. Have volunteers select a card, read aloud the heading, and summarize the information from the section that applies to the heading.

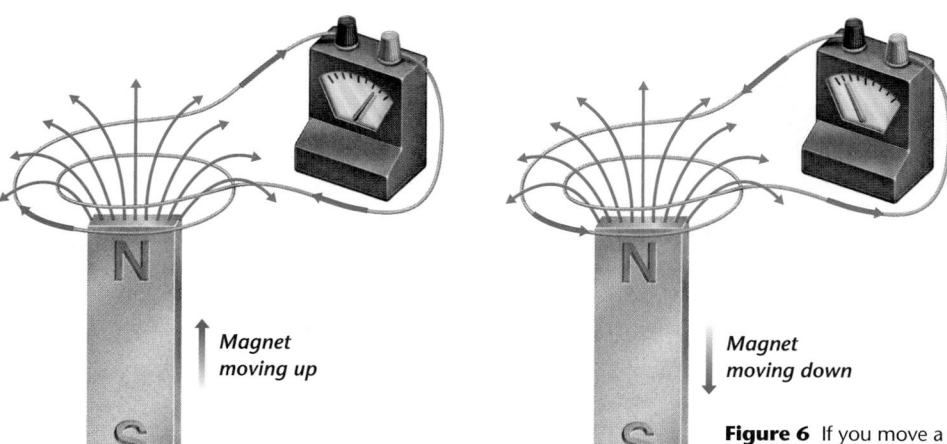

Magnet moving up

Magnet moving down

Figure 6 If you move a magnet up or down through a coil of wire, a current is induced in the wire.
Interpreting Diagrams How does the direction in which you move the magnet affect the current?

If the wire is held still, the galvanometer does not register any current. But if the wire is moved up or down, the galvanometer indicates an electric current flowing in the wire. The current is produced without a battery or other voltage source! You saw this for yourself if you did the Discover activity.

Figure 6 shows a similar experiment in which a magnet is moved instead of a wire. The result is the same as before. An electric current is produced in the wire.

The key to using a magnet to produce a current in a conductor, such as the wire, is motion. **An electric current will be produced in a conductor when the conductor moves across the lines of a magnetic field.** Either the conductor can move through the field of a magnet or the magnet itself can move. If the circuit is closed, a current flows in both cases.

Electromagnetic induction is the process of generating an electric current from the motion of a conductor through a magnetic field. The resulting current is an induced current.

✓ Checkpoint *What are the two ways that a wire and a magnet can produce an induced current?*

Alternating and Direct Current

The direction of an induced current depends on the direction in which the wire or magnet moves. If, for example, the wire in Figure 5 is moved upward, the current travels in one direction. But if the wire is moved downward, the current travels in the opposite direction. **The flow of an induced current may be constant, or may change direction.**

Induction of Electric Current

Using the Visuals: Figures 5 and 6

Ask students to examine Figure 5. Ask: **How is the current produced?** (*The coil of wire is moved up and down between two magnets.*) As students examine Figure 6, ask: **In which diagram in the figure is the current moving clockwise? Counter-clockwise?** (*left; right*) Then ask: **What do the arrows above the magnet represent?** (*The magnetic field*) **learning modality: visual**

Inquiry Challenge

Materials *bar magnet, electromagnet (wire-wrapped nail), galvanometer*
Time 30 minutes

ACTIVITY

Have groups design experiments to demonstrate electromagnetic induction. Each student should perform a task, such as reading the galvanometer or moving the objects. (*Sample: Stroke the magnet along the nail while observing the meter.*) Ask: **What happens when the number of coils is doubled?** (*Current increases.*) **cooperative learning**

Alternating and Direct Current

Building Inquiry Skills: Communicating

Ask: **How can you change the direction of an induced current?** (*Change the direction in which the wire or magnet producing the current moves.*) **learning modality: verbal**

Program Resources

- **Unit 3 Resources** 10-2 Lesson Plan, p. 69; 10-2 Section Summary, p. 70
- **Guided Reading and Study Workbook** Section 10-2

Media and Technology

 Transparencies "Induction of Electric Current," Transparency 37

Answers to Self-Assessment

Caption Question
Figure 6 The direction of current changes when the direction in which the magnet moves changes.

✓ Checkpoint
Electric current can be induced in a conductor when a coil of wire is moved in a magnetic field, or when a magnet is moved through a coil of wire.

Ongoing Assessment

Oral Presentation Ask students to list materials they would need to generate an induced current.

Alternating and Direct Current, continued

Skills Focus interpreting data

Materials *1-m wire, galvanometer or multimeter, bar magnet*

Time 20 minutes

Tips Suggest students record their findings in data tables. Tell students they can increase the strength of the field by using more than one magnet.

Interpreting Data The results are affected by the number of loops, the strength of the field, the direction of the magnet, and how fast the magnet moves.

Extend Using the materials from the activity, challenge students to combine as many factors as they can in order to create the strongest current. **learning modality: kinesthetic**

Addressing Naive Conceptions

Students may believe that direct current is produced by a battery in the same way as a current is induced by a magnetic field. Explain that induced currents are produced when the energy of motion through a magnetic field is converted to electrical energy. Batteries do not involve motion or magnets; they convert chemical energy to electrical energy. **learning modality: verbal**

Generators

Demonstration

Materials *bicycle, bicycle dynamo*

Time 20 minutes

Have students compare the parts of the dynamo to the parts of the generator in Figure 7. Ask: **What causes the axle on the dynamo to turn?** *(The moving pedals of the bicycle)* Have students predict what happens when the pedals turn the axle. *(Sample: Electricity is generated.)* Rotate the pedals quickly so that the dynamo turns the bicycle light on. **learning modality: visual**

318

Keeping Current

What factors affect an induced current?

1. Obtain a wire about one meter long with the insulation removed from both ends.
2. Coil the wire into about 15 loops.
3. Connect the ends of the wire to a galvanometer or multimeter.
4. Move the end of a bar magnet halfway into the coil. Observe the meter.
5. One at a time, change the following and observe the galvanometer: the number of loops, the strength of the magnet, the direction of the magnet, and how far and how fast you move the magnet into the coil.

Interpreting Data Which variables affect your results the most? The least? Explain your observations.

What would happen if a wire in a magnetic field were moved up and down repeatedly? The induced current in the wire would reverse direction repeatedly as well. This kind of current is called **alternating current,** or AC. A current consisting of charges that move back and forth in a circuit is an alternating current. The electric current in the circuits in your home is alternating current.

A current consisting of charges that flow in one direction only is called **direct current,** or DC. A battery produces direct current. When a battery is placed in a circuit, electrons move away from one end of the battery, around the circuit, and into the other end of the battery.

Generators

An **electric generator** converts mechanical energy into electrical energy. An electric generator is the opposite of an electric motor. **An electric motor uses an electric current to produce motion. A generator uses motion to produce an electric current.**

AC Generators A simple AC generator is shown in Figure 7. As the axle is turned, the loop of wire rotates in the magnetic field. One side of the loop moves up, and the other side moves down. This motion induces a current in the wire. The current travels up one side of the loop and down the other.

After the loop turns halfway, each side of the loop reverses direction in the magnetic field. The side that moved up now moves down, and vice versa. As a result, the current in the wire changes direction as well. In this way the generator produces an alternating current.

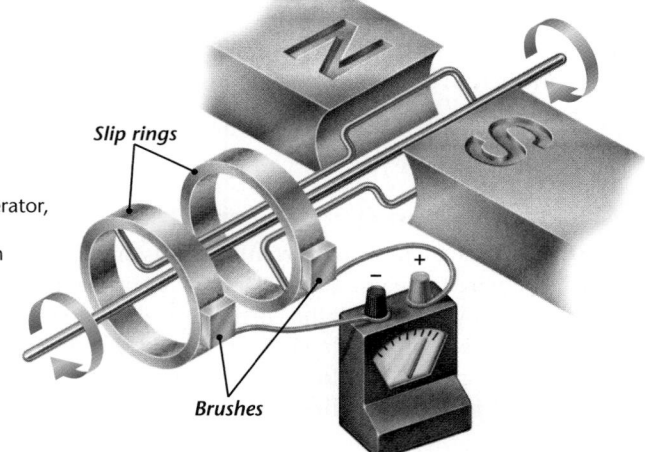

Figure 7 In a simple AC generator, a loop of wire is rotated in a magnetic field. This induces an electric current in the wire. *Applying Concepts How many times does the current reverse direction each time the loop of wire rotates?*

Slip rings

Brushes

Background

Facts and Figures Piezoelectricity is another way to change mechanical energy into electrical energy. Piezoelectricity is caused by the attraction of positive and negative charges on opposite sides of a crystal that is not a good electrical conductor, such as a thin slab of quartz. The crystal must be placed under pressure for the opposite charges to appear. When the piezoelectric effect occurs, the crystal undergoes a physical change, deforming slightly in shape due to the attraction of the opposite charges. By alternating the electric field, the crystal's deformation is also altered. Alternating electric fields cause mechanical vibrations. These vibrations can convert an electric signal into sound waves. Piezoelectricity has been used in phonograph pickups, and is used in electronic equipment, clocks, and watches.

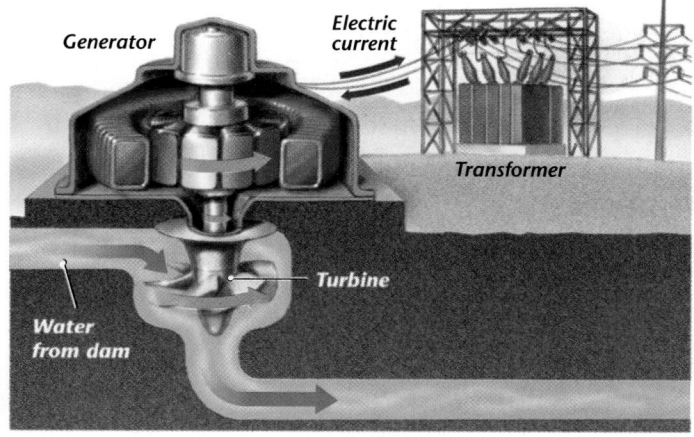

Figure 8 In most generators, a source of mechanical energy turns huge turbines such as this one. The turbine is attached to the armature of a generator, which then produces electric current.

How does the current travel to the rest of the circuit as the axle turns? **Slip rings** are attached to the ends of the wire loop in a generator. As the loop turns, the slip rings turn with it. The slip rings make contact with the brushes. The brushes are connected to the rest of the circuit, just as they are in an electric motor. The slip rings and brushes allow the loop to turn freely, yet still allow current to travel from the loop to the rest of the circuit. Large generators use armatures similar to those in a motor. They contain hundreds of loops of wire wrapped around an iron core.

DC Generators A DC generator is like an AC generator, except that it contains a commutator instead of slip rings. Replacing the slip rings in the generator in Figure 7 will make it look just like the DC motor in Section 1. In fact, a DC generator and a DC motor are the same thing. If you run electricity through a DC motor, it will spin. But if you spin the motor, you will produce electricity. The motor becomes a DC generator.

✓ *Checkpoint* *What is an electric generator?*

Turbines

A generator converts mechanical energy into electrical energy. When an electric company generates electricity, this mechanical energy usually involves huge turbines that turn. A **turbine** is a circular device made up of many blades. The turbine shown in Figure 8 is just like a propeller turned by water.

Not all turbines are turned by water. **Flowing water from a dam, wind, steam from the burning of fuels, and even the ocean's tides can be used to turn turbines.** Several sources of energy are shown in *Exploring Energy Resources* on the next two pages.

Sharpen your Skills

Classifying   ACTIVITY

1. Connect the wires from two hand generators to each other.
2. Have a partner hold one generator as you turn the crank on the other.
3. Now hold your generator as your partner turns the crank on the other one. Do not crank both generators at the same time.

Which hand generator acts like a motor and which acts like a generator? How do you know?

Media and Technology

 Transparencies "AC Generator," Transparency 38

Answers to Self-Assessment

Caption Question

Figure 7 Twice

✓ *Checkpoint*

An electric generator is a device that uses motion to produce electric current.

Sharpen your Skills

Classifying

Materials *2 identical hand generators*

Time 10 minutes

Tips Place the generators at one station and allow partners to take turns cranking. If the second generator does not crank, make sure the wire connections are tight.

Expected Outcome As one generator is cranked, the other crank also turns. As one is reversed, the other is also reversed.

Classifying The hand generator being cranked acts as a generator; it converts mechanical energy to electrical energy. The hand generator that is turned by the current acts as a motor; it converts electrical energy to mechanical energy.

Extend Ask: **How could you determine whether all the energy is converted to mechanical energy by the motor?** (*Turn the first crank 20 times and count the number of times the second crank turns. Usually some energy is lost to friction, so the second crank may turn slightly less than 20 times.*) **learning modality: kinesthetic**

Turbines

Including All Students

Materials *pinwheel*

Time 5 minutes

To help students understand how moving air can create enough power to spin a turbine, have students blow gently on pinwheels. (*The pinwheel spins slowly.*) Then ask: **What will happen if you blow harder?** (*The pinwheel will spin faster.*) Finally, have students infer what would happen if the pinwheel were connected to the armature of a generator. (*The faster the pinwheel spins, the more electricity will be generated.*) **limited English proficiency**

Ongoing Assessment

Drawing Ask students to draw and label the parts of a motor.

Turbines, continued

EXPLORING

Energy Resources

As students read about each energy source, have them identify the kind of energy that is used to provide electrical energy. For example, ask students

◆ **How does tidal energy turn a turbine?** *(When the tide moves large amounts of water, the water pushes the turbine.)* **What kind of energy is this?** *(Mechanical energy)*

◆ **What energy conversions take place when the sun's rays bounce off the reflective material and heat the water?** *(Light energy is converted into heat. The steam from the boiling water provides mechanical energy to turn the turbine and produce electrical energy.)*

Have students describe how fossil fuel energy can be converted into electrical energy. Ask: **What are the energy conversions that change fossil fuel energy into electrical energy?** *(Fossil fuel energy is chemical energy that is converted to heat; heat is converted to mechanical energy; mechanical energy is converted to electrical energy.)*

Extend Challenge groups of students to make flowcharts that show the energy conversions carried out by each energy resource. **learning modality: visual**

Portfolio Students can save their flowcharts in their portfolios.

EXPLORING Energy Resources

Electric power can be produced in several ways. Each kind of generating plant converts a particular kind of energy into electrical energy.

Solar Energy
The sun's rays can be focused on a tower by large mirrors to boil water. The resulting steam then turns a turbine. One type of solar cell can also collect the sun's energy and convert it directly into electrical energy.

Nuclear Energy
A tremendous amount of energy is stored in the nucleus of an atom. When the nucleus is split, the energy that is released is used to heat water. The water turns into steam, which expands and turns a turbine.

Energy From Falling Water
Hydroelectric plants near the bases of dams or waterfalls use water to turn turbines.

Background

History of Science The oldest dam known was built along the Nile River in Egypt about 5,000 years ago to supply water for the city of Memphis. When the Romans conquered parts of Spain, they left dams behind. Two of these, built with stone faces and filled with earth, still function. Few technological advances in dam construction appeared until the Industrial Revolution. By the mid-nineteenth century, scientists began to apply

an understanding of structural engineering and the geological properties of soils and rocks to build taller, longer-lasting dams. As the physical structure of dams became more resistant to the forces of flood waters and shifting soils, new designs were developed; but the principal materials for building dams has remained the same. Most modern dams are still constructed out of stone masonry, concrete, and soil.

Geothermal Energy
In a few locations on Earth, underground water heated by molten rock turns to steam. This steam, which can be obtained through steam vents or drilling, is then used to turn a turbine.

Energy From Fossil Fuels
Coal, natural gas, and oil can be burned in generating plants to produce steam. The steam pushes against the blades of a turbine, causing it to turn.

Energy From Wind
A windmill is essentially a turbine. As the wind blows, it turns the blades of the windmill, which then turn a generator.

Tidal Energy
As tides move in and out in a basin behind a dam, the moving water can be used to turn a turbine.

Social Studies Connection

Challenge students to find out how electrical energy is generated in your area. Suggest students find out by calling the local power company or your city services department. Place a local map in the classroom, and have students place colored pins or flags where the power plants are located. Ask students to infer why your community chose a particular type of power plant for generating electricity. *(Samples: A large river or dam is available to generate hydroelectric power; plentiful fossil fuels are available for a fossil-fuel plant; steam vents are abundant to generate power geothermally.)* **learning modality: verbal**

Including All Students

Ask students to name different electrical devices they used this morning. Prompt them by asking questions such as: **Did you use an alarm clock to wake up? Did you use a hairdryer?** Suggest they also think about household appliances and toys. Then encourage students to discuss how their routines would change if the local power plant announced a severe power shortage due to lack of a nonrenewable resource. On the board, create lists of high-priority and low-priority uses for electricity in homes, as well as for the whole community.
learning modality: verbal

Media and Technology

 Concept Videotape Library
Adventures, Tape 2, "Generating Electricity"; "Wired to the Sun"

Ongoing Assessment

Oral Presentation Ask each student to describe two ways to produce electric power.

Generating Electricity

Using the Visuals: Figure 9

Have students examine the circle graph and Figure 10 below it. Ask: **According to the graph, which energy source is used the most?** *(coal)* Based on the pros and cons listed in Figure 10, have students infer why this is the most common energy source. *(Coal is inexpensive and abundant.)* Have students determine which sources on the graph are used the least. *(Natural gas, hydroelectric, petroleum, and other)* Ask: **What types of energy sources fall in the "other" category on the graph?** *(Wind, sun, geothermal, and tides)* Next have students identify the sources that can be used with the least damage to the environment. *(Tides, sun, wind)* Ask students to infer why these energy sources are not commonly used. *(Sample: They are costly to set up or impractical in some areas.)* **learning modality: logical/mathematical**

Integrating Environmental Science

Ask students: **Which of the energy sources in Figure 9 are renewable? Nonrenewable?** *(Renewable: hydroelectricity, wind, sun, geothermal power, tides; nonrenewable: coal, oil, natural gas, nuclear power)* **learning modality: verbal**

Building Inquiry Skills: Classifying

Encourage students to identify the ultimate source of the stored chemical energy in fossil fuels. *(The sun)* Then use student input to draw a flowchart on the board that shows the flow of energy from the sun to natural processors *(Plant and animal life)*, to fossil fuels *(Coal, natural gas, and oil)*, to man-made processors *(Electricity-generating stations and oil refineries)*, and finally to principal users *(Industrial power, heating, cooling, lighting, transportation, etc.)*. **learning modality: verbal**

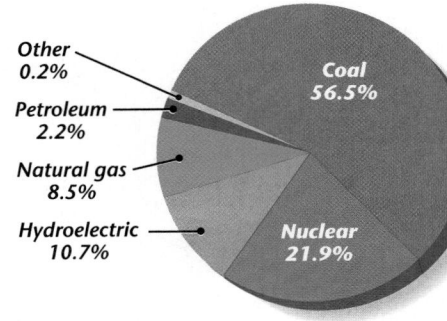

Energy Resources

- Other 0.2%
- Petroleum 2.2%
- Natural gas 8.5%
- Hydroelectric 10.7%
- Coal 56.5%
- Nuclear 21.9%

Figure 9 This circle graph shows which energy resources are used most commonly to generate electricity in the United States.

Generating Electricity

The leading resources for generating electricity in the United States are shown in the graph in Figure 9. Energy resources are limited by their availability on Earth. So not all energy resources are used as readily as others. Some resources have very small roles in generating electricity. Unless you live in certain parts of the United States, you may never have seen an array of windmills, solar mirrors, or even a dam. One thing to remember about the graph is that it shows only resources used to generate electricity. The gasoline that is burned in cars, and the natural gas that heats houses, are not shown here.

Cost is a very important factor in the generation of electricity. But the cost in dollars and cents is not the only thing to consider. Figure 10 summarizes some of the major positive and negative features of these energy resources.

Figure 10 No energy resource is ideal. All have positive and negative features.
Interpreting Tables What are the cons of hydroelectric energy?

Pros and Cons of Energy Resources

Resource	Pros	Cons
Coal	Moderate cost, large supply	Large deposits are localized. Mining damages land and water and is hazardous to miners. Burning coal produces air pollution.
Oil	Moderate cost, adequate supply	Large deposits are localized, and prices are variable. Oil spills damage land and water.
Natural gas	Moderate cost, adequate supply	Large deposits are localized.
Nuclear power	No air pollution	Construction of reactors is expensive. Waste disposal is an unsolved problem. There is a threat of nuclear accidents.
Hydroelectricity	Low cost, no wastes	Unused sites for dams are rare. Dams flood large areas and disturb wildlife in rivers.
Wind	Moderate cost, no wastes, inexhaustible supply	Winds are variable. Wind farms require large areas of land.
Sun	No wastes, inexhaustible supply	Solar generating plants are expensive. Sunlight varies with weather and time of day. Generating plants require large areas of land.
Geothermal power	Moderate cost, low operating costs	Geothermal sites are uncommon. Air pollution may be produced along with steam.
Tides	No wastes	Tidal sites are very uncommon. Power varies with tides. Construction is expensive.

Background

Integrating Science Burning fossil fuels release gases and particles into the air. In large quantities, these substances can endanger human health as well as the health of nearby ecosystems. Fossil-fuel combustion waste products, such as carbon monoxide, react in the presence of sunlight to form a brownish haze called smog. In Mexico City, smog and air pollution can reach levels in which simply breathing the outside air can be damaging. Climatic conditions can also increase air pollution problems. For example, during temperature inversions, Denver, Colorado, experiences a persistent cloud of smog that stalls over the city because the Rocky Mountains block the air from circulating. Using low-pollutant fuels, cleaning industrial smokestacks to remove particle pollutants, and moving to renewable energy resources for generating electricity will help to clean up air pollution.

One factor that does not appear in the table is carbon dioxide. Burning any fossil fuel releases carbon dioxide into the atmosphere. Scientists believe that the release of carbon dioxide may cause climates all over the world to become warmer. This climate change is called global warming. Reducing the use of fossil fuels would reduce the risk of climate change.

 INTEGRATING ENVIRONMENTAL SCIENCE Some sources of energy in Figure 10 are said to be renewable. A **renewable resource** is one that can be replaced in nature at a rate close to the rate at which it is used. In other words, the supply of a renewable resource is not fixed. Water is a renewable resource because the water supply is continually replaced by rain. Wind energy, tidal energy, geothermal energy, and solar energy are renewable resources as well.

Other sources of energy are said to be nonrenewable. A **nonrenewable resource** is one that exists in a fixed amount. The supply of a nonrenewable resource is limited. The supply cannot be replaced once it is used up. Fossil fuels, such as coal, oil, and natural gas, are nonrenewable resources. As you can see in Figure 9, coal leads all other sources in importance.

It is unlikely that the world's nonrenewable energy supplies will run out in your lifetime. Deposits of coal, in particular, are quite large. The United States has about one fifth of the world's coal. But fossil fuels cannot be replaced. Eventually even the largest deposits will be used up. For this reason, and to reduce the risk of global warming, the world's energy sources will probably shift away from fossil fuels.

Figure 11 A house like this one does not need to be connected to an electrical generating plant. Solar cells produce all of its electricity.

Section 2 Review

1. What is induction of electric current?
2. Compare and contrast a motor and a generator.
3. How is alternating current different from direct current?
4. Describe the different ways of spinning turbines to generate electricity.
5. **Thinking Critically** **Comparing and Contrasting** What is the difference between a renewable and a nonrenewable energy source? Give an example of each.

Check Your Progress CHAPTER PROJECT 10
After one week, add the numbers in the row indicating the daily use for each appliance. This will tell you the number of hours the appliance was used in a week. (*Hint:* Convert minutes to decimal portions of hours. For example, 6 minutes = 0.1 hour.)

Program Resources

◆ **Unit 3 Resources** 10-2 Review and Reinforce, p. 71; 10-2 Enrich, p. 72

Answers to Self-Assessment

Caption Question

Figure 10 The cons of hydroelectricity are that power sites are rare, and dams flood large areas and disturb wildlife in rivers.

3 Assess

Section 2 Review Answers

1. Induction is the process of producing a current from the motion of a loop of wire in a magnetic field.
2. A motor and a generator both have a magnet, a rotating armature, a complete electrical circuit, and a commutator. A motor uses electrical energy to produce motion, while a generator uses motion to produce electricity.
3. Alternating current changes direction repeatedly. Direct current moves in only one direction.
4. A turbine can be spun by water falling, wind power, the motion of the tides, steam produced from burning fossil fuels, geothermal energy, solar energy, or nuclear energy.
5. A renewable resource, such as water, can be replaced in nature at a rate close to the rate at which it is used. A nonrenewable resource, such as fossil fuel, exists in a fixed amount.

Check Your Progress CHAPTER PROJECT 10
Make sure students make daily entries into their data tables. As they begin to total the amount of time each appliance was in use, help them convert minutes to decimal hours so they can compare results more easily. For example:
6 min = 6 min ÷ (60 min/h) = 0.1 h

Performance Assessment

Drawing Have groups of students design simple electrical power plants that use one energy resource. They should label the energy source, the turbine, and the generator.

 Students can save their designs in their portfolios.

SECTION 3 Using Electric Power

Objectives

After completing the lesson, students will be able to
- define and calculate electric power and usage of electrical energy;
- describe how transformers increase and decrease the voltage of electric current;
- describe the transmission of electric current from power stations to users.

Key Terms power, transformer, step-up transformer, step-down transformer

1 Engage/Explore

Activating Prior Knowledge

Have students brainstorm simple ways that people can save money on their electric bills. *(Samples: Turn down the thermostat in winter; turn off lights when you leave the room.)* Then ask: **Why will doing these things save you money?** *(Because you have to pay for the electricity you use, using less electricity will save you money.)*

 DISCOVER

Skills Focus posing questions
Materials *light bulb in socket, hand generator, 1-m insulated copper wire*
Time 15 minutes
Tips Test the bulb in advance to determine how rapidly students can crank the generator without burning the bulb out; caution students not to exceed that amount. Prepare the wire by removing the insulation from the ends. This activity can be set up in stations that students visit in turn.
Think It Over The faster you crank the generator, the brighter the bulb shines. Sample question: Is there a speed below which no light is produced?

SECTION 3 Using Electric Power

DISCOVER · ACTIVITY

How Can You Make a Bulb Burn More Brightly?

1. Attach a light bulb in its socket to a hand generator as shown.
2. Slowly crank the generator. Observe the brightness of the bulb.
3. Crank the generator a little faster and again observe the bulb.
4. Crank the generator quickly and observe the bulb once more.

Think It Over
Posing Questions How does the speed at which you crank the generator affect the brightness of the bulb? What questions do you need to ask to explain how the rate of generating electrical energy is related to the brightness of the bulb?

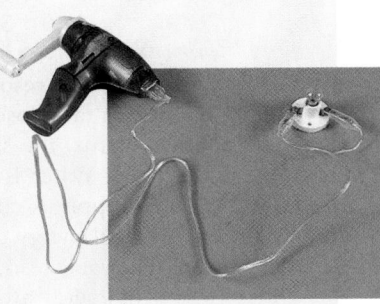

GUIDE FOR READING

- How can you calculate power and energy use?
- What is the function of a transformer?
- What makes alternating current suitable for long-distance transmission of energy?

Reading Tip As you read, use the headings in the section as an outline. Take notes in order to add details to your outline.

When you turn on an electrical appliance such as a toaster, stove, or microwave oven, you are using electrical energy. Each of these appliances converts electrical energy into heat. You can feel the heat given off as the appliance and its contents warm up. When you want heat, you usually want to convert a large amount of electrical energy in a short time. This is the same as saying you want a high rate of energy conversion.

Figure 12 Arc welding produces a white-hot glow as electrical energy is converted into heat.

READING STRATEGIES

Reading Tip Suggest that students preview the section and use the headings to prepare the outline in advance, leaving space below each heading to add details. Outlines will begin as shown.

I. Using Electric Power
   A. Electric Power
      1. Power Ratings
      2. Calculating Power
   B. Paying for Energy
   C. Transformers
   D. Changing Voltage
   E. The War of the Currents

Electric Power

The rate at which energy is converted from one form into another is known as **power.** The unit of power is the watt (W), named for inventor James Watt. Watt made important improvements to the steam engine in the 1700s.

Power Ratings You are already familiar with different amounts of electric power. The power rating of a bright light bulb, for example, might be 100 W. The power rating of a dimmer bulb might be 60 W. The bright light bulb converts (or uses) electrical energy at a faster rate than a dimmer bulb.

Calculating Power The power used by a bulb or appliance depends on two factors: voltage and current. **You can calculate power by multiplying voltage by current.**

$$Power = Voltage \times Current$$

or

$$Watts = Volts \times Amps$$

Using the symbols P for power, V for voltage, and I for current, this equation can be rewritten.

$$P = V \times I$$

You can rearrange this equation to solve for current.

$$I = \frac{P}{V}$$

Current is equal to power divided by voltage. As long as you have any two of the values in the equation, you can solve for the third.

Power Ratings for Common Appliances

Appliance	Power (W)
Stove	6,000
Clothes dryer	5,400
Water heater	4,500
Washing machine	1,200
Dishwasher	1,200
Hair dryer	1,200
Iron	1,100
Microwave oven	1,000
Coffee maker	1,000
Toaster	850
Food processor	500
Fan	240
Color television	100
Clock radio	12

Figure 13 Electrical appliances use energy at different rates. *Applying Concepts How many microwave ovens use the same amount of power as one stove?*

Sample Problem

A household light bulb has approximately 0.5 amps of current flowing through it. Since the standard household voltage is 120 volts, what is the power rating for this bulb?

Analyze. You know the current and the voltage. You need to find the power.

Write the formula. $P = V \times I$

Substitute and solve. $P = V \times I = 120 \text{ volts} \times 0.5 \text{ amps} = 60 \text{ watts}$

Think about it. The answer is reasonable, because 60 watts is a common rating for household light bulbs.

Practice Problems
1. A flashlight bulb uses two 1.5-volt batteries in series to create a current of 0.5 amps. What is the power rating of the bulb?
2. A hair dryer has a power rating of 1,200 watts and uses a standard voltage of 120 volts. What is the current through the hair dryer?

Program Resources

◆ **Unit 3 Resources** 10-3 Lesson Plan, p. 73; 10-3 Section Summary, p. 74
◆ **Guided Reading and Study Workbook** Section 10-3

Answers to Self-Assessment

Caption Question
Figure 13 six

2 Facilitate

Electric Power

Real-Life Learning

Materials *2 light bulbs of different wattages, lamp*
Time 10 minutes

Some light bulb manufacturers produce bulbs with power ratings slightly lower than standard wattages. Have students compare the brightness of a bulb of standard wattage and one of slightly lower wattage, which uses less energy and costs less to operate. Ask: **Is the reduction in power noticeable?** (*Not usually*) Then ask: **Are the low-wattage bulbs a good buy?** (*Yes; the difference is minimal and the bulbs cost less to operate.*) **learning modality: visual**

Sample Problem

Write $P = V \times I$ on the board. Have a volunteer translate the symbols into words. (*Power equals voltage times current.*) Ask: **How would you change the equation to find the value for current?** ($I = P \div V$) Then ask: **What equation would you use to solve the first practice problem?** ($P = V \times I$) **What should you substitute for the V?** (*1.5 V + 1.5 V = 3 V*) Then ask: **What should you substitute for the I?** (*0.5 amps*)

Practice Problems
1. 3 volts $\times$ 0.5 amps = 1.5 watts
2. 1,200 watts $\div$ 120 volts = 10 amps
learning modality: logical/ mathematical

Ongoing Assessment

Skills Check Have students calculate the power rating for a battery-powered radio that uses six 1.5-V batteries and creates a current of 0.5 amps.
(*9 V $\times$ 0.5 amps = 4.5 watts*)

Paying for Energy

Real-Life Learning

Show students a copy of an electric bill or obtain a sample bill from the power company. Have students use the equation to find the amount of energy used and the cost of each kilowatt-hour, and then compare their results to the total on the bill. In some communities, the rate charged for electric power varies depending on the time of day when it is used. Allow interested students to use several months' bills to determine the average use or to compare how the seasons affect electrical use. **limited English proficiency**

Including All Students

Students who need additional challenges may enjoy calculating how much it costs to a operate a clothes dryer for 2 hours if the electric company charges 4¢ per kWh. Students can refer to the table in Figure 13 to determine how many watts are used per hour by a dryer. *(5,400 watts × 2 h = 10,800 watts × h; 10,800 watts × h = 10.8 kWh; 10.8 kWh × 4¢/kWh = 43.2¢)* **learning modality: logical/ mathematical**

Transformers

Building Inquiry Skills: Applying Concepts

Have students describe the high-voltage power lines that deliver electric current to their homes. Ask: **Is the voltage of these lines the same as the voltage in the wires in your house?** *(Students should realize that the voltage in outside lines is much higher.)* Encourage students to talk about the dangers presented by the high-voltage lines. *(Students may discuss the danger of being electrocuted by touching the wires or by being near wires that fall down during storms or by accident.)* **learning modality: verbal**

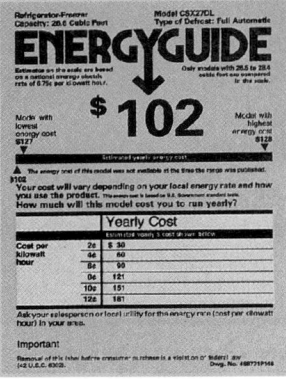

Figure 14 The total electrical energy consumption for your home can be read from a meter like this one.

Figure 15 Most large electrical appliances have labels showing the amount of energy they consume in a year. A typical refrigerator uses more than 700 kWh per year, or about 2 kWh per day.

Paying for Energy

The electric bill that comes to your home charges for energy use, not power. Energy use depends on both power and time. Different appliances convert electrical energy at different rates. And you use some appliances more than others. **The total amount of energy used by an appliance is equal to the power consumption multiplied by the time the appliance is in use.**

$$Energy = Power \times Time$$

$$E = P \times T$$

Electric power is usually measured in thousands of watts, or kilowatts (kW). And time is measured in hours. So the unit of electrical energy is the kilowatt-hour (kWh).

$$Kilowatt\text{-}hours = Kilowatts \times Hours$$

Ten 100-watt light bulbs turned on for one hour use 1,000 watt-hours, or 1 kilowatt-hour, of energy.

The electrical energy that flows into your home is measured by a meter. As more lights and appliances are turned on, you can observe the meter turning more rapidly. The electric company uses the meter to keep track of the number of kilowatt-hours used. You pay a few cents for each kilowatt-hour.

Transformers

Generating electricity costs money, and so your electric company is very interested in efficient ways of transmitting current. The most efficient way to transmit current over long distances is to maintain very high voltages—from about 11,000 volts to 765,000 volts. But electricity is used at much lower voltages (about 120 volts in the United States). How is this problem solved?

Voltage must be increased before it is sent out over the wires from a generating plant. Then it must be reduced again before it is distributed to customers. **A device that increases or decreases voltage is called a transformer.** A **transformer** consists of two separate coils of insulated wire wrapped around an iron core. One coil, called the primary coil, is connected to a circuit in which an alternating current flows. The other coil, the secondary coil, is connected to a separate circuit that does not contain a voltage source.

326

Background

Integrating Science One application of step-up transformers is electron microscopes. A scanning electron microscope is designed to scan the surface of extremely tiny objects, such as single-celled organisms. To form the image, a 5- to 25-kilovolt beam of electrons is aimed at the object. The electrons that bounce off the object are then converted to light, and the light is converted to an electric signal that forms a highly magnified image, up to 10,000 times larger than the actual object.

Ordinary transmission electron microscopes send out a beam of electrons with a voltage of 200–300 kilovolts. These electrons pass through the specimen and are collected on a photographic plate, yielding a magnification of up to 250,000 times.

When a current flows in the primary coil, it produces a magnetic field. The magnetic field changes as the current alternates. This changing magnetic field is like a moving magnetic field. It induces a current in the secondary coil.

Can a transformer work with direct current? The answer is no. A transformer works only if the current in the primary coil is changing. If the current does not change, the magnetic field does not change. No current will be induced in the secondary coil.

☑ *Checkpoint* *What are the parts of a transformer?*

Changing Voltage

How does a transformer change voltage? The answer has to do with the number of loops in the coils. If the number of loops in the primary and secondary coils are the same, the induced voltage is the same as the original voltage. However, if there are more loops in the secondary coil than in the primary coil, the voltage in the secondary coil will be greater. A transformer that increases voltage is called a **step-up transformer.**

Suppose there are fewer loops in the secondary coil than in the primary coil. The voltage in the secondary coil will be less than in the primary coil. A transformer that decreases voltage is called a **step-down transformer.**

Step-down Transformer

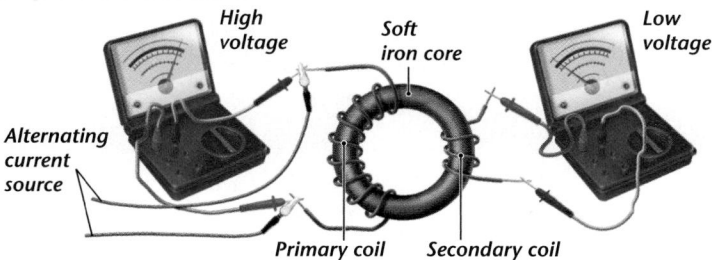

Step-up Transformer

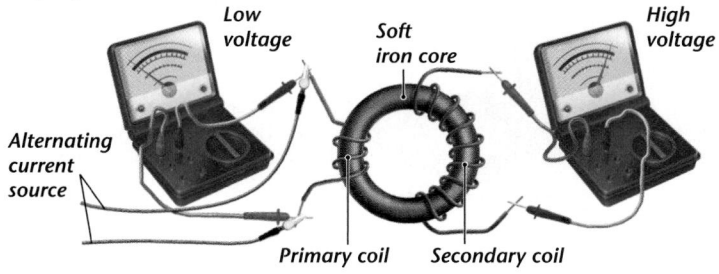

Figure 16 A step-up transformer increases voltage. A step-down transformer decreases voltage.
Comparing and Contrasting Compare the two transformers. Which transformer has a greater number of loops in the primary coil? In the secondary coil?

Sharpen your Skills

Observing

Materials *household appliances such as toasters, microwaves, mixers, and blenders*
ACTIVITY
Time 10 minutes
Tips Review the meaning of AC (alternating current), DC (direct current), W (watts of power), mA (milliamps of current), and V (volts). Some appliances will indicate 110–120 V because household voltage varies within that range. The notation 60 Hz indicates 120 V goes back and forth 60 times/second. Devices that list voltage lower than 120 V may have a step-down transformer. Some appliances adapt current from AC to DC; these may list input as 120 V AC and output as 12 V DC.
Expected Outcome Appliances with high power ratings produce heat.
Extend Have students determine whether the appliances with the lowest power ratings have similar uses.

Changing Voltage

Building Inquiry Skills: Interpreting Illustrations

After students study Figure 16, have them describe how the current in the primary loop creates current in the secondary loop. *(As the current in the primary loop alternates, the magnetic field around the wire changes. This changing field induces a current in the secondary coil.)* Ask: **Could a transformer be made that uses DC instead of AC?** *(No, current must change to induce current.)*
learning modality: visual

Answers to Self-Assessment

Caption Question

Figure 16 The secondary coil has the greater number of loops in a step-up transformer. The primary coil has the greater number of loops in a step-down transformer.

☑ *Checkpoint*

A transformer consists of two separate coils of wire wrapped around an iron core.

Ongoing Assessment

Writing Have students describe the steps necessary to convert 120 V AC to 5 V DC. *(First use a step-down transformer; then convert AC to DC.)*

Changing Voltage, continued

Building Inquiry Skills: Applying Concepts

Ask students: **What kind of appliances need to have step-up transformers?** *(Devices that produce high-voltage outputs)* Then ask: **What kinds of devices need to have step-down transformers?** *(Devices that require less than the input voltage)* Have students brainstorm devices that they think might contain step-up or step-down transformers. Students can read the input/output voltages on the device labels to check their predictions. **learning modality: verbal**

SCIENCE & History

Have students discuss how each development built on the previous ones. Encourage students to think about how experimentation contributed to these discoveries. Ask students to calculate how many years it took from the discovery of electromagnetism to the development of the household current we use today. *(68 years)*

Extend Have students find out what voltage and frequency are used in different parts of the world, such as Germany *(230 V, 50 Hz)*, Japan *(100 V, 50/60 Hz)*, Israel *(230 V, 50 Hz)*, and Argentina *(220 V, 50 Hz)*.

In Your Journal Provide materials for students to learn more about the scientists. Encourage students to be imaginative and include details in their letters. Students may want to describe the scientists' personalities as well as their work. **learning modality: verbal**

Some electrical devices contain tranformers of their own. For example, fluorescent lights, televisions, and X-ray machines require higher voltages than house current. So they contain step-up transformers. Other devices such as doorbells, electronic games, and answering machines, require lower voltages. They contain step-down transformers.

The War of the Currents

Modern electric companies use alternating current and transformers to distribute electric power. But about 100 years ago, there was a great deal of controversy over AC and DC.

The History of Electric Power

Several scientists were responsible for bringing electricity from the laboratory into everyday use.

1820
Electromagnetism

Hans Christian Oersted discovers that an electric current creates a magnetic field. The relationship between electricity and magnetism is called electromagnetism.

1800	1820	1840

1830–1831
Electric Induction

Michael Faraday and Joseph Henry each discover that an electric current can be induced by a changing magnetic field. Understanding induction makes possible the development of motors and generators.

328

Thomas Edison set up one of the first electric companies, the Edison Electric Light Company, in New York City. It supplied direct current at about 120 volts. Current traveling through long wires at that voltage would lose much of its energy in warming the wires. So Edison expected power generating plants to be small and quite close together.

A young immigrant from Croatia, Nikola Tesla, worked for Edison as an engineer for a short time. Tesla felt strongly that distribution of electricity to homes could be done safely and far more efficiently using alternating current. Generating plants could be located far apart. Step-up and step-down transformers

In Your Journal

Find out more about the work of Michael Faraday, Joseph Henry, or Hans Christian Oersted. Write a letter to a friend in which you describe your work as a research assistant for the scientist you choose. Include descriptions of his experimental procedures and the equipment he uses. Tell how his work has led to surprising discoveries.

1893

World's Columbian Exposition

Nikola Tesla's system of alternating current is used to light the world's fair in Chicago.

1860	1880	1900

1882

Direct Current

Thomas Edison opens his generating plant in New York City. The Pearl Street Station consists of six DC generators, serving an area of about 2.6 square kilometers.

1888

Alternating Current

Nikola Tesla receives patents for a system of distributing alternating current.

Chapter 10 **329**

The War of the Currents

Building Inquiry Skills: Posing Questions

Invite students to imagine that they could interview both Tesla and Edison. Have them write ten interview questions to ask each inventor. Encourage students to ask science and technology questions rather than questions of a personal nature. Then pair students and invite them to pretend that they are either Edison or Tesla. Students should try to answer each other's interview questions based on the work of the inventor. Encourage students to find the answers to any questions they have after the activity. **cooperative learning**

Real-Life Learning

Take students outside and have them locate the power line that connects your school to the city electrical supply. Challenge students to identify the transformer on the power line closest to your school. **CAUTION:** *Make sure students do not go near the power lines or transformer.* Have students infer whether the transformer is a step-up transformer or a step-down transformer and explain their inferences. *(Sample: This is a step-down transformer, because it must change the electricity from the high voltage that is carried through the power line to the lower voltage that is used in the building.)* **learning modality: verbal**

Ongoing Assessment

Skills Check Have students create compare/contrast tables showing the advantages and drawbacks associated with using DC or AC to transmit electricity from a power plant to their homes.

3 Assess

Section 3 Review Answers

1. Electric power is the rate at which electrical energy is converted to another form of energy. It is calculated by multiplying voltage by current.

2. Electric companies calculate energy by multiplying the power of an appliance by the time it is used. Electric meters measure energy in kilowatt-hours.

3. A transformer increases or decreases the voltage of an induced current. A transformer consists of two coils of wire wrapped around an iron core. An alternating current through one coil induces a current in the second coil.

4. Step-up transformers are used to increase voltage generated at a power plant, so that the voltage will be transmitted with minimal energy loss. Step-down transformers are used to reduce voltage from power lines to buildings; the lower voltage is safer for people to use.

5. 0.5 kWh = 500 watt-hours. 500 watt-hours ÷ 15 watts = 33.3 hours

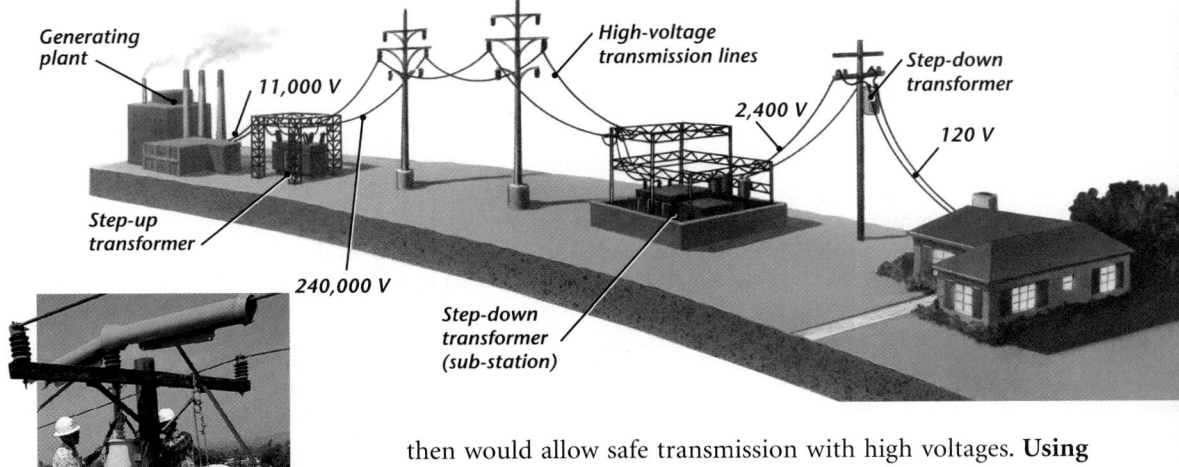

Check Your Progress

CHAPTER PROJECT 10

Appliances such as refrigerators, electric clothes dryers, furnaces, and air conditioners may have inaccessible appliance plates. Suggest students compile a class list of such appliances and contact the manufacturer or a local repair shop to find out the voltages and wattages.

Figure 17 Voltage is increased and decreased as alternating current is transmitted from its source to your home. This photo shows a transformer like the ones you might see in your neighborhood.

then would allow safe transmission with high voltages. **Using alternating current with transformers would reduce energy losses in the long transmission wires.** Tesla invented, among other devices, the first alternating current motor.

Edison thought that high voltages were dangerous. He also wanted to protect his investments in DC generating equipment.

For about 15 years, disagreement raged over which form of current was best. Tesla and the industrialist George Westinghouse eventually won the battle. In 1893 Tesla and Westinghouse were invited to light the World's Columbian Exposition in Chicago using alternating current. The lighting was spectacular! Tesla and Westinghouse were then given a contract for an alternating current system to harness the energy of Niagara Falls. Alternating current was so successful that eventually Edison's own company converted to alternating current as well. Alternating current has been used ever since.

Section 3 Review

1. What is electric power and how is it calculated?
2. How do electric companies calculate electrical energy?
3. How does a transformer work?
4. Explain why transformers are used in the transmission of electricity.
5. **Thinking Critically   Problem Solving** One jelly-filled donut contains an amount of energy equal to about 0.5 kilowatt-hours. If that energy could be converted into electrical energy, how long would it keep a 15-watt night light lit?

Check Your Progress

CHAPTER PROJECT 10

Determine the power ratings, in kilowatts, of the devices you listed. If power is not indicated on the device, you can calculate it from current and voltage. Find the amount of energy used by multiplying the power by the number of hours the device was used in a week. **CAUTION:** Get permission and adult help before looking for this information, especially on large appliances.

SECTION 4 Batteries

DISCOVER

Can You Make Electricity With Spare Change?

1. Clean a penny with vinegar. Wash your hands.

2. Cut a 2-cm × 2-cm square from a paper towel and a similar square from aluminum foil.

3. Stir salt into a glass of warm water until the salt begins to sink to the bottom. Then soak the paper square in the salt water.

4. Put the penny on your desktop. Place the wet paper square on top of it. Then place the piece of aluminum foil on top of the paper.

5. Set a voltmeter to read DC volts. Touch the red lead to the penny and the black lead to the foil. Observe the reading on the voltmeter.

Think It Over

Observing What happened to the voltmeter? What type of device did you construct?

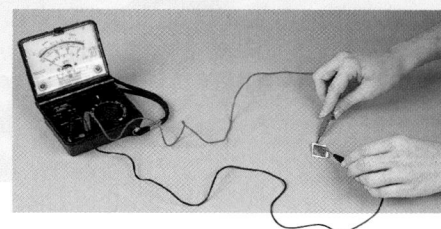

E lectric generators are excellent sources of electrical energy. But what do you do if you need electrical energy on the go? Researchers have put a tracking device on the moose in Figure 18. The moose will carry the device deep into the wilderness. Fortunately, the tracking device contains a battery. Batteries are useful in many devices, such as portable radios, flashlights, toys, and calculators, to name just a few. In this section, you'll find out how a battery produces electrical energy.

GUIDE FOR READING

◆ How can chemical reactions generate electricity?

◆ How does a battery differ from an electrochemical cell?

Reading Tip As you read, write a phrase or sentence defining each boldfaced term, using your own words.

Figure 18 A battery-powered transmitter will allow researchers to study the movements of this brown-eyed, handsome moose.

Chapter 10 **331**

READING STRATEGIES

Reading Tip Before students begin reading, provide them with note cards. Instruct them to write boldfaced terms on one side of the card and definitions on the other side. When students have finished reading, partners can use the cards to quiz each other on the terms.

Program Resources

◆ **Unit 3 Resources** 10-4 Lesson Plan, p. 77; 10-4 Section Summary, p. 78
◆ **Guided Reading and Study Workbook** Section 10-4

SECTION 4 Batteries

Objectives

After completing the lesson, students will be able to
◆ describe how chemical reactions in electrochemical cells produce electric current;
◆ explain how electrochemical cells can be combined to make a battery.

Key Terms chemical energy, chemical reaction, electrochemical cell, electrode, electrolyte, terminal, battery, wet cell, dry cell, rechargeable battery

1 Engage/Explore

Activating Prior Knowledge

Ask students to name the different sizes of batteries that they can buy. *(Samples: D, A, AA, AAA)* Then ask: **What do you think the sizes indicate?** *(All of the samples listed here are 1.5 V; the size indicates length of battery life.)* Students learn more about batteries in this section.

DISCOVER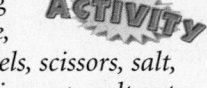

Skills Focus observing
Materials *penny, dime, metal polish, paper towels, scissors, salt, water, stirring rod, mixing cup, voltmeter*
Time 15 minutes
Tips Make sure students mix the salt thoroughly with the water. The paper towel squares should be thoroughly soaked.
Expected Outcome The voltmeter will show a reading of about 3 volts when connected to the circuit.
Think It Over The voltmeter needle moved. Students should recognize that the device they constructed is an energy source for a circuit. Some students may recognize this energy source is a battery.

2 Facilitate

The First Battery

Health Connection

Tell students that doctors and physical therapists often manipulate muscles with electric current. Electric current is now used to treat people paralyzed by injuries or illnesses. A microcomputer is programmed to stimulate muscles in the same way that the nerve impulses normally do. Then in the treatment, microcomputers send electrical impulses into specific muscles. This allows patients to move their limbs to perform tasks such as sitting, standing, and walking. This new treatment is still in the experimental phase, but doctors are hopeful that it will allow patients to be restored to a full range of movement. **learning modality: verbal**

Building Inquiry Skills: Developing a Hypothesis

Ask students to write down Galvani's and Volta's hypotheses as "If . . . then . . ." statements. *(Galvani—If there is electricity present in living tissue, then it will conduct electricity to metals. Volta—If a chemical reaction occurs between two different metals and the salty solution in the frog's leg, then an electrical effect will occur.)* Ask: **What is the major difference between the hypotheses?** *(Galvani believed that the frog itself produced the electrical effect. Volta believed that a chemical reaction took place between the metals and the frog.)* **learning modality: logical/mathematical**

The First Battery

A generator converts energy from one form into another, and so does a battery. Instead of mechanical energy, however, batteries start with chemical energy. **Chemical energy** is energy stored in chemical compounds.

Luigi Galvani The research that led to the development of the battery came about by accident. In the late 1700s, an Italian physician named Luigi Galvani was studying the anatomy of a frog. He was using a brass hook to hold a leg muscle in place. As he touched the hook to an iron railing, he noticed that the leg twitched. Galvani hypothesized that there was some kind of "animal electricity" present only in living tissue. This hypothesis was later proven to be incorrect.

Alessandro Volta An Italian scientist named Alessandro Volta argued that the electrical effect Galvani observed was actually a result of a chemical reaction. A **chemical reaction** is a process in which substances change into new substances with different properties. In this case, Volta believed that a chemical reaction occurred between the two different metals (the iron railing and the brass hook) and the salty fluids in the frog's leg muscle.

To prove his hypothesis, Volta placed a piece of silver on top of a piece of zinc. On top of the silver he added a piece of paper that had been soaked in salt water. Then he repeated the layers: zinc, silver, paper, zinc, and so on. Volta found that if he connected wires to the metals, current flowed. When he added more layers, more current flowed. If you did the Discover activity, you constructed a stack similar to Volta's.

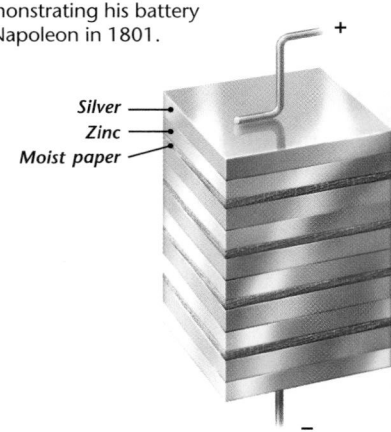

Figure 19 Alessandro Volta stacked metal plates and paper, making the first battery. Volta is shown demonstrating his battery to Napoleon in 1801.

Silver
Zinc
Moist paper
+
−

Background

Facts and Figures Cars powered by batteries were developed in the late 1880s. Up until the 1920s, battery-powered cars were popular because they were easy to maintain and quiet to operate. When Henry Ford introduced the concept of mass production of automobiles, gasoline-powered cars became relatively inexpensive and electric cars became scarce. In the 1960s, the limited supply of fossil fuels spurred engineers to reinvent the electric car. Some modern electric cars use batteries or a battery coupled with a small internal combustion engine. A special motor controller regulates the flow of energy from the battery to the motor, so that the cars can accelerate and slow down. Most cars can drive between 40 and 120 miles before recharging their batteries. Electric cars can operate on a variety of batteries including lead-acid, nickel-metal hybrid, and lithium-ion.

Volta had designed and built the first electric battery. In the year 1800, Volta made his discovery public. Although his battery was much weaker than those made today, it produced a current for a relatively long period of time. It was the basis of more powerful modern batteries.

✓ *Checkpoint* *What metals were used in Volta's experiments on electricity?*

Electrochemical Cells

In Volta's setup, each pair of metal pieces separated by paper soaked in salt water acted as an electrochemical cell. An **electrochemical cell** is a device that converts chemical energy into electrical energy. An electrochemical cell consists of two different metals called **electrodes.** The electrodes are partially immersed in a substance called an electrolyte. An **electrolyte** is a substance that conducts electric current. Volta used silver and zinc as electrodes and salt solution as his electrolyte.

A Simple Cell Look at the electrochemical cell in Figure 20. In this particular cell, the electrolyte is dilute sulfuric acid. Dilute means that the sulfuric acid has been mixed with water.

One of the electrodes in this cell is made of copper and the other is made of zinc. The part of an electrode above the surface of the electrolyte is called a **terminal.** The terminals are used to connect the cell to a circuit.

Chemical reactions occur between the electrolyte and the electrodes in an electrochemical cell. These reactions cause one electrode to become negatively charged and the other electrode to become positively charged. In this case, the zinc electrode becomes negatively charged and the copper electrode becomes positively charged. Because the electrodes have opposite charges, there is a voltage between them. Recall that voltage causes charges to flow. If the terminals are connected by a wire, electrons will flow from one terminal to the other. In other words, the electrochemical cell produces an electric current in the wire. Charges flow back through the electrolyte to make a complete circuit.

How do you know which metal will become the positive terminal and which will become the negative terminal? The answer depends on the metal strips used. Some metals, such as zinc and aluminum, are more likely to release electrons into the wire than other metals, such as copper and silver.

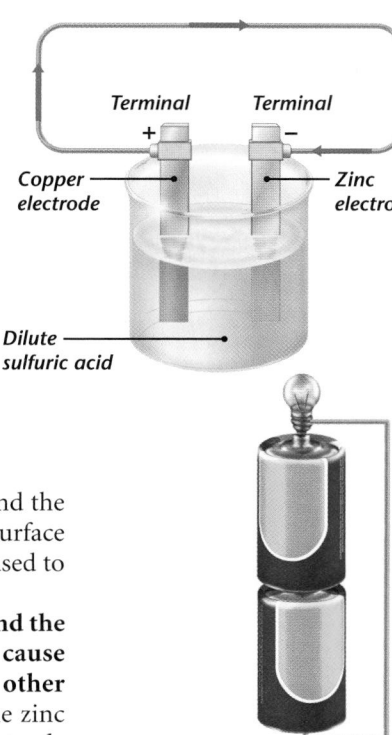

Figure 20 An electrochemical cell consists of two electrodes made of different metals, and an electrolyte. *Predicting What would you expect the voltage to be if you connected two cells together as in a flashlight?*

Inquiry Challenge
Materials *lemon, copper bar, zinc bar, connecting wires, galvanometer*
Time 30 minutes

Challenge small groups of students to design and build an electrochemical cell using a lemon. Ask students to speculate what part of a cell the lemon might be. *(The electrolyte)* Then have students determine how they will use the other materials to build the cell. *(A copper bar and a zinc bar can be electrodes; they will be connected by wires and tested with a galvanometer.)* After students gather their materials, allow them to assemble a circuit using the electrochemical cell. They can test for current by connecting the circuit to a galvanometer. Then ask: **How can you apply your understanding about electrochemical cells to test whether a particular solution would be a useful electrolyte?** *(Place the electrodes in the solution and see if they produce enough current to register on the galvanometer.)*
learning modality: kinesthetic

Answers to Self-Assessment

Caption Question

Figure 20 The voltage would be equal to the sum of the voltages of the cells.

✓ *Checkpoint*
Volta used silver and zinc in his experiment.

Ongoing Assessment

Writing Have students name the parts of an electrochemical cell and describe what each part does. *(Electrodes and an electrolyte; Electrodes are two different metals that are partially immersed in the electrolyte. The electrolyte is a substance that conducts electric current.)*

Electrochemical Cells, continued

Demonstration

Materials *flashlight that requires two dry cells, batteries*

Time 10 minutes

Show students the flashlight. Ask: **What will happen if the flashlight has only one dry cell?** (*The flashlight will not light.*) Flip the switch on the flashlight to test students' predictions. Then ask: **Why didn't the flashlight turn on?** (*The circuit needs the second battery to be complete.*) **learning modality: kinesthetic**

Real-Life Learning

Materials *at least three brands of batteries, battery-powered device*

Time 10 minutes planning and setup, several days for observation

Have small groups of students design and carry out experiments to determine which brand of battery lasts the longest. To help students design their experiments, ask: **What variables must you control?** (*Use batteries of the same voltage and test them in the same device under the same conditions.*) Suggest students test the batteries in devices such as battery-powered radios or flashlights. Caution students not to continuously run a device that produces heat, since that may present a fire hazard. Students can record the results of their experiments in data tables. **limited English proficiency**

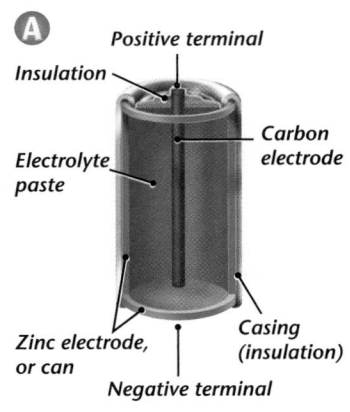

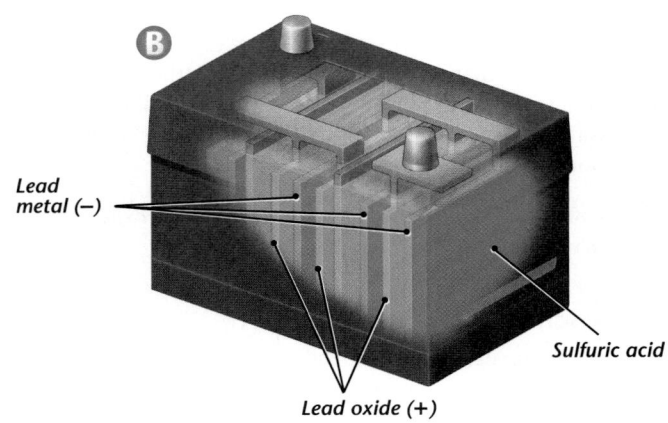

Figure 21 Electrochemical cells can be dry or wet. **A.** This diagram shows the parts of a typical dry cell. The electrolyte of a dry cell is a paste. **B.** A car battery is made up of several wet cells. A wet cell uses a liquid electrolyte.

Combining Electrochemical Cells Several electrochemical cells can be stacked together to form a battery. A **battery** is a combination of two or more electrochemical cells in a series. Today, single cells are often referred to as batteries. So the "batteries" you use in your flashlight are technically cells rather than batteries.

In a battery, two or more electrochemical cells are connected in series. The positive terminal of one cell is connected to the negative terminal of the next. The voltage of the battery is the sum of the voltages of the cells. You connect two cells in this way when you insert them into a flashlight. The total voltage of a battery is found by adding the voltages of the individual cells. If you use two 1.5-volt cells in your flashlight, the total voltage is 3 volts.

Wet Cells and Dry Cells There are two kinds of electrochemical cells: dry cells and wet cells. An electrochemical cell in which the electrolyte is a liquid is a **wet cell**. Volta's battery consisted of wet cells because the electrolyte was salt water. The six-volt automobile battery in Figure 21B consists of three wet cells. In this case, the electrolyte is sulfuric acid. Twelve-volt batteries, which are more common, consist of six wet cells.

For many devices, it would not be convenient to have cells full of liquid that can spill or leak. Flashlights and many other devices use dry cells instead. A **dry cell** is an electrochemical cell in which the electrolyte is not really dry, but a paste. The dry cell in Figure 21A consists of a zinc can with a carbon rod down the center. The can is filled with a thick electrolyte paste. Metal caps are attached at each end for terminals and the cell is wrapped in a plastic coating.

Background

History of Science Although we remember Volta for his invention of the first electrochemical cell, a lesser-known French inventor developed the first truly portable battery—the dry cell. In 1866, Georges Leclanché (1839–1882) was working in Paris as an engineer. He coupled an electrolytic solution of ammonium chloride with a negative zinc terminal and a positive manganese dioxide terminal. The materials Leclanché used were inexpensive, and producing large numbers of the dry cells was relatively easy. As a result, Leclanché's battery became a commercial success. The least expensive dry cells available today are made using the same materials as Leclanché's battery.

Dead and Rechargeable Batteries

An electrochemical cell will continue to produce a current until the electrodes and electrolyte are used up. During the reaction in an electrochemical cell, the original substances, known as the reactants, are changed into different substances. The new substances are known as products. A battery in which the reactants have run out is a dead battery.

Can you turn the products back into reactants in order to keep a battery going? In some cells, you can. In these cells the useless products can be converted back into the valuable reactants. Such cells are said to be rechargeable. A battery made of these cells is a **rechargeable battery.** Not every type of battery can be recharged. The electrodes must be carefully chosen so that a reverse reaction is possible.

A reverse chemical reaction in which products change into reactants does not happen on its own. Electrical energy, however, can cause the reaction. A rechargeable battery uses electric current to convert the products of its chemical reaction back into reactants.

Have you ever seen someone turn on a laptop computer without plugging it in? The battery on a laptop computer is rechargeable. Once the battery has run down, the computer can be plugged into a wall socket. Electrical energy from the wall socket causes a reverse reaction in the battery. When this reverse reaction is complete, the battery is fully charged.

In one type of rechargeable battery, the reactants are nickel and cadmium. Nickel-cadmium, or NiCad, batteries are popular in cordless and cellular telephones, radios, compact disc players, and other devices that require extended use.

Figure 22 Unlike other batteries that must be discarded after they become dead, rechargeable batteries can be re-used many times before they wear out.

Section 4 Review

1. Describe the components of an electrochemical cell and explain how they produce voltage.
2. Explain how cells are arranged to make a battery.
3. How does a wet cell differ from a dry cell?
4. What is a rechargeable battery?
5. **Thinking Critically** Applying Concepts What would you tell an engineer who has suggested a design for a new battery using silver for both electrodes?

Science at Home

Can you revive a dead battery? Try the following with two old D cells and a flashlight. Test the flashlight with the old D cells and observe its brightness. Then ask a family member to remove the D cells and place them in direct sunlight to warm up. After an hour or more, use the cells to test the flashlight. How does the brightness of the bulb compare in the two tests? Explain to your family how a cell works. Then discuss what your observations indicate about the chemical reactions in the battery.

Dead and Rechargeable Batteries

Building Inquiry Skills: Inferring

Ask students: **Is recharging a battery a chemical reaction? Explain.** (*Yes. The electricity used to recharge the battery converts the products of the chemical reaction back to the reactants.*) **learning modality: verbal**

3 Assess

Section 4 Review Answers

1. An electrochemical cell consists of strips of two unlike metals placed in an electrolyte. Chemical reactions occur between the electrolyte and the electrodes. One electrode becomes negatively charged, and the other becomes positively charged.
2. The positive terminal of one cell touches the negative terminal of the next. The voltages combine.
3. A wet cell uses a liquid electrolyte. A dry cell uses a paste-like electrolyte.
4. A rechargeable battery has cells with products that can be converted back into reactants.
5. A battery must have two different metals to function.

Science at Home

Materials *2 old D cells, flashlight*

After warming, the battery will light the bulb brightly, but the bulb may quickly dim again. Chemical reactions occur faster at higher temperatures, so the warm D cell produces more current, quickly depleting the energy of the D cell as the chemical reactions occur.

Program Resources

◆ **Unit 3 Resources** 10-4 Review and Reinforce, p. 79; 10-4 Enrich, p. 80

Media and Technology

Transparencies "Dry Cell and Car Battery," Transparency 40

Concept Videotape Library *Adventures, Tape 2,* "Batteries"

Performance Assessment

Writing Have students explain how chemical reactions can produce electrical energy.

 Students can save their explanations in their portfolios.

Electricity Grows on Trees

Preparing for Inquiry

Key Concept Electrochemical cells use chemical reactions to produce electrical energy.

Skills Objectives Students will be able to
◆ solve problems by applying the concepts learned in this chapter;
◆ draw conclusions about the operation of the wet-cell circuit.

Time 30 minutes

Advance Planning To save time, remove the insulation from the ends of the wire ahead of time.

Alternative Materials
◆ If calculators powered solely by a 1.5-volt dry cell are not available, use a dual-powered calculator (solar and dry cell) and cover the solar cells with a piece of black electrical tape.
◆ A wooden dowel the same length and diameter as a 1.5-volt dry cell can be fitted directly into the battery compartment after attaching a wire to each end with a small, flat-headed screw. The other ends of these wires would then be connected to the free nail and copper wire in the apples.
◆ The clothespins can be eliminated by using wires fitted with alligator clips.

Guiding Inquiry

Invitation Remove the dry cell from the calculator and have the students examine the empty compartment. Ask them to give examples of design features the calculator has for making good electrical contact with both ends of the dry cell. *(Springy metal terminals, snug fit for the dry cell)* Ask students if they believe that they will be able to run the calculator by plugging it into an apple instead of a battery.

Introducing the Procedure

For clarity, the electrodes in the photos are shown far apart. Tell students, however, that the nail and the copper piece in each piece of fruit should be as close as possible to each other without

An electrochemical cell changes chemical energy into electrical energy. In this lab, you will practice the skill of drawing conclusions as you make a simple electrochemical cell starting with an apple.

Problem

How can you make a simple wet cell out of common household materials?

Materials

2 galvanized (zinc coated) nails about 10 cm long
2 pieces of copper about the same size as the nails
4 30-cm pieces of insulated wire with about 2 cm of insulation removed from each end
2 marble-size lumps of clay
4 clothes pins (the "pinch" type with springs)
2 apples
calculator powered by one 1.5-volt dry cell

Procedure ✂

Part 1 Single Apple Power

1. Use the calculator to do some calculations to be sure it works.
2. Remove the dry cell from the calculator.
3. Stick a galvanized nail into an apple so that about three or four centimeters of the nail are showing. Stick a piece of stiff copper wire into the apple as well. **CAUTION:** *Take care handling sharp nails.*

4. Connect a piece of wire to the free end of the nail. Connect another piece of wire to the free end of the copper wire. Use clothespins to keep the connections tight.
5. Connect the free ends of the two wires to the open terminals of the calculator. Secure the connections with clothespins or pieces of clay.
6. Try using the calculator. If it doesn't work, be sure the connections are tight.
7. Reverse the connections. Again, be sure the connections are tight.

actually touching. This arrangement reduces internal resistance. The nail and copper wire should be stuck into the fruit as far as possible in order to maximize the current. Emphasize the need for tight connections everywhere in the circuit.

Troubleshooting the Experiment
◆ Rinse the nails and copper wires with clean water to prevent corrosion after they have been used. If clay is used to make

connections, care should be taken that it does not clog the terminals.
◆ You may need to help students connect the apples in series. Connect the wire from the nail on one apple to the copper on the other apple. Then the free nail and the free copper piece should be connected to the terminals of the calculator.
◆ Warn students to use care when handling sharp nails.

8. If you get the calculator to work, try using it to do some calculations. If not, continue on.

Part 2 Double Apple Power

9. Make another apple cell by repeating Steps 3 and 4 with a second apple, nail, piece of copper, and two pieces of wire.

10. Experiment with different ways of connecting the second cell until the calculator works. Once you get the calculator to work, switch the connections to the calculator and see if it still works.

11. Do you think the apple cell will work if you use two galvanized nails in each apple instead of using copper? Design an experiment to find out. Get your teacher's approval for your design, then carry out your experiment.

Analyze and Conclude

1. Draw circuit diagrams for the arrangements from Parts I and II.
2. Relate the parts of the apple cell to a typical electrochemical cell.
3. How does the calculator perform when powered by one apple? By two apples? How can you account for any differences?
4. Does the calculator work as well with the apple as it does with a dry cell?
5. Did the apple cell work with two nails? Explain why or why not.

6. What parts of the apple battery correspond to the positive end and the negative end of a dry cell? How do you know?
7. **Think About It** What was the result of reversing the connections? Why do you think this happened?

More to Explore

Are apples the only fruit that can be used to make enough electricity to power a calculator? Try oranges, lemons, tomatoes, or other fruits. Are there other instruments or appliances that can be powered with apple wet cells? Try small toys, electronic games, or electronic clocks. (*Hint:* The apple cells generate a low voltage.)

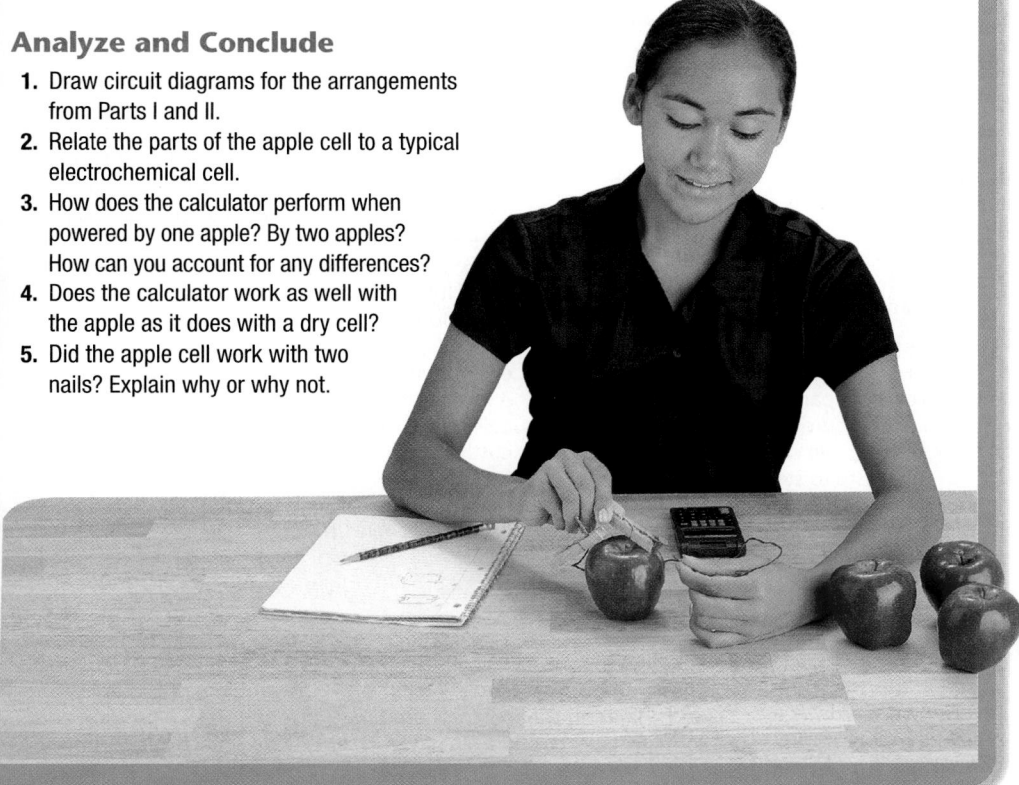

Analyze and Conclude

1. Circuit diagrams should show the Part I diagram with one cell, and the Part II diagram with two.
2. The nail and the copper are the electrodes. The liquid in the apple is the electrolyte. Because the electrolyte is liquid, the apple cell is a wet cell.
3. If one apple is used, the calculator does not operate. The calculator requires 1.4 volts; one apple must provide less voltage than that. The calculators work when two apples are used.
4. yes
5. No. The electrodes must be different metals.
6. The nail electrode is the negative electrode and it corresponds to the flat end of the dry cell. The copper wire electrode is the positive electrode, and it corresponds to the protruding end of the dry cell. If the wires are connected in the opposite orientation, the calculator will not operate. It requires a direct current that flows in one specific direction.
7. Reversing the connections caused the electrons to flow in the opposite direction. The calculator will work with the electrons flowing in one direction but not in the opposite direction.

Extending the Inquiry

More to Explore Tomatoes, potatoes, lemons, oranges, and other moist edibles can be used in place of the apples. Explain that the acid in fruit acts as the electrolyte of the cell. If citrus fruits are used, squeeze them first to loosen up the juice. The juice in citrus fruits is confined to small capsules separated from one another. Squeezing the fruit breaks the capsules.

Safety

Caution students not to eat the apples. Warn them to use care handling sharp nails. Review the safety guidelines in Appendix A.

Program Resources

◆ **Unit 3 Resources** Skills Lab blackline masters, pp. 84–85

Media and Technology

 Lab Activity Videotape *Tape 2*

Disposing of Batteries—Safely

Purpose

To provide students with an understanding of the problems associated with the disposal of common household batteries.

Debate

Time one class period for research and preparation; 30 minutes to conduct the debate

◆ Tell students they will debate the proposition "Household batteries should not be thrown away because they can cause environmental damage." Inform them that in a debate, two groups discuss a proposition by presenting reasons that support their positions.

◆ Organize the class into two groups: one to support the proposition, the other to oppose it. Have groups investigate the issue from their points of view.

◆ Groups should critically and constructively support their viewpoints. The group that supports throwing away batteries can explore ideas such as using nontoxic types of batteries. Encourage students in the other group to offer alternatives for those affected by a trash ban.

◆ Remind students to pay attention to the tone of the debate. Arguments should be clear without using harsh language.

Extend Have students contact a local landfill supervisor or environmental expert to obtain relevant background information. Encourage them to prepare questions in advance.

You Decide

Have groups of students complete the first two steps before the debate to prepare their arguments. After the debate, direct students to write their speeches using the points they raised during the debate.

Disposing of Batteries—Safely

Americans use more than 2 billion batteries each year, for everything from flashlights and toys to cameras and computers. When batteries wear out, people throw most of them into the trash. The dead batteries end up buried in landfills or burned in incinerators.

The trouble with throwing away batteries is that they contain poisonous metals, such as mercury and cadmium. Mercury harms the nervous system, and cadmium can cause cancer. As batteries break down in landfills, they can release these metals into the soil. Eventually the metals can enter the water supply. Burning batteries in incinerators isn't any better, because the metals are released into the air as the batteries are burned. So what's the safest way to dispose of batteries?

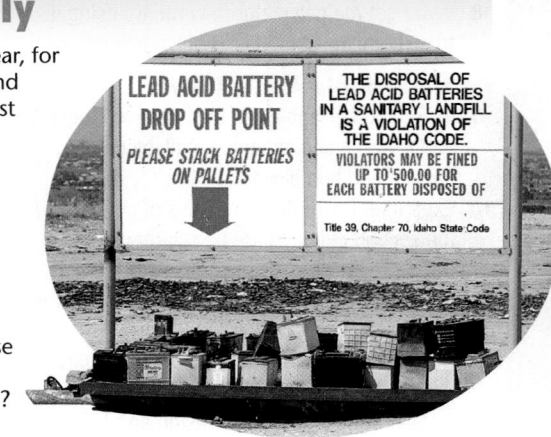

LEAD ACID BATTERY DROP OFF POINT
PLEASE STACK BATTERIES ON PALLETS

THE DISPOSAL OF LEAD ACID BATTERIES IN A SANITARY LANDFILL IS A VIOLATION OF THE IDAHO CODE.
VIOLATORS MAY BE FINED UP TO $500.00 FOR EACH BATTERY DISPOSED OF
Title 39, Chapter 70, Idaho State Code

The Issues

What Type of Battery Is Best? Alkaline batteries are used in toys, flashlights, radios, and watches. These batteries contain mercury. Even though there are some rechargeable alkaline batteries, most are thrown away once they are dead.

Nickel-cadmium (Ni-Cad) batteries are often used in hand-held video games and cordless telephones. These batteries contain cadmium. Ni-Cad batteries are rechargeable. One Ni-Cad battery can last as long as 12 single-use alkaline batteries. Yet they still don't last forever. Eventually they wear out and must be disposed of.

Where Should People Dispose of Batteries? Health experts say that batteries should be collected separately from ordinary trash and disposed of in secure, hazardous-waste landfills. These sites have clay or other materials underneath the waste to stop poisons from leaking into soil and water.

Some cities collect batteries at collection centers. Some stores also provide for special disposal or recycling. However, even when battery collection is offered, many people throw batteries into the trash simply because it's easier.

What Can People Do? Some government officials want laws that require manufacturers to reduce the amount of poisonous metals in batteries. At present, most states do not have such a law. In the last 20 years, manufacturers have lowered the amount of mercury used in alkaline batteries by 70 percent.

Local governments could fine people who don't follow the rules for disposal of batteries. But enforcing battery disposal rules would be expensive. It also would involve checking everyone's trash—a violation of people's privacy. A few states do require battery manufacturers to collect and recycle batteries. But this process is costly for companies and results in higher prices for batteries.

While people search for solutions, batteries continue to pile up.

You Decide

1. Identify the Problem
In your own words, explain the problem of safe battery disposal.

2. Analyze the Options
Examine the pros and cons of changing disposal regulations and changing the materials used to make batteries. In each case, who would the change affect?

3. Find a Solution
Your community is debating the problem of battery disposal. Take a position and write a speech supporting your opinion.

Background

Facts and Figures The toxic effect of leaking chemicals from household batteries has prompted new areas of research. One less damaging alternative to traditional batteries is the lithium battery. It has a much longer life span than conventional batteries and produces more voltage. It eventually discharges, and the breakdown of its components can harm ground water systems near landfills. However, fewer of these batteries will end up in landfills.

The most ecologically promising new batteries are portable solar-powered batteries that rely only on a light source to produce voltage. Solar batteries are now used in laptop computers. They are expensive, but as more economical solar batteries are produced, the need for the traditional nickel-cadmium battery may eventually be eliminated altogether.

Electricity, Magnetism, and Motion

Key Ideas

◆ A magnetic field exerts a force on a wire carrying current, causing the wire to move.

◆ A galvanometer uses the magnetic force on a current-carrying wire to turn a pointer on a scale. The scale can then be used to measure current.

◆ An electric motor converts electrical energy into mechanical energy.

Key Terms

energy   electric motor
electrical energy   commutator
mechanical energy   brushes
galvanometer   armature

 Generating Electric Current

Key Ideas

◆ A current is induced in a wire in a moving or changing magnetic field.

◆ Current that moves in one direction only is called direct current. Current that reverses direction is called alternating current.

◆ A generator converts mechanical energy into electric energy.

◆ Mechanical energy is required to move a turbine. That energy can be supplied by falling water, the burning of fossil fuels, the wind, the sun, the tides, or steam from within Earth.

Key Terms

electromagnetic   slip rings
  induction   turbine
alternating current   renewable resource
direct current   nonrenewable
electric generator   resource

 Using Electric Power

Key Ideas

◆ Power is the rate at which energy is converted.

◆ A transformer increases or decreases voltage.

◆ The voltage of alternating current can be stepped up and stepped down.

Key Terms

power   step-up transformer
transformer   step-down transformer

Batteries

INTEGRATING **CHEMISTRY**

Key Ideas

◆ An electrochemical cell consists of two different metals, called electrodes, and a substance through which charges can flow, called an electrolyte.

◆ In a battery, two or more electrochemical cells are connected in series to increase the voltage.

Key Terms

chemical energy   electrolyte   dry cell
chemical reaction   terminal   rechargeable
electrochemical cell battery   battery
electrode   wet cell

Organizing Information

Concept Map Copy the concept map about electromagnetism onto a separate sheet of paper. Then complete the concept map and add a title. (For more about concept maps, see the Skills Handbook.)

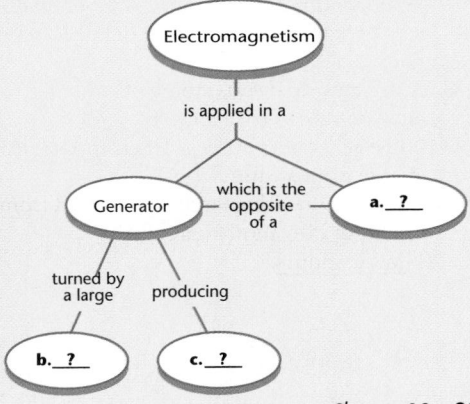

Organizing Information

Concept Map a. Motor b. Turbine c. Current or Electrical Energy
Sample title: Generating Electric Current

Program Resources

◆ **Unit 3 Resources** Chapter 10 Project Scoring Rubric, p. 64

◆ **Performance Assessment** Chapter 10, pp. 31–33

◆ **Chapter Tests** Chapter 10 Test, pp. 39–42

Media and Technology

Computer Test Bank
Chapter 10 Test

Reviewing Content

Multiple Choice

1. a 2. c 3. b 4. a 5. b

True or False

6. true 7. true 8. electrochemical cell or battery 9. true 10. power

Checking Concepts

11. Similar: Both convert electrical energy to mechanical energy. Different: The loop in a galvanometer can only turn half way, the loop in a motor can turn full circle. A motor uses commutators and brushes to reverse the direction of current in the loop.

12. A commutator-brush arrangement changes the direction of current in a DC motor. A commutator consists of two halves of a ring, each of which rubs past two stationary brushes. As the loop of wire in the motor rotates, the halves of the commutator switch from one brush to the other, changing the direction of current through the circuit.

13. In an AC generator, a loop (or many loops) of wire is turned in a magnetic field by mechanical means. As the loop turns, a current is induced in the wire. The direction of the current changes with each half revolution of the loop.

14. Both consist of moving electric charges. Alternating current changes direction. Direct current moves in one direction only.

15. A turbine is turned by a source of mechanical energy; the turbine is attached to the armature of a generator, which produces current.

16. Coal: pros—moderate cost, large supply; cons—mining and burning coal damage the environment. Wind power: pros—moderate cost, no wastes; cons—winds are variable, requires large area of land. Nuclear: pros—no air pollution; cons—reactors are expensive to build, there are no satisfactory methods of waste disposal.

17. The voltage is increased by a step-up transformer as it leaves the utility company. It is decreased by a step-down transformer before reaching its destination.

18. In chemical reaction, new substances are produced. Batteries contain electrochemical cells that use chemical reactions

Reviewing Content

Multiple Choice

Choose the letter of the answer that best completes each statement.

1. Electrical energy is converted into mechanical energy in a
   a. motor.   b. generator.
   c. transformer.   d. battery.
2. Mechanical energy is converted into electrical energy in a
   a. motor.   b. galvanometer.
   c. generator.   d. commutator.
3. Power is equal to
   a. energy × time.
   b. voltage × current.
   c. energy × current.
   d. current ÷ voltage.
4. A device that changes the voltage of alternating current is a
   a. transformer.   b. motor.
   c. generator.   d. galvanometer.
5. The metal plates in an electrochemical cell are called
   a. electrolytes.   b. electrodes.
   c. armatures.   d. brushes.

True or False

If the statement is true, write true. If it is false, change the underlined word or words to make the statement true.

6. The production of an electric current by a changing magnetic field is known as induction.
7. Several loops of wire wrapped around an iron core form the armature of an electric motor.
8. A generator converts stored chemical energy into electrical energy.
9. Large generators often get their mechanical energy from steam.
10. The rate at which energy is converted from one form into another is called kilowatt-hours.

Checking Concepts

11. How is a galvanometer similar to a motor? How is it different?
12. What is the role of the commutator and brushes in an electric motor?
13. Describe the operation of an AC generator.
14. Compare and contrast alternating and direct current.
15. What is the purpose of a turbine in generating electricity?
16. What are the pros and cons of coal, wind power, and nuclear power?
17. Explain how transformers are used to carry electricity from the utility company to your home.
18. What is a chemical reaction? How are chemical reactions related to batteries?
19. **Writing to Learn** Sometimes you may think that everything that could possibly be invented already exists. Many people thought the same thing during the 1800s. Write an article for a modern newspaper describing new uses for generators and motors.

Thinking Critically

20. **Problem Solving** The voltage of a car battery is 12 volts. When the car is started, the battery produces a 40-amp current. How much power does it take to start the car?
21. **Comparing and Contrasting** Compare the cost of using the following two bulbs. Assume that each one is used for 5 hours a day for 360 days per year. The cost of electricity is 8 cents/kWh.
    a. A 100-watt light bulb that costs $1.00
    b. A fluorescent bulb that costs $9 but provides equal brightness with only 20 watts
22. **Applying Concepts** How could you modify a battery to produce a higher voltage?
23. **Making Diagrams** Make a diagram of a wire loop in a magnetic field. Show how the direction of a current in the wire is related to the direction of rotation of the loop

---

between the electrodes and electrolyte to produce electric current.

19. Students should be creative in imagining life before electricity. They should note that motors can be used to do tasks previously done by people or animals. Generators can be used to provide electricity.

Thinking Critically

20. 12 V × 40 A = 480 watts
21. a. Find time in hours: 5 hours/day × 360 days = 1,800 hours. Then convert the given

power to kilowatts: 0.1 kW. Next find energy by $E = Pt$: $E = 0.1$ kW × 1,800 h = 180 kWh. Multiply the energy by the price: Cost = 180 kWh × $0.08/kWh = $14.40. Finally, add in the cost of the bulb: $14.40 + $1.00 = $15.40
b. Power = 0.02 kW, so $E = 0.02$ kW × 1,800 h = 36 kWh; 36 kWh × $0.08/kWh = $2.88. Add the cost of the bulb: $2.88 + $9 = $11.88.
22. You could add more cells in series.
23. Diagrams should show that the direction of rotation changes with the direction of current.

Applying Skills

Use the illustration to answer Questions 24–26.

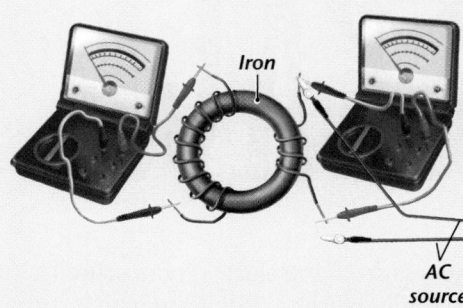

Iron

AC source

24. **Classifying** What type of transformer is shown in the illustration? How do you know?

25. **Inferring** Which coil is the primary coil and which is the secondary coil?

26. **Predicting** What will the two voltmeters show when the circuit on the right side of the diagram is completed?

Performance Assessment
CHAPTER PROJECT 10

Project Wrap Up Present the results of your energy audit to the class in a visual format. You might make a bar, circle, or line graph showing the appliances and the energy they used. What appliance uses the most electrical energy in a week? Compare the appliances that are rated at 800 watts and higher. What do they have in common? How might this conclusion be helpful to a consumer who is interested in paying the least for electricity?

Record and Reflect In your journal, write about how you calculated energy use. What problems did you have? What information couldn't you collect?

Test Preparation
Use these questions to prepare for standardized tests.

Study the table. Then answer Questions 27–30.

Appliance	Power (W)
Stove	6,000
Clothes dryer	5,400
Water heater	4,500
Washing machine	1,200
Hair dryer	1,200
Iron	1,100
Coffee maker	1,000
Food processor	500

27. If all of these appliances were used for one hour, which would use the greatest amount of energy?
   a. food processor   **b.** hair dryer
   c. clothes dryer   **d.** stove

28. Which device uses energy at the same rate as ten 100-watt light bulbs?
   a. food processor
   b. coffee maker
   c. washing machine
   d. stove

29. If standard household voltage is 120 volts, what is the current through the stove?
   a. 0.05 amp
   b. 20 amps
   c. 50 amps
   d. 750 amps

30. An electric company charges $0.25 for every kilowatt-hour of energy. How much does it cost to run a water heater for 2 hours?
   a. $0.50   **b.** $1.13
   c. $2.25   **d.** $4.50

Applying Skills

24. Step-up; the primary coil has fewer loops than the secondary coil.
25. The primary coil is on the right, and the secondary coil is on the left.
26. The meter on the right will show a lower voltage than the meter on the left.

Performance Assessment
CHAPTER PROJECT 10

Project Wrap Up Help students make visual displays of their data. Provide samples for them to refer to; power companies may have consumer information that includes graphical displays. Encourage them to prepare bar graphs of weekly electricity use in kilowatt-hours per appliance. They should present their graphs to the class as they describe the appliances in their home that use the most electricity.

Reflect and Record Students should analyze the project and should identify problems such as not being able to accurately record the time some appliances, such as furnaces, heat pumps, and refrigerators, are using electrical energy. Students' journal entries should describe how accurate students think their results are based on the problems they identified.

Test Preparation
27. d 28. b 29. c 30. c

Program Resources

- **Inquiry Skills Activity Book** Provides teaching and review of all inquiry skills
- **Prentice Hall Assessment System** Provides standardized test practice
- **Reading in the Content Area** Provides strategies to improve science reading skills
- **Teacher's ELL Handbook** Provides multiple strategies for English language learners

An Electrical Engineer in Outer Space

Focus on Engineering

This four-page feature highlights the process of scientific inquiry by involving students in a high-interest article about a working scientist, astronaut Dr. Ellen Ochoa. Using Dr. Ochoa's varied engineering work in the space program as an example, the feature focuses on persistence, determination, and a passion for science as key elements of scientific inquiry.

Scientific Inquiry

◆ Before students read the article, let them read the title, examine the pictures, and read the captions on their own. Then ask: **What questions came into your mind as you looked at these pictures?** *(Students might suggest questions such as "Who determines which astronauts get to fly on a mission? What is the RMS? Why did Ellen take her flute? Is it more difficult to play a flute in weightlessness?")* Point out to students that just as they had questions about what they were seeing, scientists too have questions about what they observe.

AN ELECTRICAL ENGINEER IN OUTER SPACE

Ellen Ochoa was born and raised in California. She earned a doctorate in electrical engineering from Stanford University and became an astronaut in 1991. She has flown on two space-shuttle missions. Currently she is a Spacecraft Communicator, an astronaut at Mission Control who talks with other astronauts while they are in space. She is a talented flute player who has taken her flute with her on the shuttle. She hopes to be aboard more missions in space soon.

When she was studying electricity in school science classes, Ellen Ochoa didn't know that some day her studies would help take her into space. "I just always liked math and science," the California-born Dr. Ochoa says. Today she is an astronaut and has flown on two space-shuttle missions. Trained as an electrical engineer, she is an expert in the uses of electricity. This is the important skill she brings to the astronaut team.

Astronaut Ochoa has worked in the testing and training process for robotics — humanlike machines that can carry out complicated tasks in space. On her shuttle flights, Ellen had the key job of controlling one of these machines, the Remote Manipulator System, or RMS. "The RMS is a robotic arm that reaches out of the spacecraft," she explains. "We use electricity to operate it. The RMS is about 50 feet long. On my flights, we used it to pick up a satellite that was in the shuttle payload bay and put it in orbit. Then a few days later, we'd come back and retrieve the satellite and put it back in the spacecraft cargo area." One of the satellites was used by scientists to gather information about the sun and its effects on Earth. Another was used to study Earth's atmosphere.

"We have a work station with two hand controllers. One is sort of like a joystick on a kid's game. The other is like a square knob that you hold. You push and pull, or move up and down or left and right, to move the electrical RMS arm to the correct position."

Background

Engineering is the application of math and science knowledge to the effective use of materials and forces in nature. There are numerous branches of engineering; however, because the branches are interrelated, an engineer specializing in any field needs to have some understanding of the other fields and how they relate.

Electrical engineering is divided into four fields: electric power, electronics, communications, and computers. Engineers studying the generation of electricity, like Ellen Ochoa, design and operate systems that generate, transmit, and distribute electrical power.

Talking with Dr. Ellen Ochoa

◀ Ellen Ochoa training on Earth with the RMS

◀ A satellite in the grasp of the RMS arm of the space shuttle *Atlantis*

This diagram of the RMS arm shows its three joints and mechanical hand (at the right). The arm is about 15 meters long.

Q *How did you become interested in science?*

A I got into science because I liked math. I always enjoyed math and did well at it. I was interested in finding out about all the ways that people could use math. So I studied physics at college. I didn't know until then that I would have a career in science.

Q *Did you follow the space program when you were young?*

A Oh sure. It was a very big thing in the 1960s when I was in elementary school. At the time, the Apollo program was sending astronauts to the moon. But it wasn't until I was in graduate school in electrical engineering that I learned how to apply for the space program and what they were looking for in selecting astronauts.

Q *What happened when you applied to the space program?*

A The first time I applied in 1985 I was not selected. So I tried again in 1990 and was chosen. That's been the case with many astronauts. Persistence is one of our qualities.

Q *How do astronauts use electricity in the space shuttle?*

A We use electrical power for many of the systems on board the shuttle. It's used for the computers and for the sensors and detectors to make sure

343

- ◆ Ask: **What qualifications do you think you need to be an astronaut?** *(Answers will vary. Samples: a doctorate in the sciences)* Ask students how many of them want to be astronauts and why. If students want to know more about astronaut program requirements, share with them the background information below. Also suggest that they consult library books to learn more about the space shuttle. (See Further Reading, page 345).
- ◆ Challenge interested students to research more about what the satellites were studying.
- ◆ Ask: **What skills do you think you need to operate the RMS?** *(Good coordination, good concentration, patience)* **Why is it important to be careful while operating the RMS?** *(If you were careless, you could damage the RMS, the satellite, or maybe even the shuttle.)*
- ◆ Ask students who follow the space program closely to share the latest news from the space program with the class. Ask them about Mars explorations as well as developments on the International Space Station.
- ◆ Ask: **Why did Ellen reapply after she was turned down?** *(She was determined to be admitted to the program. Perhaps she already knew that it was common to be turned down the first time you applied.)*

Background

The minimum requirements to be an astronaut are: excellent physical condition, a bachelor's degree in engineering, science, or mathematics, and usually some years of related experience beyond the degree. Preference is given to applicants with advanced degrees.

There are about 20 job openings every two years. NASA typically receives about 4,000 applications for those 20 openings.

343

◆ Ask: **The shuttle uses electricity. Where does the electricity come from?** *(Answers may vary. Samples: solar panels, generated by the engine, batteries)* Point out that there is not room in the shuttle for huge numbers of batteries, so astronauts have to generate their own electricity once they get into space.

◆ Ask: **What does the life-support system do?** *(Answers may vary. Samples: Keeps the astronauts warm. Keeps fresh air inside the shuttle and removes the stale air.)* If students want to know more about some of the systems on the shuttle, share with them the background information below.

◆ Ask: **Why do they use very cold oxygen and hydrogen?** *(Students may or may not know enough chemistry to answer this question. Very cold gases usually take up far less room than warm gases.)*

◆ Explain that in this book students will learn about Earth's magnetic field. They will also learn that when an electric current passes through a wire, it creates a small magnetic field around the wire. Scientists have also found out that if you pull a wire through a magnetic field, you generate an electric current in the wire. Astronauts used this discovery to experiment with generating current for the shuttle.

that the life-support systems are working correctly. Many of our instruments for research use other forms of energy related to electricity, like light or radio waves. We can use these instruments, for instance, to measure the chemicals in the atmosphere that affect climate and weather. And, of course, we use radio for communicating with the ground crew.

Ellen Ochoa at the controls of the RMS arm with astronaut Donald R. McMonagle

Q *Where does the electricity you use come from?*

A We have fuel cells on board. We bring up cryogenic (very cold) oxygen and hydrogen. Then we allow the two chemicals to mix together in the fuel cells. Fuel cells use chemical reactions, like batteries. The chemical reactions in fuel cells produce both electricity and water, which we use on board. We would like to carry up more oxygen and hydrogen fuel cells, to make more electric power. But more fuel cells would mean we could carry less of other things, such as the equipment for the scientific experiments we do.

Q *Are you studying other ways to make electricity?*

A We've had two shuttle flights that experimented with tethered satellites. Basically, the idea was to drag a satellite through space on a tether—a long conducting cable. As the conductor passes through Earth's magnetic field, electric current is generated. Tethered satellites are just at the research stage now.

**Ellen Ochoa entertains other crew ►
members during a flight.**

344

Background

The space shuttle is equipped with as many of the tools and systems that astronauts might need as is possible. Astronauts heat up meals in a kitchen area similar to that on an aircraft. Minor illnesses and injuries can be treated using the onboard medical system. Radiation from solar flares is a concern, so astronauts have to monitor how much radiation they are subjected to. Sleeping bags with restraints keep astronauts from colliding with equipment and each other while trying to sleep. Temporary and permanent foot restraints, handholds, ladders, and rails help astronauts stay in place or move around. To stay in shape, astronauts work out on a specially designed treadmill.

Students with Internet access can read about the shuttle in detail at **http://spaceflight.nasa.gov**.

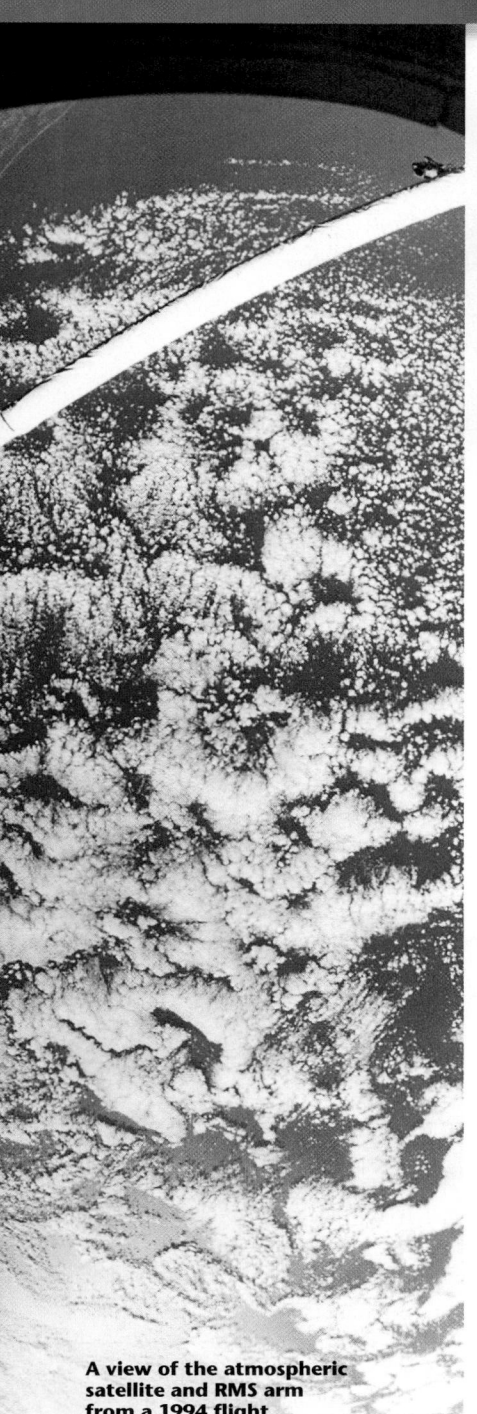

A view of the atmospheric satellite and RMS arm from a 1994 flight

An artist's concept of the space shuttle and tethered satellite

But eventually, we'd like to use power from tethers to move satellites up and down in orbit without using up precious fuel.

Q *What parts of working as an astronaut do you enjoy?*

A I think the whole flight is fun—the launch, viewing Earth from space, and living in weightlessness, although that can be frustrating, too. Doing the activities we've been trained for is hard work, but it's really enjoyable as well. There are a lot of interesting, exciting careers for people with backgrounds in science and math. Being an astronaut is just one of them.

In Your Journal

Ellen talks about persistence, a quality that helped her become an astronaut. Think of a time when you succeeded in doing something after many attempts. Describe what happened. How did persistence and determination help you? Why would these qualities be important for scientists to have?

♦ Ask: **Do you think NASA would let you take any musical instrument into space?** *(No; they would probably let you take only something small, like Ellen's flute.)*

♦ Ask: **What do you think could be frustrating about living in weightlessness?** *(Accept all reasonable answers. Sample: When you drop something, it floats away; you have to tie yourself to your bed.)*

♦ Ask: **Did Ellen intend to be an astronaut when she was young?** *(No; she was interested in science but didn't apply for the space program until after she was in college.)*

In Your Journal To prompt student thinking, ask students why they kept trying. As an alternative, suggest that students write a letter to a friend who gives up quickly, giving them advice about why they should be more persistent.

READING STRATEGIES

Further Reading

♦ Joels, Kerry Mark and Gregory P. Kennedy. *The Space Shuttle Operators Manual.* Ballantine Books, 1988.
♦ Bondar, Barbara and Roberta Bondar. *On the Shuttle: Eight Days in Space.* Owl Communications, 1993.
♦ Brown, Robert A. *Endeavour Views the Earth.* Cambridge University Press, 1996.

CHAPTER 11 Plate Tectonics

Sections	Time	Student Edition Activities	Other Activities	
CHAPTER PROJECT 11 **Cut-Away Earth** p. 347	Ongoing (3 weeks)	Check Your Progress, p. 356, 371, 379 Project Wrap Up, p. 383	TE	Chapter 11 Project Notes, pp. 346–347
1 Earth's Interior pp. 348–356 ◆ 11.1.1 Describe what geologists do. ◆ 11.1.2 List the characteristics of Earth's crust, mantle, and core.	1 period/ $\frac{1}{2}$ block	**Discover** How Do Scientists Determine What's Inside Earth?, p. 348 **Sharpen Your Skills** Creating Data Tables, p. 353	TE TE TE TE TE TE	Inquiry Challenge, p. 350 Using the Visuals, p. 351 Building Inquiry Skills: Comparing and Contrasting, p. 352 Demonstration, p. 353 Demonstration, p. 354 Integrating Physics, p. 355
2 **INTEGRATING PHYSICS** **Convection Currents and the Mantle** pp. 357–359 ◆ 11.2.1 Explain how heat is transferred. ◆ 11.2.2 Identify what causes convection currents.	1 period/ $\frac{1}{2}$ block	**Discover** How Can Heat Cause Motion in a Liquid?, p. 357 **Science at Home,** p. 359	TE TE	Demonstration, p. 358 Building Inquiry Skills: Observing, p. 358
3 Drifting Continents pp. 360–364 ◆ 11.3.1 Describe the theory of continental drift. ◆ 11.3.2 List the evidence used by Alfred Wegener to form his theory and why other scientists rejected it.	1 period/ $\frac{1}{2}$ block	**Discover** How Are Earth's Continents Linked Together?, p. 360 **Try This** Reassembling the Pieces, p. 363 **Science at Home,** p. 364	TE	Integrating Life Science, p. 363
4 Sea-Floor Spreading pp. 365–373 ◆ 11.4.1 Describe the process of sea-floor spreading. ◆ 11.4.2 List the evidence for sea-floor spreading. ◆ 11.4.3 Explain the process of subduction.	2 periods/ 1 block	**Discover** What Is the Effect of a Change in Density?, p. 365 **Try This** Reversing Poles, p. 369 **Skills Lab: Making Models** Modeling Sea-Floor Spreading, pp. 372–373	TE TE TE TE TE	Including All Students, p. 366 Including All Students, p. 367 Integrating Physics, p. 368 Including All Students, p. 369 Including All Students, p. 370
5 The Theory of Plate Tectonics pp. 374–380 ◆ 11.5.1 Explain the theory of plate tectonics. ◆ 11.5.2 Describe the three types of plate boundaries.	2 periods/ 1 block	**Discover** How Well Do the Continents Fit Together?, p. 374 **Sharpen Your Skills** Predicting, p. 375 **Skills Lab: Observing** Hot Plates, p. 380	TE TE TE TE LM	Inquiry Challenge, p. 375 Demonstration, p. 376 Using the Visuals, p. 376 Inquiry Challenge, p. 377 11, "Mapping a Future World"
Study Guide/Assessment pp. 381–383	1 period/ $\frac{1}{2}$ block		ISAB	Provides teaching and review of all inquiry skills

For Standard or Block Schedule The Resource Pro® CD-ROM gives you maximum flexibility for planning your instruction for any type of schedule. Resource Pro® contains Planning Express®, an advanced scheduling program, as well as the entire contents of the Teaching Resources and the Computer Test Bank.

Key: **CTB** Computer Test Bank
CT Chapter Tests
ELL Teacher's ELL Handbook

CHAPTER PLANNING GUIDE

Program Resources	Assessment Strategies	Media and Technology
UR Chapter 11 Project Teacher Notes, pp. 2–3 UR Chapter 11 Project Overview and Worksheets, pp. 4–7	TE Performance Assessment: Chapter 11 Project Wrap Up, p. 383 TE Check Your Progress, pp. 356, 371, 379 UR Chapter 11 Project Scoring Rubric, p. 8	Science Explorer Internet Site Audio CDs, Section Summaries
UR 11-1 Lesson Plan, p. 9 UR 11-1 Section Summary, p. 10 UR 11-1 Review and Reinforce, p. 11 UR 11-1 Enrich, p. 12	SE Section 1 Review, p. 356 TE Ongoing Assessment, pp. 349, 351, 353, 355 TE Performance Assessment, p. 356	Concept Videotape Library, *Adventures, Tape 4,* "A Trip Through the Earth" Presentation Pro, "Continental Drift"; "Earth's Interior" Transparency 41, "Exploring Earth's Interior"
UR 11-2 Lesson Plan, p. 13 UR 11-2 Section Summary, p. 14 UR 11-2 Review and Reinforce, p. 15 UR 11-2 Enrich, p. 16	SE Section 2 Review, p. 359 TE Performance Assessment, p. 359	Concept Videotape Library, *Adventures, Tape 3,* "Hot Is Hot, Cold Is Not" Concept Videotape Library, *Adventures, Tape 3,* "The Power of Heat"
UR 11-3 Lesson Plan, p. 17 UR 11-3 Section Summary, p. 18 UR 11-3 Review and Reinforce, p. 19 UR 11-3 Enrich, p. 20	SE Section 3 Review, p. 364 TE Ongoing Assessment, pp. 361, 363 TE Performance Assessment, p. 364	Concept Videotape Library, *Adventures, Tape 3,* "The Drifters" Transparency 42, "Evidence for Continental Drift"
UR 11-4 Lesson Plan, p. 21 UR 11-4 Section Summary, p. 22 UR 11-4 Review and Reinforce, p. 23 UR 11-4 Enrich, p. 24 UR Skills Lab blackline masters, pp. 29–31	SE Section 4 Review, p. 371 SE Analyze and Conclude, p. 373 TE Ongoing Assessment, pp. 367, 369 TE Performance Assessment, p. 371	Concept Videotape Library, *Adventures, Tape 3,* "Journey to the Bottom of the Sea" Transparencies 43, "Magnetic Stripes Along the Mid-Ocean Ridge"; 44, "Sea-floor Spreading and Subduction" Lab Activity Videotape, *Tape 3*
UR 11-5 Lesson Plan, p. 25 UR 11-5 Section Summary, p. 26 UR 11-5 Review and Reinforce, p. 27 UR 11-5 Enrich, p. 28 UR Skills Lab blackline masters, pp. 32–33	SE Section 5 Review, p. 379 SE Analyze and Conclude, p. 380 TE Ongoing Assessment, pp. 375, 377 TE Performance Assessment, p. 379	Concept Videotape Library, *Adventures, Tape 3,* "Everything on Your Plate" Transparencies 45, "Earth's Lithospheric Plates"; 46, "Exploring Plate Tectonics"; 47, "Continental Drift Since Pangaea" Lab Activity Videotape, *Tape 3*
GRSW Provides worksheets to promote student comprehension of content RCA Provides strategies to improve science reading skills ELL Provides multiple strategies for English language learners	SE Study Guide/Assessment, pp. 381–383 PA Performance Assessment, pp. 34–36 CT Chapter 11 Test, pp. 43–46 CTB Chapter 11 Test PHAS Provides standardized test preparation	Computer Test Bank, Chapter 11 Test

GRSW Guided Reading and Study Workbook
ISAB Inquiry Skills Activity Book
LM Laboratory Manual

PA Performance Assessment
PHAS Prentice Hall Assessment System
PLM Probeware Lab Manual

RCA Reading in the Content Area
SE Student Edition

TE Teacher's Edition
UR Unit Resources

Meeting the National Science Education Standards and AAAS Benchmarks

National Science Education Standards	Benchmarks for Science Literacy	Unifying Themes

Science As Inquiry (Content Standard A)

◆ **Develop descriptions, explanations, predictions, and models using evidence** Students build a model that shows Earth's surface and interior. Students model sea-floor spreading. (*Chapter Project; Skills Labs*)

Physical Science (Content Standard B)

◆ **Transfer of energy** The three types of heat transfer are radiation, conduction, and convection. Students observe a model of convection currents in Earth's mantle. (*Section 2; Skills Lab*)

Earth and Space Science (Content Standard D)

◆ **Structure of the Earth system** The crust, mantle, and core are the three main layers of Earth's interior. Molten material from the mantle rises at mid-ocean ridges and old crust sinks back into the mantle at deep-ocean trenches. Plate tectonics explains the formation, movement, and subduction of Earth's crust. (*Sections 1, 4, 5*)

◆ **Earth's History** Wegener used evidence from landforms, fossils, and climate to support his hypothesis of continental drift. About 260 million years ago the continents were joined together. (*Sections 3, 5*)

1A The Scientific World View Discovery of the mid-ocean ridge caused scientists to reconsider Wegener's hypothesis. (*Sections 4, 5*)

1B Scientific Inquiry Wegener gathered evidence to support his hypothesis of continental drift. (*Section 3*)

1C The Scientific Enterprise Geologists study the forces that make and shape Earth. (*Section 1*)

3A Technology and Science Scientists used sonar, submersibles, and other technology to gather evidence to support sea-floor spreading. (*Section 4*)

4C Processes That Shape the Earth Students build a model to show how Earth's interior affects its surface. The crust, mantle, and core are the three main layers of Earth. Heat inside Earth causes convection currents in the mantle. Molten material from the mantle rises at mid-ocean ridges and old crust sinks back into the mantle at deep-ocean trenches. Plate tectonics explains the formation, movement, and subduction of Earth's crust. Students investigate the movement of plates by convection currents. (*Chapter Project; Sections 1, 2, 4, 5; Skills Labs*)

4E Energy Transformation Heat is transferred by radiation, conduction, and convection. Convection currents in the mantle cause movement of Earth's plates. (*Sections 2, 5; Skills Lab*)

◆ **Energy** Heat is transferred by radiation, conduction, and convection. The movement of Earth's plates is probably caused by convection currents in the mantle. (*Sections 2, 5; Skills Lab*)

◆ **Evolution** Plate tectonics explains how Earth's crust has changed. (*Section 5*)

◆ **Modeling** Students build a model of Earth and show sea-floor spreading and convection currents in Earth's mantle. (*Chapter Project; Skills Labs*)

◆ **Patterns of Change** Temperature and pressure increase as you approach Earth's center. Earth's magnetic poles reverse themselves about once every 600,000 years. (*Section 1*)

◆ **Scale and Structure** Earth's interior is made up of crust, mantle, and core. All the continents were once joined together in a single landmass. The lithosphere is broken into a number of plates. (*Sections 1, 3, 5*)

◆ **Stability** The formation of new crust at mid-ocean ridges is balanced by the destruction of old crust at deep-ocean trenches. (*Section 4; Skills Lab*)

◆ **Systems and Interactions** No plate can move without affecting other plates. Convection currents in the mantle probably cause the movement of Earth's plates. (*Section 5; Skills Lab*)

Take It to the Net

The **www.phschool.com** Web site provides you with multiple opportunities to incorporate the internet into your instruction. Go to **www.phschool.com** and click on the Science icon. Then select Science Explorer Integrated.

Internet Activities provide opportunities for students to review, extend, or assess a concept from the chapter.

■ Have students use the chapter Self-Test to get instant feedback.

■ Hot Links and Reference Links provide opportunities for online research.

STAY CURRENT with **SCIENCE NEWS** ®

Find out the latest research and information about earthquakes, volcanoes, and plate tectonics at: **www.phschool.com**

ACTIVITY	Time (minutes)	Materials *Quantities for one work group*	Skills
Section 1			
Discover, p. 348	10	**Consumable** masking tape **Nonconsumable** 3 film canisters with tops, 3 different materials, permanent marker, scale	Inferring
Sharpen Your Skills, p. 353	15	No special materials are required.	Creating Data Tables
Section 2			
Discover, p. 357	10	**Consumable** hot water, cold water, food coloring **Nonconsumable** shallow pan, clear plastic cup, plastic dropper	Inferring
Science at Home, p. 359	home	No special materials are required.	Observing
Section 3			
Discover, p. 360	15	**Nonconsumable** globe that shows physical features	Posing Questions
Try This, p. 363	15	**Consumable** 1 sheet of newspaper	Making Models
Science at Home, p. 364	home	**Consumable** 1 piece of tracing paper **Nonconsumable** scissors	Communicating
Section 4			
Discover, p. 365	10	**Consumable** water **Nonconsumable** sink or large dishpan, washcloth	Observing
Try This, p. 369	15	**Consumable** audiotape, plastic tape **Nonconsumable** scissors, metric ruler, bar magnet	Making Models
Skills Lab, pp. 372–373	30	**Consumable** 2 sheets of unlined paper **Nonconsumable** scissors, metric ruler, colored marker	Making Models, Observing, Inferring
Section 5			
Discover, p. 374	20	**Consumable** tracing paper, sheet of paper, tape **Nonconsumable** world map in an atlas, scissors	Drawing Conclusions
Sharpen Your Skills, p. 375	10	No special materials are required.	Predicting
Skills Lab, p. 380	40	**Consumable** aluminum roasting pan, 2 10-cm-long candles, 2 L water **Nonconsumable** modeling clay, 6 bricks, 2 medium-sized kitchen sponges, 10 map pins	Observing, Making Models, Inferring

A list of all materials required for the Student Edition activities can be found beginning on page T23. You can obtain information about ordering materials by calling 1-800-848-9500 or by accessing the Science Explorer Internet site at: **www.phschool.com**

Cut-Away Earth

When most students think of what's under the surface of Earth, they generally think of a static ball of dirt and rock, unchanging through time. In this chapter, they will be introduced to the concepts of layers of Earth and plate tectonics. The Chapter 11 Project will reinforce their understanding of the relationship between Earth's interior and its surface features.

Purpose Students will make sketches of Earth's interior, plates, and plate boundaries. Then, within a group they will come to a final design for a model of Earth and build it to scale. In doing so, they will gain a better understanding of the structure of Earth.

Skills Focus After completing the Chapter 11 Project, students will be able to

◆ apply the concepts learned in the chapter to a model of Earth's interior;
◆ interpret data to make their model to scale;
◆ design and make a model of Earth's interior and features of the surface;
◆ communicate the features of their model in a presentation to the class.

Project Time Line The entire project will require about three weeks. Depending on how much class time students can spend working on the project each day, about two days may be required for each of the following phases.

◆ Make individual sketches of a possible three-dimensional model of Earth's interior.
◆ Take the sketches to a group meeting, in which all sketches can be considered in thinking about a final design.
◆ Discuss with the group possible materials in making the model.
◆ Experiment with possible materials and decide which might work best.
◆ Make individual sketches of how the model could incorporate the concept of sea-floor spreading.
◆ Take the second set of sketches to a group meeting, come to a consensus on a model design, and make the base of the model.

◆ Incorporate plate boundaries into the design and complete the construction of the model.
◆ Make a presentation to the class, explaining what the model shows about the structure of Earth.

For more detailed information on planning and supervising the chapter project, see Chapter 11 Project Teacher Notes, pages 2–3 in Unit 4 Resources.

Suggested Shortcuts You can make this project shorter and less involved in one of the following ways.

◆ Have students make their individual sketches and then design a model in their groups. Then invite the class as a whole to decide on a final design, incorporating the best aspects of all the plans. Have volunteers make the actual model in their free time.
◆ Have students individually complete the two worksheets and make a detailed sketch of Earth's interior.
◆ Challenge groups to make a detailed, color poster of Earth's interior instead of a three-dimensional model.

346

CHAPTER 11 Plate Tectonics

This is a satellite image of the San Francisco Bay area. The row of lakes below marks the line of the San Andreas fault, a crack in Earth's crust.

WEB ACTIVITY www.phschool.com

Integrating Physics

SECTION 1 Earth's Interior
Discover How Do Scientists Determine What's Inside Earth?
Sharpen Your Skills Creating Data Tables

SECTION 2 Convection Currents and the Mantle
Discover How Can Heat Cause Motion in a Liquid?

SECTION 3 Drifting Continents
Discover How Are Earth's Continents Linked Together?
Try This Reassembling the Pieces

346

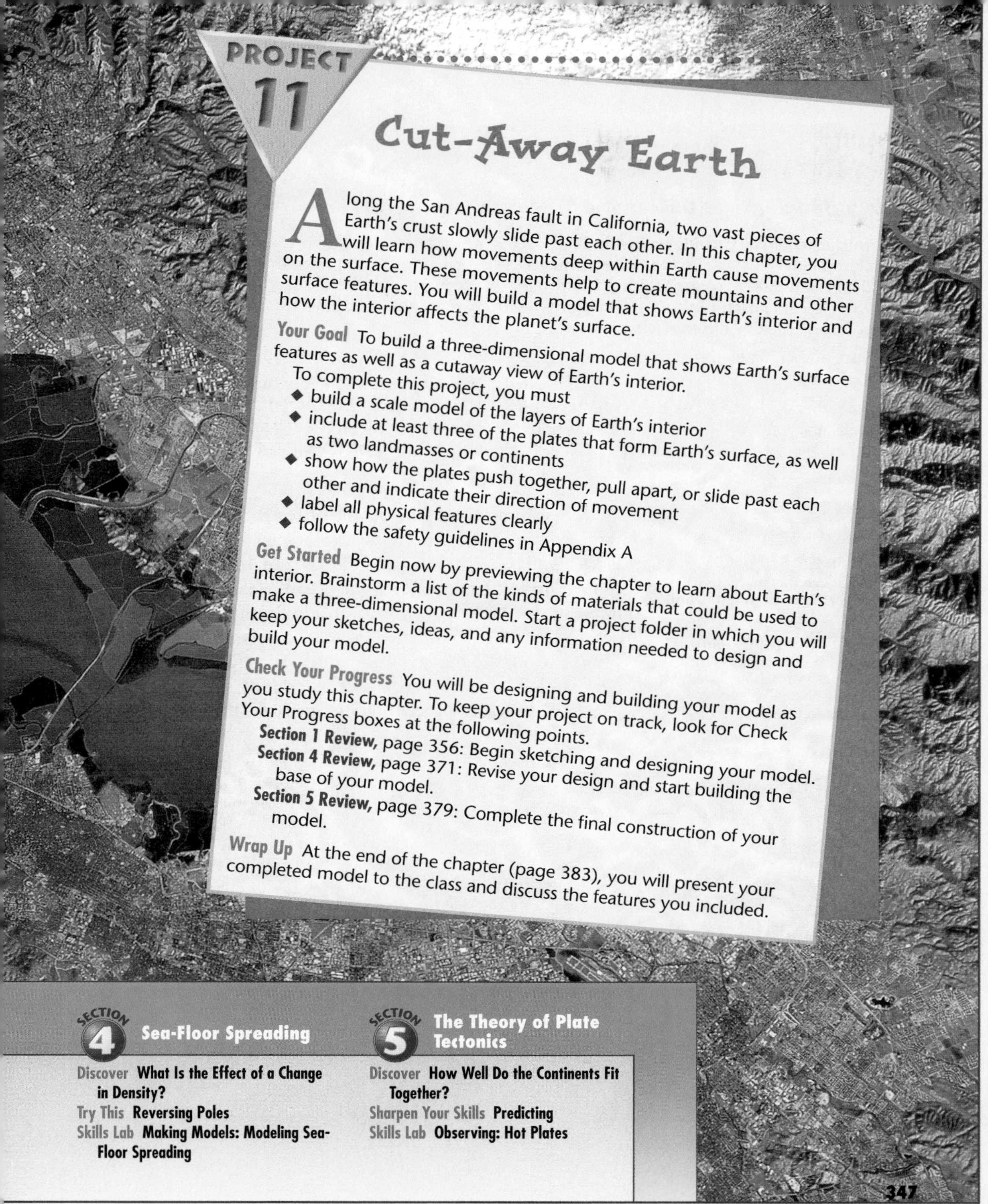

Cut-Away Earth

Along the San Andreas fault in California, two vast pieces of Earth's crust slowly slide past each other. In this chapter, you will learn how movements deep within Earth cause movements on the surface. These movements help to create mountains and other surface features. You will build a model that shows Earth's interior and how the interior affects the planet's surface.

Your Goal To build a three-dimensional model that shows Earth's surface features as well as a cutaway view of Earth's interior.

To complete this project, you must
- build a scale model of the layers of Earth's interior
- include at least three of the plates that form Earth's surface, as well as two landmasses or continents
- show how the plates push together, pull apart, or slide past each other and indicate their direction of movement
- label all physical features clearly
- follow the safety guidelines in Appendix A

Get Started Begin now by previewing the chapter to learn about Earth's interior. Brainstorm a list of the kinds of materials that could be used to make a three-dimensional model. Start a project folder in which you will keep your sketches, ideas, and any information needed to design and build your model.

Check Your Progress You will be designing and building your model as you study this chapter. To keep your project on track, look for Check Your Progress boxes at the following points.

Section 1 Review, page 356: Begin sketching and designing your model.

Section 4 Review, page 371: Revise your design and start building the base of your model.

Section 5 Review, page 379: Complete the final construction of your model.

Wrap Up At the end of the chapter (page 383), you will present your completed model to the class and discuss the features you included.

347

Program Resources

- **Unit 4 Resources** Chapter 11 Project Teacher Notes, pp. 2–3; Project Overview and Worksheets, pp. 4–7; Project Scoring Rubric, p. 8

Media and Technology

 Audio CDs Section Summaries

 **www.phschool.com**

You will find an Internet activity, chapter self-tests for students, and links to other chapter topics at this site.

Possible Materials A variety of materials could be used for the base of the model. These include papier-mâché, modeling clay, chicken wire, cardboard, plywood, and wood blocks. Groups may also think of other materials to use. To bring the models to life, paints, paint brushes, and permanent markers will also be necessary.

Launching the Project To introduce this project, show students a large world globe and ask: **If the inside of this globe reflected Earth's interior as well as it reflects Earth's surface, what would it show when cut in half?** (*Students might mention dirt, water, and rock.*) Tell them that in this chapter, they will learn that Earth's interior has several layers, each with different characteristics. Also point out that movements within the interior affect processes on the surface of the planet. Explain that in this project, they will work in groups to make a model of Earth's interior that shows a relationship between the surface and what's below. Then ask: **What kinds of materials are good for making three-dimensional models?** (*Students might mention a variety of materials, including clay and papier mâché.*) Then mention that they should be thinking of such materials in order to contribute to a group design for a model of Earth's interior. To help students get started, distribute Chapter 11 Project Overview and Worksheets, pages 4–7 in Unit 4 Resources. You may also wish to distribute the Chapter 11 Project Scoring Rubric, page 14, at this time.

Performance Assessment

Use the Chapter 11 Project Scoring Rubric to assess students' work. Students will be assessed on
- how well they make their sketches and plan their models;
- how well they incorporate the required features and create an attractive model of Earth's interior;
- how effectively they present the model and explain its features to the class;
- how well they work in the group and how much they contribute to the group's effort.

Objectives

After completing the lesson, students will be able to
◆ describe what geologists do;
◆ list the characteristics of Earth's crust, mantle, and core.

Key Terms geologist, rock, geology, constructive force, destructive force, continent, seismic wave, pressure, crust, basalt, granite, mantle, lithosphere, asthenosphere, outer core, inner core

1 Engage/Explore

Activating Prior Knowledge

Begin by having students recall times when they've dug a hole in the ground. Ask: **If you dig down far enough through the dirt, what does your shovel hit?** (*Most students will suggest that below the dirt is rock.*) **Other than rock, what else do you think is below the surface of Earth?** (*Students might mention oil and water.*) Remind them that Earth is large, and digging a hole or a well barely scratches the surface. Then challenge them to speculate about what Earth is like at its center.

DISCOVER

Skills Focus inferring
Materials *3 film canisters with tops, 3 different materials, masking tape, permanent marker, scale*
Time 10 minutes
Tips The different materials that could be used in the canisters include practically anything that will fit in the canisters. Try to include both liquids and solids and vary them in viscosity, density, size, and other physical characteristics.
Think It Over Answers will vary depending on the materials used. Some students may determine the contents of one or more canisters. Accept any reasonable explanation about how scientists gather evidence about Earth's interior.

DISCOVER .... ACTIVITY

How Do Scientists Determine What's Inside Earth?

1. Your teacher will provide you with three closed film canisters. Each canister contains a different material. Your goal is to determine what is inside each canister—even though you can't directly observe what it contains.

2. Stick a label made from a piece of tape on each canister.

3. To gather evidence about the contents of the canisters, you may tap, roll, shake, or weigh them. Record your observations.

4. What differences do you notice between the canisters? Apart from their appearance on the outside, are the canisters similar in any way? How did you obtain this evidence?

Think It Over

Inferring Based on your observations, what can you infer about the contents of the canisters? How do you think scientists gather evidence about Earth's interior?

GUIDE FOR READING

◆ What does a geologist do?
◆ What are the characteristics of Earth's crust, mantle, and core?

Reading Tip Before you read, rewrite the headings in the section as what, how, or why questions. As you read, look for answers to these questions.

In November 1963, the people of Iceland got to see how the world begins in fire. With no warning, the waters south of Iceland began to hiss and bubble. Soon there was a fiery volcanic eruption from beneath the ocean. Steam and ash belched into the sky. Molten rock from inside Earth spurted above the ocean's surface and hardened into a small island. Within the next several years, the new volcano added 2.5 square kilometers of new, raw land to Earth's surface. The Icelanders named the island "Surtsey." In Icelandic mythology, Surtsey is the god of fire.

Figure 1 The island of Surtsey formed in the Atlantic Ocean.

READING STRATEGIES

Reading Tip Students should rewrite the first heading of the section as the question, What is the science of geology? Encourage students to use this and subsequent questions as study aids by writing an answer to each question using information from the text. A typical answer to the first question might be: The science of geology is the study of planet Earth, including the forces that make and shape the planet.

Vocabulary Some students may have difficulty in both understanding and pronouncing the terms *lithosphere* and *asthenosphere.* Break the words apart and focus on the meaning and sound of *sphere,* an object in the shape of a ball. Both layers surround the rest of the planet. Thus the asthenosphere is a ball within the ball formed by the lithosphere.

The Science of Geology

Newspapers reported the story of Surtsey's fiery birth. But much of what is known about volcanoes like Surtsey comes from the work of geologists. **Geologists** are scientists who study the forces that make and shape planet Earth. Geologists study the chemical and physical characteristics of **rock,** the material that forms Earth's hard surface. They map where different types of rock are found on and beneath the surface. Geologists describe landforms, the features formed in rock and soil by water, wind, and waves. **Geologists study the processes that create Earth's features and search for clues about Earth's history.**

The modern science of **geology,** the study of planet Earth, began in the late 1700s. Geologists of that time studied the rocks on the surface. These geologists concluded that Earth's landforms are the work of natural forces that slowly build up and wear down the land.

Studying Surface Changes Forces beneath the surface are constantly changing Earth's appearance. Throughout our planet's long history, its surface has been lifted up, pushed down, bent, and broken. Thus Earth looks different today from the way it did millions of years ago.

Today, geologists divide the forces that change the surface into two groups: constructive forces and destructive forces. **Constructive forces** shape the surface by building up mountains and landmasses. **Destructive forces** are those that slowly wear away mountains and, eventually, every other feature on the surface. The formation of the island of Surtsey is an example of constructive forces at work. The ocean waves that wear away Surtsey's shoreline are an example of destructive forces.

Two hundred years ago, the science of geology was young. Then, geologists knew only a few facts about Earth's surface. They knew that Earth is a sphere with a radius at the equator of more than 6,000 kilometers. They knew that there are seven great landmasses, called **continents,** surrounded by oceans. They knew that the continents are made up of layers of rock.

Figure 2 The work of geologists often takes them outdoors—from mountainsides to caves beneath the surface. *Observing What are the geologists in each picture doing?*

Program Resources

◆ **Unit 4 Resources** 11-1 Lesson Plan, p. 9; 11-1 Section Summary, p. 10
◆ **Guided Reading and Study Workbook** Section 11-1

Answers to Self-Assessment

Caption Question

Figure 2 The geologists in the top picture are studying the characteristics of a cave. The geologist in the bottom picture is investigating rock layers.

---

2 Facilitate

The Science of Geology

Using the Visuals: Figure 1

Use the figure to reinforce the concept that the surface of Earth is constantly changing. Ask: **What are some other ways that Earth's surface is changed over time?** (*A typical answer might mention earthquakes, erosion, flooding, and glaciers.*) **Does the interior of Earth also change over time?** (*Accept any reasonable response.*) Explain that although this section is about the interior of the planet, students will learn that what occurs in the interior has a great effect on processes that shape the surface. **learning modality: visual**

Real-Life Learning

Invite a professional geologist to speak to the class about what a geologist does. This could be a teacher from a local university or a geologist from government or private industry. Mining and oil companies often hire geologists to help locate natural resources. Encourage students to make a list of questions to ask before the speaker comes to class. **learning modality: verbal**

Including All Students

To help students who have not mastered written English, have pairs of students of differing abilities work together to make a list of constructive forces and a list of destructive forces. Emphasize that their lists need not be confined to geologic forces. Then review the lists in a whole-class discussion. **cooperative learning**

Ongoing Assessment

Writing Have students write a short paragraph that explains in their own words what a geologist does.

 Students can save their paragraphs in their portfolios.

The Science of Geology, continued

Building Inquiry Skills: Posing Questions

To start students thinking about the structure of Earth, have each student write down three questions that he or she would like answered about the structure and geologic forces of planet Earth. After giving them time to write their questions, have students share them in small groups. Then have each group read their questions. Discuss how students might find the answers. **learning modality: logical/mathematical**

Using the Visuals: Figure 3

Ask students: **Who has ever visited a cave?** (*Some students may have visited local caverns or national parks with caves.*) Encourage students to relate their experiences to the class. Ask: **Why would a geologist study the interior of a cave?** (*To examine the materials below ground and try to determine the processes that formed the cave.*) Point out that even the deepest caves do not come close to reaching the center of Earth. **learning modality: logical/mathematical**

Inquiry Challenge

Materials *2-L bowl, small glass jar or bottle, pencil, water*
Time 15 minutes

To give students some idea of how geologists use seismic waves to investigate Earth's interior, have them investigate how an object in water changes the direction of waves. First, students might use the eraser end of a pencil to create waves in a bowl of water and observe how the waves move through the water. Then students could place a small jar or bottle in the middle of the bowl of water and predict how that jar or bottle will affect waves in the bowl. Students should sketch what they see happens to the waves produced and also write a description of how the changes in the waves show the location of the jar or bottle. **learning modality: kinesthetic**

Figure 3 This cave in Georgia may seem deep. But even a deep cave is only a small nick in Earth's surface.

These layers can sometimes be seen on the walls of canyons and the sides of valleys. However, many riddles remained: How old is Earth? How has Earth's surface changed over time? Why are there oceans, and how did they form? For 200 years, geologists have tried to answer these and other questions about the planet.

Finding Indirect Evidence One of the most difficult questions that geologists have tried to answer is, What's inside Earth? Much as geologists might like to, they cannot dig a hole to the center of Earth. The extreme conditions in Earth's interior prevent exploration far below the surface. The deepest mine in the world, a gold mine in South Africa, reaches a depth of 3.8 kilometers. But it only scratches the surface. You would have to travel more than 1,600 times that distance—over 6,000 kilometers—to reach Earth's center.

Geologists cannot observe Earth's interior directly. Instead, they must rely on indirect methods of observation. Have you ever hung a heavy picture on a wall? If you have, you know that you can knock on the wall to locate the wooden beam underneath the plaster that will support the picture. When you knock on the wall, you listen carefully for a change in the sound.

When geologists want to study Earth's interior, they also use an indirect method. But instead of knocking on walls, they use seismic waves. When earthquakes occur, they produce **seismic waves** (SYZ mik). Geologists record the seismic waves and study how they travel through Earth. The speed of these seismic waves and the paths they take reveal how the planet is put together. Using data from seismic waves, geologists have learned that Earth's interior is made up of several layers. Each layer surrounds the layers beneath it, much like the layers of an onion.

✓ *Checkpoint* What kind of indirect evidence do geologists use to study the structure of Earth?

Background

Facts and Figures In studying Earth's interior, scientists use the principle that the speed and direction of a seismic wave depends on the material it travels through. For example, the crust and the mantle are composed of different materials. One type of seismic wave (P waves) travels through crust material at about 6 km/sec but travels through mantle material at 8 km/sec. As a result, a wave that travels through the mantle could reach a recording station faster than a wave that travels more directly through the crust. When moving from one type of material into another, seismic waves refract, or bend. Such changes of direction are evidence of different materials. One type of seismic wave (S waves) will not travel through a liquid. By studying those waves, scientists know that the outer core is liquid.

A Journey to the Center of the Earth

If you really could travel through these layers to the center of Earth, what would your trip be like? To begin, you will need a vehicle that can travel through solid rock. The vehicle will carry scientific instruments to record changes in temperature and pressure as you descend.

Temperature As you start to tunnel beneath the surface, you might expect the rock around you to be cool. At first, the surrounding rock is cool. Then at about 20 meters down your instruments report that the surrounding rock is getting warmer. For every 40 meters that you descend from that point, the temperature rises 1 Celsius degree. This rapid rise in temperature continues for several kilometers. After that, the temperature increases more slowly, but steadily.

Pressure During your journey to the center of Earth, your instruments also record an increase in pressure in the surrounding rock. The deeper you go, the greater the pressure. **Pressure** is the force pushing on a surface or area. Because of the weight of the rock above, pressure inside Earth increases as you go deeper.

As you go toward the center of Earth, you travel through several different layers. **Three main layers make up Earth's interior: the crust, the mantle, and the core. Each layer has its own conditions and materials.** You can see these layers in *Exploring Earth's Interior* on pages 354–355.

Language Arts
CONNECTION

Imagine taking a trip to the center of Earth. That's what happens in a novel written by Jules Verne in 1864. At that time, scientists knew almost nothing about Earth's interior. Was it solid or hollow? Hot or cold? People speculated wildly. Verne's novel, called *Journey to the Center of the Earth*, describes the adventures of a scientific expedition to explore a hollow Earth. On the way, the explorers follow caves and tunnels down to a strange sea lit by a miniature sun.

In Your Journal

Write a paragraph that describes the most exciting part of your own imaginary journey to Earth's center.

Depth
0

Pressure Increases

.5m

1m

1.5m

2m

Figure 4 The deeper this swimmer goes, the greater the pressure from the surrounding water. *Comparing and Contrasting How is the water in the swimming pool similar to Earth's interior? How is it different?*

Answers to Self-Assessment

✓ *Checkpoint*

Geologists record seismic waves and study how they travel through Earth.

Caption Question

Figure 4 The deeper the water in the pool, the greater the pressure, just as pressure is greater the deeper you go beneath the surface of Earth. The water in the pool does not have layers, though.

A Journey to the Center of the Earth

Using the Visuals: Figure 4

Materials *water, bucket, 2-L plastic soft-drink bottle, small plastic soft-drink bottle*

ACTIVITY

Time 15 minutes

Ask students: **How can you show that pressure increases with depth, as suggested in the figure?** (*Students may mention using gauges to measure pressure at various depths.*) Then divide the class into small groups and challenge them to devise an experiment that would demonstrate the concept. One way to show the concept is to immerse a small plastic soft-drink bottle with a cap on into a bucket filled with water. At the bottom of the bucket, the bottle will begin to collapse. **cooperative learning**

Language Arts
CONNECTION

French writer Jules Verne (1828–1905) wrote tales of adventure that often remarkably anticipated the scientific inquiries of the twentieth century. Many libraries have the works in a form adapted especially for young people. Encourage students to read an adaptation of *Journey to the Center of the Earth* and make a report to the class.

In Your Journal Before students begin to write, have them study the *Exploring Earth's Interior* feature on pages 354–355. Then encourage them to use both that information and their imaginations to write a description of an exciting incident that might happen on a journey to the center of Earth. **learning modality: verbal**

Ongoing Assessment

Drawing Have students draw a diagram that shows a cross section of Earth with an indication of how pressure and temperature change with depth.

The Crust

Building Inquiry Skills: Comparing and Contrasting

Materials *small sample of basalt, small sample of granite, hand lens*

Time 10 minutes

Before students read the descriptions of basalt and granite, give them the opportunity to compare and contrast a small sample of each. Place the samples on a table at a central location. Students can then examine a sample of each and write a paragraph that compares and contrasts the two rocks in terms of color, density, and texture. **learning modality: visual**

Addressing Naive Conceptions

Some students may misunderstand the idea that continental crust and oceanic crust consist mainly of granite and basalt, respectively. Display a piece of granite and ask: **Are all the rocks you see on land granite?** (*A typical answer might suggest that most do not look like granite.*) Explain that soil, water, and various other kinds of rocks cover much of the surface of the crust. Granite is the most common rock in the continental crust. **learning modality: verbal**

The Mantle

Including All Students

To help students who are having trouble understanding the boundaries between the various layers, draw three circles on the board to represent the crust, mantle, and core. Invite a volunteer to label Earth's three main layers. Call on another volunteer to use white chalk to shade the area that represents the lithosphere. (*The student should shade in the crust and the uppermost part of the mantle.*) Then invite another volunteer to use a different color of chalk to shade the area that represents the asthenosphere. (*The student should make a shaded circle just inside the lithosphere, wider than the lithosphere but still leaving most of the mantle unshaded.*) **learning modality: visual**

Figure 5 Two of the most common rocks in the crust are basalt and granite. **A.** The dark rock is basalt, which makes up much of the oceanic crust. **B.** The light rock is granite, which makes up much of the continental crust.

The Crust

Your journey to the center of Earth begins in the crust. The **crust** is a layer of rock that forms Earth's outer skin. On the crust you find rocks and mountains. But the crust also includes the soil and water that cover large parts of Earth's surface.

This outer rind of rock is much thinner than what lies beneath it. In fact, you can think of Earth's crust as being similar to the paper-thin skin of an onion. The crust includes both the dry land and the ocean floor. It is thinnest beneath the ocean and thickest under high mountains. The crust ranges from 5 to 40 kilometers thick.

The crust beneath the ocean is called oceanic crust. Oceanic crust consists mostly of dense rocks such as basalt. **Basalt** (buh SAWLT) is dark, dense rock with a fine texture. Continental crust, the crust that forms the continents, consists mainly of less dense rocks such as granite. **Granite** is a rock that has larger crystals than basalt and is not as dense. It usually is a light color.

The Mantle

Your journey downward continues. At a depth of between 5 and 40 kilometers beneath the surface, you cross a boundary. Above this boundary are the basalt and granite rocks of the crust. Below the boundary is the solid material of the **mantle,** a layer of hot rock.

The crust and the uppermost part of the mantle are very similar. The uppermost part of the mantle and the crust together form a rigid layer called the **lithosphere** (LITH uh sfeer). In Greek, *lithos* means "stone." The lithosphere averages about 100 kilometers thick.

352

Figure 6 At the surface, Earth's crust forms peaks like these in the Rocky Mountains of Colorado. Soil and plants cover much of the crust.

Next you travel farther into the mantle below the lithosphere. There your vehicle encounters material that is hotter and under increasing pressure. In general, temperature and pressure in the mantle increase with depth. The heat and pressure make the part of the mantle just beneath the lithosphere less rigid than the rock above. Like road tar softened by the heat of the sun, the material that forms this part of the mantle is somewhat soft—it can bend like plastic.

This soft layer is called the **asthenosphere** (as THEHN uh sfeer). In Greek, *asthenes* means "weak." Just because asthenes means weak, you can't assume this layer is actually weak. But the asthenosphere is soft. The material in this layer can flow slowly.

The lithosphere floats on top of the asthenosphere. Beneath the asthenosphere, solid mantle material extends all the way to Earth's core. The mantle is nearly 3,000 kilometers thick.

☑ *Checkpoint* How does the material of the asthenosphere differ from the material of the lithosphere?

The Core

After traveling through the mantle, you reach the core. Earth's core consists of two parts—a liquid outer core and a solid inner core. The metals iron and nickel make up both parts of the core. The **outer core** is a layer of molten metal that surrounds the inner core. In spite of enormous pressure, the outer core behaves like a thick liquid. The **inner core** is a dense ball of solid metal. In the inner core, extreme pressure squeezes the atoms of iron and nickel so much that they cannot spread out and become liquid.

The outer and inner cores make up about one third of Earth's mass, but only 15 percent of its volume. The inner and outer cores together are just slightly smaller than the moon.

Sharpen your Skills

Creating Data Tables

Imagine that you have invented a super-strong vehicle that can resist extremely high pressure as it bores a tunnel deep into Earth's interior. You stop several times on your trip to collect data using devices located on your vehicle's outer hull. To see what conditions you would find at various depths on your journey, refer to *Exploring Earth's Interior* on pages 354–355. Copy the table and complete it.

Depth	Name of Layer	What Layer Is Made Of
20 km		
150 km		
2,000 km		
4,000 km		
6,000 km		

Answers to Self-Assessment

☑ *Checkpoint*
The material of the asthenosphere is somewhat soft and can bend like plastic, while the material of the lithosphere is solid and rigid.

Demonstration

Materials *2 cans of window glazing, small pan, water, hot plate*
Time 10 minutes

Keep a can of window glazing—a puttylike material used to hold glass in place—in a refrigerator overnight. Invite students to touch the glazing to observe that it does not flow. Ask: **Is this substance a solid or a liquid?** *(Most students will say that it is a solid.)* Provide another can of glazing that you have heated beforehand in a pan of water on a hot plate. Invite students to observe how much more pliable the heated glazing is than the cold glazing. Ask: **How is the heated glazing like the material that makes up the mantle?** *(The heated glazing still has characteristics of a solid but can be shaped like plastic.)* **learning modality: kinesthetic**

The Core

Sharpen your Skills

Creating Data Tables

Time 15 minutes
Expected Outcome
A typical completed table may include the following information. At a depth of 20 km, the layer is the crust, which is made of solid rock, mostly granite and basalt. At 150 km, the layer is the asthenosphere, made of soft material that can flow slowly. At 2,000 km, the layer is the mantle, which at this depth is hot but solid material. At 4,000 km, the layer is the outer core, which is molten iron and nickel. At 6,000 km, the layer is the inner core, which is solid iron and nickel.
Extend Pairs of students could quiz each other using such depths as 5 km, 30 km, 1,000 km, and 5,000 km. **learning modality: logical/mathematical**

Ongoing Assessment

Oral Presentation Ask students to prepare a short oral presentation on the physical characteristics of the crust, mantle, inner core, and outer core. Then call on students at random to each give a description of one of the layers.

EXPLORING
Earth's Interior

Direct students' attention to the leftmost cutaway view of Earth's interior and invite volunteers to read the annotations about the three layers. Ask: **Does Earth's interior have three or four layers?** *(Three layers, with the core having two sublayers called the inner and outer core.)* **What characteristic causes geologists to consider the inner and outer cores as part of one layer instead of as two separate layers?** *(They both consist of the same materials, iron and nickel.)* Then turn students' attention to the cross-section from surface to center. Explain that scientists believe the elements separated during Earth's formation about 4.6 billion years ago. Lighter elements rose toward the surface while certain heavier elements sank toward the center. Ask: **What general statement can you make about the change in temperature through Earth's interior?** *(Temperature increases as depth increases.)* **What about pressure?** *(Pressure also increases as depth increases.)* Finally, turn students' attention to what distinguishes the lithosphere from the asthenosphere. Make sure they understand that the lithosphere includes all of the crust and the topmost part of the mantle.
learning modality: visual

Demonstration

Materials *apple, knife*
Time 5 minutes

Show students an apple and ask: **How is this apple like Earth?** *(They are both round.)* Then cut the apple in half and repeat the question. Students should be able to see the similarities. Both have layers, with a thin crust, a large middle layer, and a core. **learning modality: visual**

EXPLORING *Earth's Interior*

Earth's interior is divided into layers: the crust, mantle, outer core, and inner core. Although Earth's crust seems stable, the extreme heat of Earth's interior causes changes that slowly reshape the surface.

CRUST
The crust is Earth's solid and rocky outer layer, including both the land surface and the ocean floor. The crust averages 32 km thick. At the scale of this drawing, the crust is too thin to show up as more than a thin line.

Composition of crust:
oxygen, silicon, aluminum, calcium, iron, sodium, potassium, magnesium

Inner core
Outer core
Mantle
Crust
1,200 km
2,250 km
2,900 km
5–40 km

MANTLE
A trip through Earth's mantle goes almost halfway to the center of Earth. The chemical composition of the mantle does not change much from one part of the mantle to another. However, physical conditions in the mantle change because pressure and temperature increase with depth.

Composition of mantle:
silicon, oxygen, iron, magnesium

CORE
Scientists estimate that temperatures within Earth's outer core and inner core, both made of iron and nickel, range from about 2,000°C to 5,000°C. If these estimates are correct, then Earth's center may be as hot as the sun's surface.

Composition of core:
iron, nickel

Background

Facts and Figures Have students consider these facts and figures about Earth's interior.

◆ Suppose you could drive a car at 100 km/hr (62 mi/hr) from Earth's surface to the center of the core. At that speed, the car would take about half an hour to drive through most continental crust, about another 29 hours to drive through the mantle, and about an additional 35 hours to drive to the center of the core.

◆ The mantle makes up about 80 percent of Earth's total volume.

◆ Pressure at the center of the inner core may be more than 1 million times greater than air pressure at sea level.

◆ Crust material is 2.5–3.0 times denser than water; mantle material is 3.3–5.5 times denser than water; core material is 10–13 times denser than water.

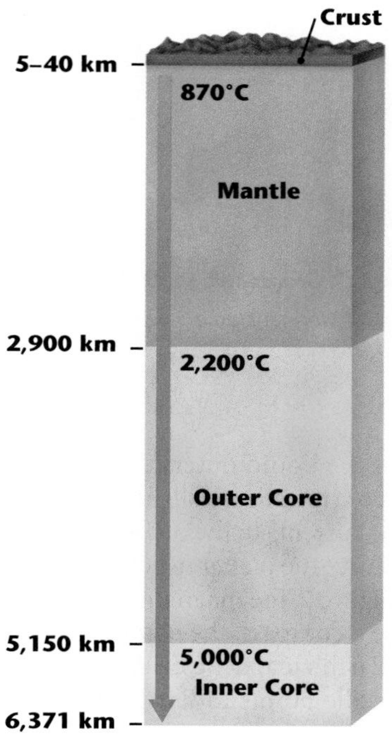

Crust

5–40 km —

870°C

◄ **CROSS-SECTION FROM SURFACE TO CENTER**
From Earth's surface to its center, the layers of Earth's interior differ in their composition, temperature, and pressure. Notice how temperature increases toward the inner core.

Mantle

2,900 km —

2,200°C

Outer Core

CRUST-TO-MANTLE
The rigid crust and lithosphere float on the hot, plastic material of the asthenosphere. Notice that continental crust, made mostly of granite, is several times thicker than oceanic crust, made mostly of basalt. ▼

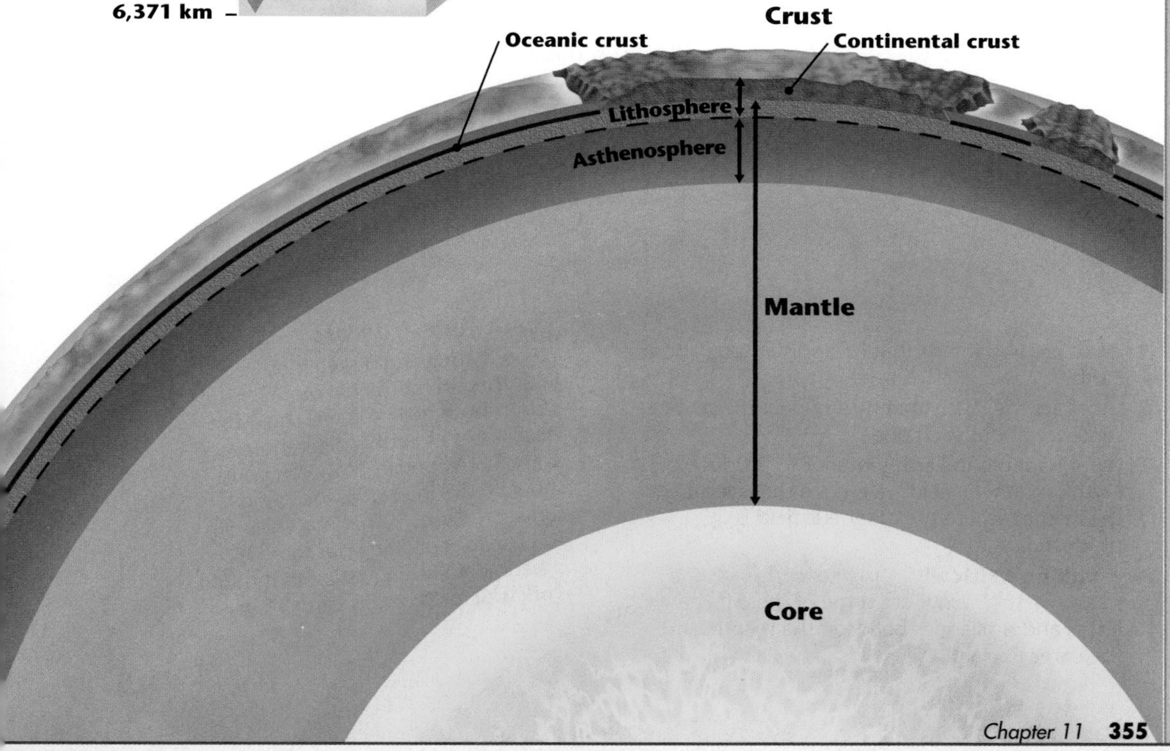

5,150 km —

5,000°C
Inner Core

6,371 km —

Crust

Oceanic crust

Continental crust

Lithosphere

Asthenosphere

Mantle

Core

Media and Technology

 Transparencies "Exploring Earth's Interior," Transparency 41

Building Inquiry Skills: Measuring

Explain that the drawings of Earth's interior shown in *Exploring Earth's Interior* were done to scale, except for the thickness of the crust in the figures on page 355, which is slightly exaggerated. Ask: **Why should scientific illustrations be drawn to a scale?** (*Drawn to scale, the proportions between parts are accurate.*) Challenge students to determine what scale was used in preparing the cutaway view on the left and the cross-section view on the upper right. To determine the scale of a drawing, students must measure the distance from the outside boundary to the center, and then divide the distance in kilometers by that number. Students should find that the cutaway view uses a scale of about 1 cm = 1,300 km, and that the cross-section view uses a scale of about 1 cm = 750 km. **learning modality: logical/ mathematical**

Earth's Magnetic Field

 Integrating Physics

Materials *bar magnet, iron filings in a paper cup, sheet of paper*
Time 10 minutes

Ask students: **What is the shape of a bar magnet's magnetic field?** Then divide the class into pairs and give each pair the basic materials with which to investigate that question. The most common way to use these materials is to lay the bar magnet on a table, place the sheet of paper over it, and then sprinkle the iron filings over the sheet of paper. Make sure students do not place the iron filings directly on the magnet. Students should make a drawing of what they see.
learning modality: kinesthetic

Ongoing Assessment

Drawing Have students make a diagram showing the layers of Earth, with brief descriptive phrases about each layer.

3 Assess

Section 1 Review Answers

1. Geologists study the processes that create Earth's features and search for clues about Earth's history.

2. Answers may vary. Students should write a sentence derived from the text about the crust, mantle, outer core, and inner core.

3. Currents in the liquid outer core force the solid inner core to spin at a different rate than the rest of the planet, causing the planet to act like a giant bar magnet. The outer core is a layer of molten material, while the inner core is a dense ball of solid metal.

4. Both the mantle and core are divided into layers. The mantle has part of the rigid lithosphere, the soft asthenosphere, and the lower mantle; the core has the molten outer core and the solid inner core. The core is much hotter than the mantle, and pressure is much greater there. Both the mantle and core contain iron, but the mantle also contains silicon, oxygen, and magnesium and the core also contains nickel.

Check Your Progress
CHAPTER PROJECT 11

A review of the sketches in each student's folder will help you assess which students are having difficulty with the concepts involved, as well as give you an idea of what each student will contribute to the group's design. Then talk with each group during its initial meeting. Encourage students to brainstorm a list of possible materials for the model. Point out that the interior layers should be made to scale, while the surface features may be exaggerated for effect. Encourage groups to begin collecting materials and experimenting with a design.

Performance Assessment

Skills Check Have each student make a compare/contrast table that includes information about all the layers of Earth's interior.

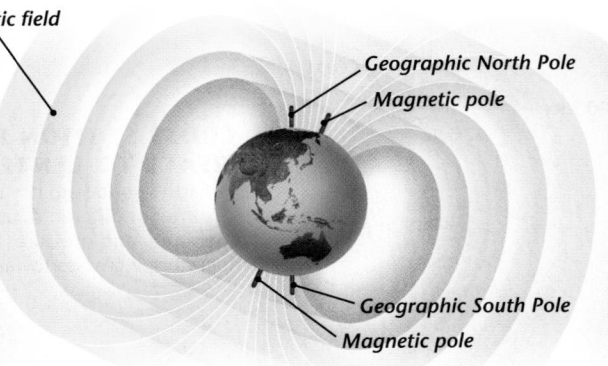

Earth's magnetic field

Geographic North Pole
Magnetic pole

Geographic South Pole
Magnetic pole

Figure 7 A. The pattern of iron filings was made by sprinkling them on paper placed over a bar magnet. **B.** Like a magnet, Earth's magnetic field has north and south poles. *Relating Cause and Effect If you shifted the magnet beneath the paper, what would happen to the iron filings?*

Earth's Magnetic Field

 INTEGRATING PHYSICS Currents in the liquid outer core force the solid inner core to spin at a slightly faster rate than the rest of the planet. These currents in the outer core create Earth's magnetic field, which causes the planet to act like a giant bar magnet. As you can see in Figure 7, the magnetic field affects the whole Earth. When you use a compass, the compass needle aligns with the lines of force in Earth's magnetic field. The north-seeking end of the compass needle points to Earth's magnetic north pole.

Consider an ordinary bar magnet. If you place it beneath a piece of paper and sprinkle iron filings on the paper, the iron filings line up with the bar's magnetic field. If you could cover the entire planet with iron filings, they would form a similar pattern.

Section 1 Review

1. What are two things that geologists study about Earth?

2. What are the layers that make up Earth? Write a sentence about each one.

3. What happens in Earth's interior to produce Earth's magnetic field? Describe the layers of the interior where the magnetic field is produced.

4. **Thinking Critically Comparing and Contrasting** What are some of the differences and similarities between the mantle and the core? Explain.

Check Your Progress
CHAPTER PROJECT 11

Begin by drawing a sketch of your three-dimensional model. Think about how you will show the thicknesses of Earth's different layers at the correct scale. How can you show Earth's interior as well as its surface features? What materials can you use for building your model? Experiment with materials that might work well for showing Earth's layers.

Answers to Self-Assessment

Caption Question

Figure 7 The iron filings would move with the magnet, again forming the same pattern above the magnet's new position.

Program Resources

◆ **Unit 4 Resources** 11-1 Review and Reinforce, p. 11; 11-1 Enrich, p. 12

SECTION 2 Convection Currents and the Mantle

DISCOVER .... ACTIVITY

How Can Heat Cause Motion in a Liquid?

1. ⚠️ Carefully pour some hot water into a small, shallow pan. Fill a clear, plastic cup about half full with cold water. Place the cup in the pan.

2. Allow the water to stand for two minutes until all motion stops.

3. Fill a plastic dropper with some food coloring. Then, holding the dropper under the water surface and slightly away from the edge of the cup, gently squeeze a small droplet of the food coloring into the water.

4. Observe the water for one minute.

5. Add another droplet at the water surface in the middle of the cup and observe again.

Think It Over

Inferring How do you explain what happened to the droplets of food coloring? Why do you think the second droplet moved in a way that was different from the way the first droplet moved?

Earth's molten outer core is nearly as hot as the surface of the sun. To explain how heat from the core affects the mantle, you need to know how heat is transferred in solids and liquids. If you have ever touched a hot pot accidentally, you have discovered for yourself (in a painful way) that heat moves. In this case, it moved from the hot pot to your hand. The movement of energy from a warmer object to a cooler object is called **heat transfer**.

Heat is always transferred from a warmer substance to a cooler substance. For example, holding an ice cube will make your hand begin to feel cold in a few seconds. But is the coldness in the ice cube moving to your hand? Since cold is the absence of heat, it's the heat in your hand that moves to the ice cube! **There are three types of heat transfer: radiation, conduction, and convection.**

Radiation

The transfer of energy through empty space is called **radiation.** Sunlight is radiation that warms Earth's surface. Heat transfer by radiation takes place with no direct contact between a heat source and an object. Radiation enables sunlight to warm Earth's surface. Other familiar forms of radiation include the heat you feel around a flame or open fire.

GUIDE FOR READING

◆ How is heat transferred?

◆ What causes convection currents?

Reading Tip As you read, draw a concept map of the three types of heat transfer. Include supporting ideas about convection.

Chapter 11 **357**

SECTION 2 Convection Currents and the Mantle

Objectives

After completing the lesson, students will be able to
◆ explain how heat is transferred;
◆ identify what causes convection currents.

Key Terms heat transfer, radiation, conduction, convection, density, convection current

1 Engage/Explore

Activating Prior Knowledge

Ask students: **In a room in a drafty house, why is it colder near the floor than near the ceiling?** (*Cold air sinks, while hot air rises.*) Students should understand that the air in such a room circulates as drafts of cold air move over the floor and warmer air rises. Point out that differences in temperature cause the circulation.

.... DISCOVER ....

Skills Focus inferring
Materials *shallow pan, clear plastic cup, hot water, cold water, plastic dropper, food coloring*
Time 10 minutes
Expected Outcome When students add the first droplet, food coloring should move toward the center, down to the bottom, and then upward along the edges of the cup toward the surface. When students add the second droplet, the coloring should move quickly to the bottom, spread out toward the edges of the cup, and then back upward.
Think It Over Heat is transferred from the hot water in the pan to the cold water in the cup. As the water in the bottom of the cup warms up, it becomes less dense and rises. The colder water at the top of the cup sinks, setting currents in the water in motion. The two droplets moved differently because they entered the currents at different places.

2 Facilitate

Radiation

Demonstration

Materials *heat lamp*
Time 5 minutes

Turn on a heat lamp and invite all students to walk within a meter of it. Ask: **How is energy transferred from the lamp to your body?** (*The energy moves across the space by means of invisible rays.*) Challenge students to name other examples of heat transfer by radiation. (*Heat from the sun, a fire, and radiators*) **learning modality: kinesthetic**

Conduction

Real-Life Learning

Show students a meat thermometer and have a volunteer describe how and why it is used. Then ask: **How does this instrument measure the heat of a piece of meat?** (*The heat from the meat is transferred to the thermometer through direct contact, or conduction.*) Then challenge students to analyze whether a medical thermometer and a weather thermometer work in the same fashion. (*They all measure heat through conduction.*) **learning modality: logical/mathematical**

Convection

Building Inquiry Skills: Observing

Materials *beaker or clear*
glass saucepan, instant chicken soup mix, water, hot plate, oven mitt
Time 10 minutes

Have small groups of students heat chicken soup in a beaker or saucepan on a hot plate. (**CAUTION:** *Students should wear goggles and aprons and handle hot materials very carefully.*) They should start with the soup cold, and use medium heat to prolong the process. (*Students should observe convection currents as the soup heats up.*) **learning modality: visual**

Figure 8 In conduction, the heated particles of a substance transfer heat to other particles through direct contact. That's how the spoon and the pot itself heat up.

Figure 9 In this pot, the soup close to the heat source is hotter and less dense than the soup near the surface. These differences in temperature and density cause convection currents.

358

Conduction

Heat transfer by direct contact of particles of matter is called **conduction.** What happens as a spoon heats up in a pot of soup? Heat is transferred from the hot soup and the pot to the particles that make up the spoon. The particles near the bottom of the spoon vibrate faster as they are heated, so they bump into other particles and heat them, too. Gradually the entire spoon heats up. When your hand touches the spoon, conduction transfers heat from the spoon directly to your skin. Then you feel the heat. Look at Figure 8 to see how conduction takes place.

Convection

Conduction heats the spoon, but how does the soup inside the pot heat up? Heat transfer involving the movement of fluids—liquids and gases—is called convection. **Convection** is heat transfer by the movement of a heated fluid. During convection, heated particles of fluid begin to flow, transferring heat energy from one part of the fluid to another.

Heat transfer by convection is caused by differences of temperature and density within a fluid. **Density** is a measure of how much mass there is in a volume of a substance. For example, rock is more dense than water because a given volume of rock has more mass than the same volume of water.

When a liquid or gas is heated, the particles move faster. As the particles move faster, they spread apart. Because the particles of the heated fluid are farther apart, they occupy more space. The density decreases. But when a fluid cools, its particles move more slowly and settle together more closely. As the fluid becomes cooler, its density increases.

If you look at Figure 9, you can see how convection occurs when you heat soup on a stove. As the soup at the bottom of the pot gets hot, it expands and therefore becomes less dense. The warm, less dense soup moves upward and floats over the cooler, denser soup. At the surface, the warm soup spreads out and cools, becoming denser. Then, gravity pulls this cooler, denser soup back down to the bottom of the pot, where it is heated again.

A constant flow begins as the cooler soup continually sinks to the bottom of the pot and the warmer soup rises. A **convection current** is the flow that transfers heat within a fluid.

Background

Integrating Science Over time, Earth's total amount of thermal energy has diminished as some heat is given off to space. Eventually, the core will be no hotter than the rest of the planet and will no longer produce convection in the mantle. Without convection in the mantle, movement of Earth's plates will come to a stop.

Media and Technology

 Concept Videotape Library
Adventures, Tape 3, "The Power of Heat"; "Hot Is Hot, Cold Is Not"

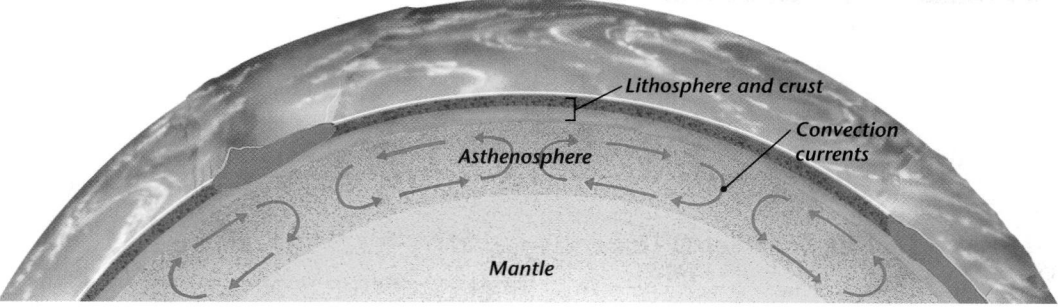

Lithosphere and crust

Convection currents

Asthenosphere

Mantle

The heating and cooling of the fluid, changes in the fluid's density, and the force of gravity combine to set convection currents in motion. Convection currents continue as long as heat is added. What happens after the heat source is removed? Without heat, the convection currents will eventually stop when all of the material has reached the same temperature.

✓ *Checkpoint* What is convection?

Convection in Earth's Mantle

Like soup simmering in a pot, Earth's mantle responds to heat. Notice in Figure 10 how convection currents flow in the asthenosphere. The heat source for these currents is heat from Earth's core and from the mantle itself. Hot columns of mantle material rise slowly through the asthenosphere. At the top of the asthenosphere, the hot material spreads out and pushes the cooler material out of the way. This cooler material sinks back into the asthenosphere. Over and over, the cycle of rising and sinking takes place. Convection currents like these have been moving inside Earth for more than four billion years!

Figure 10 Heat from Earth's mantle and core causes convection currents to form in the asthenosphere. Some geologists think convection currents extend throughout the mantle. *Applying Concepts* What part of Earth's interior is like the soup in the pot? What part is like the burner on the stove?

 Section 2 Review

1. What are the three types of heat transfer?
2. Describe how convection currents form.
3. In general, what happens to the density of a fluid when it becomes hotter?
4. What happens to convection currents when a fluid reaches a constant temperature?
5. **Thinking Critically** **Predicting** What will happen to the flow of hot rock in Earth's mantle if the planet's core eventually cools down? Explain your answer.

Science at Home

Convection currents may keep the air inside your home at a comfortable temperature. Air is made up of gases, so it is a fluid. Regardless of the type of home heating system, heated air circulates through a room by convection. You may have tried to adjust the flow of air in a stuffy room by opening a window. When you did so, you were making use of convection currents. With an adult family member, study how your home is heated. Look for evidence of convection currents.

Program Resources

◆ **Unit 4 Resources** 11-2 Review and Reinforce, p. 15; 11-2 Enrich, p. 16

Answers to Self-Assessment

Caption Question

Figure 10 The asthenosphere is like the soup in the pot. The core and mantle are like the burner on the stove.

✓ *Checkpoint*

Convection is heat transfer by the movement of a heated fluid.

Convection in Earth's Mantle

Using the Visuals: Figure 10

Explain that each of the circular currents shown in the figure is called a convection cell. Ask: **Where in the convection cell is the densest material?** *(At the bottom, just as the material turns to move horizontally.)* **Where is the material the coolest?** *(At the top, where the cell turns downward.)* **learning modality: visual**

3 Assess

Section 2 Review Answers

1. Radiation, conduction, and convection
2. The heating and cooling of a fluid, changes in a fluid's density, and the force of gravity combine to set convection currents in motion.
3. In general, when a fluid is heated, its density decreases.
4. When a fluid reaches a constant temperature, the convection currents stop.
5. The flow of hot rock would slow and eventually stop because the heat from the core is what sets convection currents in the asthenosphere in motion.

Science at Home

Outcomes will vary depending on the type of **ACTIVITY** heating system in a student's home. Students should be able to see that convection plays a part in all heating systems, though fans may also help circulate the air. They also may conclude that heating units or vents are best located near the floor, so that heat rises throughout the room.

Performance Assessment

Drawing Have students draw labeled diagrams that show how heat is transferred by radiation, conduction, and convection.

Objectives

After completing the lesson, students will be able to
◆ describe the theory of continental drift;
◆ list the evidence used by Alfred Wegener to form his theory and explain why other scientists rejected it.

Key Terms Pangaea, continental drift, fossil

1 Engage/Explore

Activating Prior Knowledge

Ask students: **What is a continent?** *(A continent is a one of Earth's seven large landmasses.)* **Can you name the continents?** *(Asia, Africa, North America, South America, Europe, Australia, Antarctica)* Then have students speculate about whether the continents have always had the same shape and been in the same place as they are today.

· · · · · · · DISCOVER · · · · · · ·

Skills Focus posing questions
Materials *globe that shows physical features*
Time 15 minutes
Tips Place several globes throughout the classroom where students can gather around them in small groups. Have students write the answers to the questions contained within the steps of the activity. *(Step 2: more than one third; Northern Hemisphere Step 3: at the North Pole; at the South Pole Step 4: through Europe and Asia)*
Think It Over Students' questions may vary. Accept any reasonable questions about the distribution of Earth's oceans, continents, and mountains.

DISCOVER · ACTIVITY · · ·

How Are Earth's Continents Linked Together?

1. Find the oceans and the seven continents on a globe showing Earth's physical features.

2. How much of the globe is occupied by the Pacific Ocean? Does most of Earth's "dry" land lie in the Northern or Southern hemisphere?

3. Find the points or areas where most of the continents are connected. Find the points at which several of the continents almost touch, but are not connected.

4. Examine the globe more closely. Find the great belt of mountains running from north to south along the western side of North and South America. Can you find another great belt of mountains on the globe?

Think It Over
Posing Questions What questions can you pose about how oceans, continents, and mountains are distributed on Earth's surface?

GUIDE FOR READING

◆ What is continental drift?
◆ Why was Alfred Wegener's theory rejected by most scientists of his day?

Reading Tip As you read, look for evidence that supports the theory of continental drift.

World map drawn by
Juan Vespucci in 1526. ▶

360

Five hundred years ago, the sea voyages of Columbus and other explorers changed the map of the world. The continents of Europe, Asia, and Africa were already known to mapmakers. Soon mapmakers were also showing the outlines of the continents of North and South America. Looking at these world maps, many people wondered why the coasts of several continents matched so neatly.

Look at the modern world map in Figure 11. Notice how the coasts of Africa and South America look as if they could fit together like jigsaw-puzzle pieces. Could the continents have once been a single landmass? In the 1700s, the first geologists thought that the continents had remained fixed in their positions throughout Earth's history. Early in the 1900s, however, one scientist began to think in a new way about this riddle of the continents. His theory changed the way people look at the map of the world.

READING STRATEGIES

Reading Tip Encourage students to keep a list of supporting evidence that includes the type of evidence, the reason why it supports the theory, and the page of their text that the evidence is on. Tell students that the section headings should help them in this process. This list will eventually serve as a study guide to the chapter.

Vocabulary Call students' attention to the boldfaced term *Pangaea*. Have students look up the term *panacea* in a dictionary and compare the use of the prefix *pan*. Explain that *gaea* was an ancient Greek word for both "Earth" and the "goddess of the Earth," the personification of Earth.

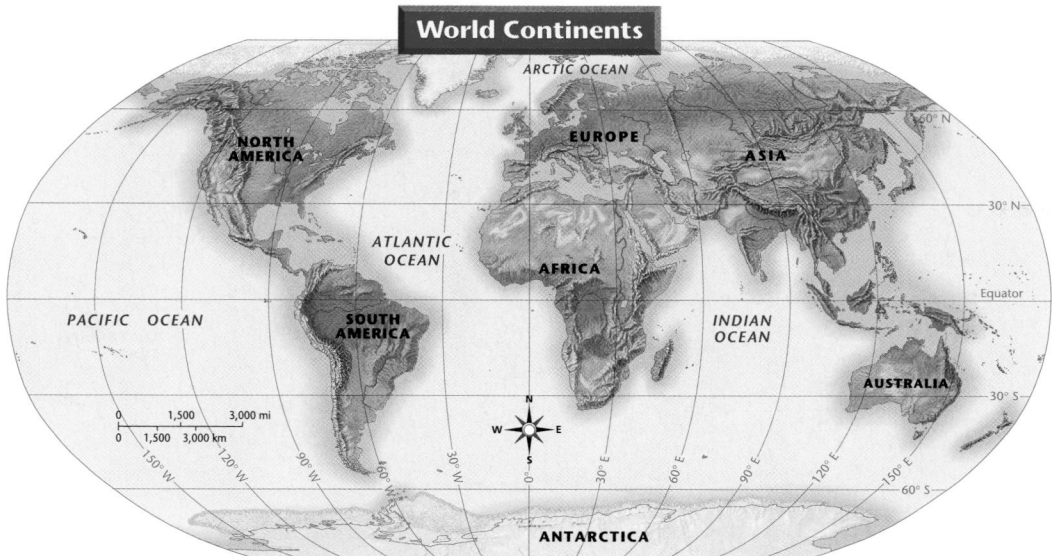

World Continents

Figure 11 Today's continents provide clues about Earth's history. *Observing Which coastlines of continents seem to match up like jigsaw-puzzle pieces?*

The Theory of Continental Drift

In 1910, a young German scientist named Alfred Wegener (VAY guh nur) became curious about the relationship of the continents. He formed a hypothesis that Earth's continents had moved! **Wegener's hypothesis was that all the continents had once been joined together in a single landmass and have since drifted apart.**

Wegener named this supercontinent **Pangaea** (pan JEE uh), meaning "all lands." According to Wegener, Pangaea existed about 300 million years ago. This was the time when reptiles and winged insects first appeared. Great tropical forests, which later formed coal deposits, covered large parts of Earth's surface.

Over tens of millions of years, Pangaea began to break apart. The pieces of Pangaea slowly moved toward their present-day locations, becoming the continents as they are today. Wegener's idea that the continents slowly moved over Earth's surface became known as **continental drift**.

Have you ever tried to persuade a friend to accept a new idea? Your friend's opinion probably won't change unless you provide some convincing evidence. Wegener gathered evidence from different scientific fields to support his ideas about continental drift. In particular, he studied landforms, fossils, and evidence that showed how Earth's climate had changed over many millions of years. Wegener published all his evidence for continental drift in a book called *The Origin of Continents and Oceans*, first published in 1915.

Program Resources

◆ **Unit 4 Resources** 11-3 Lesson Plan, p. 17; 11-3 Section Summary, p. 18
◆ **Guided Reading and Study Workbook** Section 11-3

Answers to Self-Assessment

Caption Question

Figure 11 The continents of Africa and South America best match up like jigsaw-puzzle pieces.

2 Facilitate

The Theory of Continental Drift

Using the Visuals: Figure 11

To understand the rest of this chapter, it is important for students to have a clear understanding of the distribution of land on Earth's surface. Have pairs of students quiz each other about the continents and the oceans that separate them. Identify students who have trouble with the basic geography of the world and give them a list of questions to answer by using a world map or globe. **learning modality: visual**

Including All Students

To help students place Wegener's theory in context, provide students with access to a geologic time scale. All encyclopedias and most geology books also contain a detailed time scale of Earth's history. Then have students write a description of what Earth was like when Pangaea existed, using what they find on the time scale. **learning modality: verbal**

 Students can keep their paragraphs in their portfolios.

Building Inquiry Skills: Developing Hypotheses

Ask students: **What force could have broken apart Pangaea and moved the continents into their present-day positions?** Challenge students in small groups to discuss this question and then develop a hypothesis that might answer it. Have each group read aloud its hypothesis to the class. Encourage questions and analysis of these hypotheses, though at this time do not make judgments about their validity. **cooperative learning**

Ongoing Assessment

Writing Have each student write in his or her own words what Alfred Wegener's hypothesis was.

The Theory of Continental Drift, continued

Using the Visuals: Figure 12

Have students compare the coal beds indicated on the larger map with those indicated on the inset map. Ask: **What is different about these two maps?** *(The continents are pushed together in the inset map.)* **How does that make the location of coal beds important evidence?** *(The beds seem spread out at random in the map of present-day continents. When the continents are together, the coal beds create a pattern.)* Emphasize that this map shows three different types of evidence. Alone, each type may not prove the hypothesis. Taken together, though, they helped Wegener make a strong case.
learning modality: visual

TRY THIS

Skills Focus making models
Materials *1 sheet of newspaper*
Time 15 minutes
Tips Provide pages of newspaper that are covered completely with lines of print, such as pages from a classified-ad section.
Expected Outcome When the lines of print line up correctly, the newspaper becomes readable and thus confirm that the pieces are reassembled correctly. The torn pieces of newspaper are like the continents that had drifted apart. Just as the print on the paper provides evidence that the paper was once one piece, the landforms on the continents provide evidence that the continents were once joined together.
Extend Students can make a bulletin board that explains Wegener's theory. For the continents, they can cut the shapes from one newspaper sheet.
learning modality: visual

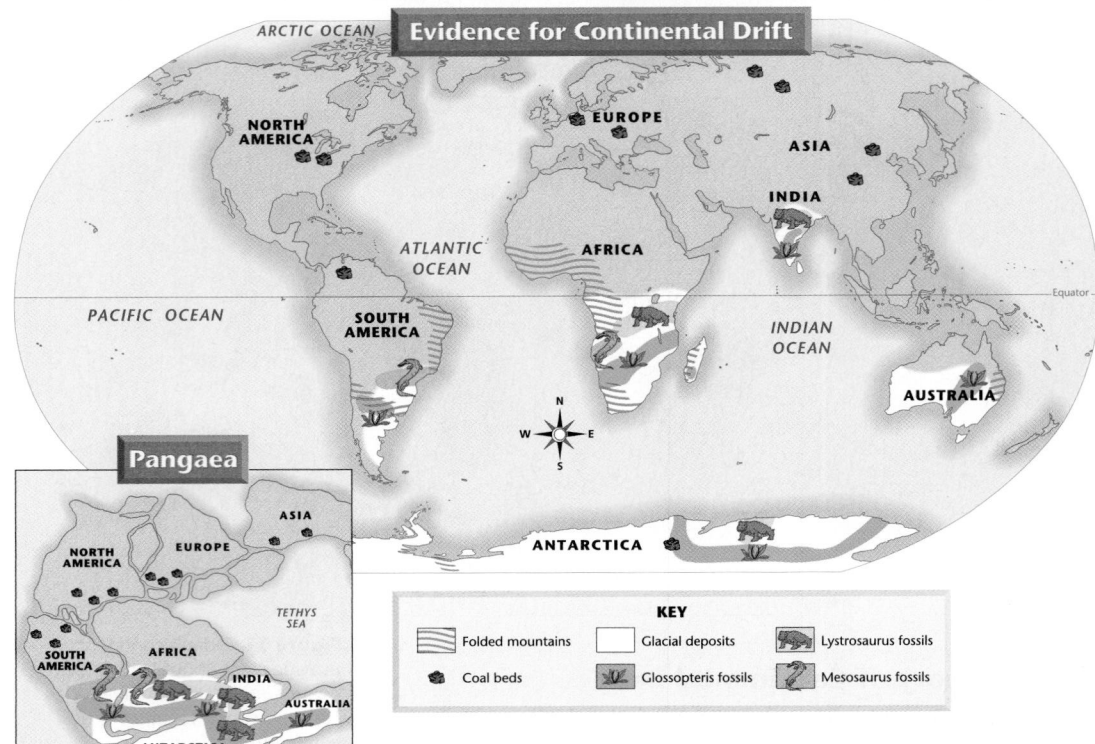

Evidence for Continental Drift

Pangaea

KEY
- Folded mountains
- Coal beds
- Glacial deposits
- Glossopteris fossils
- Lystrosaurus fossils
- Mesosaurus fossils

Figure 12 Wegener used several types of evidence to support his idea that the continents were once joined in a single landmass called Pangaea. *Inferring According to Wegener's theory, what does the presence of similar mountain ranges in Africa and South America indicate?*

Figure 13 Fossils of the freshwater reptile *Mesosaurus* found in Africa and South America provide evidence of continental drift.

Evidence from Landforms Mountain ranges and other features on the continents provided evidence for continental drift. When Wegener pieced together maps of Africa and South America, he noticed that a mountain range in South Africa lines up with a mountain range in Argentina. European coal fields match up with similar coal fields in North America. Wegener compared matching these features to reassembling a torn-up newspaper. If the pieces could be put back together, the "words" would match.

Evidence From Fossils Wegener also used fossils to support his argument for continental drift. A **fossil** is any trace of an ancient organism that has been preserved in rock. For example, fossils of the reptiles *Mesosaurus* and *Lystrosaurus* have been found in places now separated by oceans. Neither reptile could have swum great distances across salt water. It is therefore likely that these reptiles lived on a single landmass that has since split apart. Another example is *Glossopteris* (glaw SAHP tuh ris), a fernlike plant that lived 250 million years ago. *Glossopteris* fossils have been found in rocks in Africa, South America, Australia, India, and Antarctica. The occurrence of *Glossopteris* on these widely separated landmasses convinced Wegener that the continents had once been united.

Background

History of Science Strong evidence for Wegener's theory is the geological similarities on both sides of the Atlantic, including how well mountain belts line up. "It is just as if we were to refit the torn pieces of a newspaper by matching their edges and then check whether the lines of print ran smoothly across," Wegener wrote. "If they do, there is nothing left but to conclude that the pieces were in fact joined this way. If only one line was available for the test, we would still have found a high probability for the accuracy of fit, but if we have *n* lines, this probability is raised to the *n*th power." That is, the more evidence of a fit there can be found, the more the likelihood that the pieces were once joined together.

Figure 14 Fossils of *Glossopteris* are found on continents in the Southern Hemisphere and in India.

 INTEGRATING LIFE SCIENCE The seedlike structures of *Glossopteris* could not have traveled the great distances that separate the continents today. The "seeds" were too large to have been carried by the wind and too fragile to have survived a trip by ocean waves. How did *Glossopteris* develop on such widely separated continents? Wegener inferred that the continents at that time were joined as the supercontinent Pangaea.

Evidence From Climate Wegener used evidence of climate change to support his theory—for example, from the island of Spitsbergen. Spitsbergen lies in the Arctic Ocean north of Norway. This island is ice-covered and has a harsh polar climate. But fossils of tropical plants are found on Spitsbergen. When these plants lived about 300 million years ago, the island must have had a warm and mild climate. According to Wegener, Spitsbergen must have been located closer to the equator.

Thousands of kilometers to the south, geologists found evidence that at the same time it was warm in Spitsbergen, the climate was much colder in South Africa. Deep scratches in rocks showed that continental glaciers once covered South Africa. Continental glaciers are thick layers of ice that cover hundreds of thousands of square kilometers. But the climate of South Africa is too mild today for continental glaciers to form. Wegener concluded that, when Pangaea existed, South Africa was much closer to the South Pole.

According to Wegener, the climates of Spitsbergen and South Africa changed because the positions of these places on Earth's surface changed. As a continent moves toward the equator, its climate becomes warmer. As a continent moves toward the poles, its climate becomes colder. But the continent carries with it the fossils and rocks that formed at its previous location. These clues provide evidence that continental drift really happened.

☑ *Checkpoint* *What were the three types of evidence Wegener used to support his theory of continental drift?*

Reassembling the Pieces

Assembling a puzzle can reveal a hidden meaning.

1. Working with a partner, obtain one sheet of newspaper per person.
2. Tear your sheet of newspaper into six to eight large pieces. Trade your pieces with your partner.
3. Try to fit the pieces of newspaper together.

Making Models What evidence did you use to put the pieces together? How do your pieces of newspaper serve as a model of the theory of continental drift?

Integrating Life Science

Materials *variety of plant seeds*
Time 15 minutes

Bring a collection of seeds to class and allow students to examine them closely. Ask: **How are the different seeds moved from place to place?** Divide students in small groups and have them consider that question for each seed. Have each group make a list of the seeds and how they might be moved from one place to another. Groups should especially consider whether any seeds could have moved across an ocean. **learning modality: kinesthetic**

Building Inquiry Skills: Drawing Conclusions

Divide students into small groups and invite each group to evaluate Wegener's evidence in terms of whether each piece is convincing and whether they add up to a proof of the hypothesis. Encourage each group to think of some aspect that would need to be proved before the hypothesis could be totally accepted as true. **learning modality: logical/mathematical**

Media and Technology

📺 **Transparencies** "Evidence for Continental Drift," Transparency 42

📼 **Concept Videotape Library** *Adventures, Tape 3,* "The Drifters"

Answers to Self-Assessment

Caption Question

Figure 12 The presence of similar mountain ranges indicates that Africa and South America were once joined.

☑ *Checkpoint*

Evidence from landforms, evidence from fossils, and evidence from climate

---

Ongoing Assessment

Oral Presentation Call on students at random to explain the various kinds of evidence that Wegener put forward to support his hypothesis of continental drift.

Scientists Reject Wegener's Theory

Building Inquiry Skills: Observing

Several days before class, place an apple in a sunny place or over a heating duct, so that it dries quickly. Show students the apple. Ask: **Are the wrinkles on the apple's skin like the mountains on Earth? Would you expect that similar processes produced the wrinkles and mountains?** Students can discuss these questions in small groups. **learning modality: logical/mathematical**

3 Assess

Section 3 Review Answers

1. The continents had once been joined together in a single landmass.
2. Fossil leaves of *Glossopteris* are found in rocks in Africa, South America, Australia, India, and Antarctica. The "seeds" of that plant could not have been carried by wind or waves.
3. Wegener could not provide a satisfactory explanation for the force that pushes or pulls continents.
4. Coal is formed over time from plant material. Such plants could not have grown in the polar climate of present-day Antarctica. Either Earth's climate was much warmer or the continent was once closer to the equator.

Science at Home

Encourage students to do this activity at home. Then "debrief" them in a class discussion. Students can recount how receptive family members and others were to this idea and what any skeptics said in response.

Performance Assessment

Writing Challenge students to write a newspaper article reporting scientists' reactions to Wegener's theory.

Figure 15 Although scientists rejected his theory, Wegener continued to collect evidence on continental drift and to update his book. He died in 1930 on an expedition to explore Greenland's continental glacier.

Scientists Reject Wegener's Theory

Wegener did more than provide a theory to answer the riddle of continental drift. He attempted to explain how drift took place. He even offered a new explanation for how mountains form. Wegener thought that when drifting continents collide, their edges crumple and fold. The folding continents slowly push up huge chunks of rock to form great mountains.

Unfortunately, Wegener could not provide a satisfactory explanation for the force that pushes or pulls the continents. Because Wegener could not identify the cause of continental drift, most geologists rejected his idea. In addition, for geologists to accept Wegener's idea, they would need new explanations of what caused continents and mountains to form.

Many geologists in the early 1900s thought that Earth was slowly cooling and shrinking. According to this theory, mountains formed when the crust wrinkled like the skin of a dried-up apple. Wegener said that if the apple theory were correct, then mountains should be found all over Earth's surface. But mountains usually occur in narrow bands along the edges of continents. Wegener thought that his own theory better explained where mountains occur and how they form.

For nearly half a century, from the 1920s to the 1960s, most scientists paid little attention to the idea of continental drift. Then new evidence about Earth's structure led scientists to reconsider Wegener's bold theory.

Section 3 Review

1. What was Wegener's theory of continental drift?
2. How did Wegener use evidence based on fossils to support his theory that the continents had moved?
3. What was the main reason scientists rejected Wegener's theory of continental drift?
4. **Thinking Critically Inferring** Coal deposits have also been found beneath the ice of Antarctica. But coal only forms in warm swamps. Use Wegener's theory to explain how coal could be found so near the poles.

Science at Home

You can demonstrate Wegener's idea of continental drift. Use the map of the world in Figure 11. On a sheet of tracing paper, trace the outlines of the continents bordering the Atlantic Ocean. Label the continents. Then use scissors to carefully cut the map along the eastern edge of South America, North America, and Greenland. Next, cut along the western edge of Africa and Europe (including the British Isles). Throw away the Atlantic Ocean. Place the two cut-out pieces on a dark surface and ask family members to try to fit the two halves together. Explain to them about the supercontinent Pangaea and its history.

Program Resources

◆ **Unit 4 Resources** 11-3 Review and Reinforce, p. 19; 11-3 Enrich, p. 20

DISCOVER .... **ACTIVITY**

What Is the Effect of a Change in Density?

1. Partially fill a sink or dishpan with water.
2. Open up a dry washcloth in your hand. Does the washcloth feel light or heavy?
3. Moisten one edge of the washcloth in the water. Then gently place the washcloth so that it floats on the water's surface. Observe the washcloth carefully (especially at its edges) as it starts to sink.
4. Remove the washcloth from the water and open it up in your hand. Is the mass of the washcloth the same as, less than, or greater than when it was dry?

Think It Over
Observing How did the washcloth's density change? What effect did this change in density have on the washcloth?

D eep in the ocean, the temperature is near freezing. There is no light, and living things are generally scarce. Yet some areas of the deep-ocean floor are teeming with life. One of these areas is the East Pacific Rise, a region of the Pacific Ocean floor off the coasts of Mexico and South America. Here, ocean water sinks through cracks, or vents, in the crust. The water is heated by contact with hot material from the mantle and then spurts back into the ocean.

Around these hot-water vents live some of the most bizarre creatures ever discovered. Giant, red-tipped tube worms sway in the water. Nearby sit giant clams nearly a meter across. Strange spiderlike crabs scuttle by. Surprisingly, the geological features of this strange environment provided scientists with some of the best evidence for Wegener's theory of continental drift.

> **GUIDE FOR READING**
>
> ◆ What is the process of sea-floor spreading?
> ◆ What happens to the ocean floor at deep ocean trenches?
>
> *Reading Tip* Before you read, preview the art and captions looking for new terms. As you read, find the meanings of these terms.

Figure 16 Tube worms cluster near hot water vents in the ocean floor.

365

READING STRATEGIES

Reading Tip Students will likely list sonar, mid-ocean ridge, and oceanic crust. Suggest that students write each new term on a piece of paper, leaving room to fill in definitions.

Program Resources

◆ **Unit 4 Resources** 11-4 Lesson Plan, p. 21; 11-4 Section Summary, p. 22
◆ **Guided Reading and Study Workbook** Section 11-4

Objectives

After completing the lesson, students will be able to
◆ list the evidence for sea-floor spreading;
◆ describe the process of subduction.

Key Terms mid-ocean ridge, sonar, sea-floor spreading, deep-ocean trench, subduction

1 Engage/Explore

Activating Prior Knowledge

Ask students: **At what places does material from Earth's interior flow out onto the surface?** (*At volcanoes*) Most students know that lava flows from a volcano and hardens to form a type of rock. Ask: **What causes the lava to harden?** (*It hardens as it cools.*) Have students speculate on whether there are any places where the opposite occurs, where material from the surface moves into Earth's interior and melts. Have students think about the consequences if there were no such areas.

.... DISCOVER ....

Skills Focus observing **ACTIVITY**
Materials *sink or large dishpan, water, washcloth*
Time 10 minutes
Tips Review with students the difference between mass and density. The washcloth is about the same volume whether dry or wet, though it has more mass when wet. Therefore, the wet washcloth is denser than the dry washcloth.
Expected Outcome The washcloth should float for a short time on the water's surface. As it becomes soaked, the washcloth will gradually sink into the water. When removed from the water, the washcloth will be heavier than when dry.
Think It Over The washcloth's density increased as it became soaked with water. The increased density made the washcloth sink.

Mapping the Mid-Ocean Ridge

Using the Visuals: Figure 18

After students have studied the map, ask: **How is the mid-ocean ridge different under the Atlantic Ocean than it is under the Pacific Ocean?** *(It runs down the middle under the Atlantic, while it seems to outline the Pacific.)* Challenge students to think of any reason why this difference might be significant. *(Some students might infer that earthquakes and volcanoes are more common along the Pacific coasts than along the Atlantic coasts.)* **learning modality: visual**

Including All Students

For students who have difficulty seeing, provide a relief map or globe that includes the ocean floor. Give them the opportunity to trace the path of the mid-ocean ridge around the world. Ask: **Does the mid-ocean ridge always go through the middle of oceans?** *(No, sometimes it is closer to land.)* **learning modality: kinesthetic**

Building Inquiry Skills: Communicating

Bring several baseballs to class and pass them out to students, allowing each to see and feel the seam that circles the ball. Then have each student write a short paragraph that explains why the mid-ocean ridge is like the seam on a baseball. *(Most students will realize that the seam is continuous on a baseball, as the ridge is practically continuous around Earth.)* **learning modality: verbal**

Portfolio Students can keep their paragraphs in their portfolios.

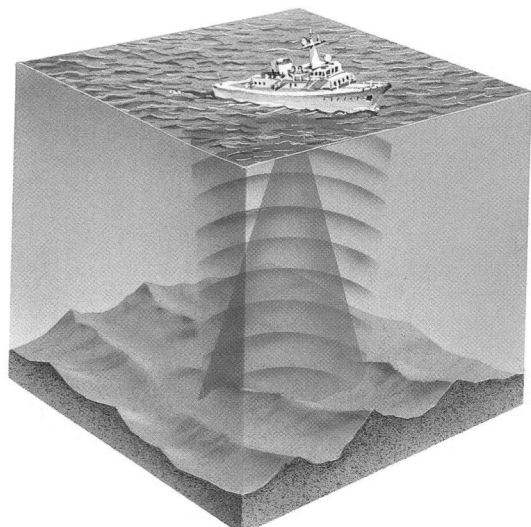

Figure 17 Scientists use sonar to map the ocean floor.

Mapping the Mid-Ocean Ridge

The East Pacific Rise is just one part of the **mid-ocean ridge,** the longest chain of mountains in the world. In the mid-1900s, scientists mapped the mid-ocean ridge using sonar. **Sonar** is a device that bounces sound waves off underwater objects and then records the echoes of these sound waves. The time it takes for the echo to arrive indicates the distance to the object.

The mid-ocean ridge curves like the seam of a baseball along the sea floor, extending into all of Earth's oceans. Most of the mountains in the mid-ocean ridge lie hidden under hundreds of meters of water. However, there are places where the ridge pokes above the surface. For example, the island of Iceland is a part of the mid-ocean ridge that rises above the surface in the North Atlantic Ocean. A steep-sided valley splits the top of the mid-ocean ridge for most of its length. The valley is almost twice as deep as the Grand Canyon. The mapping of the mid-ocean ridge made scientists curious to know what the ridge was and how it got there.

☑ *Checkpoint* *What device is used to map the ocean floor?*

Figure 18 The mid-ocean ridge is more than 50,000 kilometers long.

Earth's Ocean Floor

ASIA · NORTH AMERICA · EUROPE · ASIA · ATLANTIC OCEAN · PACIFIC OCEAN · AFRICA · SOUTH AMERICA · INDIAN OCEAN · AUSTRALIA · ANTARCTICA

KEY
— Mid-ocean ridge
— Deep-ocean trench

Background

Integrating Science The tube worms shown in Figure 16 are part of an extraordinary ecosystem that scientists have discovered around the hydrothermal vents of the mid-ocean ridge. Water at that depth normally has a temperature of about 2°C. The water from the vents is about 350°C. It doesn't boil because of the immense pressure at that depth. The warm water creates an environment with population densities that exceed those of warm coastal waters.

No sunlight penetrates to these depths, so no photosynthesis occurs. At the beginning of the food chain are bacteria that can generate energy from sulfur compounds in the water around the vents. The tube worms play a vital role in this process. The bacteria live inside the tube worms, which provide the bacteria with sulfides. The bacteria provide the tube worms with nutrients.

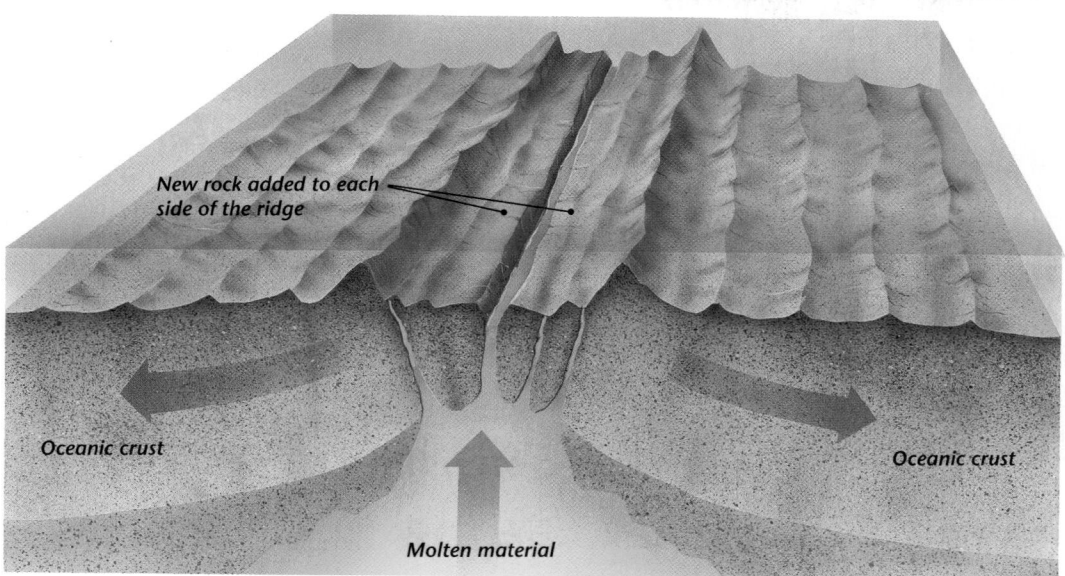

New rock added to each side of the ridge

Oceanic crust

Oceanic crust

Molten material

Figure 19 Molten material erupts though the valley that runs along the center of the mid-ocean ridge. This material hardens to form the rock of the ocean floor. *Applying Concepts What happens to the rock along the ridge when new molten material erupts?*

Evidence for Sea-Floor Spreading

Harry Hess, an American geologist, was one of the scientists who studied the mid-ocean ridge. Hess carefully examined maps of the mid-ocean ridge. Then he began to think about the ocean floor in relation to the problem of continental drift. Finally, he reconsidered an idea that he previously had thought impossible: Maybe Wegener was right! Perhaps the continents do move.

In 1960, Hess proposed a radical idea. He suggested that the ocean floors move like conveyor belts, carrying the continents along with them. This movement begins at the mid-ocean ridge. The mid-ocean ridge forms along a crack in the oceanic crust. **At the mid-ocean ridge, molten material rises from the mantle and erupts. The molten material then spreads out, pushing older rock to both sides of the ridge.** As the molten material cools, it forms a strip of solid rock in the center of the ridge. Then more molten material flows into the crack. This material splits apart the strip of solid rock that formed before, pushing it aside.

Hess called the process that continually adds new material to the ocean floor **sea-floor spreading.** He realized that the sea floor spreads apart along both sides of the mid-ocean ridge as new crust is added. Look at Figure 19 to see the process of sea-floor spreading.

Several types of evidence from the oceans supported Hess's theory of sea-floor spreading—evidence from molten material, magnetic stripes, and drilling samples. This evidence also led scientists to look again at Wegener's theory of continental drift.

Evidence for Sea-Floor Spreading

Using the Visuals: Figure 19

After students have studied the figure and read the caption, ask: **What part of the mantle contains molten material?** *(the asthenosphere)* **Therefore, the crack in the oceanic crust extends down through what layer?** *(the lithosphere)* **Through what other landforms on Earth does molten material rise to the surface?** *(volcanoes)* Point out that the mid-ocean ridge is like a huge string of volcanoes circling the planet. These volcanoes, though, don't generally erupt in the explosive way that people think of eruptions of volcanoes on land, and they are not cone-shaped like many volcanic mountains. **learning modality: visual**

Including All Students

To help students better understand the process of sea-floor spreading, place two chairs about a meter apart at the front of the room. Then have students form two lines to the back of the room. At your word, they should move in pairs through the opening and then turn away from each other, spreading out horizontally to the edges of the room. Ask: **What do the chairs represent?** *(the mid-ocean ridge)* **What does the space between the chairs represent?** *(the valley in the center of the ridge)* **What do you students represent?** *(First, the molten material from the mantle; then the spreading sea floor.)* **learning modality: kinesthetic**

Answers to Self-Assessment

☑ *Checkpoint*

Sonar is used to map the ocean floor.

Caption Question

Figure 19 The spreading molten material pushes the older rock to both sides of the ridge.

Ongoing Assessment

Drawing Pass out a sheet that contains the outlines of the world's continents and challenge students to draw the mid-ocean ridge on the map. Then have them check their drawings against the map in Figure 18 and make any corrections as necessary.

Evidence for Sea-Floor Spreading, continued

Building Inquiry Skills: Designing Experiments

Have students work in small groups to design an experiment that geologists could use to prove that rock "pillows" are an indication of molten material hardening underwater. (*A typical experiment might entail collecting rock from near a volcano, melting it in a furnace, and then allowing some to harden under water and some to harden out of water.*) Have groups compare and critique their experimental designs in a class discussion. **cooperative learning**

Using the Visuals: Figure 21

Show students a magnetic compass and have a volunteer explain how it's used. Then ask: **What does the indication "normal" refer to in Figure 21?** (*The magnetic field as it is today, in which a compass needle points to the magnetic North Pole.*) **Where would the compass needle point when Earth's magnetic field was reversed?** (*It would point to the magnetic South Pole.*) To illustrate this, flip the poles of a bar magnet held next to the compass, thereby causing the compass needle to reverse direction. Finally, ask a student to review for the class why Earth has a magnetic field, as explained in Section 1. **learning modality: verbal**

 Integrating Physics

Have the class again act out the process of sea floor spreading, using two chairs a meter apart at the front of the room to represent the mid-ocean ridge. This time, though, announce every two or three pairs that Earth's magnetic field has reversed. At the announcement, the pair going through the "ridge" should turn to walk backwards. Each succeeding pair should also walk through backwards until you announce another reversal. **learning modality: kinesthetic**

Figure 20 The submersible *Alvin* photographed pillow lava along the mid-ocean ridge. These "pillows" form under water when cold ocean water causes a crust to form on erupting molten material. Each pillow expands until it bursts, allowing molten material to flow out and form the next pillow.

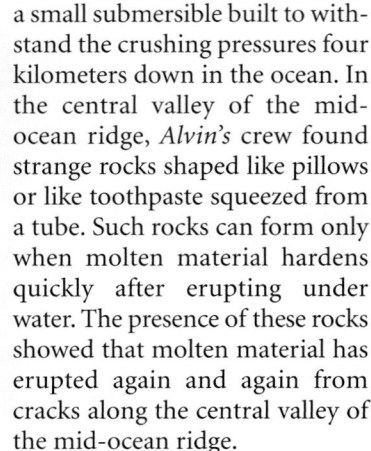

Evidence From Molten Material In the 1960s, scientists found evidence that new material is indeed erupting along the mid-ocean ridge. The scientists dived to the ocean floor in *Alvin*, a small submersible built to withstand the crushing pressures four kilometers down in the ocean. In the central valley of the mid-ocean ridge, *Alvin's* crew found strange rocks shaped like pillows or like toothpaste squeezed from a tube. Such rocks can form only when molten material hardens quickly after erupting under water. The presence of these rocks showed that molten material has erupted again and again from cracks along the central valley of the mid-ocean ridge.

Evidence From Magnetic Stripes When scientists studied **INTEGRATING PHYSICS** patterns in the rocks of the ocean floor, they found more support for sea-floor spreading. In Section 1 you read that Earth behaves like a giant magnet, with a north pole and a south pole. Evidence shows that Earth's magnetic poles have reversed themselves. This last happened 780,000 years ago. If the magnetic poles suddenly reversed themselves today, you would find that your compass needle pointed south. Scientists discovered that the rock that makes up the ocean floor lies in a pattern of magnetized "stripes." These stripes hold a record of reversals in Earth's magnetic field.

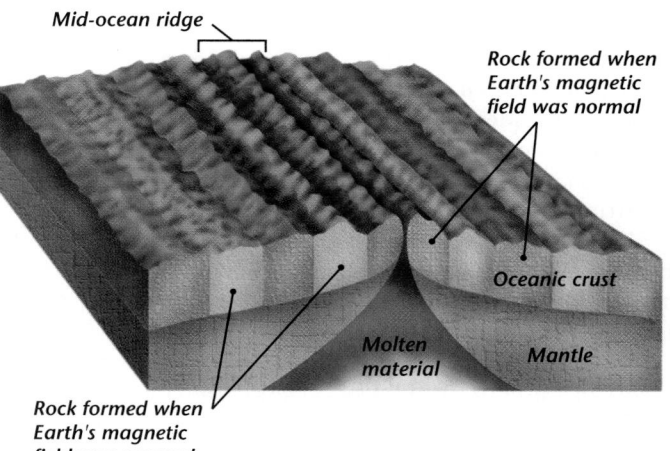

Mid-ocean ridge

Rock formed when Earth's magnetic field was normal

Oceanic crust

Molten material

Mantle

Rock formed when Earth's magnetic field was reversed

Figure 21 Magnetic stripes in the rock of the ocean floor show the direction of Earth's magnetic field at the time the rock hardened. *Interpreting Diagrams How are these matching stripes evidence of sea-floor spreading?*

368

The rock of the ocean floor, which contains iron, began as molten material. As the molten material cooled, the iron bits inside lined up in the direction of Earth's magnetic poles. When the rock hardened completely, it locked the iron bits in place, giving the rocks a permanent "magnetic memory." You can think of it as setting thousands of tiny compass needles in cement.

Using sensitive instruments, scientists recorded the magnetic memory of rocks on both sides of the mid-ocean ridge. They found that a stripe of rock that shows when Earth's magnetic field pointed north is followed by a parallel stripe of rock that shows when the magnetic field pointed south. As you can see in Figure 21, the pattern is the same on both sides of the ridge. Rock that hardens at the same time has the same magnetic memory.

Evidence From Drilling Samples The final proof of sea-floor spreading came from rock samples obtained by drilling into the ocean floor. The *Glomar Challenger*, a drilling ship built in 1968, gathered the samples. The *Glomar Challenger* sent drilling pipes through water six kilometers deep to drill holes in the ocean floor. This feat has been compared to using a sharp-ended wire to dig a hole into a sidewalk from the top of the Empire State Building.

Samples from the sea floor were brought up through the pipes. Then the scientists determined the age of the rocks in the samples. They found that the farther away from the ridge the samples were taken, the older the rocks were. The youngest rocks were always in the center of the ridges. This showed that sea-floor spreading really has taken place.

☑ *Checkpoint* What evidence did scientists find for sea-floor spreading?

Figure 22 The *Glomar Challenger* was the first research ship designed to drill samples of rock from the deep-ocean floor.

Reversing Poles

1. Cut six short **ACTIVITY** pieces, each about 2.5 cm long, from a length of audiotape.

2. Tape one end of each piece of audiotape to a flat surface. The pieces should be spaced 1 cm apart and line up lengthwise in a single line.

3. Touch a bar magnet's north pole to the first piece of audiotape. Then reverse the magnet and touch its south pole to the next piece.

4. Repeat Step 3 until you have applied the magnet to each piece of audiotape.

5. Sweep one end of the magnet about 1 cm above the line of audiotape pieces. Observe what happens.

Making Models What characteristic of the ocean floor did you observe as you swept the magnet along the line of audiotape pieces?

Answers to Self-Assessment

Caption Question

Figure 21 The pattern of stripes is the same on both sides of the ridge, indicating that the sea floor has spread from the mid-ocean ridge.

☑ *Checkpoint*

Evidence from molten material, evidence from magnetic stripes, and evidence from drilling samples

---

Skills Focus making models

Materials *audiotape, scissors, metric ruler, plastic tape, bar magnet*

Time 15 minutes

Tips Students can tape the pieces of audiotape to a desk or table. Advise them to tape only one end of each piece. Also, have them tape the pieces at least 1 cm apart so that the bar magnet will not accidentally magnetize an adjacent piece when magnetizing every other piece. Students should hold the magnet vertically in Step 5.

Expected Outcome Because every other piece of audiotape has been magnetized to an opposite pole than the one before, every piece will react differently than the pieces on either side. The pieces magnetized to the like pole will be attracted, while the pieces magnetized to the opposite pole will be repelled. The characteristic of the ocean floor modeled is its pattern of magnetic stripes.

Extend Have students write a paragraph that details the analogy suggested by this activity. **learning modality: kinesthetic**

Including All Students

Some students may have difficulty understanding the evidence from drilling samples. Have them draw a line down the middle of a piece of paper. The line represents the mid-ocean ridge, and the paper the ocean floor. Then have them mark three "drilling holes" at intervals away from each side of the line. Next, they should label the two "drilling holes" closest to the line as *1990*, the two middle ones *1980*, and the two outside ones *1970*. Explain that these dates are when the rock formed. Ask: **If you found these data in your research, what might you conclude about the process that created this ocean floor?** (*New floor periodically pushed the old floor aside on both sides of the ridge.*) **learning modality: visual**

Ongoing Assessment

Skills Check Have students make a cause and effect chart to explain the processes that produced the three types of evidence discussed on these pages.

Subduction at Deep-Ocean Trenches

Using the Visuals: Figure 23

Ask students: **Where on this figure is the oceanic crust densest? Explain your reasoning.** *(It's densest near the trenches, because there it is as old as it can get, and oceanic crust becomes denser as it cools and ages.)* Then have students recall that continental crust and oceanic crust are composed of different materials. Ask: **Which is denser, continental crust or oceanic crust?** *(Oceanic crust is denser because it is composed mostly of basalt, while continental crust is composed of the less dense granite.)* Explain that these differences in density are important for them to remember when they read the next section. **learning modality: verbal**

Building Inquiry Skills: Relating Cause and Effect

Ask: **If the effect is the subduction of oceanic crust at a deep-ocean trench, what is the cause or causes?** Challenge each student to write a paragraph that answers this question. Explain that all the causes can be found in their text. *(Some students may correctly mention three causes: (1) a push from the rising molten material at the mid-ocean ridge, (2) a push from the convection currents underneath the lithosphere, and (3) a pull from gravity on the older, denser oceanic crust far away from the mid-ocean ridge.)* **learning modality: logical/mathematical**

Subduction and Earth's Oceans

Including All Students

Provide students with a relief map of the world that includes the ocean floor. Challenge them to find the locations of as many deep-ocean trenches as they can, keeping a record as they go. Seeing-impaired students can work with sighted students to find and record trenches. Ask: **Where do you find the most trenches? The least?** *(Most are in the Pacific basin; very few are in the Atlantic basin.)* **learning modality: kinesthetic**

Subduction at Deep-Ocean Trenches

How can the ocean floor keep getting wider and wider? The answer is that the ocean floor generally does not just keep spreading. Instead, the ocean floor plunges into deep underwater canyons called **deep-ocean trenches.** A deep-ocean trench forms where the oceanic crust bends downward.

Where there are deep-ocean trenches, subduction takes place. **Subduction** (sub DUK shun) is the process by which the ocean floor sinks beneath a deep-ocean trench and back into the mantle. Convection currents under the lithosphere push new crust that forms at the mid-ocean ridge away from the ridge and toward a deep-ocean trench.

New oceanic crust is hot. But as it moves away from the mid-ocean ridge, it cools and becomes more dense. Eventually, as shown in Figure 23, gravity pulls this older, denser oceanic crust down beneath the trench. The sinking crust is like the washcloth in the Discover activity at the beginning of this section. As the dry washcloth floating on the water gets wet, its density increases and it begins to sink.

At deep-ocean trenches, subduction allows part of the ocean floor to sink back into the mantle, over tens of millions of years. You can think of sea-floor spreading and subduction together as if the ocean floor were moving out from the mid-ocean ridge on a giant conveyor belt.

Figure 23 Oceanic crust created along the mid-ocean ridge is destroyed at a deep-ocean trench. In the process of subduction, oceanic crust sinks down beneath the trench into the mantle. *Drawing Conclusions Where would denser oceanic crust be found?*

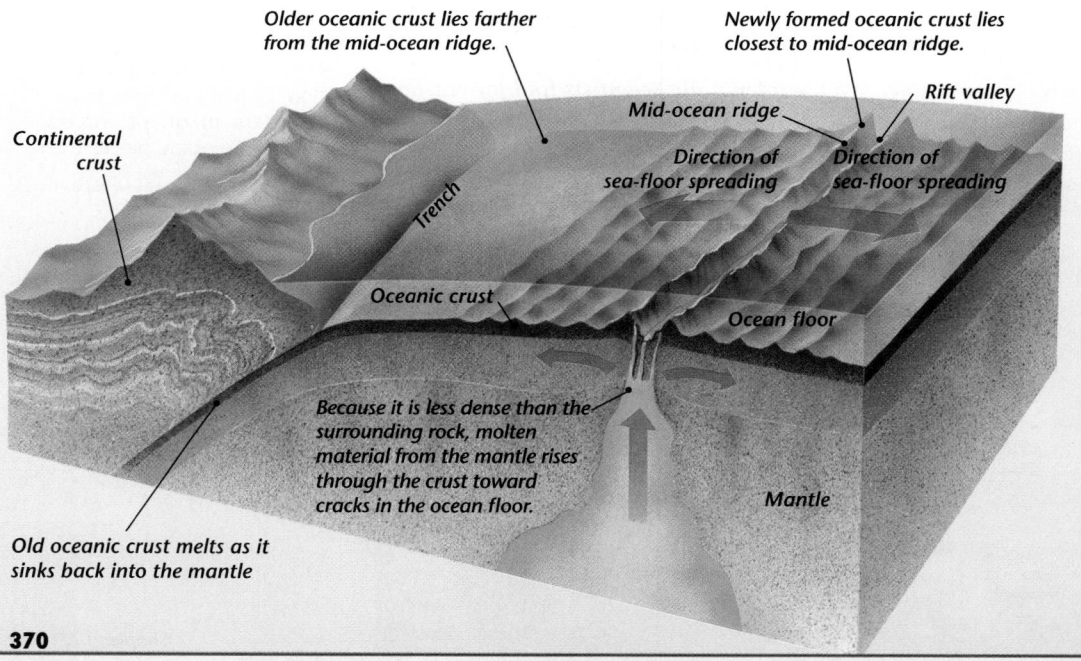

Older oceanic crust lies farther from the mid-ocean ridge.

Newly formed oceanic crust lies closest to mid-ocean ridge.

Continental crust

Trench

Oceanic crust

Old oceanic crust melts as it sinks back into the mantle

Because it is less dense than the surrounding rock, molten material from the mantle rises through the crust toward cracks in the ocean floor.

Mid-ocean ridge

Rift valley

Direction of sea-floor spreading

Direction of sea-floor spreading

Ocean floor

Mantle

Background

Facts and Figures Most deep-ocean trenches are found on the margins of the Pacific Ocean. Deep-ocean trenches are usually 8–10 km deep and thousands of kilometers long. The deepest known part of the ocean is Challenger Deep, which bottoms out at nearly 12 km below sea level. This is in the Mariana Trench, under the Pacific Ocean north of the island of New Guinea. If Mt. Everest, the world's highest mountain, were placed inside Challenger Deep, its summit would still be more than 2 km under water.

Subduction and Earth's Oceans

The processes of subduction and sea-floor spreading can change the size and shape of the oceans. Because of these processes, the ocean floor is renewed about every 200 million years. That is the time it takes for new rock to form at the mid-ocean ridge, move across the ocean, and sink into a trench.

Subduction in the Pacific Ocean The vast Pacific Ocean covers almost one third of the planet. And yet it is shrinking. How could that be? Sometimes a deep ocean trench swallows more oceanic crust than the mid-ocean ridge can produce. Then, if the ridge does not add new crust fast enough, the width of the ocean will shrink. This is happening to the Pacific Ocean, which is ringed by many trenches.

Subduction in the Atlantic Ocean The Atlantic Ocean, on the other hand, is expanding. Unlike the Pacific Ocean, the Atlantic Ocean has only a few short trenches. As a result, the spreading ocean floor has virtually nowhere to go. In most places, the oceanic crust of the Atlantic Ocean floor is attached to the continental crust of the continents around the ocean. So as the Atlantic's ocean floor spreads, the continents along its edges also move. Over time, the whole ocean gets wider. The spreading floor of the North Atlantic Ocean and the continent of North America move together like two giant barges pushed by the same tugboat.

Figure 24 It is cold and dark in the deep ocean trenches where subduction occurs. But even here, scientists have found living things, such as this angler fish.

Section 4 Review

1. What is the role of the mid-ocean ridge in sea-floor spreading?
2. What is the evidence for sea-floor spreading?
3. Describe the process of subduction at a deep-ocean trench.
4. **Thinking Critically** **Relating Cause and Effect** Where would you expect to find the oldest rock on the ocean floor? Explain your answer.
5. **Thinking Critically** **Predicting** As you can see in Figure 18, the mid-ocean ridge extends into the Red Sea between Africa and Asia. What do you think will happen to the Red Sea in the future? Explain your answer.

Check Your Progress

CHAPTER PROJECT 11

Now that you have learned about sea-floor spreading, draw a revised sketch of your model. Include examples of sea-floor spreading and subduction on your sketch. Show the features that form as a result of these processes. How will you show what happens beneath the crust? Improve your original ideas and add new ideas. Revise your list of materials if necessary. Begin building your model.

Modeling Sea-Floor Spreading

Preparing for Inquiry

Key Concept Sea-floor spreading at the mid-ocean ridge continually adds new material to the ocean floor.

Skills Objectives Students will be able to:
◆ make a model of sea-floor spreading.
◆ observe how material rises through a center opening and sinks down through openings at the edges.
◆ infer how sea-floor spreading adds new crust and how that crust moves back down into the mantle.

Time 30 minutes

Advance Planning Gather all the materials at least one day prior to the activity. Prepare two sample sheets: a sheet with stripes predrawn, and a sheet folded and marked as in steps 3 and 4.

Alternative Materials Instead of small groups making several models, you could divide the class into larger groups and have each make a large model using butcher-block paper.

Guiding Inquiry

Invitation Help students focus on the key concept by asking: **What happens at the mid-ocean ridge?** *(Molten material rises from the mantle and erupts.)* **What forms when the molten material hardens?** *(New ocean floor)* **What happens as that new floor spreads out from the ridge?** *(It pushes older rock on both sides of the ridge.)* **How are magnetic stripes evidence of this process?** *(The magnetic stripes show that material has been pushed away from the ridge over time.)* **What happens at deep-ocean trenches?** *(Oceanic crust sinks back down into the mantle.)*

Introducing the Procedure

◆ Have students read through the entire activity. Then ask: **What is the purpose of this activity?** *(To make a model of sea-floor spreading)*

Skills Lab

MODELING SEA-FLOOR SPREADING

Along the entire length of Earth's mid-ocean ridge, the sea floor is spreading. Although this process takes place constantly, it is difficult to observe directly. You can build a model to help understand this process.

Problem

How does sea-floor spreading add material to the ocean floor?

Materials

scissors
metric ruler
2 sheets of unlined paper
colored marker

Procedure ✀

1. Draw stripes across one sheet of paper, parallel to the short sides of the paper. The stripes should vary in spacing and thickness.
2. Fold the paper in half lengthwise and write the word "Start" at the top of both halves of the paper. Using the scissors, carefully cut the paper in half along the fold line to form two strips.
3. Lightly fold the second sheet of paper into eighths. Then unfold it, leaving creases in the paper. Fold this sheet in half lengthwise.

4. Starting at the fold, draw lines 5.5 cm long on the middle crease and the two creases closest to the ends of the paper.

5. Now carefully cut along the lines you drew. Unfold the paper. There should be three slits in the center of the paper.

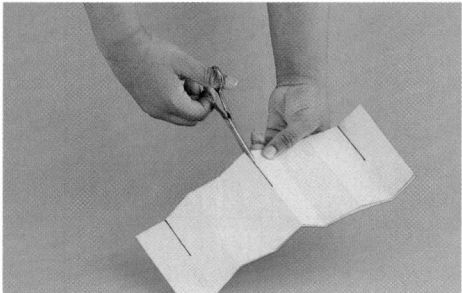

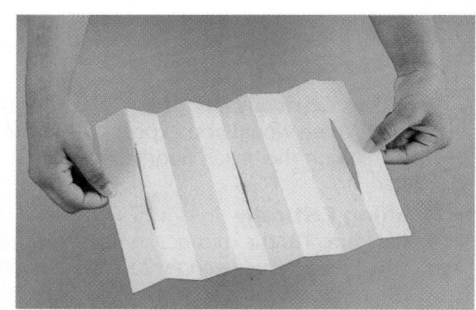

372

◆ **Why do you cut the first sheet in half?** *(The sea floor spreads out in both directions from the mid-ocean ridge. Cutting the sheet in half allows the model to represent movement on both sides of the ridge.)*

◆ **After you've cut the sheet in half, how does the pattern of stripes on one half sheet compare with the pattern on the other half?** *(The pattern is the same on each half.)*

Troubleshooting the Experiment

◆ Demonstrate how to begin to make each of the two sheets. Then show students your samples of the finished products. Allow them to refer to these sheets as they make their own.

◆ Check to see that students make the slits large enough to pull the paper through easily. They should cut a little more than halfway through the width of the sheet.

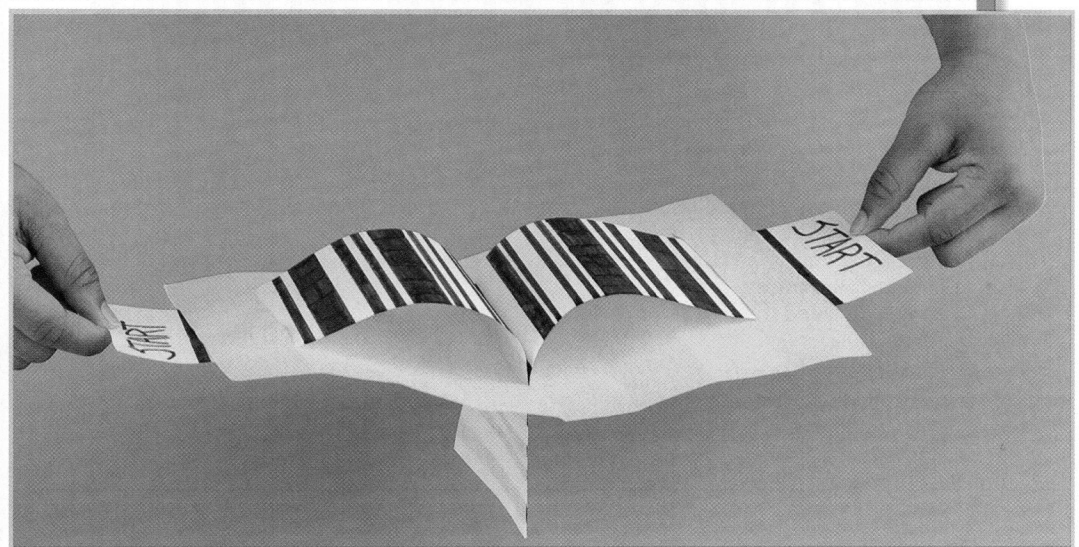

6. Put the two striped strips of paper together so their Start labels touch one another. Insert the Start ends of the strips up through the center slit and then pull them toward the side slits.

7. Insert the ends of the strips into the side slits. Pull the ends of the strips and watch what happens at the center slit.

8. Practice pulling the strips through the slits until you can make the two strips come up and go down at the same time.

Analyze and Conclude

1. What feature of the ocean floor does the center slit stand for? What prominent feature of the ocean floor is missing from the model at this point?

2. What do the side slits stand for? What does the space under the paper stand for?

3. How does the ocean floor as shown by the part of a strip close to the center slit differ from the ocean floor as shown by the part near a side slit? How does this difference affect the depth of the ocean?

4. What do the stripes on the strips stand for? Why is it important that your model have an identical pattern of stripes on both sides of the center slit?

5. Explain how differences in density and temperature provide some of the force needed to cause sea-floor spreading and subduction.

6. **Think About It** Use your own words to describe the process of ocean-floor spreading. What parts of the process were not shown by your model?

More to Explore

Imagine that so much molten rock erupted from the mid-ocean ridge that an island formed there. How could you modify your model to show this island? How could you show what would happen to it over a long period of time?

Program Resources

◆ **Unit 4 Resources** Skills Lab blackline masters, pp. 29–31

Media and Technology

 Lab Activity Videotape
Tape 3

Safety

Caution students to use care when working with sharp instruments such as scissors. Review the safety guidelines in Appendix A.

Expected Outcome

Students will build a model that shows eruption of material through the mid-ocean ridge, the spreading of the sea floor on both sides of the ridge, and the subduction of the floor at deep-ocean trenches.

Analyze and Conclude

1. The center slit stands for the central valley of the mid-ocean ridge. The feature that is missing is the mountainous ridge.
2. The side slits stand for deep-ocean trenches. The space under the paper stands for the part of the mantle called the asthenosphere.
3. The ocean floor as shown by the strip near the center slit is younger, hotter, and less dense than ocean floor farther away. As the floor moves away from the ridge, it cools and becomes denser. The ocean floor as shown by the part near a side slit is older, cooler, and denser. The increased density causes the depth of the ocean to increase.
4. The stripes stand for the magnetic stripes in the rock of the ocean floor. The pattern of magnetic stripes is the same on both sides of the mid-ocean ridge.
5. Temperature differences in the mantle cause convection currents. These currents cause molten rock to erupt through the valley that runs along the center of the mid-ocean ridge. As more material erupts, the sea floor spreads, cools, and becomes denser. The denser material sinks back into the mantle when it reaches a trench.
6. Answers may vary. A typical answer should mention the eruption of molten material at the mid-ocean ridge, the spreading of the sea floor, and the subduction of oceanic crust at deep-ocean trenches. Parts of the process not shown by the model include changes in density and the melting of the crust as it sinks back into the mantle.

Extending the Inquiry

More to Explore Answers may vary. A typical answer might suggest drawing an island near the Start label on one of the strips. Then, through the movement of the strip through the model, the island's position would change, and it would eventually be subducted.

SECTION 5 The Theory of Plate Tectonics

Objectives

After completing the lesson, students will be able to
- explain the theory of plate tectonics;
- describe the three types of plate boundaries.

Key Terms plate, scientific theory, plate tectonics, fault, transform boundary, divergent boundary, rift valley, convergent boundary

1 Engage/Explore

Activating Prior Knowledge

Ask students: **What is a plate?** (*A typical answer will describe a dinner plate.*) Challenge students to think of other contexts in which the word is used, such as metal plates that cover machinery, home plate in baseball, the plates or scales that cover a reptile, and the plates of photographs in a textbook. Help students form a general definition for *plate*, such as a broad, flat sheet of material.

••••••• DISCOVER ••••••

Skills Focus drawing conclusions
Materials *world map in an atlas, tracing paper, scissors, sheet of paper, tape*
Time 20 minutes
Tips To shorten the activity, provide students with a photocopy of the continent outlines.
Expected Outcome Students should be able to easily fit some of the continents together, such as South America and Africa. It may be more difficult to imagine how the other continents fit together. Accept all plausible configurations.
Think It Over Answers may vary. A typical answer might mention that some of the continents fit together quite well while others did not. The general fit between some continents suggests that the continents may once have been joined.

DISCOVER •••••••••••••••••••••••••••••• ACTIVITY

How Well Do the Continents Fit Together?

1. Using a world map in an atlas, trace the shape of each continent and Madagascar on a sheet of paper. Also trace the shape of India and the Arabian Peninsula.

2. ✂ Carefully cut apart the landmasses, leaving Asia and Europe as one piece. Separate India and the Arabian Peninsula from Asia.

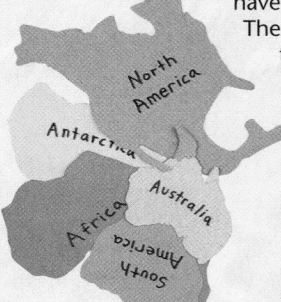

3. Piece together the continents as they may have looked before the breakup of Pangaea. Then attach your reconstruction of Pangaea to a sheet of paper.

Think It Over
Drawing Conclusions How well did the pieces of your continents fit together? Do your observations support the idea that today's landmasses were once joined together? Explain.

GUIDE FOR READING

- What is the theory of plate tectonics?
- What are the three types of plate boundaries?

Reading Tip Before you read, preview *Exploring Plate Tectonics* on pages 378–379. Write a list of any questions you have about plate tectonics. Look for answers as you read.

Have you ever dropped a hard-boiled egg? If so, you may have noticed that the eggshell cracked in an irregular pattern of broken pieces. Earth's lithosphere, its solid outer shell, is not one unbroken layer. It is more like that cracked eggshell. It's broken into pieces separated by jagged cracks.

A Canadian scientist, J. Tuzo Wilson, observed that there are cracks in the continents similar to those on the ocean floor. In 1965, Wilson proposed a new way of looking at these cracks. According to Wilson, the lithosphere is broken into separate sections called **plates.** The plates fit closely together along cracks in the lithosphere. As shown in Figure 26, the plates carry the continents or parts of the ocean floor, or both.

Figure 25 The Great Rift Valley in east Africa is a crack in Earth's crust where two pieces of crust are pulling apart.

374

READING STRATEGIES

Reading Tip Typical questions students might write include, What are plates? What are convergent and divergent boundaries? What is a rift valley? Advise students to leave enough space between each question to write the answers when they find them in the text.

Program Resources

- **Laboratory Manual** 11, "Mapping a Future World"

A Theory of Plate Motion

Wilson combined what geologists knew about sea-floor spreading, Earth's plates, and continental drift into a single theory—the theory of plate tectonics (tek TAHN iks). A **scientific theory** is a well-tested concept that explains a wide range of observations. **Plate tectonics** is the geological theory that states that pieces of Earth's lithosphere are in constant, slow motion, driven by convection currents in the mantle. **The theory of plate tectonics explains the formation, movement, and subduction of Earth's plates.**

How can Earth's plates move? The plates of the lithosphere float on top of the asthenosphere. Convection currents rise in the asthenosphere and spread out beneath the lithosphere. Most geologists think that the flow of these currents causes the movement of Earth's plates.

No plate can budge without affecting the other plates surrounding it. As the plates move, they collide, pull apart, or grind past each other, producing spectacular changes in Earth's surface. These changes include volcanoes, mountain ranges, and deep-sea trenches.

Sharpen your Skills

Predicting

Study the map **ACTIVITY** of Earth's plates in Figure 26. Notice the arrows that show the direction of plate movement. Now find the Nazca plate on the map. Which direction is it moving? Find the South American plate and describe its movement. What do you think will happen as these plates continue to move?

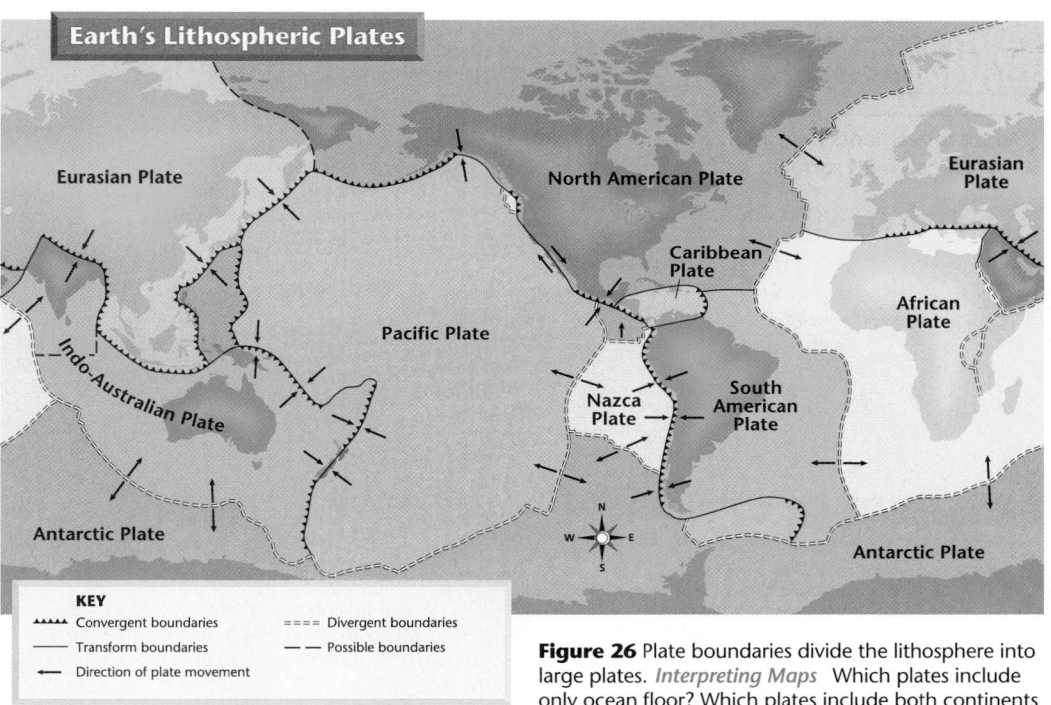

Earth's Lithospheric Plates

Eurasian Plate
North American Plate
Eurasian Plate
Caribbean Plate
African Plate
Pacific Plate
Indo-Australian Plate
Nazca Plate
South American Plate
Antarctic Plate
Antarctic Plate

KEY
▲▲▲ Convergent boundaries
==== Divergent boundaries
— Transform boundaries
— — Possible boundaries
→ Direction of plate movement

Figure 26 Plate boundaries divide the lithosphere into large plates. *Interpreting Maps* Which plates include only ocean floor? Which plates include both continents and ocean floor?

A Theory of Plate Motion

Inquiry Challenge

Materials *large clear bowl, water, block of rigid plastic foam slightly smaller than diameter of bowl, sand or gravel, metric ruler*
Time 15 minutes
Ask students: **Do you think plates with high mountains float higher or lower on the asthenosphere than those without mountains?** Then encourage students to investigate this question by using the plastic foam block to represent a plate, water to represent mantle material, and sand or gravel to create "mountains." *(Students should find that an area of a plate with mountains floats lower.)* **learning modality: kinesthetic**

Sharpen your Skills

Predicting

Time 10 minutes
Challenge students to make their prediction after they have learned about all three types of boundaries. The Nazca plate is moving east, while the South American plate is moving west. Thus, this is a convergent plate boundary. Because the Nazca plate carries dense oceanic crust and the South American plate carries less dense continental crust, the Nazca plate plunges beneath the South American plate.
Extend Challenge students to describe each of the boundaries associated with the North American plate and predict what will happen at each. **learning modality: logical/mathematical**

Program Resources

◆ **Unit 4 Resources** 11-5 Lesson Plan, p. 25; 11-5 Section Summary, p. 26
◆ **Guided Reading and Study Workbook** Section 11-5

Media and Technology

 Transparencies "Earth's Lithospheric Plates," Transparency 45

Answers to Self-Assessment

Caption Question
Figure 26 Plates that include only ocean floor include the Nazca Plate and the two smaller unlabeled plates near South America. All the other labeled plates in the figure include both continents and ocean floor.

Ongoing Assessment

Writing Have each student write a paragraph explaining in his or her own words the theory of plate tectonics.

Plate Boundaries

Demonstration

Materials *2 large wooden blocks*
Time 10 minutes

Introduce the three types of plate boundaries by demonstrating each type using wooden blocks. For a transform boundary, slide one block past the other. For a divergent boundary, pull two blocks away from each other. For a convergent boundary, push two blocks together. For each type, encourage students to make a drawing with labels and arrows showing the direction of each block's movement. **learning modality: visual**

Using the Visuals: Figure 27

Materials *large, flat rock*
Time 10 minutes

Before class, break a large, flat rock into two pieces. Invite students to examine the boundary between the two pieces and then model two plates slipping past each other. Students will observe that the process is far from smooth, as the two pieces grind against one another. Emphasize that this likely would be a jerky process, in which the boundary would catch for a moment and then let go. Ask: **Why do you think earthquakes occur frequently at transform boundaries?** *(The plates cannot move smoothly past one another because of the irregular nature of faults.)* **learning modality: kinesthetic**

Addressing Naive Conceptions

Many students may be misled into thinking that geologists can observe movements at plate boundaries, just as a person might observe other forces of nature, such as hurricanes and volcanoes. Ask: **How fast do you think Earth's plates are moving?** *(Only a few centimeters per year)* Emphasize that the movements involved in plate tectonics occur over millions of years. Geologists infer what processes are occurring by studying evidence of the past. **learning modality: verbal**

Plate Boundaries

The edges of different pieces of the lithosphere—Earth's rigid shell—meet at lines called plate boundaries. Plate boundaries extend deep into the lithosphere. **Faults**—breaks in Earth's crust where rocks have slipped past each other—form along these boundaries. There are three kinds of plate boundaries: transform boundaries, divergent boundaries, and convergent boundaries. For each type of boundary, there is a different type of plate movement.

Transform Boundaries Along transform boundaries, crust is neither created nor destroyed. A **transform boundary** is a place where two plates slip past each other, moving in opposite directions. Earthquakes occur frequently along these boundaries. Look at Figure 27 to see the type of plate movement that occurs along a transform boundary.

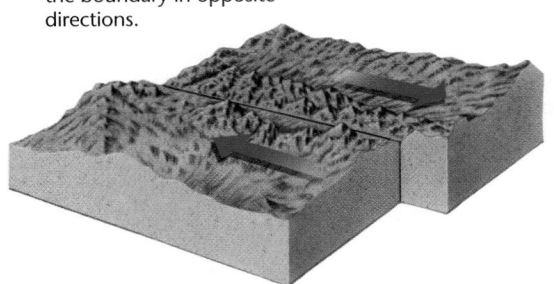

Figure 27 At a transform boundary, two plates move along the boundary in opposite directions.

EXPLORING *Plate Tectonics*

Plate movements have built many of the features of Earth's land surfaces and ocean floors.

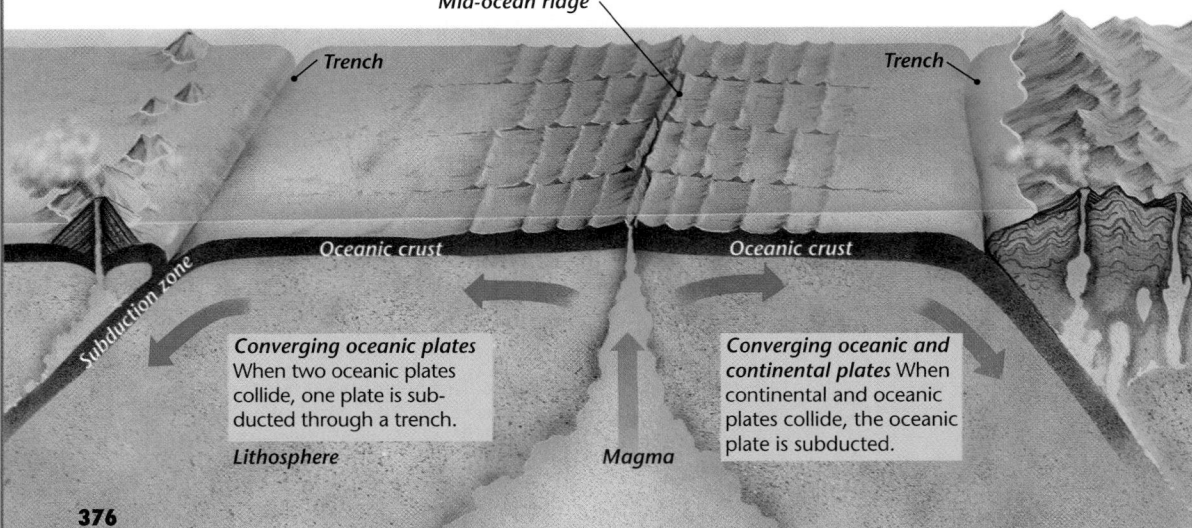

Diverging oceanic plates
The mid-ocean ridge marks a divergent boundary where plates move apart.

Mid-ocean ridge

Trench

Trench

Subduction zone

Oceanic crust

Oceanic crust

Converging oceanic plates
When two oceanic plates collide, one plate is subducted through a trench.

Lithosphere

Magma

Converging oceanic and continental plates When continental and oceanic plates collide, the oceanic plate is subducted.

376

Background

Facts and Figures

◆ The San Andreas Fault is an example of a transform boundary. The Pacific plate is sliding past the North American plate.
◆ The Rio Grande rift is a divergent boundary on land that extends from central Colorado to El Paso, Texas.
◆ The Appalachian Mountains formed as a result of a convergent boundary in which two continental plates collided.

Media and Technology

 Concept Videotape Library
Adventures, Tape 2, "Isto What?"

Divergent Boundaries The place where two plates move apart, or diverge, is called a **divergent boundary** (dy VUR junt). Most divergent boundaries occur at the mid-ocean ridge. In Section 4, you learned how oceanic crust forms along the mid-ocean ridge as sea-floor spreading occurs.

Divergent boundaries also occur on land. When a divergent boundary develops on land, two of Earth's plates slide apart. A deep valley called a **rift valley** forms along the divergent boundary. For example, the Great Rift Valley in east Africa marks a deep crack in the African continent that runs for about 3,000 kilometers. Along this crack, a divergent plate boundary is slowly spreading apart. The rift may someday split the eastern part of Africa away from the rest of the continent. As a rift valley widens, its floor drops. Eventually, the floor may drop enough for the sea to fill the widening gap.

☑ *Checkpoint* *What is a rift valley? How are rift valleys formed?*

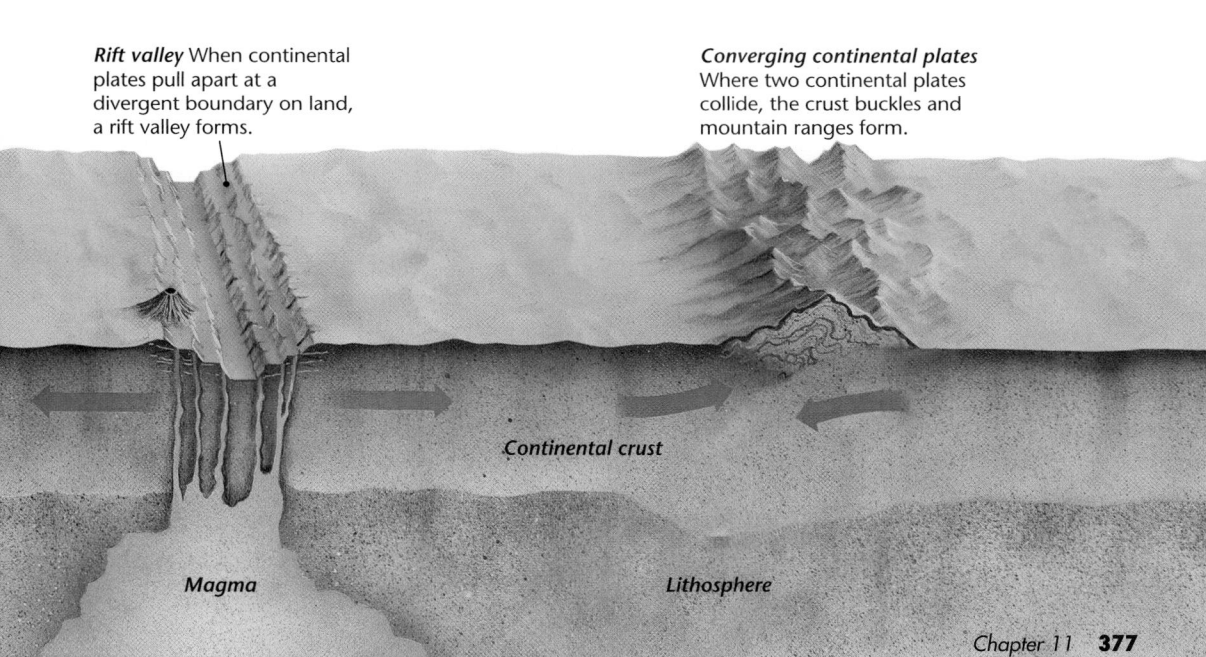

Rift valley When continental plates pull apart at a divergent boundary on land, a rift valley forms.

Converging continental plates Where two continental plates collide, the crust buckles and mountain ranges form.

Continental crust

Magma

Lithosphere

Give students a chance to study the visual essay and then call on students to read the annotations. Ask: **What is magma?** (*Some students will know that magma is hot, molten material from beneath Earth's surface.*) **Where is the magma coming from that is shown erupting through the mid-ocean ridge and the rift valley?** (*The magma comes from the asthenosphere, the part of the mantle that can flow.*) Point out that most of what is shown they already know from learning about sea-floor spreading. Ask: **What new processes are shown?** (*Movements on land, including divergent boundaries on land and converging continental plates.*) **learning modality: visual**

Inquiry Challenge

Materials *candy bar, paper towel*
Time 10 minutes

Have all students wash their hands. Then give pairs of students a candy bar with a thick chocolate top and caramel and nougat layers below. As a model, the chocolate represents the crust, the caramel represents the mantle part of the lithosphere, and the nougat represents the asthenosphere. Ask: **How can you use this candy bar to model what happens at divergent and convergent boundaries?** Students will find that when pulled apart, a valley will form between the break in the chocolate top. When pushed together, the chocolate top will buckle and form a ridge. Have students make sketches of what they see. (**CAUTION:** *Check for allergies to chocolate if you allow students to eat the candy bars.*) **learning modality: kinesthetic**

Answers to Self-Assessment

☑ *Checkpoint*
A rift valley is a deep valley that forms along a divergent boundary on land. Rift valleys form as plates slide apart.

Ongoing Assessment

Oral Presentation Call on students at random to explain what occurs at each of the different types of plate boundaries.

Plate Boundaries, continued

Including All Students

Ask students: **When two continental plates collide, why isn't one subducted beneath the other?** *(Both are approximately the same density and also less dense than the mantle, so neither one sinks beneath the other.)* Point out that not all mountains form this way, but many do. The Appalachian Mountains in the United States are another example of what results when continental plates collide. Ask: **When these plates collide, can local people hear a crash?** *(Of course not, since this collision occurs over millions of years.)* **learning modality: verbal**

Building Inquiry Skills: Comparing and Contrasting

Have students make a table that compares and contrasts the three types of plate boundaries. Their tables should include all the possibilities of what could happen at each kind of boundary, including two possibilities at divergent boundaries and three possibilities at convergent boundaries. **learning modality: verbal**

The Continents' Slow Dance

Using the Visuals: Figure 29

Call on students at random to read the annotations for each map in the sequence. Then ask: **What evidence of sea-floor spreading can you see on these maps occurring from 135 million years ago to today?** *(The Atlantic Ocean formed during that period as the sea floor spread at the mid-ocean ridge.)* **From what has occurred in the past, what do you predict will happen to the Atlantic and Pacific oceans in the future?** *(The Atlantic Ocean will expand, and the Pacific Ocean will shrink.)* **learning modality: visual**

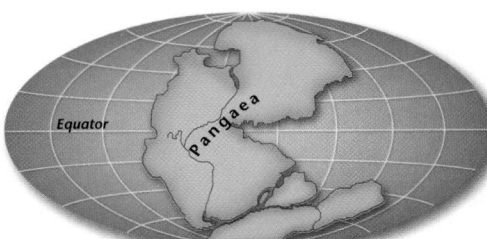

225 million years ago All Earth's major landmasses were joined in the super-continent Pangaea before plate movements began to split it apart.

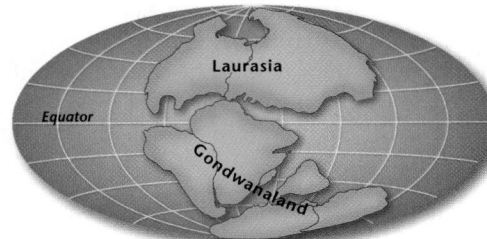

180–200 million years ago Pangaea continued to split apart, opening narrow seas that later became oceans.

Figure 29 It has taken about 225 million years for the continents to move to their present locations. *Posing Questions* What questions would you need to answer in order to predict where the continents will be in 50 million years?

Figure 28 A collision between two continental plates produced the majestic Himalayas. The collision began 50 million years ago, when the plate that carries India slammed into Asia.

Convergent Boundaries The place where two plates come together, or converge, is called a **convergent boundary** (kun VUR junt). When two plates converge, the result is called a collision. Collisions may bring together oceanic crust and oceanic crust, oceanic crust and continental crust, or continental crust and continental crust.

When two plates collide, the density of the plates determines which one comes out on top. Oceanic crust, which is made mostly of basalt, is more dense than continental crust, which is made mostly of granite. And oceanic crust becomes cooler and denser as it spreads away from the mid-ocean ridge.

Where two plates carrying oceanic crust meet at a trench, the plate that is more dense dives under the other plate and returns to the mantle. This is the process of subduction that you learned about in Section 4.

Sometimes a plate carrying oceanic crust collides with a plate carrying continental crust. The less dense continental crust can't sink under the more dense oceanic crust. Instead, the oceanic plate begins to sink and plunges beneath the continental plate.

When two plates carrying continental crust collide, subduction does not take place. Both continental plates are mostly low-density granite rock. Therefore, neither plate is dense enough to sink into the mantle. Instead, the plates crash head-on. The collision squeezes the crust into mighty mountain ranges.

☑ *Checkpoint* What types of plate movement occur at plate boundaries?

Background

Integrating Science Scientists measure the movement of plates using two technologies. In Satellite Laser Ranging, scientists bounce laser pulses off satellites orbiting Earth. By timing how long the laser pulse takes to reach the satellite and return to a station on Earth, scientists can calculate any movement of that station over time. In Very Long Baseline Interferometry, scientists use radio telescopes to record signals from quasars billions of light-years away at two stations on Earth. Over time, any change in the difference of when the same signal arrives at the two stations indicates that the stations are moving in relation to each other. Using these methods, scientists have determined, for example, that the state of Maryland is moving away from England at a rate of 1.7 cm/yr. And Hawaii is moving toward Japan at a rate of 8.3 cm/yr.

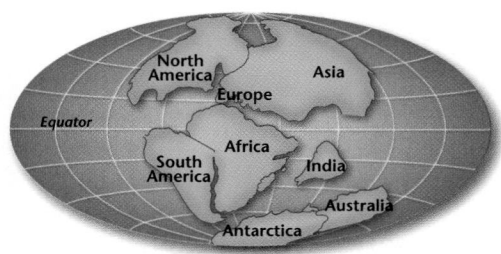

135 million years ago Gradually, the landmasses that became today's continents began to drift apart.

Earth today Note how far to the north India has drifted—farther than any other major landmass.

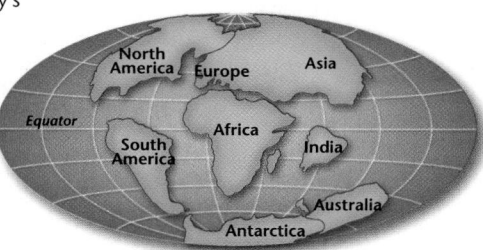

65 million years ago India was still a separate continent, charging toward Asia, while Australia remained attached to Antarctica.

The Continents' Slow Dance

The plates move at amazingly slow rates: from about one to ten centimeters per year. The North American and Eurasian plates are floating apart at a rate of 2.5 centimeters per year—that's about as fast as your fingernails grow. This may not seem like much, but these plates have been moving for tens of millions of years.

About 260 million years ago, the continents were joined together in the supercontinent that Wegener called Pangaea. Then, about 225 million years ago, Pangaea began to break apart. Figure 29 shows how Earth's continents and other landmasses have moved since the break-up of Pangaea.

Section 5 Review

1. What is the theory of plate tectonics?
2. What are the different types of boundaries found along the edges of Earth's plates?
3. What major event in Earth's history began about 225 million years ago? Explain.
4. **Thinking Critically** **Predicting** Look at Figure 26 on page 375 and find the divergent boundary that runs through the African plate. Predict what could eventually happen along this boundary.

Check Your Progress
CHAPTER PROJECT 11

Now that you have learned about plate tectonics, add examples of plate boundaries to your model. If possible, include a transform boundary, a convergent boundary, and a divergent boundary. Complete the construction of your model by adding all the required surface features. Be sure to label the features on your model. Include arrows that indicate the direction of plate movement.

Program Resources

◆ **Unit 4 Resources** 11-5 Review and Reinforce, p. 27; 11-5 Enrich, p. 28

Media and Technology

 Transparencies "Continental Drift Since Pangaea," Transparency 47

Caption Question

Figure 29 You would need answers to how fast and in what direction each plate is moving.

☑ *Checkpoint*

Plates slip past each other at transform boundaries, move apart at divergent boundaries, and come together at convergent boundaries.

3 Assess

Section 5 Review Answers

1. The theory of plate tectonics explains the formation, movement, and subduction of Earth's plates.
2. Transform boundaries, divergent boundaries, and convergent boundaries
3. The supercontinent Pangaea began to break apart.
4. If the rift valley continues to grow, it could someday split the eastern part of Africa away from the rest of the continent, forming a new ocean.

Check Your Progress
CHAPTER PROJECT 11

Discuss with each group how they can incorporate plate boundaries and the movement of plates in their model. Review their designs and give them feedback about the materials they might use. Then encourage them to make any changes necessary and construct the model of a cut-away Earth. Also, give them some guidelines of how they could best make their presentation to the class.

Performance Assessment

Drawing Divide students into small groups and give each group a piece of posterboard. Encourage each group to make a poster that includes all the information they've learned about sea-floor spreading and plate tectonics. They could use colored pencils, chalk, or water paints to make their posters.

Hot Plates

Preparing for Inquiry

Key Concept Convection currents in the mantle cause the movement of Earth's plates.

Skills Objectives Students will be able to:

◆ make a model of two layers of Earth's interior.

◆ observe how convection currents can move objects on the surface of a liquid.

◆ infer how similar convection currents in the mantle move Earth's plates.

Time 40 minutes

Advance Planning Gather the materials at least a day in advance. Buy disposable roasting pans at a grocery store. Then try out the activity. Pay close attention to how best to position the sponges together in the pan so that this can be demonstrated to students. Also, time how long it takes the sponges to reach the pan's edges with your setup.

Alternative Materials Books can be used instead of bricks. The length of the candles is dependent on the height of the pan; shorter candles should be used if the pan is raised less than three bricks high. The tip of the candle flame should be 2–3 cm below the bottom of the pan. To nudge the sponges together in Step 5, a pencil or ruler is helpful, because it disturbs the water less than hands do.

Guiding Inquiry

Invitation Help students think of prior experiences with convection currents by asking: **What happens to noodles and other solids in soup as the water heats up?** *(The solids begin to move around.)* **What causes this movement?** *(The solids move with the movement of water in convection currents, which are created by the heat of a stove's burner.)*

Introducing the Procedure

◆ Have students read through the entire activity. Then ask: **What is the purpose of the map pins?** *(They prevent the sponges from sticking together.)*

◆ Ask: **After you light the candles, where will the water in the pan be hottest and coolest?** *(The water will be hottest at the bottom of the pan and coolest at the surface.)*

Troubleshooting the Experiment

◆ Demonstrate how to place the pins in the sponges. Only about 0.5 cm of each pin should stick out of the sponge.

◆ Check that students have the pan at the right height, with the bricks positioned at the edges and the candles just inside the bricks.

HOT PLATES

In this lab, you will observe a model of convection currents in Earth's mantle.

Problem

How do convection currents affect Earth's plates?

Materials

1 aluminum roasting pan
2 candles, about 10 cm long
clay to hold the candles up
6 bricks
2 medium-sized kitchen sponges
10 map pins
2 L water

Procedure

1. Stick ten pins about halfway into a long side of one of the sponges.

2. Place an aluminum pan on top of two stacks of bricks. **CAUTION:** *Position the bricks so that they fully support both ends of the pan.*

3. Fill the pan with water to a depth of 4 cm.

4. Moisten both sponges with water and float them in the pan.

5. Slowy nudge the two sponges together with the row of map pins between them. (The pins will keep the sponges from sticking together.)

6. Carefully let go of the sponges. If they drift apart, gently move them back together again.

7. Once the sponges stay close together, place the candles under opposite ends of the pan. Use clay to hold up the candles.

8. Draw a diagram of the pan, showing the starting position of the sponges.

9. Carefully light the candles. Observe the two sponges as the water heats up.

10. Draw diagrams showing the position of the sponges 1 minute and 2 minutes after placing the candles under the pan.

Analyze and Conclude

1. What happens to the sponges as the water heats up?

2. What can you infer is causing the changes you observed?

3. What material represents the mantle in this activity? What represents Earth's plates?

4. What would be the effect of adding several more candles under the pan?

5. **Think About It** How well did this activity model the movement of Earth's plates? What type of plate movement did you observe in the pan? How could you modify the activity to model plate movement more closely?

More to Explore

You can observe directly the movement of the water in the pan. To do this, squeeze a single drop of food coloring into the pan. After the drop of coloring has sunk to the bottom, place a lit candle under the pan near the colored water. How does the food coloring move in the water? How does this movement compare with convection currents in the mantle?

Safety

Caution students to be careful when placing the pins into the sponges and to be very careful with the candle flames. Review the safety guidelines in Appendix A.

Media and Technology

 Lab Activity Videotape
Tape 3

SECTION 1 — Earth's Interior

Key Ideas
- Earth's interior is divided into the crust, the mantle, the outer core, and the inner core.
- The lithosphere includes the crust and the rigid upper layer of the mantle; beneath the lithosphere lies the asthenosphere.

Key Terms

geologist	seismic wave	lithosphere
rock	pressure	asthenospere
geology	crust	outer core
constructive force	basalt	inner core
destructive force	granite	
continent	mantle	

SECTION 2 — Convection Currents and the Mantle

INTEGRATING PHYSICS

Key Ideas
- Heat can be transferred in three ways: radiation, conduction, and convection.
- Differences of temperature and density within a fluid cause convection currents.

Key Terms

heat transfer	convection
radiation	density
conduction	convection current

SECTION 3 — Drifting Continents

Key Ideas
- Alfred Wegener developed the idea that the continents were once joined and have since drifted apart.
- Most scientists rejected Wegener's theory because he could not identify a force that could move the continents.

Key Terms
Pangaea
continental drift
fossil

SECTION 4 — Sea-Floor Spreading

Key Ideas
- In sea-floor spreading, molten material forms new rock along the mid-ocean ridge.
- In subduction, the ocean floor sinks back to the mantle beneath deep ocean trenches.

Key Terms

mid-ocean ridge	deep-ocean trench
sonar	subduction
sea-floor spreading	

SECTION 5 — The Theory of Plate Tectonics

Key Ideas
- The theory of plate tectonics explains plate movements and how they cause continental drift.
- Plates slip past each other at transform boundaries, move apart at divergent boundaries, and come together at convergent boundaries.

Key Terms

plate	transform boundary
scientific theory	divergent boundary
plate tectonics	rift valley
fault	convergent boundary

Organizing Information

Cycle Diagram To show the processes that link a trench and the mid-ocean ridge, copy the cycle diagram into your notebook and fill in the blanks.

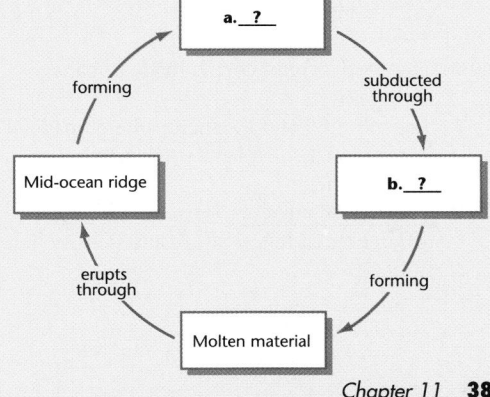

a. **?**
subducted through
forming
Mid-ocean ridge
b. **?**
forming
erupts through
Molten material

Program Resources

- **Unit 4 Resources** Skills Lab blackline masters, pp. 32–33
- **Unit 4 Resources** Chapter 11 Project Scoring Rubric, p. 8
- **Performance Assessment** Chapter 11, pp. 34–36
- **Chapter Tests** Chapter 11 Test, pp. 43–46

Media and Technology

 Computer Test Bank
Chapter 11 Test

- Remind students not to move the pans once they have been filled, since any movement will likely cause a collapse.
- Demonstrate how to nudge the sponges together. Encourage students to do this as delicately as possible—the less movement the better.

Expected Outcome
As the candles heat the water on the bottom of the pan, convection currents will form throughout the pan. The currents will carry the sponges from the center to the edges of the pan.

Analyze and Conclude
1. The sponges begin to move apart to the edges of the pan.
2. The heat from the candles has heated the water, creating convection currents. The convection currents carry the sponges to the edges of the pan.
3. The water represents the mantle; the sponges represent Earth's plates.
4. Answers may vary. A typical answer may suggest that adding candles near to the original candles would heat the water faster and thus create faster currents. The result would be that the sponges would move apart faster.
5. Answers may vary. A typical answer may suggest that the activity models the movement of Earth's plates well. The movement in the pan models divergent plate movement. Some ways to modify the experiment would be to use a thicker liquid than water in which to create convection currents, reposition the candles to get the plates to converge, and have several irregularly shaped sponge "continents."

Extending the Inquiry

More to Explore Encourage students to repeat the activity after a class discussion that explores the techniques of groups that had the most success. Then give each group access to a drop of food coloring so that they can observe the convection currents that move the sponges. The food coloring should move up to the top and then out to the sides, finally sinking back down at the edges of the pan. The basic movement is quite similar to the currents in the mantle.

Organizing Information

Cycle Diagram a. oceanic crust
b. deep-ocean trenches

Reviewing Content

Multiple Choice

1. a 2. d 3. d 4. b 5. b

True or False

6. crust 7. inner core 8. true 9. deep-ocean trenches 10. diverge

Checking Concepts

11. The inner core is a dense ball of solid iron and nickel that spins. The outer core, by contrast, is a layer of molten iron and nickel that behaves like a thick liquid.

12. Heat from Earth's core and the mantle itself create convection currents in the asthenosphere. Hot columns of soft mantle material rise slowly. At the top of the asthenosphere, the material spreads out and pushes cooler material out of the way. This cooler material then sinks.

13. Evidence includes fossils of tropical plants found in polar regions and scratches made by continental glaciers found in places with mild climates.

14. The importance of that discovery is that it supported the theory of sea-floor spreading. It also led scientists to look again at Wegener's theory of continental drift.

15. Iron bits inside molten material lock in place as rock hardens, showing the direction of the magnetic field at that time. Rock magnetized in one direction forms along the mid-ocean ridge until Earth's magnetic poles reverse themselves from time to time. Then rock magnetized in the opposite direction forms a new stripe of rock along each side of the mid-ocean ridge.

16. Oceanic crust is more dense than continental crust. As a result, when a plate carrying oceanic crust collides at a convergent boundary with a plate carrying continental crust, the oceanic plate begins to sink and plunges beneath the continental plate.

17. Answers may vary. A typical interview should include mention of a variety of evidence that supports Wegener's theory, including evidence from landforms, fossils, and climate. Students should also mention evidence for the more modern theories of sea-floor spreading and plate tectonics.

Reviewing Content

Multiple Choice

Choose the letter of the answer that best completes each statement.

1. The layer of the upper mantle that can flow is the
   a. asthenosphere.
   b. lithosphere.
   c. inner core.
   d. continental crust.
2. Most scientists rejected Wegener's theory of continental drift because the theory failed to explain
   a. coal deposits in Antarctica.
   b. formation of mountains.
   c. climate changes.
   d. how the continents move.
3. Subduction of the ocean floor takes place at
   a. the lower mantle.
   b. mid-ocean ridges.
   c. rift valleys.
   d. trenches.
4. The process that powers plate tectonics is
   a. radiation.   b. convection.
   c. conduction.   d. subduction
5. Two plates collide with each other at
   a. a divergent boundary
   b. a convergent boundary
   c. the boundary between the mantle and the crust.
   d. a transform boundary.

True or False

If the statement is true, write true. If it is false, change the underlined word or words to make the statement true.

6. The Earth's <u>outer core</u> is made of basalt and granite.
7. The spinning of the <u>asthenosphere</u>, made of iron and nickel, explains why Earth has a magnetic field.
8. <u>Convection currents</u> form because of differences of temperature and density in a fluid.

9. <u>Magnetic stripes</u> on the ocean floor are places where oceanic crust sinks back to the mantle.
10. When two continental plates <u>converge</u>, a rift valley forms.

Checking Concepts

11. How is the inner core different from the outer core?
12. Why are there convection currents in the mantle? Explain.
13. What evidence of Earth's climate in the past supports the theory of continental drift?
14. What was the importance of the discovery that molten rock was coming out of cracks along the mid-ocean ridge?
15. How do magnetic stripes form on the ocean floor? Why are these stripes significant?
16. What happens when a plate of oceanic crust collides with a plate of continental crust? Why?
17. **Writing to Learn** Imagine that Alfred Wegener is alive today to defend his theory of continental drift. Write a short interview that Wegener might have on a daytime talk show. You may use humor.

Thinking Critically

18. **Classifying** Classify these layers of Earth's crust as liquid, solid, or solid but able to flow slowly: crust, lithosphere, asthenosphere, outer core, inner core.
19. **Comparing and Contrasting** How are oceanic and continental crust alike? How do they differ?
20. **Relating Cause and Effect** What do many geologists think is the driving force of plate tectonics? Explain.
21. **Making Generalizations** State in one sentence the most significant discovery that geologists established through their study of plate tectonics.

Thinking Critically

18. Crust, lithosphere, inner core—solid; asthenosphere—solid but able to flow slowly; outer core—liquid

19. Both continental crust and oceanic crust are part of Earth's outer layer. Continental crust consists mainly of less dense rocks such as granite, while oceanic crust consists mainly of denser rock such as basalt. Oceanic crust is denser than continental crust.

20. Heat from Earth's core is the driving force of plate tectonics. The plates float on top of the partially molten asthenosphere. The heat of Earth's core causes convection currents in the asthenosphere. The flow of those currents causes the movement of the plates.

21. Answers may vary. A typical answer: Pieces of Earth's lithosphere are in constant, slow motion, driven by convection currents in the mantle.

Applying Skills

Geologists think that a new plate boundary is forming in the Indian Ocean. The part of the plate carrying Australia is twisting away from the part of the plate carrying India.

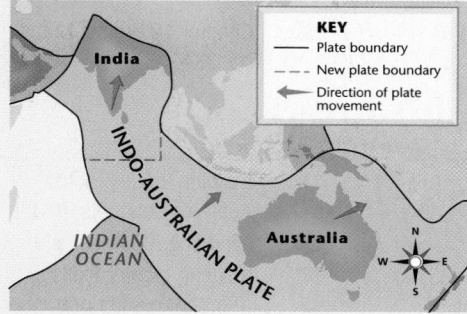

KEY
— Plate boundary
– – – New plate boundary
← Direction of plate movement

22. Interpreting Maps Look at the arrows showing the direction of plate motion. In what direction is the part of the plate carrying Australia moving? In what direction is the part carrying India moving?

23. Predicting As India and Australia move in different directions, what type of plate boundary will form between them?

24. Inferring On the map you can see that the northern part of the Indo-Australian plate is moving north and colliding with the Eurasian plate. What features would occur where these plates meet? Explain.

Performance ▼ CHAPTER PROJECT 11 Assessment

Project Wrap Up Present your model to the class. Point out the types of plate boundaries on the model. Discuss the plate motions and landforms that result in these areas. What similarities and differences exist between your model and those of your classmates?

Reflect and Record In your journal, write an evaluation of your project. What materials would you change? How could you improve your model?

Test Preparation
Use these questions to prepare for standardized tests.

Use the diagram to answer Questions 25–28.

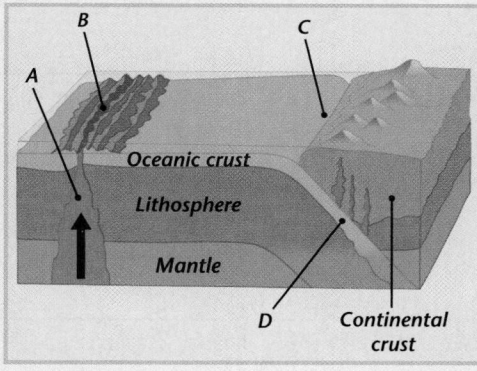

Oceanic crust
Lithosphere
Mantle
Continental crust

25. The arrow at A represents
 a. a transform boundary.
 b. continental crust.
 c. a subduction zone.
 d. molten magma rising from the mantle.

26. What is occurring at the feature labeled B?
 a. New rock is being added to the oceanic plate.
 b. The ocean floor is sinking.
 c. Subduction is occurring.
 d. Two plates are colliding.

27. As sea-floor spreading occurs, the oceanic plate
 a. does not move.
 b. moves from C toward B.
 c. moves from B toward C.
 d. floats higher on the mantle.

28. What is occurring at D?
 a. New material is rising from the mantle.
 b. The oceanic plate is melting as it sinks into the mantle.
 c. Sedimentary rock is being added to the plate.
 d. The oceanic plate is pushing the continental plate into the mantle.

Program Resources

◆ **Inquiry Skills Activity Book** Provides teaching and review of all inquiry skills
◆ **Prentice Hall Assessment System** Provides standardized test practice
◆ **Reading in the Content Area** Provides strategies to improve science reading skills
◆ **Teacher's ELL Handbook** Provides multiple strategies for English language learners

---

Applying Skills

22. The part carrying Australia is moving to the northeast; the part carrying India is moving to the north.
23. Because the parts are moving in different directions, a divergent plate boundary will form between them.
24. Students should infer that this is a convergent plate boundary where two plates made of continental crust are colliding. When the plates converge, the collision squeezes the crust into mountain ranges.

Performance ▼ CHAPTER PROJECT 11 Assessment

Project Wrap Up As each group presents its model of a cut-away Earth, assess how well the model reflects the concepts of Earth's layers, sea-floor spreading, and plate tectonics. Also assess how attractive and well-constructed the model is. Students should explain what their model shows and how Earth's interior relates to the surface.

Reflect and Record In assessing the accuracy and attractiveness of the group's model, students should compare it with other groups' models. If the materials and designs differ, they should consider how those differences might have affected the final product. They should include in their reflections which concepts were difficult to show in the model, what materials worked best, what design elements had to be revised in the process of making the model, and what improvements could be made to make a better model. Have students write their reflections in their journals.

Test Preparation
25. d **26.** a **27.** c **28.** b

383

CHAPTER 12 Earthquakes

Sections	Time	Student Edition Activities	Other Activities	
CHAPTER PROJECT 12 **Shake, Rattle, and Roll** p. 385	Ongoing (2–3 weeks)	Check Your Progress, p. 393, 401, 413 Project Wrap Up, p. 417	TE	Chapter 12 Project Notes, pp. 384–385
1 Earth's Crust in Motion pp. 386–395 ◆ 12.1.1 Describe how stress forces affect rock. ◆ 12.1.2 Describe the types of faults, why faults form, and where they occur. ◆ 12.1.3 Describe how movement along faults changes Earth's surface.	2 periods/ 1 block	**Discover** How Does Stress Affect Earth's Crust?, p. 386 **Try This** It's a Stretch, p. 387 **Sharpen Your Skills** Measuring, p. 391 **Skills Lab: Making Models** Modeling Movement Along Faults, pp. 394–395	TE TE TE TE TE	Building Inquiry Skills: Applying Concepts, p. 388 Including All Students, p. 389 Building Inquiry Skills: Comparing and Contrasting, p. 390 Real-Life Learning, p. 391 Inquiry Challenge, p. 392
2 Measuring Earthquakes pp. 396–403 ◆ 12.2.1 Describe how the energy of an earthquake travels through Earth. ◆ 12.2.2 Identify the different kinds of seismic waves. ◆ 12.2.3 Name the scales used to measure the strength of an earthquake.	2 periods/ 1 block	**Discover** How Do Seismic Waves Travel Through Earth? p. 396 **Try This** Recording Seismic Waves, p. 398 **Real-World Lab: Careers in Science** Locating an Epicenter, pp. 402–403	TE TE LM	Building Inquiry Skills: Observing, p. 397 Demonstration, p. 400 12, "Investigating the Speed of Earthquake Waves"
3 Earthquake Hazards and Safety pp. 404–409 ◆ 12.3.1 Describe how earthquakes cause damage and the kinds of damage they cause. ◆ 12.3.2 Explain what can be done to reduce earthquake hazards to buildings and to people.	1 period/ ½ block	**Discover** Can Bracing Prevent Building Collapse?, p. 404 **Sharpen Your Skills** Calculating, p. 406 **Science at Home,** p. 409	TE TE TE	Inquiry Challenge, p. 405 Building Inquiry Skills: Comparing and Contrasting, p. 406 Building Inquiry Skills: Predicting, p. 408
4 INTEGRATING TECHNOLOGY Monitoring Faults pp. 410–414 ◆ 12.4.1 Describe how geologists monitor faults. ◆ 12.4.2 Explain how geologists determine earthquake risk.	1 period/ ½ block	**Discover** Can Stress Be Measured?, p. 410	TE	Inquiry Challenge, p. 411
Study Guide/Assessment pp. 415–417	1 period/ ½ block		ISAB	Provides teaching and review of all inquiry skills

 For Standard or Block Schedule The Resource Pro® CD-ROM gives you maximum flexibility for planning your instruction for any type of schedule. Resource Pro® contains Planning Express®, an advanced scheduling program, as well as the entire contents of the Teaching Resources and the Computer Test Bank.

Key: **CTB** Computer Test Bank
CT Chapter Tests
ELL Teacher's ELL Handbook

CHAPTER PLANNING GUIDE

Program Resources	Assessment Strategies	Media and Technology
UR Chapter 12 Project Teacher Notes, pp. 34–35 **UR** Chapter 12 Project Overview and Worksheets, pp. 36–39	**TE** Performance Assessment: Chapter 12 Project Wrap Up, p. 417 **TE** Check Your Progress, pp. 493, 401, 413 **UR** Chapter 12 Project Scoring Rubric, p. 40	Science Explorer Internet Site Audio CDs, Section Summaries
UR 12-1 Lesson Plan, p. 41 **UR** 12-1 Section Summary, p. 42 **UR** 12-1 Review and Reinforce, p. 43 **UR** 12-1 Enrich, p. 44 **UR** Skills Lab blackline masters, pp. 57–58	**SE** Section 1 Review, p. 393 **SE** Analyze and Conclude, p. 395 **TE** Ongoing Assessment, pp. 387, 389, 391 **TE** Performance Assessment, p. 393	Concept Videotape Library, *Adventures, Tape 3,* "Why Worry?" Transparencies 48, "Shearing, Tension, and Compression"; 49, "Strike-Slip, Normal, and Reverse Faults" Lab Activity Videotape, *Tape 3*
UR 12-2 Lesson Plan, p. 45 **UR** 12-2 Section Summary, p. 46 **UR** 12-2 Review and Reinforce, p. 47 **UR** 12-2 Enrich, p. 48 **UR** Real-World Lab blackline masters, pp. 59–61	**SE** Section 2 Review, p. 401 **SE** Analyze and Conclude, p. 403 **TE** Ongoing Assessment, pp. 397, 399 **TE** Performance Assessment, p. 401	Concept Videotape Library, *Adventures, Tape 3,* "Waves in the Earth" Presentation Pro, "Earthquakes"; "Faults" Transparency 50, "Earthquakes and Seismic Waves" Lab Activity Videotape, *Tape 3*
UR 12-3 Lesson Plan, p. 49 **UR** 12-3 Section Summary, p. 50 **UR** 12-3 Review and Reinforce, p. 51 **UR** 12-3 Enrich, p. 52	**SE** Section 3 Review, p. 409 **TE** Ongoing Assessment, pp. 405, 407 **TE** Performance Assessment, p. 409	Concept Videotape Library, *Adventures, Tape 3,* "Rock and Roll" Transparency 51, "Exploring an Earthquake-Safe House"
UR 12-4 Lesson Plan, p. 53 **UR** 12-4 Section Summary, p. 54 **UR** 12-4 Review and Reinforce, p. 55 **UR** 12-4 Enrich, p. 56	**SE** Section 4 Review, p. 413 **TE** Ongoing Assessment, pp. 411 **TE** Performance Assessment, p. 413	
GRSW Provides worksheets to promote student comprehension of content **RCA** Provides strategies to improve science reading skills **ELL** Provides multiple strategies for English language learners	**SE** Study Guide/Assessment, pp. 415–417 **PA** Performance Assessment, pp. 37–39 **CT** Chapter 12 Test, pp. 47–50 **CTB** Chapter 12 Test **PHAS** Provides standardized test preparation	Computer Test Bank, Chapter 12 Test

GRSW Guided Reading and Study Workbook
ISAB Inquiry Skills Activity Book
LM Laboratory Manual

PA Performance Assessment
PHAS Prentice Hall Assessment System
PLM Probeware Lab Manual

RCA Reading in the Content Area
SE Student Edition

TE Teacher's Edition
UR Unit Resources

Meeting the National Science Education Standards and AAAS Benchmarks

National Science Education Standards	Benchmarks for Science Literacy	Unifying Themes

Science As Inquiry (Content Standard A)

◆ **Use appropriate tools and techniques to gather, analyze, and interpret data** Students locate an epicenter. *(Real-World Lab)*

Physical Science (Content Standard B)

◆ **Transfer of energy** Stress is a force that acts on rock. Seismic waves carry energy from an earthquake through Earth. *(Sections 1, 2)*

Earth and Space Science (Content Standard D)

◆ **Structure of the Earth system** Earthquakes result from the movement of rock beneath Earth's surface. Movement of rock along a fault causes changes in the land surface. *(Section 1, 2; Skills Lab)*

Science and Technology (Content Standard E)

◆ **Design a solution or product** Students design a model earthquake-resistant structure. *(Chapter Project)*

Science in Personal and Social Perspectives (Content Standard F)

◆ **Natural hazards** Earthquakes can cause great damage. *(Section 3; Science and Society)*

◆ **Science and technology in society** Structures can be designed to reduce earthquake damage. Geologists have invented instruments to monitor faults. Students analyze the risk of an earthquake. *(Chapter Project; Sections 3, 4; Science and Society)*

3A Technology and Science A seismograph records ground movements. Structures can be designed to reduce earthquake damage. Geologists have invented instruments to monitor faults. *(Sections 2, 3, 4)*

3B Design and Systems Students design a model earthquake-resistant structure. *(Chapter Project)*

4C Processes That Shape the Earth Earthquakes result from movement of rock beneath Earth's surface. Movement of rock along a fault causes changes in the land surface. *(Sections 1, 3; Skills Lab)*

4E Energy Transformation Stress is a force that acts on rock. Earthquakes create vibrations called seismic waves. *(Sections 1, 2)*

4F Motion Seismic waves carry the energy of an earthquake away from the focus. Seismologists use seismic waves to locate an epicenter. *(Section 2; Real-World Lab)*

7D Social Trade-Offs Students analyze the risk of an earthquake. *(Science and Society)*

11B Models Students make a model of an earthquake-resistant structure. Students model movements along faults. *(Chapter Project; Skills Lab)*

11C Constancy and Change Stress builds up along a fault until an earthquake releases it. *(Section 1)*

12B Computation and Estimation Students locate an epicenter. *(Real-World Lab)*

◆ **Energy** Stress is a force that acts on rocks. Seismic waves carry the energy of an earthquake away from the focus. Earthquakes can cause great damage. *(Sections 1, 2, 3)*

◆ **Evolution** Over time, fault movement can create mountains and valleys. *(Section 1)*

◆ **Modeling** Students design a model of an earthquake-resistant structure. Students model movement along faults. *(Chapter Project; Skills Lab)*

◆ **Patterns of Change** Stress causes rock to deform in various ways. A seismograph records ground movements. Seismologists use seismic waves to locate an epicenter. Geologists use various instruments to monitor ground movements. *(Sections 1, 2, 4; Skills Lab; Real-World Lab)*

◆ **Scale and Structure** Earthquakes vary in intensity. Structures can be made earthquake-resistant. *(Sections 2, 3; Chapter Project)*

◆ **Stability** An area can appear stable, but still have the risk of an earthquake. *(Science and Society)*

◆ **Systems and Interactions** An earthquake occurs when there is movement along a fault. The energy of an earthquake produces seismic waves. Earthquakes can cause great damage. *(Sections 1, 2, 3)*

◆ **Unity and Diversity** Shearing, tension, and compression are different types of stress that produce different types of faults. P waves, S waves, and surface waves are the three types of seismic waves. *(Sections 1, 2; Skills Lab; Real-World Lab)*

Take It to the Net

The **www.phschool.com** Web site provides you with multiple opportunities to incorporate the internet into your instruction. Go to **www.phschool.com** and click on the Science icon. Then select Science Explorer Integrated.

Internet Activities provide opportunities for students to review, extend, or assess a concept from the chapter.

■ Have students use the chapter Self-Test to get instant feedback.

■ Hot Links and Reference Links provide opportunities for online research.

STAY CURRENT with **SCIENCE NEWS** ®

Find out the latest research and information about earthquakes, volcanoes, and plate tectonics at: **www.phschool.com**

ACTIVITY	Time (minutes)	Materials Quantities for one work group	Skills
Section 1			
Discover, p. 386	5	**Consumable** popsicle stick	Predicting
Try This, p. 387	10	**Nonconsumable** plastic putty	Classifying
Sharpen Your Skills, p. 391	10	**Consumable** masking tape **Nonconsumable** small weight, spring scale, sandpaper	Measuring
Skills Lab, pp. 394–395	40	**Consumable** modeling clay in two or more colors **Nonconsumable** marking pen, plastic butter knife	Making Models, Inferring, Classifying
Section 2			
Discover, p. 396	10	**Nonconsumable** spring toy	Observing
Try This, p. 398	10	**Consumable** paper strip 1 m long **Nonconsumable** large book, pencil, pen	Observing
Real-World Lab, pp. 402–403	35–40	**Consumable** outline map of the United States **Nonconsumable** drawing compass with pencil	Interpreting Data, Drawing Conclusions
Section 3			
Discover, p. 404	10	**Consumable** 5 straws, tape	Predicting
Sharpen Your Skills, p. 406	10	**Consumable** paper **Nonconsumable** pencil (calculator optional)	Calculating
Science at Home, p. 409	home	**Nonconsumable** two small towels, various-sized books	Making Models
Section 4			
Discover, p. 410	5	**Consumable** facial tissue **Nonconsumable** ruler	Drawing Conclusions

A list of all materials required for the Student Edition activities can be found beginning on page T23. You can obtain information about ordering materials by calling 1-800-848-9500 or by accessing the Science Explorer Internet site at: **www.phschool.com**

Shake, Rattle, and Roll

Students may not realize that the design of a building or other structure and the materials of which it is made affect the amount of damage it sustains in an earthquake. This project will give students an opportunity to model and test ways to reduce structural damage during a quake.

Purpose This project is designed to enhance students' knowledge of design features and materials that make structures more earthquake-resistant. Students will research how earthquakes cause damage to structures and will learn how actual structures are designed and built to reduce damage. They will build model structures, test them in simulated earthquakes, improve the structures to make them stronger, and retest them. Finally, students will demonstrate their models in a class presentation and communicate what they have learned about building design.

Skills Focus After completing the Chapter 12 Project, students will be able to

◆ make a model structure that incorporates construction methods and materials used to reduce damage to actual structures during an earthquake;

◆ relate cause and effect to evaluate "earthquake" damage to their model;

◆ apply concepts from the text to improve their model;

◆ communicate how the design and materials of their model help to make it earthquake-resistant;

◆ predict how well an actual structure built on the model's design would survive an earthquake.

Project Time Line The project requires two to three weeks to complete. Each student should first sketch a preliminary design for his or her model structure, choose materials for making the model, and discuss his or her design with classmates. Students should complete the first design based on what they have learned, discuss possible improvements with classmates, build the model, and test it in a simulated earthquake, making

CHAPTER
12 Earthquakes

Nearly 2,000 years ago, the ancient Chinese invented this instrument to detect earthquakes.

WEB ACTIVITY
www.phschool.com

SECTION
1 Earth's Crust in Motion
Discover **How Does Stress Affect Earth's Crust?**
Try This **It's a Stretch**
Sharpen Your Skills **Measuring**
Skills Lab **Modeling Movement Along Faults**

SECTION
2 Measuring Earthquakes
Discover **How Do Seismic Waves Travel Through Earth?**
Try This **Recording Seismic Waves**
Real-World Lab **Locating an Epicenter**

SECTION
3 Earthquake Hazards and Safety
Discover **Can Bracing Prevent Building Collapse?**
Sharpen Your Skills **Calculating**

384

note of any design flaws. Students should use what they have learned to improve their models, then retest them and make any final changes. Each student should then prepare a class presentation of the model. See Chapter 12 Project Teacher Notes on pages 34–35 in Unit 4 Resources for more detailed instructions.

Possible Materials

◆ Provide a wide variety of materials for making the model structures, including popsicle sticks, pretzels, toothpicks, straws, wooden dowels, very thin crackers (such as crispbread), wooden dowels, uncooked pasta, bread sticks, tissue paper, pieces cut from plastic bottles, foam-plastic, aluminum foil, tape, glue, rubber cement, gumdrops, small marshmallows, clay, staples, paper clips, foam rubber, rubber washers, cotton batting, pieces of carpet padding, and small springs. Discourage students from using materials that would not behave realistically in a simulated earthquake—for example, modeling walls with index cards that would

PROJECT 12

Shake, Rattle, and Roll

The ground shakes ever so slightly. A bronze dragon drops a ball into the mouth of the frog below. Nearly 2,000 years ago in China, that's how an instrument like this one would have detected a distant earthquake. Earthquakes are proof that our planet is subject to great forces from within. Earthquakes remind us that we live on the moving pieces of Earth's crust. In this chapter, you will design a structure that will withstand earthquakes.

Your Goal To design, build, and test a model structure that is earthquake resistant.

Your model should
- ◆ be made of materials that are approved by your teacher
- ◆ be built to specifications agreed on by your class
- ◆ be able to withstand several simulated earthquakes of increasing intensity
- ◆ be built following the safety guidelines in Appendix A

Get Started Before you design your model, find out how earthquakes cause damage to structures such as homes, office buildings, and highway overpasses. Preview the chapter to find out how engineers design structures to withstand earthquakes.

Check Your Progress You will be working on this project as you study this chapter. To keep your project on track, look for Check Your Progress boxes at the following points.

Section 1 Review, page 393: Design your model.
Section 2 Review, page 401: Construct, improve, and test your model.
Section 4 Review, page 413: Test your model again, and then repair and improve it.

Wrap Up At the end of the chapter (page 417), you will demonstrate how well your model can withstand the effects of a simulated earthquake and predict whether a building that followed your design could withstand a real earthquake.

SECTION **4** *Integrating Technology* 🌐
Monitoring Faults

Discover **Can Stress Be Measured?**

385

Program Resources

- ◆ **Unit 4 Resources** Chapter 12 Project Teacher Notes, pp. 34–35; Project Overview and Worksheets, pp. 36–39; Project Scoring Rubric, p. 40

Media and Technology

 Audio CDs Section Summaries

 **www.phschool.com**

You will find an Internet activity, chapter self-tests for students, and links to other chapter topics at this site.

---

not tear when the structure is shaken. Also students should not use construction toys such as Legos™ and Tinker Toys™, as these would make the structures too solid.
- ◆ To simulate earthquakes, students could place their model structures on a cafeteria tray, piece of plywood, small table, or other base, hold the base at opposite ends, and shake it back and forth.

Launching the Project To introduce the project, let each student build a very simple structure using toothpicks and tape, subject it to a simulated earthquake, and observe what happens to it. Ask: **How could you improve your structure so it would be stronger in an earthquake?** *(Accept all responses at this time, and encourage creative thinking.)*

Allow time for students to read the project description on page 385. At this time, you might hand out Chapter 12 Project Overview on pages 36–37 in Unit 4 Resources. Encourage discussion of the different kinds of structures they could model and the materials they could use. Also discuss and agree on a list of specifications for the models.

Performance Assessment

The Chapter 12 Project Scoring Rubric on page 40 in Unit 4 Resources will help you evaluate how well students complete the Chapter 12 Project. You may want to share the scoring rubric with your students so they are clear about what will be expected of them. Students will be assessed on
- ◆ designing their models, including the selection of appropriate building materials and effective construction methods;
- ◆ their creativity and neatness in building the models;
- ◆ how well they work with others in testing the models and devising improvements;
- ◆ how well they present their models to the class.

Earth's Crust in Motion

Objectives

After completing the lesson, students will be able to

- describe how stress forces affect rock;
- describe the types of faults, why faults form, and where they occur;
- describe how movement along faults changes Earth's surface.

Key Terms earthquake, stress, shearing, tension, compression, deformation, fault, strike-slip fault, normal fault, hanging wall, footwall, reverse fault, fault-block mountain, folds, anticline, syncline, plateau

1 Engage/Explore

Activating Prior Knowledge

Encourage any students who have experienced an earthquake to describe the event—where they were at the time, how they first became aware that an earthquake was occurring, what happened to buildings and objects around them, how they felt during and after the quake, and so on. If students have not experienced an earthquake, let them relate what they have learned from television reports, movies, newspaper and magazine articles, and other sources.

 **DISCOVER**

Skills Focus predicting
Materials *popsicle stick*
Time 5 minutes
Tips In Step 2, advise students to increase the pressure on the stick slowly and gradually. In Step 3, caution students to maintain a firm grip on one end of the popsicle stick as they release the pressure so the stick does not fly off into the air and cause injury.
Expected Outcome When students release the pressure in Step 3, the stick will spring back to straighten. As they continue bending in Step 4, the stick will break.
Think It Over The crust will break.

Properties of Minerals

DISCOVER •• *ACTIVITY*

What Is the True Color of a Mineral?

1. Examine samples of magnetite and black hematite. Both minerals contain iron. Describe the color and appearance of the two minerals. Are they similar or different?

2. Rub the black hematite across the back of a porcelain or ceramic tile. Observe the color of the streak on the tile.

3. Wipe the tile clean before you test the next sample.

4. Rub the magnetite across the back of the tile. Observe the color of the streak on the tile.

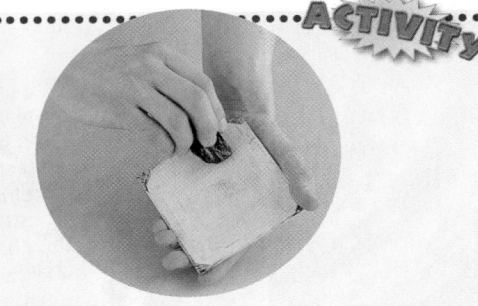

Think It Over
Observing Does the color of each mineral's streak match its color? How could this streak test be helpful in identifying them as two different minerals?

GUIDE FOR READING

- What are the characteristics of a mineral?
- How are minerals identified?

Reading Tip As you read, use the headings to make an outline showing what minerals are and how they can be identified.

If you visit a science museum, you might wander into a room named the "hall of minerals." There you would see substances you have never heard of. For example, you might see deep-red crystals labeled "sphalerite" (SFAL uh ryt). You might be surprised to learn that sphalerite is a source of zinc and gallium. These metals are used in products from "tin" cans to computer chips! Although you may never have seen sphalerite, you are probably familiar with other common minerals. For example, you have probably seen turquoise, a blue-green mineral used in jewelry.

Figure 1 The Hall of Minerals at the American Museum of Natural History in New York City contains one of the world's largest collections of minerals.

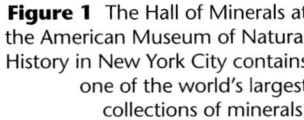 **READING STRATEGIES**

Reading Tip Encourage students to allow space in their outlines for adding detail as they read. Students can use their completed outlines as a study guide.

I. Earth's Crust in Motion
  A. Stress in the Crust
  B. Types of Stress
  C. Kinds of Faults
  D. Friction Along Faults

  E. Mountain Building
    1. Mountains Formed by Faulting
    2. Mountains Formed by Folding
    3. Anticlines and Synclines
    4. Plateaus

Types of Stress

Three different kinds of stress occur in the crust—shearing, tension, and compression. **Shearing, tension, and compression work over millions of years to change the shape and volume of rock.** These forces cause some rocks to become brittle and snap. Other rocks tend to bend slowly like road tar softened by the heat of the sun.

Stress that pushes a mass of rock in two opposite directions is called **shearing.** Shearing can cause rock to break and slip apart or to change its shape.

The stress force called **tension** pulls on the crust, stretching rock so that it becomes thinner in the middle. The effect of tension on rock is somewhat like pulling apart a piece of warm bubble gum. Tension occurs where two plates are moving apart.

The stress force called **compression** squeezes rock until it folds or breaks. One plate pushing against another can compress rock like a giant trash compactor.

Any change in the volume or shape of Earth's crust is called **deformation.** Most changes in the crust occur so slowly that they cannot be observed directly. But if you could speed up time so a billion years passed by in minutes, you could see the deformation of the crust. The crust would bend, stretch, break, tilt, fold, and slide. The slow shift of Earth's plates causes this deformation.

☑ *Checkpoint* How does deformation change Earth's surface?

Figure 2 Deformation pushes, pulls, or twists the rocks in Earth's crust.
Relating Cause and Effect Which type of deformation tends to shorten part of the crust?

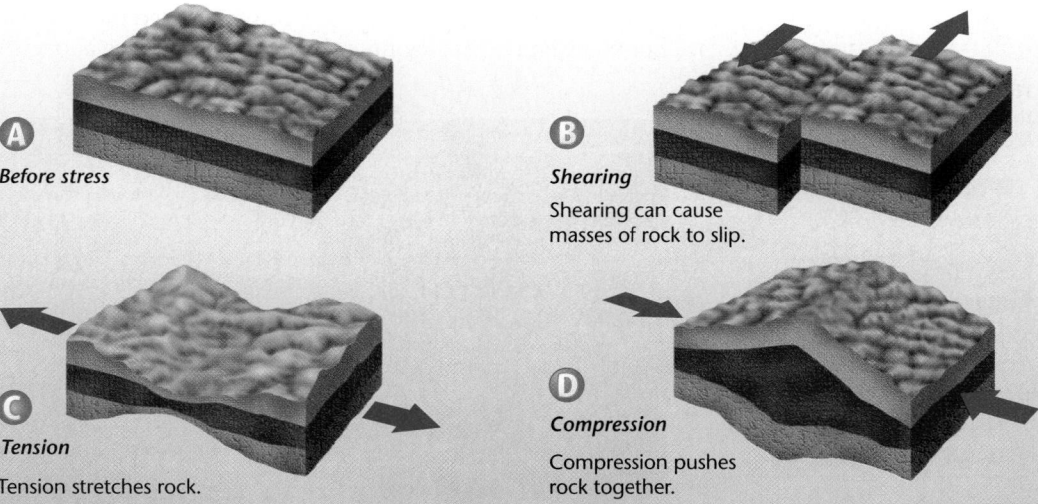

A *Before stress*

B *Shearing*
Shearing can cause masses of rock to slip.

C *Tension*
Tension stretches rock.

D *Compression*
Compression pushes rock together.

Chapter 12 **387**

TRY THIS

It's a Stretch

You can model the stresses that create faults. **ACTIVITY**

1. Knead a piece of plastic putty until it is soft.
2. Push the ends of the putty toward the middle.
3. Pull the ends apart.
4. Push half of the putty one way and the other half in the opposite direction.

Classifying Which types of stress do Steps 2, 3, and 4 represent?

---

2 Facilitate

Stress in the Crust

Including All Students

If students did the Discover activity, ask: **When you bent the popsicle stick the first time and held it in an arch shape, what was happening?** *(Energy—the "push" applied by the hands—was being transferred to the stick and stored in it.)* **What would have happened if you had suddenly let go of one end of the bent stick, and why?** *(The stick would have sprung back to its original shape because the stored energy was quickly released.)* **Where did this stored energy go?** *(It was released as energy in the form of heat.)* **learning modality: logical/mathematical**

Types of Stress

TRY THIS

Skills Focus classifying **ACTIVITY**
Materials *plastic putty*
Time 10 minutes
Tips After students soften the putty in Step 1, tell them to form it into a tube shape before they do each subsequent step.
Expected Outcome Step 2 represents compression, Step 3 represents tension, and Step 4 represents shearing.
Extend Let students repeat the activity with a stiffer material, such as modeling clay, and compare the results.
learning modality: kinesthetic

Program Resources

◆ **Unit 4 Resources** 12-1 Lesson Plan, p. 41; 12-1 Section Summary, p. 42
◆ **Guided Reading and Study Workbook,** Section 12-1

Media and Technology

 Transparencies "Shearing, Tension, and Compression," Transparency 48

Answers to Self-Assessment

☑ *Checkpoint*
It causes it to bend, stretch, break, tilt, fold, and slide.

Caption Question
Figure 2 Compression is the type of deformation that may shorten part of the crust by pushing it together.

Ongoing Assessment

Oral Presentation Ask each student to explain with the aid of a diagram how the directions of force differ in compression, tension, and shearing.

387

Kinds of Faults

Using the Visuals: Figure 3

Make sure students understand that the fault is the irregular, shadowed line running up the middle of the photograph. Point out the road running left-to-right at the bottom of the photograph and ask: **If a strong earthquake occurred, what do you think would happen to the road where it crosses the fault? Why?** *(The road would be bent out of alignment or broken because the two slabs of crust on opposite sides of the fault are moving in different directions.)* **What other things might be deformed or broken at a fault?** *(Fences, rivers and streams, bridges, driveways, straight rows of trees or crops, and the like)* **learning modality: logical/mathematical**

Building Inquiry Skills: Applying Concepts

ACTIVITY

As students read the description of each type of fault and examine its accompanying diagram, ask: **How could you use your hands to show a strike-slip fault?** *(Hold the edges of the open hands against each other with the palms down, the fingers pointing away from the body, and the thumbs tucked below, then slide one hand away from the body and the other hand toward the body.)* **A normal fault?** *(Hold the open hands with the fingers pointing toward each other, lay the fingers of one hand over the fingers of the other hand, then move the hands away from each other.)* **A reverse fault?** *(Hold the hands as described for a normal fault, but move them toward each other.)* **learning modality: kinesthetic**

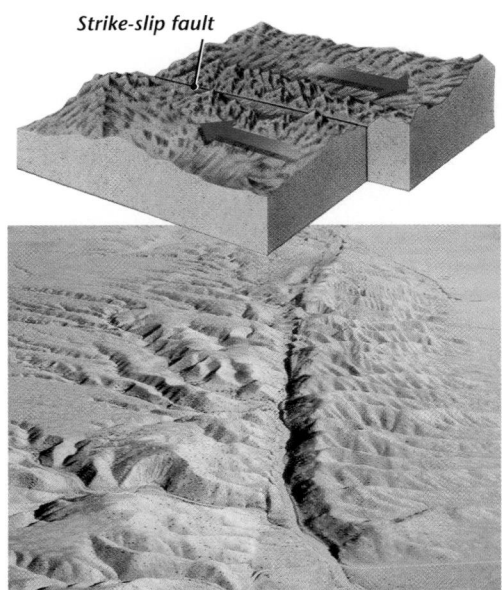

Strike-slip fault

Figure 3 A strike-slip fault that is clearly visible at the surface is the San Andreas Fault in California.

Kinds of Faults

If you try to break a caramel candy bar in two, it may only bend and stretch at first. Like a candy bar, many types of rock can bend or fold. But beyond a certain limit, even these rocks will break. And it takes less stress to snap a brittle rock than it does to snap one that can bend.

When enough stress builds up in rock, the rock breaks, creating a fault. A **fault** is a break in Earth's crust where slabs of crust slip past each other. The rocks on both sides of a fault can move up or down or sideways. **Faults usually occur along plate boundaries, where the forces of plate motion compress, pull, or shear the crust so much that the crust breaks.** There are three main types of faults: strike-slip faults, normal faults, and reverse faults.

Strike-Slip Faults Shearing creates strike-slip faults. In a **strike-slip fault,** the rocks on either side of the fault slip past each other sideways with little up-or-down motion. Figure 3 shows the type of movement that occurs along a strike-slip fault. A strike-slip fault that forms the boundary between two plates is called a transform boundary. The San Andreas fault in California is an example of a strike-slip fault that is a transform boundary.

Normal Faults Tension forces in Earth's crust cause normal faults. In a **normal fault,** the fault is at an angle, so one block of rock lies above the fault while the other block lies below the fault. The half of the fault that lies above is called the **hanging wall.** The half of the fault that lies below is called the **footwall.** Look at Figure 4 to see how the hanging wall lies above the

Figure 4 A normal fault created the Sandia Mountains in New Mexico.

Footwall

Hanging Wall

Normal fault

Key
→ Force deforming the crust
→ Movement along the fault

Background

Facts and Figures The terms *hanging wall* and *footwall* are believed to have originated with miners who excavated shafts to reach ore deposits in fault zones. As they worked, the miners walked on the rocks below the fault (the footwall) and hung their lanterns on the rocks above the fault (the hanging wall).

Normal and reverse faults are types of *dip-slip faults.* The movement in dip-slip faults is largely vertical, with the displacement (the "slip") occurring along the tilt (the "dip") of the fault plane.

A fourth type of fault, not named in the student text, is the *thrust fault.* A thrust fault is similar to a reverse fault in that the hanging wall moves upward. However, the tilt of the fault plane is not as steep as in a dip-slip fault.

footwall. When movement occurs along a normal fault, the hanging wall slips downward. Tension forces create normal faults where plates diverge, or pull apart. For example, normal faults occur along the Rio Grande rift valley in New Mexico, where two pieces of Earth's crust are diverging.

Reverse Faults Compression forces produce reverse faults. A **reverse fault** has the same structure as a normal fault, but the blocks move in the opposite direction. Look at Figure 5 to see how the rocks along a reverse fault move. As in a normal fault, one side of a reverse fault lies at an angle above the other side. The rock forming the hanging wall of a reverse fault slides up and over the footwall. Reverse faults produced part of the Appalachian Mountains in the eastern United States.

A type of reverse fault formed the majestic peaks in Glacier National Park in Montana shown in Figure 5. Over millions of years, a huge block of rock slid along the fault, moving up and over the surface rock. Parts of the overlying block then wore away, leaving the mountain peaks.

☑ *Checkpoint* What are the three types of fault? What force of deformation produces each?

Key
Force deforming the crust ➡️
Movement along the fault ↘️

Footwall   Hanging Wall

Reverse fault

Figure 5 A reverse fault formed Mt. Gould in Glacier National Park, beginning 60 million years ago.
Inferring Which half of the reverse fault slid up and across to form this mountain, the hanging wall or the footwall? Explain.

Answers to Self-Assessment

☑ *Checkpoint*

The three types of faults are strike-slip faults, produced by shearing; normal faults by tension; and reverse faults by compression.

Caption Question

Figure 5 The hanging wall slipped up and across. If the footwall had moved up, the fault would be called a normal fault.

Including All Students

The San Andreas fault is particularly interesting *ACTIVITY* because the deformations it produces in surface features are so clearly visible. Encourage students who need additional challenges to look through books and magazines to find photographs of such deformations and make multiple photocopies for the class to examine. Using evidence in the photographs, students could locate and mark the fault line in each photograph and draw arrows to indicate the directions in which the two opposing rock slabs moved. **learning modality: visual**

Building Inquiry Skills: Inferring

Instruct students to look back at Figure 26 in Chapter 11 on page 375. Ask: **What are some places on or near land where plates are converging—moving toward each other?** *(At the boundaries between the Eurasian and Indo-Australian plates, the Eurasian and Pacific plates, the Indo-Australian and Pacific plates, the Nazca and South American plates, and the Pacific and North American plates)* **What do you think happens to Earth's crust in those places as the plates move toward each other?** *(Students should be able to reason that over long periods of time, the crust compresses, forming mountains and other landforms.)* **What do you think happens to the solid rock?** *(It breaks to form faults.)* **What type of stress force is occurring along those boundaries between plates?** *(compression)* **What type of fault would you expect to find there?** *(reverse faults)* Point out that there are other faults in those areas besides the major fault along the plate boundary. **learning modality: logical/mathematical**

Ongoing Assessment

Drawing Have each student make a simple sketch of each type of fault without referring to the diagrams on these pages, add arrows to show the block movements, and label each sketch with the name of the type of fault it shows.

 Students can save their labeled drawings in their portfolios.

389

Friction Along Faults

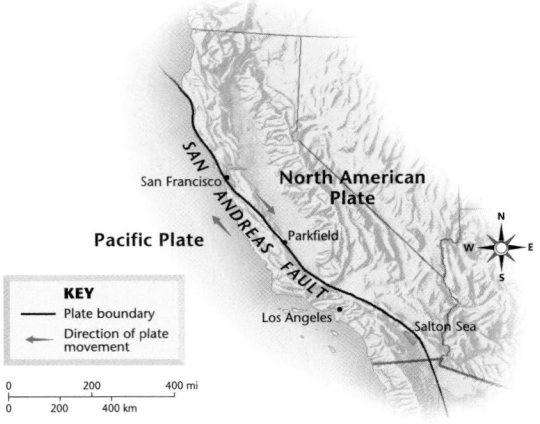

Figure 6 The San Andreas fault extends from the Salton Sea in southern California to the point in northern California where the plate boundary continues into the Pacific Ocean.

Friction Along Faults

INTEGRATING PHYSICS How rocks move along a fault depends on how much friction there is between the opposite sides of the fault. Friction is the force that opposes the motion of one surface as it moves across another surface. Friction exists because surfaces are not perfectly smooth.

Where friction along a fault is low, the rocks on both sides of the fault slide by each other without much sticking. Where friction is moderate, the sides of the fault jam together. Then from time to time they jerk free, producing small earthquakes. Where friction is high, the rocks lock together and do not move. In this case, stress increases until it is strong enough to overcome the friction force.

The San Andreas fault forms a transform boundary between the Pacific plate and the North American plate. In most places along the San Andreas fault, friction is high and the plates lock. Stress builds up until an earthquake releases the stress and the plates slide past each other.

Mountain Building

The forces of plate movement can build up Earth's surface. **Over millions of years, fault movement can change a flat plain into a towering mountain range.**

Mountains Formed by Faulting When normal faults uplift a block of rock, a **fault-block mountain** forms. You can see a diagram of this process in Figure 7. How does this process begin?

Figure 7 Two normal faults can form fault-block mountains, such as the Teton Range near the border of Wyoming and Idaho.

Normal faults

Key
Movement along normal faults ➡

390

Where two plates move away from each other, tension forces create many normal faults. When two of these normal faults form parallel to each other, a block of rock is left lying between them. As the hanging wall of each normal fault slips downward, the block in between moves upward. When a block of rock lying between two normal faults slides downward, a valley forms.

If you traveled by car from Salt Lake City to Los Angeles you would cross the Great Basin, a region with many ranges of fault-block mountains separated by broad valleys, or basins. This "basin and range" region covers much of Nevada and western Utah.

Mountains Formed by Folding Under certain conditions, plate movement causes the crust to fold. Have you ever skidded on a rug that wrinkled up as your feet pushed it across the floor? Much as the rug wrinkles, rock stressed by compression may bend slowly without breaking. **Folds** are bends in rock that form when compression shortens and thickens part of Earth's crust.

The collisions of two plates can cause compression and folding of the crust. Some of the world's largest mountain ranges, including the Himalayas in Asia and the Alps in Europe, formed when pieces of the crust folded during the collision of two plates. Such plate collisions also lead to earthquakes, because folding rock can fracture and produce faults.

Individual folds can be only a few centimeters across or hundreds of kilometers wide. You can often see small folds in the rock exposed where a highway has been cut through a hillside.

Sharpen your Skills

Measuring

You can measure the force of friction.

1. Place a small weight on a smooth, flat tabletop. Use a spring scale to pull the weight across the surface. How much force is shown on the spring scale? (*Hint*: The unit of force is newtons.)

2. Tape a piece of sandpaper to the tabletop. Repeat Step 1, pulling the weight across the sandpaper.

Is the force of friction greater for a smooth surface or for a rough surface?

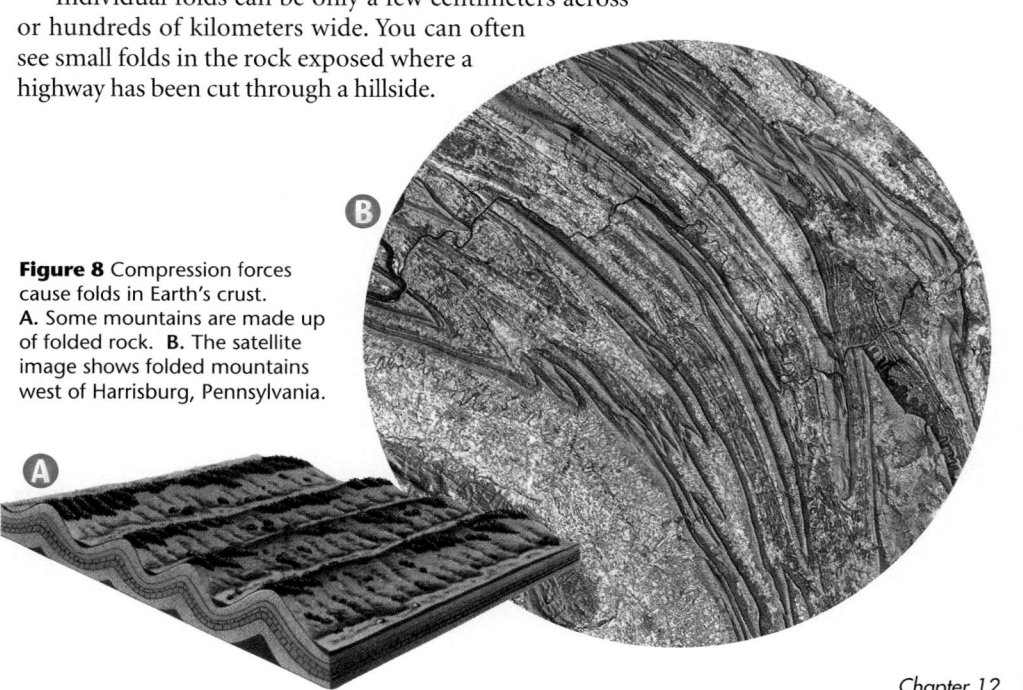

Figure 8 Compression forces cause folds in Earth's crust. **A.** Some mountains are made up of folded rock. **B.** The satellite image shows folded mountains west of Harrisburg, Pennsylvania.

Media and Technology

📼 **Concept Videotape Library**
Adventures, Tape 3, "Why Worry?"

Sharpen your Skills

Measuring

Materials *small weight, spring scale, sandpaper, masking tape*
Time 10 minutes
Tips If necessary, let students first practice using the spring scale by weighing several small objects and reading the measurements on the scale. Remind them to calibrate the scale to zero when no weight is added. Point out that when they do the activity, they must read the measurement while they are pulling the weight across the surface.
Expected Outcome The force of friction (the scale reading) is greater for a rough surface.
Extend Students could repeat the activity with other materials taped to the surface, such as waxed paper, aluminum foil, and a terrycloth towel. **learning modality: logical/mathematical**

Mountain Building

Real-Life Learning

Encourage students to look for actual examples of rock folds. (Draw students' attention to Figure 9 on the next page.) Roadways cut through rocky hillsides often have exposed folds. Tell students to note the locations of the folds they find and to sketch the fold patterns they see. In a follow-up class session, let students share their observations and drawings.
learning modality: visual

Ongoing Assessment

Writing Have students write a brief explanation, in their own words, of why earthquakes are so common—and so often violent—along the San Andreas fault.

391

Mountain Building,
continued

Inquiry Challenge

Challenge students to use any simple materials available in the classroom to model the folding process that produces anticlines and synclines. *(Students can use any material that buckles and folds when compressed, such as a stack of several sheets of construction paper of different colors to represent different rock layers. To model an anticline, lay the stack on a desktop and push the two short ends toward each other; the stack will bend upward in the middle. To model a syncline, lay the stack across a space between two desks and push the ends; the stack will bend downward in the middle.)*
learning modality: kinesthetic

Cultural Diversity

Display a detailed regional map that includes South Dakota and also shows the locations of Indian reservations in the Black Hills area. (Map 4, "The North Central States," in The National Geographic Society's *Close-Up: U.S.A.* map set is an excellent choice.) Let students first locate the Black Hills along the boundary between South Dakota and Wyoming. Explain that since ancient times, Native Americans living in that region have regarded the Black Hills as a sacred place. However, the Black Hills were taken from the native peoples when valuable minerals, including gold, were discovered there. Invite students to locate and name the present-day Indian reservations in the area and find out the name of the Native American tribe living there. *(The Pine Ridge and Rosebud reservations are home to the Oglala Sioux.)* Encourage interested students to find out more about the history of this area and how the type of geology there made it easy for people to find gold and other minerals. Students could also find pictures and descriptions of famous tourist attractions in the Black Hills, including the Mount Rushmore National Memorial and the Crazy Horse Memorial being carved on Thunderhead Mountain. **learning modality: visual**

Anticlines and Synclines Geologists use the terms anticline and syncline to describe upward and downward folds in rock. You can compare anticlines and synclines in the diagram in Figure 9. A fold in rock that bends upward into an arch is an **anticline.** A fold in rock that bends downward in the middle to form a bowl is a **syncline**. Anticlines and synclines are found on many parts of Earth's surface where compression forces have folded the crust.

One example of an anticline is the Black Hills of South Dakota. The Black Hills began to form about 65 million years ago. At that time, forces in Earth's crust produced a large dome-shaped anticline. Over millions of years, a variety of processes wore down and shaped the rock of this anticline into the Black Hills.

You may see a syncline where a valley dips between two parallel ranges of hills. But a syncline may also be a very large feature, as large as the state of Illinois. The Illinois Basin is a syncline that stretches from the western side of Indiana about 250 kilometers across the state of Illinois. The basin is filled with soil and rock that have accumulated over millions of years.

Figure 9 A. Over millions of years, compression and folding of the crust produce anticlines, which arch upward, and synclines, which dip downward. **B.** The folded rock layers of an anticline can be seen on this cliff on the coast of England.

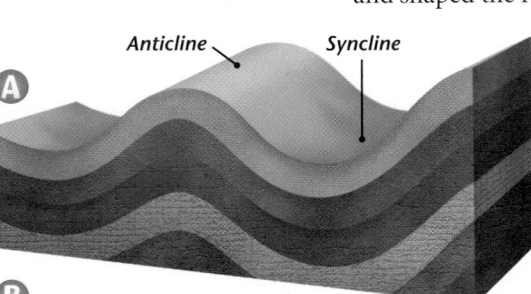

Anticline   Syncline

Ⓐ

Ⓑ

392

Plateaus The forces that raise mountains can also raise plateaus. A **plateau** is a large area of flat land elevated high above sea level. Some plateaus form when vertical faults push up a large, flat block of rock. Like a fancy sandwich, a plateau consists of many different flat layers, and is wider than it is tall.

Forces deforming the crust uplifted the Colorado Plateau in the "Four Corners" region of Arizona, Utah, Colorado, and New Mexico. The Colorado Plateau is a roughly circular area of uplifted rock more than 500 kilometers across. This vast slab of rock once formed part of a sea floor. Today, much of the plateau lies more than 1,500 meters above sea level.

Figure 10 The flat land on the horizon is the Kaibab Plateau, which forms the North Rim of the Grand Canyon in Arizona. The Kaibab Plateau is part of the Colorado Plateau.

 **Section 1 Review**

1. What are the three main types of stress in rock?
2. Describe the movements that occur along each of the three types of faults.
3. How does Earth's surface change as a result of movement along faults?
4. **Thinking Critically Predicting** If plate motion compresses part of the crust, what landforms will form there in millions of years? Explain.

Check Your Progress

CHAPTER PROJECT 12

Discuss with your classmates the model you plan to build. What materials could you choose for your earthquake-resistant structure? Sketch your design. Does your design meet the guidelines provided by your teacher? How will you use your materials to build your model? (*Hint:* Draw the sketch of your model to scale).

3 Assess

Section 1 Review Answers

1. Shearing, tension, and compression
2. *Strike-slip fault:* The rocks on either side of the fault slip sideways past each other with little up-or-down motion. *Normal fault:* The hanging wall slips downward past the footwall. *Reverse fault:* The hanging wall slides up and over the footwall.
3. Movement along faults can create mountains and valleys.
4. Compression produces reverse faults, upward folds called anticlines, and downward folds called synclines. Over time, faulting and folding create mountains, plateaus, and valleys.

Check Your Progress

CHAPTER PROJECT 12

Provide graph paper so students can draw their models to scale. Suggest that they list the materials they plan to use and attach the list to the scale drawing. Allow time for students to show their drawings to classmates and explain how they plan to build the models. Encourage the other students to comment on the plans, ask questions, and offer suggestions. If any students are having difficulty devising a plan, meet with those students individually to offer guidance. Also encourage them to talk with classmates to get ideas.

Performance Assessment

Skills Check To evaluate students' understanding of different types of faults and their ability to represent those concepts in a model, have each student use two dry kitchen sponges to show the movements involved in strike-slip, normal, and reverse faulting and explain the processes as they demonstrate them.

Modeling Movement Along Faults

Preparing for Inquiry

Key Concept The directions of stress forces are different for strike-slip, normal, and reverse faults.

Skills Objectives Students will be able to

◆ make a simple model to show block movements in a strike-slip fault, a normal fault, and a reverse fault;

◆ infer how faulting can change the land surface;

◆ classify deformations in surface features caused by different types of faults.

Time 40 minutes

Guiding Inquiry

Invitation Remind students of the three fault models they made with their hands in Building Inquiry Skills, page 388. Ask: **What was different about the directions of movement in the three types of faults?** (*In the strike-slip fault, movement was sideways and in opposite directions; in the normal fault, the hanging wall moved down; in the reverse fault, the hanging wall moved up.*)

Introducing the Procedure

Tell students that in this activity, they will be using blocks of clay to represent Earth's crust. Ask: **How will blocks of clay more closely resemble real blocks of rock than your hands did?** (*They can show several layers of rock and the actual shape of the hanging wall and footwall.*)

Troubleshooting the Experiment

Have students first cover the desktop with a sheet of waxed paper to protect it.

◆ In Step 2, make sure students cut the squares in half from one side to the opposite side, not from corner to corner.

◆ In Step 4, if any students cut the block straight down instead of at an angle, have them press the two pieces firmly back together and recut the block.

MODELING MOVEMENT ALONG FAULTS

Faults are cracks in Earth's crust where masses of rock move over, under, or past each other. In this lab, you will make a model of the movements along faults.

Problem

How does the movement of rock along the sides of a fault compare for different types of faults?

Materials

Clay in two or more colors
Marking pen
Plastic butter knife

Procedure

1. Mold some clay into a sheet about 0.5 centimeter thick and about 6 centimeters square. Then make another sheet of the same size and thickness, using a different color.

2. Cut each square in half and stack the sheets on top of each other, alternating colors. **CAUTION:** *To avoid breaking the plastic knife, do not press too hard as you cut.* The sheets of clay stand for different layers of rock. The different colors will help you see where similar layers of rock end up after movement occurs along the model fault.

3. Press the layers of clay together to form a rectangular block that fits in the palm of your hand.

4. Use the butter knife to slice carefully through the block at an angle, as shown in the photograph.

5. Place the two blocks formed by the slice together, but don't let them stick together.

6. Review the descriptions and diagrams of faults in Section 1. Decide which piece of your block is the hanging wall and which is the footwall. Using the marking pen, label the side of each block. What part of your model stands for the fault itself?

7. What part of the model stands for the land surface? Along the top surface of the two blocks, draw a river flowing across the fault. Also draw an arrow on each block to show the direction of the river's flow. The arrow should point from the footwall toward the hanging wall.

8. Make a table that includes the headings Type of Fault, How the Sides of the Fault Move, and Changes in the Land Surface.

Type of Fault	How the Sides of the Fault Move	Changes in the Land Surface

---

◆ In Step 6, the hanging wall is the block with the larger surface area on top and the footwall is the lower block. The fault is the cut between the two blocks.

◆ In Step 7, the land surface is the top surface. Make sure students draw the arrows to show the river flowing *toward* the fault on the surface of the footwall and *away from* the fault on the surface of the hanging wall.

◆ In Step 9, the blocks should be moved sideways, with no up or down movement. In Step 10, the upper block should be moved

down. In Step 11, the upper block should be moved up.

Expected Outcome

In Step 9, the riverbed will be displaced horizontally in a zig-zag shape. In Step 10, the downstream part of the river on the surface of the upper block will be displaced downward so it is lower than the upstream part. In Step 11, the downstream part will be displaced upward so it is higher than the upstream part.

9. Using your blocks, model the movement along a strike-slip fault. Record your motion and the results on the data table.
10. Repeat Step 9 for a normal fault.
11. Repeat Step 9 for a reverse fault.

Analyze and Conclude

Refer to your data table to draw a chart that will help you answer questions 1 through 4.

1. On your chart, show the direction in which the sides of the fault move for each type of fault.
2. On your chart, show how movement along a strike-slip fault is different from movement along the other two types of fault.
3. Add to your chart a column that shows how the river on the surface might change for each type of fault.
4. Assuming that the river is flowing from the footwall toward the hanging wall, which type of fault could produce small waterfalls in the surface river? (*Hint:* Recall how you tell which block is the hanging wall and which block is the footwall).
5. If you could observe only the land surface around a fault, how could you tell if the fault is a strike-slip fault? A normal fault?
6. If you slide the hanging wall of your fault model upward in relation to the footwall, what type of fault forms? If this movement continues, where will the slab of rock with the hanging wall end up?

7. From an airplane, you see a chain of several long, narrow lakes along a fault. What type of fault would cause these lakes to form?
8. **Think About It** In what ways does the model help you picture what is happening along a fault? In what ways does the model not accurately reflect what happens along a fault? How is the model still useful in spite of its inaccuracies?

More to Explore

On Earth's surface, individual faults do not exist all by themselves. With one or more of your classmates, combine your models to show how a fault-block mountain range or a rift valley could form. (*Hint:* Both involve normal faults.) How could you combine your models to show how reverse faults produce a mountain range?

Sample Data Table

Type of Fault	How Hanging Wall Moves	Changes in the Land Surface
Strike-slip fault	sideways	Riverbed is broken and moved sideways.
Normal Fault	down	Downstream part of river drops below upstream part.
Reverse fault	up	Downstream part of river may form a lake where it meets hanging wall.

Program Resources

◆ **Unit 4 Resources** Skills Lab blackline masters, pp. 57–58

Media and Technology

Lab Activity Videotape, *Tape 3*

Analyze and Conclude

1. *Strike-slip fault:* The hanging wall moves sideways. *Normal fault:* The hanging wall moves downward. *Reverse fault:* The hanging wall moves upward.
2. Students' charts should indicate that there is no upward or downward movement along a strike-slip fault.
3. *Strike-slip fault:* The continuous line of the riverbed would be broken and displaced horizontally. *Normal fault:* The downstream part of the river would drop below the upstream part, creating a waterfall at the fault. *Reverse fault:* The downstream part of the river would be thrust above the upstream part; water would collect at the fault to form a lake.
4. A normal fault
5. A strike-slip fault would be indicated by sideways displacement of a feature where it crossed the fault. A normal fault would be indicated by a break in the feature where the two blocks slipped past each other at the fault; the part of the feature on the surface of the hanging wall would be lower than the part on the surface of the footwall.
6. A reverse fault; above the footwall
7. A reverse fault or strike-slip fault
8. The model demonstrates actual rock movements. The model's fault is much more regular and smooth than real faults between rock surfaces, so the model's movements involve far less friction and are less abrupt and "jerky." The model enables you to see block movements that are hidden underground in real faulting.

Extending the Inquiry

More to Explore Encourage students to model fault-block mountains and rift valleys. They can refer to Figure 7, Page 390, for fault-block mountains and *Exploring Plate Tectonics*, pages 376–377, for a rift valley.

Safety

Students should handle the knife carefully during this activity. Review the safety guidelines in Appendix A.

Objectives

After completing the lesson, students will be able to

◆ describe how the energy of an earthquake travels through Earth;

◆ identify the different kinds of seismic waves;

◆ name the scales used to measure the strength of an earthquake.

Key Terms focus, epicenter, seismic waves, P waves, S waves, surface waves, seismograph, magnitude, Mercalli scale, Richter scale, moment magnitude scale

1 Engage/Explore

Activating Prior Knowledge

Ask: **What kinds of waves have you observed?** (*Students will probably mention ocean waves and waves in a lake, pond, swimming pool, or even a bathtub.*) **How do waves move in water?** (*They will probably say that the waves move outward from a "push" on the water.*)

DISCOVER

Skills Focus observing
Materials *spring toy*
Time 10 minutes
Tips Advise students to hold both ends of the spring securely as they make the waves. If they have difficulty observing differences in the two wave types, let them repeat each step several times.
Expected Outcome In Step 2, the coils will move forward and backward along the spring in a straight line. In Step 3, the coils will move sideways.
Think It Over In Step 2, the coils move forward and back as a wave moves from the compressed end of the spring to the other end in a straight line. In Step 3, the coils move from side to side as a wave moves in a bulge from the jerked end of the spring to the other end.

396

DISCOVER .... ACTIVITY

How Do Seismic Waves Travel Through Earth?

1. Stretch a spring toy across the floor while a classmate holds the other end. Do not overstretch the toy.

2. Gather together about 4 coils of the spring toy and release them. In what direction do the coils move?

3. Once the spring toy has stopped moving, jerk one end of the toy from side to side once. In what direction do the coils move? Be certain your classmate has a secure grip on the other end.

Think It Over

Observing Describe the two types of wave motion that you observed in the spring toy.

GUIDE FOR READING

◆ How does the energy of an earthquake travel through Earth?

◆ What are the different kinds of seismic waves?

◆ What are the scales used to measure the strength of an earthquake?

Reading Tip Before you read, rewrite the headings in the section as what, how, or why questions. As you read, look for answers to these questions.

Earth is never still. Every day, worldwide, there are about 8,000 earthquakes. Most of them are too small to notice. But when an earthquake is strong enough to rattle dishes in kitchen cabinets, people sit up and take notice. "How big was the quake?" and "Where was it centered?" are two questions just about everyone asks after an earthquake.

To know where an earthquake was centered, you need to know where it began. Earthquakes always begin in rock below the surface. Most earthquakes begin in the lithosphere within 100 kilometers of Earth's surface. An earthquake starts at one particular point. The **focus** (FOH kus) is the point beneath Earth's surface where rock that is under stress breaks, triggering an earthquake. The point on the surface directly above the focus is called the **epicenter** (EHP uh sen tur).

Seismic Waves

If you have ever played a drum, you know that the sound it makes depends on how hard you strike it. Like a drumbeat, an earthquake produces vibrations called waves. These waves carry energy as they travel outward through solid material. During an earthquake, seismic waves race out from the focus in all directions. **Seismic waves** are vibrations that travel through Earth carrying the energy released during an earthquake. The seismic waves move like ripples in a pond. Look at Figure 11 to see how seismic waves travel outward in all directions from the focus.

396

READING STRATEGIES

Reading Tip Typical questions that students might write include "What are the different types of seismic waves?" "How do seismic waves move?" "How is the strength of an earthquake measured?" and "How can scientists locate the epicenter of an earthquake?"

Vocabulary Students may wonder where the terms *seismic, seismograph, seismologist,* and *seismology* came from. Encourage students to look up the origin of the root word *seism.* (*From* seismos, *the Greek word for earthquake, derived from* seiein, *meaning "to shake"*) Also discuss the meanings of the suffixes -graph (*"a device that writes or records"*), -ology (*"the study of" something*), and -ologist (*"a person who studies" something*).

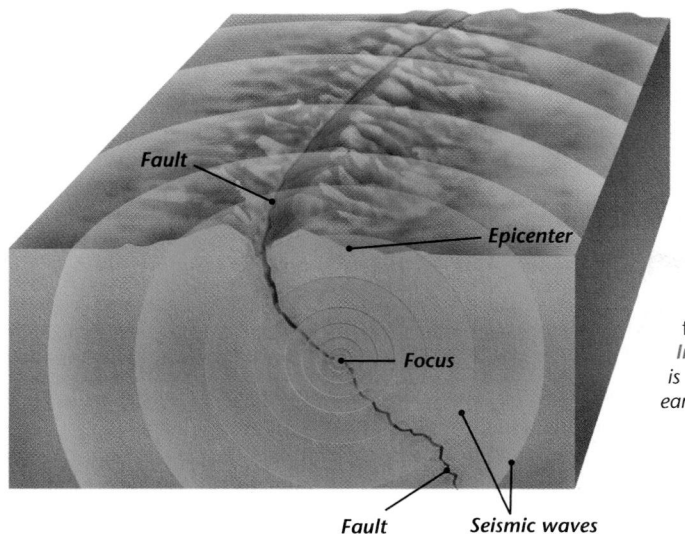

Fault

Epicenter

Focus

Fault Seismic waves

Figure 11 An earthquake occurs when rocks fracture at the focus, deep in Earth's crust. *Interpreting Diagrams What point is directly above the focus of the earthquake?*

Seismic waves carry the energy of an earthquake away from the focus, through Earth's interior, and across the surface. The energy of the seismic waves that reach the surface is greatest at the epicenter. The most violent shaking during an earthquake, however, may occur kilometers away from the epicenter. The types of rock and soil around the epicenter determine where and how much the ground shakes. You will learn more about the effects of seismic waves in Section 3.

There are three categories of seismic waves: P waves, S waves, and surface waves. An earthquake sends out two types of waves from its focus: P waves and S waves. When these waves reach Earth's surface at the epicenter, surface waves develop.

Primary Waves The first waves to arrive are primary waves, or P waves. **P waves** are earthquake waves that compress and expand the ground like an accordion. P waves cause buildings to contract and expand. Look at Figure 12 to compare P waves and S waves.

Secondary Waves After P waves come secondary waves, or S waves. **S waves** are earthquake waves that vibrate from side to side as well as up and down. They shake the ground back and forth. When S waves reach the surface, they shake structures violently. Unlike P waves, which travel through both solids and liquids, S waves cannot move through liquids.

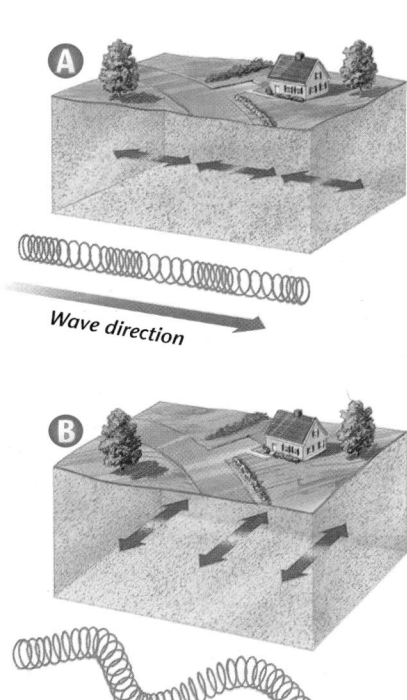

A

Wave direction

B

Wave direction

Figure 12 A. In P waves, the particles of the crust vibrate forward and back along the path of the wave. **B.** In S waves, the particles of the crust vibrate from side to side and up and down.

Chapter 12 **397**

Chapter 12 **397**

Answers to Self-Assessment

Caption Question

Figure 11 the epicenter

Program Resources

◆ **Unit 4 Resources** 12-2 Lesson Plan, p. 45; 12-2 Section Summary, p. 46
◆ **Guided Reading and Study Workbook**, Section 12-2

---

2 Facilitate

Seismic Waves

Building Inquiry Skills: Observing

Materials *dishpans or other wide, shallow containers; water; pebbles*  **Time** 10 minutes

Set up several learning centers, each with several pebbles and a container filled about 6–8 cm deep with water. Let students drop pebbles into the water and observe the waves that are formed. Then ask: **How did the waves move when a pebble hit the water?** *(The waves moved outward from the pebble in concentric rings.)* **learning modality: visual**

Using the Visuals: Figure 11

Draw students' attention to the pattern of seismic waves shown in the diagram and ask: **How are seismic waves like the waves you made when you dropped pebbles into water?** *(Seismic waves also move outward in concentric rings.)* **How are they different?** *(Seismic waves move outward three-dimensionally in all directions, whereas the water waves moved only on the surface. Seismic waves move through solid materials.)* **learning modality: visual**

Including All Students

Remind students of their experience creating waves with the spring toy in the Discover activity. Ask: **When the wave moved straight ahead along the spring, which type of earthquake wave did it model?** *(a P wave)* **When the spring moved from side to side, which type of wave did it model?** *(an S wave)* **When you used the spring, where was the focus of the model earthquake?** *(At the end that was compressed and jerked)* **learning modality: logical/mathematical**

Ongoing Assessment

Writing Have each student describe the major difference between P waves and S waves.

397

Seismic Waves, continued

Building Inquiry Skills: Inferring

After students read about surface waves, ask: **Why do you think surface waves produce more severe ground movements than P waves and S waves do?** *(Students should infer that because the surface consists of loose soil, sand, gravel, mud, small rocks, and the like rather then solid rock, it is susceptible to greater movement as the particles shift and slide.)* **learning modality: logical/ mathematical**

Detecting Seismic Waves

Skills Focus observing
Materials *large book, pencil, paper strip 1 m long, pen*
Time 10 minutes
Tips Make sure students hold the pencil and rolled strip *parallel* to the book and tabletop.
Expected Outcome The pen will first draw a straight line, then a jagged back-and-forth line as the book is jiggled. The line's spikes will be larger with stronger jiggling.
Extend Encourage students to try different types of "earthquakes"—long, slow movements; strong, abrupt movements; a strong quake followed by calm and then a smaller quake (an aftershock); and so forth. **learning modality: kinesthetic**

Using the Visuals: Figure 13

After students have studied the figure and read the caption, ask: **Which type of seismograph did you model in Try This?** *(A mechanical seismograph)* **What similarities do you see between the real seismograph record (also called a seismogram) and the marks you made on the paper strip?** *(Students should mention the back-and-forth jiggles in the line and the different sizes of the spikes caused by different strengths of the movements.)* **learning modality: visual**

Recording Seismic Waves

ACTIVITY

You and two classmates can simulate a seismograph.

1. Place a big book on a table.
2. With one hand, hold a pencil with a strip of paper about one meter long wound around it.
3. In your other hand, hold a pen against the paper.
4. As you hold the pen steady, have one student slowly pull on the paper so it slides across the book.
5. After a few seconds, have the other student jiggle the book for 10 seconds—first gently, then strongly.

Observing How did the line on the paper change when the earthquake began? When it grew stronger?

Surface Waves When P waves and S waves reach the surface, some of them are transformed into surface waves. **Surface waves** move more slowly than P waves and S waves, but they produce the most severe ground movements. Some surface waves make the ground roll like ocean waves. Other surface waves shake buildings from side to side.

☑ *Checkpoint* What are the three types of seismic waves?

Detecting Seismic Waves

To record and measure the vibrations of seismic waves, geologists use instruments called seismographs. A **seismograph** (SYZ muh graf) records the ground movements caused by seismic waves as they move through the Earth.

Until recently, scientists used mechanical seismographs. As shown in Figure 13, a mechanical seismograph consists of a heavy weight attached to a frame by a spring or wire. A pen connected to the weight rests its point on a rotating drum. When the drum is still, the pen draws a straight line on paper wrapped around the drum. During an earthquake, seismic waves cause the drum to vibrate. Meanwhile, the pen stays in place and records the drum's vibrations. The height of the jagged lines drawn on the seismograph's drum is greater for a more severe earthquake.

Today, scientists use electronic seismographs that work according to the same principle as the mechanical seismograph. The electronic seismograph converts ground movements into a signal that can be recorded and printed.

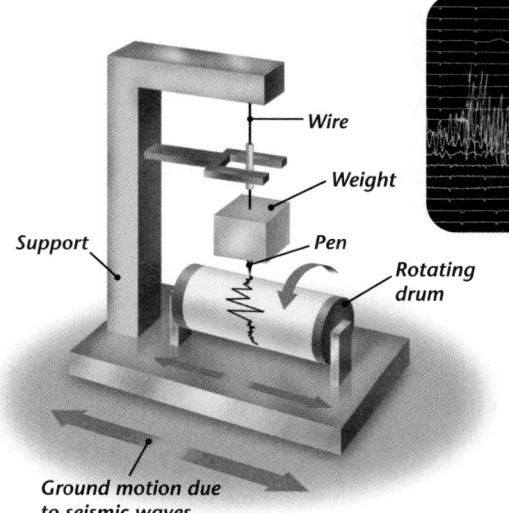

Wire

Weight

Support

Pen

Rotating drum

Figure 13
The mechanical seismograph records seismic waves. The record made by a seismograph shows the arrival times of different types of seismic waves.

Ground motion due to seismic waves

Background

History of Science Early seismic instruments, known as seismoscopes, detected the occurrence of an earthquake but created no written record of the event. The first seismoscope—the bronze dragon-and-frog device pictured on pages 384–385—was invented by Chinese astronomer and geographer Chang Heng in A.D. 132. In 1795, Italian naturalist and clockmaker Ascanio Filomarino invented a seismoscope in which

an earthquake rang small bells and made a clock tick.

The first seismograph was invented by Italian scientist Luigi Palmieri in the 1850s. One part of the device was designed to detect earthquakes, another part to print a record. Using his seismograph, Palmieri observed that small earthquakes sometimes occurred before larger ones and that quakes also were associated with volcanic eruptions.

The Mercalli Scale

Earthquake Intensity	Earthquake Effects
I–II	Almost unnoticeable
III–IV	People notice vibrations like those from a passing truck. Unstable objects disturbed.
V–VI	Dishes and windows rattle. Books knocked off shelves. Slight damage.
VII–VIII	People run outdoors. Moderate to heavy damage.
IX–X	Buildings jolted off foundations or destroyed. Cracks appear in ground and landslides occur.
XI–XII	Severe damage. Wide cracks appear in ground. Waves seen on ground surface.

Figure 14 An earthquake in 1997 damaged the tower of this city hall in Foligno, Italy (left). The Mercalli scale (right) uses Roman numerals to rank earthquakes by how much damage they cause.
Applying Concepts How would you rate the damage to the Foligno city hall on the Mercalli scale?

Measuring Earthquakes

When geologists want to know the size of an earthquake, they must consider many factors. As a result, there are at least 20 different measures for rating earthquakes, each with its strengths and shortcomings. Three ways of measuring earthquakes, the Mercalli scale, the Richter scale, and the moment magnitude scale, are described here. **Magnitude** is a measurement of earthquake strength based on seismic waves and movement along faults.

The Mercalli Scale Early in the twentieth century, the **Mercalli scale** was developed to rate earthquakes according to their intensity. An earthquake's intensity is the strength of ground motion in a given place. The Mercalli scale is not a precise measurement. But the 12 steps of the Mercalli scale describe how earthquakes affect people, buildings, and the land surface. The same earthquake can have different Mercalli ratings because it causes different amounts of damage at different locations.

The Richter Scale The **Richter scale** is a rating of the size of seismic waves that was once measured by a type of mechanical seismograph. The Richter scale was developed in the 1930s. Geologists all over the world used this scale for about 50 years. Eventually, electronic seismographs replaced the mechanical seismographs used for the Richter scale. The Richter scale provides accurate measurements for small, nearby earthquakes. But the scale does not work well for large or distant earthquakes.

Media and Technology

 Concept Videotape Library
Adventures, Tape 3, "Waves in the Earth"

Answers to Self-Assessment

☑ *Checkpoint*
The three types of seismic waves are P waves, S waves, and surface waves.

Caption Question
Figure 14 The damage would probably rate VII–VIII.

Measuring Earthquakes

Including All Students

Students may wonder how the Mercalli and Richter scales got their names. Explain that the scales were named after the men who developed them—Italian volcanologist Giuseppe Mercalli and American seismologist Charles Richter. Then ask: **How are the Mercalli scale and the Richter scale similar?** (*Both describe the "strength" of an earthquake.*) **How are they different?** (*The Mercalli scale describes an earthquake's strength in terms of its effects—to what extent people notice it and the amount of damage it causes. The Richter scale describes an earthquake's strength in terms of the size of its seismic waves; it is a precise measurement.*) **On which scale would an earthquake's strength vary from one place to another, and why?** (*The Mercalli scale; the amount of shaking that people would feel and the damage to objects would be greater in a place closer to the quake's epicenter and less in a place farther away, so the intensity ratings in the two places would be different.*) **learning modality: verbal**

Building Inquiry Skills: Classifying

Direct students to examine the photograph of the 1906 San Francisco earthquake in Figure 16 on the next page. Ask: **Where do you think this earthquake rated on the Mercalli scale?** (*Probably IX or X*) Ask volunteers to find photographs of other areas damaged by earthquakes, including moderate quakes as well as severe ones, and make photocopies of the pictures for the class to examine. Let students try to estimate each quake's Mercalli rating based on evidence they see in the photograph. (*Students may have some difficulty differentiating between categories VII–VIII and IX–X and between categories IX–X and X–XII. Accept all reasonable responses.*) **learning modality: visual**

Ongoing Assessment

Drawing Have each student draw and label a simple diagram explaining how a mechanical seismograph works.

Locating the Epicenter

Demonstration

Time 10–15 minutes

Do the following activity in a roomy area such as a gym. Choose two students to roleplay a P wave and an S wave. Position both students at a starting point, and position a third student some distance away to represent a seismograph. When you say "Earthquake!" the two students should start walking toward the third student, with the "P wave" student taking long forward strides and the "S wave" student taking shorter steps in a waddling gait to represent the side-to-side vibration of S waves. After a few seconds, say "Stop" and ask: **Which wave is closer to the seismograph?** *(The P wave)* Repeat the activity with six students roleplaying three pairs of P and S waves. Assign a number to each pair, and have all three pairs start walking at your signal. Say "One, stop," "Two, stop," and "Three, stop" at intervals. Have the students who are observing compare the distances between the P-wave and S-wave students in the three pairs. Ask: **Are all three distances the same?** *(No)* **How do they vary?** *(The P and S students who were walking for the shortest time are the closest together, while the P and S students who were walking for the longest time are the farthest apart.)* **How would this difference help a geologist tell how far away an earthquake's epicenter is?** *(If the S waves arrive at a seismograph a very short time after the P waves, the epicenter is close to the seismograph; the longer the interval between the arrival times of the P and S waves, the farther away the epicenter is.)* **learning modality: kinesthetic**

Integrating Mathematics

Ask: **Why would drawing only two circles not be enough to locate the earthquake's epicenter?** *(Two circles would intersect at two points, not one, and identify two possible epicenters. If students have difficulty visualizing this, let them lay a sheet of tracing paper over the map in Figure 17, trace each circle in a different color, and mark the two points where each pair of circles intersect.)* **learning modality: logical/mathematical**

Earthquake Magnitudes	
Earthquake	**Moment Magnitude**
San Francisco, California, 1906	7.7
Southern Chile, 1960	9.5
Anchorage, Alaska, 1964	9.2
Loma Prieta, California, 1989	7.2
Northridge/ Los Angeles, California, 1994	6.7

Figure 15 The table lists the moment magnitudes for some of the twentieth century's biggest earthquakes.

The Moment Magnitude Scale Today, geologists use the **moment magnitude scale,** a rating system that estimates the total energy released by an earthquake. **The moment magnitude scale can be used to rate earthquakes of all sizes, near or far.** You may hear news reports that mention the Richter scale. But the magnitude number they quote is almost always the moment magnitude for that earthquake.

To rate an earthquake on the moment magnitude scale, geologists first study data from modern electronic seismographs. The data show what kinds of seismic waves the earthquake produced and how strong they were. The data also help geologists infer how much movement occurred along the fault and the strength of the rocks that broke when the fault slipped. Geologists combine all this information to rate the earthquake on the moment magnitude scale.

Earthquakes with a magnitude below 5.0 on the moment magnitude scale are small and cause little damage. Those with a magnitude above 5.0 can produce great destruction. A magnitude 6.0 quake releases 32 times as much energy as a magnitude 5.0 quake, and nearly 1,000 times as much as a magnitude 4.0 quake.

☑ *Checkpoint* *What are three scales for measuring earthquakes?*

Locating the Epicenter

Geologists use seismic waves to locate an earthquake's epicenter. Seismic waves travel at different speeds. P waves arrive first at a seismograph, with S waves following close behind. To tell how far the epicenter is from the seismograph, scientists measure the difference between the arrival times of the P waves and S waves.

Figure 16 In terms of magnitude, the 1906 San Francisco earthquake was not the strongest of the century. But it toppled buildings and caused fires that devastated the city.

Background

Facts and Figures Students might be interested to learn that American astronauts placed seismographs on the moon. These instruments recorded moonquakes caused by the impact of meteorites on the lunar surface as well as moonquakes that occur when the moon's orbit brings it closest to Earth.

Program Resources

◆ **Laboratory Manual** 12, "Investigating the Speed of Earthquake Waves"

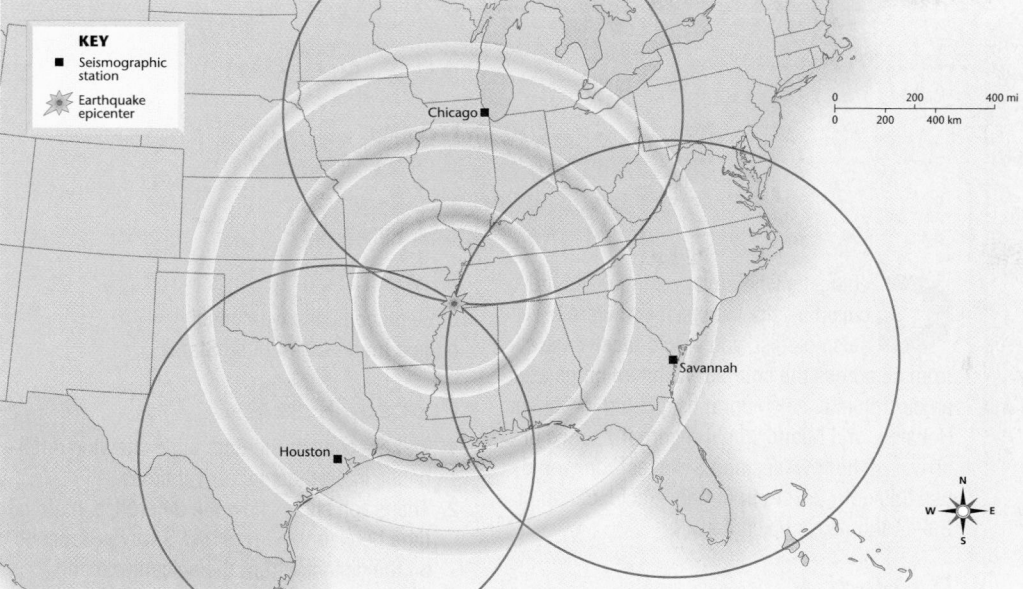

KEY
■ Seismographic station
✷ Earthquake epicenter

Chicago

Savannah

Houston

0   200   400 mi
0   200   400 km

N
W   E
S

Figure 17 The map shows how to find the epicenter of an earthquake using data from three seismographic stations. *Measuring Use the map scale to determine the distances from Savannah and Houston to the epicenter. Which is closer?*

The farther away an earthquake is, the greater the time between the arrival of the P waves and the S waves.

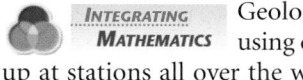
INTEGRATING MATHEMATICS Geologists then draw at least three circles using data from different seismographs set up at stations all over the world. The center of each circle is a particular seismograph's location. The radius of each circle is the distance from the seismograph to the epicenter. The point where the three circles intersect is the location of the epicenter. If you look at Figure 17, you can see why two circles would not give enough information to pinpoint the epicenter.

Section 2 Review

1. How does the energy from an earthquake reach Earth's surface?
2. Describe the three types of seismic waves.
3. What system do geologists use today for rating the magnitude of an earthquake?
4. **Thinking Critically Relating Cause and Effect** Describe how energy released at an earthquake's focus, deep inside Earth, can cause damage on the surface many kilometers from the epicenter.

Check Your Progress
Now it is time to complete your design and construct your model. From what you have learned about earthquakes, what changes will you make in your design? Have a classmate review your model and make suggestions for improvements. When you have made the changes, test your model's ability to withstand an earthquake. Take notes on how well it withstands the quake.

CHAPTER PROJECT 12

Program Resources

◆ **Unit 4 Resources** 12-2 Review and Reinforce, p. 47; 12-2 Enrich, p. 48

Answers to Self-Assessment

✓ *Checkpoint*
Three scales for measuring earthquakes are the Mercalli scale, the Richter scale, and the moment magnitude scale.

Caption Question
Figure 17 Houston (about 800 km compared with about 900 km for Savannah)

3 Assess

Section 2 Review Answers

1. Seismic waves carry the energy of an earthquake away from the focus. Some of those waves reach the surface and become surface waves.
2. *P waves:* Travel straight outward from the focus; compress and expand the ground; move through solids and liquids; are the fastest-moving seismic waves. *S waves:* Vibrate from side to side and up and down as they travel; move only through solids. *Surface waves:* Move along the surface; move more slowly than P and S waves; can produce violent ground movements.
3. Data from electronic seismographs, which convert ground movements into signals that can be recorded and printed, are used to rate the strength of earthquakes on the moment magnitude scale.
4. P waves, S waves, and surface waves can all cause damaging ground movements at the surface many kilometers from epicenter. In addition, the types of rock and soil around an earthquake's epicenter can affect where and how much the ground shakes.

Check Your Progress
CHAPTER PROJECT 12
Encourage volunteers to describe any changes they made in their initial design based on what they learned from the text and from other students. Have the class review their agreed-upon criteria for simulating earthquakes so all models are subjected to the same degree of shaking. Emphasize that they should take notes about any damage their models sustain and any weaknesses that are revealed.

Performance Assessment

Drawing Have each student draw and label a sketch, without referring to figures 11 or 12, showing an earthquake's focus underground, its epicenter on the surface, the different motions of P waves and S waves moving outward from the focus, and surface waves moving outward from the epicenter.

Locating an Epicenter

Preparing for Inquiry

Key Concept Data from seismographs in three different locations can be used to identify an earthquake's epicenter.

Skills Objectives Students will be able to

◆ interpret data to determine the distances of three seismographs from an earthquake's epicenter;

◆ draw a conclusion about the location of the earthquake's epicenter.

Time 35–40 minutes

Advance Planning Make a photocopy of the map for each student.

Guiding Inquiry

Invitation Ask: **Why is it important for scientists to know where an earthquake's epicenter is located?** *(Accept all reasonable responses, such as the usefulness of this information in predicting future earthquakes.)* Then have students look back at Figure 17 on the previous page. Explain that they will use the same technique in this activity to find an earthquake's epicenter.

Introducing the Procedure

Before students begin, review the use of a drawing compass and a map scale. Ask: **What do the numbers on the compass represent?** *(The distance in centimeters between the compass's metal point and pencil point.)* **If you set the compass at 7 and drew a circle, what would the circle's diameter be?** *(14 cm)* **What would its radius be?** *(7 cm)*

Next, ask: **What does a map scale show?** *(The distance on the map that represents a certain number of kilometers or miles on the real land surface)* **What is this map's scale?** *(Each centimeter on the map represents 300 km on land. If students cannot answer your question, have them lay a metric ruler along the scale line to see how many kilometers are represented by each centimeter.)* **Suppose you wanted to show a distance of 1800 km from Denver on this map. How would you**

Locating an Epicenter

Geologists who study earthquakes are called seismologists. If you were a seismologist, you would receive data from all across the country. Within minutes after an earthquake, seismographs located in Denver, Houston, and Miami would record the times of arrival of the P waves and S waves. You would use this data to zero in on the exact location of the earthquake's epicenter.

Problem

How can you locate an earthquake's epicenter?

Skills Focus

interpreting data, drawing conclusions

Materials

drawing compass with pencil
outline map of the United States

Procedure

1. Make a copy of the data table showing differences in earthquake arrival times.

2. The graph shows how the difference in arrival time between P waves and S waves depends on the distance from the epicenter of the earthquake. Find the difference in arrival time for Denver on the *y*-axis of the graph. Follow this line across to the point at which it crosses the curve. To find the distance to the epicenter, read down from this point to the *x*-axis of the graph. Enter this distance in the data table.

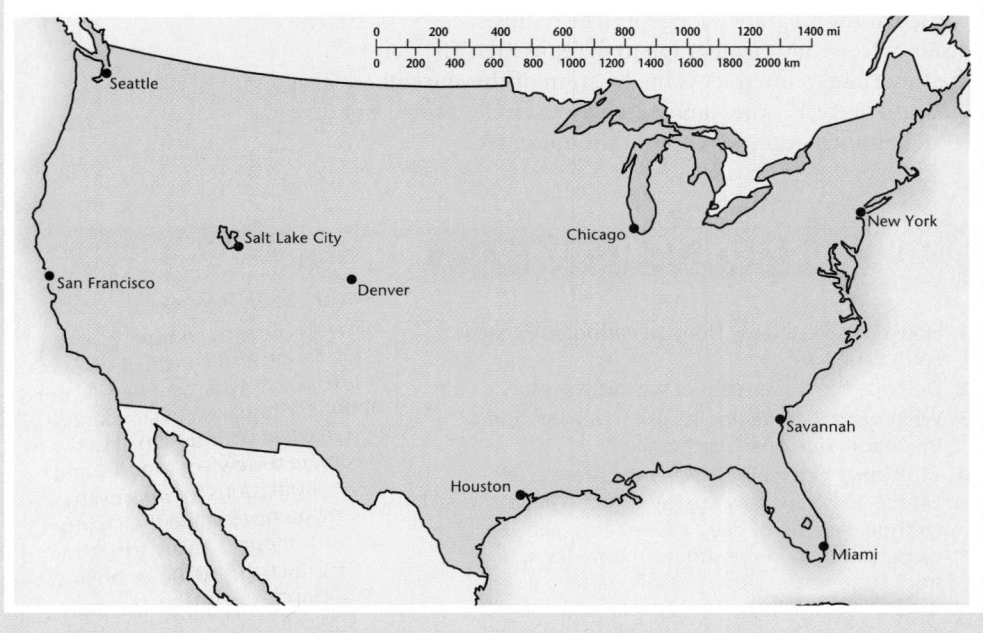

---

figure out the length of that map measurement in centimeters? *(Divide the distance you want to show by the number of kilometers represented by 1 cm on the map: 1800 km ÷ 300 km = 6 cm on the map.)* Then ask: **How would you use the compass to measure that distance?** *(Set the compass arm at 6 cm, hold the metal point on the dot for Denver, and draw a circle. To determine the compass setting, students also could hold the metal point on the 0 end of the scale line and adjust the compass arm so the pencil point is at 1800 km on the line.)*

What does the circle show? *(All the points 1800 km from Denver)* If students need more practice, give them additional examples, not including the distances they will use in the activity.

Troubleshooting the Experiment

◆ In Step 2, point out that the arrival-time differences listed in the table include seconds as well as minutes, whereas the labels on the *y*-axis give only whole minutes. Thus, students will need to use the

Data Table

City	Difference in P and S Wave Arrival Times	Distance to Epicenter
Denver, Colorado	2 min 10 s	
Houston, Texas	3 min 55 s	
Miami, Florida	5 min 40 s	

3. Repeat Step 2 for Houston and Miami.
4. Set your compass at a radius equal to the distance from Denver to the earthquake epicenter that you recorded in your data table.
5. Draw a circle with the radius determined in Step 4, using Denver as the center. Draw the circle on your copy of the map. (*Hint:* Draw your circles carefully. You may need to draw some parts of the circles off the map.)
6. Repeat Steps 4 and 5 for Houston and Miami.

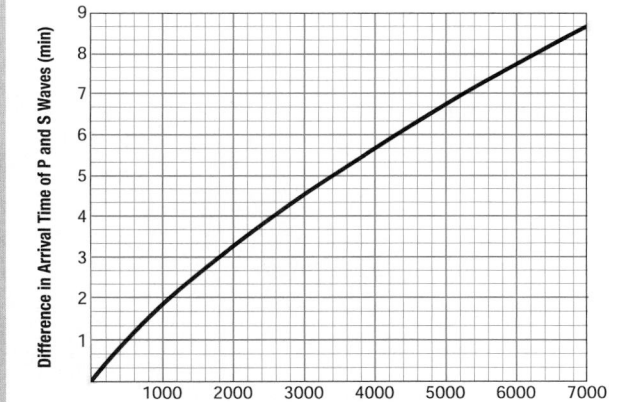

Analyze and Conclude

1. Observe the three circles you have drawn to locate the earthquake's epicenter.
2. Which city on the map is closest to the earthquake epicenter? How far, in kilometers, is this city from the epicenter?
3. In which of the three cities listed in the data table would seismographs detect the earthquake first? Last?
4. When you are trying to locate an epicenter, why is it necessary to know the distance from the epicenter for at least three recording stations?
5. About how far is the epicenter that you found from San Francisco? What would the difference in arrival times of the P waves and S waves be for a recording station in San Francisco?
6. What happens to the difference in arrival times between P waves and S waves as the distance from the earthquake increases?
7. **Apply** Working as a seismologist, you find the epicenters of many earthquakes in a region. What features of Earth's crust would you expect to find in this region?

More to Explore

You have just located an earthquake's epicenter. Find this earthquake's location on the earthquake risk map on page 413. Judging from the map, was this earthquake a freak event? What is the risk of earthquakes in the area of this quake? Now look at the map of Earth's plates on page 375. What conclusions can you draw from this map about the cause of earthquakes in this area?

---

lighter lines on the graph to estimate the partial-minute differences as closely as they can. (Since there are three lighter lines dividing each whole-minute interval, each lighter line represents 20 seconds.)
◆ Remind students that they must use the map scale to determine where to set the compass arm for each distance in steps 4 and 6.

Expected Outcome
The correct compass settings are 4 cm for Denver, 8.4 cm for Houston, and 13.3 cm for Miami. The point on the map at which all three circles intersect will be about 600 km south southeast of Seattle.

Analyze and Conclude
1. The epicenter is located about 600 km south southeast of Seattle.
2. Seattle; 600 km
3. *First:* Denver; *Last:* Miami
4. Using three recording stations enables you to identify one epicenter location, whereas using only two stations identifies two possible epicenter locations
5. 650 km from San Francisco; 1 min 20 s
6. The difference in arrival times also increases.
7. You would expect to find faults in Earth's crust in the region.

Extending the Inquiry

More to Explore This earthquake was not a freak event, as it occurred in an area of moderate risk. Earthquakes in this area are caused by movement along the boundary between the Pacific and North American plates.

Safety

Students should take care with the compass point in this activity. Review the safety guidelines in Appendix A.

Sample Data Table

City	Difference in P and S Wave Arrival Times	Distance to Epicenter
Denver, Colorado	2 min 10 s	1,200 km
Houston, Texas	3 min 55 s	2,600 km
Miami, Florida	5 min 40 s	4,000 km

Program Resources
◆ **Unit 4 Resources** Real-World Lab blackline masters, pp. 59–61

Media and Technology

 **Lab Activity Videotape**
Tape 3

Objectives

After completing the lesson, students will be able to
◆ describe how earthquakes cause damage and the kinds of damage they cause;
◆ explain what can be done to reduce earthquake hazards to buildings and people.

Key Terms liquefaction, aftershock, tsunamis, base-isolated building

1 Engage/Explore

Activating Prior Knowledge

Ask: **What kinds of structures have you seen used to make buildings, bridges, and highway overpasses stronger?** *(Students may mention heavy wooden or steel beams, supporting buttresses, diagonal beams, and the like.)* **Do you think these structures would help protect against damage in an earthquake? Why, or why not?** *(Accept all reasonable answers. Encourage students to rely on their own direct observations or on what they have seen in news reports and documentary films.)*

 **DISCOVER**

Skills Focus predicting **ACTIVITY**
Materials *5 straws, tape*
Time 10 minutes
Tips In Step 3, make sure students tape the fifth straw roughly halfway up the square.
Expected Outcome In Step 2, the frame will collapse sideways. In Step 3, it will remain standing for a time but will fall over if more pressure is exerted.
Think It Over The fifth straw provided additional support to the frame. Cardboard would provide even stronger support. Without additional supporting structures, a house's frame would probably collapse in an earthquake.

DISCOVER •• **ACTIVITY**

Can Bracing Prevent Building Collapse?

1. Tape four straws together to make a square frame. Hold the frame upright on a flat surface in front of you.

2. Hold the bottom straw down with one hand while you push the top straw to the left with the other. Push it as far as it will go without breaking the frame.

3. Tape a fifth straw horizontally across the middle of the frame. Repeat Step 2.

Think It Over

Predicting What effect did the fifth straw have? What effect would a piece of cardboard taped to the frame have? Based on your observations, how would an earthquake affect the frame of a house?

GUIDE FOR READING

◆ What kinds of damage does an earthquake cause?

◆ What can be done to reduce earthquake hazards?

Reading Tip Before you read preview the headings of the section. Then predict some of the ways that people can reduce earthquake hazards.

O
n a cold, bleak morning in January 1995, a powerful earthquake awoke the 1.5 million residents of Kobe, Japan. In 20 terrifying seconds, the earthquake collapsed thousands of buildings, crumpled freeways, and sparked about 130 fires. More than 5,000 people perished.

Most of the buildings that toppled were more than 20 years old. Many were two-story, wood-frame houses with heavy tile roofs. These top-heavy houses were about as stable in an earthquake as a heavy book supported by a framework of pencils. In contrast, many of the more modern buildings remained standing. The newer buildings had been designed to withstand intense shaking.

Figure 18 Many buildings in Kobe, Japan, could not withstand the magnitude 6.9 earthquake that struck in 1995.

READING STRATEGIES

Reading Tip Students will likely predict that earthquake hazards can be reduced by choosing a location away from faults and by building stronger structures. After students have read the section, have them review their predictions and make any needed corrections. Encourage students to note answers to these questions as they read.

How Earthquakes Cause Damage

When a major earthquake strikes, it can cause great damage. **The severe shaking produced by seismic waves can damage or destroy buildings and bridges, topple utility poles, and fracture gas and water mains.** S waves, with their side-to-side and up-and-down movement, can cause severe damage near the epicenter. As the twisting forces of S waves sweep through the ground, the S waves put enough stress on buildings to tear them apart. Earthquakes can also trigger landslides or avalanches. In coastal regions, giant waves pushed up by earthquakes can cause more damage.

Local Soil Conditions When seismic waves move from hard, dense rock to loosely packed soil, they transmit their energy to the soil. The loose soil shakes more violently than the surrounding rock. The thicker the layer of soil, the more violent the shaking will be. This means a house built on solid rock will shake less than a house built on sandy soil.

Liquefaction In 1964, when a powerful earthquake roared through Anchorage, Alaska, cracks opened in the ground. Some of the cracks were 9 meters wide. The cracks were created by liquefaction. **Liquefaction** (lik wih FAK shun) occurs when an earthquake's violent shaking suddenly turns loose, soft soil into liquid mud. Liquefaction is likely where the soil is full of moisture. As the ground gives way, buildings sink and pull apart.

Liquefaction can also trigger landslides. During the 1964 Anchorage earthquake, liquefaction caused a landslide that swept an entire housing development down a cliff and into the sea. Figure 19 shows the damage liquefaction can cause.

Aftershocks Sometimes, buildings weakened by an earthquake collapse during an aftershock. An **aftershock** is an earthquake that occurs after a larger earthquake in the same area. Aftershocks may strike hours, days, or even months later.

Figure 19 An earthquake caused the soil beneath this house to liquefy. Liquefaction caused by seismic waves can change solid soil to liquid mud within seconds. *Posing Questions What are some questions people might ask before building a house in an area that is at risk for earthquakes?*

Program Resources

◆ **Unit 4 Resources** 12-3 Lesson Plan, p. 49; 12-3 Section Summary, p. 50
◆ **Guided Reading and Study Workbook** Section 12-3

Answers to Self-Assessment

Caption Question

Figure 19 Students might suggest the following questions: Will the house be built on dense rock or loose soil? What is the slope of the land? Have other houses in the area been damaged by earthquakes? What building techniques helped protect the houses that were not damaged?

---

2 Facilitate

How Earthquakes Cause Damage

Cultural Diversity

After students have read the section opening, point out that in addition to being top-heavy with tile roofs, traditional Japanese homes are built of wood with paper walls. Ask: **How do you think this kind of construction would stand up to an earthquake?** *(Lightweight wood and paper would be more easily damaged than stronger building materials.)* **learning modality: logical/mathematical**

Inquiry Challenge

Materials *small containers such as storage boxes, shoe boxes, and baking pans; sandy soil; building materials such as index cards, popsicle sticks, straws, cardboard, paper clips, and tape*
Time 20 minutes

Challenge small groups of students to devise a model showing that structures built on loose soil shake more violently in an earthquake than structures built on solid rock. *(To model an earthquake's effects on a structure built on loose soil, students can make a small model building, put it on top of soil in a container, then shake the container. To model the effects on a structure built on solid rock, students can tape the model building directly to a desktop, then shake the desk with the same intensity.)* In a follow-up class discussion, let students describe their models and the effects they observed. **cooperative learning**

Ongoing Assessment

Writing Have each student describe, in his or her own words, the different ways in which earthquakes cause damage. *(Students should describe how shaking caused by seismic waves, local soil conditions, liquefaction, aftershocks, and tsunamis contribute to earthquake damage.)*

How Earthquakes Cause Damage, continued

Using the Visuals: Figure 20

To help students understand why tsunami waves are so high when they strike a coast, ask: **What do you see happening to the *length* of the waves as they move through shallow water?** *(The length decreases.)* **What do you see happening to the wave *height* as the length decreases?** *(The height increases.)* **learning modality: visual**

Building Inquiry Skills: Comparing and Contrasting

Materials *long, narrow, clear-plastic box; clay; water; ruler or other flat object*
Time 5 minutes

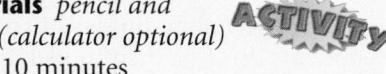

Set up the following learning station so students can observe how wave height increases as wavelength decreases. Place the box on a flat surface. Use clay to create a sloping "beach" at one end of the box. Fill the "ocean" end of the box about one-third full of water. Let pairs of students take turns making waves in the "ocean" by repeatedly pushing a ruler or other flat object toward the "beach." As one partner makes the waves, the other should watch the waves from the side. **learning modality: kinesthetic**

Sharpen your Skills

Calculating

Materials *pencil and paper (calculator optional)*
Time 10 minutes
Tips If students are uncertain about what math operations to use, lead them through the steps. *To calculate time for seismic waves to reach Hawaii:* 3,600 km ÷ 560 km/min = 6.429 (6.5) min. *To calculate time for tsunami to reach Hawaii:* 3,600 km ÷ 640 km/hr = 5.625 hrs (5 hrs, 37.5 min)
Expected Outcome Hawaii will have about $5\frac{1}{2}$ hrs advance warning (5 hrs, 37.5 min−6.5 min).
Extend Ask: **What should people in Hawaii do during that time to prepare for the tsunami? learning modality: logical/mathematical**

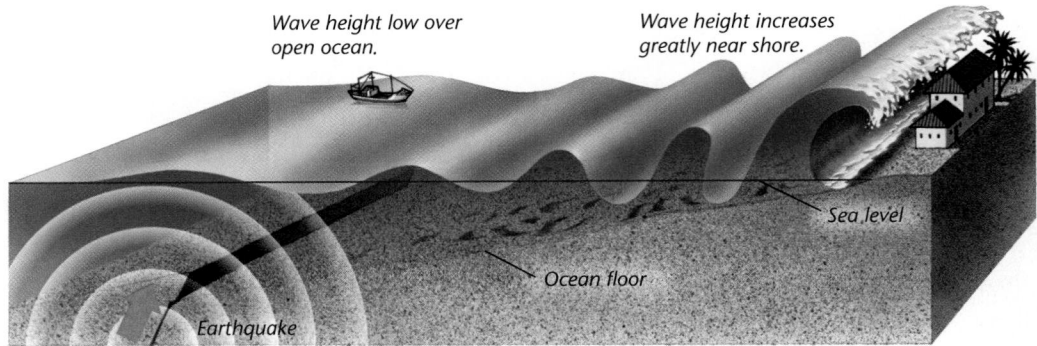

Wave height low over open ocean.

Wave height increases greatly near shore.

Sea level

Ocean floor

Earthquake

Figure 20 A tsunami begins as a low wave, but turns into a huge wave as it nears the shore.

Sharpen your Skills

Calculating ACTIVITY

The Tsunami Warning System alerts people who live near the Pacific Ocean. When geologists detect an earthquake on the ocean floor, they notify coastal areas.

An earthquake in the Gulf of Alaska occurs 3,600 kilometers from Hawaii. The quake's seismic waves travel about 560 kilometers per *minute*. The quake triggers a tsunami that travels at 640 kilometers per *hour*. The seismic waves arrive in Hawaii within minutes and are recorded on seismographs. The seismic waves' arrival warns of the dangerous tsunami that may follow. About how much advance warning will Hawaii have that a tsunami is on the way?

Tsunamis When an earthquake jolts the ocean floor, plate movement causes the ocean floor to rise slightly and push water out of its way. If the earthquake is strong enough, the water displaced by the quake forms large waves, called **tsunamis** (tsoo NAH meez). Figure 20 follows a tsunami from where it begins on the ocean floor.

A tsunami spreads out from an earthquake's epicenter and speeds across the ocean. In the open ocean, the distance between the waves of a tsunami is a very long—between 100 and 200 kilometers. But the height of the wave is low. Tsunamis rise only half a meter or so above the other waves. However, as they approach shallow water near a coastline, the waves become closer together. The tsunami grows into a mountain of water. Some are the height of a six-story building.

☑ *Checkpoint* **What are the major causes of earthquake damage?**

Making Buildings Safer

Most earthquake-related deaths and injuries result from damage to buildings or other structures. **To reduce earthquake damage, new buildings must be made stronger and more flexible. Older buildings must be modified to withstand stronger quakes.** A structure must be strong in order to resist violent shaking in a quake. It must also be flexible so it can twist and bend without breaking. *Exploring an Earthquake-Safe House* shows how a house can be made safer in an earthquake.

Choice of Location The location of a building affects the type of damage it may suffer during an earthquake. Steep slopes pose the danger of landslides. Filled land can shake violently. Therefore, people should avoid building on such sites. People should also avoid building structures near earthquake faults. As seismic waves pass through the earth, their strength decreases. So the farther a structure is from a fault, the less strong the shaking will be.

Background

Facts and Figures Although tsunamis are commonly called "tidal waves," their cause has nothing to do with tidal action. For this reason, scientists prefer the Japanese word *tsunami,* meaning "harbor wave."

Tsunamis can cause horrendous damage. For example, the explosive eruption of Krakatau volcano in Indonesia in 1883 caused tsunamis up to 30 m high. The tsunamis destroyed coastal villages on the nearby islands of Java and Sumatra and killed about 36,000 people.

Although tsunamis pose the greatest hazard around the Pacific Ocean, they can occur elsewhere as well. In 1755, for example, a major earthquake destroyed much of the city of Lisbon on Portugal's Atlantic coast. Tsunamis produced by the quake destroyed Lisbon's harbor and killed thousands of people.

EXPLORING an Earthquake-Safe House

People can take a variety of steps to make their homes safer in an earthquake. Some steps strengthen the house itself. Others may help to keep objects from tipping or falling.

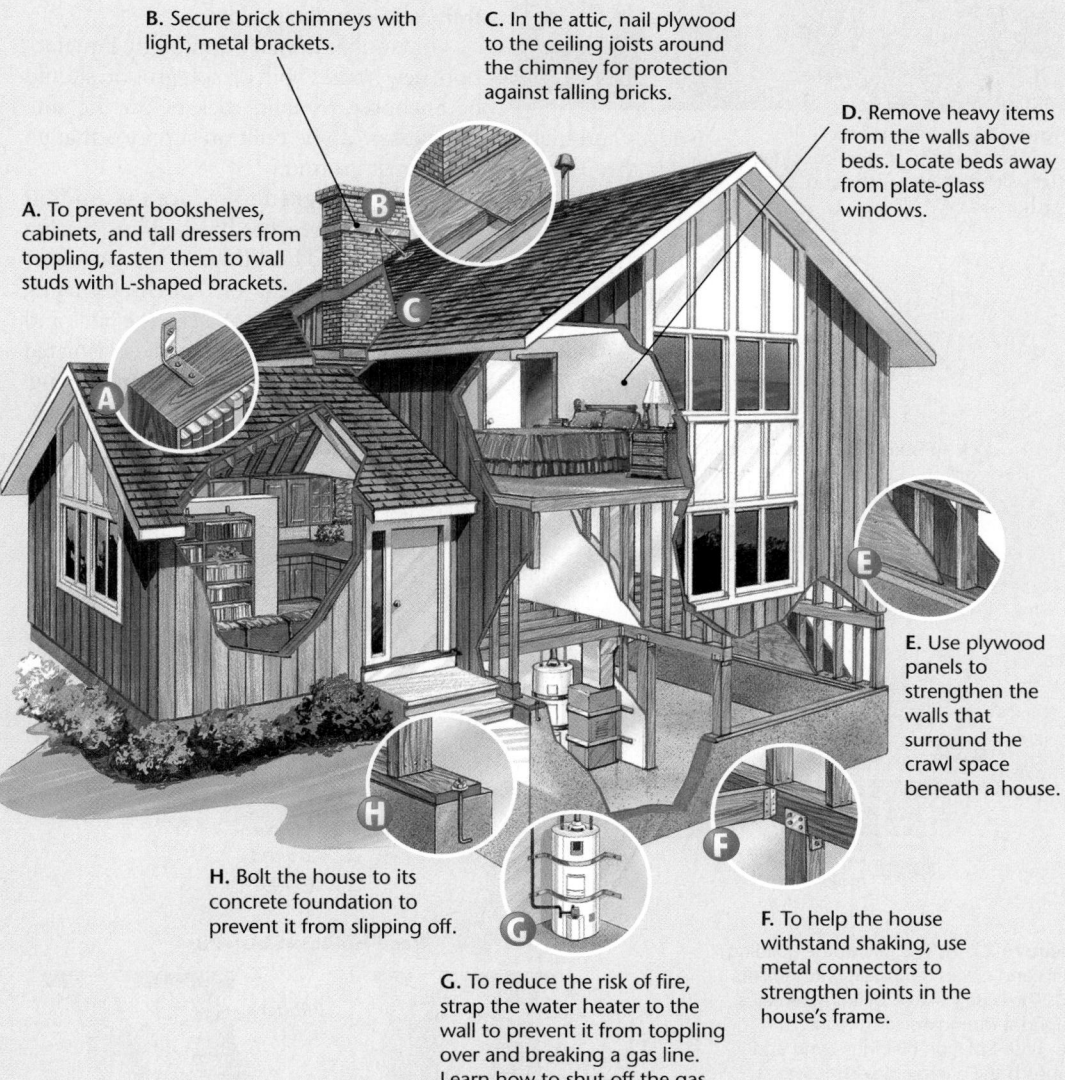

B. Secure brick chimneys with light, metal brackets.

C. In the attic, nail plywood to the ceiling joists around the chimney for protection against falling bricks.

D. Remove heavy items from the walls above beds. Locate beds away from plate-glass windows.

A. To prevent bookshelves, cabinets, and tall dressers from toppling, fasten them to wall studs with L-shaped brackets.

E. Use plywood panels to strengthen the walls that surround the crawl space beneath a house.

H. Bolt the house to its concrete foundation to prevent it from slipping off.

G. To reduce the risk of fire, strap the water heater to the wall to prevent it from toppling over and breaking a gas line. Learn how to shut off the gas, water, and electricity.

F. To help the house withstand shaking, use metal connectors to strengthen joints in the house's frame.

Media and Technology

 Transparencies "Exploring an Earthquake-Safe House," Transparency 51

 Concept Videotape Library *Adventures, Tape 3,* "Rock and Roll"

Answers to Self-Assessment

☑ *Checkpoint*

The major causes of earthquake damage are the shaking caused by seismic waves as well as local soil conditions (loose soil underlying buildings), liquefaction, aftershocks, and tsunamis.

Making Buildings Safer

EXPLORING

An Earthquake-Safe House

Review each step with the class and encourage students to infer the reasoning for each precautionary measure. Then ask: **Which of these steps could easily be done after the house is built?** *(All but steps F and H)* If students live in an area that is at risk for earthquakes, encourage them to review these precautions with their families, make a safety survey of their homes, and implement as many steps as they can. **learning modality: logical/mathematical**

Including All Students

Have students look back at the map of the San Andreas fault in Figure 6 on page 390 and compare that map with a political map of California. Ask: **You've just read that people should avoid building near earthquake faults. Have the people in California followed that safety guideline?** *(No; many cities, towns, bridges, highways, and smaller roads are close to the fault.)* **Have any of these structures ever been damaged in an earthquake?** *(Students saw a photograph of the effects of the 1906 San Francisco quake on page 68 and may have seen pictures of the damage caused by the quakes that struck San Francisco in 1989 and Northridge in 1994.)* **Now that people have already built structures near the San Andreas fault, what could be done to protect those structures in an earthquake?** *(Accept all reasonable responses, such as adding support beams to buildings and rebuilding destroyed highway overpasses so they are more earthquake-resistant.)* **learning modality: visual**

Ongoing Assessment

Writing or Drawing Have each student list or draw a simple sketch to show three ways in which his or her own home could be made safer in the event of an earthquake.

Making Buildings Safer, continued

Building Inquiry Skills: Predicting

Materials *5 straws, scissors, tape*

Time 10 minutes

Instruct students to repeat Step 3 of the Discover activity at the beginning of this section, this time placing the fifth straw diagonally across the square from corner to corner. Before students test the reinforced frame, ask: **How do you think this support will affect the frame's strength?** *(The diagonal support will greatly increase the frame's resistance to a lateral force.)* Encourage students to make use of this observation as they build their model structures for the chapter project. **learning modality: kinesthetic**

 ### Integrating Technology

After students have read about base-isolated buildings and have examined Figure 22, ask: **If you were going to build a base-isolated building for the chapter project, what kind of material could you use for the shock-absorbers?** *(Students might suggest small springs, pieces of foam rubber or spongy plastic, silicone putty, and the like.)* **learning modality: logical/mathematical**

Protecting Yourself During an Earthquake

 ### Integrating Health

Ask: **Where would you store emergency supplies so they'd be easy to reach but also protected from being buried by debris or ruined in a quake?** *(Students may suggest storing them inside a metal box or in a basement.)* **What other supplies would you add to the kit?** *(Accept all reasonable suggestions, such as candles and matches, flashlights and batteries, and blankets.)* **Besides earthquakes, for what other natural disasters would an emergency kit be useful?** *(Tornadoes, hurricanes, blizzards, floods)* **learning modality: logical/mathematical**

Figure 21 Architects and engineers work to design buildings that will be able to withstand earthquakes.

Construction Methods The way in which a building is constructed determines whether it can withstand an earthquake. During an earthquake, brick buildings as well as some wood-frame buildings may collapse if their walls have not been reinforced, or strengthened. Sometimes plywood sheets are used to strengthen the frames of wooden buildings.

To combat damage caused by liquefaction, new homes built on soft ground should be anchored to solid rock below the soil. Bridges and highway overpasses can be built on supports that go down through soft soil to firmer ground.

INTEGRATING TECHNOLOGY A building designed to reduce the amount of energy that reaches the building during an earthquake is called a **base-isolated building.** As you can see in Figure 22, a base-isolated building rests on shock-absorbing rubber pads or springs. Like the suspension of a car, the pads and springs smooth out a bumpy ride. During a quake, a base-isolated building moves gently back and forth without any violent shaking.

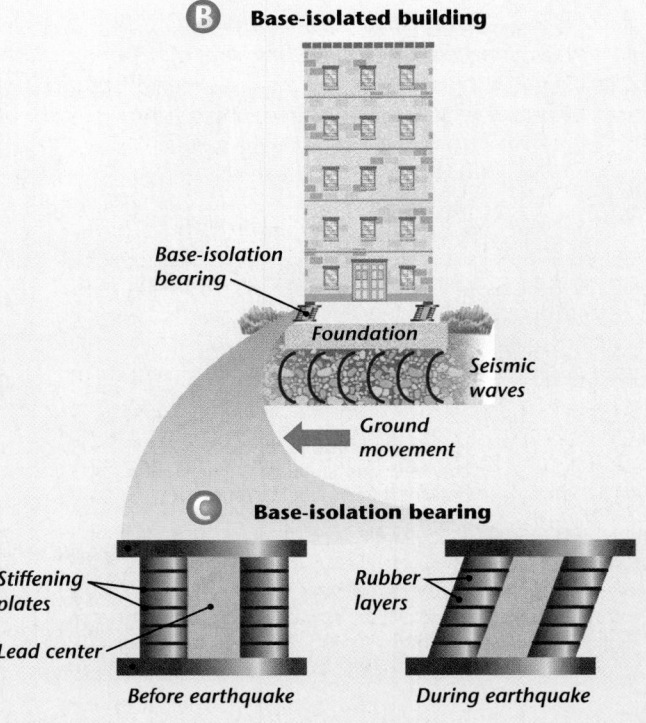

A Fixed-base building

Foundation

← *Ground movement*

B Base-isolated building

Base-isolation bearing

Foundation

Seismic waves

← *Ground movement*

C Base-isolation bearing

Stiffening plates

Lead center

Rubber layers

Before earthquake — *During earthquake*

Figure 22 **A.** The fixed-base building tilts and cracks during an earthquake. **B.** The base-isolated building remains upright during an earthquake. **C.** Base-isolation bearings bend and absorb the energy of seismic waves. *Inferring How does a base-isolation bearing absorb an earthquake's energy?*

408

Integrating Science Architect Frank Lloyd Wright was an innovator in designing buildings that could resist earthquakes. For example, Wright designed the Imperial Hotel in Tokyo, which withstood that city's severe 1923 earthquake with only minor damage.

Many modern cities located in earthquake-prone areas have enacted building codes designed to reduce damage to structures and resulting injury or death. Architects often go beyond these codes to further insure public safety. For example, the Transamerica Pyramid in San Francisco has features built into its base that are designed to reduce dramatically the amount that the building will sway during an earthquake. The building is also stronger than required by the city's building code.

Much earthquake damage is not the direct result of shaking. Earthquakes indirectly cause fire and flooding when gas pipes and water mains break. Flexible joints can be installed in gas and water lines to keep them from breaking. Automatic shut-off valves also can be installed on these lines to cut off gas and water flow.

Protecting Yourself During an Earthquake

What should you do if an earthquake strikes? The main danger is from falling objects and flying glass. **The best way to protect yourself is to drop, cover, and hold.** This means you should crouch beneath a sturdy table or desk and hold on to it so it doesn't jiggle away during the shaking. The desk or table will provide a barrier against falling objects. If no desk or table is available, crouch against an inner wall, away from the outside of a building, and cover your head and neck with your arms. Avoid windows, mirrors, wall hangings, and furniture that might topple.

If you are outdoors, move to an open area such as a playground. Avoid vehicles, power lines, trees, and buildings, especially ones with brick walls or chimneys. Sit down to avoid being thrown down.

INTEGRATING HEALTH After a major earthquake, water and power supplies may fail, food stores may be closed, and travel may be difficult. People may have to wait several days for these services to be restored. To prepare for such an emergency, families living in a region at high risk for damaging quakes may want to put together an earthquake kit. The kit should contain canned food, water, and first aid supplies and should be stored where it is easy to reach.

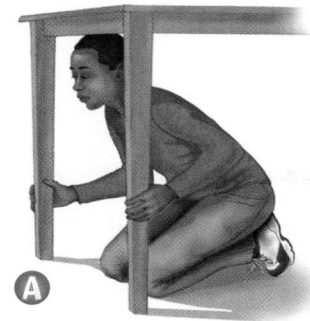

Figure 23 Drop, cover, and hold to protect yourself indoors during an earthquake. **A.** If possible, crouch under a desk or table. **B.** Or, crouch against an interior wall and cover your head and neck with your hands.

Section 3 Review

1. Explain how liquefaction occurs and how it causes damage during an earthquake.
2. What can residents do to reduce the risk of earthquake damage to their homes?
3. Describe safety measures you can take to protect yourself during an earthquake.
4. **Thinking Critically** **Problem Solving** You are a builder planning a housing development where earthquakes are likely. What types of land would you avoid for your development? Where would it be safe to build?

Science at Home

Show your family how an earthquake can affect two different structures—one with more weight on top, the other with more weight on the bottom. Make a model of a fault by placing two small, folded towels side by side on a flat surface. Pile a stack of books on the fault by placing the light books on the bottom and the heaviest ones on top. Then, gently pull the towels in opposite directions until the pile topples. Repeat the process, but this time with the heavier books on the bottom. Discuss with your family which makes a more stable structure.

Answers to Self-Assessment

Caption Question

Figure 22 The bearing acts as a shock-absorber that smooths out vibrations.

---

3 Assess

Section 3 Review Answers

1. An earthquake's shaking turns loose, soft, moist soil into liquid mud that gives way, causing buildings to sink and tear apart. Liquefaction can also trigger a landslide.
2. Students may mention any of the steps presented in the visual essay on page 407.
3. Drop, cover, and hold; students may also cite other precautions described on this page.
4. Avoid building on loose, sandy soil and on hillsides. Construct buildings on solid rock in flat areas. In coastal areas, buildings should be located away from places that might be exposed to tsunamis.

Science at Home

Tell students to make a tall stack of about **ACTIVITY** 10 books—first with several light books such as paperbacks on the bottom, several medium-size books next, and several large, heavy books (such as dictionaries, one-volume encyclopedias, and cookbooks) on top, then reversing the order. Demonstrate the procedure in class so students understand what to do when they try the activity at home. With the heavier books on top, the stack will topple when the towels are pulled in opposite directions. With the heavier books at the bottom, the stack will wobble a bit but remain intact.

Performance Assessment

Drawing Have each student draw and label a sketch showing three ways to make the model building for the chapter project more earthquake-resistant.

 Portfolio Students can save their drawings in their portfolios.

INTEGRATING TECHNOLOGY

SECTION
4 Monitoring Faults

SECTION 4 Monitoring Faults

Objectives

After completing the lesson, students will be able to
◆ describe how geologists monitor faults;
◆ explain how geologists determine earthquake risk.

1 Engage/Explore

Activating Prior Knowledge

Ask: **Why is it important for scientists to develop ways to predict earthquakes?** *(A warning would allow people who live in the area to protect themselves by reinforcing buildings and other structures, preparing emergency supplies, and the like.)* **Do you think earthquake predictions will ever be very accurate? Why, or why not?** *(Accept divergent responses so long as students support their views with well-reasoned explanations.)*

DISCOVER

Skills Focus drawing conclusions
Materials *facial tissue, ruler*
Time 5 minutes
Tips To make the measuring process easier, have students lay the ruler along the tissue's lower edge and grasp the tissue just above its two lower corners.
Expected Outcome Depending on the flexibility of the tissue used, it may lengthen by 1.5–2 cm when it is stretched. The tissue will suddenly tear when tugged.
Think It Over The tissue is like the ground along a fault in that both absorb some degree of tension force without breaking but snap suddenly when an abrupt, strong force is applied. The more stress that builds up in the ground, the greater the likelihood of a sudden earthquake.

DISCOVER ●●●●●●●●●●●●●●●●●●●●●● ACTIVITY

Can Stress Be Measured?

1. Unfold a facial tissue and lay it flat on your desk.
2. Measure the length of the tissue with a ruler.
3. Grasping the ends of the tissue with both hands, gently pull it. As you are stretching it, hold the tissue against the ruler and measure its length again.
4. Stretch the tissue once more, but this time give it a hard tug.

Think It Over
Drawing Conclusions How is the tissue like the ground along a fault? How might measuring stress in the ground help in predicting an earthquake?

GUIDE FOR READING

◆ How do geologists monitor faults?
◆ How do geologists determine earthquake risk?

Reading Tip As you read, make a list of devices for monitoring earthquakes. Write a sentence about each.

The small town of Parkfield, California, lies on the San Andreas fault about halfway between Los Angeles and San Francisco. Geologists are fascinated by Parkfield because the town had a strong earthquake about every 22 years between 1857 and 1966. Scientists have not found any other place on Earth where the time from one earthquake to the next has been so regular.

In the early 1980s, geologists predicted that a strong earthquake was going to occur in Parkfield between 1985 and 1993. The geologists eagerly set up their instruments—and waited. They waited year after year for the predicted earthquake. But it didn't happen. Finally, several medium-sized earthquakes rumbled along the San Andreas fault near Parkfield in 1993–1994.

Did these quakes take the place of the larger earthquake that geologists had expected? Or had the San Andreas fault itself changed, breaking the pattern of 22 years between quakes? Geologists still don't know the answers to these questions. Nonetheless, geologists continue to monitor the San Andreas fault. Someday, they may find a way to predict when and where an earthquake will occur.

Figure 24 This laser beam detects movement along the San Andreas Fault in Parkfield, California.

READING STRATEGIES

Reading Tip Student lists should include creep meters, laser-ranging devices, tiltmeters, and satellites. Encourage students to describe each monitoring device in their own words rather than copy the text information. Let students share their sentences in a follow-up class discussion. Guide students to agree on one "best sentence" for each device that incorporates the most important points mentioned in students' sentences.

Caption Writing Ask each student to write a new caption for Figure 24 that briefly describes how a laser-ranging device works and explains why detecting movement along a fault may help geologists predict future earthquakes in that area.

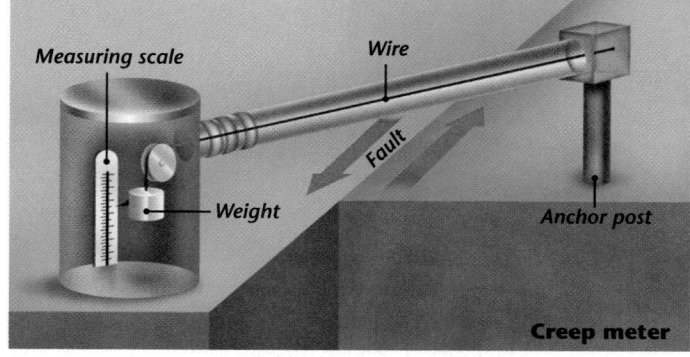

Figure 25 A creep meter can be used to measure movement along a strike-slip fault.

Devices that Monitor Faults

In trying to predict earthquakes, geologists have invented instruments to record the ground movements that occur along faults. **To observe these changes, geologists put in place instruments that measure stress and deformation in the crust.** Geologists hypothesize that such changes signal an approaching earthquake.

Unfortunately, earthquakes almost always strike without warning. The only clue may be a slight rise or fall in the elevation and tilt of the land. Instruments that geologists use to monitor these movements include creep meters, laser-ranging devices, tiltmeters, and satellites.

Creep Meters A creep meter uses a wire stretched across a fault to measure horizontal movement of the ground. On one side of the fault, the wire is anchored to a post. On the other side, the wire is attached to a weight that can slide if the fault moves. Geologists can measure the amount that the fault has moved by measuring how much the weight has moved against a measuring scale.

Laser-Ranging Devices A laser-ranging device uses a laser beam to detect even tiny fault movements. The device calculates any change in the time needed for the laser beam to travel to a reflector and bounce back. Thus, the device can detect any change in distance to the reflector.

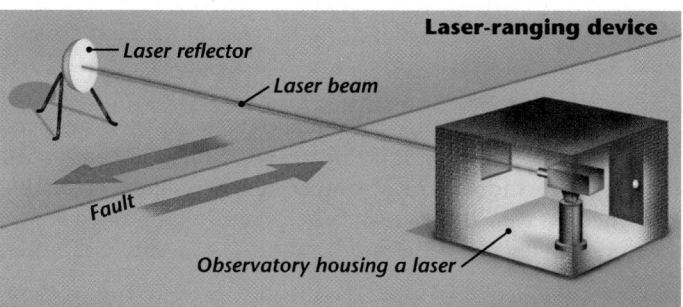

Figure 26 A laser-ranging device monitors fault movement by bouncing a laser beam off a reflector on the other side of the fault. *Comparing and Contrasting How are a laser-ranging device and a creep meter (shown above) similar? How are they different?*

---

2 Facilitate

Devices that Monitor Faults

Including All Students

After students read about monitoring faults, ask: **What might be happening deep under the ground to cause small changes in the elevation or tilt of the land surface before an earthquake?** *(The blocks of rock might be moving just slightly along a normal or reverse fault. In a normal fault, the hanging wall's surface would fall. In a reverse fault, its surface would rise.)* **What types of changes might indicate movement along a strike-slip fault?** *(Sideways distortions in objects that cross the fault, such as roads, fences, and so forth)* **learning modality: logical/mathematical**

Inquiry Challenge

Materials *clay or other material to represent fault blocks; popsicle sticks, wooden matchsticks, or paper clips for posts; metal washer or other small weight; string or wire; mirror; penlight*
Time *20 minutes*

Challenge students to devise a simple model of a creep meter or a laser-ranging device based on a description and diagram on this page. Let students use the model to demonstrate how the device indicates land movements along a strike-slip fault, a normal fault, and a reverse fault. **learning modality: logical/mathematical**

Program Resources

◆ **Unit 4 Resources** 12-4 Lesson Plan, p. 53; 12-4 Section Summary, p. 54
◆ **Guided Reading and Study Workbook** Section 12-4

Answers to Self-Assessment

Caption Question

Figure 26 *Similarity:* Both measure movement along a fault. *Differences:* A creep meter measures horizontal movement only; a laser-ranging device measures any change in distance from the reflector. A creep meter provides gross measurements; a laser-ranging device provides precise measurements.

Ongoing Assessment

Oral Presentation Have students explain how measuring changes in the land along a fault might help scientists predict earthquakes.

Devices that Monitor Faults, continued

Integrating Space Science

Ask: Which of the other three kinds of fault-monitoring devices is a satellite monitor like, and why? *(A laser-ranging device; both involve bouncing a signal off something.)* **What other kinds of measurements are made by bouncing a signal off something?** *(Students may be familiar with sonar and radar used to measure the depths and contours of the ocean floor.)* **learning modality: logical/mathematical**

Language Arts
CONNECTION

Provide newspaper articles about one or more major earthquakes, and have students circle the words or phrases that identify Who, What, Where, When, and Why.

In Your Journal Let students share their bulletins by role-playing newscasters and reading them aloud.

Monitoring Risk in the United States

Including All Students

Encourage interested students to research the locations and dates (and magnitudes, if known) of notable earthquakes that have occurred in the continental United States, Alaska, and Hawaii during the past 200 years. Suggest that they compile the data chronologically in a class master chart. Let students label a large U.S. map with tags identifying the earthquake locations, dates, and magnitudes. Students could also compare the locations of the earthquakes that occurred in the continental U.S. with the risk areas shown in Figure 28. **cooperative learning**

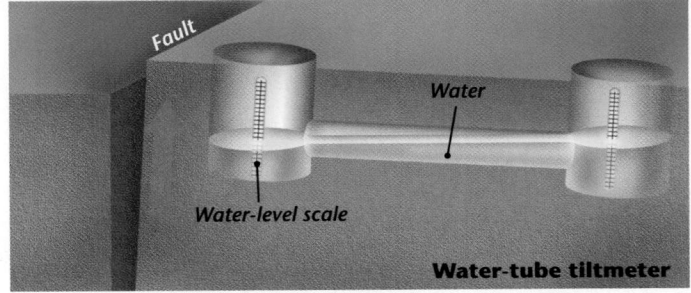

Water-tube tiltmeter

Figure 27 A tiltmeter monitors vertical movement along a fault.

Tiltmeters A tiltmeter measures tilting of the ground. If you have ever used a carpenter's level, you have used a type of tiltmeter. The tiltmeters used by seismologists consist of two bulbs that are filled with a liquid and connected by a hollow stem. Look at the drawing of a tiltmeter in Figure 27. Notice that if the land rises or falls even slightly, the liquid will flow from one bulb to the other. Each bulb contains a measuring scale to measure the depth of the liquid in that bulb. Geologists read the scales to measure the amount of tilt occurring along the fault.

INTEGRATING SPACE SCIENCE **Satellite Monitors** Besides ground-based instruments, geologists use satellites equipped with radar to make images of faults. The satellite bounces radio waves off the ground. As the waves echo back into space, the satellite records them. The time it takes for the radio waves to make their round trip provides precise measurements of the distance to the ground. The distance from the ground to the satellite changes with every change in the ground surface. By comparing different images of the same area taken at different times, geologists detect small changes in elevation. These changes in elevation result when stress deforms the ground along a fault.

✓ *Checkpoint* **What do fault-monitoring instruments measure?**

Monitoring Risk in the United States

Even with data from many sources, geologists can't predict when and where a quake will strike. Usually, stress along a fault increases until an earthquake occurs. Yet sometimes stress builds up along a fault, but an earthquake fails to occur. Or, one or more earthquakes may relieve stress along another part of the fault. Exactly what will happen remains uncertain—that's why geologists cannot predict earthquakes.

Geologists do know that earthquakes are likely wherever plate movement stores energy in the rock along faults. **Geologists can determine earthquake risk by locating where faults are active and where past earthquakes have occurred.** In the United States, the risk is highest along the Pacific coast in the states of California,

Language Arts
CONNECTION

In an emergency broadcast, the television newscaster must not only provide information on the disaster, but also grab the viewer's attention. To state the facts as briefly as possible, journalists use the 5 W's: Who, What, Where, When, and Why.

In Your Journal

You are a local newscaster presenting the news. During your broadcast, you receive information that a major earthquake has struck a city in another part of the country. You must interrupt the regular news to present an emergency news bulletin. Write that bulletin, following the 5 W's.

Background

Facts and Figures One of the very few examples of successful short-range earthquake prediction occurred in 1975, when Chinese seismologists forecast a large earthquake that was about to hit Liaoning Province. Many residents were evacuated from a major city, sparing thousands of lives.

In the 1980s, the U.S. Geological Survey predicted the long-range probability of earthquakes along the San Andreas fault for the period from 1988 to 2018. The section of the fault around Parkfield had the highest probability of producing a serious earthquake—about 90 percent. But in 1994, a 6.7 magnitude quake struck near Los Angeles at Northridge, about 50 km from the San Andreas fault. This quake caused seismologists to recognize that deeply buried faults adjacent to the San Andreas fault also pose a hazard to the region.

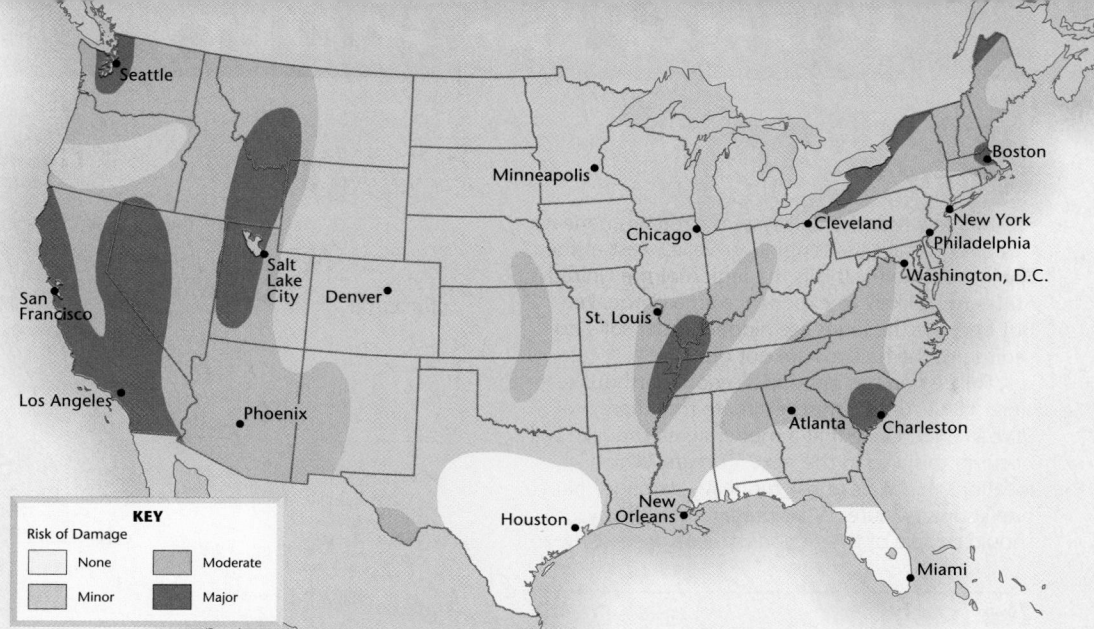

KEY

Risk of Damage

None	Moderate
Minor	Major

Figure 28 The map shows areas of the United States, excluding Alaska and Hawaii, where earthquakes are likely to occur and the relative damage they are likely to cause. *Interpreting Maps Where are damaging earthquakes least likely to occur? Most likely to occur?*

Washington, and Alaska. The risk of quakes is high because that's where the Pacific and North American plates meet.

Other regions of the United States also have some risk of earthquakes. Serious earthquakes are rare east of the Rockies. Nonetheless, the region has experienced some of the most powerful quakes in the nation's history. Scientists hypothesize that the continental plate forming most of North America is under stress. This stress could disturb faults that formed millions of years ago. Today, these faults lie hidden beneath thick layers of soil and rock. Find your state in Figure 28 to determine your area's risk of a damaging quake.

 Section 4 Review

1. What equipment do geologists use to monitor the movement of faults?
2. What two factors do geologists consider when determining earthquake risk for a region?
3. Explain how satellites can be used to collect data on earthquake faults.
4. **Thinking Critically   Making Generalizations** Why can't scientists predict the exact time and place an earthquake is going to occur?

Check Your Progress

CHAPTER PROJECT
12

Use what you have learned about making buildings earthquake resistant to repair and improve your structure. Test your model again. Are your changes successful in preventing damage? Make additional repairs and improvements to your structure.

Answers to Self-Assessment

☑ *Checkpoint*

The movement of the ground along a fault—horizontal movement, tilting, and changes in elevation

Caption Question

Figure 28 *Least likely:* areas on the map with no shading; *Most likely:* areas on the map with the darkest shading.

---

3 Assess

Section 4 Review Answers

1. Creep meters, laser-ranging devices, tiltmeters, satellites
2. The locations of active faults and the locations of past earthquakes
3. The satellite bounces radio waves off the ground and measures the time required for a round trip. If the ground elevation changes, the time for the bounce-back will change. By comparing bounce-back times, scientists can detect small changes in elevation.
4. Fault-block movements occur deep under ground, and instruments monitor only surface movements. Scientists do not fully understand the relationship between slight deformations in the land surface and the likelihood of an earthquake. Not every area throughout the world is monitored with instruments. (Accept other reasonable explanations.)

Check Your Progress

CHAPTER PROJECT
12

Encourage students to make use of the information in Section 3 as they consider improvements to their models— particularly ways to convert them to base-isolated structures. Remind students to test their improvements and, if necessary, make repairs and further changes before they settle on a final design for the class presentation.

Performance Assessment

Oral Presentation Have students name the four types of fault-monitoring devices described in this section and describe how they work.

What's the Risk of an Earthquake?

Purpose

To challenge students to identify the drawbacks and benefits of modifying structures located in areas where there is some possibility of serious earthquake damage, even though major earthquakes are infrequent, and develop an earthquake-preparedness plan for critical structures.

Panel Discussion

Time 80–90 minutes

After students have read the introductory text and the three paragraphs under The Issues, ask: **If you owned a house in the New Madrid fault area, would you want to renovate your house to protect it against possible earthquake damage? Why, or why not?** Let students discuss this issue freely until opposing viewpoints are clear. Then ask: **What if you were a contractor who was building a new housing development? Would you make the houses more earthquake-proof?** After students discuss this question, list *home-owners* and *building contractors* on the board, and ask: **What other groups of people would be interested in earthquake preparedness?** *(Students may mention community officials, safety associations such as the Red Cross, directors of utility companies, hospital directors, highway engineers, and the like. Add these groups to the list as students identify them.)* Divide the class into as many groups as are listed on the board. Provide time for each group to meet and discuss the pros and cons of spending funds on earthquake preparedness from that group's viewpoint. Ask each group to select one representative to serve on an "Earthquake-Preparedness Committee" to discuss and decide on how to spend the funds that the community has received.

What's the Risk of an Earthquake?

The New Madrid fault system stretches beneath the central Mississippi River Valley. East of the Rocky Mountains, this is the region of the United States most likely to experience an earthquake. But because the faults are hidden under soil and sediment, the hazards are not obvious.

This region has not had a serious earthquake since 1812. Yet scientists estimate that there is a 90 percent chance that a moderate earthquake will occur in this area in the next 50 years. Which locations might be at risk for heavy damage? No one knows for sure. What preparations, if any, should people of this region make?

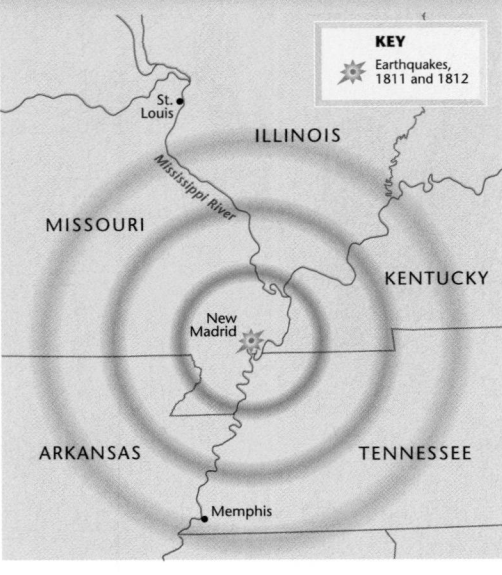

KEY
Earthquakes, 1811 and 1812

The Issues

How Much Money Should People Spend? In areas where earthquakes are rare, such as the New Madrid fault region, communities face hard choices. Should they spend money for earthquake preparation now in order to cut costs later? Or should they save the money and risk the consequences?

Which Buildings Should Be Modified? It's clear that the best way to save lives is to make buildings that can withstand severe shaking. Since damaged or collapsing buildings cause most injuries and deaths during earthquakes, modifying existing buildings could save lives. Unfortunately building renovations are costly.

Most new houses can withstand moderate earthquakes. But many older houses—especially brick or masonry houses—are not safe.

Unfortunately, few homeowners can afford the cost of making their houses safer. They might need financial aid or a tax break to help them make these changes.

What Other Structures Need Improvement? Imagine what would happen if your community were without utility stations and lines for electricity, gas, and water, or without bridges, schools, and hospitals. Engineers who understand earthquake hazards have worked out design standards to reduce damage to these structures. Today, many cities follow these standards in their building codes. But not all structures can be made earthquake-safe. Furthermore, some structures are more crucial for public health and safety than others.

You Decide

1. Identify the Problem
Summarize the dilemma that communities face in regard to earthquake preparations. Which structures in a community are most important to make earthquake-resistant?

2. Analyze the Options
Consider what would happen if communities spent more money, less money, or nothing on earthquake preparations. In each case, who would benefit? Who might be harmed?

3. Find a Solution
Your community near the New Madrid fault system has received a large sum of money to spend on earthquake preparedness. Develop a plan for building and modifying structures. Explain and defend your use of funds.

Background

Facts and Figures The central Mississippi River valley is considered to be an area of high earthquake risk. It was along the New Madrid fault that three severe earthquakes occurred in 1811 and 1812.

The area shaken by the New Madrid earthquakes extended across much of the United States and into Canada. In the region around the earthquakes' epicenters, the quakes uplifted the land surface by several meters, changed the course of the Mississippi River, and resulted in the formation of lakes, such as Reelsfoot Lake in Tennessee. These quakes caused no deaths as far as anyone knows because the region most strongly affected had very few inhabitants at the time.

SECTION 1 Earth's Crust in Motion

Key Ideas

◆ Stresses on Earth's crust produce compression, tension, and shearing in rock.
◆ Faults are cracks in Earth's crust that result from stress.
◆ Faulting and folding of the crust cause mountains and other features to form on the surface.

Key Terms

earthquake	hanging wall
stress	footwall
shearing	reverse fault
tension	fault-block mountain
compression	folds
deformation	anticline
fault	syncline
strike-slip fault	plateau
normal fault	

 SECTION 2 Measuring Earthquakes

Key Ideas

◆ As seismic waves travel through Earth, they carry the energy of an earthquake from the focus to the surface.
◆ Earthquakes produce two types of seismic waves, P waves and S waves, that travel out in all directions from the focus of an earthquake.
◆ Today, the moment magnitude scale is used to determine the magnitude of an earthquake. Other scales that geologists have used to rate earthquakes include the Mercalli scale and the Richter scale.

Key Terms

focus	seismograph
epicenter	magnitude
seismic waves	Mercalli scale
P waves	Richter scale
S waves	moment magnitude scale
surface waves	

 SECTION 3 Earthquake Hazards and Safety

Key Ideas

◆ Earthquakes can damage structures through tsunamis, landslides or avalanches, and shaking or liquefaction of the ground.
◆ New buildings can be designed to withstand earthquakes; old buildings can be modified to make them more earthquake-resistant.
◆ For personal safety indoors during an earthquake, drop, cover, and hold under a desk or table, or against an interior wall.

Key Terms

liquefaction	tsunamis
aftershock	base-isolated building

 SECTION 4 Monitoring Faults

INTEGRATING TECHNOLOGY

Key Ideas

◆ Geologists use instruments to measure deformation and stress along faults.
◆ Scientists determine earthquake risk by monitoring active faults and by studying faults where past earthquakes have occurred.

Organizing Information

Concept Map Copy the concept map about stress on a separate piece of paper. Then complete it and add a title. (For more on concept maps, see the Skills Handbook.)

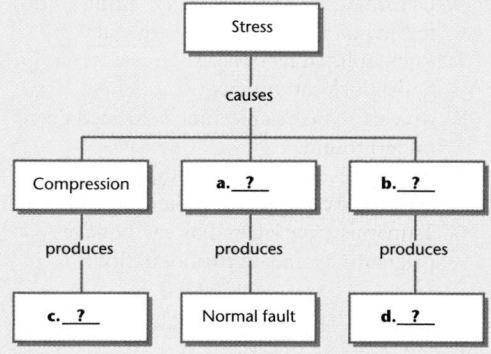

Extend

Suggest that students contact their local government representatives to find out whether the community has any plans in place for dealing with earthquake preparedness.

You Decide

1. Students' summaries should include the major points presented in the text. Students should list structures related to public health and safety as the most important to protect against damage.
2. Encourage students to carefully think through the repercussions of more, less, and no funding for earthquake preparedness from the viewpoints of the groups they identified in their initial discussion.
3. Students may rely on the points identified in the panel discussion or may present their own ideas. In either case, make sure each student gives a well-reasoned rationale for use of the funds.

Organizing Information

Concept Map Sample title: *Stress Forces in Earth's Crust* **a.** Tension **b.** Shearing **c.** Reverse fault **d.** Strike-slip fault

Program Resources

◆ **Unit 4 Resources** Chapter 12 Project Scoring Rubric, p. 40
◆ **Performance Assessment** Chapter 12, pp. 37–39
◆ **Chapter Tests** Chapter 12 Test, pp. 47–50

Media and Technology

Computer Test Bank
Chapter 12 Test

Reviewing Content
Multiple Choice
1. b 2. c 3. c 4. d 5. b

True or False
6. stress 7. normal faults 8. focus
9. P waves 10. true

Checking Concepts

11. Stress changes the crust's volume or shape through compression, tension, and shearing.

12. Where two plates move away from each other, tension forces create many normal faults. When two normal faults form parallel to each other, a block of rock is left lying between them. As the hanging wall of each normal fault slips downward, the block in between moves upward, forming a fault-block mountain.

13. Compression forms folded mountains. Compression shortens and thickens the crust so it bends slowly without breaking. If the fold bends upward into an arch, the fold is called an anticline. If the fold bends downward to form a bowl, the fold is called a syncline.

14. A plateau is a large area of flat land that is elevated high above sea level. A plateau may form when vertical faults push up a large, flat block of rock.

15. An earthquake occurs when rock along a fault suddenly breaks at a point beneath the surface called the focus. This releases the stress stored in the rock as seismic waves. The seismic waves travel outward from the focus in all directions. They reach the surface at the epicenter.

16. Both the moment magnitude scale and the Richter scale measure earthquake strength. The Richter scale rates the size of seismic waves as measured by a mechanical seismograph. The moment magnitude scale estimates the total energy released by an earthquake. The Richter scale provides accurate measurements for small, nearby earthquakes but does not work well for large or distant earthquakes. The moment magnitude scale can be used to rate earthquakes of all sizes and at all distances.

17. Geologists use fault-monitoring devices to measure stress and deformation in the crust—horizontal

Reviewing Content
Multiple Choice
Chose the letter of the answer that best completes each statement.

1. Shearing is the force in Earth's crust that
   a. squeezes the crust together.
   b. pushes the crust in opposite directions.
   c. forces the crust to bend and fold.
   d. stretches the crust apart.

2. When the hanging wall of a fault slips down with respect to the footwall, the result is a
   a. reverse fault.   b. syncline.
   c. normal fault.   d. strike-slip fault.

3. A seismograph measures
   a. the depth of an earthquake.
   b. friction forces along a fault.
   c. ground motion during an earthquake.
   d. movement along a fault.

4. Geologists use the difference in the arrival times of P waves and S waves at a seismograph to determine
   a. the magnitude of the earthquake.
   b. the depth of the earthquake's focus.
   c. the strength of the surface waves.
   d. the distance to the epicenter.

5. To monitor the upward movement along a fault, geologists would probably use a
   a. laser-ranging device.   b. tiltmeter.
   c. seismograph.   d. creep meter.

True or False
If the statement is true, write true. If it is false, change the underlined word or words to make the statement true.

6. Deformation is the breaking, tilting, and folding of rocks caused by <u>liquefaction</u>.

7. Rock uplifted by <u>strike-slip faults</u> creates fault-block mountains.

8. An earthquake's <u>epicenter</u> is located deep underground.

9. As <u>S waves</u> move through the ground, they cause it to compress and then expand.

10. <u>Tsunamis</u> are triggered by earthquakes originating beneath the ocean floor.

movement along a strike-slip fault and tilting, upward movement, or downward movement along normal or reverse faults.

18. Students' letters should include a brief description of what a fault is and why earthquakes commonly occur along faults. Evaluate students' recommendations on the basis of their practicality, benefits, and attention to critical structures such as hospitals, highways, and utilities.

Checking Concepts

11. How does stress affect Earth's crust?
12. Explain the process that forms a fault-block mountain.
13. What type of stress in the crust results in the formation of folded mountains? Explain your answer.
14. What are plateaus and how do they form?
15. Describe what happens along a fault beneath Earth's surface when an earthquake occurs.
16. Explain how the moment magnitude and Richter scales of earthquake measurement are similar and how they are different.
17. When geologists monitor a fault, what kinds of data do they collect? Explain.
18. **Writing to Learn** You are a geologist studying earthquake risk in an eastern state. Your data show that a major earthquake might happen there within 10 years. Write a letter to the governor of your state explaining why there is an earthquake hazard there and recommending how your state should prepare for the earthquake.

Thinking Critically

19. **Classifying** How would you classify a fault in which the hanging wall has slid up and over the footwall?
20. **Comparing and Contrasting** Compare and contrast P waves and S waves.
21. **Predicting** A community has just built a street across a strike-slip fault that has frequent earthquakes. How will movement along the fault affect the street?
22. **Applying Concepts** If you were building a house in an earthquake-prone area, what steps would you take to limit potential damage in an earthquake?
23. **Making Generalizations** How can filled land and loose, soft soil affect the amount of damage caused by an earthquake? Explain.
24. **Relating Cause and Effect** A geologist is monitoring a fault using radar waves bounced off Earth's surface by a satellite. If the satellite detects a change in elevation near the fault, what does this indicate? Explain.

Thinking Critically

19. It should be classified as a reverse fault.
20. Both P waves and S waves are seismic waves sent out from the earthquake's focus deep under ground. P waves arrive first at a seismograph. They compress and expand the ground like an accordion. P waves travel through both solids and liquids. S waves arrive second at a seismograph. They vibrate from side to side and up and down. S waves cannot move through liquids.

Applying Skills

The graph shows the seismograph record for an earthquake. The y-axis of the graph shows the up-and-down shaking in millimeters at the seismograph station. The x-axis shows time in minutes.

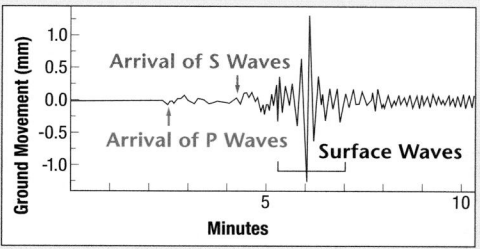

25. Interpreting Diagrams In what order do the seismic waves arrive at the seismograph station? Which type of seismic wave produces the largest ground movement?

26. Interpreting Diagrams What is the difference in arrival times for the P waves and S waves?

27. Predicting What would the seismograph record look like several hours after this earthquake? How would it change if an aftershock occurred?

28. Drawing Conclusions If the difference in arrival times for P waves and S waves is 5 minutes longer at a second seismograph station than at the first station, what can you conclude about the location of the second station?

Performance CHAPTER PROJECT **12 Assessment**

Project Wrap Up Before testing how your model withstands an earthquake, explain to your classmates how and why you changed your model. When your model is tested, make notes of how it withstands the earthquake.

Reflect and Record How would a real earthquake compare with the method used to test your model? If it were a real building, could your structure withstand an earthquake? How could you improve your model?

Test Preparation

Use these questions to prepare for standardized tests.

Use the diagram of a fault to answer Questions 29–33.

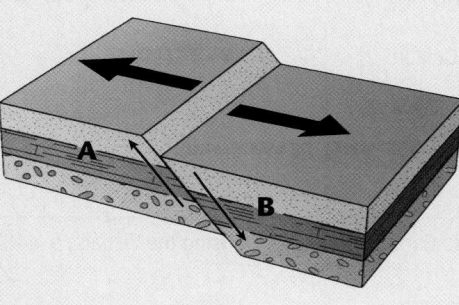

29. The rock on the side of the fault labeled B is the
   a. footwall.   b. shearing wall.
   c. hanging wall.   d. seismic wall.

30. The rock on the side of the fault labeled A is the
   a. hanging wall.   b. strike-slip wall.
   c. reverse wall.   d. footwall.

31. The thick arrows in the diagram stand for forces in Earth's crust pulling apart the two slabs of rock. This force is called
   a. shearing.   b. compression.
   c. elevation.   d. tension.

32. In the fault shown, the footwall
   a. does not move.
   b. moves down relative to the hanging wall.
   c. moves up relative to the hanging wall.
   d. slides sideways along the hanging wall.

33. The fault in the diagram is a(n)
   a. normal fault.   b. strike-slip fault.
   c. reverse fault.   d. inactive fault.

---

21. The street will break where it crosses the fault, and the two sides will be moved horizontally in opposite directions.

22. Build the home on solid rock and in a flat area rather than on loose soil and on a hillside. Build as far as possible from the fault itself and away from coastal areas that might be exposed to tsunamis. Use brackets to secure brick chimneys. Use connectors to strengthen joints in the house's frame. Use plywood panels to strengthen cripple walls beneath the house and

---

Program Resources

- **Inquiry Skills Activity Book** Provides teaching and review of all inquiry skills
- **Prentice Hall Assessment System** Provides standardized test practice
- **Reading in the Content Area** Provides strategies to improve science reading skills
- **Teacher's ELL Handbook** Provides multiple strategies for English language learners

---

on ceiling joists around the chimney to protect against falling bricks. Bolt the house to its foundation.

23. In general, filled land and loose, soft soil increase the amount of damage caused by an earthquake. During an earthquake, the loosely packed soil of the filled land shakes more violently than the surrounding rock. Also, an earthquake can cause liquefaction. Liquifaction turns soft soil with a high moisture content into liquid mud.

24. Changes in the elevation of the land surface along a fault indicate that stress is building up in the ground. Stress causes deformation of the land surface. For example, the land may bulge upward, producing the change in elevation detected by a satellite.

Applying Skills

25. P waves arrive first, then S waves, and finally surface waves. Surface waves produce the largest ground movement.

26. approximately 1 minute and 50 seconds

27. The up-and-down spikes of the waves would be much less jagged, perhaps almost smooth. If an aftershock occurred, the spikes would resume again.

28. The second station is farther away from the earthquake's epicenter.

Performance CHAPTER PROJECT **12 Assessment**

Project Wrap Up Give each student an opportunity to explain any changes made to the model based on the results of previous tests. Then let students test their models for the last time and make final changes before their class presentations. Remind students to note any further improvements they might want to make.

Reflect and Record Use the two questions in the student text as the basis for a whole-class discussion. Then let students write in their journals.

Test Preparation

29. c **30.** d **31.** d **32.** c **33.** a

Sections	Time	Student Edition Activities	Other Activities	
CHAPTER PROJECT 13 **Volcanoes and People** p. 419	Ongoing (2–3 weeks)	Check Your Progress, p. 423, 439, 444 Project Wrap Up, p. 447	TE	Chapter 13 Project Notes, pp. 418–419
1 Volcanoes and Plate Tectonics pp. 420–424 ◆ 13.1.1 Identify where Earth's volcanic regions are found, and explain why they are found there.	2 periods/ 1 block	**Discover** Where Are Volcanoes Found on Earth's Surface?, p. 420 **Try This** Hot Spot in a Box, p. 423 **Skills Lab** Mapping Earthquakes and Volcanoes, p. 424	TE	Including All Students, p. 422
2 Volcanic Activity pp. 425–434 ◆ 13.2.1 Describe what happens when a volcano erupts. ◆ 13.2.2 Explain how the two types of volcanic eruptions differ depending on the characteristics of magma. ◆ 13.2.3 Identify some hazards of volcanoes. ◆ 13.2.4 Identify types of volcanic activity other than eruptions.	1 period/ $\frac{1}{2}$ block	**Discover** What Are Volcanic Rocks Like?, p. 425 **Try This** Gases in Magma, p. 426 **Science at Home,** p. 434	TE TE TE TE LM	Building Inquiry Skills: Inferring, pp. 426–433 Inquiry Challenge, p. 428 Building Inquiry Skills: Comparing and Contrasting, p. 428 Demonstration, p. 431 13, "Predicting Lava Flows"
3 Volcanic Landforms pp. 435–441 ◆ 13.3.1 Identify landforms that lava and other volcanic materials create on Earth's surface. ◆ 13.3.2 Explain how magma that hardens beneath the surface creates landforms.	2 periods/ 1 block	**Discover** How Can Volcanic Activity Change Earth's Surface?, p. 435 **Real-World Lab: How It Works** Gelatin Volcanoes, pp. 440–441	TE	Inquiry Challenge, p. 437
4 **INTEGRATING SPACE SCIENCE** **Volcanoes in the Solar System** pp. 442–444 ◆ 13.4.1 Explain how volcanoes on Mars and Venus compare with volcanoes on Earth. ◆ 13.4.2 Describe the volcanic activity found on the moons of Jupiter and Neptune.	1 period/ $\frac{1}{2}$ block	**Discover** What Forces Shaped the Surface of Io?, p. 442	TE	Using the Visuals, p. 443
Study Guide/Assessment pp. 445–447	1 period/ $\frac{1}{2}$ block		ISAB	Provides teaching and review of all inquiry skills

For Standard or Block Schedule The Resource Pro® CD-ROM gives you maximum flexibility for planning your instruction for any type of schedule. Resource Pro® contains Planning Express®, an advanced scheduling program, as well as the entire contents of the Teaching Resources and the Computer Test Bank.

Key: **CTB** Computer Test Bank
CT Chapter Tests
ELL Teacher's ELL Handbook

CHAPTER PLANNING GUIDE

Program Resources	Assessment Strategies	Media and Technology
UR Chapter 13 Project Teacher Notes, pp. 62–63 **UR** Chapter 13 Project Overview and Worksheets, pp. 64–67	**TE** Performance Assessment: Chapter 13 Project Wrap Up, p. 447 **TE** Check Your Progress, pp. 423, 439, 444 **UR** Chapter 13 Project Scoring Rubric, p. 68	Science Explorer Internet Site Audio CDs, Section Summaries
UR 13-1 Lesson Plan, p. 69 **UR** 13-1 Section Summary, p. 70 **UR** 13-1 Review and Reinforce, p. 71 **UR** 13-1 Enrich, p. 72 **UR** Skills Lab blackline masters, pp. 85–87	**SE** Section 1 Review, p. 423 **SE** Analyze and Conclude, p. 424 **TE** Ongoing Assessment, p. 421 **TE** Performance Assessment, p. 423	Presentation Pro, "Geography of Volcanoes"; "Volcanoes" Transparencies 52, "Earth's Active Volcanoes"; 53, "Volcanoes at Converging Boundaries" Lab Activity Videotape, *Tape 3*
UR 13-2 Lesson Plan, p. 73 **UR** 13-2 Section Summary, p. 74 **UR** 13-2 Review and Reinforce, p. 75 **UR** 13-2 Enrich, p. 76	**SE** Section 2 Review, p. 434 **TE** Ongoing Assessment, pp. 427, 429, 431, 433 **TE** Performance Assessment, p. 434	Transparency 54, "Exploring a Volcano"
UR 13-3 Lesson Plan, p. 77 **UR** 13-3 Section Summary, p. 78 **UR** 13-3 Review and Reinforce, p. 79 **UR** 13-3 Enrich, p. 80 **UR** Real-World Lab blackline masters, pp. 88–89	**SE** Section 3 Review, p. 439 **SE** Analyze and Conclude, p. 441 **TE** Ongoing Assessment, p. 437 **TE** Performance Assessment, p. 439	Concept Videotape Library, *Adventures, Tape 3,* "Flying Over America" Transparency 55, "Exploring Volcanic Mountains" Lab Activity Videotape, *Tape 3*
UR 13-4 Lesson Plan, p. 81 **UR** 13-4 Section Summary, p. 82 **UR** 13-4 Review and Reinforce, p. 83 **UR** 13-4 Enrich, p. 84	**SE** Section 4 Review, p. 444 **TE** Ongoing Assessment, p. 443 **TE** Performance Assessment, p. 444	
GRSW Provides worksheets to promote student comprehension of content **RCA** Provides strategies to improve science reading skills **ELL** Provides multiple strategies for English language learners	**SE** Study Guide/Assessment, pp. 445–447 **PA** Performance Assessment, pp. 40–42 **CT** Chapter 13 Test, pp. 51–54 **CTB** Chapter 13 Test **PHAS** Provides standardized test preparation	Computer Test Bank, Chapter 13 Test

GRSW Guided Reading and Study Workbook
ISAB Inquiry Skills Activity Book
LM Laboratory Manual

PA Performance Assessment
PHAS Prentice Hall Assessment System
PLM Probeware Lab Manual

RCA Reading in the Content Area
SE Student Edition

TE Teacher's Edition
UR Unit Resources

Meeting the National Science Education Standards and AAAS Benchmarks

National Science Education Standards	Benchmarks for Science Literacy	Unifying Themes
Science As Inquiry (Content Standard A) ◆ **Develop descriptions, explanations, predictions, and models using evidence** Students interpret data to find a pattern in the locations of earthquakes and volcanoes. Students model the flow of magma inside a volcano. *(Skills Lab; Real-World Lab)* ◆ **Communicate scientific procedures and explanations** Students make a documentary about life in a volcanic region. *(Chapter Project)* **Earth and Space Science** (Content Standard D) ◆ **Structure of the Earth system** Most volcanoes occur along diverging plate boundaries or in subduction zones. A volcano erupts when magma breaks through Earth's crust and lava flows over the surface. Volcanoes create a variety of landforms. *(Sections 1, 2, 3; Skills Lab)* ◆ **Earth in the solar system** Space probes show evidence of volcanic activity on other planets and moons. *(Section 4)* **Science in Personal and Social Perspectives** (Content Standard F) ◆ **Natural hazards** A volcanic eruption can cause great damage. Volcanic eruptions have affected the land and people around them. *(Section 2; Science & History)* ◆ **Risks and benefits** Students research how volcanoes have affected people in volcanic regions. *(Chapter Project)*	**1B Scientific Inquiry** Students research how volcanoes have affected people in volcanic regions. Students interpret data to find a pattern in the locations of earthquakes and volcanoes. Students investigate the flow of magma inside a volcano. *(Chapter Project; Skills Lab; Real-World Lab)* **4A The Universe** Space probes show evidence of volcanic activity on other planets and moons. *(Section 4)* **4C Processes That Shape the Earth** Most volcanoes occur along diverging plate boundaries or in subduction zones. A volcano erupts when magma breaks through Earth's crust and lava flows over the surface. Volcanic eruptions have greatly affected the land and people around them. Volcanoes create a variety of landforms. Magma inside a volcano generally moves in an upward direction. *(Sections 1, 2, 3; Skills Lab; Science & History; Real-World Lab)* **11B Models** Students use a model to investigate the flow of magma inside a volcano. *(Real-World Lab)* **12D Communication Skills** Students make a documentary about life in a volcanic region. Students locate earthquakes and volcanoes on a map using coordinates. *(Chapter Project; Skills Lab)*	◆ **Energy** A hot spot is where magma from the mantle melts through the crust. During a volcanic eruption, gases dissolved in magma rush out, carrying magma with them. *(Sections 1, 2)* ◆ **Evolution** A volcano passes through three stages: active, dormant, extinct. *(Section 2)* ◆ **Patterns of Change** Most volcanoes occur along diverging plate boundaries or in subduction zones. Earthquake zones and volcanic belts are located along plate boundaries. The buildup of lava and magma creates landforms on or beneath Earth's surface. *(Sections 1, 3; Skills Lab)* ◆ **Scale and Structure** All volcanoes have a magma chamber, pipe, and vent. *(Section 2)* ◆ **Systems and Interactions** Students research how volcanoes have affected people living in volcanic regions. A volcano erupts when magma from the mantle breaks through the crust and lava flows over the surface. Volcanic eruptions have affected the land and people around them. Students investigate how magma flows inside a volcano. *(Chapter Project; Section 2; Science & History; Real-World Lab)* ◆ **Unity and Diversity** The silica content of magma helps to determine whether a volcanic eruption is quiet or explosive. Volcanoes create a variety of landforms. There are volcanoes on other planets and moons. *(Sections 2, 3, 4)*

Take It to the Net

The **www.phschool.com** Web site provides you with multiple opportunities to incorporate the internet into your instruction. Go to **www.phschool.com** and click on the Science icon. Then select Science Explorer Integrated.

- Have students use the chapter Self-Test to get instant feedback.

- Hot Links and Reference Links provide opportunities for online research.

WEB ACTIVITY www.phschool.com

STAY CURRENT with **SCIENCE NEWS** ®

Internet Activities provide opportunities for students to review, extend, or assess a concept from the chapter.

Find out the latest research and information about earthquakes, volcanoes, and plate tectonics at: **www.phschool.com**

ACTIVITY	Time (minutes)	Materials Quantities for one work group	Skills
Section 1			
Discover, p. 420	10	No special materials are required.	Developing Hypotheses
Try This, p. 423	15–20	**Consumable** cold water, hot water, red food coloring **Nonconsumable** plastic box, small narrow-necked bottle, flat piece of plastic foam	Making Models
Skills Lab, p. 424	40	**Consumable** outline world map showing longitude and latitude (Unit 4 Resources page 87) **Nonconsumable** 4 pencils of different colors	Interpreting Data, Observing, Inferring
Section 2			
Discover, p. 425	5–10	**Nonconsumable** samples of pumice and obsidian, hand lens	Developing Hypotheses
Try This, p. 426	10–15	**Consumable** 10 g baking soda, 65 mL water, 6 raisins, 65 mL vinegar **Nonconsumable** 1- or 2-liter plastic bottle	Making Models
Science at Home, p. 434	home	**Consumable** cold water, hot water, matches **Nonconsumable** 2 cups, candle	Making Models
Section 3			
Discover, p. 435	10–15	**Consumable** tape, balloon, damp sand, straw **Nonconsumable** box	Making Models
Real-World Lab, pp. 440–441	40	**Consumable** unflavored gelatin mold in bowl, aluminum pizza pan, red food coloring and water, unlined paper **Nonconsumable** plastic cup, plastic knife, tray or shallow pan, plastic syringe 10 cc, three small cardboard oatmeal boxes, rubber gloves	Developing Hypotheses, Making Models, Observing
Section 4			
Discover, p. 442	5	No special materials are required.	Posing Questions

A list of all materials required for the Student Edition activities can be found beginning on page T23. You can obtain information about ordering materials by calling 1-800-848-9500 or by accessing the Science Explorer Internet site at: **www.phschool.com**

Volcanoes and People

When students first consider volcanoes, they will undoubtedly think of fiery eruptions and the death, injury, and destruction they cause. As significant as those effects are, other aspects of volcanoes are also important, including their influence on the art, history, and literature of the people living near them, important products obtained or produced from volcanic materials, and the effects of volcanic activity on soil fertility and agriculture. This project encourages students to consider such aspects as well.

Purpose This project will give students an opportunity to investigate a variety of ways in which people have been affected by volcanoes. Student groups will each choose a specific volcanic region and a particular topic for research. Based on their research, the group will prepare a multimedia documentary about the volcanic region for presentation to the rest of the class.

Skills Focus After completing the Chapter 13 Project, students will be able to
◆ classify the type of volcano chosen for the project;
◆ draw conclusions from a variety of source materials about the volcano's effects on people living near it;
◆ communicate how the volcano has affected the people living in a volcanic region in a documentary presentation, using a variety of media.

Project Time Line The project requires two to three weeks to complete. Each group should first choose a volcanic region and investigate possible topics related to its effects on people in the area. After choosing one topic, group members should research information on that topic and take relevant, well-organized notes. (Chapter 13 Project Worksheet 2 on page 67 in Unit 4 Resources reviews how to take research notes.) Students then should create a storyboard showing each step in the presentation, including the media materials that will be used. Posters, transparencies, videos, and other media should then be prepared—and refined, if

WEB ACTIVITY www.phschool.com

needed—and the entire documentary rehearsed before presentation to the class. See Chapter 13 Project Teacher Notes on pages 62–63 in Unit 4 Resources for more hints and detailed directions.

Possible Materials
◆ Provide a wide variety of age-appropriate source materials for students to use in their research, including encyclopedias, nonfiction library books, magazine articles, and films on videocassette and CD-ROM. If students have access to the internet in school or at

home, encourage them to use that source as well. One appropriate website is Volcano World, at: **volcano.und.nodak.edu**
◆ Also provide index cards for taking notes and self-stick removable tags for flagging appropriate information in books.
◆ When students are ready to prepare their multimedia materials, supply a variety of materials and devices—poster paper, art supplies, acetate sheets for making overhead transparencies, videocameras, and tape recorders for taping songs, background

Volcanoes and People

The frequent eruptions of Mount Kilauea can be spectacular. And they can be dangerous. Yet volcanoes and people have been closely connected throughout history, not only in Hawaii, but around the world. People often live near volcanoes because of the benefits they offer, from rich soil to minerals to hot springs. In your chapter project, you will research how volcanoes have affected the people living in a volcanic region.

Your Goal To make a documentary about life in a volcanic region.

Your project must
◆ describe the type of volcano you chose and give its history
◆ focus on one topic, such as how people have benefited from living near the volcano or how people show the volcano in their art and stories
◆ use a variety of media in your documentary presentation

Get Started Brainstorm with a group of other students which geographic area you would like to learn about. Your teacher may suggest some volcanic regions for you to check out. What research resources will your group need? Start planning what media you want to use to present your documentary. You might consider video, computer art, overhead transparencies, a rap song, a skit, or a mural. Be creative!

Check Your Progress You'll be working on this project as you study this chapter. To keep your project on track, look for Check Your Progress boxes at the following points.
Section 1 Review, page 423: Select the topic and region you will investigate and begin collecting information.
Section 3 Review, page 439: Use storyboards to organize your materials.
Section 4 Review, page 444: Prepare your visuals and narration.

Wrap Up At the end of the chapter (page 447), practice your presentation and then present your documentary to your class.

Kilauea volcano is on Hawaii, the largest of the Hawaiian Islands.

Integrating Space Science
SECTION 4 **Volcanoes in the Solar System**
Discover What Forces Shaped the Surface of Io?

419

Program Resources

◆ **Unit 4 Resources** Chapter 13 Project Teacher Notes, pp. 62–63; Project Overview and Worksheets, pp. 64–67; Project Scoring Rubric, p. 68

Media and Technology

🎧 **Audio CDs** Section Summaries

WEB ACTIVITY www.phschool.com

You will find an Internet activity, chapter self-tests for students, and links to other chapter topics at this site.

Launching the Project

To introduce the project, suggest that students preview Science & History on pages 432–433. Then ask: **What are some ways that each of these volcanoes may have affected the people living nearby?** *(Accept all responses at this time, and encourage creative thinking.)*

Allow time for students to read the project description on page 87 and the Chapter 13 Project Overview on pages 64–65 in Unit 4 Resources. Encourage discussion of the different topics students could focus on and the types of source materials they could use for their research. Also answer any initial questions that students may have.

Emphasize that although they may divide responsibilities among group members so only some prepare the visuals, *all* members of the group should take part in planning the visuals and be prepared to answer questions about them.

Distribute Chapter 13 Project Worksheet 1 on page 66 in Unit 4 Resources, which lists a number of volcanoes and specific topics that students might want to consider as subjects for the project. Make clear, though, that they may choose any volcanic region they wish, so long as they are able to find adequate source material for their research.

Performance Assessment

The Chapter 13 Project Scoring Rubric on page 68 in Unit 4 Resources will help you evaluate how well students complete the Chapter 13 Project. Students will be assessed on
◆ their ability to identify the type of volcano they have chosen and summarize its history;
◆ how well they have focused both their research and their presentation on a single topic related to the volcano's effect on people living in the area;
◆ their creativity in making use of a variety of media to support the narrative part of their presentation;
◆ how well they present their documentary to the rest of the class.

SECTION
1 Volcanoes
and Plate
Tectonics

Objective

After completing the lesson, students will be able to

♦ identify where Earth's volcanic regions are found, and explain why they are found there.

Key Terms volcano, magma, lava, Ring of Fire, island arc, hot spot

1 Engage/Explore

Activating Prior Knowledge

Ask students: **Have you ever seen a volcano in person or on TV? Was it erupting? What was happening? What effects did you see? How were people affected?** (*Answers will vary depending on students' experience. Encourage students to share their observations.*)

DISCOVER

Skills Focus developing hypotheses
Time 10 minutes
Tips Direct students' attention to the map's key to answer the questions in Step 1.
Expected Outcome **1.** Triangles symbolize active volcanoes; solid lines symbolize plate boundaries. **2.** Yes, there is a pattern: volcanoes seem to be related to plate boundaries.
Think It Over *Possible hypothesis:* Volcanoes are concentrated along plate boundaries. *Exceptions:* A few volcanoes occur within plates.

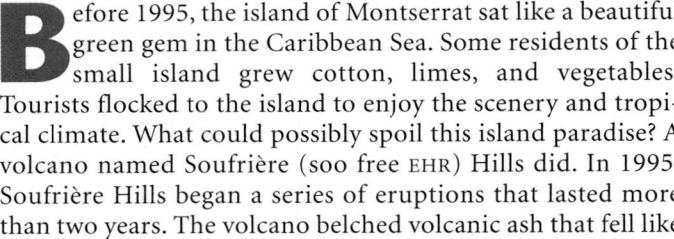
DISCOVER **ACTIVITY**

Where Are Volcanoes Found on Earth's Surface?

1. Look at the map of Earth's volcanoes on page 89. What symbols are used to represent volcanoes? What other symbols are shown on the map?

2. Do the locations of the volcanoes form a pattern? Do the volcanoes seem related to any other features on Earth's surface?

Think About It
Developing Hypotheses Develop a hypothesis to explain where Earth's volcanoes are located. Are there any volcanoes on the map whose location cannot be explained by your hypothesis?

GUIDE FOR READING

♦ Where are Earth's volcanic regions found, and why are they found there?

Reading Tip Before you read, preview the headings in this section. Predict where volcanoes are likely to be located.

Before 1995, the island of Montserrat sat like a beautiful green gem in the Caribbean Sea. Some residents of the small island grew cotton, limes, and vegetables. Tourists flocked to the island to enjoy the scenery and tropical climate. What could possibly spoil this island paradise? A volcano named Soufrière (soo free EHR) Hills did. In 1995, Soufrière Hills began a series of eruptions that lasted more than two years. The volcano belched volcanic ash that fell like snow on roofs and gardens. Residents were evacuated as the volcano continued to erupt, and heavy falls of ash buried entire towns on the southern half of the island.

What Is a Volcano?

The eruption of a volcano is among the most dangerous and awe-inspiring events on Earth. A **volcano** is a weak spot in the crust where molten material, or magma, comes to the surface. **Magma** is a molten mixture of rock-forming substances, gases, and water from the mantle. When magma reaches the surface, it is called **lava**. After lava has cooled, it forms solid rock. The lava released during volcanic activity builds up Earth's surface. Volcanic activity is a constructive force that adds new rock to existing land and forms new islands.

◄ **Soufrière Hills volcano**

420

READING STRATEGIES

Reading Tip Based on the headings alone, students should be able to determine that volcanoes are likely to be located in three main areas: at the boundaries between diverging plates, at the boundaries between converging plates (subduction zones), and in other areas called "hot spots."

Outlining Have students list the three main areas they identified in the Reading Tip on a sheet of paper and label these headings I, II, and III. Tell students to leave space below each heading so that as they read the section, they can add main ideas (labeled A, B, C, and so forth) below each main heading and supporting details (labeled 1, 2, 3, and so forth) below each main idea. Check students' outlines to make sure they have differentiated correctly between main ideas and supporting details and have included all important information.

Location of Volcanoes

There are about 600 active volcanoes on land. Many more lie beneath the sea. Figure 1 is a map that shows the location of Earth's volcanoes. Notice how volcanoes occur in belts that extend across continents and oceans. One major volcanic belt is the **Ring of Fire,** formed by the many volcanoes that rim the Pacific Ocean. Can you find other volcanic belts on the map?

Volcanic belts form along the boundaries of Earth's plates. At plate boundaries, huge pieces of the crust diverge (pull apart) or converge (push together). Here, the crust is weak and fractured, allowing magma to reach the surface. **Most volcanoes occur along diverging plate boundaries, such as the mid-ocean ridge, or in subduction zones around the edges of oceans.** But there are exceptions to this pattern. Some volcanoes form at "hot spots" far from the boundaries of continental or oceanic plates.

Volcanoes at Diverging Plate Boundaries

Volcanoes form along the mid-ocean ridge, which marks a diverging plate boundary. Recall from Chapter 11 that the ridge is a long, underwater rift valley that winds through the oceans. Along the ridge, lava pours out of cracks in the ocean floor. Only in a few places, as in Iceland and the Azores Islands in the Atlantic Ocean, do the volcanoes of the mid-ocean ridge rise above the ocean's surface.

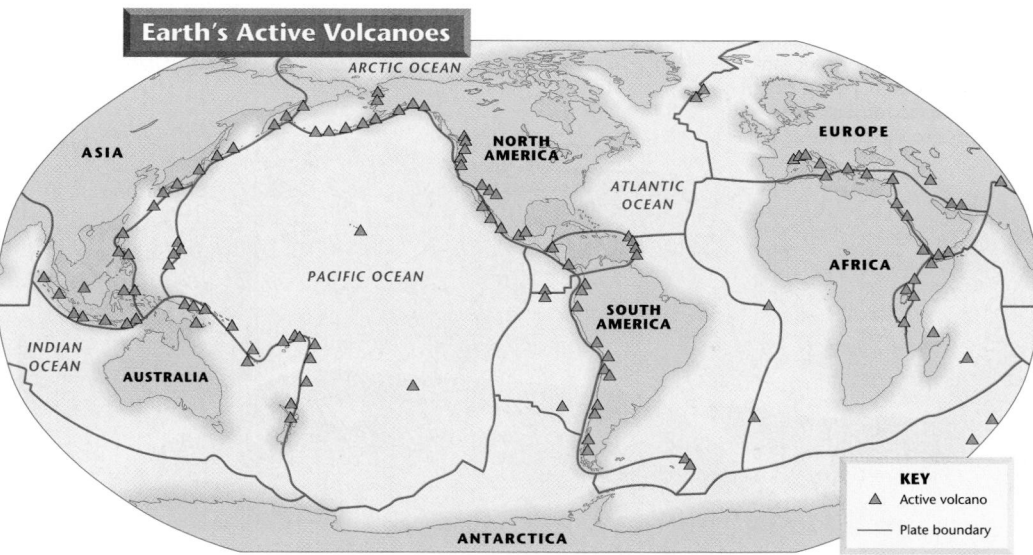

Figure 1 The Ring of Fire is a belt of volcanoes that circles the Pacific Ocean.
Observing What other patterns can you see in the locations of Earth's volcanoes?

Chapter 13 **421**

Program Resources

- **Unit 4 Resources** 13-1 Lesson Plan, p. 69; 13-1 Section Summary, p. 70
- **Guided Reading and Study Workbook** Section 13-1

Media and Technology

 Transparencies "Earth's Active Volcanoes," Transparency 52

Answers to Self-Assessment

Caption Question

Figure 1 Volcanic belts also occur along other plate boundaries.

---

2 Facilitate

What Is a Volcano?

Including All Students

For students whose primary language is not English, suggest that they start a personal glossary of vocabulary terms, with each term and its definition in English on one side of an index card and in the student's primary language on the other side. Encourage students to add to their glossaries as they study other sections in this chapter. **limited English proficiency**

Location of Volcanoes

Language Arts
CONNECTION

Provide a map of the Mediterranean region so students can locate Sicily and Mount Etna. Encourage students to find and read a myth about Vulcan.

In Your Journal *Plutonic* refers to rock formed when magma cools and solidifies deep below Earth's surface. Pluto was the name of the Roman god of the underworld. **learning modality: verbal**

Volcanoes at Diverging Plate Boundaries

Using the Visuals: Figure 1

Ask: **What other volcanic belts besides the Ring of Fire do you see on the map?** *(Along the boundaries between Europe and Africa and between Africa and the Saudi Arabian peninsula; within Africa; in the eastern Caribbean; along the islands between Australia and Asia)* **learning modality: visual**

Ongoing Assessment

Oral Presentation Call on students to explain what accounts for the volcanic belt known as the Ring of Fire.

Volcanoes at Converging Boundaries

Including All Students

Display a large world map, and invite  volunteers to locate and trace the six major island arcs mentioned in the third paragraph. Let students compare these locations with the plate boundaries shown in Figure 1 on the previous page. Repeat this procedure with the two volcanic belts mentioned in the last paragraph. Have students draw the plates and belts on a map. **learning modality: visual**

Hot Spot Volcanoes

TRY THIS

Skills Focus making models

Materials *plastic box, cold water, hot water, red food coloring, small narrow-necked bottle, flat piece of plastic foam*

Time 15–20 minutes

Tips Tell students to make sure the water in the box is deeper than the height of the bottle.

Expected Outcome The "magma" rises out of the bottle and to the water's surface, where it hits the "tectonic plate" in a spot directly above the bottle. When the plate is moved in one direction, the magma hits it in a spot behind the original spot. If the plate continued to move in the same direction, magma would hit it in a series of spots, with the newer volcanoes closer to the "hot spot" and the older volcanoes farther away from it.

Extend Suggest that students continue the plate movement and number the volcanoes to show the sequence in which the volcanoes form. **learning modality: kinesthetic**

Volcanoes at Converging Boundaries

Many volcanoes form near the plate boundaries where oceanic crust returns to the mantle. Subduction causes slabs of oceanic crust to sink through a deep-ocean trench into the mantle. The crust melts and forms magma, which then rises back toward the surface. When the magma from the melted crust erupts as lava, volcanoes are formed. Figure 2 shows how converging plates produce volcanoes.

Many volcanoes occur on islands, near boundaries where two oceanic plates collide. The older, denser plate dives under the other plate, creating a deep-ocean trench. The lower plate sinks beneath the deep-ocean trench into the asthenosphere. There it begins to melt, forming magma. Because it is less dense than the surrounding rock, the magma seeps upward through cracks in the crust. Eventually, the magma breaks through the ocean floor, creating volcanoes.

The resulting volcanoes create a string of islands called an **island arc**. The curve of an island arc echoes the curve of its deep-ocean trench. Major island arcs include Japan, New Zealand, Indonesia, the Caribbean islands, the Philippines, and the Aleutians.

Subduction also occurs where the edge of a continental plate collides with an oceanic plate. Collisions between oceanic and continental plates produced both the volcanoes of the Andes mountains on the west coast of South America and the volcanoes of the Pacific Northwest in the United States.

✓ *Checkpoint How can oceanic crust eventually become magma?*

Figure 2 Converging plates often form volcanoes when two oceanic plates collide or when an oceanic plate collides with a continental plate. In both situations, oceanic crust sinks through a deep-ocean trench, melts to form magma, and then erupts to the surface as lava.

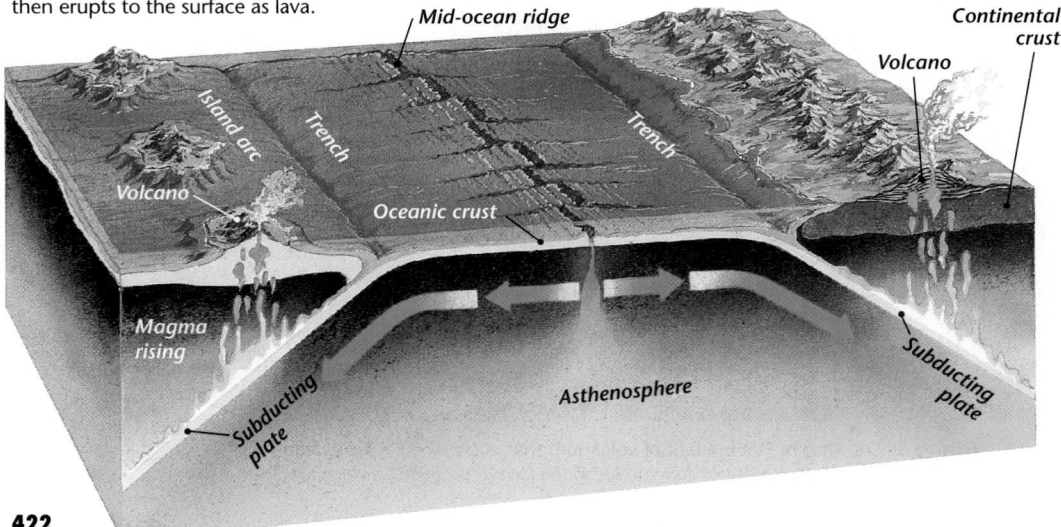

422

Background

Facts and Figures As plates diverge along the mid-ocean ridge, pressure on underlying rock decreases. The reduced pressure lowers the melting point of the rock, producing huge quantities of magma that rise upward. Some magma reaches the ocean floor, where it erupts in extensive lava flows. Flows can pile up to form volcanic cones, some rising above sea level. The island of Surtsey off Iceland's coast formed this way in 1963.

Media and Technology

 Transparencies "Volcanoes at Converging Boundaries," Transparency 53

Figure 3 Hawaii sits on the moving Pacific plate. Beneath it is a powerful hot spot. Eventually, the plate's movement will carry the island of Hawaii away from the hot spot. *Inferring Which island on the map formed first?*

Hot Spot Volcanoes

Some volcanoes result from "hot spots" in Earth's mantle. A **hot spot** is an area where magma from deep within the mantle melts through the crust like a blow torch. Hot spots often lie in the middle of continental or oceanic plates far from any plate boundaries. Unlike the volcanoes in an island arc, the volcanoes at a hot spot do not result from subduction.

A hot spot volcano in the ocean floor can gradually form a series of volcanic mountains. For example, the Hawaiian Islands formed one by one over millions of years as the Pacific plate drifted over a hot spot.

Hot spots can also form under the continents. Yellowstone National Park in Wyoming marks a major hot spot under the North American plate. The last volcanic eruption in Yellowstone occurred about 75,000 years ago.

Section 1 Review

1. Where do most volcanoes occur on Earth's surface?
2. What process forms island arcs?
3. What causes hot spot volcanoes to form?
4. **Thinking Critically** **Predicting** What will eventually happen to the active volcano on the island of Hawaii, which is now over the hot spot?

Check Your Progress **CHAPTER PROJECT 13**

Start by selecting the volcanic region you will study. Possible topics to investigate are myths and legends about volcanoes, the importance of volcanic soils, mineral resources from volcanoes, tourism, and geothermal power. Choose the topic that interests you the most. Begin your research and take notes on the information you collect.

TRY THIS

Hot Spot in a Box

ACTIVITY

1. Fill a plastic box half full of cold water. This represents the ocean.
2. Mix red food coloring with hot water in a small, narrow-necked bottle to represent magma.
3. Hold your finger over the mouth of the bottle as you place the bottle in the center of the box. The mouth of the bottle must be under water.
4. Float a flat piece of plastic foam on the water to model a tectonic plate. Make sure the "plate" is floating above the bottle.
5. Take your finger off the bottle and observe what happens to the "magma."

Making Models Move the plastic foam slowly along. Where does the magma touch the "plate"? How does this model a hot spot volcano?

---

3 Assess

Section 1 Review Answers

1. Most volcanoes occur along diverging plate boundaries, such as the mid-ocean ridge, or in subduction zones around the edges of the oceans.
2. When converging plates collide, the older, denser plate dives under the other plate and sinks into the asthenosphere. There it melts and forms magma, which seeps upward, creating volcanoes that can result in an island arc.
3. Magma from deep within the mantle rises and melts through the crust above it, often far from plate boundaries.
4. The volcano will no longer be active as the island of Hawaii moves with the Pacific plate and is carried away from the hot spot.

Check Your Progress **CHAPTER PROJECT 13**

To avoid duplication, check each group's choice of a volcanic region. You may want to allow two groups to choose the same region so long as they focus on different specific topics. Other possible topics besides those suggested in this Check Your Progress are listed on Chapter 13 Project Worksheet 1. You may also distribute Chapter 13 Project Worksheet 2 at this time, which provides support for helping students take notes as they do their research.

Program Resources

◆ **Unit 4 Resources** 13-1 Review and Reinforce, p. 71; 13-1 Enrich, p. 72

Answers to Self-Assessment

☑ *Checkpoint*

The oceanic crust sinks through a deep-ocean trench into the mantle, where it melts to form magma.

Caption Question

Figure 3 Kauai formed first.

Performance Assessment

Writing Have each student explain, in his or her own words, why volcanoes commonly occur along the boundaries of converging plates.

 Portfolio Students can save written explanations in their portfolios.

Mapping Earthquakes and Volcanoes

Preparing for Inquiry

Key Concept Earthquakes and volcanoes are concentrated together in belts.

Skills Objectives Students will be able to
- interpret data to plot the locations of earthquakes and volcanoes on a world map;
- observe areas in which earthquakes and volcanoes are concentrated;
- infer that earthquakes and volcanoes occur together in certain areas.

Time 40 minutes

Advance Planning Photocopy an outline world map for each student. (*Note:* A map is provided in Unit 4 Resources, page 87.)

Guiding Inquiry

Introducing the Procedure Review the terms *longitude* and *latitude* and how to use those lines on the map to determine precise locations. Make sure students know how to determine longitudes and latitudes that fall between lines.

Troubleshooting the Experiment When students have plotted all locations, display a copy of the map that you have marked so students can check their work.

Expected Outcome The marked map should indicate belts in which *both* volcanoes *and* earthquakes occur.

Analyze and Conclude
1., 2. Both earthquakes and volcanoes are concentrated in definite zones.
3. Earthquakes and volcanoes tend to occur in the same areas.
4. The west coast of North America has the greatest risk of both earthquake and volcano damage. Urban planners, engineers, and builders should use this

information when placing and designing structures.

Extending the Inquiry

More to Explore Provide copies of a U.S. map that includes insets for Alaska and Hawaii and have students research and plot active volcanoes and recent earthquakes in the United States.

Mapping Earthquakes and Volcanoes

In this lab, you will interpret data on the locations of earthquakes and volcanoes to find patterns.

Problem

Is there a pattern in the locations of earthquakes and volcanoes?

Materials

outline world map showing longitude and latitude
4 pencils of different colors

Procedure

1. Use the information in the table to mark the location of each earthquake on the world map. Use one of the colored pencils to draw a letter E inside a circle at each earthquake location.
2. Use a pencil of a second color to mark the locations of the volcanoes on the world map. Indicate each volcano with the letter V inside a circle.
3. Use a third pencil to lightly shade the areas in which earthquakes are found.
4. Use a fourth colored pencil to lightly shade the areas in which volcanoes are found.

Analyze and Conclude

1. How are earthquakes distributed on the map? Are they scattered evenly over Earth's surface? Are they concentrated in zones?
2. How are volcanoes distributed? Are they scattered evenly or concentrated in zones?
3. From your data, what can you infer about the relationship between earthquakes and volcanoes?

4. **Apply** Based on the data, which area of the North American continent would have the greatest risk of earthquake damage? Of volcano damage? Why would knowing this information be important to urban planners, engineers, and builders in this area?

More to Explore

On a map of the United States, locate active volcanoes and areas of earthquake activity. Determine the distance from your home to the nearest active volcano.

Earthquakes		Volcanoes	
Longitude	Latitude	Longitude	Latitude
120° W	40° N	150° W	60° N
110° E	5° S	70° W	35° S
77° W	4° S	120° W	45° N
88° E	23° N	61° W	15° N
121° E	14° S	105° W	20° N
34° E	7° N	75° W	0°
74° W	44° N	122° W	40° N
70° W	30° S	30° E	40° N
10° E	45° N	60° E	30° N
85° W	13° N	160° E	55° N
125° E	23° N	37° E	3° S
30° E	35° N	145° E	40° N
140° E	35° N	120° E	10° S
12° E	46° N	14° E	41° N
75° E	28° N	105° E	5° S
150° W	61° N	35° E	15° N
68° W	47° S	70° W	30° S
175° E	41° S	175° E	39° S
121° E	17° N	123° E	38° N

Program Resources

- **Unit 4 Resources** Skills Lab blackline masters, pp. 85–87

Media and Technology

 Lab Activity Videotape
Tape 3

SECTION 2 Volcanic Activity

DISCOVER

Pumice ▼

▲ Obsidian

ACTIVITY

What Are Volcanic Rocks Like?

Volcanoes produce lava, which hardens into rock. Two of these rocks are pumice and obsidian.

1. Observe samples of pumice and obsidian with a hand lens.

2. How would you describe the texture of the pumice? What could have caused this texture?

3. Observe the surface of the obsidian. How does the surface of the obsidian differ from pumice?

Think It Over

Developing Hypotheses What could have produced the difference in texture between the two rocks? Explain your answer.

In Hawaii, there are many myths about Pele (PAY lay), the fire goddess of volcanoes. In these myths, Pele is the creator and the destroyer of the Hawaiian islands. She lives in the fiery depths of erupting volcanoes. According to legend, when Pele is angry, she releases the fires of Earth through openings on the mountainside. Evidence of her presence is "Pele's hair," a fine, threadlike rock formed by lava. Pele's hair forms when lava sprays out of the ground like water from a fountain. As it cools, the lava stretches and hardens into thin strands.

How Magma Reaches Earth's Surface

Where does this fiery lava come from? Lava begins as magma in the mantle. There, magma forms in the asthenosphere, which lies beneath the lithosphere. The materials of the asthenosphere are under great pressure.

Magma Rises Because liquid magma is less dense than the surrounding solid material, magma flows upward into any cracks in the rock above. Magma rises until it reaches the surface, or until it becomes trapped beneath layers of rock.

GUIDE FOR READING

◆ What happens when a volcano erupts?

◆ How do the two types of volcanic eruptions differ?

◆ What are some hazards of volcanoes?

Reading Tip Before you read, preview *Exploring a Volcano* on page 427. Write a list of any questions you have about how a volcano erupts.

Figure 4 Pele's hair is a type of rock formed from lava. Each strand is as fine as spun glass.

READING STRATEGIES

Reading Tip Suggest that students write their questions on a sheet of paper, leaving space below each question to write the answer as they read the section. Questions may include, "How do side vents form?" and "How far can lava flow before it hardens?"

Program Resources

◆ **Unit 4 Resources** 13-2 Lesson Plan, p. 73; 31-2 Section Summary, p. 74

◆ **Guided Reading and Study Workbook** Section 13-2

Objectives

After completing the lesson, students will be able to

◆ describe what happens when a volcano erupts;

◆ explain how the two types of volcanic eruptions differ depending on the characteristics of magma;

◆ identify some hazards of volcanoes;

◆ identify types of volcanic activity other than eruptions.

Key Terms magma chamber, pipe, vent, lava flow, crater, silica, pahoehoe, aa, pyroclastic flow, active, dormant, extinct, hot spring, geyser, geothermal energy

1 Engage/Explore

Activating Prior Knowledge

Ask students: **What does lava look like when it comes out of a volcano?** (*Based on photographs or videos they have seen, students may describe lava as red-hot and thick or gooey.*) **What else comes out of a volcano when it erupts?** (*Students may mention steam and dark clouds of volcanic dust. Accept all responses without comment at this time.*)

DISCOVER

Skills Focus developing hypotheses

ACTIVITY

Materials *samples of pumice and obsidian, hand lens*

Time 5–10 minutes

Tips Help students with the correct pronunciations of *pumice* (PUHM is) and *obsidian* (ob SID ee un).

Expected Outcome The obsidian is smooth and glassy, whereas the pumice is rough and porous. (CAUTION: Advise students to handle the obsidian with care because it sometimes has sharp edges.)

Think It Over The lava that produced the pumice had more gas (air) in it than the lava that produced the obsidian. Obsidian formed when lava cooled very quickly.

2 Facilitate

How Magma Reaches Earth's Surface

Building Inquiry Skills: Inferring

Materials *2 clear, capped, plastic bottles of soda water; hand lens*
Time 5 minutes

Provide each pair of students with the materials. One student should closely watch a bottle with the hand lens while the other student slowly uncaps it. Students can then switch places and repeat with the second bottle. Ask: **What did you see in the bottle as the cap was removed?** *(Bubbles formed.)* **Why did that happen?** *(At some point, enough pressure was released to allow the carbon dioxide gas to come out of solution and form bubbles.)* **What do you think releases the pressure on gases trapped in magma?** *(When magma reaches Earth's surface, it is no longer confined to a limited space.)*
learning modality: visual

TRY THIS

Skills Focus making models
Materials *1- or 2-liter plastic bottle, 10 g baking soda, 65 mL water, 6 raisins, 65 mL vinegar*
Time 10–15 minutes
Tips You may want to supply funnels for pouring the materials into the bottle.
Expected Outcome The vinegar reacts with the baking soda solution to produce carbon dioxide gas. Bubbles of gas adhere to the raisins causing the raisins to rise to the surface, where the bubbles pop. The raisins sink again, and the cycle repeats. The raisins represent magma; the bubbles represent gases trapped in the magma. In this model, the raisins and gas bubbles are not under great pressure, as magma and gases are in a real volcano. Also, magma, unlike raisins, doesn't go up and down in a volcano, but rather goes up and out.
Extend Students could repeat the activity using raisins and clear carbonated soda.
learning modality: kinesthetic

426

Figure 5 Molten lava from Kilauea volcano in Hawaii.

TRY THIS

Gases in Magma

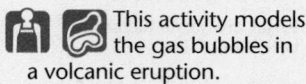 This activity models the gas bubbles in a volcanic eruption.

1. In a 1- or 2-liter plastic bottle, mix 10 g of baking soda into 65 mL of water.
2. Put about six raisins in the water.
3. While swirling the water and raisins, add 65 mL of vinegar and stir vigorously.
4. Once the liquid has stopped moving, observe the raisins.

Making a Model What happens after you add the vinegar? What do the raisins and bubbles represent? How is this model similar to the way magma behaves in a volcano?

426

A Volcano Erupts Just like the carbon dioxide trapped in a bottle of soda pop, the dissolved gases trapped in magma are under tremendous pressure. You cannot see the carbon dioxide gas in a bottle of soda pop because it is dissolved in the liquid. But when you open the bottle, the pressure is released. The carbon dioxide forms bubbles, which rush to the surface.

As magma rises toward the surface, the pressure decreases. The dissolved gases begin to separate out, forming bubbles. A volcano erupts when an opening develops in weak rock on the surface. **During a volcanic eruption, the gases dissolved in magma rush out, carrying the magma with them.** Once magma reaches the surface and becomes lava, the gases bubble out.

Inside a Volcano

All volcanoes have a pocket of magma beneath the surface and one or more cracks through which the magma forces its way. You can see these features in *Exploring a Volcano.* Beneath a volcano, magma collects in a pocket called a **magma chamber.** The magma moves through a **pipe,** a long tube in the ground that connects the magma chamber to Earth's surface. Molten rock and gas leave the volcano through an opening called a **vent.** Often, there is one central vent at the top of a volcano. However, many volcanoes also have other vents that open on the volcano's sides. A **lava flow** is the area covered by lava as it pours out of a vent. A **crater** is a bowl-shaped area that may form at the top of a volcano around the volcano's central vent.

✓ *Checkpoint* How does magma rise through the lithosphere?

Background

Integrating Science Students may wonder how geologists are able to determine what the inside of a volcano is like when they cannot observe it directly. Some evidence is indirect. For example, geologists can determine that magma is present underground by measuring delays in the arrival times of seismic waves from faroff earthquakes.

Other evidence is more direct. The erosion of some ancient volcanoes has exposed their "roots," enabling geologists to examine the dikes and pipes that once linked underground magma chambers to the surface vents. Also, magma sometimes breaks off pieces of the mantle as it rises. These fragments, called ultramafic nodules, are found in lava flows. The composition of these nodules provides support for geologists' theories about Earth's interior.

426

EXPLORING a Volcano

A volcano forms where magma breaks through Earth's crust and lava flows over the surface.

Crater
Lava collects in the crater, the bowl-shaped area that forms around the volcano's vent.

Vent
The point on the surface where magma leaves the volcano's pipe is called the vent.

Side vent
Sometimes magma forces its way out of a volcano through a side vent.

Lava
Magma that reaches the surface is called lava.

Lava flow
The river of lava that pours down a volcano and over the land is called a lava flow.

Pipe
A pipe is a narrow, almost vertical crack in the crust through which magma rises to the surface.

Magma
Magma is extremely hot, molten material that also contains dissolved gases including water vapor.

Magma chamber
As magma rises toward the surface, it forms a large underground pocket called a magma chamber.

Scientists prepare the robot Dante II for its descent into the crater of a volcano in Alaska.

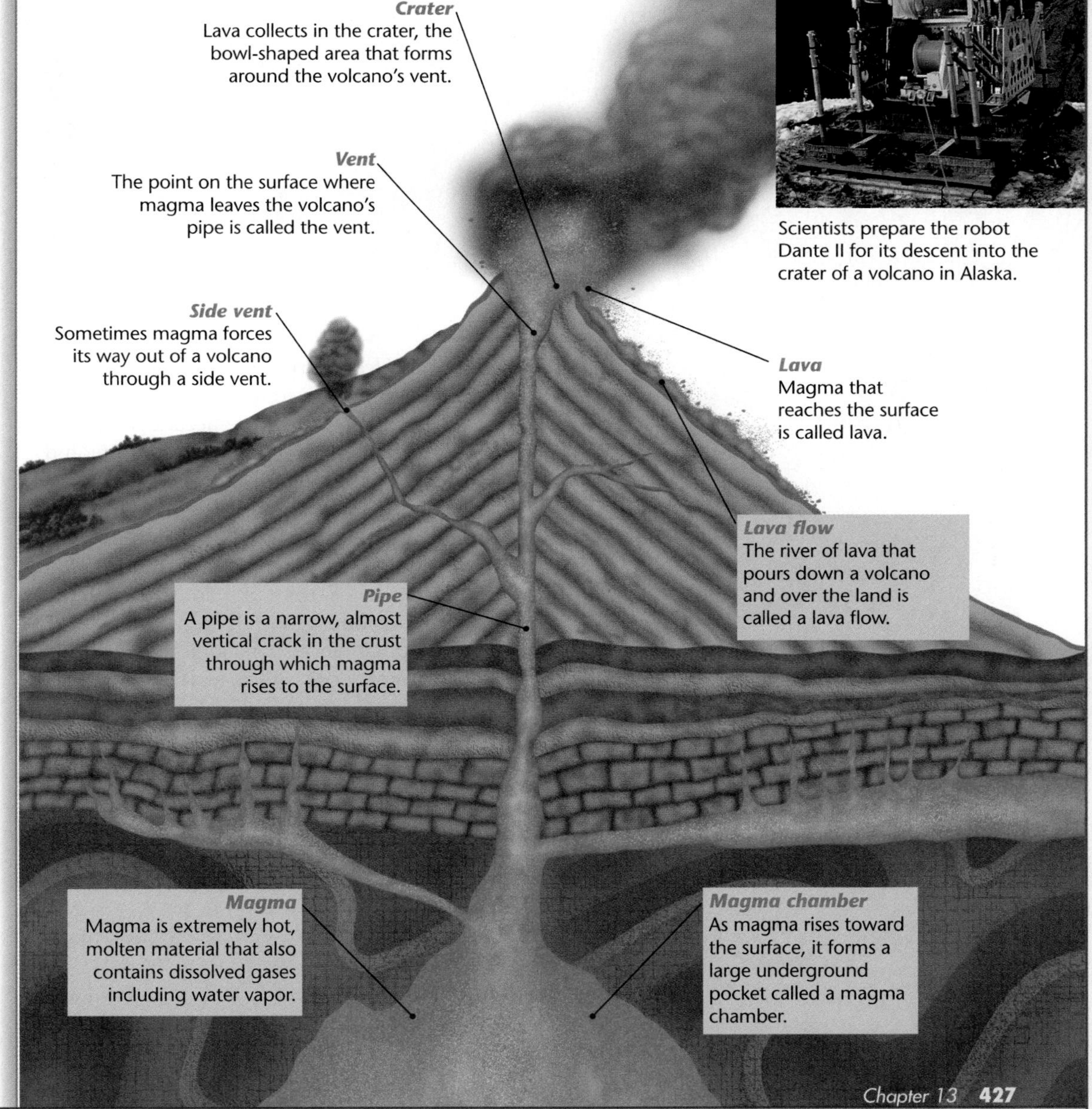

Inside a Volcano

EXPLORING a Volcano

After students have examined the diagram and read the captions on their own, call on students in turn to describe the movement of magma during an eruption, starting with the magma chamber and moving upward through the pipe to the vent and then out onto the surface in a lava flow. Make sure students notice the side vent as well. Ask: **Why would magma flow to a side vent?** *(A crack in the rock layers might offer less resistance to the magma's flow than the magma-filled main pipe.)* Point out the two bodies of magma to the right and left of the pipe just above the magma chamber. Ask: **What happened to the magma there?** *It flowed sideways away from the pipe, then smaller amounts flowed upward from those bodies.)* When students read about dikes and sills in the next section, have them look back at this diagram to review how they are formed.

Draw students' attention to the photograph and caption at the upper right. Ask: **Why would scientists use a robot to explore a volcano's crater?** *(Gases, extreme heat, steep or slippery slopes, and other conditions make exploring the crater too hazardous for people to do themselves.)* **Why was the robot named "Dante"?** *("Dante" refers to Dante Alighieri, the Italian poet who wrote* The Divine Comedy, *the first book of which is* The Inferno, *a description of hell. Students probably will not know; encourage volunteers to consult an encyclopedia and report back to the class.)* **Why is "Dante" a good name for a robot that explores volcanoes?** *(With their fire, heat, and noxious fumes, volcanoes resemble people's images of hell.)*
learning modality: visual

Answers to Self-Assessment

☑ Checkpoint

Liquid magma in the asthenosphere is less dense than the rock in the lithosphere above it, so it flows upward through cracks in the rock. It continues upward until it reaches the surface or is trapped beneath layers of rock.

Ongoing Assessment

Drawing Have each student draw a simple cross-sectional diagram of a volcano and label the magma chamber, pipe, vent, crater and lava without referring to the diagram on this page.

Characteristics of Magma

Inquiry Challenge

Materials *fluids of different thicknesses, jars with secure tops, board covered with waxed paper, other materials of students' choice*

Time 15 minutes

Ask students: **What are some thick liquids?** *(Examples include maple syrup, hand lotion, shampoo, and liquid detergent.)* **What are some thin liquids?** *(Water, milk, juice, vinegar, and so forth)* Then challenge students with the following question: **How could you test how thick or thin a liquid is and compare it with another liquid?** *(Students' ideas will vary. They could put a small amount of each liquid in a jar, turn the jar over, and observe how quickly the liquid flows to the other end. They also could pour liquids down an inclined surface, such as a board, and time its flow rate. Accept other ideas as well.)* Allow time for students to test their ideas and report their results to the rest of the class.
learning modality: logical/ mathematical

Building Inquiry Skills: Comparing and Contrasting

Materials *2 small paper cups, molasses, small paper cup with warmed molasses, small paper cup with chilled molasses.*

Time 15 minutes

Give each student an empty cup and an identical cup half-filled with molasses at room temperature. Let students pour the molasses from one cup to the other, observing its rate of flow. Let students repeat the pouring activity and compare the flow rate of warmed molasses and then the chilled molasses with the flow rate of the room-temperature molasses. Ask: **How did the temperature of the molasses affect its thickness?** *(The lower the molasses' temperature, the thicker it was.)* Emphasize that although magma is thousands of degrees hotter than the molasses used in this activity, its thickness also varies with temperature.
learning modality: kinesthetic

Figure 6 Rhyolite (top) forms from high-silica lava. Basalt (bottom) forms from low-silica lava. When this type of lava cools, it sometimes forms six-sided columns like the ones in the picture.

Characteristics of Magma

The force of a volcanic eruption depends partly on the amount of gas dissolved in the magma. But gas content is not the only thing that affects an eruption. How thick or thin the magma is, its temperature, and its silica content are also important factors.

Some types of magma are thick and flow very slowly. Other types of magma are fluid and flow almost as easily as water. Magma's temperature partly determines whether it is thick or fluid. The hotter the magma, the more fluid it is.

The amount of silica in magma also helps to determine how easily the magma flows. **Silica,** which is a material that is formed from the elements oxygen and silicon, is one of the most abundant materials in Earth's crust and mantle. The more silica magma contains, the thicker it is.

Magma that is high in silica produces light-colored lava that is too sticky to flow very far. When this type of lava cools, it forms the rock rhyolite, which has the same composition as granite. Pumice and obsidian, which you observed if you did the Discover activity, also form from high-silica lava. Obsidian forms when lava cools very quickly, giving it a smooth, glossy surface. Pumice forms when gas bubbles are trapped in cooling lava, leaving spaces in the rock.

Magma that is low in silica flows readily and produces dark-colored lava. When this kind of lava cools, rocks such as basalt are formed.

428

Background

History of Science Kilauea's quiet eruptions sometimes feature fountains of lava that shoot hundreds of meters into the air. But these lava fountains usually last only a short time, and much of the lava splashes down into a lava pool.

The Hawaiian Volcanoes Observatory has been able to operate safely on the volcano's summit since 1912, in spite of numerous eruptions. A major eruption of Kilauea began in 1983 and still continues today.

In 1986 eruptions formed a lava lake on the volcano's slope. When the lake overflowed, pahoehoe lava flows destroyed homes, buried a highway, and flowed into the ocean. There, the lava cooled and solidified, enlarging the islands' land area.

Types of Volcanic Eruptions

A volcano's magma influences how the volcano erupts. **The silica content of magma helps to determine whether the volcanic eruption is quiet or explosive.**

Quiet Eruptions A volcano erupts quietly if its magma flows easily. In this case, the gas dissolved in the magma bubbles out gently. Thin, runny lava oozes quietly from the vent. The islands of Hawaii and Iceland were formed from quiet eruptions. On the Big Island of Hawaii, lava pours out of the crater near the top of Mount Kilauea (kee loo AY uh), but also flows out of long cracks on the volcano's sides. Quiet eruptions like the ones that regularly take place on Mount Kilauea have built up the Big Island over hundreds of thousands of years. In Iceland, lava usually emerges from gigantic fissures many kilometers long. The fluid lava from a quiet eruption can flow many kilometers from the volcano's vent.

Quiet eruptions produce two different types of lava: pahoehoe and aa. **Pahoehoe** (pah HOH ee hoh ee) is fast-moving, hot lava. The surface of a lava flow formed from pahoehoe looks like a solid mass of wrinkles, billows, and ropelike coils. Lava that is cooler and slower-moving is called **aa** (AH ah). When aa hardens, it forms a rough surface consisting of jagged lava chunks. Figure 7 shows how different these types of lava can be.

☑ *Checkpoint* *What types of lava are produced by quiet eruptions?*

Figure 7 Both pahoehoe and aa can come from the same volcano.
A. Pahoehoe flows easily and hardens into a rippled surface.
B. Aa hardens into rough chunks.
Inferring *What accounts for the differences between these two types of lava?*

Chapter 13 **429**

Types of Volcanic Eruptions

Including All Students

Many excellent films are available—on both videocassette and CD-ROM—showing different types of volcanic eruptions and lava flows, including slow-moving aa flows from Kilauea advancing on and consuming homes. Try to obtain one or more such films so students can observe actual volcanoes in action. "Live" footage of lava flows, pyroclastics, fissure eruptions, and the fiery volcanic clouds known as *nuée ardente* will give students a far greater appreciation of the awesome power and drama of volcanic activity. **learning modality: visual**

Cultural Diversity

Write the terms *pahoehoe* and *aa* on the board, and tell students how to pronounce them (pah HOH ee hoh ee, AH ah). Then ask: **Where do you think these words come from?** *(They are the native Hawaiian words for these two types of lava. If students cannot make this inference on their own, remind them that Mount Kilauea is on the island of Hawaii.)* Suggest that students do research to find other native Hawaiian terms related to volcanoes. They might also enjoy reading myths about Pele, the Hawaiian goddess of volcanoes.
learning modality: verbal

Program Resources

◆ **Laboratory Manual** 13, "Predicting Lava Flows"

Answers to Self-Assessment

☑ *Checkpoint*

Quiet eruptions produce two types of lava: pahoehoe (a fast-moving, hot lava) and aa (a cooler, slower-moving lava).

Caption Question

Figure 7 The temperature of the lava and the speed at which it flows.

Ongoing Assessment

Writing Have each student write a brief explanation of how the temperature and silica content of magma affects its thickness.

429

Using the Visuals: Figure 8

Explain that Mount St. Helens is part of the Cascade Range, which runs north-south through Washington, Oregon, and northern California. Let students find the Cascades on a map of the Northwest. Ask: **What volcanic belt are the Cascades part of?** *(The Ring of Fire; let students look back at Figure 1, page 421, if necessary.)* If possible, share with students some first-hand accounts of the eruption of Mount St. Helens from books, magazines, or videos. **learning modality: visual**

Social Studies
CONNECTION

Display a large map of the Mediterranean region, and let students find Mount Vesuvius and Pompeii in Italy. You may wish to provide various source materials for students to use for their research.

In Your Journal Provide photographs showing excavated areas of Pompeii and artists' illustrations depicting daily life in the city. Encourage students to use these pictures to help them imagine what life in Pompeii was like. **learning modality: verbal**

Including All Students

Write the term *pyroclastic* on the board, and draw a line between the two word parts. Choose volunteers to find the meaning of each part in a dictionary. *(pyro: "fire"; clastic: "made of fragments")* Ask: **Why is pyroclastic a good word for a volcanic explosion?** *(The lava is fiery and is broken into pieces.)* **learning modality: verbal**

Figure 8 Mount St. Helens erupted at 8:30 A.M. on May 18, 1980. **A.** A large bulge that had formed on the north side of the mountain crashed downward.

B. As the mountainside collapsed, bottled up gas and magma inside began to escape.

Social Studies
CONNECTION

In A.D. 79, Mount Vesuvius in Italy erupted. A thick layer of ash from Vesuvius buried the Roman city of Pompeii, which lay between the volcano and the Mediterranean Sea. Beginning in the 1700s, about half of the buried city was dug out, and we now know the following: Pompeii was a walled city with shops, homes, paved streets, a forum (or public square), temples, and public baths. Perhaps 20,000 people lived there.

In Your Journal

Research Pompeii to find out what scientists have learned about daily life in the city. Write a paragraph summarizing your findings.

Explosive Eruptions If its magma is thick and sticky, a volcano erupts explosively. The thick magma does not flow out of the crater and down the mountain. Instead, it slowly builds up in the volcano's pipe, plugging it like a cork in a bottle. Dissolved gases cannot escape from the thick magma. The trapped gases build up pressure until they explode. The erupting gases push the magma out of the volcano with incredible force.

The explosion breaks the lava into fragments that quickly cool and harden into pieces of different sizes. The smallest pieces are volcanic ash—fine, rocky particles as small as a grain of sand. Cinders are pebble-sized particles. Larger pieces, called bombs, may range from the size of a baseball to the size of a car. A **pyroclastic flow** (py roh KLAS tik) occurs when an explosive eruption hurls out ash, cinders, and bombs as well as gases.

Look at Figure 8 to see the 1980 eruption of Mount St. Helens in the state of Washington. It was one of the most violent explosive eruptions that has ever occurred in the United States.

☑ *Checkpoint* **What causes an explosive eruption?**

Stages of a Volcano

The activity of a volcano may last from less than a decade to more than 10 million years. Most long-lived volcanoes, however, do not erupt continuously. Geologists often describe volcanoes with terms usually reserved for living things, such as sleeping, awakening, alive, and dead. An **active,** or live, volcano is one that is erupting or has shown signs that it may erupt in the near future. A **dormant,** or sleeping, volcano is like a sleeping bear. Scientists expect a dormant volcano to awaken in the future and become active. However, there may be thousands of years between eruptions. An **extinct,** or dead, volcano is unlikely to erupt again.

430

Background

Facts and Figures The explosive eruption of Mount St. Helens on May 18, 1980, destroyed the north face of the mountain and lowered its overall elevation by about 400 m. The eruption flattened stands of timber like matchsticks, leaving the trees stripped of branches. About 60 people died—in many cases as a result of the heat, ash, and gases of the pyroclastic flow that accompanied the eruption.

Mount St. Helens is one of 15 major volcanoes in the Cascade Range. Eight volcanoes in this group have erupted within the last several centuries. For example, Mount St. Helens was active as recently as 1857. Scientists think that several other volcanoes in the Cascade Range could also become active again, including Mount Baker, Mount Rainier, Mount Hood, Mount Shasta, and Lassen Peak.

C. Shattered rock and pyroclastic flows blasted out sideways from the volcano.

D. The blast traveled outward, leveling the surrounding forest and causing mudflows that affected a wide area around the volcano.

Other Types of Volcanic Activity

Hot springs and geysers are two examples of volcanic activity that do not involve the eruption of lava. These features may occur in any volcanic area—even around an extinct volcano.

A **hot spring** forms when groundwater heated by a nearby body of magma rises to the surface and collects in a natural pool. (Groundwater is water that has seeped into the spaces among rocks deep beneath Earth's surface.) Water from hot springs may contain dissolved gases and other substances from deep within Earth.

Sometimes, rising hot water and steam become trapped underground in a narrow crack. Pressure builds until the mixture suddenly sprays above the surface as a geyser. A **geyser** (GY zur) is a fountain of water and steam that erupts from the ground.

INTEGRATING TECHNOLOGY In volcanic areas, water heated by magma can provide a clean, reliable energy source called **geothermal energy.** The people of Reykjavik, Iceland, pipe this hot water directly into their homes for warmth. Geothermal energy is also a source of electricity in Iceland as well as northern California and New Zealand. Steam from deep underground is piped into turbines. Inside a turbine, the steam spins a wheel in the same way that blowing on a pinwheel makes the pinwheel turn. The moving wheel in the turbine turns a generator that changes the energy of motion into electrical energy.

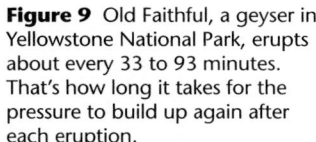

Figure 9 Old Faithful, a geyser in Yellowstone National Park, erupts about every 33 to 93 minutes. That's how long it takes for the pressure to build up again after each eruption.

431

Answers to Self-Assessment

☑ *Checkpoint*

Magma that is thick and sticky causes a volcano to erupt explosively.

431

Monitoring Volcanoes

Building Inquiry Skills: Applying Concepts

Prompt students to recall what they learned about tiltmeters and laser-ranging devices in the previous chapter by asking: **How are changes in the land surface along a fault detected with a tiltmeter? A laser-ranging device?** (*A tiltmeter uses two connected liquid-filled bulbs to measure the rise or fall of land surfaces along a fault. A laser-ranging device placed on one side of a fault bounces a laser beam off a reflector on the other side to measure changes in distance. If students have difficulty recalling this information, let them look back at pages 411–412.*) Then ask: **How do you think each of these instruments is used to detect signs of a possible volcanic eruption?** (*Accept all reasonable responses. Example: Both devices could be set up on the side of a volcanic mountain to detect bulges caused by magma rising to the surface.*) **learning modality: logical/mathematical**

SCIENCE & History

Focus students' attention on the introductory statement that volcanic eruptions "have greatly affected the land and the people around them." Ask: **How do you think each of these eruptions affected the people in the area?** (*Some eruptions killed people; people lost their homes and possessions; they may have had to evacuate the area; crops were destroyed when fields were covered with ash and other volcanic materials; and so forth.*)

In Your Journal Provide age-appropriate resource books so students can research these eruptions. Also remind students that if their group has chosen one of these volcanoes as the subject of its chapter project, they can add this research to their report. **learning modality: verbal**

Monitoring Volcanoes

Geologists have been somewhat more successful in predicting volcanic eruptions than in predicting earthquakes. Changes in and around a volcano usually give warning a short time before the volcano erupts. Geologists use tiltmeters, laser-ranging devices, and other instruments to detect slight surface changes in elevation and tilt caused by magma moving underground. Geologists monitor the local magnetic field, water level in a volcano's crater lake, and any gases escaping from a volcano. They take the temperature of underground water to see if it is getting hotter—a sign that magma may be nearing the surface.

Geologists also monitor the many small earthquakes that occur in the area around a volcano before an eruption.

SCIENCE & History

The Power of Volcanoes

Within the last 150 years, major volcanic eruptions have greatly affected the land and people around them.

1883 Indonesia
The violent eruption of Krakatau volcano threw 18 cubic kilometers of ash skyward. The blast was heard 5,000 kilometers away.

1912 Alaska, U.S.A.
Today, a river in Alaska cuts through the thick layer of volcanic ash from the eruption of Mount Katmai. Mount Katmai blasted out almost as much ash as Krakatau.

1850

1900

1902 Martinique
Mount Pelée, a Caribbean volcano, spewed out a burning cloud of hot gas and pyroclastic flows. Within two minutes of the eruption, the cloud had killed the 29,000 residents of St. Pierre, a city on the volcano's flank. Only two people survived.

432

Background

Facts and Figures Of the six volcanic eruptions presented in the time line on these pages, two—Krakatau in 1883 and Mount Pelée in 1902—are among the five most destructive volcanic eruptions since 1700. The remaining three are Unzen, Japan, in 1792; Mt. Tambora, Indonesia, in 1815; and Nevada del Ruiz, Colombia, in 1985.

As evidence of a volcano's varying hazards, 80,000 of the 92,000 people killed as a result of the 1815 Mt. Tambora eruption died not from the volcanic activity itself but from starvation afterward. Ninety percent of Krakatau's 36,000 victims were killed by a tsunami. Pyroclastic flows claimed about 30,000 lives in the Mount Pelée eruption. Mudflows killed about 25,000 people in the Nevada del Ruiz eruption. Clearly, lava flows and collapsing cones are not the only volcanic hazards.

The movement of magma into the magma chamber and through the volcano's pipe triggers these quakes.

All these data help geologists predict that an eruption is about to occur. But geologists cannot be certain about the type of eruption or how powerful it will be.

Volcano Hazards

The time between volcanic eruptions may span hundreds of years. So people living near a dormant volcano may be unaware of the danger. Before 1980, the people who lived, worked, and vacationed in the region around Mount St. Helens viewed it as a peaceful mountain. Few imagined the destruction the volcano would bring when it awakened from its 123-year slumber.

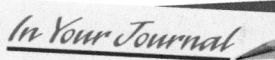

In Your Journal

People have written eye-witness accounts of famous volcanic eruptions. Research one of the eruptions in the time line. Then write a letter describing what someone observing the eruption might have seen.

1991 Philippines

Mount Pinatubo was dormant for hundreds of years before erupting in June 1991. Pinatubo spewed out huge quantities of ash that rose high into the atmosphere and also buried the surrounding countryside.

1950   **2000**

1980 Washington, U.S.A.

When Mount St. Helens exploded, it blasted one cubic kilometer of rock fragments and volcanic material skyward. The eruption was not unexpected. For months, geologists had monitored releases of ash, small earthquakes, and a bulge on the mountain caused by the buildup of magma inside.

1995 Montserrat

For more than two years, eruptions of volcanic ash from the Soufrière Hills volcano poured down on this small Caribbean island. Geologists anxiously waited for the eruption to run its course, not knowing whether it would end in a huge explosion.

Chapter 13   **433**

433

Section 2 Review Answers

1. Magma deep underground flows upward through cracks in rock. As the magma rises, the pressure decreases, and dissolved gases in the magma begin to separate out and form bubbles. When an opening develops in weak rock on the surface, the gases and magma erupt out of the volcano.

2. Quiet eruptions occur if the magma is thin and runny. The gases dissolved in the magma bubble out gently, and the lava oozes from the vent. Explosive eruptions occur if the magma is thick and sticky. The magma slowly collects in the volcano's neck and plugs it, trapping the gases. Pressure builds up until the gases explode, pushing the magma out of the volcano with great force.

3. Hazards include lava flows; hot, burning clouds of gas; cinders and bombs; volcanic ash; and landslides and mudflows. Accept other reasonable answers as well.

4. Pahoehoe; produced by thin lava. The speed is high, and smooth ripples are characteristic of pahoehoe.

Science at Home

Materials *2 cups, cold water, hot water, candle, matches*

You may want to let students do this activity in class before they present it at home. (CAUTION: Handle the lighted candle yourself; do not let students do so.) The wax in cold water will solidify more quickly and form a more rounded shape than the wax in hot water, with a greater temperature difference between the two cups producing more dramatic results. The model shows that quickly cooling lava forms distinct "lumps," whereas slowly cooling lava continues to spread out and forms a flatter mass.

Performance Assessment

Drawing Have each student draw and label a sketch to identify the parts of a volcano and describe what happens underground to cause an eruption.

Figure 10 **A.** Mudflows were one of the hazards of Mt. Pinatubo's 1991 eruption. **B.** People around Mt. Pinatubo wore masks to protect themselves from breathing volcanic ash.

Although quiet eruptions and explosive eruptions involve different volcano hazards, both types of eruption can cause damage far from the crater's rim. During a quiet eruption, lava flows pour from vents, setting fire to and then burying everything in their path. During an explosive eruption, a volcano can belch out hot, burning clouds of volcanic gases as well as cinders and bombs.

Volcanic ash can bury entire towns, damage crops, and clog car engines. If it becomes wet, the heavy ash can cause roofs to collapse. If a jet plane sucks ash into its engine, the engine may stall. Eruptions can also cause landslides and avalanches of mud, melted snow, and rock. Figure 10 shows some effects of mud and ash from Mount Pinatubo's eruption. When Mount St. Helens erupted, gigantic mudflows carried ash, trees, and rock fragments 29 kilometers down the nearby Toutle River.

Section 2 Review

1. What are the stages that lead up to a volcanic eruption?
2. Compare and contrast quiet and explosive eruptions.
3. Describe some of the hazards posed by volcanoes.
4. **Thinking Critically** **Drawing Conclusions** A geologist times a passing lava flow at 15 kilometers per hour. The geologist also sees that lava near the edge of the flow is forming smooth-looking ripples as it hardens. What type of lava is this? What type of magma produced it? Explain your conclusions.

Science at Home

Place cold water in one cup and hot tap water in another. **CAUTION:** Handle the cup containing the hot water carefully to avoid spilling. Ask members of your family to predict what will happen when some melted candle wax drops into each cup of water. Have an adult family member drip melted wax from a candle into each cup. Explain how this models what happens when lava cools quickly or more slowly.

434

Program Resources

◆ **Unit 4 Resources** 13-2 Review and Reinforce, p. 75; 13-2 Enrich, p. 76

DISCOVER ···································· ACTIVITY

How Can Volcanic Activity Change Earth's Surface?

1. Use tape to secure the neck of a balloon over one end of a straw.
2. Place the balloon in the center of a box with the straw protruding.
3. Partially inflate the balloon.
4. Put damp sand on top of the balloon until it is covered.
5. Slowly inflate the balloon more. Observe what happens to the surface of the sand.

Think It Over
Making Models This activity models one of the ways in which volcanic activity can cause a mountain to form. What do you think the sand represents? What does the balloon represent?

Volcanoes have created some of Earth's most spectacular landforms. For example, the perfect volcanic cone of Mt. Fuji in Japan and the majestic profile of snow-capped Mt. Kilimanjaro rising above the grasslands of East Africa are famous around the world.

Some volcanic landforms arise when lava flows build up mountains and plateaus on Earth's surface. Other volcanic landforms are the result of the buildup of magma beneath the surface.

Landforms From Lava and Ash

Rock and other materials formed from lava create a variety of landforms including shield volcanoes, composite volcanoes, cinder cone volcanoes, and lava plateaus. Look at *Exploring Volcanic Mountains* on page 437 to see the similarities and differences among these features.

◀ Mt. Fuji, Japan

Chapter 13 **435**

GUIDE FOR READING

◆ What landforms does lava create on Earth's surface?

◆ How does magma that hardens beneath the surface create landforms?

Reading Tip As you read, make a table comparing volcanic landforms. Include what formed each landform—lava, ash, or magma—as well as its characteristics.

READING STRATEGIES

Reading Tip Columns in students' tables should have the heads *Landform, Shape,* and *How It Forms.* Under *Landform,* students should list shield volcanoes, cinder cone volcanoes, composite volcanoes, lava plateaus, calderas, volcanic necks, dikes, sills, batholiths, and dome mountains.

Program Resources

◆ **Unit 4 Resources** 13-3 Lesson Plan, p. 77; 13-3 Section Summary, p. 78
◆ **Guided Reading and Study Workbook** Section 13-3

SECTION
3 Volcanic Landforms

Objectives

After completing the lesson, students will be able to
◆ identify landforms that lava and other volcanic materials create on Earth's surface;
◆ explain how magma that hardens beneath the surface creates landforms.

Key Terms shield volcano, cinder cone, composite volcano, caldera, volcanic neck, dike, sill, batholith

1 Engage/Explore

Activating Prior Knowledge

Ask students: **What shape is a volcano?** Choose several volunteers to come to the board and draw what they think a volcano looks like. (*Students will most likely draw cone-shaped mountains.*) **Are all volcanoes shaped like this?** (*Accept all responses without comment at this time.*)

········· DISCOVER ·········

Skills Focus making models

Materials *tape, balloon, straw, box, damp sand*
Time 10–15 minutes
Tips Make sure the box is large enough for the balloon to fit when it is fully inflated. Tell students to inflate the balloon slowly in Step 5.
Expected Outcome As the balloon is inflated, a dome will form in the sand.
Think It Over The sand represents Earth's crust. The balloon represents a filling magma chamber.

2 Facilitate

Landforms From Lava and Ash

Building Inquiry Skills: Classifying

Suggest that students look for photographs of the volcanoes mentioned but not pictured on these pages and of other volcanoes that exemplify the three mountain shapes. Point out to students that Kilauea—pictured on pages 418–419 and whose gentle eruptions they learned about on page 429—is a shield volcano. Encourage students to photocopy the pictures they find, label each one to identify the volcano type, and then use the pictures to create a bulletin board display, with all the pictures showing the same type of volcano grouped together.
learning modality: visual

Addressing Naive Conceptions

Students may think that the terms *crater* and *caldera* are used interchangeably to refer to the same structure. Help them differentiate between the two by asking: **What is a crater?** *(A bowl-shaped area around a volcano's vent; if students cannot recall this information, direct their attention back to the visual essay on page 427.)* **What happens to change a crater into a caldera?** *(The vent and magma chamber empty during an eruption, and the top of the volcano collapses inward.)*
limited English proficiency

Shield Volcanoes At some places on Earth's surface, thin layers of lava pour out of a vent and harden on top of previous layers. Such lava flows gradually build a wide, gently sloping mountain called a **shield volcano.** Shield volcanoes rising from a hot spot on the ocean floor created the Hawaiian Islands.

Cinder Cone Volcanoes A volcano can also be a **cinder cone,** a steep, cone-shaped hill or mountain. If a volcano's lava is thick and stiff, it may produce ash, cinders, and bombs. These materials pile up around the vent in a steep, cone-shaped pile. For example, Paricutín in Mexico erupted in 1943 in a farmer's cornfield. The volcano built up a cinder cone about 400 meters high.

Composite Volcanoes Sometimes, lava flows alternate with explosive eruptions of ash, cinder, and bombs. The result is a composite volcano. **Composite volcanoes** are tall, cone-shaped mountains in which layers of lava alternate with layers of ash. Examples of composite volcanoes include Mount Fuji in Japan and Mount St. Helens in Washington state.

Lava Plateaus Instead of forming mountains, some eruptions of lava form high, level areas called lava plateaus. First, lava flows out of several long cracks in an area. The thin, runny lava travels far before cooling and solidifying. Again and again, floods of lava flow on top of earlier floods. After millions of years, these layers of lava can form high plateaus. One example is the Columbia Plateau, which covers parts of Washington, Oregon, and Idaho.

Figure 11 Crater Lake in Oregon fills the caldera formed after an eruption that destroyed the top 2,000 meters of Mount Mazama nearly 7,000 years ago.
Developing Hypotheses Develop a hypothesis to explain the formation of Wizard Island, the small island in Crater Lake.

Calderas Enormous eruptions may empty the main vent and the magma chamber beneath a volcano. The mountain becomes a hollow shell. With nothing to support it, the top of the mountain collapses inward. The huge hole left by the collapse of a volcanic mountain is called a **caldera** (kal DAIR uh). The hole is filled with the pieces of the volcano that have fallen inward, as well as some lava and ash. In Figure 11 you can see one of the world's largest calderas.

☑ *Checkpoint* *What are the three types of volcanic mountains?*

Background

Facts and Figures Shield volcanoes derive their name from the shape of a warrior's shield. Over roughly one million years, five shield volcanoes, including Mauna Loa, slowly built up the island of Hawaii. Rising about 5,000 meters from the ocean floor, and another 4,000 meters above sea level, Mauna Loa and its companion Mauna Kea, overall, are higher than Mount Everest. Shield volcanoes also formed Midway Island and the Galapagos Islands.

Composite volcanoes, also called stratovolcanoes because of their layering, produce the most violent eruptions. Most active composite volcanoes are located in the Ring of Fire.

Cinder cones are small in comparison with shield volcanoes and composite volcanoes. They often form on or near larger volcanoes. Because loose volcanic cinders remain stable on a slope of 30–40 degrees, cinder cones have very steep slopes.

EXPLORING Volcanic Mountains

Volcanic activity is responsible for building up much of Earth's surface. Lava from volcanoes cools and hardens into three types of mountains.

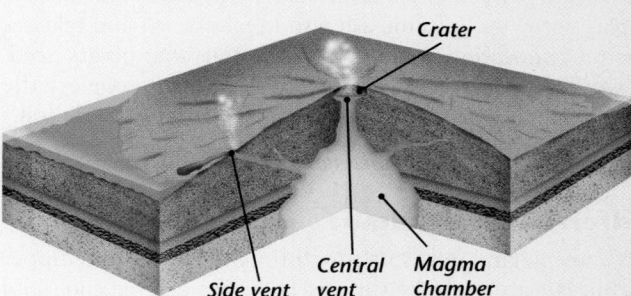

Crater

Side vent Central vent Magma chamber

Shield Volcano
Repeated lava flows during quiet eruptions gradually build up a broad, gently sloping volcanic mountain known as a shield volcano.

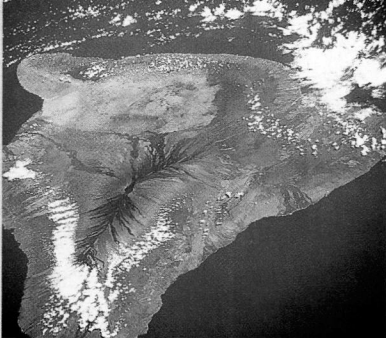

▲ Mauna Loa is one of the shield volcanoes that built the island Hawaii.

Cinder Cone Volcano
When cinders erupt explosively from a volcanic vent, they pile up around the vent, forming a cone-shaped hill called a cinder cone.

▲ Sunset Crater is an extinct cinder cone in Arizona.

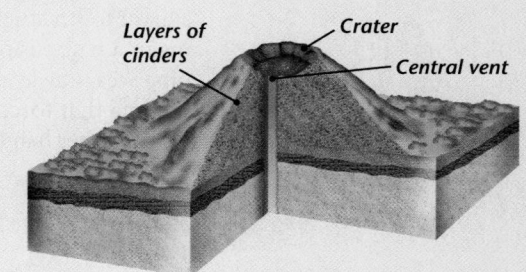

Layers of cinders Crater Central vent

Composite Volcano
Layers of lava alternate with layers of ash, cinders, and bombs in a composite volcano, which has both quiet and explosive eruptions.

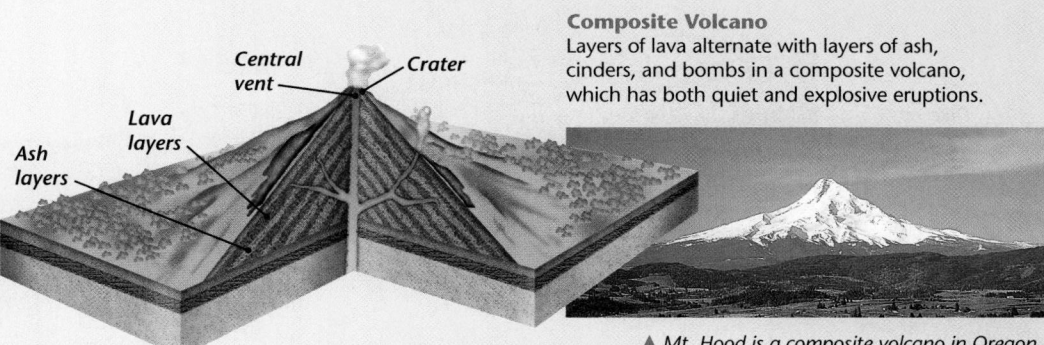

Central vent Crater Lava layers Ash layers

▲ Mt. Hood is a composite volcano in Oregon.

EXPLORING

Volcanic Mountains

After students have examined the visual essay, ask: **How do the shapes of these mountains differ?** *(The cinder cone volcano is very steep-sided. The composite volcano is also steep-sided but has a wider base. The shield volcano has a very gradual slope and is not as high as the other two.)* **What causes these differences?** *(The type of material that erupts from each volcano; pyroclastic materials—ash, cinders, and bombs— seem to create a steeper slope.)* **learning modality: visual**

Inquiry Challenge

Materials *clay, fine sand, coarse sand, small pebbles, plaster of Paris or wheat paste*
Time 30 minutes

Challenge small groups to design a model that shows how a composite volcano builds up in alternating layers over time. Then allow groups to build the models with materials you provide or materials of their own choice. *(Beginning with a small hill made of clay as the "core," students could add a layer of mixed fine sand, coarse sand, and pebbles to represent ash, cinder, and bombs, then pour plaster of Paris or wheat paste over it to represent lava and let it harden, and repeat these layers alternately to build up a composite cone.)* **cooperative learning**

Answers to Self-Assessment

Caption Question

Figure 11 Wizard Island is a small cinder cone that formed after the collapse of Mount Mazama. Accept all reasonable hypotheses.

✓ Checkpoint

The three types of volcanic mountains are shield volcanoes, cinder cone volcanoes, and composite volcanoes.

Ongoing Assessment

Drawing Have each student draw cross-sectional views of the three volcano types, label each with its name, and add a brief explanation of how it is formed.

 Students could save their sketches in their portfolios.

Soils from Lava and Ash

Integrating Environmental Science

Obtain (or ask students to find) photographs of the area around Mount St. Helens soon after the 1980 eruption and at intervals in the years afterward. (A good source is *Mount St. Helens, Eruption and Recovery of a Volcano* by Rob Carson, Sasquatch Books, 1990.) Let students examine the photographs to find evidence of regrowth in the area—first of small, scattered "settler" plants, then of wider areas of larger plants and saplings, and finally stands of maturing trees. Ask: **Where do you think the new plants came from?** *(Accept all reasonable answers. Examples: Seeds blew in from other, undamaged areas. Tree roots that were not destroyed grew new sprouts.)* **Were plants the only organisms that returned to the area? Why?** *(No, animals returned too because the regrowth provided food, shelter, and the like.)* **learning modality: visual**

Landforms from Magma

Building Inquiry Skills: Inferring

Ask students: **If magma is rising through the upper crust, why would it fail to reach the surface?** *(It might become trapped under a solid rock layer, or there might not be enough pressure to keep forcing the magma up. Accept other reasonable responses.)* **learning modality: logical/mathematical**

Including All Students

After students have read about domes, ask: **Where have you seen a bulging landform like this before?** *(In the Discover activity at the beginning of this section, when the inflated balloon made the sand bulge upward)* Review with students that the balloon in the model represented rising magma and the sand represented layers of rock in the upper crust. **learning modality: visual**

Soils from Lava and Ash

 INTEGRATING ENVIRONMENTAL SCIENCE The lava, ash, and cinders that erupt from a volcano are initially barren. Over time, however, the hard surface of the lava flow breaks down to form soil. As soil develops, plants are able to grow. Some volcanic soils are among the richest soils in the world. Saying that soil is rich means that it's fertile, or able to support plant growth. Volcanic ash also breaks down and releases potassium, phosphorus, and other materials that plants need. Why would anyone live near an active volcano? People settle close to volcanoes to take advantage of the fertile volcanic soil.

☑ *Checkpoint* *How does volcanic soil form?*

Landforms from Magma

Sometimes magma forces its way through cracks in the upper crust, but fails to reach the surface. There the magma cools and hardens into rock. Or the forces that wear away Earth's surface—such as flowing water, ice, or wind—may strip away the layers of rock above the magma and finally expose it. **Features formed by magma include volcanic necks, dikes, and sills, as well as batholiths and dome mountains.**

Volcanic Necks, Dikes, and Sills A volcanic neck looks like a giant tooth stuck in the ground. A **volcanic neck** forms when magma hardens in a volcano's pipe. The softer rock around the pipe wears away, exposing the hard rock of the volcanic neck. Magma that forces itself across rock layers hardens into a **dike.** On the other hand, when magma squeezes between layers of rock, it forms a **sill.**

Figure 12 Magma that hardens beneath the surface may form volcanic necks, dikes, and sills. *Compare and Contrast What is the difference between a dike and a sill?*

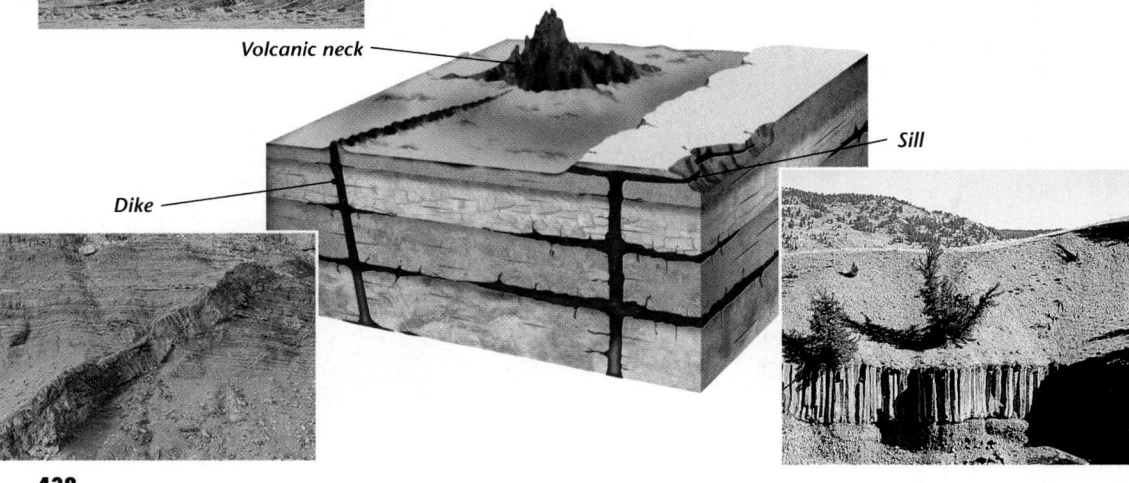

Volcanic neck

Sill

Dike

Background

Facts and Figures Like all landforms, volcanic mountains are subjected to weathering and erosion. Because they are composed of loose materials, cinder cones erode easily. Thus, cinder cones are most apt to produce volcanic necks.

As erosion continues over millions of years, the looser materials surrounding the hardened magma in the pipe are worn away,

leaving the more-resistant rock standing above the surrounding land long after the cone has disappeared.

One example of a volcanic neck is Ship Rock in New Mexico, shown in Figure 12. Ship Rock stands about 420 m high. Many volcanic necks dot the deserts of the American Southwest. In time, even these necks will be worn away.

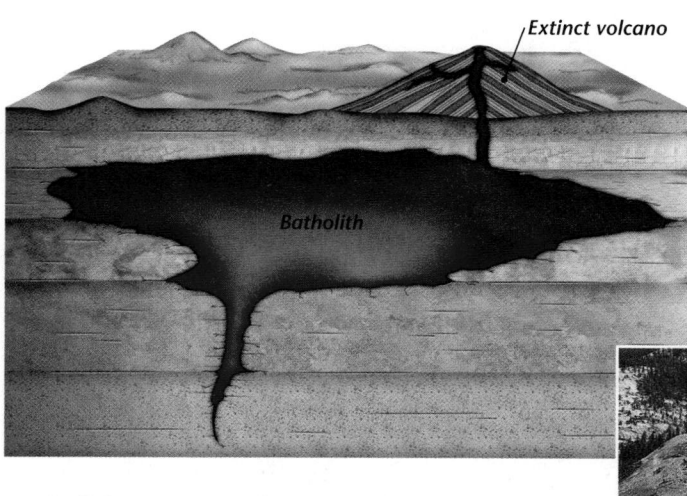
Extinct volcano

Figure 13 A batholith forms when magma cools inside the crust. One of the largest batholiths in North America forms the core of the Sierra Nevada mountains in California. These mountains in Yosemite National Park are part of that granite batholith.

Batholith

Batholiths Large rock masses called batholiths form the core of many mountain ranges. A **batholith** (BATH uh lith) is a mass of rock formed when a large body of magma cools inside the crust. The diagram in Figure 13 shows how a batholith looks when it forms. The photograph shows how it looks when the layers of rock above it have worn away.

Dome Mountains Other, smaller bodies of magma can create dome mountains. A dome mountain forms when rising magma is blocked by horizontal layers of rock. The magma forces the layers of rock to bend upward into a dome shape. Eventually, the rock above the dome mountain wears away, leaving it exposed. This process formed the Black Hills in South Dakota.

 Section 3 Review

1. Describe five landforms formed from lava and ash.
2. Describe the process that creates a lava plateau.
3. What features form as a result of magma hardening beneath Earth's surface?
4. Describe how a dome mountain can eventually form out of magma that hardened beneath Earth's surface.
5. **Thinking Critically** **Relating Cause and Effect** Explain the formation of a volcanic landform that can result when a volcano uses up the magma in its magma chamber.

Check Your Progress

CHAPTER PROJECT 13

By now you should have collected information about what it's like to live in a volcanic region. Do you need to do more research? Now begin to plan your presentation. One way to plan a presentation is to prepare storyboards. In a storyboard, you sketch each major step in the presentation on a separate sheet of paper. Decide who in your group is presenting each portion.

Chapter 13 **439**

Program Resources

◆ **Unit 4 Resources** 13-3 Review and Reinforce, p. 79; 13-3 Enrich, p. 80

Media and Technology

 Concept Videotape Library
Adventures, Tape 3, "Flying Over America"

Answers to Self-Assessment

Caption Question

Figure 12 A dike cuts across rock layers while a sill squeezes between rock layers.

3 **Assess**

Section 3 Review Answers

1. Students should describe shield volcanoes, cinder cone volcanoes, composite volcanoes, lava plateaus, and calderas using information from pages 436–437.
2. Thin, runny lava flows out of several long, horizontal cracks and travels far in all directions before cooling and hardening. Over time, layers of lava build up, forming a plateau.
3. Volcanic necks, dikes, sills, batholiths, dome mountains
4. Magma forces its way upward through cracks in the crust, but overlying rock layers keep the magma from reaching the surface. The magma forces the rock layers to bend upward into a dome shape. When the rock layers wear away, the dome is exposed.
5. A huge eruption can empty a volcano's magma chamber. Without magma to support it, the top of the mountain collapses inward, forming a caldera.

Check Your Progress

CHAPTER PROJECT 13

Consult with each group to determine whether the members were able to find all the information that they want to include in their documentary. If not, suggest or provide additional source materials. Discuss the storyboarding technique with the entire class to make sure each group knows what to do. Instruct students to include in their storyboards notes about the media materials they plan to use. Review each group's storyboard to make sure it includes all the required elements and to provide any help that students may need in organizing the information they have collected.

Performance Assessment

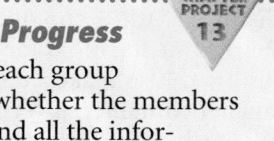

Oral Presentation Call on students to name one of the landforms discussed in this section and explain how it is formed.

Gelatin Volcanoes

Preparing for Inquiry

Key Concept Magma inside a volcano generally flows vertically to form dikes.

Skills Objectives Students will be able to
- develop a hypothesis about how magma flows inside a volcano;
- make a model volcano to test their hypothesis;
- observe how "magma" flows inside their model.

Time 40 minutes

Advance Planning

Gelatin molds: At least five hours before students will do this lab, make a gelatin mold for each student group. You can use bowls ranging from $2\frac{1}{2}$ cups to 2 quarts in capacity. For a $2\frac{1}{2}$-cup bowl (such as a plastic margarine container), mix one 7-oz envelope of unflavored gelatin with $\frac{1}{2}$ cup of room-temperature water. Add $1\frac{1}{2}$ cups of boiling water and stir until the gelatin is completely dissolved. Add $\frac{1}{3}$ cup of cold water. Refrigerate the mold for 3–5 hours or until set. Also make a test mold in a smaller container. After 3 hours, check the hardness of the test mold by removing it from its container. If it is not completely set, refrigerate the large molds for at least another 2 hours. You may want to practice removing one mold from its bowl beforehand to make sure you can demonstrate the technique successfully to the class.

Pizza pan: Use an aluminum pizza pan with holes punched in it with a nail at 2.5-cm intervals. Drive the nail *downward* through the tray so the upper surface stays smooth and the gelatin mold will not snag on the holes' edges.

Syringe: Use plastic bird-feeding syringes, which will pass through the holes in the pizza pan and pierce the gelatin by at least 1 cm.

Layered volcano (Design an Experiment): Fill a bowl only half full with gelatin solution, and set aside the rest at room temper-ature. Add the second layer to the bowl after the first layer has been refrigerated for two hours.

Gelatin Volcanoes

Does the magma inside a volcano move along fractures, or through tubes or pipes? How does the eruption of magma create features such as dikes and sills? You can use a gelatin volcano model and red-colored liquid "magma" to find answers to these questions.

Problem

How does magma move inside a volcano?

Skills Focus

developing hypotheses, making models, observing

Materials

plastic cup
tray or shallow pan
plastic knife
aluminum pizza pan with holes punched at 2.5-cm intervals
unflavored gelatin mold in bowl
red food coloring and water
plastic syringe, 10 cc
3 small cardboard oatmeal boxes
rubber gloves
unlined paper

Procedure

1. Before magma erupts as lava, how does it travel up from underground magma chambers? Record your hypothesis.
2. Remove the gelatin from the refrigerator. Loosen the gelatin from its container by briefly placing the container of gelatin in a larger bowl of hot water.
3. Place the pizza pan over the gelatin so the mold is near the center of the pizza pan. While holding the pizza pan against the top of the mold, carefully turn the mold and the pizza pan upside down.
4. Carefully lift the bowl off the gelatin mold to create a gelatin volcano.
5. Place the pizza pan with the gelatin mold on top of the oatmeal boxes as shown in the photograph.
6. Fill the syringe with the red water ("magma"). Remove air bubbles from the syringe by holding it upright and squirting out a small amount of water.
7. Insert the tip of the syringe through a hole in the pizza pan near the center of the gelatin volcano. Inject the magma into the gelatin very slowly. Observe what happens to the magma.
8. Repeat steps 6 and 7 as many times as possible. Observe the movement of the magma each time. Note any differences in the direction the magma takes when the syringe is inserted into different parts of the gelatin volcano. Record your observations.
9. Look down on your gelatin volcano from above. Make a sketch of the positions and shapes of the magma bodies. Label your drawing "Top View."
10. Carefully use a knife to cut your volcano in half. Separate the pieces and examine the cut surfaces for traces of the magma bodies.
11. Sketch the positions and shapes of the magma bodies on one of the cut faces. Label your drawing "Cross Section."

Alternative Materials Instead of a pizza pan, each group could use a pegboard square. Use pegboard with holes 5 mm in diameter. Cut the pegboard into squares about 10 cm wider than the tops of the bowls.

Guiding Inquiry

Invitation Ask: **What are dikes and sills made of?** (*Hardened magma*) **What is the major difference between a dike and a sill?** (*Dikes are vertical; sills are horizontal.*)

Introducing the Procedure

Have students read the entire procedure and examine the picture of the lab setup. Ask if they have any questions before they begin.

Troubleshooting the Experiment

- Demonstrate the mold-removal process described in steps 2–5.
- Have students wear rubber gloves in steps 6–8 to keep their hands from being stained by the food coloring.
- In Step 6, have students lightly tap the

Analyze and Conclude

1. Describe how the magma moved through your model. Did the magma move straight up through the center of your model volcano or did it branch off in places? Explain why you think the magma moved in this way.

2. What knowledge or experience did you use to develop your hypothesis? How did the actual movement compare with your hypothesis?

3. Were there differences in the direction the magma flowed when the syringe was inserted in different parts of the gelatin volcano?

4. **Apply** How does what you observed in your model compare to the way magma moves through real volcanoes?

Design an Experiment

Plan to repeat the experiment using a mold made of two layers of gelatin. Before injecting the magma, predict what effect the layering will have on magma movement. Record your observations to determine if your hypothesis was correct. What volcanic feature is produced by this version of the model? Can you think of other volcanic features that you could model using gelatin layers?

Chapter 13   **441**

syringe before they squirt water out.

◆ Before students begin injecting colored water in Step 7, make sure they have put a tray under the pizza pan to catch any water that drains out of the mold.

◆ If colored water dribbles down the syringe in steps 7 and 8, students can wrap a folded paper towel around it.

◆ In Step 10, make sure students cut the volcano in half *from top to bottom*, not across its diameter.

Expected Outcome

With a slow, steady injection rate, the colored water will create thin, vertical dikes inside the gelatin.

Analyze and Conclude

1. The magma spread vertically from the point of injection into a fan-shaped dike that gradually grew until it broke through the surface of the volcano. With repeated injections, dikes may have branched off into other vertical planes. The magma moved in this way because there was upward pressure on it from the syringe.

2. Answers will vary. Students should base their answers on what they have already learned about how magma flows through a volcano and how dikes are formed in a vertical or near-vertical plane.

3. When injected into the center, the magma flowed radially outward in any direction. When injected near the edge, magma flowed to the closest surface point, following a path of least resistance.

4. The colored water flowed vertically in the direction of least resistance, much like a flow of magma in an actual volcano.

Extending the Inquiry

Design an Experiment Horizontal sills will form along the joint between the layers. Students might also be able to model dome mountains or batholiths.

Safety

Students should wear a lab apron during this lab to protect their clothing from food coloring. Review the safety guidelines in Appendix A.

SECTION 4 Volcanoes in the Solar System

Objectives

After completing the lesson, students will be able to

◆ explain how volcanoes on Mars and Venus compare with volcanoes on Earth;

◆ describe the volcanic activity found on the moons of Jupiter and Neptune.

1 Engage/Explore

Activating Prior Knowledge

Ask: **What are the names of the planets in our solar system in order from the one closest to the sun to the one farthest away?** *(Mercury, Venus, Earth, Mars, Jupiter, Saturn, Uranus, Neptune, Pluto; if students cannot recall all the names in their correct order, teach them the following mnemonic device: My Very Easy Method: Just Stand Under North Pole.)*

•••••• DISCOVER ••••••

Skills Focus posing questions

Time 5 minutes

Tips Suggest that students compare these photographs to other photographs in this chapter showing volcanic activity.

Expected Outcome Accept all plausible answers when students speculate about the nature of the cloud in the top photo. Clearly, something is erupting into Io's atmosphere. In the bottom photo, some sort of material seems to have erupted from inside Io and flowed across its surface, much like a lava flow on Earth. Volcanoes on Io erupt molten sulfur.

Think It Over Students' questions will vary. *Examples:* What kind of material is erupting in the top photo? What material formed the riverlike flows in the bottom photo? Does the location in the top photo show repeated eruptions over time? Are more flows added to the location in the bottom photo?

442

SECTION 4 Volcanoes in the Solar System

DISCOVER •••••••••••••••••••••••• ACTIVITY

What Forces Shaped the Surface of Io?

Io is a moon of Jupiter. Pictures taken by the *Voyager* space probe as it passed by Io in 1979 show signs of unusual features and activity on Io.

1. Observe the blue cloud rising above the rim of Io in the top photo. What do you think it could be?

2. Look at the feature on Io's surface shown in the bottom photo. What do you think it looks like?

Think It Over

Posing Questions Is the volcanic activity on Io similar to that on Earth? State several questions that you would like to answer in order to find out.

GUIDE FOR READING

◆ How do volcanoes on Mars and Venus compare with volcanoes on Earth?

◆ What volcanic activity is found on the moons of Jupiter and Neptune?

Reading Tip Before you read, preview the headings in the section. Then predict where, besides Earth, volcanoes are found in the solar system.

Earth is not the only body in the solar system to show signs of volcanic activity. Pictures taken by space probes show evidence of past volcanic activity on Mercury, Venus, and Mars. These planets—like Earth and its moon—have rocky crusts. Scientists think these planets once had hot, molten cores. The heat caused volcanic activity. But because these planets are smaller than Earth, their cores have cooled, bringing volcanic activity to an end.

Geologists are eager for information about other planets and moons. By comparing other bodies in the solar system with Earth, geologists can learn more about the processes that have shaped Earth over billions of years.

Earth's Moon

If you looked at the full moon through a telescope you would notice that much of the moon's surface is pockmarked with light-colored craters. Other, darker areas on the moon's surface look unusually smooth. The craters mark where meteorites have smashed into the moon over billions of years. The smooth areas are where lava flowed onto the moon's surface more than three billion years ago.

Figure 14 The dark areas on the moon's surface are flat plains made of basalt, a type of rock formed from lava.

READING STRATEGIES

Reading Tip Students will likely list Earth's moon, Venus, Mars, and the moons of other planets. Suggest that students check off each correct prediction as they read. Other than Earth, the names of the planets in our solar system are derived from Greek and Roman mythology. Encourage students to find out who the mythological gods and characters mentioned in this section were. (**Mercury:**

the Roman god of trade and travel, messenger of the gods; **Venus:** *the Roman goddess of love and beauty;* **Mars:** *the Roman god of war;* **Jupiter:** *the supreme Roman god;* **Saturn:** *the Roman god of agriculture, father of Jupiter;* **Uranus:** *a Greek god personifying the sky;* **Neptune:** *the Roman god of the sea;* **Pluto:** *the Roman god of the dead, ruler of the underworld.)*

Volcanoes on Venus

Geologists were excited about the results of the space probe *Magellan's* mission to Venus in 1990. Venus shows signs of widespread volcanic activity that lasted for billions of years. Venus has thousands of volcanoes. There are about 150 large volcanoes measuring between 100 and 600 kilometers across and about half a kilometer high. The largest volcano on Venus, Theia Mons, is 800 kilometers across and 4 kilometers high. Scientists are trying to find evidence that volcanoes on Venus are still active.

Like Earth, Venus has volcanic mountains and other features that are probably made of thin, runny lava. Such lava produces gently sloping shield volcanoes with broad bases, as well as long, riverlike lava flows. One of the lava flows on Venus is more than 6,800 kilometers long!

☑ *Checkpoint* *What type of volcano is most common on Venus?*

Volcanoes on Mars

Mars is a planet with a long history of volcanic activity. However, there are far fewer volcanoes on Mars than on Venus. Volcanoes are found in only a few regions of Mars' surface.

Mars has a variety of volcanic features. **On Mars there are large shield volcanoes similar to those on Venus and Earth, as well as cone-shaped volcanoes and lava flows.** Mars also has lava plains that resemble the lava flows on the moon.

The biggest volcano on Mars is the largest mountain in the solar system. This volcano, Olympus Mons, is a shield volcano similar to Mauna Loa on the island of Hawaii, but much, much bigger! Olympus Mons covers an area as large as Ohio. This huge volcano, shown in Figure 16, is over eight times taller than Theia Mons on Venus.

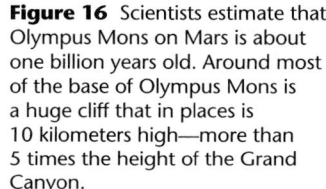

Figure 15 The space probe *Magellan* observed volcanoes on Venus, but no recent or ongoing eruptions.

Figure 16 Scientists estimate that Olympus Mons on Mars is about one billion years old. Around most of the base of Olympus Mons is a huge cliff that in places is 10 kilometers high—more than 5 times the height of the Grand Canyon.

Chapter 13 **443**

Answers to Self-Assessment

☑ *Checkpoint*
Gently sloping shield volcanoes are most common on Venus.

2 Facilitate

Earth's Moon

Using the Visuals: Figure 14

Point out to students that this photograph shows **ACTIVITY** the side of the moon that always faces Earth. Suggest that they take their book outside on the next evening when there is a full moon and compare the photograph with the real moon. Have them sketch what they see. **learning modality: visual**

Volcanoes on Venus

Using the Visuals: Figure 15

Draw students' attention to the caption and ask: **Are the volcanoes on Venus active, dormant, or extinct? How do you know?** *(Either dormant or extinct; Magellan's photographs did not show any recent or ongoing eruptions on the planet.)* **learning modality: logical/mathematical**

Volcanoes on Mars

Building Inquiry Skills: Inferring

Ask students: **If a planet has active volcanoes erupting lava on its surface, what does that tell you about the planet's interior?** *(It must be hot, like Earth's mantle.)* **If a planet shows signs of active volcanoes in the far-distant past but no evidence of recent eruptions, what does that tell you about the planet's interior?** *(It must have cooled so there is no longer any hot magma below the surface.)* **learning modality: logical/mathematical**

Ongoing Assessment

Writing Have each student briefly describe the volcanoes on Venus and Mars.

Volcanoes on Distant Moons

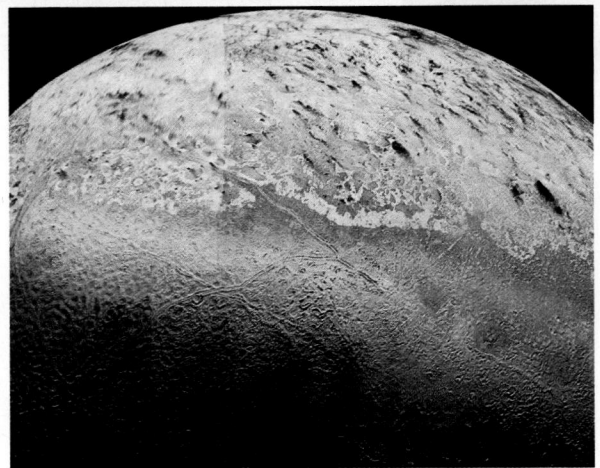

Figure 17 The surface of Neptune's moon Triton has areas covered by frozen "lava lakes" that show where liquid material erupted from inside Triton. *Posing Questions Imagine that you are observing Triton from a spacecraft. What questions would you want to answer about volcanic activity there?*

Scientists estimate that volcanic activity on Mars probably goes back about 3.5 billion years, to about the same time as the volcanic activity on the moon. Martian volcanoes don't seem to be active. Lava flows on Olympus Mons may be more than 100 million years old.

Volcanoes on Distant Moons

Besides Earth, there are only two other bodies in the solar system where volcanic eruptions have been observed: Io, a moon of the planet Jupiter, and Triton, a moon of the planet Neptune. *Voyager 1* photographed eruptions on these moons as it sped past them in 1979. Geologists on Earth were amazed when they saw these pictures. **Io and Triton have volcanic features very different from those on Earth, Mars, and Venus.** On Io, sulfur volcanoes erupt like fountains or spread out like umbrellas above the colorful surface.

The eruptions on Triton involve nitrogen. On Earth, nitrogen is a gas. Triton is so cold, however, that most of the nitrogen there is frozen solid. Scientists hypothesize that Triton's surface, which is made up of frozen water and other materials, absorbs heat from the sun. This heat melts some of the frozen nitrogen underneath Triton's surface. The liquid nitrogen then expands and erupts through the planet's icy crust.

Other moons of Jupiter, Saturn, and Neptune show signs of volcanic activity, but space probes have not observed any eruptions in progress on these moons.

Section 4 Review

1. Describe volcanic features found on Venus and Mars. Do volcanic features on these planets resemble volcanic features on Earth? Explain.
2. How is volcanic activity on the moons of Jupiter and Neptune different from volcanic activity on Earth?
3. What is the largest volcano in the solar system? What type of volcano is it?
4. **Thinking Critically Comparing and Contrasting** How do the volcanoes on Venus compare with the volcanoes on Mars?

Check Your Progress
CHAPTER PROJECT 13

By this time, your group should have planned your documentary and know what materials you will need. Put the finishing touches on your presentation. Make sure any posters, overhead transparencies, or computer art will be easy for your audience to read. If you are using video or audio, make your recordings now. Revise and polish any narrative, rap, or skit. (*Hint:* Check the length of your presentation.)

 SECTION 1 **Volcanoes and Plate Tectonics**

Key Ideas

◆ A volcano is an opening on Earth's surface where magma escapes from the interior. Magma that reaches Earth's surface is called lava.

◆ The constructive force of volcanoes adds new rock to existing land and forms new islands.

◆ Most volcanoes occur near the boundaries of Earth's plates and along the edges of continents, in island arcs, or along mid-ocean ridges.

Key Terms

volcano	lava	island arc
magma	Ring of Fire	hot spot

SECTION 2 **Volcanic Activity**

Key Ideas

◆ An eruption occurs when gases trapped in magma rush through an opening at the Earth's surface, carrying magma with them.

◆ Volcanoes can erupt quietly or explosively, depending on the amount of dissolved gases in the magma and on how thick or runny the magma is.

◆ When magma heats water underground, hot springs and geysers form.

◆ Volcano hazards include pyroclastic flows, avalanches of mud, damage from ash, lava flows, flooding, and deadly gases.

Key Terms

magma chamber	pyroclastic flow
pipe	active
vent	dormant
lava flow	extinct
crater	hot spring
silica	geyser
pahoehoe	geothermal energy
aa	

 SECTION 3 **Volcanic Landforms**

Key Ideas

◆ Lava and other volcanic materials on the surface create shield volcanoes, cinder cones, composite volcanoes, and plateaus.

◆ Magma that hardens beneath the surface creates batholiths, dome mountains, dikes, and sills, which are eventually exposed when the covering rock wears away.

Key Terms

shield volcano	caldera	sill
cinder cone	volcanic neck	batholith
composite volcano	dike	

SECTION 4 **Volcanoes in the Solar System**

INTEGRATING SPACE SCIENCE

Key Ideas

◆ Venus and Mars both have extinct volcanoes similar to volcanoes on Earth.

◆ Spacecraft have photographed volcanic activity on moons of Jupiter and Neptune.

Organizing Information

Concept Map Copy the concept map about types of volcanic mountains onto a separate sheet of paper. Then complete it and add a title. (For more on concept maps, see the Skills Handbook.)

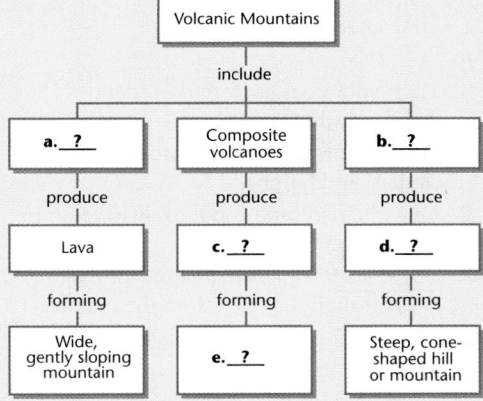

Organizing Information

Concept Map Sample Title: *Volcanic Mountains and Their Characteristics*
a. shield volcano **b.** cinder cone volcano
c. lava flows alternating with explosive eruptions of ash, cinder, and bombs
d. lava that hardens into ash, cinders, and bombs **e.** a tall, cone-shaped mountain

Program Resources

◆ **Unit 4 Resources** Chapter 13 Project Scoring Rubric, p. 68

◆ **Performance Assessment** Chapter 13, pp. 40–42

◆ **Chapter Tests** Chapter 13 Test, pp. 51–54

Media and Technology

 Computer Test Bank
Chapter 13 Test

Reviewing Content

Multiple Choice

1. c 2. d 3. c 4. d 5. c

True or False

6. true 7. lava plateaus or shield volcanoes 8. true 9. true 10. Mars

Checking Concepts

11. A volcanic belt formed by volcanoes that rim the Pacific Ocean

12. The mid-ocean ridge marks a diverging plate boundary, and lava pours out of cracks in the ocean floor.

13. In the middle of plates, often far from plate boundaries

14. The amount of silica in magma helps determine how easily the magma flows. Magma high in silica produces light-colored lava that is too sticky to flow very far and forms rhyolite, pumice, and obsidian. Magma low in silica flows readily and produces dark-colored lava that forms basalt.

15. There are three stages in a volcano's life-cycle. An active volcano is one that has erupted in the recent past and that is likely to erupt in the near future. A dormant volcano is one that is currently inactive, but may someday become active again. An extinct, or dead, volcano is unlikely to erupt again.

16. Hot springs form when groundwater heated by a body of magma rises to the surface and collects in a pool. A geyser forms when rising hot water and steam are trapped underground in a narrow crack until pressure builds and the mixture suddenly sprays to the surface.

17. Aa; forms from cooler, slower-moving lava

18. Lava repeatedly flows out of a wide fissure and hardens to form thin layers, gradually building up a wide, gently sloping mountain.

19. Many small earthquakes can occur in the area around a volcano before it erupts. These quakes are triggered by movement of magma into the magma chamber and through the pipe.

20. Students may base part of their reports on the photographs of the Mount St. Helens eruption on pages 430–431, adding details such as the sound and smell of the eruption and its effects on people, plants, and animals living in the area.

Reviewing Content

Multiple Choice

Choose the letter of the best answer.

1. When two oceanic plates collide, the result may be
   a. volcanoes on the edge of a continent.
   b. a hot spot volcano.
   c. volcanoes in an island arc.
   d. a volcano along the mid-ocean ridge.

2. The force that causes magma to erupt at the surface is provided by
   a. heat.
   b. the shape of the pipe.
   c. geothermal energy.
   d. dissolved gases under pressure.

3. An eruption of thin, fluid lava would most likely be
   a. a cinder-cone eruption.
   b. an explosive eruption.
   c. a quiet eruption.
   d. a pyroclastic eruption.

4. Alternating layers of lava and volcanic ash are found in
   a. dome mountains.
   b. dikes and sills.
   c. shield volcanoes.
   d. composite volcanoes.

5. Which of the following has active volcanoes?
   a. Venus   b. Mars
   c. Triton   d. Earth's moon

True or False

If the statement is true, write true. If it is false, change the underlined word or words to make the statement true.

6. Many volcanoes are found in <u>island arcs</u> that form where two oceanic plates collide.

7. Thin, runny lava usually hardens into <u>ash, cinders, and bombs</u>.

8. An <u>extinct</u> volcano is not likely to erupt in your lifetime.

9. <u>Hot spots</u> form where a plume of magma rises through the crust from the mantle.

10. The volcano Olympus Mons is on <u>Venus</u>.

Checking Concepts

11. What is the Ring of Fire?

12. How does plate tectonics explain the volcanoes that form along the mid-ocean ridge?

13. Where are hot spot volcanoes located in relation to Earth's plates?

14. What effect does silica content have on the characteristics of magma?

15. Describe the three stages in the "life-cycle" of a volcano.

16. How do hot springs and geysers form?

17. While observing a lava flow from a recently active volcano, you notice an area of lava with a rough, chunky surface. What type of lava is this and how does it form?

18. How does a shield volcano form?

19. Why can earthquakes be a warning sign that an eruption is about to happen?

20. **Writing to Learn** Pretend you are a newspaper reporter in 1980. You have been assigned to report on the eruption of Mount St. Helens. Write a news story describing your observations.

Thinking Critically

21. **Applying Concepts** Is a volcanic eruption likely to occur on the east coast of the United States? Explain your answer.

22. **Comparing and Contrasting** Compare the way in which an island arc forms with the way in which a hot spot volcano forms.

23. **Making Generalizations** How might a volcanic eruption affect the area around a volcano, including its plant and animal life?

24. **Relating Cause and Effect** Why doesn't the type of eruption that produces a lava plateau produce a volcanic mountain instead?

25. **Making Generalizations** What is one major difference between volcanic activity on Earth and volcanic activity on Mars, Venus, and the moon? Explain.

Thinking Critically

21. No. Figure 1 on page 421 shows that the eastern United States lacks active volcanoes. (Students may also recall, based on the plate map on page 375, that this part of the North American plate is far removed from any plate boundaries. Volcanoes most often occur along the boundaries of converging plates where subduction occurs.)

22. An island arc forms at a converging boundary where one oceanic plate subducts under the other at a deep-ocean trench. A hot spot volcano forms in a continental or oceanic plate where magma from deep within the mantle melts through the crust. Hot spot volcanoes often lie far from plate boundaries and do not result from subduction.

23. Accept all reasonable responses. *Examples:* Plants and animals could be killed by lava flows, pyroclastic flows, clouds of suffocating gases, mudflows, or avalanches. The land surface would also be changed, and new landforms created. Nutrient-rich lava, ash, and cinders would in time form fertile soil.

Applying Skills

Refer to the diagram to answer Questions 26–29.

26. Classifying What is this volcano made of? How do geologists classify a volcano made of these materials?

27. Developing Hypotheses What is the feature labeled A in the diagram? What is the feature labeled B? How do these features form?

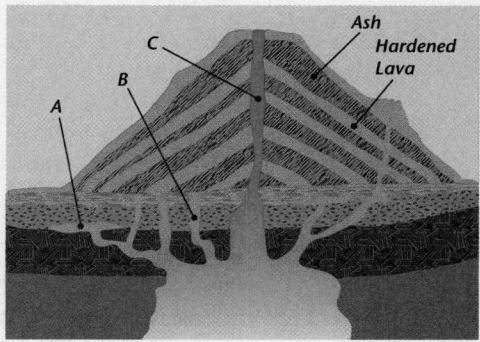

28. Inferring This volcano is located where oceanic crust is subducted under continental crust. Would the volcano erupt quietly or explosively? Give reasons for your answer.

29. Predicting What is the feature labeled C in the diagram? If this feature becomes plugged with hardened magma, what could happen to the volcano? Explain.

Performance CHAPTER PROJECT **13** **Assessment**

Project Wrap Up Rehearse your documentary with your group before presenting it to the class. All group members should be able to answer questions about the visuals.

Reflect and Record In your journal, evaluate how well your documentary presented the information you collected. As you watched the other documentaries, did you see any similarities between how people in different regions live with volcanoes?

Test Preparation

Use these questions to prepare for standardized tests.

Read the passage. Then answer Questions 30–33.

Newsflash! At 8:30 A.M. today, May 8, 1980, Mount St. Helens in Washington State erupted. It blew away 400 meters of its top. A pyroclastic flow roared out of the volcano and burned leaves on trees 20 kilometers away. The volcano also blasted a cloud of ash 25 kilometers into the atmosphere. The cloud is drifting across several northwestern states, dumping a thick carpet of ash.

What led to this eruption? For 123 years, the snow-capped volcano had stood quietly. People thought it was dormant. But in March, the volcano began to rumble with small earthquakes. Scientists knew this meant magma was moving inside the volcano. In the weeks before the eruption, part of the mountain's northeastern slope also began to bulge. Then, in a moment, Mount St. Helens changed forever.

30. A good title for this passage is
   a. "Volcanoes of Washington State."
   b. "The Dramatic Eruption of Mount St. Helens."
   c. "The Danger of Volcanic Ash."
   d. "A Dormant Volcano."

31. The series of small earthquakes before the eruption of Mount St. Helens was the result of
   a. movement along nearby faults.
   b. water building up inside the volcano.
   c. movement of magma inside the volcano.
   d. the formation of a new caldera.

32. In the weeks before Mount St. Helens erupted, the volcano
   a. let off some steam.   **b.** was very quiet.
   c. glowed at night.   **d.** began to bulge.

33. Farm crops in nearby states would have been most affected by the volcano's
   a. ash.   **b.** lava flows.
   c. cinders and bombs.   **d.** pyroclastic flow.

Applying Skills

24. Lava plateaus develop where thin, runny lava flows out of long cracks in the ground. Because the lava is so fluid and does not erupt from a central vent, it spreads out over a wide area. Many eruptions gradually build up a lava plateau.

25. Earth still has many active volcanoes, but Mars, Venus, and the moon apparently do not. Scientists think that volcanic activity on Mars and the moon ended long ago. There may still be volcanic activity on Venus, but so far none

Program Resources

◆ **Inquiry Skills Activity Book** Provides teaching and review of all inquiry skills
◆ **Prentice Hall Assessment System** Provides standardized test practice
◆ **Reading in the Content Area** Provides strategies to improve science reading skills
◆ **Teacher's ELL Handbook** Provides multiple strategies for English language learners

---

has been observed.

26. Alternating layers of lava and ash; a composite volcano

27. A is a sill; B is a dike. A sill forms when magma squeezes between rock layers and hardens. A dike forms when magma forces its way across rock layers and hardens.

28. Explosively; the volcanic cone has layers of ash, so we know that pyroclastic materials were erupted; such eruptions are explosive, not quiet.

29. The pipe; pressure might build up to the point where the entire top of the mountain blows off in a violent explosion, or if there were cracks in the layers, a new pipe might form leading to the side of the cone. (Accept other reasonable responses.)

Performance CHAPTER PROJECT **13** **Assessment**

Project Wrap Up You may want to provide time for groups to practice their presentations. Inform students how much time each group will have for its presentation. Tell them that if their practice presentation runs too long, they should find ways to cut its length without jeopardizing its content or flow.

Reflect and Record Give students time to record their thoughts individually, then encourage them to discuss their ideas with the other members of their group. Let students respond to the last question in a whole-class discussion. Emphasize the similarities that students identify by listing them on the board or an overhead transparency.

Test Preparation

30. b **31.** c **32.** d **33.** a

CHAPTER 14 Minerals

Sections	Time	Student Edition Activities	Other Activities	
CHAPTER PROJECT 14 **Growing a Crystal Garden** p. 449	Ongoing (2 weeks)	Check Your Progress, p. 458, 464 Project Wrap Up, p. 475	**TE**	Chapter 14 Project Notes, pp. 448–449
1 Properties of Minerals pp. 450–459 ◆ 14.1.1 Identify the characteristics of a mineral. ◆ 14.1.2 Identify the properties of minerals and explain how minerals are identified.	2 periods/ 1 block	**Discover** What Is the True Color of a Mineral?, p. 450 **Sharpen Your Skills** Classifying, p. 453 **Try This** Crystal Hands, p. 457 **Skills Lab: Measuring** The Density of Minerals, p. 459	**TE** **TE** **TE** **TE** **TE** **TE** **TE** **LM**	Building Inquiry Skills: Classifying, pp. 451, 455 Building Inquiry Skills: Comparing and Contrasting, p. 453 Inquiry Challenge, p. 454 Building Inquiry Skills: Observing, p. 454 Including All Students, p. 457 Demonstration, p. 457 Inquiry Challenge, p. 457 14, "How Tesselating!"
2 How Minerals Form pp. 460–465 ◆ 14.2.1 Describe the processes by which minerals form.	1 period/ $\frac{1}{2}$ block	**Discover** How Does the Rate of Cooling Affect Crystals?, p. 460	**TE** **TE** **TE**	Building Inquiry Skills: Designing Experiments, p. 461 Building Inquiry Skills: Inferring, p. 462 Demonstration, p. 463
3 *INTEGRATING TECHNOLOGY* **Mineral Resources** pp. 466–472 ◆ 14.3.1 Describe how minerals are used. ◆ 14.3.2 List the three types of mines. ◆ 14.3.3 Explain how ores are processed to obtain metals.	2 periods/ 1 block	**Discover** How Are Minerals Processed Before They Are Used?, p. 466 **Science at Home,** p. 470 **Real-World Lab: Careers in Science** Copper Recovery, p. 472	**TE** **TE** **TE** **TE**	Real-Life Learning, p. 467 Building Inquiry Skills: Comparing and Contrasting, p. 467 Real-Life Learning, p. 470 Demonstration, p. 470
Study Guide/Assessment pp. 473–475	1 period/ $\frac{1}{2}$ block		**ISAB**	Provides teaching and review of all inquiry skills

For Standard or Block Schedule The Resource Pro® CD-ROM gives you maximum flexibility for planning your instruction for any type of schedule. Resource Pro® contains Planning Express®, an advanced scheduling program, as well as the entire contents of the Teaching Resources and the Computer Test Bank.

Key: **CTB** Computer Test Bank
CT Chapter Tests
ELL Teacher's ELL Handbook

CHAPTER PLANNING GUIDE

Program Resources	Assessment Strategies	Media and Technology
UR Chapter 14 Project Teacher Notes, pp. 90–91 **UR** Chapter 14 Project Overview and Worksheets, pp. 92–95	**TE** Check Your Progress, pp. 458, 464 **TE** Performance Assessment: Chapter 14 Project Wrap Up, p. 475 **TR** Chapter 14 Project Scoring Rubric, p. 96	Science Explorer Internet Site Audio CDs, Section Summaries
UR 14-1 Lesson Plan, p. 97 **UR** 14-1 Section Summary, p. 98 **UR** 14-1 Review and Reinforce, p. 99 **UR** 14-1 Enrich, p. 100 **UR** Skills Lab blackline masters, pp. 109–111	**SE** Section 1 Review, p. 458 **SE** Analyze and Conclude, p. 459 **TE** Ongoing Assessment, pp. 451, 453, 455, 457 **TE** Performance Assessment, p. 458	Presentation Pro, "Properties of Minerals" Transparency 56, "Properties and Uses of Minerals" Lab Activity Videotape, *Tape 3*
UR 14-2 Lesson Plan, p. 101 **UR** 14-2 Section Summary, p. 102 **UR** 14-2 Review and Reinforce, p. 103 **UR** 14-2 Enrich, p. 104	**SE** Section 2 Review, p. 464 **TE** Ongoing Assessment, pp. 461, 463 **TE** Performance Assessment, p. 464	Transparency 57, "Formation of Mineral Deposits on Ocean Floor"
UR 14-3 Lesson Plan, p. 105 **UR** 14-3 Section Summary, p. 106 **UR** 14-3 Review and Reinforce, p. 107 **UR** 14-3 Enrich, p. 108 **UR** Real-World Lab blackline masters, pp. 112–113	**SE** Section 3 Review, p. 470 **SE** Analyze and Conclude, p. 472 **TE** Ongoing Assessment, pp. 467, 469 **TE** Performance Assessment, p. 471	Concept Videotape Library, *Adventures, Tape 3,* "What a Gem!" Concept Videotape Library, *Adventures, Tape 3,* "Ore What?" Presentation Pro, "Mineral Resources" Transparency 58, "Exploring Smelting Iron Ore" Lab Activity Videotape, *Tape 3*
GRSW Provides worksheets to promote student comprehension of content **RCA** Provides strategies to improve science reading skills **ELL** Provides multiple strategies for English language learners	**SE** Study Guide/Assessment, pp. 473–475 **PA** Performance Assessment, pp. 43–45 **CT** Chapter 14 Test, pp. 55–58 **CTB** Chapter 14 Test **PHAS** Provides standardized test preparation	Computer Test Bank, Chapter 14 Test

GRSW Guided Reading and Study Workbook
ISAB Inquiry Skills Activity Book
LM Laboratory Manual

PA Performance Assessment
PHAS Prentice Hall Assessment System
PLM Probeware Lab Manual

RCA Reading in the Content Area
SE Student Edition

TE Teacher's Edition
UR Unit Resources

Meeting the National Science Education Standards and AAAS Benchmarks

National Science Education Standards	Benchmarks for Science Literacy	Unifying Themes

Science As Inquiry (Content Standard A)

◆ **Use appropriate tools and techniques to gather, analyze, and interpret data** Students create a crystal garden. Students measure and compare the density of different minerals. Students recover copper from a solution. *(Chapter Project; Skills Lab; Real-World Lab)*

Physical Science (Content Standard B)

◆ **Properties and changes of properties in matter** A mineral is a naturally occurring, inorganic solid that has a crystal structure and a definite chemical composition. *(Sections 1, 2)*

Earth and Space Science (Content Standard D)

◆ **Structure of the Earth system** Some minerals form as magma cools inside Earth's crust or as lava hardens on the surface. *(Section 2)*

Science and Technology (Content Standard E)

◆ **Understandings about science and technology** After miners remove ore from a mine, smelting is necessary to remove the metal from the ore. *(Section 3)*

Science in Personal and Social Perspectives (Content Standard F)

◆ **Science and technology in society** Students examine the issue of who owns the ocean's minerals. *(Science and Society)*

1B Scientific Inquiry Students create a crystal garden. Students measure and compare the density of different minerals. Students recover copper from a solution. *(Chapter Project; Skills Lab; Real-World Lab)*

3A Technology and Science After miners remove ore from a mine, smelting is necessary to remove the metal from the ore. *(Section 3)*

3C Issues in Technology Students examine the issue of who owns the ocean's minerals. *(Science and Society)*

4C Processes That Shape the Earth Some minerals form as magma cools inside Earth's crust or as lava hardens on the surface. *(Section 2)*

4D Structure of Matter A mineral is a naturally occurring, inorganic solid that has a crystal structure and a definite chemical composition. Minerals can form through crystallization of melted materials and through crystallization of materials dissolved in water. *(Sections 1, 2)*

◆ **Energy** Magma heats water to a high temperature beneath Earth's surface. Smelting is necessary to remove the metal from an ore. *(Sections 2, 3)*

◆ **Scale and Structure** The repeating pattern of a mineral's particles forms a solid called a crystal. *(Sections 1, 2)*

◆ **Stability** Each mineral has its own specific properties that can be used to identify it. *(Section 1; Skills Lab)*

◆ **Systems and Interactions** Students create a crystal garden. Minerals form through crystallization of melted materials and through crystallization of materials dissolved in water. Metals are removed from ores through the process of smelting. Students remove copper from a solution. *(Chapter Project; Sections 2, 3; Real-World Lab)*

◆ **Unity and Diversity** Minerals are identified by properties such as color, luster, hardness, streak, crystal shape, cleavage, and fracture. Each mineral has a characteristic density. Minerals are formed from magma and from hot water solutions. The three types of mines are strip mines, open pit mines, and shaft mines. *(Sections 1, 2, 3; Skills Lab)*

Take It to the Net

The **www.phschool.com** Web site provides you with multiple opportunities to incorporate the internet into your instruction. Go to **www.phschool.com** and click on the Science icon. Then select Science Explorer Integrated.

■ Have students use the chapter Self-Test to get instant feedback.

■ Hot Links and Reference Links provide opportunities for online research.

Internet Activities provide opportunities for students to review, extend, or assess a concept from the chapter.

STAY CURRENT with **SCIENCE NEWS** ®

Find out the latest research and information about rocks and minerals at: **www.phschool.com**

ACTIVITY	Time (minutes)	Materials *Quantities for one work group*	Skills
Section 1			
Discover, p. 450	15	**Consumable** paper towel **Nonconsumable** samples of black hematite and magnetite, porcelain or ceramic tile	Observing
Sharpen Your Skills, p. 453	10	**Nonconsumable** penny; samples of talc, calcite, and quartz	Classifying
Try This, p. 457	15; 10	**Consumable** table salt, Epsom salts, water, piece of black construction paper **Nonconsumable** 2 pitchers, 2 shallow pans, hand lens	Observing
Skills Lab, p. 459	40	**Consumable** water **Nonconsumable** 100-mL graduated cylinder; balance; samples of pyrite, quartz, and galena	Measuring, Drawing Conclusions
Section 2			
Discover, p. 460	15	**Consumable** salol, plastic spoon, candle, matches, ice cube **Nonconsumable** 2 microscope slides, tongs, hand lens	Relating Cause and Effect
Section 3			
Discover, p. 466	10	**Nonconsumable** samples of bauxite and graphite, aluminum can, pencil	Posing Questions
Science at Home, p. 470	home	**Consumable** 3 iron nails, petroleum jelly, clear nail polish, water, vinegar **Nonconsumable** clear glass	Communicating
Real-World Lab, p. 472	30	**Consumable** 3 g copper sulfate, water, 5 iron nails **Nonconsumable** triple-beam balance, 400-mL beaker, 100-mL graduated cylinder	Measuring, Observing, Drawing Conclusions, Inferring, Predicting

A list of all materials required for the Student Edition activities can be found beginning on page T23. You can obtain information about ordering materials by calling 1-800-848-9500 or by accessing the Science Explorer Internet site at: **www.phschool.com**

Growing a Crystal Garden

When students think of minerals and their crystals, they likely think of something solid and unchanging. They may not realize that the forming of mineral crystals is one of the constructive processes that is continuous in Earth's crust.

Purpose In this project, students will design and create a crystal garden using at least two different crystal-growth solutions. During the project, they will observe and record the growth rate of the different crystals in their gardens. By doing this project, students will gain a better understanding of how mineral crystals form in Earth's crust.

Skills Focus Students will be able to
◆ measure and prepare a chemical solution;
◆ observe and sketch the various types of crystals that grow;
◆ compare and contrast the growth of different kinds of crystals;
◆ create a data table to record crystal growth rates;
◆ communicate results to the class.

Project Time Line The entire project will take about two weeks. Students can individually make crystal gardens or work in small groups. During the project, students may need some class time to carry out the following tasks. After the initial design and preparation, students can observe and record crystal growth at various times during the school day.
◆ Design and gather materials to create the garden scene.
◆ Prepare a solution with which to begin crystal growth in the garden scene.
◆ Use additional teacher-made solutions to add to their crystal gardens.
◆ Make a sketch of the crystal garden to keep track of which crystals are where.
◆ Record the growth rate of each kind of crystal in their gardens
◆ Make sketches of the crystals grown in their gardens.
◆ Present their crystal gardens to the class.

CHAPTER 14 Minerals

448

For more detailed information on planning and supervising the chapter project, see Chapter 14 Project Teacher Notes, pages 90–91 in Unit 4 Resources.

Suggested Shortcuts
◆ You can make this project shorter by simply having individual students grow one kind of crystal on a simple base, such as a sponge in a clear glass. Different students could grow different kinds of crystals from prepared solutions.

◆ For a class project, have students design and create one elaborate garden scene in an aquarium tank or similar container. Then have small groups grow different kinds of crystals at different places in the garden.

Possible Materials Possibly the best type of container in which to grow a crystal garden is a plastic shoe box, though students may find other containers that will work as well. Base materials in the garden include charcoal, brick pieces, porous rocks such as sandstone, plastic foam of various shapes, pipe cleaners, cotton

Growing a Crystal Garden

Everyone has wondered at the beauty of minerals. Minerals occur in an amazing variety of colors and crystal shapes—from clear, tiny cubes of halite (table salt) to precious rubies and sapphires. Some crystals look like dandelion puffs. In this project, you will grow crystals to see how different types of chemicals form different crystal shapes.

Your Goal To design and grow a crystal garden.
To complete this project successfully, you must

◆ create a three-dimensional garden scene as a base on which to grow crystals
◆ prepare at least two different crystal-growth solutions
◆ observe and record the shapes and growth rates of your crystals
◆ follow the safety guidelines in Appendix A.

Get Started Begin by deciding what materials you will use to create your garden scene. Your teacher will suggest a variety of materials and also describe the types of crystal-growth solutions that you can use.

Check Your Progress You'll be working on this project as you study this chapter. To keep your project on track, look for Check Your Progress boxes at the following points.
Section 1 Review, page 458: Design and build a setting for your crystal garden and add the solutions.
Section 2 Review, page 464: Observe and record the growth of the crystals.

Wrap Up At the end of the chapter (page 475), display your finished crystal garden to your class. Be prepared to describe your procedure, observations, and conclusions.

These aurichalcite (oh rih KAL syt) crystals were found in a copper mine in Mexico. This mineral is formed from the metals zinc, copper, and other elements.

449

swabs, and small kitchen sponges. Various chemicals can be used to create different crystalline structures, including salt (sodium chloride), sugar (sucrose), Epsom salts, alum (aluminum potassium sulfate), and magnesium sulfate. You may have to order some of these chemicals from a pharmacy a couple of weeks in advance of the start of the project. To vary the color of crystals, use dye powder, liquid bluing, or food coloring. Students will also need a hand lens to observe the crystals.

Launching the Project To introduce this project, show students pictures of mineral crystals from geology books. Then explain that they will be growing similar crystals in garden scenes that they build and design. Ask: **What are some materials you could use to build such a garden scene?** *(Practically any porous material could serve as a substrate for crystal growth.)* Explain that students will create these garden scenes, which will be the first step in creating their crystal gardens. To help students get started, hand out Chapter 14 Project Overview and Worksheets, on pages 92–95 in Unit 4 Resources. You may also wish to hand out the Chapter 14 Project Scoring Rubric, page 96, at this time.

Program Resources

◆ **Unit 4 Resources** Chapter 14 Project Teacher Notes, pp. 90–91; Project Overview and Worksheets, pp. 92–95; Project Scoring Rubric, p. 96

WEB ACTIVITY www.phschool.com

You will find an Internet activity, chapter self-tests for students, and links to other chapter topics at this site.

Media and Technology

 Audio CDs Section Summaries

Performance Assessment

Use the Chapter 14 Project Scoring Rubric to assess students' work. Students will be assessed on
◆ how well they create a three-dimensional crystal garden;
◆ how well they observe and record the growth of crystals in their crystal garden;
◆ how effectively they present their crystal garden and growth data to the class;
◆ their participation in their groups.

Objectives

After completing the lesson, students will be able to
◆ identify the characteristics of a mineral;
◆ identify the properties of minerals and explain how minerals are identified.

Key Terms mineral, inorganic, crystal, element, compound, Mohs hardness scale, streak, luster, cleavage, fracture, fluorescence

1 Engage/Explore

Activating Prior Knowledge

Ask students: **What are minerals?** (*Some students may know that minerals are the chemical compounds that make up rocks, but many students will probably mention dietary minerals, such as iron and calcium.*) **Where do you think you could find minerals in nature?** (*A few students may know that some minerals, such as sulfur and copper, occur in deposits and are mined. Students might suggest minerals are found in rocks.*)

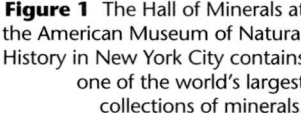 **DISCOVER**

Skills Focus observing
Materials *samples of black hematite and magnetite, porcelain or ceramic tile, paper towel*
Time 15 minutes
Tips Use black hematite rather than red. Demonstrate how to make a streak on the tile and then wipe it clean.
Expected Outcome Both hematite (Fe_2O_3) and magnetite (Fe_3O_4) are types of iron ore, and they are both dark and similar in appearance. Hematite leaves a reddish-brown streak, while magnetite leaves a black streak.
Think It Over The streak of magnetite matches its color, but the streak of black hematite does not. This streak test could be used to identify them as two different minerals.

DISCOVER •••••••••••••••••••••••••••••••• ACTIVITY

What Is the True Color of a Mineral?

1. Examine samples of magnetite and black hematite. Both minerals contain iron. Describe the color and appearance of the two minerals. Are they similar or different?

2. Rub the black hematite across the back of a porcelain or ceramic tile. Observe the color of the streak on the tile.

3. Wipe the tile clean before you test the next sample.

4. Rub the magnetite across the back of the tile. Observe the color of the streak on the tile.

Think It Over
Observing Does the color of each mineral's streak match its color? How could this streak test be helpful in identifying them as two different minerals?

GUIDE FOR READING

◆ What are the characteristics of a mineral?

◆ How are minerals identified?

Reading Tip As you read, use the headings to make an outline showing what minerals are and how they can be identified.

I f you visit a science museum, you might wander into a room named the "hall of minerals." There you would see substances you have never heard of. For example, you might see deep-red crystals labeled "sphalerite" (SFAL uh ryt). You might be surprised to learn that sphalerite is a source of zinc and gallium. These metals are used in products from "tin" cans to computer chips! Although you may never have seen sphalerite, you are probably familiar with other common minerals. For example, you have probably seen turquoise, a blue-green mineral used in jewelry.

Figure 1 The Hall of Minerals at the American Museum of Natural History in New York City contains one of the world's largest collections of minerals.

READING STRATEGIES

Reading Tip Remind students that an outline helps you organize information. In textbooks, information is organized under headings. As a guide, begin the outline on the chalkboard and let students complete it.
I. Properties of Minerals
   A. What Is a Mineral?
      1. Naturally Occuring
      2. Inorganic

Figure 2 A. Red crystals of the mineral sphalerite are called ruby zinc. **B.** Borax is a mineral that forms in dry lake beds. **C.** Coal is not a mineral because it is made of the remains of ancient plants. *Comparing and Contrasting How are sphalerite and borax similar? How are they different?*

What Is a Mineral?

Sphalerite and turquoise are just two of more than 3,000 minerals that geologists have identified. Of all these minerals, only about 100 are common. Most of the others are harder to find than gold. About 20 minerals make up most of the rocks of Earth's crust. These minerals are known as rock-forming minerals. Appendix B at the back of this book lists some of the most common rock-forming minerals.

A mineral is a naturally occurring, inorganic solid that has a crystal structure and a definite chemical composition. For a substance to be a mineral, it must have all five of these characteristics. In Figure 2, you can compare sphalerite with another mineral, borax, and with coal, which is not a mineral.

Naturally Occurring To be classified as a mineral, a substance must occur naturally. Cement, brick, steel, and glass all come from substances found in Earth's crust. However, these building materials are manufactured by people. Because they are not naturally occurring, such materials are not considered to be minerals.

Inorganic A mineral must also be **inorganic.** This means that the mineral cannot arise from materials that were once part of a living thing. For example, coal forms naturally in the crust. But geologists do not classify coal as a mineral because it comes from the remains of plants and animals that lived millions of years ago.

Solid A mineral is always a solid, with a definite volume and shape. The particles that make up a solid are packed together very tightly, so they cannot move like the particles that make up a liquid. A solid keeps its shape because its particles can't flow freely.

Program Resources

◆ **Unit 4 Resources** 14-1 Lesson Plan, p. 97; 14-1 Section Summary, p. 98
◆ **Guided Reading and Study Workbook** Section 14-1

Answers to Self-Assessment

Caption Question

Figure 2 Both are minerals. Therefore, each is a naturally occurring, inorganic solid with a crystal structure and a definite chemical composition. They are different in color and in where they form.

2 Facilitate

What Is a Mineral?

Using the Visuals: Figure 2

Ask students: **Which characteristics of a mineral does coal have and which does it not have?** (*It is naturally occurring, is a solid, and has a definite chemical composition. Some students may know that it has a crystal structure. But it is not inorganic.*) Then have students find sphalerite on the table of common minerals in Appendix B. Ask: **What property of this mineral can you confirm by looking at its picture?** (*Its color, brown to light yellow*) Explain that the other properties in the table will be explained later in the section. **learning modality: visual**

Building Inquiry Skills: Classifying

Materials *mineral samples such as quartz, calcite, halite, and feldspar; nonmineral objects such as brick, rubber ball, lump of coal, and bottle of water*
Time 10 minutes

To help students understand the difference between minerals and nonminerals, place mineral samples and examples of nonminerals on a table in random order. Then challenge students to classify each object as either a mineral or a nonmineral using their knowledge of the five characteristics that a substance must have to be a mineral. Allow students to handle and examine all objects and then classify each by making two lists on a piece of paper. **learning modality: logical/mathematical**

Ongoing Assessment

Oral Presentation Call on students at random to explain why various examples are or are not minerals, including gold, oil, cement, borax, and coal. Then call on other students to list the five characteristics of a mineral.

What Is a Mineral?, continued

Addressing Naive Conceptions

To help students differentiate between the common term crystal and the mineral characteristic, show them a piece of quartz crystal. Ask: **What is this called?** *(Many students will identify it as a "crystal.")* Explain that a common name for the crystals of the mineral quartz is simply "crystal" or "rock crystal." But quartz crystals are not the only kind of crystals. All minerals have a crystal structure, in a variety of shapes.
learning modality: verbal

Using the Visuals: Figure 3

Ask students: **What color do you get if you mix the colors silver and yellow?** *(A typical answer might suggest light yellow.)* **What color is the mineral that is composed of silver mercury and yellow sulfur?** *(red)* Point out that the mineral cinnabar is not a mixture but a compound, in which elements have been chemically combined to form a new substance. Explain that the new substance, cinnabar, has the chemical formula HgS, which means that a molecule of cinnabar is made of 1 atom of mercury and 1 atom of sulfur.
learning modality: visual

Integrating Chemistry

Provide students with access to the Periodic Table of the Elements. Focus students' attention on the symbol for each element. Then review how a chemical formula uses symbols and numbers to represent a chemical compound. Ask: **What does the formula for fluorite, CaF_2, tell you about that mineral?** *(A molecule of fluorite is composed of 1 atom of calcium and 2 atoms of fluorine.)* Emphasize that each mineral has its own formula and the properties of each compound the formulas represent differ from all other compounds. Then have students use the Periodic Table to write the number and name of the elements that compose these minerals: halite, NaCl; Magnetite, Fe_3O_4; Pyrite, FeS_2; Chalcopyrite, $CuFeS_2$; Galena, PbS; and Corundum, Al_2O_3. **learning modality: logical/mathematical**

Crystal Structure The particles of a mineral line up in a pattern that repeats over and over again. The repeating pattern of a mineral's particles forms a solid called a **crystal.** A crystal has flat sides, called faces, that meet at sharp edges and corners.

Sometimes, the crystal structure is obvious from the mineral's appearance. In other minerals, however, the crystal structure is visible only under a microscope. A few minerals, such as opal, are considered minerals even though their particles are not arranged in a crystal structure.

Definite Chemical Composition A mineral has a definite chemical composition. This means that a mineral always contains certain elements in definite proportions. An **element** is a substance composed of a single kind of atom. All the atoms of the same element have the same chemical and physical properties.

Almost all minerals are compounds. In a **compound,** two or more elements are combined so that the elements no longer have distinct properties. The elements that make up a compound are said to be chemically joined. For example, a crystal of the mineral quartz has one atom of silicon for every two atoms of oxygen. Each compound has its own properties, which usually differ greatly from the properties of the elements that form it. Figure 3 compares the mineral cinnabar to the elements that make it up.

Figure 3 Minerals are usually a compound of two or more elements. **A.** Mercury is a metal that is a silvery liquid at room temperature. **B.** The element sulfur is bright yellow. **C.** The mineral cinnabar is a compound of the elements mercury and sulfur. Cinnabar has red crystals.

Background

Facts and Figures Some 40–50 new minerals are identified each year. Two elements, oxygen and silicon, make up about 75 percent of Earth's crust. Those two elements in combination with other elements—such as iron, aluminum, calcium, and sodium—comprise the group of minerals known as the *silicates.* Silicates make up 95 percent of the volume of Earth's crust. They include such minerals as feldspar, quartz, mica, olivine, and hornblende.

Minerals that do not contain silicon are called *nonsilicates.* They include such minerals as hematite, corundum, gypsum, pyrite, cinnabar, halite, calcite, and dolomite. The elements that occur in nature in pure form are called *native elements.* These minerals, all nonsilicates, include gold, copper, diamond, sulfur, graphite, silver, and platinum.

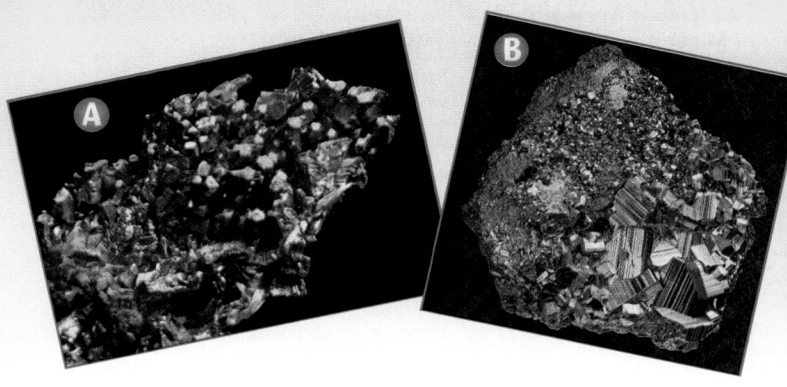

Some elements occur in nature in a pure form, not as part of a compound with other elements. These elements, such as copper, silver, and gold, are considered to be minerals. Almost all pure elements are metals.

☑ *Checkpoint* *What does it mean to say that a mineral has a definite chemical composition?*

Identifying Minerals

During the California Gold Rush of 1849, thousands of people headed west to find gold in the California hills. Some found gold, but most found disappointment. Perhaps the most disappointed of all were the ones who found pyrite, or "fool's gold." All three minerals in Figure 4 look like gold, yet only one is the real thing.

Because there are so many different kinds of minerals, telling them apart can be a challenge. The color of a mineral alone often provides too little information to make an identification. **Each mineral has its own specific properties that can be used to identify it.** When you have learned to recognize the properties of minerals, you will be able to identify many common minerals around you.

You can see some of the properties of a mineral just by looking at a sample. To observe other properties, however, you need to conduct tests on that sample. As you read about the properties of minerals, think about how you could use them to identify a mineral.

Hardness When you identify a mineral, one of the best clues you can use is the mineral's hardness. In 1812, Friedrich Mohs, an Austrian mineral expert, invented a test to describe and compare the hardness of minerals. Called the **Mohs hardness scale,** this scale ranks ten minerals from softest to hardest. Look at the

Figure 4 An old saying warns "All that glitters is not gold." **A.** Real gold can occur as a pure metal. **B.** Pyrite, or fool's gold, contains iron and sulfur. **C.** Chalcopyrite is a compound of copper, iron, and sulfur. *Observing These minerals are similar in color. But do you notice any differences in their appearance?*

Sharpen your Skills

Classifying

ACTIVITY

1. Use your fingernail to try to scratch talc, calcite, and quartz. Record which minerals you were able to scratch.

2. Now try to scratch the minerals with a penny. Were your results different? Explain.

3. Were there any minerals you were unable to scratch with either your fingernail or the penny?

4. How would you classify the three minerals in order of increasing hardness?

Building Inquiry Skills: Comparing and Contrasting

Materials *mineral samples, hand lens*
Time 10 minutes

Invite students to examine several different mineral samples. Then have each student list properties that could be used to distinguish between types of minerals.
learning modality: kinesthetic

Using the Visuals: Figure 4

Circulate samples of pyrite through the class. Ask: **Could you be fooled into thinking this is gold?** *(Many will say yes.)* Then have students turn to the table in Appendix B, find the entries for pyrite and gold, and compare these two minerals' properties. Point out the difference in their formulas. Guide students into understanding that the only property both have in common is color. **learning modality: visual**

Sharpen your Skills

Classifying

Materials *penny, samples of talc, calcite, quartz*
Time 10 minutes
Tips Divide students into pairs, pairing students of differing abilities
Expected Outcome A fingernail scratches talc but not calcite or quartz. A penny scratches talc and calcite but not quartz. Quartz, then, cannot be scratched by either a fingernail or a penny. Therefore, the minerals in order of increasing hardness are: talc, calcite, quartz.
Extend Have students test other materials in the classroom, including chalk, wood, plastics, and various metals. At the end, have students collaborate on a hardness scale for all materials tested.
learning modality: kinesthetic

Ongoing Assessment

Writing Write this question on the board: Why does each mineral have its own specific properties? Have each student write an answer, which should mention that each mineral has a different chemical composition.

Answers to Self-Assessment

Caption Question

Figure 4 Gold is brighter and occurs as nuggets; pyrite contains angular, blocklike crystals; chalcopyrite includes particles of a darker substance.

☑ *Checkpoint*

A mineral always contains the elements in certain definite proportions.

Identifying Minerals, continued

Using the Visuals: Figure 5

After students are familiar with the scale, ask: **What is the hardness of your fingernail? Explain your answer.** *(Because a fingernail can scratch gypsum but not calcite, its hardness is somewhere between the two, or about 2.5).* **What is the hardness of a steel knife? Explain.** *(Because a steel knife can scratch apatite but not feldspar, its hardness is somewhere between the two, or about 5.5).* **learning modality: logical/mathematical**

Inquiry Challenge

Materials *metal nail file, penny, glass baby-food jar, scrap piece of steel, mineral samples such as quartz, pyrite, magnetite, galena, and halite*

Time 20 minutes

Divide students into small groups. Then challenge each group to give each of the mineral samples a hardness rating and place the samples in a sequence from softest to hardest, using the Mohs hardness scale for reference. After all groups have completed their work, invite a member of each to write the results on the board. Discuss any differences. **cooperative learning**

Building Inquiry Skills: Observing

Materials *hand lens, unglazed porcelain tile, numbered samples of various minerals*

Time 10 minutes

Ask students: **How does the color of a mineral compare to the color of its streak?** *(The streak color and the mineral color are often different.)* Invite students to make a data table, list the mineral samples by number, and record the color and streak characteristic of each sample. Then have students use Appendix B to identify the samples. **learning modality: visual**

Figure 5 Mohs hardness scale rates the hardness of minerals on a scale of 1 to 10. *Drawing Conclusions You find a mineral that can be scratched by a steel knife, but not by a copper penny. What is this mineral's hardness on the Mohs scale?*

Mohs Hardness Scale		
Mineral	**Rating**	**Testing Method**
Talc	1	Softest known mineral. It flakes easily when scratched by a fingernail.
Gypsum	2	A fingernail can easily scratch it.
Calcite	3	A fingernail cannot scratch it, but a copper penny can.
Fluorite	4	A steel knife can easily scratch it.
Apatite	5	A steel knife can scratch it.
Feldspar	6	Cannot be scratched by a steel knife, but it can scratch window glass.
Quartz	7	Can scratch steel and hard glass easily.
Topaz	8	Can scratch quartz.
Corundum	9	Can scratch topaz.
Diamond	10	Hardest known mineral. Diamond can scratch all other substances.

table in Figure 5 to see which mineral is the softest and which is the hardest. A mineral can scratch any mineral softer than itself, but will be scratched by any mineral that is harder. How would you determine the hardness of a mineral not listed on the Mohs scale, such as sphalerite? You could try to scratch sphalerite with talc, gypsum, or calcite. But you would find that none of them scratch sphalerite. Apatite, the mineral rated 5 on the scale, does scratch sphalerite. Therefore, you would conclude that sphalerite's hardness is about 4 on Mohs hardness scale.

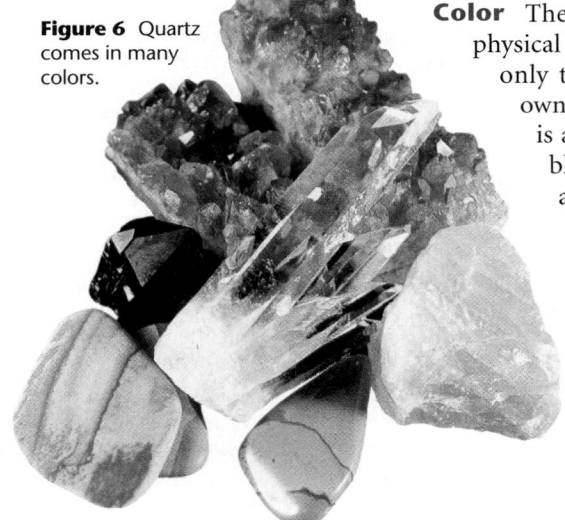

Figure 6 Quartz comes in many colors.

Color The color of a mineral is an easily observed physical property. But color can be used to identify only those few minerals that always have their own characteristic color. The mineral malachite is always green. The mineral azurite is always blue. No other minerals look quite the same as these. Many minerals, however, like the quartz in Figure 6, can occur in a variety of colors.

Streak A streak test can provide a clue to a mineral's identity. The **streak** of a mineral is the color of its powder. You can observe a streak by rubbing a mineral against a piece of unglazed tile called a streak plate. Even though the color of the mineral may vary, its streak does not. Surprisingly, the streak color

454

Background

History of Science When Friedrich Mohs (1773–1839) developed his hardness scale, he arbitrarily assigned the number 10 to diamond because that was the hardest mineral known. He then arbitrarily assigned numbers to other common minerals in descending order of hardness, assigning the number 1 to the softest mineral known, talc. Thus, the numbers of his scale do not represent any units of hardness. For

example, topaz is much harder than fluorite but not exactly twice as hard, as their numbers might suggest.

Facts and Figures Quartz can occur in a variety of different colors because of impurities. Pure quartz, colorless and transparent, is often called rock crystal. Impurities can cause it to be yellow, black, red, banded, and other colors.

Figure 7 **A.** Galena, which contains lead, has a metallic luster. **B.** Malachite, which contains copper, has a silky luster.

and the mineral color are often different. For example, although pyrite has a gold color, it always produces a greenish black streak. Real gold, on the other hand, produces a golden yellow streak.

Luster Another simple test to identify a mineral is to check its luster. **Luster** is the term used to describe how a mineral reflects light from its surface. Minerals containing metals are often shiny. For example, galena is an ore of lead that has a bright, metallic luster. Look at Figure 7 to compare the luster of galena with the luster of malachite. Other minerals, such as quartz, have a glassy luster. Some of the other terms used to describe luster include earthy, waxy, and pearly.

Density Each mineral has a characteristic density. Recall from Chapter 11 that density is the mass in a given space, or mass per unit volume. No matter what the size of a mineral sample, the density of that mineral always remains the same.

You can compare the density of two mineral samples of about the same size. Just pick them up and heft them, or feel their weight, in your hands. You may be able to feel the difference between low-density quartz and high-density galena. If the two samples are the same size, the galena is almost three times as heavy as the quartz.

But heft provides only a rough measure of density. When geologists measure density, they use a balance to determine precisely the mass of a mineral sample. The mineral is also placed in water to determine how much water it displaces. The volume of the displaced water equals the volume of the sample. Dividing the sample's mass by its volume gives the density of the mineral.

☑ *Checkpoint* How can you determine a mineral's density?

Language Arts
CONNECTION

Geologists use adjectives such as glassy, dull, pearly, silky, greasy, and pitchlike to describe the luster of a mineral. When writers describe the surfaces of objects other than minerals, they also use words that describe luster. Luster can suggest how a surface looks. A new car, for example, might look glassy; an old car might look dull.

In Your Journal

Think of a familiar scene to describe—a room, building, tree, or street. Make a list of objects in your scene and a list of adjectives describing the surfaces of these objects. You might use some of the adjectives that geologists use to describe luster. Now write a paragraph using sensory words that make the scene seem real.

Language Arts
CONNECTION

Other words geologists use to describe luster include earthy, resinous, vitreous, and waxy. These terms are meant to be self-explanatory, calling to mind other common materials of the same look.

In Your Journal Before students write their paragraphs, read a description of a natural setting by a nature writer, such as in an outdoors magazine or a book of nature essays. Discuss with students the descriptive words that helped them form an image in their minds of the scene the writer described. **learning modality: verbal**

Building Inquiry Skills: Classifying

Materials *samples of metallic minerals such as pyrite, copper, silver, galena; samples of nonmetallic minerals such as olivine, hornblende, quartz, feldspar*

ACTIVITY

Time 10 minutes

Place several mineral samples in random order on a table, identifying each only by a number. Then challenge students to classify each sample as a mineral with either metallic or nonmetallic luster. After all students have classified the samples, provide the names of each mineral sample and invite students to check their classifications using the table in Appendix B. **learning modality: visual**

Answers to Self-Assessment
Caption Question
Figure 5 The mineral's hardness is 4.

☑ *Checkpoint*
First, find the mass of the mineral with a balance. Second, find its volume by determining how much water it displaces. Finally, divide the mineral's mass by its volume.

Ongoing Assessment

Skills Check Have each student make a table that lists each mineral property, a description of each property, and a description of the test for the property.

Identifying Minerals, continued

Using the Visuals: Figure 8

Emphasize that each mineral has its own unique combination of properties. Ask: **Why does each mineral have its own properties, different from the properties of all other minerals?** *(Each mineral has a unique chemical composition and crystal structure that is different from all other minerals.)* Point out that this chart includes one example for each of the six crystal systems.
learning modality: verbal

TRY THIS

Skills Focus observing
Materials *table salt, Epsom salts, water, 2 pitchers, 2 shallow pans, piece of black construction paper, hand lens*
Time 15 minutes the first day; 10 minutes for observation a day later
Tips Prepare ahead of time supersaturated solutions of salt and Epsom salts by adding those substances to separate pitchers of hot water, allowing the water to cool, and then adding more salt or Epsom salts. To simplify the activity, also pour the solutions into the shallow pans ahead of time, filling each to a depth of 1–2 cm. Provide a place for the hand prints to dry overnight.
Expected Outcome The water in the solutions will evaporate overnight, leaving solid crystals as hand prints. Students will observe that the halite crystals are cubic, while the Epsom salts crystals are orthorhombic, or prism-shaped. Which hand prints have more crystals can vary, depending on the conditions of the experiment.
Extend Have students make drawings of the two different types of crystals they observe. **learning modality: kinesthetic**

Crystal Systems The crystals of each mineral grow atom by atom to form that mineral's particular crystal structure. Geologists classify these structures into six groups based on the number and angle of the crystal faces. These groups are called crystal systems. For example, all halite crystals are cubic. Halite crystals have six sides that meet at right angles, forming a perfect cube. Sometimes you can see that a crystal has the particular crystal structure of its mineral. Crystals that grow in an open space can be almost perfectly formed. But crystals that grow in a tight space are often incompletely formed. Figure 8 shows minerals that belong to each of the six crystal systems.

Figure 8 This chart lists some common minerals and their properties. *Interpreting Data Which mineral is lowest in density and hardness? Which mineral could you identify by using a compass?*

Properties and Uses of Minerals

Name	Magnetite	Quartz	Rutile	Sulfur	Azurite	Microcline Feldspar
Hardness	6	7	$6 - 6\frac{1}{2}$	2	$3\frac{1}{2} - 4$	6
Color	Black	Transparent or in a range of colors	Black or reddish brown	Lemon yellow to yellowish brown	Blue	Green, red-brown, pink, or white
Streak	Black	Colorless	Light brown	White	Pale blue	Colorless
Crystal System	Cubic	Hexagonal	Tetragonal	Orthorhombic	Monoclinic	Triclinic
Luster	Metallic	Glassy	Metallic or gemlike	Greasy	Glassy to dull or earthy	Glassy
Special Properties	Magnetic	Fractures like broken glass	Not easily melted	Melts easily	Reacts to acid	Cleaves well in two directions
Density (g/cm³)	5.2	2.6	4.2–4.3	2.0–2.1	3.8	2.6
Uses	A source of iron used to make steel	Used in making glass and electronic equipment, or as a gem	Contains titanium, a hard, light-weight metal used in aircraft and cars	Used in fungicides, industrial chemicals, and rubber	A source of copper metal; also used as a gem	Used in pottery glaze, scouring powder, or as a gem

456

Background

Facts and Figures The hardness of a mineral greatly depends on the strength of the bonds that hold its atoms together. For example, both diamond and graphite are pure carbon, but the strongly bonded atoms of a diamond make it much harder than graphite.

Students doing further research on minerals may find that geology books list *specific gravity* among the properties instead of density. A mineral's specific gravity is its weight compared to the weight of an equal volume of water. Since specific gravity is a ratio, it is not expressed in units, and that is why it is favored by geologists. But because 1 cm³ of water has a mass of 1 g, the value for specific gravity and density is the same. For example, quartz has a specific gravity of 2.65 and a density of 2.65 g/cm³. Thus, to translate a figure for specific gravity into density, just add the unit to the value.

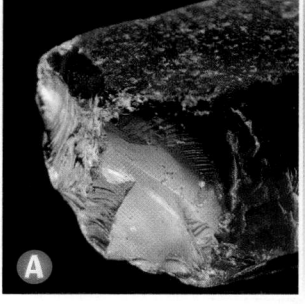

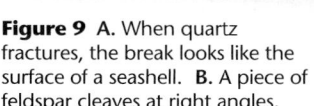

Figure 9 A. When quartz fractures, the break looks like the surface of a seashell. **B.** A piece of feldspar cleaves at right angles. **C.** Mica cleaves into thin, flat sheets that are almost transparent.
Applying Concepts How would you test a mineral to determine its cleavage and fracture?

Cleavage and Fracture The way a mineral breaks apart can help to identify it. A mineral that splits easily along flat surfaces has the property called **cleavage.** Whether a mineral has cleavage depends on how the atoms in its crystals are arranged. Depending on the arrangement of atoms in the mineral, it will break apart more easily in one direction than another. Look at the minerals in Figure 9. Mica separates easily in only one direction, forming flat sheets. Feldspar splits at right angles, producing square corners. These minerals have cleavage.

Most minerals do not split apart evenly. Instead, they have a characteristic type of fracture. **Fracture** describes how a mineral looks when it breaks apart in an irregular way. Geologists use a variety of terms to describe fracture. For example, quartz has a shell-shaped fracture. When quartz breaks, it produces curved, shell-like surfaces that look like chipped glass. Pure metals, like copper and iron, have a hackly fracture—they form jagged points. Some soft minerals that crumble easily like clay have an earthy fracture. Minerals that form rough, irregular surfaces when broken have an uneven fracture.

☑ *Checkpoint* *How are cleavage and fracture similar? How are they different?*

Crystal Hands

You can grow two different kinds of salt crystals.

ACTIVITY

1. Put on your goggles.
2. ☠ Pour a solution of halite (table salt) into one shallow pan and a solution of Epsom salts into another shallow pan.
3. Put a large piece of black construction paper on a flat surface.
4. Dip one hand in the halite solution. Shake off the excess liquid and make a palm print on the paper. Repeat with your other hand and the Epsom salt solution, placing your new print next to the first one. **CAUTION:** *Do not do this activity if you have a cut on your hand. Wash your hands after making your hand prints.*
5. Let the prints dry overnight.

Observing Use a hand lens to compare the shape of the crystals. Which hand prints have more crystals?

Program Resources

◆ **Laboratory Manual** 14, "How Tesselating!"

Media and Technology

 Transparencies "Properties and Uses of Minerals," Transparency 56

Answers to Self-Assessment

Caption Questions

Figure 8 Sulfur; magnetite
Figure 9 You would break a mineral apart to determine its cleavage and fracture.

☑ *Checkpoint*

Cleavage refers to when a mineral splits easily along a flat surface. Fracture describes how a mineral looks when it breaks apart in an irregular way.

Including All Students

Materials *2 paper towels*
Time 10 minutes

To reinforce the concept of cleavage, provide each student with a paper towel. Ask: **In which direction does a paper towel split, or tear, evenly?** Students should find that the towel tears evenly from top to bottom but not from left to right. This is similar to a mineral with cleavage that breaks apart easily in one direction but not in another. **learning modality: kinesthetic**

Demonstration

Materials *samples of halite and hematite, modeling compound, razor blade, hammer, hand lens*
Time 10 minutes

Demonstrate cleavage in halite and fracture in hematite by showing students how each breaks apart. Place a piece of halite on modeling compound to hold the halite in place. Then position the sharp edge of the razor blade on the halite and tap the blade with a hammer until the mineral breaks. It should split easily along flat surfaces. Repeat with the hematite. When it breaks, it should break irregularly. **learning modality: visual**

Inquiry Challenge

Materials *unglazed porcelain tile, mineral samples such as pyrite, galena, hornblende, feldspar, talc, hematite, quartz, olivine*
Time 20 minutes

Provide each small group with 6 to 8 mineral samples. Then challenge each group to identify the properties of each mineral, including color, streak, luster, density, and cleavage/fracture. For density, they can heft each sample and place them in order from least dense to densest. For cleavage/fracture, they can closely examine the breaks and edges of each sample. Each group should make a table to record all their findings. **cooperative learning**

Ongoing Assessment

Drawing Have students make drawings of the six crystal systems, using Figure 8 as a reference.

3 Assess

Section 1 Review Answers

1. A mineral must be a naturally occurring, inorganic solid that has a crystal structure and a definite chemical composition.

2. To determine hardness, do a scratch test and use Mohs hardness scale. To determine density, divide the mineral's mass by its volume. To determine streak, rub the mineral against a piece of unglazed tile called a streak plate.

3. An element is a substance composed of a single type of atom, while in a compound two or more elements are combined.

4. Water in its liquid form is not a mineral because it is not solid. But water as ice is classified as a mineral because it is a naturally occurring, inorganic solid with a crystal structure and a definite chemical composition.

5. Two minerals could have one or more properties that are similar or the same, such as minerals with the same color or hardness. The more tests or properties considered, the more likely it becomes to make an identification.

Check Your Progress

CHAPTER PROJECT 14

Make sure that each student has completed Chapter 14 Project Worksheet 1. Review the materials and designs, and encourage students to be creative. Help students get started with making crystals.

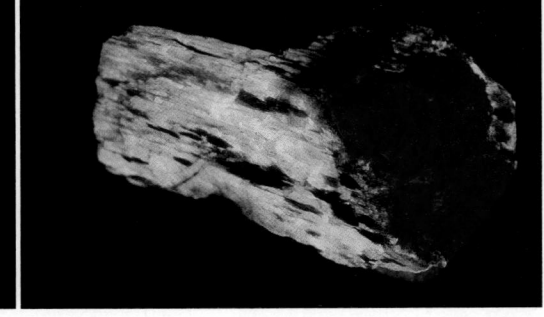

Figure 10 Scheelite looks quite ordinary in daylight, but glows with brilliant color under ultraviolet light.

Special Properties Some minerals can be identified by special physical properties. For example, minerals that glow under ultra-violet light have a property known as **fluorescence** (floo RES uns). The mineral scheelite is fluorescent. Magnetism occurs naturally in a few minerals. Lodestone, which is a form of magnetite, acts as a natural magnet. Early magnets—such as compass needles—were made by striking a piece of iron with lodestone. Uraninite and a few other minerals are radioactive. They set off a Geiger counter. Some minerals react chemically to acid. Calcite, a compound of calcium, carbon, and oxygen, fizzes and gives off carbon dioxide when a drop of vinegar is placed on it.

A few minerals, such as quartz, have electrical properties. Pressure applied to these crystals produces a small electric current. In addition, these crystals vibrate if they come in contact with an electric current. Because of these properties, quartz crystals are used in microphones, radio transmitters, and watches.

Section 1 Review

1. What characteristics must a substance have to be considered a mineral?
2. Describe how you can test a mineral to determine its hardness, density, and streak.
3. What is the major difference between an element and a compound?
4. **Thinking Critically Classifying** According to the definition of a mineral, can water be classified as a mineral? Explain your answer.
5. **Thinking Critically Making Generalizations** Explain why you can't rely on any single test or property when you are trying to identify a mineral.

Check Your Progress

CHAPTER PROJECT 14

Select a container for your crystal garden such as a plastic shoe box or a large-mouth jar. Make a sketch showing the shapes and locations of the "plants" you plan to grow. When you have designed your garden, decide what materials to put in the box for the crystals to grow on. Decide what crystal-growth solutions you will use. Halite, Epsom salts, and alum are possibilities. Check with your teacher to make sure the chemicals you plan to use are safe.

Performance Assessment

Oral Presentation Play a game using information in Appendix B. Choose a mystery mineral and begin by mentioning a property of that mineral, such as its streak color. Challenge students to identify the mineral. Announce more properties one by one until someone identifies the mineral.

Background

Facts and Figures Many minerals can be identified by their special properties. Gold is particularly malleable, which means it can easily be shaped. Clay minerals have an earthy odor. Talc feels soapy, and graphite feels greasy. The "greasiness" of graphite is useful in "dry" graphite-based lubricants. A transparent piece of calcite has the property of "double refraction." When it is placed over print, for example, the letters look to be doubled.

Program Resources

◆ **Unit 4 Resources** 14-1 Review and Reinforcement, p. 99; 14-1 Enrich, p. 100

Media and Technology

Lab Activity Videotape
Tape 3

THE DENSITY OF MINERALS

I n this lab, you will use water to help you measure the density of minerals.

Problem

How can you compare the density of different minerals?

Materials (per student)

graduated cylinder, 100 mL
3 mineral samples: pyrite, quartz, and galena
water
balance

Procedure

1. Check to make sure the mineral samples are small enough to fit in the graduated cylinder.
2. Copy the data table into your notebook. Place the pyrite on the balance and record its mass in the data table.
3. Fill the cylinder with water to the 50-mL mark.
4. Carefully place the pyrite into the cylinder of water. Try not to spill any of the water.
5. Read the level of the water on the scale of the graduated cylinder. Record the level of the water with the pyrite in it.
6. Calculate the volume of water displaced by the pyrite. To do this, subtract the volume of water without the pyrite from the volume of water with the pyrite. Record your answer.
7. Calculate the density of the pyrite by using this formula.

$$\text{Density} = \frac{\text{Mass of mineral}}{\text{Volume of water displaced by the mineral}}$$

(Note: Density is expressed as g/cm^3. One mL of water has a volume of 1 cm^3.)

8. Remove the water and mineral from the cylinder.
9. Repeat steps 2–8 for quartz and galena.

Analyze and Conclude

1. Which mineral had the highest density? The lowest density?
2. How does finding the volume of the water that was displaced help you find the volume of the mineral itself?
3. Why won't the procedure you used in this lab work for a substance that floats or one that dissolves in water?
4. **Apply** Pyrite is sometimes called "fool's gold" because its color and appearance are similar to real gold. How could a scientist determine if a sample was real gold?
5. **Think About It** Does the shape or size of a mineral sample affect its density? Explain.

More to Explore

Repeat the activity by finding the density of other minerals or materials. Then compare the densities of these materials with pyrite, quartz, and galena.

DATA TABLE

	Pyrite	Quartz	Galena
Mass of Mineral (g)			
Volume of Water without Mineral (mL)	50	50	50
Volume of Water with Mineral (mL)			
Volume of Water Displaced (mL)			
Volume of Water Displaced (cm^3)			
Density (g/cm^3)			

Safety

Have students wear safety goggles. Review the safety guidelines in Appendix A.

Program Resources

◆ **Unit 4 Resources** Skills Lab blackline masters, pp. 109–111

Analyze and Conclude

1. Galena, the highest; quartz, the lowest
2. The volume of water displaced equals the volume of the mineral itself.
3. One that floats would not displace a volume of water equal to itself; one that dissolves would not displace any water.
4. First determine the density of the sample, and then compare that to the known density of gold.
5. Neither affects density because each mineral has a characteristic density.

Measuring

The Density of Minerals

Preparing for Inquiry

Key Concept Each mineral has a characteristic density.

Skills Objectives Students will be able to
◆ measure the density of minerals;
◆ draw conclusions about how density helps identify minerals.

Time 40 minutes

Advance Planning Collect enough mineral samples. Make sure each sample will fit into a graduated cylinder. Students may need calculators to calculate the density of the samples.

Guiding Inquiry

Introducing the Procedure

◆ Ask: **What is density?** (*A measure of how much mass there is in one unit volume of a substance*) Then have students relate that definition to the formula for density in Step 7.

Troubleshooting the Experiment

◆ Emphasize that spilling any water when placing a sample in the graduated cylinder will distort the calculation of density.
◆ Demonstrate finding mass and volume of one mineral sample, and then do an example calculation on the board, using the formula given in Step 7.

Expected Outcome

In students' data tables, figures for Volume of Water with Mineral and Volume of Water Displaced will vary depending on the sample sizes. Students' calculations of density should be close to these: galena, 7.4–7.6 g/cm^3; pyrite, 5.0 g/cm^3; quartz, 2.6 g/cm^3.

Extending the Inquiry

More to Explore Challenge students to find the density of other mineral samples and then check the densities they find with the figures in Appendix B.

SECTION 2 — How Minerals Form

Objective

After completing the lesson, students will be able to

◆ describe the processes by which minerals form.

Key Terms solution, vein

1 Engage/Explore

Activating Prior Knowledge

Invite students to describe diamonds and other gems they have seen. Point out that all these gems are minerals mined from Earth's crust. Then ask: **What processes do you think are involved in the formation of a diamond?** (*A typical answer might mention high temperatures and pressures deep underground.*) Tell students that they will learn about the formation of minerals in this section.

DISCOVER

Skills Focus relating cause and effect

Materials *salol, plastic spoon, 2 microscope slides, tongs, candle, matches, ice cube, hand lens*

Time 15 minutes

Tips Obtain salol (phenyl salicylate) from a drugstore or a chemical supply house. Students should wear goggles to make sure they do not get salol in their eyes. Caution students not to overheat the slide, especially the one placed on ice because it might break. Moving the slide from side to side over the flame will prevent overheating. Keep the slides on which the salol has hardened for remelting by other classes.

Expected Outcome The crystals that form on the two slides will be of different sizes. On the first slide, the crystals should be larger, because of the slower cooling. On the second slide, the crystals should be smaller, because of the more rapid cooling.

Think It Over The first sample should have larger crystals. The crystals formed by rapid cooling should have small crystals.

SECTION 2 — How Minerals Form

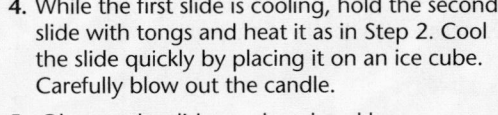

DISCOVER ···························· ACTIVITY

How Does the Rate of Cooling Affect Crystals?

1. ☠ Put on your goggles. Use a plastic spoon to place a small amount of salol near one end of each of two microscope slides. You need just enough to form a spot 0.5 to 1.0 cm in diameter.

2. 🔥🧤 Carefully hold one slide with tongs. Warm it gently over a lit candle until the salol is almost completely melted. **CAUTION:** *Move the slide in and out of the flame to avoid cracking the glass.*

3. Set the slide aside to cool slowly.

4. While the first slide is cooling, hold the second slide with tongs and heat it as in Step 2. Cool the slide quickly by placing it on an ice cube. Carefully blow out the candle.

5. Observe the slides under a hand lens. Compare the appearance of the crystals that form on the two slides.

6. Wash your hands when you are finished.

Think It Over
Relating Cause and Effect
Which sample had larger crystals? If a mineral forms by rapid cooling, would you expect the crystals to be large or small?

GUIDE FOR READING

◆ What are the processes by which minerals form?

Reading Tip Before you read, rewrite the headings of the section as how, why, or what questions. As you read, look for answers to these questions.

Imagine digging for diamonds. At Crater of Diamonds State Park in Arkansas, that's exactly what people do. The park is one of the very few places in the United States where diamonds can be found. Visitors are permitted to prospect, or search, for diamonds. Since the area became a park in 1972, visitors have found more than 20,000 diamonds!

How did the diamonds get there? Millions of years ago, a volcanic pipe formed in the mantle at a depth of 120 kilometers or more. At that depth, great

Diamonds ▶

READING STRATEGIES

Reading Tip The headings translate into these questions: What processes form minerals? How do minerals form from magma? How do minerals form from hot water solutions? How do minerals form by evaporation? Where are minerals found? Encourage students to use these questions as a study guide for the section. For each question, they should write a short paragraph that answers it succinctly but completely.

Vocabulary Remind students that a solution is a type of homogenous mixture in which substances are equally mixed throughout. The dissolved substance, called the solute, is mixed evenly throughout the dissolving substance, called the solvent. In the cases discussed in this section, the solvent is water and the solutes are elements or compounds in magma.

pressure and heat changed carbon atoms into the hardest known substance—diamond. Then the pipe erupted, carrying diamonds and other materials toward the surface. Today, geologists recognize this type of volcanic pipe as an area of unusual bluish-colored rock made up of a variety of minerals, including diamond. Volcanic pipes containing diamonds are found in only a few places on Earth. Most occur in South Africa and Australia, where many of the world's diamonds are mined today.

Processes That Form Minerals

You probably have handled products made from minerals. But you may not have thought about how the minerals formed. The minerals that people use today have been forming deep in Earth's crust or on the surface for several billion years. **In general, minerals can form in two ways: through crystallization of melted materials, and through crystallization of materials dissolved in water.** Crystallization is the process by which atoms are arranged to form a material with a crystal structure.

Minerals From Magma

Minerals form as hot magma cools inside the crust, or as lava hardens on the surface. When these liquids cool to the solid state, they form crystals. The size of the crystals depends on several factors. The rate at which the magma cools, the amount of gas the magma contains, and the chemical composition of the magma all affect crystal size.

When magma remains deep below the surface, it cools slowly over many thousands of years. Slow cooling leads to the formation of large crystals. If the crystals remain undisturbed while cooling, they grow by adding atoms according to a regular pattern.

Magma closer to the surface cools much faster than magma that hardens deep below ground. With more rapid cooling, there is no time for magma to form large crystals. Instead, small crystals form. If magma erupts to the surface and becomes lava, the lava will also cool quickly and form minerals with small crystals.

Figure 11 This crystal of the mineral spodumene is 24 cm long. But it's not the largest crystal. Spodumene crystals the size of telephone poles have been found in South Dakota. *Inferring Under what conditions did such large crystals probably form?*

Program Resources

◆ **Unit 4 Resources** 14-2 Lesson Plan, p. 101; 14-2 Section Summary, p. 102
◆ **Guided Reading and Study Workbook** Section 14-2

Answers to Self-Assessment

Caption Question

Figure 11 The large crystals probably formed deep below the surface, where magma cooled slowly over many thousands of years.

---

2 Facilitate

Processes That Form Minerals

Addressing Naive Conceptions

Many students may believe that mineral crystallization always results in perfectly formed crystals. In reality, fully formed crystals are relatively rare. Most crystals only partially form because they form at the same time as crystals of the same and other minerals. Pass around pieces of granite, and point out that granite is composed of such minerals as quartz, feldspar, and hornblende. Ask: **Can you see any fully formed quartz crystals in this rock?** (*No, only fragments of crystals can be seen.*) Emphasize that crystallization indicates the formation of a crystalline solid but not necessarily a complete crystal. **learning modality: visual**

Minerals From Magma

Building Inquiry Skills: Designing Experiments

Time 20 minutes

ACTIVITY

Ask: **What experiment could test the hypothesis that the rate at which a substance cools affects the size of the crystals that form?** Divide students into small groups and challenge each group to design an experiment that would test the hypothesis. (*A typical experiment would involve cooling two identical solutions at different rates and then comparing the crystals that form.*) Once groups have designed their experiments, examine them in a class discussion. Then help interested students carry out one of the experiments and report their findings to the class.

Ongoing Assessment

Skills Check Call on students to infer whether the formation of diamonds occurs through crystallization of melted materials or of materials dissolved in water. (*Material that erupts through a volcano is melted material, and thus diamonds form through crystallization of melted materials.*)

Minerals From Magma, continued

Building Inquiry Skills: Inferring

Materials *hand lens, rock samples of granite and rhyolite*

Time 10 minutes

Invite students to examine samples of granite and rhyolite. Explain that both rocks are composed mostly of the same minerals, including feldspar and quartz. Then ask: **What can you infer about the conditions under which each formed?** *(Students should infer that the granite cooled slower than the rhyolite because it has larger mineral crystals. Few if any crystals can be seen in rhyolite.)* Explain that granite forms when magma cools slowly underground and rhyolite forms when lava cools quickly on the surface.

learning modality: visual

Minerals From Hot Water Solutions

Using the Visuals: Figure 12

Ask students: **In the solutions described in the caption, what is the solvent and what are the solutes?** *(Water is the solvent, and minerals are the solutes.)* Explain that both the water and the minerals were part of the magma. After many other minerals have crystallized, such solutions are left. The minerals in these cases are often metals, such as silver and gold. Ask: **What are other kinds of veins you know about?** *(Veins that carry blood in the body.)* Point out that a mineral vein is visually similar to a vein in the body. The difference is that a fluid flows through a vein in the body, while a mineral vein is solid and stable, at least once the mineral has crystallized.

learning modality: verbal

Figure 12 A. Silver sometimes occurs as a pure metal, forming delicate, treelike crystals. B. Solutions containing dissolved metals form veins like the ones in this silver mine in Idaho.

Minerals From Hot Water Solutions

Sometimes, the elements that form a mineral dissolve in hot water. Magma has heated the water to a high temperature beneath Earth's surface. These dissolved minerals form solutions. A **solution** is a mixture in which one substance dissolves in another. When a hot water solution begins to cool, the elements and compounds leave the solution and crystallize as minerals. The silver shown in Figure 12A formed by this process.

Pure metals that crystallize underground from hot water solutions often form veins. A **vein** is a narrow channel or slab of a mineral that is much different from the surrounding rock. Deep underground, solutions of hot water and metals often follow cracks within the rock. Then the metals crystallize into veins that resemble the streaks of fudge in vanilla fudge ice cream. Figure 12B shows a vein of silver in a mine.

Many minerals form from solutions at places where tectonic plates spread apart along the mid-ocean ridge. First, ocean water

Figure 13 Many minerals form at chimneys along the mid-ocean ridge. Chimneys occur in areas where sea-floor spreading causes cracks in the oceanic crust. *Interpreting Diagrams What is the energy source for this process?*

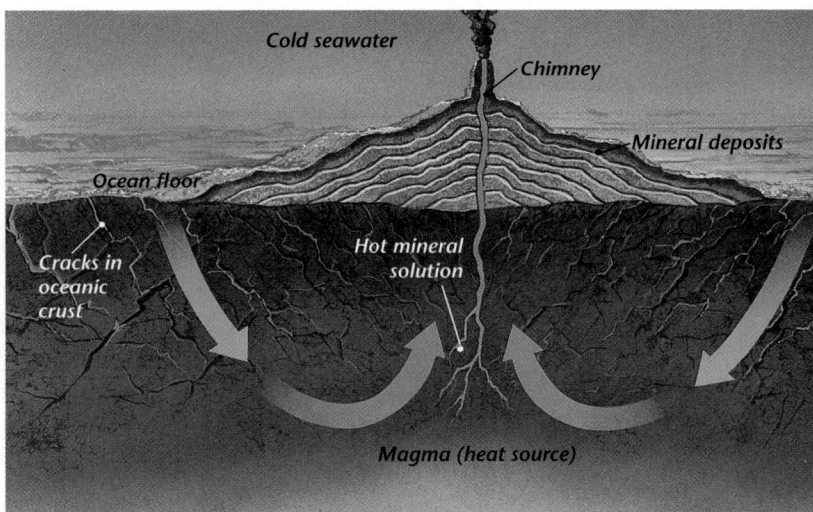

Cold seawater

Chimney

Mineral deposits

Ocean floor

Hot mineral solution

Cracks in oceanic crust

Magma (heat source)

462

Background

Facts and Figures The explanation for the multitude of minerals is that different minerals crystallize at different temperatures as magma cools. For example, olivine crystallizes at 1200°C, while quartz crystallizes at 700°C. Thus, a complicated process occurs as magma cools. Certain minerals crystallize at certain temperatures, and as they do, they tend to deplete the magma of the elements they use, changing the makeup of the magma that remains. One reason quartz tends to crystallize late in the process is because, by that time, a lot of silicon and oxygen are left in the magma. Also left at the end are rare metals such as gold and silver, and they flow into fractures with the water that's also left over, eventually crystallizing into veins.

After students have examined the figure and read the caption, ask: **What layer of Earth does the magma come from and why is it hot?** *(Magma comes from the mantle. It is hot because the mantle is heated by Earth's core.)* Explain that some materials dissolve better the higher the temperature of the solvent water. Ask: **What happens to the temperature of the heated water once it belches out of the chimneys?** *(The temperature drops very quickly as the water flows into the almost freezing ocean water.)* As a consequence of the sudden temperature change, the minerals crystallize and settle to the ocean floor. **learning modality: visual**

seeps down through cracks in the crust. There, the water comes in contact with magma that heats it to a very high temperature. The heated water dissolves minerals from the crust and rushes upward. This hot solution then billows out of vents, called "chimneys." When the hot solution hits the cold sea, minerals crystallize and settle to the ocean floor.

Figure 14 In Death Valley, California, water carries dissolved minerals from the surrounding mountains into the valley. When the water evaporates under the blazing desert sun, the minerals form a crust on the valley floor.

Minerals Formed by Evaporation

Minerals can also form when solutions evaporate. You know that if you stir salt crystals into a beaker of water, the salt dissolves, forming a solution. But if you allow the water in the solution to evaporate, it will leave salt crystals on the bottom of the beaker. In a similar way, thick deposits of the mineral halite formed over millions of years when ancient seas slowly evaporated. In the United States, such halite deposits occur in the Midwest, the Southwest, and along the Gulf Coast.

Several other useful minerals also form by the evaporation of seawater. These include gypsum, used in making building materials; calcite crystals, used in microscopes; and minerals containing potassium, used in making fertilizer.

Minerals Formed by Evaporation

Demonstration

Materials *salt, water, large glass bowl, measuring cup, spoon*
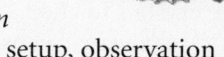

Time 5 minutes for setup, observation over 2 weeks

To model how salt deposits form, set up this demonstration as students begin the chapter. Prepare a saturated salt solution by stirring 30 mL of salt into 125 mL of water. Then set the bowl in a sunny place and allow the water to evaporate. Periodically call students' attention to changes in the bowl. When the water has completely evaporated, a deposit of salt crystals will be left. Ask: **What natural process does this demonstration model?** *(The formation of halite deposits by evaporation of seawater)* **learning modality: visual**

Chapter 14 **463**

Ongoing Assessment

Skills Check Have students make three flowcharts: one that shows how veins form, one that shows how minerals form near the mid-ocean ridge, and one that shows how minerals form through evaporation.

Where Minerals Are Found

Using the Visuals: Figure 15

Have students turn back to the map of Earth's plates in Chapter 11, Section 5, and compare the location of plate boundaries with the distribution of metals shown on this map. Ask: **What pattern do you see when you compare maps?** (*The distribution of metals roughly matches the location of plate boundaries.*) **What can you infer from this?** (*Metals are formed near plate boundaries.*) **learning modality: visual**

3 Assess

Section 2 Review Answers

1. Through crystallization of melted materials and crystallization of materials dissolved in water

2. The slower the cooling rate, the larger the crystals formed.

3. Ocean water seeps through cracks in the crust. Magma heats the water to high temperatures. Heated water dissolves minerals in the crust, rushes upward, and billows out of "chimneys." In the cold sea, minerals crystallize and settle.

4. Deep underground, a solution of hot water and silver followed a fracture within rock. When the solution cooled, the silver crystallized into a vein.

Check Your Progress

CHAPTER PROJECT 14

Make sure students are recording observations, including written descriptions, drawings of crystals, and measurements of growth. Students can make line graphs comparing the growth of different crystals.

Performance Assessment

Skills Check Have each student make a concept map entitled The Formation of Minerals. The map should include the two general ways in which minerals form and then branch out into specific ways and details.

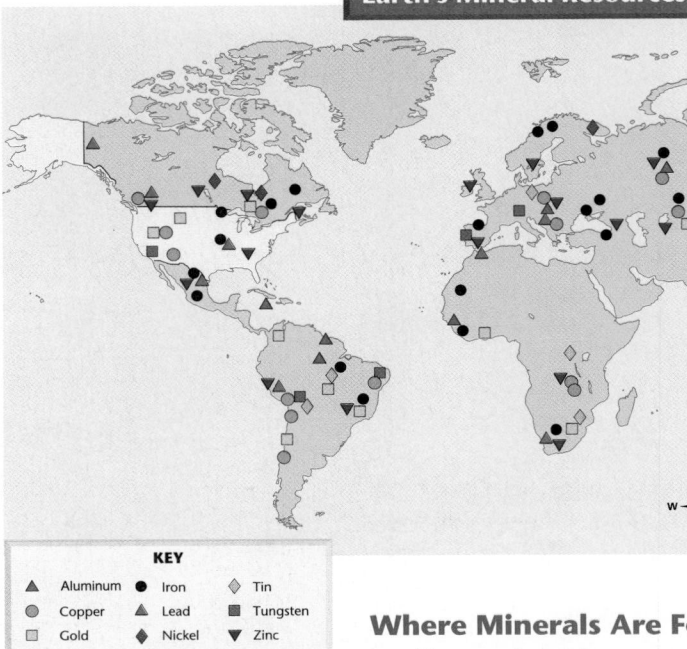

Earth's Mineral Resources

KEY

▲	Aluminum	● Iron	◆ Tin
●	Copper	▲ Lead	■ Tungsten
■	Gold	◆ Nickel	▼ Zinc

Figure 15 The map shows where important mineral resources are found throughout the world. *Interpreting Maps Which metals are found in the United States? Which ones must be imported from other countries?*

Where Minerals Are Found

Earth's crust is made up mostly of the common rock-forming minerals combined in various types of rock. Less common and rare minerals, however, are not distributed evenly throughout the crust. Instead, there are several processes that concentrate minerals, or bring them together, in deposits. Look at the map of the world's mineral resources in Figure 15. Do you see any patterns in the distribution of minerals such as gold and copper? Many valuable minerals are found in or near areas of volcanic activity and mountain building. For example, rich copper deposits are found along the Andes mountains in Chile.

Section 2 Review

1. What are the two main ways in which minerals form?
2. Describe how the cooling rate of magma affects the size of the mineral crystals formed.
3. What are the steps by which mineral deposits form along mid-ocean ridges?
4. **Thinking Critically Relating Cause and Effect** A miner finds a vein of silver. Describe a process that could have formed the vein.

Check Your Progress

CHAPTER PROJECT 14

Remember to record your daily observations of how your crystal garden grows. Sketch the shapes of the crystals and describe how the crystals grow. Compare the shapes and growth rates of the crystals grown from the various solutions. (*Hint:* If crystals do not begin growing, add more of the correct solution.)

Answers to Self-Assessment

Caption Question

Figure 15 Metals found in the United States include copper, gold, iron, lead, tungsten, and zinc. Therefore, bauxite, nickel, and tin must be imported.

Program Resources

◆ **Unit 4 Resources** 14–2 Review and Reinforcement, p. 103; 14–2 Enrich, p. 104

Who Owns the Ocean's Minerals?

Rich mineral deposits lie on and just beneath the ocean floor. Many nations would like to mine these deposits. Coastal nations already have the right to mine deposits near their shores. Today, they are mining materials such as tin, titanium, diamonds, and sulfur from the continental shelf—the wide area of shallow water just off the shores of continents.

But the ocean floor beyond the continental shelves is open for all nations to explore. Mineral deposits in volcanic areas of the ocean floor include manganese, iron, cobalt, copper, nickel and platinum. Who owns these valuable underwater minerals?

▲ This sample from the floor of the Pacific Ocean near New Guinea may contain copper and gold.

The Issues

Who Can Afford to Mine? Although the ocean floor is open to all for exploration, mining the ocean floor will cost a huge amount of money. New technologies must be developed to obtain mineral deposits from the ocean floor.

Only wealthy industrial nations such as France, Germany, Japan, and the United States will be able to afford these costs. Industrial nations that have spent money and effort on mining think that they should be allowed to keep all the profits. However, developing nations that lack money and technology disagree. Landlocked nations that have no coastlines also object.

What Rights Do Other Nations Have? As of 1996, 87 nations had signed the Law of the Sea treaty. Among other things, this treaty stated that ocean mineral deposits are the common property of all people. It also stated that mining profits must be shared among all nations.

Some people think that, because of the treaty, wealthy nations should share their technology and any profits they get from mining the ocean floor.

How Can the Wealth Be Shared? What can nations do to prevent conflict over mining the ocean floor? They might arrange a compromise. Perhaps wealthy nations should contribute part of their profits to help developing or landlocked nations. Developing nations could pool their money for ocean-floor mining. Whatever nations decide, some regulations for ocean-floor mining are necessary. In the future, these resources will be important to everyone.

You Decide

1. **Identify the Problem** In your own words, state the controversy about ocean mineral rights.

2. **Analyze the Options** Compare the concerns of wealthy nations with those of developing nations. How could you reassure developing nations that they will not be left out?

3. **Find a Solution** Look at a map of the world. Who should share the mineral profits from the Pacific Ocean? From the Atlantic Ocean? Write one or two paragraphs stating your opinion. Support your ideas with facts.

You Decide

1. Statements will vary. A typical statement should mention that the minerals on the ocean floor are valuable resources and there are differing opinions about who owns those resources.

2. Answers will vary. A typical answer might suggest that the wealthy nations have a much better opportunity to exploit the ocean's resources than do developing nations. One solution is to require that wealthy nations share any profits from mining of those resources.

3. Solutions will vary. Accept any solution as long as it shows the student has thought about the problem.

Science and Society

Purpose

Students will develop and express opinions about the difficult issue of ownership of the ocean's mineral resources.

Debate

Time 20 minutes for preparation, 20 minutes for debate

Have students read the feature and answer the You Decide questions individually as a homework assignment. The next day, divide the class into small groups for discussion. Have students consider these questions: Who should own the minerals on the ocean floor? Do the people of wealthy nations have any obligation to share profits from mining of these minerals with people from developing nations? Do private companies from any nation have an obligation to share profits with all the nations of the world?

◆ Divide the class into two groups. Arbitrarily assign one group to argue that wealthy nations and companies have no obligation to share profits from the mining of these minerals. Assign the other group to argue that the wealth should be shared equally among nations. Alternately call on students from each group to state its position or refute an idea someone from the other group has put forward.

Extend Encourage interested students to write to the U.S. State Department and to the U.S. Ambassador to the United Nations to find out about the current government's position on the ownership and use of the ocean's mineral resources. A first step might be to find these agencies' web pages on the Internet. The inquiry could then be made via e-mail, which might expedite a reply.

SECTION 3 Mineral Resources

Objectives

After completing the lesson, students will be able to
◆ describe how minerals are used;
◆ list the three types of mines;
◆ explain how ores are processed to obtain metals.

Key Terms gemstone, ore, smelting, alloy

1 Engage/Explore

Activating Prior Knowledge

Ask students: **Which things that you use every day are made of minerals?** *(Answers will vary. A typical answer might mention metallic things, such as bicycles, autos, and coins.)* **What process do you think could turn a mineral mined from the ground into a shiny piece of steel?** *(Some students may describe a steel mill, in which ore is melted in furnaces.)* Explain that this section will give some answers to these questions.

 DISCOVER

Skills Focus posing questions
Materials *samples of bauxite and graphite, aluminum can, pencil*
Time 10 minutes
Tips Place samples of bauxite and graphite, as well as the aluminum can, on a table in a central location. Have students make notes of their observations.
Think It Over While bauxite is brown, crumbly, and of a dull luster, the aluminum can is silver, hard, and of a metallic luster. The graphite sample and pencil lead are much more alike, with both being soft, dark, greasy, and of almost a metallic luster. Students should pose questions about the processes involved in turning these minerals into finished products.

466

SECTION 3 Mineral Resources

DISCOVER .... ACTIVITY

How Are Minerals Processed Before They Are Used?

1. Examine a piece of the mineral bauxite and use your knowledge of the properties of minerals to describe it.

2. Examine an aluminum can. (The metal aluminum comes from bauxite.) Compare the properties of the aluminum can with the properties of bauxite.

3. Examine a piece of the mineral graphite and describe its properties.

4. Examine the lead in a pencil. (Pencil "lead" is made from graphite.) Compare the properties of the pencil lead with the properties of graphite.

Think It Over
Posing Questions How is each mineral similar to or different from the object made from it? What questions would you need to answer to understand how bauxite and graphite are made into useful materials?

GUIDE FOR READING

◆ How are minerals used?
◆ What are the three types of mines?
◆ How are ores processed to obtain metals?

Reading Tip As you read, draw a concept map that explains how metal ores are located, mined, and smelted.

Figure 16 The copper to make this Hopewell ornament may have come from an area in Michigan that is still a source of copper ore.

More than a thousand years ago, the Hopewell people lived in the Mississippi River valley. These ancient Native Americans are famous for the mysterious earthen mounds they built near the river. There these people left beautiful objects made from minerals: tools chipped from flint (a variety of quartz), the shape of a human hand cut out of a piece of translucent mica, or a flying bird made from a thin sheet of copper.

To obtain these minerals, the Hopewell people traded with peoples across North America. The copper, for example, came from near Lake Superior. There, copper could be found as a pure metal. Because copper is a soft metal, this copper was easy to shape into ornaments or weapons.

The Uses of Minerals

Like the Hopewell people, people today use minerals. You are surrounded by materials that come from minerals—for example, the metal body and window glass of a car. **Minerals are the source of metals, gemstones, and other materials used to make many products.** Are you familiar with any products that are made from minerals? You might be surprised at how important minerals are in everyday life.

466

READING STRATEGIES

Reading Tip Review with students how to make a concept map. They should link information on a main topic with specific related information that clarifies the main topic.

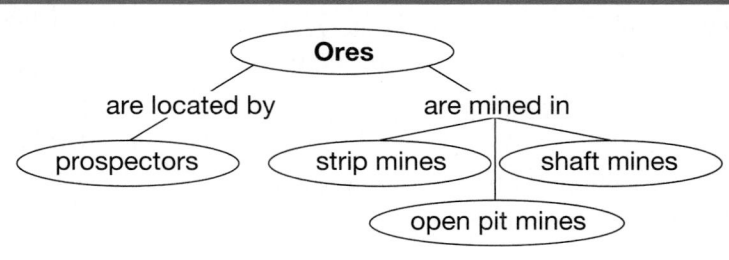

Gemstones Beautiful gemstones such as rubies and sapphires have captured the imagination of people throughout the ages. Usually, a **gemstone** is a hard, colorful mineral that has a brilliant or glassy luster. People value gemstones for their color, luster, and durability—and for the fact that they are rare. Once a gemstone is cut and polished, it is called a gem. Gems are used mainly for jewelry and decoration. They are also used for mechanical parts and for grinding and polishing.

Metals Some minerals are the sources of metals such as aluminum, iron, copper, or silver. Metals are useful because they can be stretched into wire, flattened into sheets, and hammered or molded without breaking. Metal tools and machinery, the metal filament in a light bulb, even the steel girders used to frame office buildings—all began as minerals inside Earth's crust.

Other Useful Minerals There are many other useful minerals besides metals and gems. People use materials from these minerals in foods, medicines, fertilizers, and building materials. The very soft mineral talc is ground up to make talcum powder. Fluorite is important in making aluminum and steel. Clear crystals of the mineral calcite are used in optical instruments such as microscopes. Quartz, a mineral found in sand, is used in making glass as well as in electronic equipment and watches. Kaolin occurs as white clay, which is used for making high-quality china and pottery. Gypsum, a soft, white mineral, is used to make wallboard, cement, and stucco. Corundum, the second hardest mineral after diamond, is often used in polishing and cleaning products.

☑ *Checkpoint* *What is a gemstone? Why are gemstones valuable?*

Ores

A rock that contains a metal or economically useful mineral is called an **ore**. Unlike the copper used by the Hopewell people, most metals do not occur in a pure form. A metal usually occurs as a mineral that is a combination of that metal and other elements. Much of the world's copper, for example, comes from ores containing the mineral chalcopyrite (kal kuh PY ryt). Before metals, gemstones, and other useful minerals can be separated from their ores, however, geologists must find them.

Figure 17 Gems like these red rubies and blue and yellow sapphires are among the most valuable minerals. These precious gems are varieties of the mineral corundum.

Program Resources

◆ **Unit 4 Resources** 14-3 Lesson Plan, p. 105; 14-3 Section Summary, p. 106
◆ **Guided Reading and Study Workbook** Section 14-3

Answers to Self-Assessment

☑ *Checkpoint*
Usually, a gemstone is a hard, colorful mineral that has a brilliant or glassy luster. They are valuable for their color, luster, and durability and because they are rare.

---

2 Facilitate

The Uses of Minerals

Real-Life Learning

Ask other teachers, staff, and other adults who  work at the school to stop by your classroom and show students gems they own and wear. (An alternative is to provide catalogues selling jewelry for students to examine.) These gems might include diamonds as well as emerald (beryl), ruby (corundum), sapphire (corundum), amethyst (quartz), jade (jadite), opal (opal), topaz (topaz), and turquoise (turquoise). Have students examine the gems, make notes about shape and color, and then find the mineral source in a dictionary or encyclopedia. **learning modality: visual**

Ores

Building Inquiry Skills: Comparing and Contrasting

Materials *cast-iron skillet, samples of magnetite and hematite*
Time 15 minutes

Display a cast-iron skillet and samples of iron ore. Explain to students that the skillet is a form of almost pure iron and that the two minerals are used as iron ore. Then have each student make a compare/contrast table that includes the name, formula, color, luster, and texture of the cast iron and the two minerals. **learning modality: visual**

Ongoing Assessment

Skills Check Encourage students to begin a table that lists all minerals in the left column and their uses in the right column. They should begin by including minerals and uses discussed on this page and continue the table by including all the minerals and uses they learn about during their study of the chapter.

 Students can save their tables in their portfolios.

Prospecting

Addressing Naive Conceptions

From movies and television shows, students may believe that "prospectors" are grizzled old men who pan for silver and gold in the mountains of the West. Ask: **What image comes to mind when you hear about a prospector?** *(Many students will describe the stereotypical prospector.)* Explain that only a few people fit that image. Most modern prospectors are geologists who use modern techniques and technology to find ore deposits. **learning modality: verbal**

Mining

Real-Life Learning

Bring to class pictures of mines from geology books and old magazines. These should include strip mines, open-pit mines, and shaft mines. The largest copper mine in the world is the open-pit mine at Bingham Canyon, Utah, and photos of it are common in texts. Photos of strip mines and shaft mines are often of coal rather than mineral mines, but they will serve to illustrate the basic types of mines. Show the pictures to students and have them write a description of what they observe. **learning modality: visual**

 ### Integrating Environmental Science

Encourage student volunteers to contact their state's Environmental Protection Agency (EPA) by telephone or e-mail to ask about requirements and regulations for mine operators. Students should ask what the operators need to do to prevent pollution and to repair the land after use. The state EPA may be able to send pamphlets or brochures. If not, have students take notes and report to the class. **learning modality: verbal**

Prospecting

A prospector is anyone who searches, or prospects, for an ore deposit. Geologists prospect for ores by looking for certain features on Earth's surface. These geologists observe what kind of rocks are on the land surface. They examine plants growing in an area and test stream water for the presence of certain chemicals.

Geologists also employ some of the tools used to study Earth's interior. In one technique, they set off explosions below ground to create shock waves. The echoes of these shock waves are used to map the location, size, and shape of an ore deposit.

Mining

The geologist's map of an ore deposit helps miners decide how to mine the ore from the ground. **There are three types of mines: strip mines, open pit mines, and shaft mines.** In strip mining,

Advances in Metal Technology

For thousands of years, people have been inventing and improving methods for smelting metals and making alloys.

4000 B.C. Cyprus

The island of Cyprus was one of the first places where copper was mined and smelted. In fact, the name of the island provided the name of the metal. In Latin, *aes cyprium* meant "metal of Cyprus." It was later shortened to *cuprum*, meaning "copper." The sculptured figure is carrying a large piece of smelted copper.

4000 B.C.	2500 B.C.	1000 B.C.

3500 B.C.
Mesopotamia

Metalworkers in Sumer, a city between the Tigris and Euphrates rivers, made an alloy of tin and copper to produce a harder metal—bronze. Bronze was poured into molds to form statues, weapons, or vessels for food and drink.

1500 B.C.
Turkey

The Hittites learned to mine and smelt iron ore. Because iron is stronger than copper or bronze, its use spread rapidly. Tools and weapons could be made of iron. This iron dagger was made in Austria several hundred years after the Hittites' discovery.

468

Background

Facts and Figures A mineral is classified as an ore only if it can be mined at a profit. For example, aluminum constitutes a little over 8 percent of Earth's crust. For an aluminum deposit to be considered an ore, it must be concentrated to about four times that, or about 32 percent of the crust of an area. By contrast, copper constitutes only about 0.0135 percent of the crust. To be considered an ore, it must be concentrated to about 100 times that amount. Yet it would still be only about 1 percent of the crust.

History of Science Bronze was the first alloy worked, or shaped, into tools and weapons. Historians date the Bronze Age from about 3500–1200 B.C. in the Middle East and 2000–500 B.C. in Europe. The Bronze Age followed the Stone Age and preceded the Iron Age.

earthmoving equipment scrapes away soil to expose ore. In open pit mining, miners use giant earthmoving equipment to dig a tremendous pit. Miners dig an open pit mine to remove ore deposits that may start near the surface, but extend down for hundreds of meters. Some open pit mines are more than a kilometer wide and nearly as deep. For ore deposits that occur in veins, miners dig shaft mines. Shaft mines often have a network of tunnels that extend deep into the ground, following the veins of ore.

 INTEGRATING ENVIRONMENTAL SCIENCE Mining for metals and other minerals can harm the environment. Strip mining and pit mining leave scars on the land. Waste materials from mining can pollute rivers and lakes. In the United States, laws now require that mine operators do as little damage to the environment as possible. To restore land damaged by strip mining, mine operators grade the surface and replace the soil.

In Your Journal

When people discover how to use metals in a new way, the discovery often produces big changes in the way those people live. Choose a development in the history of metals to research. Write a diary entry telling how the discovery happened and how it changed people's lives.

A.D. 1860s
England

Steel-making techniques invented by Henry Bessemer and William Siemens made it possible to produce steel cheaply on a large scale. Siemens' invention, the open-hearth furnace, is still widely used, although more modern methods account for most steel production today.

A.D. 500 **A.D. 2000**

A.D. 600s
Sri Lanka

Sri Lankans made steel in outdoor furnaces. Steady winds blowing over the top of the furnace's front wall created the high temperatures needed to make steel. Because their steel was so much harder than iron, the Sri Lankans were able to trade it throughout the Indian Ocean region.

A.D. 1960s TO THE PRESENT
United States

Scientists working on the space program have developed light and strong alloys for use in products ranging from bicycles to soda cans. For example, a new alloy of nickel and titanium can "remember" its shape. It is used for eyeglasses that return to their original shape after being bent.

Chapter 14 **469**

Smelting

SCIENCE & History

Materials *common objects made of metal, such as copper pot, bronze candle holder, cast-iron skillet, steel tool, bendable eyeglasses frame*

ACTIVITY

Time 20 minutes

Invite volunteers to read the annotations for the entries on the time line. For each entry, display an object that is made of the metal described. Allow students to handle each object and compare characteristics. Ask: **Are there important characteristics of these useful metals that improved over time?** *(Most students will recognize that bronze is harder and more durable than copper, iron is harder and more durable than bronze, and so on.)* **What characteristic is particularly useful in modern alloys, such as those used in bicycle frames?** *(Modern alloys are lightweight as well as strong.)*

In Your Journal In doing their research, students might begin by finding out about the Bronze Age, the Iron Age, or the Industrial Revolution. Some students may want to concentrate on more modern advances, including those first developed for space travel. In their paragraphs, students should mention a specific process and a specific application that changed people's lives.

Extend Have interested students make a bulletin board showing how the development of metal technology changed the world. **learning modality: verbal**

EXPLORING

Smelting Iron Ore

Have students look up the formulas for magnetite (Fe_3O_4) and hematite (Fe_2O_3) in Appendix B. Both are a compound of iron and oxygen. Then ask volunteers to read the annotations for each step in the smelting process. Ask: **What is the purpose of smelting?** *(To separate the iron from the oxygen in iron ore)* **What is added to the ore to accomplish this purpose?** *(coke and limestone)* The product of smelting can be made into either cast-iron objects or used to make steel. **learning modality: verbal**

Real-Life Learning

Bring to class something made of cast iron, such as a cast-iron skillet. Also bring something made of steel, such as a pan or a tool, and something made of stainless steel, such as utensils. Invite students to touch, visually examine, and compare the characteristics of each. Then ask students to list the major differences they observed.
learning modality: kinesthetic

Demonstration

Materials *black copper oxide, powdered charcoal, test tube, test-tube holder, Bunsen burner, jar, water*
Time 15 minutes

To help students understand how another metal can be separated from an ore, demonstrate how to extract copper from copper oxide. First, mix copper oxide with bits of charcoal at the bottom of a test tube. Then, holding the test tube with a test-tube holder and wearing goggles, heat the mixture over a Bunsen burner. Finally, pour the heated mixture into a jar of cold water. Students should see that pieces of shiny orange copper fall to the bottom of the jar, while the charcoal floats. Explain that the heating of the mixture freed the copper from the oxygen in copper oxide. Explain that copper oxide ores are smelted in a similar way, through heating the ore in a blast furnace with materials that will free the copper from the oxygen.
learning modality: visual

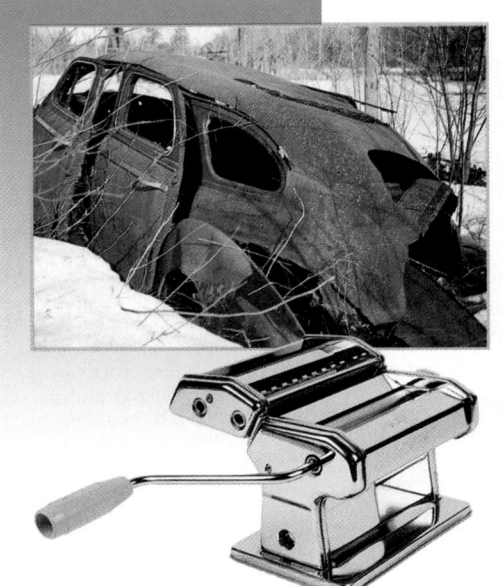

Figure 18 Plain steel rusts easily. But stainless steel—an alloy of iron, chromium, and nickel—doesn't rust. The chromium and nickel slow down the process by which the oxygen in the air combines with iron in the steel to form iron oxide, or rust.

Smelting

Ores must be processed before the metals they contain can be used. **After miners remove ore from a mine, smelting is necessary to remove the metal from the ore.** In the process of **smelting,** an ore is melted to separate the useful metal from other elements the ore contains. People around the world have used smelting to obtain metals from ores. Look at the time line in *Science and History* to see how this technology has developed from ancient times to the present.

How does smelting separate iron metal from hematite, a common form of iron ore? In general, smelting involves mixing an ore with other substances and then heating the mixture to a very high temperature. The heat melts the metal in the ore. The heat also causes the metal to separate from the oxygen with which it is combined. Metalworkers can then pour off the molten metal. Follow the steps in *Exploring Smelting Iron Ore.*

After smelting, additional processing is needed to remove impurities from the iron. The result is steel, which is harder and stronger than iron. Steel is an **alloy,** a solid mixture of two or more metals. Steelmakers mix iron with other elements to create alloys with special properties. For stronger steel, the metal manganese and a small amount of carbon are added. For rust-resistant steel, the metals chromium and nickel are added. You can compare plain steel with rust-resistant stainless steel in Figure 18.

Section 3 Review

1. What are some of the ways that people use gems and metals?
2. Describe three different kinds of mines.
3. What process is used to separate useful metals from ores?
4. What are alloys, and why are they useful?
5. **Thinking Critically** **Relating Cause and Effect** In smelting, what causes a metal to separate from its ore?

Science at Home

You can demonstrate to your family how rust damages objects that contain iron. Obtain three iron nails. Coat one of the nails with petroleum jelly and coat the second nail with clear nail polish. Do not put anything on the third nail. Place all the nails in a glass of water with a little vinegar. (The vinegar speeds up the rusting process.) Allow the nails to stand in the glass overnight. Which nails show signs of rusting? Explain these results to your family.

Background

Facts and Figures You might want to share with students these facts and figures about smelting iron ore.
◆ Iron ore often contains only 30 percent iron.
◆ A blast furnace produces about 375 tons of molten iron per hour.
◆ The molten iron poured, or "tapped," from a blast furnace is commonly referred to as *pig iron.* The name probably

originated long ago as a term describing a mold, shaped something like a baby pig, in which molten iron was cooled.
◆ Some of the pig iron is cooled to a solid and sold to foundries, which melt it and mold it into "cast iron" products. Most of the pig iron, though, remains liquid. It is carried by hot-metal "bottle" or "submarine" cars to a steel-making building.

EXPLORING *Smelting Iron Ore*

Iron usually occurs as the ores hematite or magnetite. Iron ores must be smelted to separate the iron from the oxygen and other substances in the ores. Then the iron is refined and processed into steel.

1. Iron ore is crushed and then mixed with crushed limestone and coke (baked coal), which is rich in carbon.

2. The coke and iron ore mixture is placed in a blast furnace, where extremely hot air is blown through, making the coke burn easily.

3. As the coke burns, chemical changes in the mixture produce carbon dioxide gas and molten iron.

4. The iron sinks to the bottom of the furnace. Impurities left in the ore combine with the limestone to create slag.

5. The slag and molten iron are poured off through taps in the blast furnace.

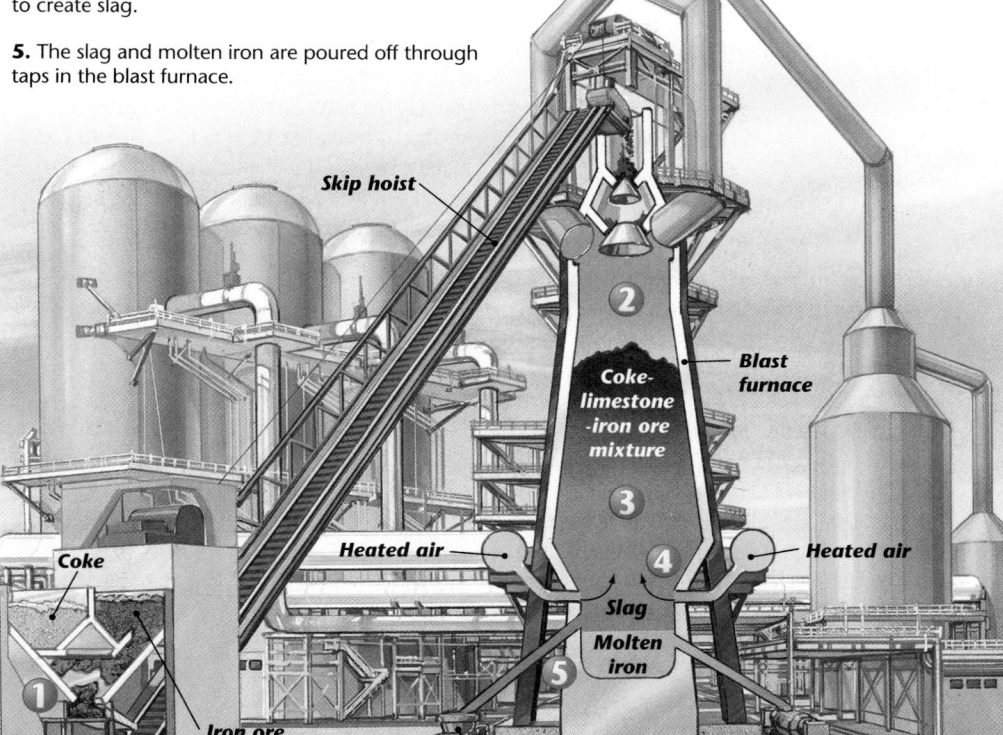

Skip hoist

Blast furnace

Coke-limestone-iron ore mixture

Coke

Heated air

Heated air

Iron ore and limestone

Slag

Molten iron

Slag ladle

Hot metal car

Section 3 Review Answers

1. Answers will vary. A typical answer might mention uses of gems in jewelry and in industry, as well as uses of metals in tools and machinery, metal filaments in light bulbs and steel girders.

2. In a strip mine, ore is exposed by scraping away the soil. An open pit mine is a tremendous pit. A shaft mine often has a network of tunnels that extends deep underground.

3. Smelting separates useful metal from other elements in ore.

4. An alloy is a solid mixture of two or more metals. Alloys have special properties that pure metals may not have.

5. The heating of the ore causes the metal to melt and separate from the oxygen it is combined with. Because the metal is heavy, it sinks to the bottom of the furnace.

Science at Home

Materials *3 iron nails, petroleum jelly, clear nail polish, clear glass, water, vinegar* **ACTIVITY**
Family members will notice that the uncoated nail shows signs of rusting after a night in water, while the coated nails do not. Remind students also to mention that stainless steel does not readily rust because it is a steel alloy that includes iron, chromium, and nickel.

Program Resources

◆ **Unit 4 Resources** 14-3 Review and Reinforcement, p. 107; 14-2 Enrich, p. 108

Media and Technology

Transparencies "Exploring Smelting Iron Ore," Transparency 58

Performance Assessment

Skills Check Have students make a flowchart that includes information about the processes involved from the formation of an ore to its use in a manufactured process. The flowchart, then, should include a process that formed the ore as well as the processes of locating, mining, and smelting the ore.

Copper Recovery

Preparing for Inquiry

Key Concept The processing of copper ore can be made more efficient by recovering copper from the waste water produced.

Skills Objectives Students will be able to

- measure amounts of copper sulfate and water to make a solution;
- observe changes in nails after adding them to the solution;
- infer that the nails draw copper from the solution;
- predict how a mine could recover copper from mine waste water;
- draw a conclusion about why a mine operator would try to collect copper from waste water.

Time 30 minutes

Advance Planning You can simplify the procedure by making the solution yourself before class. Place it in a container from which students can pour into their beakers. If students are to remove the nails from the solutions as part of disposal, provide gloves and possibly tongs.

Alternative Materials Any small pieces of iron will do in place of the nails, as long as they fit into the beaker. Avoid steel alloys, though, since they include other elements as well as iron.

Guiding Inquiry

Invitation Help students focus on the key concept by asking: **How are most minerals mined?** (*A typical answer might suggest that mining involves digging ore from the ground.*) **Could a metal also be obtained from a solution?** (*Most students will not know if that is possible.*) Explain that copper is one mineral that can be extracted from a solution and this lab will demonstrate one such method.

COPPER RECOVERY

I f you were a mining engineer, one of your tasks would be to make mining and processing ores more efficient. When copper ore is processed at copper mines, waste water containing copper sulfate is produced. Mining engineers have invented a way to recover copper metal from the waste water. They make the waste water flow over scrap iron.

Problem

How is copper recovered from a solution?

Skills Focus

observing, inferring, drawing conclusions

Materials

copper sulfate, 3 g	beaker, 400 mL
triple-beam balance	5 iron nails
graduated cylinder, 100 mL	water

Procedure

1. Place 3 g of copper sulfate in a beaker. **CAUTION:** *Copper sulfate is poisonous. Handle it with care.*
2. Add 50 mL of water to the beaker to dissolve the copper sulfate. Observe the color of the solution.
3. Add the iron nails to the beaker. The nails act as scrap iron. Describe the color of the solution after the nails have been added to the solution.
4. Follow your teacher's instructions for proper disposal. Wash your hands when you are finished.

Analyze and Conclude

1. What happened to the nails after you placed them in the solution? What is the material on the nails? Explain your answer.

2. How does the material on the nails compare with the copper sulfate?
3. Develop a plan that describes how a mine might recover copper from mine water using the method that you have just tried.
4. What additional step would you have to perform to obtain copper useful for making copper wire or pennies?
5. **Apply** Why do you think the operator of a copper mine would want to collect copper from the waste water?

Move to Explore

Repeat the experiment. This time test the solution with litmus paper both before and after you add the nails. Litmus paper indicates if a solution is acidic, basic, or neutral. Record your results. Why do you think a mining engineer would test the water from this process before releasing it into the environment?

Program Resources

- **Unit 4 Resources** Real-World Lab blackline masters, pp. 112–113

Media and Technology

📼 **Lab Activity Videotape**
Tape 3

Safety

Caution students to be careful with the copper sulfate, because it's poisonous. Since students will be working with breakable glass, they should wear goggles. Make sure they dispose of the solution per your instructions. Review the safety guidelines in Appendix A.

SECTION 1 Properties of Minerals

Key Ideas

◆ A mineral is a naturally occurring inorganic solid that has a distinct chemical composition and crystal shape.

◆ Each mineral can be identified by its own physical and chemical properties.

◆ Some of the properties of minerals include hardness, color, streak, luster, density, cleavage and fracture, and crystal structure. Hardness is measured by the Mohs hardness scale.

◆ Minerals usually consist of two or more elements joined together in a compound.

Key Terms

mineral	Mohs hardness scale
inorganic	streak
crystal	luster
element	cleavage
compound	fracture
	fluorescence

SECTION 2 How Minerals Form

Key Ideas

◆ Minerals form inside Earth through crystal-lization as magma or lava cools.

◆ Minerals form on Earth's surface when materials dissolved in water crystallize through evaporation.

◆ Mineral deposits form on the ocean floor from solutions heated by magma. The hot-water solutions containing minerals erupt through chimneys on the ocean floor, then crystallize when they come in contact with cold sea water.

Key Terms

solution
vein

SECTION 3 Mineral Resources

INTEGRATING TECHNOLOGY

Key Ideas

◆ Minerals are useful as the source of all metals, gemstones, and of many other materials.

◆ Geologists locate ore deposits by prospecting—looking for certain features on and beneath Earth's surface.

◆ Ores can be removed from the ground through open pit mines, strip mines, or shaft mines.

◆ Smelting is the process of heating an ore to extract a metal.

Key Terms

gemstone
ore
smelting
alloy

Organizing Information

Venn Diagram Copy the Venn diagram comparing the mineral hematite and the human-made material brick onto a separate piece of paper. Then complete it and add a title. (For more on Venn diagrams, see the Skills Handbook.)

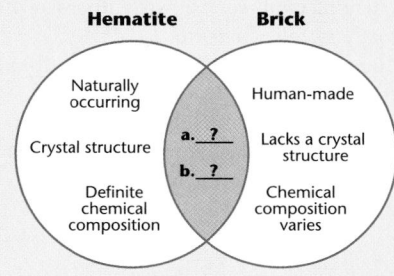

Hematite		Brick
Naturally occurring		Human-made
Crystal structure	a. ?	Lacks a crystal structure
	b. ?	
Definite chemical composition		Chemical composition varies

Introducing the Procedure

◆ **What is scrap iron?** (*Fragments of discarded iron materials*)

◆ **What could produce a change in color in a copper sulfate solution?** (*A chemical reaction caused by the addition of another substance*)

Troubleshooting the Experiment

◆ Demonstrate how to add water without splashing or spilling the solution.

◆ Allow about 10 minutes between the time students add the nails and the time when they note their observations.

Expected Outcome

Students will observe that the copper in the copper sulfate solution will coat the nails. This occurs because iron from the nails replaces the copper in a chemical reaction represented by this equation:

$$CuSO_4 + Fe = FeSO_4 + Cu$$

Analyze and Conclude

1. The nails were coated with a layer of some material. Students may correctly infer that this substance is copper, the result of a chemical reaction between the nails and the solution.

2. The material on the nails is a different color than the color of the copper sulfate before the nails were added. When the nails were added, the solution became colorless.

3. Plans may vary. A typical plan might suggest that iron materials, such as scrap iron, could be used to recover copper from the mine water.

4. The copper-coated iron would need to be processed further to remove the copper coating and obtain pure copper.

5. Copper is valuable, and allowing it to leave with the water is lost money.

Extending the Inquiry

More to Explore Students will discover that before the nails are added the solution is neutral, as indicated by no change in the color of the litmus paper. After the nails are added, the solution becomes acidic, as indicated by the paper turning blue. A mining engineer would test the water because releasing acidic water into the environment could harm living things.

Organizing Information

Venn Diagram Sample title: *Comparing Hematite and Brick* **a.** Inorganic **b.** Solid

Reviewing Content

Multiple Choice

1. b **2.** b **3.** c **4.** c **5.** d

True or False

6. true **7.** streak **8.** large **9.** true
10. mining

Checking Concepts

11. Most minerals are compounds, composed of atoms of two or more elements. A pure element is composed of atoms of a single element.

12. Although the color of a mineral may vary, the color of a mineral's streak is always the same.

13. Cleavage is when a mineral splits easily along flat surfaces. Fracture, by contrast, describes how a mineral breaks apart when it does not split evenly.

14. In general, minerals can form through crystallization of melted materials and crystallization of materials dissolved in water. In the first way, minerals form as hot magma cools deep inside the crust or as lava hardens on the surface. In the second way, minerals crystallize as solutions cool or evaporate.

15. The process of extracting a metal from hematite ore is called smelting. It involves crushing the hematite, heating it with such materials as coke and limestone, and then separating the iron in the hematite from oxygen. The metal obtained at the end of the process is iron.

16. Answers will vary. A typical letter might mention examining the rocks of an area, testing streams for the presence of chemicals, and using explosions to map the location, size, and shape of an ore deposit. The next step would be to test for the correct properties of gold as distinct from other minerals, such as fool's gold. If gold were found, the prospector would probably feel elated.

Thinking Critically

17. Color and luster are similar in that they are both visually observable properties. There are fewer kinds of luster, however, than there are colors. Luster is also different in that it can describe the surface texture of a mineral.

18. Since obsidian does not have a crystal structure, one of the five

Reviewing Content

Multiple Choice

Choose the letter of the answer that best completes each statement.

1. In a mineral, the particles line up in a repeating pattern to form
  a. an element.   **b.** a crystal.
  c. a mixture.   **d.** a compound.

2. The softest mineral in the Mohs hardness scale is
  a. quartz.   **b.** talc.
  c. apatite.   **d.** gypsum.

3. Halite is a mineral formed by
  a. chimneys on the ocean floor.
  b. cooling of magma.
  c. evaporation.
  d. cooling of lava.

4. Metals are useful for tools because they
  a. are compounds.
  b. have a metallic luster.
  c. are hard yet can be easily shaped.
  d. are elements.

5. Minerals from which metals can be removed in usable amounts are called
  a. gemstones.
  b. crystals.
  c. alloys.
  d. ores.

True or False

If the statement is true, write true. If it is false, change the underlined word or words to make the statement true.

6. <u>Luster</u> is the term that describes how a mineral reflects light from its surface.

7. A piece of unglazed tile is used to test a mineral's <u>hardness</u>.

8. If magma cools very slowly, minerals with <u>small</u> crystals will form.

9. Minerals form from <u>hot-water solutions</u> at chimneys on the ocean floor.

10. The process of removing an ore deposit from the ground is known as <u>prospecting</u>.

Checking Concepts

11. What is the difference in composition between most minerals and a pure element?

12. How can the streak test be helpful in identifying minerals?

13. Compare cleavage and fracture.

14. Describe two different ways that minerals can form.

15. Describe the process used to extract metal from hematite ore. What metal would be obtained?

16. **Writing to Learn** You are a prospector searching for gold. In a letter home, describe where you plan to look, how you will know if you have found gold, and how you will feel about your discovery.

Thinking Critically

17. **Comparing and Contrasting** Color and luster are both properties of minerals. How are these properties similar? How are they different? How can each be used to help identify a mineral?

18. **Classifying** Obsidian forms when magma cools very quickly, creating a type of glass. In glass, the particles are not arranged in an orderly pattern as in a crystal. Obsidian is a solid, inorganic substance that occurs naturally in volcanic areas. Should it be classified as a mineral? Explain why or why not.

19. **Relating Cause and Effect** Describe how a vein of ore forms underground. What is the energy source for this process?

20. **Applying Concepts** Explain the roles of elements, solutions, and compounds in the process that forms minerals around chimneys on the ocean floor.

21. **Predicting** What would happen if steelmakers forgot to add enough chromium and nickel to a batch of stainless steel?

characteristics of a mineral, it cannot be classified as a mineral.

19. Deep underground, a solution of hot water and metals follows a fracture within rock. When the solution cools, the metals crystallize into a vein. The energy source for the process is heat from hot magma, which is heated by Earth's core.

20. The elements and compounds that form minerals in oceanic crust dissolve in water heated by magma. The solutions that result, then, are rich in minerals. These solutions

belch out of chimneys, and the minerals they contain crystallize on the ocean floor.

21. Without enough chromium and nickel in the steel, iron oxide could form on the steel; that is, the steel could rust.

Applying Skills

22. The color of the sample of wulfenite is yellowish orange, the luster is shiny and gemlike, and the crystal structure appears to be rectangular, with angled edges (tetragonal).

Applying Skills

Working as a geologist, you have found a sample of the mineral wulfenite. Testing the wulfenite reveals that it has a hardness of about 3 on the Mohs hardness scale and a density of 6.8 grams per cubic centimeter. You also determine that the mineral contains oxygen as well as the metals lead and molybdenum.

Wulfenite

22. Observing Describe wulfenite's color, luster, and crystal structure.

23. Inferring Did the wulfenite form slowly or quickly? Explain your answer.

24. Drawing Conclusions Is wulfenite hard enough for use as a gem? What would you use these crystals for? Explain.

Performance ▼ Assessment
CHAPTER PROJECT 14

Project Wrap Up Before you present your crystal garden to the class, share it with a classmate. Can your classmate identify which solution created which crystals? Do your data show differences in crystal growth rates? What conclusions can you draw from your data? Now you are ready to present your project to your class.

Reflect and Record In your journal, identify any changes that would improve your crystal garden. Which materials worked best for crystals to grow on? Which ones did not work well?

Project Wrap Up Talk with each student or group before the presentation. Make suggestions and give words of encouragement. Assess the presentations on the quality of the garden scenes, the growth of the crystals in the garden, the growth data kept by the students, and the coherence of the presentation.

Reflect and Record In assessing their crystal gardens, students should reflect on the materials used, the quality and attractiveness of the scenes they made, and the growth rate of the different kinds of crystals. They should assess how their gardens compared with others in the class and suggest ways in which they could have improved their own outcome.

Test Preparation

25. d **26.** a **27.** b **28.** a **29.** c

Test Preparation

Use these questions to prepare for standardized tests.

Study the table. Then answer Questions 25–29.

Properties of Six Minerals

Mineral	Hardness	Density (g/cm³)	Luster	Streak
Corundum	9.0	4.0	glassy	white
Quartz	7.0	2.6	glassy	white
Magnetite	6.0	5.2	metallic	black
Copper	2.8	8.9	metallic	red
Galena	2.5	7.5	metallic	lead gray
Talc	1.0	2.8	pearly	white

25. Which mineral in the table could be scratched by all the others?
 a. quartz **b.** galena
 c. copper **d.** talc

26. The mineral in the table with the greatest density is
 a. copper. **b.** galena.
 c. magnetite. **d.** talc.

27. To be suitable as a gemstone, a mineral usually must be very hard and have a glassy luster. Which mineral on the list would probably make the best gemstone?
 a. copper **b.** corundum
 c. magnetite **d.** galena

28. Quartz and talc have a similar density. What property or properties could you easily test to tell them apart?
 a. hardness and luster
 b. streak only
 c. density only
 d. none of the above

29. Suppose that you have found a dense, dark-colored mineral with a metallic luster. What property would you test quickly and easily to determine if the mineral were copper rather than galena?
 a. hardness **b.** luster
 c. streak **d.** density

---

23. The fairly large size of the crystals indicates that the wulfenite formed slowly.

24. A hardness of 3 is very low on the Mohs hardness scale. Since most gems are relatively hard, wulfenite would not be hard enough to be used as a gem. These crystals might be used as an ore for the metals they contain, lead and molybdenum.

Program Resources

- ◆ **Inquiry Skills Activity Book** Provides teaching and review of all inquiry skills
- ◆ **Prentice Hall Assessment System** Provides standardized test practice
- ◆ **Reading in the Content Area** Provides strategies to improve science reading skills
- ◆ **Teacher's ELL Handbook** Provides multiple strategies for English language learners

CHAPTER 15 Rocks

Sections	Time	Student Edition Activities	Other Activities	
CHAPTER PROJECT 15 **Collecting Rocks** p. 477	Ongoing (3 weeks)	Check Your Progress, pp. 481, 490, 493, 501 Project Wrap Up, p. 505	TE	Chapter 15 Project Notes, pp. 476–477
1 **Classifying Rocks** pp. 478–481 ◆ 15.1.1 List the characteristics used to identify rocks. ◆ 15.1.2 Identify and describe the three major groups of rocks.	1 period/ ½ block	**Discover** How Are Rocks Alike and Different?, p. 478	TE TE TE	Using the Visuals: Figure 2, p. 479 Including All Students, p. 479 Observing, p. 480
2 **Igneous Rocks** pp. 482–485 ◆ 15.2.1 Identify the characteristics used to classify igneous rocks.	1 period/ ½ block	**Discover** How Do Igneous Rocks Form?, p. 482 **Sharpen Your Skills** Building Inquiry Skills: Observing, p. 484 **Science at Home,** p. 485	TE	Building Inquiry Skills: Comparing and Contrasting, p. 483
3 **Sedimentary Rocks** pp. 486–490 ◆ 15.3.1 Describe how sedimentary rocks form. ◆ 15.3.2 List and describe the three major types of sedimentary rocks.	1 period/ ½ block	**Discover** How Does Pressure Affect Particles of Rock?, p. 486 **Try This** Rock Absorber, p. 488	TE TE	Building Inquiry Skills: Making Models, p. 487; Classifying, p. 488 Integrating Life Science, p. 489
4 **INTEGRATING LIFE SCIENCE** **Rocks From Reefs** pp. 491–493 ◆ 15.4.1 Describe the formation of coral reefs. ◆ 15.4.2 Explain how coral reefs become organic limestone deposits on land.	1 period/ ½ block	**Discover** What Can You Conclude From the Way a Rock Reacts to Acid?, p. 491	TE LM	Building Inquiry Skills: Making Models, p. 492 15, "Making Models of Sedimentary Rocks"
5 **Metamorphic Rocks** pp. 494–497 ◆ 15.5.1 Describe the conditions under which metamorphic rocks form. ◆ 15.5.2 Identify the ways in which geologists classify metamorphic rocks.	2 periods/ 1 block	**Discover** How Do the Grain Patterns of Gneiss and Granite Compare?, p. 494 **Try This** A Sequined Rock, p. 495 **Science at Home,** p. 496 **Skills Lab: Classifying** Mystery Rocks, p. 497		
6 **The Rock Cycle** pp. 498–502 ◆ 15.6.1 Describe the rock cycle. ◆ 15.6.2 Explain the role played by plate tectonics in the rock cycle.	2 periods/ 1 block	**Discover** Which Rock Came First?, p. 498 **Sharpen Your Skills** Classifying, p. 499 **Real-World Lab: You, the Consumer** Testing Rock Flooring, p. 502	TE	Exploring the Rock Cycle, p. 500
Study Guide/Assessment pp. 503–505	1 period/ ½ block		ISAB	Provides teaching and review of all inquiry skills

For Standard or Block Schedule The Resource Pro® CD-ROM gives you maximum flexibility for planning your instruction for any type of schedule. Resource Pro® contains Planning Express®, an advanced scheduling program, as well as the entire contents of the Teaching Resources and the Computer Test Bank.

Key: **CTB** Computer Test Bank
CT Chapter Tests
ELL Teacher's ELL Handbook

CHAPTER PLANNING GUIDE

Program Resources	Assessment Strategies	Media and Technology
UR Chapter 15 Project Teacher Notes, pp. 114–115 UR Chapter 15 Project Overview and Worksheets, pp. 116–119	TE Perf. Assessment: Project Wrap Up, p. 505 TE Check Your Progress, pp. 481, 490, 493, 501 UR Chapter 15 Project Scoring Rubric, p. 120	🌐 Science Explorer Internet Site 🎧 Audio CDs, Section Summaries
UR 15-1 Lesson Plan, p. 121 UR 15-1 Section Summary, p. 122 UR 15-1 Review and Reinforce, p. 123 UR 15-1 Enrich, p. 124	SE Section 1 Review, p. 481 TE Ongoing Assessment, p. 479 TE Performance Assessment, p. 481	💽 Presentation Pro, "Rocks"
UR 15-2 Lesson Plan, p. 125 UR 15-2 Section Summary, p. 126 UR 15-2 Review and Reinforce, p. 127 UR 15-2 Enrich, p. 128	SE Section 2 Review, p. 485 TE Ongoing Assessment, p. 483 TE Performance Assessment, p. 485	
UR 15-3 Lesson Plan, p. 129 UR 15-3 Section Summary, p. 130 UR 15-3 Review and Reinforce, p. 131 UR 15-3 Enrich, p. 132	SE Section 3 Review, p. 490 TE Ongoing Assessment, pp. 487, 489 TE Performance Assessment, p. 490	📼 Concept Videotape Library, *Adventures, Tape 3,* "Fossils" 🎞 Transparency 59, "Formation of Sedimentary Rocks"
UR 15-4 Lesson Plan, p. 133 UR 15-4 Section Summary, p. 134 UR 15-4 Review and Reinforce, p. 135 UR 15-4 Enrich, p. 136	SE Section 4 Review, p. 493 TE Performance Assessment, p. 493	
UR 15-5 Lesson Plan, p. 137 UR 15-5 Section Summary, p. 138 UR 15-5 Review and Reinforce, p. 139 UR 15-5 Enrich, p. 140 UR Skills Lab blackline masters, pp. 145–147	SE Section 5 Review, p. 496 SE Analyze and Conclude, p. 497 TE Ongoing Assessment, p. 495 TE Performance Assessment, p. 496	📼 Concept Videotape Library, *Adventures, Tape 3,* "The Earth Library" 📼 Lab Activity Videotape, *Tape 3*
UR 15-6 Lesson Plan, p. 141 UR 15-6 Section Summary, p. 142 UR 15-6 Review and Reinforce, p. 143 UR 15-6 Enrich, p. 144 UR Real-World Lab blackline masters, pp. 148–149	SE Section 6 Review, p. 501 SE Analyze and Conclude, p. 502 TE Ongoing Assessment, p. 499 TE Performance Assessment, p. 501	🎞 Transparency 60, "Exploring the Rock Cycle" 📼 Lab Activity Videotape, *Tape 3*
GRSW Provides worksheets to promote student comprehension of content RCA Provides strategies to improve science reading skills ELL Provides multiple strategies for English language learners	SE Study Guide/Assessment, pp. 503–505 PA Performance Assessment, pp. 46–48 CT Chapter 15 Test, pp. 59–62 CTB Chapter 15 Test PHAS Provides standardized test preparation	💽 Computer Test Bank, Chapter 15 Test

GRSW Guided Reading and Study Workbook
ISAB Inquiry Skills Activity Book
LM Laboratory Manual

PA Performance Assessment
PHAS Prentice Hall Assessment System
PLM Probeware Lab Manual

RCA Reading in the Content Area
SE Student Edition

TE Teacher's Edition
UR Unit Resources

Meeting the National Science Education Standards and AAAS Benchmarks

National Science Education Standards	Benchmarks for Science Literacy	Unifying Themes
Science As Inquiry (Content Standard A) ◆ **Design and conduct a scientific investigation** Students investigate what kind of stone makes the best flooring. *(Real-World Lab)* ◆ **Use appropriate tools and techniques to gather, analyze, and interpret data** Students collect, classify, and display rocks.*(Chapter Project; Skills Lab)* **Life Science** (Content Standard C) ◆ **Populations and ecosystems** Coral animals build shells that grow together to form a coral reef. *(Section 4)* **Earth and Space Science** (Content Standard D) ◆ **Structure of the Earth system** There are three major groups of rocks: igneous, sedimentary, and metamorphic. Igneous rocks form from magma or lava. Sedimentary rocks generally form from particles deposited by water and wind. Heat and pressure can change any rock into metamorphic rock. Forces inside Earth and at the surface produce a rock cycle that builds, destroys, and changes the rocks in the crust. *(Sections 1, 2, 3, 4, 5, 6)* **Science and Technology** (Content Standard E) ◆ **Understandings about science and technology** Humans use rocks in different ways. *(Sections 2, 3, 5; Real-World Lab)*	**1B Scientific Inquiry** Students collect, classify, and display rocks. Students use the properties of rocks to classify them. Students investigate what kind of stone makes the best flooring. *(Chapter Project; Skills Lab; Real-World Lab)* **3A Technology and Science** Humans use rocks in different ways. *(Sections 2, 3, 5; Real-World Lab)* **4C Processes That Shape the Earth** There are three major groups of rocks: igneous rock, sedimentary rock, and metamorphic rock. Igneous rocks form from magma or lava. Sedimentary rocks form from particles deposited by water and wind. Coral buried by sediments can turn into limestone. Heat and pressure deep beneath Earth's surface can change any rock into metamorphic rock. Forces inside Earth and at the surface produce a rock cycle that builds, destroys, and changes the rocks in the crust. *(Sections 1, 2, 3, 4, 5, 6)* **5A Diversity of Life** Coral animals build shells that grow together to form a coral reef. *(Section 4)*	◆ **Energy** Igneous rocks form from hot magma or lava. Limestone that began as coral can be found in places where uplift has raised ancient sea floors. Heat and pressure deep beneath Earth's surface can change any rock into metamorphic rock. Forces inside Earth and at the surface produce a rock cycle that builds, destroys, and changes rocks in the crust. *(Sections 1, 2, 4, 5, 6)* ◆ **Evolution** The remains of living things may be preserved as fossils in sedimentary rock. In the rock cycle, rocks change over time. *(Sections 3, 6)* ◆ **Patterns of Change** Molten rock cools to form igneous rock. Compaction and cementation change sediments into sedimentary rock. The processes of the rock cycle cause rocks to change continuously from one form to another. *(Sections 2, 3, 6)* ◆ **Scale and Structure** Rocks are made of minerals. *(Section 1; Chapter Project; Skills Lab)* ◆ **Systems and Interactions** Plate movements drive the rock cycle. *(Sections 2, 3, 5, 6; Real-World Lab)* ◆ **Unity and Diversity** Rocks are classified as igneous, sedimentary, or metamorphic. Igneous rocks are classified as extrusive or intrusive. Sedimentary rocks are classified as clastic, organic, or chemical. Metamorphic rocks are classified as foliated or nonfoliated. The rock cycle can follow many different pathways. *(Sections 1, 2, 3, 4, 5, 6; Chapter Project; Skills Lab)*

Take It to the Net

The **www.phschool.com** Web site provides you with multiple opportunities to incorporate the internet into your instruction. Go to **www.phschool.com** and click on the Science icon. Then select Science Explorer Integrated.

■ Have students use the chapter Self-Test to get instant feedback.

■ Hot Links and Reference Links provide opportunities for online research.

Internet Activities provide opportunities for students to review, extend, or assess a concept from the chapter.

STAY CURRENT with **SCIENCE NEWS**®

Find out the latest research and information about rocks and minerals at: **www.phschool.com**

ACTIVITY	Time (minutes)	Materials *Quantities for one work group*	Skills
Section 1			
Discover, p. 478	10	**Nonconsumable** samples of marble and conglomerate, hand lens, penny	Observing
Section 2			
Discover, p. 482	10	**Nonconsumable** samples of granite and obsidian, hand lens	Inferring
Sharpen Your Skills, p. 484	10	No special materials are required.	Observing
Science at Home, p. 485	Home	No special materials are required.	Communicating
Section 3			
Discover, p. 486	15	**Consumable** sheet of paper, 2 slices of bread **Nonconsumable** stack of books, plastic knife	Observing
Try This, p. 488	15; 10	**Consumable** water **Nonconsumable** samples of sandstone and shale, hand lens, balance, pan	Drawing Conclusions
Section 4			
Discover, p. 491	15	**Consumable** dilute (5%) hydrochloric acid, running water **Nonconsumable** samples of limestone and coquina, plastic dropper	Drawing Conclusions
Section 5			
Discover, p. 494	15	**Nonconsumable** samples of gneiss and granite, hand lens	Inferring
Try This, p. 495	15	**Consumable** modeling compound, 25 sequins, 30-cm string **Nonconsumable** metric ruler, 2 blocks of wood	Making Models
Science at Home, p. 496	Home	No special materials are required.	Observing
Skills Lab, p. 497	30	**Nonconsumable** 1 nonrock solid object such as brick or bone, 2 igneous rock samples such as granite and basalt, 2 sedimentary rock samples such as sandstone and conglomerate, 2 metamorphic rock samples such as gneiss and slate, hand lens	Observing, Creating Data Tables, Classifying
Section 6			
Discover, p. 498	10	**Consumable** 3 index cards **Nonconsumable** colored pencils	Developing Hypotheses
Sharpen Your Skills, p. 499	10	No special materials are required.	Classifying
Real-World Lab, p. 502	40	**Consumable** water, materials that form stains such as ink and paint, greasy materials such as butter and crayons **Nonconsumable** steel nail; plastic dropper; wire brush; hand lens; samples of igneous, sedimentary, and metamorphic rocks with flat surfaces	Designing Experiments, Forming Operational Definitions, Drawing Conclusions

A list of all materials required for the Student Edition activities can be found beginning on page T23. You can obtain information about ordering materials by calling 1-800-848-9500 or by accessing the Science Explorer Internet site at: **www.phschool.com**

Collecting Rocks

Rocks are such a major part of the environment that for most students they remain mostly unseen, and certainly largely undifferentiated. Collecting rocks in the field will enrich student's understanding of the natural world.

Purpose In this project, students will collect rock samples in their own community, as well as classify and identify the rocks collected. They will also create a display of their collection to be presented to the class. By doing this project, students will gain a first-hand understanding of the three major groups of rocks.

Skills Focus In completing the Chapter 15 Project, students will be able to:
◆ observe rocks in the field and choose interesting samples to collect;
◆ classify each rock sample based on its characteristics into one of the three major groups of rocks;
◆ draw conclusions about the identity of specific rocks by using a field guide;
◆ communicate what they have learned by creating a display of the rock collection and making a presentation to the class.

Project Time Line The entire project will require about three weeks. Students can do this project either individually or in small groups. Some class time may be needed for planning as well as for creating the display and preparing the presentation. The bulk of the time, though, should be spent by students in the field, collecting rocks at various locations in their community. Students can complete the project by doing the following.
◆ Brainstorm locations where rocks could be collected safely and legally.
◆ Plan excursions to parks and other places where they are likely to find many kinds of rocks.
◆ Collect rocks at several locations.
◆ Examine the collected rocks, classifying and identifying each sample through observation and tests.
◆ Create a display of the rock collection.
◆ Make a presentation to the class, explaining how each sample was classified.

CHAPTER
15 Rocks

WEB ACTIVITY   www.phschool.com

SECTION 1 **Classifying Rocks**	SECTION 2 **Igneous Rocks**	SECTION 3 **Sedimentary Rocks**
Discover How Are Rocks Alike and Different?	Discover How Do Igneous Rocks Form? Sharpen Your Skills Observing	Discover How Does Pressure Affect Particles of Rock? Try This Rock Absorber

476

For more detailed information on planning and supervising the chapter project, see Chapter 15 Project Teacher Notes, pages 114–115 in Unit 4 Resources.

Suggested Shortcuts
◆ You may wish to divide the class into small groups to carry out this project.
◆ You can make this project shorter and less involved by having pairs of students collect only two or three rocks and bring the rocks to class. Then, either small groups or the class as a whole can classify and identify the most interesting samples. Those rocks can then be made into a display.

Possible Materials For the collection phase of the project, students will need a heavy bag in which to carry the rock samples. A canvas bag is traditional for this purpose, but an old book backpack would serve the same purpose. Resealable plastic sandwich bags are good for storing individual rock samples. For examination in the lab, students will need a hand lens and a fingernail file to do a scratch test. It may also be desirable for students to break apart

Hikers cross a landscape of rock in the Cascade Range, a mountain range in Washington state.

Collecting Rocks

Each rock, whether a small pebble or a giant boulder, tells a story. By observing a rock's characteristics, geologists learn about the forces that shaped the portion of Earth's crust where the rock formed. The rocks in your own community tell the story of Earth's crust in your area.

In this chapter, you will learn how three different types of rocks form. You can apply what you learn about rocks to create your own rock collection and explore the properties of these rocks.

Your Goal To make a collection of the rocks in your area.

To complete this project, you must
- collect samples of rocks, keeping a record of where you found each sample
- describe the characteristics of your rocks, including their color, texture, and density
- classify each rock as igneous, sedimentary, or metamorphic
- create a display for your rock collection
- follow the safety guidelines in Appendix A

Get Started With your classmates and teacher, brainstorm locations in your community where rocks are likely to be found. Are there road cuts, outcroppings of bedrock, riverbanks, or beaches where you could safely and legally collect your rocks?

Check Your Progress You will be working on this project as you study the chapter. To keep your project on track, look for Check Your Progress boxes at the following points.
Section 1 Review, page 481: Plan your rock-hunting expeditions.
Section 3 Review, page 490: Collect your rocks.
Section 4 Review, page 493: Begin to describe, test, and catalog your rock collection.
Section 6 Review, page 501: Classify your rocks and plan your presentation.

Wrap Up At the end of the chapter (page 505), prepare a display of your rock collection. Be prepared to discuss the properties of the rocks you collected, how the rocks formed, and how people can use them.

Integrating Life Science

SECTION 4 Rocks From Reefs

Discover What Can You Conclude From the Way a Rock Reacts to Acid?

SECTION 5 Metamorphic Rocks

Discover How Do the Grain Patterns of Gneiss and Granite Compare?
Try This A Sequined Rock
Skills Lab Mystery Rocks

SECTION 6 The Rock Cycle

Discover Which Rock Came First?
Sharpen Your Skills Classifying
Real-World Lab Testing Rock Flooring

Program Resources

- **Unit 4 Resources** Project Teacher Notes, pp. 114–115; Project Overview and Worksheets, pp. 116–119; Project Scoring Rubric, p. 120

Media and Technology

🎧 **Audio CDs** Section Summaries

WEB ACTIVITY www.phschool.com

You will find an Internet activity, chapter self-tests for students, and links to other chapter topics at this site.

---

some of the samples. A hammer and goggles are necessary for this purpose. For creating a display, students will need egg cartons or some other container with compartments, with cotton padding added to each compartment. In addition, rock and mineral guidebooks are necessary if students are to identify specific rocks in their collection.

Launching the Project To introduce the project, show students a rock collection in a professional display. At this stage, students may know very little about how rocks are classified. Point out that the display shows various kinds of rocks, each with a specific name. Then ask: **Where in our community are some good places to collect different kinds of rocks?** *(A typical answer might mention parks, roadcuts, and stream beds.)* Explain that in the Chapter 15 Project they will collect rock samples from such places, classify and identify as many samples as they can, and then create a display similar to the professional one. Emphasize that students should collect rocks only where it is safe and legal. To help students get started, hand out Chapter 15 Project Overview and Worksheets, pages 116–119 in Unit 4 Resources. You may also wish to hand out the Chapter 15 Project Scoring Rubric, page 120, at this time.

Performance Assessment

Use the Chapter 15 Project Scoring Rubric to assess students' work. Students will be assessed on
- how many rock samples they collect and describe;
- how well they classify and identify their rock samples, as well as how well they create an attractive display;
- how effectively they present their rock collections to the class;
- their participation in a group, if they worked in groups.

Objectives

After completing the lesson, students will be able to
◆ list the characteristics used to identify rocks;
◆ identify and describe the three major groups of rocks.

Key Terms texture, grain, igneous rock, sedimentary rock, metamorphic rock

1 Engage/Explore

Activating Prior Knowledge

Encourage students to share their knowledge of rocks and rock types. For example, ask students about two types of rocks that they could probably recognize: **How would you describe the difference between sandstone and marble?** (*A typical answer might describe a difference in texture—sandstone is grainy, while marble is smooth.*) **What could the feel of a rock's surface tell a geologist about how that rock formed?** (*Answers will vary. Some students might suggest that marble formed farther underground than sandstone.*)

⋯⋯⋯ DISCOVER ⋯⋯⋯

Skills Focus observing
Materials *samples of marble and conglomerate, hand lens, penny*
Time 10 minutes
Tips If you have only a few samples of each kind of rock, pair samples of about the same size and place pairs at strategic places around the classroom. Then invite students to examine the pair closest to them.
Think It Over Students should discover that marble is a fine-grained rock, with a crystalline texture that can easily be seen. Conglomerate has a rough texture and is clearly composed of small rocks and other materials, such as shells. Marble is harder and denser than conglomerate. Both marble and conglomerate vary in color.

DISCOVER ⋯⋯⋯⋯⋯⋯⋯⋯⋯⋯⋯⋯⋯⋯⋯ ACTIVITY ⋯

How Are Rocks Alike and Different?

1. Look at samples of marble and conglomerate with a hand lens.
2. Describe the two rocks. What is the color and texture of each?
3. Try scratching the surface of each rock with the edge of a penny. Which rock seems harder?
4. Hold each rock in your hand. Allowing for the fact that the samples aren't exactly the same size, which rock seems denser?

Think It Over
Observing Based on your observations, how would you compare the physical properties of marble and conglomerate?

GUIDE FOR READING

◆ **What characteristics are used to identify rocks?**
◆ **What are the three major groups of rocks?**

Reading Tip Before you read, use the headings to make an outline about rocks. Then fill in details as you read.

B etween 1969 and 1972, the Apollo missions to the moon returned to Earth with pieces of the moon's surface. Space scientists eagerly tested these samples. They wanted to learn what the moon is made of. They found that the moon's surface is made of material very similar to the material that makes up Earth's surface—rock. Some moon samples are dark rock called basalt. Other samples are light-colored rock made mostly of the mineral feldspar.

Figure 1 Geology students collect and study samples of rocks.

How Geologists Classify Rocks

For both Earth and its moon, rocks are important building blocks. On Earth, rock forms mountains, hills, valleys, beaches, even the ocean floor. Earth's crust is made of rock. Rocks are made of mixtures of minerals and other materials, although some rocks may contain only a single mineral. Granite, shown in Figure 2, is made up of the minerals quartz, feldspar, mica, and hornblende, and sometimes other minerals.

Geologists collect and study samples of rock in order to classify them. Imagine that you are a geologist exploring a mountain range for the first time. How would you study a particular type of rock found in these mountains? You might use a camera or notebook to record

---

READING STRATEGIES

Reading Tip Students should use the main headings: "How Geologists Classify Rocks," "Texture," "Mineral Composition," and "Origin." As students read the material under each heading, they should summarize the main points in a few words and add these to their outlines. Suggest that they use the sideheads under "Texture" as subheadings and write a few words under each. The finished outline can serve as a study guide for section review.

Vocabulary Have students brainstorm a list of words they commonly use to describe the feel of the surface of something, such as *rough, smooth, grainy, gritty, coarse, oily, silky, bumpy,* and *waxy.* Then point out the key term *texture* in their text. Explain that the words in their list are descriptive words of texture and they probably classify objects by texture all the time.

Figure 2 Granite is made up of quartz, mica, feldspar, and hornblende. It may also contain other minerals. *Observing* Which mineral seems most abundant in the sample of granite shown?

Granite

Quartz

Feldspar

Mica

Hornblende

information about the setting where the rock was found. (In classifying a rock, it's important for a geologist to know what other types of rock occur nearby). Then, you would use a chisel or the sharp end of a rock hammer to remove samples of the rock. Finally, you would break open the samples with a hammer to examine their inside surfaces. You must look at the inside of a rock because the effects of water and weather can change the outer surface of a rock.

When studying a rock sample, geologists observe the rock's color and texture and determine its mineral composition. Using these characteristics, geologists can classify a rock according to its origin, or where and how it formed.

Texture

As with minerals, color alone does not provide enough information to identify a rock. A rock's texture, however, is very useful in identifying the rock. To a geologist, a rock's **texture** is the look and feel of the rock's surface. Some rocks are smooth and glassy. Others are rough or chalky. Most rocks are made up of particles of minerals or other rocks, which geologists call **grains.** A rock's grains give the rock its texture. To describe a rock's texture, geologists use a number of terms based on the size, shape, and pattern of the rock's grains.

Program Resources

◆ **Unit 4 Resources** 15-1 Lesson Plan, p. 121; 15-1 Section Summary, p. 122
◆ **Guided Reading and Study Workbook** Section 15-1

Answers to Self-Assessment

Caption Question

Figure 2 Answers may vary, though most students should observe that feldspar makes up the greatest proportion of granite.

2 Facilitate

How Geologists Classify Rocks

Using the Visuals: Figure 2

Materials *hand lens, sample of granite, samples of the minerals quartz, pink feldspar, hornblende, mica*

Time 15 minutes

To help students understand the relationship between minerals and rocks, provide them with a granite sample and separate samples of the primary minerals in the rock. Have students make a labeled drawing of the granite sample, with pointers to prominent crystals of each kind of mineral. **learning modality: visual**

Texture

Including All Students

Materials *samples of cloth with different kinds of weaves*

Time 15 minutes

Explain that the term texture is derived from a Latin word meaning "to weave," as is the word *textile*, another word for "cloth." Then pass around several pieces of cloth with different weaves, or textures. Have students write a description of each piece of cloth, using adjectives that describe the weaves. Call on students to share the words they used to describe the texture of each piece. Then ask: **Does color or type of thread used affect a cloth's texture?** (*The color of the cloth does not affect its texture. The kind of thread or yarn used may affect texture.*) Likewise, texture, color, and mineral composition are separate qualities in a rock. **learning modality: kinesthetic**

Ongoing Assessment

Oral Presentation Call on students at random to name and describe one of the three characteristics geologists use to identify rocks—color, texture, and mineral composition.

Texture, continued

Using the Visuals: Figure 3

Ask students: **What do "nonbanded" and "banded" refer to in the examples of quartzite and gneiss shown?** (*Those words refer to the grain pattern of each rock. The grains of gneiss are arranged in a pattern that looks like bands, or thin layers. The grains of quartzite appear to have no bands but occur randomly throughout the rock.*) **learning modality: visual**

Mineral Composition

Building Inquiry Skills: Observing

Materials *microscope, prepared slides of thin sections of various kinds of rock, including granite, basalt, obsidian, limestone, shale, sandstone, marble, slate, schist, gneiss*
Time 15 minutes

ACTIVITY

Set up microscopes at three locations around the classroom, one each for igneous rocks, sedimentary rocks, and metamorphic rocks. Have students observe the slides and make drawings of what they see, labeling each drawing with the name of the rock. Challenge students to identify specific minerals. Give students the opportunity to observe the slides again as they learn more about differences in rocks. **learning modality: visual**

Figure 3 Texture helps geologists classify rocks. *Forming Operational Definitions* Looking at the rocks below, describe the characteristics of a rock that help you to define what a rock's "grain" is.

Fine-grained
Slate

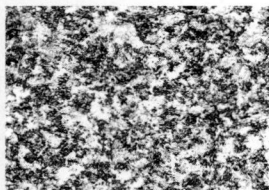
Coarse-grained
Diorite

No visible grain
Flint

Grain Size Often, the grains in a rock are large and easy to see. Such rocks are said to be coarse-grained. In other rocks, the grains are so small that they can only be seen with a microscope. These rocks are said to be fine-grained. Notice the difference in texture between the fine-grained slate and the coarse-grained diorite at left.

Grain Shape The grains in a rock vary widely in shape. Some grains look like tiny particles of fine sand. Others look like small seeds or exploding stars. In some rocks, such as granite, the grain results from the shapes of the crystals that form the rock. In other rocks, the grain shape results from fragments of other rock. These fragments can be smooth and rounded, like the fragments in conglomerate, or they can be jagged, like the fragments in breccia. You can compare conglomerate and breccia below.

Grain Pattern The grains in a rock often form patterns. Some grains lie in flat layers that look like a stack of pancakes. Other grains form wavy, swirling patterns. Some rocks have grains that look like rows of multicolored beads, as in the sample of gneiss shown below. Other rocks, in contrast, have grains that occur randomly throughout the rock.

No Visible Grain Some rocks have no grain, even when they are examined under a microscope. Some of these rocks have no crystal grains because when they form, they cool very quickly. This quick cooling gives these rocks the smooth, shiny texture of a thick piece of glass. Other rocks with no visible grain are made up of extremely small particles of silica that settle out of water. One familiar rock that forms in this manner is flint.

☑ *Checkpoint* **What terms describe a rock's texture?**

Rounded grain
Conglomerate

Jagged grain
Breccia

Nonbanded
Quartzite

Banded
Gneiss

Background

Facts and Figures Grain size in igneous rocks depends on how slowly or rapidly the minerals in magma or solution crystallized. Grain size in metamorphic rocks is affected by the degree of metamorphism—how high the temperature or great the pressure. Low-grade metamorphism often results in a rock with smaller grains. More intense metamorphism causes some minerals to recrystallize and form larger grains. Many metamorphic rocks, such as gneiss, have a texture similar to a coarse-grained igneous rock. The size of the grains in clastic sedimentary rocks is also an indication of the conditions in which the rocks formed, though it's environmental conditions that are indicated. The large particles of conglomerate, for example, might have been deposited by a fast-moving stream.

Mineral Composition

Often, geologists must look more closely at a rock to determine its mineral composition. By looking at a small sliver of a rock under a microscope, a geologist can observe the shape and size of crystals in the rock and identify the minerals it contains. To prepare a rock for viewing under the microscope, geologists cut the rock very thin, so that light can shine through its crystals.

In identifying rocks, geologists also use some of the tests that are used to identify minerals. For example, testing the rock's surface with acid determines whether the rock includes minerals made of compounds called carbonates. Testing with a magnet detects the elements iron or nickel.

Origin

There are three major groups of rocks: igneous rock, sedimentary rock, and metamorphic rock. These terms refer to how the rocks in each group formed.

Rock belonging to each of these groups forms in a different way. **Igneous rock** forms from the cooling of molten rock—either magma below the surface or lava at the surface. Most **sedimentary rock** forms when particles of other rocks or the remains of plants and animals are pressed and cemented together. Sedimentary rock forms in layers below the surface. **Metamorphic rock** is formed when an existing rock is changed by heat, pressure, or chemical reactions. Most metamorphic rock forms deep underground.

Figure 4 A scientist is preparing to cut a thin slice from a piece of moon rock. He will then examine it under a microscope to determine its composition.

Section 1 Review

1. What three characteristics do geologists use to identify a rock sample?
2. What are the three groups into which geologists classify rocks?
3. What is a rock's texture?
4. What methods do geologists use to determine the mineral composition of a rock?
5. **Thinking Critically Comparing and Contrasting** What do the three major groups of rocks have in common? How are they different?

Check Your Progress

CHAPTER PROJECT 15

Your neighborhood might be a good place to begin your rock collection. Look for gravel and crushed rock in flower beds, driveways or parking lots, and beneath downspouts. **CAUTION:** *If the area you choose is not a public place, make sure that you have permission to be there.* Begin to collect samples of rocks with different colors and textures. Plan with your teacher or an adult family member to visit other parts of your community where you could collect rocks.

Program Resources

◆ **Unit 4 Resources** 15-1 Review and Reinforce, p. 123; 15-1 Enrich, p. 124

Answers to Self-Assessment

Caption Question

Figure 3 Characteristics include grain size, grain shape, and grain pattern.

✓ *Checkpoint*

Texture is described with terms based on grain size, including fine-grained and coarse-grained; grain shape, including smooth and jagged; and grain pattern, including banded and nonbanded.

Origin

Including All Students

For students who are still mastering English, explain that *origin* refers to the source or beginning of something, in this case the formation of each of the major rock groups. Ask: **Some of the rocks of which group have their origin at the surface of Earth rather than underground?** (*Some igneous rocks form at the surface.*) **limited English proficiency**

3 Assess

Section 1 Review Answers

1. Color, texture, and mineral composition
2. Igneous rock, sedimentary rock, and metamorphic rock
3. A rock's texture is the look and feel of the rock's surface.
4. Geologists look at a small sliver of a rock under a microscope to observe its crystals and identify the minerals it contains. They also use tests to identify minerals, including the scratch test for hardness, an acid test for carbon compounds, and a magnet to detect iron or nickel.
5. Rocks in each group make up Earth's crust and are composed of minerals and other materials. They are different in the way they are formed.

Check Your Progress

CHAPTER PROJECT 15

Review each student's or group's list of places to collect rocks. Caution students that they should always work in the field in pairs or small groups, unless an adult is available to go along.

Performance Assessment

Writing Have students explain in their own words what characteristics geologists use to identify rocks.

Objective

After completing the lesson, students will be able to
♦ identify the characteristics used to classify igneous rocks.

Key Terms extrusive rock, intrusive rock, porphyritic texture

1 Engage/Explore

Activating Prior Knowledge

Help students recall the knowledge they gained from earlier chapters about molten material from the mantle and where it rises into Earth's crust. Ask: **At what places does molten material rise to Earth's surface?** (*Volcanoes, hot spots, mid-ocean ridge*) **What happens to molten material from the mantle when it rises close to or onto the surface?** (*It hardens, or crystallizes.*) Help students recall how cooling rates affect the size of mineral crystals.

·····DISCOVER·····

Skills Focus inferring
Materials *samples of granite and obsidian, hand lens*
Time 10 minutes
Tips If samples of granite and obsidian are unavailable, use any two igneous rocks with similar composition but obviously different textures, such as gabbro and basalt or diorite and andesite.
Expected Outcome Granite and obsidian are very similar in composition but have different textures because granite forms from magma and obsidian forms from lava. Students should observe that the granite has coarse-grained crystals, while the glassy obsidian has no crystals.
Think It Over Students should infer that the granite formed as magma slowly cooled deep beneath Earth's surface, while the obsidian formed as lava cooled quickly on the surface.

SECTION ② Igneous Rocks

DISCOVER ·····················ACTIVITY····

How Do Igneous Rocks Form?

1. Use a hand lens to examine samples of granite and obsidian.
2. Describe the texture of both rocks using the terms coarse, fine, or glassy.
3. Which rock has coarse-grained crystals? Which rock has no crystals or grains?

Think It Over
Inferring Granite and obsidian are igneous rocks. Given the physical properties of these rocks, what can you infer about how each type of rock formed?

GUIDE FOR READING

♦ What characteristics are used to classify igneous rocks?

Reading Tip As you read, make a list of the characteristics of igneous rocks. Write one sentence describing each characteristic.

Figure 5 A lava flow soon cools and hardens to form igneous rock.

Y ou are in a spacecraft orbiting Earth 4.6 billion years ago. Do you see the blue and green globe of Earth that astronauts today see from space? No—instead, Earth looks like a glowing piece of charcoal from a barbecue, or a charred and bubbling marshmallow heated over the coals.

Soon after Earth formed, the planet became so hot that its surface was a glowing mass of molten material. Hundreds of millions of years passed before Earth cooled enough for a crust to solidify. Then lava probably flowed from Earth's interior, spread over the surface, and hardened. The movement of magma and lava has continued ever since.

482

READING STRATEGIES

Reading Tip Point out that the subheadings "Origin," "Texture," and "Mineral Composition" provide students with three main characteristics of igneous rocks. Thus, they should write one sentence for each of those characteristics. Each sentence should sum up the information under the subheading.

Vocabulary After students have read about the derivation of the term *igneous,* point out that they may use two words that are derived from the same Greek word. When you *ignite* charcoal, for example, you set it on fire. Figuratively, you can *ignite* a crowd with a "fiery" speech. Also, when you start a car, you turn the key in the *ignition* switch. Explain that turning the switch causes an electric current to *ignite* the fuel mixture that powers the engine.

Characteristics of Igneous Rock

The first rocks to form on Earth probably looked much like the igneous rocks that harden from lava today. Igneous rock (IG nee us) is any rock that forms from magma or lava. The name "igneous" comes from the Latin word *ignis*, meaning "fire."

Most igneous rocks are made of mineral crystals. The only exceptions to this rule are the different types of volcanic glass—igneous rock that lacks minerals with a crystal structure. **Igneous rocks are classified according to their origin, texture, and mineral composition.**

Origin Geologists classify igneous rocks according to where they formed. **Extrusive rock** is igneous rock formed from lava that erupted onto Earth's surface. Basalt is the most common extrusive rock. Basalt forms much of the crust, including the oceanic crust, shield volcanoes, and lava plateaus.

Igneous rock that formed when magma hardened beneath Earth's surface is called **intrusive rock.** Granite is the most abundant intrusive rock in continental crust. Recall from Chapter 13 that granite batholiths form the core of many mountain ranges.

Texture The texture of an igneous rock depends on the size and shape of its mineral crystals. Igneous rocks may be similar in mineral composition and yet have very different textures. The texture of an igneous rock may be fine-grained, coarse-grained, glassy, or porphyritic. Rapid cooling lava forms fine-grained igneous rocks with small crystals. Slow cooling magma forms coarse-grained rock with large crystals.

Intrusive and extrusive rocks usually have different textures. Intrusive rocks have larger crystals than extrusive rocks. If you examine a coarse-grained rock such as granite, you can easily see that the crystals vary in size and color.

Some intrusive rocks have a texture that looks like a gelatin dessert with chopped-up fruit mixed in. A rock with large crystals scattered on a background of much smaller crystals has a **porphyritic texture** (pawr fuh RIT ik). How can a rock have two

Figure 6 Igneous rocks can vary greatly in texture.
A. Rhyolite is a fine-grained igneous rock with a mineral composition similar to granite.
B. Pegmatite is a very coarse-grained variety of granite.
C. Porphyry has large crystals surrounded by fine-grained crystals.
Relating Cause and Effect What conditions caused rhyolite to have a fine-grained texture?

Program Resources

◆ **Unit 4 Resources** 15-2 Lesson Plan, p. 125; 15-2 Section Summary, p. 126
◆ **Guided Reading and Study Workbook** Section 15-2

Answers to Self-Assessment

Caption Question

Figure 6 Rapid cooling on Earth's surface caused rhyolite to have a fine-grained texture.

---

2 Facilitate

Characteristics of Igneous Rocks

Using the Visuals: Figure 6

Ask students: **Which of these rocks is intrusive and which is extrusive?** *(Rhyolite is fine-grained, and thus is extrusive. Pegmatite is coarse-grained, and thus is intrusive. Porphyry has a porphyritic texture, and therefore must be an intrusive rock that cooled in two stages.)* **learning modality: visual**

Building Inquiry Skills: Comparing and Contrasting

Materials *hand lens, samples of granite and basalt*

Time 15 minutes

Explain that granite and basalt are the two most common igneous rocks. Then have students turn back to Chapter 11, Section 1, to review the text description of Earth's crust and Figure 5 of Chapter 11. Ask: **Which parts of the crust are composed mostly of one or the other of these igneous rocks?** *(Oceanic crust is composed mostly of rock such as basalt, while continental crust is composed mostly of rock such as granite.)* Then invite students to examine and handle samples of each kind of rock. Have them make sketches of mineral grains and write a description of each. In their descriptions, students should mention origin, texture, any minerals they can identify, color, and density (heft). **learning modality: kinesthetic**

 Students can keep their sketches and descriptions in their portfolio.

Ongoing Assessment

Writing Have students explain in their own words how the location where rock cools affects its texture.

Characteristics of Igneous Rocks, continued

Using the Visuals: Figure 7

Have students closely examine the figure and also re-examine the photographs in Figure 2. Then ask: **Can you identify specific mineral grains in this photograph of granite?** (*Students should be able to identify the glassy grains as quartz, the pink grains as feldspar, the dark grains as mica or hornblende.*) **Can you see the grains of this rock without the aid of a microscope?** (*Yes, because granite is an intrusive, coarse-grained rock.*) **learning modality: visual**

Sharpen your Skills

Observing

Time 10 minutes
Expected Outcome

Students should be able to conclude that feldspar is the most abundant mineral in the example either by estimating or by counting mineral grains of approximately equal size. Similarly, they may conclude that either mica or quartz is the least abundant mineral in the example.
Extend Provide students with samples of gabbro or other igneous rock to practice observing an igneous rock's mineral composition. **learning modality: visual**

Integrating Chemistry

Some students may confuse the chemical composition of minerals, which are exact and never-changing, with the mineral composition of rocks, which can vary somewhat. To address this difference, find pictures of different varieties of granite, such as pegmatite, biotite granite, and muscovite granite, in geology texts or field guides. Explain that each of the major igneous rocks, including granite and basalt, actually encompass a range of rocks with similar but not identical mineral compositions. Geologists often talk about "granitic" rocks or the "granite family." **learning modality: visual**

Sharpen your Skills

Observing

You can learn about a rock's mineral composition by looking at a thin section.

1. The diagram shows a thin section of an igneous rock. The key identifies different minerals. Which mineral makes up most of this rock? How did you decide?

2. Which mineral is present in the smallest amount?

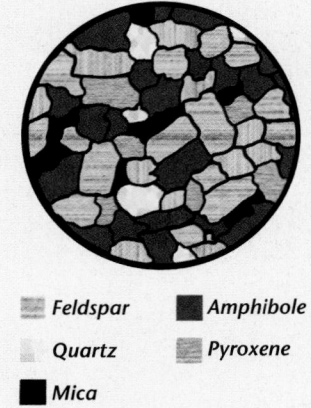

Feldspar   Amphibole

Quartz   Pyroxene

Mica

Figure 7 This thin slice of granite, viewed under a microscope, contains quartz, feldspar, mica, and other minerals.

textures? Porphyritic rocks form when intrusive rocks cool in two stages. As the magma begins to cool, large crystals form slowly. The remaining magma, however, cools more quickly, forming small crystals. The change in the rate of cooling may occur as magma moves nearer to the surface.

Extrusive rocks have a fine-grained or glassy texture. Basalt is an extrusive rock. It consists of crystals too small to be seen without a microscope.

Mineral Composition Recall from Chapter 13 that the silica content of magma and lava affects how easily the magma or lava will flow. Lava that is low in silica usually forms dark-colored rocks such as basalt. Basalt contains feldspar as well as certain dark-colored minerals, but does not contain quartz.

INTEGRATING CHEMISTRY Magma that is high in silica usually forms light-colored rocks, such as granite. However, granite comes in many shades and colors. Granite can be dark to light gray, red, and pink. Granite's color changes along with its mineral composition. Granite that is rich in reddish feldspar is a speckled pink. But granite rich in hornblende and dark mica is light gray with dark specks. Quartz crystals in granite add light gray or smoky specks. Geologists can make thin slices of granite and study each type of crystal in the rock to determine its mineral composition more exactly.

☑ *Checkpoint* How do igneous rocks differ in origin, texture, and mineral composition?

Background

Facts and Figures About 95 percent of Earth's crust is composed of igneous rocks or metamorphic rocks formed from igneous rocks. There are six major kinds of igneous rocks: the intrusive rocks granite, diorite, and gabbro; and the extrusive rocks rhyolite, andesite, and basalt.

History of Science In the early 1800s, Scottish geologist James Hall (1761–1832) showed that magma could cool to become

crystalline rock. At the time, many geologists thought that magma would always harden to a glassy texture and thus most rocks had to have crystallized from a water solution. Hall melted rocks in a glass-factory furnace and then allowed them to cool. The melted rocks that cooled quickly did have a glassy texture, but the ones that cooled slowly formed crystalline solids.

Uses of Igneous Rocks

Many igneous rocks are hard, dense, and durable. For this reason, people throughout history have used igneous rock for tools and building materials. For example, ancient Native Americans used obsidian for making very sharp tools for cutting and scraping.

Granite, one of the most abundant igneous rocks, has a long history as a building material. More than 3,500 years ago, the ancient Egyptians used granite for statues like the one shown in Figure 8. About 600 years ago, the Incas of Peru carefully fitted together great blocks of granite and other igneous rocks to build a fortress near Cuzco, their capital city. In the United States during the 1800s and early 1900s, granite was widely used to build bridges and public buildings and for paving streets with cobblestones. Thin, polished sheets of granite are still used in decorative stonework, curbstones, and floors.

Igneous rocks such as basalt, pumice, and obsidian also have important uses. Basalt is crushed to make gravel that is used in construction. The rough surface of pumice makes it a good abrasive for cleaning and polishing. Perlite, formed from the heating of obsidian, is often mixed with soil for starting vegetable seeds.

Figure 8 The ancient Egyptians valued granite for its durability. These statues at a temple in Luxor, Egypt, were carved in granite.

Section 2 Review

1. What are the three major characteristics that geologists use to identify igneous rocks?
2. What is the difference between extrusive and intrusive rocks? Give an example of each.
3. Explain what causes an igneous rock to have a fine-grained or coarse-grained texture.
4. Why are some igneous rocks dark and others light?
5. **Thinking Critically** **Comparing and Contrasting** How are basalt and granite different in their origin, texture, and mineral composition? How are they similar?

Science at Home

When you and a family member visit a pharmacy or large food store, observe the various foot-care products. What kinds of foot products are available that are made from pumice? How do people use these products? Check other skin and body care products to see if they contain pumice or other igneous rocks. Explain to your family how pumice is formed.

Program Resources

◆ **Unit 4 Resources** 15-2 Review and Reinforce, p. 127; 15-2 Enrich, p. 128

Answers to Self-Assessment

☑ *Checkpoint*

Igneous rocks form either from lava that erupted onto Earth's surface or from magma that hardened below the surface. They differ in texture according to the size and shape of their mineral grains. They differ in mineral composition depending on how much silica and other minerals are present in magma and lava.

Uses of Igneous Rocks

Real-Life Learning

Have student volunteers call local city or county offices to ask if there are any large granite buildings or other structures in the area. Then invite the volunteers to provide a short list of these granite structures to the class. Encourage students to visit these places with their families and closely examine the texture of the stone.
learning modality: kinesthetic

3 Assess

Section 2 Review Answers

1. Origin, texture, and mineral composition
2. Extrusive rock, such as basalt, forms from lava that has erupted onto Earth's surface. Intrusive rock, such as granite, forms when magma hardens beneath Earth's surface.
3. Rapid cooling causes an igneous rock to have a fine-grained texture. Slow cooling causes an igneous rock to have a coarse-grained texture.
4. Dark igneous rocks form from magma or lava low in silica content, while light igneous rocks form from magma or lava high in silica content.
5. Basalt is an extrusive rock with a fine-grained texture and low silica content. Granite is an intrusive rock with a coarse-grained texture and high silica content. Both are igneous rocks that began as molten material inside Earth.

Science at Home

Remind students that pumice forms when gas bubbles are trapped in cooling lava. Students should find that a number of foot products include pumice, especially those used to care for calluses, rough skin, and corns. Pumice is also used in some soaps.

Performance Assessment

Skills Check Have students compare and contrast granite and basalt.

Objectives

After completing the lesson, students will be able to
◆ describe how sedimentary rocks form;
◆ list and describe the three major types of sedimentary rocks.

Key Terms sediment, erosion, deposition, compaction, cementation, clastic rock, organic rock, chemical rock

1 Engage/Explore

Activating Prior Knowledge

Invite students to think of a sandy beach along an ocean or lake. Then ask: **What could cause the sand to harden into sandstone?** *(A typical answer might suggest that the weight of sand piled on that sand could provide pressure enough to harden it into a rock. Some students might suggest that there would have to be something to glue the sand particles together.)*

DISCOVER

Skills Focus observing
Materials *sheet of paper, 2 slices of bread, stack of books, plastic knife*
Time 15 minutes
Tips To keep the bread from sticking to the tabletop, have students fold the sheet of paper and place the slice of bread inside the fold. The amount of change in the bread will depend on how long the books are left in place. Have one student leave the bread under the books overnight, and then have all students observe the results.
Think It Over Students should observe that the weight of the books compressed the bread and that the bread's texture is rougher and harder than before. A typical prediction might suggest that pressure would affect rock particles similarly.

SECTION 3 Sedimentary Rocks

DISCOVER · ACTIVITY · · ·

How Does Pressure Affect Particles of Rock?

1. Place a sheet of paper over a slice of soft bread.
2. Put a stack of several heavy books on the top of the paper. After 10 minutes, remove the books. Observe what happened to the bread.
3. Slice the bread so you can observe its cross section.
4. Carefully slice a piece of fresh bread and compare its cross section to that of the pressed bread.

Think It Over
Observing How did the bread change after you removed the books? Describe the texture of the bread. How does the bread feel? What can you predict about how pressure affects the particles that make up sedimentary rocks?

GUIDE FOR READING

◆ How do sedimentary rocks form?
◆ What are the three major types of sedimentary rocks?

Reading Tip Before you read, preview the headings in the section and predict how you think sedimentary rocks form.

Visitors to Arches National Park in Utah see some of the strangest scenery on Earth. The park contains dozens of natural arches sculpted in colorful rock that is layered like a birthday cake. The layers of this cake are red, orange, pink, or tan. One arch, named Landscape Arch, is nearly 90 meters across and about 30 meters high. Delicate Arch looks like the legs of a striding giant. The forces that wear away rock on Earth's surface have been carving these arches out of solid rock for 100 million years. The arches are made of sandstone, one of the most common sedimentary rocks.

◄ Delicate Arch, Arches National Park, Utah

486

From Sediment to Rock

Sedimentary rocks form from particles deposited by water and wind. If you have ever walked along a stream or beach you may have noticed tiny sand grains, mud, and pebbles. These are some of the sediments that form sedimentary rock. **Sediment** is small, solid pieces of material that come from rocks or living things. Water, wind, and ice can carry sediment and deposit it in layers. But what turns these sediments into solid rock?

READING STRATEGIES

Reading Tip Have students write their predictions on a sheet of paper. Encourage students to check their predictions as they read. Students with prior knowledge of erosion may connect this term with the formation of sedimentary rocks and predict that the rock is made up of particles that become stuck together.

Program Resources

◆ **Unit 4 Resources** 15-3 Lesson Plan, p. 129; 15-3 Section Summary, p. 130
◆ **Guided Reading and Study Workbook** Section 15-3

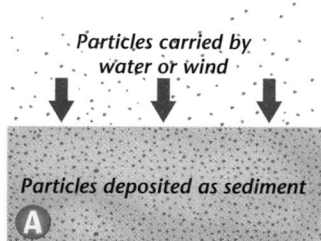

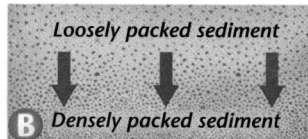

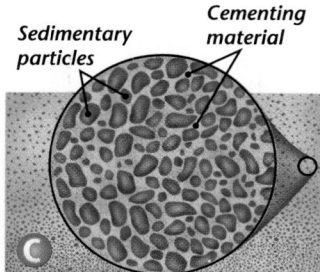

Figure 9 Sedimentary rocks form through the deposition, compaction, and cementation of sediments. **A.** Water or wind deposits sediment. **B.** The heavy sediments press down on the layers beneath. **C.** Dissolved minerals flow between the particles and cement them together.
Relating Cause and Effect What conditions are necessary for sedimentary rock to form?

Erosion Destructive forces are constantly breaking up and wearing away all the rocks on Earth's surface. These forces include heat and cold, rain, waves, and grinding ice. **Erosion** occurs when running water or wind loosen and carry away the fragments of rock.

Deposition Eventually, the moving water or wind slows and deposits the sediment. If water is carrying the sediment, rock fragments and other materials sink to the bottom of a lake or ocean. **Deposition** is the process by which sediment settles out of the water or wind carrying it. **After sediment has been deposited, the processes of compaction and cementation change the sediment into sedimentary rock.**

In addition to particles of rock, sediment may include shells, bones, leaves, stems, and other remains of living things. Over time, any remains of living things in the sediment may slowly harden and change into fossils trapped in the rock.

Compaction At first the sediments fit together loosely. But gradually, over millions of years, thick layers of sediment build up. These layers are heavy and press down on the layers beneath them. Then compaction occurs. **Compaction** is the process that presses sediments together. Year after year more sediment falls on top, creating new layers. The weight of the layers further compacts the sediments, squeezing them tightly together. The layers often remain visible in the sedimentary rock.

Cementation While compaction is taking place, the minerals in the rock slowly dissolve in the water. The dissolved minerals seep into the spaces between particles of sediment. **Cementation** is the process in which dissolved minerals crystallize and glue particles of sediment together. It often takes millions of years for compaction and cementation to transform loose sediments into solid sedimentary rock.

 Checkpoint *What are the processes that change sediment to sedimentary rock?*

Answers to Self-Assessment

Caption Question

Figure 9 Water or wind must be present for deposition to occur, and water must continue to be present for dissolved materials to cement particles together.

Checkpoint

Compaction and cementation change sediment to sedimentary rock.

---

2 Facilitate

From Sediment to Rock

Using the Visuals: Figure 9

Ask students: **What force is responsible for the compaction of sediment?** (*The weight of overlying sediment compacts underlying sediment. Therefore, the force of gravity is responsible.*) **For cementation to occur, what change must occur in the solution of water and dissolved minerals between particles of sediment?** (*The water must evaporate, leaving the minerals as solids between the particles.*)
learning modality: verbal

Building Inquiry Skills: Making Models

Materials *plaster of Paris, sand, pebbles of various colors, bowl, 2-L pop bottle with top cut off, scissors*
Time 20 minutes; 10 minutes 3–4 days later

ACTIVITY

Students can make a model of how sedimentary rock forms by building layers of sand and pebbles in a plastic bottle. In a bowl, students should mix sand, pebbles of one color, plaster of Paris, and a small amount of water. This mixture should be poured into the bottle. Repeating that process with different colors of pebbles, students can make several layers, one on top of the other. Once the layers have been prepared, the bottle should be placed in a warm, sunny place for several days to dry. When the layers have dried, have students cut the plastic away from the hardened "rock." Students should notice that the plaster has cemented the sediment together and that the bottom layers are more compressed than the top layers.
learning modality: kinesthetic

Ongoing Assessment

Writing Have students write a description in their own words of how sedimentary rock forms.
 Students can keep their descriptions in their portfolios.

Types of Sedimentary Rock

Building Inquiry Skills: Classifying

Materials *hand lens, samples of sedimentary rocks, including sandstone, conglomerate, breccia, shale, organic limestone, gypsum*
Time 15 minutes

Before students have read about specific sedimentary rocks, provide small groups with representative samples of the three major groups of sedimentary rock. Challenge each group to generate a rationale for classifying the samples into three different types. **learning modality: logical/mathematical**

Clastic Rocks

TRY THIS

Skills Focus drawing conclusions

Materials *samples of sandstone and shale, hand lens, balance, pan, water*
Time 15 minutes for setup; 10 minutes the next day
Tips Samples need to be at least 25 g to show a significant change in mass. If there are not enough samples for every student, divide the class into small groups. Make sure the pans will hold enough water to totally immerse the samples provided. Set up one or more balances in a central location so students can take each sample to a balance to find its mass. Advise students to make a data table to record the mass of each sample before and after immersing it in water.
Expected Outcome Students should observe that sandstone is rough and coarse-grained, while shale is smooth and fine-grained. The mass of each rock will vary depending on the samples used. Students should find that the mass of the shale changes little or not at all after being submerged overnight, while the mass of the sandstone increases substantially. They should conclude that sandstone has spaces between particles to absorb water, while shale does not.
Extend Have students perform the same activity with other rock samples.
learning modality: logical/ mathematical

488

Rock Absorber

Find out if water can soak into rock.

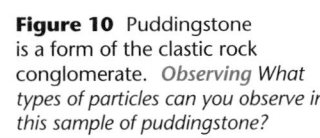

1. Using a hand lens, observe samples of sandstone and shale. How are they alike? How are they different?
2. Use a balance to measure the mass of each rock.
3. Place the rocks in a pan of water. Observe the samples. Which sample has bubbles escaping? Predict which sample will gain mass.
4. Leave the rocks submerged in the pan overnight.
5. The next day, remove the rocks from the pan and find the mass of each rock.

Drawing Conclusions How did the masses of the two rocks change after soaking? What can you conclude about each rock based on your observations?

Types of Sedimentary Rock

Geologists classify sedimentary rocks according to the type of sediments that make up the rock. **There are three major groups of sedimentary rocks: clastic rocks, organic rocks, and chemical rocks.** Different processes form each of these types of sedimentary rocks.

Clastic Rocks

Most sedimentary rocks are made up of the broken pieces of other rocks. A **clastic rock** is a sedimentary rock that forms when rock fragments are squeezed together. These fragments can range in size from clay particles too small to be seen without a microscope to large boulders too heavy for you to lift. Clastic rocks are grouped by the size of the rock fragments, or particles, of which they are made.

Shale One common clastic rock is shale. Shale forms from tiny particles of clay. For shale to form, water must deposit clay particles in very thin, flat layers, one on top of another. No cementation is needed to hold clay particles together. Even so, the spaces between the particles in the resulting shale are so small that water cannot pass through them. Shale feels smooth, and splits easily into flat pieces.

Sandstone Sandstone forms from the sand on beaches, on the ocean floor, in riverbeds, and in sand dunes. Sandstone is a clastic rock formed from the compaction and cementation of small particles of sand. Most sand particles consist of quartz. Because the cementation process does not fill all the spaces between sand grains, sandstone contains many small holes. Sandstone can easily absorb water through these holes.

Conglomerate and Breccia Some sedimentary rocks contain a mixture of rock fragments of different sizes. The fragments can range in size from sand and pebbles to boulders. If the fragments have rounded edges, they form a clastic rock called conglomerate. A rock made up of large fragments with sharp edges is called breccia (BRECH ee uh).

Figure 10 Puddingstone is a form of the clastic rock conglomerate. *Observing What types of particles can you observe in this sample of puddingstone?*

Background

Facts and Figures Clastic rocks contain a great variety of rock fragments and other materials, but clay minerals and quartz particles generally make up most of these sedimentary rocks. Clay minerals are abundant because they result from the chemical weathering of such silicates as feldspar. Quartz particles are abundant because they are so hard that they resist chemical weathering.

The time it takes for compaction and cementation to produce sedimentary rock varies greatly. Much depends on the availability of water and its dissolved minerals, which are necessary to cement the sediments together. Sediments in the Rocky Mountains, for example, became sedimentary rock in less than 20,000 years. But sand and gravel found today in western Montana were deposited 30–40 million years ago and still haven't become rock.

Organic Rocks

  Not all sedimentary rocks are made from particles of other rocks. **Organic rock** forms where the remains of plants and animals are deposited in thick layers. The term "organic" refers to substances that once were part of living things or were made by living things. Two important organic sedimentary rocks are coal and limestone.

Coal Coal forms from the remains of swamp plants buried in water. As layer upon layer of plant remains build up, the weight of the layers squeezes the decaying plants. Over millions of years, they slowly change into coal.

Limestone The hard shells of living things produce some kinds of limestone. How does limestone form? In the ocean, many living things, including coral, clams, oysters, and snails, have shells or skeletons made of calcite. When these animals die, their shells pile up as sediment on the ocean floor. Over millions of years, these layers of sediment can grow to a depth of hundreds of meters. Slowly, the pressure of overlying layers compacts the sediment. Some of the shells dissolve, forming a solution of calcite that seeps into the spaces between the shell fragments. Later, the dissolved material comes out of solution, forming calcite. The calcite cements the shell particles together, forming limestone.

Everyone knows one type of limestone: chalk. Chalk forms from sediments made of the skeletons of microscopic living things found in the oceans.

✓ *Checkpoint* *What are two important organic sedimentary rocks?*

Figure 11 When broken apart, a piece of shale from a coal mine may reveal the impression of an ancient plant. Geologists estimate that it takes about 20 meters of decayed plants to form a layer of coal about one meter thick.

Figure 12 These limestone cliffs are along the Eleven Point River in Missouri.

Organic Rocks

Integrating Life Science

Materials *pieces of lignite or subbituminous coal, paper towels, needles, hand lens, piece of wood, modeling compound*

Time 15 minutes

Have students examine pieces of soft coal, using paper towels to handle the coal. Point out that coal is a sedimentary rock composed of layers. Have students count the layers. Then take one piece of coal and separate its layers. Flatten the modeling compound on the piece of wood and press the coal into the compound, which will hold the coal in place. Then insert needles between the layers of the coal and pry the layers apart. (If students handle the needles, caution them to be careful.) Continue prying apart layers until you find an impression of a leaf or twig. Have students examine the fossil with a hand lens. **learning modality: visual**

Chemical Rocks

Real-Life Learning

Bring to class an alabaster vase or ornament and have students note its qualities. Explain that alabaster is a fine-grained form of gypsum often carved into vases and ornaments. Ask: **What do you know about gypsum that would make this rock easy to carve?** (*Gypsum has a rating of 2 on Mohs hardness scale, and thus is a relatively soft rock.*) **How did the alabaster in this vase originally form?** (*It formed as water evaporated, leaving the minerals dissolved in the water as crystals.*) **learning modality: verbal**

Answers to Self-Assessment

Caption Question

Figure 10 Answers may vary. A typical answer will mention rock fragments of various sizes, most with rounded edges.

✓ *Checkpoint*
Coal and limestone

Ongoing Assessment

Skills Check Challenge students to draw a conclusion about whether the process shown in Figure 9 better describes the formation of clastic rocks or organic rocks. (*Students should conclude that the first step, concerning sediment carried by water or wind, only relates to clastic rocks.*)

Uses of Sedimentary Rocks

Including All Students

Invite students who need additional challenges to find out what brownstone is and what "a brownstone" refers to in some American cities, especially New York City. *(Students should learn that brownstone is a reddish brown sandstone. It was once widely used in building houses and apartment buildings, hence the name "brownstone" for many older buildings in New York City and elsewhere.)* **learning modality: verbal**

3 Assess

Section 3 Review Answers

1. The processes of compaction and cementation
2. Clastic rocks, organic rocks, and chemical rocks
3. Limestone can form when shells pile up as sediment on the ocean floor and then compaction and cementation change the sediment into organic rock. Limestone can also form when calcite dissolved in lakes, seas, or underground water comes out of solution and crystallizes to form chemical rock.
4. Shale forms from tiny particles of clay deposited in flat layers. No cementation is needed to hold the particles together. Sandstone forms from the compaction and cementation of sand particles.

Check Your Progress
CHAPTER PROJECT 15

Check that students are beginning to collect rocks and bring them to class. Provide a place where each student or group can store their rocks. Encourage students to begin classifying and identifying their rocks.

Performance Assessment

Skills Check Have students make a compare/contrast table that includes all the sedimentary rocks discussed in the section. The table should have columns for name, major group, and characteristics.

Figure 13 These rock "towers" in Mono Lake, California, are made of tufa, a type of limestone. Tufa forms from solutions containing dissolved minerals. *Classifying What type of sedimentary rock is tufa?*

Chemical Rocks

Chemical rock forms when minerals that are dissolved in a solution crystallize. For example, limestone can form when calcite that is dissolved in lakes, seas, or underground water comes out of solution and forms crystals. This kind of limestone is considered a chemical rock.

Chemical rocks can also form from mineral deposits left when seas or lakes evaporate. Rock salt is a chemical rock made of the mineral halite, which forms by evaporation. Gypsum is another chemical rock formed by evaporation. Large deposits of rocks formed by evaporation form only in dry climates.

Uses of Sedimentary Rocks

For thousands of years, people have used sandstone and limestone as building materials. Both types of stone are soft enough to be easily cut into blocks or slabs. You may be surprised to learn that the White House in Washington, D.C., is built of sandstone. Builders today use sandstone and limestone for decorating or for covering the outside walls of buildings.

Limestone also has many industrial uses. Recall from Chapter 4 that limestone is important in smelting iron ore. Limestone is also used in making cement.

Section 3 Review

1. Once sediment has been deposited, what processes change it into sedimentary rock?
2. What are the three major kinds of sedimentary rocks?
3. Describe two ways in which limestone can form.
4. Thinking Critically **Comparing and Contrasting** Compare and contrast shale and sandstone. Include what they are made of and how they form.

Check Your Progress
CHAPTER PROJECT 15

With an adult, visit an area where you can collect samples of rocks. As you collect your samples, observe whether the rock is loose on the ground, broken off a ledge, or in a stream. Begin to classify your rocks into groups. Do any of your rocks consist of a single mineral? Do you recognize any of the minerals in these rocks? Notice the texture of each rock. Did you find any rocks made of pieces of other rocks?

Answers to Self-Assessment

Caption Question
Figure 13 Tufa is a chemical rock, because it forms when dissolved minerals come out of solution.

Program Resources

◆ **Unit 4 Resources** 15-3 Review and Reinforce, p. 131; 15-3 Enrich, p. 132

SECTION 4 Rocks From Reefs

DISCOVER · ACTIVITY

What Can You Conclude From the Way a Rock Reacts to Acid?

1. Using a hand lens, observe the color and texture of samples of limestone and coquina.

2. Put on your goggles and apron.

3. [icon] Obtain a small amount of dilute hydrochloric acid from your teacher. Hydrochloric acid is used to test rocks for the presence of the mineral calcite.

4. Using a plastic dropper, place a few drops of dilute hydrochloric acid on the limestone. **CAUTION**: *Hydrochloric acid can cause burns.*

5. Record your observations.

6. Repeat Steps 2 through 4 with the sample of coquina and observe the results.

7. Rinse the samples of limestone and coquina with lots of water before returning them to your teacher. Wash your hands.

Think It Over
Drawing Conclusions
How did the color and texture of the two rocks compare? How did they react to the test? A piece of coral reacts to hydrochloric acid the same way as limestone and coquina. What could you conclude about the mineral composition of coral?

O ff the coast of Florida lies a "city" in the sea. It is a coral reef providing both food and shelter for many sea animals. The reef shimmers with life—clams, sponges, sea urchins, starfish, marine worms and, of course, fish. Schools of brilliantly colored fish dart in and out of forests of equally colorful corals. Octopuses lurk in underwater caves, scooping up crabs that pass too close. A reef forms a sturdy wall that protects the shoreline from battering waves. This city was built by billions of tiny, soft-bodied animals that have outer skeletons made of calcite.

GUIDE FOR READING

◆ How do coral reefs form?

◆ How do coral reefs become organic limestone deposits on land?

Reading Tip As you read, make a list of main ideas and supporting details about coral.

Figure 14 A coral reef in the Florida Keys provides food and shelter for many different kinds of living things.

Chapter 15 **491**

READING STRATEGIES

Reading Tip Encourage students to write one main idea for each main heading and then list two or three supporting details for each. Main ideas: "Corals are animals whose skeletons grow together to form a coral reef." "When coral animals die, their skeletons remain, and new corals build on top of them." "Limestone that began as coral can be found in places where uplift has raised ancient sea floors above sea level."

Program Resources

◆ **Unit 4 Resources** 15-4 Lesson Plan, p. 133; 15-4 Section Summary, p. 134

◆ **Laboratory Manual** 15, "Making Models of Sedimentary Rocks"

◆ **Guided Reading and Study Workbook** Section 15-4

 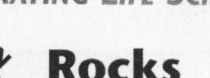

SECTION 4 Rocks From Reefs

Objectives

After completing the lesson, students will be able to
◆ describe the formation of coral reefs;
◆ explain how coral reefs become organic limestone deposits on land.

Key Terms coral reef, atoll

1 Engage/Explore

Activating Prior Knowledge

Encourage students to share their knowledge of coral reefs, either from direct experience or nature shows on television. Ask: **Where are coral reefs found?** *(In warm ocean waters, such as in the Caribbean)* **How would you describe the structure of a coral reef?** *(A typical answer might describe an underwater plantlike structure.)*

· · · · · · · · DISCOVER · · · · · · · ·

Skills Focus drawing conclusions
Materials *samples of limestone and coquina, dilute hydrochloric acid, plastic dropper, running water*
Time 15 minutes
Tips Coquina is a clastic rock composed of shells and shell fragments. A fossil shell can be used as an alternative. Coral itself is not recommended for this activity because of conservation concerns. Caution students that the dilute (5%) hydrochloric acid needs to be handled with extreme care. You could use white vinegar, which is a weak acid, in place of the dilute HCl, though the effect will not be as strong.
Think It Over The color and texture of the rocks will vary depending on the samples used. Students should observe that hydrochloric acid fizzes where it comes in contact with limestone and coquina, thus testing positive for the mineral calcite. Students should conclude that coral also contains calcite in its composition.

2 Facilitate

Living Coral

Including All Students

For students who need extra help, review some of the basic concepts related to biology that need to be understood to grasp how coral reefs originate. Explain that photosynthesis is a process carried out by plants, algae, and some other organisms that uses the energy of sunlight to produce a sugar. Then have students use dictionaries, encyclopedias, and biology books to write descriptions of corals and algae. **learning modality: verbal**

How a Coral Reef Forms

Using the Visuals: Figure 16

Ask students: **What is a fringe on a dress or shirt?** (*A border of different material that serves as an ornament*) Point out that a fringing reef is a fringe around an island. **What part of this picture will remain once the volcano is worn away?** (*The circular fringe around the volcano.*) Explain that an atoll is sometimes large enough to be inhabited, as some are in the equatorial Pacific Ocean. The middle of an atoll, where a volcano once was, becomes a lagoon at the center of the island. **learning modality: visual**

Building Inquiry Skills: Making Models

Materials *wooden board, modeling compound*
Time 15 minutes

Challenge pairs of students to make a model of a reef, randomly assigning one of the three types to each pair. Students can form their clay models on a wooden board. When all groups have finished, have students compare the different models, analyzing which models best represent the three types of coral reefs. **learning modality: kinesthetic**

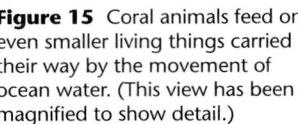

Figure 15 Coral animals feed on even smaller living things carried their way by the movement of ocean water. (This view has been magnified to show detail.)

Figure 16 The island of Bora Bora in the South Pacific Ocean is ringed by a fringing reef. Someday, erosion will wear away the island, leaving an atoll. *Inferring As the sea floor beneath an atoll sinks, what happens to the living part of the coral reef?*

492

Living Coral

Coral animals are tiny relatives of jellyfish that live together in vast numbers. Most coral animals are the size of your fingernail, or even smaller. Each one looks like a small sack with a mouth surrounded by tentacles. These animals use their tentacles to capture and eat microscopic creatures that float by. They produce skeletons that grow together to form a structure called a **coral reef.**

Coral reefs form only in the warm, shallow water of tropical oceans. Coral animals cannot grow in cold water or water low in salt. Reefs are most abundant around islands and along the eastern coasts of continents. In the United States, only the coasts of southern Florida and Hawaii have coral reefs.

Tiny algae grow within the body of each coral animal. The algae provide substances that the coral animals need to live. In turn, the coral animals provide a framework for the algae to grow on. Like plants, algae need sunlight. Below 40 meters, not enough light penetrates the water for the algae to grow. For this reason, almost all growth in a coral reef occurs within 40 meters of the water's surface.

How a Coral Reef Forms

Coral animals absorb the element calcium from the ocean water. The calcium is then changed into calcite and forms their skeletons. **When coral animals die, their skeletons remain, and more corals build on top of them.** Over thousands of years, reefs may grow to be hundreds of kilometers long and hundreds of meters thick. Reefs usually grow outward toward the open ocean. If the sea level rises or if the sea floor sinks, the reef will grow upward, too.

Background

Integrating Science The relationship between corals and the green alga Zooxanthella is a type of symbiosis called *mutualism,* in which two species live together in such a way that both benefit. The corals provide the algae with a place to live as well as the carbon dioxide needed to carry out photosynthesis. The algae help the corals produce the calcite that makes up the coral animals' skeletons. The algae may also supply some nutrients to the coral animals. Nearly all of the body of a coral animal is transparent, allowing sunlight to penetrate to the algae. One square centimeter of coral may contain as many as 1 million individual algae cells. Corals do eat other organisms, mostly microscopic protists, by capturing them with their tentacles.

There are three types of coral reefs: fringing reefs, barrier reefs and atolls. Fringing reefs lie close to shore, separated from land by shallow water. Barrier reefs lie farther out, at least 10 kilometers from the land. The Great Barrier Reef that stretches 2,000 kilometers along the coast of Australia is a barrier reef. An **atoll** is a ring-shaped coral island found far from land. An atoll develops when coral grows on top of a volcanic island that has sunk beneath the ocean's surface. How can a volcanic island sink? As the oceanic crust moves away from the mid-ocean ridge, it cools and becomes more dense. This causes the sea floor to sink.

☑ *Checkpoint* What are the three types of coral reefs?

Limestone Deposits From Coral Reefs

Over time, coral buried by sediments can turn into limestone. Like modern-day coral animals, ancient coral animals thrived in warm, tropical oceans. Their limestone fossils are among the most common fossils on Earth. **Limestone that began as coral can be found on continents in places where uplift has raised ancient sea floors above sea level.**

In parts of the United States, reefs that formed under water millions of years ago now make up part of the land. The movement of Earth's plates slowly uplifted the ocean floor where these reefs grew until the ocean floor became dry land. There are exposed reefs in Wisconsin, Illinois, and Indiana, as well as in Texas, New Mexico, and many other places.

Figure 17 A striking band of white rock tops El Capitan Peak in the Guadalupe Mountains of Texas. This massive layer of limestone formed from coral reefs that grew in a warm, shallow sea more than 250 million years ago.

Section 4 Review

1. Explain how coral reefs form.
2. How does coral become limestone?
3. Why are living coral animals only found in water that is less than 40 meters deep?
4. **Thinking Critically Predicting** The Amazon is a great river that flows through the tropical forests of Brazil. The river dumps huge amounts of fresh water, made cloudy by particles of sediment, into the South Atlantic Ocean. Would you expect to find coral reefs growing in the ocean near the mouth of the Amazon? Explain your answer.

Check Your Progress

CHAPTER PROJECT 15

Begin to make an information card for each of your rocks, and decide how to store the rocks. Each rock's card should include the following information: where and when the rock was found; the type of geologic feature where you found the rock; a description of the rock's texture; a description of the minerals that make up the rock; and the results of any tests you performed on the rock. Are any of your rocks organic rocks? How could you tell?

Program Resources

◆ **Unit 4 Resources** 15-4 Review and Reinforce, p. 135; 15-4 Enrich, p. 136

Answers to Self-Assessment

Caption Question

Figure 16 As the island sinks more than 40 meters below the water's surface, the living part of the coral grows upward to remain within 40 meters of the surface.

☑ *Checkpoint*

Fringing reefs, barrier reefs, and atolls

Limestone Deposits From Coral Reefs

Using the Visuals: Figure 17

After students have examined the figure, have them turn back to Figure 29, on pages 378–379, in Chapter 11. Ask: **How has the land we call Texas changed in the last 250 million years?** (*Texas was once part of the supercontinent Pangaea. Since then, plate movements have changed its position dramatically.*) **learning modality: visual**

3 Assess

Section 4 Review Answers

1. Coral reefs form as the shells of coral animals grow together. When coral animals die, their shells remain, and new corals build on top of them.
2. Coral buried by sediments turns into limestone. Eventually, the limestone may be uplifted above sea level.
3. Living corals depend upon tiny algae within their bodies. Like plants, these algae need sunlight. Below 40 meters, not enough sunlight penetrates the water for the algae to live. Therefore, coral animals cannot live below 40 meters deep.
4. You would not expect coral animals to grow near the mouth of the Amazon because the particles of sediment would block the sunlight needed by the algae in the body of corals. The fresh water from the river would lower the salt content of the water, and the coral animals could not survive.

Check Your Progress

CHAPTER PROJECT 15

Make sure students understand how to make an information card on each of their rocks. You may want to make a sample card and display it on a bulletin board.

Performance Assessment

Writing Have students write a description of how each of the three types of coral reefs form.

Objectives

After completing the lesson, students will be able to

◆ describe the conditions under which metamorphic rocks form;

◆ identify the ways in which geologists classify metamorphic rocks.

Key Term foliated

1 Engage/Explore

Activating Prior Knowledge

Help students recall forces that could change rocks beneath Earth's surface. For example, ask: **What occurs at convergent plate boundaries?** *(Plates collide, resulting in subduction, mountain building, and volcanic activity.)* **What effect do you think plate collisions would have on the rocks involved or on rocks in the area?** *(Students might mention increases in pressure and temperature that could deform or change rocks.)*

⋯⋯⋯ DISCOVER ⋯⋯⋯

Skills Focus inferring
Materials *samples of gneiss and granite, hand lens*
Time 15 minutes
Tips Since the color of both gneiss and granite varies, try to obtain samples of each that are of similar color in order to focus students' attention on the more relevant characteristic of texture.
Expected Outcome Students should observe that both granite and gneiss are coarse-grained. In granite, the grains are more angular than those in gneiss. The grains in gneiss appear flattened and more compact. Students' sketches should reflect these differences.
Think It Over Answers may vary. A typical answer might suggest that tremendous pressure and heat could cause such a change to occur.

DISCOVER ⋯⋯⋯⋯⋯⋯⋯⋯⋯ ACTIVITY

How Do the Grain Patterns of Gneiss and Granite Compare?

1. Using a hand lens, observe samples of gneiss and granite. Look carefully at the grains or crystals in both rocks.

2. Observe how the grains or crystals are arranged in both rocks. Draw a sketch of both rocks and describe their textures.

Think It Over

Inferring Within the crust, some granite becomes gneiss. What do you think must happen to cause this change?

GUIDE FOR READING

◆ Under what conditions do metamorphic rocks form?

◆ How do geologists classify metamorphic rocks?

Reading Tip Before you read, rewrite the headings in the section as questions. As you read, look for answers to those questions.

Every metamorphic rock is a rock that has changed its form. In fact, the word *metamorphic* comes from the Greek words *meta*, meaning "change," and *morphosis*, meaning "form." But what causes a rock to change into metamorphic rock? The answer lies inside Earth.

How Metamorphic Rocks Form

Heat and pressure deep beneath Earth's surface can change any rock into metamorphic rock. When rock changes into metamorphic rock, its appearance, texture, crystal structure, and mineral content change. Metamorphic rock can form out of igneous, sedimentary, or other metamorphic rock.

Collisions between Earth's plates can push the rock down toward the heat of the mantle. Pockets of magma rising through the crust also provide heat that can produce metamorphic rocks.

The deeper rock is buried in the crust, the greater the pressure on that rock. Under pressure hundreds or thousands of times greater than at Earth's surface, the minerals in a rock can change into other minerals. The rock has become a metamorphic rock.

Figure 18 Great heat and pressure can change one type of rock into another. Granite becomes gneiss, shale becomes slate, and sandstone changes to quartzite. *Observing* How does quartzite differ from sandstone?

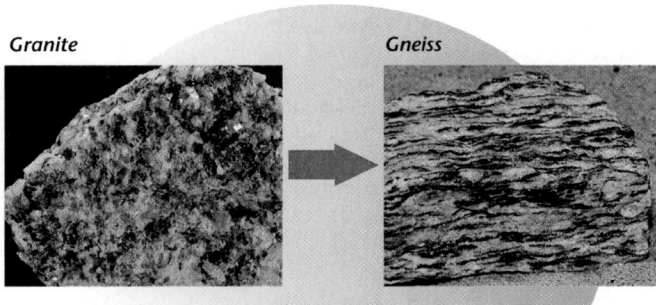

Granite   *Gneiss*

READING STRATEGIES

Reading Tip Sample questions derived from the section headings are: "How do metamorphic rocks form?" "How are metamorphic rocks classified?" "What are some uses of metamorphic rock?" Encourage students to answer each question in two to three sentences just as if these were questions on a quiz. Students can later use their questions and answers for review.

Program Resources

◆ **Unit 4 Resources** 15-5 Lesson Plan, p. 137; 15-5 Section Summary, p. 138

◆ **Guided Reading and Study Workbook** Section 15-5

Classifying Metamorphic Rocks

While metamorphic rocks are forming, high temperatures change the size and shape of the grains, or mineral crystals, in the rock. In addition, tremendous pressure squeezes rock so tightly that the mineral grains may line up in flat, parallel layers. **Geologists classify metamorphic rocks by the arrangement of the grains that make up the rocks.**

Metamorphic rocks that have their grains arranged in parallel layers or bands are said to be **foliated.** The term *foliated* comes from the Latin word for "leaf." It describes the thin, flat layering found in most metamorphic rocks. Foliated rocks—including slate, schist, and gneiss—may split apart along these bands. In Figure 18, notice how the crystals in granite have been flattened to create the foliated texture of gneiss.

One common foliated rock is slate. Heat and pressure change the sedimentary rock shale into slate. Slate is basically a denser, more compact version of shale. During the change, new minerals such as mica and hornblende form in the slate.

Sometimes metamorphic rocks are nonfoliated. The mineral grains in these rocks are arranged randomly. Metamorphic rocks that are nonfoliated do not split into layers. Marble and quartzite both have a nonfoliated texture. Quartzite forms out of sandstone. The weakly cemented quartz particles in the sandstone recrystallize to form quartzite, which is extremely hard. Notice in Figure 18 how much smoother quartzite looks than sandstone.

☑ *Checkpoint* What is a foliated rock?

A Sequined Rock

ACTIVITY

1. Make three balls of clay about 3 cm in diameter. Gently mix about 25 sequins into one ball.

2. Use a 30-cm piece of string to cut the ball in half. How are the sequins arranged?

3. Roll the clay with the sequins back into a ball. Stack the three balls with the sequin ball in the middle. Set these on a block of wood. With another block of wood, press slowly down until the stack is about 3 cm high.

4. Use the string to cut the stack in half. Observe the arrangement of the sequins.

Making a Model What do the sequins in your model rock represent? Is this rock foliated or nonfoliated?

Shale

Slate

Sandstone

Quartzite

Chapter 15 **495**

Media and Technology

 Concept Videotape Library
Adventures, Tape 3, "The Earth Library"

Answers to Self-Assessment

Caption Question

Figure 18 Quartzite looks much smoother than sandstone because heat and pressure have caused the weakly cemented particles in sandstone to recrystallize.

☑ *Checkpoint*

A foliated rock is a metamorphic rock whose grains are arranged in parallel layers or bands.

---

2 *Facilitate*

How Metamorphic Rocks Form

Using the Visuals: Figure 18

Ask students: **How could you tell the difference between granite and gneiss?** *(The grains in granite occur randomly, while the grains in gneiss occur in bands or layers; that is, gneiss is foliated, while granite is not.)* **Are all rocks classified as metamorphic foliated?** *(No. Quartzite is an example of a nonfoliated metamorphic rock.)* **learning modality: visual**

Classifying Metamorphic Rocks

Skills Focus making models

ACTIVITY

Materials *modeling compound, metric ruler, 25 sequins, 30-cm string, 2 blocks of wood*

Time 15 minutes

Tips Cut string ahead of time. Experiment to find how much modeling compound each student will need, and then prepare the appropriate number of mounds of compound.

Expected Outcome When students cut the ball in half, they should observe that the sequins are spread randomly. When they cut the stack in half, they should observe that the sequins are arranged in a layer or band. Students should infer that the sequins model rock grains and that the model rock made after flattening represents a foliated rock.

Extend Ask: **What did you model when you pressed down on the clay?** *(Pressing down modeled the pressure that changes rock into metamorphic rock.)* **learning modality: kinesthetic**

Ongoing Assessment

Drawing Challenge students to make two drawings—one of a foliated metamorphic rock and one of an nonfoliated metamorphic rock.

Uses of Metamorphic Rock

Visual Arts CONNECTION

Architects often use symmetry and repetition. A likely example is the front of the school building; there is often a central door with the same number of windows and other structures on either side.

In Your Journal Suggest that students write a letter of at least one paragraph. They should mention the use of symmetry and repetition as well as the effect that a surface of polished marble has on the observer. **learning modality: verbal**

3 Assess

Section 5 Review Answers

1. Heat and pressure caused by plate collisions, rising magma, or the weight of the crust can cause metamorphic rocks to form.
2. The arrangement of the grains that make up the rocks
3. As a rock becomes metamorphic, its appearance, texture, crystal structure, and mineral content may change.
4. Pressure can change the minerals in a rock into other minerals and cause the grains to line up in layers.
5. The temperature and pressure that cause metamorphic rock to form would likely destroy any fossils that were in the parent sedimentary rock.

Science at Home

Review the characteristics **ACTIVITY** of marble, granite, limestone, and sandstone so students can recognize these rocks. Invite volunteers to present their findings to the class.

Performance Assessment

Skills Check Challenge students to create a flowchart that describes how sandstone forms and becomes quartzite.

Figure 19 The pure white marble for the Taj Mahal came from a quarry 300 kilometers away. It took 20,000 workers more than 20 years to build the Taj Mahal.

Visual Arts CONNECTION

The architect of the Taj Mahal used symmetry and repetition to design a beautiful building. Notice how the left side mirrors the right side, creating balance. Also notice how different parts of the building, such as domes, arches, and minarets (towers), are repeated. Repetition of these shapes creates rhythms as you look at the building.

In Your Journal

Write a letter to a friend describing what you feel walking toward the Taj Mahal. Explain how the building's symmetry and other features help to create this effect.

Uses of Metamorphic Rock

Marble and slate are two of the most useful metamorphic rocks. Marble usually forms when limestone is subjected to heat and pressure deep beneath the surface. Because marble has a fine, even grain, it is relatively easy to cut into thin slabs. And marble can be easily polished. These qualities have led architects and sculptors to use marble for many buildings and statues. For example, one of the most beautiful buildings in the world is the Taj Mahal in Agra, India. An emperor of India had the Taj Mahal built during the 1600s as a memorial to his wife, who had died in childbirth. The Taj Mahal, shown in Figure 19, is made of gleaming white marble.

Slate, because it is foliated, splits easily into flat pieces that can be used for flooring, roofing, outdoor walkways, or chalkboards. Like marble, slate comes in a variety of colors, including gray, black, red, and purple, so it has been used as trim for stone buildings.

Section 5 Review

1. Describe the process by which metamorphic rocks form.
2. What characteristics are used to classify metamorphic rocks?
3. Which properties of a rock may change as the rock becomes metamorphic?
4. How does pressure change rock?
5. **Thinking Critically** **Relating Cause and Effect** Why are you less likely to find fossils in metamorphic rocks than in sedimentary rocks?

Science at Home

How are rocks used in your neighborhood? Take a walk with your family to see how many uses you can observe. Identify statues, walls, and buildings made from rocks. Can you identify which type of rock is used? Look for limestone, sandstone, granite, and marble. Share a list of the rocks you found with your class. For each rock, include a description of its color and texture, where you observed the rock, and how it was used.

Background

Facts and Figures Pure limestone is composed of a single mineral, calcite. When this sedimentary rock is metamorphosed, its small calcite crystals combine, or recrystallize, to form large, interlocking crystals. The result is marble. Marble is white when the limestone is pure calcite. Impurities in the original sedimentary rock can make the marble pink, green, gray, or black.

Program Resources

◆ **Unit 4 Resources** 15-5 Review and Reinforce, p. 139; 15-5 Enrich, p. 140

Media and Technology

Lab Activity Videotape
Tape 3

MYSTERY ROCKS

Problem

What properties can be used to classify rocks?

Materials

1 "mystery rock"   hand lens
2 unknown igneous rocks
2 unknown sedimentary rocks
2 unknown metamorphic rocks

Procedure

1. For this activity, you will be given six rocks and one sample that is not a rock. They are labeled A through G.
2. Copy the data table into your notebook.
3. Using the hand lens, examine each rock for clues that show the rock formed from molten material. Record the rock's color and texture. Observe if there are any crystals or grains in the rock.
4. Use the hand lens to look for clues that show the rock formed from particles of other rocks. Observe the texture of the rock to see if it has any tiny, well-rounded grains.
5. Use the hand lens to look for clues that show the rock formed under heat and pressure. Observe if the rock has a flat layer of crystals or shows colored bands.
6. Record your observations in the data table.

Analyze and Conclude

1. Infer from your observations which group each rock belongs in.
2. Decide which sample is not a rock. How did you determine that the sample you chose is not a rock? What do you think the "mystery rock" is? Explain.
3. Which of the samples could be classified as igneous rocks? What physical properties do these rock share with the other samples? How are they different?
4. Which of the samples could be classified as sedimentary rocks? How do you think these rocks formed? What are the physical properties of these rocks?
5. Which of the samples could be classified as metamorphic rocks? What are their physical properties?
6. **Think About It** What physical property was most useful in classifying rocks? Why?

More to Explore

Can you name each rock? Use a field guide to rocks and minerals to find the specific name of each rock sample.

Sample	Color (dark, medium, light, or mixed colors)	Texture (fine, medium, or coarse-grained)	Foliated or Banded	Rock Group (igneous, metamorphic, sedimentary)
A				
B				

Analyze and Conclude

1. Students should classify two rocks each as igneous, sedimentary, and metamorphic.
2. Students' reasons for identifying the nonrock will depend on what it is.
3. Answers may vary. Students might say all the rocks have grains. These rocks have no evidence of sediment or metamorphic change.
4. Answers may vary. Students might mention evidence of sediments or cementation. Students should describe in general terms how sedimentary rocks form.

5. Answers may vary. Students might mention foliation or evidence of pressure and heat.
6. Answers may vary. Students might suggest that texture was most useful because it reflects how rocks form.

Program Resources

◆ **Unit 4 Resources** Skills Lab blackline masters, pp. 145–147

Skills Lab

Classifying

Mystery Rocks

Preparing for Inquiry

Key Concept Properties of rocks can be used to classify rock samples as igneous, sedimentary, or metamorphic.

Skills Objectives Students will be able to
◆ observe properties of each rock sample;
◆ create a data table to organize their observations;
◆ classify each rock sample as one of the three major groups of rocks.

Time 30 minutes

Advance Planning Select and label the samples ahead of time. Suggested rock samples and labels: A. sandstone, B. gneiss, D. granite, E. conglomerate, F. slate, G. basalt. Also label as C the "mystery rock," an object that is not a rock. This could be a piece of brick, bone, wood, or pottery. Number the samples by painting a small spot of correcting fluid on each and then using a marker to write the number on the spot. Provide each group or student with a complete set of seven samples.

Guiding Inquiry

Introducing the Procedure

◆ **Why is a hand lens helpful in observing the texture of rocks?** (*The individual grains of fine-grained rocks are too small to be seen with the naked eye.*)

Troubleshooting the Experiment

◆ Demonstrate how to examine a rock sample and record observations in a data table using a sample not included in the students' samples, such as a sample of marble.

Extending the Inquiry

More to Explore Provide rock and mineral field guides for students to use to identify their samples. Have students share results and resolve differences.

SECTION 6 The Rock Cycle

Objectives

After completing the lesson, students will be able to

- describe the rock cycle;
- explain the role played by plate tectonics in the rock cycle.

Key Term rock cycle

1 Engage/Explore

Activating Prior Knowledge

Encourage students to brainstorm a list of Earth processes that affect rock in Earth's crust. (*Weathering, erosion, volcanic activity, and plate tectonics*) **Do you think rocks are ever completely destroyed?** (*Yes, when oceanic plates are subducted and become part of the mantle and when rocks are completely weathered and form soil.*) Point out that these forces affect all rocks in the crust, and thus no rock is permanent.

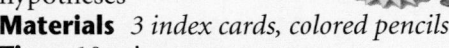 **DISCOVER**

Skills Focus developing hypotheses
Materials *3 index cards, colored pencils*
Time 10 minutes
Tips If possible, provide samples of quartzite, granite, and sandstone to give students real objects to examine and draw.
Expected Outcome Students' sketches should reflect the colors and textures of the rocks pictured in their text. They should identify quartzite as metamorphic, granite as igneous, and sandstone as sedimentary.
Think It Over Answers may vary. A typical answer might suggest that granite formed first from cooling magma. Weathering, erosion, deposition, compaction, and cementation then formed sandstone from granite particles. Pressure and high temperatures then changed the sandstone into quartzite. Some students may also suggest that both quartzite and sandstone could melt in the mantle and form again as granite or that quartzite could weather and its particles could form into sandstone.

498

SECTION 6 The Rock Cycle

DISCOVER

Which Rock Came First?

1. Referring to the photos below, make sketches of quartzite, granite, and sandstone on three index cards.

2. In your sketches, try to portray the color and texture of each rock. Look for similarities and differences.

3. To which major group does each rock belong?

Think It Over
Developing Hypotheses How are quartzite, granite, and sandstone related? Arrange your cards in the order in which these three rocks formed. Given enough time in Earth's crust, what might happen to the third rock in your series?

Quartzite

Granite

Sandstone

GUIDE FOR READING

- What is the rock cycle?
- What is the role of plate tectonics in the rock cycle?

Reading Tip Before you read, preview *Exploring the Rock Cycle* on page 500. Write a list of questions you have about the rock cycle. Then look for answers to the questions as you read.

The enormous granite dome that forms Stone Mountain in Georgia looks as if it will be there forever. The granite formed hundreds of millions of years ago as a batholith—a mass of igneous rock beneath Earth's surface. But this rock has stood exposed to the weather for millions of years. Bit by bit, the granite is flaking off. Washed away in streams, the bits of granite will eventually be ground down into sand. But that's not the end of the story. What will become of those sand particles from Stone Mountain? They are part of a series of changes that happen to all the rocks of Earth's crust.

A Cycle of Many Pathways

Earth's rocks are not as unchanging as they seem. **Forces inside Earth and at the surface produce a rock cycle that builds, destroys, and changes the rocks in the crust.** The **rock cycle** is a series of processes on Earth's surface and inside the planet that slowly change rocks from one kind to another. What drives the rock cycle? Earth's constructive and destructive forces—including plate tectonics—move rocks through the rock cycle.

The rock cycle can follow many different pathways. You can follow the rock of Stone Mountain along one of the pathways of the rock cycle.

498

READING STRATEGIES

Reading Tip Students' questions will vary. Typical questions might include these: "Do rocks always continue through the complete cycle?" "What causes rocks to melt?" and "What causes rocks to follow alternate pathways?" Students may write questions that are not answered in their text. In such cases, invite others in the class to answer the questions with what they have learned in this and previous chapters. If the question is still not answered, encourage students to do research in other books to find the answer.

Vocabulary Point out that this section focuses on a *cycle* in nature. Explain that a cycle is a series of events or processes that regularly recur and usually lead back to a starting point. A good synonym for *cycle* is *wheel*.

One Pathway Through the Rock Cycle

In the case of Stone Mountain, the rock cycle began millions of years ago. First, a granite batholith formed beneath Earth's surface. Then the forces of mountain building slowly pushed the granite upward. Over millions of years, water and weather began to wear away the granite of Stone Mountain. Today, particles of granite still break off the mountain and become sand. Streams carry the sand to the ocean.

Over millions of years, layers of sediment will pile up on the ocean floor. Slowly, the sediments will be compacted by their own weight. Dissolved calcite in the ocean water will cement the particles together. Eventually, the quartz that once formed the granite of Stone Mountain will become sandstone, a sedimentary rock.

More and more sediment will pile up on the sandstone. As sandstone becomes deeply buried, pressure on the rocks will increase. The rock will become hot. Pressure will compact the particles in the sandstone until no spaces are left between them. Silica, the main ingredient in quartz, will replace the calcite as the cement holding the rock together. The rock's texture will change from gritty to smooth. After millions of years, the sandstone will have changed into the metamorphic rock quartzite.

What will happen next? You could wait tens of millions of years to find out how the quartzite completes the rock cycle. Or you can trace alternative pathways in *Exploring the Rock Cycle*.

Figure 20 Stone Mountain, near Atlanta, Georgia, rises 210 meters above the surrounding land.

Classifying

Some metamorphic rocks form out of igneous rocks, and other metamorphic rocks form out of sedimentary rocks.

1. If you find a fine-grained metamorphic rock with thin, flaky layers, from which group of rocks did it probably form? Explain.

2. If you find a metamorphic rock with distinct grains of different colors and sizes arranged in parallel bands, from which group of rocks did it probably form? Explain.

Chapter 15 **499**

Program Resources

◆ **Unit 4 Resources** 15-6 Lesson Plan, p. 141; 15-6 Section Summary, p. 142
◆ **Guided Reading and Study Workbook** Section 5-6

Media and Technology

 Transparencies Transparencies "Exploring the Rock Cycle," Transparency 60

2 Facilitate

A Cycle of Many Pathways

Including All Students

Challenge students to describe other natural cycles. These might include the cycle of seasons, the cycle of night and day, the water cycle, and the carbon-oxygen cycle. Point out that these cycles are continuous, with no beginning or end, just as the rock cycle is. **learning modality: verbal**

One Pathway Through the Rock Cycle

Classifying

Time 10 minutes
Expected Outcome
1. Such a metamorphic rock probably formed from sedimentary rock, because sedimentary rocks form in layers. Some students might suggest that this description fits the metamorphic rock slate, which forms from the sedimentary rock shale. **2.** Answers may vary. Such a metamorphic rock probably formed from igneous rock, because igneous rocks have distinct grains of different colors and sizes. Some students, though, may correctly suggest that such a rock could form from conglomerate, a sedimentary rock.
Extend Ask: **Could igneous rock form from sedimentary rock?** (*Yes. Through the process of subduction at convergent plates, sedimentary rock melts and becomes part of the mantle. That mantle material could then rise as magma and harden into igneous rock.*) **learning modality: logical/mathematical**

Ongoing Assessment

Writing Have students explain in their own words how grains in the granite of Stone Mountain eventually became part of quartzite.

499

EXPLORING
The Rock Cycle

Materials *3 crayons of different colors, pocket pencil sharpener, aluminum foil, large piece of wood, hot plate, pan*

Time 20 minutes; 5 minutes the next day

After students have examined the feature, demonstrate a model of the rock cycle using crayons. Explain to students that the three crayons represent different kinds of rock. Then use the pencil sharpener to shave the crayons, one after another, onto a piece of aluminum foil so that the shavings create three layers. Ask: **What does this process represent?** *(Weathering, erosion, deposition, and the formation of sedimentary rock)* Then fold the aluminum foil over the shavings, place the piece of wood on top, and press moderately. Show students the compressed results. Ask: **What does this represent?** *(The formation of metamorphic rock)* Then place the "rock" and aluminum foil into a pan and heat the pan on the hot plate. Ask: **What does this process represent?** *(The melting of rock at a convergent plate boundary)* Allow the crayon material to harden overnight, and show students the results. Ask: **What does this hardening represent?** *(The formation of igneous rock)* To conclude, call on students to explain how the demonstration represented the rock cycle. **learning modality: visual**

The Rock Cycle and Plate Tectonics

Using the Visuals: Figure 21

Ask students: **Through what processes did the fossil trilobite—once a sea creature—become part of a rock in a mountain?** *(Movement of material in the asthenosphere caused crustal plates to move. Plate collisions resulted in an uplift of the land on a continental plate, raising the ocean floor above sea level to become part of a mountain.)* **learning modality: verbal**

EXPLORING *the Rock Cycle*

Earth's constructive and destructive forces build up and wear down the crust. Igneous, sedimentary, and metamorphic rocks change continuously through the rock cycle. Rocks can follow many different pathways. The outer circle shows a complete cycle. The arrows within the circle show alternate pathways.

500

Background

Facts and Figures The rock cycle is simply a way to express the concept that all rocks are impermanent over geologic time. A diagram of the cycle could actually be more complex than that shown on this page. For instance, some sedimentary rock is neither melted nor metamorphosed. Rather, it is weathered, eroded, and reformed as sedimentary rock. A further complexity might be to show the cycle as two interlocking subcycles, one for continental crust and one for oceanic crust. The subcycle for continental crust would look much like the one here. The subcycle for oceanic crust, though, would be simpler, as magma rises from the mantle, becomes igneous rock, and then is subducted to the mantle at trenches.

The Rock Cycle and Plate Tectonics

The changes of the rock cycle are closely related to plate tectonics. Recall that plate tectonics causes the movement of sections of Earth's lithosphere called plates. **Plate movements drive the rock cycle by pushing rocks back into the mantle, where they melt and become magma again. Plate movements also cause the folding, faulting, and uplift of the crust that move rocks through the rock cycle.** At least two types of plate movement advance the rock cycle. One type is a collision between subducting oceanic plates. The other type is a collision between continental plates.

Subducting Oceanic Plates Consider what could happen to the sand grains that once were part of Stone Mountain. The sand may become sandstone attached to oceanic crust. On this pathway through the rock cycle, the oceanic crust carrying the sandstone drifts toward a deep-ocean trench. At the trench, subduction returns some of the sandstone to the mantle. There, it melts and forms magma, which eventually becomes igneous rock.

Colliding Continental Plates Collisions between continental plates can also change a rock's path through the rock cycle. Such a collision can squeeze some sandstone from the ocean floor. As a result, the sandstone will change to quartzite. Eventually, the collision could form a mountain range or plateau. Then, as the mountains or plateaus containing quartzite are worn away, the rock cycle continues.

Figure 21 This fossil trilobite lived on an ocean floor about 500 million years ago. As plate tectonics moved pieces of Earth's crust, the rock containing this fossil became part of a mountain.

Section 6 Review

1. What process gradually changes rocks from one form to another?
2. How can plate movements move rocks through the rock cycle?
3. What rock comes before quartzite in the rock cycle? What rock or rocks could come just after quartzite in the rock cycle? Explain your answer.
4. **Thinking Critically** Applying Concepts Begin with a grain of sand on a beach. Describe what happens as you follow the grain through the rock cycle until it returns to a beach as a grain of sand again.
5. **Thinking Critically** Making Judgments In your opinion, at what point does the rock cycle really begin? Give reasons for your answer.

Check Your Progress

CHAPTER PROJECT 15

Now that you have collected, described, tested, and recorded your rocks, classify them as igneous, sedimentary, or metamorphic. Are any of your rocks foliated? Try to identify specific types of rock. Compare your rock samples with pictures of rocks in a field guide or other library reference sources.

Chapter 15 **501**

Program Resources

◆ **Unit 4 Resources** 15-6 Review and Reinforce, p. 143; 15-6 Enrich, p. 144

3 Assess

Section 6 Review Answers

1. The rock cycle
2. Subducting oceanic plates can return rock to the mantle. There, it melts and forms magma, which eventually becomes igneous rock. Collisions between continental plates can also change rocks. A collision can cause sandstone to become quartzite. It can also form mountains or plateaus. Then, as the mountains or plateaus are worn away, the rock cycle continues.
3. Sandstone comes before quartzite, since quartzite is formed from sandstone. Quartzite could change into either a sedimentary rock or an igneous rock, depending on which pathway it took in the rock cycle.
4. Answers may vary. A typical answer will describe the formation of the sedimentary sandstone, a change into the metamorphic quartzite, a change into an igneous rock through plate movement, weathering of the igneous rock to form sand, and erosion of the sand to a beach.
5. Answers may vary. Some students may argue that the cycle must begin with the formation of igneous rocks as minerals in magma crystallize. Others can logically argue that the rock cycle has no beginning or end.

Check Your Progress

CHAPTER PROJECT 15

Help students or groups organize their rocks into a display. Make sure that each has the necessary materials, and provide suggestions for those who seem to be having trouble. Some students may still be having difficulty in using the field guides. Help them understand how such guides are organized.

Performance Assessment

Oral Presentation Call on students at random and name one of the three major groups of rocks. Then challenge the student to describe a path in the rock cycle that rock might follow to eventually become the same type of rock again.

501

Testing Rock Flooring

Preparing for Inquiry

Key Concept Different kinds of rocks have different properties that determine how useful each is in specific situations.

Skills Objectives Students will be able to:
- design an experiment to determine which building stones are easiest to maintain and keep clean;
- form operational definitions using observations gained from testing various building stones;
- draw conclusions about which building stones would make the best flooring.

Time 40 minutes

Advance Planning Gather enough rock samples to provide each group with at least one igneous, sedimentary, and metamorphic rock. Granite, slate, sandstone, and marble are good choices, though sedimentary rocks such as sandstone are rarely used commercially as flooring. If your samples are limited, you could assign different rock samples to each group. In addition, provide a variety of stains and greasy materials.

Alternative Materials If rock samples are in short supply, provide commercial products such as brick, ceramic, or vinyl flooring. Make sure, though, that all groups test at least two rock samples.

Guiding Inquiry

Invitation Show students a commercial square tile. Then ask: **If this material were on your kitchen floor, how well do you think it would hold up under normal use?** *(Answers may vary depending on the material. In answering, students should begin to think about what sort of abuse a floor tile takes.)*

Helping Design a Plan
- Divide students into pairs or small groups, and encourage them to brainstorm qualities of good flooring.
- Encourage students to write down a procedure that details how they will perform each type of test on their rock samples.

Real-World Lab

You, the Consumer

TESTING ROCK FLOORING

You are building your own house. For the kitchen floor, you want to use some building stones such as granite, marble, or limestone. You need to know which material is easiest to maintain and keep clean.

Problem

What kind of building stone makes the best flooring?

Skills Focus

designing experiments, forming operational definitions drawing conclusions

Suggested Materials

steel nail   wire brush   water
plastic dropper   hand lens
samples of igneous, sedimentary, and metamorphic rocks with flat surfaces
materials that form stains, such as ink and paints
greasy materials such as butter and crayons

Procedure

1. Brainstorm with your partner the qualities of good flooring. For example, good flooring should resist stains, scratches, and grease marks, and be safe to walk on when wet.
2. Predict what you think is the best building stone for a kitchen floor. Why?
3. Write the steps you plan to follow to answer the problem question. As you design your plan, consider the following factors:
   - What igneous, sedimentary, and metamorphic rocks will you test? (Pick at least one rock from each group.)
   - What materials or equipment will you need to acquire, and in what amounts?
   - What tests will you perform on the samples?
   - How will you control the variables in each test?
   - How will you measure each sample's resistance to staining, grease, and scratches?
   - How will you measure slipperiness?
4. Review your plan. Will it lead to an answer to the problem question?
5. Check your procedure and safety plan with your teacher.
6. Create a data table that includes a column in which you predict how each material will perform in each test.

Analyze and Conclude

1. Which material performed the best on each test? Which performed the worst on each test?
2. Which material is best for the kitchen flooring? Which material would you least want to use?
3. Do your answers support your initial prediction? Why or why not?
4. The person installing the floor might want stone that is easy to cut to the correct size or shape. What other qualities would matter to the flooring installer?
5. **Apply** Based on your results for flooring, what materials would you use for kitchen counters? How might the qualities needed for countertops differ from those for flooring?

More to Explore

Find out the cost per square meter of some materials used to build kitchen floors in your community. How does cost influence your decision on which material to use? What other factors can influence the choice of materials?

Evaluating Student Plans
- Make sure each group has developed a procedure for performing tests for staining, grease, scratch, and slipperiness.

Troubleshooting the Experiment
- Observe each pair or group as they test one of their rock samples.
- Make sure that the results of each test are recorded in the data table.

Safety

Caution students to be careful when performing the scratch test and to wear their lab aprons when testing with grease or stains. Review the safety guidelines in Appendix A.

SECTION 1 — Classifying Rocks

Key Ideas
- A rock is a hard piece of Earth's crust.
- Geologists classify rocks according to their color, texture, mineral composition, and origin.
- The three kinds of rocks are igneous, sedimentary, and metamorphic.

Key Terms
texture   igneous rock   metamorphic rock
grain   sedimentary rock

SECTION 2 — Igneous Rocks

Key Ideas
- Igneous rocks form from magma or lava.
- Igneous rocks are classified according to their origin, texture, and composition.

Key Terms
extrusive rock   intrusive rock   porphyritic texture

SECTION 3 — Sedimentary Rocks

Key Ideas
- Most sedimentary rocks form from sediments that are compacted and cemented together.
- The three types of sedimentary rocks are clastic rocks, organic rocks, and chemical rocks.

Key Terms
sediment   compaction   organic rock
erosion   cementation   chemical rock
deposition   clastic rock

SECTION 4 — Rocks From Reefs

INTEGRATING LIFE SCIENCE

Key Idea
- When corals die, their skeletons remain. More corals grow on top of them, slowly forming a reef.

Key Terms
coral reef   atoll

SECTION 5 — Metamorphic Rocks

Key Ideas
- In a process that takes place deep beneath the surface, heat and pressure can change any type of rock into metamorphic rock.
- Geologists classify metamorphic rock according to whether the rock is foliated or nonfoliated.

Key Term
foliated

SECTION 6 — The Rock Cycle

Key Idea
- The series of processes on and beneath Earth's surface that change rocks from one type of rock to another is called the rock cycle.

Key Term
rock cycle

Organizing Information

Cycle Diagram Construct a cycle diagram that shows one pathway through the rock cycle. Include the following steps in your diagram in the correct order: sediments build up; igneous rock wears away; sedimentary rock forms; igneous rock forms from magma and lava; lava erupts. (For tips on making cycle diagrams, see the Skills Handbook.)

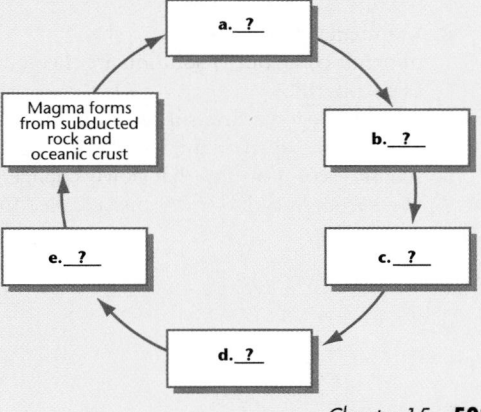

Chapter 15 **503**

Program Resources
- **Unit 4 Resources** Real-World Lab blackline masters, pp. 148–149
- **Unit 4 Resources** Chapter 15 Project Scoring Rubric, p. 120
- **Performance Assessment** Chapter 15, pp. 46–48
- **Chapter Tests** Chapter 15 Test, pp. 59–62

Media and Technology
- **Lab Activity Videotape** *Tape 3*
- **Computer Test Bank** Chapter 15 Test

Expected Outcome
The harder, smoother rocks will prove more resistant to scratches, stains, and grease but will be slipperier when wet.

Analyze and Conclude
1. Answers will vary depending on the samples tested. In a stain test, granite, slate, and marble are hard to stain, while limestone and sandstone are easy to stain. In a scratch test, all rock samples will scratch, though granite and marble may be the hardest to scratch. Limestone and sandstone should scratch easily. In a slipperiness test, the smoothest rocks, such as marble, are more slippery than more porous rocks, such as sandstone. In a grease test, porous rocks are much harder to clean than smoother rocks.
2. Answers may vary. Most students will mention marble, granite, or slate as best for kitchen flooring and sandstone or limestone as least desirable. But because of the slipperiness factor, some students may decide that sandstone, for example, may be a good choice.
3. Answers will vary depending on students' predictions. Students should cite results from their tests to explain why or why not their answers supported their predictions.
4. Answers may vary. Students might suggest that brittleness and weight would be qualities that would matter to a floor installer. Cost and availability would also be important considerations.
5. Answers may vary. Of the qualities tested, resistance to staining and grease would be more important than slipperiness or resistance to scratches.

Extending the Inquiry

More to Explore Suggest that students call retail stores that sell building materials, ask what rock flooring is available, and record the cost. Students will likely have to convert cost per square foot to cost per square meter. Most students will answer that cost would influence their decision about which material to use. They may also suggest that such considerations as color and luster might also influence their decision.

Organizing Information

Cycle Diagram Sample title: *The Rock Cycle* **a.** Lava erupts **b.** Igneous rock forms. **c.** Igneous rock wears away. **d.** Sediments build up. **e.** Sedimentary rock forms.

Reviewing Content
Multiple Choice
1. c **2.** d **3.** c **4.** b **5.** c

True or False
6. mineral composition **7.** coarse-grained
8. chemical rocks **9.** atoll **10.** true

Checking Concepts

11. An igneous rock with a glassy or fine-grained texture cooled rapidly near the surface. An igneous rock with coarse-grained texture cooled slowly deep underground. An igneous rock with a porphyritic texture cooled in two stages, first far below the surface and then nearer to the surface.

12. Water can pass through sandstone because the cementation process does not fill all the spaces between sand grains, leaving small connected holes. In shale, the spaces between the clay particles are too small for water to pass through.

13. A rock can form by evaporation when a sea or lake evaporates, leaving mineral deposits. Rock salt and gypsum are examples of rocks formed by evaporation.

14. When rock changes into metamorphic rock, its appearance, texture, crystal structure, and mineral content change.

15. Forces inside Earth push rock down toward the heat of the mantle. Pockets of magma rising through the crust also provide heat that can produce metamorphic rock.

16. The remains of a dead fish could have been covered by sediment before the fish decayed. The sediments could then have hardened into sedimentary rock. Forces inside Earth then could have lifted the land, resulting in mountain building.

Thinking Critically

17. The tremendous pressure and heat that creates metamorphic rock packs the grains closer together than in sedimentary rock. Therefore, the metamorphic marble and quartzite resist being worn away better than the sedimentary limestone and sandstone.

18. The environment was probably swampy, since coal forms from swamp plants buried in water. The shale is further evidence of a wet environment,

---

Reviewing Content
Multiple Choice
Choose the letter of the best answer.

1. Which of the following sedimentary rocks is a chemical rock?
  a. shale
  b. sandstone
  c. rock salt
  d. breccia

2. Metamorphic rocks can be formed from
  a. igneous rocks.
  b. sedimentary rocks.
  c. metamorphic rocks.
  d. all rock groups.

3. The rock formed when granite changes to a metamorphic rock is
  a. marble. **b.** basalt.
  c. gneiss. **d.** pumice.

4. Which of the following helps create both metamorphic and sedimentary rocks?
  a. cementation **b.** pressure
  c. evaporation **d.** heat

5. Millions of years ago, a deposit of organic limestone was probably
  a. a swampy forest. **b.** a lava flow.
  c. a coral reef. **d.** an intrusive rock.

True or False
If the statement is true, write true. If it is false, change the underlined word or words to make the statement true.

6. Igneous rocks are classified by their origin, texture, and <u>shape</u>.

7. Granite is a <u>fine-grained</u> igneous rock.

8. Sedimentary rocks that form when minerals come out of solution are classified as <u>porphyritic</u>.

9. A <u>barrier reef</u> is a ring-shaped coral island found in the open ocean.

10. The series of processes that slowly change rocks from one kind to another is called the <u>rock cycle</u>.

Checking Concepts

11. What is the relationship between an igneous rock's texture and where it was formed?

12. Why can water pass easily through sandstone but not through shale?

13. Describe how a rock can form by evaporation. What type of rock is it?

14. How do the properties of a rock change when the rock changes to metamorphic?

15. What are the sources of the heat that helps metamorphic rocks to form?

16. **Writing to Learn** You are a camp counselor taking your campers on a mountain hike. One of your campers cracks open a rock and finds a fossil fish inside. The camper wants to know how a fish fossil from the sea floor ended up on the side of a mountain. What explanation would you give the camper?

Thinking Critically

17. **Applying Concepts** The sedimentary rocks limestone and sandstone are used as building materials. However, they wear away more rapidly than marble and quartzite, the metamorphic rocks that are formed from them. Why do you think this is so?

18. **Inferring** As a geologist exploring for rock and mineral deposits, you come across an area where the rocks are layers of coal and shale. What kind of environment probably existed in this area millions of years ago when these rocks formed?

19. **Comparing and Contrasting** How are clastic rocks and organic rocks similar? How are they different?

20. **Relating Cause and Effect** In the rock cycle, igneous, metamorphic, and sedimentary rocks can all become magma again. What step in the rock cycle causes this to happen? Explain your answer.

---

since it forms from clay particles deposited by water.

19. Clastic rocks and organic rocks are similar in that they are both sedimentary rocks composed of sediments deposited in layers. They are different in that clastic rocks are formed when rock fragments are squeezed together, while organic rocks are formed when the remains of plants and animals are deposited in layers.

20. Melting is the step in the rock cycle by which rocks become magma again. Melting

occurs when forces inside Earth push rocks deep beneath the surface. The rocks melt and form magma. When magma cools, it produces new igneous rock.

Applying Skills

21. Students should describe rock A as being a foliated rock with a coarse-grained texture, rock B as having a coarse-grained texture, and rock C as having coarse-grained crystals mixed with fine-grained crystals.

Applying Skills

Answer Questions 21–23 using the photos of three rocks.

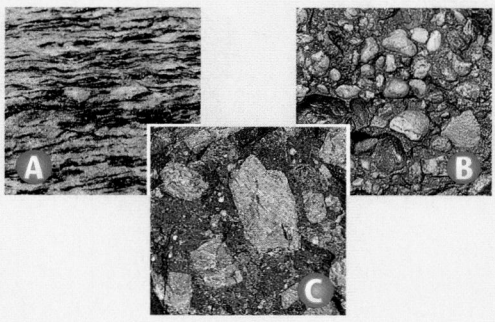

21. **Observing** How would you describe the texture of each rock?
22. **Classifying** Which of the three rocks would you classify as a metamorphic rock? Explain your answer.

23. **Inferring** A rock's texture gives clues about how the rock formed. What can you infer about the process by which rock B formed?

Performance CHAPTER PROJECT 15 Assessment

Project Wrap Up Construct a simple display for your rocks. Your display should clearly give your classification for each of your rock samples. In your presentation, describe where you went hunting for rocks and what kinds of rocks you found. Describe which of your discoveries surprised you the most.

Reflect and Record In your journal, write about how you developed your rock collection. Were there any rocks that were hard to classify? Did you find rocks from each of the three major groups? Can you think of any reason why certain types of rocks would not be found in your area?

Test Preparation

Use these questions to prepare for standardized tests.

Use the diagram to answer Questions 24–28.

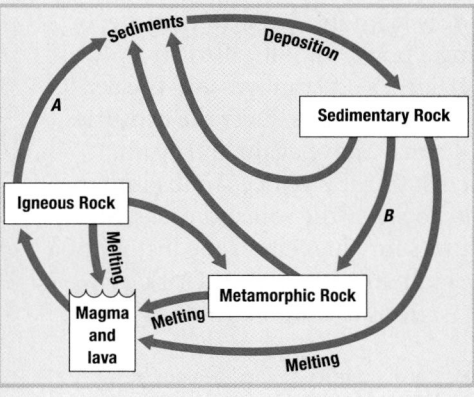

24. A good title for this diagram is
   a. Different Kinds of Rock
   b. Deposition of Sediment
   c. How Metamorphic Rock Forms
   d. Pathways of the Rock Cycle

25. The process shown by letter A is called
   a. extrusion.   **b.** crystallization.
   c. erosion.   **d.** intrusion.
26. The process shown by letter B involves
   a. cementation only.
   b. heat and pressure.
   c. erosion and deposition.
   d. compaction only.
27. According to the diagram, metamorphic rock forms from
   a. igneous rock and sedimentary rock.
   b. sedimentary rock only.
   c. magma and lava.
   d. melting rock.
28. According to the diagram, magma and lava may form through the melting of
   a. any type of rock.
   b. metamorphic rock only.
   c. sediments.
   d. igneous rock only.

Performance CHAPTER PROJECT 15 Assessment

Project Wrap Up As each student or group presents the rock collection, assess how well the rocks are displayed and how effectively the rocks were classified and identified. For example, students should give reasons for classifying a rock as igneous or identifying a rock as sandstone. These reasons might be related to observation or to tests performed on the rock.

Reflect and Record In writing about how the rock collection was developed, the student should describe where and how the rocks were collected, what observations and tests led to classification and identification of the rocks, and how the display was constructed. Some students may not have collected metamorphic rocks. If so, they might conclude that the reason is that they live far away from plate boundaries or that such rocks are probably buried deep underground.

Test Preparation
24. d 25. c 26. b 27. a 28. a

---

22. Rock A is a metamorphic rock because it is the only one of the three that is foliated.
23. From the texture of rock B, students can infer that it is a sedimentary rock formed from rounded pieces of other rocks that were cemented together.

Program Resources

♦ **Inquiry Skills Activity Book** Provides teaching and review of all inquiry skills
♦ **Prentice Hall Assessment System** Provides standardized test practice
♦ **Reading in the Content Area** Provides strategies to improve science reading skills
♦ **Teacher's ELL Handbook** Provides multiple strategies for English language learners

Focus on Faults

Focus on Seismology

This four-page feature highlights the process of scientific inquiry by involving students in a high-interest, magazine-like account of an actual working scientist, geologist Carol Prentice. Using Dr. Prentice's investigation of ancient earthquakes and faults as an example, the article focuses on the dual skills of observing and making inferences as key elements of scientific inquiry.

Scientific Inquiry

◆ Before students read the feature, let them examine the pictures and read the captions on their own. Then ask: **What do the pictures on pages 507–509 focus on?** *(Cracks in Earth's surface)* **Why are cracks like these important?** *(They show where earthquakes occurred in the past.)*

◆ Ask: **How do you think geologists know what Earth looks like deep underground, as in the figure on page 509?** *(Based on the photograph on page 508, some students may think that geologists have dug trenches far below Earth's surface and have directly observed deep faults. Other students may suggest that geologists make "an educated guess" about what soil and rock look like deep underground. Accept all responses without comment at this time.)*

FOCUS ON FAULTS

"When I was about fourteen, my family was living in Taiwan," Geologist Carol Prentice recalls. "One day I was playing pinball, and a little earthquake happened. It tilted my pinball machine."

Unlike most people experiencing their first quake, her reaction was not fright but fascination. *"What in the world is that?* I wondered. That was the first time I consciously remember thinking that earthquakes were something interesting." Later, she recalls, "When I was teaching earth science in high school, I realized that my favorite section to teach was on earthquakes and faults."

During an earthquake, forces from inside Earth fracture, or break, Earth's crust, producing a powerful jolt called an earthquake. As Earth's crust moves and breaks, it forms cracks called faults. Over the centuries, the faults may move again and again. Geologist Carol Prentice climbs into these faults to study the soil and rocks. She hunts for clues about the history of a fault and estimates the risk of a serious earthquake in the future.

Carol Prentice studied geology at Humboldt State University and the California Institute of Technology. She is currently a Research Geologist for the United States Geological Survey in Menlo Park, California.

506

Background

Geology is traditionally divided into two broad areas: physical geology and historical geology. Physical geology examines the materials that compose Earth and the processes that operate on and below its surface. Seismology, one of the many disciplines within physical geology, involves the study of the forces within Earth that create earthquakes and faults. Historical geology focuses on Earth's origins and the development of the planet through its 4.6-billion-year history. Paleoseismology, Dr. Prentice's specialty, combines these two broad areas.

Since the forces operating deep within Earth's crust cannot be observed directly, seismologists must rely on data gathered by seismographs and fault-monitoring devices. The seismologists then interpret the data to make inferences about Earth's interior.

Finding Clues to Ancient Earthquakes

Today, Dr. Prentice is an expert in the field of paleoseismology. *Paleo* means "ancient" and *seismology* is "the study of earthquakes." So it's the study of ancient earthquakes. "Paleoseismologists search for evidence of earthquakes that happened hundreds or thousands of years ago," explains Dr. Prentice.

There are written records about earthquakes that happened years ago. But the real story of a quake is written in the rocks and soil. Years after an earthquake, wind, rain, and flowing water can wear the fault lines away from Earth's surface. Then the evidence of the quake is buried under layers of sediment. But the fault is still there.

The cracks of recent earthquakes, such as the Gobi-Altay fault shown here, are sometimes visible for hundreds of kilometers. Because this quake happened in the Mongolian desert, it is especially easy to see.

Choosing a Site

How do you pick a site to research? "First we study aerial photographs, geological maps, and satellite images of the fault line," Dr. Prentice explains. "We will have some sites in mind. Then, we go out and look at the sites and do some digging with a shovel to get samples."

"We look for places where sediments, such as sand and gravel, have been building up. If sediments have been depositing there for many thousands of years, you're likely to have a good record of prehistoric earthquakes at that site. When you dig, you're likely to see not only the most recent earthquake buried and preserved in the sediments, but also earlier earthquakes. That's a really good site." Once the site is established, the geological team begins digging a trench across the fault.

Earthquakes in Mongolia

RUSSIA

1905
1905
MONGOLIA
1957

CHINA

NORTH KOREA

SOUTH KOREA

SEA OF JAPAN

JAPAN

EAST CHINA SEA

PACIFIC OCEAN

0   250   500 mi
0   250   500 km

KEY
Major earthquakes since 1900

507

◆ To give students an idea of how deep and narrow the trenches are, take them to a high wall inside the school building (such as in a gymnasium) or an outside wall of the building, and let each small group use a carpenter's metal tape measure to measure 4–5 meters (13–16½ feet) high on the wall. Encourage them to imagine themselves standing between two walls of that height and only about 1.25 meters apart (roughly the width of the trench shown in the photograph on this page). Emphasize that the trench walls are not stable, like the school's walls, but are made of gravel, sand, and other sediments packed tightly together. Ask: **How do you think you'd feel if you were working down in the trench? Why?** (*Let students share their thoughts about these dangerous working conditions.*)

◆ After students have read Looking at the Gobi-Altay Quake, have them turn back to the previous page and find the quake site on the map. Ask: **If the Gobi-Altay fault is in such a remote and unpopulated place, why are geologists so interested in it?** (*Its faults are similar to faults in other earthquake areas. By studying the Gobi-Altay earthquakes, geologists can learn about earthquakes that occur in heavily populated areas.*) Have students examine the map on page 390 showing the location of the San Andreas Fault and the photograph on page 388 showing an aerial view of the fault's surface.

◆ Before students read Interpreting the Data, ask: **What does *interpret* mean?** (*Translate, make sense of, figure out the meaning of*) After students have read the section, ask: **What specific kinds of data does Dr. Prentice collect?** (*Measurements that tell her when layers of rock and sediments formed and when they split and how fast the opposite sides of the fault are moving past each other*) **When she interprets the data, what does she find out?** (*Measurements about the formation and splitting of the layers tell her when and how frequently earthquakes occurred at that place in the past; measurements of the slip rate tell*

Working in the Trenches

What's it like to work in a spot where Earth's surface ruptured? Does Carol Prentice ever think that an earthquake might occur when she is digging in the fault? "It's always in the back of your mind when you are working in the trench," she admits.

But, she says, "The trenches are dangerous, not so much because there might be an earthquake while you are working there but because the trench can cave in. If a trench is 4 to 5 meters deep, or just over your head, it needs shores—braces and supports— or it might cave in. When sediments are soft, and the trench is deep, it's more likely to cave in. That could happen in a place like Mongolia."

Carol (in back) and another geologist in a deep trench.

String grid lines are used to map out sections of the trench.

Shores support the trench walls.

In Mongolia, in northeast Asia, it's difficult for geologists to find the right materials to support a deep trench. It could cave in while someone is in it. "That would be very frightening," she says.

Looking at the Gobi-Altay Quake

Carol Prentice travels to earthquake sites around the world—Dominican Republic, Thailand, Mongolia—as well as to the San Andreas fault in California. One of Dr. Prentice's most recent research expeditions was to the site of the monster Gobi-Altay earthquake of 1957 in the Mongolian desert. In earthquakes like this one, the faults are easy to see. "We're taking a look at this Gobi Altay earthquake and seeing whether the next-to-last earthquake had the same pattern," Dr. Prentice says.

The faults of the Gobi-Altay earthquake are similar in some ways to the San Andreas fault and to the faults of other earthquakes in the United States. That's one of the reasons the Gobi-Altay is so interesting to geologists.

Interpreting the Data

When Dr. Prentice finds evidence of several earthquakes in one spot, she takes measurements that tell her when the layers of rocks, sand, and gravel were deposited and when they split. From that she knows when and how frequently earthquakes have occurred there.

She also determines how fast the opposite sides of the fault are slipping past each other. "Those two pieces of information— the dates of prehistoric earthquakes and the slip rate—are very, very important in trying to

508

Background

The vast Gobi Desert is one of the most sparsely populated areas on Earth. Despite its remote location, desolation, and fierce wind and sand storms, the Gobi is of intense interest to scientists. Artifacts of Bronze Age and earlier peoples have been found there, as well as fossilized dinosaur eggs from the Mesozoic Era, 245–65 million years ago.

Paleontologists working in the Gobi in 1993 discovered the fossil of a 2.7-meter-long oviraptor (an ostrich-like dinosaur) squatting over an egg-filled nest—the strongest evidence to date that birds inherited brooding behavior from dinosaurs. In 1997 scientists reported finding bits of fur in 60-million-year-old fossilized dung deposits discovered in the Gobi—evidence that mammals developed hair millions of years earlier than scientists had thought.

An earthquake is caused by movement on a fault deep beneath Earth's surface. If this movement is large enough, it can cause cracks in the ground surface. Over the years, layers of sediment are deposited on top of the crack. The next earthquake causes a new crack in the surface, and new sediments are deposited. By studying evidence of the cracks in these layers of sediment, geologists learn about past earthquakes along the fault.

figure out how dangerous a particular fault is," Dr. Prentice explains.

Since faults don't move every year, but over thousands of years, you can figure out the average slip per year and make some predictions. The faster the fault is moving, the greater the danger. "We can look at the landforms around a fault.

> ❝ . . . the real story of a quake is written in the rocks and soil. ❞

We can look at what our instruments record, and say: This is an active fault. Someday it might produce a big earthquake, but what we really want to know is when. Is that earthquake likely to happen in the next fifty years, in the next hundred years, or is it going to be a thousand years before the next big earthquake?"

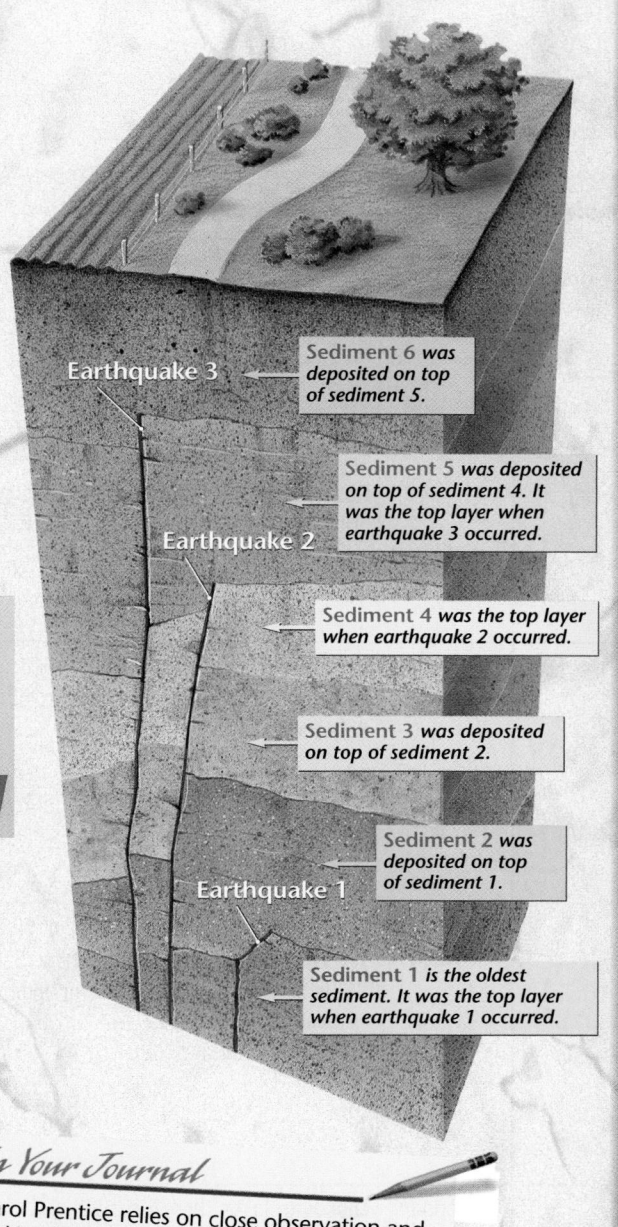

Earthquake 3

Sediment 6 *was deposited on top of sediment 5.*

Sediment 5 *was deposited on top of sediment 4. It was the top layer when earthquake 3 occurred.*

Earthquake 2

Sediment 4 *was the top layer when earthquake 2 occurred.*

Sediment 3 *was deposited on top of sediment 2.*

Sediment 2 *was deposited on top of sediment 1.*

Earthquake 1

Sediment 1 *is the oldest sediment. It was the top layer when earthquake 1 occurred.*

In Your Journal

Carol Prentice relies on close observation and making inferences in her study of earthquakes. Write a paragraph describing some of the other skills that Dr. Prentice needs to do her work as a paleoseismologist.

509

her how active—and thus how dangerous—the fault is.) **How do geologists use this information?** *(They try to determine the risk of future earthquakes along known faults.)*

◆ Direct students' attention to the diagram on this page, and ask: **How did geologists arrive at the idea behind this diagram?** *(Some things they observed when they examined trench walls or faults that have been exposed; other things they inferred from measurements and other data.)*

In Your Journal Students' paragraphs will vary. Most will probably describe the skills of measuring, recording data in an organized manner, calculating, and predicting. Students may also mention comparing and contrasting (of the slip rates along different faults, for example) and making inferences ("educated guesses") based on observable evidence.

The Atmosphere

Sections	Time	Student Edition Activities		Other Activities
CHAPTER PROJECT 16 **Watching the Weather** p. 511	Ongoing (2 weeks)	Check Your Progress, pp. 515, 534 Project Wrap Up, p. 537	TE	Chapter 16 Project Notes, pp. 510–511
1 **The Air Around You** pp. 512–517 ◆ 16.1.1 State how the atmosphere is important to living things. ◆ 16.1.2 Identify the gases that are present in Earth's atmosphere.	2 periods/ 1 block	**Discover** How Long Will the Candle Burn?, p. 512 **Try This** Breathe In, Breathe Out, p. 514 **Real-World Lab: You and Your Environment** How Clean Is the Air?, pp. 516–517	TE	Building Inquiry Skills: Inferring, p. 514
2 *INTEGRATING ENVIRONMENTAL SCIENCE* **Air Quality** pp. 518–522 ◆ 16.2.1 Name the main sources of air pollution. ◆ 16.2.2 Explain how photochemical smog and acid rain form.	1 period/ ½ block	**Discover** What's On the Jar?, p. 518 **Sharpen Your Skills** Predicting, p. 520 **Science at Home,** p. 521	TE TE TE LM	Demonstration, p. 519 Integrating Chemistry, p. 520 Inquiry Challenge, p. 520 16, "Examining Acid Rain"
3 **Air Pressure** pp. 523–528 ◆ 16.3.1 Identify some of the properties of air. ◆ 16.3.2 Name instruments that are used to measure air pressure. ◆ 16.3.3 Explain how increasing altitude affects air pressure and density.	2 periods/ 1 block	**Discover** Does Air Have Mass?, p. 523 **Try This** Soda-Bottle Barometer, p. 525 **Skills Lab: Measuring** Working Under Pressure, pp. 526–527 **Science at Home,** p. 528	TE TE TE	Including All Students, p. 524 Including All Students, p. 525 Real-Life Learning, p. 524
4 **Layers of the Atmosphere** pp. 529–534 ◆ 16.4.1 Describe the characteristics of the main layers of the atmosphere.	1 period/ ½ block	**Discover** Is Air There?, p. 529	TE TE	Exploring Layers of the Atmosphere, p. 531 Building Inquiry Skills: Modeling, p. 533
Study Guide/Assessment pp. 535–537	1 period/ ½ block		ISAB	Provides teaching and review of all inquiry skills

For Standard or Block Schedule The Resource Pro® CD-ROM gives you maximum flexibility for planning your instruction for any type of schedule. Resource Pro® contains Planning Express®, an advanced scheduling program, as well as the entire contents of the Teaching Resources and the Computer Test Bank.

Key: **CTB** Computer Test Bank
     CT Chapter Tests
     ELL Teacher's ELL Handbook

CHAPTER PLANNING GUIDE

Program Resources	Assessment Strategies	Media and Technology
UR Chapter 16 Project Teacher Notes, pp. 2–3 **UR** Chapter 16 Project Overview and Worksheets, pp. 4–7	**TE** Performance Assessment: Chapter 16 Project Wrap Up, p. 532 **TE** Check Your Progress, pp. 515, 534 **UR** Chapter 16 Project Scoring Rubric, p. 8	Science Explorer Internet Site Audio CDs, Section Summaries
UR 16-1 Lesson Plan, p. 9 **UR** 16-1 Section Summary, p. 10 **UR** 16-1 Review and Reinforce, p. 11 **UR** 16-1 Enrich, p. 12 **UR** Real-World Lab blackline masters, pp. 25–27	**SE** Section 1 Review, p. 515 **SE** Analyze and Conclude, p. 517 **TE** Ongoing Assessment, p. 513 **TE** Performance Assessment, p. 515	Concept Videotape Library, *Adventures, Tape 4,* "Air Today, Gone Tomorrow"; "A Trip Through the Earth" Presentation Pro, "The Atmosphere" Transparency 61, "Gases in Dry Air" Lab Activity Videotape, *Tape 4*
UR 16-2 Lesson Plan, p. 13 **UR** 16-2 Section Summary, p. 14 **UR** 16-2 Review and Reinforce, p. 15 **UR** 16-2 Enrich, p. 16	**SE** Section 2 Review, p. 521 **TE** Ongoing Assessment, p. 519 **TE** Performance Assessment, p. 521	Exploring Earth Science Videodisc, Unit 6 Side 2, "Caution: Breathing May Be Hazardous to Your Health"; "Space Shuttle Air Systems" Transparency 62, "Effects of Air Pollutants on Humans"
UR 16-3 Lesson Plan, p. 17 **UR** 16-3 Section Summary, p. 18 **UR** 16-3 Review and Reinforce, p. 19 **UR** 16-3 Enrich, p. 20 **UR** Skills Lab blackline masters, pp. 28–29	**SE** Analyze and Conclude, p. 527 **SE** Section 3 Review, p. 528 **TE** Ongoing Assessment, p. 525 **TE** Performance Assessment, p. 529	Exploring Earth Science Videodisc, Unit 6 Side 2, "Racing Hot Air Balloons" Presentation Pro, "Air Pressure" Transparency 63, "Density of Air at Two Altitudes" Lab Activity Videotape, *Tape 4*
UR 16-4 Lesson Plan, p. 21 **UR** 16-4 Section Summary, p. 22 **UR** 16-4 Review and Reinforce, p. 23 **UR** 16-4 Enrich, p. 24	**SE** Section 4 Review, p. 534 **TE** Ongoing Assessment, pp. 531, 533 **TE** Performance Assessment, p. 534	Exploring Earth Science Videodisc, Unit 6 Side 2, "A Trip Through the Earth" Transparency 64, "Layers of the Atmosphere"
GRSW Provides worksheets to promote student comprehension of content **RCA** Provides strategies to improve science reading skills **ELL** Provides multiple strategies for English language learners	**SE** Study Guide/Assessment, pp. 535–537 **PA** Performance Assessment, pp. 49–51 **CT** Chapter 16 Test, pp. 63–66 **CTB** Chapter 16 Test **PHAS** Provides standardized test preparation	Computer Test Bank, Chapter 16 Test

GRSW Guided Reading and Study Workbook
ISAB Inquiry Skills Activity Book
LM Laboratory Manual

PA Performance Assessment
PHAS Prentice Hall Assessment System
PLM Probeware Lab Manual

RCA Reading in the Content Area
SE Student Edition

TE Teacher's Edition
UR Unit Resources

Meeting the National Science Education Standards and AAAS Benchmarks

National Science Education Standards	Benchmarks for Science Literacy	Unifying Themes
Science As Inquiry (Content Standard A) ◆ **Design and conduct a scientific investigation** Students investigate particles in air. *(Real-World Lab)* ◆ **Use the appropriate tools and techniques to gather, analyze, and interpret data** Students use a barometer to measure air pressure. *(Skills Lab)* ◆ **Develop descriptions, explanations, predictions, and models using evidence** Students gather and interpret weather data and predict weather conditions. *(Chapter Project)* **Physical Science** (Content Standard B) ◆ **Properties and changes of properties in matter** Some gases in air are chemically active. Smog and acid rain form when certain substances in the air combine. Density and pressure are two properties of air. *(Sections 1, 2, 3)* **Earth and Space Science** (Content Standard D) ◆ **Structure of the Earth system** Earth's atmosphere is a mixture of gases and is in four layers. *(Sections 1, 4)* **Science and Technology** (Content Standard E) ◆ **Design a solution or product** Students consider the issue of air polluted by cars. *(Science and Society)*	**1B Scientific Inquiry** Students gather and interpret weather data and predict weather. Students investigate particles in air. *(Chapter Project; Real-World Lab)* **3A Technology and Science** Students use a barometer to measure air pressure. Technology has helped scientists explore the atmosphere. *(Skills Lab; Science & History)* **3C Issues in Technology** Some human activities cause air pollution. Students consider the issue of air polluted by cars. *(Section 2; Science and Society)* **4B The Earth** Earth's atmosphere is a mixture of various gases and is divided into four main layers. *(Sections 1, 4)* **4D Structure of Matter** Earth's atmosphere is made up of molecules of various gases. Smog and acid rain form when certain substances in the air combine. Density and pressure are two properties of air. *(Sections 1, 2, 3)* **4E Energy Transformation** Earth's atmosphere is heated by the sun. *(Section 4)* **8C Energy Sources and Use** Most air pollution is caused by burning fossil fuels. *(Section 2; Science and Society)* **12D Communication Skills** Students create drawings, graphs, and tables to summarize their weather observations. *(Chapter Project)*	◆ **Energy** Fossil fuels are an important source of energy. Photochemical smog is caused by the action of sunlight on chemicals. Earth's atmosphere is heated by the sun. *(Sections 2, 4; Science and Society)* ◆ **Patterns of Change** Students use their weather observations to predict weather conditions. Weather factors affect the number of particles in the air. Air pressure and density decrease as altitude increases. Students construct a barometer and use it to measure air pressure. *(Chapter Project; Real-World Lab; Section 3; Skills Lab)* ◆ **Scale and Structure** Earth's atmosphere is made up of nitrogen, oxygen, and various other gases and is divided into four main layers. *(Sections 1, 4)* ◆ **Stability** The composition of the atmosphere remains fairly constant. The layers of the atmosphere are classified by their characteristic temperatures. *(Sections 1, 4)* ◆ **Systems and Interactions** Earth's atmosphere makes conditions on Earth suitable for living things. Most air pollution is caused by burning fossil fuels. Cars add to air pollution. *(Sections 1, 2; Science and Society)*

Take It to the Net

The **www.phschool.com** Web site provides you with multiple opportunities to incorporate the internet into your instruction. Go to **www.phschool.com** and click on the Science icon. Then select Science Explorer Integrated.

www.phschool.com

Internet Activities provide opportunities for students to review, extend, or assess a concept from the chapter.

■ Have students use the chapter Self-Test to get instant feedback.

■ Hot Links and Reference Links provide opportunities for online research.

STAY CURRENT with **SCIENCE NEWS** ®

Find out the latest research and information about weather and climate at: **www.phschool.com**

ACTIVITY	Time (minutes)	Materials Quantities for one work group	Skills
Section 1			
Discover, p. 512	15	**Consumable** modeling clay, short candle, matches **Nonconsumable** aluminum pie pan, small glass jar, stopwatch or watch with second hand, large glass jar	Inferring
Try This, p. 514	10	**Consumable** limewater, straw **Nonconsumable** glass	Developing Hypotheses
Real World Lab, pp. 516–517	20,10,10, 10,10	**Consumable** coffee filters **Nonconsumable** vacuum cleaner with intake hose (1 per class), rubber band, thermometer, low-power microscope	Measuring, Interpreting Data
Section 2			
Discover, p. 518	10	**Consumable** modeling clay, aluminum foil, candle, matches **Nonconsumable** glass jar	Observing
Sharpen Your Skills, p. 520	10	No special materials are required.	Predicting
Science at Home, p. 521	home	**Nonconsumable** flashlight	Observing
Section 3			
Discover, p. 523	10	**Consumable** balloon **Nonconsumable** balance	Drawing Conclusions
Try This, p. 525	15	**Consumable** water, long straw, modeling clay **Nonconsumable** 2-liter soda bottle	Inferring
Skills Lab, pp. 526–527	40,10,10	**Consumable** large rubber balloon, white glue, 12- to 15-cm drinking straw, modeling clay, 10 cm x 25 cm cardboard strip, tape **Nonconsumable** blunt scissors, wide-mouthed glass jar, rubber band, metric ruler, pencil	Measuring, Observing, Inferring
Science at Home, p. 528	home	**Consumable** tap water **Nonconsumable** glass, piece of heavy cardboard	Communicating
Section 4			
Discover, p. 529	10	**Nonconsumable** heavy rubber band, plastic bag, wide-mouthed glass jar	Predicting

A list of all materials required for the Student Edition activities can be found beginning on page T23. You can obtain information about ordering materials by calling 1-800-848-9500 or by accessing the Science Explorer internet site at: **www.phschool.com**

Chapter 16 The Atmosphere

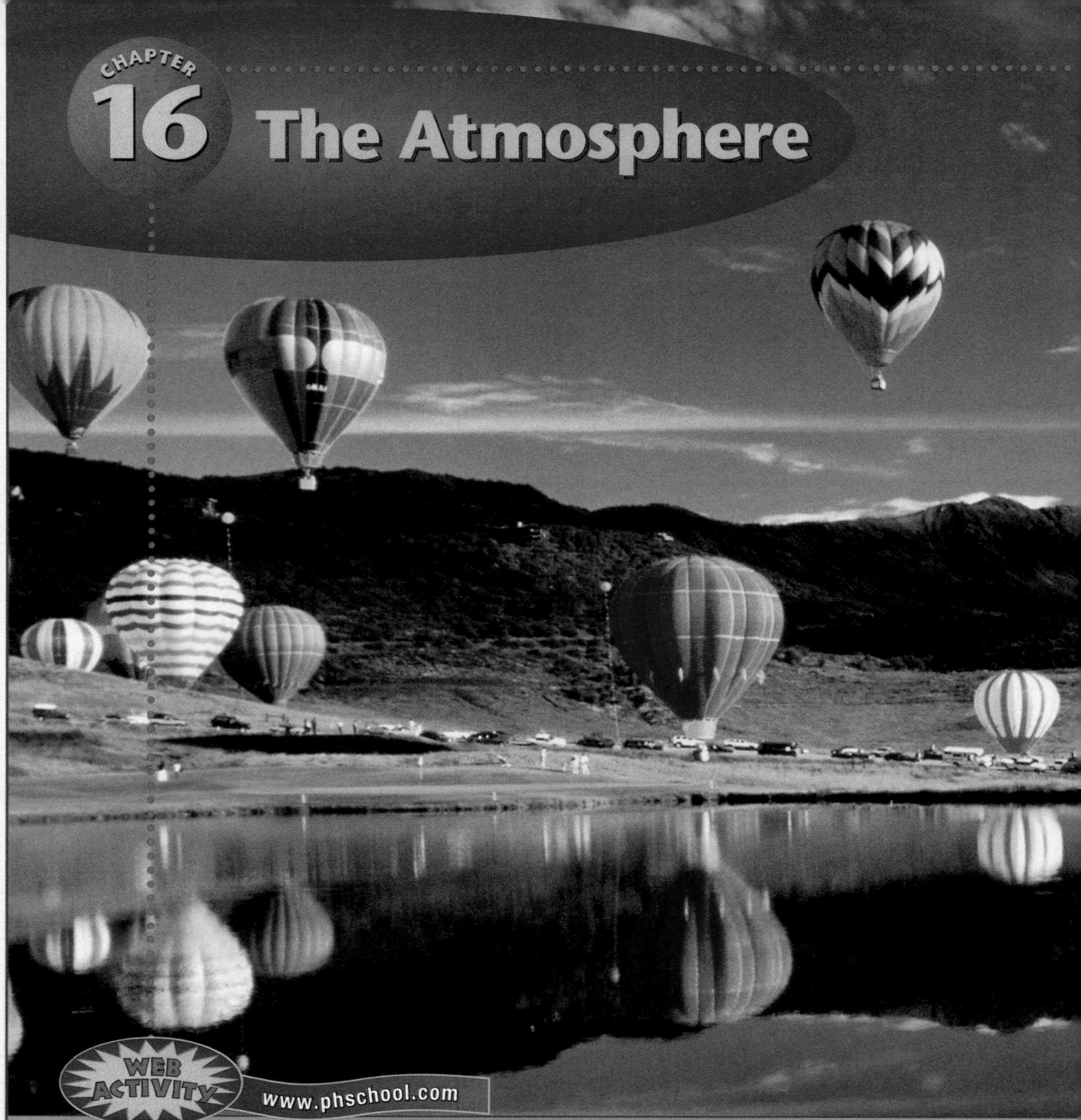

WEB ACTIVITY
www.phschool.com

Integrating Environmental Science

Section 1 The Air Around You
Discover How Long Will the Candle Burn?
Try This Breathe In, Breathe Out
Real-World Lab How Clean Is the Air?

Section 2 Air Quality
Discover What's On the Jar?
Sharpen Your Skills Predicting

Section 3 Air Pressure
Discover Does Air Have Mass?
Try This Soda-Bottle Barometer
Skills Lab Working Under Pressure

Chapter Project 16 Watching the Weather

Most people make observations about the weather almost every day of their lives, but they might not be very aware of specific weather conditions and how they change. Of course they notice when a storm is raging, but they might not notice the red clouds at sunset that may indicate a storm is coming. Most students may not think much about the conditions that make up the weather. If they think about the weather at all, they may just think of it as good or bad.

Purpose In this project, students will become more aware of the weather and the variables such as temperature, precipitation, and wind speed that make up weather conditions. Students also will develop ways of observing weather variables.

Skills Focus Students will be able to
- design and implement a plan for observing and recording daily weather conditions;
- look for patterns in their observations that will help them understand the weather and how it changes;
- create data tables and other means of displaying their observations for the rest of the class.

Project Time Line The entire project will take a minimum of two weeks. The longer students make and record weather observations, the more likely they are to see trends in their data. On the first day, allow class time for introducing the project and brainstorming how students can use their senses to describe the weather. Students should decide as soon as possible which weather variables they will observe and how they will observe them. Students also must devise a way to record their observations. Additional class time will be necessary during the two-week period to monitor students' progress and give extra guidance to students who are having difficulty. At the end of the project, students will need time to review and organize their data and present their results to the rest of the class. For more detailed information on planning and supervising the chapter project, see Chapter 16 Project Teacher Notes, pages 2–3 in Unit 5 Resources.

Suggested Shortcuts To reduce the amount of time students spend on the project, you may assign each student or group of students just one weather variable, such as temperature or precipitation, to monitor. Then, at the end of the project, students can pool their results and the whole class can work together to look for patterns in the data.

Possible Materials Each student will need a log for recording his or her observations, but no other materials or equipment are needed. In fact, you should stress to students that they are to rely only on their senses and not instruments such as thermometers or wind vanes. However, students will need to depend on various materials in their environment, such as the

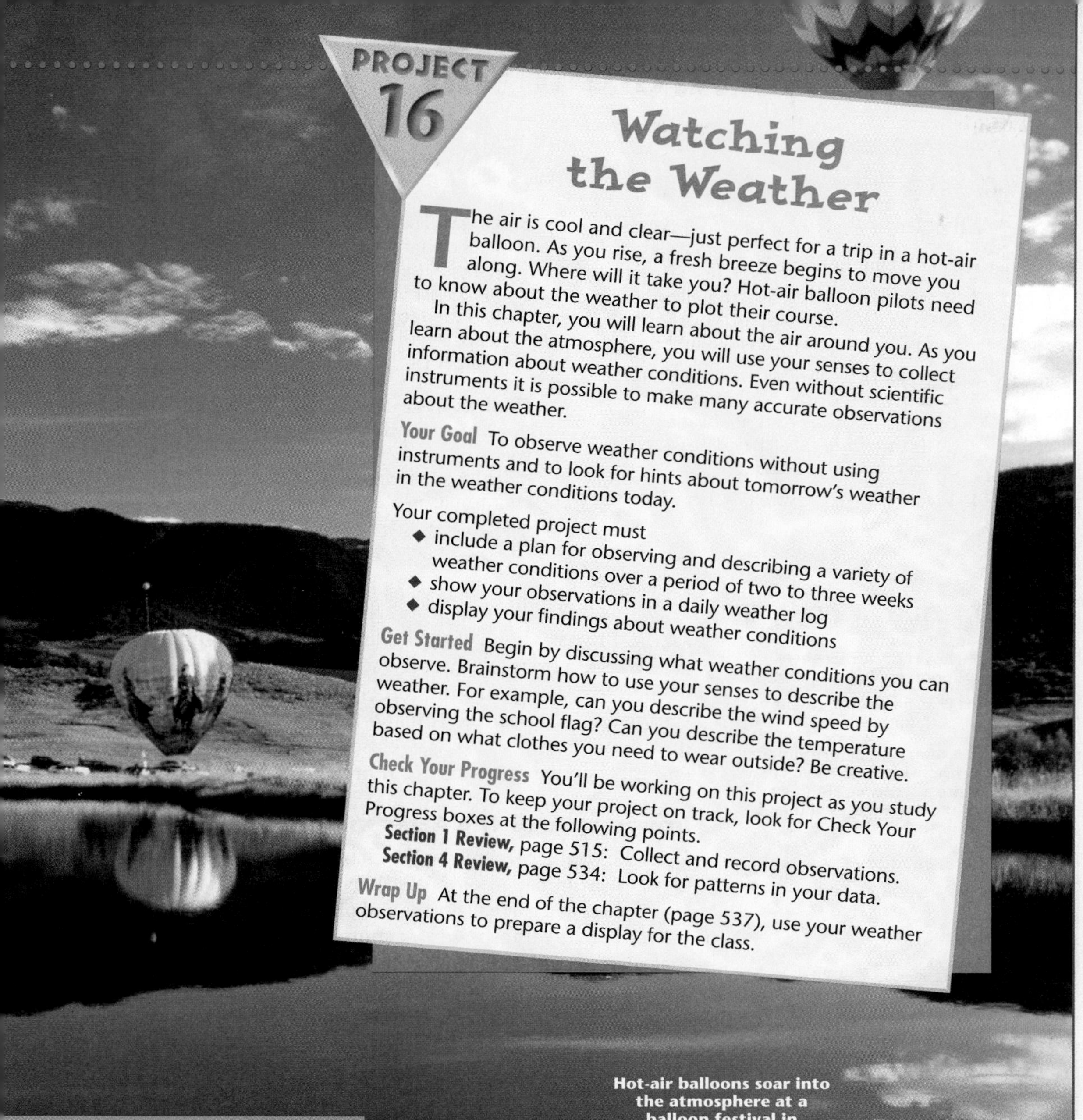

Watching the Weather

The air is cool and clear—just perfect for a trip in a hot-air balloon. As you rise, a fresh breeze begins to move you along. Where will it take you? Hot-air balloon pilots need to know about the weather to plot their course.

In this chapter, you will learn about the air around you. As you learn about the atmosphere, you will use your senses to collect information about weather conditions. Even without scientific instruments it is possible to make many accurate observations about the weather.

Your Goal To observe weather conditions without using instruments and to look for hints about tomorrow's weather in the weather conditions today.

Your completed project must
- include a plan for observing and describing a variety of weather conditions over a period of two to three weeks
- show your observations in a daily weather log
- display your findings about weather conditions

Get Started Begin by discussing what weather conditions you can observe. Brainstorm how to use your senses to describe the weather. For example, can you describe the wind speed by observing the school flag? Can you describe the temperature based on what clothes you need to wear outside? Be creative.

Check Your Progress You'll be working on this project as you study this chapter. To keep your project on track, look for Check Your Progress boxes at the following points.
Section 1 Review, page 515: Collect and record observations.
Section 4 Review, page 534: Look for patterns in your data.

Wrap Up At the end of the chapter (page 537), use your weather observations to prepare a display for the class.

Hot-air balloons soar into the atmosphere at a balloon festival in Snowmass, Colorado.

SECTION 4 Layers of the Atmosphere

Discover Is Air There?

Program Resources

- **Unit 5 Resources** Chapter 16 Project Teacher Notes, pp. 2–3; Project Overview and Worksheets, pp. 4–7; Project Scoring Rubric, p. 8

WEB ACTIVITY www.phschool.com

You will find an Internet activity, chapter self-tests for students, and links to other chapter topics at this site.

Media and Technology

Audio CDs Section Summaries

---

school flag or the clothes people are wearing, to observe weather conditions. Urge students to be creative in the materials they use for their observations. Smoke rising from chimneys, for example, can reveal the direction and speed of the wind as well as flags flying from poles can.

Launching the Project To help students start thinking of weather variables they might observe, hand out copies of newspaper weather reports. On the chalkboard, have a volunteer list the weather variables given in the reports, such as temperature, humidity, barometric pressure, and wind speed and direction. Then challenge students to think of ways these weather variables could be observed without instruments. For example, ask: **If a thin skin of ice forms on puddles during the day, what does that tell you about the temperature?** (It has fallen below the freezing point of water.) **If the school flag is flying straight out from its pole, what does that tell you about the wind?** (It is blowing at a high speed.) Urge students to think of other observations that could give them information about weather conditions.

Performance Assessment

The Chapter 16 Project Scoring Rubric on page 8 in Unit 5 Resources will help you evaluate how well students complete the Chapter 16 Project. You may wish to share the scoring rubric with your students so they know what will be expected of them. Students will be assessed on
- how thoroughly they collect and record observations of a variety of different weather conditions;
- how accurately they interpret their data to predict weather conditions and identify weather trends;
- how complete and creative their presentation of results are;
- if they work in groups, how much they contribute to their group's effort.

SECTION 1 The Air Around You

Objectives

After completing the lesson, students will be able to
- state how the atmosphere is important to living things;
- identify the gases that are present in Earth's atmosphere.

Key Terms weather, atmosphere, ozone, water vapor

1 Engage/Explore

Activating Prior Knowledge

Ask students to recall the fire triangle, which many will have learned about in fire safety demonstrations. After drawing a large triangle on the chalkboard, ask: **What is the fire triangle?** (*A triangle representing the three components needed for fire to burn: fuel, heat, and air*) As students explain, label the sides of the triangle on the chalkboard. Then relate the fire triangle to the composition of air by asking: **What is in air that fire needs to burn?** (*oxygen*) Point out that living things also need oxygen, and oxygen is just one of the components of air they will learn about in this section.

·····• DISCOVER ·····•

Skills Focus inferring
Materials *modeling clay, aluminum pie pan, short candle, matches, small glass jar, stopwatch or watch with second hand, large glass jar*
Time 15 minutes
Tips You can use beakers instead of jars for this activity. You may wish to have students practice using stopwatches before they begin the activity.
Expected Outcome Students should observe that the candle quickly burns out under the small jar and that it burns somewhat longer under the large jar.
Think It Over The gas needed for the candle to burn is oxygen. The candle burned longer under the large jar because the large jar contained more oxygen.

DISCOVER  ·····ACTIVITY·····

How Long Will the Candle Burn?

1. Put on your goggles.
2. Stick a small piece of modeling clay onto an aluminum pie pan. Push a short candle into the clay. Carefully light the candle.
3. Hold a small glass jar by the bottom. Lower the mouth of the jar over the candle until the jar rests on the pie pan. As you do this, start a stopwatch or note where the second hand is on a clock.
4. Watch the candle carefully. How long does the flame burn?
5. Wearing an oven mitt, remove the jar. Relight the candle and then repeat Steps 3 and 4 with a larger jar.

Think It Over
Inferring How would you explain any differences between your results in Steps 4 and 5?

GUIDE FOR READING

- How is the atmosphere important to living things?
- What gases are present in Earth's atmosphere?

Reading Tip Before you read, preview Figure 2. As you read, write a sentence about each of the major gases in the atmosphere.

As you walk home from school, the air is warm and still. The sky is full of thick, dark clouds. In the distance you see a bright flash. A few seconds later, you hear a crack of thunder. As you turn the corner onto your street, raindrops start to fall. You begin to run and reach your home just as the downpour begins. That was close! From the shelter of the entrance you pause to catch your breath and watch the storm.

Importance of the Atmosphere

Does the weather where you live change frequently, or is it fairly constant from day to day? **Weather** is the condition of Earth's atmosphere at a particular time and place. But what is the atmosphere? Earth's **atmosphere** (AT muh sfeer) is the layer of gases that surrounds the planet. To understand the relative size of the atmosphere, imagine that the planet Earth is the size of an apple.

Figure 1 When seen from space, Earth's atmosphere appears as a thin layer near the horizon. The atmosphere makes life on Earth possible.

READING STRATEGIES

Reading Tip Make sure students understand how the two parts of Figure 2 are related by pointing out that the table shows the gases that make up the tiny wedge of the circle that is not nitrogen or oxygen. After students have read the section and written their sentences, suggest that they form pairs, read their sentences to each other, and try to identify which gas each sentence describes. Also urge them to work together to resolve any factual errors they detect in each other's sentences. Possible student sentences include, "The most abundant gas in air is nitrogen. Air is 21 percent oxygen."

Study and Comprehension Before students read the section, have them use the main headings and subheadings to make an outline. Then, as they read the section, have them write down at least one important fact under each heading on their outline.

If you breathe on the apple, a thin film of water will form on its surface. Earth's atmosphere is like that water on the apple—a thin layer of gases on Earth's surface.

Earth's atmosphere makes conditions on Earth suitable for living things. The atmosphere contains oxygen and other gases that you and other living things need to live. In turn, living things affect the atmosphere. The atmosphere is constantly changing, with atoms and molecules of gases moving around the globe and in and out of living things, the land, and the water.

Living things also need warmth and liquid water. By trapping energy from the sun, the atmosphere keeps most of Earth's surface warm enough for water to exist as a liquid. In addition, Earth's atmosphere protects living things from dangerous radiation from the sun. It also prevents Earth's surface from being hit by most meteoroids, or chunks of rock from outer space.

☑ *Checkpoint* What would conditions on Earth be like without the atmosphere?

Composition of the Atmosphere

The atmosphere is made up of a mixture of atoms and molecules of different kinds of gases. An atom is the smallest unit of a chemical element that can exist by itself. Molecules are made up of two or more atoms. **Earth's atmosphere is made up of nitrogen, oxygen, carbon dioxide, water vapor, and many other gases, as well as particles of liquids and solids.**

Nitrogen As you can see in Figure 2, nitrogen is the most abundant gas in the atmosphere. It makes up a little more than three fourths of the air we breathe. Each nitrogen molecule consists of two nitrogen atoms.

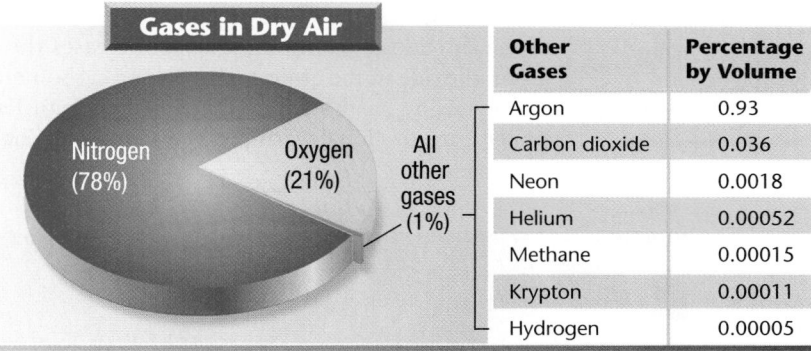

Gases in Dry Air

Nitrogen (78%) Oxygen (21%) All other gases (1%)

Other Gases	Percentage by Volume
Argon	0.93
Carbon dioxide	0.036
Neon	0.0018
Helium	0.00052
Methane	0.00015
Krypton	0.00011
Hydrogen	0.00005

Figure 2 Dry air in the lower atmosphere always has the same composition of gases. *Interpreting Data What two gases make up most of the air?*

The word *atmosphere* comes from two Greek words: *atmos*, meaning "vapor," and *sphaira*, meaning "ball," or "globe." So the atmosphere is the vapors or gases surrounding a globe—in this case, Earth.

In Your Journal

As you read this chapter, write down all the words that end in *-sphere*. Look up the roots of each word in a dictionary. How does knowing the roots of each word help you understand its meaning?

Program Resources

◆ **Unit 5 Resources** 16-1 Lesson Plan, p. 9; 16-1 Section Summary, p. 10
◆ **Guided Reading and Study Workbook** Section 16-1

Media and Technology

 Transparencies "Gases in Dry Air," Transparency 61

Answers to Self-Assessment

☑ *Checkpoint*

Water could not exist as a liquid on Earth's surface. Earth would also be exposed to meteoroids and dangerous radiation from the sun. There would be no life on Earth without the oxygen and other gases that living things need.

Caption Question

Figure 2 Nitrogen and oxygen

---

2 *Facilitate*

Importance of the Atmosphere

Language Arts
CONNECTION

Point out that many scientific terms are based on Greek words. Ask: **Why do you think English borrowed many scientific terms from Greek?** (*The Greeks were among the first Western people to study and write about the natural world. The words they used were passed on to people throughout Europe.*)

In Your Journal Other words ending in *-sphere* are terms for the layers of the atmosphere. For each term, have students write the meaning of the prefix. **learning modality: verbal**

Composition of the Atmosphere

Building Inquiry Skills: Making Models

Earth's atmosphere is composed largely of just a few gases, but even gases present in small amounts may be important to life. Also, the gases in Earth's atmosphere are present in the same proportions below about 80 kilometers. To reinforce these concepts, invite students to explain how a cake models the composition of the atmosphere. Provide a simple cake recipe first. Ask: **In what ways are the ingredients in a cake like the gases in Earth's atmosphere?** (*A cake is made up largely of just a few ingredients, especially flour. Ingredients, such as baking powder, included in small amounts may be essential for the cake. The ingredients in the cake are always in the same proportions.*) **learning modality: logical/mathematical**

Ongoing Assessment

Oral Presentation Call on students at random to state ways that the atmosphere contributes to life on Earth.

Composition of the Atmosphere, continued

Integrating Life Science

The text gives just a short summary of the nitrogen cycle. Divide the class into groups and challenge each group to research the nitrogen cycle further and then make an illustrated flowchart of it. Each student in the group should take responsibility for learning about and illustrating one part of the cycle. Urge groups to share their flowcharts and work together to resolve any discrepancies. Display their best efforts in the classroom. **cooperative learning**

Building Inquiry Skills: Inferring

Materials *tall glass jar, large cake pan, clean steel wool, water, tape*

Time 5 minutes one day; 5 minutes the next day

Estimate the amount of oxygen in the atmosphere by having students follow these instructions: Fill a cake pan almost full of water. Push steel wool down into the bottom of a tall glass jar so it will not fall out when the jar is turned over. (**CAUTION:** Remind students to handle glass carefully.) Fill the jar with water, cover the mouth with a hand, and place the jar upside down in the cake pan. Remove the hand and tilt the jar slightly to let out enough water so that the water level in the jar is just above the water level in the pan. Mark the water level in the jar with a piece of tape and leave the jar where it is. Have students check the water level the next day. It should be about one fifth higher than it was. Explain that oxygen in the air combines with iron in steel wool to form rust. Ask: **From this experiment, how can you tell how much oxygen there is in air?** *(About one fifth of the air is used up, so the air must be about one fifth oxygen.)*
learning modality: logical/ mathematical

Breathe In, Breathe Out ACTIVITY

How can you detect carbon dioxide in the air you exhale?

1. Put on your goggles.
2. Fill a glass or beaker halfway with limewater.

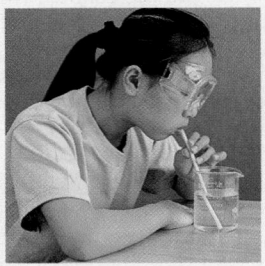

3. ☠ Using a straw, slowly blow air through the limewater for about a minute. **CAUTION:** *Do not suck on the straw or drink the limewater.*
4. What happens to the limewater?

Developing Hypotheses What do you think would happen if you did the same experiment after jogging for 10 minutes? If you tried this, what might the results tell you about exercise and carbon dioxide?

INTEGRATING LIFE SCIENCE Nitrogen is essential to living things. Proteins and other complex chemical substances in living things contain nitrogen. You and all other organisms must have nitrogen in order to grow and to repair body cells.

Most living things cannot obtain nitrogen directly from the air. Instead, some bacteria convert nitrogen into substances called nitrates. Plants then absorb the nitrates from the soil and use them to make proteins. To obtain proteins, animals must eat plants or other animals.

Oxygen Most oxygen molecules have two oxygen atoms. Even though oxygen is the second-most abundant gas in the atmosphere, it makes up less than one fourth of the volume. Plants and animals take oxygen directly from the air and use it to release energy from food in a usable form.

Oxygen is also involved in other important processes. Any fuel you can think of, from the gasoline in a car to the candles on a birthday cake, uses oxygen as it burns. Without oxygen, a fire will go out. Burning uses oxygen rapidly. During other processes, oxygen is used slowly. For example, steel in cars and other objects reacts slowly with oxygen to form iron oxide, or rust.

Have you ever noticed a pungent smell in the air after a thunderstorm? This is the odor of ozone, which forms when lightning interacts with oxygen in the air. **Ozone** is a form of oxygen that has three oxygen atoms in each molecule instead of the usual two.

Carbon Dioxide Each molecule of carbon dioxide has one atom of carbon and two atoms of oxygen. Even though the atmosphere contains only a small amount of carbon dioxide, it is essential to life. Plants must have carbon dioxide to produce food. Animals, on the other hand, give off carbon dioxide as a waste product.

When fuels such as coal and gasoline are burned, they release carbon dioxide. Burning these fuels increases the amount of carbon dioxide in the atmosphere. Rising carbon dioxide levels may be raising Earth's temperature. The issue of Earth's rising temperature, or global warming, is discussed in Chapter 19.

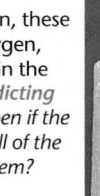

Figure 3 To burn, these candles need oxygen, one of the gases in the atmosphere. *Predicting What would happen if the candles used up all of the oxygen around them?*

514

Background

History of Science Scientists began searching for the components of air more than 300 years ago. In the 1600s, an English scientist named Robert Boyle discovered that air contains a substance needed for life when he noted that living things died if deprived of air. He called this substance "vital air." We now call it oxygen.

Almost 100 years later, Joseph Black, a Scottish medical student, found that limestone mixed with acid gives off a substance that puts out flames. He called it "fixed air." We now know it as carbon dioxide.

About 15 years later, one of Black's students, Daniel Rutherford, used a liquid to absorb vital air and fixed air. The substance that remained he called "noxious air," because it put out flames and killed living things. We now know it as nitrogen.

Other Gases Oxygen and nitrogen together make up 99 percent of dry air. Carbon dioxide and argon make up most of the other one percent. The remaining gases are called trace gases because only small amounts of them are present.

Water Vapor The composition of the air discussed so far has been for dry air. In reality, air is not dry because it contains water vapor. **Water vapor** is water in the form of a gas. Water vapor is invisible—it is not the same thing as steam, which is made up of tiny droplets of liquid water. Each water molecule contains two atoms of hydrogen and one atom of oxygen.

The amount of water vapor in the air varies greatly from place to place and from time to time. Air above a desert or polar ice sheet may contain almost no water vapor. In tropical rain forests, on the other hand, as much as five percent of the air may be water vapor.

Water vapor plays an important role in Earth's weather. Clouds form when water vapor condenses out of the air to form tiny droplets of liquid water or crystals of ice. If these droplets or crystals become large enough, they can fall as rain or snow.

Particles Pure air contains only gases. But pure air exists only in laboratories. In the real world, air also contains tiny solid and liquid particles of dust, smoke, salt, and other chemicals. Sometimes you can see particles in the air around you, but most of them are too small to see.

Figure 4 This lush vegetation grows in a rain forest in Costa Rica. The percentage of water vapor in the air in a rain forest may be as high as five percent.

Section 1 Review

1. Describe two ways in which the atmosphere is important to life on Earth.
2. What are the four most common gases in dry air?
3. Why are the amounts of gases in the atmosphere usually shown as percentages of dry air?
4. **Thinking Critically** Applying Concepts How would the amount of carbon dioxide in the atmosphere change if there were no plants? If there were no animals?

Check Your Progress CHAPTER PROJECT 16
Have you determined *how, where,* and *when,* you will make your observations? Organize a notebook to record them. Think of ways to compare weather conditions from day to day. Make your observations without weather instruments or TV weather reports. (*Hint:* You can estimate how much of the sky is covered by clouds.) For your own safety, do not try to make observations during storms.

Chapter 16 **515**

Answers to Self-Assessment

Caption Question

Figure 3 Their flames would go out.

TRY THIS

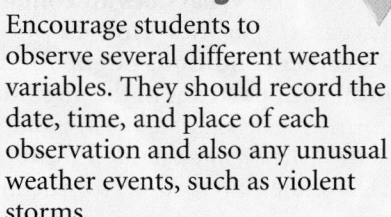

Skills Focus developing hypotheses
Materials *glass, limewater, straw*
Time 10 minutes
Tips Make sure students are careful not to splash or ingest any of the limewater.
Expected Outcome Students should observe that the limewater becomes cloudy when they blow into it because of carbon dioxide in their breath. After exercise, more carbon dioxide is exhaled, causing the limewater to get cloudier.
Extend Invite students to detect carbon dioxide in carbonated water by adding some of it to the limewater. **learning modality: kinesthetic**

3 Assess

Section 1 Review Answers

1. *Any two:* Provides oxygen and other gases living things need, traps energy from the sun to keep Earth's surface warm, and protects from meteoroids and radiation from the sun
2. Nitrogen, oxygen, argon, carbon dioxide
3. Because the amount of water vapor in air varies greatly
4. Without plants there would be less oxygen and more carbon dioxide; without animals there would be less carbon dioxide and more oxygen.

Check Your Progress CHAPTER PROJECT 16
Encourage students to observe several different weather variables. They should record the date, time, and place of each observation and also any unusual weather events, such as violent storms.

Performance Assessment

Writing Have students write a paragraph identifying the three most important gases in air for living things, the percentage of each, and why the gas is important.

How Clean Is the Air?

Preparing for Inquiry

Key Concept The number of particles in air is affected by the weather.

Skills Objectives Students will be able to
◆ measure the number of particles in samples collected from the air;
◆ interpret how the number of particles is affected by weather factors.

Time 20 minutes the first day; 10 minutes a day for four days

Advance Planning If possible, students should collect particle samples outside. If they do, the vacuum cleaner may need an extension cord. However, they should not collect samples outside in wet weather. Instead, have students collect the samples as soon as possible after a rainfall. If you use only one vacuum cleaner, plan sufficient time for each group of students to use it.

Alternative Materials A portable vacuum cleaner is easier to carry outside than a regular vacuum cleaner. Instead of coffee filters, you can use paper towels for filters, but they are less effective because they let more particles pass through.

Guiding Inquiry

Invitation To help students focus on the key concept, ask: **What does air contain besides gases?** *(particles)* **How do you think weather conditions might affect the number of particles in the air?** *(Rain might wash particles out of the air, and wind might stir them up or blow them away.)* Save their predictions so students can compare them with their results.

Introducing the Procedure

Have students read through the complete procedure and copy the data table in their notebook. Then ask: **Why do people in some occupations, such as wood-working, wear protective masks?** *(Because they work where there are high levels of particles in the air, and protective masks trap the particles so they do not breathe them in)* Mention some devices students may be familiar with, including motor vehicles and furnaces, that have filters to trap particles in the air that flows through them. You might want to ask the school custodian to show students how air in the classrooms is filtered or the industrial arts teacher to show them how wood and dust particles are filtered from the air in the shop. Tell students that in this lab they will trap particles in the air by running a vacuum cleaner with a paper filter placed over the end of the hose.

How Clean Is the Air?

Sometimes you can actually see the atmosphere! How? Since air is normally transparent, it can only be visible because it contains particles. In this activity, you will use a vacuum cleaner to gather particles from the air.

Problem

How do weather factors affect the number of particles in the air?

Skills Focus

measuring, interpreting data

Materials

coffee filters
rubber band
thermometer
low-power microscope
vacuum cleaner with
intake hose (1 per class)

Procedure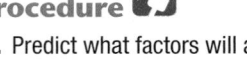

1. Predict what factors will affect the number of particles you collect. How might different weather factors affect your results?
2. In your notebook, make a data table like the one below.
3. Place the coffee filter over the nozzle of the vacuum cleaner hose. Fasten the coffee filter securely to the hose with a rubber band. Make sure the air passes through the coffee filter before entering the vacuum cleaner.
4. You will take air samples in the same place each day for five days. If possible, find a place outdoors. Otherwise, you can run the vacuum cleaner out a classroom window. **CAUTION:** *Do not use the vacuum cleaner outdoors on wet or rainy days.* If it is wet or rainy, collect the sample as soon as possible after it stops raining.
5. Hold the vacuum nozzle at least one meter above the ground each time you use the vacuum. Turn on the vacuum. Run the vacuum for 30 minutes. Shut off the vacuum.

DATA TABLE

Date and Time	Temperature	Amount of Precipitation	Wind Direction	Wind Speed	Number of Particles

Troubleshooting the Experiment

◆ If possible, have students run the vacuum cleaner for 30 minutes each time. However, if the air is very dirty, 20 minutes each time may be enough.
◆ Because a vacuum cleaner is noisy, it may be necessary to run it outside of class time.
◆ Stress that samples should be taken in the same place each day to help control other variables besides weather conditions that might influence the number of particles collected, such as proximity to a dusty playing field.

6. While the vacuum is running, observe the weather conditions. Measure the temperature. Estimate the amount of precipitation, if any, since the previous observation. Note the direction from which the wind, if any, is blowing. Also note whether the wind is heavy, light, or calm. Record your observations.

7. Remove the coffee filter from the nozzle. Label the filter with the place, time, and date. Draw a circle on the filter to show the area that was over the vacuum nozzle.

8. Place the coffee filter on the stage of a microscope (40 power). Be sure that the part of the filter that was over the vacuum nozzle is directly under the microscope lens. Without moving the coffee filter, count all the particles you see. Record the number in your data table.

9. Repeat Steps 3–8 each clear day.

Analyze and Conclude

1. Was there a day of the week when you collected more particles?

2. What factors changed during the week that could have caused changes in the particle count?

3. Did the weather have any effect on your day-to-day results? If so, which weather factor do you think was most important?

4. Make a list of some possible sources of the particles you collected. Are these sources natural, or did the particles come from manufactured products?

5. How could you improve your method to get more particles out of the air?

6. **Apply** Identify areas in or around your school where there may be high levels of dust and other particles. What can people do to protect themselves in these areas?

Design an Experiment

Do you think time of day will affect the number of particles you collect? Develop a hypothesis and a plan for testing it. Could you work with other classes to get data at different times of the day? Before carrying out your plan, get your teacher's approval.

Sample Data Table

Date and Time	Temp.	Amt. of Precipitation	Wind Direction	Wind Speed	# of Particles
Oct. 1, 2 P.M.	18°C	none	SW	calm	60
Oct. 2, 2 P.M.	19°C	none	SW	light breeze	55
Oct. 3, 2 P.M.	11°C	1 cm	W	moderate wind	18
Oct. 4, 2 P.M.	12°C	5 cm	W	strong wind	10
Oct. 5, 2 P.M.	13°C	5 cm	W	strong wind	11

Program Resources

◆ **Unit 5 Resources** Real-World Lab blackline masters, pp. 25–27

Media and Technology

 Lab Activity Videotape
Tape 4

Expected Outcome

Using the microscope, students should be able to see and count the particles collected on the filters. The number of particles may vary greatly from one sample to another.

Analyze and Conclude

1. The particle count may vary from day to day depending on human activities and the weather.

2. The particle count is likely to be higher later in the week as particles given off by motor vehicles and factories and produced by other human activities accumulate in the air. Changing weather conditions also may cause changes in the particle count.

3. Weather factors most likely to affect day-to-day results are wind speed and recent precipitation.

4. Particles can come from many different sources. Natural sources include flowering plants, bare ground, and forest fires. Manufactured products that produce particles include motor vehicles, factories, and power plants.

5. Possible ways to get more particles out of the air include using a more powerful vacuum cleaner or a vacuum cleaner with a wider hose, running the vacuum cleaner longer each time, and using a finer filter.

6. **Apply** The cafeteria, gymnasium, and shop may have more particles than the classrooms. Playing fields and parking lots may have more particles than lawn areas. Wearing dust masks and using special air filters can help protect people from high levels of particles in the air.

Extending the Inquiry

Design an Experiment Students may hypothesize that particles build up in the air during the day as the result of increased human activity, such as driving vehicles and construction.

Safety

Emphasize the importance of not using the vacuum cleaner around water because of electrical shock. Review the safety guidelines in Appendix A.

SECTION 2 Air Quality

Objectives

After completing the lesson, students will be able to
- ◆ name the main sources of air pollution;
- ◆ explain how photochemical smog and acid rain form.

Key Terms pollutant, photochemical smog, acid rain

1 Engage/Explore

Activating Prior Knowledge

Guide students in recalling weather reports they may have seen or heard that included an air quality index or pollen count. Alternatively, share copies of newspaper weather reports that include these measures. Then ask: **Why do weather reports include warnings about air pollution and pollen in the air?** *(Because high levels of pollution and pollen in the air can make people sick)* **What is the source of pollen in the air?** *(plants)* **What are some sources of pollution in the air?** *(cars and factories)*

······· DISCOVER ·······

Skills Focus observing
Materials *modeling clay, aluminum foil, candle, matches, glass jar*
Time 10 minutes
Tips Before students light their candles, be sure the candles are firmly in place in the modeling clay. When students put their jars near the flame, caution them to avoid touching the wax or wick.
Expected Outcome Students should see black powder collect on the part of the jar just above the flame. In addition to soot, students may see condensation form on the jar from water vapor in the air.
Think It Over The black powder on the jar is soot, which came from the incomplete burning of the wax candle.

SECTION 2 Air Quality

DISCOVER ···················· ACTIVITY····

What's On the Jar?

1. Put on your goggles.
2. Put a small piece of modeling clay on a piece of aluminum foil. Push a candle into the clay. Light the candle.
3. Wearing an oven mitt, hold a glass jar by the rim so that the bottom of the jar is just above the flame.

Think It Over
Observing What do you see on the jar? Where did it come from?

GUIDE FOR READING

- ◆ What are the main sources of air pollution?
- ◆ How do photochemical smog and acid rain form?

Reading Tip As you read, look for evidence to support this statement: Most air pollution is caused by human activities. What facts support this statement? What facts do not support it?

One hundred years ago, the city of London, England, was dark and dirty. Factories burned coal, and most houses were heated by coal. The air was full of soot. In 1905, the term *smog* was created by combining the words *smoke* and *fog* to describe this type of air pollution. Today, people in London burn much less coal. As a result, the air in London now is much cleaner than it was 100 years ago.

Air Pollution

As you are reading this, you are breathing without even thinking about it. Breathing brings air into your lungs, where the oxygen you need is taken into your body. You may also breathe in tiny particles or even a small amount of harmful gases. In fact, these particles and gases are a concern to people everywhere.

If you live in a large city, you probably already know what air pollution is. You may have noticed a brown haze or an unpleasant smell in the air. Even if you live far from a city, the air around you may be polluted. Harmful substances in the air, water, or soil are known as **pollutants**. Figure 5 shows some of the effects of air pollution on human health.

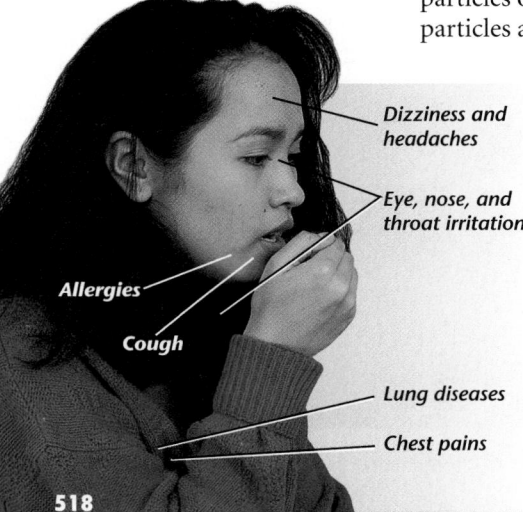

Dizziness and headaches

Eye, nose, and throat irritation

Allergies

Cough

Lung diseases

Chest pains

Figure 5 Air pollution can cause many different problems. Some air pollutants are natural, but most are caused by human activities. *Interpreting Photographs* What parts of the body are most affected by air pollution?

READING STRATEGIES

Reading Tip Evidence supporting the statement that air pollution is caused by human activities includes the fact that most air pollution is the result of burning fossil fuels. Evidence contradicting the statement includes the fact that many natural processes add particles to the air. Some particles from natural sources are ocean salt, molds, plant pollen, soil, and ashes from forest fires and volcanoes.

Program Resources

- ◆ **Unit 5 Resources** 16-2 Lesson Plan, p. 13; 16-2 Section Summary, p. 14
- ◆ **Guided Reading and Study Workbook** Section 16-2
- ◆ **Laboratory Manual** 16, "Examining Acid Rain"

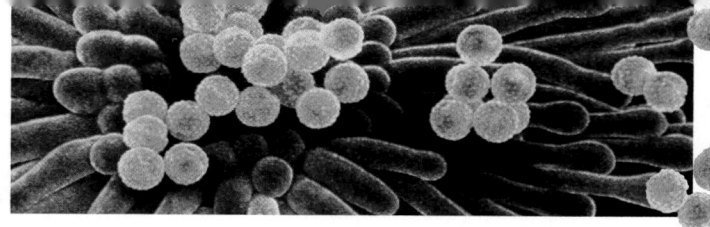

Figure 6 These pollen grains from a ragweed flower have been greatly magnified to show detail. Pollen can cause people who are allergic to it to sneeze.

Some air pollution occurs naturally, but much of it is caused by human activities. **Most air pollution is the result of burning fossil fuels such as coal, oil, gasoline, and diesel fuel.** Almost half of the air pollution from human activities comes from cars and other motor vehicles. A little more than one fourth comes from factories and power plants that burn coal and oil. Burning fossil fuels produces a number of air pollutants, including particles and gases that can form smog and acid rain.

☑ ***Checkpoint*** *What are two sources of air pollution that you see every day?*

Particles

As you know, air contains particles along with gases. When you draw these particles deep into your lungs, the particles can be harmful. Particles in the air come from both natural sources and human activities.

Natural Sources Many natural processes add particles to the atmosphere. When ocean waves splash salt water against rocks, some of the water sprays into the air and evaporates. Tiny salt particles stay in the air. The wind blows particles of molds and plant pollen. Forest fires, soil erosion, and dust storms add particles to the atmosphere. Erupting volcanoes spew out clouds of dust and ashes along with poisonous gases.

INTEGRATING HEALTH Even fairly clean air usually contains particles of dust and pollen. Figure 6 shows pollen, a fine, powdery material produced by many plants. The wind carries pollen not only to other plants, but also to people. One type of allergy, popularly called "hay fever," is caused by pollen from plants such as ragweed. Symptoms of hay fever include sneezing, a runny nose, red and itchy eyes, and headaches. Weather reports often include a "pollen count," which is the average number of pollen grains in a cubic meter of air.

Human Activities When people burn fuels such as wood and coal, particles made mostly of carbon enter the air. These particles of soot are what gives smoke its dark color. Farming and construction also release large amounts of soil particles into the air.

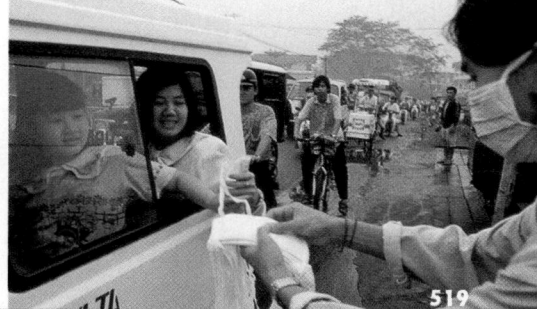

Figure 7 These people in Pontianak, Indonesia, are being given dust masks to protect them from smoke caused by widespread forest fires. *Inferring What effects do you think this smoke might have had on the people who live in this area?*

519

2 Facilitate

Air Pollution

Demonstration

ACTIVITY

Materials *cotton ball, fingernail polish remover, glass jar with lid, rayon cloth, tape*
Time 5 minutes one day; 5 minutes the next day

Point out that air pollution is bad for clothing and other materials as well as for people. To show students the effect of air pollution on cloth, saturate a cotton ball with fingernail polish remover, which contains acetone, and place it in the bottom of a glass jar. Tape a small piece of rayon to the inside of the jar lid and put the lid on tightly. Place another small piece of rayon beside the jar and leave both overnight. The next day, invite students to compare the two pieces of cloth. Ask: **Why did the cloth in the jar weaken?** *(The fingernail polish produced acetone vapors that attacked fibers in the cloth.)* Add that similar vapors pollute the air over cities. **learning modality: kinesthetic**

Particles

Integrating Health

Invite students to learn more about allergies such as hay fever by working in groups to conduct a survey. Each group member should ask family members, friends, and neighbors if they suffer from hay fever or other allergies. Then group members should pool their results and use the data to identify the frequency of such allergies. **cooperative learning**

Media and Technology

Transparencies "Effects of Air Pollutants on Humans," Transparency 62

Answers to Self-Assessment

Caption Questions

Figure 5 The respiratory system, including the nose, throat, and lungs
Figure 7 It might have caused respiratory and other health problems.

☑ ***Checkpoint***

Motor vehicles and factories or power plants that burn coal or oil

Ongoing Assessment

Concept Mapping Have students make a concept map of particles found in the air, including sources and examples.

Smog

Integrating Chemistry

Materials *two small glass bottles, pan of hot water, bowl of ice, matches*
Time 10 minutes

Point out that smog is trapped near the ground when the air near the ground is cooler than the air above it. Demonstrate by placing a small glass bottle in a shallow pan of hot water and another in a bowl of ice. Then drop a smoking match into each bottle. Smoke will rise from the bottle of warm air but not from the bottle of cold air. Ask: **Why does smoke stay in the bottle of cold air?** (*Because cold air is denser than warm air and does not rise*) **learning modality: logical/mathematical**

Sharpen your Skills

Predicting

Time 10 minutes
Expected Outcome The amount of pollutants may vary by time of day and day of week. Cars and trucks produce the most pollution during morning and evening rush hours, and factories and plants produce pollutants throughout the workday. Thus, pollution levels are likely to be higher late in the day and on Fridays after pollutants have accumulated.
Extend Have students predict how pollutants in air might vary by season.
learning modality: logical/ mathematical

Acid Rain

Inquiry Challenge

Materials *two saucers, two pennies, tap water, vinegar*
Time 10 minutes one day; 5 minutes the next day

Challenge small groups to brainstorm a way to use the materials to show the effects of acid rain on metal. (*The most likely way is to place each penny on a saucer, cover one penny with vinegar and the other with water, and let them stand overnight.*)
cooperative learning

520

Sharpen your Skills

Predicting

Are the amounts of pollutants in the air always at the same level, or do they change from time to time? At what time of the day do you think the major sources of air pollution— cars, trucks, power plants, and factories— might produce the most pollution? Overall, do you think there is more air pollution in the morning or in the evening? On Mondays or on Fridays? On what did you base your prediction?

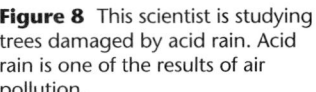

Figure 8 This scientist is studying trees damaged by acid rain. Acid rain is one of the results of air pollution.

520

Smog

London-type smog forms when particles in coal smoke combine with water droplets in humid air. Fortunately, London-type smog is no longer common in the United States. Today sunny cities like Los Angeles often have another type of smog. The brown haze that forms in cities is called **photochemical smog**. The *photo-* in photochemical means "light." Photochemical smog is caused by the action of sunlight on chemicals.

Integrating Chemistry

Photochemical smog is formed by a complex process. All fossil fuels contain hydrocarbons, which are substances composed of carbon and hydrogen. When fossil fuels are burned, some hydrocarbons are not burned completely and escape into the air. At the same time, the high temperatures that accompany burning cause some of the nitrogen in the air to react with oxygen to form nitrogen oxides. **The nitrogen oxides, hydrocarbons, and other air pollutants then react with each other in the presence of sunlight to form a mix of ozone and other chemicals called photochemical smog.** The ozone in photochemical smog irritates breathing passages, harms plants, and damages rubber, paint, and some plastics.

Checkpoint How do natural conditions combine with human activities to create photochemical smog?

Acid Rain

One result of air pollution is acid rain. The burning of coal that contains a lot of sulfur produces substances composed of oxygen and sulfur called sulfur oxides. **Acid rain forms when nitrogen oxides and sulfur oxides combine with water in the air to form nitric acid and sulfuric acid.**

Background

Facts and Figures The 99.9% of the atmosphere that is made up of nitrogen, oxygen, and argon has remained relatively stable for the past 100 million years. Chemical interactions among fewer than 0.1% of molecules in the atmosphere are the cause of all the air quality problems facing us today, including smog and acid rain.

The average pH of rain water is about 4.2, which means that it is weakly acidic. Rain in remote areas little affected by pollution is less acidic and may have a pH as high as 4.8. Considerably more acidic water is found in the smog over Los Angeles. It may have a pH as low as 1.8. To put these values in perspective, consider that tomato juice has a pH of 4.3, vinegar a pH of 2.8, and battery acid a pH of 0.8.

Rain, sleet, snow, fog, and even dry particles carry these two acids from the air to trees, lakes, and buildings. Rain is naturally slightly acidic, but rain that contains more acid than normal is known as **acid rain.** Acid rain is sometimes strong enough to damage the surfaces of buildings and statues.

As Figure 8 shows, needle-leafed trees such as pines and spruce are especially sensitive to acid rain. Acid rain may make tree needles turn brown or fall off. It also harms lakes and ponds. Acid rain can make water so acidic that plants, amphibians, fish, and insects can no longer survive in it.

Improving Air Quality

The United States government and state governments have passed a number of laws and regulations to reduce air pollution. For example, pollution-control devices are required equipment on cars. Factories and power plants must install filters in smokestacks to remove pollutants from smoke before it is released into the atmosphere. These filters are called scrubbers.

Air quality in this country has generally improved over the past 30 years. The amounts of most major air pollutants have decreased. Newer cars cause less pollution than older models. Recently built power plants are less polluting than power plants that have been in operation for many years.

However, there are now more cars on the road and more power plants burning fossil fuels than in the past. Unfortunately, the air in many American cities is still polluted. Many people think that stricter regulations are needed to control air pollution. Others argue that reducing air pollution is very expensive and that the benefits of stricter regulations may not be worth the costs.

 Section 2 Review

1. How is most air pollution produced?
2. Name two natural and two artificial sources of particles in the atmosphere.
3. How is photochemical smog formed? What kinds of harm does it cause?
4. What substances combine to form acid rain?
5. **Thinking Critically** **Inferring** Do you think that photochemical smog levels are higher during the winter or during the summer? Explain.

Science at Home

It's easy to see particles in the air. Gather your family members in a dark room. Open a window shade or blind slightly, or turn on a flashlight. Can they see tiny particles suspended in the beam of light? Discuss with your family where the particles came from. What might be some natural sources? What might be some human sources?

Chapter 16 **521**

Answers to Self-Assessment

✓ *Checkpoint*

Pollutants in the air produced by human activities react with each other in the presence of sunlight to form photochemical smog.

Program Resources

◆ **Unit 5 Resources** 16-2 Review and Reinforce, p. 15; 16-2 Enrich, p. 16

Improving Air Quality

Building Inquiry Skills: Inferring

Point out that nitrogen dioxide and sulfur dioxide emissions in the U.S. have decreased over the past 30 years. Ask: **How do you think the level of acid in rain has been affected by these trends in air pollutants?** *(Nitrogen dioxide and sulfur dioxide cause acid rain, so the amount of acid in rain probably has decreased as well.)* **learning modality: logical/mathematical**

3 Assess

Section 2 Review Answers

1. By the burning of fossil fuels
2. Natural: ocean salt, molds, plant pollen, forest fires, soil erosion, volcanoes; Artificial: burning of fossil fuels, farming, and construction
3. It forms when nitrogen oxides, hydrocarbons, and other pollutants react in the presence of sunlight. It can irritate breathing passages, harm plants, and damage rubber, paint, and some plastics.
4. Nitrogen oxides, sulfur oxides, and water in the air
5. During the summer, because the production of photochemical smog requires sunlight and the sun's rays are more direct and the hours of daylight are longer then

Science at Home

Materials *flashlight*
Students will see more particles if they stir up dust first. Point out that most particles in the air are too small to be seen without a microscope. Natural sources include plant pollens and molds. Human sources include soot from burning fossil fuels and soil from farming.

Performance Assessment

Writing Challenge students to write letters to a newspaper to raise peoples' awareness of the causes and dangers of air pollution.

Cars and Clean Air

Purpose

To help students learn ways that pollution from cars can be reduced and make a reasonable judgment about the best ways to do this.

Panel Discussion

Time one day to prepare; 30 minutes for panel discussion

After students have read the feature, ask for volunteers to form a panel to discuss the issues. Have each panel member assume one of the following roles: a car manufacturer, a person who commutes 50 miles a day to work, a person who lives near a busy intersection, a lawmaker, and a public health official. Students should take the point of view of the individual they represent and present relevant facts and opinions for that individual. Following the panel discussion, take a class vote on which methods of reducing pollution seem most effective and whether the methods should be voluntary or enforced.

Extend Challenge students to learn about alternative means of transportation in their community and report on the costs and availability of each.

You Decide

1. Even the least polluting cars cause some air pollution, and there are more cars on the road each year. More cars also mean more traffic jams, which produce more pollution than does driving on the open road. Automobiles pollute the air with particles such as soot and gases that contribute to smog and acid rain.

2. Driving cars that are more efficient and produce less pollution, and driving less

3. Students should illustrate more than one way to help reduce pollution from cars. Their captions should demonstrate that they understand how the solutions address the problem.

Cars and Clean Air

New technology and strict laws have brought cleaner air to many American cities. But in some places the air is still polluted. Cars and trucks still cause about half the air pollution in cities. And there are more cars on the road every year!

Worldwide, there are about 500 million cars. More cars will mean more pollution and more traffic jams. Unfortunately, cars stuck in traffic produce three times as much pollution as cars on the open road. What can people do to reduce air pollution by cars?

The Issues

Can Cars Be Made To Pollute Less?
In the past 20 years, cars have become more fuel-efficient and pollution levels have been lowered. Now engineers are running out of ways to make cars run more efficiently and produce less pollution. But technology does offer other answers.

Some vehicles use fuels other than gasoline. For instance, natural gas can power cars and trucks. Burning natural gas produces less pollution than burning gasoline.

Battery-powered electric cars produce no air pollution. However, the electricity to charge the batteries often comes from power plants that burn oil or coal. So electric cars still produce some pollution indirectly. Car makers have produced a few electric cars, but they are expensive and can make only fairly short trips.

Should People Drive Less? Many car trips are shorter than a mile—an easy distance for most people to walk. For longer trips, people might consider riding a bicycle. Many cars on the road carry just one person. Some people might consider riding with others in car pools or taking buses or subways.

Are Stricter Standards or Taxes the Answer? Some state governments have led efforts to reduce pollution. The state of California, for example, has strict anti-pollution laws. These laws set standards for gradually reducing pollutants released by cars. Stricter laws might make some old cars illegal.

Another approach is to make driving more expensive so that people use their cars less. That might mean higher gasoline taxes or fees for using the roads at busy times.

You Decide

1. Identify the Problem
In your own words, explain why automobiles make it hard to improve air quality. What kinds of pollution are caused by automobiles?

2. Analyze the Options
What are some ways to reduce the pollution caused by cars? Should these actions be voluntary, or should governments require them?

3. Find a Solution
How would you encourage people to try to reduce the pollution from cars? Create a visual essay from newspaper and magazine clippings. Write captions to explain your solution.

Background

Young teens tend to see things in all-or-nothing terms. They may think that any method of reducing pollution from cars should be adopted and enforced. Help students appreciate that most methods of reducing pollution from cars have drawbacks by citing these two examples.

Catalytic converters convert unburned hydrocarbons in car exhaust into nonpoisonous gases. These devices have been required by law for many years on all new cars sold in the United States. However, catalytic converters also result in a higher production of sulfuric acid, which contributes to acid rain.

Cars that are more fuel-efficient burn less gas and produce fewer pollutants per mile driven. However, the number of cars on the road and the number of miles people drive every year are both increasing.

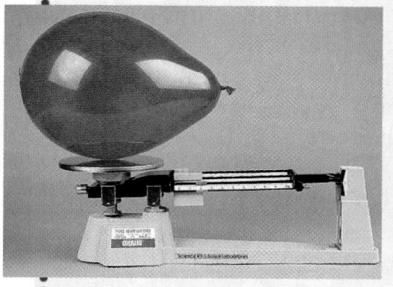

DISCOVER · ACTIVITY · · ·

Does Air Have Mass?

1. Use a balance to find the mass of a deflated balloon.

2. Blow up the balloon and tie the neck closed. Do you think the mass of the inflated balloon will differ from the mass of the deflated balloon?

3. Find the mass of the inflated balloon. Compare this mass to the mass of the deflated balloon. Was your prediction correct?

Think It Over

Drawing Conclusions Did the mass of the balloon change after it was inflated? What can you conclude about whether air has mass?

O ne of the best parts of eating roasted peanuts is opening the jar. When a jar of peanuts is "vacuum packed," most of the air is pumped out, creating low pressure inside. When you break the seal, the "whoosh" you hear is air from the outside rushing into the jar. The "whoosh" is the result of a difference in pressure between the outside of the jar and the inside.

Properties of Air

It may seem to you that air has no mass. However, air consists of atoms and molecules, which have mass. So air must have mass. **Because air has mass, it also has other properties, including density and pressure.**

Density The amount of mass in a given volume of air is its **density**. You can calculate density by dividing mass by volume.

$$\text{Density} = \frac{\text{Mass}}{\text{Volume}}$$

If there are more molecules in a given volume of air, the density is greater. If there are fewer molecules, the density decreases.

Pressure The force pushing on an area or surface is known as **pressure**. A denser substance has more mass per unit volume than a less dense one. So denser air exerts more pressure than less dense air.

To understand pressure, think of carrying a heavy backpack. The weight presses the straps into your shoulders just as the pack does to the hiker in the photo.

> ### GUIDE FOR READING
>
> ◆ What are some of the properties of air?
>
> ◆ What instruments are used to measure air pressure?
>
> ◆ How does increasing altitude affect air pressure and density?
>
> *Reading Tip* As you read this section, use the headings to make an outline about air pressure.

523

READING STRATEGIES

Reading Tip Suggest to students that they summarize the main points under each heading in a few words and add these to their outline. Student outlines might begin as follows:
I. Properties of Air
   A. Density
   B. Pressure
II. Measuring Air Pressure
   A. Mercury Barometer

Program Resources

◆ **Unit 5 Resources** 16-3 Lesson Plan, p. 17; 16-3 Section Summary, p. 18

◆ **Guided Reading and Study Workbook** Section 16-3

SECTION
3 Air Pressure

Objectives

After completing the lesson, students will be able to
◆ identify some of the properties of air;
◆ name instruments that are used to measure air pressure;
◆ explain how increasing altitude affects air pressure and density.

Key Terms density, pressure, air pressure, barometer, mercury barometer, aneroid barometer, altitude

1 Engage/Explore

Activating Prior Knowledge

Introduce students to the concept of air pressure by asking: **Did your ears ever "pop" when you rode in an elevator or airplane?** (*Many students probably have had this experience.*) Explain that as one goes higher, the pressure of the air outside the body decreases while the pressure of the air inside the body, including the ears, stays the same. The popping sensation is air escaping from inside the ears into the throat to even out the pressure. Tell students they will learn more about air pressure and other properties of air in this section.

· · · · · · · · · DISCOVER · · · · · · · ·

Skills Focus drawing conclusions
Materials *balance, balloon*
Time 10 minutes
Tips You may want to review how to use the balance before students begin the activity. The larger the balloon, the greater the difference in mass will be. Inflatable balls may be substituted for balloons.
Expected Outcome The balloon should have a greater mass after it is inflated.
Think It Over Students should say that the mass of the balloon increased after it was inflated and conclude from this that air has mass.

2 Facilitate

Properties of Air

Including All Students

Materials *two sink plungers*
Time 5 minutes

To help students appreciate how much pressure air exerts, give pairs of students two sink plungers and show them how to put the plungers together by matching the ends. Then have the students try to pull the plungers apart. Relate this to air pressure by asking: **Why are the plungers hard to pull apart?** *(Because air is pressing on the outside of the two plungers and holding them together)*
learning modality: kinesthetic

Measuring Air Pressure

Building Inquiry Skills: Predicting

Reinforce students' understanding of how a mercury barometer works by asking: **Why must there be a vacuum in the tube of a mercury barometer?** *(So the mercury can rise inside the tube)* **What do you predict would happen if the tube was filled with air?** *(The column of mercury would not rise as high because of the pressure from the air in the tube. The barometer would give an incorrect reading.)* **learning modality: verbal**

Real-Life Learning

Materials *copies of newspaper weather reports*
Time 15 minutes

Help students appreciate how barometer readings relate to weather. First, explain that the average air pressure worldwide is 29.9212 inches. A drop of less than an inch can be a sign of a major storm, and a rise of less than an inch a sign of fair weather. Then show students newspaper weather reports for several different days. Have them observe how changes in barometric pressure are related to weather conditions. **learning modality: logical/mathematical**

524

When you take off a backpack, it feels as if all the pressure has been taken off your shoulders. But has it? The weight of the column of air above you remains, as shown in Figure 9.

Air pressure is the result of the weight of a column of air pushing down on an area. The weight of the column of air above your desk is about the same as the weight of a large school bus! So why doesn't air pressure crush your desk? The reason is that the molecules in air push in all directions—down, up, and sideways. So the air pushing down on the top of your desk is balanced by the air pushing up on the bottom of the desk.

Figure 9 There is a column of air above you all the time. The weight of the air in the atmosphere causes air pressure.

Measuring Air Pressure

Have you ever heard a weather report say that the air pressure is falling? Falling air pressure usually indicates that a storm is approaching. Rising air pressure usually means that the weather is clearing. A **barometer** (buh RAHM uh tur) is an instrument that is used to measure changes in air pressure. **There are two kinds of barometers: mercury barometers and aneroid barometers.**

Mercury Barometers The first barometers invented were mercury barometers. Figure 10 shows how a mercury barometer works. A **mercury barometer** consists of a glass tube open at the bottom end and partially filled with mercury. The space in the tube above the mercury is almost a vacuum—it contains no air. The open end of the tube rests in a dish of mercury. The air pressure pushing down on the surface of the mercury in the dish is equal to the

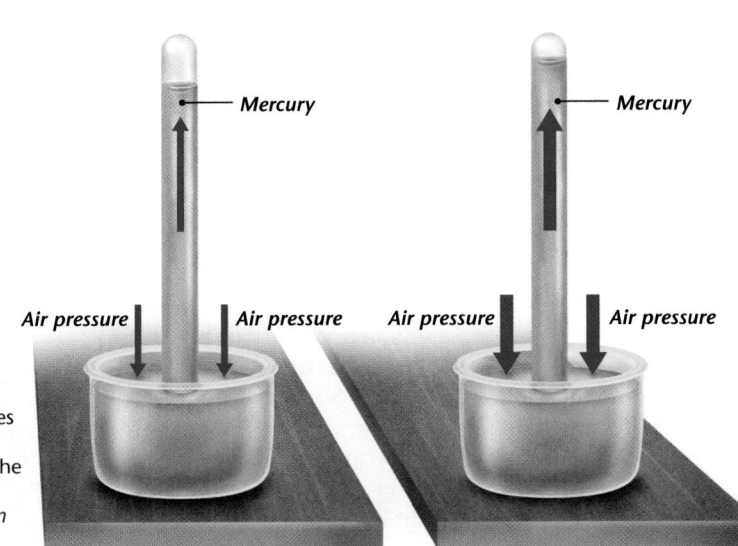

Figure 10 Air pressure pushes down on the surface of the mercury in the dish, causing the mercury in the tube to rise. *Predicting What happens when the air pressure increases?*

524

Background

History of Science The first mercury barometer was invented in 1643 by an Italian physicist named Evangelista Torricelli. Torricelli was studying why liquids rise only to a certain height in a column. Because mercury is so heavy, he thought it would rise to a lower height than water and be more convenient to study. He filled a long glass tube with mercury, blocked the open end with his finger, and turned the tube upside down in a container of mercury. The mercury in the glass tube went down to about 76 cm. Torricelli experimented with different-sized tubes, but the height of the mercury stayed the same. From this Torricelli concluded that the height of the mercury in the tube was directly related to the pressure of the air on the mercury in the container. Thus, he had invented a way to measure air pressure.

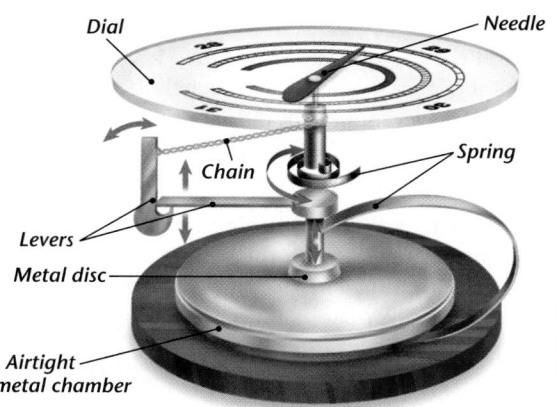

Dial — Needle — Spring — Chain — Levers — Metal disc — Airtight metal chamber

Figure 11 Changes in air pressure cause the walls of the airtight metal chamber to flex in and out. The needle on the dial indicates the air pressure.

weight of the column of mercury in the tube. At sea level the mercury column is about 76 centimeters high, on average.

When the air pressure increases, it presses down more on the surface of the mercury. Greater air pressure forces the column of mercury higher. What will happen to the column of mercury if the air pressure decreases? The column will fall.

Aneroid Barometers If you have a barometer on a desk or wall at home, it is probably an aneroid barometer. The word *aneroid* means "without liquid." An **aneroid barometer** (AN uh royd) has an airtight metal chamber, as shown in Figure 11. The metal chamber is sensitive to changes in air pressure. When air pressure increases, the thin walls of the chamber are pushed in. When the pressure drops, the walls bulge out. The chamber is connected to a dial by a series of springs and levers. As the shape of the chamber changes, the needle on the dial moves.

Aneroid barometers are smaller than mercury barometers and don't contain a liquid. Therefore, they are portable and often more practical for uses such as airplane instrument panels.

Units of Air Pressure Weather reports use several different units for air pressure. Most weather reports for the general public use inches of mercury. For example, if the column of mercury in a mercury barometer is 30 inches high, the air pressure is "30 inches of mercury" or just "30 inches."

National Weather Service maps indicate air pressure in millibars. One inch of mercury equals approximately 33.87 millibars, so 30 inches of mercury is approximately equal to 1,016 millibars.

✓ *Checkpoint* *Name two common units used to measure air pressure.*

Soda-Bottle Barometer

Here's how to build a device that shows changes in air pressure.

1. Fill a 2-liter soda bottle one-half full with water.

2. Lower a long straw into the bottle so that the end of the straw is in the water. Seal the mouth of the bottle around the straw with modeling clay.

3. Squeeze the sides of the bottle. What happens to the level of the water in the straw?

4. Let go of the sides of the bottle. Watch the level of the water in the straw.

Inferring Explain your results in terms of air pressure.

Materials *calculator*
Time 10 minutes

Invite students who need additional challenges to do this activity. It will give them a better appreciation of how air pressure is measured. First, tell students that if you laid a quarter on a table, it would exert a pressure of 0.00013 kg per cm². Then say that the pressure exerted by the atmosphere at sea level is 1.03 kg per cm². Ask: **How many quarters would you need to stack on top of each other for the quarters to exert the same pressure as the air at sea level?** *(1.03 kg ÷ 0.00013 kg = 7,923)* **If six quarters are about 1 cm thick, how high would the stack of quarters be?** *(7,923 ÷ 6 = 1,321 cm, or about 1.3 km)* **learning modality: logical/mathematical**

Skills Focus inferring
Materials *2-liter soda bottle, water, long straw, modeling clay*
Time 15 minutes
Tips Before students seal the mouth of the bottle with clay, make sure the straw is in the water but not touching the bottom of the bottle.
Expected Outcome When students squeeze the sides of the bottle, the water level rises in the straw. When they let go of the sides, the water level falls in the straw. Students should infer that the water rises in the straw because air pressure increases in the bottle when the sides of the bottle are squeezed.
Extend Ask: **What do you think would happen if you heated the air in the bottle?** *(The air would expand and make the water rise in the straw.)* **learning modality: logical/mathematical**

Answers to Self-Assessment

Caption Question

Figure 10 When the air pressure increases, the column of mercury in the tube of a mercury barometer goes up.

✓ *Checkpoint*

Two common units used to measure air pressure are inches and millibars.

Ongoing Assessment

Skills Check Challenge students to make a table comparing and contrasting mercury barometers and aneroid barometers.

Working Under Pressure

Preparing for Inquiry

Key Concept A flexible wall of a sealed container will expand and contract with changes in the pressure of the outside air.

Skills Objectives Students will be able to
- measure air pressure with a simple barometer that they construct;
- observe daily weather conditions;
- infer from their data the kinds of weather conditions that are associated with high and low air pressure.

Time 40 minutes the first day; 10 minutes each day for the next two days

Advance Planning You may wish to have students work in pairs for this activity, because it is easier for two people to assemble the barometer. If possible, bring a commercial aneroid barometer to class to familiarize students with air pressure readings before they begin the activity. You may want to leave the barometer so students can compare their readings with the readings on the commercial barometer. When students record weather conditions during the lab, at a minimum they should record whether the sky is cloudy or fair. You may want them to record additional factors, including temperature. If so, place an outdoor thermometer in a shady location where students can see it from the classroom.

Alternative Materials Students can use beakers instead of wide-mouthed glass jars, rubber dental dams instead of balloons, and rulers instead of cardboard strips.

Guiding Inquiry

Invitation Show students a commercial aneroid barometer and then ask: **How does the aneroid barometer work?** (*Changes in air pressure cause slight movements in or out of the walls of a box, and these movements are measured on a scale.*) Tell students that they will make a barometer that works the same way as a commercial aneroid barometer. However, their barometer will be less accurate.

Increasing Altitude

The air pressure at the top of Alaska's Mount McKinley—more than 6 kilometers above sea level—is less than half the air pressure at sea level. **Altitude,** or elevation, is the distance above sea level, the average level of the surface of the oceans. **Air pressure decreases as altitude increases. As air pressure decreases, so does density.**

Altitude Affects Air Pressure Imagine a stack of ten books. Which book has more weight on it, the second book from the top or the book at the bottom? The second book from the top has only the weight of one book on top of it. The book at the bottom

Skills Lab

Measuring

Working Under Pressure

Air pressure changes are related to changing weather conditions. In this lab, you will build and use your own barometer to measure air pressure.

Problem

How can a barometer detect changes in air pressure?

Materials

modeling clay	scissors
white glue	tape
pencil	wide-mouthed glass jar
metric ruler	rubber band

large rubber balloon
drinking straw, 12–15 cm long
cardboard strip, 10 cm x 25 cm

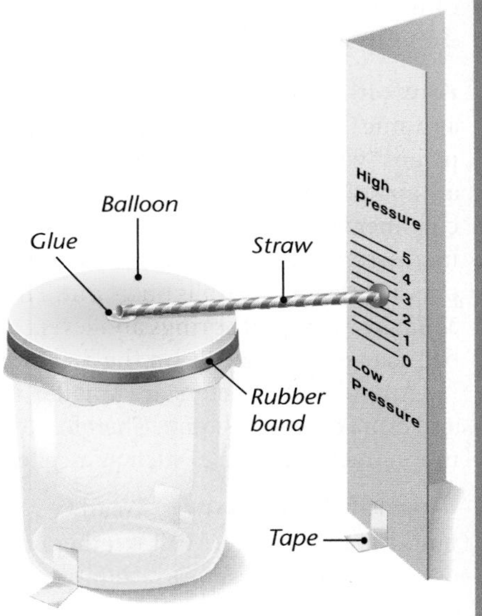

Procedure

1. Cut off the narrow opening of the balloon.
2. Fold the edges of the balloon outward. Carefully stretch the balloon over the open end of the glass jar. Use a rubber band to hold the balloon on the rim of the glass jar.
3. Place a small amount of glue on the center of the balloon top. Attach one end of the straw to the glue. Allow the other end to extend several centimeters beyond the edge of the glass jar. This is your pointer.

Diagram labels: Glue, Balloon, Straw, High Pressure, 5 4 3 2 1 0, Low Pressure, Rubber band, Tape

526

Introducing the Procedure

Have students read the entire procedure. Then ask: **What part of your barometer is like the flexible sides of the metal box in a commercial aneroid barometer?** (*The balloon stretched across the jar*) Point out that the balloon will expand when the air pressure falls. Ask: **Why does the expanding balloon make the pointer in your barometer fall?** (*Students may think that the pointer should rise, not fall, as the balloon expands.*) Explain that the pointer resting on the jar is like a seesaw. The rim of the jar acts like a fulcrum, and the clay weights down the free end of the straw. The free end falls when the expanding balloon causes the other end of the straw to rise.

Troubleshooting the Experiment
- Before students cut their balloon, suggest they inflate it to stretch the rubber.
- Caution students to avoid making holes in the balloon when they cut it. Once the balloon is in place, they should make sure it does not leak air.

of the stack has the weight of all the other books pressing on it.

Air at sea level is like the bottom book. Recall that air pressure is the weight of the column of air pushing down on an area. Sea-level air has the weight of the whole atmosphere pressing on it. So air pressure is greatest at sea level. Air near the top of the atmosphere is like the second book from the top. There, the air has less weight pressing on it, and thus has lower air pressure.

DATA TABLE

Date and Time	Air Pressure	Weather Conditions

4. While the glue dries, fold the cardboard strip lengthwise and draw a scale along the edge with marks 0.5 cm apart. Write "High pressure" at the top of your scale and "Low pressure" at the bottom.
5. After the glue dries, add a pea-sized piece of modeling clay to the end of the pointer. Place your barometer and its scale in a location that is as free from temperature changes as possible. Arrange the scale and the barometer as shown in the diagram. Note that the pointer of the straw must just reach the cardboard strip.
6. Tape both the scale and the barometer to a surface so they do not move during your experiment.

7. In your notebook, make a data table like the one at the left. Record the date and time. Note the level of the straw on the cardboard strip.
8. Check the barometer twice a day. Record your observations in your data table.
9. Record the weather conditions for each day.

Analyze and Conclude

1. What change in atmospheric conditions must occur to cause the free end of the straw to rise? What change must occur for it to fall?
2. According to your observations, what kind of weather is usually associated with high air pressure? With low air pressure?
3. If the balloon had a tiny hole in it, what would happen to the accuracy of your barometer?
4. **Think About It** What effect, if any, would a great temperature change have on the accuracy of your barometer?

More to Explore

Compare changes in air pressure shown by your barometer with high and low air pressure readings shown on newspaper weather maps during the same time period. How do your readings compare with the readings in the newspapers?

Sample Data Table

Date and Time	Air Pressure	Weather Conditions
April 2, 10:00 A.M.	1	rainy, 24°C
April 2, 2:00 P.M.	2	cloudy, 23°C
April 4, 10:00 A.M.	4	sunny, 18°C
April 4, 2:00 P.M.	5	sunny, 19°C

Program Resources

◆ **Unit 5 Resources** Skills Lab blackline masters, pp. 28–29

Media and Technology

 Lab Activity Videotape
Tape 4

Expected Outcome

When the air pressure outside is low, the higher air pressure inside the jar pushes up on the balloon, causing the pointer to fall. When the air pressure outside is high, it pushes down on the balloon, causing the pointer to rise. Low air pressure is likely to be followed by cloudy or even stormy weather conditions. High air pressure is likely to be followed by fair weather conditions.

Analyze and Conclude

1. Air pressure must rise for the free end of the straw to rise. Air pressure must fall for the free end of the straw to fall.
2. Clear, dry weather usually is associated with high air pressure. Cloudy, wet, or stormy weather usually is associated with low air pressure.
3. A tiny hole in the balloon would cause the barometer not to work because air would leak in or out to equalize the air pressure inside and outside the jar.
4. **Think About It** A great increase in temperature would cause the air inside the barometer to expand and a large decrease in temperature would cause it to contract, affecting the readings.

Extending the Inquiry

More to Explore Students' air pressure readings should agree in general with high and low air pressure readings given in the newspaper. If the readings do not agree, it may be because students' barometers are faulty. Balloons may leak air or not be stretchy enough, or the lumps of clay may be too large. Also, students' barometers are not likely to be accurate enough to reflect minor fluctuations in air pressure. In addition, the readings reported in the newspaper may have been taken at a different time of day when air pressure was lower or higher.

Safety

In Step 2, to reduce chances of the jar breaking, suggest that one student hold the jar while the other stretches the balloon and rubber band over it. Review the safety guidelines in Appendix A.

Increasing Altitude

 Integrating Life Science

People who live at high altitudes have developed adaptations to the low pressure and density of oxygen in the air around them. Ask: **What kinds of adaptations would allow people to live successfully at high altitudes?** *(A larger chest and lungs would allow a person to take in more air.)* **learning modality: logical/mathematical**

3 Assess

Section 3 Review Answers

1. It increases its pressure.
2. Air presses down on the mercury in the bottom of the barometer, and this forces the mercury up into the sealed tube. The greater the air pressure, the higher the mercury rises and the higher the air pressure reading.
3. Because it has low pressure and density, there are fewer oxygen molecules in each lungful of air.
4. You would expect to see the air pressure increase above the value for sea level, because the column of air pressing down on the barometer would be taller.

Materials *glass, tap water, piece of heavy cardboard*

Students should fill the glass until the level of water bulges over the rim and then slide the cardboard *completely* over the rim, being careful not to let any air bubbles under the cardboard. Some water may overflow the glass, so students should do this over a sink.

Performance Assessment

Skills Check Call on volunteers to infer why an inflated balloon flies around the room when it is released. *(The force of the air escaping the balloon propels the balloon.)*

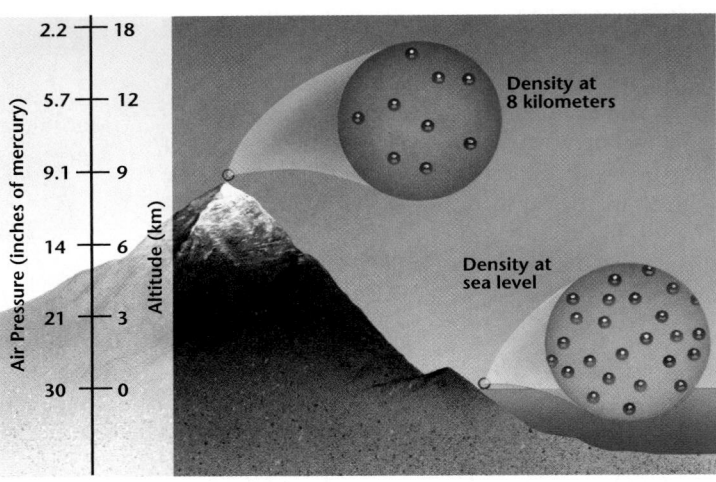

Figure 12 The density of air decreases as altitude increases. Air at sea level has more gas molecules in each cubic meter than air at the top of a mountain.

Altitude Also Affects Density If you were near the top

 INTEGRATING LIFE SCIENCE of Mount McKinley and tried to run, you would get out of breath quickly. Why would you have difficulty breathing at high altitudes?

As you go up through the atmosphere, the air pressure decreases. As air pressure decreases, the density of the air decreases. So density decreases as altitude increases, as shown in Figure 12.

Whether air is at sea level or at 6 kilometers above sea level, the air still contains 21 percent oxygen. However, since the air is less dense at a high altitude, there are fewer oxygen molecules to breathe in each cubic meter of air than there are at sea level. You are taking in less oxygen with each breath. That is why you get out of breath quickly.

Section 3 Review

1. How does increasing the density of a gas affect its pressure?
2. Describe how a mercury barometer measures air pressure.
3. Why is the air at the top of a mountain hard to breathe?
4. **Thinking Critically** **Predicting** What changes in air pressure would you expect to see if you carried a barometer down a mine shaft? Explain.

Science at Home

Here's how you can show your family that air has pressure. Fill a glass with water. Place a piece of heavy cardboard over the top of the glass. Hold the cardboard in place with one hand as you turn the glass upside down. **CAUTION:** *Be sure the cardboard does not bend.* Now remove your hand from the cardboard. What happens? Explain to your family that the cardboard doesn't fall because the air pressure pushing up on it is greater than the weight of the water pushing down.

Media and Technology

 Transparencies "Density of Air at Two Altitudes," Transparency 63

 Concept Videotape Library *Adventures, Tape 4,* "Racing Hot Air Balloons"

Program Resources

◆ **Unit 5 Resources** 16-3 Review and Reinforce, p. 19; 16-3 Enrich, p. 20

SECTION 4 Layers of the Atmosphere

DISCOVER ·············· ACTIVITY ····

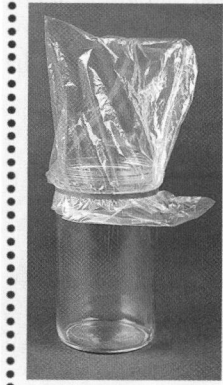

Is Air There?

1. Use a heavy rubber band to tightly secure a plastic bag over the top of a wide-mouthed jar.

2. Gently try to push the bag into the jar. What happens? Is the air pressure higher inside or outside of the bag?

3. Remove the rubber band and line the inside of the jar with the plastic bag. Use the rubber band to tightly secure the edges of the bag over the rim of the jar.

4. Gently try to pull the bag out of the jar with your fingertips. What happens? Is the air pressure higher inside or outside of the bag?

Think It Over

Predicting Explain your observations in terms of air pressure. How do you think differences in air pressure would affect a weather balloon as it traveled up through the atmosphere?

I magine taking a trip upward into the atmosphere in a hot-air balloon. You begin on a warm beach near the ocean, at an altitude of 0 kilometers.

You hear a roar as the balloon's pilot turns up the burner to heat the air in the balloon. The balloon begins to rise, and Earth's surface gets farther and farther away. As the balloon rises to an altitude of 3 kilometers, you realize that the air is getting colder. As you continue to rise, the air gets colder and colder. At 6 kilometers you begin to have trouble breathing. The air is becoming less dense. It's time to go back down.

What if you could have continued your balloon ride up through the atmosphere? As you rose farther up through the atmosphere, the air pressure and temperature would change dramatically. **The four main layers of the atmosphere are classified according to changes in temperature. These layers are the troposphere, the stratosphere, the mesosphere, and the thermosphere.**

The Troposphere

You live in the inner, or lowest, layer of Earth's atmosphere, the **troposphere** (TROH puh sfeer). *Tropo-* means "turning" or "changing"; conditions in the troposphere are more variable than in the other layers. The troposphere is where Earth's weather occurs.

GUIDE FOR READING

◆ What are the characteristics of the main layers of the atmosphere?

Reading Tip Before you read, preview *Exploring Layers of the Atmosphere.* Make a list of unfamiliar words. Look for the meanings of these words as you read.

Chapter 16 **529**

READING STRATEGIES

Reading Tip Students lists might include the names of the layers of the atmosphere, as well as terms such as *meteoroid* and *aurora borealis*. Suggest that, as they read and encounter the words on their list, students record their meanings.

Program Resources

◆ **Unit 5 Resources** 16-4 Lesson Plan, p. 21; 16-4 Section Summary, p. 22
◆ **Guided Reading and Study Workbook** Section 16-4

Media and Technology

 **Transparencies** "Layers of the Atmosphere," Transparency 64

SECTION 4 Layers of the Atmosphere

Objective

After completing this lesson, students will be able to
◆ describe the characteristics of the main layers of the atmosphere.

Key Terms troposphere, stratosphere, mesosphere, thermosphere, ionosphere, aurora borealis, exosphere

1 Engage/Explore

Activating Prior Knowledge

Ask: **Did you ever see a shooting star?** *(Most students probably will say yes.)* **What is a shooting star?** *(A meteor burning up because of friction as it falls through Earth's atmosphere)* Point out that most shooting stars are visible from about 50 to 80 km above Earth in a layer of the atmosphere called the mesosphere. This layer protects us from being bombarded by shooting stars and other space debris. The mesosphere is just one of four major layers of the atmosphere students will read about in this section.

········ **DISCOVER** ········

Skills Focus predicting **ACTIVITY**
Materials *heavy rubber band, plastic bag, wide-mouthed glass jar*
Time 10 minutes
Tips Make sure the rubber band is tight and the plastic bag does not have holes in it. Caution students to push gently on the bag to avoid breaking the bag or the jar.
Expected Outcome Students should find it difficult to push the bag into or pull it out of the jar.
Think It Over Trying to push the bag into the jar decreases the volume and increases the air pressure inside the jar. Trying to pull the bag out of the jar increases the volume and decreases the air pressure inside the jar. As a weather balloon traveled up, it would expand until it burst as the air pressure outside the balloon became lower than the air pressure inside.

2 Facilitate

The Troposphere

Building Inquiry Skills: Graphing

Challenge students to calculate the temperature for every 1,000 m above Earth's surface in the troposphere, starting at sea level and ending at 10,000 m. They should assume that the temperature is 15.0°C at sea level and decreases 6.5 Celsius degrees for each 1,000-m increase in altitude. Then have students draw a graph that shows the relationship between altitude and temperature in the troposphere. **learning modality: logical/mathematical**

The Stratosphere

Addressing Naive Conceptions

In Section 2, students read that ozone is a harmful chemical in smog. In this section, they read that ozone is a natural component of the atmosphere that protects Earth from solar radiation. Students may wonder if ozone is harmful or not. Explain that the ozone in the stratosphere absorbs, and thus protects us from, too much sunlight. Ozone in this layer occurs naturally. However, ozone in the troposphere harms our health and contributes to photochemical smog. Ozone in this layer is caused by pollution. **limited English proficiency**

The Mesosphere

Building Inquiry Skills: Inferring

Challenge students to explain why there is a temperature reversal between the stratosphere and mesosphere. Ask: **Why is the mesosphere generally colder than the stratosphere?** (*Because it contains no ozone molecules to absorb solar radiation and convert the radiation into heat*) **learning modality: logical/ mathematical**

Figure 13 This weather balloon will carry a package of instruments to measure weather conditions high in the atmosphere. *Applying Concepts Which is the first layer of the atmosphere the balloon passes through on its way up?*

Although hot-air balloons cannot travel very high into the troposphere, other types of balloons can. To measure weather conditions, scientists launch weather balloons that carry instruments up into the atmosphere. The balloons are not fully inflated before they are launched. Recall that air pressure decreases as you rise through the atmosphere. Leaving the balloon only partly inflated gives the gas inside the balloon room to expand as the air pressure outside the balloon decreases.

The depth of the troposphere varies from more than 16 kilometers above the equator to less than 9 kilometers above the North and South Poles. Even though it is the shallowest layer of the atmosphere, the troposphere contains almost all of the mass of the atmosphere.

As altitude increases in the troposphere, the temperature decreases. On average, for every 1-kilometer increase in altitude the air gets about 6.5 Celsius degrees cooler. At the top of the troposphere, the temperature stops decreasing and stays constant at about −60°C. Water here forms thin, feathery clouds of ice.

☑ *Checkpoint* *Why are clouds at the top of the troposphere made of ice crystals instead of drops of water?*

The Stratosphere

The **stratosphere** extends from the top of the troposphere to about 50 kilometers above Earth's surface. *Strato-* is similar to *stratum*, which means "layer" or "spreading out."

The lower stratosphere is cold, about −60°C. You might be surprised to find out that the upper stratosphere is warmer than the lower stratosphere. Why is this? The upper stratosphere contains a layer of ozone, the three-atom form of oxygen. When the ozone in the stratosphere absorbs energy from the sun, the energy is converted into heat, warming the air.

As a weather balloon rises through the stratosphere, the air pressure outside the balloon continues to decrease. The volume of the balloon increases. Finally, the balloon bursts, and the instrument package falls back to Earth's surface.

The Mesosphere

Above the stratosphere, a drop in temperature marks the beginning of the next layer, the **mesosphere.** *Meso-* means "middle," so the mesosphere is the middle layer of the atmosphere. The mesosphere begins 50 kilometers above Earth's surface and ends at 80 kilometers. In the outer mesosphere temperatures approach −90°C.

Background

Facts and Figures You may wish to share the following facts and figures about the mesosphere with students.

◆ The mesosphere is the coldest part of the atmosphere. Temperatures there reach lows that are as cold as the lowest temperatures ever recorded anywhere on Earth.

◆ Oddly, air temperatures in the mesosphere are colder in summer than in winter. Temperatures there also are colder over the equator than over the North and South poles.

◆ The clouds that form in the mesosphere are unlike any other clouds in the atmosphere. They are formed of ice crystals and are called noctilucent clouds because they are visible only at night.

EXPLORING Layers of the Atmosphere

The atmosphere is divided into four layers: the troposphere, the stratosphere, the mesosphere, and the thermosphere. The thermosphere is further divided into the ionosphere and the exosphere.

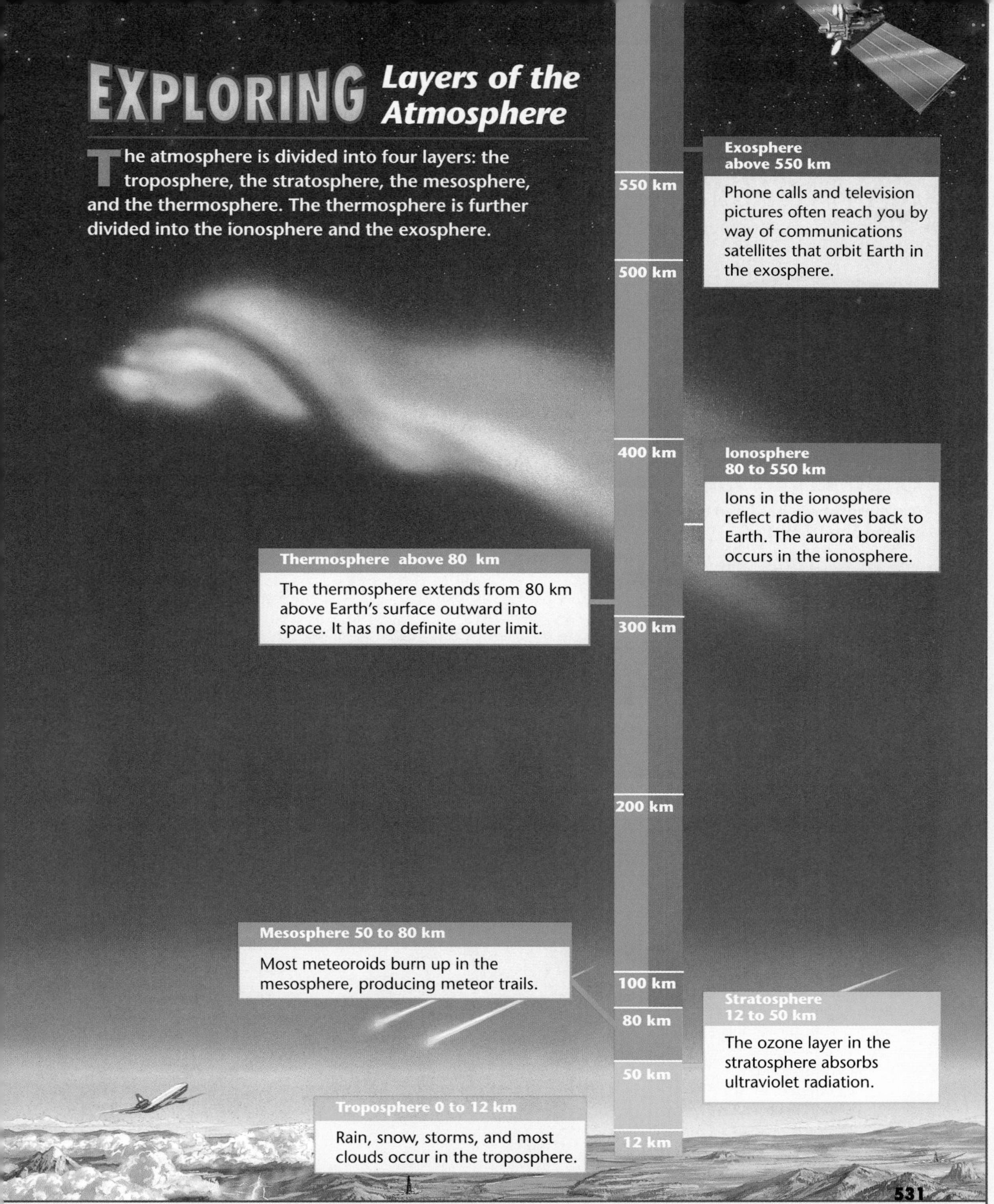

550 km
500 km
400 km
300 km
200 km
100 km
80 km
50 km
12 km
Exosphere above 550 km
Phone calls and television pictures often reach you by way of communications satellites that orbit Earth in the exosphere.
Ionosphere 80 to 550 km
Ions in the ionosphere reflect radio waves back to Earth. The aurora borealis occurs in the ionosphere.
Thermosphere above 80 km
The thermosphere extends from 80 km above Earth's surface outward into space. It has no definite outer limit.
Mesosphere 50 to 80 km
Most meteoroids burn up in the mesosphere, producing meteor trails.
Stratosphere 12 to 50 km
The ozone layer in the stratosphere absorbs ultraviolet radiation.
Troposphere 0 to 12 km
Rain, snow, storms, and most clouds occur in the troposphere.

EXPLORING

Layers of the Atmosphere

Materials *posterboard, colored markers, index cards, buttons and other small objects for game pieces*
Time 30 minutes

ACTIVITY

Divide the class into groups and have each group use the information presented in the feature to create a board game. The object of the game should be to get from the ground to the top of the atmosphere. Reaching the objective might involve overcoming various obstacles in the different layers of the atmosphere, such as clouds and storms in the troposphere, very high temperatures in the stratosphere, meteoroids in the mesosphere, electrically charged ions in the ionosphere, and orbiting satellites in the exosphere. To advance through the layers of the atmosphere, players might be required to correctly answer questions about each layer, such as the layer's temperature or height above Earth's surface. Group members should work together to brainstorm the objectives and rules of the game. The actual work of constructing the game board and other parts of the game should be divided up among individual group members. Suggest that the groups exchange games and try them out. **cooperative learning**

Media and Technology

Concept Videotape Library
Adventures, Tape 4, "A Trip Through the Earth"

Answers to Self-Assessment

Caption Question

Figure 13 The first layer is the troposphere.

Checkpoint

Because the temperature at that altitude is always below the freezing point of water

Ongoing Assessment

Writing Challenge students to write a short story describing their imaginary ascent up through the troposphere and stratosphere in a hydrogen balloon. They should describe the conditions they pass through in each layer.

Portfolio Students can save their stories in their portfolios.

The Mesosphere, continued

Integrating Space Science

Stress that the mesosphere protects Earth from meteoroids that are pulled toward the planet by gravity. Tell students that the moon has gravity, too, but no atmosphere to protect it from meteoroids. As a result, meteoroids crash on the moon's surface, forming large depressions called craters. Challenge students to draw labeled diagrams showing what happens to meteoroids that fall toward the moon as compared with those that fall toward Earth.
limited English proficiency

SCIENCE & History

Point out that exploring the atmosphere is difficult because it requires scientists or their instruments to reach high altitudes. Ask: **What are some ways explorers of the atmosphere have made scientific observations at high altitudes?** (*By climbing to the tops of mountains, ascending in hydrogen balloons, flying kites, and attaching instruments to balloons and satellites*)
What have these explorers learned through these means? (*That air pressure decreases with altitude, that lightning is a form of electricity, how the sun influences the atmosphere, and the temperature, air pressure, and humidity at various altitudes*)

In Your Journal Ask volunteers to read their paragraphs aloud to the class. The items students would take with them should show they understand how the atmosphere changes with altitude. For example, warm clothing would be necessary above an altitude of just a few kilometers because temperature declines steadily with increasing altitude. Also, a supply of oxygen would be needed above about 7 km. Instruments should include at least a thermometer for measuring changes in temperature and a barometer for measuring changes in air pressure.
learning modality: verbal

INTEGRATING SPACE SCIENCE If you watch a shooting star streak across the night sky, you are seeing a meteoroid burn up as it enters the mesosphere. The mesosphere protects Earth's surface from being hit by most meteoroids, which are chunks of stone and metal from space. What you see as a shooting star, or meteor, is the trail of hot, glowing gases the burning meteoroid leaves behind.

☑ *Checkpoint* **What is the depth of the mesosphere?**

The Thermosphere

Near the top of the atmosphere, the air is very thin. The air 80 kilometers above Earth's surface is only about 0.001 percent as dense as the air at sea level. It's as though you took a cubic

SCIENCE & History

Explorers of the Atmosphere

The atmosphere has been explored from the ground and from space.

1746
Franklin's Experiment with Electricity

American statesman and inventor Benjamin Franklin and some friends in Philadelphia experimented with electricity in the atmosphere. To demonstrate that lightning is a form of electricity, Franklin flew a kite in a thunderstorm. However, Franklin did not hold the kite string in his hand, as this historical print shows.

| 1600 | 1700 | 1800 |

1643
Torricelli Invents the Barometer

Italian physicist and mathematician Evangelista Torricelli improved existing scientific instruments and invented some new ones. In 1643 he invented the barometer, using a column of mercury 1.2 meters high.

1804
Gay-Lussac Studies the Upper Troposphere

French chemist Joseph-Louis Gay-Lussac ascended to a height of about 7 kilometers in a hydrogen balloon to study the upper troposphere. Gay-Lussac studied pressure, temperature, and humidity.

532

Background

Facts and Figures At sea level, an air molecule can travel just a fraction of a centimeter before colliding with another, whereas in the upper thermosphere it can travel as far as 10 km before colliding with another. Because of their very high temperatures, air molecules in the upper thermosphere move at speeds of up to 40,000 km per hour, allowing many to escape into outer space. Therefore, where the thermosphere ends and outer space begins is arbitrary. Air molecules become farther and farther apart as you travel higher above Earth's surface until, somewhere thousands of kilometers above the surface, there are no more air molecules.

meter of air at sea level and expanded it into 100,000 cubic meters at the top of the mesosphere. The outermost layer of the atmosphere, the **thermosphere**, extends from 80 kilometers above Earth's surface outward into space. It has no definite outer limit. The atmosphere does not end suddenly at the outer edge of the thermosphere. Gas atoms and molecules there are so far apart that the air blends gradually with outer space.

The *thermo-* in thermosphere means "heat." Even though the air in the thermosphere is thin, it is very hot, up to 1,800°C. The temperature in the thermosphere is actually higher than the temperature in a furnace used to make steel! But why is the thermosphere so hot? Energy coming from the sun strikes the thermosphere first. Nitrogen and oxygen molecules convert energy from the sun into heat.

In Your Journal

Imagine you were one of the first people to go up into the atmosphere in a balloon. What would you need to take? Find out what the early explorers took with them in their balloons. Write at least two paragraphs about what you would take, and why.

1931
Piccard Explores the Stratosphere

Swiss-Belgian physicist Auguste Piccard made the first ascent into the stratosphere. He reached a height of about 16 kilometers in an airtight cabin attached to a huge hydrogen balloon. Piccard is shown here with the cabin.

1900   **2000**

1960
First Weather Satellite Launched

TIROS-1, the first weather satellite equipped with a camera to send data back to Earth, was put into orbit by the United States. As later weather satellites circled Earth, they observed cloud cover and recorded temperatures and air pressures in the atmosphere.

1994
Space Shuttle Investigates the Atmosphere

The NASA space shuttle *Atlantis* traveled to a height of 300 kilometers in the thermosphere. *Atlantis* carried the ATLAS–3 research program, which observed the sun's influence on the atmosphere.

Chapter 16 **533**

Answers to Self-Assessment

☑ *Checkpoint*

The mesosphere extends from 50 to 80 km above Earth's surface, so it has a depth of 30 km.

The Thermosphere

Building Inquiry Skills: Modeling

Time 5 minutes

Challenge a group of student volunteers to pretend they are atoms and molecules and to demonstrate the density and speed of atoms and molecules in the atmosphere, first at sea level, then in the thermosphere. *(For sea level, students should stand close together and move very slowly. For the thermosphere, they should stand as far apart as possible and move very quickly.)* Point out that the classroom would have to be much larger for them to be as far apart as atoms and molecules really are in the thermosphere. Ask: **How much larger would the classroom have to be?** *(Almost 100,000 times larger)* **learning modality: kinesthetic**

Including All Students

To help students whose native language is not English remember that the defining characteristic of the thermosphere is its high temperature, stress that the prefix *thermo-* means "heat." Ask: **What are some other words that start with this prefix?** *(thermometer, thermostat, thermal, thermos)* Have students explain how each of the terms is related to heat. **limited English proficiency**

Ongoing Assessment

Oral Presentation Call on students to describe density, temperature, and pressure of air in the thermosphere as compared with the troposphere. Call on other students to explain why the thermosphere has these characteristics.

Integrating Technology

Help students understand why satellites orbit Earth at such high altitudes. First point out that molecules in air create resistance that can slow down objects orbiting Earth. Then ask: **What happens to the density of molecules in air as you go higher above Earth's surface?** (*It decreases.*) **Why do you think satellites orbit Earth at such high altitudes?** (*The lower density of air molecules creates less resistance to slow down orbiting satellites.*) **learning modality: logical/ mathematical**

3 Assess

Section 4 Review Answers

1. Answers may vary. The troposphere is where weather occurs. The stratosphere contains the ozone layer. The mesosphere is where most meteoroids burn up. The thermosphere is very hot.
2. A shooting star, or meteor, is a trail of hot, glowing gas left by a meteoroid as it burns up in the atmosphere. You would see it in the mesosphere.
3. A glowing light display caused when energy from the sun causes gas molecules to become electrically charged; it occurs in the lower layer of the thermosphere.
4. Because it does not absorb much energy from the sun

Check Your Progress
CHAPTER PROJECT 16

Students may observe such trends in their observations as cooler temperatures after a storm and fair weather after an increase in air pressure. Which weather conditions changed most will depend partly on how precisely the variables were measured. Also, some weather variables, such as temperature and wind speed, have a greater range than others, including air pressure.

Figure 14 The aurora borealis, seen from Fairbanks, Alaska, creates a spectacular display in the night sky.

Despite the high temperature, however, you would not feel warm in the thermosphere. An ordinary thermometer would show a temperature well below 0°C. Why is that? Temperature is the average amount of energy of motion of each molecule of a substance. The gas molecules in the thermosphere move very rapidly, so the temperature is very high. However, the molecules are spaced far apart in the thin air. And there are not enough of them to collide with a thermometer and warm it very much. So an ordinary thermometer would not detect the molecules' energy.

The Ionosphere The thermosphere is divided into two layers. The lower layer of the thermosphere, called the **ionosphere** (eye AHN uh sfeer), begins 80 kilometers above the surface and ends at 550 kilometers. Energy from the sun causes gas molecules in the ionosphere to become electrically charged particles called ions. Radio waves bounce off ions in the ionosphere and then bounce back to Earth's surface.

The brilliant light displays of the **aurora borealis**—the Northern Lights—also occur in the ionosphere. The aurora borealis is caused by particles from the sun that enter the ionosphere near the North Pole. These particles strike oxygen and nitrogen atoms in the ionosphere, causing them to glow.

The Exosphere *Exo-* means "outer," so the **exosphere** is the *INTEGRATING TECHNOLOGY* outer layer of the thermosphere. The exosphere extends from 550 kilometers outward for thousands of kilometers. When you make a long-distance phone call or watch television, the signal may have traveled up to a satellite orbiting in the exosphere and then back down to your home. Satellites are also used for watching the world's weather and carrying telescopes that look deep into space.

Section 4 Review

1. Describe one characteristic of each of the four main layers of the atmosphere.
2. What is a shooting star? In which layer of the atmosphere would you see it?
3. What is the aurora borealis? In which layer of the atmosphere does it occur?
4. **Thinking Critically** **Drawing Conclusions** Why is the mesosphere the coldest part of the atmosphere?

Check Your Progress
CHAPTER PROJECT 16

At this point, review your weather log. What do you notice about the weather on one day that might allow you to predict the next day's weather? What weather conditions changed the most from day to day? Continue to record your observations and start thinking about how you will present them.

Background

Facts and Figures Another sphere around Earth, called the magnetosphere, extends above the atmosphere to more than 65,000 km above Earth's surface. It is a magnetic field that traps charged particles from the sun. The trapped particles follow the lines of magnetic force and bounce back and forth from one pole to the other, sometimes breaking through into the ionosphere to produce auroras.

Program Resources

◆ **Unit 5 Resources** 16-4 Review and Reinforce, p. 23; 16-4 Enrich, p. 24

SECTION 1 The Air Around You

Key Ideas

- Earth's atmosphere makes conditions on Earth suitable for living things.
- Earth's atmosphere is made up of molecules of nitrogen, oxygen, carbon dioxide, and water vapor, as well as some other gases and particles of liquids and solids.

Key Terms

weather   ozone
atmosphere   water vapor

SECTION 2 Air Quality

INTEGRATING ENVIRONMENTAL SCIENCE

Key Ideas

- Most air pollution results from the burning of fossil fuels such as coal and oil.
- Nitrogen oxides, hydrocarbons, and other air pollutants react with one another in the presence of sunlight to form a mix of ozone and other chemicals called photochemical smog.
- Acid rain forms when nitrogen oxides and sulfur oxides combine with water in the air to form nitric acid and sulfuric acid.

Key Terms

pollutant   acid rain
photochemical smog

SECTION 3 Air Pressure

Key Ideas

- Properties of air include mass, density, and pressure.
- Air pressure is the result of the weight of a column of air pushing down on an area.
- Air pressure is measured with mercury barometers and aneroid barometers.
- Air pressure decreases as altitude increases. As air pressure decreases, so does density.

Key Terms

density   barometer   altitude
pressure   mercury barometer
air pressure aneroid barometer

SECTION 4 Layers of the Atmosphere

Key Ideas

- The four main layers of the atmosphere are classified according to changes in temperature. These layers are the troposphere, the stratosphere, the mesosphere, and the thermosphere.
- Rain, snow, storms, and most clouds occur in the troposphere.
- Ozone in the stratosphere absorbs energy from the sun.
- Most meteoroids burn up in the mesosphere, producing meteor trails.
- The aurora borealis occurs in the ionosphere.
- Communications satellites orbit Earth in the exosphere.

Key Terms

troposphere   thermosphere   aurora borealis
stratosphere   ionosphere   exosphere
mesosphere

Organizing Information

Concept Map Copy the air pressure concept map onto a separate sheet of paper. Then complete it and add a title. (For more on concept maps, see the Skills Handbook.)

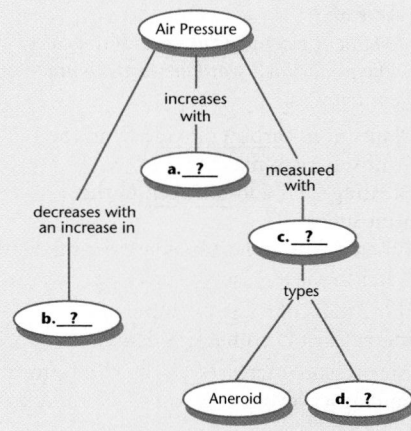

Organizing Information

Concept Map Sample title: Air Pressure **a.** Density **b.** Altitude **c.** Barometers **d.** Mercury

Program Resources

- **Unit 5 Resources** Chapter 16 Project Scoring Rubric, p. 8
- **Performance Assessment** Chapter 16, pp. 49–51
- **Chapter Tests** Chapter 16 Test, pp. 63–66

Media and Technology

 Computer Test Bank
Chapter 16 Test

Performance Assessment

Writing Challenge students to write crossword puzzles using all the bold-faced terms in the section. Then have students exchange crossword puzzles with a partner and try to solve their partner's puzzle.

535

Reviewing Content
Multiple Choice
1. d 2. d 3. c 4. b 5. b

True or False
6. true 7. carbon dioxide (Other possible answers: nitrogen oxides, sulfur oxides, soot) 8. acid rain 9. more 10. decreases

Checking Concepts
11. Carbon dioxide is added to the atmosphere through the respiration of animals and the burning of fossil fuels.
12. It is difficult to include water vapor in a graph that shows the percentages of different gases in the atmosphere because the percentage of water vapor varies greatly.
13. Photochemical-type smog is caused by the action of sunlight on chemicals in the air. It forms over sunny cities like Los Angeles today. London-type smog was caused by particles in coal smoke combining with water droplets in humid air. It once blanketed industrial cities like London but is no longer common.
14. Acid rain may make lake and pond water so acidic that many types of plants and animals can no longer live in it. Acid rain may also cause damage to tree needles and the surfaces of buildings and statues.
15. Moving upward from Earth's surface, the layers are troposphere, stratosphere, mesosphere, thermosphere.
16. As you move upward through the troposphere, the temperature decreases by about 6.5°C for each 1,000-meter increase in altitude.
17. Students' letters should demonstrate a thorough understanding of their chosen layer of the atmosphere.

Thinking Critically
18. You would experience a decrease in temperature and also in the pressure and density of the air. You would feel cold unless you dressed appropriately. You would also feel the effects of low oxygen pressure and density. For example, you might be short of breath and tire easily.

Reviewing Content
Multiple Choice
Choose the letter of the answer that best completes each statement.

1. The most abundant gas in the atmosphere is
   a. ozone.   b. carbon dioxide.
   c. oxygen.   d. nitrogen.
2. Most air pollution is caused by
   a. dust and pollen.
   b. acid rain.
   c. erupting volcanoes.
   d. the burning of fossil fuels.
3. A barometer is used to measure
   a. temperature.   b. smog.
   c. air pressure   d. density.
4. The layers of the atmosphere are classified according to changes in
   a. altitude.
   b. temperature.
   c. pressure.
   d. density.
5. The inner layer, or "weather layer," of the atmosphere is called the
   a. mesosphere.
   b. troposphere.
   c. thermosphere.
   d. stratosphere.

True or False
If the statement is true, write true. If it is false, change the underlined word or words to make the statement true.

6. Plants need <u>carbon dioxide</u> from the atmosphere to make food.
7. Burning fuels add <u>nitrogen</u> to the atmosphere.
8. When sulfur and nitrogen oxides mix with water in the air, they form <u>smog</u>.
9. If the mass of a fixed volume of air increases, it becomes <u>less</u> dense.
10. Air pressure <u>increases</u> as you climb from land at sea level to the top of a mountain.

Checking Concepts
11. Name two ways in which carbon dioxide is added to the atmosphere.
12. Explain why it is difficult to include water vapor in a graph that shows the percentages of various gases in the atmosphere.
13. What is the difference between photochemical smog and London-type smog?
14. Describe some of the problems caused by acid rain.
15. List the following layers of the atmosphere in order moving up from Earth's surface: thermosphere, stratosphere, troposphere, mesosphere.
16. Describe the temperature changes that occur as you move upward through the troposphere.
17. **Writing to Learn** You are a scientist who has a chance to join a research mission to explore the atmosphere. To win a place on this mission, write a persuasive letter telling which layer of the atmosphere you want to research and why you chose it.

Thinking Critically
18. **Predicting** Describe the changes in the atmosphere that you would experience while climbing a mountain four or more kilometers high. How might these changes affect you physically?
19. **Applying Concepts** Why can an aneroid barometer be used to measure elevation as well as air pressure?
20. **Relating Cause and Effect** How can burning high-sulfur coal in a power-generating plant harm a forest hundreds of kilometers away?
21. **Classifying** Which sources of air pollution occur naturally, and which are caused by humans?

19. Air pressure decreases as elevation or altitude increases. An aneroid barometer can be calibrated to show the change in air pressure as a change in altitude.
20. Burning high-sulfur coal can produce sulfur oxides and other air pollutants that may lead to the formation of acid rain hundreds of kilometers away, where it might harm a forest.
21. Natural sources of air pollution include molds, dust, pollen, salt from ocean spray, and particles from forest fires, soil erosion, dust storms, and volcanoes. Human sources of air pollution include soot and carbon dioxide and other gases from the burning of fuels, such as wood, coal, oil, and gas, and dust particles from farming and construction.

Applying Skills

The table below shows the temperature at various altitudes above Omaha, Nebraska, on a day in January. Use the table to answer the questions that follow.

Altitude (kilometers)	0	1.6	3.2	4.8	6.4	7.2
Temperature (°C)	0	−4	−9	−21	−32	−40

22. Graphing Make a line graph of the data in the table. Put temperature on the horizontal axis and altitude on the vertical axis. Label your graph.

23. Interpreting Graphs At about what height above the ground was the temperature −15°C?

24. Interpreting Graphs What was the approximate temperature 2.4 kilometers over Omaha?

25. Calculating Suppose an airplane was about 6.8 kilometers above Omaha on this day. What was the approximate temperature at 6.8 kilometers? How much colder was the temperature at 6.8 kilometers above the ground than at ground level?

Performance CHAPTER PROJECT 16 **Assessment**

Project Wrap Up For your class presentation, prepare a display of your weather observations. Include drawings, graphs, and tables that summarize the weather you observed. Practice presenting your project to your group. Do you need to make any improvements? If so, make them now.

Reflect and Record In your journal, write how you might improve your weather log. What weather conditions would you like to know more about? What factors could you have measured more accurately using instruments?

Test Preparation   *Use these questions to prepare for standardized tests.*

Study the graph. Then answer Questions 26–29.

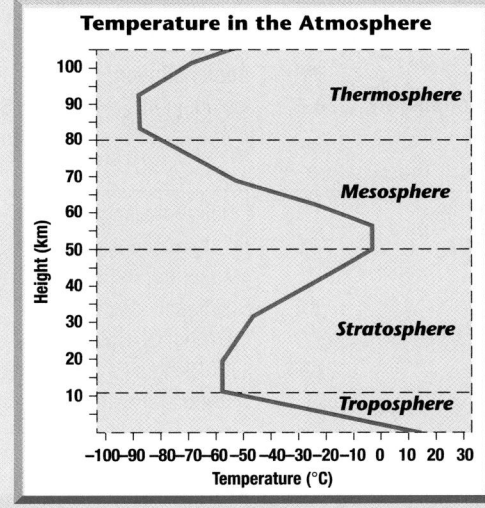

Temperature in the Atmosphere

26. Name the layer of the atmosphere that is closest to Earth's surface.
   a. thermosphere   **b.** troposphere
   c. stratosphere   **d.** mesosphere

27. Which layer of the atmosphere has the lowest temperature?
   a. thermosphere   **b.** troposphere
   c. stratosphere   **d.** mesosphere

28. The range of temperatures found in the stratosphere is about ____ Celsius degrees.
   a. 100   **b.** 0
   c. 30   **d.** 60

29. Which of the following best describes how temperature changes as altitude increases in the troposphere?
   a. steadily increases
   b. increases then decreases
   c. steadily decreases
   d. decreases then increases

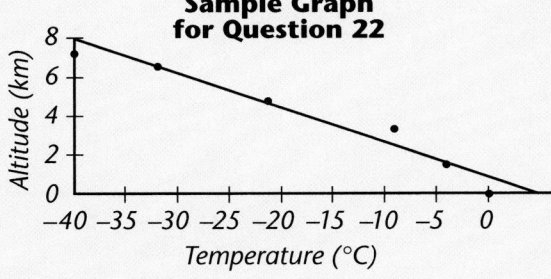

Sample Graph for Question 22

Program Resources

- ◆ **Inquiry Skills Activity Book** Provides teaching and review of all inquiry skills
- ◆ **Prentice Hall Assessment System** Provides standardized test practice
- ◆ **Reading in the Content Area** Provides strategies to improve science reading skills
- ◆ **Teacher's ELL Handbook** Provides multiple strategies for English language learners

---

Applying Skills

22. Students' graphs should show a line with a negative slope, that is, a line that slopes downward to the right. See sample graph below.

23. The temperature was -15°C at about 4 kilometers above the ground.

24. At 2.4 kilometers over Omaha, the approximate temperature was -6.5°C.

25. The approximate temperature at 6.8 kilometers above Omaha was -36°C, which was about 36° colder than the temperature at ground level.

Performance CHAPTER PROJECT 16 **Assessment**

Project Wrap Up Displays should show how, where, and when observations were made and what scale was used to categorize each weather variable. Encourage students to present their observations in creative ways, such as weather centers, bulletin boards, or newspaper or television weather reports. Students should be prepared to discuss any trends they have identified in their observations.

Reflect and Record Students may be able to improve their weather logs by observing more weather variables or making more frequent or detailed observations. Encourage students to look at other students' logs for additional ideas. Weather factors that are not directly observable, such as temperature and air pressure, could be measured more accurately using instruments.

Test Preparation

26. b **27.** a **28.** d **29.** c

Weather Factors

Sections	Time	Student Edition Activities		Other Activities
CHAPTER PROJECT 17 **Your Own Weather Station** p. 539	Ongoing (2–3 weeks)	Check Your Progress, pp. 549, 558, 568 Project Wrap Up, p. 571	TE	Chapter 17 Project Notes, pp. 538–539
1 **Energy in the Atmosphere** pp. 540–545 ◆ 17.1.1 State in what form energy travels from the sun to Earth. ◆ 17.1.2 Explain what happens to energy from the sun when it reaches Earth.	2 periods/ 1 block	**Discover** Does a Plastic Bag Trap Heat?, p. 540 **Science at Home,** p. 543 **Skills Lab: Developing Hypotheses** Heating Earth's Surface, pp. 544, 545 (Probeware version available) **PLM** Provides instructions for the probeware version of the lab	TE TE	Integrating Physics, p. 541 Exploring Energy in the Atmosphere, p. 542
2 *INTEGRATING PHYSICS* **Heat Transfer** pp. 546–549 ◆ 17.2.1 Describe how temperature is measured. ◆ 17.2.2 Explain the three ways heat is transferred.	1 period/ ½ block	**Discover** What Happens When Air Is Heated?, p. 546 **Try This** Temperatures at Two Heights, p. 548	TE TE TE	Demonstration, p. 547 Building Inquiry Skills: Calculating, p. 547 Inquiry Challenge, p. 548
3 **Winds** pp. 550–558 ◆ 17.3.1 Explain what causes winds. ◆ 17.3.2 Distinguish between local winds and global winds. ◆ 17.3.3 Describe the major global wind belts and where they are located.	2 periods/ 1 block	**Discover** Which Way Does the Wind Turn?, p. 550 **Try This** Build a Wind Vane, p. 551 **Real-World Lab: You and Your Community** Where's the Wind?, pp. 552–553	TE TE TE TE	Demonstration, p. 551 Including All Students, p. 554 Demonstration, p. 555 Including All Students, p. 556
4 **Water in the Atmosphere** pp. 559–564 ◆ 17.4.1 Describe how relative humidity is measured. ◆ 17.4.2 Explain how clouds form. ◆ 17.4.3 Name the three main types of clouds.	1 period/ ½ block	**Discover** How Does Fog Form?, p. 559 **Sharpen Your Skills** Interpreting Data, p. 561 **Science at Home,** p. 564	TE TE TE LM	Inquiry Challenge, p. 560 Building Inquiry Skills: Measuring, p. 561 Building Inquiry Skills: Inferring, p. 562 17, "Using a Psychrometer to Determine Relative Humidity"
5 **Precipitation** pp. 565–568 ◆ 17.5.1 Identify the main types of precipitation. ◆ 17.5.2 Describe how precipitation is measured and ways that it might be controlled.	1 period/ ½ block	**Discover** How Can You Make Hail?, p. 565 **Sharpen Your Skills** Calculating, p. 567	TE TE	Building Inquiry Skills: Observing, p. 566 Building Inquiry Skills: Measuring, p. 567
Study Guide/Assessment pp. 569–571	1 period/ ½ block			

For Standard or Block Schedule The Resource Pro® CD-ROM gives you maximum flexibility for planning your instruction for any type of schedule. Resource Pro® contains Planning Express®, an advanced scheduling program, as well as the entire contents of the Teaching Resources and the Computer Test Bank.

Key: **CTB** Computer Test Bank
CT Chapter Tests
ELL Teacher's ELL Handbook

CHAPTER PLANNING GUIDE

Program Resources	Assessment Strategies	Media and Technology
UR Chapter 17 Project Teacher Notes, pp. 30–31 **UR** Chapter 17 Project Overview and Worksheets, pp. 32–35	**TE** Performance Assessment: Chapter 17 Project Wrap Up, p. 571 **TE** Check Your Progress, pp. 549, 558, 568 **UR** Chapter 17 Project Scoring Rubric, p. 36	Science Explorer Internet Site Audio CDs, Section Summaries
UR 17-1 Lesson Plan, p. 37 **UR** 17-1 Section Summary, p. 38 **UR** 17-1 Review and Reinforce, p. 39 **UR** 17-1 Enrich, p. 40 **UR** Skills Lab blackline masters, pp. 57–59 **PLM** Probeware blackline masters	**SE** Section 1 Review, p. 543 **SE** Analyze and Conclude, p. 545 **TE** Ongoing Assessment, p. 541 **TE** Performance Assessment, p. 543	Concept Videotape Library, *Adventures, Tape 4,* "Why Is the Sky Blue?"; "Never Put Up the Umbrella Until It Starts to Rain" Presentation Pro, "Energy in the Atmosphere" Transparency 65, "Energy in the Atmosphere" Lab Activity Videotape, *Tape 4*
UR 17-2 Lesson Plan, p. 41 **UR** 17-2 Section Summary, p. 42 **UR** 17-2 Review and Reinforce, p. 43 **UR** 17-2 Enrich, p. 44	**SE** Section 2 Review, p. 549 **TE** Ongoing Assessment, p. 547 **TE** Performance Assessment, p. 549	Concept Videotape Library, *Adventures, Tape 4,* "A Wave Is a Wave Is a Wave"; "As Hot As a Desert"; "Hot is Hot, Cold is Not"; "The Power of Heat" Transparency 66, "Types of Heat Transfer"
UR 17-3 Lesson Plan, p. 45 **UR** 17-3 Section Summary, p. 46 **UR** 17-3 Review and Reinforce, p. 47 **UR** 17-3 Enrich, p. 48 **UR** Real-World Lab blackline masters, pp. 60–61	**SE** Analyze and Conclude, p. 553 **SE** Section 3 Review, p. 558 **TE** Ongoing Assessment, pp. 551, 555, 557 **TE** Performance Assessment, p. 557	Presentation Pro, "Winds" Transparency 67, "Global Winds" Lab Activity Videotape, *Tape 4*
UR 17-4 Lesson Plan, p. 49 **UR** 17-4 Section Summary, p. 50 **UR** 17-4 Review and Reinforce, p. 51 **UR** 17-4 Enrich, p. 52	**SE** Section 4 Review, p. 564 **TE** Ongoing Assessment, pp. 561, 563 **TE** Performance Assessment, p. 564	Transparency 68, "The Water Cycle"; Transparency 69, "Clouds"
UR 17-5 Lesson Plan, p. 53 **UR** 17-5 Section Summary, p. 54 **UR** 17-5 Review and Reinforce, p. 55 **UR** 17-5 Enrich, p. 56	**SE** Section 5 Review, p. 568 **TE** Ongoing Assessment, p. 567 **TE** Performance Assessment, p. 568	
GRSW Provides worksheets to promote student comprehension of content **RCA** Provides strategies to improve science reading skills **ELL** Provides multiple strategies for English language learners	**SE** Study Guide/Assessment, pp. 569–571 **PA** Performance Assessment, pp. 52–54 **CT** Chapter 17 Test, pp. 67–70 **CTB** Chapter 17 Test **PHAS** Provides standardized test preparation	Computer Test Bank, Chapter 17 Test

GRSW Guided Reading and Study Workbook
ISAB Inquiry Skills Activity Book
LM Laboratory Manual

PA Performance Assessment
PHAS Prentice Hall Assessment System
PLM Probeware Lab Manual

RCA Reading in the Content Area
SE Student Edition

TE Teacher's Edition
UR Unit Resources

Meeting the National Science Education Standards and AAAS Benchmarks

National Science Education Standards	Benchmarks for Science Literacy	Unifying Themes

Science As Inquiry (Content Standard A)

◆ **Use appropriate tools and techniques to gather, analyze, and interpret data** Students create a weather station. Students investigate wind patterns. *(Chapter Project; Real-World Lab)*

◆ **Think critically and logically to make the relationships between evidence and explanations** Students compare heating and cooling rates of sand and water. *(Skills Lab)*

Physical Science (Content Standard B)

◆ **Transfer of energy** Energy travels to Earth from the sun as electromagnetic waves. Different materials absorb radiation at different rates. Heat is transferred by radiation, conduction, and convection. *(Sections 1, 2; Skills Lab)*

Earth and Space Science (Content Standard D)

◆ **Structure of the Earth system** The movement of air between the equator and the poles produces global winds. Water moves between the atmosphere and Earth's surface in the water cycle. Precipitation is any form of water that falls to Earth. *(Sections 3, 4, 5)*

◆ **Earth in the solar system** Nearly all the energy in Earth's atmosphere comes from the sun. Winds are caused by unequal heating of the atmosphere by the sun. As the sun heats Earth's surface, the amount of water in the atmosphere changes. *(Sections 1, 3, 4)*

1B Scientific Inquiry Students create a weather station. Students investigate heating and cooling rates of sand and water. Students investigate wind patterns. *(Chapter Project; Skills Lab; Real-World Lab)*

3A Technology and Science Students use instruments to measure weather conditions. Students measure wind to determine the best location for a door on a building. *(Chapter Project; Real-World Lab)*

4B The Earth Nearly all the energy in Earth's atmosphere comes from the sun. The movement of air between the equator and the poles produces global winds. Water moves between the atmosphere and Earth's surface in the water cycle. Precipitation is any form of water that falls from clouds to Earth's surface. *(Sections 1, 3, 4, 5)*

4E Energy Transformation The direct transfer of energy by electromagnetic waves is called radiation. Different materials absorb radiation at different rates. Heat is transferred by radiation, conduction, and convection. Winds are caused by unequal heating of the atmosphere. *(Sections 1, 2, 3; Skills Lab)*

4F Motion Visible light is a mixture of all the colors of the rainbow. *(Section 1)*

12C Manipulation and Observation Students measure weather conditions using various instruments. *(Chapter Project)*

◆ **Energy** Nearly all the energy in Earth's atmosphere comes from the sun. Different materials absorb radiation at different rates. The energy transferred from a hotter object to a cooler one is referred to as heat. Wind is the movement of air. *(Sections 1, 2, 3; Skills Lab)*

◆ **Modeling** Students create a weather station. Students make a simple anemometer. *(Chapter Project; Real-World Lab)*

◆ **Patterns of Change** Students look for patterns in their weather data. Monsoons change direction with the seasons. Students investigate wind patterns around a building. *(Chapter Project; Section 3; Real-World Lab)*

◆ **Systems and Interactions** When Earth's surface is heated, it radiates some of the heat back into the atmosphere. Winds are caused by the unequal heating of Earth and its atmosphere. Water moves between the atmosphere and Earth's surface in the water cycle. *(Sections 1, 3, 4)*

◆ **Unity and Diversity** Most light reaches Earth in the form of visible light, infrared radiation, and ultraviolet radiation. Heat is transferred by radiation, conduction, and convection. Both local winds and global winds are caused by differences in air pressure. The three main types of clouds are cumulus, stratus, and cirrus. Rain, sleet, freezing rain, hail, and snow are types of precipitation. *(Sections 1, 2, 3, 4, 5)*

Take It to the Net

The **www.phschool.com** Web site provides you with multiple opportunities to incorporate the internet into your instruction. Go to **www.phschool.com** and click on the Science icon. Then select Science Explorer Integrated.

www.phschool.com

Internet Activities provide opportunities for students to review, extend, or assess a concept from the chapter.

■ Have students use the chapter Self-Test to get instant feedback.

■ Hot Links and Reference Links provide opportunities for online research.

STAY CURRENT with **SCIENCE NEWS** ®

Find out the latest research and information about weather and climate at: **www.phschool.com**

ACTIVITY	Time (minutes)	Materials *Quantities for one work group*	Skills
Section 1			
Discover, p. 540	10	**Consumable** plastic bag, 2 small pieces of paper, tape **Nonconsumable** 2 thermometers	Measuring
Science at Home, p. 543	home	No special materials required.	Observing
Skills Lab, pp. 544–545	40	**Consumable** 300 mL water, string, 300 mL sand, graph paper **Nonconsumable** 2 thermometers or temperature probes, 2 400-mL beakers, metric ruler, ring stand and two ring clamps, lamp with 150-W bulb, clock or stopwatch	Developing Hypotheses, Measuring, Creating Data Tables, Drawing Conclusions
Section 2			
Discover, p. 546	10	**Consumable** aluminum pie plate, thread, candle **Nonconsumable** heavy scissors, hot plate or incandescent light	Inferring
Try This, p. 548	10, 10, 10, 20	**Consumable** graph paper **Nonconsumable** 2 thermometers, metric tape measure, watch or clock	Interpreting Data
Section 3			
Discover, p. 550	10	**Consumable** heavy-duty tape **Nonconsumable** pencil, large smooth ball, marker	Making Models
Try This, p. 551	15	**Consumable** construction paper, soda straw, tape, straight pin **Nonconsumable** scissors, metric ruler, pencil with eraser	Observing
Real-World Lab, pp. 552–553	40	**Consumable** 15 cm x 20 cm corrugated cardboard sheet, round toothpick, 2 wooden coffee stirrers, narrow masking tape **Nonconsumable** pen, wind vane, meter stick	Measuring, Interpreting Data, Drawing Conclusions
Section 4			
Discover, p. 559	10	**Consumable** hot tap water, 2 ice cubes, cold tap water **Nonconsumable** narrow-necked plastic bottle	Developing Hypotheses
Sharpen Your Skills, p. 561	10	No special materials required.	Interpreting Data
Science at Home, p. 564	home	**Consumable** cold water, ice cubes **Nonconsumable** large glass	Communicating
Section 5			
Discover, p. 565	15	**Consumable** 15 g salt, 50 mL water, 15 mL cold water, crushed ice **Nonconsumable** beaker, stirrer, clean test tube, watch or clock	Inferring
Sharpen Your Skills, p. 567	15	**Nonconsumable** funnel, narrow straight-sided glass jar, metric ruler, calculator	Calculating

A list of all materials required for the Student Edition activities can be found beginning on page T23. You can obtain information about ordering materials by calling 1-800-848-9500 or by accessing the Science Explorer Internet site at: **www.phschool.com**

In this chapter, students will learn more about specific weather factors, how they are related, and how they can be measured with instruments. The Chapter 17 Project gives students an opportunity to use instruments to take measurements of each of the weather factors.

Purpose In this project, students will set up a weather station and use instruments to measure weather factors over a two-week period. At the end of the project, students will look for patterns in their data and use them to try to predict the weather. Doing the project will give students a better understanding of weather factors and how they can be used to predict the weather.

Skills Focus After completing this project, students will be able to
- plan and create a model weather station;
- use their weather station to measure weather factors;
- record the data in a weather log;
- graph their data and analyze it for trends;
- use the trends to try to predict the weather and compare their predictions with actual weather conditions;
- communicate their findings to the rest of the class.

Project Time Line The entire project will take about three weeks. On the first day, introduce the project and hand out the Chapter 17 Project Overview, pages 32–33 in Unit 5 Resources. Allow time for class discussion of the project rules and for students to brainstorm weather factors, how they can be measured, and ways to record the measurements.

Distribute the Chapter Project 17 Worksheet 1, page 34 in Unit 5 Resources, to help students plan their weather station, and Worksheet 2, page 35 in Unit 5 Resources, to show students a way to measure cloud cover. You also may wish to distribute the Chapter 17 Project Scoring Rubric, page 36 in the Unit 5 Resources.

Give students a day or two to plan their weather station and assemble the instruments and other materials they will need. Allow one class period for students

538

CHAPTER 17 Weather Factors

WEB ACTIVITY www.phschool.com

Integrating Physics

SECTION 1 Energy in the Atmosphere
Discover Does a Plastic Bag Trap Heat?
Skills Lab Heating Earth's Surface

SECTION 2 Heat Transfer
Discover What Happens When Air Is Heated?
Try This Temperatures at Two Heights

SECTION 3 Winds
Discover Which Way Does the Wind Turn?
Try This Build a Wind Vane
Real-World Lab Where's the Wind?

538

to set up their weather station and practice using the instruments. You may wish to give students enough class time each day over the next two weeks to measure and record weather data. At the end of two weeks, give students a day or two to graph and analyze their data. Finally, set aside a class period at the end of the project for students to make their presentations and discuss the results.

For more detailed information on supervising the chapter project, see Chapter 17 Project Teacher Notes, pages 30–31 in Unit 5 Resources.

Suggested Shortcuts You can streamline the project by having students make and share a single weather station. If you assemble the instruments and materials for the shared weather station yourself, you will save another day or two. You can streamline the project even more by doing the project as a class project. Assign different students to make the weather observation each day and have them record the observations on a large weather log posted in the classroom.

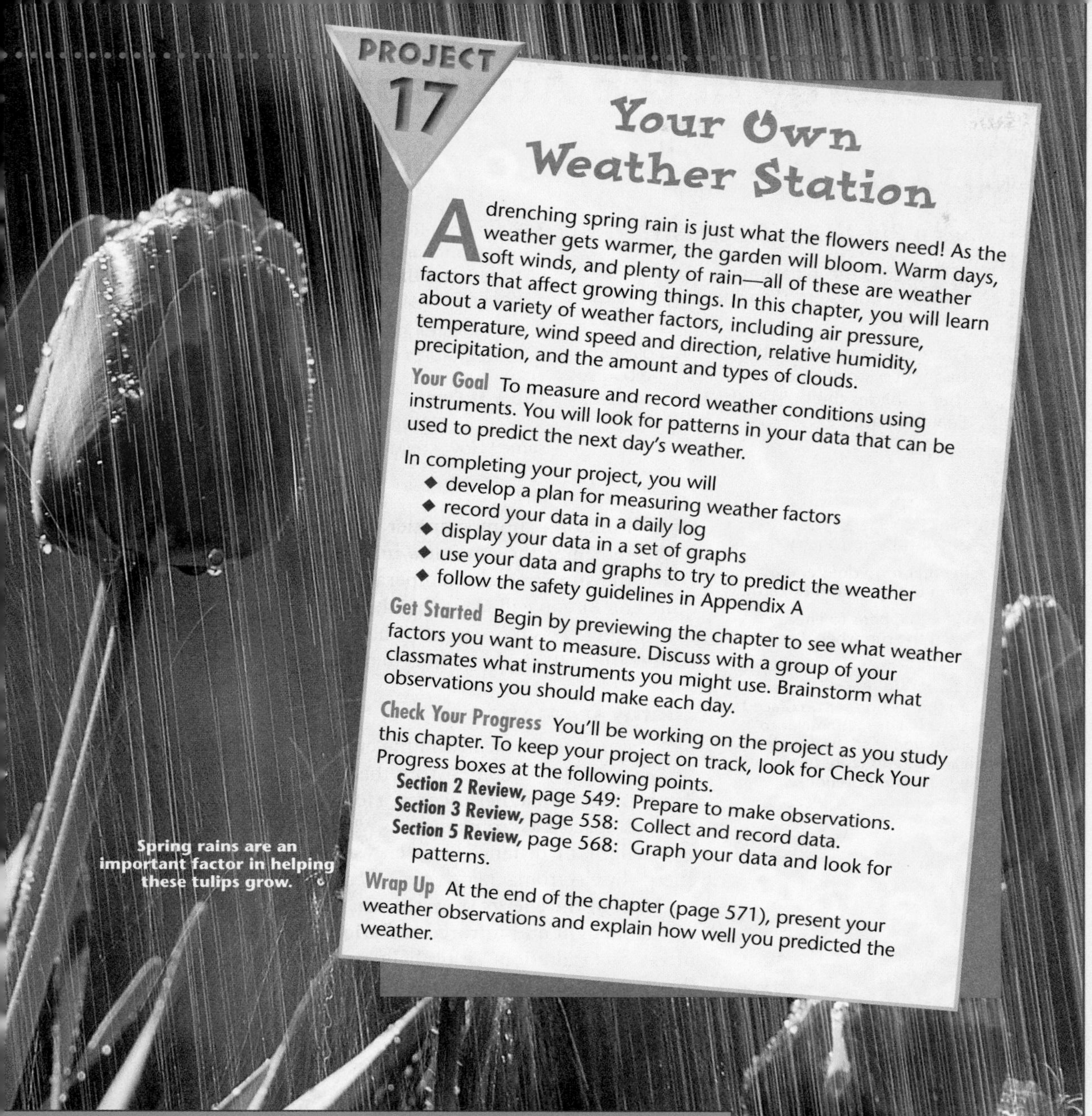

Your Own Weather Station

A drenching spring rain is just what the flowers need! As the weather gets warmer, the garden will bloom. Warm days, soft winds, and plenty of rain—all of these are weather factors that affect growing things. In this chapter, you will learn about a variety of weather factors, including air pressure, temperature, wind speed and direction, relative humidity, precipitation, and the amount and types of clouds.

Your Goal To measure and record weather conditions using instruments. You will look for patterns in your data that can be used to predict the next day's weather.

In completing your project, you will
◆ develop a plan for measuring weather factors
◆ record your data in a daily log
◆ display your data in a set of graphs
◆ use your data and graphs to try to predict the weather
◆ follow the safety guidelines in Appendix A

Get Started Begin by previewing the chapter to see what weather factors you want to measure. Discuss with a group of your classmates what instruments you might use. Brainstorm what observations you should make each day.

Check Your Progress You'll be working on the project as you study this chapter. To keep your project on track, look for Check Your Progress boxes at the following points.
Section 2 Review, page 549: Prepare to make observations.
Section 3 Review, page 558: Collect and record data.
Section 5 Review, page 568: Graph your data and look for patterns.

Wrap Up At the end of the chapter (page 571), present your weather observations and explain how well you predicted the weather.

Spring rains are an important factor in helping these tulips grow.

539

Program Resources

◆ **Unit 5 Resources** Chapter 17 Project Teacher Notes, pp. 30–31; Project Overview and Worksheets, pp. 32–35; Project Scoring Rubric, p. 36

WEB ACTIVITY www.phschool.com

You will find an Internet activity, chapter self-tests for students, and links to other chapter topics at this site.

Media and Technology

 Audio CDs Section Summaries

Possible Materials A weather station requires a sheltered place outdoors, such as the slatted wooden box described in Worksheet 1. Several different instruments are needed, including a thermometer, psychrometer, barometer, wind vane, anemometer, and rain gauge. Useful additions to the weather station are a device for measuring cloud cover (see Worksheet 2 for materials) and a chart showing cloud types.

Students will need commercial thermometers and psychrometers. They can use the barometer they made in the Skills Lab in Chapter 16, pages 526–527 in the text. They also can make their own wind vane (Try This, page 551 in the text), anemometer (Real-World Lab, pages 552–553 in the text), and rain gauge (Sharpen Your Skills, page 567 in the text). However, commercial versions of these instruments will give more accurate readings and should be used if possible.

Launching the Project Introduce the project by discussing weather stations. Ask: **If you were going to visit another city, what would you want to know about the weather?** (*Students may say they would want to know how hot or cold it was and if it was raining or snowing.*) **How could you find out what the weather conditions in the city were?** (*Students may say they would watch a national weather report on television or look at a national weather map in a newspaper.*) Point out that weather information for specific locations is collected and recorded by weather stations. Tell students that in this project they will make their own weather station and observe and record weather factors

Performance Assessment

To assess students' performance in this project, use the Chapter 17 Project Scoring Rubric on page 36 in Unit 5 Resources. Students will be assessed on their
◆ weather observations and weather log;
◆ graphical presentation and interpretation of weather data;
◆ presentation of the results to the class;
◆ group participation, if they worked in groups.

Objectives

After completing the lesson, students will be able to
◆ state in what form energy travels from the sun to Earth;
◆ explain what happens to energy from the sun when it reaches Earth.

Key Terms electromagnetic wave, radiation, infrared radiation, ultraviolet radiation, scattering, greenhouse effect

1 Engage/Explore

Activating Prior Knowledge

Encourage students to think about the way the sun heats Earth's surface by asking: **Which is cooler on a hot, sunny day, a lawn or a parking lot?** (*a lawn*) Point out that even without trees, a grass-covered surface stays cooler than a surface covered by blacktop. Ask: **Why doesn't the lawn get as hot as the parking lot?** (*Students may not know.*) Tell students that grass absorbs less light than pavement even when both surfaces receive the same amount of sun. As a result, the grass does not get as hot. Add that such differences in the heating of Earth's surface, on a large scale, are the major cause of Earth's weather.

•••••••• **DISCOVER** ••••••••

Skills Focus measuring
Materials ACTIVITY
2 thermometers, plastic bag, 2 small pieces of paper, tape
Time 10 minutes
Tips Make sure the bulbs of both thermometers are shaded by the pieces of paper from direct rays of light or both may show equally high temperatures.
Expected Outcome The thermometer in the bag should show a higher temperature.
Think It Over The plastic bag trapped the heat inside it from the sun, and this caused the thermometer in the bag to show a higher temperature.

540

DISCOVER ••••••••••••••••••••••••••••**ACTIVITY**••••

Does a Plastic Bag Trap Heat?

1. Record the initial temperatures on two thermometers. (You should get the same readings.)

2. Place one of the thermometers in a plastic bag. Put a small piece of paper in the bag so that it shades the bulb of the thermometer. Seal the bag.

3. Place both thermometers on a sunny window ledge or near a light bulb. Cover the bulb of the second thermometer with a small piece of paper. Predict what you think will happen.

4. Wait five minutes. Then record the temperatures on the two thermometers.

Think It Over
Measuring Were the two temperatures the same? How could you explain any difference?

GUIDE FOR READING

◆ In what form does energy from the sun travel to Earth?

◆ What happens to energy from the sun when it reaches Earth?

Reading Tip Before you read, skim the section for boldfaced words that are unfamiliar to you. As you read, find their meanings and write them down in your notebook.

Think of a sunny summer day. When you get up in the morning, the sun is low in the sky and the air is cool. As the sun rises, the temperature increases. By noon it is quite hot. As you will see in this chapter, heat is a major factor in the weather. The movement of heat in the atmosphere causes temperatures to change, winds to blow, and rain to fall.

Energy from the Sun

INTEGRATING PHYSICS Nearly all the energy in Earth's atmosphere comes from the sun. This energy travels to Earth as **electromagnetic waves,** a form of energy that can travel through space. Electromagnetic waves are classified according to wavelength, or distance between waves. The direct transfer of energy by electromagnetic waves is called **radiation.**

Most of the energy from the sun reaches Earth in the form of visible light and infrared radiation, and a small amount of ultraviolet radiation. Visible light is a mixture of all of the colors that you see in a rainbow: red, orange, yellow, green, blue, and violet. The different colors are the result of different wavelengths

540

READING STRATEGIES

Reading Tip Suggest that students make a list of unfamiliar boldfaced words and then fill in their meanings as they read.
Study and Comprehension Suggest that students use ROY G. BV to remember the order of colors in the spectrum of visible light, going from longer to shorter wavelengths. The colors represented by the letters are red, orange, yellow, green, blue, and violet.

Media and Technology

 Concept Videotape Library
Adventures, Tape 4, "Why Is the Sky Blue?"

 Concept Videotape Library
Adventures, Tape 4, "Never Put Up the Umbrella Until It Starts to Rain"

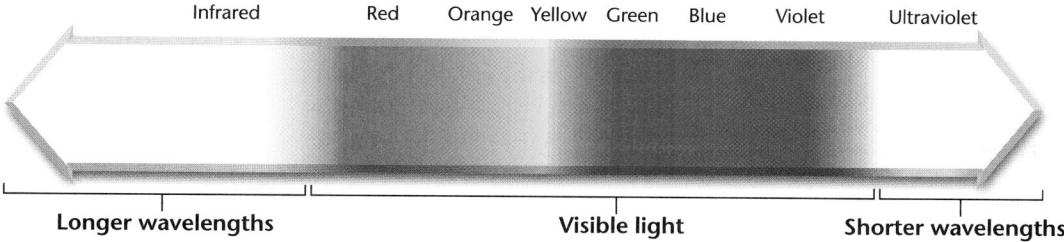

| Infrared | Red | Orange | Yellow | Green | Blue | Violet | Ultraviolet |

Longer wavelengths — **Visible light** — **Shorter wavelengths**

of visible light. Red and orange light have the longest wavelengths, while blue and violet light have the shortest wavelengths.

Infrared radiation is a form of energy with wavelengths that are longer than red light. Infrared radiation is not visible, but can be felt as heat. Heat lamps used to keep food warm in restaurants give off both visible red light and invisible infrared radiation. The sun also gives off **ultraviolet radiation,** which has wavelengths that are shorter than violet light. Sunburns are caused by ultraviolet radiation. This radiation can also cause skin cancer and eye damage.

☑ *Checkpoint* *Which color of visible light has the longest wavelengths?*

Energy in the Atmosphere

Before the sun's rays can reach Earth's surface, they must pass through the atmosphere. The path of the sun's rays is shown in *Exploring Energy in the Atmosphere* on the following page.

Some of the energy from the sun is absorbed within the atmosphere. Water vapor and carbon dioxide absorb some infrared radiation. The ozone layer in the stratosphere absorbs most of the ultraviolet radiation. Clouds, dust, and other gases also absorb energy from the sun.

Some of the sun's rays are reflected. Clouds in the atmosphere act like mirrors, reflecting some solar energy back into space. In addition, dust particles and molecules of gases in the atmosphere reflect light from the sun in all directions.

Figure 1 Electromagnetic waves include infrared radiation, visible light, and ultraviolet radiation.
Interpreting Diagrams What type of radiation has wavelengths that are shorter than visible light? What type has wavelengths that are longer?

Program Resources

◆ **Unit 5 Resources** 17-1 Lesson Plan, p. 37; 17-1 Section Summary, p. 38
◆ **Guided Reading and Study Workbook** Section 17-1

Media and Technology

 Transparencies "Energy in the Atmosphere," Transparency 65

Answers to Self-Assessment

Caption Question

Figure 1 Ultraviolet radiation has wavelengths that are shorter than visible light. Infrared radiation has wavelengths that are longer than visible light.

☑ *Checkpoint*
Red light has the longest wavelengths.

---

2 Facilitate

Energy from the Sun

 Integrating Physics

Materials *prism*
Time 5 minutes

Show students a prism and explain that its angled sides bend the different colors in sunlight by different amounts, splitting the light into a rainbow. Demonstrate by placing the prism in sunlight. Then ask: **Where does light have the shortest wavelength and where does light have the longest wavelength?** *(The end with violet light is the shortest, and the end with red light is the longest.)* **learning modality: visual**

Energy in the Atmosphere

Building Inquiry Skills: Inferring

Describe the following hypothetical situation to the class. City A is located where the ozone layer of the stratosphere has become very thin. City B is located where the ozone layer is still relatively thick. Ask: **How do you think the two cities compare in terms of the ultraviolet radiation they receive?** *(City A would get more ultraviolet radiation than City B because less of the ultraviolet radiation would be absorbed by ozone in the stratosphere.)* **learning modality: logical/mathematical**

Ongoing Assessment

Drawing Have students draw a representation of the visible spectrum, showing the different colors of visible light in order by wavelength.

Including All Students

Remind students that the moon, unlike Earth, has no atmosphere. Then ask: **If you were standing on the moon during the day, what color would the sky appear to be?** (*Students may know from photographs that the sky would appear to be black.*) **Why wouldn't the sky appear to be blue?** (*Because without an atmosphere on the moon there are no gas molecules to scatter the light and make it look blue*) **learning modality: logical/mathematical**

EXPLORING

Energy in the Atmosphere

Materials *several sheets of light- and dark-colored construction paper, bandanas or other material for blindfolds*

Time 10 minutes

Point out to students that all parts of Earth's surface are not heated equally by energy from the sun. Demonstrate this point by placing several pieces of construction paper in direct sunlight. Use white, black, and at least one or two other light and dark colors. After the papers have been in the sun for at least five minutes, ask volunteers to put on blindfolds. Then rearrange the order of the papers and have the volunteers try to tell which papers are light colored and which are dark colored based on how warm or cool they feel to the touch. Ask: **Why do the dark-colored papers feel warmer than the light-colored papers?** (*Dark-colored surfaces absorb more of the light that strikes them, whereas light-colored surfaces reflect more of the light that strikes them.*) **Which surfaces on Earth do you think reflect more of the sun's light back into space?** (*Light-colored surfaces such as sand or snow*) **Which surfaces absorb more of the sun's light?** (*Dark-colored surfaces such as bare soil or blacktop pavement*) **learning modality: kinesthetic**

Reflection of light in all directions is called **scattering.** When you look at the sky, the light you see has been scattered by gas molecules in the atmosphere. Gas molecules scatter short wavelengths of visible light (blue and violet) more than long wavelengths (red and orange). Scattered light is therefore bluer than ordinary sunlight, which is why the daytime sky looks blue.

When the sun is rising or setting, light from the sun passes through a greater thickness of the atmosphere than when the sun is higher in the sky. More light from the blue end of the spectrum is removed by scattering before it reaches your eyes. The remaining light from the sun contains mostly red and orange light. The sun looks red, and clouds around it become very colorful.

☑ *Checkpoint* *Why would particles from volcanic eruptions make sunsets and sunrises more red?*

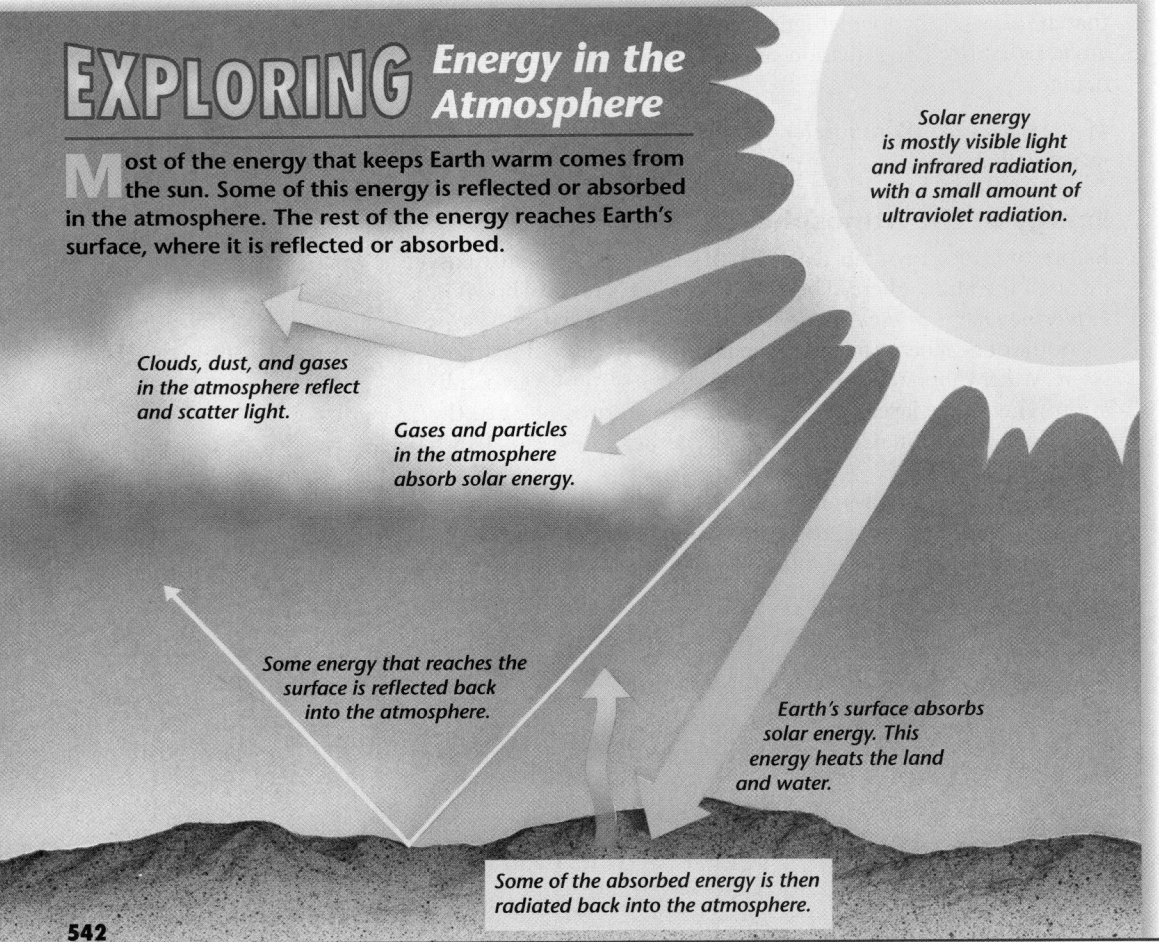

EXPLORING Energy in the Atmosphere

Most of the energy that keeps Earth warm comes from the sun. Some of this energy is reflected or absorbed in the atmosphere. The rest of the energy reaches Earth's surface, where it is reflected or absorbed.

Solar energy is mostly visible light and infrared radiation, with a small amount of ultraviolet radiation.

Clouds, dust, and gases in the atmosphere reflect and scatter light.

Gases and particles in the atmosphere absorb solar energy.

Some energy that reaches the surface is reflected back into the atmosphere.

Earth's surface absorbs solar energy. This energy heats the land and water.

Some of the absorbed energy is then radiated back into the atmosphere.

542

Background

Facts and Figures The amount of energy produced by the sun is amazing. An area of the sun's surface the size of a postage stamp gives off enough energy to power 500 60-watt light bulbs. Although only one part in two billion of the total amount of solar energy reaches Earth, this is still a huge amount. If the amount of solar energy reaching Earth in just one hour could be used, it would meet the world's total energy needs for a year. If

the amount of solar energy reaching Earth in a day could be used, it would take 700 billion tons of coal to match it.

A tiny fraction of the sun's energy actually is trapped and used for power. Solar energy plants collect sunlight with mirrors and focus it with lenses on tubes filled with fluid. The fluid heats up, and the heat is used to boil water into steam that powers electric generators.

Energy at Earth's Surface

Some of the sun's energy reaches Earth's surface and is reflected back into the atmosphere. Some of the energy, however, is absorbed by the land and water and changed into heat.

When Earth's surface is heated, it radiates some of the energy back into the atmosphere as infrared radiation. Most of this infrared radiation cannot travel all the way through the atmosphere back into space. Instead, much of it is absorbed by water vapor, carbon dioxide, methane, and other gases in the air. The energy from the absorbed radiation heats the gases in the air. These gases form a "blanket" around Earth that holds heat in the atmosphere. The process by which gases hold heat in the air is called the **greenhouse effect.**

Have you ever been inside a greenhouse during the winter? Even on a cold day, a greenhouse is warm. Greenhouses trap heat in two ways. First, infrared radiation given off in the interior cannot easily pass through glass and is trapped inside. Second, warm air inside the greenhouse cannot rise because the glass blocks the movement of air. What happens in Earth's atmosphere is similar to the first way that greenhouses trap heat.

The greenhouse effect is a natural process that keeps Earth's atmosphere at a temperature that is comfortable for most living things. Human activities over the last 200 years, however, have increased the amount of carbon dioxide in the atmosphere, which may be warming the atmosphere. You will learn more about the greenhouse effect in Chapter 19.

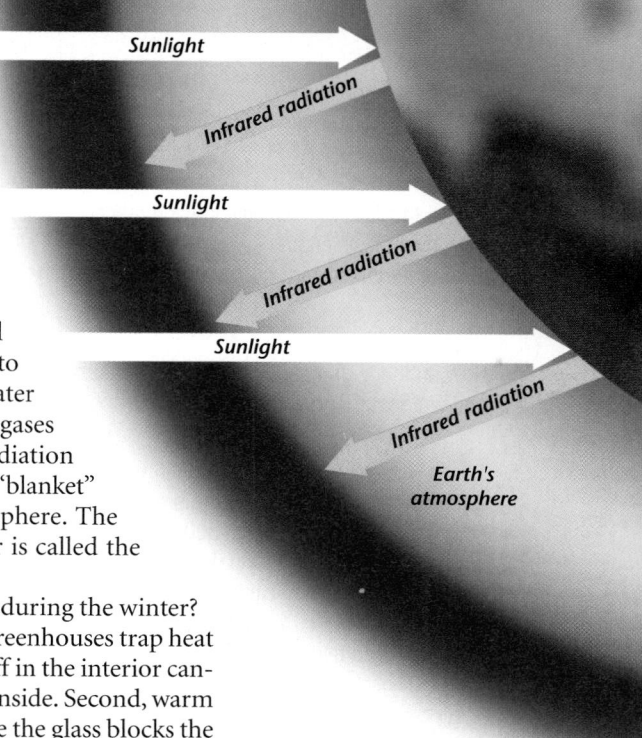

Sunlight

Infrared radiation

Sunlight

Infrared radiation

Sunlight

Infrared radiation

Earth's atmosphere

Figure 2 Sunlight travels through the atmosphere to Earth's surface. Earth's surface then gives off infrared radiation. Much of this energy is held by the atmosphere, warming it.

Section 1 Review

1. List three forms of radiation from the sun. How are these alike? How are they different?
2. What happens to the energy from the sun that is absorbed by Earth's surface?
3. Why is the sky blue? Why are sunsets often red?
4. **Thinking Critically** **Applying Concepts** What might conditions on Earth be like without the greenhouse effect?

Science at Home

With an adult family member, explore the role radiation plays in heating your home. Are some rooms warmer and sunnier in the morning? Are other rooms warmer and sunnier in the afternoon? How does opening and closing curtains or blinds affect the temperature of a room? Explain your observations to your family.

3 Assess

Section 1 Review Answers

1. Visible light, infrared radiation, and ultraviolet radiation; they differ in their wavelengths.
2. It is changed into heat.
3. The sky is blue because short-wavelength blue light is scattered more by gas molecules in the atmosphere. Sunsets are often red because the light from the setting sun passes through a greater thickness of the atmosphere than when the sun is higher in the sky, and more blue light is removed by scattering, leaving mostly red light to reach your eyes.
4. Without the greenhouse effect, more infrared radiation radiated back from Earth's surface would escape into space instead of being held in the atmosphere, so Earth's surface would be much colder.

Science at Home

Suggest to students that they try to do this activity **ACTIVITY** on a sunny day, preferably when the furnace or other source of artificial heat is not operating.

Answers to Self-Assessment

☑ *Checkpoint*

The particles would scatter more light from the sun. This would remove more light from the blue end of the spectrum, causing the remaining light to look mostly red.

Performance Assessment

Oral Presentation Call on students to explain in their own words one of the various things that can happen to sunlight that reaches Earth's atmosphere.

Heating Earth's Surface

Preparing for Inquiry

Key Concept Sand heats and cools more quickly than water.

Skills Objectives Students will be able to

- develop hypotheses about how quickly sand and water heat and cool;
- measure the temperature of sand and water while they are heating and cooling;
- create a data table to record their measurements;
- conclude from their data whether sand or water heats and cools more quickly.

Time 40 minutes

Advance Planning To be sure students have enough class time to record temperatures for a full 30 minutes, you may wish to set up the equipment and measure out the sand and water ahead of time. Make sure the sand is dry. Both sand and water should be at room temperature when the lab begins.

If using probeware, refer to the *Probeware Lab Manual.*

Alternative Materials Students can use small wide-mouthed glass jars instead of beakers, as long as both jars are the same size and shape. They also can substitute sugar for sand. If ring stands and clamps are not available, you can substitute two 2-L soda bottles placed about 30 cm apart and connected by a ruler placed across the tops. The thermometers can be suspended from the ruler.

Guiding Inquiry

Invitation To help students formulate hypotheses about the heating and cooling of sand and water, have them recall walking barefoot on a beach. Ask: **Did you ever walk barefoot on the beach on a sunny day? What was the temperature of the sand like?** *(The sand was probably hot.)* **When you reached the water, how did it feel by comparison to the hot sand?** *(much cooler)* **If you ever walked barefoot on the beach after dark, which felt warmer, the sand or the water?** *(the water)* Challenge students to

---

Skills Lab

Heating Earth's Surface

In this lab, you will develop and test a hypothesis about how quickly different materials absorb radiation.

Problem

How do the heating and cooling rates of sand and water compare?

Materials

2 thermometers or temperature probes
2 beakers, 400 mL   sand, 300 mL
water, 300 mL   lamp with 150-W bulb
metric ruler   clock or stopwatch
string   graph paper
ring stand and two ring clamps

Procedure

1. Do you think sand or water will heat up faster? Record your hypothesis. Then follow these steps to test your hypothesis.
2. Copy the data table into your notebook. Add enough rows to record data for 15 minutes.
3. Fill one beaker with 300 mL of dry sand.
4. Fill the second beaker with 300 mL of water at room temperature.
5. Arrange the beakers beneath the ring stand.
6. Place one thermometer in each beaker. If you are using a temperature probe, see your teacher for instructions.
7. Suspend the thermometers from the ring stand with string. This will hold the thermometers in place so they do not fall.

8. Adjust the height of the clamp so that the bulb of each thermometer is covered by about 0.5 cm of sand or water in a beaker.
9. Position the lamp so that it is about 20 cm above the sand and water. There should be no more than 8 cm between the beakers. **CAUTION:** *Be careful not to splash water onto the hot light bulb.*
10. Record the temperature of the sand and water in your data table.
11. Turn on the lamp. Read the temperature of the sand and water every minute for 15 minutes. Record the temperatures in the Light On column in the data table.
12. Which material do you think will cool off more quickly? Record your hypothesis. Again, give reasons why you think your hypothesis is correct.
13. Turn the light off. Read the temperature of the sand and water every minute for another 15 minutes. Record the temperatures in the Light Off column (16–30 minutes).

DATA TABLE

Temperature with Light On (°C)			Temperature with Light Off (°C)		
Time (min)	Sand	Water	Time (min)	Sand	Water
Start			16		
1			17		
2			18		
3			19		
4			20		
5			21		

---

think of other past observations that might help them formulate their hypotheses.

Introducing the Procedure
Have students read through the steps of the procedure. Clarify any steps they do not understand. Emphasize the importance of following each step of the procedure precisely. For example, students should use exactly the same amount of sand as water and place both beakers exactly the same distance from the lamp. Explain that by making these factors the

same for both the sand and water they will be controlling other variables that might affect the outcome of the experiment.

Troubleshooting the Experiment
- To reduce the number of setups needed, divide the class into groups and have each group use one setup.
- Make sure that each lamp is positioned so it shines evenly on the two beakers. If one beaker receives more direct rays than the other, it may bias the results. Also check that

Analyze and Conclude

1. Draw two line graphs to show the data for the temperature change in sand and water over time. Label the horizontal axis from 0 to 30 minutes and the vertical axis in degrees Celsius. Draw both graphs on the same piece of graph paper. Use a dashed line to show the temperature change in water and a solid line to show the temperature change in sand.

2. Calculate the total change in temperature for each material.

3. Based on your data, which material had the greater increase in temperature?

4. What can you conclude about which material absorbed heat faster? How do your results compare with your hypothesis?

5. Review your data again. In 15 minutes, which material cooled faster?

6. How do these results compare to your second hypothesis?

7. **Think About It** If your results did not support either of your hypotheses, why do you think the results differed from what you expected?

8. **Apply** Based on your results, which do you think will heat up more quickly on a sunny day: the water in a lake or the sand surrounding it? Which will cool off more quickly after dark?

More to Explore

Do you think all solid materials heat up as fast as sand? For example, consider gravel, crushed stone, or different types of soil. Write a hypothesis about their heating rates as an "If . . . then. . . ." statement. With the approval and supervision of your teacher, develop a procedure to test your hypothesis. Was your hypothesis correct?

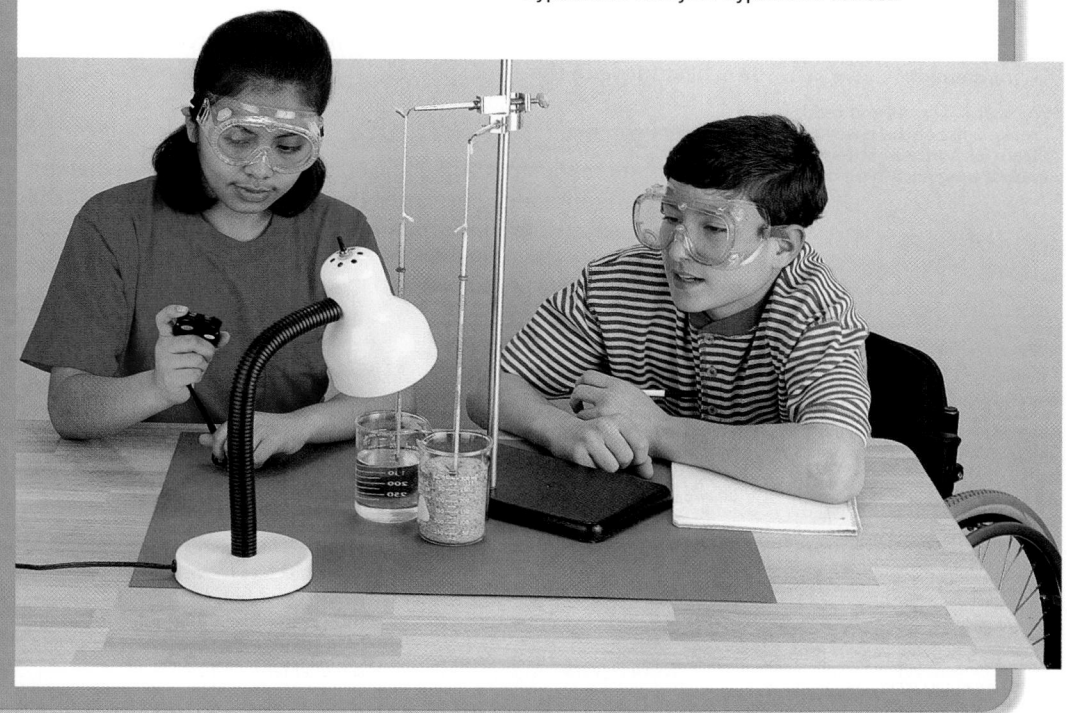

Safety

Caution students to be careful not to touch the light bulb or splash water on it. Review the safety guidelines in Appendix A.

Program Resources

◆ **Unit 5 Resources** Skills Lab blackline masters, pp. 57–59
◆ **Probeware Lab Manual** Blackline masters

Media and Technology

 Lab Activity Videotape
Tape 4

---

both thermometers are positioned the same distance below the surface and held in an upright position by the string.

Expected Outcome
Students should find that the sand heats and cools more quickly than the water.

Analyze and Conclude
1. Both graphs should rise steadily during the first 15 minutes and then decline steadily during the second 15 minutes. The line for sand temperature should rise and fall more steeply than the line for water temperature, indicating a greater rate of change in temperature for sand than water.
2. Exact answers will vary depending on the specific temperatures recorded. However, the sand should show a greater total change in temperature than the water.
3. The data should show that the sand had a greater increase in temperature.
4. Students should conclude that the sand absorbed heat faster than the water. These results may or may not agree with their hypothesis.
5. The data should show that the sand cooled faster.
6. These results may or may not agree with their second hypothesis.
7. Answers may vary. One possible answer is that they expected both the sand and water to heat and cool at the same rate because there were equal amounts of the two substances.
8. Based on their results, students should say that the sand surrounding a lake will heat up more quickly on a sunny day and cool off more quickly after dark than the water in the lake.

Extending the Inquiry

More to Explore Students may think that solids with a different texture, made of different materials, or having different colors might heat up at different rates than sand. For example, students may think that rock would heat up faster than sand because it is more solid. Students may hypothesize that soil will heat up faster than sand because it is darker in color. They can test their hypothesis by repeating the skills lab and substituting soil or other materials for water.

SECTION 2 Heat Transfer

Objectives

After completing the lesson, students will be able to
- describe how temperature is measured;
- explain the three ways heat is transferred.

Key Terms thermal energy, temperature, thermometer, heat, conduction, convection

1 Engage/Explore

Activating Prior Knowledge

Introduce students to the concept of heat transfer by helping them recall the shimmery effect produced by heated air rising from hot pavement. Ask: **On a hot sunny day, did you ever see cars, buildings, or other objects appear to shimmer or waver on the other side of a street or parking lot?** (*Most students probably will say yes.*) **What causes this effect?** (*Hot air rising from the pavement*) Explain that the sun heats up the ground more quickly than the air, especially if the surface of the ground is dark colored. The heated air then rises and bends light waves as they pass through it, making objects on the other side shimmer.

•••••• DISCOVER ••••••••

Skills Focus inferring
Materials *aluminum pie plate, heavy scissors, thread, candle or hot plate or incandescent light*
Time 10 minutes
Tips You may want to poke the holes in the flat parts yourself.
Expected Outcome The spiral will spin.
Think It Over The spiral spun because warm air rose from the heat source and pushed against the spiral.

SECTION 2 Heat Transfer

DISCOVER •••••••••••••••••••••••• ACTIVITY••••

What Happens When Air Is Heated?

1. Use heavy scissors to cut the flat part out of an aluminum pie plate. Use the tip of the scissors to poke a small hole in the middle of the flat part.
2. Cut the part into a spiral shape, as shown in the photo. Tie a 30-centimeter piece of thread to the middle of the spiral.
3. Hold the spiral over a source of heat, such as a candle, hot plate, or incandescent light bulb.

Think It Over
Inferring What happened to the spiral? Why do you think this happened?

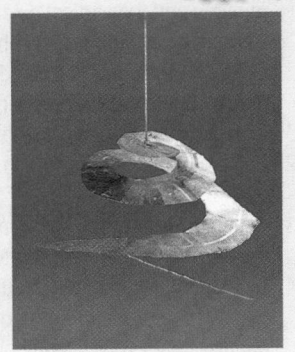

GUIDE FOR READING

- How is temperature measured?
- In what three ways is heat transferred?

Reading Tip As you read, make a list of the types of heat transfer. Write a sentence about how each type occurs.

You know that energy from the sun is absorbed by Earth's surface. Some energy is then transferred from the surface to the atmosphere in the form of heat. The heat then moves from place to place within the atmosphere. But how does heat move in the atmosphere?

Energy and Temperature

Gases are made up of small particles, called molecules, that are constantly moving. The faster the molecules are moving, the more energy they have. Figure 3 shows how the motion of

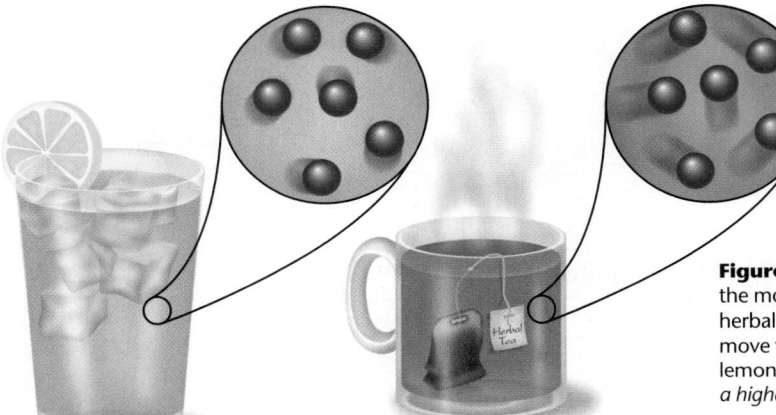

Figure 3 The lemonade is cold, so the molecules move slowly. The herbal tea is hot, so the molecules move faster than the molecules in the lemonade. *Inferring* Which liquid has a higher temperature?

READING STRATEGIES

Reading Tip Student lists should include radiation, conduction, and convection. Their sentences should explain that radiation occurs by direct transfer of heat by one substance touching another, and that convection occurs as the result of the movement of fluids.

Program Resources

- **Unit 5 Resources** 17-2 Lesson Plan, p. 41; 17-2 Section Summary, p. 42
- **Guided Reading and Study Workbook** Section 17-2

molecules is related to the amount of energy they hold. The total energy of motion in the molecules of a substance is called **thermal energy.** On the other hand, **temperature** is the *average* amount of energy of motion of each molecule of a substance. That means that temperature is a measure of how hot or cold a substance is.

Measuring Temperature

Ask someone what the weather is like. The answer will probably include the temperature. Temperature is one of the most important elements of weather. **Air temperature is usually measured with a thermometer.** A **thermometer** is a thin glass tube with a bulb on one end that contains a liquid, usually mercury or colored alcohol.

Thermometers work because liquids expand when they are heated and contract when they are cooled. When the air temperature increases, the liquid in the bulb expands and rises up the column. What happens when the temperature decreases? The liquid in the bulb contracts and moves down the tube.

Temperature is measured in units called degrees. The two most common scales are shown in Figure 4. Scientists use the Celsius scale. On the Celsius scale, the freezing point of pure water is 0°C (read "zero degrees Celsius"). The boiling point of pure water is 100°C. Weather reports in the United States use the Fahrenheit scale. On the Fahrenheit scale, the freezing point of water is 32°F and the boiling point is 212°F.

☑ *Checkpoint How many degrees Celsius are there between the freezing point of water and the boiling point of water?*

Figure 4 Scientists use the Celsius scale to measure temperature. However, weather reports use the Fahrenheit scale. *Measuring According to this thermometer, what is the air temperature in degrees Celsius?*

How Heat Is Transferred

The energy transferred from a hotter object to a cooler one is referred to as **heat.** The types of heat transfer are shown in Figure 5 on the next page. **Heat is transferred in three ways: radiation, conduction, and convection.**

Radiation Have you ever felt the warmth of the sun's rays on your face? You were feeling energy coming directly from the sun as radiation. Recall that radiation is the direct transfer of energy by electromagnetic waves. The heat you feel from the sun or a campfire travels directly to you as infrared radiation. You cannot see infrared radiation, but you can feel it as heat.

Energy and Temperature

Demonstration

Materials *glass jar with lid, black and white sheets of construction paper, toothpick, thread, glue, tape, scissors*
Time 15 minutes

Make a radiometer to show students that heat increases the movement of air molecules. Cut four 2-cm squares from white construction paper and four from black construction paper. Glue each black square to a white square. Holding a toothpick vertically, glue one edge of each square to the shaft of the toothpick, like feathers sticking out from the shaft of an arrow. Arrange the squares so that colors alternate between black and white. Tape the end of a piece of thread to one end of the toothpick. Tape the other end of the thread to the inside of a jar lid. Put the lid on the jar, making sure the toothpick dangles freely, and place the jar in sunlight. Soon the toothpick will start to spin. When it does, ask: **What causes the toothpick to spin?** *(The black squares heat up faster than the white squares, and this heats the air molecules close to them. The heated air molecules bounce off the black squares, pushing the toothpick around in a circle.)* **learning modality: visual**

Measuring Temperature

Building Inquiry Skills: Calculating

Materials *calculator*
Time 10 minutes

Help students become more familiar with the Celsius scale by having them convert several Fahrenheit temperatures to their Celsius equivalents, using the formula °C = (°F - 32) x 5/9. **learning modality: logical/mathematical**

Ongoing Assessment

Skills Check Have students compare and contrast the terms *thermal energy, temperature,* and *heat.*

547

Media and Technology

 Transparencies "Types of Heat Transfer," Transparency 66

Answers to Self-Assessment

Caption Questions

Figure 3 The herbal tea has a higher temperature.

Figure 4 The air temperature is about 20 degrees Celsius.

☑ *Checkpoint*

Between the freezing point of water and the boiling point of water there are 100 Celsius degrees.

How Heat Is Transferred

Inquiry Challenge

Materials *ball*
Time 5 minutes

Challenge students to model the three different types of heat transfer by using a ball to represent heat and students to represent air molecules. Then have students move the ball around the classroom in different ways to model radiation, conduction, and convection. Ask: **How would you move the ball to represent radiation?** *(Toss or roll it.)* **How would you move the ball to represent conduction?** *(Pass it from one student to another.)* **How would you move the ball to represent convection?** *(Have one student walk with it.)*
learning modality: kinesthetic

Heat Transfer in the Troposphere

TRY THIS

Skills Focus interpreting data

Materials *2 thermometers, metric tape measure, watch or clock, graph paper*
Time 10 minutes per day for 3 days; 20 minutes to graph and analyze data
Tips Doing this activity on sunny days will lead to greater differences in temperatures at the two heights.
Expected Outcome Students should find that the temperature 1 cm above the ground varies more than the temperature 1.25 m above the ground. The ground heats up during the day as it absorbs sunlight. It cools quickly at night as it radiates the heat back into the air. Heat is not effectively transferred through air, so air close to the ground will be more affected by these variations in ground temperature than air farther above the ground.
Extend Have students repeat the activity in a shady location and then compare the data obtained from the two locations. They should find less variation in the shady-location readings. Challenge students to explain why. **learning modality: logical/mathematical**

Temperatures at Two Heights

How much difference do you think there is between air temperatures near the ground and air temperatures higher up? Give reasons for your prediction.

1. Take all of your measurements at a location that is sunny all day.

2. Early in the morning, measure the air temperature 1 cm and 1.25 m above the ground. Record the time of day and the temperature for both locations. Repeat your measurements late in the afternoon.

3. Record these measurements in the morning and afternoon for two more days.

4. Graph your data for each height with temperature on the vertical axis and time on the horizontal axis. Draw both lines on the same piece of graph paper using the same axes. Label both lines.

Interpreting Data At which height did the temperature vary the most? How can you explain the difference?

Conduction   Have you ever walked barefoot on hot sand? Your feet felt hot because heat moved directly from the sand into your feet. When a fast-moving molecule bumps into a nearby slower-moving molecule, it transfers some of its energy. The direct transfer of heat from one substance to another substance that it is touching is called **conduction.** The molecules that gain energy can in turn pass the energy along to other nearby molecules. When you walk on hot sand, the fast-moving molecules in the sand transfer heat into the slower-moving molecules in your feet.

The closer together the molecules in a substance are, the more effectively they can conduct heat. Conduction works well in some solids, such as metals, but not as well in liquids and gases. Air and water do not conduct heat very well.

Convection   How can you dry your boots over a hot-air vent, even though the furnace is in another room? Air from the furnace carries the heat to your boots. In fluids (liquids and gases), molecules can move from place to place. As the molecules move, they take their heat along with them. The transfer of heat by the movement of a fluid is called **convection.**

☑ *Checkpoint* *Give at least one example each of radiation, conduction, and convection in your daily life.*

Heat Transfer in the Troposphere

Radiation, conduction, and convection work together to heat the troposphere. When Earth's surface absorbs solar energy during the day, the surface of the land becomes warmer than the air. Air near Earth's surface is warmed by radiation and conduction of heat from the surface to the air. However, heat is not easily conducted from one air molecule to another. Only the first few meters of the troposphere are heated by conduction. Thus, the air close to the ground is usually warmer than the air a few meters up.

Convection causes most of the heating of the troposphere. When the air near the ground is heated, the molecules have more energy. Because they have more energy, the molecules move

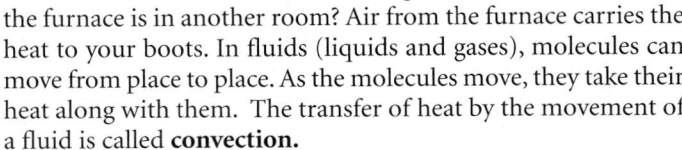

Heat transfer by convection

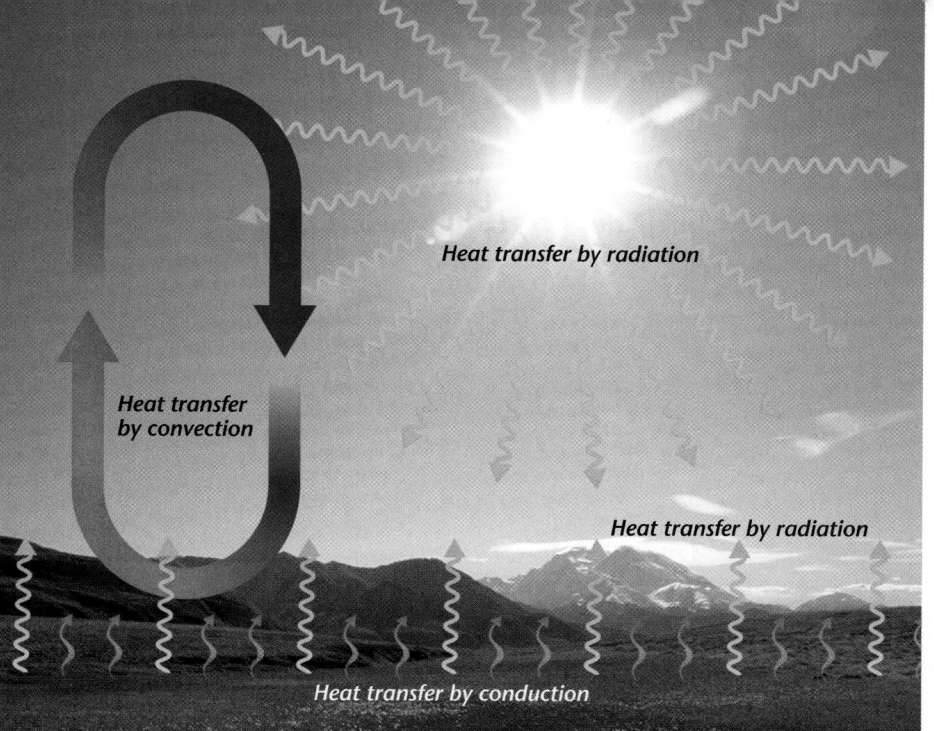

Heat transfer by radiation

Heat transfer by convection

Heat transfer by radiation

Heat transfer by conduction

faster. As the molecules in the heated air move, they bump into each other and move farther apart. The air becomes less dense. Cooler, denser air sinks, forcing the warmer, less dense air to rise.

The upward movement of warm air and the downward movement of cool air form convection currents. Convection currents move heat throughout the troposphere.

Figure 5 All three types of heat transfer—radiation, convection, and conduction—occur near Earth's surface.

Section 2 Review

1. What is temperature?
2. Describe how a thermometer works.
3. Name three ways that heat can be transferred. Briefly explain how the three work together to heat the troposphere.
4. **Thinking Critically** **Applying Concepts** When you light a fire in a fireplace, warm air rises by convection and goes up the chimney. How, then, does a fireplace heat a room? Why do only the people directly in front of the fireplace feel the warmth of the fire?

Check Your Progress

CHAPTER PROJECT 17

Gather the instruments you will need to measure the weather factors. (*Hint:* Make sure you know how to take accurate measurements.) Plan when and where to measure weather factors. Be sure to take your measurements at the same location and at the same time of day.

Chapter 17 **549**

Using the Visuals: Figure 5
Call students' attention to the illustration and have them locate the arrows showing each of the three types of heat transfer. Point out that radiation occurs from Earth's surface as well as from the sun.
learning modality: visual

3 Assess

Section 2 Review Answers

1. The average amount of energy of motion in the molecules of a substance
2. When the air temperature increases, the liquid in the bulb of a thermometer expands and rises up the column. When the air temperature decreases, the liquid contracts and moves down the column.
3. Heat can be transferred by radiation, conduction, and convection. Air near Earth's surface is warmed by radiation and by conduction of heat from the surface to the air. When the air near the ground is heated, it becomes less dense and rises in convection currents.
4. A fireplace heats a room by radiation. Only people sitting directly in front of the fire feel its warmth because radiation is the direct transfer of energy and does not effectively heat areas of the room out of the direct line of the fireplace.

Check Your Progress

CHAPTER PROJECT 17

Check that students have all the instruments they need and know how to use them. Make sure that the place they plan to take their measurements is suitable. Remind students to take their measurements in the same place and at the same time each day.

Media and Technology

 Concept Videotape Library
Adventures, Tape 4, "A Wave Is a Wave Is a Wave"; "As Hot As a Desert"; "Hot is Hot, Cold is Not"; "The Power of Heat"

Answers to Self-Assessment

☑ *Checkpoint*

Possible examples might include heat radiating from a campfire, heat being conducted through the bottom of a metal pot on a stove, and heat flowing in convection currents through a house heated by a furnace.

Performance Assessment

Drawing Have students draw a diagram to show how heat is transferred from Earth's surface to the atmosphere.

Objectives

After completing the lesson, students will be able to

♦ explain what causes winds;

♦ distinguish between local winds and global winds;

♦ describe the major global wind belts and where they are located.

Key Terms wind, anemometer, wind-chill factor, local wind, sea breeze, land breeze, monsoons, global wind, Coriolis effect, latitude, jet stream

1 Engage/Explore

Activating Prior Knowledge

Introduce students to winds by helping them recall a time when they flew a kite. Ask: **What made the kite fly in the air?** *(the wind)* **What is wind?** *(the movement of air)*. Then remind students how hard it can be to hold on to a kite against the force of a strong wind. Stress that even though air is an invisible gas, it still consists of molecules, and their movement, especially at high speeds, can exert a lot of force. Tell students they will learn more about wind in this section.

DISCOVER

Skills Focus making models

Materials *heavy-duty tape, pencil, large smooth ball, marker*

Time 10 minutes

Tips Make sure students spin the ball in a counterclockwise direction before their partner draws on it with the marker. You might want to have students also draw a line from the "South Pole" to the "Equator" to see what direction winds blow in the Southern Hemisphere due to Earth's rotation.

Expected Outcome The lines students draw should veer to the west as the marker goes from the "North Pole" to the "Equator" of the ball.

Think It Over The movement of cold air from Canada to the United States would turn toward the west.

550

DISCOVER •••••••••••••••••••••••••••••• ACTIVITY

Which Way Does the Wind Turn?

Do this activity with a partner. Think of the ball as a model of Earth and the marker as representing wind.

1. Using heavy-duty tape, attach a pencil to a large smooth ball so that you can spin the ball from the top without touching it.

2. One partner should hold the pencil. Slowly turn the ball counterclockwise when seen from above.

3. While the ball is turning, the second partner should use a marker to try to draw a straight line from the "North Pole" to the "equator" of the ball. What shape does the line form?

Think It Over

Making Models If cold air were moving south from Canada into the United States, how would its movement be affected by Earth's rotation?

GUIDE FOR READING

♦ What causes winds?

♦ What are local winds and global winds?

♦ Where are the major global wind belts located?

Reading Tip Before you read, preview the illustrations and read their captions. Write down any questions you have about winds. As you read, look for answers to your questions.

The highest point in the north-eastern United States, at 1,917 meters above sea level, is Mount Washington in New Hampshire. Sometimes winds near the top of this mountain are so strong that hikers cannot safely reach the summit! The greatest wind speed ever measured at Earth's surface—370 kilometers per hour—was measured on April 12, 1934, at the top of Mount Washington. What causes this incredible force?

What Causes Winds?

Because air is a fluid, it can move easily from place to place. The force that makes air move is caused by a difference of air pressure. Fluids tend to move from areas of high pressure to areas of low pressure. A **wind** is the horizontal movement of air from an area of high pressure to an area of lower pressure. **All winds are caused by differences in air pressure.**

READING STRATEGIES

Reading Tip Student questions might include: Why does the wind blow? What is a monsoon? How are winds connected to the energy of the sun? Encourage students to record the answers to their questions as they encounter them in their reading.

Vocabulary Urge students to look up the word *doldrums* in a dictionary. In addition

to being the name for the equatorial zone of calm winds, students will find that it also means "a period of inactivity or stagnation." Call students' attention to the explanation given in the text for the name *horse latitudes*. Knowing the rather memorable story behind it will help them remember that the *horse latitudes* also are zones of calm.

Most differences in air pressure are caused by unequal heating of the atmosphere. As you learned in the previous section, convection currents form when an area of Earth's surface is heated by the sun's rays. Air over the heated surface expands and becomes less dense. As the air becomes less dense, its air pressure decreases. If a nearby area is not heated as much, the air above the less-heated area will be cooler and denser. The cool, dense air has a higher air pressure so it flows underneath the warm, less dense air. This process forces the warm air to rise.

Measuring Wind

Winds are described by their direction and speed. Wind direction is determined with a wind vane. The wind swings the wind vane so that one end points into the wind. The name of a wind tells you where the wind is coming from. For example, a south wind blows from the south toward the north. A north wind blows to the south.

Wind speed is measured with an **anemometer** (an uh MAHM uh tur). An anemometer has three or four cups mounted at the ends of spokes that spin on an axle. The force of the wind against the cups turns the axle. A speedometer attached to the axle shows the wind speed.

A cool breeze can be very refreshing on a warm day. However, during the winter, a similar breeze can make you feel uncomfortably cold. The wind blowing over your skin removes body heat. The stronger the wind, the colder you feel. The increased cooling that a wind can cause is called the **wind-chill factor.** Thus a weather report may say, "The temperature is 20 degrees Fahrenheit. But with a wind speed of 30 miles per hour, the wind-chill factor makes it feel like 18 degrees below zero."

☑ *Checkpoint* *Toward what direction does a west wind blow?*

Build a Wind Vane

Here's how to build your own wind vane.

ACTIVITY

1. ✂ Use scissors to cut out a pointer and a slightly larger tail fin from construction paper.
2. Make a slit 1 cm deep in each end of a soda straw.
3. Slide the pointer and tail fin into place on the straw, securing them with small pieces of tape.

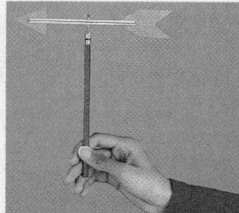

4. Hold the straw on your finger to find the point at which it balances.
5. Carefully push a pin through the balance point and into the eraser of a pencil. Move the wind vane back and forth to make sure it can spin freely.

Observing How can you use your wind vane to tell the direction of the wind?

Figure 6 The wind vane on the left points in the direction the wind is blowing from. The anemometer on the right measures wind speed. The cups catch the wind, turning faster when the wind blows faster.

Program Resources

◆ **Unit 5 Resources** 17-3 Lesson Plan, p. 45; 17-3 Section Summary, p. 46
◆ **Guided Reading and Study Workbook** Section 17-3

Answers to Self-Assessment

☑ *Checkpoint*
A west wind blows toward the east.

2 Facilitate

What Causes Winds?

Demonstration

Materials *pinwheel, lamp with incandescent light bulb* **ACTIVITY**
Time 10 minutes

Show students how differences in temperature cause air movement by holding a pinwheel over a lamp. First hold the pinwheel over the lamp with the light bulb turned off. The pinwheel will remain stationary. Then hold the pinwheel over the lamp with the light bulb turned on. Once the light bulb gets hot, the pinwheel will start to spin. Ask: **Why did the pinwheel start spinning after the lightbulb was turned on?** (*The hot light bulb heated the air around it, which rose and turned the pinwheel.*)
learning modality: visual

Measuring Wind

Skills Focus observing **ACTIVITY**
Materials *scissors, construction paper, metric ruler, soda straw, tape, straight pin, pencil with eraser*
Time 15 minutes
Expected Outcome Students should find when they take their wind vane outside in the wind or blow on it that the wind vane points in the direction from which the wind is coming.
Extend If students set their wind vane in the center of a compass, it will show them whether it is an east, west, north, or south wind. Remind students that winds are named for the direction from which they blow. **learning modality: kinesthetic**

Ongoing Assessment

Drawing Have students make a simple drawing with arrows and labels to show how differences in air temperature cause wind.

 Students can keep their drawings in their portfolios.

Where's the Wind?

Preparing for Inquiry

Key Concept Obstacles such as buildings can change the speed and direction of the wind.

Skills Objectives Students will be able to

◆ measure the direction and speed of the wind on all sides of the school building;

◆ interpret their data to determine which side of the building is less windy than the other sides;

◆ conclude from the data which side of the building provides the best location for a door.

Time 40 minutes

Advance Planning Follow weather reports when scheduling the lab so students take their measurements on a day when the wind is blowing steadily, not in gusts, and from its usual direction (west in most of the United States). Students can make the anemometers one day and measure wind speed and direction another day. You may want to have a fan or hair dryer for students to use to test their anemometers.

Alternative Materials If you do not have a wind vane, students can measure wind direction by observing the direction that flags are flying or smoke is drifting. Instead of using a corrugated cardboard sheet to make the anemometer, students may use a piece of plastic foam cut from the bottom of a plastic foam plate. Also, wooden craft sticks may be used in place of wooden stirrers. Other types of tape, such as adhesive or electrical tape, will work as well as masking tape.

Guiding Inquiry

Invitation Help students focus on the problem in the lab by asking: **Which two factors do you need to know to determine wind patterns?** *(Wind direction and wind speed)* **How can you measure wind direction?** *(With a wind*

Local Winds

Have you ever flown a kite at the beach on a hot summer day? Even if there is no wind inland, there may be a cool breeze blowing in from the water toward the beach. This breeze is an example of a local wind. **Local winds** are winds that blow over short distances. **Local winds are caused by unequal heating of Earth's surface within a small area.** Local winds form only when no winds are blowing from farther away.

WHERE'S THE WIND?

Your city is planning to build a new community center. You and your classmates want to be sure that the doors will not be hard to open or close on windy days. You need to know which side of the building will be sheltered from the wind. You decide to measure wind speeds around a similar building.

Problem

How can you determine wind patterns around a building?

Skills Focus

measuring, interpreting data, drawing conclusions

Materials

pen
wind vane
meter stick
corrugated cardboard sheet, 15 cm x 20 cm
round toothpick
2 wooden coffee stirrers
narrow masking tape

Procedure

1. You'll begin by making a simple anemometer that uses wooden coffee stirrers to indicate wind speed. On your piece of cardboard, draw a

curved scale like the one shown in the diagram. Mark it in equal intervals from 0 to 10.

2. Carefully use the pen to make a small hole where the toothpick will go. Insert the toothpick through the hole.

3. Tape the wooden coffee stirrers to the toothpick as shown in the diagram, one on each side of the cardboard.

4. Copy the data table into your notebook.

5. Take your anemometer outside the school. Stand about 2–3 m away from the building and away from any corners or large plants.

552

---

vane or by observing the direction in which objects are blowing in the wind) **How can you measure wind speed?** *(With an anemometer)* Point out to students that in this lab they will make a simple anemometer. Then they will use a wind vane to measure wind direction and their anemometer to measure wind speed. Making the measurements on all sides of their school building will let them determine wind patterns around it and from this decide on the best location for a door.

Introducing the Procedure

Have students read through the entire procedure. Explain that the second coffee stirrer added to the anemometer provides a balance for the stirrer that measures wind speed. Point out that the numbers on the dial do not represent actual units, such as kilometers per hour. However, they do allow wind speeds to be quantified for comparison. Stress the importance of taking all measurements the same distance from the building. Suggest that they select a spot near

Unequal heating often occurs on land that is next to a large body of water. It takes more energy to warm up a body of water than it does to warm up an equal area of land. This means that as the sun heats Earth's surface during the day, the land warms up faster than the water. The air over the land becomes warmer than the air over the water. The warm air expands and rises, creating a low-pressure area. Cool air blows inland from the water and moves underneath the warm air. A wind that blows

DATA TABLE

Location	Wind Direction	Wind Speed

6. Use the wind vane to find out what direction the wind is coming from. Hold your anemometer so that the card is straight, vertical, and parallel to the wind direction. Observe which number the wooden stirrer is closest to. Record your data.
7. Repeat your measurements on all the other sides of the building. Record your data.

Analyze and Conclude

1. Was the wind stronger on one side of the school building than the other sides? How can you explain your observation?
2. Do your classmates' results agree with yours? What might account for any differences?
3. **Apply** Based on your data, which side of the building provides the best location for a door?

More to Explore

What effect do plants have on the wind speed in an area? Could bushes and trees be planted so that they reduce the wind speed near the doors? What measurements could you make to find out?

553

Sample Data Table

Location	Wind Direction	Wind Speed
East side of building	W	1
South side of building	NW	4
West side of building	W	3
North side of building	SW	6

Program Resources

◆ **Unit 5 Resources** Real-World Lab blackline masters, pp. 60–61

Media and Technology

 **Lab Activity Videotape**
Tape 4

the middle of each side about 2 to 3 m from the building.

Troubleshooting the Experiment

◆ Have students test their anemometers before they take them outside to measure wind speed. They can use a fan or hair dryer set on low or simply blow on them. They should make sure the coffee stirrers blow freely in the wind and adjust them if necessary.
◆ Check that students are holding their anemometers parallel to wind direction. Otherwise, the wind will be less effective at moving the coffee stirrer and the anemometer will give a reading that is too low.

Expected Outcome

Students will probably find that one side of the building had winds blowing at a lower speed than the other sides. If a west wind was blowing, then the east side of the building probably was the least windy. Students also may find that wind direction is different from one side of the building to another.

Analyze and Conclude

1. Students probably will find that the wind was stronger on the side of the building that the wind was coming from. Students should explain their observations by saying that the building blocked and slowed the wind on the other sides of the building.
2. Classmates' results may or may not agree. Differences may be due to students measuring the wind at somewhat different locations around the building, wind gusts, or slight differences in how the anemometers were made or used.
3. Students should conclude that the best location is the side of the building that has winds with the lowest speed.

Extending the Inquiry

More to Explore Students may say that plants can block the wind and reduce its speed near the doors. They could find out by determining wind patterns around bushes and trees, as they did around the school building, to see how these obstacles affect wind direction and speed.

Safety

Do not do this lab on a day when there is danger of lightning or high winds. Review the safety guidelines in Appendix A.

Local Winds

554

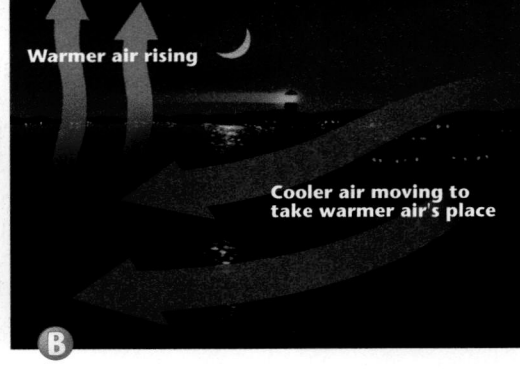

Warmer air rising

Warmer air rising

Cooler air moving to take warmer air's place

Cooler air moving to take warmer air's place

A

B

Figure 7 **A.** During the day, cool air moves from the sea to the land, creating a sea breeze. **B.** At night, cooler air moves from the land to the sea. *Forming Operational Definitions* What type of breeze occurs at night?

from an ocean or lake onto land is known as a **sea breeze** or a lake breeze. Figure 7A shows a sea breeze.

At night, the situation is reversed. Land cools more quickly than water, so the air over the land becomes cooler than the air over the water. As the warmer air over the water rises, cooler air moves from the land to take its place. The flow of air from land to a body of water is called a **land breeze.**

Monsoons

A process similar to land and sea breezes can occur over wider areas. In the summer in South and Southeast Asia, the land gradually gets warmer than the ocean. A large "sea breeze" blows steadily inland from the ocean all summer, even at night. In the winter, the land cools and becomes colder than the ocean. A "land breeze" blows steadily from the land to the ocean.

Sea and land breezes over a large region that change direction with the seasons are called **monsoons.** The summer monsoon in South Asia and Southeast Asia is very important for the crops grown there. The air blowing from the ocean during the rainy season is very warm and humid. As the humid air rises over the land, the air cools, producing heavy rains that supply the water needed by rice and other crops.

Figure 8 This heavy rain in Nepal is part of the summer monsoon, which blows from the ocean to the land. In the winter, the monsoon reverses and blows from the land to the ocean.

554

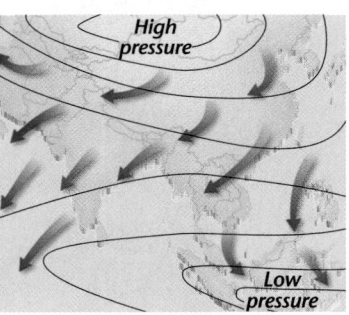

Summer Monsoon

Low pressure

High pressure

Winter Monsoon

High pressure

Low pressure

Global Winds

Winds that blow steadily from specific directions over long distances are called **global winds**. Like local winds, global winds are created by unequal heating of Earth's surface. Refer to Figure 9 to see how sunlight strikes Earth's surface. In the middle of the day near the equator, the sun is almost directly overhead. The direct rays from the sun heat Earth's surface intensely. Near the North Pole or South Pole, the sun's rays strike Earth's surface at a lower angle, even at noon. The sun's energy is spread out over a larger area, so it heats the surface less. As a result, temperatures near the poles are much lower than they are near the equator.

Global Convection Currents Temperature differences between the equator and the poles produce giant convection currents in the atmosphere. Warm air rises at the equator, and cold air sinks at the poles. Therefore air pressure tends to be lower near the equator and greater near the poles, causing winds at Earth's surface to blow from the poles toward the equator. Higher in the atmosphere, air flows away from the equator toward the poles. **The movement of air between the equator and the poles produces global winds.**

The Coriolis Effect If Earth did not rotate, global winds would blow in a straight line from the poles toward the equator. Because Earth is rotating, global winds do not follow a straight path. As the winds move, Earth rotates from west to east underneath them, making it seem as if the winds have curved. The way Earth's rotation makes winds curve is called the **Coriolis effect** (kawr ee OH lis). It is named for the French mathematician who studied and explained it in 1835.

In the Northern Hemisphere, all global winds gradually turn toward the right. As you can see in Figure 10, a wind blowing toward the north gradually turns toward the northeast. In other words, a south wind gradually changes to a southwest wind. In the Southern Hemisphere, winds curve toward the left. A south wind becomes an southeast wind, and a north wind becomes a northwest wind.

☑ *Checkpoint* What happens to a wind blowing toward the south in the Northern Hemisphere? What would you call this wind?

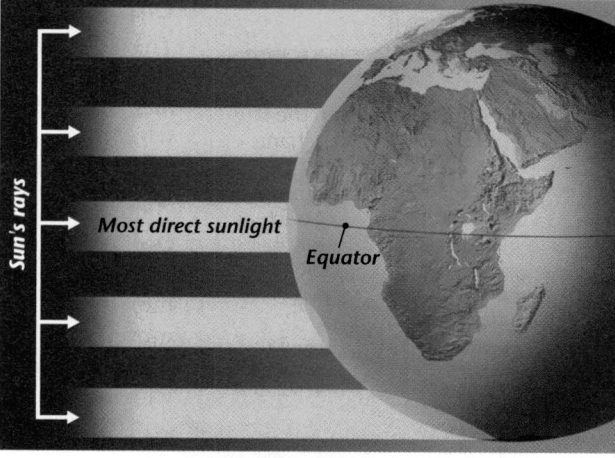

Figure 9 Near the equator, energy from the sun strikes Earth almost directly. Near the poles, the same amount of energy is spread out over a larger area.

Figure 10 As Earth rotates, the Coriolis effect turns winds in the Northern Hemisphere toward the right. *Interpreting Diagrams Which way do winds turn in the Southern Hemisphere?*

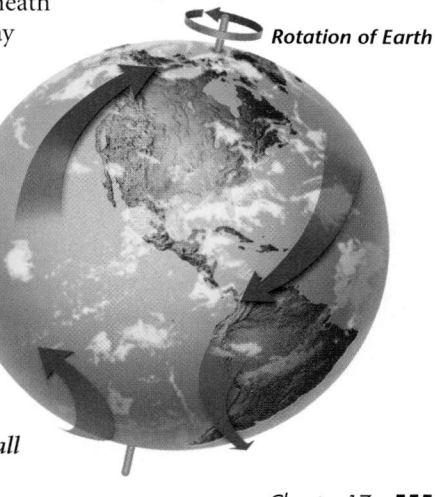

Rotation of Earth

Demonstration

Materials *globe, small flashlight*
Time 5 minutes

Challenge a pair of students to model Earth and the sun using a globe and flashlight. *(One student should hold the globe, and the other student should shine the light on the equator, with the room lights dimmed.)* Call students' attention to the fact that the light is direct and bright over the equator but angled and dim at the poles. Ask: **How do these differences in energy cause global winds?** *(The more concentrated energy falling directly on the equator causes air over the equator to be warmer than air over the poles, leading to the convection currents that cause global winds.)*
learning modality: visual

Answers to Self-Assessment

Caption Questions

Figure 7 A land breeze occurs at night.
Figure 10 In the Southern Hemisphere, winds turn toward the left.

☑ *Checkpoint*

A wind blowing toward the south in the Northern Hemisphere gradually turns toward the right. You would call it a northeast wind.

Ongoing Assessment

Drawing Have students make a sketch in their journals to show how the Coriolis effect influences global winds.

Global Wind Belts

Including All Students

Materials *globe*
Time 10 minutes

Give students who need extra help a chance to spin a globe in a west to east direction while moving their finger over its surface from north to south. Ask: **How does the path you traced on the globe model global winds?** *(The path of global winds curves to the right in the same way.)* Then have students use the globe to locate a city or country that interests them. Ask: **Which major wind belt flows over that location?** *(Answers will vary depending on locations students choose.)* Suggest that students find the latitude of their location to determine which global wind belt flows over it.
learning modality: kinesthetic

Social Studies
CONNECTION

Make sure students realize that for the time period in question, ships had sails and depended on the wind to move. Suggest that they refer to the illustration on page 557 when doing this feature. From the figure, students should be able to identify which winds they would have used to sail east *(prevailing westerlies)* and which they would have used to sail west *(trade winds)*.

In Your Journal Students should see from the figure on page 557 that making use of the trade winds to go west requires a more southern route across the Atlantic. They should write in their letter that the journey west takes almost twice as many weeks because the southern route is less direct and longer.
learning modality: verbal

Social Studies
CONNECTION

From colonial days to the late 1800s, American merchants traded new ships, lumber, cotton, tobacco, and furs for manufactured goods, such as textiles, from England. The eastbound voyage in the early 1800s took about three weeks. However, the westbound passage took almost twice as long—five to six weeks.

In Your Journal

Imagine that you are a sea captain making the voyage to England and back to America. Your family doesn't understand why your journey home takes almost twice as long as your journey to England. Write a letter to your family explaining why you have to travel farther south to take advantage of the prevailing winds on your return voyage.

Global Wind Belts

The Coriolis effect and other factors combine to produce a pattern of calm areas and wind belts around Earth. The calm areas include the doldrums and the horse latitudes. **The major global wind belts are the trade winds, the prevailing westerlies, and the polar easterlies.** As you read about each area, find it in *Exploring Global Winds.*

Doldrums Near the equator, the sun heats the surface strongly. Warm air rises steadily, creating an area of low pressure. Cool air moves into the area, but is warmed rapidly and rises before it moves very far. There is very little horizontal motion, so the winds near the equator are very weak. Regions near the equator with little or no wind are called the doldrums.

Horse Latitudes Warm air that rises at the equator divides and flows both north and south. **Latitude** is the distance from the equator, measured in degrees. At about 30° north and south latitudes, the air stops moving toward the poles and sinks. In each of these regions, another belt of calm air forms. Hundreds of years ago, sailors becalmed in these waters ran out of food and water for their horses and had to throw the horses overboard. Because of this, the latitudes 30° north and south of the equator are called the horse latitudes.

Trade Winds When the cold air over the horse latitudes sinks, it produces a region of high pressure. This high pressure causes surface winds to blow both toward the equator and away from it. The winds that blow toward the equator are turned west by the Coriolis effect. As a result, winds in the Northern Hemisphere between 30° north latitude and the equator blow generally from the northeast. In the Southern Hemisphere between 30° south latitude and the equator, the winds blow from the southeast. These steady easterly winds are called the trade winds. For hundreds of years, sailors relied on them to carry cargoes from Europe to the West Indies and South America.

Figure 11 The bark *Patriot*, built in 1809, carried goods to many parts of the world. *Applying Concepts How much effect do you think the prevailing winds have on shipping today?*

Background

Integrating Science Like global winds, the surface currents of oceans are deflected by the Coriolis effect. They flow to the right in the Northern Hemisphere and to the left in the Southern Hemisphere.

The prevailing winds blow the surface waters of the oceans and contribute to the deflection of ocean currents caused by the Coriolis effect. For example, the prevailing westerlies, which blow across most of the United States, help make the Gulf Stream the largest, strongest surface current in the North Atlantic Ocean. The Gulf Stream flows from the Caribbean Sea northeast along the east coast of the United States until it reaches North Carolina. Then it veers off into the Atlantic Ocean. Eventually the Gulf Stream reaches the western coast of Europe, where its warm waters bring relatively mild, humid weather.

EXPLORING Global Winds

A series of wind belts circles Earth. Between the wind belts are calm areas where air is rising or falling.

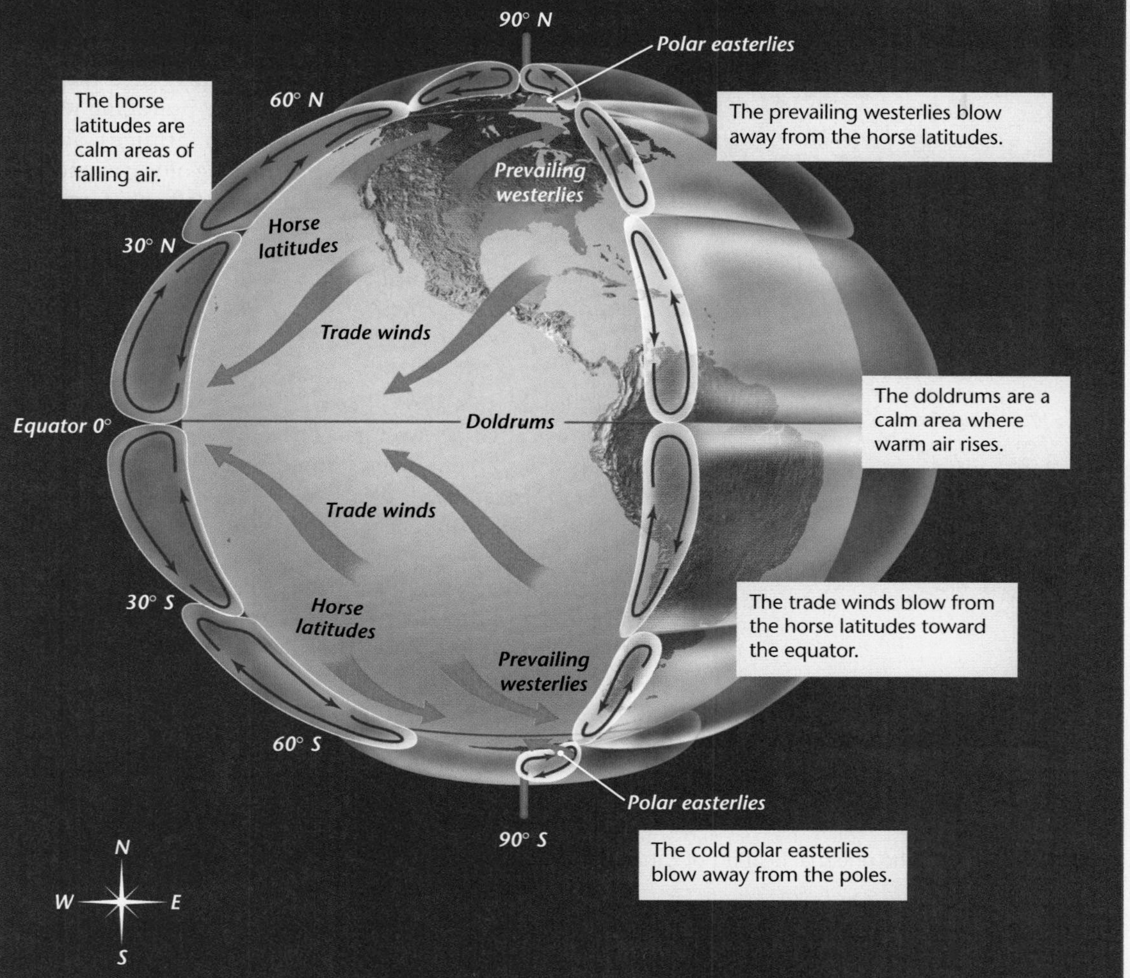

The horse latitudes are calm areas of falling air.

The prevailing westerlies blow away from the horse latitudes.

The doldrums are a calm area where warm air rises.

The trade winds blow from the horse latitudes toward the equator.

The cold polar easterlies blow away from the poles.

90° N
Polar easterlies
60° N
Prevailing westerlies
Horse latitudes
30° N
Trade winds
Equator 0°   Doldrums
Trade winds
30° S
Horse latitudes
Prevailing westerlies
60° S
Polar easterlies
90° S

N
W   E
S

Make sure students understand that the spin of the planet in the figure is from left to right, or counterclockwise as seen from the North Pole. Check to see that students understand how the two different types of arrows are used in the diagram. Ask: **What do the small blue arrows pointing straight north or straight south represent?** (*The general direction of convection currents in the atmosphere due to unequal heating*) **What do the large red arrows represent?** (*The direction in which global winds blow because of the Coriolis effect*)

Tell students to assume they are planning a sailing trip from California to the tip of South America. Have them use the figure to trace with a finger the route they would take. Ask: **Which winds would help speed you on your way?** (*In the Northern Hemisphere the trade winds and in the Southern Hemisphere the prevailing westerlies*) **Which winds would slow you down?** (*In the Northern Hemisphere the prevailing westerlies and in the Southern Hemisphere the trade winds*)

Students may not understand why the two major global wind belts in each hemisphere blow in opposite north/south directions, even though both are turned in the same east/west direction by Earth's rotation. Explain that they blow in opposite directions because the convection currents that produce them flow in opposite directions. Point out in the figure how, in the Northern hemisphere, the convection currents in the region of the prevailing westerlies flow to the north, whereas in the region of the trade winds, the convection currents flow to the south. **learning modality: visual**

Media and Technology

Transparencies "Global Winds," Transparency 67

Answers to Self-Assessment

Caption Question

Figure 11 Answers may vary. The most likely answer is that prevailing winds have little effect on shipping today because ships no longer depend on the winds to move.

Ongoing Assessment

Oral Presentation Call on students at random to explain in their own words similarities and differences between the prevailing westerlies and the trade winds.

Jet Streams

Building Inquiry Skills: Inferring

Point out that the jet stream follows the boundary between the prevailing westerlies and polar easterlies. Ask: **Why do you think the jet stream is farther south in the winter?** *(As the sun's direct rays move south, the global wind belts also shift south.)* **learning modality: logical/mathematical**

3 Assess

Section 3 Review Answers

1. Unequal heating of air above Earth's surface causes winds because the warm air rises and cool air moves in to take its place.

2. Both local and global winds are caused by unequal heating of Earth's surface. Local winds cover small areas; global winds circle the globe. Local winds often change direction; global winds do not.

3. The major wind belts are trade winds, prevailing westerlies, and polar easterlies. Students' drawings should show the winds as pictured on page 557.

4. The pilot should set a course to the southeast because Earth's rotation will result in the plane going west relative to cities on the ground.

Check Your Progress
CHAPTER PROJECT 17

Check that students continue to take accurate measurements. Make sure they are recording all the measurements in their weather log, including the units for each measurement.

Performance Assessment

Writing/Drawing Have students write a paragraph explaining what causes global winds and why they flow in the direction they do. Have them accompany their explanation with a clearly labeled diagram.

Figure 12 By traveling east in a jet stream, pilots can save time and fuel. *Predicting What would happen if a plane flew west in a jet stream?*

Prevailing Westerlies In the mid-latitudes, winds that blow toward the poles are turned toward the east by the Coriolis effect. Because they blow from the west to the east, they are called prevailing westerlies. The prevailing westerlies blow generally from the southwest between 30° and 60° north latitudes and from the northwest between 30° and 60° south latitudes. The prevailing westerlies play an important part in the weather of the United States.

Polar Easterlies Cold air near the poles sinks and flows back toward lower latitudes. The Coriolis effect shifts these polar winds to the west, producing winds called the polar easterlies. The polar easterlies meet the prevailing westerlies at about 60° north and 60° south latitudes, along a region called the polar front. The mixing of warm and cold air along the polar front has a major effect on weather changes in the United States.

☑ *Checkpoint* In what region do the polar easterlies meet the prevailing westerlies?

Jet Streams

About 10 kilometers above Earth's surface are bands of high-speed winds called **jet streams.** These winds are hundreds of kilometers wide but only a few kilometers deep. Jet streams blow from west to east at speeds of 200 to 400 kilometers per hour. As jet streams travel around Earth, they wander north and south along a wavy path.

Airplanes are aided by a jet stream when traveling east. Pilots can save fuel and time by flying east in a jet stream. However, airplanes flying at jet stream altitudes are slowed down when traveling west against the jet stream winds.

Section 3 Review

1. How does the unequal heating of Earth's surface cause winds?
2. How are local winds and global winds similar? How are they different?
3. Name and draw the three major wind belts.
4. **Thinking Critically** **Applying Concepts** Imagine you are flying from Seattle to San Francisco, which is almost exactly due south of Seattle. Should the pilot set a course due south? Explain your answer.

Check Your Progress
CHAPTER PROJECT 17

Check with your teacher to be sure you are using the weather instruments correctly. Are you recording units for each measurement? Collect and record measurements each day.

Answers to Self-Assessment

☑ *Checkpoint*

The polar easterlies meet the prevailing westerlies at about the 60° north and 60° south latitudes.

Caption Question

Figure 12 If a plane flew west in a jet stream, it would be slowed down by the winds flowing east.

Program Resources

◆ **Unit 5 Resources** 17-3 Review and Reinforce, p. 47; 17-3 Enrich, p. 48

DISCOVER · · · · · · · ·

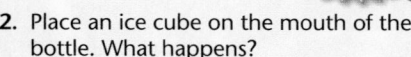

How Does Fog Form?

1. Fill a narrow-necked plastic bottle with hot tap water. Pour out most of the water, leaving about 3 cm at the bottom. **CAUTION:** *Avoid spilling hot water. Do not use water that is so hot that you cannot safely hold the bottle.*

2. Place an ice cube on the mouth of the bottle. What happens?

3. Repeat Steps 1 and 2 using cold water instead of hot water. What happens?

Think It Over

Developing Hypotheses How can you explain your observations? Why is there a difference between what happens with the hot water and with the cold water?

D uring a rainstorm, the air feels moist. On a clear, cloudless day, the air may feel dry. As the sun heats the land and oceans, the amount of water in the atmosphere changes. Water is always moving between the atmosphere and Earth's surface.

This movement of water between the atmosphere and Earth's surface, called the water cycle, is shown in Figure 13. Water vapor enters the air by evaporation from the oceans and other bodies of water. **Evaporation** is the process by which water molecules in liquid water escape into the air as water vapor. Water vapor is also added to the air by living things. Water enters the roots of plants, rises to the leaves, and is released as water vapor.

As part of the water cycle, some of the water vapor in the atmosphere condenses to form clouds. Rain and other forms of precipitation fall from the clouds toward the surface. The water then runs off the surface, or moves through the ground, back into the oceans, lakes, and streams.

GUIDE FOR READING

◆ How is relative humidity measured?

◆ How do clouds form?

◆ What are the three main types of clouds?

Reading Tip Before you read, write a definition of "cloud." Revise your definition as you read about clouds.

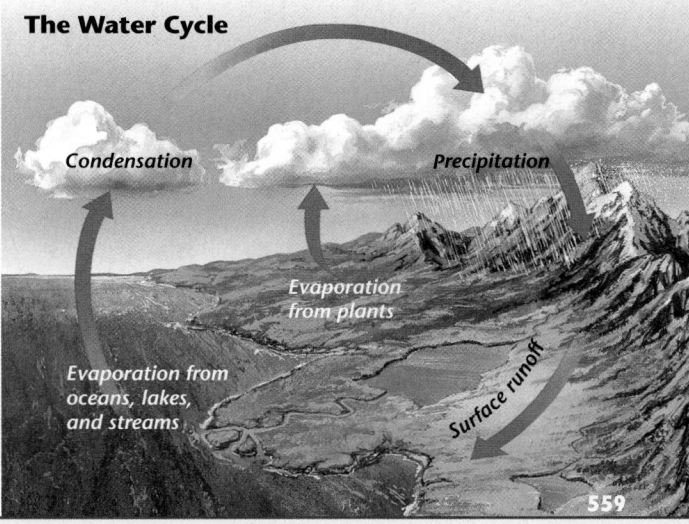

The Water Cycle

Condensation

Precipitation

Evaporation from plants

Evaporation from oceans, lakes, and streams

Surface runoff

559

Figure 13 In the water cycle, water moves from lakes and oceans into the atmosphere and falls back to Earth.

READING STRATEGIES

Reading Tip Encourage students to base their initial definition of "cloud" on what they have observed or experienced. Their revised definition should describe a cloud as consisting of drops of liquid water or ice crystals in the air.

Program Resources

◆ **Unit 5 Resources** 17-4 Lesson Plan, p. 49; 17-4 Section Summary, p. 50

◆ **Guided Reading and Study Workbook** Section 17-4

Media and Technology

Transparencies "The Water Cycle," Transparency 68

Objectives

After completing the lesson, students will be able to

◆ describe how relative humidity is measured;

◆ explain how clouds form;

◆ name the three main types of clouds.

Key Terms evaporation, humidity, relative humidity, psychrometer, condensation, dew point, cumulus, stratus, cirrus

1 Engage/Explore

Activating Prior Knowledge

Help students recall seeing water vapor condense out of the air. Ask: **Have you ever noticed when you take a shower that the bathroom mirror clouds up?** *(Most students will have had this experience.)* **Do you know what causes this?** *(Students may say it is caused by moisture in the air from the shower.)* Explain that when warm moist air from the shower comes into contact with the cool surface of the mirror, the air cools and can hold less water vapor. As a result, water vapor condenses on the mirror. Point out that clouds form the same way: water vapor condenses when warm moist air cools in the atmosphere.

· · · · · · · DISCOVER · · · · · · ·

Skills Focus developing hypotheses

Materials *narrow-necked plastic bottle, hot tap water, 2 ice cubes, cold tap water*

Time 10 minutes

Tips Make sure students let the bottle cool before repeating Steps 1 and 2 with cold water.

Expected Outcome Fog will form in the bottle when it contains hot water but not when it contains cold water.

Think It Over Fog forms in the bottle when warm moist air rises from the surface of the hot water and condenses as it cools near the ice cube. This does not occur when there is cold water in the bottle because the cold water does not produce warm moist air.

2 Facilitate

Humidity

Integrating Life Science

Help students appreciate how evaporation can cool the body by asking: **Did you ever step out of a swimming pool on a hot day and feel cold, even though the air was warmer than the water?** *(Most students will have experienced this.)* **Why did you feel cold?** *(As the water evaporated, it took heat from the body.)* Then help students appreciate the effect of high relative humidity on evaporative cooling. Ask: **What happens when you exercise on a hot, humid day?** *(You get wet with sweat, but the sweat doesn't evaporate and cool you down.)* **learning modality: verbal**

Measuring Relative Humidity

Inquiry Challenge

Materials *human hair, drinking straw, tape, glue, clay, shoebox, or other materials of students' choice*

Time 20 minutes for setup; 5 minutes for later observations

Tell students that human hair shrinks when the humidity is low and stretches when the humidity is high. Then challenge students to use a human hair to indicate changes in humidity. One way students might do this is by setting a shoebox on one of its long sides and taping one end of a drinking straw to the inside of this long side. The unattached end of the straw should be close, but not touching, the inside of a short side of the shoebox. Then attach a long human hair to the straw and to the inside of the opposite (top) long side of the shoebox so it suspends the unattached end of the straw, making it a pointer. Plug this end of the straw with a little clay so the hair remains taut. Students can calibrate this hair hygrometer by observing the straw pointer move up and down with changes in humidity. **learning modality: logical/mathematical**

Humidity

Humidity is a measure of the amount of water vapor in the air. The percentage of water vapor in the air compared to the maximum amount the air could hold is called the **relative humidity.** For example, at 10°C, 1 cubic meter of air can hold a maximum of 8 grams of water vapor. If there actually were 8 grams of water vapor in the air, then the relative humidity of the air would be 100 percent. If the air held 4 grams of water vapor, the relative humidity would be half, or 50 percent. The amount of water vapor that the air can hold depends on its temperature. Warm air can hold more water vapor than cool air.

 "It's not the heat, it's the humidity." What does this common expression mean? Even on a hot day, you can still feel comfortable if the air is dry. Evaporation of moisture from your skin removes heat and helps to keep your body's temperature comfortable. You feel less comfortable on a hot day if the relative humidity is high. When the relative humidity is high, evaporation slows down. Evaporation therefore has less cooling effect on your body.

Measuring Relative Humidity

Relative humidity can be measured with a psychrometer. A **psychrometer** (sy KRAHM uh tur) has two thermometers, a wet-bulb thermometer and a dry-bulb thermometer. The bulb of the wet-bulb thermometer has a cloth covering that is moistened with water. Air is then blown over both thermometers. Because the wet-bulb thermometer is cooled by evaporation, its reading drops below that of the dry-bulb thermometer.

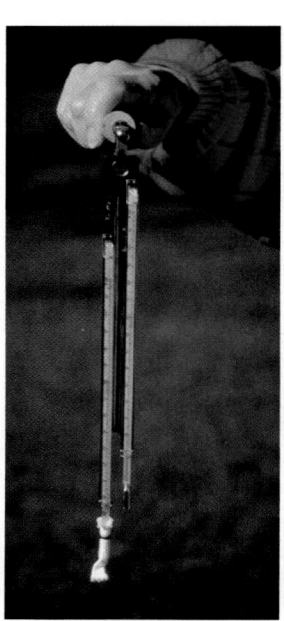

Relative Humidity					
Dry-Bulb Reading (°C)	**Difference Between Wet- and Dry-Bulb Readings (°C)**				
	1	**2**	**3**	**4**	**5**
10	88	76	65	54	43
12	88	78	67	57	48
14	89	79	69	60	50
16	90	80	71	62	54
18	91	81	72	64	56
20	91	82	74	66	58
22	92	83	75	68	60
24	92	84	76	69	62
26	92	85	77	70	64
28	93	86	78	71	65
30	93	86	79	72	66

Figure 14 A sling psychrometer is used to measure relative humidity. First, find the wet-bulb and dry-bulb temperatures. Then find the dry-bulb temperature in the left column of the table. Find the difference between the wet- and dry-bulb temperatures across the top of the table. The number in the table where these two readings intersect indicates the relative humidity in percent.

560

Background

Facts and Figures The heat stress index tells you how much hotter it feels because of high humidity. For example, a temperature of 38°C (100°F) combined with a relative humidity of 50% gives a heat stress index of 49°C (120°F). In other words, the humidity makes it feel like it is 11°C (20°F) hotter than it actually is.

The dew point is a good indicator of relative humidity, because the higher the temperature at which water vapor starts condensing out of the air, the more saturated the air must be. When the dew point is 27°C (80°F) or higher, humidity is extremely high. When the dew point is around 10°C (50°F), humidity is moderate. When the dew point is below 4°C (40°F), humidity is very low.

If the relative humidity is high, the water on the wet bulb will evaporate slowly and the wet-bulb temperature will not change much. If the relative humidity is low, the water on the wet bulb will evaporate rapidly and the wet-bulb temperature will drop. The relative humidity can be found by comparing the temperatures of the wet-bulb and dry-bulb thermometers on a table like the one in Figure 14.

☑ *Checkpoint* *What is the difference between humidity and relative humidity?*

How Clouds Form

What do clouds remind you of? They can look like people, animals, countries, and a thousand other fanciful forms. Of course, not all clouds are fluffy and white. Storm clouds can be dark and cover the whole sky.

Clouds of all kinds form when water vapor in the air becomes liquid water or ice crystals. The process by which molecules of water vapor in the air become liquid water is called **condensation.** How does water condense? As you know, cold air can hold less water vapor than warm air. As air cools, the amount of water vapor it can hold decreases. Some of the water vapor in the air condenses to form droplets of liquid water.

The temperature at which condensation begins is called the **dew point.** If the dew point is below the freezing point, the water vapor may change directly into ice crystals. When you look at a cloud, you are seeing millions of tiny ice crystals or water droplets.

For water vapor to condense, tiny particles must be present so the water has a surface on which to condense. Most of these particles are salt crystals, dust from soil, and smoke. Sometimes water vapor condenses onto solid surfaces, such as blades of grass, instead of particles. Water that condenses from the air onto a cold surface is called dew. Frost is ice that has been deposited directly from the air onto a cold surface.

Clouds form whenever air is cooled to its dew point and particles are present. But why does the air cool? If air is warmed near the ground, it

Figure 15 Dew forms when water vapor condenses out of the air onto a solid surface, such as this flower.

Sharpen your *Skills*

Interpreting Data

At lunchtime you use a psychrometer and get readings of 26°C on the dry-bulb thermometer and 21°C on the wet-bulb thermometer. Use Figure 14 to find the relative humidity.

Later in the day you use the psychrometer again and this time get readings of 20°C on the dry-bulb thermometer and 19°C on the wet-bulb thermometer. Find the new relative humidity. Is the relative humidity increasing or decreasing?

Sharpen your *Skills*

Interpreting Data

Time 10 minutes
Tips Remind students to subtract the wet-bulb reading from the dry-bulb reading and then find the difference between the two readings in the table.
Expected Outcome The first value for relative humidity is 64%, the second is 91%; relative humidity is increasing.
Extend Use the table to help students understand the relationship between temperature and relative humidity. Ask: **When the difference between wet- and dry-bulb readings is small, is the relative humidity high or low?** (high) **How is this relationship affected by air temperature?** (*The higher the air temperature, the higher the relative humidity for a given difference between wet- and dry-bulb readings.*) **learning modality: logical-mathematical**

How Clouds Form

Building Inquiry Skills: Measuring

Materials *beaker, room-temperature water, ice cubes, stirring rod, thermometer*
Time 10 minutes

Have students find the dew point in the classroom. Have them fill a beaker with room-temperature water and measure and record the water temperature. Then have them add a few ice cubes to the beaker and stir the ice water. As soon as moisture condenses on the outside of the beaker, have students measure and record the temperature of the water again. This temperature represents the dew point in the classroom. Ask: **Would the dew point be the same if you did this experiment on a different day?** (*Probably not, because the dew point depends on the temperature and relative humidity*) **learning modality: logical/mathematical**

Ongoing Assessment

Writing Have students explain in their own words how temperature, humidity, and dew point are related.

Answers to Self-Assessment

☑ *Checkpoint*
Humidity is a measure of the amount of water vapor in the air. Relative humidity is the percentage of water vapor in the air compared to the maximum amount the air could hold.

How Clouds Form,
continued

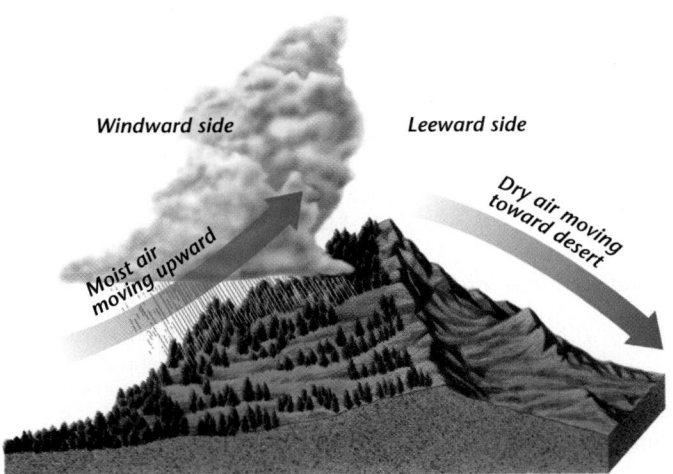

Windward side   Leeward side

Moist air moving upward

Dry air moving toward desert

Figure 16 Humid air cools as it is blown up the side of a mountain. *Predicting What happens when water vapor condenses out of the air?*

becomes less dense and rises in a convection current. When the rising air expands and becomes cooler, clouds may form.

When wind strikes the side of a hill or mountain, the air is forced upward. As the air rises along the slope, the air cools. Rain or snow falls on the windward side of the mountains, the side facing the on-coming wind.

By the time the air reaches the other side of the mountains, it has lost much of its water vapor. The air is cool and dry. The land on the leeward side of the mountains—downwind—is in a rain shadow. Just as very little light falls in a sun shadow, very little rain falls in a rain shadow. Not only has the air lost its water vapor while crossing the mountains, but the air has also grown warmer while flowing down the mountainside. This warm, dry air often creates a desert on the leeward side of the mountains.

✓ *Checkpoint* Why are the tops of some mountains almost always covered by clouds?

Types of Clouds

As you know, clouds come in different shapes. **Meteorologists classify clouds into three main types: cumulus, stratus, and cirrus.** Clouds are also classified by their altitude. Each type of cloud is associated with a different type of weather.

Clouds that look like fluffy, rounded piles of cotton are called **cumulus** (KYOO myuh lus) clouds. The word *cumulus* means "heap" or "mass." Cumulus clouds form less than 2 kilometers above the ground, but may grow in size and height until they extend upward as much as 18 kilometers. Cumulus clouds usually indicate fair weather. Towering clouds with flat tops, called cumulonimbus clouds, often produce thunderstorms. The suffix *-nimbus* comes from a Latin word meaning "rain."

Clouds that form in flat layers are called **stratus** (STRAT us) clouds. *Strato* means "spread out." Stratus clouds usually cover all or most of the sky. As stratus clouds thicken, they may produce drizzle, rain, or snow. They are then called nimbostratus clouds.

Wispy, feathery clouds are called **cirrus** (SEER us) clouds. Cirrus clouds form only at high levels, above about 6 kilometers, where temperatures are very low. As a result, cirrus clouds are made of ice crystals.

EXPLORING Clouds

The main types of clouds are cumulus, stratus, and cirrus. A cloud's name contains clues about its height and structure.

Cirrus clouds
Cirrus, cirrostratus, and cirrocumulus clouds are made up of ice crystals.

Cumulonimbus clouds
Thunderstorms come from cumulonimbus clouds. For this reason cumulonimbus clouds are also called thunderheads.

Nimbostratus clouds
Nimbostratus clouds may produce rain or snow.

Cumulus clouds
Cumulus clouds are usually a sign of fair weather.

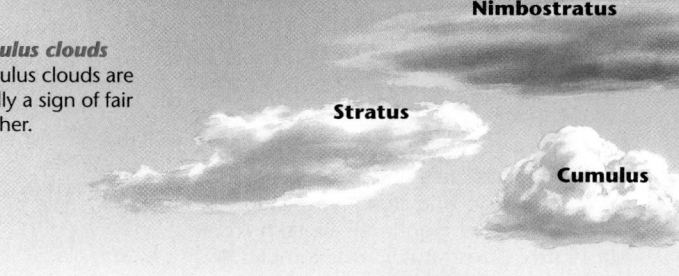

Cirrus

Cirrocumulus

Altocumulus

Altostratus

Cumulonimbus

Nimbostratus

Stratus

Cumulus

Fog

Answers to Self-Assessment

Caption Question

Figure 16 When water vapor condenses out of the air, clouds form.

☑ *Checkpoint*

When warm, moist air moves upward over a mountain, it cools. This causes water vapor to condense out of the air and form clouds.

EXPLORING
Clouds

Extend the information in the Exploring feature by calling students' attention to each of the clouds pictured on the left, starting with cumulus clouds, and explaining how each type of cloud is formed. This will help students understand why the different cloud types have the shapes and other characteristics they do. Explain that cumulus clouds form during clear weather when warm air rises over small regions of Earth, such as plowed fields or paved parking lots, because these areas are heated more by the sun. Nimbostratus clouds are formed by warm air rising over a wide area, so they tend to cover the whole sky. Cumulonimbus clouds are formed when a lot of hot air rises very fast and towers upward for several kilometers. Strong winds at the bottom of the stratosphere flatten the tops of cumulonimbus clouds to give them their characteristic anvil shape. Cirrus clouds are formed high up in the atmosphere where it is very cold and there is little water vapor, making them thin and wispy. **learning modality: visual**

Building Inquiry Skills: Forming Operational Definitions

If students are having difficulty keeping cloud names straight, have them play a quiz game called "Name that Cloud." First have students find and list the definitions of basic cloud names (cumulus, stratus, cirrus, nimbus) and cloud prefixes (alto-, nimbo-, cirro-) on a set of index cards. Then have students use the definitions as the basis for the game. Students should provide a definition of a specific cloud type, and their partner must correctly name the cloud. The person with the most correct responses wins the game. **cooperative learning**

Ongoing Assessment

Drawing Have students draw and label each of the three main cloud types.

563

Types of Clouds, continued

Real-Life Learning

Point out that how large a cloud appears is a good indicator of its altitude. Tell students that in general fist-sized clouds are cumulus clouds, thumb-sized clouds altocumulus, and little-fingernail-sized clouds cirrocumulus. **learning modality: kinesthetic**

3 Assess

Section 4 Review Answers

1. The instrument is a psychrometer. It works by comparing the temperatures on a wet-bulb and a dry-bulb thermometer.
2. For clouds to form, air must be cooled to its dew point and particles must be present in the air.
3. Cumulus clouds look like fluffy, rounded piles of cotton. Stratus clouds form in flat layers. Cirrus clouds are wispy and feathery.
4. Low-level clouds are fog, cumulus, stratus, and nimbostratus. Medium-level clouds are altocumulus and altostratus. High-level clouds are cirrostratus and cirrus.

Science at Home

Materials *large glass, cold water, ice cubes*

Tips Tell students to use cold tap water for the activity, not cold water from the refrigerator, which may be cold enough to make water condense on the outside of the glass without adding ice. Students should explain that the water on the outside of the glass condensed from water vapor in the air. It only appeared after ice was added because water vapor condenses out of the air when the temperature falls below the dew point.

Performance Assessment

Skills Check Have students infer why they can see their breath on a cold day. *(Students should infer that water droplets condense out of their warm, moist breath when it hits the cold air.)*

564

Figure 17 Fog often forms at night over cool lakes. *Predicting What will happen as the sun rises and warms the air above the lake?*

Cirrus clouds that have feathery "hooked" ends are sometimes called mare's tails. Cirrocumulus clouds, which look like rows of cotton balls, often indicate that a storm is on its way.

Part of a cloud's name may be based on its height. The names of clouds that form between about 2 and 6 kilometers above Earth's surface have the prefix *alto-*, which means "high." The two main types of these clouds are altocumulus and altostratus.

Clouds that form at or near the ground are called fog. Fog often forms when the ground cools at night after a warm, humid day. The ground cools the air just above the ground to the air's dew point. The next day the heat of the morning sun "burns" the fog off as its water droplets evaporate.

Section 4 Review

1. What instrument is used to measure relative humidity? How does it work?
2. What conditions are needed for clouds to form?
3. Describe each of the three main types of clouds.
4. **Thinking Critically Classifying** Classify each of the following cloud types as low-level, medium-level, or high-level: altocumulus, altostratus, cirrostratus, cirrus, cumulus, fog, nimbostratus, and stratus.

564

Science at Home

Fill a large glass half-full with cold water. Show your family members what happens as you add ice cubes to the water. Explain to your family that the water that appears on the outside of the glass comes from water vapor in the atmosphere. Also explain why the water on the outside of the glass only appears after you add ice to the water in the glass.

Answers to Self-Assessment

Caption Question

Figure 17 The fog will "burn" off as its water droplets evaporate.

Program Resources

◆ **Unit 5 Resources** 17-4 Review and Reinforce, p. 51; 17-4 Enrich, p. 52

DISCOVER ···················· ACTIVITY····

How Can You Make Hail?

1. Put on your goggles.
2. Put 15 g of salt into a beaker. Add 50 mL of water. Stir the solution until most of the salt is dissolved.
3. Put 15 mL of cold water in a clean test tube.
4. Place the test tube in the beaker.
5. Fill the beaker almost to the top with crushed ice. Stir the ice mixture every minute for six minutes.

6. Remove the test tube from the beaker and drop an ice chip into the test tube. What happens?

Think It Over
Inferring Based on your observation, what conditions are necessary for hail to form?

I n Arica, Chile, the average rainfall is less than 1 millimeter per year. Many years pass with no precipitation at all. On the other hand, the average rainfall on Mount Waialeale on the island of Kauai in Hawaii is about 12 meters per year. That's more than enough to cover a three-story house! As you can see, rainfall varies greatly around the world.

Water evaporates into the air from every water surface on Earth and from living things. This water eventually returns to the surface as precipitation. **Precipitation** (pree sip uh TAY shun) is any form of water that falls from clouds and reaches Earth's surface.

Precipitation always comes from clouds. But not all clouds produce precipitation. For precipitation to occur, cloud droplets or ice crystals must grow heavy enough to fall through the air. One way that cloud droplets grow is by colliding and combining with other cloud droplets. As the droplets grow larger, they fall faster and collect more and more small droplets. Finally, the droplets become heavy enough to fall out of the cloud as raindrops.

Types of Precipitation

In warm parts of the world, precipitation is almost always rain or drizzle. In colder regions, precipitation may fall as snow or ice. **Common types of precipitation include rain, sleet, freezing rain, hail, and snow.**

GUIDE FOR READING

◆ What are the main types of precipitation?

◆ How is precipitation measured?

Reading Tip As you read, make a list of the types of precipitation. Write a sentence describing how each type forms.

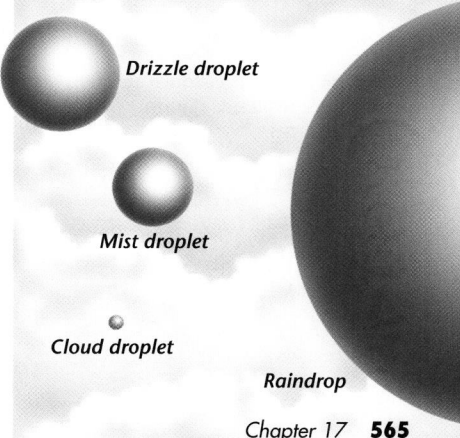

Drizzle droplet

Mist droplet

Cloud droplet

Raindrop

Figure 18 Droplets come in many sizes. Believe it or not, a raindrop has about one million times as much water in it as a cloud droplet.

Chapter 17 **565**

READING STRATEGIES

Reading Tip Students lists should include rain, sleet, freezing rain, hail, and snow. Suggest to students that they save their sentences and use them as a study guide. Tell students that knowing how each type of precipitation forms will help them understand its characteristics.

Program Resources

◆ **Unit 5 Resources** 17-5 Lesson Plan, p. 53; 17-5 Section Summary, p. 54
◆ **Guided Reading and Study Workbook** Section 17-5

Objectives

After completing the lesson, students will be able to
◆ identify the main types of precipitation;
◆ describe how precipitation is measured and ways that it might be controlled.

Key Terms precipitation, rain gauge, droughts

1 Engage/Explore

Activating Prior Knowledge

Stimulate students to think about precipitation by asking: **Did you ever hear the expression, "It's raining cats and dogs"?** (*Most students will say yes.*) **Do you know what it means?** (*That it's raining very hard*) **Where do you think the expression comes from?** (*Students probably will not know.*) Explain that the expression may come from old Norse myths, in which cats were identified with rain and dogs with winds. Tell the class they will learn more about rain and other types of precipitation in this section.

········· DISCOVER ·········

Skills Focus inferring
Materials *15 g salt, beaker, 50 mL water, stirrer, 15 mL cold water, clean test tube, crushed ice, watch or clock*
Time 15 minutes
Tips The inside of the test tube must be very clean. Have students measure the temperature of the water in the test tube before they add the ice chip. They may be surprised to find it is less than 0°C. (The freezing point of salt water is less than 0°C, the freezing point of fresh water.)
Expected Outcome When the ice chip is dropped into the test tube, the cold water in the test tube will crystalize into ice around it.
Think It Over For hail to form, it must be very cold and there must be particles on which water can crystalize into ice.

565

2 Facilitate

Types of Precipitation

Building Inquiry Skills: Observing

Materials *transparent plastic lid, dropper, pencil, water*
Time 10 minutes

Have student pairs do this activity to observe how tiny water droplets in clouds merge to form larger drops of water until the drops are heavy enough to fall as precipitation. Students should fill the dropper with water and squeeze many separate drops onto the inside of a transparent plastic lid. Then they should quickly turn the lid over and, holding it in the air by one side, use the point of a pencil from underneath the lid to move the tiny drops of water together. When the drops touch, they will appear to leap together to form larger drops, and when the drops get large enough they will fall like rain. Ask: **What causes the water drops in clouds to move around and bump into each other so they can merge into larger drops?** *(wind and gravity)* **learning modality: kinesthetic**

Using the Visuals: Figure 19

Call students' attention to the devastation caused by freezing rain that is shown in photo B. Ask: **How did freezing rain cause this kind of damage?** *(The weight of the accumulated ice broke tree branches and downed power lines.)* **How would the street pictured in the photo look if, instead of freezing rain, the same amount of snow or hailstones had fallen?** *(Snow is lighter than ice so it probably would not have broken branches or power lines, although it might have blocked the street. Hailstones, depending on their size, might have broken twigs and small branches and even the windshield of the car, but it probably would not have blocked the street with large branches or downed power lines.)* **learning modality: visual**

Figure 19 **A.** Snowflakes form in clouds that are colder than 0°C. **B.** Freezing rain coats objects with a layer of ice. **C.** Hailstones are formed inside clouds during thunderstorms.

Rain The most common kind of precipitation is rain. Drops of water are called rain if they are at least 0.5 millimeter in diameter. Precipitation made up of smaller drops of water is called mist or drizzle. Mist and drizzle usually fall from nimbostratus clouds.

Sleet Sometimes raindrops fall through a layer of air below 0°C, the freezing point of water. As they fall, the raindrops freeze into solid particles of ice. Ice particles smaller than 5 millimeters in diameter are called sleet.

Freezing Rain At other times raindrops falling through cold air near the ground do not freeze in the air. Instead, the raindrops freeze when they touch a cold surface. This is called freezing rain. In an ice storm, a smooth, thick layer of ice builds up on every surface. The weight of the ice may break tree branches onto power lines, causing power failures. Freezing rain and sleet can make sidewalks and roads slippery and dangerous.

Hail Round pellets of ice larger than 5 millimeters in diameter are called hailstones. Hail forms only inside cumulonimbus clouds during thunderstorms. A hailstone starts as an ice pellet inside a cold region of a cloud. Strong updrafts in the cloud carry the hailstone up and down through the cold region many times. Each time the hailstone goes through the cold region, a new layer of ice forms around the hailstone. Eventually the hailstone becomes heavy enough to fall to the ground. If you cut a hailstone in half, you can often see shells of ice, like the layers of an onion. Because hailstones can grow quite large before finally falling to the ground, hail can cause tremendous damage to crops, buildings, and vehicles.

566

Background

History of Science For centuries people have tried to increase the amount of precipitation that falls. From praying and dancing to sending up explosives into clouds, they have searched for ways to make rain. It wasn't until the 1940s, however, that Vincent Schaefer discovered how to make rain by seeding clouds. He discovered that a grain of dry ice dropped into a cloud led to the formation of millions of ice crystals,

often leading to precipitation. Shortly after this discovery, Bernard Vonnegut discovered that silver iodide led to the production of even more ice crystals than dry ice. Since then, no other process has been found that is better at making rain than their cloud-seeding method. Rainmaking companies still use this method in many parts of the world.

Snow Often water vapor in a cloud is converted directly into ice crystals called snowflakes. Snowflakes have an endless number of different shapes and patterns, all with six sides or branches. Snowflakes often join together into larger clumps of snow in which the six-sided crystals are hard to see.

☑ *Checkpoint* How do hailstones form?

Measuring Precipitation

Meteorologists measure rainfall with a rain gauge. A rain gauge is an open-ended can or tube that collects rainfall. The amount of rainfall is measured by dipping a ruler into the water or by reading a marked scale. To increase the accuracy of the measurement, the top of a rain gauge may have a funnel that collects ten times as much rain as the tube alone. The funnel collects a greater depth of water that is easier to measure. But to get the actual depth of rain, it is necessary to divide by ten.

Snowfall is measured using a ruler or by melting collected snow and measuring the depth of water it produces. On average, 10 centimeters of snow contains about the same amount of water as 1 centimeter of rain. Of course, light, fluffy snow contains far less water than heavy, wet snow.

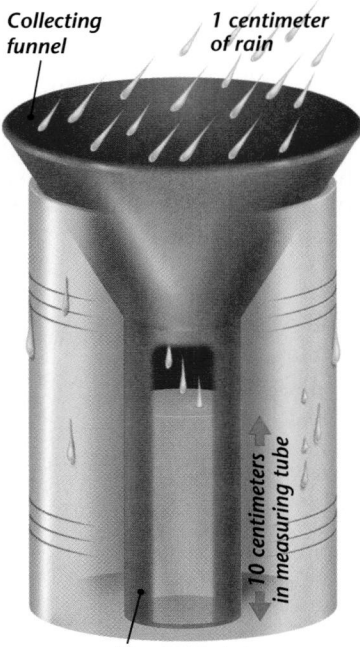

Collecting funnel

1 centimeter of rain

10 centimeters in measuring tube

Measuring tube
1/10 area of funnel

Figure 20 A rain gauge measures the depth of rain that falls. *Observing How much rain was collected in the measuring tube of this rain gauge?*

Sharpen your Skills

Calculating

Make your own rain gauge by putting a funnel into a narrow, straight-sided glass jar. Here's how to calculate how much more rain your funnel collects than the jar alone.

1. First measure the diameter of the top of the funnel and square it.
   Example: $4 \times 4 = 16$

2. Then measure the diameter of the top of the jar and square it.
   Example: $2 \times 2 = 4$

3. Divide the first square by the second square.
   Example: $\dfrac{16}{4} = 4$

4. To find the actual depth of rain that fell, divide the depth of water in the jar by the ratio from Step 3.
   Example: $\dfrac{8 \text{ cm}}{4} = 2 \text{ cm}$

Answers to Self-Assessment

☑ Checkpoint

Hailstones form when pellets of ice inside cumulonimbus clouds are carried up and down many times, each time adding a new layer of ice, until they become heavy enough to fall to the ground.

Caption Question

Figure 20 Though one cm of rain fell into the gauge, 10 cm were collected.

Building Inquiry Skills: Measuring

Materials *shallow pan, flour, sieve*

ACTIVITY

Time 10 minutes to collect raindrops; 10 minutes to compare sizes

On a day when it is raining and there is no danger of lightning, challenge students to catch raindrops and estimate their size. Have each student hold a shallow pan containing a smooth layer of flour out in the rain for a second or two, just long enough for several raindrops to land in the pan and form little lumps in the flour. After at least 15-20 minutes when the lumps have dried, have students pour the flour through a sieve to separate the lumps. Ask: **How big are the raindrops you caught?** (*Students should estimate the size of the raindrops from the size of the lumps. The bigger the lumps, the larger the raindrops.*)
learning modality: visual

Measuring Precipitation

Sharpen your Skills

Calculating

ACTIVITY

Time 15 minutes

Tips Explain that the amount of rain collected in the jar is the amount that fell over an area the size of the funnel opening. The calculations show how much smaller the area of the jar opening is than the area of the funnel opening. The total amount of rain collected must be reduced by this ratio to show how much would have fallen into the jar alone. Be sure students do not get confused by Figure 20, which shows a different ratio.

Expected Outcome Students should work through the calculations to make sure they also get a final answer of 2 cm.

Extend Ask: **What is the actual depth of the rain that fell if the diameter of the top of the funnel is 6 cm and the depth of water in the jar is 8 cm?** (*8 cm ÷ 36/4 = 0.89 cm*) **learning modality: logical/mathematical**

Ongoing Assessment

Drawing Have students draw diagrams showing how rain, sleet, and freezing rain form.

Controlling Precipitation

Integrating Technology

Point out that rain-making technology could not be developed until scientists discovered how rain actually forms in clouds. In the early 1900s, a scientist named Alfred Wegener hypothesized that almost all precipitation, even rain, starts out as ice crystals. Explain that the condensation of water alone is a much slower process, and this is why Wegener believed correctly that it could not account for most precipitation. Ask: **How does Wegener's hypothesis relate to the cloud-seeding technology?** *(Clouds are seeded with crystals of dry ice and silver iodide because this quickly leads to the formation of ice crystals large enough to fall as precipitation.)* **learning modality: verbal**

3 Assess

Section 5 Review Answers

1. Rain, sleet, freezing rain, hail, and snow
2. rain gauge
3. Cloud droplets or ice crystals must grow heavy enough to fall through the air.
4. Cumulonimbus clouds produce hail.
5. The can with the larger diameter would collect more rain. However, the depth of the water in the two cans would be the same.

Check Your Progress

CHAPTER PROJECT 17

Suggest that students experiment with different types of graphs to display their weather data. Also require that they graph all or most of the weather factors on the same graph so they can see how the weather factors change together. This will help them see patterns in the data.

Performance Assessment

Skills Check Have students make a table comparing and contrasting the five common types of precipitation.

Figure 21 The corn in this photo was damaged by a long drought. *Applying Concepts How can cloud seeding be used to reduce the effect of droughts?*

Controlling Precipitation

In some regions, there may be periods that are much drier than usual. Long periods of unusually low precipitation are called **droughts.** Droughts can cause great hardship. In the farming regions of the Midwest, for example, droughts may cause entire crops to fail. The farmers suffer from lost income and consumers suffer from high food prices. In some less-developed countries, droughts can cause widespread hunger, or famine.

 INTEGRATING TECHNOLOGY In recent years, scientists have been trying to produce rain during droughts. The most common method is called cloud seeding. In cloud seeding, tiny crystals of dry ice (solid carbon dioxide) and silver iodide are sprinkled into clouds from airplanes. Many clouds contain supercooled water droplets, which are actually below 0°C. The droplets don't freeze because there aren't enough particles around which ice crystals can form. Water vapor can condense on the particles of silver iodide, forming rain or snow. Dry ice works by cooling the droplets even further, so that they will freeze without particles being present.

Cloud seeding has also been used with some success to clear fog from airports. Dry ice is sprinkled into the fog, causing ice crystals to form. This removes some of the fog so pilots can see the runways. Unfortunately, cloud seeding clears only cold fogs, so its use for this purpose is limited.

Section 5 Review

1. Name the five common types of precipitation.
2. What device is used to measure precipitation?
3. What must happen before precipitation can fall from a cloud?
4. What kind of cloud produces hail?
5. **Thinking Critically Applying Concepts** If two open cans of different diameters were left out in the rain, how would the amount of water they collected compare? How would the depth of water in the cans compare?

568

Check Your Progress

CHAPTER PROJECT 17

Now you should be ready to begin graphing your weather data. Look for patterns in your graphs. Use your data to predict what the next day's weather will be. Compare your predictions with what actually happens the next day. Are you able to predict the weather with confidence?

Answers to Self-Assessment

Caption Question

Figure 21 Cloud seeding can be used to lessen the effect of droughts by sprinkling clouds with particles around which water droplets can condense to form rain.

Program Resources

◆ **Unit 5 Resources** 17-5 Review and Reinforce, p. 55; 17-5 Enrich, p. 56

SECTION 1 Energy in the Atmosphere

Key Ideas
◆ Energy from the sun travels to Earth as electromagnetic waves—mostly visible light, infrared radiation, and ultraviolet radiation.
◆ When Earth's surface is heated, it radiates some of the energy back into the atmosphere in the form of longer-wavelength radiation.

Key Terms
electromagnetic waves   ultraviolet radiation
radiation   scattering
infrared radiation   greenhouse effect

SECTION 2 Heat Transfer
INTEGRATING PHYSICS

Key Ideas
◆ The energy of motion in the molecules of a substance is called thermal energy.
◆ Three forms of heat transfer—radiation, conduction, and convection—work together to heat the troposphere.

Key Terms
thermal energy   thermometer   conduction
temperature   heat   convection

SECTION 3 Winds

Key Ideas
◆ All winds are caused by differences in air pressure, which are the result of unequal heating of Earth's surface.
◆ Local winds are caused by unequal heating of Earth's surface within a small area.
◆ The movement of air between the equator and the poles produces global winds.

Key Terms
wind   monsoon
anemometer   global wind
wind-chill factor Coriolis effect
local wind   latitude
sea breeze   jet stream
land breeze

SECTION 4 Water in the Atmosphere

Key Ideas
◆ Relative humidity is the percentage of water vapor in the air compared to the amount of water vapor the air could hold. It can be measured with a psychrometer.
◆ Clouds of all kinds form when water vapor in the air becomes liquid water or solid ice.
◆ Meteorologists classify clouds into three main types: cumulus, stratus, and cirrus.

Key Terms
evaporation   psychrometer   cumulus
humidity   condensation   stratus
relative humidity dew point   cirrus

SECTION 5 Precipitation

Key Ideas
◆ Common types of precipitation include rain, sleet, freezing rain, hail, and snow.
◆ Rain is measured with a rain gauge.
◆ Scientists have used cloud seeding to produce rain and to clear fog from airports.

Key Terms
precipitation
rain gauge
drought

Organizing Information

Concept Map Construct a concept map about winds on a separate sheet of paper. Be sure to include the following terms: local winds, global winds, monsoons, sea breezes, land breezes, prevailing westerlies, polar easterlies, tradewinds, and the two types of monsoon. (For more on concept maps, see the Skills Handbook.)

Organizing Information

Concept Map Answers will vary. A typical concept map is shown below.

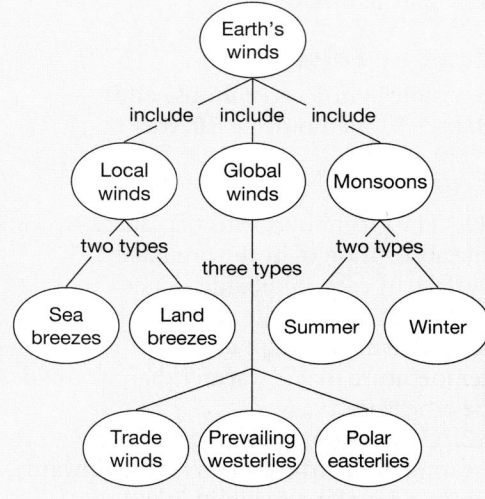

Program Resources

◆ **Unit 5 Resources** Chapter 17 Project Scoring Rubric, p. 36
◆ **Performance Assessment** Chapter 17, pp. 52–54
◆ **Chapter Tests** Chapter 17 Test, pp. 67–70

Media and Technology

 Computer Test Bank
Chapter 17 Test

569

Reviewing Content
Multiple Choice
1. a **2.** b **3.** b **4.** c **5.** c

True or False
6. visible light **7.** greenhouse effect
8. true **9.** anemometer **10.** true

Checking Concepts
11. The greenhouse effect is caused by the absorption of heat from Earth's surface by carbon dioxide, water vapor, and other gases in the atmosphere. It keeps Earth's atmosphere at a temperature that is warmer than it would be otherwise.

12. Convection causes most of the heating of the troposphere as the upward movement of warm air and the downward movement of cool air form convection currents.

13. Like local land and sea breezes, monsoons occur because of unequal heating of land and nearby bodies of water. Unlike local land and sea breezes, monsoons occur over a wide region and change direction with the seasons.

14. Warm air rises at the equator and flows toward the poles. Cold air sinks at the poles and spreads out toward the equator. The movement of air between the equator and the poles produces global winds.

15. When wind strikes the windward side of a mountain range, it is forced upward. As air rises, it becomes cooler. Since cool air can hold less water vapor than warm air, the moisture in the air often precipitates as snow or rain on the windward side of the mountain, leaving little to fall on the leeward side.

16. Clouds usually form high in the air instead of at Earth's surface because the air must be cold for water vapor to condense and form clouds and air at high altitudes usually is colder than air near the surface.

17. Sleet forms when raindrops fall through a layer of air below 0°C and freeze into small particles of ice. Hail forms when an ice pellet in a cumulonimbus cloud is carried up and down through the cold region of the cloud by strong updrafts, each time gathering another layer of ice until the

Reviewing Content
Multiple Choice
Choose the letter of the best answer.

1. Energy from the sun travels to Earth's surface by
   a. radiation.
   b. convection.
   c. evaporation.
   d. conduction.
2. Rising warm air transports heat energy by
   a. conduction.
   b. convection.
   c. radiation.
   d. condensation.
3. A psychrometer is used to measure
   a. rainfall.
   b. relative humidity.
   c. temperature.
   d. humidity.
4. Clouds form because water vapor in the air
   a. warms.   b. conducts.
   c. condenses.   d. evaporates.
5. Rain, sleet, and hail are all forms of
   a. evaporation.
   b. condensation.
   c. precipitation.
   d. convection.

True or False
If the statement is true, write true. If it is false, change the underlined word or words to make the statement true.

6. Infrared radiation and <u>ultraviolet radiation</u> make up most of the energy Earth receives from the sun.
7. The process by which gases hold heat in the atmosphere is called the <u>wind-chill factor</u>.
8. Water molecules in liquid water escape into the atmosphere as water vapor in the process of <u>evaporation</u>.
9. The instrument used to measure wind speed is a <u>thermometer</u>.
10. Clouds that form near the ground are called <u>fog</u>.

Checking Concepts
11. What causes the greenhouse effect? How does it affect Earth's atmosphere?
12. What form of heat transfer is most important in heating the troposphere?
13. What are monsoons? How are they like land and sea breezes? How are they different?
14. Describe how the movements of hot air at the equator and cold air at the poles produce global wind patterns.
15. Why are deserts often found on the leeward side of mountain ranges?
16. Why do clouds usually form high in the air instead of near Earth's surface?
17. Describe sleet, hail, and snow in terms of how each one forms.
18. **Writing to Learn** Imagine you are a drop of water in the ocean. Write a diary describing your journey through the water cycle. How do you become a cloud? What type of conditions cause you to fall as precipitation? Use descriptive words to describe your journey.

Thinking Critically
19. **Relating Cause and Effect** What circumstances could cause a night-time land breeze in a city near the ocean?
20. **Problem Solving** If you use a psychrometer and get the same reading on both thermometers, what is the relative humidity?
21. **Comparing and Contrasting** How are hail and sleet alike? How are they different?
22. **Classifying** Classify the different types of clouds by the kind of weather associated with each type.
23. **Relating Cause and Effect** What is the source of the energy that powers Earth's winds?

hailstone is heavy enough to fall to the surface. Snow forms when water vapor in a cloud is converted directly into ice crystals.

18. Students' diary entries will vary, but they should reflect students' knowledge of the water cycle and include the terms *evaporation, condensation,* and *precipitation.*

Thinking Critically
19. A nighttime land breeze in a city near the ocean would be caused by the land cooling off more quickly than the water at night so that as warm air rose over the water, cool air would flow from the land to take its place.

20. The relative humidity is 100 percent because since both temperatures were the same, the water on the wet bulb must not have been able to evaporate, which would happen only when the relative humidity is that high.

21. Hail and sleet are both frozen rain. Sleet is smaller than 5 millimeters in diameter, while hail is larger than 5 millimeters in diameter. Sleet forms anytime rain falls through a layer of air below 0°C; hail forms only inside

Applying Skills

Use the table below to answer Questions 24–27.

Average Monthly Rainfall

Month	Rainfall	Month	Rainfall
January	1 cm	July	49 cm
February	1 cm	August	57 cm
March	1 cm	September	40 cm
April	2 cm	October	20 cm
May	25 cm	November	4 cm
June	52 cm	December	1 cm

24. **Graphing** Use the information in the table to draw a bar graph that shows the rainfall each month at this location.
25. **Calculating** What is the total amount of rainfall each year at this location?
26. **Classifying** Which months of the year would you classify as "dry"? Which months would you classify as "wet"?

27. **Drawing Conclusions** The place represented by the rainfall data is in Southeast Asia. What do you think accounts for the extremely heavy rainfall that occurs during some months?

Performance | CHAPTER PROJECT 17 | **Assessment**

Project Wrap Up Develop a way to present your findings to the class. For example, you could put your graphs and predictions on a poster. Are your graphs neatly drawn and easy to understand? Practice your presentation and make any needed improvements.

Reflect and Record How could you improve the accuracy of your observations? What did you learn about how easy or difficult it is to predict the weather?

Test Preparation   *Use these questions to prepare for standardized tests.*

Study the graph. Then answer Questions 28–31.

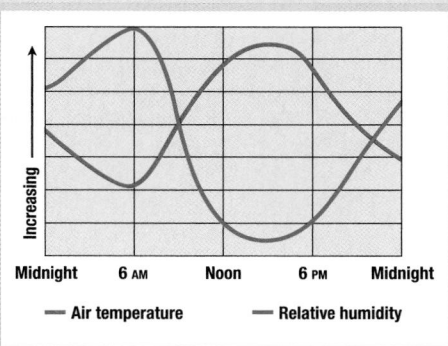

— Air temperature   — Relative humidity

28. The greatest change in air temperature occurred during the period from
    a. midnight to 6 A.M.
    b. 6 A.M. to noon.
    c. noon to 6 P.M.
    d. 6 P.M. to midnight.

29. The graph indicates that as air temperature increases, relative humidity
    a. increases.
    b. sometimes increases and sometimes decreases.
    c. decreases.
    d. stays about the same.

30. Condensation is most likely to occur at approximately
    a. 6 A.M.   b. noon.
    c. 3 P.M.   d. 6 P.M.

31. Assuming that the amount of water vapor in the air stayed constant through the day, one could infer from the graph that
    a. cool air can hold more water vapor than warm air.
    b. cool air can hold less water vapor than warm air.
    c. cool air and warm air can hold the same amount of water vapor.
    d. cool air cannot hold water vapor.

---

cumulonimbus clouds during thunderstorms when layers of ice form around ice pellets as they are carried up and down through cold regions of a cloud.
22. Cumulus clouds are associated with fair weather. Cumulonimbus clouds are associated with thunderstorms. Nimbostratus clouds are associated with drizzle, mist, rain, or snow.
23. Earth's winds are powered by unequal heating of Earth's atmosphere by the sun.

Program Resources

- ◆ **Inquiry Skills Activity Book** Provides teaching and review of all inquiry skills
- ◆ **Prentice Hall Assessment System** Provides standardized test practice
- ◆ **Reading in the Content Area** Provides strategies to improve science reading skills
- ◆ **Teacher's ELL Handbook** Provides multiple strategies for English language learners

---

Applying Skills

24. Student's graphs should have one axis labeled "Month" and the other axis labeled "Average Monthly Rainfall (centimeters)." The bars should range from 1 centimeter in height (January, February, March, and December) to 57 centimeters in height (August).
25. 253 centimeters
26. *Dry:* January, February, March, April, November, and December; *Wet:* May, June, July, August, September, and October
27. Monsoons

Performance | CHAPTER PROJECT 17 | **Assessment**

Project Wrap Up Make sure students have clearly drawn graphs or other visuals to use for their presentations. Advise them to include in their presentations a description of when and where their measurements were made and the instruments that were used. They also should include a discussion of any patterns they see in their data.

Reflect and Record If students used instruments they made themselves, they may be able to improve the accuracy of their observations by using commercial instruments. Students probably will find that it is difficult to predict the weather because some of the patterns they observe in their data may not be significant for prediction. Help students focus on the most significant factors for predicting the weather, including air pressure, clouds, and wind direction.

Test Preparation

28. b   29. c   30. a   31. b

CHAPTER 18 Weather Patterns

Sections	Time	Student Edition Activities	Other Activities	
CHAPTER PROJECT 18 **The Weather Tomorrow** p. 573	Ongoing (2–3 weeks)	Check Your Progress, pp. 580, 596, 603 Project Wrap Up, p. 607	TE	Chapter 18 Project Notes, pp. 572–573
1 Air Masses and Fronts pp. 574–580 ◆ 18.1.1 Identify the major types of air masses that affect the weather in North America. ◆ 18.1.2 Name and describe the main types of fronts. ◆ 18.1.3 Define cyclones and anticyclones.	1 period/ $\frac{1}{2}$ block	**Discover** How Do Fluids of Different Densities Behave?, p. 574 **Sharpen Your Skills** Classifying, p. 579	TE TE TE TE	Inquiry Challenge, p. 577 Including All Students, p. 577 Demonstration, p. 578 Including All Students, p. 579
2 Storms pp. 581–592 ◆ 18.2.1 List the main kinds of storms and explain how they form. ◆ 18.2.2 Describe measures you can take to ensure safety in a storm.	2 periods/ 1 block	**Discover** Can You Make a Tornado?, p. 581 **Try This** Lightning Distances, p. 582 **Science at Home,** p. 589 **Real-World Lab: Careers in Science** Tracking a Hurricane, pp. 590–591	TE TE	Demonstration, p. 582 Including All Students, p. 583
3 **INTEGRATING HEALTH** **Floods** pp. 593–596 ◆ 18.3.1 Identify the causes of flooding. ◆ 18.3.2 Explain how the dangers of floods can be reduced.	1 period/ $\frac{1}{2}$ block	**Discover** What Causes Floods?, p. 593 **Sharpen Your Skills** Communicating, p. 594	TE	Using the Visuals: Figure 15, p. 594
4 Predicting the Weather pp. 597–604 ◆ 18.4.1 Explain how technology helps forecasters predict the weather. ◆ 18.4.2 Describe the types of information shown on weather maps. ◆ 18.4.3 Describe El Niño and its effects.	1 period/ $\frac{1}{2}$ block	**Discover** What's the Weather?, p. 597 **Sharpen Your Skills** Interpreting Data, p. 600 **Skills Lab: Interpreting Data** Reading a Weather Map, p. 604	TE TE TE TE LM	Inquiry Challenge, p. 599 Real-Life Learning, p. 602 Building Inquiry Skills: Calculating, p. 602 Exploring Newspaper Weather Maps, p. 603 18, "Investigating Weather Maps"
Study Guide/Assessment pp. 605–607	1 period/ $\frac{1}{2}$ block			

 For Standard or Block Schedule The Resource Pro® CD-ROM gives you maximum flexibility for planning your instruction for any type of schedule. Resource Pro® contains Planning Express®, an advanced scheduling program, as well as the entire contents of the Teaching Resources and the Computer Test Bank.

Key: **CTB** Computer Test Bank
CT Chapter Tests
ELL Teacher's ELL Handbook

CHAPTER PLANNING GUIDE

Program Resources	Assessment Strategies	Media and Technology
UR Chapter 18 Project Teacher Notes, pp. 62–63 **UR** Chapter 18 Project Overview and Worksheets, pp. 64–67	**TE** Performance Assessment: Chapter 18 Project Wrap Up, p. 67 **TE** Check Your Progress, pp. 580, 596, 603 **UR** Chapter 18 Project Scoring Rubric, p. 68	Science Explorer Internet Site Audio CDs, Section Summaries
UR 18-1 Lesson Plan, p. 69 **UR** 18-1 Section Summary, p. 70 **UR** 18-1 Review and Reinforce, p. 71 **UR** 18-1 Enrich, p. 72	**SE** Section 1 Review, p. 580 **TE** Ongoing Assessment, pp. 575, 577, 579 **TE** Performance Assessment, p. 580	Presentation Pro, "Air Masses and Fronts" Transparencies 70, "North American Air Masses"; 71, "Cold Front"; 72, "Warm Front"; 73, "Occluded Front"
UR 18-2 Lesson Plan, p. 73 **UR** 18-2 Section Summary, p. 74 **UR** 18-2 Review and Reinforce, p. 75 **UR** 18-2 Enrich, p. 76 **UR** Real-World Lab blackline masters, pp. 85–87	**SE** Section 2 Review, p. 589 **SE** Analyze and Conclude, p. 591 **TE** Ongoing Assessment, pp. 583, 585, 587 **TE** Performance Assessment, p. 589	Concept Videotape Library, *Adventures, Tape 4,* "Never Put Up the Umbrella Until It Starts to Rain"; "Violent Storms" Presentation Pro, "Storms" Transparency 74, "Clouds and Winds in a Hurricane" Lab Activity Videotape, *Tape 4*
UR 18-3 Lesson Plan, p. 77 **UR** 18-3 Section Summary, p. 78 **UR** 18-3 Review and Reinforce, p. 79 **UR** 18-3 Enrich, p. 80	**SE** Section 3 Review, p. 596 **TE** Ongoing Assessment, p. 595 **TE** Performance Assessment, p. 596	
UR 18-4 Lesson Plan, p. 81 **UR** 18-4 Section Summary, p. 82 **UR** 18-4 Review and Reinforce, p. 83 **UR** 18-4 Enrich, p. 84 **UR** Skills Lab blackline masters, pp. 88–89	**SE** Section 4 Review, p. 603 **SE** Analyze and Conclude, p. 604 **TE** Ongoing Assessment, pp. 599, 601 **TE** Performance Assessment, p. 603	Presentation Pro, "Weather Maps" Transparencies 75, "Weather Map"; 76, "Newspaper Weather Map" Lab Activity Videotape, *Tape 4*
GRSW Provides worksheets to promote student comprehension of content **RCA** Provides strategies to improve science reading skills **ELL** Provides multiple strategies for English language learners	**SE** Study Guide/Assessment, pp. 605–607 **PA** Performance Assessment, pp. 55–57 **CT** Chapter 18 Test, pp. 71–74 **CTB** Chapter 18 Test **PHAS** Provides standardized test preparation	Computer Test Bank, Chapter 18 Test

GRSW Guided Reading and Study Workbook
ISAB Inquiry Skills Activity Book
LM Laboratory Manual

PA Performance Assessment
PHAS Prentice Hall Assessment System
PLM Probeware Lab Manual

RCA Reading in the Content Area
SE Student Edition

TE Teacher's Edition
UR Unit Resources

Meeting the National Science Education Standards and AAAS Benchmarks

National Science Education Standards	Benchmarks for Science Literacy	Unifying Themes

Science As Inquiry (Content Standard A)

◆ **Use appropriate tools and techniques to gather, analyze, and interpret data** Students make weather forecasts. Students use data to predict the path of a hurricane. Students interpret a weather map. (*Chapter Project; Real-World Lab; Skills Lab*)

Earth and Space Science (Content Standard D)

◆ **Structure of the Earth system** An air mass is a huge body of air that has similar temperature, humidity, and air pressure throughout. A storm is a violent disturbance in the atmosphere. Floods occur when so much water pours into a stream or river that it overflows its banks. (*Sections 1, 2, 3*)

Science in Personal and Social Perspectives (Content Standard F)

◆ **Personal health** There are various measures to take to ensure safety during storms and floods. (*Sections 2, 3*)

◆ **Natural hazards** Unanticipated storms have even changed the course of history. (*Science & History*)

◆ **Risks and benefits** Students analyze the controversy around hurricane evacuations. (*Science and Society*)

◆ **Science and technology in society** Technology helps meteorologists predict the weather. (*Section 4*)

1B Scientific Inquiry Students make weather forecasts. Students use data to predict the path of a hurricane. Students interpret a weather map. (*Chapter Project; Real-World Lab; Skills Lab*)

3A Technology and Science Technology helps meteorologists predict the weather. (*Section 4*)

4B The Earth An air mass is a huge body of air that has similar temperature, humidity, and air pressure throughout. A storm is a violent disturbance in the atmosphere. Floods occur when so much water pours into a stream or river that it overflows its banks. (*Sections 1, 2, 3*)

6E Physical Health There are various measures to take to ensure safety during storms and floods. (*Sections 2, 3*)

7C Social Change Unanticipated storms have even changed the course of history. (*Science & History*)

7D Social Trade-Offs Students analyze the controversy around hurricane evacuations. (*Science and Society*)

◆ **Energy** A storm is a violent disturbance in the atmosphere. Rushing water in a flood has tremendous power. (*Sections 2, 3*)

◆ **Patterns of Change** Students look for patterns in the weather to make weather forecasts. As an air mass moves into an area, it changes the weather there. Students use data to predict the path of a hurricane. Meteorologists interpret weather data to prepare weather forecasts. (*Chapter Project; Sections 1, 4; Real-World Lab*)

◆ **Scale and Structure** An air mass is a huge body of air that has similar temperature, humidity, and air pressure throughout. A typical hurricane is about 600 kilometers across. (*Sections 1, 2*)

◆ **Systems and Interactions** Four major types of air masses influence the weather in North America. Different atmospheric conditions cause different kinds of storms. A warm-water event, known as El Niño, affects global weather. Students interpret a weather map to describe weather conditions. (*Sections 1, 2, 4; Skills Lab*)

◆ **Unity and Diversity** Air masses are classified as tropical, polar, maritime, or continental and fronts as cold, warm, stationary, or occluded. Four kinds of storms are thunderstorms, tornadoes, hurricanes, and winter storms. (*Sections 1, 2*)

Take It to the Net

The **www.phschool.com** Web site provides you with multiple opportunities to incorporate the internet into your instruction. Go to **www.phschool.com** and click on the Science icon. Then select Science Explorer Integrated.

■ Have students use the chapter Self-Test to get instant feedback.

■ Hot Links and Reference Links provide opportunities for online research.

Internet Activities provide opportunities for students to review, extend, or assess a concept from the chapter.

STAY CURRENT with **SCIENCE NEWS** ®

Find out the latest research and information about weather and climate at: **www.phschool.com**

ACTIVITY	Time (minutes)	Materials Quantities for one work group	Skills
Section 1			
Discover, p. 574	10	**Consumable** cardboard divider, red food coloring, 1 L warm water, 100 mL table salt, blue food coloring, 1 L cold water **Nonconsumable** plastic shoe box, apron	Developing Hypotheses
Sharpen Your Skills, p. 579	home	No special materials required.	Classifying
Section 2			
Discover, p. 581	10	**Consumable** water, liquid dish detergent **Nonconsumable** large plastic jar with lid, penny or marble	Observing
Try This, p. 582	10	**Nonconsumable** watch with second hand	Calculating
Science at Home, p. 589	home	No special materials required.	Communicating
Real-World Lab, pp. 590–591	40	**Consumable** tracing paper **Nonconsumable** ruler; red, blue, green, and brown pencils	Interpreting Data, Predicting, Making Judgements
Section 3			
Discover, p. 593	10	**Consumable** water **Nonconsumable** cup, funnel, basin	Inferring
Sharpen Your Skills, p. 594	10	No special materials required.	Communicating
Section 4			
Discover, p. 597	10	**Nonconsumable** local newspaper weather report	Observing
Sharpen Your Skills, p. 600	10	No special materials required.	Interpreting Data
Skills Lab, p. 604	30	No special materials required.	Interpreting Data, Drawing Conclusions

A list of all materials required for the Student Edition activities can be found beginning on page T23. You can obtain information about ordering materials by calling 1-800-848-9500 or by accessing the Science Explorer Internet site at: **www.phschool.com**

The Weather Tomorrow

People often complain about the unreliability of weather forecasts. Yet predicting the weather is something that interests most people because the weather influences so many things that we do. In this chapter, students will learn what causes changes in the weather and how the information recorded on weather maps can be used to make weather predictions.

Purpose In this project, students will get a chance to predict the weather and then evaluate how well they have done compared with the actual weather and with professional forecasts.

Skills Focus After completing this project, students will be able to
◆ interpret the symbols in newspaper weather maps;
◆ compare weather maps from day to day to find patterns in the weather;
◆ predict the weather for tomorrow based on the weather today;
◆ draw weather maps to show their weather predictions;
◆ compare their own predictions with professional forecasts and the next day's weather.

Project Time Line The entire project will take at least two weeks. Students should start collecting newspaper weather maps immediately. They should also read about weather maps in Section 4, paying special attention to *Exploring Newspaper Weather Maps* on page 603. As soon as students have finished reading Section 1 on air masses and fronts, they can start analyzing their weather maps. They should be looking for patterns in the weather by comparing the maps from day to day. Check students' progress at this point and give extra guidance to any students who are having problems.

Students should continue collecting and comparing weather maps over the next week or so. Check their progress when they finish Section 3 by having them predict the next day's weather at their own location and two other locations of their choice that are at least 1,000 km apart. Students should draw a weather map to show their weather predictions. After a week of predicting

CHAPTER 18 Weather Patterns

A lightning bolt tears through the dark sky, illuminating a field of wheat.

WEB ACTIVITY www.phschool.com

SECTION 1 Air Masses and Fronts
Discover **How Do Fluids of Different Densities Behave?**
Sharpen Your Skills **Classifying**

SECTION 2 Storms
Discover **Can You Make a Tornado?**
Try This **Lightning Distances**
Real-World Lab **Tracking a Hurricane**

Integrating Health
SECTION 3 Floods
Discover **What Causes Floods?**
Sharpen Your Skills **Communicating**

572

the weather in this way, have students compare their own predictions to the next days' weather maps and to professional forecasts.

When students have finished reading the chapter, give them a day or two to organize their presentations. They should display their newspaper weather maps and the weather maps they made to predict the weather. They should also include commentary, written or oral, about the patterns they observed in the weather and how they made their predictions.

For more detailed information on planning

and supervising the chapter project, see Chapter 18 Project Teacher Notes, pages 62–63 in Unit 5 Resources.

Suggested Shortcuts You can reduce the scope of the project by requiring students to select just one location instead of three. Another shortcut is to have students work in groups. If you do, make sure that each student makes a significant contribution to the overall effort. Urge groups to divide tasks according to students' specific abilities and interests, if possible.

The Weather Tomorrow

When the sky turns dark and threatening, it's not hard to predict the weather. A storm is on its way. But wouldn't you rather know about an approaching storm before it actually arrives?

In this chapter you will learn about weather patterns, including the kinds of patterns that cause strong thunderstorms like this one. As you work through this chapter, you will get a chance to make your own weather forecasts and compare them to the forecasts of professionals. Good luck!

Your Goal To predict the weather for your own community and two other locations in the United States.

To complete the project you will
◆ compare weather maps for several days at a time
◆ look for repeating patterns in the weather
◆ draw maps to show your weather predictions

Get Started Begin by previewing Section 4 to learn about weather maps and symbols. Start a project folder to hold daily national weather maps from your local newspaper and a description of the symbols used on the maps. Choose two locations in the United States that are at least 1,000 kilometers away from your community and from each other.

Check Your Progress You'll be working on this project as you study this chapter. To keep your project on track, look for Check Your Progress boxes at the following points.
Section 1 Review, page 580: Collect weather maps and look for patterns.
Section 3 Review, page 596: Predict the next day's weather.
Section 4 Review, page 603: Compare your predictions to professional forecasts and to the actual weather.

Wrap Up At the end of the chapter (page 607), you will present your weather maps and discuss how well you predicted the weather.

SECTION 4 Predicting the Weather

Discover What's the Weather?
Sharpen Your Skills Interpreting Data
Skills Lab Reading a Weather Map

573

Program Resources

◆ **Unit 5 Resources** Chapter 18 Project Teacher Notes, pp. 62–63; Project Overview and Worksheets, pp. 64–67; Project Scoring Rubric, p. 68

Media and Technology

 Audio CDs Section Summaries

 **www.phschool.com**

You will find an Internet activity, chapter self-tests for students, and links to other chapter topics at this site.

This chapter project can also be done as a class project. Spend a few minutes at the beginning of class each day reviewing with students that day's newspaper weather map. If possible, make an overhead transparency of the map so you can point out details on the map as you discuss it. Also spend a few minutes each day comparing that day's weather map with the one from the day before. At the end of a week, have students start to predict the next day's weather.

Possible Materials Newspaper weather maps are readily available and easy to work with as long as students always use the same source so the maps have the same format. This makes them easier to compare and creates less confusion. A good source for weather maps regardless of where you live is *USA Today*.

Launching the Project Introduce students to weather maps by handing out copies of a national weather map showing today's weather. Have students find their own state on the map, and then challenge them to use the map to learn as much as they can about their state's weather. For example, ask: **What does the map tell you about the temperature in our state today?** Make sure all the students know how to find this and other weather factors for their state on the map. If necessary, call their attention to the map key and point out the relevant symbols and numbers on the map. Tell students they will be collecting and comparing maps like this one for the Chapter 18 Project. They will use the maps to learn how weather changes and how to predict tomorrow's weather. Point out, however, that students will make their weather predictions without using the weather forecasts that are often included in newspapers and on radio and television.

Performance Assessment

To assess students' performance in this project, use the Chapter 18 Project Scoring Rubric on page 68 of Unit 5 Resources.
Students will be assessed on
◆ their collection and interpretation of weather maps;
◆ their weather predictions;
◆ their class presentation;
◆ their group participation, if they worked in groups.

Objectives

After completing the lesson, students will be able to
◆ identify the major types of air masses that affect the weather in North America;
◆ name and describe the main types of fronts;
◆ define cyclones and anticyclones.

Key Terms air mass, tropical, polar, maritime, continental, front, occluded, cyclone, anticyclone

1 Engage/Explore

Activating Prior Knowledge

Help students recall the properties of air they learned about in Chapter 17. Ask: **Which is denser, warm air or cold air?** *(cold air)* **What do you think would happen if a large mass of cold air came into contact with a large mass of warm air?** *(The cold air would sink and the warm air would rise.)* Tell students that large masses of cold and warm air often do meet in the atmosphere. Point out that the meeting of large air masses with different temperatures causes most of our weather.

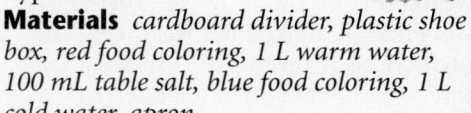

DISCOVER

Skills Focus developing hypotheses
Materials *cardboard divider, plastic shoe box, red food coloring, 1 L warm water, 100 mL table salt, blue food coloring, 1 L cold water, apron*
Time 10 minutes
Tips The more salt students use, the denser the cold water will be and the more obvious the outcome.
Expected Outcome The red water and the blue water will not mix. Instead, they will form separate layers, with the blue water on the bottom and the red water on top.
Think It Over Students should hypothesize that the cold air mass would move underneath the warm air mass and the warm air mass would rise.

574

SECTION 1 Air Masses and Fronts

DISCOVER .... ACTIVITY

How Do Fluids of Different Densities Behave?

1. Put on your apron. Place a cardboard divider across the middle of a plastic shoe box.

2. Add a few drops of red food coloring to a liter of warm water. Pour the red liquid, which represents low-density warm air, into the shoe box on one side of the divider.

3. Add about 100 mL of table salt and a few drops of blue food coloring to a liter of cold water. Pour the blue liquid, which represents high-density cold air, into the shoe box on the other side of the divider.

4. What do you think will happen if you remove the divider?

5. Now quickly remove the divider. Watch carefully from the side. What happens?

Think It Over
Developing Hypotheses Based on this activity, write a hypothesis stating what would happen if a mass of cold air ran into a mass of warm air.

GUIDE FOR READING

◆ What are the major types of air masses that affect the weather in North America?

◆ What are the main types of fronts?

◆ What are cyclones and anticyclones?

Reading Tip Before you read, use the headings to make an outline about air masses and fronts. Leave space to fill in details as you read.

574

Listen to the evening news and you may hear a weather forecast like this: "A huge mass of Arctic air is moving our way, bringing freezing temperatures." Today's weather is influenced by air from thousands of kilometers away—perhaps from Canada or the Caribbean Sea. A huge body of air that has similar temperature, humidity, and air pressure throughout it is called an **air mass.** A single air mass may spread over an area of millions of square kilometers and be up to 10 kilometers high.

Types of Air Masses

Scientists classify air masses according to two characteristics: temperature and humidity. Whether an air mass is warm or cold depends on the temperature of the region over which the air mass forms. **Tropical,** or warm, air masses form in the tropics and have low air pressure. **Polar,** or cold, air masses form north of 50° north latitude and south of 50° south latitude. Polar air masses have high air pressure.

Whether an air mass is humid or dry depends on whether it forms over water or land. **Maritime** air masses form over oceans. Water evaporates from the oceans, so the air can become very humid. **Continental** air masses form over land, in the middle of continents, and are dry.

READING STRATEGIES

Reading Tip Review with students the outline format. If necessary, provide a model outline on the board to remind students how to arrange numerals and letters. Student outlines might begin as follows:

I. Types of Air Masses
  A. Tropical
    1. Maritime Tropical
    2. Continental Tropical
  B. Polar

Vocabulary Point out to students that the term *cyclone,* as it is used in this section, has a somewhat different meaning than its common usage. Many people use the term *cyclone* to mean a tornado, a type of severe storm students will learn about in Section 2. In this section, the term *cyclone* is used to refer to any large, swirling air mass that has low pressure at the center. Unlike a tornado, a cyclone may cover thousands of kilometers.

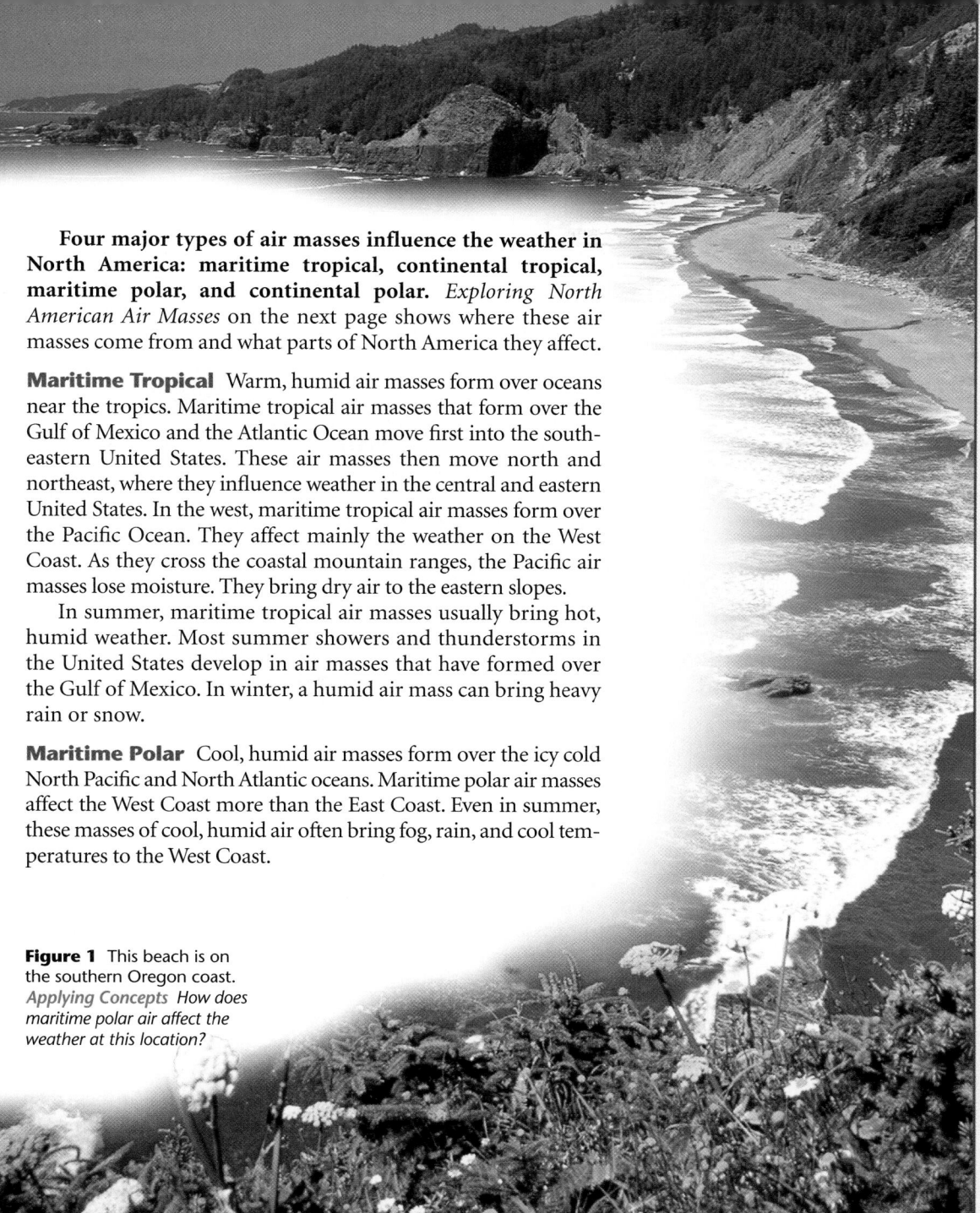

Four major types of air masses influence the weather in North America: maritime tropical, continental tropical, maritime polar, and continental polar. *Exploring North American Air Masses* on the next page shows where these air masses come from and what parts of North America they affect.

Maritime Tropical Warm, humid air masses form over oceans near the tropics. Maritime tropical air masses that form over the Gulf of Mexico and the Atlantic Ocean move first into the southeastern United States. These air masses then move north and northeast, where they influence weather in the central and eastern United States. In the west, maritime tropical air masses form over the Pacific Ocean. They affect mainly the weather on the West Coast. As they cross the coastal mountain ranges, the Pacific air masses lose moisture. They bring dry air to the eastern slopes.

In summer, maritime tropical air masses usually bring hot, humid weather. Most summer showers and thunderstorms in the United States develop in air masses that have formed over the Gulf of Mexico. In winter, a humid air mass can bring heavy rain or snow.

Maritime Polar Cool, humid air masses form over the icy cold North Pacific and North Atlantic oceans. Maritime polar air masses affect the West Coast more than the East Coast. Even in summer, these masses of cool, humid air often bring fog, rain, and cool temperatures to the West Coast.

Figure 1 This beach is on the southern Oregon coast. *Applying Concepts How does maritime polar air affect the weather at this location?*

Program Resources

◆ **Unit 5 Resources** 18-1 Lesson Plan, p. 69; 18-1 Section Summary, p. 70
◆ **Guided Reading and Study Workbook** Section 18-1

Answers to Self-Assessment

Caption Question

Figure 1 It causes the weather to be cool and humid and often foggy and rainy.

---

2 Facilitate

Types of Air Masses

Building Inquiry Skills: Applying Concepts

Some students may need to review concepts covered in earlier chapters to understand the material presented in this section. Check their comprehension of relevant concepts by asking: **How does warm ocean water or a warm land surface heat the air above it?** *(By radiation and conduction of heat from the surface to the air above it and by convection, which carries the heated air high up into the atmosphere in air currents)* **Which type of air mass would you expect to contain more moisture, a maritime air mass or a continental air mass?** *(A maritime air mass, because it forms over the ocean)* **Would a maritime tropical air mass or a maritime polar air mass have more moisture?** *(A maritime tropical air mass, because it is warmer and warm air can hold more moisture than cold air)* **learning modality: verbal**

Including All Students

Help students distinguish among the different types of air masses covered in this section. Challenge them to create crossword puzzles incorporating the terms *tropical, polar, maritime,* and *continental.* After students have created their puzzles, urge them to exchange puzzles with a partner and try to solve them. **learning modality: limited English proficiency**

Ongoing Assessment

Writing Have students explain the similarities and differences between polar and tropical air masses and between maritime and continental air masses.

Types of Air Masses, continued

EXPLORING

North American Air Masses

Invite students to apply the information in the feature by having them identify the types of air masses that affect different locations, such as different regions of the United States, different states, or different cities. Include the location where students live. For each location, ask: **What type of air are you likely to find there, and where does it come from?** (*Answers will depend on the locations chosen. For example, northern California receives cool, humid air due to maritime polar air masses from the northern Pacific Ocean.*) **learning modality: visual**

Building Inquiry Skills: Predicting

Point out that when air masses move from where they originate, they tend to be modified by the terrain they pass over. For example, the cold, dry air of continental polar air masses is warmed and moistened when it passes over the Great Lakes. Ask: **How would you predict that the other three North American air masses would be modified by the terrain they usually pass over?** (*Continental tropical air masses would be cooled, maritime polar air masses would be warmed and dried, maritime tropical air masses would be cooled and dried.*) **learning modality: logical/ mathematical**

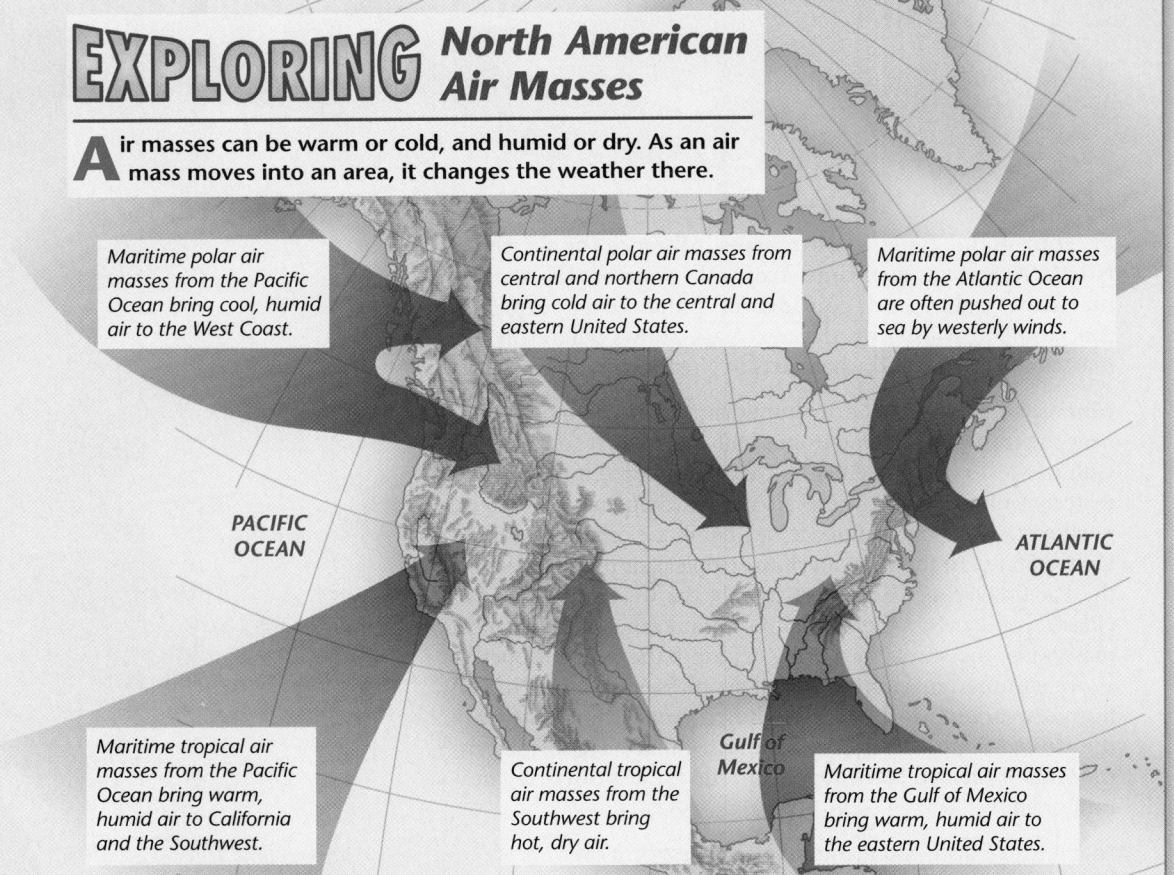

EXPLORING North American Air Masses

Air masses can be warm or cold, and humid or dry. As an air mass moves into an area, it changes the weather there.

Maritime polar air masses from the Pacific Ocean bring cool, humid air to the West Coast.

Continental polar air masses from central and northern Canada bring cold air to the central and eastern United States.

Maritime polar air masses from the Atlantic Ocean are often pushed out to sea by westerly winds.

PACIFIC OCEAN

ATLANTIC OCEAN

Maritime tropical air masses from the Pacific Ocean bring warm, humid air to California and the Southwest.

Continental tropical air masses from the Southwest bring hot, dry air.

Gulf of Mexico

Maritime tropical air masses from the Gulf of Mexico bring warm, humid air to the eastern United States.

Continental Tropical Hot, dry air masses form only in summer over dry areas of the Southwest and northern Mexico. Continental tropical air masses cover a smaller area than other air masses. They occasionally move northeast, bringing hot, dry weather to the southern Great Plains.

Continental Polar Large continental polar air masses form over central and northern Canada and Alaska. As you would expect, continental polar air masses bring cool or cold air. In winter, continental polar air masses bring clear, cold, dry air to much of North America. Air masses that form near the Arctic Circle can bring bitterly cold weather with very low humidity. In summer, storms may occur when continental polar air masses move south and meet maritime tropical air masses moving north.

☑ *Checkpoint* Where do continental polar air masses come from?

576

Background

History of Science Up until the early 1900s, scientists thought that storms were caused by low air pressure. This conclusion was based on the fact that storms always seemed to occur in low-pressure areas. Then, in the early twentieth century, a Norwegian meteorologist named Vilhelm Bjerknes and a group of his colleagues deduced that storms are caused by the collision of large air masses that differ from one another in temperature and humidity. Although storms do occur in low-pressure areas, the low pressure is not their cause. Rather, low pressure areas, like storms, are a result of the collision of different air masses. This finding is now accepted as one of the most important principles of modern meteorology, and it is the basic principle underlying weather forecasting today.

How Air Masses Move

Recall that the prevailing westerlies are the major wind belts in the continental United States. The prevailing westerlies generally push air masses from west to east. For example, maritime polar air masses from the Pacific Ocean are blown onto the West Coast, bringing heavy rain or snow. Continental polar air masses from central Canada enter the United States between the Rocky Mountains and the Great Lakes. These cold, dry air masses are then blown east, where they affect the weather of the central and eastern United States.

Fronts

As huge masses of air move across the land and the oceans, they bump into each other. But the air masses do not easily mix. Why don't they? Think about a bottle of oil-and-vinegar salad dressing. The less dense oil floats on top of the more dense vinegar.

Something similar happens when two air masses with different temperatures and densities collide. The area where the air masses meet and do not mix becomes a **front**. The term *front*, which is borrowed from military language, means a battle area where opposing armies meet to fight. When air masses meet at a front, the collision often causes storms and changeable weather. A front may be 15 to 200 kilometers wide and extend as much as 10 kilometers up into the troposphere.

There are four types of fronts: cold fronts, warm fronts, stationary fronts, and occluded fronts. The kind of front that develops depends on the characteristics of the air masses and how they are moving. How does each type of front affect your local weather?

Figure 2 A cold front forms when cold air moves underneath warm air, forcing the warm air to rise.

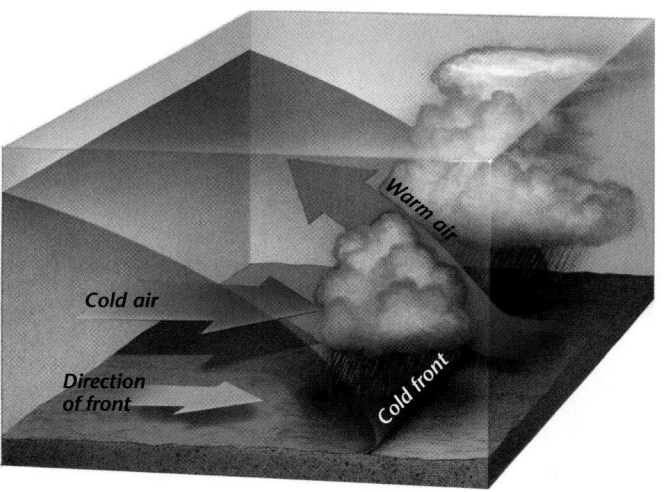

Inquiry Challenge

Material *world map or globe*

Time 10 minutes

Based on what they have just learned about the movement of air masses in North America, challenge students to infer which types of air masses are likely to affect the weather of Europe. First provide students with a world map or globe, and then ask: **Where do you think air masses come from that move over the European continent?** (*The Atlantic Ocean, northern Eurasia, and the African continent*) **What type of air do you think they bring to Europe?** (*Cool humid air from the Atlantic Ocean, cold dry air from northern Eurasia, and hot dry air from Africa*) **learning modality: logical/mathematical**

Fronts

Including All Students

Materials *red and blue modeling clay*

Time 5 minutes

Give hands-on learners an opportunity to model the formation of warm and cold fronts using wedges of red and blue modeling clay to represent warm and cold air masses, respectively. For each type of front that students model, ask: **In which direction is the front moving?** (*For the cold front, toward the warm air mass; for the warm front, toward the cold air mass*) **learning modality: kinesthetic**

Answers to Self-Assessment

☑ *Checkpoint*
Continental polar air masses come from central and northern Canada and Alaska.

Ongoing Assessment

Oral Presentation Call on students to name the four types of air masses that influence weather in North America. Then call on other students to state where each type of air mass forms, whether it is warm or cold, and whether it is humid or dry.

Fronts, continued

Using the Visuals: Figure 3

Help students understand the similarities and differences between warm and cold fronts by having them compare and contrast illustrations of each type of front. Ask: **How does Figures 3, which shows the formation of a warm front, differ from Figure 2, which shows the formation of a cold front?** *(In Figure 3, the warm air mass moves up over the cold air mass; in Figure 2, the cold air mass moves underneath the warm air mass.)* **How are the two figures similar?** *(In both cases, the warm air rises and cools, causing water vapor to condense out of it and form clouds.)* **learning modality: visual**

Demonstration

Materials *tall heat-resistant jar or beaker, cold water, pepper, stirrer, container of hot water, food coloring, candle, matches*
Time 15 minutes

Do this demonstration to show students how fronts form. Half-fill a tall, heat-resistant jar or beaker with cold water. Stir pepper into the water until it is mixed throughout. Add food coloring to a container of hot water, mix well, and then gently pour the hot water into the jar of cold water. The two layers of water should remain separate and mix only slightly. Light a candle and hold the jar above it. As the cold water in the bottom of the jar heats up, the pepper will move upward due to convection. However, the pepper will not penetrate the top layer of colored water but instead collect at the "front" between the two layers of water. Ask: **Why doesn't the pepper rise up through the top layer of water?** *(Because the top layer of water is warmer and will not mix with the cooler layer of water containing the pepper)* **learning modality: visual**

Cold Fronts As you know, cold air is dense and tends to sink. Warm air is less dense and tends to rise. When a rapidly moving cold air mass runs into a slowly moving warm air mass, the denser cold air slides under the lighter warm air. The warm air is pushed upward, as shown in Figure 2. The front that forms is called a cold front.

As the warm air rises, it cools. Remember that warm air can hold more water vapor than cool air. The rising air soon reaches the dew point, the temperature at which the water vapor in the air condenses into droplets of liquid water. Clouds form. If there is a lot of water vapor in the warm air, heavy rain or snow may fall. What will happen if the warm air mass contains only a little water vapor? In this case, the cold front may be accompanied by only cloudy skies.

Cold fronts move quickly, so they can cause abrupt weather changes, including violent thunderstorms. After a cold front passes through an area, cool, dry air moves in, often bringing clear skies and cooler temperatures.

Warm Fronts Clouds, storms, and rain also accompany warm fronts. At a warm front, a moving warm air mass collides with a slowly moving cold air mass. Because cold air is more dense than warm air, the warm air moves over the cold air, as shown in Figure 3. If the warm air is humid, showers and light rain fall along the front where the warm and cold air meet. If the warm air is dry, scattered clouds form. Because warm fronts move more slowly than cold fronts, the weather may be rainy or foggy for several days. After a warm front passes through an area, the weather is likely to be warm and humid. In winter, warm fronts bring snow.

Figure 3 A warm front forms when warm air moves over cold air.
Interpreting Diagrams What kind of weather forms at a warm front?

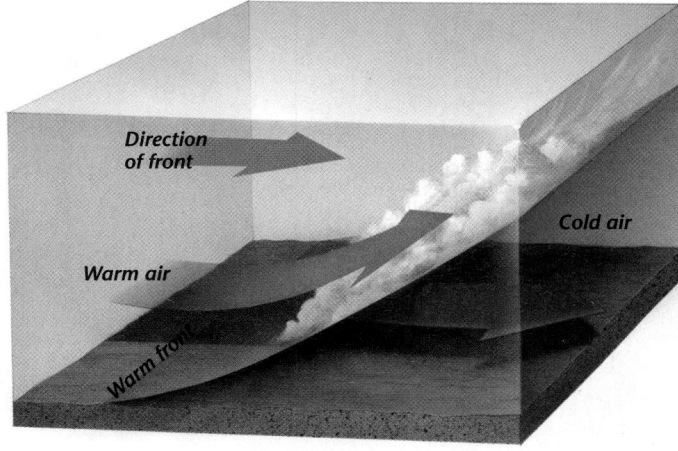

578

Background

Facts and Figures Like fingerprints or snowflakes, no two fronts are exactly alike. For example, the slope of a front can vary considerably, from about 1:100 (1 km of vertical distance covers 100 km of horizontal distance) for a cold front to about 1:200 for a warm front.

The slope of a front is an important determinant of the type of weather the front brings. A cold front with a very steep slope is likely to bring a narrow band of violent storms extending less than 100 km. A warm front with a very gradual slope, on the other hand, is likely to bring cloudy weather but no storms. However, the area affected by the cloudy weather may extend for many hundreds of kilometers.

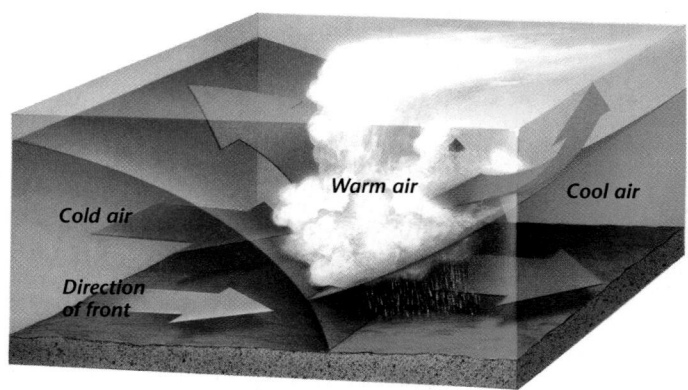

Figure 4 When a cold air mass and a cool air mass come together, the warm air caught between them is forced upward. The result is an occluded front.

Stationary Fronts Sometimes cold and warm air masses meet, but neither one has enough force to move the other. The two air masses face each other in a "standoff." In this case, the front is called a stationary front. Where the warm and cool air meet, water vapor in the warm air condenses into rain, snow, fog, or clouds. If a stationary front remains stalled over an area, it may bring many days of clouds and precipitation.

Occluded Fronts The most complex weather situation occurs at an occluded front, shown in Figure 4. At an occluded front, a warm air mass is caught between two cooler air masses. The denser cool air masses move underneath the less dense warm air mass and push it upward. The two cooler air masses meet in the middle and may mix. The temperature near the ground becomes cooler. The warm air mass is cut off, or **occluded,** from the ground. As the warm air cools and its water vapor condenses, the weather may turn cloudy and rainy or snowy.

☑ *Checkpoint* *What type of front forms when two air masses meet and neither one can move?*

Cyclones and Anticyclones

If you look at a weather map, you will see areas marked with an L. The L is short for "low," and indicates an area of relatively low air pressure. A swirling center of low air pressure is called a **cyclone,** from a Greek word meaning "wheel."

As warm air at the center of a cyclone rises, the air pressure decreases. Cooler air blows toward this low-pressure area from nearby areas where the air pressure is higher. Winds spiral inward toward the center of the system. Recall that in the Northern Hemisphere the Coriolis effect deflects winds to the right.

Sharpen your Skills

Classifying

ACTIVITY

At home, watch the weather forecast on television. Make a note of each time the weather reporter mentions a front. Classify the fronts mentioned or shown as cold, warm, stationary, or occluded. Also, note what type of weather is predicted to occur when the front arrives. Is each type of front always associated with the same type of weather?

Chapter 18 **579**

Answers to Self-Assessment

Caption Question

Figure 3 Clouds, storms, and precipitation form at a warm front.

☑ *Checkpoint*

A stationary front forms when two air masses meet and neither one can move.

3 Assess

Section 1 Review Answers

1. temperature and humidity
2. A front is the area where two air masses meet and do not mix. A cold front forms when cold air moves underneath warm air. A warm front forms when warm air moves over cold air. A stationary front forms when a warm and a cold air mass meet but neither can move the other. An occluded front forms when a warm air mass is caught between two cool air masses and cut off from the ground.
3. A swirling center of low air pressure; storms and precipitation
4. Because East Coast maritime polar air masses are blown out to sea by prevailing westerlies
5. Maritime tropical and polar air masses are humid; continental tropical and polar air masses are dry.

Check Your Progress

CHAPTER PROJECT 18

Check that each student has started to collect weather maps. Comparisons of weather in the three locations should include all the weather factors represented on the maps.

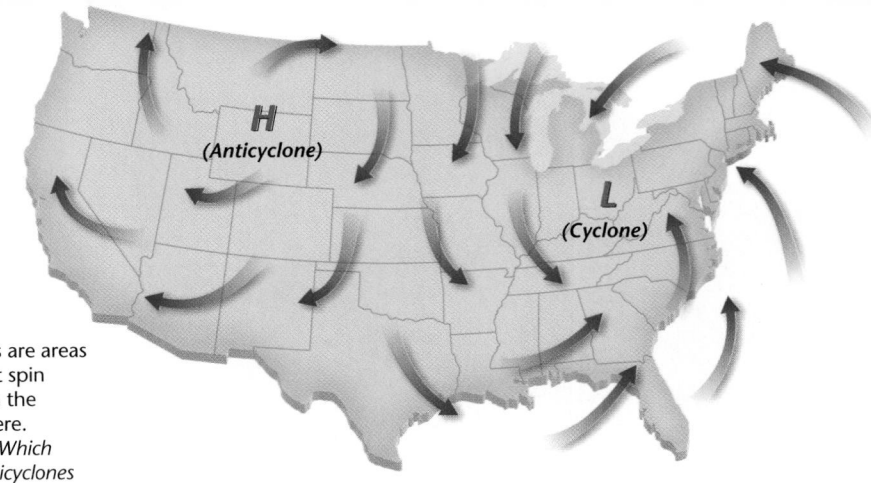

Figure 5 Cyclones are areas of low pressure that spin counterclockwise in the Northern Hemisphere. *Interpreting Maps Which way do winds in anticyclones spin?*

Because of this, winds in a cyclone spin counterclockwise in the Northern Hemisphere, as shown in Figure 5.

Cyclones play a large part in the weather of the United States. As air rises in a cyclone, the air cools, forming clouds and precipitation. **Cyclones and decreasing air pressure are associated with storms and precipitation.**

As its name suggests, an anticyclone is the opposite of a cyclone in most ways. **Anticyclones** are high-pressure centers of dry air. Anticyclones are also called "highs"—H on a weather map. Winds spiral outward from the center of an anticyclone, moving toward areas of lower pressure. Because of the Coriolis effect, winds in an anticyclone spin clockwise in the Northern Hemisphere. Because air moves out from the center of the anticyclone, cool air moves downward from higher in the troposphere. As the cool air falls, it warms up, so its relative humidity drops. The descending air in an anticyclone causes dry, clear weather.

Section 1 Review

1. What two main characteristics are used to classify air masses?
2. What is a front? Name and describe four types of fronts.
3. What is a cyclone? What type of weather does it bring?
4. Why do maritime polar air masses have more effect on the West Coast than the East Coast?
5. **Thinking Critically Classifying** Classify the four major types of air masses according to whether they are dry or humid.

Check Your Progress

CHAPTER PROJECT 18

Collect newspaper weather maps for about a week, and arrange them in order. Look carefully at how symbols on the map have moved from one day to the next. What patterns do you see from day to day in different weather factors? How does the weather in your community differ from the weather in the two other locations you selected?

Answers to Self-Assessment

Caption Question

Figure 5 Winds in anticyclones spin clockwise in the Northern Hemisphere.

Program Resources

◆ **Unit 5 Resources** 18-1 Review and Reinforce, p. 71; 18-1 Enrich, p. 72

Performance Assessment

Skills Check Have students describe the direction of winds in cyclones and anticyclones in the Southern Hemisphere.

DISCOVER

Can You Make a Tornado?

1. Fill a large jar three-quarters full with water. Add a drop of liquid dish detergent and a penny or marble.
2. Put the lid on the jar tightly. Now move the jar in a circle until the water inside begins to spin.

Think It Over

Observing What happens to the water in the jar? Describe the pattern that forms. How is it like a tornado? Unlike a tornado?

Early in 1998, a series of powerful tornadoes roared through central Florida. With winds as high as 210 miles per hour, the tornadoes dropped cars into living rooms, crumpled trailers, and destroyed businesses and school buildings. They were the deadliest tornadoes ever to hit Florida. These tornadoes were not the only violent weather that year. In California the problem was rain. Record rainfalls brought devastating floods and mudslides.

What was causing these disasters? Meteorologists had an answer: El Niño. El Niño is a weather pattern related to the temperature of the water in the tropical Pacific Ocean. When temperatures there rise, they set off a series of events that can influence weather half a world away.

Have you ever experienced a tornado, hurricane, or other severe storm? When rain pours down, thunder crashes, or snowdrifts pile up, it may be hard to think about the actions of air pressure and air masses. Yet these are the causes of severe storms as well as the weather you experience every day.

A **storm** is a violent disturbance in the atmosphere. Storms involve sudden changes in air pressure, which in turn cause rapid air movements. Conditions that bring one kind of storm often cause other kinds of storms in the same area. For example, the conditions that cause thunderstorms can also cause tornadoes.

GUIDE FOR READING

◆ What are the main kinds of storms? How do they form?
◆ What measures can you take to ensure safety in a storm?

Reading Tip As you read, create a table comparing thunderstorms, tornadoes, hurricanes, and snowstorms. Include temperature, precipitation, and safety rules.

Figure 6 Tornadoes caused tremendous damage in Florida and other parts of the southeastern United States in 1998.

581

READING STRATEGIES

Reading Tip There should be a column for each kind of storm. In addition to rows for temperature, precipitation, and safety, students may add rows to their tables for recording such factors as wind speed, size of storm, length of time the storm lasts, and the type of damage it does. Have students save their tables for review.

Program Resources

◆ **Unit 5 Resources** 18-2 Lesson Plan, p. 71; 18-2 Section Summary, p. 72
◆ **Guided Reading and Study Workbook** Section 18-2

Objectives

After completing the lesson, students will be able to
◆ list the main kinds of storms and explain how they form;
◆ describe measures they can take to ensure safety in a storm.

Key Terms storm, lightning, tornado, hurricane, storm surge, evacuate

1 Engage/Explore

Activating Prior Knowledge

Introduce students to tornadoes and other storms by asking: **Did you ever see a dust devil, a spinning wind that picks up and carries dust, dead leaves, and other debris?** (*Most students probably will say "yes."*) **What did it look like?** (*a funnel*) **What do think causes dust devils?** (*Air swirling in a circle*) Point out that dust devils resemble small tornadoes. Explain that they are caused by hot air rising rapidly from the heated ground. As the hot air rises, the wind blows it into a spinning motion and it picks up loose material. Add that most dust devils last just a few seconds, rise only a few meters, and cause no damage. Tell students that a similar type of air movement also causes tornadoes, as they will learn in this section.

DISCOVER

Skills Focus observing
Materials *large plastic jar with lid, water, liquid dish detergent, penny or marble, water*
Time 10 minutes
Tips Tell students not to shake the jar or slosh the water back and forth to create bubbles. Instead, they should swirl the water gently with a circular motion.
Expected Outcome The water should swirl around in the jar like a tornado.
Think It Over Students should say that the water swirls in a funnel-shaped spiral. It is like a tornado because the water spins around in a circle. It is unlike a tornado because it occurs in water instead of air.

2 Facilitate

Thunderstorms

Demonstration

Materials *bottle with plastic cap, copper wire, aluminum foil, plastic comb, wool fabric*

Time 10 minutes

Show the class how lightning occurs with this demonstration. Push a short piece of copper wire through a small hole in the cap of a bottle. Form the bottom end of the wire into a hook and hang a small strip of aluminum foil over it. Put the cap on the bottle with the hook and foil inside. Rub a comb on wool fabric to give it an electrical charge and then touch the comb to the end of the wire protruding from the top of the bottle cap. Students will see the ends of the foil strip move apart from one another. Ask: **Why did the ends of the foil strip move?** *(Students may not know.)* Explain that the foil became charged with electricity, which was transmitted through the wire from the comb, causing the two ends of the foil strip to repel each other. Ask: **How is this like lightning?** *(A charge is built up when particles in clouds rub together, and when the electricity is discharged from one part of the cloud to another or to the ground, lightning occurs.)* **learning modality: visual**

TRY THIS

Skills Focus calculating

Materials *watch with second hand*

Time 10 minutes

Expected Outcome The number of seconds between the lightning flash and the sound of the thunder will depend on how far away the lightning is. If the lightning is very close, the thunder will occur just a split second later. If the lightning is very far away, the thunder may not even be audible. If the length of time between the lightning and thunder is increasing, the storm is moving away from you. If the length of time is decreasing, the storm is moving toward you. **learning modality: logical/mathematical**

582

Figure 7 The anvil shape of this cloud is typical of cumulonimbus clouds that produce thunderstorms. *Applying Concepts Why do cumulonimbus clouds often form along cold fronts?*

TRY THIS

Lightning Distances

Because light travels faster than sound, you see a lightning flash before you hear the clap of thunder. Here's how to calculate your distance from a thunderstorm.

CAUTION: *Do this activity inside a building only.*

1. Count the number of seconds between the moment when you see the lightning and when you hear the thunder.

2. Divide the number of seconds you counted by three to get the distance in kilometers. Example:

$$\frac{15 \text{ s}}{3 \text{ s/km}} = 5 \text{ km}$$

Calculating Wait for another flash of lightning and calculate the distance again. How can you tell whether a thunderstorm is moving toward you or away from you?

582

Thunderstorms

Do you find thunderstorms frightening? Exciting? A little of both? As you watch the brilliant flashes of lightning and listen to long rolls of thunder, you have probably wondered what caused them.

How Thunderstorms Form Thunderstorms are heavy rainstorms accompanied by thunder and lightning. **Thunderstorms form within large cumulonimbus clouds, or thunderheads.** Most cumulonimbus clouds and thunderstorms form when warm air is forced upward at a cold front. Cumulonimbus clouds also form on hot, humid afternoons in the spring and summer. In both cases, the warm, humid air rises rapidly. As the air rises, it cools, forming dense thunderheads. Heavy rain falls, sometimes along with hail.

Thunderstorms produce strong upward and downward winds—updrafts and downdrafts—inside clouds. When a downdraft strikes the ground, the air spreads out in all directions, producing bursts of wind called wind shear. Wind shear has caused a number of airplane accidents during takeoff or landing.

Lightning and Thunder During a thunderstorm, areas of positive and negative electrical charges build up in the storm clouds. **Lightning** is a sudden spark, or energy discharge, as these charges jump between parts of a cloud, between nearby clouds, or between a cloud and the ground. Lightning is similar to the shocks you sometimes feel when you touch a metal object on a very dry day, but on a much larger scale.

What causes thunder? A lightning bolt can heat the air near it to as much as 30,000°C, much hotter than the surface of the sun. The rapidly heated air expands suddenly and explosively. Thunder is the sound of the explosion. Because light travels faster than sound, you see lightning before you hear thunder.

Background

Facts and Figures Just how serious a threat do thunderstorms pose? At any given moment, about 1,800 thunderstorms are occurring somewhere on Earth. That's a total of 16 million thunderstorms a year worldwide, of which an estimated 100,000 occur in the United States. Every second about 100 bolts of lightning strike Earth's surface. About 80 people in the United States are killed by lightning each year (more than are typically killed each year by tornadoes). Over the last 10 years, lightning started more than 15,000 fires in the United States and caused hundreds of millions of dollars in damage each year and the destruction of two million acres of forest. The high winds that often accompany thunderstorms can be even more damaging. Thunderstorm winds can exceed 160 km/h, which is as fast as the winds of a hurricane.

Thunderstorm Safety When lightning strikes

the ground, the hot, expanding air can shatter tree trunks or start forest fires. When lightning strikes people or animals, it acts like a powerful electric shock. Being struck by lightning can cause unconsciousness, serious burns, or even heart failure.

What should you do to remain safe if you are caught outside during a thunderstorm? **During thunderstorms, avoid touching metal objects because they can conduct electricity from lightning into your body.** Lightning usually strikes the tallest nearby object, such as a tree, house, or flagpole. To protect buildings from lightning, people install metal lightning rods at the highest point on a roof. Lightning rods intercept a lightning stroke and conduct the electricity through cables safely into the ground.

In open spaces, such as a golf course, people can be in danger because they are the tallest objects in the area. It is equally dangerous to seek shelter under a tree, because lightning may strike the tree and you at the same time. Instead, find a low area away from trees, fences, and poles. Crouch with your head down and your hands on your knees. If you are swimming or in a boat, get to shore and find shelter away from the water.

If you are inside a house during a thunderstorm, avoid touching telephones, electrical appliances, or plumbing fixtures, all of which can conduct electricity into the house. It is usually safe to stay in a car with a hard top during a thunderstorm because the electricity will move along the metal skin of the car and jump to the ground. However, do not touch any metal inside the car.

☑ *Checkpoint* *Why is lightning dangerous?*

Tornadoes

A tornado is one of the most frightening and destructive types of storms. A **tornado** is a rapidly whirling, funnel-shaped cloud that reaches down from a storm cloud to touch Earth's surface. If a tornado occurs over a lake or ocean, it is known as a waterspout. Tornadoes are usually brief, but can be deadly. They may touch the ground for 15 minutes or less and be only a few hundred meters across, but wind speeds may approach 480 kilometers per hour.

Figure 8 Lightning occurs when electricity jumps within clouds, between clouds, or between a cloud and the ground.

Media and Technology

 Concept Videotape Library
Adventures, Tape 4, "Never Put Up the Umbrella Until It Starts to Rain"; "Violent Storms"

Answers to Self-Assessment

Caption Question

Figure 7 Cumulonimbus clouds often form along cold fronts because warm air is forced upward. As the warm air rises, it cools, forming dense thunderheads.

☑ *Checkpoint*

Lightning acts like a powerful shock and can cause unconsciousness, serious burns, or even heart failure.

 ## Integrating Health

There are many naive conceptions about lightning that may cause people to take needless risks in thunderstorms. Address some of these naive conceptions by first asking: **Do you think the old saying is true that lightning never strikes twice in the same place?** *(Students may say "yes".)* Tell students that the chance of lightning striking the same place twice is very small, but there is no reason it cannot happen. In fact, some buildings and even people have been struck by lightning repeatedly. Other myths about lightning include that there is no danger from lightning if it is not raining and that rubber-soled shoes will protect you from being struck by lightning.
learning modality: verbal

Tornadoes

Including All Students

Materials *raw potato, plastic drinking straw*
Time 5 minutes

Tell students that the force of the wind in a tornado may be great enough to drive a drinking straw through a board. If students find this hard to believe, this activity will help them appreciate just how strong the wind can be. Have students place the end of a plastic drinking straw against a raw potato and push as hard as they can. The straw will bend and scarcely penetrate the potato. Now have students hold the straw at least half a meter away from the potato and drive it into the potato as fast as possible. This time the straw will penetrate the potato without bending. Ask: **Why did the straw go through the potato when you drove it in from a distance?** *(It was pushed harder.)* Add that winds in a tornado can push with such force that a blade of grass may be driven into a tree trunk.
learning modality: kinesthetic

Ongoing Assessment

Writing Challenge students to write a public service announcement for television or radio that spells out the precautions people should take to remain safe in a thunderstorm.

Tornadoes, continued

Call students' attention to the feature and then ask: **What types of storms are described in the feature?** *(Thunderstorms and hurricanes)* Point out that tornadoes are not included, and then ask: **Why might tornadoes have less impact on history?** *(A tornado's path of destruction tends to be narrow and short lived.)* Inform students that there are some notable exceptions to the brief, local nature of most tornadoes. For example, the Great Tri-State Tornado of March 18, 1925, killed almost 700 people in three states, and the Superoutbreak Tornadoes of April 3–4, 1974, killed more than 300 people and injured over 5,500 others in 12 states in 24 hours. Add that, unlike thunderstorms and hurricanes, exactly when and where a tornado will touch down is still difficult to predict. Suggest to students who need an extra challenge that they research other examples of tornadoes, thunderstorms, and hurricanes that had an impact, great or small, on the course of history. Urge them to share what they learn with the rest of the class.

In Your Journal Students' paragraphs will vary depending on the specific event they choose. If they choose the storms that affected the *Mayflower*, for example, they may say that, with advance warning, the settlers might have delayed their landing until the storms had passed and then settled in what is now New York City instead of Plymouth. **learning modality: verbal**

584

How Tornadoes Form **Tornadoes develop in low, heavy cumulonimbus clouds—the same clouds that bring thunderstorms.** Tornadoes are most likely to occur when thunderstorms are likely—in spring and early summer, often late in the afternoon when the ground is warm. The Great Plains often have the kind of weather pattern that is likely to create tornadoes: a warm, humid air mass moves north from the Gulf of Mexico into the lower Great Plains. A cold, dry air mass moves south from Canada. When the air masses meet, the cold air moves under the warm air, which rises. A squall line of thunderstorms is likely to form, with storms traveling from southwest to northeast. A single squall line can cause 10 or more tornadoes.

Tornadoes occur more often in the United States than in any other country. About 800 tornadoes occur in the United States

SCIENCE & History

Weather That Changed History

Unanticipated storms have caused incredible damage, killed numbers of people, and even changed the course of history.

1281 Japan
In an attempt to conquer Japan, Kublai Khan, the Mongol emperor of China, sent a fleet of ships carrying a huge army. A hurricane from the Pacific brought high winds and towering waves that sank the ships. The Japanese named the storm *kamikaze*, meaning "divine wind."

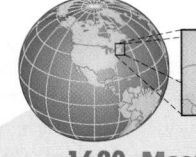

1620 Massachusetts
English Pilgrims set sail for the Americas in the *Mayflower*. They had planned to land near the mouth of the Hudson River, but turned back north because of rough seas and storms. When the Pilgrims landed farther north, they decided to stay and so established Plymouth Colony.

| 1300 | 1400 | 1500 | 1600 |

1588 England
King Philip II of Spain sent the Spanish Armada, a fleet of 130 ships, to invade England. Strong winds in the English Channel trapped the Armada near shore. Some Spanish ships escaped, but storms wrecked most of them.

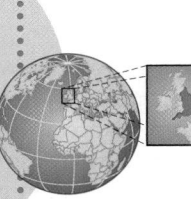

584

Background

Facts and Figures Tornadoes are commonly classified according to the following scale, which is called the Fujita-Pearson Tornado Intensity Scale after its inventors:
F0 Light (under 116 km/h)
F1 Moderate (116–180 km/h)
F2 Considerable (181–253 km/h)
F3 Severe (254–332 km/h)
F4 Devastating (333–419 km/h)

F5 Incredible (over 419 km/h)
The winds of tornadoes have done some amazing things. In Bedfordshire, England, in May of 1950, a tornado is reported to have plucked the feathers off several chickens, who amazingly were otherwise unharmed. Tornadoes also have lifted frogs and fish from ponds and then dropped them elsewhere, leading to the saying, "a tornado may rain frogs."

every year. Weather patterns on the Great Plains result in a "tornado alley," shown in Figure 9, that runs from north-central Texas across central Oklahoma, Kansas, and Nebraska. However, tornadoes can and do occur in nearly every part of the United States.

☑ *Checkpoint* **Where do tornadoes form?**

Tornado Safety A tornado can level houses on one street, but **INTEGRATING HEALTH** leave neighboring houses standing. Tornado damage comes from both strong winds and flying debris. The low pressure inside the tornado sucks up dust and other objects into the funnel. Tornadoes can move large objects—sheds, trailers, cars—and scatter debris many miles away. One tornado tore off a motel sign in Broken Bow, Oklahoma, and dropped it 30 miles away in Arkansas!

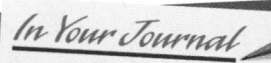

In Your Journal

Some of these events happened before forecasters had the equipment to predict weather scientifically. Choose one of the events in the time line. Write a paragraph describing how history might have been different if the people involved had had accurate weather predictions.

1870 Great Lakes

Learning that more than 1,900 boats had sunk in storms on the Great Lakes in 1869, Congress decided to set up a national weather service, the Army Signal Corps. In 1891 the job of issuing weather warnings and forecasts went to a new agency, the U.S. Weather Bureau.

| 1700 | 1800 | 1900 |

1837 North Carolina

The steamship *Home* sank during a hurricane off Ocracoke, North Carolina. In one of the worst storm-caused disasters at sea, 90 people died. In response, the U.S. Congress passed a law requiring seagoing ships to carry a life preserver for every passenger.

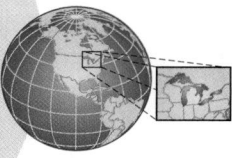

1915 Texas

When a hurricane struck the port city of Galveston in 1900, it killed 6,000 people and destroyed much of the city. As a result, a seawall 5 meters high and 16 kilometers long was built. When another hurricane struck in 1915, the seawall greatly reduced the amount of damage.

Chapter 18 **585**

Tornadoes, continued

Using the Visuals: Figure 9

Use the map in Figure 9 to help students understand why the central part of the United States has so many tornadoes. Ask: **What is the reddish shaded area called?** *(Tornado Alley)* **Why is it called that?** *(More tornadoes occur there than anywhere else in the United States.)* **Why do you think so many tornadoes occur there?** *(Because cold and warm air masses meet there)* **learning modality: visual**

Addressing Naive Conceptions

Ask students if the following statements are true or false: **If you don't have a basement, the safest place in your home in the event of a tornado is the southwest corner.** *(False. The safest place is a small windowless room or closet in the center of the house.)* **If a tornado catches you on the road, it is best to stay in your car.** *(False. A tornado can overturn a car or pick it up and drop it elsewhere. You should leave the car and go to a well-built building or lie flat in a low place with your head covered.)* Based on how students respond, discuss any misconceptions they may hold. For example, if students believe that the safest place in a home without a basement is an outside corner, explain that an outside room is more at risk of damage from the wind, and windows in outside rooms put you at risk of flying glass. **learning modality: verbal**

Hurricanes

Including All Students

Explain to students that hurricanes are given names according to certain rules. They are named alphabetically, alternating between masculine and feminine names. For example, in 1999, the first storm of the season was named Arlene, the second Bret, the third Cindy, and so on. Challenge the class to come up with their own list of names for 15 hurricanes. Give each student a number from 1 to 15 and have the student apply the rules to name the hurricane of that number. **limited English proficiency**

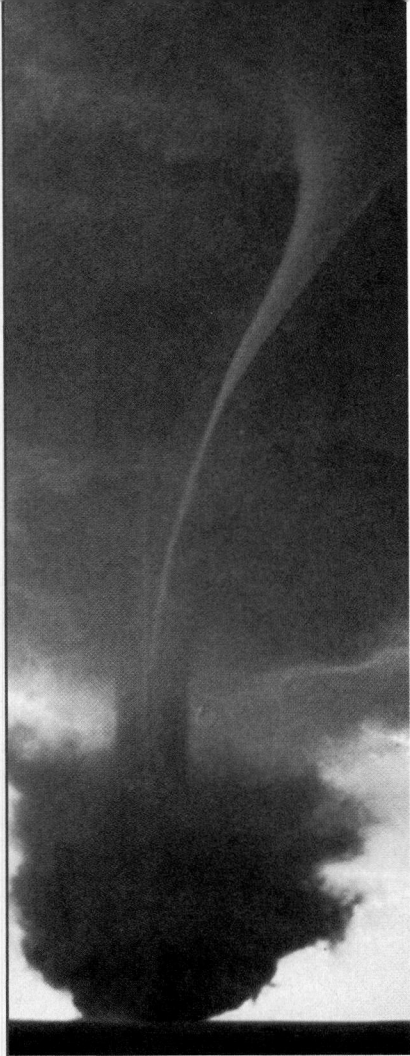

Figure 9 A tornado can cause a lot of damage in a short period of time. The map shows where tornadoes are most likely to occur in the United States.
Interpreting Maps Which states are partially located in "tornado alley"?

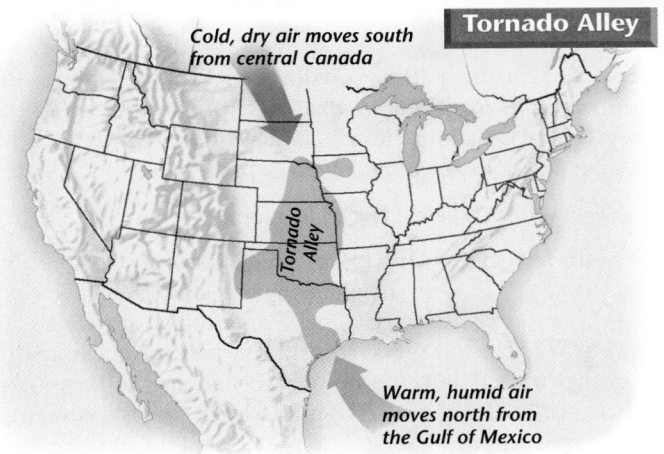

Tornado Alley

Cold, dry air moves south from central Canada

Tornado Alley

Warm, humid air moves north from the Gulf of Mexico

What should you do if a tornado is predicted in your area? A "tornado watch" is an announcement that tornadoes are possible in your area. Watch for approaching thunderstorms. A "tornado warning" is an announcement that a tornado has been seen in the sky or on weather radar. If you hear a tornado warning, move to a safe area as soon as you can. Do not wait until you actually see the tornado.

The safest place to be during a tornado is in the basement of a well-built building. If the building you are in does not have a basement, move to the middle of the ground floor. Stay away from windows and doors that could break and fly through the air. Lie on the floor under a sturdy piece of furniture, such as a large table. If you are outdoors or in a car or mobile home, move to a building or lie flat in a ditch.

☑ *Checkpoint What is the difference between a tornado watch and a tornado warning?*

Hurricanes

Between June and November, people who live in the eastern United States hear weather reports much like this: "A hurricane warning has been issued for the Atlantic coast from Florida to North Carolina. Hurricane Michael has winds of over 160 kilometers per hour and is moving north at about 65 kilometers per hour." A **hurricane** is a tropical storm that has winds of 119 kilometers per hour or higher. A typical hurricane is about 600 kilometers across.

Hurricanes also form in the Pacific and Indian oceans. In the western Pacific Ocean, hurricanes are called typhoons. Although hurricanes may be destructive, they bring much-needed rainfall to South Asia and Southeast Asia.

586

How Hurricanes Form A typical hurricane that strikes the United States forms in the Atlantic Ocean north of the equator in August, September, or October. **A hurricane begins over warm water as a low-pressure area, or tropical disturbance.** If the tropical disturbance grows in size and strength, it becomes a tropical storm, which may then become a hurricane.

A hurricane gets its energy from the warm, humid air at the ocean's surface. As this air rises and forms clouds, more air is drawn into the system. As with other storm systems, winds spiral inward toward the areas of low pressure. Inside the storm are bands of very high winds and heavy rains. The lowest air pressure and warmest temperatures are at the center of the hurricane. The lower the air pressure at the center of a storm, the faster the winds blow toward the center. Hurricane winds may be as strong as 320 kilometers per hour.

The Eye of the Hurricane The center of a hurricane is a ring of clouds surrounding a quiet "eye," as shown in Figure 10. If you were in the path of a hurricane, you would notice that the wind gets stronger as the eye approaches. When the eye arrives, the weather changes suddenly. The winds grow calm and the sky may clear. After the eye passes, the storm resumes, but the wind blows from the opposite direction.

How Hurricanes Move Hurricanes last longer than other storms, usually a week or more. Hurricanes that form in the Atlantic Ocean are steered by easterly trade winds toward the Caribbean islands and the southeastern United States. After a hurricane passes over land, it no longer has warm, moist air to draw energy from. The hurricane gradually slows down and loses strength, although heavy rainfall may continue for a number of days.

Figure 10 In a hurricane, air moves rapidly around a low-pressure area called the eye. *Observing Where is the eye of the hurricane in the photograph?*

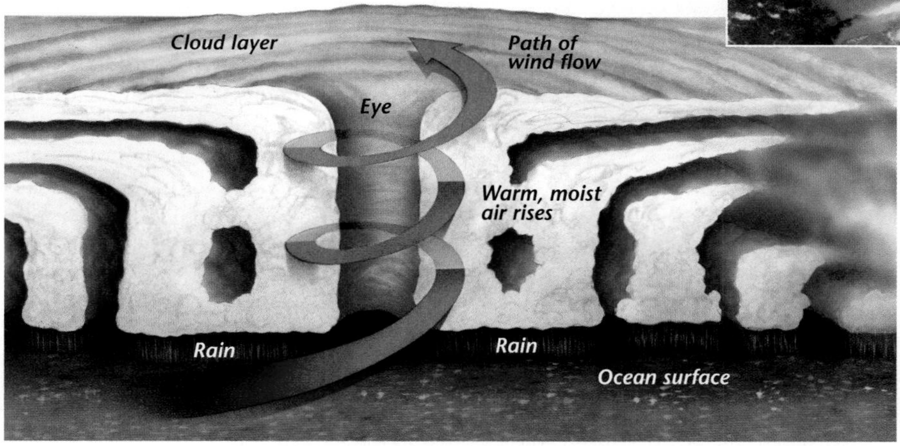

Cloud layer

Path of wind flow

Eye

Warm, moist air rises

Rain

Rain

Ocean surface

Chapter 18 **587**

Answers to Self-Assessment

☑ *Checkpoint*

Tornado watch: tornadoes are possible. Tornado warning: a tornado has been seen in the sky or on weather radar.

Caption Questions

Figure 9 South Dakota, Iowa, Nebraska, Kansas, Missouri, Oklahoma, Texas, New Mexico, Arkansas

Figure 10 In the center of the clouds

Real-Life Learning

If it is hurricane season, have groups of students monitor tropical disturbances, watch for those that develop into hurricanes, and note where the hurricanes reach land. Groups should gather information from newspapers, television, or the Internet and, at the end of hurricane season, present the information to the class. Challenge groups to use a diversity of ways to record and present the information. **cooperative learning**

Using the Visuals: Figure 10

Call students' attention to the figure, then check to be sure that they understand how the two parts of the figure are related, by asking: **In which illustration are you looking down at a hurricane from above?** (*The photograph on the right*) **From which direction are you looking at the hurricane in the drawing?** (*From the side*) **In which direction is the wind blowing in both illustrations?** (*Counterclockwise around the eye of the hurricane*) **learning modality: visual**

Building Inquiry Skills: Problem Solving

Challenge students to solve the following problem. Tell them to assume they have been caught in the path of a hurricane and the eye of the storm is predicted to pass over their town. Now, after two days of high winds and waves and severe thunderstorms with torrential rain, the storm has died down and the sky has cleared. Ask: **Should you assume the storm has passed and start unboarding the windows and cleaning up the debris? Why or why not?** (*No, because this may be a temporary calm due to the eye of the storm. If so, after the eye passes, the storm will return.*) **How could you find out?** (*Listen to weather bulletins on radio or television*) **learning modality: logical/mathematical**

Ongoing Assessment

Oral Presentation Call on students at random to name the parts of the country where hurricanes occur. Call on other students to explain in their own words why hurricanes occur only in those places.

587

Hurricanes, continued

Integrating Health

Divide the class into groups and challenge the groups to brainstorm a list of actions people in hurricane-prone areas should take: (1) at the beginning of hurricane season (*Trim dead branches from trees, learn safe routes inland*); (2) if a hurricane watch is issued (*Keep tuned to radio or television for storm updates, check radio and flashlight for batteries, stock up on canned food*); and (3) if a hurricane warning is issued (*Leave mobile homes, unplug appliances and turn off gas tanks, board up glass windows and doors, listen to radio or television for orders to evacuate and do so immediately when instructed*). When groups have completed their lists, have them share their ideas with the class. **cooperative learning**

Winter Storms

Visual Arts CONNECTION

Challenge students talented in art to create their own artwork depicting a snowstorm or other storm. Invite them to share their artwork with the class.

In Your Journal Students should comment on how well the words made them see, hear, and feel a snowstorm. **learning modality: visual**

Building Inquiry Skills: Inferring

Towns in the Rocky Mountains get even more snow than Buffalo and Rochester, New York. **Why do you think the high mountain areas of the West receive so much snow?** (*Because warm, moist air from the Pacific Ocean is cooled and drops its moisture as snow when it rises up over the Rocky Mountains*) **How are the Rocky Mountains similar to areas bordering the Great Lakes that receive lake-effect snow?** (*Both areas receive warm, moist west winds that are cooled to produce large amounts of snow.*) **learning modality: logical/mathematical**

Visual Arts CONNECTION

Weather and storms are favorite subjects for artists. "Snow Storm" is an oil painting by English artist J.M.W. Turner (1775–1851). To convey a mood or feeling, artists choose certain colors and textures. How does Turner's choice of colors enhance the mood of the painting? What texture do you see in the sea and sky? How does the texture support the feeling of the painting?

In Your Journal

Write a paragraph or two about the mood of this painting. Describe how you would feel being out in the wind and waves. Before you begin writing, jot down words that describe what you would see, hear, touch, taste, and smell. Exchange your descriptive writing with a partner to get feedback.

Hurricane Damage When a hurricane comes ashore, it brings high waves and severe flooding as well as wind damage. Hurricanes uproot trees, smash buildings, and destroy power lines. Heavy rains flood roads.

One of the most dangerous features of a hurricane is the storm surge. The low pressure and high winds of the hurricane over the ocean raise the level of the water up to six meters above normal sea level. The result is a **storm surge,** a "dome" of water that sweeps across the coast where the hurricane lands. As the hurricane comes onshore, the water comes with it. Storm surges can cause great damage, washing away beaches and destroying buildings along the coast.

Hurricane Safety Until the 1950s, a fast-moving hurricane could strike with little warning. Since then, **INTEGRATING HEALTH** advances in communications and satellite tracking have made hurricanes less deadly. People now receive information well in advance of an approaching hurricane.

A "hurricane watch" is an announcement that hurricane conditions are *possible* in your area within the next 36 hours. People should be prepared to **evacuate** (ee VAK yoo ayt), or move away temporarily.

A "hurricane warning" means that hurricane conditions are *expected* within 24 hours. **If you hear a hurricane warning and are told to evacuate, leave the area immediately.** If you must stay in a house, move to the interior of the building, away from windows.

☑ *Checkpoint* *What is a storm surge?*

Winter Storms

In the winter in the northern United States, much precipitation falls as snow. **Snow falls when humid air cools below 0°C.** Heavy snowfalls can block roads, trapping people in their homes and making it hard for emergency vehicles to move. Extreme cold can damage crops and cause water pipes to freeze and burst.

Figure 11 The British artist J.M.W. Turner painted "Snow Storm" in 1842.

Background

Integrating Science Two serious health dangers of winter storms are frostbite and hypothermia. Frostbite is damage to body tissue, usually in the nose, ears, fingers, or toes, due to freezing of the tissue. Symptoms include a loss of feeling and a white appearance in the affected area. If you think you have frostbite, slowly rewarm the affected area and get medical help right away.

Hypothermia is a fall in body temperature below normal. Symptoms include shivering, disorientation, slurred speech, and drowsiness. Hypothermia is a life-threatening emergency. If someone shows signs of hypothermia, seek medical help immediately.

Lake-effect Snow Two of the snowiest cities in the United States are Buffalo and Rochester in upstate New York. On average, nearly three meters of snow falls on each of these cities every winter. Why do Buffalo and Rochester get so much snow?

Study Figure 12. Notice that Buffalo is located to the east of Lake Erie, and Rochester is located to the south of Lake Ontario. In the fall and winter, the land near these lakes cools much more rapidly than the water in the lakes. Although the water in these lakes is cold, it is still much warmer than the surrounding land and air. When a cold, dry air mass moves from central Canada southeast across one of the Great Lakes, it picks up water vapor and heat from the lake. As soon as the air mass reaches the other side of the lake, the air rises and cools again. The water vapor condenses and falls as snow, usually within 40 kilometers of the lake.

Snowstorm Safety Imagine being out in a snowstorm when

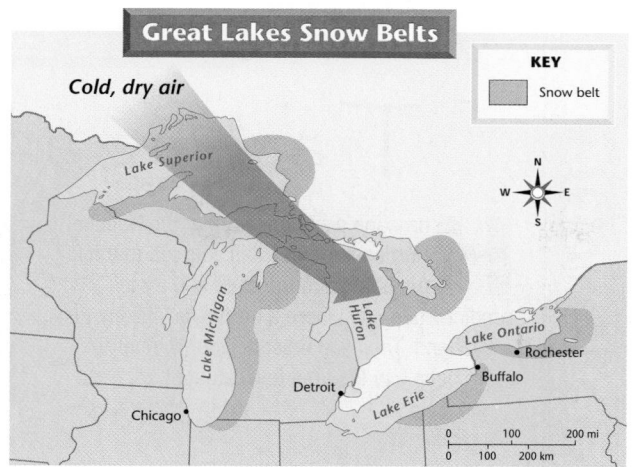

Great Lakes Snow Belts

Cold, dry air

KEY
Snow belt

Lake Superior
Lake Michigan
Lake Huron
Lake Ontario • Rochester
Detroit • Buffalo
Chicago •
Lake Erie

0   100   200 mi
0   100   200 km

Figure 12 As cold dry air moves across the warmer water, it picks up water vapor. When the air reaches land and cools, lake-effect snow falls. *Interpreting Maps Which two cities receive large amounts of snow?*

the wind suddenly picks up. High winds can blow falling snow sideways or pick up snow from the ground and suspend it in the air. This situation can be extremely dangerous because the blowing snow makes it easy to get lost. Also, strong winds cool a person's body rapidly. **If you are caught in a snowstorm, try to find shelter from the wind.** Cover exposed parts of your body and try to stay dry. If you are in a car, the driver should keep the engine running only if the exhaust pipe is clear of snow.

INTEGRATING HEALTH

Section 2 Review

1. What weather conditions are most likely to cause thunderstorms and tornadoes?
2. What is the most common path for the hurricanes that strike the United States?
3. What safety precautions should you take if a tornado is predicted in your area? If a hurricane is predicted?
4. **Thinking Critically** **Applying Concepts** In the winter, cool, humid air from the Pacific Ocean blows across the cold land of southern Alaska. What kind of storm do you think this causes?

Science at Home

Interview a family member or other adult about a dramatic storm that he or she has experienced. Before the interview, make a list of questions you would like to ask. For example, how old was the person when the storm occurred? When and where did the storm occur? Write up your interview in a question-and-answer format, beginning with a short introduction.

Program Resources

◆ **Unit 5 Resources** 18-2 Review and Reinforce, p. 75; 18-2 Enrich, p. 76

Answers to Self-Assessment

☑ *Checkpoint*

A storm surge is a "dome" of water that sweeps across the coast where a hurricane lands.

Caption Question

Figure 12 Buffalo and Rochester in upstate New York receive large amounts of snow.

Integrating Health

Tell students that the winds of snowstorms make them even more dangerous because they lead to low wind-chill temperatures. Wind chill is how cold it feels because of the wind. For example, if the air temperature is -8°C and the wind is blowing at 50 km/h, the wind-chill temperature is -31°C. Ask: **Why does the wind make you feel colder than the cold air temperature alone?** *(Because it blows the heat away from your body)* **learning modality: logical/mathematical**

3 Assess

Section 2 Review Answers

1. Warm air being forced upward at a cold front to form large cumulonimbus clouds
2. From the Atlantic Ocean westward toward the Caribbean islands and the southeastern United States
3. If a tornado is predicted, go to the basement of a well-built building. If a hurricane is predicted, leave the area immediately.
4. A heavy snowstorm, because the moisture in the cool humid air from the Pacific would condense and fall as snow when it reached the cold land of southern Alaska

Science at Home

Encourage students to tape record or video-tape their interview. They might want to present it to the class in the form of a newspaper article or television news report. Suggest that they use drawings or photographs to illustrate their presentation.

Performance Assessment

Skills Check Have students make a table comparing and contrasting thunderstorms, tornadoes, hurricanes, and snowstorms.

Tracking a Hurricane

Preparing for Inquiry

Key Concept The path of a hurricane is not always easy to predict, making it difficult to issue hurricane warnings.

Skills Objectives Students will be able to

◆ interpret data on a map representing the location of a hurricane at repeated intervals;

◆ interpret additional data in tables to plot the continued path of the hurricane;

◆ use the data to predict when and where the hurricane will come ashore;

◆ make a judgement about when and for what area a hurricane warning should be issued.

Time 40 minutes

Advance Planning Students will have to press down hard to mark clearly on the tracing paper with the colored pencils, so have a pencil sharpener and extra pencils on hand. Students may need to trace additional maps, so have extra sheets of tracing paper on hand as well. You may wish to make a copy of the map from the student text as an overhead transparency. Use it to show students how to read latitude and longitude and plot the path of the hurricane.

Alternative Materials Instead of having students use tracing paper to trace the map in their text, you may want to provide each student with a photocopy of the map to mark on directly. If so, make copies of the map in advance.

Guiding Inquiry

Invitation To give the lab a context, point out that today hurricanes cause an average of only 17 deaths each year in the United States. Explain that the relatively low death rate is due to early warnings of when and where hurricanes are coming ashore. Earlier in this century, before the knowledge and technology needed for early warnings were available, the death rate from hurricanes was much higher. Add that one of the main jobs of some

---

Tracking a Hurricane

Hurricane alert! You work at the National Hurricane Center. It is your job to track the paths of hurricanes and try to predict when and where a hurricane is likely to strike land. Then you must decide whether to warn people in the area to evacuate.

Problem

How can you predict when and where a hurricane will come ashore?

Skills Focus

interpreting data, predicting

Materials

ruler
red, blue, green, and brown pencils
tracing paper

Procedure

1. Look at the plotted path of the hurricane on the map. Each dot represents the location of the eye of the hurricane at six-hour intervals. The last dot shows where the hurricane was located at noon on August 30.

2. Predict the path you think the hurricane will take. Place tracing paper over the map below. Using a red pencil, place an X on your tracing paper where you think the hurricane will first reach land. Next to your X, write the date and time you think the hurricane will come ashore.

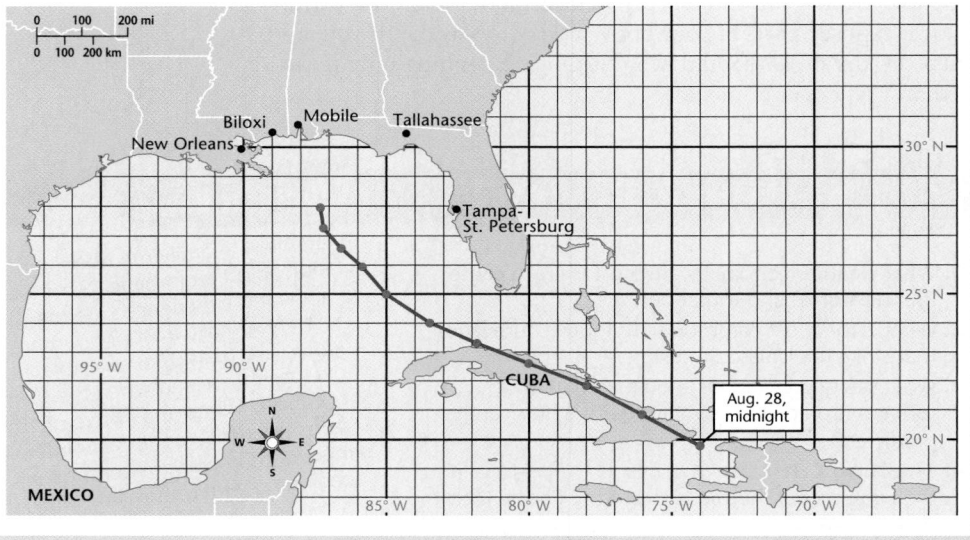

---

meteorologists during hurricane season is to track the storms so warnings can be issued in time to save lives.

Introducing the Procedure

Have students read through the steps of the procedure. Clear up any questions they may have. If necessary, review how to find latitude and longitude. Emphasize to students that they will be plotting the eye of the hurricane as it travels across the water. Ask: **How far on either side of the eye of the hurricane is the storm**

likely to extend? *(A typical hurricane is 600 km wide, so the storm may extend 300 km on either side of the eye.)* **Why is this important to know for issuing a hurricane warning?** *(The area affected by the hurricane when it comes ashore will be as wide as the storm, and this is the area for which a hurricane warning should be issued.)*

3. Hurricane warnings are issued for an area that is likely to experience a hurricane within 24 hours. On your tracing paper, shade in red the area for which you would issue a hurricane warning.

4. Using the following data table, plot the next five positions for the storm using a blue pencil. Use your ruler to connect the dots to show the hurricane's path.

Date and Time	Latitude	Longitude
August 30, 6:00 P.M.	28.3° N	86.8° W
August 31, midnight	28.4° N	86.0° W
August 31, 6:00 A.M.	28.6° N	85.3° W
August 31, noon	28.8° N	84.4° W
August 31, 6:00 P.M.	28.8° N	84.0° W

5. Based on the new data, decide if you need to change your prediction of where and when the hurricane will come ashore. Mark your new predictions in blue pencil on your tracing paper.

6. During September 1, you obtain four more positions. (Plot these points only after you have completed Step 5.) Based on these new data, mark in green pencil when and where you now think the hurricane will come ashore.

Date and Time	Latitude	Longitude
September 1, midnight	28.8° N	83.8° W
September 1, 6:00 A.M.	28.6° N	83.9° W
September 1, noon	28.6° N	84.2° W
September 1, 6:00 P.M.	28.9° N	84.8° W

7. The next day, September 2, you plot four more positions using a brown pencil. (Plot these points only after you have completed Step 6.)

Date and Time	Latitude	Longitude
September 2, midnight	29.4° N	85.9° W
September 2, 6:00 A.M.	29.7° N	87.3° W
September 2, noon	30.2° N	88.8° W
September 2, 6:00 P.M.	31.0° N	90.4° W

Analyze and Conclude

1. Describe in detail the complete path of the hurricane you tracked. Include where it came ashore and identify any cities that were in the vicinity.
2. How did your predictions in Steps 2, 5, and 6 compare to what actually happened?
3. What was unusual about your hurricane's path?
4. How do you think hurricanes with a path like this one affect the issuing of hurricane warnings?
5. Why do you have to be so careful when issuing warnings? What problems might be caused if you issued an unnecessary hurricane warning? What might happen if a hurricane warning were issued too late?
6. **Think About It** In this activity you only had data for the hurricane's position. If you were tracking a hurricane and issuing warnings, what other types of information would help you make decisions about the hurricane's path?

More to Explore

With your teacher's help, search the Internet for more hurricane tracking data. Map the data and try to predict where the hurricane will come ashore.

Troubleshooting the Experiment
◆ Point out to students that the lines of latitude and longitude on the map are in one-degree increments. Therefore, students will have to estimate where to plot the points because these are given in tenths of a degree of latitude or longitude.
◆ Use an overhead transparency of the map to show students how to plot the first point in the table as an example.
◆ If students think they are plotting incorrectly, advise them that hurricanes can change direction.

Program Resources
◆ **Unit 5 Resources** Real-World Lab blackline masters, pp. 85–87

Media and Technology
 Lab Activity Videotape
Tape 4

◆ As the hurricane changes direction, students' maps may become too crowded and difficult to read. If so, suggest that they trace a new map.

Expected Outcome
Students' maps should show that the hurricane changed direction twice, once to the east and then to the west, before finally coming ashore near Biloxi, Mississippi, on September 2.

Analyze and Conclude
1. The hurricane first appeared to be moving north toward southern Louisiana. It then turned east toward central Florida, before reversing direction and heading northwest toward the panhandle of Florida. It continued to move west or northwest until it came ashore near Biloxi, Mississippi.
2. Students' predictions will vary. They are likely to have predicted that the storm would come ashore near Mobile in Step 2, between Tallahassee and Tampa-St. Petersburg in Step 5, and near New Orleans in Step 6. The hurricane actually came ashore somewhat east of New Orleans at Biloxi.
3. The path of the hurricane was unusual because it reversed direction.
4. Hurricanes with a path like this one make it difficult to issue accurate warnings because where the hurricane actually comes ashore is different from where it appears to be headed.
5. You have to be careful when you issue hurricane warnings because unnecessary warnings can disrupt lives, put people in danger, and cause economic losses, whereas warnings that come too late can result in needless loss of life and damage to property.
6. Other types of information that would help you make decisions about the hurricane's path and when and where to issue hurricane warnings would include how fast the hurricane is moving, the speed of its winds, and other indicators of the severity of the storm.

Extending the Inquiry
More to Explore A good Internet site for hurricane tracking data is the National Hurricane Center at: www.nhc.noaa.gov

Hurricane Alert: To Stay or Not To Stay?

Purpose To inform students of the pros and cons of evacuation in a hurricane and help them decide whether or not the government should have the power to force people to evacuate.

Role-Play

Time a day to prepare; 15 minutes for role-play

Choose several students to role-play a family discussion in which family members argue over whether or not they should evacuate after a hurricane warning has been issued. Instruct some of the students to take the position that the family should evacuate and others to take the opposite position. Urge students to support their arguments with facts from the feature.

Extend Before the role-play is presented to the class, take a poll of students to see how many would and how many would not evacuate in a hurricane. After the role-play has been presented, take the poll again. Call on any students who changed their minds to explain why.

You Decide

1. The government can order but not enforce evacuations in a hurricane. Some people do not want to evacuate. Other people believe that the government should have the right to force people to evacuate for public safety.

2. Forcing people to evacuate may prevent injuries and save lives by getting people to safety. People who benefit are those who would have been killed or injured had they not been evacuated. People who might be harmed include people who need to protect their homes, businesses, or animals. Government officials might try to increase public awareness of the dangers of not evacuating. Citizens could become better informed about the reasons for evacuating.

3. Make sure students' arguments are well reasoned.

Hurricane Alert: To Stay or Not To Stay?

When a hurricane sweeps in from the ocean, the National Hurricane Center tracks the storm's course. Radio stations broadcast warnings. Sirens blow, and people in the storm path take steps to protect their homes and families.

State and local governments may try to keep people safe by closing state offices, setting up emergency shelters, and alerting the National Guard. As the danger increases, a state's governor can order the evacuation of people from dangerous areas. These actions are meant to protect public safety.

But not everyone wants to evacuate. Some people believe they have the right to stay. And officials cannot make people obey an evacuation order. How much can—or should—the government do to keep people safe?

The Issues

Why Play It Safe? Hurricanes can be extremely dangerous. High winds blow off roofs and shatter windows. Flash floods and storm surges can wash away houses. Even after the storm blows away, officials may need to keep people from returning home because of flooded sewers or broken power lines and gas mains.

In recent years, earlier and more accurate forecasts have saved lives. People now have time to prepare and to get out of the hurricane's path. Emergency officials urge people—especially the elderly, sick, or disabled—to leave early while the weather is still good. Most casualties happen when people are taken by surprise or ignore warnings. Those who decide to stay may later have to be rescued by boat or helicopter. These rescues add to the expense of the storm and may put the lives of rescuers in danger.

Why Ride Out the Storm? People have different reasons for not wanting to evacuate. Some want to protect their homes or businesses. Others don't want to leave pets or farm animals or go to public shelters. Store owners may stay open to sell disaster supplies. In addition, warnings may exaggerate the potential danger, urging people to leave when they might actually be safe. Since leaving can be expensive and disruptive, residents have to carefully evaluate the risks.

Is It a Matter of Rights? Should a government have the power to make people evacuate? Some citizens argue that the government should not tell them what to do as long as they are not harming others. They believe that individuals should have the right to decide for themselves. What do you think?

You Decide

1. Identify the Problem

In your own words, explain the controversy around hurricane evacuations.

2. Analyze the Options

Review and list the pros and cons of forcing people to evacuate. What people benefit? Who might be harmed? What more, if anything, should government officials do? What more could citizens do?

3. Find a Solution

Imagine that the radio has broadcast a hurricane warning. Write a dialogue in which you and members of your family discuss the options and decide whether or not to evacuate.

Background

Many of the severe hurricanes that struck the United States earlier in the twentieth century had high fatality rates. For example, in 1900, a hurricane that struck Texas killed 6,000 people. In 1919, a hurricane that struck the Florida Keys killed 900 people. More recent hurricanes have led to less loss of life, primarily because of early warnings. For example, in 1989, hurricane Hugo killed fewer than 30 people in the United States, even though it was a severe storm. However, recent hurricanes have caused huge amounts of property damage. Hugo, for example, caused an estimated $10.5 billion worth of damage. The increased cost of hurricanes is partly due to an influx of population to the coast. With more houses, businesses, and other types of property along the shore, there is much greater potential for property damage due to hurricanes.

INTEGRATING HEALTH

SECTION 3 Floods

DISCOVER

ACTIVITY

What Causes Floods?

1. Fill a cup with water. Hold a funnel above a basin and pour the water very slowly into the funnel.
2. Refill the cup with the same amount of water you used in Step 1. Hold the funnel above the basin and this time pour the water rapidly into the funnel. What happens?

Think It Over

Inferring How is a funnel like a river valley? What do you think would happen if a large amount of water entered a river valley in a short period of time?

Antelope Canyon in the northern Arizona desert is only a few meters wide in places. On August 12, 1997, a group of 12 hikers entered the dry, narrow canyon. That afternoon a severe thunderstorm dropped several inches of rain on the Kaibeto Plateau, 24 kilometers away. Dry stream channels that drain into Antelope Canyon quickly filled with rainwater. The water rushed into the canyon, creating a wall of water over 3 meters high. Tourists at the top of the canyon watched in horror as the water swept the hikers away. Only one hiker survived.

Are you surprised that floods can occur in a desert? Actually, floods like this are more common in the dry Southwest than in areas with more rain.

GUIDE FOR READING

- What causes flooding?
- How can the dangers of floods be reduced?

Reading Tip As you read, draw a flowchart showing what can happen during a flood and how people should respond to it.

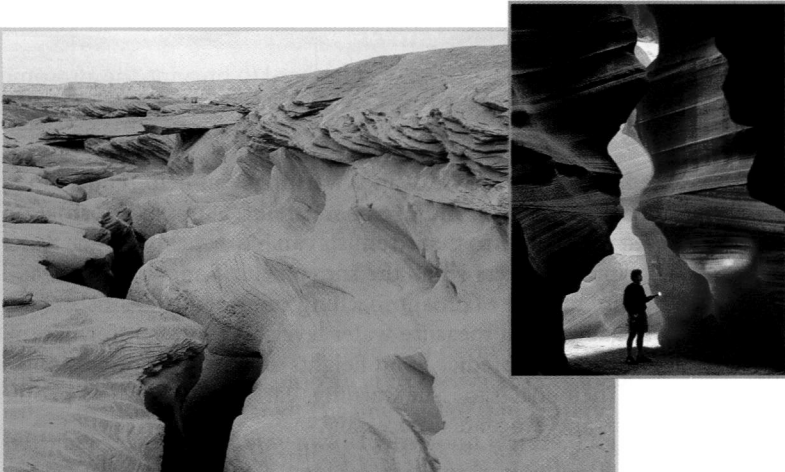 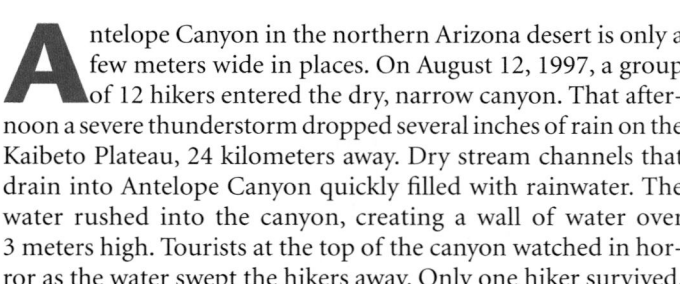

Figure 13 From the top, Antelope Canyon looks like a narrow slit in the ground.

Chapter 18 **593**

READING STRATEGIES

Reading Tip A sample flowchart is: rain falls→river rises→land floods→people evacuate. You might want to have students add the words *dam* and *ice jam* to their flowcharts as additional causes of floods.

Study and Comprehension As students read the last two pages of the section, have them summarize flood safety rules in two brief lists, one a list of what *to* do, the other a list of what *not* to do, in a flood.

Program Resources

- **Unit 5 Resources** 18-3 Lesson Plan, p. 77; 18-3 Section Summary, p. 78
- **Guided Reading and Study Workbook** Section 18-3

Caption Question

Figure 15 It is dangerous to stay in a car in a flood because the water can wash the car away.

INTEGRATING HEALTH

SECTION 3 Floods

Objectives
After completing the lesson, students will be able to
- identify the causes of flooding;
- explain how the dangers of floods can be reduced.

Key Term flash flood

1 Engage/Explore

Activating Prior Knowledge
Introduce the section by having students apply what they know about watches and warnings to floods. Ask: **What do you think is the difference between a flood watch and a flood warning?** (*Students may say a flood watch means floods are possible and a flood warning means floods have already started to occur.*) **What should people do if a flood watch has been issued?** (*Stay tuned to radio or television.*) **What should people do if a flood warning has been issued?** (*Listen for further instructions, evacuate if ordered to do so.*)

DISCOVER

Skills Focus inferring
Materials *cup, water, funnel, basin*
Time 10 minutes
Tips The funnel should be smaller than the cup so it overflows when students fill it rapidly.
Expected Outcome In Step 1, all the water will flow through the funnel. In Step 2, some of the water will overflow the funnel.
Think It Over Both a funnel and a river valley are narrow channels that collect water from much larger areas. The river might overflow its banks, similar to the way the water overflowed the funnel, and this would create a flood.

593

Oral Presentation Call on various students to describe in their own words one of the ways that flash floods can occur.

595

① *Heavy rain falls on the plateau*

Flash Floods

Although movies feature the violent winds of tornadoes and hurricanes, floods are the most dangerous weather-related events in the United States. **Floods occur when**

19 Climate and Climate Change

Sections	Time	Student Edition Activities		Other Activities
CHAPTER PROJECT 19 **Investigating Microclimates** p. 609	Ongoing (3 weeks)	Check Your Progress, pp. 617, 636 Project Wrap Up, p. 643	TE	Chapter 19 Project Notes, pp. 608–609
1 What Causes Climate? pp. 610–619 ◆ 19.1.1 Identify the factors that influence temperature and precipitation. ◆ 19.1.2 Explain what causes the seasons.	2 periods/ 1 block	**Discover** How Does Earth's Shape Affect Climate Zones?, p. 610 **Sharpen Your Skills** Inferring, p. 613 **Skills Lab: Controlling Variables** Sunny Rays and Angles, pp. 618–619 (Probeware version available) **PLM** Provides instructions for the probeware version of the lab	TE TE TE TE TE	Demonstration, p. 612 Inquiry Challenge, p. 612 Building Inquiry Skills: Observing, p. 613; Inferring, p. 614 Including All Students, p. 614, 615 Exploring the Seasons, p. 616
2 Climate Regions pp. 620–631 ◆ 19.2.1 Identify factors used to define climates. ◆ 19.2.2 Describe the different types of climate regions.	1 period/ ½ block	**Discover** What Are Different Climate Types?, p. 620 **Try This** Modeling a Humid Climate, p. 625 **Sharpen Your Skills** Classifying, p. 627 **Science at Home,** p. 629 **Real-World Lab: Careers in Science** Cool Climate Graphs, pp. 630–631	TE TE TE LM	Real-Life Learning, p. 623 Inquiry Challenge, p. 625 Including All Students, p. 628 19, "Investigating Differences in Climate"
3 Long-Term Changes in Climate pp. 632–636 ◆ 19.3.1 Identify how scientists can learn about ancient climates. ◆ 19.3.2 Describe how Earth's surface changes during an ice age. ◆ 19.3.3 Explain the theories that have been proposed to explain natural climate change	1 period/ ½ block	**Discover** What Story Can Tree Rings Tell?, p. 632	TE TE	Including All Students, p. 634 Including All Students, p. 636
4 ⬤ *INTEGRATING ENVIRONMENTAL SCIENCE* **Global Changes in the Atmosphere** pp. 637–640 ◆ 19.4.1 Describe the greenhouse effect and how human activities might be affecting the temperature of Earth's atmosphere. ◆ 19.4.2 Describe how human activities have affected the ozone layer.	1 period/ ½ block	**Discover** What Is the Greenhouse Effect?, p. 637 **Try This** It's Your Skin!, p. 639 **Science at Home,** p. 640		
Study Guide/Assessment pp. 641–643	1 period/ ½ block		ISAB	Provides teaching and review of all inquiry skills

For Standard or Block Schedule The Resource Pro® CD-ROM gives you maximum flexibility for planning your instruction for any type of schedule. Resource Pro® contains Planning Express®, an advanced scheduling program, as well as the entire contents of the Teaching Resources and the Computer Test Bank.

Key: **CTB** Computer Test Bank
CT Chapter Tests
ELL Teacher's ELL Handbook

CHAPTER PLANNING GUIDE

Program Resources	Assessment Strategies	Media and Technology
UR Chapter 19 Project Teacher Notes, pp. 90–91 **UR** Chapter 19 Project Overview and Worksheets, pp. 92–95	**TE** Performance Assessment: Chapter 19 Project Wrap Up, p. 643 **TE** Check Your Progress, pp. 617, 636 **UR** Chapter 19 Project Scoring Rubric, p. 96	Science Explorer Internet Site Audio CDs, Section Summaries
UR 19-1 Lesson Plan, p. 97 **UR** 19-1 Section Summary, p. 98 **UR** 19-1 Review and Reinforce, p. 99 **UR** 19-1 Enrich, p. 100 **UR** Skills Lab blackline masters, pp. 113–115 **PLM** Probeware blackline masters	**SE** Section 1 Review, p. 617 **SE** Analyze and Conclude, pp. 618–619 **TE** Ongoing Assessment, pp. 611, 613, 615 **TE** Performance Assessment, p. 617	Concept Videotape Library, *Adventures, Tape 4,* "Sunny Days" Transparency 77, "The Seasons" Lab Activity Videotape, *Tape 4*
UR 19-2 Lesson Plan, p. 101 **UR** 19-2 Section Summary, p. 102 **UR** 19-2 Review and Reinforce, p. 103 **UR** 19-2 Enrich, p. 104 **UR** Real-World Lab blackline masters, pp. 116–117	**SE** Section 2 Review, p. 629 **SE** Analyze and Conclude, p. 631 **TE** Ongoing Assessment, pp. 621, 623, 625, 627 **TE** Performance Assessment, p. 629	Concept Videotape Library, *Adventures, Tape 4,* "Climate in the U.S." Presentation Pro, "Climate Regions" Transparencies 78, "World Climate Regions"; 79, "Climate Graph for Washington, D.C." Lab Activity Videotape, *Tape 4*
UR 19-3 Lesson Plan, p. 105 **UR** 19-3 Section Summary, p. 106 **UR** 19-3 Review and Reinforce, p. 107 **UR** 19-3 Enrich, p. 108	**SE** Section 3 Review, p. 636 **TE** Ongoing Assessment, pp. 633, 635 **TE** Performance Assessment, p. 636	Concept Videotape Library, *Adventures, Tape 4,* "Changes in Climate" Presentation Pro, "Climate Change" Transparency 80, "Extent of Northern Hemisphere Glaciation"
UR 19-4 Lesson Plan, p. 109 **UR** 19-4 Section Summary, p. 110 **UR** 19-4 Review and Reinforce, p. 111 **UR** 19-4 Enrich, p. 112	**SE** Section 4 Review, p. 640 **TE** Ongoing Assessment, p. 639 **TE** Performance Assessment, p. 641	Concept Videotape Library, *Adventures, Tape 4,* "The Greenhouse Effect"
GRSW Provides worksheets to promote student comprehension of content **RCA** Provides strategies to improve science reading skills **ELL** Provides multiple strategies for English language learners	**SE** Study Guide/Assessment, pp. 641–643 **PA** Performance Assessment, pp. 58–60 **CT** Chapter 19 Test, pp. 75–78 **CTB** Chapter 19 Test **PHAS** Provides standardized test preparation	Computer Test Bank, Chapter 19 Test

GRSW Guided Reading and Study Workbook
ISAB Inquiry Skills Activity Book
LM Laboratory Manual

PA Performance Assessment
PHAS Prentice Hall Assessment System
PLM Probeware Lab Manual

RCA Reading in the Content Area
SE Student Edition

TE Teacher's Edition
UR Unit Resources

Meeting the National Science Education Standards and AAAS Benchmarks

National Science Education Standards	Benchmarks for Science Literacy	Unifying Themes
Science As Inquiry (Content Standard A) ◆ **Design and conduct a scientific investigation** Students investigate how the angle of a light source affects the rate of temperature change on a surface. (*Skills Lab*) ◆ **Use appropriate tools and techniques to gather, analyze, and interpret data** Students investigate microclimates. Students analyze climate graphs. (*Chapter Project; Real-World Lab*) **Life Science** (Content Standard C) ◆ **Populations and ecosystems** There are five main climate regions, each with typical plants and animals. (*Section 2*) **Earth and Space Science** (Content Standard D) ◆ **Structure of the Earth system** The climate of a region is determined mainly by temperature and precipitation. (*Sections 1, 2*) ◆ **Earth's history** Scientists study fossils, tree rings, and pollen records to learn about ancient climates. (*Section 3*) ◆ **Earth in the solar system** The seasons are caused by the tilt of Earth's axis. (*Section 1*) **Science in Personal and Social Perspectives** (Content Standard F) ◆ **Science and technology in society** Human activities are affecting Earth's climate and atmosphere. (*Section 4*)	**1B Scientific Inquiry** Students investigate microclimates. Students examine how the angle of a light source affects the rate of temperature change of a surface. (*Chapter Project; Skills Lab*) **3C Issues in Technology** Two important worldwide issues are global warming and thinning of the ozone layer. (*Section 4*) **4B The Earth** The seasons are caused by the tilt of Earth's axis. Scientists classify climates according to temperature and precipitation. Throughout Earth's history, climates have gradually changed. (*Sections 1, 2, 4*) **4C Processes That Shape the Earth** Human activities have had an effect on Earth's climate and atmosphere. (*Section 4*) **5D Interdependence of Life** There are five main climate regions, each with its own particular plants and animals. (*Section 2*) **9B Symbolic Relationships** Students compare climate data for four cities. (*Real-World Lab*) **12D Communication Skills** Students present data on the microclimates they studied. (*Chapter Project*)	◆ **Energy** Latitude, altitude, distance from large bodies of water, and ocean currents influence temperature. Students investigate how the angle of a light source affects the rate of temperature change. Global warming is a gradual increase in the temperature of Earth's atmosphere. (*Sections 1, 4; Skills Lab*) ◆ **Scale and Structure** A small area with its own climate is a microclimate. Earth has three main temperature zones. Earth has five main climate regions. (*Chapter Project; Sections 1, 2*) ◆ **Stability** Climate regions are determined on the basis of average temperature and precipitation. Although weather can vary from day to day, climates change more slowly. (*Sections 2, 3*) ◆ **Systems and Interactions** Students relate microclimates to the plants and animals found there. The seasons are caused by the tilt of Earth's axis. Students investigate how the angle of the sun's rays affects the amount of energy absorbed by different parts of Earth's surface. Human activities have had an effect on Earth's climate and atmosphere. (*Chapter Project; Sections 1, 4; Skills Lab*) ◆ **Unity and Diversity** Each hemisphere has a polar zone, temperate zone, and tropical zone. Each climate region has a characteristic average temperature and precipitation. Students compare climate data for four cities. (*Sections 1, 2; Real-World Lab*)

Take It to the Net

The www.phschool.com Web site provides you with multiple opportunities to incorporate the internet into your instruction. Go to www.phschool.com and click on the Science icon. Then select Science Explorer Integrated.

www.phschool.com

Internet Activities provide opportunities for students to review, extend, or assess a concept from the chapter.

■ Have students use the chapter Self-Test to get instant feedback.

■ Hot Links and Reference Links provide opportunities for online research.

STAY CURRENT with **SCIENCE NEWS** ®

Find out the latest research and information about weather and climate at: www.phschool.com

ACTIVITY	Time (minutes)	Materials Quantities for one work group	Skills
Section 1			
Discover, p. 610	15	**Consumable** cash register or adding machine paper, clear tape, empty toilet paper roll **Nonconsumable** globe, pencil, flashlight, metric ruler	Observing
Sharpen Your Skills, p. 613	10	No special materials required.	Inferring
Skills Lab, pp. 618–619	40	**Consumable** black construction paper, clear tape, graph paper **Nonconsumable** scissors, ruler, 3 thermometers or temperature probes, protractor, books, 100-W incandescent lamp, watch or clock, pencil	Controlling Variables, Collecting Data, Graphing, Inferring
Section 2			
Discover, p. 620	15	**Consumable** magazines or newspapers **Nonconsumable** scissors	Forming Operational Definitions
Try This, p. 625	10, 5	**Consumable** water, clear plastic wrap **Nonconsumable** 2 small plastic bowls, 2 rubber bands	Inferring
Sharpen Your Skills, p. 627	10	No special materials required.	Classifying
Science at Home, p. 629	home	No special materials required.	Classifying
Real-World Lab, pp. 630–631	40	**Consumable** 3 pieces of graph paper **Nonconsumable** calculator, ruler, black pencil, blue pencil, red pencil, green pencil, climate map on pages 622–623, U.S. map with city names and latitude lines	Graphing, Interpreting Data, Drawing Conclusions
Section 3			
Discover, p. 632	10	**Nonconsumable** Figure 16 on page 633, magnifying lens	Inferring
Section 4			
Discover, p. 637	15, 5	**Consumable** 2 pieces of black construction paper, 2 shoe boxes, clear plastic wrap, masking tape **Nonconsumable** 2 thermometers, lamp	Inferring
Try This, p. 639	15	**Consumable** ultraviolet-sensitive paper, 3 plastic sandwich bags, 2 sunscreens with different SPF numbers **Nonconsumable** black marking pen	Drawing Conclusions
Science at Home, p. 640	home	**Nonconsumable** calculator	Comparing and Contrasting

A list of all materials required for the Student Edition activities can be found beginning on page T23. You can obtain information about ordering materials by calling 1-800-848-9500 or by accessing the Science Explorer Internet site at: **www.phschool.com**

All students notice daily weather conditions, but many are not aware that these daily patterns determine the climate in which they live. Even more subtle are the various microclimates located in an area. These microclimates support different organisms based on slightly different daily weather conditions.

Purpose In this project, students will gather weather data and observe the organisms living in three different areas to determine their microclimates. In doing so, they will be able to conclude that climates in very small areas can be different from each other, even though these areas are located near each other.

Skills Focus After completing the Chapter 19 Project, students will be able to
- develop hypotheses about how microclimates in three areas will differ;
- create data tables for weather data and environmental factors;
- graph weather data and analyze the data for patterns;
- relate each microclimate to the plants and animals found there;
- communicate the project results in a class presentation.

Project Time Line The entire project will require about three weeks. Begin by distributing Chapter 19 Project Overview and Worksheets and Scoring Rubric on pages 92–96 in Unit 5 Resources. See Chapter 19 Project Teacher Notes on pages 90–91 in Unit 5 Resources for more information.

Divide the class into groups and allow time for them to choose their three microclimates. For convenience, these areas should be relatively close to the school. Make sure each group chooses areas that have different environmental conditions.

At this point, students can use Worksheet 1 to help them organize their group logbook. Review how to use various weather instruments, if necessary. Students can use Worksheet 2 to practice analyzing weather data. Then students will be ready to gather data in each area for two weeks. Students should collect data from the same location at the

CHAPTER **19** Climate and Climate Change

WEB ACTIVITY www.phschool.com

608

same time each day for consistent results. Students will also need time to prepare graphs for their class presentations.

Suggested Shortcuts You can simplify this project by asking each student group to collect data from only one microclimate. The entire class can compare and contrast the data collected by each group. Students could also collect data for only one week instead of two.

Possible Materials Students will need instruments that measure weather data such as thermometers, anemometers, wind vanes, wet and dry bulb thermometers, rain gauges, and light meters. If you don't have class sets of these instruments, schedule their use for each group throughout the day, or students can use the weather instruments they have made for activities in Chapter 17. Students will also need

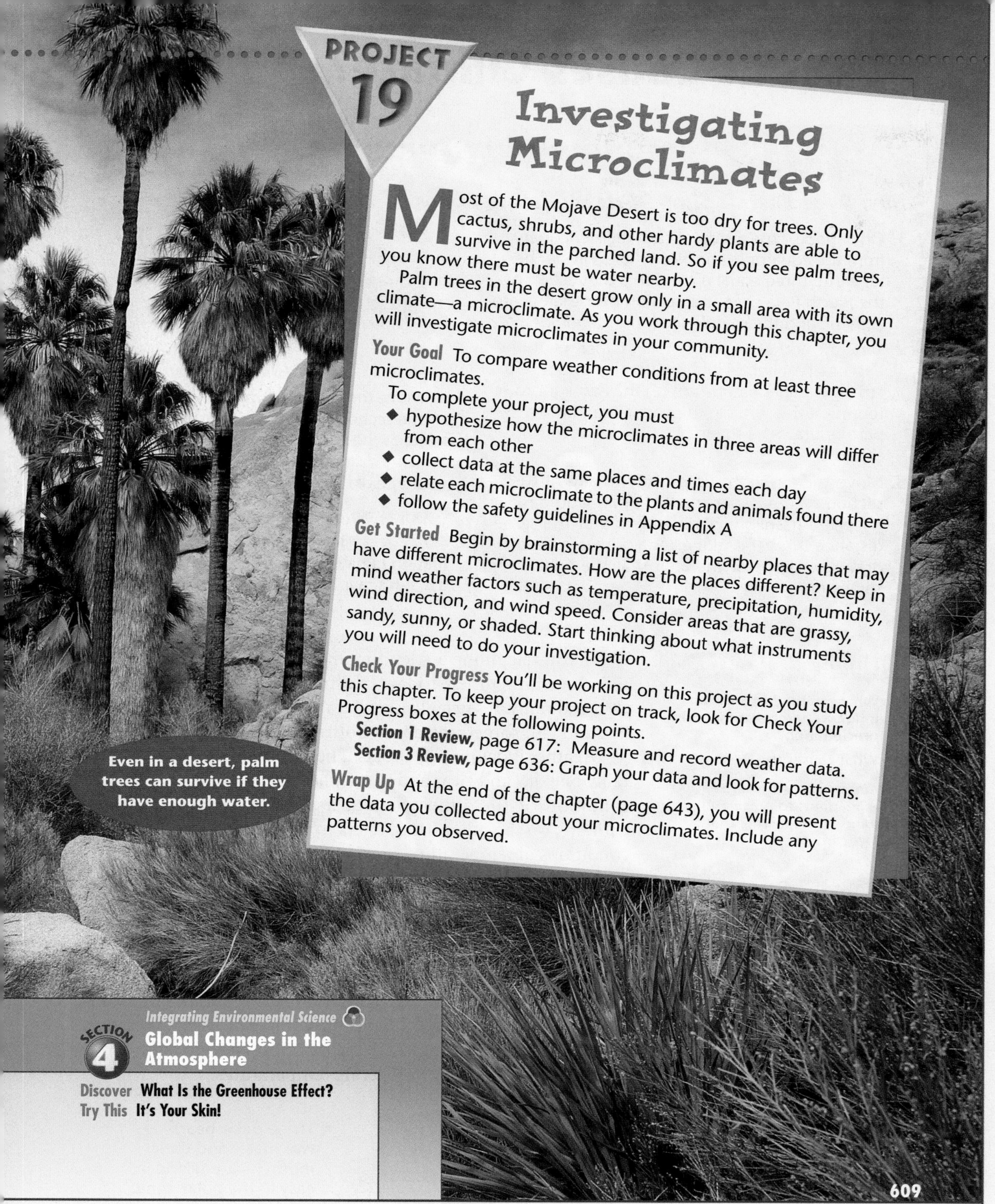

Investigating Microclimates

Most of the Mojave Desert is too dry for trees. Only cactus, shrubs, and other hardy plants are able to survive in the parched land. So if you see palm trees, you know there must be water nearby. Palm trees in the desert grow only in a small area with its own climate—a microclimate. As you work through this chapter, you will investigate microclimates in your community.

Your Goal To compare weather conditions from at least three microclimates.

To complete your project, you must
◆ hypothesize how the microclimates in three areas will differ from each other
◆ collect data at the same places and times each day
◆ relate each microclimate to the plants and animals found there
◆ follow the safety guidelines in Appendix A

Get Started Begin by brainstorming a list of nearby places that may have different microclimates. How are the places different? Keep in mind weather factors such as temperature, precipitation, humidity, wind direction, and wind speed. Consider areas that are grassy, sandy, sunny, or shaded. Start thinking about what instruments you will need to do your investigation.

Check Your Progress You'll be working on this project as you study this chapter. To keep your project on track, look for Check Your Progress boxes at the following points.
Section 1 Review, page 617: Measure and record weather data.
Section 3 Review, page 636: Graph your data and look for patterns.

Wrap Up At the end of the chapter (page 643), you will present the data you collected about your microclimates. Include any patterns you observed.

Even in a desert, palm trees can survive if they have enough water.

SECTION 4
Integrating Environmental Science
Global Changes in the Atmosphere

Discover What Is the Greenhouse Effect?
Try This It's Your Skin!

609

Program Resources

◆ **Unit 5 Resources** Chapter 19 Project Teacher Notes, pp. 90–91; Project Overview and Worksheets, pp. 92–95; Project Scoring Rubric, p. 96

Media and Technology

🎧 **Audio CDs** Section Summaries

WEB ACTIVITY www.phschool.com

You will find an Internet activity, chapter self-tests for students, and links to other chapter topics at this site.

---

hand lenses to observe organisms and field guides to identify them, a logbook, and graph paper.

Launching the Project To introduce this project, take the class on a walk around the school grounds or neighborhood. Call students' attention to the plants and animals found in specific places. Focus on the environmental conditions these organisms need to survive. For example, moss grows only in moist areas. Encourage students to offer comments and to ask questions about the organisms and the environmental conditions that they observe.

Give students time to read the description of the Chapter 19 Project in their text and in the Chapter 19 Project Overview on pages 92–93 in Unit 5 Resources. Encourage students to begin thinking of nearby places with different microclimates and the conditions that make each place different.

Performance Assessment

The Chapter 19 Project Scoring Rubric on page 96 of Unit 5 Resources will help you evaluate how well students complete the Chapter 19 Project. Students will be assessed on
◆ how completely and accurately they collect data from their microclimate areas,
◆ how neat, thorough, and accurate their logbooks are,
◆ how thorough and interesting their class presentations are,
◆ how well they worked together in their groups.

By sharing the Chapter 19 Project Scoring Rubric with students at the beginning of the project, you will make it clear to them what they are expected to do.

Objectives

After completing the lesson, students will be able to
- identify the factors that influence temperature and precipitation;
- explain what causes the seasons.

Key Terms climate, tropical zone, polar zone, temperate zone, marine climate, continental climate, windward, leeward, microclimate

1 Engage/Explore

Activating Prior Knowledge

Ask students: **What is the weather like today?** Then ask: **Is today's weather typical of the weather we usually have at this time of year?** (*Accept all answers without comment.*) Explain that the average, year-after-year weather conditions is climate.

DISCOVER

Skills Focus observing

Materials *globe, cash register or adding machine paper, clear tape, pencil, flashlight, empty toilet paper roll, metric ruler*

Time 15 minutes

Advance Preparation Cut the cash register paper into lengths that are slightly longer than the distance between the equator and the North Pole on the globe.

Tips Have students label the paper before they tape it to the globe. One student should hold the flashlight the same distance from the globe, but move it up in a straight line perpendicular to the globe for each drawing.

Expected Outcome The shapes will change from a perfect circle at the equator to an elongated oval at the North Pole.

Think It Over The shape is a perfect circle at the equator, an oval at the mid-latitudes, and an elongated, faded oval at the poles. The sun's rays heat Earth unevenly because the light rays from the sun hit Earth's surface at different angles.

SECTION 1 What Causes Climate?

DISCOVER ········· ACTIVITY

How Does Earth's Shape Affect Climate Zones?

1. On a globe, tape a strip of cash register paper from the equator to the North Pole. Divide the tape into three equal parts. Label the section near the North Pole *poles*, the section near the equator *equator*, and the middle section *mid-latitudes*.

2. Tape the end of an empty toilet paper roll to the end of a flashlight. Hold the flashlight about 30 cm from the equator. Turn on the flashlight to represent the sun. On the paper strip, have a partner draw the shape of the area the light shines on.

3. Move the flashlight up slightly to aim at the section of the paper marked "mid-latitudes." Keep the flashlight horizontal and at the same distance from the globe. Again have a partner draw the shape of the area that the light shines on.

4. Move the flashlight up again to shine on the section of the paper marked "poles." Keep the flashlight horizontal and at the same distance from the globe. Draw the shape of the area that the light shines on.

Think It Over

Observing How does the shape of the area that is illuminated change? Do you think the sun's rays heat Earth's surface evenly?

GUIDE FOR READING

- What are the factors that influence temperature and precipitation?
- What causes the seasons?

Reading Tip As you read, use the headings to make an outline of the factors that affect climate.

I f you telephone a friend in another state and ask, "What's the weather there today?" she might answer: "It's gray, cool, and rainy. It's usually like that this time of year." Your friend has told you something about both weather and climate.

Weather is day-to-day events. The weather may be cloudy and rainy one day and clear and sunny the next. Weather refers to the condition of the atmosphere at a particular place and time. **Climate,** on the other hand, refers to the average, year-after-year conditions of temperature, precipitation, winds, and clouds in an area. How would you describe the climate where you live?

Two main factors—temperature and precipitation—determine the climate of a region. A climate region is a large area with similar climate conditions throughout. For example, the climate in the southeastern United States is humid, with moderate temperatures.

◄ These polar bears— two males and their mother—are taking it easy in the polar zone.

610

READING STRATEGIES

Reading Tip Suggest to students that they skim the section first before making their outlines. Students should use the section title as the title for their outlines. They should use the main heads of the section as the main headings in their outlines and the section subheads as the subheadings. Students can fill in details under outline headings as they read the section. Students can use their outlines as study aids.

Student outlines might begin as follows:

I. Factors Affecting Temperature
   A. Latitude
   B. Altitude
   C. Distance from Large Bodies of Water
   D. Ocean Currents
II. Factors Affecting Precipitation
   A. Prevailing Winds
   B. Mountain Ranges

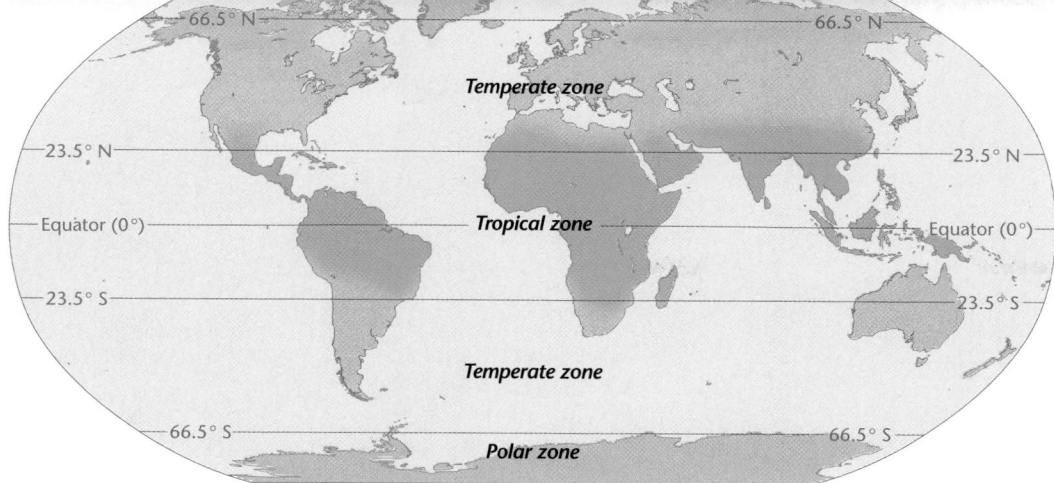

Figure 1 Earth has three main temperature zones.
Interpreting Maps In which temperature zone is most of the United States located?

Factors Affecting Temperature

Tropical countries, such as Panama, are usually hot. Northern countries, such as Finland, are usually cold. Why are some places warm and others cold? **The main factors that influence temperature are latitude, altitude, distance from large bodies of water, and ocean currents.**

Latitude In general, climates of locations farther from the equator are cooler than climates of areas closer to the equator. Why is this? As you found out if you tried the Discover activity, the sun's rays hit Earth's surface most directly at the equator. At the poles, the same amount of solar radiation is spread out over a larger area, and therefore brings less warmth.

Recall that latitude is the distance from the equator, measured in degrees. Based on latitude, Earth's surface can be divided into the three temperature zones shown in Figure 1. The **tropical zone** is the area near the equator, between about 23.5° north latitude and 23.5° south latitude. The tropical zone receives direct or nearly direct sunlight all year round, making climates there warm.

In contrast, the sun's rays always strike at a lower angle near the North and South poles. As a result, the areas near both poles have cold climates. These **polar zones** extend from about 66.5° to 90° north and 66.5° to 90° south latitudes.

The **temperate zones** are between the tropical and the polar zones—from about 23.5° to 66.5° north and 23.5° to 66.5° south latitudes. In summer, the sun's rays strike the temperate zones more directly. In winter, the sun's rays strike at a lower angle. As a result, the weather in the temperate zones ranges from warm or hot in summer to cool or cold in winter.

2 Facilitate

Factors Affecting Temperature

Using the Visuals: Figure 1

Review latitude with students. Ask: **What does latitude measure?** *(The distance from the equator)* Instruct students to find the equator in Figure 1. Then ask: **At what degree of latitude is the North Pole?** *(90° north latitude)* Draw a circle on the board and show students that 360° is a full circle and 180° is a half circle. Ask: **How many degrees are equal to one-fourth of a circle?** *(90°)* Relate these measurements of a circle to degrees of latitude. **learning modality: logical/ mathematical**

Cultural Diversity

Students can learn how climate affects the culture of a group of people by comparing and contrasting types of clothing, housing, and customs of people living in different temperature zones. Encourage groups of students to choose a group of people to study. Groups may choose native cultures or modern cultures from around the world or from different areas of the United States. Monitor the groups' choices so that each is studying a different culture. Groups should divide the research tasks and the preparation for a class presentation. Challenge students to find creative ways to present the culture of the people they studied. **cooperative learning**

Media and Technology

 Concept Videotape Library
Adventures, Tape 4, "Sunny Days"

Program Resources

◆ **Unit 5 Resources** 19-1 Lesson Plan, p. 97; 19-1 Section Summary, p. 98
◆ **Guided Reading and Study Workbook** Section 19-1

Answers to Self-Assessment

Caption Question
Figure 1 the temperate zone

Ongoing Assessment

Drawing Instruct students to make a diagram that shows the different angles at which the sun's rays strike Earth in each temperature zone.
 Students can save their diagrams in their portfolios.

Factors Affecting Temperature, continued

Demonstration

Materials *small black mat, desk lamp with high intensity bulb, 2 thermometers, 2 ring stands with clamps for thermometers*
Time 15–20 minutes

To demonstrate why air temperature is colder at higher altitudes, shine the light directly on the black mat for 10 minutes. During this time, set up the ring stands so that one holds the bulb of one thermometer 5 cm above the mat and the other holds the thermometer 20 cm above the mat. When you turn out the light, place the thermometers over the black mat. Read the thermometers right away, then every minute until the temperature stops rising. Encourage students to infer why the lower thermometer had a higher temperature reading than the higher thermometer. *(The black mat absorbed the light energy from the light as heat, then radiated the heat into the air above it.)*
learning modality: visual

Inquiry Challenge

With the knowledge that large bodies of water greatly moderate the temperatures of nearby land, challenge small groups of students to devise a plan that would help them cool off on a hot summer day. After checking each group's plan, help them gather the materials they will need to implement it. *(One possible plan: set up a fan so that it blows across ice water.)*
cooperative learning

Figure 2 Mount Kilimanjaro in Tanzania, Africa, is near the equator. *Applying Concepts Why is there snow on top of the mountain?*

Altitude The peak of Mount Kilimanjaro towers high above the African plains. At nearly 6 kilometers above sea level, Kilimanjaro is covered in snow all year round. Yet it is located near the equator, at 3° south latitude. Why is Mount Kilimanjaro so cold?

In the case of high mountains, altitude is a more important climate factor than latitude. Recall from Chapter 16 that the temperature of the troposphere decreases about 6.5 Celsius degrees for every 1-kilometer increase in altitude. As a result, highland areas everywhere have cool climates, no matter what their latitude. At nearly 6 kilometers, the air at the top of Mount Kilimanjaro is about 39 Celsius degrees colder than the air at sea level at the same latitude.

Distance From Large Bodies of Water Oceans or large lakes can also affect temperatures. Oceans greatly moderate, or make less extreme, the temperatures of nearby land. Water heats up more slowly than land; it also cools down more slowly. Therefore, winds from the ocean keep coastal regions from reaching extremes of hot and cold. Much of the west coasts of North America, South America, and Europe have mild **marine climates,** with relatively warm winters and cool summers.

The centers of North America and Asia are too far inland to be warmed or cooled by the oceans. Most of Canada and Russia, as well as the central United States, have **continental climates.** Continental climates have more extreme temperatures than marine climates. Winters are cold, while summers are warm or hot.

Background

Facts and Figures Like altitude, large bodies of water and ocean currents can be as important in influencing the temperature of a location as latitude. For example, Bergen, Norway, is a coastal city located over 2,000 km north of Omaha, Nebraska. Based only on latitude, one would assume that Bergen would have a colder climate. However, the average January temperature in Bergen is higher than that of Omaha, and on average, Bergen is cooler than Omaha in July.

The seasonal temperatures in Bergen are directly influenced by its proximity to the ocean and the North Atlantic drift. The ocean acts as a huge reservoir of heat energy due to its great depth and volume, and its ability to absorb large amounts of solar radiation.

Ocean Currents Many marine climates are influenced by ocean currents, streams of water within the oceans that move in regular patterns. In general, warm ocean currents carry warm water from the tropics toward the poles. Cold currents bring cold water from the polar zones toward the equator. The surface of the water warms or cools the air above it. The warmed or cooled air then moves over the nearby land. So a warm current brings warm air to the land it touches. A cold current brings cool air.

As you read about the following currents, trace their paths on the map in Figure 3. The best-known warm-water current is the Gulf Stream. The Gulf Stream begins in the Gulf of Mexico, then flows north along the east coast of the United States. When it crosses the North Atlantic, it becomes the North Atlantic Drift. This warm current gives Ireland and southern England a mild, wet climate despite their relatively high latitude.

In contrast, the cool California Current flows from Alaska southward down the West Coast. The California Current makes climates of places along the West Coast cooler than you would expect at their latitudes.

✓ *Checkpoint* **What effect do oceans have on the temperatures of nearby land areas?**

Inferring ACTIVITY

Look at the currents in the South Pacific, South Atlantic, and Indian oceans. What pattern can you observe? Now compare currents in the South Atlantic to those in the North Atlantic. What might be responsible for differences in the current patterns?

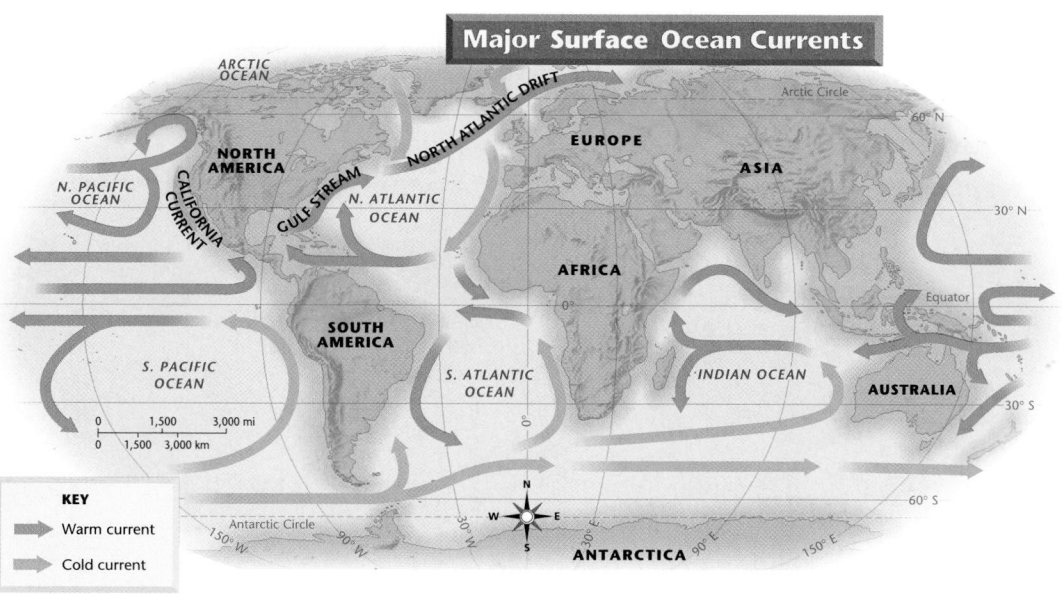

Major Surface Ocean Currents

KEY
➡ Warm current
➡ Cold current

Figure 3 On this map, warm currents are shown in red and cold currents in blue.

Answers to Self-Assessment

Caption Question

Figure 2 The top of the mountain is at a higher altitude, so the air there is much cooler than the air at the bottom.

✓ *Checkpoint*

The surface of the water warms or cools the air above it. The warmed or cooled air then moves over nearby land, affecting the temperatures there.

Building Inquiry Skills: Observing

Materials *heat-resistant pan, water, ice, bricks, bunsen burner or candle, food coloring*

Time 15 minutes

🔥 Have students observe how differences in water temperature cause currents. First, they should fill a shallow pan with water and place ice cubes in the center of the pan. Then they should elevate the pan with bricks so that a bunsen burner or candle will fit under the pan. They should heat one side of the pan and place a few drops of food coloring in the water. Students should observe the movement of the colored water in the pan. Ask: **What is causing the water to move?** (*As the water warms, it becomes less dense and rises. The cold water, which is denser, sinks and pushes the warmer water out of the way.*) Encourage students to relate their observations to the movement of ocean currents. **learning modality: kinesthetic**

Sharpen your Skills

Inferring ACTIVITY

Time 10 minutes

Students should observe that the currents in the South Pacific, South Atlantic, and Indian oceans move south toward Antarctica. Students should infer that movement of cold water from the poles toward the equator pushes warm water at the equator toward the poles. Wind direction and the location of land masses also affect the direction of currents. Students may also note the clockwise rotation of currents in the northern hemisphere and the counterclockwise rotation in the southern hemisphere.

Extend Challenge students to trace the changes in Figure 3 when an El Niño occurs. **learning modality: visual**

Ongoing Assessment

Writing Instruct students to write a description of how the temperature of a climate is affected by altitude, distance from large bodies of water, and ocean currents.

Factors Affecting Precipitation

Including All Students

Materials *2 sponges, water*

Time 10 minutes

Students can use sponges to model prevailing winds that blow inland from oceans and those that blow from over land. Allow students to completely saturate a sponge with water. Have them describe what type of prevailing wind it represents. *(Humid wind blowing inland from an ocean)* Then instruct them to compare the saturated sponge with a dry sponge. Ask: **Which sponge can absorb more water?** *(the dry sponge)* **Which sponge represents wind blowing from over land?** *(the dry sponge)* **Which sponge represents the kind of wind that blows over the Sahara?** *(the dry sponge)* **learning modality: kinesthetic**

Building Inquiry Skills: Inferring

Materials *physical map of the United States, map of global wind patterns*

Time 20 minutes

Challenge students to work together in small groups to make inferences about the amount of precipitation in different regions of the United States. Groups can compare wind patterns with topography. Invite groups to share their inferences with the rest of the class. You might wish to record each group's inferences and revisit them as you study climate regions in the next section. Help students determine why they might have inferred incorrectly. **cooperative learning**

Factors Affecting Precipitation

The amount of rain and snow that falls in an area each year determines how wet or dry its climate is. But what determines how much precipitation an area gets? **The main factors that affect precipitation are prevailing winds and the presence of mountains.**

Prevailing Winds As you know, weather patterns depend on the movement of huge air masses. Air masses are moved from place to place by prevailing winds, the directional winds that usually blow in a region. Air masses can be warm or cool, dry or humid. The amount of water vapor in the air mass influences how much rain or snow will fall.

Warm air can carry more water vapor than cold air can. When warm air rises and cools, water comes out of the air as precipitation. For example, surface air near the equator is generally hot and humid. As the air rises and cools, heavy rains fall, nourishing thick tropical forests. In contrast, sinking cold air is usually dry. Because the air becomes warmer as it sinks, it can hold more water vapor. The water vapor stays in the air and little or no rain falls. The result may be a desert.

The amount of water vapor in prevailing winds also depends on where the winds come from. Winds that blow inland from oceans carry more water vapor than winds that blow from over land. For example, the Sahara in Africa is near both the Atlantic Ocean and the Mediterranean Sea. Yet the Sahara is very dry. This is because few winds blow from the oceans toward this area. Instead, the prevailing winds are the dry northeast trade winds. The source of these winds is cool, sinking air from southwest Asia.

Figure 4 The prevailing winds that blow across the Sahara begin far inland. Since the air is dry, the Sahara gets very little rain.

614

Background

Facts and Figures The dry prevailing winds that blow across the Sahara absorb any water that is present on land, rather than bring rain. Because of this, these winds are sometimes called evaporating winds.

An evaporating wind in northwestern United States, called a chinook, is a westerly wind that blows down the eastern slope of the Rocky Mountains. This wind is made up of warm Pacific air that has lost much of its water vapor on the western slope of the Rockies. It is so warm and dry that it melts snow in the valleys during winter.

Mountain Ranges A mountain range in the path of prevailing winds can also influence where precipitation falls. As you have learned, when humid winds blow from the ocean toward coastal mountains, they are forced to rise up to pass over the mountains. The rising warm air cools and its water vapor condenses, forming clouds. Rain or snow falls on the **windward** side of the mountains, the side the oncoming wind hits.

By the time the air reaches the other side of the mountains, it has lost much of its water vapor, so it is cool and dry. The land on the **leeward** side of the mountains—downwind—is in a rain shadow.

The Owens Valley in California, shown in Figure 5, is in the rain shadow of the Sierra Nevada, about 80 kilometers west of Death Valley. Humid winds blow eastward from the Pacific Ocean. In the photo, you can see that this humid air has left snow on top of the mountains. Then the air flowed down the leeward side of the mountains. As it moved downward, the air became warmer. The desert in the Owens Valley, on the eastern side of the Sierra Nevada, was formed by this hot, dry air.

☑ *Checkpoint* Why does precipitation fall mainly on the windward sides of mountains?

Figure 5 The Sierra Nevada runs through eastern California, parallel to the Pacific coast. To the east of the Sierras is the Owens Valley, shown above. *Inferring Is the Owens Valley on the windward or leeward side of the mountains?*

Microclimates

Have you ever noticed that it is cooler and more humid in a grove of trees than in an open field? The same factors that affect large climate regions also affect smaller areas. A small area with specific climate conditions may have its own **microclimate.** Inland mountains, lakes, forests, and other natural features can influence climate nearby, resulting in a microclimate.

You might find a microclimate in a downtown area with clusters of tall buildings, or on a windy peninsula jutting out into the ocean. Even a small park, if it is usually sunnier or windier than nearby areas, may have its own microclimate. The grass on a lawn can be covered in dew and produce conditions like a rain forest, while the pavement in the parking lot is dry, like a desert.

Including All Students

Allow students to make shadows on the wall with **ACTIVITY** a flashlight in the darkened classroom or outside on a sunny day. Then ask: **What is a shadow?** *(An area that doesn't receive light because something is blocking the light)* Relate this idea to a rain shadow by explaining that a rain shadow is an area that doesn't receive rain because a mountain range is blocking the rain. Ask: **Which side of a mountain is in a rain shadow?** *(the leeward side)* **limited English proficiency**

Microclimates

Real-Life Learning

Challenge students to identify the locations of microclimates around the school grounds. Lead them to identify microclimates as small as the north side of the school building compared to the south side. They should compare the climates of the microclimates they identify. Ask: **What climate factors cause the microclimates to exist?** *(Students should explain how the amount of precipitation and the temperature are affected in the microclimates.)* **learning modality: logical/mathematical**

Answers to Self-Assessment

Caption Question

Figure 5 the leeward side

☑ *Checkpoint*

Winds are forced to rise up and over mountains. As the air rises it cools, and the water vapor condenses and falls as rain or snow. When the air drops down the leeward side, it's dry because it lost most of its water vapor.

Ongoing Assessment

Oral Presentation Have several students describe the factors that affect the amount of precipitation in an area, and challenge others to relate temperature and precipitation to microclimates.

The Seasons

 Integrating Space Science

Draw on the chalkboard Earth's orbit around the sun. Draw Earth so that its poles are perpendicular to its orbit. Ask students: **How long does it take Earth to revolve around the sun?** *(365 days, or one year)* Remind students that Earth spins on its axis, or rotates, once every 24 hours. Explain that the hours of daylight would equal the hours of nighttime if Earth had a straight axis. Then draw Earth with a tilted axis. Ask: **How does the tilted axis affect the length of day and night on Earth?** *(The tilt causes the length of day and night to be different, depending on where Earth is in its orbit.)* **How does the tilted axis affect how the sun's rays strike different parts of Earth?** *(The tilt causes the sun's rays to strike one hemisphere more directly at the equator than the other at different times of the year.)* **learning modality: visual**

Math TOOLBOX

Time 10 minutes
Tips Have students set up the fraction by writing 23.5/90. When students divide the numbers, they should find that Earth's tilt is about 0.26, or just over one quarter, of a right angle. **learning modality: logical/mathematical**

EXPLORING the Seasons

Materials *flashlight, balloon, marker*
Time 10 minutes

Challenge students to use a flashlight and a balloon to observe the effect of Earth's tilted axis on the seasons. One student should hold a round balloon at a tilt similar to Earth's axis while another student shines a flashlight on it. A third student can use a permanent marker to outline the darkened area of the balloon and label the dark side, the light side, the North Pole, the South Pole, and the equator. Then have students compare their balloons to the diagram in *Exploring the Seasons.* **learning modality: kinesthetic**

Math TOOLBOX

Angles

Light from the sun strikes Earth's surface at different angles. An angle is made up of two lines that meet at a point. Angles are measured in degrees. A full circle has 360 degrees.

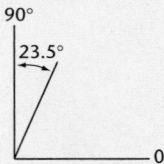

When the sun is directly overhead near the equator, it is at an angle of 90° to Earth's surface. A 90° angle is called a right angle. It is one fourth of a circle.

When the sun is near the horizon, it is at an angle of close to 0° to Earth's surface.

Earth's axis is tilted at an angle of 23.5°. About what fraction of a right angle is this?

The Seasons

 INTEGRATING SPACE SCIENCE Although you can describe the average weather conditions of a climate region, these conditions are not constant all year long. Instead, most places on Earth outside the tropics have four seasons: winter, spring, summer, and autumn.

You might think that Earth is closer to the sun during the summer and farther away during winter. If this were true, every place on Earth would have summer at the same time. Actually, when it is summer in the Northern Hemisphere it is winter in the Southern Hemisphere. So the seasons are *not* a result of changes in the distance between Earth and the sun.

Tilted Axis *Exploring the Seasons* on page 617 shows how Earth's axis is tilted in relation to the sun. **The seasons are caused by the tilt of Earth's axis as Earth travels around the sun.** The axis is an imaginary line through Earth's center that passes through both poles. Earth turns, or rotates, around this axis once each day. Earth's axis is not straight up and down, but is tilted at an angle of 23.5°. The axis always points in the same direction—toward the North Star. As Earth travels around the sun, the north end of the axis is pointed away from the sun for part of the year and toward the sun for part of the year.

Winter or Summer Look at *Exploring the Seasons* on the next page. Which way is the north end of Earth's axis tilted in June? Notice that the Northern Hemisphere receives more direct rays from the sun. Also, in June the days in the Northern Hemisphere are longer than the nights. The combination of more direct rays and longer days makes Earth's surface warmer in the Northern Hemisphere than at any other time of the year. It is summer.

In June, when the north end of Earth's axis is tilted toward the sun, the south end of the axis is tilted away from the sun. The Southern Hemisphere receives fewer direct rays from the sun. The days are shorter than the nights. As a result, the Southern Hemisphere is experiencing winter.

Now look at the situation in December, six months later. Which way is the north end of Earth's axis tilted now? The Northern Hemisphere receives fewer direct rays from the sun and has shorter days. It is winter in the Northern Hemisphere and summer in the Southern Hemisphere.

Twice during the year, in March and September, neither end of Earth's axis is tilted toward the sun. At both of these times, one hemisphere has spring while the other has autumn.

Background

Facts and Figures The equator does not have the same seasonal changes as other latitudes because the length of day at the equator changes very little through the year and the sun's rays always hit the equator almost directly. Because of this, the equator receives about the same amount of energy from the sun all year long. At higher latitudes, the length of day changes because of Earth's tilted axis. This is seen in the extreme at the poles, where six months of continuous daylight are followed by six months of continuous darkness. Even during continuous daylight, temperatures at the poles are very cold because the poles do not receive much of the sun's energy. The sun's energy that reaches the poles is spread over a larger area than at the equator, and much of that sunlight is reflected off the ice and snow near the poles.

EXPLORING the Seasons

The seasons are a result of Earth's tilted axis. The seasons change as the amount of energy each hemisphere receives from the sun changes.

December
The south end of Earth's axis is tilted toward the sun. The Southern Hemisphere receives more energy from the sun. It is summer in the Southern Hemisphere and winter in the Northern Hemisphere.

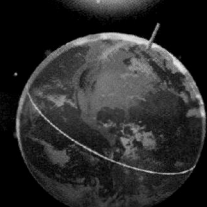

June
As the north end of Earth's axis is tilted toward the sun, the Northern Hemisphere receives more energy. It is summer in the Northern Hemisphere and winter in the Southern Hemisphere.

March and September
Neither end of Earth's axis is tilted toward the sun. Both hemispheres receive the same amounts of energy.

 Section 1 Review

1. Name the four main factors that influence the temperature of an area.
2. How do prevailing winds affect the amount of precipitation an area receives?
3. On which side of mountains—leeward or windward—does precipitation fall?
4. How does the tilt of Earth's axis cause the seasons?
5. **Thinking Critically** *Developing Hypotheses* How might Earth's climates be different if Earth were not tilted on its axis?

Check Your Progress

CHAPTER PROJECT 19

Have you chosen your microclimate study sites? If your sites are on private property, get permission. Set up a logbook so that you can record your data. How do you think the conditions in these sites will differ? Write down your hypotheses. Now you are ready to measure daily weather conditions for your microclimates. (*Hint:* Be sure to take your measurements at the same time each day.)

Program Resources

◆ **Unit 5 Resources** 19-1 Review and Reinforce, p. 99; 19-1 Enrich, p. 100

Media and Technology

 Transparencies "The Seasons," Transparency 77

---

3 Assess

Section 1 Review Answers

1. Latitude, altitude, distance from large bodies of water, and ocean currents
2. Prevailing winds that carry more water vapor will cause more precipitation in an area. Prevailing winds that carry warmer air will also cause more precipitation than winds carrying cooler air.
3. windward
4. As Earth travels around the sun, the north end of the axis points toward the sun for part of the year and away from the sun for part of the year. When the north end points toward the sun, the Northern Hemisphere receives more energy than the Southern Hemisphere receives. The seasons change as the amount of energy each hemisphere receives from the sun changes.
5. There would not be seasons, so there would not be the seasonal changes in the climate that many parts of Earth experience now.

Check Your Progress

CHAPTER PROJECT 19

Meet with each group and review their chosen study sites. If they have chosen a site located on private property, make sure they have permission from the property owners. Review their logbooks. Find out when they plan to measure the daily weather conditions at their study sites. Remind them to take measurements at the same time each day. Invite students to demonstrate how to operate the weather instruments they plan to use. Correct their techniques if necessary.

Performance Assessment

Drawing Challenge students to draw a diagram or map that shows how the factors that affect climate affect their local climate. Students should include all the factors that affect temperature and precipitation that are appropriate for their area.

617

Sunny Rays and Angles

Preparing for Inquiry

Key Concept The angle at which the sun's rays hit Earth affects the amount of energy absorbed by Earth's surface.

Skills Objectives Students will be able to

◆ control variables to determine the effect of the angle of light rays on temperature;

◆ collect temperature data by reading thermometers;

◆ graph temperature data that they collected;

◆ infer which thermometer or temperature probe represents certain regions of Earth's surface.

Time 40 minutes

Alternative Materials If you wish to save time, you can make the construction paper pockets for students ahead of time.

 If using probeware, refer to the *Probeware Lab Manual.*

Guiding Inquiry

Invitation Remind students of their results from the Discover activity. Ask: **On what part of Earth's surface do the sun's rays hit straight on?** *(at the equator)* **Where do the sun's rays hit Earth at the lowest angle?** *(at the poles)* Challenge students to explain how the angle at which the sun's rays hit Earth affects the temperature of each climate zone.

Introducing the Procedure

◆ Have students read the entire procedure. Then ask: **What part of the experimental setup represents the sun?** *(the lamp)* **What represents Earth's surface?** *(the paper pockets)*

◆ Point out in the photo how the books are used to hold the thermometers at a 45° and a 90° angle. Demonstrate how to use the protractor.

Skills Lab

Controlling Variables

Sunny Rays and Angles

In this lab, you will investigate how the angle of the sun's rays affects the amount of energy absorbed by different parts of Earth's surface.

Problem

How does the angle of a light source affect the rate of temperature change of a surface?

Materials

books	graph paper	pencil
watch or clock	ruler	clear tape
3 thermometers or temperature probes		protractor
100-W incandescent lamp		scissors
black construction paper		

Procedure

1. Cut a strip of black construction paper 5 cm by 10 cm. Fold the paper in half and tape two sides to form a pocket.

2. Repeat Step 1 to make two more pockets.

3. Place the bulb of a thermometer inside each pocket. If you're using a temperature probe, see your teacher for instructions.

4. Place the pockets with thermometers close together, as shown in the photo. Place one thermometer in a vertical position (90° angle), one at a 45° angle, and the third one in a horizontal position (0° angle). Use a protractor to measure the angles. Support the thermometers with books.

5. Position the lamp so that it is 30 cm from each of the thermometer bulbs. Make sure the lamp will not move during the activity.

6. Copy a data table like the one below into your notebook.

7. In your data table, record the temperature on all three thermometers. (All three temperatures should be the same.)

8. Switch on the lamp. In your data table, record the temperature on each thermometer every minute for 15 minutes. **CAUTION:** *Be careful not to touch the hot lampshade.*

9. After 15 minutes, switch off the lamp.

Analyze and Conclude

1. In this experiment, what was the manipulated variable? What was the responding variable? How do you know which is which?

2. Graph your data. Label the horizontal axis and vertical axis of your graph as shown on the sample graph. Use solid, dashed, and dotted lines to show the results from each thermometer, as shown in the key.

3. Based on your data, at which angle did the temperature increase the most?

4. At which angle did the temperature increase the least?

DATA TABLE

Time (min.)	Temperature (°C)		
	0° Angle	45° Angle	90° Angle
Start			
1			
2			
3			
4			
5			

Troubleshooting the Experiment

◆ Show students one completed thermometer pocket to help them construct the pockets properly.

◆ Make sure students place all three of the thermometer bulbs near each other so that each one is the same distance from the lamp.

◆ Remind students to record the temperature from each thermometer before they turn on the lamp.

Expected Outcome

The thermometer at the 0° angle will show the highest increase in temperature. The thermometer at the 90° angle will show the lowest increase in temperature. The thermometer at the 45° angle will show a moderate temperature increase.

5. What part of Earth's surface does each thermometer represent?

6. Why is air at the North Pole still very cold in the summer even though the Northern Hemisphere is tilted toward the sun?

7. **Think About It** In this experiment, what variables were held constant?

Design an Experiment

Design an experiment to find out how the results of this investigation would change if the lamp were placed farther from the thermometers. Then design another experiment to find out what would happen if the lamp were placed closer to the thermometers.

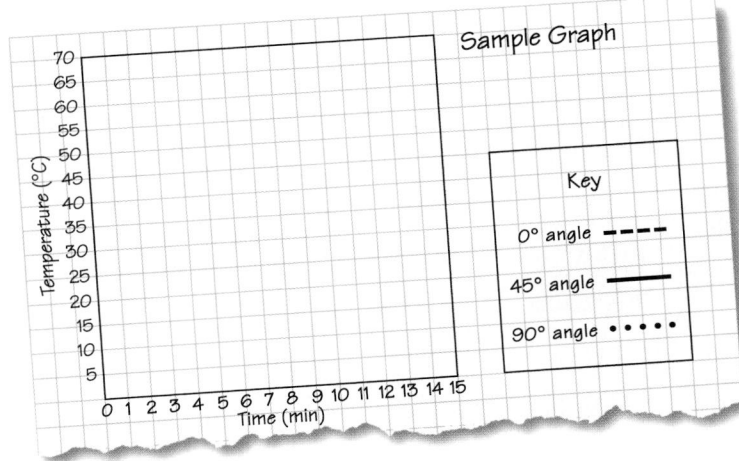

Sample Graph

Temperature (°C) — 70, 65, 60, 55, 50, 45, 40, 35, 30, 25, 20, 15, 10, 5

Time (min) — 0 1 2 3 4 5 6 7 8 9 10 11 12 13 14 15

Key

0° angle ----

45° angle ——

90° angle •••••

Analyze and Conclude

1. The manipulated variable is the angle of the thermometer. The responding variable is the rate of temperature change. The responding variable is affected by the changes in the manipulated variable.

2. All three lines of the graph should show an increase in temperature over time. However, the line for the thermometer at 0° should show a greater temperature increase than the thermometer at 45°, which should show a greater temperature increase than the thermometer at 90°.

3. at the 0° angle

4. at the 90° angle

5. The thermometer at 0° represents the tropical zone, the thermometer at 45° represents the temperate zone, and the thermometer at 90° represents the polar zone.

6. Because the angle at which the sun's rays strike the North Pole in summer is still very low

7. Variables that were held constant include the thermometers, the heat source, the distance of the heat source from the thermometer bulbs, and the type of heat-absorbing material that enclosed the thermometer bulbs.

Extending the Inquiry

Design an Experiment Students should use the same procedure, except they should change the distances between the thermometers and the lamp.

Program Resources

◆ **Unit 5 Resources** Skills Lab blackline masters, pp. 113–115
◆ **Probeware Lab Manual** Blackline masters

Media and Technology

 Lab Activity Videotape
Tape 4

Safety

Caution students to be careful when handling the lamp, because the lightbulb and the lampshade get hot. Review the safety guidelines in Appendix A.

Objectives

After completing the lesson, students will be able to
- identify factors used to define climates;
- describe the different types of climate regions.

Key Terms rain forest, savanna, desert, steppe, humid subtropical, subarctic, tundra, permafrost

1 Engage/Explore

Activating Prior Knowledge

Invite students to describe places to which they have traveled, read about, or seen in movies. Elicit details about the weather and the kinds of plants and animals that live there. Challenge students to compare the climate and the plants and animals of these places and their home. Ask: **What climate factors cause the climate at home to be different from the places you visited or learned about?** *(Any of the climate factors from Section 1 will cause places to have different climates and organisms.)*

DISCOVER

Skills Focus forming operational definitions
Materials *magazines or newspapers, scissors*
Time 15 minutes
Tips To save class time, assign students to collect magazine pictures for homework, or you could provide the pictures. Before students look at the pictures, encourage them to list some characteristics of various climates.
Expected Outcome Students should sort the pictures into categories such as desert, forest, mountain, and prairie. However, students might sort the pictures based on other climate factors.
Think It Over Accept all answers that are based on some logical classification system. Some students might use actual climate names to describe their pictures.

DISCOVER .... ACTIVITY

What Are Different Climate Types?

1. Collect pictures from magazines and newspapers of a variety of land areas around the world.
2. Sort the pictures into categories according to common weather characteristics.

Think It Over
Forming Operational Definitions Choose several words that describe the typical weather for each of your categories. What words would you use to describe the typical weather where you live?

GUIDE FOR READING

- What factors are used to define climates?
- What are the five main climate regions?

Reading Tip **Before you read, preview** *Exploring Climate Regions.* **Write a list of any questions you have about climate regions.**

When the Spanish settlers came to California in the 1700s, they brought with them plants from home. The padres, or priests, who established missions planted vineyards and orchards. They found that grapes, figs, and olives grew as well in California as they had in Spain. What do Spain and California have in common? They have similar climates.

Classifying Climates

The Spanish padres traveled a long distance but found a familiar climate. Suppose you traveled from your home to a place where the weather, the sunlight, and even the plants and trees were very different from what you are used to. Would you know what caused those differences?

Scientists classify climates according to two major factors: temperature and precipitation. They use a system developed around 1900 by Wladimir Köppen (KEP un). This system identifies broad climate regions, each of which has smaller subdivisions.

There are five main climate regions: tropical rainy, dry, temperate marine, temperate continental, and polar. Note that there is only one category of dry climates, whether hot or cold. These climate regions are shown in *Exploring Climate Regions* on pages 622–623.

◀ Olive trees

READING STRATEGIES

Reading Tip Encourage students to use what they learned in the first section as a basis for writing questions about climate regions. Some questions that students might ask: **How are climate regions defined?** *(By temperature and precipitation)* **How many climate regions are there?** *(Five in the Köppen system, six including highlands)*

Do certain plants and animals live in certain climate regions? *(Yes, climate regions have very different plants and animals that are especially adapted to living there.)*

Vocabulary Show students that in the word *permafrost*, the prefix *perma* is short for *permanent*. Explain that permafrost is soil that is permanently frozen.

Exploring Climate Regions also shows a sixth type of climate: highlands. Recall that temperatures are cooler at the tops of mountains than in the surrounding areas. So a highland climate can occur within any of the other zones.

Maps show boundaries between the climate regions. In the real world, of course, no clear boundaries mark where one climate region ends and another begins. Each region blends gradually into the next.

☑ *Checkpoint* *What are the five main climate regions?*

Tropical Rainy Climates

The tropics have two types of rainy climates: tropical wet and tropical wet-and-dry. Trace the equator on *Exploring Climate Regions* with your finger. Tropical wet climates are found in low-lying lands near the equator. If you look north and south of tropical wet climates on the map, you can see two bands of tropical wet-and-dry climates.

Tropical Wet In areas that have a tropical wet climate, many days are rainy, often with afternoon thunderstorms. With year-round heat and heavy rainfall, vegetation grows lush and green. Dense rain forests grow in these rainy climates. **Rain forests** are forests in which plenty of rain falls all year-round. Tall trees such as teak and mahogany form the top layer, or canopy, while smaller bushes and vines grow near the ground. There are also many animals in the rain forest, including colorful parrots and toucans, bats, insects, frogs, and snakes.

In the United States, only the windward sides of the Hawaiian islands have a tropical wet climate. Rainfall is very heavy—over 10 meters per year on the windward side of the Hawaiian island of Kauai. The rain forests in Hawaii have a large variety of plants, including ferns, orchids, and many types of vines and trees.

Figure 6 Lush tropical rain forests grow in the tropical wet climate. *Relating Cause and Effect What climate factors encourage this growth?*

Chapter 19 **621**

Program Resources

◆ **Unit 5 Resources** 19-2 Lesson Plan, p. 101; 19-2 Section Summary, p. 102
◆ **Guided Reading and Study Workbook** Section 19-2

Answers to Self-Assessment

☑ *Checkpoint*
Tropical rainy, dry, temperate marine, temperate continental, and polar

Caption Question
Figure 6 Large amounts of rain and warm temperatures

2 Facilitate

Classifying Climates

Addressing Naive Conceptions

Question students to find out what ideas they have about climates in other parts of the world. Ask: **Do you think that other parts of the world have similar climates to areas of the United States?** *(Some students may not think so.)* To make sure students understand that many parts of the world have similar climates, direct them to study the map in *Exploring Climate Regions*. Challenge them to find different countries that share similar climates. Ask: **What factors cause these different regions of the world to have similar climates?** *(These regions share similar factors that affect temperature and precipitation. Such factors include latitude, altitude, prevailing winds, and distance from large bodies of water.)*
learning modality: visual

Tropical Rainy Climates

Using the Visuals: Figure 6

Direct students to study the plants in the photo and ask: **How do you know this photo shows a tropical wet climate?** *(the lush vegetation)* **How would you describe the temperature of this climate region** *(warm all year long)* **The precipitation?** *(a large amount of precipitation)* Challenge students to identify the climate factors that affect precipitation and temperature in a tropical wet climate. *(Low altitude, near the equator, windward side of mountains, warm and moist prevailing winds)*
learning modality: visual

Ongoing Assessment

Writing Instruct students to list the six climate regions. Then have them write a description of a tropical wet climate that includes temperature and precipitation.

621

EXPLORING
Climate Regions

Instruct student pairs to read aloud the map key and the descriptions of the climate regions to each other. Encourage them to talk about how the climate region definitions on the map are similar to and different from the Köppen system. *(Highland region added and more detailed divisions of the five climate regions)* Then have pairs identify the climate region they live in and the climate region in which their family originated, if they know where. Challenge them to find other places that have the same climates. **learning modality: verbal**

Including All Students

Have students make a flip book of the climate regions using index cards held together with string or a binder ring. This activity will be especially helpful to students with limited English proficiency. Instruct students to write the name of each climate region on one index card. Then have students write a brief description of each region. These descriptions should include precipitation and temperature information. Encourage students with limited English to add illustrations or words from their native language to help them understand the terms. **limited English proficiency**

Portfolio Students can save their flip books in their portfolios.

EXPLORING Climate Regions

Climate regions are classified according to a combination of temperature and precipitation. Climates in highland regions change rapidly as altitude changes.

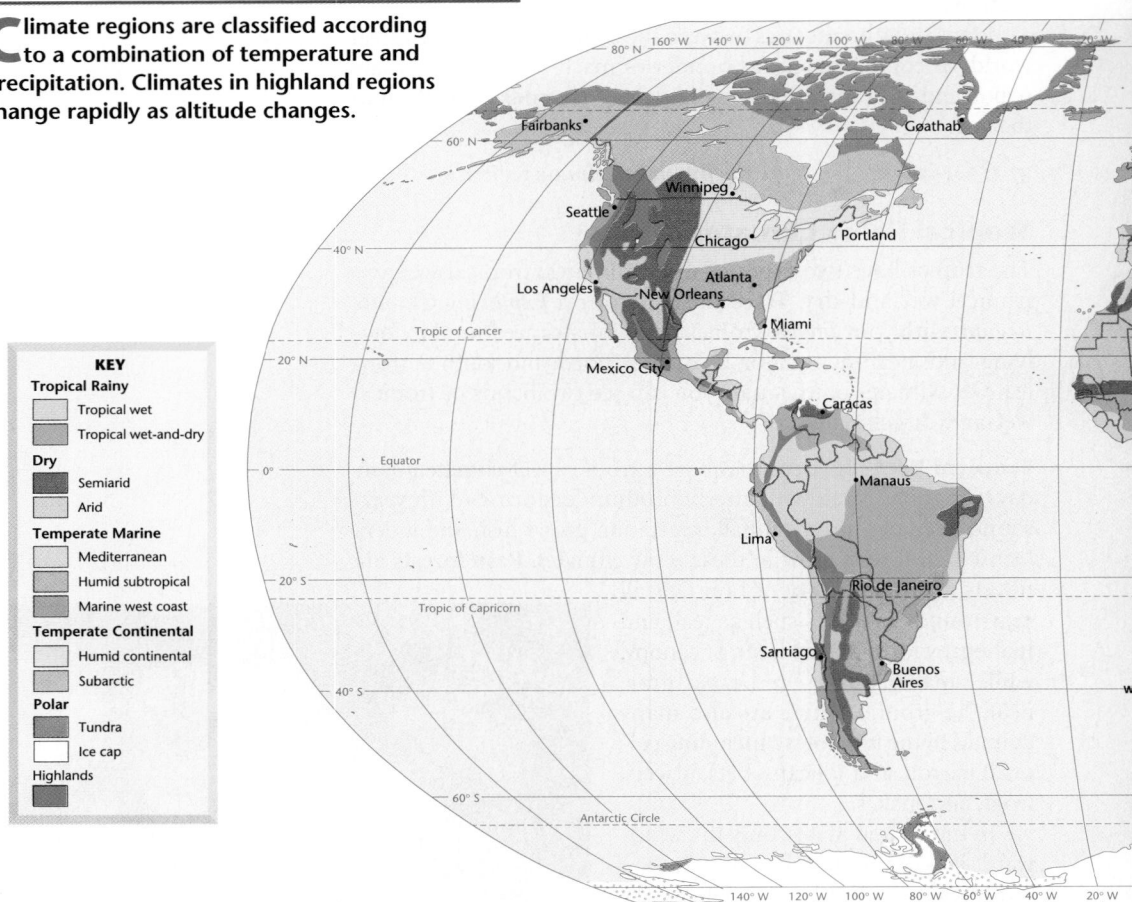

KEY

Tropical Rainy
- Tropical wet
- Tropical wet-and-dry

Dry
- Semiarid
- Arid

Temperate Marine
- Mediterranean
- Humid subtropical
- Marine west coast

Temperate Continental
- Humid continental
- Subarctic

Polar
- Tundra
- Ice cap

Highlands

Tropical Rainy
Temperature always 18°C or above.

Tropical wet *Always hot and humid, with heavy rainfall (at least 6 centimeters a month) all year round.*
Tropical wet-and-dry *Always hot, with alternating wet and dry seasons; heavy rainfall in the wet season.*

Dry
Occurs wherever potential evaporation is greater than precipitation. May be hot or cold.

Arid *Desert, with little precipitation, usually less than 25 centimeters a year.*
Semiarid *Dry but receives about 25 to 50 centimeters of precipitation a year.*

Temperate Marine
Average temperature 10°C or above in the warmest month, between −3° and 18°C in the coldest month.

Mediterranean *Warm, dry summers and rainy winters.*
Humid subtropical *Hot summers and cool winters.*
Marine west coast *Mild winters and cool summers, with moderate precipitation year round.*

622

Background

Integrating Science Plant growth is influenced by genetics and the environment. All plants have different requirements for growth, based on their genetic makeup. Environmental requirements include sunlight, climate, and soil condition. Some plants grow best in sun, others in shade. Plants also differ in the amount of light and water they require for growth.

Wladimir Peter Köppen became

interested in the influence of climate on plants while he was a student. He recognized that plants required more rainfall at higher temperatures. From these observations of plants and his knowledge as a meteorologist, Köppen introduced a system to classify climates based on rainfall and temperature. He used monthly rainfall amounts and average monthly temperatures to define the five major climate regions.

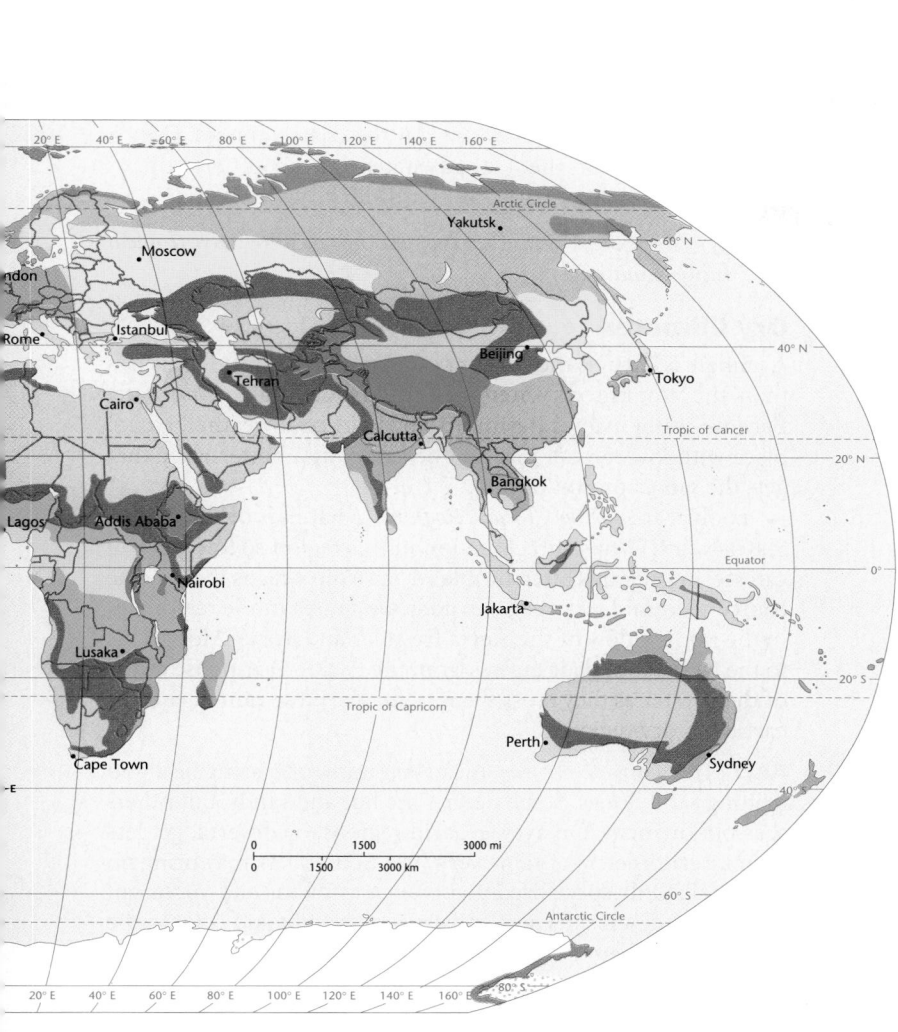

Temperate Continental
Average temperature 10°C or above in the warmest month, –3°C or below in the coldest month.

Humid continental *Hot, humid summers and cold winters, with moderate precipitation year round.*
Subarctic *Short, cool summers and long, cold winters. Light precipitation, mainly in summer.*

Polar
Average temperature below 10°C in the warmest month.

Tundra *Always cold with a short, cool summer—warmest temperature about 10°C.*
Ice cap *Always cold, average temperature at or below 0°C.*

Highlands
Generally cooler and wetter than nearby lowlands, temperature decreasing with altitude.

Challenge small student groups to assume the role of a travel agency. Groups should choose one destination and use the climate regions map to identify its climate. Then have groups assemble a travel brochure that describes the destination, its climate, and what travelers would expect to see there. Display actual travel brochures to give students ideas about what to include in their own brochures. Invite groups to share their brochures with the class. You might wish to use the brochures for a bulletin board display. **cooperative learning**

Building Inquiry Skills: Creating Data Tables

As students continue this section, they will learn more about the different climate regions. To help them organize this information, instruct students to create a data table or chart in which they record the characteristics of each climate region. Encourage students to identify climate factors that they will use to organize their tables. Explain that these factors will help them classify each climate region. Students can use the information in *Exploring Climate Regions* to help them organize their tables.
learning modality: logical/mathematical

Students can save their data tables in their portfolios.

Program Resources

◆ **Laboratory Manual** 19, "Investigating Differences in Climate"

Media and Technology

Transparencies "World Climate Regions," Transparency 78

Concept Videotape Library *Adventures, Tape 4,* "Climate in the U.S."

Ongoing Assessment

Writing Challenge students to write an outline about the climate regions. In the outline, they should include the temperature and precipitation factors that are used to classify each climate region.

Using the Visuals: Figure 7

Instruct students to compare the photo in Figure 7 with the one in Figure 6. Ask: **What climate factor do both climate regions have in common?** *(hot temperatures)* **What climate factor differs in these climate regions?** *(the amount and frequency of precipitation)* Challenge students to infer how the difference in the amounts of precipitation can have such a visible affect on a climate. *(Plants with different water requirements live in each climate region. A rain forest plant would not survive in a savanna because there is not enough precipitation.)* **learning modality: visual**

Dry Climates

Including All Students

To help students with the vocabulary terms, invite them to write each of the words, *rain forest, savanna, steppe,* and *desert* on separate index cards. Suggest that students write the definitions of the words on the cards and any other words, phrases, or illustrations that will help them to remember the meanings of the words. Some students might also find it helpful to write the phonetic pronunciation of the words. Students can add their cards to their flip books. **limited English proficiency**

Figure 7 A reticulated giraffe gazes across the grasses and shrubby trees of the African savanna. Savannas are found in tropical wet-and-dry climates.

Tropical Wet-and-Dry Tropical wet-and-dry climates get slightly less rain than tropical climates and have distinct dry and rainy seasons. Instead of rain forests, there are tropical grasslands called **savannas.** Scattered clumps of trees that can survive the dry season dot the coarse grasses. Only a small part of the United States—the southern tip of Florida—has a tropical wet-and-dry climate.

☑ *Checkpoint* What parts of the United States have tropical rainy climates?

Dry Climates

A climate is "dry" if the amount of precipitation that falls is less than the amount of water that could potentially evaporate. Because water evaporates more slowly in cool weather, a cool place with low rainfall may not be as dry as a hotter place that gets the same amount of rain.

Look at *Exploring Climate Regions.* What part of the United States is dry? Why is precipitation in this region so low? As you can see, dry regions often lie inland, far from oceans that are the source of humid air masses. In addition, much of the region lies in the rain shadow of the Sierra Nevadas and Rocky Mountains to the west. Humid air masses from the Pacific Ocean lose much of their water as they cross the mountains. Little rain or snow is carried to dry regions.

Arid The word *desert* may make you think of blazing heat and drifting sand dunes. Some deserts are hot and sandy, but others are cold or rocky. On average, arid regions, or **deserts,** get less than 25 centimeters of rain every year. Some years may bring no rain at all. Only specialized plants such as cactus and yucca can survive the desert's dryness and extremes of hot and cold. In the United States there are arid climates in portions of California, the Great Basin, and the southwest.

Figure 8 Dry-land wheat farming is common in the steppe region of the Great Plains. *Comparing and Contrasting How are steppes similar to savannas, shown in Figure 7? How are they different?*

Integrating Science Plants adapted to living in dry climates have special ways to collect and store water. Desert plants are spread apart so that they don't compete for the small amount of water available. Many cactus plants have roots that spread over a large area just below the surface to capture as much rainwater as possible. The mesquite tree has very deep roots that absorb water from sources deep below the surface.

Plants also store water in their roots, stems, and leaves. A barrel cactus swells after a rainfall because of the water it stores in its stem. Jade plants store water in their leaves. Many desert cacti and succulents open their pores only at night, when the air is cooler and less water can evaporate.

Semiarid Locate the semiarid regions on *Exploring Climate Regions*. As you can see, large semiarid areas are usually located on the edges of deserts. A steppe is dry but gets enough rainfall for short grasses and low bushes to grow. For this reason, a **steppe** may also be called a prairie or grassland.

The Great Plains are the steppe region of the United States. Many kinds of short grasses and wildflowers grow here, along with scattered forests. Livestock grazing is an important part of the economy of the Great Plains. Beef cattle, sheep, and goats graze on the short grasses of the region. Farm crops include grains, such as wheat and oats, and sunflowers.

Temperate Marine Climates

Look at *Exploring Climate Regions*, along the coasts of continents in the temperate zones. You will find the third main climate region, temperate marine. There are three kinds of temperate marine climates. Because of the moderating influence of oceans, all three are humid and have mild winters.

Marine West Coast The coolest temperate marine climates are found on the west coasts of continents north of 40° north latitude and south of 40° south latitude. Humid ocean air brings cool, rainy summers and mild, rainy winters.

In North America, the marine west coast climate extends from northern California to southern Alaska. In the Pacific Northwest of the United States, humid air from the Pacific Ocean rises as it hits the western slopes of the Coastal Ranges. As the air cools, large amounts of rain or snow fall on the western slopes.

Because of the heavy precipitation, thick forests of tall trees grow in this region, including coniferous, or cone-bearing, trees such as Sitka spruce, Douglas fir, redwoods, and Western red cedar. One of the main industries of this region is harvesting and processing wood for lumber, paper, and furniture.

Figure 9 Seattle, Washington, is in the marine west coast climate region. Here the summers are cool and rainy, and winters are wet and mild.

Modeling a Humid Climate

ACTIVITY

Here's how you can create humidity.

1. Put the same amount of water in each of two small plastic bowls.
2. Place a sheet of transparent plastic wrap over each bowl. Secure each sheet with a rubber band.
3. Place one bowl on a warm, sunny windowsill or near a radiator. Put the other bowl in a cool location.
4. Wait a day and then look at the two bowls. What do you see on the plastic wrap over each bowl?

Inferring Would you expect to find more water vapor in the air in a warm climate or in a cool one? Why? Explain your results in terms of solar energy.

Answers to Self-Assessment

☑️ *Checkpoint*

The windward sides of the Hawaiian Islands and the southern tip of Florida have tropical rainy climates.

Caption Question

Figure 8 Both steppes and savannas are flat regions where grasses grow. Savannas have clumps of trees while steppes do not.

Inquiry Challenge

Materials *cactus plant, jade plant, various grasses, magnifying lens, forceps*
Time 20 minutes

Challenge students to identify the adaptations that enable these plants to live in a desert or steppe. Encourage students to use a magnifying lens to examine all parts of the plants, including the roots, stems, and leaves. You can use a scalpel or razor blade to slice some cross-sections of leaves, stems, and roots for students to examine. Then have students explain how such adaptations allow the plants to survive in their climates. **learning modality: logical/mathematical**

Temperate Marine Climates

Skills Focus inferring
Materials *2 small plastic bowls, water, clear plastic wrap, 2 rubber bands*
Time 10 minutes for set up, 5 minutes for later observation
Tips Have students find their own locations to place the bowls. Or, to save time, choose the locations yourself.
Expected Outcome Students will observe more water drops on the plastic wrap of the warm bowl than on the plastic wrap of the cool bowl.

More water vapor is present in the air of warm climates because solar energy warms water, causing it to evaporate into the air.
Extend Instruct students to keep the bowls in the same places, but remove the plastic wrap. Have them check the bowls everyday for one week to find out which bowl has less water at the end of the week. **learning modality: visual**

Ongoing Assessment

Writing Have students describe an air mass in a dry climate and one in a temperate marine climate. *(Air masses in dry climates have little water vapor and air masses in temperate marine climates have a lot of water vapor.)*

Temperate Marine Climates, continued

Including All Students

Give each student a blank map of the United States that has the state borders indicated. Instruct students to shade in the climate regions using a different colored pencil for each climate region. Also have students make a map key. **learning modality: kinesthetic**

 Students can save their maps in their portfolios.

Real-Life Learning

Help students relate the economy of a region to its climate by asking: **How does the climate of each temperate marine climate affect the industry of that region?** (*The climate enables certain plants to grow that have either an agricultural use or are used for lumber, paper, or furniture.*) Challenge students to infer how these industries are affected in a year when the weather is extreme. (*Farmers may lose money because the weather doesn't permit the usual crops to grow, or the crops are damaged.*) **learning modality: logical/mathematical**

Building Inquiry Skills: Comparing and Contrasting

Reinforce that the marine west coast climate, the Mediterranean climate, and the humid subtropical climate are three kinds of temperate marine climates. Have students compare and contrast the three kinds of temperate marine climates. Then challenge students to devise a means of presenting this information. Students might create a table, a map, a diagram, or even a poem. Encourage students to be creative. Invite them to present their comparisons to the class. **learning modality: logical/ mathematical**

Figure 10 A. Much of Italy has a Mediterranean climate, with warm, dry summers and cool, rainy winters. **B.** Rice is a major food crop in places with a humid subtropical climate, as in parts of China. *Comparing and Contrasting How are Mediterranean and humid subtropical climates similar? How do they differ?*

Mediterranean A coastal climate that is drier and warmer than west coast marine is known as Mediterranean. Find the Mediterranean climates in *Exploring Climate Regions.* In the United States, the southern coast of California has a Mediterranean climate. This climate is mild, with two seasons. In winter, marine air masses bring cool, rainy weather. Summers are somewhat warmer, with little rain.

Mediterranean climates have two main vegetation types. One is made up of dense shrubs and small trees, called chaparral (chap uh RAL). The other vegetation type includes grasses with a few oak trees.

Agriculture is an important part of the economy of California's Mediterranean climate region. Some crops, including olives and grapes, were originally introduced by Spanish settlers. With the help of irrigation, farmers grow many different crops, including rice, oranges, and many vegetables, fruits, and nuts.

Humid Subtropical The warmest temperate marine climates are on the edges of the tropics. **Humid subtropical** climates are wet and warm, but not as constantly hot as the tropics. Locate the humid subtropical climates in *Exploring Climate Regions.*

The southeastern United States has a humid subtropical climate. Summers are hot, with much more rainfall than in winter. Maritime tropical air masses move inland, bringing tropical weather conditions, including thunderstorms and occasional hurricanes, to southern cities such as Houston, New Orleans, and Atlanta. Winters are cool to mild, with more rain than snow. However, polar air masses moving in from the north can bring freezing temperatures and severe frosts.

Mixed forests of oak, ash, hickory, and pines grow in the humid subtropical region of the United States. Cotton was once the most important crop grown in this region. Other crops, including oranges, grapefruits, peaches, peanuts, sugar cane, and rice, are now more important to the economy.

☑ *Checkpoint* What is the main difference between a humid subtropical climate and a tropical climate?

Background

Facts and Figures The chaparral biome, or plant and animal community, is very typical of Mediterranean climates. The chaparral is characterized by dense growth of evergreen shrubs and small trees. Chaparral plants have small, thick, waxy leaves. These plants are dormant in the hot, dry summer and spring to life with the first rainfall in winter.

The chaparral is a fire-dependent biome.

Fires wipe out dead plant material, recycle nutrients, thin old growth, and stimulate new growth from seeds and sprouts. Chaparral plants have adapted to fire by producing seeds early in their life cycles that are either resistant to fire or require fire for germination. Many chaparral plants also produce volatile oils that are highly flammable.

Temperate Continental Climates

Temperate continental climates are found on continents in the Northern Hemisphere. Because they are not influenced very much by oceans, temperate continental climates have extremes of temperature. Why do continental climates occur only in the Northern Hemisphere? The parts of continents in the Southern Hemisphere south of 40° south latitude are not far enough from oceans for dry continental air masses to form.

Humid Continental Shifting tropical and polar air masses bring constantly changing weather to humid continental climates. In winter, continental polar air masses move south, bringing bitterly cold weather. In summer, tropical air masses move north, bringing heat and high humidity. Humid continental climates receive moderate amounts of rain in the summer. Smaller amounts of rain or snow fall in winter.

What parts of the United States have a humid continental climate? The eastern part of the region—the Northeast—has a range of forest types, from mixed forests in the south to coniferous forests in the north. Much of the western part of this region—the Midwest—was once tall grasslands, but is now farmland. Farmers in the Midwest grow wheat, corn, other grains, and soybeans. These crops are used as food for people and for hogs, poultry, and beef cattle.

Subarctic The **subarctic** climates lie north of the humid continental climates. The world's largest subarctic regions are in Russia, Canada, and Alaska. Summers in the subarctic are short and cool. Winters are long and bitterly cold.

In North America, coniferous trees such as spruce and fir make up a huge northern forest that stretches from Alaska to Canada's east coast. Many large mammals, including bears, wolves, and moose, live in the forest. Small mammals such as beavers, porcupines, and red squirrels, and birds such as grouse and owls also live in the forest. Wood products from the northern forest are an important part of the economy.

Sharpen your Skills

Classifying

The table shows some climate data for three cities.

	City A	City B	City C
Average January Temperature (°C)	12.8	18.9	−5.6
Average July Temperature (°C)	21.1	27.2	20
Annual Precipitation (cm)	33	152	109

Describe the climate you would expect each city to have. Identify which city is Miami, which is Los Angeles, and which is Portland, Maine. Use *Exploring Climate Regions* on pages 622–623 to help identify each city's climate.

Figure 11 Subarctic climates have cool summers and cold winters. Parts of this region are called "spruce-moose belts."

Temperate Continental Climates

Building Inquiry Skills: Applying Concepts

Invite students to compare and contrast the characteristics of humid continental and subarctic climates. List their similarities and differences on the board. Then ask: **What factor or factors affecting climate causes the differences between subarctic and humid continental climates?** (*primarily latitude*) **What climate factor or factors causes the similarities between these two climates?** (*Distance from large bodies of water and prevailing winds*) **learning modality: logical/mathematical**

Sharpen your Skills

Classifying

Time 10 minutes
Expected Outcome City A is Los Angeles. Its warm and dry climate is a Mediterranean climate. City B is Miami. Its hot and humid climate is a tropical wet-and-dry climate. City C is Portland, Maine. With hot summers and cool winters, it is a humid continental climate.

Extend Challenge students to classify the climates of Seattle, Atlanta, and Chicago. Ask: **Which of these cities has climates similar to City A, City B, or City C?** (*Chicago is like City C, Portland, Maine.*) **Which do not?** (*Seattle has a marine west coast climate, and Atlanta has a humid subtropical climate.*) **learning modality: logical/mathematical**

Ongoing Assessment

Writing Have students summarize the differences between a temperate continental climate and a temperate marine climate.

627

Polar Climates

Cultural Diversity

The Inuit and the Pueblo are two Native American groups that live in extreme climates. Show students pictures of the climates these groups live in. Help students locate where these groups live on the map in *Exploring Climate Regions* on pages 622–623. Then challenge student groups to learn how these two groups have adapted to their environments. You might assign groups to study one aspect of their traditional cultures, such as housing, food, dress, customs, social structure, communication, and art. Have groups present their findings to the class. **cooperative learning**

Highlands

Including All Students

Students can make models of a highland climate using salt dough or papier-mâché. They may base their models on the description of the Rocky Mountains in the text, or they can choose a different mountain range. Their models should show how the climate changes as altitude increases. Encourage students to be creative. Not only could they color-code the various climate regions on the mountain, but they could also add models of the plants and animals that live there. **learning modality: kinesthetic**

Figure 12 Emperor penguins live on the ice cap of Antarctica.

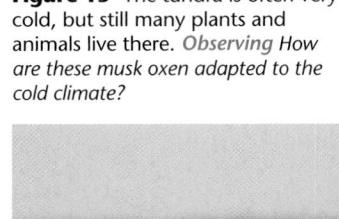

Figure 13 The tundra is often very cold, but still many plants and animals live there. *Observing How are these musk oxen adapted to the cold climate?*

Polar Climates

The polar climate is the coldest climate region. Ice cap and tundra climates are found only in the far north and south, near the North and South poles.

Ice Cap As you can see in *Exploring Climate Regions*, ice cap climates are found mainly on Greenland and in Antarctica. With average temperatures always at or below freezing, the land in ice cap climate regions is covered with ice and snow. Intense cold makes the air dry. Lichens and a few low plants may grow on the rocks.

Tundra The **tundra** climate region stretches across northern Alaska, Canada, and Russia. Short, cool summers follow bitterly cold winters. Because of the cold, some layers of the tundra soil are always frozen. This permanently frozen tundra soil is called **permafrost.** Because of the permafrost, water cannot drain away, so the soil is wet and boggy in summer.

It is too cold on the tundra for trees to grow. Despite the harsh climate, during the short summers the tundra is filled with life. Mosquitoes and other insects hatch in the ponds and marshes above the frozen permafrost. Mosses, grasses, lichens, wildflowers, and shrubs grow quickly during the short summers. Herds of caribou and musk oxen eat the vegetation and are in turn preyed upon by wolves. Some birds, such as the white-tailed ptarmigan, live on the tundra year-round. Others, such as the arctic tern and many waterfowl, spend only the summer there.

☑ *Checkpoint* *What type of vegetation is found on the tundra?*

Background

Facts and Figures The alpine tundra, which is the tundra found in a highland climate, is somewhat different from the arctic tundra of a polar climate. The main differences are that the alpine tundra does not have permafrost and receives much more precipitation. Most alpine tundra has well-drained soil. However, bare rock-covered ground is also very common. Low-growing plants, mosses, and lichens characterize both the arctic and the alpine tundras. The alpine tundra plants include more mat-growing plants that are adapted to the gusty winds, heavy snowfalls, and fluctuating temperatures found at mountaintops. Common alpine tundra animals include mountain goats, big-horned sheep, pikas, and marmots. Butterflies, beetles, and grasshoppers are also common, whereas flies and mosquitoes are more rare.

Highlands

Why are highlands a distinct climate region? Remember that temperature falls as altitude increases, so highland regions are colder than the regions that surround them. Increasing altitude produces climate changes similar to the climate changes you would expect with increasing latitude. In the tropics, highlands are like cold islands overlooking the warm lowlands.

The climate on the lower slopes of a mountain range is like that of the surrounding countryside. The foothills of the Rocky Mountains, for instance, share the semiarid climate of the Great Plains. But as you go higher up into the mountains, temperatures become lower. Climbing 1,000 meters up in elevation is like traveling 1,200 kilometers north. The climate higher in the mountains is like that of the subarctic: cool with coniferous trees. Animals typical of the subarctic zone—such as moose and porcupines—live in the mountain forest.

Above a certain elevation—the tree line—no trees can grow. The climate above the tree line is like that of the tundra. Only low plants, mosses, and lichens can grow there.

Figure 14 The top of this mountain is too cold and windy for trees to grow. *Classifying What climate zone does this mountaintop resemble?*

Section 2 Review

1. What two factors are used to classify climates?
2. Briefly describe each of the five main climate types.
3. Give three examples of how the climate of a region affects what plants and animals can live there.
4. **Thinking Critically** Applying Concepts Which of these two places has more severe winters—central Russia or the west coast of France? Why?
5. **Thinking Critically** Classifying Classify the main climate regions according to whether or not trees usually grow in each one.

Science at Home

Describe to your family the characteristics of each of the climate regions found in the United States. Which climate region does your family live in? What plants and animals live in your climate region? What characteristics do these plants and animals have that make them well-adapted to living in your climate region?

Chapter 19 **629**

Program Resources

◆ **Unit 5 Resources** 19-2 Review and Reinforce, p. 103; 19-2 Enrich, p. 104

Answers to Self-Assessment

Caption Questions

Figure 13 They have thick, long coats.
Figure 14 tundra

✓ *Checkpoint*

Mosses, grasses, lichens, wildflowers, and shrubs

3 Assess

Section 2 Review Answers

1. Temperature and precipitation
2. Tropical: hot and rainy; dry: little precipitation; temperate marine: humid with mild winters; temperate continental: warm or cool summers and cold winters, moderate precipitation; polar: cool summers and very cold winters, little precipitation
3. Answers may vary. Students should give examples that show how the climate affects what plants or animals live in a region or what types of farming, ranching, or forestry are important.
4. Central Russia has more severe winters because it is at a higher latitude than France in the center of the continent and has a continental climate; the climate of the coast of France is west coast marine and is more moderate.
5. Trees: tropical rainy, temperate marine, temperate continental, highlands; no trees: dry, polar

Science at Home

To ensure students identify their climate correctly, encourage volunteers to identify your climate region and explain what climate factors your community has. Help students identify the special factors of your climate to which plants and animals must adapt. For example, in a temperate continental climate, animals need some kind of adaptation to survive the change of seasons. Encourage students to interview family members about other climate regions they have visited.

Performance Assessment

Organizing Information Instruct students to make a table in which they list the climate factors and types of living things for each of the six climate regions they studied. Students should also include in their tables information about the subtypes of climate regions, such as ice cap and tundra climates.

629

Cool Climate Graphs

Preparing for Inquiry

Key Concept Factors in addition to latitude, such as the proximity of large bodies of water, altitude, and the presence of mountains, also help to determine the climate of a region.

Skills Objectives Students will be able to

♦ graph the monthly average precipitation, high temperature, and low temperature for three different cities;

♦ interpret data to determine which city matches which climate graph;

♦ draw conclusions about which city has the best climate for different types of recreational facilities.

Time 40 minutes

Advance Planning Depending on the level of your students, you may want to distribute copies of graphs with the axes already marked. An overhead transparency of a climate graph will help instruct students on making their own.

Guided Inquiry

Invitation To help students relate to the lab, ask: **How does climate affect your life?** *(Students should explain how they have to change their lifestyle based on the yearly weather changes.)* Discuss what kinds of activities students can or cannot do because of the climate.

Introducing the Procedure

Instruct students to look over the climate graph shown in their text. Discuss what kinds of information are being graphed. Ask: **Why is this type of graph useful?** *(A visual picture of monthly temperatures and precipitation makes it easier to compare the climates among different cities.)*

Cool Climate Graphs

You are a land-use planner who has been hired by a company that builds recreational facilities. Your company is considering buying land near at least one of four cities, all at about the same latitude. Your job is to decide which of the cities would be the best place to build a water park and which is the best place to build a ski-touring center.

Problem

Based on climate data, which city is the best place for each type of recreational facility?

Skills Focus

graphing, interpreting data, drawing conclusions

Materials

calculator
ruler
3 pieces of graph paper
black, blue, red, and green pencils
climate map on pages 124–125
U.S. map with city names and latitude lines

Procedure

1. Work in groups of three. Each person should graph the data for a different city, A, B, or C.

2. On graph paper, use a black pencil to label the axes as on the climate graph below. Title your climate graph City A, City B, or City C.

3. Use your green pencil to make a bar graph of the monthly average amount of precipitation. Place a star below the name of each month that has more than a trace of snow.

4. Use a red pencil to plot the average monthly maximum temperature. Make a dot for the temperature in the middle of each space for the month. When you have plotted data for all 12 months, connect the points into a smooth curved line.

5. Use a blue pencil to plot the average monthly minimum temperature for your city. Use the same procedure as in Step 4.

6. Calculate the total average annual precipitation for this city and include it in your observations. Do this by adding the average precipitation for each month.

Washington, D.C., Climate Averages

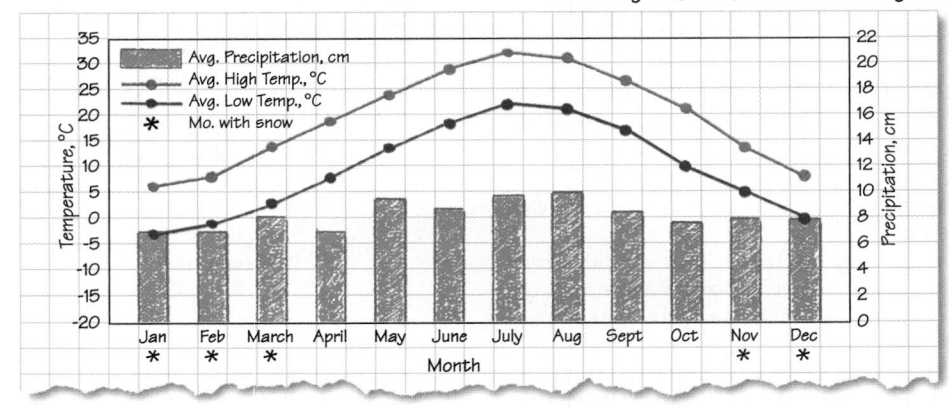

Troubleshooting the Experiment

♦ If necessary, review with students the factors that affect climate from Section 1.

♦ Walk around the room as students are graphing to help with any problems they might be having.

♦ Using maps that show the names of cities and the physical geography will help students match their climate graphs with the proper cities.

♦ Encourage students to list the climate criteria for a water-slide park and a cross-country ski touring center.

Expected Outcome

Students should determine the climate type of each city and the identity of each city based on their climate graphs and their U.S. maps.

Climate Data

Washington, D.C.	Jan	Feb	Mar	April	May	June	July	Aug	Sept	Oct	Nov	Dec
Average High Temp. (°C)	6	8	14	19	24	29	32	31	27	21	14	8
Average Low Temp. (°C)	-3	-2	3	8	14	19	22	21	17	10	5	0
Average Precipitation (cm)	6.9	6.9	8.1	6.9	9.4	8.6	9.7	9.9	8.4	7.6	7.9	7.9
Months With Snow	*	*	*	trace	—	—	—	—	—	trace	*	*

City A	Jan	Feb	Mar	Apr	May	Jun	July	Aug	Sept	Oct	Nov	Dec
Average High Temp. (°C)	13	16	16	17	17	18	18	19	21	21	17	13
Average Low Temp. (°C)	8	9	9	10	11	12	13	13	13	11	8	8
Average Precipitation (cm)	10.4	7.6	7.9	3.3	0.8	0.5	0.3	0.3	0.8	3.3	8.1	7.9
Months With Snow	trace	trace	trace	—	—	—	—	—	—	—	—	trace

City B	Jan	Feb	Mar	Apr	May	Jun	July	Aug	Sept	Oct	Nov	Dec
Average High Temp. (°C)	5	7	10	16	21	26	29	27	23	18	11	6
Average Low Temp. (°C)	−9	−7	−4	1	6	11	14	13	8	2	−4	−8
Average Precipitation (cm)	0.8	1.0	2.3	3.0	5.6	5.8	7.4	7.6	3.3	2.0	1.3	1.3
Months With Snow	*	*	*	*	*	—	—	—	trace	*	*	*

City C	Jan	Feb	Mar	Apr	May	Jun	July	Aug	Sept	Oct	Nov	Dec
Average High Temp. (°C)	7	11	13	18	23	28	33	32	27	21	12	8
Average Low Temp. (°C)	−6	−4	−2	1	4	8	11	10	5	1	−3	−7
Average Precipitation (cm)	2.5	2.3	1.8	1.3	1.8	1	0.8	0.5	0.8	1	2	2.5
Months With Snow	*	*	*	*	*	trace	—	—	trace	trace	*	*

Analyze and Conclude

Compare your climate graphs and observations. Use all three climate graphs, plus the graph for Washington, D.C., to answer these questions.

1. Which of the four cities has the least change in average temperatures during the year?
2. In which climate region is each city located?
3. Which of the cities listed below matches each climate graph?

Colorado Springs, Colorado	latitude 39° N
San Francisco, California	latitude 38° N
Reno, Nevada	latitude 40° N
Washington, D.C.	latitude 39° N

4. Even though these cities are at approximately the same latitude, why are their climate graphs so different?
5. **Apply** Which city would be the best location for a water slide park? For a cross-country ski touring center? What other factors should you consider when deciding where to build each type of recreational facility? Explain.

More to Explore

What type of climate does the area where you live have? Find out what outdoor recreational facilities your community has. How is each one particularly suited to the climate of *your* area?

Analyze and Conclude

1. City A
2. Washington, D.C.: humid subtropical; City A: Mediterranean; City B: semiarid; City C: arid
3. Colorado Springs: City B; San Francisco: City A; Reno: City C
4. Other climate factors, such as distance from large bodies of water, altitude, and mountain ranges, affect the climate of these cities.
5. Washington, D.C., would be the best choice for a water-slide park because it has fewer months with snow and very warm summertime temperatures, even though it has relatively high amounts of precipitation. Colorado Springs would be the best choice for a cross-country ski touring center because it has the most months with enough snow. Other factors to consider include water supply, local economy, building sites, numbers of tourists, roads, and the amount of taxes. These factors will affect the cost of building and maintaining the facility and whether there are enough people to use the facility so that it will make money.

Extending the Inquiry

More to Explore Help students identify and list the recreational facilities in and around your community. Some facilities in your community might include parks, ice skating rinks, pools, amusement parks, water slide parks, ski hills, golf courses, and toboggan runs. Students should describe how the climate requirements of the recreation facilities match the climate factors in your community.

Program Resources

◆ **Unit 5 Resources** Real-World Lab blackline masters, pp. 116–117

Media and Technology

 Lab Activity Videotape
Tape 4

 Transparencies "Climate Graph for Washington, D.C.," Transparency 79

Objectives

After completing the lesson, students will be able to

◆ identify how scientists can learn about ancient climates;

◆ describe how Earth's surface changes during an ice age;

◆ explain the theories that have been proposed to explain natural climate change.

Key Terms ice age, sunspot

1 Engage/Explore

Activating Prior Knowledge

To find out what students know about ancient climates ask: **What do you know about climate changes in Earth's past?** *(Some students might mention past ice ages or climate changes that might have caused the extinction of dinosaurs.)* **How do you think these climate changes might have affected plants and animals?** *(Students might mention that plants and animals would die out if they couldn't move or adapt to the climate changes. Accept all answers without comment.)*

DISCOVER

Skills Focus inferring
Materials *Figure 16 from student text, magnifying lens*
Time 10 minutes
Tips Make a photocopy of Figure 16 and enlarge the photo of the tree rings. Students can label on the photocopy thick and thin tree rings. If possible, provide students with cross-sections of tree trunks to examine.
Expected Outcome Students should observe that tree rings are not all the same thickness. Students might infer that temperature and precipitation affect the thickness of tree rings.
Think It Over Students should infer that the relative thickness of tree rings tells about weather conditions in the past.

DISCOVER · ACTIVITY

What Story Can Tree Rings Tell?

1. Look at the photo of tree rings on page 135. Tree rings are the layers of new wood that form as a tree grows each year.

2. Look closely at the tree rings. Note whether they are all the same thickness.

3. What weather conditions might cause a tree to form thicker or thinner tree rings?

Think It Over
Inferring How could you use tree rings to tell you about weather in the past?

GUIDE FOR READING

◆ What principle do scientists follow in studying ancient climates?

◆ What changes occur on Earth's surface during an ice age?

◆ What theories have been proposed to explain natural climate change?

Reading Tip Before you read, preview the art and photos and read the captions. Write a prediction about how Earth's climate has changed through time.

One of the greatest Native American cultures in the American Southwest was the Ancestral Pueblos. These farming people built great pueblos, or "apartment houses," of stone and sun-baked clay, with hundreds of rooms. By about the year 1000, the Ancestral Pueblos were flourishing. They grew crops of corn, beans, and squash and traded extensively with other groups of people. But in the late 1200s, the climate became drier, reducing the size of their crops. After a long period of drought, the Ancestral Pueblos migrated to other areas.

Although weather can vary from day to day, climates usually change more slowly. But climates do change, both in small areas and throughout the world. Although climate change is usually slow, its consequences are great. Climate changes have affected many civilizations, including the Ancestral Pueblos.

Figure 15 The Ancestral Pueblos lived in these buildings, now in Mesa Verde National Park in southwestern Colorado, about 1,000 years ago.

632

READING STRATEGIES

Reading Tip Students may predict that Earth's climate is warmer than it was in the past. Encourage students to share and explain their predictions.
Study and Comprehension Encourage students to look over the section before they read it to identify the main topics. Suggest that they use the topic heads from the section to organize an outline. Then students can use their completed outlines as a study guide.

Studying Climate Change

In studying ancient climates, scientists follow an important principle: If plants or animals today need certain conditions to live, then similar plants and animals in the past also required those conditions. For example, today magnolia and palm trees grow only in warm, moist climates. Scientists assume that the ancestors of these trees required similar conditions. Thus, 80-million-year-old fossils of these trees in Greenland are good evidence that the climate of Greenland was warm and moist 80 million years ago.

Tree rings can also be used to learn about ancient climates. Every summer, a tree grows a new layer of wood under its bark. These layers form rings when seen in a cross section, as shown in Figure 16. In cool climates, the amount the tree grows—the thickness of a ring—depends on the length of the warm growing season. In dry climates, the thickness of each ring depends on the amount of rainfall. By looking at cross sections of trees, scientists can count backward from the outer ring to see whether previous years were warm or cool, wet or dry. A thin ring indicates that the year was cool or dry. A thick ring indicates that the year was warm or wet.

A third source of information about ancient climates is pollen records. Each type of plant has a particular type of pollen. The bottoms of some lakes are covered with thick layers of mud and plant material, including pollen, that fell to the bottom of the lake over thousands of years. Scientists can drill down into these layers and bring up cores to examine. By looking at the pollen present in each layer, scientists can tell what types of plants lived in the area. The scientists can then infer that the climate that existed when the pollen was deposited was similar to the climate where the same plants grow today.

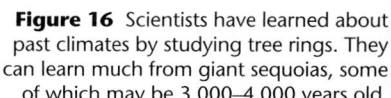

Figure 16 Scientists have learned about past climates by studying tree rings. They can learn much from giant sequoias, some of which may be 3,000–4,000 years old.

633

Program Resources

◆ **Unit 5 Resources** 19-3 Lesson Plan, p. 105, 19-3 Section Summary, p. 106
◆ **Guided Reading and Study Workbook** Section 19-3

2 Facilitate

Studying Climate Change

Including All Students

Help students organize the information in the text by asking: **What three sources of information do scientists use in studying ancient climates?** *(Fossil evidence, tree rings, pollen records)* **What important principle do scientists follow while studying ancient climates?** *(Ancient plants and animals probably required the same living conditions as similar plants and animals living now.)* **learning modality: verbal**

Building Inquiry Skills: Drawing Conclusions

Explain to students that scientists have found fossils of brachiopods and trilobites in southeastern Wisconsin. These fossils are about 400 million years old. Encourage students to use encyclopedias to learn more about trilobites and brachiopods, or display pictures or fossils of these organisms and help students infer their habitats. Challenge students to use this information to draw a conclusion about the climate of southeastern Wisconsin about 400 million years ago. *(Brachiopods and trilobites are organisms that lived on the bottom of warm, shallow seas. The presence of these fossils in southeastern Wisconsin indicates that this area was covered by warm, shallow seas about 400 million years ago.)* **learning modality: logical/mathematical**

Ongoing Assessment

Oral Presentation Call on various students to describe the three sources of information that scientists use to study ancient climates.

Ice Ages

Using the Visuals: Figure 17

Invite students to use Figure 17 to determine whether your area was covered by glaciers 18,000 years ago. Ask: **What could you conclude if a fossil of a mammoth were found north of the mammoth steppe region shown on the map?** *(That the size of the glaciers changed over time, and the mammoth steppe region changed accordingly.)* Elicit suggestions about why woolly mammoths and scimitar-toothed cats are extinct. Discuss how the changing climate might have affected these animals. **learning modality: visual**

Building Inquiry Skills: Inferring

Challenge students to infer what your community might have looked like during the last ice age. Then have students draw a picture showing how the street on which they live might have looked about 18,000 years ago. **learning modality: visual**

Including All Students

Materials *shallow pan, damp sand, ice cubes or crushed ice, water, toothpicks*

Time 20 minutes, 5 minutes

Students can construct models to show why the ocean level rises as ice sheets melt. Instruct students to use the damp sand to mold a land mass in the shallow pan. Suggest that they include depressions, mountains, and coastal areas. Students should add water to the pan to simulate the ocean. Then they can pack the ice on the land masses to represent glaciers and ice sheets. Have students mark the water level at various places on their land masses with toothpicks. Ask students to predict what will happen to the ice sheets and oceans in their models. *(The ice sheets will melt, and the ocean level will rise.)* (Note: Keep pans in a cool, shady area overnight to minimize evaporation.) The next day, have students observe the changes in ice and water in their models. Discuss why oceans are lower during the ice ages than they are now. **learning modality: kinesthetic**

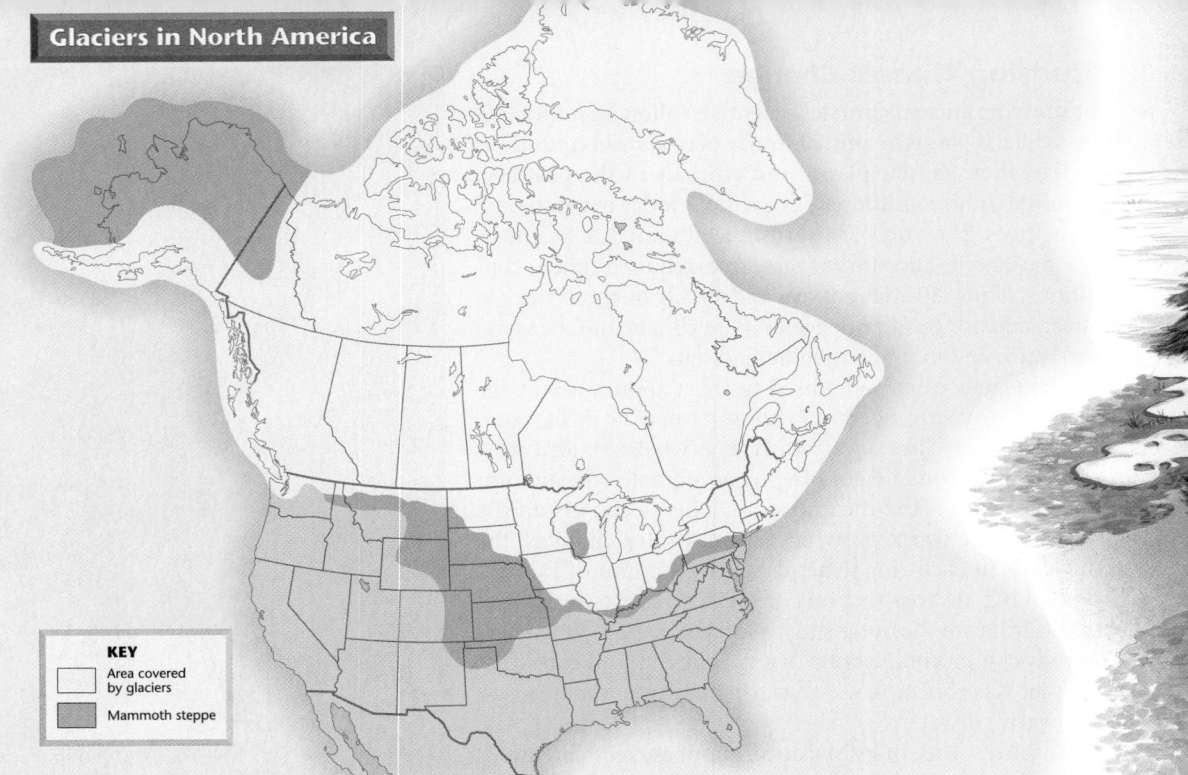

Glaciers in North America

KEY
- Area covered by glaciers
- Mammoth steppe

Figure 17 The map shows the parts of North America that were covered by glaciers 18,000 years ago. On the steppe near the glaciers lived many mammals that are now extinct, including woolly mammoths and scimitar-toothed cats.

Ice Ages

Throughout Earth's history, climates have gradually changed. Over millions of years, warm periods have alternated with cold periods known as **ice ages,** or glacial episodes. **During each ice age, huge sheets of ice called glaciers covered large parts of Earth's surface.**

From fossils and other evidence, scientists have concluded that in the past two million years there have been at least four major ice ages. Each one lasted 100,000 years or longer. Long, warmer periods known as interglacials occurred between the ice ages. Some scientists think that we are now in a warm period between ice ages.

The most recent major ice age ended only about 10,500 years ago. Ice sheets covered much of northern Europe and North America, reaching as far south as present-day Iowa and Nebraska. In some places, the ice was more than 3 kilometers thick. So much water was frozen in the ice sheets that the average sea level was much lower than it is today. When the ice sheets melted, the rising oceans flooded coastal areas. Inland, large lakes formed.

✓ *Checkpoint* Why were the oceans lower during the ice ages than they are now?

Background

Integrating Science All planets, including Earth, revolve around the sun in elliptical orbits. Because its orbit is not circular, Earth is not the same distance from the sun at all points in its orbit. About January 3, Earth is nearest the sun at a point called the perihelion. About July 4, Earth is farthest from the sun at the aphelion. Since planets move faster when they are closer to the sun, the time interval from the March equinox to the September equinox is longer than the interval between September and March. If Earth's orbit shifts so that its perihelion is in July, the winter season in the Northern Hemisphere will be longer because Earth will be moving more slowly between September and March. This could cause the climate to become cooler, setting the stage for an ice age.

Social Studies
CONNECTION

To help students think about how their lives might change, ask: **How would a colder climate affect the plants and animals living in our environment?** *(Some plants might not survive. Animals that depend on them for food also might not survive. Some animals might migrate.)* Explain that the climate in an ice age would be similar to subarctic, tundra, or ice cap climates. Discuss how these climates are different from your current climate.

In Your Journal Provide time for students to make their lists. Encourage students to share their lists in a class discussion. **learning modality: verbal**

Causes of Climate Change

Why do climates change? Scientists have formed several hypotheses. **Possible explanations for major climate changes include variations in the position of Earth relative to the sun, changes in the sun's energy output, and the movement of continents.**

Earth's Position Changes in Earth's position relative to the sun may have affected climates. According to one hypothesis, as Earth revolves around the sun, the time of year when Earth is closest to the sun shifts from January to July and back again over a period of about 26,000 years.

The angle at which Earth's axis tilts and the shape of Earth's orbit around the sun also change slightly over long periods of time. The combined effects of these changes in Earth's movements may be the main cause of ice ages.

INTEGRATING SPACE SCIENCE **Solar Energy** Short-term changes in climate have been linked to changes in the number of **sunspots**—dark, cooler regions on the surface of the sun. Sunspots increase and decrease in regular 11-year cycles. Sunspot cycles could in turn be caused by changes in the sun's energy output.

Social Studies
CONNECTION

Prehistoric people who lived during the last ice age faced a harsh environment. To endure the cold, they learned to make clothing from animal skins. They also used fires for warmth and cooking.

In Your Journal

Make a list of five ways your life would change if the climate suddenly became colder.

Media and Technology

 Transparencies "Extent of Northern Hemisphere Glaciation," Transparency 80

 Concept Videotape Library *Adventures,* Tape 4, "Changes in Climate"

Answers to Self-Assessment

☑ *Checkpoint*
Much of the water on Earth was frozen in ice sheets that covered the land.

Ongoing Assessment

Writing Have students explain what an ice age is and how one might occur.

Causes of Climate Change, continued

Including All Students

Give students a photocopied map of the world. Tell them to cut out the continents and India, but leave Europe and Asia together as one continent. Then challenge them to fit the continents together to form Pangaea. **learning modality: kinesthetic**

3 Assess

Section 3 Review Answers

1. Fossil evidence, tree rings, and pollen records

2. The temperature was colder and huge sheets of ice covered large parts of Earth.

3. Earth's position relative to the sun, changes in the sun's energy output, and the movement of continents

4. A volcanic eruption would send ash and other particles into the air that would block the sun's energy from Earth's surface. The climate would become cool, but the change would not be permanent. Over time, the volcanic ash and dust would settle out of the air.

Check Your Progress
CHAPTER PROJECT 19

Groups should be finished collecting weather data and starting to graph the data. Encourage students to look critically at the data for any similarities and differences. Besides graphing their data, suggest that students construct tables or charts to help them compare and contrast their observations. Encourage students to think about which climate factors caused the weather data to be different in each microclimate.

Performance Assessment

Skills Check Have students make a cause and effect table showing causes for climate change and the effects.

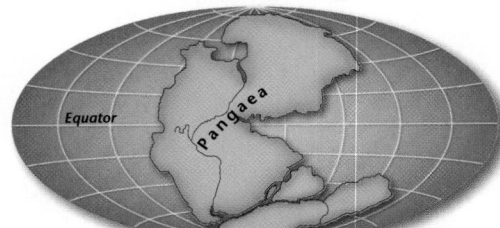

225 million years ago

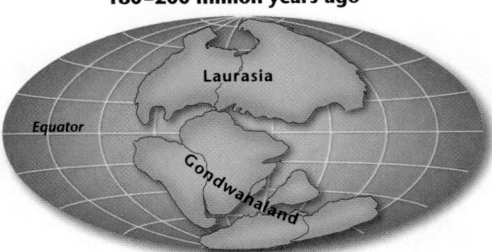

180–200 million years ago

Figure 18 The continents have moved over millions of years. *Interpreting Maps Which present-day continents broke away from Gondwanaland? Which broke away from Laurasia?*

Recently, satellite measurements have shown that the amount of energy the sun produces increases and decreases slightly from year to year. These changes may cause Earth's temperature to increase and decrease. More observations are needed to test this hypothesis.

Movement of Continents Earth's continents have not always been located where they are now. About 225 million years ago, most of the land on Earth was part of a single continent called Pangaea (pan JEE uh).

As Figure 18 shows, most continents were far from their present positions. Continents that are now in the polar zones were once near the equator. This movement explains how tropical plants such as magnolias and palm trees could once have grown in Greenland.

Over millions of years, the continents broke away and gradually moved to their present positions. The movements of continents over time changed the locations of land and sea. These changes affected the global patterns of winds and ocean currents, which in turn slowly changed climates. And as the continents continue to move, climates will continue to change.

Section 3 Review

1. What types of evidence do scientists use to study changes in climate?

2. How was the climate during an ice age different from the climate today?

3. List three factors that could be responsible for changing Earth's climates.

4. Thinking Critically Predicting What kinds of climate changes might be caused by a volcanic eruption? Would these changes be permanent? Explain.

Check Your Progress
CHAPTER PROJECT 19

What types of weather conditions have you measured at each site? Have you been recording all the data in your logbook? You should now be ready to graph and analyze your data. Are the weather conditions at all of your test areas similar, or do you see differences? What do you think causes the different conditions? What organisms did you observe at your sites?

Answers to Self-Assessment

Caption Question

Figure 18 South America, Africa, Australia, and Antarctica broke away from Gondwanaland; North America, Europe, and Asia broke away from Laurasia.

Program Resources

◆ **Unit 5 Resources** 19-3 Review and Reinforce, p. 107; 19-3 Enrich, p. 108

SECTION 4 Global Changes in the Atmosphere

DISCOVER •••ACTIVITY••••

What Is the Greenhouse Effect?

1. ✂ Cut two pieces of black construction paper to fit the bottoms of two shoe boxes.

2. 🌡 Place a thermometer in one end of each box. Read the temperatures on the thermometers. (They should be the same.) Cover one box with plastic wrap.

3. Place the boxes together where sunlight or a light bulb can shine on them equally. Make sure the thermometers are shaded by the sides of the boxes.

4. What do think will happen to the temperatures on the thermometers? Wait 15 minutes and read the thermometers again. Record the temperatures.

Think It Over

Inferring How can you explain the temperature difference between the box with the plastic wrap and the open box? Why does the inside of a car left in direct sunlight get so warm?

Have you ever seen a headline like the one below? If you hate cold winters and love summer sports, you may wonder what would be wrong with a slightly warmer world. Some experts agree with you, but many scientists are worried about such climate change.

> ❂ ANYWHERE U.S.A. DAILY NEWS ❂
> **Earth's Average Temperature Expected to Increase by 3 Celsius Degrees**

Most changes in world climates are caused by natural factors. In the last hundred years, however, human activities have also had an effect on Earth's climate and atmosphere. Two of the most important worldwide issues are global warming and thinning of the ozone layer.

Global Warming

Over the last 120 years, the average temperature of the troposphere has risen by about 0.5 Celsius degree. Was this increase part of natural variations, or was it caused by human activities? What effects could higher temperatures have? Scientists have done a great deal of research to try to answer these questions.

GUIDE FOR READING

◆ How might human activities be affecting the temperature of Earth's atmosphere?

◆ How have human activities affected the ozone layer?

Reading Tip As you read, draw a concept map showing how human activities can cause changes in the atmosphere and climate.

Chapter 19 **637**

READING STRATEGIES

Reading Tip Suggest that students look over the section before they read it so they can choose a title and the major concepts for their concept maps. Concept maps might begin as follows:

```
        ( human activities )
               |
      can add to the atmosphere
         /              \
( greenhouse gases )   ( CFCs )
```

Program Resources

◆ **Unit 5 Resources** 19-4 Lesson Plan, p. 109; 19-4 Section Summary, p. 110
◆ **Guided Reading and Study Workbook** Section 19-4

INTEGRATING ENVIRONMENTAL SCIENCE

SECTION 4 Global Changes in the Atmosphere

Objectives

After completing the lesson, students will be able to
◆ describe the greenhouse effect and how human activities might be affecting the temperature of Earth's atmosphere;
◆ describe how human activities have affected the ozone layer.

Key Terms greenhouse gas, global warming, chlorofluorocarbon

1 Engage/Explore

Activating Prior Knowledge

Invite students to explain what they think of when they hear about global warming and the depletion of the ozone layer. Then elicit their ideas of how the actions of people might affect climate. Record students' remarks on the board. As they study this section, refer to these comments and encourage students to modify the remarks, if necessary.

•••••••• DISCOVER ••••••••

Skills Focus inferring
Materials *2 pieces of black construction paper, 2 shoe boxes, 2 thermometers, plastic wrap, masking tape, source of sunlight or lamp*
Time 15 minutes, 5 minutes
Tips Tape the plastic wrap tightly to the box so that the box is air tight. The thermometers must be shaded. If not, they will give artificially high readings.
Expected Outcome The box covered with plastic wrap will be warmer.
Think It Over Light rays that enter both boxes radiate as heat from the box bottom. Heat is trapped inside the box with plastic wrap; heat escapes from the box without. The temperature inside a car increases as the heat from sunlight entering the car builds up and cannot escape.

2 Facilitate

Global Warming

Using the Visuals: Figure 19

If students have done the Discover activity, encourage them to compare their plastic covered box with the greenhouse in Figure 19. Then help students understand the analogy of a greenhouse to the greenhouse effect. Ask: **What part of Earth's atmosphere acts like a greenhouse roof?** *(Certain gases in the atmosphere—water vapor, carbon dioxide, and methane)* **What affect do these gases have on Earth's atmosphere?** *(They trap energy in the atmosphere.)* **Why are some scientists concerned about greenhouse gases?** *(As these gases increase in the atmosphere, they may trap more energy and cause global temperatures to increase.)* **learning modality: verbal**

Sunlight

Infrared radiation cannot easily pass through the greenhouse roof

Figure 19 Sunlight enters the greenhouse and is absorbed. The interior of the greenhouse radiates back energy in the form of infrared radiation, or heat. The heat is trapped and held inside the greenhouse, warming it. *Applying Concepts What gases in Earth's atmosphere can trap heat like a greenhouse?*

The Greenhouse Effect Recall that gases in Earth's atmosphere hold in heat from the sun, keeping the atmosphere at a comfortable temperature for living things. The process by which gases in Earth's atmosphere trap solar energy is called the greenhouse effect.

Gases in the atmosphere that trap solar energy are called **greenhouse gases.** Water vapor, carbon dioxide, and methane are some of the greenhouse gases. **Human activities that add greenhouse gases to the atmosphere may be warming Earth's atmosphere.** For example, the burning of wood, coal, oil, and natural gas adds carbon dioxide to the air. If the increased carbon dioxide traps more heat, the result could be **global warming,** a gradual increase in the temperature of Earth's atmosphere.

The amount of carbon dioxide in the atmosphere has been steadily increasing. Some scientists predict that if the level of carbon dioxide doubles by the year 2100, the average global temperature could go up by 1.5 to 3.5 Celsius degrees.

Another Hypothesis Not everyone agrees about the causes of global warming. Some scientists think that the 0.5 Celsius degree rise in global temperatures over the past 120 years may be part of natural variations in climate rather than a result of increases in carbon dioxide.

Background

Facts and Figures Much of the carbon dioxide produced by burning fossil fuels is absorbed instead of staying in the atmosphere. Plants absorb carbon dioxide from the air and use it to make food in the process of photosynthesis. Rain forests absorb large amounts of carbon dioxide from the atmosphere. Not only is the destruction of rain forests reducing the amount of carbon dioxide that can be absorbed from the atmosphere, but burning them also increases the amount of carbon dioxide added to it.

Earth's oceans also absorb much of the extra carbon dioxide in the atmosphere. Carbon dioxide from the air enters water by simple diffusion. As long as the concentration of carbon dioxide in ocean water is less than that of the air, carbon dioxide gas will diffuse into the water.

As you learned in Section 3, satellite measurements have shown that the amount of energy the sun produces increases and decreases from year to year. These changes in solar energy could be causing periods of warmer and cooler climates. Or climate change could be a result of changes in both carbon dioxide levels and amounts of solar energy.

Possible Effects Global warming has some potential advantages. Farmers in cool areas could plant two crops a year. Places that are too cold for farming today could become farmland. However, many effects of global warming are likely to be less positive. Higher temperatures would cause water to evaporate from exposed soil, such as plowed farmland. Dry soil blows away easily. Thus some fertile fields might become "dust bowls."

A rise in temperatures of even a few degrees could warm up water in the oceans. As ocean surface temperatures increased, the number of hurricanes might increase.

As the water warmed, it would expand, raising sea levels around the world. Glaciers and polar ice caps might partially melt, which would also increase sea levels. Sea levels have already risen by 10 to 20 centimeters over the last 100 years, and could rise another 25 to 80 centimeters by the year 2100. Even such a small rise in sea levels would flood low-lying coastal areas.

 Checkpoint *What are three possible effects of global warming?*

Ozone Depletion

Another global change in the atmosphere involves the ozone layer, which you learned about in Chapter 16. Ozone in the stratosphere filters out much of the harmful ultraviolet radiation from the sun.

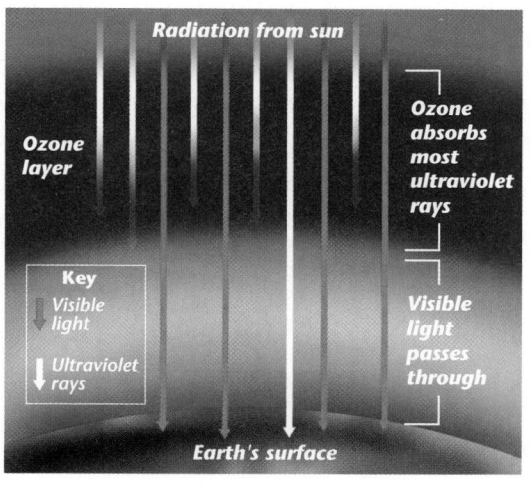

Figure 20 The ozone layer blocks much of the ultraviolet radiation coming from the sun. Visible light can pass through the ozone layer.

It's Your Skin!

How well do sunscreens block out ultraviolet rays? Here's how to compare sunscreens.

1. Close the blinds or curtains in the room. Place one square of sun-sensitive paper inside each of three plastic sandwich bags.
2. Place three drops of one sunscreen on the outside of one bag. Spread the sunscreen as evenly as possible. Label this bag with the SPF number of the sunscreen.
3. On another bag, repeat Step 2 using a sunscreen with a different SPF. Wash your hands after spreading the sunscreen. Leave the third bag untreated as a control.
4. Place the bags outside in direct sunlight. Bring them back inside after 3 minutes or after one of the squares of paper has turned completely white.

Drawing Conclusions Did both of the sunscreens block ultraviolet radiation? Did one of the sunscreens block more ultraviolet radiation than the other one? Explain your results.

Real-Life Learning

Challenge student groups to make a plan for personally reducing carbon dioxide. Direct groups to first brainstorm a list of sources of carbon dioxide. (You might provide various resources to help groups identify these sources.) Then groups should identify the carbon-dioxide producing activities in which they are involved. Finally, groups should formulate a plan to reduce their carbon dioxide output. Encourage groups to present their plans to the class.
cooperative learning

Ozone Depletion

Skills Focus drawing conclusions
Materials *ultraviolet-sensitive paper, 3 plastic sandwich bags, 2 sunscreens with different SPF numbers, black marking pen*
Time 15 minutes
Tips Results will be more obvious if students use sunscreens with highly different SPF numbers. Obtain ultraviolet-sensitive paper from toy or craft stores (called "Sunprint Kit"). Save class time by precutting the paper.
Expected Outcome The paper without sunscreen will show the most color change, and the paper covered with the higher SPF sunscreen will show the least.
Answers Since the untreated paper showed the most color change, the sunscreens did block ultraviolet radiation. The sunscreen with the lower SPF number blocked less ultraviolet radiation because it showed more color change than the paper covered with the higher SPF sunscreen.
Extend Encourage students to return the bags with sunscreen to direct sunlight and monitor them to find out how long the sunscreen is effective.
learning modality: kinesthetic

Ongoing Assessment

Drawing Challenge students to draw their own diagrams showing how greenhouse gases trap heat energy from sunlight in Earth's atmosphere.
 Students can save their diagrams in their portfolios.

Media and Technology

Concept Videotape Library
Adventures, Tape 4, "The Greenhouse Effect"

Answers to Self-Assessment

Caption Question
Figure 19 Water vapor, carbon dioxide, methane

Checkpoint
Areas too cold for farming today could become farmland, some fertile fields could become "dust bowls," the number of hurricanes could increase, and sea levels could rise and flood low-lying coastal areas.

Ozone Depletion,
continued

Addressing Naive Conceptions

Some students might be confused about why the depletion of the ozone layer is harmful when many metropolitan areas have Ozone Action Days to reduce air pollution. Ask: **Do you know why ozone is harmful to people?** *(Some students may not.)* Explain that ozone is part of smog. Ozone forms when sunlight irradiates the emissions from gasoline engines. Smog reduces visibility, irritates the respiratory system, causes eye irritations, and can damage plants. Point out that the concentration of ozone found in the ozone layer would be harmful for people to breathe. However, the ozone layer protects us from the ultraviolet radiation from the sun.
learning modality: verbal

3 Assess

Section 4 Review Answers

1. The burning of wood, coal, oil, and natural gas
2. More carbon dioxide in the air traps more heat in the atmosphere, which causes a gradual increase in global temperatures.
3. chlorofluorocarbons
4. Depending on where they live, students might mention milder winters, longer growing seasons, coastal flooding, more hurricanes, and heat waves.

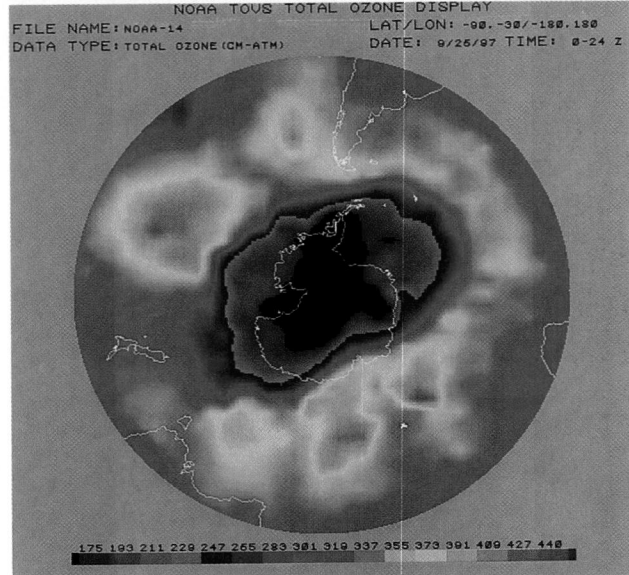

```
NOAA TOVS TOTAL OZONE DISPLAY
FILE NAME: NOAA-14          LAT/LON: -90.-30/-180,180
DATA TYPE: TOTAL OZONE (CM-ATM)   DATE: 9/26/97 TIME: 0-24 Z
```

`175 193 211 229 247 265 283 301 319 337 355 373 391 409 427 440`

Figure 21 This satellite image shows the concentration of ozone in the air over the South Pole. The dark area shows where the ozone layer is the thinnest.

In the 1970s, scientists noticed that the ozone layer over Antarctica was growing thinner each spring. By 1992, the area of thinner ozone was more than twice as large as the continental United States. What created the ozone hole? **Chemicals produced by humans have been damaging the ozone layer.**

The main cause of ozone depletion is a group of chlorine compounds called **chlorofluorocarbons,** or CFCs. CFCs were used in air conditioners and refrigerators, as cleaners for electronic parts, and in spray cans. Most chemical compounds released into the air eventually break down. CFCs, however, can last for decades and rise all the way to the stratosphere. In the stratosphere, ultraviolet radiation breaks down the CFC molecules into atoms, including chlorine. The chlorine atoms then break ozone down into oxygen atoms.

Because ozone blocks ultraviolet radiation, a decrease in ozone means an increase in the amount of ultraviolet radiation that reaches Earth's surface. If you have ever been sunburned, you can understand one effect of stronger ultraviolet radiation! Ultraviolet radiation can also cause eye damage and several kinds of skin cancer.

In the late 1970s, the United States and many other countries banned the use of CFCs in spray cans. In 1990, many nations agreed to end the production and use of CFCs by 2000. Because ozone depletion affects the whole world, such agreements must be international to be effective.

Section 4 Review

1. What human actions increase the amount of carbon dioxide in Earth's atmosphere?
2. How could increases in carbon dioxide in the air affect world temperatures?
3. What chemicals are the major cause of ozone depletion in the stratosphere?
4. **Thinking Critically** **Predicting** How might global warming change conditions where you live? How would this affect your life?

Science at Home

Visit a drugstore with your family. Compare the SPF (sun protection factor) of the various sunscreens for sale. Explain why it is important to protect your skin from ultraviolet radiation. Ask your family members to determine the best value for their money in terms of SPF rating and price.

640

Program Resources

◆ **Unit 5 Resources** 19-4 Review and Reinforce, p. 111; 19-4 Enrich, p. 112

SECTION 1 — What Causes Climate?

Key Ideas
◆ The climate of a region is determined by its temperature and precipitation.
◆ The main factors that influence temperature are latitude, altitude, distance from large bodies of water, and ocean currents.
◆ The main factors that affect precipitation are prevailing winds and the presence of mountains.
◆ The different seasons are a result of the tilt of Earth's axis as Earth travels around the sun.

Key Terms

climate	continental climate
tropical zone	windward
polar zone	leeward
temperate zone	microclimate
marine climate	

SECTION 2 — Climate Regions

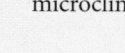

Key Ideas
◆ Climates are classified according to temperature and precipitation.
◆ There are five main climate regions: tropical rainy, dry, temperate marine, temperate continental, and polar. Highlands are often considered to be a sixth climate region.

Key Terms

rain forest	steppe	tundra
savanna	humid subtropical	permafrost
desert	subarctic	

SECTION 3 — Long-Term Changes in Climate

Key Ideas
◆ During each ice age, huge sheets of ice covered much of Earth's surface.
◆ Possible explanations for major climate changes include movement of continents, variations in the position of Earth relative to the sun, and changes in the sun's energy output.

Key Terms
ice age   sunspot

SECTION 4 — Global Changes in the Atmosphere

INTEGRATING ENVIRONMENTAL SCIENCE

Key Ideas
◆ Human activities that add greenhouse gases to the atmosphere may be warming Earth's atmosphere.
◆ Chemicals produced by humans have been damaging the ozone layer.

Key Terms
greenhouse gas
global warming
chlorofluorocarbons

Organizing Information

Concept Map Copy the concept map about climate onto a separate sheet of paper. Then complete it and add a title. (For more on concept maps, see the Skills Handbook.)

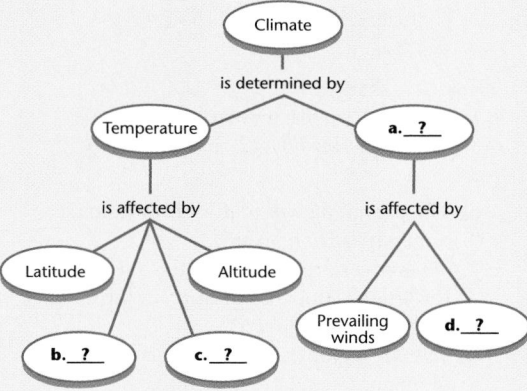

Climate
is determined by
Temperature — a. ?
is affected by — is affected by
Latitude — Altitude
b. ? — c. ?
Prevailing winds — d. ?

Science at Home

ACTIVITY

To make sure that students can explain to their families the importance of using sunscreen, ask: **Why is it important to protect your skin from ultraviolet radiation?** *(Ultraviolet radiation can cause sunburn and several kinds of skin cancer.)* To help prepare students for comparison-shopping, suggest that they take calculators with them to the drugstore and calculate the price per ounce of the sunscreens they are comparing. After they compare the prices of equal quantities, then they can begin to determine which sunscreens are a better value based on their SPF numbers.

Organizing Information

Concept Map *Sample Title:* Factors Affecting Climate **a.** precipitation **b.** or **c.** distance from large bodies of water or ocean currents **d.** mountain ranges

---

Program Resources

◆ **Unit 5 Resources** Chapter 19 Project Scoring Rubric, p. 96
◆ **Performance Assessment** Chapter 19, pp. 58–60
◆ **Chapter Tests** Chapter 19 Test, pp. 75–78

Media and Technology

 Computer Test Bank
Chapter 19 Test

Performance Assessment

Writing Challenge students to write a news article that describes what global warming and ozone depletion are and how human activities have affected the atmosphere.

 Students can save their news articles in their portfolios.

Reviewing Content

Multiple Choice

1. b 2. c 3. b 4. d 5. a

True or False

6. precipitation 7. winter 8. true 9. true
10. carbon dioxide

Checking Concepts

11. Water heats up and cools down more slowly than land. Oceans and other large bodies of water generally moderate the temperature of nearby land areas.

12. The seasons are caused by the tilt of Earth's axis.

13. Most of the United States is in the temperate zone; Hawaii and southern Florida are in the tropical zone; much of Alaska is in the polar zone.

14. Dry climates occur where potential evaporation is greater than precipitation. The two types of dry climates differ in the amount of precipitation they receive. Steppes get more precipitation than deserts.

15. Present-day continents were once at different latitudes and had different climates. As the continents moved from their original positions, their latitudes changed, global patterns of wind and ocean currents changed, and mountains formed, all of which affect climate.

16. Ozone depletion affects the whole world, and the actions of people around the world affect the ozone. For this reason, everyone around the world must work together to prevent ozone depletion.

17. Answers should show that students have accurately observed their local climate factors and have successfully related them to the concepts in the chapter.

Thinking Critically

18. Answers may vary. *Sample answer:* Large bodies of water moderate the climates of nearby land; warm and cold ocean currents influence the climate of coastal areas; the amount of precipitation is a factor in wet and dry climates.

19. Global warming caused by an increase in greenhouse gases is the result of human activities and can be controlled. Earlier changes in climate were the result of natural forces.

Reviewing Content

Multiple Choice

Choose the letter of the best answer.

1. Temperatures are highest in the tropical zone because
   a. the land is flat.
   b. the sun's rays strike most directly.
   c. Earth's axis is tilted toward the sun.
   d. ocean currents warm the region.

2. Continental climates are found
   a. on every continent.
   b. only near the equator.
   c. only in the Northern Hemisphere.
   d. only in the Southern Hemisphere.

3. In a wet-and-dry tropical climate, the most common vegetation is
   a. coniferous forests.
   b. savanna grasslands.
   c. tropical rain forest.
   d. steppe grasslands.

4. Extremely cold periods in Earth's history have resulted in huge
   a. tree rings.
   b. sunspots.
   c. pollen deposits.
   d. glaciers.

5. Chlorofluorocarbons, or CFCs, are the main cause of
   a. ozone depletion.
   b. global warming.
   c. the greenhouse effect.
   d. ice ages.

True or False

If the statement is true, write true. If it is false, change the underlined word or words to make it true.

6. The prevailing winds affect how much <u>sunlight</u> falls on an area.

7. When the north end of Earth's axis is tilted toward the sun, it is <u>summer</u> in the Southern Hemisphere.

8. Climate regions are classified according to temperature and <u>precipitation</u>.

9. A <u>thin</u> tree ring indicates that a year was cool or dry.

10. An increase in <u>nitrogen</u> in the atmosphere may be making world temperatures increase.

Checking Concepts

11. Explain how distance from large bodies of water can affect the temperature of nearby land areas.

12. What causes Earth's seasons?

13. Identify the parts of the United States that are located in each of the three temperature zones.

14. How are "dry" climates defined? How do the two types of dry climate differ?

15. How does the movement of continents explain major changes in climate over time?

16. To be effective, why must agreements aimed at preventing or reducing ozone depletion be international?

17. Writing to Learn In what climate region do you live? Write a description of your local climate and identify some of the things—such as latitude, bodies of water, or wind patterns—that affect the climate.

Thinking Critically

18. Relating Cause and Effect Describe three ways in which water influences climate.

19. Comparing and Contrasting How is global warming different from earlier changes in Earth's climate?

20. Making Judgments What is the most important thing that needs to be done about global warming?

21. Relating Cause and Effect Why do parts of the United States have a semiarid climate while neighboring areas have a humid continental climate?

---

20. Answers may vary. Some students might suggest the most important thing to do is to study the problem more to find definitive answers. Other students might say reduce the amount of carbon dioxide released into the atmosphere.

21. Air that passes over the steppe in a semiarid climate has lost its water vapor as it passed over mountain ranges, so the air is drier. Some of the air that passes over humid continental areas comes from the oceans and doesn't cross mountain ranges, so the air carries more moisture.

Applying Skills

22. Zone A, polar zone; Zone B, temperate zone; Zone C, tropical zone; Zone D, temperate zone; Zone E, polar zone

23. tropical zone; 47 degrees of latitude

24. Zone B

Applying Skills

Use the map of world temperature zones to answer Questions 22–24.

22. **Interpreting Maps** Name each of the five zones shown on the map.

23. **Measuring** What is the name of the temperature zone that includes the equator? How many degrees of latitude does this zone cover?

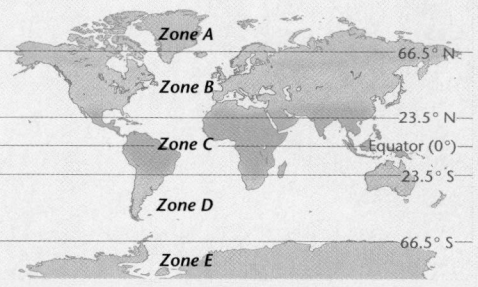

24. **Interpreting Data** Which of the five zones shown on the map has the greatest amount of land area suitable for people to live?

Performance CHAPTER PROJECT 19 **Assessment**

Project Wrap Up Decide how to present your project. You could use a written report, oral presentation, or a bulletin board. Do your graphs compare the conditions in the different microclimates? What conditions favor plants or animals in some areas? After you present your project to the class, discuss what you think causes different microclimates.

Reflect and Record In your journal, describe how you could improve your investigation. Are there factors you did not study? Did you notice any organisms that live only in certain microclimates? What additional information about microclimates would you like to find?

Test Preparation

Use these questions to prepare for standardized tests.

Study the graph. Then answer Questions 25–30.

25. Which of the following months has the widest range of temperatures during the year?
   a. September **b.** June
   c. May **d.** April

26. Which month shown on the graph is the warmest on average?
   a. August **b.** June
   c. July **d.** May

27. Which month is the coldest on average?
   a. January **b.** December
   c. March **d.** February

28. What is the average temperature in April?
   a. about −21°C **b.** about −17°C
   c. about 0°C **d.** about −30°C

29. What is the average temperature in December?
   a. about −20°C **b.** about −26°C
   c. about 0°C **d.** about −30°C

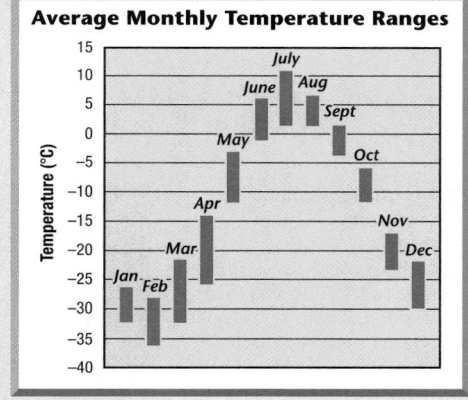

Average Monthly Temperature Ranges

30. What kind of climate is indicated by the graph?
   a. polar
   b. temperate continental
   c. temperate marine
   d. tropical rainy

Performance CHAPTER PROJECT 19 **Assessment**

Project Wrap Up Find out from groups how they intend to present their projects. Have bulletin board space available for those groups who choose to use it. Groups giving oral presentations could use an overhead projector to display their graphs. Each group should present graphs that compare the weather conditions in the different microclimates they studied. In their presentations, groups should draw conclusions about the kinds of conditions that favor certain plants and animals. After groups have presented their reports, discuss the factors that cause different microclimates. Begin by prompting students to recall the climate factors that affect temperature and precipitation.

Reflect and Record Encourage students to be objective as they evaluate their investigations. For their journals, suggest that they reflect on the concepts they learned in this chapter and what they could have added to their investigation.

Test Preparation

25. d **26.** c **27.** d **28.** a **29.** b **30.** a

Program Resources

◆ **Inquiry Skills Activity Book** Provides teaching and review of all inquiry skills
◆ **Prentice Hall Assessment System** Provides standardized test practice
◆ **Reading in the Content Area** Provides strategies to improve science reading skills
◆ **Teacher's ELL Handbook** Provides multiple strategies for English language learners

Eyes on Earth

Focus on Meteorology

This four-page feature provides students with an insider's view of the process of scientific inquiry. It introduces a young research meteorologist who studies severe storms, including hurricanes. The feature describes how he became interested in meteorology, attained his career goals, and now uses sophisticated technology to gather and analyze weather data in order to predict severe storms.

Scientific Inquiry

◆ Before students read the feature, have them preview the photos and captions on pages 644 and 645. Then ask: **What is meteorology?** *(The correct response is "the study of weather." Some students may logically think that meteorology is "the study of meteors.")* Inform students that both *meteor* and *meteorology* have the same Greek root, which means "atmosphere." Explain that weather is caused by disturbances in the atmosphere. Finally, introduce the feature by telling students that it is about a meteorologist, or scientist who studies the weather.

◆ Call students' attention to the paragraph that opens the feature, then ask: **Besides satellite launches, what are some reasons people might want to know what the weather will be in the future?** *(Responses might include: in order to make outdoor plans and plan what to wear.)* Point out that predicting severe weather is especially important because knowledge of an approaching storm often prevents loss of life and property. Add that some severe storms in the past have killed thousands of people and caused billions of dollars worth of damage. Conclude by saying that better weather prediction is one of the main goals of meteorological research.

Eyes On EARTH

At the Kennedy Space Center on the east coast of Florida, a crew prepares to launch a satellite into space. They know that a thunderstorm may be moving toward them. Should they launch the mission or delay? Before deciding, the crew contacts meteorologists for the latest weather forecast.

The Kennedy Space Center is about 100 kilometers east of the center of the state. More summer thunderstorms occur in central Florida than nearly any other area in the world. Predicting when severe storms will develop and where they will move is one of the most demanding jobs for a meteorologist. One of the best people at this job is J. Marshall Shepherd.

J. Marshall Shepherd
The son of two school principals, J. Marshall Shepherd was born in 1969 and raised in the small town of Canton, Georgia. Today he works for NASA as a research meteorologist for Mission to Planet Earth. He's an expert on the development of powerful thunderstorms. He studied meteorology at Florida State University.

TRMM
Tropical Rainfall Measuring Mission

644

Background

The Greek philosopher Aristotle is given credit for coining the term *meteorology*. His manuscript titled *Meteorologica,* written around 340 B.C., is the oldest known description of weather phenomena. One of the first people to study weather using scientific methods was Galileo. In 1593, he invented a device called a thermoscope for measuring temperature. Throughout the next three centuries, many advances in meteorological theory were made, and a number of new instruments for measuring weather factors were invented, including the barometer for measuring air pressure and the hygrometer for measuring relative humidity. However, the history of modern weather technology didn't really begin until 1949, when radar was first used to gather weather data. Then technology advanced rapidly, and by 1960 the first weather satellite had been launched.

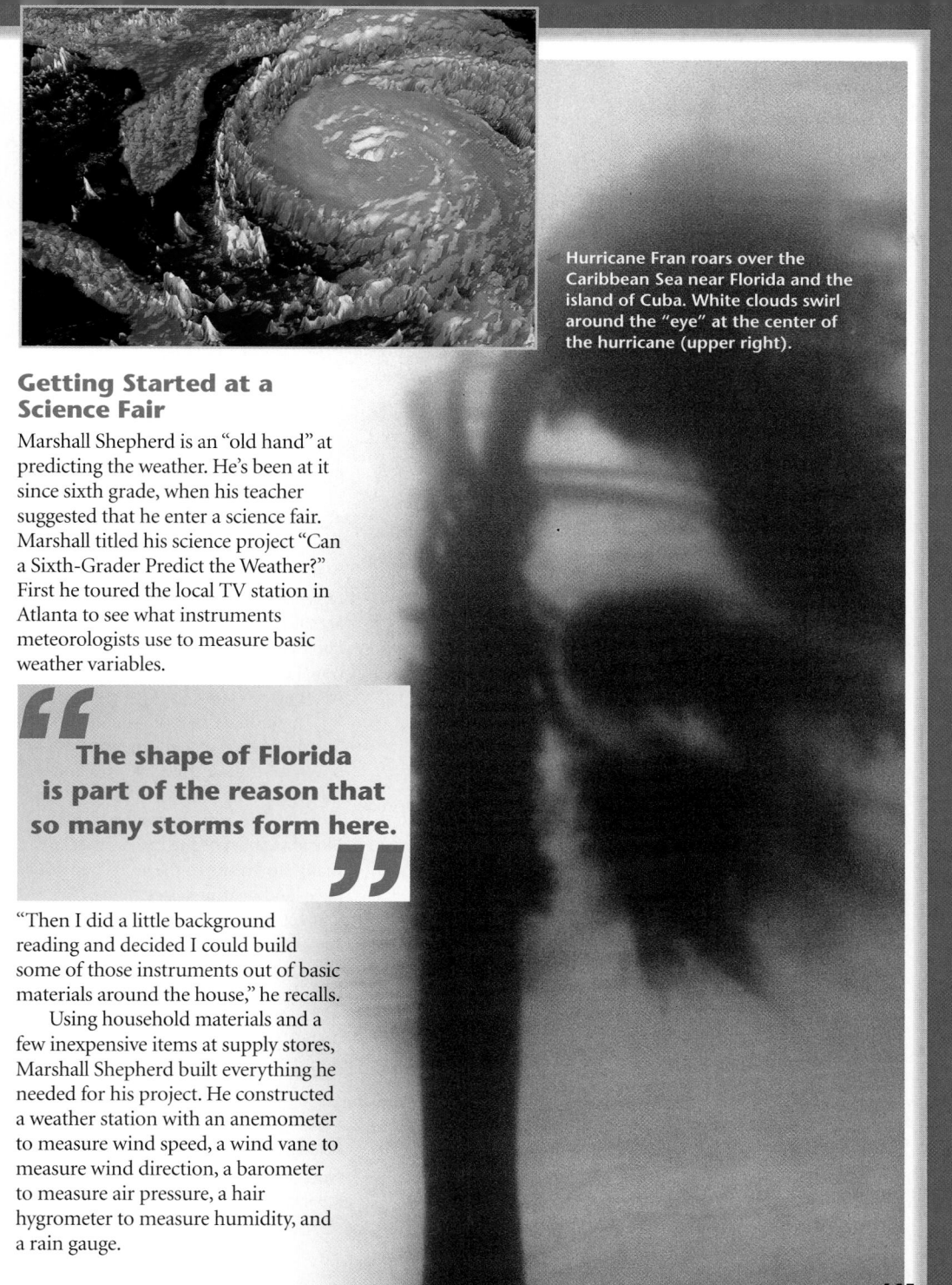

Hurricane Fran roars over the Caribbean Sea near Florida and the island of Cuba. White clouds swirl around the "eye" at the center of the hurricane (upper right).

Getting Started at a Science Fair

Marshall Shepherd is an "old hand" at predicting the weather. He's been at it since sixth grade, when his teacher suggested that he enter a science fair. Marshall titled his science project "Can a Sixth-Grader Predict the Weather?" First he toured the local TV station in Atlanta to see what instruments meteorologists use to measure basic weather variables.

> ❝ **The shape of Florida is part of the reason that so many storms form here.** ❞

"Then I did a little background reading and decided I could build some of those instruments out of basic materials around the house," he recalls.

Using household materials and a few inexpensive items at supply stores, Marshall Shepherd built everything he needed for his project. He constructed a weather station with an anemometer to measure wind speed, a wind vane to measure wind direction, a barometer to measure air pressure, a hair hygrometer to measure humidity, and a rain gauge.

645

◆ Emphasize that Marshall Shepherd's sixth-grade science fair project was the initial impetus for his interest in meteorology. Ask: **Did any of your strong interests develop in a similar way, that is, because of a single positive experience? Explain what happened.** (*Students may say, for example, that they developed an interest in cooking or horses through a 4-H project, an interest in sports through playing on an intramural team or watching the Olympic games on television, or an interest in camping through their first scout camp experience.*) **How did Shepherd's science fair experience change his life?** (*From then on, he did science projects in school and, by the end of high school, he knew that he wanted to be a research scientist at NASA, a goal he pursued and accomplished.*)

◆ Point out to students that, starting with his first science project and continuing through his present job as a NASA research meteorologist, Marshall Shepherd has been interested in collecting weather data. Use this fact to introduce students to the importance of data collection in scientific inquiry. Tell students that scientists depend on data to test and either confirm or reject hypotheses. To make this point clearer, relate the following example to the class. In 1856, an American meteorologist named William Ferrel hypothesized, on theoretical grounds alone, that winds in the Northern Hemisphere blow in a counterclockwise direction around areas of low air pressure and in a clockwise direction around areas of high air pressure. Then, just a few months later, a Dutch meteorologist named Buys Ballot collected the data on wind direction and air pressure needed to test Ferrel's hypothesis. The data confirmed the hypothesis, and it is now known as Buys Ballot's law.

Background

The goal of NASA's Mission to Planet Earth (MTPE) is to collect the data needed to study planet-wide environmental problems, such as ozone depletion, deforestation, and global warming. MTPE, in turn, includes several different projects and programs. The Upper Atmosphere Research Satellite (UARS), for example, collects data on the chemistry of the upper atmosphere. The space shuttle's Atmospheric Laboratory for Applications and Science (ATLAS) investigates how solar radiation and pollution affect the upper atmosphere. The Earth Probes program involves several specialized satellites, including the Tropical Rainfall Measuring Mission (TRMM) satellite described on page 646. In 1998, the Earth Observing System (EOS) program began launching a total of 17 spacecraft, each of which will study a different aspect of climate change.

◆ Have students examine the illustration of TRMM, a satellite that gathers the tropical rainfall data Marshall Shepherd helps analyze. Also have students read the caption under the illustration. Then contrast the TRMM satellite with a geostationary weather satellite. Explain that a geostationary satellite orbits Earth at the same speed as Earth's rotation. Because of this, it stays over the same spot on Earth each day, which is why it is called *geostationary*. TRMM, in contrast, passes over many different places on Earth each day, providing a wealth of information on rainfall. You may want to share with students the additional information about the TRMM satellite at the bottom of page 647. Emphasize that measuring tropical rainfall, as TRMM does, is crucial to understanding and predicting global climate.

◆ Encourage students to share what they may already know about hurricanes. Ask: **What is a hurricane?** *(A kind of storm that produces very high winds)* **Where do hurricanes usually occur in the United States?** *(In Florida and other southeastern states bordering on the Atlantic Ocean)* Point out that hurricanes develop over the ocean and then usually move rather slowly toward the coast. Add that it often is possible to predict in advance where a hurricane will strike land. This is important so people can prepare themselves for the storm by boarding up windows, trimming dead tree branches, and taking other steps to secure property. If necessary, they also can temporarily leave the area to prevent injury and loss of life.

◆ Remind students that Marshall Shepherd works at NASA where he contributes to Mission to Planet Earth. Share with students the additional information about Mission to Planet Earth on the bottom of page 645. Point out that Marshall Shepherd's specialty is "remote sensing." Ask: **Why is Marshall Shepherd's specialty so relevant to Mission to Planet Earth?** *(Because Mission to Planet Earth focuses on collecting and analyzing weather observations from*

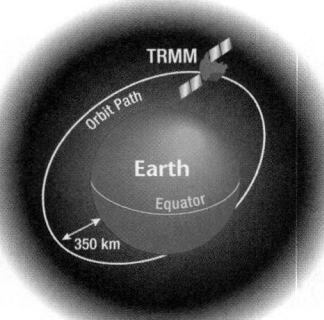

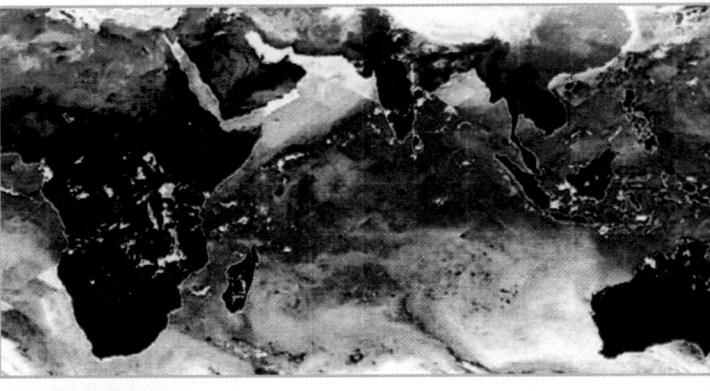

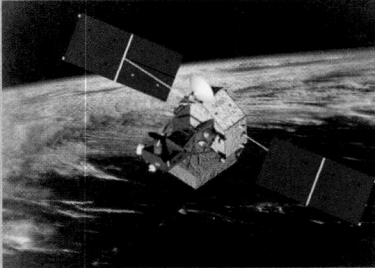

▲ TRMM, a device that records weather conditions from space, orbits Earth at an altitude of 350 kilometers. It flies over each position on Earth at a different time each day.

TRMM observatory is about the size of a small room and weighs as much as a medium-sized truck. It contains two solar panels and instruments to record weather data.

"From these basic instruments, I took weather observations around my neighborhood," he explains. "I developed a model of day-to-day weather over a six-month period and found some very interesting and accurate results." Marshall's instruments and scientific work on this project won prizes for him at local, district, and state science fairs.

"From that point on, I was involved with science projects," he recalls. By the time he graduated from high school, he had a definite goal. "One day, I planned to be a research scientist at NASA (National Aeronautics and Space Administration)," he stated.

Predicting Severe Storms

Hurricane Andrew—the most powerful hurricane ever to strike Florida—swept through Southern Florida and Louisiana in 1992. Marshall was in college at the time. "My college research paper was on hurricane tracking using radar. I actually did some work with Hurricane Andrew," he says. "That's how I got interested in tropical weather."

In graduate school, Marshall Shepherd investigated the way powerful thunderstorms form and move, especially those in central Florida. The long, narrow shape of Florida is part of the reason that so many storms form there. "When you have land heating faster than water, you get something called sea-breeze circulation," he explains. "On a typical summer day, a sea-breeze forms on both the west coast and the east coast of Florida. They tend to move toward the center. When they collide, you get intense thunderstorm development."

Designing New Instruments

Now Marshall Shepherd works at NASA, where his projects contribute to NASA's Mission to Planet Earth.

646

remote places—high in the atmosphere and space—using satellites and spacecraft)

◆ After students have read Looking Ahead, ask: **What does Marshall Shepherd plan to do after Mission to Planet Earth?** *(From the ground, he wants to conduct Earth-directed meteorological research from the international space station. He also wants "to reach out, inspire, and expose students to science.")*

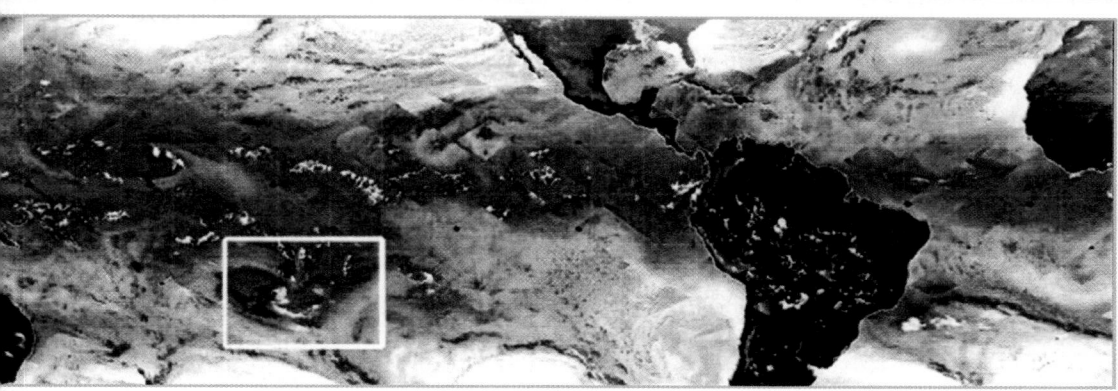

This map was generated by TRMM. The white rectangle identifies a cyclone.

This long-term program uses information from satellites, aircraft, and ground studies to explore environmental changes around the world.

Marshall Shepherd's knowledge of thunderstorms is especially valuable in interpreting data from TRMM (Tropical Rainfall Measuring Mission), a device that measures tropical and subtropical rainfall. Rainfall cycles in tropical regions affect weather throughout the world.

Marshall Shepherd's work involves both observation and calculation. As he did in sixth grade, he designs and builds instruments. But now his devices are some of the most advanced in the world. He no longer takes his instruments into a neighborhood to measure weather conditions directly. Instead, his specialty is "remote sensing"—making observations of weather conditions (rainfall, water vapor, and so on) from a distance.

After collecting data, Marshall uses a computer to analyze it. He and others have designed a computer program that uses the data to predict the development of severe storms. So

when a crew at the Kennedy Space Center must decide whether or not to launch a rocket, they rely on predictions from programs similar to ones that Marshall Shepherd has worked on.

Looking Ahead

Marshall Shepherd's personal goals go beyond Mission to Planet Earth. "With the upcoming international space station, scientists are going to have the opportunity to do research from space. My goal is to conduct Earth-directed meteorological research from the space station as well as from the ground. I'll use some of the new instruments we are currently developing." He describes another important goal back home on Earth—"to reach out, inspire, and expose students to science."

In Your Journal

Marshall Shepherd credits his success to having detailed goals. "I always write down goals, and check them off as they happen," he says. Think of an important task that you would like to accomplish over the next year. Identify the steps and note target dates you will need to meet in order to reach your goal. How do those steps help bring you closer to achieving your goal?

Background

The Tropical Rainfall Measuring Mission, or TRMM, is run by the Goddard Space Flight Center in Maryland for NASA. The TRMM satellite orbits Earth between 35°N and 35°S latitude and measures tropical and subtropical rainfall.

Why is measuring tropical rainfall so important? Tropical rainfall makes up more than two thirds of global rainfall, and it is the main heat source that drives global air

circulation. Variation in tropical rainfall can affect the weather in places thousands of kilometers away. The best known influence of tropical weather on global weather is El Niño, which students read about in Chapter 18. Despite the importance of tropical rainfall patterns, until TRMM our knowledge of tropical rainfall, especially over the oceans, was very limited.

CHAPTER 20 Living Resources

Sections	Time	Student Edition Activities	Other Activities
CHAPTER PROJECT 20 **Variety Show** p. 649	Ongoing (2–3 weeks)	Check Your Progress, pp. 655, 674 Project Wrap Up, p. 677	Chapter 20 Project Notes, pp. 648–649
1 Environmental Issues pp. 650–656 ◆ 20.1.1 Identify the main types of environmental issues. ◆ 20.1.2 Define environmental science. ◆ 20.1.3 Describe how decision makers balance different needs and concerns related to environmental issues.	2 periods/ 1 block	**Discover** How Do You Decide?, p. 650 **Sharpen Your Skills** Communicating, p. 655 **Real-World Lab: You and Your Environment** Is Paper a Renewable Resource?, p. 656	TE Building Inquiry Skills: Graphing, p. 651 TE Including All Students, p. 652 TE Science and History, p. 653
2 Forests and Fisheries pp. 657–662 ◆ 20.2.1 Describe different ways that forests can be managed to provide resources. ◆ 20.2.2 Describe different ways that fisheries can be managed to provide resources.	2 periods/ 1 block	**Discover** What Happened to the Tuna?, p. 657 **Sharpen Your Skills** Calculating, p. 660 **Science at Home,** p. 661 **Skills Lab: Interpreting Data** Tree Cookie Tales, p. 662	TE Inquiry Challenge, p. 659 TE Real-Life Learning, p. 660 LM 20, "Managing Fisheries"
3 Biodiversity pp. 663–671 ◆ 20.3.1 Identify the factors that affect biodiversity. ◆ 20.3.2 Explain the value of biodiversity. ◆ 20.3.3 Name some human activities that threaten biodiversity. ◆ 20.3.4 List some ways that biodiversity can be protected.	1 period/ $\frac{1}{2}$ block	**Discover** How Much Variety Is There?, p. 663 **Science at Home,** p. 671	TE Building Inquiry Skills: Observing, pp. 664, 673; Communicating, pp. 662, 670; Making Models, p. 667 TE Demonstration, pp. 665, 670 TE Addressing Naive Conceptions, p. 666 TE Inquiry Challenge, p. 669 TE Real-Life Learning, p. 670
4 *INTEGRATING HEALTH* **The Search for New Medicines** pp. 672–674 ◆ 20.4.1 Explain why many rain forest plants are sources of medicines.	1 period/ $\frac{1}{2}$ block	**Discover** How Are Plant Chemicals Separated?, p. 672	TE Real-Life Learning, p. 673 TE Building Inquiry Skills: Observing, p. 673
Study Guide/Assessment pp. 675–677	1 period/ $\frac{1}{2}$ block		ISAB Provides teaching and review of all inquiry skills

 For Standard or Block Schedule The Resource Pro® CD-ROM gives you maximum flexibility for planning your instruction for any type of schedule. Resource Pro® contains Planning Express®, an advanced scheduling program, as well as the entire contents of the Teaching Resources and the Computer Test Bank.

Key: **CTB** Computer Test Bank
CT Chapter Tests
ELL Teacher's ELL Handbook

CHAPTER PLANNING GUIDE

Program Resources	Assessment Strategies	Media and Technology
UR Chapter 20 Project Teacher Notes, pp. 2–3 **UR** Chapter 20 Project Overview and Worksheets, pp. 4–7	**TE** Check Your Progress, pp. 655, 674 **TE** Performance Assessment: Chapter 20 Project Wrap Up, p. 677 **UR** Chapter 20 Project Scoring Rubric, p. 8	Science Explorer Internet Site Audio CDs, Section Summaries
UR 20-1 Lesson Plan, p. 9 **UR** 20-1 Section Summary, p. 10 **UR** 20-1 Review and Reinforce, p. 11 **UR** 20-1 Enrich, p. 12 **UR** Real-World Lab blackline masters, pp. 25–27	**SE** Section 1 Review, p. 655 **SE** Analyze and Conclude, p. 656 **TE** Ongoing Assessment, pp. 651, 653 **TE** Performance Assessment, p. 655	Concept Videotape Library, *Adventures, Tape 5,* "Can We Still Get What We Need?" Lab Activity Videotape, *Tape 5*
UR 20-2 Lesson Plan, p. 13 **UR** 20-2 Section Summary, p. 14 **UR** 20-2 Review and Reinforce, p. 15 **UR** 20-2 Enrich, p. 16 **UR** Skills Lab blackline masters, pp. 28–29	**SE** Section 2 Review, p. 661 **SE** Analyze and Conclude, p. 662 **TE** Ongoing Assessment, p. 659 **TE** Performance Assessment, p. 663	Lab Activity Videotape, *Tape 5* Transparency 81, "Logging Methods"
UR 20-3 Lesson Plan, p. 17 **UR** 20-3 Section Summary, p. 18 **UR** 20-3 Review and Reinforce, p. 19 **UR** 20-3 Enrich, p. 20	**SE** Section 3 Review, p. 671 **TE** Ongoing Assessment, pp. 665, 667, 669 **TE** Performance Assessment, p. 671	Concept Videotape Library, *Adventures, Tape 5,* "Can We Save the Tigers?"; "Extinction"; "It's All Happening at the Zoo" Presentation Pro, "Biodiversity"
UR 20-4 Lesson Plan, p. 21 **UR** 20-4 Section Summary, p. 22 **UR** 20-4 Review and Reinforce, p. 23 **UR** 20-4 Enrich, p. 24	**SE** Section 4 Review, p. 674 **TE** Ongoing Assessment, p. 673 **TE** Performance Assessment, p. 675	Concept Videotape Library, *Adventures, Tape 5,* "A Question of Balance"
GRSW Provides worksheets to promote student comprehension of content **RCA** Provides strategies to improve science reading skills **ELL** Provides multiple strategies for English language learners	**SE** Study Guide/Assessment, pp. 676–677 **PA** Performance Assessment, pp. 61–63 **CT** Chapter 20 Test, pp. 79–82 **CTB** Chapter 20 Test **PHAS** Provides standardized test preparation	Computer Test Bank, Chapter 20 Test

GRSW Guided Reading and Study Workbook
ISAB Inquiry Skills Activity Book
LM Laboratory Manual

PA Performance Assessment
PHAS Prentice Hall Assessment System
PLM Probeware Lab Manual

RCA Reading in the Content Area
SE Student Edition

TE Teacher's Edition
UR Unit Resources

Meeting the National Science Education Standards and AAAS Benchmarks

National Science Education Standards	Benchmarks for Science Literacy	Unifying Themes

Science as Inquiry (Content Standard A)
◆ **Design and conduct an investigation** Students observe diversity of organisms. (*Chapter Project*)
◆ **Develop descriptions, explanations, predictions, and models using evidence** Students model paper recycling. Students observe a tree cross section to draw conclusions about how the tree grew. (*Real-World Lab; Skills Lab*)

Life Science (Content Standard C)
◆ **Diversity and adaptions of organisms** The number of different species in an area is called biodiversity. Plants in many ecosystems produce chemicals that protect them. (*Chapter Project; Sections 3, 4*)

Science in Personal and Social Perspectives (Content Standard F)
◆ **Populations, resources, and environments** Human activities can threaten biodiversity. (*Section 3*)
◆ **Science and technology in society** Environmental issues include resource management, population growth, and pollution. (*Section 1*)

History and Nature of Science (Content Standard G)
◆ **History of science** Certain individuals have influenced the viewpoints of others toward the environment. (*Science & History*)

1B Scientific Inquiry Students survey a plot of land to observe the diversity of organisms, model paper recycling, and observe a tree cross section to draw conclusions about the conditions in which the tree grew. (*Chapter Project; Real-World Lab; Skills Lab*)
1C The Scientific Enterprise Certain individuals have influenced the viewpoints of many others toward environmental issues. (*Science & History*)
3A Technology and Society Students model the process of recycling paper. Some chemicals rainforest plants produce to protect their leaves and bark can also be used to fight human diseases. (*Real-World Lab; Section 4*)
3C Issues in Technology The three main types of environmental issues are resource management, population growth, and pollution. Some methods of logging and fishing are harmful to the environment. Human activities can threaten biodiversity. (*Sections 1, 2, 3*)
4B The Earth Forests and fisheries are renewable resources if managed properly. (*Section 2*)
5A Diversity of Life The number of different species in an area is called biodiversity. Many plants produce chemicals that protect them from predators, parasites, and disease. (*Chapter Project; Sections 3, 4*)

◆ **Evolution** Extinction is the disappearance of all members of a species from Earth. (*Section 3*)
◆ **Modeling** Students model paper recycling. (*Real-World Lab*)
◆ **Patterns of Change** Any change to the environment that has a negative effect on the environment is called pollution. If fish are caught at a faster rate than they can breed, the population of a fishery decreases. (*Sections 1, 2*)
◆ **Scale and Structure** Each pair of light and dark rings in a tree cross section represents one year's growth. (*Skills Lab*)
◆ **Stability** Managing forests and fisheries helps conserve these living resources for the future. (*Section 2*)
◆ **Systems and Interactions** Environmental science is the study of the natural processes that occur in the environment and how humans can affect them. Factors that affect biodiversity in an ecosystem include area, climate, and diversity of niches. Some plants produce chemicals that protect them from predators, parasites, and diseases. (*Sections 1, 3, 4*)
◆ **Unity and Diversity** The three main types of environmental issues are resource management, population growth, and pollution. (*Section 1*)

Take It to the Net

The **www.phschool.com** Web site provides you with multiple opportunities to incorporate the internet into your instruction. Go to **www.phschool.com** and click on the Science icon. Then select Science Explorer Integrated.

- Have students use the chapter Self-Test to get instant feedback.
- Hot Links and Reference Links provide opportunities for online research.

Internet Activities provide opportunities for students to review, extend, or assess a concept from the chapter.

STAY CURRENT with **SCIENCE NEWS** ®

Find out the latest research and information about natural resources and pollution at: **www.phschool.com**

ACTIVITY	Time *(minutes)*	Materials *Quantities for one work group*	Skills
Section 1			
Discover, p. 650	15	No special materials are required.	Forming Operational Definitions
Sharpen Your Skills, p. 655	20	No special materials are required.	Communicating
Real-World Lab, p. 656	15; 40; 10	**Consumable** newspaper, water, plastic wrap **Nonconsumable** microscope, microscope slide, eggbeater, square pan, screen, heavy book, mixing bowl	Observing, Designing Experiments
Section 2			
Discover, p. 657	15	**Consumable** graph paper **Nonconsumable** ruler, pencil	Inferring
Sharpen Your Skills, p. 660	15	**Nonconsumable** calculator	Calculating
Science at Home, p. 661	home	No special materials are required.	Classifying
Skills Lab, p. 662	40	**Nonconsumable** tree cookie (tree cross section), metric ruler, hand lens, colored pencils, calculator (optional)	Observing, Measuring, Drawing Conclusions
Section 3			
Discover, p. 663	20	**Nonconsumable** two different seed mixtures, two cups, paper plate	Inferring
Science at Home, p. 671	home	**Nonconsumable** map of community or state	Communicating
Section 4			
Discover, p. 672	15	**Consumable** strip of filter paper, water, tape **Nonconsumable** black marking pen, clear plastic cup, pencil	Observing

A list of all materials required for the Student Edition activities can be found beginning on page T23. You can obtain information about ordering materials by calling 1-800-848-9500 or by accessing the Science Explorer Internet site at: **www.phschool.com**

Variety Show

The Chapter 20 Project is designed to develop students' appreciation for the rich diversity of living things that can be found in even a very small plot of land. The project also provides an opportunity for students to apply methods and skills that are used by field biologists.

Purpose After marking study plots of land, students will observe their plots regularly and record observations and data in a notebook. To conclude the project, students will communicate their findings in a class presentation.

Skills Focus After completing the Chapter 20 Project, students will be able to

◆ observe, compare and contrast, and classify organisms;
◆ infer relationships among organisms and between organisms and the abiotic factors in their environment;
◆ create a data table for recording observations;
◆ communicate observations and conclusions to others.

Project Time Line The Chapter 20 Project requires two to three weeks to complete. Each small group of students will begin by staking out a 1.5-by-1.5 meter plot of land and preparing a notebook for recording observations, including notes and drawings of the organisms observed, and the date, time, air temperature, and weather conditions during each observation. The major portion of the project involves making regular observations and recording data. During this time, students can use field guides to identify organisms. At the conclusion of the observation period, each group will prepare a class presentation that may include support materials such as photographs, drawings, videos, or computer displays.

Possible Materials

◆ To mark the plot, each group will need a meter stick or metric tape measure, four small stakes, a hammer, surveyor's tape or sturdy string, and a directional compass.
◆ When students observe their plots, each group will need a thermometer, hand lenses, rulers, and trowels.

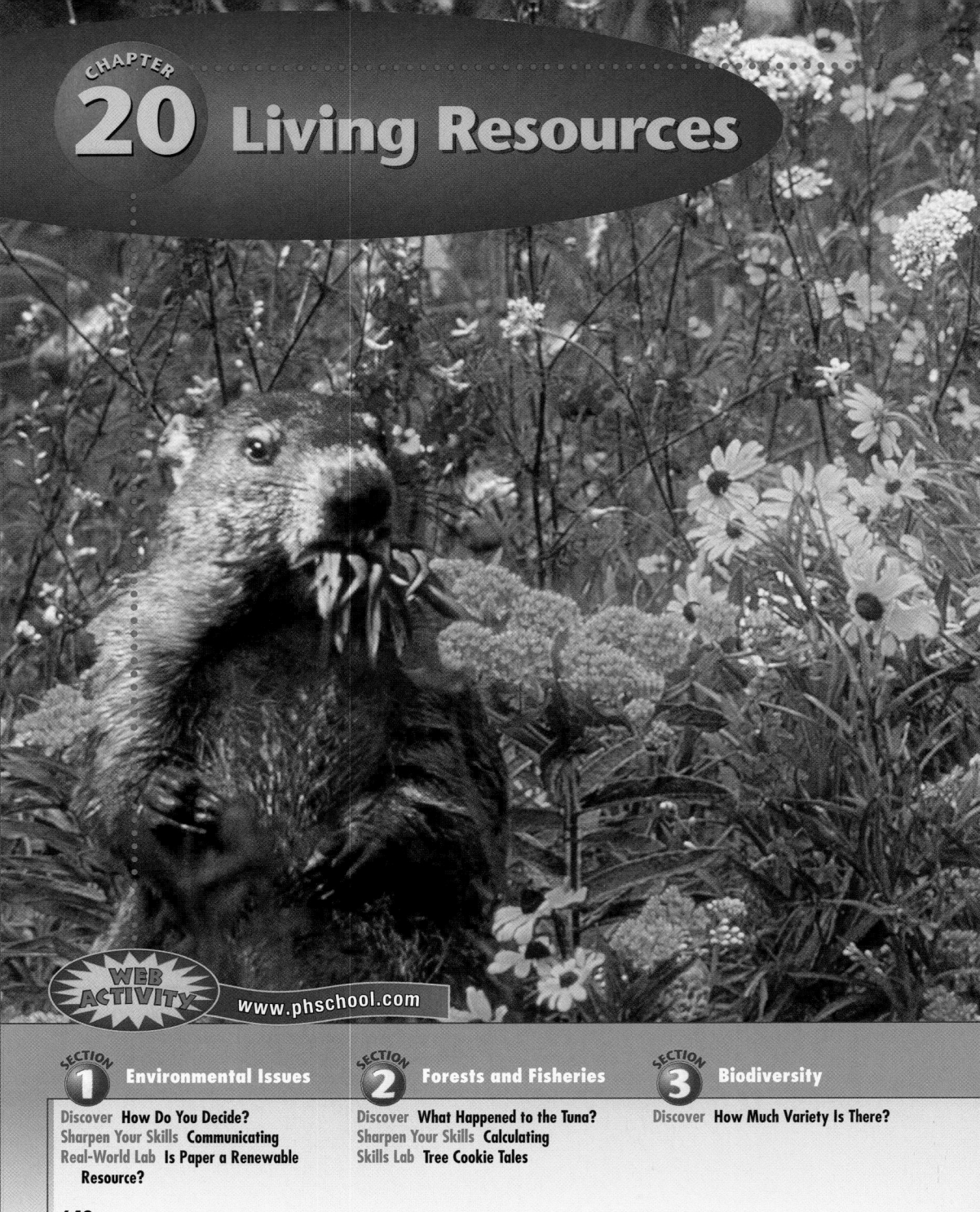

CHAPTER 20 Living Resources

WEB ACTIVITY   www.phschool.com

SECTION 1 Environmental Issues
Discover **How Do You Decide?**
Sharpen Your Skills **Communicating**
Real-World Lab **Is Paper a Renewable Resource?**

SECTION 2 Forests and Fisheries
Discover **What Happened to the Tuna?**
Sharpen Your Skills **Calculating**
Skills Lab **Tree Cookie Tales**

SECTION 3 Biodiversity
Discover **How Much Variety Is There?**

648

◆ Provide a variety of field guides so students can research the names and classification of any unfamiliar organisms they observe. A field guide to animal tracks will also be helpful for students who find trace evidence of organisms that have visited the plot.
◆ When students are ready to prepare their class presentations, provide art supplies and audiovisual equipment such as cameras and videocassette recorders, if available.

Advance Preparation Before introducing the Chapter 20 Project, survey the grounds around your school so that you can guide students to areas where they are likely to find a good variety of organisms. If the school grounds are not appropriate, locate a nearby field, park, vacant lot, or other natural area to which you can take the class during school hours. Obtain permission to use the land, if necessary.

Launching the Project Invite students to read the project description on page 649. Then guide a class brainstorming session about nearby areas that might be good for setting up the study plots. Share what you know about

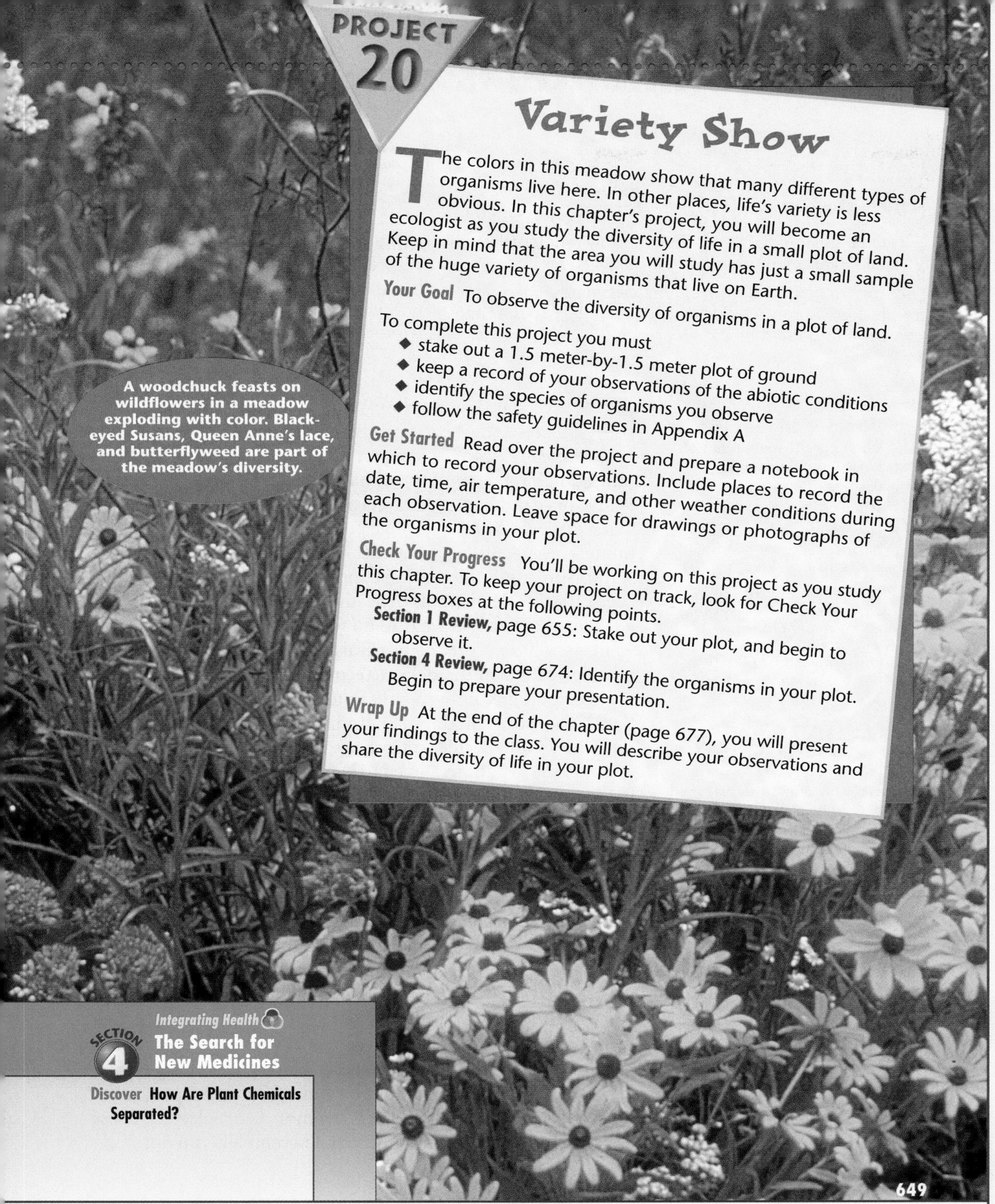

Variety Show

The colors in this meadow show that many different types of organisms live here. In other places, life's variety is less obvious. In this chapter's project, you will become an ecologist as you study the diversity of life in a small plot of land. Keep in mind that the area you will study has just a small sample of the huge variety of organisms that live on Earth.

Your Goal To observe the diversity of organisms in a plot of land.

To complete this project you must
◆ stake out a 1.5 meter-by-1.5 meter plot of ground
◆ keep a record of your observations of the abiotic conditions
◆ identify the species of organisms you observe
◆ follow the safety guidelines in Appendix A

Get Started Read over the project and prepare a notebook in which to record your observations. Include places to record the date, time, air temperature, and other weather conditions during each observation. Leave space for drawings or photographs of the organisms in your plot.

Check Your Progress You'll be working on this project as you study this chapter. To keep your project on track, look for Check Your Progress boxes at the following points.
Section 1 Review, page 655: Stake out your plot, and begin to observe it.
Section 4 Review, page 674: Identify the organisms in your plot. Begin to prepare your presentation.

Wrap Up At the end of the chapter (page 677), you will present your findings to the class. You will describe your observations and share the diversity of life in your plot.

A woodchuck feasts on wildflowers in a meadow exploding with color. Black-eyed Susans, Queen Anne's lace, and butterflyweed are part of the meadow's diversity.

SECTION 4 *Integrating Health*
The Search for New Medicines
Discover How Are Plant Chemicals Separated?

649

Program Resources

◆ **Unit 6 Resources** Chapter 20 Project Teacher Notes, pp. 2–3; Project Overview and Worksheets, pp. 4–7; Project Scoring Rubric, p. 8

Media and Technology

 Audio CDs Section Summaries

WEB ACTIVITY www.phschool.com

You will find an Internet activity, chapter self-tests for students, and links to other chapter topics at this site.

possible areas. Help students agree on appropriate areas. Suggest that students may select an area near their homes where they can carry out observations.

Distribute Chapter 20 Project Overview on pages 4–5 in Unit 6 Resources. Have students review the project rules and procedures. Encourage students' questions. Clarify whether students will be given class time for observing the plots or they must carry out the observations on their own time.

Divide the class into groups of four to six students each. Explain that each group's members may divide the project responsibilities among themselves. However, every member should help plan the notebook, stake out the plot, make and record observations, and develop the group's presentation and be prepared to answer questions. You may also wish to offer the option for students to work alone near their homes if space in the schoolyard is an issue.

To get students started, allow time for groups to meet and begin planning the project notebook. Distribute Worksheet 1, which provides instructions and a grid for making a scale drawing of the study plot. At the end of Section 1, distribute Worksheet 2, which provides guidance for recording information about the organisms that students observe.

Additional information on guiding the project is provided in Chapter 20 Project Teacher Notes on pages 2–3 in Unit 6 Resources.

Objectives

After completing the lesson, students will be able to
- identify the main types of environmental issues;
- define environmental science;
- describe how decision makers balance different needs and concerns related to environmental issues.

Key Terms renewable resources, nonrenewable resources, pollution, development viewpoint, preservation viewpoint, conservation viewpoint

1 Engage/Explore

Activating Prior Knowledge

Ask students: **What is an "issue"?** *(Students' responses should include the idea of a problem or question on which people have different viewpoints.)* **What are some examples of issues that you've heard about?** *(Sample answers: Should a run-down historic building in town be restored or demolished? Should owners of beachfront property be allowed to restrict public access to beaches? Should the federal government fund daycare facilities?)*

·······DISCOVER·······

Skills Focus forming operational definitions ⚡ACTIVITY⚡
Time 15 minutes
Tips As students identify general issues such as "air pollution," encourage them to think of specific, *debatable* questions such as "Should car manufacturers be forced to build more efficient engines so our air is cleaner?"
Expected Outcome Decisions regarding the most important issue will vary.
Think It Over Students' definitions will vary but should include the idea of environment-related questions or problems on which people have different viewpoints.

SECTION 1 Environmental Issues

DISCOVER ·································ACTIVITY

How Do You Decide?

1. On a sheet of paper, list the three environmental issues you think are most important.

2. Form a group with three other classmates. Share your lists. As a group decide which one of the issues is the most important.

Think It Over
Forming Operational Definitions
Based on your group's discussion, how would you define the term *environmental issue?*

GUIDE FOR READING

- **What are the main types of environmental issues?**
- **What is environmental science?**
- **How do decision makers balance different needs and concerns?**

Reading Tip Before you read, make a list of ways that humans depend on the environment. As you read, add examples from the text.

Figure 1 This leopard seal's habitat could be affected if oil drilling is allowed in Antarctica. This tradeoff is an example of an environmental issue.

650

Here's a puzzle for you: What is bigger than the United States and Mexico combined; is covered with two kilometers of ice; is a source of oil, coal, and iron; and is a unique habitat for many animals? The answer is Antarctica. People once thought of Antarctica as a useless, icy wasteland. But when explorers told of its huge populations of seals and whales, hunters began going to Antarctica. Then scientists set up research stations to study the unique conditions there. They soon discovered valuable minerals beneath the thick ice.

Now the puzzle is what to do with Antarctica. Many people want its rich deposits of minerals and oil. Others worry that mining will harm the delicate ecosystems there. Some people propose building hotels, parks, and ski resorts. But others feel that Antarctica should remain undisturbed. It is not even obvious who should decide Antarctica's fate.

In 1998, 26 nations agreed to ban mining and oil exploration in Antarctica for at least 50 years. As resources become more scarce elsewhere in the world, the debate will surely continue. What is the best use of Antarctica?

Types of Environmental Issues

People have always used Earth's resources. But as the human population has grown, so has its effect on the environment. People compete with each other and with other living things for Earth's limited resources. Disposing of wastes created by people can change ecosystems. And while people are continuing to take resources from the environment, many resources cannot be replaced. These resources could eventually run out.

Figure 2 Cherries are a renewable resource. After they are harvested, new cherries will grow in their place. In contrast, the aluminum and iron used to make these kitchen tools are nonrenewable resources.

The three main types of environmental issues are resource use, population growth, and pollution. These issues are all connected, making them very difficult to solve.

Resource Use Anything in the environment that is used by people is a natural resource. Some natural resources, called **renewable resources,** are naturally replaced in a relatively short time. Renewable resources include sunlight, wind, and trees. But it is possible to use up some renewable resources. For example, if people cut down trees faster than they can grow back, the supply of this resource will decrease.

Natural resources that are not replaced as they are used are called **nonrenewable resources.** Most nonrenewable resources, such as coal and oil, exist in a limited supply. As nonrenewable resources are used, the supply may eventually be depleted.

Population Growth Figure 3 shows how the human population has changed in the last 3,000 years. You can see that the population grew very slowly until about A.D. 1650. Around that time, improvements in medicine, agriculture, and sanitation enabled people to live longer. The death rate decreased. But as the population has continued to grow, the demand for resources has also grown.

Pollution Any change to the environment that has a negative effect on living things is called **pollution.** Pollution is an issue because it is often the result of an activity that benefits humans. For example, generating electricity by burning coal can result in air pollution. Some pesticides used to kill insects that eat crops are harmful to other animals.

☑ *Checkpoint* *What is a natural resource?*

Figure 3 If two's company, six billion is certainly a crowd! The human population has grown rapidly in the last few centuries. *Calculating How much has the population grown since 1650?*

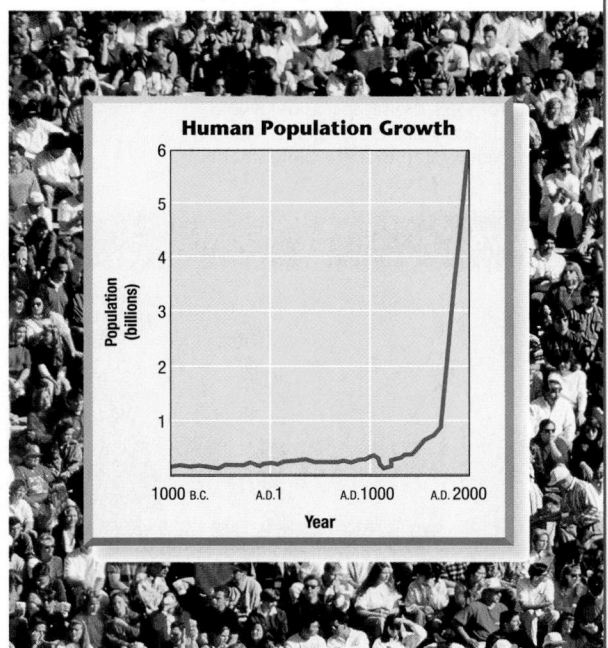

Human Population Growth

(graph: Population (billions) on y-axis from 0 to 6; Year on x-axis from 1000 B.C., A.D.1, A.D.1000, A.D.2000)

Answers to Self-Assessment
Caption Question
Figure 3 By more than 5 million people (from about 750 thousand to about 6 million)
☑ *Checkpoint*
A natural resource is anything in the environment that is used by people.

---

2 *Facilitate*

Types of Environmental Issues

Building Inquiry Skills: Graphing

Materials *graph paper, ruler, pencil, world map*
Time 15 minutes

ACTIVITY

Point out that Figure 3 shows the entire world population and that growth rates and population sizes vary among different regions and countries of the world. Give students the current populations of several countries listed below, and have each student make a bar graph to compare the population sizes. Then have students use their graphs to answer the following questions: **Which country has the largest population?** *(China)* **The next largest?** *(India)* **How many times larger than Japan's population is the U.S. population?** *(About twice as large)* Have students compare the United States' and Japan's land areas on a world map, and ask: **Which country has a higher population density?** *(Japan; if needed, help students recall the term* population density *from Chapter 1.)* **learning modality: logical/mathematical**

1998 Population of Selected Countries	
Brazil	165,200,000
China	1,255,100,000
Great Britain	58,200,000
India	975,800,000
Indonesia	207,400,000
Japan	125,900,000
Mexico	95,800,000
Nigeria	121,800,000
Russia	147,200,000
United States	270,000,000

Ongoing Assessment

Writing Have each student explain why the world's human population has grown so dramatically in the past 350 years.

Approaches to Environmental Issues

Real-Life Learning

Ask students: **What things that you do now or could start doing would help protect the environment if a lot of other people did them, too?** *(Accept all reasonable responses, such as recycling soft-drink cans instead of throwing them in the trash or putting on a sweater instead of turning up the heat at home.)* As students suggest actions, list each one on the board and ask: **How does this help solve environmental problems?** *(Sample answers: Recycling cans reduces our need to mine more aluminum, which is a nonrenewable resource. Putting on a sweater instead of turning up the heat reduces our use of heating fuel, another nonrenewable resource, and the air pollution that is released when fuels are burned.)* **learning modality: logical/mathematical**

Including All Students

Materials *current newspapers and magazines, scissors, large sheet of construction paper, tape or glue, markers*

ACTIVITY

Time *20–40 minutes*

For students who need additional challenges, provide a variety of magazines and local and national newspapers. Let students work in groups of two or three to look through the sources and find articles about environmental issues in their community, state, or region. Suggest that each group choose one issue to use as the subject of a poster that summarizes the problem in the students' own words, briefly describes different viewpoints on or proposed solutions to the problem, and includes a photograph, graph, or other visual related to the issue. Display the completed posters in the classroom. Allow time for students to review one another's posters and discuss their ideas and views about the issues. **learning modality: verbal**

Approaches to Environmental Issues

Dealing with environmental issues means making choices. These choices can be made at personal, local, national, or global levels. Whether to ride in a car, take a bus, or ride your bicycle to the mall is an example of a personal choice. Whether to build a land-fill or an incinerator for disposing of a town's wastes is a local choice. Whether the United States should allow oil drilling in a wildlife refuge is a national choice. How to protect Earth's atmosphere is a global choice.

Choices that seem personal are often part of much larger issues. Choices of what you eat, what you wear, and how you travel all affect the environment in a small way. When the choices made by millions of people are added together, each person's actions can make a difference.

SCIENCE & History

Making a Difference

Can one individual change the way people think? The leaders featured in this time line have influenced the way that many people think about environmental issues.

1892
California writer John Muir founds the Sierra Club. The group promotes the setting aside of wild areas as national parks. Muir's actions lead to the establishment of Yosemite National Park.

1905
Forestry scientist Gifford Pinchot is appointed the first director of the United States Forest Service. His goal is to manage forests scientifically to meet current and future lumber needs.

1875 **1900** **1925**

1903
President Theodore Roosevelt establishes the first National Wildlife Refuge on Pelican Island, Florida, to protect the brown pelican.

Theodore Roosevelt (left) and John Muir (right)

Background

History of Science Students could also research these people for *In Your Journal.*

◆ **Jacques Cousteau** Through his many TV films, marine explorer Cousteau educated millions about ocean life and environmental damage caused by humans.

◆ **Dian Fossey** A zoologist known for her field studies of the rare mountain gorilla in east-central Africa, Fossey urged the preservation of this endangered species.

◆ **Jane Goodall** This animal behaviorist's multigenerational studies discovered meat eating and tool use among wild chimpanzees and increased our knowledge of the ecology of nonhuman primates.

◆ **Chico Mendes** Brazilian rubber tapper Mendes fought to prevent the destruction of rain forests and to establish extractive reserves where products could be harvested without causing ecological damage.

The first step in making environmental decisions is to understand how humans interact with the environment. **Environmental science is the study of the natural processes that occur in the environment and how humans can affect them.**

When people make decisions about environmental issues, the information provided by environmental scientists is a starting point. The next step is to decide what to do with the information. But environmental decisions also involve discussions of values, not just facts and figures. Environmental decisions usually require considering many different points of view. Most of these viewpoints fall into one of these three categories: development, preservation, or conservation.

☑ *Checkpoint* *What is an example of a local choice about an environmental issue?*

In Your Journal

Find out more about one of the people featured in this time line. Write a short biography of the person's life explaining how he or she became involved in environmental issues. What obstacles did the person overcome to accomplish his or her goal?

1949

Naturalist Aldo Leopold publishes *A Sand County Almanac.* This classic book links wildlife management to the science of ecology.

1969

At the age of 79, journalist Marjory Stoneman Douglas founds Friends of the Everglades. This grassroots organization is dedicated to preserving the unique Florida ecosystem. She continues to work for the Everglades until her death in 1998.

1950 **1975** **2000**

1962

Biologist Rachel Carson writes *Silent Spring*, which describes the harmful effects of pesticides on the environment. The book raises awareness of how human activities can affect the environment.

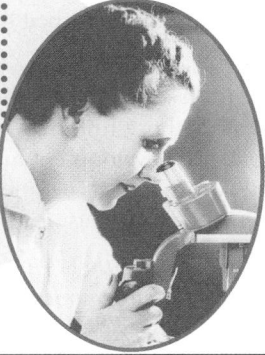

1977

Biologist Wangari Maathai founds the Green Belt Movement. This organization encourages restoring forests in Kenya and other African nations.

Chapter 20 **653**

Answers to Self-Assessment

☑ *Checkpoint*

Answers will vary. *Sample answer:* Whether to build a landfill or an incinerator for disposing of a town's wastes

Approaches to Environmental Issues, continued

Building Inquiry Skills: Classifying

After students have read about development, preservation, and conservation viewpoints, direct their attention to an environmental issue in the text or from your local area, and ask: **What would be the development viewpoint on this issue?** (*Wildlife refuge example: We need to use all possible new sources of oil in the United States.*) **The preservation viewpoint?** (*Wildlife refuges must be kept natural and unspoiled by human activity.*) **The conservation viewpoint?** (*We need to find ways to use less oil in this country so we don't have to risk damaging natural areas to get it.*) Continue the same procedure using several other issues as examples.
learning modality: logical/ mathematical

Weighing Costs and Benefits

Sharpen your Skills

Communicating

Time 20 minutes
Tips The three students in each group should represent the development, preservation, and conservation viewpoints.
Expected Outcome *Similarities:* All three viewpoints recognize that Antarctica has valuable resources and unique conditions. *Differences:* The development viewpoint gives priority to people's need for Antarctica's rich supply of oil and mineral resources; the preservation viewpoint gives priority to the needs of the organisms that live in Antarctica; the conservation viewpoint tries to strike a balance between the other two viewpoints.
Extend Let each group choose a local issue and create a compare/contrast table from the same three viewpoints.
learning modality: verbal

Economic value
The hills are a source of resources such as lumber and minerals.

Recreational value
The river is a good place to canoe and raft. Hikers can enjoy the surrounding hills.

Scenic value
The river valley is a beautiful and peaceful area.

Ecological value
The river valley is home to many plants, animals, and other organisms.

Health value
The river is a source of clean drinking water.

Figure 4 The environment is valued for many different reasons. *Applying Concepts In what other ways might this area be valuable?*

Development The belief that humans should be able to freely use and benefit from all of Earth's resources is referred to as the **development viewpoint.** This viewpoint considers the environment in terms of economics. Economics involves business, money, and jobs. According to the development viewpoint, the most valuable parts of the environment are those resources that are most useful to human beings.

Preservation The belief that all parts of the environment are equally important, no matter how useful they are to humans, is the **preservation viewpoint.** This viewpoint considers humans to be the caretakers of nature. Preservationists feel that Earth and its resources should be a source of beauty, comfort, and recreation. The preservation viewpoint is that living things and ecosystems should not be disturbed for the benefit of people.

Conservation The **conservation viewpoint** is the belief that people should use resources from the environment as long as they do not destroy those resources. Conservationists feel that people must balance development and preservation. The conservation viewpoint is that people should manage Earth's resources for the future, not just for today.

☑ *Checkpoint* What are three viewpoints about how humans should interact with the environment?

Background

History of Science Should oil exploration be allowed in the Arctic National Wildlife Refuge? Visitors to this vast preserve of boreal forest and tundra in northeastern Alaska can see wildlife ranging from polar bears and musk oxen to arctic foxes and caribou. Opponents of exploration worry that oil exploration and production could damage the refuge's fragile ecosystems. Proponents argue that the United States needs to produce more oil domestically, rather than import it from other countries, to meet the nation's energy needs. In 1995, the Department of the Interior issued a study concluding that oil drilling would adversely affect the refuge's ecosystems. Nonetheless, Congress passed a bill to permit oil exploration there. President Clinton vetoed that measure, but the controversy over the refuge continues.

Weighing Costs and Benefits

Lawmakers work with many different government agencies to make environmental decisions. Together they must consider the needs and concerns of people with many different viewpoints. **To help balance these different opinions, decision makers weigh the costs and benefits of a proposal.**

Costs and benefits are often economic. Will a proposal provide jobs? Will it cost too much money? But costs and benefits are not only measured in terms of money. For example, building an incinerator might reduce the beauty of a natural landscape (a scenic cost). But the incinerator might be safer than an existing open dump site (a health benefit). It is also important to consider short-term and long-term effects. A proposal's short-term costs might be outweighed by its long-term benefits.

Consider the costs and benefits of drilling for oil in Antarctica. Drilling for oil would have many costs. It would be very expensive to set up a drilling operation in such a cold and distant place. Transporting the oil would be difficult and costly. An oil spill in the seas around Antarctica could harm the fish, penguins, and seals there.

On the other hand, there would be many benefits to drilling in Antarctica. A new supply of oil would provide fuel for heat, electricity, and transportation. The plan would create many new jobs. There would be a greater opportunity to study Antarctica's ecosystems. Do the benefits of drilling outweigh the costs? This is the kind of question lawmakers ask when they make environmental decisions.

Sharpen your Skills

Communicating
ACTIVITY

Form a group with two other students. Each person will be assigned a different viewpoint toward the environment. Hold a panel discussion in which each person proposes how the continent of Antarctica should be used. What similarities and differences are there among your responses?

Section 1 Review

1. List the three main types of environmental issues.
2. Define environmental science.
3. What is one way to balance different viewpoints on an environmental issue?
4. How has the growth of the human population affected the environment?
5. List three costs and three benefits of drilling for oil on Antarctica.
6. **Thinking Critically Comparing and Contrasting** Compare renewable and nonrenewable resources. Give an example of each type of resource.

Check Your Progress
CHAPTER PROJECT 20

Stake out a square plot measuring 1.5 meters on each side. Record the date, time, temperature, and weather. Observe the organisms in your plot, and record them with notes and drawings. Include enough detail so that you can identify any unfamiliar organisms later. (*Hint:* Also note evidence such as feathers or footprints that shows that other organisms may have visited the plot.)

Program Resources

◆ **Unit 6 Resources** 20-1 Review and Reinforce, p. 11; 20-1 Enrich, p. 12

Answers to Self-Assessment

Caption Question

Figure 4 Accept all reasonable responses. *Sample answer:* The valley might be the source of fish or other animals used for food.

☑ *Checkpoint*

The three viewpoints are development, preservation, and conservation.

3 Assess

Section 1 Review Answers

1. Resource management, population growth, pollution
2. The study of natural processes that occur in the environment and how humans can affect those processes
3. Weigh the costs and benefits of a proposal
4. As the population has grown, people have used more and more of Earth's resources. They have also produced more wastes.
5. *Costs:* Setting up drilling operations and transporting the oil would be difficult and expensive. Oil spills could damage ecosystems. *Benefits:* New oil supplies would provide fuel for heating, generating electricity, and transportation. Drilling for and transporting the oil would provide new jobs. Setting up oil operations in Antarctica would allow people to study its ecosystems and plan ways to protect its wildlife.
6. Renewable resources are those that are replaced naturally within a fairly short time as they are used, such as trees, sunlight, and wind. Nonrenewable resources are those that are not replaced within a short time as they are used, such

Check Your Progress
CHAPTER PROJECT 20

If students' plots are grouped in the same area, make sure they leave enough space between the plots so they can move around without walking on another group's plot. In this and subsequent observation sessions, encourage students to note any animal behaviors they see, such as feeding, fighting, or cooperating in some way—for example, ants collecting food.

Performance Assessment

Skills Check Have each student choose one action related to an environmental issue and create a table with the costs of the action listed in one column and its benefits in a second column.

Is Paper a Renewable Resource?

Preparing for Inquiry

Key Concept Paper is a renewable resource because it can be recycled.

Skills Objectives Students will be able to
- observe and compare dry newspaper and recycled paper made from newspaper pulp;
- design an experiment to recycle other types of paper.

Time *Day 1:* 15 minutes; *Day 2:* 40 minutes; *Day 3:* 10 minutes

Advance Planning Gather an ample supply of old newspapers.

Guiding Inquiry

Introducing the Procedure
- Have students read the entire procedure. Clarify that they will do the lab on three different days: Steps 1–2 on Day 1, Steps 3–6 on Day 2, and Step 7 on Day 3.

Troubleshooting the Experiment
- *Day 1:* In Step 1, ask: What do you see in the paper? (*fibers*)
- *Day 2:* Have students reread Steps 3–6. Remind them to replace the newspaper under the screen each day if it is wet.
- *Day 3:* Make sure the pulp is completely dry before handling it.

Expected Outcome
The dried pulp will be rough, stiff, and grayish—like cardboard egg cartons. Cellulose fibers will be visible.

Analyze and Conclude
1. Fibers; they are made of plant material and come from the plants used to make the paper.
2. When the paper is soaked and mashed, the fibers are broken up. When the pulp is flattened and dried, the fibers intertwine again.
3. After two or three recyclings, the fibers become too short or too fragile to intertwine again.

Real-World Lab

You and Your Community

Is Paper a Renewable Resource?

Recycling is a common local environmental issue. In this lab, you will explore how well paper can be recycled.

Problem

What happens when paper is recycled?

Skills Focus

observing, designing experiments

Materials

newspaper	microscope	water
eggbeater	square pan	screen
plastic wrap	mixing bowl	heavy book
microscope slide		

Procedure

1. Tear off a small piece of newspaper. Place the paper on a microscope slide and examine it under a microscope. Record your observations.
2. Tear a sheet of newspaper into pieces about the size of postage stamps. Place the pieces in the mixing bowl. Add enough water to cover the newspaper. Cover the bowl and let the mixture stand overnight.
3. The next day, add more water to cover the paper if necessary. Use the eggbeater to mix the wet paper until it is smooth. This thick liquid is called paper pulp.
4. Place the screen in the bottom of the pan. Pour the pulp onto the screen, spreading it out evenly. Then lift the screen above the pan, allowing most of the water to drip into the pan.
5. Place the screen and pulp on several layers of newspaper to absorb the rest of the water. Lay a sheet of plastic wrap over the pulp. Place a heavy book on top of the plastic wrap to press more water out of the pulp.
6. After 30 minutes, remove the book. Carefully turn over the screen, plastic wrap, and pulp. Remove the screen and plastic wrap. Let the pulp sit on the newspaper for one or two more days to dry. Replace the newspaper layers if necessary.
7. When the pulp is dry, observe it closely. Record your observations.

Analyze and Conclude

1. What kind of structures did you observe when you examined torn newspaper under a microscope? What are these structures made of? Where do they come from?
2. What do you think happens to the structures you observed when paper is recycled?
3. Based on your results, predict how many times a sheet of newspaper can be recycled.
4. **Apply** Should paper be classified as a renewable or nonrenewable resource? Explain.

Design an Experiment

Using procedures like those in this lab, design an experiment to recycle three different types of paper, such as shiny magazine paper, paper towels, and cardboard. Find out how the resulting papers differ. Obtain your teacher's approval for your plans before you try your experiment.

4. Renewable; paper can be recycled, and new trees can be planted.

Extending the Inquiry

Design an Experiment Students' plans should be similar to the lab procedure.

Safety

Students should handle the microscope slide carefully to avoid breakage. Review the safety guidelines in Appendix A.

Program Resources

- **Unit 6 Resources** Real-World Lab blackline masters, pp. 25–27

Media and Technology

Lab Activity Videotape
Tape 5

SECTION 2 Forests and Fisheries

SECTION 2 Forests and Fisheries

DISCOVER ······· ACTIVITY

What Happened to the Tuna?

1. Use the data in the table to make a line graph. Label the axes of the graph and add a title. (To review graphing, see the Skills Handbook.)
2. Mark the high and low points on the graph.

Think It Over

Inferring How did the tuna population change during this period? Can you suggest a possible reason for this change?

Year	Western Atlantic Bluefin Tuna Population
1970	240,000
1975	190,000
1980	90,000
1985	60,000
1990	45,000
1994	60,000

At first glance, a bluefin tuna and a pine tree may not seem to have much in common. One is an animal and the other is a plant. One lives in the ocean and the other lives on land. However, tuna and pine trees are both living resources. Tuna are a source of food for people. People don't eat pine trees, but they do use them to make lumber, paper, and turpentine. People also use pine needles as mulch in gardens.

Every day you use many different products that are made from living organisms. In this section, you will read about two major types of living resources: forests and fisheries. As you read, think about how they are similar and how they are different.

Forest Resources

Forests are a resource because they contain valuable materials. Many products are made from the flowers, fruits, seeds, and other parts of forest plants. Some of these products, such as maple syrup, rubber, and nuts, come from living trees. Other products, such as lumber and pulp for paper, require cutting trees down. Conifers, including pine and spruce, are used for construction and for making paper. Hardwoods, such as oak, cherry, and maple, are used for furniture because of their strength and beauty.

Trees and other plants produce oxygen that other organisms need to survive. They also absorb carbon dioxide and many pollutants from the air. Trees also help prevent flooding and control soil erosion. Their roots absorb rainwater and hold the soil together.

GUIDE FOR READING

◆ How can forests and fisheries be managed?

Reading Tip As you read, make a list of ways to conserve forests and fisheries.

Figure 5 One important use of forest resources is for building housing.

657

Objectives

After completing the lesson, students will be able to
◆ describe different ways that forests can be managed to provide resources;
◆ describe ways that fisheries can be managed to provide resources.

Key Terms clear-cutting, selective cutting, sustainable yield, fishery, aquaculture

1 Engage/Explore

Activating Prior Knowledge

Invite students to look around the classroom and identify as many products as they can that are derived from trees. (*Examples include writing paper, cardboard, posterboard, paper towels, wood furniture, pencils, rulers, and plywood.*)

DISCOVER

Skills Focus inferring
Materials *graph paper, ruler, pencil*
Time 15 minutes
Expected Outcome Increments used for the vertical axis may vary.
Sample Graph

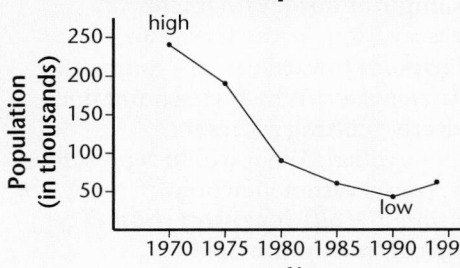

Changes in Western Atlantic Bluefin Tuna Population

Think It Over The tuna population declined steadily from 1970 to 1990, then increased from 1990 to 1994. The decline was probably due to overfishing of tuna; the rebound may have resulted from limits on tuna fishing.

READING STRATEGIES

Reading Tip Students' lists may vary. *Sample lists of ways to conserve forests:* selective cutting, replanting trees, plan frequency of cutting, log small patches of forest in stages. *Sample list of ways to conserve fisheries:* set fishing limits, control size of fish harvested, close fishery until it recovers, regulate fishing methods, develop aquaculture techniques, fish for new species.

Program Resources

◆ **Unit 6 Resources** 20-2 Lesson Plan, p. 13; 20-2 Section Summary, p. 14
◆ **Guided Reading and Study Workbook** Section 20-2

Forest Resources

Including All Students

Ask students to name kinds of trees that grow in their region of the country. If any are grown commercially, discuss with students the uses of those trees. **learning modality: verbal**

Managing Forests

Social Studies CONNECTION

Provide a picture of a small village with a commons, such as ones found in England or New England. To help students understand how this problem could arise, ask them to put themselves in the place of the local people. Would they stop bringing their cattle to the commons for the greater good, or would they expect others to stop?

In Your Journal Volunteers can share their ideas in a class discussion. Encourage students to comment on each idea's feasibility. **learning modality: verbal**

Building Inquiry Skills: Classifying

After students have read about the two logging methods, ask: **Is clear-cutting an example of the development, preservation, or conservation viewpoint toward the environment?** *(development)* **Which viewpoint does selective cutting represent?** *(conservation)* **What would represent the preservation viewpoint?** *(Not cutting the forest at all)* **learning modality: logical/mathematical**

Figure 6 Clear-cutting has left large portions of these hillsides bare. *Interpreting Photographs What problems might clear-cutting cause?*

Social Studies CONNECTION

Many of the world's living resources are owned by no one—they are shared by everyone. A word that is sometimes used to describe such a shared resource is a "commons." This word comes from a time when villages were built around common areas of open land. All the town's residents grazed their cattle on the commons. This worked well as long as there weren't too many people. But as more and more people brought their cattle to the commons, the area would become overgrazed. There would not be enough pasture to feed even one cow—the "tragedy of the commons."

In Your Journal

Suppose you live in a farming community with a central commons. Propose a solution that will allow residents to use the commons while protecting it from overuse.

Managing Forests

There are about 300 million hectares of forests in the United States. That's nearly a third of the nation's area! Many forests are located on publicly owned land. Others are owned by private timber and paper companies or by individuals. Forest industries provide jobs for 1.5 million people.

Because new trees can be planted to replace trees that are cut down, forests can be renewable resources. The United States Forest Service and environmental organizations work with forestry companies to conserve forest resources. They try to develop logging methods that maintain forests as renewable resources.

Logging Methods There are two major methods of logging: clear-cutting and selective cutting. **Clear-cutting** is the process of cutting down all the trees in an area at once. Cutting down only some trees in a forest and leaving a mix of tree sizes and species behind is called **selective cutting.**

Each logging method has advantages and disadvantages. Clear-cutting is usually quicker and cheaper than selective cutting. It may also be safer for the loggers. In selective cutting, the loggers must move the heavy equipment and logs around the remaining trees in the forest. But selective cutting is usually less damaging to the forest environment than clear-cutting. When an area of forest is clear-cut, the habitat changes. Clear-cutting exposes the soil to wind and rain. Without the protection of the tree roots, the soil is more easily blown or washed away. Soil washed into streams may harm the fish and other organisms that live there.

Sustainable Forestry Forests can be managed to provide a sustained yield. A **sustainable yield** is a regular amount of a renewable resource such as trees that can be harvested without

---

Background

Integrating Science Forests can have a profound effect on climate. Scientists think that deforestation contributes to changes in climate at regional and global scales. Through transpiration, trees add huge amounts of water vapor to the atmosphere. In fact, a tree returns to the air about 97 percent of the water that the tree's roots absorb from the ground. This water eventually falls back to Earth through the water cycle. Removal of a forest may cause the rainfall in a region to decline and increase the frequency of droughts.

The deforestation of tropical rain forests, so prevalent in recent years, may contribute to an increase in global temperatures. Burning the felled trees adds carbon dioxide to the atmosphere. The higher the concentration of CO_2 in the atmosphere, the more heat the atmosphere holds in and does not radiate back into space.

reducing the future supply. This works sort of like a book swap: as long as you donate a book each time you borrow one, the total supply of books will not be affected. Planting a tree to replace one being cut down is like donating a book to replace a borrowed one.

Part of forest management is planning how frequently the trees must be replanted to keep a constant supply. Different species grow at different rates. Trees with softer woods, such as pines, usually mature faster than trees with harder woods, such as hickory, oak, and cherry. Forests containing faster-growing trees can be harvested and replanted more often. For example, pine forests may be harvested every 20 to 30 years. On the other hand, some hardwood forests may be harvested only every 40 to 100 years. One sustainable approach is to log small patches of forest. This way, different sections of forest can be harvested every year.

Certified Wood Forests that are managed in a sustainable way can be certified by the Forest Stewardship Council. Once a forest is certified, all wood logged from that forest may carry a "well-managed" label. This label allows businesses and individuals to select wood from forests that are managed for sustainable yields.

☑ *Checkpoint* *What is a sustainable yield?*

Figure 7 Two logging methods are clear-cutting and selective cutting. **A.** After clear-cutting, the new trees are usually all the same age and species. **B.** Selective cutting results in a more diverse forest.

Original forest   *Clear-cutting*   *Replanted growth*

Original forest   *Selective cutting*   *Diverse regrowth*

Inquiry Challenge

Materials *colored plastic chips, construction paper squares, or similar objects*
Time 15 minutes

Tell students that another sustainable forestry practice is to harvest all the mature trees in an area at intervals—a practice known as shelterwood cutting. In the first harvest, all the unwanted tree species and dead or diseased trees are cut down. The forest is then left alone so the remaining trees can continue to grow and new seedlings can become established. After a period of time, many of the mature trees are removed in a second harvest, and the forest is again left alone to grow. In a third harvest, the remaining mature trees are cut down. By this time, though, the seedlings have grown into young trees, and more new seedlings are growing. Challenge small groups of students to devise a simple model of shelterwood cutting. Team students who have difficulty seeing or whose movements are limited with students who do not have these disabilities. *(Sample model: Use green paper squares to represent mature trees and brown squares to represent unwanted trees. For the "first harvest," remove all brown squares. Add red squares to represent seedlings. In the "second harvest," remove some of the green squares. Replace the red squares with yellow squares to represent the growth of the seedlings into young trees, and add more red squares. In the "third harvest," remove the remaining green squares, replace the yellow squares with green squares and the red squares with yellow squares, and add more red squares.)* Have each group describe their model in writing. Ask: **How does shelterwood cutting provide a sustainable yield?** *(The forest constantly replenishes itself.)* **learning modality: kinesthetic**

Answers to Self-Assessment

Caption Question

Figure 6 The soil on the hill may erode, and silt may clog streams. Without tree roots to absorb water, areas may flood. Many organisms would lose their habitat.

☑ *Checkpoint*

A regular amount of a renewable resource that can be harvested without reducing the future supply

Ongoing Assessment

Skills Check Have each student construct a table comparing the advantages and disadvantages of clear-cutting and selective cutting.

 Students could save their tables in their portfolios.

Fisheries

Sharpen your Skills

Calculating

In a recent year, the total catch of fish in the world was 112.9 million metric tons. Based on the data below, calculate the percent of this total each country caught.

Country	Catch (millions of metric tons)
China	24.4
Japan	6.8
United States	5.6
Peru	8.9

Figure 8 A fishing boat returns to harbor at the end of a long day. Overfishing has forced the crews of many boats to find other work until the fisheries recover.

Fisheries

Until recently, the oceans seemed like an unlimited resource. The waters held such huge schools of fish, it seemed impossible that they could ever disappear. And fish reproduce in incredible numbers. A single codfish can lay as many as nine million eggs in a single year! But people have discovered that this resource has limits. After many years of big catches, the number of sardines off the California coast suddenly declined. The same thing happened to the huge schools of cod off the New England coast. What caused these changes?

An area with a large population of valuable ocean organisms is called a **fishery.** Some major fisheries include the Grand Banks off Newfoundland, Georges Bank off New England, and Monterey Canyon off California. Fisheries like these are valuable renewable resources. But if fish are caught at a faster rate than they can breed, the population decreases. This situation is known as overfishing.

Scientists estimate that 70 percent of the world's major fisheries have been overfished. But if those fish populations are allowed to recover, a sustainable yield of fish can once again be harvested. **Managing fisheries for a sustainable yield includes setting fishing limits, changing fishing methods, developing aquaculture techniques, and finding new resources.**

Fishing Limits Laws can help protect individual fish species. Laws may also limit the amount that can be caught or require that fish be at least a certain size. This ensures that young fish

Background

History of Science In 1994, a section of the Georges Bank fishery was closed because of overfishing. A 1998 study of the area found that there were more than three times the number of scallops there than in areas where fishing had continued. Based on these findings, scallopers wanted regulators to let them back into the closed area. However, scallopers can catch 70 to 80 percent of the scallops in areas that are open to fishing.

Taking this many scallops could swiftly decimate the scallop population on Georges Bank again. Scallopers' dredges also catch groundfish, endangering those populations.

Some scallop researchers advocate another approach: closing selected scallop beds from time to time to let the scallop populations regenerate, much as areas of forest are allowed to regrow after being cut.

survive long enough to reproduce. Also, setting an upper limit on the size of fish caught ensures that breeding fish remain in the population. But if a fishery has been severely overfished, the government may need to completely ban fishing until the populations can recover.

Fishing Methods Today fishing practices are regulated by laws. Some fishing crews now use nets with a larger mesh size to allow small, young fish to escape. Some methods have been outlawed. These methods include poisoning fish with cyanide and stunning them by exploding dynamite underwater. These techniques kill all the fish in an area rather than selecting certain fish.

Aquaculture The practice of raising fish and other water-dwelling organisms for food is called **aquaculture**. The fish may be raised in artificial ponds or bays. Salmon, catfish, and shrimp are farmed in this way in the United States.

However, aquaculture is not a perfect solution. The artificial ponds and bays often replace natural habitats such as salt marshes. Maintaining the farms can cause pollution and spread diseases into wild fish populations.

New Resources Today about 9,000 different fish species are harvested for food. More than half the animal protein eaten by people throughout the world comes from fish. One way to help feed a growing human population is to fish for new species. Scientists and chefs are working together to introduce people to deep-water species such as monkfish and tile fish, as well as easy-to-farm freshwater fish such as tilapia.

Figure 9 As fishing limits become stricter, aquaculture is playing a larger role in meeting the worldwide demand for fish. This fish farm in Hawaii raises tilapia.

Section 2 Review

1. Describe one example of a sustainable forestry practice.
2. What are three ways fisheries can be managed so that they will continue to provide fish for the future?
3. Why are forests considered renewable resources?
4. **Thinking Critically Comparing and Contrasting** Describe the advantages and disadvantages of clear-cutting and selective cutting.

Science at Home

With a family member, conduct a "Forest and Fishery" survey of your home. Make a list of all the things that are made from either forest or fishery products. Then ask other family members to predict how many items are on the list. Are they surprised by the answer?

Program Resources

◆ **Unit 6 Resources** 20-2 Review and Reinforce, p. 15; 20-2 Enrich, p. 16
◆ **Laboratory Manual** 20, "Managing Fisheries"

---

3 Assess

Section 2 Review Answers

1. *Any one:* replant trees, plan frequency of cutting, log small patches of forest in stages
2. *Any three:* Fishing limits can be imposed; nets with a larger mesh size can be used; dynamiting, poisoning, and other fishing methods that kill all the fish in an area can be outlawed; aquaculture can replace fishing in natural areas.
3. New trees can be planted to replace trees that are cut down.
4. Clear-cutting is quicker, cheaper, and may be safer for loggers, but selective cutting is less damaging to the environment.

Science at Home

Encourage students to look beyond the most obvious products, such as wood and paper from forests, and salt and seafood from oceans, and check labels closely to see if they can find the names of other items. Examples include nuts, spices, tree bark and salt hay for mulch, seaweeds (used both as food and in shampoos and other products), and cuttlebone for pet birds.

Performance Assessment

Oral Presentation Call on students at random to name a way to conserve forests or fisheries.

Tree Cookie Tales

Preparing for Inquiry

Key Concept Growth rings provide information about a tree's age and the growing conditions during its life.

Skills Objectives Students will be able to
- observe growth rings in a tree cookie to determine a tree's age;
- draw conclusions from their observations about conditions that affected the tree's growth.

Time 40 minutes

Advance Planning Purchase or prepare a tree cookie for each group. Inexpensive classroom sets of tree cookies are available from biological supply houses. The tree cookies should come from trees that were more than 10 years old. You can also make tree cookies by sawing a tree trunk into cross sections 1.5–2.5 cm thick. To preserve homemade tree cookies, spray or paint all surfaces with clear polyurethane or other clear sealant.

Guiding Inquiry

Troubleshooting the Experiment
Clarify that each year's growth is shown by a pair of rings—a light ring for spring and a dark ring for summer.

Expected Outcome
Results will vary depending on the particular tree cookies used.

Analyze and Conclude
1. Ages will vary. The tree's age is equal to the number of annual rings.
2. Answers will vary. The largest proportion of tree growth usually occurs during a tree's early years.
3. Observations may vary. Spring rings are usually wider, as trees undergo a burst of new growth in the spring when it is usually wetter followed by slower growth in the summer when it is usually drier.
4. Growth rings reflect weather conditions. Generally, rings are wider during years when temperatures are warmer and rainfall is plentiful.
5. Answers will vary. In addition to the tree's age and weather-related growth

patterns, students may note holes made by insects or birds, blackening due to fire or lightning, a hollow pith due to disease, or cracks or gashes from tools.
6. You could look for annual growth patterns indicating the weather conditions and additional evidence of fire, disease, or other environmental conditions.

Extending the Inquiry

More to Explore Answers will depend on the specific tree cookies used.

Tree Cookie Tales

Tree cookies aren't snacks! They're slices of a tree trunk that contain clues about the tree's age, past weather conditions, and fires that occurred during its life. In this lab, you'll interpret the data hidden in a tree cookie.

Pith

Summer ring

Spring ring

Bark

Problem

What can tree cookies reveal about the past?

Materials

tree cookie   metric ruler   hand lens
colored pencils   calculator (optional)

Procedure

1. Use a hand lens to examine your tree cookie. Draw a simple diagram of your tree cookie. Label the bark, tree rings, and center, or pith.
2. Notice the light-colored and dark-colored rings. The light ring results from fast springtime growth. The dark ring, where the cells are smaller, results from slower summertime growth. Each pair of light and dark rings represents one year's growth, so the pair is called an annual ring. Observe and count the annual rings.
3. Compare the spring and summer portions of the annual rings. Identify the thinnest and thickest rings.
4. Measure the distance from the center to the outermost edge of the last summer growth ring. This is the radius of your tree cookie. Record your measurement.
5. Measure the distance from the center to the outermost edge of the 10th summer growth ring. Record your measurement.
6. Examine your tree cookie for any other evidence of its history, such as damaged bark or burn marks. Record your observations.

Analyze and Conclude

1. How old was your tree? How do you know?
2. What percent of the tree's growth took place during the first 10 years of its life? (*Hint:* Divide the distance from the center to the 10th growth ring by the radius. Then multiply by 100. This gives you the percent of growth that occurred during the tree's first 10 years.)
3. How did the spring rings compare to the summer rings for the same year? Suggest a reason.
4. Why might the annual rings be narrower for some years than for others?
5. Using evidence from your tree cookie, summarize the history of the tree.
6. **Think About It** Suppose you had cookies from two other trees of the same species that grew near your tree. How could you verify the interpretations you made in this lab?

More to Explore

Examine and compare several tree cookies. Record any similarities and differences you observe. Do you think any of the tree cookies came from trees growing in the same area? Support your answer with specific evidence.

Program Resources

- **Unit 6 Resources** Skills Lab blackline masters, pp. 28–29

Media and Technology

 Lab Activity Videotape
Tape 5

DISCOVER · ACTIVITY · · · ·

How Much Variety Is There?

1. You will be given two cups of seeds and a paper plate. The seeds in Cup A represent the trees in a section of tropical rain forest. The seeds in Cup B represent the trees in a section of deciduous forest.

2. Pour the seeds from Cup A onto the plate. Sort the seeds by type. Count the different types of seeds. This number represents the number of different kinds of trees in that type of forest.

3. Pour the seeds back into Cup A.

4. Repeat Steps 2 and 3 with the seeds in Cup B.

5. Share your results with your class. Use the class results to calculate the average number of different kinds of seeds in each type of forest.

Think It Over
Inferring How does the variety of trees in the tropical rain forest compare with the variety of trees in a deciduous forest? Can you suggest any advantages of having a wide variety of species?

N o one knows exactly how many species live on Earth. So far, more than 1.7 million species have been identified. The number of different species in an area is called its **biodiversity.** It is difficult to estimate the total biodiversity on Earth because many areas of the planet have not been thoroughly studied. Some experts think that the deep oceans alone could contain 10 million new species! Protecting this diversity is a major environmental issue today.

Factors Affecting Biodiversity

Biodiversity varies from place to place on Earth. **Factors that affect biodiversity in an ecosystem include area, climate, and diversity of niches.**

Area Within an ecosystem, a large area will contain more species than a small area. For example, suppose you were counting tree species in a forest. You would find far more tree species in a 10-square-meter area than in a 1-square-meter area.

> **GUIDE FOR READING**
>
> ◆ What factors affect an area's biodiversity?
> ◆ Which human activities threaten biodiversity?
> ◆ How can biodiversity be protected?
>
> *Reading Tip* Before you read, use the headings to make an outline on biodiversity.

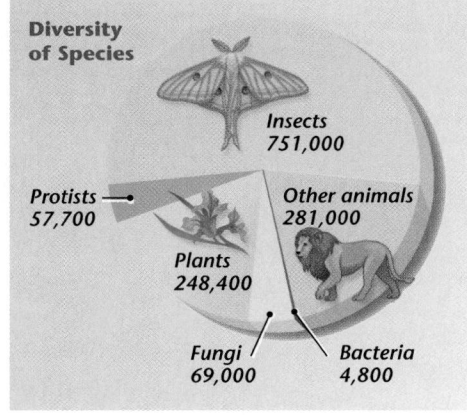

Figure 10 Organisms of many kinds are part of Earth's biodiversity.
Interpreting Graphs Which group of organisms has the greatest number of species?

Diversity of Species

Insects 751,000
Protists 57,700
Other animals 281,000
Plants 248,400
Fungi 69,000
Bacteria 4,800

READING STRATEGIES

Reading Tip Students' outlines may vary slightly. *Sample Outline (partial):*

I. Factors Affecting Biodiversity
   A. Climate
   B. Niche Diversity
II. The Value of Biodiversity
   A. Economic Value
   B. Value to the Ecosystem

Answers to Self-Assessment

Caption Question
Figure 10 insects

Program Resources

◆ **Unit 6 Resources** 20-3 Lesson Plan, p. 17; 20-3 Section Summary, p. 18
◆ **Guided Reading and Study Workbook** Section 20-3

Objectives

After completing the lesson, students will be able to
◆ identify the factors that affect biodiversity;
◆ explain the value of biodiversity;
◆ name some human activities that threaten biodiversity;
◆ list some ways that biodiversity can be protected.

Key Terms biodiversity, keystone species, genes, extinction, endangered species, threatened species, habitat destruction, habitat fragmentation, poaching, captive breeding

1 Engage/Explore

Activating Prior Knowledge

Ask students: **What organisms are native to our area?** (*Answers will vary. Encourage students to consider a wide variety of organism types, including insects, worms, mosses, algae, and bacteria, as well as mammals, birds, fish, reptiles, and amphibians.*) Write the name of each organism on the chalkboard, and after students have finished naming organisms, ask: **Would you say there is very much diversity of species living here?** (*Answers may vary, but in most cases students will say there is.*)

· · · · · · · · · DISCOVER · · · · · · · · ·

Skills Focus inferring
Materials *two labeled cups containing different seed mixtures, paper plate*
Time 20 minutes
Advance Preparation Use a mixture of at least ten types of seeds for Cup A and four or five types for Cup B.
Expected Outcome The average number of different kinds of seeds should be greater for the tropical rain forest.
Think It Over The tropical rain forest has a greater variety of trees than the deciduous forest. The wider variety of tree species supports a wider variety of other organisms that depend on the trees for habitat and food.

Factors Affecting Biodiversity

Building Inquiry Skills: Observing

Materials *books and magazines with photographs of coral reefs*
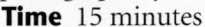
Time 15 minutes

To illustrate the rich diversity of life on coral reefs, encourage small groups of students to examine other photographs similar to Figure 12, choose a "favorite" photo, and list all the organisms shown in the photo and named in its caption or accompanying text. In a follow-up class discussion, list the number of species on the board for each group. **learning modality: visual**

How Diverse Are Tropical Ecosystems?

In Costa Rica, which is half the size of Tennessee, there are 850 species of birds—200 more than in all the rest of North America.

A 10-hectare area of forest in Borneo contains 700 species of trees, as many as all of North America.

A single river in Brazil contains more species than all of the rivers in the United States combined.

Figure 11 Tropical ecosystems tend to be more diverse than those further from the equator.

Figure 12 Coral reefs are the second most diverse ecosystems. *Applying Concepts What is one reason why coral reefs are so diverse?*

664

Climate In general, the number of species increases from the poles toward the equator. The tropical rain forests of Latin America, southeast Asia, and central Africa are the most diverse ecosystems in the world. These forests cover about 7 percent of Earth's land surface and contain over half of the world's species.

The reason for the great biodiversity in the tropics is not fully understood. Many scientists hypothesize that it has to do with climate. For example, tropical rain forests have fairly constant temperatures and large amounts of rainfall throughout the year. Many plants in these regions have year-round growing seasons. This means that food is available for other organisms year-round.

Niche Diversity Coral reefs make up less than 1 percent of the oceans' area. But reefs are home to 20 percent of the world's saltwater fish species. Coral reefs are the second most diverse ecosystems in the world. Found only in shallow, warm waters, coral reefs are often called the rain forests of the sea. A reef supports many different niches for organisms that live under, on, and among the coral. This enables more species to live in the reef than in a more uniform habitat such as a flat sandbar.

☑ *Checkpoint* *What is one possible reason that tropical regions have the greatest biodiversity?*

The Value of Biodiversity

Perhaps you are wondering how biodiversity is important. Does it matter whether there are 50 or 5,000 species of ferns in some faraway rain forest? Is it necessary to protect every one of these species?

Background

Facts and Figures Scientists have not yet studied most species of plants, animals, fungi, and microorganisms to determine whether they might be useful to humans. Of approximately 250,000 known plant species, only about 25,000 have been investigated.

Insects are one example of an often overlooked biological resource. Insects play a major role in pollinating crops, controlling weeds, and even in controlling some insects that are pests. And other insects produce unusual chemical compounds for which humans may find some use. For example, scientists have found a compound made by fireflies that has potential as an antiviral agent in humans. A fungicide produced by centipedes to protect their eggs might also protect crops from fungus attack.

There are many reasons why preserving biodiversity is important. The simplest reason is that wild organisms and ecosystems are a source of beauty and recreation.

Economic Value Many plants, animals, and other organisms are essential for human survival. In addition to providing food and oxygen, these organisms supply raw materials for clothing, medicine, and other products. No one knows how many other useful species have not yet been identified.

Ecosystems are economically valuable, too. For example, many companies now run wildlife tours in rain forests, savannas, mountain ranges, and other locations. This ecosystem tourism, or "ecotourism," is an important source of jobs and money for nations such as Brazil, Costa Rica, and Kenya.

Value to the Ecosystem All the species in an ecosystem are connected to one another. Species may depend on each other for food and shelter. A change that affects one species will surely affect all the others.

Some species play a particularly important role. A species that influences the survival of many other species in an ecosystem is called a **keystone species.** If a keystone species disappears, the entire ecosystem may change. For example, the sea stars in Figure 14 are a keystone species in their ecosystem. The sea stars prey mostly on the mussels that live in tide pools. When researchers removed the sea stars from an area, the mussels began to outcompete many of the other species in the tide pool. The sea star predators had kept the population of mussels in check, allowing other species to live. When the keystone species disappeared, the balance in the ecosystem was destroyed.

Figure 13 Ecosystem tours such as safaris can provide income for local people. These tourists are observing giraffes in Botswana.

Figure 14 These sea stars on the Washington coast are an example of a keystone species. By preying on mussels, the sea stars keep the mussels from taking over the ecosystem.

Chapter 20 **665**

The Value of Biodiversity

Building Inquiry Skills: Communicating

Time 20 minutes

ACTIVITY

Divide the class into small groups, and pose the following hypothetical environmental issue for each group to debate: **A chemical for making a new drug has been discovered in a plant species growing in the Amazon rain forest. Several rare species of butterflies depend on the plant for food. To harvest the chemical for human use, the plants have to be cut down and removed from the forest. Should people make use of this new resource, and if so, how?** Encourage each group to try to reach consensus on the issue. After students have debated for a time, let each group report its decision and the reasoning behind it to the rest of the class. **learning modality: verbal**

Demonstration

Materials *model architectural building blocks or photo of arch with keystone*
Time 5–10 minutes

ACTIVITY

Use model architectural building blocks to construct an arch with a keystone. (If such blocks are not available, use a photo of an arch with a keystone.) Point to the keystone, and ask: **What do you predict will happen if I remove this block?** (*Some may predict the arch will fall.*) Remove the keystone to confirm students' predictions. Explain that the block you removed is called a keystone. Ask: **Why is a keystone a good analogy for a keystone species?** (*Because when a keystone species is removed, the entire ecosystem may collapse*) **learning modality: visual**

Ongoing Assessment

Writing Have each student identify and briefly explain the three major factors that affect an ecosystem's biodiversity.

 Students can save their work in their portfolios.

Gene Pool Diversity

Building Inquiry Skills: Predicting

Ask students: **What is cloning?** *(Making an exact duplicate of an organism—more precisely, using genes taken from an organism's cells to create a new individual that is genetically identical to the original organism)* Pose the following question: **Suppose scientists found an easy and inexpensive way to create large herds of sheep, cattle, and other domestic animals through cloning. Do you think this would be a good idea? Why or why not?** *(Some students may say that cloned herds could have traits that increase our supply of meat, milk, wool, leather, and other products. However, students should realize that entire herds of genetically identical animals could increase susceptibility to disease.)* **learning modality: logical/mathematical**

Extinction of Species

Addressing Naive Conceptions

ACTIVITY

Materials *large sheet of construction paper, colored markers, source books*

When students consider extinction, they usually think of dinosaurs and other species that became extinct in the distant past. Explain that many species have become extinct in relatively recent times. Let each pair of students research one species that became extinct in the past 300 years. Examples include the quagga, dodo, moa, Tasmanian wolf (thylacine), dusky seaside sparrow, Santa Barbara song sparrow, Greek auk, Hawaii oo, passenger pigeon, Abingdon tortoise, blue pike, Tecopa pupfish, and Sampson's pearly mussel. Suggest that one student in each pair draw a picture of the organism and the other student write a brief, first-person description of it—for example, *I'm a quagga, a variety of zebra. I used to live in huge, wild herds in South Africa, but I was hunted for my hide. I became extinct in 1883.* **learning modality: verbal**

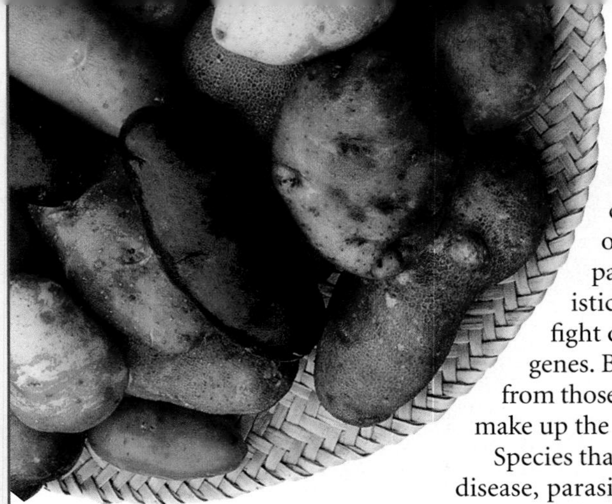

Figure 15 Just as diversity of species is important to an ecosystem, diversity of genes is important within a species. Diverse genes give these potatoes their rainbow of colors.

Gene Pool Diversity

The organisms in a healthy population have a diversity of traits. These traits are determined by genes. **Genes** are the structures in an organism's cells that carry its hereditary information. Every organism receives a combination of genes from its parents. Genes determine the organism's characteristics, from its size and appearance to its ability to fight disease. The organisms in one species share many genes. But each organism also has some genes that differ from those of other individuals. These individual differences make up the total gene "pool" of that species.

Species that lack a diverse gene pool are less able to adapt to disease, parasites, or drought. For example, most agricultural crops, such as wheat and corn, have very little diversity. These species are bred to be very uniform. If a disease or parasite attacks, the whole population could be affected. A fungus once wiped out much of the corn crop in the United States in this way. Fortunately, there are many wild varieties of corn that have slightly different genes. At least some of these plants contain genes that make them more resistant to the fungus. Scientists were able to breed corn that was not affected by the fungus. Keeping a diverse gene pool helps ensure that crop species can survive such problems.

☑ *Checkpoint* *What do an organism's genes determine?*

Extinction of Species

The disappearance of all members of a species from Earth is called **extinction.** Extinction is a natural process. Many species that once lived on Earth, from dinosaurs to dodos, are now extinct. But in the last few centuries, the number of species becoming extinct has increased dramatically.

Once a population drops below a certain level, the species may not be able to recover. For example, millions of passenger pigeons once darkened the skies in the United States. People hunted the birds for sport and food, killing many hundreds of thousands. This was only part of the total population of passenger pigeons. But at some point, there were not enough birds to reproduce and increase the population. Only after the birds disappeared did people realize that the species could not survive without its enormous numbers.

Species in danger of becoming extinct in the near future are considered **endangered species.** Species that could become endangered in the near future are considered **threatened species.**

Background

History of Science In the past 100 years, scientists have greatly increased the yields of crops such as corn and wheat by creating highly productive but genetically uniform varieties. With genetic uniformity, however, goes decreased resistance to certain diseases and pests. To restore resistance to these crop varieties, scientists cross them with other, often wild, varieties that retain genetic diversity. Scientists used this approach to create a type of corn that could resist the corn blight fungus described in the student text. They crossed genetically uniform varieties susceptible to the blight with Mexican varieties that possessed the genes needed to be blight resistant. Because the cultivation and domestication of corn (or maize) began in Mexico thousands of years ago, Mexican varieties are ancestral to modern varieties and have greater genetic diversity.

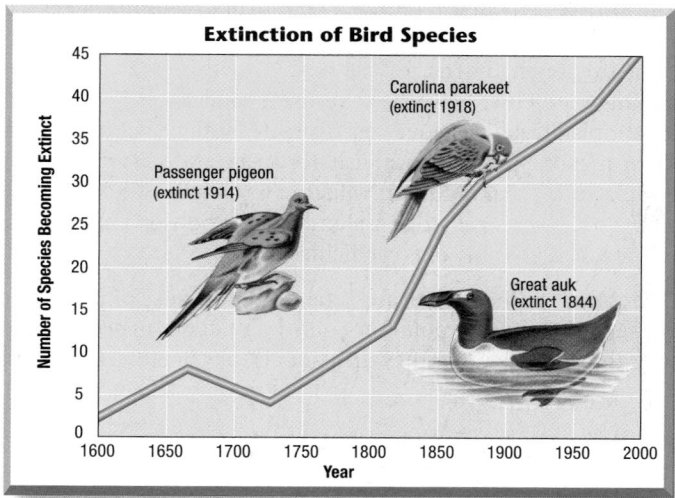

Extinction of Bird Species

Y-axis: Number of Species Becoming Extinct
X-axis: Year

Passenger pigeon (extinct 1914)

Carolina parakeet (extinct 1918)

Great auk (extinct 1844)

Figure 16 This graph shows the rate of extinction of bird species in the last 400 years.
Interpreting Graphs How many bird species became extinct in 1750? In 1850? In 1950?

Threatened and endangered species are found on every continent and in every ocean. Some are well-known animals such as Africa's black rhinoceros. Others are little known, such as hutias, rodents that live on only a few Caribbean islands. Ensuring that these species survive is one way to protect Earth's biodiversity.

Causes of Extinction

A natural event, such as an earthquake or volcano, can damage an ecosystem, wiping out populations or even some species. **Human activities can also threaten biodiversity. These activities include habitat destruction, poaching, pollution, and introduction of exotic species.**

Habitat Destruction The major cause of extinction is **habitat destruction,** the loss of a natural habitat. This can occur when forests are cleared to build towns or create grazing land. Plowing grasslands or filling in wetlands greatly changes those ecosystems. Some species may not be able to survive such changes to their habitats.

Breaking larger habitats into smaller, isolated pieces, or fragments, is called **habitat fragmentation.** For example, building a road through a forest disrupts habitats. This makes trees more vulnerable to wind damage. Plants may be less likely to successfully disperse their seeds. Habitat fragmentation is also very harmful to large mammals. These animals usually need large areas of land to find enough food to survive. They may not be able to obtain enough resources in a small area. They may also be injured trying to cross to another area.

Figure 17 Building this subdivision caused the habitats in the area to change. Open land was replaced by houses, streets, and yards.
Inferring How would these changes affect species in this area?

Causes of Extinction

Building Inquiry Skills: Making Models

Materials *sheet of graph paper ruled in centimeters, pencil, calculator (optional)*
Time 10–15 minutes

Use the following activity to demonstrate habitat fragmentation. Have each student draw a rounded rectangle, roughly 20 by 25 cm, on a sheet of graph paper. Explain that the rectangle represents a rain forest in Indonesia and that each centimeter on the graph paper represents 10 m on the actual land. Ask: **How much land does each square centimeter represent?** *(100 m²)* Have students calculate the forest's approximate area. *(50,000 m²)* Next, have students draw a 9-cm by 8-cm rectangle in the middle of one side of the forest, to represent land that was cleared for farming, and a 1-cm-wide "road" through the middle of the forest along the cleared area, dividing the forest into three smaller pieces. Let students calculate the area of each smaller piece and the total area remaining. *(6,300 m² + 4,500 m² + 30,000 m² = 40,800 m²)* Pose the following question: **Suppose orangutans live in this rain forest. Each one needs 10,000 m² of land area to survive. How many orangutans could have lived in the original forest?** *(5)* **How many can live in the remaining forest?** *(3)* **Why not four?** *(The two smaller pieces of forest are too small to support any orangutans at all.)* **learning modality: logical/mathematical**

Answers to Self-Assessment

☑ Checkpoint

Genes determine an organism's traits.

Caption Questions

Figure 16 1750–6; 1850–24; 1950–37
Figure 17 Organisms could no longer meet their food and shelter needs from their surroundings. The number of species probably decreased.

Ongoing Assessment

Writing Have students explain why gene pool diversity is so important to a species' survival.

Causes of Extinction, continued

EXPLORING
Endangered Species

Make sure students realize that all of the species shown in this feature are native to the United States. Locate and label the area where each species is found on a large wall map. (Grizzly bear–northern and western U.S.; piping plover–east coastal areas; Eureka Valley primrose–Oregon; whooping crane–central and southwestern U.S.) Encourage interested students to research the names and locations of other endangered species in the United States and add them to the map. Then challenge students to create a large table on the chalkboard listing all the endangered species and the reason why each is endangered. **learning modality: visual**

Real-Life Learning

Point out to students that the tropical fish and parrots sold in reputable pet shops in this country are specifically bred for the pet trade, not imported illegally. Invite a local pet store owner or manager to speak to students about obtaining fish, parrots and other birds, exotic reptiles, and other nonnative species. **learning modality: verbal**

Poaching The illegal killing or removal of wildlife species is called **poaching.** Many endangered animals are hunted for their skin, fur, teeth, horns, or claws. These things are used for making medicines, jewelry, coats, belts, and shoes.

People illegally remove organisms from their habitats to sell them as exotic pets. Tropical fish, tortoises, and parrots are very popular pets, making them valuable to poachers. Endangered plants may be illegally dug up and sold as houseplants. Others are poached to be used as medicines.

Pollution Some species are endangered because of pollution. Substances that cause pollution, called pollutants, may reach animals through the water they drink or air they breathe. Pollutants

EXPLORING *Endangered Species*

Abroad range of species and habitats are represented on the endangered list in the United States.

Grizzly bear ▷ This omnivore needs a large area to obtain food. Shrinking wilderness areas have limited its numbers.

Piping plover The ▷ population of this tiny, active, coastal bird is recovering as a result of increased protection of its sand dune nesting sites.

◁ **Eureka valley evening primrose** This flower, which blooms for only one night, must compete for water with exotic plants.

may also settle in the soil. From there they are absorbed by plants, and build up in other organisms through the food chain. Pollutants may kill or weaken organisms or cause birth defects.

Exotic Species Introducing exotic species into an ecosystem can threaten biodiversity. When European sailors began visiting Hawaii hundreds of years ago, rats from their ships escaped onto the islands. Without any predators in Hawaii, the rats multiplied quickly. They ate the eggs of the nene goose. To protect the geese, people brought the rat-eating mongoose from India to help control the rat population. Unfortunately, the mongooses preferred eating eggs to rats. With both the rats and the mongoose eating its eggs, the nene goose is now endangered.

◄ **Steller's sea lion** This mammal competes with fishermen for its prey along the Pacific coast.

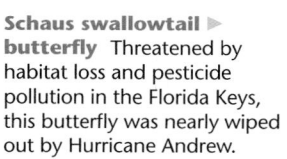

**Schaus swallowtail ►
butterfly** Threatened by habitat loss and pesticide pollution in the Florida Keys, this butterfly was nearly wiped out by Hurricane Andrew.

▲ **Whooping crane** Threatened by habitat destruction and disease, half of the remaining population of this wading bird is in captivity. The species seems to be recovering well since its lowest point in the 1940s.

◄ **New Mexico ridgenose rattlesnake** Illegal collectors have reduced the population of this rare snake, the largest known group of which lives in a single canyon.

Media and Technology

 Concept Videotape Library
Adventures, Tape 5, "Can We Save the Tigers?"; "Extinction"

Inquiry Challenge

Materials *plastic chips or paper squares*
Time 10 minutes

Challenge students to work together to devise a model showing how pollutants build up as organisms feed on each other in a food chain. *(Sample model: One student represents a top-level consumer such as a hawk, five students represent first-level consumers such as rabbits, and the rest of the students represent producers such as clover plants. Each "clover plant" holds a plastic chip representing a unit of a toxic chemical sprayed on a field. Each "rabbit" eats several clover plants by taking their chips. Then each "hawk" eats two or three rabbits by taking all of the chips they collected from the clover plants. The two hawks between them will have all of the toxic chemical chips.)* Ask: **Why do you think pollutants build up in organisms?** *(Their bodies cannot break the pollutants down into harmless materials or get rid of them as waste products.)* **cooperative learning**

Including All Students

Encourage students who need additional challenges to research other examples of exotic species that have been introduced to the United States that compete with native species, and what has happened to the native species as a result. Examples include the blue water hyacinth, purple loosestrife, kudzu, leafy spurge, Eurasian milfoil, tamarisk tree, flathead catfish, sea lamprey, green crab, zebra mussel, gypsy moth, brown tree snake, and starling. Let students share their findings in a class discussion. **learning modality: verbal**

Ongoing Assessment

Skills Check Have each student draw a concept map identifying and explaining the four human causes of extinction described in the text.

 Students can save their concept maps in their portfolios.

Protecting Biodiversity

Real-Life Learning

Take the class on a field trip to visit a zoo with a captive-breeding program or invite a zoologist to speak to the class. Before students visit the zoo or listen to the speaker, instruct them to write down two or three questions about captive breeding and endangered species.
learning modality: verbal

Building Inquiry Skills: Communicating

Time 15 minutes

After students read about the California condor, share the following information: In 1973, the federal government listed the gray wolf (timber wolf) as endangered after its population dropped to a few hundred in Minnesota and almost zero in the other lower-48 states. This protected gray wolves from hunting and trapping. In addition, captive breeding programs released more gray wolves into the wild. Biologists estimate that there are now 2,380 wolves in Minnesota and Wisconsin. In 1998 the government recommended removing the gray wolf from the endangered species list. Divide the class into groups to debate the issue of hunting and trapping bans from two viewpoints—that of farmers and ranchers who are losing animals to gray wolf predation, and that of people who support continued protection of the species. **learning modality: verbal**

Demonstration

Materials *aquarium, sand, water, 2 crayfish, several cans and/or boards*

Time 15 minutes for initial set-up

Explain that people can help preserve biodiversity by constructing artificial habitats to replace ones that were destroyed or damaged. Let students help you create an "artificial" habitat: Set up an aquarium with only sand in the bottom, and add two crayfish. Have students observe the crayfish for a day or two. Then add several cans and/or boards to the aquarium to provide hiding places. Let students continue to observe the crayfish. **learning modality: visual**

Protecting Biodiversity

Many people are working to preserve the world's biodiversity. Some focus on protecting individual endangered species, such as the giant panda or the Florida panther. Others try to protect entire ecosystems, such as the Great Barrier Reef in Australia. **Many programs to protect biodiversity combine scientific and legal approaches.**

Captive Breeding One scientific approach to protecting severely endangered species is captive breeding. **Captive breeding** is the mating of animals in zoos or wildlife preserves. Scientists care for the young to increase their chance of survival. These offspring are then released back into the wild.

A captive breeding program was the only hope for the California condor. California condors are the largest birds in North America. They became endangered as a result of habitat destruction, poaching, and pollution. By the mid-1980s there were fewer than ten California condors in the wild. Fewer than 30 were in zoos. Scientists captured all the wild condors and brought them to the zoos. Soon afterward, the first California condor chick was successfully bred in captivity. Today, there are more than 100 California condors in zoos. Some condors have even been returned to the wild. Though successful, this program has cost more than $20 million. It is not possible to save many species in this costly way.

Laws and Treaties Laws can help protect individual species. Some nations have made it illegal to sell endangered species or products made from them. In the United States, the Endangered Species Act of 1973 prohibits importing or trading products made from threatened or endangered species. This law also requires the development of plans to save endangered species.

Figure 18 Captive breeding programs use a scientific approach to protect endangered species.
A. California condor chicks raised in captivity need to learn what adult condors look like. Here, a scientist uses a puppet to feed and groom a chick.
B. These young green turtles were hatched in the laboratory. Now a researcher is releasing the turtles into their natural ocean habitat.

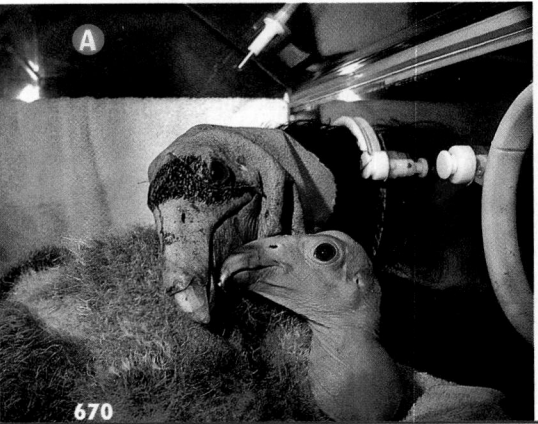

American alligators, Pacific gray whales, and green sea turtles are just a few of the species that have begun to recover as a result of legal protection.

The most important international treaty protecting wildlife is the Convention on International Trade in Endangered Species. Eighty nations signed this treaty in 1973. This treaty lists nearly 700 threatened and endangered species that cannot be traded for profit. Laws like these are difficult to enforce. Even so, they have helped to reduce the poaching of many endangered species, including African elephants, snow leopards, sperm whales, and mountain gorillas.

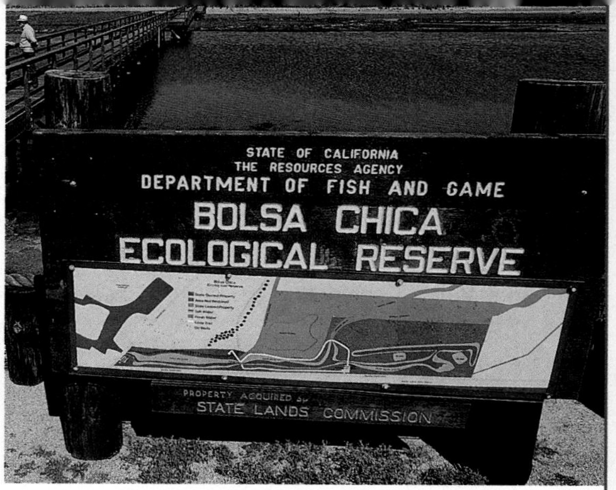

Habitat Preservation The most effective way to preserve biodiversity is to protect whole ecosystems. Preserving whole habitats saves not only endangered species, but also other species that depend on them.

Beginning in 1872 with Yellowstone National Park, the world's first national park, many countries have set aside wildlife habitats as parks and refuges. In addition, private organizations have purchased millions of hectares of endangered habitats throughout the world. Today, there are about 7,000 nature parks, preserves, and refuges in the world.

To be most effective, reserves must have the characteristics of diverse ecosystems. For example, they must be large enough to support the populations that live there. The reserves must contain a variety of niches. And of course, it is still necessary to keep the air, land, and water clean, remove exotic species, and control poaching.

Figure 19 Preserving whole habitats is probably the most effective way to protect biodiversity.

Section 3 Review

1. What are three factors that affect biodiversity?
2. List four possible causes of extinction.
3. Give an example of a legal approach and a scientific approach to preventing extinction.
4. Which are the most diverse ecosystems on Earth?
5. Identify three ways in which biodiversity is important.
6. **Thinking Critically Making Generalizations** Explain how the statement "In the web of life, all things are connected" relates to keystone species.

Science at Home

Obtain a map of your community or state. With a family member, identify any city, state, or national parks, reserves, or refuges in your area. Create a travel brochure highlighting one of these areas. Describe the habitats there. Find out whether any endangered or threatened species live in the park. Include their pictures in your brochure.

Program Resources

◆ **Unit 6 Resources** 3-3 Review and Reinforce, p. 19; 3-3 Enrich, p. 20

Media and Technology

Concept Videotape Library *Adventures, Tape 5,* "It's All Happening at the Zoo"

3 Assess

Section 3 Review Answers
1. Area, climate, and diversity of niches
2. Habitat destruction, poaching, pollution, and exotic species
3. *Legal approach:* Laws such as the Endangered Species Act and the Convention on International Trade in Endangered Species; *Scientific approach:* captive breeding in zoos or wildlife preserves, habitat preservation
4. Tropical rain forests and coral reefs
5. Biodiversity is important for beauty and recreation, economic reasons, the health of ecosystems, and genetic diversity.
6. A keystone species is one that influences the survival of many other species in an ecosystem. If something happens to the keystone species, all other species in the ecosystem are affected.

Science at Home

Besides looking at maps, students can contact their state's Environmental Protection Agency, a local chapter of the National Audubon Society, or their town's parks department. Students' brochures should describe the habitats of endangered or threatened species in the area.

Performance Assessment

Writing Have each student identify and briefly describe the four causes of extinction presented in the text.

Students can save their work in their portfolios.

SECTION 4 The Search for New Medicines

Objective

After completing the lesson, students will be able to

◆ explain why many rain forest plants are sources of medicines.

Key Term taxol

1 Engage/Explore

Activating Prior Knowledge

Before students read the introductory text on this page, ask: **Where are temperate rain forests located?** (*Along the northwest coast of the United States*)

DISCOVER

Skills Focus observing
Materials *black marking pen, strip of filter paper, water, clear plastic cup, tape, pencil*
Time 15 minutes
Tips If filter paper is not available, use paper towels cut into strips.
Expected Outcome Water will carry the dissolved black ink up the strip, where the individual colors will separate out.
Think It Over The specific colors that separate from the black ink will depend on the marker used. Different colors will advance up the strip at different rates: blue the fastest, yellow slightly slower, and red much slower.

SECTION 4 The Search for New Medicines

DISCOVER ACTIVITY

How Are Plant Chemicals Separated?

1. Using a black marking pen, draw a dot about 2 centimeters from the end of a strip of filter paper.
2. Pour a few centimeters of water into a clear plastic cup.
3. Tape the top edge of the filter paper strip to a pencil. Place the pencil across the top of the cup so that the ink dot hangs just below the water surface. If necessary, turn the pencil to adjust the length of the paper.

4. Observe what happens to the black dot.

Think It Over
Observing How many different colors of ink did you separate from the black ink? This process models one method of separating individual chemicals contained in plants.

GUIDE FOR READING

◆ Why are many rain forest plants sources of medicines?

Reading Tip As you read, identify statements that show how biodiversity is related to human health.

Pacific yew tree

You lace up your hiking boots, and sling your collecting bag over your shoulder. It's time to head out for another day of searching in the cool, damp forest. Stepping carefully to avoid mud, you walk beneath the giant evergreens. Their needle-covered branches form a thick roof above your head. Rotting logs covered with ferns, seedlings, and brightly colored fungi line your path. You scan the ground for telltale signs of the object of your search. What are you looking for in this forest? A plant that can save lives!

This ancient forest is the temperate rain forest of the Pacific Northwest. Many of its giant trees are more than 200 years old. Like tropical rain forests, temperate rain forests are diverse ecosystems. They contain many species that are found nowhere else. Some of these species are threatened or endangered, including the bull trout, Olympic salamander, and the life-saving plant you are looking for—the Pacific yew tree.

Plants and Medicines

People have always valued plants for their ability to heal wounds and fight diseases. For example, aspirin was originally made from the bark of the willow tree. The active chemical in aspirin can now be made in a laboratory.

READING STRATEGIES

Reading Tip Some statements that show how biodiversity is related to human health that students might identify include: *People have always valued plants for their ability to heal wounds and fight diseases. Some chemicals rain forest plants produce to protect their leaves and bark can also be used to fight human diseases. Almost half of all medicines sold today contain chemicals originally found in wild organisms.*

Summarizing To ensure that students understand the sequence of events in the development of taxol as an anticancer drug, have them summarize the text in The Story of Taxol and A Threatened Supply of Taxol on pages 673–674. Tell students to write one sentence that summarizes the main idea of each paragraph. When the sentences are read in order, they will provide a summary of the text.

Figure 20 Scientists studied Pacific yew tree seedlings to learn more about the cancer-fighting substance taxol. In the closeup, a researcher examines taxol crystals.

The ability to fight disease is a result of the plants' adaptations to their environment. Plants in many ecosystems produce chemicals that protect them from predators, parasites, and diseases. This is particularly true in rain forests, where so many organisms make their living by eating plants. **Some chemicals that rain forest plants produce to protect their leaves and bark can also be used to fight human diseases.**

The Story of Taxol

The Pacific yew tree is very resistant to diseases and insects. Scientists began studying the bark of the Pacific yew to find out why it was so hardy. They separated chemicals from the bark. During this analysis, the scientists discovered unusual crystals in the bark. These crystals are made from a chemical called **taxol,** the substance that protects the Pacific yew tree.

Scientists next experimented with taxol in the laboratory. They discovered that taxol crystals affect cancer cells in an unusual way. Typically, cancer cells grow and divide very rapidly. This quick growth forms a mass of cells called a tumor. When cancer cells are exposed to taxol, the taxol forms structures that look like tiny cages around each cancer cell. These structures prevent the cancer cells from dividing. As a result, the cancer cannot grow and spread.

After more research, doctors were ready to test taxol on cancer patients. The taxol treatments often were able to shrink certain types of tumors. Sometimes they even stopped the cancer from spreading in the body. Taxol is now used to treat more than 12,000 cancer patients each year.

✓ *Checkpoint* How is taxol helpful to Pacific yew trees?

Answers to Self-Assessment

✓ *Checkpoint*

Taxol makes the trees resistant to diseases and insects.

---

2 *Facilitate*

Plants and Medicines

Real-Life Learning

Materials *packages from herbal teas and dietary supplements*
Time 15 minutes

Tell students that many traditional folk remedies are still used today. As examples, supply empty packages from a variety of herbal teas and dietary supplements such as chamomile, St. John's wort, ginseng, kava kava, echinacea, ginkgo biloba, goldenseal, and cat's claw. Let students examine the labels and identify the herb each product contains and its purported benefits. Point out the notice on each supplement's label that the product is not approved by the FDA for medical use. Also encourage students to ask older family members about traditional remedies that were commonly used in the past. **learning modality: verbal**

The Story of Taxol

Building Inquiry Skills: Observing

Materials *small branches from yew shrubs*
Time 10 minutes

Provide each pair or small group of students with a small branch clipped from a variety of yew (*Taxus*) that is commonly used for landscaping. Let students examine the needles and the thin, scaly bark. Explain that the Pacific yew is related to these shrubs but is a large tree that grows up to 14 m tall with a wide trunk. Before taxol was discovered, wood from the Pacific yew was used to build furniture. **learning modality: kinesthetic**

Ongoing Assessment

Writing Have each student explain how protective chemicals are helpful to plants.

A Threatened Supply of Taxol

Building Inquiry Skills: Calculating

Point out that the text says more than 12,000 cancer patients are treated with taxol each year. Ask: **How many yew trees would have to be cut down to supply the drug to those people?** *(36,000 per year)* **learning modality: logical/mathematical**

Biodiversity and Medicine

Cultural Diversity

Explain that many scientists are learning about the medicinal qualities of wild organisms from native peoples. These groups often still depend on plants and animals for medicines. For example, cat's claw (Uña de Gato), a traditional herbal medicine in Peru, has a high alkaloid content. Limited studies have found that alkaloids may help bolster the disease-fighting function of white blood cells. **learning modality: verbal**

3 Assess

Section 4 Review Answers

1. Many of these plants produce chemicals that protect them against predators, parasites, and diseases.
2. Temperate rain forests, which are cool, damp, and heavily shaded
3. Taxol encloses each cancer cell in a cage that keeps the cell from dividing.
4. The company would be interested in testing new species to determine whether they might have any medical uses.

Check Your Progress

CHAPTER PROJECT 20

As students observe their plots, encourage them to draw the organisms in detail so they can identify them later using field guides. Remind students to make notes about abiotic factors as well. Check each group's notebook occasionally to make sure students are recording data.

Figure 21 This researcher is pressing leaves as part of a species survey in a forest reserve.

A Threatened Supply of Taxol

The demand for taxol as a cancer treatment has grown rapidly. Now many scientists have become concerned about the supply of Pacific yew trees. It takes the bark of three Pacific yew trees to produce enough pure taxol for one cancer patient's treatment. If the bark is removed from a yew tree, the tree cannot survive. And by the time researchers discovered taxol's value as a cancer-fighting drug, a large portion of the yew trees' temperate rain forests were gone.

Taxol has a very complex chemical structure. Chemists have been working for many years to reproduce this structure. In 1996, chemists successfully created taxol in the laboratory for the first time. This discovery could help protect the remaining Pacific yew trees for future generations.

Biodiversity and Medicine

Almost half of all medicines sold today contain chemicals originally found in wild organisms. What other medicines are growing undiscovered in the forests of the world? So far, only about 2 percent of the world's known plant species have been studied for possible medical use. In 1995 the American Medical Association called for the protection of Earth's biodiversity. Their goal was to preserve the undiscovered medicines that may exist in nature. Governments, scientists, and private companies are working together to find new species all over the world. Perhaps they will find new sources of cancer-fighting drugs.

Section 4 Review

1. What adaptations of rain forest plants make them a likely source of medicines?
2. Describe the ecosystem in which Pacific yew trees are found.
3. How does taxol affect cancer cells?
4. **Thinking Critically** **Inferring** Suppose a group of scientists is planning an expedition to identify new species in the South American rain forest. Why might a company that manufactures medicines be interested in supporting their expedition?

Check Your Progress

CHAPTER PROJECT 20

Visit your plot regularly to make observations. Use field guides to identify the plants, animals, and other organisms you observe. Record their locations within your plot along with their common and scientific names. By now you should also be planning how to present your findings. Consider using a series of drawings, a flip chart, a computer presentation, or a video of your plot with closeups of the species you have identified. (*Hint:* Be sure to include the data you collected on abiotic factors.)

Background

Integrating Science Taxol was first tested in women with severe ovarian cancer that had not responded to chemotherapy and radiation. Ovarian tumors in 40 percent of the women shrank to half their original size. When taxol was later given to women with breast cancer, more than half the patients experienced partial remission.

Program Resources

◆ **Unit 6 Resources** 20-1 Review and Reinforce, p. 37; 20-1 Enrich, p. 38

SECTION 1 Environmental Issues

Key Ideas
◆ Three types of environmental issues are resource use, population growth, and pollution.
◆ Making environmental decisions requires balancing different viewpoints and weighing the costs and benefits of proposals.

Key Terms
renewable resources
nonrenewable resources
pollution
development viewpoint
preservation viewpoint
conservation viewpoint

SECTION 2 Forests and Fisheries

Key Ideas
◆ Because new trees can be planted to replace those that are cut down, forests can be renewable resources.
◆ Managing fisheries involves setting fishing limits, changing fishing methods, using aquaculture, and finding new resources.

Key Terms
clear-cutting
selective cutting
sustainable yield
fishery
aquaculture

SECTION 3 Biodiversity

Key Ideas
◆ Factors that affect biodiversity include area, climate, and diversity of niches.
◆ Human activities that threaten biodiversity include habitat destruction, poaching, pollution, and introduction of exotic species.
◆ Three techniques for protecting biodiversity are regulating capture and trade, captive breeding, and habitat preservation.

Key Terms
biodiversity
keystone species
genes
extinction
endangered species
threatened species
habitat destruction
habitat fragmentation
poaching
captive breeding

SECTION 4 The Search for New Medicines

INTEGRATING HEALTH

Key Ideas
◆ Many plants make chemicals that protect them from predators, parasites, and disease. These chemicals may fight human diseases.
◆ The cancer-fighting drug taxol comes from Pacific yew trees, which have been affected by logging of the forests where they grow.
◆ The possible discovery of other medicines is one reason to protect biodiversity.

Key Term
taxol

Organizing Information

Concept Map Copy the biodiversity concept map below onto a sheet of paper. Complete it and add a title. (For more on concept maps, see the Skills Handbook.)

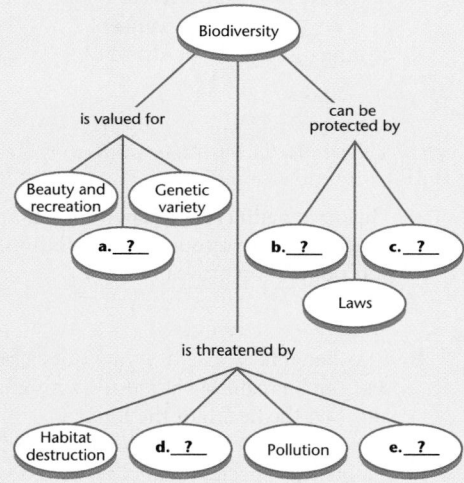

Organizing Information

Concept Map **a.** Economic value; **b., c.** Captive breeding, Habitat preservation; **d., e.** Poaching, Exotic species. Sample title: Facts About Biodiversity

Program Resources

◆ **Unit 6 Resources** Chapter 20 Project Scoring Rubric, p. 8
◆ **Performance Assessment** Chapter 20, pp. 61–63
◆ **Chapter Tests** Chapter 20 Test, pp. 79–81

Media and Technology

Computer Test Bank
Chapter 20 Test

Performance Assessment

Writing Have students explain why it is important to be able to duplicate taxol in a laboratory.

Reviewing Content
Multiple Choice
1. b **2.** d **3.** a **4.** b **5.** b

True or False
6. true **7.** renewable **8.** true **9.** keystone
10. preservation

Checking Concepts
11. *Sample answers: personal/local issue*—deciding whether to recycle materials; *national/global issue*—setting aside land for wildlife refuges

12. By considering the viewpoints of many different people and weighing the costs and benefits of different solutions

13. Clear-cutting exposes soil to erosion by wind and water, damages streams with eroded silt, and destroys forest habitats. Selective cutting is less damaging to the forest environment and maintains diversity.

14. *Any one:* Set limits on the amount and/or size of fish that can be caught; use nets with a larger mesh size; outlaw fishing methods that kill all the fish in an area rather than selected species; raise fish on farms (aquaculture)

15. Species lose the places where they feed, breed, and nest. If they cannot find a substitute niche, they must move to a new location to survive. If they cannot relocate, they will not survive.

16. Each student's editorial should demonstrate understanding of the viewpoint he or she has chosen: development (using resources freely to benefit people), preservation (not disturbing the environment), or conservation (using resources without destroying them).

Thinking Critically
17. As the number of humans increases, they compete with other species for space, food, water, and other resources. More humans also create more pollution and develop more land, which in turn destroys natural habitats. Pollution and habitat destruction can threaten the survival of some species.

18. An exotic species may compete with native species for limited resources. If the exotic species has no natural predators in its new habitat, it may outcompete the native species.

Reviewing Content
Multiple Choice
Choose the letter of the best answer.

1. The viewpoint that humans should be able to benefit from all of Earth's resources is the
   a. conservation viewpoint.
   b. development viewpoint.
   c. scientific viewpoint.
   d. preservation viewpoint.
2. The most diverse ecosystems in the world are
   a. coral reefs.   b. deserts.
   c. grasslands.   d. tropical rain forests.
3. If all members of a species disappear from Earth, that species is
   a. extinct.   b. endangered.
   c. nonrenewable.   d. threatened.
4. The illegal removal from the wild or the killing of an endangered species is called
   a. habitat destruction.
   b. poaching.
   c. pollution.
   d. captive breeding.
5. Taxol, which comes from Pacific yew trees, is a medicine that is used to fight
   a. heart disease.   b. cancer.
   c. lung disease.   d. diabetes.

True or False
If the statement is true, write true. If it is false, change the underlined word or words to make the statement true.

6. The three main types of environmental issues today are resource use, pollution, and <u>population growth</u>.
7. Forests and fisheries are examples of <u>nonrenewable</u> resources.
8. A <u>sustainable yield</u> is a number of trees that can be regularly harvested without affecting the health of the forest.
9. A species that influences the survival of many other species in an ecosystem is called a(n) <u>endangered</u> species.
10. The most effective way to protect biodiversity is through habitat <u>fragmentation</u>.

Checking Concepts
11. Give an example of a personal or local environmental issue and an example of a national or global environmental issue.
12. Describe how environmental decisions are made.
13. Compare the effects of clear-cutting and selective cutting on forest ecosystems.
14. Describe one way that overfishing can be prevented.
15. Explain how habitat destruction affects species.
16. **Writing to Learn** You are a member of the county land use commission. Hundreds of people are moving to your county every day. You must make a decision regarding how to manage a 5,000-hectare woodland area in your county. Choose one point of view: development, preservation, or conservation. Write an editorial for a newspaper explaining your position.

Thinking Critically
17. **Relating Cause and Effect** Explain how human population growth affects other species on Earth.
18. **Making Generalizations** Describe how an exotic species can threaten other species in an ecosystem.
19. **Predicting** How could the extinction of a species today affect your life 20 years from now?
20. **Making Judgments** Suppose you were given a million dollars toward saving an endangered turtle species. You could use the money to start a captive breeding program for the turtles. Or you could use the money to purchase and protect part of the turtle's habitat. How would you spend the money? Explain your answer.
21. **Relating Cause and Effect** Explain why many human medicines are made from chemicals that come from plants.

19. *Sample answers:* The species might have been the source of a medicine or had another use that is unknown today. The species might have been the source of genes for rare traits that could help other species survive.

20. Accept all reasonable responses so long as students support their choices with well-reasoned arguments that include why the method has a greater chance of success or can achieve more for the money invested.

21. Many plants produce chemicals that ward off disease and parasites. These chemicals often have disease-fighting properties in humans.

Applying Skills

One study identifies the reasons that mammal and bird species are endangered or threatened. Use the table to answer Questions 22–24.

Reason	Mammals	Birds
Poaching	31%	20%
Habitat loss	32%	60%
Exotic species	17%	12%
Other causes	20%	8%

22. Graphing Make a bar graph comparing the reasons that mammals and birds are endangered and threatened. Show percents for each animal group on the vertical axis and reasons on the horizontal axis.

23. Interpreting Data What is the major reason that mammals become endangered or threatened? What mainly endangers or threatens birds?

24. Developing Hypotheses Suggest explanations for the differences between the data for mammals and birds.

Performance **CHAPTER PROJECT 20** Assessment

Project Wrap Up In your presentation, describe the biodiversity in your plot. Suggest an explanation for any patterns you observed. Make sure each person in your group has a role in the presentation. Before the presentation day, brainstorm questions your classmates might ask. Then prepare answers for them.

Reflect and Record In your journal, write what you learned from observing a single location. Which of your findings were surprising? What was the hardest part of this project? What would you do differently if you did this project again?

Test Preparation

Use these questions to prepare for standardized tests.

Read the passage. Then answer Questions 25–27.

Starting in the late 1940s, the pesticide DDT was used to kill insects that spread disease and damaged crops. At first, DDT seemed to have no effect on other organisms. Over time, however, people noticed that the numbers of bald eagles and other large fish-eating birds were declining.

Ecologists discovered that DDT settled into the soil and eventually found its way into rivers and lakes. The DDT contaminated tiny organisms in the water, which were then eaten by small fishes. As bigger fishes ate the small fishes, and large birds ate the bigger fishes, they took the DDT into their bodies at higher and higher concentrations.

The DDT caused the eagles to lay eggs with very thin shells, which broke before hatching. Eagle populations began to decline steadily. In the 1970s, the use of DDT was banned in the United States. Since then, the populations of bald eagles and other affected birds have begun to recover.

25. What is the main idea of this passage?
   a. DDT has been used to kill harmful insects.
   b. The use of DDT was banned in the 1970s.
   c. The use of DDT led to a decline in the number of bald eagles.
   d. DDT found its way into rivers and lakes.

26. According to this passage, what effect does DDT have on bald eagles?
   a. DDT kills adult bald eagles.
   b. DDT affects the formation of eggshells, so fewer young are hatched.
   c. DDT kills the organisms that bald eagles prey upon.
   d. DDT has no effect on bald eagles.

27. Based on this passage, predict what might have happened if DDT had not been banned.
   a. Crop damage might have increased.
   b. Bald eagle populations might have increased.
   c. DDT might have stopped flowing into rivers and lakes.
   d. Bald eagles might have become endangered.

Applying Skills

22. See bottom left.
23. Habitat loss is the major cause for both birds and mammals. Poaching is almost as significant for mammals.
24. *Sample answer:* Areas where birds tend to nest and breed, such as wetlands, are particularly threatened by habitat destruction.

Performance **CHAPTER PROJECT 20** Assessment

Project Wrap Up Before groups give their presentations to the entire class, meet with each group briefly to review students' plans. Suggest any questions that may not have occurred to them.
Reflect and Record Let each group reconvene to discuss their answers to these questions, then encourage all groups to share their ideas in a class discussion.

Test Preparation

25. c **26.** b **27.** d

Applying Skills

22.

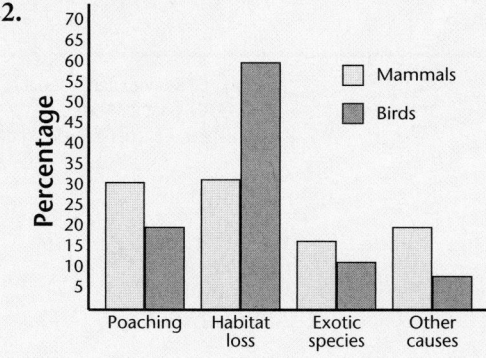

Program Resources

◆ **Inquiry Skills Activity Book** Provides teaching and review of all inquiry skills
◆ **Prentice Hall Assessment System** Provides standardized test practice
◆ **Reading in the Content Area** Provides strategies to improve science reading skills
◆ **Teacher's ELL Handbook** Provides multiple strategies for English language learners

Land and Soil Resources

Sections	Time	Student Edition Activities	Other Activities
CHAPTER PROJECT 21 **What's in a Package?** p. 679	Ongoing (2 weeks)	Check Your Progress, pp. 685, 700 Project Wrap Up, p. 703	Chapter 20 Project Notes, pp. 678–679
1 Conserving Land and Soil pp. 680–686 ◆ 21.1.1 Describe major forms of land use. ◆ 21.1.2 Identify problems that occur when soil is not properly managed.	2 periods/ 1 block	**Discover** How Does Mining Affect the Land?, p. 680 **Skills Lab: Controlling Variables** Save That Soil, p. 686	TE Integrating Earth Science, p. 682 TE Building Inquiry Skills: Observing, p. 682 TE Inquiry Challenge, p. 683
2 Solid Waste pp. 687–695 ◆ 21.2.1 Name and describe three ways of dealing with solid waste. ◆ 21.2.2 List the four major types of recyclable waste. ◆ 21.2.3 Describe methods for managing solid waste.	2 periods/ 1 block	**Discover** What's in the Trash?, p. 687 **Sharpen Your Skills,** Graphing, p. 689 **Try This** It's in the Numbers, p. 691 **Science at Home,** p. 693 **Real-World Lab: How It Works** Waste, Away!, pp. 694–695	TE Demonstration, p. 688 TE Building Inquiry Skills: Making Models, p. 689 TE Integrating Technology, p. 690 TE Building Inquiry Skills: Calculating, p. 690 TE Real-Life Learning, p. 691 TE Building Inquiry Skills: Communicating, p. 692 LM 21, "Choosing Packing Materials"
3 *INTEGRATING CHEMISTRY* **Hazardous Wastes** pp. 696–700 ◆ 21.3.1 List and describe the categories of hazardous wastes. ◆ 21.3.2 Explain how hazardous wastes affect human health. ◆ 21.3.3 Identify methods for managing hazardous wastes.	1 period/ ½ block	**Discover** What's Hazardous?, p. 696	TE Building Inquiry Skills: Classifying, p. 697 TE Real-Life Learning, p. 697 TE Integrating Health, p. 698 TE Inquiry Challenge, p. 698 TE Building Inquiry Skills: Communicating, p. 699 TE Using the Visuals: Figure 16, p. 700
Study Guide/Assessment pp. 701–703	1 period/ ½ block		ISAB Provides teaching and review of all inquiry skills

 For Standard or Block Schedule The Resource Pro® CD-ROM gives you maximum flexibility for planning your instruction for any type of schedule. Resource Pro® contains Planning Express®, an advanced scheduling program, as well as the entire contents of the Teaching Resources and the Computer Test Bank.

Key: **CTB** Computer Test Bank
CT Chapter Tests
ELL Teacher's ELL Handbook

CHAPTER PLANNING GUIDE

Program Resources	Assessment Strategies	Media and Technology
UR Chapter 21 Project Teacher Notes, pp. 30–31 **UR** Chapter 21 Project Overview and Worksheets, pp. 32–35	**TE** Check Your Progress, pp. 685, 700 **TE** Performance Assessment: Chapter 21 Project Wrap Up, p. 703 **UR** Chapter 21 Project Scoring Rubric, p. 36	Science Explorer Internet Site Audio CDs, Section Summaries
UR 21-1 Lesson Plan, p. 37 **UR** 21-1 Section Summary, p. 38 **UR** 21-1 Review and Reinforce, p. 39 **UR** 21-1 Enrich, p. 40 **UR** Skills Lab blackline masters, pp. 49–50	**SE** Section 1 Review, p. 685 **SE** Analyze and Conclude, p. 686 **TE** Ongoing Assessment, pp. 681, 683 **TE** Performance Assessment, p. 685	Concept Videotape Library, *Adventures, Tape 5,* "Is Our Soil Endangered?" Transparency 82, "Soil Layers" Lab Activity Videotape, *Tape 5*
UR 21-2 Lesson Plan, p. 41 **UR** 21-2 Section Summary, p. 42 **UR** 21-2 Review and Reinforce, p. 43 **UR** 21-2 Enrich, p. 44 **UR** Real-World Lab blackline masters, pp. 51–53	**SE** Section 2 Review, p. 693 **SE** Analyze and Conclude, p. 695 **TE** Ongoing Assessment, pp. 689, 691 **TE** Performance Assessment, p. 693	Concept Videotape Library, *Adventures, Tape 5,* "Where Does Your Garbage Go?"; "It Really Isn't Garbage" Transparency 83, "Exploring a Landfill" Lab Activity Videotape, *Tape 5*
UR 21-3 Lesson Plan, p. 45 **UR** 21-3 Section Summary, p. 46 **UR** 21-3 Review and Reinforce, p. 47 **UR** 21-3 Enrich, p. 48	**SE** Section 3 Review, p. 700 **TE** Ongoing Assessment, pp. 697, 699 **TE** Performance Assessment, p. 700	
GRSW Provides worksheets to promote student comprehension of content **RCA** Provides strategies to improve science reading skills **ELL** Provides multiple strategies for English language learners	**SE** Study Guide/Assessment, pp. 701–703 **PA** Performance Assessment, pp. 64–66 **CT** Chapter 21 Test, pp. 83–86 **CTB** Chapter 21 Test **PHAS** Provides standardized test preparation	Computer Test Bank, Chapter 21 Test

GRSW Guided Reading and Study Workbook
ISAB Inquiry Skills Activity Book
LM Laboratory Manual

PA Performance Assessment
PHAS Prentice Hall Assessment System
PLM Probeware Lab Manual

RCA Reading in the Content Area
SE Student Edition

TE Teacher's Edition
UR Unit Resources

Meeting the National Science Education Standards and AAAS Benchmarks

National Science Education Standards	Benchmarks for Science Literacy	Unifying Themes
Science as Inquiry (Content Standard A) ◆ **Design and conduct a scientific investigation** Students investigate how rainfall can cause erosion. *(Skills Lab)* ◆ **Develop descriptions, explanations, predictions, and models using evidence** Students model landfills to see how they work. *(Real-World Lab)* **Earth and Space Science** (Content Standard D) ◆ **Structure of the Earth system** Soil is a complex system made up of living and nonliving things. *(Section 1)* **Science and Technology** (Content Standard E) ◆ **Evaluate completed technological designs or products** Students analyze product packaging. *(Chapter Project)* **Science in Personal and Social Perspectives** (Content Standard F) ◆ **Personal health** Exposure to hazardous wastes can affect health. *(Section 3)* ◆ **Natural hazards** Poor soil management can result in erosion, nutrient depletion, and desertification. *(Section 1; Skills Lab)* ◆ **Science and technology in society** Solid waste can be buried, burned, or recycled. *(Chapter Project; Section 2)*	**1B Scientific Inquiry** Students analyze product packaging, investigate how different land surfaces are affected by rainfall, and model different kinds of landfills to see how they work. *(Chapter Project; Skills Lab; Real-World Lab)* **3A Technology and Science** Some farming methods can help reduce soil erosion. A well-designed sanitary landfill contains the waste and prevents it from polluting the surrounding land and water. Scientists have developed several methods of hazardous waste disposal. *(Sections 1, 2, 3; Real-World Lab)* **3C Issues in Technology** Poor soil management can result in erosion, nutrient depletion, and desertification. The basic ways to deal with solid waste are to bury it, burn it, or recycle it. Hazardous waste is any material that can be harmful to human health or the environment if it is not properly stored, transported, treated, or disposed of. *(Sections 1, 2, 3; Chapter Project; Skills Lab)* **4B The Earth** Three uses that change the land are agriculture, development, and mining. A wide range of materials can be recycled. *(Sections 1, 2)*	◆ **Energy** The burning of solid waste is called incineration. Recycling saves energy. *(Sections 1, 2 ; Skills Lab)* ◆ **Modeling** Students model different land surfaces to see how they are affected by rainfall and different kinds of landfills to see how they work. *(Skills Lab; Real-World Lab)* ◆ **Patterns of Change** Agriculture, development, and mining change the land. A substance that can be broken down and recycled by natural decomposers is biodegradable. *(Sections 1, 2)* ◆ **Scale and Structure** Soil is a complex system made up of living and nonliving things. *(Section 1)* ◆ **Stability** The process of restoring land to a more natural, productive state is called land reclamation. *(Sections 1, 3)* ◆ **Systems and Interactions** Some farming methods can help reduce erosion. The basic ways to deal with solid waste are to bury it, burn it, or recycle it. *(Sections 1, 2, 3; Chapter Project)* ◆ **Unity and Diversity** Most recycling focuses on four major categories of products: metal, glass, paper, and plastic. Hazardous wastes can be toxic, explosive, flammable, or corrosive. Radioactive wastes also need special disposal. *(Sections 2, 3)*

Take It to the Net

The **www.phschool.com** Web site provides you with multiple opportunities to incorporate the internet into your instruction. Go to **www.phschool.com** and click on the Science icon. Then select Science Explorer Integrated.

■ Have students use the chapter Self-Test to get instant feedback.

■ Hot Links and Reference Links provide opportunities for online research.

Internet Activities provide opportunities for students to review, extend, or assess a concept from the chapter.

STAY CURRENT with **SCIENCE NEWS** ®

Find out the latest research and information about natural resources and pollution at: **www.phschool.com**

Activity	Time (minutes)	Materials — Quantities for one work group	Skills
Section 1			
Discover, p. 680	10	**Consumable** mixture of sand and soil, 10–15 sunflower seeds **Nonconsumable** pan, pencil, tweezers, spoon	Predicting
Skills Lab, p. 686	40	**Consumable** newspaper, loose soil, water, sod **Nonconsumable** 2 blocks, 2 unbreakable pans, "rainmaker"	Developing Hypotheses, Controlling Variables, Observing
Section 2			
Discover, p. 687	20	**Consumable** trash bag, 10–15 items commonly found in household waste, plastic gloves, graph paper **Nonconsumable** ruler	Interpreting Data
Sharpen Your Skills, p. 689	15	**Nonconsumable** protractor, drawing compass	Graphing
Try This, p. 691	10	**Nonconsumable** pieces of plastic products with recycling codes	Classifying
Science at Home, p. 693	home	**Consumable** household trash collected for one week **Nonconsumable** scale, calculator (optional)	Calculating
Real-World Lab, pp. 694–695	40; 20	**Consumable** plastic wrap, heavy-duty plastic bag, 12 small sponge cubes, cheesecloth, water, red food coloring, soil, newspaper **Nonconsumable** measuring cup, small pebbles, 5 rubber bands, 3 transparent wide-mouthed jars, metric ruler, scissors, tweezers	Making Models, Drawing Conclusions
Section 3			
Discover, p. 696	10	**Nonconsumable** labels from common hazardous household products	Forming Operational Definitions

A list of all materials required for the Student Edition activities can be found beginning on page T23. You can obtain information about ordering materials by calling 1-800-848-9500 or by accessing the Science Explorer Internet site at: **www.phschool.com**

What's in a Package?

The Chapter 21 Project provides an opportunity for students to examine product packaging, determine the various materials used and their functions, and investigate what happens to the materials when the packages are discarded.

Purpose Students will identify the materials used in a package; infer the purpose of each material for the product's producers, retailers, and consumers; find out what happens to each type of material in the community's waste-disposal system; and communicate findings in a display.

Skills Focus After completing the Chapter 21 Project, students will be able to
◆ classify the types of materials used in product packages;
◆ infer the purpose of each material;
◆ draw conclusions about what happens to each type of material when it is discarded;
◆ communicate their findings.

Project Time Line The Chapter 21 Project requires about two weeks to complete. This project is most appropriate as an individual activity, though students could work cooperatively to research what happens to the various materials when they are discarded. As the class studies Section 1, each student should choose a product package and begin analyzing the materials used in it. The major portion of the project involves finding out what happens to each material when the package is discarded and then preparing a class display.

Advance Preparation You may wish to contact the municipal department or private company that handles waste collection and recycling in the students' community, and arrange to have a representative speak to the class when students are ready to research waste disposal. If a visit to the class is not possible, arrange to have a designated representative available to answer students' questions on the phone. Other sources of information include municipal waste department fact sheets and town Web sites.

WEB ACTIVITY www.phschool.com

SECTION **1** Conserving Land and Soil	SECTION **2** Solid Waste	SECTION **3** Hazardous Wastes
Discover **How Does Mining Affect the Land?** Skills Lab **Save That Soil**	Discover **What's in the Trash?** Sharpen Your Skills **Graphing** Try This **It's in the Numbers** Real-World Lab **Waste, Away!**	Integrating Chemistry Discover **What's Hazardous?**

678

Possible Materials

◆ Let each student choose a package for the project. Encourage students to choose packages that include two or more different materials. Alternatively, you may wish to collect appropriate packages and assign them to students. CAUTION: *Tell students to make sure the packages are empty before they bring them to school. If students select cans, bottles, and plastic containers for foods, advise them to wash the containers thoroughly with hot, soapy water before bringing them to class. Do not allow students to use packaging for raw chicken, ground beef, or any other uncooked meats or fish. Be particularly aware of your school's policy regarding students bringing over-the-counter medicines, vitamin pills, and similar items to school, as empty packages may be misinterpreted by administrators or other teachers.*

◆ Students will need scissors to take their packages apart.

◆ Provide posterboard, tape, colored markers, and other supplies for product displays.

What's in a Package?

The next time you're in the supermarket, take a look at all the different kinds of packages. There are glass bottles, plastic bottles, metal cans, cardboard boxes, plastic bags, paper wrappers, and more! Different kinds of packages are used for different kinds of products.

Many of these packages are opened and then thrown away. But where is "away"? In this chapter, you will read about what happens to wastes after they are discarded. While you study the chapter, you will be analyzing the anatomy of a package.

Your Goal To analyze and display information about a product package.

Your display must

◆ Include a cutaway portion of the package with the different materials labeled.
◆ Identify the purpose of each part of the package.
◆ Describe what happens to each part of the package after it is thrown away in your community.

Get Started Obtain a product package to study. Empty the package and clean it out.

Check Your Progress You'll be working on this project as you study this chapter. To keep your project on track, look for Check Your Progress boxes at the following points.

Section 1 Review, page 685: Cut the package open and identify the materials from which it is made.
Section 3 Review, page 700: Investigate what happens to the materials that make up the package.

Wrap Up At the end of the chapter (page 703), you will assemble your product display and present it to your class.

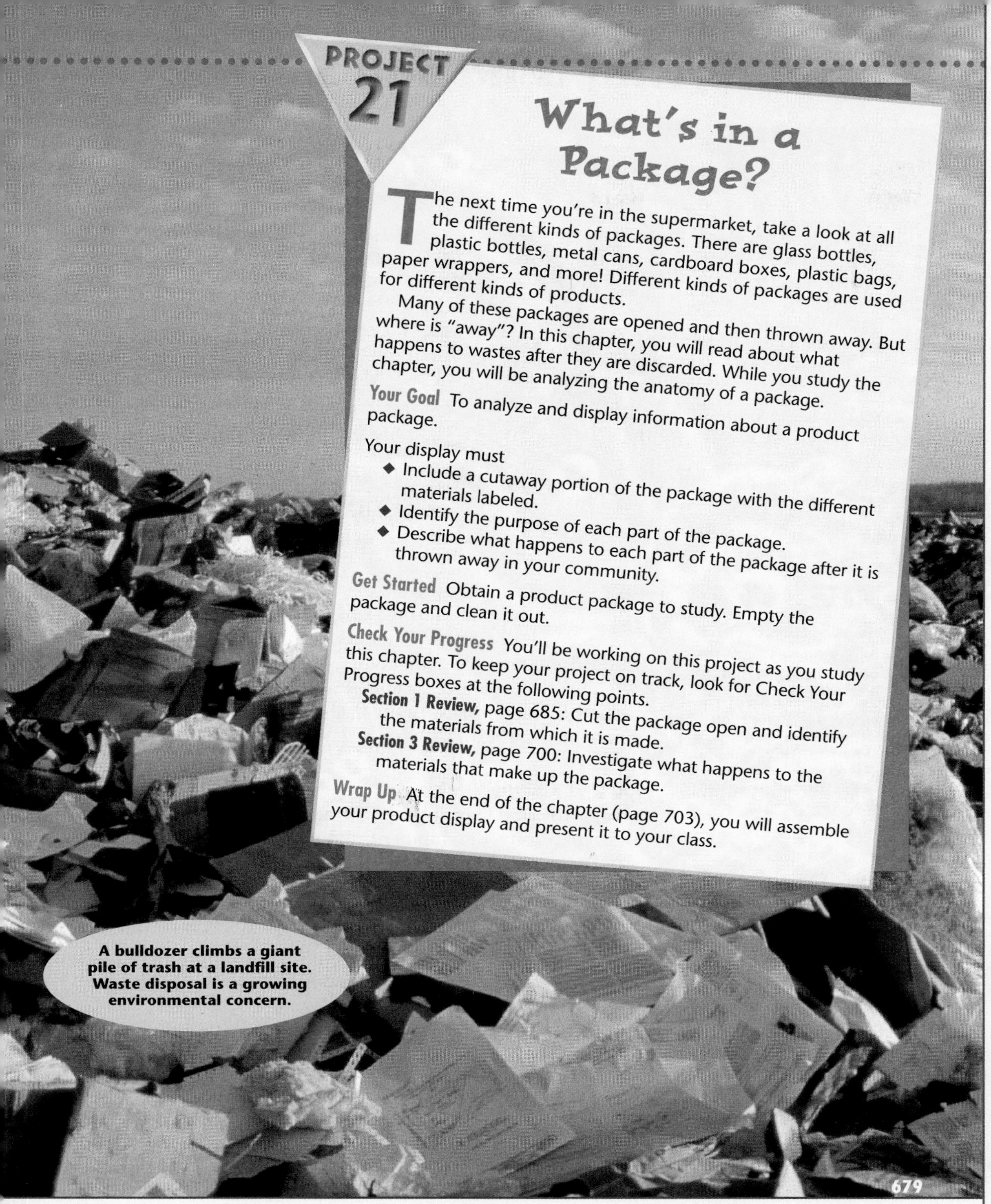

A bulldozer climbs a giant pile of trash at a landfill site. Waste disposal is a growing environmental concern.

679

Program Resources

◆ **Unit 6 Resources** Chapter 21 Project Teacher Notes, pp. 30–31; Project Overview and Worksheets, pp. 32–35; Project Scoring Rubric, p. 36

Media and Technology

 Audio CDs Section Summaries

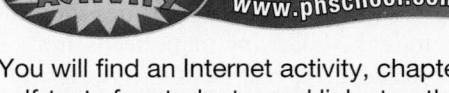 **www.phschool.com**

You will find an Internet activity, chapter self-tests for students, and links to other chapter topics at this site.

Launching the Project Invite students to read the Chapter 21 Project description on page 679. Lead the class in brainstorming types of packaging materials they know of, and list their ideas on the board. Ask students how the materials might be grouped.

Discuss some purposes of packaging materials—for example, keeping the product from spoiling, keeping it from breaking or being damaged during shipment, displaying the product attractively, preventing theft, and making the product convenient for consumers to store and use. Ask students to suggest which packaging materials might be best for each purpose.

Distribute Chapter 21 Project Overview on pages 32–33 of Unit 6 Resources, and have students review the project rules and procedures. Encourage students' questions and comments. Also distribute Worksheet 1 on page 34 of Unit 6 Resources, which lists a wide variety of possible products.

At the end of Section 1, distribute Worksheet 2 on page 35 of Unit 6 Resources, which provides a format for analyzing a package's components.

Additional information on guiding the project is provided in Chapter 21 Project Teacher Notes on pages 30–31 in Unit 6 Resources.

Performance Assessment

The Chapter 21 Project Scoring Rubric on page 36 in Unit 6 Resources will help you evaluate how well students complete the Chapter 21 Project. You may want to share the scoring rubric with students so they are clear about what will be expected of them. Students will be assessed on

◆ their completeness and accuracy in classifying the types of materials used in a product package;
◆ their ability to infer the purpose of each packaging material;
◆ their thoroughness in researching what happens to each type of material when the package is discarded in their community;
◆ how well they have communicated their findings to the class.

679

Conserving Land and Soil

Objectives

After completing the lesson, students will be able to

◆ describe major forms of land use;
◆ identify problems that occur when soil is not properly managed.

Key Terms development, litter, topsoil, subsoil, bedrock, erosion, nutrient depletion, fallow, crop rotation, desertification, land reclamation

1 Engage/Explore

Activating Prior Knowledge

To determine what students already know about soil, ask: **What is soil made of?** *(Rock that was broken down into very small pieces over time; accept other reasonable responses without comment at this time.)* **What else does soil contain?** *(Students may mention minerals, nutrients, dead and decaying organisms, and living organisms.)*

DISCOVER

Skills Focus predicting
Materials *pan, mixture of sand and soil, 10–15 sunflower seeds, pencil, tweezers, spoon*
Time 10 minutes
Advance Preparation For each student or small group, prepare a model mining site by filling a pan about half full with a mixture of sand and soil, burying 10–15 sunflower seeds in the mixture, then smoothing the surface to hide the seeds. CAUTION: *Students should wash their hands when they finish.*
Tips Let students use any method they wish to locate and extract the seeds.
Expected Outcome The site will have many holes and mounds of dirt.
Think It Over Students should realize that the land is changed significantly when a site is mined. Restoring it is difficult; holes must be filled, the excavated soil replaced and regraded, and the land replanted.

Conserving Land and Soil

DISCOVER •• ACTIVITY

How Does Mining Affect the Land?

1. You will be given a pan filled with sand and soil representing a mining site. There are at least 10 deposits of "ore" (sunflower seeds) buried in your mining site.
2. Your goal is to locate and remove the ore from your site. You may use a pencil, a pair of tweezers, and a spoon as mining tools.

3. After you have extracted the chunks of ore, break them open to remove the "minerals" inside. **CAUTION:** Do not eat the sunflower seeds.
4. Observe your mining site and the surrounding area after your mining operations are finished.

Think It Over
Predicting How did mining change the land at your mining site? Predict whether it would be easy or difficult to restore the land to its original state. Explain.

GUIDE FOR READING

◆ How do people use land?
◆ What kinds of problems occur when soil is not properly managed?

Reading Tip Before you read, use the section headings to make an outline about land and soil conservation. Leave space in the outline to take notes.

Less than a quarter of Earth's surface is dry land. Except for a small amount formed when volcanoes erupt, new land cannot be created. All the people on Earth must share this limited amount of land to produce their food, build shelter, and obtain other resources. Land is a precious resource. As the American author Mark Twain once said about land, "They don't make it anymore."

Types of Land Use

People use land in many ways. **Three uses that change the land are agriculture, development, and mining.** Examples of these land uses are shown in Figure 1.

680

READING STRATEGIES

Reading Tip Students' outlines should include the following main heads and subheads: *I. Types of Land Use*, *A. Agriculture*, *B. Development*, *C. Mining*, *II. Protecting the Soil*, *A. Erosion*, *B. Nutrient Depletion*, *C. Desertification*, *III. Restoring the Land*. Students might include *Soil Layers* as the first subhead below *Protecting the Soil*. Encourage students to include vocabulary terms and definitions in their outlines.

Study and Comprehension After students have examined Exploring Soil Conservation on page 683, have them write new captions for the photographs, paraphrasing the text captions in their own words. Tell students to make sure their captions explain what each farming practice involves and how it helps reduce soil erosion.

Agriculture Land is the source of most food. Crops such as wheat, rice, and potatoes require large areas of fertile land. But less than a third of Earth's land can be farmed. The rest is too dry, too wet, too salty, or too mountainous. To provide food for the growing population, new farmland must be created by clearing forests, draining wetlands, and irrigating deserts. When people make these changes, organisms that depended on the natural ecosystem must find new homes.

Many crops are grown to feed livestock such as hogs, chicken, and cattle. Other land serves as pasture or rangeland for grazing animals.

Development People settled the first villages in areas that had good soil and were near a source of fresh water. As population grew, these settlements became towns and cities. People built more houses and paved roads. The construction of buildings, roads, bridges, dams, and other structures is called **development.**

In the United States, about a million hectares of farmland (an area half the size of New Jersey) are developed each year. Development not only reduces the amount of farmland, but can also destroy wildlife habitats.

Mining Mining is the removal of nonrenewable resources such as iron, copper, and coal from the land. Resources just below the surface are strip mined. Strip mining involves removing a strip of land to obtain the minerals and then replacing the strip. Strip mines expose the soil. It can then be blown or washed away more easily. Strip-mined areas may remain barren for years before the soil becomes rich enough to support the growth of plants again.

For resources located deep underground, it is necessary to dig a tunnel, or shaft. The minerals are carried up through the shafts. This process is called underground mining.

☑ *Checkpoint* *Why isn't all land suitable for farming?*

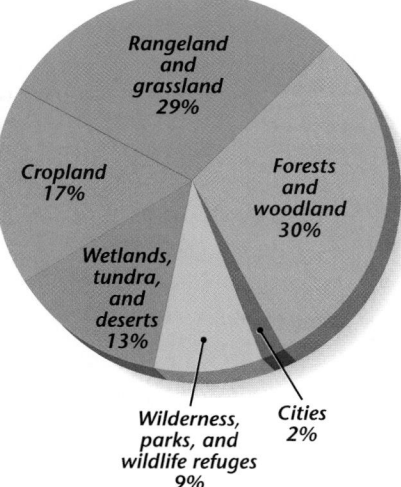

Land Use in the United States

- Rangeland and grassland 29%
- Forests and woodland 30%
- Cropland 17%
- Wetlands, tundra, and deserts 13%
- Wilderness, parks, and wildlife refuges 9%
- Cities 2%

Figure 1 Land in the United States is used in many ways. *Classifying Which of these land uses change the natural ecosystems of the land?*

Figure 2 Three major uses of land are agriculture, development, and mining.

Chapter 21 **681**

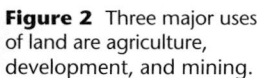

Answers to Self-Assessment

Caption Question

Figure 1 Cropland, cities, and rangeland

☑ *Checkpoint*

Much of Earth's land is too dry, too wet, too salty, or too mountainous to be farmed.

---

2 *Facilitate*

Types of Land Use

Using the Visuals: Figure 1

Have students answer the caption question in a class discussion. Students should readily recognize that both the cities (an example of development) and the cropland (agriculture) are uses that change natural ecosystems. Some students may also realize that in the rangeland and grassland section of the graph, rangeland—land that is used for grazing domestic animals—is another use that changes natural ecosystems. **learning modality: logical/ mathematical**

Real-Life Learning

After students have examined the photographs in Figure 2 and read the caption, ask: **What examples of these three types of land uses have you seen for yourself? How was the land changed?** (*Answers will vary depending on students' location.*) Use prompting questions to help students describe the changes in detail and consider the effects of those changes on both the land itself and the organisms that lived in the area. **learning modality: verbal**

Ongoing Assessment

Oral Presentation Call on students at random to describe the various kinds of land use and tell how they affect the natural ecosystems of the land.

Protecting the Soil

Integrating Earth Science

Materials *glass jar with screw-on lid, water, soil sample, hand lens*

Time *Day 1:* 5 minutes; *Day 2:* 10 minutes

To illustrate the materials in topsoil, ask each student to collect and bring in about 500 mL of soil from a location near home. (Advise students to remove any visible living organisms and leave them at the location.) Have each student put his or her sample in a jar, add water to cover the soil well, screw the lid on tightly, then shake the jar gently until the soil and water are thoroughly mixed. (Remind students to wash their hands.) Have students leave their jars undisturbed overnight and examine them the next day. Ask: **What do you see in the jar now?** (*The soil components have settled in layers, with the largest and most dense particles at the bottom and the finest particles at the top; lightweight organic matter is floating on the surface.*)
learning modality: kinesthetic

Building Inquiry Skills: Observing

Materials *small potted plants such as ivy, geraniums, or begonias, hand lens, craft stick, newspaper*
Time 10 minutes

Provide a small potted plant to each group of students. Instruct students to carefully remove the plant from the pot. Then have students examine the roots with a hand lens, paying particular attention to how the roots wrap around and hold onto the soil particles. Instruct students to shake the plant over a sheet of newspaper and gently flick the roots with their fingers to dislodge as much soil as they can. When they examine the roots again, they will see fine particles of soil still clinging to the roots. (Remind students to wash their hands.) When they are done, students should repot the plants with fresh soil. **learning modality: visual**

Protecting the Soil

INTEGRATING EARTH SCIENCE Do you think of soil only as something that has to be washed off your hands or swept off the floor? Then you may not realize how much you depend on soil! Soil is a complex system made up of living and nonliving things. It contains the minerals and nutrients that plants need to grow. Soil also absorbs, stores, and filters water. Bacteria, fungi, and other organisms that live in soil break down the wastes and remains of living things. These decomposers recycle the chemical substances that are necessary for life.

Figure 3 shows the structure of fertile soil. Notice that it is composed of several layers. The very top layer of dead leaves and grass is called **litter.** The next layer, **topsoil,** is a mixture of rock fragments, nutrients, water, air, and decaying animal and plant matter. The water and nutrients are absorbed by the many plant roots located in this layer. Below the topsoil is the **subsoil.** The subsoil also contains rock fragments, water, and air, but has less animal and plant matter than the topsoil.

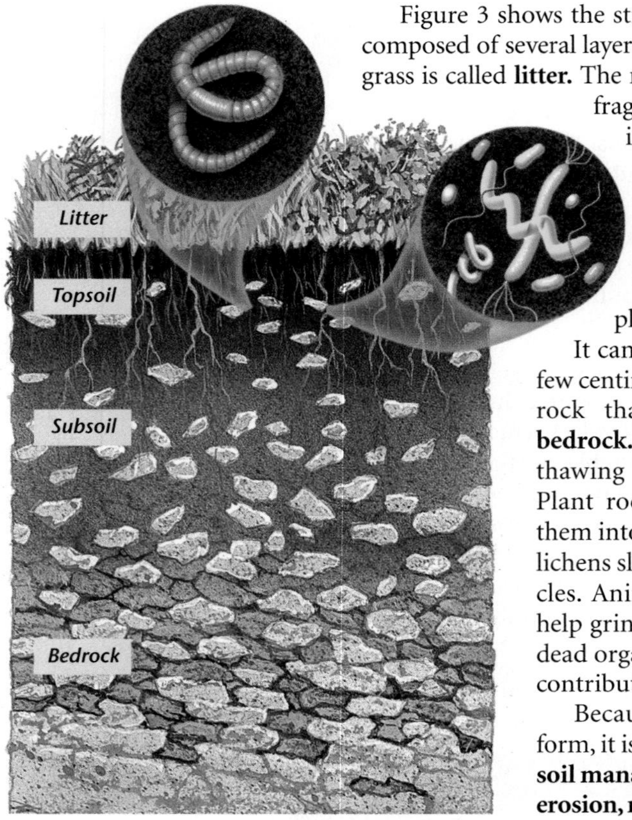

It can take hundreds of years to form just a few centimeters of new soil. All soil begins as the rock that makes up Earth's crust, called **bedrock.** Natural processes such as freezing and thawing gradually break apart the bedrock. Plant roots wedge between rocks and break them into smaller pieces. Chemicals released by lichens slowly break the rock into smaller particles. Animals such as earthworms and moles help grind rocks into even smaller particles. As dead organisms break down, their remains also contribute to the mixture.

Because rich topsoil takes a long time to form, it is important to protect Earth's soil. **Poor soil management can result in three problems: erosion, nutrient depletion, and desertification.**

Erosion The process by which water, wind, or ice moves particles of rocks or soil is called **erosion.** Normally, plant roots hold soil in place. But when soil is exposed to wind and water, erosion occurs more rapidly. Many uses of land, including logging, mining, and farming, expose the soil and can cause erosion. Some farming methods that help reduce erosion are described in *Exploring Soil Conservation.*

Figure 3 Soil consists of several layers. *Applying Concepts In which layer are most plant roots located? What do the roots absorb there?*

Litter
Topsoil
Subsoil
Bedrock

Background

Integrating Science In addition to leaving fields fallow and rotating crops, many farmers today use organic farming to reduce nutrient depletion.

Instead of manufactured fertilizers, organic farmers use natural fertilizers such as manure and composted plant matter. Instead of herbicides, they weed with physical methods. And instead of pesticides, they use insect-eating organisms such as praying mantises, ladybugs, birds, and bats.

Nutrient Depletion Plants make their own food through photosynthesis. But plants also require a variety of nutrients from the soil. Just as your body needs iron, zinc, and calcium to grow and function properly, plants need nitrogen, potassium, phosphorus, and other nutrients. Decomposers supply these nutrients to the soil as they break down the remains of dead organisms.

Sometimes, a farmer plants the same crops in a field year after year. As a result, the plants use more nutrients than the decomposers can replace. The soil becomes less fertile, a situation that is called **nutrient depletion.**

One way to prevent nutrient depletion is to periodically leave fields **fallow,** or unplanted with crops. A second way to prevent nutrient depletion is to leave the unused parts of crops, such as cornstalks and watermelon vines, in the fields rather than

EXPLORING Soil Conservation

These farming practices can help reduce soil erosion.

Conservation plowing ▼
Rather than plowing fields and leaving them bare, farmers use machines that break up only the subsoil. This method leaves the dead stalks and weeds from the previous year's crop in the ground to hold the topsoil in place.

◄ **Strip cropping and contour plowing**
Farmers alternate strips of tall crops, such as corn, with short crops, such as squash. The short crops prevent soil from washing out of the tall crop rows, which are less protected. Crops are planted in curving rows that follow the slope, or contour, of the land. Contour plowing can reduce soil erosion as much as 50 percent on gently sloping land.

▲ **Windbreaks**
Rows of trees are planted along the edges of fields. These windbreaks block the wind and also trap eroding soil. Using fruit or nut trees as windbreaks provides an extra benefit for the farmer and wildlife.

Terracing ▶
Steep hillsides are built up into a series of flat "terraces." The ridges of soil at the edges of the terraces slow down runoff and catch eroding soil.

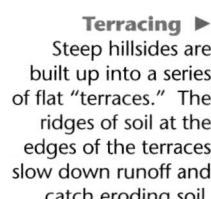

Chapter 21 **683**

Media and Technology

 Transparencies "Soil Layers," Transparency 82

 Concept Videotape Library *Adventures, Tape 5,* "Is Our Soil Endangered?"

Answers to Self-Assessment

Caption Question

Figure 3 Topsoil; the roots absorb water and nutrients.

EXPLORING
Soil Conservation

Discuss the various farming practices described in the feature, with particular attention to how each helps to reduce soil erosion. If students live in or have visited an agricultural area, encourage them to describe examples of these farming practices that they have seen. Challenge students to find other photographs of these practices—particularly of terracing, which is not often done in the United States but is common in hilly countries with limited fertile land. **learning modality: verbal**

Inquiry Challenge

Materials *2 deep pans or plastic storage containers, mixture of sand and soil, water*
Time 20 minutes

Challenge small groups of students to create a model showing how either contour plowing or terracing helps reduce soil erosion compared with straight-row plowing or planting on an unterraced hillside. *(Each group should use one container to model the "non-conservation" practice and the other container to model the erosion-reducing practice. Students could compare the results subjectively by describing the amount of erosion they observe in the two containers. To quantify the effects of each practice, students could measure the amount of water that collects at the bottom of the hill in each container and/or the amount of soil that is washed downhill.)* **cooperative learning**

Ongoing Assessment

Drawing Have each student draw and label a simple diagram showing the layers found in the soil.

Portfolio Students can save their drawings in their portfolios.

683

Protecting the Soil,
continued

Cultural Diversity

Display a map of Africa and point out the location of the Sahel, just south of the Sahara, the world's largest desert. Explain that the Sahel is a dry grassland. Many parts of the Sahel are experiencing desertification due to repeated droughts and overgrazing. People in the Sahel face continuing food shortages and many other problems caused by the loss of land that can be farmed. Encourage volunteers to find out more about the Sahel and report to the class. **learning modality: verbal**

Restoring the Land

Including All Students

Support students who need more help by encouraging them to relate the text's description of land reclamation to their own direct experience. If students did the Discover at the beginning of the section, ask: **What did your mining site look like when you finished?** (*The site was full of holes and piles of soil.*) Have students recall their predictions about how easy or difficult it would be to restore the land. Then ask: **Now that you've read about restoring the land, were there any problems or costs that you didn't think of earlier?** (*Students may not have realized that the subsoil and topsoil would have to be replaced after the mining operation or that new trees would need to be planted.*) **learning modality: logical/mathematical**

clearing them away. The stalks and vines decompose in the fields, adding nutrients to the soil.

Another method of preventing nutrient depletion is crop rotation. In **crop rotation,** a farmer plants different crops in a field each year. Different types of plants absorb different amounts of nutrients from the soil. Some crops, such as corn and cotton, absorb large amounts of nutrients. The next year, the farmer plants crops that use fewer soil nutrients, such as oats, barley, or rye. The year after that, the farmer sows legumes such as alfalfa or beans to restore the nutrient supply. Another benefit of crop rotation is that it limits the growth of pest populations from year to year.

☑ *Checkpoint* *What causes nutrient depletion?*

Desertification Plants cannot grow without the moisture and nutrients in fertile soil. The advance of desertlike conditions into areas that previously were fertile is called **desertification.** In the past 50 years, desertification has occurred on about five billion hectares of land.

One cause of desertification is climate. During periods of drought, crops fail. Without plant cover, the exposed soil easily blows away. Overgrazing of grasslands by cattle and sheep also exposes the soil. Cutting down trees for firewood can also cause desertification.

Desertification is a very serious problem. People cannot grow crops and graze livestock where desertification has occurred. People may face famine and starvation as a result. In central Africa, where desertification is severe, millions of rural people are moving to the cities because they can no longer support themselves on the land.

Figure 4 Large areas of the world are at risk of desertification. One cause is overgrazing. Without grass to hold the soil in place, the Senegal plain is becoming a barren desert.

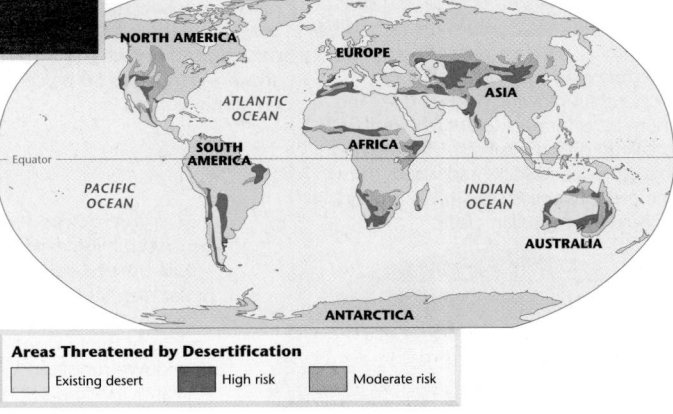

Areas Threatened by Desertification
Existing desert · High risk · Moderate risk

Background

Facts and Figures Most grasslands are located in semiarid areas. These areas have long periods of drought. The aboveground parts of plants die, but their roots remain alive and hold the soil in place. In this way, the native grasses survive droughts. The roots send up new shoots when the droughts end.

However, when overgrazing occurs during a drought, wind erodes the soil due to the absence of ground cover. The land is so stripped of fertile soil that it cannot recover. Water erosion removes any topsoil that remains, leaving only sand that is blown into dunes.

According to the United Nations, about 135 million people are in danger of displacement because of this desertification process.

Figure 5 It's hard to believe that cows now graze on the same hillside that used to be an open mine. Thanks to land reclamation practices, many mining areas are being restored for other uses.

Restoring the Land

Fortunately, it is often possible to restore land damaged by erosion or mining. The process of restoring an area of land to a more natural, productive state is called **land reclamation.** In addition to restoring lands for agriculture, land reclamation can restore habitats for wildlife. Many different types of land reclamation projects are currently underway all over the world. But it is generally more difficult and expensive to restore damaged land and soil than it is to protect them in the first place.

Figure 5 shows an example of land reclamation. When the mining operation in the first scene was completed, the mine operators smoothed out the sides of the mining cuts. Then they carefully replaced the subsoil and topsoil that had been removed before mining. Finally, they planted grass. The former mine is now agricultural land.

Section 1 Review

1. List three ways that people use land.
2. What are three problems that can occur when topsoil is not properly managed?
3. Describe the effects of strip mining on the land.
4. Why is it important to protect topsoil?
5. Describe two methods for reducing soil erosion.
6. **Thinking Critically Relating Cause and Effect** How may human activities be related to desertification?

Check Your Progress

CHAPTER PROJECT 21

Cut your package open so that you can observe its construction. Create a data table identifying each part of the package, the material it is made of, and its purpose. What properties of these materials make them desirable as packaging? (*Hint:* Packaging benefits include protecting a product from breakage, preventing spoilage, making it more attractive, or making it easier to use. Can you think of other benefits of the materials in your package?)

Section 1 Review Answers

1. Agriculture, development, and mining
2. Erosion, nutrient depletion, and desertification
3. Removing a strip of land exposes the soil to erosion by wind and water. The area may remain barren for years before the soil becomes rich enough again to support plant growth.
4. Topsoil contains the minerals and nutrients that plants need, and it takes a long time for fertile topsoil to form.
5. Students can describe two of the following: conservation plowing, strip cropping, contour plowing, terracing, and planting windbreaks.
6. To meet the needs of the growing human population, people raise large herds of grazing animals, cut down trees, and carry out strip mining, all of which contribute to desertification.

Check Your Progress

CHAPTER PROJECT 21

CAUTION: *Make sure students handle scissors carefully. Review the safety guidelines in Appendix A.* Give each student a copy of Chapter 21 Project Worksheet 2 on page 35 in Unit 6 Resources. Explain that the worksheet will help them analyze the packaging materials and infer the purpose of each one. Remind students to keep a sample of each material for use in their product displays.

Program Resources

◆ **Unit 6 Resources** 21-1 Review and Reinforce, p. 39; 21-1 Enrich, p. 40

Answers to Self-Assessment

☑ *Checkpoint*

If a farmer plants the same crop in a field year after year, the plants use more nutrients than decomposers in the soil can replace, and the soil becomes less fertile.

Performance Assessment

Skills Check Have each student create a concept map that identifies and briefly explains the three major problems that occur when soil is not managed well.

 Students can save their concept maps in their portfolios.

Save That Soil

Preparing for Inquiry

Key Concept Plants help reduce erosion by holding soil with their roots.

Skills Objectives Students will be able to
- develop a hypothesis about how different land surfaces are affected by rainfall;
- control all variables except land surface;
- observe erosion by water of two different land surfaces.

Time 40 minutes

Advance Planning Purchase enough aluminum or plastic pans for each group to have two. For each group, cut one piece of sod to fit a pan. Obtain enough loose soil for each group to partially fill one pan.

Guiding Inquiry

Troubleshooting the Experiment

- If students have limited experience with controlling variables, discuss what a variable is.
- Some ways students might devise a "rainmaker" are to punch holes in the bottom of a paper cup or to use a sprinkler top for a soda bottle.
- Before Step 4, ask students how they will control the amount and flow of "rainfall."
- In Step 5, remind students to examine not only the soil left at the upper end of each pan but the runoff water at the lower end. Muddier water indicates more erosion.

Expected Outcome

The loose soil will erode easily. The sod will lose very little soil.

Analyze and Conclude

1. "Rain" washed away the loose soil more easily than the soil in the sod.
2. Loose soil erodes more easily than soil growing plants. A farmer can conserve topsoil by keeping the land planted.
3. The amounts of eroded soil can be compared only if the original amounts of soil and "rainfall" were the same.

Save That Soil

In this lab, you'll decide how to control variables as you investigate the way rainfall causes soil erosion.

Problem

How are different types of land surfaces affected by rainfall?

Materials

newspaper	2 unbreakable pans
2 blocks	sod
loose soil	"rainmaker"
water	

Procedure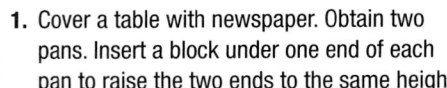

1. Cover a table with newspaper. Obtain two pans. Insert a block under one end of each pan to raise the two ends to the same height.
2. Read over the rest of the lab. Write a hypothesis that you will test. Pay careful attention to the variables you must control.
3. Place loose soil in the raised end of one pan. Place a small square of sod (soil with grass growing in it) in the raised end of the second pan. One variable is the amount of soil in each pan. Find a way to make the two amounts of soil the same. Record your procedures.
4. Create a "rainmaker" that controls the amount of water and the way it falls on the two soil samples. Then use your rainmaker to test the effect of the same amount of "rain" on the two kinds of soil. Record the results.
5. Review your experiment and your results. Do you see any procedure you wish to change? If so, get your teacher's permission to try the lab again with your revised procedures.

Analyze and Conclude

1. What effects did the "rainwater" produce on each type of soil you tested?
2. This experiment models soil erosion. What can you conclude about actual soil erosion caused by rain? How could a farmer use the information gained from this experiment to conserve topsoil?
3. **Think About It** Why was it essential for you to control the amounts of soil and "rainfall" in the two pans?

Design an Experiment

How does soil erosion caused by a gentle, steady rain compare with that caused by a heavy downpour? Design an experiment to find out. Be sure to control the way you imitate the two types of rain. Obtain your teacher's permission before conducting this experiment.

Extending the Inquiry

Design an Experiment To compare erosion by different kinds of "rainfall," loose soil should be used in both pans.

Safety

Students should wear safety goggles and lab aprons. Review the safety guidelines in Appendix A.

Program Resources

- **Unit 6 Resources** Skills Lab blackline masters, pp. 49–50

Media and Technology

 Lab Activity Videotape
Tape 5

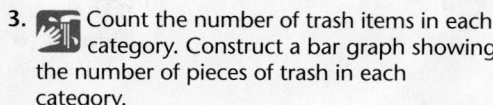

DISCOVER · ACTIVITY

What's in the Trash?

Your teacher will give you a trash bag. The items in the bag represent the most common categories of household waste in the United States.

1. Before you open the bag, predict what the two most common categories are.

2. Put on some plastic gloves. Open the bag and sort the trash items into categories based on what they are made of.

3. Count the number of trash items in each category. Construct a bar graph showing the number of pieces of trash in each category.

Think It Over

Interpreting Data Based on your graph, what are the two most common types of household waste? Was your prediction correct?

How much trash does your family throw away in a year? If it's your job to take the trash out, you might say that it's a large amount. But the amount of trash produced in the United States may be even greater than you think. Consider these facts:

◆ The average person produces about 2 kilograms of trash daily.

◆ Every hour, people throw away 2.5 million plastic bottles.

◆ Every year, people throw away enough white paper to build a wall 4 meters high that stretches from coast to coast.

◆ Every year, people throw away 1.6 billion pens, 2.9 million tons of paper towels, and 220 million automobile tires.

You can see why people call the United States a "throw-away society"! Disposable products can be cheap and convenient. But they have created a big problem—what to do with all the trash.

GUIDE FOR READING

◆ What can be done with solid waste?

◆ What are the four major types of waste that can be recycled?

◆ What are the "three R's"?

Reading Tip Before you read, preview *Exploring a Landfill* on page 688. Make a list of any unfamiliar words in the diagram. Look for the meanings of these words as you read.

687

Objectives

After completing the lesson, students will be able to

◆ name and describe three ways of dealing with solid waste;

◆ list the four major types of recyclable waste;

◆ describe methods for managing solid waste.

Key Terms municipal solid waste, leachate, sanitary landfill, incineration, recycling, biodegradable, resins, composting

1 Engage/Explore

Activating Prior Knowledge

Ask students: **What kinds of things does your family throw away?** (*Used paper, metal cans, glass jars, plastic milk jugs, and so on*) **How does your family get rid of its trash?** (*Trash may be collected in the students' community, or families may bring it to a "dump" themselves. Some families may recycle part of their trash.*)

· · · · · · · · DISCOVER · · · · · · · ·

Skills Focus interpreting data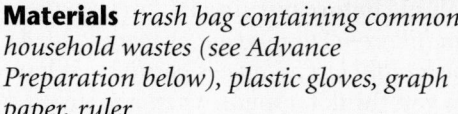

Materials *trash bag containing common household wastes (see Advance Preparation below), plastic gloves, graph paper, ruler*

Time 20 minutes

Advance Preparation For each group of students, prepare a trash bag containing the following items: 4 paper items; 2 items of yard waste such as leaves; 1 piece of rubber, cloth, or wood waste; 1 soda can or other metal item; 1 glass jar or bottle; 1 plastic item; 1 food-waste item such as an orange peel.

Tips Have students work on the floor so glass containers do not fall and break.

Expected Outcome Students should sort the items into the seven categories above.

Think It Over Paper and yard waste

The Problem of Waste Disposal

Demonstration

Materials *various trash items, bathroom scale, plastic gloves*

Time 10 minutes

Point out the text statement that each day, the average person produces about 2 kg of waste. Tell students that 1 kg equals 2.2 pounds, and let them calculate how many pounds 2 kg equal. *(4.4)* Have a volunteer calculate the daily total for a family of four. *(17.6 lbs)* Have another volunteer help you add trash to the bag until the scale indicates about 17 pounds. Pass the bag around so each student can lift it and get a sense of its weight.

learning modality: kinesthetic

EXPLORING
a Landfill

Ask different volunteers to read the captions aloud. Ask: **What is special about this landfill?** *(It is designed to prevent it from polluting the surrounding environment.)* Then ask: **Why do landfill operators want to reduce the waste's volume before burying it?** *(To keep the landfill from running out of space; to make the landfill last as long as possible.)* **What do you think happens when a town's landfill runs out of space?** *(The town has to build a new landfill; the trash has to be trucked to another town's landfill or maybe even out of state; the town has to find another way to dispose of its trash, perhaps by building an incinerator.)*

learning modality: logical/ mathematical

The Problem of Waste Disposal

In their daily activities, people generate many types of waste, including used paper, empty packages, and food scraps. The waste materials produced in homes, businesses, schools, and other places in a community are called **municipal solid waste.** Other sources of solid waste include construction debris and certain agricultural and industrial wastes. **Three methods of handling solid waste are to bury it, to burn it, or to recycle it.** Each method has advantages and disadvantages.

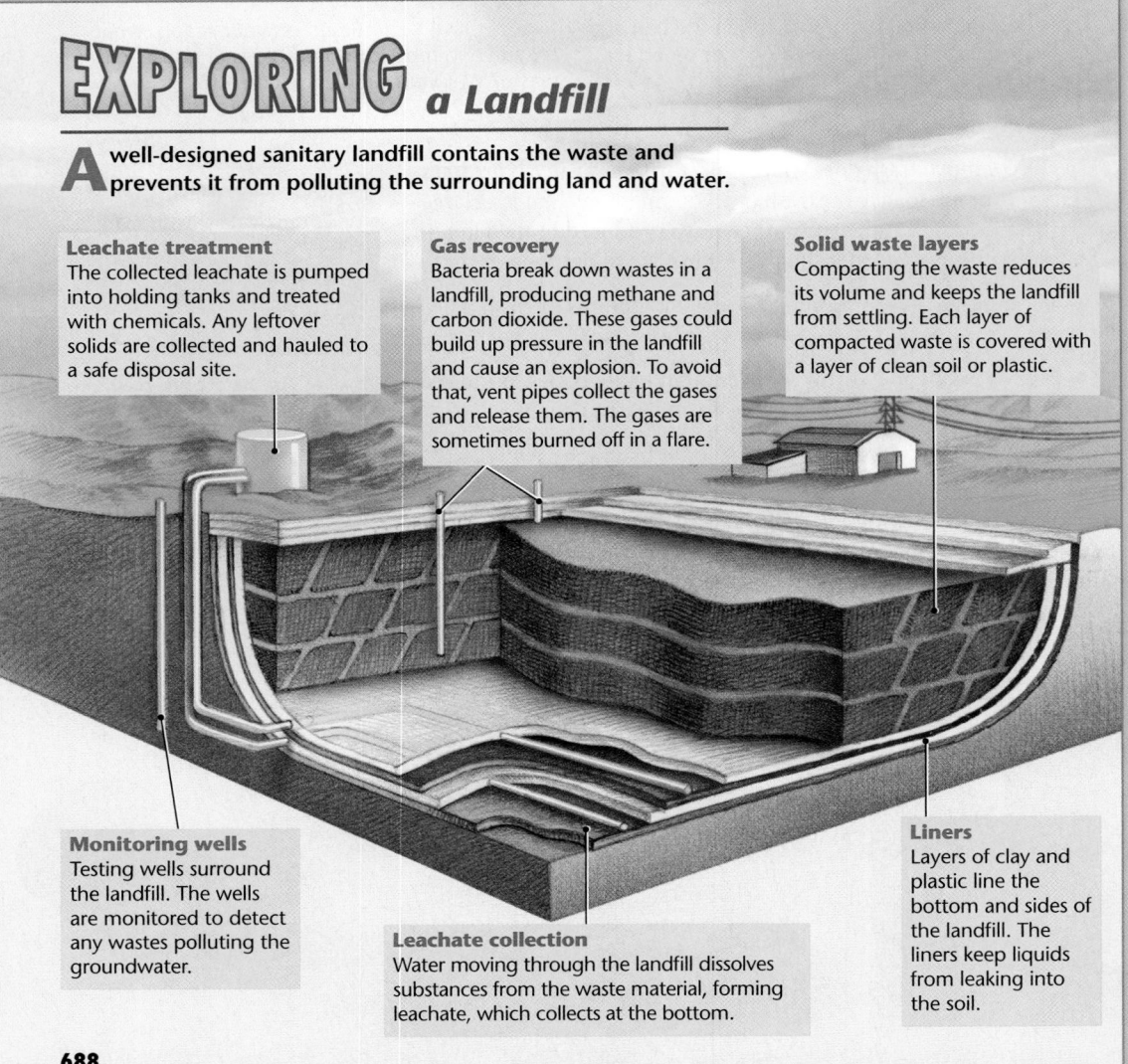

EXPLORING a Landfill

A well-designed sanitary landfill contains the waste and prevents it from polluting the surrounding land and water.

Leachate treatment
The collected leachate is pumped into holding tanks and treated with chemicals. Any leftover solids are collected and hauled to a safe disposal site.

Gas recovery
Bacteria break down wastes in a landfill, producing methane and carbon dioxide. These gases could build up pressure in the landfill and cause an explosion. To avoid that, vent pipes collect the gases and release them. The gases are sometimes burned off in a flare.

Solid waste layers
Compacting the waste reduces its volume and keeps the landfill from settling. Each layer of compacted waste is covered with a layer of clean soil or plastic.

Monitoring wells
Testing wells surround the landfill. The wells are monitored to detect any wastes polluting the groundwater.

Leachate collection
Water moving through the landfill dissolves substances from the waste material, forming leachate, which collects at the bottom.

Liners
Layers of clay and plastic line the bottom and sides of the landfill. The liners keep liquids from leaking into the soil.

688

Background

History of Science Sanitary landfills are a vast improvement over open dumps, but they are not an ideal solution. Many of the materials that fill up landfills are organic and could biodegrade. But little of the paper, grass clippings, and food waste in a sanitary landfill actually decomposes. That's because the soil used to cover the landfill limits the availability of the oxygen needed for the organic wastes to decompose.

One solution is municipal solid waste composting. With this technique, all the organic wastes that a community produces can be composted. As much as three fourths of all household waste by weight could be composted. This would dramatically reduce the volume of waste disposed in sanitary landfills. One drawback of this type of composting is that heavy metals and toxic pesticide residues may be left in the compost.

Landfills Until fairly recently, people usually disposed of waste in open holes in the ground. But these open dumps were dangerous and unsightly. Rainwater falling on the wastes dissolved chemicals from the waste, forming a polluted liquid called **leachate.** Leachate could run off into streams and lakes, or trickle down into the groundwater below the dump.

In 1976, the government banned open dumps. Now much solid waste is buried in landfills that are constructed to hold the wastes more safely. A **sanitary landfill** holds municipal solid waste, construction debris, and some types of agricultural and industrial waste. *Exploring a Landfill* shows the parts of a well-designed sanitary landfill. Once a landfill is full, it is covered with a clay cap to keep rainwater from entering the waste.

However, even well-designed landfills still pose a risk of polluting groundwater. And while capped landfills can be reused in certain ways, including as parks and sites for sports arenas, they cannot be used for other needs, such as housing or agriculture.

Incineration The burning of solid waste is called **incineration** (in sin ur AY shun). Incineration has some advantages over the use of landfills. The burning facilities, or incinerators, do not take up as much space. They do not pose a risk of polluting groundwater. The heat produced by burning solid waste can be used to generate electricity. These "waste-to-energy" plants supply electricity to many homes in the United States.

Unfortunately, incinerators do have drawbacks. Even the best incinerators release some pollution into the air. And although incinerators reduce the volume of waste by as much as 90 percent, some waste still remains. This waste needs to be disposed of somewhere. Finally, incinerators are much more expensive to build than sanitary landfills. Many communities cannot afford to replace an existing landfill with an incinerator.

✓ *Checkpoint* *What is a waste-to-energy plant?*

Figure 6 This waste-to-energy plant generates electricity while disposing of municipal solid waste.

Sharpen your Skills

Graphing

What happens to trash? Use the data in the table below to construct a circle graph of methods of municipal solid waste disposal in the United States. Give your circle graph a title. (For help making a circle graph, see the Skills Handbook.)

Method of Disposal	Percentage of Waste
Landfills	56%
Recycling	27%
Incineration	17%

Sharpen your Skills

Graphing

Materials *protractor, drawing compass*
Time 15 minutes

Students should determine the size of each wedge of the circle graph by multiplying 360° by each percentage. *(Landfills = 202°, Recycling = 97°, Incineration = 61°) Sample title:* Methods of Waste Disposal in the U.S.

Extend Have students make a second circle graph to show what would happen if 15% of the total waste were recycled instead of being sent to landfills. *(Landfills = 148°, Recycling = 151°)*
learning modality: logical/mathematical

Building Inquiry Skills: Making Models

Materials *glass or plastic jar, coffee filter, rubber band, soil, food coloring, beaker, water*
Time 10 minutes

Have each group of students make a simple model of leachate, as follows: Put a coffee filter over the mouth of a jar, letting it hang into the jar, and secure it in place with a rubber band. Fill the filter about halfway with soil. Put several drops of food coloring on the soil, then pour water into the jar. When students have finished, ask: **What do you see in the bottom of the jar?** *(Colored water)* **Where did the color come from?** *(The food coloring)* **What does the food coloring represent in this model?** *(Chemicals on the soil's surface)* **In a real landfill, where do chemicals come from?** *(The wastes in the landfill)*
learning modality: kinesthetic

Media and Technology

🖳 **Transparencies** "Exploring a Landfill," Transparency 83

📼 **Concept Videotape Library** *Adventures, Tape 5,* "Where Does Your Garbage Go?"

Answers to Self-Assessment

✓ *Checkpoint*
A power plant that uses the heat from burning solid waste to generate electricity

Ongoing Assessment

Skills Check Have each student construct a compare/contrast table that identifies the advantages and disadvantages of sanitary landfills and incinerators.

Portfolio Students can save their tables in their portfolios.

Recycling

Figure 7 Metal and glass are two frequently recycled materials. **A.** Crumpled aluminum cans ride up a conveyor belt in a recycling center. **B.** A giant mound of crushed glass awaits recycling. *Predicting Without recycling, what might eventually happen to the supply of aluminum?*

Recycling

 *INTEGRATING TECHNOLOGY* The process of reclaiming raw materials and reusing them is called **recycling.** Recycling reduces the volume of solid waste. Recycling enables people to use the materials in wastes again, rather than discarding those materials. As you know, matter in ecosystems is naturally recycled through the water cycle, carbon cycle, and other processes. A substance that can be broken down and recycled by bacteria and other decomposers is **biodegradable** (by oh dih GRAY duh bul).

Unfortunately, many of the products people use today are not biodegradable. Plastic containers, metal cans, rubber tires, and glass jars are examples of products that do not naturally decompose. Instead, people have developed techniques to recycle the raw materials in these products.

A wide range of materials, including motor oil, tires, and batteries, can be recycled. **Most recycling focuses on four major categories of products: metal, glass, paper, and plastic.**

Metal In your classroom, you are surrounded by metal objects that can be recycled. Your desk, scissors, staples, and paper clips are probably made of steel. Another very common metal, aluminum, is used to make soda cans, house siding, window screens, and many other products.

Metals such as iron and aluminum can be melted and reused. Recycling metal saves money and causes less pollution than making new metal. With recycling, no ore needs to be mined, transported to factories, or processed. In addition, recycling metals helps conserve these nonrenewable resources.

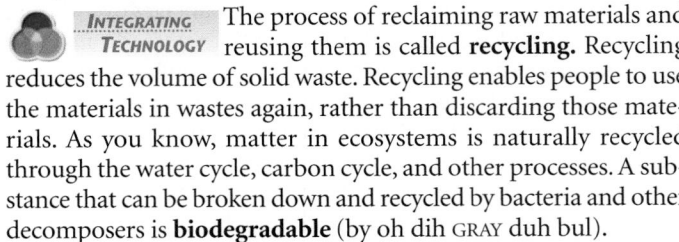

Background

Facts and Figures In the United States and other developed countries, the average computer is replaced every three years—not because it is broken but because rapid technological advances and new generations of software make it obsolete. Although they may still be in working order, old computers have little resale value and are even difficult to give away. As a result, they are frequently discarded in the trash.

According to an estimate by researchers at Carnegie Mellon University, by 2005 there will be 55 million computers discarded in landfills around the world. Nearly 150 million computers will be recycled for their usable components and recyclable materials. These include plastics and metals such as aluminum, copper, tin, nickel, palladium, silver, and gold.

Glass Glass is made from sand, soda ash, and limestone mixed together and heated. Glass is one of the easiest products to recycle because glass pieces can be melted down over and over to make new glass containers. Recycled glass is also used to make fiberglass, bricks, tiles, and the reflective paints on road signs.

Recycling glass is less expensive than making glass from raw materials. Because the recycled pieces melt at a lower temperature than the raw materials, less energy is required. Recycling glass also reduces the environmental damage caused by mining for sand, soda, and limestone.

☑ *Checkpoint* *Why is it easy to recycle glass?*

Paper It takes about 17 trees to make one metric ton of paper. Paper mills turn wood into a thick liquid called pulp. Pulp is spread out and dried to produce paper. Pulp can also be made from used paper such as old newspapers. The newspapers must be washed to remove the inks and dyes. The paper is then mixed with more water and other chemicals to form pulp.

Most paper products can only be recycled a few times. Recycled paper is not as smooth or strong as paper made from wood pulp. Each time paper is recycled to make pulp, the new paper is rougher, weaker, and darker.

Plastic When oil is refined to make gasoline and other petroleum products, solid materials called **resins** are left over. Resins can be heated, stretched, and molded into plastic products. Have you ever noticed a symbol like the ones in Figure 8 on a plastic container? This number indicates what type of plastic a container is made of. For example, plastics labeled with a *1* or a *2* are made from plastics that are often recycled. Common products made from these types of plastic include milk jugs, detergent containers, and soda bottles.

It's in the Numbers

Sort pieces of plastic products into groups according to their recycling numbers. Compare and contrast the pieces in each group with each other and with those in other groups.

Classifying Write a sentence describing characteristics of the plastics in each group.

Figure 8 These plastic bottles have numbers indicating the type of plastic they are made of. Plastics must be sorted by type before they are recycled.

Chapter 21 **691**

Answers to Self-Assessment

Caption Question

Figure 7 The supply of aluminum would decrease or be used up.

☑ *Checkpoint*

Glass pieces can be melted down over and over to make new glass containers and other products.

TRY THIS

Skills Focus classifying
Materials *pieces of plastic products (see Advance Preparation below)*
Time 10 minutes
Tips Assemble a set of plastic pieces by selecting several examples from each of these recycling categories: **1** (polyethylene terphthalate), soft-drink bottles; **2** (high-density polyethylene), milk and water jugs; **3** (vinyl), shampoo bottles; **4** (low-density polyethylene), ketchup bottles; **5** (polypropylene), squeeze bottles; **6** (polystyrene), fast-food containers and coffee cups; **7** (all other resins and layered multi-materials). To reduce preparation time, assemble one set of plastic pieces and let students take turns sorting the pieces.
Expected Outcome Students should be able to sort the plastics into at least four or five groups according to the plastics' color/clarity and rigidity.
Extend Have students make a compare/contrast table listing the types, descriptions, and uses of the different groups of plastics. **learning modality: logical/mathematical**

Real-Life Learning

Materials *used item that could be reused by converting it into another useful item*
Time 15 minutes

Collect used glass, plastic, and metal containers and paper items such as old greeting cards. Make sure all containers are empty and clean. Give each student one item. Tell students to think of a way to convert the item into something that would be useful at home or in school. Let students describe and/or carry out their ideas. *(Examples: A jar could be made into a pencil holder or a bank for saving change. A used greeting card could be cut to make gift tags.)* **learning modality: kinesthetic**

Ongoing Assessment

Oral Presentation Call on students at random to explain why metal, glass, and plastic should be recycled instead of being discarded in landfills.

Solid Waste Management

Real-Life Learning

To help students relate the text's concepts on recycling to their own lives, ask: **What ways to recycle have you seen?** (*Students may mention some of the examples described in the text as well as other examples, such as dry cleaners providing bins for customers to return plastic bags or supermarkets offering a slight price reduction if customers bring in their own bags for packing their groceries.*) **Why do some people not recycle?** (*Accept all reasonable answers, such as that recycling takes effort.*) **Can you suggest any ways to increase the number of people who recycle?** (*Accept all reasonable responses.*) **learning modality: verbal**

What Can You Do?

Building Inquiry Skills: Communicating

Challenge students individually or in small groups to think of a creative way to communicate the "three R's" to their community. For example, students could create posters, public service announcements, skits, rap songs, or poems. At a specified time, have each student or group present its product to the class for critique. Then after students have made their revisions, let them present their products in a community forum, such as a parent-teacher meeting, parents' night at school, or a community civic association meeting. **learning modality: verbal**

Energy Savings in Manufacturing	
Material	**Using Recycled Rather Than Raw Materials**
Aluminum	90–97 %
Glass	4–32 %
Paper	23–74 %

Figure 9 As this table shows, some kinds of recycling save more energy than others.
Interpreting Data Which type of recycling saves the most energy?

When they are recycled, they take on very different forms: as fiber filling for sleeping bags and jackets, carpeting, park benches, shower stalls, floor tiles, trash cans, or dock pilings!

Is Recycling Worthwhile? In addition to conserving resources, recycling saves energy. Figure 9 shows how much energy can be saved by using recycled materials instead of raw materials.

Recycling is not a complete answer to the solid waste problem. Many materials can be recycled. But scientists have not found good ways to recycle other materials, such as plastic-coated paper and plastic foam. There are not enough uses for some recycled products, such as low-quality recycled newspaper. Finally, all recycling processes require energy and create some pollution.

✓ *Checkpoint* **What are some advantages and disadvantages of recycling?**

Solid Waste Management

In the past few decades, people have become more aware of the solid waste problem. Many communities now collect recyclable items along with other household trash. Many supermarkets recycle paper and plastic grocery bags. Many states charge deposit fees on certain glass, metal, and plastic containers. When people return the containers to be recycled, they get their deposit back. This return system encourages people to recycle the containers instead of throwing them away. You might have seen recycling bins for metal and glass drink containers in movie theaters, parks, and other public areas. Consumers can also choose to buy products made with recyclable materials.

Figure 10 These students are sorting materials for a school recycling project.

Facts and Figures The number of U.S. communities with recycling programs increased dramatically during the 1990s. Today, the average American family of four annually recycles more than 450 kg of aluminum and steel cans, plastic containers, glass jars and bottles, newspapers, and cardboard. More than 100 million people now live in areas with curbside-collection recycling programs. In other communities, trash is collected and taken to resource recovery facilities, where it is sorted by hand or separated using technologies that include magnets, screens, and conveyor belts—like the one shown in Figure 7 on page 690. The United States currently recycles about a quarter of its municipal solid waste.

As a result of these efforts, the amount of municipal solid waste that is recycled has increased. But most municipal solid waste in the United States still goes to landfills. Yet as usable land becomes more scarce, it will be even more critical to reduce the need for landfills.

What Can You Do?

The good news is that there are lots of ways individuals can help control the solid waste problem. **These are sometimes called the "three R's"—reduce, reuse, and recycle.** *Reduce* refers to creating less waste in the first place. For example, you can use a cloth shopping bag rather than a disposable paper or plastic bag. *Reuse* refers to finding another use for an object rather than discarding it. For example, you could refill plastic drink bottles with drinking water or juice you mix instead of buying drinks in new bottles. And *recycle* refers to reclaiming raw materials to create new products. You can make sure you recycle at home, and you can also encourage others to recycle. How about starting a used paper collection and recycling program at your school?

One way to significantly reduce the amount of solid waste your family produces is to start a compost pile. **Composting** is the process of helping the natural decomposition processes break down many forms of waste. Compost piles can be used to recycle yard trash such as grass clippings and raked leaves, and food waste such as fruit and vegetable scraps, eggshells, and coffee grounds. Some farms use compost piles to naturally recycle animal manure. Compost is an excellent natural fertilizer for plants.

Figure 11 Many communities have neighborhood compost bins like this one in Brooklyn, in New York City. *Applying Concepts How does composting help solve the solid waste problem?*

Section 2 Review

1. What happens to most solid waste in the United States?
2. List the four major categories of solid waste that are most often recycled.
3. Name and define the "three R's" of solid waste management.
4. Give an example of a way in which communities can reduce their solid waste.
5. What is composting?
6. **Thinking Critically Comparing and Contrasting** Compare the recycling of metal and paper. How are they similar? How are they different?

Science at Home

For one week, have your family collect their household trash in large bags. Do not include food waste. At the end of the week, hold a trash weigh-in. Multiply the total amount by 52 to show how much trash your family produces in a year. Together, can you suggest any ways to reduce your family trash load?

Program Resources

♦ **Unit 6 Resources** 21-2 Review and Reinforce, p. 43; 21-2 Enrich, p. 44

Answers to Self-Assessment

Caption Question

Figure 9 Recycling aluminum
Figure 11 It reduces the solid waste discarded in landfills or incinerated.

✓ Checkpoint

Reduces need for raw materials and landfill space, saves energy; some products not suitable, some recycled materials not in demand

Section 2 Review Answers

1. It goes to landfills.
2. Metal, glass, plastic, paper
3. *Reduce* means creating less waste in the first place. *Reuse* means finding another use for an object instead of discarding it. *Recycle* means reclaiming raw materials to create new products.
4. Answers may vary. *Sample answer:* By creating community composting programs
5. The process of helping the natural decomposition processes break down many forms of waste
6. The recycling of both metals and paper reclaims raw materials for new products. Metals can be recycled many times, whereas paper products can be recycled only a few times before quality is reduced.

Science at Home

If students' families already recycle, tell students to weigh the materials being recycled separately from the other materials. Let students report their findings in class.

Performance Assessment

Writing Have each student briefly explain the benefits of recycling compared with discarding waste materials in landfills or burning them in incinerators.

Portfolio Students can save their explanations in their portfolios.

693

Waste, Away!

Preparing for Inquiry

Key Concept A sanitary landfill prevents groundwater pollution more effectively than a poorly designed landfill or an open dump does.

Skills Objectives Students will be able to
- make models of a sanitary landfill, a poorly designed landfill, and an open dump;
- draw conclusions about the environmental benefits of sanitary landfills.

Time 40 minutes on Day 1; 20 minutes on Day 2

Advance Preparation Cut the cheesecloth and plastic pieces large enough to overlap the top of the jar when they are suspended in it, as shown in the photo. Cut extra pieces in case some tear when students add pebbles to them. Check the plastic pieces to make sure there are no holes in them.

Alternative Materials If supplies are limited, have one third of the groups construct System 1, one third construct System 2, and one third construct System 3.

Guiding Inquiry

Invitation Hold up a transparent drinking glass of clean tap water, then drop a few small pieces of household waste into it. Ask: **Would you want to drink water with trash in it? Why not?** (*Chemicals in the trash pollute the water.*)

Introducing the Procedure
- Invite students to read the entire lab procedure. Answer any questions they have.
- Explain that the models will represent three different types of landfills, but at this point do not discuss which type each model represents.

Troubleshooting the Experiment
- Circulate among the groups as they build the models to make sure the cheesecloth and plastic pieces are draped well down into the jars and are secured tightly with rubber bands.

Waste, Away!

About two thirds of municipal solid waste ends up in a landfill. In this lab, you'll investigate how landfills are constructed to be most effective and safe.

Problem

How do different kinds of landfills work?

Skills Focus

making models, drawing conclusions

Materials

measuring cup	metric ruler	soil
small pebbles	cheesecloth	scissors
plastic wrap	water	newspaper
5 rubber bands	red food coloring	tweezers

heavy-duty plastic bag
12 small sponge cubes
3 transparent, wide-mouthed jars

Procedure

1. Read over the rest of the procedure to preview the three landfill systems you will model. Determine which parts of the models represent potential drinking water, rainfall, solid waste, leachate, and the landfill systems themselves. Write a prediction about the way each system will respond to the test you'll conduct in Part 2.

Part 1 Modeling Three Landfill Systems

2. Obtain 3 identical jars. Label them *System 1, System 2,* and *System 3.* Pour clean, clear water into each jar to a depth of 5 cm.

3. Add equal amounts of small pebbles to each jar. The pebbles should be just below the surface of the water.

4. For System 1, cover the pebble and water mixture with 2.5 cm of soil.

5. For System 2, suspend a piece of cheesecloth in the jar about 5 cm above the water line, as shown in the photograph. Hold the cheesecloth in place with a rubber band around the outside mouth of the jar. Gently pour a handful of small pebbles into the cheesecloth.

6. For System 3, suspend a plastic bag in the jar about 5 cm above the water line. Hold the bag in place with a rubber band around the outside mouth of the jar. Gently pour a handful of small pebbles into the plastic bag.

7. Observe the water and pebbles at the bottom of each system. Record your observations.

Part 2 Testing the Systems

8. Soak 12 identical sponge cubes in water tinted with red food coloring. Use tweezers to place four soaked sponge cubes onto the top surface in each jar.

9. Cover the sponge cubes in Systems 2 and 3 with a thin layer of soil. Leave the sponge cubes in System 1 uncovered.

- In Steps 5 and 6, caution students to add the pebbles gently so they do not tear the cheesecloth and plastic.
- When students draw the systems in Step 10, they should label the following elements: *groundwater* (water at bottom of jar); *soil; liner* (cheesecloth and plastic pieces); and *trash* (colored sponge cubes). Students could also label the pebbles *permeable layer.*

Expected Outcome

The groundwater in Systems 1 and 2 will turn red with "leachate"—food coloring from the sponge cubes. The water may also be cloudy with dissolved soil particles that have washed out of the landfills. The groundwater in System 3 will remain clear, with all of the leachate contained by the plastic liner.

10. Make a labeled drawing of each system. Explain what each part of the model represents.
11. Pour 150 mL of water over each system. Then cover each jar with plastic wrap, and hold the wrap in place with a rubber band. Let the systems stand overnight.
12. Observe each landfill system. Note especially any changes in the color or clarity of the "groundwater." Record your observations.

Analyze and Conclude

1. Explain how your models represent three common types of landfills: a well-designed, or sanitary, landfill; a landfill with a poor design; and an open dump. Compare the way the three systems work.
2. Which part of the model represented the leachate? How well did each landfill system protect the groundwater from the leachate?

3. Do you think a community's water supply is protected when waste is placed in landfills that are not immediately above groundwater sources? Explain.
4. **Apply** Based on your results, which landfill system is safest for the environment? Explain your answer.

Design an Experiment

Solid waste can be compacted (crushed into smaller pieces) and have liquid removed before it is placed in a landfill. Does preparing the waste in this way make it safer for the environment? Write a hypothesis, then use the ideas and procedures from this lab to test your hypothesis. Obtain your teacher's permission before trying your experiment.

Analyze and Conclude

1. In System 1, an open dump, there is no barrier to separate waste from the soil and keep leachate from seeping into the groundwater. In System 2, a poorly designed landfill, the permeable liner contains the waste but allows leachate to seep into the groundwater. In System 3, a well-designed sanitary landfill, the plastic liner contains the leachate and keeps it from seeping into the groundwater.
2. The red-tinted water represented the leachate. Only System 3 protected the groundwater.
3. Locating a landfill in an area that is not immediately above groundwater is safer. However, groundwater can still become contaminated if surface runoff from the landfill carries leachate to nearby rivers and streams or to permeable soil layers above groundwater supplies.
4. A well-designed sanitary landfill (like System 3) is safest because it protects groundwater the best.

Extending the Inquiry

Design an Experiment Compacting the waste takes less space and extends the life of the landfill but does not remove harmful substances from the waste. It also keeps the wastes from settling inside the landfill. Removing liquid from the waste could reduce the amount of leachate produced. Students could model reduced-liquid waste by soaking the sponge cubes in food coloring, then squeezing the liquid out and allowing the cubes to dry thoroughly before placing them in the landfill models.

Program Resources

◆ **Unit 6 Resources** Real-World Lab blackline masters, pp. 49–50

Media and Technology

 Lab Activity Videotape
Tape 5

Safety

Remind students to wear lab aprons and safety goggles and handle the glass jars carefully. Review the safety guidelines in Appendix A.

SECTION 3 Hazardous Wastes

Objectives

After completing the lesson, students will be able to
- list and describe the categories of hazardous wastes;
- explain how hazardous wastes affect human health;
- identify methods for managing hazardous wastes.

Key Terms hazardous waste, toxic, explosive, flammable, corrosive, radioactive

1 Engage/Explore

Activating Prior Knowledge

Ask students: **What kinds of activities can be hazardous?** (*Sample answers: riding a bicycle in traffic, driving on icy roads, using a chainsaw, climbing a tall ladder*) **When you're involved in a hazardous activity, what do you do to protect yourself?** (*Be very careful, follow safety guidelines, wear protective clothing or equipment, and so forth*)

DISCOVER

Skills Focus forming operational definitions
Materials *labels from common hazardous household products, such as pesticides, herbicides, cleaning agents, nail polish remover and other solvents, spray lacquers*
Time 10 minutes
Tips Tell students to look for the word *Warning* on the labels and carefully read the information that follows it. Keep the labels for use in other activities.
Expected Outcome Students will find warnings such as *Causes eye and skin irritations; Harmful if swallowed; Do not use near fire or flame;* and *Use outdoors or in a well-ventilated area.*
Think It Over Students' definitions should focus on the risk of harm or injury to people and other living organisms.

SECTION 3 Hazardous Wastes

DISCOVER ⋯⋯⋯⋯⋯⋯⋯⋯⋯⋯⋯⋯ ACTIVITY

What's Hazardous?

1. Your teacher will give you labels from some common hazardous household products.
2. Read the information on each label. Identify the word or words that tell why the product is hazardous.

Think It Over
Forming Operational Definitions Based on your observations of the product labels, write a definition of the term *hazardous.*

GUIDE FOR READING

- What are the categories of hazardous wastes?
- How can hazardous wastes affect human health?
- What techniques can be used to manage hazardous wastes?

Reading Tip Before you read, rewrite the headings in each section as *how, what,* or *where* questions. As you read, look for answers to these questions.

Figure 12 This school in Love Canal was abandoned because of pollution.

In the early 1950s, the city of Niagara Falls, New York, bought an area of land around an old canal. The canal had been filled with chemical wastes from nearby industries. On top of this land, the city built a new neighborhood and elementary school. The neighborhood was named Love Canal.

Then strange things began to happen. Children playing in muddy fields developed skin rashes. Wooden fence posts rotted and turned black. People reported colored liquid seeping into their basements. Babies were born with birth defects. Adults developed epilepsy, liver disease, and nerve disorders. The neighborhood was finally declared a federal emergency disaster area. More than two hundred families were moved away.

What was behind these strange events at Love Canal? Building the neighborhood had caused the clay cover on the old canal dump site to crack. Rainwater seeped into the buried wastes through the cracks. The construction caused chemicals to leak from the underground storage containers. Over time, water mixed with the chemicals to form a dangerous leachate. This leachate polluted the soil and the groundwater and leaked into people's basements.

The Love Canal problem was the first time a federal emergency was declared in an area because of hazardous wastes. It helped people realize that certain chemicals can remain dangerous in soil and water for many years. As a result, new laws were passed to find and clean up other dangerous waste sites.

READING STRATEGIES

Reading Tip Students' questions might include *What are some types of hazardous wastes?, What are the health effects of hazardous wastes?, What problems are involved in the disposal of hazardous wastes?, How do people locate disposal sites?,* and *How can people reduce hazardous waste?*

Vocabulary To help students recall the major categories of hazardous wastes, suggest that each student make a set of cards, each with the name of a category and its symbol (copied from Figure 13) on the front of the card and, on the back, the textbook's definition paraphrased in the student's own words.

Types of Hazardous Wastes

Many people picture hazardous wastes as bubbling chemicals, thick fumes, or oozing slime. But even some harmless-looking, common materials such as window cleaner, radio batteries, and nail polish remover can become hazardous wastes. **Hazardous waste** is any material that can be harmful to human health or the environment if it is not properly disposed of.

Hazardous wastes are created during the manufacture of many household products. Many more are produced as a result of agriculture, industry, military operations, and research at hospitals and scientific laboratories.

Hazardous wastes are classified into four categories: toxic, explosive, flammable, and corrosive. Figure 13 gives some examples of these types of waste. **Toxic** wastes, or poisonous wastes, are wastes that can damage the health of humans and other organisms. **Explosive** wastes are wastes that react very quickly when exposed to air or water, or that explode when they are dropped. Explosive wastes are also called reactive wastes. **Flammable** wastes catch fire easily and can begin burning at fairly low temperatures. **Corrosive** wastes are wastes that dissolve or eat through many materials.

Other wastes that require special disposal are radioactive wastes. **Radioactive** wastes are wastes that contain unstable atoms. These unstable atoms give off radiation that can cause cancer and other diseases. There are two types of radioactive wastes: high-level waste and low-level waste. An example of high-level radioactive waste is the used fuel from nuclear reactors. Low-level radioactive wastes are produced when radioactive minerals such as uranium are mined. They are also produced at some medical and scientific research sites. Radioactive waste can remain dangerous for thousands of years.

Figure 13 Vehicles transporting dangerous materials must use signs like these to alert people of the potential dangers of their loads.

Category: Radioactive
Examples: Uranium, plutonium

Category: Flammable
Example: Kerosene

Category: Toxic
Examples: Chlorine, PCBs, mercury

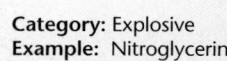

Category: Explosive
Example: Nitroglycerin

Category: Corrosive
Examples: Hydrochloric acid, sodium hydroxide

Chapter 21 **697**

Program Resources

◆ **Unit 6 Resources** 21-3 Lesson Plan, p. 45; 21-3 Section Summary, p. 46
◆ **Guided Reading and Study Workbook** Section 21-3

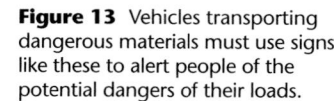

2 Facilitate

Types of Hazardous Wastes

Building Inquiry Skills: Classifying

Materials *labels from common hazardous household products (See Discover activity on page 696.)*
Time 10 minutes

Challenge students to sort the labels into four of the categories described on this page—toxic, explosive, flammable, and corrosive—plus a fifth group for products whose warnings indicate more than one type of hazard. Ask: **How many labels do you have in each group? What kinds of products do those labels represent?** *(Answers will vary, but students may find that many, if not most, hazardous products fall into more than one category.)* **learning modality: verbal**

Real-Life Learning

Time 5 minutes

Encourage students to copy the symbols from Figure 13. Then instruct students to cut out the individual symbols and tape the appropriate ones to hazardous products they find in the classroom, other areas of the school (the art room or shop area, for example), and at home. In a follow-up class discussion, ask: **Were you surprised by the number of hazardous products you found?** *(Students may not have realized that so many common, everyday products contain hazardous substances.)* **learning modality: kinesthetic**

Ongoing Assessment

Writing Have each student name the categories of hazardous wastes and define each category in his or her own words.

 Students can save their work in their portfolios.

Health Effects of Hazardous Wastes

Integrating Health

Materials *labels from common hazardous household products (See Discover activity on page 696.)*

ACTIVITY

Time 10 minutes

Have students examine the labels to look for wording that indicates the specific health hazards of the products. Also point out that labels often include first-aid instructions in case the user needs immediate treatment after exposure to a hazardous ingredient in a product. Encourage students to look for those instructions as well and read them aloud. As students read the first-aid procedures, list on the board the names of any antidotes or medications that people should have in their homes in case of an emergency—for example, syrup of ipecac to induce vomiting. Suggest that students copy the list and check their own homes to see if their families have these materials on hand. **learning modality: verbal**

Disposal of Hazardous Wastes

Inquiry Challenge

Time 15 minutes

ACTIVITY

Divide the class into small groups, and pose the following problem: **Many years ago, containers of toxic chemicals were buried in a vacant field. Now the containers are leaking, and the wastes are soaking into the soil. How can you make a model to show what is happening?** Let each group discuss possible models, agree on one, draw it on a large sheet of paper, and then describe it to the rest of the class. *(Example: Fill a small jar with colored water, punch a pinhole in the jar's lid, then bury the jar on its side in a dishpan filled with sand.)* Also ask groups to explain what they could do to model how the "wastes" could be cleaned up. If time allows, have students build and demonstrate their models. **cooperative learning**

Health Effects of Hazardous Wastes

 INTEGRATING HEALTH A person can be exposed to hazardous wastes by breathing, eating or drinking, or touching them. Many factors determine the effects of a hazardous substance on a person. One factor is how harmful the substance is. Another factor is how much of the substance a person is exposed to. A third factor is how long the exposure lasts. A person may be exposed for a short time, such as a child accidentally drinking antifreeze. Or a person may be exposed for many years, as were the residents of Love Canal. Finally, a person's age, weight, and health all influence how a substance affects that person.

In general, short-term exposure to hazardous wastes may cause irritation or more severe health problems. These health problems can include breathing difficulties, internal bleeding, paralysis, coma, and even death. **Long-term exposure to hazardous wastes may cause diseases, such as cancer, and may damage body organs, including the brain, liver, kidneys, and lungs.** These effects may eventually be life threatening.

Disposal of Hazardous Wastes

It is hard to safely dispose of hazardous wastes. Burying them can pollute the soil or groundwater. Releasing wastes into lakes or rivers can pollute surface water. Burning hazardous wastes can pollute the air. You can see the problem!

Methods of hazardous waste disposal include burial in landfills, incineration, and breakdown by living organisms. Another method involves storing liquid wastes in deep rock layers.

Figure 14 Hazardous wastes can pollute the soil, water, and air. The chemical drums on the left were illegally dumped in a field. Below, environmental scientists in protective gear test the contents of an old storage tank.

Background

History of Science Two federal laws dictate the management of hazardous waste. The Resource Conservation and Recovery Act covers hazardous waste currently being produced. The Comprehensive Environmental Response, Compensation, and Liability Act, commonly known as Superfund, provides for cleanup of abandoned and inactive hazardous waste sites.

The federal government estimates that the United States has more than 300,000 old hazardous waste sites. At many such sites, hazardous chemicals have seeped deep into the soil and polluted groundwater. Sites that pose the greatest threat to public health and the environment are placed on the Superfund National Priorities List; the federal government will assist in their cleanup.

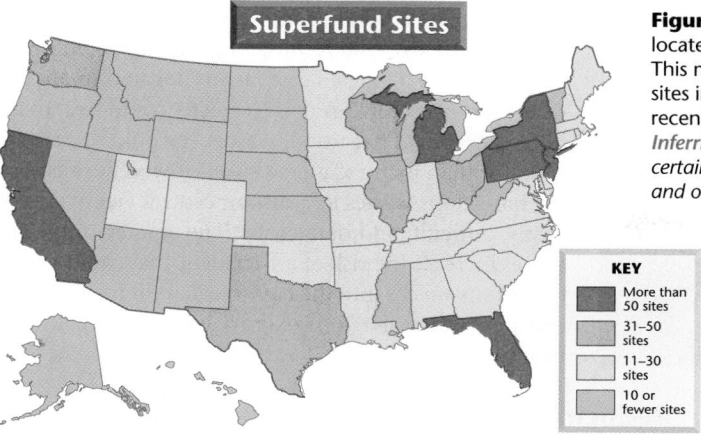

Superfund Sites

Figure 15 Superfund sites are located all over the country. This map shows the number of sites in different states in a recent year.
Inferring Why do you think certain states have many sites and others have few?

KEY
- More than 50 sites
- 31–50 sites
- 11–30 sites
- 10 or fewer sites

Hazardous wastes are most often disposed of in carefully designed landfills. These landfills are lined with clay and plastic to keep chemicals from leaking into the soil and groundwater. A clay and plastic cover prevents rainwater from seeping into the wastes.

Scientists have developed some other methods for disposing of hazardous waste. For example, wastes can be incinerated at very high temperatures. Incineration often breaks down harmful compounds into less harmful ones. Bacteria, algae, and fungi can break down some hazardous chemicals. Another disposal method involves pumping liquid wastes into a layer of sandstone or limestone thousands of meters underground. The wastes spread throughout this soft rock layer. But the wastes cannot move through the thicker, harder layers of rock above and below. A few types of hazardous waste, such as motor oil and lead-acid car batteries, can even be recycled.

Scientists have not been able to develop completely safe methods for disposing of radioactive waste. Some techniques used today are mixing the waste with concrete or sealing it in abandoned mine shafts. High-level radioactive wastes are currently stored in vaults dug hundreds of meters underground or in concrete and steel containers above ground. But these storage areas are temporary. Scientists are still searching for methods that will provide safe, permanent disposal of radioactive wastes.

☑ *Checkpoint* **How are most hazardous wastes disposed of?**

Locating Disposal Sites

Besides deciding how to dispose of hazardous wastes, communities must also decide *where* to dispose of them. Should there be fewer, larger disposal sites, or many smaller ones? Each answer has costs and benefits.

Social Studies
CONNECTION

In 1980, Congress passed a law creating a hazardous waste site cleanup program called the Superfund. The law determines who should pay for the cleanup. This can include any businesses or people that have ever owned or operated the property, or have ever contributed wastes to it.

In Your Journal

Most industries did not purposely pollute the air, land, and water. In the past, people were largely unaware that some industrial wastes were hazardous, and that these substances could have serious effects many years later. Should these industries still be responsible for paying for the cleanup? If not, where should this money come from? Write a paragraph explaining your opinion.

Social Studies
CONNECTION

For additional information about Superfund, see Background on the previous page.

In Your Journal Accept divergent views on the questions posed in the text, as long as students support their positions with sound reasoning. Encourage students to share their views in a class discussion. **learning modality: verbal**

Locating Disposal Sites

Building Inquiry Skills: Communicating

Time 20–30 minutes

Ask students to imagine their community's government has just announced that it wants the residents to vote on whether to allow a private company to build a landfill in the community for hazardous wastes trucked in from all over the state. Residents would receive a tax benefit plus job opportunities if the landfill is built. Then divide the class into small groups, and assign one of the following viewpoints to each group: *We should vote for the landfill because . . .*, or *We should vote against the landfill because. . . .* Allow time for each group to discuss the issue from its assigned viewpoint. Then choose one student from each group to participate in a debate in front of the rest of the class. At the conclusion of the debate, have students vote on the issue. **learning modality: logical/ mathematical**

Answers to Self-Assessment

Caption Question

Figure 15 *Sample answers:* States with many sites may have large-scale industry and/or mining that produced more hazardous wastes than states with fewer sites.

☑ *Checkpoint*

Most are buried in landfills.

Ongoing Assessment

Drawing Have each student draw and label a simple diagram showing how a landfill for hazardous wastes is constructed.

Portfolio Students can save their drawings in their portfolios.

Burn a citronella candle in the classroom while students are involved in another activity. When the aroma is noticeable, ask: **What's that odor?** (*Some students may be familiar with the odor of citronella candles.*) Point out the photograph's caption. Suggest that students examine labels in stores to find examples of other products that can be used in place of hazardous chemicals. Let them report their findings in class. **learning modality: verbal**

3 Assess

Section 3 Review Answers

1. *Toxic wastes* can affect the health of humans and other organisms. *Explosive wastes* react very quickly when exposed to air or water or explode when they are dropped. *Flammable wastes* catch fire easily and begin burning at fairly low temperatures. *Corrosive wastes* dissolve or eat through many materials.

2. Short-term exposure may cause irritation or more severe health problems such as breathing difficulties, internal bleeding, paralysis, coma, and death. Long-term exposure may cause diseases such as cancer and may damage body organs.

3. One method is to bury hazardous wastes in landfills lined and sealed with plastic and clay. Other disposal methods include incineration at very high temperatures, exposure to organisms that break the wastes down, pumping the wastes deep underground, and recycling them.

4. For the first time in U.S. history, a national emergency was declared because of hazardous wastes. The problem helped people realize how long certain chemicals can remain dangerous in soil and water. As a result, new laws were passed to find and clean up other dangerous waste sites.

Figure 16 The scent of these citronella candles naturally repels insects and creates less hazardous waste than bug spray.

Most people don't want to live or work near a hazardous waste disposal facility. In general, people would prefer to have a single large facility located in an area where few people live. A central facility could treat many different types of hazardous wastes. It would be easier to monitor than many scattered sites. However, transporting hazardous wastes to a distant central facility can be costly, difficult, and dangerous. The greater travel distances increase the risk of an accident that could release hazardous wastes into the environment. It may be safer, cheaper, and easier to transport wastes to small local facilities instead.

Reducing Hazardous Waste

The best way to manage hazardous wastes is to produce less of them in the first place. Industries are eager to develop safe alternatives to harmful chemicals. For example, some brands of furniture polishes are now made from lemon oil and beeswax instead of petroleum oils. Many products such as air fresheners, plastic dishes and countertops, carpets, and curtains used to be made with the chemical formaldehyde, which gradually leaked out of these products into the air. Companies have developed alternatives to formaldehyde to use in their products. For instance, the next time you are in a supermarket or hardware store, look for air fresheners that are labeled "formaldehyde-free."

At home, you can find substitutes for some hazardous household chemicals. For example, instead of using insect spray, use harmless materials that naturally repel insects, such as the citronella candles shown in Figure 16. Many household cleaners also now come in biodegradable forms.

Section 3 Review

1. List and define the four categories of hazardous waste.
2. Describe the short-term and long-term effects of hazardous substances on human health.
3. Describe one method used to dispose of hazardous wastes.
4. What was the significance of the events at Love Canal?
5. Explain why radioactive wastes are particularly difficult to manage.
6. **Thinking Critically Making Judgments** Do you think hazardous wastes should be treated and disposed of at one central facility or at many small local facilities? Give reasons for your answer.

Check Your Progress

By now you should be investigating what happens to the different materials in your package when it is thrown away. You will need to find out what types of waste your community recycles, and how it handles other solid waste. (*Hint:* The town engineer or Department of Public Works may be a good source of this information. Be sure to check with your teacher before contacting anyone.)

Program Resources

◆ **Unit 6 Resources** 21-3 Review and Reinforce, p. 47; 21-3 Enrich, p. 48

SECTION 1 Conserving Land and Soil

Key Ideas

◆ Land is a nonrenewable resource. All the people on Earth must share this limited resource for agriculture, development, mining, and other uses.

◆ Soil is a complex system that takes a very long time to form.

◆ Poor soil management can cause erosion, nutrient depletion, and desertification.

◆ There are many farming techniques to help prevent erosion and nutrient depletion.

Key Terms

development	nutrient depletion
litter	fallow
topsoil	crop rotation
subsoil	desertification
bedrock	land reclamation
erosion	

SECTION 2 Solid Waste

Key Ideas

◆ Wastes are produced in the making and using of many products.

◆ Three ways of handling solid waste are to bury it, to burn it, or to recycle it.

◆ Most municipal solid waste in the United States is buried in sanitary landfills.

◆ The main types of municipal solid waste that are recycled are metal, glass, paper, and plastic.

◆ Recycling can conserve both resources and energy. However, there are not always many ways to use recycled materials.

◆ One way to help solve the solid waste problem is to practice the "three R's"—reduce, reuse, and recycle.

Key Terms

municipal solid waste	recycling
leachate	biodegradable
sanitary landfill	resins
incineration	composting

SECTION 3 Hazardous Wastes

INTEGRATING **CHEMISTRY**

Key Ideas

◆ Hazardous wastes are materials that can threaten human health and safety or can be harmful to the environment if they are not properly disposed of.

◆ Hazardous wastes include toxic, explosive, flammable, and corrosive wastes. Radioactive wastes also require special disposal.

◆ How a person is affected by a hazardous substance depends on several factors, including the amount of the substance, the length of time the person is exposed, and how the substance enters the person's body.

◆ It is very difficult to find safe ways to dispose of hazardous wastes and good places to store them. A good way to manage hazardous wastes is to produce less of them.

Key Terms

hazardous waste	flammable
toxic	corrosive
explosive	radioactive

Organizing Information

Compare/Contrast Table On a separate sheet of paper, copy the table below about ways to dispose of municipal solid waste. Then complete it and add a title. (For more on compare/contrast tables, see the Skills Handbook.)

	Landfill	Incinerator
Cost		
Pollution		
Attractiveness		
Usefulness to Community		

Program Resources

◆ **Unit 6 Resources** Chapter 21 Project Scoring Rubric, p. 36

◆ **Performance Assessment** Chapter 21, pp. 64–66

◆ **Chapter Tests** Chapter 21 Test, pp. 83–86

Media and Technology

 Computer Test Bank
Chapter 21 Test

5. Radioactive wastes can remain dangerous to humans and other organisms for thousands of years.

6. Answers may vary. A central facility might dispose of hazardous waste more efficiently, would not expose as many people to the potential dangers of spills and leaks, and would be easier to monitor than many scattered sites. However, transporting hazardous waste to a central facility would be costly, difficult, and potentially dangerous. Small local facilities could be cheaper and safer.

Check Your Progress

CHAPTER PROJECT 21

Ask the representative you contacted earlier to present information in a class visit. (See page 678.) If a visit is not possible, designate two or three volunteers to call and collect information for the rest of the class. Remind students to take notes during the visit or phone call so they will have all the information they need for their final presentations and displays.

Organizing Information

Compare/Contrast Table

Students' tables should include the following information: Landfills are cheaper to build but may be more expensive to operate; can cause pollution of soil and groundwater; are not attractive while in operation; provide jobs and produce methane that can be captured for use as fuel. Incinerators are more expensive to build but cheaper to operate; can cause air pollution and also create some solid waste that must be disposed of elsewhere; could be more attractive than an operating landfill; provide jobs and could be used to generate electricity. Sample title: Landfills versus Incinerators

Performance Assessment

Oral Presentation Call on students at random to give reasons why it is important to dispose of hazardous wastes safely.

Reviewing Content

Multiple Choice

1. a 2. c 3. a 4. c 5. c

True or False

6. true 7. topsoil 8. true 9. true
10. groundwater

Checking Concepts

11. *Living:* bacteria, earthworms, fungi, insects, plant roots; *Nonliving:* minerals, water, air
12. *Any one:* Contour plowing: Rows of crops along the slope of the land prevent soil from washing away. Terracing: Flat steps cut into a hillside with ridges along their edges slow runoff and catch eroding soil. Conservation plowing: Machines break up the deeper subsoil layer without disturbing the topsoil. Windbreaks: Rows of trees are planted along the edges of fields to block the wind and trap eroding soil.
13. *Any two:* Leaving fields fallow (unplanted with crops); leaving crop wastes in the fields; rotating crops
14. The type of plastic the container is made of and how it can be recycled
15. *Any one:* Institute curbside recycling with trash pickup; place recycling bins in public places
16. Composting is the process of helping the natural decomposition processes break down many forms of waste. Biodegradable materials—yard wastes, food wastes, paper, and so on—can be composted.
17. The substance might have leached out of waste in a landfill and seeped into groundwater, thus contaminating people's water supply.
18. Students should draw on what they learned in Section 3 about hazardous substances in common household products.

Thinking Critically

19. Students should suggest contour plowing or terracing, both of which reduce soil erosion caused by water flowing down slopes.
20. The topsoil and subsoil could be replaced in their original order. Then the area could be replanted.
21. Accept all answers so long as students provide well-reasoned

---

Reviewing Content

Multiple Choice

Choose the letter of the best answer.

1. The advance of desertlike conditions into areas that previously were fertile is called
   a. desertification.
   b. crop rotation.
   c. nutrient depletion.
   d. land reclamation.
2. Water containing dissolved chemicals from a landfill is called
   a. resin.
   b. litter.
   c. leachate.
   d. compost.
3. Solid wastes are burned in the process of
   a. incineration.
   b. composting.
   c. erosion.
   d. recycling.
4. Which of the following is a biodegradable waste?
   a. a glass jar   b. a metal can
   c. an apple core   d. a plastic bag
5. Wastes that contain unstable atoms are called
   a. corrosive.   b. flammable.
   c. radioactive.   d. explosive.

True and False

If the statement is true, write true. If it is false, change the underlined word or words to make the statement true.

6. Three major types of land use are agriculture, development, and <u>mining</u>.
7. The layer of soil that contains the most animal and plant matter is the <u>subsoil</u>.
8. Fields that are left unplanted with crops are called <u>fallow</u>.
9. Most of the municipal solid waste generated in the United States is disposed of in <u>landfills</u>.
10. Liners prevent the waste in landfills from polluting the <u>air</u>.

Checking Concepts

11. List two living things and two nonliving things that are found in topsoil.
12. Choose one of the following techniques and explain how it can reduce soil erosion: contour plowing, terracing, conservation plowing, or windbreaks.
13. Give examples of two techniques for preventing nutrient depletion.
14. What does the number on a plastic container indicate?
15. Describe one way communities can encourage residents to produce less solid waste.
16. What is composting? What kinds of materials can be composted?
17. Explain how a person might be exposed to a hazardous substance that was buried underground many years ago.
18. **Writing to Learn** Write a public service announcement to inform people about household hazardous wastes. Begin with a "hook" to catch your listener's attention. Be sure to explain what makes a waste hazardous. Also give examples of household hazardous wastes, and tell people what to do with these substances.

Thinking Critically

19. **Applying Concepts** If you owned a large farm on a hill, how would you prevent soil erosion? Explain your answer.
20. **Problem Solving** In strip mining, a layer of soil is removed to expose a resource, such as coal, underneath. What methods could be used to restore this damaged land?
21. **Making Judgments** Suppose you go to the store to buy some juice. You can choose from juice sold in an aluminum, glass, or plastic container, all for the same price. Which would you choose? Explain your answer.
22. **Applying Concepts** Why is it unsafe to bury or incinerate radioactive waste?

---

arguments for their choices.

22. Radioactive waste remains dangerous for thousands of years. Burying it in an open dump or sanitary landfill or burning it in an incinerator would not protect people and other organisms from the hazards of radioactivity. Burning the waste might pollute the air, and burying the waste could pollute the groundwater or incorporate radioactive substances in the food chain.

Applying Skills

23.

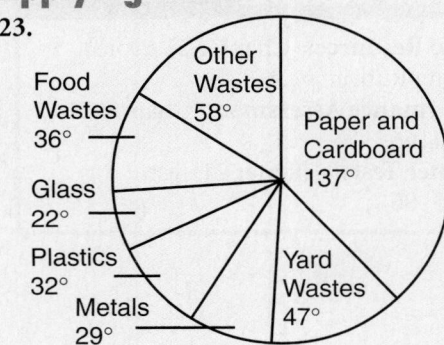

Food Wastes 36°
Glass 22°
Plastics 32°
Metals 29°
Other Wastes 58°
Paper and Cardboard 137°
Yard Wastes 47°

Applying Skills

Use the following data on municipal solid waste in the United States to answer Questions 23–25.

Type of Waste	Percent of Total
Paper and cardboard	38%
Food wastes	10%
Yard wastes	13%
Metals	8%
Plastics	9%
Glass	6%
Other wastes	16%

23. **Graphing** Use the data to create a circle graph. (To review circle graphs, see the Skills Handbook.)
24. **Classifying** Which of the types of waste shown are recyclable? Which include wastes that can be composted?

25. **Developing Hypotheses** Why do you think paper makes up the largest percent of solid waste?

Performance CHAPTER PROJECT 21 **Assessment**

Project Wrap Up As you finish work on your project, share it with one or more classmates. Ask: Does the display clearly explain what the package is made of? Are the benefits of the package identified? Does the display describe what happens to each material? If you need to make any revisions to your display, do so now.

Reflect and Record In your project notebook, describe the most surprising information you learned during this project. What questions might you ask before purchasing a product like the one you studied?

Test Preparation Use these questions to prepare for standardized tests.

Study the information below. Then answer Questions 26–28.

The graph shows how rain can wash away certain compounds that plants need.

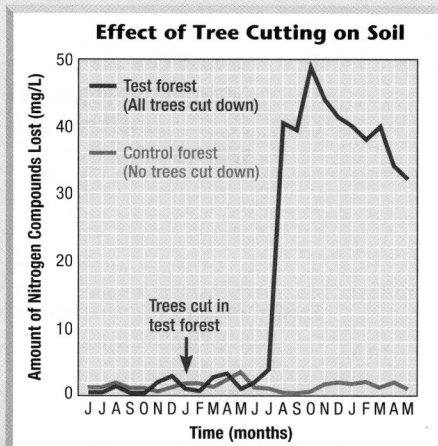

Effect of Tree Cutting on Soil

26. Before trees were cut down, the loss of nitrogen compounds was
    a. unknown.
    b. about the same in both forests.
    c. greater in the test forest.
    d. greater in the control forest.
27. During the second year, the amount of nitrogen compounds lost in the test forest was
    a. about the same as in the first year.
    b. about 2 times greater than in the first year.
    c. about 20 times greater than in the first year.
    d. about 20 times less than in the first year.
28. According to the graph, cutting down trees
    a. caused the death of other trees.
    b. had no effect on the loss of nitrogen compounds.
    c. caused more nitrogen compounds to be lost.
    d. caused nitrogen compounds to increase.

---

24. Paper and cardboard, metals, plastics, and glass are recyclable. Yard wastes and food wastes can be composted.
25. *Sample answer:* Paper is used to make more products and product packages that are discarded than any other type of material.

Program Resources

◆ **Inquiry Skills Activity Book** Provides teaching and review of all inquiry skills
◆ **Prentice Hall Assessment System** Provides standardized test practice
◆ **Reading in the Content Area** Provides strategies to improve science reading skills
◆ **Teacher's ELL Handbook** Provides multiple strategies for English language learners

Performance CHAPTER PROJECT 21 **Assessment**

Project Wrap Up Remind students that their displays should also include a cut-away view of the package and a sample of each material used in it. Having every student present his or her display to the entire class might be time-consuming and tedious. Instead, assign students to small groups or have two poster sessions where half the class displays their projects to the other half.

Reflect and Record Invite students to share their reflections on the project in a class discussion.

Test Preparation

26. b 27. c 28. c

CHAPTER 22 Air and Water Resources

Sections	Time	Student Edition Activities	Other Activities
CHAPTER PROJECT 22 **Pollution vs. Purity** p. 705	Ongoing (2 weeks)	Check Your Progress, pp. 719, 724 Project Wrap Up, p. 727	Chapter 22 Project Notes, pp. 704–705
1 Air Pollution pp. 706–714 ◆ 22.1.1 Identify and describe outdoor and indoor air pollutants. ◆ 22.1.2 Explain the importance of ozone in the upper atmosphere. ◆ 22.1.3 Describe the greenhouse effect and explain how it affects climate.	2 periods/ 1 block	**Discover** How Does the Scent Spread?, p. 706 **Try This** How Acid Is Your Rain?, p. 709 **Sharpen Your Skills** Communicating, p. 710 **Science at Home,** p. 713 **Real-World Lab: You and Your Environment** How Does the Garden Grow?, p. 714	TE Addressing Naive Conceptions, p. 707 TE Building Inquiry Skills: Observing, p. 708 TE Real-Life Learning, p. 709 TE Math Toolbox, p. 711 TE Inquiry Challenge, p. 711 TE Integrating Earth Science, p. 712
2 The Water Supply pp. 715–720 ◆ 22.2.1 Identify factors that make most of Earth's water not useful to people. ◆ 22.2.2 Identify human sources of water pollution.	2 periods/ 1 block	**Discover** How Does the Water Change?, p. 715 **Try This** Getting Clean, p. 716 **Skills Lab: Measuring** Concentrate on This!, p. 720	TE Building Inquiry Skills: Graphing, p. 716 TE Inquiry Challenge, p. 717 TE Building Inquiry Skills: Making Models, p. 718
3 *INTEGRATING TECHNOLOGY* **Finding Pollution Solutions** pp. 721–724 ◆ 22.3.1 Describe ways that technology can help control air pollution. ◆ 22.3.2 Describe ways that technology can help control water pollution.	1 period/ $\frac{1}{2}$ bloc	**Discover** Can You Remove the Tea?, p. 721 **Sharpen Your Skills** Graphing, p. 722	TE Real-Life Learning, p. 723 TE Cultural Diversity, p. 723 TE Real-Life Learning, p. 724 LM 22, "Pollution Prevention With Rocks"
Study Guide/Assessment pp. 725–727	1 period/ $\frac{1}{2}$ block		ISAB Provides teaching and review of all inquiry skills

 For Standard or Block Schedule The Resource Pro® CD-ROM gives you maximum flexibility for planning your instruction for any type of schedule. Resource Pro® contains Planning Express®, an advanced scheduling program, as well as the entire contents of the Teaching Resources and the Computer Test Bank.

Key: **CTB** Computer Test Bank
CT Chapter Tests
ELL Teacher's ELL Handbook

CHAPTER PLANNING GUIDE

Program Resources	Assessment Strategies	Media and Technology
UR Chapter 22 Project Teacher Notes, pp. 54–55 UR Chapter 22 Project Overview and Worksheets, pp. 56–59	TE Check Your Progress, pp. 719, 724 TE Performance Assessment: Chapter 22 Project Wrap Up, p. 727 UR Chapter 22 Project Scoring Rubric, p. 60	🌐 Science Explorer Internet Site 🎧 Audio CDs, Section Summaries
UR 22-1 Lesson Plan, p. 61 UR 22-1 Section Summary, p. 62 UR 22-1 Review and Reinforce, p. 63 UR 22-1 Enrich, p. 64 UR Real-World Lab blackline masters, pp. 73–74	SE Section 1 Review, p. 713 SE Analyze and Conclude, p. 714 TE Ongoing Assessment, pp. 707, 709, 711 TE Performance Assessment, p. 713	📼 Concept Videotape Library, *Adventures, Tape 5,* "The Greenhouse Effect"; "Our Passion for Driving"; "A Better Cool" 💿 Presentation Pro, "Air Pollution" 📽 Transparencies 84, "Temperature Inversion"; 85, "The Ozone Cycle"; 86, "The Greenhouse Effect"; 87, "Exploring Climate Predictions" 📼 Lab Activity Videotape, *Tape 5*
UR 22-2 Lesson Plan, p. 65 UR 22-2 Section Summary, p. 66 UR 22-2 Review and Reinforce, p. 67 UR 22-2 Enrich, p. 68 UR Skills Lab blackline masters, pp. 75–77	SE Section 2 Review, p. 719 SE Analyze and Conclude, p. 720 TE Ongoing Assessment, p. 717 TE Performance Assessment, p. 719	📼 Concept Videotape Library, *Adventures, Tape 5,* "What's in Our Tap?" 📼 Lab Activity Videotape, *Tape 5*
UR 22-3 Lesson Plan, p. 69 UR 22-3 Section Summary, p. 70 UR 22-3 Review and Reinforce, p. 71 UR 22-3 Enrich, p. 72	SE Section 3 Review, p. 724 TE Ongoing Assessment, p. 723 TE Performance Assessment, p. 724	📼 Concept Videotape Library, *Adventures, Tape 5,* "Xeriscape"
GRSW Provides worksheets to promote student comprehension of content RCA Provides strategies to improve science reading skills ELL Provides multiple strategies for English language learners	SE Study Guide/Assessment, pp. 725–727 PA Performance Assessment, pp. 67–69 CT Chapter 22 Test, pp. 87–90 CTB Chapter 22 Test PHAS Provides standardized test preparation	💿 Computer Test Bank, Chapter 22 Test

GRSW Guided Reading and Study Workbook
ISAB Inquiry Skills Activity Book
LM Laboratory Manual

PA Performance Assessment
PHAS Prentice Hall Assessment System
PLM Probeware Lab Manual

RCA Reading in the Content Area
SE Student Edition

TE Teacher's Edition
UR Unit Resources

Meeting the National Science Education Standards and AAAS Benchmarks

National Science Education Standards	Benchmarks for Science Literacy	Unifying Themes
Science as Inquiry (Content Standard A) ◆ **Design and conduct a scientific investigation** Students investigate how pollutants affect seed growth. *(Real-World Lab)* ◆ **Use appropriate tools and techniques to gather, analyze, and interpret data** Students compare concentrations of a pollutant. *(Skills Lab)* ◆ **Communicate scientific procedures and explanations** Students communicate the importance of protecting air or water quality. *(Chapter Project)* **Earth and Space Science** (Content Standard D) ◆ **Structure of the Earth system** Air is a mixture of nitrogen, oxygen, carbon dioxide, water vapor, and other gases. Earth has a limited supply of fresh water. *(Sections 1, 2)* **Science and Technology** (Content Standard E) ◆ **Understandings about science and technology** Technology can help control pollution. *(Chapter Project; Sections 1, 2, 3)* **Science in Personal and Social Perspectives** (Content Standard F) ◆ **Personal health** Pollution can affect the health of humans. *(Sections 1, 2)* ◆ **Risks and benefits** Small changes in people's behavior can help reduce pollution. *(Chapter Project; Section 3)*	**1B Scientific Inquiry** Students investigate how pollutants affect seed growth and compare different concentrations of a pollutant in water. *(Real-World Lab; Skills Lab)* **3A Technology and Science** Technology can help control pollution. *(Section 3)* **3B Designs and Systems** The engines of motor vehicles release emissions into the air. Most pollution is the result of human activities, including agriculture, industry, construction, and mining. *(Chapter Project; Sections 1, 2)* **3C Issues in Technology** In the United States, laws help to reduce pollution. *(Section 3)* **4B The Earth** Air is a mixture of nitrogen, oxygen, carbon dioxide, water vapor, and other gases. Earth has a limited supply of fresh water. *(Sections 1, 2)* **6E Physical Health** Pollution can affect the health of humans. *(Sections 1, 2)* **7D Social Trade-Offs** Important human activities can cause air and water pollution. *(Chapter Project; Sections 1, 2)* **12D Communication Skills** Students communicate about air or water quality to younger students. *(Chapter Project)*	◆ **Energy** Obtaining and using energy resources can result in pollution. The theory of global warming predicts that increases in carbon dioxide will cause the average temperature to rise. The addition of heat can have a negative effect on a body of water. *(Chapter Project; Sections 1, 2)* ◆ **Modeling** Most scientists base their climate predictions on computer models. Students use models to observe the effects of pollutants on seed growth and compare the concentrations of a pollutant in water. *(Section 1; Real-World Lab; Skills Lab)* ◆ **Patterns of Change** Pollution can affect the health of humans and other living things. The theory of global warming predicts that increases in carbon dioxide will cause the average temperature to rise. *(Sections 1, 2)* ◆ **Scale and Structure** The ozone layer is a layer of the upper atmosphere about 30 kilometers above Earth's surface. Pollution can affect areas far from its source. *(Sections 1, 2)* ◆ **Stability** Earth's supply of fresh water is renewable. *(Section 2)* ◆ **Systems and Interactions** The engines of motor vehicles release emissions that cause air pollution. Most pollution is the result of human activities, including agriculture, industry, construction, and mining. Technology can help reduce pollution. *(Chapter Project; Sections 1, 2, 3)*

Take It to the Net

The **www.phschool.com** Web site provides you with multiple opportunities to incorporate the internet into your instruction. Go to **www.phschool.com** and click on the Science icon. Then select Science Explorer Integrated.

■ Have students use the chapter Self-Test to get instant feedback.

■ Hot Links and Reference Links provide opportunities for online research.

WEB ACTIVITY www.phschool.com

Internet Activities provide opportunities for students to review, extend, or assess a concept from the chapter.

STAY CURRENT with **SCIENCE NEWS** ®

Find out the latest research and information about natural resources and pollution at: **www.phschool.com**

ACTIVITY	Time (minutes)	Materials Quantities for one work group	Skills
Section 1			
Discover, p. 706	5	**Nonconsumable** bottle of perfume (for teacher only)	Inferring
Try This, p. 709	10	**Consumable** rainwater, pH paper, pH chart, lemon juice **Nonconsumable** two plastic cups	Measuring
Sharpen Your Skills, p. 710	15	No special materials are required.	Communicating
Science at Home, p. 713	home	**Consumable** petroleum jelly **Nonconsumable** 2 empty glass jars	Predicting, Observing
Real-World Lab, p. 714	30; 5 x 5 days	**Consumable** potting soil, 20 radish seeds, detergent solution, day-old tap water, acid solution, oil solution, salt solution, masking tape **Nonconsumable** 2 plastic petri dishes with lids, metric ruler, wax pencil	Controlling Variables, Measuring, Interpreting Data
Section 2			
Discover, p. 715	5	**Consumable** water, milk **Nonconsumable** flashlight, clear plastic cup, plastic dropper	Observing
Try This, p. 716	10; 5 x 3 days	**Consumable** water, food coloring, sugar **Nonconsumable** plastic cup, spoon, graduated cylinder	Making Models
Skills Lab, p. 720	40	**Consumable** food coloring, water **Nonconsumable** 9 test tubes, test tube rack, 10-mL graduated cylinder	Measuring, Calculating, Observing
Section 3			
Discover, p. 721	10	**Consumable** cooled herbal tea, paper filter, crushed charcoal **Nonconsumable** 2 plastic cups, funnel	Developing Hypotheses
Sharpen Your Skills, p. 722	20	**Consumable** graph paper **Nonconsumable** 2 pens or pencils of different colors	Graphing

A list of all materials required for the Student Edition activities can be found beginning on page T23. You can obtain information about ordering materials by calling 1-800-848-9500 or by accessing the Science Explorer Internet site at: **www.phschool.com**

Chapter 22 focuses on the causes and effects of air and water pollution and on methods of protecting air and water quality. The Chapter 22 Project will give students an opportunity to explore chapter concepts in greater depth and to convey their understanding to others.

Purpose For the Chapter 22 Project, students will research a specific topic related to air or water quality, then create a book, game, video, or other educational tool to communicate their findings and ideas to younger students. The project is suitable as either an individual or a small-group activity.

Skills Focus After completing the Chapter 22 Project, students will be able to
◆ relate the causes and effects of specific forms of air or water pollution;
◆ make judgments about ways that individuals can help reduce those forms of pollution;
◆ communicate information about air or water quality to younger students using age-appropriate materials and methods.

Project Time Line The Chapter 22 Project requires about two weeks to complete, depending on the amount of time you allot for the research phase of the project. As students study Sections 1 and 2, they will choose a specific topic for study, conduct their research, and organize the information they gather. During Section 3, students will design and create the final product. At the conclusion of the chapter, students will present their products to younger students and evaluate the products' appeal and effectiveness in conveying information about air or water quality.

Possible Materials
◆ Provide appropriate materials for creating the final products that students have chosen—posterboard and art supplies for making board games, video cameras for creating videos, and the like. Encourage students to use materials from home as well.

Advance Preparation Check your school and town libraries to make sure

WEB ACTIVITY www.phschool.com

SECTION
1 Air Pollution

Discover **How Does the Scent Spread?**
Sharpen Your Skills **Communicating**
Try This **How Acid Is Your Rain?**
Real-World Lab **How Does the Garden Grow?**

SECTION
2 The Water Supply

Discover **How Does the Water Change?**
Try This **Getting Clean**
Skills Lab **Concentrate on This!**

SECTION
Integrating Technology
3 Finding Pollution Solutions

Discover **Can You Remove the Tea?**
Sharpen Your Skills **Graphing**

students will have access to ample research materials for the project. Contact teachers of younger students to arrange for your students to present their final products at the conclusion of the chapter. Try to provide a range of age/grade possibilities so your students can choose among them.

Launching the Project Invite students to read the Chapter 22 Project description on page 705. Then ask: **What kinds of things did you enjoy doing in school when you were younger? What made learning fun?** Encourage students

to keep these ideas in mind as they work on this project, particularly when they plan their final products.

Distribute Chapter 22 Project Overview on pages 56–57 of Unit 6 Resources, and have students review the project rules and procedures. Invite questions and comments. Emphasize that the final product should be designed for their specific target audience. Advise students to think about the target audience's age range, skills, interests, and previous learning when they develop the final

Pollution vs. Purity

Pollution is a change to the environment that has a harmful effect on humans and other living things. Pollution can come from a single smokestack or from many different sources all over the world.

As you study this chapter, your project is to help communicate the importance of preventing pollution and protecting air or water quality.

Your Goal To create a book, game, or video that educates younger students about air or water quality.

Your product should
- present facts about the causes and effects of a form of pollution
- engage your audience while informing them about the topic
- include steps that the students can take to be part of the "pollution solution"

Get Started Survey the chapter to see what types of pollution are discussed. Begin thinking about which topic you would like to study. Discuss with your teacher what age group your product should be designed for. Decide which form your product will take.

Check Your Progress You'll be working on the project as you study this chapter. To keep your project on track, look for Check Your Progress boxes at the following points.

Section 2 Review, page 719: Gather information on your topic and organize it.

Section 3 Review, page 724: Design and create your product.

Wrap Up At the end of the chapter (page 727), you will present your product to younger students and get their feedback.

Smoke billows from a row of smokestacks at an automobile plant.

705

Program Resources

◆ **Unit 6 Resources** Chapter 22 Project Teacher Notes, pp. 54–55; Project Overview and Worksheets, pp. 56–59; Project Scoring Rubric, p. 60

Media and Technology

 Audio CDs Section Summaries

 www.phschool.com

You will find an Internet activity, chapter self-tests for students, and links to other chapter topics at this site.

product. Encourage students to consider students in special-needs classes, as well as younger students.

If you prefer to have students do the project as a small-group activity, divide the class into groups of two to four students each. Let the groups meet briefly to brainstorm ideas for specific topics and products. Whether the project is done individually or in groups, monitor students' choices of topics, products, and target audiences.

When students are ready to make their final products, distribute Chapter 22 Project Worksheet 1, which provides guidelines for creating a board game, video, or skit. At the end of the chapter, distribute Worksheet 2, which provides a format for students to obtain the younger students' feedback on the products' appeal and effectiveness.

Additional information on guiding the project is provided in Chapter 22 Project Teacher Notes on pages 54–55 of Unit 6 Resources.

Performance Assessment

The Chapter 22 Project Scoring Rubric on page 60 in Unit 6 Resources will help you evaluate how well students complete the Chapter 22 Project. You may want to share the scoring rubric with students so they are clear about what will be expected of them. Students will be assessed on
- ◆ their ability to identify the causes and effects of one specific type of air or water pollution and organize the information;
- ◆ their ability to create an age-appropriate product to teach younger students about air or water quality and present the product to the target audience;
- ◆ their participation in their group, if they worked in groups.

SECTION 1 Air Pollution

Objectives

After completing the lesson, students will be able to
- identify and describe outdoor and indoor air pollutants;
- explain the importance of ozone in the upper atmosphere;
- describe the greenhouse effect and explain how it affects climate.

Key Terms air pollution, emissions, photochemical smog, ozone, temperature inversion, acid rain, ozone layer, chlorofluorocarbons, greenhouse effect, global warming

1 Engage/Explore

Activating Prior Knowledge

Encourage students to describe specific examples of air pollution that they have seen, such as smog hanging over a city, smoke coming from factory smokestacks, and grime or pollen settling on cars parked outdoors. Ask: **What kinds of materials pollute the air we breathe?** *(Accept all responses without comment at this time.)*

········ DISCOVER ·········

Skills Focus inferring
Materials *bottle of perfume*
Time 5 minutes
Tips Make sure students are evenly spaced throughout the room so the scent will reach different students at different times.
Expected Outcome Students closest to you will smell the perfume first, and those standing farthest away will smell it last.
Think It Over Students will see a "wave" of raised hands traveling from you to the farthest parts of the room. Students should infer that molecules of perfume traveled across the room in the air.

DISCOVER

How Does the Scent Spread?

1. Choose a place to stand so that you and your classmates are evenly spread around the room.
2. Your teacher will open a bottle of perfume in one corner of the room.
3. Raise your hand when you first smell the perfume.

Think It Over
Inferring Describe the pattern you observed as people raised their hands. How do you think the smell traveled across the room?

GUIDE FOR READING

- What causes photochemical smog?
- How is the ozone layer important?
- What are climate predictions based on?

Reading Tip As you read, make a list of different types of air pollution. Write a sentence about the effect of each type.

Figure 1 The air supply aboard the space station *Mir* was threatened by a collision during docking.

706

June 25, 1997, began as an ordinary day aboard the Russian space station *Mir.* The three crew members were busy with their usual tasks. One checked on the various scientific experiments. Another was exercising. The third cosmonaut was skillfully guiding a supply ship as it docked with *Mir.*

Suddenly, the crew members heard a frightening sound—the crumpling of collapsing metal. The space station jolted from side to side. The pressure gauges indicated an air leak! One crew member hurried to prepare the emergency evacuation vehicle. Meanwhile, the other two managed to close the airtight door between the damaged area and the rest of the space station. Fortunately, the pressure soon returned to normal. A disaster had been avoided. There was no need to abandon ship.

Closing the door preserved the most valuable resource on *Mir*—the air. Although you probably don't think about the air very often, it is just as important on Earth as it is on a space station. Air is a resource you use every minute of your life.

What's in the Air?

Though you can't see, taste, or smell it, you are surrounded by air. Air is a mixture of nitrogen, oxygen, carbon dioxide, water vapor, and other gases. Almost all living things depend on these gases to carry out their life processes.

Nitrogen, oxygen, and carbon dioxide cycle between the atmosphere and living things. These cycles ensure that the air supply on Earth will not run out. But they don't guarantee that the air will always be clean. A change to the atmosphere that has harmful effects is called **air pollution.** Substances that cause pollution are called pollutants. Pollutants can be solid particles,

---

Reading Tip Students could list the following types of air pollution: emissions (particles and gases) from factories, power plants, and automobiles; photochemical smog; acid rain; cigarette smoke; carbon monoxide from incomplete burning of fuels; radon; and chlorofluorocarbons. Their sentences should describe or explain the source of each type.

Caption Writing Distribute photocopies of Figure 4, and suggest that each student write a new caption that identifies each source of indoor pollution shown. Then have each student add another source of air pollution to the drawing. Have students exchange cartoons and expand the caption to include the pollution source that was added.

such as ash, or gases, such as chlorine. Air pollution can affect the health of humans and other living things. Pollution can even impact the climate of the whole planet.

What causes air pollution? If you're like many people, you probably picture a factory smokestack, belching thick black smoke into the sky. Until the mid-1900s, factories and power plants that burned coal produced most of the air pollution in the United States. Solid particles and gases that are released into the air are called **emissions.** Today, there is an even larger source of emissions that cause air pollution: motor vehicles such as cars, trucks, and airplanes. The engines of these vehicles release gases such as carbon monoxide, an invisible toxic gas.

Though most air pollution is the result of human activities, there are some natural causes as well. For example, an erupting volcano sends an enormous load of soot, ash, sulfur, and nitrogen oxide gases into the atmosphere.

☑ *Checkpoint* **What are some examples of air pollutants?**

Smog

Have you ever heard a weather forecaster talk about a "smog alert"? A smog alert is a warning about a type of air pollution called photochemical smog. **Photochemical smog** is a thick, brownish haze formed when certain gases in the air react with sunlight. When the smog level is high, it settles as a haze over a city. Smog can make people's eyes burn and irritate their throats.

The major sources of photochemical smog are the gases emitted by automobiles and trucks. Burning gasoline in a car engine releases some gases into the air. These gases include hydrocarbons (compounds containing hydrogen and carbon) and nitrogen oxides. The gases react in the sunlight and produce a form of oxygen called **ozone.** Ozone, which is toxic, is the major chemical found in smog.

Language Arts
CONNECTION

People sometimes coin, or invent, a word to express a specific idea. For example, Londoners coined the word *smog* to describe the heavy gray air formed when coal smoke mixed with ocean fog.

In Your Journal

Can you guess the meaning of these coined words?

- brunch
- chortle
- squinched
- liger

Try coining a few descriptive words of your own. Exchange your words with a classmate and see if you can guess the meanings of the other's words.

Figure 2 A haze of photochemical smog hangs over this city's skyline. *Interpreting Photographs What is the source of the smog?*

707

Program Resources

- **Unit 6 Resources** 22-1 Lesson Plan, p. 61; 22-1 Section Summary, p. 62
- **Guided Reading and Study Workbook** Section 22-1

Answers to Self-Assessment

☑ *Checkpoint*

Air pollutants include solid particles such as ash, and gases such as chlorine and carbon monoxide.

Caption Question

Figure 2 The source of smog is the gases emitted by automobiles and trucks in the city.

2 *Facilitate*

What's in the Air?

Addressing Naive Conceptions

Materials *drawing compass, calculator*
Time 10–15 minutes

Ask: **Which gas do you think is most common in the air we breathe?** *(Accept all responses without comment.)* Then provide the following data: nitrogen 78%; oxygen 21%; argon 0.9%; other gases, including carbon dioxide and water vapor, 0.1%. Ask: **Was your prediction correct, or were you surprised?** *(Students may have thought that oxygen is the most common gas or that carbon dioxide is present in a much higher proportion.)* Challenge each student to use these data to create a circle graph. *(Nitrogen 281°, oxygen 75.5°, argon 3°, other gases 0.5°)* **learning modality: logical/mathematical**

Smog

Language Arts
CONNECTION

To clarify how the word smog was created, write *smoke + fog* on the board, erase *oke* and *f*, and write = *smog*.

In Your Journal As a class, discuss suggestions for each word. (*Brunch:* a meal midway between breakfast and lunch; *chortle:* to chuckle and snort; *squinch:* to squint or squeeze and pinch; *liger:* the offspring of a lion and a tiger) The word *chortle* was coined by British author Lewis Carroll, who coined many terms in his famous poem "Jabberwocky." Students may enjoy identifying other coined words in the poem. **learning modality: verbal**

Ongoing Assessment

Oral Presentation Call on students to each name one source of particles or gases that contribute to air pollution.

Integrating Health

Some respiratory problems, such as asthma, bronchitis, and emphysema are caused or worsened by breathing polluted air. A local hospital, nursing association, or pediatric practice may be able to provide pamphlets or a speaker on these topics. Encourage students to use the information they receive to make posters that include a labeled diagram of the respiratory system (or parts of it) and a brief description of how the system is affected. **learning modality: verbal**

Acid Rain

Building Inquiry Skills: Observing

Materials *plastic cup, scissors, piece of nylon stocking fabric, tape, hand lens*

ACTIVITY

Time 10–15 minutes for setup plus follow-up observations

Have students examine nylon stocking fabric with a hand lens and draw what they see. Also have students pull and twist the fabric to test its strength and flexibility. Then have each student make an "acid rain tester" by cutting out the bottom of a plastic cup and taping a piece of stocking over the opening. Take students outdoors to hang the testers where they will be exposed to air and rain. At the end of a week, have students reexamine the fabric, compare it with their original drawings, retest its strength and flexibility, and look for broken fibers and other signs of damage. Encourage students to consider what could have caused any damage. Point out that polluting gases in the air, such as sulfur oxides and nitrogen oxides, also affect the nylon. **learning modality: visual**

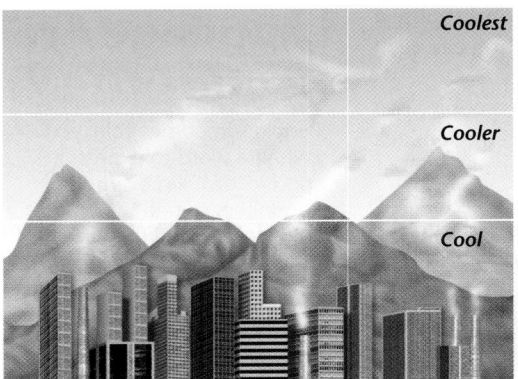 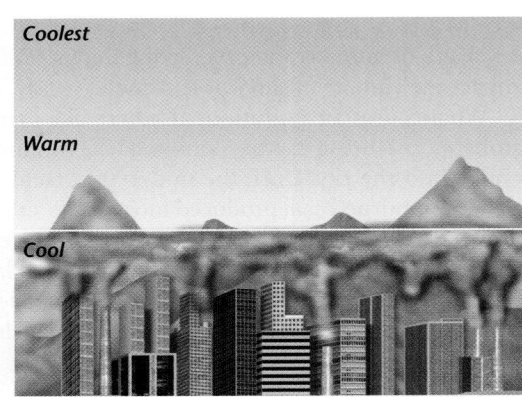

Figure 3 Normally, pollutants rise high in the air and blow away (left). But during a temperature inversion, a layer of warm air traps pollutants close to the ground (right).

Temperature Inversion Pollutants usually blow away from the place where they are produced. Normally, air close to the ground is heated by Earth's surface. As the air warms, it rises into the cooler air above it. The pollutants are carried higher into the atmosphere where they blow away. But certain weather conditions cause a condition known as a temperature inversion. During a **temperature inversion,** a layer of warm air prevents the rising air from escaping. The polluted air is trapped and held close to Earth's surface. The smog becomes more concentrated and dangerous.

Health Effects of Smog The effects of smog can be more serious than itchy, watery eyes and a scratchy throat. The ozone in smog can cause lung problems and harm the body's defenses against infection. When smog levels reach a certain point, a city issues a smog alert. During a smog alert, you should avoid exercising outdoors. People who have asthma or other conditions that affect their breathing should be particularly careful.

Checkpoint *What happens during a temperature inversion?*

Acid Rain

Another type of air pollution is caused by power plants and factories that burn coal and oil. These fuels produce nitrogen oxides and sulfur oxides when they are burned. These gases react with water vapor in the air, forming nitric acid and sulfuric acid. The acids return to Earth's surface dissolved in precipitation. Precipitation that is more acidic than normal is called **acid rain.** Acid rain can be in the form of snow, sleet, or fog as well as rain.

As you can imagine, acid falling from the sky has some negative effects. When acid rain falls into a pond or lake, it changes

Background

Facts and Figures Ordinary rainwater contains dissolved carbon dioxide and other compounds of natural origin that form weak acid solutions. Normally, the pH of rainwater is about 5 to 6. But rain in the northeastern United States usually has a pH of about 4. Sometimes the rain in this region is at least as acidic as vinegar, which has a pH of 3.

One factor that makes acid rain such a complex problem is that it occurs far from the source of the gases that cause it. For example, gases from coal-burning power plants in England are blown eastward and cause acid rain in Sweden and Norway. In the United States, midwestern and eastern states produce much of the acid rain that falls in New England and southeastern Canada.

the conditions there. Many fish, and particularly their eggs, cannot survive in more acidic water. Acid rain that falls on the ground can damage plants by affecting the nutrient levels in the soil. Whole forests have been destroyed by acid rain. Fortunately, some of the effects of acid rain are reversible. Badly damaged lakes have been restored by adding substances such as lime that neutralize the acid.

Acid rain doesn't just affect living things. The acid reacts with stone and metal in buildings and statues. Automobiles rust more quickly in areas with acid rain. These effects are not reversible.

Indoor Air Pollution

You might think that you could avoid air pollution by staying inside. But in fact, the air inside buildings can be polluted, too. Many substances can cause indoor air pollution. Some, such as dust, pet hair, and air fresheners, bother only those people who are allergic to them. Other pollutants have more widespread effects. Asbestos, a building material common in older buildings, can cause lung disease. Products such as oil-based paints, glues, and cleaning supplies may give off toxic fumes. Read the label whenever you use any of these products. You may need to open a window or use the chemical outdoors.

If you have been near someone smoking a cigarette, you know how the smell stays in your clothes and hair even after you leave the room. The smoke reached your lungs every time you inhaled near the smoking person. Research has shown that cigarette smoke can damage the lungs and heart. Now smoking is banned in many places such as restaurants, airports, and stadiums.

How Acid Is Your Rain?

In this activity you will test whether rain in your area is more or less acidic than lemon juice (citric acid).

1. Collect some rainwater in a clean plastic cup.
2. Indoors, dip a piece of pH paper into the cup. Compare the color of the paper to the chart on the package to find the pH. (The lower the pH of a substance, the more acidic it is.)
3. Pour a little lemon juice into a plastic cup. Repeat Step 2 with the lemon juice.

Measuring What is the pH of the rainwater? How does it compare to the pH of the lemon juice?

Figure 4 Air inside buildings can be polluted, too. *Observing How many sources of pollution can you spot in this room?*

Chapter 22 **709**

Media and Technology

 Transparencies "Temperature Inversion," Transparency 84

Answers to Self-Assessment

☑ *Checkpoint*

A layer of warm air prevents cooler air below it from rising, trapping polluted air close to Earth's surface.

Caption Question

Figure 4 *Samples:* Smoking, dusting, burning wood in the fireplace, cat hair, bird feathers, flower pollen, carpet fumes

---

Skills Focus measuring
Materials *rainwater, 2 plastic cups, pH paper, pH chart, lemon juice*
Time 10 minutes
Tips You might want to collect rainwater ahead of time for this activity.
Expected Outcome Rainwater is normally slightly acidic (pH 5–6); a pH lower than 5 indicates acid rain. Lemon juice's pH is 2.
Extend Have students measure the pH of tap water and compare it with their pH measurements of rainwater and lemon juice. **learning modality: logical/mathematical**

Indoor Air Pollution

Real-Life Learning

Materials *containers of various products such as oil-based paints, glues, and cleaning supplies that give off toxic fumes*
Time 10 minutes

Display the products for students to examine their labels. (CAUTION: *Instruct students to not open any container.*) Have volunteers read aloud cautionary statements on the labels. Then ask: **How could you use these products safely?** (*Instructions may vary. Usually such products can be used safely outside or in well-ventilated areas.*) **How should such products be stored?** (*They should be stored in a secure area, away from small children and pets, and the containers should be closed tightly.*) **How should such products be disposed of?** (*Most such products should be taken to a hazardous waste site.*) **learning modality: verbal**

Ongoing Assessment

Drawing Have each student draw and label a diagram to explain how acid rain forms.

 Students can save their drawings in their portfolios.

Indoor Air Pollution, continued

Including All Students

For students who need additional help with language skills, write *carbon dioxide* and *carbon monoxide* on the board and ask: **What difference do you see between these terms?** *(The prefixes di- and mon-; draw a box around each prefix.)* **What do these word parts mean?** *(Di- means "two," mon- means "one.")* **What do you think *dioxide* and *monoxide* mean?** *("Two oxygens" and "one oxygen")* Write CO_2 and CO below the terms, and draw a simple diagram of each molecule. Explain that CO_2, a harmless gas, has two oxygen atoms in each molecule, while CO has only one. CO is deadly because it is absorbed by red blood cells more easily than oxygen (O_2) is. When a person breathes CO, it replaces the O_2 in the body, causing suffocation. Stress the value of detectors in preventing CO poisoning. **learning modality: verbal**

Sharpen your Skills

Communicating

Time 15 minutes
Tips Have students work in groups of three. Establish a time limit of 30 or 45 seconds for the announcement. Let each group tape-record its announcement.
Expected Outcome Play the announcements in class, and have students assess each one for the elements cited in the text, including "listener appeal."
Extend Let the class choose the most effective announcement. Arrange to have it broadcast over the school's PA system.
learning modality: verbal

Figure 5 Installing a carbon monoxide detector in a home can save lives. Because carbon monoxide has no color or odor, it cannot be detected by sight or smell.

Carbon Monoxide One particularly dangerous type of indoor air pollution is carbon monoxide. Carbon monoxide is a colorless, odorless gas that forms when wood, coal, oil, or gas are incompletely burned. When carbon monoxide builds up in an enclosed space such as a basement, apartment, or house, it can be deadly. Because carbon monoxide cannot be detected by sight or smell, its victims have no warning that the level is dangerously high. Any home heated by wood, coal, oil, or gas should have a carbon monoxide detector. The detector sounds a warning alarm when the gas is present.

Radon Another type of pollution that is difficult to detect is radon. Radon is a colorless, odorless gas that is radioactive. It is formed naturally by certain types of rocks underground. Radon can enter homes through cracks in basement walls or floors. Research indicates that breathing radon gas over many years may cause lung cancer and other health problems. But the level of radon necessary to cause these effects is unknown. To be safe, many homeowners have installed ventilation systems to prevent radon from building up in their homes.

☑ *Checkpoint* Why is it important to install carbon monoxide detectors in homes?

The Ozone Layer

If you have ever had a sunburn, you have experienced the painful effects of the sun's ultraviolet radiation. But did you know that such burns would be even worse without the protection of the ozone layer? The **ozone layer** is a layer of the upper atmosphere about 30 kilometers above Earth's surface. Actually, the concentration of ozone in this layer is very low—only a few parts per million.

Communicating

Write a radio public service announcement to inform people about either carbon monoxide or radon. Think about how the announcement could catch your listeners' attention. Describe the source and effects of the pollutant. Suggest how listeners can protect themselves.

Background

Integrating Science The ozone layer is located in the upper atmosphere, in the stratosphere. In 1985, meteorologists brought a strange discovery to the attention of other scientists: there was a "hole" in the ozone layer. They had observed a large area in the stratosphere over Antarctica where the ozone layer had become much thinner. The area of the hole in the mid-1990s was about 23.3 million km^2, roughly as big as North America. There is also evidence of a smaller hole in the ozone layer above the Arctic.

CFCs are the primary cause of the depletion of the stratospheric ozone layer. Ultraviolet radiation from the sun breaks the CFCs apart, forming chlorine. Chlorine reacts with ozone, thereby destroying the ozone molecules.

Yet even the small amount of ozone in the ozone layer protects people from the effects of too much ultraviolet radiation. These effects include sunburn, eye diseases, and skin cancer.

Since you read earlier that ozone is a pollutant, the fact that ozone can be helpful may sound confusing. The difference between ozone as a pollutant and ozone as a helpful gas is its location. Ozone close to Earth's surface in the form of smog is harmful. Higher in the atmosphere, where people cannot breathe it, ozone protects us.

The Source of Ozone Ozone is constantly being made and destroyed. When sunlight strikes an ozone molecule, the energy of the ultraviolet radiation is partly absorbed. This energy causes the molecule to break apart into an oxygen molecule and an oxygen atom, as shown in Figure 6. The oxygen atom soon collides with another oxygen molecule. They react to form a new ozone molecule. Each time this cycle occurs, some ultraviolet energy is absorbed. That energy does not reach Earth's surface.

The Ozone Hole In the late 1970s, scientists observed that the amount of ozone in the ozone layer seemed to be decreasing. What was to blame for this loss of ozone?

One problem was a group of gases containing chlorine and fluorine, called **chlorofluorocarbons,** or "CFCs." CFCs had been used instead of smelly, toxic ammonia in refrigerators and air conditioners. CFCs were also used in fire extinguishers and aerosol spray cans. Then scientists discovered that CFCs react with ozone molecules. The CFCs block the cycle that absorbs ultraviolet radiation. In 1990, many nations signed an agreement to ban the use of almost all CFCs by the year 2000. Unfortunately, the CFC molecules are very stable. They have remained in the atmosphere for a long time. But scientists predict that if the ban is maintained, the ozone layer will gradually recover.

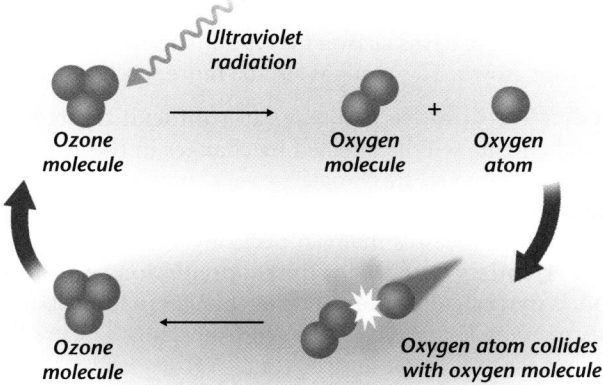

Ultraviolet radiation

Ozone molecule → Oxygen molecule + Oxygen atom

Ozone molecule ← Oxygen atom collides with oxygen molecule

Figure 6 When ultraviolet radiation from the sun strikes an ozone molecule, some energy is absorbed by the ozone molecule. This energy causes the ozone molecule to split into an oxygen molecule and a free oxygen atom. *Interpreting Diagrams What happens when the free oxygen atom collides with an oxygen molecule?*

Math TOOLBOX

Concentration

Levels of pollutants are often written as concentrations. A concentration is a ratio that compares the amount of one substance to a certain amount of another substance. For example, suppose that the concentration of ozone in a part of the atmosphere is 3 parts per million. This means that there are 3 molecules of ozone in 1,000,000 molecules of air. This ratio can also be written in three other ways:

3 : 1,000,000 or

3 to 1,000,000 or

$$\frac{3}{1,000,000}$$

Math TOOLBOX

Materials *graph paper ruled in tenths of an inch*
Time 10 minutes

Give each student a sheet of graph paper ruled in tenths of an inch, and have students calculate the total number of small squares in an 8- by 10-inch block on the sheet. *(8,000)* Tell students to darken any four small squares on the sheet. Ask: **What is the concentration of black squares?** *(4 parts per 8,000)* Have four volunteers come to the board and write the four ways to express this ratio. *(4 parts per 8,000; 4:8,000; 4 to 8,000; and 4/8,000)* For students who need an additional challenge, ask: **How many parts per thousand is that?** *(0.5)* **per million?** *(500)* **per billion?** *(500,000)* **learning modality: logical/ mathematical**

Inquiry Challenge

Materials *clay or other materials of students' choice; flashlight or lamp*
Time 10 minutes

Challenge pairs of students to create a model to demonstrate the ozone cycle. *(Sample model: Shape three balls from clay to represent oxygen atoms. Stick the three balls together to represent an ozone molecule. Shine light at the ozone molecule and detach one oxygen atom. Then there is an oxygen molecule and a single oxygen atom. To create an ozone molecule, stick the single ball to the two attached balls, returning to the first step in the cycle.)* **cooperative learning**

Answers to Self-Assessment

☑ *Checkpoint*

Carbon monoxide cannot be seen or smelled, so detectors are needed to warn people when it is present at dangerous levels.

Caption Question

Figure 6 An ozone molecule is formed.

Ongoing Assessment

Writing Have each student explain how ozone forms in the atmosphere and why this process protects organisms on Earth.

 Students can save their work in their portfolios.

Global Climate Change

Integrating Earth Science

Materials *2 small glass aquaria; 2 thermometers; 2 rulers; string; paper cup cut in half lengthwise; tape; glass aquarium cover or plastic wrap*
Time 10 minutes

Put two glass aquaria on a sunny windowsill, and lay a ruler across each one. Suspend a thermometer from each ruler with the numbered side facing toward the classroom and away from the window. Shade each thermometer by taping a cup half behind it. Ask a volunteer to read both thermometers and record these starting temperatures on the board. Then cover one aquarium with a glass cover or a piece of plastic wrap taped to the sides. At regular intervals, have other volunteers take new readings and record the temperatures and times on the board. In a follow-up class discussion, ask: **What happened to the air temperature in the uncovered aquarium?** *(It should have increased a bit at first, then stayed the same.)* **What happened to the air temperature in the covered aquarium?** *(It kept increasing.)* **What does the air inside the aquaria represent in this model?** *(The air near Earth's surface)* **What does the cover on the aquarium represent?** *(The gases that trap heat and keep it from escaping into space)* **What is this process called?** *(The greenhouse effect)* **learning modality: logical/mathematical**

EXPLORING
Climate Predictions

Point out that the questions posed in the captions are ones that scientists ask as they study Earth's climate and try to predict long-term changes. Emphasize that there are no "right" answers to questions such as these. In a class discussion or in small groups, let students offer their own ideas in response to the questions. **learning modality: verbal**

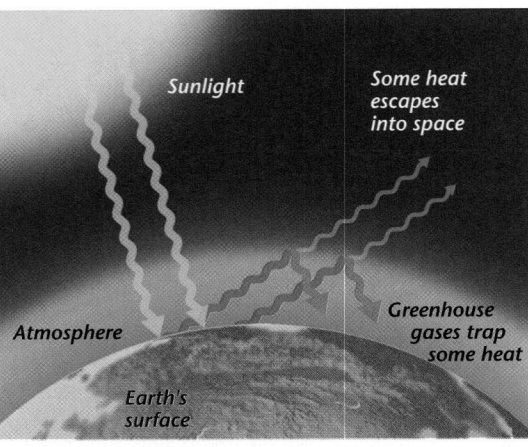

Figure 7 When energy in the form of sunlight strikes Earth's surface, it changes to heat. Certain gases in the atmosphere trap some of the heat, preventing it from escaping back into space. This trapping of heat is known as the greenhouse effect.
Applying Concepts What gases in the atmosphere trap heat near Earth's surface?

Global Climate Change

Some changes to the atmosphere affect the climate of the whole planet. To understand why, you need to know more about the atmosphere.

The Greenhouse Effect Think about the sun shining through a window on a cool day. The window lets light enter the room. The light strikes objects in the room and is converted to heat. But the closed windows trap the warm air inside, so the room becomes warmer.

In the atmosphere, water vapor, carbon dioxide, and certain other gases act like windows. These gases allow sunlight to reach Earth's surface, but they prevent the heat from escaping back into space. The trapping of heat near Earth's surface is called the **greenhouse effect**. Without the greenhouse effect, Earth would be much colder—about 33°C colder on average.

Global Warming Since the 1800s, coal and oil have been the main sources of energy in most of the world. As you have read, burning these substances produces carbon dioxide. During this time, the amount of carbon dioxide in the atmosphere has increased from 280 parts per million to 350 parts per million. This amount is increasing more quickly every year.

Does increasing carbon dioxide cause the greenhouse effect to become stronger? One theory, called **global warming**, predicts that the increase in carbon dioxide will cause the average temperature to continue to rise. Scientists have estimated that the increase in the next century could be as much as 3 to 8 Celsius degrees. Although that may not sound like a big change, it could have a huge impact. Parts of the Antarctic ice cap would melt, raising the level of the oceans. The temperature change would affect climate patterns all over the world. This would affect where crops are grown. There might also be more severe storms.

Predicting Climate Change It is difficult to predict how Earth's climate will be affected by changes in the atmosphere. The systems that create climate are very complex. Scientists have studied these systems for less than a century, a very short time to learn about processes that can occur over thousands of years. **Most scientists base their climate predictions on computer models that calculate the effects of changes in the atmosphere.** As *Exploring Climate Predictions* shows, making these predictions requires many types of information.

EXPLORING Climate Predictions

Many factors affect the complex systems that create climate. Good predictions must consider as many of these factors as possible.

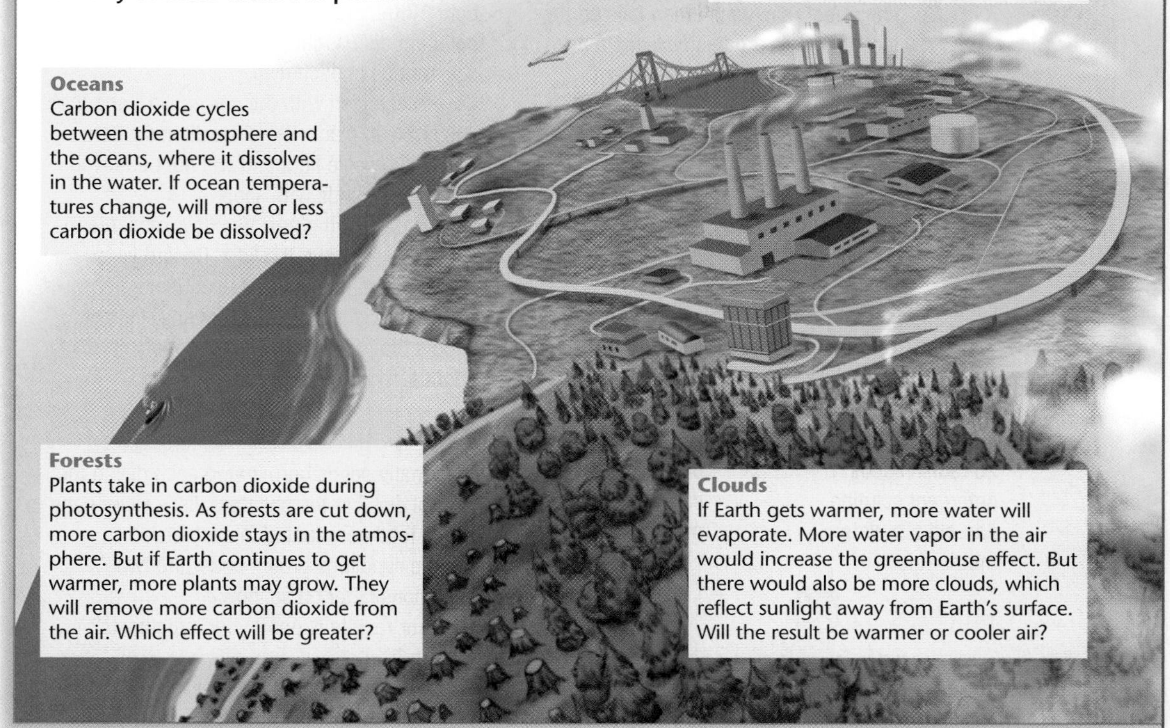

Emissions
Power plants, factories, and vehicles produce gases that increase the greenhouse effect. Will there be more emissions in the future, or will ways be found to reduce them? Will people change their habits to use less energy?

Oceans
Carbon dioxide cycles between the atmosphere and the oceans, where it dissolves in the water. If ocean temperatures change, will more or less carbon dioxide be dissolved?

Forests
Plants take in carbon dioxide during photosynthesis. As forests are cut down, more carbon dioxide stays in the atmosphere. But if Earth continues to get warmer, more plants may grow. They will remove more carbon dioxide from the air. Which effect will be greater?

Clouds
If Earth gets warmer, more water will evaporate. More water vapor in the air would increase the greenhouse effect. But there would also be more clouds, which reflect sunlight away from Earth's surface. Will the result be warmer or cooler air?

 Section 1 Review

1. How does photochemical smog form?
2. How does the ozone layer protect people?
3. How do scientists make climate predictions?
4. Give three examples of indoor air pollutants and list their sources.
5. **Thinking Critically** **Predicting** One possible result of global warming is that melting ice could cause ocean levels to rise. What effects might this have?

Science at Home

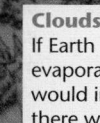

Outside Wed. 11/5

What solid particles are in your air? With a family member, set up two particle collectors. Smear petroleum jelly on the inside of two clean, empty glass jars. Place one inside your home and the other outside. Make sure both jars are in locations where they will not be disturbed. Predict what you will find if you leave the jars in place for a few days. Compare the solid particles in each jar. How similar are they? Can you identify any of the particles?

Chapter 22 **713**

---

3 Assess

Section 1 Review Answers

1. Hydrocarbons and nitrogen oxides react in sunlight to produce ozone, the major chemical in photochemical smog.
2. The ozone layer absorbs some of the harmful ultraviolet energy in sunlight and prevents it from reaching Earth's surface.
3. Most scientists base their climate predictions on computer models that calculate the effects of changes in the atmosphere.
4. *Any three:* dust, pet hair, and air fresheners; asbestos from building materials; oil-based products; gases and particles in cigarette smoke; carbon monoxide from burning wood, coal, oil, or gas as fuel; radon gas that enters buildings from rocks underground
5. *Sample answer:* Rising ocean levels would flood coastal areas, destroying cities, farms, and habitats.

Science at Home

Materials *2 clean, empty glass jars; petroleum jelly*

Suggest that students place the inside jar in a busy room, such as the kitchen or living room, and the outside jar in their yard or close to a driveway or street. Depending on the time of year, students may observe pollen grains as well as dust, pet hair, soot, and the like.

Media and Technology

 Transparencies "The Greenhouse Effect," 86, and "Exploring Climate Predictions," 87

 Concept Videotape Library *Adventures, Tape 5, "A Better Cool"*

Answers to Self-Assessment

Caption Question
Figure 7 Water vapor, CO_2, and others

Program Resources

◆ **Unit 6 Resources** 22-1 Review and Reinforce, p. 63; 22-1 Enrich, p. 64

Performance Assessment

Drawing Have each student draw and label a diagram to explain one of the following processes: the formation of photochemical smog, the formation of acid rain, the ozone cycle, or the greenhouse effect.

 Students can save their diagrams in their portfolios.

How Does the Garden Grow?

Preparing for Inquiry

Key Concept Pollutants in water reduce seed germination and injure growing plants.

Skills Objectives Students will be able to
◆ measure given amounts of plain water and a polluted solution as the manipulated variable in an experiment;
◆ control all other variables;
◆ interpret data on seed germination and plant growth.

Time *Day 1:* 30 minutes; *Days 2–6:* 5 minutes each

Advance Planning Let tap water stand uncovered for 24–48 hours to allow chlorine to dissipate. Prepare each polluted solution by mixing 5 mL of the pollutant with 100 mL water (for acid use vinegar, for oil use vegetable oil).

Guiding Inquiry

Troubleshooting the Experiment
◆ Advise students to make sure the hypothesis is a testable statement.
◆ Monitor students' choices of places to put the two dishes.

Expected Outcome
All or most seeds in the control dish should germinate within two or three days and grow well. Some or all seeds in the pollutant dish will fail to germinate, and any sprouts will not grow well.

Analyze and Conclude
1. Answers will vary. Pollutants usually reduce the number of seeds that germinate.
2. Yes; seedlings in the pollutant dish did not grow as well as those in the control dish.
3. Answers will depend on hypotheses.
4. *Sample answer:* Fewer seeds would germinate, and the seedlings that did sprout would not grow into healthy plants.

HOW DOES THE GARDEN GROW?

Air pollution doesn't just affect the air. It can affect rain, which then falls on the land, harming organisms living there. In this lab you will investigate how pollutants affect plants.

Problem

How do pollutants affect seed growth?

Skills Focus

controlling variables, measuring, interpreting data

Materials

2 plastic petri dishes with lids
potting soil
20 radish seeds
detergent solution
day-old tap water
metric ruler
wax pencil
acid solution
oil solution
salt solution
masking tape

Procedure

1. Read all the steps of the lab. Choose a pollutant to investigate. Write a hypothesis about the effect of this pollutant. Then copy the data table into your notebook. Write the name of the pollutant in the data table.
2. Write your initials on the lids of the petri dishes. Then write "Control" on one lid. Label the other lid with the name of your pollutant.
3. Fill each dish with potting soil. Do not pack down the soil.
4. Pour 10 mL of water into the control dish. Pour 10 mL of the pollutant solution into the pollutant dish. Lightly scatter 10 seeds on the soil surface in each dish.
5. Cover each dish with the correct lid. Tape the lids firmly in place. Store the dishes where they will receive light and will not be moved. Wash your hands with soap.
6. Once a day for the next five days, observe the seeds (do not open the lids). Record your observations in the data table. Use a metric ruler to measure the length of any roots or shoots that develop. If you do not observe any change, record that observation.

Analyze and Conclude

1. How many seeds germinated each day in the control dish? In the pollutant dish? How many seeds total germinated in each dish?
2. Did the seedlings grown under the two conditions differ? If so, how?
3. Did your results support your hypothesis? Explain.
4. **Apply** Predict what the effect would be if the pollutant you investigated reached a vegetable garden or farm.

Design an Experiment

Do you think the pollutant you studied has the same effect on all types of plants? Write a hypothesis, and design an experiment to test it. With your teacher's approval, carry out your plan.

DATA TABLE				
Date	Number of Seeds That Germinated		Condition of Seedlings	
	Control	Pollutant	Control	Pollutant

Extending the Inquiry

Design an Experiment Students' plans should involve controlling all variables except the types of plants.

Safety

Students should wear safety goggles and wash their hands well with soap after handling the seeds and soil. Review the safety guidelines in Appendix A.

Program Resources
◆ **Unit 6 Resources** Real-World Lab blackline masters, pp. 73–74

Media and Technology
 Lab Activity Videotape
Tape 5

DISCOVER • ACTIVITY

How Does the Water Change?

1. Shine a flashlight through a clear plastic cup of water.

2. Add 6 drops of milk to the water and stir.

3. Shine the flashlight through the cup again. Note any differences.

Think It Over

Observing Where in the cup of water is the milk located? Could you easily separate the milk from the water?

Most of Earth's surface is covered by some form of water. Oceans cover nearly three fourths of Earth's surface. Around the poles are vast sheets of ice. From space you cannot even see many parts of Earth because they are hidden behind clouds of tiny water droplets. It's hard to believe that water is a scarce resource in much of the world.

A Limited Supply

How can water be scarce when there is so much of it on Earth's surface? **The reason is that most of the water on Earth—about 97 percent—is salt water. Salt water cannot be used for drinking or watering crops.** People need fresh water for these purposes.

In addition, about three quarters of the fresh water on Earth is in the form of ice. This water is not available for people to use. Finally, the supplies of liquid fresh water that do exist are not always close to where people live. For example, many cities in the southwestern United States draw their drinking water from rivers hundreds of kilometers away. About half the people in the United States use **groundwater,** water stored in layers of soil and rock beneath Earth's surface.

GUIDE FOR READING

◆ Why is fresh water a limited resource?

◆ What are the major sources of water pollution?

Reading Tip As you read, identify sentences that support this statement: *Water is a scarce resource that must be protected.*

Figure 8 A view from space shows the abundance of water on Earth.

715

SECTION
2 The Water Supply

Objectives

After completing the lesson, students will be able to

◆ identify factors that make most of Earth's water not useful to people;

◆ identify human sources of water pollution.

Key Terms groundwater, drought, water pollution, sewage, fertilizer, pesticide, sediments

1 Engage/Explore

Activating Prior Knowledge

Display a world map or globe, and ask: **How much of Earth's surface is covered by oceans?** (*Nearly 75%; accept all reasonable estimates.*) **Where else does some form of water exist?** (*In glaciers and polar ice, in freshwater lakes and rivers, in soil, deep underground in aquifers, and in the air as vapor. Record students' responses on the board, but do not comment on any omissions at this time.*)

• • • • • • • • DISCOVER • • • • • • • •

Skills Focus observing
Materials *flashlight, clear plastic cup, water, plastic dropper, milk*
Time 5 minutes
Tips In Step 3, encourage students to shine the light downward at the cup and from different angles.
Expected Outcome The mixture will appear cloudy; solid particles in the milk will reflect the light so the beam does not pass easily through the cup.
Think It Over The milk is scattered evenly throughout the water and cannot be easily separated from it. (Students may realize that the milk's solid particles can be separated by evaporating the mixture.)

715

2 Facilitate

A Limited Supply

Building Inquiry Skills: Graphing

Materials *drawing compass, calculator (optional)*
Time 10–15 minutes

Provide students with the following data: salt water 97%; ice caps and glaciers 2.3%; groundwater 0.67%; other fresh water (lakes, rivers, soil, atmosphere) 0.03%. Then have each student use these data to create a circle graph. *(Salt water 349.2°, ice caps and glaciers 8.3°, groundwater 2.4°, other fresh water 0.1°; the "other" section should be only as wide as a pencil line.)* Students will readily see that usable fresh water—groundwater plus other fresh water—is only a small portion of all the water on Earth.
learning modality: logical/mathematical

TRY THIS

Skills Focus making models
Materials *15 mL water, plastic cup, spoon, graduated cylinder, food coloring, half teaspoon sugar*
Time 10 minutes plus 5 minutes for follow-up observations on several days
Tips Supply room-temperature water, not hot water, as hot water will produce a super-saturated solution.
Expected Outcome Sugar crystals and a tint from the food coloring will remain in the cup. These materials represent dissolved substances that are left behind when water evaporates in the water cycle. The liquid water changes to water vapor.
Extend Let students repeat the activity using other substances in the water, such as milk, salt, and baking soda. **learning modality: visual**

Figure 9 People obtain and store water in many ways. At left, a tower holds the water supply of a community in Bucks County, Pennsylvania. At right, women in the Yucatán in Mexico draw water from a well.

TRY THIS

Getting Clean

In this activity you will see how Earth's fresh water is purified in the water cycle.

1. Pour 15 mL of water into a plastic cup.
2. Add a few drops of food coloring and half a teaspoon of sugar. Stir until the sugar is dissolved.
3. Put the cup in the sunlight in a place where it will not be disturbed.
4. Check on the cup twice a day until all the water has evaporated. Observe what remains in the cup.

Making Models What do the sugar and food coloring represent? What happens to the water in this activity?

Renewing the Supply Fortunately, Earth's supply of fresh water is renewable. Water continually moves between the atmosphere and Earth's surface in the water cycle. Water evaporates from oceans, lakes, and rivers, becoming water vapor in the atmosphere. As the water evaporates, any dissolved substances are left behind. The pure water vapor condenses into tiny droplets which form clouds. When the droplets become large and heavy enough, they fall as precipitation.

Water Shortages Water shortages occur when people use water in an area faster than the water cycle can replace it. This is more likely to happen during a **drought,** a period when less rain than normal falls in an area. During a drought, people have to limit their water use. All unnecessary water uses may be banned. If the drought is severe, crops may die from lack of water.

Due to growing populations, many places in the world never receive enough rain to meet their water needs. They must obtain water from distant sources or by other means. For example, the desert nation of Saudi Arabia obtains more than half its fresh water by removing salt from ocean water.

☑ *Checkpoint* What is a drought?

Water Pollution

When fresh water supplies are scarce, pollution can be devastating. Any change to water that has a harmful effect on people or other living things is called **water pollution.** Some pollutants, such as iron and copper, make water unpleasant to drink or wash in. Other pollutants, such as mercury or benzene, can cause sickness or even death.

Background

Facts and Figures Scientists estimate that Earth has enough fresh water to meet the needs of its human population. However, Earth's usable water is not always found where and when it is needed. In many regions, there is a substantial amount of precipitation. But usable runoff in rivers and streams can vary greatly over the course of a year. For example, in India, 90% of the precipitation occurs during a wet season from June to September. During the rest of the year, there may be little runoff available for human use.

In other regions, longer periods of recurring drought are the problem. Droughts are frequent in the Sahel, a vast belt of semiarid grassland that lies south of the Sahara in Africa.

Most pollution is the result of human activities. Many activities—including agriculture, industry, construction, and mining—produce wastes that can end up in water.

If you did the Discover activity, you saw that a few drops of milk quickly spread throughout a cup of water. You could not tell where the milk first entered the water. In the same way, pollutants dissolve and move throughout a body of water. This is how pollution can affect areas far from its source.

Sewage The water and human wastes that are washed down sinks, toilets, and showers are called **sewage.** If sewage is not treated to kill disease-causing organisms, they quickly multiply. If untreated sewage mixes with water used for drinking or swimming, these organisms can make people very ill.

Even treated sewage can pollute. The wastes in the sewage can feed bacteria living in the water. As the bacteria multiply, they use up the oxygen in the water. Other organisms that need the oxygen, such as fish, cannot survive.

Agricultural Wastes Animal wastes and farm chemicals are also sources of pollution. Two examples are fertilizers and pesticides. **Fertilizers** are chemicals that provide nutrients to help crops grow better. But rain can wash fertilizers into ponds, where they cause algae to grow quickly. The algae soon cover the pond, blocking light from reaching plants in the pond. **Pesticides** are chemicals that kill crop-destroying organisms such as beetles or worms. However, pesticides can also harm other animals such as birds that feed in the sprayed fields.

Because agricultural chemicals are usually spread over a large, open area, it is hard to keep them from polluting nearby water. Even low levels of chemicals in the water can build up to harmful concentrations as they move through the food chain.

Figure 10 This plane is spraying crops with pesticides. *Relating Cause and Effect How might pesticides sprayed on a field affect fish that live in a nearby pond?*

717

Media and Technology

Concept Videotape Library
Adventures, Tape 5, "What's in Our Tap?"

Answers to Self-Assessment

☑ *Checkpoint*

A drought is a period when less rain than normal falls in an area.

Caption Question

Figure 10 The pesticides might be carried into the pond in runoff, poisoning the fish directly or poisoning organisms on which the fish depend for food.

Water Pollution

Including All Students

Some students may need more help in organizing the information on water pollution. Create a table on the chalkboard with these headings: *Type of Pollution, Examples of Pollutants, Effects.* Encourage students to review each subsection under the heading, Water Pollution, and then volunteer to help fill in the table. When the table is complete, students can make a copy of it to use as a study guide. **learning modality: verbal**

Inquiry Challenge

Materials *long tray or plastic box, sod, powdered drink mix, water, sprinkling can*
Time 15–20 minutes

Challenge small groups of students to create a model showing how agricultural chemicals that are spread on the ground can reach and pollute nearby bodies of fresh water. *(Sample model: Elevate one end of a tray slightly. Use sod to make a hill that slopes gently from the high end of the tray to the low end. Pour water into the low end to represent a lake. Scatter powdered drink mix over the sod to represent fertilizer or pesticide. Sprinkle water on the sod to represent rain. The lake will become tinted with the color of the drink mix.)* **cooperative learning**

Ongoing Assessment

Skills Check Have each student create a concept map that identifies the two types of agricultural pollutants described in the text, defines each term, and describes how the pollutant affects other organisms.

 Students can save their concept maps in their portfolios.

Water Pollution,
continued

Real-Life Learning

Encourage students to share with the class any observations they have made of examples of water pollution in their community. Have students describe the extent of the pollution and suggest possible sources for it. Then challenge all students to brainstorm ways to reduce each example of pollution. Encourage volunteers to write letters to the appropriate officials, identifying the incidents of pollution and offering suggestions for reducing the pollution.
learning modality: verbal

Building Inquiry Skills: Making Models

Materials *plastic margarine tub or other small bowl, water, cooking oil, plastic dropper, 2 paper towels, graduated cylinder or small plastic cup calibrated in mL*

ACTIVITY

Time 15 minutes

To demonstrate how difficult it is to clean up an oil spill, have each student fill a small bowl halfway with water, add 25 mL of cooking oil, and then try to remove the oil using a dropper and a paper towel. Tell students to wipe out the small cup with one paper towel, discard that towel, and then put the oil they recover back into the cup so they can see how much they remove from the water. After students have worked for about 10 minutes, ask: **How much oil have you removed?** (*Answers will vary, but students probably will have recovered very little oil.*) **Is there still oil on the water? How can you tell?** (*Yes; the water surface still has an oily sheen.*) Remind students that unlike the cooking oil they are using in this model, crude oil is thick and sticky. (Soak up any remaining oil and oily water with paper towels, and place all disposable materials from the activity in a plastic bag for trash pickup.) **learning modality: kinesthetic**

Figure 11 Industrial processes and mining are two sources of chemical pollutants. At left, a chemical plant spills wastes into a river. At right, dissolved copper from a mine turns a stream turquoise.

Industry and Mining Chemical plants, paper and textile mills, and factories that use metals produce wastes that can pollute water. Mining sites are another source of metal wastes. Chemicals and metals can harm the living things in the polluted bodies of water. In addition, humans that drink the water or feed on these organisms are exposed to the pollution.

Sediments When water runs off bare ground, it turns a muddy brown color. This color is due to particles of rock, silt, and sand called **sediments.** Water that flows through places where the ground is disturbed, such as building sites and mines, can pick up large loads of sediments.

As sediments wash into bodies of water, the particles cover up the food sources, nesting sites, and eggs of organisms. By blocking sunlight in the water, the sediments prevent algae and plants from growing. This affects other organisms that rely on the algae and plants for food.

Oil and Gasoline One of the most dramatic forms of water pollution is an oil spill. You may have seen news reports showing beaches covered with tarry black oil, or of volunteers cleaning globs of oil from the feathers of birds. It can take many years for an area to recover from such a spill.

Background

Integrating Science To monitor water pollution, scientists sometimes observe the effects of pollution on organisms such as mollusks, birds, and fish. For example, analysis of mussels taken from coastal waters provides U.S. government scientists clues about toxic compounds in the water. In the Great Lakes region, Canadian scientists test the eggs of herring gulls for toxins.

Surprisingly, a species of tropical fish is used to monitor water pollution in England's Stour River. The fish normally emit 300–500 electric pulses per minute as a sensory aide. In polluted water, the fish increase the pulses to 1,000 per minute. Scientists keep the fishes in separate tanks, pump river water through the tanks, and then observe whether the fishes' emissions increase.

Another pollution problem is caused by oil and gasoline that leak out of underground storage tanks. Think of how many gas stations there are in your area. Each one has storage tanks below the street level to hold the gasoline. In the past, these tanks were often made of steel. Over time, they rusted and developed small holes. As the gasoline leaked out, it soaked into the soil and polluted the groundwater. The pollution was sometimes carried very far away from the leaking tank. Controlling this type of pollution has been difficult because the sources are hidden underground.

Heat Pollution is usually thought of as a substance added to water. But the addition of heat can also have a negative effect on a body of water. Sometimes factories or power plants release water that has been used to cool machinery. This heated water changes the temperature of the stream or lake into which it is released. This temperature change can kill plants, animals, and other organisms in the body of water. If you have ever kept an aquarium, you know that fish can only survive within a small temperature range. Today most power plants have cooling towers that release steam rather than hot water. In the next section, you will read about some other methods of preventing both water and air pollution.

Figure 12 A sheen of oil swirls around a maple leaf in a puddle. *Observing What characteristics of oil make it difficult to clean up?*

Section 2 Review

1. Why isn't most of the water on Earth's surface available for people to use?
2. Name four types of human activities that can be sources of water pollution.
3. Explain why finding the source of water pollution can be difficult.
4. What is sewage? Why should sewage be treated before being released to the environment?
5. **Thinking Critically Relating Cause and Effect** In what way can heat pollute a body of water?

Check Your Progress

CHAPTER PROJECT 22

By now you should be gathering information to include in your product. Consider including the story of a historical event related to your topic in order to get your audience's interest. As you collect information, begin putting it in a logical order. Using an outline or a storyboard can help you organize your thoughts. (*Hint:* Be sure to keep your topic well focused. Air and water quality are very broad topics! Focusing your topic will help you stay on task and manage your time.)

Program Resources

◆ **Unit 5 Resources** 22-2 Review and Reinforce, p. 67; 22-2 Enrich, p. 68

Answers to Self-Assessment

Caption Question
Figure 12 Oil is thick, sticky, and "tarry."

3 Assess

Section 2 Review Answers

1. Most of the water on Earth is salty, and much of the fresh water is ice.
2. Agriculture, industry, construction, mining
3. The source may be far from the polluted water. Pollutants can dissolve and move throughout a body of water. Sources such as gasoline tanks may be hidden underground.
4. Sewage is the water and human wastes that are washed down sinks, toilets, and showers. Sewage contains disease-causing organisms that can mix with water used for drinking or swimming and make people ill.
5. Heated water from factories or power plants raises the temperature of bodies of water into which it is released. The temperature increase can kill plants, animals, and other organisms.

Check Your Progress

CHAPTER PROJECT 22

Students may need some help in narrowing their choices of topics to ones that will be suitable for their target audiences and for which there are adequate resource materials available. To help students organize the information they collect, review outlining procedures with the class.

Performance Assessment

Oral Presentation Call on students at random to name a type of water pollution. Call on other students to give examples and effects.

Concentrate on This!

Preparing for Inquiry

Key Concept Very low concentrations of pollutants may not be visible to the eye.
Skills Objectives Students will be able to
◆ measure given amounts of water and food coloring representing a pollutant;
◆ calculate the pollutant's concentration at different dilutions;
◆ observe solutions to determine whether the pollutant can be detected by sight.
Time 40 minutes

Guiding Inquiry

Troubleshooting the Experiment
Students may need some help with the math calculations.

Expected Outcome
See Sample Data Table below.

Analyze and Conclude
1. The tint becomes lighter until it disappears (usually in Test Tube 5 or 6).
2. Yes; the food coloring molecules are so widely scattered that no tint is visible.
3. A "part" is 1 mL of food coloring.
4. *Million:* Tube 6; *billion:* Tube 9
5. *Sample answer:* Pollutants are often present in very low concentrations.

Extending the Inquiry

Design an Experiment Students may answer the first question by doing a calculation. *(5 ppm)* Make sure students' plans include one tube with a concentration of 5 ppm and one with a concentration of 10 parts per 10 million (1 ppm).

Concentrate on This!

Many pollutants have harmful effects even at very low concentrations. In this lab you will compare different concentrations of a pollutant in water.

Problem

Can you detect a pollutant in water at a very low concentration?

Materials

9 test tubes   test tube rack
water   food coloring
10-mL graduated cylinder

Procedure

1. Read through the entire procedure. Write a prediction about the results you expect. Then copy the data table into your notebook.
2. Label nine test tubes 1 through 9.
3. Use a 10-mL graduated cylinder to add 9 mL of water to each test tube.
4. Add 1 mL of food coloring to Test Tube 1. Record the volume of liquid now in the test tube. Swirl the test tube gently to mix.
5. The concentration of food coloring in Test Tube 1 is 1 mL in 10 mL, or 1 part per 10. Record that concentration in the data table.
6. Now transfer 1 mL of the mixture from Test Tube 1 into Test Tube 2. Swirl Test Tube 2 to mix its contents.

7. Record the concentration in Test Tube 2. [*Hint:* The mL you just added had a concentration of 1 part per 10. When you dilute (water down) that mL to 1/10 of its strength, the new concentration is 1 part per (10 × 10).]
8. For test tubes 3 through 9, add 1 mL from the previous test tube. Record each new concentration in the data table.
9. Observe the water in each test tube. Record your observation. If you do not observe any color in a test tube, write "colorless."

Analyze and Conclude

1. How does the appearance of the water change from test tubes 1 through 9?
2. Food coloring consists of molecules of dye. Are there any food coloring molecules remaining in Test Tube 9? Explain.
3. What is meant by a "part" in this lab?
4. Which test tube has a concentration of 1 part per million? Which test tube has a concentration of 1 part per billion?
5. **Think About It** Why is parts per million a useful form of measurement when discussing environmental issues?

Design an Experiment

Which is more concentrated, a mixture with 5 parts per million, or 10 parts per 10 million? How different do the two mixtures appear? Use the ideas from this lab to design a plan to find out. Check your plan with your teacher.

DATA TABLE

Test Tube	Total Volume Added (mL)	Concentration of Food Coloring	Color
1			
2			

Sample Data Table

Test Tube	Total Drops Added	Concentration of Food Coloring	Color
1	10	1:10	very dark
2	10	1:100	dark
3	10	1:1,000	light
4	10	1:10,000	very light
5	10	1:100,000	hint of color
6	10	1:1,000,000	colorless
7	10	1:10,000,000	colorless
8	10	1:100,000,000	colorless
9	10	1:1,000,000,000	colorless

Program Resources
◆ **Unit 6 Resources** Skills Lab blackline masters, pp. 75–77

Media and Technology
 Lab Activity Videotape
Tape 5

SECTION 3 Finding Pollution Solutions

DISCOVER

ACTIVITY

Can You Remove the Tea?

1. Pour some cooled herbal tea into a plastic cup. Observe the color of the tea.
2. Place a paper filter in a funnel. Fill it halfway with crushed charcoal. Put the funnel on top of another plastic cup.
3. Slowly pour the tea through the funnel so that it collects in the cup.
4. Observe the filtered liquid.

Think It Over
Developing Hypotheses Suggest an explanation for any changes you observe in the tea after pouring it through the funnel.

Only 50 years ago, the French Broad River in North Carolina was a river to avoid. Its color changed daily, depending on the dyes being used at a nearby blanket factory. Towns dumped raw sewage into the water. Sediment and fertilizers from farms washed into the river with every rainfall. The few fish were unhealthy and covered with sores. Mostly, the river was a home for wastes and bacteria—certainly not a place for people to play. Today, however, the river is a popular white-water rafting spot. Fish thrive in the clear water. The blanket factory and other plants have stopped releasing wastes into the river. The towns have sewage treatment plants. And ponds catch the runoff from farm fields before it reaches the river.

This story shows that pollution problems can be solved. People near the river still carry out the same activities—farming, building houses, and even making blankets. But by changing the way they do these things, they have stopped the pollution.

In the United States, laws regulate the amount of certain pollutants that can be released into the environment. Laws also state how these pollutants must be handled. The major federal laws that control air and water quality are the Clean Air Act and the Clean Water Act. These laws also encourage the development of new technology to reduce pollution.

GUIDE FOR READING

◆ How can technology help control air pollution?
◆ How can technology help control water pollution?

Reading Tip Before you read, use the section headings to make an outline. Leave space in your outline to take notes.

Rafters enjoying the clean water of the French Broad River

721

READING STRATEGIES

Reading Tip Students' outlines should include the following headings: *I. Reducing Air Pollution; A. Emissions Controls; B. CFC Substitutes; II. Cleaning Up the Water; A. Sewage Treatment; B. Oil and Gasoline; C. Industrial and Agricultural Chemicals; III. What Can You Do?* Suggest that students also include the vocabulary terms below the appropriate headings.

Program Resources

◆ **Unit 6 Resources** 22-3 Lesson Plan, p. 69; 22-3 Section Summary, p. 70
◆ **Guided Reading and Study Workbook** Section 22-3

SECTION 3 Finding Pollution Solutions

Objectives

After completing the lesson, students will be able to
◆ describe ways that technology can help control air pollution;
◆ describe ways that technology can help control water pollution.

Key Terms scrubber, catalytic converter, primary treatment, secondary treatment

1 Engage/Explore

Activating Prior Knowledge

Ask students: **What happens to the waste water from your family's home?** (*Students' houses or apartment buildings may be connected to a municipal sewage system or have a private septic system. If students do not know, encourage them to find out.*)

DISCOVER

Skills Focus developing hypotheses
ACTIVITY
Materials *cooled herbal tea, 2 plastic cups, paper filter, funnel, crushed charcoal*
Time 10 minutes
Tips Use a tea that has a distinct color, and brew a strong solution. Using powdered iced tea mix in cool water is effective.
Expected Outcome The filtered tea will be lighter in color than the unfiltered tea.
Think It Over The charcoal and paper filter trapped tiny particles in the tea, making its color lighter.

2 Facilitate

Reducing Air Pollution

Sharpen your Skills

Graphing

Materials *graph paper, 2 pens or pencils of different colors*

Time *20 minutes*

Tips Point out that chlorine is the active ingredient in ordinary household bleach. If students question how chlorine gets into the atmosphere, let them review the last paragraph on page 145. Explain that when CFC molecules drift high into the atmosphere, the sun's ultraviolet radiation destroys them, releasing chlorine in the process. This chlorine affects the ozone layer.

Expected Outcome *Sample paragraph:* With the ban, the chlorine level in 2005 is predicted to be less than 1.5 times the level in 1985. Without the ban, the 2005 level would be 5 times the 1985 level and nearly 3 times the 2005 level with the ban. Although the level increased from 1985 to 1995 with the ban, it is expected to decrease through 2005.

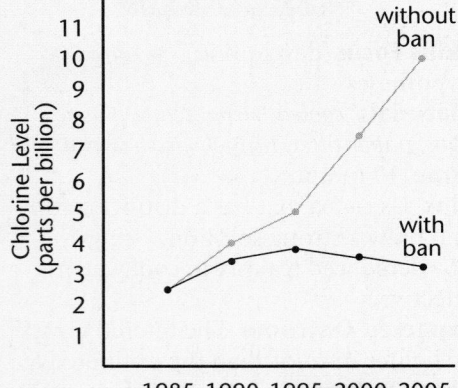

Extend Suggest that students calculate the percentage of increase or decrease each year with and without the ban. Also ask: **Why is a line graph, not a bar graph, appropriate for these data?** (*A line graph shows changes in one thing over time; a bar graph compares different things at the same point in time.*)

learning modality: logical/ mathematical

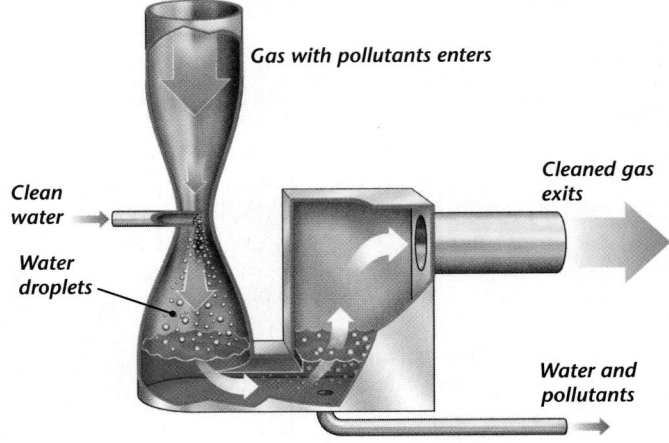

Figure 13 A smokestack scrubber removes pollutants such as sulfur dioxide from emissions. The dirty gas passes through a tube containing water droplets. Pollutants dissolve in the water, leaving clean gas to flow out of the chamber. The dirty water still must be properly disposed of.

Sharpen your Skills

Graphing ACTIVITY

The table below shows a scientist's predictions of chlorine levels in the atmosphere with and without the ban on CFCs. Make a line graph of the data, using two different colors. Write a short paragraph describing the results.

Year	Chlorine Level (parts per billion)	
	With Ban	**Without Ban**
1985	2.5	2.5
1990	3.5	4.0
1995	3.8	5.0
2000	3.6	7.5
2005	3.4	10.0

Reducing Air Pollution

The Clean Air Act has resulted in the development of technology to control air pollution. **The major role of technology in controlling air pollution is to reduce emissions.**

Emissions Controls At one time, industries dealt with emissions by building tall smokestacks. The stacks released wastes high in the air, where they could blow away. But the pollutants still ended up somewhere. Now factories place devices in the stacks to treat emissions. For example, a filter can trap particles of ash. The device in Figure 13, called a **scrubber,** removes pollutants from emissions using a stream of water droplets. Pollutants dissolve in the water and fall into a container.

Cars and trucks now contain pollution control devices. For example, a **catalytic converter** is a device that reduces emissions of carbon monoxide, hydrocarbons, and nitrogen oxides. This device causes the gases to react, forming less harmful carbon dioxide and water.

Laws can ensure that people use pollution-control devices. For example, in many states, cars must pass emissions tests. The state of California's strict emissions-testing laws have helped reduce the smog problem in Los Angeles in recent years.

CFC Substitutes When a pollutant is banned by law, people must find substitutes for the banned substance. For example, in 1990 many nations agreed to stop using most CFCs by the year 2000. Scientists immediately began to search for substitutes for these chemicals. Refrigerators and air conditioners were redesigned to use less harmful substances. Researchers developed new ways to make products such as plastic foam without using CFCs. As a result of this work, fewer CFCs should enter the atmosphere after 2000 than in the past.

Background

History of Science Mexico City, one of the world's largest cities, has the worst air pollution of any city. In 1990, the city instituted a plan to improve air quality. According to the plan, vehicles equipped with catalytic converters and burning unleaded fuel would replace older vehicles. The city also implemented periodic checks of exhaust emissions and driving restrictions for periods when air quality is especially bad.

Although levels of lead, sulfur dioxide, and carbon monoxide in the air have been reduced, the city's plan has not been a complete success. Critics charge that the city government does not enforce the laws that combat air pollution strictly enough. Unfortunately, Mexico City's air quality in 1996 was worse than it had been a decade earlier.

Cleaning Up the Water

Technology can also help control water pollution. **Two ways to reduce water pollution are to treat wastes so that they are less harmful, and to find substitutes for pollutants.**

Sewage Treatment Most communities treat wastewater before returning it to the environment. A typical sewage plant handles the waste in several steps. **Primary treatment** removes solid materials from the wastewater. During primary treatment, the water passes through filters. Then it is held in tanks where heavy particles settle out. **Secondary treatment** involves using bacteria to break down wastes. Finally, the water is treated with chlorine to kill disease-causing organisms.

The town of Arcata, California, treats sewage in a creative way. Wastewater flows into ponds containing algae that begin to break down the sewage. Then the water flows into artificial marshes lined with cattails and bulrushes. These plants and the bacteria in the marsh filter and clean the water. These marshes are also habitats for many mollusks, fish, and birds. Trails for walking and biking encourage people to enjoy the marshes as well. After two months in this system, the wastewater is cleaner than the bay into which it is released!

Oil and Gasoline Oil is a pollutant that nature can handle in small amounts. Bacteria that break down oil live in the ocean. When oil is present, the bacteria multiply quickly as they feed on it. As the oil disappears, the bacteria population dies down. But in the case of a very large spill, many organisms are affected before the balance in the ecosystem is restored.

Gasoline or oil that leaks from an underground tank is hard to clean up. If the pollution has not spread far, the soil around the tank can be removed. But pollution that reaches groundwater may be carried far away. Groundwater can be pumped to the surface, treated, and then returned underground. This can take many years.

Figure 14 A bicyclist in Arcata, California, may not even be aware that this peaceful marsh is also a sewage treatment system. *Applying Concepts What are the two major sewage treatment steps?*

Figure 15 Workers struggle to clean oil from a rocky beach.

Answers to Self-Assessment

Caption Question

Figure 14 The two steps are primary treatment, which removes solid materials, and secondary treatment, which uses bacteria to break down wastes.

Cleaning Up the Water

Real-Life Learning

Take the class on a field trip to visit your community's wastewater treatment plant. Before the visit, have students brainstorm a list of questions they would like to have answered. Ask the plant guide to pay particular attention to those questions during the tour. **learning modality: visual**

Cultural Diversity

Time 15–30 minutes

Point out to students that emission controls, wastewater treatment plants, and other technological devices to reduce air and water pollution are very expensive. Individuals and businesses in the United States and other developed countries are more able to afford these devices than those in developing countries, where people must work very hard simply to supply their most basic needs. In developing countries, pollution control may seem like a luxury. As one example, share the information in Background on the previous page. Then pose the following question to the class: **Imagine you're a taxi driver in Mexico City. You have to work twelve hours a day, seven days a week, just to earn enough money to pay for your family's food, clothing, housing, and other basic needs. Now city officials tell you that you have to replace your old taxi with a newer one that doesn't release so much pollution. How would you feel? What would you do?** Divide the class into small groups, and let students discuss the issue from the viewpoints of both the taxi driver and the officials who are trying to improve air quality. Have students share their ideas in a follow-up class discussion. **learning modality: verbal**

Ongoing Assessment

Drawing Have each student draw a flowchart to identify and describe the steps in the sewage treatment process. Students can save their flowcharts in their portfolios.

What Can You Do?

Real-Life Learning

Suggest that students find out whether their community has a hazardous waste collection day or drop-off location. If it does, encourage students to find out about it. If the community does not have a hazardous waste disposal program, encourage students to write letters to the editor recommending that a program be implemented. **learning modality: verbal**

ACTIVITY

3 Assess

Section 3 Review Answers

1. The major role is to reduce emissions.
2. Treat wastes so they are less harmful and find substitutes for pollutants
3. A filter traps particles of soot and ash. A scrubber removes pollutants using a stream of water droplets.
4. Bacteria that live in the ocean can feed on the oil and break it down.
5. *Sample answer:* Laws can regulate the amount of certain pollutants that can be released into the environment and encourage new technology to reduce pollution.

Check Your Progress
CHAPTER PROJECT 22

Many students are likely to underestimate the amount of time it will take to complete their final products. Check with students regularly to answer questions, provide assistance regarding the skill and interest levels of the target audiences, and ensure they are making steady progress.

Performance Assessment

Writing Have each student identify and explain one practice that he or she could implement at home to help reduce air or water pollution.

Figure 16 These teens are planting trees in a park in Austin, Texas. Planting trees is one way to improve air quality. Trees absorb carbon dioxide from the air and produce oxygen.

Industrial and Agricultural Chemicals Instead of releasing wastes to the environment, industries can recycle their wastes to recover useful materials. Once such programs are underway, companies often find they save money as well as reduce pollution. Others change their processes to produce less waste or less harmful waste. For example, some industries use natural fruit acids as cleaning agents rather than toxic solvents. Likewise, many farmers are finding alternatives to toxic pesticides and fertilizers for their crops.

What Can You Do?

You may not think there is much you can do to reduce air and water pollution. But in fact, some small changes in people's behavior can make a big difference.

You can help reduce air pollution by reducing certain types of energy use. Much air pollution is a result of fuels that are burned to provide electricity and transportation. Using less energy conserves fuel resources and also reduces pollution. When you take public transportation, walk, or ride a bicycle, there is one fewer car on the road. This means there are fewer emissions that contribute to smog and the greenhouse effect. In the next chapter, you will read how you can use less energy for these purposes.

It is also easy to prevent water pollution at home. Some common household water pollutants are paint and paint thinner, motor oil, and garden chemicals. You can avoid causing water pollution by never pouring these chemicals down the drain. Instead, save these materials for your community's next hazardous household waste collection day.

Section 3 Review

1. What role does technology usually play in controlling air pollution?
2. In what two basic ways can technology help control water pollution?
3. Describe one smokestack device that can help reduce emissions from factories.
4. Explain how small oil spills can be cleaned up naturally.
5. **Thinking Critically** **Making Generalizations** Explain how laws can play a part in reducing pollution.

Check Your Progress
CHAPTER PROJECT 22

Now you are ready to make your finished product using the information you have gathered. Keep in mind the age group of your audience when you are considering word choice, number and style of pictures, music, and other parts of your product. (*Hint:* Don't forget to include steps that members of your audience can take to be part of the solution. Make sure these suggestions are appropriate for their age.)

724

Program Resources

◆ **Unit 6 Resources** 22-3 Review and Reinforce, p. 71; 22-3 Enrich, p. 72

SECTION 1 — Air Pollution

Key Ideas

◆ Air pollutants can be in the form of solid particles or gases.

◆ The major sources of photochemical smog are the gases emitted by motor vehicles.

◆ Sources of indoor air pollution include smoke, dust, pet hair, asbestos, and other substances. Two dangerous pollutants that are very difficult to detect are carbon monoxide and radon.

◆ Certain gases in Earth's atmosphere prevent heat from escaping back into space.

◆ The ozone layer protects people and other living things from the effects of too much ultraviolet radiation.

◆ Most scientists base their climate predictions on computer models that calculate the effects of changes in the atmosphere.

Key Terms

air pollution   acid rain
emissions   ozone layer
photochemical smog   chlorofluorocarbons
ozone   greenhouse effect
temperature inversion   global warming

SECTION 2 — The Water Supply

Key Ideas

◆ Most of Earth's water—about 97 percent—is salt water.

◆ People and many other organisms require fresh water to carry out their life processes.

◆ Although there are some natural sources of water pollution, most pollution is the result of human activities. Agriculture, industry, construction, and mining all produce wastes that can end up in water.

Key Terms

groundwater   fertilizer
drought   pesticide
water pollution sediments
sewage

SECTION 3 — Finding Pollution Solutions

INTEGRATING TECHNOLOGY

Key Ideas

◆ The major role of technology in controlling air pollution is to reduce emissions.

◆ Two basic ways to reduce water pollution are to treat wastes so that they are less harmful, and to find substitutes for pollutants.

Key Terms

scrubber   primary treatment
catalytic converter   secondary treatment

Organizing Information

Concept Map Copy the concept map below onto a sheet of paper. Then complete it and add a title.

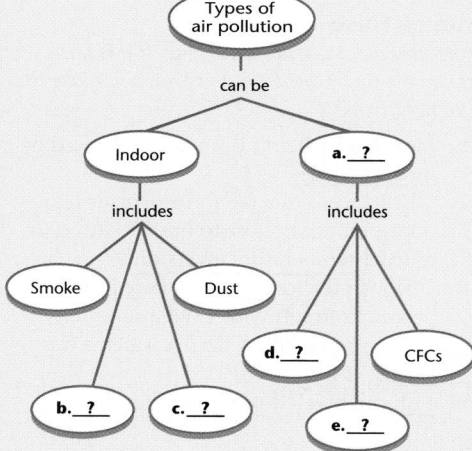

Organizing Information

Concept Map

a. outdoor b. and c. *Any two:* carbon monoxide, radon, pet hair/feathers, asbestos, fumes from carpets or furniture d. and e. *Any two:* smog, acid rain, ash, carbon monoxide, nitrogen oxide, ozone, nitric acid, sulfuric acid. Sample title: Air Pollution

Program Resources

◆ **Unit 6 Resources** Chapter 22 Project Scoring Rubric, p. 60

◆ **Performance Assessment** Chapter 22, pp. 67–69

◆ **Chapter Tests** Chapter 22 Test, pp. 87–90

Media and Technology

Computer Test Bank
Chapter 22 Test

Reviewing Content
Multiple Choice
1. b **2.** b **3.** c **4.** b **5.** b

True or False
6. true **7.** true **8.** upper **9.** salt
10. bacteria

Checking Concepts
11. Photochemical smog can cause breathing and lung problems and harm the body's defenses against infection.
12. Coal and oil produce nitrogen oxides and sulfur oxides when they are burned. These gases react with water vapor in the air to form nitric acid and sulfuric acid. The acids return to Earth's surface dissolved in precipitation.
13. Water vapor and carbon dioxide act like windows, allowing sunlight to reach Earth's surface but preventing the heat from escaping back into space.
14. A drought is a period when less rain than normal falls on an area. During a drought, people have to limit their water use. If the drought is severe, people may have to travel long distances to get water, and crops may die.
15. Runoff from rain can wash fertilizers into lakes, rivers, ponds, and streams, where they cause an overgrowth of algae.
16. Motor vehicles can be equipped with catalytic converters, which reduce carbon monoxide emissions.
17. Bacteria that normally live in the ocean feed on the oil and break it down.
18. Students' newscasts should focus on the points presented in *Exploring Climate Predictions,* page 713.

Thinking Critically
19. Both radon and carbon monoxide are gases that pollute indoor air and are difficult to detect. Carbon monoxide forms when wood, coal, oil, or gas is incompletely burned. Radon is formed naturally by certain types of rocks underground and is radioactive. Carbon monoxide can kill people if it reaches certain levels. Radon is thought to cause cancer over long periods of time.
20. More ultraviolet light would be blocked and prevented from reaching Earth's surface. Sunburn and cases of eye diseases and cancer caused by ultraviolet radiation would decrease.

Reviewing Content
Multiple Choice
Choose the letter of the best answer.

1. Solid particles and gases released into the air are
   a. sewage.   b. emissions.
   c. scrubbers.   d. acid rain.
2. A deadly gas formed when fuels are incompletely burned is
   a. ozone.
   b. carbon monoxide.
   c. photochemical smog.
   d. CFCs.
3. Which gas is thought to be the cause of global warming?
   a. radon   b. ozone
   c. carbon dioxide   d. carbon monoxide
4. The water and waste materials washed down toilets and sinks are called
   a. pesticides.
   b. sewage.
   c. industrial chemicals.
   d. fertilizers.
5. A technology that reduces carbon monoxide emissions from vehicles is a
   a. scrubber.
   b. catalytic converter.
   c. filter.
   d. CFC substitute.

True or False
If the statement is true, write true. If it is false, change the underlined word or words to make the statement true.

6. Most photochemical smog is produced by <u>motor vehicles</u>.
7. The presence of a layer of warm air that traps pollutants close to Earth's surface is called a <u>temperature inversion</u>.
8. Ozone in the <u>lower</u> atmosphere protects people from ultraviolet radiation.
9. About 97 percent of Earth's water is <u>fresh</u> water.
10. <u>Fish</u> can break down oil in the ocean.

Checking Concepts
11. Describe some possible health effects of photochemical smog.
12. How does acid rain form?
13. What role do water vapor and carbon dioxide play in the greenhouse effect?
14. What is a drought? What effects could a drought have on people?
15. Explain how fertilizers from a farm might pollute a nearby river.
16. What is one way to reduce emissions from cars and trucks?
17. How can a small oil spill in the ocean be naturally cleaned up?
18. **Writing to Learn** Write a television newscast explaining how one of the following factors is related to climate predictions: clouds, forests, oceans, emissions.

Thinking Critically
19. **Comparing and Contrasting** How are radon and carbon monoxide alike? How are they different?
20. **Predicting** What effect might a sudden increase in the amount of ozone in the ozone layer have?
21. **Making Generalizations** Would you expect the levels of photochemical smog to be worse in cities or in rural areas? Explain your answer.
22. **Applying Concepts** Suppose someone says that the heat cannot cause water pollution because heat is not a substance. What could you say to show that the person is wrong? Include examples of the possible effects of heat pollution in your response.
23. **Problem Solving** Write a summary of a plan you could follow to evaluate your school's air quality.

21. In cities; the major sources of photochemical smog are the gases emitted by motor vehicles, which are more concentrated in cities than in rural areas.
22. Adding heat to water can damage the environment just as a polluting substance does. The heat can kill organisms living in the water and may also harm other organisms living nearby.

23. Students may suggest using tools to detect dangerous gases or substances that cause allergies, or measuring temperatures at different times of the day in different locations.

Applying Skills

Use the graph to answer Questions 24–26.

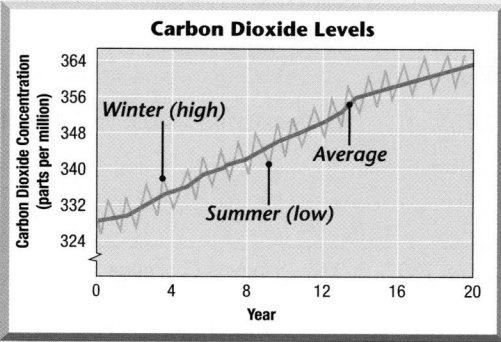

Carbon Dioxide Levels

24. **Interpreting Data** What was the average level of carbon dioxide in the atmosphere at the beginning of the study? What was the average level of carbon dioxide in Year 20 of the study?

25. **Calculating** How much did the average level of carbon dioxide increase during the study period?

26. **Developing Hypotheses** In each year of the study, the winter level of carbon dioxide was higher than the summer level. Suggest an explanation for this.

Performance **CHAPTER PROJECT 22** **Assessment**

Project Wrap Up Share your finished project with a group of younger students. As the children view or play with the product, notice what parts they find most interesting. After they are finished, ask them what they liked and didn't like about the product. What do they remember most?

Reflect and Record In your project notebook, write a short evaluation of your product. What parts of the product do you feel worked best? Which ones did you find the most difficult? What challenges did you face in communicating information in the form you chose to work with?

Test Preparation

Use these questions to prepare for standardized tests.

The map below shows one prediction of the possible effects of global warming. Use the map to answer Questions 27–29.

Effects of Global Warming

KEY
- Soil wetter than now
- Soil drier than now
- Decreased crop yield
- Increased crop yield
- Threatened by rising ocean levels

27. According to the map, global warming might cause the total amount of available land to
   a. increase.   c. remain the same.
   b. decrease.   d. increase, then decrease.

28. The map shows that the land areas most threatened by rising ocean levels are
   a. restricted to North America.
   b. located under the ozone hole.
   c. mainly on the east coasts of North America and South America.
   d. mainly on the west coasts of North America and South America.

29. The map shows that global warming will cause crop yields to
   a. be unaffected.
   b. be affected the same way everywhere.
   c. increase in some areas and decrease in other areas.
   d. decrease everywhere.

Applying Skills

24. *Beginning:* 328 ppm; *Year 20:* 363 ppm
25. By 35 ppm
26. *Sample answers:* In the summer, more plants are growing and removing carbon dioxide from the air. Also, more heating fuels are burned in the winter, so carbon dioxide emissions increase.

Performance **CHAPTER PROJECT 22** **Assessment**

Project Wrap Up Before they present their final products to younger students, let students present them to another group of students as a "trial run." Encourage students to offer positive comments and tactful suggestions for improvement. This practice session will also give you an opportunity to assess students' work. Distribute Chapter 22 Project Worksheet 2, page 59 in Unit 6 Resources, so students can elicit feedback from the younger students.

Reflect and Record Encourage students to incorporate comments from Worksheet 2 into their self-evaluations.

Test Preparation

27. b   28. c   29. c

Program Resources

- ◆ **Inquiry Skills Activity Book** Provides teaching and review of all inquiry skills
- ◆ **Prentice Hall Assessment System** Provides standardized test practice
- ◆ **Reading in the Content Area** Provides strategies to improve science reading skills
- ◆ **Teacher's ELL Handbook** Provides multiple strategies for English language learners

Sections	Time	Student Edition Activities	Other Activities
CHAPTER PROJECT 23 **Energy Audit** p. 729	Ongoing (2–3 weeks)	Check Your Progress, pp. 736, 744, 751 Project Wrap Up, p. 759	Chapter 23 Project Notes, pp. 728–729
1 **Fossil Fuels** pp. 730–736 ◆ 23.1.1 Explain how fuels provide energy. ◆ 23.1.2 List the three major fossil fuels. ◆ 23.1.3 Explain why fossil fuels are considered nonrenewable resources.	1 period/ $\frac{1}{2}$ block	**Discover** What's in a Piece of Coal?, p. 730 **Sharpen Your Skills** Graphing, p. 732	TE Inquiry Challenge, p. 732 TE Building Inquiry Skills: Classifying, p. 733; Observing, p. 734; Calculating, p. 735
2 **Renewable Sources of Energy** pp. 737–746 ◆ 23.2.1 Explain how the sun provides energy and describe ways to collect this energy. ◆ 23.2.2 Identify and describe various sources of energy not dependent on fossil fuels.	2 periods/ 1 block	**Discover** Can You Capture Solar Energy?, p. 737 **Real-World Lab: How It Works** Cooking With Sunshine, p. 745	TE Integrating Technology, p. 738 TE Real-Life Learning, p. 739 TE Building Inquiry Skills: Making Models, p. 741 TE Demonstration, p. 743 LM 23, "Solar Heating"
3 *INTEGRATING CHEMISTRY* **Nuclear Energy** pp. 747–751 ◆ 23.3.1 Describe nuclear fission and nuclear fusion reactions. ◆ 23.3.2 Explain how a nuclear power plant produces electricity.	1 period/ $\frac{1}{2}$ block	**Discover** Why Do They Fall?, p. 747 **Try This** Shoot the Nucleus, p. 748 **Sharpen Your Skills** Calculating, p. 749	TE Building Inquiry Skills: Making Models, p. 748 TE Real-Life Learning, p. 750 TE Inquiry Challenge, p. 750
4 **Energy Conservation** pp. 752–756 ◆ 23.4.1 List two ways to ensure that there will be enough energy for the future. ◆ 23.4.2 Identify things that individuals can do to conserve energy.	2 periods/ 1 block	**Skills Lab: Designing Experiments** Keeping Comfortable, p. 752 **PLM** Provides instructions for the probeware version of the lab **Discover** Which Bulb Is More Efficient?, p. 753 **Science at Home,** p. 756	TE Building Inquiry Skills: Calculating, p. 754 TE Building Inquiry Skills: Observing, p. 755
Study Guide/Assessment pp. 757–759	1 period/ $\frac{1}{2}$ block		ISAB Provides teaching and review of all inquiry skills

For Standard or Block Schedule The Resource Pro® CD-ROM gives you maximum flexibility for planning your instruction for any type of schedule. Resource Pro® contains Planning Express®, an advanced scheduling program, as well as the entire contents of the Teaching Resources and the Computer Test Bank.

Key: **CTB** Computer Test Bank
  CT Chapter Tests
  ELL Teacher's ELL Handbook

CHAPTER PLANNING GUIDE

Program Resources	Assessment Strategies	Media and Technology
UR Chapter 23 Project Teacher Notes, pp. 78–79 **UR** Chapter 23 Project Overview and Worksheet, pp. 80–83	**TE** Check Your Progress, pp. 736, 744, 751 **TE** Performance Assessment: Chapter 23 Project Wrap Up, p. 759 **UR** Chapter 23 Project Scoring Rubric, p. 84	Science Explorer Internet Site Audio CDs, Section Summaries
UR 23-1 Lesson Plan, p. 85 **UR** 23-1 Section Summary, p. 86 **UR** 23-1 Review and Reinforce, p. 87 **UR** 23-1 Enrich, p. 88	**SE** Section 1 Review, p. 736 **TE** Ongoing Assessment, pp. 731, 733, 735 **TE** Performance Assessment, p. 736	Concept Videotape Library, *Adventures, Tape 5,* "Our Passion for Driving"; "Power for the People" Presentation Pro, "Energy Resources" Transparency 88, "An Electric Power Plant"
UR 23-2 Lesson Plan, p. 89 **UR** 23-2 Section Summary, p. 90 **UR** 23-2 Review and Reinforce, p. 91 **UR** 23-2 Enrich, p. 92 **UR** Real-World Lab blackline masters, pp. 101–102	**SE** Section 2 Review, p. 744 **SE** Analyze and Conclude, p. 745 **TE** Ongoing Assessment, pp. 739, 741, 743 **TE** Performance Assessment, p. 744	Concept Videotape Library, *Adventures, Tape 5,* "Wired to the Sun" Presentation Pro, "Renewable Energy" Transparencies 89, "Exploring a Solar House"; 90, "A Geothermal Power Plant" Lab Activity Videotape, *Tape 5*
UR 23-3 Lesson Plan, p. 93 **UR** 23-3 Section Summary, p. 94 **UR** 23-3 Review and Reinforce, p. 95 **UR** 23-3 Enrich, p. 96	**SE** Section 3 Review, p. 751 **TE** Ongoing Assessment, p. 749 **TE** Performance Assessment, p. 751	Presentation Pro, "Nuclear Energy" Transparencies 91, "Nuclear Fission"; 92, "A Nuclear Power Plant"; 93, "Nuclear Fusion"
UR 23-4 Lesson Plan, p. 97 **UR** 23-4 Section Summary, p. 98 **UR** 23-4 Review and Reinforce, p. 99 **UR** 23-4 Enrich, p. 100 **UR** Skills Lab blackline masters, pp. 103–105	**SE** Analyze and Conclude, p. 752 **SE** Section 4 Review, p. 756 **TE** Ongoing Assessment, p. 755 **TE** Performance Assessment, p. 756	Lab Activity Videotape, *Tape 5*
GRSW Provides worksheets to promote student comprehension of content **RCA** Provides strategies to improve science reading skills **ELL** Provides multiple strategies for English language learners	**SE** Study Guide/Assessment, pp. 757–759 **PA** Performance Assessment, pp. 70–72 **CT** Chapter 23 Test, pp. 91–94 **CTB** Chapter 23 Test **PHAS** Provides standardized test preparation	Computer Test Bank, Chapter 23 Test

GRSW Guided Reading and Study Workbook
ISAB Inquiry Skills Activity Book
LM Laboratory Manual

PA Performance Assessment
PHAS Prentice Hall Assessment System
PLM Probeware Lab Manual

RCA Reading in the Content Area
SE Student Edition

TE Teacher's Edition
UR Unit Resources

Meeting the National Science Education Standards and AAAS Benchmarks

National Science Education Standards	Benchmarks for Science Literacy	Unifying Themes

National Science Education Standards

Science as Inquiry (Content Standard A)

◆ **Design and conduct a scientific investigation** Students investigate how solar energy can be used to cook food and compare how well different materials stop heat transfer. (*Real-World Lab; Skills Lab*)

◆ **Use appropriate tools and techniques to gather, analyze, and interpret data** Students evaluate energy use in their school. (*Chapter Project*)

Physical Science (Content Standard B)

◆ **Transfer of energy** Fuel provides energy as the result of a chemical change. Nuclear reactions convert matter into energy. (*Sections 1, 3*)

Science and Technology (Content Standard E)

◆ **Understandings about science and technology** The energy stored in fuels can be used to generate electricity. Technologies to capture and use solar energy, wind and water power, and alternative fuels help meet energy needs. Nuclear fission can be used to generate electricity. (*Sections 1, 2, 3*)

Science in Personal and Social Perspectives (Content Standard F)

◆ **Science and technology in society** Students evaluate the benefits and costs of hydroelectric dams. (*Science and Society*)

Benchmarks for Science Literacy

1B Scientific Inquiry Students evaluate energy use in their school, investigate how solar energy can be used to cook food, and compare how well different materials stop heat transfer. (*Chapter Project; Real-World Lab; Skills Lab*)

3A Technology and Science People have developed technologies that improve energy efficiency and reduce energy use. (*Section 4; Science & History*)

3B Designs and Systems Control rods are used to control fission reactions in nuclear reactors. Certain materials can slow the transfer of heat. (*Section 3; Skills Lab*)

3C Issues in Technology Students suggest ways to save energy in their school. Students evaluate the benefits and costs of hydroelectric dams. Reducing energy use is called energy conservation. (*Chapter Project; Science and Society; Section 4*)

8C Energy Sources and Use The three major fossil fuels are coal, oil, and natural gas. The sun, wind, water, tides, biomass material, Earth's interior, and hydrogen are renewable sources of energy. Controlled nuclear fission reactions can be used to generate electricity. (*Sections 1, 2, 3; Real-World Lab*)

Unifying Themes

◆ **Energy** Students evaluate energy use in their school. The sun, wind, water, tides, biomass material, Earth's interior, and hydrogen are renewable sources of energy. Nuclear reactions convert matter into energy. (*Chapter Project; Sections 2, 3,; Real-World Lab; Science & History*)

◆ **Patterns of Change** Over time, heat and pressure changed dead organisms into fossil fuels. When a neutron hits a nucleus, the nucleus splits apart into two smaller nuclei and three neutrons. (*Sections 1, 3*)

◆ **Scale and Structure** Hydrocarbons are energy-rich chemical compounds that contain carbon and hydrogen atoms. The central core of an atom that contains protons and neutrons is called a nucleus. (*Sections 1, 3*)

◆ **Stability** A renewable source of energy is one that is constantly being supplied. Radioactive wastes remain dangerous for many thousands of years. (*Sections 2, 3*)

◆ **Systems and Interactions** Electric power plants generate electricity by converting energy from one form to another. People have developed technologies that improve energy efficiency and reduce energy use. (*Sections 1, 4; Science and Society*)

◆ **Unity and Diversity** Energy sources can be renewable or nonrenewable. (*Sections 1, 2*)

Take It to the Net

The **www.phschool.com** Web site provides you with multiple opportunities to incorporate the internet into your instruction. Go to **www.phschool.com** and click on the Science icon. Then select Science Explorer Integrated.

■ Have students use the chapter Self-Test to get instant feedback.

■ Hot Links and Reference Links provide opportunities for online research.

www.phschool.com

Internet Activities provide opportunities for students to review, extend, or assess a concept from the chapter.

STAY CURRENT with **SCIENCE NEWS** ®

Find out the latest research and information about energy and energy resources at: **www.phschool.com**

ACTIVITY	Time (minutes)	Materials Quantities for one work group	Skills
Section 1			
Discover, p. 730	10	**Nonconsumable** lignite coal, hand lens	Observing
Sharpen Your Skills, p. 732	15	**Nonconsumable** drawing compass, protractor, calculator (optional)	Graphing
Section 2			
Discover, p. 737	10; 5	**Consumable** 500 mL water **Nonconsumable** 2 sealable clear plastic bags, 2 thermometers	Developing Hypotheses
Real-World Lab, p. 745	40	**Consumable** glue, tape, marshmallows, 3 sheets aluminum foil, 3 sheets oaktag paper **Nonconsumable** scissors, 3 thermometers, 3 dowels or pencils, clock or watch	Predicting, Designing Experiments, Forming Operational Definitions
Section 3			
Discover, p. 747	10	**Nonconsumable** 15 dominoes	Inferring
Try This, p. 748	10	**Nonconsumable** 12 marbles	Making Models
Sharpen Your Skills, p. 749	5	**Nonconsumable** calculator (optional)	Calculating
Section 4			
Skills Lab, p. 752	40	**Consumable** ice water, hot water **Nonconsumable** thermometers, beakers, watch or clock, containers and lids made of paper, plastic foam, plastic, glass, and metal	Measuring, Designing Experiments
Discover, p. 753	20	**Nonconsumable** 60-watt incandescent light bulb and 15-watt compact fluorescent light bulb in packages, lamp, thermometer, clock or watch	Inferring
Science at Home, p. 756	home	No special materials are required.	Observing

A list of all materials required for the Student Edition activities can be found beginning on page T23. You can obtain information about ordering materials by calling 1-800-848-9500 or by accessing the Science Explorer Internet site at: **www.phschool.com**

Energy Audit

Chapter 23 covers the sources and uses of energy and ways to conserve energy. The Chapter 23 Project is designed to provide real-life application of chapter concepts.

Purpose The Chapter 23 Project will give students an opportunity to examine energy uses in their school and suggest ways to reduce the school's energy consumption. Each student group will choose one area of the school to study, identify the types of energy used in that area, and determine the amount of each type of energy used. As students collect and record data, they will consider ways to reduce each type of energy use. Each group will prepare a written report that describes the students' findings and lists their ideas for reducing energy uses in the area they studied. The class as a whole will then prepare a proposal for conserving energy throughout the school.

Skills Focus After completing the Chapter 23 Project, students will be able to

◆ create a data table for recording the types and amounts of energy uses in the area selected for study;

◆ make observations and record data;

◆ interpret data and draw conclusions as the basis for recommending ways to reduce energy use;

◆ communicate findings and recommendations in a written report.

Project Time Line The Chapter 23 Project requires two to three weeks to complete, depending on how long a period of time you want to have students collect and evaluate numerical data, including the school's utility bills and readings of electric meters and fuel gauges. Most observations can be made during a class period. For purposes of comparison, making observations of the same area on different days and at different times of day should help students detect average and unusual uses, such as increased use of heating fuel during a cold spell.

Possible Materials

No special materials are required. Students will find it helpful to use calculators.

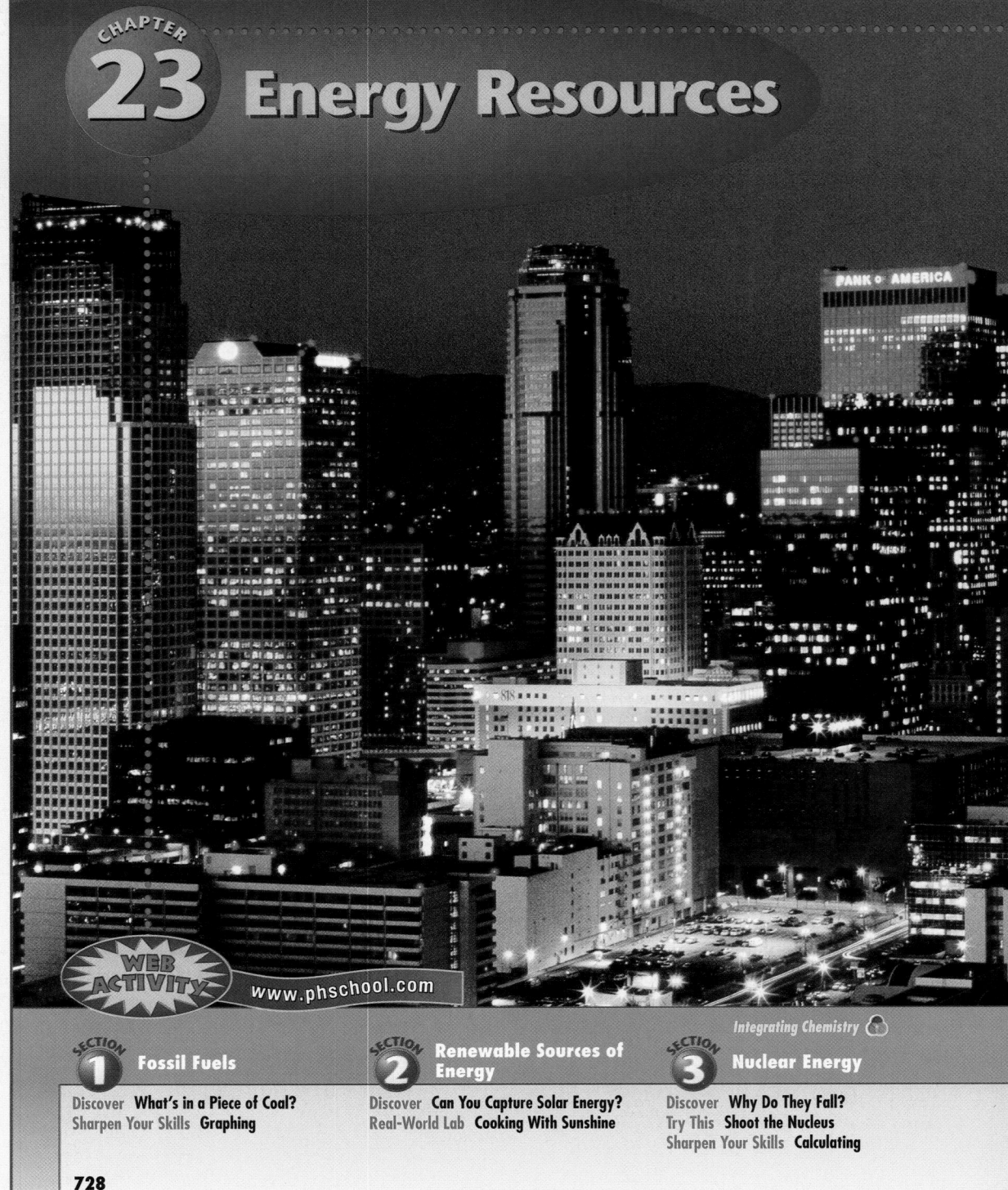

CHAPTER 23 Energy Resources

WEB ACTIVITY www.phschool.com

SECTION **1** Fossil Fuels	SECTION **2** Renewable Sources of Energy	*Integrating Chemistry* SECTION **3** Nuclear Energy
Discover What's in a Piece of Coal? **Sharpen Your Skills** Graphing	**Discover** Can You Capture Solar Energy? **Real-World Lab** Cooking With Sunshine	**Discover** Why Do They Fall? **Try This** Shoot the Nucleus **Sharpen Your Skills** Calculating

728

Advance Preparation

◆ Discuss with your school principal what students will be doing in this project, and obtain approval for students to enter areas that are usually off-limits to them, such as the utility room, or the cafeteria's kitchen. If necessary, arrange to have the school custodian or another adult accompany students to these areas.

◆ Obtain copies of the school's utility and fuel bills for students' use in determining the amounts of energy used.

Launching the Project Invite students to read the Chapter 23 Project description on page 729. Lead students in brainstorming a list of areas in the school that they could study.

Take the class on a tour of the school building and grounds. Encourage students to keep track of the different energy uses they observe—electricity for lighting, fuel oil or natural gas for heating, electricity or natural gas for cooking, gasoline for the school buses, and the like.

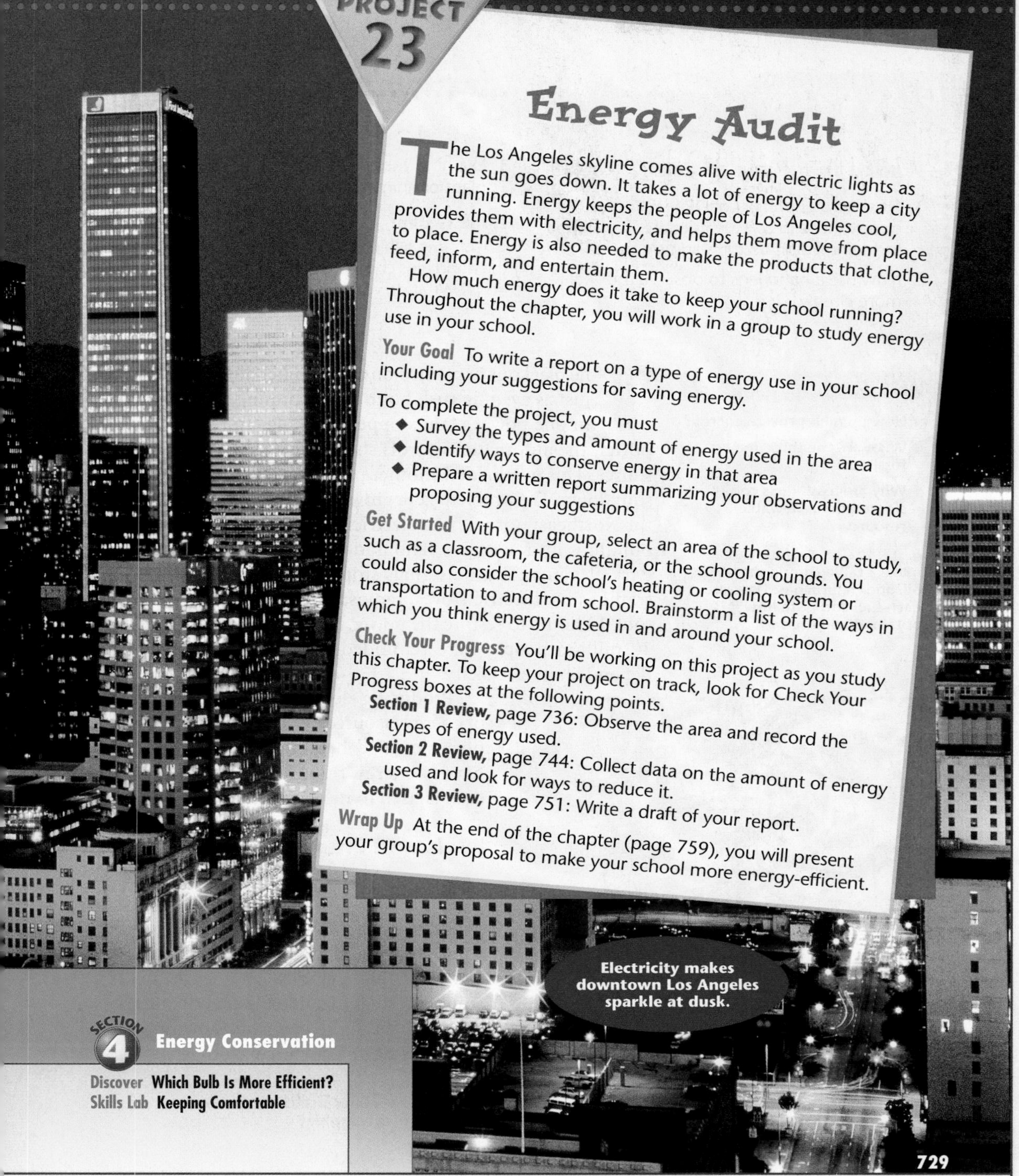

PROJECT 23

Energy Audit

The Los Angeles skyline comes alive with electric lights as the sun goes down. It takes a lot of energy to keep a city running. Energy keeps the people of Los Angeles cool, provides them with electricity, and helps them move from place to place. Energy is also needed to make the products that clothe, feed, inform, and entertain them.

How much energy does it take to keep your school running? Throughout the chapter, you will work in a group to study energy use in your school.

Your Goal To write a report on a type of energy use in your school including your suggestions for saving energy.

To complete the project, you must
◆ Survey the types and amount of energy used in the area
◆ Identify ways to conserve energy in that area
◆ Prepare a written report summarizing your observations and proposing your suggestions

Get Started With your group, select an area of the school to study, such as a classroom, the cafeteria, or the school grounds. You could also consider the school's heating or cooling system or transportation to and from school. Brainstorm a list of the ways in which you think energy is used in and around your school.

Check Your Progress You'll be working on this project as you study this chapter. To keep your project on track, look for Check Your Progress boxes at the following points.
Section 1 Review, page 736: Observe the area and record the types of energy used.
Section 2 Review, page 744: Collect data on the amount of energy used and look for ways to reduce it.
Section 3 Review, page 751: Write a draft of your report.

Wrap Up At the end of the chapter (page 759), you will present your group's proposal to make your school more energy-efficient.

Electricity makes downtown Los Angeles sparkle at dusk.

SECTION
4 Energy Conservation

Discover Which Bulb Is More Efficient?
Skills Lab Keeping Comfortable

729

Program Resources

◆ **Unit 6 Resources** Chapter 23 Project Teacher Notes, pp. 78–79; Project Overview and Worksheets, pp. 80–83; Project Scoring Rubric, p. 84

Media and Technology

 Audio CDs Section Summaries

WEB ACTIVITY www.phschool.com

You will find an Internet activity, chapter self-tests for students, and links to other chapter topics at this site.

Distribute Chapter 23 Project Overview on pages 80–81 of Unit 6 Resources, and have students review the project rules and procedures. Also distribute Chapter 23 Project Worksheet 1 on pages 82–83 of Unit 6 Resources. This worksheet provides instructions on how to read electric and gas meters and provides equivalents for converting different energy units (kilowatt-hours, gallons, and so forth) into the common unit of BTUs.

Divide the class into groups of three or four, and let the groups meet briefly to choose areas to study. Monitor the groups' choices to avoid duplication. As an alternative, you could assign an area to each group.

Tell students that each group's members may divide the project responsibilities among themselves in any way they wish. However, emphasize that *every* group member should take part in identifying the types and amounts of energy uses in the area the group has chosen, recording and analyzing data, and developing the written report, and should be prepared to answer questions about the project.

Additional information on guiding the project is provided in Chapter 23 Project Teacher Notes on pages 79–80 of Unit 6 Resources.

Performance Assessment

The Chapter 23 Project Scoring Rubric on page 84 in Unit 6 Resources will help you evaluate how well students complete the Chapter 23 Project. You may want to share the scoring rubric with students so they are clear about what will be expected of them. Students will be assessed on
◆ their ability to identify and evaluate all the types of energy used in the area studied;
◆ their ability to make recommendations for reducing those energy uses and to communicate their findings and recommendations to others;
◆ their participation in their group.

729

SECTION 1 Fossil Fuels

Objectives

After completing the lesson, students will be able to

♦ explain how fuels provide energy;

♦ list the three major fossil fuels;

♦ explain why fossil fuels are considered nonrenewable resources.

Key Terms combustion, fossil fuels, hydrocarbons, reserves, petroleum, refinery, petrochemicals

1 Engage/Explore

Activating Prior Knowledge

Ask students: **What is energy?** *(Answers will vary depending on students' prior science learning. Responses may include "strength," "power," "something that makes something else happen," and the like. If necessary, point out that the scientific definition of energy is "the capacity to do work.")*

DISCOVER

Skills Focus observing
Materials *lignite coal, hand lens*
Time 10 minutes
Tips Lignite—the second stage of coal formation after peat—is the only form of coal that may contain recognizable plant remains.
Expected Outcome Students may or may not find fossils of plant remains in the coal samples. If fossils are present, they will be more noticeable with a hand lens.
Think It Over The lignite's texture, layering, and fossils (if present) can be seen more clearly with a hand lens. If fossils are visible, students should be able to infer that coal is made of plant remains.

SECTION 1 Fossil Fuels

DISCOVER · ACTIVITY

What's in a Piece of Coal?

1. Observe a chunk of coal. Record your observations in as much detail as possible, including color, texture, and shape.

2. Now use a hand lens to observe the coal more closely.

3. Examine your coal for fossils, imprints of plant or animal remains.

Think It Over

Observing What did you notice when you used the hand lens compared to your first observations? What do you think coal is made of?

GUIDE FOR READING

♦ How do fuels provide energy?

♦ What are the three major fossil fuels?

♦ Why are fossil fuels considered nonrenewable resources?

Reading Tip As you read, make a table comparing coal, oil, and natural gas. Describe each fuel and note how it is obtained and used.

The blackout happened on a November afternoon in 1965, just as evening rush hour was beginning. One small part in one power plant stopped working. To replace the lost power, the automatic controls shifted electricity from another source. This overloaded another part of the system, causing it to shut down. The problem kept growing. Within minutes, much of the Northeast was without electricity! Lights went out, plunging buildings into darkness. Thousands of people were trapped in dark elevators. Traffic signals stopped working, causing huge traffic jams. Electric stoves, radios, clocks—nothing worked. It took 13 hours to restore the power. During that time, more than 30 million people were reminded just how much their lives depended on electricity.

Producing electricity is an important use of energy resources. Other uses include transportation and heating. As you read about Earth's energy resources, think about how each is used to meet people's energy needs.

Fuels and Energy

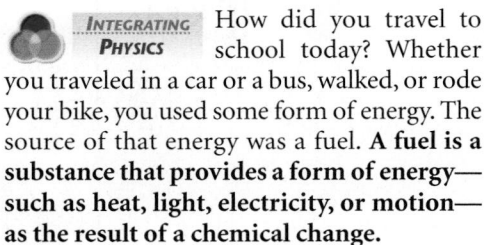 **INTEGRATING PHYSICS** How did you travel to school today? Whether you traveled in a car or a bus, walked, or rode your bike, you used some form of energy. The source of that energy was a fuel. **A fuel is a substance that provides a form of energy—such as heat, light, electricity, or motion—as the result of a chemical change.**

◀ Electric power lines stretch against the evening sky.

730

READING STRATEGIES

Reading Tip Students' tables should consist of columns for coal, oil, and natural gas. The comparisons should be listed down the side: description, method of obtaining fuel, and use. Students may wish to add further rows to compare advantages and disadvantages or other criteria.

Program Resources

♦ **Unit 6 Resources** 23-1 Lesson Plan, p. 85; 23-1 Section Summary, p. 86

♦ **Guided Reading and Study Workbook** Section 23-1

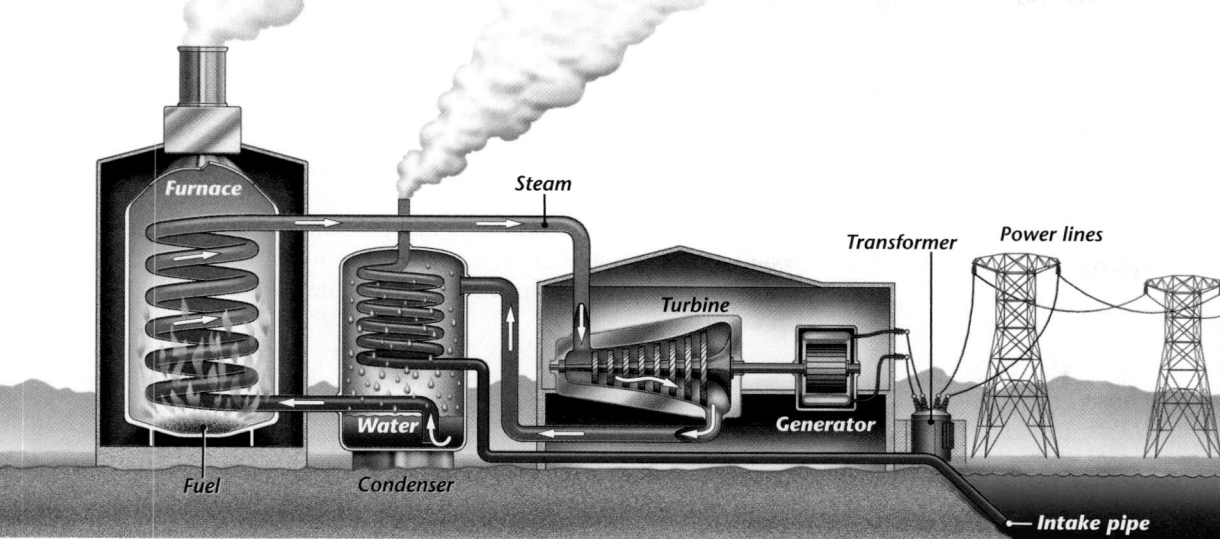

Figure 1 Electric power plants generate electricity by converting energy from one form to another. In the furnace, fuel is burned, releasing thermal energy. This energy is used to boil water and make steam. The mechanical energy of the moving steam turns the blades of a turbine. The turbine turns the shaft of the generator, producing an electric current.

Energy can be converted from one form to another. To see how, rub your hands together quickly for several seconds. Did you feel them become warmer? When you moved your hands, they had mechanical energy, the energy of motion. The friction of your hands rubbing together converted some of this mechanical energy to thermal energy, which you felt as heat.

Combustion Fuels contain stored chemical energy, which can be released by burning. The process of burning a fuel is called **combustion.** For example, the fuel used by most cars is gasoline. When gasoline is burned in a car engine, it undergoes a chemical change. The gasoline combines with oxygen, producing carbon dioxide and water. The combustion of gasoline also converts some of the stored chemical energy into thermal energy. This thermal energy is converted to mechanical energy that moves the car.

Production of Electricity The energy stored in fuels can be used to generate electricty. In most power plants, the thermal energy produced by burning fuel is used to boil water, making steam, as shown in Figure 1. The mechanical energy of the steam turns the blades of a turbine. The shaft of the turbine is connected to a generator. The generator consists of powerful magnets surrounded by coils of copper wire. As the shaft rotates, the magnets turn inside the wire coil, producing an electric current. The electric current flows through power lines to homes and industries.

☑ *Checkpoint* *What are three energy conversions that might occur in a power plant?*

Fuels and Energy

 Integrating Physics

After students have read about energy conversion and rubbed their hands together, give some other examples of energy conversions and challenge students to infer the energy changes that are occurring. Some examples include a toaster (*Electrical energy is changed to heat energy.*), light bulb (*Electrical energy is changed to light and heat energy.*), power saw (*Electrical energy is changed to mechanical and heat energy.*), and candle (*Chemical energy is changed to light and heat energy.*). **learning modality: logical/mathematical**

Real-Life Learning

Invite a local auto mechanic or students who are particularly interested in automobiles to bring in and explain diagrams showing how an internal combustion engine works. Suggest that students who need an additional challenge create posters based on the diagrams. Ask: **Besides cars, trucks, buses, and other automobiles, what other devices contain an internal combustion engine?** (*Gasoline-powered lawnmowers, snowblowers, chainsaws, portable generators, and the like*) **learning modality: visual**

Media and Technology

 Transparencies "An Electric Power Plant," Transparency 88

Answers to Self-Assessment

☑ *Checkpoint*

When fuel is burned, chemical energy is converted to thermal energy (heat). Some of the thermal energy is converted to the mechanical energy of moving steam. In a power plant, the mechanical energy is then converted to electrical energy.

Ongoing Assessment

Oral Presentation Call on students at random to identify the energy conversions shown in Figure 1 in the order in which they occur.

731

What Are Fossil Fuels?

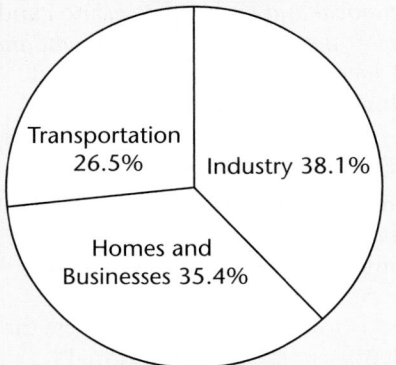
Sharpen your Skills

Graphing ACTIVITY

Use the data in the table below to make a circle graph showing the uses of energy in the United States. (To review circle graphs, see the Skills Handbook.)

End Use of Energy	Percent of Total Energy
Transportation	26.5
Industry	38.1
Homes and businesses	35.4

What Are Fossil Fuels?

Most of the energy used today comes from organisms that lived hundreds of millions of years ago. As these plants, animals, and other organisms died, their remains piled up. Layers of sand, rock, and mud buried the dead organisms. Over time, heat and pressure changed the material into other substances. **Fossil fuels** are the energy-rich substances formed from the remains of once-living organisms. **The three major fossil fuels are coal, oil, and natural gas.**

Fossil fuels are made of hydrocarbons. **Hydrocarbons** are energy-rich chemical compounds that contain carbon and hydrogen atoms. During combustion, the carbon and hydrogen combine with oxygen in the air to form carbon dioxide and water. This process releases energy in the forms of heat and light.

Fossil fuels have more hydrocarbons per kilogram than most other fuels. For this reason, they are an excellent source of energy. Combustion of one kilogram of coal, for example, provides twice as much heat as burning one kilogram of wood. Oil and natural gas provide three times the energy of wood.

☑ *Checkpoint* Why do fossil fuels yield more energy than other fuels?

Coal

Coal is a solid fossil fuel formed from plant remains. People have burned coal to produce heat for thousands of years. But coal was only a minor source of energy compared to wood until the 1800s. As Europe and the United States entered the Industrial Revolution, the need for fuel increased rapidly.

Figure 2 Coal is formed from the remains of trees and other plants that grew in swamps hundreds of millions of years ago.

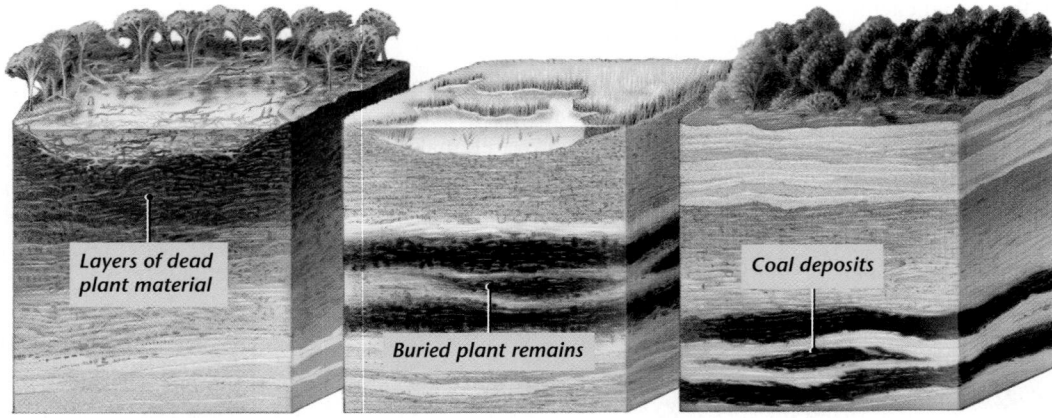

Layers of dead plant material

Buried plant remains

Coal deposits

200 million years ago   **50 million years ago**   **Present**

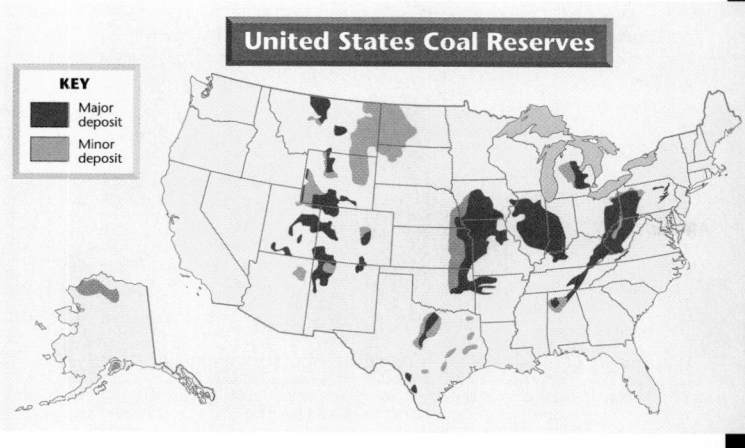

United States Coal Reserves

KEY
- Major deposit
- Minor deposit

As forests were cut down, firewood became more expensive. It became worthwhile to find, mine, and transport coal. Coal fueled the huge steam engines that powered trains, ships, and factories during the Industrial Revolution.

Today, coal provides 23 percent of the energy used in the United States. The major use of coal is to fuel electric power plants.

Coal Mining Before it can be used to produce energy, coal has

 INTEGRATING TECHNOLOGY to be removed from the ground, or mined. Some coal is located very deep underground or is mixed with other materials, making it too difficult to obtain. Known deposits of coal (and other fossil fuels) that can be obtained using current technology are called **reserves.**

A century ago, miners had to break the coal apart with hand tools. Today they use machines to chop the coal into chunks and lift it to the surface. The coal is then cleaned to remove rocks, sand, and other materials that do not burn. Removing them also makes the coal lighter, reducing the cost of transporting it.

Coal as an Energy Source Coal is the most plentiful fossil fuel in the United States. It is fairly easy to transport, and provides a lot of energy when burned. But coal also has some disadvantages. Coal mining can increase erosion. Runoff from mines can cause water pollution. Finally, burning most types of coal results in more air pollution than other fossil fuels.

In addition, coal mining can be a dangerous job. Thousands of miners have been killed or injured in accidents in the mines. Many more suffer from "black lung," a disease caused by years of breathing coal dust. Fortunately, the mining industry has been working hard to improve conditions. New safety procedures and better equipment, including robots and drills that produce less coal dust, have made coal mining safer.

Figure 3 The map shows the locations of coal reserves in the United States. In the photograph, a miner obtains hard coal from a shaft deep underground. *Interpreting Maps Which states have major deposits of coal?*

Figure 4 A farmer in Ireland turns over blocks of soft peat. Peat is formed in the early stages of the process of coal formation.

Oil

Building Inquiry Skills: Observing

Materials *2 small paper cups, 30 mL dark molasses, paper towel, aluminum pan*

Time 10 minutes

CAUTION: *If you are concerned about spills, have a few volunteers perform this activity as a demonstration for the other students.* Give each student or group a paper towel, a small paper cup containing about 30 mL of dark molasses, and an empty cup. Explain that molasses is very similar to crude oil in consistency. Invite students to pour the molasses from one cup to the other over the pan, try to pick some up with the paper towel, and touch some between the thumb and index finger. Students will find that the molasses is too thick to pour readily, is not absorbed by the towel, and is sticky. Ask: **How easy do you think it would be to clean up crude oil that spilled on a beach?** *(Extremely difficult)* **learning modality: kinesthetic**

Using the Visuals: Figure 5

Let students answer the caption question, then ask: **Which of the named nations has the smallest oil reserve?** *(United States)* **Does this mean the United States is the nation with the smallest oil reserves in the world?** *(No, it has the eleventh largest. All nations other than those named have smaller reserves than the United States.)* **learning modality: logical/mathematical**

Integrating Technology

Ask students: **Do you know of any other examples where sound waves are used to locate objects or materials?** *(Students may know how sonar is used to map the ocean floor.)* **learning modality: verbal**

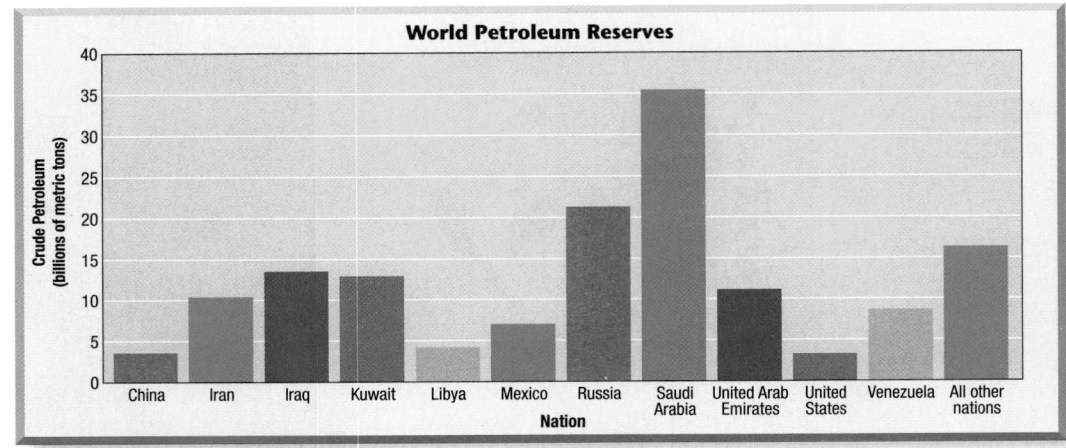

World Petroleum Reserves

Figure 5 Known petroleum deposits, called reserves, are located in many parts of the world. *Interpreting Graphs Which two nations have the largest reserves?*

Oil

Oil is a thick, black, liquid fossil fuel. It formed from the remains of small animals, algae, and protists that lived in oceans and shallow inland seas hundreds of millions of years ago. **Petroleum** is another name for oil, from the Latin words *petra* (rock) and *oleum* (oil). Most oil deposits are located underground in tiny holes in sandstone or limestone. The oil fills the holes somewhat like water trapped in the holes of a sponge.

Petroleum accounts for more than one third of the energy produced in the world. Fuel for most cars, airplanes, trains, and ships comes from petroleum. Many homes are heated by oil.

The United States consumes about one third of all the oil produced in the world. But only three percent of the world's supply is located in this country. The difference must be purchased from countries with large oil supplies.

Locating Oil Deposits Because it is usually located deep below the surface, finding oil is difficult. Scientists can use sound waves to test an area for oil without drilling. This technique relies on the fact that sound waves bounce off objects and return as echoes. Scientists send pulses of sound down into the rocks below ground. Then they measure how long it takes the echoes to return. The amount of time depends on whether the sound waves must travel through solid rock or liquid oils. This information can indicate the most likely places to find oil. However, only about one out of every six wells drilled produces a usable amount of oil.

Figure 6 An oil rig bobs up and down as it pumps oil from a Texas oil field.

Background

Facts and Figures In addition to refined petroleum, gasoline contains many different additives. These include antiknock compounds, metal deactivators and antioxidants, antirust and anti-icing agents, detergents, lubricants, and dyes.

For many years, tetraethyl lead was added to gasoline to improve its combustion characteristics. Lead reduces or eliminates "knocking" caused by premature ignition in high-compression engines and lubricates close-fitting engine parts where oil tends to wash away or burn off. However, because lead is highly toxic, the government phased out and finally banned the use of lead as a gasoline additive. As a result, the amount of lead in the atmosphere decreased by about 98 percent between 1970 and 1996.

Refining Oil When oil is first pumped out of the ground, it is called crude oil. Crude oil can be a runny or a thick liquid. In order to be made into useful products, crude oil must undergo a process called refining. A factory where crude oil is separated into fuels and other products by heating is called a **refinery.**

In addition to gasoline and heating oil, many products you use every day are made from crude oil. **Petrochemicals** are compounds that are made from oil. Petrochemicals are used in plastics, paints, medicines, and cosmetics.

☑ *Checkpoint* *How is petroleum used?*

Natural Gas

The third major fossil fuel is natural gas, a mixture of methane and other gases. Natural gas forms from the same organisms as petroleum. Because it is less dense than oil, natural gas often rises above an oil deposit, forming a pocket of gas in the rock.

Pipelines transport the gas from its source to the places where it is used. If all the gas pipelines in the United States were connected, they would reach to the moon and back—twice! Natural gas can also be compressed into a liquid and stored in tanks as fuel for trucks and buses.

Natural gas has several advantages. It produces large amounts of energy, but lower levels of many air pollutants than coal or oil. It is also easy to transport once the network of pipelines is built. One disadvantage of natural gas is that it is highly flammable. A gas leak can cause a violent explosion and fire.

Gas companies help to prevent dangerous explosions from leaks. If you use natural gas in your home, you probably are familiar with the "gas" smell that alerts you whenever there is unburned gas in the air. You may be surprised to learn that natural gas actually has no odor at all. What causes the strong smell? The gas companies add a chemical with a distinct smell to the gas before it is piped to homes and businesses so that any leaks will be noticed.

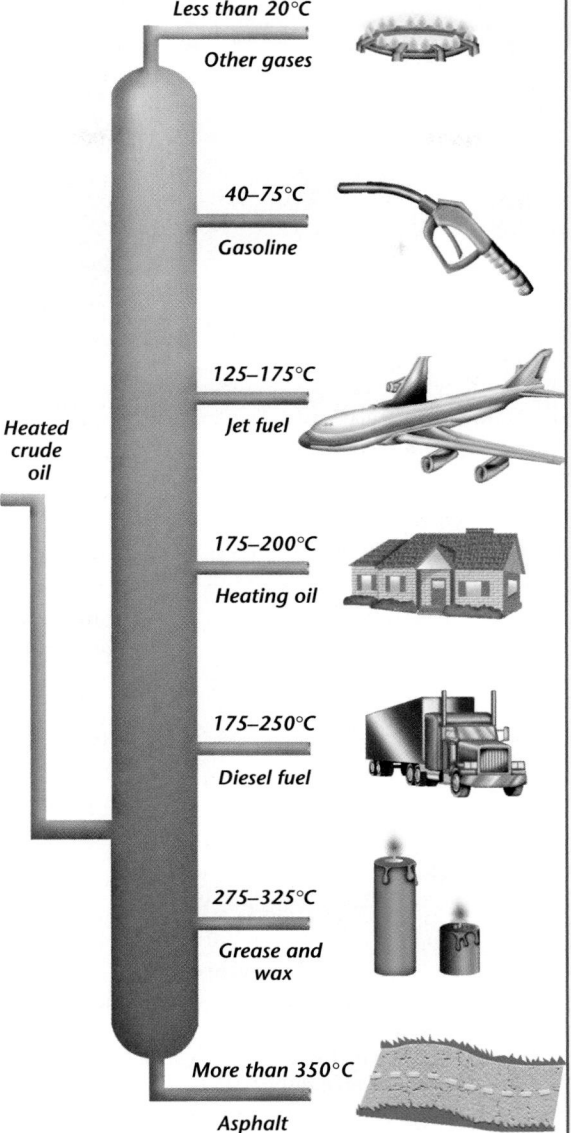

Less than 20°C — Other gases
40–75°C — Gasoline
125–175°C — Jet fuel
175–200°C — Heating oil
175–250°C — Diesel fuel
275–325°C — Grease and wax
More than 350°C — Asphalt

Heated crude oil

Figure 7 Crude oil is refined to make many different products. In the refining process, heat causes the different molecules in crude oil to separate. Different substances vaporize at specific temperatures.

Natural Gas

Building Inquiry Skills: Calculating

Materials *calculator*
Time 5 minutes

Point out the text statement "If all the gas pipelines in the United States were connected, they would reach to the moon and back—twice!" Have students use the moon's average distance from Earth *(384,392 km)* to calculate the total length of U.S. gas pipelines. *(384,392 × 4 = 1,537,568 km)* They can extend this activity by comparing this distance to another reference, such as the width of their state. **learning modality: logical/mathematical**

Real-Life Learning

Companies that supply natural gas usually publish materials to teach customers about safety issues when dealing with gas appliances and gas lines. Some companies also can provide a representative to speak to your class about gas safety. Contact your local gas company to request materials and, if available, a speaker. **learning modality: verbal**

Fuel Supply and Demand

Building Inquiry Skills: Inferring

Tell students that in 1973, 36 percent of all the oil used in the United States was imported from other countries; in 1993, 51 percent of the oil used was imported. Ask: **What do those percentages tell you?** *(The United States became more dependent on imported oil.)* **Why do you think that happened?** *(The country's oil consumption increased, but production did not increase enough to keep up with the demand.)* **learning modality: logical/mathematical**

Answers to Self-Assessment

Caption Question

Figure 5 Saudi Arabia and Russia

☑ *Checkpoint*

Petroleum is refined to make fuels and other products, including plastics.

Ongoing Assessment

Skills Check Have each student create a simple, three-column table listing the advantages and disadvantages of each type of fossil fuel.

Portfolio Students can save their tables in their portfolios.

3 Assess

Section 1 Review Answers

1. Fuels contain stored chemical energy. When they are burned, the chemical energy is converted into other forms of energy.

2. *Coal* is a solid fossil fuel formed from decaying plant matter that was changed by heat and pressure. *Oil* is a thick, black liquid fossil fuel formed from the remains of small animals, algae, and protists. *Natural gas* is a mixture of methane and other gases formed from the same organisms as oil.

3. Because fossil fuels take hundreds of millions of years to form, they can be easily used up faster than they can be replaced.

4. *Advantages:* produces lower levels of many air pollutants; is easy to transport. *Disadvantage:* is highly flammable, so a leak can cause a violent explosion and fire.

5. *Sample answers:* Not all oil deposits have been located; countries may not want to reveal the size of their oil reserves.

Check Your Progress
CHAPTER PROJECT 23

Point out that the school's meters and gauges show the amount of fuel used for the entire building. To estimate the amount used in each area, students can count the number of rooms in the school (including the cafeteria, gym, auditorium, and so forth) and divide the total amount of fuel used by the number of rooms. Students should suggest whether energy use in this area is above or below average.

Performance Assessment

Writing Have each student explain why it is important for the United States to become less dependent on fossil fuels.

Figure 8 During the gasoline crisis, people frequently had to wait in long lines to buy gas. *Relating Cause and Effect What caused the gasoline shortage?*

Fuel Supply and Demand

The many advantages of using fossil fuels as an energy source have made them essential to modern life. **But remember that fossil fuels take hundreds of millions of years to form. For this reason, fossil fuels are considered a nonrenewable resource.** For example, Earth's known oil reserves took 500 million years to form. One fourth of this oil has already been used. If fossil fuels continue to be used more rapidly than they are formed, the reserves will eventually be used up.

Many of the nations that consume large amounts of fuel have very limited reserves of their own. They have to buy oil, natural gas, and coal from the regions that have large supplies. The uneven distribution of fossil fuel reserves has often been a cause of political problems in the world. For example, in the 1970s, a group of oil-exporting nations decided to reduce their oil exports to the United States. As the supply of gasoline fell, prices rose very rapidly. People sometimes waited in line for hours to buy gasoline. This shortage reminded Americans of their dependence on oil imported from other nations.

New sources of energy are needed to replace the decreasing fossil fuel reserves. The rest of this chapter will describe some other sources of energy, as well as ways to make current fuel resources last longer.

Section 1 Review

1. Explain how fuels provide energy.
2. Name the three major fossil fuels and briefly describe each.
3. Explain why fossil fuels are classified as nonrenewable resources.
4. List two advantages and one disadvantage of natural gas as an energy source.
5. **Thinking Critically** **Applying Concepts** Why is it impossible to know exactly how large the world's oil reserves are?

Check Your Progress
CHAPTER PROJECT 23

With your team, observe your selected area of the school. Determine which types of energy use take place in this area: heating, cooling, lighting, mechanical devices, electronic equipment, or moving vehicles. Record the specific types and amounts of energy use in a data table. To find the amounts, you will need to collect data from electric meters or fuel gauges. (*Hint:* Observe your area at several different times of the day, since the pattern of energy use may vary.)

736

Program Resources

◆ **Unit 6 Resources** 23-1 Review and Reinforce, p. 87; 23-1 Enrich, p. 88

Answers to Self-Assessment

Caption Question

Figure 8 A group of oil-exporting nations reduced oil exports to the United States.

2 Renewable Sources of Energy

DISCOVER · ACTIVITY · · · ·

Can You Capture Solar Energy?

1. Pour 250 milliliters of water into each of two sealable, clear plastic bags.

2. Measure and record the water temperature in each bag. Seal the bags.

3. Put one bag in a dark or shady place. Put the other bag in a place where it will receive direct sunlight.

4. Predict what the temperature of the water in each bag will be after 30 minutes.

5. Measure and record the ending temperatures.

Think It Over

Developing Hypotheses How did the water temperature in each bag change? What could account for these results?

As the sun rises over the rim of the canyon where your family is camping, you feel its warmth on your face. The night's chill disappears quickly. A breeze stirs, carrying with it the smell of the campfire. Maybe you'll take a morning dip in the warm water of a nearby hot spring.

This relaxing scene is far from the city, with its bustling cars and trucks, factories and power plants. But there are energy resources all around you here, too. The sun warms the air, the wind blows, and heat from inside Earth warms the waters of the spring. These sources of energy are all renewable—that is, they are constantly being supplied. You can see why people are trying to find ways to use these renewable resources instead of fossil fuels. As you read about each source of renewable energy, think about how it could help meet people's energy needs.

Energy From the Sun

The warmth you feel on a sunny day is **solar energy,** energy from the sun. **The sun constantly gives off energy in the form of light and heat.** Solar energy is the source, directly or indirectly, of most other renewable energy resources. In one day, Earth receives enough solar energy to meet the energy needs of the entire world for 40 years. Solar energy does not cause pollution, and it will not run out for billions of years.

So why hasn't solar energy replaced fossil fuels? One reason is that solar energy is only available when the sun is shining. A backup energy source must be available on cloudy days and at night. Another problem is that

GUIDE FOR READING

◆ How does the sun provide energy?

◆ What are some renewable sources of energy?

Reading Tip Before you read, preview the headings in this section. Predict some sources of energy that are renewable.

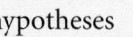
737

2 Facilitate

Energy From the Sun

Including All Students

Ask students to estimate the number of sunny days there are each year in your region of the country. If an almanac is available, provide students with data on number or percent of days that are sunny. Using this information, have students evaluate the feasability of using solar energy in your region. **learning modality: logical/mathematical**

Solar Technologies

Integrating Technology

Materials *several examples of solar cells and small solar-powered motors (available from home-electronics stores)*

Let students examine the solar cells and motors. Encourage them to use the cells and motors to make simple devices that will operate when placed in sunlight— for example, a solar-powered toy boat or car. Ask: **What energy conversions are taking place?** *(Solar energy to electrical energy to mechanical energy)* **learning modality: kinesthetic**

Figure 9 Aimed at the sun, these mirrors provide power to an electric plant in New South Wales, Australia. *Inferring How does the shape of these mirrors make them more effective?*

although Earth receives a lot of energy from the sun every day, this energy is very spread out. To obtain enough power, it is necessary to collect this energy from a huge area.

Solar Technologies

INTEGRATING TECHNOLOGY Improving technologies to capture and use solar energy will help meet future energy needs. Some current solar technologies are described below.

Solar Plants One way to capture the sun's energy involves using giant mirrors. In a solar plant, rows of mirrors focus the sun's rays to heat a tank of water. The water boils, making steam that can be used to generate electricity.

Solar Cells Solar energy can be converted directly into electricity in a solar cell. A solar cell consists of a "sandwich" of very thin layers of the element silicon and other materials. The upper and lower parts of the sandwich have a negative and a positive terminal, like a battery. When light hits the cell, electrons move across the layers, producing an electric current.

The amount of electricity produced by solar cells depends on the area of the cell and the amount of light available. Solar cells are used to power calculators, lights, telephones, and other small devices. However, it would take more than 5,000 solar cells the size of your palm to produce enough electricity for a typical American home. Building solar cells on a large scale is very expensive. As a result, solar cells are used mostly in areas where fossil fuels are difficult to transport.

☑ *Checkpoint* *What are solar cells made of and how do they work?*

738

Background

Integrating Science The solar cells described in the student text are made of crystalline silicon and are also known as photovoltaic (PV) cells. Although suitable for use in calculators and watches, these cells are not very efficient at converting solar energy to electricity and are expensive to produce. A new kind of solar cell made from a thin film of semiconductor material may prove to be more efficient and less expensive.

Media and Technology

 Transparencies "Exploring a Solar House," Transparency 89

 Concept Videotape Library *Adventures, Tape 5,* "Wired to the Sun"

Solar Heating Systems Solar energy can be used to heat buildings. As shown in *Exploring a Solar House,* there are two types of solar heating systems: passive and active.

A **passive solar system** converts sunlight into thermal energy without using pumps or fans. If you have ever stepped into a car on a sunny day, you have experienced passive solar heating. Solar energy passes through the car's windows as light. The sun's rays heat the seats and other parts of the car, which then transfer heat to the air. The heated air is trapped inside, so the car gets warmer. The same principle can be used to heat a home.

An **active solar system** captures the sun's energy, then uses fans and pumps to distribute the heat. Light strikes the black metal surface of a solar collector. There, it is converted to thermal energy. Water is pumped through pipes in the solar collector to absorb the thermal energy. The heated water flows to a storage tank. Pumps and fans distribute the heat throughout the building.

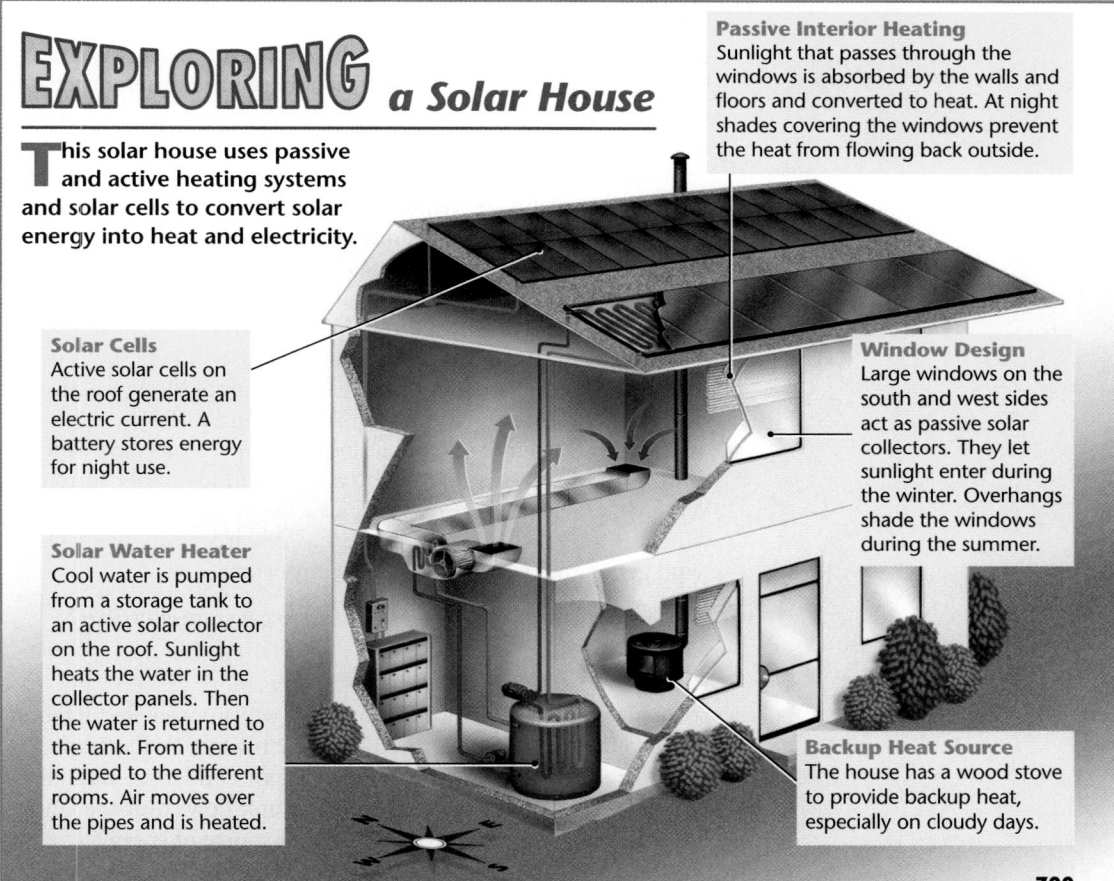

EXPLORING *a Solar House*

This solar house uses passive and active heating systems and solar cells to convert solar energy into heat and electricity.

Solar Cells
Active solar cells on the roof generate an electric current. A battery stores energy for night use.

Solar Water Heater
Cool water is pumped from a storage tank to an active solar collector on the roof. Sunlight heats the water in the collector panels. Then the water is returned to the tank. From there it is piped to the different rooms. Air moves over the pipes and is heated.

Passive Interior Heating
Sunlight that passes through the windows is absorbed by the walls and floors and converted to heat. At night shades covering the windows prevent the heat from flowing back outside.

Window Design
Large windows on the south and west sides act as passive solar collectors. They let sunlight enter during the winter. Overhangs shade the windows during the summer.

Backup Heat Source
The house has a wood stove to provide backup heat, especially on cloudy days.

739

Answers to Self-Assessment

Caption Question

Figure 9 The curved shape concentrates the sun's rays by reflecting them toward the center of the dish.

☑ *Checkpoint*

They are made of layers of silicon and other materials. When light hits the cell, electrons move across the layers, producing an electric current.

EXPLORING
a Solar House

After students have reviewed the figure, ask: **Which of these solar systems do you have in your own home?** *(Most students will probably identify the two passive systems, passive interior heating and window design.)* If any students say that their homes are equipped with active solar systems, invite those students to describe the devices and their operation to the rest of the class. **learning modality: verbal**

Real-Life Learning

Materials *2 thermometers, large glass jar*
Time 10 minutes

Give students an opportunity to directly observe passive solar heating. On a sunny day, take the class outdoors to a place that receives direct sunlight, but away from pavement. Have students read the two thermometers and note the temperatures. Then put one thermometer in an upside-down glass jar and the other thermometer in open air. Have students compare the temperatures after several minutes. Ask: **Why is the temperature higher inside the glass jar?** *(The glass allows light to pass into the jar but traps heat inside the jar.)* **learning modality: logical/mathematical**

Ongoing Assessment

Oral Presentation Call on students at random to each describe one example of technology that captures solar energy for use by people.

Capturing the Wind

Using the Visuals: Figure 10

Tell students that people have used windmills for over a thousand years. Display a photograph of a large "old-fashioned" windmill, and have students compare it with the modern windmills shown in the photograph. Ask: **How are modern windmills different from old windmills?** *(Modern windmills are more streamlined, do not have a building as the base, have fewer blades, and the blades are metal instead of wood.)* **Why do you think wind farms use streamlined windmills like these instead of the old-fashioned type?** *(Modern windmills are stronger and also more sensitive to light winds.)* Encourage interested students to find out about the history and technology of windmills. **learning modality: visual**

The Power of Flowing Water

Social Studies
CONNECTION

Use Figure 11 to help students understand how a water wheel is used to capture energy. Ask: **What energy conversion takes place at the mill?** *(Kinetic energy is converted to mechanical energy.)*

In Your Journal Remind students that a news story focuses on factual information, particularly the "five Ws"—*Who, What, Where, When,* and *Why.* Divide the class into groups of three to write the stories, with each student writing about one of the three topics mentioned in the text. Have groups share their stories by reading them aloud. **cooperative learning**

Figure 10 This wind farm in the Mojave Desert is one of many in the state of California. *Making Generalizations What are some advantages of wind power?*

Capturing the Wind

The sun is one source of renewable energy. **Other renewable sources of energy include wind, water, tides, biomass material, Earth's interior, and hydrogen.**

Wind energy is actually an indirect form of solar energy. The sun heats Earth's surface unevenly. As a result of this uneven heating, different areas of the atmosphere have different temperatures and air pressure. The differences in pressure cause winds as air moves from one area to another.

Wind can be used to turn a turbine and generate electricity. Wind power plants or "wind farms" consist of many windmills. Together, the windmills generate large amounts of power.

Although wind now provides less than one percent of the world's electricity, it is the fastest-growing energy source. Wind energy is free and does not cause pollution. In places where fuels are difficult to transport, such as Antarctica, wind energy is the major source of power. In the remote grasslands of Mongolia, electricity is obtained from more than 70,000 wind turbines.

Wind energy is not ideal for all locations. Few places have winds that blow steadily enough to be a worthwhile energy source. Wind generators are noisy and can be destroyed by very strong winds. But as fossil fuels become more scarce and expensive, wind generators will become more important.

✓ *Checkpoint* How can wind be used to generate electricity?

The Power of Flowing Water

Solar energy is also the indirect source of water power. Recall that in the water cycle, energy from the sun heats water on Earth's surface, forming water vapor. The water vapor condenses and falls back to Earth as rain and snow. As the water flows over the land into lakes and oceans, it provides another source of energy.

740

Background

History of Science The first known windmills were used in Persia (now Iran) in the seventh century A.D. By the twelfth century, their use had spread throughout Europe. They were used for irrigation and to grind grain. In the late 1800s, thousands of windmills were in use in the rural United States.

Flowing water can turn a turbine and generate electricity in the same way as steam or wind. A dam across a river blocks the flow of water, creating an artificial lake called a reservoir. Water flows through tunnels at the bottom of the dam. As the water moves through the tunnels, it turns turbines connected to a generator.

Hydroelectric power is electricity produced by flowing water. This type of power is the most widely used source of renewable energy in the world today. Once a dam and power plant are built, producing the electricity is inexpensive. Another benefit is that hydroelectric power does not create air pollution. Unlike wind or solar energy, flowing water provides a steady supply of energy.

But hydroelectric power does have limitations. In the United States, for example, most of the suitable rivers have already been dammed. And dams can have negative effects on the environment. You can read more about the pros and cons of hydroelectric dams in *Science and Society* on page 746.

Tidal Energy

Another source of moving water is the tides. The gravity of the moon and sun causes the water on Earth's surface to regularly rise and fall on its shores. Along some coastlines, enormous amounts of water move into bays at the high tide. The water flows out to sea again when the tide goes out.

A few tidal power plants have been built to take advantage of this regular motion. A low dam across the entrance to a shallow bay holds water in the bay at high tide. As the tide goes out, water flowing past turbines in the dam generate electricity, as in a hydroelectric power plant.

Only a few coastal areas in the world are suitable for building tidal power plants. A dam across a bay also blocks boats and fish from traveling up the river. For these reasons, tidal power will probably never become a major source of energy.

☑ *Checkpoint* *How are tidal power plants similar to hydroelectric power plants? How are they different?*

Figure 11 Flowing water provides the power to turn the water wheel of this historic mill in Tennessee.

Social Studies CONNECTION

Early settlers in the eastern United States often built mills along streams. The mills captured the power of flowing water at dams or waterfalls, where the water turned water wheels connected to machines. Saw mills sawed logs into boards, and grist mills ground wheat into flour. A mill site often formed the center of a new town.

In Your Journal

Suppose you are writing a news story about an old mill. Describe the mill's early importance to the settlers, how a town grew up around it, and how it is used today.

Building Inquiry Skills: Making Models

Materials *large, empty thread spool; 8 self-adhesive index tabs or duct tape and tabs cut from heavy acetate; unsharpened pencil or dowel*
Time 15 minutes

Let students make model waterwheels by attaching tabs around the outside of a thread spool with the tabs parallel to the spool's axis. They can insert a pencil through the spool's hole, making sure the spool turns freely. Allow students to test their waterwheels under a running faucet. Holding the wheel above the stream so the water hits the lower tabs demonstrates an "undershot" waterwheel. Holding the wheel below the stream so the water hits the upper tabs demonstrates an "overshot" wheel. The water-driven turbines used in hydroelectric power plants today are more complicated—and much more efficient— than old waterwheels, but they operate in much the same way. **learning modality: kinesthetic**

Tidal Energy

Real-Life Learning

If students live in or have visited a coastal area, invite them to describe what they have seen and felt as tides moved in and out. Prompt their descriptions by asking questions such as the following: **How far did the waterline move from low tide to high tide?** *(Answers will vary.)* **What did the water flow feel like to you when the tide was coming in or going out?** *(Answers will vary, but students should be able to describe feeling the force of the water against their legs or bodies.)* Point out that it is this force of moving water that is tapped by tidal power plants. **learning modality: verbal**

Ongoing Assessment

Writing Have each student describe one advantage of water power over wind power in generating electricity.

Answers to Self-Assessment

Caption Question
Figure 10 The wind itself doesn't cost anything and is renewable; wind power is available in remote places where it would be difficult to transport fossil fuels.

Answers to Self-Assessment

☑ *Checkpoint*
p. 740: Wind can be used to turn a turbine.
p. 741: Both use moving water as the energy source and have turbines that generate electricity. A hydroelectric plant uses fresh water in a river or stream; a tidal plant uses ocean tides. Hydroelectric plants are built on rivers; tidal plants are built in bays.

Biomass Fuels

Building Inquiry Skills: Predicting

Ask students: **Would burning wood or plant wastes in an open fire be a good way to make use of biomass fuels? Why, or why not?** *(No; open burning allows heat to escape and releases pollutants into the atmosphere.)* **How do you think biomass materials must be burned in order to be efficient and nonpolluting fuels?** *(In some sort of closed incinerator that captures harmful waste products and captures all or most of the heat)* **What else would have to be part of the equipment to generate electricity with the heat of the burning fuel?** *(Water to make steam to drive a turbine)* **learning modality: logical/mathematical**

Including All Students

For students who need help with language skills, write the two words on the board, draw boxes around *gas* in *gasoline* and *ohol* in *alcohol,* draw a plus sign between the two boxes, and ask: **What word do these two parts make when you put them together?** *(gasohol)* **limited English proficiency**

Biomass Fuels

The oldest fuel used for heat and light is wood. As trees carry out photosynthesis, they use the sun's energy to convert carbon dioxide and water into more complicated molecules. Burning wood breaks down these molecules again and releases energy.

Wood is one of a group of fuels, called **biomass fuels,** made from living things. Other biomass fuels include leaves, food wastes, and even manure. As fossil fuel supplies shrink, people are taking a closer look at biomass fuels. For instance, when oil prices rose in the early 1970s, Hawaiian sugar-cane farmers thought of a way to use sugar-cane wastes. They began burning the wastes to generate electricity instead of discarding the wastes in landfills. Now almost one fourth of the electricity used on the island of Kauai comes from biomass material.

Biomass materials can be also converted into other fuels. For example, corn, sugar cane, and other crops can be used to make alcohol. Adding the alcohol to gasoline forms a mixture called **gasohol.** Gasohol can be used as fuel for cars. When bacteria decompose wastes, they convert the wastes into methane gas. The methane produced in some landfills is used to heat buildings.

Alcohol and methane are renewable resources. But producing them in large quantities is more expensive than using fossil fuels. And though wood is renewable, it takes time for new trees to grow and replace those that have been cut down. As a result, biomass fuels are not widely used today in the United States. But as fossil fuels become scarcer, biomass fuels may play a larger role in meeting energy needs.

Figure 12 This corn field is a rich source of biomass fuel. After the corn is harvested, the stalks and leaves can be burned to provide energy. *Comparing and Contrasting How are biomass fuels similar to energy sources such as wind and water? How are these fuels different?*

742

Background

Facts and Figures Besides reducing our dependence on fossil fuels, using biomass fuels helps reduce our waste-disposal problems. In one case in California, the Mesquite Lake Resource Recovery Project, an electric power plant burns cow manure to produce enough electricity for thousands of homes. The manure would otherwise pose a disposal problem because of its high salt content and the presence of seeds that make it undesirable for use as fertilizer.

Some problems are associated with the use of biomass materials. Growing the crops often used as biomass fuels takes up land that could be used for growing food crops. And removing all the stalks, leaves, and roots from a field for use as biomass fuel means that these crop wastes will not decay and enrich the soil. Unprotected soil is also more susceptible to erosion.

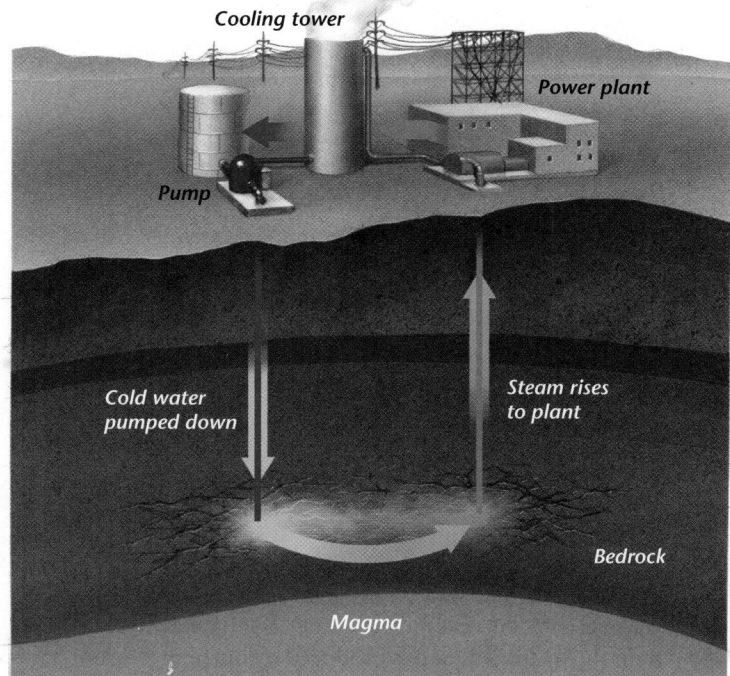

Figure 13 A geothermal power plant uses heat from Earth's interior as an energy source. Cold water is piped deep into the ground, where it is heated by magma. The resulting steam can be used for heat or to generate electricity.

Cooling tower

Power plant

Pump

Cold water pumped down

Steam rises to plant

Bedrock

Magma

Tapping Earth's Energy

Below Earth's surface are pockets of very hot, liquid rock called magma. In some places, magma is found very close to the surface. It may even erupt out of the ground as volcanic lava. The intense heat from Earth's interior that warms the magma is called **geothermal energy.**

In certain regions, such as Iceland and New Zealand, the magma heats underground water to the boiling point. The hot water and steam are valuable sources of energy. In Reykjavik, Iceland, 90 percent of homes are heated by water warmed underground in this way. Geothermal energy can also be used to generate electricity, as shown in Figure 13.

Geothermal energy is an unlimited source of cheap energy. But it has disadvantages, just like every other energy source. There are only a few places where magma comes close to Earth's surface. Elsewhere, a very deep well is required to tap this energy. Drilling deep wells is very expensive. Even so, geothermal energy is likely to play a part in meeting energy needs in the future.

☑ *Checkpoint* *How can geothermal energy be used to generate electricity?*

Using the Visuals: Figure 13

Have students work in pairs to create cycle diagrams of the process shown in the figure. Ask: **What do you think the cooling tower is used for?** (*After the steam has been used to turn turbines in the power plant, it is cooled to turn it into liquid water.*) **learning modality: visual**

Including All Students

Support students who need more help in comprehending the term *geothermal*. Write the term *geothermal* on the board and draw a vertical line between the two word parts. Invite volunteers to look up the meaning of each part in a dictionary and read the meanings aloud (*geo*, "Earth"; *thermal*, "heat"). Ask: **What does "geothermal" mean?** (*Earth-heat, or heat inside Earth*) **limited English proficiency**

Hydrogen Power

Demonstration

Materials *electrolysis apparatus, matches*
Time 10 minutes

 Use an electrolysis apparatus to show students that hydrogen can be obtained by passing an electric current through water. (If you are not familiar with the electrolysis setup and procedure, ask a physical science teacher to show you or to do the demonstration for the class.) At the end of the demonstration, emphasize that more energy is used in producing the electricity needed for electrolysis than is provided by the hydrogen. **learning modality: visual**

Answers to Self-Assessment

Caption Question

Figure 12 They all derive their energy from the sun and are renewable. Using biomass materials to produce alcohol and methane is expensive, and though they are renewable, it takes time for them to grow.

☑ *Checkpoint*

Geothermal energy can be used to produce steam to turn a turbine.

Ongoing Assessment

Writing Have each student briefly describe the two different ways in which biomass materials can be used as fuels.

 Students can save their work in their portfolios.

Section 2 Review Answers

1. Energy from the sun
2. Winds are created by uneven heating of the atmosphere by the sun. Flowing water is part of the water cycle, which is driven by the sun's energy.
3. Active solar systems convert solar energy to thermal energy and then use fans and pumps to distribute the heat. Passive solar systems convert solar energy to thermal energy but do not distribute it.
4. *Any three:* wood, leaves, food wastes, manure, sugar-cane wastes, corn, alcohol, methane
5. Geothermal energy is available only where magma is close to Earth's surface.
6. Accept a variety of responses. Students should support their answers with reasons that take into account the geographic features of their area.

Check Your Progress
CHAPTER PROJECT 23

Check each group's data table to make sure students are collecting and recording data. Provide some copies of the school's fuel and utility bills so students can determine the amount and actual cost of each type of energy used. If a group is studying energy used for transportation, encourage them to survey other students about transportation to school. They also may need to contact your district's central office or the private company that owns and operates the school buses for information.

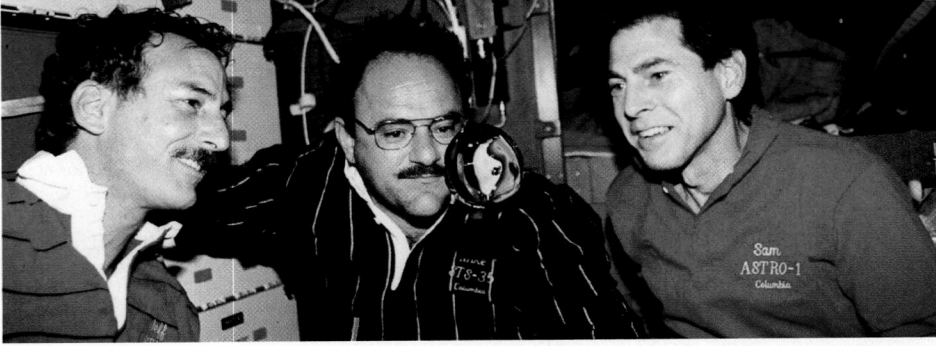

Figure 14 The object fascinating these three astronauts is a bubble of water—the harmless by-product of the hydrogen fuel cells used on the space shuttle.

Hydrogen Power

Now that you have read about so many energy sources, consider a fuel with this description: It burns cleanly, forming only water as a by-product. It creates no smoke, smog, or acid rain. It can be handled and transported through pipelines, much like natural gas. This fuel exists on Earth in large supply.

This ideal-sounding fuel is real—it's hydrogen. However, there is an obstacle. Almost all the hydrogen on Earth is combined with oxygen in the form of water. Pure hydrogen can be obtained by passing an electric current through water. But it takes more energy to obtain the hydrogen than is produced by burning it again.

Scientists aren't ruling out hydrogen as a good fuel for the future. At present, hydroelectric plants decrease their activity when the demand for electricity is low. Instead, they could run at full power all the time, using the excess electricity to produce hydrogen. Similarly, solar power plants often generate more electricity than is needed during the day. This extra electricity could be used to produce hydrogen. If a way can be found to produce hydrogen cheaply, it could someday be an important source of energy.

Section 2 Review

1. What is solar energy?
2. How are the energy of wind and flowing water each related to solar energy?
3. How are active and passive solar heating systems different?
4. List three examples of biomass fuels.
5. What limits the use of geothermal energy?
6. **Thinking Critically** **Predicting** Which of the renewable sources of energy do you think is most likely to be used in your community in 100 years? Give reasons to support your answer.

Check Your Progress
CHAPTER PROJECT 23

Continue to collect data on how much energy is used in your group's area of the school. Begin to brainstorm ideas for reducing energy usage in this area. For example, is there a way to use some electrical devices for shorter periods of time? (*Hint:* Interviewing some adults who are responsible for the operation of the school building may give you some good ideas. Be sure to check with your teacher before interviewing anyone.)

Performance Assessment

Skills Check Have each student create a compare/contrast table that includes at least five of the renewable energy sources discussed in this section and identifies one advantage and one disadvantage of each source.

Portfolio Students can save their tables in their portfolios.

Program Resources

◆ **Unit 6 Resources** 23-2 Review and Reinforce, p. 91; 23-2 Enrich, p. 92

Cooking With Sunshine

In the future, will you cook your meals with sunshine instead of electricity? That's certainly a possibility. In this lab, you'll investigate how solar energy can be used to cook food.

Problem

What is the best shape for a solar cooker?

Skills Focus

predicting, designing experiments, forming operational definitions

Suggested Materials

scissors	glue	3 thermometers
3 dowels	tape	marshmallows
3 sheets of aluminum foil		clock or watch
3 sheets of oaktag paper		

Procedure

Part 1 Capturing Solar Energy

1. Read over the entire lab. Then predict which shape will produce the largest temperature increase when placed in the sun.
2. Glue a sheet of aluminum foil, shiny side up, to each sheet of oaktag paper. Before the glue dries, gently smooth out any wrinkles in the foil.
3. Bend one sheet into a V shape. Bend another sheet into a U shape. Leave the last sheet flat.
4. Place the aluminum sheets in direct sunlight, using wood blocks or books to hold the U- and V-shapes in position.
5. Tape a dowel to each thermometer. Record the starting temperature on each thermometer.
6. Use the dowels to hold the thermometer bulbs in the center of the aluminum shapes. After 15 minutes, record the final temperature on each thermometer.

Part 2 Designing a Solar Cooker

7. Use the results from Step 6 to design a solar cooker that can toast a marshmallow. Prepare a written description of your plan for your teacher's approval. Include an operational definition of a "well-toasted" marshmallow.
8. After your teacher has approved your plan, test your design by placing a marshmallow on a wooden dowel. Record the time it takes to toast the marshmallow.

Analyze and Conclude

1. What was the role of the aluminum foil in this investigation? What other materials could you have used instead? Explain.
2. Which of the three shapes—V, U, or flat—produced the largest increase in temperature? Propose an explanation for this result.
3. What other variables might have affected your results? Explain.
4. **Apply** What are some possible advantages of a solar cooker based on this design? What are some possible disadvantages?

More to Explore

Try adapting your design to heat water. Show your new design to your teacher before trying it.

Extending the Inquiry

More to Explore Have students use a small volume of water. Encourage them to consider the kind of material to use for the water container.

Safety

Students should wear safety goggles and use caution in handling glass thermometers. Review the safety guidelines in Appendix A.

Program Resources

◆ **Unit 6 Resources** Real-World Lab blackline masters, pp. 101–102

Media and Technology

 Lab Activity Videotape
Tape 5

Real-World Lab

How It Works

Cooking With Sunshine

Preparing for Inquiry

Key Concept A solar cooker that focuses the sun's rays in its center works best.
Skills Objectives Students will be able to
◆ predict which of three designs will produce the greatest temperature increase in a solar cooker;
◆ design an experiment to test how the shape of a solar cooker affects how it functions;
◆ form an operational definition of a "well-toasted" marshmallow.
Time 40 minutes
Advance Planning Identify a sunny area for the solar cookers.

Guiding Inquiry

Introducing the Procedure
◆ Have students work in groups of three.
◆ If needed, review the meaning of "operational definition."

Troubleshooting the Experiment
◆ In Step 3, make sure students have the foil side on the inside of the U or V.
◆ In Step 6, make sure students hold the thermometers with their bulbs at the same distance from the foil.

Expected Outcome
Specific temperatures will vary, but the U-shaped cooker should produce the largest temperature increase and the flat cooker the smallest increase.

Analyze and Conclude
1. The foil reflected the sun's rays. Other reflective materials such as mirrors or shiny metal could be used.
2. The U shape; it reflects the sun's rays into the center of the cooker.
3. Variables include time of day, distance between the thermometer bulbs and the cookers' surface, and air movement.
4. *Advantages:* simple design, ease of use, inexpensive, no polluting fumes. *Disadvantages:* cannot be used on a cloudy day or at night; slow; not efficient for cooking large items.

Hydroelectric Dams: Are They All Here to Stay?

Purpose
Evaluate the benefits and costs of removing hydroelectric dams, and recommend removing, adapting, or relicensing a dam.

Role-Play

Time 40 minutes

- After students have read the feature, ask: **Why should people try to protect fish species?** (*Accept a variety of reasons, including the economic value of commercial fishing.*) **Why are hydroelectric dams an important source of energy?** (*They reduce use of fossil fuels, produce electricity at low cost, and don't cause pollution.*)
- Point out that there are *three* possible recommendations: relicense the dam, remove it, or find ways to enable fish to bypass it. Let students discuss the issue freely.
- Divide the class into small groups, with each group member representing a different viewpoint—for example, the company that owns the dam, local industries that rely on the electricity produced by the dam, fisheries, ecologists, and citizens. Provide time for the groups to discuss the options.

Extend Suggest that students research the costs of electricity produced by hydroelectric dams and by burning fossil fuels. They could also investigate the effectiveness of fish ladders.

You Decide

- Students' answers to Identify the Problem and Analyze the Options should use the points in the text.
- In response to Find a Solution, students may rely on issues raised in their discussions or present new ideas. Each student should give a well-reasoned rationale for his or her recommendation.

Hydroelectric Dams: Are They All Here to Stay?

There are hundreds of hydroelectric dams on United States rivers. These dams provide electricity for millions of people. Hydroelectric dams provide clean, inexpensive, and renewable energy. They are a good source of power.

Recently, however, people have learned that dams can have negative effects on river ecosystems. Some people have even suggested removing certain dams. But is this wise? When do the benefits of dams outweigh the problems?

The Issues

How Do Dams Affect the Environment? Because dams change water depth and flow, they can alter the temperature of a river. The water may become too cold or too warm for fish that normally live there. A change in temperature can also reduce the number of algae in a river. This affects other organisms in the river food web.

Some species of fish, such as salmon, herring, and menhaden, hatch in rivers but then travel to the ocean. To breed, they must return to the river. Dams can block the movement of these fish populations. For example, the Columbia River Basin, which has more than 50 dams, once contained more than 10 million salmon. Today it is home to only 2 million salmon.

What Are the Effects of Removing Dams? Some people say that the only way to restore ecosystems is to remove dams. However, these dams supply a small but important part of the nation's electricity. Removing them could force the United States to use more nonrenewable fossil fuels. Fossil fuels also produce more pollution than hydroelectric plants.

The reservoirs behind hydroelectric dams supply water for irrigation and drinking. These supplies would be difficult to replace. In addition, a series of dams on a river can reduce flooding downstream during heavy rains.

What Can People Do? Removing dams might restore some river ecosystems. For example, Edwards Dam on the Kennebec River in Maine was removed in 1999 to allow several threatened fish species to spawn. Edwards Dam provided only a small percent of Maine's electric power. This small amount was easier to replace than the power provided by a much larger dam.

There are other ways to protect migrating fish. Fish ladders, for example, are step-like waterways that help fish pass over dams. Fish can even be carried around dams in trucks. Still, these methods are costly and not always successful.

The government issues licenses for hydroelectric dams. In considering license renewals, officials examine environmental impact as well as energy production.

You Decide

1. Identify the Problem
In your own words, explain some of the major issues surrounding hydroelectric dams.

2. Analyze the Options
Examine the pros and cons of removing dams. What are the benefits? What are the costs? Who will be affected by the change?

3. Find a Solution
The license of a nearby dam is up for review. The dam provides electricity, but also blocks the migration of fish. What do you recommend? Explain.

Background

History of Science In November 1997, the Federal Energy Regulatory Commission for the first time refused to renew the license for a hydroelectric dam—the Edwards Dam on the Kennebec River in Maine. The dam produced only a very small amount of electricity, but prevented salmon and other anadromous fish, which travel up river, from spawning in the river.

The owners of hydroelectric dams upstream on the Kennebec contributed millions of dollars toward the costs of removing the dam and restoring 17 miles of spawning grounds in exchange for having their deadlines extended to install fish ladders on the upstream dams.

SECTION 3 Nuclear Energy

DISCOVER .... ACTIVITY

Why Do They Fall?

1. Line up 15 dominoes to form a triangle, as shown.

2. Knock over the first domino so that it falls against the second row of dominoes. Observe the results.

3. Set up the dominoes again, but then remove the dominoes in the third row from the lineup.

4. Knock over the first domino again. Observe what happens.

Think It Over

Inferring Suppose each domino produced a large amount of energy when it fell over. Why might it be helpful to remove the dominoes as you did in Step 3?

Wouldn't it be great if people could use the same method as the sun to produce energy? In a way, they can! The kind of reactions that power the sun involve the central cores of atoms. The central core of an atom that contains the protons and neutrons is called the **nucleus** (plural nuclei). The reactions that involve nuclei, called nuclear reactions, involve tremendous amounts of energy. Two types of nuclear reactions are fission and fusion.

Fission Reactions and Energy

Nuclear reactions convert matter into energy. In 1905, Albert Einstein developed a formula that described the relationship between energy and matter. You have probably seen this famous equation, $E = mc^2$. In the equation, the E represents energy and the m represents mass. The c, which represents the speed of light, is a very large number. This equation states that when matter is changed into energy, an enormous amount of energy is released.

Nuclear fission is the splitting of an atom's nucleus into two smaller nuclei. The fuel for the reaction is a large atom that has an unstable nucleus, such as uranium-235 (U-235). A neutron is shot at the U-235 atom at high speed. **When the neutron hits the U-235 nucleus, the nucleus splits apart into two smaller nuclei and two or more neutrons.** The total mass of all these particles is a bit less than the mass of the original nucleus. The small amount of mass that makes up the difference has been converted into energy—a lot of energy, as described by Einstein's equation.

GUIDE FOR READING

◆ What happens during fission and fusion reactions?

◆ How does a nuclear power plant produce electricity?

Reading Tip As you read, create a Venn diagram to compare and contrast nuclear fission and nuclear fusion.

Figure 15 Albert Einstein, shown here in 1930, described the relationship between energy and matter.

747

SECTION 3 Nuclear Energy

Objectives

After completing the lesson, students will be able to

◆ describe nuclear fission and nuclear fusion reactions;

◆ explain how a nuclear power plant produces electricity.

Key Terms nucleus, nuclear fission, reactor vessel, fuel rods, control rods, meltdown, nuclear fusion

1 Engage/Explore

Activating Prior Knowledge

Ask several students to come to the board, draw what they think an atom looks like, and label its parts. Encourage the rest of the class to discuss the drawings and suggest corrections or additions. You can return to the diagrams later in the section.

.... DISCOVER ....

Skills Focus inferring
Materials *15 dominoes*
Time 10 minutes
Tips Make sure students place the dominoes with less than a domino-length space between rows.
Expected Outcome In Step 2, all 15 dominoes will topple as those in one row fall back against those in the next row. With the third row removed in Step 4, the last two rows will remain standing.
Think It Over Removing the third row would stop the production of energy after a certain point.

READING STRATEGIES

Reading Tip Review the format of a Venn diagram: two overlapping circles with likenesses noted in the overlap area and differences noted in the outer areas.

Vocabulary To help students differentiate between fission and fusion, explain that the term *fusion* comes from the root "fuse." Ask students to explain what it means to fuse things together.

Program Resources

◆ **Unit 6 Resources** 23-3 Lesson Plan, p. 93; 23-3 Section Summary, p. 94

◆ **Guided Reading and Study Workbook** Section 23-3

2 Facilitate

Fission Reactions and Energy

Building Inquiry Skills: Making Models

Materials *sheet of paper*
Time 5 minutes

Give each student a sheet of paper, and tell the class to think of the paper as the nucleus of a U-235 atom. To model the nucleus splitting into two smaller nuclei and three neutrons, have students tear the paper into five pieces—two larger and three smaller—and label the two larger pieces "smaller nucleus" and the three smaller pieces "neutron." Then have students tear a tiny piece off each "smaller nucleus" and set these tiny pieces aside. Explain that the tiny pieces represent the tiny amount of matter that is converted into energy in a fission reaction. **learning modality: kinesthetic**

TRY THIS

Skills Focus making models
Materials *12 marbles*
Time 10 minutes
Tips Caution students not to walk around during this activity so they do not step on the marbles.
Expected Outcome The single marble represents a neutron being shot at an atom's nucleus. When it strikes the cluster, it scatters the marbles, similar to the breaking apart of the nucleus when it is struck by a neutron.
Extend After students have read about nuclear fusion on pages 750–751, challenge them to adapt this activity to model fusion. **learning modality: kinesthetic**

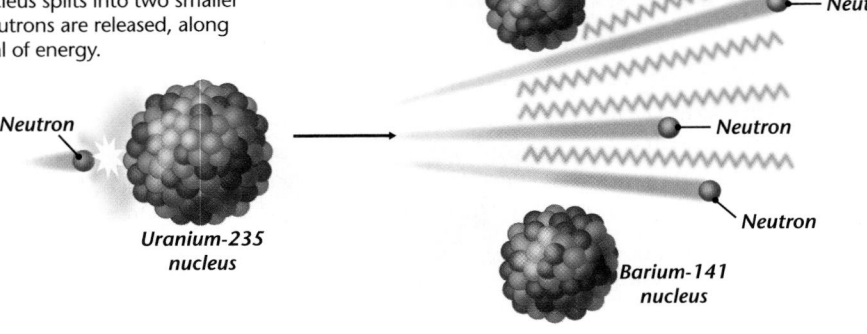

Figure 16 In a nuclear fission reaction, a neutron "bullet" strikes a U-235 nucleus. As a result, the nucleus splits into two smaller nuclei. More neutrons are released, along with a great deal of energy.

Shoot the Nucleus

In an open area of your classroom, make a model of a nuclear fission reaction. Place a handful of marbles on the floor in a tight cluster, so that they touch one another. Step back about a half-meter from the marbles. Shoot another marble at the cluster.

Making Models What does the marble you shot at the cluster represent? What effect did the marble have on the cluster? How is this similar to a nuclear fission reaction?

748

Meanwhile, the fission reaction has produced three more neutrons. If any of these neutrons strikes another nucleus, the fission reaction is repeated. More neutrons and more energy are released. If there are enough nuclei nearby, the process continues over and over in a chain reaction, just like a row of dominoes falling. In a nuclear chain reaction, the amount of energy released increases rapidly with each step in the chain.

What happens to all the energy released by these fission reactions? If a nuclear chain reaction is not controlled, the released energy causes a huge explosion. The explosion of an atomic bomb is an uncontrolled nuclear reaction. A few kilograms of matter explode with more force than several thousand tons of a nonnuclear explosive such as dynamite. However, if the chain reaction is controlled, the energy is released as heat, which can be used to generate electricity.

Nuclear Power Plants

Controlled nuclear fission reactions take place inside nuclear power plants. **In a nuclear power plant, the heat released from the reactions is used to change water into steam. As in other types of power plants, the steam then turns the blades of a turbine to generate electricity.** Look at the diagram of a nuclear power plant in Figure 17. In addition to the generator, it has two main parts: the reactor vessel and the heat exchanger.

Reactor Vessel The **reactor vessel** is the section of a nuclear reactor where nuclear fission occurs. The reactor contains rods of U-235, called **fuel rods.** When several fuel rods are placed close together, a series of fission reactions occurs. The reactions are controlled by placing **control rods** made of the metal cadmium between the fuel rods. The cadmium absorbs the neutrons

---

Background

Integrating Science Investigation of the Chernobyl accident revealed two basic causes. First, the reactor was not housed in a containment building and was extremely unstable at low power. This type of reactor is not used commercially in North America or Western Europe because nuclear engineers consider it too unsafe. Second, many of the plant's operators lacked scientific or technical expertise and made major errors when dealing with the initial problem.

The long-term health effects of the Chernobyl disaster are still being studied. Increases in birth defects and thyroid cancer in children have been documented. Other cancers are not expected to increase until 20 or more years after the accident.

released during the fission reactions. As the cadmium control rods are removed, the fission reactions speed up. If the reactor vessel starts to get too hot, the control rods are moved back in place to slow the chain reaction.

Heat Exchanger Heat is removed from the reactor vessel by water or another fluid that is pumped through the reactor. This fluid passes through a heat exchanger. There, the fluid boils water to produce steam, which runs the electrical generator. The steam is condensed again and pumped back to the heat exchanger.

☑ *Checkpoint* *How are fission reactions controlled?*

The Risks of Nuclear Fission

When it was first demonstrated, people thought that nuclear fission would provide an almost unlimited source of clean, safe energy. Today nuclear power plants generate much of the world's electricity—about 20 percent in the United States and more than 70 percent in France. But these plants have some problems.

In 1986, in Chernobyl, Ukraine, the reactor vessel in a nuclear power plant overheated. The fuel rods generated so much heat that they started to melt, a condition called a **meltdown.** The excess heat increased the steam pressure in the generator. A series of explosions blew parts of the roof off and injured or killed dozens of plant workers and firefighters. Radioactive materials escaped into the environment. Today, the soil in an area the size of Florida remains contaminated with radioactive waste.

Sharpen your Skills

Calculating

A single pellet of U-235 the size of a breath mint can produce as much energy as 615 liters of fuel oil. An average home uses 5,000 liters of oil a year. How many U-235 pellets would be needed to supply the same amount of energy?

Figure 17 In a nuclear plant, uranium fuel undergoes fission, producing heat. The heat boils water, and the resulting steam drives the turbines that generate electricity. *Interpreting Diagrams From which part of the power plant is heat released to the environment?*

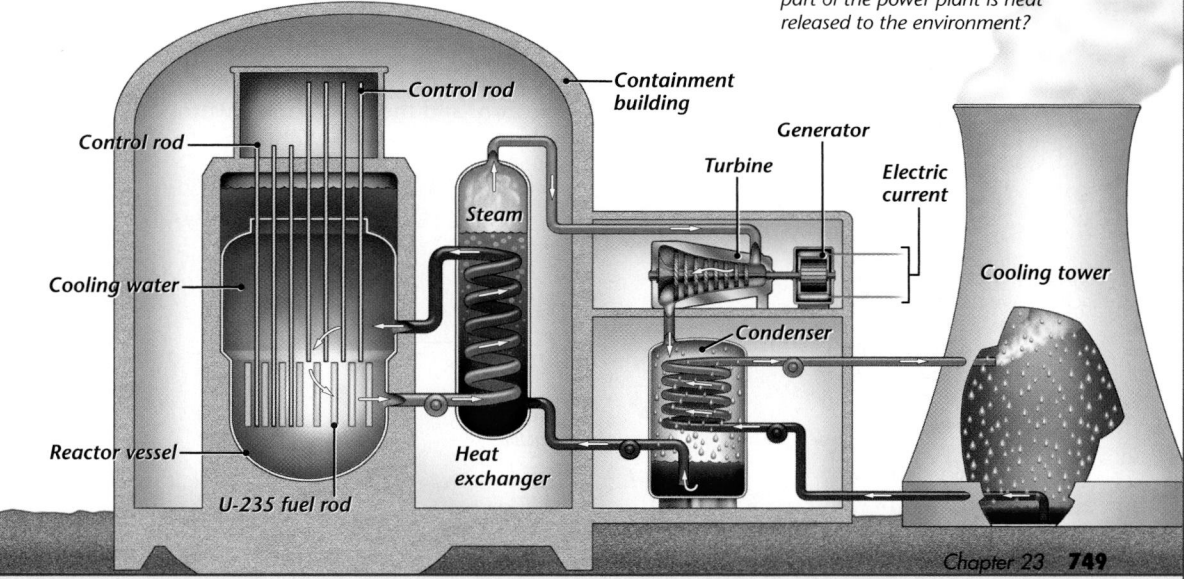

Control rod
Control rod
Containment building
Generator
Turbine
Electric current
Steam
Cooling tower
Cooling water
Condenser
Reactor vessel
Heat exchanger
U-235 fuel rod

Chapter 23 **749**

Answers to Self-Assessment

☑ *Checkpoint*

Fission reactions are controlled by placing cadmium control rods between the fuel rods to absorb neutrons.

Caption Question

Figure 17 The cooling tower

Nuclear Power Plants

Sharpen your Skills

Calculating

Materials *calculator* *(optional)*
Time 5 minutes
Tips If needed, help students determine how to calculate the answer (divide 5,000 by 615).
Expected Outcome About 8 (8.13) pellets would be needed.
Extend Suggest that each student estimate how many homes are in his or her neighborhood, then calculate how many pellets would be needed to supply energy to all those homes for a year.
learning modality: logical/ mathematical

The Risks of Nuclear Fission

Building Inquiry Skills: Inferring

Display a large world map, and let volunteers locate Chernobyl (51°N, 30°E, about 130 km north of Kiev). Tell students that the force of the 1986 explosion carried radioactive materials high into the atmosphere, where they spread across the Northern Hemisphere and then settled back to Earth in what is called "fallout." The heaviest fallout occurred in Ukraine, Belarus, Sweden, Norway, Denmark, France, and Switzerland. In addition, Finland, Lithuania, Germany, Poland, the Czech Republic, Slovakia, Austria, Hungary, Italy, and Great Britain suffered moderate fallout. Let students find all these countries on the map. Ask: **What does this tell you about the dangers of nuclear power plants?** (*An accident can affect a huge area.*) **learning modality: visual**

Ongoing Assessment

Oral Presentation Call on students at random to each explain a step in the process of how a nuclear power plant converts nuclear energy to electricity.

The Risks of Nuclear Fission, continued

Figure 18 One problem with nuclear power is disposal of the used radioactive fuel rods. In this plant in France, the fuel rods are stored in a deep pool of water.

Chernobyl and less-serious accidents at other nuclear power plants have led to public concerns about nuclear plant safety.

The danger of a meltdown is a serious concern. However, a meltdown can be avoided by careful planning. A more difficult problem is the disposal of radioactive wastes produced by power plants. Radioactive wastes remain dangerous for many thousands of years. Scientists must find a way to safely store these wastes for a long period of time. Finally, nuclear power has turned out to be a much more costly source of power than was originally expected. The safety features required for nuclear plants make the plants very expensive.

☑ *Checkpoint* *What are three problems with using nuclear fission as an energy source?*

The Quest to Control Fusion

A second type of nuclear reaction is fusion. **Nuclear fusion** is the combining of two atomic nuclei to produce a single larger nucleus. **As shown in Figure 19, two kinds of hydrogen nuclei are forced together in a fusion reaction.** One kind (hydrogen-2) has one proton and one neutron, and the other kind (hydrogen-3) has one proton and two neutrons. The tremendous heat and pressure

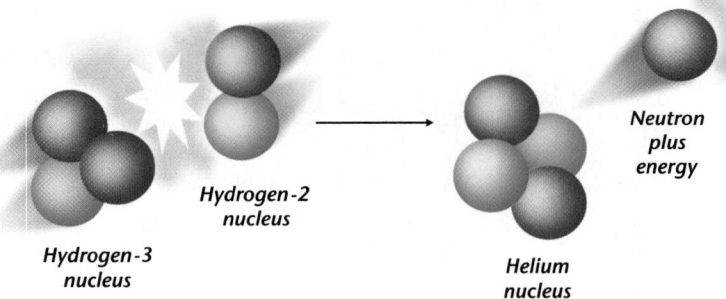

Figure 19 In a nuclear fusion reaction, two nuclei combine to form a single larger nucleus. *Interpreting Diagrams What is released during a fusion reaction?*

Hydrogen-3 nucleus

Hydrogen-2 nucleus

Helium nucleus

Neutron plus energy

cause them to combine and create a helium nucleus with two protons and two neutrons. This helium nucleus has slightly less mass than the total mass of the two hydrogen nuclei. The difference is converted to energy.

Nuclear fusion would have many advantages as an energy source. Fusion can produce much more energy per atom than nuclear fission. The fuel for a nuclear fusion reactor is also readily available. Water, which is plentiful in Earth's oceans, contains one of the kinds of hydrogen needed for fusion. Fusion should be safer and less polluting than nuclear fission. You can see why scientists are eager to find a way to build a nuclear fusion reactor!

Although some fusion bombs have been exploded, scientists have not yet been able to control a large-scale fusion reaction. The biggest problem is temperature. In the sun, nuclear fusion occurs at 15 million degrees Celsius. Such conditions are almost impossible to create on Earth. Very great pressure would also work to contain a fusion reaction. But no material has been found that could serve as a reactor vessel under such high pressure. Extremely powerful magnetic fields can contain a fusion reaction. However, it takes more energy to generate these fields than the fusion reaction produces.

Although many more years of research are expected, some scientists believe that they will eventually be able to control fusion reactions. If they succeed, the quest for a clean, cheap energy source may be over at last.

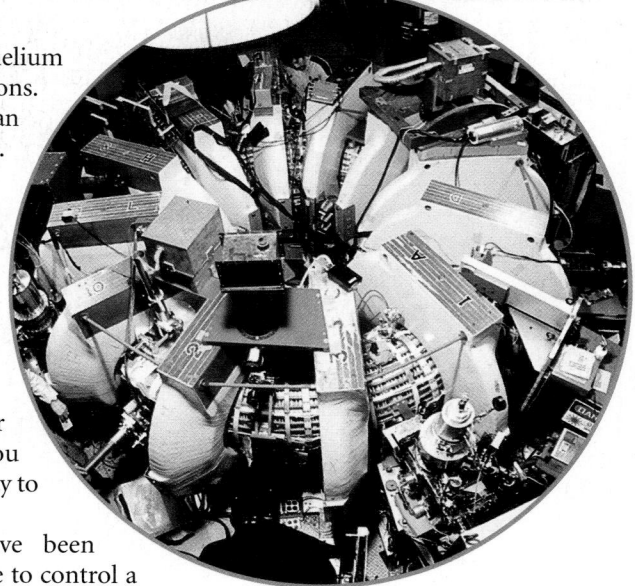

Figure 20 Researchers at Los Alamos National Laboratory in New Mexico are studying fusion as an energy source. This machine creates strong magnetic fields that allow fusion to occur for short periods of time.

Section 3 Review

1. Draw and label a simple diagram of a nuclear fission reaction. Include the following labels: U-235 nucleus, neutrons, smaller nuclei, and energy.
2. How can the energy released in a fission reaction be used to produce electricity?
3. Explain the purpose of control rods.
4. Give two reasons that people have not been able to use nuclear fusion as an energy source.
5. **Thinking Critically Classifying** Is nuclear fission a renewable or nonrenewable energy source? Is nuclear fusion renewable or nonrenewable? Explain.

Check Your Progress CHAPTER PROJECT 23
By now you should begin preparing the written report of your findings about energy use in your group's area of the school. Your report should include the major ways energy is used in your chosen area. You should also include recommendations on how energy use might be reduced.

Section 3 Review Answers

1. Students' diagrams should show the U-235 nucleus being struck by one neutron, then splitting to form two smaller nuclei, three neutrons, and energy. (See Figure 16.)
2. The heat energy released by a fission reaction can be used to boil water, producing steam that turns the blades of a turbine to generate electricity.
3. Control rods absorb excess neutrons and control the fission reactions.
4. Fusion reactions cannot be controlled; more energy is needed to produce a fusion reaction than is produced by the reaction itself.
5. Nuclear fission is considered a nonrenewable resource because it depends on uranium, which is a nonrenewable element. Nuclear fusion is considered a renewable resource because Earth's water is abundant and is renewed in natural processes.

Check Your Progress CHAPTER PROJECT 23
Encourage students to make their reports concise, focusing on the major points and, when appropriate, using visual displays (such as a neat copy of the data table). Also suggest that they explain how each recommendation would reduce energy use.

Program Resources

◆ **Unit 6 Resources** 23-3 Review and Reinforce, p. 95; 23-3 Enrich, p. 96

Media and Technology

 Transparencies Transparencies "Nuclear Fusion," Transparency 93

Answers to Self-Assessment

✓ *Checkpoint*
An accident can cause serious damage, injury, and death. Radioactive wastes are difficult to dispose of safely. Nuclear power is costly.

Caption Question
Figure 19 A neutron plus energy

Performance Assessment

Skills Check Have each student create a table that compares the advantages and disadvantages of nuclear fission and nuclear fusion as energy sources. Students can save their tables in their portfolios.

751

Skills Lab

Designing Experiments

Keeping Comfortable

NOTE: This lab is placed before its related section.

Preparing for Inquiry

Key Concept Different materials lessen the transfer of heat to different degrees.
Skills Objectives Students will be able to
◆ measure temperature changes of water in a paper cup for use as a baseline;
◆ design an experiment to compare how different materials slow heat transfer.
Time 40 minutes
Advance Planning Prepare hot and ice water ahead of time, and keep them in insulated containers. CAUTION: *Do not use water hot enough to cause scalding.*
If using probeware, refer to the *Probeware Lab Manual.*

Guiding Inquiry

Helping Design a Plan
◆ Ask: **What is the purpose of doing Part 1?** (*To determine a standard for comparing materials*)

Troubleshooting the Experiment
◆ Have students discuss the questions in Step 5 before writing their plans.
◆ Make sure students control all variables and record temperatures at regular intervals.

Expected Outcome
Plastic foam is most effective for stopping heat transfer; metal, least effective.

Analyze and Conclude
1. Temperatures will vary. Heat flowed from the hot water to the cold water, as shown by the temperature changes.
2. *Rooms:* cold water; *outdoor weather:* hot water; *walls:* paper cup
3. *Most effective:* plastic foam. *Least effective:* metal. Plastic foam kept the cold water close to its starting temperature for the longest time, while metal let the starting temperature increase the most.
4. Other issues, such as strength, durability, and cost, must be considered.

Skills Lab

Keeping Comfortable

Two ways to use less energy are to keep heat *out* of your home during hot weather, and *in* during cold weather. In this lab, you will investigate how to do this.

Problem

How well do different materials stop heat transfer?

Suggested Materials

watch or clock
beakers
ice water
hot water
thermometers or temperature probes
containers and lids made of paper, plastic foam, plastic, glass, and metal

Design a Plan

Part 1 Measuring Temperature Changes

1. Use a pencil to poke a hole in the lid of a paper cup. Fill the cup about halfway with cold water.
2. Put the lid on the cup. Insert a thermometer into the water through the hole. (If you are using a temperature probe, see your teacher for instructions.) When the temperature stops dropping, place the cup in a beaker. Add hot water to the beaker until the water level is about 1 cm below the lid.
3. Record the water temperature once every minute until it has increased by 5°C. Use the time it takes for the temperature to increase 1°C as a measure of the effectiveness of the paper cup in preventing heat transfer.

Part 2 Comparing Materials

4. Use the ideas from Part 1 to design a controlled experiment to rank the effectiveness of different materials in preventing heat transfer.
5. Use these questions to help you plan your experiment:
   ◆ What hypothesis will you test?
   ◆ Which materials do you predict will be the best and worst at preventing heat transfer?
   ◆ What will your manipulated, responding, and controlled variables be?
   ◆ What step-by-step procedures will you use?
   ◆ What kind of data table will you use?
6. After your teacher has reviewed your plans, make any necessary changes in your design. Then perform your experiment.

Analyze and Conclude

1. In Part 1, what was the starting temperature of the hot water? What was the starting temperature of the cold water? In which direction did the heat flow? How do you know?
2. If the materials in Part 1 are used to represent your home in very hot weather, which material would represent the rooms in your home? The outdoor weather? The building walls?
3. Which material was most effective at preventing the transfer of heat? Which was the least effective? Explain.
4. **Think About It** Would experiments similar to this one provide you with enough information to choose materials to build a home? Explain.

Design an Experiment

Design an experiment to compare how well the materials would work if the hot water were inside the cup and the cold water were outside. With your teacher's permission, carry out your plan.

Extending the Inquiry

Design an Experiment Students' plans should be similar to those they developed in Part 2.

Safety

Students should use caution in handling the thermometers, hot water, and glass containers. Review the safety guidelines in Appendix A.

Program Resources

◆ **Unit 6 Resources** Skills Lab blackline masters, pp. 103–105
◆ **Probeware Lab Manual** Blackline masters

Media and Technology

 Lab Activity Videotape
Tape 5

DISCOVER · ACTIVITY

Which Bulb Is More Efficient?

1. Record the light output (listed in lumens) from the packages of a 60-watt incandescent light bulb and a 15-watt compact fluorescent bulb.

2. [icons] Place the fluorescent bulb in a lamp socket.
   CAUTION: *Make sure the lamp is unplugged.*

3. Plug in the lamp and turn it on. Hold the end of a thermometer about 8 centimeters from the bulb.

4. Record the temperature after 5 minutes.

5. Turn off and unplug the lamp. When the bulb is cool, remove it. Repeat Steps 2, 3, and 4 with the incandescent light bulb.

Think It Over
Inferring The 60-watt bulb uses 4 times more energy than the 15-watt bulb. How does the light output of these bulbs compare with the energy they use? How can the difference in efficiency be explained?

Imagine what would happen if the world ran out of fossil fuels today. Eighty percent of the electric power would disappear. Most buildings would lose their heating and cooling. Forests would disappear as people began to burn wood for heat and cooking. Almost all transportation would stop. Cars, buses, trains, airplanes, and ships would be stranded wherever they ran out of fuel. Since radios, televisions, computers, and telephones depend on electricity, communication would be greatly reduced.

Although fossil fuels won't run out immediately, they also won't last forever. Most people think that it makes sense to start planning now to avoid a fuel shortage in the future. **One approach to the problem is to find new sources of energy. The second way is to make the fuels that are available now last as long as possible while other solutions are being developed.**

Conservation and Efficiency

Reducing energy use is called **energy conservation.** For example, if you walk to the store instead of getting a ride, you are conserving the gasoline needed to drive to the store. Reducing energy use is a solution to energy problems that will help no matter what form of energy is used in the future.

> ### GUIDE FOR READING
>
> ◆ What are two ways to make sure there will be enough energy for the future?
>
> ◆ How does insulation help conserve energy?
>
> *Reading Tip* Before you read, list ways to conserve energy. As you read, add to the list.

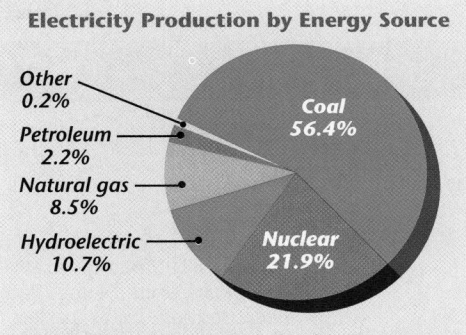

Electricity Production by Energy Source

- Other 0.2%
- Petroleum 2.2%
- Natural gas 8.5%
- Hydroelectric 10.7%
- Coal 56.4%
- Nuclear 21.9%

Figure 21 Nonrenewable fossil fuels generate over two thirds of the nation's electricity.

Chapter 23 **753**

Background

Reading Tip To provide structure and prompt students' thinking, suggest that they list types of energy uses (electricity for lights and appliances, oil or natural gas for heating, gasoline for cars, and so forth) as headings across the top of a page and then list ways to reduce each use below the headings.

Program Resources

◆ **Unit 6 Resources** 23-4 Lesson Plan, p. 97; 23-4 Section Summary, p. 98

◆ **Guided Reading and Study Workbook** Section 23-4

SECTION
4 Energy Conservation

Objectives

After completing the lesson, students will be able to

◆ list two ways to ensure that there will be enough energy for the future;

◆ identify things that individuals can do to conserve energy.

Key Terms energy conservation, efficiency, insulation

1 Engage/Explore

Activating Prior Knowledge

Point out the section's title and ask:
What does the term energy conservation mean? (*Accept all reasonable responses, such as "not wasting energy."*)
What are some examples of wasting energy? (*Setting a thermostat too high, leaving lights on in an unoccupied room, running a dishwasher with only a small load, and the like.*)

· · · · · · · · DISCOVER · · · · · · · ·

Skills Focus inferring
Materials *60-watt incandescent light bulb and 15-watt compact fluorescent light bulb in packages, lamp, thermometer, clock or watch*
Time 20 minutes
CAUTION: *Students should use caution when handling the bulbs and lamp plug.*
Tips Compact fluorescent bulbs, widely available in supermarkets and hardware stores, screw into a regular bulb socket.
Expected Outcome The fluorescent bulb will produce a lower temperature because it converts more electricity to light and less to heat.
Think It Over Light output varies among bulbs. Of a 15-W fluorescent bulb that gives off 825 lumens and a 60-W incandescent bulb that gives off 900 lumens, the fluorescent bulb is about 4 times more efficient (825 lumens/15 W compared to 900 lumens/60 W). The incandescent bulb is less efficient because it converts so much energy into heat.

Conservation and Efficiency

Building Inquiry Skills: Calculating

Materials *packages from 60-watt incandescent light bulb and 15-watt compact fluorescent light bulb, calculator (optional)*
Time 10 minutes

Explain that the number of watts printed on a light bulb and its package tells how much electrical energy is needed to light the bulb for one second (1 watt = 1 joule per second). Have students examine the packages and identify the wattage of each bulb. *(Incandescent bulb 60 watts, fluorescent bulb 15 watts)* Ask: **How many times more electrical energy does the incandescent bulb use to produce the same amount of light as the fluorescent bulb?** *(4 times as much)* **What is the expected life of each bulb?** *(Answers will depend on brands of bulbs used; examples: incandescent bulb 1,000 hours, fluorescent bulb 10,000 hours)* **How many incandescent bulbs would you need to equal the life of one fluorescent bulb?** *(10)* **How much would 10 incandescent bulbs cost compared with the cost of one fluorescent bulb?** *($7.50 [10 × 75¢] compared with $20.00; prices may vary)* **How much more than 10 incandescent bulbs would the fluorescent bulb cost over its life?** *($12.50)* **Do you think the fluorescent bulb is worth its higher cost?** *(Accept all answers at this point.)* **According to the fluorescent bulb's package, how much would you save in electricity costs by using that one bulb instead of 10 incandescent bulbs for 10,000 hours?** *($45.00)* **What would your total savings be over the life of the fluorescent bulb?** *($45.00 − $12.50, or $32.50)* **So which type of bulb is better, and why?** *(The fluorescent bulb, because it costs less in the long term and conserves electricity.)*
learning modality: logical/ mathematical

A way to get as much work as possible out of fuels is to use them efficiently. **Efficiency** is the percentage of energy that is actually used to perform work. The rest of the energy is "lost" to the surroundings, usually as heat. People have developed many ways to increase energy efficiency.

Lighting Lights can use as much as 10 percent of the electricity in your home, but much of that electricity is wasted. An incandescent light bulb converts less than 10 percent of the electricity it uses into light. The rest is given off as heat. You can prove this to yourself by holding your hand close to an incandescent light bulb. But don't touch it! Compact fluorescent bulbs, on the other hand, use only about one fourth as much energy to provide the same amount of light.

✓ *Checkpoint* **Which type of light bulb is more energy-efficient?**

SCIENCE & History

Energy-Efficient Devices

Scientists and engineers have developed many technologies that improve energy efficiency and reduce energy use.

1932 Fiberglass Insulation

Long strands of glass fibers trap air and keep buildings from losing heat. Less fuel is used for heating.

1958 Solar Cells

More than 150 years ago, scientists discovered that silicon can convert light into electricity. The first useful application of solar cells was to power the radio on a satellite. Now solar cells are even used on experimental cars like the one below.

| 1930 | 1940 | 1950 |

1936 Fluorescent Lighting

Fluorescent bulbs were introduced to the public at the 100th anniversary celebration of the United States Patent Office. Because these bulbs use less energy than incandescent bulbs, most offices and schools use fluorescent lights.

754

Background

Facts and Figures Energy-efficient devices like those shown in the timeline have helped conserve energy. For example, "superinsulated" homes can use from 70 to 95 percent less energy for heating than homes with conventional insulation. These homes are surrounded by an "envelope" of insulation and have airtight construction.

Because of lighter materials and designs that reduce air drag, the fuel efficiency of passenger cars has improved dramatically, from an average of 6.8 km/L in 1981 to 9.1 km/L in 1994.

The National Appliance Energy Conservation Act sets energy-efficiency standards for refrigerators, washing machines, water heaters, and other appliances. As a result of this law, refrigerators built in the mid-1990s use more than 80 percent less energy than those built in the early 1980s.

Heating and Cooling One method of increasing the efficiency of heating and cooling systems is insulation. **Insulation** is a layer of material that helps block the transfer of heat between the air inside and outside a building. You have probably seen insulation made of fiberglass, which looks like fluffy pink cotton candy. The mat of thin glass fibers trap air. **This layer of trapped air helps keep the building from losing or gaining heat from the outside.** A layer of fiberglass 15 centimeters thick insulates a room as well as a brick wall 2 meters thick or a stone wall almost 6 meters thick!

Buildings lose a lot of heat around the windows. Look at the windows in your school or home. Was the building built after 1980? Have the windows been replaced recently? If so, you will most likely see two panes of glass with space between them. The air between the panes of glass acts as insulation.

In Your Journal

Design an advertisement for one of the energy-saving inventions described in this time line. The advertisement may be a print, radio, or television ad. Be sure that your advertisement clearly explains the benefits of the invention.

1967
Microwave Ovens

The first countertop microwave oven for the home was introduced. Microwaves cook food by heating the water the food contains. The microwave oven heats only the food, not the air, racks, and oven walls as in a conventional oven. Preheating is also not required, saving even more energy.

1997
Smart Roads

The Department of Transportation demonstrated that cars can be controlled by computers. Sensors built into the road control all the cars, making traffic flow more smoothly. This uses less energy.

| 1970 | 1980 | 1990 | 2000 |

1981
High-Efficiency Window Coatings

Materials that reflect sunlight were first used to coat windows in the early 1980s. This coating reduces the air conditioning needed to keep the inside of the building cool.

Chapter 23 **755**

Answers to Self-Assessment

☑ *Checkpoint*
A compact fluorescent bulb is more energy-efficient.

What You Can Do

Real-Life Learning

Create a class list on the board from students' lists they started if they did the Reading Tip on page 753. Pay particular attention to any ideas that are not covered in the text. Encourage students to copy the list so they can use it in the Science at Home activity below.

learning modality: verbal

3 Assess

Section 4 Review Answers

1. Find new sources of energy, and make the fuels we have now last as long as possible.

2. Insulation traps air so heat is not lost to the outside in cold weather and is kept outside in hot weather, reducing use of the building's heating and cooling systems.

3. Several people sharing one car uses less fuel than each person driving separately.

4. The building with only incandescent lights has higher energy bills because incandescent bulbs are less energy-efficient than fluorescent bulbs; most of the electrical energy used by incandescent bulbs is converted to heat, not light.

Science at Home

Encourage students to look for simple energy-saving ideas that they and their family members can implement easily and inexpensively—for example, wrapping an older, less efficient water heater with an insulating material rather than replacing the heater.

ACTIVITY

Performance Assessment

Oral Presentation Have each student describe one energy-saving idea that he or she will take responsibility for implementing at home.

Figure 22 A single city bus can transport dozens of people, reducing the number of cars on the roads and saving energy. *Applying Concepts How does riding a bus conserve energy?*

Transportation Engineers have improved the energy efficiency of cars by designing better engines and tires. Another way to save energy is to reduce the number of cars on the road. In many communities, public transit systems provide an alternative to driving. Other cities encourage carpooling. If four people travel together in one car, they use much less energy than they would by driving separately. Many cities now set aside lanes for cars containing two or more people.

In the future, cars that run on electricity may provide the most energy savings of all. Electric power plants can convert fuel into electricity more efficiently than a car engine converts gasoline into motion. Therefore, a car that runs on electricity is more energy-efficient than one that runs directly on fuel.

What You Can Do

You can reduce your personal energy use by changing your behavior in some simple ways.

◆ Keep your home cooler in winter and warmer in summer. Instead of turning up the heat, put on a sweater. Use fans instead of air conditioners.

◆ Use natural lighting instead of electric lights when possible.

◆ Turn off the lights or television when you leave a room.

◆ Walk or ride a bike for short trips. Ride buses and trains.

◆ Recycle, especially metal products. Recycling an aluminum can uses only 5 percent of the energy making a new can uses!

The items in this list are small things, but multiplied by millions of people they add up to a lot of energy saved for the future.

Section 4 Review

1. What are two ways to make energy resources last longer?
2. Explain how putting insulation in a building conserves energy.
3. How does carpooling conserve energy?
4. **Thinking Critically** **Predicting** An office building contains only incandescent lights. The building next door contains fluorescent lights. Predict which building has higher energy bills. Explain your answer.

756

Science at Home

With an adult family member, conduct an energy audit of your home. Look for places where energy is being lost, such as cracks around windows and doors. Also look for ways to reduce energy use, such as running the dishwasher only when it is full. Together, create a list of energy-saving suggestions for your family. Post the list where everyone can see it.

Program Resources

◆ **Unit 6 Resources** 23-4 Review and Reinforce, p. 99; 23-4 Enrich, p. 100

Answers to Self-Assessment

Caption Question

Figure 22 A bus uses less fuel than all the individual cars that would be driven by the bus passengers.

SECTION 1 Fossil Fuels

Key Ideas

◆ A fuel is a substance that provides a form of energy as a result of a chemical change.

◆ Energy can be converted from one form to another.

◆ The three major fossil fuels are coal, oil, and natural gas. These fuels release more energy when they are burned than most other substances do.

◆ Because fossil fuels take hundreds of millions of years to form, they are considered nonrenewable resources.

Key Terms

combustion   petroleum
fossil fuels   refinery
hydrocarbons   petrochemicals
reserves

SECTION 2 Renewable Sources of Energy

Key Ideas

◆ Solar energy is plentiful and renewable, and does not cause pollution. However, a backup energy source is needed.

◆ Because the sun causes winds and drives the water cycle, wind power and water power are considered indirect forms of solar energy.

◆ Biomass fuels, geothermal energy, and hydrogen power are other renewable energy sources that are currently in limited use.

Key Terms

solar energy   biomass fuels
passive solar system   gasohol
active solar system   geothermal energy
hydroelectric power

SECTION 3 Nuclear Energy

INTEGRATING **CHEMISTRY**

Key Ideas

◆ Nuclear reactions include fission reactions and fusion reactions.

◆ In a fission reaction, an atom's nucleus is split into two smaller nuclei and two or more neutrons, releasing energy.

◆ In a nuclear power plant, the thermal energy released from controlled fission reactions is used to generate electricity.

Key Terms

nucleus   fuel rods   meltdown
nuclear fission   control rods   nuclear fusion
reactor vessel

SECTION 4 Energy Conservation

Key Ideas

◆ To avoid an energy shortage in the future, people must find new energy sources and conserve available fuels now.

◆ Insulation keeps a building from losing heat to, or gaining heat from, the outside.

Key Terms

energy conservation   efficiency   insulation

Organizing Information

Compare/Contrast Table Copy the table about types of energy onto a separate sheet of paper. Then complete the table and add a title.

Energy Type	Advantages	Disadvantages
Coal		
Petroleum		
Solar		
Wind		
Water		
Geothermal		
Nuclear		

Organizing Information

Compare/Contrast Table
Students' tables should include information similar to the following. Sample title: Energy Sources

Coal: *(column 1, "Advantages")* Produces large amount of energy; easy to transport. *(column 2, "Disadvantages")* Causes air pollution when burned; difficult to mine.

Petroleum: Produces large amount of energy; can be used to produce plastics and other products. Causes air pollution when burned; difficult to find; must be refined.

Solar: Free; renewable; does not cause pollution. Not available on cloudy days or at night; is very spread out.

Wind: Free; renewable; does not cause pollution. Not available in many places; generators are noisy and can be destroyed by very strong winds.

Water: Free; renewable; does not cause pollution. Most of the suitable rivers in the United States have already been dammed; dams can have negative effects on the environment.

Geothermal: Free; renewable; does not cause pollution. Available in only a few places; drilling deep wells is expensive.

Nuclear: Produces huge amount of energy. Creates radioactive waste; risk of meltdown; costly.

Program Resources

◆ **Unit 6 Resources** Chapter 23 Project Scoring Rubric, p. 84

◆ **Performance Assessment** Chapter 23, pp. 70–72

◆ **Chapter Tests** Chapter 23 Test, pp. 91–94

Media and Technology

 Computer Test Bank
Chapter 23 Test

Reviewing Content
Multiple Choice
1. b **2.** c **3.** c **4.** a **5.** d

True or False
6. petrochemicals **7.** true **8.** renewable
9. solar cells **10.** true

Checking Concepts
11. The coal must be broken out of the surrounding rock and transported to the surface, often from deep underground. Coal creates dust that is unhealthy to breathe.

12. As plants die and decay, their remains pile up and are buried by layers of sand, rock, and mud. Over millions of years, heat and pressure change the decaying remains into coal.

13. Possible answers include overhangs to shade the windows in summer, positioning the house to receive maximum sunlight in winter, solar cells on the roof to provide electricity, and a backup energy source.

14. Wind can turn a turbine, which rotates an electromagnet to create electricity.

15. Very few locations have tides that are large enough to provide a power source.

16. By placing control rods made of cadmium between the fuel rods to limit chain reactions

17. Energy efficiency is the percentage of energy actually used to perform work; *examples:* insulation, fluorescent light bulbs, window coatings, microwave ovens

18. Responses will vary but should include ways of traveling, preparing meals, and obtaining light and heat.

Thinking Critically
19. *Likenesses:* All form from the remains of organisms, contain hydrocarbons, and produce a large amount of energy when burned. *Differences:* Coal forms from plant remains; oil and natural gas form from the remains of small animals, algae, and protists. Coal is solid, oil is liquid, and natural gas is a gas. Natural gas causes less air pollution than coal and oil.

20. Students should support their predictions with references to local weather patterns, including the frequency of sunny days and days with

Reviewing Content
Multiple Choice
Choose the letter of the best answer.

1. Which of the following is *not* a fossil fuel?
   a. coal   b. wood
   c. oil   d. natural gas
2. Wind and water energy are both indirect forms of
   a. nuclear energy.
   b. electrical energy.
   c. solar energy.
   d. geothermal energy.
3. Which of the following is *not* a biomass fuel?
   a. methane
   b. gasohol
   c. hydrogen
   d. sugar-cane wastes
4. The particle used to start a nuclear fission reaction is a(n)
   a. neutron.
   b. nucleus.
   c. proton.
   d. atom.
5. A part of a nuclear power plant that undergoes a fission reaction is called a
   a. turbine.
   b. control rod.
   c. heat exchanger.
   d. fuel rod.

True or False
If the statement is true, write true. If it is false, change the underlined word or words to make the statement true.

6. Products made from petroleum are called <u>hydrocarbons</u>.
7. The process of burning a fuel for energy is <u>combustion</u>.
8. Geothermal energy is an example of a <u>nonrenewable</u> energy source.
9. Solar energy is harnessed to run calculators using <u>solar satellites</u>.
10. Most of the energy used in the United States today comes from <u>fossil fuels</u>.

Checking Concepts
11. Explain why coal mining is a difficult task.
12. Describe how coal forms.
13. Describe three features of a solar home. (Your answer may include passive or active solar systems.)
14. Explain how wind can be used to generate electricity.
15. What factors limit the use of tides as an energy source?
16. How is a nuclear fission reaction controlled in a nuclear power plant?
17. Define *energy efficiency*. Give three examples of inventions that increase energy efficiency.
18. **Writing to Learn** Suppose you had no electricity. Write a journal entry describing a typical weekday, including your meals, classes, and after-school activities. Explain how you might get things done without electricity.

Thinking Critically
19. **Comparing and Contrasting** Discuss how the three major fossil fuels are alike and how they are different.
20. **Predicting** Do you think you will ever live in a solar house? Explain your prediction using specific information about the area where you live.
21. **Classifying** State whether each of the following energy sources is renewable or nonrenewable: coal, solar power, methane, hydrogen. Give a reason for each answer.
22. **Making Judgments** Write a short paragraph explaining why you agree or disagree with the following statement: "The United States should build more nuclear power plants to prepare for the future shortage of fossil fuels."
23. **Problem Solving** Find out what major sources of energy provide electricity to your area. Describe what families in your location can do to conserve energy.

extreme temperatures.

21. Coal is nonrenewable because it takes so long to form. Solar power is renewable because its supply is unlimited. Methane is renewable because it is produced as wastes decompose. Hydrogen is renewable because it can be obtained from water, which is abundant on Earth.

22. Accept both "agree" and "disagree" responses. Students should support their views

with explanations that cite the advantages and disadvantages of nuclear power as an energy source.

23. Students may want to look for useful references. To avoid having them deluge local utilities for information, choose volunteers to obtain materials from the various public relations departments. Libraries will also be useful.

Applying Skills

The table below shows how the world's energy production changed between 1973 and 1995. Use the information in the table to answer Questions 24–26.

Source of Energy	Energy Units Produced 1973	Energy Units Produced 1995
Coal	1,498	2,179
Gas	964	1,775
Hydroelectric	107	242
Nuclear	54	646
Oil	2,730	3,228
TOTAL Energy Units	5,353	8,070

24. **Interpreting Data** How did the total energy production change between 1973 and 1995?
25. **Calculating** What percentage of the total world energy production did nuclear power provide in 1973? In 1995?

26. **Classifying** Classify the different types of energy according to whether they are renewable or nonrenewable. How important was renewable energy to the world's energy production in 1995?

Project Wrap Up Share your report with another group. The group should review the report for clarity, organization, and detail. Make revisions based on feedback from the other group. As a class, discuss each group's findings. Prepare a class proposal with the best suggestions for conserving energy in your school.

Reflect and Record In your notebook, explain what types of energy use were the hardest to measure. What other information would have helped you make your recommendations? Record your overall opinion of energy efficiency in your school.

Test Preparation

Use these questions to prepare for standardized tests.

Use the graph to answer Questions 27–30.

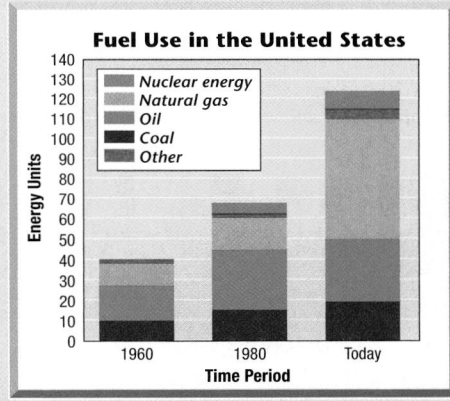

Fuel Use in the United States

27. Most of the fuel sources used in the U.S. are classified as
    a. renewable fuels.   c. fossil fuels.
    b. nuclear fuels.   d. solar energy.
28. Which source provides most of the energy used in 1980?
    a. coal   c. nuclear energy
    b. natural gas   d. oil
29. Which statement about fuel use in the United States is best supported by the information shown in the graph?
    a. Natural gas has become the most widely used source of energy.
    b. Nuclear energy is not used today because it is unsafe.
    c. Coal is becoming the main source of fuel.
    d. The amount of oil being used today has greatly decreased since 1980.

Project Wrap Up Encourage groups to give each other specific suggestions for improving the reports and to avoid making overly general criticisms. In the whole-class discussion, give each group an opportunity to summarize its findings, then focus on the groups's suggestions for reducing energy use. Ask students for their ideas about how the proposal should be organized and presented. You may want to have a group of volunteers compile the final proposal and present it to the entire class for further discussion.

Reflect and Record Specific responses to the questions and issues raised in this paragraph will vary. Allow time for students to share the answers and ideas they recorded.

Test Preparation

27. c 28. d 29. a

Applying Skills

24. It increased from 5,353 units to 8,070 units.
25. *1973:* 1%; *1995:* 8%
26. *Renewable:* hydroelectric; *nonrenewable:* coal, gas, nuclear, oil. Renewable energy (hydroelectric power) was not very important to the world's energy production in 1995, representing only 3% of the total energy units produced.

Program Resources

- **Inquiry Skills Activity Book** Provides teaching and review of all inquiry skills
- **Prentice Hall Assessment System** Provides standardized test practice
- **Reading in the Content Area** Provides strategies to improve science reading skills
- **Teacher's ELL Handbook** Provides multiple strategies for English language learners

Antarctica

This interdisciplinary feature focuses on the weather and climate of Antarctica, the world's coldest, driest, and windiest continent. The perspectives of four different disciplines—social studies, science, mathematics, and language arts—show students how the content they have learned in Unit 6 relates to other sciences and to other subjects they are studying in school. This feature is particularly suitable for team teaching and is a good springboard for extra-credit projects for students needing extra challenges.

1 Engage/Explore

Activating Prior Knowledge

Point out to students that they will be reading about Antarctica, the continent on which the South Pole is located. Help students recall what they learned in Chapter 19 about polar climates. Ask: **What would you expect the climate of Antarctica to be like?** (*Students are likely to say extremely cold; they also may say snowy.*) **What makes it so cold there?** (*The sun's rays strike the ground at a low angle year round, so it never heats up there.*) Point out that Antarctica actually receives very little snow. In fact, the continent receives less than 5 cm of precipitation each year. Ask: **Why do you think Antarctica gets so little precipitation?** (*The very cold air cannot hold much moisture.*)

Introducing the Unit

Have students look at the picture on page 761, which shows the landscape of Antarctica and people exploring there. Call students' attention to the way the people are dressed. Then have students try to imagine being in Antarctica themselves. Ask: **What do you think it would be like to live and work in**

ANTARCTICA

What kind of weather do you expect in July—hot and sunny? Brace yourself—July in Antarctica will surprise you!

On July 21, 1983, the temperature at the Russian research station Vostok dropped to a world record low: –89°C.

WELCOME TO ANTARCTICA!

Because Antarctica is in the Southern Hemisphere, July is midwinter there. But the temperature isn't very warm in summer, either. The average summer temperature at Vostok is –33°C. Antarctica's climate is unusual in other ways. It's the windiest continent as well as the coldest. Even though Antarctica is covered with snow and ice, it's also the driest continent—a snowy desert. Less than five centimeters of precipitation falls in the interior in a year. Antarctic blizzards are terrifying, but they don't bring much new snow. They just blow drifts from one place to another.

In spite of its extremes, Antarctica is both beautiful and fascinating. As you can see on the map, many countries have set up research stations there to study climate, temperature, and the atmosphere. Scientists in Antarctica also research wildlife and geology.

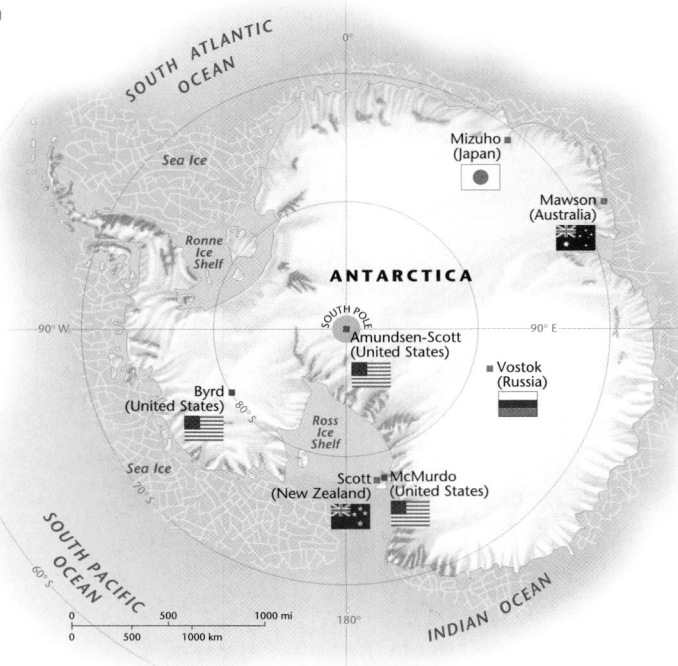

The map shows major research stations in Antarctica.

A huge dome covers buildings at the U.S. Amundsen-Scott station at the South Pole.

760

Antarctica? (*Correct any serious misconceptions students may reveal by their comments.*) Point out to the class that, even though cruise ships now take tourists to Antarctica, it is still a difficult and dangerous place to visit because of the harshness of its climate.

Program Resources

◆ **Unit 6 Resources** Interdisciplinary Explorations, Social Studies, pp. 106–108; Science, pp. 109–112; Mathematics, pp. 113–115; Language Arts, pp. 116–117

Race to the South Pole

Would you brave the darkness and cold of Antarctica? In the early 1900s, several famous explorers began a "race to the pole." Their attempts to reach the South Pole produced stories of heroism—and tragedy.

Robert F. Scott (above center) and his men reached the South Pole, but lost the race.

In October 1911, the British explorer Robert Falcon Scott traveled to the South Pole. He started overland with dog teams, motorized sleds, and ponies. He and four other explorers reached the South Pole in January 1912—only to find that a Norwegian expedition led by Roald Amundsen had beaten them there by a month! Scott's team had lost the race!

Soon after, Scott and his crew started back. But they were trapped in blizzards. All of them died. Searchers later found their tent, Scott's diary, and photographs. Scott's team had been only 18 kilometers from a supply camp.

A few years later, Sir Ernest Shackleton was the hero of an incredible Antarctic survival story. In 1914, Shackleton tried a new route to the South Pole. On the way, ice trapped and crushed his ship, the *Endurance*. He and his men escaped across the ice to Elephant Island. Leaving 22 men there, Shackleton and five others sailed in a small whaleboat to find help. Amazingly, everyone was rescued.

In the 1920s, airplanes brought a new way to explore Antarctica. American pilot and explorer Richard E. Byrd led the first flight over the South Pole in 1929. Later, Byrd set up research stations at Little America.

International Cooperation

In 1957–1958, during the International Geophysical Year, scientists from countries around the world established research stations in Antarctica and shared their scientific findings. In 1959, twelve nations signed the Antarctic Treaty to guarantee "freedom of scientific investigation." The original signers were (from top left) Argentina, Australia, Belgium, Chile, France, Japan, New Zealand, Norway, the Soviet Union, South Africa, the United Kingdom, and the United States.

Social Studies Activity

Create a time line of important events in Antarctica. Find photos or draw sketches to illustrate the events.
Include the following events:
- early expeditions
- "race to the pole" in the early 1900s
- International Geophysical Year
- Antarctic Treaty
- new research stations

Why did it take courage and endurance to try to reach the South Pole in the early 1900s?

761

2 Facilitate

◆ Discuss why people have been so determined to explore or do research in Antarctica. Ask: **Why would people put their lives at risk to explore Antarctica or do research there?** *(Antarctica was the last great unexplored frontier. It is of great research interest because of its uniqueness.)* Add that exploration of Antarctica began as early as 1820 and, by 1992, 17 different countries had a total of 37 research stations in Antarctica.

Social Studies Activity

Urge students to go beyond the information provided in the feature to find important events and illustrations for their time lines, such as the First (1882–1883) and Second (1932–1933) International Polar Years. You also may want to share with the class the information on early explorations given in the Background on the bottom of this page. **Unit 6 Resources** These worksheets correlate with this page: Plotting Points on a Map, pp. 160–107, Locating Physical Features on a Map, p. 108.

3 Assess

Activity Assessment

Students' time lines should show they have mastered the content of the feature by including important events in correct chronological order. Make sure students know more than just the date of each event they include. *(For example, the International Polar Years were held to coordinate scientific research in both the Arctic and Antarctic.)* You may want to give students a place to display their time lines. In their answers, students should reveal their understanding of the rigors and dangers of working in the polar climate and remoteness of Antarctica, especially given the technological limitations of the early 1900s.

2 Facilitate

- Relate the content of this page to Chapter 17. Ask: **Why does the ocean make coastal regions of Antarctica warmer than inland areas?** (*The water retains its heat longer than the land and warms the air over the coast.*) **Why does a covering of snow make most areas of Antarctica colder?** (*Snow, because it is white, reflects most of the sunlight that strikes it, so snowy areas are not heated up by the sun as much as areas of bare land, which are darker.*)

- Make sure students understand the rationale for wearing multiple layers of clothing to stay warm. Ask: **Why do many layers of clothes keep you warmer than one thick layer?** (*Each layer has a different purpose. Also, the multiple layers trap air between them, providing extra insulation.*)

Science Activity

Caution students to be very careful handling the hot water. Check students' understanding of the need to control variables by asking: **Why is it important for all the jars to start out at the same temperature?** (*So any differences in water temperature after 30 minutes will be due only to differences in the rate of cooling because of the socks*)

Unit 6 Resources The following worksheets correlate with this page: Designing an Experiment, page 109; Plotting Weather Station Data, pages 11–111; and Interpreting Temperature Data, page 112.

3 Assess

Activity Assessment

Students should find that the jar in the nylon sock cooled fastest, whereas the jars in the natural-fiber socks, particularly the wool sock, retained more heat.

Continent of Extremes

Why is Antarctica so cold? Its high latitude and months of darkness are important reasons. In addition, the broad expanses of white snow and icy glaciers reflect back sunlight before much heat is absorbed.

As on every continent, climates vary from place to place. Warmer parts of Antarctica are at lower elevations, at lower latitudes, or near the coast. Coastal areas are warmer because the nearby ocean moderates temperatures. These areas also have bare land, which absorbs heat.

Summer weather patterns in Antarctica are different from winter patterns. The short summer warm-up starts in October. The warmest temperatures are from mid-December to mid-January. Then temperatures drop suddenly. So by mid-March, the beginning of winter, the temperature has fallen to winter levels. Over the next six months Antarctica remains very cold—and dark.

How do polar explorers and researchers stay warm? The secret is wearing layers of clothing that keep body heat from escaping. ▼

An insulated hood, a hat with earflaps, or a face mask protects against wind. Sunglasses or goggles reduce the glare of sunlight and protect eyes from freezing.

Boots and gloves are layered, too. A layer of fleece may be sealed inside a waterproof rubber layer.

- An **inner layer** of long underwear (silk, wool, or synthetic) carries moisture away from the skin.

- A fluffy **insulating layer,** such as fleece or down, traps pockets of air that are warmed by body heat.

- The **outer shell layer** protects against wind and water.

762

Science Activity

Staying warm is essential for life in the Antarctic. Set up an experiment to test how well different materials keep heat from escaping. Use socks made of nylon, silk, cotton, and wool. You will need a jar for each material plus one jar as a control.

- 🧤 📖 Fill jars with equal amounts of very hot water. The water in each jar should be the same temperature.
- Record the temperature of each jar and screw each cap on.
- Place each jar, except the control, inside a sock. Refrigerate all the jars for 30 minutes.
- Remove the jars and record the water temperature of each.

Which jar cooled fastest? Which materials retained the heat best?

Background

Facts and Figures Although the climate of Antarctica is too frigid for humans to live there without insulating clothing, stoves, and other technological support, that doesn't mean that there is no life in Antarctica. More than 40 different species of birds spend the summer there, including albatrosses, terns, and gulls. Sea animals are also abundant. They include seals, penguins, whales, squid, and about 100 species of fish. Many different species of animals also live on the land, although all of them are invertebrates, mostly insects. There is a greater variety of plant life on the land, with a total of about 800 plant species. Close to half of the plant species are lichens, but mosses, grasses, liverworts, and a few other types of plants are also found. In addition to animals and plants, Antarctica is home to bacteria, molds, yeast, algae, and fungi.

Sky Watch

It's March 21—the beginning of winter—and you're watching the sun set very, very slowly. It takes 30 hours—more than a day—for the sun to disappear below the horizon. Once it's gone, you won't see sunshine again until September! April and early May aren't completely dark, but there is hardly enough light to cast a shadow. Then it's dark for two months. In August, light begins again. The sky brightens quickly until the polar sunrise.

The tilt of Earth on its axis affects the hours of daylight and darkness from season to season. At the poles, midsummer brings the "midnight sun," which circles around the sky but does not set. Midwinter brings almost total darkness.

Lingering
Antarctic sunset

The table shows hours of daylight on ▶ the 15th of each month. It shows readings at two different Antarctic locations—the Amundsen-Scott station and Japan's Mizuho station.

HOURS OF DAYLIGHT IN ANTARCTICA
(sunrise to sunset, rounded to nearest hour)

Month	Mizuho Station 70° S	Amundsen-Scott Station 90° S
January	24	24
February	18	24
March	14	24
April	9	0
May	3	0
June	0	0
July	0	0
August	7	0
September	11	0
October	16	24
November	22	24
December	24	24

Math Activity

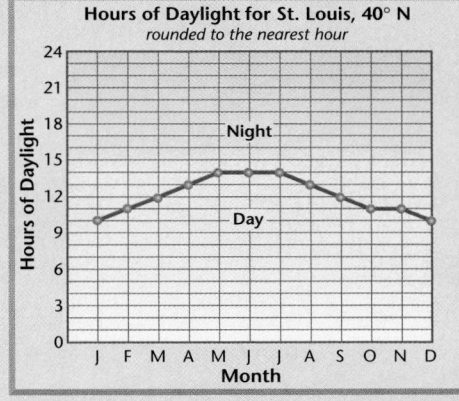

Hours of Daylight for St. Louis, 40° N
rounded to the nearest hour

(Graph with vertical axis "Hours of Daylight" marked 0, 3, 6, 9, 12, 15, 18, 21, 24; horizontal axis "Month" marked J F M A M J J A S O N D; labels "Night" and "Day")

This line graph shows the year-round pattern of daylight for St. Louis, Missouri, located at about 40° north latitude. Readings were taken on the fifteenth of each month. Use the table to make another line graph that shows hours of daylight for Mizuho station, Amundsen-Scott station, and St. Louis.

◆ On the horizontal axis of the table, list the months.

◆ On the vertical axis, mark off spaces for 0 to 24 hours.

◆ Choose a different color marker for each latitude. Above each month for each location, place a colored dot at the correct hour mark. Connect the dots to show changes in daylight at each place during a year.

◆ How are the changes in darkness and daylight in Antarctica like those you see at home? How are they different?

763

Background

Facts and Figures Antarctica is the world's fifth-largest continent. With an area of more than 13 million km², it makes up almost one tenth of Earth's land surface. However, more than 98 percent of Antarctica is under a thick layer of ice, in some places 3 km thick. Because of the ice, scientists have had to learn about the shape of the land surface by beaming radio-echo soundings down through the ice.

Much of the ice-free land in Antarctica lies along the coast, but the greatest continuous stretches of ice-free land on the continent lie in three major valleys. Because extremely dry winds blow down into these valleys, no precipitation has fallen in them for over two million years. Any snow that blows into them simply evaporates because the air is so dry.

2 Facilitate

◆ Check that students understand the effect of latitude on hours of daylight by asking: **How many hours of daylight do you predict a station at 80°S latitude would have in March? In November?** *(About 19 hours of daylight in March and 23 hours in November)*

◆ Help students appreciate the importance in their lives of a regular cycle of day and night. First have them compare the number of hours of daylight for the current month where they live with the number for the same month at 90°S latitude. Then ask: **How would your everyday life and activities be different if your location had the same number of hours of daylight as the South Pole?** *(Answers may range from trouble sleeping when it is light all night to the cancellation of outside events when it is dark all day. Accept all reasonable answers without comment.)*

Math Activity

Before students start plotting points on their graphs, check to see that they have labeled both axes correctly. You can extend the activity by asking: **How many hours of daylight do you predict there would be at the equator?** *(About 12 hours a day year round)*

Unit 6 Resources The following worksheets correlate with this page: Using a Model, page 113; Reading a Table, page 114; and Making a Graph, page 115.

3 Assess

Activity Assessment

Students may say that the changes in darkness and daylight both in Antarctica and at home vary in a regular way from month to month. However, in Antarctica the changes are more extreme, and the months with the most hours of daylight are different—June and July at home as compared with December and January in Antarctica.

2 Facilitate

- Provide students with a context for Byrd's memoir by telling them that the excerpt was written during the second of five expeditions that Byrd led to Antarctica. During the second expedition, Byrd spent more than four months alone at his research station because he wanted to see what it would be like. Share the additional information provided in the background material below. Invite students who need extra challenges to research Byrd's later expeditions to Antarctica and share what they learn with the rest of the class.

- Call students' attention to the month the Byrd excerpt was written. *(April)* Point out that Little America, where Byrd set up research stations, is not the same as Byrd Station shown on the map on page 760. Little America was located in the Ross Ice Shelf at about 80°S latitude. Then have students determine from the table on page 763 about how many hours of daylight each day Byrd would have had during April at that latitude. *(From just a few hours a day to no daylight)* Ask: **How do you think long periods of darkness would have affected Byrd's solitary stay in Antarctica?** *(Students may say that long periods of darkness would have made it much harder to cope with the loneliness, barren landscape, frigid cold, and other hardships.)*

Language Arts Activity

Help students appreciate how Byrd uses concrete, sensory details to communicate to the reader the extreme cold of Antarctica. Point out that all three paragraphs describe the cold, then ask: **What images does Byrd use to convey to the reader how extremely cold it is in Antarctica?** *(Possible answers include so cold that tomato juice shatters in its bottles, your breath sounds like Chinese firecrackers, the flame of a lamp dries up on the wick, and rubber turns brittle.)* Encourage students to use similar concrete sensory details in their descriptive writing.

Alone in Antarctica

Admiral Richard Byrd worked in the Antarctic for nearly 30 years after his flight over the South Pole. He led several expeditions and set up research stations at Little America. Byrd's book *Alone* is based on the journal he kept while spending the winter of 1934 alone at a weather station outpost. During his four-and-a-half-month stay, Byrd nearly gave up mentally and physically. He endured, however, and kept up his weather research until help arrived in August.

In this memoir of his days in early April, 1934, Byrd describes some of the problems of working in the intense cold.

Admiral Byrd tries to keep warm in his small shack at Little America. ▶

Coastal view of Antarctica ▼

At times I felt as if I were the last survivor of an Ice Age, striving to hold on with the flimsy tools bequeathed by an easy-going, temperate world. Cold does queer things. At 50° Fahrenheit below zero a flashlight dies out in your hand. At −55° Fahrenheit kerosene will freeze, and the flame will dry up on the wick. At −60° Fahrenheit rubber turns brittle. One day, I remember, the antenna wire snapped in my hands when I tried to bend it to make a new connection. Below −60° Fahrenheit cold will find the last microscopic touch of oil in an instrument and stop it dead. If there is the slightest breeze, you can hear your breath freeze as it floats away, making a sound like that of Chinese firecrackers. . . . And if you work too hard and breathe too deeply, your lungs will sometimes feel as if they were on fire.

Cold—even April's relatively moderate cold— gave me plenty to think about. . . . Two cases of tomato juice shattered their bottles. Whenever I brought canned food inside the shack I had to let it stand all day near the stove to thaw. . . . Frost was forever collecting on the electrical contact points of

Background

History Byrd's second expedition to Antarctica in 1933–1935 is considered one of Antarctica's greatest and most adventure-filled scientific expeditions. Byrd had to be rescued from his solitary encampment in August of 1934 because of carbon monoxide fumes from his camp stove. The expedition became famous because of live radio broadcasts. This led to greater interest in Antarctica. Byrd went on to lead three more

Antarctic expeditions.

Byrd founded the Little America station during his second expedition. Little America served as a research station until 1960, when it was abandoned because the ice beneath it had become unstable and the station started floating out to sea on an iceberg. Later, the United States built McMurdo, a station on McMurdo Sound. It is now the largest research station in Antarctica.

the wind vane and wind cups. Some days I climbed the twelve-foot anemometer pole two and three times to clean them. It was a bitter job, especially on blustery nights. With my legs twined around the slender pole, my arms flung over the cleats, and my free hands trying to scrape the contact point clean with a knife and at the same time hold a flashlight to see, I qualified for the world's coldest flagpole sitter. I seldom came down from that pole without a frozen finger, toe, nose, or cheek.

The shack was always freezingly cold in the morning. I slept with the door open [for ventilation]. When I arose the inside temperature (depending upon the surface weather) might be anywhere from 10° to 40° Fahrenheit below zero. Frost coated the sleeping bag where my breath had condensed during the night; my socks and boots, when I picked them up, were so stiff with frozen sweat that I first had to work them between my hands. A pair of silk gloves hung from a nail over the bunk, where I could grab them the first thing. Yet, even with their protection, my fingers would sting and burn from the touch of the lamp and stove as I lighted them.

Language Arts Activity

From this passage, what can you conclude about Byrd's attitude toward his research? Although you've probably never traveled to Antarctica, you may have had an outdoor adventure—at summer camp or even in a city park. Use descriptive writing to recapture that experience. Remember to include concrete, sensory details like those in Byrd's journal. If you prefer, write about an imaginary event or adventure in the outdoors.

Plan a Cool Expedition

You're on your way to Antarctica! Good planning is the key to a successful expedition. Work in small groups to plan your expedition. When your group has finished planning, meet with your class to present your program. Consider these questions and issues in making your plan:

◆ What research will you do—weather, wildlife, geology, or another topic?

◆ Where will you work? Will you work near the coast? Will you join an existing research station?

◆ Will you travel? Plot your travel course and location on a map of Antarctica.

◆ How long do you plan to stay?

◆ What equipment will you take—climbing gear to cross glaciers, boats and kayaks, tents for camping?

◆ What clothing will you need? Check the illustration of protective clothing.

◆ What supplies will you take? Plan the kinds and amounts of food that you will take.

765

Unit 6 Resources The following worksheets correlate with these pages: Comparing Descriptive Writing, page 116, and Reading for Content, page 117.

3 Assess

Activity Assessment

Based on the hardships and dangers Byrd endured, students are likely to conclude that he was very serious about his research and very devoted to it. In their descriptive writing, students should describe an adventure, either real or imaginary, using concrete sensory details. For example, instead of saying simply that they were frightened by a bear outside their tent on a camping trip, they might describe how they imagined the bear was a monster and how the shadow it cast on their tent made it look as big as King Kong.

Tie It Together

Time 1 day for groups to develop plans, 1 day for class presentations

Tips Tell students that where they plan to work, whether they plan to travel, how long they plan to stay, and what equipment they plan to take will all depend largely on the nature of the research they plan to do. Therefore, they must first decide what their research topic will be, what data they will collect, and how they will collect it. Encourage groups to develop specific research topics. If students are having difficulty thinking of topics, you might suggest such topics as the ozone hole over Antarctica and Antarctica's active volcanoes. When groups present their plans to the class, encourage other students to suggest any items they think have been overlooked and to offer other helpful suggestions.

Extend Challenge students to pretend they have undertaken the planned expedition. Have them write journal entries to record their observations and experiences. Ask volunteers to read some of their journal entries aloud to the class.

Developing scientific thinking in students is important for a solid science education. To learn how to think scientifically, students need frequent opportunities to practice science process skills, critical thinking skills, as well as other skills that support scientific inquiry. The *Science Explorer* Skills Handbook introduces the following key science skills:

◆ Science Process Skills
◆ SI Measuring Skills
◆ Skills for Conducting a Scientific Investigation
◆ Critical Thinking Skills
◆ Information Organizing Skills
◆ Data Table and Graphing Skills

The Skills Handbook is designed as a reference for students to use whenever they need to review a science skill. You can use the activities provided in the Skills Handbook to teach or reinforce the skills.

Think Like a Scientist

Observing

ACTIVITY

Before students look at the photograph, remind them that an observation is what they can see, hear, smell, taste, or feel. Ask: **Which senses will you use to make observations from this photograph?** (*Sight is the only sense that can be used to make observations from the photograph.*) **What are some observations you can make from the photograph?** (*Answers may vary. Sample answers: The boy is wearing sneakers, sports socks, shorts, and a T-shirt; the boy is sitting in the grass holding something blue against his knee; the boy is looking at his knee; there is a soccer ball laying beside the boy.*) List the observations on the board. If students make any inferences or predictions about the boy at this point, ask: **Can you be sure your statement is accurate from just observing the photograph?** Help students understand how observations differ from inferences and predictions.

Inferring

ACTIVITY

Review students' observations from the photograph. Then ask: **What inferences can you make from your observations?** (*Students may*

Think Like a Scientist

Although you may not know it, you think like a scientist every day. Whenever you ask a question and explore possible answers, you use many of the same skills that scientists do. Some of these skills are described on this page.

Observing

When you use one or more of your five senses to gather information about the world, you are **observing.** Hearing a dog bark, counting twelve green seeds, and smelling smoke are all observations. To increase the power of their senses, scientists sometimes use microscopes, telescopes, or other instruments that help them make more detailed observations.

An observation must be an accurate report of what your senses detect. It is important to keep careful records of your observations in science class by writing or drawing in a notebook. The information collected through observations is called evidence, or data.

Inferring

When you interpret an observation, you are **inferring,** or making an inference. For example, if you hear your dog barking, you may infer that someone is at your front door. To make this inference, you combine the evidence—the barking dog—and your experience or knowledge—you know that your dog barks when strangers approach—to reach a logical conclusion.

Notice that an inference is not a fact; it is only one of many possible interpretations for an observation. For example, your dog may be barking because it wants to go for a walk. An inference may turn out to be incorrect even if it is based on accurate observations and logical reasoning. The only way to find out if an inference is correct is to investigate further.

Predicting

When you listen to the weather forecast, you hear many predictions about the next day's weather—what the temperature will be, whether it will rain, and how windy it will be. Weather forecasters use observations and knowledge of weather patterns to predict the weather. The skill of **predicting** involves making an inference about a future event based on current evidence or past experience.

Because a prediction is an inference, it may prove to be false. In science class, you can test some of your predictions by doing experiments. For example, suppose you predict that larger paper airplanes can fly farther than smaller airplanes. How could you test your prediction?

ACTIVITY Use the photograph to answer the questions below.

Observing Look closely at the photograph. List at least three observations.

Inferring Use your observations to make an inference about what has happened. What experience or knowledge did you use to make the inference?

Predicting Predict what will happen next. On what evidence or experience do you base your prediction?

---

say that the boy hurt his knee playing soccer and is holding a coldpack against his injured knee.) **What experience or knowledge helped you make this inference?** (*Students may have experienced knee injuries from playing soccer, and they may be familiar with coldpacks like the one the boy is using.*) **Can anyone suggest another possible interpretation for these observations?** (*Answers may vary. Sample answer: The boy hurt his knee jogging, and he just happened to sit beside a soccer ball his sister left in the yard.*) **How can you find out whether an inference is correct?** (*by further investigation*)

Predicting

ACTIVITY

After students come to some consensus about the inference that the boy hurt his knee, encourage them to make predictions about what will happen next. (*Students' predictions may vary. Sample answers: The boy will go to the doctor. A friend will help the boy home. The boy will get up and continue playing soccer.*)

Classifying

Could you imagine searching for a book in the library if the books were shelved in no particular order? Your trip to the library would be an all-day event! Luckily, librarians group together books on similar topics or by the same author. Grouping together items that are alike in some way is called **classifying.** You can classify items in many ways: by size, by shape, by use, and by other important characteristics.

Like librarians, scientists use the skill of classifying to organize information and objects. When things are sorted into groups, the relationships among them become easier to understand.

Classify the objects in the photograph into two groups based on any characteristic you choose. Then use another characteristic to classify the objects into three groups. **ACTIVITY**

Making Models

This student is using a model to demonstrate what causes day and night on Earth. What do the flashlight and the tennis ball represent in the model? **ACTIVITY**

Have you ever drawn a picture to help someone understand what you were saying? Such a drawing is one type of model. A model is a picture, diagram, computer image, or other representation of a complex object or process. **Making models** helps people understand things that they cannot observe directly.

Scientists often use models to represent things that are either very large or very small, such as the planets in the solar system, or the parts of a cell. Such models are physical models—drawings or three-dimensional structures that look like the real thing. Other models are mental models—mathematical equations or words that describe how something works.

Communicating

Whenever you talk on the phone, write a letter, or listen to your teacher at school, you are communicating. **Communicating** is the process of sharing ideas and information with other people. Communicating effectively requires many skills, including writing, reading, speaking, listening, and making models.

Scientists communicate to share results, information, and opinions. Scientists often communicate about their work in journals, over the telephone, in letters, and on the Internet. They also attend scientific meetings where they share their ideas with one another in person.

On a sheet of paper, write out clear, detailed directions for tying your shoe. Then exchange directions with a partner. Follow your partner's directions exactly. How successful were you at tying your shoe? How could your partner have communicated more clearly? **ACTIVITY**

767

On what did you base your prediction? *(Scientific predictions are based on knowledge and experience.)* Point out that in science, predictions can often be tested with experiments.

Classifying **ACTIVITY**

Encourage students to think of other common things that are classified. Then ask: **What things at home are classified?** *(Clothing might be classified in order to place it in the appropriate dresser drawer; glasses, plates, and silverware are grouped in different parts of the kitchen; screws, nuts, bolts, washers, and nails might be separated into small containers.)* **What are some things that scientists classify?** *(Scientists classify many things they study, including organisms, geological features and processes, and kinds of machines.)* After students have classified the different fruits in the photograph, have them share their criteria for classifying them. *(Some characteristics students might use include shape, color, size, and where they are grown.)*

Making Models **ACTIVITY**

Ask students: **What are some models you have used to study science?** *(Students may have used human anatomical models, solar system models, maps, stream tables.)* **How did these models help you?** *(Models can help you learn about things that are difficult to study, because they are either too big, too small, or complex.)* Be sure students understand that a model does not have to be three-dimensional. For example, a map in a textbook is a model. Ask: **What do the flashlight and tennis ball represent?** *(The flashlight represents the sun, and the ball represents Earth.)* **What quality of each item makes this a good model?** *(The flashlight gives off light, and the ball is round and can be rotated by the student.)*

Communicating **ACTIVITY**

Challenge students to identify the methods of communication they've used today. Then ask: **How is the way you communicate with a friend similar to and different from the way scientists communicate about their work to other scientists?** *(Both may communicate using various methods, but scientists must be very detailed and precise, whereas communication between friends may be less detailed and precise.)* Encourage students to communicate like a scientist as they carry out the activity. *(Students' directions should be detailed and precise enough for another person to successfully follow.)*

Making Measurements

Measuring in SI

Review SI units in class with students. Begin by providing metric rulers, graduated cylinders, balances, and Celsius thermometers. Use these tools to reinforce that the meter is the unit of length, the liter is the unit of volume, the gram is the unit of mass, and the degree Celsius is the unit for temperature. Ask: **If you want to measure the length and width of your classroom, which SI unit would you use?** *(meter)* **Which unit would you use to measure the amount of matter in your textbook?** *(gram)* **Which would you use to measure how much water a drinking glass holds?** *(liter)* **When would you use the Celsius scale?** *(To measure the temperature of something)* Then use the measuring equipment to review SI prefixes. For example, ask: **What are the smallest units on the metric ruler?** *(millimeters)* **How many millimeters are there in 1 cm?** *(10 mm)* **How many in 10 cm?** *(100 mm)* **How many centimeters are there in 1 m?** *(100 cm)* **What does 1,000 m equal?** *(1 km)*

Length
(Students should state that the shell is 4.6 centimeters, or 46 millimeters, long.) If students need more practice measuring length, have them use meter sticks and metric rulers to measure various objects in the classroom.

Liquid Volume
(Students should state that the volume of water in the graduated cylinder is 62 milliliters.) If students need more practice measuring liquid volume, have them use a graduated cylinder to measure different volumes of water.

Making Measurements

When scientists make observations, it is not sufficient to say that something is "big" or "heavy." Instead, scientists use instruments to measure just how big or heavy an object is. By measuring, scientists can express their observations more precisely and communicate more information about what they observe.

Measuring in SI

The standard system of measurement used by scientists around the world is known as the International System of Units, which is abbreviated as SI (in French, *Système International d'Unités*). SI units are easy to use because they are based on multiples of 10. Each unit is ten times larger than the next smallest unit and one tenth the size of the next largest unit. The table lists the prefixes used to name the most common SI units.

Common SI Prefixes

Prefix	Symbol	Meaning
kilo-	k	1,000
hecto-	h	100
deka-	da	10
deci-	d	0.1 (one tenth)
centi-	c	0.01 (one hundredth)
milli-	m	0.001 (one thousandth)

Length To measure length, or the distance between two points, the unit of measure is the **meter (m)**. The distance from the floor to a doorknob is approximately one meter. Long distances, such as the distance between two cities, are measured in kilometers (km). Small lengths are measured in centimeters (cm) or millimeters (mm). Scientists use metric rulers and meter sticks to measure length.

Common Conversions
1 km = 1,000 m
1 m = 100 cm
1 m = 1,000 mm
1 cm = 10 mm

The larger lines on the metric ruler in the picture show centimeter divisions, while the smaller, unnumbered lines show millimeter divisions. How many centimeters long is the shell? How many millimeters long is it?

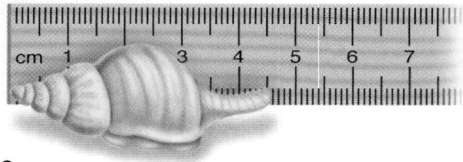

Liquid Volume To measure the volume of a liquid, or the amount of space it takes up, you will use a unit of measure known as the **liter (L).** One liter is the approximate volume of a medium-size carton of milk. Smaller volumes are measured in milliliters (mL). Scientists use graduated cylinders to measure liquid volume.

Common Conversion
1 L = 1,000 mL

The graduated cylinder in the picture is marked in milliliter divisions. Notice that the water in the cylinder has a curved surface. This curved surface is called the *meniscus*. To measure the volume, you must read the level at the lowest point of the meniscus. What is the volume of water in this graduated cylinder?

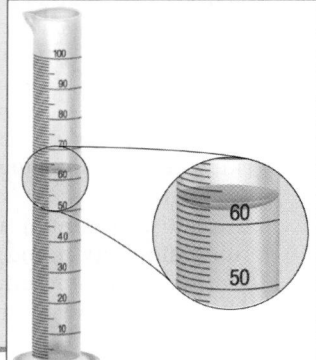

Mass To measure mass, or the amount of matter in an object, you will use a unit of measure known as the **gram (g)**. One gram is approximately the mass of a paper clip. Larger masses are measured in kilograms (kg). Scientists use a balance to find the mass of an object.

Common Conversion

1 kg = 1,000 g

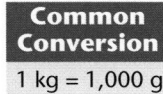

The mass of the apple in the picture is measured in kilograms. What is the mass of the apple? Suppose a recipe for applesauce called for one kilogram of apples. About how many apples would you need?

Temperature
To measure the temperature of a substance, you will use the **Celsius scale**. Temperature is measured in degrees Celsius (°C) using a Celsius thermometer. Water freezes at 0°C and boils at 100°C.

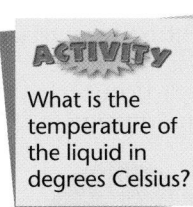

ACTIVITY
What is the temperature of the liquid in degrees Celsius?

Converting SI Units

To use the SI system, you must know how to convert between units. Converting from one unit to another involves the skill of **calculating**, or using mathematical operations. Converting between SI units is similar to converting between dollars and dimes because both systems are based on multiples of ten.

Suppose you want to convert a length of 80 centimeters to meters. Follow these steps to convert between units.

1. Begin by writing down the measurement you want to convert—in this example, 80 centimeters.

2. Write a conversion factor that represents the relationship between the two units you are converting. In this example, the relationship is *1 meter = 100 centimeters*. Write this conversion factor as a fraction, making sure to place the units you are converting from (centimeters, in this example) in the denominator.

3. Multiply the measurement you want to convert by the fraction. When you do this, the units in the first measurement will cancel out with the units in the denominator. Your answer will be in the units you are converting to (meters, in this example).

Example

80 centimeters = _____?_____ meters

$$80 \text{ centimeters} \times \frac{1 \text{ meter}}{100 \text{ centimeters}} = \frac{80 \text{ meters}}{100}$$

$$= 0.8 \text{ meters}$$

Convert between the following units.
1. 600 millimeters = _?_ meters
2. 0.35 liters = _?_ milliliters
3. 1,050 grams = _?_ kilograms

769

Conducting a Scientific Investigation

Posing Questions

Before students do the activity on the next page, walk them through the steps of a typical scientific investigation. Begin by asking: **Why is a scientific question important to a scientific investigation?** *(It is the reason for conducting a scientific investigation.)* **What is the scientific question in the activity at the bottom of the next page?** *(Is a ball's bounce affected by the height from which it is dropped?)*

Developing a Hypothesis

Emphasize that a hypothesis is a possible explanation for a set of observations or answer to a scientific question, but it is *not* a guess. Ask: **On what information do scientists base their hypotheses?** *(Their observations and previous knowledge or experience)* Point out that a hypothesis does not always turn out to be correct. Ask: **In that case, do you think the scientist wasted his or her time? Explain your answer.** *(No, because the scientist probably learned from the investigation and may be able to develop another hypothesis that could be supported.)*

Designing an Experiment

Have a volunteer read the Experimental Procedure in the box. Then call on students to identify the manipulated variable *(amount of salt added to water)*, the variables that are kept constant *(amount and starting temperature of water, placing containers in freezer)*, the responding variable *(time it takes water to freeze)*, and the control *(Container 3)*.

Ask: **How might the experiment be affected if Container 1 had only 100 mL of water?** *(It wouldn't be a fair comparison with the containers with that have more water.)* **What if Container 3 was not included in the experiment?** *(You wouldn't have anything to compare the other two containers with to know if their freezing times were faster or slower than normal.)* Help students understand the importance of keeping all variables constant except the manipulated variable.

Conducting a Scientific Investigation

In some ways, scientists are like detectives, piecing together clues to learn about a process or event. One way that scientists gather clues is by carrying out experiments. An experiment tests an idea in a careful, orderly manner. Although experiments do not all follow the same steps in the same order, many follow a pattern similar to the one described here.

Posing Questions

Experiments begin by asking a scientific question. A scientific question is one that can be answered by gathering evidence. For example, the question "Which freezes faster— fresh water or salt water?" is a scientific question because you can carry out an investigation and gather information to answer the question.

Developing a Hypothesis

The next step is to form a hypothesis. A **hypothesis** is a possible explanation for a set of observations or answer to a scientific question. In science, a hypothesis must be something that can be tested. A hypothesis can be worded as an *If … then …* statement. For example, a hypothesis might be *"If I add salt to fresh water, then the water will take longer to freeze."* A hypothesis worded this way serves as a rough outline of the experiment you should perform.

770

Also, be sure they understand the role of the control. Then ask: **What operational definition is used in this experiment?** *("Frozen" means the time at which a wooden stick can no longer move in a container.)*

Designing an Experiment

Next you need to plan a way to test your hypothesis. Your plan should be written out as a step-by-step procedure and should describe the observations or measurements you will make.

Two important steps involved in designing an experiment are controlling variables and forming operational definitions.

Controlling Variables

In a well-designed experiment, you need to keep all variables the same except for one. A **variable** is any factor that can change in an experiment. The factor that you change is called the **manipulated variable.** In this experiment, the manipulated variable is the amount of salt added to the water. Other factors, such as the amount of water or the starting temperature, are kept constant.

The factor that changes as a result of the manipulated variable is called the responding variable. The **responding variable** is what you measure or observe to obtain your results. In this experiment, the responding variable is how long the water takes to freeze.

An experiment in which all factors except one are kept constant is a **controlled experiment.** Most controlled experiments include a test called the control. In this experiment, Container 3 is the control. Because no salt is added to Container 3, you can compare the results from the other containers to it. Any difference in results must be due to the addition of salt alone.

Forming Operational Definitions

Another important aspect of a well-designed experiment is having clear operational definitions. An **operational definition** is a statement that describes how a particular variable is to be measured or how a term is to be defined. For example, in this experiment, how will you determine if the water has frozen? You might decide to insert a stick in each container at the start of the experiment. Your operational definition of "frozen" would be the time at which the stick can no longer move.

EXPERIMENTAL PROCEDURE

1. Fill 3 containers with 300 milliliters of cold tap water.

2. Add 10 grams of salt to Container 1; stir. Add 20 grams of salt to Container 2; stir. Add no salt to Container 3.

3. Place the 3 containers in a freezer.

4. Check the containers every 15 minutes. Record your observations.

Interpreting Data

The observations and measurements you make in an experiment are called data. At the end of an experiment, you need to analyze the data to look for any patterns or trends. Patterns often become clear if you organize your data in a data table or graph. Then think through what the data reveal. Do they support your hypothesis? Do they point out a flaw in your experiment? Do you need to collect more data?

Drawing Conclusions

A conclusion is a statement that sums up what you have learned from an experiment. When you draw a conclusion, you need to decide whether the data you collected support your hypothesis or not. You may need to repeat an experiment several times before you can draw any conclusions from it. Conclusions often lead you to pose new questions and plan new experiments to answer them.

Is a ball's bounce affected by the height from which it is dropped? Using the steps just described, plan a controlled experiment to investigate this problem. **ACTIVITY**

Interpreting Data

Emphasize the importance of collecting accurate and detailed data in a scientific investigation. Ask: **What if you forgot to record some data during your investigation?** *(They wouldn't be able to completely analyze their data to draw valid conclusions.)* Then ask: **Why are data tables and graphs a good way to organize data?** *(They often make it easier to compare and analyze data.)* You may wish to have students review the Skills Handbook pages on Creating Data Tables and Graphs at this point.

Drawing Conclusions

Help students understand that a conclusion is not necessarily the end of a scientific investigation. A conclusion about one experiment may lead right into another experiment. Point out that in scientific investigations, a conclusion is a summary and explanation of the results of an experiment.

Tell students to suppose that for the Experimental Procedure described on this page, they obtained the following results: Container 1 froze in 45 minutes, Container 2 in 80 minutes, and Container 3 in 25 minutes. Ask: **What conclusions can you draw about this experiment?** *(Students might conclude that the more salt that is added to fresh water, the longer it takes the water to freeze. The hypothesis is supported, and the question of which freezes faster is answered—fresh water.)*

You might wish to have students work in pairs to plan the controlled experiment. **ACTIVITY** *(Students should develop a hypothesis, such as "If I increase the height from which a ball is dropped, then the height of its bounce will increase." They can test the hypothesis by dropping balls from varying heights (the manipulated variable). All trials should be done with the same kind of ball and on the same surface (constant variables). For each trial, they should measure the height of the bounce (responding variable).)* After students have designed the experiment, provide rubber balls and invite them to carry out the experiment so they can collect and interpret data and draw conclusions.

Thinking Critically

Comparing and Contrasting

Emphasize that the skill of comparing and contrasting often relies on good observation skills, as in this activity. *(Students' answers may vary. Sample answer: Similarities—both are dogs and have four legs, two eyes, two ears, brown and white fur, black noses, pink tongues; Differences—smooth coat vs. rough coat, more white fur vs. more brown fur, shorter vs. taller, long ears vs. short ears.)*

Applying Concepts

Point out to students that they apply concepts that they learn in school in their daily lives. For example, they learn to add, subtract, multiply, and divide in school. If they get a paper route or some other part-time job, they can apply those concepts. Challenge students to practice applying concepts by doing the activity. *(Antifreeze lowers the temperature at which the solution will freeze, and thus keeps the water in the radiator from freezing.)*

Interpreting Illustrations

Again, point out the need for good observation skills. Ask: **What is the difference between "interpreting illustrations" and "looking at the pictures"?** *("Interpreting illustrations" requires thorough examination of the illustrations, captions, and labels, while "looking at the pictures" implies less thorough examination.)* Encourage students to thoroughly examine the diagram as they do the activity. *(Students' paragraphs will vary, but should describe the internal anatomy of an earthworm, including some of the organs in the earthworm.)*

Thinking Critically

Has a friend ever asked for your advice about a problem? If so, you may have helped your friend think through the problem in a logical way. Without knowing it, you used critical-thinking skills to help your friend. Critical thinking involves the use of reasoning and logic to solve problems or make decisions. Some critical-thinking skills are described below.

Comparing and Contrasting

When you examine two objects for similarities and differences, you are using the skill of **comparing and contrasting.** Comparing involves identifying similarities, or common characteristics. Contrasting involves identifying differences. Analyzing objects in this way can help you discover details that you might otherwise overlook.

Compare and contrast **ACTIVITY** the two animals in the photo. First list all the similarities that you see. Then list all the differences.

Applying Concepts

When you use your knowledge about one situation to make sense of a similar situation, you are using the skill of **applying concepts.** Being able to transfer your knowledge from one situation to another shows that you truly understand a concept. You may use this skill in answering test questions that present different problems from the ones you've reviewed in class.

You have just learned **ACTIVITY** that water takes longer to freeze when other substances are mixed into it. Use this knowledge to explain why people need a substance called antifreeze in their car's radiator in the winter.

Interpreting Illustrations

Diagrams, photographs, and maps are included in textbooks to help clarify what you read. These illustrations show processes, places, and ideas in a visual manner. The skill called **interpreting illustrations** can help you learn from these visual elements. To understand an illustration, take the time to study the illustration along with all the written information that accompanies it. Captions identify the key concepts shown in the illustration. Labels point out the important parts of a diagram or map, while keys identify the symbols used in a map.

Upper blood vessel
Reproductive organs
Arches
Brain
Mouth
Bristles
Digestive tract
Lower blood vessel
Nerve cord
Waste-removal organs
Intestine

▲ Internal anatomy of an earthworm

Study the diagram above. Then write **ACTIVITY** a short paragraph explaining what you have learned.

Relating Cause and Effect

If one event causes another event to occur, the two events are said to have a cause-and-effect relationship. When you determine that such a relationship exists between two events, you use a skill called **relating cause and effect.** For example, if you notice an itchy, red bump on your skin, you might infer that a mosquito bit you. The mosquito bite is the cause, and the bump is the effect.

It is important to note that two events do not necessarily have a cause-and-effect relationship just because they occur together. Scientists carry out experiments or use past experience to determine whether a cause-and-effect relationship exists.

> **ACTIVITY**
> You are on a camping trip and your flashlight has stopped working. List some possible causes for the flashlight malfunction. How could you determine which cause-and-effect relationship has left you in the dark?

Making Generalizations

When you draw a conclusion about an entire group based on information about only some of the group's members, you are using a skill called **making generalizations.** For a generalization to be valid, the sample you choose must be large enough and representative of the entire group. You might, for example, put this skill to work at a farm stand if you see a sign that says, "Sample some grapes before you buy." If you sample a few sweet grapes, you may conclude that all the grapes are sweet—and purchase a large bunch.

> **ACTIVITY**
> A team of scientists needs to determine whether the water in a large reservoir is safe to drink. How could they use the skill of making generalizations to help them? What should they do?

Making Judgments

When you evaluate something to decide whether it is good or bad, or right or wrong, you are using a skill called **making judgments.** For example, you make judgments when you decide to eat healthful foods or to pick up litter in a park. Before you make a judgment, you need to think through the pros and cons of a situation, and identify the values or standards that you hold.

> **ACTIVITY**
> Should children and teens be required to wear helmets when bicycling? Explain why you feel the way you do.

Problem Solving

When you use critical-thinking skills to resolve an issue or decide on a course of action, you are using a skill called **problem solving.** Some problems, such as how to convert a fraction into a decimal, are straightforward. Other problems, such as figuring out why your computer has stopped working, are complex. Some complex problems can be solved using the trial and error method—try out one solution first, and if that doesn't work, try another. Other useful problem-solving strategies include making models and brainstorming possible solutions with a partner.

773

Relating Cause and Effect

Emphasize that not all events that occur together have a cause-and-effect relationship. For example, tell students that you went to the grocery and your car stalled. Ask: **Is there a cause-and-effect relationship in this situation? Explain your answer.** (*No, because going to the grocery could not cause a car to stall. There must be another cause to make the car stall.*) Have students do the activity to practice relating cause and effect. (*Students should identify that the flashlight not working is the effect. Some possible causes include dead batteries, a burned-out light bulb, or a loose part.*)

Making Generalizations

Point out the importance of having a large, representative sample before making a generalization. Ask: **If you went fishing at a lake and caught three catfish, could you make the generalization that all fish in the lake are catfish? Why or why not?** (*No, because there might be other kinds of fish you didn't catch because they didn't like the bait or they may be in other parts of the lake.*) **How could you make a generalization about the kinds of fish in the lake?** (*By having a larger sample*) Have students do the activity in the Student Edition to practice making generalizations. (*The scientists should collect and test water samples from a number of different parts of the reservoir.*)

Making Judgments

Remind students that they make a judgment almost every time they make a decision. Ask: **What steps should you follow to make a judgment?** (*Gather information, list pros and cons, analyze values, make judgment*) Invite students to do the activity, and then to share and discuss the judgments they made. (*Students' judgments will vary, but should be supported by valid reasoning. Sample answer: Children and teens should be required to wear helmets when bicycling because helmets have been proven to save lives and reduce head injuries.*)

Problem Solving **ACTIVITY**

Challenge student pairs to solve a problem about a soapbox derby. Explain that their younger brother is building a car to enter in the race. The brother wants to know how to make his soapbox car go faster. After student pairs have considered the problem, have them share their ideas about solutions with the class. (*Most will probably suggest using trial and error by making small changes to the car and testing the car after each change. Some students may suggest making and manipulating a model.*)

Organizing Information

Concept Maps

Challenge students to make a concept map with at least three levels of concepts to organize information about types of transportation. All students should start with the phrase *types of transportation* at the top of the concept map. After that point, their concept maps may vary. *(For example, some students might place* private transportation *and* public transportation *at the next level, while other students might have* human-powered *and* gas-powered. *Make sure students connect the concepts with linking words. Challenge students to include cross-linkages as well.)*

Compare/ Contrast Tables

Have students make their own compare/contrast tables using two or more different sports or other activities, such as playing musical instruments. Emphasize that students should select characteristics that highlight the similarities and differences between the activities. *(Students' compare/contrast tables should include several appropriate characteristics and list information about each activity for every characteristic.)*

Organizing Information

As you read this textbook, how can you make sense of all the information it contains? Some useful tools to help you organize information are shown on this page. These tools are called *graphic organizers* because they give you a visual picture of a topic, showing at a glance how key concepts are related.

Concept Maps

Concept maps are useful tools for organizing information on broad topics. A concept map begins with a general concept and shows how it can be broken down into more specific concepts. In that way, relationships between concepts become easier to understand.

A concept map is constructed by placing concept words (usually nouns) in ovals and connecting them with linking words. Often, the most general concept word is placed at the top, and the words become more specific as you move downward. Often the linking words, which are written on a line extending between two ovals, describe the relationship between the two concepts they connect. If you follow any string of concepts and linking words down the map, it should read like a sentence.

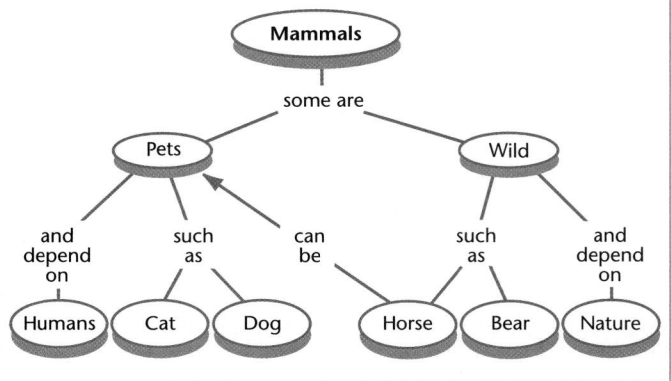

Some concept maps include linking words that connect a concept on one branch of the map to a concept on another branch. These linking words, called cross-linkages, show more complex interrelationships among concepts.

Compare/Contrast Tables

Compare/contrast tables are useful tools for sorting out the similarities and differences between two or more items. A table provides an organized framework in which to compare items based on specific characteristics that you identify.

To create a compare/contrast table, list the items to be compared across the top of a table. Then list the characteristics that will form the basis of your comparison in the left-hand

Characteristic	Baseball	Basketball
Number of Players	9	5
Playing Field	Baseball diamond	Basketball court
Equipment	Bat, baseball, mitts	Basket, basketball

column. Complete the table by filling in information about each characteristic, first for one item and then for the other.

Venn Diagrams

Another way to show similarities and differences between items is with a Venn diagram. A Venn diagram consists of two or more circles that partially overlap. Each circle represents a particular concept or idea. Common characteristics, or similarities, are written within the area of overlap between the two circles. Unique characteristics, or differences, are written in the parts of the circles outside the area of overlap.

To create a Venn diagram, draw two overlapping circles. Label the circles with the names of the items being compared. Write the

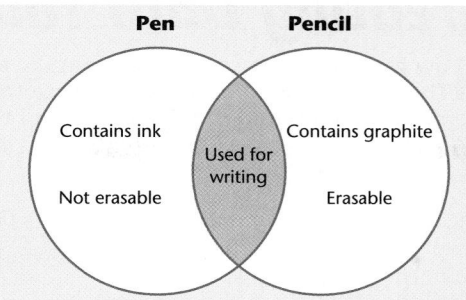

unique characteristics in each circle outside the area of overlap. Then write the shared characteristics within the area of overlap.

Flowcharts

A flowchart can help you understand the order in which certain events have occurred or should occur. Flowcharts are useful for outlining the stages in a process or the steps in a procedure.

To make a flowchart, write a brief description of each event in a box. Place the first event at the top of the page, followed by the second event, the third event, and so on. Then draw an arrow to connect each event to the one that occurs next.

Preparing Pasta

Boil water → Cook pasta → Drain water → Add sauce

Cycle Diagrams

A cycle diagram can be used to show a sequence of events that is continuous, or cyclical. A continuous sequence does not have an end because, when the final event is over, the first event begins again. Like a flowchart, a cycle diagram can help you understand the order of events.

To create a cycle diagram, write a brief description of each event in a box. Place one event at the top of the page in the center. Then, moving in a clockwise direction around an imaginary circle, write each event in its proper sequence. Draw arrows that connect each event to the one that occurs next, forming a continuous circle.

Steps in a Science Experiment

Pose a question → Develop a hypothesis → Design an experiment → Interpret data → Draw conclusions → (back to Pose a question)

Venn Diagrams

ACTIVITY

Students can use the same information from their compare/contrast tables to create a Venn diagram. Make sure students understand that the overlapping area of the circles is used to list similarities and the parts of the circles outside the overlap area are used to show differences. If students want to list similarities and differences among three activities, show them how to add a third circle that overlaps each of the other two circles and has an area of overlap for all three circles. *(Students' Venn diagrams will vary. Make sure they have accurately listed similarities in the overlap area and differences in the parts of the circles that do not overlap.)*

Flowcharts

ACTIVITY

Encourage students to create a flowchart to show the things they did this morning as they got ready for school. Remind students that a flowchart should show the correct order in which events occurred or should occur. *(Students' flowcharts will vary somewhat. A typical flowchart might include: got up → ate breakfast → took a shower → brushed teeth → got dressed → gathered books and homework → put on jacket.)*

Cycle Diagrams

ACTIVITY

Review that a cycle diagram shows a sequence of events that is continuous. Then challenge students to create a cycle diagram that shows how the weather changes with the seasons where they live. *(Students' cycle diagrams may vary, though most will include four steps, one for each season.)*

Creating Data Tables and Graphs

Data Tables

Have students create a data table to show how much time they spend on different activities during one week. Suggest that students first list the main activities they do every week. Then they should determine the amount of time they spend on each activity each day. Remind students to give this data table a title. *(Students' data tables will vary. A sample data table is shown below.)*

Bar Graphs

Students can use the data from the data table they created to make a bar graph showing how much time they spend on different activities during a week. The vertical axis should be divided into units of time, such as hours. Remind students to label both axes and give their graph a title. *(Students' bar graphs will vary. A sample bar graph is shown below.)*

Creating Data Tables and Graphs

How can you make sense of the data in a science experiment? The first step is to organize the data to help you understand them. Data tables and graphs are helpful tools for organizing data.

Data Tables

You have gathered your materials and set up your experiment. But before you start, you need to plan a way to record what happens during the experiment. By creating a data table, you can record your observations and measurements in an orderly way.

Suppose, for example, that a scientist conducted an experiment to find out how many Calories people of different body masses burn while doing various activities. The data table shows the results.

Notice in this data table that the manipulated variable (body mass) is the heading of one column. The responding variable (for Experiment 1, the number of Calories burned while bicycling) is the heading of the next column. Additional columns were added for related experiments.

CALORIES BURNED IN 30 MINUTES OF ACTIVITY			
Body Mass	Experiment 1 Bicycling	Experiment 2 Playing Basketball	Experiment 3 Watching Television
30 kg	60 Calories	120 Calories	21 Calories
40 kg	77 Calories	164 Calories	27 Calories
50 kg	95 Calories	206 Calories	33 Calories
60 kg	114 Calories	248 Calories	38 Calories

Bar Graphs

To compare how many Calories a person burns doing various activities, you could create a bar graph. A bar graph is used to display data in a number of separate, or distinct, categories. In this example, bicycling, playing basketball, and watching television are three separate categories.

To create a bar graph, follow these steps.

1. On graph paper, draw a horizontal, or *x*-, axis and a vertical, or *y*-, axis.
2. Write the names of the categories to be graphed along the horizontal axis. Include an overall label for the axis as well.
3. Label the vertical axis with the name of the responding variable. Include units of measurement. Then create a scale along the axis by marking off equally spaced numbers that cover the range of the data collected.
4. For each category, draw a solid bar using the scale on the vertical axis to determine the

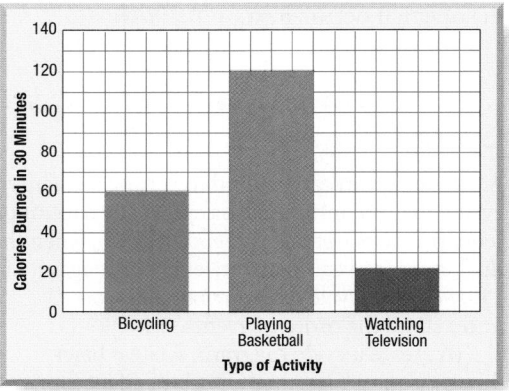

Calories Burned by a 30-kilogram Person in Various Activities

appropriate height. For example, for bicycling, draw the bar as high as the 60 mark on the vertical axis. Make all the bars the same width and leave equal spaces between them.
5. Add a title that describes the graph.

Time Spent on Different Activities in a Week

	Going to Classes	Eating Meals	Playing Soccer	Watching Television
Monday	6	2	2	0.5
Tuesday	6	1.5	1.5	1.5
Wednesday	6	2	1	2
Thursday	6	2	2	1.5
Friday	6	2	2	0.5
Saturday	0	2.5	2.5	1
Sunday	0	3	1	2

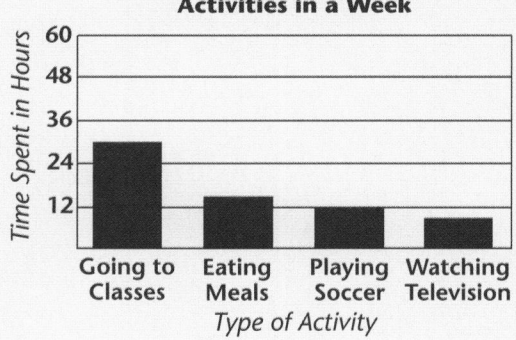

Time Spent on Different Activities in a Week

Line Graphs

To see whether a relationship exists between body mass and the number of Calories burned while bicycling, you could create a line graph. A line graph is used to display data that show how one variable (the responding variable) changes in response to another variable (the manipulated variable). You can use a line graph when your manipulated variable is *continuous*, that is, when there are other points between the ones that you tested. In this example, body mass is a continuous variable because there are other body masses between 30 and 40 kilograms (for example, 31 kilograms). Time is another example of a continuous variable.

Line graphs are powerful tools because they allow you to estimate values for conditions that you did not test in the experiment. For example, you can use the line graph to estimate that a 35-kilogram person would burn 68 Calories while bicycling.

To create a line graph, follow these steps.

1. On graph paper, draw a horizontal, or *x*-, axis and a vertical, or *y*-, axis.
2. Label the horizontal axis with the name of the manipulated variable. Label the vertical axis with the name of the responding variable. Include units of measurement.
3. Create a scale on each axis by marking off equally spaced numbers that cover the range of the data collected.
4. Plot a point on the graph for each piece of data. In the line graph above, the dotted lines show how to plot the first data point (30 kilograms and 60 Calories). Draw an imaginary vertical line extending up from the horizontal axis at the 30-kilogram mark. Then draw an imaginary horizontal line extending across from the vertical axis at the 60-Calorie mark. Plot the point where the two lines intersect.

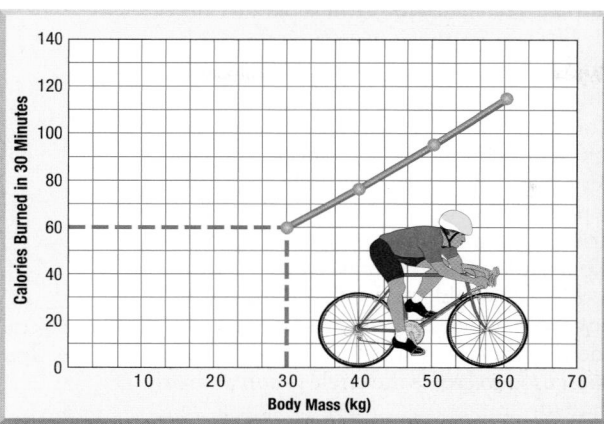

Effect of Body Mass on Calories Burned While Bicycling

5. Connect the plotted points with a solid line. (In some cases, it may be more appropriate to draw a line that shows the general trend of the plotted points. In those cases, some of the points may fall above or below the line. Also, not all graphs are linear. It may be more appropriate to draw a curve to connect the points.)
6. Add a title that identifies the variables or relationship in the graph.

> **ACTIVITY**
> Create line graphs to display the data from Experiment 2 and Experiment 3 in the data table.

> **ACTIVITY**
> You read in the newspaper that a total of 4 centimeters of rain fell in your area in June, 2.5 centimeters fell in July, and 1.5 centimeters fell in August. What type of graph would you use to display these data? Use graph paper to create the graph.

777

Line Graphs

Walk students through the steps involved in creating a line graph using the example illustrated on the page. For example, ask: **What is the label on the horizontal axis? On the vertical axis?** *(Body Mass (kg); Calories Burned in 30 Minutes)* **What scales are used on each axis?** *(3 squares per 10 kg on the x-axis and 2 squares per 20 calories on the y-axis)* **What does the second data point represent?** *(77 Calories burned for a body mass of 40 kg)* **What trend or pattern does the graph show?** *(The number of Calories burned in 30 minutes of cycling increases with body mass.)*

Have students follow the steps to carry out the first activity. *(Students should make a different graph for each experiment with different y-axis scales to practice making scales appropriate for data. See sample graphs below.)*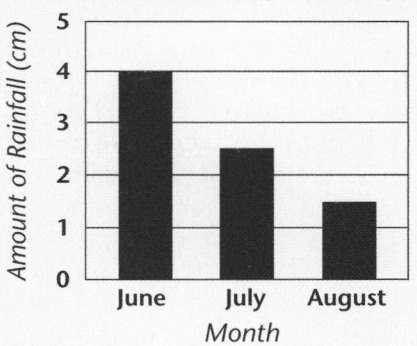

Have students carry out the second activity. *(Students should conclude that a bar graph would be best for displaying the data. A sample bar graph for these data is shown below.)*

Rainfall in June, July, and August

Effect of Body Mass on Calories Burned While Playing Basketball

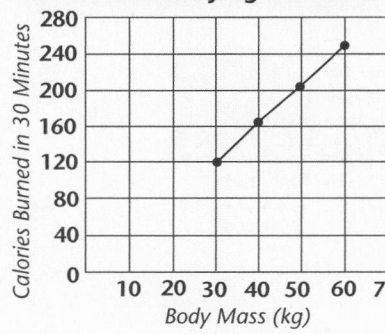

Effect of Body Mass on Calories Burned While Watching Television

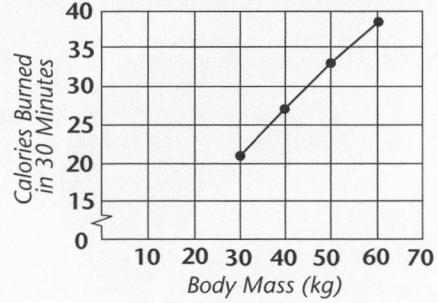

Circle Graphs

Emphasize that a circle graph has to include 100 percent of the categories for the topic being graphed. For example, ask: **Could the data in the bar graph titled "Calories Burned by a 30-kilogram Person in Various Activities" (on the previous page) be shown in a circle graph? Why or why not?** *(No, because it does not include all the possible ways a 30-kilogram person can burn Calories.)* Then walk students through the steps for making a circle graph. Help students to use a compass and a protractor. Use the protractor to illustrate that a circle has 360 degrees. Make sure students understand the mathematical calculations involved in making a circle graph.

You might wish to have students work in pairs to complete the activity. *(Students' circle graphs should look like the graph below.)*

Circle Graphs

Like bar graphs, circle graphs can be used to display data in a number of separate categories. Unlike bar graphs, however, circle graphs can only be used when you have data for *all* the categories that make up a given topic. A circle graph is sometimes called a pie chart because it resembles a pie cut into slices. The pie represents the entire topic, while the slices represent the individual categories. The size of a slice indicates what percentage of the whole a particular category makes up.

The data table below shows the results of a survey in which 24 teenagers were asked to identify their favorite sport. The data were then used to create the circle graph at the right.

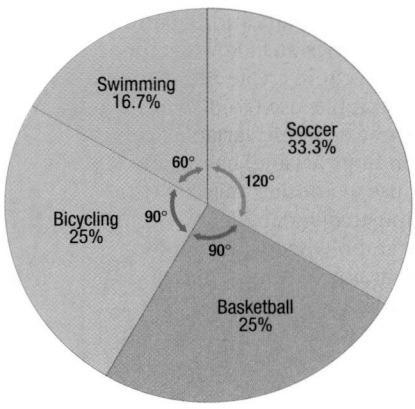

Sports That Teens Prefer

FAVORITE SPORTS	
Sport	Number of Students
Soccer	8
Basketball	6
Bicycling	6
Swimming	4

To create a circle graph, follow these steps.

1. Use a compass to draw a circle. Mark the center of the circle with a point. Then draw a line from the center point to the top of the circle.

2. Determine the size of each "slice" by setting up a proportion where x equals the number of degrees in a slice. (NOTE: A circle contains 360 degrees.) For example, to find the number of degrees in the "soccer" slice, set up the following proportion:

$$\frac{\text{students who prefer soccer}}{\text{total number of students}} = \frac{x}{\text{total number of degrees in a circle}}$$

$$\frac{8}{24} = \frac{x}{360}$$

Cross-multiply and solve for x.

$$24x = 8 \times 360$$
$$x = 120$$

The "soccer" slice should contain 120 degrees.

3. Use a protractor to measure the angle of the first slice, using the line you drew to the top of the circle as the 0° line. Draw a line from the center of the circle to the edge for the angle you measured.

4. Continue around the circle by measuring the size of each slice with the protractor. Start measuring from the edge of the previous slice so the wedges do not overlap. When you are done, the entire circle should be filled in.

5. Determine the percentage of the whole circle that each slice represents. To do this, divide the number of degrees in a slice by the total number of degrees in a circle (360), and multiply by 100%. For the "soccer" slice, you can find the percentage as follows:

$$\frac{120}{360} \times 100\% = 33.3\%$$

6. Use a different color to shade in each slice. Label each slice with the name of the category and with the percentage of the whole it represents.

7. Add a title to the circle graph.

ACTIVITY

In a class of 28 students, 12 students take the bus to school, 10 students walk, and 6 students ride their bicycles. Create a circle graph to display these data.

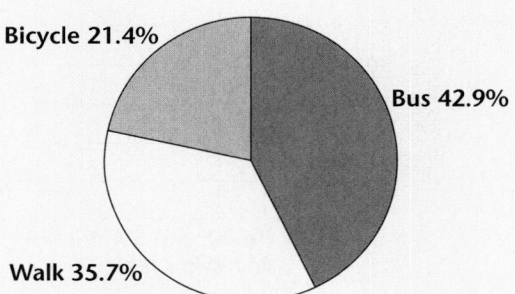

Ways Students Get to School

Bicycle 21.4%
Bus 42.9%
Walk 35.7%

Laboratory Safety

Safety Symbols

These symbols alert you to possible dangers in the laboratory and remind you to work carefully.

Safety Goggles Always wear safety goggles to protect your eyes in any activity involving chemicals, flames or heating, or the possibility of broken glassware.

Lab Apron Wear a laboratory apron to protect your skin and clothing from damage.

Breakage You are working with materials that may be breakable, such as glass containers, glass tubing, thermometers, or funnels. Handle breakable materials with care. Do not touch broken glassware.

Heat-resistant Gloves Use an oven mitt or other hand protection when handling hot materials. Hot plates, hot glassware, or hot water can cause burns. Do not touch hot objects with your bare hands.

Heating Use a clamp or tongs to pick up hot glassware. Do not touch hot objects with your bare hands.

Sharp Object Pointed-tip scissors, scalpels, knives, needles, pins, or tacks are sharp. They can cut or puncture your skin. Always direct a sharp edge or point away from yourself and others. Use sharp instruments only as instructed.

Electric Shock Avoid the possibility of electric shock. Never use electrical equipment around water, or when the equipment is wet or your hands are wet. Be sure cords are untangled and cannot trip anyone. Disconnect the equipment when it is not in use.

Corrosive Chemical You are working with an acid or another corrosive chemical. Avoid getting it on your skin or clothing, or in your eyes. Do not inhale the vapors. Wash your hands when you are finished with the activity.

Poison Do not let any poisonous chemical come in contact with your skin, and do not inhale its vapors. Wash your hands when you are finished with the activity.

Physical Safety When an experiment involves physical activity, take precautions to avoid injuring yourself or others. Follow instructions from your teacher. Alert your teacher if there is any reason you should not participate in the activity.

Animal Safety Treat live animals with care to avoid harming the animals or yourself. Working with animal parts or preserved animals also may require caution. Wash your hands when you are finished with the activity.

Plant Safety Handle plants in the laboratory or during field work only as directed by your teacher. If you are allergic to certain plants, tell your teacher before doing an activity in which those plants are used. Avoid touching harmful plants such as poison ivy, poison oak, or poison sumac, or plants with thorns. Wash your hands when you are finished with the activity.

Flames You may be working with flames from a lab burner, candle, or matches. Tie back loose hair and clothing. Follow instructions from your teacher about lighting and extinguishing flames.

No Flames Flammable materials may be present. Make sure there are no flames, sparks, or other exposed heat sources present.

Fumes When poisonous or unpleasant vapors may be involved, work in a ventilated area. Avoid inhaling vapors directly. Only test an odor when directed to do so by your teacher, and use a wafting motion to direct the vapor toward your nose.

Disposal Chemicals and other laboratory materials used in the activity must be disposed of safely. Follow the instructions from your teacher.

Hand Washing Wash your hands thoroughly when finished with the activity. Use antibacterial soap and warm water. Lather both sides of your hands and between your fingers. Rinse well.

General Safety Awareness You may see this symbol when none of the symbols described earlier appears. In this case, follow the specific instructions provided. You may also see this symbol when you are asked to develop your own procedure in a lab. Have your teacher approve your plan before you go further.

779

Laboratory Safety

Laboratory safety is an essential element of a successful science class. It is important for you to emphasize laboratory safety to students. Students need to understand exactly what is safe and unsafe behavior, and what the rationale is behind each safety rule.

Review with students the Safety Symbols and Science Safety Rules listed on this and the next two pages. Then follow the safety guidelines below to ensure that your classroom will be a safe place for students to learn science.

◆ Post safety rules in the classroom and review them regularly with students.
◆ Familiarize yourself with the safety procedures for each activity before introducing it to your students.
◆ Review specific safety precautions with students before beginning every science activity.
◆ Always act as an exemplary role model by displaying safe behavior.
◆ Know how to use safety equipment, such as fire extinguishers and fire blankets, and always have it accessible.
◆ Have students practice leaving the classroom quickly and orderly to prepare them for emergencies.
◆ Explain to students how to use the intercom or other available means of communication to get help during an emergency.
◆ Never leave students unattended while they are engaged in science activities.
◆ Provide enough space for students to safely carry out science activities.
◆ Keep your classroom and all science materials in proper condition. Replace worn or broken items.
◆ Instruct students to report all accidents and injuries to you immediately.

Laboratory Safety

Additional tips are listed below for the Science Safety Rules discussed on these two pages. Please keep these tips in mind when you carry out science activities in your classroom.

General Precautions

- For open-ended activities such as Chapter Projects, go over general safety guidelines with students. Have students submit their procedures or design plans in writing and check them for safety considerations.
- In an activity where students are directed to taste something, be sure to store the material in clean, *nonscience* containers. Distribute the material to students in *new* plastic or paper dispensables, which should be discarded after the tasting. Tasting or eating should never be done in a lab classroom.
- During physical activity, make sure students do not overexert themselves.
- Remind students to handle microscopes and telescopes with care to avoid breakage.

Heating and Fire Safety

- No flammable substances should be in use around hot plates, light bulbs, or open flames.
- Test tubes should be heated only in water baths.
- Students should be permitted to strike matches to light candles or burners *only* with strict supervision. When possible, you should light the flames, especially when working with younger students.
- Be sure to have proper ventilation when fumes are produced during a procedure.
- All electrical equipment used in the lab should have GFI switches.

Using Chemicals Safely

- When students use both chemicals and microscopes in one activity, microscopes should be in a separate part of the room from the chemicals so that when students remove their goggles to use the microscopes, their eyes are not at risk.

Science Safety Rules

To prepare yourself to work safely in the laboratory, read over the following safety rules. Then read them a second time. Make sure you understand and follow each rule. Ask your teacher to explain any rules you do not understand.

Dress Code

1. To protect yourself from injuring your eyes, wear safety goggles whenever you work with chemicals, burners, glassware, or any substance that might get into your eyes. If you wear contact lenses, notify your teacher.
2. Wear a lab apron or coat whenever you work with corrosive chemicals or substances that can stain.
3. Tie back long hair to keep it away from any chemicals, flames, or equipment.
4. Remove or tie back any article of clothing or jewelry that can hang down and touch chemicals, flames, or equipment. Roll up or secure long sleeves.
5. Never wear open shoes or sandals.

General Precautions

6. Read all directions for an experiment several times before beginning the activity. Carefully follow all written and oral instructions. If you are in doubt about any part of the experiment, ask your teacher for assistance.
7. Never perform activities that are not assigned or authorized by your teacher. Obtain permission before "experimenting" on your own. Never handle any equipment unless you have specific permission.
8. Never perform lab activities without direct supervision.
9. Never eat or drink in the laboratory.
10. Keep work areas clean and tidy at all times. Bring only notebooks and lab manuals or written lab procedures to the work area. All other items, such as purses and backpacks, should be left in a designated area.
11. Do not engage in horseplay.

First Aid

12. Always report all accidents or injuries to your teacher, no matter how minor. Notify your teacher immediately about any fires.
13. Learn what to do in case of specific accidents, such as getting acid in your eyes or on your skin. (Rinse acids from your body with lots of water.)
14. Be aware of the location of the first-aid kit, but do not use it unless instructed by your teacher. In case of injury, your teacher should administer first aid. Your teacher may also send you to the school nurse or call a physician.
15. Know the location of emergency equipment, such as the fire extinguisher and fire blanket, and know how to use it.
16. Know the location of the nearest telephone and whom to contact in an emergency.

Heating and Fire Safety

17. Never use a heat source, such as a candle, burner, or hot plate, without wearing safety goggles.
18. Never heat anything unless instructed to do so. A chemical that is harmless when cool may be dangerous when heated.
19. Keep all combustible materials away from flames. Never use a flame or spark near a combustible chemical.
20. Never reach across a flame.
21. Before using a laboratory burner, make sure you know proper procedures for lighting and adjusting the burner, as demonstrated by your teacher. Do not touch the burner. It may be hot. And never leave a lighted burner unattended!
22. Chemicals can splash or boil out of a heated test tube. When heating a substance in a test tube, make sure that the mouth of the tube is not pointed at you or anyone else.
23. Never heat a liquid in a closed container. The expanding gases produced may blow the container apart.
24. Before picking up a container that has been heated, hold the back of your hand near it. If you can feel heat on the back of your hand, the container is too hot to handle. Use an oven mitt to pick up a container that has been heated.

Using Glassware Safely

- Use plastic containers, graduated cylinders, and beakers whenever possible. If using glass, students should wear safety goggles.
- Use only nonmercury thermometers with anti-roll protectors.
- Check all glassware periodically for chips and scratches, which can cause cuts and breakage.

Using Chemicals Safely

25. Never mix chemicals "for the fun of it." You might produce a dangerous, possibly explosive substance.
26. Never put your face near the mouth of a container that holds chemicals. Many chemicals are poisonous. Never touch, taste, or smell a chemical unless you are instructed by your teacher to do so.
27. Use only those chemicals needed in the activity. Read and double-check labels on supply bottles before removing any chemicals. Take only as much as you need. Keep all containers closed when chemicals are not being used.
28. Dispose of all chemicals as instructed by your teacher. To avoid contamination, never return chemicals to their original containers. Never simply pour chemicals or other substances into the sink or trash containers.
29. Be extra careful when working with acids or bases. Pour all chemicals over the sink or a container, not over your work surface.
30. If you are instructed to test for odors, use a wafting motion to direct the odors to your nose. Do not inhale the fumes directly from the container.
31. When mixing an acid and water, always pour the water into the container first and then add the acid to the water. Never pour water into an acid.
32. Take extreme care not to spill any material in the laboratory. Wash chemical spills and splashes immediately with plenty of water. Immediately begin rinsing with water any acids that get on your skin or clothing, and notify your teacher of any acid spill at the same time.

Using Glassware Safely

33. Never force glass tubing or thermometers into a rubber stopper or rubber tubing. Have your teacher insert the glass tubing or thermometer if required for an activity.
34. If you are using a laboratory burner, use a wire screen to protect glassware from any flame. Never heat glassware that is not thoroughly dry on the outside.
35. Keep in mind that hot glassware looks cool. Never pick up glassware without first checking to see if it is hot. Use an oven mitt. See rule 24.
36. Never use broken or chipped glassware. If glassware breaks, notify your teacher and dispose of the glassware in the proper broken-glassware container. Never handle broken glass with your bare hands.
37. Never eat or drink from lab glassware.
38. Thoroughly clean glassware before putting it away.

Using Sharp Instruments

39. Handle scalpels or other sharp instruments with extreme care. Never cut material toward you; cut away from you.
40. Immediately notify your teacher if you cut your skin when working in the laboratory.

Animal and Plant Safety

41. Never perform experiments that cause pain, discomfort, or harm to animals. This rule applies at home as well as in the classroom.
42. Animals should be handled only if absolutely necessary. Your teacher will instruct you as to how to handle each animal species brought into the classroom.
43. If you know that you are allergic to certain plants, molds, or animals, tell your teacher before doing an activity in which these are used.
44. During field work, protect your skin by wearing long pants, long sleeves, socks, and closed shoes. Know how to recognize the poisonous plants and fungi in your area, as well as plants with thorns, and avoid contact with them. Never eat any part of a plant or fungus.
45. Wash your hands thoroughly after handling animals or a cage containing animals. Wash your hands when you are finished with any activity involving animal parts, plants, or soil.

End-of-Experiment Rules

46. After an experiment has been completed, turn off all burners or hot plates. If you used a gas burner, check that the gas-line valve to the burner is off. Unplug hot plates.
47. Turn off and unplug any other electrical equipment that you used.
48. Clean up your work area and return all equipment to its proper place.
49. Dispose of waste materials as instructed by your teacher.
50. Wash your hands after every experiment.

Using Sharp Instruments

◆ Always use blunt-tip safety scissors, except when pointed-tip scissors are required.

Animal and Plant Safety

◆ When working with live animals or plants, check ahead of time for students who may have allergies to the specimens.
◆ When growing bacteria cultures, use only disposable petri dishes. After streaking, the dishes should be sealed and not opened again by students. After the lab, students should return the unopened dishes to you. Students should wash their hands with antibacterial soap.
◆ Two methods are recommended for the safe disposal of bacteria cultures. *First method:* Autoclave the petri dishes and discard without opening. *Second method*: If no autoclave is available, carefully open the dishes (never have a student do this) and pour full-strength bleach into the dishes and let stand for a day. Then pour the bleach from the petri dishes down a drain and flush the drain with lots of water. Tape the petri dishes back together and place in a sealed plastic bag. Wrap the plastic bag with a brown paper bag or newspaper and tape securely. Throw the sealed package in the trash. Thoroughly disinfect the work area with bleach.
◆ To grow mold, use a new, sealable plastic bag that is two to three times larger than the material to be placed inside. Seal the bag and tape it shut. After the bag is sealed, students should not open it. To dispose of the bag and mold culture, make a small cut near an edge of the bag and cook in a microwave oven on high setting for at least 1 minute. Discard the bag according to local ordinance, usually in the trash.
◆ Students should wear disposable nitrile, latex, or food-handling gloves when handling live animals or nonliving specimens.

End-of-Experiment Rules

◆ Always have students use antibacterial soap for washing their hands.

Identifying Common Minerals

GROUP 1
Metallic Luster, Mostly Dark-Colored

Mineral/Formula	Hardness	Density (g/cm³)	Luster	Streak	Color	Other Properties/Remarks
Pyrite FeS_2	6–6.5	5.0	Metallic	Greenish, brownish black	Light yellow	Harder than chalcopyrite and pyrrhotite; called "fool's gold," but harder than gold and very brittle
Magnetite Fe_3O_4	6	5.2	Metallic	Black	Iron black	Very magnetic; important iron ore; some varieties known as "lodestone"
Hematite Fe_2O_3	5.5–6.5	4.9–5.3	Metallic or earthy	Red or red brown	Reddish brown to black; also steel gray crystals	Most important ore of iron; known as "red ocher"; often used as red pigment in paint.
Pyrrhotite FeS	4	4.6	Metallic	Gray black	Brownish bronze	Less hard than pyrite: slightly magnetic
Sphalerite ZnS	3.5–4	3.9–4.1	Resinous	Brown to light yellow	Brown to yellow	Most important zinc ore
Chalcopyrite $CuFeS_2$	3.5–4	4.1–4.3	Metallic	Greenish black	Golden yellow, often tarnished	Most important copper ore; softer than pyrite and more yellow; more brittle than gold
Bornite Cu_5FeS_4	3	4.9–5.4	Metallic	Gray black	Copper, brown; turns to purple and black	Important copper ore; known as "peacock ore" because of iridescent purple color when exposed to air for a time
Copper Cu	2.5–3	8.9	Metallic	Copper red	Copper red to black	Can be pounded into various shapes and drawn into wires; used in making electrical wires, coins, pipes
Gold Au	2.5–3	19.3	Metallic	Yellow	Rich yellow	Can be pounded into various shapes and drawn into wires; does not tarnish; used in jewelry, coins, dental fillings
Silver Ag	2.5–3	10.0–11.0	Metallic	Silver to light gray	Silver white, tarnishes to black	Can be pounded into various shapes and drawn into wires; used in jewelry, coins, electrical wire
Galena PbS	2.5	7.4–7.6	Metallic	Lead gray	Lead gray	Main ore of lead; used in shields against radiation
Graphite C	1–2	2.3	Metallic to dull	Black	Black	Feels greasy; very soft; used as pencil "lead" and as a lubricant

GROUP 2
Nonmetallic Luster, Mostly Dark-Colored

Mineral/Formula	Hardness	Density (g/cm³)	Luster	Streak	Color	Other Properties/Remarks
Corundum Al_2O_3	9	3.9–4.1	Brilliant to glassy	White	Usually brown	Very hard; used as an abrasive; transparent crystals used as gems called "ruby" (red) and "sapphire" (blue and other colors)
Garnet $(Ca,Mg,Fe)_3$ $(Al,Fe,Cr)_2(SiO_4)_3$	7–7.5	3.5–4.3	Glassy to resinous	White, light brown	Red, brown, black, green	A group of minerals used in jewelry, as a birthstone, and as an abrasive
Olivine $(Mg,Fe)_2SiO_4$	6.5–7	3.3–3.4	Glassy	White or gray	Olive green	Found in igneous rocks; sometimes used as a gem
Augite $Ca(Mg,Fe,Al)$ $(AlSi)_2O_6$	5–6	3.2–3.4	Glassy	Greenish gray	Dark green to black	Found in igneous rocks
Hornblende $NaCa_2(Mg,Fe,Al)_5$ $(Si,Al)_8O_{22}(OH)_2$	5–6	3.0–3.4	Glassy, silky	White to gray	Dark green to brown, black	Found in igneous and metamorphic rocks
Apatite $Ca_5(PO_4)_3F$	5	3.1–3.2	Glassy	White	Green, brown, red, blue, violet, yellow	Sometimes used as a gem; source of the phosphorus needed by plants
Azurite $Cu_3(CO_3)_2(OH)_2$	3.5–4	3.8	Glassy to dull	Pale blue	Intense blue	Ore of copper; used as a gem
Biotite $K(Mg,Fe)_3AlSiO_{10}$ $(OH)_2$	2.5–3	2.8–3.4	Glassy or pearly	White to gray	Dark green, brown, or black	A type of mica, sometimes used as a lubricant
Serpentine $Mg_6Si_4O_{10}(OH)_8$	2–5	2.2–2.6	Greasy, waxy, silky	White	Usually green	Once used in insulation but found to cause cancer; used in fireproofing; can be in the form of asbestos
Limonite Mixture of hydrous iron oxides	1–5.5	2.8–4.3	Glassy to dull	Yellow brown	Brown black to brownish yellow	Ore of iron, also known as "yellow ocher," a pigment; a mixture that is not strictly a mineral
Bauxite Mixture of hydrous aluminum oxides	1–3	2.0–2.5	Dull to earthy	Colorless to gray	Brown, yellow, gray, white	Ore of aluminum, smells like clay when wet; a mixture that is not strictly a mineral

GROUP 3
Nonmetallic Luster, Mostly Light-Colored

Mineral/ Formula	Hardness	Density (g/cm³)	Luster	Streak	Color	Other Properties/Remarks
Diamond C	10	3.5	Brilliant	White	Colorless and varied	Hardest known substance; used in jewelry, as an abrasive, in cutting instruments
Topaz $Al_2SiO_4(F,OH)_2$	8	3.5–3.6	Glassy	White	Straw yellow, pink, bluish, greenish	Valuable gem
Quartz SiO_2	7	2.6	Glassy, greasy	White	Colorless, white; any color when not pure	The second most abundant mineral; many varieties are gems (amethyst, cat's-eye, bloodstone, agate, jasper, onyx); used in making glass
Feldspar (K,Na,Ca) $(AlSi_3O_8)$	6	2.6	Glassy	Colorless, white	Colorless, white, various colors	As a family, the most abundant of all minerals; the different types of feldspar make up over 60 percent of Earth's crust
Fluorite CaF_2	4	3.0–3.3	Glassy	Colorless	Purple, light, green, yellow, bluish green, other colors	Some types are fluorescent (glow when exposed to ultraviolet light); used in making steel
Dolomite $CaMg(CO_3)_2$	3.5–4	2.8	Glassy or pearly	White	Colorless, white, pinkish, or light tints	Used in making concrete and cement; fizzes slowly in dilute hydrochloric acid
Calcite $CaCO_3$	3	2.7	Glassy	White to grayish	Colorless, white, pale tints	Easily scratched; bubbles in dilute hydrochloric acid; frequently fluorescent
Halite NaCl	2.5	2.1–2.6	Glassy	White	Colorless or white	Occurs as perfect cubic crystals; has salty taste
Gypsum $CaSO_4 \cdot 2H_2O$	2	2.3	Glassy, pearly, silky	White	Colorless, white, light tints	Very soft; used in manufacture of plaster of Paris; form known as alabaster used for statues
Sulfur S	2	2.0–2.1	Resinous to greasy	White	Yellow to yellowish brown	Used in making many medicines, in production of sulfuric acid, and in vulcanizing rubber
Talc $Mg_3Si_4O_{10}(OH)_2$	1	2.7–2.8	Pearly to greasy	White	Gray, white, greenish	Very soft; used in talcum powder; found mostly in metamorphic rocks; also called "soapstone"

Glossary

A

aa A slow-moving type of lava that hardens to form rough chunks; cooler than pahoehoe. (p. 429)

absolute dating A technique used to determine the actual age of a fossil. (p. 92)

acceleration The rate at which velocity changes. (p. 132)

acid rain Precipitation that is more acidic than normal. (pp. 521, 708)

active Said of a volcano that is erupting or has shown signs of erupting in the near future. (p. 430)

active solar system A method of capturing the sun's energy and distributing it using pumps and fans. (p. 739)

actual mechanical advantage The mechanical advantage that a machine provides in a real situation. (p. 213)

adaptation A trait that helps an organism survive and reproduce. (p. 81)

aftershock An earthquake that occurs after a larger earthquake in the same area. (p. 405)

air mass A huge body of air that has similar temperature, pressure, and humidity throughout. (p. 574)

air pollution A change to the atmosphere that has harmful effects. (p. 706)

air pressure A force that is the result of the weight of a column of air pushing down on an area. (p. 524)

air resistance The fluid friction experienced by objects falling through the air. (p. 157)

alleles The different forms of a gene. (p. 21)

alloy A solid mixture of two or more metals. (p. 470)

alternating current Current consisting of charges that move back and forth in a circuit. (p. 318)

altitude Elevation above sea level. (p. 526)

ammeter A device used to measure current in a circuit. (p. 292)

amniocentesis A technique by which a small amount of the fluid that surrounds a developing baby is removed; the fluid is analyzed to determine whether the baby will have a genetic disorder. (p. 60)

anemometer An instrument used to measure wind speed. (p. 551)

aneroid barometer An instrument that measures changes in air pressure without using a liquid. Changes in the shape of an airtight metal box cause a needle on the barometer dial to move. (p. 525)

anticline An upward fold in rock formed by compression of Earth's crust. (p. 392)

anticyclone A high-pressure center of dry air. (p. 580)

aquaculture The practice of raising fish and other water organisms for food. (p. 661)

Archimedes' principle The rule that the buoyant force on an object is equal to the weight of the fluid displaced by that object. (p. 189)

armature The moving part of an electric motor, consisting of dozens or hundreds of loops of wire wrapped around an iron core. (p. 313)

asthenosphere The soft layer of the mantle on which the lithosphere floats. (p. 353)

atmosphere The layer of gases that surrounds Earth. (p. 512)

atoll A ring-shaped coral island found far from land. (p. 493)

atom The smallest particle of an element that has the properties of that element. (p. 250)

aurora A glowing region produced by the interaction of charged particles from the sun and atoms in the atmosphere. (p. 260)

aurora borealis A colorful, glowing display in the sky caused when particles from the sun strike oxygen and nitrogen atoms in the ionosphere; also called the Northern Lights. (p. 534)

B

balanced forces Equal forces acting on an object in opposite directions. (p. 144)

barometer An instrument used to measure changes in air pressure. (p. 524)

basalt A dark, dense, igneous rock with a fine texture, found in oceanic crust. (p. 352)

base-isolated building A building mounted on bearings designed to absorb the energy of an earthquake. (p. 408)

batholith A mass of rock formed when a large body of magma cooled inside the crust. (p. 439)

battery A combination of two or more electrochemical cells in series. (p. 334)

bedrock Rock that makes up Earth's crust. (p. 682)

Bernoulli's principle The rule that a stream of fast-moving fluid exerts less pressure than the surrounding fluid. (p. 196)

biodegradable Capable of being broken down by bacteria and other natural decomposers. (p. 690)

biodiversity The number of different species in an area. (p. 663)

biomass fuel Fuel made from living things. (p. 742)

branching tree A diagram that shows how scientists think different groups of organisms are related. (p. 100)

brushes The contact points connected to a current source and the commutator of a motor. (p. 313)

buoyant force The upward force exerted by a fluid on a submerged object. (p. 189)

caldera The large hole at the top of a volcano formed when the roof of a volcano's magma chamber collapses. (p. 436)

captive breeding The mating of endangered animals in zoos or preserves. (p. 670)

carrier A person who has one recessive allele for a trait and one dominant allele, but does not have the trait. (p. 54)

cast A type of fossil that forms when a mold becomes filled in with minerals that then harden. (p. 90)

catalytic converter A device that reduces carbon monoxide emissions from vehicles. (p. 722)

cementation The process by which dissolved minerals crystallize and glue particles of sediment together into one mass. (p. 487)

centripetal force A force that causes an object to move in a circle. (p. 169)

chemical energy The energy stored in chemical compounds. (p. 332)

chemical reaction A process in which substances change into new substances with different properties. (p. 332)

chemical rock Sedimentary rock that forms when minerals crystallize from a solution. (p. 490)

chlorofluorocarbons Gases containing chlorine and fluorine, formerly used in air conditioners, refrigerators, and spray cans. (pp. 640, 711)

cinder cone A steep, cone-shaped hill or mountain made of volcanic ash, cinders, and bombs piled up around a volcano's opening. (p. 436)

circuit breaker A safety device that uses an electromagnet to shut off a circuit when the current becomes too high. (p. 303)

cirrus Wispy, feathery clouds made mostly of ice crystals that form at high levels, above about 6 kilometers. (p. 562)

clastic rock Sedimentary rock that forms when rock fragments are squeezed together under high pressure. (p. 488)

clear-cutting The process of cutting down all the trees in an area at once. (p. 658)

cleavage A mineral's ability to split easily along flat surfaces. (p. 457)

climate The average, year-after-year conditions of temperature, precipitation, winds, and clouds in an area. (p. 610)

clone An organism that is genetically identical to the organism from which it was produced. (p. 66)

codominance A condition in which neither of two alleles of a gene is dominant or recessive. (p. 30)

combustion The burning of a fuel. (p. 731)

commutator A device that controls the direction of the flow of current through an electric motor. (p. 313)

compaction The process by which sediments are pressed together under their own weight. (p. 487)

compass A device with a magnetized needle that can spin freely; a compass needle always points north. (p. 256)

composite volcano A tall, cone-shaped mountain in which layers of lava alternate with layers of ash and other volcanic materials. (p. 436)

composting Helping the natural decomposition process to break down certain wastes. (p. 693)

compound A substance in which two or more elements are chemically joined. (p. 452)

compound machine A device that combines two or more simple machines. (p. 226)

compression Stress that squeezes rock until it folds or breaks. (p. 387)

condensation The process by which molecules of water vapor in the air become liquid water. (p. 561)

conduction A method of charging an object by allowing electrons to flow directly from one object to another object (p. 281); also, the direct transfer of heat from one substance to another substance that it is touching. (pp. 358, 548)

conductor A material through which electrons move freely, forming an electric current. (p. 264)

conservation of charge The law that states that charges are neither created nor destroyed. (p. 282)

conservation viewpoint The belief that people should use natural resources as long as they do not destroy those resources. (p. 654)

constructive force A force that builds up mountains and landmasses on Earth's surface. (p. 349)

continent A great landmass surrounded by oceans. (p. 349)

continental (air mass) A dry air mass that forms over land. (p. 574)

continental climate The climate of the centers of continents, with cold winters and warm or hot summers. (p. 612)

continental drift The hypothesis that the continents slowly move across Earth's surface. (p. 361)

controlled experiment An experiment in which all variables except one are kept constant. (pp. 6, 771)

control rod Cadmium rod used in a nuclear reactor to absorb neutrons from fission. (p. 748)

convection The transfer of heat by the movement of a fluid. (pp. 358, 548)

convection current The movement of a fluid, caused by differences in temperature, that transfers heat from one part of the fluid to another. (p. 358)

convergent boundary A plate boundary where two plates move toward each other. (p. 378)

coral reef A structure of calcite skeletons built up by coral animals in warm, shallow ocean water. (p. 492)

Coriolis effect The way Earth's rotation makes winds in the Northern Hemisphere curve to the right and winds in the Southern Hemisphere curve to the left. (p. 555)

corrosive Able to dissolve or break down many other substances, such as an acid. (p. 697)

crater A bowl-shaped area that forms around a volcano's central opening. (p. 426)

crop rotation The planting of different crops in a field each year. (p. 684)

crust The layer of rock that forms Earth's outer surface. (p. 352)

crystal A solid in which the atoms are arranged in a pattern that repeats again and again. (p. 452)

cumulus Clouds that form less than 2 kilometers above the ground and look like fluffy, rounded piles of cotton. (p. 562)

cyclone A swirling center of low air pressure. (p. 579)

data The facts, figures, and other evidence collected in an experiment. (pp. 7, 766)

deep-ocean trench A deep valley along the ocean floor through which oceanic crust slowly sinks towards the mantle. (p. 370)

deformation A change in the volume or shape of Earth's crust. (p. 387)

density The amount of mass in a given space; mass per unit volume. (pp. 192, 358, 523)

deposition The process by which sediment settles out of the water or wind that is carrying it. (p. 487)

desert A region that gets less than 25 centimeters of rain a year. (p. 624)

desertification The advance of desertlike conditions into areas that previously were fertile. (p. 684)

destructive force A force that slowly wears away mountains and other features on the surface of Earth. (p. 349)

development The construction of buildings, roads, dams, and other structures. (p. 681)

development viewpoint The belief that humans should be able to freely use and benefit from all of Earth's resources. (p. 654)

dew point The temperature at which condensation begins. (p. 561)

dike A slab of volcanic rock formed when magma forces itself across rock layers. (p. 438)

direct current Current consisting of charges that flow in only one direction in a circuit. (p. 318)

divergent boundary A plate boundary where two plates move away from each other. (p. 377)

dominant allele An allele whose trait always shows up in the organism when the allele is present. (p. 21)

dormant Said of a volcano that does not show signs of erupting in the near future. (p. 430)

drought A period of less rain than normal. (pp. 568, 716)

dry cell An electrochemical cell in which the electrolyte is a paste. (p. 334)

earthquake The shaking that results from the movement of rock beneath Earth's surface. (p. 386)

efficiency The percentage of the input work that is converted to output work. (pp. 212, 754)

El Niño An event that occurs every two to seven years in the Pacific Ocean, during which winds shift and push warm surface water toward the coast of South America; it can cause dramatic climate changes. (p. 600)

electric charge A property of electrons and protons; electrons carry a negative charge, and protons carry a positive charge. (p. 262)

electric circuit A complete path through which electric charges can flow. (p. 264)

electric current The flow of electric charges through a material. (p. 263)

787

electric field The field around charged particles that exerts a force on other charged particles. (p. 279)

electric generator A device that converts mechanical energy into electrical energy. (p. 318)

electric motor A device that converts electrical energy to mechanical energy to turn an axle. (p. 312)

electrical energy The energy of moving electrical charges. (p. 311)

electrical potential The potential energy per unit of electric charge. (p. 288)

electrochemical cell A device that converts chemical energy into electrical energy. (p. 333)

electrode A metal part of an electrochemical cell, which gains or loses electrons. (p. 333)

electrolyte A liquid or paste that conducts electricity. (p. 333)

electromagnet A strong magnet that can be turned on and off; a solenoid with a ferromagnetic core. (p. 271)

electromagnetic induction The process of generating an electric current from the motion of a conductor through a magnetic field. (p. 317)

electromagnetic wave A form of energy that can travel through space. (p. 540)

electron A negatively charged particle that orbits the nucleus of an atom. (p. 250)

electroscope An instrument used to detect electric charge. (p. 285)

element A substance in which all the atoms are alike; one of about 100 basic materials that make up all matter. (pp. 250, 452)

emissions Solid particles and gases released into the air from a smokestack or motor vehicle. (p. 707)

endangered species A species in danger of becoming extinct in the near future. (p. 666)

energy The ability to move an object some distance. (p. 311)

energy conservation The practice of reducing energy use. (p. 753)

epicenter The point on Earth's surface directly above an earthquake's focus. (p. 396)

erosion The destructive process in which water or wind loosen and carry away fragments of rock. (pp. 487, 682)

evacuate To move away temporarily. (p. 588)

evaporation The process by which water molecules in liquid water escape into the air as water vapor. (p. 559)

evolution The gradual change in a species over time. (p. 81)

exosphere The outer layer of the thermosphere, extending outward into space. (p. 534)

explosive Capable of reacting very quickly when exposed to air or water or of exploding when dropped. (p. 697)

extinct A species that does not have any living members (p. 92); also, said of a volcano that is unlikely to erupt again. (p. 430)

extinction The disappearance of all members of a species from Earth. (p. 666)

extrusive rock Igneous rock that forms from lava on Earth's surface. (p. 483)

fallow Left unplanted with crops. (p. 683)

fault A break in Earth's crust where slabs of rock slip past each other. (pp. 376, 388)

fault-block mountain A mountain that forms where a normal fault uplifts a block of rock. (p. 390)

ferromagnetic material A material that is strongly attracted to a magnet, and which can be made into a magnet. (p. 251)

fertilizer A chemical that provides nutrients to help crops grow better. (p. 717)

fishery An area with a large population of valuable ocean organisms. (p. 660)

flammable Capable of catching fire easily and burning at low temperatures. (p. 697)

flash flood A sudden, violent flood that occurs within a few hours, or even minutes, of a heavy rainstorm. (p. 594)

fluid A substance that can easily change shape. (p. 178)

fluid friction Friction that occurs as an object moves through a fluid. (p. 155)

fluorescence The property of a mineral in which the mineral glows under ultraviolet light. (p. 458)

focus The point beneath Earth's surface where rock breaks under stress and causes an earthquake. (p. 396)

fold A bend in rock that forms where part of Earth's crust is compressed. (p. 391)

foliated Term used to describe metamorphic rocks whose grains are arranged in parallel layers or bands. (p. 495)

footwall The block of rock that forms the lower half of a fault. (p. 388)

force A push or pull exerted on an object. (p. 142)

fossil The preserved remains or traces of an organism that lived in the past. (pp. 89, 362)

fossil fuel An energy-rich substance (such as coal, oil, or natural gas) formed from the remains of organisms. (p. 732)

fossil record The millions of fossils that scientists have collected. (p. 92)

fracture The way a mineral looks when it breaks apart in an irregular way. (p. 457)

free fall The motion of a falling object when the only force acting on it is gravity. (p. 156)

friction A force that is exerted when two substances are rubbed together; electrons can be transferred by the rubbing. (pp. 154, 281)

front The area where air masses meet and do not mix. (p. 577)

fuel rod Uranium rod that undergoes fission in a nuclear reactor. (p. 748)

fulcrum The fixed point around which a lever pivots. (p. 219)

fuse A safety device with a thin metal strip that will melt if too much current passes through a circuit. (p. 302)

galvanometer A device that uses an electromagnet to detect small amounts of current. (p. 311)

gasohol A mixture of gasoline and alcohol. (p. 742)

gears Two or more wheels linked together by interlocking teeth. (p. 226)

gemstone A hard, colorful mineral that has a brilliant or glassy luster. (p. 467)

gene A segment of DNA on a chromosome that codes for a specific trait; a structure in an organism's cells that carries its hereditary information. (pp. 21, 666)

gene therapy The insertion of working copies of a gene into the cells of a person with a genetic disorder in an attempt to correct the disorder. (p. 68)

genetic disorder An abnormal condition that a person inherits through genes or chromosomes. (p. 57)

genetic engineering The transfer of a gene from the DNA of one organism into another organism, in order to produce an organism with desired traits. (p. 66)

genetics The scientific study of heredity. (p. 18)

genome All of the DNA in one cell of an organism. (p. 70)

genotype An organism's genetic makeup, or allele combinations. (p. 30)

geologist A scientist who studies the forces that make and shape planet Earth. (p. 349)

geology The study of planet Earth. (p. 349)

geothermal energy Heat from Earth's interior; energy from water or steam that has been heated by magma. (pp. 431, 743)

geyser A fountain of water and steam that builds up pressure underground and erupts at regular intervals. (p. 431)

global warming A gradual increase in the temperature of Earth's atmosphere; the theory that increasing carbon dioxide in the atmosphere will raise Earth's average temperature. (pp. 638, 712)

global winds Winds that blow steadily from specific directions over long distances. (p. 555)

gradualism The theory that evolution occurs slowly but steadily. (p. 96)

grain A particle of mineral or other rock that gives a rock its texture. (p. 479)

granite A usually light-colored rock that is found in continental crust. (p. 352)

gravity The force that pulls objects toward each other. (p. 156)

greenhouse effect The process by which heat is trapped in the atmosphere by water vapor, carbon dioxide, methane, and other gases that form a "blanket" around Earth. (pp. 543, 712)

greenhouse gases Gases in the atmosphere that trap heat. (p. 638)

grounded Allowing charges to flow directly from the circuit to the ground connection. (p. 301)

groundwater Water stored in underground layers of soil and rock. (p. 715)

habitat destruction The loss of a natural habitat. (p. 667)

habitat fragmentation The breaking of a habitat into smaller, isolated pieces. (p. 667)

half-life The time it takes for half of the atoms in a radioactive element to break down. (p. 92)

hanging wall The block of rock that forms the upper half of a fault. (p. 388)

hazardous waste A material that can be harmful if it is not properly disposed of. (p. 697)

heat The energy transferred from a hotter object to a cooler one. (p. 547)

heat transfer The movement of energy from a warmer object to a cooler object. (p. 357)

heredity The passing of traits from parents to offspring. (p. 18)

heterozygous Having two different alleles for a trait. (p. 30)

homologous structures Body parts that are structurally similar in related species; provide evidence that the structures were inherited from a common ancestor. (p. 98)

homozygous Having two identical alleles for a trait. (p. 30)

hot spot An area where magma from deep within the mantle melts through the crust above it. (p. 423)

hot spring A pool formed by groundwater that has risen to the surface after being heated by a nearby body of magma. (p. 431)

humid subtropical A wet and warm climate area on the edge of the tropics. (p. 626)

humidity A measure of the amount of water vapor in the air. (p. 560)

hurricane A tropical storm that has winds of 119 kilometers per hour or higher; typically about 600 kilometers across. (p. 586)

hybrid An organism that has two different alleles for a trait; an organism that is heterozygous for a particular trait. (p. 22)

hybridization A selective breeding method in which two genetically different individuals are crossed. (p. 65)

hydraulic system A system that multiplies force by transmitting pressure from a small surface area through a confined fluid to a larger surface area. (p. 186)

hydrocarbon A compound that contains carbon and hydrogen atoms. (p. 732)

hydroelectric power Electricity produced using the energy of flowing water. (p. 741)

hypothesis A possible explanation for a set of observations or answer to a scientific question; must be testable. (pp. 6, 770)

ice ages Cold time periods in Earth's history, during which glaciers covered large parts of the surface. (p. 634)

ideal mechanical advantage The mechanical advantage that a machine would have without friction. (p. 213)

igneous rock A type of rock that forms from the cooling of molten rock at or below the surface. (p. 481)

inbreeding A selective breeding method in which two individuals with identical or similar sets of alleles are crossed. (p. 65)

incineration The burning of solid waste. (p. 689)

inclined plane A flat surface with one end higher than the other. (p. 217)

induction A method of electrically charging an object by means of the electric field of another object. (p. 282)

inertia The tendency of an object to resist any change in its motion. (p. 146)

inference An interpretation based on observations and prior knowledge. (p. 5)

infrared radiation A form of energy with wavelengths that are longer than visible light. (p. 541)

inner core A dense sphere of solid iron and nickel in the center of Earth. (p. 353)

inorganic Not formed from living things or the remains of living things. (p. 451)

input force The force exerted on a machine. (p. 209)

insulation Building material that blocks heat transfer between the air inside and outside. (p. 755)

insulator A material through which the charges of an electric current are not able to move. (p. 264)

International System of Units (SI) A system of measurement based on multiples of ten and on established measures of mass, length, and time. (p. 117)

intrusive rock Igneous rock that forms when magma hardens beneath Earth's surface. (p. 483)

ionosphere The lower part of the thermosphere, where electrically charged particles called ions are found. (p. 534)

island arc A string of islands formed by the volcanoes along a deep ocean trench. (p. 422)

isobars Lines on a map joining places that have the same air pressure. (p. 600)

isotherms Lines on a map joining places that have the same temperature. (p. 600)

jet streams Bands of high-speed winds about 10 kilometers above Earth's surface. (p. 558)

joule A unit of work equal to one newton-meter. (p. 207)

karyotype A picture of all the chromosomes in a cell arranged in pairs. (p. 61)

keystone species A species that influences the survival of many others in an ecosystem. (p. 665)

land breeze The flow of air from land to a body of water. (p. 554)

land reclamation The process of restoring land to a more natural state. (p. 685)

latitude The distance from the equator, measured in degrees. (p. 556)

lava Liquid magma that reaches the surface; also the rock formed when liquid lava hardens. (p. 420)

lava flow The area covered by lava as it pours out of a volcano's vent. (p. 426)

law of conservation of momentum The rule that the total momentum of objects in an interaction does not change. (p. 166)

leachate Water that has passed through buried wastes in a landfill. (p. 689)

leeward The downwind side of mountains. (p. 615)

lever A rigid object that pivots about a fixed point. (p. 219)

lightning A sudden spark, or energy discharge, caused when electrical charges jump between parts of a cloud or between a cloud and the ground. (p. 582)

lightning rod A metal rod on a building connected to a grounding wire; meant to protect a building from lightning damage. (p. 302)

liquefaction The process by which an earthquake's violent movement suddenly turns loose soil into liquid mud. (p. 405)

lithosphere A rigid layer made up of the uppermost part of the mantle and the crust. (p. 352)

litter Layer of dead leaves and grass on top of the soil. (p. 682)

local winds Winds that blow over short distances. (p. 552)

luster The way a mineral reflects light from its surface. (p. 455)

machine A device that changes the amount of force exerted or the direction in which force is exerted. (p. 208)

magma The molten mixture of rock-forming substances, gases, and water from the mantle. (p. 420)

magma chamber The pocket beneath a volcano where magma collects. (p. 426)

magnetic declination The angle between geographic north and the north to which a compass needle points. (p. 258)

magnetic domain A region in which the magnetic fields of all atoms are lined up in the same direction. (p. 251)

magnetic field The region around a magnet where the magnetic force is exerted. (p. 249)

magnetic field lines Lines that map out the magnetic field around a magnet. (p. 249)

magnetic pole The ends of a magnetic object, where the magnetic force is strongest. (p. 247)

magnetism The force of attraction or repulsion of magnetic materials. (p. 247)

magnetosphere The region of Earth's magnetic field shaped by the solar wind. (p. 259)

magnitude The measurement of an earthquake's strength based on seismic waves and movement along faults. (p. 399)

manipulated variable The one factor that a scientist changes during an experiment. (pp. 6, 771)

mantle The layer of hot, solid material between Earth's crust and core. (p. 352)

marine climate The climate of some coastal regions, with relatively warm winters and cool summers. (p. 612)

maritime (air mass) A humid air mass that forms over oceans. (p. 574)

mass The amount of matter in an object. (p. 147)

mechanical advantage The number of times the force exerted on a machine is multiplied by the machine. (p. 211)

mechanical energy The energy an object has due to its movement or position. (p. 311)

meiosis The process that occurs in sex cells (sperm and egg) by which the number of chromosomes is reduced by half. (p. 36)

meltdown A dangerous condition caused by overheating inside a nuclear reactor. (p. 749)

Mercalli scale A scale that rates earthquakes according to their intensity and how much damage they cause. (p. 399)

mercury barometer An instrument that measures changes in air pressure, consisting of a glass tube partially filled with mercury, with its open end resting in a dish of mercury. Air pressure pushing on the mercury in the dish forces the mercury in the tube higher. (p. 524)

mesosphere The middle layer of Earth's atmosphere; the layer in which most meteoroids burn up. (p. 530)

messenger RNA RNA that copies the coded message from DNA in the nucleus and carries the message into the cytoplasm. (p. 41)

metamorphic rock A type of rock that forms from an existing rock that is changed by heat, pressure, or chemical reactions. (p. 481)

meteorologists Scientists who study the causes of weather and try to predict it. (p. 598)

meter The basic SI unit of length. (p. 117)

microclimate The climate characteristic of a small, specific area; it may be different from the climate of the surrounding area. (p. 615)

mid-ocean ridge The undersea mountain chain where new ocean floor is produced; a divergent plate boundary. (p. 366)

mineral A naturally-occurring, inorganic solid that has a crystal structure and a definite chemical composition. (p. 451)

Mohs hardness scale A scale ranking ten minerals from softest to hardest; used in testing the hardness of minerals. (p. 453)

mold A type of fossil formed when a shell or other hard part of an organism dissolves, leaving an empty space in the shape of the part. (p. 90)

moment magnitude scale A scale that rates earthquakes by estimating the total energy released by an earthquake. (p. 400)

momentum The product of an object's mass and velocity. (p. 165)

monsoons Sea and land breezes over a large region that change direction with the seasons. (p. 554)

motion The state in which one object's distance from another is changing. (p. 115)

multiple alleles Three or more forms of a gene that code for a single trait. (p. 51)

municipal solid waste Waste produced in homes, businesses, and schools. (p. 688)

natural selection The process by which individuals that are better adapted to their environment are more likely to survive and reproduce than other members of the same species. (p. 82)

net force The overall force on an object when all the individual forces acting on an object are added together. (p. 144)

newton A unit of measure that equals the force required to accelerate one kilogram of mass at 1 meter per second per second. (p. 151)

nonrenewable resource A natural resource that is not replaced as it is used. (pp. 323, 651)

normal fault A type of fault where the hanging wall slides downward; caused by tension in the crust. (p. 388)

nuclear fission The splitting of an atom's nucleus into smaller nuclei. (p. 747)

nuclear fusion The combining of two atomic nuclei into a single larger nucleus. (p. 750)

nucleus The central core of an atom that contains the protons and neutrons. (pp. 250, 747)

nutrient depletion The situation that arises when more soil nutrients are used than the decomposers can replace. (p. 683)

observation Using one or more senses to gather information. (pp. 5, 766)

occluded Cut off, as the warm air mass at an occluded front is cut off from the ground by cooler air beneath it. (p. 579)

Ohm's law Resistance equals voltage divided by current. (p. 292)

operational definition A statement that describes how a particular variable is to be measured or a term is to be defined. (p. 771)

ore Rock that contains a metal or economically useful mineral. (p. 457)

organic rock Sedimentary rock that forms where remains of organisms are deposited in thick layers. (p. 489)

outer core A layer of molten iron and nickel that surrounds the inner core of Earth. (p. 353)

output force The force exerted on an object by a machine. (p. 209)

ozone A form of oxygen that has three oxygen atoms in each molecule instead of the usual two; a toxic form of oxygen. (pp. 514, 707)

ozone layer The layer of the atmosphere that contains a higher concentration of ozone than the rest of the atmosphere. (p. 710)

P wave A type of seismic wave that compresses and expands the ground. (p. 397)

pahoehoe A hot, fast-moving type of lava that hardens to form smooth, ropelike coils. (p. 429)

Pangaea The name of the single landmass that broke apart 200 million years ago and gave rise to today's continents. (p. 361)

parallel circuit An electric circuit with multiple paths. (p. 298)

pascal A unit of pressure equal to one newton per square meter. (p. 177)

Pascal's principle The rule that when force is applied to a confined fluid, the increase in pressure is transmitted equally to all parts of the fluid. (p. 185)

passive solar system A method of converting solar energy into heat without pumps or fans. (p. 739)

pedigree A chart or "family tree" that tracks which members of a family have a particular trait. (p. 55)

permafrost Permanently frozen soil found in the tundra climate region. (pp. 68, 628)

permanent magnet A magnet made of material that keeps its magnetism. (p. 252)

pesticide A chemical that kills crop-destroying organisms. (p. 717)

petrified fossil A fossil formed when minerals replace all or part of an organism. (p. 90)

petrochemical Compound made from oil. (p. 735)

petroleum Liquid fossil fuel; oil. (p. 734)

phenotype An organism's physical appearance, or visible traits. (p. 30)

photochemical smog A brownish haze that is a mixture of ozone and other chemicals, formed when nitrogen oxides, hydrocarbons, and other pollutants react with each other in the presence of sunlight. (pp. 520, 707)

pipe A long tube through which magma moves from the magma chamber to Earth's surface. (p. 426)

plate One of the major pieces that make up Earth's upper layer; a section of the lithosphere that slowly moves over the asthenosphere, carrying pieces of continental and oceanic crust. (pp. 126, 374)

plate tectonics The theory that pieces of Earth's lithosphere are in constant motion, driven by convection currents in the mantle. (p. 375)

plateau A large area of flat land elevated high above sea level. (p. 393)

poaching Illegal hunting of wildlife. (p. 668)

polar (air mass) A cold air mass that forms north of 50° north latitude or south of 50° south latitude and has high air pressure. (p. 574)

polar zones The areas near both poles, from about 66.5° to 90° north and 66.5° to 90° south latitudes. (p. 611)

pollutants Harmful substances in the air, water, or soil. (p. 518)

pollution A change to the environment that has a negative effect on living things. (p. 651)

porphyritic texture An igneous rock texture in which large crystals are scattered on a background of much smaller crystals. (p. 483)

potential difference The difference in electrical potential between two places; measured in volts. (p. 289)

power The rate at which one form of energy is converted into another; the unit of power is the Watt; Watts = Volts × Amps. (p. 325)

precipitation Any form of water that falls from clouds and reaches Earth's surface. (p. 565)

preservation viewpoint The belief that all parts of the environment are equally important, no matter how useful they are to humans. (p. 654)

pressure The force exerted on a surface divided by the total area over which the force is exerted; the amount of force pushing on a surface or area. (pp. 177, 351, 523)

primary treatment The removal of solid materials from wastewater. (p. 723)

probability The likelihood that a particular event will occur. (p. 26)

projectile An object that is thrown. (p. 156)

proton A positively charged particle that is part of an atom's nucleus. (p. 250)

psychrometer An instrument used to measure relative humidity, consisting of a wet-bulb thermometer and a dry-bulb thermometer. (p. 560)

pulley A grooved wheel around which is wrapped a rope, chain, or cable. (p. 224)

punctuated equilibria The theory that species evolve during short periods of rapid change. (p. 96)

Punnett square A chart that shows all the possible combinations of alleles that can result from a genetic cross. (p. 28)

purebred An organism that always produces offspring with the same form of a trait as the parent. (p. 19)

pyroclastic flow The expulsion of ash, cinders, bombs, and gases during an explosive volcanic eruption. (p. 430)

radiation The direct transfer of energy by electromagnetic waves; the transfer of energy through empty space. (pp. 357, 540)

radioactive Containing unstable atoms. (p. 697)

radioactive element An unstable particle that breaks down into a different element. (p. 92)

rain forest A forest in the tropical wet climate zone that gets plenty of rain all year. (p. 621)

rain gauge An instrument used to measure the amount of precipitation, consisting of an open-ended can topped by a collecting funnel and having a collecting tube and measuring scale inside. (p. 567)

reactor vessel The part of a nuclear reactor where nuclear fission occurs. (p. 748)

recessive allele An allele that is masked when a dominant allele is present. (p. 21)

rechargeable battery A battery in which the products of the electrochemical reaction can be turned back into reactants to be reused. (p. 335)

recycling The process of reclaiming and reusing raw materials. (p. 690)

reference point A place or object used for comparison to determine if an object is in motion. (p. 116)

refinery A factory where crude oil is separated into fuels and other products. (p. 735)

relative dating A technique used to determine which of two fossils is older. (p. 91)

relative humidity The percentage of water vapor in the air compared to the maximum amount the air could hold at that temperature. (p. 560)

renewable resource A natural resource that can be replaced in nature at a rate close to the rate at which it is used. (pp. 323, 651)

reserve A known deposit of fuels. (p. 733)

resin Solid material produced during oil refining that can be used to make plastics. (p. 691)

resistance The opposition to the movement of electric charges flowing through a material. (p. 266)

resistor A device in an electric circuit that uses electrical energy as it interferes with the flow of electric charge. (p. 266)

responding variable The factor that changes as a result of changes to the manipulated variable in an experiment. (pp. 6, 771)

reverse fault A type of fault where the hanging wall slides upward. (p. 389)

Richter scale A scale that rates seismic waves as measured by a particular type of mechanical seismograph. (p. 399)

rift valley A deep valley that forms where two plates move apart. (p. 377)

Ring of Fire A major belt of volcanoes that rims the Pacific Ocean. (p. 421)

rock The material that forms Earth's hard surface. (p. 349)

rock cycle A series of processes on the surface and inside Earth that slowly change rocks from one kind to another. (p. 498)

rolling friction Friction that occurs when an object rolls over a surface. (p. 155)

S wave A type of seismic wave that moves the ground up and down or side to side. (p. 397)

sanitary landfill A landfill that holds nonhazardous waste such as municipal solid waste and construction debris. (p. 689)

satellite Any object that travels around another object in space. (p. 169)

savanna A tropical grassland with scattered clumps of trees; found in the tropical wet-and-dry climate zone. (p. 624)

scattering Reflection of light in all directions. (p. 542)

science A way of looking at the natural world and the knowledge gained in that process. (p. 4)

scientific inquiry The ways in which scientists study the world around them. (p. 4)

scientific law A statement that describes what scientists expect to happen every time under a particular set of conditions. (p. 10)

scientific theory A well-tested concept that explains a wide range of observations. (pp. 10, 81, 375)

screw An inclined plane wrapped around a central cylinder to form a spiral. (p. 219)

scrubber A device that uses water droplets to clean smokestack emissions. (p. 722)

sea breeze The flow of air from an ocean or lake to the land. (p. 554)

sea-floor spreading The process by which molten material adds new oceanic crust to the ocean floor. (p. 367)

secondary treatment The use of bacteria to break down wastes in wastewater. (p. 723)

sediment Small, solid pieces of material that comes from rocks or organisms; particles of rock and sand. (p. 486, 719)

sedimentary rock A type of rock that forms when particles from other rocks or the remains of plants and animals are pressed and cemented together. (pp. 90, 481)

seismic wave A vibration that travels through Earth carrying the energy released during an earthquake. (pp. 350, 396)

seismograph A device that records ground movements caused by seismic waves as they move through Earth. (p. 398)

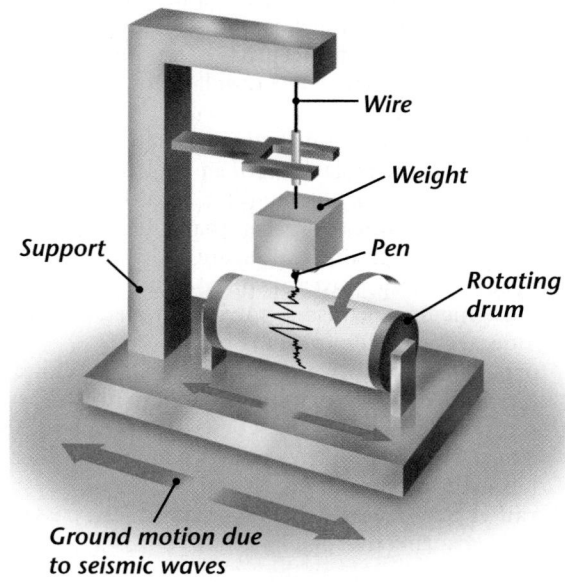

Wire

Weight

Support

Pen

Rotating drum

Ground motion due to seismic waves

selective breeding The process of selecting a few organisms with desired traits to serve as parents of the next generation. (p. 64)

selective cutting The process of cutting down only some trees in an area. (p. 658)

series circuit An electric circuit with a single path. (p. 297)

sewage The water and human wastes that are washed down sinks and toilets. (p. 717)

sex-linked gene A gene that is carried on the X or Y chromosome. (p. 54)

shearing Stress that pushes a mass of rock in opposite directions. (p. 387)

shield volcano A wide, gently sloping mountain made of layers of lava and formed by quiet eruptions. (p. 436)

short circuit An electrical connection that allows current to take an unintended path. (p. 300)

silica A material that is formed from the elements oxygen and silicon; silica is found in magma. (p. 428)

sill A slab of volcanic rock formed when magma squeezes between layers of rock. (p. 438)

sliding friction Friction that occurs when one solid surface slides over another. (p. 155)

slip rings The parts of a generator that rotate with the armature and make contact with the brushes. (p. 319)

smelting The process by which ore is melted to separate the useful metal from other elements. (p. 470)

solar wind Streams of electrically charged particles flowing at high speeds from the sun; solar wind pushes against Earth's magnetic field and surrounds it. (p. 259)

solenoid A current-carrying coil of wire with many loops that acts as a magnet. (p. 271)

solution A mixture in which one substance is dissolved in another. (p. 462)

sonar A device that determines the distance of an object under water by recording echoes of sound waves. (p. 366)

species A group of similar organisms that can mate with each other and produce fertile offspring. (p. 79)

speed The distance an object travels in one unit of time. (p. 118)

static discharge The loss of static electricity as electric charges move off an object. (p. 282)

static electricity A buildup of charges on an object. (p. 281)

step-down transformer A transformer that decreases voltage. (p. 327)

steppe A prairie or grassland found in the semiarid climate region. (p. 625)

step-up transformer A transformer that increases voltage. (p. 327)

storm A violent disturbance in the atmosphere. (p. 581)

storm surge A dome of water that sweeps across the coast where a hurricane lands. (p. 588)

stratosphere The second-lowest layer of Earth's atmosphere; the ozone layer is located in the upper stratosphere. (p. 530)

stratus Clouds that form in flat layers. (p. 562)

streak The color of a mineral's powder. (p. 454)

stress A force that acts on rock to change its shape or volume. (p. 386)

strike-slip fault A type of fault where rocks on either side move past each other sideways with little up-or-down motion. (p. 388)

subarctic A climate zone that lies north of the humid continental climate zone, with short, cool summers and long, bitterly cold winters. (p. 627)

subduction The process by which oceanic crust sinks beneath a deep-ocean trench and back into the mantle at a convergent plate boundary. (p. 370)

subsoil Layer of soil below topsoil. (p. 682)

sunspots Dark, cooler regions on the surface of the sun. (p. 635)

superconductor A material that has no electrical resistance. (p. 267)

surface wave A type of seismic wave that forms when P waves and S waves reach Earth's surface. (p. 398)

sustainable yield A regular amount of a renewable resource that can be harvested without reducing the future supply. (p. 658)

syncline A downward fold in rock formed by compression in Earth's crust. (p. 392)

taxol Chemical in Pacific yew tree bark that has cancer-fighting properties. (p. 673)

temperate zones The area between the tropical and polar zones, from about 23.5° to 66.5° north and 23.5° to 66.5° south latitudes. (p. 611)

temperature The average amount of energy of motion in the molecules of a substance. (p. 547)

temperature inversion Condition in which a layer of warm air traps polluted air close to Earth's surface. (p. 708)

tendon A band of connective tissue that attaches a muscle to a bone. (p. 230)

tension Stress that stretches rock so that it becomes thinner in the middle. (p. 387)

terminal The part of an electrode above the surface of the electrolyte. (p. 333)

terminal velocity The maximum velocity a falling object can achieve. (p. 157)

texture The look and feel of a rock's surface, determined by the size, shape, and pattern of a rock's grains. (p. 479)

thermal energy The energy of motion in the molecules of a substance. (p. 547)

thermometer An instrument used to measure temperature, consisting of a thin, glass tube with a bulb on one end that contains a liquid (usually mercury or alcohol). (p. 547)

thermosphere The outermost layer of Earth's atmosphere. (p. 533)

third prong The round prong of a plug which connects the metal shell of an appliance to the safety grounding wire of a building. (p. 301)

threatened species A species that could become endangered in the near future. (p. 666)

topsoil An upper layer of soil consisting of rock fragments, organisms, nutrients, water, air, and decaying matter. (p. 682)

tornado A rapidly whirling, funnel-shaped cloud that reaches down from a storm cloud to touch Earth's surface, usually leaving a destructive path. (p. 583)

toxic Damaging to the health of humans or other organisms; poisonous. (p. 697)

trait A characteristic that an organism can pass on to its offspring through its genes. (p. 18)

transfer RNA RNA in the cytoplasm that carries an amino acid to the ribosome and adds it to the growing protein chain. (p. 41)

transform boundary A plate boundary where two plates move past each other in opposite directions. (p. 376)

transformer A device that increases or decreases voltage. (p. 326)

tropical (air mass) A warm air mass that forms in the tropics and has low air pressure. (p. 574)

tropical zone The area near the equator, between about 23.5° north latitude and 23.5° south latitude. (p. 611)

troposphere The lowest layer of Earth's atmosphere, where weather occurs. (p. 529)

tsunami A large wave produced by an earthquake on the ocean floor. (p. 406)

tundra A polar climate region, found across northern Alaska, Canada, and Russia, with short, cool summers and bitterly cold winters. (p. 628)

turbine A circular device with many blades that is turned by water, wind, steam, or tides. (p. 319)

ultraviolet radiation A form of energy with wavelengths that are shorter than visible light. (p. 541)

unbalanced force A nonzero net force, which changes an object's motion. (p. 144)

Van Allen belts Two doughnut-shaped regions 1,000–25,000 kilometers above Earth that contain electrons and protons traveling at high speeds. (p. 259)

variable Any factor that can change in an experiment. (pp. 6, 771)

variation Any difference between individuals of the same species. (p. 83)

vein A narrow slab of a mineral that is sharply different from the surrounding rock. (p. 462)

velocity Speed in a given direction. (p. 121)

vent The opening through which molten rock and gas leave a volcano. (p. 426)

volcanic neck A deposit of hardened magma in a volcano's pipe. (p. 438)

volcano A weak spot in the crust where magma has come to the surface. (p. 420)

voltage Potential difference; measured by a voltmeter. (p. 289)

voltage source Creates a potential difference in an electric circuit; batteries and generators are voltage sources. (p. 290)

voltmeter A device used to measure voltage, or potential difference. (p. 292)

water pollution A change to water that has a harmful effect. (p. 716)

water vapor Water in the form of a gas. (p. 515)

weather The condition of Earth's atmosphere at a particular time and place. (p. 512)

wedge An inclined plane that moves. (p. 218)

weight The force of gravity on an object at the surface of a planet. (p. 157)

wet cell An electrochemical cell in which the electrolyte is a liquid. (p. 334)

wheel and axle Two circular or cylindrical objects that are fastened together and rotate about a common axis. (p. 222)

wind The horizontal movement of air from an area of high pressure to an area of lower pressure. (p. 550)

wind-chill factor Increased cooling caused by the wind. (p. 551)

windward The side of mountains that faces the oncoming wind. (p. 615)

work Force exerted on an object that causes it to move. (p. 204)

Index

pipe 426, 427, 433, 460
piping plover 668
pistil 19
plants
   cloning of 66
   fossil record of 93
   genetic engineering in 68
   selective breeding of 64–65
plasmid 67
plate 126–129, 374, 375, 388, 390, 421–422
   calculating movement 127–128
plate boundary 376–378
plate tectonics 126–127, 375, 501
plateau 393
poaching 668, 670, 671
polar 574
polar climate 628
polar easterlies 556, 557, 558
polar zone 611
pollen 19, 519, 633
pollination 19
   cross-pollination 19
   self-pollination 19
pollutant 518, 519, 520, 657, 668, 669, 706, 708, 709, 716, 721, 722
pollution 518–519, 651, 668–669, 670, 719, 740
   air 518–519, 520, 521, 522, 651, 706–707, 708, 709–710, 733
   solutions 721–724
   water 716–719, 733
Pompeii 430
population growth 651
porphyritic texture 483
porphyry 483
potential difference 289, 290, 300
potential energy 288
power 323, 324
   calculating 323
Pre-Cambrian time 93–94
precipitation 559, 565–567, 579, 588, 610, 614–615, 622, 624, 625, 716
   controlling 568
   measuring 567
Prentice, Carol 506, 507, 508, 509
preservation viewpoint 654
pressure 176–178, 185, 196, 198, 351, 354, 523
   air 179–180, 523–524
   balanced 179–180
   fluid 178
   water 181
prevailing westerlies 556, 557, 558, 577
prevailing wind 614, 615
primary treatment 723
probability 26, 27, 28, 29, 50, 65
   of genetic disorders 61, 62–63
   genetics and 26–33
   Mendel and 28, 29
   predicting 29
   principles of 27
   Punnett squares 28–29, 31, 36
projectile 156–157
protein 39, 40–41, 58, 67, 514
protein synthesis 40–43

proton 250, 259, 278–279, 280, 281, 747, 750, 751
psychrometer 560
puddingstone 488
punctuated equilibria, theory of 96
Punnett Square 28–29, 31, 36, 50, 51, 53, 55, 61
pulley 216, 222, 224-225
purebred 19, 65, 107
pyrite 453, 455
pyroclastic flow 430

quartz 454, 455, 456, 457, 458, 479, 484, 499
quartzite 495
Quaternary Period 95

radiation 357, 540, 547, 548, 549
   infrared 541, 542, 543
   ultraviolet 541, 542
radioactive element 92
radon 710
ragweed 519
rain 566
rain forest 621
rain gauge 567, 645
reactor vessel 748
recessive allele 21, 23, 51, 54, 55, 58, 59
rechargeable battery 333
recycling 656, 690–692
red blood cell 58
Red River 596
reference point 116
refinery 735
relative dating 91
relative humidity 560–561
remote manipulator system (RMS) 342, 343
renewable resource 321, 651, 658
research chemist 13
reserves 733
resistance 266, 267, 290–291, 292, 297, 299, 300, 301, 303, 304
resistor 265, 266, 292–293
resources 321, 651
   fisheries 660–661
   forest 657–659
   nonrenewable 321, 651
   renewable 321, 651, 658
responding variable 6
reverse fault 389
rhyolite 483
ribosome 42
Richter scale 399, 400
rift valley 377
Ring of Fire 421
RNA 41
   messenger 41, 42
   transfer 41, 43
robotics 342
rock 349, 478–479
   chemical 488, 490
   classifying 478–481
   clastic 488
   extrusive 483, 484

   igneous 481, 482, 483–485, 498, 500
   intrusive 483, 484
   metamorphic 481, 494–496, 499, 500
   organic 488, 489
   sedimentary 90, 91, 481, 486–490, 499, 500
rock cycle 498–501
rocket 168–169
Rocky Mountains 353
rolling friction 155
Roosevelt, Theodore 652

S wave 397–398, 400, 401, 405
safety 10, 304, 407
   earthquake 407, 409
   electrical 304
   flood 594–595
   hurricane 588, 592
   laboratory 10
   snowstorm 589
   thunderstorm 583
Sahara 614
Sally light-foot crab 79
San Andreas fault 388, 390, 410, 508
Sandia Mountains 388
sandstone 488, 495, 499
satellite 169–170, 342, 343
   tethered 344–345
satellite monitor 412
savanna 624
scattering 542
Schaus swallowtail butterfly 669
scheelite 458
science 4
   branches of 12
scientific inquiry 4-5
scientific law 10
scientific theory 10, 81, 375
screw 219, 223
scrubber 722
sea breeze 554
sea-floor spreading 367, 369, 370–371
sea star 665
season 616–617
Seattle, Washington 625
secondary treatment 723
sediment 89–90, 486, 487, 489, 499, 507, 509, 718
sedimentary rock 90, 91, 481, 486–490, 499, 500
seismic wave 350, 396–397, 398, 405, 406
seismograph 398, 399, 400, 401
selective breeding 64–65
selective cutting 658, 659
self-pollination 19
series circuit 297, 299
sex cell 34, 36, 37, 57
sex-linked gene 54
sex-linked trait 54, 55
sewage 717
   treatment 723
shaft mine 468–469
shale 488, 495
shearing 387
Shepherd, J. Marshall 644, 645, 646, 647

803

Acknowledgments

Staff Credits

The people who made up the Prentice Hall **Integrated Science** team—representing design, editorial, editorial services, electronic publishing technology, manufacturing & inventory planning, marketing, marketing services, market research, online services & multimedia development, production services, product planning, project office, publishing processes—are listed below. Bold type denotes core team members.

Carolyn Belanger, Suzanne Biron, Peggy Bliss, Patricia Cully, Bob Craton, **Patricia Fromkin,** Jennifer Muncharian, **Phyllis Hawkes,** Roberto Portocarrero, **Richard Stakun-Pickering,** Jennifer Teece, Char Lyn Yeakley.

Illustration

Carol Barber: 358
Kathleen Dempsey: 372, 380, 394, 402, 424, 440, 497, 502
John Edwards & Associates: 166–167, 170, 179, 186(t), 258(t), 259, 320, 406, 528, 542, 554, 577, 578, 579, 587, 617, 638, 688, 713, 722, 731, 732, 739, 743, 749
Chris Forsey: 359, 366(t), 367, 370, 376, 377, 432, 509(t)
Robert Fuller: 78–79
GeoSystems Global Corporation: 87, 108–109, 127, 258(b), 361, 362, 363, 375, 383, 390(t), 401, 402(b), 413, 414, 421, 464, 586, 589, 590, 601(t), 613, 622–623, 634, 684, 699, 733, 762
Andrea Golden: 236, 646, 765
Jared Lee: 709, 764
Martucci Design: 122, 136, 177, 194, 403(b), 417, 447, 513, 521, 541, 601(b), 619, 630, 651, 681, 727, 734, 753, 776, 777, 778
Matt Mayerchak: 73, 103, 137, 199, 273, 307, 381, 415, 445, 456, 474, 503, 535, 641, 676, 726, 775
Karen Minot: 663
Albert Molnar: 372
Morgan Cain & Associates: 37, 40–41, 42–43, 92, 139, 158, 169, 173(t), 178, 182, 185, 186(b), 189, 192, 198, 201, 109, 218, 219, 224, 225, 235, 237, 238, 249, 250, 251, 253, 270, 271, 272, 279, 280, 281, 285, 290, 291, 299, 307, 354, 355, 356, 368, 369, 383, 387, 392, 397(tl), 398, 408, 409, 411, 412, 427, 437, 438, 484, 487, 505, 524(b), 525, 526, 537, 543, 546, 548–549, 552, 555, 557, 565, 567, 571, 638, 708, 711, 712, 735, 748, 750, 752, 768 (bl, br), 769(tl, bl)
Ortelius Design Inc.: 1, 128–129, 222–223, 378, 379, 432, 433, 468, 469, 507(m), 515, 554(b), 580, 584–585, 607, 611, 614, 636, 643
Judith Pinkham: 656, 686, 694, 745, 752(t)
Matthew Pippin: 397(br), 407, 422, 462, 470, 524(t), 531, 559, 563, 594, 682 (soil)
Pond and Giles: 658
Precision Graphics: 311, 312, 314, 316, 317, 318, 319, 327, 332, 333, 334, 339, 341
Proof Positive/Farrowlune Associates, Inc.: 763
John Sanderson/Horizon Design: 576
Rob Schuster: 197
Walter Stuart: 635
J/B Woolsey Associates: 25, 29, 31, 36, 51, 53, 56, 67, 75, 94–95, 96, 98, 101, 139, 157, 163, 173(b), 187, 197(insets), 101, 135, 261, 283, 289, 296, 297, 298, 307, 376, 388, 389, 390(b), 391, 417, 562, 595, 615, 643, 667, 682 (spots), 703, 727, 759, 772

Photography

Cover Design Studio Montage and Prentis Hall
Photo Credits Ferris wheel: EyeWire Collection/ Getty Images
lizard: Corel Stock Photo Library
desert: David Muench Photography

Nature of Science
Page xxii m, Courtesy of Wind Engineering Research Center, Texas Tech University; **xxii–1,** Annie Griffiths Belt/National Geographic; **1 t, 1 b, 2, 3 all,** Courtesy of Wind Engineering Research Center, Texas Tech University.

What is Science?
Page 4 t, Stone/Dave Bjorn; **4 b,** Nancy Sheehan Photography; **5,** Manfred Gottschalk/Tom Stack & Associates; **9,** Tsado/NCDC/NOAA/Tom Stack & Associates; **10, 11,** Richard Haynes; **12 l,** Paula Lerner/Index Stock Imagery; **12 r,** Peter Menzel/Stock Boston; **13 t,** Frank Pederick/The Image Works; **13 b,** Kim Steele/PhotoDisc; **14,** Tsado/NCDC/NOAA/Tom Stack & Associartes.

Chapter 1
Pages 16–17, Ron Kimball; **18,** Mike Rothwell/Stone; **18,** Corbis-Bettmann; **19,** Barry Runk/Grant Heilman Photography; **22 both,** Meinrad Faltner/The Stock Market; **23,** Inga Spence/The Picture Cube; **26–27,** Image Stop/Phototake; **30,** Hans Reinhard/Bruce Coleman; **33,** Richard Haynes; **34 l,** David M. Phillips/Photo Researchers; **34 r,** University "La Sapienza," Rome/Science Photo Library/Photo Researchers; **35 l,** Jonathan D. Speer/Visuals Unlimited; **35 r,** M. Abbey/Photo Researchers; **39,** AP/Wide World Photos; **44,** William E. Ferguson; **45,** Mike Rothwell/Stone.

Chapter 2
Pages 48–49, Herb Snitzer/Stock Boston; **50,** Richard Haynes; **52,** Camille Tokerud/TSI; **53 t, b,** Biophoto Associates/Science Source/Photo Researchers; **54,** Andrew McClenaghan/Science Photo Library/Photo Researchers; **56,** Superstock; **57 t,** CNRI/Science Photo Library/Photo Researchers; **57 t,** Lawrence Migdale/TSI; **58 t,** Simon Fraser/RVI, Newcastle-upon-TYNE/Science Photo Library/Photo Researchers; **58 b,** Stanley Flegler/Visuals Unlimited; **59,** Corbis-Bettmann; **60 l,** CNRI/Science Photo Library/Photo Researchers; **60 r,** Mugshots/The Stock Market; **61,** Will and Deni McIntyre/Photo Researchers Inc.; **62,** Richard Haynes; **64,** AP/Wide World Photos; **66,** Tim Barnwell/Stock Boston; **66,** Patricia J. Bruno/Positive Images; **67,** LeLand Bobbe/TSI; **68,** Gary Wagner/Stock Boston; **69,** AP/Wide World Photos; **70,** U.S. Department of Energy/Human Genome Management Information System, Oak Ridge National Laboratory; **71,** David Parker/Science Photo Library/Photo Researchers; **72,** Michael Newman/PhotoEdit.

Chapter 3
Pages 76–77, Bill Varie/Westlight; **78 t,** Portrait by George Richmond/Down House, Downe/The Bridgeman Art Library; **78 b,** Corbis-Bettmann; **79 t, b,** Tui De Roy/Minden Pictures; **79 m,** Frans Lanting/Minden Pictures; **80 l,** Zig Leszczynski/Animals Animals; **80 r,** Tui De Roy/Minden Pictures; **81,** Dr. Jeremy Burgess/Science Photo Library/Photo Researchers; **82,** Mitsuaki Iwago/Minden Pictures; **83,** Jeff Gnass Photography/The Stock Market; **85,** Richard Haynes; **86 l, r,** Breck P. Kent; **87 l, r,** Pat & Tom Leeson/Photo Researchers; **88 t,** John Cancalosi/Tom Stack & Associates; **88 b,** Tom McHugh/Photo Researchers; **89 t,** James L. Amos/Photo Researchers; **89 b,** Sinclair Stammers/Science Photo Library/Photo Researchers; **93,** Robert Landau/Westlight; **97,** Richard Haynes; **99 l,** Keith Gillett/Animals Animals; **99 m,** George Whiteley/Photo Researchers; **99 r,** David Spears Ltd./Science Photo Library/Photo Researchers; **100 l,** Gary Milburn/Tom Stack & Associates; **100 r,** Daryl Balfour/TSI.

Interdisciplinary Exploration
Page 106 t, Tim Fitzharris/Minden Pictures; **106 b,** Bridgeman Art Library; **107,** Ron Kimball; **108 tr,** Charles Philip/Westlight; **108 b,** Jack Daniels/TSI; **108 tl, ml, mr,** Corel Corp.; **108ml,** C. Jeanne White/Photo Researchers; **109 all others,** Corel Corp.; **110 t,** Peter Cade/TSI; **110 b,** AP/ Wide World Photos; **110–111,** Nick Meers/Panoramic Images.

Chapter 4
Pages 112–113, Frans Lanting/Minden Pictures; **114 t,** Richard Haynes; **114 bl,** Bob Abraham/The Stock Market; **114 br,** Roy Morsch/The Stock Market; **115 t,** D. Roundtree/The Image Bank; **115 b,** Steve Maslowski/Photo Researchers; **116,** NASA; **117 l,** Chuck Zsymanski/International Stock; **117 r,** Robert Maier/Animals Animals; **118,** Mike Agliolo/International Stock; **119,** John Kelly/The Image Bank; **120,** National Motor Museum, Beaulieu, England; **121 t,** Topham/The Image Works; **121 b,** David Barnes/The Stock Market; **122,** Marc Romanelli/The Image Bank; **123,** A.T. Willet/The Image Bank; **125,** Richard Haynes; **126 t,** Russ Lappa; **126 b,** Image Makers/The Image Bank; **129,** Richard Haynes; **130,** Richard Haynes; **131,** Lou Jones/The Image Bank; **132 t,** Richard Haynes; **132 b,** Mike Hewitt/Allsport; **133 l,** Tracy Frankel/The Image Bank; **133 m,** Tim DeFrisco/Allsport; **133 r,** Yann Guichaoua/Agence Vandystadt/ Allsport; **134 t,** Addison Geary/Stock Boston; **134 inset,** Corel Corp.; **135,** Corel Corp.; **137,** Mike Agliolo/International Stock.

Chapter 5

Pages 140–141, David Stoecklein/The Stock Market; **142 t,** Russ Lappa; **142 bl,** Calimberti/Liaison International; **142 br,** Alain Ernoult/The Image Bank; **143,** Richard Thom/Visuals Unlimited; **144,** Elisabeth Weiland/Photo Researchers; **145 all,** Richard Haynes; **146,** Bilderberg/The Stock Market; **147 t,** Russ Lappa; **147 b, 149, 150,** Richard Haynes; **152,** Richard Haynes; **153,** Russ Lappa; **154 t,** Jan Hinsch/Science Photo Library/Photo Researchers; **154 b,** B & C Alexander/Photo Researchers; **155 tl,** The Photo Works/Photo Researchers; **155 tr,** Welzenbach/The Stock Market; **155 b,** Russ Lappa; **156 t,** Jack Novak/Superstock; **156 bl,** Megna/Peticolas/Fundamental Photographs; **156 br,** Richard Megna/ Fundamental Photographs; **159,** NASA; **160,** Richard Haynes; **161,** Ken O'Donaghue; **162 t,** Richard Haynes; **162 b,** Ed Young/Science Photo Library/Photo Researchers; **163,** Bob Woodward/The Stock Market; **164 l,** Syracuse/Dick Blume/The Image Works; **164 r,** Michael Devin Daly/The Stock Market; **166,** Russ Lappa; **168 t,** Richard Haynes; **168 b,** Corel Corp.; **169,** Jeff Hunter/The Image Bank.

Chapter 6

Pages 174–175, Rana Clamitans/Visuals Unlimited; **176 t,** Richard Haynes; **176 bl,** Chlaus Lotscher/ Stock Boston; **176 br,** Milton Feinberg/Stock Boston; **180 l, 180 r,** Richard Megna/Fundamental Photographs; **181,** Russ Lappa; **182,** Benn Mitchell/The Image Bank; **183,** Russ Lappa; **184 t,** Richard Haynes; **184 b,** Chris Sheridan/ Monkmeyer; **187 l,** Stuart Westmorland/Photo Researchers; **187 inset,** Andrew Mertiner/Photo Researchers; **188 t,** Russ Lappa; **188 b,** Ken Marshall/Madison Press Limited; **189,** Russ Lappa; **191,** Richard Haynes; **192,** Russ Lappa; **193,** Runk/Schoenberger/Grant Heilman Photography, Inc.; **195 t,** Richard Haynes; **195 b,** Mercury Archives/The Image Bank; **196 t,** Richard Haynes; **196 b,** Patti McConville/The Image Bank; **198 t,** Russ Lappa; **198 b,** Richard Haynes; **199 bl,** Chlaus Lotscher/ Stock Boston; **199 br,** Milton Feinberg/Stock Boston.

Chapter 7

Pages 202–203, Belinda Banks/Tony Stone Images; **204 all,** Richard Haynes; **205 t,** David A. Jentz/Photo Network; **205 b,** Fotopic/Omni-Photo Communications; **207,** Stephen McBrady/Photo Edit; **208 t,** Richard Haynes; **208 b,** Skjold/Photo Edit; **209,** Skjold/Photo Edit; **210,** Siegfried Tauquer/Leo De Wys; **211 t,** David Young-Wolff/Photo Edit; **211 b,** Richard Haynes; **212,** Russ Lappa; **215,** Richard Haynes; **216 t,** Richard Haynes; **216 b,** Russ Lappa; **217,** John Akhtar/Vivid Images Phtg., Inc.; **218 t,** Tony Freeman/Photo Edit; **218 b, 219,** Russ Lappa; **220 t,** Museum of Modern Art, New York/©FPG International 1991; **221 t,** Russ Lappa; **221 l,** Jerry Wachter/Photo Researchers; **221 r,** Elliot Smith/International Stock; **222 t,** Sylvain Grandadam/Tony Stone Images; **222 b,** Gerard Champion/The Image Bank; **223 t,** Jeffrey Aaronson/Network Aspen; **223 r,** G.B. Archives/Sygma; **224,** John Elk/Stock Boston; **226 t,** David R. Frazier; **226 b,** Tony Freeman/Photo Edit; **227,** Jeff Smith/The Image Bank; **228,** Cleo Freelance Photo/New England Stock; **229,** Richard Haynes; **230,** Russ Lappa; **231 all,** Richard Haynes; **232 t,** Ken Karp; **232 m, b,** Richard Haynes.

Interdisciplinary Exploration

Page 236 t, IFA/Peter Arnold; **236–237 m,** John Higginson/TSI; **236–237 b** Chris Warren /International Stock; **238–239** Bob Kramer/Stock Boston; **239 t,** Joseph Pobereskin/TSI; **239 b,** Richard Haynes; **240 tl, 240 b,** Corbis-Bettmann; **240 tm, 240 tr,** The Granger Collection, NY; **241,** Corbis-Bettmann; **242–243,** Richard Weiss/Peter Arnold.

Chapter 8

Pages 244–245, Dick Durrance II/The Stock Market; **246 t,** Richard Haynes; **246 b,** Marcello Bertinetti/Photo Researchers; **247 t,** Paul Silverman/ Fundamental Photographs; **247 b,** Russ Lappa; **248 both, 249 l,** Richard Megna/Fundamental Photographs; **249 r,** Phil Degginger/Color-Pic, Inc.; **250 both,** Richard Megna/Fundamental Photographs; **252 t,** Russ Lappa; **252 b,** Richard Haynes; **254,** Aaron Rezny/The Stock Market; **255 both,** Richard Haynes; **256 t,** Russ Lappa; **256 b,** Sisse Brimberg/National Geographic Image; **257,** National Geographic Society/NGS Image; **260,** Lionel F. Stevenson/Photo Researchers; **262 t,** Russ Lappa; **262 b,** Corbis-Bettmann; **263 b,** Richard Megna/Fundamental Photographs; **263 all others,** Russ Lappa; **264,** Fred McKinney/FPG International; **265,** Corel Corp.; **265 inset,** Russ Lappa; **266 l,** Russ Lappa; **266 r,** Richard Megna/Fundamental Photographs; **267,** AT&T Bell Labs/ Science Photo Library/Photo Researchers; **268,** Kevin Cruff/FPG International; **269, 270 t,** Richard Haynes; **270 b, 271,** Richard Megna/ Fundamental Photographs; **272,** Applied Superconductivity Center at the University of Wisconsin-Madison; **273,** Lionel F. Stevenson/Photo Researchers.

Chapter 9

Pages 276–277, Telegraph Colour Library/FPG International; **278 t,** Richard Haynes; **278 b,** Mark C. Burnett/Photo Researchers; **281,** Hank Morgan/ Rainbow; **282,** Russ Lappa; **283 both,** Richard Haynes; **284,** Richard Kaylin/TSI; **286, 287,** Richard Haynes; **288 t,** Russ Lappa; **288 b,** Craig Tuttle, The Stock Market; **289,** Bob Daemmrich/Stock Boston; **291, 292,** Russ Lappa; **293,** M. Antman/The Image Works; **294,** Mark Burnett/Stock Boston; **295,** Richard Haynes; **296,** James Dwyer/Stock Boston; **297, 298, 300,** Russ Lappa; **301 t,** Joel Page/AP Wide World Photos; **301 b,** Russ Lappa; **302,** Armen Kachaturian/Liaison International; **303 l,** Russ Lappa; **303 r,** M. Antman/The Image Works; **304,** Ross Harrison Koty/TSI; **305,** Russ Lappa.

Chapter 10

Pages 308–309, John Henley/The Stock Market; **310 t,** Russ Lappa; **310 b,** Jon Chomitz; **313, 315 t,** Russ Lappa; **315 b,** Telegraph Colour Library/FPG International; **316,** Richard Haynes; **320 t,** Peter Menzel/Stock Boston; **320 b,** Martin Rogers/TSI; **320 bkgd,** Peter/Stef Lamberti/TSI; **321 t,** Adam Woolfitt/Woodfin Camp & Associates; **321 m,** Roger Ball/The Stock Market; **321 b,** Stephen J. Krasemann/ Photo Researchers; **321 bkgd,** Manfred Gottschalk/Tom Stack & Associates; **323,** Alison Wright/Stock Boston; **324 t,** Russ Lappa; **324 b,** Frank Siteman/Stock Boston; **326 l,** Toni Michaels; **326 r,** B. Daemmrich/The Image Works; **327,** Russ Lappa; **328 t,** The Granger Collection, NY; **328 b,** Corbis-Bettmann; **329 t,** The Granger Collection, NY; **329 bl, br,** Corbis-Bettmann; **330,** Montes De Oca, Art 1998/FPG International; **331 t,** Russ Lappa; **331 b,** William Johnson/Stock Boston; **332,** J-L Charmet/ Science Photo Library/Photo Researchers; **335,** Jose Pelaez/The Stock Market; **336 t,** David Barnes/TSI; **336 b,** Russ Lappa; **337,** Richard Haynes; **338,** David R. Frasier/TSI; **339,** Peter Menzel/Stock Boston.

Nature of Science

Page 342, 343 t, inset, NASA; **343 b,** SPAR Aerospace/SPAR Space Systems; **344–345, 344t,** NASA; **344b,** Courtesy of Ellen Ochoa; **345,** NASA.

Chapter 11

Pages 346–347, Earth Satellite Corporation/Science Photo Library/Photo Researchers; **348,** Gardar Palsson/Mats Wibe Lund; **349 t, b,** M. W. Franke/Peter Arnold; **350,** Michael Nichols/Magnum; **351,** Tracy Frankel/The Image Bank; **352–353 t,** Linde Waidhofer/Liaison International; **352 m,** E. R. Degginger; **352 b,** Breck P. Kent; **356,** Runk/ Schoenberger/Grant Heilman; **357,** Richard Haynes; **360 t,** Russ Lappa; **360 b,** The Granger Collection, NY; **363,** Breck P. Kent; **364,** Bildarchiv Preussischer Kulturbesitz; **365,** Emory Kristof/National Geographic Image Collection; **368 tl,** Woods Hole Oceanographic Institute/Sygma; **368 tr,** USGS/HVO 3cp/U. S. Geological Survey; **369,** SCRIPPS Oceanographic Institute; **371,** Norbert Wu; **372 all,** Richard Haynes; **373 t,** Richard Haynes; **374 t,** Russ Lappa.

Chapter 12

Pages 384–385, Science Museum/Michael Holford; **386,** Ben S. Kwiatkowski/ Fundamental Photographs; **388 t,** David Parker/Science Photo Library/Photo Researchers; **388 b,** David Muench Photography; **389,** Sharon Gerig/Tom Stack & Associates; **390,** Stan Osolinski/TSI; **391,** Phillips Petroleum; **392–393,** Tom Bean; **395 b, inset,** Richard Haynes; **396, 398 t,** Richard Haynes; **398 b,** Russell D. Curtis/Photo Researchers; **399,** Leonetto Medici/AP Photo; **400,** EERC/Berkeley; **404 t,** Richard Haynes; **404 b,** Natsuko Utsumi/Gamma Liaison; **405,** EERC/Berkeley; **408,** Esbin-Anderson/The Image Works; **410,** Terraphotographics/BPS.

Chapter 13

Pages 418–419, Soames Summerhays/Photo Researchers; **420,** Savino/Sipa Press; **425 all,** Breck P. Kent; **426,** E. R. Degginger; **427,** B. Ingalls/NASA/Liaison International; **428 t,** Ed Reschke/Peter Arnold; **428 b,** E. R. Degginger; **429 l,** Dave B. Fleetham/Tom Stack & Associates; **429 r,** William Felger/Grant Heilman Photography; **430 l, r,** Alberto Garcia/Saba Press; **431 l, r,** Alberto Garcia/Saba Press; **431 b,** Norbert Rosing/Animals Animals/Earth Scenes; **432 tl,** North Wind; **432 tr,** Kim Heacox/Peter Arnold; **432 b,** Robert Fried Photography; **433,** Alberto Garcia/Saba Press; **434 l,** Pat Roqua/AP/Wide World; **434 r,** Antonio Emerito/Sipa Press; **435 t,** Richard Haynes; **435 b,** Hela Lade/Peter Arnold; **436,** Greg Vaughn/Tom Stack & Associates; **437 t,** Picture Perfect; **437 b,** Manfred Gottschalk/Tom Stack & Associates; **438 tl,** Brownie Harris/The Stock Market; **438 bl,** Tom Bean/DRK Photo; **438 br,** David Hosking/Photo Researchers; **439,** Bob Newman/Visual Unlimited; **441,** Richard Haynes; **442 t, m,** NASA; **442 b,** Chris Bjornberg/Photo Researchers; **443 t, b, 444,** NASA.

Chapter 14

Pages 448–449, Thomas R. Taylor/Photo Researchers; **450 t,** Richard Haynes; **450 b,** Richard B. Levine; **451 t,** Mark A. Schneider/Visuals Unlimited; **451 m,** Ben Johnson/Science Photo Library/Photo Researchers; **451 b,** E.R. Degginger; **452 l,** Richard Treptow/Visuals Unlimited; **452 r,** Gregory G. Dimijian/Photo Researchers; **452 m,** McCutcheon/Visuals Unlimited; **453 l,** Arne Hodalic/Corbis; **453 r,** Breck P. Kent; **454,** Paul Silverman/Fundamental Photographs; **455 l, r,** Breck P. Kent; **456 sulfur,** E. R. Degginger; **456 all others,** Breck P. Kent; **457 l,** A. J. Copley/Visuals Unlimited; **457 tr,** Paul Silverman/Fundamental Photographs; **458 l, r,** E. R. Degginger; **460 t,** Richard Haynes; **460 b,** Gerhard Gscheidle/Peter Arnold; **461,** Jeffrey Scovil; **462 l,** Ken Lucas/Visuals Unlimited; **462 r,** Ted Clutter/Photo Researchers; **463,** Jay Syverson/Stock Boston; **465,** Nautilus Minerals Corp.; **466,** C. M. Dixon; **467 t,** Runk/Schoenberger from Grant Heilman; **467 b,** Mike Husar/DRK photo; **468 t,** C. M. Dixon; **468 bl,** Scala/Art Resource, NY; **468 br,** C. M. Dixon; **469,** The Granger Collection, NY; **470 t,** Charles D. Winters/Photo Researchers; **470 b,** Russ Lappa; **471,** Visuals Unlimited; **472,** Richard Haynes; **473 t, b, 475,** Breck P. Kent.

Chapter 15

Pages 476–477, Jim Nelson/Adventure Photo; **478 t, m,** Breck P. Kent; **478 b,** Jeff Zaroda/The Stock Market; **479 tl, bl,** E. R. Degginger; **479 tr, m,** Breck P. Kent; **479 br,** Barry L. Runk/Grant Heilman; **480 slate, gneiss,** E. R. Degginger; **480 quartzite,** Jeff Scovil; **480 all others,** Breck P. Kent; **481,** Martin Rogers/Stock Boston; **482 tl,** Breck P. Kent; **482 tr,** Doug Martin/Photo Researchers; **482 b,** Greg Vaughn/Tom Stack & Associates; **483 tl, tm,** Breck P. Kent; **483 tr,** E. R. Degginger; **484,** Alfred Pasieka/Science Photo Library/Photo Researchers; **485,** Michele & Tom Grimm/TSI; **486,** Clyde H. Smith/Peter Arnold; **488,** Specimen from North Museum/Franklin and Marshall College/Grant Heilman Photography; **489 t,** E. R. Degginger; **489 b,** Kevin Sink/Midwestock; **490,** Grant Heilman/Grant Heilman Photography; **491 t,** Ted Clutter/Photo Researchers; **491 b,** Stephen Frink/Waterhouse; **492,** Norbert Wu/The Stock Market; **492 b,** Jean-Marc Truchet/TSI; **493,** Grant Heilman/Grant Heilman Photography; **494 tl,** E. R. Degginger; **494 bl,** Barry L. Runk/Grant Heilman Photography; **494 br, 495 bl,** Andrew J. Martinez/Photo Researchers; **496,** David Hosking/Photo Researchers; **498 tl, tr,** Jeff Scovil; **498 tm,** Breck P. Kent; **499,** Corbis; **500 tl,** Tom Algire/Tom Stack & Associates; **500 bl,** Breck P. Kent; **500 br,** N.R.Rowan/Stock Boston; **501,** Breck P. Kent; **502 t, m, b,** Russ Lappa; **505 l, r,** E. R. Degginger; **505 m,** Breck P. Kent.

Nature of Science

Page 506, 508, Paul Mann; **507,** Carol Prentice/US Geological Survey.

Chapter 16

Pages 510–511, Jay Simon/TSI; **512 t,** Russ Lappa; **512 b,** NASA/Photo Researchers; **514 b,** Russ Lappa; **514 t,** Richard Haynes; **515 r,** George G. Dimijian/Photo Researchers; **516 tl,** Eric Horan/Liaison International; **517,** Richard Haynes; **518 t,** Russ Lappa; **518 b,** Aaron Haupt/Photo Researchers; **519 b,** Paul Lowe/Magnum Photos; **519 t,** Biophoto Associates/Photo Researchers; **520,** Will McIntyre/Photo Researchers; **522,** Steve Casimiro/Liaison International; **523 t,** Russ Lappa; **523 b,** Eric A. Kessler; **525 t,** Ivan Bucher/Photo Researchers; **527,** Russ Lappa; **529 t,** Russ Lappa; **529 b,** Steve Vidler/Superstock; **530,** Mark C. Burnett/Photo Researchers; **532 b,** Corbis-Bettmann; **532 t,** The Granger Collection, NY; **533 b,** NASA; **533 t,** The National Archives/Corbis; **534,** Jack Finch/Science Photo Library/Photo Researchers.

Chapter 17

Pages 538–539, William Johnson/Stock Boston; **540–541,** Photo Researchers; **545,** Richard Haynes; **546,** Russ Lappa; **547,** Russ Lappa; **548–549,** Daniel Cox/Allstock/PNI; **550 t,** Russ Lappa; **550 bl,** Victoria Hurst/Tom Stack & Associates; **550–551,** Gary Retherford/Photo Researchers; **551 r,** Richard Haynes; **553,** Richard Haynes; **554,** Steve McCurry/Magnum Photos; **556,** Scala/Art Resource, NY; **558,** Ken McVey/TSI; **559,** Russ Lappa; **560,** E.J. Tarbuck; **561,** Peter Arnold; **563 t,** Michael Gadomski/GADOM/Bruce Coleman; **563 tm,** Phil Degginger/Bruce Coleman; **563 bm,** E.R. Degginger; **563 b,** John Shaw/Bruce Coleman; **564,** Wendy Shattil/Bob Rozinski/Tom Stack & Associates; **565,** Richard Haynes; **566 t,** AP/Wide World; **566 b,** Nuridsany et Perennou/Photo Researchers; **566 inset,** Gerben Oppermans/TSI; **568,** Bill Frantz/TSI; **569,** Victoria Hurst/Tom Stack & Associates.

Chapter 18

Pages 572–573, Pete Turner/The Image Bank; **574 t,** Russ Lappa; **574 b,** Russ Lappa; **575,** Jim Corwin/TSI; **581 t,** Russ Lappa; **581 b,** Dirck Halstead/Liaison International; **582,** Dan Sudia/Photo Researchers; **583,** Schuster/Superstock; **584 b,** The Granger Collection, NY; **584 t,** The Granger Collection, NY; **585 l,** North Wind Picture Archives; **586,** Sheila Beougher/Liaison International; **587,** NASA-Goddard Laboratory for Atmospheres; **588,** Clore Collection, Tate Gallery, London/Art Resource, NY; **590,** NOAA; **592,** Tony Freeman/Photo Edit; **593 t,** Richard Haynes; **593 bl,** Keith Kent/Science Photo Library/Photo Researchers; **593 br,** Grant V. Faint/The Image Bank; **596,** AP Photo/Pool/David J. Phillip; **597 t,** Larry Lawfer; **597 b,** Corel Corp.; **598,** AP Photo/David Umberger; **599,** NOAA; **601,** NOAA; **602–603,** AccuWeather, Inc.; **605,** Schuster/Superstock;.

Chapter 19

Pages 608–609, David Muench; **610 t,** Richard Haynes; **610 b,** Thomas D. Mangelsen/Peter Arnold; **612,** David Madison/Bruce Coleman; **614,** Duncan Wherrett/TSI; **615,** Chris Cheadle/TSI; **619,** Richard Haynes; **620 t,** Russ Lappa; **620 b,** Charlie Waite/TSI; **621,** Geogory G. Dimigian/Photo Researchers; **624 t,** Thomas D. Mangelsen/Peter Arnold; **624 b,** Alex S. MacLean/Peter Arnold; **625,** Stephen Johnson/TSI; **626 t,** Ann Duncan/Tom Stack & Associates; **626 b,** Margaret Gowan/TSI; **627,** Kennan Ward Photography/Corbis; **628 t,** Art Wolfe/TSI; **628 b,** Thomas Kitchin/Tom Stack & Associates; **629,** Photodisc, Inc.; **632,** 1996 Ira Block; **633 r,** Tony Craddock/Science Photo Library/Photo Researchers; **633 inset,** George Godfrey/Animals Animals; **640,** NOAA; **641,** Tony Craddock/Science Photo Library/Photo Researchers.

Nature of Science

Page 644, Jane Love/NASA; **645 r,** Jose L. Pelaez/The Stock Market; **645 l,** NASA/Photo Researchers; **646 b,** NASA; **646–647 t,** NASA

Chapter 20

Pages 648–649, Gay Bumgarner/TSI; **650,** Frans Lanting/Minden Pictures; **651 l,** Inga Spence/Tom Stack & Associates; **651 r,** Charles D. Winters/Photo Researchers; **651 b,** Key Sanders/TSI; **652 t,** UPI/corbis-Bettmann; **652 b,** Corbis-Bettmann; **653 t,** UPI/Corbis-Bettmann; **653 bl,** Underwood & Underwood/Corbis-Bettmann; **653 br,** William Campbell/Peter Arnold; **654,** Jeff Gnass/The Stock Market; **656,** Russ Lappa; **657,** Martin Rogers/Stock Boston; **658,** Gary Braasch/TSI; **660,** Tom Stewart/The Stock Market; **661,** Greg Vaughn/Tom Stack & Associates; **662,** Russ Lappa; **663,** Richard Haynes; **664 tl,** Dave Watts/Tom Stack & Associates; **664 tm,** Frans Lanting/Minden Pictures; **664 tr,** George G. Dimijian/Photo Researchers; **664 b,** Fred Bavendam/Minden Pictures; **665 t,** Frans Lanting/Minden Pictures; **665 b,** Jim Zipp/Photo Researchers; **666,** D. Cavagnaro/DRK Photo; **667,** Randy Wells/TSI; **668 l,** John Shaw/Tom Stack & Associates; **668 m,** Dan Suzio/Photo Researchers; **668 tr,** Stephen J. Krasemann/DRK Photo; **668–669,** Phil A. Dotson/Photo Researchers; **669 tm,** Frans Lanting/Minden Pictures; **669 m,** David Liebman, **669 r,** Lynn M. Stone/DRK Photo; **670 l,** Roy Toft/Tom Stack & Associates; **670 r,** Frans Lanting/Minden Pictures; **671,** Tom McHugh/Photo Researchers; **672 t,** Richard Haynes; **672 b,** Greg Vaughn/Tom Stack & Associates; **673 l, r,** G. Payne/Liaison International; **674,** D. Cavagnaro/DRK Photo; **675,** Gary Braasch/TSI.

Chapter 21

Pages 678–679, Nick Vedros, Vedros & Assoc./TSI; **680 t,** Richard Haynes; **680 bl,** Bertrand Rieger/TSI; **680 br,** Chad Slattery/TSI; **681,** Jacques Jangoux/TSI; **683 tl,** Kevin Horan/TSI; **683 tr,** Tom Bean 1994/DRK Photo; **683 bl,** Larry Lefever/Grant Heilman Photography; **683 br,** Martin Benjamin/The Image Works; **684,** Chris Sattleberger/Panos Pictures; **685 l, r,** Wally McNamee/Woodfin Camp & Associates; **686,** Richard Haynes; **687,** Russ Lappa; **689,** Hank Morgan/Science Source/Photo Researchers; **690 l,** David Joel/TSI; **690 r,** Hank Morgan/Science Source/Photo Researchers; **691,** Russ Lappa; **692,** David Lassman/The Image Works; **693,** Ray Pfortner/Peter Arnold; **694,** David Young Wolff/PhotoEdit; **695,** Richard Haynes; **696 t,** Russ Lappa; **696 b,** Galen Rowell/Peter Arnold; **697 all,** Russ Lappa; **698 l,** Fred Hirschmann/TSI; **698 r,** Stephen Agricola/The Image Works; **700,** Russ Lappa, **701,** Fred Hirschmann/TSI.

Chapter 22

Pages 704–705, G. Randall/FPG International; **706 t,** Russ Lappa; **706 b,** NASA/Liaison International; **707,** Conor Caffrey/SPL/Photo Researchers; **710, 713,** Russ Lappa; **715 t,** Richard Haynes; **715 b,** NASA/The Stock Market; **716 l,** Ed Wheeler/The Stock Market; **716 r,** Robert Fried/Stock Boston; **717,** Bilderberg/The Stock Market; **718 l,** Suzi Moore/Woodfin Camp & Associates; **718 r,** Jeffrey Muir Hamilton/Stock Boston; **719,** Randy Duchaine/The Stock Market; **721 t,** Richard Haynes; **721 b,** Mike Booher/Transparencies, Inc.; **723 t,** Courtesy of city of Arcata, CA; **723 b,** Stephen Rose/Rainbow; **724,** Bob Daemmrich/Stock Boston; **725 t,** Conor Caffrey/SPL/Photo Researchers; **725 b,** Randy Duchaine/The Stock Market.

Chapter 23
Pages 728–729, Yamada Toshiro/TSI; **730,** M. L. Sinibaldi/The Stock Market; **733 t,** Mike Abrahams/TSI; **733 b,** Paul Harris/TSI; **734,** Jbboykin Oil Prod./The Stock Market; **736,** UPI/Corbis-Bettmann; **737,** Chad Ehlers/International Stock; **738,** Nadia MacKenzie/TSI; **740,** A & L Sinibaldi/TSI; **741,** Larry Ulrich/DRK Photo; **742,** Carlie Waite/TSI; **744,** NASA; **745,** Richard Haynes; **746,** Herb Swanson; **747 t,** Russ Lappa; **747 b,** Photograph by Johan Hagemeyer, courtesy AIP Emilio Segre Visual Archives; **750,** Y. Arthus-Bertrand/Peter Arnold; **751,** U.S. Dept. of Energy/Science Photo Library/Photo Researchers; **753,** Richard Haynes; **754 l,** Mitch Kezar/TSI; **754 r,** Leonard Lessin/Peter Arnold; **759,** Yves Marcoux/TSI; **760,** Wolf/Monkmeyer; **761 l,** Nadia MacKenzie/TSI; **761 r,** Yves Marcoux/TSI.

Interdisciplinary Exploration
Page 760, Galen Rowell/Corbis; **761,** The Granger Collection, NY; **763,** AE Zuckerman/Photo Edit; **764 inset,** Corbis-Bettmann; **764–765,** AE Zuckerman/Photo Edit.

Skills Handbook
Page 766, Mike Moreland/Photo Network; **767 t,** Foodpix; **767 m,** Richard Haynes; **767 b,** Russ Lappa; **770,** Richard Haynes; **772,** Ron Kimball; **773,** Renee Lynn/Photo Researchers.